INTEGRATIVE THEOLOGY

HISTORICAL • BIBLICAL • SYSTEMATIC • APOLOGETIC • PRACTICAL

Three Volumes in One

GORDON R. LEWIS & BRUCE A. DEMAREST

ZONDERVAN™

GRAND RAPIDS, MICHIGAN 49530

ZONDERVAN™

Integrative Theology
Copyright © 1996 by Gordon R. Lewis and Bruce A. Demarest
Integrative Theology, Volume 1
Copyright © 1987 by Gordon R. Lewis and Bruce A. Demarest
Integrative Theology, Volume 2
Copyright © 1990 by Gordon R. Lewis and Bruce A. Demarest
Integrative Theology, Volume 3
Copyright © 1994 by Gordon R. Lewis and Bruce A. Demarest

Requests for information should be addressed to:

Zondervan, *Grand Rapids, Michigan 49530*

ISBN 0-310-20915-3

Library of Congress Cataloging-in-Publication Data

Demarest, Bruce A.   Integrative theology.

    Vol. 1-3 by Gordon R. Lewis and Bruce A. Demarest
      Includes bibliographical references and index.
      Contents: v. 1. Knowing ultimate reality. The living God—v. 2. Our primary need. Christ's atoning provisions.—v. 3. Spirit-given life
      1. Theology, Doctrinal. 2. Theology—Methodology. I. Lewis, Gordon Russell, 1926–. II. Title.

BT75.2.D37   1987   230
                                       86-24564

ISBN: 0-310-39230-6 (v. 1)
ISBN: 0-310-39240-3 (v. 2)
ISBN: 0-310-59830-3 (v. 3)
This edition: 0-310-20915-3

01 02 03 04 05 06 07 /❖ DC/ 14 13 12 11 10 9 8 7 6 5

VOLUME I

VOLUME II

VOLUME III

VOLUME I

INTEGRATIVE THEOLOGY

CONTENTS

Preface

Coherent thinking and authentic living in the modern world require that a person view life holistically rather than in fragments. For some people a meaningful world view is provided by the data of lived experience, while for others empirical analysis of the external world supplies the "big picture." Christians, however, believe that a coherent understanding of reality begins with God's perspective mediated by general and special revelation. In order to develop a comprehensive view of the real, the true, and the valuable and so to arrive at viable convictions by which to live and serve, we propose that Christians consider the paradigm of integrative theology.

Bernard Ramm, in his book *After Fundamentalism,* argues that Evangelicals must devise a new paradigm for doing theology in the post-Enlightenment world. The traditional approach to doing theology, he argues, will not suffice for the future. Ramm believes that Evangelicals "have not developed a theological method that enables them to be consistently evangelical in their theology and to be people of modern learning. That is why a new paradigm is necessary."[1] Ramm chooses the method of Karl Barth as the preferred model for doing theology in the future. "Barth's paradigm has resulted in an authentic methodology," he claims.[2] In response to such felt needs for a new theological methodology, we propose the paradigm of integrative theology. This approach, we believe, follows a more reliable method than that of Barth and yields results that are more consistent with Scripture and the historic Christian faith.

The approach we call integrative theology involves six successive stages. The first involves identification of the problem under consideration. The investigator delineates the parameters of the theological problem and senses its significance for personal and societal existence.

Second, one identifies the various solutions to the problem that have been suggested in the history of Christian thought. Devout and gifted minds may have acquired insights that later Christians have not considered. But since equally competent scholars differ on many issues, we should view the alternative proposals as hypotheses to be tested by the primary biblical data.

Third, one goes behind the secondary testimony of history to the prime source of theological knowledge—inspired and inerrant Scripture. Following the method of biblical theology and employing a responsible hermeneutic, one finds the relevant teachings of the Old and New Testaments in their chronological development. This stage also involves relating one portion of Scripture to other portions that deal with the same subject in the progress of revelation.

Fourth, the investigator orders the relevant data of general and special revelation into a coherent doctrine and relates the same to the other doctrines similarly derived. The person commits himself to the thesis that satisfies the test for truth with the fewest number of difficulties. The commended test for truth is threefold: (1) logical consistency, (2) agreement with the data of revelation, and (3) existential viability.

Fifth, the Christian defends this doctrinal position in interaction with contrary positions in theology, philosophy, and new religions. At this stage the offensive component of an integrative theology becomes evident as the truth encounters and challenges alien ideologies. The goal of theology is to bring every dimension of thought and action under the lordship of the sovereign God.

Sixth, theology is applied to specific life situations in the world. This final stage assumes (1) that truth does not terminate in abstract contemplation and (2) that faithful living flows from truth as water flows from a fountain. It is imperative that Christians live by their convictions authentically before God, in relationship with others, and in service to the world. The ethical dimension of theology is apparent in this final stage.

The integrative approach to theology proposed in this volume thus may be summarized by six key phrases: The Problem; Historical Hypotheses; Biblical Teaching; Systematic Formulation; Apologetic Interaction; and Relevance for Life and Ministry. Due to space limitations each of these sections will be less than exhaustive and can only initiate thought in the given area.

Our contention is that integrative theology as implemented in this series offers more promise than alternative theological methods practiced in the past. It is superior to *confessional theology,* which presents the tenets that constitute a particular ecclesiastical tradition and invites adherence on that basis. The difficulty with confessional theology is that frequently few reasons are given why one tradition (Reformed, Lutheran, Anabaptist) is held to be superior to another. Such an approach seems to be closed rather than open to new insights from special or general revelation.

The integrative approach would also appear superior to *fideistic theology,* which enjoins belief on the authority of the speaker who claims to possess God's Word. It may not be clear to the hearer of such a presentation that the claimant does in fact possess the truth of God. The element of unsubstantiated dogmatism present in the fideistic approach likewise may hinder the reception of the message.

The approach of integrative theology may be superior to traditional *systematic theology* for several reasons. The latter (1) usually does not develop a comprehensive history of the doctrine with a view to identifying hypotheses to be tested; (2) often does not follow the method of biblical theology but relies on proof-texting without the developmental context; (3) may not employ a comprehensive test for truth and thus not attain a high degree of objective validity in deciding which proposal is true and which views are spurious; (4) may not defend each doctrine in interaction with opposing views; and (5) may not show the relevance of each doctrinal issue for Christian life in the church and in the world.

Integrating our thoughts is something that we must do for ourselves— others cannot do it for us. These volumes provide several sets of data that should be coherently related in our minds. They also indicate ways in which the authors express their attempts at a coherent formulation. In the final analysis, however, we cannot organize your thoughts for you. Readers are urged to digest the material and to begin integrating their own thinking. If that seems discouraging at first, do not be surprised. Integrating our thoughts and then living by the convictions based on this integration is a life-time challenge. If a good start is made in that direction, the purpose of these volumes will have been achieved.

The method of integrative theology herein set forth is biblically grounded, historically related, culturally sensitive, person-centered, and profoundly related to life. Its goal is to set forth a comprehensive picture of the cosmos, of persons, and of history that is logically consistent, factually adequate, and capable of maximizing personal meaning and fulfillment. We propose a method for doing theology that follows a coherent research method, that avoids callous indoctrination, and that encourages the learner to come to his or her own conclusions and create his or her own commitments face-to-face with the Word of God and under the gentle guidance of the Holy Spirit. Our hope is that this approach may enable theology to overcome the impasse in which it finds itself in the contempo- rary situation, and that it might enable theology once again to speak convincingly to a church in need of instruction and to a world in need of God's liberating truth and light.

After reviewing a few chapters of *Integrative Theology*, you may find yourself asking some of the following questions:

Question: Should the problem addressed in the first section of each chapter focus more directly on the urgent cultural problems of our times?

The immediate issues of a given culture provide valuable conversa- tional starting points, but the study of each basic Christian doctrine begins with a problem of permanent, transcultural significance. A theological treatment of the multitudes of specific issues in each culture and subculture is important, but that can best be done by Christians who have specialized in the areas of the sciences, history, psychology, sociology, etc. Furthermore multitudes of contemporary issues may pass out of date almost as quickly as daily newspapers. The classical issues and doctrines have exhibited universal and permanent relevance because they are common to all men and women from the Near East, the Far East, and the West, in the two-thirds world and the one-third world, in rural areas and the large cities.

Question: Before looking at the "alternative proposals in the church" regarding a problem, should not theological research examine the biblical teaching? Would it not be wise to examine biblical truth inductively without theological biases?

Attempts to begin inductive research with the "objective" biblical evidence overlook the impossibility of obtaining complete objectivity in any comprehensive field. Nothing has become more evident recently than that all researchers and writers in any field have presuppositions. The ideal of objectivity is worthy and not in question here. The problem is to find a critical method by which to move toward greater objectivity. The most effective way we know for students of the Bible to identify their biases is to survey the alternative perspectives and so become aware of their own assumptions. By stating the alternative doctrines as mere hypotheses to be tested we not only become aware of the similarities and differences between our perspectives and those of others, but also of the need of verifying our own doctrine. This critical approach is necessary if we are to get out of our closed hermeneutical circles and in a spirit of openness do genuine research with any hope of making some progress. We make no claim to exhaustiveness but have attempted to state succinctly the most significant options from the beginning of the history of a given doctrine to the present time as a means of exposing assumptions so that they can be tested for their consistency and adequacy with the biblical evidence.

Question: Must a person adopt only one of the alternative views or can he be eclectic?

The section Systematic Formulation seeks to develop with clarity and some creativity a coherent interpretation of the primary biblical data in the space allotted—an interpretation that encompasses elements of truth from several of the different historical views and avoids their weaknesses. Beginning students may tend to take one of those views and reject everything in the others. Only where the others contradict a biblical position must they logically be dismissed. Often there is something to learn from views that have had major historical or contemporary influence. From their own historical and biblical studies professors and students may wish to formulate their conclusions with different emphases. So the formulation presented may serve as the springboard for further discussion.

Question: Could other views be considered in the sections under Apologetic Interaction?

The apologetic interaction sections are generally more concerned with the major non-Christian contemporary contradictory options than with fine tuning the evangelical position adopted as against other evangelical versions. It is our view that within the framework of an evangelical position there may be freedom to vary in specifics. Teachers and students in different traditions should feel free to focus in greater detail on the intramural refinements as they wish. Having tried to incorporate the values of the alternative options in the section Systematic Formulation, it is important not to undermine those elements of truth while opposing the nonbiblical elements or the system in general.

Question: Can other points of personal and social relevance be noted?

Readers are encouraged to supplement the section Relevance for Life and Ministry with their own applications of the doctrine. Teachers and students are free to consider other ways in which the revealed truth can make a difference in their own specific life situations and vocations. Keep in mind that the ministry here envisioned is not just that of ordained ministers, but more generally that of all Christians in their service to others, whether vocationally or avocationally.

Question: How can the review questions at the end of each chapter be used?

The review questions may help readers determine how well they can recall and express the major ideas of each section. The review questions may also stimulate discussions among students in larger or smaller groups. And they may be used as examination questions for essay tests.

Question: Can you briefly explain the relationship between the sections of each chapter? They are closely related as logically ordered steps in a verificational method of researching one basic issue. The verificational method of devising truth is not purely inductive, nor deductive. Rather, it is an abductive or retroductive method often called the hypothetical, critical, or scientific method of reasoning. The diagram on page 12 may clarify this.[3]

After a problem has been delimited, the verificational method does not begin with an allegedly blank mind (as in inductive methods), or with a confessional statement presupposed to be true (as in deductive methods), but with several historical and contemporary answers as hypotheses to be tested. These proposals are evaluated and confirmed or disconfirmed by the primary biblical evidence. Then the elements confirmed are formulated topically and logically in a consistent way that accounts for the biblical teaching. The section Apologetic Interaction indicates how the opposing hypotheses are inconsistent and inadequate in accounting for the evidence. Finally, the section Relevance for Life and Ministry indicates some of the viability of the conclusion for life and ministry.

Please note: because of the important connections of the sections of each chapter to each other in this verificational approach, no single section can be taken out of its context in the entire chapter to stand by itself as a

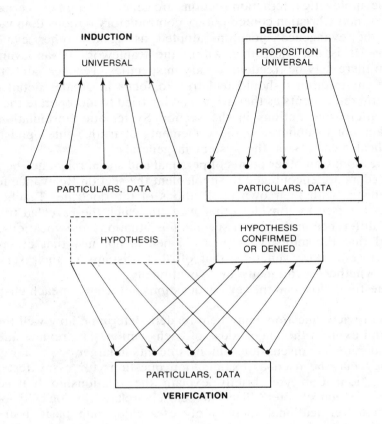

INDUCTION

DEDUCTION

UNIVERSAL

PROPOSITION
UNIVERSAL

PARTICULARS, DATA

PARTICULARS, DATA

HYPOTHESIS

HYPOTHESIS
CONFIRMED
OR DENIED

PARTICULARS, DATA

VERIFICATION

Three Methods of Justifying Beliefs
This diagram was taken from Gordon R. Lewis, "Schaeffer's Apologetic Method" in *Reflections on Francis Schaeffer*, ed. Ronald W. Ruegsegger (Grand Rapids: Zondervan, 1986), 71. Used by permission.

complete discussion of any topic or school of thought. If, for example, people want to study the neoorthodox view of special revelation, it will not be sufficient to look at the references to it in just one section of the chapter. That view is stated in Alternative Proposals (section two), is tested in Biblical Teaching, its strengths and weaknesses may be incorporated in Systematic Formulation, and its lack of consistency or adequacy reflected in Apologetic Interaction.

Each part of this integrative work, particularly, must be read in the broader context of its chapter with understanding of the contribution of each section to the overall method. Many analytical works on theological words have been written. The purpose of this integrative work is to construct a more synthetic, big picture. We ask the patience of the analytically inclined who try to pursue this synthetic work. Before judging a given specific discussion of a topic or view in any one section of a chapter, readers are urged to integrate it with the teaching of the entire chapter. To help with this the review questions at the end of each chapter are provided.

Question: How did the authors work together in writing this work?

After the authors agreed on the basic approach and the issues, Bruce Demarest contributed the first half of each chapter, defining the problem, surveying the historical views, and summing up the relevant biblical evidence. Gordon Lewis contributed the second half of each chapter, formulating the doctrine systematically, defending it, and applying it to life and ministry. Then we interacted with each other's materials and with several readers' and editors' suggestions, making revisions accordingly.

Question: Who else significantly contributed to the production of this publication?

Innumerable people have contributed to our lives and thinking through the years. We are particularly indebted to our stimulating colleagues at Denver Seminary and to the administration's thoughtful policy on sabbaticals. Special thanks go to Zondervan editors Stanley Gundry and Gerard Terpstra. We benefited also from the suggestions of several readers—above all, from those of Daniel B. Wallace of Probe Ministries. In the production of the manuscript we express our gratitude to the skillful and cheerful assistance of Doris Haslam, our secretary at Denver Seminary.

Question: Can you suggest other ways to help people become involved in doing theology?

Many have been helped to struggle with some of the issues, interpret some relevant passages for themselves, and formulate their own conclusions by doing studies in Gordon R. Lewis, *Decide for Yourself: A Theological Workbook* (Downers Grove: InterVarsity, 1970). This workbook has been widely used by lay people and by college, seminary, and extension-seminary students. For some classes the workbook may appropriately serve as a student manual, and *Integrative Theology* as a teacher's manual.

Abbreviations

AB	*The Anchor Bible*, ed. W. F. Albright and D. N. Freedman
BAGD	Walter Bauer, William F. Arndt, F. Wilbur Gingrich, and Frederick W. Danker, *A Greek-English Lexicon of the New Testament* (Chicago: University of Chicago Press, 1979)
CD	Karl Barth, *Church Dogmatics*, ed. G. W. Bromiley and T. F. Torrance, 13 vols. (Edinburgh: T. & T. Clark, 1936–69)
CGTC	*The Cambridge Greek Testament Commentary*, ed. C. F. D. Moule
EBC	*The Expositor's Bible Commentary*, ed. Frank E. Gaebelein (Grand Rapids: Zondervan, 1976–)
EDT	*Evangelical Dictionary of Theology*, ed. Walter A. Elwell (Grand Rapids: Baker, 1984)
EP	*Encyclopedia of Philosophy*, ed. Paul Williams, 8 vols. (New York: Macmillan, 1967)
HNTC	*Harper's New Testament Commentary*, ed. Henry Chadwick
ICC	*The International Critical Commentary*, ed. J. A. Emerton and C. E. B. Cranfield
ISBE	*The International Standard Bible Encyclopedia*, ed. G. W. Bromiley, 4 vols. (Grand Rapids: Eerdmans, 1979–)
LCC	*Library of Christian Classics*, 25 vols. (Philadelphia: Westminster, 1953–69)
LW	*Luther's Works*, ed. J. Pelikan and H. T. Lehman, 55 vols. (St. Louis: Concordia and Philadelphia: Fortress, 1955–76)
NBCRev	*The New Bible Commentary*, revised. (London: Inter-Varsity, 1970)
NBD	*New Bible Dictionary* (Wheaton, Ill.: Tyndale, 1982)
NCBC	*New Century Bible Commentary*, 6 vols. (Grand Rapids: Eerdmans, 1980–84)
NICNT	*The New International Commentary of the New Testament*, ed. F. F. Bruce. 17 vols. (Grand Rapids: Eerdmans, 1952–84)
NICOT	*The New International Commentary of the Old Testament*, ed. R. K. Harrison (Grand Rapids: Eerdmans, 1965–82)
NIDNTT	*The New International Dictionary of New Testament Theology*, ed. Colin Brown, 4 vols. (Grand Rapids: Zondervan, 1975–78)

NIGTC   *New International Greek Testament Commentary*, 4 vols. (Grand Rapids: Eerdmans, 1978–82)

NLBC   *The New Layman's Bible Commentary*, ed. G. C. D. Howley, F. F. Bruce, and H. L. Ellison (Grand Rapids: Zondervan, 1979)

OTL   *The Old Testament Library*, ed. G. Ernest Wright, John Bright, James Barr, and Peter Ackroyd

SCG   Thomas Aquinas, *Summa Contra Gentiles*, 4 vols. (Notre Dame: Notre Dame University Press, 1975)

ST   Thomas Aquinas, *Summa Theologica*, 22 vols. (London: R. & T. Washbourne, 1912–25)

TDNT   *Theological Dictionary of the New Testament*, ed. G. Kittel and G. Friedrich, 9 vols. (Grand Rapids: Eerdmans, 1965)

TDNTAbr   *Theological Dictionary of the New Testament*, ed. G. Kittel and G. Friedrich and abridged in one volume by G. W. Bromiley (Grand Rapids: Eerdmans, 1985)

TDOT   *Theological Dictionary of the Old Testament*, ed. G. Johannes Botterweck and H. Ringgren, 6 vols. (Grand Rapids: Eerdmans, 1977)

TI   Karl Rahner, *Theological Investigations*, 14 vols. (New York: Seabury: 1974–76)

TNTC   *Tyndale New Testament Commentaries*, ed. R. V. G. Tasker (Grand Rapids: Eerdmans, 1975–83)

TOTC   *Tyndale Old Testament Commentaries*, ed. D. J. Wiseman, 17 vols. (Downers Grove, Ill.: InterVarsity, 1968–84)

TWOT   *Theological Wordbook of the Old Testament*, ed. R. Laird Harris, Gleason L. Archer, Jr., and Bruce K. Waltke, 2 vols. (Chicago: Moody, 1980)

WA   *D. Martin Luthers Werke: Kritische Gesamptausgabe* (Weimar, 1883–)

WBC   *Word Biblical Commentary*, ed. David A. Hubbard and Glenn W. Barker (Waco: Word, n.d.)

ZPEB   *Zondervan Pictorial Encyclopedia of the Bible*, ed. Merrill C. Tenney, 5 vols. (Grand Rapids: Zondervan, 1976)

PART ONE

KNOWING
ULTIMATE REALITY

CHAPTER 1

THEOLOGY'S CHALLENGING TASK

Theology's Challenging Task

INTRODUCTION

The Need for Integrative Thinking

We seldom find time to put all the bits and pieces of our learning together in a meaningful whole. The rapid growth of knowledge makes it difficult to keep up in one field, let alone develop a unified world view encompassing all fields of knowledge.

The diversity of experiences and cultures accessible to us adds to the difficulty of comprehensive knowledge. The radically different kinds of experiences of people in East and West, North and South complicate the challenge of relating areas of learning cohesively on a shrinking globe. And even within the same culture people's interests vary greatly.

Difficult as it may be for us, with a multiplicity of experiences and interests in an exploding information age, to "put it all together," we need to relate our thinking about our particular specialty to reliable thought about other areas. The importance of seeing life whole is illustrated in ecology. Before unnecessarily exhausting a limited source of energy for personal profit, a person ought to consider, as far as possible, the potential effect on the earth's whole ecological system.

A coherent world view and way of life provides a necessary context for our ethical decision making in general. Without the "big picture" it is difficult to determine wisely what values are worth living and dying for in a fast-moving, pluralistic world. Francis Schaeffer diagnosed the basic problem of Christians in America in this way: "They have seen things in bits and pieces instead of totals."[1] In the social issues of life it is important to be able to detect the underlying assumptions about reality (metaphysics) and about how we know reality (epistemology).

Not all those who reject skepticism and try to make sense out of life accept the existence of special revelation as their starting point. A variety of unifying principles are proposed. Many naturalists find the ultimate integrative factor in nature's energy-matter and its uniform laws. For secular humanists the highest reality that gives meaning to everything else is not impersonal, but personal: humanity. Pantheists think the supreme being is an impersonal god: the dynamic underlying energy of nature and our inner being.

Theists on the other hand see every-

21

thing in the cosmos as the creation of a personal God who is distinct from the world but active in it. And Christian theists find that the existence, meaning, and purpose of energy, nature, and persons derive from the purposes of the transcendent Lord of all, disclosed in Jesus Christ and the Bible.

Developing a theology that relates biblically revealed truth to humanity and nature is not an elective for Christians who believe in the Lord of all, but a requirement. God knows, sustains, and gives purpose to all that is. God provides a focal point not only for our limited personal experiences or special interests but for all thought. The question for Christians is not whether they will relate all their fields of knowledge to God's purposes, but whether they, as stewards of God's truth, will do so poorly or well.

Entry Points for Serious Thinking About Revealed Truth

As new Christians begin to further their understanding of what changed their lives, language functions not only to communicate vague feelings but to define the experienced reality. Usually new believers express the same beliefs about God and his purposes as those held by the people who were most influential in their conversion to Christ.

Denominationally, their earliest influences may have come from Baptists, Pentecostalists, Nazarenes, Presbyterians, Methodists, Episcopalians, Roman Catholics, or independents. Transdenominationally, the earliest influences may have come from systems of theology primarily evangelical, liberal, neoorthodox, ecumenical, liberation, process, fundamentalist, or charismatic.

Whatever our original enthusiasm and psychological certitude, subsequent experiences may cause us to think more carefully about particular beliefs. In this shrinking, pluralistic world we discover other Christians with quite different and even contradictory views. Our relatives, co-workers, neighbors, or friends may have significantly different perspectives, and their loyalties challenge us to know why we should maintain beliefs that until now we accepted without question.

There are many points in life at which we are forced to think more deeply about what we believe and why. While each of us has his or her specific "entry points" for serious thinking about revealed truth, there are some broad areas of experience that provide the "entry points" for many. Involved in church *outreach* programs, we confront people involved in non-Christian philosophies, religions, and cults. Dialogue with non-Christians may raise difficult issues that motivate further study. Compassion for people genuinely struggling with issues of basic beliefs may also motivate the search for answers.

Christians who have dedicated their lives to *vocational service* must decide in which doctrinal tradition they can serve with intellectual integrity and fervent commitment. A preliminary form of that decision may be the choice of a college or seminary. In training, courses in church history present many alternative theological traditions. Other challenging issues may be raised by studies in psychology and counseling, sociology, philosophy of religions, and crosscultural missions. Even the study of the Old and New Testaments discloses conflicting beliefs among knowledgeable and dedicated interpreters of the biblical languages. And responsible courses in theology involve the student in comparing and contrasting live options in the field. In order to establish normative beliefs to guide life and ministry, people considering Christian vocations will evaluate the relevance of alleged biblical evidence and the cogency of the arguments drawn from it.

Members of committees and boards of various organizations are often called on to discern the implications of doctrine that may determine the future of organizations and their personnel. The vitality of churches may depend on the theological discernment of pulpit committees who must make a choice from among candidates with radically different doctrinal loyalties to recommend for their pastorate. For the integrity of their mission agencies and schools board members must determine what beliefs are nonnegotiable.

A well-founded, personally appropriated faith becomes crucial when one is experiencing serious *illness* and facing *death*. Do the anxieties of a seemingly meaningless life, real guilt, and death have an answer that stands examination? In times of crisis it may not be enough to hunt for a verse here and there. When pressures gang up on us we need well-formulated, well-founded convictions that will not let us down. Even under the more ordinary pressures of life we need well-established convictions by which to live in a faithful, loving relation to God and others.

Experiences at some of these "entry points" motivate Christians to investigate the work others have done in theology and to become involved in the discipline themselves. Throughout our lives we need the guidance of revealed truths. Our spiritual Master asked us to grow, not only in grace, but also in knowledge of him and his revealed purposes (Eph. 4:15; 2 Peter 3:18).

Developing *intellectual maturity* takes Christians through at least four stages. (1) As they become aware of other religions, philosophies, and theologies, they can think and speak of them fairly. (2) Then they grow in an ability to evaluate alternative doctrines objectively by reliable criteria of truth. (3) Mature people do not remain in an undecided state but decide in favor of the most coherent account of the relevant data with the fewest difficulties. (4) Having personally accepted a well-founded conviction, they grow in their ability to live by it authentically, state it clearly, defend it adequately, and communicate it effectively.

SYSTEMATIC FORMULATION

Systematic Theology

The root meaning of the word "theology" is the "organized study (*logos*) of God (*theos*)." However, in this work we do not claim to know anything about God apart from God's disclosure of himself in nature and in Scripture. As used here, therefore, *theology* is the topical and logical study of God's revealed nature and purposes.

Theology is more comprehensive than the study of separate doctrines. *Doctrinal studies* consider individual biblical topics without logically relating them to other biblical or nonbiblical tenets in a developing belief system. *Systematic theology* not only derives coherent doctrines from the entirety of written revelation but also systematically relates them to each other in developing a comprehensive world view and way of life.

Systematic theology differs from *biblical theology* in its aim and organizing principle. Both systematic and biblical theology derive their data from the same primary source, the Bible. But biblical theology, aiming to be a descriptive science, is organized around the chronological and cultural development of a given biblical writer's own terms, categories, and thought forms in his historical and cultural context. Systematic theology, on the other hand, aims to produce normative guidelines to spiritual reality for the present generation; it organizes the material of divine revelation topically and logically, developing a coherent and comprehensive world view and way of life.[2]

During centuries of attempts to develop systematics, the discipline has met with much opposition, as is true of any ethical or social attempt to state normative principles that people *ought* to accept and live by unhypocritically. But the opposition has targeted particularly systematic theology's *method of reasoning*. The discipline of systematics has sometimes been dominated by a given philosophical emphasis and paid insufficient attention to the history of doctrine and to biblical teaching in its literary, historical, and cultural contexts.

Not only biblical and historical scholars but also philosophers opposed (and oppose) premature systematizing. Some of the most influential recent philosophies (such as positivism, linguistic analysis, existentialism, and pragmatism) abandoned all hope of developing coherent and comprehensive world views. A similarly based antisystematic temper is also evident in influential twentieth-century theologies such as liberalism, neoorthodoxy, and biblical theology.

Instead of systematic theology, graduate schools and publishers by and large emphasized psychology of religion, philosophy of religion, comparative religions, Old Testament studies, the faith of Israel (as evidenced in stories or case studies), New Testament studies, and the faith of the church. Even Karl Barth, who tried to call liberalism back to the transcendent God of the Bible, failed to regard the Bible itself as a coherent, divine revelation and wrote his extensive series of volumes on *church* dogmatics rather than systematic theology.

Charges Against Systematic Theology

These trends produced some very powerful charges against the discipline of systematic theology, and these charges led many to think it presumptuous and arrogant even to attempt coherence in all our thought about God, humanity, history, and nature. These charges, described below, cannot be overlooked by anyone approaching the field today.

1. Systematic theology organized a system of Christian thought around one central theme (such as sovereignty, freedom, covenant, dispensation, or kingdom) chosen a priori and imposed on the rest of revelation in a contrived interrelatedness.

2. Systematic theology failed to do justice to the multiplicity of relevant lines of biblical information seen in their cultural and historical contexts.

3. Systematic theology paid insufficient attention to the history of doctrine in the church.

4. Systematic theology tended to regard a system of theology as closed rather than open to new discoveries from God's Word or God's world.

5. Systematic theology passed its teachings on to the next generation by sheer indoctrination—an unworthy approach to education.

6. Finally, systematic theology failed to display the relevance of its content to the burning personal and social issues of its day.

Responses of Systematic Theologians

In spite of the measure of validity and power in criticisms like these, some evangelical theologians have made few methodological changes, while others have made major changes without explicitly formulating a new method of decision making.

Apparently unmoved by charges like those above are presuppositionalists (such as Cornelius Van Til and Rousas Rushdoony)[3] and the deductive rationalists (such as Gordon Clark and Carl Henry).[4] Valuable as the contributions of these writers have been in many ways, their presuppositional and axiomatic methodologies remain unchanged. Consequently, charges of a priori assumptions of the things to be proved, eisegesis, insufficient attention to the history of the doctrines, closed-mindedness, indoctrination, and insufficient relevance continue to limit the extent of their outreach and impact.

A change from such presuppositional approaches is evident in Millard Erickson's *Christian Theology*. Called "systematic theology" in chapter 1, this work displays a heightened consciousness of biblical contexts, the history of doctrine, an openness to investigation, avoidance of sheer indoctrination, and a meeting of contemporary needs. Some of these advantages are reflected in Erickson's definition of systematic theology as "that discipline which strives to give a coherent statement of the doctrines of the Christian faith, based primarily on the Scriptures, placed in the context of culture in general, worded in contemporary idiom, and related to issues of life."[5]

Although Erickson devotes valuable chapters to methodology, biblical criticism, and philosophy, his systematic theology is not explicitly developed on the basis of a distinctive method of decision making. (A similar weakness appears in the helpful work of John Jefferson Davis.)[6] Commendable as the elements discussed in Erickson's chapter on methodology and related chapters are, a procedure by which a reader might be expected to relate these elements to each other is not explicitly outlined. The telling criticisms leveled against systematic theology seem to require a more developed methodological proposal than either Erickson or Davis offers.

Contemporary theologians generally announce their intention to do justice to historical, biblical, contemporary, and practical aspects. However, the data may not always be made available to students who want to evaluate the evidence for themselves, and the relationship between the data and the decision-making process may not always be clear. Assuming a participatory philosophy of education in such a comprehensive field, a methodological paradigm becomes an essential tool for both research and teaching.

Integrative Theology

The Meaning of "Integrative Theology"

Integrative theology utilizes a distinctive verificational method of decision making as it defines a major topic, surveys influential alternative answers in the church, amasses relevant biblical data in their chronological development, formulates a comprehensive conclusion, defends it against competing alternatives, and exhibits its relevance for life and ministry.

Integrative theology is a *science*. On the basis of the entirety of special and general revelation, it develops a comprehensive, noncontradictory set of convictions on topics significant for Christian life and service. As a comprehensive science, integrative theology, like synthetic philosophy, tries to draw upon relevant lines of evidence from God's external world as responsibly interpreted by the empirical sciences, and from internal experience as responsibly interpreted by psychology, axiology, ethics, epistemology, and ontology.

Like other sciences, integrative theology works with *interrelated criteria* of truth (logical noncontradiction, empirical adequacy, and existential viability), accepting only those hypotheses that upon testing are discovered to be (1) noncontradictory, (2) supported by adequate evidence, and (3) affirmable without hypocrisy.

Integrative theology is not only a comprehensive science but also an *art* that requires student participation. It is one thing to learn a field by reading the research of others. It is quite another thing to do theological research for oneself. The art of research in integrative theology employs a consciously chosen methodology that answers the charge of starting with a priori presuppositions and imposing these on Scripture. The use of a research methodology assumes that Christians are illumined by the Holy Spirit, not only in preaching and teaching but also in their stewardship of Bible college and seminary assignments and in personal study. We seek to provide the data that will enable readers to follow these steps and integrate their own thinking for themselves. In the final analysis, no one can integrate other people's thinking for them.

The method used here seeks to involve the reader in six distinct steps: (1) defining and distinguishing one distinct topic . or problem for inquiry; (2) learning alternative approaches to it from a survey of Spirit-led scholars in the history of the church; (3) discovering and formulating from both the Old and the New Testament a coherent summary of relevant biblical teaching by making use of sound principles of hermeneutics, worthy commentaries, and biblical theologies; (4) formulating on the basis of the relevant data a cohesive doctrine and relating it without contradiction to other biblically founded doctrines and other knowledge; (5) defending this formulation of revealed truth in interaction with contradictory options in theology, philosophy, science, religion, and cults; and (6) applying these convictions to Christian life and ministry in the present generation.[7] These six steps provide the outline for each of the following chapters: The Problem; Historical Hypotheses; Biblical Teaching; Systematic Formulation; Apologetic Interaction; and Relevance for Life and Ministry.

Integrative Theology and Systematic Theology

Consider how integrative theology preserves the values of systematics and avoids its weaknesses:

1. If systematic theology involves reading an a priori central organizing idea into the Bible, an integrated, verificational approach, by contrast, seeks coherence at the *end* of its investigation, not by eisegesis, but by exegesis. The methodology of integrative theology does not start with indefensible presuppositions or axioms. The logical starting point in verificational research discovers alternative hypotheses to be tested. It will accept only those proposals that cohere with adequate evidence from special revelation or general revelation. Several *checks and balances* in the method help a person avoid a contrived interrelatedness (historical surveys of alternatives, surveys of relevant biblical evidence, and interaction with conflicting views). The criteria are designed to permit only as much integration as the data of Scripture and experience permit.

Erickson's central motif is "the magnificence of God."[8] Although his emphasis on the greatness of God's natural and moral attributes is intended to center all of life and theology on God, this could be accomplished more explicitly if we formulate the central and all-important theme of divine revelation in a more comprehensive way. The overarching *great idea* of divine revelation focuses on the *Father's* eternal purposes revealed in *promises* to do gracious things for *his redeemed people* and *through them* individually and collectively for the *whole world.*[9]

This verificationally derived central theme of Scripture integrates such basic doctrines as trinitarianism, decrees, grace, revealed promises or covenants, Christ's atonement, the Holy Spirit's work, and the mission of people in the world, both as persons and as members of such social institutions as families, the Israelite nation, and churches.

2. If systematic theology fails to distinguish human interpretations of the divine revelation from the revelation as given, integrative theology's method requires this distinction. This integrative approach to theology assumes (from the argumentation of apologetics and evidence concerning revelation) that God can reveal information to people who are created in his image to think his thoughts after him. Nevertheless, the method emphasizes the difference between what is *given* in divine revelation and what is *taken from* it by human interpreters. We seek to avoid premature claims to finality of interpretations, or conclusiveness on every point beyond reasonable doubt. Interpretive conclusions have degrees of probability according to the extent and the present state of clarity of their supporting evidence. Thus *the attempt to state our partial understanding of revealed truth without logical contradiction involves no claim to our full comprehension of any complex reality such as God, humans, historical events, or the church.*

3. If systematic theology begins a study of each doctrine presupposing the conclusion, integrative theology begins by surveying the historical and contemporary options as hypotheses. Hypotheses may be confirmed or invalidated upon testing. This survey of options helps people to interact consciously with alternatives other than the one most influential in their lives up to this point. And it asks people to consider their own position as one among many hypotheses to be verified or invalidated.*

4. If systematic theology involves a closed system, integrative theology does not. Integrative theology can never be completely finished and its content as presently formulated can never become a final and closed system. It is always open to new discoveries about the significance of God's Word and God's world. The verificational method sees all truth as God's truth, wherever it is found. And all truth is ours (1 Cor. 3:21–23). On this approach one need not fear the reexamination of any doctrine. If what has been held is not true, it ought to be revised; if what has been held is true, it will stand reexamination.

5. If systematic theology is taught by indoctrination, integrative theology is not. Given its methodology, it cannot be communicated by sheer indoctrination, but only by challenging the coming generation to become sharers of the adventure of doing theology for themselves. The appropriate philosophy of education for communicating integrative theology calls for the participation of students in each step of the research methodology. To gain most from their study of theology, students will struggle with the issues, consider alternative answers, examine the relevant data, arrive at their own conclusions, and think through the import of these con-

*The importance of reexamining the biblical data may be seen in the following statement by a noted Presbyterian in another context, "In this [formulation of the doctrine of God], as in most other matters, the truly original contributions of the Reformation are not to be found in 'classic Protestantism' (Lutheranism, Calvinism, Anglicanism), but in the thinkers of 'radical or sectarian Protestantism' (Baptists, Congregationalists, Quakers, etc., and later Methodists) who sought to press behind theological formulations of the centuries and recover the 'pure' faith of primitive Christianity. However, only in the present period has their influence begun to become significant within the mainstream of Protestantism." Henry P. Van Dusen, in *A Handbook of Christian Theology*, ed. Marvin Halvorson (New York: Meridian, 1958), 148–49.

clusions for their own lives and ministries.

6. If systematic theology fails to exhibit its relevance, integrative theology has a built-in demand to do so. The approach endeavors to exhibit the practical significance for Christian life and service of the doctrines it establishes. It endeavors to display the contemporary relevance of the doctrines formulated without reducing theology to a trendy tract for the fleeting times.

Integrative Theology: Benefits and Limitations

Practicing the art of doing theology for oneself has many *benefits*. The discipline of doing his or her own theological research along with us will help the student to (1) relate the teaching of one portion of Scripture to others on the same subject; (2) integrate the distinct doctrines of Scripture into a coherent whole; (3) develop a biblical view of the real, the true, and the valuable; (4) compare and contrast a biblical world view and way of life with nonbiblical perspectives; (5) apply criteria of truth to distinguish authentic from counterfeit religious experiences; (6) develop personal and social convictions and values worth living and dying for; (7) build confidence to speak up in favor of his or her experience with the God who is there, acting and speaking; and (8) teach biblically based, historic Christian doctrine with its moral significance to children, young people, and adults. The art of integrative theology involves skill at each of these steps.

Integrative theology also has its evident *limitations*. It is no simple task to build a full-orbed world view and way of life based on God's universal revelation in nature, humanity, and history; on God's special revelation in the life and teachings of Christ; and on the thirty-nine Old Testament books and twenty-seven New Testament books, and the history of doctrine derived from them. The best we can do is to work *toward* comprehensiveness and adequacy, *toward* an integrative theology. None can even come close to God's omniscient understanding, and most certainly this limited work does not. It seeks only to make a significant attempt in the direction of an integrative comprehensiveness of five fields: the historical, biblical, systematic, apologetic, and practical. Others are more qualified to add substantial sections on psychology and sociology and all the other lines of relevant data from the diverse fields of knowledge.

Given the vast and varied amount of material available to Christians, it is not surprising that Spirit-illumined people from all different backgrounds organize and apply it in quite different ways. Some consider certain facts of history and teachings of Scripture more important and determinative than others for organizing purposes (as the historical surveys show). The remarkable thing is that Christian theologians in very different cultures and using very different methodologies through the history of the church have reflected such agreement on basic Christian doctrines.

The Contribution of Other Fields to Integrative Theology

Apologetics: The Defense of Theological Presuppositions. In an increasingly complicated world, no discipline, and certainly not a comprehensive discipline, can put it all together by itself. In doing theology it is therefore necessary to assume what has been established particularly in apologetics.

Apologetics, having examined epistemological issues and alternatives with an openness to all sources of knowledge, establishes reliable criteria by which to evaluate truth claims in religion. Accepted as true are those hypotheses about reality that are logically noncontradictory, factually adequate, and existentially viable.

After examining numerous alternative world views, apologists argue that logical, empirical, and existential data are best accounted for by the Christian theistic world view.[10] The basic tenets of Christian theism affirm (1) the existence of the God of creation disclosed in (2) the Jesus of history and (3) the teaching of Scripture. Since that threefold conclusion is defended in apologetics, we here presuppose that God has acted and spoken in creation, Christ, and Scripture. The challenging theological task is to explicate the enriching world view and way of life that follows from those presuppositions for people individually and collectively.

Biblical Studies: The Primary Source of Theological Information. A philosophy student who plans to devote his life to teaching the thought of Plato's classic Dialogues must learn what other experts from ancient to modern times have taught about Plato's philosophy. But a thorough student will not be satisfied with second-hand interpretations. From the Dialogues themselves, preferably in the original Greek and from the best manuscripts, he must find out for himself what Plato taught. Similarly, people who devote their lives to teaching and preaching a biblical message must know what the most influential scholars in the history of the church have said about it. But beyond these secondary sources, they must determine what the primary source, the Bible itself, teaches.

The student of Plato regards the varied interpretations as alternative hypotheses to be tested. He critically determines which writings are indeed Plato's and how well the text has been preserved through the centuries. To relate the thought of the Dialogues to each other, their dates must be determined as far as possible. And the more thorough the knowledge of Greek culture and history of Plato's time, the

better the milieu for understanding the famous philosopher's objectives and meaning. Similarly, in a lifelong study of Scripture, textual, linguistic, historical, critical, and cultural studies are valuable. Students who lack a background in the biblical languages, logic (critical thinking), history, and culture sooner or later may regret their lack of resources for determining what is genuinely biblical.

But critical studies are not an end in themselves. They are a means to identifying the divinely inspired writings in order that they may be studied, lived, taught, and preached. The content of the inspired writings, as other chapters and apologetics extensively support, is the primary source and only inerrant norm of Christian theology.

Christians confident of biblical revelation minister, like the apostle Paul, not only to the "foolish" but also to the "wise" (Rom. 1:14). They have a secure base from which to dialogue daily with skeptics, naturalists, pantheists, and other kinds of theists (Acts 17:1, 17; 18:4, 19). Christian ministers who hold "firmly to the trustworthy message" can not only "encourage others by sound doctrine" but also "refute those who oppose it" (Titus 1:9).

With all the stress on Christianity's relevance to alternative world views and ways of life, evangelical theology is grounded in the teaching of Scripture, God's written Word. Through all critical and philosophical interpretation, what the Bible teaches remains the primary source and final court of appeal. And in all decisions between biblical interpreters and theologians, reflective commitment is granted to the position coherently taught in the only writings that are inerrant.

Hermeneutics: Antidote to Theological Subjectivism. Supporting theological positions from Scripture is not as simple as it often appears to beginning students. All references to the Bible in support of a theological position involve interpretations, as the egregious use and open abuse of biblical quotations in cultic movements show. Listing a reference does not necessarily mean that one's interpretation of it is faithful to the biblical meaning.

After hearing a Bible study or sermon on a controversial theme, a listener may say, "But that is just your interpretation!" And after listening to the critic, the speaker may reply, "And that is just *your* interpretation!" Any resolution of such a conflict between those holding opposing views is hopeless if there is no escape from *eisegesis*, from reading their own ideas into the Bible. To engage in *exegesis*, the deriving of ideas *from* the Bible, both need to acknowledge that their views are hypotheses to be tested. Both need to be willing to submit their views to the test of standard logical criteria of truth and hermeneutical principles for interpreting literature in general and the literature of the Bible in particular. Without respect for hermeneutical guidelines, doctrinal differences among even those who believe the Bible may lack any hope of resolution. Some of those standards of responsible interpretation follow.

1. The meaning of a biblical statement is the ordinary, or normal, meaning of the statement (usually literal with some figures of speech) in terms of its context and the author's purpose. "Jesus died" is a cognitive assertion that is either true or false in fact. The assertion is not merely emotive, nor is it merely of spiritual significance (as Christian Science alleges). The fact of Christ's death (and the deaths of others) cannot be changed to fit the assumption that in reality there is no death. Assumptions must be changed to fit the given facts of Scripture about nature and history.

2. The meaning of a biblical statement fits the historical and cultural setting of the writer and the first readers. Their frame of reference cannot be ignored and replaced by one foreign to them. For example, a Hindu cyclical view of history cannot be introduced into the Jewish-Christian linear view of history. Given the present stress on the differences between cultures, one of the major theological issues today focuses on the question of what teaching applies only to the one culture addressed and what applies to all people of all times. In supporting a doctrine as authoritative today, one of the basic questions that must be answered is, "How does the normative teaching of this passage in its immediate context fit into the total pattern of God's progressive revelation relevant to this subject?"[11] But while we must take cultural differences seriously, we must remember that human beings in all times and places are human beings with more commonalities than differences. All peoples of all cultures are created in the image of God and fallen, inclined to all the works of the flesh, dependent upon God, obligated to God, alienated from God, in all justice guilty before God's moral norms, and in need of mercy and grace, etc.[12]

3. The meaning of a sentence is the one most coherent with the writer's own context. The author's usage of a word as traced throughout his writings is a stronger indication of its meaning than the derivation of the word. A word should not be interpreted apart from its sentence, the basic unit of the writer's thought. Then the sentence should be understood in its paragraph and the paragraph in its place in the progress of thought in the book. Each book of the Bible needs to be understood in relation to the other books in its Testament. And the two Testaments need to be related to each other.

4. The meaning of any single biblical statement is not contradictory to any teaching of other Scripture on the sub-

ject. God's Word, presumably, does not affirm and deny the same thing at the same time in the same respect. So a verse should be taken in accord with the broader theological context. This is involved in the Reformers "analogy of faith." Scripture interprets Scripture.

5. The intended meaning is the one, literal, historical, grammatical, contextual meaning, not a "deeper" or "secret" meaning. Although the applications of a passage are many, the meaning in context is one. Many groups today, such as Theosophy, Divine Science, and the New Age movements in general, assume plural meanings in biblical statements. They regard the normal, literal meaning as the simple meaning, to be superceded by the "deeper" meaning, which turns out to teach an unbiblical monism and support mystical, metaphysical, or occult practices. For examples of this, see Unity's *Metaphysical Bible Dictionary* or the "Glossary" in Mary Baker Eddy's *Science and Health with Key to the Scriptures*.[13]

6. Extensive passages on a subject take priority for theological purposes over brief allusions. We are more likely to misinterpret a single sentence than a whole series of statements on a topic in a paragraph. For example, on the subject of what is necessary for salvation it is unwise to base the eternal life of millions on a single allusion to baptism for the dead (1 Cor. 15:29).

7. Doctrinal passages have initially a greater importance than historical narratives that may report ideas and practices not normative for others. Hence the meaning of the baptism of the Spirit is more clearly defined in the teaching of 1 Corinthians 12:13 than in references to the practice in Acts (1:5; 2:4; 8:14–17; 10:44–48). The allusion to the Jerusalem believers having everything in common and selling their possessions (Acts 2:44–45) does not take priority over the general exhortation to work, to

have something (private ownership), and to share with those in need as generous stewards (Eph. 4:28).

8. What is central in scriptural teaching should be central in our theologies and ministries. The basic human problem throughout the world is sin against our Creator and against others. The universal prescription to resolve the problem is justification through faith on the basis of Christ's death for our sins. Christ's atonement was anticipated throughout the Old Testament, achieved in the Gospels, proclaimed in Acts, and explicated in the rest of the New Testament. To give preeminence to any other teaching, however good, is to distort the central message of special revelation to which the Holy Spirit witnesses.[14]

Logic: A Tool to Sharpen Theological Thinking. Students of theology often misunderstand each other's view and interpretation of the primary biblical source. The same words may be used with different meanings, or very different words may be used for the same belief. Merely verbal disputes are counterproductive. So it is important to avoid hasty labeling of one another and to define terms with increasing precision. Diligence is needed to develop proficiency in the discipline of logic. This discipline specializes, for one thing, in how to define terms. Introductory logic texts explain that good definitions are not circular, figurative, negative, or synonymous attempts at explaining meaning. Rather, a concept to be defined is placed under the next more general genus (kind) and then distinguished from other things of the same kind. So it becomes important to know the varieties of genus common in a biblical world view, and the varieties within each.[15]

If biologists and other scientists give careful thought to logical classifications and definitions, surely theologians can and must do so. Knowing when humankind originated on earth, for example, depends on how theologians and scientists define humanness. We cannot limit ourselves to existential truth, truth about our own passionate existence, important as that is. We can know both existential truth and essential truth. Without knowledge of the essence of humanity, we have no way to know which creatures deserve respect as humans and have distinctively human rights and which are not made in the image of God.

Early theologians, seriously seeking to distinguish Christian truth from non-Christian opinions, carefully chose and defined their terms. At great cost, the early Christian thinkers explained the respect in which God is one and the respect in which God is threefold. Similarly they worked hard and long to explain the respect in which Jesus Christ was human and the respect in which he was divine. Contemporary carelessness in clarifying trinitarian distinctions and the ontological deity and humanity of Christ has contributed to many leaving churches with classical Christian teaching for those with unorthodox teaching and for other religions and cults. Much unnecessary ambiguity and debate can be avoided if people speaking and writing about Christian theology will discipline themselves to define their terms as they use them.

Logic also helps people who think about the God of the Bible to realize that the final authority includes not only what the Bible explicitly asserts but also what biblical assertions presuppose. Many important controversial issues today are not addressed explicitly in Scripture, but guidance concerning these issues may come from understanding the presuppositions of Christ and the biblical writers. The biblical record does not indicate that Jesus asserted explicitly that all people are sinners. But from his concern to seek and to save the lost, we may argue that Jesus presupposed that all are sinful.

Logical presuppositions may be not only of content but also of method, or principles of reasoning. Acquaintance with the methods of logical reasoning used in certain passages can also provide data to aid students in their theological reasoning. Paul, arguing that Israel's election was by grace, not works, says, "If it were [by works], grace would no longer be grace" (Rom. 11:6). Here Paul presupposes classical logic's three laws of thought: (1) the principle of *identity*: A is A, grace is (unmerited) grace; (2) the principle of the *excluded middle*: A is not non-A, (unmerited) grace is not nongrace (or works with merit); and (3) the principle of *noncontradiction*: a thing cannot be both A and non-A, God's choice cannot be according to both grace and nongrace (works).

Some modern logicians regard these three laws as mere tautologies, but their objective validity and general applicability is presupposed by Paul's inspired argument and reflected in their usefulness for over two thousand years in all fields of disciplined thought and meaningful communication. Opponents' arguments against these laws of thought cannot be understood or even given an appearance of validity unless these three laws of thought hold for their words and sentences. Not even one side of a paradox or dialectical antithesis can mean what it says if the three laws do not hold.[16]

Given the truth of biblical assertions, logic helps students of theology draw valid inferences from them. Logically one may draw an immediate inference from a universal affirmative proposition ("all people are sinners") to a particular affirmative proposition ("John Jones is a sinner"). The Bible does not list each sinner by name. All who try to help others see the need for Christ's salvation depend on the logical validity of this inference from the truth of the universal proposition in Scripture to its truth for each particular person.[17]

The basic need for logic in religion and Christian theology is often challenged. Mystics think it inhibits experience—but logic only asks that they make sense when they interpret their experience and speak about it to others. Some biblical theologians think it is alien to the Jewish mind. But it was not alien to Paul's mind or to the thinking of other biblical writers. Differences between the Hebrew and Greek cultures may be exaggerated. Both the Hebrew Old Testament and the Greek New Testament assert that God is not a man that he should lie. Basic principles of logic may have been discovered and formulated by Aristotle, but they were not invented by Aristotle.

Logical principles, like moral principles, are rooted ultimately in the mind and nature of the Creator. Common intellectual grids enable people from vastly different cultures to overcome initial difficulties and eventually communicate with each other. Logic is as indispensable to meaningful thought as grammar is to understandable language. In this God has made no exceptions, not even for born-again students of theology. Life can become very complicated and thought confused, but it will not help in those difficult periods to throw away such a valuable tool as logic. We may need to slow down, call for division of the question, and deal with one issue at a time.

The persistent may allege that "consistency is the mark of a small mind." But as one scholar aptly replied, "Better a small mind than none at all!" No theologian claims fully to comprehend human beings, atoms, or the Bible, let alone God. But Christians who believe that God revealed truth in the Bible's sentences have a basis for speaking about that truth in coherent sentences. We know in part, as Paul said. When speaking or writing about the part we do know, Christians studying theology seek to make sense. People cannot follow our preaching or teaching if we contradict ourselves.

Like any other instrument, logical reasoning can be used either for the ultimate glory of God or for the glorification of created beings. The misuse of reason by people who made logic or something in creation their God need not keep others from responsible use of the tool in support of God's revealed purposes in the church and throughout the world. Logic is not an invention of unbelieving philosophers, but a reflection of God's mind in minds made in his image. Our ability to reason, like every other capacity, has been affected by our fallen sensuality and pride, but it has not been destroyed. The Holy Spirit renews the minds of believers so that they grow not only in grace, but also in knowledge (Col. 3:10). We will never fully comprehend God or his purposes, but we can and ought to know God and his purposes in part.

Logical reasoning helps God's will get done on earth in at least three additional ways: (1) Logical thinking helps display the coherence of the world view and way of life based on revealed truth. (2) Logically developed sermons and Bible studies help people know unequivocally what is expected of them as they face appealing contradictory options. (3) Also living consistently by a coherent belief system helps avoid hypocrisy and exemplifies Christianity's relevance for contemporary ethical and social issues.[18]

Previous Theologies: Secondary Sources With Provisional Authority. The challengin⸢ task of integrative theology cannot be accomplished by one person alone. Each theologian depends on many others, for in divine providence many have been enabled to make significant contributions to the field for nearly two thousand years. Whether ancient or recent, their interpretations, insights, syntheses, and applications are ignored to our loss. Doctrinal studies, Old or New Testament theologies, biblical theologies, and systematic theologies of others may suggest hypotheses that we would otherwise not consider. These hypotheses may deserve to be tested by the primary biblical data and, if more coherent than contradictory alternatives, applied in life and ministry.

Fortunately, some of the finest work in the past has been summed up through painstaking efforts in confessions of faith and creeds recognized in the church as being in harmony with the biblical standard. These deserve special attention as representative of a wide scholarly consensus and serve as provisional authorities for Christians as yet unable to do theological research for themselves. In this Protestant approach, creeds are not rules that rule Scripture (*norma normans*), but they are ruled by Scripture (*norma normata*).[19]

Particularly when new in the faith, like young children under the authority of their parents, Christians wisely depend rather heavily on their received traditions. But valuable as well-founded traditions in classical Christianity are, at best they can serve only as provisional authorities. They function as authorities until we have been able to check out their faithfulness to Scripture for ourselves. To the extent that they provide the most coherent account of the biblical data, they will continue to serve as consciously chosen authorities. But, and here is the provision, to the extent that received traditions do not measure up to the primary scriptural materials, they will no longer serve as norms. The only nonnegotiable authority in theology is Scripture quoted in an appropriate context from a reliable text or translation. With the Protestant Reformers, we affirm that although there are many sources of theological knowledge, there is but one inerrant, final authority: *sola scriptura*. In seeking to integrate biblical truth with other knowledge, we constantly face, for example, the issue of whether the biblical or the scientific has the priority. The liberal tradition tended to accommodate the biblical to the psychological or philosophical in order to communicate to contemporary society. Natural theology corrected scriptural theology.[20] In the process, the essence of revealed truth was lost. We must adapt our communication of theology to our generation but be alert to the great danger of accommodating the message to its errors. As Fulton J. Sheen once said, "He who marries the spirit of the age will become a widower in the age to come."

We may hope that educated young people will mature to the place of doing research for themselves. And educated Christians who desire to minister to others will mature to the place of examining alternative doctrinal hypotheses, responsibly evaluating them, and arriving at their own reflective commitments. To decide for ourselves does not mean that our conclusions will be entirely new. It does mean that they should be entirely ours.

Research Methodology: Key to Responsible Theological Decision Making. Sound theology does not arise from wishful thinking, naïve gullibility, or arbitrary leaps into the dark. Nor does it come from a haphazard quoting of creeds, Scriptures, or favorite Bible-conference speakers. Too often people have sought to do theology without giving sufficient attention to research methodology. Some such surveys of historical and contemporary theologies have left many in an anchorless sea of relativism.

How can anyone determine religious

truth in our times? Even in biblical hermeneutics many have been influenced by the impact of relativism. No one can be objective, we are told, for all come to a subject with pre-understandings. Anthony Thiselton's *The Two Horizons* contrasts the presuppositional horizon of the biblical writers and the presuppositional horizon of biblical interpreters some two thousand years later.[21] Charles Kraft's *Christianity in Culture* complicates the issue further, and properly so, by adding a third horizon, that of the people to whom we present the biblical message.[22] In the midst of at least three different sets of cultural presuppositions (not to mention possible generation gaps or subcultural perspectives within each), how can anyone know any normative propositional truth, let alone presume to declare God's truth to others with very different horizons?[23]

Admittedly no one is free from pre-understandings in any field, including Old Testament, New Testament, and theology. In all knowing, the knower actively participates, a point sometimes overlooked by pure empiricists. There is an element of subjectivity in all human knowing. Karl Marx showed that as active knowers we bring with us to any field an ideological taint. Our economic status as "haves" or "have nots" influences our outlook on life, including our theological or philosophical world views. According to Sigmund Freud, our belief system is also influenced by psychological factors resulting from early childhood experiences. John Dewey underlined the impact of early educational experiences on a scholar in any discipline. Anthropologists and missionaries have pointed to the varying influences of cultures and subcultures on Christians seeking to take essentials of the gospel to the people of these cultures for the first time.

The cumulative impact of all of these and other disciplines has led many toward a total relativism, pragmatism, and functionalism, even in theology. People are said to be not only culturally influenced but culturally determined to think and believe as they do. If God did give absolute truth in Scripture centuries ago to people with an entirely different set of preunderstandings than ours, we are hopelessly removed from that truth. And some think these considerations make it impossible even for God to have given changelessly true affirmations of truth to biblical writers in human propositions expressed in sentences in human languages.

Note on the Cultural Factor in Interpretation

People are the essentially human and fallen in all places and all times and in all cultures, but there are also real differences of art forms, music, diets, ceremonies, family customs, and governmental forms. Some imagine everything always the same; others, always totally different.

Careful interpreters of biblical literature must do justice to the similarities and the differences. They will acknowledge both the normative principles universally applicable to all people of all times and some principles normative only for a specific person or group in a specific situation. In certain situations an action may not be governed by principle but merely by wisdom or consideration of others. In delineating principles in biblical teaching, seek the biblical author's *reason* for the given principle.[24]

1. Is the reason for the principle rooted in the unchanging nature of God? (Love others because God first loved you [1 John 4:19]?) God's nature, transcending all cultural variables and racial prejudices, does not change.

2. Is the reason for the principle rooted in the uniform nature of creation, mankind, or moral law? Natural

laws, essential humanness, and creation mandates are not altered by cultural differences. However distorted or suppressed the universal requirements of the Ten Commandments—written by God on human hearts, given by Moses, and repeated in the New Testament—may be, they are universally binding (though the Sabbath need not be on the seventh day).

3. Is the principle rooted in the unchanging redemptive principles of God's plan of salvation (sheer grace, faith, the righteousness provided by the Messiah)? These do not change with the passing of a changing institution such as circumcision.

4. Is the principle rooted in character traits of Jesus Christ and produced by the Holy Spirit? Humility may be expressed in other cultures in a different way than by washing one another's feet in a society where people walked on dirt roads (John 13:12–16).

5. Are Old Testament principles reiterated in the New Testament? If so, they transcend the earlier cultures and express absolute norms (e.g., condemnation of occult practices of all sorts). But the Old Testament dietary requirements are not repeated in the New Testament and so would not be normative, though in some similar conditions (e.g., lack of refrigeration) they might be wise.

6. Even culturally specific principles may apply to others because a culture may be similar to other cultures in many respects. Eugene Nida observed that in choosing the Jewish people, God chose the greatest number of world cultures (*Message and Missions*). Also the Greek language and culture was inherited by great sectors of the human family.

To respond to the challenge of relativism we need more than a set of hermeneutical principles. Those principles themselves are in question. We need a reliable method for research derived from a reliable epistemology that has successfully interacted with relativism. Assuming a critical realism,* we hasten to point out that the

---

*Critical realism as here used is a theory of human knowing about what is (metaphysics). It maintains the reality of persons, things, and events independent of knowing them to the extent that hypotheses concerning them are confirmed by a critical (verificational) method of justifying beliefs. Critical realism is not naïve realism. For naïve realists, the oar halfway in the water is believed to be bent in reality as well as in appearance. And naïve realists believe that the railroad tracks not only appear to meet in the distance, but actually do meet. Reality is as they uncritically see it.

Neither is critical realism to be confused with common-sense (Scottish) realism. Not all the intuitions or "natural judgments" of "common sense" are true even though our minds have been made by God to know and govern reality. For finite and fallen minds to know which of our impressions conform to what is real requires a testing of hypotheses by reliable criteria of truth. A critical or verificational method is needed to distinguish actual persons, things, and events from illusions, dreams, fantasies, and hallucinations, however common (e.g., flat earth, rising sun).

Again, critical realism is not to be confused with idealism. Idealists think that since all our knowledge involves ideas, there is no reality independent of human or divine perceiving of them. However, the fire in the fireplace is not recreated when I come into the room after an hour's absence. Neither is it sustained only in the mind of the divine Perceiver during the absence of a human observer. But idealists are correct in holding that ideas (as distinct from things) are involved in all knowing. Critical realism concedes to idealism that whenever a thing is perceived, it is an object for the mind, but it does not conclude that things have no existence except in the mental perception.

The difference critical realists make between objects known and data derived from them in the mind explains several important aspects of experience. That difference makes memory

fact of multiple influences on human knowers presents an insufficient basis for concluding that we know *nothing but* our own subjective opinions. A political crisis may be reported from a variety of perspectives in *The World Press Review,* but it does not follow that its readers know nothing about the facts or events that stirred up such conflicting opinions. Furthermore, some of the reports may be better informed of the relevant data than others. While no journalist can claim total objectivity, all may agree on certain elements. Critically trained, morally responsible political observers and scientific historians may significantly overcome economic, psychological, cultural, and linguistic hurdles to write on a crisis with commendable objectivity and substantial truth.

Analogously, the fact that no theologian can claim complete objectivity does not mean that no theological statement conveys any truth. We must, however, develop our ability to identify how we have been influenced by our background and environment and consider our preunderstandings as tentative hypotheses that must be tested as severely as other people's preunderstandings in the light of objective criteria in order to arrive at responsible conclusions.

To contribute toward the ends of objective validity and maturity in doing theology, the following verificational method is proposed. Growing out of a critically realistic epistemology, it provides many checks and balances to avoid naïve, unsupported "horizons" or preunderstandings from overruling relevant principles and data. In our writing we seek to adhere to this demanding methodology in the development of each doctrine. We hope that the product will therefore be more than an exercise in bias or tradition and that it will have a higher degree of objective validity than theologies less conscious of these methodological checks and balances. But none can be more aware than we that we have not attained!

The verificational method includes five steps:

1. Genuine inquiry begins with defining a problem to be researched and becoming aware of its significance. It is impossible to work effectively on everything at once. So we must limit the scope of each doctrinal study. If too much is attempted initially, it may become necessary to divide the question into two or more studies. If the problem is to understand a scriptural passage relating to a subject, it is also helpful to try to feel what the writer felt in accord with his purpose for this writing. To research existentialist emphases on authenticity, students need to feel their disgust for hypocrisy and its effects throughout christendom. To engage in a genuine inquiry of neoorthodox emphases on God's distinctness from na-

possible and explains differences of appearances under different conditions, such as a distant light in a fog or an oar halfway submerged in water. This difference between a thing and mental data derived from it also accounts for different interpretations of the same events, and it accounts for error or illusions (for example, of a person on drugs).

In sum, critical realism retains the belief of common-sense realism in independent things but admits that these are not directly and homogeneously presented to very different knowers in very different or even similar perceptual situations. Hence a critical procedure becomes indispensable to verify or disconfirm any religious beliefs, whether derived from common sense, sensory observation, mystical intuition, rational intuition, or Holy Spirit–illumined *interpretation* of Scripture on any subject.

For further thoughts on this subject, see Elton Trueblood, *General Philosophy* (Grand Rapids: Baker, 1963), 29–45; Antony Flew, *A Dictionary of Philosophy* (New York: St. Martin's, 1979), 77; D. F. Kelly, "Scottish Realism," in *EDT, 990–91.*

ture and humanity, scholars need to feel Barth's disillusionment with liberalism's unrealistic view of human nature, its unfounded faith in the inevitability of progress, and its humanistic worship and service of the self. People need to feel poverty and powerlessness to appreciate Latin American liberation theology, seemingly endless chauvinism to begin to understand feminist theology, and discrimination and slavery to research black theology. The motivation for painstaking theological research often comes from enigmatic and even traumatic experiences in life. Sheltered students need to do their best to identify with the experiences and motivations of the leaders who shape the thinking of the theological world.

2. The theological method then discovers alternative answers to the problem by surveying relevant literature or interviewing theologians from many perspectives. No limits are placed on sources of possible hypotheses to be tested. Stimulation of thought may come from the whole spectrum of theologies, religions, philosophies, new consciousness groups, cults, and the occult. Creative contextualizations of the Christian faith may come from any cultural horizon in any country in the world. An objective survey of varied perspectives helps students become aware of their own presuppositions, much like travel overseas helps them become conscious of assumptions taken for granted as universal in their own culture. Elements of the different answers that do not contradict teachings of Scripture or each other may be combined in new syntheses.

3. All hypotheses, even those whose truth we have assumed for years, must be tested for their coherence and viability on standard criteria of truth. If they are true, we need not fear reexamination. True doctrines will not be found self-contradictory, or unrelated to reality in the external or internal worlds of human experience. Sound interpretations of a disputed passage of Scripture will without self-contradiction account for all the relevant lines of evidence: the author's purpose, grammar, and word usage; the immediate biblical context; and the broader theological context. Fitting the external givens, the hypotheses should also fit the internal givens. That is, one should be able to live by it without disillusionment or inauthenticity.

These criteria derive, not from one theological tradition, but from the Creator, his image in humanity, and common grace. On these bases we insist that however great the cultural, educational, economic, social, political, religious, and theological differences people may have, they are still human. All human beings have this in common that they all deserve respect, have inalienable rights, and ought to be treated fairly or justly as self-determined, responsible agents, not as mere victims of their environments. Furthermore, truth for all human beings is equally related to the data of reality, including logical principles of meaningful thought and communication. Among the most significant givens in human experience is the Bible. It cannot be erased from human experience, history, literature, philosophy, or theology. Every world view must give some account of its teachings. And for Christians, every theological hypothesis considered true must without contradiction account for all the relevant biblical lines of evidence.

4. After resolving preliminary or subordinate issues between alternatives that are live options, we seek to formulate the overall conclusion to the issue under inquiry. The most coherent and viable position is stated in a way faithful to the revealed truth and at the same time clear and significant for the present generation of Christians and the unreached people we serve.

5. The method applies the conclusion to the burning issues of life by determining worthy ends and values in life and service and, when possible, by suggesting more concrete ways in which to implement the conclusions as persons in families, churches, and nations.

Without a theological method of this kind, liberals and Evangelicals, Baptists and Roman Catholics will not break out of their hermeneutical circles and will fail to reduce the misunderstanding and carnal divisiveness that threaten our world.[25] Important as piety is in the doing of theology, spirituality will not by itself settle conflicting presuppositions and truth claims. Faith is indispensable to progress in any field, but fideism alone will not change the conflicting claims made by believers. Although the object of faith may be unseen, the evidence for a belief is seen and needs to be examined with sound methodology.

Without the witness of the Holy Spirit to the truth of the gospel and our appropriation of its benefits, Christian theology is about an alien universe. But the Spirit witnesses to truth discovered in evidence. Apart from evidence of truth about reality in general or special revelation, the Holy Spirit does not provide a method for resolving conflicting theological claims. The Spirit of truth guides people into truth through illumined, accountable uses of the mental capacities he gave the church.

Intuitive insights may come from God or other sources independently of historical and scriptural evidence. Any intuitive insights alleged to be from God must fit together into a consistent whole that squares with Scripture and reality as we face it daily. Carefully interpreted scriptural teaching must test intuitions, not the other way around (1 John 4:1–3).

Much spiritual-life teaching today seems to make intuition not only a source of truth but also the highest test of truth. Watchman Nee's trichotomy elevates the intuitive capacity to the highest "part" of a human being (the spirit) and demotes the reasoning capacity to a lower "part" (the soul).[26] On this analysis, direct intuitions ("word of knowledge," "prophecies," etc.) are often believed to constitute a higher, "spiritual knowledge" than knowledge that comes through a reasoned exegesis of Scripture: Reasoning from nature or the Scriptures is considered "soulish." However, depravity has seriously affected not only our reasoning capacities but also our intuitive capacities. Ideas derived intuitively can be as carnal as those derived by misuse of reasoning from the Scriptures. Either source of knowledge may be deceptive. If there is to be growth in grace and knowledge, the entire person, including the intuitive abilities, must be brought into harmony with the truth of the Creator-God revealed in the historic Christ and the inspired Scriptures. And the God of nature, Christ, and Scripture is maturely known through some method such as that outlined in the five steps above, not merely through direct intuitions without checks and balances.

All who would do more than report the theology of others, must determine whether in controversial issues the final court of appeal is immediate intuitive insight independent of scriptural study or thorough research of the issue in a verificational method. Faithful stewards of divine revelation have found no successful substitute for the disciplined use of a fruitful research method. The sooner gifted young people devote their best intellectual efforts to such a systematic study of the Word with faithful prayer, the sooner they will meet qualifications for ministry and lead thinking people and churches to greater piety, faith, Spirit-attested truth, and wholesome spirituality. The ultimate key to spirituality is not our own immediate experience, however sincere, life-transforming, and important that may be, but divinely revealed truth. Truth is not falsified by our lack of experience but the authenticity of our experience is tested by truth.

Summation

We can now succinctly state what integrative theology is ideally and what it is not. The significance of these points will become increasingly clear in the development of subsequent chapters.

Integrative theology seeks to be human, not humanistic; person-related, not merely relational; situation-related, not situation-bound; biblical, not biblicistic; subjective, not subjectivistic; historically related, not culture-bound or historicistic; verifiable, not positivistic; experience-related, not experience-bound; critically realistic, not naïvely realistic; rational, not rationalistic; classically relevant, not relativistic; normative, not merely descriptive; presuppositionally conscious, not uncritical; scientific, not scientistic; assertive, not arbitrary; systematic, not omniscient; coherent, not fully comprehended; substantially viable, not liveable to perfection in this life.

APOLOGETIC INTERACTION

Influenced by the analytic approaches of the twentieth century, both biblical scholars and philosophers tended to abandon integrative syntheses of thought such as systematic theologies and comprehensive philosophies. Can some of their antisystematic reasoning be answered from an integrative approach?

Is an Integrative Theology Possible Philosophically?

Among the philosophies arrayed against systematic and integrative theology are logical positivism, philosophical analysis, nontheistic existentialism, pragmatism, and Marxism-Leninism. In their opposition to developing a theological *Weltanschauung* (world view) they form a kind of secular humanist consensus. Opposition also arises from a humanist consensus of Eastern Hindu and Buddhist, occult, and the new-consciousness movements. It is impossible to respond here to each of these, but we can give a brief indication of directions answers might take.

The powerful impact of the positivists' verifiability criterion of meaning and truth led Clark Pinnock to say, "The question of questions for our time is the very possibility of any theology at all."[27] An invisible divine Spirit cannot be verified according to a strict interpretation of the verifiability criterion, and thus talk about God is meaningless. Theological definitions are either tautologies or merely the venting of feelings. Testimonies of religious experiences, said A. J. Ayer, provide interesting material for abnormal psychology.[28]

However, the positivists' own division of sentences into but two categories, meaningful and meaningless, turned out to be nonsense because it is unverifiable. Verifiability "died the death of a thousand qualifications." In these times of nuclear proliferation anyone who declares nonsensical sentences about justice (also invisible), cannot be taken seriously. In 1980 A. J. Ayer himself signed the Secular Humanist Declaration, which contains a number of invisible and unverifiable values. For example, the statement about the value of the scientific method ("We believe the scientific method, though imperfect, is still the most reliable way of understanding the world") cannot be verified by the five senses in a laboratory experiment. It is more a philosophical or epistemological judgment than a scientific statement. People who accept the case of logical positivism or scientism against theology must on the same grounds be prepared to give up *all* of the highest values in life.

The end result of mere empiricism is the loss of the empiricist's self. Limiting all knowledge to mere sensory impressions, David Hume received no impression of his soul or self receiving impressions. This led to the loss of inner dignity and responsibility. In an attempt to enhance human worth, secular humanism tends to destroy the self-determining, personal agent who was to have dominion over his environment rather than be determined by it. One total empiricist vainly trying to live by the philosophy greeted another one morning, saying, "You are fine; how am I?"

Existentialists sought to overcome the tragic oversight of the self in empiricism by giving priority to the individual, existing person. We must first become aware that the full responsibility of our existence rests on ourselves. No fixed human nature limits human freedom. No God, Jean-Paul Sartre insists, prescribes values or issues commands. We cannot abstract a universal essence of goodness from good acts, nor a universal essence of humanness from a number of persons. The slogan "Existence precedes essence" means, among other things, that no essences can be known.

It follows that, if there is no God and if there are no objectively valid ethical principles, there can be not only no normative theology but no objectively valid statements about anything. Why then should Sartre expect us to consider the assertion, "Existence precedes essence" as anything more than an expression of his own feeling? Has that statement any value beyond a description of his subjectivism? We have acknowledged an element of subjectivity in our knowledge of objectively valid truths. If Sartre wants an element of objectivity in his basic theses, then objective validity is possible. Other truths that are true for everyone may eventually be found and related to one another coherently so that a synthesis of these truths might gradually develop. We may even find that such changeless truths rest ultimately in a changeless mind, the Logos of God!

Marx reacted against Hegel's talk of empty consciousness and spoke persuasively of practical activity in real life. If theology or philosophy is viewed as an independent branch of activity apart from the taintedness of economics and dialectical determinations, it has no value whatever.

Opposing abstraction as much as Marx did, William James, psychologist and pragmatist, even dismissed the notion of "truth" as an abstraction. The question "What is truth?" is not a real question because it is not relative to any conditions. The concept of truth, James said, is a mere abstraction from truths (in the plural). Mistakenly, James thought that if one system was right, every other must be wrong. He failed to allow for elements of truth in systems that need be logically wrong only where they contradicted the Christian faith. Needless to say, William James rejected those elements of other philosophies that contradicted the presuppositions of pragmatism, implying the objective validity of the law of noncontradiction.

If William James or John Dewey had adequately defined pragmatism, the definition would constitute an abstraction that all ought to accept. If all knowledge must operationally work for us, satisfy us, or promote our adaptation to our environment, we have some normative abstractions (depending on the definition of "work" and "satisfy" and whether the "environment" includes eternal surroundings) according to which a system develops. The writings of James and Dewey were basically consistent with their assumptions, except for their claim to avoid abstractions from particulars in universal and normative truths. An absolute relativism is self-contradictory. Some truths are known and advanced as valid for all. What we know we need to understand and communicate coherently. In doing that, like it or not, we are involved in culture-transcending systems of thought.

Another attack on integrative syntheses has come from a very different perspective, that of Eastern and occult monism. Hinduism in its countless forms has affirmed the ultimate reality of Brahman, but allegedly no true statements can be made about that transcendent being. Although alleged to be beyond all thought, Brahman can be experienced in an ineffable, temporary, passive, mystical union. In this union distinctions between the knower and the known, subject and object become meaningless. All is one. No duality can be maintained in reality, even between good and evil. Distinctions are made only in *maya* (appearance). Illusory propositional truth *seems* to be of value, but in reality it is not of value. Any theology claiming propositional revelation true for God and humanity is consigned to the illusions of maya. And any theology based on a distinction between good and evil that holds for God and dependent man becomes illusory.

The Buddhist doctrine of maya, Alan Watts found, has remarkable similarity to the Western doctrine of relativism. It alleges that things, events, and persons are delineated not by nature, but by human description, and the way in which we divide or describe them is relative to our varying illusory points of view. We can know no distinct thing or person in reality. A thing or person can be said to be nothing more than the sum total of these relationships, dependencies, influences, effects, and determinations. Things in themselves cannot be known. Only relationships can be known. Personal identity has slipped into the "reality" of the shining sea, never to be distinguished again.

Those who on the basis of Eastern relativistic assumptions oppose systematic doctrines about God as he is revealed to be in himself need to remember that the same assumptions rule out any knowledge of themselves, others, and things. No universals can be known, only changing relationships, whatever these may be or, rather, become. Not even ideals can survive. So Watts writes, "Be not concerned with right and wrong. The conflict between right and wrong is the sickness of the mind."[29] Instead, cultivate a bland indifference. Decide without having the faintest understanding of how you do it. Yet Alan Watts published 222 relatively coherent pages about unspeakable religious experience in *Beyond Theology: The Art of Godmanship*, in addition to numerous other books.[30]

The self-contradictions inherent in these challenges to systematic thought in general, and systematic thought in theology in particular, are evident. Their relativism and amorality does not adequately fit the facts of human valuational or moral experience. The perspectives underlying these challenges are impossible to live by without assuming our continuous identity and responsibility. But that responsibility would be meaningless if there were no moral Judge to whom we will give account.

We need not reject coherent thought in order to find existentially, pragmatically, and mystically significant experience. Rather, fulfilling Christian experience of the living God comes through a growing appreciation of the coherent truth and vital relevance of his revelation in the person of Christ and the teachings of Scripture.

Is an Integrative Theology Possible Biblically?

Much recent "biblical theology" opposes generalizations or abstractions from the Scripture's immediate historical and cultural contexts and considers systematic theology impossible and illegitimate. The Bible's message, many biblical theologians argue, is timebound and limited to the events to which it refers in their historical, cultural contexts. Of relative validity only, the writers' messages cannot be harmonized with each other or generalized with normative authority for all people of all times and places. The practical outcome for ministers is that they can present only a situational theology from case studies in "expository" messages and not normative doctrinal messages with legitimate authority for all situations.

John Bright, for example, in *The Authority of the Old Testament* claims that the normative authority does not rest in the Bible's timeless abstract teachings but in its events. Bright's Bible as such has no final authority and is not given by God.[31] It is not to be used as a compendium of doctrine, since a harmonious system of biblical teaching is considered impossible.[32] Not even Paul's letters justify systematics, for their propositions are not revelation, nor are the sentences conveying them verbally inspired.[33] Paul's letters simply summon people to new life in Christ.[34]

Bright's caricature of systematic theology bears little resemblance to the discipline here presented. Except for affirming that the Bible is fully inspired in all its parts, Bright's notion of theology deserves rejection. According to Bright, systematic theology quotes verses in a mechanical way to set forth what is intelligible to the individual theologian or his denomination. It introduces categories foreign to the Bible's historical nature and terminology that is not part of the faith of its writers in their own times and cultures.

The conventional rubrics—God, man, sin, and salvation—force the biblical materials into a Procrustean bed of nonbiblical, Greek philosophical origin.[35]

Bright's inductive approach to the historical events is as incapable of discovering changeless kerygmatic truth as scientism is of discovering moral absolutes. Behind the varieties of biblical expression, the biblical theologian finds one common center of unity, namely, that history is the theater of God's purposive activity. But beliefs are not to be identified with the biblical expressions.[36] These beliefs do not permit metaphysical or ontological knowledge of God, for Bright's horizon is limited to the phenomenal realm of history.

Bright's approach raises some of the most basic issues between biblical and systematic theology. Is it possible to abstract normative principles for all times from the detailed historical and cultural context of biblical narratives? In the diversity of biblical writings addressing a variety of situations, can we find unified teaching on basic topics or do we have many conflicting christologies and soteriologies? Is there a noncontradictory harmony of biblical doctrines contained in the biblical text? Is a biblically rooted theology totally discontinuous with philosophy or is there some common ground?

In response to these questions Bright has overlooked scriptural examples of condensed, transferable statements of duty and doctrine. The Bible itself on occasion abstracts generalizations applicable in every context in all times and places. Apparently the extensive legislation of the Pentateuch could be summed up in the Book of the Covenant (Exod. 20–24) and condensed further in the Ten Commandments (Exod. 20:1–17). Jesus even further condensed the ten into two (Matt. 22:36–40). The writer of Hebrews abstracted several elementary teachings from their historical contexts: repentance from acts of laying on of hands, the resurrection of the dead, and eternal judgment (Heb.

6:1–2). These doctrines may summarize emphases of the previous Jewish dispensation preparing the way for Christ's coming. Whether they reflect pre-Christian or early Christian teaching, or both, the point is the same: a condensed statement of doctrines abstracted from their initial settings in literary narrative is not contrary to biblical precedent.

The New Testament also recognizes certain coherent patterns of gospel teachings in faithful words. The supposition that early Christians had no fixed pattern of teachings that regulated thought and practice is entirely alien to the apostle's ethic.[37] Paul summed up the core of the gospel that was according to the Scriptures, not merely behind them in events (1 Cor. 15:3–4). And Paul judged people's lives by what was "contrary to the sound doctrine that conforms to the glorious gospel of the blessed God," which God had entrusted to him (1 Tim. 1:10–11). The gospel was expressed in faithful sayings passed on to Timothy (1 Tim. 1:15), and these sayings were worth defending (1 Tim. 1:18; 2 Tim. 1:13–14) and transmitting to other reliable men (2 Tim. 2:1–2).

Paul praised members of the church at Rome for wholeheartedly obeying the form (*typos,* pattern) of teaching received (Rom. 6:17). The Thessalonians' faith in "the Lord's message" was well known (1 Thess. 1:7), and Paul exhorted them to "hold to" and "live according to the teaching" received from the apostles" (2 Thess. 3:6).

Just as the tabernacle was built according to a pattern (*typos,* Heb. 8:5), so faith and life conformed to a pattern of sound doctrine. The same pattern applied not only in different geographical areas but to both Jews and Greeks (Acts 20:21), showing that the gospel message conveyed in human language transcended prejudicial cultural boundaries and did not fluctuate in different cultural settings. Of greater concern

than life itself to Paul was "testifying to the gospel of God's grace" (Acts 20:24). And in his parting plea to pastors Paul called on them to guard the gospel, the word of God's grace (Acts 20:28–32).

Granting that the Bible summarizes and abstracts both law and gospel from their original historical situations, do we depart from Scripture when we consider how law and gospel relate to each other? If it is proper to do so within the work or works of one writer, is it impossible to find a coherent teaching on law and gospel in all the different summations of them by all the writers in the same Testament? And then would there not be value in relating teaching on law and on the gospel in both Testaments? Might it then not also be helpful to consider the relation of law and gospel to the law written on all human hearts (Rom. 2:14–15)? Would it be departing from Scripture (or too "philosophical") to consider the relation of all that revelation teaches on law to all that it teaches on gospel?

For integrative theology to "put all Scripture on a subject together" is no less biblical than for biblical theologians who accept propositional revelation to do the same with a selected part of the biblical corpus. The Scriptures are the primary source of information for systematic theology as much as for biblical theology. The main difference between the two types of theology lies in their organizing principles, which are chronological and logical respectively. Biblical theology stresses the concepts of law and gospel in different writers at their particular stage in the progress of revelation. Systematic theology synthesizes the teaching of all the biblical writers on basic topics in a logical order.

Can either discipline accomplish its purpose while limiting itself to biblical words and categories of thought alone? With due respect for the Holy Spirit's inspiration of the original wording, must we stay with the original languages? To be obliged to stay with the words of Scripture alone would destroy all exposition and interpretation of Scripture, not systematic theology alone. What interpreters take from Scripture must be distinguished from what is given by Scripture, as the differences among commentators and biblical theologians indicate. If different wordings cannot be used, interpreters cannot make clear in what way they are taking the Bible's teaching. Furthermore, truth is not merely a matter of words but of propositional content, and the same assertion can be made in different words in different languages, or in the same language in direct or indirect quotations or active and passive moods.

To allege that we must use the same words as Scripture does would render useless all preaching and teaching of the Bible. A minister or teacher could do nothing but read Scripture. Authors could not write about Scripture. A Calvinist could not be distinguished from an Arminian or a Pelagian, nor a trinitarian from a nontrinitarian. Sometimes a given word is used with different meanings in different biblical contexts. Only by expressing the sense of the context can the meanings of even biblical terms be clear. The contextual sense can be determined only by the wording, but its expression is not limited to the wording of a sentence, paragraph, or book.

Biblical theologians suggest that systematic theologians often introduce categories alien to the Scriptures. Can we use different general ways of thinking in systematics? Existentialist and neo-orthodox theologians speak of authenticity as persons and of personal encounters. Relational theologians emphasize personal relationships. Process theologians limit themselves to process forms of thought. Functional theologians speak repeatedly of functions. Orthodox theologians have for centuries spoken also of substances or essences and attributes of things and of persons in relationships.

All students of theology must determine which ways of thinking are validly inferred from Scripture, and none can avoid the use of categories of thought in understanding and communicating its teaching. Often fundamentalists, Barthians, and biblical theologians who imagine themselves most free from philosophical categories are subconsciously influenced by them. Biblical theologians who attack systematic theologians as too influenced by philosophy exhibit the phenomenalistic and antiabstractionist tendencies of certain modern philosophies. Thinkers cannot avoid categories. But categories are not explicitly set forth in Scripture. So theologians, whether organizing their material chronologically or logically, use "philosophical" categories such as existence, being, person, relationship, or function. The only questions are whether they choose their categories consciously or unconsciously and whether the choice is based on valid scriptural inferences or not.

In summary, biblical theology interprets passages relevant to a given topic and abstracts the teaching of those passages for a given writer or period of Old Testament or New Testament history. Having summed up the teaching for different periods of biblical history, some may abstract further to the teaching of all the biblical materials in progressive revelation on a given topic in a logical manner.

Biblical theology brings out differences of emphasis in the concepts by different writers at different periods, and ideally it does so without doing injustice to their unity. Systematic theology shows the unity of the teaching throughout the Scriptures, and ideally it does so without doing injustice to the differences at different stages in the progress of revelation.

Systematic theology then relates the different doctrines to each other coherently. This it does by presenting a unified view of theology proper, humanity, moral law, sin, Christ, the atonement, the gospel, the Spirit and the experience of salvation, and the church and its mission.

If in their initial steps biblical theologians do not limit themselves to biblical language and categories, why should systematic theologians in the next stage of abstraction be considered unbiblical? If generalizations are possible in dealing with individual books, writers, and periods of biblical history, why not for all the periods together? If the abstractions of biblical theologians can be documented from Scripture without a charge of proof-texting, may not also those of systematic theologians?

The case against systematics from the side of biblical theology has provided a healthy warning to avoid biblically unjustified importations into integrative theology. But the case either proves too much and so also destroys biblical theology or it fails to justify a bias against all verificationally derived systematic thinking about scriptural revelation. The challenging task remains, then, for people in integrative theology to derive from the primary and secondary sources a coherent world view and way of life in harmony with the explicit and implicit teaching of Scripture.

RELEVANCE FOR LIFE AND MINISTRY

Integrative theology contributes to healthy spiritual experience and service to others in a number of ways.

Truth Essential to Spirituality

Truth is not spirituality, but without it authentic spiritual experience is impossible. Spirituality is not merely a feeling of dependence on God (as Schleiermacher taught). Neither is spirituality merely a life poured out in service to others (as Paul Van Buren declared in his view of secular theology). Genuine spirituality is not an ecstatic experience of union with a nonpersonal Ground of Being (as held by Paul Tillich and Eastern mysticism). Distinctively Christian spiritual experience is not merely encountering a person believed without evidence to be divine (as neoorthodoxy and relational theology maintain). Christian spirituality is experience directed away from idols and demons to the living God by revealed scriptural truths. By reliable biblical doctrine those who are wise test the spirits to see whether they are of God. Then they enjoy personal fellowship with the God of the Bible and, dependent on his grace, pour out their lives in service to others.

Truth Important to Fellowship Between Persons

Truth expressed in words is a means of fellowship between persons. Words are utterances of spirit. Although there may be nonverbal indications of fellowship, through words spirits hold the most meaningful fellowship with spirits. As Andrew Murray said long ago, "In a man's words he reveals himself to the one who receives his promise. In his commands he sets forth his will."[38] Analogously, Murray said of God:

When God speaks forth Himself in His words, He does indeed give Himself, His love, His life, His will and His power to those who receive these words, in a reality passing comprehension. In every promise He puts Himself in our power to share with Him His will, His Holiness, His perfection. In God's Word is nothing less than the Eternal Son, Jesus Christ. And so all Christ's words and God's words are full of a Divine quickening life and power.[39]

Truth a Vehicle of Life and Power

Jesus himself is not the only dynamic source of spiritual life. The truth of the Old Testament, Jesus maintained, will remain, though heaven and earth disappear (Matt. 5:17, 18). Jesus, endued with the Holy Spirit, quoted the Old Testament and withstood Satan's three great temptations (Matt. 4:1–11). Of his own words Jesus said, "The *words* I have spoken to you are spirit and they are life" (John 6:63). Jesus later said, "If you hold to my teaching, you are really my disciples. Then you will know the truth, and the truth will set you free" (John 8:31–32). The words of Scripture need not become an idol standing between a person and the living God. They are vehicles of enduring meaning that the Spirit illumines in order to convey to mankind life, truth, power, and freedom.

Truth an Ingredient in Personal Faithfulness

"Truth" can mean both instruction and faithfulness.[40] As instruction it conveys a witness concerning what is and ought to be. Thus, Jesus taught in words what was and what ought to be. He also exemplified the personal fidelity of one who knows ultimate reality and God's ethical demands. Jesus not only taught the truth, he is the truth. In the mind truth is reliable information; in the life truth is faithfulness to the realities of which it speaks.

Truth the Criterion of Authentic Spiritual Experiences

The key to authentic spiritual experiences is assent to God's revelation as reliably informative about what is in reality and what ought to be. Then life can be faithfully devoted to the truly real and the most significant.

Without reliable information one may expend his life for nothing; without faithfulness to the highest values, one may be a hypocrite. On the one hand a merely doctrinaire view of truth may lead to an empty idealism or an arrogant legalism. On the other hand, an undirected commitment may lead to a blind emotionalism, a frustrated activism, or a tragic discontinuity with what is or ought to be.[41]

So it is by doctrinal truth concerning Christ that we must test encountered spirits to see whether they are of God (1 John 4:1–3).

It has been in vogue to say that today the important thing is not Christianity's truth but its relevance. That is like saying to the sick that the important point is not the accuracy of the prescription, but taking the medicine. In determining which of the innumerable kinds of medicine to take, how much, and how often, nothing is more important than the accuracy of the doctor's prescription. In the taking of the proper medicine in the proper amounts at the proper times, nothing is more important than faithfulness. If we choose between accurate information and fidelity, we do so to our own harm. *Both* are crucial for their respective purposes. One is not a good substitute for the other. Accurate information from reliable Scriptures concerning authentic spirituality and faithfulness to it are both necessary to a healthy spiritual life.

Truth Indispensable to Distinctively Christian Service

Sound theological understanding underlies distinctively Christian ministry. Servants who understand their master's purposes have a clearer sense of mission. Theological perception of God's program in the world helps formulate long-range goals in life for those who would do his will on earth. Servants who know who they are can function more freely with a sense of identity as not only metaphysical but also moral and spiritual children of God.

Theology determines whether the world needs to be evangelized, whether evangelism is urgent, and why. Theological considerations are important to formulating the message that is initially to be proclaimed to non-Christians. It helps Christian servants understand their roles in relation to the work of the Holy Spirit as they endeavor to lead people to faith in Christ. Theological reflection enables Christians to determine priorities in a maturing Christian life.

Theology contributes to determining whether a church is necessary and what is needed to make a church what it ought to be. From a theological base we determine what is essential to a Christian church, whether conditions of membership, reasons for discipline, ordinances, offices, and ministries and mission in the world today.

The theologically reflective grow in seeing all of life, individually and collectively, from the perspective of God's revealed truth. As they do so they respond with gratitude in devotional commitment to God. "Christian discipleship focuses on the authentic meaning of faith; Christian mission focuses on its consequences for life." Again, "If action lacks rootage in a characteristic Christian motivation, it will lose its identity as witness to the gospel and becomes simply our own good works. . . . There is only one remedy for this malaise: a conscious recovery of the life principle of the church, Christian devotion."[42]

ALTERNATIVE APPROACHES TO THEOLOGY IN THE CHURCH

The Patristic Period

Systematic theology first found expression in the East, particularly in Alexandria, where in 185 a Christian catechetical school was founded. In that cosmopolitan center Clement (c. 155–c. 200) used Greek philosophy to show on the one hand that Christianity is the one rational philosophy and to expose on the other hand the fallacies of Gnosticism. Ordering his theology around the doctrine of the Logos, Clement stressed the eternal preexistence, incarnation, and redemptive work of the Word. Against heretics who claimed an esoteric *gnosis,* Clement insisted that Christianity is the true *gnosis* and that followers of Christ are the true gnostics. Clement's theology is set forth in three works: *Address to the Greeks, The Tutor,* and *Miscellanies.*

Origen (c. 185–c. 254), who taught at catechetical schools in Alexandria and Caesarea, was described by Jerome as "a teacher second only to the great Apostle." A gifted philologist, exegete, dogmatician, and apologist, Origen is regarded as the leading theologian of the early church. His work *On First Principles* (218–230) was the first major systematic formulation of Christian doctrine. Origen's theology represents a synthesis of scriptural teaching (often allegorically derived) and contemporary Greek philosophy.

The school of Asia Minor is represented by Irenaeus (c. 130–c. 202), the anti-Gnostic theologian. In his classic work *Against Heresies* (181–189) Irenaeus refuted Gnostic doctrines and expounded the leading tenets of the Christian system. He asserted the unity of the Godhead against the Gnostic demiurges, the incarnation of God in flesh, redemption through the God-man, and the future resurrection of the body. Compared with the Logos theology of earlier fathers, Irenaeus's theology is a theology of the historic Christ.

During this golden age of exegesis and theology, the main doctrines of the Christian faith were refined through the process of refuting sundry errors. Athanasius (296–373), bishop of Alexandria, defended for fifty years the deity of the incarnate Word against the Arians. His classic essay *The Incarnation of the Word* (318) discusses the fall of the race and the dilemma this posed for God. In order to destroy sin and redeem the creature, God became man in Jesus of Nazareth. To be an effectual Savior, Jesus Christ had to be coequal, coeternal, and consubstantial with God the Father. Athanasius's exposition of the Trinity is one of the outstanding theological essays of all time.

The three Cappadocian theologians Basil of Caesarea (c. 329–379), Gregory of Nazianzus (330–389), and Gregory of Nyssa (c. 334–395) were largely responsible for the formula that settled the Arian controversy. Gregory of Nazianzus, acclaimed "The Theologian," preached five celebrated *Theological Orations* against the Arians, in which he argued for the equality of the Father and the Son and the consubstantiality of the Spirit with the Father and the Son. Gregory of Nyssa wrote an important *Catechetical Oration* (383)—a manual for new converts—that expounded the essential Christian doctrines: God, Creation, Fall, the Incarnation of Christ, the Atonement, the sacraments, and eschatology. John of Damascus (c. 675–c. 794), the last of the Greek fathers, wrote *The Orthodox Faith* in one hundred chapters. This work served as the classic statement of Greek patristic theology.

In the West, Hilary of Potiers (315–386) wrote *On the Trinity,* an important treatise against the Arians. Ambrose (340–397), the leading churchman of the fourth century, drafted several theological treatises dealing with the Incarnation, the Resurrection, and the Holy Spirit. Jerome, the great biblical scholar, wrote many exegetical commentaries and numerous letters, some of which were rich in theological content. The greatest Latin theologian and the towering figure of Christendom's first 750 years was Augustine (354–430), bishop of Hippo. Augustine wrote profound theological treatises against the Manichaeans, Donatists, Arians, and Pelagians. His monumental essay *On the Trinity* (399–419) summarized patristic teaching and advanced his own understanding of the Godhead. His *Enchiridion,* or *Handbook,* outlined, via an exposition of the Apostles' Creed, the main features of Augustine's theology. *The City of God* presents the first comprehensive philosophy of history within an explicitly theological framework. Augustine's views on church and sacraments reflected a growing trend toward Roman theology, whereas his emphases on universal inherited guilt, the bondage of the will, election, and the effectual grace of God in salvation was a catalyst for the thought of Luther and Calvin.

Medieval Theology

During the medieval era, patristic authorities were collected and arranged according to preestablished categories. In time, tradition was placed on a par with the Bible as the source of theology. Medieval theology also reflected a shift from the spirituality of the fathers to an external sacramentalism. The theology of the Eucharist, for example, developed into the dogma of transubstantiation and the Mass. Medieval Catholic theology also became increasingly Pelagian, thus provoking the protest of the sixteenth-century Reformers. The twelfth century saw the rise, the thirteenth the zenith, and the fourteenth and fifteenth centuries the decline of medieval scholasticism.

Because of the speculative and dialectical character of his theology, Anselm of Canterbury (c. 1033–1109) earned the title "the father of medieval scholasticism." Anselm's *Monologion* and *Proslogion* set forth, respectively, the bishop's cosmological and ontological arguments for God's existence. *Cur Deus Homo* (*Why God Became Man*), perhaps the greatest work on the Atonement ever written, propounds a biblical rationale for Christ's work on the cross. Another important scholastic theologian, Peter Abelard (1079–1142), emphasized the role of reason in theology: "A doctrine is believed not because God has said it, but because it has been proven to be so." His chief work, *Yes and No*, presents seemingly contradictory views from the fathers on a wide range of doctrines and practices. Abelard also wrote an *Introduction to Theology* in three books (1136). A third leading theologian of the period was Peter Lombard (c. 1100–60), bishop of Paris. His *Four Books of Sentences* (c. 1150) brought together sayings from the fathers ordered around the main theological headings, namely, the Trinity, Creation, Redemption, and the Sacraments and Last Things. The *Sentences*, Aristotelian in orientation, became a leading textbook for several hundred years.

Stimulated by the rise of the universities and the revival of Aristotelianism in the West via Latin translations of Arabic texts, the thirteenth century is known as "the golden age of scholasticism." In this period was Thomas Aquinas, the chief theologian of the second 750 years of the church. The "Angelic Doctor" affirmed a rational ontology that drew a sharp distinction between philosophy and theology, between nature and grace. Thomas's Aristotelian theology is set forth in *Summa Contra Gentiles* (1261–64) and in the seventeen large volumes of the unfinished *Summa Theologica* (1265–72). For centuries it has remained the classic treatment of medieval Roman Catholic theology.

The decline of medieval theology in the fourteenth and fifteenth centuries need not long detain us. William of Ockham (c. 1280–1349), the English commentator on Peter Lombard's *Sentences*, attacked the scholastic procedure of wedding Aristotelian philosophy to Christian theology. God is known, not by rational inference, but by reception of divine revelation by faith. The nominalist theology of Ockham and of Gabriel Biel (1420–95) further asserted the power of human free will and weakened the operation of divine grace. The gradual demise of speculative theology prompted the renewed medieval quest for God through mystical experience. Thus Meister Eckhart (c. 1260–1327), John Tauler (c. 1300–61), and Henry Suso (c. 1300–66) promoted in sermons and tracts the merger of the human soul into the reality of God. Suso, for example, strove to become one with God "as a drop of water mingles with a cask of wine."

Era of the Reformation

During the medieval era Roman Catholic theology became corrupted with the doctrine of salvation by works, the veneration of relics, the idea of a treasury of merit, and the sale of indulgences. Abuses such as these led to the protest movement known as the Reformation. Guided by the themes *sola scriptura, sola gratia,* and *sola fide,* the Protestant Reformers forged a return to the teachings of the Bible as the primary authority.

Martin Luther (1483–1546), the Augustian monk and Wittenberg professor, turned from legalistic works and guilt to the Bible, where he discovered the theme of justification by grace through faith. Luther's theology followed the main outlines of Augustianism. A churchman and biblical scholar, Luther wrote no systematic theology. His doctrinal distinctives are set forth in numerous treatises, particularly in two epoch-making commentaries, *Lectures on Romans* (1515) and *Lectures on Galatians* (1535). Philip Melanchthon

(1497–1560) was the leading theologian of the Lutheran wing of the Reformation. His work *Leading Conceptions in Theology* (*Loci communes*, 1521) was the first systematic theology of the Reformation, focusing on the authority of the Bible, law and Gospel, justification by faith, and the forgiveness of sins.

Ulrich Zwingli (1484–1531) was the first of the Reformed theologians. From his humanistic background Zwingli wrestled with the issues of original sin, predestination, the work of Christ, the nature of the church, and the two sacraments. A succinct statement of Zwingli's position is preserved in his *Sixty-Seven Theses* (1523) and in *An Exposition of the Faith* (1529). The leading theologian of the modern era is John Calvin (1509–64). Melanchthon designated St. Paul as "the apostle," St. Thomas as "the philosopher," and Calvin as "the theologian." As Luther stressed the doctrine of justification by faith, Calvin emphasized the sovereignty of God and his inscrutable will. Calvin's theological treatises, commentaries, and sermons (some eight hundred in all) occupy fifty-nine quarto volumes. Calvin's *Institutes of the Christian Religion* (1559) engaged the Reformer's energies for thirty years. Calvin's purpose in the *Institutes* was to expound the "Christian philosophy" that God gave in the Bible. It has been said that "no system exceeds it in comprehensiveness, precision, lucidity, and literary elegance."[43]

The Protestant Reformation forced Rome to reexamine and redefine its own doctrinal stance. At the Council of Trent (1545–63) the diverse strands of medieval theology were woven together into a tapestry of authoritative dogma. Trent established (1) Scripture (the Apocrypha included) and tradition as coequal authorities; (2) the Roman Catholic church as the authoritative determiner of the canon and interpreter of Scripture; (3) the doctrine of justification by faith and subsequent works; and (4) the validity of the seven sacraments through which saving grace is mediated. In addition, at Trent the dogma of transubstantiation and the practice of indulgences were commended to the faithful.

Modern Theology

Protestant orthodoxy in the seventeenth century produced numerous dogmatic theologies from both Lutheran and Reformed perspectives. Energetic theologians strove to consolidate the theological positions of the Reformers. There is some validity in the criticism that rational definition of doctrines tended to supplant the freshness and vigor of Reformational theology. Scholasticizing tendencies appear in the writings of both Lutheran and Reformed theologians of the period.[44]

The leading dogmatician of Lutheran orthodoxy, John Gerhard of Jena (1582–1637), prepared the massive *Theological Commonplaces* in twenty-three volumes (1610–22). Although it emphasized Aristotelian categories and terminology, the work became the classic of Lutheran theology. Abraham Calov (1612–86), the prodigious Wittenberg theologian, wrote the twelve-volume *System of Theological Themes* (1655–77). Calov's militant passion for orthodoxy is reflected in his prayer, "Fill me, O Lord, with hatred of heretics."[45] Dogmatic texts with a decided scholastic bent were prepared by J. A. Quenstedt (1617–88), J. W. Baier (1647–95), and David Hollaz (1707).

For Reformed theology the seventeenth century was an era of controversy. Jacob Arminius of Leyden (1560–1609) protested the extreme supralapsarianism of Theodore Beza (1519–1605). Arminius's followers published the *Five Articles of the Remonstrants* (1610) that limited the salvific decree to those whom God foresaw would trust Christ. The Synod of Dort (1618–19) settled the dispute in favor of the majority Reformed party. Not a few of the Remonstrants (free-spirited successors to the Arminians) lapsed into Socinianism or rationalism (e.g., Grotius, Limborch, Wettstein).

In the mainstream of Calvinist orthodoxy Johannes Wollebius (1586–1629) prepared *Compendium of Christian Theology* (1626), a classic work developed under the two headings, "The Knowledge of God" and "The Service of God." Gisbert Voetius of Holland (1589–1676) wrote the pious yet polemical five-volume dogmatics *Selected Theological Disputations* (1648–69), while Johannes Cocceius (1602–69) forged a new direction by ordering theology about the poles of the covenant of works and the covenant of grace. In Geneva Francis Turretin's (1623–87) four-volume *Institutio Theologiae Elencticae* (1688) exercised much influence on Reformed theology, especially on nineteenth-century American Presbyterianism. Meanwhile in France, Moise Amyraut (1596–1664) of the Saumur Academy propounded in *Treatise on Predestination* (1634) the theory of hypothetical universalism that was opposed by both the *Formula Consensus Helvetica* (1675) and the Zurich theologian J. H. Heidegger (1633–98) in *Body of Christian Theology* (1700).

The Puritans in England and America were preacher-theologians who viewed theology practically as the act of living unto God. Thus, rather than being pure scholars, the Puritans practiced the craft of practical exegesis by applying Bible and theology to Christian faith and life. The Puritans upheld the full authority of the Bible, the mystery of sovereign election, the moral corruption of the sinner, and the finality of Christ and his saving work on the cross. The Puritans are known primarily for their excellent biblical commentaries and theological treatises on nearly every aspect of the faith. Leading Puritan theologians include Thomas Manton (1620–77), John Owen (1616–83), Stephen Charnock (1628–80), Jonathan Edwards (1703–58), and Samuel Hopkins (1721–1803).

The pietistic movement in eighteenth-century Europe arose as a lively reaction to the dry intellectualism of Protestant scholasticism. The Pietists replaced dogmatics with practical instruction in the spiritual life. They emphasized the necessity of conversion, devotional study of the Bible, the priesthood of believers, and foreign missions. The Pietists often gathered in homes in cell groups that later developed into movements that were known as "inner missions." Leading Pietist spokesmen include Philip J. Spener (1635–1705), the "Father of Pietism" who wrote *Pious Longings;* A. H. Francke (1663–1727), the Halle theologian; and J. A. Bengel (1687–1752), the Wittenberg exegete whose *Gnomon of the New Testament* (1742) remains one of the finest word-by-word expositions of the Greek Testament.

The Romantic movement in the eighteenth and nineteenth centuries arose in reaction to the sterility of theological rationalism, which viewed reason as the all-sufficient system builder. According to the Romantic theologians, the source of theology resided in the feelings and in the imagination of the human agent. F. D. E. Schleiermacher (1768–1834), acclaimed the greatest theologian between Calvin and Barth, may be viewed as the father of modern theology. His work *The Christian Faith* (1821) was the most influential theology of the nineteenth century. Schleiermacher played on the fringes of pantheism, for he viewed God as the creative Eros immanent in all things. Religion is not a collection of dogmas certified by some external authority; rather, it is a set of convictions that arise from a person's feelings of absolute dependence on God.

In the latter half of the nineteenth century a new impulse was generated by Albrecht Ritschl (1822–89), whose theology was heavily influenced by Kant's *Critique of Practical Reason*. In his three-volume doctrinal work *The Christian Doctrine of Justification and Reconciliation* (1870–74), Ritschl, the antimetaphysical theologian, rejected as "fact" the traditional doctrines of Christ's incarnation and resurrection, original sin, and forensic justification. His theory of "moral value" focused on the gradual realization of the kingdom of God via actualization of the ethic of Jesus. Ritschl had a profound influence on the social gospel in America. Disciples of Ritschl include J. W. Herrmann (1846–1922), who outlined his moralistic theology in *The Communion of the Christian With God* (1886) and a posthumous *Systematic Theology* (1925), and Adolf Harnack (1851–1930) who, in *What Is Christianity?* (1901), substituted the fatherhood of God and the infinite value of the human soul for the so-called culturally conditioned doctrines of Christianity. Walter Rauschenbusch (1861–1918), the author of *A Theology for the Social Gospel* (1917), was an influential Ritschlian theologian in America.

The Contemporary Period

Neoorthodoxy, also known as the "theology of crisis" or "dialectical theology," was a vehement protest against various immanentalistic theologies prominent around the turn of the present century. Neoorthodox theologians, while certain that the faith of the Reformers required reworking in the light of modern critical knowledge, sought to forge a return to the theology of the Reformation.

Karl Barth (1886–1968), driven back to the Scriptures and to Calvin by the practical inadequacies of liberal theology, launched neoorthodox theology with his monumental *Romans* commentary (1919). The Swiss scholar's main work is the unfinished thirteen-volume *Church Dogmatics* (1935–67), larger than Thomas's *Summa Theologica* and nine times the size of Calvin's *Institutes*. Barth's theology emphasizes the freedom and transcendence of God, the threefold form of the Word, and the radical sinfulness of the creature. Somewhat to the left of Barth was his Swiss colleague Emil Brunner (1889–1966), who wrote the three-volume *Dogmatics* (1946–60). Brunner differed from Barth in that he accepted a preliminary revelation of God in nature and history and the sinner's retention of the *imago Dei*. Unlike Barth, Brunner denied the virgin birth of Christ. Reinhold Niebuhr (1893–1971) moved in the direction of Barthianism from the early liberalism of his teachers. Niebuhr made insightful observations on the human condition and its social and political consequences. His most systematic work is *The Nature and Destiny of Man* (1941). H. Richard Niebuhr (1894–1962), the younger brother of Reinhold, articulated a relativistic view of the divine self-disclosure in *The Meaning of Revelation* (1941) and wrestled with the Christian's relation to the modern world in *Christ and Culture* (1951).

John Henry Newman (1801–90), the Anglican convert to Catholicism, anticipated recent developments in the church with his programmatic essay *Development of Christian Doctrine* (1845). The Cardinal challenged the notion of fixed and inviolable dogmas by asserting that through the course of history truth undergoes development. Moreover, since Scripture does not contain the whole of revelation the Bible must be supplemented by insights gleaned from experience. The rise of Catholic modernism around the turn of the century enlarged the distance between traditional theology and the new ideas. George Tyrrell (1861–1909), in *Christianity at the Cross-Roads* (1909), argued that Christians should retain Jesus' religious spirit but abandon many of the dogmas that have grown up around him. Alfred Loisy (1857–1940), the leader of Catholic modernism in France, insisted that traditional dogmas must be revised or rejected in the light of new knowledge. His book *The Gospel and the Church* (1902) boldly claims that the Roman church has departed from the way of Christ. The Catholic modernist movement was condemned by Pius X in the encyclical *Pascendi* (1907). The new impulses in Catholic theology came to the fore at the Second Vatican Council (1962–65), summoned by Pope John XXIII. Vatican II was traditional on such matters as papal infallibility, Mary, the Mass, and purgatory. But in other important areas liberal and radical perspectives prevailed. The notion of "dogmatic relativism" was endorsed by the Council, thus throwing open the door to many new ideas. Vatican II acknowledged that, since the reality of God naturally wells up within, all people possess "implicit faith." Moreover, the exclusivity of the Roman church as the only means of salvation was denied. Non-Christians and atheists were said to be recipients of saving grace. The missionary task thus was envisaged as announcing the news that God has accepted the world in Christ.

A leading spokesman for the new Catholicism is Karl Rahner (b. 1904), the German Jesuit author of the fourteen-volume *Theological Investigations* (1974–76), whom some rank on a par with Barth. Rahner propounds a system of "transcendental Thomism," which is a reinterpretation of Aquinas guided by insights from Kant, Heidegger, and Marechal, the Belgian Jesuit (d. 1944). Central to Rahner's theology is the "supernatural existential," the dynamic impulse that drives the person toward the immediate presence of God. Since all people subconsciously are oriented toward the Absolute, the entire world is an "anonymous Christianity."[46] The most outspoken critic of traditional Catholic polity and theology is Hans Küng (b. 1927), the Swiss-born theologian who in 1979 was disqualified as an official Catholic teacher by Pope John Paul II. In *The Church* (1967) Küng charges that both the papacy and its claim of infallibility are without biblical warrant. Küng describes his *On Being a Christian* (1976) as "a kind of small 'Summa' of the Christian faith."[47] Küng's theology begins with the human situation, redefines the God-idea, asserts the fallibility of the Bible and its doctrines, and claims that the non-Christians are part of God's plan for the salvation of the world. Rahner charges Küng with speaking like a "liberal Protestant." Edward Schillebeeckx (b. 1914), the Flemish Catholic theologian, synthesizes insights from Thomism, existentialism, and linguistic philosophy to forge new directions in Christology, the phenomena of human existence, and the church as agent of social change.

The religious existentialism of Heidegger and Kierkegaard had a substantial impact on twentieth-century Protestant theology. One of the most prominent existentialists was Paul Tillich (1886–1965), whose "existential-ontological theism" sought to forge a middle way between supernaturalism and naturalism. Tillich insisted that modern theology must affirm the "God beyond God"[48] or "the God above the God of theism."[49] Tillich's mystical system of Being-Itself, set forth in his *Systematic Theology* (1951–63) encouraged later secular theologians to pronounce God dead. Rudolf Bultmann (1884–1976) was an existentially oriented biblical theologian who shared common ground with dialectical theology. In his 1941 programmatic essay, "New Testament and Mythology," Bultmann, on the basis of form-critical analysis, distinguished between the pure kernel of revelation and the more extensive husk of Jewish and Gnostic myths that allegedly had encrusted the simple Christian message. In Bultmann's mind Christ's incarnation, miracles, sacrificial atonement, resurrection, and second coming are nonhistoric myths. The German scholar launched the program of demythologization, interpreting the alleged biblical myths via an existential hermeneutic. The main outlines of Bultmann's system are set forth in *New Testament Theology* (1949–53; ET: 1952–55). The leading systematic theology based on philosophical existentialism is *Principles of Christian Theology* (1977) by the English theologian John Macquarrie (b. 1919). Stimulated by Bonhoeffer, Tillich, and Bultmann, J. A. T. Robinson (b. 1919) radically redefined the Christian faith in *Honest to God* (1963) and *The Human Face of God* (1973).

Two turbulent but short-lived liberal impulses from the 1960s were the so-called secular theology and the death-of-God movement. The former was stimulated in part by Dietrich Bonhoeffer's enigmatic expressions "man come of age" and "religionless Christianity." Paul van Buren (b. 1924) left his early Barthian theology after concluding that the word "God" makes little sense to the modern mind. *The Secular Meaning of the Gospel* (1963) expounds a nonmetaphysical view of the religion of the historical Jesus. Meanwhile Harvey Cox (b. 1929) in *The Secular City* (1965) argues that industrialization and urbanization offer a fruitful context in which modern man lives before God with a mature sense of this-worldiness. More radical yet, Thomas J. J. Altizer (b. 1927) in *The Gospel of Christian Atheism* (1967) and Altizer and William

Hamilton in *Radical Theology and the Death of God* (1966) claimed that at the Incarnation God died. Yet the Good News is that God, though dead, lives on in the man Jesus. In the death-of-God movement, religious skepticism came to its logical end. God is eliminated, but Jesus is retained as a figure who offers some measure of spiritual solace.

Process theology is an influential form of philosophical theology indebted to the thought of A. N. Whitehead (1861–1947) and Charles Hartshorne (b. 1897). Process thought postulates that reality consists not of bits of substance but of subatomic moments of experience called "actual occasions" or "occasions of experience." With great rapidity each actual occasion "prehends" (i.e., grasps or feels) prior actual occasions, incorporating these into its own universe, thus forming a creative and novel synthesis. In process theology, also known as neoclassical theism, God is a special kind of energy event continually being shaped by relations with other actual occasions. Moreover, each person apprehends God in every moment of human experience in a manner not unlike ESP or mental telepathy. John B. Cobb, Jr., outlines the main features of process theology in *A Christian Natural Theology* (1965), as does Norman Pittenger in *God in Process* (1967) and *The Divine Triunity* (1977).

Heightened social, political, and economic tensions in the modern world have prompted the rise of a broad movement known as political theology. An early form, the theology of hope, was developed by the German theologian Jürgen Moltmann in *Theology of Hope* (1964). Indebted to Hegel, Marx, and the Marxist Ernst Bloch, Moltmann maintains that humanity's hope lies in openness to a future that has been given meaning by the resurrection of Jesus. Moltmann stresses that the Christian hope must be worked out in radical political and social action. A similar emphasis is enunciated by Johannes Metz (b. 1928), the leading Catholic political theologian in Germany.

A second from of political theology, the theology of liberation, was developed in Latin America in the late 1960s. The systematic charter of the liberation movement is *A Theology of Liberation* (1971; ET: 1973) by the Peruvian Catholic theologian Gustavo Gutièrrez (b. 1928). Other titles from this perspective include *Revolutionary Theology Comes of Age* (1975), by Jose Miguiz Bonino and Juan Luis Segundo's *The Liberation of Theology* (1977). Theology, according to the liberationists, consists not in meditative reflection on supernaturally revealed truths but in *praxis*, namely, involvement in the plight of the poor and powerless of this world. Much of liberation theology is indebted to the Marxist critique of society and its program of violent revolution. Black theologians such as James Cone (*A Black Theology of Liberation* [1970] and *God of the Oppressed* [1975]) undertake a similar program from the Black American perspective. In a similar vein feminist theologies address the alleged oppression of women in Western culture (e.g., Georgia Harkness, *Women in Church and Society* [1971]; Mary Daley, *Beyond God the Father* [1973]; and Philis Trible, *God and the Rhetoric of Sexuality* [1978]).

The aim of this final section is to identify several more or less conservative theologies of the last hundred years or so. Charles Hodge (1797–1878), who taught at Princeton Seminary for fifty years, is the most prominent nineteenth-century American theologian. His three-volume *Systematic Theology* (1871–73) that defended the Calvinism of the old Princeton school is still referred to today. His son A. A. Hodge (1823–86) is the author of the useful *Outlines of Theology* (1878). The scholarly three-volume *Dogmatic Theology* of W. G. T. Shedd is rich in philosophi-

cal interaction. The Presbyterian B. B. Warfield (1851–1921), who succeeded A. A. Hodge at Princeton, wrote no systematic theology; yet his scores of books and essays on biblical theological subjects are widely read and highly valued.

On the Continent Abraham Kuyper (1837–1920), described by one authority as "the greatest Calvinist since Calvin,"[50] wrote the three-volume *Encyclopedia of Sacred Theology* (1894). The Dutch theologian successfully integrated the theological enterprise with human achievements in science, government, and the arts. An equally staunch defender of the Reformed faith was Herman Bavinck (1854–1921), who wrote the erudite four-volume *Reformed Dogmatics* in Dutch (1895–1901). A one-volume English synopsis bears the title *Our Reasonable Faith* (1956).

G. C. Berkhouwer (b. 1903), author of the thirteen-volume series *Studies in Dogmatics* (1949–67), professes a confessional method in theology but in recent times appears to have adopted a relational neoorthodox understanding of revelation and knowledge (see especially his *Holy Scripture* [1967; ET: 1975]). Hendrikus Berkhof's *Christian Faith* (1973; ET: 1979) interacts in depth with the world of critical theological scholarship. Louis Berkhof has written a succinct and widely read *Systematic Theology* (1941). J. O. Buswell's two-volume *Systematic Theology of the Christian Religion* (1962–65) contains extensive exegetical sections and represents a premillennial position. Thomas F. Torrance (b. 1913), the Edinburgh dogmatician, is an important modern thinker who seeks to unify the worlds of theology and science. *Theology in Reconstruction* (1965) represents his most unified theological work. Donald Bloesch (b. 1928), in the two-volume *Essentials of Evangelical Theology* (1978–79), attempts to articulate "a

Catholic Evangelicalism'' that takes issue with both fundamentalism and liberalism. The readable work reflects a special sympathy for Barth and elements of Roman Catholic theology.

In the Lutheran tradition Francis Pieper (1852–1931) wrote the modern classic theology (three volumes plus index) under the title *Christian Dogmatics* (1917–24; ET: 1950–57). A one-volume condensation of Pieper bearing the same title (1934/55) was prepared by John Theodore Mueller. A noteworthy modern dogmatics is Helmut Thielicke's (b. 1908) three-volume *The Evangelical Faith* (1968–78; ET: 1974–82). Thielicke's broadly evangelical theology incorporates some features from the thought of Kant, Kierkegaard, and Barth. Thielicke is guided by the salutary premise that "the value of dogmatics depends upon whether it can be preached." Wolfhart Pannenberg (b. 1928), in *Revelation as History* (1961), argues that God reveals himself in universal history, the whole of which is summed up in the resurrection of Jesus. His *Jesus, God and Man* (1964; ET: 1968) develops a Christology from below from the data of Jesus' life, death, and resurrection.

Representing the Wesleyan-Arminian tradition, John Miley (1813–95) has left the church a thorough, albeit traditional, *Systematic Theology* (1892–94) in two volumes. H. Orton Wiley, writing from a Nazarene standpoint, prepared the equally scholarly *Christian Theology* (1940–43) in three volumes. *A Contemporary Wesleyan Theology* (1983), a two-volume work edited by Charles W. Carter, expounds the main features of Wesleyan doctrine and ministry.

The Baptist theologian A. H. Strong (1836–1921) wrote the often-reprinted *Systematic Theology* (1886) that upholds evolution as the mode of God's working in nature. The Southern Baptist theologian Edgar Y. Mullins, who wrote *The Christian Religion in Its Doctrinal Expression* (1917), shaped in nontechnical language a theology that mediates between Calvinism and Arminianism, while focusing on evangelical experience. More recently from the same tradition Dale Moody has written the scholarly work *The Word of Truth* (1981), which makes concessions to critical liberal scholarship in the areas of revelation, the person of Christ, and the justification of the sinner.

The Anglican tradition in modern times has made only minor contributions to systematic theology. A. C. Headlam, whose *Christian Theology* (1934) covers only revelation and theology proper, offers the following observation: "It is one of the characteristics of the English church that it has never produced a great work on systematic theology. English people do not love system, or order, or completeness."[51] The conservative Anglican W. H. G. Thomas has provided a theological exposition of the Thirty-Nine Articles of the Church of England in *The Principles of Theology* (1930).

Within the broad evangelical movement Louis Sperry Chafer (1871–1952) provided the classic exposition of the older dispensationalism (from a modified Calvinist perspective) in his eight-volume *Systematic Theology* (1947–48). Recent reformulations of the dispensationalist position have rendered Chafer's work increasingly obsolete. *Lectures in Systematic Theology* by Henry C. Thiessen (1949–79) is a nontechnical work written from a moderate dispensational point of view. The revised edition is more Calvinistic than the original.

Finally, but not least in importance, Carl F. H. Henry (b. 1913) has produced the six-volume opus *God, Revelation and Authority* (1976–83) that covers the limited areas of prolegomena, revelation, and the Godhead. The incisive analyses and penetrating criticisms that Henry offers represent mature evangelical scholarship. Millard J. Erickson in *Christian Theology* (1983–85) offers a fresh restatement of the Christian faith from a baptistic perspective.

REVIEW QUESTIONS

To Help Relate Each Section of This Chapter to Doing Theology

1. Explain why integrative thinking is needed in a diversified world.

2. What entry points for serious thinking about divinely revealed truth have you experienced in your own life?

3. List the charges that have been brought against the discipline of systematic theology recently and indicate how other theologians responded?

4. What is integrative theology?

5. How does integrative theology relate to systematic theology and how does it answer charges against systematics?

6. Explain the relationship of integrative theology to other fields such as the following:

    apologetics
    biblical studies
    hermeneutics
    logic
    historical theology
    research methodology

7. How is integrative theology possible philosophically?

8. How is integrative theology possible biblically?

9. How does integrative theology compare and contrast with alternative approaches to doing theology in the history of the church?

10. In what ways are well-founded, well-formulated theological truths relevant for your life and service to others?

CHAPTER 2

DIVINE REVELATION TO ALL PEOPLE OF ALL TIMES

Divine Revelation
to All People of All Times

THE PROBLEM: DOES EVERY RATIONAL PERSON COMPREHEND SOMETHING OF GOD?

Christianity differs from religion, commonly understood, in that it involves God's gracious quest for the person rather than the person's groping search for God. Central to the Christian way is the claim that God has taken the initiative and has, in intelligible ways, disclosed himself to people. It is of fundamental importance, however, to understand to whom God reveals himself, at what times, and in what ways. Has God given a revelation of himself and his will only to his covenant people Israel and the Christian church, or has the Creator somehow disclosed himself to all people who have ever lived? Did God first make a meaningful disclosure of himself in Jesus Christ, or has there been a valid revelation since the beginning of time? Moreover, is God revealed only through mighty signs and miracles, or has he made a disclosure in the ordinary operations of nature and in the course of history? Does only the reader of the Bible or the believer in Christ know God, or does every rational person comprehend something of the reality of God?

To clarify these issues, Christian theology has made a distinction between two kinds of revelation: general and special. *General revelation* refers to the disclosure of God in nature, in providential history, and in the moral law within the heart, whereby all persons at all times and places gain a rudimentary understanding of the Creator and his moral demands. *Special revelation* refers to God's self-disclosure through signs and miracles, the utterances of prophets and apostles, and the deeds and words of Jesus Christ, whereby specific people at particular times and places gain further understanding of God's character and a knowledge of his saving purposes in his Son.

On the one hand, a denial that knowledge of God is mediated through general revelation appears to undermine the basis for enduring moral values and the meaningfulness of human existence; for the Christian it would also mean the elimination of common ground in witness to the unsaved. On the other hand, an overestimation of the value of general revelation might imply that saving knowledge of God is available to all people quite apart from the gospel message about Jesus Christ.

The issues surrounding God's general disclosure thus involve the spiritual condition of people who make no profession of Christ, be they our friends and relatives or far-off pagans who have not heard the gospel. The issues raised also relate to the current debate over the value of the non-Christian religions as vehicles for mediating knowledge of God and salvation. Thus even the missionary enterprise has a profound stake in these basic theological considerations.

It is no exaggeration to say that the foundational issue in Christian theology deals with the nature and scope of divine revelation. A. C. Headlam has rightly maintained that "the primary question in theology must be, what is the source of our knowledge of God."[1] Hence it is appropriate and necessary that our study of Christian theology should begin with these chapters on revelation.

ALTERNATIVE PROPOSALS IN THE CHURCH

In the history of the Christian church, several influential answers have been given to the question as to whether all people know God and, if so, to what extent and with what consequences?

Aquinas and the Thomistic Tradition

Thomists maintain that rational induction from the data of nature leads to a demonstration of God's existence and the infinity of his perfections. Saving knowledge of God, however, comes only through Scripture and church teachings. Thomas Aquinas, rejecting the Platonic scheme of innate ideas, favored the Aristotelian method of rational induction from temporal effects. Aquinas created a metaphysical model consisting of two realms (nature and grace), two kinds of knowledge (natural and revealed), and two independent methods of knowing (reason and faith). The "Angelic Doctor" came to theology with three presuppositions, by virtue of which he judged the human mind competent to reason its way to knowledge of God: (1) human beings, made in the image of God, are endowed with the power of a rational mind; (2) the intellect was not seriously affected by the Fall; and (3) God's existence is analogous to human existence (analogy of being), hence the former is not totally other to the latter.

With regard to the realm of nature, Aquinas argued that the empirical data of the sensible world interpreted by the principle of cause and effect lead to proof of God's existence and the infinity of his perfections. Via rational induction from created effects, he sought to prove both that God exists (the famous Five Ways) and that God is infinite, eternal, incorporeal, immutable, intelligent, and so on. This general disclosure in the cosmos, quite apart from propositional revelation, leads to a substantial natural theology or philosophical science. He was quite clear, however, that this corpus of natural theology is inadequate to save a person. Only God's revelation in Christ and the Scriptures imparts the knowledge necessary for salvation—knowledge of God's being and purpose (e.g., Trinity, Incarnation, and Atonement). Concerning the way of rational ascent and the way of revelational descent, Aquinas concludes: "We have a more perfect knowledge of God by grace than by natural reason."[2]

Empirically Orientated Liberalism

Liberals of an empirical bent argue that knowledge of God is obtained by rational evaluation of the so-called assured results of the natural and social sciences. The insights afforded by modern learning are judged superior to those possessed by prescientific biblical writers. Henry Van Dusen argues that knowledge of God is gained through the study of the universe and of persons. The empirical sciences shed considerable light on nature, whereas philosophy, sociology, and the psychology of religion impart understanding of persons and human values. According to Van Dusen, modern learning is "an all-sufficient interpreter of reality and guide for life."[3] He argues that the disciplines of human knowledge correct the fallible teachings of the Bible concerning God, man, and the universe. Van Dusen and other liberals stress the continuity between general and special revelation, between natural and supernatural knowledge, and between reason and faith.

Similarly, L. H. DeWolf, who affirms "the powers of human thought to find and recognize the truth,"[4] postulates the universal availability of a substantial corpus of natural theology. The data of experience, interpreted by reason and tested by the principle of comprehensive coherence, affords a considerable knowledge of God and of human destiny. DeWolf insists that the traditional distinction between general and special revelation is difficult to sustain; human experience of the world and reflection are caused by God and are expressive of his thought. Thus "the line cannot be drawn between nature and the Bible on the ground of the more direct, unmediated character of the latter."[5] Indeed, DeWolf prefers to speak of the difference between usual and unusual, or spectacular, forms of revelation. The latter might include a rainbow, a particularly bright and starry sky, or a sudden flash of intuition. In the liberal scheme, then, knowledge of God and his will is secured by rational observation and is available to all persons of sound mind.

Existentially Orientated Liberalism

Liberals in the existential tradition, assuming the unity of being and knowing, postulate the knowability of all being—including Being-itself (God)—via an immediate, illuminatory preapprehension. Thus human beings, *qua* human beings, know God in a mystical, life-changing experience of grace. Schleiermacher, an important precursor of this emphasis, taught that through the noncognitive faculty of feeling or ineffable intuition the human soul is brought into immediate contact with the Soul of the universe. Thus God is not found in the external world through the modalities of natural revelation. Rather, through the "feeling of absolute dependence" or the intuition of immediate self-consciousness, in which the subject-object duality is overcome, the human soul is united with the Soul of the universe. Since the sense and taste for the Infinite is universal, it follows that all people everywhere "know God." Argued Schleiermacher: "This feeling of absolute dependence . . . is therefore not an accidental element, or a thing which varies from person to person, but a universal element of life."[6]

In the twentieth century, Paul Tillich replaced the categories of general and special revelation with "primary revelation" and "secondary revelation." In primary revelation the focus is not the objective cosmos or history but the reflection of Being-itself within the person's awareness of Primal Reality that transcends the subject-object duality. Tillich describes this experience as a moment of the gnostic insight in which human eyes are opened to "the abysmal element in the ground of Being."[7] Thus all people are said to know God via primary revelation, namely, through the experience of being grasped by "ultimate, unconditional, total, infinite concern."[8] Clearly, Tillich has propounded a natural theology of ecstatic religious experience centering on the mystical intuition of Being-itself within the depths of the person's own being. Secondary revelation, according to Tillich, involves the formal representation of this mystical experience in the symbols and myths of religion.

Karl Rahner, by means of a Heideggerian interpretation of Aquinas, reaches roughly the same conclusions as Tillich. Since, Rahner argues, an a priori transcendental relationship exists between the human person and God, in every moment of consciousness human beings find their life oriented toward the life of God; the dynamic impulse that drives every person toward the immediate presence of God is the "supernatural existential."[9] By virtue of this preconceptual encounter with Being-itself, all people possess an experienced, albeit unthematic, knowledge of God. According to Rahner, those who permit the supernatural existential to shape their existence are Christians, even though they may reject the name. Indeed, since all people respond positively to this transcendental experience, the entire world constitutes an "anonymous Christianity."[10] Rahner's vision of the person as transcendental consciousness continually shaped by holy Mystery eliminates the objective basis of revelation in favor of a mysticism of the emotions. Revelation imparts no new knowledge, only a new consciousness. Thus, according to the transcendental Thomism of Rahner and other contemporary Catholic thinkers, nature and grace have merged. The old Catholic scholastic theology is viewed as an antiquated anachronism.

The Neoorthodox Tradition

Karl Barth and many neoorthodox theologians deny the existence of any revelation outside of God's radical address through the Word. The wholly otherness of the Creator and the thoroughgoing sinfulness of the creature mandate that God can be known only through God. Thus, against liberalism's assertion of a natural theology derived either from science or from the religious affections and against medieval Catholicism's postulate of a natural theology established by reason, Karl Barth affirmed that God reveals himself solely through his threefold Word of address.

Barth's polemic against natural knowledge of God from below was rooted in three assumptions: (1) The infinite qualitative difference between God and persons; time and eternity are viewed as two mutually exclusive realms without any natural connecting links. (2) The annihilation of the *imago Dei* by the Fall; corrupted reason is incapable of apprehending the transcendent Majesty. (3) Rejection of an analogy of being (*analogia entis*) between the Creator and the creature; Barth boldly characterized the latter Thomistic tenet as an "invention of the Antichrist."[11]

Thus Barth intoned that no general revelation is given "in reason, in conscience, in the emotions, in history, in nature, and in culture and its achievements."[12] No knowledge is mediated by the modalities of so-called general revelation, for God is known only in his entirety, namely, in his Trinitarian nature. The meeting between God and persons must be actualized entirely from God's side—and particularly through his reconciling grace in Christ. Any alleged disclosure that does not involve the unveiling of grace to the sinner is not revelation. Thus we see that Barth upheld a rigorous Christomonism of revelation: "Revelation means the incarnation of the Word of God."[13]

To maintain consistency with his thesis, Barth radically reinterprets Romans 1:18–20. This text, according to Barth, affirms nothing about Gentiles gaining knowledge of God's invisible nature from created effects. When Paul states, "What may be known about God is plain to them, because God has made it plain to them" (Rom. 1:19), Barth appeals to the immediately preceding context (vv. 15–17), which discusses the apostolic proclamation of the gospel. Thus, according to Barth, the revelation discussed in verses 18–20 is not a general disclosure in nature; rather it is the message of God's supernatural revelation in Christ. Argues Barth, "We cannot isolate what Paul says about the heathen in Romans 1:19–20 from the context of the apostolic preaching, from the incarnation of the Word."[14] But how, on this showing, does Barth interpret Paul's repeated insistence that the Gentiles *know* God (vv. 19–21)? Barth's answer is that the pagan *theoretically* knows God on the basis of God's universal election of humankind in Christ, even though *in actual fact* the pagan is not conscious of such knowledge.[15] For Barth, the burden of Romans 1:18–20 is the paradox of election!

Dutch Reformed Theology

Most Dutch Reformed theologians postulate the reality of general revelation and a knowledge of God implanted within the sinner's moral and psychological constitution. But because sin has blinded the mind, natural human beings attain no knowledge of God by reflection on the *indicia* of the space-time universe. Abraham Kuyper argues that sin has bolted shut the door to general knowledge of God; only those who approach nature and history with regenerate eyes and minds find the cosmos to be a legible book.

G. C. Berkouwer maintains that Scripture touches on the subject of a general knowledge of God mediated by the cosmos only incidentally and infrequently. The clear thrust of biblical

teaching on the subject is the sinner's thoroughgoing *ignorance* of God (Gal. 4:8; 1 Thess. 4:5; 2 Thess. 1:8). According to Berkouwer, Paul in Romans 1 teaches only that sinners *confront* or *make contact with* revelation in nature. Paul's saying that the Gentiles "knew God" (Rom. 1:21) must be viewed as hyperbole. General revelation is *there,* and natural man encounters it. But, due to epistemic inability, it fails to register in one's mind as knowledge. Insists Berkouwer, "The Christian church, in speaking of general revelation, never intended to assert that *true* knowledge of God is possible through the natural light of reason."[16] Following Kuyper, Berkouwer claims that knowledge of God as Creator is possible only on the basis of prior knowledge of God as Redeemer.

Cornelius Van Til arrives at a similar conclusion from an involved epistemological analysis. He argues that there are two schemes for viewing reality: the Christian and the non-Christian. The former postulates the triune God of the Bible as its universal, while the latter centers on rebellious, autonomous man. If a person wants to know anything about God, he or she must adopt the correct referent by presupposing the God revealed in authoritative Scripture. But sinful human beings, consistently dismissing God from their lives, are incapable of drawing right conclusions about God from nature or any other source. Thus general revelation affords the sinner no knowledge. Epistemologically, all the unsaved are atheists.[17] The God of the Bible is known only by those persons who renounce the reckless quest for autonomy and who presuppose the truth of the Bible and its interpretation of human life and experience.

Many Fathers, Reformers, and Evangelicals

A significant number of Fathers, Reformers, and evangelical theologians maintain that the rational mind intuits God as a first principle and thereafter draws further conclusions about God's character and moral requirements by contemplating the magnitude and precision of the universe. This nonsalvific knowledge of God establishes human responsibility and provides the basis for God's redemptive revelation in Christ and in the Scriptures.

Thus the Apologists, in defending the faith against pagan assaults, appealed to what any person concludes about God from the surrounding world. Theophilus argued that "God cannot be seen by human eyes, but is beheld and perceived through His providence and works."[18] Clement argued that "there always was a natural manifestation of the one Almighty God among all right-thinking men."[19] Tertullian, who polemicized against philosophical speculation, argued that knowledge of God is innate in the soul and subsequently enlarged by rational inspection of created things.[20] Many Fathers—e.g., Origen, Athanasius, Cyril of Jerusalem, and Gregory of Nyssa—insisted that although human beings cannot behold God's essence, they can observe the clear imprint of Deity from the design of the universe and from the works of providence.[21]

Augustine argued that God's universal self-disclosure affords all people a rudimentary knowledge of himself. The knowledge of God that all possess is first of all a priori. Enabled by a divine general illumination, the person effably intuits eternal changeless principles, including the reality of God. By virtue of this immediate act of "seeing" facilitated by the Logos (John 1:4, 9), none can justly claim to be atheists. This a priori meeting of the soul with God is subsequently enlarged by a knowledge content that is a posteriori. From the signs or data displayed in nature and in providential history, the rational mind, blessed by common grace, draws further conclusions about the character and moral demands of the Creator God. By these two means, Augustine argued, "Noble philosophers looked and knew the Maker from His handiwork."[22] But instead of cultivating the preliminary knowledge of God ("wisdom") thus provided, the sinner moves to dismiss God and thus sinks into moral debauchery. Augustine clearly insisted that general revelation does not save. Rather, it serves only to establish the person's accountability to the Judge of the universe. Redemptive knowledge ("saving wisdom") is acquired by faith in (assent to) the incarnate Christ, whose atoning death and saving life are recorded in Holy Scripture.

Luther likewise propounded a twofold scheme of revelation and knowledge, under the rubric "general knowledge of God" (which he also called "legal" and "left-handed" knowledge) and "particular knowledge of God" (or "evangelical" and "right-handed" knowledge). On the basis of immediate intuition of the divine Being and reflection on the data of nature, "all men have the general knowledge, namely that God is, that He has created heaven and earth, that He is just, that He punishes the wicked, etc."[23] This universal general knowledge that establishes a person's accountability to God is incomplete, and so it cannot save.

Calvin's twofold understanding of revelation is set forth in the first two books of his *Institutes,* which bear the titles "The Knowledge of God the Creator" and "The Knowledge of God the Redeemer." God is known as Creator by general revelation and by the added light of special revelation. General revelation mediates knowledge of God as Creator by an immediate intuition (which Calvin calls the universal "sense of divinity" and "seed of religion"), by the moral law implanted in the heart, and by the imprint of Deity on nature, the human frame, and providential history. Of the revelation of God in nature Calvin asserts, "Even wicked men are forced, by the mere view of the earth and sky, to rise to the Creator."[24] Calvin, therefore, believed that all persons know God as Creator—both from within themselves and from the world without. General revelation, however, does not save; it only serves to condemn. Hence, God graciously grants to sinners his Word, whereby the elect know him as efficacious Redeemer.

The same Reformational stance on general revelation appears in Article II of the French Confession of Faith (1559), Article II of the Belgic Confession (1561/1619), and Article I.1 of the Westminster Confession of Faith (1647). Evangelical authorities who support the mediation of a limited knowledge of God by the modalities of general revelation include Charles Hodge,[25] Carl F. H. Henry,[26] Henry C. Thiessen,[27] Dale Moody,[28] and Millard J. Erickson.[29]

BIBLICAL TEACHING

We cannot subscribe to all the conflicting views on universal revelation, but we can examine them in terms of their conformity to the primary, biblical sources.

Pentateuch

"In the beginning God . . ." (Gen. 1:1). The very first statement of the Bible assumes the reality of the living, active, powerful God. Thirty-five times in the first chapter of Genesis, with no attempt to explain his reality, Moses identifies *Elohim* as the Creator and Sovereign of all that is. There is no definition of God, no explication of his character, no proof of his existence. *Elohim* simply is *there*—a universal given—the living God! Whether we treat the early chapters of Genesis as history or as "a proclamation of God's

decisive dealing with His creation,"[30] the idea of the Creator is assumed.[31] The forthright manner in which God is presented in the first chapter of the Bible leads us to believe that the fundamental concept of God was the common property of all people from the very beginning.

Poetry and Wisdom

Elihu's speech to Job (esp. Job 36:24–37:24) sheds further light on God's revelation to all persons at all times and places. The clouds and rain that faithfully water the earth (Job 36:27–28), the clap of thunder and flash of lightning that strike terror in the heart (36:29–37:5), the snow and ice of winter that remind humans that they are dependent creatures (37:6–10), the fury of a howling thunderstorm (37:11–15), and the sun that, following the storm, shines brilliantly through the windswept sky (37:21–22) amply attest the power, majesty, goodness, and severity of the God of creation. Elihu observes that God's revelation of himself in nature is not limited to those who possess a prior faith: "All mankind has seen it; men gaze on it from afar" (36:25).

God's retort to Job (Job 38:1–39:30) elaborates on the revelation of God in the created order. The vast expanse of earth and sea (38:4–11), the daily rising of the sun (38:12–15), snow and hail, wind and rain, frost and ice (38:22–30), the mighty constellations that grace the heavens (38:31–38), and the incredible complexity and harmonious interrelationships of the animal kingdom (38:39–39:30) clearly reflect the infinite Mind that created and orders all these phenomena. The burden of this section of Job is that both the inanimate and the animate worlds attest the existence and glory of God.[32] Through the medium of a magnificent cosmos the observer plainly perceives the reality of the God who made and who upholds all that is.

Several so-called "nature psalms" (e.g., Pss. 8, 19, 29, 65, 104, 148) uphold the reality of a general revelation of God in the created order. But since many of these psalms are songs to God from the perspective of faith, our attention turns to two psalms that speak to the issue of God's self-disclosure in a more didactic manner. According to Psalm 14:1 (cf. Ps. 53:1), "The fool says in his heart, 'There is no God.'" The fool (nābāl; cf. 1 Sam. 25:25; Rom. 1:22) is the person who deliberately and volitionally closes the mind to God and his instruction. The psalmist is persuaded that the person who utters the sentence "There is no God" is afflicted with a certain perversity, since the reality of God inexorably impresses itself on all right-minded people at all times. That is to say, the knowledge of God is divinely implanted in all and is strengthened by daily contemplation of the natural world. On the basis of a general, universal revelation of God, all mankind confronts God as supreme Creator and Judge. Hence, the one who affirms the contrary, namely, the non-existence of God, is properly a "fool." The psalmist proceeds to underscore the fact that those who defiantly deny God's existence inevitably sink to a life of moral corruption (Ps. 14:1b–3).

Psalm 19 mainly teaches that the natural order displays the existence and glory of God. This psalm of David consists of two books: the book of nature (vv. 1–6)—which teaches that God reveals himself to all people as Elohim, the God of creation—and the book of the law (vv. 7–13)—which states that God reveals himself as Yahweh to the covenant community. The modalities of God's self-disclosure in nature are the starry heavens (vv. 1–4a) and, more particularly, the sun (vv. 4b–6). With respect to the former the psalmist makes two direct assertions that establish the validity of a general revelation of God in nature: "The

heavens declare the glory of God" (v. 1a) and "the skies proclaim the work of his hands"(v. 1b). The verbs "declare" (mᵉsappᵉrîm) and "proclaim" (maggîd) are participles that indicate that the revelatory activity is continuous. That which the heavens declare is the divine glory (kābôd), namely, the external manifestation of God's character. David affirms of the revelation of God's glory through the heavens that it is uninterrupted and perpetual (v. 2), that it is wordless, being cast, not in language, but in sensations perceptible to the senses (v. 3), and that it is universal, extending to the ends of the earth (v. 4).

The psalmist saw in the sun a second testimony to the existence and glory of God, even if his knowledge of earth's nearest star was limited. Surely the psalmist David would have echoed the conviction recorded by the prophet Isaiah, "The whole earth is full of his glory" (Isa. 6:3). The psalmist in particular and the Jewish people in general believed that God is displayed in nature and that—in rudimentary fashion, at least—he is known there. As expressed in Wisdom of Solomon 13:5, "The greatness and beauty of created things give us a corresponding idea of their Creator."

Primitive Christianity/Acts

In their remarks to the largely Gentile audience in the Roman colony of Lystra (Acts 14:15–17), Paul and Barnabas appealed to two factors from the realm of everyday experience with which their hearers were familiar: (1) God is Creator of all (v. 15) and (2) he is the providential Provider of basic human needs (v. 17). Even though they had distorted the knowledge of God and worshiped idols, the pagan people of Lystra were not strangers to "the living God, who made heaven and earth and sea and everything in them" (v. 15).

The works of the Creator God were displayed with sufficient clarity to be seen by all. Similarly, by the providential supply of the means for the maintenance of life, God did "not leave himself without testimony" (*amartyron*)— that is, unattested or unknown. God's witness to himself consisted in doing good (*agathourgon*) to all by sending rain, ordering the cycle of the seasons, providing full harvests, and filling the people's hearts with gladness (v. 17). Behind these providential provisions, people should have apprehended the living God who governs the nations. Their fall into idolatry and spiritual confusion was their own fault.

In his Areopagus address to sophisticated Athenian pagans (Acts 17:24–31), Paul, as was his custom, sought for a meaningful point of contact with his audience. Before proclaiming specific redemptive truths (v. 31), the apostle sought to establish areas of agreement between his hearers and himself. The common ground Paul chose here was the elementary knowledge of God that the Stoics possessed on the basis of common grace and general revelation. Although their knowledge was partial and distorted, the Athenians were aware of a number of things about God on the basis of his universal self-disclosure: (1) God is the invisible Creator and Sovereign of the universe (v. 24); (2) God is self-sufficient and dependent on the creature for nothing (v. 25a); (3) God is the source of life and everything humans value as good (v. 25b); (4) God is an intelligent Being, for he has established the times and bounds of man's habitation on the earth (v. 26); (5) God is immanent in the world (v. 27); and (6), amplifying the idea advanced in verse 25b, God is the very ground of human existence (v. 28). Gärtner, in his definitive study of the Acts 17 text, draws the following conclusion: "Creation and history provide a revelation of God apprehensible by man and imparting to him a certain knowledge of what God is."[33] The Athenians had sufficient knowledge of God to move to a relationship of dependence and obligation. But because they chose to extinguish the light God had given to them, Paul described their condition as one of "ignorance" (*agnoia,* v. 30) and moral culpability (v. 31).

A brief additional comment is warranted in connection with verse 28, where the apostle cites two pieces of Stoic wisdom; namely, "In him we live and move and have our being" and "We are his offspring." The Stoics believed that divine Reason, or the Logos, was immanent in man. Paul turned that belief around, insisting that the whole of man's life is grounded in God.[34] The continual existence of mankind's physical life and the exercise of intellectual and emotional faculties are so dependent on God that the apostle could say that all persons exist "in him." Moreover, Paul's second citation refutes the supposition of pantheism and conveys his conviction that human beings by creation bear the image and likeness of the Creator. Synthesizing these two lines of thought, we arrive at Paul's conviction that, made in the image of God and sustained in rationality by God's common grace, humans as humans cognitively apprehend the reality of God as an inviolable datum. Therefore, although they know God as Creator, they are motivated by a sinful heart and repress this elemental knowledge and give themselves to the worship of idols (v. 23).

The Pauline Literature

The classic text that treats the universal revelation of God in nature is Romans 1:18–21. Paul's thesis in this passage is that the human race is judicially guilty; for although all people know God from his works, all have willfully excluded him from their lives. The larger passage, Romans 1:18–32, makes four principal assertions concerning revelation and the knowability of God:

1. All people everywhere acquire a rudimentary knowledge of God as Creator (vv. 18–21). Paul's opening statement is clear: "What may be known [*to gnōston*] about God is plain to them [*en autois*], because God has made it plain to them" (v. 19). Moreover, "God's invisible qualities—his eternal power and divine nature—have been clearly seen" and "understood" (v. 20). What is perceived and grasped by the mind are God's "eternal power" and his "divine nature" (*theiotēs*). The latter term signifies the aggregate of God's invisible attributes or perfections. Yet again, lest he be misunderstood, the apostle states the conclusion: "They knew God" (*gnontes ton theon*, v. 21).

2. Knowledge of God as Creator is acquired by rational reflection on created effects (v. 20). Many biblical scholars (e.g., Godet, Hodge, Hughes, Litton) believe that the general statement of verse 19 ("What may be known about God is plain to them, because God has made it plain to them") includes both knowledge of God intuited as a first truth and knowledge gained by rational contemplation of the natural world. Yet in the next verse Paul plainly asserts that God's invisible qualities are discerned "from what has been made" (v. 20). Twice (vv. 19, 21) the apostle uses the verb *ginōskō* ("to know"), which involves the idea of perceiving with the senses and grasping with the mind. In verse 32 he uses the intensive form of the verb, *epiginōskō*, which means to "know exactly, completely, through and through"[35]; and in verse 28 we find the intensive noun form, *epignōsis*. If further evidence were needed, Paul adds in verse 20 that the divine perfections "have been clearly seen," the verb *kathoraō* denoting the process of observation and perception by the senses. In addition, the phrase "being understood" (*nooumena*) signifies the acquisition of knowledge by the workings of the rational mind. We concur with the conclusion of Murray, Kant notwithstanding, that "phenomena disclose the noumena of God's transcendent perfection and specific divinity."[36]

3. The sinful heart consistently suppresses the knowledge, derived from nature, of God as Creator (vv. 21–22, 28). Although the knowledge of God was impressed on human hearts and minds, Paul asserts that "they did not think it worthwhile to retain the knowledge of God" (v. 28). The verb *dokimazō* suggests the idea of testing or proving. People tasted the knowledge of God as Sovereign and Judge, found it not to their liking, and thus summarily dismissed it from their lives. Determined to seek meaning apart from God, they proceeded to fashion lifeless idols in the form of birds, animals, and reptiles (v. 23). The result of this rejection of the light of general revelation is that they "exchanged the truth of God for a lie, and worshiped and served created things rather than the Creator" (v. 25). Wherefore three times (vv. 24, 26, 28) Paul insists that "God gave them over" to the impulses of their lower nature. Rejection of the knowledge of God as Creator resulted in defilement of the human body (vv. 24–27), chiefly in the form of sexual perversions, and in defilement of the human spirit (vv. 28–32), namely, in the form of a host of crimes against the neighbor and the community.

4. Finally, humanity's deliberate repudiation of the light of the knowledge of God establishes human guiltworthiness before the bar of divine justice (v. 20). All people, having perceived God's eternal power and divine nature and having rejected it, are said to be "without excuse" (*anapologētos*), that

is, lacking any defense against an accusation. The divine revelation in nature thus is an instrument not of salvation but of judgment. Because the knowledge of God (both innate and acquired) is trampled underfoot, God justly sentences all to death (v. 32).

In Romans 2:14–15, the apostle Paul teaches that all people at all times and places possess an intuitive knowledge of God's moral law. Apart from any contact with the written law of God, humans *qua* humans instinctively know that God requires goodness and abhors evil. In the wider context of Romans 2:12–16, the apostle states that all people stand condemned before God, since all have violated his holy laws. The Jews are guilty because they have transgressed the law given through Moses; and the Gentiles, who have not the Mosaic Law, are likewise guilty because they have violated the unwritten law of God inscribed on their hearts. "The requirements of the law" (*to ergon tou nomou*, v. 15), said by Paul to be written on the Gentiles' hearts, should be understood not as the set of moral values that the sinner learns from a religious and social milieu (the so-called affects of the law).[37] Rather, the phrase signifies the statutory dimension of the law engraved on the heart by virtue of which all people know the difference between good and evil. The apostle in verses 14–15 draws a precise parallel between the written law of Moses accessible to the Jews and the unwritten law implanted on the hearts of the Gentiles. Paul concludes his discussion by affirming that conscience (*syneidēsis*, co-knowing), the universal faculty of moral judgment, testifies to each person's compliance or noncompliance with the moral law within. Although a person's conscience may be hardened or seared, the accusations of conscience nevertheless convey the realization that there is a supreme Lawgiver and Judge who rewards good and requites evil. In sum, the moral law implanted within and the testimony of conscience provide additional means by which all people gain a rudimentary knowledge of God and his moral requirements.

The Johannine Literature

John's contribution to the issue focuses on the illuminatory operation of the Logos. John affirms of the eternal Word, "In him was life, and that life was the light of men" (John 1:4). Moreover, the Word is "the true light that gives light to every man who comes into the world" (John 1:9).[38] John's use of the Logos represents the synthesis of the Old Testament Word of the Lord (*debār Yahweh*) and Hellenistic (Stoic) usage that finds many parallels in the Wisdom motif in late Judaism. The Stoics saw in the Logos the divine power that pervades all things and that undergirds rational and moral life. The Book of Proverbs semihypostatizes and portrays Wisdom (the parallel Jewish motif) as the first of all created entities. In the Wisdom of Solomon 7:22–9:18, wisdom, among other functions, leads people to the attainment of knowledge of God. Thus in late Jewish thought, Wisdom is analogous to the power of God—operative in the world, creating, enlightening, and renewing. An identical pattern is found in John's use of the Logos motif in the fourth Gospel. The eternal Word created the universe (John 1:3), illumines human intellectual and moral faculties (John 1:4, 9), and, having become incarnate, renews spiritually those who believe in him (John 3:3, 16). Thus it seems clear that in John 1:4, 9 the apostle teaches that through the universal operation of the Logos the mind of every person is divinely illumined so as to perceive God as the inescapable datum of human existence. All people, by virtue of the general illumination of the Logos, reflect—in the manner of Calvin's "sense of divinity" or "seed of religion"—awareness of the reality of God within their hearts or minds. Tasker, among other exegetes, agrees with this interpretation, claiming that "the source of man's intellectual and spiritual perception, his conscience as well as his consciousness, is the divine Word."[39] Plummer concurs, adding the perceptive observation, "The Light illumines every man, but not every man is better for it; that depends on himself."[40]

SYSTEMATIC FORMULATION

After gathering primary biblical data and secondary historical views of a subject, the next task of a student of theology is to organize those data coherently and to develop a comprehensive biblical doctrine.

Information Revealed to All (General Revelation)

What God Has Universally Revealed

As we have seen, the reality of a universal revelation through creation is clear from such passages as Psalm 19 and Romans 1–2. Exactly what has God made known to all people in and through creation?

1. God is one. In spite of the diversity of peoples and cultures, the evident unity of mankind indicates one source (Acts 17:26), and the order of the cosmos similarly indicates one sustainer God (Ps. 19:1–5; Rom. 1:20).

2. The Creator, who has life in himself, is the source of all that has life (Acts 17:25).

3. God is eternal and independent of everything else (Ps. 93:2; Rom. 1:20; Acts 17:25).

4. God is invisible and powerful (Rom. 1:20).

5. God is personal and wise (Ps. 104:24).

6. Although distinct from the universe, God is active in it (Acts 17:24, 26–27).

7. The Creator of mankind is the continuous source of earth's life-support system (Acts 14:15–16; 17:24–28).

8. The living and relating God is moral and just in himself and in his judgment of people and nations (Acts 14:17; Rom. 1:32; 2:14–15).

9. God alone, as the ultimate source and support of values, is of supreme worth and deserving of ultimate concern and worship. Idolaters exchange this truth for a lie (Acts 14:15; 17:23; Rom. 1:25).[41]

It is important to see that there are no redemptive truths here! What *is* revealed through nature is the heart of a theistic world-and-life view. "Theism signifies belief in one God (*theos*) who is (1) personal, (2) worthy of adoration, and (3) separate from the world, but (4) continuously active in it."[42] The ultimate reality is not an impersonal Thatness or energy, but a personal, knowing, and active God. The world is not a part or a mode of God, as pantheists and panentheists think, but a temporal creation of an eternal God distinct from it. People are not divine and cannot hope to become like God. Although distinct from the world (transcendent), God is also continuously relating to it (immanent). God did not create the world and then leave it to run on its own, as deists think.

The truths revealed universally imply an irreducible twofold nature of reality that must not be overlooked in the quest for a unified world-and-life view. Reality is not all of one kind. Ever since Creation there has been a *metaphysical dualism:* the eternal Creator cannot be reduced to the level of any part of creation, and creatures ought never to confuse themselves with deity (Rom. 1:20–25). Furthermore, an *ethical dualism* is presupposed in the truths of universal revelation (Rom. 2:14–15):

Never call evil good or good evil. Similarly implied is an ineradicable *epistemological dualism* between truth and falsehood (Rom. 1:25): truth ought not be reduced to error, and error ought never be regarded as true.

This latter difference between truth and falsehood relates to the fact that revealed truth concerning God can be asserted in universally significant propositions expressed in sentences. "A proposition is an assertion which proposes or denies something, and is capable of being judged true or false."[43] A proposition is expressed in indicative sentences with a subject (S), some form of the verb "to be" (e.g., is), and a predicate nominative (P); a proposition thus has the general form "S is P." Although in ordinary conversation people may not emphasize such indicative sentences, when their deepest beliefs about what is real and important are challenged, propositions become crucial. The languages in which the assertion is expressed may be as diverse as English, Sanskrit, or Chinese, but the logical content affirmed can in essence be the same. The meaning of the nine propositions listed above is made known universally, whatever the language in which it is spoken or written, and can be understood even by the nonliterate.

It also follows that, since these propositions are true, their contradictories are false, or "lies" (as Paul calls them in Rom. 1:25), presupposing the validity of the logical law of noncontradiction (i.e., both the affirmation and the denial of the same thing cannot be true at the same time and in the same respect). The law of noncontradiction is important in evaluating the claim that it does not matter what one calls God so long as one worships God. Names for God convey meanings ascribed to the ultimate reality. Divine names are not mere signs without significance. Names for God in any language or religion are acceptable logically if they convey the meanings listed above or are not contradictory to them, other considerations being equal. But divine names designating concepts contradictory to the content of general revelation cannot be accepted on logical principle. If one's ultimate concern is the Creator, it cannot be temporal process, evolution, "mother nature," or one's own inner self viewed as divine. Our ultimate loyalties ought not be to gurus, witch doctors, teachers, rabbis, preachers, parents, political leaders, or any historical institutions or processes.

Not every difference of thought or wording is a logical contradiction, however. Only logical contradictions of revealed truths must necessarily be rejected on logical principles. Theists may profitably study comparative religions, anthropology, the psychology of religious experience, and philosophy of religion with an openness to learn from varieties of thought and expression that supplement or confirm but do not flatly contradict what God has disclosed to be true.

In view of this data supporting a universal cognitive revelation of the essence of theism, we conclude that existentialist and Barthian hypotheses insofar as they deny a universal revelation fail to fit the relevant facts.

Where God's Universal Revelation May Be Seen

Granting that God has made his existence, power, and moral demands known in creation, where, more specifically, may these truths be perceived? God's universal revelation is made known in (1) the universal human consciousness of dependence on a higher being, (2) the universal capacity to distinguish right from wrong, (3) the order, regularity and intelligibility of nature, and (4) the continuous judgments in history on persons and nations.

73

First, God has revealed his presence *in human consciousness of dependence on a higher being*. Millions of Hindus sense an inner awareness of the "thatness" beyond themselves and the observable world. Life touches on a reality beyond itself. People from varied cultures through the centuries have testified to a sense of dependence on something greater than they, even though this sense of dependence may not be perceived as a distinctly religious experience. Schleiermacher referred to a universal consciousness or feeling of "unqualified dependence,"[44] and many who try to suppress this awareness are haunted by the feeling that "there must be something more." Augustine's attempt to suppress this sense of dependence led to increasing anxiety and a feeling of emptiness. Out of years of unfulfilled experience he prayed, "Thou hast created us for thyself, and our hearts are restless until they find their rest in thee."

Second, God discloses his moral nature *in human conscience with its sense of obligation or "oughtness."*[45] People in cultures throughout the world acknowledge a difference between what is just and what is unjust, particularly if they are treated unjustly themselves. People *ought* not treat other people unfairly. Researchers *ought* not represent their findings dishonestly. People *ought* to respect honesty. The universality and necessity of such norms indicate that these norms are more than the results of public opinion polls and more than the probable conclusions of social scientists. No one ought ever to treat others unjustly or dishonestly, not teachers, students, judges, legislators, law-enforcement people, parents, children, spouses, or neighbors.

Normative moral distinctions, however different in application in different cultures, permeate every culture. Expectations of moral decency within nations and among nations and cultures presuppose the objective validity of moral distinctions. The biblical explanation that a transcendent God has "written" the requirements of moral law on our hearts (Rom. 2:14–15) accounts most adequately for the nonnegotiable principles of justice that ought to be maintained without respect of persons.

Third, God reveals his intelligence, power, and personal qualities *in nature's intelligibility and awesome power and in life, especially human life*. Indications of the divine existence are seen, not only in subjective human consciousness and conscience, but also in objective givens in the universe. The world we observe is not self-derived, self-explanatory, or self-sufficient. It points to a source beyond itself, the Source already known in humanity's moral experience. Both the world's raw materials and its form come from God. God is both creative will and Logos, both the source of vitality and the source of conceptual meaning.[46] Nature exists but is not eternal. Nature has a beginning in the finite past: God created it all out of nothing (*ex nihilo*). Nature displays order on the microscopic and macroscopic levels, as well as on the levels of ordinary human experience. Nature displays an exceptional amount of power; and nature presents us with life, not only plant and animal life, but also human, personal life. In view of these data, it is improbable that nature's source is nonintelligent and purposeless, nonliving and nonpersonal. Nature makes more explicit the revelation in human consciousness that God is both transcendent and immanent, wise and powerful. And since persons are the highest reality in nature, their most likely source is also intelligent, powerful, and personal.

Fourth, God reveals his moral uprightness *in history's judgment of people and nations*. Human history is not merely a record of humanity's quest for God or of increasingly adequate definitions of God. It is rather the record of the tendency of persons and nations to rebel against creatureliness and dependence on God. People seek to be as independent, as secure, and as autonomous as God. Having received the truths of general revelation, they sometimes do by nature the things required by God's law. But more often, their knowledge is better than their actions. Knowing the requirements of God's just principles, they fail to live by them, and then they experience the deserved consequences.

Given these lines of internal and external human experience, we concur with Aquinas, Schleiermacher, Tillich, and Rahner (against Barth) on theological significance in empirical, historical, moral, and spiritual experience.

Human Perception of Universal Revelation (Natural Theology)

The Scriptures teach both that God makes reliable information available to people and that people universally perceive it. *General revelation* is God's activity of making known to people his eternal existence, and *natural theology* as used here is the people's activity of perceiving this truth. In other contexts, "natural theology" often refers only to Thomas Aquinas's five arguments from the sensory observation of nature, but here it refers to knowledge of God from creation derived from any sort of inner as well as external experience and any valid form of interpretation or argument utilizing those data.

The reality of natural theology, though devalued or denied in some Barthian and Reformed thinking, is explicitly and repeatedly taught in Scripture. As we have seen in the previous section, several times in Romans 1 the ungodly are said to know God. They are not held guilty for rejecting the gospel they did not know but for

disbelieving and disobeying the Creator they *did* know. The ungodly must have been aware of the Creation truths in order to have "suppressed the truth" (Rom. 1:18). Indeed, the presence of these truths is the basis of their culpability in disobedience to God and his moral principles.

The texts often used by Barth and Reformed theologians to deny the actuality of a natural knowledge of God fail to take sufficiently into account the two kinds of knowledge of God required by the respective contexts: knowledge of a moral theism and knowledge of God's redemptive plan. Passages of Scripture that state that people do not know God deny, not a knowledge of theism, but a knowledge of *God's redemptive plan* in the incarnate, crucified, and risen Christ. Before Paul says that the Galatians formerly did not know God (Gal. 4:8), he spoke of their being sons of God through faith in Jesus Christ (Gal. 3:26), and he said that having the witness of the Holy Spirit in the heart one is a child of God spiritually (Gal. 4:1–7). Although no one is by nature a spiritually reborn child of God, everyone is by nature a child of the Creator, deriving life and breath from him (Acts 17:28). The lack of redemptive sonship does not deny the reality of a metaphysical creaturely sonship.

Does the teaching that some truth can be known through the creation contradict the teaching that depraved minds cannot understand the things of God apart from faith in Christ (1 Cor. 2:14)? Again, the context has to do with redemptive truth—the message of the Cross (1 Cor. 1:18), Jesus Christ and him crucified (1 Cor. 2:2). If by some effort we extend depravity to include the absence of any knowledge of God's existence, then it is important to recall the Augustinian emphasis on a universal as well as a special work of divine illumination.[47] God's Logos, through whom all things were made, gave people life, and "that life was the light of men" (John 1:4). And "the true light that gives light to every man was coming into the world" (John 1:9). Even more explicitly, Paul argues that the ungodly have a knowledge of theism "because God has made it plain to them" (Rom. 1:19). Thus, in addition to the divine activity of general revelation and the human activity of learning from this revelation, there is another divine activity that enables fallen, fleshly minds clearly to see and understand the theistic content that has been revealed.

It is true, of course, that the nature psalms and Romans 1 were written by people of faith. Can it be inferred from this that what is taught in these passages can apply only to believers? No. What is taught is the universal, continuous, and clear revelation to all, the perception of all, and the accountability of all. One might as well affirm that Paul's description of the basis of condemnation (Rom. 3:9–20) still holds for believers because the passage was written by a believer. If believers today can discuss the status of unbelievers before God, surely biblical writers could.

The teaching of Scripture that all human beings do know the truths of theism and inexcusably fail to live up to them does not automatically support any particular type of argument for God's existence and moral administration of the world. People asked to state the reasons for their belief in God give quite different arguments. But with different starting points, intermediate steps, degrees of probability, and psychological certitude, all conclude that God exists.

Prior to faith in Christ, some theists have only a vague feeling of a Creator, others a rational intuition. Many have followed the five arguments of Aquinas from observed data to an adequate cause. Some simply testify to their own mystical experiences of God. Others presuppose God's existence and show how that assumption lends meaning to everything else. People propose the hypothesis of God's existence and find it verified rather than disconfirmed by many converging lines of external and internal data.

The Bible does not support any one of these forms of argument explicitly. It simply asserts that, from the things made, people do know (by whatever type of reasoning) God's eternal power and personhood. Although one may find one argument for concluding that God exists more convincing than another, we may need to recognize the cumulative impact of all external and internal data and the valid elements in all lines of reasoning based on them. For the weighing of strengths and weaknesses of each type of reasoning, it is wise to examine textbooks on Christian apologetics.[48]

The Dutch Reformed and Barthian hypotheses denying natural knowledge of God do not account for this evidence as adequately as the Augustinian evangelical doctrine does.

Human Accountability for Universal Revelation

God's intention in the giving of universal revelation, as in the giving of the Mosaic Law, was that any who would live in accordance with it would be right with him. "God did this so that men would seek him and perhaps reach out for him and find him" (Acts 17:27). People who perfectly and continuously keep the requirements written on their own heart (Rom. 2:14–15) or in the Mosaic Law, or who worship and serve the Creator more than the creature (Rom. 1:25), need not fear divine condemnation.

The question is whether anyone ever meets these just requirements continuously and perfectly all of his or her life. The Scriptures clearly teach that no one does. Righteousness before God cannot be achieved by depraved sinners attempting to keep God's moral law. All non-Jews (Gentiles) are accountable before God's general revelation (Rom. 1:18–2:16). All Jews are accountable in addition before the written law of Moses (Rom. 2:17–3:8). On the basis of what they *know*, God finds all Gentiles and Jews without respect of persons to be "under sin" (Rom. 3:9–18). God's standard is "holy, just and good" (Rom. 7:12). The problem is not with the divine demands but with fallen human nature, with what the "flesh" cannot do (Rom. 8:3). Hence, it is descriptively a fact that all who have not by faith received the gift of Christ's perfect righteousness remain under condemnation (John 3:18, 36).

But, in view of the teaching of Romans 1–3, it is simply inaccurate to affirm that rejection of Christ is the only reason anyone will ever be found guilty by God. The present-tense verbs throughout Romans 1 indicate that the universal revelation is continuous and actually perceived. On that basis an omniscient and uncompromisingly moral Judge finds all people inexcusably idolatrous in relation to himself and unjust in relationships with other people, regardless of whether they have heard of Christ or not.

The universality of moral accountability, of failure to attain the moral ideal, and of divine condemnation often raises the objection that God is unjust. Dale Moody asks the hard question, which no one can sidestep: "But what kind of God is he who gives man enough knowledge to damn him but not enough to save him?"[49] Moody argues that the possibilities resulting from general revelation must be positive as well as negative, redemptive as well as condemnatory. Hypothetically, he is right. Anyone who could keep the moral law continuously and perfectly would not be justly found guilty of any injustice. Prior to the Fall, general revelation was

indeed both redemptive and condemnatory: Adam and Eve could have obeyed God, and had they done so, the result would have been positive and not negative. But reality for us is the fallen human condition: no one born of the flesh with a fleshly nature (John 3:6) loves God and neighbors perfectly. God wrote the requirements of morality on our hearts that we might find him, not that we might be condemned. We, of our own will, have rebelled against those requirements. Moody's inference that it is unjust of God to demand justice because we may be condemned by those standards reminds one of a college dean who argued that the students should have no rules so that they would not feel guilty for breaking them.

Granting the propensities toward evil in the fallen race and the pervasiveness of greed, hate, murder, lust, and rape— even in the presence of the restraints imposed by God's universal moral law—we can imagine how intolerable and impossible life would be without a universal sense of uncompromising justice and fair play. As a restraint on flagrant evils, the revelation of moral principles to all constitutes a manifestation of God's universal concern for the well-being of all. How could God remain just, we ask, and not call injustice wrong?

The God of the Bible does not arbitrarily condemn anyone but judges according to people's works, according to the truth they knew. These principles hold true without respect of persons, not only within certain subcultures (such as evangelicalism) or cultures (such as that of North America), but for all nations and peoples in the world. And we need not fear that the all-knowing Judge of all the earth will not do right. None will be punished more than they deserve.

Thus the fundamental significance of the revelation in creation is this: that through it man as man is a *person*, a responsible being, a being related to God, "standing before" him; and also that by this revelation man is responsible for his sin, and is therefore inexcusable. This is why it is the presupposition of the saving revelation in Jesus Christ, although in itself it has no saving significance.[50]

One question that remains in debate is whether the Holy Spirit brings conviction of sin and repentance to people who never hear the message about Jesus Christ. Evangelicals know that no one lives up to the light he or she has received through general revelation or the law of Moses. No one is absolved of real guilt, changed in nature, and restored to fellowship with God by trying to be as good as possible or by being as good as or better than others.

However, some suggest that although no one is perfectly good, a person can repent of sin without having heard of Christ. They believe that those who realize their guilt and throw themselves on the mercy of the divine court with a sincerity that shows in their lives will find mercy because of the cross of Christ, even though they have never heard of it.[51] Others believe that probably no such people exist. The latter view appears to be more in harmony with the overall teaching of Scripture. Repentance, like every other good gift, is from above, the result of a preliminary work of the Holy Spirit in bringing people to Christ. Faith comes by hearing, through a human instrument (Rom. 10:9–14). All who receive the preliminary work of the Spirit leading to a repentant heart (rather than merely a temporary intention) in God's providence hear the gospel in some way, whether it be through a believer, literature, or the media. That is why the Savior left his disciples with the unforgettable words of the Great Commission as recorded by Luke: "Repentance and forgiveness of sins will be preached in his [Christ's] name to all nations, beginning in Jerusalem. You are my witnesses of these things" (Luke 24:47–48).[52]

APOLOGETIC INTERACTION

Those who accept a universal revelation and knowledge of God's existence and moral demands will need to be prepared for rejection on the basis that the doctrine does not fit the facts of experience. Can we claim a universal knowledge of a personal God when atheists and pantheists explicitly deny his existence? Liberal and other universalist thinkers who regard natural knowledge of God sufficient for relating to God challenge the conclusion that universal knowledge of God's existence and moral demands does not put people morally and spiritually right with God. Then Barthian theologians flatly deny that either Scripture or experience justifies belief in any universal revelation and knowledge of the true God.

One caution before investigating the data of human experience to determine whether the biblical teachings fit the facts. The biblical hypothesis asserts not only a general revelation and natural theology but also the universal tendency in sinful people to suppress this truth.

We ought not expect, then, that Gallup polls will disclose that 100 percent of respondents affirm belief in the one true God or that those who do affirm it live up to his moral norms. Rather, if the scriptural position is in harmony with the experience of mankind, we should expect to find in each generation traces of a prior awareness of the truths revealed: (1) some consciousness of a higher power on which life depends, (2) a sense of a real difference between right and wrong, (3) a consciousness of moral purpose and accountability in history, and, at the same time, (4) indications of sinful rebellion against these truths in atheistic suppressions and religious distortions. These four points together coherently account for the elements of truth and of error in the world's philosophies and religions.

Atheistic Suppression

We do not claim that atheists are believers in disguise, but rather that, having cognitive knowledge of God, it is foolish for them to say in their hearts that God is nonexistent (Ps. 53:1). Knowing better, they are foolish not to yield themselves to God and to claim that assertions about God are meaningless (according to logical-positivist or existentialist categories). An atheist can neither live meaningfully as a human being nor understand himself without adhering to some ultimate loyalty and concern.

Nontheists, for example, will often pledge loyalty to many of the same values as theists: the dignity of man; human rights; the obligation to remove racial, social, and economic injustices; the promotion of understanding and peace among nations; and the alleviation of natural evils such as earthquakes and moral evils such as alcoholism. But if ultimate reality is nonmoral and reducible to a quantifiable scientific explanation, then there is no *nonnegotiable* basis for these values. Thus secular humanist presuppositions tend to suppress the truth that their inherent value derives from a higher source. Nontheists cannot account for the universality and necessity of principles of justice.

What amazes theists is not that nontheists have no ultimate concerns, but that they find it possible to worship and serve. Corliss Lamont, author of *The Philosophy of Humanism*, finds it unreasonable to worship a personal God distinct from the world, but he does find it reasonable to call the scientific method "an instrument of infinite power."[53] He accepts the impersonal, nonpurposive universe as "self-existing" and history as "a continuous process" (eternal).[54] Could this be worship and service of the creature rather than the Creator (Rom. 1:25)?

Pantheistic Distortions

Scholars studying world religions find differently worded but rather similar vestiges of original general revelation and natural theology in the world's religions. S. H. Kellogg lists four basic similarities among the world's theistic, pantheistic, nontheistic, and animistic religions. First, all religions "assume the existence of a Power (or powers) superior to man, on which he is dependent, and which is able to influence his destiny." Second, "because of man's relation to this Supreme Power, certain things are obligatory on him, and other things must be avoided at the peril of suffering." Third, "between man and the Supreme Power or powers, something is wrong." Fourth, "there is for man a state of being after death; and the consequence of wrongdoing or rightdoing in this present life will follow a man after death."[55] Kellogg's findings include both the theistic consciousness and its distortions in pantheistic worship of the creation.

Aldous Huxley's portrayal of "the perennial philosophy" in various forms in culture after culture over a period of twenty-five centuries slants these truths toward monistic pantheism.[56] At the core of the perennial philosophy Huxley finds four fundamental doctrines:

First, the phenomenal world of matter and of individualized consciousness . . . is the manifestation of a Divine Ground . . . apart from which they would be nonexistent. Second: human beings are capable not merely of knowing about the Divine Ground by inference; they can also realize its existence by a direct intuition. . . . This immediate knowledge unites the knower with that which is known. Third: men possess a double nature, a phenomenal ego and an eternal Self, which is the inner man, the spirit, the spark of divinity within the soul. Fourth: man's life on earth has only one end and purpose: to identify himself with his eternal Self and so to come to unitive knowledge of the Divine Ground.[57]

Huston Smith prefers to speak of "the primordial tradition" rather than the "perennial religion," because he thinks these beliefs express less an intellectual philosophy than a tradition. The author of *The Religions of Man* wrote *Forgotten Truth: The Primordial Tradition* to show that beyond the quantifiable limits of science people have found values, purposes, and meanings in life through the tradition, which includes the recognition of infinite being, infinite awareness, and infinite bliss.[58] Smith moves toward Vedanta Hinduism when he says that theism is "true," but not the final truth. God's personal mode is not the final reality, he thinks, because the final reality is spoken of literally only in negative terms, and in positive terms only analogically and paradoxically.[59]

Smith's typical allegation that conceptual knowledge limits God confuses assertions with their referents. Do we limit Niagara Falls by defining water? And Smith has failed to show the superiority of impersonal analogies of God to personal ones. Smith also misses the mark of truth when he supposes that the human mind was made for knowing facts and fictions but not ultimates.[60] The mind of man was and is renewed to know God in part (1 Cor. 13:12; Col. 3:10). In the first use of language reported in Scripture, God communicated with man (Gen. 1:28–30; 2:16). Univocal knowledge is denied whenever the realm of time, space, and human thought is consigned to the relative and changing and whenever God is said to be totally different. Indeed God is changeless, but God created mankind to think his thoughts after him, using analogies with univocally valid points, as shown above in the propositional content of universal revelation.

C. S. Lewis observes that people generally prefer to distort the theistic belief in a concrete, choosing, commanding, prohibiting God with determinate character and purposes into a pantheistic being in general, about which nothing can be truly asserted, who does nothing and demands nothing, who is there if you wish for him, like a book on a shelf, but will not pursue you. But the point of general revelation is that God is "the fountain of facthood." God invents, acts, and creates. He creates concrete, individual, determinate things that do exist: things like flamingoes, lovers, pineapples, comets, and kangaroos. This concreteness is not accounted for by abstractions of logic or scientific law. "If God is the ultimate source of all concrete, individual things and events, then God Himself must be concrete and individual in the highest degree."[61]

The impulse of fallen humanity toward pantheism has been revitalized today in the rejuvenation of Eastern religions, the New Age movement, new-consciousness groups, and human potential movements. "Yet by a strange irony, each new relapse into this immemorial 'religion' is hailed as the last word in novelty and emancipation."[62] Pantheists—however perennial, traditional, or "new" their religion may seem to be—distort the original, theistic revelation and worship and serve created energy rather than the Creator (Rom. 1:25).

Liberal Theology's Inflation

Liberalism traditionally assumed a naturalistic, evolutionary view of the world, an optimistic view of man as inherently good, and a reductive view of Scripture as little more than a collection of minute segments written and compiled by children of their respective times. Mankind having no supernaturally inspired propositions from above, DeWolf's natural theology "corrects" the Bible.[63] No distinctive special revelation remains. Redemption is unnecessary. Revelation in nature is made the determinative revelation.

Here is a crucial issue with liberalism. Do the traditions of the world religions and philosophies represent the final truth by which to correct Scripture, or do the Scriptures (when validly interpreted) represent the final truth by which to correct the religious philosophies? Because the data of experience can be readily misinterpreted, the more specific biblical corrective is needed and was "breathed out" by God.

Misinterpretations of Scripture may be corrected by responsibly interpreted data from history and the sciences. And irresponsible historical and scientific interpretations can be corrected by responsibly interpreted Scripture.

Given the best efforts at adhering faithfully to sound scientific, historical, epistemological, and hermeneutical principles, we may nevertheless be confronted with contradictory assertions from nature and Scripture. When this happens, the view that is drawn from sound exegesis of Scripture and confirmed by people of varied cultural perspectives throughout the creedal history of the church is the least likely to be the one in error. Even apart from the supernatural inspiration of Scripture, linguistic statements permit greater precision in communication than nonverbal types of communication. We are less likely to misinterpret language on a subject than mere objects or events. Special revelation must not be demoted and understood as inferior to general revelation.

Neoorthodox Denials

Karl Barth represents one of the most vigorous recent writers in opposition to both universal revelation and natural theology. He speaks for a host of experience-oriented people from varied theological perspectives who consider divine revelation essentially noninformational. What God reveals is himself, we are told, and not information *about* himself.[64] This concept of revelation is based on extreme views of God's transcendence,[65] making God's mind totally different from the human mind, thus undercutting the fact that our minds are made in the image of God's (Col. 3:10).[66] Barth also fails to distinguish nonredemptive knowledge of God from redemptive knowledge, confusing revelation with redemption and imagining that there is no revelation if there is no positive human response (which contradicts Romans 1).[67] Barth and others also think that a direct Person-to-person encounter excludes information from the essence of revelation. However, the author of Psalm 19 appreciated both the way God's written Word "revives the soul" (vv. 7–10) and the way nature "declares God's glory" (vv. 1–6). And Paul, who so personally met Christ on the Damascus road (Acts 9:1–19), fully appreciated the knowledge of God's existence and moral norms mediated through nature (Rom. 1:18–25; 2:14–15).

Barth also denied general revelation and natural theology because he feared that any belief taken to be propositionally true in itself would become an idol (antichrist) and stand between a person and a personal relationship with Christ.[68] All who hold to objectively valid religious truths ought to share this concern. A system of theistic beliefs can become our ultimate concern rather than a means to lead us away from idols to a personal relationship with the One of whom the belief system speaks. But the belief system of theism is necessary to lead us away from the idols of materialism and pantheism to seek the Most High God. Such reliable assertions led people at Thessalonica away from idols to the living God (1 Thess. 1:9; 2:13). Conceptual truth is not an end in itself but a means to the end of avoiding worship and service of the unreal, the visible material creation, and the invisible demonic hosts.

On the basis of his presuppositions Barth considered the teaching of passages like Psalm 19 and Romans 1 incidental and contradictory to the major biblical teaching that unbelievers do not know God (1 Cor. 1:20–21). Commenting on the statement "The invisible things of God are clearly seen" (Rom. 1:20) Barth wrote, "And what does this mean but that we know nothing of God. . . ?"[69] However, it is hardly incidental to the teaching of Romans and other Scripture to affirm the essentials of a theistic world-and-life view in which all people are dependent on and accountable to God. Redemptive knowledge of God teaches the just basis on which God can forgive all who have failed to worship and serve him faithfully all of their lives. Moral knowledge helps people see their need for the gospel. Hence the moral law within and the knowledge of its source, the moral Creator, is not rendered unnecessary by the gospel. Natural theology and morality are the forerunners of the gospel.

An objectively valid revelation of God, then, is in fact true and important, not as an end in itself, but as a means of avoiding the worship and service of idols. It also provides a means of thankful acknowledgment of our dependence on God and of our obligation to the ultimate Source who created us in his image. The inexorable moral judgments within, like Moses' written law, become a strict teacher, enabling us to realize our need for a just amnesty and for the restoration of right relationships with God, ourselves, and our neighbors. General revelation must not be stripped of its significance by special revelation.

Of the historical and contemporary options available, an Augustinian-Reformed-Evangelical view provides the most coherent and viable account of the relevant biblical and experiential data with the fewest difficulties.

RELEVANCE TO LIFE AND MINISTRY

It would be advantageous if people working for a better world did so from a sound theological base and if well-grounded theologians were at the same time actively involved in promoting just relationships in the family, church, and society.

Assuming the validity of practicing what we know, preach, and teach, we here introduce some suggestions in application of the truth of a universal revelation. We make little attempt to delineate strategies and methods of influencing human life, leaving that to specialists in related fields (such as ethics, education, legislation, practical theology, and missions). But we try to highlight some practical ends and goals worth living, ministering, and dying for.

A universal revelation and a universal knowledge of God by common grace at this point is no longer a mere hypothesis. Its truth has been confirmed by Scripture and experience. What, then, are the values and purposes for life and ministry that follow from the truth about the reality of God's general revelation?

Pro-Life Universally

The above research has shown that the giving of rain, crops, food, and joy are "testimonies" to God's "kindness" (Acts 14:17). Can those who worship the *King* as Lord of all be unkind to their neighbors? Since our God "gives life and breath and everything else" (Acts 17:25) to all mankind, shall we unnecessarily pollute the air and waste planet earth's life support resources? Believing that God supports human life universally, we will be pro–human life in the broadest sense of the words. Regardless of economic, political, cultural, racial, educational, or religious differences, understanding theists, like their God, will be known for their kindness to all other persons as persons.

Among the values of people under God is the desire that all people should have the resources for a happy life. Theists whose resources have been met experience the joy of giving generously for the sake of those who lack the necessities of life. Persons, families, and communities who share God's objectives will contribute and work that all people may have adequate resources to pursue happiness.

Nontheists imagine that to believe in a personal God is to lose happiness. But among the values of believers in the great personal Giver of every good gift is the joy of giving.[70] By serving ends in harmony with those of the wise giver of the entire life-support system, theists discover the most lasting joy. Experience indicates that human happiness is seldom found when it is pursued as an end in itself.[71] Our highest and most lasting happiness is experienced when we do not make our happiness, but the well-being of others among our highest values.

Whatever else we may lose in this changing life, if we serve changeless God-given norms, our highest values cannot be taken away. Total relativists, materialists, and naturalists of all sorts face the loss of their highest loyalties, none of which is absolute or enduring. But God and the moral values of God's nature and law are incorruptible. Whatever losses occur in this fallen world,

those who serve the living God's values cannot lose the final source of inner joy. So in God's universal revelation theists discover a more enduring ground for supporting human values than humanists who are naturalists or atheists. However tragically some theists may have failed to realize this pro-life truth in history, theistic humanism better motivates and more permanently sustains human values than naturalistic or pantheistic humanisms.

Pro-Truth Universally

Although human knowers have their varied perspectives as relativists have so emphasized, a universal ability to *know* some objective truth about creation and the Creator is implied in a natural theology as a product of common grace. We know the difference between being in the presence of a person and being in the presence of a thing. We know that we ought to respect the rights of human beings. We know that we ought to treat people justly as we would be treated. We know that there is a real difference between right and wrong. Such knowledge is necessary to morally responsible behavior.

All the ordered, intelligible relationships or criteria in the world come from the creative mind of God. Beyond the multitudes of varying opinions in the world are unchanging principles of thought (logic), communication, education, aesthetics (rhyme, verse, proportion, scales, harmony), arithmetic, geometry, astronomy, physics, nuclear energy, anthropology, sociology, and psychology. By these principles we evaluate claims concerning these areas. Some theories in these fields are found to be better informed and closer to reality than others. Valid truths in a university's different departments and colleges are not ultimately irreconcilable.

Confidence in the theistic basis for unifying research in all fields motivated many of the early scientists and the founders of the great *uni*versities. Unfortunately the exaggerated individualism and total relativism of recent times has shattered confidence in a comprehensive world view and philosophy of life. Relativistic scientists have become so absorbed in the differences between revolutionary models and paradigms that they have forgotten the similarities. Many of the first scientists worked creatively because they were guided by the conviction that "the enduring rationality of the cosmos made sense only so long as the world, its laws and its constants were *given* in the deepest ontological sense."[72]

Pro-Justice Universally

A universal natural morality by common grace is part of a natural theology. "Conscience," whether clear or guilty, bears witness to the requirements of God's moral law inscribed on human hearts (Rom. 2:14–15). Humans universally discriminate between right and wrong. In their hearts, all human beings understandably demand justice and know that they ought to treat others fairly. The basic requirements of God's universal moral law were expressed by Moses. If we were to sum up the moral law of God, the Ten Commandments, in one word, God expects from all people justice. The prophets constantly called people back to basic morality under God. "And what does the LORD require of you? To act justly . . . and to walk humbly with your God" (Mic. 6:8).

What is just or unjust is not decided by the moral consensus. Fifty-one percent of a society may be wrong, as in the Nazi regime. What *is* does not decide what *ought* to be. A total relativism is inadequate to account for the universal sense of obligation to be a just person and act justly. Can theists who preach and teach a universal moral revelation, think that they will escape judgment for their injustice to their spouses? to their children? to neighbors? to students? to administrators? to faculty? to employees? to employers? Justice as an absolute is nonnegotiable. And the Administrator of Justice judges without respect of persons.

After examination of injustice in their own lives, contemporary theists, like the prophets of old, may be prepared to challenge the injustice and immorality in others whether in high or low places. Can theists place their highest values in the Lord of all and remain uninvolved with injustice to the poor, widows, orphans, prisoners, and refugees? However popular relativism may become, is there no objective and real difference between right and wrong? Is there no objective difference between helping a person and hurting a person? Even in the name of "law and order" it is wrong to oppress and exploit others! And even in the name of "liberation" it is wrong to seek personal vindictive vengeance. Freedom does not mean license to violate and destroy others.[73] Theists challenge immorality and injustice in high places when these threaten the well-being of creatures made in God's image.[74]

Pro–Human Accountability Universally

Talk about justice is cheap if no Administrator of Justice can be found. Unenforced moral norms in human hearts are of little use in a fallen world. But the doctrine of universal revelation shows that all people are not only dependent on God but also obligated to God the giver of every good. People are stewards of God's resources. He is their ultimate owner. Temporarily we are stewards accountable for sharing these resources for the benefit of all. Unfaithful stewardship fails to conserve the earth's finite life support resources, to develop them fully, and to distribute them generously.[75]

In a day of increasing disrespect for private property it seems relevant to note that half of the commandments are prohibitions against theft of what belongs to another. I must not covet anything that belongs to my neighbor or rob him of his life, wife, property, or reputation. I cannot deprive him of God's purpose through nature to provide my neighbor with freedom to grow crops, harvest them, and give to assist the less fortunate. Injustices resulting from private or state ownership come from attempts to be independent of the Creator who knows our thoughts and acts. Permanent improvements in economic and social situation will not come from communist programs that deceive people into thinking themselves to be autonomous and unaccountable to God. Correctives to selfish abuses of private ownership in accord with the moral law of God do not abolish private ownership, but they should abolish the irresponsibility and thanklessness of private owners who disregard the universal revelation (Rom. 1:21). Thankful theists, knowing that they are accountable to God, will exhibit generous, risk-taking stewardship of whatever they have from God's common grace.[76]

Accountability to God becomes essential for improved conditions in all realms. Whatever the form of government, no branch of government and no person in power may usurp ultimate authority or be given our ultimate loyalty. Whether in legislative, administrative, or executive branches, every leader has power under God. Every leader in any country ought to recognize his accountability to the highest Ruler of all. Given human experience, any form of political power can be corrupted. But absolute power is corrupted absolutely. No human being, as Plato's *Republic* vividly showed, is wise enough or good enough to be given

unaccountable power. Even where human accountability is built into political structures, the fullest alleviation of political injustice will not come without ultimate accountability to the all-knowing God.

The major objective of a pastor-teacher may not be to change political structures as such, if these structures have built-in checks and balances against the leader's absolute pretensions. But the major responsibility of Christian ministers is to call political leaders to accountable stewardship before the God on whom they depend for their life and breath. Under God human leaders are accountable in their governing to provide for their subjects a just ability to procure food and drink, the right to justice, and the freedom to pursue happiness. Like Paul at Athens, we must deliver the divine summons to repent to leaders who are inexcusable for not living up to the moral and spiritual truth they ought to see clearly.

Similarly theists will work for universal justice in education. More ultimate than school buildings and strategies and methods of teaching is the acknowledgment of dependence on the Creator and obligation to the moral Lawgiver and Administrator. All school teachers, administrators, and staff members are inexcusable for intellectual dishonesty. All educators will give account of prejudices that deprive qualified students of their right to learn. Public schools cannot justly serve only one segment of a pluralistic society. Does not the principle of justice indicate that since theists pay taxes equally, that theists' children should be able to hear a theistic interpretation of any field of learning in the curriculum as well as naturalistic and pantheistic interpretations? If so, justice works in the other direction also. Public schools cannot be made exclusively theistic if others besides theists pay for them. Academic freedom implies academic responsibility to the basic world views of the community served.

Although ministers and average church leaders as general practitioners may not be specialists in economics, politics, and education, they have an important contribution to make in each of these and other fields. If they know that all people in all fields are dependent on God, accountable to God, and guilty before God, they can call all people everywhere to repent.

In calling people to repent of injustice and to treat others justly as they would be treated, no church leaders need fear that they are thus imposing denominational, evangelical, or even distinctively Christian standards on non-Christians. This appeal to universal moral law is based on human nature and universal revelation, not on revelation to some persons and not on sectarian values. A Christian theist simply calls on people everywhere to uncover the nonnegotiable original requirements of God's law in their own hearts, however suppressed. Although evangelical theists may not be able to cooperate with nonevangelicals for evangelistic and missionary purposes, they may consistently cooperate with other theists (liberal Christian, Jewish, etc.) for concerted religious efforts for greater justice in school districts, neighborhoods, cities, states, and nations. And in the political arena theists may also, on the ground of the universal revelation and knowledge of justice, cooperate with nontheists who happen at the moment to be working for just causes.

Pro–Moral Education Universally

Another implication of a universal natural theology by common grace is the universal capacity in normal human beings for moral education to action on the basis of moral principles (derived from the nature and revelation of God). Before young people assume responsibilities in business, education, and government, they need to be morally mature and responsible. Increasing crime rates in high places have led to a concern for clarifying values and helping children to own them. The recent work of Lawrence Kohlberg has served as a catalyst for many studies on this subject.[77] Kohlberg found that children may justify or condemn their own actions in various ways: (1) They may choose to do something for a reward or to avoid punishment. (2) They may choose on mere pragmatic considerations. (3) They may be motivated by conventional approval or (4) by authoritative law and order considerations. (5) They may develop a respect for social contracts and legal concerns. Finally, (6) they may justify their moral actions by their harmony with universal ethical principles.

Where do children and adults get the capacity for deciding right and wrong on the basis, not of what is being done by their peers, but of universal moral principles? Nontheistic total relativism fails to provide an adequate answer. On the hypothesis of a universal implantation of the requirements of the moral law on human hearts, theists have an adequate explanation. Moral education brings students to a level at which they recall the moral principles God incorporated in their being.

Beyond accounting for absolute moral principles of justice, theists add an even higher motive—the ultimate motive—for deciding and acting on principle: not legalistic necessity, but thankful love. In church and family education theists will seek to develop in their children love for the Source and Support of moral values. And with love for God will come love for all people, to whom God universally gives life and breath.

The moral education of people on the basis of universal revelation takes logical precedence over their spiritual education on the basis of redemptive revelation to prophets and apostles. Before young children are asked to believe in Jesus' saving provision for them, they need to understand their ultimate dependence on the Creator, their obligation to his moral laws and their guilt before his just judgment. Children of all ages need to know that there is a real or objective difference between right and wrong, truth and falsehood. And they need to learn well that they will give account to God for what they choose to think, say, and do. Christian parents, child evangelists, and youth ministers need to remember this order. General revelation precedes special revelation.

Only after coming to an age of moral accountability for their actions can children be expected to understand what it is to be sinners guilty of injustice before God and in need of the Savior. After children are old enough to realize real guilt before divine justice, they are old enough to realize their need for the Savior. Then they can grasp to some degree that the sinless Jesus, who came from God, gave his life a just payment for the forgiveness of all their sins and their complete acceptance with God.

In a pluralistic world frantically seeking to suppress the truth of dependence on God and obligation to God, parents and teachers will start early to help children understand that important and loved as they are, they are not the center of the universe. God is. God-centered moral development also emphasizes that with our rights as persons come as many responsibilities before God and mankind.

Pro–Common Ground for Apologetic Purposes

A universal revelation and theology in a pluralistic world makes cross-philosophical communication possible. When people from other world views challenge the truth of Christianity, can Christians discover any points of contact on which both can agree? As Christians begin conversations with non-Christians, are there any common principles of sound thought or valid argument to which both can appeal? Are there any ground rules in common by which they can engage in a respectable debate?

Although nontheists may suppress and distort the truths of universal revelation and misuse the perceptual and reasoning capacities that make them possible, the doctrine of universal revelation implies common ground in several respects. Non-Christians as well as Christians are dependent on adequate provisions of air, food, and water to live. Both demand justice and can rediscover the moral law within them. Both are themselves moral-lawbreakers. Both are accountable to know the reality God created and to use the laws of sound reasoning that come from God. Both need to consciously affirm the truth that Someone cares about them, and both need love.

However different Christian and non-Christian prescriptions for restoring moral and spiritual fellowship may be, there is common ground in metaphysical dependence on God, moral accountability to God, and need for acceptance by God. While Dutch Reformed thinkers fear that acknowledgments of common ground make unsaved people independent of God, in fact no atheist exists apart from God's common grace. To deny that he is dependent makes him no less dependent. Again the fear that common ground makes humans autonomous is unfounded, for the admission of a common principle of justice does not make non-Christian philosophers independent of God's moral demands, but accountable to universal principles of morality.[78]

Christians speaking up for their faith may count on common ground as did Paul, the apostle to the pagans (nontheistic Gentiles) at Athens. Although in preaching to the Jews in the synagogues Paul reasoned out of the Scriptures (Acts 17:2), with pretheists and pre-Christians he reasoned out of God's revelation in nature, history, and the human heart. Addressing the atheistic Epicurean materialists, Stoic pantheists, and idolaters, Paul presented the truth about the God they worshiped as unknown (vv. 22–23). Although his points about God were in accord with Old Testament Scripture, Paul did not quote the Old Testament as of divine authority. Rather, he reminded the educated Athenians that their life and breath depended on the personal God (vv. 24–29) and that they were accountable to God, guilty before God, and in need of repentance (v. 30).

Paul at Athens established the truth about God as Creator and as giver of the moral law by recovering distorted common ground in the writings of one of the Stoic pantheists' own poets (v. 28). Paul's use of the common ground did not make the Athenians independent of God or autonomous. It made them more responsible for what they knew. Paul's approach began with theism and moved to the gospel of the crucified and risen Christ. Although some sneered and some put off deciding, Paul's approach was highly successful. Well-known leaders Dionysius and Damaris and several others came to believe in Christ (v. 34). And, according to church history, Dionysius became the first pastor of a Christian church in that influential ancient city. Paul, especially called and prepared for presenting the gospel to the pagans, first built on common ground to help naturalistic, pantheistic, and idolatrous people recover the truths of theism from general revelation. Paul's approach to the Athenians provides the most extensive New Testament example of reasoning with nontheistic unbelievers. The multiplying numbers of naturalists and

pantheists in post-Christian cultures need to believe that God is (Heb. 11:6) before they are asked to believe the gospel of the Lord Jesus Christ.

Pro–Common Ground Crossculturally in Missiology

A universal revelation and theology by common grace in a pluralistic world provides the basis for crosscultural communication. Christian missions, as observed by Lit-sen Chang in the Far East, reflected diminished effectiveness when missionaries failed to understand the importance of the distinctive content of universal revelation or confused it with the redemptive message of special, redemptive revelation.

On one extreme, liberal missionaries in the Far East tended to magnify the universal revelation into the entirety of revelation. Finding elements of theism and morality in non-Christian religions, liberals tended to regard theists as Christians. But if a moral theism were the whole essence of the Christian faith, then it would never have become distinct from Judaism's moral theism.[79] It would have been one more sect like those of the Pharisees and the Sadducees. The gospel message concerning the redemptive provisions of Christ's atonement differed not merely in degree but also in kind from the teaching of meritorious works in Eastern religions. It set forth, not what we must do to be just, but what Christ did for the best of people who come short of absolute justice.

Paul understood the theism that Judaism and Christianity held in common. But as one who had come to grasp the redemptive provision of Jesus as the Messiah, he considered his Jewish relatives and friends zealous, but unsaved (Rom. 10:1–2). The more they emphasized the justice of the law, the more they should have realized how short they themselves came from meeting it themselves. By trying to establish their own righteousness, they did not receive Christ's perfect righteousness as a gift by faith (vv. 3–4).

Similarly, liberal Christianity has missed the distinctive importance of Christ's once-for-all objective provision by which God remains just and justifies the ungodly who believe. Liberal missionaries found so much in common with non-Christians because they lost the heart of the good news about the incarnate, crucified, and risen Christ they came to present. So liberalism also lost the urgency to present the gospel of God's grace. The research above shows that missionary outreach is urgent. No fallen person has perfectly satisfied God's absolute justice by trying to live up to the moral law within. Given only general revelation, the best of us is not good enough.

Some Evangelicals seek to alleviate the awesome urgency to reach the un-reached with the gospel by suggesting that people who never heard the gospel may be acceptable to God, not on the basis of works, but on the basis of their repentance for insufficient meritorious works. Even though they have never heard of Christ or his atonement and its provisions, this view suggests, they may be accepted through repentance without faith.[80] We ask, however, whether the Holy Spirit ever convicts of sin to bring about authentic repentance without also providentially directing missionaries so that the permanently repentant may hear and believe the gospel of Christ?

Of course God is free to bring the gospel to anyone at any time independently of human missionary agents, and we must not limit him. But we must respect what God has revealed about his freely chosen way of bringing a knowledge of Christ's provisions to the unreached. Although the end of Romans 10 alludes to the hearing of the universal revelation (vv. 18–20), the earlier verses make clear that people must call on Christ to be saved (v. 13) and so must believe in Christ and hear about Christ from a preacher in order to believe (v. 14).[81]

On the other extreme in the Far East were pietistic fundamentalists and neoorthodox missionaries who urgently proclaimed the person of Christ and the gospel but failed to have a point of contact with non-Christians. Fundamentalism has characteristically neglected to develop a doctrine of universal revelation. So fundamentalist missionaries were isolated from contact with the people they sought to reach. They failed to capitalize on their common knowledge and to learn of cultural points of contact. This led to one-directional communication and insensitivity to people's needs. As a result, the Christian message seemed meaningless and irrelevant. Reacting against ecumenical missions, some fundamentalists sought "to serve the Creator by ignoring his creation."[82]

Christian missionaries (and what Christian in this shrinking world does not communicate crossculturally?) need general revelation for points of contact with people in every culture on earth. But since general revelation is law, not gospel, every missionary urgently needs to preach the good news of grace in Christ, not the message of salvation by works.

What is the relationship between general and special revelation? It is not one of sheer contrast and opposition, as B. B. Warfield saw it, but "rather one of supplement and completion."[83] "All religion and all morality which has ever been in the world is of God. Whether natural or revealed, it is he who has given it; and it is he alone who has maintained it, yea, and will maintain it, enlarge and enriched to meet sinful man's clamant needs and renewed man's deeper desires. Both religion and morality are rooted in God, live in God, and in all the states of their development, and phases of their manifestation alike reflect man's essential relations to God—relations of dependence and obligation."[84]

As Lit-sen Chang more succinctly put it, "Although we thoroughly realize the absolute insufficiency of general revelation for salvation, nevertheless, we should also realize that general revelation has certain value for the Christian religions and that there is a close relationship between the two. Special revelation has incorporated, corrected, and interpreted general revelation."[85]

The specially revealed gospel is *not* suspended in air, so to speak; it presupposes the order of nature and speaks to life everywhere in the world at its ultimate level. Special revelation itself shows the connection between common and special grace, between the order of nature and the order of redemptive grace.

Not everything practiced in a non-Christian culture need be given up, then, as people receive Christ's perfect righteousness. All that evangelical missionaries need to ask people to give up is their sin. All the true and good elements of the former religion and culture by common grace can be incorporated in a Christian world view and way of life. The Christ who saves is the Christ who created and sustains all that is, whether visible or invisible, and by him all things "hold together" (Col. 1:16–17). So evangelical Christian missionaries need not limit themselves to the special revelation contained in Scripture or to Christian sources like Paul, Apollos or Cephas. "All things are yours, . . . the *world* or life or death or the present or the future—all are yours, and you are of Christ, and Christ is of God" (1 Cor. 3:21–23).

Evangelical Christian missionaries have a basis in general revelation for drawing as many nonredemptive analogies from a culture as possible for illustrating the truths of metaphysical dependence on God and moral accountability to God. And although illustrations of aspects of the gospel may be found in a culture, it may be misleading to call the analogies redemptive as has become popular since the exciting account of *Peace Child*. No analogies are in themselves redemptive, and to speak of "redemptive analogies" from nature and culture may be misleading in terms of the conclusions drawn above.

REVIEW QUESTIONS

To Help Relate and Apply Each Section in This Chapter

1. *Briefly state the classical problem* this chapter addresses and indicate reasons why genuine inquiry into it is important for your world view and your existence personally and socially.

2. *Objectively summarize the influential answers* given to this problem in history as hypotheses to be tested. Be able to compare and contrast their real similarities and differences (not merely verbal similarities or differences).

3. *Highlight the primary biblical evidence* on which to decide among views—evidence found in the relevant teachings of the major divisions of Scripture—and decide for yourself which historical hypothesis (or synthesis of historical views) provides the most consistent and adequate account of the primary biblical data.

4. *Formulate in your own words your doctrinal conviction* in a logically consistent and adequate way, organizing your conclusions in ways you can explain clearly, support biblically, and communicate effectively to your spouse, children, friends, Bible class, or congregation.

5. *Defend your view* as you would to adherents of the alternative views, showing that the other views are logi-

cally less consistent and factually faced with more difficulties than your view in accounting for the givens, not only of special revelation but also of human experience in general.

6. *Explore the differences the viability of your conviction can make in your life.* Then test your understanding of the viability of your view by asking, "Can I live by it authentically (unhypocritically) in relation to God and to others in my family, church, vocation, neighborhood, city, nation, and world?"

MINISTRY PROJECTS

To Help Communicate This Doctrine in Christian Service

1. *Memorize one major verse or passage* that in its context teaches the heart of this doctrine and may serve as a text from which to preach, teach, or lead small group studies on the topic. The memorized passages from each chapter will build a body of content useful also for meditation and reference in informal discussions.

2. *Formulate the major idea of the doctrine in one sentence* based on the passage memorized. This idea should be useful as the major thesis of either a lesson for a class (junior high to adult) or a message for a church service.

3. *State the specific purpose or goal of your doctrinal lesson or message.* Your purpose should be more than informative. It should show why Christians need to accept this truth and live by it (unhypocritically). For teaching purposes, list indicators that would show to what extent class members have grasped the truth presented.

4. *Outline your message or lesson in complete sentences.* Indicate how you would support the truth of the doctrine's central ideas and its relevance to life and service. Incorporate elements from this chapter's historical, biblical, systematic, apologetic, and practical sections selected according to the value they have for your audience.

5. *List applications of the doctrine* for communicating the difference this conviction makes in life (for sermons, lessons, small-group Bible studies, or family devotional Bible studies). Applications should make clear what the doctrine is, why one needs to know it, and how it will make differences in thinking. Then show how the difference in thought will lead to differences in values, priorities, attitudes, speech, and personal action. Consider also the doctrine's possible significance for family, church, neighborhood, city, regional, and national actions.

6. *Start a file and begin collecting illustrations* of this doctrine's central idea, the points in your outline, and your applications.

7. *Write out your own doctrinal statement on this subject in one paragraph* (in half a page or less). To work toward a comprehensive doctrinal statement, collect your formulations based on a study of each chapter of *Integrative Theology.* As your own statement of Christian doctrine grows, you will find it personally strengthening and useful when you are called on for your beliefs in general and when you apply for service with churches, mission boards, and other Christian organizations. Any who seek ordination to Christian ministry will need a comprehensive doctrinal statement that covers the broad scope of theology.

CHAPTER 3

DIVINE REVELATION THROUGH CHRIST, PROPHETS, AND APOSTLES

Divine Revelation Through Christ, Prophets, and Apostles

THE PROBLEM: HOW DOES A MAN, WOMAN, OR CHILD, CREATED AND LOVED BY GOD, COME TO KNOW THE LORD OF THE UNIVERSE IN A PERSONAL, SAVING RELATION?

In the preceding chapter we showed that by means of general revelation God reveals himself to all people at all times and in all places so that his existence and something of his character and moral demands are known. No person, we have shown, is without a rudimentary knowledge of God and the moral law. But we have also seen that due to the debilitating effects of sin on the mind and will, God's revelation in nature, history, and the implanted moral law fails to accomplish the purpose for which it was given. Scripture plainly testifies that, motivated by a darkened heart, sinners repudiate the rudimentary knowledge of God mediated by general revelation and devote themselves to idols. Thus in the end, general revelation does not save; it serves only to condemn.

Consequently, if anyone is to be saved, the sovereign God must move to communicate further dimensions of his hidden person and redemptive plan. No amount of inductive inference from God's past activity can bring to light his inner purposes. No amount of deduction from permanent principles of operation can make known salvific grace. Since manifestly not all people are saved, a number of important questions follow. To whom does God disclose his redemptive grace? Furthermore, what is it that God reveals? Does he disclose himself alone? Or does he disclose his saving plan as well? The problem for the thoughtful Christian, then, is to determine by what means God has made known his saving purposes and how finite, alienated persons can identify and appropriate the several modes of special revelation.

A further issue of considerable importance today is whether God in the present continues to give added special revelation to his people. Did special revelation end with the exaltation of Christ and the close of the canon of Scripture, or does God continue to reveal heretofore undisclosed aspects of his redemptive purposes through specially appointed spokespersons?

The tendency in recent theology, both Protestant and Roman Catholic, has been to deny that objective knowledge or intellectual concepts are revealed by God and to insist that saving revelation takes the form of ineffable encounters. One authority, for example, states, "Nowhere in the Bible is revelation the disclosure of a transcendental mystery, or an element of information."[1] What is revealed, most nonevangelical scholars assert, is not information about God, but God himself in ecstatic experience. Thus a primary issue in regard to special revelation is whether God's self-disclosure is propositional or nonpropositional, or perhaps something of both.

Clearly special revelation is foundational to the entire Christian scheme of things. It constitutes the prerequisite for the formulation of a theology that is properly Christian. Moreover, it forms the basis whereby a person comes to know God savingly, to worship him, and to serve him meaningfully in life.

ALTERNATIVE PROPOSALS IN THE CHURCH

The sources of information about God's redemptive plan are so important to every person that it is not surprising that over the centuries strong differences about them have arisen in the church.

Roman Catholic Scholasticism

Traditional Roman Catholic theologians taught that natural knowledge of God is supplemented by a supernatural knowledge mediated by the teachings of the prophets, apostles, and Jesus Christ. God's redemptive revelation preserved in Scripture is enriched by oral tradition and interpreted by the teaching office of the church.

Thomas Aquinas postulated both an ascent to God by the light of reason and nature and a descent by God in the form of revelation to be received by faith. Revelation transcends but does not contradict truths about God secured by

reason. Aquinas affirmed that God gave saving revelation in the events of sacred history, in the words of chosen prophets and apostles, and supremely in the enfleshment of God's eternal Son. The permanent record of saving revelation was inerrantly recorded on the pages of the Bible. Aquinas stressed the cognitive character of special revelation. What God supernaturally revealed for faith's acceptance is described as "truths that exceed reason," "knowledge," "doctrine," and "sacred science." Aquinas, however, held that the Bible and the teachings of the church constitute two sources (*principia*) of Christian belief. Later Roman Catholic authorities were more insistent that church tradition represents a second source of revelation.

The Council of Trent opposed the *sola scriptura* principle of the Protestant Reformers and insisted that divine revelations were preserved both in Scripture and in ecclesiastical tradition. Thus the Council stated that the gospel, which is "the source of all saving truth and rule of conduct," is contained "in the written and unwritten traditions that have come down to us, having been received from the apostles from the mouth of Christ Himself, or from the apostles by the dictation of the Holy Spirit, and have been transmitted as it were from hand to hand . . . and preserved in continuous succession in the Catholic church."[2]

Enlightenment Skepticism

Enlightenment theologians and their modern disciples deny the possibility and necessity of supernatural revelation. Human reason, experience, and the scientific method are judged sufficient to provide modern people with the knowledge needed to forge their future. Spinoza, a pantheist, attacked the Christian concept of propositional revelation. The Word of God, he argued, cannot be captured in a book, in paper and ink. Enlightenment skepticism regarding special revelation was greatly abetted by Hume's rejection of miracles and his radical empiricist claim that theological statements, being non-verifiable by the senses, lack meaning. Moreover, Kant's denial of theoretical or metaphysical knowledge of God in favor of practical knowledge struck at the very foundations of the classical model of special revelation.

The consistent deists denied the reality of special revelation. Following the lead of Lord Herbert of Cherbury, they maintained that divine revelation to specific people at certain times conflicts with God's all-sufficient revelation in the Creation. As put by Matthew Tindal, "Can revelation . . . add anything to a religion thus absolutely perfect, universal, and immutable?"[3] Special revelation was judged unnecessary, since the rational mind and the scientific method could uncover all truth.

The German rationalists, following the deductive reasoning of Leibnitz and Wolff, likewise undermined the validity of special revelation. G. E. Lessing, for example, claimed: "All revealed religion is nothing but a reconfirmation of the religion of reason. Either it has no mysteries, or, if it does, it is indifferent whether the Christian combines them with one another, or with none at all."[4] Lessing envisaged revelation as the natural process whereby God effects his educative program for the human race.

In his book, *Has Christianity a Revelation?* F. Gerald Downing protests the intellectualist position that argues for the attainment of clear knowledge of God. Downing insists that from the biblical perspective God cannot be said to have revealed himself. "If God intended to 'reveal himself' in Christ, in the events of his life and death and resurrection and in his teaching, he failed."[5] The word "revelation" is best reserved for the future consummation.

Kierkegaard and Neoorthodoxy

Neoorthodox authorities and proponents of the so-called "biblical theology" maintain that God's saving purposes are revealed through mighty acts in the history of Israel and the church, and supremely in the Christ-event. In the present, revelation consists in the event of God speaking to a person in Jesus Christ through the medium of the biblical witness.

Kierkegaard inaugurated this emphasis with his postulate of the "infinite qualitative difference" between God and man, which implied the incomprehensibility of God to finite minds. Since God is unfathomable to discursive reason and the emotions, Kierkegaard insisted that the abyss between eternity and time must be closed by God himself. Thus the focus of God's revelation was said to be the Incarnation of the God-man in the form of a servant. God is known, not by an analysis of nature or history, but by the radical inbreaking of God in Jesus Christ. But given the severe chasm between eternity and time, Jesus Christ appears to the mind as an offense and a scandal, indeed, as the absolute paradox. Thus God's revelation must be received by a radical and passionate leap of faith.

Barth, following Kierkegaard, insisted that the transcendent Word is the only revelation. God discloses himself, not through propositional information, but only as the Ineffable breaks into a person's existence in an experience of crisis, evoking the response of decision and trust. In Barth's own words:

> Real revelation puts man in God's presence. . . . It is the revelation which is attested to ourselves. . . . An objective revelation as such, a revelation which consists statically only in its sign-giving, in the objectivity of Scripture, preaching and sacrament, a revelation which does not penetrate to man: a revelation of this

kind is an idol like all the rest, and perhaps the worst of idols.[6]

Barth grants that God worked through mighty events in the history of Israel and the church. But he posits revelation, not in the bare historical events (*Historie*), but in the events interpreted according to the faith response of the believer (*Geschichte*). Thus for Barth revelation is a noncognitive inner confrontation with the Divine, rather than the rational communication of information. Moreover, revelation is an ongoing event in the believer's experience, rather than a "frozen" deposit from the past. Consequently the Bible is not itself revelation, but is only a fallible witness to revelatory events and encounters. Barth concludes that "when divine revelation meets us and we respond in faith and obedience the Bible becomes the Word of God."[7]

Brunner developed in greater detail the notion of revelation as an "I-Thou" personal encounter. "Divine revelation is not a book or a doctrine; the revelation is God Himself in His self-manifestation within history. Revelation is something that happens."[8] Through the fallible biblical witness to past revelations (i.e., theophanies, dreams, visions, words of prophets and apostles, and the life of Christ), God sovereignly brings the individual face to face with himself as Lord and as Love. In that moment of personal encounter the individual participates in the mysterious event of revelation. For Brunner, as for Barth, the human, errant Bible becomes the Word of God as the Sovereign graciously speaks to people through it.

H. Richard Niebuhr forged a path between neoorthodoxy and liberalism in *The Meaning of Revelation* (1941). Rejecting the classical view as formal and static, Niebuhr viewed revelation as relational, contextual, and relative. Revelation is relational in that its locus is the "I-Thou" encounter that invites the person's trust and devotion. Revelation is contextual in the sense that Jesus and the biblical writers were sufficiently bound by their culture to teach falsehoods. Finally, revelation is relative in that, because culturally skewed, it is not objectively true for all people of all times. "Such a theology of revelation is objectively relativistic, proceeding with confidence in the independent reality of what is seen, though recognizing that its assertions about that reality are meaningful only to those who look upon it from the same standpoint."[9]

Hans Küng maintains that God revealed himself to believers in Israel and the church as "I," thus becoming for them a "Thou"—i.e., a subject rather than a predicate. The biblical writers were "witnesses of faith" to their revelatory encounters with the "Wholly Other." The Scriptures therefore are not divine revelation; they are human testimonies ("unequivocally man's word") to past revelatory experiences. Nevertheless man's word in the Bible *becomes* God's Word for those who submit in faith to its testimony. "For someone who accepts the invitation . . . the Bible does not remain man's word, but—despite all the problems—becomes God's assisting, liberating, saving Word."[10]

Pannenberg's Revelation as History

Wolfhart Pannenberg proposes that God has provided revelation in the course of world history and chiefly in the resurrection of Christ, both of which are explicated by the historical method. Against the position of his mentor Barth that faith is suprahistorical, Pannenberg strives to ground faith in the verifiable basis of universal world history. Appealing to Hegel's vision of world history as an indirect revelation of God, Pannenberg insists that the only permissible revelation is the single revelation that is identical with the totality of history. *Heilsgeschichte*, he argues, created a false dichotomy between the narrow stream of special redemptive history and the broader stream of secular history. Pannenberg thus defines revelation as the temporal process of a history that is not yet completed, open to all, and open to a future that is anticipated in the history and teachings of Jesus. Pannenberg maintains that the end of history had its "advance-enactment" in the life and resurrection of Jesus Christ. Through Christ's resurrection the God of Israel has substantiated his Deity in an ultimate way and so is manifest as the God of all mankind.

Theistic Existentialism

Existentialist theologians such as Bultmann and Macquarrie view revelation as an ongoing process in which a person, when confronted with the mythical kerygma, realizes the meaning of Being and is thereby transformed to a condition of authentic existence. Following Heidegger, Bultmann rejects both "objective knowledge" that involves an "I-It" relation and "personal knowledge" that centers on the "I-Thou" relation in favor of "primordial knowledge" that corresponds to the demands of being (as understood by the existentialist tradition). Revelation consequently is not the transmission of information (orthodoxy) nor the soul's meeting with God (neoorthodoxy). Revelation is the encounter one has with the kerygma, whereby human eyes are opened to the possibility of true being. Argues Bultmann:

> What has been revealed? Nothing at all, so far as the question concerning revelation asks for doctrines—doctrines, say, that no man could have discovered for himself—or for mysteries that become known once for all as soon as they are communicated. On the other hand, however, *everything has been revealed insofar as man's eyes are opened concerning*

his own existence and he is once again able to understand himself.[11]

In the existentialist schema, revelation is entirely horizontal. It is an experience that occurs *within* the human subject as self-understanding and a new mode of being are grasped by faith. Moreover, revelation is never completed, for the encounter and resultant insight may be repeated again and again.

Most Church Fathers, Reformers, and Evangelicals

Many leading authorities within the church insist that God has revealed himself to particular persons at specific times through personal encounters and miraculous deeds that are explicated by inspired, truth-bearing propositions. The Bible, as the record of God's purposes in deeds and words among men, is an authoritative revelation of God's heart.

Like many other church fathers, Irenaeus posited revelation in the theophanies of the Old Testament, the law of Moses, the utterances of prophets and apostles, the person of Christ, and the Rule of Faith. The pinnacle of redemptive revelation was Christ incarnate, who mediated sure knowledge of God. Athanasius observed that since general revelation was insufficient to lead people to salvation, God made a higher disclosure. He noted that if the subjects of a king should go astray, "he warns them by letters, and often sends to them friends, or if need be, he comes in person to put them to rebuke in the last resort by his presence."[12] Likewise God has revealed himself to sinners by giving the law, by sending prophets and apostles to deliver heavenly instruction, and supremely, by his self-manifestation in Christ. Consequently, "they who would not know him from his providence and rule over all things, may even from the works done by his actual body know the Word of God which is in the body, and through him the Father."[13]

Augustine noted that God specially revealed himself to the patriarchs, to Moses in the burning bush and the giving of the law, and to the Old Testament prophets. In the fullness of time, however, God laid bare his person and his saving purposes through the observable life, death, and resurrection of Christ. Spirit-illumined prophets and apostles bore witness to Christ, and their testimony is inerrantly recorded in Holy Scripture. Said Augustine, "We were too weak by unaided reason to find out the truth, and for this cause needed the authority of holy writings."[14] For Augustine, reason (ratio) illumined by the Logos attains from the inscripturated data of special revelation a fund of knowledge (sapientia) about God's hidden character and redemptive purposes. This knowledge about God's saving provision in the incarnate Christ (scientia) provides the objective basis for faith's decision. Faith, according to Augustine, is not blind but rests on knowledge of the object to be believed and the reasons why one is to believe.

Calvin similarly held that God revealed himself to the Fathers by means of oracles and visions, through the law of Moses, by the preaching of prophets and apostles, and paramountly through the living Word, Jesus Christ. The sum of saving wisdom is recorded in Holy Scripture, which descended, as it were, from God in heaven. "We must come to the Word, where God is truly and vividly described to us from his works, while these very works are appraised not by our depraved judgment but by the rule of eternal truth."[15] Only through the written Word that testifies to Christ, the living Word, does the sinner gain knowledge of God as Redeemer.

Carl F. H. Henry describes revela-

tion as the "critical center" of the crisis in modern theology.[16] Revelation, defined as God's free and personal communication of himself that offers persons privileged communication with the Creator, flows entirely from God's free purpose and grace. The modalities of special revelation include unique saving acts in the history of Israel and the church, the communication of the meaning of such events to chosen prophets and apostles, and consummately the incarnation, crucifixion, and resurrection of Christ. Holy Scripture, which contains the inspired interpretation of all God's disclosures, is itself supernatural revelation. Henry underscores the rational intelligibility of the oral and written special revelation: "God's revelation is rational communication conveyed in intelligible ideas and meaningful words, that is, in conceptual-verbal form."[17]

Further discussion of special revelation from an Evangelical perspective can be found in the writings of B. B. Warfield,[18] and Millard J. Erickson.[19] Valuable monographs on the subject include Bernard Ramm's *Special Revelation and the Word of God*[20] and Ronald Nash's *The Word of God and the Mind of Man*.[21]

BIBLICAL TEACHING

Pentateuch

Divine revelation to specific persons at particular times and places began immediately following Adam and Eve's fall into sin. In Eden God announced the goal of all ensuing revelations, namely, the person and mission of Jesus Christ (Gen. 3:15). The *protoevangelium*, as this declaration is called, attests the fact that the religion of Israel and the church would be rooted in special revelation.

An important modality of special revelation in the Pentateuch is *divine speech.* When irreligion was rife, God spoke to Noah and divulged his plan to destroy the world by a mighty flood (Gen. 6:13). God supernaturally communicated the design of the ark and told Noah how to use it to preserve life during the forty-day deluge. Later God called Abram to Canaan and gave him promises that served as the core of subsequent Old Testament revelations (Gen. 12:1–4). At Horeb God spoke to Moses from the burning bush and communicated his intention to deliver the Israelites from Egyptian bondage (Exod. 3:1–4:17). At Sinai God not only communicated verbally the Ten Commandments (Exod. 20:3–17) but also gave Moses the extensive Law code (Exod. 20:22–23:33) and instructions for building and furnishing the tabernacle (Exod. 25–27).

In the Pentateuch God also disclosed himself through dreams, visions, and theophanies. The dream (*ḥªlôm*) was a common mode of revelation in the patriarchal era when written revelation did not exist. Thus Jacob had a dream at Bethel in which God confirmed the covenant made with Abraham (Gen. 28:10–17). Joseph dreamed a dream that depicted his prominence over his brothers (Gen. 37:5–9). Revelatory dreams were also given to non-Israelites, viz., Abimelech (Gen. 20:3–6), Laban (Gen. 31:24), and Pharaoh (Gen. 41:1–7). Far from being abstruse mystical experiences, these dreams, when rightly interpreted, conveyed objective knowledge of God's unfolding purposes.

Whereas the dream generally occurred during sleep, the revelatory vision (*ḥazôn*) commonly was given to one awake. Visions were given almost exclusively to holy men in the service of God. In visions God confirmed his covenant with Abraham (Gen. 15:1), directed Jacob to go down to Egypt, and promised him that he would bring Israel out as a nation (Gen. 46:2–4).

God gave Balaam a vision that conveyed divine guidance and instruction (Num. 22:31–35).

A higher modality of revelation was the theophany, or visible manifestation of God. The angel of the Lord told Hagar of the fortunes of her soon-to-be-born son Ishmael (Gen. 16:7–13). It is clear from verse 13 that the angel of the Lord was Yahweh in his self-manifestation. The three men who conversed with Abraham at the entrance to his tent (Gen. 18:1–5) were likewise a theophany. The men are plainly identified as "the LORD" (vv. 10, 13–14), yet two of the men are further designated as "angels" (Gen. 19:1) sent by God to execute his purposes (Gen. 19:13). The identity of the angel who encountered Moses in the flaming fire at Horeb is given as "the God of Abraham, the God of Isaac and the God of Jacob" (Exod. 3:6). The Lord who visibly manifested himself unfolded to his servant plans for Israel's deliverance from Egypt (vv. 7–22). The theophany was thus accompanied by intelligible words of command and encouragement. The pillar of cloud and the pillar of fire that guided Israel on their journey through Sinai (Exod. 13:21–22; cf. 24:16–17) likewise were visible symbols of God's presence with his people. When God said to Moses, "My Presence will go with you" (Exod. 33:14), Scripture identifies the "Presence" (*pānîm*) as the angel of the Lord (Isa. 63:9), that is, as God himself mediated to the human senses.

Special revelation in the Old Testament also came in the form of mighty acts wrought on the stage of Israel's history. All events, in a certain sense, are revealing. But God was operative in Israel's history in a way that he is not at work in the general history of the world.

God specially revealed himself and his saving purposes through the plagues meted out on Egypt (Exod. 7–10). Nine times God did "miraculous signs" (*môsᵉtîm*) and "wonders" (*'ôtôt*) that Pharaoh and his magicians were powerless to oppose (Exod. 7:3).²² Israel's passage through the Sea of Reeds (Exod. 14:13–31) after their release from Egypt was another instance of revelation as miraculous event. Yahweh announced in advance that the purpose of the miracle was that "the Egyptians will know that I am the LORD" (Exod. 14:4, 18). As the sea retreated, allowing the Israelites safe passage, and as the same waters caved in on the pursuing Egyptians, God's power, holiness, and salvation were openly displayed.

The judgments God meted out on his disobedient people during their sojourn in the Sinai peninsula (Num. 11:1–3; 12:10–12) were revelatory of God's justice and hatred of sin. Likewise, the forty years of wandering in the wilderness was a revelatory event (Num. 14:33).

Historical Books

In the historical books, God gave commands, provided information, and communicated promises. His special revelations to Joshua are introduced by the formula "The LORD said to Joshua" (Josh. 1:1; 3:7; 4:1, et al.). The Lord also spoke to Samuel and instructed him to anoint Saul as Israel's first king. Later, when the disobedient Saul was rejected as king, God directed Samuel to identify David as Israel's next king (1 Sam. 16:1–12). When David sought to build the temple, the Lord told Nathan that David's son Solomon would construct it, but God promised David a dynasty that would endure forever. The account closes with the words "Nathan reported to David all the words of this entire revelation" (1 Chron. 17:15).

In the same period revelation also came in the form of theophany. Near

Jericho, Joshua saw standing before him with drawn sword "the commander of the LORD's army" (Josh. 5:13–15). This military figure, identified by the text as "the LORD" (*Yahweh*, Josh. 6:2), delivered instructions to Joshua concerning the march his forces were to make around Jericho. Gideon likewise was comforted by an angel of the Lord (Judg. 6:11–24), whom the Hebrew warrior designates as the "Sovereign LORD" (v. 22). The Lord, through the modality of the theophany, imparted a message to encourage Gideon in his battle with the Midianites.

The historical books also attest revelation in the form of space-time events with accompanying interpretation. The miracle that parted the flood waters of the Jordan (Josh. 3:14–4:18) took place so that people might fear the all-powerful God (Josh. 4:24). Israel's defeat by the Canaanites at Ai (Josh. 7:1–24), together with God's interpretation of the disaster, revealed the heinousness of sin. The contest on Carmel between Elijah and the prophets of Baal (1 Kings 18:16–39), in which the man of God called the fire of God down from heaven, prompted the confession of the onlookers, "The LORD—he is God! The LORD—he is God!" (1 Kings 18:39). Israel's exile at the hand of Assyria (2 Kings 17) and Judah's captivity at the hand of Babylon (2 Kings 24–25), as the commentary on the judgments attests, were revelatory events in which Yahweh's holiness and anger were openly displayed.

Wisdom and Poetry

The Book of Job makes clear that finite beings of themselves cannot penetrate the hidden reality of God. Thus Zophar poses the question, "Can you fathom the mysteries of God? Can you probe the limits of the Almighty? They are higher than the heavens—what can we do? They are deeper than the depths of the grave—what can you know?" (Job 11:7–8). Since people cannot find God by themselves (Job 23:8–9), God must initiate contact through his special self-disclosure.

Commonplace in the Psalms is the theme of God's redemptive revelation to Israel through mighty acts of deliverance and judgment. Thus Psalms 77–78, 103, and 105–107 rehearse God's manifold saving acts, such as the giving of the Law at Sinai, the career of Joseph, the plagues on Egypt, the passage through the Sea of Reeds, the miraculous guidance in the wilderness, and the capture of Canaan. In describing these saving events the singers of Israel use such words as "wonders" (*môpᵉtîm*, Pss. 78:43; 105:27), "miracles" (*pᵉlā'îm*, Pss. 77:11; 78:12), "judgments" (*mišpātîm*, Pss. 97:8; 105:5, 7), "wonderful deeds" (*niplā'ôt*, twenty-seven times in the Psalms, e.g., Pss. 26:7; 75:1; 106:22), "miraculous signs" (*'ôtôt*, Pss. 78:43; 105:27), and "awesome deeds" (*nôrā'ôt*, Pss. 65:5; 106:22). Through these works God's character and will were powerfully impressed on the hearts of his people.

God revealed his purposes to Israel by the direct disclosure of laws, statutes, and commands (Ps. 78:5). God distinguished Israel from all the other nations by disclosing his word to them. "He has revealed his word to Jacob, his laws and decrees to Israel. He has done this for no other nation; they do not know his laws" (Ps. 147:19–20). God's specially revealed precepts and ordinances effect spiritual revitalization in the believer (Pss. 19:7; 119:93), impart spiritual understanding (Pss. 19:7; 119:104, 130), give peace to troubled consciences (Ps. 119:165), and implant the hope of final salvation (Ps. 119:81).

The Prophets

Of old God gave his word to chosen prophets. Thus the prophetic literature contains frequent introductory formulas, such as, "The LORD came to me" (Jer. 1:2, 4; Jonah 1:1; Zech. 1:1, 7). While worshiping in the temple Isaiah heard the exalted Lord say, "Whom shall I send? And who will go for us?" (Isa. 6:8). When Isaiah volunteered, the Lord spoke to the prophet the message he wanted delivered to the people. God spoke to Jeremiah, conveying his call, purposes, and message (Jer. 1:4–2:3; 11:1–23, et al.). Likewise, God spoke his word to other prophetic messengers (Ezek. 2:1–3, 8; Hos. 1:2–11; Hab. 1:5–11). God spoke in the Old Testament both audibly and inaudibly. The important point is that his revelation through speech involved the communication of objective knowledge. Biblical faith affirms, with Amos, "The Sovereign LORD has spoken" (Amos 3:8)!

Not only did God speak *to* the prophets, he also spoke *through* them. The utterances of the prophets constitute the final modality of special revelation in the Old Testament. The prophets predicted events that would come to pass in the future (Isa. 42:9; Amos 5:27; Obad. 19), but they also proclaimed the Word and the will of God (Deut. 18:18). Thus the prophetic ministry involved both foretelling and forthtelling. With respect to the latter aspect of the prophet's ministry, God put his words in Jeremiah's mouth (Jer. 1:9) so that they became to him as "a burning fire" (Jer. 20:9). Similarly God sent Ezekiel to the obstinate Israelites armed with his message (Ezek. 2:4). Ezekiel must eat the scroll on which were written the words of God (Ezek. 3:1–3). This symbolism teaches that the Word of God was so much a part of Ezekiel's being that the prophet's message and God's message were one and the same.

When Hosea opened his mouth he said, "Hear the word of the LORD, you Israelites" (Hos. 4:1). Joel's prophetic message is identified as "The word of the LORD that came to Joel" (Joel 1:1).

So also, Amos's message to the northern kingdom was punctuated by the oft-repeated phrase, "This is what the LORD says" (Amos 1:3, 6, 9, et al.). Similar epithets from Obadiah, Nahum, Micah, Haggai, and Zechariah prove that the proclamation of the prophets was identical with the Word of God. The prophecies of Nahum (1:1) and Habakkuk (1:1) are specifically designated an "oracle" (*dābār*), namely, an utterance from the mouth of God himself.

"Word of God" in the Old Testament thus evolved into a technical term for the prophetic proclamation of God's truth. This word was first spoken by the Spirit-anointed prophets and later set down in writing. Hence not only the prophetic utterances but also the prophets' writings are forms of special revelation. In the same era Nebuchadnezzar had dreams (Dan. 2:1; 4:5–18), the meaning of which was revealed to Daniel in a night vision (Dan. 2:19, 31–45). Later God gave Daniel a revelatory dream and vision (Dan. 7) in which four beasts came out of the sea, representing the four world empires that would precede the eternal kingdom of the Son of Man. Through visions God called persons to a prophetic vocation (Isa. 6:1–10), communicated the content of the prophets' message (Isa. 1:1; Jer. 1:11–17; Amos 7:1–9), pointed out the sinfulness of the nation (Ezek. 8:1–18), and comforted God's people (Zech. 1:8–17; 2:1–5). In both dreams and visions specific truths were imparted.

The prophets testify that God made himself known through mighty deeds in Israel's history. God's preservation of Daniel in the den of lions (Dan. 6:16–27) was a miraculous work that elicited a remarkable confession from Darius the Persian king (Dan. 6:26–27). Moreover, God's holy name would be vindicated when the sovereign Lord established his people back in the land.

Israel's return from exile thus was a revelatory event (Ezek. 36:24–38).

Although rich in content, special revelation in the Old Testament was preparatory and incomplete (1 Peter 1:10–12). The consummate revelation of God's saving purposes awaited the coming of Christ, the living Word of God.

Synoptic Gospels

The modalities of special revelation in the synoptic Gospels are diverse. First, there is the direct revelation of God through dreams, visions, and theophanies. An angel of the Lord (identified as Gabriel) appeared to Zechariah bearing the message that his wife Elizabeth would bear a son John and that this Spirit-anointed servant would pave the way for the coming of the Lord (Luke 1:11–20). The same angel appeared to Mary and told her that she would conceive through the power of the Spirit and give birth to the Son of God (Luke 1:26–38). An angel of the Lord appeared to Joseph in a dream (Matt. 1:20–24) and to shepherds near Bethlehem (Luke 2:9–15), communicating additional messages. When Jesus was baptized by John, the Spirit of God descended on him in the form of a dove and the Father spoke the audible words, "This is my Son, whom I love; with him I am well pleased" (Matt. 3:16–17).

Second, God revealed himself to specific persons at particular times and places through Jesus' miracles. In the prologue to his Gospel, Luke wrote, "Many have undertaken to draw up an account of the things [*ta pragmata*, i.e., events or deeds] that have been fulfilled among us" (Luke 1:1). In her song of praise Mary uttered the words "The Mighty One has done great things [*megala*] for me" (Luke 1:49). Peter later declared to the Jews that Jesus was "accredited by God to you by miracles [*dynameis*], wonders [*terata*] and signs [*sēmeia*]" (Acts 2:22). Jesus demonstrated his power over nature by the miracle of calming the storm on the Sea of Galilee (Mark 4:37–41), over the consequences of sin by healing people of numerous afflictions and diseases (Mark 5:22–29; 8:22–25), and over sin itself by exorcising demons and forgiving offenses against God (Matt. 9:2–8; Mark 5:2–13). The Gospels attest that the miracles done by Jesus affirmed his compassion for people, his mighty power, and his heavenly authority. Some who witnessed his mighty revelatory works confessed him to be the Son of God (Matt. 14:33). The supreme event that demonstrated Jesus to be the all-powerful Son of God (cf. Rom. 1:4) was his resurrection from death and the grave (Matt. 28:1–10 and parallels).

Third, special revelation in the Synoptics also took the form of a direct communication of truth from God. The Holy Spirit disclosed (*chrēmatizō*, to "impart a revelation")[23] to Simeon that he would live to see the Christ of God (Luke 2:26). After his pronouncement of judgment on the unrepentant cities Jesus praised the Father because he had "hidden these things from the wise and learned, and revealed [*apokalyptō*] them to little children" (Matt. 11:25). After Peter had confessed Jesus as the Christ and the Son of God, the Lord commended him with the words, "This was not revealed [*apokalyptō*] to you by man, but by my Father in heaven" (Matt. 16:17). The verb *apokalyptō*, which occurs twenty-six times in the New Testament, signifies the removal of a covering and hence the disclosure of what was previously hidden or unknown.

Fourth, the Synoptics represent Jesus and his teaching as an important modality of special revelation. Filled with the Holy Spirit, Simeon cradled the infant Jesus in his arms and described him as "a light for revelation [*apokalypsis*] to the Gentiles and for

glory to your people Israel" (Luke 2:32). The noun *apokalypsis* occurs eighteen times in the New Testament in the sense of a divine disclosure or revelation. In language reminiscent of John's Gospel, Matthew observes that by virtue of Jesus' filial relation to God he is eminently capable of revealing the Father to those he chooses (Matt. 11:27). When Jesus in the synagogue read from Isaiah 61:1–2 and applied to himself the words "The Spirit of the LORD is on me, because he has anointed me to preach good news to the poor," we conclude that both his teaching and his deeds were vehicles of special revelation (cf. Acts 3:22).

Primitive Christianity/Acts

An important modality of revelation in Acts is the vision, often accompanied by messages mediated by an angel of the Lord or the Holy Spirit. In Acts 10:3–8 Cornelius had a vision of an angel of God (described as "a man in shining clothes," v. 30) who instructed him to send for Peter. The next day Peter had a vision and heard the voice of God telling him not to despise what God had made clean (10:9–16; cf. v. 28). While Peter was reflecting on this vision, the Holy Spirit told him to receive the messengers who were sent to him (vv. 19–20; cf. 11:12). When Peter arrived at Caesarea, Cornelius urged him to relate "everything the Lord has commanded you to tell us" (v. 33). Whereupon Peter replied, "You know the message God sent to the people of Israel" (v. 36).

Elsewhere in Acts Stephen had a revelatory vision of the heavenly Jesus (Acts 7:55–56), and Saul had a vision of the glorified Christ who told him of his purpose to make him an apostle (9:3–6; 22:6–11). Thereafter God gave Ananias a vision and instructed him to lay hands on Saul so that the latter might receive the Holy Spirit (9:10–18). Later Paul had a vision of a man of Macedonia urging the apostle to preach the gospel in that region (16:9–10). When certain Jews opposed Paul's ministry in Corinth, the Lord spoke to the missionaries in a vision with words of spiritual encouragement (18:9–10).

In the ministry of the apostolic church an angel of the Lord gave instructions to the apostles who were freed from jail (Acts 5:19–20), spoke to Philip (8:26–29), and gave words of assurance to Paul aboard the storm-tossed ship (27:23–26). Similarly the Holy Spirit instructed the church at Antioch to set apart Barnabas and Saul for the work of the ministry (13:2, 4) and warned Paul of impending hardships (20:23). The Lord himself spoke to Paul in Jerusalem, informing the apostle of what lay in store for him in Rome (23:11).

A second modality of special revelation in Acts is found in the miracles God wrought through the apostles. Luke reports that "The apostles performed many miraculous signs [sēmeia] and wonders [terata] among the people" (Acts 5:12; cf. 4:30; 6:8). The outpouring of the Holy Spirit at Pentecost (2:1–4), accompanied by strong winds, tongues of fire, and spontaneous utterances in foreign languages, was a striking revelation of the power and holiness of God. When the Jews assembled in Jerusalem heard the Spirit-anointed Christians speak, they remarked, "we hear them declaring the wonders [ta megaleia] of God in our own tongues" (2:11). Peter stated that these things happened in fulfillment of the prophecy of Joel (2:28–32), namely, that in the latter days God "will show wonders [terata] in the heaven above and signs [sēmeia] on the earth below" (2:19). Thus Peter's healing of the crippled beggar (3:1–8), the judgment meted out on Ananias and Sapphira (5:1–11), and the resuscitation of Eutychus at Troas (20:7–10) were miraculous works that

certified Jesus as the Son of God and the apostles as his authoritative spokesmen.

Finally, the Spirit-given message of the apostles was itself revelatory. Luke relates that after being filled with the Holy Spirit the early Christians "spoke the Word of God boldly" (Acts 4:31). The preaching of Peter and John in Samaria (8:25), the teaching and preaching of Barnabas and Paul on Cyprus (13:7), in Pisidian Antioch (13:46), and at Syrian Antioch (15:35) are all designated as "the word of God." Luke describes the content of the apostles' preaching and teaching as "God's salvation" (28:28). The oral teaching of the apostles in due course was set down in writing and valued equally with the Old testament Scriptures.

The Pauline Corpus

Nothing is more certain than the fact that Paul's ministry was rooted in supernatural revelation. Divine revelation to Paul was first of all subjective in character. Reflecting on his Damascus road experience, Paul asked, "Have I not seen Jesus our Lord?" (1 Cor. 9:1; cf. 15:8). Some six or eight years after his conversion Paul was taken up by the Spirit into Paradise where he was given visions and revelations from the Lord and "heard inexpressible things, things that man is not permitted to tell" (2 Cor. 12:1–4). But Paul's teaching also focused on revelation that was objective in character. Defending his apostleship, Paul claimed that the gospel he preached was received by revelation from Christ (Gal. 1:12). A theme often enunciated in Paul is that God disclosed to him "the mystery hidden for long ages past" (Rom. 16:25). Specifically what God revealed to Paul was that believing Gentiles would be given equal status with believing Jews in the body of Christ in fulfillment of the promise (Eph. 3:6). But in the larger sense the mystery is synonymous with the gospel of God's grace in Jesus Christ. In this sense "the mystery is the total meaning of God's redemptive purpose, which he has accomplished in Christ."[24] Thus it is clear that God disclosed to Paul both himself as a person and his Word and will. Revelation encompasses not only the messenger but also the message.

It follows that the Spirit-guided teaching and preaching of the apostle was revelation. Paul testified that "the message [*logos*] of the cross," while appearing foolish to the unsaved, is in truth to the believer "the power [*dynamis*] of God" (1 Cor. 1:18). Moreover, Paul spoke "in words taught by the Spirit, expressing spiritual truths in spiritual words" (1 Cor. 2:13). Elsewhere Paul's preaching is identified as "the word of God" (2 Cor. 2:17; 4:2; 1 Thess. 2:13) since, as the apostle testifies, Christ was speaking through him (2 Cor. 13:3).

Paul believed that the historical Jesus Christ was the pinnacle of all God's revelations to mankind. The apostle described the eternal second person of the Trinity as "the image [*eichōn*] of the invisible God" (Col. 1:15). In Koine Greek, *eichōn* could refer to, among other things, a portrait. A soldier on duty in a remote outpost, for example, could write to his sweetheart, "I send you an *eichōn* of myself." Christ, then is the portrait of the ineffable God sent to finite, feeble-sighted people. Repeatedly the apostle affirms that at the Incarnation the invisible God took visible form in Jesus of Nazareth. As the fragment of a hymn of the early church put it, "He [God] appeared in a body" (1 Tim. 3:16; cf. Titus 2:11; the aorist tense in both texts points to the event of the Incarnation). Likewise, "in Christ all the fullness [*plēroma*] of the Deity [*theotēs*] lives in bodily form" (Col. 2:9; cf. 1:19). The verb "lives" (*katoikei*) is

present continuous tense, signifying that the reflection of the divine essence through Jesus of Nazareth was a continuous mode of revelation as long as he lived on earth.

Not only the Incarnation but also the visible return of Christ to consummate the present age was viewed by Paul as a modality of special revelation. The apostle denotes the Second Advent as an unveiling (*apokalypsis*, 1 Cor. 1:7; 2 Thess. 1:7) and as a shining appearance (*epiphaneia*, 1 Tim. 6:14; 2 Tim. 4:1; Titus 2:13). This application of revelation language to Christ's first advent as well as his second advent prompts one authority to conclude: "To speak of revelation in the fullest biblical sense is to speak of Jesus Christ."[25] Just as Christ's first coming was a powerful revelation of God's grace, so his second coming will be a potent revelation of God's unsurpassing glory.

The Johannine Literature

Special revelation, according to John, was given in the first instance through various "miraculous signs" (*sēmeia*, John 6:30; 11:47; 12:37; 20:30) and "miracles" (*ergo*, John 7:3, 21; 10:25, 32) wrought by Jesus. Thus John describes Jesus' miracle of changing water to wine at Cana (John 2:1–11) as "the first of his miraculous signs," the healing of the royal official's son (John 4:46–54) as the "second miraculous sign," and so on. Rightly Jesus said to the unbelieving Jews, "I have shown you many great miracles [*ergo*] from the Father" (John 10:32). Appropriately the victorious saints in the Book of Revelation sing the song, "Great and marvelous are your deeds [*erga*], Lord God Almighty" (Rev. 15:3). Jesus' revelatory works were performed for several purposes: (1) to demonstrate that the Father sent him into the world (John 5:36), (2) to validate his extraordinary claims (10:25), (3) to affirm the unique relationship that exists between him and the Father (10:38), and (4) to engender the faith in himself that issues in eternal life (20:30–31). In sum, Jesus performed mighty revelatory works to manifest (*phaneroō*) his eternal glory (2:11).

Given the strong christological focus of John's Gospel and Epistles, it is natural that Jesus Christ is upheld as the supreme embodiment of special revelation. Throughout his writings John implies that God is known by the coming of a personal representative. Thus in the theologically pregnant prologue to the fourth Gospel John teaches that the Word (*logos*), coeternal and coequal with the Father, became a man and dwelt in our midst. Adds John, "We have seen his glory, the glory of the One and Only, who came from the Father, full of grace and truth" (John 1:14). The historical Jesus thus was the revelation of the *shekinah* glory of God.

John continues by saying that the fleshly eye has never seen God (v. 18). But by virtue of the unique relationship the Son sustains to the Father, Christ has made God known (*exēgeomai*). This verb is variously translated in the New Testament as "tell" (Acts 10:8; 15:12), "describe" (15:14), and "report in detail" (21:19). It is the verb from which comes the English word "exegete," which means to interpret or unfold the meaning of a thing. The eternal Son thus most fully "exegetes" for mortals the reality of the invisible God. It is he who tells us who God is and what God is like. Hence the culminating Word of all God's words is Jesus Christ who has become man in our space and time. The third chapter of John's Gospel adds that Jesus, who has come from the Father in heaven (John 3:13), testifies to what he has seen and heard there (v. 32). Commissioned by God and anointed by the Spirit he "speaks the words of God" (v. 34). Later in the Upper Room Peter asked Jesus to show them the Father, perhaps hoping to be given a theophany. Jesus' answer was powerful in its simplicity: "Anyone who has seen me has seen the Father" (John 14:9). Our Lord's character, deeds, and words provided a perfect revelation of the Father to the world (John 17:6, 26). This role of our Lord as the revelation of God is confirmed by the titles John ascribes to him: "faithful witness" (Rev. 1:5; 3:14), the "divine glory" (John 1:14; 17:24), "light of the world" (8:12; 9:5); "teacher" (11:28; 13:13); and "prophet" (7:40; 9:17).[26]

Other New Testament Writings

A powerful text that identifies Christ as God's final, redemptive revelation is Hebrews 1:1–2. The writer affirms that under the old economy revelation had a long history ("at many times") and came in a multiplicity of modes ("in various ways"). This revelation, which was chiefly a "speaking," was a gradually unfolding reality. But at the juncture between the old and the new eras God "has spoken [*elalēsen*] to us by his Son" (Heb. 1:2). The aorist tense of the verb "to speak" (*laleō*) signifies that God's revelation through Christ is full and complete. Except for the apostolic explication of the gospel, God's final word of revelation was spoken through the total reality of the Son's incarnation, death, resurrection, and second coming (so the anarthrous *en huiō*). As the supreme modality of special revelation the Son is the visible outshining (*apaugasma*) of God's glory and the exact expression (*charaktēr*) of God's invisible reality (v. 3). The same verse asserts that God's final disclosure through the Son is a saving revelation, for it involves "purification for sins." Peter, moreover, identifies Christ's second coming as a specifically revelatory datum. To this immanent eschatological event he applies the verb *apokalyptō*

(1 Peter 1:5) and the noun *apokalypsis* (v. 7). The revelation of Christ at his second coming is likened to the rising of the morning star and the dawning of a new day (2 Peter 1:19).

SYSTEMATIC FORMULATION

A distinctively Christian doctrine of special revelation begins with a distinctively Christian view of God. Skeptics, deists, and liberals often find a cognitive communication from God in time unthinkable because their concept of eternity makes it impossible. And neoorthodox ministers consider God so totally other that any relation to people in history becomes paradoxical or dialectical. So people who would communicate information from God today need first to make clear both *who* the eternal God is and *how* this God has related to the spokesmen he especially appointed in time.

God's Word in Eternity

A Christian understanding of eternity begins with the triune God: Holy Father, Holy Word, and Holy Spirit. The ultimate Revealer expressed his very nature in his Word and in his Spirit. From eternity communication was normal and enhanced the relationships of the three divine persons.

Before the world was, "the Word was with God" (John 1:1). God was never *alogos*, without reason or speech like the animals (2 Peter 2:12; Jude 10). Within the divine Being, John's personal Logos was face to face ("with") the Father, in significant communication with him (cf. John 17:5, 24). The Holy Spirit, like Jesus, was a person "whom" he would send from the Father (John 15:26). Based on biblical data like this, the early confessions affirm trinitarianism against a mere divine singularity. The unbroken fellowship of the three persons before the

foundation of the world involved intercession (Rom. 8:26). Meaningful communication thus is not foreign to God. Communication is inherent in the triune God eternally. Transcending the limits of space and time in the Godhead are personal relationships involving contentful communication.[27]

In the eternal Word, furthermore, were the patterns or forms of everything that would be created. "Through him [the eternal Word] all things were made; without him nothing was made that has been made" (John 1:3). Since God made nothing without reason, the divine "Word" or "Son" gives the whole world figuratively "light" (John 1:3–5; cf. 8:12), or knowability. The creation is not chaotic, but an ordered cosmos with regular laws because everything received its intelligible nature from God. Eternal "wisdom" served as "the craftsman" at God's side during creation (Prov. 8:22–31). Hence we see that "wisdom" personified speaks what is worthy, right, true, just, and faultless (Prov. 8:6-9).

"If anyone denies the existence of this eternal wisdom [*sapienta*]," St. Augustine explained, "then logically— if a plan of Creation was not present to God—He must hold that without any plan God made what He made, or that, either when He made it or before He made it, He did not know what He made or would make."[28]

God's eternal Logos not only gave meaning to the things in the world but also gave purpose to the course of events in history. God planned to create men and women to share his fellowship and his rule of creation. And God made the world to be ruled by people. It follows that categories that exist in the mind of God, though not limited like those of finite, fallen people, are not totally removed from theirs or totally different in every respect. God is not impersonal energy. God is not nonrational. Rational meaning and purpose is

109

not an afterthought but prior to creation. Existence is not prior to essence, as Jean-Paul Sartre alleged, but essences are prior in the mind of God (not abstract concepts as in Plato's world of ideas).[29] The archetypes of knowledge of principles of physics, music, morality, and thought (logic) are in the divine mind. Our ectypal knowledge is true when it corresponds with God's original and more complete knowledge.[30]

God disclosed himself to be "faithful and true" (Isa. 65:16; John 3:33; 16:13; 17:17; Rom. 3:5–7). He who is "faithful" (Heb. 10:23) "remains faithful forever" (Ps. 146:6). Hence we can depend on the fact that God is "faithful to all his promises" (Ps. 145:13). One's concept of revelation reflects one's concept of God. The God of the Bible speaks only in accord with truth. No discrepancy can be found between God's statements and his acts. It is impossible for God to err or "lie" (Heb. 6:17–18). In other words, because God in himself, in his eternal Son, is faithful, his word in eternity is true (inerrant) and reliable (infallible).[31]

God's Word in Time

Theological relativists may grant absolute truth in God but find impossible the communication of God's undistorted truth to errant sinners conditioned by a given culture in space and time. In an age of conceptual relativism those who would minister God's revealed truth must prepare to address the difficulties raised by different cultural, conceptual, and linguistic influences in time. On the basis of the extensive biblical data above, we here propose that in addition to a universal revelation God has communicated objectively valid truths to specific people in particular cultures at specific places and times.

Formally *defined,* "special revelation" refers to the eternal God's disclo-sure of his redemptive purposes in the Near East (1) supremely *through* Jesus Christ's character, life, and conceptual teachings (in human words) confirmed by miraculous acts, and also (2) in various ways *to* prophetic and apostolic spokesmen whose teachings from God in human words were confirmed by their consistency with one another and by signs, wonders, and mighty acts.

God's Word Incarnate

The eternal Logos or second person of the Trinity "became flesh and made his dwelling among us" (John 1:14). He came to make God known (1:18) to people in the Near East in the first century and through them to the whole world in every generation (Matt. 28:19; Heb. 1:3).

Jesus Christ entered history not as a mere symbol of divine love, but as an actual demonstration of transcendent love. He was truly human as well as truly divine. The account of Jesus' birth is not a myth analogous to the birth of Krishna and many other Hindu avatars. Jesus literally lived, atoned for sin, and rose from the dead. Because of his once-for-all signs, wonders, and mighty acts, he ranks above all mere religious leaders and indeed above the angels (Heb. 1:5–14). "In Christ all the fullness of the Deity lives in bodily form" (Col. 2:9).

For all people of all times and cultures Jesus of Nazareth vividly displayed the fact that the living God is personal, wise, caring, intelligent, and purposive. Jesus displayed a holiness from beyond fallen human history. Jesus' judgments, like the Father's, were "faithful and true" (Rev. 3:7; 16:5, 7; 19:2, 11). Jesus disclosed an objectively valid universal purpose of God to satisfy justice and deliver sinners from the slave markets of selfishness by giving his life a ransom in their place (Mark 2:9–10). Jesus demonstrated a transcendent *agapē* love as the friend of tax collectors and sinners (Luke 7:34). No greater love could have been displayed than the laying down of his life for others (John 15:13). And the power that raised Christ from the dead clearly came from above and hence normatively declares with power that the son of David was indeed the Son of God (Rom. 1:3–4). The first Christians confessed on the basis of many confirming signs, wonders, and mighty acts, not only that Jesus exemplified the eternal Christ in time, but that Jesus *was* the Christ (John 20:31).

What did Jesus Christ teach about his own teaching, either by direct statement or by implication?[32] Many who emphasize revelation only in the person of Christ seem to ignore this crucial question. Emphasizing nonconceptual "encounters" with Christ's person or his "mighty acts," people may neglect what he taught in human categories and words. It is hard to find a discussion of his teaching about his own doctrine. Let us return to one of the most important questions of contemporary theology: What did Jesus teach his first-century disciples about his own teaching? From Jesus' teaching what implications can be drawn about the possibility of stating the Father's eternal truth in history in human thought forms and languages?

1. Jesus' teaching *originated*, not with himself, but *with God the Father*. When the amazed Jews asked, "How did this man get such learning without having studied?" Jesus replied, "My teaching is not my own. It comes from him who sent me" (John 7:15–16). In his high priestly prayer, Jesus could say, "I have revealed you to those whom you gave me. . . . Now they know that everything you have given me comes from you" (John 17:6–8). May we not infer that the conceptual content of Jesus' teaching in history conformed to the Father's in eternity?

2. Jesus taught that divine revelation could be communicated *in human concepts and words.* "For I gave them the words you gave me" (John 17:8). Jesus did not speak a special heavenly language, but the Aramaic or Greek of the common people. May we not infer that the propositional content of Jesus' teaching could be expressed verbally in culturally influenced human languages?

3. Jesus also taught that human words reveal a person's inner heart. Just as a tree can be recognized by its fruit, so good or evil persons can be recognized by the "fruit" of their lips (Matt. 12:35; 7:15–20): "Out of the overflow of the heart the mouth speaks" (Matt. 12:34). Jesus spoke out of the overflow of his own heart and therefore not only his deeds but also his words disclose his inner divine nature. Concepts and words enhance personal, heartfelt relationships. May we not infer that Jesus' words revealed his personal, inner convictions, feelings, and purposes, enriching personal relationships with those who received them?

4. The information Jesus taught in human concepts and languages was conceptually true—consistent and factual. In humbling himself to become a human, Jesus adapted himself to the human level, but did not accommodate himself to human sin or error. In prayer to the Father he exclaimed, "I gave them the words you gave me. . . . Your word is truth" (John 17:8, 17).

Although Christ emphasized eternal life, he taught reliable assertions about a great variety of subjects: the Pharisees, God's moral law in the Sermon on the Mount, the demonic, illness, the kingdom of God, the new birth, faith, the cost of discipleship, paying taxes, offending children, riches, his coming betrayal and denial and death, signs of the end of the age, and the Great Commission. Jesus' teaching on all of these and other matters conformed to reality and the mind of God the Father. May we not infer that Jesus taught no error on any subject of which he spoke (his plenary inerrancy)?

5. The teaching of Jesus was not only conceptually true but also existentially viable and effectual. Far from a static hindrance to vitality, his teaching was rejuvenating. It served as a viable instrument of the Holy Spirit to give spiritual life. "The Spirit gives life; the flesh counts for nothing. The words I have spoken to you are spirit and they are life" (John 6:63). People also found Jesus' conceptual truth to be liberating. It served as an instrument of the Holy Spirit to free people from moral and spiritual slavery to sinful desires. Jesus said, "If you hold to my teaching, you are really my disciples. Then you will know the truth, and the truth will set you free" (John 8:31–32).

Further, Jesus' teaching was sanctifying. As an instrument of the Holy Spirit in the disciples' lives, it helped them become spiritually mature. Jesus prayed, "Sanctify them by the truth; your word is truth" (John 17:17). May we not infer that Jesus' teaching was infallible in accomplishing the ends for which it was given?

6. All that Jesus affirmed on any subject was not only true and viable, but also authoritative for his immediate and subsequent disciples, as follows from the evidence in statements 1 through 5. Furthermore, the Father granted him "authority over all people that he might give eternal life . . . " (John 17:2).

His hearers recognized his authority; the people in the town of Capernaum "were amazed at his teaching, because his message had authority" (Luke 4:31–32). At the conclusion of the Sermon on the Mount "the crowds were amazed at his teaching, because he taught as one who had authority, and not as their teachers of the law" (Matt. 7:28–29).

Before ascending to the Father Jesus said, "All authority in heaven and on earth has been given to me." On that basis he asked them to make disciples, "teaching them to obey *everything*" he had commanded them (Matt. 28:18–20). May we not infer that all of Jesus' teaching had normative authority in his own time?

7. Jesus' teaching was *not time-bound, but classically time-related.* "Heaven and earth will pass away," Jesus said, "but my words will never pass away" (Mark 13:31). Disciples today may need the best critical procedures to determine what indeed Jesus said, and what he meant by what he said, but any teaching known to be from the first-century incarnate Christ remains normative for authentic disciples until his return. Remember his words, "If anyone loves me, he will obey my teaching" (John 14:23). May we not infer that Jesus' teaching had normative authority for all times and cultures?

The biblical data thus support Jesus' revelation of himself, the Father, and the Holy Spirit in human concepts and languages. He communicated truth in two major senses:[33] (1) His teaching conveyed reliable information concerning what is and normative principles concerning what ought to be, and (2) his life reflected fidelity to the ultimate reality, God the Father, and his will on earth. He affirmed what is the case essentially, and he lived by it existentially. Those who find the supreme revelation of God in Jesus Christ need put no distance between propositional and relational truth. In Christ essential and existential truth are inseparable. Barth's and Bultmann's views are less adequate insofar as they separate the conceptual from the experiential.

God's Word Through Prophetic Spokesmen

Just as Jesus' teachings originated with God the Father, *true prophets' teachings originated with God* and *were given by the supernatural power of the Holy Spirit.* The problem is not how a totally other God could possibly speak with finite and fallen people in concepts and words. A conceptual communication is possible because the living God made mankind to think his thoughts after him. As Jesus' teaching has demonstrated, God's truth can be communicated in human, culturally influenced categories and languages.

Is it not one thing, however, for the incarnate Christ to convey truth in human languages and another for finite, fallen sinners to do so? Indeed! How could authentic prophets transcend the limits of their finiteness and the corruption of their sinfulness to convey objectively valid truth from God? God providentially prepared them for this task (Jer. 1:5) and then supernaturally enabled them to overcome their innate propensities to err in receiving and speaking God's truth through sentences in human language (Zech. 7:12). That the Spirit's work on their behalf should be supernatural is not strange. The Logos entered the fallen world as God's Son (the Holy One) by supernatural conception (Luke 1:35). So also the Logos entered the fallen world of the prophets as God's Word by supernatural mental conceptions.

The Spirit of God disclosed divine truth to prophets in different ways: (1) by means of an audible voice (Exod. 19:3–6), though God as spirit (John 4:24) has no physical body or larynx (John 5:37); (2) through internal suggestion or silent hearing of the Word by a prophet but not by others around him (1 Kings 13:18–22; Isa. 7:3–4); (3) by presenting a vision or imaginary picture (Ezek. 37; Micah 4:1–4); and (4) through an opening of the prophet's eyes to see realities otherwise invisible (Num. 22:31; 2 Kings 6:15–17).[34] However varied the modes, the *point* of the figurative visions (et al.) could be stated in unfigurative language.

The basic problem was distinguishing between two kinds of prophets. *Presumptuous prophets* claimed to speak for God, but in fact did not (Deut. 18:20). They would wag their own tongues but say, "The Lord declares . . . " (Jer. 23:31), and they could "speak visions from their own minds, not from the mouth of the LORD" (Jer. 23:16) and so distort the words of the living God and raise false hopes. In that situation "every man's own word becomes his oracle" (Jer. 23:36).

True prophets received the content of their messages from God as Aaron did from Moses. Aaron served as "prophet" or spokesman for Moses, and Moses was to Aaron as "God" (Exod. 7:1; 4:16). True prophets did not just give fallible advice (cf. 2 Sam. 7:1–3), they also spoke on behalf of God (cf. vv. 4–17). They were not mere automata but real persons facing real situations to which they spoke for God. As finite, the prophets were limited in knowledge; as fallen, they could make mistakes or intentionally deceive. But when prophets received messages from God and conveyed them to the people, they functioned as God's spokesmen inerrantly. God, the all-knowing and all-wise, did not make untrustworthy promises. His Word did not err in what it affirmed of objective reality or subjective feelings. And God's Word through the prophets infallibly achieved its objectives.

The crucial issue for the people was not deciding what to accept and reject from among the prophets' teachings, but whether the alleged prophets communicated truth from God or spoke presumptuously. The people naturally cried out, "How can we know when a message has not been spoken by the LORD?" (Deut. 18:21). God's people were not condemned for asking that question, but were given *criteria* to use for detecting religious deceivers.

First, the alleged prophet's *signs must take place* as predicted (Deut. 18:22). God's predictions never fail to come true as foreseen. One who speaks for God does not misrepresent reality but presents assertions that fit the facts (sustained and known by God). God does not raise false hopes, but teaching from God conforms to reality. Special revelation involved more than words and concepts; it included also signs, wonders, and mighty acts supernaturally performed by God in support of his redemptive program.

Second, the alleged prophet's *teaching concerning God must be consistent* with what has been given by previous revelation, whether through Moses or other prophets. Whatever signs and wonders might occur, if a prophet asked the Israelites to follow other gods and worship idols, God's people ought not listen to the words of that prophet (Deut. 13:3–4). God does not deny himself nor contradict himself. Any self-contradictory religious teaching not only cannot be meaningfully communicated but neither can it originate with the living God, who is faithful.

Only after a prophet's credentials had been verified should his message be accepted as from God. God still wants his people to use their critical capacities for distinguishing true from false religious claims. In a day of many prophets, the people had to "inquire, probe and investigate [them] thoroughly" (Deut. 13:14).

Once the credentials of Moses, for example, were verified, his teaching was to be received as true on his authority and obeyed as God's teaching. The prophet's teaching was not merely a fallible witness to a noncognitive divine act, encounter, or relationship. What an accredited prophet taught was the *normative* Word of God. It ought to be received as true and obeyed. The tendency today seems to encourage criticism of revealed content (in theology) to the neglect of critical examination of the credentials of the alleged divine representatives (in apologetics).

God made known his redemptive plans and purposes in various ways (Heb. 1:1), including (1) revealed assertions in sentences, (2) miraculous deeds, and (3) the prophet's personal experiences of God. Personal encounters (Isa. 6:1–5), mighty acts (Exod. 14:13, 31), and propositional assertions (1 Sam. 2:27; 3:21) were intertwined as the prophets called people to a life of fellowship with God and service for God. Their faith, hope, and love was not fraudulently evoked but motivated by truth concerning God's nature, purposes, and acts.

The basic element of revealed conceptual truth is not an isolated concept or single word but an assertion expressed in an indicative sentence. Of course, the sentence ordinarily occurs in a paragraph, and the paragraph in a series of such units of thought. Hence a word communicated by a prophet was understood in the context of its sentence, paragraph, and broader cultural and theological world view.

Like Christ's teaching, the prophetic teaching was not only coherent, but also *permanently viable and authoritative*. Jesus said, "Do not think that I have come to abolish the Law or the Prophets; I have not come to abolish them but to fulfill them. I tell you the truth, until heaven and earth disappear, not the smallest letter, not the least stroke of a pen, will by any means disappear from the Law until everything is accomplished" (Matt. 5:17–18). In the subsequent points of the Sermon on the Mount Jesus refuted not only the teaching of the Old Testament prophets but also the misunderstandings of them in Pharisaic legalism.

By way of summary and definition,

then, prophets were providentially prepared people of God whose claims to receive messages from God were accredited and who affirmed with divine authority and power reliable information about significant events in the past, present, and future and normative principles about how people ought to relate to God and one another.

God's Word Through Apostolic Spokesmen

Jesus as an "apostle" sent by the Father "was faithful to the one who appointed him" (Heb. 3:1–2). As Jesus preached with the Father's delegated authority, so Jesus appointed apostles to preach with his delegated *authority* (Mark 6:7) and Spirit-endued *power* (John 20:21; Acts 1:8; 2:4). Hence Peter asked people to remember not only the words spoken in the past by the holy prophets but also "the command given by our Lord and Savior through your apostles" (2 Peter 3:2).

What was the *source* of the prophetic and apostolic message? Peter insisted that "prophecy never had its origin in the will of man, but men spoke from God as they were carried along by the Holy Spirit" (2 Peter 1:21). Paul claimed to speak "not in words taught us by human wisdom but in words taught by the Spirit, expressing spiritual truths in spiritual words" (1 Cor. 2:13), even when giving his own judgment on subjects on which no quotation from Jesus was available (1 Cor. 7:25; 14:37). And Paul thanked God that the Thessalonians "received the word of God," which they heard from the apostles "not as the word of men, but as it actually is, the word of God" (1 Thess. 2:13).

By what *criteria* could people in the first century know whether an alleged apostle was speaking for God or speaking presumptuously? The tests of a true apostle were similar to those of a true prophet. The first-century Christians had every reason to expect that Saul should give evidence of being transformed into Paul, the apostle to the Gentiles. In defense of his apostolic ministry Paul stressed the consistency of his one gospel with that of the other apostles (Gal. 1:9–11; 2:7–9). Paul also had become an eyewitness of the risen Christ, a requirement for an apostle (Acts 1:22–23; 1 Cor. 15:7). And Paul's miracles came to pass. "The things that mark an apostle—signs, wonders and miracles—were done among you with great perseverance" (2 Cor. 12:12; Heb. 2:4).

God's people needed to be critical rather than gullible, for there were already many false apostles in the first century. Not all that was supernatural was of God. First-century Christians were not to believe every spirit but to "test the spirits to see whether they [were] from God" (1 John 4:1). This major test was doctrinal. "Every spirit that acknowledges that Jesus Christ has come in the flesh is from God, but every spirit that does not acknowledge Jesus is not from God" (1 John 4:2–3). Anyone who departs from the teaching of (about) Christ does not have God (2 John 9). Revelation allegedly from God that comes through people who deny the deity of Christ is clearly not from the Most High but from a lesser source.

What an accredited apostle taught, God taught. The *contents* of the apostles' messages were not subject to critical testing and possible acceptance or rejection, because the apostles' *credentials* had been verified. The early Christians did not think of rejecting the apostolic teaching. The teaching of the apostles was all normative for establishing doctrine, making value judgments in life, overseeing the church, and disciplining church members.

Like the messages of Christ, the apostle's messages originated with God the Father, came through human concepts and words, were supernaturally kept from error by the power of the Holy Spirit, taught only truth authoritatively and effectually, and were not time-bound, but classically time-related and relevant.

APOLOGETIC INTERACTION

Are There Additional Revelations Today?

Since prophets and apostles were instrumental to special revelation, the question may be restated. Do the offices of prophet and apostle continue in the church? If so, in what form? With respect to prophets, after about 400 B.C. no more prophets appeared in Israel. Three times the writer of 1 Maccabees mentions that there were no prophets in Israel (4:46; 9:27; cf. 14:41). And Josephus said that at about the time of Artaxerxes of Persia "the exact succession of the prophets" had ceased.[35] The Old Testament being completed, after four centuries of prophetic silence John the Baptist is the last of the prophets of the old covenant and the precursor of Jesus.

Since it was God's will to give another Testament presenting the accomplishment of redemption as predicted in the Old Testament, another period of prophecy would be expected. Jesus Christ is the greatest prophet (Deut. 18:15–19; Matt. 7:29). There were several prophets mentioned by name in the New Testament (Luke 1:67; Acts 11:28; 13:1; 15:32; 21:9–10). Before the New Testament had been completed many false prophets had appeared (Acts 13:6; 1 John 4:1; Rev. 2:20).

The new period of prophecy, like the earlier one, came to an end when this portion of God's Word was completed. The end of this period, when new divine revelations would no longer be given, was not immediately apparent. As in the case

of the OT, they simply ceased. The entire Bible was written. Thereafter people in the Church were called prophets only in the extended sense of presenting God's people truths received, not by direct revelation, but from careful study of the completed and infallible Word of God.[36]

The work of noncanonical prophets emphasized application of the teaching of written revelation to specific situations, not adding books to the canon of either the Old Testament or the New. The authentic successor to the prophets is the Old Testament itself, since it continues their ministry to the world and the people of God. In a secondary sense those who instruct and challenge people or encourage and comfort people from the Old or New Testament Scriptures may be said to have a prophetic ministry and may be called prophets (1 Cor. 14:3).

Is there a succession of apostles from the first century until today? The Church of England and Episcopalian terminology of apostolic succession is not found in the New Testament, and there is little evidence for the idea. One passage used emphasizes the continuity of apostolic doctrine, not the office (2 Tim. 2:2). The idea of a succession of apostles is absent in the first two centuries. There could be no more apostles in the original (revelatory) sense of the word (Acts 1:21–22). "The real successor to the apostolate is the NT itself, since it continues their ministry within the church of God. Their office was incommunicable."[37]

Since the completion of the biblical books, there is no further divine *inspiration* for the writing of Scripture. Divine *illumination* produces no new revelation; illumination opens the mind and will to the reception of revelation (1 Cor. 2:14). Jesus Christ has done all that he can do in his redemptive purposes until his return to the earth. And in the available canon we have all the truths necessary to acceptance with

God and for an abundant life. All the noncontradictory teachings of alleged recent revelations together do not add anything significant to scriptural teachings on God, mankind, sin, salvation, the church, and things to come.

The commission of the apostles was unique and nonrepeatable. The apostles were eyewitnesses of the incarnate and risen Christ. Apostolic ministry was distinguished from all other ministries, was not local but universal, and was not derived from the church, but was foundational to it.[38] Just as the enduring product of the Incarnation was the teaching of the divine-human person of Christ, the enduring product of revelation through prophets and apostles was their divine-human teaching (doctrine). The question is this: Does revelation continue today through the church?

Note that the revelation came *to* the people of God through specially gifted prophets and apostles as well as through Jesus Christ. The revelation did not come *from* the church as a whole or its permanent officers. The evidence does not support the traditional Roman Catholic position stated by Thomas Aquinas: "Revelation is the truth that God communicates through the prophets, Christ, the Apostles, *and the Church*."[39]

Church leaders (elders, pastors, bishops) serve as provisional authorities for teaching new converts and others until they can discover and relate revealed truth for themselves. Christians are all priests indwelt and illumined by the Holy Spirit in the study of special revelation. When leaders in the church stray from its teaching, the mature members can call them back to the supernaturally originated Word of God. However, they do not receive new revelation to add to the Bible.

The provisional authority of ecclesiastical leaders as *interpreters* of the Word, however, deserves respect, especially where reflected in thoroughly prepared doctrinal statements such as the creeds of the early church. Nevertheless, if contradiction appears between the explicit teaching of church authorities and responsibly interpreted revealed truth, people must obey the revelation that originated with God and was supernaturally given through the specially gifted prophets and apostles who were authenticated by supernatural signs, wonders, and mighty acts.

To preserve the unique authority of the foundational and only inerrant revelation (*sola scriptura*), Christians often challenge the pretensions of any church or cult that sees itself as an additional source of revelation for these latter days alongside the Lord, the prophets, and the apostles. Israel and the church were not *above* but *under* the authority of the Word. The tendency to speak of the church as a continuation of the incarnation must avoid the inference that it can add new revelation to the foundational truth of the prophets and apostles.

Is revelation continuous today? Facing many alleged revelations from both occult and established sources, people must develop discernment and overcome gullibility. False as well as true prophets may produce signs, wonders, and mighty acts (Matt. 24:24). Not all that is supernatural in our times is of God. Examine contemporary claims of revelation by the same criteria as in Old and New Testament times. Determine whether the advertised miracles in fact took place and whether the central teachings contradict teachings known to be from God in the Old and New Testaments.

All the alleged revelations of spiritists, Latter-Day Saints, Christian Scientists, and others put together do not add anything significant to the teaching of Scripture. Remember that Christ has completed all that can be done for the salvation of the world until he returns again to the earth. What people need now is not more revelation but more faithfulness to the Spirit-illumined applications of biblical principles to specific situations. To protect the uniqueness of biblical revelation we do not call applications "revelations," but "illuminations."

Just as the Word must always test the spirits, the Holy Spirit must always attest the Word. Although we may not anticipate additional objective truth mediated through propositions, the Holy Spirit continues to work with believers immediately, enabling them to *receive* the deep things of God's divine wisdom and to grow in understanding toward the mind of Christ (1 Cor. 2:10–16). The continuing immediate aspect of special revelation in the inner witness of the Holy Spirit is indispensable to spiritual growth. Commitment to the objective truth of redemptive revelation is no substitute for keeping in step with the Spirit or illumination (Gal. 5:25). And "abiding in the Spirit" cannot for long serve as a satisfactory substitute for adherence to objectively revealed truths.

The Particularity of Special Revelation

The occurrence of divine disclosures to specific persons at specific times and places seems unfair to those to whom no special revelation was given. However, special revelation does not preclude the reality of general revelation in the repeated laws of nature, events of history, and human consciousness universally (as established in the previous chapter). Through general revelation God justly approaches all people everywhere in the same manner.

Although special revelation underlines what all deserve equally, it focuses centrally on undeserved mercy and grace. Since justice has been served, does it follow that God could not mercifully grant certain benefits to some people and not to others? Has he not freely given some gifts to certain leaders that are not given to others?

The gifts of grace are given not for people to spend for their own pleasures, but to use for the benefit of all. The purpose of the covenant with Abraham and the choice of Israel as a nation was not to encourage their pride, arrogance, or self-indulgence, but rather that Abraham's descendants might bring blessing to the whole world (Gen. 12:2–3). Jesus ministered to the specially chosen disciples in a way he did not to others. But our Lord's ministry to the Twelve was also for their becoming equipped to make disciples throughout the world and teach all that Jesus had disclosed to them. God chose Saul to become an apostle to the Gentiles, not to provide him with selfish ease and comfort, but to give him a mission to reach the world with the gospel of grace.

If revelation was to become something more than general revelation, it would necessarily have to be given to a person in history at a particular time and place. If Jesus was to become incarnate at all, (1) it would have to be in some century—so why not the first? (2) It would have to be in some place—so why not the Near East? (3) It would necessarily be in the context of some people—so why not the Jewish people?

"What advantage, then, is there in being a Jew? . . . First of all, they have been entrusted with the very words of God" (Rom. 3:1–2). The choice of the Jewish prophets and apostles in particular was not based on some special merit on their part. All have sinned; none is deserving of divinely bestowed benefits. Paul wrote to the Corinthians, as much concerning himself as anyone else, "God chose the foolish things of the world to shame the wise; God chose the weak things of the world to shame the strong . . . so that no one may boast before him" (1 Cor. 1:27–29). Clearly, to be chosen by God to receive and communicate revelation as a prophet or apostle was not grounds for feelings of superiority. Paul could ask anyone, "What do you have that you did not receive?" (1 Cor. 4:7).

Beyond all this, the particular instrument through which divine revelation comes faces great responsibility. The Pharisees who failed to understand grace relied on the law and bragged about their relationship to God, but Paul wrote, "You, then, who teach others, do you not teach yourself? . . . God's name is blasphemed among the Gentiles because of you" (Rom. 2: 21–24). Paul's indictment of humanity concludes, "Are we any better? Not at all! We have already made the charge that Jews and Gentiles alike are all under sin" (Rom. 3:9). In the Old Testament context, Israel would receive the same judgments as the nations driven out before her if she disobeyed the Lord in the way they had.

The particularism of special revelation is not that of an ethnic or geographical favoritism, but of a redeemed remnant called out from the masses to serve them. Belief in a God who cares enough for the lost to come into the world as their Savior and to communicate the redemptive message through his prophetic and apostolic spokespeople remains essential to Christian faith. If this gracious, spiritual particularism is rejected, Christianity is rejected. God's special redemptive program takes place not in a vacuum but in the context of God's universal providential program that includes every person and every culture throughout history.

By way of contrast, if the alleged incarnation of the Hindu Krishna is not particularistic, it is because according to the myths Krishna could not have a literal body in space and time without becoming evil. According to Christian teaching, matter is not evil; it is the creation of God. Humanness also, as created, is not inherently evil. So a literal incarnation is not morally impos-

sible. Because Christianity is actually incarnational, it is uniquely particularistic and essentially so.

Although the differences between various historical periods and cultures are often emphasized and should not be overlooked, there are also many similarities in human beings of all times and places. All are persons and have inalienable human rights, all demand justice and intellectual honesty, all need mercy and love, all have to relate to reality, and all ought to speak coherently in order to understand and be understood. All have failed to live up to the norms of general revelation. Hence all need salvation by grace through faith.

So, while there is an inescapable truth in Christianity's particularism, its particularism does not render it negotiable, nor is it irrelevant to people of other times and places. Like the particularism of a classical work of art or music, special revelation speaks relevantly and normatively to people around the world in generation after generation, whether yellow, black, brown, red, or white, male or female, Eastern or Western, poor or rich, educated or uneducated.

Because of the marked differences between human cultures and even within the same culture over a period of fifteen hundred years, special revelation was *progressive*. Not everything could be taught at once and the divine spokesman is responsible only for the new element introduced at a given time. As prophet after prophet spoke, their messages did not contradict earlier communications. At times paradoxes (apparent contradictions) stimulated thought. But further investigation showed that the divine spokesmen were not affirming and denying the same thing at the same time or in the same respect. Jesus' communiques did not "destroy" but "fulfilled" earlier revelations from the prophets (Matt. 5:17–18). And the apostles, including Paul, did not destroy but carried through to completion the teaching of their Lord.[40] The spokesmen for a God who cannot deny himself did not contradict themselves. Before attributing contradictory nonsense to God's spokesmen, interpreters do well to exhaust every possible way of understanding the harmony and continuity of authority that the authors sensed in the ultimate Author's plan.

Special Revelation: Personal and Propositional

Contemporary existentialist, neoorthodox, and biblical theology has repeatedly alleged that what God reveals is himself, not information about himself. "God does not give us information by communication; He gives us Himself in communion."[41] Again, "there appears a remarkable breadth of agreement in recent discussions about revelation. It is that what is fundamentally revealed is God Himself, not propositions about God."[42]

The claim to have received propositional revelation is not to be confused with occult or magical claims to guidance from hidden spirit sources. In animistic and occult practice questions are asked requiring a yes or no answer through involuntary signs in a liver or on a Ouija board and the voluntary signs of "familiar spirits." By contrast, the propositional revelation given to prophets and apostles produced promises, covenants, unconditional predictions, conditional predictions, epistles, gospels, histories, psalms, proverbs, exhortations, doctrinal teaching, and laws. Furthermore, this has come from openly acknowledged, tested, and confirmed prophets and apostles. The happenings these people report were not done in a corner, a darkened room, or among believers only. They were observed by Egyptians, Baal worshipers, Roman guards, and other nonbelievers as well as many questioning believers and people who became believers.

A defense of propositional revelation may also be misunderstood as a claim that all revealed information came in the form of "S is P" (a subject, some form of the verb to be, and a predicate nominative). Although many revealed assertions are not in this form, propositions in logical form may be presupposed or inferred from the poetry, letters, biographical descriptions and narratives. Assumptions and inferences about God and humanity are implied in what has been stated in nonpropositional form.

Misunderstandings also occur when a "proposition" is taken to be so inflexible and static as to be inapplicable to meaningful personal existence and relationships.

In philosophy, but not in business or sexual activity, a proposition is whatever can be asserted, denied, contended, maintained, assumed, supposed, implied, or presupposed. In other words, it is that which is expressed by a typical indicative sentence.[43]

The content of a proposition needs to be distinguished from the sentence conveying it. The same assertion can appear very differently in different languages. "God knows you and cares about you" may be communicated in totally different wordings in Hebrew, Greek, Spanish, Sanskrit, Russian, Swahili, and Chinese. The same affirmation can be expressed in these and hundreds of other languages.

Truth is a quality of propositions; sentences either convey the proposition effectively or ineffectively. The proposition, "God knows and cares about you" is cognitive; that is, it is either true or false. The fact that the proposition is always and everywhere true does not make either God or you static beings, nor does it make knowing and caring a static relationship. The content of propositions ought not be confused with the realities designated. The objective validity of propositions about persons does not render personal relationships "static," as often charged, or "lifeless." Precisely the opposite is the case. If it may be equally true that "God does *not* know or care about you," then God may not be living, knowing, and caring and he may indeed be a static principle, impersonal energy, or a dumb idol.

Nevertheless, according to Karl Barth such doctrinal information could not have been revealed by God. "Revelation in fact does not differ from the person of Jesus Christ, and again does not differ from the reconciliation that took place in him. To say revelation is to say, 'The Word became flesh.' "[44] Jesus Christ alone can reveal God to us. Even assertions of prophets and apostles are not God's Word. Barth regards them witnesses and only witnesses who claim no authority at all for themselves. Barth never identifies Paul's words with God's words. "In the one case *Deus dixit*, in the other *Paulus dixit*. These are two different things."[45] No doctrinal propositions, Barth thought, could be revealed, with apparently this one exception: "The Word became flesh." Revelation presents the person of Christ, not information about Christ. But to affirm that, Barth had to allow for at least this one exceptional proposition that holds for both God and man in eternity and time. If the alleged "infinite qualitative distinction" between God's mind and human minds is not so great that one proposition can be true for both, then others may also be affirmed.

Emil Brunner similarly declared that "the Word of God is not doctrine, that God in his Word does not speak 'something true,' but himself."[46] Admittedly, doctrinal assertions are "related instrumentally to the Word of God as token and framework, serving in relation to the reality—actual personal fellowship with God, but they are not the Word of God."[47] "God can, if he so wills, speak his Word to a person even through false doctrine and correspondingly find in a false Credo-credo the right echo of his Word."[48]

The Barth-Brunner concern for personal relationship to God as the end and goal of revelation is commendably scriptural. The God-given means to that end, however, are not erroneous assertions but true assertions. True concepts lead away from idols and to the living God who is there. Conceptual truth can become an idol just as any means can become an end. Nevertheless, viewing revealed assertions as less than true does not remove that danger.

Persons relate well to other persons when there is mutual respect and trust. Personal relationships are not enhanced by untrustworthy sayings. Persons disclose their inner commitments and purposes in nonverbal ways but also with greater explicitness and precision in words.

As Jesus said, "Out of the overflow of the heart the mouth speaks" (Matt. 12:34). The audible words are simply external evidence of the heart's attitude. True statements, therefore, are not a hindrance to knowing the inner person but a help. Even a Freudian slip of the tongue may disclose something about a person.

Removal of the possibility of communication in solitary confinement is a most serious penalty. To remove a personal God from the possibility of communication in assertions conveyed by words does not enhance but hurts the possibility of personal relationships. The gift of speech shows that humanity has been made for fellowship. We cannot live fully as persons apart from our neighbors or apart from God.

Although both Barth and Brunner seek to return to a biblical perspective, their position on revelation is not sufficiently biblical at this point. For example, *Logos* refers to the person of Christ in two passages (John 1:1–14; Rev. 19:13) but to information in scores of other passages. Revelation occurs in linguistic assertions, not in the person of Christ only.

Similarly, Old and New Testament words for *revelation* make it clear that God disclosed himself not only without a verbal message but also, and far more frequently, through messages conveyed by prophets and apostles. Revelation takes place not only in events or happenings but also in interpretations of events, predictions of the significance of coming events, commandments and exhortations, judgments and blessings, promises and covenants. "Revelation" is not confined to the foundational message of Christ but includes also messages of the prophets and apostles.[49]

The terms for "speaking," "saying," and other such words support a doctrine of revelation not only in indescribable experiences that one may have with the person of the living Christ, but also in the words of Christ and God's other spokespeople. The Hebrew noun *dabar* basically means "what God said or says." Of the 242 times the phrase "the word of the Lord" occurs, the expression appears as a technical form for a communicable prophetic revelation 225 times.[50]

Summing up the biblical data, Bernard Ramm found that "revelation is both a meeting and a knowing. Something is said in revelation, and what is said is the root and ground of our knowledge of God." Ramm explained further, "Certainly the word 'revelation' is rich in meaning. God's word to the prophet is revelation; God's act is revelation; the return of Christ is revelation. The concept of revelation in Scripture is too rich to be easily schematized; *it is also rich enough to be applied to the conceptual side of revelation.*"[51]

Responding to Barth and Brunner's view, Ramm asks, "But what does it mean to disclose a person? Certainly two people who are deaf, blind, and mute can hardly have any real encounter with each other apart from touch. Real encounter in life between persons is always within the context of mutual knowledge."[52] Any noncognitive concepts of revelation, like those of the neoorthodox, mystics, and new-consciousness groups fail to fit the biblical evidence. In the next chapter we will consider how divine truth can be expressed in human ways without distortion.

RELEVANCE TO LIFE AND MINISTRY

The Chief End of Special Revelation

The comprehensive purpose of special revelation is the reestablishment of the full communion of sinful people with God. So special revelation is directed to life as a whole—to the intellect and the conscience, the emotions and the will. The divine communication seeks to move the whole person away from enticements to sin and toward spiritual life with God.

Few have expressed the objective of revelation as well as W. H. Griffith Thomas has:

The essential purpose of revelation is life: the gift of the life of God to the life of man. Its practical character is stamped on every part. The "chief end of revelation" is not philosophy, though it has a philosophy profound and worthy. It is not doctrine, though it has its experiences precious and lasting. It is not even morality, though it has its ethic unique and powerful. Christianity *has* all these, but *is* far more than them all. It is the religion of redemption, including salvation from sin, equipment for holiness, and provision for life to be lived in fellowship with God and for His glory. The "chief end" of revelation is the union [communion] of God and man, and in that union [communion] the fulfillment of all God's purposes for the world. The elements of sonship, worship, stewardship, fellowship, heirship, practically sum up the purpose of Divine revelation as it concerns man's life—a life in which he receives God's grace, realizes God's will, reproduces God's character, renders God service, and rejoices in God's presence in the Kingdom of grace below and the Kingdom of glory above.[53]

The apostle John wrote his Gospel in order that sinners might obtain spiritual life. His purpose, he said, was "that you may believe [the proposition having been attested by many signs] that Jesus is the Christ, the Son of God, and that by believing [that revealed truth] you may have life in his name" (20:31).

Truth Necessary but Not Sufficient

In bringing the whole person to life, the Holy Spirit has freely chosen to use truth as the necessary instrument. Revealed truths are necessary to direct people away from deceptive idols to the living God. But in and of themselves truths are incapable of doing that. Although necessary, the truths of the gospel are not sufficient because sinners need not only new light but also new sight. No one except the Holy Spirit can grant sight—the ability to receive redemptive doctrines. Hence the necessary condition of spiritual life is revealed truth, but truth can be "received" only by the enablement of the Holy Spirit (1 Cor. 2:14).

Christianity, as J. Gresham Machen said, is "a way of life founded on a message." The gospel "is not a mere expression of Christian experience, but on the contrary it is a setting forth of those facts upon which experience is based."[54]

Bombarded by countless claims from new-consciousness leaders, gurus, and witches of all sorts, people need dependable guidelines to lead them away from idols in their quest for personal transformation through experience of their transcendent Source. People created in God's image are unfulfilled by relativistic agnosticism. Still they want answers. Desiring authority, many have joined one cult after another. But spiritual promiscuity is no more viable than agnosticism. Spiritual fulfillment will never be permanent apart from the changeless Lord of all. The lasting key to spiritual reality is changeless gospel truth from the changeless Lord. "How, then, can they call on the one they have not believed in? And how can they hear without someone preaching to them?" (Rom. 10:14).

A Reliable Guide to Significant Worship

Because Jesus is the second person of the Trinity, he is rightly the object of *worship*. To worship and serve other spiritual masters is sinfully to worship and serve creatures rather than the Creator (Rom. 1:25). Not so when Christians worship the Logos who was with God, was God, and became flesh. The incarnate Word or Son mediates God's blessings to us and exemplifies worship in spirit and in truth.[55]

Revelation provides reliable information as an instrument of the Spirit by which all worship God. The peak worship experience is not a mindless feeling of oneness with the underlying energy of everything in nature. The peak worship experience occurs when we love God with all our minds as well as our hearts (Matt. 22:37).

We recognize the Being of greatest worth—not only with our spirits, but also our minds—by worshiping in spirit and in truth (John 4:24). The ideal is not ecstatic utterance with an unfruitful mind. Rather, Paul said, "I will pray with my spirit, but I will also pray with my mind; I will sing with my spirit, but I will also sing with my mind" (1 Cor. 14:15).

Sound conceptual guidelines in our minds direct our adoration away from the creation and to the Creator-Redeemer-Counselor who hears, speaks, and acts. Worship involves the whole person, including an actively dedicated mind. Studies of the *prayers* of people like Hannah (1 Sam. 2:1–10), David (Psalm 119), Jesus (Matt. 6:9–13; John 17), and Paul (Eph. 1:15–23; 3:14–21) show how their communion with God was shaped by profound knowledge of revealed truths or doctrines.

Many approaches to *meditation* today under the influence of Hindu and Buddhist mysticism ask that a person's mind be rid of all conceptual thought from any source whatever, including propositional revelation. That may be an appropriate way to identify with the impersonal, nonintelligent energy of the cosmos, but it is not an acceptable way to commune with the heavenly Father to whom Jesus asked us to pray without vain repetition.

Authentic spirituality is not a mere social activism (Paul Van Buren), a feeling of dependence on God (Schleiermacher), an ecstatic experience (Tillich), nor even a personal encounter with God. Authentic spirituality involves a personal response to a personal God with assent to the instruction of revelation concerning what is most ultimate and of highest value. Without reliable information one may expend his life for nothing; without faithfulness to the highest values, one may be a hypocrite. Accurate information and fidelity are both crucial for their respective purposes. Neither can substitute for the other.[56] In *A Theology of Christian Devotion* Thor Hall observed, "Spirituality without understanding is not faith; it is superstition. Faith without knowledge is not biblical devotion; it is blind fideism."[57]

A Dependable Source of Comfort and Courage

Belief in the unfailing promises of God may provide *comfort* in sorrow and *courage* in the valley of the shadow of death. At such crucial times, a servant of God who does not think any promise in human concepts and words can be reliable, or isn't sure whether revealed doctrines concerning life after death are "faithful sayings," fails to meet the deepest need of the dying and the sorrowing, who look to a minister at such a time if no other. A psychological survey of terminally ill patients by a University of Denver psychologist showed that most preferred visits by conservative ministers, who read the Bible and prayed, to visits by liberal ministers who did not. Before they officiate at a funeral, ministers need to settle whether they have reason to affirm with conviction, "I am convinced that neither death nor life, neither angels nor demons, neither the present nor the future, nor any powers, neither height nor depth, nor anything else in all creation, will be able to separate us from the love of God that is in Christ Jesus our Lord" (Rom. 8:38–39).

A Solid Base for Unity and Fellowship in the Church

Spiritual life involves reconciliation to God and membership in the church, the body of Christ. A chief end (*telos*) of revelation is spiritual fellowship (*koinonia*) with God and with his people (1 John 1:3–4). A common commitment to a divinely revealed, objectively valid belief system provides a solid base for church *unity*. Those who believed the gospel on the day of Pentecost were baptized and then devoted themselves to the apostle's teaching and to the fellowship, the breaking of bread, and of prayer (Acts 2:41–42). Those who thus preached and received the Word of God began, not another sect of Judaism, but the Christian church. By Spirit-endued belief in Christ-centered revelation they stood against the powerful persecution of the Roman government, they overcame centuries of prejudice against both the Samaritans and the Gentiles to baptize them into the one body of Christ and so into prejudice-shattering fellowship with themselves.

Enduring unity in the church today also needs to be constructed on every member's reflective commitment to the apostles' revealed doctrines. Commitment to truth does not enslave. Propositional truth liberated the early church for service and it can free the church for greater exploits today. In addition to a unity of mighty acts of God (happenings), the first Christians had a unity because of a common assent to revealed gospel beliefs and a common personal trust in the living Christ to whom they referred.

A healthy church needs strong preaching of God's revealed Word. Many ministers do not preach with authority what careful study has shown to be a spiritual reality based on a central doctrine of God's Word, but some "totally other" unknown "X" to which people of God at a certain period endeavor fallibly to point. Christians, knowing that the lordship of Christ comes to expression in Scripture, will attend and support churches that are faithful to the prophetic and apostolic revelations in preaching and practice.

Schools raised up to train people to minister God's revealed truth need to examine themselves to determine whether they are presently serving their educational *raison d'être*. It is not enough to promote the school as a seedbed of revealed thought. Contributors and friends might well ask, "Do all the faculty declare and defend an informational revelation that originated with God and was communicated through the Messiah as well as tested and confirmed prophetic and apostolic spokesmen, whose affirmations are true and not false?" What is the integrating focus of the curriculum, if any? Is every department's teaching faithful to the living God's supernatural revelation in the words of the Jesus of history, the prophets, and the apostles? Believers in propositional revelation from an omniscient God who does not deny himself have the responsibility of developing and defending the coherence of revealed teachings. To affirm that the revelation is noncontradictory and that a systematic theology is possible, is not to hold that anyone can fully comprehend all that was revealed and known. It is only to say that when we claim to know in part, one part of divine revelation will not destroy another. In developing the harmony of the content of universal and particular revelation, attempts to hold a teaching true in theology but false in philosophy or science (double truth) have not long maintained respect.[58]

A Wise Source of Standards for Church Discipline

Churches and schools today could be more glorifying to their Savior and Head if there were more *discipline*. Unfortunately in many organizations an erosion of belief in revealed truths may have made discipline of those who deny the truth nearly impossible. No ethical effort should be spared to correct such situations. Unless normative teachings are implemented by church leaders, the church becomes indistinguishable from the world.

Where discipline is impossible ecclesiastical separation may become necessary. Separation could not be avoided in Luther's day, and many today find themselves in "fellowships" without basic loyalties in common because they are without a shared revelational base.

125

When a well-researched, respectful, loving, and persistent request to return to the purposes of the organization's original documents affirming the normativity of revealed truths shows no prospect of success, the only remaining alternative may be separation with regret.

Jesus Christ holds the church responsible for maintaining doctrinal as well as moral purity (Rev. 2:2, 14, 20). Paul urged the church at Rome to "keep away from" those who caused division by doctrine "contrary to the teaching" they had learned (Rom. 16:17). And Paul left no doubt about the teaching intended, for it is "now revealed and made known through the prophetic writings by the command of the eternal God, so that all nations might believe and obey him" (Rom. 16:26).

An Authentic Exhibit of Justice Tempered With Mercy

By Spirit-endued belief in justice, mercy and love taught by Christ, prophets, and apostles, the early church made a substantial difference in the first-century world. Not only in Israel, but wherever they went, believers in special revelation improved the condition of women, men, children, masters, and slaves. Progressively they realized that every person's dignity as created in the image of God meant having inherent human rights. They called for justice without respect of persons, and honesty rather than false witness against a neighbor. When people realized their inability to live according to such universal norms fully, Christians offered the mercy and love of God for them.

The prophets and apostles warned of judgment and called people to repent of their unfaithfulness to God and others. At the same time they also called people to believe the news of the Messiah's coming atonement and resurrection, and to trust Christ himself. In societies that are far from just—whether communist, socialist, or capitalist—the message of a just amnesty created a forgiving community. Christians are not merely forgiven, they are forgiving. The unjust today cannot succeed in suppressing their guilt nor in denying the reality of their sinfulness. Psychologically and spiritually, spouses, parents, children, employers, and employees need to see the dynamic of Calvary's forgiveness that satisfies justice and graciously provides new life from above.

REVIEW QUESTIONS

To Help Relate and Apply Each Section in This Chapter

1. *Briefly state the classical problem* this chapter addresses and indicate reasons why genuine inquiry into it is important for your world view and your existence personally and socially.

2. *Objectively summarize the influential answers* given to this problem in history as hypotheses to be tested. Be able to compare and contrast their real similarities and differences (not merely verbal similarities or differences).

3. *Highlight the primary biblical evidence* on which to decide among views—evidence found in the relevant teachings of the major divisions of Scripture—and decide for yourself which historical hypothesis (or synthesis of historical views) provides the most consistent and adequate account of the primary biblical data.

4. *Formulate in your own words your doctrinal conviction* in a logically consistent and adequate way, organizing your conclusions in ways you can explain clearly, support biblically, and communicate effectively to your spouse, children, friends, Bible class, or congregation.

5. *Defend your view* as you would to

adherents of the alternative views, showing that the other views are logically less consistent and factually faced with more difficulties than your view in accounting for the givens, not only of special revelation but also of human experience in general.

6. *Explore the differences the viability of your conviction can make in your life.* Then test your understanding of the viability of your view by asking, "Can I live by it authentically (unhypocritically) in relation to God and to others in my family, church, vocation, neighborhood, city, nation, and world?"

MINISTRY PROJECTS

To Help Communicate This Doctrine in Christian Service

1. *Memorize one major verse or passage* that in its context teaches the heart of this doctrine and may serve as a text from which to preach, teach, or lead small group studies on the topic. The memorized passages from each chapter will build a body of content useful also for meditation and reference in informal discussions.

2. *Formulate the major idea of the doctrine in one sentence* based on the passage memorized. This idea should be useful as the major thesis of either a lesson for a class (junior high to adult) or a message for a church service.

3. *State the specific purpose or goal of your doctrinal lesson or message.* Your purpose should be more than informative. It should answer the question of why Christians need to accept this truth and live by it (unhypocritically). For teaching purposes list indicators that would show to what extent class members have grasped the truth presented.

4. *Outline your message or lesson in complete sentences.* Indicate how you would support the truth of the doctrine's central ideas and its relevance to life and service. Incorporate elements from this chapter's historical, biblical, systematic, apologetic, and relevance sections selected for their direct importance to your purpose for your audience.

5. *List applications of the doctrine* for communicating the difference this conviction makes in life (for sermons, lessons, small-group Bible studies, or family devotional Bible studies). Applications should make clear what the doctrine is, why one needs to know it, and how it will make differences in thinking. Then show how the difference in thought will lead to differences in values, priorities, attitudes, speech, and personal action. Consider also the doctrine's possible significance for family, church, neighborhood, city, regional, and national actions.

6. *Start a file and begin collecting illustrations* of this doctrine's central idea, the points in your outline, and your applications.

7. *Write out your own doctrinal statement on this subject in one paragraph* (in half a page or less). To work toward a comprehensive doctrinal statement, collect your formulations based on a study of each chapter of *Integrative Theology.* As your own statement of Christian doctrine grows, you will find it personally strengthening and useful when you are called on for your beliefs in general and when you apply for service with churches, mission boards, and other Christian organizations. Any who seek ordination to Christian ministry will need a comprehensive doctrinal statement that covers the broad scope of theology.

CHAPTER 4

THE BIBLE AS GIVEN BY INSPIRATION AND RECEIVED BY ILLUMINATION

The Bible
as Given by Inspiration
and Received by Illumination

THE PROBLEM: IN WHAT WAY IS THE BIBLE INSPIRED AND AUTHORITATIVE?

Having shown that God revealed to prophets and apostles not only himself but truths concerning his redemptive purposes, we now face the question of how revelation given in the distant past could be preserved and transmitted to future generations in need of his Word. Judaism and Christianity confess that by Holy Spirit inspiration God ensured the preservation of revelation in a sacred book, the Bible

Since theologians differ widely on the meaning of inspiration, it is necessary to determine what this theological concept entails. Did God inspire the biblical writer or the written document? If inspiration pertains to the prophetic or apostolic record, the question arises how finite, sinful men could state the undistorted truth of God in human language. Did God dictate his Word to the biblical writer, or did the writer, under the general guidance of the Spirit, record in ordinary human fashion the substance of what God had revealed?

It is also a question whether the inerrancy of the Bible can be upheld in the modern world. Must the writing reflect the limitations and frailties of the human author, or did God supernaturally superintend the process so that what the prophet wrote was the Word of God unalloyed by any error? Is it faithful to the teaching of Jesus and the apostles to limit inerrancy to those teachings of the Bible pertinent to salvation? Many today question whether this collection of ancient documents possesses any authority for sophisticated twentieth-century people. Christians need to know on what basis and to what extent the Bible is a binding authority in the modern world.

Many people regard the Bible as a book difficult to understand. Is it reasonable to believe that for the Bible to be properly understood the same God who inspired its contents must also illumine its message to the human mind? Finally, one must confront the issue of the canon of Scripture. How can we today be assured that all the documents God inspired have found their way into the Bible? Can the so-called apocryphal books included in some editions of the Bible be considered inspired? How should the church respond if a copy of a hitherto unknown Davidic Psalm or Pauline letter were to become unearthed?

Since the theology and life of the church is uniquely rooted in the Bible, an authentic understanding of the origin, validity, and relevance of this foundational document is essential.

ALTERNATIVE PROPOSALS IN THE CHURCH

As the issues of biblical inspiration, infallibility, and canon have been addressed in the church, several interpretations have been and continue to be influential.

Roman Catholic Scholasticism

Traditional Roman Catholic theology upheld in principle the divine origin, inspiration, and inerrancy of the Bible. Thomas Aquinas insisted that "the author of Holy Writ is God."[1] Consequently Aquinas refused to concede any errors to the inspired writers: "It is heretical to say that any falsehood whatever is contained either in the Gospels or in any canonical Scripture."[2] The Scriptures represent an incontrovertible authority, whereas the doctors of the church constitute an authority that is merely probable.

In spite of Rome's formal views on inspiration and infallibility, the authority of Scripture in practice was undermined. This was in part because Rome regarded the Bible as obscure and capable of interpretation only by the hierarchy. Thus the church's Magesterium claimed to unfold unerringly the meaning of the Word of God. The authority of the Scripture was also undermined because of the recklessly nonliteral interpretation advanced by many medieval Roman authorities. Wycliffe protested against the debasement and falsification of Scripture by incompetent persons in the Roman church. Luther said that Romanists "treat the Scriptures and make out of them what they like, as if they were a nose of wax, to be pulled about at will."[3] Add to the above the vast complex of papal decretals, conciliar judgments, and canon laws, and it is clear that the Roman church was prior to and above the Scriptures.

The Council of Trent in 1546 affirmed that Scripture and church tradition were given as "dictation by the mouth of Jesus Christ or of the Holy Ghost."[4] Inspired Scripture and inspired tradition are to be venerated "with equal piety and reverence." Trent certified longstanding trends within the Catholic church by declaring the Apocryphal books (except 1 and 2 Esdras and the Prayer of Manasses) to be inspired by God and thus part of the canonical Old Testament. Moreover, it pronounced the Latin Vulgate the authentic version of Scripture and relegated to the Magesterium the prerogative of giving the true interpretation of the Bible.

Protestant Liberalism

Liberal Protestants, for whom supernatural revelation was problematic, minimized or denied altogether the special inspiration of sacred documents. The Deists viewed Scripture as a human book and saw in it many obscurities, contradictions, and immoral prescriptions. They believed that the biblical writers were inspired only to the extent that their literary talents were elevated in moments of special creativity. Many German rationalists rejected divine inspiration altogether. J. S. Semler, for example, traced the idea of verbal inspiration to the legend of the Septuagint, whose translators were said to have been guided in the very words they used. The church appropriated the Jewish doctrine, Semler said, only when it perceived the need to guarantee the contents of the Bible.

Horace Bushnell, the father of American liberalism, likewise rejected verbal inspiration and an infallible Scripture as involving "insuperable difficulties."[5]

Neither, he argued, did God infallibly guide the church in selecting the books that would form the biblical canon. According to Bushnell, God inspired the biblical writers in the same general way that he inspires all persons for the work they perform. Walter Rauschenbusch defined inspiration as "the stirring of the prophetic spirit in living men."[6] Inspiration, so defined, did not cease with the close of the biblical canon, but will continue until the church ushers in the kingdom of God. The Bible, Rauschenbusch says, is a collection of human documents that reflects the frailty and liability to error of its human authors. "Inspiration did not involve infallibility."[7]

James Barr, following Gerhard Von Rad, views the Bible as a collection of the religious traditions of Israel and the church. By inspiration Barr means that God was with his people in the formation of their religious traditions. Since the biblical writers played a pioneering role in the formation of Judeo-Christian traditions, one may call them "inspired" in some special sense. So defined, inspiration has nothing to do with inerrancy and final authority. Indeed, Barr insists that the early church concept of inspired and authoritative Scripture was a gross mistake: it was "the clearest demonstration of the presence of original sin in the early church."[8]

Neoorthodox Theology

Neoorthodoxy views the Bible as a witness to the Word of God, a time-bound, culturally conditioned human word about past revelatory encounters. Barth regards verbal, plenary inspiration as a mechanical process that attributes too much to the Bible and too little to God himself. He judges that the Bible as defined by conservative theology has become a "paper Pope."[9] Barth believes that the biblical writers penned accounts of their revelatory encounters with the transcendent God. The precise *how* of their inscripturation of the Word, however, is an inexplicable mystery. Barth insists that one should not make the mistake of equating Scripture with the Word of God. "It is quite impossible that there should be a direct identity between the human Word of Holy Scripture and the Word of God."[10] Barth avers that to avoid a docetic view of the Bible, one must posit at least a capacity for error, both in the Bible's historical and scientific teaching and in its theological content. "The prophets and apostles . . . were real, historical men as we are, and therefore sinful in their action, and capable and actually guilty of error in their spoken and written word."[11] Nevertheless, as God graciously condescends to speak through a biblical text and the person responds in faith, the human witness acquires the dignity of the Word of God.

Brunner attacked the doctrine of verbal inspiration, calling it a fundamentalist error. "The orthodox doctrine of verbal inspiration has been finally destroyed. It is clear that there is no connection between it and scientific research and honesty; we are forced to make a decision for or against this view."[12] The written word of the Bible is equated with the Word of God only idolatrously, for the former contains "It-Truth," whereas the latter (authentic revelation) contains "Thou-Truth." According to Brunner, Scripture is merely an errant human word about Christ, the divine Word. But in spite of myriads of inconsistencies and contradictions, the Bible becomes the Word of God in that moment of crisis when the individual meets Christ through it. Inspiration connotes the divine illumination of the biblical writers that enabled them to grasp the mystery of Christ and to bear witness to him.

Vatican II Catholicism

The Vatican II Catholic view of the Bible, influenced by Protestant neoorthodoxy, limits the veracity and authority of Scripture to those teachings that pertain to salvation. The original draft of the "Dogmatic Constitution on Divine Revelation" presented to the first session of the Council expressed the traditional Catholic view that Scripture is "absolutely immune from error." This position was challenged and ultimately replaced by a more "modern" stance, the heart of which reads: "The holy books of Scripture must be acknowledged as teaching firmly, faithfully and without error that truth which God wanted to put into the sacred writings for the sake of our salvation" (no. 11). Avant-garde Catholic authorities thus insist that the so-called nonsalvific teachings of the Bible are neither inerrant nor binding on the faithful.

Hans Küng insists that historical-critical studies of the Bible have demolished the classical doctrine of verbal inspiration. The biblical writers were not divinely programmed penmen, but frail human witnesses who testified to their encounter with the divine revelation. The misleading term, inspiration of Scripture, if it be used at all, connotes only that the human witnesses were "*Spirit-pervaded* and *Spirit-filled.*"[13] But inspiration, so defined, applies equally to the totality of the apostolic life and ministry as to the apostles' literary endeavors. Therefore, Küng concludes, the Bible "is unequivocally *man's word:* collected, written down, given varied emphases, sentence by sentence by quite definite individuals and developed in different ways. Hence it is not without shortcomings and mistakes, concealment and confusion, limitations and errors."[14] Indeed, insists Küng, "there is not a single text in Scripture asserting its freedom from error."[15]

"Liberal" Evangelicals

Some Evangelicals (the so-called limited inerrantists) restrict the veracity and authority of the Scriptures to its salvific teachings. C. S. Lewis upheld the theory of degrees of inspiration when he insisted that inspiration is not "always present in the same mode and the same degree" throughout the Bible.[16] Lewis is not disturbed by the presence of errors in the biblical text: "The human qualities of the raw materials show through. Naïveté, error, contradiction, even (as in the cursing Psalms) wickedness is not removed. The total result is not 'the Word of God' in the sense that every passage, in itself gives impeccable science or history."[17] The flawed character of the Bible is seen in the fact that it contains pagan myths (the Genesis account) and nonhistorical narratives (the stories of Jonah, Job, and Esther).

Dewey Beegle speaks of different "kinds" of inspiration. The great "sent ones" of Scripture—Moses, the leading prophets, Jesus, and Paul—were recipients of a special *charismata,* whereas the lesser writers of the Bible wrote on the basis of their natural abilities and status within the covenant community. The former mode of inspiration ceased with the close of the New Testament canon, whereas the latter "process of reinterpretation and application will continue as long as man exists."[18] Two implications of this thesis follow: (1) Contemporary Christian writers are inspired to the same degree as, for example, David, Haggai, or Jude. (2) The Bible amounts to a collection of contradictory traditions, all of which do not fit into a coherent pattern. According to Beegle, the Bible is "inspired from cover to cover, human mistakes and all."[19]

G. C. Berkouwer is said to have moved through three stages in his understanding of Scripture.[20] The first, held in the 1930s before Berkouwer became acquainted with Barth, posited the entire veracity and trustworthiness of the Bible. The second, adopted in the 1940s, stressed Scripture's salvific character. And the third, embraced in the 1960s, focuses on the existential dimension of the Word. Currently Berkouwer is less concerned with such formal issues as inspiration and inerrancy (which he claims border on Docetism) than with the life-transforming message of salvation embedded in the Bible. He is not troubled by the fact that when the Word became Scripture it succumbed to the fate of all writing, that is, to time-bound notions, culturally conditioned expressions, and scientific misconceptions. But none of these imperfections cause the Bible to swerve from its central purpose, which is to uphold the truth of the gospel.

Jack Rogers follows Berkouwer in replacing verbal inspiration and inerrancy with the "organic" concept of inspiration, whereby "the function, the saving purpose, of Scripture [is] the focus of human concern rather than the form of the writing."[21] Rogers draws a distinction between the divine content, or kernel, of the biblical message and the human form, or husk, in which the message is cast. Rogers insists that the Bible is inspired only in terms of the former, i.e., "the central saving message of Scripture," and not in matters of science, history, chronology, or the male-female relation.[22] Infallibility and authority likewise are redefined in terms of the Bible's central purpose. Hence truth (viewed pragmatically, functionally, and existentially) is that which meets people's needs, and error that which willfully deceives. Insofar as the Bible makes people wise for salvation it is infallible, but because by modern standards it contains factual errors, it is not inerrant.

Protestant Fundamentalism

A fundamentalist view of the Bible, such as that advanced by John R. Rice, posits divine dictation to biblical writers who functioned as secretaries of the Holy Spirit. Rice's view of inspiration as dictation implies that God gave the very words that men wrote down in Holy Scripture. "A secretary is not ashamed to take dictation from man. Why would a prophet be ashamed to take dictation from God?"[23] Rice seeks to safeguard the human element in Scripture by maintaining that God prepared the writers in advance so that their style, vocabulary, and personality are included in the writing in accord with God's plan. What he wishes to avoid is that the biblical writers engaged in historical research, utilized oral traditions, or acquired information from eye witnesses. All Scripture came in a straight line from God to the human writers. Rice's theory of dictation borders on the docetic: "The Scriptures are fundamentally the Word of God, not the word of men, except in some incidental and controlled and limited sense."[24]

Most Fathers, Reformers, and Evangelicals

Most orthodox authorities believe that God supernaturally moved the writers of Scripture so that, although they wrote in accord with their own interests, style, and abilities, the resultant documents are his Word, authoritative in matters of faith and practice, and truthful in all they affirm. Many early Fathers stressed the divine side of Scripture by means of vivid analogies. Justin Martyr described inspiration as the process whereby the Holy Spirit worked on the biblical writers much as a musician plays on a harp or a lyre. Athenagoras maintained that the biblical writer was "a stringed instrument which the Holy Ghost put in motion, in order to draw out of it the divine harmonies of life."[25] Tertullian described individual Old Testament texts as "the commandments of God"[26] and the canon as the Scripture of the Holy Ghost.

Irenaeus in the West upheld the verbal inspiration and veracity of the entire Bible: "The Scriptures are indeed perfect, since they were spoken by the Word of God (i.e., Christ) and His Spirit."[27] Gregory of Nazianzus argued that the smallest stroke of Scripture derives from the Holy Spirit, and that even the slightest nuance of the inspired writer is not in vain. Jerome upheld verbal, plenary inspiration, as evidenced by his overstatement that "the individual sayings, syllables, phonetic markings, and punctuations in divine Scripture are filled with meanings."[28]

Irenaeus and Clement of Alexandria accepted as canonical the books of the Apocrypha. On the other hand, Origen, Athanasius, Gregory of Nazianzus, Cyril of Jerusalem, and Jerome (an authority on Hebrew) strongly opposed the extracanonical writings. Against Jerome's will the Apocrypha were included in the Latin Vulgate, yet accorded a secondary status.

Augustine was a staunch defender of the verbal inspiration of canonical Scripture. While asserting that the biblical authors wrote with an active mind, he stressed the divine initiative by stating that the apostles wrote at the command of Christ, the Lord using them "as if they were His own hands."[29] In a letter to Jerome, Augustine said of canonical Scripture, "I believe most firmly that not one of those authors has erred in any respect in writing."[30] The veracity of Scripture extends even to its discussions of natural science and history. By virtue of the divine afflatus, Holy Scripture is endowed with an indisputable authority.[31] Augustine held that the Old Testament contained forty-four books, including six Apocrypha. On certain occasions he differentiated the "canonical" Scriptures received by the Jews from others (the Apocrypha) that were not accepted by the Jews.[32] The uncertainty in Augustine's mind concerning the Apocrypha may be due to his unfamiliarity with Hebrew and his high regard for the LXX translation.

Martin Luther judged that since Scripture is from the Holy Spirit it possesses the authority of God himself. The function of the written Word is to teach Christ, the living Word. So Luther referred to the Bible as the swaddling clothes and manger in which Christ is wrapped and laid.[33] The Reformer repeatedly insisted that in both its salvific and nonsalvific teachings the Scriptures have never erred. "The Holy Spirit is not a fool or a drunkard to express one point, not to say one word, in vain."[34] Luther's German translation of the Bible eliminated the Apocryphal books inserted by Rome. However, he disputed the canonicity of Jude, Hebrews, James, and Revelation, persuaded that none of these books lays the foundations of gospel faith. Using his own criterion of canonicity—namely, that which teaches Christ—Luther assigned these four letters a secondary status in the New Testament. Luther did not hold a low view of the Bible, as critics allege. The fact is that those Scriptures Luther judged canonical he upheld as fully inspired, inerrant, and authoritative. Only his faulty criterion of canonicity caused him to question the integrity of those four books.

Calvin believed that from Genesis to Revelation, "The Bible has come down to us from the mouth of God."[35] God is the author of the words, propositions, and doctrines contained in Holy Scripture. Indeed, Calvin states that the biblical writers were "clerks,"[36] "penmen,"[37] "amanuenses,"[38] and "organs and instruments"[39] of the Holy Spirit.

By these bold metaphors Calvin did not endorse the dictation theory; rather he sought to convey in this way his conviction that God was in sovereign control of the inscripturation of his Word and that he is its ultimate Author. Calvin further believed that, having God as its author, the written Word of God is infallible or inerrant. Thus Scripture "is the certain and unerring Rule,"[40] "sacred and inviolable truth,"[41] the "sure and inviolable record,"[42] "unerring light,"[43] etc. The only errors Calvin admitted were copyists' errors in some manuscripts. Although the Bible is not a textbook of science or history, when it touches on such matters, its judgments are true.[44] Full conviction of the divine authority and veracity of Scripture is imparted by the compelling testimony of the Holy Spirit.[45]

The major branches of Protestantism uphold the high view of Scripture in their confessional statements. So the Lutheran communion in The Formula of Concord (Epitome), the Reformed in The Belgic Confession (Art. III), The Second Helvetic Confession (ch. I), and The Westminster Confession of Faith (ch. I.5, 6, 8), the Anglican tradition in The Thirty-Nine Articles (Art. XX), and the Baptists in The New Hampshire Confession (Art. I).

B. B. Warfield held that the manner of the Word's inscription is best described by the phrases "concursive operation" and "confluent authorship." That is, the human activity involving historical research and logical reasoning was mysteriously cojoined with the divine operation of the Spirit's superintendence, direction, and control. As a divine-human product, Scripture is "God-breathed" (i.e., produced by the creative breath of the Almighty), not in its thought only, but also in its words, and not in part but in full. Thus "the Bible is the Word of God in such a sense that its words, though written by men and bearing indelibly impressed on them the marks of their human origin, were written, nevertheless, under such an influence of the Holy Ghost as to be also the words of God, the adequate expression of His mind and be also the words of God, the adequate expression of His mind and will."[46] As the veritable Word of God, Scripture is inerrant: "No single error has yet been demonstrated to occur in the Scriptures as given by God to His Church."[47]

Carl F. H. Henry defines inspiration as that "supernatural influence upon divinely chosen prophets and apostles whereby the Spirit of God assures the truth and trustworthiness of their oral and written proclamation."[48] Henry stresses that Scripture is inspired in its entirety, that inspiration does not continue, even sporadically, and that the Scriptures written are the very Word of God. Henry refers *inerrancy* to the veracity of the inspired autographs and *infallibility* to the qualified perfection of the manuscript copies and translations. He urges that the term inerrancy not be dropped, but retained and carefully defined. By verbal inerrancy Henry means (1) that the Bible teaches truth in matters of history and science as well as theology and ethics; (2) that God's truth resides in the words, propositions, and sentences of the Bible; and (3) that only the original writings (autographs) are error-free. Inerrancy does not imply modern scientific precision, does not mean verbal exactitude in the apostolic quotation of Old Testament texts, and does not nullify the need for personal faith in Christ, who is the living Word of God.

The Chicago Statement on Biblical Inerrancy, produced by the International Council on Biblical Inerrancy (1978), agrees with the stance of Henry. It affirms that utilizing the distinctive personalities and literary styles of chosen men, the Spirit superintended their writing such that the sum of what was written, to the very words used, constitutes the authoritative Word of God. Since God is the author of Scripture, what is written "is inerrant, being free from all falsehood, fraud, or deceit" (Art. XII). The statement denies that the Bible could be infallible though errant in its assertions. The Statement is sensitive to the cultural contexts in which the biblical documents were written: "Although Scripture is nowhere culture-bound in the sense that its teaching lacks universal validity, it is sometimes culturally conditioned by the customs and conventions of a particular period, so that the application of its principles today calls for a different sort of action."[49]

The Evangelical position on inspired and authoritative Scripture has been further expounded in a number of recent informative studies.[50]

BIBLICAL TEACHING

To determine which historical perspective on Scripture is closest to the Bible's view of itself, we need to survey the relevant biblical materials in the context of progressive revelation.

Pentateuch

At Sinai (Exod. 24:4) Moses wrote down all the case laws and statutes (known as "the Book of the Covenant," 20:22–23:33) that God had given to Israel. Shortly after that God summoned Moses to ascend the mountain to receive the two tablets of stone on which God had written his laws and commands (24:12). The text states that on the tablets the Decalogue was "inscribed by the finger of God" (31:18; Deut. 9:10), where "finger" is a symbol for the creative power of God. Moses explains, "The tablets were the work of God; the writing was the writing of God, engraved on the tablets" (Exod. 32:16). After the tablets had been broken (v. 19), God rewrote the Ten Com-

mandments on new stone tablets that Moses had chiseled out (34:1), and God ordered that they be lodged in the ark of the Testimony (25:16, 21; Deut. 10:5). In one instance, then, a portion of the Word of God (the Decalogue) was put in writing by God himself without any human instrumentality.

Still at Sinai God commanded Moses, "Write down these words, for in accordance with these words I have made a covenant with you and with Israel" (Exod. 34:27). What Moses wrote down by the command of God (dictation?) most likely are Exodus 34:10–26 and "the Book of the Covenant," cited above. The final reference to Moses' literary endeavors, in Deuteronomy 31:24–26, indicates that "Moses finished writing in a book the words of this law from beginning to end." Jewish tradition identifies "this Book of the Law" (v. 26) as the entire Pentateuch, though other scholars limit the writing to Deuteronomy 1–30.[51] Whatever the scope of the writing, Moses ordered the Book of the Law placed with the other sacred writings by the Ark of the Covenant. What Moses wrote were not his own words, but "the commands of the LORD" (Deut. 4:2). By virtue of their divine origin and authority nothing was to be added to or subtracted from these writings accomplished by the hand of Moses (4:2; cf. 12:32).

Historical Books

As God continued to speak to his servants, their writings came to be viewed as divinely authoritative and so were deposited alongside the ark. Thus at the end of his life Joshua recorded the substance of the covenant established at Shechem "in the Book of the Law of God" (Josh. 24:25–26). Similarly Samuel "explained to the people the regulations of the kingship. He wrote them down on a scroll and deposited it before the LORD" (1 Sam. 10:25). During the reign of Josiah in the seventh century Hilkiah the high priest discovered a copy of "the Book of the Law" (2 Kings 22:8) or "the Book of the Covenant" (2 Kings 23:2). This document has been variously identified as the Pentateuch placed beside the ark (Deut. 31:26) or as the books of Exodus and Deuteronomy. The Chronicler's description of the document as "the Book of the Law of the LORD that had been given through Moses" (2 Chron. 34:14) underscores the divine-human character of this Mosaic writing. In the fifth century, following the rebuilding of the walls of Jerusalem, Ezra, Nehemiah, and the Levites interpreted to the people "the Book of the Law of Moses" (Neh. 8:1) or "the Book of the Law of God" (Neh. 8:8). The book, likely the Pentateuch, is described as both the work of Moses and the work of God.

The human side of Scripture is reflected not only in different styles of writing, but in the biblical writers' use of secular archival records, prophetic annals, collections of poetry, and the like. Uninspired sources utilized by the sacred authors in the preparation of canonical Scriptures include the Book of Jashar (2 Sam. 1:18), the book of the annals of Solomon (1 Kings 11:41), the book of the annals of the kings of Judah (1 Kings 14:29), the records of Samuel the seer (1 Chron. 29:29), the records of Nathan the prophet (1 Chron. 29:29), the records of Shemaiah the prophet and of Iddo the seer (2 Chron. 12:15), and the annotations on the book of the kings (2 Chron. 24:27).

Poetry and Wisdom

The unsurpassing excellence of Scripture, befitting its divine origin, is amply attested in the Psalms. Psalm 12:6 declares that "the words of the LORD are flawless, like silver refined in a furnace of clay, purified seven times"

(cf. Ps. 18:30; Prov. 30:5). More precious than silver purged of its dross the Word of God is unblemished truth and absolutely trustworthy. The second volume of Psalm 19 upholds the inherent perfections of the Word of the Lord and its spiritual relevance for life. Thus the Law of God, identified by the synonyms "statutes," "precepts," "commands," and "ordinances," is described as "perfect" (v. 7), or without blemish, "trustworthy" (v. 7), or firm or reliable, "right" (v. 8), or the opposite of crooked or perverse, "radiant" (v. 8), or bright as the sun, "sure" (v. 9) or fully dependable, and "altogether righteous" (v. 9), or straight and true. The conclusion of the psalmist's meditation is that the Law of the Lord is more precious than pure gold and sweeter than honey from the comb (v. 10).

Psalm 119 presents an even more extensive portrait of Scripture's impeccable qualities and spiritual benefits, in that order. Without being exhaustive the Law of the Lord is described as "righteous" (vv. 7, 62, et al.), "good" (v. 39), "trustworthy" (vv. 86, 138), "eternal" (vv. 89, 160), awe-inspiring (v. 120), "right" (vv. 128, 137), "wonderful" (v. 129), and "true" (vv. 142, 151). The psalmist explicitly ascribes several of these perfections to the totality of the written Law by means of the qualifier "all" (vv. 86, 151, 160, 172). Scripture's utility relative to the spiritual life is extensive both in its depth and in its breadth: it guards against sin (vv. 9, 11), renews and restores the life (vv. 25, 37, 40, et al.), mediates God's unfailing love (v. 41), offers encouragement in affliction (v. 92), imparts discernment and understanding (vv. 100, 104, 130, et al.), illumines life's pathway (v. 105), and imparts peace to the soul (v. 165).

The humanity of Scripture is reflected in the fact that the Book of Job accurately records the misguided judgments of Eliphaz, Bildad, and Zophar.

Whereas the Scripture affirms that Job was a "blameless and upright" man who "feared God and shunned evil" (Job 1:1), Job's three friends and Elihu erroneously judged that his suffering was a direct consequence of grievous sins he had committed (Job 4:7–9; 36:8–10). Yet at the close of the episode God vindicates Job, rebukes Eliphaz and company for their faithless counsel, and promises that Job will intercede for them! (Job 42:7–8). The point is that inspiration extends to the accurate recording of patently false counsel. A similar accurate recording of obviously uninspired wisdom occurs in the Book of Ecclesiastes. The naturalistic philosophy of the person who lives life without reference to God is faithfully reproduced in Ecclesiastes 1:2; 3:19–21; 9:1, 10.

The human side of the Bible is further seen in the emotional outbursts recorded in the imprecatory Psalms (Pss. 55, 59, 69, 79, 109, 137). The psalmist not only cries out to God, "Let death take my enemies by surprise; let them go down alive to the grave" (Ps. 55:15), but he also utters the harsh wish, "May they be blotted out of the book of life and not be listed with the righteous" (Ps. 69:28). The most violent imprecation of all was uttered against the Babylonian captors who committed atrocities against the inhabitants of Jerusalem: "Happy is he who repays you for what you have done to us—he who seizes your infants and dashes them against the rocks" (Ps. 137:8–9). The preceding statement should be understood as hyperbolic expressions of the distressed spirit who cries out in anguish against the enemies of God and who longs for the vindication of God's honor and justice.

The Book of Proverbs bears within itself clear evidence that it is a compilation (adapted and edited by Solomon) of the nobler aspects of Near Eastern wisdom. Thus in addition to sections written by Solomon himself (Prov. 10:1–22:16; 25:1–29:27), there are collections called "Sayings of the Wise" (22:17–24:22) and "Further Sayings of the Wise" (24:23–34). Proverbs thus likely represents the distillation of the wisdom—writings of many wise men (some of whom received revelation and others who did not) in various places and over a considerable period of time. On this showing, "Proverbs is the scrapbook of common grace."[52]

The Prophets

As for the rest of the Old Testament canon, God dictated a message to Isaiah that the prophet was to record on a scroll (Isa. 8:1). God ordered the writing of another oracle on a scroll that it might serve as a perpetual witness (Isa. 30:8). And the prophet claimed that his prophetic message was preserved in "the scroll of the LORD" (Isa. 34:16). The prophet Jeremiah claimed that his message was given directly by God (Jer. 1:9). Indeed, God commanded Jeremiah to write in a book the very words that the Lord would speak to him (Jer. 30:2). The procedure by which Scripture was produced is delineated in some detail in Jeremiah 36:1–6. The prophet "dictated" to Baruch "all the words the LORD had spoken to him," whereupon the scribe "wrote them on [a] scroll." Jeremiah certifies that a prophetic utterance from Obadiah (Jer. 49:14–19) and from Micah (Jer. 26:18) are the very words of God himself.

Hosea describes God's prophet as an "inspired man" (Hos. 9:7), and Micah claims to be "filled with power" and "with the Spirit of the LORD" (Mic. 3:8). Moreover, God told Habakkuk to inscribe the revelation on tablets so that its message would be plain for all to read (Hab. 2:2). God himself certifies that the written revelation "will not prove false" (Hab. 2:3).

Synoptic Gospels

That inspiration extends to the very form of a word is clear from Matthew 2:15, where God's watchful care over the infant Jesus was viewed as the fulfillment of Hosea 11:1: "When Israel was a child, I loved him, and out of Egypt I called my son" (cf. Exod. 4:22–23). The singular "son" was an unusual designation for the nation Israel (hence the LXX translation, "Out of Egypt I called his children"). Yet only "son" and not "sons" was appropriate to the Holy Spirit's application of the text to Jesus, the Son whom God would bring up out of Egypt.

Jesus unequivocally upheld the authority of the Old Testament as the Word of God in Matthew 5:17–19 (cf. Luke 16:17). In response to the charge that he sought to do away with the Law and the Prophets, Jesus insisted that his mission was to "fulfill" them (v. 17). The verb *plēroō* conveys the idea of "confirm" or "establish." Whereas Matthew emphasizes that Scripture must be filled out, Luke makes the point that Scripture will not be made void: it is impossible "for the least stroke of a pen to drop out [*pesein*] of the Law" (Luke 16:17). Indeed, Jesus insisted that the authority of Scripture extends to its most minute portions. Both the *iota,* possibly a reference to the *yod,* the smallest Hebrew letter, and the *keraia,* the smallest stroke of the pen, would stand until all God's purposes are accomplished.

In dialogue with the Pharisees and the teachers of the Law (Mark 7:5–13; Matt. 15:3–9) Jesus quoted Isaiah 29:13; Exodus 20:12; and Exodus 21:17 and described the words of Moses and Isaiah as "the commands of God." In each case the Old Testament writings as the "Word of God" were clearly differentiated from human "traditions." In Matthew 19:4–5 Jesus cites a word from Moses (Gen. 2:24). Yet instead of introducing the text with "Moses said" or "the Scripture says," Jesus used the formula, "the Creator said." On another occasion Jesus introduced his quotation of Psalm 110:1 with the claim that David spoke these words *"en pneumati"* (Matt. 22:43–44). The indefectibility of our Lord's words in Scripture is asserted in Matthew 24:35: "Heaven and earth will pass away, but my words will never pass away."

The synoptic Gospels assume that the Old Testament is authoritative in its historical teaching. Jesus treated as factual the accounts of Adam and Eve (Matt. 19:4–5), Cain and Abel (Luke 11:51), Noah and the Flood (Matt. 24:37–39; Luke 17:26–27), the destruction of Sodom and Gomorrah (Matt. 10:15; 11:23–24), the experience of Lot (Luke 17:28–32), Moses the lawgiver (Matt. 19:8; Mark 7:10), David eating the shewbread (Matt. 12:3–4; Luke 6:3–4), the splendor of Solomon (Matt. 6:29; Luke 11:31), Elijah and the widow of Zarephath (Luke 4:25–26), Elisha and Namaan the Syrian (Luke 4:27), and Jonah and the fish (Matt. 12:39–41; Luke 11:29–32).

Similarly Jesus and the Evangelists upheld the Old Testament as prophetically authoritative. Typically a contemporary event was noted, an observation was made ("This was to fulfill what was spoken through the prophet"), and the relevant Old Testament prophecy was quoted. The most important acknowledgments of fulfilled prophecy in the synoptic Gospels are: Matthew 1:22–23 (Isa. 7:14); Matthew 2:15 (Hos. 11:1); Matthew 2:17–18 (Jer. 31:15); Matthew 4:13–16 (Isa. 9:1–2); Matthew 11:10 (Mal. 3:1); Matthew 12:17–21 (Isa. 42:1–4); Matthew 13:14–15 (Isa. 6:9–10); Matthew 21:4–5 (Zech. 9:9); Matthew 24:15 (Dan. 9:27); Matthew 26:31 (Zech. 13:7); and Matthew 27:9–10 (Zech. 11:12–13; Jer. 32:6–9). Jesus summed up the authority of prophetic Scripture in this manner: "Everything must be fulfilled that is written about me in the Law of Moses, the Prophets and the Psalms" (Luke 24:44).

Jesus also regarded the Old Testament as doctrinally authoritative. A dispute over resurrection was settled by appeal to teaching from the Law (Matt. 22:29–32; Exod. 3:6). Similarly the issue of the abomination of desolation in the eschatological future (Matt. 24:15; Mark 13:14) was clarified by appeal to Daniel 9:27; 11:31; and 12:11. That Jesus viewed the Old Testament as being ethically authoritative is clear from the fact that he frequently quoted from it in making statements regarding moral values and conduct (Matt. 4:1–10; 7:12; 22:36–40).

Christ's belief in verbal inspiration and the indefectible authority of Scripture is reflected in the frequently occurring phrases: "It is written" (Matt. 4:4, 6, 7, 10; Mark 1:2; 9:13; Luke 19:46), "Have you never read?" (Matt. 21:16, 42; Mark 2:25; Luke 6:3), "This is what is written" (Luke 24:46), et al. Likewise the singular term "Scripture" (*graphē*, Mark 12:10; 15:28; Luke 4:21) and the plural "the Scriptures" (*hai graphai*, Matt. 21:42; Mark 12:24; Luke 24:27, et al.) depict the Old Testament uniformly as a book of divine oracles, every portion of which is clothed with irrefragable authority.

Whereas the foregoing data from the Gospels confirms the divinity of the entire Old Testament, the prologue to Luke's Gospel (Luke 1:1–4) sheds light on the human side as it is related to his Gospel. (1) Luke sets forth his human qualifications for writing (v. 2): although a second generation Christian, he has access to oral and written accounts by eyewitnesses. (2) Luke affirms that he has carefully researched the history to ascertain the facts (v. 3a). (3) The historian states the method he has followed in writing (v. 3b): he organizes his material in a connected whole with a set principle or

arrangement. And (4) Luke relates his humanly formed purpose (v. 4): "so that you may know the certainty of the things you have been taught." Thus it is evident that Luke "presents his Gospel as a very human composition."[53] Nevertheless it constitutes "the word" (v. 2) and hence is marked by truth and "certainty" (v. 4).

Primitive Christianity/Acts

Peter and John certify that the sovereign God in Psalm 2:1–2 "spoke by the Holy Spirit through the mouth of . . . our father David" (Acts 4:25–26). Later Paul said to leaders of the Jews (Acts 28:25), "The Holy Spirit spoke the truth to your forefathers when he said through Isaiah the prophet: 'Go to this people and say . . .'" (Isa. 6:9–10). Not only did the apostles attribute the Old Testament writings to the Holy Spirit, but they also regarded them as "truth" (Acts 28:25), unalloyed by any falsehood. Paul believed the Old Testament to be plenarily inspired, for he declared to Felix, "I believe everything that agrees with the Law and that is written in the Prophets" (Acts 24:14).

In the course of defending their ministry the apostles certified the reliability of the Old Testament history. Stephen surveyed the leading events of Old Testament history from Abraham to Solomon (Acts 7:2–47). Before the synagogue rulers at Pisidian Antioch Paul rehearsed the history of the Exodus (Acts 13:17), the wilderness wanderings (v. 18), the destruction of the Canaanite nations (v. 19), the judges (v. 20), and the kings Saul and David (vv. 20–22).

Moreover, the apostles established their preaching and teaching on the authority of Old Testament prophecy. Repeatedly they insisted that the events that had come to pass occurred in direct fulfillment of an Old Testament prediction (Acts 1:16–17; 2:16–21; 3:21–23, et al.). Likewise their ministry was guided by the authority of Old Testament theology. Thus appeal was made to Amos 9:11–12 to settle doctrinal differences at the Jerusalem Council (Acts 15:15–18). The Bereans diligently searched the Scriptures to determine the validity of Paul's gospel (Acts 17:11).

The Pauline Corpus

As shown in the previous chapter, Paul in 1 Corinthians 2:12 acknowledged that the apostles were recipients of special revelation. The following verse indicates that the very words (*logoi*) in which the Gospels were clothed were provided by the Holy Spirit: "we impart this in words not taught by human wisdom but taught by the Spirit" (1 Cor. 2:13 RSV). Verbal inspiration is also attested in Galatians 3:16, where Paul's argument rests on the singular form of "seed" (*zera´*) in the Old Testament. Thus "the promises were spoken to Abraham and to his seed. The Scripture does not say 'and to seeds,' meaning many people, but 'and to your seed,' meaning one person, who is Christ." The Holy Spirit directed Moses to use the collective "seed" in Genesis 12:7; 13:15, et al. rather than the customary plural, since the ultimate fulfillment of the promise centered on Christ.

The *locus classicus* of the doctrine of inspiration is 2 Timothy 3:16: "All Scripture is God-breathed. . . ." "All Scripture" (*pas* with the singular noun without the article) is rightly understood as each individual Scripture within the totality of Holy Writ. The metaphor "God-breathed" (*theopneustos*, from *theos* and *pneō*, to breathe) connotes origination by divine power (cf. Ps. 33:6; Isa. 40:7, 24). What is divinely spirated or breathed out, according to Paul, is not the human writer, but the written Scripture (*graphē*) itself. Some

authorities, such as the RSV margin reading, regard *theopneustos* as a qualifying adjective and translate the verse, "Every Scripture inspired by God is also profitable . . . ," the outcome being to suggest that only certain parts of Scripture are inspired and hence of spiritual profit. It is preferable, however, to take *theopneustos* as a predicate that is coordinated by the conjunction *kai* ("and") with "useful" or "profitable." This construction, commended by the AV, NIV, and others, upholds the parallelism of the two adjectives "God-breathed" and "useful."[54] Paul in these few words has propounded the doctrine of plenary inspiration: every portion of Scripture has its origin with God. And precisely because Scripture is divinely inspired it possesses spiritual utility. Hence Scripture is "useful for teaching, rebuking, correcting and training in righteousness, so that the man of God may be thoroughly equipped for every good work." Unlike some critics, the inspired apostle was not guilty of placing the functional cart (Scripture's utility) before the ontological horse (its plenary inspiration)!

The divine side of Scripture is affirmed in Romans 3:2, where the apostle maintains that the chief advantage of the Jews is that "they have been entrusted with the very words (*ta logia*) of God." *Logia*, translated "oracles" in the AV and RSV, denotes utterances from the very mouth of God.[55] Hence Paul insists that Scripture, as a book of divine oracles, is the pure and absolute Word of God.

Paul also acknowledges the unity of the Word of God inscripturated by means of the expressions "It is written" (Rom. 1:17; 4:17; 11:26; 1 Cor. 1:19; 2:9; Gal. 3:10, 13, et al.), "Scripture" (Rom. 4:3; 10:11; Gal. 3:16; 1 Tim. 5:18), and "the Holy Scriptures" (Rom. 1:2). On other occasions an Old Testament text is quoted, introduced by the word *legei* (Rom. 15:10; 2 Cor. 6:2; Eph. 4:8; 5:14), *eipē* (1 Cor. 15:27), or *phēsin* (1 Cor. 6:16)—all of which are generally translated by the impersonal "It says." However, B. B. Warfield has convincingly shown that in such texts "It says" = "the Scripture says" = "God says."[56] Once again a number of Old Testament texts are apostolically certified as direct utterances of God himself.

The Pauline corpus also attests the divine origin and authority of the then-emergent New Testament writings. Paul not only asserts that Christ was speaking through him (2 Cor. 13:3), but he describes what he *wrote* to the Corinthians as "the Lord's command" (1 Cor. 14:37) and hence endowed with "the authority of the Lord Jesus " (1 Thess. 4:2). Paul also commanded the brethren to lay hold of the traditions (*paradoseis*) taught by the apostles "whether by word of mouth or by letter" (2 Thess. 2:15). Indeed, Paul solemnly charged as with an oath (*enorkizō*) the church at Thessalonica to read his first letter to the gathered body (1 Thess. 5:27). And he urged that his letter to the Colossians be read to the church there and to the Laodiceans (Col. 4:16). Whoever failed to obey the written apostolic teaching would incur severe punishment (2 Thess. 3:14). The inspiration of a specific New Testament text was acknowledged by the apostle when he placed a saying of Jesus (Luke 10:7) on a par with a command of Yahweh through Moses (Deut. 25:4) and referred to both as "Scripture" (1 Tim. 5:18).

The writings of Paul, although replete with evidences of the divinity of Scripture, also attest its human authorship. The apostle said that beyond the household of Stephanas he did not recall if he baptized any others (1 Cor. 1:16). In the area of marital relationships on which Paul had no directive from the Lord, he gave his own opinion (1 Cor. 7:12). In other situations the apostle rendered a personal judgment (1 Cor. 7:40) and gave his own counsel (2 Cor. 8:8–10). Yet his acknowledgment, "I too have the Spirit of God" (1 Cor. 7:40) reminds us that behind his human judgments was the guidance of the Holy Spirit.

Finally, Paul added that for a person to know God as Savior the Holy Spirit must illumine the truths of Scripture and apply them to the heart. The non-Christian has little understanding of God's redemptive purposes (1 Cor. 2:8–9), for a veil covers the sinner's heart (2 Cor. 3:15). However, when the unbeliever turns to Christ, the Holy Spirit removes the veil (2 Cor. 3:16) and unfolds the things of God to the trusting soul (1 Cor. 2:10–11). Whereas spiritual truths appear foolish to the unbeliever, the Spirit imparts to the believer spiritual insight so that the verities of God's Word are understood and appropriated (1 Cor. 2:14–15). Indeed, through the teaching ministry of the Spirit believers possess "the mind of Christ" and thus evaluate life from his point of view (1 Cor. 2:16). Unlike inspiration, illumination does admit of degrees, the extent of the operation being dependent on the faith and obedience of the individual.

The Johannine Literature

According to the fourth Gospel, Jesus commissioned the apostles to be his witnesses (John 1:37–50; 21:16–17). The Lord trained them to be teachers of the New Covenant, using methods similar to those used by the rabbis to train their disciples (John 4:31–38; 6:5–12; 13:1–17, et al.). He also equipped them with the special endowment of the Holy Spirit (John 14:12; 20:21–23). Jesus gave them the words (*hrēmata*) the Father had given him (John 17:8). Moreover, after his death and exaltation Christ would send the Holy Spirit both to remind them of past teaching and to impart new revelations (John 14:26; cf. 16:13–15). Thereafter the apostolic testimony would be guided and preserved by special inspiration of the Spirit (John 15:26–27; cf. Acts 5:32). The Gospel that John wrote, as indeed the entire New Testament does, represents the fulfillment of these promises.

Several Johannine texts teach the divine inspiration and authority of Scripture. The written record of Moses (John 5:45–47) is equated with "the Scriptures" (v. 39) and designated the Father's "word" (v. 38). In John 10:34–36 the "law" of the Jews—i.e., the Old Testament—is expressly denoted "the Word of God." Moreover, Jesus' argument vis-à-vis the Jews turned on a single word in the Old Testament text. If God in Psalm 82:6 called the prophets "gods" (*'elōhîm, theoi*), why should his Jewish opponents level accusations of blasphemy when Jesus claimed to be the Son of God (*huios tou theou*)? In addition, Jesus in this text made the unqualified assertion, "the Scripture cannot be broken." The aorist infinitive passive of *luō* means "to be destroyed," i.e., to be set aside or invalidated.[57] Jesus asserts that since Scripture is the very Word of God, it cannot be deprived of its binding authority. In John 17:17 Jesus intercedes for his disciples with these words: "Sanctify them by the truth; your word is truth" (cf. 8:31–32). Truth (*alētheia*) here means judgments about an object of knowledge that conform perfectly to reality and provide the basis for facticity. As Westcott noted, "The Word of God is not only 'true' but 'truth' and had a transforming virtue."[58] Similarly in John 21:24 John claims "truth" or inerrancy for his written Gospel.

The Book of Revelation unmistakenly claims its own divine inspiration. John, in a condition of openness to the Spirit, was commanded by God to record the content of his vision in the form of letters to seven churches in Asia Minor (Rev. 1:10–11; chs. 2–3).[59] The entire Apocalypse is in view when the heavenly voice commanded John, "Write . . . what you have seen, what is now and what will take place later" (Rev. 1:19). At the close of the book (Rev. 22:18–19) John invokes a curse on anyone who in any way tampers with the text of his prophecy.

The human side of Scripture is reflected in the conclusion to John's Gospel and in the prologue to his first Letter. Concerning the Gospel, we observe (1) John's humanly former purpose, namely that his readers may know that Jesus is the Messiah, and (2) his humanly determined principle of selection, that those signs are narrated that may elicit saving faith (John 20:30–31). In the prologue of his first letter (1 John 1:1–4), against the background of an incipient Docetism, we may discover (1) John's competence for writing, namely, he was an eyewitness of Christ (so he had "heard," "seen," and "touched" him, vv. 1–2); (2) his aim vis-à-vis those tempted by false teaching: that they might have fellowship with the apostles (v. 3); and (3) the personal benefit John expected to derive from writing: "to make our joy complete" (v. 4).

Other New Testament Writings

In the first chapter of Hebrews seven Old Testament texts are quoted by means of the formulae *legei, eipen,* and *eirēken* and are identified as the sayings of God (Heb. 1:5–8, 10, 13). Later words of Moses (Heb. 4:4) and David (4:7; 7:21) are cited as spoken by God himself. On three occasions texts from the Psalms and Jeremiah are quoted and attributed to the mouth of the Holy Spirit (Heb. 3:7–11; 10:15–16; 10:17). And contemplating the Old Testament the author of Hebrews wrote, "You

145

need someone to teach you the elementary truths of God's word all over again" (5:12). Hence not only is the Old Testament regarded as a collection of divine utterances, but it is also shown to possess a relevance and an authority for believers in the present age.

First Peter 1:10–12 affirms that the Old Testament prophets testified of Christ's sufferings and glorification through "the Spirit of Christ in them." Likewise the New Testament apostles were moved by the influence of the same Holy Spirit when they communicated the gospel. Because of the inspiration of both bodies of writings, Old and New Testaments enjoy the same canonical status (cf. 2 Peter 3:2). Second Peter 3:15–16 indicates that Paul wrote "with the wisdom that God gave him." Peter then juxtaposed all Paul's "letters" with "the other Scriptures," thus indicating that the Pauline Epistles were regarded as equally authoritative with the canon of the Old Testament.

The most important Petrine text relative to the inspiration of Scripture is 2 Peter 1:19–21. The phrase "prophecy of Scripture" refers to the entire Old Testament, whose content is broadly prophetic (Acts 3:21–25; Rom. 16:26). Peter teaches that prophetic Scripture did not originate "by the prophet's own interpretation" (the latter word *epilysis,* meaning the unraveling of a problem). Or as Warfield put it, the Scripture "is not the result of human investigation into the nature of things."[60] Unlike the false prophets the Old Testament prophetic writers did not invent the substance of their writing. Rather, "men spoke from God as they were carried along by the Holy Spirit." The term *pheromenoi* (present passive participle of *pherō*) means to be borne or carried along. It is used in Acts 27:15, 17 of a sailing ship being borne along by the wind. "The prophets raised their sails, so to speak (they were obedient and receptive), and the Holy Spirit filled them and carried their craft along in the direction He wished."[61] The text makes clear that the impulse and the enablement to write was of God the Spirit. Yet the conscious instrumentality of holy writers is fully preserved.

These and other texts that speak to the issue of the Bible's divine inspiration, authority, and illumination bring to mind Warfield's "avalanche of texts" analogy.[62] Warfield observed that an adroit walker might be able to sidestep a limited number of stones that rolled down upon him from above. But one could hardly escape the force of an avalanche of boulders. Analogously, Warfield argued, the number of texts in support of biblical inspiration are so numerous that the Bible reader cannot possibly avoid the sheer force of their demonstration.

SYSTEMATIC FORMULATION

Before determining which of the historical views most coherently and viably accounts for the extensive biblical data, it will help to organize the biblical givens topically on some of the most controversial issues.

Jesus, the supreme revelation of God in history, has ascended to heaven. About four centuries earlier the line of Jewish prophets had ceased. No apostles (as eyewitnesses of Christ) survived the first century. Granted that prophets and apostles articulated divinely revealed truths to the people of their times, how can they help us centuries later? Their revealed teachings have been preserved for successive generations in writing. Given their ability to express truths from God in audible symbols, there can be no a priori objection to the expression of God's words in visible symbols.

The Inscripturation of Revelation by Inspired Prophets

Although Jesus himself did not leave us any writings, the information he constantly derived from the *Old Testament* remains available to us as it was to him. God instructed prophets not only to speak, but also to write. The writing of the Old Testament was *commissioned by God*. Among those commissioned to write were: Moses (Exod. 17:14; 34:27), Joshua (Josh. 24:25–26), Samuel (1 Sam. 10:25), Isaiah (Isa. 30:8), Jeremiah (Jer. 30:2; 36:2, 17, 28–29), Ezekiel (Ezek. 43:11), and Habakkuk (Hab. 2:2). The writings of prophets with credentials were preserved alongside the ark of the covenant in which Moses placed the Ten Commandments (1 Kings 8:9; Deut. 31:24–26; Josh. 24:25–26; 1 Sam. 10:25; Isa. 8:20; 29:18; 34:16).

The prophets' written words served, not as a fallible human witness to their ineffable experiences of the transcendent, but as a nonnegotiable *divine witness against Israel* (Deut. 31:26). In the realistic world view of the Bible, God and the prophets knew that even the people of God tended to rebel against the Lord (vv. 26–27), become unfaithful to God's guidance (Josh. 24:25–27), and instead follow mediums and spiritists (Isa. 8:19).

Given the well-verified fact of human depravity, what Israel needed was not a collection of errant human pointers, but supernaturally inspired standards for reference. "They . . . would not listen to the law or to the words that the LORD Almighty had sent by his Spirit through the earlier prophets" (Zech. 7:12). The inference drawn from human depravity does *not* imply, as many contemporary theologians do, that divinely inspired prophets distort revealed truth by writing it. Rather, the tendency to unfaithfulness underscores the need for the prophets' undistorted truth from God in a public, written form. When people refused to repent and become faithful, God's Spirit-inspired Scripture provided a just basis for their accountability before God and their peers.

Jesus Christ recognized the final authority of the Spirit-inspired prophetic writings. He resisted satanic temptations by quoting the Old Testament, introducing the quotations with "It is written" (Matt. 4:1–10). He said that the Law and the Prophets could not be abolished. All must be fulfilled (Matt. 5:17–18) and ought to be believed (Luke 24:25). All, according to Paul, originated with God (2 Tim. 3:16) and not, according to Peter, with the writers (2 Peter 1:20–21).

The Canon of Prophetic Writings

By what *criteria* were such unimpeachable writings distinguished from others? The primary factor in recognizing the divine authority of these books was *authorship by a tested and verified prophet*. Merely human writings were not invested with divine authority by decision of a council, but books originating with God were recognized as of final authority immediately, upon knowing their authors' authenticity as prophetic spokesmen.

Jesus Christ recognized the entire *Jewish canon* as from God. The Lord referred to each of its three divisions: the Law of Moses, the Prophets, and the Writings (Luke 24:44; the Psalms is the largest book of the Writings). Sometimes he referred to the entire canon as "the Law and the Prophets" (Matt. 5:17), or to the entire Old Testament as "the Law" (as when quoting a Psalm, John 10:34). The Jewish canon at the time of Christ was the same as our Protestant canon; it did not include the apocryphal additions.[63]

Augustine approved the apocryphal books for edifying reading, but not for establishing authoritative doctrine. Jerome, in Augustine's time, about A.D. 400, Gregory the Great, Bishop of Rome (Pope), 590–604, and Cardinal Cajetan (1517–34) at the time of the Reformation, opposed the inclusion of

147

those books in the canon, "the rule for confirming those things which are of faith." The authors of the apocryphal additions to the Old Testament were not recognized prophets inspired of God. Nevertheless, following the Protestant Reformation in 1546 the Roman Catholic Council of Trent declared that anyone who did not receive as canonical these books entire, with all their parts, was anathema![64]

THE TEXT OF THE PROPHET'S INSPIRED WRITINGS

Granting that the thirty-nine books of the Old Testament were supernaturally inspired and authoritative when written, can we know that we have reliable manuscripts of the Old Testament books Jesus approved? A painstaking examination of extant manuscripts, including the Dead Sea Scrolls and the Cairo Geniza, lead to the conclusion that "the material for the establishment of the OT text is many times as great as that for establishing the text for any other ancient document, except the NT. The agreement in the consonantal text of the various MSS is most remarkable, and the great bulk of the very extensive material that has now been found from before the time of Christ agrees very closely with the consonantal text of the MT [Masoretic Text]."[65]

The manuscripts our translators use are generally so accurate that we can say that what those manuscripts teach, God teaches. But because our surviving Hebrew texts have some variations in wordings, careful students of the Old Testament need to compare Scripture with Scripture and not base a doctrine on one verse. Although a given verse may contain a copyist's mistake, the probability that two or more verses on a subject in different contexts each conceal the same error is so small as to be negligible.[66]

In claiming any teaching to be re-

vealed truth, students of theology who are not equipped to evaluate the different manuscripts will avoid some of the dangers of quoting a poorly supported reading by documenting their claim from more than one biblical assertion. No doctrine important for Christian faith or life is drawn from a single passage. When a doctrinal proposition is well-founded in several Old Testament passages, responsibly translated from the Hebrew and Aramaic, and interpreted according to sound principles of hermeneutics, the probability of abusing the revealed message is reduced.

Summing up, the data show that the Old Testament is more than a human witness to revelation—it is (written) revelation. It is a supernaturally inspired inscripturation of information ultimately given by God in various ways to verified prophetic spokesmen divinely commissioned to write its thirty-nine books as a divine witness by which God would evaluate their lives. The teachings of these faithfully copied books were endorsed by the Lord Jesus Christ as conveying objectively valid (inerrant) truth factually and ethically, and so authoritative and necessary to healthy Christian beliefs and experience in the world.

The Inscripturation of Revelation by Apostles

Jesus Christ not only placed his imprimatur on the Old Testament, he also prepared the way for a similar preservation of his teaching to the apostles in the New Testament. Jesus, having all authority in heaven and on earth, *delegated authority* for ministry in history *to his apostles*. The head of the church commissioned and authorized them in his place to prescribe belief and action to the church. No longer mere learners, but apostles, they substituted for their King; witnessed to his life, death, and resurrection; served his purposes; and spoke for him with final authority. As Jesus Christ gave the apostles the right, the Holy Spirit (beginning at Pentecost) gave them the power, the boldness, and the freedom to command, rule, and expect obedience from all who call Jesus Lord and Savior.[67]

Jesus also gave the apostles reason to anticipate further revelation. The Lord said, "I have much more to say to you, more than you can now bear" (John 16:12). The promised Spirit would not only remind them of everything Jesus taught (John 14:26), but also guide the apostles into all truth (John 16:13), tell them what was yet to come, and take from Christ (as he had from the Father) and make it known to them (John 16:13–15).

The apostles, authorized by their Lord, ministered, not only in teaching and preaching, but also in *writing*. Paul's letters were to be read publicly in the churches (1 Thess. 5:25). Paul admonished the Thessalonians saved "through belief in the truth," to "stand firm and hold to the teachings we passed on to you, whether by word of mouth or by letter" (2 Thess. 2:13, 15). The apostle's authority was such that he could add, "If anyone does not obey our instruction in this letter, take special note of him. Do not associate with him, in order that he may feel ashamed. Yet do not regard him as an enemy, but warn him as a brother" (3:14–15). Disobedience to Paul's letters reflected disobedience to God's Word and required disciplinary action.

In an epistle in which Paul had to deal with issues on which he could not quote Jesus Christ, he had to give his own judgment (1 Cor.7:12, 25). However, he maintained that his judgment was "trustworthy" (7:25). Adequate grounds are not given in 1 Corinthians 7 for arguing that Paul disclaims authority for his writings. In the same epistle he insists, "If anybody thinks he is a prophet or spiritually gifted, let him acknowledge that what I am writing to you is the Lord's command" (1 Cor. 14:37).

The view that the apostles were simply missionaries and not apostles with divine authority does not fit the facts. Paul said he was not ashamed of "the authority the Lord gave" the apostles for building up the body of Christ (2 Cor. 10:8). He warned the church at Corinth in writing so that when present he would not have to be harsh in the use of his God-given authority (2 Cor. 13:10). Anyone who preached a "gospel" contradicting that of Paul could be anathematized, because, as he said, "The gospel I preached is not something that man made up. I did not receive it from any man, nor was I taught it; rather, I received it by revelation from Jesus Christ" (Gal. 1:11–12).

The evidence indicates that Paul's written contributions in the New Testament originated with God, and although expressed in human categories of thought and the common Greek language, conveyed objectively valid and normatively authoritative truth by the inspiration of the Holy Spirit, whom Jesus Christ had promised to send for this purpose.

Peter put Paul's letters on a par with the Old Testament Scriptures (2 Peter 3:15–16). Although Luke was not an apostle, he was a close associate of Paul, traveling with him on his second missionary journey. Luke's Gospel reflects Paul's apostolic authority, and Luke 10:7 was quoted as Scripture alongside a passage from the Old Testament (1 Tim. 5:18). The introduction to the Gospel of Luke shows not only how the writers, supervised by the Holy Spirit, were active in research, but also that Luke consulted all available apostles (eyewitnesses) as he "carefully investigated everything from the beginning" (Luke 1:2–3). Luke's association with Paul also lends Paul's apostolic authority to the Book of Acts.

Peter also identifies himself as an apostle of Jesus Christ (1 Peter 1:1; 2 Peter 1:1). Although Mark was not a disciple, as a close associate of Peter, his gospel presents its material with Peter's authority through his associate. New Testament books not written by apostles were written by apostolic associates and carry apostolic endorsement.

Truth and Error in Apostolic Writings

The apostles commend their writings to us, not only on the basis of the Lord's delegated authority, but also on their *veracious authority*, the authority of truth. True ideas from Jesus Christ conform to the mind of God and to reality, and ought therefore to be believed in order to guide conduct to desirable ends. By what criteria do we know when our affirmations conform to God's thinking and to existence as it is? Three signs of true affirmations are characteristic of apostolic teaching. True statements convey propositions that are (1) empirically reliable, (2) existentially viable, and (3) logically noncontradictory. It follows, then, that *error* is failure to meet these three standards. Because scholars holding a merely dynamic or functional view of inspiration deny that these criteria are biblical it is necessary to document their use in the New Testament especially.

1. The teaching of John's epistles is presented as *empirically reliable*. "That which was from the beginning, which we have heard, which we have seen with our eyes, which we have looked at and our hands have touched—this we proclaim concerning the Word of life" (1 John 1:1). John also stressed empirical verification in his Gospel by recording many visible "signs" indicating that Jesus was the Christ, and especially the visible, audible, and tangible signs of the Lord's risen body. Christ's appearances convinced skeptical Thomas and the fishermen who, upon arriving at shore, ate a breakfast the risen Lord had prepared for them (John 20–21). The gospel Paul preached had not only been given to him by revelation from Jesus Christ, but also had been verified by many witnesses on many different occasions, including over five hundred at once, who were still living when he wrote (1 Cor. 15:1–11). The hypothesis that factual assertions in Scripture may not be reliable does not fit the factual emphasis of passages like these, and undercuts the gospel itself.

2. John also commends his written message as *existentially viable*. John writes his second Epistle with the authority of an "elder" who experientially knows and loves the truth that lives in us and will be with us forever (2 John 1:1–2). Knowing personally the joy of living the truth, John urges people to walk in the truth (v. 4) and continue in the teaching of Christ, without which they do not have God (vv. 9, 11). In his third Epistle, John appeals to those he loves in the truth, to walk in the truth, and work together for the truth (3 John 1, 3, 4, 8). Clearly in the New Testament truth can be lived, and was personally experienced.

3. The apostles commend New Testament teaching as true, furthermore, because its sayings are faithful, or *logically noncontradictory*. In teaching about faithfulness to oaths made to the Lord, the Master had asked that his followers not swear by heaven, earth, Jerusalem, or their own heads. "Simply let your 'Yes' be 'Yes,' and your 'No,' 'No'; anything beyond this comes from the evil one" (Matt. 5:33–37). James, concerned about a responsible use of the tongue, echoed the Lord's words, saying, "Let your 'Yes' be yes, and your 'No,' no, or you will be condemned" (James 5:12). This teaching of

Christ and James provides background for Paul's second Letter to the Corinthians.

To the Corinthians Paul wrote that his plans were not made "in a worldly manner" so that in the same breath he would say "Yes, yes" and "No, no" (2 Cor. 1:17). Then, of his letter, Paul said, "But as surely as God is faithful, our message to you is not 'Yes' and 'No.' For the Son of God, Jesus Christ, who was preached among you by me and Silas and Timothy, was not 'Yes' and 'No,' but in him it has always been 'Yes.' For no matter how many promises God has made, they are 'Yes' in Christ" (2 Cor. 1:18–20).

Paul warned Timothy about "false doctrines," myths, endless genealogies, meaningless talk and "whatever else is contrary to the sound doctrine that conforms to the glorious gospel of the blessed God, which he entrusted to me" (1 Tim.1:3–11). No contradiction of the revealed message, not even in the name of "profound" or "existentially relevant" theology, could be given assent. So Paul warned Timothy to "guard" the sound doctrine that had been entrusted to his care, avoiding "opposing" ("antithetical" RSV) ideas of what is falsely called knowledge (1 Tim. 6:20).

In view of these New Testament criteria of truth, its words are *faithful,* not only existentially but also factually and logically. The emphasis on not contradicting faithful sayings was not so much based on Aristotle's formulation of the law of noncontradiction as rooted in God's faithful nature: "He who promised is faithful" (Heb. 10:23; cf. Rev. 19:2, 9, 11; 21:5; 22:6). Thus the logical integrity of the inscripturated Word is not imported from Greek philosophy but inherent in the meaning of "faithfulness" on the part of the God who speaks through prophets and apostles. No infinite qualitative distinction between the divine and human minds makes necessary dialectical reasoning in which theologians must say "Yes" and "No" to every relationship between God and humanity. What the Father gave Jesus, he taught, and what Jesus gave the apostles the Holy Spirit inspired them to write. Hence we can confidently rely on their teaching without either intellectual denial or personal disillusionment (Rom. 10:11). People who announce their belief in biblical inerrancy and hold that a biblical affirmation may be contradicted elsewhere in Scripture, miss the mark of a biblical view of personal faithfulness expressed in logical consistency. They also render their belief in inerrancy meaningless. If the contradictory of a biblical affirmation may be true, then no Scripture is dependable.

The Supernaturalness of Apostolic Inspiration

How could finite, forgetful, often uneducated people with sinful biases faithfully teach the truth without error? On their own, these truly human and fallen writers could not. By the Spirit's ordinary illumination, they could not. The issue is not so much the humanness of the writers. Their varied styles, vocabularies, cultural conditionedness, historical standpoints, finite limitations, and sinful tendencies have been thoroughly emphasized from all sides. The additional issue is whether the Spirit's work with them was the ordinary work of illumining all God's people or an extraordinary work for divine spokesmen, a supernatural inspiration.

Does a providential or a miraculous inspiration account most coherently for the relevant data? The New Testament authors were enabled to convey Christ's teachings with fidelity and add their wisdom from above where he had not spoken, by the *supernatural inspiration* of the Holy Spirit. The Spirit overshadowed in both the content

151

taught and the wording conveying it. Christ had endorsed the Spirit-directed writings of the prophets and promised the Spirit to the apostles. Although those promises may have broader applications to all believers, they most certainly apply in a special way to those apostolic men to whom he addressed them and who wrote New Testament books. The New Testament insight into the mystery of Christ was not made known to men in other generations as "it has now been revealed by the Spirit to God's holy apostles and prophets" (Eph. 3:4–5).

The doctrine of the unity of the Gentiles with the Jews in the church was communicated by apostles who were "holy" in that the Holy Spirit "set them apart" from the rest of humanity to contribute these New Testament writings (Eph. 3:3). So they may be classed along with the writers of the Old Testament as prophets. Peter thus associated the apostles with the prophets when he wrote, "I want you to recall the words spoken in the past by the holy prophets and the command given by our Lord and Savior through your apostles" (2 Peter 3:2). Such nonnegotiable authority for human words is more probably than not a supernatural work of God's Spirit.

Since Peter mentioned Paul's Epistles as Scripture (2 Peter 3:16), his teaching about the origin of Scripture holds for New Testament books as well as Old: "Above all, you must understand that no prophecy of Scripture came about by the prophet's own interpretation. For prophecy never had its origin in the will of man, but men spoke from God as they were carried along by the Holy Spirit" (2 Peter 1:20–21). Since the prophetic writings had a superhuman reliability and authority, they must have been supernaturally kept from error, and so must the New Testament books be classified along with the Old.

Paul's awareness of Luke's writings, and surely of other New Testament books toward the end of his life, means that his teaching applies not only to the Old Testament writings, but also the New, when he said that the Scriptures are able to make one wise for salvation through faith in Christ Jesus. But inspiration is not limited to the teachings on salvation. "All Scripture is God-breathed and is useful for teaching, rebuking, correcting and training in righteousness, so that the man of God may be thoroughly equipped for every good work" (2 Tim. 3:16–17).

Given not only the humanness, but also the fallenness of the writers, the point at issue is whether the Holy Spirit worked with them in an extraordinary manner to produce a result with more than fallible human authority. In view of the recognition that the New Testament books were revelation (not merely a human witness to revelation), and were in the part and the whole, of divine, nonnegotiable authority in the churches, we conclude that their inspiration must have been qualitatively different from the Spirit's illumination of other Christian literature. It produced a cognitive miracle. Without a supernatural inspiration, no portion of even the gospel could have been preserved from errancy and fallibility.

The Canon of Apostolic Writings

Granting that apostolic people wrote inspired Scripture in the first century, do we now have the proper books in the New Testament canon? The most influential factor in the recognition of a book's inspired authority was its apostolic origin.[68]

Some twenty of the twenty-seven New Testament books were immediately known to be from Authentic divine spokesmen and for these no difference of opinion occurred in the early church. On such works as Hebrews,

James, 2 Peter, 2 and 3 John, Jude, and Revelation, some question remained into the second and third centuries. For example, although Hebrews was read in many churches, second-century Western writers questioned whether Paul wrote the anonymous book. Eastern writers maintained that he did. This and other controversies "show that second-century Christians were neither credulous nor superficial in their approach to the holy books."[69] Summing up the issue of the New Testament canon, Geisler and Nix write:

> The vast majority of the New Testament books were never disputed from the beginning. Of the books originally recognized as inspired, but later questioned, all of them came to full and final acceptance by the universal church. Some other books which enjoyed wide usage and were included in local lists for a time were valuable for devotional and homiletical use but never gained canonical recognition by the church. Only the twenty-seven books of the New Testament are known to be genuinely apostolic. Only these twenty-seven have found a permanent place in the New Testament Canon.[70]

THE TEXT OF APOSTOLIC WRITINGS

Have we today the same wording in the original texts of the Greek manuscripts that the apostles wrote? The suggestion that the original apostolic writings are unreal or unimportant because they are not extant today reflects a disregard for the authority of the Savior delegated to these authors. Because every scribe, secretary, and typesetter did not have the special inspiration of the Spirit the apostles had does not diminish the evidence for their original authority for doctrine and practice.

What difference does it make if the original was inerrant since we do not have inerrant copies? Although we have not seen the autographs, others did. Tertullian, about A.D. 200, said that the originals of the New Testament could still be inspected. Have we very good copies of merely human books or of divine-human books? The nature of the Scriptures as originally given is at stake in the assertions about the Gospels and Epistles as they came from apostolic men inspired of God. The doctrine of inspiration has to do with the Bible's origin, not its transmission. To claim that one's view of the Bible's origin is unimportant (so long as it "works"), seems theologically irresponsible.

Given the original nature of the inscripturated revelation, however, its transmission to our day also has great importance. The manuscript evidence is even more abundant for the text of the New Testament than of the Old Testament. Although the different families of manuscript copies are in basic agreement, there are differences that occurred through centuries of copying. Why did the Lord permit this? Perhaps it is because the lack of the originals prevents any museum or church from treating them superstitiously as relics. The written form of God's Word was not given for purposes of bibliolatry. Christians do not worship a book, but the God who has not only acted, but also spoken, in the foundational writings of the prophets and apostles.

Variations in the extant manuscripts are generally of very small, scattered details, except for the end of the Lord's Prayer (Matt. 6:13), the conclusion of the Gospel of Mark, the story of the adulteress (John 8:1–11), Romans 16:15–17, and 1 John 5:7. However, these together amount to about one page of the entire Greek New Testament, and though all of them were found insufficiently supported by the better manuscripts, no doctrine of Scripture is affected. And most of the variations, when studied by knowledgeable scholars can be resolved. Thus the text of the originals can be established beyond reasonable doubt in the bulk of the material.

As George Ladd has said,

> It is a seldom disputed fact that critical science has to all intents and purposes recovered the original text of the New Testament. There remain indeed numerous debatable and debated readings; but if one compares our four contemporary critical texts of the New Testament, edited by E. Nestle (1963), G. D. Kilpatrick (1958), R. V. G. Tasker and Kurt Aland— M. Black—B. M. Metzger—A. Wikgren (1966), he will find them to be in substantial agreement.[71]

"From a practical view, however," said J. H. Greenlee, "the difference involved in most variants is so slight that little or no difference of meaning is involved." He agreed with Kenyon, "we have in our hands, in substantial integrity, the veritable word of God."[72]

Summing up the data on the New Testament, the Lord Jesus Christ, the supreme revelation of God, prepared the disciples for additional revelation after his departure and delegated authority to his authentic apostles to write, as well as speak, revealed truth foundational for the building of the church in every century and culture. The twenty-seven books of the New Testament, well preserved through the centuries, are not a mere human witness to a noncognitive revelation, but convey teachings ultimately from God and communicated through verified apostolic spokesmen by the supernatural inspiration of the Holy Spirit. What the New Testament teaches, God teaches. What it affirms is objectively valid truth: logically, factually, and ethically (inerrant), and so it is authoritative for Christians in the development of healthy, coherent convictions by which to live in the church and the world (infallible). In a world of relativism and

rationalization, whether accepted or not, it stands written as of self-evaluation, church discipline, and divine judgment. This view of the New Testament is not a late invention of Princeton theologians like B. B. Warfield, or Scottish realists, but the most coherent account of the primary data from the apostles and the Lord himself.

APOLOGETIC INTERACTION

Can the view of the Bible's inerrancy in all that it affirms stand examination and meet challenges? We seek here to indicate, not an answer to every question that can be raised about the Bible's teachings, but the structure of argument by which to address questions with intellectual integrity.

Some have attempted a purely *inductive* approach to the authority of scriptural claims and phenomena. Important as it is to check assumptions by the given data, a purely inductive method of reasoning is unrealistic. No one has a completely objective mind; all people from all sides have preunderstandings. As assumptions are verified or disproved people change their personal and passionate commitments to world views.

Recognizing the inescapability of assumptions, others have tried a purely *deductive* approach from their presupposition of plenary inerrancy. But this approach assumes the point to be established, committing the fallacy of circular reasoning. It is also special pleading, for the revelation claims of any other religion or cult would not be considered justifiable on this method of reasoning.

But there is a third approach, the *verificational* method, which begins with hypotheses and tests them by logical, empirical, and existential criteria. Utilizing this approach, we compare three logically distinct hypotheses that are held in the church today and determine which of them provides the most coherent and probable account of the internal and external biblical phenomena with the fewest difficulties.

Three Hypotheses to Test

The first proposal to be tested is that *the Bible is totally errant*. A number of Protestant and Roman Catholic scholars regard God's mind so totally different from spatially and temporally limited and morally depraved human minds that none of the assertions of the Bible can be cognitively true in and of themselves. The Bible's teachings may be accepted only when confirmed by other disciplines such as archaeology or the psychology of religious experience. At no point do holders of this view identify the assertions of Scripture with divinely revealed, reliable information. So secular humanists holding this view summarily dismiss the Bible as self-contradictory, unreliable, and irrelevant.

The dismissal of cognitive truth in religious language in general, and the Bible in particular, does not keep others from using the Bible for religious experiences of different kinds. Religious secularists and mystics continue to use if for its relevant emotive and experiential values. The allegedly errant scriptural witness is "inspired" when inspiring (to liberals), calling existentialists to become authentic individuals, or becoming the occasion for encounters with God (for the neoorthodox and relational theologians), or when it occasions an immediate, nonpersonal, mystical absorption into God (for mystics).

On any of these "dynamic" perspectives what the Bible affirms is not to be confused with true (objectively, or logically valid) information revealed from God himself. Although G. C. Berkouwer, for example, thinks that Scripture is composed of the relative conceptions of time-bound humans, he thinks that its words "mysteriously" introduce people to the eternal Christ. The func-

tion of biblical language is not so much to inform, Berkouwer says, as to point or witness to something beyond itself.[73] It is indeed "mysterious" how the Holy Spirit witnesses to the truth of falsehoods and through them leads people to the real Christ. Faith, then, is not an act of the mind assenting to all scriptural teachings, he claims, but exclusively a matter of choice and trust.[74]

A second hypothesis proposes that some of the Bible's affirmations are errant and some are inerrant; that is, there is *a partial biblical errancy and a partial biblical inerrancy*. Partial inerrancy theories distinguish what is cognitively true from what is not, generally less by subjective experiences and more by rational or doctrinal considerations. G. C. Berkouwer makes an exception to the alleged time-boundedness of all biblical statements about Christ's resurrection. For biblical teaching on the resurrection he declares objective validity by some exceptional "mystery."[75] Some will say that the Bible makes no false or misleading statements on matters of *faith and practice*, redemptive matters, or "saving truth."[76] However, on other subjects (assuming the Bible teaches things that are not important for faith and practice in some direct or indirect way) the Bible may assert falsehoods and mislead.[77] Faith, then, involves sifting the true from the false in Scripture, and God's Spirit illumines both truth and falsehood to direct us away from idols and lead believers to himself. Belief involves assent only to those matters one finds to be essential to "faith and practice," which may vary considerably from person to person.

A third hypothesis proposes a *plenary inerrancy*. This stance asserts the truth, the objective validity, or the inerrancy of all that the biblical autographs affirm on any subject. All Scripture originated with God, and the Holy Spirit uses only truth to lead people away from idols to himself. Faith, then, need not critically distinguish true from false affirmations in Scripture. The critical function is crucial for interpretive purposes, for determining the precise content asserted by the biblical sentences. An inquiry into the meaning of the authors' manuscripts also follows a verification procedure. Acknowledging subjectivity in preunderstandings, we seek as much objectivity as possible. Some interpretations are better informed than others. We survey the interpretive hypotheses, and assent to the best informed interpretation according to standard criteria of truth and to sound principles of hermeneutics.[78]

Comparisons

Similarities may be seen in that all three views affirm in one way or another that Scripture can be and has been a *dynamic* instrument of the Spirit to renew lives. In our terms, all hold that the Bible is "infallible" in that the Holy Spirit witnesses to it to accomplish the purposes for which God sent it (Isa. 55:11). In Christian theology Spirit-illumined biblical teaching serves as the primary means by which people come into fellowship with the living God, who not only created, but also redeems. People who stress the dynamic power of Spirit-illumined Scripture often portray the plenary view as if it displaced the Spirit's power with a "static" body of truths. What is affirmed is that the Spirit's ability to change lives and societies through scriptural teaching depends on its Spirit-inspired truthfulness.

The three views are also similar in that none of the hypotheses has been *completely demonstrated*. There are several reasons for this. Biblical teaching about invisible realities and the meanings of events are by nature unobservable. Even many of the observable events are no longer verifiable because some left no remains at all, and the

visible remains left from others through the centuries has been destroyed. So none of the three hypotheses has been, or can be, completely confirmed or invalidated.

No plenary errantist has verified that *every* biblical statement about the infinite and holy God is false. Dogmatists (sic!) against the truth of religious language and biblical statements in particular support their views by tautologous or stipulative definitions of an alleged "infinite qualitative distinction" between "God's infinite mind" and "human finite minds," and reductively functional or existentialist perspectives of "religious truths," "revelation," and "faith."

Partial inerrantists have not confirmed all of those biblical statements that they hold to be true nor disconfirmed all that they hold to be false. Neither have they succeeded in defining or clarifying a criterion by which adequately to distinguish the one from the other. Agreement has not been reached in distinguishing those statements essential to salvation or "faith and practice" from those with no relation to these purposes. Which are "saving truths" and which are not?

Plenary inerrantists have not verified, nor can they verify, that *every* biblical assertion is true. A doctrine of plenary inerrancy is based on evidence of the view of Jesus Christ as Lord of all, and on the authority of prophets and apostles who had the credentials of supernaturally called spokesmen for God, inspired to write, not merely a human testimony to God, but a divine testimony to man. These lines of evidence are also supported by the classical view in the church and by standard Christian evidences.

A Matter of Probabilities

None of the three views of Scripture has been, or can be "proven" in a complete intellectual sense. The issue becomes, where different, Which of the three hypotheses provides the *most probable* (coherent and viable) account of the relevant lines of evidence with the fewest difficulties? The issue at this point is *not* psychological certitude. Some theological decisions in this complex world are like some political decisions in which we must opt for the proposal with the less severe problems. This being the case, a single historical or scientific difficulty, as is often alleged, does not in itself destroy the plenary inerrancy position. The question for systematic and integrative purposes calls for a judgment only after the court has heard the many relevant lines of evidence—both pro and con. Only then can the jury assess which proposal carries the highest probability with the fewest difficulties. We cannot go into extensive detail again, but seek only to outline a verificational approach to a concept of the Bible's inspiration.

Major Lines of Relevant Evidence

What are the major lines of given *data* that any view must explain? (1) Jesus Christ's view of Scripture; (2) the claims of the prophets; (3) the claims of the apostles (assuming on nos. 1–3 only that the record is of general historical reliability, not of inspired authority for this purpose); (4) the dominant view of the Scriptures throughout the varied history of the church; (5) the humanness (both finiteness and fallenness) of the writers; (6) problem phenomena: difficulties of apparent historical, chronological, and scientific discrepancies; and (7) the positive phenomena: such as the standard "Christian evidences" of fulfilled prophecy and miracles confirming the office and messages of divine spokesmen.

Some errantists tend to sidestep distinctively Christian evidences. However, the fulfillment of specific predictions made scores or hundreds of years in advance still displays a transcendent, divine knowledge. And the "signs and wonders" still exhibit a transcendent, divine power. Scholarly objectivity calls for consideration of such positive indications as well as the negative phenomena.

Evaluation

How well, then, do the three hypotheses account for all seven lines of evidence?

Briefly, although a noncognitive, total errancy hypothesis does seem to fit the finiteness and fallenness of the writers and their passages presenting problem phenomena, it does not provide an adequate account of the other five lines of data presented by Christ, prophets, apostles, Christian evidences, or the history of the doctrine in the church.

Similarly, a partial-inerrancy hypothesis has little problem with the humanness of the writers and their apparent discrepancies, but it fails to provide an adequate account of the view held by Christ, the prophets, and the apostles, as confirmed by signs and wonders and attested by most authorities throughout church history.

A plenary-inerrancy hypothesis has a coherent and adequate explanation of the final authority of Scripture held by Jesus Christ, the prophets, and the apostles and of their confirmation by supernatural signs and wonders and their attestation throughout the history of the church, but it does not have a full explanation of every historical, scientific, or literary difficulty that can be raised.

If the pattern of reasoning, or paradigm, is now clear, we must look more closely at the consistency, adequacy, and viability of each view.

A belief that the Bible is wholly

subject to errancy resolves all tensions between biblical and other sources of knowledge, but it does so at too great a cost. To relinquish the authority of the Bible merely for the sake of harmony with the prevailing voices in the academic community is too great a price to pay. The view loses the relevance of biblical teaching to anything but a noncognitive relationship to what is felt to be God.

This belief supplies no cognitive criteria by which to distinguish the true God from idols or the personal God of Christian theism from the impersonal God of pantheistic monism. If scriptural doctrine cannot convey truth about the transcendent realm, mystics, occultists, and others have no way to test the spirits to see whether they are of Christ or Antichrist, of God or Satan.

It makes God's thoughts so "totally other" than human thoughts that God himself cannot communicate with the creature he created in his image for the purpose of communicating and working together. In this, it fails to fit the revealed facts concerning the image of God in humanity, including the human mind (Col. 3:10).

In its desire to free the faith from intellectual difficulties with reversible models of scientific knowledge, it commits intellectual suicide. It reduces intellectual content of Scripture to a merely human emotional, functional, relational, and mystical witness. Having done so, its adherents must not be surprised if people who desire to distinguish God from idols and worship God with their minds as well as their hearts, find the view intellectually uncritical, naïve, and dangerous. Inscripturated revelation has to do essentially with the created cosmos and historical events.

The God of the hypothesis that the Bible is wholly subject to errancy is too small to overcome the limitations of human finiteness and fallenness. James Barr, for example, does not identify the Bible with revelation but calls it an errant human witness to revelation (Jesus Christ). "The entire Bible is a human word, subject to the strains, weaknesses and errors of any other book and deserves, indeed requires, to be studied with just the same methods as any other."[79] Ignoring Jesus' teaching about his own teaching as well as that of the prophets, Barr says that "the Spirit's work with the prophets and apostles was not essentially different in kind from the mode in which he is with his people today."[80] Barr's hypothesis may seem to cohere with the problem phenomena and the humanness of the writers, but it fails to account for the overwhelming data from Christ, the prophets, the apostles, the church and the "signs and wonders" in their support.

According to the view of limited inerrancy, "salvific" teaching in Scripture is to be relied on, while other teaching is not. For such a view to be valid, "saving" must be given clear content. If the charge of insufficient definition applies to total inerrantists with respect to "inerrancy," the charge holds with greater force against the lack of definition of what is "soteriological" in the limited-inerrancy view. If it so prescribes the referents of reliable biblical teaching to "faith and practice" that it never can be in opposition to the facts of contemporary historical and scientific interpretations, it faces all the major problems of the belief that the Bible is wholly subject to errancy. The benefit of freedom from conflicts with science and history is won at great cost—the loss of theism and Christianity at its heart and essence.

If the definition of redemptive truth becomes broad enough to include the historical events that founded the Christian faith, then observable matters of fact are reliably true (inerrant) as well as subjective, experiential matters. The nature of Christianity's redemptive message involves truth about the created and fallen world and historical provisions for its redemption. Mystics may divorce Christian faith from science and history, but evangelical Christians will not do so. The mighty acts of God in the world are no mere myths or symbols, but observable events that have made a difference in time, space, and human lives. To suggest that assertions about redemption are inerrant but that matters of history are not shows a dreadful lack of understanding concerning distinctively Christian faith. Christianity is a matter of facts as well as of relations and experiences.

Inadequate guidelines are given for what is essential to believe and practice or what is soteriological. Hence the concept may be too broad and assert the inerrancy of everything taught in Scripture, or it may be too narrow and fail to include all that has been supernaturally inspired for various purposes of church administration, church discipline, etc.

Divine revelation has more than one single "saving" purpose. The Lord of redemption is the Lord of all. Granted that the highest purpose for us is salvation, a personal, moral, and spiritual communion with God is not the sole end for which each paragraph of Scripture was written. Some units of thought tell us about ultimate origins, the Fall, society's need for government, the judgment that falls on evildoers, and the coming divine wrath to overtake the ungodly. If the Bible is partially errant and if all of this is for salvation (faith and practice), then all that the Bible teaches is subject to errancy and the definition of partial inerrancy is inadequate.

The same arguments by which partial inerrantists regard some scriptural teaching errant (the human authors' finiteness and fallenness) apply to all scriptural affirmations. All teachings, including those on faith and practice, are written by finite, fallen persons in human categories of thought expressed in human languages of a given period and culture. Unless a clearly supernatural inspiration of the inerrant portions is affirmed, it is simply a matter of time until the arguments for partial errancy will be extended to the gospel.

Partial inerrancy fights a losing battle because the rules of the contest are set up by the prevailing standards of modernity (in the fields of history, science, etc.) rather than by revealed truths of general or special revelation. A biblical authority dependent on the gaps in present secular knowledge, may gradually evaporate. It is far from the inherent, unshakable revealed authority of which Jesus Christ, the prophets, and the apostles taught.

The appeal of the errantist positions should not be overlooked, however. Whether one believes that the Bible is wholly subject to errancy or that it is only partially so, he seeks to remove even apparent conflict between Christian faith and contemporary knowledge, fluctuating as that is. Because the Bible's authority does not hold except where they define it to hold, however, their view can never be disconfirmed. It is true by their stipulated authority in matters of faith and practice. So the ultimate authority becomes the standard of the historian or scientist rather than the Scripture. However, in the final analysis Scripture must judge science and history, not vice versa.

Improbable indeed is the hypothesis that the Holy Spirit uses erroneous human teachings more dynamically than supernaturally revealed true teachings expressed in faithful words. Untrue teachings lead to idols and dream castles of unreality. The Spirit of truth has chosen to use true concepts to lead people away from idols and illusions to the living God who hears, speaks, and acts. Of course the sovereign Lord has the power to overrule human errors in

159

preaching, but no evidence indicates that the sovereign God chooses to reveal himself and his purposes by originating ("breathing out") errors.

Although restricting the view of the Bible's authority, the partial inerrancy view fails sufficiently to restrict the theologians' authority. "Once historical criticism was seriously applied to the Bible," wrote A. T. and R. P. C. Hanson, "the old doctrines of inspiration and inerrancy were no longer tenable. They vanished like shadows in the light of the day."[81] The Hanson brothers admit that their view is not that of the historic church: "We must candidly reject the ancient oracular view of the Bible and substitute for it the concept of the Bible as witness or testimony."[82] Nevertheless they believe that the biblical compilation of literature gives sufficient evidence for people "to understand and embrace the Way of Life."[83]

With all the frailties of the Hansons' Bible, it functions inexplicably as a norm of doctrine in Christian churches! But they use "norm" and "rule" in a very "restricted" sense. "What the Bible supplies us with is the raw material for doctrine, not the finished product itself."[84] Unfortunately, the Hansons' "finished product" may become more authoritative in practice than the Scriptures themselves. Although their hypotheses may account for some critical problems and the writers' humanness, it faces far more severe problems with the repeated teaching of Christ, the prophets, the apostles, and the church as supported by Christian evidences.

The *plenary inerrancy* view, although not straining to account for most of the major lines of evidence, has been charged by some with (1) unsatisfactory definition of its terms, (2) an insufficient account of the biblical writers' humanness, and (3) an inadequate explanation of the problem phenomena. In intellectual honesty it cannot ignore the difficulties. Plenary inerrantists who overlook these difficulties reflect more about their own intentions (not to admit any difficulties), as a kind of procedural rule, than they inform about the Scriptures themselves. But those who understand the verificational methodology used here cannot justifiably charge that it dismisses logical or factual considerations a priori. How it can meet some major charges against it is outlined in the next three sections.

Inerrancy: Not Defined? or Defined Away?

Opponents of plenary biblical inerrancy often insist either that no one ever defined inerrancy (truth) to their satisfaction or that the definitions proposed were so complex as to die the death of a thousand qualifications. As the following definitions are proposed for consideration and acceptance, the reader may assess the validity of such objections.

By "inerrancy" we mean that as a product of supernatural inspiration the information affirmed by the sentences of the original autographs of the sixty-six canonical books of the Bible is true.[85]

By "true" content we mean propositions that correspond to the thought of God and created reality because they are logically noncontradictory, factually reliable, and experientially viable. Therefore, as given, the Bible provides a reliable guide for healthfully experiencing the physical, mental, moral, and spiritual realities that people face in time and eternity.

To grasp the truth that was *given*, as fully as possible, a passage of Scripture must be *taken* (interpreted) by a believer in accord with its author's purpose; degrees of precision appropriate to that purpose at that time; and its grammatical, historical, cultural, and theological contexts (all under the illumination of the Holy Spirit who inspired it).

"Infallible" sentences are units of thought faithfully copied from the canonical autographs that convey the content God intended to communicate through his spokesmen and accomplish their divinely intended purpose.[86]

By "plenary" inspiration we mean that as a result of the Holy Spirit's supernatural supervision, all of the parts of the canon equally are God's Word, infallible in wording and inerrant in teaching. Belief in plenary inspiration does not mean that all passages are equally important for answering any given question (How do you receive eternal life? How do you discipline a wayward church member?). It does mean that all that the Scriptures teach is important for some purpose and contributes in some way to the process of becoming thoroughly furnished to every good work (2 Tim. 3:16–17) in God's universal kingdom with its cultural mandate as well as in the redemptive kingdom with its Great Commission.

By the "perspicuity of the Scriptures" we affirm that they were written with sufficient clarity that readers or hearers are accountable for their response to the content conveyed. People without special training may respect the provisional authority of Christians who have given their lives to a study of the Word, but not grant them ultimate allegiance. Even the most gifted teachers are errant and fallible. But whatever the errors of ill-trained or presumptuous interpreters, the Bible's visual symbols in print adequately convey the truth God intended to reveal. And all who can read or hear the Bible are responsible to read it, assent to its teaching, and live by it.

What are thought to be difficulties concerning biblical inerrancy may be difficulties of the Bible's interpreters. Qualifications put on interpreters of Scripture (as taken) are not to be thought to be on the inerrancy of the Bible (as given). If it is thought objectionable that inerrantists qualify interpretation in terms of the writer's purpose, standards of accuracy appropriate to that purpose at that time, and a responsible use of principles of hermeneutics, then the objection may remain. If it be considered strained harmonization to carefully apply criteria of truth and logical principles utilized in the New Testament (differentiating contradictions from subcontraries and merely verbal differences), then objections there must be. Would errantists, however, commend interpretations of their own writings that failed to take account of their purpose, their intended level of technicality, or their context? Is it irresponsible interpretation, not inerrancy as here defined, that has died the death of a thousand qualifications?

Much fuzzy thinking has suggested that biblical inerrancy is meaningless because it is "tied up" with hermeneutics. Inerrancy and hermeneutics are related, but they are as distinct as the important difference between *what is given* by inspiration and *what is taken* by illumination. It is the difference between the content the inspired biblical writers conveyed and the extent to which their readers for two thousand years have grasped it with the help of sound principles of hermeneutics and growing skills in applying them.

No amount of interpretive abuse can change the nature of the biblical message as it was originally given. But "ignorant and unstable people" may distort it "to their own destruction" (2 Peter 3:16). There are crucial questions of interpretation; there are also crucial questions about the nature of the book to be interpreted. The meaning of the Bible's inspiration and inerrancy cannot be reductively treated as one of a hermeneutical wax nose, to be twisted at will. The one type of question does not rule out the other. There is the question of the Bible as given and the question of the Bible as taken. We can confidently assert that the Bible was entirely inerrant when it was written, without claiming that any individual defender of plenary inerrancy holds all aspects of that truth in his own mind and teaching today. "We know in part" (1 Cor. 13:9).

Plenary Inerrancy and the Writers' Humanness

Many contemporary theologians stress the biblical authors' humanness to the point of errancy. They argue that scriptural authors were time-bound and their writings, though not necessarily true, are of functional value. Some of these are Reformed writers such as G. C. Berkouwer and Harry Boer, evangelical writers like Jack Rogers and Charles Kraft, and Roman Catholic writers like Charles Davis, Hans Küng, and Leslie Dewart.[87]

But just as Jesus Christ was truly divine and truly human without sin, so the Scriptures are truly divine and truly human without error. The inerrancy of finite, fallen human authors makes sense within the cultural context in which Scripture was given, the context of a theistic world view that includes orthodox doctrines of God, creation, providence, and miracles. In such a setting it is clear that human writers would not be abstracted from their relationship of dependence on God and treated autonomously. They lived and moved and had their being in the all-wise Lord of all. Created by God in his image, they had a capacity of self-transcendence enabling them to receive changeless truths by general and special revelation. Although physically time-bound, as image-bearers of the divine, they were created with the capacity to receive truths from beyond time by revelation.

Providentially prepared by God in their unique personalities, they also had, of course, characteristics common to all other human persons in all times and cultures. Categories of thought concerning essential human existence, as well as divinely revealed ideas transcending historical flux could be immutable. Beyond that, truth about a unique, once-for-all event in history remains true always. Their teaching, whether common or uniquely theirs, originated not with their own wills, but God's and came to them through a variety of means: audible voice, inner insights, visions, reading, and research. The use of other human sources is not excluded in universal divine providence. What is excluded is the single-cause fallacy operative in much higher-critical thought—that if an author researched and used other sources, his message was not ultimately from God. God in his sovereignty chose to work through means, not only providentially in everything that comes to pass, but also miraculously in overseeing the production of, say, Luke's Gospel (1:1–4) and in the use of other canonical and noncanonical sources.

In all their research, writers were supervised by the Holy Spirit. Just as Jesus was kept from human depravity by a moral miracle at his virgin conception, so the writers of Scripture were kept from human error by an epistemological miracle at their teaching's conception and birth in written form. The Spirit's work with the writers is not appropriately thought analogous to impersonal, mechanical relationships, but rather like worthy personal relationships. They were moved by the Spirit as one wise, loving person influences another alert, teachable, person in innumerable conscious and unconscious ways.

What stands written in human languages, therefore, is not merely human, but also divine. What the sentences convey, God and his spokesmen wanted to convey. What the content teaches, God and his spokesmen teach. The affirmations conform to the mind of God and to the reality God created. In that sense the content is true or inerrant. And in conveying that content the wording is effectual or infallible. The Bible's teachings are objectively normative for all people of all times and cultures whether these teachings are received or not.

Why does the Bible function effectively to bring sinners to Christ and thoroughly equip them for every good work? Because it is God-breathed (divinely originated) and trustworthy in all that it teaches (2 Tim. 3:15–17).[88]

Plenary Inerrancy and Problem Phenomena

Before accepting a challenge to the truth of a scriptural assertion from any field, it is wise to determine what *canons of scientific evaluation* or *criteria of truth* are used. The reign of the strict logical positivist's verificational principle has been brought down. Historical claims cannot be dismissed as meaningless a priori because they are not repeatable or verifiable by the scientific method at present. The highest values of life (such as justice and love) are unverifiable in that narrow sense and many of the most significant events in the world are not repeatable under controlled conditions (e.g., the death of Abraham Lincoln).

Because there are so many conflicting presuppositions from which to understand the past and even to define "history" and other sciences, we need to develop a healthy skepticism regarding claims that "all critics agree. . . ." Universal agreement in our pluralistic world, even among professionals in the same field, seems highly unlikely. Often this claim covers up a hidden premise: "All who agree with me are critical

scholars, all who differ with me are obscurantists."

Because of an insufficiently critical skepticism among Christian people in the nineteenth and twentieth centuries, a movement of critical thinkers starting with naturalistic, evolutionary assumptions developed an imposing consensus in prominent Christian institutions. Nevertheless, there has continued a historic train of "classical criticism" with different presuppositions that faced the same problems with quite different results.

As early as St. Augustine, problems of the similarities and differences in the synoptic Gospels, for example, were faced and found not irreconcilable with the Bible's view of its own origin and nature. Given the distinction between the content asserted and the linguistic vehicle conveying those affirmations, the wording in the three Gospels need not be identical, only the meanings must be noncontradictory. Different sentences can convey the same content from the different perspectives of different witnesses of such events as the resurrection and the healing of a blind person.[89]

A comparison of the evangelical and nonevangelical presuppositions influential in scientific, historical, anthropological, and biblical interpretations has seemed to confine people to reasoning in "hermeneutical circles." However, we need not orbit forever in one or the other set of presuppositions. Difficult as it may be to break out of longstanding assumptions, the following steps applying our verificational methodology make genuine knowledge and exegesis (rather than eisegesis) possible. (1) Increase the consciousness of one's influential presuppositions and hypotheses. (2) Delimit the issue by focusing initially on the meaning of the scriptural teaching as given. (3) Acknowledge that presuppositions are not beyond examination, but are

163

truth-claims or hypotheses to be reexamined. (4) Build on common ground available as human beings in a threatened world avoiding violence and mind-control. (5) Utilize sound criteria of truth in assessing all of the relevant hermeneutical data. (6) Make a fresh, objective examination of the relevant data with a willingness to accept the set of assumptions that without contradiction accounts for the many diverse lines of relevant grammatical, historical, cultural, theological, and experiential data with the fewest difficulties.[90]

With The International Council on Biblical Inerrancy in its Chicago Statement on Biblical Hermeneutics, "WE AFFIRM that any preunderstandings which the interpreter brings to Scripture should be in harmony with scriptural teaching and subject to correction by it. WE DENY that Scripture should be required to fit alien preunderstandings inconsistent with itself, such as naturalism, evolutionism, scientism, secular humanism and relativism."[91]

People concerned about the problem phenomena of the Bible need to be aware that the preponderance of discovery has tended to support the historical specifics asserted in Scripture, turning some who started with errantist perspectives toward more conservative views of Scripture (Sir William Ramsay and William Foxwell Albright). Rather than tending to shatter confidence in the wording of biblical manuscripts, textual criticism has built confidence in it. Higher criticism—concerned with matters of sources, date, and authorship—has had to revise late dates for biblical books in view of recent discoveries. Although many difficult questions have been raised, the Bible's credibility has been enhanced. "After more than two centuries of facing the heaviest guns that could be brought to bear, the Bible has survived, and is perhaps better for the siege. Even on the critics' own terms—historical fact—the Scriptures

seem more acceptable now than they did when the rationalists began the attack."[92]

Just as in issues regarding science and the Bible a moderate concordism is well supported, so in matters of history, and cultural anthropology, the basic characteristics are in harmony with Scripture, and the remaining difficulties may or may not be cleared up by further study, in our lifetimes. Being finite, we must accept the most probable hypothesis with the fewest difficulties. Many difficulties have been helpfully addressed by the better commentators. Also Gleason Archer, in his *Encyclopedia of Bible Difficulties,* proposes resolutions of numerous difficulties.[93]

Attempts to hold to the truth of the Bible in matters of spiritual life, but not in matters of fact are unsuccessful. The Bible itself is in major segments a set of assertions about historical facts. God created and sustains and governs history. The Exodus occurred in history. Jesus became flesh, lived and taught, died and rose again in history. He builds a church that continues to make world history. He understood the Old Testament to teach literal history. Without history Christianity is not Christianity, but some otherworldly mysticism. Theologians who regard the incarnation as mere mythology have missed the central, unique message of the faith.

Granting that some true biblical history is necessary to faith, where is the criterion by which we can decide which biblical history is necessary and true and which historical passages in Scripture are not necessary and may not be true? From Feuerbach, Harnack, and Schleiermacher on, attempts to define the essence of the Christian faith have had far from universal agreement. If a criterion by which to distinguish among true and false historical records in Scripture were proposed, would it not then be a more ultimate authority than the Scriptures themselves? Everyone believes some things in Scripture, like the Golden Rule. Some also believe biblical history that has been confirmed by extrabiblical historical evidence. Others accept biblical references to nature confirmed by science. They do not believe the Bible as such. They accept only those judgments with which they agree on some other ground.

The Bible's purpose is primarily redemptive, but the same bases for our faith in the central redemptive message (which itself involves historical facts—for example, Jesus is the Christ, he died for our sins, he was buried, he rose again), indicate that all that it teaches on other subjects as well is true.

Whether all or part of the biblical history is in view, Colin Brown effectively argued, "If the truth claims of a purported revelation can be shown to be false on a factual level, we can hardly claim it to represent the truth about God and man on any other level."[94]

RELEVANCE TO LIFE AND MINISTRY

The Book With Life-Transforming Power

A French naturalist, Emile Cailliet, had time to think while recovering from wounds of war, but could find "no light beyond the curtain" of his meaningless life. His favorite literary and philosophical works could not speak to the condition that asked, "Who was I anyway? Nay, what was I?" Upon reading the Bible for the first time in his life, he suddenly realized, "This was the Book that would understand me!" He found its pages "animated by the Presence of the Living God and the power of his mighty acts." As Cailliet prayed and read the opening chapters of the Gospel of John, he responded to the person of the gospel and life became meaningful. It was no longer a miserable sequence

of broken vows and vain resolutions. It is a life of love, and power because it is a redeemed and fully surrendered life, a life in line with the will of God. A man of power does not give the impression of strain and effort, but what he does God does in him. God's presence issues in Christlikeness and worship. Worship because the power of the Presence is not a mere duty; rather it is "a delectation wherein a Christian's destiny finds its fulfillment."[95]

The Only Inerrant Guide for Decision Making

What are the most valuable sources of guidance for people in a pluralistic world? They are not horoscopes, Ouija boards, good feelings, inner experiences, or altered states of consciousness. Mindless attempts to grasp ultimate reality sooner or later need to be conceptually interpreted in relation to all knowledge. Feelings and experiences do not come with tags giving their significance in the long run. Uninterpreted experience does not supply guidance. Knowledge by which to guide life includes the data of experience plus interpretation. Then, of course, the question is whose interpretation is most coherent?

How then shall Christians interpret the varied experiences of life? What goals are worth striving for? How do you know? Whatever experiences and feelings a Christian may have, and whatever may be learned from all other fields of knowledge, the teaching of Scripture provides the primary source of reliable information for guidance in life. It takes priority over counsel from any other field of knowledge and rules out any advice that contradicts it.

Biblical revelation stands out like a "light shining in a dark place" until Christ returns (2 Peter 1:19). Knowing that he will soon leave his body (1:13–14), Peter reminds God's people of the exceptional experience of the apostles who saw Christ transfigured (1:16–18). But he does not ask believers to seek a similar, "mountain top" experience! Even more certain than those eyewitness reports of living apostles, is "the word of the prophets . . . you will do well to pay attention to it. . . . For prophecy never had its origin in the will of man, but men spoke from God as they were carried along by the Holy Spirit" (1:19–21).

Biblical teaching has the divine right decisively to determine beliefs and behaviors. This one Book has this *authority* above all other books, for it is different in kind, not merely in degree. No other writing deserves the reading, the meditation, the study that this volume does. But belief in biblical inerrancy does not make biblical interpretation easy for decision making.

Given plenary inerrancy, a sufficient reason for a belief is that the Bible teaches it normatively for all humanity. However, not everything the Bible records is directly exemplary or normative today. Scripture presents not only general principles, but also narrative about particular people and events in particular cultural circumstances. General revelation presented basic truths about the changeless character of God and his moral demands for all people everywhere. And universal moral law is amplified in some biblical passages. But other passages present laws distinctively for the Jewish commonwealth not directly applicable in the same way to all other nations or to churches. In addition the lies of Satan, the grumbling of the people in the wilderness, the sins of many otherwise great leaders, must be distinguished in context for what they are (according to the most coherent account of all the relevant grammatical, historical, cultural, theological data).[96]

By what criteria can we distinguish universal from particular teachings in applying the biblical teaching to our daily lives? Teachings that are true can generally be recognized if they are given in a context that indicates their (1) universality; (2) necessity or unqualified "oughtness" or normativity for all people, for all people of God, for all in national Israel, or for all in Christian churches; and (3) changelessness. Nine commandments, at least, illustrate such absolute truths (the nine of the ten commandments repeated in the New Testament and written on all people's hearts) for all human beings of all time.

Indicative sentences about particular, irrepeatable events are also permanently true. The fact that events rapidly change does not mean that the truth about a given event itself changes. Truths about particular persons or events are not relative nor less true as time passes or as they are communicated around the world.

In one of these ways or another, through scriptural instruction, the Lord Jesus Christ instructs his discerning church. Apart from adherence to the Bible's guidance, talk about Christ as the head of the church can be manipulated in any direction. A Christian church in which the ultimate operative authority is not God's living Word through the written Word is like a body without a head.

Ned Stonehouse said, "Apart from clarity and unity in understanding the Lordship of Jesus Christ as coming to expression in the Holy Scripture, there can be no theological wholeness and no lasting assurance of advancement in theological education."[97]

The Dependable Means to Fellowship With the Living Word

Through the written Word we learn of the living Word: his eternal existence with the Father, his unique incarnation, his matchless life, his inerrant teaching (which renews, liberates, and sanctifies), his mighty miracles, his atoning death, his triumphant resurrection, his ascension, his intercession on our behalf and his coming again in glory and power. If we turn from the Christ of the written Word, to whom shall we go? To Marx? To Lenin? To Mao? To gurus from the Eastern religions? To gurus of the Western new-consciousness techniques? The Christ of the written Word remains incomparable! Are you bowing to the scriptural Christ as Master of your knowing, loving, and serving (epistemologically, affectively, and ethically)?

"The Christian who wants to encounter God without listening to what he has to say," Richard Lovelace writes, "may remain in the condition of a smilingly subliterate and disobedient two-year old. Sanctification of the mind is of pivotal importance in sanctification of the whole life, and sanctification of the mind involves an increasing ability to think biblically under the empowering of the Spirit."[98]

The key to authentic spiritual experience is assent to God's Word as true, that is, as informative concerning what is in reality, and what ought to be. With that guidance, life can be faithfully devoted to the really real and the most significant. "Without reliable information one may expend his life for nothing: without faithfulness to the highest values, one may be a hypocrite. On the one hand, a merely doctrinaire view of truth may lead to an empty idealism or an arrogant legalism. On the other hand, an undirected commitment may lead to a blind emotionalism, a frustrated activism, or a tragic discontinuity with what is and ought to be."[99]

The Truth to Which the Holy Spirit Witnesses

Because the Bible is God's Word it ought to command belief and action; because readers of it are finite and sinful, they need the aid of the Holy Spirit to relate productively to its ultimate Author and his dynamic purposes in the world. Although doctrine is a reliable indicator of the kind of spiritual life or motivating force within a person or movement, Richard Lovelace has emphasized, it does not necessarily guarantee spiritual life or force within a person or movement (2 Tim. 3:5; 1 Cor. 13:1; Rev. 2:2–4).[100]

If a sound interpretation of Scripture is necessary, but not sufficient to give spiritual vitality, what is? The Scripture properly interpreted by a believer with the *illumination of the Holy Spirit* who inspired it is able to give spiritual vitality. The mind of sinners, according to some, is blind, and divine illumination provides new sight. The will of sinners, according to others, is rebellious and would not accept the biblical verdict of guilt nor the gospel of grace if it could "see" it. A third view suggests that both are correct and the whole person—the thinking, feeling, and willing self—though active in relation to himself and the world, is unresponsive to the truths of special revelation. The Holy Spirit's illumining activity frees a person's capacities in relation to spiritual things. Renewing the capacities to know, love, and obey God, illumination enables sinners to understand that the gospel is objectively true, to assent to its truth for themselves personally, and to commit themselves to the Savior.

The Spirit's activity of illumination for all believers does not reveal new information to be added to the canon of Scripture, nor does it make any believer, however sincere, inerrant or infallible. Neither does it by internal persuasion apart from examination of the evidence settle questions of which books belong in the canon or which reading of a text has the best manuscript support. The witness of the Spirit does not settle controversies about the meaning of a controversial passage apart from study of the text with sound hermeneutics. Nor does illumination displace the need for objective evidences and sound apologetic arguments based on them in preevangelism.

The witness of the Spirit attests the objective truth and meaning of special revelation, beginning at its heart, the gospel. The Spirit inspired the content of the gospel in the Scriptures, and now the Spirit persuades sinners of its truth objectively for all and internally for themselves. In this persuasion the Spirit may use different amounts of the relevant exegetical, historical, literary, and cultural data discovered by long hours of hard study by the inquirer or the ones ministering the Word to him. Hence the gospel appears no longer as foolishness or a stumbling block. The mind, desires, and will are opened to Christ and then one makes the commitment to him as Savior and Lord (1 Cor. 2:14; 12:3).

As a result of the Spirit's witness, believers develop assurance of their identity as children in God's spiritual family and joint heirs with Christ of all his resources for an abundant life (Rom. 8:15–16; Gal. 4:6). Enabled by the Spirit, believers trust and experience God's purposes of redemptive grace (1 Cor. 2:12). They are no longer in bondage to the values of the natural man (v. 14) and grow in evaluating things according to the revealed mind of Christ (vv. 15–16; 1 John 2:20–22, 27).[101]

People do not have to receive the Bible for it to become the Word of God. It *is* the Word of God objectively whether received as such or not. To reject its teaching is to be judged by its teaching. Christians who enjoy the Bible's benefits, receive it and act on it as the oracles of God. God's Spirit abides with believers, enabling them to receive the things that come from him (1 Cor. 2:14). That applies particularly to the Spirit-revealed and Spirit-inspired Scriptures. Receivers enabled by the Spirit delight, not merely in the Bible's verbal sentences, indispensable vehicles that they are, but especially in the great truths they teach and the awesome realities and events to which they refer.

It is the Spirit through the Word who enables receivers to walk faithfully with the Lord they love. When people are unreceptive, the Spirit's presence convicts them of yielding to fleshly desires, however delightful the temporary pleasures of sin may seem. Although some nonredemptive truths are revealed in nature, the necessary instrument of redemptive truth—since the completion of the canon until Christ himself returns—is scriptural teaching received as God's living voice.

Spiritual disciplines helpful in receiving the prophetic-apostolic message include reading it, studying it, memorizing it, and meditating on its application to life. "Be diligent in these matters; give yourself wholly to them so that everyone may see your progress. Watch your life and doctrine closely. Persevere in them, because if you do, you will save both yourself and your hearers" (1 Tim. 4:15).

An Unfailing Stimulus to Faith

Although suffering as a prisoner for proclaiming the gospel, Paul was not disillusioned or in despair. Why? Because of his faith. As he testifies to his faith, its essential elements become clear. "And of this gospel I was appointed a herald and an apostle and a teacher. That is why I am suffering as I am. Yet I am not ashamed, because I *know* whom I have believed, and am *convinced* that he is able to guard what I have *entrusted* to him for that day" (2 Tim. 1:11–12). Truth about God can be known. Zeal for God without knowledge (of the Redeemer) did not suffice for monotheistic and moral Jews (Rom.

10:1–2). Neither did worship of an "unknown God" atone for the cultured Athenians (Acts 17:23–31). In contrast, Abraham was "fully persuaded that God had power to do what he had promised" (Rom. 4:21).

The faith that saves is directed away from human educational, cultural, and religious achievements to the Creator, whose redemptive plan has been preserved and publicized in Scripture. Faith comes by *hearing* the message of special revelation now affirmed by the written Word of God, the hearer *being convinced* that "Jesus is Lord" and *trusting* in him (Rom. 10:4, 8–11, 14). Faith involves knowledge (*notitia*), persuasion (*assensus*), and commitment (*fiducia*). These three elements of faith are operative, not only when one first believes the gospel and trusts the Savior, but also in a growing faith throughout the Christian life.

An Indestructible Weapon for Victory in Spiritual Warfare

How did Christ, who was tempted in every way as we are (Heb. 4:15), avoid yielding to temptation? By quoting Scripture! Starved after forty days of fasting, Jesus was challenged by the Devil to change stones to bread. Jesus answered, "It is written: 'Man does not live on bread alone, but on every word that comes from the mouth of God'" (Matt. 4:4; Deut. 8:3). Jesus also countered the next two temptations with "It is written . . ." and then the Devil left him (Matt. 4:7, 10–11). Satan flees from nothing else like the Word of the Most High. Those who reduce any part of God's inscripturated Word to a mere human witness subject themselves and those they teach to spiritual warfare without some of their most effective weapons.

Although Christ won the decisive victory against Satan, the great dragon continues to tempt, primarily through our own fleshly desires and those of the unregenerate world, to lie, murder, and not hold to the truth (John 8:44). How can we counteract the works of the flesh such as sexual immorality, idolatry, witchcraft, hatred, jealousy, rage, selfish ambition, envy, drunkenness, and orgies (Gal. 5:19–21)? The scriptural instructions concerning these and an unforgiving spirit were given "in order that Satan might not outwit us. For we are not unaware of his schemes" (2 Cor. 2:5–11).

Christians who would take their stand against the Devil's schemes put on the full armor of God (Eph. 6:11). "For our struggle is not against flesh and blood, but against the rulers, against the authorities, against the powers of this dark world and against the spiritual forces of evil in the heavenly realms" (v. 12). In addition to the defensive armor, the one offensive weapon for this spiritual conflict is "the sword of the Spirit, which is the word of God" (6:17). The Word, as always, is accompanied by praying in the Spirit (6:18).

Whether the attraction to displease God is indirect or more directly present, "basic to all victory of the believer over Satan," said a Baptist pastor experienced in a deliverance ministry, "is the absolute truth of Bible doctrine. . . . Satan backs off from nothing but the absolute truth and fact of God's Word. . . . Seeing this truth is perhaps the single greatest key (to victory) in warfare against Satan."[102]

REVIEW QUESTIONS

To Help Relate and Apply Each Section in This Chapter

1. *Briefly state the classical problem* this chapter addresses and indicate reasons why genuine inquiry into it is important for your world view and your existence personally and socially.

2. *Objectively summarize the influ-*

ential answers given to this problem in history as hypotheses to be tested. Be able to compare and contrast their real similarities and differences (not merely verbal similarities or differences).

3. *Highlight the primary biblical evidence* on which to decide among views—evidence found in the relevant teachings of the major divisions of Scripture—and decide for yourself which historical hypothesis (or synthesis of historical views) provides the most consistent and adequate account of the primary biblical data.

4. *Formulate in your own words your doctrinal conviction* in a logically consistent and adequate way, organizing your conclusions in ways you can explain clearly, support biblically, and communicate effectively to your spouse, children, friends, Bible class, or congregation.

5. *Defend your view* as you would to adherents of the alternative views, showing that the other views are logically less consistent and factually faced with more difficulties than your view in accounting for the givens, not only of special revelation but also of human experience in general.

6. *Explore the differences the viability of your conviction can make in your life.* Then test your understanding of the viability of your view by asking, "Can I live by it authentically (unhypocritically) in relation to God and to others in my family, church, vocation, neighborhood, city, nation, and world?"

MINISTRY PROJECTS

To Help Communicate This Doctrine in Christian Service

1. *Memorize one major verse or passage* that in its context teaches the heart of this doctrine and may serve as a text from which to preach, teach, or lead small group studies on the topic. The memorized passages from each chapter will build a body of content useful also for meditation and reference in informal discussions.

2. *Formulate the major idea of the doctrine in one sentence* based on the passage memorized. This idea should be useful as the major thesis of either a lesson for a class (junior high to adult) or a message for a church service.

3. *State the specific purpose or goal of your doctrinal lesson or message.* Your purpose should be more than informative. It should show why Christians need to accept this truth and live by it (unhypocritically). For teaching purposes, list indicators that would show to what extent class members have grasped the truth presented.

4. *Outline your message or lesson in complete sentences.* Indicate how you would support the truth of the doctrine's central ideas and its relevance to life and service. Incorporate elements from this chapter's historical, biblical, systematic, apologetic, and practical sections selected according to the value they have for your audience.

5. *List applications of the doctrine* for communicating the difference this conviction makes in life (for sermons, lessons, small-group Bible studies, or family devotional Bible studies). Applications should make clear what the doctrine is, why one needs to know it, and how it will make differences in thinking. Then show how the difference in thought will lead to differences in values, priorities, attitudes, speech, and personal action. Consider also the doctrine's possible significance for family, church, neighborhood, city, regional, and national actions.

6. *Start a file and begin collecting illustrations* of this doctrine's central idea, the points in your outline, and your applications.

7. *Write out your own doctrinal statement on this subject* in one paragraph (in half a page or less). To work toward a comprehensive doctrinal statement,

collect your formulations based on a study of each chapter of *Integrative Theology*. As your own statement of Christian doctrine grows, you will find it personally strengthening and useful when you are called on for your beliefs in general and when you apply for service with churches, mission boards, and other Christian organizations. Any who seek ordination to Christian ministry will need a comprehensive doctrinal statement that covers the broad scope of theology.

PART TWO

THE LIVING GOD

CHAPTER 5

GOD: AN ACTIVE, PERSONAL SPIRIT

God: An Active, Personal Spirit

THE PROBLEM: HOW SHALL WE VIEW THE REALITY OF GOD ONTOLOGICALLY?

Having shown that God has revealed himself to all persons via general revelation and to specific persons via special revelation preserved in inspired Scripture, we explore in this chapter what God has disclosed about his own person and character. Kant's critical philosophy maintained that the being of God, as a suprasensible reality is beyond the reach of theoretical knowledge. Having forfeited intellectual knowledge of God, Kant claimed that God, or the purposive Mind, is a postulate of the moral life. Beyond this, the moral Ruler and Lawgiver is inscrutable to persons bound to the phenomenal world. Living in the shadow of Kant, can we claim to know anything about God as he is in himself? Furthermore, given the modern aversion to metaphysics, can we represent God as a being (i.e., "One who is" as opposed to becoming or change) who dwells beyond the world? Does Scripture speak of God in essentialist categories, and if so, how valid are such representations? Can the Greek conception of God as the absolute, timeless being be reconciled with the popular Christian notion of God as Savior, Father, and Friend? Moreover, in an age when ultimate reality is viewed in terms of impersonal principles or pulses of energy, can Christians continue to maintain that God is properly a personal being? If such is the case, as evangelical Christians claim, how do the special qualities of maleness and femaleness apply to God?

Given the biblical claim of the unity and indivisibility of God, how shall we understand the relationship between God's being and his attributes? In this regard the proposals of realists, nominalists, and others will be examined. The present chapter searches for a meaningful and fresh way of arranging the perfections of God as presented in Scripture. In addition, we will inquire into the meaning and relevance of the statement that metaphysically God is self-existent, eternal, unchanging, and omniscient.

When considering the being and character of God, certain crucial problems need to be addressed. Is God an impassible being, as some classical authorities maintained, or does God possess authentic emotions in relation to the creature? Does God feel with persons when they grieve, sorrow, or hurt?

Moreover, how can God's immutability be reconciled with events in Scripture in which God appears to alter his dealings with persons, as for example, when he replaces blessing with cursing and vice versa?

ALTERNATIVE PROPOSALS IN THE CHURCH

The following represent the principal interpretations advanced by Christendom concerning the being of God and his metaphysical perfections.

Scholastic Thomism

Aquinas and later Thomists, having wedded Aristotelian philosophy to Christian truth, defined God as first unmoved mover, first efficient cause, and absolutely necessary being. By definition altogether immutable and thus lacking beginning and end, God is an eternal being in the sense that his reality is the permanent now. As both eternal and necessary being, God is "pure act (*actus purus*) without any potentiality."[1] It follows that as absolute being God is simple and not composite: "God is His essence, quiddity, or nature."[2] Thomas insists that nothing can be added to God's essence in an accidental way. And because he is simple being, he has both intelligence and a will. Hence God is a living person who contains within himself all the perfections of being. Furthermore, Thomas's immutable God never experiences passions of sorrow, pain, or fear, for God as an incorporeal being has no sensitive appetites. Nevertheless, Thomas's God knows the joy and delight that is rooted in His own nature. Yahweh ("he who is"), the special name of God, "denominates the infinite ocean of substance"[3] and represents God in his divine immutability and eternity. As the soul indwells every part of the body, so God is everywhere in the threefold sense of his presence, his power, and his substance. God's ubiquity as Spirit does not exclude the co-presence of other entities.

Hegelian Idealism

Hegel viewed God, the Absolute Spirit, as that immanent reality in the world process that continually unfolds itself through opposing forces in history. The German idealist brought together epistemology and ontology to arrive at a "developmental pantheism." For Hegel, truth (i.e., the Absolute) is the whole, which essentially reaches its completeness through the process of its own development, called Spirit (*Geist*). God, then, is Absolute Spirit, which, like the bud◆blossom◆fruit sequence, is a living process of negation and mediation. The Absolute is neither above nor with the universe; it is the eternal totality. Ultimate reality is becoming (Being◆Nothing◆Becoming), hence the Absolute Spirit unfolds itself developmentally through the process of conflicting and contradictory forces in history. God is neither independent nor self-existent, but a total process of self-expression in and through the finite. Although God is "living," he is not personal, for this would limit the Absolute to a particular mode of being. In short, God is impersonal historical oneness, of which the whole process of reality is a teleological movement toward the realization of Absolute Spirit.

Influenced by Hegel, Schleiermacher developed a pantheistic idealism that envisages God as the personification of the "Spirit of the universe." The Absolute, who is never an object of rational thought, nevertheless is a postulate of the creature's sense of dependence. The divine attributes, which place objective reality in God, give expression to the various dimensions of the Christian self-consciousness or feeling of absolute dependence. Following Hegel, Schleiermacher denied immutability in favor of a God who is eternally becoming.

Protestant Liberalism

The older liberalism rejected traditional metaphysical theology as an alien Greek construct and denied that God is a remote, self-sufficient, and unfeeling being. Walter Rauschenbusch affirmed that there are only two concepts of God: the despotic and the democratic. The former view, espoused by classical and Reformation theology, was stimulated by the totalitarian state. It holds that God is sufficient unto himself, remote, and insulated from human suffering. Rauschenbusch insisted that modern theology must democratize its concept of God by viewing him as a Father who feels and suffers with humankind. Given Rauschenbusch's concept of God as the infinite spirit that undergirds the movement for social progress (cf. Hegel), some authorities accuse him of pantheism.

W. A. Brown, who taught at Union Theological Seminary in New York, likewise rejected the classical approach which he perceived begins with abstract notions of God's absoluteness from which are derived such metaphysical qualities as aseity, eternity, and immutability. The liberal theologian began rather with the personality and character of God as loving Father displayed humanwise in Jesus. The attributes are descriptive of God not as he is in himself, but of the Father's relationship with his people. They are a peculiar construct of the Christian thought of God in the mind. God's absoluteness, for example, signifies that "the holy and loving personality whom Christ has revealed is really master of the universe."[4] His omnipresence means that one cannot drift away from God's love and care.

Barthian Neoorthodoxy

Karl Barth followed Kierkegaard in stressing the infinite qualitative difference between God and human beings. The eternal, ineffable "Wholly Other" reveals himself through the Word as a living, personal God who loves in freedom.

Contrary to the immanent God of liberal theology, Barth emphasized the irrevocable otherness of the God of the Bible. Since God and humans are metaphysical opposites, the invisible and ineffable God is known only by his gracious self-revelation in Christ. Barth's conviction that the sovereign God is known only on the basis of his free decision to engage man is reflected in such statements as, "God's being is absolutely His act"[5] and "the operation of God is the essence of God."[6] Revelation indicates that the living, personal, spiritual God is the eternal being who loves in freedom. Barth divides the divine attributes (God *is* his perfections) into two categories: (1) perfections of the divine loving, and (2) perfections of the divine freedom. In the latter category Barth places God's ubiquity, constancy, and eternity. The first of these signifies not God's inactive extension through the universe, but his sovereign dominion over all space. He is everywhere present as Lord, i.e, generally in creation, especially in revelation and reconciliation, and preeminently in Jesus Christ. Constancy signifies not that God is immobile, but that he is true to himself or self-consistent. God is not moved by impulses external to himself; rather his affections of sympathy, compassion, and anger are self-generated from within his innermost being. Finally, eternity connotes that God is "the One who is and rules before time, in time, and again after time, the One who is not conditioned by time, but conditions it absolutely in His freedom."[7]

Protestant and Roman Catholic
Neoliberalism

Recent Protestant and Roman Catholic liberals redefine theism along existentialist lines. God is not a supreme being who dwells in some heavenly realm independent of the world. Above the limiting categories of being and personality, God is said to be the ground and power of being or the infinite horizon of human existence. The relation between God and the world is viewed in terms of the panentheistic model: the reality of God includes within itself the world, but is not exhausted by it.

From an idealistic and anthropological perspective, Tillich transforms the idea of God by upholding "the God above the God of theism."[8] God is not a being alongside of or above other beings, for as such he would be a creature of time and space. Rather God is being-itself (*ipsum esse*) or the creative ground and power of being. More simply put, God represents the depths of one's life or one's ultimate concern— what one takes seriously without any reservation.[9] Thus, according to Tillich, "God does not exist. He is being-itself beyond essence and existence."[10] Indeed, "It is as atheistic to affirm the existence of God as it is to deny it."[11] Tillich claims that the Ultimate or the Unconditioned is not *a person*, but *personal*, where the latter is defined as "the concreteness of man's ultimate concern."[12] To the foregoing *absolute* characteristics are added several *symbolic* descriptions of the Mystery of being: God is living in that he is the ground of life, eternal in that he conquers the nonbeing of temporality, and omnipresent in that by creative participation in the existence of his creatures insecurity and anxiety are overcome.

John Macquarrie likewise opposes the classical theistic model in favor of an existentialist approach along the lines proposed by Heidegger. Thus God, the most ultimate reality, is not a being (*ens*) beyond the world, but the dynamic "act of being (*esse*)."[13] Thus "Being always includes becoming, and . . . the essence of Being is the dynamic act of letting-be."[14] Macquarrie's "organic" model by his own admission is panentheistic: God is related to the world as form is to matter. Macquarrie's God is hardly self-sufficient, for the organic model involves a reciprocity in which God and the world are dependent upon each other. With his emphasis on becoming, Macquarrie joins other authorities in rejecting the divine impassibility. Rather than being immutable, God is said to be "consistent," or preferably, "faithful."

Much of recent Roman Catholic thought, persuaded that classical theology adopted an alien hellenistic cultural form, likewise doubts that God is properly a supreme being. If God is not a *res* (thing), if God has no essence (a scholastic category), then it can be argued that God does not exist. Are Christians then atheists? No, some avant-garde Catholics respond, for Christians do experience the presence of a reality *beyond* being. Given this development, doubts are raised about God's personality, as customarily defined. Thus Hellwig acknowledges that not a few recent Catholic writers view God as "beyond personality."[15] Moreover, with the traditional distinction between the natural and the supernatural being seriously questioned, Catholic "progressives" tend to view the relation between God and the world in terms of the panentheistic model.

Retreating from the idea of a supreme being or transcendent Deity who exists independently of the world, Hans Küng adopts the panentheistic perspective of "God in this world and this world in God."[16] Thus God "is certainly not an infinite, still less a finite, *alongside* or *above* finite things. He is the infinite *in* all that is finite, being itself in all that is."[17] Küng wants to retain the values of a personal God and so asserts that "he is a God with a human face."[18] Yet Küng insists that the primal reason, support, and meaning of all reality is not a discrete person alongside other persons. Since God is not a being, "It is better . . . to describe him not as personal or impersonal, but as transpersonal, superpersonal."[19] The attributes of God, moreover, describe God not intrinsically or independently, but in terms of his relationship to persons and the world.

Leslie Dewart, in *The Future of Belief*, which bears the subtitle *Theism in a World Come of Age*, insists that traditional notions of God's personality, eternity, immutability, and impassibility entered Christian theology by a process of hellenization. If theism is to prove relevant to the modern world, a dehellenization of the doctrine of God must occur. Dewart believes that personality no longer should be predicted of God. "God is, rather than a center of being to which we are drawn, an expansive *force* [italics added] which impels persons to go out from and beyond themselves."[20] In fact, Dewart completely radicalizes the doctrine of God by suggesting that the supernatural is not essential to Christian faith.

> I suggest that in the future we may not feel the need to conceive God as a supernatural being. If we discard the hellenic view of nature, the Christian God no longer must, in order to remain free, be graciously and freely self-giving, perform supernatural feats, undertake supernatural functions and roles, or enjoy supernatural status.[21]

Process Theology

The process theism of Whitehead, Hartshorne, and their followers firmly rejects the God of classical theism, which it describes as an Oriental despot, a static sovereign, and an unrelational idol. The proponents of neoclassical theism view the essence of reality as becoming, not being, i.e., as a series of nonsensory experiences or energy events. Hence all reality (including God) is processive, relational, and pragmatic. Thus God cannot be objectified as an existent or a substantial self. Rather, God is a moving pattern of events, or as Cobb puts it, "an occurrence of thinking, willing, feeling, and loving."[22] More specifically, process theology confounds the divine simplicity by positioning a metaphysical dualism wherein God is said to be bipolar. God's abstract or potential nature—eternal, absolute, unconscious, and unchanging—is said to provide the initial aim or intentional purpose for every actual occasion. On the other hand, God's concrete or actual nature—temporal, dependent, relative, and constantly changing—is the composite nature that prehends all actual occasions and assimilates them into its own reality. But since process thinkers plead that to be real is to be actual ("process is reality"), the primordial pole of God is a pure abstraction, a philosophical construct that possesses no reality whatever. With the collapse of the abstract pole God is shorn of most of the perfections traditionally ascribed to God. Thus the Deity is not a person, for personality is said to limit God.[23] Neither is God self-sufficient, for his consequent nature is dependent on the world for its actuality. And God is certainly not changeless, for Yahweh ("I will be what I will be") continually surpasses himself through the myriad experiences of creative becoming. God is omnipresent in the radical sense that all things are taken into or occur within the divine reality. Process theology, in short, postulates an impersonal "God" who is the creative movement in nature.

Protestant Orthodoxy

Most Fathers, Reformers, and Evangelicals view God as an uncreated, noncontingent, living, and active spirit who, on the basis of propositional revelation, can be partially yet truthfully represented in analogical language. This God is invisible, timeless, everywhere present, and impassible in the sense that he is not moved by external forces contrary to his will.

In the midst of pagan polytheism, the early Fathers depicted God as the one uncreated, invisible, immortal, imperishable, and immutable Being. In spite of the Hellenistic language of many early church authorities (e.g., God as unbegotten, absolute Being—*ho ōn*), they consistently viewed God as related to his creation. So Theophilus describes God as constantly "running, moving, active, nourishing, governing, and making things alive."[24]

Clement of Alexandria, influenced by the Platonic idea of the Absolute, affirms that Deity is incomprehensible to the human mind: "God is invisible and beyond expression by words."[25] Unable to say what God *is*, the creature can only assert what God *is not*: i.e., he is unbegotten, invisible, immutable, and imperishable. God even transcends the abstract conceptions the mind frames of him: the One, Good, Mind, Absolute Being, Lord. Although Clement's God is ontologically remote, he nevertheless is relationally near in his power, providence, and love.

Ontological considerations took on fresh importance during the period of the christological and trinitarian controversies. From the revealed name Yahweh (Exod. 3:14), Athanasius conceived of God as the One, the incomprehensible being (*akatalēptos ousia*) or essence. "When it is said, 'I am that I am,' ..., we understand nothing else than the very simple, and blessed, and incomprehensible essence itself of Him that is."[26] The famous formula of Athanasius—three persons (*hypostaseis*) in one essence (*ousia*)—communicates in Greek philosophical language the conviction that in his most intrinsic being God "is a concrete reality, not a fiction or abstraction."[27]

Augustine insisted that the inexhaustible and ineffable God cannot be fully grasped by human thought and language. The name Yahweh offers the most fundamental representation of what God is in himself—the only real being or substance. Borrowing elements from Neoplatonism, Augustine claimed that God is simple and therefore cannot be differentiated from his attributes. Hence, "in God to be is the same as to be strong, or to be just, or to be wise, or whatever is said of that simple multiplicity or multifold simplicity."[28] Whereas other entities admit of accidents and therefore are subject to change, Yahweh—"I am he who never changes"—is the only immutable essence. Not only God's nature but also his knowing, willing, and decreeing undergo no mutability. Moreover, according to Augustine, in God there can be no suffering. "Be it far from us to surmise that the impassible nature of God is liable to any molestation."[29]

As the real and unchanging being, God is also eternal. Augustine conceives of eternity not so much as endless time (time being a created entity), but as that higher level of existence free of change where there exists no sequence of yesterday, today, and tomorrow. While denying that God is diffused through space as air or light, Augustine affirms that God is wholly everywhere and is contained in no place. "He is not distributed through space by size so that half of Him should be in half of the world and half in the other half of it. He is wholly present in all of it in such wise as to be wholly in heaven alone and wholly in earth alone, and wholly in heaven and earth together; not confined in any place, but wholly in Himself everywhere."[30] Although he used Greek categories of thought, from start to finish Augustine regarded God not as the abstract Absolute, but as a living and active divine person. Thus God is "always working, . . . sustaining, pervading, and protecting; creating, nourishing, and developing; seeking and yet possessing all things."[31]

Melanchthon, the first systematic theologian of the Reformation, viewed God as a unified, uncreated spiritual being who is eternal, incorruptible, and independent. Being (Germ. *Wesen*, Gk. *ousia*) for Melanchthon "means something that definitely exists in and of itself, and is not dependent on some other foundation, as a contingent thing is."[32] Moreover, God's attributes of power, wisdom, righteousness, etc., are one with his essence. "Divine being is divine power, wisdom and righteousness, and these virtues are not to be separated from the Being."[33]

John Calvin was acutely conscious of the glory and majesty of God: "God is incomprehensible, a Spirit above all spirit, light above all light."[34] The name Yahweh denotes the "incomprehensible essence"[35] of the God who is invisible both to the naked eye and to the human mind. On the basis of revelation God is spoken humanwise as a living and active Spirit. Far from the first cause or unmoved mover of scholastic theology, Calvin upheld a God of "a watchful, effective, active sort, engaged in ceaseless activity."[36] The self-existent God is eternal, and because eternal he is unchanging both in his essence and in his purposes. Scriptures that speak of God as repenting or changing his mind pertain not to God as he is in himself, but to our finite understanding of him. God "cannot be touched with repentance, and his heart cannot undergo change. To imagine such a thing would be impiety."[37] A familiar refrain

in Calvin is that the eternal God remains ever like himself.

The Reformed confessions articulate a full-orbed vision of God. The Second Helvetic Confession (1566) declares: "God is one in essence or nature, subsisting by Himself, all-sufficient in Himself, invisible, without a body, infinite, eternal" (ch. III). The Westminster Shorter Catechism (1647) contemplates God as "infinite, eternal, and unchangeable" in his being and perfections. According to the Westminster Confession of Faith (1647), "There is but one only living and true God, who is infinite in being and perfection, a most pure spirit, without body, parts, or passions, immutable, immense, eternal, incomprehensible. . ." (ch. II.1).

Stephen Charnock in his classic book, *The Existence and Attributes of God*, regards God, the first and independent being, as "a pure act, nothing but vigor and act."[38] The proper name Yahweh signifies both his eternity ("I am") and his unchangeableness ("that I am"). The former denotes the duration of the divine essence without beginning, without end, and without succession. The latter signifies that God's essence, perfections, purposes, and promises endure eternally without any variation. The biblical assertions of repentance and passion involve no changes in God himself. Repentance connotes a change in God's external relations, whereas passions of anger, grief, and joy are anthropopathisms adapted to human minds.

W. G. T. Shedd affirms that the fundamental aspects of God are substantiality (essence or substance) and personality (self-conscious being). Because God is both substance and a person, he can possess and exert attributes. Like Hodge, Shedd insists that the attributes are objectively real qualities in God. God is not essence and attributes, but essence in attributes. "The whole essence is in each attribute, and the attribute in the essence."[39] Shedd insists that God is "without passions" in the sense that he is not passively wrought upon by finite entities external to himself. Although independent of the creation and thus impassive, God nevertheless has feelings and emotions. Literally attributes to the Divine are love (*agapē*) and wrath (*orge*). And as the soul is present in every part of the body, so the whole essence of God is present at every point of space as a simple and undivided unity.

Other evangelical discussion of the being of God and the metaphysical attributes include Ronald Nash,[40] Millard J. Erickson,[41] and Carl F. H. Henry.[42]

Protestant Liberalism

BIBLICAL TEACHING

In order to determine which hypothesis is preferred we now turn to the teachings of Scripture, which constitute our primary authority.

Pentateuch

In the opening chapters of the Old Testament, God made himself known through word and deed as a living and active personal Spirit. With the concreteness that characterizes the Hebrew mind the Pentateuch depicts God as the sovereign personal agent who creates man from the dust of the earth and breathes into his nostrils the breath of life (Gen. 1:27; 2:7). Subsequently God planted a garden in Eden, placed Adam and Eve in it to work it, and entered into personal relations with the first couple. The same God disclosed himself to Noah and caused a flood to cover the earth, thereby destroying those who had violated his holy laws. No passive unrelated being, God entered into personal covenant relations with Abraham, Isaac, and Jacob.

When Israel languished in Egypt, God came to Moses at the burning bush (Exod. 3:1–6). The flame of fire in which the angel of the Lord appeared symbolizes the glory and majesty of the invisible God, whereas the fact that the bush was not consumed suggests that God is self-sustaining or life itself. When God disclosed his plan to bring Israel out of Egypt, Moses asked the name of the One who was behind so bold a venture. God's response to Moses was the profound statement "I AM WHO I AM" (*'ehyeh 'ašer 'ehyeh*, Exod. 3:14). Moreover, Moses was to tell the people, "I AM [*'ehyeh*] has sent me to you." The imperfect tense of the verb "to be" or "to exist" denotes that he ever continues to be Yahweh. The Hebrew expression provides no basis for a projection into the future in the sense of "I shall be what I shall be." The self-designation connotes that the God of Israel is the living, awe-inspiring one who is always active in every experience of his people. "I AM" or Yahweh (LXX, *ho ōn*) thus implies (1) that the faithful God is self-existent, in the sense that he possesses his very nature; (2) that he is eternal ("This is my name for ever," 3:15); and (3) that he is unchanging in his person and purposes.[43]

That God is a living and active Deity is seen in the series of nine plagues that released Israel from Egyptian bondage (Exod. 7–10) and in the miraculous passage through the Sea of Reeds (Exod. 14). On the latter occasion Moses told Israel, "The LORD will fight for you" (Exod. 14:14). God's approach to Moses in a dense cloud (Exod. 19:9) at Sinai symbolizes his invisibility and glory. The accompanying fire and smoke (Exod. 19:18) signifies his spirituality; and the thunder, lightning, and earthquake (19:16, 18) signifies his awesome majesty and power (cf. Exod.

24:15–17; Deut. 5:24). The second commandment, which prohibits the making of corporeal representations of God (Exod. 20:4; cf. 34:17), attests the fact that God is an invisible spirit being. Moses later reminded the people, "You saw no form [*t*ᵉ*mûnāh*] of any kind the day the LORD spoke to you at Horeb out of the fire" (Deut. 4:15). God's "Presence" (e.g., his glorious person, *pānîm*) would accompany Israel (Exod. 33:14–16); but as God said to Moses, "You cannot see my face (*pānîm*), for no one may see me and live" (Exod. 33:20).

The Pentateuchal theophanies—e.g., the angel who dialogued with Hagar (Gen. 16:7–13) and the three men who conversed with Abraham (18:1–5)—were shown in chapter 3 to be visible representations of God. These temporary manifestations of Deity in forms accessible to the senses no more vitiate the spirit-nature of God than did the later incarnation of Christ. Anthropomorphisms, which figuratively ascribe to God human features such as a face, hands, back (Exod. 33:23), arm (6:6), and finger (Deut. 9:10); humanlike sentiments of grief (Gen. 6:6), anger (Exod. 15:7), hatred (Deut. 12:31), jealousy (Exod. 20:5), and vengeance (Deut. 32:35); and humanlike actions such as knowing (Gen. 18:21), purposing (50:20), choosing (Deut. 7:6–7), performing (Gen. 21:1), and disciplining (Deut. 8:5) confirm that God is not an impersonal force but a personal being endowed with intellect, emotions, and the power of self-determination. Moses justifiably represented God as "the living One" (*ḥay*, Gen. 16:14) and the living God (*ᵉlōhîm ḥayyîm*, Deut. 5:26)—a judgment that God himself confirmed (Num. 14:21, 28).

In Oriental cultures a person's name is richly descriptive of his character and significance. Hence, the biblical names of God, no less than the acts of God, are revelatory instruments that disclose who God is. To know God's name is to know God himself (Exod. 3:13–15; cf. Isa. 52:6). The most common name of God, *ᵉlōhîm*, occurs more than two thousand times in the Hebrew Bible. A designation for the gods of the Semitic peoples, *ᵉlōhîm* likely was derived from the root meaning "to reverence," or "to fear." Thus, in meaning and context *ᵉlōhîm* connotes "the Mighty One or "he that is to be feared." Since *ᵉlōhîm* overwhelmingly governs pronouns and verbs in the singular, its plural form should be viewed as a plural of intensity or majesty.[44]

Yahweh, the self-existent, eternal, and unchanging "I AM," is the God of grace who enters into covenant relations with his chosen people (Deut. 5:2). The glorious incommunicable name that the Jews superstitiously refused to pronounce (cf. Lev. 24:16) is descriptive of none but the God of Israel. Since the name Yahweh occurs some 150 times in Genesis, one meets with initial surprise Yahweh's saying to Moses (Exod. 6:3): "I appeared to Abraham, to Isaac and to Jacob as God Almighty [*ēl šadday*], but by my name the LORD (Yahweh) I did not make myself known to them." No contradiction in the pentateuchal traditions need be posited. Rather Exodus 6:3 affirms that whereas God formerly had been addressed as Yahweh, only at Sinai was the full import of that "glorious name" (Deut. 28:58) made known.

In addition to his names, God's character is known by the ascription to him of specific attributes. The opening statement of the Bible, "In the beginning God . . ." (Gen. 1:1), suggests an existence that is absolute and not contingent on any other being or power. God's self-existence or aseity is also affirmed in the revelation of the divine name at Sinai (Exod. 3:14). Yahweh thus is upheld as the One who has life in himself, the One who most fundamentally *is*.

The eternity of God is amply affirmed in the five books of the Law. Abraham "called upon the name of the LORD, the Eternal God" (Gen. 21:33). Moreover, implicit in the "I AM" of Exodus 3:14 is the postulate of the divine eternity. In addition, both Moses and Yahweh testify that the Lord will live and reign forever (Exod. 15:18; Deut. 32:40), a fact that is a source of hope and comfort for the godly (Deut. 33:27). The divine eternality suggests (1) that God's existence had no beginning and will have no end, (2) that God transcends the limitations of time ("I AM"), and (3) that God is the cause and ground of time (cf. John 1:3).

A consequent of the divine aseity and eternity is God's immutability. "I AM WHO I AM" (Exod. 3:14) dwells above the flux of the contingent universe. Similarly the oracle of Balaam reads: "God is not a man, that he should lie, nor a son of man, that he should change his mind [nāham]. Does he speak and then not act? Does he promise [dābar] and not fulfill?" (Num. 23:19). Moreover, the God who is unchanging in his being, character, and counsel is given the title of "Rock" (Deut. 32:4, 15, 18, et al.). As the solid material of which mountains are formed, Rock (ṣûr) points up the stability, unchangeableness, and reliability of Israel's God. The fact that in Noah's day God was grieved (Niphal of nāham, "be sorry," "mourn over") and purposed to destroy sinners from the face of the earth (Gen. 6:6), does not invalidate the divine immutability. Neither did his decision to stay his hand of judgment following the golden-calf incident (Exod. 32:12–14) and to withhold his judgment of fire against the murmuring Israelites (Num. 11:1, 10) effect any change in God's being, character, or strategic purpose. Rather, God consistently dealt with people on the basis of his changeless character and their moral responses, and these dealings he had

omnisciently included in his overall plan. That God experienced authentic emotions of regret (Gen. 6:6), anger (Num. 11:10), hatred (Deut. 12:31), jealousy (Exod. 20:4–5), and vengeance (Deut. 32:35) demonstrates that the personal God enjoys a healthy and controlled emotional life. Not moved by forces external to himself, God remains himself in the fullness of his own nature.

Historical Books

God is depicted in the documents chronicling Israel's history as a living, active, and personal God. So Joshua describes the One who led Israel to the Promised Land as "the living God ['ēl ḥay] among you" (Josh. 3:10; cf. 1 Sam. 17:26, 36). The historical books depict a God of consummate intelligence and purpose who performs mighty works on behalf of his people. Thus Yahweh's parting of the waters of the Jordan (Josh. 3:14–17) and his toppling of the walls of Jericho (Josh. 6:1–27) further establish him as a living and active God. Similarly Elijah's triumph by the power of the Lord over the 450 prophets of Baal on Mount Carmel evoked this response from the assembled throng: "The LORD—he is God! The LORD—he is God!" (1 Kings 18:39). Numerous other works were wrought in Israel's history by the personal, living God, such as Elijah's rapture in a whirlwind and the rout of the Syrian army that had besieged Samaria. The fall and resettlement of Jerusalem illustrates the working of the living God. The Lord sent numerous messengers to warn his people of their wicked ways. But when the inhabitants of Jerusalem scoffed at the warnings, the Lord "brought up against them the king of the Babylonians . . . and handed all of them over to Nebuchadnezzar" (2 Chron. 36:17). After the people had been held captive for seventy years, "the LORD moved the heart of Cyrus king of Persia" to free the Jewish exiles and permit them to rebuild the temple in Jerusalem (Ezra 1:1–4).

The historical literature also affirms the immutability of Israel's God: "He who is the Glory of Israel does not lie or change his mind; for he is not a man, that he should change his mind" (1 Sam. 15:29). Also the unique title for God, "the Glory of Israel" (nēṣaḥ yiśrā'ēl, where nēṣaḥ connotes endurance or constancy), admirably attests that God's character and will are unalterable. Nevertheless, in the face of Saul's deliberate disobedience, not only was God grieved (the Niphal of nāḥam) that he had made Saul king (vv. 11, 35), but he also rejected Saul as king of Israel (v. 23). Far from altering his eternal counsel, God in wisdom adapted his immediate response to the then-existing situation. Changes in God's emotional attitudes and tactical responses, consistent with his overall immutability, are also evident in Judges 2:18–23; 2 Samuel 24:16; 2 Chronicles 12:12; 30:8–10.

The first explicit mention of omnipresence—that the totality of God is present everywhere in the universe—occurs in 1 Kings 8:27 (cf. 2 Chron. 2:6), where Solomon acknowledged in prayer, "The heavens, even the highest heaven, cannot contain you. How much less this temple I have built!" The infinite God cannot be confined to an earthly building, for his Spirit-being pervades, indeed transcends, the entire created order.

Poetry and Wisdom

Job contemplates God as an incorporeal spirit being: "When he passes me, I cannot see him; when he goes by, I cannot perceive him" (Job 9:11). Since God is invisible, Job adds, "If I go to the east, he is not there; if I go to the west, I do not find him" (23:8). The

invisible God, however, is no mere cosmic force or energy, but a conscious personal agent. The Hebrew plural noun pānîm (rendered in the AV by "face," "presence," and "countenance") is symbolic of the person and his attitudes, sentiments, moods, and actions.[45] Accordingly, God causes his face to shine on the saints (Pss. 4:6; 31:16), and sets his face against evildoers (34:16). Believers seek his face (27:8; 105:4) and will dwell in his presence (140:13), whereas God-haters flee from his face (68:2).

That God is properly personal is seen in the fact that he possesses intelligence, emotions, and a will. Job (12:13) teaches that God possesses wisdom (ḥokmāh), counsel ('ēṣāh), and understanding (tᵉbûnāh). God's counsel is formulated, not arbitrarily, but according to a consistent, intelligent plan (Job 38:2). God also possesses the full range of emotions attributed to personality: compassion (Pss. 103:13; 111:4), jealousy (Ps. 78:58), anger (Job 9:13; 19:11), and wrath (Job 21:20). Finally, God possesses a will, or the power of personal choice. He devised an eternal counsel (Ps. 33:11) that cannot be thwarted (Job 42:1) and chose a people for himself (Ps. 135:4).

That God is the "living God" ('ēl ḥay, Ps. 84:2) actively engaged in the affairs of his people is plainly seen in several psalms that survey the history of Israel (Pss. 78, 105, 106, 136). Together these psalms form a mosaic of the mighty deeds of the living God on behalf of his people, including the creation, the making of covenants with the patriarchs, the plagues in Egypt, deliverance through the Sea of Reeds, divine guidance in the wilderness and the conquest of Canaan.

Several names of God are found in the poetic and wisdom literature. Apparently derived from a root meaning to be strong, 'ēl connotes the God of power, greatness, and awe. Uncompounded in Job (5:8; 8:3; 9:2, et al.), '*ēl* is frequently linked with other epithets in the Psalms: "God of glory" (Ps. 29:3), "God of truth" (31:5), "the God of heaven" (136:26), et al. The name '*ēlôah*, which occurs forty-one times in Job (3:4; 4:9; 5:17, et al.), denotes the God of power and comfort. Derived from the verb '*ālāh* ("to go up"), '*elyôn* depicts God as majestic, exalted, and all-powerful. The name also appears in the compounds "God Most High" ('*ēl* '*elyôn*, Ps. 78:35; '*ĕlōhîm* '*elyôn*, Pss. 57:2; 78:56), and "LORD Most High" (*Yahweh* '*elyôn*, Ps. 47:2). The title ('*ēl šadday*) occurs forty-eight times in the Old Testament. God revealed himself to the patriarchs by this compound name (cf. Exod. 6:3), but as *šadday* alone he is known thirty-one times in Job (5:17; 6:4, 14, et al.). The name probably comes from the Akkadian word for mountain, and thus connotes the omnipotent, invincible God, who is the source of all comfort. A shortened form of Yahweh, namely, *yāh*, occurs most frequently (thirty-nine times) in the Psalms (77:11; 89:8; 94:7, et al.).

Although the hymnbook of Israel is chiefly practical, Psalm 36:9 asserts the self-existence of the Lord: "With you is the fountain of life (*mᵉqôr ḥayyîm*)." Like a spring that brings forth a constant supply of water, God is the unfailing source of life. "All life flows forth from Him, who is the absolutely existing and happy One."[46] Moreover, eternity, in the sense of infinite continuation of existence, is affirmed of God in Job 36:26 ("The number of his years is past finding out") and in Psalm 90:2 ("From everlasting to everlasting you are God"). Psalm 139:7–12 uses dramatic imagery to affirm the divine ubiquity. If one should ascend to the highest heaven, descend to the lowest depths, or fly from East to West with the speed of light, escape from God's personal presence and care is impossible, for he is everywhere.

Prophetic Literature

When Isaiah repaired to the temple to ponder the fate of Judah he experienced a life-transforming vision of the glory of God (Isa. 6:1–5). Isaiah saw with spiritual eyes the Lord seated on a throne, high and exalted, the train of his robe filling the temple. Accompanying phenomena such as the foundations that shook and the smoke that filled the temple (v. 4) recall the revelation of the majestic God at Sinai. Likewise Ezekiel's call to ministry was preceded by an equally magnificent vision of the glory of God (Ezek. 1:1–28). In the midst of a violent thunderstorm the prophet beheld a fiery chariot formed by four living creatures, and above the chariot he saw a throne of sapphire occupied by the figure of a man glowing with fire and surrounded by brilliant light. Prostrated by the awesomeness of the vision, Ezekiel concluded, "This was the appearance of the likeness of the glory of the LORD" (1:28). That God is a personal spirit is seen in Isaiah's ascription to him (Isa. 11:2) of intelligence, specifically "wisdom" (*ḥokmāh*, discernment), "understanding" (*bînāh*, intelligence), "counsel" ('*ēṣāh*, the ability to plot a strategy), and "knowledge" (*da'at*, insight). So also Isaiah 40:14, 28 and Jeremiah 51:15. In the prophetic literature, God possesses a full range of emotions, including pity (Jer. 16:5; Ezek. 5:11), grief (Isa. 63:10; Jer. 42:10), jealousy (Nah. 1:2; Zech. 1:14), and anger (Isa. 5:25; Jer. 7:20). Isaiah 54:7–8 brings together the profound emotions of burning "anger" (*qeṣep*), "deep compassion" (*raḥᵃmîm*), and "kindness" (*ḥesed*). That God possesses conscious purpose or a will is seen in the fact that he formulates rational intentions (*maḥᵃšābôt*, Isa. 55:8—"My thoughts are not your thoughts"), and purposes (*'ēṣôt*, Isa. 46:10—"My purpose will stand, and I will do all that I please."

A common title for God in the prophets is "LORD," which signifies God's sovereign authority, dominion, and rule over persons and nations. The singular noun with the article, *hā-'ādôn*, is applied to God in such texts as Isaiah 1:24; 3:1; Micah 4:13; Malachi 3:1. The plural form (a plural of majesty similar to *'elōhîm*) with the first person singular suffix, *'adōnāy*, occurs more than three hundred times in the Old Testament and always with respect to God. It is most frequent in the prophetic writings (e.g., Isa. 3:17; Jer. 50:31; Amos 1:8). Very common is the combined name *'adōnāy-Yahweh*, rendered "LORD God" (AV) or "Sovereign LORD" (NIV), e.g., in Isaiah 7:7; Ezekiel 2:4; 4:14; Amos 1:8. The title *Yahweh ṣebā'ôt*, rendered "LORD of Hosts" (AV) or "LORD Almighty" (NIV), occurs nearly three hundred times in the Old Testament, frequently in the prophets (e.g., Isa. 1:9; Jer. 6:6; Mic. 4:4; Zech. 1:3). The title "the Holy One of Israel" (*qedôš yiśra'ēl*) signifies God's absolute moral perfection and separation from evil. It is most common in the prophets, especially in Isaiah (1:4; 5:19; 17:7, et al.). The title "Father" (*'āb*) is used sparingly in the Old Testament. It denotes God as creator (Mal. 2:10), founder of the nation Israel (Isa. 63:16; 64:8), and the One who entered into a saving, covenantal relationship with his people (Jer. 3:19; 31:9).

Although God appears to change his tactical responses to specific situations (Jer. 18:8, 10; 26:3, 13, 19; Jonah 3:9–10), he remains steadfastly immutable in his purposes (Isa. 14:24; 46:10), word (Isa. 31:2), character (Isa. 54:10), and very being (Mal. 3:6—"I the LORD do not change"). Amos affirms that sinful Israel cannot escape God's judgment, for there is no place where he is not (Amos 9:1–4). Whether his people climb to the heavens or seek refuge in a deep pit, hide in Carmel's caves or sink to the bottom of the sea, God is wholly present to execute punishment (cf. Jer. 23:23–24).

Synoptic Gospels

The synoptic Gospels, like the rest of the New Testament, depict God as a God of exceeding glory. The Greek word *doxa*, analogous to the Hebrew *kābôd*, connotes the plenitude of God's perfections or the luminous manifestation of his person. It signifies those fundamental qualities of majesty, splendor, and grandeur that radiate from the sovereign universe.[47] The glory of God is most dramatically portrayed in the Transfiguration event (Matt. 17:1–8). On the mountain Jesus displayed his glorified state as the God-man. Thus Jesus' "face shone like the sun" (Matt. 17:2), where the verb *lampō* signifies to gleam or shine as a bright light. Moreover, according to Mark (9:3), "his clothes became dazzling white" (*stilbonta leuka lian*); the verb *stilbō*, "to gleam," or "glitter," often was used of polished metal surfaces.[48] Or as Luke puts it (9:29), "His clothes became as bright as a flash of lightning" (*leukos exastraptōn*). The narrative closes with the observation that the disciples were enveloped by "a bright cloud" (*nephelē phōteinē*), which is further manifestation of the brilliance or radiance of the glory of God (Matt. 17:5). Whereas the shining of Moses' countenance at Horeb (Exod. 34:29, 35) was a reflected glory, the dazzling whiteness of Jesus' transfiguration represented an effulgence from the source itself, which is none other than the God of glory (cf. 2 Cor. 3:12–18; 2 Peter 1:16–18).

That the God of the synoptic Gospels is a personal, living, and active God is beyond dispute. Luke attests that God hears prayer (1:13), gives gifts to those who ask (11:11–13), supplies the necessities of life (12:14–28), and works justice on behalf of the oppressed (18:7–8). Mary, in her song of praise, gratefully acknowledges God's operations on behalf of his people: "He has performed mighty deeds with his arm" (Luke 1:51); "He has brought down rulers from their thrones" (v. 52); "He has filled the hungry with good things" (v. 53); and "He has helped his servant Israel" (v. 54).

In addition to the common names for God, *theos* and *kyrios*, the synoptic Gospels attest several less common titles of Deity. "The Most High" (*hypsistos*), the correlate of *'elyôn,* affirms the supreme dignity of the God of the Bible over all other gods. Alone (Luke 1:32, 35, 76) or in combination with *theos* (Mark 5:7; Luke 8:28), *hypsistos* was the customary Gentile title for the God of the Jews (cf. Acts 7:48; 16:17). God was addressed in prayer as "Sovereign Lord" (*despotēs*), a title that designates God as owner and ruler of all (Luke 2:29; cf. Acts 4:24; Rev. 6:10). A title that affirms the transcendent power of God is "the Mighty One" (*ho dynatos*), which occurs only in Luke's Gospel (1:49; cf. 22:69).

Primitive Christianity/Acts

Luke the historian and theologian, although primarily concerned with the work of the Holy Spirit, did not neglect the doctrine of God. The active nature of God is attested by his manifold works. God created the world and everything in it (Acts 14:15), sends rain to water the crops (14:17), and supplies food to sustain life (14:17). God made covenants with (3:25) and gave promises to (2:30) the Fathers of old. He raised Jesus from the grave (2:24), poured out the Holy Spirit (2:17), sovereignly calls people to missionary work (16:10), forgives sins (3:19), works miracles through his servants (19:11), and rescues those who serve him (12:11).

God afflicted his adversaries with deadly diseases (12:23), punishes nations (7:11), and one day will bring about the eschatological restoration (3:21). Appropriately, therefore, he is called "the living God" (Acts 14:15).

In the context of the expansion of the apostolic church, Acts focuses on the purposive will of the personal God. Thus Luke writes of "God's set purpose and foreknowledge" (Acts 2:23), "the whole will of God" (20:27), and of David who "served God's purpose in his own generation" (13:36). The Greek word *boulē*, translated "purpose" or "will" in the preceding verses, signifies a counsel that originates from God's deliberate predetermination. Moreover, Paul's companions said in regard to Paul: "The Lord's will be done" (21:14), and Ananias declared, "The God of our fathers has chosen you [Paul] to know his will" (22:14). *Thelēma*, "will," in these verses connotes the plan or design of the all-wise Deity (cf. Eph. 3:1–13).

Preaching to Gentiles at Athens, Paul affirmed God's self-existence or aseity. Since God is a noncontingent, perfect being, he needs no provision the creature may bring to him (Acts 17:25). Moreover, Paul's recitation of a piece of Stoic wisdom—"In him we live and move and have our being" (Acts 17:28)—suggests that whereas humans possess a life that is derived from God, the Lord has life absolutely in himself. He is the source and fount of life itself. When Paul adds that God "is not far from each one of us" (Acts 17:27), he asserts God's presence everywhere in the world (ubiquity), while rejecting the Stoic view that regarded God as identical with the world's order (a kind of pantheism).

Pauline Literature

Paul knew nothing of a static sovereign or a deistical deity; rather, the apostle's God is vitally living and dynamically active (2 Cor. 6:16; 1 Tim. 4:10). God's activity of creation, providence, and redemption is summed up in Paul's observation (1 Thess. 1:9) that the Thessalonians turned from idols to serve "the living and the true God" (*theos zōn kai alēthinos*). The absence of the article before "God" stresses God's nature rather than his person. So understood, his "nature is to be God living and true"[49]—living instead of inert, and true instead of unreal. The apostle reminds us that "in all things God works for the good [*synergei*] of those who love him" (Rom. 8:28). Indeed, "there are different kinds of working (*energēmatōn*), but the same God works all of them in all men" (1 Cor. 12:6).

Significantly, Paul levied no ontological embargo in his speech about God. He affirmed not only God's existential relevance but also his ontological reality. Thus in Romans 1:20 the apostle maintains that general revelation mediates to man a rudimentary knowledge of "God's invisible qualities—his eternal power and divine nature [*theiotēs*]." Moreover, according to Colossians 2:9, "in Christ all the fullness of the Deity [*theotēs*] lives in bodily form." The latter term, *theotēs*, focuses on the perfections or attributes that inhere in the divine being.[50] In Philippians 2:6, Paul does not hesitate to speak of the "very nature [of] God," where *morphē theou* denotes the spiritual and incorporeal form or essence that manifests itself outwardly in the divine glory. The "equality with God" [*isa theō*] that Paul attributes to Christ connotes equality of being or "parity in possession of this form of God."[51]

The most common New Testament title for God is *theos*, which in the Septuagint translates the Hebrew *'elōhîm* and, to a lesser extent, Yahweh. Thus *theos* designates the all-powerful, eternal, and self-originated Deity, who alone is to be feared. The name *kyrios*—which occurs in every New Testament book except Titus and the letters of John, but most frequently in Paul—translates the Hebrew Yahweh (Rom. 4:8; 10:16), *'ādôn* (Matt. 22:44), and *'ᵃdônāy* (Matt. 1:22). *Kyrios* denotes God as the Ruler and Sovereign who exercises legal authority over all things.[52] A title that occurs most commonly in the Pastorals (six times) is *sōtēr* (1 Tim. 1:1; 2:3; 4:10, et al.), which depicts God as the redeemer and deliverer from sin. Twice in the Pauline corpus (1 Tim. 1:17; 6:15) God is addressed as *basileus*, or "king," although the reality of God's kingdom (*basileia*) is more frequently upheld (Rom. 14:17; 1 Cor. 6:10; Col. 4:11). Implicit in the title is the affirmation of God's sovereign rule, royal power, and dominion.

Paul views God's eternity not in the sense of timelessness, but in the sense that his person endures through an endless series of ages. This is expressed by the phrase "forever" (lit. "unto the ages," Rom. 11:36), by "for ever and ever" (lit. "unto the ages of the ages," 1 Tim. 1:17), and by the remarkable compound phrase that literally reads, "to the generations of the ages of the ages" (Eph. 3:21). In 1 Timothy 6:16 Paul speaks of God's immortality (*athanasia*) and in Romans 1:20 of God's "eternal power," where *aidios* connotes steadiness or unalterability through all times. God's unchangeableness follows logically from his eternity. According to 2 Timothy 2:13, God "cannot disown himself," i.e., act in a way contrary to his nature. And Paul's teaching in Romans 11:29 that "God's gifts and his call are irrevocable" (note the emphatic position of *ametamelēta*) is a claim for the unchangeableness of the divine purpose. Yet the immutability of God's person and purpose in no wise means that he fails to experience a healthy and controlled emotional life (e.g., Jer. 9:24).

The Johannine Literature

No New Testament writer tells us more about the nature of God than does John. In brief, God is light (1 John 1:5), God is spirit (John 4:24), and God is love (1 John 4:8). Light (*phōs*, thirty-three times) is one of the great themes of the Johannine literature. Applied to God, the metaphor of light "suggests ubiquity, brightness, happiness, intelligence, truth, purity, holiness. It suggests excellence without limit and without taint."[53] The notion of glory (*doxa*, thirty-five times in the Johannine writings) is closely related to that of light. *Doxa* signifies the manifestation of God's incomparable brightness and splendor. It is the luminous display of God's very being and attributes. Jesus in John 17:5, 22, 24 spoke of the supratemporal glory that was his by virtue of his eternal relation with the Father. Later, in his apocalyptic visions, John saw the heavenly temple "filled with smoke from the glory of God and from his power" (Rev. 15:8). The new Jerusalem that came down from heaven "shone with the glory of God, and its brilliance was like that of a very precious jewel, like a jasper, clear as crystal" (Rev. 21:11). The city has no need of sun or moon, "for the glory of God gives it light" (Rev. 21:23).

In the second place, Jesus asserts that "God is spirit" (John 4:24). The absence of the article before *pneuma* affirms that God is spirit in his intrinsic nature, and the fact that the word occupies first place in the sentence suggests that he is so absolutely. Because there is no materiality in God, carnal worship is forbidden. It follows that God the Spirit is wholly invisible (John 6:46; 1 John 4:12). Thus it is recorded that Jesus replied to the Jews,

"You have never . . . seen his form" (*eidos*, John 5:37).[54]

Third, by affirming that "God is love" (1 John 4:8, 16), the apostle attests not only that God's essential nature is *agapē*, but also that he is a vital personal agent endowed with volition. So God loves the Son (John 3:35; 5:20), the disciples (John 14:23; 1 John 3:1), and the entire sinful world (John 3:16). That God executes his "will" (*thelēma*, John 6:38–40; Rev. 4:11) and his "purpose" (*gnōmē*, i.e., decision, Rev. 17:17) provides further proof that God is a rational personal agent rather than a blind, impersonal force.

In the fourth place, John declares that God is "the living Father" (John 6:57), and "eternal life" (1 John 5:20). The apostle's assertion that "the Father has life in himself" (John 5:26), conveys the truth that God is the absolutely living One, the spring and source of the vital force called *zōē*. Life is inextricably linked with vitality, and so Jesus makes the claim, "My Father is always at his work to this very day" (John 5:17). The verb *ergazomai* ("to work, perform") suggests that from creation to the present God has been ceaselessly operative in preservation and redemption.

A concomitant of all the above is that God is eternal and unchangeable. John represents the God of the Apocalypse as "the Alpha and the Omega" (Rev. 1:8; 21:6; 22:13), "the First and the Last" (Rev. 1:17; 2:8), the One "who is, and who was, and who is to come" (Rev. 1:4, 8; 4:8). The ascription, "who is" recalls the "I AM" of Exodus 3:14— the self-existent, eternal, unchanging God who is absolute beginning and end. The God of majesty and judgment who occupies the throne "lives for ever and ever" (Rev. 4:9–10; 10:6).

John uses several distinctive titles of God. "The Alpha and the Omega," as mentioned above, denotes the sovereign and immutable Lord of all ages.

"Lord [God] Almighty," *kyrios (ho theos) ho pantokrator* (Rev. 4:8; 11:17; 15:3, et al.), is the Greek equivalent of *Yahweh ṣᵉbā'ôt* and depicts God as the unrivaled and all-powerful ruler of the cosmos. The title "Father," sparingly used of God in the Old Testament, assumes greater importance in the New Testament revelation. Whereas outside the Johannine corpus Father (*patēr*) is used of God as creator and originator (Matt. 6:25–27, 32; 1 Cor. 8:6; Heb. 12:9), John some eighty times refers to God as the Father of Jesus Christ (e.g., John 5:19–22; 11:41; 17:1). Jesus' relation to God the Father was unoriginated and essential. Furthermore, by regeneration and adoption God has become the Father of believers in Christ. The term *patēr* thus signifies the new relation of life and love that Christians enjoy with God (John 4:23; 20:17; 1 John 2:13; 3:1). The Aramaic term *abba*, "dear Father" (Rom. 8:15; Gal. 4:6), is a title of special intimacy found on the lips of a young child.

Other New Testament Books

In the context of his argument for the superiority of Christ and the new covenant the writer of Hebrews extols the glory and majesty of God. Thus he asserts that Christ is "the radiance of God's glory" (*apaugasma tēs doxēs*, Heb. 1:3), where glory is viewed as the brilliant effulgence from a luminous body (cf. Heb. 9:5). The Epistle of Jude concludes (v. 25) with a doxological ascription to "the only God our Savior be glory [*doxa*], majesty [*megalosunē*], power [*kratos*] and authority [*exousia*]." Moreover, the noun *megalosynē*, that speaks of God's majesty, greatness, and dignity, appears in Hebrews as a title of God—namely, "the Majesty in heaven" (Heb. 1:3; 8:1). Consistent with the spirit of the Old Testament on which Hebrews builds, the God of glory and majesty is

upheld as invisible (Heb. 11:27), living (Heb. 10:31), and dynamically active (Heb. 10:30–31). The General Epistles also stress the divine volition in the sense of God's permission (Heb. 6:3), his intention (2 Peter 3:9), and his deliberate design (James 1:18; 1 Peter 4:2).

That an ontological theology constitutes the warp and woof of biblical revelation is seen in Hebrews' assertion that Christ is "the exact representation of his [God's] being" (Heb. 1:3). *Hypostasis*, from *hyphistēmi* (reflexive), "to stand under," signifies that which is the basis of something, as, for example, the foundation of a building or the bottom of the sea. Applied to God, *hypostasis* connotes his substantial nature, essence, or actual being. It is that foundational spirit reality in which the divine attributes inhere.[55] On the other hand, Peter's reference to the believer's participation in "the divine nature" (*theias physeōs*, 2 Peter 1:4) should be viewed as a periphrasis for entrance into the blessings of salvation in Christ (cf. John 1:12; 1 Peter 5:1).

Finally, Hebrews affirms God's unoriginated self-existence (Heb. 2:10), his eternality (Heb. 1:8, 12; 9:14), and the immutability of both his person (Heb. 1:11–12; 6:18) and his purpose (Heb. 6:17). James attests the divine constancy with the claim that the Father "does not change like shifting shadows" (James 1:17): "God never changes (*parallagē*) nor is changed (darkened by a shadow from change)."[56]

SYSTEMATIC FORMULATION

Although finite, fallen people on earth are incapable of inventing the truth about the inner nature of the highest Being, God has chosen to make known some truths about his being and purposes. Biblically revealed information teaches that God is an invisible, personal, and living Spirit, distinguished from all other spirits not only because he is personal, but also because he is self-existent, eternal, and unchanging. Hence God's being is not continuous with the being of any one or thing in creation. Metaphysically, God transcends all people, animals, events, processes, and principles in the cosmos.

Speaking About the Most High

Is it possible to systematize one's thought about the supreme Being "on the other side" of the divide between the eternal and the temporal? Scientists are still working on a unified field theory of physics, and psychologists have yet to complete a systematic view of human consciousness. Can theologians presume to propose a coherent account of the divine Being?

Mystics consider it impious or unspiritual to fine-tune vague notions about higher powers beyond our control, or the highest Power of all. It is more pious, mystics say, to experience God, than to define God. Impressive as that sounds in devotional literature, the inspired Scriptures wisely advise people to know whom they experience beyond themselves because evil as well as good spirits may be encountered. Mystics generally assume that all is one, all is God, and God is good. Hence there are no demonic beings to encounter. Anything or anyone pantheists meet they presuppose to be inwardly divine.

Not all that transcends observable phenomena is of God. Before dismissing conceptual knowledge for religious purposes, pietists should determine (conceptually!) whether ultimate reality is pantheistic or theistic. If in fact not all is God and we are faced with a present dualism (though not an eternal dualism) between God and Satan, good and evil, right and wrong, then we do well to determine whether the spirits' doctrines are of God or not.

How ludicrous it is to choose for either experience or conceptual truth about God! Distinctively human experience is not irrational or unknowing. And knowing takes place in conjunction with experience. Knowledge and experience, therefore, are inseparable, and each is crucial to meaningful life. On the conceptual level nothing is more important than knowing with what or with whom we have ultimately to do, the cosmos—humanity, the demonic or God. On the experiential level nothing is more important than being properly related to the cosmos and to the living God "on the other side" of the cosmos. Existential experience is no substitute for conceptual knowing, and conceptual knowing cannot displace the need for relating experientially.

Some refrain from giving a clear definition of God for fear of confining God to human concepts. That reasoning, however, confuses words and meanings with their referents in experience. Clarity in thought about God no more restricts the Almighty than defining water as H_2O diminishes the power of Niagara Falls. Since the word "God" has been used in so many diverse ways, it is imperative that a speaker or writer indicate which of those uses he has in mind. We need not fear that our definitions will put God in a straight jacket![57]

Of which God do we here speak? To define anything is to state the essential qualities that make it what it is, as distinct from other, similar things. The essence of anything, as "essence" is defined here, equals its being (substance) plus its attributes, not merely the sum of the attributes. Following Kant's skepticism concerning knowing anything in itself (its essence), many philosophers and theologians have limited their categories or general ways of speaking about God to describing the phenomena of Jewish or Christian religious experience. Abandoning categories of essence, substance, and attribute, they speak exclusively in terms of Person-to-person encounters, mighty acts of God (happenings, or events), divine functions, or divine processes in history. Indeed, God is active in all of these ways, but is not a speechless mime. Inscripturated revelation discloses some truth not only about God's acts but also about his spiritual being and his attributes. We should not be too quick to give up categories of substance and attributes. Revealed truth discloses not only what God does, but also who God is.

God's Being: An Invisible, Personal, Living Spirit

Jesus explained to the Samaritan woman at the well why she should worship God, not at this mountain or that, but in spirit and in truth. "God," Christ said, "is spirit" (John 4:24). Although some interpreters take "spirit" as an attribute, the term "spirit" in Jesus' statement is not an adjective, but a substantive. The noun "spirit" occurs first in the sentence for emphasis. And a substantive interpretation fits best with the cultural context. In the pre-Kantian, first-century world of the biblical authors, spirits were not dismissed with an a priori agnosticism or skepticism. Jesus taught that God is a real nonphysical entity, substance, or being. Skepticisms come and go, but Jesus' teaching that God is spirit will not pass away. Undoubtedly the majority of the world's population, including animists and others, believe in the reality of spirits. Often that belief includes a conception of one supreme Spirit.

As a spiritual entity, God is *invisible*. No one has ever seen God or ever will (1 Tim. 6:16). People in Old Testament history from time to time saw visions of God, temporary physical manifestations of God, theophanies, and mighty acts of God, but they did not literally see God. The resurrected Jesus explained to the startled disciples that a spirit or a ghost "does not have flesh and bones," as they saw he had (Luke 24:39). Worshipers of the invisible God, therefore, ought not "think that the divine being is like gold or silver or stone—an image made by man's design and skill" (Acts 17:29; cf. Exod. 20:3–4; Rom. 1:23–25). The tendency of many, not just Latter-Day Saints, to think of a flesh-and-bones God (an old man with a long white beard, a glorified police officer, a rock star, or olympic hero) contradicts revealed truth of God's transcendence and invisibility and leads away from the God who is there and leads rather to idolatry. Idolatry, in turn, leads to disillusionment, and despair.

As spirit, furthermore, God is *personal*. Although thinkers in the neo-Platonic and Hegelian traditions use "spirit" to designate an impersonal Absolute, in the biblical context the divine Spirit exhibits personal capacities of self-consciousness, and self-determination. These capacities are inferred from the abundance of Scripture concerning the Spirit's knowing, feeling, and acting, as seen in the preceding discussion. In thinking about God as personal, it is important to deny any moral or spiritual misuse of these capacities. In addition, we have already emphasized the necessity of divesting our understanding of a personal God from any finite, physical limitations.

Distinct from the physical aspects of human personhood, God transcends the physical aspects of both maleness and femaleness. However, since God created both male and female in his image, we may think of both as like God in their distinctively nonphysical, personal male and female qualities. Both male and female are personal in the likeness of God who is personal. From this

195

perspective, scriptural uses of masculine personal pronouns for God (and other male designations such as "Father") primarily convey the connotation of God's personal qualities. Secondarily, the masculine pronouns and titles in some contexts may indicate whatever distinctive functional roles and responsibilities males have in social relationships.

In the Lord's Prayer and elsewhere Jesus' unique emphasis on God as Father becomes meaningless if God is not indeed personal. Similarly, the great doctrines of mercy, grace, forgiveness, imputation, justification, and intercession can be meaningful only if God is genuinely personal. God can hear the sinner's cry for mercy, be moved by it, decide to act, and save the lost. Because God is essentially personal, furthermore, he may be even superpersonal or tripersonal—Father, Son, and Holy Spirit. Whether we are referring to God's oneness or to his threeness, we may think of him as personal. Add to the biblical evidence of God's personhood the astounding fact of persons in the world, and it is most unlikely that hypotheses of God as impersonal can account for the evidence as adequately as the view that God is personal.

The oneness of the divine Being or personal Spirit means that he is *indivisible* or simple. This characteristic is inferred from the first-century cultural understanding of spirit in the context of the biblical teaching about God's oneness. Neither the real personal distinctions of trinitarianism nor the multiple attributes divide the essential unity of the divine Being. The ontological oneness as essential is not torn apart even by the Incarnation, nor even by the death of Jesus. Relationally, or functionally, the incarnate Jesus on the Cross was separated from the Father, who imputed to him the guilt and punishment of human sin. The incarnate, suffering Christ gave up the glory of his heavenly status to provide a just salvation for sinful humans but did not empty himself of his essential divine nature. As God, he could not deny himself. How the divine attributes relate to the divine being without shattering God's unity is explored in the next section.[58]

As spirit, furthermore, God is *living and active*. In contrast to the passive ultimates of Greek philosophies, "we have put our hope in the living God" (1 Tim. 4:10). The God of Abraham, Elijah, David, Christ, and Paul, actively creates, sustains, covenants with his people, preserves the Messiah's line of descent in Israel, commissions prophet after prophet, sends his Son into the world, provides the atoning sacrifice to satisfy his own righteousness, raises Christ from the dead, builds the church, and judges all justly. Far from being a passive entity like a building, the God of the Bible is an active architect, builder, freedom fighter, advocate of the poor and oppressed, an empathetic counselor, a suffering servant, and a triumphant deliverer.

A living God is no mere passive object of human investigation. Writers like Pascal, Kierkegaard, Barth, and Brunner have helpfully reminded Christians that knowing God is not like knowing soils. However, these writers go too far in claiming that God is merely a revealing subject. To emphasize personal relationships with God they unjustifiably deny the reliability of scriptural information about God. Members of a creative artist's family may know the artist not only with passionate, personal subjectivity, but also with some objective validity through an examination of the artist's portfolio and résumé. Similarly, God is known, not only in passionate commitment, but also by careful study of his creative works (general revelation), written communiques (in Scripture), and, in a lesser way, through theological "résumés" of divine words and works.

In summary, "God is spirit" means that God is one invisible, personal, living, and active being. There are, however, many spirits. To distinguish God more fully from other spirits, attention must be given to distinctively divine attributes.

Relating God's Attributes to God's Being

Before considering the meaning of each attribute, it helps to consider the relationship of God's essential characteristics to God's being. Attributes are not accidentals but essential characteristics. According to Scripture, God's attributes are not outside of God but are predicated of him. God *is* holy, God *is* love. These qualities do not simply describe what God does or how God functions. They define who it is who speaks and acts. The nature of the tree, Jesus emphasized, determines the fruit it bears. What God is determines what God says and does. Scripturally, essence is prior to existential activity. The phenomena of divine relationships are ultimately what they are because they issue from God's "heart," or innermost essence.

Does the fact that there are different attributes shatter God's indivisibility? The essential characteristics are not mere names for human use with no referent in the divine Spirit (nominalism). Nor are the attributes separate from each other within the divine being so that they could conflict with each other (realism). The attributes all equally qualify the entirety of the divine being and each other (modified realism). God is love, and God is holy. Preserving the simplicity of God's being, then, God's love is always holy love, and God's holiness is always loving holiness. It follows that arguments for the superiority of one attribute over another are futile. Every attribute is equally essential in the divine Being.

One characteristic may be more important for our specific purposes at a particular time, but cannot be more essential than another in an uncompounded, unextended, simple, being.

Inseparable from the divine being, then, the attributes govern every divine activity. Because God is wise, he cannot speak or act arbitrarily or foolishly. Since God is faithful and true, he cannot lie. Inasmuch as God is just, he cannot treat people unfairly. Given the fact that God is holy, he cannot be pleased with moral evil. Because God is love, he cannot act toward people apart from their best interests. Since God is eternal, he cannot die. Again, since God is self-existent, it follows that God cannot become dependent on any person, denomination, or nation. Given that God is immutable, he cannot deny himself. By way of contrast, if, for example, the Muslim God can act arbitrarily (condemning the just and rewarding the evil), the Christian God cannot. The sovereignty and freedom of the God of the Bible involves free self-determination according to his nature, but not self-destruction.

Interpreting and Classifying the Divine Attributes

How should people in space and time interpret the divine attributes? Some thinkers who deny a cognitive revelation believe that God is so totally other than humanity that all alleged knowledge of God must be interpreted *equivocally*. Human thought about attributes of God so distorts the way they are that talk about them may amount to nothing more than talk about characteristics of mankind. To imagine that we can span the heavens is to equivocate. As Pope said, "The proper study of mankind is man." Interpretations reducing biblical teaching about God to equivocal teaching about man destroys the nature of a cognitive revelation by an interpretive principle inconsistent with the avalanche of data on revelation and inspiration, and on the cognitive image of God in mankind by creation and regeneration.

Other theologians, often following Thomas Aquinas, hold that our understanding of God's characteristics is to be taken *analogically* or figuratively. God's love or holiness is not exactly like ours at any point because God is so much greater than we are. Much of our knowledge is analogical or figurative where the Bible uses figures of speech. Even then, however, the point illustrated can be stated in nonfigurative language. A univocal point of understanding, the same for God and man, is necessary to determine which figures are appropriately used of God and which are not. Similarly, the ability to determine in what respect an illustration applies to God, and in what respects it does not, presupposes some nonfigurative knowledge of God's nature in itself.

In seeking to define the divine attributes, then, we seek to discover the element of truth that God intended to disclose and that illumined and informed people can understand *univocally,* that is, with one voice, or one nonfigurative, cognitive meaning. Some points of univocal understanding of divine attributes, such as holiness and love, do not imply full comprehension of them, for now we know only in part. But insofar as our assertions about God's holiness and love faithfully represent conceptually revealed meanings, they are true of God and conform in part to God's understanding. Otherwise, God in the unknown "parts" of himself may be unholy and unloving, and revelation becomes irresponsible deception (a hypothesis that does not fit the relevant data).

Our partial knowledge of the incomprehensible God is not like knowledge of an apple, of which one bite may be good and the next have a worm in it. Rather, our limited knowledge of God is better illustrated in a young child's initial knowledge of a triangle in contrast to a geometry professor's knowledge of the triangle. The child learns that a triangle is a three-sided, plane figure. That simple definition applies to the entire triangle and holds good for the professor's lifetime of teaching geometry. The professor may know many more things about sides, planes, figures, and angles, and how to infer from the degrees of two angles what the third is, etc. However advanced in geometry the professor becomes, he never denies that a triangle is a three-sided, plane figure. Our knowledge of God's revealed attributes may be like that of the child. But as univocal, it was, is, and always will be true of God's entire nature as God is and knows himself to be. However advanced knowledge may become in this life or the next, we will not learn that God is not holy or loving.

Theologians have organized their discussions of God's attributes in different ways to help in relating and remembering them. Classifications of divine attributes have been quite diverse, and each has its strengths and weaknesses. We may distinguish those attributes that are absolute and immanent (A. H. Strong); incommunicable and communicable (Louis Berkhof); metaphysical and moral (John Gill); absolute, relative, and moral (H. Orton Wiley); or personal and constitutional (L. S. Chafer). Advantages and disadvantages of these may be seen in their respective theologies.[59] We find it more meaningful to classify God's characteristics in the following important ways: metaphysically, intellectually, ethically, emotionally, volitionally, and relationally.

Metaphysically, God Is Self-existent, Eternal, and Unchanging

Other spirits also are invisible, personal, living, and active. How does the divine Spirit differ from them? Of the significant differences in several respects, we look first at the distinctive metaphysical attributes.

God is uniquely self-existent. All other spirits are created, and so there was a time when they did not exist. They owe their existence to another. God does not depend on the world or anyone in it for his existence. The cosmos depends on God for its existence.

Contrary to the view that we can know nothing in itself (metaphysically), Jesus disclosed the fact that God "has life in himself" (John 5:26). The ground of God's being is not in others; nothing is more ultimate. God is uncaused by anything other than himself. God is the one who always is (Exod. 3:14). To ask, "Who caused God?" is to ask a self-contradictory question, or to fail to understand who Yahweh is. When we say that every effect must have a cause (other than itself), we mean that every finite, limited effect must have its cause in something else. But God is unlimited or infinite and "laws" describing regular relations of finite things do not necessarily apply to him.

To express this truth, the church fathers, writing in Latin, said God's existence was *a se*, from himself. The English term derived from the Latin is "aseity." An understanding of God's self-existence helps one appreciate why God is not dependent on anything. God is unlimited, free, and self-determined both because he is prior to creation and because he is not contingent on any creature unless he has decreed such contingency (as in being moved by our prayers). Anyone who grasps the fact that God has life in himself (whether his understanding is on a popular or on a more technical, philosophical level), has already broken through the anti-metaphysical prejudice of much contemporary philosophy and theology, such as the tendency of process theology to regard God dependent upon natural and historical processes.

God is also eternal and omnipresent. The essential difference between eternity and time, Augustine held, is the difference between the changeless and the changing. With all the flux of history, God in nature, knowledge, and purpose is the same. Transcendent to temporal change, God as eternal is immutable.

Transcendent to temporal change, God is also quantitatively changeless, or everlasting. God has no beginning, growth, old age, or death. The Lord is enthroned as King forever (Ps. 29:10). And "this God is our God for ever and ever" (Ps. 48:14).

Transcendent to temporal change, the eternal God is unlimited by time in his knowledge. God does not learn line upon line, or observation after observation, or conclusion after premise. God is simultaneously conscious of past and future as well as the present. Since God is not limited by the succession of events in time, his knowledge is not contingent on history. Although God is not limited by changes in time, he created time and sustains the succession of events.

Exalted above all limitations of time and change, God has eternal purposes for time and is vitally active to fulfill them in time. According to his changeless purposes, he created changing creatures and time—past, present, and future. Future aeons are not viewed, as in Barth, totally other than the present age, and in them God may be said to have endless time, or unlimited time. But Oscar Cullmann's attempt to reduce eternity to infinitely extended time bounded by creation and eschatological events fails to fit revelation on God's transcendence.

The changing world, although not as important as God, has permanent significance in God's grand design. Because contingent and changing, it is not to be considered unreal, or, as in some Hinduism, maya. No person, family, subculture, tribe, city, or nation is valueless to the omnipresent Lord of all. History is the product of God's eternally wise planning, creative purposes, providential preservation, and common grace. God fills space and time with his presence, sustains history, and gives the temporal realm lasting value. The transcendent One is Lord of history. God does not negate time, but sustains, guides, and brings it to meaningful fulfillment of wise, gracious and just purposes. To fulfill his redemptive purposes God brought the Messiah into the world "when the time had fully come" (Gal. 4:4).

In sum, God is eternal, or everlasting, in his transcendent being and changeless in his universal purposes and knowledge of past, present and future.

Metaphysically, then, God is not only self-existent, and eternal, but also unchanging or immutable. To affirm that God is changeless is not to contradict the truth that the divine Spirit is living and active. It is to say that all the uses of divine vitality and power are consistent with his attributes and purposes. Although some uses may be for reasons wholly within himself, rather than for revealed considerations, God's acts are never arbitrary, fickle, or capricious. Underlying each judgment of the wicked and each pardon of the repentant is his changeless purpose concerning sin and conversion.

The changelessness of God's purposes does not exclude human instrumentality. Sovereignly, God chooses to accomplish some things independently of any human agency and to accomplish other things through the use of human means. These will be not be achieved without the participation of human instruments. As God purposely achieves some things through human instrumentality, the immutability of God's purposes does not imply the insignificance of personal involvement, but just the opposite. Human agency in many respects finds an important place in God's changeless plans for history.

Unlike the Stoic concept of divine immutability, God is not indifferent to human activity and need. Rather, we can always count on God's concern for human righteousness and well-being. God changelessly answers prayer in accord with his desires and purposes of holy love. From the standpoint of human experience it appears (in the phenomenological language of Scripture) that God repents, but in reality it is the ungodly who have changed their minds in respect to sin. When the people of Nineveh repented, God "relented" and in compassion did not bring on them the destruction he had "threatened" (Jonah 3:9–10). God's basic purposes toward the unrepentant and the repentant in Nineveh remained unchanged; only God's activity changed in accord with changes in the spiritual attitudes of the Ninevites.

Even though everything in creation becomes old like a garment, God is the same (Ps. 102:25–27). Because Jesus Christ was no mere part of creation, the passage from Psalm 102 was quoted also of him. The Son of God remains the same (Heb. 1:10–12). "Jesus Christ is the same yesterday and today and forever" (Heb. 13:8).

The meaning of immutability is vividly illustrated throughout Christ's past active ministry on earth. While moving from weddings to funerals, from greedy tax collectors to the poor and powerless, from harlots to self-righteous Pharisees, from the ill to the demonized, he changelessly remained just, loving, and wise. Deeply moved by experiences of caring, temptations, and tragedies, Christ never lost his integrity. Amid the pressures of an active life in history, he exhibited the dependability of the Father, whose immutability deserves our praise, faith, and trust (Heb. 6:17–18).

APOLOGETIC INTERACTION

The Idol of "Mother Nature"

A high school French teacher asked her young nephew, "Is not God merely mother nature?" Unfortunately, the high school student was not well prepared to answer that rather common question. Had he been more conversant with God's distinctive metaphysical characteristics, he could have pointed out how unattributable they are to "mother nature." The world is not self-existent; God has life in himself. The cosmos had a beginning in the finite past and will eventually come to an end; God is eternal. The useful energy of nature is being depleted; God is tireless, he never slumbers nor sleeps (Ps. 121:4). The world constantly changes; God is immutable.

Contradictory characteristics cannot belong to the same reality. The same entity cannot be self-existent and not self-existent, eternal and not eternal, immutable and not immutable. Hence God cannot be equated with "mother nature," atomic energy, natural laws, human beings, or the sum total of the dependent, temporal, changing universe.

In Athens, the university center of the ancient world, Paul exemplified a Christian approach to Gentiles with unsound views of God. The nontheistic Epicureans considered atoms and space the ultimate reality. The pantheistic Stoics regarded the usual order of natural law (an immanent, impersonal Logos) the highest metaphysical reality with which people have to do. Then, of course, there were the agnostics who worshiped and served an "unknown God."[60]

The confusion of the Creator with the creatures continues to be one of the most prominent problems in contemporary Gentile and Jewish thinking. Many speak out in behalf of atheistic humanism, pantheistic mysticism, and religious agnosticism. If a personal God is distinct from the world and is worthy of worship, then people in pluralistic societies need to speak out on behalf of Christian theism. At any level in public educational systems proud of their "academic freedom" little may be said to represent the classical theism of the Judeo-Christian tradition fairly. Like Paul at Athens, theists today need to (1) earn the right to be heard, (2) address the board of education with respect, (3) appeal to any common ground that can be found, (4) proclaim the truth about the living God, and (5) call people to repent of their idolatrous secular humanism, pantheistic mysticism, or religious agnosticism.[61]

The Idol of Energy (Atoms in Space and Time)

With the mushroom cloud has come not only a concern about the future of humanity, but also a preoccupation with energy. People in a desperate quest for lasting meaning think that their ultimate concern has to do with the finite energy of the universe. Then, with energy as their ultimate object of trust, they attribute divine qualities to it.

The energy of the cosmos, rather than God, has come to be regarded as self-existent. From early ideas that energy was "a force," scientists began to think of it rather as "capability to do work." Then science discovered the interconvertibility of energy with matter ($E = MC^2$) and the conservation of the sum total. From this, the philosopher of science M. Jammer leaps to belief in "the emancipation of energy as an autonomous existent." In place of an autonomous God, Jammer worships and serves "autonomous energy." Following Ostwald, not only has energy become the universal currency of physics, but "all the phenomena of nature were merely manifestations of energy and its manifold transformations." Energy, Jammer maintains, is substance, and "the only substance."[62]

This "dissolution of matter" into energy was welcomed by monistic thinkers because it suggested a unified conception of the universe with energy as the ubiquitous god. New Consciousness and New Age thinkers with Paul Davies in *God and the New Physics* claim that the end result of the new physics is "more like mysticism than materialism."[63] Davies remarks about the "strong holistic flavour to the quantum aspects of the nature of matter" with "everything somehow made up of everything else and yet displaying a hierarchy of structure."[64]

"The Force" is not just for children at the movies. Forms of monism, pantheism, or panentheism underlie many new religious trends in human potential, new consciousness, altered states of consciousness, and the occult. If the inner energy of all humans is divine, then all have infinite potential and anyone may evolve to the next stage in cultural or religious evolution (often imagined to be like an avatar or god). All people are thought to be "spiritually" connected by this energy. Illness is considered an imbalance of energy, a by-product of an unenlightened consciousness. If you will only "eat" of this theory, as the Deceiver said to Eve and Adam, "you will be like God" (Gen. 3:4).

Valuable as modern physical discoveries have been, the energy of the universe is not the unlimited, personal God of the Bible: (1) Energy loses its usefulness, God does not. (2) The energy of the universe had a beginning and will have an end; God does not. (3) The energy of the universe is impersonal; God is personal. (4) The energy of the universe is amoral; God is moral. (5) The energy of the universe can be manipulated by human engineering; God will not be manipulated by physicists or mediums.

God alone sovereignly rules over all the finite energy in the cosmos. The cosmos is not "all that ever was or ever will be." Sagan exclaims, "Passage from the Chaos of the Big Bang to the Cosmos that we are beginning to know is the most awesome transformation of matter and energy that we have been privileged to glimpse."[65] But that awesome transformation of energy cannot compare with power of the Word of the living Lord who spoke energy-matter into existence and sustains it! How like the wisdom of this fallen world, however, to value mother's cooking more than mother, and created energy more than its Creator!

The Idol of "Being Itself"

To think of God as personal, according to Paul Tillich, is idolatrous, because it makes God a limited, finite being. Tillich thought he avoided idolatry by taking the symbol "God" to stand for "being itself" beyond essence and existence. So he could not speak of the existence of God or the essence of the God who is. He thought it idolatrous even to appeal to evidence for the existence of a personal God. The night before he died, Tillich was pleased to learn that he had "fathered" T. J. Altizer's death-of-God theology.

Although rejecting the God of biblical theism, Tillich said he was not an atheist. His god was the power of being (like energy) enabling all things that are to exist. And he insisted that he was not a pantheist. His god was not the universal essence of all forms. Tillich thought that the ground of all that is transcended the essence of existing things in every respect. This, he says, is what the philosophers teach literally and what the biblical writers also teach if interpreted symbolically. Tillich took only one statement about God to be literally true: "God is being itself, not a being."[66] God is beyond all other cognitive, literal assertions. Religious language generally is more like poetry evoking ecstatic religious experience than like scientific or philosophical language. Faith involved no belief of propositions (other than the one) but was an existential leap into the dark to overcome the anxieties resulting from the apparent meaninglessness of life, guilt, and despair in the face of death.

As devout and strategic as Tillich's view may appear, it fails to do justice to the scriptural revelation concerning God. Even when figurative or symbolic language is used of God, the figure illustrates a point that can be expressed in nonfigurative language. Scripturally more than one proposition can be cognitively asserted of God. God is a living, spiritual being who thinks, feels, wills, and is self-existent, eternal, and unchanging. One can have a personal relationship with the God of the Bible, but not with being itself.

Does a personal concept of God, as Tillich thought, make God finite? Specifically we have established that the Creator is not contingent on, or limited by, space, time, or change. God is personal in a far greater way than humans are. As an infinite, or unlimited, personal being, God far supersedes Tillich's unknown, impersonal being itself. Although Tillich claims that "being itself" transcends personhood, he can literally know nothing about the characteristics of being itself. Therefore Tillich cannot know that "greater than personal" (whatever that is) is a more appropriate symbol for his Unknown of ultimate concern than "personal infinite" or "unlimited personal being."[67]

To the extent that Tillich views the orthodox doctrine of God, a finite God,

he is not addressing the view actually held. On the classical understanding, God is unlimited by time, space, and anything else in all creation, except as in his sovereignty he chose to limit himself. Tillich's abstract being itself cannot respond to intercession or act supernaturally on the world. The abstract Ground of Being could not raise Christ from the dead, answer prayer, or, as Billy Graham used to say, "bless you real good."

The question children ask continues to disturb mature clergymen, "Where is God?" As far as possible replies do well to avoid spatial language ("up there," "out there," or "in us" after J. A. T. Robinson's *Honest to God*), for God is spirit. But answers incorporate a nonphysical element of truth that may have been intended in all these perspectives. Aided by biblical revelation, rather than to assert that God is "up there," we may affirm that God is Lord of all (distinct from all and over all). God is not physically "out there," but active in everything that is and happens, in accord with his providential purposes in space and time. And God is not the inner energy of people but is active with his believing people in accord with his redemptive purposes for the present age.

John Gill helpfully distinguished God's glorious presence in heaven (1 Kings 8:27; Ps. 103:19; Isa. 57:15; Heb. 9:24), his providential presence throughout the universe (Ps. 103:19; Jer. 23:22, 24), and his redemptive presence in the bodies of believers now the dwelling place of God (2 Cor. 6:16; 1 Cor. 6:19, 20).[68] Biblical analyses never blur the distinction between Creator and creature. God is not nature nor people, not even redeemed people or their leaders. The God who transcends people continuously acts by his Holy Spirit to conform believers from the inside out to become more like the Lord Jesus Christ in heaven.

The Idol of Evolution

Another influential confusion of the creation with the transcendent Creator absolutizes evolution. Pierre Teilhard de Chardin (1881–1955) sought to synthesize love for God and love for the world, the internal and the external, theology and science. His organizing key was not merely biological evolution, but an expanded, cosmic evolution of the universe. The matter-energy reality, he suggested, had a psychic aspect. So the geosphere evolved into living organisms, the biosphere. After several hundred thousand years, mind appeared developing the neosphere. Later life was hominized with the appearance of humanity.

As life becomes increasingly complex, de Chardin's humanity evolves on a planetary scale of increasing socialization. That would provide personality the power to develop to its fullest and best. This end is not guaranteed, since humanity is free, and so we must work with faith in man and the world toward our ultimate destination or omega point.

An impersonal omega point as a condition or state will not provide sufficient motivation to overcome every obstacle to evolutionary progress. Christianity provides the personalized, motivating omega point in the return of Christ at the end of the age. We may prepare for Christ's return by unifying all people around Christ and loving our neighbors. When humanity is unified, we will have passed from the neosphere to the Christosphere. With Henri Bergson, de Chardin thinks that the universe is "a machine for making gods." It is not surprising, then, that the new consciousness movements frequently quote Teilhard de Chardin's spiritualized version of evolutionary development.

Teilhard's evolutionary scheme has extrapolated from any limited, actual data of development (within the biblical "kinds") to a total philosophy of evolu-

tion, which is far from scientific. He assumes a now-controversial Lamarkian development by acquired characteristics from the simple to the complex. (Further evaluation of evolution may be found in the chapter on creation.)

The supreme consciousness at the end of de Chardin's development is far from the transcendent personal God of Christ and Scripture. Like Brahman in Hinduism, Teilhard's evolutionary God seems to depersonalize human beings. At the end they all appear to be absorbed in the divine consciousness.

Teilhard's religious evolution occurs for many or most without benefit of a reception of Christ's once-for-all redemptive provisions by the regeneration of the Holy Spirit. In gaining the cosmic Christ Teilhard has returned to the nature religions and lost the supernatural Savior of the Scriptures. However dedicated, worship and service of evolution rather than the transcendent Lord of all, is idolatrous.[69]

The Idol of Process

Process theology takes dynamic processes in time in much the same way that Teilhard de Chardin took evolution. Philosopher Alfred North Whitehead combined the growing belief in evolution with the newly conceived concept of relativity in his *Process and Reality* (1929). A dynamic world, said Whitehead, could not have a static creator. God, like all other beings, is in some respects incomplete and a companion of man in the creative advance toward perfection.

God, according to Norman Pittenger, is the inescapable energy that moves through all things. That creative energy

is nothing other than love, pure, unbounded love, sharing, participating, giving and receiving. That is the very heart of deity. Cosmic love is present in all creaturely occasions, enfolding them in its concern and working to bring them to actualization. God is the tender lover, the fellow sufferer who understands, the participant in all human experience whether joyful or painful. There is that in every person which will not let go. And that is what we mean by God. It faithfully acts by lure, persuasion, solicitation and attraction to secure the free consent of people to this purpose of good.[70]

Process thought misrepresents a biblical view of God. The God of the Bible has been found to be far from immobile, static, or unconcerned in relation to nature and human history. The Greek philosopher Parmenides may have held such a view of Being, but not biblically informed Christian theologians. We need not reject God's changelessness in essence and purpose in order to emphasize God's dynamic activity in human history. "The biblical God is not static but inexhaustibly dynamic on his own terms, not ours."[71]

Process thought loses any persevering identity of God. The same living God, however, related dynamically to Abraham, David, Christ, Paul, Augustine, Luther, and Billy Graham. Although changeless in essence and purpose, the divine Spirit is changing in specific activities and relationships with changing persons.

Process thinkers miss the mark of the personal God of Scripture who transcends temporal processes as self-existent and eternal. The Lord of all freedom is free from dependence on the temporal, changing world. A God in process does not know the future and is not sovereign. Limited by time, God is not sovereignly in charge, but indebted to all. Human experience is a mode of God's becoming. Again humans are in danger of confusing themselves with deity. Divine grace is replaced by an inherent optimism born of an unfounded faith in cosmic evolution.

The changing process is unworthy of our worship, as Emil Brunner argued. "Were God one who is 'becoming,'

then everything would founder on the morass of relativism. We can measure nothing by changing standards; changeable norms are no norms at all; a God who is constantly changing is not a God whom we can worship. He is a mythological being for whom we can only feel sorry."[72]

Process thinking about God provides some helpful insights into the activities and relationships of God in history but fails to fit the biblical data of God's changeless being. There is no question that the biblical God is engaged in history, but, as Royce Gruenler, a former process theologian, has concluded, "The limitation of God to time and space has to be considered a modern idolatry."[73]

The Idol of Humanism

Humanists regard the highest manifestation of energy, evolution or process to be found in mankind. The ultimate goal according to Humanist Manifesto II (1973) is "the fulfillment of the potential for growth in each human personality." Among the greatest obstacles to achieving this goal are the promises of immortal salvation in the traditional religions. Ethics needs no theological or ideological sanction because it is considered "autonomous" and "situational." Yet Corliss Lamont seems to present an objectively valid propositional truth when he writes in *The Philosophy of Humanism*: "The chief end of thought and action is to further this-earthly human interests on behalf of the greater glory of man"[74]

Not only is the highest goal autonomous human happiness, but also the highest knowledge and power are human. Humanism aims to realize "as close an approach as possible to human omniscience and omnipotence."[75] Human nature is thought to be neither essentially bad nor good, but essentially flexible and educable.[76] But one who is too autonomous is subject to another of the great aims of humanism, "the transformation and socialization of human motives."[77] Why should this be necessary? Each individual has an "unending debt to the collective culture of mankind and his corresponding obligation to serve the common good."[78] Whence arise these universal and necessary obligations when all is relative?

It becomes clear that humanists, who do not worship and serve the God of the Bible, do not stop worshiping and serving. Instead they are "saved" by, and for, the good of universal humanity, however that may be defined by the humanists in power.

That abstract god, even when associated with nature and given the attributes that belong to God alone, lacks the example, the teaching, and the atonement that Christ provides. It also ignores the human disposition to selfishness and the power of the Holy Spirit, the only One who can transform sinful human nature. Abandoning the illusory hope that education and science will solve the world's problems, many naturalistic and secular humanists today realize the need for a transcendent power to deliver human beings individually and collectively.[79]

Making Idols of Biblical Words

Can biblical theologians wisely limit themselves to terms used in Scripture when other words such as *substance, essence, attributes, personhood, transcendence,* and *relationships* are so essential to adequately represent biblical teaching in view of the antimetaphysical temper of the age?

Without question the initial work of exegesis in the Old or New Testament must start with studies of the inspired words. But the concepts conveyed by those words two millennia or more ago may not be conveyed in the same way today. In the light of today's controversies the point of biblical figures of speech may need to be stated nonfiguratively, and communication of the coherent teaching of all the Scriptures about God may call for more technical terms.

For example, George Ladd's chapter "The God of the Kingdom" in *The Theology of the New Testament,* fails to provide an adequate basis for determining whether God is an invisible Spirit, Energy manifest as matter, Being itself, Evolution, Process, or Humanity. Ladd's four headings are "The Seeking God," "The Inviting God," "The Fatherly God," and "The Judging God." But unless Ladd defines God, he may as well speak of the seeking, inviting, fatherly, judging unknown *x.* Are these four Gods or one? If one, one what? Who or what is engaged in these activities? Are they personifications referring to aspects of mother nature's activities? Or, is God one transcendent personal Spirit who seeks, invites, cares, and judges? A biblical theologian today cannot escape the responsibility of clarifying the agency or agencies responsible for the selected activities regarded divine. In the confusion of a pluralistic society, nothing can be taken for granted. Ladd's descriptive purpose may excuse him from giving the point of biblical figures in nonfigurative language and from defining terms. But his work, as far as it goes, points up the need for an integrative theology.[80]

John Bright's ultimate concern seemed to focus on Israel's faith, rather than the nature of the God in whom they believed. His undefined *x,* or Yahweh, elected a special people, and exercised sovereign lordship over them through covenants and promises.[81] Again we are told of activities, but not who, or what, acts in these ways. Is the agent beyond nature or is it nature itself? Is the agent personal or merely a literary personification? If biblical theology cannot answer questions like these, for fear of philosophy (the love of wisdom), it lacks the courage of the writers of the biblical revelation. If there is a danger that much theology today may become unscriptural by using extrabiblical words, the same danger haunts biblical theologians who stress biblical verbs and overlook the nouns revealing God's substantive nature.[82]

RELEVANCE FOR LIFE AND MINISTRY

The renewal of Christian witness and mission requires constant examination of the assumptions shaping the church's life. Today, an apparent loss of a sense of the transcendent is undermining the church's ability to address with clarity and courage the urgent tasks to which God calls it in the world.

Eighteen Protestant, Catholic, and Orthodox theologians meeting at Hartford Seminary in 1975 said that the lack of theological affirmation has serious secular and naturalistic implications. The sole purpose of worship becomes the promotion of self-realization and human community. Emphasis on God's transcendence is considered at least a hindrance to, and perhaps incompatible with, Christian social concern and action.[83] In contrast, J. I. Packer considers knowing the transcendent God to provide at once "a foundation, shape and goal for our lives, plus a principle of priorities and a scale of values."[84]

Against Relativizing the Absolute

Those who worship the God of the Bible in spirit and in truth need to be careful not to reduce the Most High to nature, being, evolution, process, humanity, or even religious experiences. The radical biblical distinction between the transcendent Creator and the creature does not permit a monism, even for devotional purposes. Theists may be attracted by the simplicity and neatness of monism but ought not yield to the temptation to blur the distinction between the Creator and the creature. Their worship and service take place in the context of a dualistic world view. The truth of God's transcendence leads their meditation beyond the physical, visible, audible, changing, temporal idols to the God who is, acts, and speaks. Before Jesus ministered to people's needs, he withdrew from them and communicated with his Father in heaven. Failure to understand God's transcendent being can turn one's worship and service into idolatry. "The essence of idolatry," A. W. Tozer said, "is the entertainment of thoughts about God that are unworthy of Him."[85] No church can long serve the God of truth with an untrue and diminished view of who he is. "The first step down for any church," Tozer observed, "is taken when it surrenders its high opinion of God."[86]

Against Absolutizing the Relative

Because God is uniquely one, he cannot be compared to anything else. People either bow to God as Lord of all or devalue him. No one, Jesus taught, can serve two spiritual masters or ultimates. To have divided loyalties at the highest level, is to distort our entire scale of values and our consequent living. The Christian theists' ultimate concern and commitment is to none other than the living God. "A right conception of God is basic not only to systematic theology but to practical Christian living as well. It is to worship what the foundation is to the temple; where it is inadequate or out of plumb the whole structure must sooner or later collapse."[87]

Meditation on nature is radically different for theists than for pantheists. On the one hand, theists look at the beauty and vastness of the Rocky Mountains and appreciate more fully God's transcendent creative wisdom and power. Theists worship the God whose being is distinct from the being of nature. On the other hand, pantheists and panentheists look at the same mountain range and regard it as a partial expression of God's being.

Unfortunately Richard Foster encourages meditation on nature with Evelyn Underhill's statement, "To elude nature, to refuse her friendship, and attempt to leap the river of life in the hope of finding God on the other side, is the common error of a perverted mysticality." Only on a pantheistic or panentheistic hypothesis is worship of God on the other side of nature a "perversion." The transcendent Creator of the cosmos is not to be confused with it. Foster, quoting Underhill, continues, "So you are to begin with that first form of contemplation which the old mystics sometimes called the 'discovery of God in His creatures.' "[88] Theists may also begin meditation on nature, but in doing so they move from its changing being subject to entropy to the unchanging being of God, who neither slumbers nor sleeps (Ps. 121:4).

What, then, is the top priority on the agenda of the church today? According to A. W. Tozer, it is neither in science nor in the arts.

The heaviest obligation lying upon the Christian Church today is to purify and elevate her concept of God until it is once more worthy of Him—and of her. In all her prayers and labors this should have first place. We do the greatest service to the next generation of Christians by passing on to them undimmed and undiminished the noble concept of God which we received from our Hebrew and Christian fathers of generations past. This will prove of greater value to them than anything that are of science can devise.[89]

Against Visualizing God

Because God as spirit is invisible, no images drawn from visible things will enrich our worship of him. No one ever has seen God nor can see him (1 Tim. 6:16). Physical images are forbidden in worship by the second commandment: "You shall not make for yourself an idol in the form of anything in heaven above or the earth beneath or in the waters below" (Exod. 20:4). Material images, however skillfully done (even on the Sistine Chapel ceiling), fail to convey the truth about God's spiritual being and may lead attention away from the God who is worthy of worship and service. J. I. Packer argues that images dishonor God, for they obscure his glory and mislead people.[90] With the Reformers we suggest the use of imaginative pictures in teaching to illustrate some facets of truth but decry their use in worship. Fantasies may helpfully entertain and illustrate well-founded cognitive truths. But they do not lead to deeper relationships with the God who, as spirit, transcends mountain ranges, oceans, bulls, snakes, elephants, Venus, Hercules, and any saints who are pictured in the classic art of the Christian church.

Since Jesus became incarnate and visible to the senses, it cannot be wrong for teaching purposes to picture Jesus Christ's humanity and his activities in the Gospels on behalf of sinners. Unwisely Richard Foster's *Celebration of Discipline* is criticized for use of the imagination (in a nonmanipulative sense) in meditating on the incarnate Christ. Can we be obedient to the Scriptures, however, and accept Foster's suggestions to use visualization in achieving the objective of "deep inner communion with the Father" when "you look at Him and He looks at you."[91] However well intended, does not worship or meditation that pictures the Father's face violate the second commandment? Has Foster's teaching, beneficial though it is in may respects, lived up to his desire to make Scripture "the central reference point by which all other meditations are kept in proper perspective"?[92]

Pro–Communion, Not Ontological Union, With God

Because God is personal and transcendent to humans on earth and in heaven, the objective in all forms of worship is not absorption into God, nor any form of ontological union of the finite and fallen with the infinite and holy One. According to Scripture, for mere humans, however "enlightened," to consider themselves continuous with Deity is blasphemy.

Only in pantheism are all persons ontologically one. In theism persons are distinct beings created as unique individuals for fellowship with a personal God. The loyalty of persons to one another in families, churches, and nations can reflect a significant solidarity of values, commitments, and relationships, but not a sameness of being.

Although made like God in some respects, humans are not God. God's distinctive ontological attributes are not communicable to human beings. We are not eternal or immutable, and we are not to seek continuity with the incomparable One who is. We become "partakers of the divine nature" (2 Peter 1:4), not ontologically, but in participating in such communicable characteristics as justice and loving personal relationships in God's kingdom. The goal of worship, then, needs to be clarified frequently in societies that do not teach theism in the public schools and are post-theistic as well as post-Christian. The goal in every worship service is not noncognitive mystical union, but communion. "Our fellowship is with the Father and with his Son, Jesus Christ" (1 John 1:3). The teaching and preaching of divine revelation is intended to lead people away from fellowship with darkness (2 Cor. 6:14) and into the fellowship of light (1 John 1:7).

Pro–Change Consistent With God's Revealed Plans

Given the fact that God is living and active, he is not food in the cupboard, passively there until you go for it. We ought not be surprised if God takes the initiative like a woman who has lost a coin or a shepherd who has lost a sheep, or a father whose son is prodigal. Those who imagine that God transcends the personal in such a way that their deity is more like a vapor or a gas diffused throughout the universe may seem philosophically profound, but unfortunately, are profoundly wrong. God is more like a faithful lifeguard or an all-wise personnel manager than an impersonal "Force." A purely contemplative life, inactive in meeting the needs of the spiritually lost and physically deprived, is not godly.

Although Jesus Christ is the same yesterday, today, and forever (in character and purpose), he may use different strategies or methods.

As relational theologian Bruce Larson observed, God "is always changing in his strategy. God is a God of change in both the Old and New Testament." The prophets challenged those who lived in the past. "Forget the former things; do not dwell on the past. See I am doing a new thing!" (Isa. 43:18–19).

"If God is in the business of perfecting his people," Bruce Larson argued, "then change must be in order." Since hope, with faith and love, is one of the three great verities in life, "we must deal with the fact that hope is an attitude about a future state which can only be ushered in by change." Difficult as it is for conservative mentalities to live with changes in strategy and method emotionally, "Christians need to be excited by change, expectant about it. Indeed, Christians should feel at home in change, for God is the initiator of much change."[93] The changes God initiates, and Christians eagerly anticipate, do not contradict his nature and purposes. God's actions are never out of character.

As self-existent, God does not depend on persons or processes in time and space, but uniquely deserves their worship. God does not need our works for his own well-being. He does not lack anything that we can give. God created people in order to give the undeserved benefits of his common and special grace to them, not to fill up some lack in himself. None can compare to the God who has life in himself. So none deserve the same honor, tribute, and praise as the Lord of Life.

As eternal, God is always there desiring personal relationships with his people, sustaining and governing the world, supporting all that is real, good, beautiful, and true. Beyond the limits of time, the fellowship believers have with God continues beyond the grave and beyond history itself. As eternal, God graciously gives sinners the gift of eternal life, life from his transcendent self, from above all temporal sources and resources. The transformations achieved by other agencies or new consciousness powers within ourselves can never have the permanence of the eternal life from above. In the midst of new-age thinking, which declares that people have infinite potential within themselves, ministers of the gospel need to make clear that the source of authentically eternal life transcends all temporal techniques for changing consciousness.

What difference does it make if in nature and purposes God is eternally immutable? However tragic the developments in history may seem, never will God be unfaithful to his plan of redemption. His wisdom, holiness, and love are not affected by entropy or fatigue. None of God's purposes of grace can flicker and fail. The objective validity of God's truth will hold good though heaven and earth pass away.

God will never break faith with those who trust him.

Pro–Freedom Under God

Whether or not we bow to an unpredictably active Lord of all who is distinct from the world is as much a matter of our wills as our intellects. Are we willing to find our freedom under the Almighty? Or do we imagine that to be free we must deny the existence of a living God distinct from the world?

Consider the insightful analysis of one who was for ten years a process theologian and has now returned to faith in the sovereign God of biblical theism. Along with many penetrating criticisms of process thought, Royce Gordon Gruenler says:

> At the heart, I am convinced, the system sets out not so much to defend God against the problem of evil . . . but is designed to assure that we are free from the despotic control of a sovereign God, such as confronts us in the Judeo-Christian Scriptures. . . . In order to be completely free to choose without external compulsion from a sovereign God, other persons . . . must be completely alone on the very edge of creativity . . . like one of Gottfried Wilhelm Leibniz's windowless monads.[94]

The god of process theologians cannot even know the future. To preserve their self-defined freedom, reality itself and God's experience of it must remain open. Starting with human-centered freedom, an evangelical Arminian attracted to process thought argued, "Either the future is open for God, or I am not really free."[95] But the highest freedom delivers us from ultimate loyalty to finite creatures who wish to be gods, including ourselves. Rebels against the omniscient God, as Jesus said, find themselves idolatrously enslaved to sin (John 8:34).

Pro–Transcendent Authority

Paul Tillich's views also seem to reflect rebellion against objective truths delivered from a transcendent God outside of himself. Tillich's world view is motivated by his opposition to "heteronomy," the rule of a law from another than himself. He also rejects "autonomy"—that is, living by the rational structure of one's own mind. Instead, Tillich favored "theonomy," the law of "Being itself" within one's self. Committed to the inner principles of the universe, Tillich did not deny the self nor distinguish the sacred from the secular. His experience of being itself contributed to his sense of wholeness. In the name of ecstatic union with the depth of his own (and others') being, Tillich revolted against the transcendent Lord of all. He, being a man, blasphemously called his own perspective "theonomy." A more descriptive term for anyone whose "ultimate concern" is within himself, however "inexhaustible" the ground of his being, might be "being-onomy." Medically speaking, we might consider it the disease of "being-itus."[96]

A sign in a physician's office reads, "Whether you get well or not may depend upon which of us is the doctor." Whether we find and minister moral and spiritual health or not, may depend on whether we esteem as divine the depth of our inner selves or the transcendent God (uniquely disclosed in Christ and Scripture).

Reason for a Resistance Movement

Eventually a king will come who "will do as he pleases. He will exalt and magnify himself above every god and will say unheard-of things against the God of gods" (Dan. 11:36). Having desecrated the temple and abolished the sacrifices, he will set up the abomination that causes desolation (v. 31).

"With flattery he will corrupt those who have violated the covenant, but the people who know their God will firmly resist him" (v. 32).

Before Daniel's predicted abomination comes to pass, shortly before the Lord Jesus Christ returns to judge the world (Matt. 24:15), Christian theists ought to stand against the burgeoning consensus of movements committed to worship and service of the creation rather than the Creator. Preaching and teaching must prepare people to defend theism and live and work for the glory of God. Throughout the different areas of society, theists need to speak out, in psychology, education, medicine, and politics. As the source of all truth about reality, the transcendent God cannot wisely be dismissed in any area of life.

REVIEW QUESTIONS

To Help Relate and Apply
Each Section in This Chapter

1. *Briefly state the classical problem* this chapter addresses and indicate reasons why genuine inquiry into it is important for your world view and your existence personally and socially.

2. *Objectively summarize the influential answers* given to this problem in history as hypotheses to be tested. Be able to compare and contrast their real similarities and differences (not merely verbal similarities or differences).

3. *Highlight the primary biblical evidence* on which to decide among views—evidence found in the relevant teachings of the major divisions of Scripture—and decide for yourself which historical hypothesis (or synthesis of historical views) provides the most consistent and adequate account of the primary biblical data.

4. *Formulate in your own words your doctrinal conviction* in a logically consistent and adequate way, organizing your conclusions in ways you can ex-

plain clearly, support biblically, and communicate effectively to your spouse, children, friends, Bible class, or congregation.

5. *Defend your view* as you would to adherents of the alternative views, showing that the other views are logically less consistent and factually faced with more difficulties than your view in accounting for the givens, not only of special revelation but also of human experience in general.

6. *Explore the differences the viability of your conviction can make in your life.* Then test your understanding of the viability of your view by asking, "Can I live by it authentically (unhypocritically) in relation to God and to others in my family, church, vocation, neighborhood, city, nation, and world?"

MINISTRY PROJECTS

To Help Communicate This Doctrine in Christian Service

1. *Memorize one major verse or passage* that in its context teaches the heart of this doctrine and may serve as a text from which to preach, teach, or lead small group studies on the topic. The memorized passages from each chapter will build a body of content useful also for meditation and reference in informal discussions.

2. *Formulate the major idea of the doctrine in one sentence* based on the passage memorized. This idea should be useful as the major thesis of either a lesson for a class (junior high to adult) or a message for a church service.

3. *State the specific purpose or goal of your doctrinal lesson or message.* Your purpose should be more than informative. It should show why Christians need to accept this truth and live by it (unhypocritically). For teaching purposes, list indicators that would show to what extent class members have grasped the truth presented.

4. *Outline your message or lesson in complete sentences.* Indicate how you would support the truth of the doctrine's central ideas and its relevance to life and service. Incorporate elements from this chapter's historical, biblical, systematic, apologetic, and practical sections selected according to the value they have for your audience.

5. *List applications of the doctrine* for communicating the difference this conviction makes in life (for sermons, lessons, small-group Bible studies, or family devotional Bible studies). Applications should make clear what the doctrine is, why one needs to know it, and how it will make differences in thinking. Then show how the difference in thought will lead to differences in values, priorities, attitudes, speech, and personal action. Consider also the doctrine's possible significance for family, church, neighborhood, city, regional, and national actions.

6. *Start a file and begin collecting illustrations* of this doctrine's central idea, the points in your outline, and your applications.

7. *Write out your own doctrinal statement on this subject in one paragraph* (in half a page or less). To work toward a comprehensive doctrinal statement, collect your formulations based on a study of each chapter of *Integrative Theology.* As your own statement of Christian doctrine grows, you will find it personally strengthening and useful when you are called on for your beliefs in general and when you apply for service with churches, mission boards, and other Christian organizations. Any who seek ordination to Christian ministry will need a comprehensive doctrinal statement that covers the broad scope of theology.

GOD'S MANY-SPLENDORED CHARACTER

God's Many-Splendored Character

THE PROBLEM: HOW SHALL WE VIEW THE CHARACTER OF GOD INTELLECTUALLY, ETHICALLY, EMOTIONALLY, VOLITIONALLY, AND RELATIONALLY?

In chapter 5 we emphasized the kind of being God is ontologically—a living, active, personal Spirit, who is self-sufficient, eternal, unchanging, and omnipresent. In this chapter we inquire primarily about the capacities and characteristics of the divine being intellectually, ethically, emotionally, volitionally, and relationally. A number of questions and issues are faced in this chapter. For instance: What is included in the claim that God is all-knowing? Does God's knowledge include both his own purposes and the future free acts of persons? How does God's wisdom differ from his omniscience? Does the fact that God shows mercy on some persons but punishes others eternally invalidate the assertion that he is just? How shall we understand the relation between God's justice and his mercy? Moreover, what is involved in the rich claim that "God is love [*agapē*]"? The reality of God's love (as well as human love) will be shown to be more volitional than emotional.

In the modern world can God's anger and wrath toward persons made in his image be reconciled with his love? Does the claim that God is a jealous and angry God cast any shadow over his holy character? In the day of judgment will God's compassion and mercy prevail over his hatred of evil? Furthermore, what light might contemporary interest in personal authenticity shed on the character of God? Does the perfection of omnipotence mean that God can make a square circle, tell a lie, or destroy himself? How can the belief that God is transcendent be reconciled with the notion that he is immanent in the world in terms of his presence and operations? Does the claim of transcendence cast God in the role of a ruthless despot, as liberals claim? Or is such a notion entirely consistent with an understanding of the supreme Being?

ALTERNATIVE INTERPRETATIONS IN THE CHURCH

The character or perfections of God have been variously interpreted within the Christian tradition, broadly conceived. The following represents a summary of the principal ways in which God's attributes have been understood.

Marcion and the Gnostics

Marcionite and Gnostic dualism drew a radical distinction between the inferior god of the Old Testament (the demiurge or creator) and the greater God revealed in the New Testament (the Redeemer). The former, who created the material world, was a god of anger, mighty in war; he was one who took vengeance on his enemies. Since the creator permitted the Fall, Marcion reasoned, he could not be good, all-knowing, and all-powerful. Several early Fathers, including Tertullian, responded that Marcion's creator god was the Devil of hell. The Redeemer, Marcion continued, was a God of pure love and mercy who revealed himself in Christ. This Most High God never became angry and never inflicted punishment. According to Marcion, the God of grace fought against and vanquished the god of law and justice and so opened the way to salvation for all who trust him. Clearly, Marcion ruptured the unity of God by assuming that the good God could not be just and the merciful God could not be angry.

Scholastic Thomism

The Thomistic school arrived at a fairly traditional understanding of the divine attributes by the special method of rational deduction from the notion of God as first unmoved mover, first efficient cause, and absolutely necessary being. Aquinas reasoned a priori that such a being contains within himself all the excellencies of perfection. Since infinite perfection includes intelligence, there must exist in God the most perfect knowledge. God perfectly knows himself ("necessary knowledge") and all things outside of himself ("knowledge of vision"). Indeed, God knows all things—past, present, and future contingent—not in a temporal succession but simultaneously in the vision of his eternal now. From the attribute of will (also necessary to perfection) Thomas argued that God is perfect love. Human love is motivated by perceived goodness in its object. God's love, on the contrary, freely creates goodness in all finite things. Since there are not passions in an absolutely perfect being, Thomas understood the emotional attributes of anger, compassion, and jealousy in a metaphorical sense. He argued that what God actually does (creation, preservation, etc.) he accomplishes by his "ordinary power." God's omnipotence—his "absolute power"—exceeds his actual operations in our particular order. Thus, "God's power is not limited to some particular effect, but He is able to do absolutely all things; in other words, He is omnipotent."[1] On closer inspection, it appears that, following Pseudo-Dionysius and others, Thomas arranged the attributes in two categories: those by way of negation (eliminating characteristics that do not apply to the perfect first cause—e.g., *im*material, *in*visible, *in*finite) and those by way of eminence (infinitely elevating perfections found in finite creatures—e.g., *omni*scient, *omni*potent, *all*-loving).

Deism and Socinianism

Deists, who succumbed to the rationalism of the seventeenth and eighteenth centuries, posited a transcendent God who is the first cause of the created order and governs the universe from a distance, much like an indifferent clockmaker who made a clock and then let it run on its own. With their emphasis on the divine transcendence, Deists effectively denied that God is immanent in providential and in redemptive activity. Thus the Deists allowed no special revelation, no fulfilled prophecy, no miracles, and no active providence. They conceded that God is infinitely wise and good and that he righteously rewards good and punishes evil. But, given their denial of God's continued involvement in the universe, they seriously compromised God's love and mercy. Concluding that belief in an all-knowing and all-powerful God would be inconsistent with evil in the world, they also limited his attributes of omniscience and omnipotence.

The rationalistic Socinians (F. Socinus, J. Crell) emasculated the divine omniscience by insisting that God has an imperfect knowledge of future conditional events. Since free human acts are uncertain as to their actualization, it is impossible that God should infallibly foreknow them. The Socinians also assailed the notion of God's retributive justice. "There is no such justice in God that requires absolutely and inexorably that sin be punished."[2] The divine justice was viewed as general moral excellence, on the basis of which God frees sinners from punishment.

Schleiermacher and Ritschl

Schleiermacher prepared the way for the liberal interpretation by viewing God's attributes as explications of the human religious consciousness. This Romantic theologian divided the divine perfections into three categories: (1) the absolute attributes that arise from one's sense of dependence (eternity, omnipresence, omnipotence, and omniscience), (2) the moral attributes, which arise from consciousness of sin (holiness, justice, and mercy), and (3) those attributes that arise from the person's experience of grace (love and wisdom). Schleiermacher insisted that God's knowledge and power are limited to what actually transpires in the world. Since the real world is the complete expression of the divine will and power, nature reflects all there is of God. Schleiermacher regarded justice the causal link by which sin results in

suffering; little place was found in his system for God's wrath.

Schleiermacher's reduction of the divine attributes was carried to more radical ends by Ritschl, an antisupernaturalist theologian who regarded God's moral attributes as fundamental and insisted that the only adequate view of God is love. "There is no other conception of equal worth beside this which need to be taken into account."[3] He maintained that holiness, justice, and wrath are alien to the divine being. The notion of God's distributive justice and anger against sin were particularly opposed. In Ritschl, retribution and punishment were swallowed up by the divine goodness and grace.

Modern Protestant Liberalism

Twentieth-century Protestant liberalism, in its quest to make God relevant to modern minds, so stressed the divine immanence as to equate God with the world order. In general, God's attributes were identified by magnifying the noble qualities of persons. For example, Walter Rauschenbusch claimed that the classical doctrine of transcendence and power represents a totalitarian concept of God, whereas the model of immanence upholds the democratic view. Jesus, he argued, fought against the totalitarian view, by which God was imagined to be remote from humanity, interfering in human affairs only when necessary, and exacting punishment according to a capricious will. By democratizing the God-concept, Jesus upheld God as the Father of all spirits, infinitely loving, and close to all persons. Rauschenbusch was willing to think of God as less than omnipotent and omniscient if such a model would further the kingdom.

A. C. Knudson polemicized against the idea of retributive justice, where the divine righteousness rewards or punishes in accord with one's deeds.

The old view of God as an "unfeeling judge" must be replaced by the modern conception of God as "forgiving love." Claims Knudson, "There would seem to be no principle in the divine nature that requires that rewards and punishments be meted out to men in strict accordance with their deserts. . . . No atonement in the ordinary sense of the term is necessary before the forgiving love of God can become operative."[4]

W. A. Brown claims that all the emotions attributed to God in the Bible are manifestations of love. This is true not only of God's mercy and long-suffering but also of his jealousy and anger. Both sets of attributes reflect God's "desire to win men for himself, and his opposition to any obstacle which stands in the way of his realizing his loving end."[5] Wrath is merely a form of redeeming love. Some scholars also deny anger and wrath in God. Walter Eichrodt, an Old Testament specialist, insists that "wrath never forms one of the permanent attributes of the God of Israel; it can only be understood . . . as a footnote to the will to fellowship of the covenant God."[6] On the New Testament side, C. H. Dodd viewed wrath not as a divine attribute but as the impersonal process of retribution. "We cannot think with full consistency of God in terms of the highest human ideals of personality and yet attribute to him the irrational passion of anger."[7]

Barthian Neoorthodoxy

Against the radical immanentalism of liberal theology, neoorthodoxy stresses the radical otherness of God and the vast gulf that allegedly exists between Creator and creature. Karl Barth, operating from the premise that the attributes of God describe, not his essence but his acts, represents God as "the One who loves in freedom."[8] That is, love constitutes the foreground and

freedom the background of all God's operations. Love is that perfection in God that seeks the creation of fellowship without any regard to worth in the object loved. Freedom means that God is determined and moved by himself and not by anything from without. Viewed as ontic independence, it means that the sovereign God is free to speak or to keep silent, free to adopt or to reject, free to illumine or to blind.

Barth enumerates the perfections of the divine *loving* as grace counterbalanced by holiness, as mercy counterbalanced by righteousness, and as patience counterbalanced by wisdom. The divine righteousness means that violations of God's holiness will incur terrible wrath and punishment. The divine patience means that God does not immediately destroy, but he gives people opportunity to repent. The perfections of the divine *freedom* Barth enumerates as unity and omnipresence, constancy and omnipotence, and eternity and glory. With respect to omnipotence, God's power is not a neutral or a purely physical power; rather, it is a supremely moral power—"the power both to do the sum of whatever is possible for him and therefore genuinely possible, and also not to do what is impossible for him and therefore completely impossible."[9] Omnipotence includes both omniscience and omnivolence. Barth means by the latter that God's will embraces and controls all other wills. Nothing can hinder the will of the God who is capable of willing everything but the absurd. Finally, Barth upholds the unconditioned transcendence of the "wholly Other"; an absolute gulf exists between God and all created beings. Immanence, to Barth, means relatedness to the world through the incarnate Word, Jesus Christ.

Protestant and Roman Catholic Neoliberalism

Recent expressions of Protestant and Roman Catholic liberalism tend to view

God as the creative power immanent in human life and history (panentheism). Traditional notions of omnipresence, omniscience, retributive justice, and wrath are denied as unworthy of the real God. John A. T. Robinson, following Paul Tillich, attacks the classical notion of transcendence that views God as a discrete personal being wholly other to man. To affirm the transcendence of God is to acknowledge "the transcendent, unconditional element in all our relationships, and supremely in our relationships with other people."[10] For John Macquarrie, a Christian existentialist, omnipotence means that "Being itself" is the source and horizon of all possibilities. God's wrath is viewed as positive rather than punitive; it connotes "a transforming of evil into good, a healing of injuries, a restoring of what has been destroyed or blighted."[11]

Process theology affirms that as to his primordial nature, God is supremely absolute and transcendent—the source of all ideals and possibilities—but according to his consequent nature, God is supremely relative and immanent—a participant in the world's evolutionary advance. This increasingly popular form of neoclassical theism insists that God is supremely "creative-responsive Love."[12] The creative side of love (a function of the primordial nature) produces positive transformation in creatures, whereas the responsive side (a function of the consequent nature) ensures that God is changed and enriched through interaction with the world. Process theology wages war against the notion of divine omnipotence, claiming that God works by the solicitation of love rather than by the coercion of power. In addition, followers of Whitehead insist that God does not know future contingent events. Rather, God knows "the purpose He entertains, the potentialities of the created order, and his own ability to overrule for good."[13] Finally, process theology pays little

attention to God's moral attributes (e.g., holiness, justice, truth), choosing rather to stress his feeling qualities (e.g., empathy, patience, tenderness) and aesthetic (e.g., imagination, creativity, refreshment). As Whitehead, the father of process thought, put it, the love of God "is a little oblivious to morals."[14]

On the Roman Catholic side, consistent with the claim that the entire world has been forgiven, Karl Rahner says little about God's justice, anger, and judgment. Thus, "we have more reason to praise his mercy than to fear his justice, because He has allowed his grace to overflow and not his anger."[15] Hans Küng likewise stresses God's benevolence at the expense of his justice and wrath: "He does not demand but gives, does not oppress but raises up, does not wound but heals. . . . He forgives instead of condemning, liberates instead of punishing, permits the unrestricted rule of grace instead of law."[16] In reaction to the distant and unrelated God of the Greeks, Küng stresses the immanence and radical haveability of the ultimate Reality who indwells persons and history. Leslie Dewart avers that the divine omnipotence must be abandoned as a threat to creaturely freedom. God deals with persons, not by "acting upon" them with limitless power, but in terms of "being with" them in reciprocal relations. People today "find themselves compelled by their Christian faith to *disbelieve* in a supreme Being, in a God behind whose kindness and generosity to man stands a supreme, omnipotent and eternal will."[17]

Protestant Orthodoxy

The Fathers, the Reformers, Protestant orthodox theologians, and Evangelicals posit a God who is all-knowing, holy, and loving, who justly rewards good and punishes evil, who detests sin and yet is long-suffering and compassionate with sinners, who is free, authentic, and all-powerful, and who is transcendent in being (as the exalted One) and yet immanent (as the related One) in providential and redemptive activity.

The apologist Theophilus represented God's character by saying what it is not: "In glory he is incomparable, in wisdom unrivalled, in goodness inimitable, in kindness unutterable."[18] To the question "Is God angry?" Theophilus responds, "Yes, He is angry with those who act wickedly, but He is good and kind and merciful to those who love and fear him. For He is a chastener of the godly . . . but He is a judge and punisher of the impious."[19] In the East, Clement upheld God's omniscience by affirming that God comprehends all things past, present, and future in a single glance. Against Marcion he insisted that the good God is both righteous and just. "Being a lover of men, He is a hater of the wicked, entertaining a perfect aversion to all villany."[20] Clement pointed out that the God who is ontologically transcendent, being beyond space and time, is dynamically near through the immanent operations of the Logos. In the West, Tertullian argued that God would not be wholly good unless he were an enemy of evil. The righteous God "knows how to *heal*, but also how to *strike*."[21] Gregory of Nazianzus argued that mercy is God's natural work, whereas anger is his unnatural work. God is naturally inclined to the former but compelled by sin to the latter. Gregory adds that it is impossible for God to be evil or to cause two plus two to equal ten, "for this would be indicative of weakness in God rather than of strength."[22]

Augustine claims that the omniscient God comprehends all things past, present, and future in his single timeless contemplation.[23] The divine foreknowledge connotes not merely prescience

but the ordination that ensures things will eventuate in accord with the will of God. One of Augustine's favorite designations for God is that of "truth." God is true (1) in the metaphysical sense that he is the genuine essence; (2) in the ethical sense of a perfect correspondence between his being, deeds, and words; and (3) in the logical sense that he knows things as they really are. The bishop found no inconsistency between the divine justice and mercy. In justice, God rewards good for good and evil for evil; in mercy, he, through justifying grace, rewards good for evil. Emotionally, God "is jealous without any darkening of spirit, wrathful without any perturbation, pitiful without any pain, and patient without any passion."[24] God's anger is not a disturbing emotion; it is his just retribution against sin. Volitionally, Augustine stresses that God is free to do whatever he pleases in heaven or on earth. Apart from any external compulsion, God is free to create, to confer mercy, and to punish. God is omnipotent, not that he can do anything at all (he cannot die, sin, deny himself, etc.), but that he is able to do whatever he wills—God's will and power being inseparable from his essence. Finally, Augustine insists that God is both transcendent and immanent—transcendent above space as the exalted One, immanent in space as the Actuality that fills everything with his being and power.[25]

With Luther, several attributes of God came in for special attention. In his innermost heart, God is "nothing but burning love and a glowing oven full of love."[26] According to Luther, God's love is neither kindled by any worth, nor quenched by any unworthiness, in its object. Further, if love is God's "proper work," being identical with his nature, wrath is that "alien work," contrary to his nature, that is provoked by wickedness. Noteworthy in Luther is the contrast between transcendence and immanence—i.e., between God in himself and God manifested in Christ, between God hidden (*Deus absconditus*) and God revealed (*Deus revelatus*), between the naked God (*Deus nudus*) and God clothed in his promises.[27] To view God as majesty and law breeds despair; to view him as revealed in Christ opens the door to justification.

Calvin argues that the attributes of God that are most important for us to know are his lovingkindness, righteousness, and judgment.[28] God's fundamental disposition toward the elect is gratuitous love. In spite of our corrupt natures and depraved conduct, "He still finds something in us which in lovingkindness He can love."[29] Righteousness connotes that God's will is the supreme standard of justice and equity. "He must naturally love justice and abhor injustice."[30] As for judgment, the wicked are the special objects of God's severity and wrath. "As God is the fountain of all righteousness, He must necessarily be the enemy and judge of man so long as he is a sinner."[31] Whereas Luther stressed the divine condescension, Calvin emphasized God's transcendence, majesty, and freedom. Although God is infinite in majesty, nevertheless he is immanent in his providential and redemptive operations.

The Protestant confessions clearly articulate the divine perfections. The Belgic Confession (1619) affirms that God is "incomprehensible, invisible, immutable, infinite, almighty, perfectly wise, just, good, and the overflowing fountain of all good" (art. 1). According to the Westminster Confession of Faith (1647), God is "almighty, most wise, most holy, most free, most absolute, . . . most loving, gracious, merciful, long-suffering, abundant in goodness and truth, forgiving iniquity, transgression and sin; the rewarder of them that diligently seek him; and withal most just and terrible in his judgments" (ch. 2).

Charles Hodge and William G. T. Shedd rehearse the consensus of Evangelical opinion on the divine perfections. God's holiness connotes absolute moral perfection—entire freedom from moral evil. His justice is both rectoral and distributive. The former connotes that God has laid down laws that are holy, just, and good. The latter implies that God rewards everyone according to his works. Distributive justice is remunerative in that it rewards virtue; it is retributive in that it punishes evil. "In every instance of transgression, the penalty of law must be inflicted, either personally or vicariously; either upon the transgressor or upon his substitute."[32] Yet the God of the Bible is equally a God of grace and mercy. Grace is God's benevolent compassion toward the person as a guilty sinner, and mercy is his compassion toward the one in misery and wretchedness.

Recent monographs by J. I. Packer,[33] Ronald Nash,[34] and Stephen Davis[35] helpfully discuss the character of God from an Evangelical perspective.

THE BIBLICAL TEACHING

In order to determine which interpretation of the character of God is to be admitted, we turn now to the primary scriptural data.

Pentateuch

God's perfect, all-inclusive knowledge of everything in the universe is attested by Hagar's name for Deity— "the God who sees me" (*ēl rā'î*, Gen. 16:13), and by the fact that Israel's suffering in Egypt was completely transparent to him (Exod. 3:7). God has unerring knowledge of the future, a knowledge that embraces his own actions (Exod. 9:18–20) and the free choices of human agents. Concerning the latter, God knew in advance that Pharaoh would decide to release Israel from Egypt (Exod. 6:1; 11:1) and that once they were in the land Israel would profane the covenant and worship idols (Deut. 31:20–21). There is no suggestion in these texts that God's foreknowledge is the efficient cause of the object of knowledge.

In the patriarchal history, Abraham's servant (Gen. 24:27) and Jacob (Gen. 32:10) praised God for his faithfulness (*'emet*) to them. At Sinai Yahweh revealed himself to Moses as "abounding in . . . faithfulnesss" (Exod. 34:6). Moses in turn represented God as wholly dependable or reliable: "He is the Rock [*ṣûr*] . . . a faithful [*'emûnāh*] God who does no wrong" (Deut. 32:4). A prominent theme of the Pentateuch is Yahweh's unswerving faithfulness to his covenant with Israel. Hence Moses' reminder: "He is the faithful [Niphal participle of *'āman*, to be firm] God, keeping his covenant of love to a thousand generations of those who love him and keep his commands" (Deut. 7:9; cf. Gen. 9:16; Exod. 2:24; Deut. 4:31).

When Moses testified of Yahweh, "All his ways are just (*mišpāt*). . . . Upright and just (*ṣaddîq*) is he" (Deut. 32:4), he affirmed that God consistently acts in accord with his righteous character. God shows no partiality or unfairness in his dealings; he gives to each what is his due. Thus, in the record of the Fall, God inflicted just penalties on the serpent, on Eve, and on Adam (Gen. 3:14–24). He justly punished Cain for his murder of Abel (Gen. 4:10–13) and executed justice by the destruction of the Flood (Gen. 6:5–7). When God unleashed the plagues on Egypt, Pharaoh confessed, "The LORD is in the right" (*ṣaddîq*, Exod. 9:27). God acted justly in sentencing faithless Israel to forty years of wilderness wandering and in permitting only Caleb and Joshua of that generation to enter the promised land (Num. 14:26–35).

Mercy in Scripture connotes God's goodness to those in distress or deserving judgment. At Sinai, God revealed himself as "a God merciful [*raḥûm*] and gracious" (Exod. 34:6, RSV), who freely exercises mercy (*rāḥam*) on whom he will (Exod. 33:19). Later Moses warned Israel that after committing idolatry in Canaan their unity would be dissolved. Yet if they repented, the merciful God would renew the covenant and relieve their misery (Deut. 4:27–31). God's standing promise was that whenever Israel returned from her idolatrous liaisons, he would turn from his anger and "show mercy" (Deut. 13:17).

Prominent in the Pentateuch is the unfailing love (*hesed*, 245 times in the OT) of the Lord who is loyal to his covenant. Thus, Yahweh disclosed himself to Israel as a loving God: "showing love to a thousand generations of those who love me and keep my commandments" (Exod. 20:6; cf. 34:6–7; Num. 14:18–19). God chose Israel and delivered them from the power of Pharaoh simply by virtue of his love (*'ahʾbāh*) for them (Deut. 7:7–8; cf. 4:37). If Israel would be faithful to his covenant of love (*habᵉrît wᵉhahesed*, Deut. 7:9), God would love (*'āhēb*) and bless them (Deut. 7:13).

The word "holiness" (*qōdeš*) likely derives from the root meaning "to cut" or "to separate."[36] Thus God is holy in the twofold sense that he is separate (1) from all that is finite and earthly and (2) from all that is unclean and defiled. The first dimension of the divine holiness connotes God's transcendence over the creation, the second the ethical perfection of his character. Holiness in the sense of greatness and sovereignty is affirmed in Exodus 15:11: "Who is like you—majestic in holiness, awesome in glory, working wonders?" The word "holy" (*qādōš*) and cognates occur more than 150 times in Leviticus,[37] chiefly in the sense of ethical purity. Thus, the offerings an Israelite must bring if he would approach God (Lev. 1–7), the special priesthood to mediate access to God (8–10), and the laws concerning purity (11–15) all attest the absolute moral perfection of God's character. The leitmotif of the Book of Leviticus is the divine command "Be holy because I, the Lord your God, am holy" (19:2; cf. 11:44–45).

The history of Israel illustrates God's intense hatred of evil. God's anger was unleashed against Israel for worshiping the golden calf at Sinai (Exod. 32:10–12; cf. Deut. 9:7–8; 19–20), for their discontent with the provision of manna and quail (Num. 11:33), and for their veneration of the fertility god Baal (25:3–9). That God's wrath was kindled by the idolatry of his covenant people is a frequent theme of Deuteronomy (4:25–26; 6:14–15; 29:22–28, et al.). Yet God's anger was tempered by a patience that grants the sinner opportunity to repent—so the Lord is described as being "slow to anger" (*'erek 'appayîm*, Exod. 34:6; Num. 14:18). God repeatedly promised Israel that if they would turn from foreign gods, he would "have compassion" (*rāham, nāham*) on them (Deut. 13:17; 30:3). To the oppressed, God promises, "I will hear, for I am compassionate" (Exod. 22:27). God's compassion thus represents his love and pity for the weak and unfortunate. Emotionally God is also depicted as jealous or endowed with a righteous possessiveness. Since God reserves for himself the worship of his people (19:5–6), his jealousy is aroused when the redeemed forsake the covenant and cleave to foreign gods (20:5; Deut. 4:24; 32:16). Yahweh himself said, "Do not worship any other god, for the Lord, whose name is Jealous [*qannā'*], is a jealous God" (Exod. 34:14).

Freedom, a quality close to sovereignty, means that God has power to determine his own self according to his nature and purposes. Thus, God is depicted as a sovereign agent who freely creates (Gen. 1:1), freely grants finite people a measure of freedom (2:16–17), freely plans redemption (3:15), freely chooses a special people (12:1–3), freely reveals himself (Exod. 3:2–15) and his moral law (20:2–17), and freely redeems (14:21–30). God is capable of performing these works, since he is "God Almighty" (Gen. 17:1; Exod. 6:3) and "the Mighty One of Jacob" (Gen. 49:24). In the exercise of his omnipotence, God sometimes works directly, without secondary causes, as in the judgment at Babel (Gen. 11:5–9) and the birth of Isaac (Gen. 21:1–2; cf. 17:17). More frequently, God exercises his power through secondary causes, such as may be the case in the destruction of Sodom and Gomorrah (Gen. 19), several of the plagues against Pharaoh (Exod. 7:11), and Israel's passage through the Sea of Reeds (Exod. 14). In the words of Moses, God is "majestic in power . . . , awesome in glory, working wonders" (Exod. 15:6, 11). Nothing is too hard for the Lord (Gen. 18:14).

The God of the patriarchs is transcendent in being, and this means that he is distinct from all that he has created. The divine transcendence is commonly expressed in spatial terms; e.g., he is "the Most High" (Num. 24:16; Deut. 32:8) and "God Most High" (Gen. 14:18–20). The terrifying phenomena of thunder, lightning, fire, and smoke were visible when God descended to the top of Mount Sinai (Exod. 19:18, 20). The biblical view unites the transcendence and immanence of the divine Being, as in Deuteronomy 4:39: "The Lord is God in heaven above and on the earth below." God is also immanent in providential activity, in the sense that he unceasingly directs the affairs of people and nations to their appointed ends (Gen. 39:2–3; 45:7–8; 50:20; Deut. 2:7). The God of Israel likewise is immanent in redemptive activity, manifesting himself with Israel to redeem and comfort (Exod. 3:8; 15:13; Num. 9:15–23).

Historical Books

The accounts of Israel's history attest that God instantly and all-inclusively knows people's thoughts (1 Chron. 28:9), deeds (1 Sam. 2:3), and comings and goings (2 Kings 19:27). God inerrantly knows not only all actualities (2 Chron. 16:9) but also all future contingencies—i.e., yet unrealized events whose occurrence depends on the free choices of human agents. Thus, God knew in advance that David would vanquish the Philistine forces at Keilah (1 Sam. 23:4–5) and that he would be betrayed to Saul if he remained in the area (vv. 10–13). God is also presented as absolutely faithful to his promises (Josh. 23:14) and to his covenant of love established with Israel (1 Kings 8:23; Neh. 1:5). When Israel was oppressed by pagan neighbors, God in fidelity to his covenant preserved his chosen people (2 Kings 13:23). The name Rock (*ṣûr*), commonly ascribed to God (1 Sam. 2:2; 2 Sam. 22:32, 47), connotes both the strength and faithfulnesss of Israel's God.

That God is "righteous" (*ṣaddîq*) connotes his right behavior or holiness in action (Ezra 9:15; Neh. 9:8). God is just (same word, *ṣaddîq*) in that with absolute equity he apportions to each what is his due (2 Chron. 12:6; Neh. 9:33). Hence David's song celebrating God's deliverance: "To the faithful you show yourself faithful, to the blameless you show yourself blameless, to the pure you show yourself pure, but to the crooked you show yourself shrewd" (2 Sam. 22:26–27). "With the LORD our God there is no injustice or partiality" (2 Chron. 19:7). In some cases a slight offense against his holiness incurs swift punishment (1 Sam. 6:19–20). Yet even when God punishes, he does not utterly abandon his people, for the Lord is "a

gracious and merciful God" (Neh. 9:31). The Lord steadfastly maintains his covenant of love (*ḥesed*, 1 Kings 8:23; 2 Chron. 6:14).

The history of Israel is replete with God's hatred of evil. Thus, "the LORD's anger burned" against Israel on account of Achan's sin (Josh. 7:1) and against Uzzah for his careless handling of the ark (2 Sam. 6:6–7). God's anger also burned against Israel for serving false gods (1 Kings 14:9, 15; 16:26), for acts of divination and sorcery (2 Kings 17:17), for consulting mediums and spiritists (2 Kings 21:6)—in short, for disobeying the law of God (2 Kings 22:13). Israel's sins stirred up God's righteous possessiveness or jealousy (Josh. 24:19). Thus his response to spiritual infidelity was "jealous anger" (1 Kings 14:22). Nevertheless, God did not impulsively punish, for he also is "slow to anger" (*'erek 'appayîm*, Neh. 9:17). Indeed, in fidelity to the covenant, God dealt with his wayward people with grace and compassion (2 Kings 13:23).

The plenitude of God's power is seen in the mighty works he performed in Israel. The staying of the waters of the Jordan (Josh. 3), the toppling of the walls of Jericho (Josh. 6), Elijah's victorious contest with the 450 prophets of Baal (1 Kings 18), and the killing of 185,000 Assyrian warriors by the angel of the Lord (2 Kings 19) demonstrate that the Yahweh of Israel is "the great, mighty and awesome God" (Neh. 9:32; cf. 1 Chron. 29:11–12). No person, no force can withstand his power (2 Chron. 20:6).

Poetry and Wisdom

In Israel's devotional literature, God knows people's thoughts and motives (Prov. 24:12), their "secret sins" (Ps. 90:8), their hurts and anxieties (Ps. 56:8), and their every action (Job 31:4; Prov. 5:21).[38] Job describes God as "perfect in knowledge" (*dē'āh*, Job

36:4; 37:16). Psalm 139 affirms that God knows every aspect of the psalmist's being: his actions (vv. 2a, 3), his mind (v. 2b), and his unformed words (v. 4). David concludes, "Such knowledge [da'at, God's intimate knowledge of him] is too wonderful for me, too lofty for me to attain" (v. 6). Divine wisdom (hokmāh, tebûnāh)—the application of knowledge to the realization of moral ends—is a common theme (Job 9:4; 12:13), particularly in connection with the creation and preservation of the universe (Ps. 104:24; Prov. 3:19–20). In Proverbs 8:22–31, God's attribute of wisdom is personified and set forth in highly descriptive language.[39] God's faithfulnesss, a common theme in the Psalter, is limitless (Pss. 36:5; 57:10), inviolable (Ps. 89:33–34), and eternal (Pss. 117:2; 146:6).

Equally common are assertions of God's righteousness and justice. As elsewhere in the Old Testament, justice connotes the principles of retribution whereby God rewards the faithful and punishes the wicked (Ps. 11:5–7; Prov. 24:12). In the Psalms, righteousness frequently signifies God's deliverance of oppressed saints in fulfillment of his covenantal faithfulnesss (Pss. 5:8; 51:14; 71:15–16, et al.). In this latter sense, ṣedāqāh is equivalent to the salvation of the Lord (Ps. 69:27). God's mercy—the concrete manifestation of pity to the weak and afflicted (Ps. 69:14–17)—results in deliverance from trouble (Ps. 40:11) and forgiveness of sins (Pss. 51:1; 79:8). In the Psalms God's covenant love (hesed) is richly represented as infinite (Ps. 57:10), "unfailing" (Ps. 107:8), everlasting (Ps. 136), and the saint's chief delight (Ps. 63:3). In the Song of Songs, the love ('ahabāh) of God is irresistible in attractive power (8:6) and absolutely indestructible (v. 7).

God, moreover, is endowed with the titles "the Holy One" (Job 6:10; Ps. 22:3; Prov. 9:10) and "the Holy One of Israel" (Pss. 78:41; 89:18). Indeed, the attribute of holiness develops into a synonym for Deity, so that God swearing by his holiness is equivalent to God swearing by himself (Ps. 89:35). Psalm 99, where holiness is thrice ascribed to God (vv. 3, 5, 9), affirms the two aspects of his holiness—i.e., transcendent majesty (vv. 1–3) and absolute moral perfection (vv. 4–5).

The literature also upholds God's severe hatred of wickedness (Ps. 45:7) and of the sinner himself. Concerning the latter, God is said to "hate" (śānē') the evildoer (Ps. 5:4–6).[40] Proverbs 6:16–19 enumerates seven abominations (tô'ēbāh), i.e., the attitudes, thoughts, speech, and actions that the Lord hates. Furthermore, "the sacrifice of the wicked" (Prov. 15:8), "the way of the wicked" (Prov. 15:9), "the thoughts of the wicked" (15:26), and the "prayers" of the wicked (28:9) are abominations to the Lord. God responds to evil by unleashing his "burning anger" (harôn 'ap, Job 20:23), furious wrath (Job 40:11), and angry rage (za'am, Ps. 69:24). Psalm 78, a rehearsal of Israel's history from Egypt to the Davidic kingdom, attests God's indignation against his people's stubbornness and disobedience (vv. 21, 31, 49, 58, 59, 62). No less real, however, is the fact that the compassionate God (Pss. 51:1; 86:15) is slow to anger ('erek 'appayîm, Pss. 86:15; 145:8)—i.e., God takes a long deep breath before venting his wrath.

Volitionally, God is free to execute his purposes in nature and history (Job 12:13–25). "Our God is in heaven; he does whatever pleases him" (Ps. 115:3). He is authentic or true in the sense that his words are in harmony with his being and actions ("the God of truth," Ps. 31:5). So his word likewise is veracious and sure ('emet, Ps. 119:142, 151, 160). Job was captivated by the power of God, i.e., that he is able to do all that he wills to do (Job 9:4, 19; 36:5, 22). Hence

225

his acknowledgment, "I know that you can do all things; no plan of yours can be thwarted" (Job 42:2). The psalmist confesses that God's power has no equal in the entire universe (Pss. 65:6; 66:3). God's will is his power; all that he wills to do, he performs (Ps. 115:3).

God's transcendence, i.e., his otherness vis-à-vis the finite world, is evidenced by the titles "God Most High" (Pss. 57:2; 78:35) and "the LORD Most High" (Ps. 47:2). The God of Israel is "the Most High over all the earth" (Pss. 83:18; 97:9). In a vivid use of spatial language the psalmist states that God is "enthroned so high, he needs to stoop to see the sky and earth" (Ps. 113:4–5, JB). The Psalms correspondingly acknowledge God's immanence in providential activity (Pss. 36:6; 65:9–13) and his immanence in redemptive activity (Pss. 23:4, 6; 78:52–55).

Prophetic Literature

The divine omniscience is the presupposition of all trustworthy prophecy. Because God's knowledge is complete and perfect, through prophets he declares future occurrences (Isa. 42:9; 48:3, 5). So perfect is God's knowledge (*da'at*) and understanding (*t*ebûnāh) that he has complete cognizance of all future contingent events (Jer. 38:17–18), particularly the course of world history (Dan. 2, esp. v. 28). The prophets also testify that God is absolutely faithful to the covenant and the promises made with Israel (Jer. 32:37–40; Ezek. 16:60; Dan. 9:4). Habakkuk 2:4 states that "the righteous will live by his faithfulness" (*'emûnāh*, i.e., God's moral steadfastness or fidelity to his holy character).[41] In spite of God's stern judgment, Jeremiah could say, "Great is your faithfulness" (Lam. 3:23).

The prophets dwell much on God's righteousness and justice. God is righteous (*ṣaddîq*) in that he consistently

acts in accord with his holy will and character (Jer. 12:1; Dan. 9:7, 14). God is just in the sense that he apportions to each what is his due, i.e., blessings for obedience and punishment for disobedience (Mic. 7:9; Nah. 1:3). Isaiah 53:4–6 teaches that the punishment justice demands would be vicariously inflicted on the Messiah. The frequent combination "justice and righteousness" (*mišpāt* and *ṣedeq/ṣ*edāqāh, Isa. 33:5; Jer. 9:24; Hos. 2:19) indicates that God's dealings with people are always characterized by "high principles" and "irreproachable conduct."[42] Such righteous demands are explicable for the reason than that God is the "Holy One" (Isa. 10:17; 40:25; Hos. 11:9, 12), the "Holy One of Jacob" (Isa. 29:23), and the "Holy One of Israel" (thirty times in Isa.; Jer. 51:5; Ezek. 39:7). God's holiness is most clearly displayed in Isaiah's temple vision (Isa. 6:1–5). The winged seraphim in worship, the shaking of the foundations, the darkness, the smoke, the prophet's cry of unworthiness, and the threefold ascription to God ("Holy, holy, holy is Yahweh, ṣ*bā'ôt*") affirm the majesty, transcendence, and absolute moral perfection of Israel's God. God's holiness in action is evidenced by his judging sin (Ezek. 28:22), by bringing Israel back from captivity (thus preserving the honor of his name, Ezek. 36:20–23; 39:27), and by punishing Israel's oppressors (Hab. 1:12–13).

God's character as love is affirmed with particular force by the prophets, especially Hosea. God's covenant love (*ḥesed*) for his people is more unshakable than the mountains—the emblem of stability. They will be moved, but his love shall stand forever (Isa. 54:10). Hosea views God's love (*ḥesed*) in terms of a faithful husband's love for his faithless wife (Hos. 3:1). When Israel persisted in apostasy and rebellion, God poured out on them a love that was free, unmerited, and overflowing (Hos. 14:4). Even though Israel spurned him, God refused to give them up (Hos. 11:7–9). The prophet promises that God will renew Israel with his love (Zeph. 3:17).

"The wrath of God is described in the Old Testament with terrible severity, especially by the prophets."[43] Since sin and its perpetrator are inextricably linked, God is said to hate (i.e., despise or detest) the sinner (Hos. 9:15; Mal. 1:3). God's emotional response to violations of his holy law is described in the strongest possible terms: "fiery anger" (Ezek. 21:31), "burning anger" (Isa. 13:13), "fierce anger" (Jer. 4:8, 26), and "indignation" (Nah. 1:6). God's fury against sin is expressed in the most dramatic imagery. As a farmer thrashes his field, so the Lord slashes his sickle across the nations (Hab. 3:12). In anger God gathers sinful humanity into a fiery furnace, much as a smelter melts unrefined metals in a crucible (Ezek. 22:17–22). And God's judgment of sinners is like the ferocity of an angry lion who tears its prey to pieces and carries them off (Hos. 5:14). Nevertheless, the execution of wrath and punishment is God's "strange work," and "his alien task" (Isa. 28:21), in the sense that God takes delight in healing rather than in destroying (Ezek. 18:32). The prophets depict God as jealous (*qānā'*) for the holiness of his name profaned by Israel's defeat (Ezek. 39:25), for his chosen people (Zech. 1:14), and for the holy land (Joel 2:18). Notwithstanding God's hatred and jealousy provoked by sin, God is "slow to anger" (Joel 2:13; Jonah 4:2), in that he sent messengers with repeated warnings (Jer. 7:13, 25) and postponed his judgments (Isa. 48:9). The prophets depict a deeply compassionate God (Hos. 11:8), whose tenderness for his people is more profound than a mother's love for her child (Isa. 49:15). God's compassion—love modified by the wretchedness of people—moved

him to restore captive Israel to the land (Isa. 54:7–8; Jer. 30:18).

God's freedom to actualize his own will is affirmed in Isaiah 46:10: "My purpose will stand, and I will do all that I please." God freely chose Cyrus of Persia to bring Israel back from captivity (Isa. 44:28). When challenged as to his choice of this pagan ruler, God responded with the parable of the potter who freely shapes the clay as he sees fit (Isa. 45:9–13). His is the sovereignty, the freedom, and the power (cf. Dan. 4:35). By his limitless power, God fashioned the heavens and earth (Jer. 10:12; Amos 4:13). The myriad of stars testify to "his great power and mighty strength" (Isa. 40:26). Truly there is nothing that the Lord is incapable of performing (Jer. 32:17, 27), except that which is contrary to his character and will—e.g., condone evil or tolerate wrong (Hab. 1:13).

Synoptic Gospels

Jesus taught that God knows the acts (e.g., giving, praying, and fasting, Matt. 6:4, 6, 18) that people perform in secret. He knows people's needs (Matt. 6:8, 32), their hearts (Luke 16:15), and the minutest details of their lives (Matt. 10:29–30). God has knowledge of future contingencies, for he knew that Tyre and Sidon (Matt. 11:21) and even Sodom (v. 23) would have repented if certain miracles had been performed in their midst. God knows in advance the exact time of Christ's return to earth (Matt. 24:36). In sum, God knows all that possibly can be known.

Jesus also upheld God's justice, or the righteous impartiality of all his ways. In the parable of the persistent widow (Luke 18:1-8), he reasoned that if a corrupt judge works justice, would not God execute justice for his chosen ones? Most assuredly God "will see that they get justice [*ekdikēsis*, just recompense], and quickly" (v. 8).

God's distributive justice is taught in the parable of the talents (Matt. 25:14–29). The first two servants who executed their duties obediently were amply rewarded, whereas the third servant who proved faithless was severely punished. Even a criminal on the cross acknowledged that God administers punishment in accord with his righteous character (Luke 23:41).

Jesus' story of the fig tree (Luke 13:6–9) teaches that God is long-suffering. The vineyard pictures Israel, the cutting of the tree represents God's judgment against sin (Luke 3:9), and the caretaker's plea for an additional year in which to wait for fruit indicates God's patience, which holds his anger in abeyance. God's compassion was amply demonstrated in the ministry of Jesus. The Lord was filled with compassion at the sight of the leper (Mark 1:41), the aimless crowds in Galilee (Matt. 9:36), the widow of Nain whose only son had died (Luke 7:13), and the hungry five thousand (Matt. 14:14). The parable of the wayward son (Luke 15:11–32) teaches that God's love for the lost in Israel is like the father's concern for the prodigal.[44] In each of the above, the verb *splanchnizomai* signifies the messianic compassion of Jesus, whereby his heart was filled with loving tenderness toward those in dire need.[45]

Following the angel's announcement that she would conceive supernaturally, Mary confessed the divine omnipotence with the words "Nothing is impossible with God" (Luke 1:37). Mary's name for God is *ho dynatos*, "the Mighty One" (Luke 1:49). Jesus likewise acknowledged that God's power knows no limits, save his character and will (Matt. 19:26; Mark 14:36). Jesus' healings (Mark 1:23–26; 2:1–12; 3:1–5, et al.), resuscitations (Luke 7:11–16; 8:49–56), exorcisms (Matt. 9:32–33; Luke 8:26–39), and nature miracles (Mark 4:35–41; 6:45–52) were wrought by a mighty power from God.

The Acts of the Apostles

God's immediate knowledge of all things past, present, and future is reflected in the prophetic predictions of Christ's crucifixion and resurrection (Acts 2:23–28; cf. 3:18).[46] James testified that from eternity God knew that the house of David would be restored and the knowledge and worship of God would be opened up to the Gentiles (15:15–18). Peter, on the same occasion, claimed that God knows the secrets of people's hearts (15:8; cf. 1:24).

In his address to the Athenians, Paul declared that God will judge the world through Christ on the basis of the absolute moral equity that is his nature (Acts 17:31). Even pagan Greeks, when they witnessed the principle of retribution at work, were quick to attribute it to "justice" (*hē dikē*, 28:4). The ground of God's justice—the perfect rectitude of his nature—in Acts is seen most clearly in the person of Jesus Christ, "the Holy and Righteous One" (3:14; cf. 4:27, 30). Still, Acts affirms that God is patient in that he grants sinners time in which to repent. With an eye to the Athenians' idolatry, Paul insists that "in the past God overlooked such ignorance" (17:30)—where the verb *hyperoraō* is used in the LXX of God's postponing severe judgment. Formerly God overlooked the spiritual darkness of the pagan world, but he will do so no longer. With the threat of severe judgment, God now calls the pagan world to repent (17:31; cf. 3:19).

God's mighty power is seen in the healing of the crippled beggar (Acts 3:1–8, 12), of Aeneas the paralytic (9:33–34), and of the crippled man at Lystra (14:8–11); in the raising of Dorcas (9:36–41) and of Eutychus from the dead (20:7–10), and in the miraculous deliverance of Peter (12:6–11) and of

Paul and Silas (16:25-26) from prison. Gamaliel reminded the Sanhedrin of the futility of humans contending against the power of God (5:38–39)—the power that created the heavens, the earth, and everything therein (4:24). The main emphasis in Acts is on God's immanence in providential activity (13:17; 17:26–27) and in redemptive activity (2:1–4; 9:5, 17). Nevertheless, Luke also upholds God's ontological transcendence over the world (7:48–50; 16:17).

Pauline Epistles

Although the word "foreknowledge" primarily indicates "foreordaining mercy"[47] or "electing grace"[48] (Rom. 8:29; 11:2; cf. 1 Cor. 8:3; Gal. 4:9; 2 Tim. 2:19), it also a major ad minor, connotes God's unerring knowledge of all things in advance, for God knows what he plans. God also possesses a plenitude of wisdom (sophia), in the sense of his ability to arrange and adapt all things to the fulfillment of his holy purposes (Rom. 11:33; 16:27; Eph. 1:7–8). The zenith of God's wisdom emerges in his ingenious plan of salvation (1 Cor. 2:7; Eph. 3:10), more particularly as the chief actor in that drama—the crucified Christ (1 Cor. 1:24, 30). Paul repeatedly affirms that God is faithful (pistos, reliable or dependable), in that he fulfills all his promises (2 Cor. 1:20), provides escape from trials (1 Cor. 10:13), protects believers from the evil one (2 Thess. 3:3), and preserves the redeemed to the end (1 Cor. 1:8–9; 1 Thess. 5:23–24).

Paul describes the second person of the Godhead as the "righteous Judge" (2 Tim. 4:8) in that he embodies the perfect standard of right (i.e., "right behavior or right disposition").[49] In his dealings with people, God shows no favoritism or partiality (Rom. 2:11; Eph. 6:9). No charge of injustice can be levied against him (Rom. 3:5–6; 9:14),

for he gives to each his desert. More specifically, God's justice is remunerative (Eph. 6:8) and punitive (Rom. 1:32; 6:23; 12:19). In Paul's statement, "the wages of sin is death" (Rom. 6:23), the word opsōnion (e.g., wages or recompense) "strictly denotes payment in kind."[50]

The apostle's teaching about God's love is pervasively soteriological. The divine agapē is the raison d'être for Christ's incarnation and cross (Eph. 5:2)—indeed, for his entire redemptive mission (2 Thess. 2:16; Titus 3:4). God's active, outgoing love is also the basis of the believer's eternal election and adoption (Eph. 1:4–5; cf. Rom. 9:13), in fact, of the entire salvation experience (Eph. 2:4–7). So intense and so powerful is God's love that no person or power in the universe can sever the believer from it (Rom. 8:35–39). The chief demonstration of divine love occurred when Christ voluntarily laid down his life for his enemies (Rom. 5:6–8). Paul stands in no less awe of God's mercy (eleos)—"the emotion aroused by someone in need and the attempt to relieve the person and remove his trouble."[51] Eternal election (Rom. 9:16, 18, 23), salvation from sin (Eph. 2:4–5; Titus 3:5), and summons to service (1 Tim. 1:13, 16) are all rooted in God's free mercy and pity.

Paul was acutely conscious of God's severe displeasure toward sin, expressed as the emotional responses of anger (thymos) and wrath (orgē). The holy God responds with indignation against every violation of his righteous standards (Rom. 1:18; Eph. 5:6). Eschatologically, Paul viewed the day of the Lord as a treasure of accumulated wrath that God would execute justly (Rom. 2:5, 8; 5:9; 1 Thess. 1:10). Paul, however, uses three nouns to indicate that God delays his judgment so as to provide opportunity for repentance: paresis, "overlooking" (Rom. 3:25), implies that for a time God ignores and thus passes over sins; *anochē*, "forebearance" (2:4; 3:25), points to God's tolerance of Israel's blindness; and *makrothymia*, "patience" (2:4; 9:22), focuses on delay of the final judgment.

God is authentic in that in his unlimited self-consciousness he knows who he is, his significance, and his distinctive purpose (1 Cor. 2:11). The apostle gives manifold testimony to the omnipotence of God. In Romans 1:20, Paul identifies God's "eternal power" (*aidios dynamis*) as one of his prominent properties. God's power is seen in his role as Creator, Governor, and Consummator of all things (Rom. 11:36; 1 Cor. 8:6), in his work of spiritual "re-creation" (2 Cor. 5:17), and in his raising of Christ from the dead (1 Cor. 6:14; 2 Cor. 13:4). To describe the power of God operative in believers, Paul brings together four descriptive nouns (Eph. 1:19; cf. 3:20): *dynamis* (power), *energeia* (powerful working), *kratos* (effective might), and *ischus* (latent strength). The only qualifier to the divine omnipotence is that God cannot act contrary to his character (2 Tim. 2:13)—in particular, he cannot lie (Titus 1:2).

Johannine Literature

John upholds the divine omniscience when he affirms that God knows all things (*oida*, John 21:17), including every person's heart (*ginōskō*, 1 John 3:20). Jesus Christ, God manifest in the flesh, knew perfectly all that could be known (John 6:15, 64; 18:4; 19:28). Wisdom, moreover, is ascribed both to God the Father (Rev. 7:12) and to the Lamb (5:12).

John's declaration "God is light; in him there is no darkness at all" (1 John 1:5) affirms that God is absolute moral purity, the antithesis of evil (cf. Rev. 15:4), and absolute truth, the antithesis of falsehood (cf. John 14:6). Isaiah's threefold ascription of holiness is directed to God by the four living creatures in Revelation 4:8. Jesus, moreover, ascribes to God righteousness, or holiness in action, by the phrase "righteous Father" (John 17:25). God is absolutely just (*dikaios*) and dependable (*alēthinos*) in all his judgments (Rev. 16:7; 19:2), indeed, in all his ways (15:3). John's trenchant statement "God is love" (*ho theos agapē estin*, 1 John 4:8, 16) affirms that in his very character and activity God is infinite, self-giving affection. The greatest love one can show is to lay down one's life for a friend (John 15:13). God has done this and more, for the Father sent his own Son to die for friend and enemy alike (1 John 4:9). It is with a sacrificial love that God loves his Son (John 3:35; 5:20), Christian believers (John 16:27; 1 John 3:1), and the entire human race (John 3:16).[52]

A leading feature of John's theology is God's hatred of evil and consequent wrath against evildoers. God is said to hate (*miseō*) the idolatry and fornication of the Nicolaitans (Rev. 2:6) and to pour out his wrath (*orgē*) on all who reject the Son (John 3:36). The predominant motif in John, however, is the awesome eschatological wrath God will mete out on the Christ-rejecting world. Thus Revelation expresses God's terrible judgment under various descriptive images, viz., the wine of God's "fury" (*thymōs*) or "wrath" (*orgē*) that sinners must drink (Rev. 14:10; 16:19), as bowls filled with God's "wrath" that must be poured out (15:7; 16:1), as the reaping of a ripe harvest with a sharp sickle (14:17–19), and finally as the winepress of the fury of wrath that God must tread (14:19; 19:15). The first of John's words for anger, *orgē* (seven times), connotes the righteous wrath that arises from deliberate reflection. The more frequent word *thymōs* (ten times) denotes an emotional rage that boils, or a "burning, blistering anger."[53] John reasons that the believer's eternal salvation (John 10:29), all God's eschatological judgments (Rev. 19:1–2; 20:11–15), and his eternal reign of justice and peace (11:17) are grounded in his "great power" (11:17) or omnipotence. A common title for God in the Apocalypse is "Lord God Almighty" (4:8; 11:17; 19:6).

Other New Testament Books

The omniscience of God is asserted by the claim that "everything is uncovered and laid bare before the eyes of him to whom we must give account" (Heb. 4:13). God's trustworthiness is seen in the fact that he is faithful (*pistos*) to his Word and promises (10:23; 11:11). God is absolutely just, for as Peter testifies, he "judges each man's work impartially" (1 Peter 1:17). With respect to the law, God determined that "every violation and disobedience received its just punishment" (*misthapodosia*, recompense or retribution, Heb. 2:2). God could not do otherwise, for he is a God of consummate holiness (Heb. 12:10; 1 Peter 1:15–16).

Yet God takes greater delight in mercy than in punishment: "Mercy triumphs over judgment!" (James 2:13). God's heart overflows with mercy (*eleos*, Heb. 4:16; 1 Peter 1:3), compassion (*oiktirmos*, James 5:11), and love (*agapē*, Heb. 12:6; Jude 1, 21). But should the recipients of his grace prove disobedient, God brings forth anger and wrath as an inexorable law of retribution (Heb. 3:7–11). Still, God is patient, or long-suffering (*makrothymia*, 1 Peter 3:20; cf. 2 Peter 3:9), to the end that sinners might be saved (2 Peter 3:15). His omnipotence in this section is seen chiefly in terms of his ability to equip believers with every resource for holy living (2 Peter 1:3) and to bring saints to their heavenly destination (Jude 24). Since God's power is conditioned by his holiness, he cannot be tempted by evil (James 1:13) or lie (Heb. 6:18).

SYSTEMATIC FORMULATION

The logical organization of the historically and biblically derived thought about God's many-splendored character began in chapter 5 and continues here. For a comprehensive concept of God, both chapters must be considered together.[54] With these must be integrated chapter 7 on the Trinity.

Intellectually, God Is Omniscient, Faithful, and Wise

God differs from other spirits, not only in being, but also in knowledge. Transcendent to all else, God's intellectual capacities are unlimited by space, time, energy, laws, things, or persons. Hence, God's knowledge is *omniscient*. Immediately, consciously, and comprehensively God is aware of all eternal, changeless reality (himself, his attributes, and his purposes, as well as the decisions and acts executing them) and all of the temporal reality that ever was, is, or will be.

God knows all of nature's energy-matter, laws, animals, and finite spirits. God also knows living people. He knows not only their physical characteristics, but also their inner thoughts, struggles, motives, volitional decisions, and expressions of those determinations in words, acts, events, and happenings. God knows all things (Ps. 139:2–10; John 21:17; 1 John 3:20).

God knows the free wills he purposed to create, sustain, and utilize preceptively or permissively. He knows all the logical, mathematical, moral, spiritual, and empirical possibilities humans face. God also knows the alternative(s) people choose from among these possibilities and the extent to which they can, since the Fall, achieve their chosen goals. God also knows the future of human beings in a way that does not destroy their freedom or responsibility. From different theological perspectives (Arminian and process) it is argued that if God knows the future there can be no human freedom. However, for God to know what a person will choose to do, and the extent to which since the Fall he will be able to achieve it, is not for God to do it in the person's place. God knows what he himself is going to choose and do independently of human agency and what he will accomplish through human self-determination. God's precognition of evil choices by his creatures is not equivalent to God's predetermination of evil.

How can God know the future and not render our involvement in day-to-day experience pointless? An illustration adapted from Augustine may help. Suppose you have memorized the Shepherd Psalm and are going to listen to a member of your Bible study quote it. You know the entirety of Psalm 23 from the beginning to end. But that prior knowledge does not render meaningless the experiential knowledge of quoting it audibly for your family devotions. When you or a student in your class has quoted the first half of the Shepherd Psalm, you can distinguish what part of it is past and what remains to be quoted.[55] In a far greater way the God who is unlimited by time knows the future in its entirety, as we know the whole Psalm simultaneously. The Creator and Sustainer of time also knows what part of history is past and what is future in any time zone on earth at any given date and time.

When we are confronted with the fulfillments of detailed predictions far in advance consistent with God's purposes, we confront signs of the transcendent knowledge of divine omniscience. The prophet Isaiah dramatically pointed up a decisive difference between the God of the Bible and idols: the Lord's ability to predict the future (Isa. 44:7–8, 25–28). Although the idols could not hear or speak anything, God's prophetic spokesman predicted specific details involving many human decisions far in advance concerning Jerusalem, Judah, Cyrus, and the temple.

God is not only all-knowing; he is also intellectually *faithful and true*. Throughout Scripture, knowledge and faithfulness are inseparable. Unless knowledge learned from others comes from people with intellectual honesty, we may be deceived or mistaken in what we think we know. Because God is faithful and true (Rev. 19:11), his judgments (Rev. 19:2) and his words in human language are faithful and true (Rev. 21:5; 22:6). In God's person there is no lack of fidelity, thought, or promise. God is not hypocritical or inconsistent. Descartes's hypothesis that God may be a great deceiver does not fit the biblical facts.[56]

We may hold unswervingly to our hope because he who promised is faithful (Heb. 10:23). He is faithful to forgive our sins (1 John 1:9), sanctify believers until the return of Christ (1 Thess. 5:23–24), strengthen and protect from the evil one (2 Thess. 3:3), and not let us be tempted beyond what we can bear (1 Cor. 10:13). Even if we are faithless, he remains faithful, for he cannot disown himself (2 Tim. 2:13).

Long before God's promises were inscripturated, not one word of any of the good promises he gave through Moses failed (1 Kings 8:56). Isaiah praised the name of God, for in perfect faithfulness God did marvelous things planned long ago (Isa. 25:1). Passages like these convey a basic divine integrity not only in character, but also in thought. No hypocritical contrast can be drawn between what God is in himself and what God has revealed of himself in relation to those who trust his spoken or written Word. God does not contradict his promises in his personal relationships, works, or communications.

Teachings from this God are faithful or consistent, not irresolvably dialectical or paradoxical. The wisdom that comes from the God who is faithful takes everything into account coherently and is not limited to a paradoxical tension or mere complementarity. The interpretations taken from the faithful words of revelation may be contradictory, dialectical, paradoxical, or merely complementary in the minds of theologians. But our psychological tensions ought not be ascribed to God or his revelation as given.

Intellectually, furthermore, God is *wise*. A wise person is more than a walking encyclopedia of facts; a wise person knows how to use knowledge for worthy ends and purposes. Wisdom includes knowledge (*scientia*), but features ability to use eternal truths in abundant living and effective serving (*sapientia*). Knowledge is indispensable to wisdom, and research is indispensable to insight and intuition. Knowing all the relevant data on any subject and all the possible courses of action, God discerningly selects ends—as well as strategies and methods for achieving them—that are consistent with his purposes of holy love. Prudently God not only chooses the right ends, but also does so for the right reasons—his glory in the good of his creatures.

None of God's counsels, decrees, or predeterminations are arbitrary. In wisdom, God thinks, decides, speaks, relates, and acts in ways supportive, rather than counterproductive of his changeless character. God's activities in space, time, and human history are not unprincipled, chaotic, or helterskelter. In the cosmos, God's program for the world is wisely devised and administered both creatively and redemptively.

Because God does not act arbitrarily, we can put our trust in his justice and love in all of his purposes, strategies, and methods. Although we may not at any given time in our lives be able to see how God is wisely working things together for good (Rom. 8:28), we have sufficient reason to trust in the depth of the wisdom of the only God (Rom. 11:33; 16:27).

Ethically, God Is Holy, Just, Merciful, and Loving

God transcends his creatures, not only metaphysically and epistemologically, but also morally. The Most High is morally spotless in character and action. In essence God is upright, pure and untainted with evil desires, motives, thoughts, words, or acts. God is eternally and unchangeably *holy*. God is holy in a preethical sense, in himself the exalted source and support who is distinct from or transcendent to all that is. Consciousness of the Most High ideally results in a sense of ultimate dependence on him and obligation to him, an awesome worship of him as the Almighty, and praise to him as the Creator.

However, consciousness of God's ontological greatness quickly leads into consciousness of God's absolute moral uprightness. Free from all evil, God loves only the good and right. He values inner authenticity and takes no pleasure in hypocrisy—religious or nonreligious. God takes no pleasure in evil (Ps. 5:4) and cannot tolerate evil (Hab. 1:13). He cannot even encourage sin in any way (James 1:13–14). Desiring transparent authenticity, God hates hypocrisy. Who, then, can stand in judgment before the Holy One who knows everything?

While standing in awe of such metaphysical and moral holiness, Christians are not in awe of "The Holy" as a totally other abstraction, but of "the Holy One" who speaks to the prophets (Isa. 40:25). The Holy One is not merely an object of emotional fascination but also of intellectual understanding (in part) and volitional obedience.

With mind, will, and emotions enhanced by the Holy Spirit, people who are conscious of the presence of God may experience variously an awe, dread, fear, utter unworthiness, and unacceptability. Isaiah heard the angels crying, "Holy, holy, holy is the LORD Almighty; the whole earth is full of his glory," and he saw a vision of the Lord exalted in the temple. "Woe to me!" cried Isaiah. "I am ruined! For I am a man of unclean lips, and I live among a people of unclean lips, and my eyes have seen the King, the LORD Almighty" (Isa. 6:1–5). Nothing contradictory to holiness can be acceptable to the One of nonnegotiable moral standards.

Not solely a product of God's will, holiness is a changeless characteristic of his eternal nature. In this light, Plato's famous question needs to be reworded. Assuming a world of absolute ideas or principles independent of God, Socrates asked, Is the good good because God wills it? Or does God will it because it is good?[57]

In the context of biblical revelation, we must add a third question: "Is the good good because the very essence of God is good?" The good is not a product of an arbitrary decision of a mere will sporting about in a vacuum. Neither is it good because God's will happens to yield to an alleged higher set of (Platonic) principles to which the Creator of all is subservient. Rather, the good is good because it is consistent with God's very nature. God's self-determinations always express who he is. He cannot deny himself. God wills the good and holiness because he is good and holy. God is always displeased with evil and unholiness because in his very essence he is awesomely separate from all the evil and unholy.

In addition to being morally holy, God is morally *just* and *righteous*. Jesus addressed God as "Righteous Father" (John 17:25). So when Jesus suffered, he made no threats. "Instead, he entrusted himself to him who judges justly" (1 Peter 2:23; cf. Rev. 16:5–7). God's upright character is expressed in his moral law and in judgment according to it without respect of persons. For Christians, righteous conduct is in accord not simply with the standards of a community but, beyond that, with the standards of God. Conformity to a standard implies more than a social obligation; it involves conformity to divine authority expressed in Scripture.[58]

Divine judgment is never arbitrary or capricious, but principled and fair. As absolutely honest and just, God declares people to be what they are, sinners. Justice, in matters of merit, judges that morally responsible people should receive exactly what they deserve. Biblical writers frequently protest the injustice experienced by the poor, widows, orphans, strangers, and the godly. Although people often blame God for these circumstances, God pities the poor (Ps. 72:12, 14), and he answers, revives, and acquits them and grants them justice. In righteousness God delivers the needy from persecution and will create a new heaven and earth in which righteousness will dwell (Isa. 65:17).

Since fallen people suppress God's revealed truth and hold it down in unrighteousness, on standards of sheer merit they deserve God's wrath (Rom. 1:18–32). But a perfect righteousness from God has been revealed in the gospel, a righteousness "by faith from first to last" (Rom. 1:17; 3:21). Those who, like Abraham, are fully persuaded that God can do what he has promised (Rom. 4:21), find their faith credited to them for righteousness on the ground of Christ's atonement (Rom. 4:3, 24). The righteous One satisfies justice through mercy, grace, and love.

As *merciful*, God withholds deserved judgment. The "LORD your God is a merciful God" (Deut. 4:31). Daniel exclaims, "The Lord our God is merciful and forgiving, even though we have rebelled against him" (Dan. 9:9). Paul praises the Father of compassion (mercies) and the God of all comfort (2 Cor. 1:3). As *gracious*, God freely gives undeserved benefits to those he chooses. God is "a gracious and merciful God" (Neh. 9:31). "The LORD your God is gracious and compassionate. He will not turn his face from you if you return to him" (2 Chron. 30:9).

God is not only merciful and gracious but also *loving*, with *agapē* love. Frequently people ask, "What was lacking in God's being that made it necessary for him to create?" God "is not served by human hands, as if he needed anything, because he himself gives all men life and breath and everything else" (Acts 17:25). God created, not out of self-seeking love (*eros*), but out of self-giving love (*agapē*). He desired to give of himself for the well-being of those loved, however unlovely and undeserving they might become. God cares and loves because God *is* love (1 John 4:8).

God's great love is likened to that of a father for a son and a mother toward an unweaned baby (Isa. 49:15; 66:13). Out of love God chose Israel (Deut. 7:7) and all the elect (Eph. 1:4). And out of love for the lost world, God gave his only Son (John 3:16). In love God cares for the aged, the oppressed, the poor, orphans, widows, and the ill. God is not unmoved by people in need; he is not impassible. The God of Abraham, Ruth, Job, Jesus, Peter, and Paul suffered!

In empathy God enters into the feelings of his creatures. Beyond that, through participation God incarnate entered into our temptations and sufferings. H. Wheeler Robinson has said, "The only way in which moral evil can enter into the consciousness of the morally good [*sic*] is as suffering."[59] In all Israel's afflictions, God was afflicted (Isa. 63:9). What meaning can there be, Robinson asks, in a love that is not costly to the lover?[60] The God of the Bible is far from apathetic in regard to the vast suffering of people in the world. In love God sent his Son to die so that ultimately suffering may be done away with and righteousness may cover the earth as the waters cover the seas.

Although love involves emotions, it is not here classed primarily as an emotional characteristic of God, because it involves commitment of the whole person, initiated in the will. Love is a settled purpose of will involving the whole person in seeking the well-being of others. As the greatest commandment indicates, love is an ethical obligation (cf. Matt. 22:37). Love will normally involve the intellect and the emotions to different degrees, but love is more than emotional feeling. Since God's love does involve emotions, it is appropriate to consider divine emotions more explicitly.

Emotionally, God Detests Evil, and Is Long-suffering and Compassionate

Passibility, Thomists argued, involves potentiality, and potentiality involves change. Unrealized potential and change in the Deity seemed to contradict their understanding of God's immutability, transcendence, self-existence, and perfection. Suffering, furthermore, seemed incompatible with perfect divine blessedness. Thus, the Thirty-nine Articles of the Church of England affirm that "God is without body, parts or passions."[61] However, that view seemed to others to convey the idea that God was devoid of an affectional nature essential to personality and *agapē* love. As early as the Bishops Conference of 1786, the word "passions" was omitted. Hence Doctrines and Disciplines of the Methodist Church (1960) stops with saying God is "without body or parts" (art. i).[62]

Which of the two hypotheses, that God is impassible and that he is passible, coherently fits the data of Scripture? Unquestionably the Scripture speaks of God as passionately involved with sinners and repentant sinners. Even though its language be taken figuratively, it illustrates a nonfigurative point. God really suffers when people sinfully destroy his creation, and God literally rejoices when one sinner repents.

Indeed, God is devoid of caprice and of passions out of control. God has no selfish anger. But this is not to say that God has no passions and no righteous anger or wrath. As a person God has emotions as well as intelligence and volition, and as an ethical personal being God experiences displeasure with unrighteousness, and he is pleased with righteousness. Concerned for the well-being of his creatures, God can only be repulsed by the injustice, unrighteousness, and corruption that destroys their health physically, emotionally, mentally, and spiritually. The Bible frequently speaks of God's righteous anger with the evil that would destroy his people and their work in the world. Righteous indignation is anger aroused, not by being overcome by emotions irrationally or selfishly, but by an altruistic concern for people who are suffering from injustice, selfishness, greed, lust, envy, jealousy, and lack of self-control in any respect. In a way such as this *God detests evil.*

Jesus, and the Scriptures in general, speak often of God's wrath at injustices such as persistent mistreatment of the poor and needy. Although the Lord is slow to anger, he will in no way leave the guilty unpunished but will pour out just judgment on them (Nah. 1:3). None can withstand his indignation when it is poured out like fire and when it shatters rocks (v. 6). Apart from understanding God's wrath against evil, it is impossible to understand the extent of divine love in the Incarnation, the extent of Jesus' suffering on the cross, the propitiatory nature of his sacrifice, or the prophetic Scriptures speaking of a future day of divine wrath, the great tribulation on the ungodly in the Book of Revelation.

Fortunately, the living God is also patient and remarkably *long-suffering.* Properly jealous for the well-being of the objects of his love, God is angry with injustice done to them, but suffers without losing heart. Being long-suffering with evildoers without condoning their sin, God graciously provides them with undeserved temporal and spiritual benefits. For example, God promised the land to Abraham, but the iniquity of the Amorites was not yet full (Gen. 15:16). Only after some four hundred years of long-suffering and restraint did God allow the Israelite armies to bring just judgment on multiplying Amorite unrighteousness. When Israel worshiped the golden calf and deserved the judgment that was meted out to other idolaters, God revealed himself at the second giving of the Law as "The LORD, the LORD, a God merciful and gracious, slow to anger, and abounding in steadfast love and faithfulness" (Exod. 34:6 RSV). The psalmist could write, "But thou, O Lord, art a God merciful and gracious, slow to anger and abounding in steadfast love and faithfulness" (Ps. 86:15 RSV). However, even the day of God's grace has an end. Eventually, without respect of persons, God's just judgment fell on Israel for its persistent evils. God's long-suffering is a remarkable virtue, but it does not exclude or contradict God's justice.

Although historically many theologians have taught the impassibility of God, the Scriptures do not hesitate to call God *compassionate.* The compassionate feel so strongly for another's sorrow or hardship that they desire to help them. Because of God's great love his people are not consumed, for his compassions for them never fail (Lam. 3:22). Even after Israel's deserved captivity, God again had compassion on them (Mic. 7:19). The God of the Bible is not an apathetic God but One who deeply cares when the sparrow falls. Jesus beautifully displayed this divine-human feeling for the hungry (Matt. 15:32), the blind (Matt. 20:34), and the sorrowing (Luke 7:13). And Jesus taught the importance of divine and human compassion in the accounts of the Good Samaritan (Luke 10:33) and the father's concern for his lost son (Luke 15:20). The divine blessedness is not unrealistic concerning the evils of the world. Deeply moved by all of the depraved conduct of humanity, the omniscient God nevertheless rejoices over many like the prodigal who return to the way of faith, life, and peace.

As incarnate, Christ felt what humans feel in all respects but did not yield to the temptations involved. As God in literal human experience, Jesus wept with those who wept. He also rejoiced with those who rejoiced. The divine-human author of our salvation, however, was made perfect or complete through suffering in this life (Heb. 2:10). Because he himself suffered, he can help those who suffer and are tempted (v. 18). The God revealed in Jesus Christ is no mere apathetic, uninvolved, impersonal principle.

As Christ's holy nature and loving purposes were unchanged by his suffering, so the living God prior to the Incarnation could experience changing emotions without affecting the immutability of his nature and purposes. God's emotions are always consistent with his holiness and love. His emotions are never out of control. Acknowledging healthy emotions in God, we are as concerned to stress that the God of the Bible experiences no unworthy emotions as are those who deny them. God is changelessly just and righteous and will never go back on his word to us. The most important concerns of defenders of divine impassibility may be maintained without denying the point of a multitude of scriptural assertions to the effect that habitual sin receives divine wrath and that repentance causes rejoicing in heaven—and not only among the angels! Whether expressed in figurative language or not, the teaching of Scripture supports these principles.[63]

Volitionally, God Is Free, Authentic, and Omnipotent

Recent existentialist concerns for freedom, authenticity, and personal fulfillment should not be limited to mankind. Biblical writers seem even more concerned that God be understood to be free, authentic, and fulfilled by being able to do all that he chooses in the way he plans to do it.

God is *free*. From all eternity God is not affected by anything contrary to his purposes. Good things, as we have seen, are purposed with divine pleasure and enduement. Evil things are permitted with divine displeasure. But either way, God is self-determined. The essence of freedom is the power to determine one's self apart from external compulsion according to one's own nature and purposes. In God, freedom need not always involve a choice between contrary options. God cannot deny himself. God chooses according to his nature and has the power to pursue what he has chosen.

Given God's changeless nature and purposes, there are many things God cannot do. Although free to be himself, he cannot deny himself. Being self-existent, eternal, and unchanging, God cannot die. Being personal, God cannot be a mere projection, ideal, or impersonal principle. Being holy, God cannot take pleasure in sin. Being loving, God cannot be impatient, unkind, self-seeking, or easily angered (1 Cor. 13:4–5). Because God is love, he never fails (1 Cor. 13:8). Always God's free will exercises itself in a manner consistent with his personal, eternal, living, intellectual, ethical, emotional, volitional self. Divine freedom does not require the power of choice in these matters. Self-determination is the divine kind of freedom, the highest kind of freedom possible.

God is also *authentic*, authentically himself. The God revealed in the Christ who so unalterably opposed hypocrisy is himself no hypocrite. Earlier we emphasized God's intellectual integrity or faithfulness. Here we emphasize his integrity ethically, emotionally, and volitionally. In contrast to persons who struggle to find out who they are, God in his unlimited self-consciousness knows who he is (1 Cor. 2:11). He has a keen sense not only of his own identity but also of his unique significance and distinctive purpose. God's authenticity is displayed in the fact that his words are in harmony with his being and action. No discrepancy can be found between what God says and what he does.

If it is important for each person created by God to achieve fulfillment as a unique person and not be lost in the crowd or become depersonalized, how much more important it is that God knows himself and realizes fully his own uniqueness. As the ultimate being, God is honestly self-assertive. In reality, no one can compare with him. In calling on people to turn from idols, therefore, God in no way is asking of us anything inappropriate or out of accord with reality. In steadfastly opposing idolatry, he seeks to protect people from ultimate concerns that inevitably disillusion and disappoint. God desires our worship for our sakes, so that we will not eventually succumb to despair as one after another of our finite gods lets us down. In asking for our exclusive ultimate allegiance, God is simply being transparently honest and authentic.

The living God is also *omnipotent*. When Mary wondered how she, a virgin, could give birth to a son, and Elizabeth wondered how she could have a child (John the Baptist) in her old age, the angel declared, "Nothing is impossible with God" (Luke 1:37). God's omnipotence means that God is able to accomplish whatever he wills (e.g., the incarnation of the Son) in the way in which he wills it (the Virgin Birth).

But as we have seen, God does not will to do anything contradictory to his nature and purposes. Deeply distressed and troubled in Gethsemane, Jesus prayed that if possible the hour of death might pass from him (Mark 14:33–35). Was it possible? " '*Abba*, Father,' he said, 'everything is possible for you.' " Jesus knew that the Father was omnipotent. But in addition, he knew that the Father would not act contrary to the redemptive purpose at the Cross. So Jesus added, "Take this cup from me. Yet not what I will, but what you will" (Mark 14:36). Omnipotence does not mean that God does everything by his own immediate power without the use of angelic or human agencies. God does not will to accomplish everything by the same strategy. Some things come to pass without the use of any other agents in creation—i.e., unconditionally (Isa. 14:24–27). But most events occur through the obedience or disobedience of people to divine precepts (2 Chron. 7:14; Luke 7:30; Rom. 1:24). In either case, God's eternal purposes for history are achieved, whether preceptively, with divine pleasure, or permissively, with divine displeasure.

Some have tried to challenge the omnipotence of God by suggesting that God could not create a boulder so heavy that he could not lift it. Or God cannot create two mountains without a valley between them. The problems here do not illustrate a lack of divine power but the contradictory character of the question. God cannot create square circles because, by definition, there can be no square circles. God can do all things, but not nothings. The difficulty with the proposed illustrations is certainly not with God but with the questions.

God has not only the power to effect all his purposes in the way he purposes them but also the authority in the entire realm of his kingdom to do as he wills. God has the right to rule all his creation. God is not a subject of another dominion; he is King, or Lord of all. And by virtue of all his other attributes, God is fit for ruling well all that he created and sustains. God is a wise, holy, and gracious sovereign. Because he is just, God does not punish any sinner more than he deserves. Because he is full of grace, God freely bestows undeserved benefits and gifts as he pleases (Ps. 135:6).

Having permitted sin, God is great enough to limit its extent and to overrule it for good. God permitted evil's most hideous outbreaking in history at Calvary and transformed it into the way of salvation (Acts 4:24–28). Though all the nations and demonic hosts should rage against him, God cannot fail to achieve his purposes in history. For any of the ungodly to go their own ways independently of God's sustaining power and rightful authority is folly. Only a fool, speaking and living by God's sustaining providence, can claim that there is no God. As Cornelius Van Til put it, atheists could not slap God in the face if he did not hold them on his lap. Whether recognized or not by his dependent creatures, God remains omnipotent.

Relationally, the Transcendent Divine Being Is Immanent Universally in Providential Activity and Immanent With His People in Redemptive Activity

God, as we have indicated, is distinct from the world metaphysically, intellectually, ethically, emotionally, and existentially. Biblical theism cannot compromise the biblically founded belief in God's transcendence in pantheistic, panentheistic, or process world views. No more can they accommodate to deism, for God is continuously active throughout the world providentially. God is not so exalted that since creation he cannot know and relate to natural law in the world of everyday experience. The study of scriptural teaching on divine providence has shown that God sustains, guides, and governs all creation. The nature Psalms reflect on God's activity in relation to every aspect of the earth, the atmosphere, vegetation, and animal life (see Ps. 104). God also preserves and governs persons in human history, he judges corrupt societies and blesses the just and the unjust with temporal benefits like the sunshine, rain, nourishment, and drink. Through God's universal providential activity the cosmos holds together and his wise purposes of common grace are achieved.

But just as persons may be present to one another in varying degrees or ways, God may be present in one way to the unjust and in a richer way to the just. You may be superficially present to a stranger on a bus, revealing little about yourself. However, you may be more significantly present with your godly mother who has prayed daily for you all your life, even though she is miles away. God is graciously present in forgiving love with the converted who by faith have been forgiven, reconciled, and redeemed by Christ's precious blood. They become God's people, and he becomes their moral and spiritual Father. "For this is what the high and lofty One says—he who lives forever, whose name is holy: I live in a high and holy place, but also with him who is contrite and lowly in spirit, to revive the spirit of the lowly and to revive the heart of the contrite" (Isa. 57:15). God, who is ontologically transcendent to the world, is immanently present throughout it and related to it by his providential and redemptive activities.

APOLOGETIC INTERACTION

In the previous chapter, I defended belief in divine transcendence against idolatrous tendencies to reduce God so that he is no more than the world. In this chapter, I will defend divine immanence against unbiblical tendencies to think that God is no longer with us in significant activity here and now.

God's Transcendent Omniscience Immanently Revealed in History

Belief in transcendent divine omniscience and wisdom is of little value to mankind at present if no divine truth can be shared with human minds. Some think that God's thought is so transcendent as to be totally removed from human thought. It has become commonplace to say that God can reveal to finite and fallen human minds only himself, but not true information about himself.

Karl Barth and Rudolph Bultmann presupposed Søren Kierkegaard's teaching of infinite qualitative distinction between God and man. The claim provided an effective corrective in the minds of Barth and Bultmann against the continuity that modernism had alleged between the highest human thought and God's thought. But the view that God is totally other precluded the communication of any sound information in Scripture or elsewhere about God as he is in himself or about God's plan of redemption.

The claim that God's mind is totally removed from human minds receives additional support from Eastern mystics who deny any objective validity to conceptual thinking in reference to the eternal. Relativists from many fields also deny that any human assertions, including the Bible's, are capable of expressing the truth concerning God. Then there are the multitudes of Christian devotional writers who imagine that there is "deeper" spirituality in worshiping a God beyond doctrinal or propositional information. In these movements discursive thought (including careful exegesis and doctrinal formulation) tends to become the archenemy of mystical or spiritual experience of God.

From these perspectives people claim that human knowledge is discursive, line upon line, but God's knowledge is immediate and instantaneous without painstaking research or moving from one logical step to another. Our thought distinguishes subject from predicate in propositions (S is P), but God's mind immediately knows S and P simultaneously as SP without separating them with the verb "to be." Our theological knowledge is propositional, God's is said to be nonpropositional.

One wonders, of course, how a person can know so much about the operations of God's mind if it is totally other than ours. Leaving that consideration aside and admitting that God knows all things at once, we may be certain that his knowledge includes the step-by-step reasoning of people limited by time, their need for gathering data for research, and their use of propositions to communicate. Divine knowledge can distinguish conceptually and linguistically a subject from a predicate nominative and an intransitive verb. Even though God is not limited to temporal steps and propositional distinctions, they are not meaningless to him. He is no stranger to the human mind in time. He created and sustains it in order to communicate truth to people.

To communicate with people in time, God can ascribe appropriate qualities to a thing using one word after another without distorting the truth he knows. Whether we think of the whole of Psalm 23 simultaneously or recite it line after line does not affect the the truth in either case. Similarly, simultaneous knowledge in God's mind need be no hindrance to communication of truth to people who think concept after concept and line upon line. Simultaneous knowledge differs from propositional and discursive reasoning, but not infinitely in every respect. It is knowledge. Truth is truth for God and man, whether known immediately or arrived at discursively.

The view that God's knowledge is infinitely other than ours implies a kind of twofold truth: what is true for discursive human reasoning may be false for God, and what is false for human propositional truth may be true for God's immediate, nonconceptual knowledge. Hence, on that assumption any assertion about God in the form "God is X" is false. Then it may even be false to say that God's knowledge is immediate and simultaneous. If God's mind is "infinitely different" in every quality, those words may mean their opposite. Then God's knowledge is not immediate and simultaneous. But, in fact, truth is truth for God and man, whether arrived at immediately or discursively, whether known apart from concepts and propositions or expressed through concepts and propositions.

Truth from immediate experience of God does not contradict truth mediated by scriptural revelation. Assertions about God alleged from interpretations of mystical intuitions of God do not have a higher authority than assertions about God derived from sound interpretations of Scripture. The doctrine of double truth held that an assertion could be true in philosophy but false in theology, or true in theology and false in philosophy (which covered all other fields at that time). Such double truth was condemned in 1277 by Bishop Stephen Tempier of Paris as a denial of the law of noncontradiction for the purpose of asserting heresy.[64] Truth does not contradict truth, in philosophy (or science) and theology. No more does truth from divine revelation contradict truth from religious or mystical experience. Neither need truth in human theology, well-based in inscripturated revelation, contradict truth in the mind of God.

God's truth, in part, can be communicated without distortion to people because God created humans in his image so that he could communicate with them. Although the human mind cannot invent eternal truth, it can receive general and special revelation from the Eternal. Although the Fall has affected the human mind, it has not eradicated it. Common grace enables people to receive revelation in nature, history, and the human heart. The new birth renews the person in knowledge after the image of the Creator (Col. 3:10). This knowledge is not only of temporal things, but also of the present position and nature of the exalted Christ (1:15–20) and knowledge of God's will (1:9). With knowledge like this Christians are able to avoid the deception in merely fine-sounding arguments (2:4) and strengthen the faith they were taught in concepts and words (2:7). Thus the content of the Word of the risen and exalted Christ can inform their teaching and worship (3:16).

In these and other ways the Scriptures presuppose an informative revelation from God, verbally inspired and Spirit-illumined to minds created and renewed in the divine image for the reception of divine truth. Insofar as we have grasped the contextual meaning given by the original writers of Scripture, our biblically based assertions that God is spirit, God is holy, and God is love are true. They are true for the faith and life of Christians and churches because they are true for God as he is in himself.

Since God's omniscience is formed by all the relevant data and principles of reasoning he established in his universe, God's mind is not totally other than human minds. And our judgments are true insofar as they conform to God's by being faithful to, or coherent with, all the obtainable relevant evidence. Even though God's being is transcendent, his revealed truths are with us here and now by his activities of revelation, inspiration, and illumination. Every one of us will be judged by God's all-knowing mind for our response to his truth in our lives and ministries. God may be intellectually transcendent, but he has revealed truths that all of us are accountable to know, believe, love, and obey here and now in history.

God's Transcendent Righteousness Normative in Historical Justice

God and gurus, Hinduism tells us, are not only beyond propositional truths, but also beyond good and evil. No principles of right and wrong hold for God. All duality, including the difference between right and wrong is illusory. Hindus are taught that in reality all is one, beyond all conceptual distinctions. For the "enlightened" all opposites are either nonexistent or identical. If the Absolute is beyond good and evil and is indifferent to what people do on earth, then literally, all things are lawful. This can lead not only to "a holy indifference" to evil, as the Bhagavad-Gita may have intended, but also to a diabolical insensitivity to evil, as in the Charles Manson group. Influenced not only by drugs but also by Eastern

mysticism's monistic disparagement of propositional truth in morality, Manson could not have made a real difference between killing and the loving activities of Mother Theresa![65]

In Zen Buddhism, Alan Watts explained, "there is no good to gain and no evil to be avoided, no thoughts to be eradicated and no mind to be purified, no body to perish and no soul to be saved."[66] The view that in reality there is no distinct good and evil, that moral judgments between right and wrong are illusory, is a form of relativism.[67] Relativism pervades morality it seems, except when the qualifications of our political leaders are being examined. Reflecting the spirit of moral relativism, an advertisement for a New Age organization paradoxically declared, "It is a sin to call a person a sinner!"

In the context of relativism from the East and West, it is more important than ever to be aware of, and defend, not only God's transcendent holiness, righteousness, and justice, but also God's moral norms in all human hearts (Rom. 2:14–15) and in scriptural teaching. Good and evil are not one. They are not to be confused. "Woe to those who call evil good and good evil" (Isa. 5:20). "Let those who love the LORD hate evil" (Ps. 97:10). "Love must be sincere. Hate what is evil; cling to what is good" (Rom. 12:9). The hope of humanity rests on returning to the belief that we do know the difference between right and wrong, that it is a real difference, a difference revealed by God, a difference by which every human being will be judged. No hypothesis is more thoroughly verified by empirical experience documented in the daily news than the hypothesis that in the world there is real evil, real goodness, and a real difference between them. That difference derives from the will of the holy, righteous, and just God. The Holy One is the source and support of abiding moral values in the flux of history. And all rebellion against moral laws is ultimately against the Most High from whose nature they eternally derive.

God's Transcendent Love Immanently Active to Meet Human Need

If God is thought to be totally transcendent intellectually and morally, one wonders how he can be immanently available for personal encounters even in some nonintellectual and nonmoral sense. The exalted Lord of all is omnipresent holistically: intellectually, morally, emotionally, volitionally, existentially, and relationally. In intelligent and just love, God providentially sustains the world and redemptively atones for sin. Providentially, God in his goodness prevents evil, permits it within certain limits, accomplishes things in a fallen world otherwise impossible, and overrules it for good. Mercifully, he has not destroyed the wicked of the world. In long-suffering love, he bears with the just in spite of many failures, while they mature. While we were yet sinners, God in *agapē* love determined to send his Son to provide for our just redemption.

Often it appears that science has all the answers, that events like the Holocaust show how history has got out of hand, and that believers in God are no more involved in meeting human need than are nonbelievers. For reasons like these, William Hamilton argued in an all-night seminar on God in 1970 at the University of Colorado that God is not with us here and now. Belief in a living Lord of history has become meaningless logically and existentially. A sovereign, wise, and loving Lord of history, Hamilton concluded, "died in his times." Instead of personally experiencing in his life immanently the God of holy love, he experienced, he said, the death of such a God. We respect the honesty of a professional theologian who admits that he has not experienced

God with him in wisdom, mercy, grace, and transforming power. We can sympathize with him in his concern for intellectual honesty, moral integrity, and the social relevance of the church. But his interpretation of his experience and of the church does not coherently account for all the facts.

Had Altizer and Hamilton lived at the time of the Flood, they might have concluded that God had died in their time. But God was there in righteous judgment on the incorrigibly wicked and in matchless grace for Noah and his family. Had they been pursued by King Saul as was David, the Lord's anointed, they might well have concluded that God was dead. But God was there, and in the appointed time David became king. If any of us had been present when Israel and then Judah were taken into captivity, we might have concluded that God was dead. But God was there in just judgment on evil without respect of persons and he was there in grace, sending prophet after prophet to call his people back to significant fellowship and service.

Finally, in spite of the people's rejecting prophet after prophet, God said, "I will send my Son; surely they will hear him." And Jesus Christ "came to that which was his own, but his own did not receive him" (John 1:11). After multiple rejections, false accusations, and betrayal, Jesus suffered on the Cross. If ever it seemed that God were dead, it was at Calvary. Jesus himself cried out, "My God, my God, why have you forsaken me?" (Matt. 27:46). But the Father was there in righteous wrath judging the sins of mankind and in marvelous grace transforming history's greatest miscarriage of justice into the basis for the world's salvation. In three days Christ rose from the dead in a verifiable triumph over sin, Satan, and the grave.

After the tragedies through which any of us lives personally, nationally, and internationally, it is easy to say that it no longer makes sense to believe that the Lord of all is in control. But the truth is that the eternal, self-existent, divine Being is still with us in holy love, wisdom, and power, here and now. He acts immanently in history in varied and incomprehensible ways to accomplish authentically and sovereignly his absolutely just and gracious purposes.

As we think of his presence, we cannot abstract his love from justice, or wisdom from power, or holiness from mercy. The scriptural data assure us again and again that in all of his perfections the living God is with us here and now and will be through the end of history and eternally. God did not create the world and leave it to carry on as best it could by itself (as deists say). Any philosophy or religious teaching that denies the continuous, immanent presence and activity of the transcendent Lord of all in history does not fit the facts of biblical revelation.

RELEVANCE FOR LIFE AND MINISTRY

Because God, with all of his attributes, is present and active immanently in history, we have every reason to develop our consciousness of his presence and activity in relation to our own experience. We stand in awe of God's transcendence far beyond us; it is also significant to contemplate in awe the fact that we live and move and have our being (Acts 17:28) because of his immanent preserving and guiding activities. We are ultimately dependent on him. "He himself gives all men life and breath and everything else" (Acts 17:25). Daily, then, we do well to "practice" contemplating "the presence of God" in our own lives and responding appropriately to his immanent presence in activities all around and within us.

Contemplating God as an invisible

spiritual being, we will not expect literally to see or hear him with our physical senses. But since God is personal, we may cultivate a relationship more like our relationship to human persons than to impersonal principles or things. We are open to communication from God as mediated through the Scriptures and immediately attested in our hearts by the Holy Spirit. We enjoy fellowship or communion with God in that we who have always been part of his ontological family are now by grace through faith part of the same moral and spiritual family. We jointly participate not only in the fellowship of the redeemed family of God but also in God's purposes for the world in general and the people of God in particular. A growing appreciation of God's purposes for all humanity and for the members of the church enables us to appreciate the immanent activity of God in our lives. Although the distinct attributes be isolated from one another, it is of value to sketch briefly the import of each as we contemplate God's immanent presence and activities in our world.

The Highest Human Knowledge

Great as it is to know the universe and persons in it in many different ways, it is greater still to know the transcendent Source and Sustainer. Just as we have an exciting affinity with the minds of some people more than with the minds of others, we may develop an increasingly exciting affinity with the mind of God as disclosed in nature and in the inscripturated Word.

Knowing on biblical authority that God is *omniscient*, we may anticipate each day with the confidence that God knows the challenges we face (physically, mentally, and spiritually). Each evening we are conscious that God knows what we have done that we ought not to have done, stimulating confession and repentance. What has been done for his glory that may or may not have received human recognition God also knows. With a growing awareness that God is consistently *faithful*, whatever crises we face, we can daily and nightly confidently rely on his promises and programs. Believing that God is *wise*, however opaque the circumstances at any given time in our lives, we will not despair but trust that what God permits and appoints has a wise purpose consistent with his holy love.

How can we turn our knowledge *about* God into knowledge *of* God? "The rule for doing this is demanding but simple," said J. I. Packer. "It is that we turn each truth that we learn *about* God into matter for meditation before God, leading to prayer and praise *to* God."[68]

Life's *Summum Bonum*

Increasingly conscious of God's ethical nature, we will grow in moral discernment, love all that is good, and expend our energies for ends that please God. Aware that God is absolutely *just*, without respect of persons, we will know that we ought not even try to rationalize even momentary indulgence of fleshly desires, thoughts, words, and behavior. Daily in the presence of the uncompromising Judge we confess and forsake our sins. Increasingly conscious of God's absolute holiness and his call for us to be holy as he is holy, our ultimate concern to please him cannot be shared with another, for none is like him. When our scale of values is scrambled in the pressures of family, business, social movements, and friends, we are daily reminded that no one else, much less our fallen selves, can function as the Most High for our ultimate concern.

In a growing sense of God's *mercy* and *love* to repentant sinners, we are inwardly renewed. Because God first loved us, we respond by loving God with more of our heart, soul, strength, and mind. The chief end of forgiven and regenerated people is not only to glorify God but also to enjoy him forever. People were created not only to serve God but also for loving communion with him. We are here not only to be of influence in the world but also to love, worship, contemplate, and meditate upon God.

What God desires from us more than anything else is our love (Matt. 22:37–38). To enjoy a loving communion with God is the supreme good of every person in time and eternity. Our hearts indeed are restless until they find their fulfillment in God. The unsatisfied, homesick heart will not be satisfied without giving priority to loving God. As John Burnaby summarized this perceptive thought of Saint Augustine: "To be joined to God is the supreme good for man, because there is no human goodness that is not fruit of the marriage between the human spirit and the divine. And Charity, the love of God, is the power that cements and consummates the union."[69]

No competition need be imagined between fulfilling the first and the second greatest commandments, between loving contemplation of God and loving service to needy neighbors. Carrying through the analogy of the highest human love to love of God (common to the Song of Solomon and Christian mystics), Bernard combined the contemplative life with energetic practical activities. The voice of the Beloved says, "Arise and hasten . . . "—that is, to work for the good of others. "It is the sign of contemplation's truth and purity that the spirit which has been enkindled by the divine flame be filled ever and again with zeal to win for God others to love him in like manner."[70]

The Peak Affective Experience

Moved by daily meditation upon God's emotional characteristics, we increasingly seek by the enablement of the Holy Spirit to control our own emotional patterns so that they become more like his. Like the God in whose presence we feel, as well as think and act, we will not cultivate Stoic apathy or Buddhist indifference to reality. Having acknowledged the appropriately intense emotions of God, we should not be shocked when Christians are deeply moved in face of gross sin and repentance from it. C. S. Lewis declared that he gave up atheism because it was too boring!

Those who would be like God increasingly *detest evil*. In the face of social injustice to the poor and powerless, the godly hate oppression, discrimination, selfishness, greed, covetousness, and all the contributing evils. For those who are living consciously in the presence of the Holy One, the sin that is a stench in his nostrils should become as repulsive in their own.

Although hating sin, the devout, like God, will develop an attitude that is *long-suffering* with the sinner. We must be long-suffering with people (relatives, neighbors, fellow students, and co-workers) who are unjust, unkind, unloving, and undeserving because we want them to be long-suffering with us. But far beyond that, God is long-suffering with them and us! With a growing consciousness of God's omnipresence, we develop not only similar intellectual and ethical responses, but also similar emotional responses to God's.

Maturing Christians in a fallen world become more *compassionate*. In the presence of God and the afflicted, they, like their God, are afflicted (see Isa. 63:9). Christians living in the presence of God not only rejoice with those who rejoice but also weep with those who weep. With empathy they enter into others' sufferings and sorrows, bearing others' burdens.

The Ultimate Commitment

Existentially, as they continuously contemplate God's freedom, maturing Christians grow in a responsible and rewarding sense of being *free* by God's grace. They celebrate their liberation from all lesser creatures who may become tyrants by demanding the ultimate allegiance deserved only by God. Delivered by a higher loyalty from the loyalties that enslave, they are free to determine themselves without compulsion or duress. Under the work of God's Spirit they are enabled to accomplish what of their fleshly selves they could not do. Daily commitment to the God of grace frees us to develop the capacity for self-determination according to our new spiritual natures, not ultimately for the sake of pride or privilege but for the glory of God. Not making our own happiness our ultimate concern, we find joy as a by-product.

The freedom of determining one's self need not be sheer rebellion against conformity to the world's mold. It can, with consciousness of never being ultimately alone in the universe, become affirmatively authentic. The Christian, consciously in step with the Holy Spirit, can increasingly avoid hypocrisy and be authentically himself or herself as created, regenerated, and sanctified. The new person, though far from perfect, can become increasingly candid and transparent in relation to God, herself, relatives, neighbors, and church members. People who might otherwise be intimidating do not threaten us when we come from conscious awareness of a higher presence.

Contemplating God's omnipotence takes a huge load off our shoulders, delivering us from unrealistic notions of what we ourselves are responsible for and so freeing us to fulfill more realistic expectations. Living in the presence of the Almighty helps us not to waste energy, and so there will be more power to use for wise purposes. The universe and the church belong to God, not to us. It is God, not any one person on earth at any given time, who bears the ultimate responsibility for God's work in the world and in the church. Young people who have dedicated themselves to the Lord to change not only the church but also the world need high, but not unrealistically high ideals. Each one is but an instrument—one of many persons God has chosen to use in reaching the world and reviving the church. The recognition that it is God, not ourselves, who is omnipotent frees us from the despair of failing to attain unattainable objectives. Freed from these unnecessary frustrations about the future of humanity and of the church, God's servants do not waste energy on futile anxieties. They then discover greater strength in the use of their gifts for the fulfillment of their distinctive purposes in the world and the church.

The Greatest Relationship You Can Enjoy

Relationally, as we meditate on the presence of the transcendent God with all people in providential ways and with the church in redemptive ways, we know that no greater relationship can be enjoyed than with our awesome Creator and Redeemer.

As human beings made in God's image, we have a capacity for consciously transcending ourselves and relating meaningfully to our neighbors (everyone we come in responsible contact with). We have special relationships with colleagues or fellow workers. We may enjoy even deeper relationships with friends. Then there are those intimate family relationships of chil-

dren, parents, husbands, and wives. As fellow servants of the Lord in a church, we share still deeper spiritual commitments than with unsaved members of our families. But beyond all these is the greatest human relationship of all—an abiding, loving communion with the Lord himself. We can, by grace, transcend our selfish interests and desires and develop a more settled determination to love above all the One who will never leave nor forsake us. And by grace most of us can begin a more vital, personal relationship with God than we have previously cultivated, right where we are, right at this moment.

What, or who, is your ultimate concern? On what or on whom do you place the highest value of all? What is the dominant love, the supreme love of your life?

REVIEW QUESTIONS

To Help Relate and Apply Each Section in This Chapter

1. *Briefly state the classical problem* this chapter addresses and indicate reasons why genuine inquiry into it is important for your world view and your existence personally and socially.

2. *Objectively summarize the influential answers* given to this problem in history as hypotheses to be tested. Be able to compare and contrast their real similarities and differences (not merely verbal similarities or differences).

3. *Highlight the primary biblical evidence* on which to decide among views—evidence found in the relevant teachings of the major divisions of Scripture—and decide for yourself which historical hypothesis (or synthesis of historical views) provides the most consistent and adequate account of the primary biblical data.

4. *Formulate in your own words your doctrinal conviction* in a logically consistent and adequate way, organizing

your conclusions in ways you can explain clearly, support biblically, and communicate effectively to your spouse, children, friends, Bible class, or congregation.

5. *Defend your view* as you would to adherents of the alternative views, showing that the other views are logically less consistent and factually faced with more difficulties than your view in accounting for the givens, not only of special revelation but also of human experience in general.

6. *Explore the differences the viability of your conviction can make in your life.* Then test your understanding of the viability of your view by asking, "Can I live by it authentically (unhypocritically) in relation to God and to others in my family, church, vocation, neighborhood, city, nation, and world?"

MINISTRY PROJECTS

To Help Communicate This Doctrine in Christian Service

1. *Memorize one major verse or passage* that in its context teaches the heart of this doctrine and may serve as a text from which to preach, teach, or lead small group studies on the topic. The memorized passages from each chapter will build a body of content useful also for meditation and reference in informal discussions.

2. *Formulate the major idea of the doctrine in one sentence* based on the passage memorized. This idea should be useful as the major thesis of either a lesson for a class (junior high to adult) or a message for a church service.

3. *State the specific purpose or goal of your doctrinal lesson or message.* Your purpose should be more than informative. It should show why Christians need to accept this truth and live by it (unhypocritically). For teaching

purposes, list indicators that would show to what extent class members have grasped the truth presented.

4. *Outline your message or lesson in complete sentences.* Indicate how you would support the truth of the doctrine's central ideas and its relevance to life and service. Incorporate elements from this chapter's historical, biblical, systematic, apologetic, and practical sections selected according to the value they have for your audience.

5. *List applications of the doctrine* for communicating the difference this conviction makes in life (for sermons, lessons, small-group Bible studies, or family devotional Bible studies). Applications should make clear what the doctrine is, why one needs to know it, and how it will make differences in thinking. Then show how the difference in thought will lead to differences in values, priorities, attitudes, speech, and personal action. Consider also the doctrine's possible significance for family, church, neighborhood, city, regional, and national actions.

6. *Start a file and begin collecting illustrations* of this doctrine's central idea, the points in your outline, and your applications.

7. *Write out your own doctrinal statement on this subject in one paragraph* (in half a page or less). To work toward a comprehensive doctrinal statement, collect your formulations based on a study of each chapter of *Integrative Theology.* As your own statement of Christian doctrine grows, you will find it personally strengthening and useful when you are called on for your beliefs in general and when you apply for service with churches, mission boards, and other Christian organizations. Any who seek ordination to Christian ministry will need a comprehensive doctrinal statement that covers the broad scope of theology.

CHAPTER 7

GOD'S UNITY INCLUDES THREE PERSONS

God's Unity Includes
Three Persons

THE PROBLEM: HOW OUGHT WE UNDERSTAND THE PLURALITY OF GOD (AS FATHER, SON, AND SPIRIT), GIVEN THE FACT THAT GOD IS ONE?

Israel was repeatedly taught, against the pervasive polytheism of her pagan neighbors, that the Lord is one. Yet in her life before God Israel became aware of one called Seed, Branch, Wisdom, Prophet, and King and of another called Spirit of God and Holy Spirit. Centuries later the church became convinced that Jesus, more than a man, was a divine person come from God, and likewise that the Holy Spirit, more than an impersonal power, was himself a divine personal agent. The problem within the community of faith is how to retain belief in the unity and uniqueness of Yahweh while doing justice to the divinity of Jesus Christ and the Holy Spirit. Both of these realities appear to be established by propositional revelation and personal experience.

The doctrine of the Trinity represents the heart of both Christian theology and the Christian life. Historically, followers of Christ have affirmed that the nature of God is such that the Atonement was made by the second person of

the Trinity and salvation applied by the third person. The Trinity thus is profoundly bound up with what it means to be a Christian. Yet many influential thinkers of today question the assertion that God is multiplicity in unity. Is it true that the Trinitarian confession is a contradiction or, to put it more benignly, a paradox? In what sense is oneness ascribed to God? In what sense threeness? Can we talk about an ontological equality among members of the Trinity? What about an ordering relation? How shall we understand the longstanding conviction in the church that the Son is begotten from the Father and the Spirit proceeds from the Father (and the Son)? Moreover, how weighty are the critics' claims that the doctrine of the Trinity represents a cultural Hellenism, i.e., a metaphysical construct alien and unserviceable to the modern mind? These and other important issues will occupy our attention in the discussion to follow.

ALTERNATIVE INTERPRETATIONS IN THE CHURCH

For an issue so central and crucial to the Christian faith, the Trinity has been subjected to numerous explications.

The following views represent the main interpretations of the Trinity as it has been articulated by Christendom throughout its history.

Monarchian Formulations

Various forms of Monarchianism viewed God as an indivisible monad (i.e., Monarch) without any personal distinctions. Adoptionism or dynamic monarchism, as championed by Theodotus of Byzantium and Paul of Samosata, regarded the Logos as an impersonal power operative in the man Jesus by virtue of which he was adopted as God's Son, and it viewed the Holy Spirit equally impersonally as the grace of God in the church. Modalist Monarchianism, which claimed that the three "persons" are merely names for the several manifestations of the one God, assumed two forms. Patripassianism in the West held that the Father descended into the Virgin, was born of her, and himself suffered on the Cross. Sabellianism claimed that Father, Son, and Holy Spirit are simply designations for three different phases under which the one undivided essence operationally manifests itself. Thus it was claimed that God revealed himself as the Father in creation and the giving of the Law, as the Son in the Incarnation, and as the Holy Spirit in regeneration and sanctification. Sabellius emphatically denied that the Son and the Holy Spirit are distinct persons.

Arianism, Socinianism, and Deism

Arians in the patristic era, Socinians at the time of the Reformation, and Deists and rationalists in the seventeenth and eighteenth centuries denied multiplicity within the Godhead, while generally holding that Jesus was a man adopted by God and that the Holy Spirit was an impersonal power or influence from God. Arius, a deacon in the church at Alexandria, argued that because God is eternal, immutable, and indivisible, his essence cannot be communicated to another. Thus whatever else exists must have come into being by God's creative act. So Arius insisted that God created the Son ("Son" being merely a figure of speech) from nothing by an act of his will to be the instrument for the creation of all things. Christ, the highest mediator, neither is consubstantial nor coeternal with the Father. "The Son, begotten by the Father, created and founded before the ages, was not before he was begotten."[1] Insofar as the Holy Spirit was viewed as a quality or as an attribute of God, a strict monotheism was preserved but triunity was denied.

The conviction of the Socinians that no satisfaction is needed for the human spiritual condition prompted them to deny the Trinity and to insist that God is one both in essence and in person. "The divine essence is single only in number, and therefore there cannot be several persons in it. For a person is nothing else than intelligent, indivisible essence."[2] Failing to distinguish between "essence" and "person," the Socinians argued that if the Godhead consists of three persons, there would have to be three essences. They viewed Jesus as a man supernaturally conceived and adopted by God to serve as a moral teacher. At the completion of his mission, Jesus was elevated to heavenly power and immortality. The Spirit, likewise, was not a divine person, but only a power or influence from God. The Socinian form of Arianism thus denied the deity of the Son and the personality of the Holy Spirit.

The English deists rejected the Trinity for the reason that its mystery was said to violate the religion of nature agreeable to reason. Thomas Chubb insisted that Christ was a mere man, the Holy Spirit an enigma, and the Trinity a doctrine of a "triangular" God. German rationalists such as H. Reimarus, G. E. Lessing, and K. G. Bretschneider rejected the Trinity and the two natures of Christ. They viewed God as a loving Father, Jesus as an inspired ethical teacher, and the Spirit as the power at work in persons to effect moral development.

Hegelian Idealism

Hegel regarded the Trinity as a pictorial representation of a philosophical dialectic of process involving thesis, antithesis, and synthesis. According to Hegel, ontologically God is Spirit (*Geist*). God is also unity, i.e., the All-Containing, the Absolute, the Universal in-and-for-itself. Relationally, God is a unity-in-difference, the mediation of the moments of its own self-determination, the eternal synthesis of itself. The Trinity is the God who differentiates himself within himself, but in the process remains identical with himself. Thus God or Spirit is viewed in three forms: *Universality* (eternal being-in-and-with-itself), *Particularization* (being-for another), and *Individuality* (a return from appearance into Self)—i.e., Father, Son, and Holy Spirit, respectively. The relation between Father, Son, and Holy Spirit is merely a figurative expression. The term "Father" is referred to God as he is in himself; the One apart from creation. But just as the universal gives rise to the particular, so in theological terms the Father "begets" the Son, the Other. This is the moment of particularization, differentiation, and determination. The term "Holy Spirit" denotes the relation of the Father and the Son for which the word "love" is the fitting synonym.

Thus Hegel's Trinity is a dialectic movement wherein the thesis (Father) and the antithesis (Son) are united into the higher unity of the Spirit or Absolute Love. Hegel formulated a modern modalism—an economic, not an essential, Trinitarianism. His God is an impersonal and immanental process of Self-Realization. As such the differentiation within the Godhead only represents simultaneous moments in its continuing being, of which the Son is mere finite existence and the Spirit a mere category of expression.

Neoorthodox Theology

The neoorthodox tradition ascribes personality to the unitary essence of God and regards Father, Son, and Holy Spirit as three different modes of operation of the divine being.

For Karl Barth the central thesis of Christianity is that "God reveals himself as the Lord."[3] Moreover, the God who makes himself known through Jesus Christ is seen to be Revealer, Revelation, and Revealedness, which corresponds to Father, Son, and Holy Spirit of Scripture. Such a phenomenon, Barth argues, includes both unity and variety. The unity consists in the "numerical unity of the essence of the three 'Persons.'"[4] The variety that contributes to the "Three-in-oneness" involves, not three personalities, but three modes of being. So as to avoid the error of what he regards as tritheism, Barth ascribes personality to the undivided essence rather than to the threefold differentiation. For Barth, then, Father, Son, and Holy Spirit are "three modes of being of the *one* God subsisting in their relationships with one another."[5] Beyond that, the Trinity is an inscrutable mystery. Barth's replacement of the classical formula with "one divine subject in three different modes of being" leads us to conclude that his position is a form of idealistic modalism.[6]

Emil Brunner rejects the classical Trinitarian formula as "an aberration of theological thought."[7] Consistent with his interest in function rather than ontology, Brunner focuses on the historical revelation of the Trinity, i.e., on the one God who reveals himself to persons in the form of three operations or names—Father, Son, and Spirit. "If the name 'Father' designates the origin and content of the revelation, the Name of the 'Son' designates the historical Mediator, and the 'Holy Spirit' the present reality of this revelation."[8] Modalism enters when the Son and Spirit are viewed as mere aspects of God—the former being God's self-communication and the latter God's indwelling presence. And subordination occurs when "the three Names do not stand alongside of one another but after one another."[9] Brunner believes with Barth that a triad of three equal divine persons necessarily involves tritheism.

Roman Catholic Neoliberalism

Contemporary Roman Catholic neologists repudiate the classical ontological model as embracing an alien Greek metaphysic and follow Barth in upholding an economic Trinity. The unity of God is consistently emphasized, with plurality viewed as aspects of God's self-communication. The belief that God *is* Trinity is thus replaced by the notion that God *reveals* himself as Trinity. This restatement of the Trinity requires a new definition of the meaning of person. According to Dewart, "the different persons are different modes . . . of his self-communication."[10] Contemporary Catholic liberals seek to maintain a link with Christian tradition by formulating an economic view of the Trinity.

Karl Rahner argues that the formula "three persons in one substance" upholds a "vulgar tritheism" more dangerous than Sabellian modalism. Since, according to Rahner, there cannot be three distinct consciousnesses or centers of activity in God, one must adopt an economic approach to the Trinity. The unity of God resides in the one essence, the one cognition, the one consciousness. But since the immanent Trinity *is* the economic Trinity and vice versa, God's unity can be viewed as his one self-communication to the world. This self-communication, however, occurs in three modes. Thus Father, Son, and Spirit are said to be three self-communications of the one God vis-à-vis the world. "The Father is the incomprehensible origin and the original unity, the 'Word' his utterance into history, and the 'Spirit' the opening up of history into the immediacy of its fatherly origin and end."[11] Rahner not only avoids calling Father, Son, and Spirit "persons," but he replaces "triune" or "three-in-one" (*Dreieinigkeit*) with "the threefold God" (*Dreifaltigkeit*). Thus Rahner's modalism is openly manifest.

Hans Küng follows Rahner in renouncing the ontological Trinity (a Hellenistic distortion unintelligible to modern people) in favor of an economic Trinity. "The triadic formulas of the New Testament are meant to express not an 'immanent' but an 'economic' theology of the Trinity, not an innerdivine (immanent) essential Trinity in itself but a salvation-historical (economic) unity of the Father, Son, and Spirit in their encounter with us."[12] The unity Küng posits resides in the revelation event, and the diversity in the "roles" that Father, Son, and Spirit perform. What God is in himself is wholly inexplicable.

Protestant Neoliberalism

Contemporary Protestant liberals have generally abandoned the ontological Trinity, believing that there are no personal distinctions within the reality or being of God. The most that can be affirmed is that the Trinity sums up the threefold way in which God is known in personal experience. Suspicious of the traditional metaphysical postulates about God's inner being and relations, W. A. Brown affirms of the Trinity: "It is not a doctrine about God as He is in Himself, but concerning God as revealed. It is a summary of the different ways in which one may know God in experience."[13] Thus God discloses himself in "three aspects"—namely, as the Absolute or ultimate source of life; as the self-revealing one disclosed in nature, history, and Christ; and as the self-imparting one or indwelling Presence. Brown readily admits that his is a "Trinity of consciousness."[14] In a similar vein, Fosdick contemplated only a Trinity of experience, the substance of which is "the grace of the Lord Jesus Christ, the love of God, and the fellowship of the Holy Spirit."[15]

Process theology likewise derives its "Trinity" from the threefold experience persons have of the living God. First there is the experience of God as Creative Source, which provides each entity with its initial aim or intentional purpose. This is said to be God the Father. Second, there is the experience of God as Self-Expressive Act, which provides a person with the pattern by which to realize one's initial aim. This is God the Son. According to Pittenger, Jesus is the "visible human expression of the divine intention. He is the self-expression of the divine purpose for the human race."[16] And third, there is the experience of God as Responsive Movement, which is the power of love eliciting the response of obedience and worship. This is said to be the Holy Spirit.[17] The "Trinity" of process theology thus involves not three persons but one threefold activity. "Process theology is not interested in formulating distinctions within God for the sake of conforming with traditional Trinitarian notions."[18]

Orthodox and Evangelical Theology

The historic Christian church from earliest times—including most Fathers, medieval theologians, Reformers, and Evangelicals—maintains that God is a unitary essence consisting of three co-equal persons—Father, Son, and Holy Spirit. Although ontologically equal, the three persons evince a subordination in economy or modes of operation. Moreover, the Father is unbegotten, the Son was begotten from the eternal essence of the Father, and the Spirit proceeds from the Father and the Son (West) or the Father alone (East).

Early in the second century the *Letter of Barnabas* affirmed a Trinity comprised of God the Father, Christ the preexistent Lord and Judge, and the Holy Spirit who prepares hearts for salvation.[19] The Trinitarian formula preserved in *The Didache* 7.1 indicates that belief in the triune God was assumed by much of the second-century Christian community. Theophilus first used the term "Trinity" (*trias*) to connote within the Godhead the reality of "Father," "Logos," and "Wisdom" (i.e., the Spirit) without fully explicating the relation between the persons.[20] Irenaeus, against the Gnostics, argued that the one Creator and Redeemer God subsists as Father, Son, and Spirit. More clearly than any previous authority, Irenaeus affirmed the eternal preexistence and divinity of the Word[21] (who was eternally generated from the Father) and the Spirit.[22] Irenaeus spoke plainly of the essential Trinity and the functions each person performs in the administration of salvation.[23]

Tertullian, in his complete discussion of the Trinity, claimed that although God is one by unity of substance (*substantia*), the Father, Son, and Spirit are distinct divine persons (*personae*).[24] The first church father to employ the Latin word *trinitas*, Tertullian explained the differences between the persons in terms of their functions in the out-working of salvation.

The church at Nicea (325) and Constantinople (381) countered the Arian theology by upholding the Son's proper coeternity and consubstantiality with the Father. Christ was not created but was begotten by a timeless generation from the substance of the Father. The Council completed its Trinitarian confession by acknowledging the analogous reality of the Holy Spirit. The heart of the Nicene Creed of 381 reads:

> We believe in one God, the Father almighty . . . ; and in one Lord Jesus Christ, the only-begotten Son of God, begotten from the Father before all ages, light from light, true God from true God, begotten not made, of one substance [*homoousios*] with the Father. . . . And in the Holy Spirit, the Lord and life-giver, who proceeds from the Father. Together with the Father and the Son he is worshipped and glorified.

Athanasius insisted that only the triune God is capable of saving from the consequences of sin. Thus, as a matter of salvation, he upheld one divine being who is at once Father, Son, and Holy Spirit. Against Arius he affirmed the strict consubstantiality of the Father and the Son: "He and the Father are one . . . in the identity of the one Godhead."[25] By an inscrutable process the Word was generated eternally from the essence of God. Athanasius went beyond Nicea's simple statement of faith in the Holy Spirit to affirm that the Holy Spirit is fully eternal and in essence divine: he "is one with the Son as the Son is one with the Father."[26] Whereas the Word is begotten, the Spirit proceeds from the Father through the Son.

Basil, Gregory of Nazianzus, and Gregory of Nyssa made lasting contributions to Trinitarian theology. The Cappadocian theologians, perhaps concerned that the three *hypostaseis* might dissolve into the Platonically defined *ousia*, followed Origen in emphasizing the three distinct persons within the Godhead and the primacy of the Father.

Their Trinitarian formula was: "one divine *ousia* in three distinct *hypostaseis*." By *ousia* they meant one invisible, divine nature, and by *hypostasis* they meant mode of being or personal center with independent existence and unique characteristics. The Cappadocians distinguished the three persons (1) by their mutual relations—the Father is unbegotten, the Son begotten, and the Spirit spirated—and (2) by their activities—the Father is the source, the Son the agent, and the Spirit the consummation of all things. Gregory of Nyssa in his essay *On Not Three Gods* refuted the charge that if Peter, James, and John are one human nature but three men, then the Father, Son, and Spirit as one divine nature must be three Gods.

Augustine, in his essay *The Trinity*, began with the single divine essence and thereafter sought to comprehend how the three persons share in the one nature without dividing it. The Trinity consists of the one essence (*essentia*) that includes three distinct subsistences or persons (*personae*).[27] In fact, given his commitment to the Neo-Platonic doctrine of God's simplicity (where the One lacks all distinctions), Augustine seems to hold not merely that the divine essence includes three persons, but also that each of these persons is actually identical to the divine essence. Thus the distinction between persons is not substantial, but only relational; i.e., paternity (the Father begets), filiation (the Son is begotten), and gift (the Spirit proceeds). For Augustine, oneness of essence implies equality of perfections, unity of will, and oneness of operations. The three persons "are infinite in themselves. And so each is in each, all are in each, each is in all, all are in all, and all are one."[28] The Son is eternally begotten from the substance of the Father, whereas the Spirit proceeds eternally from the Father and the Son (*filioque*), although principally from the Father.[29]

Augustine suggested that the Spirit's procession differs from the Son's begetting: the Spirit "came forth, not as one born, but as one given."[30]

Greek theology viewed the Trinity from the standpoint of the Father as the beginning and source of the Godhead. Thus the Son was begotten and the Spirit proceeds from the person of the Father. This was the position of Athanasius, the Cappadocians, the Niceno-Constantinopolitan Creed, and John of Damascus. In the West, on the other hand, where persons were viewed as relations, the Trinity was derived from the being of the Godhead. Hence the Spirit was said to proceed from both the Father and the Son (*filioque*). The *filioque* was expressly affirmed by Hilary, Augustine, and the Athanasian Creed, and it became a major factor in the eleventh-century schism between East and West.

Calvin welcomed the early-church doctrine of the Trinity; namely, that within the unity of the unbegotten essence there exist three distinct persons or hypostases. Each of these subsistences, while related to the others by a common essence, is distinguished by its own peculiar properties, as follows: "To the Father is attributed the beginning of activity, and the fountain and wellspring of all things; to the Son, wisdom, counsel, and the ordered disposition of all things; but to the Spirit is assigned the power and efficacy of that activity."[31] Such differentiation of persons involves an economic ordering that is properly eternal: "The Father is thought of as first, then from him the Son, and finally from both the Spirit."[32] Calvin further elaborates the relation between the one God and the three persons as follows:

> Under the name of God is understood a single, simple essence, in which we comprehend three persons, or hypostases. Therefore, whenever the name of God

is mentioned without particularization, there are designated no less the Son and the Spirit than the Father; but where the Son is joined to the Father, then the relation of the two enters in; and so we distinguish among the persons. But because the peculiar qualities in the persons carry an order within them, e.g., in the Father is the beginning and the source, so often as mention is made of the Father and the Son together, or the Spirit, the name of *God* is peculiarly applied to the Father.[33]

The Protestant Confessions articulate the consensus of the church concerning God's Trinitarian being. The reader is directed to Art. 1 of the Lutheran Augsburg Confession (1530), Art. XII of The Epitome of the Formula of Concord (1577), Art. I of The Anglican Thirty-Nine Articles (1563), Art. III of the Reformed Second Helvetic Confession (1566), and chapter 2 of The Westminster Confession (1646). The heart of the latter statement reads: "In the unity of the Godhead there are three persons, of one substance, power, and eternity: God the Father, God the Son, and God the Holy Ghost. The Father is of none, neither begotten nor proceeding; the Son is eternally begotten of the Father; the Holy Ghost eternally proceeding from the Father and the Son."

Recent evangelical theology reflects the received doctrine of the Trinity in its Western form. So L. Berkhof,[34] Henry C. Thiessen,[35] and Millard J. Erickson.[36]

THE BIBLICAL TEACHING

To determine which historical interpretation is preferred, we now turn to the primary data of Scripture.

Pentateuch

The fundamental datum of Old Testament theology is the uniqueness and unity of Israel's God. Contrary to the polytheism of Israel's neighbors, Yahweh alone is the true and living God. Thus in the *Shema* Moses declared, "Hear, O Israel: The Lord our God, the Lord is one" (*'eḥād,* Deut. 6:4). If this text focuses primarily on the uniqueness of Yahweh and the obligation to worship him alone, the unity of God follows from that (cf. Exod. 26:6, 11; 36:13, where *'eḥād,* is rendered "a unit"). So Vriezen argues, "The unity and the uniqueness are . . . quite clearly related. The unity indicates that God is not divided. His uniqueness means that Yahweh alone is God."[37] Vriezen correctly urges that God's unity not be sacrificed to his uniqueness. Whereas texts such as Deuteronomy 4:35, 39; 32:39 emphasize God's uniqueness, Numbers 6:27 stresses God's unity, for his "name" (which connotes his person) is single in number.

On the other hand, the Old Testament emphasis on the unity of God's being is supplemented by a certain multiplicity suggesting distinct centers of consciousness. Thus (1) plural pronouns are used to describe the actions of the Godhead (Gen. 1:26; 3:22; 11:7). It is unlikely that the "us" in Genesis 1:26 refers to God and angels, since man alone was created in God's image (Gen. 1:27). The fact that plural pronouns were not used elsewhere in reference to God may suggest that God is calling the reader's attention to something unusual. Moreover, given the fact that the rest of Scripture depicts three persons working together in the *opera ad extra* (Ps. 33:6; John 1:3; 5:17, 19; Col. 1:16), this phenomenon of plural pronouns points to a plurality of persons in the Godhead. "It would seem most acceptable to hold to the interpretation advanced by the ancient church Fathers and universally accepted by scholars of the past, that this is a reference to the Triune God. . . . What is clearly indicated here is that God, in His unity, has a certain plurality."[38]

(2) When God is the subject, the Old Testament occasionally uses plural verbs (e.g., Gen. 35:7) where a single form of the verb would be expected. In a monotheistic context Elohim ordinarily governs verbs, adjectives, and pronouns in the singular. (3) Many early Christian authorities saw in the threefold blessing and threefold repetition of the divine Name (Num. 6:24–26) an adumbration of the Trinity that later would stimulate the explicitly triune apostolic blessing of 2 Corinthians 13:14. (4) Some authorities see in the divine name Elohim a hint of the Trinity. Thus Elohim is "a term conveying both the unity of the one God and yet allowing for a plurality of persons."[39] On balance, however, it is preferable to view this plural name for God in the sense of a plural of excellence or of majesty.[40]

Multiplicity within the divine unity is further suggested by personal entities endowed with divine qualities. (1) Genesis 3:15 refers to the "offspring," or "seed" (*zᵉra'*) of Eve, who is wounded by Satan but who ultimately destroys the evil one. Whereas the seed could be viewed as the people of God collectively (Rom. 16:20), its ultimate reference is to Eve's conquering Seed, the Lord Jesus Christ (Heb. 2:14). The message of victory, moreover, represents the first announcement of the Good News (the *Protoevangelium*). (2) Deuteronomy 18:15 refers to a "prophet" (*nābî'*) like Moses whom God would raise up from the Jews to proclaim his word. The prophet to come refers in the first instance to the succession of prophets who would continue the work of Moses,[41] but ultimately to the prophetic Messiah himself, as the New Testament clearly attests (John 1:21; Acts 3:22; 7:37). (3) Jacob's blessing ("The scepter will not depart from Judah, nor a ruler's staff from between his feet, until he comes to whom it belongs and the obedience of the nations is his," Gen. 49:10) describes the messianic descendant of Judah who would rule the nations with unrivaled authority. Numbers 24:17 similarly depicts the star of Jacob, the kingly Messiah. (4) One of the most enigmatic figures in the Old Testament is the "angel of the LORD" (*mal'ak Yahweh*). In the Hagar account (Gen. 16:7–14) the angel of the Lord is identified as "the LORD" (v. 13) and yet is different from the Lord God (v. 11b). Abraham's three visitors (Gen. 18:1–33) are described as "three men" (v. 2; cf. vv. 16, 22), of whom the first is said to be "the LORD" (vv. 1, 10, 13, et al.) and the remaining two "angels" (Gen. 19:1). Calvin, like many other authorities, judges that "the chief of the embassy" was Christ.[42] In the account of Abraham's call to sacrifice Isaac (Gen. 22:11–18), the angel of the Lord is a messenger different from the Lord whom Abraham obeyed. According to Exodus 23:20–21, God's "Name" (i.e., the Lord in his self-manifestation) was in the angel who directed Israel's wilderness journey. The angel is endowed with authority and the power to forgive sins. In God's promise to Moses (Exod. 32:34–33:16), the angel of the Lord bears within himself God's "Presence" (33:14). On balance, it seems preferable to view the *mal'ak Yahweh* as a self-manifestation of the triune God in a visible form.[43] In the light of our discussion about the "seed," "prophet," and "ruler," Jesus' saying to the Jews, "Moses . . . wrote about me" (John 5:46) gains greater clarity.

In the context of a strict monotheism, Genesis 1:2 attests the creative agency of the *rûah 'elohîm* ("the Spirit of God was hovering over the waters"). Since *rûah 'elohîm* in the Old Testament consistently indicates the Spirit of God, we do well to understand it in the same sense here. Concerning this active power who prepares the cosmos for God's further creative work, Aalders

writes, "There is no doubt that here, in the first verses of the Bible, there is a reference to the Holy Spirit."[44] According to Genesis 6:3, the Spirit of Yahweh is a divine personal agent distinct from the Lord: "The LORD said, 'My Spirit will not contend with man forever, for he is mortal.'" In the Pentateuch, God's Holy Spirit temporarily empowered leaders for the performance of specific tasks (Exod. 31:3; 35:31; Num. 24:2; Deut. 34:9).

Historical Books

Some suggest that a plurality of persons in the Godhead is attested by the humanlike figure who stood before Joshua and identified himself as "the commander of the LORD's army" (Josh. 5:15). The leader of God's angel host is represented not only as holy (v. 15) but as "the LORD" himself (6:2). Some authorities identify this remarkable figure as an appearance of the preexistent Son of God.[45] It seems better to conclude that the prince of the Lord's host was an angel of the Lord (see the discussion on Gen. 16:7–14 and 18:1–33, above).[46] Nathan's prophecy (2 Sam. 7:13–16) directed attention to David's greater Son who was at the same time the Son of the Father. David's dynasty would endure forever in the form of the kingdom reign of the Messiah (2 Sam. 7:16). Hebrews 1:5 attests that Nathan spoke of the second person of the Godhead.

The period of the Judges records many instances in which "the Spirit of the Lord" temporarily came upon people to inspire and empower them for special tasks (Judg. 3:10; 6:34; 11:29, et al.). The same Spirit-anointment occurred during the monarchy (1 Sam. 10:6, 10; 16:13–14; 1 Chron. 12:18). The Spirit also is seen as a divine person active in the composition of the songs of David (2 Sam. 23:2). "At most points . . . context approves and the analogy of the New Testament strongly suggests that the *rûaḥ YHWH* is the Holy Spirit in the fullest Christian sense."[47]

Poetry and Wisdom

Psalm 33:6 may well be a divinely designated intimation of the triune God: "By the word of the Lord were the heavens made, their starry host by the breath of his mouth." Given the fact that the background of verses 6–9 is the Genesis 1 creation account where the work of the Spirit of God is cited, and given the fact that throughout Scripture Christ is depicted as the unique agent of creation, the Christian understands Psalm 33:6 with many early Fathers in terms of the personal Word and Spirit.[48] If this is the case, an economic ordering of persons in the work of creation may be indicated.

The Psalms direct attention to a divine Messiah or "Anointed One" (*māšîaḥ*) who is clearly distinct from Yahweh. Psalm 2 provides a good example. Whereas Psalm 2:1–3 in its historical context describes ungodly rebellion against the Lord and the Davidic king, Acts 4:25–27 interprets these verses in terms of God's "holy servant Jesus." Moreover, whereas Psalm 2:7–9 depicts the installation and rule of the Davidic king, the verses prophetically anticipate the eschatological enthronement and sovereign rule of the messianic King. The saying in Psalm 2:7, "You are my Son; today I have become your Father," is applied by several New Testament writers to major moments in the experience of Jesus Christ: (1) his incarnation (Heb. 1:5), (2) his baptism (Matt. 3:17), (3) his transfiguration (Matt. 17:5; 2 Peter 1:17), (4) his resurrection from the dead (Acts 13:33), and (4) his ascension and session to the right hand of God (Heb. 1:5). The New Testament writers cited Psalm 2:7 to prove that God's promises made to David (2 Sam. 7:11–16) were being brought to fruition through Jesus Christ, the divine Messiah.

Calvin observes that the statement "Your throne, O God, will last for ever and ever" (Ps. 45:6) "is sufficient of itself to establish the eternal divinity of Christ."[49] The following verse teaches that the One above him is equally "God." In Hebrews 1:8–9 it is unequivocally clear that the first person addressed as "God" is Christ, God's very Son. Psalm 72 highlights the righteousness and universality of David's kingdom. Yet the achievements of the king and his endless reign so far exceed the capability of a human ruler that the Psalm "suggests for its fulfillment no less a person than the Messiah."[50] Beyond the immediate historical situation, the words "The Lord says to my Lord: 'Sit at my right hand until I make your enemies a footstool for your feet' " (Ps. 110:1), should be viewed as an emphatic reference to the future reign of Christ, as Peter made clear in Acts 2:34–35. When Jesus inquired (Matt. 22:44–46) how Christ could be both David's son and David's Lord, he clearly identified himself with the "my Lord" (*'ᵃdônî*) of Psalm 110:1. C. S. Lewis agrees that in addition to the primary historical meaning these Psalms "contain a second or hidden meaning . . . concerned with the Incarnation, the Passion, the Resurrection, the Ascension, and with the Redemption of man."[51] The reality of the Messiah as a person coequal but distinct from Yahweh thus is embedded in many of the Psalms.

Proverbs offers a highly suggestive portrayal of wisdom. *Hokmāh* reproves and rebukes (1:23, 30), laughs at the calamity of his rejecters (1:30), answers prayer (1:28), exercises love (8:17), and is the source of life and favor (8:35). As indicated in the previous chapter, wisdom in Proverbs is a divine attribute personified in highly descriptive language. Later, the Holy Spirit led the apostle Paul to explicate the wisdom motif christologically (1 Cor. 1:24, 30; Col. 2:3). It is not likely that the writer himself understood *ḥokmāh* as a divine being.[52]

One catches glimpses of the Spirit in the poetic books as a divine person distinct from and sent by Yahweh. Thus, David prays that God's "Holy Spirit" (*rûaḥ qōdeš*), who is "good" (Ps. 143:10), "holy" (Ps. 51:11), and ubiquitous (Ps. 139:7), performs works appropriate to a divine person—i.e., he creates (Job 33:4; cf. Ps. 33:6), renews the earth (Ps. 104:30), guides believers (Ps. 143:10), imparts understanding (Job 32:8), and may be grievously sinned against (Ps. 106:33).

Prophetic Literature

Israel's prophets upheld the same explicit monotheism affirmed by the Pentateuch. God said through Isaiah: "I am the LORD, and there is no other; apart from me there is no God" (Isa. 45:5; cf. 44:6; 46:9). Inherent in God's uniqueness is the idea of unity of his being.

A plurality of persons within the unity of the Godhead may be intimated by the juxtaposition of singular and plural pronouns in Isaiah 6:8: "Whom shall I send? And who will go for us?" A clearer indication of the multiplicity within the Godhead is found in Isaiah 11:1–2. The text reads that "the Spirit of the LORD will rest" on One called "a Branch," thereby equipping him for messianic ministry. In a related passage the Servant-King testifies: "The Spirit [*rûaḥ*] of the Sovereign LORD [*'adōnāy Yahweh*] is on me, because the LORD has anointed me to preach good news to the poor" (Isa. 61:1). Christian faith recognizes that the Son is sent by the Father and anointed for messianic service by the Spirit. Jesus applied this text from Isaiah to his own life and ministry

(Luke 4:18–19). Also, Isaiah 42:5 contains the triad "God the LORD" (*'el Yahweh*), his elect "servant" (*'ebed*), and his anointing "Spirit" (*rûaḥ*). Isaiah 32, descriptive of the righteous kingdom of the Messiah, refers to "the LORD" (v. 6), the "king" who will reign (v. 1), and to "the Spirit" poured out from on high (v. 15).

The Servant declares in Isaiah 48:16: "And now the Sovereign LORD has sent me with his Spirit." Here *'adōnāy Yahweh* sends both his Son and his Spirit in what one authority describes as "a remarkable glimpse, from afar, of the Trinity."[53] Recounting God's faithfulness to his covenant people, Isaiah speaks of "the LORD" (Isa. 63:7), "the angel of his presence" (*mal'ak pānāyw*, v. 9), and "his Holy Spirit" (vv. 10–11).

The prophets unmistakably depict the Messiah-Son as a divine preexistent person. So Isaiah 7:14 speaks of him as "Immanuel" (i.e., "God with us"), which the New Testament pointedly applies to Jesus Christ (Matt. 1:23). The Son whom God would give (Isa. 9:6) is described in terms that imply divinity: "Wonderful Counselor," "Mighty God," and "Everlasting Father [lit., father or possessor of the ages]." The "righteous Branch," the messianic Ruler whom God would raise up from the fallen house of David (cf. Isa. 4:2; 11:1), in Jeremiah 23:6 (cf. 33:15–16) is given the divine title "The LORD Our Righteousness" (*Yahweh ṣidqēnû*). Judaism understood this as a name for the Messiah.[54] Daniel in a vision saw "one like a son of man" led into the presence of "the Ancient of Days." The former was given "authority, glory and sovereign power; all peoples, nations and men of every language worshiped him. His dominion is an everlasting dominion that will not pass away . . ." (Dan. 7:13–14). Jesus understood this passage in terms of his own person (Matt.

261

26:64), and "son of man" became his favorite self-designation.

Malachi 3:1 states that God will send his "messenger" to prepare the way for "the messenger of the covenant"— figures we understand from Mark 1:1–2 to be, respectively, John the Baptist and Jesus. Yet Malachi expressly identifies the messenger of the covenant to come as "the Lord" (*hā 'ādôn*)—a divine person distinct from "the LORD Almighty" (*Yahweh ṣᵉbāôt*).

We find in the prophets intimations that the Spirit of the Lord is a personal being (Zech. 7:12; Mic. 2:7), one with the Lord (Isa. 30:1; Hag. 2:5), yet distinctly separate from Yahweh (Isa. 48:16; Ezek. 43:5) and endowed with divine perfections (Isa. 11:2; Mic. 3:8). The prophetic promises that God will pour out his Spirit in the new age (Ezek. 36:25–27; Joel 2:28–32) suggest that the Holy Spirit is a divine person sent from the Father (Acts 2:17–18, 33).

Given Israel's inveterate tendency toward polytheism, the primary purpose of the Old Testament was to impress on the chosen people God's uniqueness and unity. Nevertheless a number of texts suggest that the one God of Israel was perceived to be complex in being, even though fuller explication of the Trinity would await New Testament development. Jesus' rebuke of his disciples for their failure to understand what the prophets had written concerning himself (Luke 24:25) and his explication of the Old Testament Scriptures that testify to him (v. 27) suggest that Christ was portrayed in the Bible of the Jews with some clarity.

Synoptic Gospels

Jesus upheld the Old Testament teaching on the uniqueness and unity of God. The Lord reiterated the *Shema* of Israel (Mark 12:29) and accepted the commendation of a Jewish teacher of the Law: "You are right in saying that God is one and there is no other but him" (Mark 12:32; cf. Deut. 4:35). With the advent of Christ, however, the plurality of persons within the Godhead became more evident. Thus, the angel Gabriel's announcement to Mary (Luke 1:30–35) identified three distinct persons: "the Lord God" (v. 32), "the Son of the Most High" (v. 32) or "the Son of God" (v. 35), and "the Holy Spirit" (v. 35), each of whom from the language and context is by nature divine. Yet it is also evident that the three persons are one, for so Jesus and the Holy Spirit are designated, respectively, the "Son" and "the power of the Most High" God (vv. 32, 35). The disclosure of the angel to Joseph (Matt. 1:18–23) reveals a similar triadic pattern.

Jesus' baptism by John (Matt. 3:16–17) attests the reality of the Trinity. (1) Three distinct persons are identified—"God"; "Jesus," or God's "Son"; and "the Spirit of God." (2) Three unique signs are reported— the Father's audible voice, the Son's real flesh, and the Spirit's mystical presence. (3) Three separate actions are cited—the Father's speaking from heaven, the Son's baptism in the Jordan River, and the Spirit's descent like that of a dove. These data indicate that Father, Son, and Spirit are not merely different names for one God, but are three uniquely distinct personal agents. The unity of persons is highlighted by God's identification of Jesus as "my Son, whom I love" (v. 17). Jesus did not become the Son of God at his baptism. Rather, the Spirit came upon the Son to equip him for the messianic work he was about to begin. John's reluctance to baptize Jesus (v. 14) and his admission that *he* ought to be baptized by Jesus suggests that he knew Jesus to be the Messiah. The third person in the scenario is identified as "the Spirit of God" who descended from heaven (v. 16). Fairly has it been said, "Go to the Jordan and you will see the Trinity."[55]

The narrative of the threefold temptation of Jesus by the Devil (Matt. 4:1–10)—which identifies as separate persons "the Lord . . . God" (vv. 7, 10), "Jesus" or "the Son of God" (an assumption, not an issue of doubt, vv. 3, 6), and "the Spirit" (v. 1)—provides an unmistakable allusion to the Trinity. The fact that Satan attempted to kill Jesus as an infant (Matt. 2:13) suggests that the Devil here did not assume Jesus' deity merely for the sake of argument. Jesus' words in Matthew 12:28 reflect a similar Trinitarian pattern: "If I drive out demons by the Spirit of God, then the kingdom of God has come upon you" (cf. vv. 31–32). Our Lord's Great Commission (Matt. 28:19), however, presents a deliberately conceived Trinitarian formula: ". . . baptizing them in the name of the Father, and of the Son and of the Holy Spirit." Unity of being is suggested by the one "name" (*to onoma*) into which converts were to be baptized, and plurality of persons by the three distinct subjects—"the Father," "the Son," and "the Holy Spirit." The deliberate repetition of the article in the phrase *tou patros kai tou kuriou kai tou hagiou pneumatos* is a most concise and unambiguous representation of the coequality of the three distinct persons in being, authority, and honor. It is fitting that Jesus' earthly ministry concludes with so concise a summary of the one God who subsists in three persons.

The Gospels also unfold the unique filial relation that exists between the first two persons of the Godhead. Matthew 11:25–27 makes this point in two ways: (1) Jesus testifies, "All things [i.e., viceregency over the world; cf. Matt. 28:18] have been committed to me by my Father,"[56] and (2) the Son perfectly knows (*epiginōskō*, v. 27) the latter by virtue of an intimate relationship that was experienced both before and after his incarnation. "The saying grounds Jesus' right to be the mediator of knowledge of God to men in the exclusive relationship which a son has with his father, and thus implicitly he claims a unique filial status."[57] At the Transfiguration (Matt. 17:1–8) the Father declared of Jesus: "This is my Son, whom I love; with him I am well pleased" (v. 5). The radiant transformation of Jesus into the appearance of a supernatural figure (v. 2) attests that the Son is no less divine than the Father. Whereas the radiance of Moses (Exod. 34:29, 35) was a reflected glory, Jesus' represents an effulgence from the source—i.e., from his divine person. In Matthew 22:41–45, Jesus claimed that the designation "son of David" fell far short of explicating Christ's true reality. Since "David, speaking by the Spirit, calls him 'Lord' " (v. 43, quoting Ps. 110:1), Christ must be the very Son of God. Matthew 3:3 establishes that Jesus is identical with the Yahweh of Isaiah 40:3. Finally, when asked by the high priest whether he was "the Christ, the Son of God," Jesus responded, "Yes, it is as you say" (Matt. 26:63–64; cf. the more pointed reply in Mark 14:62, "I am").[58] In other texts, Jesus Christ is denoted the unique and beloved Son of the Father (e.g., Matt. 10:32; 16:16–20; 27:40, 43). The Gospels also indicate a functional ordering between the Father, the One who sends, and Jesus, the Son who is sent (Matt. 10:40; Mark 9:37).

Primitive Christianity/Acts

The preaching of the early Christian missionaries includes the basic elements of the Trinity. In the first sermon after Pentecost (Acts 2:14–40) Peter testified that God raised Jesus from the dead and elevated him to his own right hand, thereby attesting that the Nazarene was indeed the "Holy One" (v. 27) and the "Lord and Christ"

(v. 36). "It is especially in the title 'Lord' that the primitive *kerygma* verges toward Trinitarianism."[59] Moreover, Peter's saying that the risen Christ "has received from the Father the promised Holy Spirit and has poured out what you now see and hear" (v. 33) implies not only the unity of Father, Son, and Spirit, but also an ordering principle in their operations. Stephen's speech (Acts 7:48–52) juxtaposes "the Most High" (v. 48), "the Righteous One" (v. 52) who is "the Son of Man standing at the right hand of God" (v. 56), and "the Holy Spirit" (v. 51) whose promptings the Jews have sinfully resisted. Peter's message to Cornelius speaks of "God" (Acts 10:34, 36, 38, et al.), "Jesus Christ"— the "Lord of all" (v. 36) whom God raised from the grave and appointed as judge of humankind—and "the Holy Spirit" (vv. 38, 44). Paul also acknowledged a Trinitarian faith when he said to the Ephesian elders: "I have declared to both Jews and Greeks that they must turn to God in repentance and have faith in our Lord Jesus. And now, compelled by the Spirit, I am going to Jerusalem" (Acts 20:21–22).

The purpose of the early Christian preaching was to convince Jews and Gentiles that Jesus was the promised Messiah and personal viceregent of God. Accordingly, Jesus was designated "the Lord" (Acts 18:9; 23:11), "Lord and Christ" (2:36), "Lord of all" (10:36), "the Holy and Righteous One" (3:14), "the author of life" (3:15), and "Prince and Savior" (5:31). Moreover, the risen Jesus has taken his seat at God's right hand (connoting a dignity equal to that of the Father), sends the Holy Spirit, forgives sins, and executes judgment on all. The only conclusion warranted is that Acts "assigns to Jesus a function and status equal to those of God the Father himself."[60]

Sometimes called "the Acts of the Holy Spirit," Luke's history of the early church focuses attention on the activity of the Holy Spirit, who continues the ministry of the glorified Jesus.[61] That the Spirit is a personal agent is proven by the juxtaposition of the Holy Spirit with the apostles in Acts 15:28 ("It seemed good to the Holy Spirit and to us . . ."). Moreover, the personality and divinity of the Spirit are implied in his manifold operations— i.e., the Spirit baptized the Galilean disciples so they spoke in vernacular languages (1:5, 8), imparted spiritual power for mission (4:8–13, 31; 9:31), directed Philip to Ethiopia and after that snatched Philip away to another place (8:29, 39), gave Agabus the ability to foretell the future (11:28), directed the Antiochene church to select missionaries (13:2, 4), restrained Paul and his companions from preaching in Asia (16:6–7), and appointed overseers for the churches (20:28). The deity of the Holy Spirit is explicitly affirmed in Acts 5:3–4, where lying to the Spirit is equivalent to lying to God: "Ananias, . . . you have not lied to men but to God." We have noted that an economic ordering is implied in Acts 2:33, where the Spirit of the Father was sent, or "poured out," by the Son. In addition, the third person of the Trinity is denoted "the Spirit of the Lord" (8:39) and "the Spirit of Jesus" (16:7).

Pauline Letters

One discovers in the writings of Paul, who had avidly studied the Jewish Scriptures, a firm insistence on the unity and uniqueness of God. The apostle undoubtedly had in mind the Hebrew *Shema* (Deut. 6:4) when he insisted, "There is no God but one" (1 Cor. 8:4) and "There is but one God, the Father" (v. 6).[62] Paul's emphasis on the oneness of God is also reflected in 1 Timothy 1:17 and 2:5.

The juxtaposition of three persons, with equal prominence given to each, provides the second element of the Trinity. In Romans 1:1–4, Paul testifies to "God" the Father, "his Son. . . Jesus Christ our Lord," and "the Spirit of holiness" (a Hebraism for the Holy Spirit). A deliberate Trinitarianism (that may allude to the triple name used in baptism) is found in 1 Corinthians 6:11: ". . . in the name of the Lord Jesus Christ and by the Spirit of our God." Paul's benediction in 2 Corinthians 13:14 reflects the same close association of three coequal persons: "The grace of the Lord Jesus Christ, and the love of God, and the fellowship of the Holy Spirit be with you all."[63] The Trinity is succinctly set forth in Ephesians 4:4–6: "one Spirit . . . one Lord . . . one God and Father of all, who is over all and through all and in all." This remarkable association of persons is seen also in 1 Corinthians 12:4–6: "the same Spirit . . . the same Lord . . . the same God." Titus 3:4–6 presents a triadic pattern that includes "God our Savior," "the Holy Spirit," and "Jesus Christ our Savior." Bernard comments concerning this text: "The co-operation of all three Persons of the blessed Trinity in the work of grace is tersely and pregnantly expressed."[64] The association of three distinct persons in ways consistent with their deity occurs also in Romans 8:1–4; Ephesians 1:3–14; 5:18–20; and 2 Thessalonians 2:13–14. The fact that within the Godhead the three designations occur in various orders implies their ontological equality: God—Son—Spirit (Rom. 1:1–4; Eph. 1:3–14); God—Spirit—Christ (Titus 3:4–6); Christ—God—Spirit (2 Cor. 13:14); Christ—Spirit—God (Rom. 8:1–4; 1 Cor. 6:11); and Spirit—Christ—God (1 Cor. 12:4–6; Eph. 4:4–6; 5:18–20).

Paul specifies that each of the three persons is fully God. The first person of the Trinity, when viewed in relation to Christ, is known by the name "Father" (Rom. 1:7; Eph. 1:17, et al.) Scripture repeatedly attests that, as to

his intrinsic being, the Father is "God" (*theos*): so the first person is denoted "God the Father" (Gal. 1:1; Eph. 6:23; Phil. 2:11, et al.) and "the God and Father of our Lord Jesus Christ" (2 Cor. 1:3; Eph. 1:3; cf. 2 Cor. 11:31).

The apostle likewise believed that Jesus Christ is equally God. Many Fathers, Reformers, and modern authorities, together with the AV. RV. NASB, and NIV, take the phrase "who is God over all, forever praised!" (*ho ōn epi pantōn theos eulogētos eis tous aiōnas*, Rom. 9:5) to be in apposition to and, thus, in explication of the preceding "Christ" (*ho christos*). In that case, Paul argues that the Messiah, as to his human descent, came through the line of the patriarchs, but, as to his eternal being, he is sovereignly divine.[65] Philippians 2:6, which depicts Christ as "being in very nature God" (*en morphē theou hyparchōn*), clearly certifies the Lord's deity. The participle *hyparchōn*, ("stronger than . . . the usual verb 'to be,' . . . speaks of what was and is unchangeably His")[66] is concessive in force. As such, it indicates that although possessing the divine nature, Christ nevertheless became a man and assumed a temporary subordination to the Father. The parallel between *morphē theou* and *morphē doulou* (v. 7) implies that if Jesus Christ were truly a servant, then he was truly God. The following expression, "equality with God," refers to the glory and dignity Christ possessed as one coeternal with the Father. In verse 7 the act of emptying (*ekenōsen*) is defined by the following participial construction (*morphēn doulou labōn*). The verb *labōn* is a participle of means, indicating that Christ "emptied" himself *by* clothing his deity with humanity. The allusion to Isaiah 45:23 in verses 10–11, as well as the inverted subject-predicate nominative construction in verse 11 (suggesting that *kyrios* is definite—i.e., "the LORD" = Yahweh) also argue for the claim that Jesus Christ is true God.

The expression "the glorious appearing of our great God and Savior, Jesus Christ" (Titus 2:13) indicates in three ways that Christ is God: (1) The presence of one article before the two nonproper and singular nouns "great God" and "Savior" refers both nouns to the same person; (2) the New Testament speaks of the "appearing" of Christ but never of the Father; and (3) the adjective *megas* in "great God" makes better sense applied to Christ, since the greatness of God was assumed by all. Finally, Colossians 1:19 and 2:9 teach, against the Gnostic division of Deity among the aeons, that the totality of the divine essence (*theotēs*) resides in Christ. Even Thayer, an Arian, maintains that *theotēs* in Colossians 2:9 upholds Christ's deity.[67]

. Texts such as Romans 8:3 and Galatians 4:4, which depict the preincarnate Christ as the Son of God (a term descriptive not of function but of nature), suggest the eternal relation the second person of the Trinity has with the Father. This consideration, plus the descriptions of Christ as "the image of God" (*eikōn*, 2 Cor. 4:4; Col. 1:15), "the radiance of God's glory" (*apaugasma*, Heb. 1:3), "the exact representation of [God's] being" (*charaktēr*, 1:3), and "the Word" through whom God reveals himself (*logos*; cf. John 1:1, 14; 1 John 1:1; Rev. 19:13) have prompted many Christian authorities to postulate the eternal generation of the Son from the essence of the Father.

Paul upholds the deity of the Holy Spirit when he states, "The Lord is the Spirit" (2 Cor. 3:17; cf. v. 18). Although some identify *kyrios* as the God of the Old Testament, it seems preferable, given the immediate context (v. 14), to hold that the apostle identifies Christ and the Spirit. That being so, "The Lord and the Spirit are 'one' in the same sense that Jesus said that

He and the Father were one (John 10:30)."[68] The deity and personality of the Holy Spirit, however, are demonstrated more through his manifold activities than through specific statements about his person. Thus, the Holy Spirit mediates revelation from God (1 Cor. 2:10a; Eph. 3:5), raised Christ from the dead (Rom. 8:11), searches out the deep things of God (1 Cor. 2:10b–11) so as to interpret spiritual truths to persons (1 Cor. 2:12, 14), fills the Christian with God's love (Rom. 5:5), imparts spiritual gifts to the church (Rom. 12:6–8; 1 Cor. 12:4–11; Eph. 4:11–12), encourages believers in the struggle with the lower nature (Rom. 8:4, 9), promotes hope for the future (Gal. 5:5), and intercedes for the saints before the Father (Rom. 8:26–27).

In sum, "the New Testament thinks of the Spirit as a person, not simply a power; as 'He' not 'It'."[69] Pauline expressions such as "the Spirit who is from God" (1 Cor. 2:12), "the Spirit of God" (1 Cor. 2:14; Rom. 8:9), and "God's Spirit" (1 Cor. 3:16), appear to imply that the Holy Spirit (his person, not his essence) derives from God the Father. According to Charles Hodge, 1 Corinthians 2:10–14 teaches "the Holy Spirit as proceeding from him [i.e., God the Father] and sent by him as the instructor of men."[70] Similarly, when the apostle refers to "the Spirit of Christ" (Rom. 8:9), "the Spirit of the Lord" (2 Cor. 3:17), and "the Spirit of his Son" (Gal. 4:6), he suggests that the Holy Spirit comes forth from the Son.

Alongside the essential equality of persons there exists an economic ordering or functional subordination. Paul implies that, within the administration of the Godhead, the Father has the primacy over the Son (Rom. 8:3; 1 Cor. 15:24, 28; Phil. 2:7–8) and over the Spirit (1 Cor. 6:19; Gal. 4:6), and the Son has priority over the Spirit (Gal. 4:6). With regard to the operations of the Godhead, Father, Son, and Holy

Spirit are source, channel, and agent respectively: all things are of (*ek*) the Father who originates (1 Cor. 8:6; Eph. 2:8; 3:15), through (*dia*) the Son who mediates (Rom. 1:5; Eph. 2:13, 18), and by (*en*) the Spirit who completes the work (1 Cor. 6:11; Eph. 2:18, 22; 3:5). Texts such as 1 Corinthians 15:24, 28 (which states that, after completion of his work, Christ subjects himself to the Father that the latter "may be all in all") prove that the ordering relation is eternal and not limited to Christ's state of humiliation.

In the Pauline writings, each person of the Godhead has a dominant function attributed to him (the principle of appropriation). Thus, chiefly the Father creates (1 Cor. 8:6; 2 Cor. 4:6), the Son redeems (Eph. 1:7; Titus 3:6), and the Spirit sanctifies (Rom. 15:16; 2 Cor. 3:18; 2 Thess. 2:13). Yet by virtue of the common essence, what one divine person performs each may be said to perform (the principle of *perichorēsis*). Accordingly, the Son creates (1 Cor. 8:6; Col. 1:16) and the Spirit creates (cf. Job 33:4; Ps. 33:6); the Father redeems (2 Cor. 5:18–19; Eph. 2:4–5, 8) and the Spirit redeems (Rom. 8:4; Titus 3:5); and the Father sanctifies (Eph. 1:3–4; 1 Thess. 5:23) and the Son sanctifies (Eph. 4:15–16; 5:25–27).

Johannine Literature

The AV reading of 1 John 5:7 provides an explicit declaration of the Trinity: "There are three that bear record in heaven, the Father, the Word, and the Holy Ghost: and these three are one." However, the manuscript evidence for this reading is sufficiently weak that modern translations rightly omit it from the text of 1 John. A copyist, prompted by the triad of earthly witnesses in verse 8 (Spirit, water, blood), was no doubt reminded of the heavenly Trinity and so made the gloss in a Latin version of 1 John about the fifth century.[71]

The distinction between the three persons—the Father, Jesus, and the Spirit—is dramatically set forth in the Johannine corpus. In John 14:16–17, Jesus differentiates between himself, "the Father," and "the Spirit" (who is identified as "another Counselor" [*allos paraklētos*]). The three persons likewise are distinguished in John 14:26 and 15:26. The Holy Spirit is clearly a person, for he is named "Counsellor" or "Comforter" (AV) and he teaches the disciples and testifies to Christ. Moreover, in such texts as John 5:17–23; 6:37–40; 12:49–50 the Father and the Son are represented as distinct persons, as are Jesus and the Spirit in John 5:32 (*allos* connotes "another" rather than "an other"; that is, he is another of the same kind).

Equally clear in John is the fact that the Father, Son, and Spirit are one in being or essence. Thus, the Spirit's presence with the disciples implies the simultaneous presence of the Father and the Son (John 14:16–24). The mutual participation (*communio*) of the Father and the Son and of the Son and the Spirit within the unity of the Godhead is evident in John 16:13–15. The ontological oneness of the Father and the Son is repeatedly asserted by John. So Jesus called God his Father in a manner that implied full equality with God (John 5:18). He claimed to be "in" the Father, even as the Father was "in" him (John 10:38; 14:10–11, 20; 17:21–23). The unity of Father and Son in essence and attributes is evident in John 10:28–30. In verses 28–29 Jesus claims equal power with the Father ("my hand"—"my Father's hand"). His statement "I and the Father are one" (v. 30) was a claim to deity, for the Jews sought to stone him for what they perceived to be blasphemy.[72] The unity of being that there is between the Father and Jesus is seen also in John 14:9; 17:10; 1 John 2:23–24.

John also upholds the full deity of

each of the three persons. The statement "The Father has life in himself" (John 5:26) is an implicit claim to deity. More explicitly, the Father is called "God" in John 6:27; 17:3; 20:17; Revelation 1:6. Moreover, the Son is plainly represented as God. John 1:1 makes a threefold claim for the Word (*logos*): (1) his eternal subsistence: the Word was "in the beginning" (*en archē*); (2) his eternal intercommunion with God: "the Word was with God" (*pros ton theon*); and (3) his eternal identity with God: "the Word was God" (*theos ēn ho logos*). The fact that *theos* (God) occupies first place in the previous clause indicates that it receives the emphasis. And that *theos* lacks the article denotes that the term refers to Christ's nature—i.e., "What God was, the Word was" (NEB). The Greek text gives no support for the rendering of the *New World Translation* (of Jehovah's Witnesses): "and the Word was a god." The preferred reading of John 1:18 describes Jesus Christ as *monogenēs theos*—"only begotten God" or "the only begotten (himself) God"[73]—an uncommon expression that likely was later changed to the simpler *ho monogenēs huios*. Thomas, after observing Jesus' wounded body, cried out, "My Lord and my God!" (*ho kyrios mou kai ho theos mou*, John 20:28). Identically structured phrases separated by *kai* indicate that "Lord" and "God" both describe the risen Jesus. What John says in 1 John 5:20 ("We are in him who is true—even in his Son Jesus Christ. He is the true God [*ho alēthinos theos*] and eternal life") is fully agreeable with other Johannine ascriptions of deity to Jesus the Son (cf. John 10:33, 36; 20:31). Jesus' response to the Jews in John 8:58: "Before Abraham was born, I am" (*egō eimi*) clearly testifies to his deity. The Jews understood that Jesus claimed to be the "I AM" of Exodus 3:14, the eternally existing Yahweh, as their attempt to stone him indicates.

Commonplace in John is the claim that God the Father is the Father of Jesus Christ (e.g., John 3:35; 14:12–13; 16:25–28; 20:17). Since to the Hebrew mind, sonship involves derivation of nature, filial love, and heirship, the Father-Son conceptuality suggests the eternal generation of the Son. When John depicts Christ as "the one who was born of God" (*ho gennētheis*, 1 John 5:18), he may have contemplated the timeless relation of Christ's begetting and sonship. When applied to Christ, *mongenēs* (John 1:14, 18; 3:16; 1 John 4:9) connotes the Son's uniqueness and incomparability; Christ is in a class by himself.

In the Gospel of John, the Spirit, though not explicitly called God, is invisible (John 14:17), eternal (v. 16), omniscient (v. 26), and true (v. 17; 15:26; 16:13). Attributed to him are numerous divine works; e.g., he convicts of sin (John 16:8–11), regenerates (John 3:5–8), guides believers into the truth of God (16:13–15), and gives power for ministry (20:22–23). In sum, "this Spirit is not an agency, but an agent, who teaches and selects; who can be sinned against and grieved; and who in the New Testament, is unmistakably revealed as a distinct person."[74] John 15:26 ("When the Counselor comes, whom I will send to you from the Father, the Spirit of truth who goes out from the Father, . . .") has traditionally been interpreted in the sense of the eternal procession of the Spirit (Olshausen, Lange, Godet, Pieper, et al.). But behind the primary reference to the mission of the Spirit (*para tou patros ekporeutai*) may lie the primary relation of the Spirit to the Father and the Son. Thus Westcott notes, "The revelation of the mission of the Spirit to men (*which proceedeth, I will send*) corresponds with the revelation of the eternal relations of the Spirit (*from the Father, through the Son*)."[75]

Entirely consistent with the ontological equality of persons, John, like Paul, recognizes an ordering relation within the Godhead. Thus, in a functional sense, both in time and eternity, the Father enjoys priority vis-à-vis the Son. This voluntary subordination of the Son to the Father is evidenced in the Father's act of sending the Son into the world (John 3:34; 5:23, 37; 17:3, 18, 25; 1 John 4:9). That Jesus' will and power were always dependent on the Father (John 5:19, 30, 36; 6:38) is reflected by the fact that the Son speaks the Father's message (John 12:49; cf. 3:34), obeys his commands (John 14:31; 15:10), and accepts his purpose of suffering (John 18:11). In sum, with regard to the Son's role as the agent of creation and preservation and with regard to his voluntary humiliation in the incarnate state, Jesus declared, "The Father is greater than I" (John 14:28).

John also states that in terms of the economy of the Godhead the Father has priority vis-à-vis the Spirit, for the Father has sent the Counselor to indwell believers, thereby continuing the work of the glorified Jesus Christ (John 14:16, 26). In like manner, the Son is functionally greater than the Spirit, in that following his ascension the Son sent the Counselor to bless the church (John 16:7; 20:22). In the work of the Godhead, the Spirit faithfully testifies to Christ (John 14:26; 15:26). Finally, in one text (John 15:26) John affirms that both the Father and the Son send the Holy Spirit on his mission.

Other New Testament Literature

Given the Jewish background of the Epistle of James, one is not surprised to find the unity and uniqueness of God upheld: "You believe that God is one; you do well" (James 2:19, RV, RSV). Yet, notwithstanding his own Hebrew background, Peter acknowledged by an early formula the Trinitarian character of God: ". . . chosen according to the foreknowledge of God the Father, by the sanctifying work of the Spirit, for obedience to Jesus Christ" (1 Peter 1:2). Likewise, Jude juxtaposes the three persons as equal in dignity and divinity: "Pray in the Holy Spirit. Keep yourselves in God's love as you wait for the mercy of our Lord Jesus Christ to bring you to eternal life" (Jude 20–21). The absence of a fixed order of persons in the above texts suggests the essential coequality of Father, Son, and Spirit.

Hebrews 1:8–9, quoting Psalm 45:6–7, explicitly states that the Son of the Father is "God." Similarly, Hebrews 1:3 describes the Son as "the radiance of God's glory" (*apaugasma tēs doxēs*) and "the exact representation of his being" (*charaktēr tēs hypostaseōs autou*). The first expression indicates that the effulgence of the eternal Godhead shines forth through the historical existence of the Son, the second that the essence of the Godhead finds perfect expression in the Son, and the present participle (*on*, "being') introducing the sentence invests the Father-Son relation with a certain permanence. Peter specifically identifies the second person of the Trinity as God: ". . . through the righteousness of our God and Savior Jesus Christ" (2 Peter 1:1). According to the Granville Sharp rule, the presence of the definite article before "our God" and the absence of the article before "Savior" refers the phrase "God and Savior" to Jesus Christ.[76] Elsewhere the Son is given titles that indicate unqualified deity; e.g., "God" (*theos*, Heb. 1:8), "sovereign Lord" (*despotēs*, 2 Peter 2:1), and "only Sovereign and Lord" (*ton monon despotēn kai kyrion hēmōn*, Jude 4). The last text, Jude 4, satisfies the criteria of the Granville Sharp rule.

The deity of the Holy Spirit is indirectly acknowledged, in the sense that words spoken by him are attributed to God (Heb. 3:7–11; 10:15–17). Moreover, the Spirit performs works that are appropriate only to Deity; e.g., he energized the prophets (1 Peter 1:11), inspired the Old Testament (2 Peter 1:21; cf. Heb. 3:7; 10:15), empowered Christ for his ministry of suffering (Heb. 9: 14), quickened Christ's crucified body (1 Peter 3:18), and sanctifies believers so as to render them fit for heaven (1 Peter 1:2).

SYSTEMATIC FORMULATION

Organizing our thinking about this vast amount of biblical and historical data, we consider several basic topics in a logical order. Most basic in the context of contemporary concerns is the meaning of the biblical teaching that God is one.

The Oneness of God's Being

The Old Testament clearly and repeatedly teaches that "the LORD is one" (Deut. 6:4), denying the reality of other gods and the value of polytheistic worship. When God judges a polytheistic people, the gods in which they took refuge do not help them. "See now that I myself am He! There is no god besides me" (Deut. 32:36–39). In ultimate reality there are not many, separate divine beings. Metaphysically, we have to do with only one divine being.

Debate becomes serious, however, about whether the repeated biblical teachings on God's oneness rule out, not only polytheism, but also Trinitarianism. A priori assumptions will not resolve this issue. Only an examination of the evidence can determine whether "one" is a technical term excluding diversity in unity, as in a mathematical point, or an ordinary multiplicity in unity, as in a body.

According to the *Old Testament*, when a couple marries, the two become

"one flesh" (Gen. 2:24), *one family.* That actual oneness does not exclude but requires two distinct persons. The experienced oneness of marriage does not exclude multiplicity but requires it—and that multiplicity is a multiplicity of persons.

The Old Testament also uses the same word in reference to *one people or nation.* When Moses told the people of Israel the Lord's words and laws, "they responded with one voice" (Exod. 24:3). By that "one voice" a great multiplicity of Israelites unanimously entered into covenant with the Lord. Even though Israel and Judah would later separate and go into different captivities, Ezekiel symbolized their future reunion by joining two sticks together into one stick. So in the hand of God the two would again become one nation (Ezek. 37:19).

Israel's *one tabernacle* was made up of ten curtains (Exod. 26:1) fastened together with fifty loops and gold clasps on each end (26:5–6) so that the tabernacle was a unit (26:6, 11). Indeed, the one tabernacle was composed of many parts. Its oneness did not exclude, but required, multiplicity.

In the Old Testament usage, "oneness" is drawn from the daily experience with the unity of such things as a family, a nation, and a tabernacle. From these and many similar uses, it follows that "when the Jewish writers of the Old Testament taught that God is 'one,' they stressed God's unity while recognizing diversity within that oneness." The Old Testament as well as the New is "strictly monotheistic while at the same time teaching diversity within the unity."[77]

The *New Testament* similarly speaks of the unity of a *family,* as the passage on "one flesh" (Gen. 2:24) is quoted several times (Matt. 19:5, 6; 1 Cor. 6:16; Eph. 5:31). The complexity of one *human body* is also prominent. The "body is a unit, though it is made up of many parts" (1 Cor. 12:12). Analogously, the body portrays the multiplicity in the unity of the *church*. Hence, "in Christ we who are many form one body" (Rom. 12:5). The unity of the body of Christ, the church, includes a relational unity "in heart and mind" (Acts 4:32) and more. For amidst the disturbing differences at Corinth, the members remained in the spirtually organic unity of the body of Christ (cf. 1 Cor. 1:2 with 12:12–13).

Clearly, New Testament assertions that anything is "one," like those of the Old Testament, do not exclude a multiplicity in unity. To attribute a technical, undiversified sameness to the word "one" in the Bible shows a lack of appreciation for its meaning in its own nontechnical frame of reference.

In *everyday experience* we regularly confront diversity in a thing, an animal, or a movement. Although physical analogies fail to portray all the aspects of Trinitarianism, they effectively illustrate the commonness of multiplicity in unity and our ability to speak about it without contradiction. One electrical appliance or watch may be very complex. Essential to one atom are quite different kinds of energy such as electrons, protons, and neutrons. Water, essentially H_2O, may exist not only as a liquid but also as steam or ice. Essential to one triangle are three sides and three angles. Space has three dimensions: length, breadth, and height. Time has reference to past, present, and future. Light rays from the sun heat, illuminate, and cause chemical photosynthesis in plants. If daily we experience plurality in unity, should be be surprised to find it in God?

Although we lack full comprehension of an atom, water, space, time, light, the human body, a church, or a nation, what we do know we can communicate coherently. By distinguishing the respect in which each of these items is one and the respect(s) in which it has

elements that can be differentiated, we remove confusion. Although we lack full comprehension of the Trinity, when we choose to speak with others about the Trinity and expect them to follow us, we must communicate without self-contradiction. If the Christian doctrine of God were contradictory, it would affirm and deny one divine being, or affirm and deny three divine persons. It does not. The Christian doctrine affirms oneness in respect to essence and threeness in respect to centers of consciousness capable of fellowship, communication, and intercession with one another. Keeping the categories of being and persons distinct, we need suffer no tensions about the classical doctrine of the Trinity being contradictory. Any initial appearance of contradiction (paradox) should be handled like the measles: isolate it until the difficulty is resolved.[78]

Granting a multiplicity in divine unity, in what way is God's oneness to be interpreted? Not as a continuity in space, for God is spirit. God is one *substantially* (one spiritual being) and one *essentially* (one spiritual being with all the attributes belonging to him). (Essence = substance + attributes). The unity is not merely of genus, for there are not three gods of the same kind (genus). Only a substantial and essential oneness fits the scriptural data denying polytheism and affirming monotheism. The divine unity revealed in Scripture is not like a mystical Neo-Platonic "One" beyond all categories of human thought. The biblical oneness does not rule out distinguishable attributes and persons.

Church tradition sometimes made matters more difficult than necessary by claiming that, as simple, God can really include no distinctions at all—not between essence and existence, act and potential, person and essence, or anything else. This last requirement of the classic simplicity theory (that persons and essence in God must be identical) traditionally made the doctrine of the Trinity look incoherent. For on the one hand the doctrine of the Trinity claimed that Father, Son, and Spirit are distinct persons (a claim derived especially from the Gospel of John). On the other hand, the same doctrine seemed to imply that all three persons were actually just the same thing as the divine essence. Both the concept of simplicity above presented and the law of noncontradiction allow for differences of respect (one in essence and three in personhood) without inconsistency.

Although God may be experienced as one, the assertion of God's oneness is *not a doctrine describing phenomena* of religious experiences, or human events or relationships. It is a doctrine about ultimate reality, about God as God *is* metaphysically. Those who believe the teaching of biblical revelation cannot join the antimetaphysical temper of the times without devastating results, not only to Trinitarianism, but also to the doctrine of God's oneness. Those who deny any propositional information about God either inconsistently claim to hold that God is ontologically one or, more consistently, find themselves tending toward the new polytheism (discussed below).

Three Personal Consciousnesses in the Divine Being

If in respect to spiritual being God is one, in what respects is God diverse or multiple? We have already seen diversity of attributes, emotions, purposes, and actions. Is there sufficient evidence to add diversity in another respect, that of persons? Could the one underlying common psyche (the unconscious) have three distinguishable centers of consciousness? Like an ocean (of one substance) with three waves (modes of its existence), does the one personal, spiritual Being subsist in three personal modes?

Inscripturated revelation speaks of the one God as Father, Son, and Holy Spirit. The Bible does not use the terms "essence" and "being" but teaches the concept in other words. Similarly, it does not explicitly refer to three "persons" but its statements about God are most coherently explained by the doctrine of three persons in the one divine essence and being. Alternative views throughout the history of doctrine have failed to fit all the biblical data on God's oneness and threeness as adequately. What are some of the more prominent indications of threeness in the oneness of the divine being?

Three are addressed as essentially God and worshiped as persons. First, the Father's deity is recognized in Daniel's prayer: "O Lord, the great and awesome God, who keeps his covenant of love with all who love him and obey his commands" (Dan. 9:4). Jesus' teaching on prayer begins, "Our Father in heaven, hallowed be your name" (Matt. 6:9). Second, Jesus was called "Immanuel—which means, 'God with us'" (Matt. 1:23). Thomas could no longer doubt Jesus' deity when the risen Lord invited him to touch his wounded hands and side. In worship and dedication the doubter exclaimed, "My Lord and my God!" (John 20:28). Third, when the Israelites in the wilderness tempted the Lord (Exod. 17:2–7), they provoked the Holy Spirit (Heb. 3:7–9). And for Ananias and Sapphira to lie to the Holy Spirit (Acts 5:3) is to lie to God (v. 4). To be born of the Spirit (John 3:6, 8) is to be born of God (1 John 5:18). To pray to Father, Son, and Spirit, if they were not essentially God, would be idolatrous. The Bible consistently repudiates the worship of idols, and therefore, in encouraging worship of the Father, Son, and Spirit, it implies their deity

The name of God as used in benediction at the end of worship in the New Testament era is the threefold name of the Father, the Son, and the Holy Spirit. In the earlier Old Testament benedictions priests put the name of the Lord (singular) on the people (Num. 6:27), emphasizing God's unity. As revelation progressed, making more explicit God's triune existence, Paul's benediction placed the name of God on the people by saying, "May the grace of the Lord Jesus Christ, and the love of God, and the fellowship of the Holy Spirit be with you all" (2 Cor. 13:14). And when people confessed faith in Christ publicly by baptism, the name of God was placed on them by "baptizing them in the name [sing.] of the Father and of the Son and of the Holy Spirit" (Matt. 28:19). If the Son and Spirit were not equally God, the benedictory and baptismal formulas would have been unthinkable. The benediction and the baptismal formulas indicate that first-century believers implicitly recognized the essential deity of the Father, but also of the Son and Spirit.

Father, Son, and Spirit *possess the divine attributes*. The Father is eternal (Gen. 21:33; 1 Tim. 1:17), the Son is eternal (John 1:1; 8:58; 17:5, 24; Heb. 7:3; Rev. 22:13), and the Spirit is eternal (Heb. 9:14). The Father is omnipresent (Jer. 23:24; Acts 17:27), the Son is omnipresent (Matt. 28:20), and the Spirit is omnipresent (Ps. 139:7–10). The Father is holy (Lev. 11:45; John 17:11), the Son is holy (John 6:69; Acts 4:27), and the Spirit is holy (Rom. 1:4; Eph. 4:30). The Father is love (Ps. 136:1–26; Jer. 31:3; John 3:16; 1 John 4:8,16), the Son is love (John 15:9, 13; 1 John 3:16), the Spirit is love (Rom. 5:5; Gal. 5:22; Col. 1:8). The Father is omnipotent (Mark 14:36; Luke 1:37), the Son is omnipotent (Matt. 9:6; Luke 8:25; John 10:18), and the Spirit is omnipotent (Luke 1:35; Acts 1:8; 2:2–4, 17–21; 4:31–33). While sharing the same divine es-

sence, the Father, Son, and Holy Spirit have *personal characteristics*. The three are not just three different roles or "hats" worn by the one God of Judaism and Islam. Nor are they merely three modes of revelation to people in history as in Sabellian modalism. They are three modes of existence within the deity, with distinctive modes of relating to mankind. They are more like multiple personalities (*The Three Faces of Eve*), but all at once, not serially, and all equally righteous, wise, etc.

The Father, Son, and Spirit distinctively have *personal capacities of intellect, emotion, and will*. God the Father is a personal being with intelligent self-consciousness, emotional self-control, and volitional purposes. The Father consciously "knows" (Matt. 6:8, 32), determines himself or wills (Matt. 6:10; 12:50; 18:14), chooses (1 Peter 1:2), and feels without being out of control (Ps. 86:15; Isa. 63:9; Rom. 1:18).

God the Son also knows (John 2:24; 16:30), feels (Matt. 9:36; John 11:35), and wills (Luke 22:42; John 5:30; 6:38). An entire book has been written on the messianic consciousness of Jesus.[79] Readers of the Gospels can hardly fail to see that although Jesus had an affective nature, he was uniquely self-controlled. Furthermore, he was not "under the circumstances" or, like the Pharisees, compelled by what others thought. Rather, Jesus Christ uniquely determined his thought, words, and actions in a manner consistent with his conscious messianic purpose.

Similarly, the Holy Spirit displays intellectual capacities (John 14:26; 15:26; 16:7, 13; 1 Cor. 2:10); affective capacities (Isa. 63:10; Eph. 4:30), producing fruit involving human emotions (Gal. 5:22–23); and will (Gen. 6:3; Isa. 63:10; 1 Cor. 12:11). So each has personal capacities of intellect, emotion, and will, essential characteristics of persons. In other words, each exhibits self-consciousness, self-control, and self-determination. And, as we will see, the three interrelate as persons in "I-Thou" fellowship and intercession.

People who accept the personhood of the Father and the Son may ask, "Is the Holy Spirit personal?" This is understandable since the Old Testament word "spirit" frequently means air in motion, wind, or breath. However, "spirit" in other contexts means disposition of mind, the entire immaterial consciousness of man, a supernatural angelic being, the active power of God, and, finally, the Holy Spirit in a Trinitarian sense (cf. Isa. 48:16).[80] A similar progression of meanings may be seen in New Testament uses of the term "spirit" (*pneuma*). "Jesus understood the Holy Spirit as a personality . . . 'Paraclete,' i.e., the Comforter (Counselor, Advocate)." (John 14:16, 26; 15:26; 16:5)[81]

The Holy Spirit, as "Counselor," is referred to by personal pronouns (John 14:17), and this is not mere literary personification, since he performs personal services like "witnessing" concerning Christ (John 14:26), teaching (John 16:13), revealing (1 Cor. 2:10), and convicting (John 16:8–11). He witnesses with believers' spirits that they are children of God (Rom. 8:16). As an advocate, the Holy Spirit can intercede for believers with the Father (Rom. 8:26). An impersonal power or influence from the Father could not take the initiative and become an advocate of our cause with the Father. The most unmistakable single indication of the Spirit's personal distinctiveness from the Father is his ability to intercede on behalf of Christians with the Father.

To say that we cannot fully comprehend the meaning of "persons" in ourselves, let alone the divine being, is not to say that we do not understand anything about them. We do know that *persons* are intelligent, self-conscious, self-determined, responsible agents capable of appreciating values, choosing purposes, and sharing them with others in fellowship and action. As active subjects, not mere objects, the divine persons are not to be identified with physical bodies, finite limitations like mutual exclusiveness, or evil. The divine persons are far greater than finite persons and cannot be fully comprehended. George Smeaton argues, "Only remove from the use of the term every notion involving imperfection . . . and it must be admitted that in human language no term can be found better fitted to express the Church's meaning than the term person."[82]

The doctrine of the Trinity affirms that three such personal consciousnesses or agencies compose the oneness of the the divine being. Norman C. Bartlett pictured a "more or less subconscious nature possessed in common" and controlling three free self-consciousnesses.[83] John B. Champion stresses that as persons the Father, Son, and Spirit do not possess an exclusive self-consciousness but an "inter-consciousness" and "other-conscious."[84] John Lawson emphasizes that the most developed, loving human personalities are "not the most fiercely autonomous, but those who are most completely united in mutual accord and sympathy with other persons around them."[85] To help avoid a tritheism with a merely relational unity it is important to contemplate not only the loving interconsciousness of the three, but also something like a common subconscious or metaphysical essence in common. When Scripture speaks of God as one or as spirit, it speaks of God as personal, and this makes possible the tripersonal distinctions.

The view that God does not just function in relation to the world in three different ways but exists as three persons in one spiritual-psychical essence accounts for the varied lines of evidence with the fewest difficulties. The hypothesis of three modes of revelation accounts for evidence of functional distinctions, but such Sabellianism does not account for the scriptural data that make clear that behind the three modes of revelation to mankind in history are three transcendent, ontological modes of being, subsistences, or persons. Our critical method does not just present an unresolved oneness and threeness but decides for the hypothesis with the greatest explanatory power and the fewest difficulties.

Interpersonal Fellowship of Father, Son, and Holy Spirit

Distinguishable as each of the persons in the Trinity is, each functions harmoniously in an unbroken fellowship of love with the others. People sometimes ask, "What was God doing before he created the world?" In prayer Jesus said, "Father, glorify me in your presence with the glory I had with you before the world began" (John 17:5). Again, "Father, . . . you loved me before the creation of the world" (17:24). Before the world was, Father, Son, and Spirit enjoyed the highest of values—unbroken loving relationships.

The unbrokenness of their fellowship is rooted in the fact that each of the three persons functions in accord with the same essential attributes or perfections. Each consciously embraces wisdom, holiness, love, etc. Father, Son, and Holy Spirit will not and cannot act contrary to the common, unchanging divine nature.

The harmony of fellowship is also rooted in the holistic commitment of each of the three persons to function harmoniously with the eternal purposes for history determined from eternity, whether universal in nature and history or redemptive among the people of God. No act contradictory to these purposes can be soundly ascribed to Father, Son, or Holy Spirit.

Administrative Order Among the Three Persons

Although all three distinct persons are equal essentially and enjoy a perfect fellowship, their interrelationships may reflect a distinctive ordering of activities. In the economic ordering of things, in contrast to the essential equality, the Father is mentioned first, the Son is *of* the Father (never vice versa), and the Spirit is *of* the Father and *of* the Son (never vice versa). Why? What is the significance of their respective names "Father," "Son," and "Holy Spirit"? Do the biblical names and illustrations for the three indicate their relationships functionally?

Some people have rejected Trinitarianism on the ground that a person must have a body and three persons cannot occupy the same space at the same time. Such reasoning fails to understand that God is a spirit and transcends limitations of physics. God does not have a flesh-and-bones body. The premise of God's spiritual nature is basic to understanding not only the essential unity of the three persons and their relational communion, but also their administrative order.

In the biblical context the term "Father" is a figure of speech for the creative source of ideas, the fountainhead of planning goals, and the initiator of the mutual relationships and activities. The first person is to the second as the sun is to its brightness (Heb.1:3), an original to its exact copy (Heb.1:3), a speaker to his word (John 1:1) and a father to his unique and only son (John 3:16). The first person emanates the light, determines the nature of the copy, expresses his word, and begets his Son. In less figurative language, the first person creatively designs and initiates relationships and activities. The point illustrated is not a time of origin, but a distinctness of activity with sameness of nature. The first person initiates and purposes.

The second person's relation to the first is scripturally illustrated by the same four interesting figures. What is the point of each in nonfigurative language? First, "the Son is the *radiance of God's glory*" (Heb. 1:3). Jesus Christ is to the Father as the brightness of a ray of light emanating from the sun is to the sun. As light from the sun, Christ sustains all things (v. 3) and exhibits God's transcendent glory.[86] What is the point of the illustration? Although fire and its brightness are of the same nature, they are distinguishable and in an administrative order for operational activities (the brightness comes from and discloses the sun, not the sun the brightness).

Second, Christ is "the *exact representation* of his being" (Heb. 1:3). Again, Christ is "the image of God" (2 Cor. 4:4) and "the image of the invisible God" (Col. 1:15). This figure, like the first, indicates that although the second person is of the same nature as the first, he is distinguishable from the first, and they follow a functional order. Jesus is an exact representation of the invisible being of God. At best these temporal illustrations of the sameness of nature provide only "some slight and small resemblance" of the relationship in eternal reality.[87]

Third, the second person is to the first as a *word* is to its speaker. "In the beginning was the Word, and the word was with God, and the Word was God. He was with God in the beginning" (John 1:1–2). How does a word relate to its speaker? Jesus explained in another context that a person can be judged by his words because "out of the overflow of the heart the mouth speaks" (Matt. 12:34). Analogously, the second person as the Word audibly expresses the overflow of the Father's heart in creating and sustaining the world. He also achieves his loving purposes of redemption. By becoming flesh (John 1:14), Christ "has made him known" (1:18). Was he the Word of the Father only since his incarnation? Not according to the context. Before creation the Word was with God and was God (1:1).

The most well-known analogy pictures the relationship of the second person to the first as that of a son to his father. "For God so loved the world that he gave his one and only Son" (John 3:16). Not just the first or the highest created being (as Jehovah's Witnesses claim), Jesus is the only Son "who came from the Father" (1:14), the only Son, "who is at the Father's side" (1:18), "his one and only Son" (3:16, 18).

For purposes of systematics it is not enough simply to report that the above passages in the NIV teach the uniqueness of the second person of the Trinity. Building on biblical theology here, we must ask what the concept of uniqueness ("one and only")[88] implies and relate it to a coherent view of the interpersonal activities. We are not turning an action (begetting) into a state of being. We are asking about the point concerning the activities of the first and second persons illustrated by "Father" and "unique Son."

Interestingly, the NIV translators, while preferring to translate *monogenēs* "one and only," include "begetting" in the margin (John 1:14; 3:16, 18). Although both terms were not used in the translation (only begotten), the concepts of uniqueness and begottenness are not logically exclusive. Interpreters need not choose for one against the other. An only son is also begotten! If "begotten" is not explicitly taught in the term *monogenēs*, is it not implied in the Father-Son relationship?

Consider the points illustrated by the figure "unique son." First, the Father/unique-Son terminology illustrates a relationship that is eternal. It did not begin at Bethlehem. John does not say, "God so loved the world that he gave his one and only Son" (John 3:16; cf. 1:18; 1 John 4:9). As B. B. Warfield pointed out, the passage implies that the Son had been in a loving fellowship with the father from eternity.[89] The value of the Father's gift depended on Jesus' unique relationship to the Father prior to his physical conception. If the Word was in the beginning with God and was God (John 1:1), then the Son was in the beginning with God and was God (eternally).

Second, the Father/unique-Son terminology illustrates a relationship that is personal. The second person of the Trinity is a distinguishable person with the same essence. He was not, like the creation, merely created *by* God. Nor was he, like human persons, merely created *by* God *in* God's image. Jesus Christ alone is *of* the same divine nature as the Father's. What figure could better express this Father-Son relationship than that of one person being begotten of the other person? The Son is not merely an impersonal "radiance," "representation," and "Word." The "Son" exhibits the Father's nature as only a person born of another person could do. He is personally unique, as the early church said, because he was "begotten, not made." The point is not that the Son is physically conceived (as if the Father were flesh and bones); God is spirit. And it is not that he had a beginning in time (or had a birthday); the Son of God is eternal. We must dismiss all physical and temporal images of propagation from the figures of "Father" and "Son" (and "begotten," whether implied or read in the margin). The point is that Christ, who is of the same nature as the Father, is a distinguishable person.

Third, the Father/unique-Son relationship well illustrates the point that functionally the begotten One, without ontological inferiority has a derivative role. With respect to active roles, the begetter initiates and commissions, while the begotten lovingly carries out and provides. Eternally, as well as temporally the Father has a priority as the One who commissions and sends. The unique Son in loving fellowship responds as a faithful missionary sent by the Father to serve.

The derivative administrative role of the second person (without resultant ontological inferiority) is better illustrated by "uniquely begotten" than by "unique" or "one and only" alone. Contrary to charges, the Athanasian concept of eternal generation is far from meaningless. Where is a more significant account of the inter-Trinitarian relationship between the Father and the Son than in eternal generation?

> "Generation" makes it plain that there is a divine sonship prior to the incarnation (cf. John 1:18; 1 John 4:9), that there is thus a distinction of persons within the one Godhead (John 5:26), and that between these persons there is priority and subordination of order (cf. John 5:19; 8:28). "Eternal" reinforces the fact that the generation is not merely economic (i.e., for the purpose of human salvation as in the incarnation, cf. Luke 1:35), but essential, and that as such it cannot be construed in the categories of natural or human generation. In virtue of eternal generation, and not in spite of it, the Father and the Son are one (John 10:30).[90]

The concept of eternal generation, furthermore, accounts most coherently for Christ's frequent statements regarding his equality with the Father and his dependence on the Father. This relationship applies to our Savior's temporary condition of humiliation but also reaches far beyond the thirty-three years of his incarnation.

Note that the case for returning to the concept of the "uniquely begotten Son" is not based on nonbiblical, pagan philosophical considerations, but on interpretation of the points illustrated by the Bible's figurative expressions (such as *radiance, image, word*, and *son*) in their immediate and broader contexts. Those biblically revealed points were recognized in the historic creeds ("begotten of the Father before all worlds" [Nicene] and "begotten before the worlds" [Athanasian]). These points cannot be erased by multiplying exegetical "authorities" whose atomistic word studies and biblical positivism may even unconsciously be rooted in an antimetaphysical bias that does not permit them to interpret in nonfigurative language the truth illustrated in figures of speech about God.

Some avoid the point of the figurative language by using synonyms. Calling the Father's relation to the Son that of "paternity" only repeats the figure, however, and does not explain its point. A similar redundancy occurs when the Son's relation to the Father is called filial. Illustrations figuratively communicate a nonfigurative point that a reader must interpret for theological purposes.

Calvin rejected "eternal generation" as a continuous activity in favor of a once-for-all generation in eternity to avoid speculation about continuous generation.[91] Thus Calvin changes the speculation to how a once-for-all act meaningfully happens in an eternal relationship. To say as Calvin did that the Son "derives" from the Father seems hardly less figurative than affirming that the Son "is begotten by" the Father. But in the time of Athanasius and in any period it is crucial to the deity of Christ that he be eternally of the Father.

For summary purposes we now integrate the four biblical analogies considered above as portraying the relationship of the first two persons of the Trinity in their activities. The second person of the Trinity in eternity as well as in time radiates, models, expresses, and exhibits the Father's plans and purposes. Eternally and temporally he radiates the Father's purposes with the brilliance of the sunlight, models them with the accuracy of an exact copy, expresses them with the meaningfulness of a word, and exhibits them with the personableness of a unique Son.

Scripture does not speak as frequently regarding *the Holy Spirit's relation* to Father and Son, but it gives parallels to its teaching about the Son-Word-Image-Radiance. Why do we speak of the third person as "Spirit" rather than another Son? Relationally, the Spirit also is of (*ek*, "out from") God (1 Cor. 2:12), breathed out or spirated from him. What is the point of this illustration? It may be made in others words when Christ says that the Spirit of truth "goes out from the Father" (John 15:26). Other translations have "proceeds from" (AV), "issues from" (Moffatt), and "goes forth from" (Norlie).[92] In a continuous (present tense) "exhalation" of the third person from the first, the Spirit (the breath of God) implements his purposes. As the Word continuously expresses the "heart" of the Father in the ordering of the world, the Spirit continuously emanates from the "lungs" of the Father to bring his purposes to fulfillment.

Never is the first person *of* the third, but the other way around: "the Spirit of God" (Gen. 1:2; Matt. 3:16), "the Spirit of our God" (1 Cor. 6:11), "Spirit of the living God" (2 Cor. 3:3), "the Spirit of the LORD" (Judg. 3:10), and "the Spirit of the Sovereign LORD" (Isa. 61:1).

Does the Spirit proceed, not only from the Father, but also from the Son? The Eastern church has denied that the Spirit proceeds from the Father *and the Son* (*filioque*).[93] However, the Scriptures also refer to "the Spirit of Jesus Christ" (Phil. 1:19), "the Spirit of Jesus" (Acts 16:7), "the Spirit of

Christ" as parallel to "the Spirit of God" (Rom. 8:9), "the Spirit of his Son" (Gal. 4:6), and "the Spirit of the Lord" (Acts 5:9; 8:39). In anticipating the coming of the Spirit at Pentecost, Jesus said that the Spirit would be sent by the Father in Jesus' name (John 14:26), but also that he would send the Spirit from the Father (15:26). The Pentecostal sending of the Spirit by the Father and the Son may not be totally unique but an instance of many such operational orders. Hence scriptural precedent suggests affirming that the Holy Spirit proceeds not only from the Father but also from the Son. Although all three are spirit, the third person is distinctively the One who powerfully brings to fulfillment in our lives the redemptive transformation envisioned by the Father and provided for by the Son.

Since holiness is an attribute of all three persons, why is the third particularly called the *Holy* Spirit? Holiness is not only an attribute but also a distinctive feature of the Spirit's ministry. The third person convicts of sin, regenerates, and sanctifies. Insofar as converted sinners progressively become holy, their virtue can be traced to the Spirit's teaching, illumination, leading, abiding, and cultivating of Christlike holiness. Furthermore, it is important in cultures like those of Bible times, where people are constantly aware of the presence of evil spirits, to regularly distinguish the Holy Spirit from evil spirits.

Summing up revealed truths concerning the interpersonal relations in the Trinity, there is an unbroken fellowship of love among the Father, the Son, and the Holy Spirit. Their equality of essence and fellowship is not affected by the administrative ordering of relationships among themselves in creative (John 1:1–3) and redemptive activity. In that functional order the first person creatively initiates, the second brightly exhibits, and the third effectually brings to fulfillment.

Distinctive, but Harmonious Ministries in History

Systematic thinking requires keeping the essential and functional categories distinct. Whether we read about God in Scripture or speak about him, we must ask whether the referent is (1) God's underlying essence and being, (2) the three divine persons in their distinctive interpersonal relationships, or (3) their distinctive but harmonious ministries to people in space-time history. For example, operationally in space and time, the incarnate Jesus Christ could say, "The Father is greater than I" (John 14:28). Jehovah's Witnesses think this statement contradicts Trinitarianism, but a reference to Jesus' functional self-denial does not alter his continuous essential deity.

Although all three persons are omnipresent and consciously interrelated in all their activities, each has some distinctive historical activities. In regard to *creation*, the Father calls forth energy-matter, the Logos informs it and orders its laws of change, and the Holy Spirit leads it to develop according to its nature and achieve its destiny.[94] The work of the Spirit is to realize the glory of the Father in the life of every creature, Kuyper finds, by "impregnating" (developing) inanimate matter, animating the rational soul, and taking up his abode in the children of God.[95]

In implementing the redemptive program, all three divine persons manifested their presence in distinctive ways at the *baptism* of Jesus marking the beginning of his ministry. However, only Jesus was immersed by John. Only the Father said, "You are my Son, whom I love; with you I am well pleased." And only the Holy Spirit descended on Jesus "in bodily form like a dove" (Luke 3:22).

279

During the *temptations of Jesus*, our Lord effectively resisted Satan's temptations by conscious prayer to the Father while quoting inspired Scripture in the presence and power of the Holy Spirit.

Recall the interconnections and distinctive roles of the three divine persons in *revelation*: the Father had the creative idea for it, the Son actively expressed and exhibited it, and the Spirit inspired and illumined it.

Most succinctly, in regard to the distinctive roles of each of the three persons in the work of *salvation*, God the Father *planned* it, God the Son *provided* it, and God the Holy Spirit *applies* it.

Such harmonious functional activities of Father, Son, and Spirit reflect a deeper personal unity of conscious thinking, feeling, and willing. And that unity of mind and purpose reveals an even deeper essential oneness of being.

APOLOGETIC INTERACTION

The Many Gods of the New Polytheism

Polytheism has returned as the logical conclusion of relativistic theology done with an antimetaphysical bias. Unable to know anything about God in himself, those who deny propositional revelation limit all theology to information from changing phenomena of religious experience, events, and relationships. People consigned to the resulting total relativism have not only different perspectives of God. They have no way of knowing that they worship the same God, ultimately. In *The New Polytheism: Rebirth of the Gods and Goddesses*, acknowledging the death of a transcendent, omnipotent God and having lost the one *Logos* by whom all things were created and are sustained, David L. Miller can find no single center harnessing all our pluralistic meanings and values. Miller concludes, "Everywhere one stands is a center, . . . when the center is everywhere it is in fact multiple."[96]

God's ontological unity was argued from the universe by the best Greek philosophers (Plato and Aristotle) and from the writings of inspired Hebrew prophets and apostles by Christian theologians. Hebrew and Greek mentalities have some differences, but also some common concerns. Both traditions had good reasons to regard polytheism a hypothesis that did not cohere with the unity evident in the universe or both the universe and the teaching of the Scriptures. Although omnipresent, God cannot be divided into multiple beings. God transcends and rules the diversity of powers in the world. The hypothesis of many gods does not fit the facts of general and special revelation (above) as coherently as the hypothesis of God's oneness in essence.

The Many Spirits of Animism

The polytheist's gods and goddesses are reminiscent of the many "spirits" of animistic cultures and traditional religions.

Again, the hypothesis of many forces beyond our individual and social control simply fails to account for the data of both general and special revelation (above) concerning the *one* Lord of all. Could an animistic or polytheistic commitment also indicate willful disobedience to the one ultimate source of the countless biblical condemnations of polytheism?

The Three Gods of Tritheism

The early church found it important to make clear that in reality there were not three gods in a kind of tritheistic committee, but only one. To preserve the truth of God's ontological unity, church fathers affirmed that Christ was of the same being or substance (*homoousia*) not just of like substance (*homoiousia*) with the Father. With G. L. Prestige in his extensive study *God in Patristic Thought*, "We may therefore conclude that, down to the Council of Nicea, *homoousios* meant 'of one stuff' or 'substance'; and that when it was applied to the Divine Persons, it conveyed a metaphor drawn from material objects . . . with, however, a safeguard to the unity of God."[97] The biblical evidence on the unity of the Son with the Father is not sufficiently accounted for by affirming a relational or functional harmony, true and important as this evidence is. Only *one* transcendent God is present to the world. Only *one* Trinitarian Lord of all knows the future, speaks, and acts, as documented above.

Metaphysical Skepticism and Orthodox Confessions

Since Immanuel Kant's (1724–1804) denials of objective knowledge of anything in itself, especially God, much contemporary thought has limited religious language to the existential, pragmatic, and relational phenomena. Having dismissed all sources of changeless truth about ultimate reality, it became impossible to know even that ultimate reality is one, let alone triune. Neither Leonard Hodgson's inductions from revelatory historical acts, nor Karl Barth's analysis of revelatory activity adequately represent the biblically revealed trinity.[98]

The Episcopal bishop James A. Pike observed that the people of God had experienced God in three ways and said that "three persons in one God" was probably the best statement that the philosophers of the early church could devise, but he wanted to believe in a *big* God, one who could not be enclosed in a philosophical concept. He imagined that if he described God, he would "cabin in" God. The Apostles Creed,

Pike explained, contained several phrases he could not affirm as literal prose sentences, "but I can certainly sing them, . . . because [the creed] affirms the things basically important and true, in poetic terms."[99]

As a member of the World Council of Churches, apparently he subscribed to its basic statement of faith: "The World Council of Churches is a fellowship of churches which confess the Lord Jesus Christ as *God* and Savior according to the Scriptures and therefore seek to fulfill their common calling to the glory of the *one* God—Father, Son, and Holy Spirit."

To become a participant in the World Council and many other such organizations, is it enough to sing about the Trinity while denying the cognitive statements that God is one being existing in three persons? Will today's young seminary graduates, who have reductively empirical or existential assumptions, find it impossible to assert (however well they may sing!) the *ontological oneness* of Father, Son, and Spirit? If so, will they be accepted in churches and schools with orthodox statements of Trinitarianism?

The Anti-Trinitarianism of Jehovah's Witnesses, LDS (and Others)

Jehovah's Witnesses and Latter-Day Saints are among the most aggressive opponents of Trinitarianism whom Christians frequently meet at their door. Their challenges to Trinitarians reflect arguments common to many other groups. Ministers who fail to prepare their people to meet these challenges may expect to lose members to many such groups. After quoting the Athanasian Creed, James E. Talmadge, a leading Mormon theologian comments, "It would be difficult to conceive of a greater number of inconsistencies and contradictions expressed in words so few."[100]

Those who oppose the teaching regarding the Trinity usually have not taken sufficient time to examine what they oppose or to define the charge of contradiction, which they make against the doctrine. Trinitarians do not assert one God and three Gods, or only one person and three persons. Such assertions affirm and deny the same thing at the same time and in the same respect. But the historic doctrine affirming oneness in respect to being and threeness in respect to persons, although not fully comprehensible, is not contradictory. Attacks of Jehovah's Witnesses (and others) also confuse the basic categories of thought: ontological (what one is) and functional (what one does). Claiming that the Bible nowhere teaches the equality of the Son with the Father, Jehovah's Witness writers allege that it teaches the very opposite, that the Son is in subjection to the Father and hence inferior to him.[101] When he was preparing his disciples for his imminent death, Jesus said, "The Father is greater than I" (John 14:28). However, this statement does not contradict his other assertions of oneness with the Father in power to keep his followers from perishing (10:27–30). The Jews understood his claim to be God (v. 33) and sought to stone him for blasphemy. During the Incarnation, Jesus humbled himself as a human servant in order to provide for our salvation. While he was on earth Jesus gave up his heavenly glory and, unlike the Father, limited the use of his divine powers, for he came to suffer hunger, fatigue, and death. It is important in relation to the Trinity not to confuse what the second person is with what he does. Jesus *is* one in essence with the Father, but *functionally* he limited himself as a human to provide for mankind's salvation.

Jehovah's Witnesses (among others) also make the mistake of claiming that the doctrine of the Trinity is unbiblical because it was not fully formulated in Scripture until 350 years after the death of Jesus Christ.[102] But its elements are progressively revealed as extensively documented above. "The formulation of the doctrine," Warfield concluded, "although not made in Scripture, is not opposed to Scripture. When we assemble the *disjecta membra* into their organic unity, we are not passing from Scripture, but entering more thoroughly into the meaning of Scripture."[103]

Jehovah's Witnesses (and others, like Victor Paul Wierwille, leading writer of The Way, in *Jesus Was Not God*) also allege that Trinitarianism originated long after biblical times from pagan sources introduced into the apostate church.[104] The Christian church as a whole hardly became apostate before the apostles died! History can find no such departure from the faith when the Nicean and Athanasian statements were formulated. Rather, the early creeds express in a coherent way the complex teachings of Scripture regarding the one God—the Father, the Son, and the Holy Spirit. Doctrinal apostasy becomes apparent by departure of people and movements from the biblically derived creedal statements.[105]

Pantheistic "Trinities" in the West and in the East

Mary Baker Eddy, founder of Christian Science, considered belief in Trinitarianism a belief in polytheism rather than in one ever-present *I AM*.[106] In accord with her impersonal pantheistic assumptions, she proposed an alternative interpretation: "Life, Truth, and Love constitute the triune Person called God—that is, the triply divine Principle, Love. They represent a trinity in unity, three in one, the same in essence, though multiform in office." Mrs. Eddy explained further, "God the Father-mother; Christ the spiritual idea of sonship; divine Science the threefold, essential nature of the infinite."[107]

The Hindu *trimurti* or threefold manifestation of the Absolute—Brahman, or the universe—in its triple role as emanator, destroyer, and preserver has sometimes been thought analogous to the Christian Trinity. Note the pantheistic rather than theistic presupposition, the lack of three persons, and sheer functional modalism. The Divine Light Mission's Guru Maharaj Ji's acrostic for God: Generator, Operator, and Destroyer, even on a functional level is far from similar to a biblically rooted Trinitarianism.

The situation is similar in regard to the Buddhist *trikaya*. The three bodies emanating from the Buddha are: the primordial and ultimate body of Essence, Bliss, and Appearance, which alone is present in earthly existence.[108] Anything experienced in reality may have threeness in unity. To have a significant comparison with Trinitarianism in other religions, one would need to find a concept of a transcendent, personal God as in Judaism with three personal distinctions able to commune and intercede with one another.

Process Theology and Trinitarianism

In the antimetaphysical mood of the times, process Trinitarianism, a Western variety of thought parallel to Buddhism, rejects substantialist, essentialist, and even personalist categories of thought. With Buddhism, John B. Cobb in *Christ in a Pluralistic Age* seeks to rid his readers of attachment to personal existence as a final good.[109] Cobb's God is no longer a personal, triune, transcendent, absolute being. Father, Son, and Spirit are not eternal persons, but changing functions of the whole process in its relations and activities. In place of the historic Christian doctrine of God, Cobb puts an immanent process of eternal and relativistic

becoming. "In a system of naturalistic pantheism God has been reduced to the factor of order and value within the evolutionary process."[110] In view of all the evidence above for God's one-in-essence, three-in-persons transcendence, Cobb's hypothesis has little probability.

Muslim Anti-Trinitarianism

From a Muslim point of view belief in the Trinity is not only illogical; it is the major sin one can commit. It is a sign of infidelity! "Infidels now are they who say, 'God is the messiah, Son of Mary'." Although God is merciful with adulterers and liars, Trinitarians deserve hell. "Whoever shall join other gods with God, God shall forbid him the Garden, and his abode shall be the Fire." Why so strong? The creed, repeated many times a day, affirms, "There is no God but one God [Allah]." And the Koran continues, "The Messiah, Son of Mary, is but an apostle."[111] Christians in Muslim countries or witnessing to Muslim exchange students might suggest a study of oneness in the Old and New Testaments, human experience, and the Koran to determine whether it so summarily dismisses any complexity in the divine being. Then the Muslims may consider the extensive evidence above for the three persons in the Trinity.

A lifelong, active member of a large fundamentalist church said she had never heard an entire sermon or Sunday school class on the Trinity. It is little wonder that a veteran Jehovah's Witness, after a lengthy discussion with one who believed in the Trinity said, "I never before met a Trinitarian who actually seemed to believe the doctrine!" Christian movements will continue to lose members to anti-Trinitarian groups unless they teach their people how to handle the Scriptures that teach God's oneness and threeness.

Until a view is proposed that more coherently fits the biblical passages on both the unity and the diversity of the Godhead, we do well not only to believe and to sing about the Trinity, but also to defend Trinitarianism.

Sooner or later every world view not blind to observed diversity and unity in the world must account for both the one and the many in its ultimate reality. No one escapes this problem by abandoning the Scriptures or Christianity. Some philosophers, such as Parmenides, stress the reality of the one to the denial of the reality of the many. Others, like Heraclitus, affirm the reality of the many changing things in everyday experience and deny the reality of an unchanging unity. If the ultimate reality in a world view is one without diversity, it becomes difficult to account for the many. If the ultimate reality in the world view is many, it becomes impossible to account for the unity of the world. In the ultimate reality, the Trinity, Christianity has a coherent account of diversity in the unity in the world and so does not find it unthinkable that the universe (micro and macro) exhibits both multiplicity and unity.

RELEVANCE FOR LIFE AND MINISTRY

A. W. Tozer held that "a right conception of God is basic not only to systematic theology, but to practical Christian living as well."[112] This Christian pietist reasoned, "The essence of idolatry is the entertainment of thoughts about God that are unworthy of Him."[113] It follows that "the heaviest obligation lying upon the Christian Church today is to purify and elevate her concept of God until it is once more worthy of Him—and of her. In all her prayers and labors this should have first place."[114]

Relating to the Trinity Personally

Being made in God's image, we have the capacity to know the triune God, but because of our sins we lack the power to know him as we ought. The renewal of our minds and hearts in the new birth begins the great adventure. An esteemed former colleague a few days before his death spoke of anticipating "the great adventure." We need not wait for it until the next life. For "now begins the glorious pursuit, the heart's happy exploration of the infinite riches of the Godhead."[115]

Relationships with the three persons of the Trinity can be cultivated as with other personal beings. And the divine Father, Son, and Spirit intensely desire a growing relationship with us. God the Father desired our love from eternity; God the Son provided justly for it on the cross; and God the Holy Spirit makes available the resources for a growing personal communion. No one who calls upon the Father, the Son, or the Spirit in repentant faith is ever turned away.

So a conscious, personal awareness of the triune God's omnipresence and redemptive presence may be experienced here and now! (see 1 Cor. 2:9–10a). The awareness may differ in intensity at different times. It varies like one's awareness of a distant loved one over many busy days, months, and years, but is heightened at times by letters, phone calls, and special visits. The variation is in our conscious attention, however, not of divine presence. The triune God is omnipresent, but we may be brought into a more explicit awareness in the body of believers and at the Lord's Table. The relationship is personal or individual as well as communal. As Tozer says, "It does not come through the body of believers, as such, but is known to the individual, and to the body through the individuals who compose it."[116]

Our consciousness may emphasize, as do the Scriptures on different occasions, the divine oneness, or threeness. Initially, from our experience of nature, we may think of the ultimate source of the world and ourselves. Through the Old Testament we may emphasize the Father's personal, covenant-making grace and steadfast love. Through the Gospels we may zoom in on the incarnate Son's self-giving ministry and his death for our sins. And in the study of Acts we focus on the Holy Spirit proceeding from the Father and the Son to form the Christian church and send believers to disciple others throughout the world. The "Great Commission" and the epistles help us put the three persons together as subsistences within the oneness of the divine Being. Many Christians, as they grow in the grace and in the knowledge of the triune God, follow this historical and literary order of learning.

Putting all the teaching on the doctrine of the Trinity together, Herman Bavinck observed,

is of the utmost importance for practical religion. . . . Religion cannot afford to be satisfied with anything less than God. In Christ God himself comes to us, and in the Holy Spirit he imparts himself to us. . . . Of God, and through God, and in God are all things. . . . We know ourselves as children of the Father, redeemed by the Son, and having communion with both through the Holy Spirit.[117]

So the Trinitarian understanding of God enriches our limited grasp of the one God *above* us, *for* us, and *in* us.

Some people in these existentialist and pragmatic times may be tempted to seek the practical values of Trinitarian worship and service without knowing the true God and his Son Jesus Christ and the Holy Spirit. A writer very sympathetic to existentialism warns:

One may carry the contrast between the subjective and objective to such a point

that value or science or logic (or doctrine) is unwisely deprecated. In theology, the contrast can be drawn so sharply that faith and reason are driven unwholesomely asunder. Let us be clear that wherever existentialism undercuts the elements of rational structure which are indispensable to both metaphysics and Christian theology, it must be rejected. Properly employed, however, this mode of thinking rightly opens the way to a reformulation of philosophy and Christian doctrine which can render them vital and dramatic instead of rigid and sterile.[118]

Practicing the Presence of the Trinity

It is not uncommon for untrained Trinitarians to worship as "practical unitarians," claiming to believe in the Trinity but praying like Unitarians. Unitarians, Walter Marshall Horton showed, have emphasized at different times ideas representing all three persons. Influenced by the eighteenth-century Enlightenment, Unitarians thought of God as the ungenerated source of all things. Then, under the impact of New England Transcendentalism, stress fell on God as immanent Spirit, close at hand, dwelling in human beings. Although many turned to pure humanism, some consider God to be the Son who comes forth from himself to reveal his nature in creative and redemptive action.[119]

Practical Trinitarians in their devotional outlook ought to appreciate all three emphases at once. In thinking of the presence of God, they think of the creatively purposive Father; the incarnate, active Son; and the abiding, enabling Spirit. Christians discipline their thinking to avoid "Father Only," "Jesus Only," or "Spirit Only" reductionist tendencies. In practicing the presence of the triune God, Trinitarians consciously meditate on the distinctives of the Planner, Provider, and Enabler while aware of their functional harmony and ontological oneness. "May the grace of the Lord Jesus Christ, and the love of God, and the fellowship of the Holy Spirit be with you all" (2 Cor. 13:14).

Praying to the Triune God

Instead of addressing prayer simply to God; Allah; Jehovah; or the God of Abraham, Isaac, and Jacob, Christians may pray to any of the three persons of the Trinity. It not only follows that persons can have personal relationships, but the Scriptures exhort us to pray to the Father (Matt. 6:6) in the name of the Son (John 16:24) through or in the Holy Spirit (Jude 20). Nowhere does the Bible suggest that prayer must always end with a phrase like "in the name of Christ." Many have found it salutary to begin, "Through Jesus Christ our Lord. . . ." A variety in the order and in the use of divine names helps avoid vain repetition.

Prayer addressed to the Son is not merely a matter of inference from Trinitarianism but is also supported by biblical exhortation and example. Jesus invited prayer to himself (Matt. 11:28; John 4:10). Stephen addressed his dying requests to the "Lord Jesus" (Acts 7:59–60). All Christians call upon Christ (Acts 22:16; 1 Cor. 1:2; 1 Thess. 3:11; 2 Tim. 2:22). Throughout eternity, praise will be offered to Christ (Rev. 1:5–6).

Although prayer addressed to the Holy Spirit is not explicitly exemplified in Scripture, it may be inferred. Prayer to "the Lord of the harvest" to send out workers into the harvest field (Matt. 9:38) is most probably to the Holy Spirit, because it is the Holy Spirit who sends out missionaries (Acts 13:2–4), appoints overseers (Acts 20:28), gives gifts, leads, and empowers for harvest ministries. Since the person of the Holy Spirit dwells in believers' bodies and among believers in the church, it is most appropriate to offer "the Lord of

the harvest" thanksgiving, adoration, praise, and petitions.[120]

Relating to Others in Love Like That of the Trinity

"When we confess the faith of the Church in the Holy Trinity," C. W. Lowry perceives, "we affirm our belief that God is Himself the archetype of all community, all fellowship, all love."[121] The unity of the Godhead, because essential, is also relational. Christians are never of the same essence with one another as are Father, Son, and Spirit, but Jesus prayed that believers would have a relational unity similar to that of the Godhead: "that they may be one as we are one" (John 17:21–22).

The ultimate foundation for all community is found, not in the creatures, but in the ultimate nature of things, in the triune Creator. The final reason for families staying together is not legal agreement enforced by state or church, but demonstration of Trinitarian love and grace. And schism in the church is scripturally sinful (1 Cor. 12:25), not only because of the hurt to many members, but also because it violates their unity in Christ's body and its unity in him with the Father and the Spirit.[122]

Tracing Implications of the Simple Gospel

Although the doctrine of the Trinity is not explicitly stated to pre-Christians in the apostles' *kerygma*, it is implied (in part at least) in the acceptance of Jesus Christ as from the Father above in a unique way and as both Lord and Christ. Young children who accept Christ may not be expected to state the doctrine of the Trinity in the technical terms of one essence and three persons; however, children (of all ages!) understand that Jesus is not simply another human, but in a special way the unique Son from God. That understanding, however childlike, implies some grasp of Jesus' Trinitarian relationship to the heavenly Father. All who believe the gospel and are saved know that, in committing their lives to the Lord Jesus Christ, they are worshiping the Creator, not idolatrously worshiping another creature. Surely any brief tract presenting the plan of salvation for children or adults ought to clarify the deity of Jesus and of the Holy Spirit and relate these in some introductory way.

Testing the Doctrinal Orientation of Institutions

Any doctrinal statement for a Christian church or Christian parachurch society should include in some terms belief in the basic truth of Trinitarianism as a requirement of membership, teaching, and leadership. Unfortunately, too many are satisfied with a statement mentioning a unity, and the names of the Father, Son, and Spirit, without specifying the respects in which they are one and three. Hence a relational unity of mind and purpose may be thought sufficient. Others imagine that they hold a biblical view that the three are not coexistent persons, but merely three different modes of revelation by a unitarian deity. Binitarians affirm only two persons, thinking that the Holy Spirit is just an impersonal influence. If our Christian institutions are to remain true to all the strands of biblical teaching about God, then they must require allegiance to an *essential* unity of the three *persons*—Father, Son, and Holy Spirit.

Teaching the Fundamentals of the Faith

Trinitarian doctrine, like any other, needs only to remain untaught for one generation to be lost. Oddly enough, one of the modern movements most neglectful of the doctrine of the Trinity is modern Fundamentalism. The Fundamentalists did not include the doctrine of the Trinity in their list of the five fundamentals of the faith, nor did they explicitly formulate it in *The Fundamentals* (1912). It is assumed in B. B. Warfield's article "The Deity of Christ," G. Campbell Morgan's work on "The Purpose of the Incarnation," Robert E. Speer's essay on "God in Christ, the only Revelation of the Fatherhood of God," and R. A. Torrey's defense of "The Personality and Deity of the Holy Spirit." The ingredients are there, but not put together to form a coherent teaching about God.[123]

In a pluralistic world constantly face to face with many concepts of God, parents, Sunday school teachers, ministers, and leaders of parachurch organizations who desire the next generation to be Trinitarian, do well to exhibit the loving personal relationships that follow from it and teach Trinitarian truths on which they remain firm even though heaven and earth should pass away.

The Deepest Roots of a Missionary Theology

The very idea of missions, that of sending, is at the heart of Trinitarianism. In love the Father sent the Son. After his death and resurrection the Son says, " 'As the Father has sent me, I am sending you.' And with that he breathed on them and said, 'Receive the Holy Spirit' " (John 20:21–22). The Lord of the harvest, having come at Pentecost and having added many to the church, sent the first missionaries, Paul and Barnabas, from Antioch. Christianity begins with the heavenly mission: the Father sends the Son, and the Father and Son send the Spirit. Christianity continues as the Spirit sends the forgiven people of God to reach the unreached people in their cities and regions and in the uttermost parts of the world with the message of forgiving, sending, ministering love.[124] Gerald H. Anderson writes:

> A major cause for confusion in missions today comes from the inadequacy of the various attempts to formulate the theology of mission in recent years . . . from the culture-centered, man-centered, revelation-centered, eschatology-centered, kingdom-centered, Bible-centered, church-centered, and Christ-centered points of view.[125]

Although each of these aspects is essential, none is adequate as the central point or focus of a theology of missions. So Anderson continues, "It remains now for a major attempt to be made at formulating the theology of mission from the view of *radical trinitarian theocentrism*. When it comes, this approach may plant the seed—but only God gives the growth—for a new flowering of missionary endeavor in our time."[126]

Observing that missionary theology is not an appendix to a biblically based theology, George W. Peters takes up the challenge to produce a Trinitarian-based missions theology. His primary chapter concludes:

> The triune God in his very being as Spirit, light and love is an outgoing God, a missionary God, ever sending Himself in benevolent relations to mankind, ever searching in love to bestow Himself in blessings upon mankind, and ever spending Himself in great sacrifice to make man's salvation possible. Father, Son, and Holy Spirit are cooperating and coordinating to bring sinners back from their sinful wandering and blundering and restore them to their pristine state, purpose, destiny and glory.[127]

In another attempt to develop a Trinitarian theology of missions, Lesslie Newbigin, in his book *The Open Secret*, neatly organizes his fresh discussion of the mission of the triune God in three chapters: first, "Proclaiming the Kingdom of the Father: Mission as Faith in Action"; second, "Sharing the Life of the Son: Mission as Love in Action"; and third, "Bearing the Witness of the Spirit: Mission as Hope in Action."[128] After a thoughtful chapter on each of these, Newbigin indicates, "This threefold way of understanding the church's mission is rooted in the triune being of God himself. If any one of these is taken in isolation as the clue to the understanding of mission, distortion follows."[129]

Missionary work could be further strengthened by an even more thorough response to Anderson's call for a radical Trinitarian theocentric missionary theology. The present work should contribute to that as it considers the significance for life and ministry of the Father's grand design for human history, the Son's atoning provision for it, and its implementation at present by the Holy Spirit.

REVIEW QUESTIONS

To Help Relate and Apply Each Section in This Chapter

1. *Briefly state the classical problem* this chapter addresses and indicate reasons why genuine inquiry into it is important for your world view and your existence personally and socially.

2. *Objectively summarize the influential answers* given to this problem in history as hypotheses to be tested. Be able to compare and contrast their real similarities and differences (not merely verbal similarities or differences).

3. *Highlight the primary biblical evidence* on which to decide among views—evidence found in the relevant teachings of the major divisions of Scripture—and decide for yourself which historical hypothesis (or synthesis of historical views) provides the most consistent and adequate account of the primary biblical data.

4. *Formulate in your own words your*

doctrinal conviction in a logically consistent and adequate way, organizing your conclusions in ways you can explain clearly, support biblically, and communicate effectively to your spouse, children, friends, Bible class, or congregation.

5. *Defend your view* as you would to adherents of the alternative views, showing that the other views are logically less consistent and factually faced with more difficulties than your view in accounting for the givens, not only of special revelation but also of human experience in general.

6. *Explore the differences the viability of your conviction can make in your life.* Then test your understanding of the viability of your view by asking, "Can I live by it authentically (unhypocritically) in relation to God and to others in my family, church, vocation, neighborhood, city, nation, and world?"

MINISTRY PROJECTS

To Help Communicate This Doctrine in Christian Service

1. *Memorize one major verse or passage* that in its context teaches the heart of this doctrine and may serve as a text from which to preach, teach, or lead small group studies on the topic. The memorized passages from each chapter will build a body of content useful also for meditation and reference in informal discussions.

2. *Formulate the major idea of the doctrine in one sentence* based on the passage memorized. This idea should be useful as the major thesis of either a lesson for a class (junior high to adult) or a message for a church service.

3. *State the specific purpose or goal of your doctrinal lesson or message.* Your purpose should be more than informative. It should show why Christians need to accept this truth and live

by it (unhypocritically). For teaching purposes, list indicators that would show to what extent class members have grasped the truth presented.

4. *Outline your message or lesson in complete sentences.* Indicate how you would support the truth of the doctrine's central ideas and its relevance to life and service. Incorporate elements from this chapter's historical, biblical, systematic, apologetic, and practical sections selected according to the value they have for your audience.

5. *List applications of the doctrine* for communicating the difference this conviction makes in life (for sermons, lessons, small-group Bible studies, or family devotional Bible studies). Applications should make clear what the doctrine is, why one needs to know it, and how it will make differences in thinking. Then show how the difference in thought will lead to differences in values, priorities, attitudes, speech, and personal action. Consider also the doctrine's possible significance for family, church, neighborhood, city, regional, and national actions.

6. *Start a file and begin collecting illustrations* of this doctrine's central idea, the points in your outline, and your applications.

7. *Write out your own doctrinal statement on this subject in one paragraph* (in half a page or less). To work toward a comprehensive doctrinal statement, collect your formulations based on a study of each chapter of *Integrative Theology.* As your own statement of Christian doctrine grows, you will find it personally strengthening and useful when you are called on for your beliefs in general and when you apply for service with churches, mission boards, and other Christian organizations. Any who seek ordination to Christian ministry will need a comprehensive doctrinal statement that covers the broad scope of theology.

CHAPTER 8

GOD'S GRAND DESIGN FOR HUMAN HISTORY

God's Grand Design
for Human History

THE PROBLEM: ARE ALL EVENTS IN NATURE AND HISTORY THE FULFILLMENT OF THE SOVEREIGN PLAN OF A PERFECTLY WISE AND OMNIPOTENT GOD?

This chapter considers the question of whether the events of nature and history are related to a transcendent plan or purpose. Previous chapters have shown that God is no impersonal principle or mindless energy, but a thinking and feeling Being who, while sovereign over the cosmos, is actively involved in human life and history. Given God's ultimacy over the universe, the question arises as to how occurrences in the world, in fact, are related to ends God chose before creation. If God has an overall plan, does he determine to accomplish all of his purposes in the same way or does he determine to accomplish some of them supernaturally apart from any normal use of means and others instrumentally through "natural" forces or human agents? When working with persons made in his image, has God resolved to permit actions that displease him? Can all things, including the spread of sin and the destruction of the wicked, be said to be part of God's all-wise and loving plan in the same way? Some Christians have tried to solve such problems by distinguishing between God's decretive will and his permissive will, whereas others deny that God's relation to evil can be reduced to mere permission.

If God's will is the ultimate cause of all occurrences in nature and history, does it follow that creaturely freedom and responsibility are thereby eliminated? If God's will prevails in the world, how could a person justly be judged for his actions? Furthermore, how, if at all, do the actions of thinking and willing persons impinge on God's sovereign purpose? Can God's plan be altered by human choices? How does finite human decision making relate to God's sovereign and eternal plan? The proposals of Calvinists, Arminians, and theologians of other traditions in regard to such questions will be fairly examined. The present chapter interacts with what most Christians perceive to be true: persons are not pawns in the grip of a blind, immoral power, and ultimately life and history are not meaningless but are invested with purpose and direction by virtue of the eternal plan of a wise and loving God.

ALTERNATIVE CHURCH INTERPRETATIONS

The issue of God's eternal purpose, considered in relation to such matters as human freedom and responsibility, the existence of evil, and the perdition of the unsaved, has occasioned much controversy throughout the history of Christianity. Consequently we must carefully examine the leading interpretations of this complex problem within the church.

Pelagian and Liberal Traditions

Pelagianism and modern liberalism have severely weakened the doctrine of effectual decrees out of concern for creaturely autonomy and freedom. Pelagius and certain of his followers, such as Celestius and Julian of Eclanum, believed that the human person is the master of his own destiny and that God did not subject the creature to an inviolable will. Pelagianism thus virtually denied the notion of a supernatural decree, declaring it to be inconsistent with human autonomy and moral responsibility.

In the nineteenth century Albrecht Ritschl claimed that the quest to probe an alleged supramundane will of a hidden God follows the illegitimate method of speculative theology. His position was that the mind of God was disclosed in the history of Jesus of Nazareth. Through Jesus God is known as "loving will" who guides the world toward the realization of the kingdom.[1] The divine purpose reflected in Jesus excludes the exercise of a punitive will.

Twentieth-century liberal theology has similarly depreciated the sovereign purposes of God in its appeal to human freedom and autonomy. W. N. Clarke affirms that divine foreordination would impugn creaturely freedom, the absence of which would render meaningless human responsibility. Thus "nei-ther foreordination nor fate has slain freedom, but freedom lives."[2] Clarke's bottom line is that the church need not be bound by the picture of a God of immutable and irresistible decrees.

Other liberals argue that Graeco-Roman philosophy bequeathed to the church the idea of God as capricious and having an arbitrary will. According to Rauschenbusch, the doctrine of divine decrees represents the transference of the idea of the coercive and predatory state to the realm of religion. The "despotic" conception of God as arbitrary tyrant must be replaced by the "democratic" idea of God as benign and loving Father.[3] W. A. Brown similarly held that abstract and individualistic notions such as "secret counsel" and "arbitrary will" (as illegitimate Hellenizations) must give way to concrete and social conceptions of God's gracious kingdom purposes disclosed by Jesus of Nazareth.[4]

Process theology rejects the idea of God as the Controlling Power who determines every detail, present and future, of the world's order. Its God foreknows the future only in terms of the future's potentialities. Process theologians argue that the God of classical theism is an obstacle to the freedom, creativity, and growth of persons. Accordingly, the followers of Whitehead insist that God does not coerce or command; rather, he lovingly lures and tries to persuade entities to new opportunities and satisfactions. Indeed, God provides each actuality with a dynamic impulse called the "initial aim," which each person may choose to accept or reject. "Persuasion and not control is the divine way of doing things."[5]

Semi-Pelagian and Arminian Perspectives

Semi-Pelagians and Arminians argue that in relation to persons an effectual decree would vitiate freedom and responsibility and thereby dehumanize the individual. All God's purposes in relation to human destiny are conditional and are based on God's foresight of human decisions. Semi-Pelagians in the fourth and fifth centuries, in the medieval era, and in much of modern Catholic theology maintain that the Augustinian doctrine of decrees represents a crude fatalism. In matters of salvation Semi-Pelagians uphold the priority of the human will over the divine will and so restrict God's decree to foreknowledge of free human choices. Predestination thus is based on foreseen faith and obedience.

James Arminius, emphasizing human freedom and spontaneity, denied that God efficiently wills the actions of free agents. Thus he viewed the decree of predestination passively as a statement of how God works, namely, saving those he foresaw would believe and of judging those he foresaw would not believe.[6] Against Reformed supralapsarianism, Arminius argued that if God actively decreed the Fall, he would be the author of sin. Hence God "neither perpetrated this crime through men, nor employed against man any action either internal or external, by which He might incite him to sin."[7] Reformed theologians charged Arminius with teaching that God's will is ineffectual and mutable and that his purposes may be frustrated.

John Wesley likewise emphasized less the sovereign purpose of God than the free moral response of the human agent. The Calvinist postulate of an unchanging sovereign decree that determines a person's actions and fate would leave one as free as a stone projected from a sling or a toy in the hands of a tyrant. Thus, although Wesley upheld God's unconditional will to service, he affirmed a conditional will to salvation or perdition. God's sovereign will is not the determiner of a person's destiny. The high Calvinist decree of reproba-

tion violates God's goodness, love, and justice. Wesley argued that it depicts God as "more carnal, false, and unjust that the Devil."[8] Richard Watson, who wrote the first Methodist theology, concurred with Wesley. There are, he argued, two classes of divine decrees: "what He has Himself *determined to do*, and what He has *determined to permit* to be done by free and accountable creatures."[9] Contrary to the Reformed belief in the immutability of God's purpose, Watson insists that God's plan may be changed and even revoked: "The Scriptural doctrine . . . consists in His never changing the *principles* of His administration."[10]

Supralapsarian Hypotheses

Some medieval authorities, Reformers, and orthodox theologians uphold a supralapsarian view of the decrees, whereby all things eventuate according to the logically prior, effectual will of God. They reject the thesis of a permissive will as mere permission would undermine certainty of occurrence. The early Middle Ages witnessed the rise of extreme forms of Augustinianism. Gottschalk, the first significant proponent of double predestination, held that God foreordained to life and to death those whom he sovereignly willed. Gottschalk's supralapsarianism, by which God decreed the eternal damnation of souls prior to his decision to create the world and persons, allowed little room for creaturely freedom. For his views Gottschalk was flogged and confined for life. Similar was the position of Ratramnus: "Nothing that happens to men in this world takes place apart from the secret counsel of the Almighty. For God, foreknowing all things that are to follow, decreed before the ages how they are to be arranged through the ages."[11]

Analogous to his dualism between the "hidden God" and the "revealed

God," Luther postulated a twofold will in God, namely, his hidden and his revealed will. The former, the inscrutable purpose into which persons dare not pry, includes God's unconditional predestination of some to be saved and his reprobation of the rest to perdition. Appealing to God's hatred for Esau (Rom. 9:13) and his hardening of Pharaoh (Rom. 9:17–18), Luther affirmed that "the will of the Divine majesty purposely abandons and reprobates some to perish."[12] This will to perdition is not unjust, for the will of God is the highest authority; he is obliged to justify his ways to no one. Mortals, however, must turn from the fearsome, hidden will to God's revealed will made known through Christ and the Scriptures. Luther clearly perceives the workings of God's hidden will as supralapsarian. In addition, little room appears to have been left for a person's freedom of choice vis-à-vis God's will. "Just as we do not come into being by our own will, but by necessity, so we do not do anything by right of free choice, but as God has foreknown and as He leads us to act by His infallible and immutable counsel and power."[13] That God is not the author of sin, and that persons bear responsibility for the choices they make is a mystery embedded in the hidden will of God that only eternity will bring to light.

John Calvin likewise stressed God's comprehensive sovereign will, which allows no room for permission: "All the deeds of men are governed not by His bare permission but by His consent and secret counsel."[14] Thus creation, the fall of Adam, the coming of the Mediator, and Christ's death on the cross were all effected by the active will of the sovereign God. Calvin clearly taught double predestination. "Not all men have been created under the same conditions: some are predestined to eternal life, others to eternal damnation. And inasmuch as a man is created

to reach the one goal or the other, we say that he is predestined to life or to death."[15] Concerning the reprobation of the unrighteous, Calvin soberly remarks: "The decree is dreadful indeed, I confess."[16] Calvin, however, proceeds to distinguish between ultimate and proximate causes. Whereas God's sovereign will is the remote cause of the Fall, Adam's unbelief and rebellion is the immediate cause.[17] By appeal to proximate causes Calvin upholds the responsibility of the human agent. "Men act from their own wickedness, so that the whole fault rests on them."[18] Although Calvin's interest in the decrees was more practical than speculative, what statements he made on their logical order point in the direction of supralapsarianism.[19]

Beza's treatment of the decrees was more speculative: "Nothing in the entire world comes to pass without God's will or knowledge. Everything happens in the manner in which God ordained it from eternity. He disposed the intermediate causes in such a powerful and effective fashion that they were necessarily brought to the appointed end to which He ordained them."[20] Within the framework of double predestination, Beza insisted that the will of God is the first and efficient cause of Adam's fall. But Beza distinguished between God's *decree* of election and reprobation and the *execution* of that decree. Although God willed salvation and damnation, his decree was executed by the secondary means of faith and unbelief. By so reasoning, Beza, the supralapsarian, sought to uphold human responsibility while denying that God is the author of sin. Beza referred the above antinomies to the mysterious will of the sovereign God.

In similar manner John Owen extolled the sovereign God who effectively causes all that eventuates. Reluctant to posit mere permission, Owen argued that "God disposes the hearts of men, rules their wills, inclines their affections, and determines them freely to choose and do what He in His good pleasure has decreed shall be performed."[21] God's sovereign plan includes the coordinate poles of election to eternal life and reprobation to eternal death.

Modern Dutch Reformed theology is predominantly supralapsarian on the decrees. Bavinck, however, maintains that "the history of the universe can never be made to fit into a little scheme of logic."[22] Bavinck does insist that nothing comes to pass without first being established in the divine mind. Hence all things—Adam's fall, the rejection of Esau, the perdition of Judas—have been eternally fixed in the counsel of God and so rendered certain. If the language of permission be used at all, permission must be understood as being "positive" and "efficacious."[23] It follows that for Bavinck the decree of predestination includes both election and reprobation; each has its origin in God's sovereign good pleasure.

Barthian Neoorthodoxy

As understood by Karl Barth, God's decree focuses concretely on Jesus Christ, the beginning and sum of the divine purposes. We will see that Barth proposed a novel scheme of double predestination: God chose Christ for rejection ("No") and elected Christ for salvation ("Yes").

Barth insisted that Scripture does not direct attention to the general doctrine of decrees, with election a subfunction thereof; rather election constitutes the *sum* of the gospel, under which is subsumed all other facets of God's purposes for the world. Against liberalism Barth therefore maintained that God's elective decree is sovereign, omnipotent, and effectual.[24] Against orthodoxy he insisted that the static, abstract decree of Augustine and Calvin must be replaced by a dynamic, concrete decree that has its reality in Jesus Christ. Thus Barth claims that Jesus Christ "is God's Word, God's decree and God's beginning. He is so all-inclusively, comprehending absolutely within Himself all things and everything, enclosing within Himself the autonomy of all other words, decrees and beginnings."[25] Jesus Christ is both the beginning and the sum of the purposes of God. Barth then proceeds to affirm a doctrine of double predestination, albeit not a scheme in which election and reprobation are symmetrical decrees, as in Calvin and Beza. Negatively, in Jesus Christ God eternally elected himself for rejection, suffering, and death. In the first instance, then, "predestination is the non-rejection of man. It is so because it is the rejection of the Son of God."[26] And positively, in Jesus Christ God eternally elected sinful persons to salvation and blessedness.[27] Since God has irrevocably said no to himself and yes to humanity, Barth's logic leads to the vestibule of universalism. Hence the church witnesses to this reality: "that this choice of the godless man is void; that he belongs eternally to Jesus Christ and therefore is not rejected, but elected by God in Jesus Christ."[28] Since God's elective decree in Christ preceded all other determinations, Barth identifies his scheme as a "purified Supralapsarianism."[29]

The Infralapsarianism of Some Fathers, Medieval Authorities, Reformers, and Many Evangelicals

Although many early church fathers stressed human freedom vis-à-vis pagan fatalism, other fathers (e.g., Augustine) and medieval authorities (e.g., Anselm, Aquinas), some Reformers (the later Melanchthon), most confessional standards (e.g., Concord, Belgic, Westminster), and many orthodox and Evangelicals (e.g., Hodge, Packer, Henry) affirm that God has decreed certain things unconditionally (creation, the Incarnation, the salvation of believers) and other things conditionally (the rise of evil, the perdition of unbelievers).

Confronted with pagan astrology and the Stoic doctrine of fate (whereby a person's actions were said to be necessitated by forces beyond his control), the apologists circumstantially emphasized human freedom and responsibility rather than inevitability. Tatian insisted that sin is not due to any divine determination, but to the misuse of human free will. "We were not created to die, but we die by our own fault. Our free-will has destroyed us. . . . Nothing evil has been created by God."[30] Irenaeus, in conflict with the Gnostic doctrine of necessity, muted God's effectual will in salvation. Nevertheless, the sovereign will of God in salvation emerges here and there; e.g., "the Son, according to the Father's good pleasure, administers the Spirit charismatically as the Father will, to those whom he will."[31] On the other hand, Irenaeus maintained that God foresaw human rebellion and permitted his free creatures to walk "in the darkness which they have chosen for themselves."[32] Tertullian concluded that God rejects a person according to his desert: "It is not the mark of a good God to condemn beforehand persons who have not yet deserved condemnation.[33] Tertullian acknowledged in God the equivalent of a preceptive and a permissive will. According to the former, God sets before a person precepts to guide his actions.[34] According to the latter, God did not rescind the gift of freedom, for "He did not interfere to prevent the occurrence of what He wished to happen, in order that He might keep from harm what He wished for."[35]

Against the Pelagians Augustine insisted that the effectual and unchangeable will of God is the ground of all occurrences. Election, one component of God's unconditional will, is that secret, wise, and beneficent purpose whereby God chose out of the mass of fallen humanity a fixed number to be saved.[36] The bishop was careful to differentiate foreordination from fatalism and determinism, in that he upheld the willing agent's psychological freedom and responsibility. Indeed, "our wills are included in that order of causes which is certain to God and is embraced by His foreknowledge."[37] Augustine also postulated in God a conditional or permissive will. God does not will sins; rather, he permits persons to perpetrate wickedness out of respect for creaturely freedom and for the good he will bring about. God "judged it better to bring good out of evil than not to permit evil to exist."[38] The perdition of the ungodly Augustine ascribed not to God's decretive will, but to his foreknowledge and permission. God left the nonelect in the damnation they justly deserve.[39] Augustine occasionally wrote of God's predetermining sinners to damnation.[40] By such language he conceived of the plan of God broadly, as inclusive both of God's order and of his permission: "Nothing comes about unless God wills it so, either by permitting it to happen or himself performing it."[41] Hence for Augustine reprobation is the divine determination that abandoned sinners should pay the penalty for their own sins. Augustine's order of decrees thus was infralapsarian (or sublapsarian): God's decree of election logically follows his decree to create and to permit the Fall.

Thomas Aquinas's treatment of the decrees was Augustinian. He insisted that some events, such as creation and predestination to life, must be attributed to God's unconditional will. Other events, such as the spread of sin and the reprobation of the wicked, are due to God's permissive will.[42] Thomas explained how evil acts form part of God's overall plan. Although the particular cause of an evil deed is the free act of human persons or Satan, God willed to grant the agent freedom to commit the act. "Since the very act of the free will is traced to God as a cause, it necessarily follows that everything happening from the exercise of the free will must be subject to divine providence. For human providence is included under the providence of God, as a particular under a universal cause."[43] Is human effort or prayer incompatible with God's foreordination? No, he answers, since God's eternal purpose, executed with perfect prevision, includes second causes. "Providence [i.e., foreordination] . . . does not do away with secondary causes, but so provides effects that the order of secondary causes falls also under providence."[44]

Most of the post-Reformation Protestant confessions uphold an infralapsarian view of the divine decrees. Thus the Lutheran Formula of Concord commends an effectual divine predestination to eternal life but not to eternal death. The Westminster Confession affirms (without reconciling the paradoxes) that God is the all-determining first Cause; that he willed the means (second causes) as well as the end of all things; that human actions, although self-actualized, fall within the certainty of God's plan; and that God's will is not the effective cause of sin (Art. III.1; V.2). The Reformed Confessions (Second Helvetic, Gallic, Belgic, Dort, and Westminster) uniformly uphold a single predestination to life. Reprobation includes the twofold purpose of preterition and condemnation to a just judgment (e.g., Westminster Confession, Art. III.3,7). Typical is the Synod of Dort: "Not all, but only some, are elected, while others are passed by in the eternal decree; whom God, out of His sovereign, most just, irreprehensible and unchangeable good pleasure, hath decreed to leave in the common misery into which they have willfully plunged themselves" (Art. I.15). Most of the Reformed confessions reflect an infralapsarian outlook, less clearly so in the case of Dort and Westminster.[45]

Charles Hodge, infralapsarian on the decrees, upheld the Reformed emphasis on the God who foreordains whatever comes to pass. God's will is twofold: efficacious (in the sphere of nature and the ethically good) and permissive (in relation to sin). Hodge maintains that "God has a plan or end for which the universe was created, that the execution of that plan is not left contingent, and that whatever is embraced in the decrees of God must certainly come to pass."[46] Against detractors, Hodge insists that God is not the author of sin, that foreordination is consistent with human freedom and responsibility, and that the decrees do not discourage human effort, since God has ordained both the end and the means to it.[47]

Carl F. H. Henry insists that foreknown and permitted human acts inhere in God's eternal plan. His free, unchanging, and effectual decree imposes certainty on events, be they good or wicked. "The fact that God has foreordained human choices and that His decree renders human actions certain does not therefore negate human choice."[48]

Other recent authorities that uphold an infralapsarian or moderately Reformed stance on the decrees include Millard J. Erickson[49] and the revision of Henry C. Thiessen's theology.[50] Louis Berkhof gives more credence to God's permissive decree than do so-called hyper-Calvinists, but in the end he finds elements of truth in both the infralapsarian and the supralapsarian schemes.[51]

BIBLICAL TEACHING

Pentateuch

The opening statements of the Bible indicate that everything has its origin in

God's thought and will. The formula, "And God said, Let there be . . . " (Gen. 1:3, 6, 14; cf. 1:9, 11, 20, 24, 26) connotes creative words spoken with deliberate intention. The burden of Genesis 1 is that the existence of the universe is grounded in God's intelligent and wise purpose. The observation following each creative episode—"God saw that it was good (tôb)" (Gen. 1:10, 12, 18, 21, 25; cf. 1:31)—indicates that God's creative purpose had been realized. The adjective tôb connotes less an aesthetic judgment than the fact that "the results of His creative work fully conform to His plan and purpose."[52]

In the Garden of Eden the divine prohibition against eating from the tree of the knowledge of good and evil (Gen. 2:17) indicates that God is a God of specific intention. While the tree contained no magical powers, it served as a symbol of God's conditional purpose vis-à-vis the first pair. The threat of punishment for eating the forbidden fruit (Gen. 2:17; 3:3) implies that sin was permitted by God but not necessitated. Genesis 3 depicts God's allowing with displeasure Adam and Eve's exercise of their free agency in disobedience. The narrative suggests that God's will to permit sin renders Adam and Eve's act empirically certain by virtue of his foreknowledge, but not logically certain.[53] God's will is not the immediate cause of the disobedience of the first pair.

God's promise to give Abraham a land, a posterity, and a mission of blessing (Gen. 12:1–3), a promise later repeated to the patriarchs, is an instance of God's efficient will executed with pleasure. However, the decretive will eliminated neither Abraham's active response (Gen. 12:4; 15:6) nor his moral responsibility (Gen. 17:1; 18:19). Several examples in Genesis of apparent rejection warrant comment. God rejected Cain's offering (Gen. 4:3–5) since, unlike that of Abel, it was not

brought in faith (cf. Heb. 11:4). Similarly, Ishmael was rejected both on account of his scornful attitude (Gen. 21:9) and for the reason that not he but Isaac was chosen for blessing (Gen. 21:10). Finally, God sovereignly chose to install Jacob in the privileged line of Abraham and Isaac (Gen. 25:23; cf. Rom. 9:10–13) while bypassing Esau (but note the latter's preoccupation with merely temporal concerns, Gen. 25:30–34).

The history of Joseph sheds light on the secret workings of God's will. Having learned that God would give Joseph dominion over his brothers, the latter deliberately sold Joseph to Midianite merchants, who in turn sold him to an official in Pharaoh's administration (Gen. 37:28, 36). Yet three times the text declares that God sent Joseph to Egypt (45:5, 7–8), which suggests that the brothers' evil designs, permitted by God, were incorporated into his larger plan for the Hebrew people. The severe famine that followed (41:32) and Joseph's rise to authority in Egypt (45:9) were brought about by God. Thus at the end of the episode, Joseph declared that although the intentions of his brothers were evil, God had so overruled and ordered circumstances that his sovereign plan for Israel was actualized (50:20).

The ten or so references to God's hardening Pharaoh's heart (Exod. 4:21; 7:3; 9:12, et al.) offer no proof that God efficiently caused the Egyptian's stubbornness, nor on balance do they support the notion of divine reprobation. Prior to mention of the divine hardening, Scripture implies that Pharaoh freely determined to oppose God's purposes (Exod. 1:9–10, 16). In fact, the text plainly states that Pharaoh volitionally hardened his own heart (Exod. 8:15, 19, 32; 9:7, 34, 35, et al.; cf. 13:15; 1 Sam. 6:6). The most coherent and consistent explanation of the hardening is that God, by withdrawing his sustaining Spirit and by giving Pharaoh up to his own impulses, permitted Pharaoh to actualize his hostile designs (cf. Rom. 1:24, 26, 28).[54] A similar situation occurred in the case of Sihon, king of the Amorites, who refused to permit Israel to pass through his territory. Yet the Hebrews so attributed ultimate causality to God that Moses could say, "God had made his spirit stubborn and his heart obstinate" (Deut. 2:30; cf. Num. 21:23), even though God's involvement was limited to permission of the incident.[55]

God's preceptive will—those moral precepts or commandments that God sets before people for their obedience—is given in the Pentateuch in four major codes. (1) The Decalogue (Exod. 20:1–17) expounds God's purpose for his people in terms of their duty to him and their neighbor. The will of God imbedded in the Ten Commandments is frequently broken even by the devout believer. (2) The Book of the Testament (Exod. 20:22–23:33) provides detailed explication of the principles contained in the Decalogue. The conditional nature of the prescriptions is plainly evident throughout the code (Exod. 21:14, 20, 22; 22:1–2, 16, 23, et al.). (3) The priestly codes (large portions of Leviticus and Numbers) proposed God's wise design for the ministrations of the Aaronic priests. That the laws and decrees in these codes are preceptive and conditional is reflected in the repeated pattern "If you . . . , then I will . . ." (e.g., Lev. 26:3–45). God both permits the violation of his preceptive will and unconditionally ordains punishment for lawbreakers. (4) The Deuteronomic codes (Deut. 1–30; Num. 28–30) contain a restatement of earlier law portions. The preceptive nature of God's will emerges through the common theme of the two books, namely, that if Israel would obey God's voice, he would give them the land and expand their influence. Subsequent his-

tory shows that Israel chose to disobey God's preceptive will, that he permitted them to do so, and that God exacted punishment for their disobedience. God's threatened punishment for disobedience and anger toward sin (Num. 15:30–31; Deut. 28:15–29) suggest that he permitted sin but did not effectively cause it.

God's decretive will is illustrated by his election of Israel for special privileges and service. His choice of Israel was rooted, not in any numerical strength or intrinsic worth, but solely in his own sovereign purpose (Deut. 7:6–8; 10:15, et al.). That God's choice of Israel was made in respect of a fallen universe (Deut. 7:6) seems to point in the direction of an infralapsarian understanding of the logical order of the decrees. In Deuteronomy 29:29 Moses states, "The secret things [*hannistārōt*] belong to the LORD our God." By these words Moses refers to events yet future that are known only to God—specifically to the judgment that would fall *if* Israel persisted in their radical disobedience (see vv. 21–28). The following words, "the things revealed [*hanniglōt*] belong to us and to our children forever, that we may follow all the words of this law," refer to God's preceptive will, which if obeyed, will result in God's blessing.

Historical Books

God's decretive will is evident in the promulgation of his covenant with David (2 Sam. 7:12–16). Here God declares his intention to establish through David an eternal house (vv. 11–12), an eternal throne (v. 13), and an eternal kingdom (v. 16). Even though the Davidic kings would prove faithless and incur punishment, God's redemptive purpose would not fail (vv. 14–16). God's will is likewise seen in his purpose to punish idolatrous Israel. Whereas God justly willed that sin must be punished, the moral evil associated with Nebuchadnezzar's ravaging of Judah (2 Kings 19:25) is part of God's permissive will. The same applies to the punishment inflicted on Jerusalem and Judah by the coalition of pagan nations (2 Kings 24:2–3, 20).

The Lord likewise willed the punishment of Eli's sons by death, but it cannot be said that God was responsible for their sins. Referring to Eli's offspring, 1 Samuel 2:25 reads: "His sons, however, did not listen to their father's rebuke, for it was the LORD's will to put them to death." Two points need be made here. First, the Hebrew conjunction *kî*, translated "for," may also mean "so that," indicating the outcome or result of a situation. In addition, the verb *ḥāpēṣ* has an affective rather than volitional focus and fundamentally means "to experience emotional delight."[56] Thus whereas the Lord took great delight in Samuel, his anger toward the sons of Eli was aroused by virtue of their stubborn persistence in sin.

With regard to Eli's sons, "their failure to listen to their father or obey him functions like the hardening of Pharaoh's heart: it justifies Yahweh's death threat against them. Since they would not hear, he took pleasure in killing them."[57] When the Scripture says that an evil spirit from the Lord "tormented" Saul (1 Sam. 16:14) following the departure of the Holy Spirit from his life, we understand that God permitted the affliction as punishment for Saul's callous disobedience. Moreover, 2 Samuel 24:1 states that God "incited" (lit. "moved," *sût*) David to number the troops of Israel and Judah. Yet David acknowledged that he was morally responsible for his act (v. 10), which reflects a sinful trust in numbers. This admission by David agrees with the chronicler's testimony that "Satan . . . incited David to take a census of Israel" (1 Chron. 21:1). Satan, not

God, prompted David to sin. God's involvement in the matter was one of permission, though to the Hebrew mind God is the ultimate (i.e., final) cause of all occurrences.[58] Likewise Rehoboam's rejection of the advice of the wise elders and the defection of the ten tribes was a matter of divine permission, not causality. The outcome, however, was included in God's sovereign plan (1 Kings 12:15; cf. v. 24). We similarly understand the lying spirit that lured Ahab into attacking Ramoth Gilead (1 Kings 22:20–23). "The sending of the evil spirit is to be regarded as done by the permissive will of God instead of by His direct will. Let it be remembered that Ahab had had ample chance to know truth through Elijah, but had stubbornly resisted it."[59] The incident of God's hardening (Piel of *ḥāzaq*, "to make strong") the hearts of the Canaanite city dwellers (Josh. 11:18–20) should be understood in the sense of Pharaoh's hardening in Exodus. The Hebrew mind, which saw God as the ultimate cause of all that is, frequently spoke of God as causing what he merely permits—though self-hardening is acknowledged, as in 1 Samuel 6:6; 2 Chronicles 36:13; cf. Nehemiah 9:16–17, 29. The Hebrews thus shared little of the pagan belief that events happen by "chance" (*miqreh*, 1 Sam. 6:9). Texts that speak of God rejecting (*mā'as*) persons refer not to eternal reprobation, but to God's temporal penal judgments. God rejects those who have first rejected him (1 Sam. 15:23, 26).

Poetry and Wisdom

Job's trials taught him that God is a God of intelligent purpose (*'ēṣāh*, Job 12:13). All his dealings with nature (v. 15), persons (vv. 17–21), and nations (vv. 23–25) were carefully conceived, though not fully understood by humans (Job 42:3). The decree of God is wholly sovereign and free (Job 23:13–14). The Hebrew of Psalm 135:6 literally reads: "Everything that Yahweh willed to do [*hāpēṣ*] he did [*'āśāh*]." The "plan" (*'ēṣāh*) or "purpose" (*maḥªšābôt*) of the Lord is eternal and unchangeable (Ps. 33:11). Given his wisdom and power, God need not have any contingency plans. Moreover, God's will is effectual (Prov. 19:21), and his "plan" (*mᵉzimmāh*, Job 42:2) is absolutely invincible. God's purpose embraces all things; even the evil deeds of the wicked fit into his overarching plan (Prov. 16:4).

The poetical books acknowledge God's unconditional will. Thus the election, anointing, enthronement, and rule of David, and ultimately of Christ (Ps. 2:7–8), were effected by God's inviolable "decree" (*ḥōq*). Moreover, God willed the punishment of those who refused his grace and rebelled against him. The language of rejection, common in the Psalms and indicated by the verbs *zānaḥ* (Pss. 43:2; 44:9, 23; 60:1, et al.) and *mā'as* (Ps. 53:5; 78:59, 67; 89:38), refers to a temporal forfeiture of privileges as a result of deliberate covenant-breaking. God's work among the Egyptians—"whose hearts he turned to hate (*śāmē'*) his people" (Ps. 105:25)—must be understood in the sense of his hardening of Pharaoh's heart (for human self-hardening, see Ps. 95:8; Prov. 28:14). Scripture refuses to ascribe sin to God's efficient will, as indicated by repeated warnings of judgments against evil practices (Ps. 81:13–15; Eccl. 11:9).

God's preceptive will, which embodies his desired intentions and which may be broken, is suggested by such Hebrew words as *mišpāt* ("ordinance," "laws," Ps. 119:91, 103, 149), *tŏrāh* ("instruction," "law," or "teaching," Pss. 1:2; 19:7; 119:1), *'ēdāh* ("statute," Pss. 78:56; 93:5; 119:2, 22, 24), *miṣwāh* ("command," "precept," Pss. 19:8; 78:7; 89:31), *'ēṣāh* ("counsel," Job

38:2; Pss. 73:24; 106:13), *derek* ("way," "path," Job 21:14; 23:11; 31:7), and *rāṣôn* ("will," in the sense of delight or good pleasure, Pss. 40:8; 103:21). God desires that people obey him and realize his moral purposes for their lives (Ps. 51:6; Prov. 19:20). Yet it is clear that God's preceptive will of pleasure frequently is broken by disobedience (Ps. 107:11; Prov. 1:25, 29–30).

God's permissive will is seen in his allowing Satan to strike at Job (Job 2:3–6) and his possessions (Job 1:12). Although Satan was the effective agent of affliction (Job 2:7), Job 42:11 speaks of "all the trouble [*rā'āh*, "misfortune," "adversity"] the LORD had brought upon him" (cf. Job 1:21). Clearly here, as elsewhere, God is said to cause what he merely permits to be done. Other instances of God permitting with displeasure what was contrary to his highest purposes appear in Psalms 78:18–31 and 81:11–12. That sin entered the world by divine permission only is clear from Ecclesiastes 7:29: "God made mankind upright, but men have gone in search of many schemes" (cf. Ps. 92:15).

The Prophets

God's plan (*'ēṣāh*) in the prophets is represented as a coherent whole (Isa. 14:26). Aspects thereof, actualized in time and history, are "great" (Jer. 32:19) and inscrutable (Isa. 55:8). God's will, moreover, is sovereign and free (Dan. 4:35). The imagery of the potter and clay (Isa. 45:9–13), adduced in response to the questions, Why did God bring the captivity? and Why did God choose Cyrus to effect restoration? clearly affirms that God wills events on the basis of his sovereign pleasure. The divine purpose, in addition, is effectual and inviolable. "The LORD Almighty has purposed [*yā'aṣ*], and who can thwart him?" (Isa. 14:27; cf. 55:10–11).

God's sovereign will, effected by

human instrumentality, includes his purpose to liberate Israel from captivity by Cyrus, to repopulate Jerusalem, and to rebuild the temple (Isa. 44:28; 46:10–11; Jer. 29:11). God's word in Malachi 1:2, "I have loved Jacob" refers to God's decision to show compassion to or to sovereignly elect the younger brother to salvation. The parallel clause, "Esau I have hated" (śānē'), connotes God's relative lack of preference for, or his passing over, the firstborn, for reasons known only to himself.[60]

A prominent feature of God's will in the prophets is his decision to punish the wicked (Isa. 14:24–25; 26:21; Jer. 50:45). In the execution of the divine judgment, hostile nations freely act according to their own political and military self-interests (Isa. 23:13; Mic. 4:12–13). Habakkuk wrestles with the problem of why the people of God suffer at the hands of ruthless pagan invaders. Although the language speaks of God "raising up the Babylonians" and employing them as agents of judgment (Hab. 1:6, 12), the Hebrew mind once again ascribes to God's initiative what he merely permits to be done.[61]

In Habakkuk 1:17 the anguished prophet appears to ask God how long the Babylonians will be permitted to ravage the nations without being checked. When in the course of judgment God is said to work ra' or rā'āh (Isa. 45:7; Jer. 18:11; Amos 3:6; Zech. 8:14–15), the meaning is not that God is the author of wickedness but that his punishment takes the form of "disaster" or "calamity."

How should we understand the relation between the will of God and the Messiah's death? Isaiah 53:3–5, 7–9 prophetically depicts the deep physical and emotional sufferings of the Christ, which the Gospels indicate were administered by the Jewish religious leaders and Roman authorities. The latter, then, were the efficient agents of the Messiah's suffering and death. The text of Isaiah 53:10 is somewhat corrupt and could be translated, "But Yahweh took pleasure in his humiliated one."[62] But if the common reading be allowed to stand—"Yet it was the LORD's will to crush him and cause him to suffer" (cf. RSV, NASB, JB)—"perhaps no more is intended than the fact that the servant's anguish was in every way the fulfillment of a great divine plan."[63] That is, God's role in the death of the Messiah (Isa. 53:4, 10) was to permit the foreseen passion of the Lord and sovereignly to ordain the *saving ends* that would be achieved by his death—namely, atonement for sins, declaration of righteousness, and spiritual cleansing for all who believe (Isa. 52:15; 53:5, 10–11).

The prophets upheld God's preceptive will that included his desired intentions for his people. Isaiah 48:17 reads, "I am the LORD your God, who teaches you what is best for you, who directs you in the way you should go" (so also Ezek. 18:21; Hos. 6:6). Yet because God's will of pleasure was scorned, disaster fell upon the people of God (Isa. 1:19–20; Ezek. 18:20). The object lesson of the potter (Jer. 18:1–12), wherein the first pot became marred, prompting the potter to fashion a second pot, teaches that God's will of pleasure for his people was violated by disobedience. God does not compel a person against his will to obey his precepts; rather, with displeasure God permits people to choose their own loyalty (Jer. 2:21; 44:4–5; Hos. 6:6–7). The wicked die (Ezek. 18:23) because God has purposed to honor human decisions. What is hebraistically known as God's stupifying activity (Isa. 6:9–10) represents his permission of creaturely rejection of his Word.[64] God's rejection of his people occurred only (logically) after they had deliberately rejected him (Jer. 6:30; Hos. 4:6; 9:17).

The Synoptic Gospels

Jesus was conscious of the unconditional will of his Father. His model prayer contains the petition "Your kingdom come, your will [*thelēma*] be done on earth as it is in heaven" (Matt. 6:10). The verbs "come" and "be done"—imperatives of request that stand first in each clause in the Greek—indicate that Jesus petitioned for the historical actualization of God's eternal purpose for history—namely, the establishment of the kingdom on earth. According to Luke 12:32, God by a sovereign determination resolved (*eudokēsen*) to give his little flock the blessings of his reign. Moreover, Luke affirms that Christ's suffering, death, and resurrection—being fixed in the plan of God—were foretold in prophetic Scripture (Luke 24:46). Luke 22:22 is an important Scripture on the subject of the divine decree: "The Son of Man will go as it has been decreed [*hōrismenon*, perfect passive participle of *horizō*, "to determine," "appoint"], but woe to that man who betrays him." This text teaches that the Crucifixion was part of God's overarching decree, though the efficient and blameworthy cause of Christ's death clearly was Judas's act of betrayal (cf. Matt. 26:24). The impersonal verb *dei* ("it is necessary")[65] connotes that Jesus' preaching ministry (Luke 4:43); his suffering, death, and resurrection (Matt. 16:21; Luke 24:7, 26, 44); and the world-wide proclamation of the gospel (Mark 13:10) were aspects of God's purpose: "The necessity of the events results from the sovereign purpose of God and the inviolability of His word through the prophets."[66]

Some interpreters find in certain sayings of Jesus justification for an alleged decree of reprobation. Matthew 11:25, however, teaches that God by his "good pleasure" (*eudokia*) has chosen to reveal the significance of Christ's words and deeds to receptive hearts and to hide the same from the proud and self-sufficient. The Lord made the same point in Matthew 13:11. Jesus' parable of the sheep and the goats (Matt. 25:31–46) differentiates between the sheep on the right hand ("blessed" by the Father) and the goats on the left ("cursed" [*katēromenoi*] by him). The text states that the righteous inherit the kingdom prepared specifically for them (v. 34), whereas the accursed depart into the place of torment prepared, not for them, but for Satan and his angels (v. 41). "The distinctive element in the biblical statement is not the 'congruity' but the 'incongruity' of the 'right hand and the left hand.' "[67] The lost are those whom God has sovereignly chosen to "leave" (*aphiēmi*, Luke 17:34–35) in their self-chosen state of sinful rebellion.

God's preceptive will is set forth in Jesus' Sermon on the Mount (Matt. 5–7). Access to heaven is predicated on obedience to God's preceptive will of pleasure (*thelēma*, Matt. 7:21; 12:50). Many people, however, respond like the Jewish leaders who "rejected God's purpose for themselves" (Luke 7:30). The words "for themselves" modify the verb "rejected," thus emphasizing that persons may break God's will of pleasure and thereby incur condemnation.[68] Other instances where God's preceptive will was spurned occur in Matthew 23:37 and Luke 12:47. The Lord takes no pleasure in the death of any of his creatures (Matt. 18:14).

Jesus taught that God's permissive will is characterized by empirical certainty. According to Matthew 24:6, wars "must" (*dei*) occur, and, according to Matthew 18:7, the working of those who obstruct true faith is "inevitable" (*anankē*). Some things are rendered certain by God's decreeing their happening, others by his foreseeing their permitted occurrence. God's holy and righteous character ensures that he is not the efficient cause of greed and hatred in the world.

Primitive Christianity/Acts

The record of the church's growth in Acts gives pride of place to God's sovereign will. As in the Gospels, so in Acts Christ's rejection, death, and resurrection were grounded in God's overarching plan. So Peter testifies to the Jews: "This man was handed over to you by God's set purpose [*horismonē boulē*] and foreknowledge [*prognōsis*] and you, with the help of wicked men, put him to death by nailing him to the cross" (Acts 2:23). Peter later declared that the authorities "did what [God's] will [*boulē*] had decided beforehand [*proōrisen*] should happen" (Acts 4:28). These texts teach (1) that Christ's death in respect to its saving end or purpose was willed by God and thus certain of occurrence (cf. Acts 3:18; 17:3); (2) that God permitted the freely conceived plots of Jesus' enemies which were incorporated into his redemptive plan.[69]; and (3) that Christ's death, though part of God's plan, did not exclude Jesus' free giving of himself (Eph. 5:2)—i.e., for Jesus God's will was conditionally experienced.

God's decretive will is further illustrated by the fact that God "set [*etheto*] by his own authority" the time for the restoration of the kingdom (Acts 1:7). In addition, God not only ordained (*hōrismenos*) Jesus to be judge of the living and the dead (Acts 10:42), but he also appointed (*estēsen*) a day for the judgment of the world (Acts 17:31). The account of Paul's shipwreck (Acts 27) teaches that God's sovereign will does not discourage genuine human effort. An angel of God informed the apostle that both he and the others on the ship would survive the storm (Acts 27:22–24, 34). Yet God's purposes would be realized only as the mariners stayed with the ship (v. 31), jettisoned cargo (v. 38), and used their nautical skills to run the ship aground (vv. 39–41). Some of God's purposes are achieved by human instrumentality.

Acts recognizes, in addition to God's decretive will done with pleasure, his permissive will accomplished with his displeasure. At Lystra Paul and Barnabas said the following of God's dealings with the Gentile world: "In the past, he let [*eiasen*, "to permit," "allow"] all nations go their own way" (Acts 14:16). God did not compel obedience to his preceptive will (cf. David's obedience to the same, Acts 13:22). Rather, after issuing adequate warnings, he reluctantly allows people to follow their own desires. Paul's statement that "in the past God overlooked [*hyperidōn*] such ignorance" (Acts 17:30) conveys the same meaning.

Pauline Corpus

Paul's letters contain extensive teaching on the divine decrees. Ephesians 1:9–11 outlines the leading characteristics of God's will. (1) God has but a *single* plan. Verse 9 refers to "the mystery of his will [*thelēma*]" and verse 11 "the plan [*prothesis*] of him who works out everything in conformity with the purpose [*boulē*] of his will [*thelēma*]." (Cf. God's "purpose" in Rom. 8:28; Eph. 3:11.) (2) This plan is an *inclusive* plan; it embraces "everything" (Eph. 1:11) or "all things" (Rom. 8:28). "Everything is comprehended in his purpose, and everything is ordered by his efficient control."[70] (3) His is an *eternal* plan, as indicated by the word *protithēmi* ("to purpose," v. 9), *proorizō* ("to predestine," v. 11), and *prothesis* ("purpose," v. 11). Ephesians 3:11 pointedly speaks of God's "eternal purpose" (*prothesis tōn aiōnōn*). (4) God's plan is also a *free* plan, in that God acts not by internal constraint or by external compulsion, but strictly on the basis of "his good pleasure'' (*eudokia,* v. 9; cf. v. 5; Phil. 2:13). And (5) God's plan is an *effectual* plan; what the sovereign God wills unconditionally or conditionally comes to pass (v. 10; cf. v. 13). The end of the divine decrees is God's glory (*doxa,* Eph. 1:6), or the manifestation of the sum of his excellencies.

Elsewhere in Paul's writings it is clear that God sovereignly planned from eternity the scheme of saving sinners through Christ (1 Cor. 2:7; cf. 1:21; Eph. 1:9). The components of God's saving ''purpose'' (Rom. 8:28) are detailed in Romans 8:29–30 by a series of aorist verbs: God ''foreknew,'' ''predestined,'' ''called,'' justified,'' and ''glorified'' his people. That the glorification of the saints is put in the aorist tense indicates that the event was rendered so certain in the divine plan that Paul regards it as an accomplished fact.[71] The apostle believed that God from eternity elected individual sinners to be saved (Eph. 1:4–5, 11; 1 Thess. 5:9; 2 Thess. 2:13; 2 Tim. 1:9). Texts such as Romans 9:15; 1 Corinthians 2:7; Ephesians 1:4; and 2 Timothy 1:9 suggest that God's saving purpose was executed with respect to a fallen world order, a view that agrees with the infralapsarian order of the decrees. It is also clear that God's effectual will to save includes genuine human involvement and responsibility (Phil. 2:12–13; 2 Thess. 2:13).

Paul applies his theology of divine decrees to the historical problem of Israel's unbelief and apparent rejection by God. That the Gentiles and not Israel have found favor with God was foreshadowed by God's love for Jacob and his ''hatred'' of Esau (Rom. 9:13). The statement ''Jacob I loved'' connotes that God extended compassion toward Jacob or that he elected him in grace. On the other hand, the statement ''Esau I hated'' signifies that God purposed not to extend compassion toward Esau or that he chose not to elect him in

grace. According to Cranfield, ''God has chosen Jacob and his descendants to stand in a positive relation to the fulfillment of His gracious purpose: He has left Esau and Edom outside this relationship.''[72] The affirmation that God is merciful to whom he wills (vv. 15, 18) signifies election according to his free self-determination. On the other hand, God's hardening of Pharaoh and Israel (v. 18) connotes not reprobation, but his ratification of their own determination to steel their hearts against the divine will of pleasure. With Shedd we could say that God hardens the hearts of the unsaved in two ways: (1) by permitting the person to exercise his sinful will and (2) by withdrawing his grace so that the person's sinful lusts go unchecked.[73] Paul's statement that God ''raised up'' (*exēgeira*) Pharaoh—the Hebrew of Exodus 9:16 suggests that God merely sustained Pharaoh in life (see RSV)—was intended to point up God's use of hard-hearted Pharaoh in the out-working of his saving plan. God was not, however, the efficient cause of Pharaoh's actions.

The analogy of the potter and the clay (Rom. 9:20–21), whereby the craftsman fashions out of the same lump one vessel ''for noble purposes'' (*eis timēn*) and another ''for common use'' (*eis atimian*) registers the point made earlier that God purposes to sanctify one group of people and to leave the other in their sins. ''It should be noted that *eis atimian* implies menial use, not reprobation or destruction. The potter does not make ordinary, everyday pots in order to destroy them.''[74] Neither do verses 22–23 support a predestination to destruction. The text states that the saved were ''prepared in advance for glory'' (*proētoimasen*), whereas the lost are ''prepared for destruction'' (*katērtismena*). The fact that Paul does not here use the verb *prokatartizō* (cf. 2 Cor. 9:5) suggests that it is not God who reprobated in eternity; rather, the sinner prepared himself for destruction by his own refusal to repent. The emphasis in these verses is not God's reprobation, but the postponement of his wrath against people who are ripe for destruction. In sum, "there appears here no support for any dogma of predestination to damnation, while the parallel foreordination to glory is stated with no uncertainty."[75]

The hardening of Israel cited in Romans 11:7, 25 and their subsequent spiritual insensibility (Rom. 11:8, 10) should be understood in the sense of Romans 9:18. With pleasure God willed the salvation of "a remnant" (Rom. 11:5) within the family of Abraham, but with displeasure he permitted the majority of Israelites to reject his offer of grace (v. 12). We agree with Brunner that "there is no doctrine of a double decree in the New Testament, and still less in the Old."[76] As Paul reflects on God's sovereign and inscrutable decrees, he is compelled to worship and praise the God from whom and through whom and to whom are all things (v. 36).

Paul sees God's decretive will as providing the benefits of Christ's death on the Cross (Gal. 1:4) and as the ground of his apostleship (2 Cor. 1:1; Gal. 1:1, 15–16), the gifts granted by the Spirit to the church (1 Cor. 12:11), and the authority of civil rulers (Rom. 13:1–2).

The hortatory sections of Paul's letters admonish believers to actualize God's preceptive will for their lives. These exhortations to do God's *thelēma* (Rom. 12:2; Eph. 5:17; Col. 4:12; 1 Thess. 4:3) focus on the concrete goal of spiritual maturing or perfection in Christ. Paul's statement that God "wants [*thelei*] all [cf. *pantōn (anthrōpōn)*, vv. 1–2, 6] men to be saved and to come to a knowledge of the truth" (1 Tim. 2:4) refers, not to God's decretive will that shall be effected (so Roman Catholic and other universalists),

but to that general desire or wish of God that is constantly assailed by creaturely freedom.[77]

God's permissive will is seen in the threefold "God gave them over" (*paredōken*) cited in Romans 1:24, 26, 28. God reluctantly permitted humankind to substitute idolatry for the knowledge and worship of the living God. The element of displeasure in God's permissive will stands out in 1 Corinthians 10:5, where it is said of the Israelites who practiced idolatry and sexual immorality, "God was not pleased [*ouk eudokēsen*] with most of them." According to 2 Thessalonians 2:10, 12, the workers of iniquity perish because they refuse to embrace the truth of the gospel. The opening phrase of verse 11, *kai dia toutou* ("for this reason"), introduces the result of this self-chosen unbelief: "God sends them a powerful delusion so that they will believe the lie." Thus Peter suggests that God responds to persistent unbelief with judicial hardening. "God sends a 'working of delusion' in the sense that to be misled by falsehood is the divine judgment inevitably incurred in a moral universe by those who close their eyes to the truth."[78]

John's Writing

According to Revelation 4:11, God's will (*thelēma*) is the ground of the creation of the world and the existence of all that is. That same unconditional will planned the values and ends of Christ's death, so that John could speak of "the Lamb that was slain from the creation of the world" (Rev. 13:8). John's claim that the Father gave certain individuals to belong to the Son (John 6:37, 39) connotes God's decretive will to save. Yet it is clear that this decree of election requires the faith response of the individual ("whoever comes to me," v. 37, and "who looks to the Son and believes in him," v. 40).

Jesus' saying that he came into the world "for judgment" (John 9:39) implies no decree of reprobation, still less a supralapsarian order of the decrees. Rather, Jesus intended that his teaching and miracles would bring people to a point of decision. Those who chose to reject him passed judgment on themselves. Similarly, Jesus' description of Judas as "the one doomed to destruction" (John 17:12) focuses on Judas's self-chosen character and his inevitable end. Thus "even the fall of Judas found a place in the whole scheme of divine Providence."[79]

Jesus' burden was to do the will (*thelēma*) of the Father who sent him (John 4:34; 6:38). The major moments of Jesus' life were included in the plan of God: namely, his arrest (John 7:30; cf. 2:4), his crucifixion (the verb *dei*, John 3:14; 12:34), and his resurrection (*dei*, John 20:9). Each of these events was empirically necessary because it was foreseen by God and included in his eternal purpose.

The Book of Revelation uses the verb of necessity, *dei*, to speak of those events that "must soon take place" (Rev. 1:1; cf. 4:1; 22:6) in the overall purpose of God. The future course of the world's order includes events both planned and permitted by God. Thus God unconditionally planned the second coming of Christ, the overthrow of Satan, the millennial reign of Christ, the resurrection of the just and the unjust, and the new heavens and the new earth. On the other hand, God has permitted with displeasure the spread of apostasy, the rise of totalitarian regimes, the unleashing of Satanic oppression during the Great Tribulation, and the rebellion of Satan after the thousand-year reign. In spite of all the sin in the world, John insists that God is not the author of evil: "God is light; in him there is no darkness at all" (1 John 1:5). As light (*phōs*), God is the unimpeachable source of holiness, righteousness, and truth.

Other New Testament Literature

Hebrews attests the immutability and trustworthiness of the divine decree with the phrase "the unchanging nature of his purpose" (*boulē*, Heb. 6:17). James agrees that no variation occurs in God's willing and doing (James 1:17). This is so because the plan of God is eternal, having been formed before the creation of the world (1 Peter 1:20).

In teaching that Christ "was chosen (*proegnōsmenou*, perfect passive participle of the verb "to foreknow") before the creation of the world" (1 Peter 1:20), Peter implies that God eternally planned the end and the values of Christ's saving mission (cf. Luke 22:22; Acts 2:23). Although the great moments of Christ's ministry were included in the plan of God, Jesus' statement "I have come to do your will [*thelēma*], O God" (Heb. 10:7; cf. v. 9) indicates that from his earthly standpoint he conditionally experienced the sovereign will. According to 1 Peter 1:2, God's sovereign decree of election involves (1) the use of foreordained means ("through the sanctifying work of the Spirit") and (2) conscious human participation and responsibility ("for obedience to Jesus Christ"). Jude 4 affirms, not a decree of reprobation, but God's purpose to execute judgment (*krima*) on false teachings. Likewise 1 Peter 2:8 affirms the divinely appointed ruin of those who persistently reject the gospel. The antecedent of the clause "which is also what they were destined for" (*etethēsan*) is not the verb "they disobey" (so Calvin, Beza), but "they stumble."[80]

Hebrews 13:20–21 teaches that God desires that his preceptive will be fulfilled: "May the God of peace . . . equip you with everything good for doing his will [*thelēma*], and may he work in us what is pleasing (*euarestos*) to him, through Jesus Christ." Other references to God's will of pleasure are Hebrews 10:36 and 1 Peter 2:15; 4:2, 19. Similar to 1 Timothy 2:4 is the teaching of 2 Peter 3:9: "The Lord . . . is patient with you, not wanting [*boulomai*] anyone to perish, but everyone to come to repentance." The last two texts teach that God takes no pleasure in the death of the wicked but waits for the unsaved to turn and live (cf. Ezek. 18:23).

According to James 1:13–15 God does not tempt (*peirazō*) anyone to sin. Rather, out of respect for creaturely freedom God permits people to follow their own lusts and to sin. Hebrews' mention of Israel's hardness of heart in Egypt focuses on the individual as the cause of the hardening (Heb. 3:8, 13, 15; 4:7). Scripture suggests that continued resistance to God's grace produces a fixed habit of opposition to God that is not easily broken. One authority observes that the aorist passive subjunctive, *sklērunthē* ("that none of you may be hardened," Heb. 3:13) is best "understood as a passive of permission; i.e., 'allow or permit one's self to be hardened.' "[81] Similarly, Esau was rejected by God only after he had rejected the grace of God freely offered (Heb. 12:17).

SYSTEMATIC FORMULATION

Before seeking as far as possible to order the extensive controversial material from the primary scriptural and secondary historical sources logically, we pause to examine our preunderstandings about causal actions.

Assumptions Concerning Personal and Impersonal Causes

To understand anything, said the Greek philosopher, Aristotle, we must know not only (1) the material of which it is made and (2) the agent who made it, but also (3) the end or purpose in mind and (4) the form given it to satisfy this purpose.[82] In short, Aristotle sought four causes of events in human history and of the whole nature: material, efficient, final, and formal antecedents. The New Testament also, allowing for material factors and forms or essences in the Logos, attributes events to personal (efficient) agencies and their purposes. For centuries afterward theologians continued to investigate not only the nonpersonal materials contributing to the nature of things and events, but also personal causes and teleological ends served.

However, since Hume, Kant and many modern scientists abandoned the early theistic assumptions of scientists and philosophers and overlooked the agency of persons as efficient causes with final causes or purposes. Secular humanism's epistemology tends to limit philosophical inquiry to phenomenal description of observable causes and their forms (formulae). The choices of persons are attributed to other impersonal factors. Our actions may be held to be determined by nonintelligent antecedents. If we perform actions that appear to be uncaused, they are attributed to sheer chance. Secular science now simply describes changes in the forms of matter-energy and does not even ask, let alone answer, questions about personal agency and purpose in the cosmos at large. So, if we have been educated within the assumptions of a nontheistic world view, we may describe only event-causation and whatever meaning individual existentialist types may read into their lives at the moment.

To overcome the sense of pointlessness, non-Christians may inconsistently "borrow" or "steal" from a Christian world view a universally good "purpose" that will automatically work itself out through a Marxist economic dialectic, mere chance, or an undirected evolution. These unwarranted hopes within non-Christian world views need to be unmasked. Then Christians need to place greater emphasis on "agent causation: the notion of a person as an ultimate source of action."[83] Christians need not reject the categories of causality, as Barth does, to emphasize personal categories.

Believing with good reason that the ultimate reality is a transcendent, personal, causal Agent who knows, feels, and wills, it makes sense to inquire whether God has an overarching purpose for the world. If our heavenly Father has a goal for history and is personally involved with the world, lasting significance in human existence can make sense. And human determinations and actions may also be regarded as responsible causes. Issues related to ways in which God works out his plans in history must be reserved for the study of divine providence.

The Meaning of Divine Decrees in General

By the divine decrees we mean the eternal Father's self-determined purposes and strategies that guide his Son's and the Spirit's dynamic activities from the world's creation to history's consummation.

To help grasp the significance of this hypothesis we here briefly present some of its important facets for consideration. Some of the more controversial points will be defended at greater length in relation to soteriology.

The decrees refer to purposes our heavenly *Father* has chosen for creation and human history. Although the distinctive ministries of the Son and the Spirit are often highlighted, the Father's distinctive role may not receive equal time. One characteristic emphasis of the Scriptures attributes to the Father the primary responsibility for electing, predestining, and foreknowing (Matt. 6:10; Eph. 1:3–4). So passages in the Old and New Testaments referring the purposes to "God" (without distinguishing the persons of the Trinity) may be interpreted as meaning the Father's purposes when trinitarian distinctions are in view.

The Father's decrees were not automatically necessitated, but were *free decisions* of purposes for the universe. In making them, God was not coerced by anything outside himself, for nothing else existed beyond the triune essence. As a personal agent God has the intellectual capacity to choose among ends and the volitional ability to move toward their achievement by the strategies he chooses. On our concept of freedom these decisions were self-determined in accord with the Father's nature. It may seem tautologous to insist on a freedom with fidelity to the divine character since that should be implied in *self*-determination. But Barth and James Daane seek to divorce God's freedom from his essence. Daane opposes a decretal theology in which God "is a decreeing God in terms of his ontology, and not in terms of his freedom."[84] According to Daane, "The distinctive feature of God's decree is that it expresses the freedom of the divine will."[85] Indeed God's decrees are chosen freely, but God cannot deny himself, lie, or determine to do anything unholy or unjust. God's choice of ends was not arbitrary but in accord with attributes of wisdom, holiness, and love. The freedom of Christ's heavenly Father cannot be abstracted from his whole being. It is not a mere will that decrees, it is the whole being of God the Father who decrees. The agent choosing the divine purposes is God the Father, not just his will abstracted from him. So we insist that God's freedom does not include the power of choice contrary to his attributes, but the power of self-determination according to them. Note, please, that by holding that God is faithful to wise, holy, and loving ends, *we* do not limit God. Rather, we simply recognize that the Almighty makes decisions with integrity and authenticity. God's sovereignty is absolute, but not tyrannical.

The decrees were also *eternal decisions* giving direction to dynamic action in time. Before the creation of the world the Father envisioned creation's goals. His settled determinations secure the direction of his dynamic acts in history. The changelessness of the decrees need not imply a "fixed" and "static" view of history (as Barth charged). Clarity of purpose and strategy should not be confused with lack of activity. God is not less active for knowing where he is going. Quite the contrary, God's purposes call for the dynamic activities of his spiritual people, his Son, and the Spirit in history.

The Father determined *both purposes and strategies* (ends and means). Beginning students in this doctrine often find insuperable difficulties because they are preoccupied with the notion that God is achieving ends entirely apart from means and processes. The goal of winning a football game is one thing, the team's strategy for achieving that win in different plays is another. Both are indispensable. Thought about the ends should not ignore the strategies for attaining them. Neither should means be mistaken for ends or ends for means. The end is what is aimed at (the final cause), means are the ways the end is brought about. Purposes are intended goals; strategies are the tactics designed to achieve them. God included strategies as well as purposes in his plan.

God's purposes and strategies are *comprehensive but radically different* in relation to moral evil and good. The Father permits the work of Satan; he ordains the work of Christ. Moral evil is included in God's plan, as we shall see, not with pleasure but with displeasure.

To affirm with some Reformed theologians that all the decrees are one may raise unnecessary problems. All may be considered one if it means all God's purposes are just and his different strategies are coordinated in God's mind. If, however, the oneness of the decrees means that the Father determines human enslavement to sin unconditionally with the same pleasure as redemption from sin, that is unthinkable. If God cannot even tempt to sin (James 1:13) and takes no pleasure in death (Ezek. 18:20) its merited consequence (Rom. 6:23), theologians ought not to imply that he has purposed it or contributes to it by the same strategies as he contributes to holiness, which he efficiently encourages and which is an unmerited gift of grace.[86]

Does not the Bible itself say that God can create evil (Isa. 45:7)? Isaiah does not teach the blasphemous idea that the Lord creates sin! What the Lord, the Holy One of Israel (v. 11), initiates is punishment for sin! He created "darkness" or "disaster" (v. 7) in judgment on Egypt when it was dark for three days (Exod. 10:21–23). "He sent darkness and made the land dark—for had they not rebelled against his words?" (Ps. 105:28). So Isaiah predicted that a sudden disaster would come upon Babylon (Isa. 47:11). Amos warned Israel that God would punish her for her sins (Amos 3:2). Only in the context of judgment for sin do the prophets write, "When disaster comes to a city, has not the LORD caused it?" (v. 6).

Like a just judge, God decrees punishment for sin but he does not decree acts of sin! That radical distinction must not be forgotten when we read about "the plan of him who works out everything in conformity with the purpose of his will" (Eph. 1:11). From Paul's generalization it does not follow that God intends moral rebellion and eternal punishment with the same pleasure as moral faithfulness and heaven. What follows from Paul's statement is that in one way or another everything is teleologically related to God. Again, the fact that God "works out everything in conformity with the purpose of his will" in its broader biblical context does not imply that God is the causal agent of evil as well as good nor that he is the efficient cause of sin. Rather, God is the final cause of whatever comes to pass because from eternity God purposefully planned for it all either with pleasure or permissively. Some things he permissively allowed with displeasure and judgment, and some things he predestined with pleasure.

The Father's elective purposes are both *individual and collective*. The decrees do not stop with individuals like Adam, Abraham, and Paul, but encompass whole groups of people. God's purpose to create our original parents and permit their fall encompasses every descendant of theirs, the totality of human persons. Similarly, God's redemptive purposes include people of all times who are justified by faith. Within the category of his people are purposes for such subgroups as Israel (Deut. 7:7–8) and, since Pentecost, the church (1 Peter 1:1–2). God purposed to call these people out from fallen humanity in order that they should bless the whole world. So everyone, individually and collectively, repentant or unrepentant, is in one way or another related to God's purposes.

To speak of God's collective concerns as a corporate election is not to exclude individuals. The Father's condemnation of evil involved the condemnation of all people, Jews and Gentiles, including each person (Rom. 3:10–23). So his redemptive purpose was not directed to an empty corporation or logical class, but to the body of Christ with each of its members. Election need not be of either individuals or a class, but of both.

The election of individuals for salvation is clearly taught by our Lord's explanation of why some responded to his message and others did not (John 6:35–36; 60–71). Those given to him by the Father come to him and are received by him (v. 37) and are kept by him (vv. 39–40). "No one can come to me," Jesus explained, "unless the Father who sent me draws him" (v. 44), or enables him (v. 65). People did not believe the miracles of Jesus because they were not his sheep (John 10:26). His sheep listen to his voice and follow him, and he gives them eternal life; they shall never perish and no one can snatch them out of Christ's hand (v. 27). Since they are given to Christ by the Father, neither can anyone snatch them out of the Father's hand (v. 29). They have been chosen not only for salvation but also for service and that is why the world hates them (John 15:16–19). The Father granted the Son authority over all people that he might give eternal life to all those the Father gave to him (John 17:2). To those given to him Jesus reveals the Father, and they obey the Father's Word (v. 6); they know Jesus comes from the Father (v. 7), Jesus prays for them (v. 9), keeps them (vv. 11–12), asks that they have the full measure of his joy (v. 13), protection from the evil one (v. 15), sanctification (vv. 17–19), the fruitfulness of their message to win others to belief (vv. 20–21), and unity with one another (vv. 22–23). Jesus also anticipated seeing them in glory (v. 24). Not all were given to Jesus by the Father, but some persons clearly were.

God's redemptive purposes are intended for both *salvation and service*. In Old Testament times Abraham, Moses, David, and the prophets were justified by faith and intended to take the message of God's righteousness and grace to the world. In New Testament times Saul was called out of the world for salvation from his sin and for service as the apostle to the Gentiles. The other apostles had been called out from among the masses by Jesus for salvation (including both justification and sanctification) and service. All believers are chosen "to be holy" (Eph. 1:4), "to do good works, which God prepared in advance for us to do" (2:10), "for obedience" (1 Peter 1:2), and for the world-wide proclamation of the gospel (Matt. 28:19, 20). All have gifts for ministry to the church (1 Cor. 12:7).

The Father's elective purposes are *Christ-centered but not Christomonistic* (as in Barth's proposal). Unquestionably Christ has preeminence in the Father's plans for creation (John 1:1–3; Col. 1:15–17) and redemption (Col. 1:18–20; 2:9, 10), but he is not the only one chosen in the redemptive plan. In Christ the Father chose believing sinners in the church to be holy (Eph. 1:4), to be his spiritual children (v. 5), to be redeemed (v. 7), and to know his will (v. 9). As we have seen, these passages are both collectively of the church and individually of its members, so that the Father's plan to provide redemption in Christ includes specific persons to benefit by his provisions. "If there is no election of individuals," as Carl Henry argued against Barth's view, "election can hardly be personal good news."[87]

Furthermore, Henry added, "Unless Christian proclamation reaches the sinner as a condemned and doomed person to whom God offers redemption, it is not the good news intended by the New Testament."[88] Barth's hypothesis that all people are already condemned and already justified in Christ and are simply in need of being informed about Christ does not cohere with the Scriptures. We cannot ignore the crucial distinction between Christ's provisions for reconciliation, redemption, and forgiveness and the sinner's Spirit-enabled reception of these benefits by repentant faith. Jesus Christ was not the only

person in view in the decision to permit sin with its consequences.

According to the Bible, condemnation fell first on Adam and his descendants, individually and collectively. It is on sinners—not on the Savior—that judgment first fell. Logically, as well as historically, only after the condemnation of the entire human race can its guilt and penalty meaningfully be imputed to the dying Christ. And only after Christ has paid the penalty for our sin, can we receive his redemption.

Specific Purposes

Thoughtful children (of all ages) sometimes ask, "Why is there anything at all?" To answer simply and directly, "Because before there was anything else the heavenly Father, who always existed, lovingly planned to create all good things and persons. God decided to create, not because he had to fill up any lack in the divine being, for God is perfect (Matt. 5:48). Things exist because freely and lovingly God determined to share his goodness with other existing beings."

What more specific ends for the creation has God revealed to the prophets (Amos 3:10)? For what eternal purposes can we discover adequate evidence in revelation (explicit or implicit)? God's purposes have been amplified here beyond the minimal logical issues to point up their relevance (often thought to be purely theoretical) and to anticipate an outline of a Christian philosophy of history or theodicy.

1. In holy love God wisely planned *to create the cosmos* to function according to regular physical laws. He also planned *to create persons* to love and serve him in harmony with physical and moral laws. All things, we infer from the subsequent deed, were to be created not only by Christ but also for him (Col. 1:16)—i.e., for his glory (Rom. 11:36). That decision to create other personal

beings would mean the existence of other self-determining agents, other efficient causes of actions and events. They would not be equally ultimate with him, but necessarily persons dependent on him for their existence and persons with a beginning in time and history. As finite beings, their use of their capacity of self-determination would not always necessarily be consistent with their natures. They could changeably exercise their self-determination either morally in harmony with their upright natures, or contrary to them. Similarly people in history would be free to determine their moral choices and actions either consistently with God's precepts, or contrary to them. By choosing to create changing people in history God would create people free to choose not only in accord with their moral natures (as created), but also contrary to them.[89]

2. Although God desired people's faithfulness to himself and the order he established for human good, he planned to *permit self-determining persons to become unfaithful* to him. God did not predestine our first parent's disobedience to his moral law, but permitted it in his plan for history. God also planned to permit people who broke his precepts and covenants to suffer the just consequences of their self-determined disbelief and disobedience. As Augustine said, "There are two kinds of evil—sin and the penalty for sin."[90] There may be no explicit biblical statement to the effect that God knew before the foundation of the world that Adam and Eve would sin, but divine omniscience includes everything. If the Father did not know that Adam and Eve would sin, why did he plan in eternity to atone for sin (Acts 2:23)?

3. Before creation God planned *to send his Son* and through his atonement provide justly for *common and saving grace*. Redemption is provided by the precious blood of Christ who was "chosen before the creation of the world" (1 Peter 1:20). The Father's election of Christ was revealed at Jesus' transfiguration: "This is my Son, whom I have chosen; listen to him" (Luke 9:35). Peter could later say, "This man was handed over to you [who cried, "Crucify him!"] by God's set purpose and foreknowledge" (Acts 2:23; cf. 4:27–28; 1 Cor. 2:7–8; Rev. 13:8).

On the ground of Christ's loving provision, temporal effects of sin would be ameliorated for all in common grace. Then as repentant believers would take the gospel to all, many would be born again. At conversion the seeds of the victory over the habitual, moral, relational results of sin would also be planted.

4. From eternity God planned *to send the Holy Spirit to call out his people for eternal life* from among the human rebels. Many persons would thus repent, believe, and grow in faithfulness. God's people individually and collectively not only share his fellowship but also the mission of his kingdom. "For he chose us in him before the creation of the world to be holy and blameless in his sight . . . to be adopted as his sons . . . when the times will have reached their fulfillment—to bring all things in heaven and on earth together under one head, even Christ" (Eph. 1:4–11; cf. 3:10–11).

"This grace was given us in Christ Jesus before the beginning of time" (2 Tim. 1:9). We rest "on the hope of eternal life, which God, who does not lie, promised before the beginning of time" (Titus 1:2). However unfaithful people may have been prior to their conversion, those united to Christ by faith believe that God's Spirit will bring their lives in this world to a just and wise culmination, as the beginning of life eternal.

In this history-spanning rebuilding of God's rule, the Father planned to send the Son and the Spirit to work in, with, and through his people *collectively* through families (Noah's, Abraham's, etc.), the Israelite nation, and Christian churches.

The Father's plan included preserving the human race from extinction and self-destruction through the *family*. To Adam and Eve God said, "Be fruitful and increase in number; fill the earth and subdue it. Rule over the earth" (Gen. 1:28–30). That cultural mandate came first to a specific couple, a family. While judging the persistently evil with the destruction of the Flood, God would establish a covenant with Noah to save him and his family from destruction (Gen. 6:18).

The Father's plan also included descendants of Abraham's family in the Israelite *nation*. God covenanted with Abraham to make of him a great nation, to bless those who bless him and his descendants, and to bless all people of the earth through him (Gen. 12:2–3). God also promised him countless descendants (Gen. 15:4–5) and a land (Gen. 15:7). God planned to bring them out of slavery in Egypt through Moses (Exod. 3:7–10) and into the land through Joshua (Deut. 34:9; Josh. 1:15). Through Isaiah, God pleaded with the rebellious people in the house of Jacob: "Remember the former things, those of long ago [God's purposes fulfilled in the deliverance from Egypt]; I am God, and there is no other . . . I make known the end from the beginning, from ancient times what is still to come. I say: My purpose will stand, and I will do all that I please. From the east I summon a bird of prey; from a far-off land, a man to fulfill my purpose. What I have said, that will I bring about; what I have planned, that will I do." (Isa. 46:9–11). Earlier Isaiah had alluded to the fact that a plan for one nation involves a plan for all. "This is the plan determined for the whole world; this is the hand stretched out over all nations" (Isa. 14:26).

The primary institution God planned to use in bringing blessing to the whole world in the present era is the *church*. On earth, having become incarnate to do the Father's will, Jesus exclaimed, "I will build my church, and the gates of Hades will not overcome it" (Matt. 16:18). That the building of the church unifying Gentiles and Jews (not merely as classes, but as persons also) was in the Father's plan before creation seems even more explicit in Paul's calling (Eph. 2:15). Although God's intent was not revealed for ages before Paul, it was that the church's race-transcending unity would display the manifold wisdom of God to rulers and authorities in heavenly realms, according to his eternal purpose (Eph. 3:10–11).

5. God ultimately purposed *to unite heaven and earth under Christ*. God sovereignly determined to bring linear history to a just culmination in a final judgment of the evil ones and a climax of grace, bringing all things together in heaven and on earth under one head, even Christ (Eph. 1:10). The people of God in Israel and the churches have an underlying spiritual unity in the first to be elected, Christ. But institutionally the nation remains one kind of organization not reducible to an ecclesiastical organization. And the organized church is made up of people. Because the body of Christ is corporate, societal, and communal, it is an empty fiction without its many members. Hence it seems difficult to exclude persons from election. God's election is not solely christological, nor is it either corporate or individual. The Father elected Christ, the individuals who make up his "body," and the corporate whole of his "body," his people—Israel and the church.

Just as by God's word the heavens existed and the earth was formed, so "the present heavens and earth are reserved for fire, being kept for the day of judgment" (2 Peter 3:7). When the appointed time has come, the Lord God Almighty, who is and was, judges the dead and rewards his servants (Rev. 11:17–18). And how can we have any assurance that after all these years this is still God's purpose? "The Lord is not slow in keeping his promise" (2 Peter 3:9). Although the ungodly will be destroyed, "in keeping with his promise we are looking forward to a new heaven and a new earth, the home of righteousness" (v. 13).

Undoubtedly these promises flow from eternal purposes. The decision to create involved an awareness that in the new "home of righteousness" not only would justice be done, but also mercy and grace would be lavishly experienced. Hence history is neither open-ended nor cyclical, but linear and climactic. Evil will finally be destroyed; universal justice, peace, and love will follow.

Varied Strategies

The great designer of the cosmos is the final cause of everything, for there would be nothing at all if it had not been for his plan to create and sustain the world and life. In the final analysis God has a reason for everything, good and evil. Teleologically we incorporate an element of the supralapsarians' concern that God be sovereign over the evil as well as the good. The final cause of everything's existence, however, is not the efficient cause of everything's activities. Certainly the Holy One is not the efficient cause of morally evil acts to destroy his creatures. The Most High is not the blameworthy cause of rebellion against himself.

To illustrate the difference between being the final cause of something and being its efficient cause, think of an airline established for the final purpose of transporting people and goods from one city to another. Because the final cause or *raison d'être* of the airline is transportation, its workers serve as stewards of that goal. If the airline maintains reasonable standards of safety and competence and if a terrorist blows up one of its planes in the air, the airline company cannot be regarded as the efficient cause or the blameworthy cause of that tragedy. The terrorist's purpose of destroying the flight contradicts the purpose of the airline to complete the flight without accident. The flight's passengers would not have lost their lives in that way if it had not been for that airline company's existence, but the company as such is not the culpable cause of the tragedy. No illustration intended to make clear God's relationship to evil can be perfect, but the above illustration helps us to understand how God can be the final cause of life (even that of the terrorist) and not be culpable for destructive actions efficiently caused by sinners.

By what strategies does God attain his life-giving ends? His miraculous and providential strategies vary significantly. Ordinarily God works providentially through impersonal forces of nature and personal agents (as second causes) to achieve his temporal and preceptive ends. In extraordinary instances (usually related to preserving and establishing his creative and redemptive programs) God chooses to achieve his decretive ends directly through miracles. Consider his miraculous strategy first and then his providential strategy.

1. To achieve certain special decretive purposes God's strategy is to act miraculously, either superseding nature's laws and human agencies or using other means in extraordinary ways. For example, creation *ex nihilo* must necessarily have been achieved without the use of secondary causal factors. At the point of initial creation no other beings or things existed to play an intermediate role in that creative act. In God's

miraculous strategy he is both the final cause and the efficient cause.

Since the creation God is not the only agent and God's miraculous strategies are not always so totally removed from other means. But when means are used in miracles, they are used in an extraordinary manner, as in the following examples. Dust does not ordinarily produce human beings, but God used "dust" in the miraculous creation of man (Gen. 2:7). Ordinarily virgins do not conceive, but in an extraordinary way God enabled Mary to bring the Messiah into the world (Luke 1:35; 2:7). Clay on the eyes does not ordinarily heal blindness, but at the request of Christ it enabled the blind man to see (John 9:7). In such extraordinary uses of means, God not only chooses their final purpose, but also acts as efficient cause.

No amount of opposition from human or demonic terrorists can succeed against God's miraculous strategies. God's plans are great! "O great and powerful God, whose name is the LORD Almighty, great are your purposes and mighty are your deeds. . . . You brought your people Israel out of Egypt with signs and wonders" (Jer. 32:18–21). Kings and kingdoms cannot succeed against God's extraordinary acts. The One enthroned in the heavens laughs when the kings of the earth take their stand against him (Ps. 2:1–2). "Surely, as I have planned, so will it be, and as I have purposed, so will it stand. . . . This is the plan determined for the whole world; this is the hand stretched out over all nations" (Isa. 14:24–26). Again, "He does as he pleases with the powers of heaven and the peoples of the earth. No one can hold back his hand" (Dan. 4:35). God's miraculous strategy for achieving his *decretive will* cannot be thwarted.

2. Although we have found that God is the final cause of whatever comes to pass, ordinarily God has chosen to work through nature's impersonal forces and cognitive precepts. In God's *providential strategy* he remains the final cause of everything but makes use of nature's ordinary energies (as "material" causes) and of people as efficient causes to achieve the ends of his preceptive will. Hence in any historical event on planet earth there may be several causal factors.

In analyzing human events we must avoid the single-cause fallacy and look for many contributing factors. Under divine providence there may be multiple natural factors and one or more persons involved. Creation's laws are uniform but people's responses to God's revealed precepts occur in two radically different ways. People may either (1) believe and obey divine exhortations (as in Exod. 20:1–17) or (2) disbelieve and disobey God's precepts.

God is pleased with belief and obedience to his *preceptive will*; he is not pleased with unbelief and disobedience to his preceptive will. God's permission of disbelief and disobedience to his preceptive will may be referred to as his *permissive will*. With either obedience or disobedience, the all-knowing God is not surprised. Both responses to his instrumental strategy have been included in his all-encompassing plan.

In God's preceptive will more than the Ten Commandments are involved. The preceptive strategy includes the use of all of general revelation and special revelation. God uses the inspired Scriptures "for teaching, rebuking, correcting and training in righteousness" (2 Tim. 3:17). Reports of historical blessings and judgments are given to provide hope and warnings to the receptive, but others may ignore them. Doctrinal passages provide the materials for structuring a world view, but they may be side-stepped by unbelieving thinkers. The Bible's gospel invitations are to be received and acted on, but they may be rejected.

Neither the giving of the law nor the presentation of the gospel as such guarantees a positive response from fallen people. God sent John the Baptist to summon people to repent in preparation for the Messiah's ministry. John baptized those who repented, but "the Pharisees and experts in the law *rejected* God's purpose for themselves, because they had not been baptized by John" (Luke 7:30). The unrepentant sinners in their insolence nullified or set aside (*atheteō*) God's preceptive will (*boulē*) in which he takes pleasure. But they are still within his permissive will, receiving the displeasure of God. The Father's preceptive will not only may be opposed, but in fact the dominant tendency of sinners by nature is to thwart it. Even after God delivered his people from Egypt and miraculously fed them in the wilderness, he lamented, "But my people would not listen to me; Israel would not submit to me. So I gave them over to their stubborn hearts to follow their own devices" (Ps. 81:11–12). The fact that some of God's strategies can be resisted should not lead us to think that all of them can be resisted or thwarted. God's miraculous strategies cannot be thwarted, as we found. Two kinds of strategies, then, are required to account for the evidence: one miraculous and unconditionally effective; the other providential and, up against depraved human nature, in itself relatively ineffective.

Two kinds of strategies are required furthermore, because the evidence indicates two results to the different responses to God's providential or conditional strategy. Some people believe and obey God's preceptive will and therefore please God, and other people are permitted to disbelieve and disobey that will and, by doing so, displease God. The Scriptures imply that God permits what displeases him. Clearly he permits the death of the wicked but takes no pleasure in their death (Ezek. 18:23): "I take no pleasure in the death of anyone, declares the Sovereign LORD" (Ezek. 18:32). God permitted hypocrites to live, but said, "I desire mercy, not sacrifice" (Hos. 6:6). An evident difference occurs between what he desires and what he permits. Again, " 'I am not pleased with you,' says the LORD Almighty" (Mal. 1:10). Clearly among the prophets no contradiction was seen in holding to the permissive will of the Sovereign Lord. None of the prophets claimed to fully understand the relation between God's decretive (unconditional) will and his permissive (conditional) will, but they did recognize the two as significant for their respective purposes.

Many tend to assume that God has only one strategy for achieving his purposes—either an unconditional strategy (hyper-Calvinism) or a conditional one (Wesleyanism or Arminianism).[91] Either symmetrical hypothesis, affirming that God plans to accomplish good and evil in the same way, seems too oversimplified to account for the differences in the relevant data. The biblical evidence above (and in the biblical section) is complex, making more probable the hypothesis that the Father (1) conditionally permits sin with displeasure and (2) unconditionally (for sinners unable to meet the condition of faith) gives the gift of Christ's righteousness.

The Logical Order of Decrees

One cannot state all God's specific eternal purposes at once; so in listing them some order, though artificial, is unavoidable. A temporal order is out of the question, since time had not begun before the creation of the world. The issue is which decrees had logical priority over the others in the Father's plan. Three logical possibilities need to be clearly distinguished: Arminian double foreknowledge, supralapsarian double predestination, and an infralapsarian foreknowledge of sin and predestination to salvation.

For Arminianism God's purposes of salvation and of condemnation are both conditional; so God simply foresaw the Fall with its universal implications and he foresaw those sinners who would believe on Christ. We may call this view double foreknowledge. God foresaw who would fail to meet the condition of faith in Christ and who would meet that condition and be saved. From an Arminian perspective the order of decrees is (1) creation, (2) permission of the Fall and the condemnation of all, (3) the universal provision of Christ's atonement and prevenient grace, and (4) the election of all who meet the condition of faith in Christ. This is a type of infralapsarianism, since the election of the saved logically follows the permission of the Fall (*lapse*).

From a supralapsarian Calvinistic perspective neither purpose is conditional, so God unconditionally predestines some to be saved and some to be lost. This view is commonly called double predestination—of the lost and the saved. It is called supralapsarianism because the Father's election, determining who will be saved and who will be lost is made logically before (*supra*) the decision concerning the Fall (*lapse*) into sin. The logical agenda in God's mind was thought to include the following steps: (1) to glorify himself God predestined some people to eternal life and some to eternal death; (2) as a means to that goal, God decided to create human beings; (3) God decreed the Fall to supply some people for eternal punishment; and (4) so that the elect could be justly saved, he decreed the work of Jesus Christ.

By calling the supralapsarian decree concerning the Fall "permissive," Fred H. Klooster makes the decree of the

Fall conditional.[92] But a consistent supralapsarian position regards the decrees as unconditional. It it difficult to soften the blows of double predestination without being inconsistent. As a distinct logical alternative it requires that the decrees concerning the lost be unconditional and not permissive.

A clearly distinct infralapsarian Calvinism regards the decree concerning the lost to be conditional and the decree concerning the saved to be unconditional. God foresaw the fall of all mankind into sin but predestines the unmerited salvation of many, since the depraved will be incapable of meeting a spiritual condition. The Father's choice of the elect is not logically prior to his decision to permit the Fall, but after (*infra,* or *sub*) the Fall (*lapse*). Hence in infralapsarianism God's decrees were made along the lines of this agenda: (1) the creation of all mankind; (2) the permission of the Fall and just condemnation of all; (3) since no sinners could meet the condition of salvation, the predestination of "many" to salvation and permission of others to receive the just penalty for their sins; and (4) the provisions for salvation through the work of Christ and the application of salvation's benefits through the work of the Holy Spirit.[93]

Limiting our concern to the lost at this point, the issue is between infralapsarian permission of sin and its consequences and supralapsarian predestination of them. Is a just God glorified by unconditionally predestining some human beings to eternal punishment independent of their foreseen creation and fall? Could a judgment predestining some to be condemned be made without respect of persons? Finding the supralapsarian position unjust and irreconcilable with Scripture, infralapsarian Calvinists join with Arminians in regarding the degree concerning the Fall to be conditioned on foreseen disbelief and disobedience. It is a permissive decree with displeasure. And it is administered, not to some, but universally without respect of persons. The object of the decree is universal, not particular (Rom. 3:19–20), and its basis is foreseen works of disobedience.

Throughout Scripture just judgment is always merited; saving grace is always unmerited. That categorical difference ought to be reflected from the beginning of a theology about God's eternal purposes. Throughout Scripture punishments must fit the crimes actually committed. Jesus endorsed degrees of punishment when he said, "From everyone who has been given much, much will be demanded" (Luke 12:47–48). Jesus also said that it would be more bearable for Tyre, Sidon, and Sodom on the day of judgment than for those who had rejected him (Matt. 11:20–24). Justice is merited; grace is unmerited. Great harm is done when the distinct categories of grace and works are confused at any point in theology. When people complain that an infralapsarian view of election is unjust, they forget that no one is treated unjustly. A customer confused these categories when complaining that a photograph did not do him justice. The photographer replied, "My friend, what you need is not justice, but mercy!" All are treated justly when all are judged sinners and worthy of condemnation.

If God, by electing many to be saved, passes over some, it may be asked, Is not that the same as predestining them to their unenviable destiny? Admittedly, the end result is the same, but the radical difference is whether that punishment was deserved and whether the sentence of condemnation was justly pronounced. If the sentence was not merited by sinful works but was unconditionally decreed, as in supralapsarianism, it would seem to be unfair indeed. But given the universality of sin and the sentence, as in infralapsarianism, it was not assigned to some with partiality.

And given the degrees of punishment, no one is punished more than he or she deserves. No injustice is done to any sinner by this decree. We could wish that God had found it wise and just to give Christ's righteousness to all sinners, but that theory does not fit the biblical facts. One might more justifiably complain on behalf of the nonelect that undeserving as they are, they did get a gift that others received, though gifts are not appropriately demanded. One cannot rightly complain, however, that God has dealt with the nonelect unjustly. That complaint shows a confusion of logical categories of grace and justice or works.

After a helpful historical overview and summary of the biblical data, Paul K. Jewett, in his *Election and Predestination*, fails to find a clearly distinct infralapsarian alternative to supralapsarianism or Arminianism. Admittedly the "great majority, even in the Reformed tradition, have backed away from the supralapsarian position . . ."[94] because the Scriptures teach an unconditional election and a conditional reprobation.[95] But a Calvinist cannot hold that God simply *foresees* that the reprobate will fall, Jewett says, "without borrowing a leaf from the Arminian's book."[96] Why must Jewett as a Calvinist fear borrowing a word from Arminians if their usage is (in part) from the Bible? A study of "foreknowledge" and "foreknowing" indicates in some cases mere prescience (Acts 26:5; 2 Peter 3:17) and in others a stronger determination (Acts 2:23; Rom. 8:29; 11:2; 1 Peter 1:2, 20). The term *foreknowledge*, like most words, has more than one meaning. It can mean mere prescience of evil in some contexts and predetermination of Christ and salvation in others. Apparently unaware of the twofold usage in Scripture, Jewett returns to a supralapsarian symmetry, saying that "the reprobate are what they are [i.e., morally and spiritually blind] by the positive ordination of God."[97] Inconsistent with his own interpretation of the scriptural difference between conditional and unconditional, he claims that "supra- and infralapsarianism are but nuances of one and the same fundamental approach."[98]

Unable to reconcile the issues, Jewett confesses that for him, "when all is said and done, the problem of reprobation remains unresolved."[99] Since he cannot resolve it, he seems to think no one can, for he then adds, "it would appear, unresolvable."[100] Resorting to "the paradox of grace"[101] and "mystery,"[102] Jewett leaves the impression that any attempt to resolve his contradictions amounts to "artificially contrived compromises."[103]

On the basis of the biblical evidence above, it is far from artificial, we submit, to regard the election of the depraved as unconditional and the reprobation of all in Adam as conditional. Such a clearly distinct logical alternative as infralapsarianism provides is by far the more probable hypothesis than a contradictory one. By taking a position on this controversial doctrine, we make no claim to fully comprehend the ways of God with humans. Rather, applying our verificational method, we find a clearly distinct infralapsarian hypothesis (as here defined) to be more likely true because (1) it is not contradictory, (2) it is able to account for the relevant biblical evidence above with fewer difficulties, and (3) it is tenable without pretense or hypocrisy.

APOLOGETIC INTERACTION

Is the Heavenly Father the Author of Evil?

Although the biblical evidence indicates that God did not initiate evil, some will ask, "If God permits evil, is not God responsible for it? Did not God create people with the potential for rebellion against him?" God is responsible for creating personal agents. They turned aside from him. Not even God could create self-determining persons minus the power of determining their own actions (just as he cannot make square circles). God can be the final cause of the existence of everything without being the efficient, blameworthy cause of any evil acts.

By way of illustration, Henry Ford is the final cause of all Ford cars, for there would not be any if he had not invented them to provide transportation. But Henry Ford, who could well have envisioned misuses of his automobiles, apparently felt it wiser, in a kind of benefit-evil analysis, to invent them than not. However, when a drunken driver of a Ford car takes others' lives in a head-on collision, Henry Ford is not the efficient cause of the tragedy. Similarly, although God is the teleological (final) cause of everything that is, he is not the efficient cause of his creatures' evil choices. The Father chose to create self-determining beings and to work with them preceptively and permissively. People are responsible for their bad decisions and actions. We cannot blame our sinful choices on the Devil or on God.

Others will insist that if God knew that people would sin, he would not have escaped responsibility for their evil if he then created them. As omniscient, surely God knew that human beings, though created in his image and carefully advised to avoid evil, would alienate themselves from one another and from the triune God, would come under condemnation, and would become predisposed to selfishness, materialism, pride, and sensuality. Nevertheless God is not the blameworthy, or efficient, cause of rebellion against himself. God could foreknow with certainty that Adam and Eve would yield to temptation and sin, without himself being their tempter or inducing them to yield. But did he not know that the Tempter would enter the Garden of Eden? Yes, he knew. But God did not send Satan there. And apparently before Satan fell from his created state of perfection, there was no other creature to tempt him; the Devil fell of his own volition. No more ultimate source or explanation for sin can be found than the volition of the creature. God foreknows with certainty what his creatures will decide, but God does not make their decisions for them. When he created their natures by which they are self-determined, he made them good. Since by their own choices persons originated moral evil, God is not the author of sin. "God cannot be tempted by evil, nor does he tempt anyone" (James 1:13).

Although God has not told us specifically why he chose to create, we suggest that in infinite wisdom, taking into account all the data of omniscient foreknowledge in a kind of foreseen benefits-evils analysis, he concluded that it was better to create than not to create. Analogously, although some married couples may hesitate to bring children into a fallen world with all the known risks or evils, most do have children. Apparently they conclude that the evils are far outweighed by the inestimable values of enduring loving relationships with children (and possibly grandchildren) throughout their lives.

What are some of the values that the Father may have had in mind in permitting moral evil with its consequent suffering? Some suffering is justly judgmental. *Retributive* suffering vindicates justice or fairness, a fact that is clear to all who have been treated unjustly or unfairly. (Just laws are of little help to a society if they are not enforced.) Through suffering we receive many other benefits. *Empathic* suffering enriches personal relations. In all of Israel's afflictions, God was afflicted (Isa.

63:9). Paul wrote to the Corinthians "out of much affliction and anguish of heart and with many tears" (2 Cor. 2:4 RSV). Christians find deepening relationships in weeping with those who weep and rejoicing with those who rejoice (Rom. 12:15). Empathic suffering may lead to *vicarious* suffering, supremely exemplified by Jesus Christ on the cross. Then *testimonial* suffering may be experienced by those who follow the example of Christ. We may suffer for righteousness' sake (1 Peter 3:14), for the kingdom of God (2 Thess. 1:5), for the gospel (2 Tim. 2:9), or for bearing injustice (1 Peter 2:19). Pain may serve to prevent greater suffering as an early warning sign to avoid a more serious condition. In this way suffering serves a beneficial *educational* purpose. The greatest good of the Christian life is not freedom from pain, but Christlikeness. God planned to work all things together for good, not for our ease, but for our conformity to Christ's characteristics. So he planned to permit discipline ("for our good"), that those who are trained by it might enjoy the "peaceable fruit of righteousness" (Heb. 12:10–11 RSV). Suffering is usually involved in purification, said C. S. Lewis. And looking back over his life, Lewis mused, "Most of the real good that has been done me in this life has involved it."[104]

In sum, God is not the author of sin, for moral evil, as Augustine taught, is not a substance created by God, but a turning of creatures' wills against God.[105] Evil has no independent status; creatures brought evil into the world. Having permitted creaturely self-determination, God manages evil for the greater good through such activities as the experience of fairness, loving empathy, vicarious giving, faithful witness, and disciplined education.[106]

Do the Father's Decrees Undermine Human Responsibility?

God has chosen not to be the sole efficient cause of events, but to work ordinarily through human persons as self-determining agents. Since he plans not to be the sole efficient cause of events, others will have the privilege of a dependent self-determination and the responsibility for their choices. God has planned for our self-determination even at the cost of permitting sin with its horrid consequences.

How, then, can God know with certainty and even predict what people will do without determining what they will do? For one thing, self-determination is according to one's nature, and God knows human nature with its limited knowledge and power at different times. (1) Prefallen persons were able to determine themselves in obedience to God or the contrary, disobedience to God. (2) As enslaved to sin people are able only to sin. (3) As regenerated by the Holy Spirit believers have two natures, an old and a new, so they again have the power of contrary choice, but faithfulness to God dominates. (4) When believers are resurrected, they will have one new nature confirmed in righteousness, and so they will be able only to glorify God. God as omniscient knows each of these states of the moral nature with certainty.

God also knows the hereditary factors contributing to one's personality. God knows ahead of time, not only the givens at one's conception and birth, but also one's grandparents, great grandparents, the entire family tree. In God's plan from before the foundation of the world God chooses from among all the hereditary factors in human life that make up the specific nature of each unique person. If, for example, he wants a prophet with the basic make-up of a Moses or an Elijah, he does not start looking at the available people, but can plan the appropriate genetic factors in the progenitors. As Erickson explains, God, foreknowing the infinite possibilities, chooses to bring into existence the individual who will freely

decide to respond to every situation precisely as God intends. By so doing, God renders *certain,* but not *necessary,* the free decisions and actions of the individual."[107]

God's omniscience from eternity also anticipates environmental, cultural, and subcultural influences and pressures. In the midst of these cultural occasions for our self-determination he can anticipate whether we will succumb or resist. As responsible agents we can consent to, or rebel against, our parents' style of life and our schools and their educational philosophies. Well-known counterculture movements support this ability, as do converts from capitalism to communism, and from communism to capitalism, to new religions and cults, and from them. God knows what we will do because he knows all of the factors contributing to our moral natures and cultural influences.

God also knows what we will choose spontaneously. He made us with a power of creativity like his own. And the completeness of his knowledge does not miss the possibilities and actualities of our creative abilities. Clearly these are within the limits of our physical, mental, moral, and spiritual natures, however, and not unlimited, like his. Spontaneous acts are not nonacts, and they too are known by God. But morally accountable behavior is self-determined, whether spontaneous or routine. According to Millard Erickson's concept of freedom, "the answer to the question 'could the individual have chosen differently?' is yes, while the answer to the question, 'But would he have?' is no."[108] Some concepts of freedom would require total spontaneity or random choice. Erickson's concept of freedom (and ours) more realistically accepts the fact that in human decisions and actions nothing is completely spontaneous or random.

God's plan includes all that he foreknows of the nature of human agency and its enslaved use as fallen. He also knows how it will be used when renewed and spiritually liberated. For morally corrective purposes he may choose to do some extraordinary things to regenerate a person's moral nature and so free up the ability to know, love, and serve him. God's initiative will be required when people are enslaved to sin and neither would nor could deliver themselves. However, God's certain knowledge of what we will do, is not confused in his mind with his certain knowledge of what he will do for us. And he knows what we will do when we are left to our sinful selves and what we will do with his gracious illumination and enablement. Either way our self-determination is involved.

What we determine in and of our sinful selves we cannot blame on our parents, our teachers, the other sex, the government, the Devil, or God. Under whatever pressures, persons are responsible for their responses, from conformity to rebellion. By foreknowing which will be the case with certainty, God does not thereby become the efficient cause or render it necessary by some compulsion. God can know with certainty which of the infinite possibilities we choose without compelling our choices. For our choices we remain responsible, and we will give account to him, the righteous Judge. To the extent that any view of the divine decrees takes away one's sense of accountability to God for his own decisions and actions, that understanding is unbiblical.

How could God's prophets predict specific future events produced by the complexities of human determinations far in advance? By foreknowing all the people involved with all their ordinary and spontaneous determinations, God could anticipate an eventuality with certainty without coercion. For example, in a case like the prediction of the Flood, without altering the responsibility of the wicked for their multiplying sins, God could himself determine their just punishment and introduce for the people of faith a way of deliverance. God could foresee the evils of Joseph's brothers and overrule them for Joseph's good. But God's introduction of beneficial results in no way changed the brothers' responsibility for their jealousy and hatred. More on how this works out in history has been examined in the chapter on providence.

Far from subverting responsibility, Christianity contributes to human responsibility precisely because all people will give account to an all-knowing, holy Judge. If the ultimate reality were impersonal, as in secular and pantheistic world views, we would never give account to an all-knowing Judge of our deeds, whether they are good or bad. In those philosophies we must live with the consequences of our choices, but we need not anticipate personal judgment. Christian theism results, not only in a sense of dependence, but also in a sense of obligation to the revealed purposes of the living God before whom we ultimately stand to give account.

Does Predestination Make History Meaningless?

The prior choice of ends and strategies by a coach does not as such make a football game meaningless. The execution of the plays by responsible members of the team is indispensable. Every business has its purposes. Management without goals would not be effective. With predetermined goals and strategies the manager can get things done through people. But the clarity of objectives does not make the employees' work unnecessary or insignificant. Academic courses have objectives that render the day-by-day activity of students more, rather than less, meaningful. Long trips have planned destinations that lend significance to each day's travel. The prior choice of ends for a career in sports or the military does not make the career meaningless.

So too, the ends God wisely chose for persons, families, nations, and churches mean that our efforts are not merely full of sound and fury, signifying nothing. God's eternal purposes give meaning to history. History is not a ceaseless repetition of meaningless cycles. Nor is human history like a telephone book with a great cast of characters, but no plot! God's grand design gives the course of history a wise, just, and gracious significance not only for time, but also for eternity.

Do the divinely chosen strategies render history meaningless? If God had chosen to accomplish everything independently of human agency by supernatural means, the objection might have force. But since God has sovereignly chosen generally to work in, with, and through people, people are far from unimportant in history. That God should at times plan, in view of permitting self-determining people to fall into sin, to use supernatural remedial strategies does not counter his plan to use human agencies normally. At least insofar as God's strategy is instrumental or conditional, the significance of human choices and activities is not erased but enhanced. And even his supernatural strategy is designed to rescue humans from the results of their sin and guarantee a just culmination of history.[109]

The Futility of Fatalism

According to the fatalistic hypothesis, what will happen, will happen, and nothing we do or do not do can make any difference. An impersonal, irrational, purposeless, inescapable force determines all of the apparently free choices of life. Freedom may not be absent, but it is subjected to a meaningless necessity that has no purpose. Since fatalism implies impersonal, un-

wise, unjust, and unloving ends, then Christianity cannot be classified as fatalistic. The heavenly Father wisely chose holy and loving ends.

Since fatalism also means that human agency makes no difference in the achieving of the ends, Christianity is not fatalistic. The Father sovereignly chose to achieve predetermined objectives generally by an instrumental strategy utilizing human volition, not bypassing it. Foreseeing that human wills would become enslaved to sin, God provided for their liberation to fulfill their destiny. A planned providence provides the loving support that makes life bearable; fate, on the other hand, renders all human striving futile. Christian self-determination is not rendered pointless, but meaningful eternally in the grand design of a personal God who creates personal beings for fellowship and shared objectives in work. Under sheer fate we can only face the future with despair. Under wise, loving, and just providence, we can face it with hope.[110] Is not the theistic option more viable (as well as more coherent)?

The Senselessness of Sheer Indeterminacy or Chance

Chance events in life are uncaused by either impersonal or personal forces. If things fall out by chance, our existence is contingent on uncalculated and uncalculable convergences of atoms in space. Life is then made up of unplanned, irrational happenings. The causes of human choices are not only unknown, but they have no rational antecedents, determinations, or occasions. On this hypothesis human behavior is completely uncaused.

Charles Sanders Pierce thought that the hypothesis of chance events accounts for the diversity of the universe. And William James thought that it provided a way out of the conflict between determinism and free will. Faced with a possible conflict between God's omniscience and chance, James concluded that God knows the ends he wishes achieved, but not necessarily the means to these ends. At various points in God's plan ambiguous possibilities exist, human free will comes into play, determining the means to already determined ends.[111]

In contrast, God's acts are determined not by ambiguity or chance, but by his own holy and loving nature. Similarly when God leaves decisions to human instrumentality, he does not leave them to an arbitrary will sporting in a vacuum but to persons who, among other activities, decide among alternatives and move to accomplish their chosen ends. As the evidence above shows, human decisions are not uncaused; they are self-determined. We cannot blame chance; mature people accept responsibility for their own choices.

The Dehumanization of Naturalistic Determinism

Naturalists picture the cosmos as a most unusual machine (without a personal being inventing, manufacturing, maintaining, and running it). It follows that naturalistic determinists try to show that for everything that happens, there are conditions, such that, given them, nothing else could have happened. People's choices are determined allegedly by antecedent physical and psychological causes, including hereditary factors in the person's genetic make-up and physical condition. This theory, however, fails to account for the data of Scripture and of consciousness. It overlooks the reality of personal agency and reduces persons to events. Nontheistic determinism leaves people irresponsible and unaccountable for moral decisions. Furthermore, a secularistic determinism fails to explain adequately the human ability to rebel

against environmental and cultural influences. Environmental givens—economical, psychological, and otherwise—may preset some insuperable limits. Yet in other respects, people may be strongly influenced, but not invariably determined. Many cultural pressures may be major, but they can be rejected or changed. So in matters of moral responsibility it becomes more accurate to speak of cultural occasions of human decisions, rather than of the cultural determination of those decisions.

The hypothesis of determinism fails to account for the givens of spontaneity, deliberation, free choice, creativity, moral responsibility, and the ability to pursue ends. We are people who act, not merely people who are acted upon. We are not free when we are caused to act by an external force or compulsion. But when we are not under external compulsion, we have power over the determinations of our own wills to cause our own actions. Unlike other living things, we are self-moved and engage in creative activities.[112]

Adam and Eve could have resisted temptation; they could have said no. However culturally or satanically tempted by the thirty pieces of silver, Judas himself coveted the money and responsibly determined to betray Christ. Even spouses or mature children who allow themselves to be dominated by another family member for years may have some responsibility for giving in for so long. In God's plan we are not mere victims; we initially give in to our addictions. In his image we are self-determining, responsible agents within the limits of our created, fallen, and regenerated natures. The glorification of Christians, of course, awaits Christ's second coming.

By way of summary and conclusion, we do not claim to fully comprehend all that is involved in God's sovereign plans from eternity and what the rela-

327

tion of those plans are to human freedom in time, especially in regard to the lost. What we have here found is that, of the hypotheses surveyed, an infralapsarian Calvinist (or Arminian) decree of conditional reprobation is (1) without logical contradiction, (2) the most adequate in accounting for the relevant biblical evidence with the fewest difficulties, and (3) tenable without hypocrisy in the face of either the awful results of sin or the awesome trophies of divine grace. In connection with soteriology more will be said about the decrees concerning the saved.

RELEVANCE FOR LIFE AND MINISTRY

Great Joy in Being Chosen

Everyone who believes does so because he or she is chosen by the Father from the foundation of the world, redeemed by the atonement of Jesus Christ, and enabled by the Holy Spirit. Far from producing pride, the truth of the Father's gracious choice of a sinner who deserved only his wrath, leads to humility before him. Those who are justified by grace through faith have nothing of which to boast (Eph. 2:8–9).

For an example of how acceptance of God's elective purpose can bring blessing, consider the perspective of Charles Haddon Spurgeon, who said:

> I believe the doctrine of election, because I am quite sure that if God had not chosen me I should never have chosen Him; and I am sure He chose me before I was born, or else He never would have chosen me afterwards; and He must have elected me for reasons unknown to me, for I never could find any reason in myself why He should have looked upon me with special love. So I am forced to accept that doctrine. I am bound to the doctrine of the depravity of the human heart, because I find myself depraved in heart, and have daily proofs that there dwelleth in my flesh no good thing."[113]

In many Christian minds lurks the fear that their sanctification, if not their justification, depends on their working for Christ from morning until night. James W. Ney confessed, "When I admitted that according to the Scriptures there was no justification apart from God's loving choice, my life began to change."[114] The burden of his own stewardship was lifted. His work for Christ was no longer done out of fear or necessity, but purely out of love for being accepted though unacceptable.

Relief From the Weight of the World on Our Shoulders

Many other questions trouble young Christians, especially about their work for Christ. "What is my responsibility for the spiritual condition of the billions of people in the world? Am I the ultimately responsible person for winning every relative, friend, acquaintance, and contact to Christ? How can I overcome the constant worry and fear that if any souls perish it will be all my fault?"

Study of our heavenly Father's decrees should help us realize that the weight of the whole world is not on our shoulders. Ultimately it is on God's shoulders. And we are assured that his judgments are absolutely just. No sinners will ever be punished more than they deserve. No sinners have any claim on God's grace. He can freely give it to whom he will.

Jesus illustrated these principles in the parable of the workers in the vineyard, some of whom worked from early morning, others from morning break time, others from the beginning of the afternoon, and some only after the afternoon break (Matt. 20:1–16). No injustices were done to any of the people who worked, whether for all day or a small part of it. Those who worked all day received what they deserved; those who worked less time received the same amount—more than they deserved. Those who worked from early morning for the full day complained that they were treated unjustly (v. 12) But the landowner said, "Friend, I am not being unfair to you. Didn't you agree to work for a denarius? Take your pay and go. I want to give the man who was hired last the same as I gave you. Don't I have the right to do what I want with my own money? Or are you envious because I am generous?" (vv. 13–15). In this teaching Jesus kept the categories of justice and grace (generosity) clear. We will avoid unnecessary worry about injustice if we do not charge God with injustice for his generosity to many sinners. While treating all justly, he has a right to give good gifts generously to the elect. The ultimate responsibility for who receives salvation and who does not is not ours, but his.

True, God's strategy is to use human witnesses in presenting the way of salvation. At most, however, our responsibility is intermediate, not ultimate. The ultimate burden of who is saved and who is lost does not rest with an evangelist, a pastor, a Sunday school teacher, a parent, a missionary, a church board, or the board of a mission society (1 Cor. 3:5–6). It is God who gives the increase (though all of those mentioned above have been used in the history of the growth of the Christian church and its outreach in foreign missions). Christians who have done what they can may rest at night knowing that in the final analysis, God's sovereignty guides the mission boards and the missionaries to the people whom he will enable to respond to the gospel. Liberated from the ultimate burden and confident of being called by God, we can serve God and the lost more effectively.[115]

Many think that acceptance of a Calvinistic view of election destroys any evangelistic zeal and missionary outreach. However, for many the assurance that God has elected some to respond encourages them in the tough tasks of preevangelism and evangelism. God has chosen not only the end of salvation, but also the means—human instruments. As it pleases God he will produce the fruit of our labors.

Others imagine that belief in predestination cuts their desire to pray. If God knows who will be saved, why should we pray for the unreached people we seek to reach with the gospel of grace? The heartfelt intercession of Paul, who wrote much about God's election, pleaded that his fellow Israelites might be saved (Rom. 10:1). If God had done in prevenient grace all that he could justly do for Paul's friends (as Arminians think), there would be no point in praying further for them. In praying for the lost, we express our faith that God can without injustice graciously transform contemporary Sauls into Pauls. When all are on their knees, they seem to be Calvinists.

Similarly, college and seminary studies and sermon and Sunday-school lesson preparations may be viewed as elements in God's instrumental strategy, rather than interruptions in God's work. When God becomes the center and circumference of our theology, our lives begin to show our confidence in him. Peace and joy become realities of experience. Fellowship with the heavenly Father becomes a heartwarming reality for his children, not merely a biblical word-study or a name for a group.

A Transcendent, Changeless Source of Meaning in Life

The Scriptures do not present God's eternal purposes for his people as a source of tension or a logical problem but as a great spiritual blessing in Christ (Eph. 1:3). Indeed the Father's grand design gives purpose to Christians in the present and gives them hope for the future (vv. 8–10).

Many non-Christians have no sense of purpose in the whole of history or in their own lives. Although scientists have generally excluded personal agency and final causes from their methodology, there is continuous evidence of responsible human agencies in our daily activities. How strange to imagine that every meaningful thing we do has a purpose but that the totality of our lives has no point! Purpose in every meaningful human act reflects purpose in the universe as a whole.

Persistent attacks on teleological evidence by those who refuse to believe in the intelligent, purposeful heavenly Father, have caused some existentialist Christians to limit confident affirmation of God's revealed purposeful ends to the subjectivity of believers' hearts. However, the Scriptures are emphatic, and we too should be, that according to one strategy or another, everything in nature, history, and our lives has a purpose in God's grand design.[116]

The Only Assurance That Good Will Triumph Over Evil

People who have no transcendent, sovereign source, support, and guarantor of values, have insufficient reason for believing that history will end in a way that they could approve of.

Many alternative proposals are popular, but they all fail to certify a just end to history. "Evolution" cannot assure us of that hope. Evolution has produced no major change in essential humanness in all the years of human existence on earth. There is no evidence that quantum jumps in evolution will occur or, if they should, that they would be for the better rather than for the worse.

Dialectical materialism has failed to produce a classless, peaceful, society without need for massive military and police might to put down the rest-

lessness of the self-determining human hearts. The hypothesis that forceful revolution can produce permanent peace lacks adequate support in the history of humanity in general and in the history of Marxism-Leninism in particular. Marxism's promise of eventual peace is belied by preparation for war.

To project confidence in a pointless world, however heroic it may seem, is not the mark of intelligent commitment. Instead it represents wishful thinking contrary to the evidence of divine revelation.

Or to hold with Sartre that man is "a useless passion" with no lasting meaning does not provide freedom for significant existential involvement in the battles of life. This philosophy involves mankind in nothing more than an endless, losing fight with ultimate absurdity.[117]

In contrast to the world's unfounded hope for a just peace, Christians may confidently trust in God's changeless nature and eternal plan, which includes the triumphant return of Christ to unify the world. That hope is based on the reliable revelation of God's great purpose. "Because God wanted to make the *unchanging nature of his purpose* very clear to the heirs of what was promised, he *confirmed it with an oath*. God did this so that, by two unchangeable things in which it is impossible for God to lie, we who have fled to take hold of the hope offered to us may be greatly encouraged. We have this hope as an anchor for the soul, firm and secure" (Heb. 6:17–19, italics added).

A Paradigm of Goal-Oriented Living and Ministering

The tendency of many teachers and ministers is to be problem-oriented in serving the Lord, rather than goal-oriented. We cannot ignore problems, but they can best be met from the perspective of long-range, affirmative goals. The Father in heaven established a goal-oriented kingdom that at the same time provides for solving humanity's deepest problem—sin. So at least in our problem solving, we do well to follow our Father's example and have some positive goals encompassing our problems and more. Paul did not simply plead with Euodia and Syntyche to agree with each other in the Lord (Phil. 4:2); he first laid the groundwork for the attempt at problem solving by praying that all members of the Philippian church under Christ might share the objective of "having the same love, being one in the spirit and *purpose*" (2:2). Encouraging others to have attitudes like that of Christ, who gave up glory in heaven out of concern for the interests of others, our attempts to solve disputes among church members should be more effective if these attempts are made in the context of a constructive objective of continuous unity for all members "in spirit and purpose."

Aligning Our Purposes With God's Chosen Ends

Pastors and officers of churches, as other institutions, do well to write out the long-range goals of the institution. Those churches that aim at nothing are sure to accomplish their aim. Each church can profit from the discipline of formulating its *raison d'être* for itself in its particular location at its particular time. The stated purpose provides the reference point for periodic evaluations of the leaders in ministry and of all church officers. How well has the church done in the preceding year in accomplishing its chosen ends? In what ways is it succeeding or failing, and why? By what changes of focus or personnel can it do better?

The reasons for a particular church's existence, however detailed and specific, ought to be in harmony with the ultimate ends God has chosen for the church (both universal and local). When that is the case, there will be regard for nature and its laws as God's creation and respect for the value of self-determining people created in God's image. People's most basic problem will be seen to be moral and spiritual rebellion against God, resulting in alienation from God. And the focal point of ministry in seeking to meet that need will be the proclamation of the atoning provision of Jesus Christ. Other ministries, however beneficial in themselves, must not take the place of the divine priority for Christians individually and collectively in churches in the present age.

From God's general, transcultural exhortations, we know of other divine purposes for our lives and ministries. God desires that his people be stewards of and rule over lower forms of life. God plans to use us as witnesses, as salt, light, saints, ambassadors, co-regents in his kingdom, and co-builders in his church. He desires that we be sanctified through the truth of the Word (John 17:17–19), testify to the truth (18:37), honor God with our bodies (1 Cor. 6:20), and do all to the glory of God (10:31). God also wills that we excel in using our gifts to build up the church (14:12) so that all may reach unity in the faith and become mature in the fullness of Christ (Eph. 4:12–13). In brief, "we make it our goal to please him" (2 Cor. 5:9).

Choosing Strategies in Harmony With God's Strategies

A person or church can have the best list of ends in the world, but they are unlikely to be efficiently achieved without similar consideration of the wisest strategies for achieving them. It is also beneficial to spell out the role and responsibility that each officer fulfills in order to achieve those goals. And these ought to be consistent with the Father's strategies for attaining his ends in the world. No strategy will be attempted to accomplish what God has chosen to do miraculously without human instrumentality, though we will want to be available should the Father desire to work through us in extraordinary ways. We cannot manipulate the Almighty. But the church's primary responsibility is to set its goals for the ordinary, day-by-day responsibilities God has delegated to it.

Coercive means of programing and deprograming persons against their wills should not be used. God himself respected his self-determining creatures enough to permit them to make mistakes. People's value as creatures of God will be esteemed. The human rights of persons in God's image ought to be respected. Christian churches will use only ethically persuasive methods such as preaching, teaching, and personal dialogue. People who do not repent of sin, believe the gospel and trust Christ will not be pressured into church membership, whether younger or older, richer or poorer. Our strategies will take into account not only our good purposes but also the person's abilities to respond to them under normal circumstances. And our strategies will not be completed when justification by faith and church membership are achieved, but assistance will continue for all members in their growth toward the goals of spiritual maturity. The development of worthy ends with commendable strategies will be encouraged by the hope of the coming universal unity at the return of Christ. Until the day of Christ's return, we will recommit ourselves to faithful work toward ends consistent with God's ends, and strategies in harmony with God's strategies. We have been brought from spiritual death to life for a grand purpose. Our election is "a call to service, a summons to be a co-laborer with God in the actualization of God's elective purpose and goal."[118]

Has God a Detailed Plan for Our Lives?

In addition to the general moral and spiritual ends for all Christians, has God a detailed plan for each person, family, and church? Beyond general purposes, evidence indicates that the Father planned a number of specific matters. Apparently God chose Adam and Eve to be the first parents of the human race, Abraham to be the father of a great nation, Noah and family to sustain the race through the flood, Saul to be Israel's first king, David to rule as his successor, the prophets and apostles to be his spokesmen, and Paul to be the catalyst for uniting Gentiles with the Jews in the Christian church. To members of Christ's body the Holy Spirit gives gifts, just as he determines (1 Cor. 12:11). From such indications we might consider it probable that God has specific plans for all of his people.

If God has such detailed plans for us in his comprehensive purposes, he has not, like a travel agent, listed the various routes we are to take to the end of our journey. Instead he made us self-determining beings who can be guided by his entire revelation, both general and special. In seeking to make a decision, we do not ask for a revelation of God's will beyond what he chose to reveal, but for his leading in making a decision in harmony with his revealed purposes and strategies. A Christian way of life based on the primary data of the entirety of revelation, general and special, includes not only explicit moral teachings but many ethical inferences for life and ministry (such as we seek to exhibit briefly in each chapter of this volume).[119]

However, making decisions on matters not specifically discussed according to God's moral principles is often more difficult than it appears. Which principles apply in a given case? What is their order of priority? Exactly how do we apply them? To make decisions in accord with the moral will of God, we do well to take more fully into account the moral and ethical implications of the entirety of Scripture in the coherent manner of Christian writers in *ethics*. The study of secondary sources in moral theology ought not be ignored.[120]

Ordinarily God's promised guidance (Ps. 32:8) of repentant believers (vv. 3–5) who pray for leading (vv. 6–7) is not by the force of "bit and bridle" (v. 9). Neither is it by nonrational means like Ouija boards, witches, or cards, but through his "instruction" and "counsel" (v. 8). The Lord's instruction and counsel is found in the option that most coherently accounts for all lines of relevant data such as: (1) all that special revelation now in Scripture teaches relevant to the options (primarily, but not exclusively moral instruction) and (2) all that general revelation indicates in our experience, including (a) our recognition of our spiritual gifts, (b) the counsel of qualified persons, (c) providentially ordered experiential data and (d) our persistent desire for the option in order to glorify God.

Having gathered all these data, we arrive at a decision about the wisest course of action in accord with the *criteria of God's truth* on any other matter. Our option sufficiently corresponds with God's thoughts when (1) without any contradiction (2) it accounts for all the relevant lines of evidence (explicit and implied) and (3) we can live by it without hypocrisy. The Holy Spirit guides us in the process of decision making according to these criteria. He then witnesses with our spirits to the objective validity of the truth discovered and its personal, subjective applicability, and this gives us a sense of peace.

The degree of psychological assurance of having discovered a course of action pleasing to God depends on many intellectual factors contributing to a well-founded conviction. Intellectually the degree of probability depends on (1) the amount of relevant material from general and special revelation perused, (2) the validity of our interpretive principles and our skill in the art of applying them, (3) the soundness of our criteria of truth and skill in applying them to all the relevant areas of instruction and life, and (4) the reliability of our method of reasoning for arriving at well-founded conclusions.[121] With strong probability that a decision based on the convergence of many of these factors is right, there should develop a strong inner assurance that we have a course of action in accord with his plan.

We need all of these checks and balances because we are so easily tempted to take short cuts, prematurely claiming to know God's plans with finality when, much like presumptuous prophets, we think and speak out of our own hearts. Another reason why we need these checks and balances is that on a similar issue equally able and dedicated Christians often come to different and even opposite conclusions. In life's decisions we generally act on conclusions with degrees of intellectual probability depending on the extent of the relevant evidence and our skill in handling it (2 Tim. 2:15). But knowing God's good purposes for us and his promise to lead us in our sincere search, we endeavor to order our lives for his glory. Through this process the Holy Spirit gives the psychological assurance that he has led us with his "eye."

We ought never dictate to God what we have concluded he must will. However, assured of the Lord's leading, we will always proceed on ventures with the proviso of James, "If it is the Lord's will, we will live and do this or that'' (James 4:15). That qualification need not reflect a lack of faith on our part that what God promised he will do (Rom. 4:21). Rather, it may indicate awareness that we are not inerrant in even the best judgments of our finite minds concerning the future.

REVIEW QUESTIONS

To Help Relate and Apply Each Section in This Chapter

1. *Briefly state the classical problem* this chapter addresses and indicate reasons why genuine inquiry into it is important for your world view and your existence personally and socially.

2. *Objectively summarize the influential answers* given to this problem in history as hypotheses to be tested. Be able to compare and contrast their real similarities and differences (not merely verbal similarities or differences).

3. *Highlight the primary biblical evidence* on which to decide among views—evidence found in the relevant teachings of the major divisions of Scripture—and decide for yourself which historical hypothesis (or synthesis of historical views) provides the most consistent and adequate account of the primary biblical data.

4. *Formulate in your own words your doctrinal conviction* in a logically consistent and adequate way, organizing your conclusions in ways you can explain clearly, support biblically, and communicate effectively to your spouse, children, friends, Bible class, or congregation.

5. *Defend your view* as you would to adherents of the alternative views, showing that the other views are logically less consistent and factually faced with more difficulties than your view in accounting for the givens, not only of special revelation but also of human experience in general.

6. *Explore the differences the viabil-*

ity of your conviction can make in your life. Then test your understanding of the viability of your view by asking, "Can I live by it authentically (unhypocritically) in relation to God and to others in my family, church, vocation, neighborhood, city, nation, and world?"

MINISTRY PROJECTS

To Help Communicate This Doctrine in Christian Service

1. *Memorize one major verse or passage* that in its context teaches the heart of this doctrine and may serve as a text from which to preach, teach, or lead small group studies on the topic. The memorized passages from each chapter will build a body of content useful also for meditation and reference in informal discussions.

2. *Formulate the major idea of the doctrine in one sentence* based on the passage memorized. This idea should be useful as the major thesis of either a lesson for a class (junior high to adult) or a message for a church service.

3. *State the specific purpose or goal of your doctrinal lesson or message.* Your purpose should be more than informative. It should show why Christians need to accept this truth and live by it (unhypocritically). For teaching purposes, list indicators that would show to what extent class members have grasped the truth presented.

4. *Outline your message or lesson in complete sentences.* Indicate how you would support the truth of the doctrine's central ideas and its relevance to life and service. Incorporate elements from this chapter's historical, biblical, systematic, apologetic, and practical sections selected according to the value they have for your audience.

5. *List applications of the doctrine* for communicating the difference this conviction makes in life (for sermons, lessons, small-group Bible studies, or

family devotional Bible studies). Applications should make clear what the doctrine is, why one needs to know it, and how it will make differences in thinking. Then show how the difference in thought will lead to differences in values, priorities, attitudes, speech, and personal action. Consider also the doctrine's possible significance for family, church, neighborhood, city, regional, and national actions.

6. *Start a file and begin collecting illustrations* of this doctrine's central idea, the points in your outline, and your applications.

7. *Write out your own doctrinal state-* *ment on this subject in one paragraph* (in half a page or less). To work toward a comprehensive doctrinal statement, collect your formulations based on a study of each chapter of *Integrative Theology.* As your own statement of Christian doctrine grows, you will find it personally strengthening and useful when you are called on for your beliefs in general and when you apply for service with churches, mission boards, and other Christian organizations. Any who seek ordination to Christian ministry will need a comprehensive doctrinal statement that covers the broad scope of theology.

Notes

Preface

[1] Bernard Ramm, *After Fundamentalism: The Future of Evangelical Theology* (San Francisco: Harper & Row, 1983), 27.

[2] Ibid.

[3] For additional comparison and contrast of these three methods of decision making, see Gordon R. Lewis, "Schaeffer's Apologetic Method," in Reflections on Francis Schaeffer ed. Ronald W. Reugsegger (Grand Rapids: Zondervan, 1986), 69–104.

Chapter One

[1] Francis Schaeffer, *A Christian Manifesto* (Westchester: Crossway, 1981), 4.

[2] B. A. Demarest, "Systematic Theology," *EDT*, 1064–66; George Ladd, *A Theology of the New Testament* (Grand Rapids: Eerdmans, 1974), 25–26; David Wells, *The Search for Salvation* (Downers Grove: InterVarsity, 1978), 23–28, 36–46; Klaus Bockmuhl, "The Task of Systematic Theology," ed. Kenneth S. Kantzer and Stanley N. Gundry, *Perspectives on Evangelical Theology* (Grand Rapids: Baker, 1979), 3–14.

[3] Cornelius Van Til, *An Introduction to Systematic Theology* (Unpublished syllabus, 1971). Rousas John Rushdoony, *The Necessity for Systematic Theology* (Valliceto, Calif.: Ross House, 1979).

[4] Gordon Clark, *Karl Barth's Theological Method* (Philadelphia: Presbyterian and Reformed, 1963). Carl Henry, *God, Revelation and Authority* (Waco: Word, 1976), vol. 1.

[5] Millard J. Erickson, *Christian Theology*, 3 vols. (Grand Rapids: Baker, 1983–85), 1:21.

[6] John Jefferson Davis, *Foundations of Evangelical Theology* (Grand Rapids: Baker, 1984).

[7] Considering biblical teaching as evidence, compare the steps in a scientific method in Irving M. Copi, *Introduction to Logic*, 6th ed. (New York: Macmillan, 1982), 470–75.

[8] Erickson, *Christian Theology*, 1:78.

[9] For initial ideas in this direction from the Old Testament see Walter Kaiser, *Toward an Exegetical Theology* (Grand Rapids: Baker, 1981), 139. More will be said on this in future volumes, d.v.

[10] For criteria of truth and ways of defending the existence of the God revealed in the Jesus of history and the teaching of Scripture, see Gordon R. Lewis, *Testing Christianity's Truth Claims* (Chicago: Moody, 1976), esp. chapters 7–10, and appendix.

[11] Adapted from Henry A. Virkler, *Hermeneutics: Principles and Processes of Biblical Interpretation* (Grand Rapids: Baker, 1981), 117.

[12] On the missiological issue of contextualizing the message in terms of the hearers' horizons see John Jefferson Davis, "Contextualization and the Nature of Theology" in his *The Necessity of Systematic Theology* (Grand Rapids: Baker, 1978), 169–85.

[13] *Metaphysical Bible Dictionary* (Lee's Summit, Mo.: Unity School of Christianity, 1954); Mary Baker Eddy, *Science and Health with Key to the Scriptures* (Boston: First Church of Christ Scientist, 1932).

[14] For chapters on the doctrinal use of Scripture see Bernard Ramm, *Protestant Biblical Interpretation* (Boston: W. A. Wilde, 1956) and Berkeley Michaelsen, *Interpreting the Bible* (Grand Rapids: Eerdmans, 1963).

[15] See Copi, *Introduction to Logic*, chapter on defining terms, 138–73.

[16] William L. Reese, "Laws of Thought," in *Dictionary of Philosophy and Religion* (Atlantic Highlands, N.J.: Humanities, 1980), 297.

[17] See Copi, *Introduction to Logic*, chapter on immediate references, 177–202.

[18] See John Jefferson Davis, *Foundations of Systematic Theology* (Grand Rapids: Baker, 1984), 136.

[19] Bruce Demarest, "Christendom's Creeds: Their Relevance in the Modern World," *Journal of Evangelical Theological Society,* vol. 21, no. 4 (Dec. 1978): 345–56.

[20] L. Harold DeWolf, *The Case for Theology in a Liberal Perspective* (Philadelphia: Westminster, 1959), 19–41.

[21] Anthony Thiselton, *The Two Horizons* (Grand Rapids: Eerdmans, 1980).

[22] Charles Kraft, *Christianity in Culture* (Maryknoll: Orbis, 1979).

[23] John Jefferson Davis, "Contextualization and the Nature of Theology" in his *The Necessity of Systematic Theology* (Grand Rapids: Baker, 1978), 169–85.

[24] For reading on cultural factors in interpretation see Walter C. Kaiser, "Legitimate Hermeneutics," in *Inerrancy,* ed. Norman L. Geisler (Grand Rapids: Zondervan, 1980), 141–44; Gordon R. Lewis, "The Human Authorship of Inspired Scripture" in *Inerrancy,* 229–51; Alan Johnson, "History and Culture in the New Testament Interpretation," ed. Samuel J. Schultz and Morris Inch, in *Interpreting the Word of God* (Chicago: Moody, 1976), 128–61; R. C. Sproul, *Knowing Scripture* (Downers Grove: InterVarsity, 1977), 101–12; Henry A. Virkler, *Hermeneutics: Principles and Processes of Biblical Interpretation* (Grand Rapids: Baker, 1981), 211–32.

[25] On breaking out of the hermeneutical circles or assumptions, see Gordon R. Lewis, "A Response to Presuppositions of Non-Evangelical Hermeneutics" in *Hermeneutics, Inerrancy and the Bible,* Earl D. Radmacher and Robert D. Preus, eds. (Grand Rapids: Zondervan, 1984), 615–26.

[26] Watchman Nee, *The Spiritual Man* (New York: Christian Fellowship Publications, 1968), 3 vols.

[27] Clark Pinnock, "Prospects for Systematic Theology," ed. David F. Wells, *Toward a Theology for the Future* (Carol Stream: Creation House, 1971), 96.

[28] A. J. Ayer, *Language, Truth and Logic* (New York: Dover, 1946), 114–20.

[29] Alan Watts, *The Way of Zen* (New York: Random House, 1957), 115.

[30] Alan Watts, *Beyond Theology: The Art of Godmanship* (New York: Vintage Books, 1964).

[31] John Bright, *The Authority of the Old Testament* (Grand Rapids: Baker, 1978), 159.

[32] Ibid., 116.

[33] Ibid., 131.

[34] Ibid., 140.

[35] Ibid., 47–48, 115, 125.

[36] Ibid., 130.

[37] John Gill, *Body of Divinity* (Atlanta: Turner Lasseter, 1957), xxiv–xxv.

[38] Andrew Murray, *With Christ in the School of Prayer* (New York: Loizeaux Brothers, n.d.), 171–72.

[39] Ibid.

[40] Francis Brown, S. R. Driver, and C. A. Briggs, *A Hebrew and English Lexicon* (Oxford: Clarendon, 1907), 54; Gerhard Kittel, *TDNT,* 10 vols., 1:232–47.

[41] Gordon R. Lewis, "God's Word: Key to Authentic Spirituality" in *A Call to Christian Character,* ed. Bruce Shelley (Grand Rapids: Zondervan, 1970), 111.

[42] Thor Hall, *A Theology of Christian Devotion* (Nashville: The Upper Room, 1969), 90, 74–75.

[43] W. G. T. Shedd, *Dogmatic Theology,* 3 vols. (Grand Rapids: Zondervan, n.d.), 1:5.

[44] For an exposition and defense of post-Reformation Lutheran orthodoxy see Robert D. Preus, *The Theology of Post-Reformation Lutheranism,* 2 vols. (St. Louis: Concordia, 1970–72); for the views of Reformation and post-Reformation divines, see Heinrich Heppe, *Reformed Dogmatics* (London: Allen and Unwin, 1950).

[45] Cited in Hubert Cunliffe-Jones, *History of Christian Doctrine* (Philadelphia: Fortress, 1980), 431.

[46] Karl Rahner, *TI,* 5:115–34.

[47] Hans Küng, *On Being a Christian* (Garden City, N.Y.: Doubleday, 1976), 21.

[48] Paul Tillich, *The Courage to Be* (New Haven: Yale University Press, 1952), 179.

[49] Ibid., 177–80.

[50] Frank Vanden Berg, *Abraham Kuyper* (Grand Rapids: Eerdmans, 1960), 282.

[51] A. C. Headlam, *Christian Theology* (Oxford: Clarendon, 1934), 3–4.

Chapter Two

[1] A. C. Headlam, *Christian Theology* (Oxford: Clarendon, 1934), 7.

[2] Thomas Aquinas, *ST,* I.12.13.

[3] Henry P. Van Dusen, *The Vindication of Liberal Theology* (New York: Scribner, 1963), 77.

4 L. Harold DeWolf, *A Theology of the Living Church* (New York: Harper, 1953), 24.

5 Ibid., 65.

6 Friedrich Schleiermacher, *The Christian Faith* (Reprint, Philadelphia: Fortress, 1976), 133.

7 Paul Tillich, *Systematic Theology*, 3 vols. (Chicago: University of Chicago Press, 1951–63), 1:110.

8 Ibid., 1:12.

9 Karl Rahner, *TI*, X:36.

10 See ibid., V:115–34 for Rahner's development of this expression.

11 Cited by Henri Bouillard, *The Knowledge of God* (New York: Herder & Herder, 1967), 12–13.

12 Karl Barth, *CD*, vol. 2, pt. 1, 173.

13 Ibid., vol. 1, pt. 1, 192.

14 Ibid., vol. 1, pt. 2, 306.

15 For Barth's development of this idea, see *CD*, vol. 2, pt. 2, 306ff. and vol. 2, pt. 2, 345ff.

16 G. C. Berkouwer, "General and Special Revelation," in *Revelation and the Bible*, ed. C. F. H. Henry (Grand Rapids: Baker, 1976), 15.

17 Van Til maintains not only that the sinner cannot know God's general revelation, but that "the natural man is spiritually blind with respect to everything." *An Introduction to Systematic Theology: In Defense of the Faith* (Nutley, N.J.: Presbyterian and Reformed, 1974), 82.

18 Theophilus, *To Autolychus*, I.5; cf. Tatian, *Address to the Greeks*, IV; XII.

19 Clement of Alexandria, *Miscellanies*, V.13.

20 Tertullian, *The Apology*, XVII.6; *Against Marcion*, I.10.

21 Origen, *On First Principles*, I.1.6; Athanasius, *Against the Heather*, III.35–36; Cyril of Jerusalem, *Catechetical Lectures*, IX.16; XI.2; Gregory of Nyssa, *The Beatitudes*, sermon no. 6.

22 Augustine, *Sermons on the New Testament*, XCI.2.

23 Martin Luther, *LW*, vol. XXVI, 299.

24 John Calvin, *Institutes of the Christian Religion*, I.xvi.1.

25 Charles Hodge, *Systematic Theology* (Reprint, Grand Rapids: Eerdmans, 1973), 21–25.

26 Carl F. H. Henry, *God, Revelation and Authority*, 6 vols. (Waco: Word, 1976–83), 1:399–402; 2:69–76, 83–90.

27 Henry C. Thiessen, *Lectures in Systematic Theology* (Grand Rapids: Eerdmans, 1979), 7–10.

28 Dale Moody, *The Word of Truth* (Grand Rapids: Eerdmans, 1981), 57–77, 276–77.

29 Millard J. Erickson, *Christian Theology*, 3 vols. (Grand Rapids: Baker, 1983–85), 1:154–74.

30 Walter Brueggemann, *Genesis* (Atlanta: John Knox, 1982), 16.

31 In subsequent chapters of Genesis Moses presents a rich description of God's character, his works, and especially the unfolding of his saving purposes vis-à-vis his chosen people Israel.

32 According to Francis I. Anderson, the focus of God's universal revelation in the Job text is twofold: "So far as the world is concerned, God's wisdom is seen in its variegation and its order. So far as man is concerned, God's wisdom is expressed in his moral conduct." *Job* (Downers Grove: InterVarsity, 1976), 262.

33 Bertil Gärtner, *The Areopagus Speech and Natural Revelation* (Lund: Gleerup, 1955), 178.

34 See William Neil, *The Acts of the Apostles. NCBC*, 191.

35 *BAGD*, 291.

36 John Murray, *The Epistle to the Romans*, 2 vols. (Grand Rapids: Eerdmans, 1959), 1:40.

37 So G. C. Berkouwer, *General Revelation* (Grand Rapids: Eerdmans, 1955), 175–87. According to Berkouwer the law of God works on the human heart from without; it is not implanted in the heart as an innate endowment.

38 The NIV margin reading (so also the AV) sets forth the preferred translation. "Everyman . . . . coming into the world" is the rabbinic way of saying, "Everyone who is born." See R. V. G. Tasker, *St. John* (London: Inter-Varsity, 1960), 46.

39 Tasker, *St. John*, 42.

40 Alfred Plummer, *The Gospel According to St. John* (Grand Rapids: Baker, 1981), 68.

41 For a thorough study of the biblical content see Bruce Demarest, *General Revelation: Historical Views and Contemporary Issues* (Grand Rapids: Zondervan, 1982), 227–62. For an example of reading more into divine revelation in nature than warranted scripturally or experientially see A. H. Seiss, *The Gospel in the Stars* (Grand Rapids: Kregel, 1972). The stars are "signs" of agricultural, not redemptive significance (Gen. 1:14). In an agricultural context, the stars served as signs of "seasons," "days," and "years" for planting and

harvesting. See Basil F. C. Atkinson, *The Book of Genesis* in *The Pocket Commentary of the Bible* (Chicago: Moody, 1957), 18.

[42] H. P. Owen, "Theism," *EP*, 8:97.

[43] William Reese, *Dictionary of Philosophy and Religion: Eastern and Western* (Atlantic Highlands, N.J.: Humanities, 1980), 462.

[44] Friedrich Schleiermacher, *The Christian Faith*, ed. H. R. Machintosh and J. S. Steward (Philadelphia: Fortress, 1976), 133.

[45] Immanuel Kant, *Critique of Practical Reason*, II, Conclusion, ed. R. M. Hutchins, *Great Books of the Western World* (Chicago: Encyclopedia Britannica, 1952), 42:360.

[46] Reinhold Niebuhr, *The Nature and Destiny of Man* (New York: Scribner, 1943), 135.

[47] Gordon R. Lewis, "Faith and Reason in the Thought of St. Augustine" (Unpublished dissertation, University Microfilm Syracuse University, 1959), 25–54.

[48] Gordon R. Lewis, *Testing Christianity's Truth Claims* (Chicago: Moody, 1976) compares six systems of reasoning to the existence of the God revealed in the Jesus of history and the teachings of Scripture.

[49] Dale Moody, *The Word of Truth* (Grand Rapids: Eerdmans, 1981), 59.

[50] Emil Brunner, *Revelation and Reason*, 76.

[51] J. N. D. Anderson, *Christianity and Comparative Religion* (Downers Grove: InterVarsity, 1970), 102, 105. See also A. H. Strong, *Systematic Theology* (Philadelphia: Judson, n.d.), 843–44; W. G. T. Shedd, *Dogmatic Theology*, 3 vols. (Grand Rapids: Zondervan, n.d.), 2:704–12.

[52] Charles Hodge, *Systematic Theology* (Grand Rapids: Eerdmans, 1946), 2:646–48; Robert E. Speer, *The Finality of Jesus Christ* (Westwood, N.J.: Revell, n.d.); Gordon Lewis, *Judge for Yourself* (Downers Grove: InterVarsity, 1977), 26–35.

[53] Corliss Lamont, *The Philosophy of Humanism* (New York: Frederick Unger, 1982), 197.

[54] Ibid., 286.

[55] S. H. Kellogg, *A Handbook of Comparative Religion* (Grand Rapids: Eerdmans, 1951), 7–9.

[56] Aldous Huxley, Introduction, in *The Song of God: Bhagavad-Gita* (New York: New Americana Library, 1951), 12.

[57] Ibid., 13.

[58] Huston Smith, *Forgotten Truth: The Primordial Tradition* (New York: Harper & Row, 1976), 152.

[59] Ibid., 52–56.

[60] Ibid., 58.

[61] C. S. Lewis, *Miracles* (New York: Macmillan, 1948), 105.

[62] Ibid., 101.

[63] L. Harold DeWolf, *The Case for Theology in a Liberal Perspective* (Philadelphia: Westminster, 1959), 32.

[64] John Hick, *Philosophy of Religion* (Englewood Cliffs: Prentice-Hall, 1963), 76. Compare Barth's denials of propositional truths in revelation.

[65] On Barth's changing views of divine transcendence with his criticisms of his own earlier position, see Karl Barth, *The Humanity of God* (Richmond: John Knox, 1960), 37–65.

[66] Barth, *CD*, vol. 1, pt. 1, 252.

[67] Karl Barth, "No!" in Emil Brunner and Karl Barth, *Natural Theology*, trans. Peter Fruenkel (London: Geoffrey Bles, Centenary Press, 1946), 62.

[68] Barth, *CD*, vol. 1, pt. 1, 10.

[69] Karl Barth, *Epistle to the Romans*, trans. Edwyn C. Hoskyns (London: Oxford, 1963), 47. For a biblically based evaluation of Barth's and others' views see Demarest, *General Revelation*, 1–226.

[70] For a critique of non-Christian values and a defense of Christian values see Edward John Carnell, *A Philosophy of the Christian Religion* (Grand Rapids: Eerdmans, 1952), condensed in Gordon R. Lewis, *Testing Christianity's Truth Claims*, 210–30.

[71] Augustine, *The Happy Life*, trans. by Ludwig Schupp, *Writings of Saint Augustine*, vol. 1, *Fathers of the Church*, 43–84.

[72] Stanley L. Jaki, *The Road of Science and the Ways to God* (Chicago: University of Chicago Press, 1978), 180.

[73] Lausanne Covenant, International Congress on World Evangelization (Wheaton: Lausanne Committee on World Evangelization, 1974), Article 5.

[74] Waldron Scott, *Bring Forth Justice* (Grand Rapids: Eerdmans, 1980). For reformed ways of developing the implications of general revelation for society see H. Henry Meeter, *The Basic Ideas of Calvinism* (Grand Rapids: Kregel, 1967) and Henry R. Van Til, *The Calvinistic Concept of Culture* (Grand Rapids: Baker, 1972).

[75] David Chilton, *Productive Christians in an Age of Guilt Manipulators: A Biblical Response to Ronald Sider* (Tyler, Tex.: Institute for Christian Economics, 1981); cf. Ronald

Sider, *Justice: The Bible Speaks on Hunger and Poverty* (Downers Grove: InterVarsity, 1980).

[76] Waldron Scott, ed., *Serving Our Generation: Evangelical Strategies for the Eighties* (Colorado Springs: World Evangelical Fellowship, 1980).

[77] Brenda Munsey, *Moral Development, Moral Education and Kohlberg* (Birmingham: Religious Education Press, 1980).

[78] For discussions of points of contact with non-Christians in six systems of apologetics see Gordon Lewis, *Testing Christianity's Truth Claims*, and Gordon Lewis, "Van Til and Carnell," ed. E. R. Geehan, *Jerusalem and Athens* (Phillipsburg, N.J.: Presbyterian and Reformed, 1971), 349–68.

[79] C. F. D. Moule, *The Phenomenon of the New Testament* (Naperville, Ill.: Allenson, 1967), 19.

[80] See references in note 51.

[81] See references in note 52.

[82] Lit-sen Chang, *Strategy of Missions in the Orient: Christian Impact on the Pagan World* (Phillipsburg, N.J.: Presbyterian and Reformed, 1970).

[83] B. B. Warfield, *Selected Shorter Writings* (Phillipsburg, N.J.: Presbyterian and Reformed, n.d.), 27, 45.

[84] Ibid., 45.

[85] Lit-sen Chang, *Strategy of Missions in the Orient*, 105.

Chapter Three

[1] "Revelation," *The Encyclopedia of the Lutheran Church*, 2:2052.

[2] Council of Trent, Session IV (April 8, 1546). See Philip Schaff, *Creeds of Christendom*, 3 vols. (Grand Rapids: Baker, 1977), 2:80.

[3] Cited in Edward G. Waring, *Deism and Natural Religion* (New York: F. Unger, 1967), 109.

[4] G. E. Lessing, cited in Peter Gay, *The Enlightenment* (New York: Knopf, 1966), 330.

[5] F. Gerald Downing, *Has Christianity a Revelation?* (Philadelphia: Westminster, 1964), 238.

[6] Karl Barth, *CD*, vol. 1, pt. 2, 237.

[7] Ibid., vol. 1, pt. 1, 136.

[8] Emil Brunner, *Revelation and Reason* (London: SCM, 1947), 8.

[9] H. Richard Niebuhr, *The Meaning of Revelation* (New York: Macmillan, 1941), 16.

[10] Hans Küng, *On Being a Christian* (Garden City, N.Y.: Doubleday, 1976), 467.

[11] Rudolph Bultmann, *Existence and Faith* (London: Collins, 1960), 100.

[12] Athanasius, *The Incarnation of the Word*, XIII.

[13] Ibid., XIV.

[14] Augustine, *Confessions*, VI.5.8.

[15] John Calvin, *Institutes of the Christian Religion*, I.vi.3.

[16] Carl F. H. Henry, *God, Revelation and Authority*, 6 vols. (Waco: Word, 1976–83), 2:7.

[17] Ibid., 12.

[18] B. B. Warfield, "The Biblical Idea of Revelation," in *The Inspiration and Authority of the Bible* (Nutley, N.J.: Presbyterian and Reformed, 1970), 82–96.

[19] Millard J. Erickson, *Christian Theology*, 3 vols. (Grand Rapids: Baker, 1983–85), 1:175–98.

[20] Bernard Ramm, *Special Revelation and the Word of God* (Grand Rapids: Eerdmans, 1961).

[21] Ronald H. Nash, *The Word of God and the Mind of Man* (Grand Rapids: Zondervan, 1982).

[22] Cf. Deut. 34:11: "Moses . . . did all those miraculous signs and wonders the LORD sent him to do in Egypt—to Pharaoh and to all his officials and to his whole land." See also Deut. 7:18–19.

[23] C. Brown, "*chrēmatizō*," *NIDNTT*, 3:324.

[24] G. D. Lass, *A Theology of the New Testament* (Grand Rapids: Eerdmans, 1974), 392.

[25] B. Gärtner, "*epiphaneia*," *NIDNTT*, 3:319.

[26] Cf. Bernard Ramm, *Special Revelation and the Word of God*, 110.

[27] Robert E. Webber, *God Still Speaks: A Biblical View of Christian Communication* (Nashville: Thomas Nelson, 1979), 69–72.

[28] Augustine, "Retractions" I.3.2, trans. Robert P. Russell, in *Fathers of the Church: A New Translation*, ed. Ludwigg Schopp et al., "Writings of St. Augustine" (New York: CIMA, 1948), 1:332n.

[29] Jean Wahl, *A Short History of Existentialism* (New York: Philosophical Library, 1949), 19; Jean-Paul Sartre, *Existentialism* (New York: Philosophical Library, 1947), 15; Gordon R. Lewis, "Augustine and Existentialism" *Bulletin of the Evangelical Theological Society* vol. 8, no.1 (Winter 1965), 13–22.

[30] Edward John Carnell, *Introduction to Christian Apologetics* (Grand Rapids: Eerdmans, 1948), 60; Bernard Ramm, *Special Revelation and the Word of God* (Grand Rapids: Eerdmans, 1961), 143–54.

[31] See on the Logos: Ronald Nash, *The Word of God and the Word of Man*, 6 vols. (Grand Rapids: Zondervan, 1982), 59–69; Henry, *God, Revelation and Authority* 3:164–247.

[32] Few works on revelation consider Christ's view of his own teaching. Donald Guthrie has a brief section arguing that "of utmost importance for any approach to the authority of the NT is the attitude which Jesus took to his own teaching," but that statement seems difficult to reconcile with his earlier agreement with Cullmann that the concept of prophet and teacher "played no significant part in NT Christology." *New Testament Theology* (Downers Grove: InterVarsity, 1981), 960–61 and 269–70. Barth also had sections studying the verbs for Jesus' evangelizing, preaching, and teaching, but he did not develop Jesus' view of his own teaching. *CD*, vol. 4, pt. 2, 194–209.

[33] Francis Brown, S. R. Driver, and Charles A. Briggs, *A Hebrew and English Lexicon of the Old Testament* (Oxford: Clarendon, 1907); Rudolph Bultmann, *"alethia," TDNT*, 1:241–47; Anthony Thiselton, "Truth," *Dictionary of New Testament Theology*, ed. Colin Brown (Grand Rapids: Zondervan, 1978), 897–901.

[34] Allan A. MacRae, "Prophets and Prophecy," *ZPEB*, 4:880; Bernard Ramm, *Special Revelation and the Word of God*, 59.

[35] Josephus *Apion* I.8.

[36] A. A. MacRae, "Prophets and Prophecy," *ZPEB*, 4:903.

[37] R. E. Higginson, "Apostolic Succession," *EDT*, 73.

[38] Donald Guthrie, *New Testament Theology*, 769.

[39] Evaluated by contemporary Roman Catholic theologian Richard P. O'Brien, *Catholicism* (Minneapolis: Winston, 1980), 240.

[40] Thomas Dehany Bernard, *The Progress of Doctrine in the New Testament* (London: Macmillan, 1879), 1–207.

[41] John Baillie, *The Idea of Revelation in Recent Thought* (New York: Columbia University Press, 1956), 47.

[42] Ibid., 49.

[43] Antony Flew, *A Dictionary of Philosophy* (New York: Martin's Press, 1979), 271.

[44] Barth, *CD*, vol. 1, pt. 1, 134.

[45] Ibid., 125–27.

[46] Emil Brunner, *Truth as Encounter* (Philadelphia: Westminster, 1943), 131; for an evaluation of Brunner see Paul Jewett, *Emil Brunner's Concept of Revelation* (London: James Clarke, 1954), esp. 139–85.

[47] Emil Brunner, *Truth as Encounter*, 133.

[48] Ibid., 137.

[49] W. Mundle, "Revelation," *NIDNTT*, 3:312–16.

[50] Earl S. Kalland, *"Dābār," TWOT*, 1:180.

[51] Bernard Ramm, *Special Revelation and the Word of God*, 150–51.

[52] Ibid., 159.

[53] W. H. Griffith Thomas, "Revelation," in *Hastings Dictionary of the Bible*, ed. James Hastings (New York: Scribner, 1909, reprint 1951), 797.

[54] J. Gresham Machen, *Christianity and Liberalism* (Grand Rapids: Eerdmans, 1946), 21, 19.

[55] Geoffrey Wainwright, *Doxology: The Praise of God in Worship, Doctrine and Life: A Systematic Theology* (New York: Oxford, 1980), 86.

[56] Gordon R. Lewis, "God's Word: Key to Authentic Spirituality," in *A Call to Christian Character*, ed. Bruce Shelley (Grand Rapids: Zondervan, 1970), 105–20.

[57] Thor Hall, *A Theology of Christian Devotion* (Nashville: The Upper Room, 1969), 4.

[58] See Martin Pine, "Double Truth," in *Dictionary of the History of Ideas*, ed. Philip P. Wiener (New York: Scribner, 1973), 2:31–37.

Chapter Four

[1] Thomas Aquinas, *ST*, I.1, q. 1, art. 10.

[2] Thomas Aquinas, *Job*, XIII.1.

[3] Cited by Philip Watson, *Let God Be God!* (Philadelphia: Fortress, 1947), 12.

[4] Council of Trent, session IV, April 8, 1546.

[5] Horace Bushnell, *Nature and the Supernatural* (New York: Scribner, 1858), 33, 493.

[6] Walter Rauschenbusch, *A Theology for the Social Gospel* (New York: Macmillan, 1917), 192.

[7] Ibid., 191.

[8] James Barr, *The Bible in the Modern World* (London: SCM, 1973), 43. Later in the same book Barr asserts that from the modern point of view, the early church's doctrine of Scripture appears to be the result of "an authority neurosis." Ibid., 113.

[9] Barth, *CD*, vol. 1, pt. 2, 525.

[10] Ibid., 499.

[11] Ibid., 529. For Barth's ascription of error to the Bible, see also ibid., 507, 530, 533.

[12] Emil Brunner, *The Mediator* (Philadelphia: Westminster, 1947), 105.

[13] Hans Küng, *On Being a Christian* (Garden City, N.Y.: Doubleday, 1976), 465.

[14] Ibid., 463.

[15] Ibid., 466-67. Many contemporary Catholic authorities have adopted a lower view of inspiration. So Richard P. McBrien limits inerrancy "to those essential religious affirmations which are made for the sake of our salvation." *Catholicism* (Minneapolis: Winston, 1981), 64. Monika Hellwig asserts that God's revelation about Jesus has been transmitted through various historical channels, "none of which is free from human error and the ambiguities of history." *Understanding Catholicism* (New York: Paulist, 1981), 3. Consequently there are no formal statements that may be taken as the final authority on many matters of faith and life. Anthony Wilhelm, in his classic introduction to Catholicism, insists that "although the Catholic church reverences the Bible, the biblical authors in their writings were, like us, sinful, subject to error." *Christ Among Us: A Modern Presentation of the Catholic Faith* (New York: Paulist, 1981), 159.

[16] Cited by Norman L. Geisler, *Decide for Yourself* (Grand Rapids: Zondervan, 1982), 95-96.

[17] C. S. Lewis, *Reflections on the Psalms* (New York: Harcourt, Brace, 1958), 111-12.

[18] Dewey Beegle, *Scripture, Tradition and Infallibility* (Grand Rapids: Eerdmans, 1973), 76.

[19] Ibid., 208.

[20] See R. C. Sproul, "The Case for Inerrancy: A Methodological Analysis," in *God's Inerrant Word*, ed. John W. Montgomery, (Minneapolis: Bethany, 1974), 243-44.

[21] Jack Rogers and Donald McKim, *The Authority and Interpretation of the Bible* (San Francisco: Harper & Row, 1979), 30.

[22] Ibid., 393.

[23] John R. Rice, *Our God-Breathed Book— The Bible* (Murfreesboro, Tennessee: Sword of the Lord, 1969), 287.

[24] Ibid., 141.

[25] Athenagoras, *A Plea for the Christians*, IX.

[26] Tertullian, *A Treatise on the Soul*, XXVII.

[27] Irenaeus, *Against Heresies*, II.28.2.

[28] Jerome, *Patrologia Latina*, ed. J. P. Migne, vol. XXVI, 481; cited by Otto Weber, *Foundations of Dogmatics*, 2 vols. (Grand Rapids: Eerdmans, 1981–83), 1:232.

[29] Augustine, *Harmony of the Gospels*, I.35.54.

[30] Augustine, "Letter," LXXXII.3.

[31] "Faith will totter if the authority of Scripture begins to shake." Augustine, *On Christian Doctrine*, I.37.4.

[32] For Augustine's discussion of the value of the Apocrypha, see *On Christian Doctrine*, II.8.12–13 and *City of God*, XVIII.36.

[33] Neoorthodox authorities deny that Luther established an identity between the Word of God and the written Scriptures. They maintain that Luther viewed the Scriptures as a vehicle of the Word, i.e., as a witness to Christ. On this showing the Bible is the authoritative Word of God only as it witnesses to Christ and as the Spirit animates the text to the life. "For Luther, Scripture is not the Word, but only witness to the Word, and it is from Him whom it conveys that it derives the authority it enjoys." J. K. S. Reid, *The Authority of Scripture* (New York: Harper, 1957), 72.

[34] Martin Luther, *WA*, LIV:39.

[35] John Calvin, *Institutes*, I.18.4.

[36] John Calvin, *Harmony of the Gospels*, 1:127.

[37] John Calvin, *Psalms*, 3:205.

[38] Calvin, *Institutes*, IV.8.8–9.

[39] John Calvin, *Philippians, Colossians, I & II Thessalonians*, 87; *Minor Prophets*, 3:197; cf. *Pastoral Epistles*, 249.

[40] Calvin, *Psalms*, 1:11.

[41] Calvin, *Institutes*, III.2.6.

[42] John Calvin, *Job*, 744.

[43] Calvin, *Psalms*, 4:480.

[44] Calvin, *Psalms*, 5:184–85.

[45] Calvin, *Institutes*, I.7.5; I.8.13; *John*, 2:101. Neoorthodox authorities such as K. Barth, W. Niesel, and J. K. S. Reid deny that Calvin taught a doctrine of verbal inspiration and verbal infallibility. "Calvin is no verbal inspirationist" (Reid, *Authority of Scripture*, 36; cf. 47). According to the neoorthodox, Calvin taught that the Bible is not the Word of God, but is only a witness to the Word, i.e., to Christ himself. The written record *becomes* the Word of God as the Spirit vivifies it to the hearer or reader. So Reid, ibid., 51.

[46] B. B. Warfield, "The Real Problem of Inspiration," in *The Inspiration and Authority*

of the Bible, ed. Samuel G. Craig (Philadelphia: Presbyterian and Reformed, 1970), 173.

[47] Ibid., 225.

[48] Carl F. H. Henry, *God, Revelation and Authority,* 6 vols. (Waco: Word, 1976–83), 4:129.

[49] "Exposition," of the "Articles of Affirmation and Denial," reprinted by Henry, *God, Revelation and Authority,* 4:218. Clark Pinnock, in *The Scripture Principle* (San Francisco: Harper & Row, 1984), attempts to mediate between a conservative evangelical posture on one hand, and a liberal evangelical or neoorthodox stance on the other. Whereas in his earlier work, *Biblical Revelation* (Chicago: Moody, 1971), Pinnock vigorously insisted that the Bible is the Word of God, in *The Scripture Principle* he implies that the Bible plus the Holy Spirit is the Word of God (pp. 57, 198), or that the Bible contains the Word of God (pp. 56, 99). In his earlier work, Pinnock argued that Jesus and the biblical writers taught the full inerrancy of Scripture, and that errors in the Bible would impugn the character of God. In *The Scripture Principle,* however, Pinnock claims that neither Jesus nor the apostles taught inerrancy (p. 57): "The case for inerrancy just isn't there" (p. 58; cf. p. 59). Pinnock now argues that the Bible is infallible in its testimony to Christ, but is flawed in its teachings concerning science and history (pp. 99–100; 104–5). The Genesis record of the Fall is probably "saga" to be interpreted existentially (pp. 67–68, 116), and the Jonah story is "a didactic fiction" (p. 117). Given these admissions, it is difficult to see how Pinnock's position can be accommodated to the historic position of the church.

[50] For example, Roger R. Nicole and J. Ramsey Michaels, eds., *Inerrancy and Common Sense* (Grand Rapids: Baker, 1980); D. A. Carson and John D. Woodbridge, eds., *Scripture and Truth* (Grand Rapids: Zondervan, 1983); Ronald Youngblood, ed., *Evangelicals and Inerrancy* (Nashville: Thomas Nelson, 1984); and Gordon R. Lewis and Bruce Demarest, eds., *Challenges to Inerrancy: A Theological Response* (Chicago: Moody, 1984).

[51] Joshua refers to this Mosaic writing as "the Book of the Law of Moses" (Josh. 23:6; cf. 1:7–8).

[52] Charles G. Martin, "Proverbs," *NLBC,* 703.

[53] E. Earle Ellis, *The Gospel of Luke. NCBC,* 64.

[54] This construction is preferred by J. N. D. Kelley, *A Commentary on the Pastoral Epistles* (Grand Rapids: Baker, 1981), 203.

[55] Cf. B. B. Warfield: The Scripture as *ta logia* are "one continuous oracular deliverance from God's own lips." *Inspiration and Authority,* 404.

[56] B. B. Warfield, "'It Says:' 'Scripture Says:' " *Inspiration and Authority,* 299–348.

[57] F. Büchsel, *"luō,"* TDNT, 4:336.

[58] B. F. Westcott, *St. John* (London: John Murray, 1882), 245. Cf. A. C. Thiselton, "Truth," *NIDNTT,* 3:889–93.

[59] H. B. Swete observes that John was so steeped in the Scriptures that 278 of the 404 verses of Revelation contain references to the Old Testament. *Apocalypse of St. John* (London, 1907), cxxxv.

[60] B. B. Warfield, *Inspiration and Authority,* 136.

[61] Michael Green, *2 Peter and Jude,* TNTC (London: Tyndale, 1968), 91. K. Weiss, *"pherō,"* TDNT, 9:58, prefers to translate *pheromenoi* by the weaker term "impelled."

[62] Warfield, *Inspiration and Authority,* 119–20. Said Warfield about the biblical texts in support of the orthodox view of the Bible: "There are scores, hundreds of them: and they come bursting upon us in one solid mass. Explain them away? We should have to explain away the whole New Testament."

[63] On Jesus' view of the OT see, John W. Wenham, *Christ and the Bible* (Downers Grove: InterVarsity, 1972), 11–81.

[64] On the OT canon see R. Laird Harris, "Canon of the Old Testament," *ZPEB,* 1:709–31; R. Laird Harris, *Inspiration and Canonicity of the Bible* (Grand Rapids: Zondervan, 1957), 131–95.

[65] "Text and Manuscripts of the Old Testament," *ZPEB,* 5:696.

[66] MacRae, ibid.

[67] J. Norval Geldenhuys, *Supreme Authority: The Authority of the Lord, His Apostles and the New Testament* (Grand Rapids: Eerdmans, 1953), 16–64.

[68] Donald Guthrie, "Canon of the New Testament," *ZPEB,* 1:733.

[69] Andrew F. Walls, "The Canon of the New Testament," in *EBC,* 1:638.

[70] Norman L. Geisler and William E. Nix, *From God to Us: How We Got Our Bible* (Chicago: Moody, 1974), 125.

[71] George Ladd, *The New Testament and Criticism* (Grand Rapids: Eerdmans, 1967), 80–81.

[72] J. H. Greenlee, "Text and Manuscripts of the New Testament," *ZPEB,* 5:713.

[73] G. C. Berkouwer, *Holy Scripture* (Grand Rapids: Eerdmans, 1975), 358, 361.

[74] Ibid., 54, 279.

[75] Ibid., 253.

[76] Pinnock, *Scripture Principle,* 128.

[77] Steven T. Davis, *The Debate About the Bible* (Philadelphia: Westminster, 1977), 15. For discussions of limited inerrancy by Richard J. Coleman, J. Barton Payne, and Vern S. Pothyress, see Youngblood, ed., *Evangelicals and Inerrancy,* 161–85.

[78] For one who practices a similar approach, though with less of a structured methodology, see Millard J. Erickson, *Christian Theology,* 3 vols. (Grand Rapids: Baker, 1983–85), 199–240.

[79] James Barr, *The Scope and Authority of the Bible,* 18–20.

[80] Ibid.

[81] A. T. Hanson, and R. P. C. Hanson, *Reasonable Belief: A Survey of the Christian Faith* (New York: Oxford University Press, 1980), 42.

[82] Ibid., 43.

[83] Ibid., 45.

[84] Ibid., 46.

[85] Gordon R. Lewis, "What Does Infallibility Mean?" *Bulletin of the Evangelical Theological Society,* 6 (Winter 1963): 18–27; reprinted in Youngblood, ed., *Evangelicals and Inerrancy,* 35–48. See also Kevin J. VanHoozer's challenge of our view of propositional revelation in "The Semantics of Biblical Literature," in D. A. Carson and John D. Woodbridge, eds., *Hermeneutics, Authority, and Canon* (Grand Rapids: Zondervan, 1986), 53–104. Interacting in some measure with G. R. Lewis, "What Does Infallibility Mean?" VanHoozer seeks to preserve a cognitive communication that allows for greater appreciation of the ordinary language of Scripture and its diverse literary forms. Although he has purposes similar to ours, such as not divorcing propositional and personal revelation, his chapter has several problems: (1) It leaves the misimpression that defenders of propositional revelation regard the entire Bible as informative (p. 59), thus overlooking half of my article devoted to its expressive, directive, interrogative, exclamatory, and pictorial or imaginative uses of language. (2) His chapter fails to emphasize that diverse literary forms in ordinary language such as parables, though not propositional in form, teach a propositional point that Jesus himself on occasion "translated" into formal assertions (Matt. 13:18–23). Such "translation" did not distort the figurative purpose! No "logical gap" need be manufactured either between a parable and its propositional interpretation or between sentences' verbal signs and their meanings (the content signified). (3) In defining language acts as "*something* propounded for consideration" (p. 92), VanHoozer fails to provide a meaningful alternative to propositional content. (4) VanHoozer has not answered "the strongest argument for the existence of propositions" (p. 60), the fact that the same content can be asserted in all the different languages in which the Bible is translated. (5) He manufactures "disparate views" and alleged "confusion" between Henry, Clark, and G. R. Lewis/Obitts when admittedly all three scholars are agreed as to the general thrust of propositional revelation (p. 59). This illustrates the danger of magnifying differences of wording when on this point the thought is essentially the same. (6) VanHoozer seems to belong among those who commit the "heresy of propositional paraphrase" (p. 67), for among his three requisites for a successful speech act is a propositional condition (p. 96). Propositional conditions specify the kinds of *content* that are appropriate for various "illocutionary forces" including states of affairs and future events (p. 96). (7) In his search for a broader criterion of truth, he adopts the narrower one. At best a "correspondence" test can confirm empirical claims (not mere words, symbols), but comes far short of the breadth of a coherence test in relation to the nonempirical teachings of Scripture. (8) He has not indicated how phenomenal human speech acts can refer to the metaphysical reality of who God is. The concern for a propositional revelation was designed to counter not only noncognitive, but also antimetaphysical notions of revelation. (9) His own definition of infallibility, though different in words, is little different from ours in meaning. He writes, "Infallibility means that speech acts are performed successfully" (p. 100). (10) VanHoozer's allegation that our view is similar to Barth's (p. 58) is impossible to follow. How is a doctrine of revelation and inspiration—one that indicates that all the Bible's verbally conveyed teachings *are* divine revelation—similar to one that claims that the Bible's teachings are not revelation and errantly "point" to the living person of Christ only?

[86] Ibid.

[87] For a brief evaluation of these positions see Gordon R. Lewis, "The Human Authorship of Inspired Scripture," ed. Norman Geisler, *Inerrancy* (Grand Rapids: Zondervan, 1979), 229–40.

[88] Ibid., 240–64.

[89]Gordon R. Lewis, "A Comparison of Form Criticism and Classical Criticism of the Gospels," in *More Evidence That Demands a Verdict*, ed. Josh McDowell (Arrowhead Springs: Campus Crusade for Christ, 1975), 335–40.

[90]Gordon R. Lewis, "Non-Evangelical Hermeneutics: Response," in *Hermeneutics, Inerrancy, and the Bible*, ed. Earl D. Radmacher and Robert D. Preus (Grand Rapids: Zondervan, 1984), 613–25.

[91](Article XIX), ibid., 885–86.

[92]"The Bible: The Believers Gain," *Time Magazine* (December 30, 1974), 41.

[93]As an example of the thoroughness with which evangelical scholars have faced the issues and dealt with them, see Gleason L. Archer, *Encyclopedia of Bible Difficulties* (Grand Rapids: Zondervan, 1982).

[94]Colin Brown, "Revelation," *NIDNTT*, 3:334.

[95]Emile Cailliet, *Journey Into Light* (Grand Rapids: Zondervan, 1968), 11–18, 98, 105–6.

[96]See J. Robertson McQuilkin, "Problems of Normativeness in Scripture: Cultural Versus Permanent" and the Papers in Response by George W. Knight and Alan F. Johnson, ed. Earl D. Radmacher and Robert D. Preus, *Hermeneutics, Inerrancy, and the Bible*, 219–82; Alan F. Johnson, "History and Culture in New Testament Interpretation," in *Interpreting the Word of God*, ed. Samuel J. Schultz and Morris A. Inch (Chicago: Moody, 1976), 128–61.

[97]Ned B. Stonehouse, "Review of Theological Education in America" in *Christianity Today* (Feb. 16, 1959), 36.

[98]Richard F. Lovelace, *Dynamics of Spiritual Life* (Downers Grove: InterVarsity, 1980), 282–83.

[99]Gordon R. Lewis, "God's Word: Key to Authentic Spirituality," in *Call to Christian Character*, ed. Bruce Shelley (Grand Rapids: Zondervan, 1970), 111.

[100]Ibid., 283–84.

[101]On illumination see Bernard Ramm, *The Witness of the Spirit* (Grand Rapids: Eerdmans, 1960), 130 pp.

[102]Mark I. Bubeck, *The Adversary* (Chicago: Moody, 1975), 94.

Chapter Five

[1]Thomas Aquinas, *ST*, vol. 1, pt. 1, q. 3, art. 2.

[2]Aquinas, *Summa Contra Gentiles*, I. 21. 1.

[3]Aquinas, *ST*, vol. 1, pt. 1, q. 13, art. 11.

[4]W. A. Brown, *Christian Theology in Outline* (New York: Scribner, 1911), 113.

[5]Karl Barth, *CD*, vol. 2, pt. 1, p. 272.

[6]Ibid., vol. 1, pt. 1, p. 426.

[7]Ibid., vol. 2, pt. 2, p. 619.

[8]Paul Tillich, *The Courage to Be* (New Haven: Yale University Press, 1952), 177–78.

[9]"Whatever concerns a man ultimately becomes God for him." Paul Tillich, *Systematic Theology*, 3 vols. (Chicago: University of Chicago Press, 1951–63), 1:211.

[10]Ibid., 205.

[11]Ibid., 237.

[12]Ibid., 223.

[13]John Macquarrie, *Principles of Christian Theology* (New York: Scribner, 1977), 206.

[14]Ibid., 122. Yahweh, according to Macquarrie, means, "I cause to be," or "I bring to pass." Ibid., 196–97.

[15]Monika Hellwig, *Understanding Catholicism* (Ramsey, N.J.: Paulist, 1981), 191.

[16]Hans Küng, *On Being a Christian* (Garden City, N.Y.: Doubleday, 1976) 82, 295.

[17]Ibid., 303.

[18]Ibid., 308.

[19]Ibid., 303.

[20]Leslie Dewart, *The Future of Belief* (New York: Herder & Herder, 1966), 189.

[21]Ibid., 211.

[22]John B. Cobb, Jr., "The World and God," in Ewert H. Cousins, ed., *Process Theology* (New York: Newman, 1971), 158.

[23]According to H. N. Wieman and W. M. Horton, God "is not a personality, but God is more worthful than any personality could ever be." *The Growth of Religion* (Chicago: Willett, Clark, 1938), 362–63.

[24]Theophilus, *To Autolychus*, I.4.

[25]Clement of Alexandria,, *Miscellanies*, V.11. Cf., "God is one, and beyond the one, and above the Monad itself." *The Instructor*, I.8.

[26]Athanasius, *De Synodis*, III.35. So also Gregory of Nazianzus, *Oration*, XXX.17–18, who links Yahweh with the special, absolute name *ho ōn*.

[27]G. L. Prestige, *God in Patristic Thought* (London: SPCK, 1952). 17.

[28]Augustine, *On the Trinity*, VI.4.6.

[29]Augustine, *On Patience*, I.

30 Augustine, *Letters*, CLXXXVII.14. Cf. *Sermon on the Mount*, II.9.32; *City of God*, VII.30.

31 Augustine, *Confessions*, I.4.4.

32 Philip Melanchthon, *Loci Communes*, I; cited by Clyde L. Manschreck, ed., *Melanchthon on Christian Doctrine* (Grand Rapids: Baker, 1982), 8.

33 Ibid.

34 John Calvin, *Calvin: Theological Treatises*, ed. J. Baillie, J. T. McNeill and H. P. Van Dusen, *LCC* (Philadelphia: Westminster, 1954), XXII:302.

35 John Calvin, *Institutes of the Christian Religion*, III.xxx.40.

36 Ibid., I.xvi.3.

37 John Calvin, *Minor Prophets*, 1:402.

38 Stephen Charnock, *The Existence and Attributes of God* (Grand Rapids: Kregel, 1958), 80.

39 W. G. T. Shedd, *Dogmatic Theology*, 3 vols. (Grand Rapids: Zondervan, n.d.), 1:334.

40 Ronald Nash, *The Concept of God* (Grand Rapids: Zondervan, 1983).

41 Millard J. Erickson, *Christian Theology*, 3 vols. (Grand Rapids: Baker, 1983–85), 1:263–81.

42 Carl F. H. Henry, *God, Revelation and Authority*, 6 vols. (Waco: Word, 1976–83), 5:9–306.

43 "*Hayah* means to be, to exist and not: to be here—ready to help. God is not called the 'One who is' because He is faithful, but He is faithful because He is the 'One who is.'" Paul Heinisch, *Theology of the Old Testament* (Collegeville, Minn.: Liturgical Press, 1955), 45.

44 See Jack B. Scott, "*'elohim*," *TWOT*, 1:44–45 for a discussion of the traditional interpretation. Erickson, *Christian Theology*, 1:328–29, explores the possibility that the plural may be a "quantitative plural," which connotes diversity within the Godhead.

45 Victor P. Hamilton, "*pānîm*," *TWOT*, 2:727.

46 Franz Delitzsch, *Biblical Commentary on the Psalms*, 3 vols. (Grand Rapids: Eerdmans, 1952), 2:6.

47 According to Charles Hodge, "The glory of God is the manifested excellence of God." *A Commentary on the Epistle to the Ephesians* (Reprint, Grand Rapids: Baker, 1980), 38.

48 Fritz Rienecker and Cleon L. Rogers, Jr., *A Linguistic Key to the Greek New Testament* (Grand Rapids: Zondervan, 1982), 112.

49 Leon Morris, *The First and Second Epistles to the Thessalonians*. *NICNT* (Grand Rapids: Eerdmans, 1959), 63.

50 "*Theotes* indicates the divine essence of the Godhead, the personality of God; *theiotes*, the attributes of God, His divine nature and properties." W. E. Vine, *Expository Dictionary of New Testament Words* (Westwood, N.J.: Revell, 1961), 329.

51 John Eadie, *A Commentary on Philippians* (Reprint, Grand Rapids: Baker, 1979), 105.

52 *Kyrios* "expresses particularly his creatorship, his power revealed in history, and his just dominion." H. Bietenhard, "Lord," *NIDNTT*, 2:514.

53 Alfred Plummer, *The Epistles of St. John* (Reprint, Grand Rapids: Baker, 1980), 23.

54 *Eidos*, from *eidō*, "to see," signifies "the expression of the essence in visible form." G. Braumann, *eido*," *NIDNTT*, 1:704.

55 F. F. Bruce paraphrases *charakter tes hypostaseōs autou* as, "the very image of the substance of God—the impress of His being." *The Epistle to the Hebrews* (London: Marshall, Morgan & Scott, 1965), 5. See also J. Hering, *The Epistle to the Hebrews* (London: Epworth, 1970), 5; and B. F. Westcott, *The Epistle to the Hebrews* (London: Macmillan, 1889), 13.

56 Peter Davids, *Commentary on James*. *NTGTC* (Grand Rapids: Eerdmans, 1982), 88.

57 For a definition of God see G. R. Lewis, "God, Attributes of," *EDT*, 451.

58 On divine simplicity see Henry, *God, Revelation and Authority*, 5:127–40; Ronald Nash, *The Concept of God* (Grand Rapids: Zondervan, 1983), 85–97.

59 A. H. Strong, *Systematic Theology* (Philadelphia: Judson, 1907), 247–49; Louis Berkhof, *Systematic Theology* (Grand Rapids: Eerdmans, 1959), 55–56; John Gill, *Body of Divinity* (Atlanta, Georgia: Turner Lassetter, 1957), 34–35; H. Orton Wiley, *Christian Theology*, 3 vols. (Kansas City, Mo.: Beacon Hill, 1959), 1:325–29; Lewis Sperry Chafer, *Systematic Theology*, 8 vols. (Dallas: Dallas Seminary Press, 1947), 1:189–91, 212.

60 Kenneth F. W. Grove, *The Gospel in a Pagan Society* (Downers Grove: InterVarsity, 1975), 125 pp.

61 Gordon R. Lewis, "The Gospel on Campus" (in four parts) *His* (Oct., Nov., Dec. 1966, and Jan. 1967).

62 M. Jammer, "Energy" *EP*, 2:511–17.

63 Paul Davies, *God and the New Physics* (New York: Simon and Schuster, 1983), vii.

64 Ibid., 163.

[65] Carl Sagan, *Cosmos* (New York: Random, 1980), 4, 21.

[66] Tillich, *Systematic Theology,* 1:268.

[67] For an evangelical evaluation of Tillich see R. Allen Killen, *The Ontological Theology of Paul Tillich* (Kampen: J. H. Kok N. V., 1956), 253–57.

[68] Gill, *Body of Divinity, 43.*

[69] On Teilhard de Chardin see: J. J. Duyvene De Wit, "Pierre Teilhard de Chardin" in *Creative Minds in Contemporary Theology,* ed. Philip Edgcombe Hughes, (Grand Rapids: Eerdmans, 1966), 407–48; N. M. Wildiers, *An Introduction to Teilhard de Chardin,* trans. Hubert Hoskins (New York: Harper and Row, 1968); David Gareth Jones, *Teilhard de Chardin: An Analysis and Assessment* (Grand Rapids: Eerdmans, 1970).

[70] Norman Pittenger, "Process Theology Revisited," *Theology Today,* XXVII, 2 (July 1970): 213.

[71] Royce Gordon Gruenler, *The Inexhaustible God* (Grand Rapids: Baker, 1983), 126.

[72] Emil Brunner, *The Christian Doctrine of God* (Philadelphia: Westminster, 1950), 269.

[73] Gruenler, *The Inexhaustible God,* 105; on process theology see also Norman Geisler, "Process Theology" in *Tensions in Contemporary Theology,* ed. Stanley N. Gundry and Alan F. Johnson (Chicago: Moody, 1976), 237–84; Norman Geisler, "Process Theology and Inerrancy," ed. Gordon Lewis and Bruce Demarest, *Challenges to Inerrancy: A Theological Response* (Chicago: Moody, 1984), 247–84.

[74] Corliss Lamont, *The Philosophy of Humanism* (New York: Frederick Ungar, 1982, 6th ed.), 227.

[75] Ibid., 143.

[76] Ibid., 241.

[77] Ibid., 240.

[78] Ibid., 241.

[79] For evaluations of humanism see Norman L. Geisler, *Is Man the Measure? An Evaluation of Contemporary Humanism* (Grand Rapids: Baker, 1983); James Hitchcock, *What Is Secular Humanism?* (Ann Arbor, Mich.: Servant Books, 1982); Robert E. Webber, *Secular Humanism: Threat and Challenge* (Grand Rapids: Zondervan, 1982).

[80] George E. Ladd, *A Theology of the New Testament* (Grand Rapids: Eerdmans, 1974), 81–90.

[81] John Bright, *The Authority of the Old Testament* (Grand Rapids: Baker, 1975), 130–34.

[82] Gordon R. Lewis, "Categories in Collision?" ed. Kenneth S. Kantzer and Stanley N. Gundry, *Perspectives on Evangelical Theology* (Grand Rapids: Baker, 1979), 259–64.

[83] "The Hartford Appeal for Theological Affirmation," *Christianity and Crisis,* vol. 35, no. 12 (July 12, 1975), 168–69.

[84] J. I. Packer, *Knowing God* (Downers Grove: InterVarsity, 1974), 29.

[85] A. W. Tozer, *The Knowledge of the Holy* (New York: Harper, 1961), 11.

[86] Ibid., 12.

[87] Ibid., 10.

[88] Richard Foster, *The Celebration of Discipline* (New York: Harper, 1978), 25.

[89] Tozer, *Knowledge of the Holy,* 12.

[90] Packer, *Knowing God,* 40–41.

[91] Foster, *Celebration of Discipline,* 27.

[92] Ibid., 26.

[93] Bruce Larson, *The Relational Revolution* (Waco: Word, 1976), 94–95.

[94] Gruenler, *Inexhaustible God,* 18–19.

[95] Ibid., 38–39.

[96] See note 67.

Chapter Six

[1] Thomas Aquinas, *SCG,* II.22.8.

[2] Faustus Socinus, *Prelectiones Theologicae,* ch. 16.

[3] Albrecht Ritschl, *The Christian Doctrine of Justification and Reconciliation* (Clifton, N.J.: Reference Book Publishers, 1966), 273.

[4] Albert C. Knudson, *The Doctrine of God* (Nashville: Abingdon, 1930), 345–46.

[5] W. A. Brown, *Christian Theology in Outline* (New York: Scribner, 1941), 11.

[6] Walter Eichrodt, *Theology of the Old Testament,* 2 vols. (Philadelphia: Westminster, 1961–67), 1:262.

[7] C. H. Dodd, *Romans* (London: Hodder & Stoughton, 1946), 24.

[8] Barth, *CD,* vol. II, pt. I, pp. 257, 322, passim.

[9] Ibid., 533.

[10] J. A. T. Robinson, *Honest to God* (London: SCM, 1963), 52.

[11] John Macquarrie, *Principles of Christian Theology* (New York: Scribner, 1977), 365.

12 John B. Cobb, Jr., and David R. Griffin, *Process Theology* (Philadelphia: Westminster, 1976), 61.

13 Ewert H. Cousins, *Process Theology: Basic Writings* (New York: Newman, 1971), 27.

14 Cited with approval by Norman Pittenger in *God's Way With Men* (London: Hodder & Stoughton, 1969), 22.

15 Karl Rahner, *TI*, 9:136.

16 Hans Küng, *On Being a Christian* (Garden City, N.Y.: Doubleday, 1976), 312.

17 Leslie Dewart, *The Future of Belief* (New York: Herder & Herder, 1966), 204–5.

18 Theophilus, *To Autolychus*, I.3.

19 Ibid.

20 Clement of Alexandria, *Miscellanies*, VII.3.

21 Tertullian, *On Purity*, 2.

22 Gregory of Nazianzus, *Fourth Theological Oration*, 11.

23 Augustine said of all occurrences in the past, the present, and the future: "All of these are by Him comprehended in His stable and eternal presence." *City of God*, IX.21.

24 Augustine, *On Patience*, 1. That Augustine believed God experiences a healthy and controlled emotional life is clear from Confessions, I.4.4: "Thou knowest, but art not disturbed by passion; Thou art jealous, but free from care; Thou art repentant, but not sorrowful; Thou art angry, but calm."

25 For Augustine's interpretation of the divine transcendence and immanence, see *Confessions*, I.2–3; *Soliloquies*, I.1.3–4.

26 Martin Luther, *LW*, LI:95.

27 Luther, *LW*, I:11–14; III:138, 276; XII:312–13; *LW* Companion Volume, "Luther the Expositor," 56.

28 John Calvin, *Institutes of the Christian Religion*, I.x.2.

29 Ibid., II.xvi.3.

30 Ibid., II.xxiii.4.

31 Ibid., III.xvii.2.

32 W. G. T. Shedd, *Dogmatic Theology*, 3 vols. (Reprint, Grand Rapids: Zondervan, n.d.), 1:373.

33 J. I. Packer, *Knowing God* (Downers Grove: InterVarsity, 1973).

34 Ronald H. Nash, *The Concept of God* (Grand Rapids: Zondervan, 1983).

35 Stephen T. Davis, *Logic and the Nature of God* (Grand Rapids: Eerdmans, 1983).

36 Th. C. Vriezen argues that the root denotes the idea of brilliance, by virtue of which the person cannot behold God. *An Outline of Old Testament Theology* (Wageningen: H. Veenman, 1958), 149.

37 Gordon J. Wenham, *The Book of Leviticus. NICOT* (Grand Rapids: Eerdmans, 1979), 18. Wenham estimates that Leviticus contains 20 percent of the total occurrences of *qādōš* and cognates in the Old Testament.

38 Cf. Ps. 33:13–14: "From heaven the LORD looks down and sees [*rā'āh*] all mankind; from his dwelling place he watches [*šāqaḥ*] all who live on earth."

39 Cf. Louis Goldberg, *"hokmāh," TWOT*, 2:283: "Wisdom should not be regarded as God but it does belong to God; it is one of his attributes."

40 Gerard Van Groningen, *śānē'," TWOT*, 1:880, states that the verb *śānē'* conveys God's emotional attitude of detesting and despising both evil and the evildoer. "God's hatred for idols and feasts is also directed against people (Mal. 1:3; Pss. 5:5; 11:50). In each case the character and/or activities of the hated ones are expressed; thus God is opposed to, separates himself from, and brings the consequences of his hatred upon people not as mere people, but as sinful people."

41 R. E. H. Stephens, "Habakkuk," *NBCRev*, 770, comments that the ground or support of the righteous person's faith is God's faithfulness. "The 'faithfulness' of which he [Habakkuk] now speaks is not only moral endurance to the end, but the persistent belief that God will be true to Himself. 'Faith' in this narrower sense is an essential element in the wider fidelity, as Paul and Luther clearly saw."

42 H. C. Leupold, *Exposition of Isaiah*, 2 vols. (Grand Rapids: Baker, 1968), 1:513.

43 Vriezen, *Outline of Old Testament Theology*, 157.

44 E. Earle Ellis, *The Gospel of Luke. NCBC* (Grand Rapids: Baker, 1968), 1:513.

45 H. Köster, *"splanchnizomai," TDNT*, 7:553–55.

46 For a discussion of the relationship between the death of Jesus Christ and God's all-encompassing plan for the world, the reader is directed to chapter 8, "God's Grand Design for Human History."

47 F. F. Bruce, *Romans. TNTC* (London: Tyndale, 1963), 176.

48 Matthew Black, *Romans. NCBC* (Grand Rapids: Eerdmans, 1981), 125.

[49] William Dyrness, *Themes in Old Testament Theology* (Downers Grove: InterVarsity, 1979), 53. Cf. *TDNTAbr*, 170.

[50] F. Godet, *Commentary on St. Paul's Epistle to the Romans* (New York: Funk & Wagnalls, 1883), 262. Cf. O. Becker, *"opsonion,"* *NIDNTT*, 3:144–45.

[51] Fritz Rienecker and Cleon Rogers, Jr., *A Linguistic Key to the Greek New Testament* (Grand Rapids: Zondervan, 1980), 525.

[52] A distinction can be made between two important words for God's love. *Phileō* denotes affection, concern, and fondness resulting from a personal relationship, and in this sense it is used of God's love for the Son (John 5:20) and for Christian believers (John 16:27). *Agapaō/agapē* connotes affection or deep regard resulting from a deliberate choice, and so is used of God's love for Christ (John 3:35; 10:17; 15:9; 17:24, 26), Christian believers (John 17:23; 1 John 3:1; 4:19), and the entire human race (John 3:16). See W. Günther, "love," *NIDNTT*, 2:542, 544, 548.

[53] Rienecker and Rogers, *Linguistic Key*, 847. Cf. H. Schönweiss, "anger, wrath," *NIDNTT*, 1, 105–6.

[54] For a connected study of this approach to the divine attributes see also G. R. Lewis, "God, Attributes of," *EDT*, 451–59.

[55] Augustine, *Confessions*, XI.31.

[56] René Descartes, *Meditations*, III, ed. Hutchins, *Great Books of the Western World*, 31:82.

[57] *Euthyphro*, ed. Hutchins, *Great Books of the Western World*, 7:196.

[58] Colin Brown, "Righteousness," *NIDNTT*, 3:352–73.

[59] H. Wheeler Robinson, *Suffering: Human and Divine* (New York: Macmillan, 1939), 178.

[60] Ibid., 156.

[61] *Book of Common Prayer* (New York: Church Pension Fund, 1945), 603.

[62] *Doctrines and Disciplines of the Methodist Church*, 1960 (Nashville: Methodist Publishing House, 1960), 30.

[63] For further discussion see G. R. Lewis, "Impassibility of God," *EDT*, 553–54.

[64] Martin Pine, "Double Truth," in *Dictionary of the History of Ideas*, ed. Philip P. Wiener (New York: Scribner, 1973), 2:31–37.

[65] R. C. Zaehner, *Our Savage God: The Perverse Use of Eastern Thought* (New York: Sheed and Ward, 1974), pp. 9–17.

[66] Alan Watts, *The Way of Zen* (New York: Random, 1957), 152.

[67] Ibid., 40.

[68] J. I. Packer, *Knowing God* (Downers Grove: InterVarsity, 1974), 18.

[69] John Burnaby, *Amor Dei: A Study of the Religion of St. Augustine* (London: Hodder & Stoughton, 1938), 141.

[70] Ibid., 262.

Chapter Seven

[1] Arius, *Letter to Alexander of Alexandris*, 4.

[2] *Racovian Catechism*, 22.

[3] Karl Barth, *CD*, vol. 1, pt. 1, pp. 351, 353, 382.

[4] Ibid., 402. Here Barth argues that God's essence is his act of revelation. "God's essence and His operation are not twain but one. . . . The operation of God is the essence of God." Ibid., 426.

[5] Ibid., 366. Barth, defining person as a center of conscious individuality, concludes that in God there are not three Thou's—three personal subjects—but only one. His suborthodox understanding of the Trinity follows from this crucial judgment.

[6] So argues Sylvester P. Schilling in his book *Contemporary Continental Theologians* (Nashville: Abingdon, 1966), 36: "[Barth] definitely espouses a modalistic trinitarianism." The same conclusion is reached by Jürgen Moltmann in *The Trinity and the Kingdom* (San Francisco: Harper & Row, 1981), 139–44.

[7] Emil Brunner, *The Christian Doctrine of God* (Philadelphia: Westminster, 1949), 226. "The idea of *'una substantia'* has had a particularly disastrous influence. . . . Similarly, the idea of Three Persons is more than questionable."

[8] Ibid., 206–7.

[9] Ibid., 223.

[10] Leslie Dewart, *The Future of Belief* (New York: Herder & Herder, 1966), 148.

[11] Karl Rahner, *The Trinity* (New York: Seabury, 1974), 47.

[12] Hans Küng, *On Being a Christian* (Garden City, N.Y.: Doubleday, 1976), 475.

[13] W. A. Brown, *Christian Theology in Outline* (New York: Scribner, 1911), 156.

[14] Ibid., 157.

[15] Harry Emerson Fosdick, *The Living of These Days: An Autobiography* (New York: Harper, 1956), 64.

[16] Norman Pittenger, *The Holy Spirit* (Philadelphia: United Church Press, 1974), 123.

[17] The Spirit "is the 'responding,' the conforming, the returning of the 'amen' of God through the whole creation and in deity itself." Pittenger, *Holy Spirit*, 59.

[18] John B. Cobb, Jr., and David R. Griffin, *Process Theology: An Introductory Exposition* (Philadelphia: Westminster, 1976), 110.

[19] *Letter of Barnabas*, 2:9; 12:8 (Father); 5:5; 7:2 (Son); 6:14; 12:2; 19:7 (Holy Spirit).

[20] Theophilus, *To Autolychus*, 2.15.

[21] Irenaeus, *Against Heresies*, II.30.9; III.6.1–2; III.8.3; IV.6.6; and passim.

[22] Irenaeus, *Proof of the Preaching*, 5; idem., *Against Heresies*, V.12.2.

[23] Irenaeus, *Proof of the Preaching*, 7; idem., *Against Heresies*, V.10; IV.6.7; 20.1,4.

[24] Tertullian, *Against Praxeus*, II, V–VII, XIII; *Apology*, XXI.

[25] Athanasius, *Oration Against the Arians*, III.4; cf. IV.1.

[26] Athanasius, *Letters to Sarapion*, I.20–21; *Oration Against the Arians*, III.25.

[27] Augustine, *The Trinity*, VII.6.11. Or, "one substance or essence" subsisting in "three persons."

[28] Ibid., VI.12.12; cf. idem., *Enchiridion*, 38; *On Christian Doctrine*, I.5; *The Trinity*, V.8.9; XV.5.8.

[29] Augustine, *The Trinity*, XV.20.38; 17.29; 26.47.

[30] Ibid., V.14.15.

[31] John Calvin, *Institutes of the Christian Religion*, I.13.18.

[32] Ibid.

[33] Ibid., I.13.20.

[34] L. Berkhof, *Systematic Theology* (Grand Rapids: Eerdmans, 1941), 82–99.

[35] Henry C. Thiessen, *Lectures in Systematic Theology*, rev. by Vernon D. Doerksen (Grand Rapids: Eerdmans, 1979), 89-99.

[36] Millard J. Erickson, *Christian Theology*, 3 vols. (Grand Rapids: Baker, 1983–85) 1:321–42

[37] Th. C. Vriezen, *An Outline of Old Testament Theology* (Wageningen: Veenman & Zonen, 1958), 175. Peter C. Craigie, *The Book of Deuteronomy*. NICOT (Grand Rapids: Eerdmans, 1976), 169, concurs: "The word ['ehād] expresses not only uniqueness but also the unity of God." M. Dahood believes that God's uniqueness lies in the foreground, for he translates the verse "Obey, Israel, Yahweh. Yahweh our God is the Unique." Cited by Craigie, *Deuteronomy*, 169.

[38] G. Ch. Aalders, *Genesis*, 2 vols. (Grand Rapids: Zondervan, 1981), 2:70.

[39] Jack B. Scott, "'elōhîm," TWOT, 1:470.

[40] So *Gesenius' Hebrew Grammar*, ed. E. Kautzsch (Oxford: Clarendon, 1976), 398–99.

[41] Craigie, *Deuteronomy*, 262, comments: "The singular ('a prophet') is a collective form indicating a succession of prophets."

[42] John Calvin, *Commentary on Genesis*, 1:470.

[43] "The evidence for the view that the angel of the Lord is a preexistent appearance of Christ is basically analogical and falls short of being conclusive. . . . It is best to see the angel as a self-manifestation of Yahweh in a form that would communicate his immanence and direct concern to those to whom he ministered." Thomas E. McComiskey, "Angel of the Lord," *EDT*, 48. For extended exegetical argumentation, see William Graham MacDonald, "Christology and 'The Angel of the Lord,'" in *Current Issues in Biblical and Patristic Interpretation*, ed. Gerald F. Hawthorne (Grand Rapids: Eerdmans, 1975), 324–35. Cf. H. Bietenhard, "angel," *NIDNTT*, 1:101.

[44] Aalders, *Genesis*, 1:55. Henri Blocher claims, "The part played alongside God by His Word, which distinguishes and communicates, and by His Spirit, which is a living presence, suggests that the writer's monotheism is not as simple as might appear." *In the Beginning* (Downers Grove: InterVarsity, 1984), 70.

[45] Hugh J. Blair, "Joshua," *NBCRev*, 239.

[46] See also Martin Woudstra, *The Book of Joshua* (Grand Rapids: Eerdmans, 1981), 105.

[47] J. Barton Payne, "rûah," TWOT, 2:837.

[48] H. C. Leupold argues as follows concerning the phrase "the breath of his mouth": "in which, without any doubt, God's Holy Spirit was potently at work" to bring into being all the heavenly bodies. *Exposition of the Psalms*, 2 vols. (Columbus: Wartburn, 1959), 1:272.

[49] John Calvin, *Commentary on the Psalms*, 5 vols. (Grand Rapids: Eerdmans, 1949), 2:183. What likely was opaque to the psalmist was brought to light by the New Testament, following the Incarnation.

[50] Derek Kidner, *Psalms 1–72*. TNTC (London: Inter-Varsity, 1973), 254.

[51] C. S. Lewis, *Reflections on the Psalms* (New York: Harcourt, Brace, 1958), 99. Cf. Derek Kidner, *Psalms 73–150*. TOTC (London: Inter-Varsity, 1975), 393.

[52] Cf. Derek Kidner, *Proverbs*. TOTC (London: Tyndale, 1964), 79: "The personification

of wisdom, far from overshooting the literal truth, was a preparation for its full statement, since the agent of creation was no mere activity of God, but the Son, His eternal Word, Wisdom, and Power."

[53] Derek Kidner, "Isaiah," *NBCRev*, 616.

[54] See Charles L. Feinberg, *Jeremiah: A Commentary* (Grand Rapids: Zondervan, 1982), 163.

[55] Abraham Calov, cited by Robert D. Preuss, *The Theology of Post-Reformation Lutheranism*, 2 vols. (St. Louis: Concordia, 1970–72), 2:129.

[56] Alfred Plummer comments that "the aorist points back to a moment in eternity and implies the preexistence of the Messiah." *An Exegetical Commentary on the Gospel According to Matthew* (Reprint, Grand Rapids: Baker, 1982), 168.

[57] I. Howard Marshall, *"huios tou theou,"* *NIDNTT*, 3:641.

[58] For a complete discussion of Jesus' response to the high priest, see Plummer, *Matthew*, 378–79.

[59] R. S. Franks, *The Doctrine of the Trinity* (London: Duckworth, 1953), 10.

[60] I. Howard Marshall, *The Acts of the Apostles. TNTC* (Grand Rapids: Eerdmans, 1980), 296.

[61] "The dominating theological motif in Acts is the presence and work of the Holy Spirit." F. F. Bruce, "The Acts of the Apostles," *NBCRev*, 972.

[62] The pagan Greeks (v. 5) believed in "many 'gods' " (i.e., idols) and "many 'lords' " (i.e., mythological heroes). In contradistinction, Paul emphasizes the uniqueness of "one God, the Father" and of "one Lord, Jesus Christ" (v. 6). When Christ is separately mentioned in context, Paul denominates God as "the Father" (e.g., Rom. 1:7; 2 Cor. 1:3; Eph. 1:17).

[63] "The distinct personality and the divinity of the Son, the Father, and the Holy Spirit, to each of whom prayer is addressed, is here taken for granted. And therefore this passage is a clear recognition of the doctrine of the Trinity." Charles Hodge, *II Corinthians* (Reprint, Grand Rapids: Baker, 1980), 314.

[64] J. H. Bernard, *The Pastoral Epistles* (Reprint, Grand Rapids; Baker, 1980), 179.

[65] See F. F. Bruce, *Romans. TNTC* (London: Tyndale, 1963), 187. Also John Murray, *Romans. NICNT*, 2 vols. (Grand Rapids: Eerdmans, 1959–65), 2:246: "Grammatically or syntactically there is no reason for taking the clauses in question as other than referring to Christ." Romans 9:5 may be punctuated differently than the above have suggested (see AV, RV, RSV marg., NEB marg.), in which case the text would then make no explicit claim of deity for Christ. The orthodoxy of believing Christians who favor one of the alternative forms of punctuation ought not be impugned.

[66] F. Foulkes, "Philippians," *NBCRev*, 1132.

[67] Joseph Henry Thayer, *A Greek-English Lexicon of the New Testament* (New York: American, 1889), 288.

[68] R. V. G. Tasker, *2 Corinthians. TNTC* (London: Tyndale, 1958), 66.

[69] Leon Morris, *1 Corinthians. TNTC* (London: Tyndale, 1958), 173.

[70] Charles Hodge, *1 Corinthians* (Reprint, Grand Rapids: Baker, 1980), 40.

[71] For a discussion of the history of the *Comma Johanneum*, see Bruce M. Metzger, *The Text of the New Testament* (New York & Oxford: Oxford University Press, 1968), 101–2.

[72] B. F. Westcott comments: "It seems clear that the unity here spoken of cannot fall short of unity of essence." *The Gospel According to St. John*, 2 vols. in one (Reprint, Grand Rapids: Baker, 1980), 2:68.

[73] F. F. Bruce maintains that these two expressions best represent the meaning of *monogenēs theos* (cf. NASB), *The Gospel of John* (Grand Rapids: Eerdmans, 1983), 44. Modern lexicography judges that *monogenēs* derives from *monos* and *genos* and thus bears the meaning "one of a kind" or "unique." The NIV works a conflation of sorts by translating *monogenēs theos* as "God the only Son." Whichever translation is accepted, however, the deity of Christ is established.

[74] Charles Hodge, *Systematic Theology*; 3 vols. (Reprint, Grand Rapids: Eerdmans, 1973), 1:447.

[75] Westcott, *St. John*, 2:214.

[76] See J. H. Moulton, *A Grammar of the New Testament Greek. Vol. I: Prolegomena* (Edinburgh: T. & T. Clark, 1908), 84.

[77] Herbert Wolf, " '*ehad*," *TWOT* (Chicago: Moody, 1980), 1:30.

[78] J. Oliver Buswell, Jr., "The Place of Paradox in Our Christian Testimony," *Journal of the American Scientific Affiliation*, vol. 17, no. 1 (March 1965): 96.

[79] Geerhardus Vos, *The Self-Disclosure of Jesus* (Grand Rapids: Eerdmans, 1954).

[80] J. Barton Payne, "*rûah*," *TWOT*, 2:836–37.

[81] T. S. Caulley, "Holy Spirit," *EDT*, 523.

[82] George Smeaton, *The Doctrine of the Holy Spirit* (Edinburgh: T. & T. Clark, 1882), 100.

[83] Norman C. Bartlett, *The Triune God* (New York: American Tract Society, 1937), 81.

[84] John B. Champion, *Personality and the Trinity* (New York: Revell, 1935), 97.

[85] John Lawson, *Comprehensive Handbook of Christian Doctrine* (Englewood Cliffs, N.J.: Prentice-Hall, 1967), 123.

[86] Augustine, "Sermons on NT Lessons" LXVII, 11.

[87] Ibid.

[88] K. H. Bartells, "One," *NIDNTT*, 2:725.

[89] See B. B. Warfield, *The Lord of Glory* (Reprint, Grand Rapids: Zondervan, n.d.), 198–99; see also Gordon Clark's defense of eternal generation in his work *The Trinity* (Jefferson, Md.: Trinity Foundation, 1985), 109–26.

[90] G. W. Bromiley, "Eternal Generation," *EDT*, 368.

[91] B. B. Warfield, *Calvin and Augustine* (Philadelphia: Presbyterian and Reformed, 1956), 250.

[92] Curtis Vaughn, ed., *The New Testament From 26 Translations* (Grand Rapids: Zondervan, 1967).

[93] For a discussion of the debate see George S. Hendry, *The Holy Spirit in Christian Theology* (Philadelphia: Westminster, 1956), 30–52.

[94] Abraham Kuyper, *The Work of the Holy Spirit* (Grand Rapids: Eerdmans, 1956), 19–21. See also Dorothy Sayers, *The Mind of the Maker* (London: Methuen, 1941).

[95] Ibid., 24.

[96] David L. Miller, *The New Polytheism* (New York: Harper & Row, 1974), 11.

[97] G. L. Prestige, *God in Patristic Thought* (London: SPCK, 1952), 213.

[98] Gordon R. Lewis, "Triune God: Revelational Bases for Trinitarianism," *Christianity Today*, 7 (Jan. 4, 1963): 20–22.

[99] James A. Pike, "Three-Pronged Synthesis," *The Christian Century*, 21 (Dec. 21, 1960): 1497–98.

[100] James E. Talmadge, *Articles of Faith* (Salt Lake City: Church of Jesus Christ of Latter-Day Saints, 1952), 48.

[101] *The Truth That Leads to Eternal Life* (New York: Watchtower Bible and Tract Society, 1968), 22–23.

[102] Ibid.

[103] B. B. Warfield, "Trinity," in *ISBE*, 5:3012.

[104] *Let God Be True*, 2d ed. (New York: Watchtower Bible and Tract Society, 1946), 111.

[105] For more detailed response to the Jehovah's Witnesses see Gordon R. Lewis, *Confronting the Cults* (Phillipsburg, N.J.: Presbyterian and Reformed, 1966), 23–29; Anthony Hoekema, *The Four Major Cults* (Grand Rapids: Eerdmans, 1963), 270–76.

[106] Mary Baker Eddy, *Science and Truth With Key to the Scriptures* (Boston: The Trustees Under the Will of Mary Baker Eddy, 1906), 256.

[107] Ibid.

[108] John A. Hutchison, *Paths of Faith* (New York: McGraw-Hill, 1975), 636.

[109] John B. Cobb, *Christ in a Pluralistic Age* (Philadelphia: Westminster, 1975), 220.

[110] Bruce A. Demarest, "Process Trinitarianism" in *Perspectives on Evangelical Theology*, ed. Kenneth S. Kantzer and Stanley N. Gundry (Grand Rapids: Baker, 1979), 31.

[111] *The Koran*, CXIV, Sura V. 77, trans. M. Rodwell (New York: Dutton, 1953), 494.

[112] A. W. Tozer, *The Knowledge of the Holy* (New York: Harper, 1961), 10.

[113] Ibid., 11.

[114] Ibid., 12.

[115] A. W. Tozer, "The Pursuit of God," in *The Best of A. W. Tozer*, ed. Warren Wiersbe (Grand Rapids: Baker, 1978), 15.

[116] Ibid., 15.

[117] Herman Bavinck, *The Doctrine of God* (Grand Rapids: Eerdmans, 1955), 333.

[118] David E. Roberts, *Existentialism and Religious Belief* (New York: Oxford, 1957), 10.

[119] See Walter Marshall Horton, *Christian Theology: An Ecumenical Approach* (New York: Harper, 1955), 195.

[120] See E. H. Bickersteth, *The Trinity* (Grand Rapids: Kregel, 1959), 134–35n.

[121] C. W. Lowry, *The Trinity and Christian Devotion* (New York: Harper, 1946), 157.

[122] Bernard Piault, *What Is the Trinity?* trans. Rosemary Haughton, *Twentieth Century Encyclopedia of Catholicism* (New York: Hawthorn, 1959), 17:139.

[123] See Claude Welch, *In This Name* (New York: Scribner, 1952), 94.

[124] See Charles W. Lowry, *The Trinity and Christian Devotion*, 157.

[125]Gerald H. Anderson, "The Theology of Mission Among Protestants in the Twentieth Century," in *The Theology of Christian Mission*, ed. Gerald H. Anderson (Nashville: Abingdon, 1961), 15.

[126]Ibid.

[127]George W. Peters, *A Biblical Theology of Missions* (Chicago: Moody, 1972), 81.

[128]Lesslie Newbigin, *The Open Secret* (Grand Rapids: Eerdmans, 1978), esp. 20–72.

[129]Ibid., 72.

Chapter Eight

[1] "God is conceived as loving will, when we regard His will as set upon the bringing forth of His Son and the community of the kingdom of God; and if we abstract from that, what we conceive is not God at all." A. Ritschl, *The Christian Doctrine of Justification and Reconciliation* (Reprint, Clifton, N.J.: Reformed Book Publishers, 1966), 283.

[2] William Newton Clarke, *An Outline of Christian Theology* (Edinburgh: T. & T. Clark, 1909), 146.

[3] Walter Rauschenbusch, *A Theology for the Social Gospel* (New York: Macmillan, 1917), 174–79.

[4] William Adams Brown, *Christian Theology in Outline* (New York: Scribner, 1911), 89–95, 182–83, 190–94.

[5]John B. Cobb, Jr., and David Ray Griffin, *Process Theology: An Introductory Exposition* (Philadelphia: Westminster, 1976), 53.

[6]Arminius "believed that the sublapsarian unconditional predestination view of Augustine . . . is unscriptural." J. K. Grider, "Arminianism," *EDT*, 79.

[7]Jacob Arminius, *The Writings of Arminius* (Reprint, Grand Rapids: Baker, 1977), 4:82.

[8]John Wesley, "Sermon CXXVIII," in *The Works of John Wesley*, 14 vols. (Grand Rapids: Zondervan, n.d.), 7:383.

[9]Richard Watson, *Theological Institutes*, 2 vols. (New York: Lane & Scott, 1851), 2:423.

[10]Ibid., 426.

[11]Ratramnus, *On Predestination*, I.

[12]Martin Luther, *The Bondage of the Will*, *LW*, 33:146

[13]Luther, *Bondage of the Will*, *LW*, 33:191. For Luther's treatment of Judas's betrayal in relation to God's will, see ibid., 185, 193.

[14]John Calvin, "Articles Concerning Predestination," *LCC*, 22:180. Cf. *Institutes of the Christian Religion*, III.23.8.

[15]Calvin, *Institutes*, III.21.5. Cf. "God once established by His eternal and unchangeable plan those He long before determined once for all to receive into salvation, and those whom, on the other hand, he would devote to destruction." Ibid., III.21.7.

[16]Ibid., III.23.7. Although sovereign election to life is more prominent, Calvin regards reprobation to death as the logical consequence of the positive decree. For his treatment of reprobation see further ibid., I.18.2; II.4.1,3–5; III.22.6,11; III.23.1–10; III.24.12–14; "Articles Concerning Predestination," 179–80.

[17] "While . . . God holds the Devil and the godless subject to His will, nevertheless God cannot be called the cause of sin, nor the author of evil, nor subject to any guilt." Calvin, "Articles Concerning Predestination," 179.

[18]Calvin, "Brief Reply in Refutation of the Calumnies of a Certain Worthless Person," *LCC*, 22:342. Cf. *Institutes*, III.21.1,4; III.23.2–5.

[19]See Calvin, *Institutes*, III.23.3,7–8.

[20] Theodore Beza, *Quaestiones et responsiones* (Geneva, 1570), 107; cited by John S. Bray, *Theodore Beza's Doctrine of Predestination* (Nieuwkoop: De Graf, 1975), 88.

[21]John Owen, *The Works of John Owen*, ed. by William Gould; 16 vols. (Edinburgh: Banner of Truth Trust, 1965–68), 10:42.

[22]Herman Bavinck, *The Doctrine of God* (Reprint, Grand Rapids: Baker, 1977), 391.

[23]Ibid., 360, 386. "The final answer to the question why a thing is and why it is as it is must ever remain: 'God willed it,' according to his absolute sovereignty." Ibid., 371.

[24]Barth grants the usual distinctions between God's absolute and conditional will and between his efficient and permissive will. But since the divine decision establishes the conditions by which all things eventuate, the latter terms in each of the above pairs dissolve into his sovereign decree. *CD*, vol. 2, pt. 1, pp. 590–97.

[25]Ibid., vol. 2, pt. 2, p. 95. "Before Him and without Him God does not, then, elect or will anything." Ibid., 94.

[26]Ibid., vol. 2, pt. 2, p. 167.

[27] "God has ascribed to man . . . election, salvation, and life; and to Himself He has ascribed . . . reprobation, perdition, and death." Ibid., vol. 2, pt. 2, p. 117.

[28]Ibid., 306.

[29]Ibid., 142. For Barth's complete discussion of the supra-infra debate, see ibid., 127–145.

30 Tatian, *Address to the Greeks*, XI.

31 Irenaeus, *Proof of the Apostolic Preaching*, 7. Cf. *Against Heresies*, V.2.2.

32 Irenaeus, *Against Heresies*, V.29.2.; cf. IV.39.3–4.

33 Tertullian, *Against Marcion*, II.23. Cf. "What God has justly decreed, having no evil purpose in his decree, He decreed from the principle of justice not malevolence." Ibid., II.24.

34 Ibid., II.6.

35 Ibid., II.16.

36 Augustine, *Concerning the Predestination of the Saints*, 11, 18–19, 32–37; *On the Gift of Perseverance*, 41–42, 47; *On Admonition and Grace*, 13–14, 32.

37 Augustine, *The City of God*, V.9.

38 Augustine, *Enchiridion*, 27.

39 Augustine, *The City of God*, XXI.12; *Enchiridion*, 27; *On the Gift of Perseverance*, 16.

40 Augustine, *The City of God*, XV.1; *Enchiridion*, 26; *On the Gospel of St. John*, 43.14; 48.4,6.

41 Augustine, *Enchiridion*, 95; cf. *On the Trinity*, III.4.

42 "As predestination includes the will to confer grace and glory, so also reprobation includes the will to permit a person to fall into sin and to impose the punishment of damnation on account of that sin." Thomas Aquinas, *ST*, vol. I, pt. 1, q. 23, art. 3.

43 Ibid., q. 22, art. 2.

44 Ibid., q. 23, art. 8. Thomas adds: "Secondary causes cannot escape the order of first universal cause . . . , indeed, they execute that order." Ibid.

45 Richard A. Muller states, "The infralapsarian view is the confessional view of the Reformed churches," in *Dictionary of Latin and Greek Theological Terms* (Grand Rapids: Baker, 1985), s.v., *supra lapsum*, 292.

46 Charles Hodge, *Systematic Theology*, 3 vols. (Reprint, Grand Rapids: Eerdmans, 1973), 1:542. He also writes, "The decrees of God are in no case conditional. The event decreed is suspended on a condition, but the purpose of God is not. It is inconsistent with the nature of God to assume suspense on His part." Ibid., 1:540.

47 Ibid., 1:545–48.

48 Carl F. H. Henry, *God, Revelation and Authority*, 6 vols. (Waco: Word, 1976–83), 6:85.

49 Millard J. Erickson, *Christian Theology*, 3 vols. (Grand Rapids: Baker, 1983–85), 1:345–63.

50 Henry C. Thiessen, *Lectures in Systematic Theology*, rev. by Vernon D. Doerksen (Grand Rapids: Eerdmans, 1979), 100–110.

51 L. Berkhof, *Systematic Theology* (Grand Rapids: Eerdmans, 1941), 100–108, 115–25.

52 G. Ch. Aalders, *Genesis*; 2 vols. (Grand Rapids: Zondervan, 1981), 1:57. Cf. Claus Westermann, *Creation* (Philadelphia: Fortress, 1974), 61; Andrew Bowling, "*tob*," *TWOT*, 1:345–46.

53 Against the sweeping judgment of L. Berkhof, *Systematic Theology*, 108, and certain other Reformed theologians, to the effect that God's permissive will renders the entrance of sin into the world *logically* certain.

54 See Paul's discussion of the hardening of Pharaoh's heart under the Pauline literature, later in this section, pp. 305–6.

55 According to J. A. Thompson: "The demands of God, once rejected, became a hardening influence on Sihon's heart, so that he was unable to respond favorably to Israel's request." *Deuteronomy*. TOTC (London: Inter-Varsity, 1974), 95.

56 Leon J. Wood, "*ḥāpēṣ*," *TWOT*, 1:310.

57 Ralph W. Klein, *1 Samuel*. WBC (Waco: Word, 1983), 26.

58 "From the biblical viewpoint, all things have their ultimate source in God. Even the wrath of men and Satan ultimately further the divine purposes." Fred E. Young, *The Wycliffe Bible Commentary*, ed. Charles F. Pfeiffer and Everett F. Harrison (Chicago: Moody, 1962), 304.

59 Ibid., 339.

60 "Loved" thus connotes "preferred," and "hated" metaphorically signifies "not preferred." "The Hebrew word for 'to hate' often means to scorn, or to rank something lower than something else, while 'to love' may mean to choose something and rank it higher than something else." Th. C. Vriezen, *An Outline of Old Testament Theology* (Wageningen: Veenman & Zonen, 1960), 167. For the imagery see Genesis 29:30–31; Deuteronomy 21:15–16; Proverbs 13:24; Matthew 6:24; cf. Matthew 10:37 with Luke 14:26.

61 See Ebenezer Henderson, *The Twelve Minor Prophets* (Reprint, Grand Rapids: Baker, 1980), 298: "God is often said to do what He permits to be done by others."

62 Claus Westermann, *Isaiah 40–66*. OTL (Philadelphia: Westminster, 1969), 266.

63 H. C. Leupold, *Exposition of Isaiah*, 2 vols. (Grand Rapids: Baker 1968–71), 2:232. Cf. Edward J. Young, *The Book of Isaiah*, 3 vols. *NICOT* (Grand Rapids: Eerdmans, 1965–72), 3:354: "They were only obeying what the Lord permitted them to do." So also Alfred Martin and John Martin, *Isaiah: The Glory of the Messiah* (Chicago: Moody, 1983), 141: "What Christ suffered at the hands of men was tragic. . . . Nevertheless, in and through that tragedy God was working out His sovereign purpose of grace. Isaiah emphasizes that in verse 10."

64 In Isaiah 6:9–13, God commanded Isaiah to make the people callous through his preaching. God gave his word through the prophet, to which the people chose to respond perversely, thus provoking God's just retribution.

65 "The *dei*, as often in the Gospels, may mean 'by God's decree' (Matt. 24:6; 26:54), which is true of the good, but not of the evil." Alfred Plummer, *The Gospel According to St. Matthew* (Reprint, Grand Rapids: Baker, 1982), 250.

66 E. Earle Ellis, *The Gospel of Luke. NCBC* (Grand Rapids: Eerdmans, 1981), 277.

67 Emil Brunner, *The Christian Doctrine of God: Dogmatics* (Philadelphia: Westminster, 1950), 1:237.

68 Ellis, *Luke*, 120.

69 Some authorities such as A. H. McNeile, *The Gospel According to St. Matthew* (Reprint, Grand Rapids: Baker, 1982), 250, and I. Howard Marshall, *The Acts of the Apostles. TNTC* (Grand Rapids: Eerdmans, 1980), 75, view the divine determination and the human betrayal as an insoluble paradox. Marshall comments: "Here we have the paradox of divine predestination and human responsibility in its strongest form." We suggest that the apparent paradox is solved as one divides the problem and distinguishes between (1) God as the final cause who ordains the saving values of Christ's death and (2) the human agent (Judas) as the efficient, blameworthy cause of Christ's sufferings.

70 Charles Hodge, *Ephesians* (Reprint, Grand Rapids: Baker, 1980), 28.

71 Niger Turner points out that the verb "glorified" (*edoxasen*) is likely a proleptic aorist: "The timeless [proleptic] aorist is a suitable tense to express this projection of the future into the present as if some event had already occurred." In J. H. Mounton, ed., *A Grammar of New Testament Greek*, s.v. "syntax" (Edinburgh: T. & T. Clark, 1963), 3:74.

72 C. E. B. Cranfield, *The Epistle to the Romans*, 2 vols. *ICC* (Edinburgh: T. & T. Clark, 1975–79), 2:480. F. F. Bruce observes

that the terse statements about Jacob and Esau describe "God's choice of Jacob and passing over his brother." *Romans. TNTC* (London: Tyndale, 1963), 188. Cf. W. G. T. Shedd, *Commentary on Romans* (Reprint, Grand Rapids: Baker, 1980), 286.

73 Shedd, *Romans*, 292. We agree with Charles Bigg, *The Epistles of St. Peter and St. Jude. ICC* (New York: Scribner, 1909), 133, that the doctrine of reprobation "is irreconcilable with the idea [or character] of God."

74 Cranfield, *Romans*, 2:492.

75 F. Davidson and Ralph P. Martin, "Romans," *NBCRev*, 1035. Other texts adduced by some in support of reprobation, such as 1 Corinthians 9:27; Galatians 4:30; 2 Timothy 2:20; 3:8, are best understood as not positing an unconditional will of perdition in God.

76 Brunner, *The Christian Doctrine of God*, 331.

77 J. H. Bernard remarks, "That the divine intention may be thwarted by man's misuse of his free will is part of the great mystery of evil, unexplained and inexplicable." *The Pastoral Epistles* (Reprint, Grand Rapids: Baker, 1980), 41.

78 F. F. Bruce, *1 & 2 Thessalonians. WBC* (Waco: Word, 1982), 174. Cf. I. Howard Marshall, *1 and 2 Thessalonians. NCBC* (Grand Rapids: Eerdmans, 1983), 204: "Those who refuse to believe and accept the truth find that judgment comes upon them in the form of an inability to accept the truth."

79 B. F. Westcott, *The Gospel According to St. John;* 2 vols. in 1 (Reprint, Grand Rapids: Baker, 1980), 2:251.

80 Bigg, *St. Peter and St. Jude*, 103.

81 Fritz Rienecker and Cleon L. Rogers, Jr., *A Linguistic Key to the Greek New Testament* (Grand Rapids: Zondervan, 1982), 673. Cf. U. Becker, "hard, hardened," *NIDNTT*, 2:156: "In the NT men who do not open themselves to the Gospel are described as hardened."

82 Aristotle, *Metaphysics* I.3.

83 Alvin Plantinga, "Advice to Christian Philosophers," *Faith and Philosophy*, 1, 3 (July 1984): 266.

84 James Daane, *The Freedom of God* (Grand Rapids: Eerdmans, 1973), 60.

85 Ibid., 170.

86 For an analysis and refutation of the single decree see ibid., 45–73.

87 Henry, *God, Revelation and Authority*, 104.

[88] For an evangelical evaluation of Barth's view of election see ibid., 90–107.

[89] The concept of human free agency here presented focuses on human self-determination, not in a vacuum, but dependent on God and in accord with the different moral condition of human nature at different times. Our view differs from that of Norman Geisler and many others who fail to take into account the differing states of human nature affecting the power of self-determination (1) prior to the Fall, (2) after the Fall, (3) after regeneration, and (4) after glorification. In agreement with Geisler's chapter entitled "God Knows All Things," we affirm that before the Fall humans had the power of contrary choice and that God simply knows all things. But differing with Geisler, we state that after the Fall God foreknows that people with depraved natures use their power of self-determination only sinfully. Left to mere divine prescience, none would believe. So that many would believe and benefit by Christ's atonement, the Father chose to grant them (the elect) repentance and a radically new heart. Then with the new nature and the old, believers have the power of contrary choice again. But in heaven, they will no longer be able to sin. Hence our view of human freedom includes the strength of a view like Geisler's in relation to evil and a view like John S. Feinberg's Augustinian soft (persuasive) determinism in relation to the redemption of depraved sinners. Our view differs from Feinberg's chapter "God Ordains All Things" by holding more consistently that God does not ordain evil. For a brief comparison, if we were to write a chapter in their series, it might be entitled "God Knows All Things and Ordains Some (Redemptive) Things." For Feinberg's and Geisler's concepts see their chapter edited by David Basinger and Randall Basinger, in *Predestination and Free Will* (Downers Grove: InterVarsity, 1986), 19–43, 64–84.

[90] Augustine, *Against Fortunatus*, 15.

[91] Unfortunately most of the Arminian debate has been directed against supralapsarian double predestination, and vice versa. Inadequate focus has been given either in exposition or debate to a clear infralapsarian alternative. The infralapsarian view here developed is not answered by the critical evaluations of supralapsarianism, for example, in Clark Pinnock, ed., *Grace Unlimited* (Minneapolis: Bethany Fellowship, 1975) or in Roger Forster and V. Paul Marston, *God's Strategy in Human History* (Wheaton: Tyndale, 1973).

[92] F. H. Klooster, "Supralapsarianism," *EDT*, 1060.

[93] R. V. Schnucker, "Infralapsarianism," *EDT*, 560–61.

[94] Paul K. Jewett, *Election and Predestination* (Grand Rapids: Eerdmans, 1985), 93.

[95] Ibid., 94.

[96] Ibid., 95.

[97] Ibid., 96.

[98] Ibid.

[99] Ibid., 97.

[100] Ibid.

[101] Ibid., 106.

[102] Ibid., 108.

[103] Ibid.

[104] C. S. Lewis, *Letters to Malcolm* (New York: Harcourt, Brace and World, 1963), 109.

[105] Augustine, "The Free Choice of the Will" II, 20. cf. his *Confessions* VII, 16.

[106] For further discussion of the purposes of suffering, see Gordon R. Lewis, "Suffering and Anguish" ed. Merrill C. Tenney, *ZPEB* 5:530–33.

[107] See Erickson, *Christian Theology*, 1:368, especially note 11.

[108] Ibid., 359.

[109] See B. B. Warfield's discussion of God's miraculous strategy in "Christian Supernaturalism" in *Biblical and Theological Studies* (Philadelphia: Presbyterian and Reformed, 1952), 1–21.

[110] See Donald Bloesch, "Fate, fatalism," *EDT*, 407.

[111] See Stephen M. Cahn's discussion of Pierce and James's "Dilemma of Determinism," *EP*, 2:73.

[112] Richard Taylor, "Determinism," *EP*, 2:359–71; Norman L. Geisler, "Freedom, Free Will and Determinism," *EDT*, 428–30.

[113] Charles Haddon Spurgeon, *Lectures to My Students* (Grand Rapids: Zondervan, 1954), 80.

[114] James W. Ney, "Revolution," *His*, 21, 2 (November 1960): 35.

[115] For application of the sense of being called by God in the Christian life see Gordon MacDonald, *Ordering Your Private World* (Nashville: Nelson, 1984), 55–65.

[116] See Emile Cailliet, *The Recovery of Purpose* (New York: Harper, 1959).

[117] Jean-Paul Sartre, *Existentialism and Human Emotions* (New York: Philosophical Library, 1957), 90.

[118] Daane, *Freedom of God*, 150.

[119] Whereas all of the Bible is inspired and profitable in various ways (2 Tim. 3:16–17), Gary Friesen tends to limit the data of the Bible for decision making to "those areas specifically addressed by the Bible, and the revealed commands and principles of God." *Decision Making and the Will of God* (Portland: Multnomah, 1980), 163.

[120] See Carl F. H. Henry, *Christian Personal Ethics* (Grand Rapids: Eerdmans, 1957); idem, *Christian Social Ethics* (Grand Rapids: Eerdmans, 1964).

[121] It might help to review the steps in the method of theological decision making in chapter 1 of this book.

General Index

Aalders, G. Ch., 259
Aaron, 113
abba, 193
Abel, 141, 222, 296
Abelard, Peter, 49
Abimelech, 101
Abomination of desolation, the, 442
Abraham; and angels, 185, 259; faith of, 169; God's covenant with, 118; revelation to, 101, 142, 143, 184–86, 205, 234, 236; and the will of God, 315–16
Abram. *See* Abraham
Achan, 224
Acts, Book of, 149, 190, 229, 306, 352n.61
Adam, 77, 141; judgment of, 314; sin of, 100, 222, 296–97, 327; and the will of God, 184, 300, 313, 315–16, 322, 332
Agabus, 264
agapē, 111, 184, 192, 215, 229, 231, 235, 243, 350n.52
Agnosticism, 123, 201; relativistic, 123; on theology proper, 201
Ahab, 302
Aland, Kurt, 154
Albright, William Foxwell, 164
Altizer, Thomas J., 55, 202, 243
Ambrose, theology of, 49
Amorites, the, 236
Amos, the prophet, 189, 312
Amyraut, Moise, 52
Analogy of being, 64
"Analogy of Faith," 31
Ananias and Sapphira, 264, 272
Ananias, the disciple of Paul, 190
Ananias, the priest, 105
Anderson, Gerald H., 288
Angels: and Jesus, 110, 351n.43; rejoicing of, 237; revelation by, 101–2, 104–6, 185, 233, 238, 259, 306
Anglicanism, 27n

Animism, 195, 280
Animists. *See* Animism
Anselm of Canterbury, 49–50, 297–98
Anthropologists. *See* Anthropology
Anthropology, 35, 73
Anthropomorphisms, 185
Antichrist, the, 64, 158
Apocalypse, the, 145
Apocrypha, the, 116–17; and the canon, 147; and the church fathers, 136; and inspiration, 131, 148; and revelation, 116–17; and the Roman Catholic Church, 132
Apollos, 90
Apologetics, 28–29, 66, 76, 114, 298, 341n.78
Apologists. *See* Apologetics
Apostasy, 309
Apostles, the, 61, 146; the authority of, 149–50; the choice of, 118, 332; and Christ, 120, 144–45, 148–50; criteria for, 115; and inscripturation, 148–50; and inspiration, 131, 136, 144, 151–53, 157; and the New Testament, 150; and the Old Testament, 142–43; and revelation, 96, 98–100, 106, 110, 115, 117, 120–21, 131, 144–45; succession of, 116–17; teachings of, 127, 151, 159
Apostles Creed, the, 49, 281
Aquinas, Thomas, 53; on inerrancy, 132; and natural theology, 75; and Rahner, 54; on revelation, 64, 75–76, 96, 117; theology of, 50; on theology proper, 62, 178, 198, 216; on the will of God, 297–99, 355n.42. *See also* Thomism
Archer, Gleason L., Jr., 164
Areopagus address, the, 69
Arianism: Athanasius on, 49; on the Trinity, 49, 252–53, 256. *See also* Arius

359

Decrees of God, 356n.65; Augustine on, 295, 297, 298; Barth on, 297, 354n.24; Beza on, 296; Calvin on, 296–97; classes of, 295; and confessions, 299; definition of, 309, 311; and evangelism, 328–29; and events, 305–6, 309, 318; for salvation, 295–96, 308–29; and the glory of God, 307; Hodge on, 299, 355n.46; and human responsibility, 323–25; infralapsarian view of, 298, 299, 301, 307; and Jesus, 305; and Job, 303–4; meaning of, 311–14; in the New Testament, 305–10; in the Old Testament, 300–305; order of, 319–22; permissive vs. unconditional, 320; and responsibility, 323–25, 356n.69; of reprobation, 309, 356nn.73,75; supralapsarian view of, 295, 298, 309, 317, 320

Deism: and Scripture, 132; and special revelation, 97; on theology proper, 109, 216–17, 239, 244; on the Trinity, 252–53

Deists. *See* Deism

Demarest, Bruce, 13, 339–40n.41

Demons, 105

Descartes's view of God, 232

Despair, 195, 238

Determinism: philosophy of, 327–28; vs. the will of God, 298

Deus absconditus, 221

Devil, the. *See* Satan

Dewart, Leslie: on inerrancy, 162; on theology proper, 181, 219; on the Trinity, 254

Dewey, John, 35, 41

DeWolf, L. H., 63, 81

Dionysius, 88, 216

Disciples, the, 112, 118, 154, 195

Discipleship, 111

Discipline: in the church, 154, 159, 161; standards of, 125–26

Diseases, 104

Disillusionment, 195

Dispensationalism, 57

Divination, 224

Divine Light Mission, the, 283

Divine revelation. *See* Special revelation

Divine Science movement, 31

Divine speech, 100–101

Docetism, 138, 145

Doctrine: basic, 26; biblical, 26, 158–60, 162; in early church, 44; examination of, 23, 27–28, 148; false, 151; historic Christian, 28, 115; and institutions,

287; of life and death, 124; redemptive, 123; and revelation, 96, 117, 122; sound, 124, 151, 167; and the verificational method, 37–40

Doctrines and Disciplines of the Methodist Church, 235–36

Dodd, C.H., 218

"Dogmatic Constitution on Divine Revelation," 134

dokimazō, 70

Donatists, 49

Dorcas, 228

Dort Confession. *See* Synod of Dort

Downing, F. Gerald, 97

Dreams, and revelation, 98, 101, 104

Dreieinigkeit, Dreifaltigkeit, 254

Dutch Reformed theology, *See* Reformed theologians

dynamis, 107, 230

Eckhart, Meister, 50

'ēdāh, 303

Eddy, Mary Baker, 31, 282

Edom, 307

edoxasen, 356n.71

Education: of children, 86–87; and humanism, 206; justice in, 85; moral, 86–87; and theism, 201, 211

Educational *raison d' etre,* 125

Edwards, Jonathan, 52

Egypt. *See* Egyptians

Egyptians: hard hearts of, 102, 303; judgment on, 312; and Old Testament events, 120

Eichrodt, Walter, 218

Eisegesis, 25, 26, 30, 163

Election: biblical teaching, 301–10; Calvinism's view of, 329, 354n.15, 354n.16; decree of, 309–9, 313, 320–22; doctrine of, 298, 316, 329, 354n.27, 357n.115; eternal, 229; paradox of, 65; Puritans' view of, 52; relevance of, 332; Spurgeon's view of, 328

Eli, sons of, 302

Elihu, 67, 140

Elijah: and Ahab, 302; and the widow, 141; at Carmel, 102, 186, 224; God's plan for, 324

Eliphaz, 139

Elisha, 141

Elizabeth, 104, 238

Elohim, 67–68, 145, 185, 188–89, 258, 347n.44

Emotionalism, 167

Freud, Sigmund, 35
Functionalism, 35
Friesen, Gary, 358n.119
Fundamentalism: Bloesch on, 56–57; on inspiration, 135; and revelation, 89; on the Trinity, 287
Fundamentalists. *See* Fundamentalism

Gabriel, the angel, 104, 262
Galatians, the, 75
Gallic Confession, 299
Gallup polls, 78
Gamaliel, 229
Garden of Eden, 300, 323
Gärtner, Bertil, 69
Geisler, Norman L., 153, 357n.89
Geist, 178, 253
General revelation: accountability for, 76–78, 119; and Athenians, 69; Augustine on, 66; Barth on, 81, 121–22, 64–65, 97–98, 281; and biblical writers, 162; Calvin on, 66; and Dutch Reformed theology, 65; and Existentialism, 99; and Fundamentalism, 89; and God, 80, 95, 177, 196; forms of, 63; harmony of, 125; in nature, 63, 65–73, 80, 339n.32, 339n.41; information of, 72–75; issues of, 61–63, 80; Luther on, 66; and missions, 88–90; and Neoorthodoxy, 64–65, 81–82, 97–98; Pannenberg on, 98–99; and redemption, 95–96, 103, 108, 118; rejection of, 70; relevance of, 26, 73, 82–90, 110, 159, 166, 191, 241, 318, 332–33, 340n.74; and salvation, 67, 89, 96, 99; and skepticism, 97; vs. special revelation, 82, 87–90, 118; and theology proper, 183, 197, 203; variety of, 73–75; and world religions, 79, 88–89. *See also* Special Revelation
Gentiles, 125, 264; in the church, 152; and general revelation, 77, 87, 105–6; and knowledge of God, 64–65, 71, 201, 228; and Paul, 118, 190, 201, 314, 332; and the will of God, 306–7, 313, 316
Gerhard, John, 51
Geschichte, 98
Gethsemane, 238
Gideon, 102
Gill, John, 198, 203
Gnosticism: Clement on, 48; doctrine of necessity, 298; Irenaeus on, 48; view of God, 216, 266; view of the Trinity, 255

Goals, 47–48, 330–33
God: active nature of, 190-91, 196, 203, 205–6, 209, 233, 239, 243; attributes of, 72, 83, 177, 181, 184–200, 206, 210, 221–24, 232, 239, 311, 354n.1; being of, 195–97; communication of, 109–13, 121; comprehension of, 61–70, 75–76, 81–82, 95; concept of, 207–8, 239, 284; design for history, 293–333; and divine speech, 100–101; emotions of, 185–88, 197, 218, 220, 223, 227, 229, 235–36, 246; vs. energy, 200–201; foreknowledge of, 190, 221–22, 224–32, 240–42, 295, 300, 306; freedom of, 237, 307, 311–12; gender of, 177, 195–96; glory of, 188–89, 192–93, 208; hatred of evil, 223–25, 229–30, 232–34, 236, 349n.40; holiness of, 222, 225–26, 230–31, 233–34, 237, 244–45; immortality of, 191, 201; immutability of, 186–87, 191–92, 197, 199–201, 210, 235; infinite, 187–88; and inspiration, 131, 138, 147–48, 151, 155, 162–63; and judgment, 70–71, 102, 186, 200, 232, 356n.78; justice of, 102, 110, 118, 190, 222, 225–30, 233–34, 236, 239, 243, 245; long-suffering of, 228, 231, 236; mercy of, 222, 225, 229, 231, 235, 243, 245; and morality, 242, 245; names of, 73, 185, 187–88, 191; and nature, 67, 75, 203; omnipotence of, 223, 228–29, 230–31, 238–39, 243, 247; omnipresence of, 199–200, 280, 284; omniscience of, 226, 231, 240–42, 244, 315, 324–25; panentheistic model of, 180; in the Pentateuch, 184–86; personal, 165, 196, 203, 205, 209, 244–47, 274; relation to evil, 293, 298, 243, 302–4, 317, 322, 356n.89; relevance for life, 207–11, 244–47; self-existence of, 197–201, 205, 210; self-revelation of, 70, 72–74, 80, 89, 96–97, 100–103, 108, 110–11, 114, 166, 177, 184-86; sovereignty of, 191, 306, 311, 317; transcendence of, 199–200, 207–9, 211, 215, 217–18, 220–23, 226, 233, 240, 242, 244, 281; in the Trinity, 251–88; unfailing love, 222, 225–39, 244–45, 350n.52; will of, 293–317; wisdom of, 225, 230–33, 243–44
Godet, F., 70, 268
Goldberg, Louis, 349n.39
Golden calf, the, 223, 236

Hopkins, Samuel, 52
Horoscopes, 165
Horton, Walter Marshall, 285
Hosea, the prophet, 103, 140, 226
Hughes, Philip, 70
Humanism, 285; atheistic, 201; idol of, 205–6; naturalistic, 83; pantheistic, 83; theistic, 83. *See also* Secular Humanism
Humanist Manifesto II, 205
Humanists. *See* Secular humanism
Hume, David: on knowledge, 41; philosophy of, 96–97, 310
Humility, 36
Huxley, Aldous, 79
Hypocrite. *See* Hypocrisy
Hypocrisy, 25, 33, 37, 167, 233, 238, 319, 333
Hypostatic union, 182, 193, 256
Hypotheses, 25; alternative, 26; Barthian, 73; existentialist, 73; testing of, 27, 34, 38, 154, 156, 163

Iddo the Seer, 139
Idealism, 167; Hegelian, 253; pantheistic, 178; vs. realism, 36n
Idolaters. *See* Idolatry
Idolatry, 69, 70, 72, 82, 88, 95, 98, 114, 123, 155, 158, 159, 195, 205, 207, 232; of Athenians, 228; counteracting, 169; essence of, 284; in God's permissive will, 308; and Israel, 222, 223, 236, 302; of Nicolaitans, 230; prohibition of, 238
Illness, 23, 202
Illumination, divine, 242, 325; Brunner on, 133; and the Holy Spirit, 47, 144, 160, 168; and revelation, 116–18, 161; Warfield on, 146
Illusions, 36n–37n
Image of God, 53, 64
Images. *See* Idols
Immorality, sexual, 169, 308
Incarnation, the, 107, 108, 117, 119, 164, 166, 185, 196, 229, 237, 236, 238, 260, 276, 277, 282, 351n.49
Individualism, 84
Indoctrination, 24, 25, 27
Indulgences, 50–51
Inerrancy: definition of, 137, 160–62; and hermeneutics, 161; and the law of noncontradiction, 151; partial, 155, 156, 157–60; Pinnock on, 344n.49; plenary, 162–66; truth of, 154–55. *See also* Inspiration; Plenary Inerrancy; Plenary Inspiration

Infallibility, of Scripture, 345n.85
Infralapsarianism, 355n.45, 357n.91; and Arminians, 320; and Calvinism, 320; Jewett on, 322; order of decrees in, 320–21; and reprobation, 327–28; verification of, 322
Injustice: battle against, 86, 246; and God, 328–29; and sinners, 321. *See also* Justice
Inspiration, 131–46, 151, 157, 159–61, 345n.85; Evangelicalism's view of, 134–37; Fundamentalism's view of, 135; and God, 241; Jesus' view of, 142, 144; Liberalism's view of, 132; meaning of, 131; Neoorthodoxy's view of, 133; and the New Testament, 141–46, 152–53; and prophets, 140; Roman Catholicism's view of, 132, 134; verbal, 143. *See also* Illumination; Inerrancy; Plenary Inerrancy; Plenary Inspiration
Institutions, doctrinal statements of, 287
Integrative theology: benefits and limitations, 28; vs. "biblical" theology, 23–24, 42–46; definition of, 40; and indoctrination, 27; meaning of, 25–26; methodology of, 9, 26;, relevance of, 46–48; stages of, 7–8; and systematic theology, 26–28. *See also* Theology
Intercession, doctrine of, 109, 196. *See also* Prayer
International Council on Biblical Inerrancy, 137, 164
Intuition, in spiritual-life teaching, 39
Irenaeus: on revelation, 99, 136; theology of, 48; on the Trinity, 255; on the will of God, 298
Isaac, 259; God's choice of, 300; God's covenant with, 184
Isaiah, the prophet, 356n.64; and inspiration, 103, 140, 147, 316; on sin, 312; view of God, 68, 232, 234; vision of, 188, 230
Ishmael, 101, 300
Islam, 273; on theology proper, 197; on the Trinity, 283
Israel: afflictions of, 323; hardening of, 307–8, 310; history of, 97–98, 184, 187, 221–28, 235–36, 243, 270, 272, 301, 304; in the plan of God, 301, 313, 316; and revelation, 100–104, 118, 119, 147, 166
Israelites. *See* Israel

264–67, 269, 273; on the will of God, 306–8, 312–14, 329, 332, 355n.54; on worship, 123–24

Paul of Samosata, 252

Pelagianism, theology of, 49, 294, 298

Pelagius. *See* Pelagianism

Pentateuch, the: Bright on, 43; and special revelation, 100–102, 138; teaching about God, 184–86, 221–23, 301; theophanies in, 185; on the Trinity, 257–59; on the will of God, 299–301; writing of, 138–39

Pentecost, the, 124, 149, 263, 279, 287, 313

Peter, the apostle: ministry of, 228; on prophecy, 115, 152, 260; on revelation, 105–6, 108, 142, 146, 149, 150, 165; theology proper, 231, 264, 269, 315; on unbelief, 308; vision of, 105; on the will of God, 306, 309

Peters, George W., 288

Pharaoh: dreams of, 101; hard heart of, 296, 300–303, 307, 355n.54; and the will of God, 221–23

Pharisees, 88, 111, 119, 141, 273, 319

phileō, 350n.52

Philip, 264

Philosophers, non-Christian, 87

Philosophy, 26; definition of, 63; Graeco-Roman, 294; propositions in, 120; of religion, 73; and revelation, 122, 125, 207; synthetic, 25; and theology, 241

Physics, mysticism and, 201–2

Pieper, Francis, 57, 268

Pierce, Charles Sanders, 326

Pietistic movement, 52

Pietists, theology of, 52, 194

Piety, 39

Pike, James A., 281

Pinnock, Clark, 344n.49; on election, 257n.91; on positivism, 40

Pittenger, Norman, 204; on the Holy Spirit, 350n.17; and process theology, 55; on the Trinity, 255

Pius X, Pope. *See* Pope Pius X

Plagues, 101, 103, 184, 187, 222, 223

Plato, 85; on God, 280; philosophy of, 29, 62, 234; world of ideas, 110

Plenary inerrancy: and biblical writers, 162–64; definition of, 160–62; Jesus' view of, 112; of the New Testament, 154–57; and problem phenomena, 163–65; relevance of, 165–68. *See also* Inerrancy; Inspiration; Plenary Inspiration

Plenary inspiration: Barth on, 133; definition of, 161; and Paul, 143. *See also* Inerrancy; Inspiration; Plenary Inerrancy

Plummer, Alfred, 72, 352n.56, 356n.65

pneuma, 192, 274

Politics, and theists, 86, 211

Polytheism: and early Fathers, 182; gods of the new, 280; of Greeks, 352n.62; and Israel, 251, 257–58, 262; vs. Trinitarianism, 270–72, 282

Pope John XXIII, 54

Pope John Paul II, 54

Pope Pius X, 54

Pope, Alexander, 197

Positivism: case against theology, 40–41; philosophy of, 24, 278

Pragmatism, 35; William James on, 41; philosophy of, 24, 40–41

Prayer, 124, 200, 244; and foreordination, 299; and the Trinity, 286, 352n.63. *See also* Intercession

Prayer of Manasses, 132

Predestination, 256n.69; Barth on, 297; Calvin on, 296, 320, 355n.42; to destruction, 307–8; double, 295–96, 320, 357n.91; and evangelism, 329; and history, 325–26; Luther on, 295–96; Lutheranism's view of, 299; and the will of God, 295. *See also* Supralapsarianism

Prestige, G. L., 281

Presuppositions, 26; biblical, 32; cultural, 35; Evangelical, 163; humanist, 79; logical, 32

Presuppositionalists, 24

Principia, 96

Principle of identity, 32

Principle of noncontradiction, 32. *See also* Law of Noncontradicion

Principle of the excluded middle, 32

Priorities, 207

Process theology: criticism of, 210; issues of, 55; on theology proper, 181, 199, 204–5, 210; on the Trinity, 255, 283

Prodigal son, 228

Pro-Life position, 82–83

Proof-texting, 9, 46

Prophecy, 157, 216

Prophets, 61, 146, 157, 258, 351n.41; of Baal, 102, 186; choice of, 118, 196; false, 116–17, 146; inspiration of, 131, 140, 146–47, 151–52, 157; and Jesus, 141, 147; noncanonical, 116–17, 148; presumptuous vs. true,

Revelation, general. *See* General Revelation

Revelation, special. *See* Special Revelation

Review Questions: 58, 90, 126–27, 169–70, 211–12, 247–48, 288–89, 334

Rice, John R., 135

Righteous indignation, 236

Ritschl, Albrecht, 217; on God, 294, 354n.1; theology of, 53

Robinson, H. Wheeler, 235

Robinson, J. A. T., 55, 203, 219

Rogers, Jack, 135, 162

Roman Catholic Church. *See* Catholicism

Rushdoony, Rousas, 24

Sabbath, the, 36

Sabellianism, 252, 273, 275

Sabellius, 252

Sacramentalism, 49

Sadducees, 88

Sagan, Carl, 202

Salvation, 31, 46, 62, 110, 135, 196, 230, 251; and election, 313, 320, 329; by faith, 89; and humanism, 205; and inspiration, 134; plan of, 136, 229, 239, 243, 255, 280, 287; and revelation, 70–71, 90, 99, 103, 108, 117, 152, 156, 159; Roman Catholicism's view of, 50; universal need of, 119; and the will of God, 295–98, 307, 314

Samaritans, the, 125

Samaritan woman, 195

Samuel, the prophet, 102, 138, 139, 147, 302

Sanctification: of believers, 313–14, 328; of life, 167

Sanhedrin, the, 229

Sarte, Jean-Paul, 330; on existence, 110; on freedom, 41

Satan, 158; and evil, 169, 194, 299; and Job, 303; inciting sin, 169, 302; and Jesus, 47, 263, 279; overthrow of, 309; relation to God's plan, 312, 322–23, 355n.58; resisting, 169, 280, 323

Saul. *See* Paul

Saul, King, 102, 187, 224, 243, 332

Schaeffer, Francis, 21

Schillebeeckx, Edward, 54

Schleiermacher, Friedrich D. E.: on revelation, 63, 74–75; on spirituality, 46; on theology proper, 52–53, 124, 164, 178–79, 217

Scholasticism, 49, 52; on inspiration, 132; on revelation, 96

Schools, 125, 209

Science, 26, 80, 125, 243; and the church, 208; empirical, 63; and humanism, 206; relativistic, 83; and Scripture, 80, 134, 136, 137

Scientific method, the: and humanism, 40, 79; and revelation, 96, 97, 163, 337n.7

Scientism, 40, 164

Scientist. *See* Science

Scripture: authority of, 159; canon of, 95, 131, 167; and creeds, 34; doctrines of, 28, 153; excellence of, 139, 161; exegesis of, 39; Fundamentalism's view of, 135; and history, 164–65; humanity of, 140; illumination of, 144–45; inerrancy of, 162; and infallibility, 345n.85; inspiration of, 131–46, 152, 161, 177; interpretation of, 30–31, 38–39, 45, 81, 161, 164, 167; Liberalism's view of, 80–81, 134–35; Neoorthodoxy's view of, 98, 133; original languages of, 45; relevance of, 165–68; and revelation, 82, 96, 100–18, 196; Roman Catholicism's view of, 134; study of, 29; and theology, 34. *See also* Bible; Illumination; Inerrancy; Inspiration; Plenary Inerrancy; Plenary Inspiration

Sea of Galilee, 105

Sea of Reeds. *See* Red Sea

Second Advent, the, 107, 109, 166, 227, 309, 327, 330, 332

Second Coming, the. *See* Second Advent

Second Commandment, the, 185, 208

Second Helvetic Confession, the: on God, 183, 257; on Scripture, 137; on the will of God, 299

Second Vatican Council, The. *See* Vatican II

Secular humanism, 21, 164; on the Bible, 155; and education, 201; philosophy of, 40–41, 79, 83, 205–6, 310; on values, 40. *See also* Humanism

Secular Humanist Declaration, 40

Secular humanists. *See* Secular humanism

Segundo, Luis, 56

Self-determination: and freedom, 357n.89; in God's plan, 324–26, 332

Semi-Pelagians: on salvation, 295; on theology proper, 294–95

Semler, Johann S., 132

Septuagint, the, 132, 136

Sermon on the Mount, 111, 112, 114, 305

Scripture Index

Proverbs

VOLUME TWO

INTEGRATIVE
THEOLOGY

CONTENTS

Preface

    As we come to the last decade of the twentieth century, and influences shaping history in the twentieth century are in place, the need for understanding global humnanity's most basic predicament has never been greater.

    . A particular diagnosis of humanity's deepest need is developed in chapters 1–4. It turns on one's view of humanity's origination in the world (chap. 1), human activity in relation to God's activity providentially (chap. 2), the ontic nature of human beings (chap. 3), and a realistic assessment of our accountability and moral condition (chap. 4). Progress toward just and lasting peaceful relationships personally and socially, as well as locally and globally, can be made by candidly acknowledging our most basic moral affliction and deepest spiritual need. The relativistic doctoring of symptoms by naturalists and pantheists who deny a revealed, realistic diagnosis will continue to be a help superficially and temporarily. But humanity's deepest needs are not to attain harmony with nature's laws, or union with its inner energy, or self-justification. Given our moral perversity, we desperately need a supernatural re-creation, a supernaturally provided just basis for amnesty from all our insolence, and an authentic reconciliation to the living God, one another, and the earth's limited resources.

    Following the diagnostic bad news concerning the human condition (chaps. 1–4), we consider the prescriptive good news (chaps. 5–8). The Holy One from above has come. The eternal Son or Word of God who became flesh was supernaturally conceived by the virgin Mary (chap. 5). As the God-man, Jesus is the one Mediator who can alleviate not only mere symptoms of our human plight but also their deepest cause (chap. 6). More than a marvelous example, Jesus of Nazareth gave up his life once-for-all as a sacrifice to reverse all the tragic results of sin in human existence (chap. 7). Jesus Christ no longer hangs on the cross or lies in the grave. The risen One lives and rules today far above all other powers (chap. 8). Never was there greater need for grasping the uniqueness of this spriritual Master of masters than in our pluralistic times. The unparalleled provisions of Jesus Christ's atonement and resurrection ought to be heralded to the ends of the earth. For apart from this Prince of Peace the finest of human efforts will produce no lasting or just peace personally or socially.

For the sake of a fallen world in urgent need of guidance from divine revelation we offer this volume with the prayer that through those who proclaim its message God will graciously bring many to the abundant salvation Christ came to give. May the Lord of all be pleased to convict many of their addictive worship of drugs, alcohol, spouse, child, academic achievement, or financial success. Author of all life, turn back the counterproductive forces of evil and death. Help, we pray, those honest enough to admit that they are not all they should be to abandon superficial antidotes offered in countless "new" spiritual, social, or political movements. May many persons who know they are not all they ought to be find help toward a lifelong commitment to the supernatural Christ, who alone can justly forgive, powerfully redeem, and effectively reconcile to both God the Father and other people.

It has been rewarding to hear encouraging words from professors, pastors, youth leaders, and lay readers who have used volume 1 of *Integrative Theology*. Their anticipation of this second volume has been encouraging. We have considered carefully, not only the many positive comments about volume 1 but also proposals for strengthening the approach. Several of those constructive suggestions have significantly helped enrich the present volume, and for them we are grateful.

Readers unacquainted with volume 1 are urged to read especially its first chapter in order to understand the verificational method of reasoning we use. After defining the problem, we present alternative answers from the earliest days of Christianity to the present, survey the extensive biblical evidence relevant to the topic from Genesis to Revelation, formulate a systematic answer inclusive of the strengths of various positions, interact with the views with which we do not find reason to agree, and exhibit some of the enriching relevance of our conclusion for a Christian's life and ministry.

Although our approach has appeared to some to evince a negative attitude toward contemporary theology, what we oppose is the reductive exclusivism of relational, functional, existentialist, and naturalistic systems of thought. We often agree with what these theologies affirm but differ with what they deny of the logical, ontological, and supernatural assumptions and implications of the biblical content. The method here adopted is open to all kinds of human experience interpreted with the discernment provided by the primary scriptural sources. Our criteria of truth and method require us to employ not only logical and factual data but also existential data from ethical, axiological, psychological, and spiritual aspects. This internal experience is emphasized in the concluding section of each chapter—Relevance for Life and Ministry. The Systematic Formulation and Apologetic Interaction sections present and defend positions in a manner consistent with their personal and relational significance. For example, in volume 1 our doctrine of divine revelation was both propositional and relational, and our doctrine of God stressed both ontological and relational categories. It is the less comprehensive and less integrative approaches that are categorically more negative. Because of the contemporary impact of these anti-integrational approaches we have felt it necessary to respond to their negations of essential elements of a biblically based theology at some length.

Those who allege that we choose only passages in harmony with our conclusions fail to realize that we have not assumed the thing to be proved in a vacuum but have been genuinely involved in the research method and have chosen evidence, as in any investigation, in terms of its relevance. Since the Biblical Teaching sections are far more comprehensive in amassing the relevant biblical data than most theologies, the dangers of selective attention in the use of the evidence have been to that extent reduced. Although in some doctrines these sections approach the ideal of including every explicit text relevant to the chapter's basic issue, we do not claim to have exhausted the biblical evidence for any doctrine. Readers are encouraged to incorporate any additional biblical evidence that is relevant. We maintain only that the passages included are indeed relevant and do require assessment in coming to doctrinal conclusion on the issue of a given chapter. To counter the presented biblical evidence effectively one needs to demonstrate its irrelevance to the issue or its misinterpretation exegetically in its biblical and thological contexts.

We are indebted to too many people for us to mention all of them (such as the authors cited in the end notes), but we appreciate especially the discussions we have had with Denver Seminary colleagues on particular issues and the important contributions of instructor Charles Moore on the entire manuscript. Dr. James Beck made helpful suggestions for the chapters on humanness and sin, and Dan Davis did the same for the chapter on creation. Efficient assistance with computer difficulties and revising the manuscript in final form was always available from Denver Seminary's Director of Word Processing, Kris Smith. The faithful editorial work of Gerard Terpstra at the Zondervan Corporation has improved the volume. For the limitations that remain, however, the authors acknowledge responsibility.

Abbreviations

AB	*The Anchor Bible*, ed. W. F. Albright and D. N. Freedman
BAGD	*A Greek-English Lexicon of the New Testament*, ed. William F. Arndt and F. Wilbur Gingrich; rev. by F. Wilbur Gingrich and Frederick W. Danker. (Chicago: University of Chicago Press, 1979)
BDT	*Beacon Dictionary of Theology*, ed. Richard S. Taylor. (Kansas City, Mo.: Beacon Hill, 1984)
CD	*Church Dogmatics*, ed. G. W. Bromiley and T. F. Torrance.
CGTC	*The Cambridge Greek Testament Commentary*, ed. C. F. D. Moule
CR	*Corpus Reformatum* (Berlin et al.: C. A. Schwetschke, 101 vols., 1834–1956)
EBC	*The Expositor's Bible Commentary*, ed. Frank E. Gaebelein (Grand Rapids: Zondervan, 1976–).
EDT	*Evangelical Dictionary of Theology*, ed. Walter A. Elwell. (Grand Rapids: Baker, 1984)
EP	*Encyclopedia of Philosophy*, ed.Paul Williams. 8 vols. (New York: Macmillan, 1967)
HNTC	*Harper's New Testament Commentary*, ed. Henry Chadwick
ICC	*The International Critical Commentary*, ed. J. A. Emerton and C. E. B. Cranfield
ISBERev	*The International Standard Bible Encyclopedia*, revised, ed. Geoffrey W. Bromiley, 4 vols. (Grand Rapids: Eerdmans, 1979–88)
LCC	*Library of Christian Classics*, ed. J. A. Baillie, John T. McNeill, and Henry P. Van Dusen. 26 vols. (Philaldelphia: Westminster, 1953–69)
LKGNT	*A Linguistic Key to the Greek New Testament*, ed. Fritz Rienecker and Cleon Rogers (Grand Rapids: Zondervan, 1982).
LW	*Luther's Works*, ed. J. Pelikan and H. T. Lehman. 55 vols. (St. Louis: Concordia, and Philadelphia: Fortress, 1955–76)
NBCRev	*The New Bible Commentary: Revised*, ed. D. Guthrie and J. A. Motyer (London: Inter-Varsity, 1970)
NBD	*New Bible Dictionary*, ed. J. D. Douglas. Revised by N. Hillyer (Wheaton, Ill., Tyndale House, 1982)

11

NCBC   *The New Century Bible Commentary*, ed. R. E. Clements and M. Black

NCE   *New Catholic Encyclopedia*, ed. F. J. Corley. 15 vols. (San Francisco: McGraw-Hill, 1967)

NDT   *New Dictionary of Theology*, ed. Sinclair B. Ferguson, David F. Wright, and J. I. Packer. (Downers Grove, Ill.: InterVarsity)

NICNT *The New International Commentary on the New Testament*, ed. Ned B. Stonehouse and F. F. Bruce

NICOT *The New International Commentary on the Old Testament*, ed. R. K. Harrison

NIDNTT *The New International Dictionary of New Testament Theology*, ed. Colin Brown. 3 vols. (Grand Rapids: Zondervan, 1975–78)

NLBC   *The New Layman's Bible Commentary*, ed. G. C. D. Howley, F. F. Bruce, and H. L. Ellison (Grand Rapids: Zondervan, 1979)

NIGTC *New International Greek Testament Commentary*, ed. I. Howard Marshall and W. Ward Gasque

OTL   *The Old Testament Library*, ed. G. Ernest Wright, John Bright, James Barr, and Peter Ackroyd

SCG   Thomas Aquinas, *Summa Contra Gentiles*. 4 vols. in 5 (Notre Dame: Notre Dame University Press, 1975)

ST   Thomas Aquinas, *Summa Theologica*. 22 vols. (London: Burns, Oates and Washbourne, 1927–35)

TDNT   *Theological Dictionary of the New Testament*, ed. G. Kittel and G. Friederich. 9 vols. (Grand Rapids: Eerdmans, 1965)

TDNTAbr *Theological Dictionary of the New Testament*, abridged by G. W. Bromiley (Grand Rapids: Eerdmans, 1965)

TDOT   *Theological Dictionary of the Old Testament*, ed. G. Johannes Botterweck and H. Ringgren. 6 vols. (Grand Rapids: Eerdmans, 1977)

TI   Karl Rahner, *Theological Investigations*. 21 vols. (New York, Seabury: 1947–88)

TNTC   *Tyndale New Testament Commentaries*, ed. R. V. G. Tasker

TOTC   *Tyndale Old Testament Commentaries*, ed. D. J. Wiseman

TWOT   *Theological Wordbook of the Old Testament*, ed. R. Laird Harris; Gleason L. Archer, Jr.; and Bruce K. Waltke. 2 vols. (Chicago: Moody, 1980)

WA   *D. Martin Luthers Werke: Kritische Gesamptausgabe* (Weimar, 1883–)

WBC   *Word Biblical Commentary*, ed. David A. Hubbard and Glenn W. Barker

ZPEB   *Zondervan Pictorial Encyclopedia of the Bible*, ed. Merrill Tenney. 5 vols. (Grand Rapids: Zondervan, 1975–76)

PART ONE

OUR PRIMARY NEED

CHAPTER 1

THE ORIGIN OF THE WORLD AND HUMANITY

The Origin of
the World and Humanity

THE PROBLEM: HOW DID THE UNIVERSE, PERSONS, AND ALL LIVING FORMS AS WE NOW KNOW THEM COME INTO EXISTENCE?

This chapter considers the first of the outward operations of the triune God (creation, providence, preservation), in distinction from the inner operations considered in volume 1, chapter 7 (eternal generation of the Son and eternal procession of the Spirit). The Judeo-Christian doctrine of creation affirms the relation between the God who is and everything finite in the universe. The doctrine of creation informs us that the world is neither divine (thus avoiding idolatry) nor illusory (avoiding despair) and that people are neither demigods (negating idolatry) nor meaningless accidents (negating nihilism). The insight of Aquinas is profoundly true that one's view of the origin of creation greatly influences one's understanding of God (vol. 1, chaps. 5–7), for an inevitable correlation exists between how one pictures the universe and how one views God. Likewise one's concept of creation significantly influences one's understanding of the human person (vol. 2, chap., 3) and the meaning of

life. Questions such as who men and women are, why they are here, and where they are going all rest on the larger issues of the nature and meaning of the world. Similarly, one's view of creation significantly shapes one's attitude toward the environment and the larger issue of the utilization of earth's natural resources.

A host of questions and problems surround the origin of the universe and all living forms. Was the universe specifically created by the living God, or is it an emanation from the being of God? Did all things come into existence by a cosmic accident or by some sort of natural process? If God created the universe, as Jews and Christians claim, did he create all things in six solar days or over a long period of time, or possibly from eternity past? Are the theories of naturalistic evolution and theistic evolution supported by scientific facts and consistent with a biblical view of God and persons? Furthermore, how should Christians respond to numerous scientific findings that the universe and lower forms of life are very old? What do the data of general and special revelation indicate concerning the antiquity of the universe and human beings? Can the Genesis creation accounts be responsibly interpreted in a way that agrees with the findings of modern astronomy, geology, and paleontology? The present chapter, then, explores a problem of universal interest: how the universe, persons, and all other living forms came into existence.

ALTERNATIVE PROPOSALS IN THE CHURCH

The following is a summary of the principal ways in which the origin of the world and humanity has been understood by authorities within the church throughout history.

Pantheistic Emanationism

As affirmed by Neoplatonists, philosophical pantheists, Hegelian idealists, and certain Christian mystics, pantheistic emanationism claims that all things flow from God, the first principle of being. Thus the world is said to emerge eternally from the being of God, much as light flows from the sun. Plotinus, the founder of Neoplatonism, held that the world is the result of an eternal chain of emergences from the One or the Absolute and thus is a phenomenal manifestation of God.

One of the profoundest thinkers of the Middle Ages, John Scotus Erigena, sought to reconcile Neoplatonist emanationism with the Christian doctrine of creation. Persuaded that God's essence and operations are one, Erigena insisted that all things emanate from or flow out of God, the first principle of being. The biblical statement that God created all things *ex nihilo* means that he created the same out of himself. Thus in what was patently a pantheistic schema, Erigena held that the universe is a "theophany" or a manifestation of God. In the end all animate and inanimate things will return to the original unity of being from whence they have come. A similar theory of emanation was advanced by Meister Eckhart, sometimes called a mystical Erigena. As ideas flow from the mind, so the visible world represents the temporal unfolding of the eternal world of ideas. God, according to Eckhart, is the fountain from which the spiritual and material universe flows and to which it returns.

Eternal Creationism

So-called eternal creationists, who assume that God and the exercise of his perfections are inseparable, postulate that God's eternal existence has always been accompanied by a universe in some stage of being. In the early church Origen was the chief proponent of this theory of eternal creation. Persuaded that God could not be omnipotent or loving apart from the active exercise of his power and love, Origen concluded that God created a plurality of worlds that eternally succeed one another. "Not for the first time did God begin to work when He made this visible world; but as, after its destruction, there will be another world, so also we believe that others existed before the present world came into being."[1] Origen viewed the Genesis days as a literary form to describe the instantaneous creation of all things in logical fashion for human minds.

From a different perspective, F. D. E. Schleiermacher judged that the postulate of a beginning to God's creative activity would implicate him in change and make him a temporal being. Thus, according to the Romantic theologian, the traditional doctrine of creation means only that the world is absolutely dependent on God, a dependence that in reality cannot be restricted to an event in time. In the end, Schleiermacher reinterpreted the doctrine of creation in virtually a pantheistic sense to connote the totality of causality in nature.

William Newton Clarke, who prefers to speak of God as "the Source" rather than "Creator" in the traditional fiat sense, believes that from eternity God has always been accompanied by a universe dependent on himself. Thus God "always has about him a universe, or a sum or organized being, into which always flows the fulness of his energy and love. The divine will is eternally productive, and God has never been without a creation, and will never be alone."[2]

Rejecting the notion of God as autonomous controlling Power, process theology affirms that God and the world exist only in relation to each other. God needs the world to be God, and the world needs God to be the world. Process theologians hold to be an inexplicable mystery how all reality, including God, had its beginning. Whiteheadians insist that in the interactive process of physical prehensions it is just as true to affirm that the world creates God as to affirm that God creates the world.

The View of Augustine

This renowned church father and theologian interpreted the Genesis days allegorically and held that the "days" are not units of time but six states of cognition by the angels in heaven as they beheld God's formative activity. Augustine believed that simultaneous with the inception of time the triune God in goodness created all things out of nothing. Augustine in fact postulated two main stages in creation. First, God in the beginning instantaneously created "the heavens" (the angelic world) and "the earth" (the material universe) in an unformed state (Gen. 1:2), having impregnated all living forms with seminal reason or the seedlike principles from which the myriad forms of life would later develop. Thus "as mothers are pregnant with young, so the world itself is pregnant with the causes of things or things that are born."[3] Second, in the six days described in Genesis 1 God gradually brought to formation all living species out of the seminal forms embedded in the unformed matter. Augustine asserted that the Mosaic record that describes the full development of the original formless creation is not to be taken literally. Hence the Genesis "days" are not units of time (for there were "days" before the appearance of the sun), but rather ineffable, God-delimited "days." The Genesis "days," which "are beyond the experience and knowledge of earthbound men,"[4] may, after the allegory is set aside, translate into the boundaries of great formative epochs.

The Fathers' primitive understanding of the universe should be noted. All believed in a flat earth located at the center of the solar system. Many fathers, such as Lactantius and Augustine, rejected the notion that the other side of the globe was inhabited with Adamic people. "Is there anyone so senseless as to believe that there are men whose footsteps are higher than their heads? Or that the crops and trees grow downwards? Or that the rain, and snow, and hail fall upwards to the earth?" The philosophers falsely "thought that the world is round like a ball, and they fancied that the heaven revolves in accordance with the motion of the heavenly bodies."[5] Such beliefs remained unchallenged until the rise of modern science.

Theistic Evolution

Theistic evolutionists, both Protestant and Roman Catholic, hold that God supernaturally created the world and the beginnings of life, but ordained organic evolution as the mechanism for producing the myriads of living forms. Many hold that at a certain point in the evolutionary process God endowed an ape with a soul to produce Adam in the divine *imago*. Proponents of the view interpret the Genesis creation account more figuratively, some denying the historicity of Adam and the Fall. The latter interpret the story of Eve's creation from Adam's rib as a symbolic representation of the unity of male and female before God.

According to A. H. Strong, Genesis 1 and 2 describe both an original creation and a subsequent development that arose from energy latent within all living forms. "If science should render it certain that all the present species of living creatures were derived by natural descent from a few original germs, and that these germs were themselves an evolution of inorganic forces and materials, we should not therefore regard the Mosaic account as proven untrue."[6] Not a few British and European evangelical scholars subscribe to theistic evolution. James Orr notes that the theory of evolution has been fairly well established by the scientific community. Thus he upholds creation from within living forms and postulates a sudden genetic mutation to account for Adam. "That species should have arisen by a method of derivation from some primaeval germ (or germs) rather than by unrelated creations, is not only not inconceivable, but may even commend itself as a higher and more worthy conception of the divine working than the older hypothesis."[7] Orr, however, retains belief in the original sin and guilt of the human race.

Richard Bube and some colleagues of the American Scientific Affiliation synthesize biblical faith and evolutionary mechanisms. Bube rejects philosophical evolution (the world-view dominated by indeterminism and chance) with its denial of divine creation, the fall of the race, and humanity's need for spiritual recreation through Christ. But Bube regards the general theory of evolution well attested scientifically and the probable means God used to produce all living forms, including Adam. Bube asserts that God brought lower forms of life into being by a process of physical interaction, and he brought man and the human soul into being by a process of biological interaction. The characteristics commonly associated with spirit arose from the natural interaction of man's bodily parts. Claims Bube: "It does not matter at all whether God created man in a process of evolutionary development or whether God created man in an act of divine fiat. The only significant thing for him to know is that God *did* create him."[8] Bube designates his synthesis of biblical creation and evolutionary process as "biblical evolutionism."[9]

Teilhard de Chardin developed a unique theory of theistic evolution. Instead of a punctiliar creation in the past, God has been creating since the beginning of time through a continuous transformation from within the universe. The mechanism of creation is a special kind of evolution. It is not, however, an evolution characterized by random selection, but a unidirectional development that moves inexorably toward a predetermined goal (orthogenesis). Teilhard's "cosmic law of complexity consciousness" postulates that through time matter tends to become increasingly complex and to take on consciousness. Thus an evolutionary development proceeds from the geosphere (inorganic matter), to the biosphere (simple forms of life), to the noosphere (intelligent man), to the christosphere (Superconsciousness), to a final convergence in the Omega-Point, which represents the parousia of Christ. Teilhard concludes that Christ is the initiator, the energizer, and the final end of the cosmic evolutionary process.

The Dutch *New Catechism,* an influential authority among European Catholics, also advances an evolutionary vision of the universe. In the incalculably distant past from inorganic matter simple forms of life appeared, which in turn gave rise to the more advanced species of animals. Humans, in fact, evolved from the beasts. "Primitive man on the steppes and in the forests and in the caves had still to grow into a humane being. He had to leave the beast behind him."[10] The *New Catechism,* identifies evolution as the mechanism God employed to create the vast universe. In a similar vein, Hans Küng believes that some thirteen billion years ago the universe came into existence through a gigantic cosmic explosion or "big bang" (Gen. 1:3, "Let there be light"). Moreover, he believes that science has satisfactorily shown that the cosmos as a whole and the human being in his bodily nature has developed naturally, i.e., by an evolutionary process. Science, however, cannot answer the questions, "What existed before the fireball?" and "What is the meaning of the world process?" According to Küng, faith discerns from Scripture that God is the creator and conserver of the evolutionary structure. Thus the Lord is the "primal ground, primal support and primal meaning of everything, a creator, ruler and finisher of the evolutionary process."[11]

Neoorthodox and Theistic Existentialist View

Persuaded that the biblical world view is mythological, most neoorthodox and theistic existentialists regard the Genesis account as "myth" and "saga." Adam was not a historical person, and Genesis provides no scientific data. Scholars in the tradition subject the Genesis text to radical reinterpretation along Christological and existential lines.

Karl Barth's understanding of creation is governed by the ideas of covenant and Christology. The two Genesis accounts view creation from different perspectives and thus richly complement one another. The first account (Gen. 1:1–2:4a) expounds creation as the external basis of the covenant. That is, creation is the work of the triune God in fulfillment of the election of grace. Its purpose was to make possible the history of the covenant, whose beginning, center, and consummation is Jesus Christ. Barth's supralapsarian scheme of decrees is thus evident. "Creation is the external . . . basis of the covenant. It can be said that it makes it technically possible; that it prepares and establishes the sphere in which the institution and history of the covenant take place."[12] Since creation includes the beginning of time, Barth argues that God's creative activity eludes all historical description and thus must be expressed in the form of "saga." Neither fairy tale nor myth, saga for Barth is a poetic account of a prehistorical reality enacted *in* time and space. Hence the Genesis accounts impart no scientific or cosmological information. Barth believes that the world was not created in six days and that Adam was not an historical person. Rather, Barth interprets the creation saga typologically in terms of the history of salvation. Thus the separation of light from darkness, dry land from the seas, and day from night uphold the relationship between God's grace and his wrath. Moreover, the second creation account (Gen. 2:4b–25) affirms "the covenant as the internal basis of Creation."[13] By this Barth means that the covenant of redemption is the meaning, presupposition, and inner basis of creation.

Likewise holding that the Genesis account of creation is irreconcilable with modern science, Brunner argues that Genesis is purified ancient world-myth—a concept different from Barth's notion of saga. Thus there was no historical Adam and no historical Fall. The creation narratives, he argues, must be interpreted Christologically and existentially. Through the Genesis record God encounters me as the sovereign Creator of all things. In my own existential response I discover myself as a creature and a sinner. Faith thus posits a beginning of all things by the power of the eternal God. Science, however, suggests that the world attained its present form by the process of "creative evolution." The latter expression, borrowed from Henri Bergson, affirms the sudden appearance in the evolutionary continuum of new forms of life that cannot be explained by natural factors. Brunner believes that the Christian must acknowledge the reality of both creation and evolution. "Evolution is the mechanism of creation; creation is the spiritual source and the Final Cause of evolution."[14]

Even more radically, Bultmann claims that the Genesis story was borrowed from early Babylonian and Canaanite creation myths. That the Genesis account is nonhistorical is no loss, for only those theological statements are valid that deal with the existential relation between God and the person. For Bultmann, the Genesis record focuses on the existential situation of persons rather than on the origin of the universe. "The Old Testament doctrine of creation expresses a sense of the present situation of man. He is hedged in by the incomprehensible power of Almighty God. The real purpose of the creation story is to indicate what God is doing all the time."[15]

Creation in Six Twenty-Four-Hour Days

Many older authorities (early Fathers, Reformers, and orthodox theologians) and a few recent conservatives (F. Pieper, H. C. Leupold, and L. Berkhof) argue that God created *ex nihilo* the primal energy from which he fashioned the present universe and earth in six twenty-four-hour days in the recent past. Adherents of the "Flood Geology" movement add that

God created all things with the appearance of age in six solar days, and that all fossil remains, strata formations, and coal beds are due to the universal Noachian Flood.

Theophilus was the first church father to indicate that the creation days were literal twenty-four hour days. From a study of the Old Testament genealogies he concluded that from the creation of the world to his own time 5,698 years had passed. Theophilus calculated that God created the universe about the year 5,529 B.C. Julius Africanus claimed that the period from Adam to Jesus occupied 5,531 years, whereas for Clement of Alexandria the figure was 5,590 years. It did not occur to the Fathers that the Genesis genealogical lists might be selective rather than exhaustive. Barnabas and Irenaeus likewise held to solar days and believed on the basis of 2 Peter 3:8 that each of the six days of creation further pointed to a millennium of world history.[16] Thus the consensus of the early Fathers was that God created the earth approximately five and one-half millennia B.C., many believing that Christ would consummate history six thousand years later about A.D. 500.

Luther likewise upheld a strictly literal interpretation of the Genesis creation accounts. God created the world in six twenty-four-days about four thousand years before Christ in the spring of the year. Calvin similarly claimed that God created heaven and earth in a confused state (Gen. 1:1) some six thousand years before his time. During the six solar days that followed, God arranged the earth into its present habitable form, utilizing second causes, and he supernaturally created animal and human life. Most post-Reformation Lutheran and Reformed divines made the same distinction between God's primary creation of the formless mass of the universe and his secondary creation, which involved the shaping of the undisposed materials to form the world as we know it.

Thus up to the year 1750 a general consensus existed among Protestants that God created the universe *ex nihilo* in six solar days some six millennia ago. The Westminster Confession affirms: "It pleased God the Father, Son, and Holy Ghost, for the manifestation of the glory of his eternal power, wisdom, and goodness, in the beginning, to create or make of nothing the world and all things therein, whether visible or invisible, in the space of six days, and all very good" (art. IV.1). Some orthodox theologians chose to be more specific. Archbishop Ussher, working with the Genesis genealogical registers, concluded that there were 4,036 years from the creation of the world to Christ, and so identified the year of creation as 4,004 B.C. John Lightfoot, the Cambridge biblical scholar, declared that creation took place during the week of October 18–24, 4,004 B.C., and that God created Adam on October 23 at 9 A.M., fourth-fifth meridian time![17]

Proponents of "flood geology" or "catastrophism" claim that God created all things with a superficial appearance of age in six twenty-four-hour days only a few thousand years ago. The theory asserts that the only adequate explanation for all strata formation, fossil remains, volcanic activity, and mountain formation is a universal Noachian Flood of one year's duration. Proponents insist that catastrophism represents the theistic outlook, whereas uniformitarianism (the idea that "the present is the key to the past") is a fundamentally atheistic vision. The findings of astronomy and geology that point to an old solar system and earth are rejected as enhancing the evolutionary hypothesis. Contrary to the judgment of Warfield and other conservatives, flood geology regards issues such as the late date of Adam and Eve and the absence of any developmental mechanisms as essential to theological orthodoxy.[18]

Gap or Reconstructionist Theory

The eighteenth and nineteenth centuries produced considerable evidence from the fields of geology, astronomy, and paleontology to suggest that the earth was of great antiquity. Some Evangelical authorities such as Chalmers, Delitzsch, and the *Scofield Reference Bible* made room for an old earth by positing the Gap-Reconstructionist theory. According to this view, Genesis 1:1 describes the original creation of a perfect universe that allegedly was inhabited by a race of pre-Adamic or Old Stone Age people. Due to the rebellion of Lucifer and the sin of these pre-Adamites, God reduced the original creation to a state of ruin (Gen. 1:2; cf. Isa. 24:1; 45:18; Jer. 4:23–26). Proponents of the theory translate Genesis 1:2 as follows: "But the earth became without form and empty." Then after millions of years, about 4,000 B.C., God undertook the reconstruction of the sin-cursed earth in six twenty-four-hour days (Gen. 1:3–2:7) and created Adam as a New Stone Age man. The theory accounts for the long periods of time required by geology in the creation, destruction, and re-creation of the planet. Adherents of the theory maintain that *bārā'* in Genesis 1:1 (the orignal creation) is a strong verb meaning to "create," whereas *'āśāh* in Genesis 1:7, 16, 25, 26, 31; 2:2 (the reconstruction) is a weaker verb signifying to "remake." Advocates also claim that the verb *mālē'* in Genesis 1:28 ("fill the earth") really means to "fill up again." The Gap theory became popular in conservative circles through the influence of the *Scofield Reference Bible* (1909).[19]

23

Revelation-Day Theory

A few conservatives, such as J. H. Kurtz, P. J. Wiseman, and James M. Houston, uphold the Revelation-Day theory, which postulates that creation was revealed to Moses, not performed, in six consecutive days. Proponents of the theory view the Genesis days as vehicles of revelation or days in the life of Moses, rather than periods of actual creative activity. The purpose of Genesis 1 and 2, it is claimed, is not to teach science, but to communicate the great fact that God is Creator of all and to evoke from the reader praise and adoration to God for all his works. Wiseman, indeed, argues that the Hebrew ʿāśāh (to "make"), widely used in Genesis 1 and 2, more properly means to "show." James M. Houston comments as follows: "What then was God doing in these six days? He was speaking to man, revealing what He said to bring creation into being. . . . A statement of command to all creation, it is also a statement of revelation to man."[20]

The Framework Hypothesis

Nicholas Ridderbos, Meredith Kline, and Ronald Youngblood interpret Genesis 1 in terms of the "framework hypothesis." According to this theory, Moses carefully crafted a literary framework in which the work of creation was distributed over six "days." Proponents maintain (1) that the "days" are not time periods but literary devices to teach the theological truth that God is Creator of all and (2) that the arrangement is not chronological, but topical. Accordingly, a horizontal parallelism is pointed up, in which the work of day one parallels that of day four, the work of day two parallels that of day five, and so on. Youngblood, in addition, notes that there exists a vertical parallelism structured by the phrase "formless and empty" (Gen. 1:2). "As

it turns out, the phrase itself is the key that unlocks the literary structure of Genesis 1: The acts of separating and gathering on days 1–3 give form to the formless, and the acts of making and filling on days 4–6 give assurance that the heavens and the earth will never again be 'empty.' "[21] Ridderbos sums up as follows:

> In Genesis 1 the inspired author offers us a story of creation. It is not his intent, however, to present an exact report of what happened at creation. By speaking of the eightfold work of God he impresses the reader with the fact that all that exists has been created by God. This eightfold work he places in a framework: he distributes it over six days, to which he adds a seventh day as the day of rest.[22]

Advocates of the framework hypothesis emphasize that since the theory eliminates time sequences in Genesis, no conflict exists between the biblical record and the events proposed by modern science.

Various Day-Age Proposals

Many orthodox authorities (e.g., C. Hodge, W. G. T. Shedd, J. Miley, F. Godet, B. Ramm) seek to harmonize Genesis and science by upholding variants of the Day-Age theory, which postulates that God created heaven and earth in six epochs of indefinite duration. Others, such as J. O. Buswell, argue that the "days" are overlapping eras, thus maximizing the agreement between Scripture and recent scientific findings.

Proponents of the theory appeal to the following considerations: (1) The Hebrew word yôm in Scripture frequently connotes an extended period of time (Gen. 2:4; Joel 1:15; Zech. 12:3); (2) "evening" and "morning" sometimes are used figuratively in Scripture (Ps. 90:5–6); (3) the sun did not function as a measure of time before the fourth day (Gen. 1:14–18); (4) expressions such as "let the land produce vegetation" (Gen. 1:11) suggest a period of considerable length of time for their accomplishment; (5) the events of the sixth day would have required more than twenty-four hours (Gen. 1:24–31; 2:4–23); (6) the seventh day, the Sabbath of the Lord, continues to the consummation of the age; and (7) the Old Testament genealogies, used by some to uphold a recent creation, are selective rather than exhaustive.

Shedd's explication of the theory is typical of older interpretations. Genesis 1:1 provides a comprehensive statement of God's *ex nihilo* creation of the spiritual ("the heavens") and the material ("the earth") worlds. Genesis 1:2 describes the chaotic nature of the newly created earth. A vast period of time intervened between the original creation and the series of divine acts described in the six epochs (Gen. 1:3–31). According to Shedd, the first, second, and fourth days describe how God, working through natural laws of which he is the author, brought about the gradual penetration of light, the formation of the earth's crust, the ocean beds, and finally the full clearing of the atmosphere so that sun, moon, and stars might shine forth undiffused. Days three, five, and six describe God's special creation of vegetation, fish, birds, reptiles, animals, and finally man himself. Like Hodge and others, Shedd believes that minerals, vegetation, and animals may be very old; human life, however, goes back no more than six to eight thousand years.

Bernard Ramm affirms that Scripture tells the *Who* of creation, whereas astronomy and geology tell the *how* and the *when*. Ramm's theory of "progressive creationism" (creation in stages) mediates between what he calls the "arbitrariness" of fiat (instantaneous) creation and the "uniformitarianism" of theistic evolution. "Progressive creation is the means whereby God as world ground and the Spirit of God as World Entelechy bring to pass the divine will in nature."[23] Thus Genesis 1:1 relates the *ex nihilo* creation of the universe, Genesis 1:2 refers to the chaotic condition of the earth awaiting formation. The remainder of the chapter describes God's several acts of fiat creation to produce the root-species and the Spirit's working through natural means to effect development within physical nature and within the living "kinds." Ramm's alternative to theistic and naturalistic evolution upholds both instantaneous creative acts and lengthy processes of development. "The laws of Nature, under the direction of the Holy Spirit, actualize over a period of time and through process, the plan of God."[24] According to Ramm, science confirms that the universe is four to five billion years old and that humans are of great antiquity.

Robert C. Newman and Herman J. Eckelmann, Jr., two biblical scholars and scientists who believe that Scripture and responsible science can be harmonized, offer a variant of the Day-Age theory. Their Modified Intermittent-Day theory maintains that each of the six creative epochs was preceded by a twenty-four-hour solar day. The universe began fifteen to twenty billion years ago when God-created matter and energy, concentrated in a hot mass, expanded explosively and subsequently condensed. Genesis 1:1 relates that God created the materials that would make up the heavens and the earth. The following verses describe God's activity in forming this gaseous material into the myriads of heavenly bodies and living forms. The "days" of Genesis 1 are ordinary solar days, but not consecutive. Each twenty-four-hour day introduces a new creative epoch that overlaps the preceding ones. But since God created the universe during the epochs, what is the significance of the introductory days? The authors claim:

> God highlights these seven days, among the many actually occurring during creation, in order to set up an ordinance by which man is to commemorate creation. The six days of work remind him that he was created by God, and the seventh day of rest looks forward to God's rest, when redeemed man will rejoice with all creation in the new heavens and new earth.[25]

Additional helpful studies on creation include works by Arthur C. Custance,[26] Norman L. Geisler,[27] and Davis A. Young.[28]

BIBLICAL TEACHING

We now proceed to the primary biblical data to determine which hypothesis concerning the origin of the world and humanity best accords with the teachings of Scripture.

Pentateuch

"In the beginning God created [bārā'] the heavens and the earth" (Gen.1:1). The opening verse of the Bible immediately confronts the reader with the timeless and transcendent God who is there. Indeed, some thirty-five times in the creation narrative (Gen. 1:1–2:3) the name 'elōhîm comes to the fore. These majestic opening words of the Bible indicate that God is the transcendent source of all existence. Before any other reality came to be, 'elōhîm was present in his timeless eternity. Moreover, the universe as we know it was not always there. Genesis 1 describes the cosmos as created and temporal, not uncreated and eternal. The first seven words of the Hebrew Bible further suggest that the creation event was a free act of a sovereign will. God brought the universe into existence not of necessity, but by his own free determination.

Scholars have debated whether the first word of Genesis, berē'šît, should be taken in the construct or in the absolute state. If the former, the text would read: "When God began to create the heavens and the earth—the earth being formless and empty, and darkness being over the surface of the deep, and the Spirit of God hovering over the waters—God said, 'Let there be light.'" On this showing, the earth was empty and waste before God began to create. Creation then would describe God's transformation of preexistent matter into an organized universe. The fact that the absolute form reflects the common Hebrew usage and that all ancient versions (e.g., LXX, Vulgate) translate berē'šît as absolute suggest that Genesis 1:1 is best rendered by the familiar independent sentence: "In the beginning God created the heavens and the earth."

Although some authorities view Genesis 1:1 as a caption to the creation account that follows, it is preferable to regard this first sentence of the Bible as a comprehensive statement affirming God's creation of the energy-matter that would constitute the universe. "In the beginning," denotes the moment when, by a spoken word, God brought the universe from nonexistence to existence. With Augustine and against Cullmann, the text suggests that time and space began at the moment of God's creative act. Since the Hebrews had no word for universe, the phrase "the heavens and the earth" (cf. Gen. 2:1, 4) conveyed the intended meaning. Several factors point to God's creation of the universe out of nothing (*ex nihilo*): (1) The phrase "In the beginning," (2) the absence of any preexistent material that God might have used, (3) repeated references to the divine fiat as causative (Gen. 1:3, 6, 9), and (4) the testimony of later biblical writers. Thus, as opposed to God's subsequent creative activity that employed existing materials, Genesis 1:1 clearly depicts an immediate and instantaneous creation of the material and immaterial realms.

Attention turns in Genesis 1:2 from the initial creative act to the condition of the earth: "Now the earth was formless and empty . . ." *Hāyᵉtāh*, the third-person feminine singular of the verb "to be," should be translated "was" rather than the "became" that Gap theorists prefer. After relating the initial creative act, the text describes the gas cloud that was proto-earth as "formless and empty." The first noun, *tōhû*, denotes an amorphous, trackless waste (cf. Deut. 32:10; Job 6:18), whereas the second noun, *bōhû*, connotes an expanse of desolate, uninhabited emptiness (cf. Isa. 34:11; Jer. 4:23). The following phrase, "darkness was over the surface of the deep [*tᵉhôm*]," indicates the absence of light amidst the primal gaseous material. The phrase, "and the Spirit of God was hovering over the the waters [*mayim*]," denotes the role of the Holy Spirit in creation. The Spirit brooded (cf. Deut. 32:11) over the watery chaos preparing the world for God's further creative activity.

Genesis 1:3–13 records a series of creative fiats whereby in three "days" or stages God progressively formed the dark nebula into the vast cosmos. God's first word, "Let there be light" may refer to the massive primal explosion ("big bang") that God effected by the contraction of the created gas cloud. In this first "day" God also separated the light from the darkness, although the heavenly bodies were not yet visible. This division of light from darkness may have been caused by the gradual clearing of the atmosphere as the material produced by the "big bang" slowly cooled. Verse 5 indicates that the first creative day was bounded by "evening" and "morning," the beginning and ending of the period. The fact that

sun, moon, and stars were not "made" until the fourth day (Gen. 1:14–19) suggests that the "first day" probably was not twenty-four hours long.

In a second "day" or stage (Gen. 1:6–8) God continued to form the now-solid earth by effecting through his spoken word the separation of the waters of the atmosphere above from the waters of the earth's surface. Thus "God made [*'āśāh*] the expanse [*rāqîaʿ*] and separated the water under the expanse from the water above it" (v. 7). The common creation word *'āśāh* is a broad term meaning to "form" or to "fashion." This creative activity was followed by a second day, "evening" and "morning" referring to the boundaries of this indeterminate period.

The creative process of forming the earth continued for a third "day" or stage (Gen. 1:9–13), when by God's spoken word (fiat) the waters that covered the surface of the earth separated to form land and seas. With the forming of the shapeless earth now complete, God pronounced the result "good" (*tôb*), or suited for the purpose for which it had been prepared. Verse 12 relates that God commenced the process of filling the earth with living things. The text states that God caused the land to sprout with seed-bearing plants and fruit-bearing trees "according to their kinds." The sense of the text is not that the *élan* of plant production resided in the earth, but that plant and vegetable life sprang forth from the soil by the power of God. Thus the filling of the earth began by a secondary divine creation using existent materials. Some interpreters explain the appearance of vegetation before the full appearance of the sun by the fact that several forms of plant-life grow well in diffused light. The time required for the land to produce vegetation and the fact that the sun and moon were not yet "made" suggests that the "third day" of creation was more than twenty-four hours long.

In a fourth "day" or stage (Gen. 1:14–19), once again by his spoken word, God "made" (*'āśāh*) the sun, moon, and stars. But if, as we believe to be the case, the heavenly bodies were formed by the congealing of the material produced by the supernaturally produced big-bang, the fourth day likely describes God's work of unveiling the luminaries that were created aeons earlier. Indeed, the verb *wayya'aś* in verse 16 is better translated "had made" rather than the simple past tense. Whereas pagans deify and fear the heavenly bodies, Scripture teaches that God created the luminaries to serve several beneficient purposes: (1) to divide day and night (v. 14), (2) to distinguish seasons of the year (v. 14), and (3) to provide energy for the entire earth (v. 15). The text states that this "fourth day" or epoch was bounded by "evening" and "morning."

In a fifth "day" or stage (Gen. 1:20–23) God by divine fiat continued filling the earth by creating (*bārā'*, the second use of this verb) sea creatures, reptiles, and birds "according to their kinds." The creative utterance "Let the water teem with living creatures" (v. 20) suggests that God's creation of these living forms was mediate and may have involved a lengthy process, albeit not by evolutionary mechanisms. The "fifth day" of unspecified length was bounded by "evening" and "morning."

In a sixth "day" or stage (Gen. 1:24–31) God continued the work of filling the earth by making (*'āśāh*) domesticated animals, small creatures, and game, all "according to their kinds." Although the biological equivalent of the "kind" (*mîn*) is not identified, it is evident that development of plants and animals within well-defined limits did occur, perhaps by natural selection or some other God-ordained force. The expression "Let the land produce living creatures" (v. 24) once again points to a mediate creation effected over time. The climax of God's work over the six days was his special creation of male and female as image-bearers. "So God created [*bārā'*] man in his own image, in the image of God he created [*bārā'*] him" (v. 27). God's resolve "Let us make man" (v. 26), contrasts with his action vis-à-vis lower forms of life (viz., "Let the land produce"; "Let the water teem", vv. 11, 20) and indicates an instantaneous creation of a fully developed Adam (cf. v. 28). God's command to Adam and Eve to "fill [*mālē'*] the earth" (v. 28) does not imply replenishment, as advocates of the Gap or Reconstruction theory suggest.

The events of the sixth day were far-ranging indeed. The creation of the animals (Gen. 1:24–25), the creation of Adam (1:26–27), the planting of the garden (2:8–14), Adam's naming of the animals (2:19–20), the sleep of Adam, and the creation of Eve (2:21–23) likely were not accomplished in a single twenty-four day.[29] At the end of the six stages of forming and filling the earth, Genesis 1:31 states that "God saw all that he had made [*'āśāh*], and it was very good." God judged the individual aspects of the creation to be "good," and the whole "very good." Angelic beings must be included in the "all" that God created prior to the sixth day (cf. 2:1). Although the Mosaic record is silent on the subject, angels may have been included in the primal creation "in the beginning" (Gen. 1:1). Like the other creative epochs, the "sixth day" was bounded by "evening" and "morning."

On a seventh day (Gen. 2:2–3) God finished his work of forming and filling the earth and so "rested [*šābat*] from all his work." The divine rest involved a cessation of creative activity, not complete inactivity, for God continues his work of preservation, providence, and spiritual recreation, and one day he will fashion the universe anew. The absence of any reference to "evening" and "morning" suggests that the sabbath of God continues to the present. God's sabbath (v. 2) represents the basis and pattern for the human day of rest (v. 3). As God rested one day out of seven, so persons made in his image are enjoined to do the same.

The meaning of "day" (*yôm*) in Genesis 1 and 2 requires comment. The identical application of "evening" and "morning" to each of the six days may suggest that they were all of equal length. Yet the first three days existed before the sun, moon, and stars were "made." Moreover, as we have seen, "day" in Scripture frequently connotes a long period of time (Gen. 2:4; Job 20:28; Amos 9:11; 2 Thess. 2:3). Psalm 90:4 and 2 Peter 3:8 indicate that from God's perspective a thousand years are as one day. In addition, *yôm* in its nearly 1,300 occurrences in the Old Testament is variously translated by the AV as time, year, age, life, space, weather, etc. Carl Henry observes that "the term day in Genesis has no consistent chronological value."[30] A further consideration is that the words "evening" and "morning" often signify longer periods of time (Ps. 90:5–6; Jer. 6:4). Furthermore, Scripture seems to indicate that the seventh day continues through the present age (Heb. 4:1–11). Ultimately, responsible geology must determine the length of the Genesis days, even as science centuries earlier settled the issue of the rotation of the earth about the sun. Derek Kidner judges on the basis of empirical evidence that "a scientific account would have to speak of ages, not days."[31] Since Scripture elsewhere teaches that God *made* the universe in six days (Exod. 20:11; 31:17), it is probable that the "days" represent the creative epochs.[32]

Contrary to some critical theories, Genesis 2 is not a contradictory account of creation. Genesis 1 describes the creation of the universe chronologically and culminates in the making of man and woman in the divine *imago*. The second chapter, however, differs from the first in emphasis and order. Anticipating the account of the Fall in chapter 3, it begins with man, sets man at the center of things, and relates all else to the man and woman. Genesis 2:4a— "This is the account [*tôlᵉdôt*] . . ."— suggests that what follows in the text is a recitation of the history of the habitable world, beginning with the first man.[33] The shift from the divine name *'ᵉlōhîm* ("God") in Genesis 1 to *yahweh 'ᵉlōhîm* ("Lord God"), which occurs twenty times in Genesis 2–3, underscores God's role as the Creator who will manifest himself in the sphere of human history as Redeemer.

Genesis 2:7, which gives a fresh slant on Adam's origin, relates that "the Lord God formed [*yāṣar*] the man [*hā'ādām*] from the dust of the ground [*'ᵃdāmāh*] . . ." The description of the forming conveys the work of a craftsman, and the play on the Hebrew words for "man" and "ground" indicates that Adam's origin is earthly; God created him from the substances found in the earth's crust. The verse continues that the Lord God "breathed into his nostrils the breath of life," which means that Adam's material body received life-breath by a direct creative act of God. The final phrase of the verse, "and man became a living being [*nepeš hayyāh*]," affirms simply that Adam became a living creature, even as the lower life forms by God's power had become living creatures (Gen. 1:21, 24; cf. 9:16). Adam, of course, differed from the lower animals by virtue of his creation in the divine *imago*. Although the process of Adam's formation is not specified, the language conveys the idea of a special creation from inorganic matter, rather than a development from some extant organic form. The creation of vegetation (v. 9) after the creation of Adam (v. 7), and the forming of the animals (v. 19) after Adam, indicates that the Genesis 2 account is structured topically rather than chronologically.

According to Genesis 2:21–22, "the LORD God made [lit. "built," *bānāh*] a woman from the rib he had taken out of the man." This enigmatic act implies the ontological equality of the male and the female, as well as their intrinsic unity. The fact that God fashioned Eve from Adam's side appears to be a fatal blow to the theistic evolutionist claim that humanity was genetically derived from a nonhuman ancestor.

Genesis 5:1–2 represents a recapitulation of God's creation of humanity as male and female: "When God created [*bārā'*] man, he made [*'āśāh*] him in the likeness of God. He created [*bārā'*] them male and female and blessed them. And when they were created [*bārā'*], he called them 'man.'" This verse indicates that *bārā'* is occasionally juxtaposed with the verb *'āśāh* (cf. Gen. 2:4). But whereas *'āśāh* connotes the idea of shaping (Gen. 1:7, 16, 31; 2:18), and *yāsar* fashioning (2:7–8, 19) in the creative process, *bārā'* indicates God's supernatural initiation of something new—primal energy and matter (1:1), sea creatures, reptiles, and birds (v. 21), and man as male and female (1:27; 5:1–2).

Genesis 4:17–24 records the development of Cainite culture, with nomads building cities (v. 17), the domestication of cattle (v. 20), the development of music and art (v. 21), and the forging of implements of bronze and iron (v. 22). Most authorities locate this stage in the development of civilization toward the beginning of the neolithic or New Stone Age some eight to ten thousand years B.C. Inasmuch as this activity appears to be the work of the near descendants of Adam, it would seem that Adam should be dated close to that time. Most physical anthropologists, however, claim that humans have been on earth for a million years or more. Appeal is made, for example, to the Neanderthal cave man in Europe 50,000–100,000 years ago, to Flourisbad man in Africa some 80,000 years ago, and to Cro-Magnon man in Europe some 20,000–35,000 years ago. The most reasonable solution seems to be that these creatures were pre-Adamic anthropoids, highly developed apes, who nevertheless were not created in the image of God and thus had no covenant relation with him.

The ten-member genealogy of Genesis 5:3–32, which traces the line from Adam to Noah, was used by older scholars to date creation some four millennia B.C. It is now universally recognized that the listing is selective rather than exhaustive; not every link in the family chain is given. The purpose of the listing is more theological than exhaustively chronological; it affirms the continuance of Adam's line to the time of the Flood. The genealogy of Genesis 11:10–26, which traces the line from Shem to Abram, is likewise selective in composition.

Whereas in Genesis 1 God brought order out of chaos, in Genesis 6–9 God's judgment on unrepentant human wickedness rendered the created order a watery chaos. In the greatest judgment since the Fall, God brought a great flood upon the earth for more than a year. The face value of the language of the biblical text concerning the Flood suggests a deluge of universal extent. Thus God said, "I am going to bring floodwaters on the earth to destroy all life under the heavens, every creature that has the breath of life in it" (Gen. 6:17; cf. 7:4). Moreover, "all the high mountains under the entire heavens were covered" (Gen. 7:19; cf. 8:9). Certain scholars, however, argue that in Scripture "all" frequently signifies the whole of a part and not all possible parts (e.g., Gen. 41:54–57; Deut. 2:25;

Dan. 2:37–38) and that "the heavens" (*haššāmayim*, Gen. 6:17; 7:19) can denote only the region of the sky visible to the observer (1 Kings 18:45). Thus some maintain that Moses' language could be understood phenomenologically from the limited standpoint of his personal experience. "The Flood covered a vast area, the 'whole world' of man's early history as recounted in Genesis 2ff."[34] But if Moses described a limited flood by virtue of his restricted knowledge of the earth, his account of creation would suffer the same limitation, which cannot be. R. K. Harrison concludes, "While some arguments may suggest a limited flood, the fact that the mountains were submerged implies a more extended one (Gen. 7:19–20). Genesis thus supports arguments for both a local and a universal deluge, with traditional biblical teaching favoring the latter and regarding the flood as a punishment for unrepented wickedness (Gen. 6:5)."[35]

The sequential events of the Genesis creation week serve as a paradigm for the biblical doctrine of the sabbath rest. The fourth commandment states that since God created the universe in six days and rested (lit. "relaxed") on the seventh, humankind in God's plan should rest one day in seven (Exod. 20:11). By following this prescription, persons would realize maximal physical, emotional, and spiritual renewal. The language of Exodus 31:17 is highly anthropomorphic: "In six days the LORD made the heavens and the earth, and on the seventh day he abstained [*šābat*] from work and rested [*nāpaš*, lit., 'caught his breath']." In Exodus 23:10–11 and Leviticus 25:4–7 the creation sequence provides the basis for causing the land to lie fallow for one year after six years of cultivation. Thus the most that the Genesis creation-rest teaching establishes is the ratio of six units of labor to one unit of rest. Hence no proof for a literal twenty-four-hour

day derives from the sabbath-day injunction. "While God's seventh-day rest sanctions the sabbath day, Genesis hardly limits God's rest to a twenty-four-hour period."[36]

Poetry and Wisdom

In its hymnbook Israel repeatedly confessed a fundamental datum of its faith, namely, that the Lord is "the Maker ['*ōśēh*] of heaven and earth" (Pss. 115:15; 121:2; 124:8). A frequent refrain in the Psalms is the impotence of the pagan idols and the power of the Lord who created all things (96:5). Joyfully Israel lifted its heart heavenward and acknowledged, "You founded [*yāsad*] the world and all that is in it" (89:11; cf. 24:2; 119:90). The psalmist was careful to affirm that Yahweh is prior to and above the natural order: "Before the mountains were born or you brought forth the earth and the world, from everlasting to everlasting you are God" (90:2). The universe is not eternal, but had a discrete beginning in time (102:25). Neither is the universe an emanation from the being of God, for by a free act of the will God spoke and the cosmos came into being (148:5–6).

In Job 38, one of the great creation pericopae of the Old Testament, the Lord revealed himself to Job as the Creator of earth's vast structure (Job 38:4–7). As the Lord was founding the earth, "all the angels shouted for joy" (v. 7)—a statement that suggests that God created the angels prior to the material universe. Job continues by saying that the seas are a creation of God, called forth and controlled by him (vv. 8–11). Thus in Job, "the world is described as a vast edifice whose designer and maker is God"[37]

Many creation texts in this portion of the Old Testament prove to be poetic reflections on the Genesis creation narrative. Thus the statement that the universe was created by the Spirit of

31

God (Pss. 33:6; 104:30) corresponds to the teaching of Genesis 1:1–2. The Spirit's work of implanting in persons the breath of life (Job 33:4) reflects the language of Genesis 2:7. The statement of Psalm 33:9, "He spoke and it came to be," corresponds to the reiterated phrase "And God said . . . And it was so" of Genesis 1:6–7, 9, 11, 14–15, 24, 29–30. Moreover, the poetic image of dry land rising out of the waters (Ps. 24:2) is an allusion to Genesis 1:9–10. The discussion in Psalm 74:16–17 of the division of land and sea, the establishment of sun and moon, and the delineation of the seasons corresponds to the events of days three and four in Genesis 1. Finally, one discovers in Psalm 104 a striking correspondence to what God wrought in the six creative days of Genesis 1.

The Old Testament closely links God's creative and redemptive activities (e.g., Ps. 74:12–17). Psalm 33 relates that the God who fashioned the universe (vv. 6–9) is the same God who directs the course of saving history (vv. 10–12). Psalm 124:8 makes the point concisely: "Our help is in the name of the LORD, the Maker of heaven and earth" (cf. 121:2; 146:5–6).

Job 28:25–27 and Psalm 104:24 affirm that God's creative activity was conceived and executed in wisdom. Proverbs 3:19 makes the same point: "By wisdom [ḥokmāh] the LORD laid the earth's foundations, by understanding [tᵉbûnāh] he set the heavens in place." The most complete explication of wisdom's role in creation, however, is poetically set forth in Proverbs 8:22–31. There wisdom, inseparable from God, was with God eternally (vv. 22–26). The text depicts wisdom as God's creative agent in the forming of the universe (vv. 27–31). On balance, this text presents a personification of wisdom—an attribute of God—for the sake of poetic vividness. The author's point is that if God made nothing apart from wisdom, neither should believers act apart from divine wisdom. The apostle Paul clearly saw that the sum of God's wisdom was revealed in Christ (Col. 2:3); hence he denoted the latter "the wisdom of God" (1 Cor. 1:24; cf. v. 30).

The Psalms also state the purpose for which God created the vast universe. A subsidiary goal was the welfare of the persons God would create to inhabit his world (Ps. 115:16). The primary purpose of creation, however, was the display of God's glory, or the aggregate of the divine perfections (8:1; 19:1). The cosmos is not something to be worshiped (as if it were God), but a richly adorned created entity that would lead the beholder to the living God himself.

The Prophetic Literature

The Old Testament prophets accepted the Genesis creation doctrine and repeatedly appealed to it as proof that Yahweh is the Sovereign of the universe and the Lord of history. Compared with impotent idols, the Creator is a God of incomparable power and knowledge: "God made ['āśāh] the earth by his power; he founded the world by his wisdom and stretched out the heavens by his understanding" (Jer. 10:12; 51:15). Hezekiah's prayer indicates that since the Lord Almighty is Creator of all, he possesses absolute dominion and authority (Isa. 37:16). Jonah's creedal confession, "I worship the LORD, the God of heaven, who made ['āśāh] the sea and the land" (Jonah 1:9), implies that the world is under God's control and fulfills his purposes, as the remainder of the book plainly demonstrates. Amos declares that the sovereign, all-powerful Creator will punish Israel with captivity for their sins (Amos 4:12–13; 5:8–9), and Jeremiah states that the Creator will do the same to Judah (Jer. 27:5).

On the other hand, Isaiah declares

that the Creator God will comfort and strengthen his chosen people (Isa. 40:25–31). The God of Isaiah's message of grace and hope in chapters 40–66 is none other than "the Creator [*bôrē'*] of the ends of the earth" (Isa. 40:28). The Lord who fashioned the earth and the heavens (Isa. 44:24; 48:13) will bring his people back from captivity (Isa. 43:5–7; cf. 44:2–3). Moreover, the Lord "who stretches out the heavens, who lays the foundation of the earth, and who forms the spirit of man within him" (Zech. 12:1), as the Sovereign of history, will overthrow the enemies of Jerusalem.

In another sublime description of the omnipotent Creator, Isaiah affirms that he who created the heavens, earth, and persons (Isa. 42:5) is also the architect of human redemption (e.g., vv. 6–7). So close is the link between the two, that God's "former" work of creation springs forth to his "new" work of salvation (v. 9). And toward the end of the prophecy, in language reminiscent of Genesis 1:1, God declares that his work of creation and redemption will consummate in a newly fashioned order of righteousness and peace: "Behold, I will create [*bārā'*] new heavens and a new earth. . . . I will create [*bārā'*] Jerusalem to be a delight and its people a joy" (Isa. 65:17–18).

Gap theorists maintain that Jeremiah 4:23–26 supports the notion of a great primal cataclysm that devastated the earth. Careful examination of the context suggests that these verses point to the future and describe the desolation God would inflict on Judah at the hand of the Babylonians for their national apostasy. So destructive would be God's judgment that Jeremiah found it useful to describe it in the language of Genesis 1:2. Similarly Isaiah 24:1 refers to the final worldwide eschatological judgment. Isaiah 45:18, also cited in favor of the Gap theory, more accurately states that God created the ordered universe for a purposeful end,

namely, to provide a suitable habitation for human beings.

Synpotic Gospels

Jesus clearly endorsed the validity of the Old Testament creation doctrine. Thus in the Olivet Discourse the Lord reflected Genesis 1 language when he spoke of a coming distress "unequaled from the beginning, when God created the world" (Mark 13:19). The Greek verb for "create," *ktizō*, always has God for its subject and corresponds to the Hebrew *bārā'*. Jesus furthermore grounded monogamy and the permanence of marriage in the Genesis creation ordinance. In Matthew 19:4 (cf. Mark 10:6) the phrase "at the beginning" echoes Genesis 1:1, and the clause "the Creator [*ho ktisas*] made [*epoiēsen*] them male and female" recalls Genesis 1:27. The verb *poieō*, "to make," corresponds to the Hebrew creation verb *'āśāh*. Furthermore, Matthew 19:5 (cf. Mark 10:7–8) is a direct quotation of Genesis 2:24. Finally, the saying of Jesus, "The Sabbath was made [*egeneto*] for man" (Mark 2:27) corroborates God's hallowing of one day in seven as a time of rest and worship (cf. Gen. 2:3).

Primitive Christianity/Acts

The prayers and speeches of the early Christians reflect the Old Testament outlook on creation. The prayer of thanksgiving uttered after the release of Peter and John from prison conveys the common conviction of the church at Jerusalem: "Sovereign Lord, . . . you made [*poieō*] the heaven and the earth and the sea, and everything in them" (Acts 4:24). Stephen's speech to the Sanhedrin, quoting Isaiah 66:2, affirms that the hand of the Lord made all that is (Acts 7:50). Paul and Barnabas, in their announcement of the Good News to Gentiles at Lystra, began with the fundamental truth of religion, namely, that "the living God . . . made heaven and earth and sea and everything in them" (Acts 14:15).

Preaching to Athenians steeped in Stoic ideas, Paul began with the assertion, drawn from the Old Testament (Exod. 20:11; Neh. 9:6), that God is Creator and Lord of all (Acts 17:24). The apostle continued by claiming that God did not create out of necessity, as if he had need to complete himself in some way. Far from being a contingent being, God "himself gives all men life and breath and everything else" (v. 25; cf. Isa. 42:5). Finally, Paul acknowledged the familiar Old Testament truth that God made the entire human family from the first man Adam (v. 26).

Pauline Literature

Paul accepts as indisputable the fact of creation (*ktisis*) by the omnipotent God (Rom. 1:20). According to the apostle, God "created [*ktizō*] all things" (Eph.3:9) and he "gives life [*zōogoneō*] to everything" (1 Tim. 6:13). The apostle's saying, "from him [*ex autou*] and through him [*di autou*] and to him [*eis auton*] are all things" (Rom. 11:36; cf. Eph. 4:6), indicates that the Godhead is the source, the agent, and the end or goal of all reality. Paul insists that God's creation was wrought "in conformity with the purpose of his will" (Eph. 1:11) and infers, against incipient forms of Gnosticism that regarded matter as evil, that "everything God created [*ktizō*] is good" (1 Tim. 4:4). The latter pronouncent recalls God's words of approval in Genesis 1: "it was good" and "it was very good.'

Paul further specifies that the cosmic Christ is the Lord of creation (Col. 1:16). The clause *en autō ektisthē ta panta* ("in him all things were created") may indicate that Christ is the sphere in which the work of creation took place.

He is the *raison d'etre* for the world of visible objects and the realm of invisible spirits. The phrase "all things were created by him [*di autou*] and for him [*eis auton*]" in this verse identifies the cosmic Christ as the agent and the goal of creation. He is both the *archē* and the *telos* of the vast universe. "From start to finish the created order is bound up with the person of Christ."[38] The apostle combines the roles of Father and Son in the creation drama in 1 Corinthians 8:6: "There is but one God, the Father, from whom [*ex hou*] all things came and for whom we live; and there is but one Lord, Jesus Christ, through whom (*di hou*) all things came and through whom we live." All things thus originate from the Father through the agency of the Son. The phrases "for whom we live" and "through whom we live" attest that the Creator of the physical order is also the Recreator of the new spiritual order. This relationship is further taught in 2 Corinthians 4:6, where the spiritual light that dispels the darkness of sin is the correlate of the physical light that illumined the darkness of the primal chaos (cf. Gen. 1:3). In 2 Corinthians 5:17 Paul establishes the same relationship between the original physical creation and the new spiritual recreation.

Paul bases his teaching concerning the role of women in the church on transcultural principles deduced from the order of creation. A woman should pray with head veiled, thus acknowledging submission to her husband, (1) because "woman came from man" (1 Cor. 11:8, 12; cf. Gen. 2:22–23) and (2) because "woman [was created] for man" (v. 9; cf. Gen. 2:18). Paul's bottom line, however, is that "everything comes from God" (*panta ek tou theou*, 1 Cor. 11:12). Moreover, in 1 Timothy 2:12–14 Paul forbids a woman to teach or wield authority over a male elder or bishop in the church, because (1) "Adam was formed [aorist of *plassō*, to "form," "create"] first, then Eve" (cf. Gen. 2:7, 22) and (2) the woman succumbed to Satan's deception (cf. Gen. 3:6). Concerning the relation between male and female in the church, Guthrie concludes: "The priority of man's creation places him in a position of superiority over woman, the assumption being that the original creation, with the Creator's own imprimatur upon it, must set a precedent for determining the true order of the sexes."[39]

Johannine Literature

The beginning of John's Gospel affirms the central role of the Logos in creation. John 1:3 states that "through him [*di autou*, i.e., the Logos] all things were made [*ginomai*]." The "all things" of creation include the stars, quasars, asteriods, angels, earth, persons, animals, and vegetation. The aorist of *ginomai* signifies that all these entities "became" or "came into existence." The phrase *di autou* and its location in the sentence stress the agency of the Logos in the creative event. The second half of the sentence emphatically excludes all creative agencies other than the Christ. John, in effect, affirms that "everything that has reached existence must have passed through the will of the Logos."[40]

In the Apocalypse the twenty-four elders ascribe glory and honor to God, offering his creative wisdom as their rationale: "For you created [*ktizō*] all things, and by your will they were created [*ktizō*] and have their being" (Rev. 4:11). Here the cause of all that exists is the sovereign will of the all-powerful God. John cites God's creation of heaven and earth and all that is in them (Rev. 10:6; 14:7) as the rationale for the awesome end-time events of redemption and judgment. The Creator, as Ruler over all, is fully capable of achieving his eschatological purposes.

In fulfillment of the prophecies of Isaiah 65:17 and 66:22, Revelation 21 correlates God's primal creation with the coming new creation. God's promise "I am making everything new" (v. 5) embodies the promise of a new order in which "the first heaven and the first earth" will give way to "a new heaven and a new earth" (v. 1). In the coming renovation God will reshape the present fallen universe in such a manner as to provide the optimal dwelling place for the redeemed in the eternal state of blessedness.

Other New Testament Writings

The writer of Hebrews had a lively recognition of God as Creator. Hebrews 3:4 states that "God is the builder of everything," the verb *kataskeuazō*, to "construct," to "furnish," connoting here both God's original fashioning and his subsequent furnishing of the universe. Agreeable with Romans 11:36, Hebrews 2:10 indicates that everything exists "for" God and "through" God; that is, God is the ultimate goal or purpose of life, and he is the agent or instrument of the world's creation. Hebrews 11:3 is an important text on the subject: "By faith we understand that the universe was formed at God's command, so that what is seen was not made out of what was visible." It is significant that Hebrews' catalogue of faith (Heb. 11:3–38) begins with the foundational truth that the universe exists by God's creative fiat (*rhēma*). The faith that holds fast to changless verities posits God as the one efficient cause of the universe. The latter half of the verse denies that the universe came into being from any extant material. Hence, against prevailing Greek views, verse 3 upholds the fact of creation out of nothing (*ex nihilo*). Hebrews 3:7–4:11 finds in God's rest (*katapausis*) on the seventh day (cf. Gen. 2:2) an anticipation of the spiritual rest (*sabba-*

tismos) the believer realizes in Christ. Here again we discover the close link that exists between God's works of creation and redemption.

Analagous to John 1:3 and Colossians 1:16, Hebrews identifies Christ as the preexistent agent of creation. Thus the Son is the one "through [*dia*] whom he [i.e., God] made the universe" (Heb. 1:2). The early Christians clearly were convinced that Jesus of Nazareth who lived among them created the universe in its vast array. Thus in Hebrews 1:10, Psalm 102:25 (originally directed to God) is applied to the Son: "In the beginning, O Lord, you laid the foundations [*themelioō*] of the earth, and the heavens are the work of your hands." Similar to Revelation 21:1–5, but without the apocalyptic imagery, 2 Peter 3:13 correlates God's primal creation with the coming new creation: "We are looking forward to a new heaven and a new earth." At the end of the present age God's creative power will transform this sin-cursed world into a new order in which righteousness and peace will prevail.

SYSTEMATIC FORMULATION

We now seek to test the historical views above by the primary biblical data, consider the debated issues, and develop a coherent doctrine of origins. Does Scripture teach an original creative act? Did a series of creative acts follow? If so, are they given in chronological order? What, then, is the length of time between them?

God's Immediate Creation of Matter-Energy

Although often the Scriptures speak of "God" as the Creator, the three triune Persons contributed to creation in distinctive and harmonious ways. In accord with the Father's plan, the Logos spoke the original finite energy

(raw material) into existence (John 1:3), formed everything that was made (v. 3) and gave it life (v. 4). At the same time the Spirit "was hovering over" the original creation, bringing to fulfillment the Father's purposes in the world (Gen. 1:2).

Careful thought about the beginning of the triune God's creative activity distinguishes between the original supernatural creation out of nothing (immediate creation) and the successive supernatural creative acts forming particular kinds of things out of "raw materials" (*mediate creation*). By immediate creation we mean God's extraordinary action in the past that brought into existence out of nothing the basic raw materials of the universe—its underlying matter-energy.

In 1769 before the rise of modern science John Gill's *Body of Divinity* distinguished the mediate creations of Adam out of dust and of Eve out of Adam from the earlier immediate creation out of nothing.[41] The source of the distinction was Scripture, not scientific theory. "In the beginning God created the heavens and the earth" (Gen. 1:1). Other translations put it this way: "When God began to create" the earth was formless and empty, implying the preexistence of the unformed earth (RSV note). However, as found in the Biblical Teaching section above, the Bible's first statement is not a dependent clause, but an independent clause, as the most natural and obvious interpretation of the grammar as understood throughout both Jewish and Christian traditions.[42] The Father created *ex nihilo* the basic "raw materials" (at present called energy-matter) out of which things in the universe are made.

Several lines of evidence support a supernatural understanding of God's creative acts rather than a nonmiraculous providential direction of alleged evolutionary processes:

1. In Genesis 1:1 creation *ex nihilo*

best fits the meaning of the Hebrew term for create, *bārā'*. It differs from *yāṣar* "to fashion" in that the latter primarily emphasizes the shaping of an object while *bārā'* emphasizes the initiation of the object."[43] The word is used in the Hebrew Qal stem only of God's supernatural activity "initiating something new" (Isa. 41:20; 48:6–7), and "bringing into existence" (Isa. 43:1; Ezek. 21:30; 28:13, 15). "The limitation of this word to divine activity indicates that the area of meaning delineated by the root falls outside the sphere of human ability."[44] Although "out of nothing" is not necessarily inherent in the meaning of the word, it "never occurs with the object of the material, and since the primary emphasis of the word is on the newness of the created object, the word lends itself well to the concept of creation *ex nihilo*."[45] Where something previously created is used, as in dust for man, the term indicates God's supernatural or miraculous use of dust in producing a living being from inanimate materials.

2. The case for creation of the "raw materials," or "the substance of the universe"[46] *ex nihilo* rests with even greater weight on the fact that *everything other than God was created by God*. The creation of the heaven and earth was the actual beginning of all things. The existence of any primeval material is precluded by the object created: "the heavens and the earth," the most all-inclusive terms available to the Hebrew writer. The earth being "formless and empty" (Gen. 1:2) is the result of God's original creative act.[47] The "universe was formed" at God's command (Heb. 11:3). The Greek term for universe "includes in it all that exists under the conditions of time and space together with those conditions of time and space themselves."[48] The verb "was formed" means was "made to be and to be what we find them."[49] All the necessary ingredients and the

designs of things in the cosmos owe their existence to Almighty God.

3. Everything other than God, furthermore, had a *beginning* in the finite past, for nothing but God is eternal. Because everything other than God had a beginning in the finite past, so also did the earth's energy. "The statement 'In the beginning God created the heavens and the earth' (Gen. 1:1) is not a mere heading, nor a summary of the history of the creation, but a declaration of the primeval act of God by which the universe was called into being."[50] The eternal God existed, furthermore, when the mountains, the earth, and the world did not (Ps. 90:2).

4. That which came to be, arose *out of God* by God's will expressed in God's Word. "For from [*ex*] him and through him and to him are all things" (Rom. 11:36). In fact, "everything comes from [*ek*] God" (1 Cor. 11:12). In the biblical context all things come from God, not by a necessary pantheistic process of emanation, but *by a free act of God's will expressed in his Word*, in other words, by divine *fiat*. "By the word of the LORD were the heavens made, their starry host by the breath of his mouth. . . . For he spoke, and it came to be; he commanded, and it stood firm" (Ps. 33:6, 9; cf. 148:5). Creation by divine command (fiat) is not arbitrary. God acts in accord with his nature. The decision and command to create is a sovereign act in accord with God's wise, loving, and just purpose.

Creation out of God by his authoritative order ought not be confused with an automatic emanation from God's being. "Speaking is the revelation of thought; the creation, the realization of the thoughts of God, a freely accomplished act of the absolute Spirit, and not an emanation of creatures from the divine essence."[51] So "Through him [the Word who was with God and was God] all things were made; without him nothing was made that has been made"

37

(John 1:3). Because the Christian believes the Scriptures for good and sufficient reasons, faith is not wishful thinking. "By faith we understand that the universe was formed at God's command, so that what is seen was not made out of what was visible" (Heb. 11:3).

The world's energy was no imperfect thing at the time of creation, even though as yet the world was formless and uninhabited, for it fulfilled the Father's plan at that point. Eventually God's purpose did include inhabitants (cf. Isa. 24:1; 34:11; 45:18; Jer. 23–26). But no evidence of a "catastrophe" or divine judgment on an alleged pre-Adamic race can be found; the command to Adam and Eve was not to "replenish" the earth (AV), but to "be fruitful and increase in number; *fill* the earth and subdue it" (Gen. 1:28). The hypothesis that the formless state of the earth is the result of judgment on fallen angels who were cast out of heaven to earth, is logically possible, but not as probable because this idea is not explicitly in the text. So belief in a catastrophe ought not be made a test of belief in the Bible.

How long the earth "was formless and uninhabited" we have no way of telling. The Bible has not told us. And we do not have adequate evidence to insist on the hypothesis of a recent creation. It is possible that the earth was "formless and uninhabited" for a very long time. However great the age of energy or matter in the universe, many of those years may be included while the earth was in this unformed and uninhabited state.

The Subsequent Series of Creative Acts (Mediate Creation)

By God's *mediate creation* we mean that series of extraordinary events in the past by which God brought into existence out of the precreated raw materials (at present understood as energy-matter), light, atmosphere, water, dry land, vegetation, animals, and humanity.

Deists and theistic evolutionists may admit that Genesis informs about a single supernatural creative act but deny that it also teaches a subsequent series of creative acts during six periods of time called "days." Theistic evolutionists think that everything evolved from lower forms of life, including human beings, without any miraculous activity. But God "spoke" six different times, and several different kinds of things came to be: light (Gen. 1:3), space (v. 6), water and dry land (v. 9), vegetation (v. 11), the light of day versus the night and the seasons (v. 14), fish and birds (v. 20), land animals (v. 24), and man: male and female (vv. 26–27).

In the light of the informative purpose throughout the Book of Genesis, we take not only the original creative act cognitively, but also understand the six subsequent creative acts cognitively. Alleged contradictions between the Genesis 1–2:3 and Genesis 2:4–25 accounts do not preclude their informative purpose. The second account does not attempt another complete order of events. Since its purpose is not chronological, it cannot be regarded to be in conflict with Genesis 1 on that basis. Genesis 2 zooms in on the man and woman to set the background for the drama of sin's origin (chapter 3). Although the biblical and Babylonian accounts of origins are often alleged to have been derived from one another or a common Babylonian source, the evidence is insufficient to sustain that theory. Both allude in general to sunlight, vegetation, animals, and man, but do not have enough detailed similarities to require the derivation of one from the other, or from a third common source.

We interpret Genesis 1 and 2 not only as evocative and devotional but also as cognitive or informative for several reasons:

1. The purpose of Genesis 1 is to provide an account of the origin of each of the kinds of things in the world in order that people might worship and serve, not the gods of the sun, the moon, and the rain, but the Lord of all. The feeling of dependence evoked is drawn from the Creator's production of all the kinds of things made, not just of a part of nature.

2. Although the events take place before human written history, the passage is not an imaginary human saga about the past, but a divine revelation of a series of divine acts.

3. The writer's informative purpose in Genesis 2:4–25 is indicated by the use of the same phrase "this is the written account of" that introduces cognitive histories of subsequent lives. Just as there is an informative "written account of" the lives of Jacob (37:2); Esau (36:9); Edom (36:1); Isaac (25:19); Ishmael (25:12); Terah and Abraham (11:27); Shem (11:10); Shem, Ham, and Japheth (10:1); Noah (6:9); and Adam's line (5:1), so there is an informative "[written] account of the heavens and earth when they were created" (2:4).

4. One of the author's major informative purposes was to set the actual cultural stage and introduce the lead characters for the following informative account of the origin of sin among humans in (Genesis 3).

5. The literary genre of Genesis 1–3 as Old Testment scholar Alan A. MacRae has shown, is *not* that of Hebrew poetry.[52] There are poetical accounts of creation in the Bible, such as Psalm 104, but they contrast remarkably with the first chapter of Genesis. Informative accounts may include figures of speech and symbols, but the general frame of reference in context is literal narrative.

6. If the passage were not informative, what nonliteral purpose could there be, for example, in the paragraph of detailed description of four rivers watering the garden (Gen. 2:10–14)? That passage takes pains to locate the Garden of Eden in relation to four rivers, two of which remain with the same names to this day. Only irresponsible allegorization could lead the Jewish writer Philo to claim that the four rivers represent the four major virtues of Plato's ethics!

7. Furthermore, how can the genealogy in Genesis be taken noncognitively? The people mentioned toward the end of the genealogy are literal individuals with literal descendants. At what point early in the genealogy did a figurative father beget a literal son?

8. The Lord Jesus Christ and his apostles who wrote the New Testament by the Spirit's inspiration understood the early chapters of Genesis to be informative. Jesus said, "At the beginning the Creator 'made them male and female'" (Matt. 19:4); he also stated, "As it was in the days of Noah, so it will be at the coming of the Son of Man" (24:37). Jesus spoke of the blood shed from the beginning of the world, the blood of Abel (Luke 11:51), and of the similarity between the days of Lot in Sodom and the days before Jesus' return (17:28–30). Paul taught that Adam was the first man (1 Cor. 15:45) and that Adam was formed first, then Eve (1 Tim. 2:13–14). No stronger case can be made for a cognitive approach to the early chapters of Genesis for those who consider Christ their example and who bow to him as Lord than that from Christ's informative interpretation of the Old Testament accounts. People who deny what Jesus taught of earthly things will not long find viable the spiritual or existential values Christ drew from the Old Testament.

9. In general, biblical values, in contrast to Hindu-Buddhist values, are inseparably grounded in actual facts that take place in the flesh. The theolog-

ical meaning of Christ's incarnation, for example, evaporates if the eternal Logos (John 1:1) did not become flesh (v. 14) cognitively or factually (1 John 4:1–3).

Given a basically informative purpose, then, a normal interpretation of Genesis 1 and 2 is that, in addition to the immediate, creative act, (1) there was *a series of creative acts* on each of the six days (length undetermined as yet). (2) God created each of the living "kinds" (Genesis 1:11–12, 21, 24–25). As a word study shows, the Hebrew word for kind (*min*) designates classifiable biological beings that are capable of reproducing. "Kind" is used in describing the animals that went into Noah's ark (Gen. 6:20; 7:14), of ravens (Lev. 11:15), hawks (v. 16), herons (v. 19), locusts, catydids, crickets, grasshoppers (v. 22), and lizards (v. 29; cf. Deut. 14:13–18). (3) Living animals will reproduce "each according to its kind" (Gen. 1:24). This allows for development of varieties within the kinds, but not evolution beyond the limits of the kinds. Since the Scriptures do not define the limits of the kinds of animals other than by reproductive capability (1:11, 24), we may leave it to the actual (not imagined or constructed) empirical data to determine where the limits are.

Given a series of at least six creative acts on an informative interpretation of Genesis, the processional or developmental is not ruled out within the kinds, for several ictic (sudden or abrupt) events occurred. The great gaps in the fossil evidence and any evidence of developments (within the kinds) are not a problem. "The Christian is not embarrassed by evidence of hiatus nor evidence of link."[53]

The Order of the Series of Creative Acts

Are the days in Genesis 1 numbered so that we may understand the order of creative acts and of the appearance of things in the universe? Not according to the pictorial-day interpretation, which takes them as days of revealing activity to the writer of Genesis. The chronological element is said to designate the order in which God revealed the topics to the writer, not necessarily the order in which they came into existence. On such a revelation-day hypothesis, no problems can arise between observational knowledge of the order of origins and scripturally derived knowledge, because the Bible has nothing to say about the order in which things were created.

Although the revelation-day or pictorial-day theory alleviates all apparent difficulties with related observed data, it does not fit well with the text of Genesis. The purpose of the early chapters is to convey information about the origin, not of Genesis, but of the things in the world. The six days refer not to God's revelatory acts, but to his creative acts. The phrases "And God said . . . and it was" apply to creations, not revelations (Pss. 33:6, 9; 148:5). The subsequent summary statement reads, "For in six days the LORD *made* the heavens and the earth, the sea, and all that is in them, but he rested on the seventh day" (Exod. 20:11). Although occasionally the verb "made" means "show" (44 times, according to Wiseman), in the overwhelming majority of instances (2,240 in *Young's Complete Concordance*) it means to "do, execute, perform, work."

The seven days' works are not so many prophetic-historical tableux, which were spread before the mental eye of the seer, whether of the historian or the first man. The account before us does not contain the slightest marks of a vision, is no picture of creation, in which every line betrays the pencil of the painter rather than the pen of a historian, but is obviously a historical narrative, which we could no more transform into a vision than the account of paradise or of the fall.[54]

From considerations like these the most probable interpretation is that the six days of Genesis 1 refer to a series of creative acts occurring in the order of their numbering from one through six. Genesis 1 does teach a chronological order of origins. Therefore we may look for a general correlation of the data from nature as to when the designated aspects came into existence.

1. First, then, the Logos of God made *light* (Gen. 1:3). Although the earth's solar system was not arranged as at present until the fourth "day," God created light on the first day. The light of the first day may have come from the energy-matter of the immediate creation (Gen. 1:1). Light, heat, and electricity are different forms of energy. May it not be that God's first mediate creative command produced a big bang that would illuminate the world? Is it possible that God then invested the universe with its basic amount of energy (according to the first law of thermodynamics) and regulated the law of entropy (according to the second law of thermodynamics) governing the usefulness of energy in its forms of light, heat, and electricity? In view of the universality of energy and its relation to light this interpretation may be worth pursuing.[55]

Robert C. Newman and Herman J. Ecklemann, Jr., *Genesis One and the Origin of the Earth,* suggest that as a result of this creative act of God "the contracting gas cloud [of the original creation Gen. 1:1–2], having become dark within, eventually heats up to the point that it begins to glow" (1:3). Assuming a uniform speed of light since the first day of creation, Newman and Ecklemann seek to determine the age of our galaxy, sun, and universe. From the expansion of the observable universe since the big bang and the structure of the stars, they conclude that our galaxy is 15 billion to 20 billion years old; the sun, 5 to 10 billion years old; and the earth's solar system, about 5 billion years old. If this was not the case, then God must have created the light speeding to the earth as if from distant stars when actually it was not![56]

The phrase with each of the days— "there was evening and there was morning" (v. 5) refers to the beginning and ending of the period in which God supernaturally formed light and the time that elapsed until God's next creative act. Although in our culture we think of the day beginning with the morning, in the Hebrew culture a day began with the evening at 6:00 P.M. The first day started in darkness and ended with light, and so the analogy to the literal Hebrew days was easily drawn. As the phrase "evening and morning" occurs repeatedly, it emphasizes how each stage of God's work progressed from the beginning chaos to the order intended.

2. God then made the "expanse" of the sky, the earth's *atmosphere and space* (vv. 6–8). Just as God divided the darkness from the light, he divided the atmospheric heavens from the earth. A perfectly uniform mass would have been meaningless and boring. God's creative informing of the earth involved "pounding" or "stretching" the moisture out to separate the clouds from the ocean by something very thin. The earth's atomosphere is unique as far as human exploration has penetrated. It provides a great life-support system, supplying water, oxygen, and carbon dioxide. The atmosphere shields life on earth from the ultraviolet rays of the sun and other rays, and moderates the earth's temperatures. "Who has measured the waters in the hollow of his hand, or with the breadth of his hand has marked off the heavens?" (Isa. 40:12).[57]

3. At the Creator's command the

waters were gathered into *seas,* an occurrence that divided them from the *dry land* and made possible the *kinds of vegetation* (Gen. 1:9–13). The continents were once submerged and rose from the oceans. The division of land from water on earth did not occur by chance, blind geologic forces, or fallen angels. By this act God wisely prepared the globe for the coming human population. The land produced vegetation: seed-bearing plants and trees according to their kinds. The Bible does not ask us to believe that the incredibly complicated chemical substances that make up a tiny seed happened by chance. The highly complex structures of living plants, including trees, grains and vegetables, are not said here to have come from nothing but from the earth. The fact that the command of God is involved most probably means that the essential elements were supernaturally brought together by the intelligence of the Creator to produce living vegetation.

4. God ordered the earth's solar system uniformly to give *light and regulate time on earth.* Because there had been light since the first day, most probably on the fourth day God ordered the solar system as it is now. The sun may have been created on the first day, and on the fourth day God placed it at the right distance away healthfully to provide for light on earth and, with the moon, to mark seasons, days, nights, and years (vv. 15–19; cf. Ps. 104:19). From the perspective of relativity, one can choose either the earth or the sun as the primary reference point. The Creator has established not only the distance of the sun from the earth, but also the speed of the earth in orbit around it, etc. Here is the beginning of *time* as the marking of successions of events on earth by literal days, nights, months, seasons, and years. In a biblical context, in contrast to a Greek philosophical context, furthermore, time is not

some alien thing limiting the eternal God, but a manifestation of his free will in fulfillment of his creation purposes. On the fourth day God provided for a linear view of history and meaningful evaluation of human achievements in time. God's work on the fourth day also makes emphatic that the sun and moon are not gods as has been thought in Babylonia, Assyria, Egypt, and elsewhere; they are but parts of the craftsmanship of the one Lord of all. They are part of God's plan to provide for life and supremely human life on one planet!

5. God "created" (the second use of *bārā'*) living and moving things (v. 21), specifically, the *kinds of fish* in the seas and the *kinds of birds* in the air (vv. 20–23). The creation of self-moving living creatures required a specific command and *ex nihilo* act of God. He created the seas and the air, not purposelessly on the previous days, but to be inhabited, to sustain the life of great varieties of small and large living things. God's temporal purposes are rich and even humorous, as evidenced in aquariums and museums. Stewards of God's world will give account for treatment of these species and their habitats. Any receptive reader of Genesis 1 will refuse to worship and serve any fish or bird or any artistic likeness of it because he will recognize the Creator, who is God over all.

6. God made the *kinds of animals* (vv. 24–25), and finally, God "created" (the third use of *bārā'*) *humans* the one and only *self-moving kind in the divine image.* To humans God delegated authority to rule over the animals and the earth (vv. 26–27). Although the Hebrew for "Adam" may mean mankind universally, at the beginning mankind included one particular man. God made Adam out of the dust (2:7)—that is, in the context, nonliving matter, the ground to which the body returns at death (3:19). It is unlikely that Adam's

body was formed out of lower forms of animal life (as some theistic evolutionists suppose). To interpret the "dust" as a reference to similar chemical elements in the human body and dust introduces into the Bible's language scientific technicalities anachronistically. The point is that from the dust that was not alive God created a living man (2:7). The fact that Adam was "the first man" is foundational to progressive revelation as finally expressed in Paul's theology (1 Cor. 15:45). The first man Adam, heads the fallen race; the second man Christ, heads God's redeemed people (Rom. 5:12–19). The literal facts need emphasis here because the same interpretive assumptions that lead to denying a literal Adam have led consistent interpreters to deny a literal Christ. And to deny that the Christ came in literal flesh is a tragic error (1 John 4:1–3).

Although God created Adam first and Eve second, both the female and male were distinctly created by God; this is indicated by the third and fourth uses of *bārā'* (1:27). Both female and male were created in God's image (v. 27). Because they are made in God's image, human males and females are a unique "kind" distinct from the animals and ought never to be bestialized figuratively or literally. Furthermore, as if to answer theistic evolutionists who would have the woman as well as the man evolving from lower forms of animal life, the author repeats, "Male and female he created them" (v. 27). Clearly none of the female animals could serve as a companion for Adam nor as a mate for reproduction of humans. The animals were of different "kinds" and were to be ruled by man. In order to provide "a helper suitable for him" God created a woman, not by evolution from animals, but out of Adam (2:18, 20). That God made them male and female "at the beginning" is taught by no less than the Lord Jesus Christ, the supreme source of divine revelation (Matt. 19:4). This interpretation of the male and female in God's image is supported by the Logos and the inspired New Testament report of his words. In the context of progressive biblical revelation, then, it seems improbable that any hermeneutical device could successfully suggest that the account of God's creation of woman from man (2:23) teaches that Eve's body evolved (according to the theory of theistic evolutionists) from lower forms of animal life. Eve, no less than Adam, was created by God and created in the divine image, and so she is of no less inherent dignity and value than he.

The Length of Time Between the Creative Acts

What is at issue here is important. The question is not how long it took God supernaturally to speak things into existence. Whether God's supernatural creative acts are separated by twelve hours, twenty-four hours, or many thousands of years does not make them less miraculous. Creation did not need to take the omnipotent Creator six literal days. Any view that posits more than one divine creative act in a series in time is a progressive-creation view. A biblically based view of progressive creations with long periods intervening between, therefore, is by no means to be confused with views that may deny an actual series of supernatural creative acts (as in theistic evolution). The only issue at this point is the length of time between the supernatural creative acts.

At first reading the creation account seems to indicate that these six days of creative activity were twenty-four hours each. "Day" is usually literal, and elsewhere always so with a numeral. And the Sabbath command based on the six days of creation and one of rest seems to imply literal days (Exod. 20:11). Certainly God could have created all kinds of things in one week of seven twenty-four-hour days, or of twelve-hour days, or of one-second days. But the question is not in what time God *could* create the world, but in what time periods God in fact *did* create all the basic kinds of things in existence.

Further examination of Scripture indicates that the term "day" does not always designate twenty-four hours. The Hebrew term for "day" (*yôm*) can denote (1) the period of light in contrast to the period of darkness, (2) a period of twenty-four hours, (3) a point of time, (4) a year, or (5) a long "time." "Day" meant a month (Gen. 29:14), seven sabbaths of years (Lev. 25:8), "a long time" (forty years) in the desert (Josh. 24:7), and another "long time" when Israel was without the true God (2 Chron. 15:3).

In the context of Genesis 1 the solar system was not arranged to regulate days and nights until the fourth day, and then the "day" was not twenty-four hours, but the period of light in contrast to the darkness of the night (Gen. 1:18). This most literal use of "day" for, say, twelve hours of light as distinct from the period of darkness lacked a literal referent before the fourth creative period. Other indications in the Genesis account also suggest a period of time involved between the successive creative acts. "Let the land produce vegetation" (v. 11) and "let the water teem with living creatures" (v. 20). A period of time longer than twenty-four hours is also indicated between the creation of Adam and of Eve. Both male and female were created on the sixth "day" (v. 27). But before Eve was created, Adam's initial excitement with his new vocation of caring for the garden subsided long enough for him to become lonely (2:15, 18). And enough time then had to pass for all the kinds of animals and birds God created to pass before him for

classifying and naming (2:19–20). Only after Adam had completed the encyclopedic task of naming the animals was Eve created (2:21–23).[58]

Although references to the "evening" and the "morning" on each of the creation days (Gen. 1) has seemed to many to indicate twenty-four-hour days, the literal meaning is not invariable even after the fourth day. Sometimes the beginning of the day is evening (Est. 4:16; Dan. 8:14) and sometimes morning (Deut. 28:66–67). And clearly figurative uses for longer periods of time do, in fact, occur. The brevity of human life is like that of grass, for "in the morning it springs up new, by evening it is dry and withered" (Ps. 90:5–6). As the original *Scofield Bible* note on Genesis 1:5 explained, "The use of 'evening' and 'morning' may be held to limit 'day' to the solar day; but the frequent parabolic use of natural phenomena may warrant the conclusion that each creative 'day' was a period of time marked off by a beginning and ending."

To hold that the "days" of creation are not literal, however, is not to say that they are merely literary devices for something other than periods of time. Although biblical usage of the term shows that a "day" may refer to an indefinite period of time, word studies do not reflect figurative uses of nonchronological sorts. The most probable conclusion is that the six consecutive creative acts were separated by long periods of time.

The cognitive and chronological purposes in Genesis 1 do not necessarily exclude other purposes such as providing a pattern to facilitate memorization. As J. Oliver Buswell, Jr., suggests, the parallel pattern of Genesis 1 (in contrast to the account in chapter 2), though not poetic, may serve a *mnemonic* purpose. As in some other passages of Scripture (e.g. Jesus' genealogy in Matthew 1 and Psalm 119), the items are arranged both in chronological sequence and "in convenient symmetrical patterns for memorizing."[59]

We may conclude with Edward J. Young that Genesis 1 is trustworthy history "intentionally patterned, chronological, of indeterminable length," showing "step by step how God changed the uninhabitable and unformed earth of verse two into the well-ordered world of verse thirty-two."[60]

Recent Creation and Flood Geology

Advocates of a recent creation observe that the most common use of "day" in the Old Testament is for a twenty-four-hour period, especially when numbered. When evening and morning are mentioned, literal days are most often in view. The Sabbath commandment seemingly refers to six literal days of work and one of rest. On such biblical arguments as these, many argue for twenty-four-hour days or one literal week of creation. Usually to this is added a case for a recent date of the creation of the universe and mankind from genealogies. Although this view opposes progressive creations separated by longer periods of time, the interpretive hypothesis involves a kind of progressive creation. The omnipotent God could have created everything in one day. Clearly he did not choose to do that. Rather he chose to produce the world in a series of creative acts. But the recent creationist view regards the possible figurative use of "day" for longer periods of time as less probable than that the progressive acts of creation marked off from each other by twenty-four-hour days.

For the public-school context the recent-creation view is called "scientific creationism." A textbook by that title seeks to deal "with all the important aspects of the creation-evolution question from a strictly scientific point of view, attempting to evaluate the physical evidence from the relevant scientific fields without reference to the Bible or other religious literature."[61]

The recent-creation hypothesis involves not only creation but also the curse and the Flood (both of which are biblically derived, are they not?). This threefold hypothesis seeks to explain indications of the permanence of all things, the Fall, and uniformity following the Flood. Morris explains these three worldwide events: (1) a period of six twenty-four-hour days of God's creation and the formation of all things, the completion and permanence of which are now manifest in the law of conservation of energy; (2) the rebellion of humans and the resultant curse of God on all mankind's dominion, formalized now in the law of increasing entropy; and (3) the world-destroying flood in the days of Noah, leaving the new world largely under the domain of natural uniformity. The main key to true interpretation of the physical data of the world is found in a recognition of the effects of creation, the curse, and the flood.[62]

Although by a strict scientific method one may observe some of the relevant data, one cannot observe the connection between evidence of a wise plan and great power and six twenty-four-hour days of creation apart from the scriptural teaching. Neither can anyone by a strict scientific method verify the moral connection of entropy with God's curse on human sin. Nor can an observed uniformity be connected with the Flood by a strict scientific observation. The judgments of the Flood and the curse are parts of the hypothesis supplied by biblical revelation. Other elements of the hypothesis also are revealed: an absolutely moral, all-wise, all-powerful, and triune God. Even the case for creation by the God of theism depends on some method of reasoning beyond the strictly observed data and scientific method. Scientists as such cannot observe, repeat, or control the actual acts of creation or of judgment by the invisible God.

The doctrine of creation cannot be reduced to the physical evidence for it, nor even to the minimal elements of a doctrine of God in a theism apart from special revelation. A fully Christian doctrine of origins integrates careful interpretation of all the relevant Scriptures, a historical survey of the doctrine in the church, a systematic formulation of the Scripture's teaching, an interaction with alternative views, and an application to life and ministry. So although the scientific creationist doctrine may provide some interesting data from science, it cannot, by its own limitations, provide an alternative full-orbed *theological* position for consideration.

As appealing as recent creationism may be to people giving priority to literal biblical interpretation, several additional difficulties with it need to be noted:

1. It tends to make an inferred recent date of the earth's origin a test of faith and fellowship, though the Bible teaches no explicit date of the origin of the earth.

2. Those who make the inference that Scripture teaches a recent date of creation unwisely assume that the genealogies provide a sufficient basis for computing an approximate date of the origin of mankind. But the gaps in a comparative study of them shows that they were not intended to be complete. Benjamin Warfield wrote, "In a word, the scriptural data leave us wholly without guidance in estimating the time which elapsed between the creation of the world and the deluge, and between the deluge and the call of Abraham."[63]

3. Recent-creationists infer literal twenty-four-hour days before the fourth day when literal days were not possible. This inference overlooks the probability of longer periods, at least for the first three days and for the state of emptiness (Gen. 1:2). Only after God appointed the sun to mark days and nights could there have been literal days. By assuming literal days before literal days were possible recent-creationists assume the point to be established. They fallaciously reason in a circle.

4. Granting that Adam and Eve were created mature, they may have appeared to be something like twenty-one or thirty years old rather than one-day-old infants. But it is hardly justifiable to take this highly probable conclusion and extrapolate it into a warrant for compressing billions of years into six thousand.[64]

5. Recent-creationist attempts to undermine the results of the several scientific methods of dating are insufficient to discount these methods entirely. The data for scientific dating are drawn from many different sources and show a significant degree of agreement.[65] Even granting a large margin of error—something comparable to a ratio of one day to thirty years of age for humans, the evidence for the age of God's world is difficult to harmonize with their interpretation of God's Word. For the recent-creationist hypothesis to fit all of the relevant data coherently, a vast amount of experimental data will be needed to overthrow data to the contrary.

6. With all the work that has been done by the Creation Research Society, this organization has yet to make a sufficiently conclusive case for the hypothesis that the Flood of Noah's day was the efficient cause of the bulk of the fossils and geological formations everywhere around the world. "The vast majority of professionally engaged geologists, both Christian and non-Christian, reject the arguments for flood geology as indefensible science."[66] Although according to the biblical account, the Flood seems repeatedly and

emphatically to have been universal, scientific creationists face a stupendous task if they are adequately to support the hypothesis that the one flood accounts for all the observable geological evidence by observable evidence from all areas universally.

Common Ground Among Creationists

Regardless of their intramural differences on the dating of the origin of the world and humans, all progressive creationists have much in common and should stand together where possible. Consider some of the crucial points on which creationists from several perspectives might constructively agree: (1) The cognitive significance of the early chapters of Genesis in providing an account of origins. (2) An original immediate, supernatural creation of matter-energy out of nothing. (3) An undeterminable length of time in which the earth was formless and empty. (4) A series of subsequent creative acts producing distinct kinds of things that can reproduce themselves (progressive creations, whatever the time between). (5) Development of varieties within kinds (microevolution). As Henry Morris says, "There is certainly room for variations within each kind."[67] (6) The improbability of the philosophical hypothesis of universal evolution (macroevolution). It has not been adequately confirmed and is not scientific fact. (7) The providential uniformity of nature's laws, but not in such a manner as to forbid miracles and catastrophic judgments. (8) Some truth in the view that catastrophic judgments like those following both the Fall and the unbridled immorality at the time of Noah have made some differences in the earth and the remains of human history.

Creationists should avoid making guesses on the date of the origin of the earth or of humankind a test of orthodoxy. Since the Scriptures do not ex-plicitly teach dates for the origin of the earth or mankind, interpreters of Scripture should not make explicit dates normative. Differences on the length of the creation "days" should not become tests for dividing personal, church, or other Christian fellowships. Specifically, since "day" is used literally in Scripture, those who hold a day-age interpretation should respect those who consider the day to have been one of twenty-four hours. Similarly, since Scripture uses "day" and "evening" and "morning" figuratively and because "days" prior to the fourth could not have a literal meaning, people holding to a twenty-four-hour day ought to respect those who take it as a longer time.

APOLOGETIC INTERACTION

Relating Interpretations of God's Word and God's World

In volume 1 we found good reason for holding that what the Bible teaches God teaches, and so scriptural teaching is the final court of appeal in matters of Christian faith and practice. God also revealed some truth about himself in the things he made (Rom. 1:20). Hence *Integrative Theology* seeks to relate the truth of God's special revelation to truth of God's universal revelation. Where there appears to be contradiction between the truth of God's Word and the facts of God's world we give priority to the teaching of the inspired Scriptures. However, our initial impression of biblical teaching may not be adequately informed, as the interpretations of some church fathers show. Conflicts alleged between scientific understandings of nature and theological understandings of Scripture may be traced to misinterpretations of either nature or Scripture or both.

Students of theology need to distinguish the Scriptures as originally given (by the inspired writers) from the Scriptures as they are presently read (interpreted by readers of varying competence thousands of years later). From the hard data of scientific observation we may realize that the Bible does not teach that the earth is the center of the universe, nor that it has four corners, nor that the sun rises and sets. Theologians have been known to be wrong in their interpretations of Scripture! And all the conflicting views on creation cannot correctly match the biblical authors' intentions. That is why critical thinking in theology involves the rethinking of interpretative hypotheses, reexamining the biblical and scientific data and accepting the account that is most coherent. While doing so, we must keep in mind that the Bible was written for people generally in lay (newspaper) language, not in the technical scientific jargon of contributors to professional journals. But remember that what the Bible teaches about origins in common language is not false, but true.

Students of science must also distinguish the given data of nature from the interpretations taken from it. From reexaminations of the data, scientific theories also have been discovered to be untrue or in need of revision. Scientists have learned that the atom is complex and divisible, not uncuttable as formerly thought. Scientists differ regarding the age of human life on earth and of the age of the earth and the solar system. Scientific views that prevail today may in the future be regarded improbable. Hence we must avoid undue dogmatism concerning scientific evidence. However, revolutions in scientific paradigms, reported by Thomas S. Kuhn,[68] do not justify a total renunciation of a cognitive use of scientific evidence in favor of a sheer pragmatic use as in Gordon Clark's *Philosophy of Science and Belief in God*.[69] The reason why some theories work is that they have a relationship to reality.

Open-minded scholars in science as well as theology are always humble before new evidence and are willing to revise their prior theories in the light of more coherent explanations.

Genuine scientific advances begin with the premise that there is order or regularity throughout the universe and that critically evaluated human observations of it can be meaningful. Even though a round coin looks to be of a different shape by an observer directly above it and by an observer in some other place in the room, the relative perspectives occur in actuality and can be checked from other standpoints. Relative perspectives on a coin do not make the existence of the coin less conclusive. Naturalistic scientists merely assume an ordered world and the ability of the human mind to make sense of it. In a Christian world view those are not *ad hoc* assumptions or matters such as those of Kant's practical reason having no theoretical justification. The intelligent Creator has made humans in his image to know, love, and serve him and to rule in the world as accountable stewards. Hence we have good reason for believing that the categories of our minds are like those of the Creator's mind and world. So we have solid reasons for faith in an ordered world and in our observations of it and the reliability of our limited and correctable knowledge that is critically tested and confirmed.

By similar testing and confirmation we have identified divine revelation in Christ and the inspired Writings. When our interpretations of them, limited and correctable as they may be, have been carefully subjected to criteria of truth, we have a solid base for faith. The dangers of misinterpretation are less for the linguistic revelation than for the revelation in nature and historical events. In both fields we have the same criteria of truth, but in investigations of Scripture we have in addition a host of hermeneutical checks and balances. So if irresolvable contradictions arise, we give precedence to critical interpretations of the written Word above our critical understandings of the changing consensus in physics, geology, biology, and astronomy.

Common Ground Among Evolutionists and Creationists

Both nontheistic evolutionists and theistic creationists, because of their basic humanness, can communicate with one another about both their similarities and their differences. They have several beliefs in common: (1) The universe as we know it is not eternal; it had a beginning in the finite past, and it did not originate in 4004 B.C. (2) On the one hand, development (evolution) within the "kinds" of living organisms has occurred. On the other hand, great gaps in the evidence for transitional varieties of life remain (sometimes labeled sudden "emergences" of new species or "quantum leaps" in evolution or new creations of God). (3) Humanity is the highest form of life on earth, and some the earliest fossil finds are fully human. (4) People properly classify kinds of existing beings. (5) Both the evolutionist and the creationist comprehensive explanations of the origins of existing things do not fully explain the nature of those things.

The two accounts of origins also have important differences. Where they differ, we must ask, Does a nontheistic evolutionary theory or does a doctrine of progressive creation provide the more probable interpretation?

Ultimate Origins

Nontheistic scientists and theists differ in their approach to the question of the ultimate origin of anything at all, such as matter-energy. A pure empiricist does not even address questions beyond observation and repetition. Scientists *as scientists* properly avoid even suggesting answers to ultimate questions. Becoming philosophers or theologians, however, scientists may propose theories of ultimate sources. No scientific observer was present at the beginning, and the big bang cannot be repeated under controlled conditions according to a strict scientific method. Scientists playing unscientific roles may speculate about primeval gases or energy. But these had a beginning in the finite past and require more ultimate explanations. Ultimately naturalists have to come up with such entities out of nothing without a creator. In contrast, in apologetics and theology there are good reasons for belief in the eternal God's intelligent purpose and great power to create energy and the entire universe.

Naturalistic speculations about ultimate origins do well to avoid fantasies about ultimate origins like the contradictory nonsense of American philosopher Charles Sanders Pierce:

In the beginning—infinitely remote—there was a chaos of unpersonalized feeling, which being without connection or regularity would properly be without existence. This feeling sporting here and there in pure arbitrariness, would have started the germ of a generalizing tendency. Its other sportings would be evanescent, but this would have a growing virtue. Thus the tendency to habit would be started; and from this with the other principles of evolution, all the regularities of the universe would be evolved.[70]

The imagination may suggest hypotheses to be tested, but it is no substitute for the verifiable and verified proposals of philosophers, scientists, and theologians. A growing agreement has developed between science and theology, at least on the fact of a beginning of the universe in the finite past. Aristotle's notion that the cosmos is ungenerated and indestructible is not commonly received. And the more recent "steady state" theory has been losing ground. Most astronomers now hold that the universe had an instant of origin in a fireball explosion 15 or 20 billion years ago. The "shrapnel" from that big bang is still flying outward from the focus of the blast. One of those fragment clusters is the galaxy we call the Milky Way. One of its billions of stars is the earth's sun with its tiny orbiting planets. And one of these planets is the earth. Empirical scientists assume that every consequent has antecedents, but they fail to propose a cause of the big bang that began the universe or the orderly way in which the "fallout" fell into place. "Adopting, therefore, the big bang scenario, it would seem that we have little choice but to assume that the universe went bang in a remarkably orderly way, even though an accidental creation would, with a probability that is virtual certainty, produce a totally disordered universe."[71]

The faith and assumptions of the scientists, Robert Jastrow explains, indicate that the scientists cannot bear the thought of a natural phenomenon that cannot be explained. Their religious faith in natural causation, Jastrow argues, is violated by three lines of evidence supporting a beginning: the outward motions of the galaxies, the laws of thermodynamics, and the life story of the stars. Unable to discover with unlimited time and money the cause of the origin of the universe, the scientist as such ought to lose confidence in the exclusiveness of his method and naturalistic presuppositons.

For the scientist who has lived by his faith in the power of reason, the story ends like a bad dream. He has scaled the mountains of ignorance; he is about to conquer the highest peak; as he pulls himself over the final rock, he is greeted by a band of theologians who have been sitting there for centuries.[72]

The explanation of ultimate origins that makes the most sense is creation by an intelligent, powerful God who has life in himself.

The Origin of Life

The theistic and nontheistic hypotheses radically differ also in their accounts of the origin of life. Today many scientists think that living organisms emerged gradually from nonliving material even though all indications are that life always arises from other life. So noncreationists sometimes suggest that life arose by a kind of spontaneous generation; theists, however, propose creation by an intelligent transcendent Being.

To decide between the two hypotheses, we need to understand something of the complexity of the simplest biological life. Biomolecules contain proteins that consist of chains of amino acids linked together in a certain way. Amino acids are compounds of nitrogen, hydrogen, carbon, and oxygen that combine in various ways to form the proteins making up living matter. Eight or ten amino acids are regarded as the building blocks of the proteins that make up the bulk of the cells of the human body. To achieve the proper orderings of the amino acids, enzymes speed up the chemical reactions that make life possible for biopolymers. A typical enzyme has a chain of some two hundred links with about twenty possibilities for each link. Hence the numbers of useless arrangements for one enzyme is enormous, more than the number of atoms in all the galaxies visible in the largest telescopes. This correlation exists for one enzyme, and there are upwards of two thousand of them, mainly serving different purposes.[73] So how did the complex situation of life get to where we find it to be? A biologist faces the problem of accounting for life with a vast amount of information in a very intricate formula (involving many steps with precise timing).

The theory of spontaneous generation without intelligent planning and direction lacks evidence in its support and so is highly improbable. A theory of gradual change from simple enzymes to complex ones exacerbates the problem. The time involved in gradual change can work against life, rather than contributing to it. The vast majority of mutations are harmful to the species, not helpful to it. Hence Sir Fred Hoyle found it to be "apparent that the facts point overwhelmingly against life being of terrestrial origin."[74] Hoyle then explored an interstellar source of life, but observed, "Try as I would, I couldn't convince myself that even the whole universe would be sufficient to find life by random processes—by what are called the blind forces of nature. The thought occurred to me one day that the human chemical industry doesn't take a chance on its products by throwing chemicals at random into a stewpot. To suggest to the research department at Du Pont that it should proceed in such a fashion would be thought ridiculous."[75]

What is the simplest explanatory theory to account for the origin of life on earth? "By far the simplest way to arrive at the correct sequences of amino acids in the enzyme would be by thought, not by random processes. . . . Rather than accept the fantastically small probability of life having arisen through the blind forces of nature, it seemed better to suppose that the origin of life was a deliberate intellectual act." Hoyle concludes:

A common sense interpretation of the facts suggests that a superintellect has monkeyed with physics, as well as with chemistry and biology, and that there are no blind forces worth speaking about in nature. the numbers one calculates from the facts seem to me so overwhelming as

to put this conclusion almost beyond question.[76]

Further complicating the problems for theories of the spontaneous generation of life is entropy. Entropy expresses in a word the result of the second law of thermodynamics. The first law of thermodynamics asserts that the total energy of the universe (as a closed system) is constant, neither increasing nor decreasing with time. The second law asserts that any process decreases the amount of energy available for work. Although on earth there may be a local replacement of useful energy, it is always at the expense of an overall decrease of useful energy in the universe. The energy for useful work in the universe, including our earth, is being depleted. If energy is not fed into the universe from beyond it, the processes in the system will eventually terminate and all life on earth will be snuffed out. Nontheists assume that the universe is a closed system into which no energy is introduced by God; therefore, on their view all life will eventually suffer a cold death. Ecologists warn that humanity faces a steady decrease in energy available for conversion into work. Even recycling increases entropy. Even though it retards the loss rate, it uses more available energy in the overall environment than it replaces.

The second law of thermodynamics becomes severely problematic for any view that suggests that life arose spontaneously through the random interaction of natural forces. A mere appeal to *open* system thermodynamics on earth does little good. "What must be done is to advance a workable model of *how* the available energy can be coupled to do the required work."[77] After an examination of scientific theories, these scientists conclude, "The primary difficulty was not lack of suitable energy sources. Rather it was both a lack of sufficient energy mobilizing means to harness the energy to the specific task of building biopolymers and a lack of means to generate the proper sequence of, say, amino acids in a polypeptide to get biological function."[78] They add, "There is no hint in our experience of any mechanistic means of supplying the necessary configurational entropy work. Enzymes and human intelligence, however, do it routinely."[79] Again, "Many facts have come to light in the past three decades of experimental inquiry into life's beginning. With each passing year the criticism has gotten stronger. The advance of science itself is what is challenging the notion that life arose on earth by spontaneous (in a thermodynamic sense) chemical reactions."[80]

> Over the years a slowly emerging line or boundary has appeared which shows observationally the limits of what can be expected from matter and energy left to themselves, and what can be accomplished only through what Michael Polanyi has called "a profoundly informative intervention." When it is acknowledged that most so-called prebiotic simulation experiments actually owe their success to the crucial but *illegitimate* role of the investigator, a new and fresh phase of the experimental approach to life's origin can then be entered.[81]

These scientists conclude that "the undirected flow of energy through a primordial atmosphere and ocean is at present a woefully inadequate explanation for the incredible complexity associated with even simple living systems, and is probably wrong."[82]

Another way of understanding the difficulty atheists face is to recall that although living things today reduce the entropy of the earth's ecosystem, this does not violate the second law, because it is at the expense of an overall increase in the entropy of the universe. Living things are able to continue to process available energy and increase entropy, however, only because incredibly complex (low entropy) structures already exist that permit them to do so. An irresolvable problem faces nontheists—how to account for an initial reduction in entropy when life with its increased complexity first appeared supposedly by pure chance. As Harold F. Blum asks, "How, when no life existed, did substances come into being which today, are absolutely essential to living systems, yet which can only be formed by those systems?"[83]

Could life have formed by chance, given the addition of aeons of time? Given sufficient time, it may be argued, even wildly improbable events become virtual certainties. Tossing a coin ten times may not produce five heads in a row. But tossing the coin a hundred million times dramatically increases the probability of five heads in a row. The analogy does not fit, however, because, unlike a coin toss, the chemical reactions necessary to form a living creature are reversible. The addition of great ages of time simply increases the probability that any complex organic molecule will be destroyed. In other words, if one tosses a series of five heads, the noted outcome is irreversible. Molecular chains such as proteins, however, are relatively fragile. Without some sort of protection over a period of time they are far more likely to spontaneously disintegrate than to form. Time is the enemy, not the friend, of spontaneous abiogenesis (the origin of life from nonlife).

Despite facile appeals to "mutation steps," the problems facing the critic of creation who believes that life arose rapidly or through a series of spontaneous steps from nonliving compounds are extremely serious. Robert Jastrow has put the issue succinctly:

> Perhaps the appearance of life on earth is a miracle. Scientists are reluctant to accept that view, but their choices are

limited; either life was created on the earth by the will of a being outside the grasp of scientific understanding, or it evolved on our planet spontaneously through chemical reactions occurring in nonliving matter lying on the surface of the planet.[84]

Since none of us was there to observe the first living organism, both views involve faith in what was unseen. One can believe in spontaneous generation despite well-established natural laws that render it so highly improbable as to be unthinkable, or one can believe the well-attested revelation of the Lord of all.

The authors of *Fundamentals of Classical Thermodynamics,* Gordon J. Van Wylen and Richard E. Sonntag, cautiously raise questions about the beginning and the end of the natural world as we know it, and whether it is a closed system to which the second law of thermodynamics applies as a whole. They acknowledge that "it is impossible to give conclusive answers to these questions on the basis of the second law of thermodynamics alone." They themselves, however, see the second law of thermodynamics as "man's description of the prior and continuing work of a Creator, who also holds the answer to the future destiny of man and the universe."[85]

Another who looks at the implications of entropy for our past and future with less caution is Jeremy Rifkin. He said,

It's strange indeed that we in the modern world are willing to see the history of the universe as beginning with a perfect state and moving toward decay and chaos and yet continue to cling to the notion that earthly history follows the exact opposite course, i.e., that it is moving from a state of chaos to a "progressively" more ordered world.[86]

Although Rifkin takes notice of a Christian world view,[87] he hopes to escape the ultimate randomness of entropy by resorting to a God *within* the cosmos experienced in a collective consciousness[88] or Buddhist enlightenment.[89] He fails to see that even such a monistic reality must incorporate entropy. The more plausible account lies in a God *beyond* the cosmos with its entropy, in the transcendent Creator of all. The transcendence of the particular by union with universal energy does not escape the dismal end of entropy. For that, one needs communion with the eternal Lord over all.

Distinguishing Species

Theists and nontheists may also differ on the real divisions between species. The distinguishing line can be drawn in a way harmonious with either an evolutionary or a creation doctrine. In classifying living beings, evolutionists often emphasize similarities and magnify incidental or accidental differences in proposing a million or a million-and-half species in order to "find" intermediate forms. If, however, by "species" we mean organisms with the same essential qualities, in spite of numerous accidental variations, there could not be intermediate forms.[90]

For the crucial example, shall we classify human beings as different from animals essentially or only accidentally? Do people differ from animals only in degree or also in kind? The issue turns out to be as much a matter of principles of classification as it does of observation. Definition of the human species is as much philosophy or theology as science. And the classification may depend on a prior assumption that all reality is ultimately nonpersonal. Only the mind of humans, however, can even frame the question of an impersonal or personal Source. Only humans are responsible morally. So humans are essentially unique. The hypothesis of an ultimately impersonal universe inadequate to account for: (1) the unique personhood of the evolutionists themselves, (2) their nonnegotiable ideal of intellectual honesty, (3) their universal and necessary disapproval of injustice, and (4) their wise hesitancy to approve an ethic of the survival of the fittest in human conduct. The value of human personal existence in accord with moral norms is more adequately explained by theism.

Fossil Groupings and Gaps

Of the two hypotheses, creation and evolution, which accounts most coherently for the fossil groupings and gaps? The fossilized remains of former life indicate that all of the major groups of animals originated simultaneously, they were similar to animals of the present day, and they have maintained their relations with each other back to the time when the first evidences of life appeared. There is not the slightest evidence that any of the major phyla or groups arose from any other.[91]

A nontheistic evolutionary philosophy that believes that all living things, including humans, are derived from nonorganic energy-matter through gradual, minor changes fails to fit the facts. Seven major evolutionary assumptions, G. A. Kerkut has shown, have insufficient or no evidence supporting them: (1) Something (energy-matter) came from nothing at all. (2) Nonliving things gave rise to living things. (3) Spontaneous generation occurred only once. (4) Single-celled organisms (protozoa) developed gradually into many-celled organisms (metazoa). (5) Viruses, bacteria, plants, animals, and minerals are all interrelated. (6) The various vertebrates are interrelated. (7) Invertebrates gradually produced vertebrates. (8) Fish, amphibia, reptiles, birds, mammals, and mankind are all interrelated.[92] But humans, most evolutionists agree, are on one di-

verging branch from that of the apes, both being developed from an undiscovered allegedly common ancestor. Writing in an international science series of volumes, Kerkut found that these seven beliefs are unsupported by actual empirical evidence and are projected on extremely limited data of a circumstantial sort. More popularly, Luther D. Sunderland points up the lack of transitional forms in the macroevolutionary scheme from fish to amphibian, amphibian to reptile, reptile to bird, reptile to mammal.[93]

At each of these gaps a theistic view of origins derived from the data of special revelation provides a coherent account. (1) Something (finite energy-matter) comes from nothing (*ex nihilo*) by the power of an eternal God in accord with his intelligent plan. (2) Life is given to the kinds of organisms by the eternal Creator, who has life in himself. The kinds of living things need be created only once, for they can reproduce. (3) So God created single-cell and many-celled organisms, the basic kinds of viruses, bacteria, plants, animals—invertebrate and vertebrate. (4) and he created man—male and female. Thus God created the kinds of fish, amphibia, animals, and humans.

Sudden Novelties

Where the model of nontheistic evolution has traditionally pictured a gradual progressive process over a long period of time, a theistic model includes *both gradual development* within the limits of the kinds *and sudden creative novelty*. If questions remain about differences developing (evolving under God's providence) within the created "kinds," consider the many varieties of human beings, yet all one species (*homo sapiens*) from one set of original parents (Acts 17:26).

Even where the case for biological evolution is the strongest, in hypothesizing that all life on earth is based on essentially the same genetic code and that given the right combination of environmental influences the varieties of life will inevitably arise, it *lacks sufficient time* for the development of all the varieties of life forms that exist.

According to Darwin's gradualistic model, "it may metaphorically be said that natural selection is daily and hourly scrutinizing, throughout the world, the slightest variations; rejecting those that are bad, preserving and adding up all that are good; silently and insensibly working, *whenever and wherever opportunity offers,* at the improvement of each organic being in relation to its organic and inorganic conditions of life."[94] So gradual is this process that Darwin admits that it is unobservable. He continues by saying, "We see nothing of these slow changes in progress, until the hand of time has marked the lapse of ages, and then so imperfect is our view into long-past geological ages, that we see only that the forms of life are now different from what they formerly were."[95]

However, the fossil evidence has failed to show essential changes in the species. The earliest remains of living creatures continue to turn up with the same characteristics as they have today. Embarrassed by the quality of the fossil record in his day Darwin said, it "displayed discrete species that showed virtually no change in shape between their first and last appearances." The earliest finds fall into existing groups today. A. H. Clark has suggested that from the single cell all of the major phyla developed simultaneously and at once in every possible direction![96] Although geologists should find an abundance of missing links shunted aside by natural selection, these have not appeared. There are embarrassingly few fossil fragments, and huge gaps still exist in the fossil record. The human fossil record is the sketchiest of all.

A Punctuated Process?

In 1954 Ernst Mayr suggested that the sudden appearance of evolutionary novelties in the fossil evidence might reflect the actual pattern of evolution rather than the extreme imperfection of the record. This has led to a radically different *punctuational model* of evolution, which holds that the "budding" of one species from another may involve sudden, rather than gradual, change. Some such "speciation events," not all, accomplish major changes, and they account for most evolution in the history of life.[97]

After documenting several examples of fixed species, Stanley presents "a message to geneticists:"

> The abundant evidence that species of animals and plants have remained stable in form while groups to which they belong have experienced substantial evolutionary change can be translated into the simple language of population genetics. It is now apparent that barring its extinction, a typical established species of mammals, marine invertebrates, land plants, or insects has undergone little measurable change in form during at least one hundred thousand generations, and often a million or 10 million generations.[98]

Why has an average species undergone little evolution in the course of millions of generations? Why are well-established species resistant to change? And why, in the past forty thousand years or more in Europe has human anatomy undergone extremely little change? Darwin's gradual model of evolution provides neither the time nor the mechanism to answer this question. Others describe the phenomenon within a large evolutionary framework, but fail to answer these questions.

Spokespeople for the punctuational

model propose "evolution by sudden changes," "catastrophic selection," or "quantum speciation events."[99] We may be excused for thinking that a figurative use of "budding" and a tautologous assertion that "evolution" (essential change) is brought to pass by "sudden change" cover an astounding ignorance of any satisfactory explanatory hypothesis. It used to be popular to charge theists with believing without evidence in the "God of the gaps" in scientific knowledge. Now scientists without evidence seem to be defending an "evolution of the gaps!" Stanley continues to believe in evolution, but not a gradual evolution. A theory that essential changes occur through inexplicable, sudden catastropic phenomena remains the same as naturalistic evolutionary theories only in denying the explanatory power of God's creative plan and power. After long years of research, unbridgeable gaps remain in the scientific picture.

Robert Jastrow explained,

Theologians generally are delighted with the proof that the Universe had a beginning, but astonomers are curiously upset. Their reactions provide an interesting demonstration of the response of the scientific mind—supposedly a very objective mind—when evidence uncovered by science itself leads to a conflict with the articles of faith in our profession. It turns out that the scientist behaves the way the rest of us do when our beliefs are in conflict with the evidence. We become irritated, we pretend the conflict does not exist, or we paper it over with meaningless phrases."[100]

Henri Bergson concluded that a gradual accumulation of acquired characteristics fails to explain the sudden appearance of multicellular animals or organisms like a vertebrate eye, for which any survival or adaptation required the functional whole at once, not individual parts over a long period of time. To account for the sudden novelties in nature, Bergson turned to metaphysics. He claimed to be intuitively aware of a vital impetus (*elan vital*) pushing him on in his own development as a person with a continued identity in time. Bergson extrapolated from his interpretation of his intuitions to "an original impetus of life that pervades the whole evolutionary process." Accordingly, Bergson viewed the evolutionary process creatively rather than mechanistically.[101] However, unless the "Vital Force" has foreknowledge of alternative directions and wisdom to choose the best ends in accord with what is just and loving, there is no reason to imagine that its direction is commendable. Bergson made recalcitrant matter the source of evil that resisted the "Life Force" at every turn. He envisioned the Life Force constantly striving to transcend the physical limitations of the stage it has reached. Like the Gnostic and Hindu traditions, Bergsonian endless, impersonal, emergent evolution contradicts the data of divine revelation concerning God, matter, humanity, morality, and spirituality.

The Future of Evolution?

Even with the paucity of evidence for an all-encompassing physical evolution, some now hope for an *evolution of human consciousness*. After seven years of traveling to lecture on the implications of the new physics, Fritjof Capra reports, that the nineteen sixties and seventies have generated a whole series of social movements that all seem to go in the same direction. The rising concern with ecology, the strong interest in mysticism, the growing feminist awareness, and the rediscovery of holistic approaches to health and healing are all manifestations of the same evolutionary trend.[102]

Note the leap from physical data alleged to support biological evolution to an evolution of thought spiritually (involving mystical experience) and morally (involving feminist awareness). If a biological evolution were supported with high probability, that would not justify a moral or spiritual evolution. Studying the relation of consciousness to physics and biology, David Bohm suggested a model of all reality from a physical hologram. Each of the parts of a hologram in some sense contains the whole, the whole being enfolded in each of its parts.[103] Fallaciously, then, Fritjof Capra and others reason from that physical analogy to the pantheism of the Vedas: "I am That, you are That, and all this is That." Analogies may illustrate points otherwise confirmed, but analogies of themselves prove nothing. Physical holograms confirm nothing about the relationship of the creation to the Creator morally or spiritually.

Evolutionary theories in the New Age movements of eastern, occult, and new-consciousness contexts, abandon the classical ideal of scientific objectivity[104] and create their own world. Allegedly New Age scientists become increasingly conscious of their alleged inner divine energy while experiencing the dance of Shiva. Those who have difficulty making the transition from the former biological evolution to the evolution of the One Consciousness can be helped along the way as Carlos Castenada and Capra himself were, by "power plants."[105] Mystical experiences themselves, whether induced by mantras or drugs, are often thought to prove an evolutionary spiritualism involving pantheism and reincarnation. By definition mystical experiences are noncognitive. So the reincarnationist interpretations given them afterward are mere hypotheses subject to critical investigation. As pantheistic interpretations of human experience, they do not fit the facts as well as classical Christian theism.

From the dubious quantum leap from the new physics to mysticism comes "a radical reformulation of the most fundamental aspects of reality . . . that seemed to turn common sense on its head and find closer accord with mysticism than materialism."[106] Undermining objective truth, the relativism of Hindu and Buddhist doctrines of maya undercut scientific as well as specially revealed theological truths. The radical distinction between Creator and creature is erased encouraging selfishly inclined sinners to fall victim to narcissistic self-deification. And this "blasphemy" of these humans visualizing themselves as gods is uttered in the name of evolution to a "higher" state of consciousness!

Concluding the apologetic section, we propose that the most coherent and probable explanation of origins is a biblically based progressive series of supernatural creative acts. Since the dates of the origin of neither the earth nor humanity are conclusively settled by Scripture or science, the dates ought not be the prime emphasis. A series of creations coherently accounts for the ultimate origin of anything at all, the beginning of life, the distinctiveness and persistence of the "kinds" of beings, the continuities and novelties in the fossil evidence, and above all for the uniqueness of human beings.

RELEVANCE FOR LIFE AND MINISTRY

Bow to the Sovereign Creator

"To know the Creator," Emil Brunner explained, "means to become conscious, first and foremost, that God is sovereign Lord. Because he is absolute Lord he [Christ] is 'above' all and 'before' all. The One who originates all things and is himself originated by none; he is the one who determines all things and is determined by none." Brunner added, "Schleiermacher's phrase 'absolute dependence' is right, indeed it is excellent. . . . The idea of creation means that I, together with the whole of nature to which I belong, am absolutely dependent upon God, while he, on the other hand, is dependent neither upon me nor upon it."[107]

As dependents we bow before God in humility. "What do you have that you did not receive? And if you did receive it, why do you boast as though you did not?" (1 Cor. 4:7). We have not created even those unique abilities wherein we differ from others. Whether we are like Paul, Peter, or Apollos, we ought not take pride in one against another (1 Cor. 4:6). We all need each other's fellowship and gifts. "Every good and perfect gift is from above" (James 1:17). Humbly bow before the source of all being ontologically. "Praise God from whom all blessings flow, praise him all creatures here below."

Because God first loved you, bow before the Creator in love. The world of men and women has derived ultimately from God's *agapē* (love). God did not have to create anything. As Emil Brunner said, "God created the world because he willed to communicate himself . . . as the loving God he willed to give himself to others. . . . The love of God is the *causa finalis* of the creation."[108] How, then, should humans respond? Our Creator desires nothing from us more than our love (Matt. 22:35–38). It is the first and greatest commandment. What is your ultimate love, care, or concern? We ought not seek first our pleasure, money, or success. God made us to love him, and our hearts are restless until they find their highest fulfillment in him.

Those who love the Creator ought also love all he created in his image. Although all things were made by God, only humans were made in the divine likeness. By creation all people are "children" of God, and God is the ultimate Father of the being of all persons (Acts 17:28–29). Even though God is not the moral and spiritual Father of all (John 8:44), every human being created and sustained by God deserves to be treated with respect, justice, consideration, and love. The second greatest commandment from the Creator is to love our neighbors as ourselves (Matt. 22:39). This text allows no exception for those of different racial or social backgrounds. Indeed, as Creator God is the Father of all, and all humans are children of God (Acts 17:28–29). "So in everything, do to others what you would have them do to you, for this sums up the Law and the Prophets" (Matt. 7:12). In all human relationships creationists seek to exhibit their love for God's image-bearers by keeping that golden rule.

Refuse to Deify Nature

Although creationists love every good gift the Creator has made, they will not bow to nature as God. Pantheism and panentheism tend to idolize the world by including it within the deity. Christian theists disallow worship of any part of the universe or even the whole of it as God. We ought to value creation highly as a great achievement of the most creative Being who is. But the powers of the earth's processes and energy, whether physical or psychic, are not to be deified. Theists avoid worshiping and serving the creature rather than the Creator. The godly in Scripture never blur the line between Creator and creature. To make "mother nature" or the whole of creation our ultimate concern insults the Creator.

The prophets exposed the futility of those who were more terrified by the signs in the sky, such as astrological configurations (Jer. 10:2), than by God's Word. The endless counsel of the magicians, sorcerers, and astrologers month after month, Isaiah observed, "has only worn you out" (Isa. 47:12–

13). The prophet added that they cannot save anyone from what is coming, they are "like stubble; the fire will burn them up. They cannot even save themselves from the power of the flame. . . . Each of them goes on in his error; there is not one that can save you" (vv. 14–15). Jeremiah displayed the absurdity of worshiping our own artistic works: The idol-makers select a tree, cut it down, and shape it with a chisel. They adorn it with silver and gold, and fasten it with hammer and nails so that it will not totter. "Like a scarecrow in a melon patch, their idols cannot speak; they must be carried because they cannot walk. Do not fear them; they can do no harm nor can they do any good" (Jer. 10:3–5). In dramatic contrast the living God wisely and lovingly chooses his people, calls them out of the world, warns them of future danger, and acts in their behalf. People trusting the Creator who knows the future, hears, speaks, and acts need not fear (Isa. 44:6–10).

The creationists' ultimate concern goes beyond harmony with nature to harmony with its transcendent Creator. As appreciative as we are of a home-made pie, we do not thank the pie, we thank its maker! While seeking God's kingdom in nature, we do not confuse God with the power exhibited in the ocean, the mountains, the atom, or space. By a sound doctrine of God we must always direct our adoration beyond the things that are made to their Creator. We give our ultimate honor to the Lord of all. We ascribe the glory, not to the universe, but to its great Architect and Builder. We bow to the Ruler of all by actively aligning ourselves with his providential and redemptive purposes. From this point of view we can understand what the world is by Creation and the Fall and how God's purpose is finally revealed and recovered in Jesus Christ.[109]

Use Physical Things for Good, not Evil

At Creation God pronounced all things "good," including the bodies of both the male and the female (Gen. 1:31). Neither the matter-energy nor the desires of our bodies are inherently evil. Our bodies (*sōmata*) are not the fundamental source of our problems. With all the frustrations of our finitude, our deepest need is not to be free from our physical, spatial, temporal, and energy limitations. We need not engage in bodily aceticism or self-flaggelation. Neither need we be asexual. Our bodily abilities are like instruments that God's fallen image-bearers can use either for the ends of pride, greed, and lust or to please our Creator, who has our best interests at heart. Our perverse desires and wills spring from our depraved hearts. Our fallen nature (*sarx*, flesh) initiates unjust and immoral uses of our bodies. Although everything God created is good in itself, fallen people can use their bodies for evil as well as good.

We can use every material thing we possess also either to please or displease God. How can we use our material acquisitions in a way that will please the Creator? The general pattern comes out in the three conditions Paul taught Timothy (1 Tim. 4:4–5): "Everything God created is good, and nothing is to be rejected, if (1) it is received with thanksgiving, because (2) it is consecrated by the word of · God and (3) prayer" [parentheses mine]. Accept with thanksgiving everything you have: your food, clothing, dishes, furniture, books, magazines, television, sports equipment, and means of transportation. Determine to use all for purposes consistent with God's Word and set apart all you have to glorify God by a prayer of dedication.

Singles may choose to give up a spouse for the sake of God's kingdom (Matt. 19:12; 1 Cor. 7:25–38). But those who receive divine revelation do not *command* abstinence from sexual intercourse. The sexual union of husband and wife is neither morally evil nor shameful, but a beautiful portrayal of divine love when expressing the partners' mutual faith, love, and covenanted commitments to each other. Hence arguments for the celibacy of spiritual leaders fail whether in Hinduism or Buddhism or Roman Catholicism. People can marry to the glory of the Creator.

Some first-century people also imagined that the more spiritual ought to be vegetarians. Although created by God, animals are not God and are not made in the image of God. So it is not morally wrong to kill them for food. "Everything that lives and moves [animals and birds] will be food for you. Just as I gave you the green plants, I now give you everything" (Gen. 9:3). The sixth commandment (not to kill) does not forbid hunting animals or fighting justifiable wars through which God providentially brought deserved judgment on morally corrupt nations. This commandment is more accurately translated in the *New International Version*, "You shall not murder" (Exod. 20:13). The intentional taking of human life is immoral because "in the image of God has God made man" (Gen. 9:6).

Although creationists have liberty to eat meat, there may be occasions when they do not. People are not to eat meat that has its lifeblood still in it (Gen. 9:4). For good reasons in their situation Hebrews had dietary laws also forbidding eating meat designated "unclean" (Lev. 11; cf. Acts 10:9–16). In New Testament times, however, Christians are not to reject anything as common that God made (Acts 11:9), nor should they waste it. Although creationists are free to eat meat, Jesus taught that food was not the most important thing in life (Matt. 6:25). Paul sharply rebuked lazy gluttons (Titus 1:12–13). A "companion

of gluttons disgraces his father" (Prov. 28:7; 23:20–21). Like any other material thing, meat may be taken if received with thanksgiving, eaten moderately according to God's Word, and dedicated to purposes honoring to God. But if eating meat would cause a brother to stumble, creationists willingly give up their right to eat meat (Rom. 14:13–21; 1 Cor. 8:8–13). In India and some other countries Christians give up their right to eat meat because their Hindu relatives think they became Christians in order to become meat-eaters.

Avoid Addictions

Although some have imagined that Christians are commanded totally to abstain from wine and other "strong drinks" made from fruit or grain, wine as a creation of God is no more inherently evil than meat. Creationists have liberty to drink wine so long as it is used for good ends (1 Tim. 4:4–5). The psalmist praised God for providing wine that "gladdens the heart of man" (Ps. 104:15). For that reason wine was often used at celebrations. At the wedding in Cana Jesus turned water into wine (John 2:1–11). The Lord frequented dinners where wine was served, and this led to allegations that he was a glutton and a drunkard (Matt. 11:19). The situation of these dinners and the possibility of drunkenness makes a translation of unfermented "grape juice" improbable. Even so by eating and drinking with tax collectors and sinners Jesus did not become a glutton or a drunkard. The research of Anderson Spickard, M.D., indicates that "Nations and communities that drink only at the dinner table and do not tolerate public drunkenness do not have high rates of alcoholism."[110]

People in Old Testament times took wine beneficially also as a depressant or narcotic to alleviate pain (Prov. 31:6). In the first century wine mixed with myrrh served as an anesthetic.[111] People offered this to Jesus on the cross to ease the pain (Matt. 27:34). Paul encouraged Timothy to "use a little wine" for medicinal purposes (1 Tim. 5:23). A "little wine" may be taken, like other addictive substances, when medically advisable. Creationists should consider alcoholic drinks like other material things. Whether Christians eat or drink, they do it to the glory of God (1 Cor. 10:31).

Although alcoholic drinks in moderation can serve good purposes, "alcohol abuse" expresses voluntary disregard for God's precepts. Voluntary drunkenness violates emphatic biblical teaching (Luke 21:34; 1 Cor. 5:11; Gal. 5:21; Eph. 5:18). It reflects disrespect for the wisdom of God's commands and, like all flagrant disobedience, separates us from God's fellowship. Doubtless the Bible forbids drunkenness also because alcohol harms the abusers' minds and bodies, damages their home lives, and interferes with their jobs. For our good God disallows drunkenness. But God forgives the sin of drunkenness as he forgives disobedience to any other biblical commands when we call it the sin it is against God, others, and ourselves, repent of it, and turn from it.

Persistent alcohol abuse can develop with little if any notice into an involuntary addiction or "alcoholism," a disease that can be fatal. The disease of alcoholism affects the whole person, the outer and inner person. Hence alcoholism should be treated holistically both as a physical and psychological disease and as a spiritual problem. At least in its initial stages it is a sin against one's Creator, oneself, and one's neighbors. Alcoholics need medical and psychological help; they also need unconditional *agapē* and forgiveness. Divine enabling through providentially provided alcohol treatment centers and programs like Alcoholics Anonymous have set alcoholics free. Churches ought to be aware of these resources in their communities, help people involved in alcohol abuse to acknowledge their need, and refer them for specialized treatment.

Quite inconsistently contemporary American society accepts drunkenness at parties, but condemns driving under the influence of alcohol. This hypocritical approach to drunkenness in America has led to alcoholism for one out of every ten drinkers or ten million people.[112] "Alcohol abuse is involved in most murders, most assaults, most child abuse cases, most traffic fatalities, and most fire and drowning accidents. It is also a primary factor in the development of alcohol addiction. For both reasons we do ourselves and our society a great disservice when we laugh at drunkenness or treat it lightly."[113] Rather than get involved in the debauchery of drunkenness contemporary Christians drink of the Spirit's fullness (Eph. 5:18). Christians have a source of inner peace and lasting joy far more effective than wine.

Total abstinence from alcoholic beverages is not necessary to Christian faith and life, but Anderson Spickard, M.D., suggests reasons why all Christians and especially elders, teachers, and counselors, should give serious consideration to total abstinence: (1) If indications of addiction appear in the family history, we are wise to abstain. (2) Most of the drinkers who become alcoholics drift into the disease unconsciously; so an ounce of prevention is worth a ton of cure. (3) Drinking has a deleterious effect on the part of the brain that controls judgment and inhibits evil. In view of the temptations we face in our constant warfare with evil, the risk of lowering our ability to resist enticements to sin may be greater than we want to take.[114] The slowing effect of even two or three alcoholic drinks on mental judgment and reaction time may seriously affect the safety of autmobile drivers. So in cultures with much traffic Christians may choose to give up their right to drink to reduce the risk of maiming and killing their "neighbors." "Wine is a mocker and beer a brawler; whoever is led astray by them is not wise" (Prov. 20:1).

Overseers, elders, deacons and their wives must be "temperate, self-controlled, . . . not given to drunkenness [or] indulging in much wine" (1 Tim. 3:2–3, 8, 11). Christian leaders may choose to give up their right to temperate drinking for total abstinence because of the force of their example. Out of consideration for the special needs of alcoholics among their children, relatives, church members, and friends, they may refrain. Some leaders choose to abstain because they know that one in ten drinkers cannot take even one drink without renewing the agony of their addiction. "It is better not to eat meat or drink wine or to do anything else that will cause your brother to fall" (Rom. 14:21).

The differences between Christian nondrinkers and moderate drinkers ought not destroy personal fellowship nor split churches. On the one hand, total abstainers ought not condemn others who can drink a little wine with self-control (Col. 2:16) and not cause alcoholics to stumble. On the other hand, Christians who drink moderately ought not feel uncomfortable around Christians who choose to say, "No thank you." Both moderate drinkers and abstainers need to emphasize together that "the kingdom of God is not a matter of eating and drinking, but of righteousness, peace and joy in the Holy Spirit" (Rom. 14:17).

The Bible does not provide explicit teaching on abuse of other substances, but the principles given for alcoholic drinks may be applied. The use of any unprescribed substances that shatter one's Spirit-enabled self-control and produce addiction, altered states of consciousness, drowsiness, sleep, or less pain should be evaluated by the same principles as alcohol.

Conserve Earth's Limited Resources

The Creator delegated to his image-bearers responsibility for ruling the world. All humans will give account to God for carrying out this creation mandate well. The Creator produced the limited resources of our planet for the benefit of all human beings, including coming generations. So those who love God and their neighbors should live by a responsible conservationist ethic. As Francis Schaeffer said in *Pollution and the Death of Man:* "When people take advantage of their special relationship by taking over God's creation as their own, using it for their own ends rather than God's glory, they have broken covenant and are rebelling against God."[115]

The stewardship doctrine provides an answer to the ultimate question, "Why should I take responsibility of caring for and preserving the natural order?" That answer is "Because it is God's order." It is not for mere pragmatic reasons. If I love God, I will love what he has made. The almighty God created nature's resources and the covenant-making God entrusted human beings with the responsibility of overseeing their use.

"It comes down to a question of serving God," Jeremy Rifkin said, "or rejecting Him."[116] In a posttheistic age we must ask to which God he refers. Although Rifkin takes note of the Christian God as being distinct from the world, he does not see the blatant contradiction in founding his own future on a monistic view. If all is God, then entropy diminishes the usefulness of divine energy! So although Rifkin's pantheistic God transcends Rifkin, it is not transcendent enough or personal enough. Rifkin hopes to escape the physical plane altogether in a "collective consciousness" or Buddhist "enlightenment." But the sense of total responsibility of mankind that Rifkin seeks will not be achieved apart from the accountability of everyone to the transcendent, personal Creator.

The ultimate practical goal of Christian creationists is not, as for adherents of monistic religions, harmony with nature. Our goal is harmony not only with nature but beyond that with nature's Creator. Everything in nature has importance and worth because it was made by God for a just and loving purpose. Everything is teleologically related to the Logos. And to its Creator we shall give account of our stewardship. So Christian theists will not treat nature as if it were nothing, or illusory. Neither will they waste or pollute its resources for their own selfish gain. The responsibility of ruling over the animals and earth (Gen. 1:26, 28) is not license to waste them. Creationists will not avoidably waste gasoline or any other resource, nor will they pollute the environment; they will use created resources altruistically as good stewards.

Because we are accountable to the Creator for our dominion over nature's energy resources, we ought not ignore creation's finite limitations. Energy resources had a beginning and will have an end. Finite energy is subject to entropy. We ought not rationalize unlimited wealth for selfish reasons. Stewards dare not rationalize irresponsible individualism, unaccountable enterprise, or unlimited exploitation of limited resources. This "unaccountable theology" must be replaced by a concept of human dominion in the earth as stewards accountable to God. Energy users who are aware of the fact that they are accountable to the Lord of all and considerate of their own descendants, as well as the needy around the world, will not waste or pollute the planet's limited life-support system.

Enjoy Working Six Days a Week

Christians enjoy each day of life on earth, whether they are working or retired. Like the psalmist, they say, "This is the day the LORD has made; let us rejoice and be glad in it" (Ps. 118:24). Rather than putting their hope in riches, they "put their hope in God, who richly provides us with everything for our enjoyment" (1 Tim. 6:17).

The Creator ordained that we work: "Six days you shall labor and do all your work" (Exod. 20:8). The ultimate stimulus for the work ethic comes from God's example in creation: "For in six days the LORD made the heavens and the earth, the sea, and all that is in them" (v. 11). God created humans to share not only his fellowship, but also his work. As a general rule, when health and opportunites make it possible, we work six days a week. Theists know that they are not gods, angels, or animals, but God's image-bearers made to commune with God and work for God. More important than what we do for a livelihood is whom we live for. Whatever Christians do, they work at it ultimately for the glory of God (1 Cor. 10:31).

What is work? Negatively, work is neither an evil nor a punishment for the Fall. Affirmatively, work is the use of God-given abilities and the expenditure of God-given energy as a means to achieve good ends. We misunderstand work if we think it is an end in itself, like play. Before the Fall God gave Adam work to perform for the good of creation (Gen. 2:15). Since the Fall work may be more irksome, but it still benefits others and provides purpose and fulfillment. In losing ourselves in service for others we find ourselves. By way of *definition,* work is the expenditure of mental and physical energy to the best of our trained abilities in making quality products or doing needed services that we "may have something to share with those in need" (Eph. 4:28).

The primary goal of work is not to make money for selfish purposes but to provide the best possible service or product. It is the quality of our products and services that merits pay, not the time we put in. In order to produce a more beneficial service or product one may need to get more education or training. In education also it is the quality of the papers turned in, not the time spent on them that merits the grades. Efficiency and excellence in learning to serve well reflects faithfulness as stewards. The level of productivity in what may seem to be small things in school or in an internship may indicate whether we are ready for greater responsibilities.

No business or nation owes money to capable people who refuse to produce a needed service or a quality product when opportunity is available. If our training or work seems meaningless, we may need to realign our values. We may lack respect for ourselves as image-bearers of God and disregard our own need for fulfillment through using our gifts in servant ministries. Or we may have insufficient concern for others and for helping meet their needs well. Or we may lack love for God and a desire to serve God's righteous causes in the world. A Christian's daily work is primarily rendered to the Lord and not humans (Eph. 6:7), and it is to be done with integrity (Col. 3:22–24). People who have not become self-starters in producing quality work in their Christian churches and schools are not likely to produce self-disciplined work in Christian service.

The lowliest task on earth can be viewed as a service for others when we love God who gave us gifts for our work and when we love others for whom and with whom we work. No amount of success, fame, and private accumulation of goods will save us from the essential emptiness of selfishness. We live life with others and essentially for others' safety, health, clothing, housing, education, protection, justice, and education. And in so doing we find ourselves fulfilled. With servants' hearts like our Lord's, we live not to be served in high positions but to serve in humility (Mark 10:43–45). Our Lord did not try to get away with as little work as possible but lived as a carpenter until the beginning of his ministry (Mark 6:3).

Paul had a small business, buying skins from hunters, making tents of the skins, and selling quality merchandise in the market to people in need. The apostle worked night and day, laboring and toiling. He teaches that Christians should do something useful with their hands to (1) avoid dependence on others (1 Thess. 2:9–12; 2 Thess. 3:8), (2) provide for their own family's needs (1 Thess. 4:11, 12), and (3) to share with the needy (Eph. 4:28). As Wesley put it, "Earn all you can, save all you can, and give all you can."

God's creation mandates provide a healthy context for using our natural abilities in earning a livelihood, but Christians do not live to work. Above earning a living, Christians live to fellowship with their Redeemer and extend his church. Christians will not let earning a temporal living take the place of their redemptive vocations. God "calls" his people to repentance and faith for fellowship and service in his redemptive program. Jesus worked as a carpenter but had a redemptive calling to perform. Paul made tents but that was not what he lived for. The apostle lived to take the gospel to the Gentiles. Mechanics, secretaries, and physicians may have gifts of evangelism, teaching, administration, helping, and giving— gifts that can well be used in the church. The Christian's highest spiritual fulfillment is not met in creation work, however successful and valuable, but in their work for the redemptive kingdom. For some this means a change of creation work, but for most it may not. But God has called and endowed all members of Christ's body with gifts to help take the gospel to the whole world.[117] That meets humanity's deepest need.

Employers, in addition to meeting the requirements of other workers, ought to treat workers as they would be treated, without threats and without favoritism, knowing that they face the judgment of God (Eph. 6:9). Overseers should provide for their workers what is right and fair, for they also have a Master in heaven (Col. 4:1). If certain economic structures are inherently unfair and oppressive, they ought to be changed. The laborers whose excellent work produces greater profits for a multinational corporation, for example, should participate in profit-sharing, even though they may live in other countries. Owners and board members ought not let covetousness and greed lead them to exploit their employees. Laborers are worthy of their wages in every situation, and certainly in Christian churches, schools, or mission boards (1 Tim. 5:18).

How should Christians work? "Whatever you do, work at it with all your heart, as working for the Lord and not for men" (Col. 3:23; Eph. 6:7–8). The ultimate Owner of the universe is distinct from it, and so no private ownership of land and resources is ever ultimate, but a temporary stewardship under the Creator. God lends us some property and its resources temporarily for use in efficient service of others. God asks us not only to work, but to work energetically, giving a full day's work for a full day's pay. So God's stewards may pray: "Creator and Lord of all, thank you for my life and for trusting me temporarily with the abilities, material resources, and opportunities I have. Sharpen my discernment so that I can see ways to conserve and invest them that will help expand your rule throughout the world. May your will be done in my work on earth as it is in heaven."

Set Apart One Day in Seven

The Creator knows that those who work six days need rest! Rest from the usual work, however, need not mean total inactivity. God, who is spirit, neither slumbers nor sleeps and was not exhausted after six periods of creation so that he would have needed literal rest (John 5:17). Although God ceased creating, he remained active in sustaining the world and redeeming the lost. Analogously, one day a week we need a change. We need to devote a day a week for special personal and communal fellowship with God. Goethe well expressed the attitude of non-Christians: "Bitter week, happy festival." In contrast, Christians say, "Refreshing Sunday, fulfilling week!" Christian creationists live all week in the joy of the first day with God. That day brings not only devotion to God but also personal renewal spiritually, mentally, and physically. And it provides opportunity for fellowship with other Christians and for helping people in need.

"The Sabbath," as Jesus explained, "was made for man, not man for the Sabbath" (Mark 2:27). Since the sabbath rest was planned to meet our need for enrichment, workaholics who do not sanctify one day in seven miss its blessings. Those who overwork seven days a week may identify too much with their work and fail to realize the importance of who and what they are as persons. Workahololics devalue the importance of fellowship with their Creator and his people. God himself "blessed the Sabbath day and made it holy" (Exod. 20:11). "The sabbath is holy—not in a magical sense, but as set apart to the covenant God who is the Lord of time."[118]

The practice of keeping the Sabbath as rooted in Creation is beneficial for all, not just Israelites seeking to keep Moses' law. The Mosaic stipulations for the Sabbath were fading away in the first century (2 Cor. 3:7–11) but the principle remains. Although the New Testament repeats all other nine commandments, it does not repeat the one on the Sabbath. So some Christians think there is no longer any need to observe the Sabbath, even in principle. Other Christians believe that the fourth commandment remains inviolable and that we ought to worship on the seventh day of the week (which starts at 6:00 Friday evening).

Most Christians think that the principle of the Sabbath is now fittingly fulfilled on the first day of the week when our Redeemer victoriously fulfilled all the Old Testament ceremonies and rose from the dead. Strangely the Jewish writers of the New Testament ingrained in centuries of traditional seventh-day worship, emphasized a new time of celebration—the first day of the week. Jesus rose from the dead on the first day (John 20:1) and appeared to the disciples on that day (v. 19). One week later he appeared to the eleven disciples (v. 26). The promised coming of the Holy Spirit occurred on Sunday (Lev. 23:16). On that day Peter preached Christ's death and resurrection, and three thousand people received the gospel, were baptized, and were added to the church (Acts 2). At Troas the Christians assembled for worship on the first day of the week (20:6–7). The Corinthians brought their offerings on the first day of the week, (presumably when they met for worship) (1 Cor. 16:2). Since the Jewish Sabbath commemorated not only Creation but also the deliverance from Egypt (Deut. 5:15), it is fitting that the Christian Sabbath commemorate the deliverance Christ provided on the cross and by his triumphant resurrec-

tion. We rest from our own works on the first day in order that Christ's Spirit may do his renewing work in us. Hence the first day of the week is fittingly called "the Lord's Day" (Rev. 1:10).

Those who need to work only five days a week could conceivably celebrate two days a week! Saturdays could be set apart in special gratitude for the blessings of work and of rest. Sundays could be set aside to honor the risen Christ and his gracious provision of eternal spiritual rest. Doubtless most people will still need to combine the two purposes on Sundays. Whatever time we regard holy we must remember that Jesus did not conform to the heartless Pharisaic notions of the Sabbath that reduced it to little more than an external show. On Sabbath days Jesus healed the man with the shriveled hand (Mark 3:1–6), a woman crippled for eighteen years (Luke 13:10–17), a man suffering from dropsy (14:1–6), an invalid for thirty-eight years at the pool of Bethesda (John 5:1–18), and the man born blind (9:1–16). Healings and other acts like these not only countered Pharisaic Sabbath traditions but also exhibited Jesus' messianic consciousness. By these acts Jesus disclosed his awareness of the fact that "the Son of Man is Lord even of the Sabbath" (Mark 2:28). So Christian theists avoid judging Sabbath keeping by legalistic taboos on that day. Paul also emphasized that externals should not become a matter of judgment of one Christian by another (Rom. 13:8–10; 14:4–6, 10, 12–13; Gal. 4:9–10; Col. 2:13–17).

Only people with authentic faith in the Creator and Redeemer can keep the Lord's Day holy in motive as well as act. Believers' primary motivations in keeping Sunday different should be to (1) love their Lord who enables them to work and plans for their rest, (2) worship in spirit and truth together with others in the church, (3) give proportionately as God has prospered them

(1 Cor. 16:1–2), (4) help others who are in need, and (5) anticipate eternal rest from all their work in the world of space and time (Heb. 4:3–11).

Cooperate With Other Creationists

Creationists of the world unite! You have nothing to lose but taxation for public education without representation! In pluralistic societies one would expect public education to represent the major pluralistic worldviews. Public education would present the three major philosophical traditions—naturalism, pantheism, and theism, not just naturalism or naturalism and an exploding pantheism. The first amendment to the Constitution of the United States, for example, while prohibiting the establishment of one denomination as the state religion, guarantess freedom of religion. In schools valuing academic freedom, furthermore, the worldview of theism has as much right to representation in the textbooks and classrooms as the worldviews of naturalism and pantheism. Hence there should be freedom to teach a theistic philosophy of life, not only in courses in science, but also in courses in history, sociology, psychology, philosophy, etc. Teachers who are theists in America should not be intimidated by misinterpretations of the first amendment to the United States Constitution. It does not erect a wall between public education and religion nor limit public education in a pluralistic society to secular or pantheistic views of life. The amendment wisely forbids an established state religion while guaranteeing freedom of religion. Surely that means freedom for theists as teachers or students in public education.

Quite apart from differences on the length of the days (Gen. 1), creationists together should present a theistic-creationist point of view in free societies, not on sheer authority, whether scientific or religious, but because Creation provides a coherent account of more of the data concerning origins with fewer difficulties than naturalistic or pantheistic evolutions. In short, teachers can indicate that the theistic-creationist hypothesis makes more sense. Theism does not ask students to believe in an unfounded chance or accident in the beginning. Theism justifies the scientists' belief in an ordered world and in the ability of the human mind to know it. Science originated and thrives among theists. Science will not survive as well among naturalists without normative values such as intellectual honesty, nor among pantheistic occultists depending on the deceptions of channeling and uncritical visualizations of their own imagined quantum leaps into godhood. For the sake of freedom in education and benefits to the scientific endeavor in pluralistic societies, teachers ought to present theism at least as one of three major worldviews with which all students should have reliable knowledge.

REVIEW QUESTIONS

To Help Relate and Apply
Each Section in This Chapter

1. *Briefly state the classical problem* this chapter addresses and indicate reasons why genuine inquiry into it is important for your worldview and your existence personally and socially.

2. *Objectively summarize the influential answers* given to this problem in history as hypotheses to be tested. Be able to compare and contrast their real similarities and differences (not merely verbal similarities or differences).

3. *Highlight the primary biblical evidence* on which to decide among views—evidence found in the relevant teachings of the major divisions of Scripture—and decide for yourself which historical hypothesis (or synthesis of historical views) provides the

most consistent and adequate account of the primary biblical data.

4. *Formulate in your own words your doctrinal conviction* in a logically consistent and adequate way, organizing your conclusions in ways you can explain clearly, support biblically, and communicate effectively to your spouse, children, friends, Bible class, or congregation.

5. *Defend your view* as you would to adherents of the alternative views, showing that the other views are logically less consistent and factually faced with more difficulties than your view in accounting for the givens, not only of special revelation but also of human experience in general.

6. *Explore the differences the viability of your conviction can make in your life.* Then test your understanding of the viability of your view by asking, "Can I live by it authentically (unhypocritically) in relation to God and to others in my family, church, vocation, neighborhood, city, nation, and world?"

MINISTRY PROJECTS

To Help Communicate This Doctrine in Christian Service

1. *Memorize one major verse or passage* that in its context teaches the heart of this doctrine and may serve as a text from which to preach, teach, or lead small-group studies on the topic. The memorized passages from each chapter will build a body of content useful also for meditation and reference in informal discussions.

2. *Formulate the major idea of the doctrine in one sentence* based on the passage memorized. This idea should be useful as the major thesis of either a lesson for a class (junior high to adult) or a message for a church service.

3. *State the specific purpose or goal of your doctrinal lesson or message.* Your purpose should be more than informative. It should show why Christians need to accept this truth and live by it (unhypocritically). For teaching purposes, list indicators that would show to what extent class members have grasped the truth presented.

4. *Outline your message or lesson in complete sentences.* Indicate how you would support the truth of the doctrine's central ideas and its relevance to life and service. Incorporate elements from this chapter's historical, biblical, systematic, apologetic, and practical sections selected according to the value they have for your audience.

5. *List applications of the doctrine* for communicating the difference this conviction makes in life (for sermons, lessons, small-group Bible studies, or family devotional Bible studies). Applications should make clear what the doctrine is, why one needs to know it, and how it will make differences in thinking. Then show how the difference in thought will lead to differences in values, priorities, attitudes, speech, and personal action. Consider also the doctrine's possible significance for family, church, neighborhood, city, regional, and national actions.

6. *Start a file and begin collecting illustrations* of this doctrine's central idea, the points in your outline, and your application.

7. *Write out your doctrinal statement on this subject in one paragraph* (half a page or less). To work toward a comprehensive doctrinal statement, collect your formulations based on a study of each chapter of *Integrative Theology*. As your statement of Christian doctrine grows, you will find it personally strengthening and useful when you are asked your beliefs and when you apply for service with churches, mission boards, and other Christian organizations. Any who seek ordination to Christian ministry will need a doctrinal statement that covers the broad scope of theology.

CHAPTER 2

EXISTENCE UNDER PROVIDENTIAL DIRECTION

Existence Under Providential Direction

THE PROBLEM: TO WHAT EXTENT AND BY WHAT MEANS DOES THE ALL-WISE, ALL-LOVING, AND ALL-POWERFUL GOD GOVERN THE UNIVERSE, HISTORY, AND PERSONS TO HIS PREDETERMINED END?

In chapter 8 of volume 1 we saw that in eternity past the sovereign God devised a wise plan, both directive and permissive, for all times. Chapter 9 of volume 1 explored how God began to implement that plan by creating the cosmos, persons, and all living forms. The present chapter considers the next step in the execution of the divine plan, namely, how God sustains and guides all that he has brought into existence. A moment's reflection suggests that creation, preservation, and providence are inextricably linked, since it is unlikely, if not impossible, that a wise, loving, and omnipotent God (see vol. 1, chaps. 5 and 6) would create a vast universe without upholding it in existence and guiding it to a suitable end.

Problems arise when we relate the doctrine of providence to the actual world in which we live. Consider, first, the relation of providence to the laws of nature. Scientists inform us that the Sahara Desert creeps southward several miles each year, destroying valuable farm and grazing land, thereby displacing thousands of already impoverished African villagers. Furthermore, how does the doctrine of providence relate to powerful typhoons that seasonally wreak destruction on many poor people in Sri Lanka and Bangladesh? How does it relate to famines that tragically cut short the lives of thousands in Ethiopia? or to severe droughts that impoverish peoples in various parts of the world?

Reflect for a moment on the relation of the doctrine of providence to humanly caused evil. Is it reasonable to believe that God rules the world, given Hitler's barbarous annihilation of six million or so Jews during World War II? Can one adhere to providence in the face of the extensive human suffering inflicted by the cultural revolution in China, or by Idi Amin in devastated Uganda, or by "Papa Doc" Duvalier in poverty-ridden Haiti? How does providence relate to the present AIDS epidemic? Medical authorities, for example, predict that the entire population of several African countries will be carriers of the AIDS virus before the end of the century. In the face of such widespread human suffering, can we believe that a good and powerful God controls the world? Or is the tragedy-ridden human story merely "a tale told by an idiot, full of sound and fury, signifying nothing"?

Does the Judeo-Christian hypothesis of divine providence allow room for human freedom and meaningful involvement in the affairs of history? To what extent does God accomplish his purposes through the will and efforts of human beings such as we? How does God operate in relation to the evil intentions and acts of persons? The doctrine of providence raises the question as to whether both good and evil historical events are efficiently ordered by the sovereign God, or whether morally evil acts are merely permitted. Does God effectively limit or restrain the malicious designs of evil persons? Does God redirect the nefarious deeds of wicked persons to worthy ends unimagined by the perpetrators? In our study of providence it will be important to consider distinguishing between God's unconditional (decretive) and conditional (permissive) wills, as discussed in chapter 8 of volume 1.

Moreover, is God's governance of history accomplished solely by secondary causes (i.e., by the laws of nature and the free acts of persons), or are there grounds for believing that God can and does work through exceptional events in nature and history known as miracles? Is there sound basis for believing that God may employ immaterial angelic beings to accomplish his providential purposes? Furthermore, is belief in supernatural spiritual powers such as Satan and demons tenable in the modern world? If so, how does their activity cohere with God's providential rule of history? Finally, what effect does prayer to God have in the events of everyday life? Can people in an advanced scientific age sustain the belief that prayer effects objective changes in nature and human history?

ALTERNATIVE INTERPRETATIONS IN THE CHURCH

The data of Scripture and human experience are extensive, and the issues associated with the doctrine of divine providence are complex. Consequently a number of hypotheses have been advanced on the subject of divine providence in the history of the Christian church.

Supralapsarian Calvinist Perspectives

Consistent with their understanding of the divine decrees, supralapsarians emphasize God's absolute sovereignty and effectual working over the whole range of human (and nonhuman) activity. Authorities view the government of persons and history, not in terms of God's permissive will, but as a function of his effectual will. Supralapsarians throughout history underscore the fact that the control of the world and the outcome of history are in the hands of God, not finite persons. Theologians in the tradition are reluctant to explain the occurrence of evil in terms of bare permission. The fact that God actively governs the world and that persons nevertheless act freely and responsibly generally is viewed as a mystery incomprehensible to finite human minds.

Luther's high view of divine causality led him to conclude that God's providential operations embrace all occurrences, both good and evil. Luther understood God's word in Isaiah 45:7, "I form the light and create darkness," to mean, "I hold good fortune and misfortune in my hand."[1] In this regard Luther viewed the immediate agent of an act as the disguise under which God both works and hides himself. Thus Luther refers to "God's mask, under which he conceals himself and so marvelously exercises dominion and introduces disorder into the world.''[2] In spite of the fact that Satan and sinners are impelled by God's power, Luther stopped short of affirming that God works sin. He viewed the seeming contradiction between God's efficient governance of all things and his holiness as a mystery hidden to human reason.

Zwingli staunchly maintained that God is absolute controlling providence. His God is the efficient cause of all occurrences: ''all things are so done and disposed by the providence of God that nothing takes place without His will and command.''[3] So absolute is the divine providence that second causes, including the agency of finite persons, is denied. Since God's providence excludes human service, Zwingli avers, persons are no more than tools in the hands of the divine Majesty. ''By the providence of God, therefore, are taken away together free will and merit; for if it disposes all things, what part have we that permits us to think anything done of ourselves?''[4] This deterministic view of providence appears to make God the efficient cause of evil. Zwingli, however, denied that God is morally responsible for sinful acts, for the reason that the Sovereign transcends all temporal laws.

Closer to Luther than to Zwingli, Calvin repeatedly insists that the sovereign God actively governs all things in accordance with his secret purpose. ''Governing heaven and earth by his providence, God so regulates all things that nothing takes place without his deliberation.''[5] Again, ''God by the bridle of his providence turns every event whatever way he wills.''[6] Calvin believes that in addition to effecting the good, God also governs the plans and intentions of evildoers. Thus ''Satan and all the impious are so under God's hand and power that he directs their malice to whatever end seems good to him.''[7] In one section of the *Institutes*

(I.18.2) Calvin explains how God inspires and even impells evildoers. He suggests that God works inwardly in the impious to bend their minds and to harden their wills such that they act perversely. On the basis of Proverbs 21:1 and other texts, he concludes that ''Satan performs his part by God's impulsion.''[8] Calvin dismisses the thesis of permissive providence as a clever subterfuge. Yet Calvin (unlike Zwingli) insists that God's active governance does not nullify human agency and responsibility, for God uses intermediate causes to achieve his ends. Does the scheme of government thus proposed implicate God in sin? On the basis of the divine incomprehensibility, whereby God's ways transcend the capacity of finite minds, and on the basis of the divine holiness, whereby God remains undefiled, Calvin responds with a firm no!

The supralapsarian position on miracles, angels, and prayer is similar to that of moderately Reformed authorities discussed below.

The Arminian View

The distinctive hypothesis of the Arminian tradition is the so-called moral view of providence. Most Arminian theologians hold to (1) God's conservation of the universe by the laws of nature, (2) his preservation of the animate realm by his power, and (3) his moral government of persons. We focus on the third tenet of the Arminian view, as follows: Emphasizing the maintenance of human initiative and freedom, the Arminians argue that God's providential working is not causative but is chiefly moral. Authorities in this tradition view divine providence neither in terms of an absolute decree nor in terms of a coercive power. Rather, they believe that God exercises providential control over the world by setting before free and responsible persons moral and religious precepts that ought to be obeyed. God permits but does not cause the manifold evils in the world; he limits their effects and rules over all in love.

Jacob Arminius understood providence in the sense that God "preserves, regulates, governs and directs all things, and that nothing in the world happens fortuitously or by chance."[9] Yet Arminius quickly follows with the distinctive that would characterize the tradition that bears his name: "I place in subjection to Divine Providence both the *free will* and even *the actions of the rational creature*."[10] That is, whereas God wills and performs morally good actions, he preserves human freedom by freely permitting persons to oppose his will and perpetrate evil. Reformed contemporaries of Arminius claimed that the latter seriously limited divine providence by shifting control of history from the sovereign God to autonomous persons.

John Wesley believed that God sustains the cosmos in its existence and operations. But in the human realm providence consists of God's work of overruling human disobedience so as to achieve his saving plan for the world. Wesley wrote:

> In the natural world all things roll on in an even, uninterrupted course. But it is far otherwise in the moral world. Here evil men and evil spirits continually oppose the divine will and create numberless irregularities. Here, therefore, is full scope for the exercise of all the riches both of the wisdom and knowledge of God, in counteracting all the wickedness and folly of men and all the subtlety of Satan, to carry on his own glorious design—the salvation of lost mankind.[11]

Charles Finney likewise maintains that in the human order God's providential operations represent a moral influence exerted over free and responsible agents. Finney explicates his theory of moral government as follows: It is "the government of free will by motives

as distinguished from the government of substance by force. . . . It is a government exercised in accordance with the law of liberty, as opposed to the law of necessity. It is the administration of moral as opposed to physical law."[12] God guides the course of human affairs primarily by extending to persons the promise of rewards and the threat of punishment.

Recent Arminian writers reflect a similar emphasis. God's conservation of the physical universe and his preservation of all living forms in existence is properly effectual. Yet in respect of persons "a change in the activity of divine providence is noted. Here God's relationship is not causative, as in conservation and preservation. Rather, God's providential care and government is moral. Providence is exerted in the form of motive rather than compulsion."[13]

The Arminian tradition interprets miracles, angels, and prayer in much the same way as moderately Reformed authorities discussed below.

The Deistic Position

Deists in seventeenth- and eighteenth-century England, assuming the radical transcendence of God and the unity of nature, posited a First Cause who created the universe and who instituted universal laws by which the cosmos functions. From the beginning the Creator caused the universe to operate as a well-ordered machine, thereby eliminating the need for direct supernatural intervention in its affairs. The deists thus viewed preservation negatively as God's refusal to destroy the work of his hands, and they viewed providence positively as God's general oversight of the properties and laws by which the universe functions.

Thomas Chubb, in *A Short Dissertation on Providence* (London, 1738), advanced many reasons why God does not intervene in the world in works of special providence. Voltaire, the French deist, upheld a general providence (God's oversight of the laws by which the universe functions), but dismissed as absurd the notion of special providence (God's watchful care of individual lives). Thomas Paine, who conceived of God as "the great mechanic of the creation,"[14] had in mind divine providence when he wrote of that "system of principles as fixed and unalterable as those by which the universe is regulated and governed."[15] Since the deists viewed the universe as a vast machine, they had no cogent rationale for life's evils and disasters. Their best explanation for evil was superstition, ignorance, and the alleged sinister influence exerted by the clergy.

Given their fundamental presuppositions, the deists refused to countenance the possibility of miracles. The biblical accounts of miracles—including the incarnation and the resurrection of Christ—were variously described as "absurdities," "impossibilities," and "lying wonders." Thomas Paine wrote, "We have never seen in our time nature go out of her course."[16] The most the deists would affirm is that the remarkable orderliness of the universe, with its inviolable laws, is the most profound "miracle." The world view of the deists also precluded the efficacy of prayer. Finite creatures cannot alter the functioning of a universe that operates on the basis of fixed laws and properties.

The Classical Liberal View

Traditional liberalism, guided by the Enlightenment theme of inevitable progress, interpreted providence as the purposive force that has guided human history from crude beginnings to present heights of social cooperation, political freedom, and economic prosperity. Liberal thinkers, many of whom worked on the fringes of pantheism, denied that God actively directs particular occurrences in history. Rather, the active force or soul of the universe effects progress by means of the laws of nature, emergent evolution, and the moral achievements of persons. Liberal thinkers supplanted the direct governance of a personal God by the forces of material causality and free human actions.

Schleiermacher firmly denied any special divine governance of nature or history. The term *providence,* which the Romantic theologian used sparingly, refers to the forces of nature that the Most High has set in motion and to the free acts of responsible persons. Following Kant and Hegel, Schleiermacher upheld the notion of a relentless cosmic progress.

W. A. Brown concurs with the definition of providence as the uniform evolutionary advance within nature and history:

> Instead of confining God's activity to a series of isolated interpositions . . . , we think of him as ever at work, forming, training and perfecting the moral personalities whom he has designed for union with himself. In the gradual development which science recognizes, from the lower forms to the higher, from the more simple to the more complex, we see the slow unfolding of God's providential plan.[17]

From a similar perspective Gordon Kaufman defines providence as "the ordering of all finite being in terms of processes of development in history."[18] The Harvard theologian insists that via evolution and the flow of history the world is moving toward its final goal. In Kaufman's mind the distinction between general and special providence is unfounded. All events are explicable in terms of the ordinary operations of nature and history.

As we saw in chapter 8 of volume 1, process theology denies that God is the controlling Power that guides history to a predetermined end. Rather, by providing each entity with its initial aim, God lures or persuades entities to new opportunities and satisfactions. Indeed, with respect to his consequent nature, God is said to be part of the process itself. In sum, according to process thought, God does not order the world; he experiences or feels it.

Liberalism's quasi-pantheistic and evolutionary worldview allows no room for miracles as instruments of providence. Schleiermacher defined a miracle as any religiously significant event. Thus for the truly religious person every event is a miracle. According to Harnack, the biblical picture of miracles derived from a prescientific view of the world. Said the Ritschlian liberal, "Miracles, it is true, do not happen; but of the marvelous and the inexplicable there is no lack."[19] Modern liberalism retains the notion of miracle as any event that bears religious import.

The liberal tradition likewise dismisses angels as products of the imagination of primitive people or as poetic personifications of the powers of nature. Belief in Satan and demons as personal malignant powers is rejected as antithetic to the tradition's vision of cosmic progress. Said DeWolf, "We would best regard the belief in demons reflected in the New Testament as belonging merely to the pseudoscience of the first century."[20] Untrained in medical science, the biblical writers falsely ascribed to demons what modern enlightened people understand as diseases of the mind and nervous system.

From the perspective of its evolutionary worldview, liberalism denies that prayer effects objective change in the world. Theological liberals uniformly view prayer as the soul's personal communion with God. The chief effect of prayer is to alter the disposition and attitudes of the one who prays.

The View of Theistic Existentialists and Some Neoorthodox

As a result of the traumas of the twentieth century, existentially orientated theologians argue that no purpose or meaning can be found in nature or history. Because history is soiled with brutality and death, many thinkers limit divine providence to the hearts of believers. This means that the present rule of God is spiritual and subjective only. God's governmental dealings with the unbelieving world will be manifest only in the eschaton. Such considerations lead one authority to conclude that "Providence is the forgotten stepchild of contemporary theology."[21]

Russian theologian Nicolas Berdyaev denies that God governs the course of nature and history, given the stark reality of cruelty, barbarism, and suffering in the world. History, that narrative forged by human freedom, is a horrible tragedy and a horrendous failure. Simply put, "God does not govern this world, the world of objectivity which is under the power of its own Prince."[22] Berdyaev makes his point more fully:

> This world into which we are thrown is not God's world and in it the divine order and divine harmony cannot hold sway. God's world only breaks through into this world, the light of it shines through only in that which really exists, in living beings and their existence. . . . There is nothing of God in the dull and prosaic normality of the objective world order.[23]

The rule of God will be manifest in the historical sphere only in the age to come, when God will have the final word.

Given his emphasis on the existential summons of God to personal decision, Bultmann denies as an abstraction the doctrine that God directs the course of history: "The New Testament has no knowledge of . . . the *concept of providence*."[24] History, the continuum of the consciously willed actions of persons, possesses no meaning whatsoever. Only the particular moment has meaning, when the individual encounters God in an act of personal decision.

Brunner argues that the dual realities of the divine government of the world and human responsibility for evil deeds represent an insoluble paradox, which the thesis of permission cannot resolve. For Brunner the problems of providence and theodicy are solved, not philosophically or even theologically, but existentially. Before the cross of Christ the believer stands in the abyss, feels his own guilt and sin, and knows that God acts with justice and compassion. Thus in regard to the problem of theodicy, "the real solution lies in the acknowledgment of guilt and in the hope of redemption."[25]

Existentialists join with liberals in rejecting miracles as a negation of the uniformity of nature. Any alleged intrusion of God into the cause-effect nexus is dismissed as mythological. Bultmann argues that the real miracle (*Wunder*) is that God meets a person in grace in his concrete existence. For John Macquarrie miracle is a perfectly natural event that excites awe in a person. Existentially interpreted, miracle is "an event that opens up Being and becomes a vehicle for Being's revelation of grace or judgment."[26] Angels and demons likewise belong to a prescientific understanding of the universe. Comments Bultmann, "Now that the forces and laws of nature have been discovered, we can no longer believe in spirits, whether good or evil."[27] After being demythologized, angels depict those powers that stimulate persons to rise above earthly existence to a realm of spiritual power, and demons highlight the suprahuman and sometimes systemic character of evil in the world.

Existentialists likewise reject as mythological the view of prayer as human conversation with God. Prayer is said to be an expression of a person's finitude and frail dependence on the ground of Being. According to Bultmann, by prayer to God the believer certifies his eschatological existence. On the other hand, theistic existentialists view intercessory prayer as an expression of a person's freedom and openness to others. Heinrich Ott, Barth's successor at Basel, insists that the traditional view of prayer as verbal petition and intercession is unrealistic. Rather, prayer is a dialogical "I-Thou" relation with God that embraces the believer's total existence. "The one who prays opens himself for God, he bears himself up toward God and exposes his whole life before him." Adds Ott, "He does this . . . in that he casts his future into God."[28]

Liberation Theology

Proponents of the theology of liberation minimize God's providential working in history and stress rather the revolutionary struggles of the poor and oppressed to transform history. Gutierrez believes, not that God actively guides history, but that he is revealed in history amid human efforts (violent if necessary) to forge a just society. For the Peruvian theologian, man rather than God is the artisan of human destiny.

The "messianic humanism" proposed by Rubem Alves envisages the formation of a pact between God and persons, and in this pact both parties, as co-creators, jointly build a new society. According to Alves, God alone cannot guide the course of history, for his being, yet incomplete, requires human activity to be fully constituted. "In the context of the politics of human liberation man encounters a God who remains open, who has not yet arrived, and who is determined and helped by human activity. God needs man for the creation of his future."[29].

Advocates of a black theology of

liberation see God as more actively involved in providential activity. Albert Cleage believes that through Christ, the Black Messiah, God works in history to liberate blacks from oppression and to build a Black Nation.[30] God's operations in history are consistently for blacks and against whites. James Cone has a similar vision of the divine providence: "God is at work in the black community vindicating black people against white oppression."[31]

The various forms of political theology are generally skeptical of angels and miracles. The miracles alleged in the Bible involve no supernatural interruption of the natural order. Liberation theologians instead view miracles as momentous events, namely, as signs of liberation or the arrival of the kingdom of God. Moreover, political theologians generally hold that the traditional view of prayer as petition to God to change conditions represents an evasion of personal responsibility and a substitute for action. Thus they view prayer as a reflective exercise that sharpens conscience and so prepares a person to participate in the struggle for the political liberation of the oppressed.

Moderately Reformed Position

Many Fathers, medieval authorities, Reformers, and evangelicals maintain that God works providentially through the laws of nature, miracles, the free actions of persons, and supremely through the life, death, and resurrection of Jesus Christ. God effects some of his providential ends unconditionally, according to his decretive will, and others conditionally, according to his preceptive and permissive wills. Although God in part works permissively, he nevertheless retains control of all things by limiting (setting bounds to) evil acts and by redirecting their effects to worthy ends unintended by the doer.

The church fathers upheld God's providential governance of the cosmos and all living things through the Word, while insisting that God is in no way responsible for evil. They commonly called God's providential ordering of the whole his "economy" (*oikonomia*). Clement of Alexandria delineates the scope of God's "economy" as follows:

> Providence begins by ordering the world and the heavens, the course of the sun's orbit and the movements of the other heavenly bodies, all for the sake of man. Then it concerns itself with man himself. . . . And because it considers this as its most important work, it guides man's soul on the right path by the virtues of prudence and temperance, and equips his body with beauty and harmony. Finally, into the actions of mankind it infuses uprightness and some of its own good order.[32]

God never causes suffering and evil, although he permits such for the sake of the larger good: "We must not think that God actively produces afflictions; but we must be persuaded that he does not prevent those that cause them, but overrules for good the crimes of His enemies."[33] Athanasius emphasizes that God governs the universe through the agency of the Logos. At Christ's bidding the heavens revolve, the sun shines, the birds fly, plants grow, and persons live and die.

Against the contrary doctrines of fate and chance, Augustine maintained that God sovereignly governs the entire creation by a twofold providence. The "natural" working of providence refers to God's hidden governance of the material world according to an established order, whereas the "voluntary" working of providence pertains to his control and direction of the decisions and actions of free agents.[34] Seeking to defend the reality of second causes and to avoid the idea that God is responsible for evil, Augustine judged that God's providence embraces both his divine command and the acts of human beings.

That is, "Whatever is done in the world is done partly by divine agency and partly by our will."[35] Evil, defined as privation of the good and rebellion of the will, is permitted by God and wisely employed to serve his purposes. Thus "even what is done in opposition to his will does not defeat his will. For it would not be done did he not permit it. . . . Nor would a good Being permit evil to be done but that in his omnipotence he can turn evil into good."[36] Augustine went on to say that God employs wicked spirits and persons in his service to judge evildoers and to purify the righteous. Since the sovereign God turns evil to salutary ends, Augustine argued that specific evil deeds may be judged good when viewed in the light of the whole.

Several Reformed confessions explicate this understanding of divine providence. The Belgic Confession reads as follows:

> We believe that the same good God, after he had created all things, did not forsake them or give them up to fortune or chance, but that he rules and governs them according to his holy will, so that nothing happens in this world without his appointment; nevertheless God neither is the Author of nor can be charged with the sins that are committed. . . . This doctrine affords us unspeakable consolation, since we are . . . persuaded that he so restrains the devil and all our enemies that without his will and permission they cannot hurt us (art. XIII).

According to the Heidelberg Catechism:

> Providence is the almighty and ever-present power of God by which he upholds, as with his hand, heaven and earth and all creatures, and so rules them that leaf and blade, rain and drought, fruitful and lean years, food and drink, health and sickness, prosperity and poverty—all things, in fact, come to us not by chance but from his fatherly hand (Lord's Day 10, Q. 27).

More recently, Carl Henry maintained that God is "providential Orderer of the world, the supreme Ruler who constantly disposes nature and the history of man in a rational, purposive plan."[37] Providence is purposive in that God actively directs all things toward the realization of his eternal plan in Jesus Christ. It is furthermore all-encompassing, embracing the powers of nature, the pattern of history, evil deeds of persons (without ascribing evil to God), miraculous redemptive events, and chiefly the incarnation, death, and resurrection of Jesus Christ, who will return to lead history to its final destiny. Divine providence, moreover, is specific, in that God works out his purposes in the minutiae of life. The chief focus of providence is the believer, for whose ultimate good God lovingly rules and overrules in human affairs.

Orthodox Christian authorities maintain that miracles are not violations of nature but are purposeful exceptions to the customary way in which God works. God usually operates through the known laws of nature. But to achieve his redemptive purposes, the Almighty occasionally overrules the usual processes to produce unexpected results. Augustine affirmed that miracles cannot be contrary to nature, for God's will defines the nature of every creature. The Westminster Confession states, "God, in his ordinary providence, makes use of means, yet he is free to work without, above, and against them, at his pleasure (ch. V.3). Ramm adds, "With providence working with the theistic view of nature, a normal, natural, credible doorway was left open for God to answer prayer, work the miraculous, and even send his Son into the world with all the attendant supernatural activity the incarnation and resurrection involved."[38]

Most Christian theologians view angels as created spiritual intelligences, organized in various ranks and assisting in the providential ordering of history. According to Augustine, "God the Creator rules over all creation by means of holy spirits, his heavenly and earthly ministers."[39] Although some Fathers and medieval authorities speculated excessively about angels, most orthodox scholars view these holy ones as guiding the affairs of the nations, protecting believers, and punishing the enemies of God. On the other hand, they regard Satan as an archangel who pridefully rebelled aginst God, and they view demons as lesser angels who were carried away by Satan's apostasy. Satan and the demons oppose God and his will, oppress the people of God, incite sinners to evil, and cause mental and physical disorders. Observed Augustine, "The devil fell by pride from the beginning of time and never lived in peace and blessedness with the holy angels, but apostasized from his Creator at the very outset of his creation."[40] Some recent evangelicals, such as Yoder and Stringfellow, point out Satan's role in the formation of structural evil in the political, social, and economic realms.

Theologians in the tradition likewise view prayer as an instrument of divine providence. Understood as communion, petition, and intercession, prayer has both a subjective and an objective efficacy. As an act of worship, prayer produces godly attitudes and dispositions in the one who prays. "Prayer clears and cleanses our heart, and makes it more capable of receiving the divine gifts which are spiritually infused into us."[41] On the other hand, prayer causes things to occur in the objective world that otherwise would not have come to pass. This is generally explained in the sense that God from eternity past ordained not only the ends, but also the means for the realization of his purposes. Henry observes that prayer, as a crucial element in the realization of God's providential pur-

poses, "has more than a subjective value; it not only 'changes us' but it 'changes things.'"[42]

Additional information on this unit can be found in helpful studies by C. S. Lewis,[43] G. C. Berkouwer,[44] and Colin Brown.[45]

BIBLICAL TEACHING

To determine which historical proposal is closest to the teaching of Scripture, we proceed with a study of the relevant biblical materials on the subject of providence and the means God employs to achieve his purposes in history, namely, miracles, angels, and prayer.

Pentateuch

The doctrine of providence takes its name from a phrase in the text of Genesis 22:8. When Isaac on Mount Moriah asked Abraham where the lamb was for the burnt offering, Abraham responded, "God himself will provide the lamb for the burnt offering, my son." The Hebrew phrase is *'elōhîm yir'eh-lô*, and that of the Latin Vulgate is *Deus providebit*. The Hebrew verb *rā'āh*, to "see," here bears the extended meaning to "provide." When Abraham had thus demonstrated faith and obedience, God directed the patriarch to a ram caught by its horns in a thicket (v. 13). At the end of this remarkable episode, "Abraham called that place The LORD Will Provide" (v. 14). In the words of one scholar, "God saw! God provided! God's divine provision took care of everything."[46]

At the most basic level God accomplishes his purposes through the observable operations of nature. Thus God said after the Flood: "As long as the earth endures, seedtime and harvest, cold and heat, summer and winter, day and night will never cease" (Gen. 8:22).

More specially, divine providence

expresses itself in God's care and protection of his own people. Recalling their experiences in the wilderness, Moses reminded Israel, "The LORD your God carried you, as a father carries his son, all the way you went until you reached this place" (Deut. 1:31; cf. 7:18). The peace, protection, and safety God provides for the righteous is beautifully affirmed in Deuteronomy 33:12, 25–28. God, moreover, promises to provide his obedient people with material prosperity in the form of rain and bountiful harvests (Lev. 26:3–4) and with victory over their enemies (vv. 6–9). Although Israel had to contend against its foes, success in battle was clearly a provision of the Lord (Deut. 3:2–3).

God's providential dealings with his people include not only blessing but also discipline (Deut. 4:36; 8:5). If Israel failed to submit to God's discipline and persisted in evildoing, the Lord would send as a negative providence disease, poor harvests, famine, plagues, war, and exile among the nations (Lev. 26:23–39; Deut. 28:15–68). In the case of persistent disobedience, God would permit unfriendly nations to punish Israel with military defeats (Num. 14:43).

God providentially directs not only the great but also the small issues of life, such as the time and circumstances of a person's death. In his sovereignty God caused Moses to die on Mount Nebo without entering the Promised Land (Deut. 32:49–52; Num. 27:12–14). Likewise God prevented Aaron from entering Canaan by terminating his life also (Num. 20:22–26).

The Pentateuch attests several ways by which God exercises control over evil acts. First by a restraining kind of providence God prevents sin that otherwise would occur. When Abimilech tried to add Sarah to his harem, believing she was unmarried, God told the Philistine king not to "touch her" but to return her to her husband (Gen. 20:1–7). Since God's plan for Sarah was that she should bear a son by Abraham (Gen. 17:16–21), the Lord kept Abimelech from thwarting his plan and also from sinning (Gen. 20:6). In similar fashion God warned Laban not to harm his son-in-law Jacob in any way (Gen. 31:24), thus preventing the shedding of innocent blood.

A redirecting kind of providence, whereby the Lord channels evil acts to worthy ends unimagined by the perpetrator, occurs in the account of Judah's lust with Tamar his daughter-in-law, whom he thought to be a harlot (Gen. 38). In the plan of God, Perez, the illegitimate son of Judah and Tamar, occupies a place in the family line of the Messiah (Matt. 1:2–3; Luke 3:33).

The familiar story of Joseph provides the clearest account in the Old Testament of a redirecting providence. Joseph was thrown into a cistern by his brothers, rescued by Midianite traders, sold as a slave in Egypt, and made Pharaoh's prime minister. God informed Joseph in a dream that seven years of famine were coming and told him to set aside ample food stores for the lean times. Joseph's prudent planning saved his family from starvation when they journeyed to Egypt to buy food. In an emotional confrontation, when Joseph's brothers expressed their shame for mistreating him, Joseph reassured them three times that God had sent him to Egypt to provide for the chosen people (Gen. 45:5–8). " 'Not you . . . but God' (v. 8) expresses the fact of Providence in a typically sweeping biblical idiom."[47] Joseph's testimony, "You intended to harm me, but God intended it for good to accomplish what is now being done, the saving of many lives" (Gen. 50:20), confirms that the God who controls history redirected the brothers' evil act to a salutary end. Thus divine providence overrules and transforms the worst forms of human malice.

Exodus 1–2 relates the beautiful story of how God overruled the evil intentions of a pharaoh to spare the life of the infant Moses, who later would become the liberator of Israel from Egypt. "God's providence used natural factors: motherly love, sisterly love, a woman's pity, Israelite acumen, Egyptian culture. . . . It was precisely the commandment to throw the boys into the Nile that brought Moses to the Egyptian court."[48]

In the Old Testament, miracles—viewed as exceptional events in nature or history—contributed to the deliverance and preservation of Israel as a special people. The focal miracle of the Old Testament was the deliverance of Israel through the Sea of Reeds (Exod. 14). When Moses stretched out his right hand, the Lord drove back the sea with a strong east wind (v. 21). In his song of thanksgiving to the Lord, Moses interpreted the wind as "the blast" of Yahweh's nostrils (Exod. 15:8, 10). With Israel safely through the sea, Moses again stretched out his hand in obedience to God's command, whereupon the waters flowed back on the pursuing Egyptians destroying every last warrior. Repeatedly throughout Israel's history God led his people by miraculous events. Yet without doubt, "the miracle at the Red Sea is the paradigm of God's acting."[49]

Angels, who constitute a mighty army of spiritual beings (Deut. 33:2), are represented in Scripture as special agents by which God executes his providential purposes. Thus an angel led Israel in their flight from Egypt and protected the people against Pharaoh's pursuing army (Exod. 14:19; cf. Num. 20:16). Moreover, God used angels to guide Israel into the Promised Land and to destroy their enemies (Exod. 23:20, 23). Scripture also depicts a malignant spiritual power named Satan (*śātan,* "adversary"), who actively opposes God's purposes. Genesis 3:1–5 describes Satan's instigation of the fall of the first pair into sin. Satan, who indwelt a serpent, cast God in the role of a deceiver who sought to inhibit Adam and Eve's happiness (v. 5). "With one stroke Satan reinterpreted God as a devil, a liar possessed by jealous pride, and the way of the curse as the way to blessing."[50] Genesis 3:15 anticipates not only the struggle between Christ and Satan that would culminate in the victory of the cross, but also the agelong enmity that would exist between the people of God and the forces of Satan. Scripture, furthermore, recognizes malignant spiritual powers, or demons, who assist Satan in opposing God's providential activity. Thus in Deuteronomy 18:10–14 Moses warns against using occult powers to predict the future and communicate with the deceased. Yet in spite of God's manifold goodness, Israel abandoned God, worshiped alien gods, and sacrificed to demons (*šēdîm;* Deut. 32:17). The latter text suggests that pagan sacrifice actually represents sacrifice to demonic powers.

Scripture represents prayer as a purposeful instrument of God's providence. For example, in Genesis 24 Abraham sent his servant Eliezer to secure a wife for Isaac from among Abraham's kinfolk. Eliezer prayed earnestly that God would grant him success in the mission (vv. 12–14). Yet, according to verse 15, God answered Eliezer's prayer even before he had finished praying. As a result, the line that would lead to the Messiah was established. On the other hand, Abraham's intercession for Sodom, although uttered with persistence and compassion, yielded no tangible result (Gen. 18:22–33).

Historical Books

In his prayer celebrating the building of the temple, Ezra said of God, "You give life to everything" (Neh. 9:6). By these words Ezra acknowledged that the creator God sustains all things in existence by his power. Likewise Hannah in her prayer confessed that God guides in all the circumstances of life (1 Sam. 2:6–10).

The historical books affirm that God actively guided the affairs of the nation Israel. The Lord raised up David to be a shepherd and ruler of his people (2 Sam. 5:2; 12:7–8) and chose Solomon to succeed him as king (1 Kings 3:7; 1 Chron. 22:10). God not only selected kings, but he also rejected kings, as in the case of the wicked Saul (1 Sam. 16:1). The Scriptures relate that because of persistent idolatry, the Lord delivered the northern kingdom into the hands of Assyria (2 Kings 17:18–20). Sennacherib, in fact, was God's chosen instrument to punish Israel (2 Kings 19:25). Likewise, God delivered Judah and Jerusalem into the hands of Nebuchadnezzar, king of Babylon, who burned the temple and deported the remaining Jews to Babylon (2 Kings 24:2–3, 20; 2 Chron. 36:17–20).

In 539 B.C. the Persians conquered the Babylonian Empire. One of the first public acts of Cyrus was to issue a decree allowing the Jews to return to Jerusalem and rebuild the temple (Ezra 1:1–4). The decree of Cyrus likely was a matter of personal political expediency, for the Persian king cultivated the loyalty of subjugated peoples by granting them a measure of self-determination and by respecting their religious traditions.[51] Nevertheless, the sovereign God providentially used Cyrus' political maneuvering in a way that perpetuated the life and worship of the Jewish nation.

The providence of God is the principal theme of at least two books of the Old Testament. The Book of Ruth relates God's providential workings in the lives of ordinary people. Following the death of her husband, Ruth the Moabitess accompanied her widowed mother-in-law Naomi to Bethlehem. A poor woman, Ruth "happened" to be gleaning in a field belonging to Boaz, the kinsman of Naomi's late husband. After Ruth's nearest kinsman refused to redeem her (i.e., buy back her deceased husband's land and marry her, Ruth 4:3–6), Boaz himself purchased the property and took Ruth as his wife. Through this marriage to Boaz, Ruth entered the family of David and Jesus Christ, who centuries later was born in the same town of Bethlehem (Ruth 4:18–20; Matt. 1:1, 5).[52]

The Book of Esther tells the story of a plot to exterminate the Jews in the reign of Xerxes and of God's working to preserve his chosen people. When queen Vashti was deposed because she refused to be displayed at the king's lavish party, Esther, a Jewess, was chosen out of many aspirants to be the new queen. Meanwhile Haman, Xerxes' self-seeking prime minister, conceived a plot to kill Mordecai (Esther's cousin) and all the Jews who remained behind in Persia. One night when the king could not sleep, he read of Mordecai's role in foiling an asassination plot against himself. Ironically, through an astonished Haman, the king elevated Mordecai to a position of honor in his palace. Later, when Haman appeared to molest Esther, the king ordered Haman hung on the gallows that he, Haman, had prepared for Mordecai. Meanwhile Mordecai had urged Esther to intercede before the king on behalf of the Jews. The heart of his argument is the famous line: "And who knows but that you have come to royal position for such a time as this?" (Est. 4:14). Esther prevailed in her plea, and the king issued a second decree permitting the Jews to defend themselves against attack. Mordecai's rise to power within Xerxes' administration spared the Jews from any further persecution (9:1–4; 10:3). Clearly the Book of Esther attests God's overruling in the affairs of men and nations and his unfailing care for his people. The fact that God's name is not mentioned in the book serves to underscore God's providential working behind the scenes.[53]

Through miracles God furthered his plan for the chosen people. When Joshua made a late-night attack on the Amorites, God caused the sun to stand still (Josh. 10:12–14), thereby allowing Israel to complete the battle under cover of semi-darkness. The reduction of light may have been due to an eclipse of the sun or the result of a severe hailstorm (v. 11). Whatever the cause,[54] the point is that God miraculously lengthened the darkness to enable Israel to gain a military victory. The miracle God wrought in connection with Elijah's contest with 450 priests of Baal on Mount Carmel (1 Kings 18:17–40) demonstrated that God is the true God and that Baal is helpless. After Elijah prayed to the Lord fervently (vv. 36–37), fire fell from heaven and burned both the sacrifice and the stones of the altar.

Wisdom and Poetry

Scripture affirms that created entities are not self-sustaining, but are held in existence by the active power of God. Thus Job says of the Lord: "In his hand is the life (*nepeš*) of every creature and the breath (*rûaḥ*) of all mankind" (Job 12:10; cf. Ps. 36:6). "If [God] withdrew his spirit and breath, all mankind would perish together" (Job 34:14–15).

Job believed that God exercises providential control over the affairs of nations: "He makes nations great, and destroys them; he enlarges nations and disperses them" (Job 12:23). When the psalmist says, "The kings of the earth belong to God" (Ps. 47:9), he means that the world's rulers wittingly or

unwittingly serve God's purposes and further his ends.

A prominent theme in Job and the Psalms is God's wise governance of the inanimate and lower animate realms. According to Job 38, God controls all the operations of the natural world, namely, the earth and the sea (vv. 4–8), the daily rising of the sun (vv. 12–15), the underworld (vv. 16–18), hail and snow (vv. 22–23), storms (vv. 24–30), the stars (vv. 31–33), and clouds and lightning (vv. 34–38). The phenomena of nature are not fortuitous nor are they products of a blind force (popularly called "mother nature"), for the psalmist confesses that "lightning and hail, snow and clouds, stormy winds . . . do his bidding" (Ps. 148:8; cf. Job 37:5–13). Psalm 65:9–11 asserts that the fructification of the soil, the provision of early and latter rains, and bounteous harvests all attest God's providential supply. Psalm 104 teaches not only God's governance of the physical world (vv. 3–13), but also the marvelous way he provides for and orders the vegetable (vv. 14–17) and animal (vv. 17–22) worlds. The Lord gives food to every creature (Ps. 136:25; cf. 147:9).

The Psalms repeatedly attest God's encircling providential care for the righteous (Ps. 5:12). The Lord protects his people from danger, sustains them in time of want, delivers them from their enemies, and destroys their foes (Pss. 34:17, 19; 37:17, 28). Entire Psalms (e.g., Pss. 91, 121) praise God for his providential care in times of trouble or need. The wicked, however, are the objects of God's providential judgment (Ps. 11:6; 75:8).

In relation to evil, the psalmist acknowledges God's restraining providence when he prays that God would spare him from the bondage of "willful sins" (Ps. 19:13). Permissive providence is evident in God's determination to remove the hedge of protection around Job and allow Satan to ravage his property (Job 1:10–12). Limiting providence occurs in God's refusal to allow Satan to touch Job's person. Similarly, in Job's second test God permitted Satan to afflict Job himself short of taking his life (Job 2:6). The story of Job indicates that God establishes specific boundaries for suffering and evil in the world. God's permission of affliction for the accomplishment of spiritual goals is also evident in Psalm 119:67, 71, 75.

A redirecting kind of providence, by which God turns human sin to serve his ends, is indicated in the words of Psalm 76:10: "Surely the wrath of men shall praise thee; the residue of wrath thou wilt gird upon thee" (RSV). God takes the evil that opposes him and marvously redirects it to serve his purposes. The saying "The king's heart is in the hand of the LORD (Prov. 21:1) similarly affirms that God ultimately accomplishes his purposes in the lives of rulers (cf. Prov. 16:9; 19:21).

The Psalms indicate that the universe is populated with myriads of angels organized in the form of an "assembly" (qāhāl) or a "council" (sôd) (Ps. 89:5, 7). The cherubim appear to be a high order of angels who guard the throne of God (Pss. 18:10; 80:1), whereas the greater number of angels are lesser messengers dedicated to doing God's will (Ps. 103:20). A primary function of the common angels is to minister to the needs of the saints (Pss. 34:7; 91:11–12). Prayer in the Psalms is also seen to be a potent instrument of providence. God answers the petitions of his people with "awesome deeds of righteousness" (Ps. 65:2, 5) that inspire terror in the unsaved (Pss. 46:2; 76:7). In response to believing prayer he delivers the righteous from all their troubles (Pss. 34:17; 91:15).

Prophetic Literature

Divine providence is seen in God's selection and empowering of Jeremiah to serve as his prophet to the nations (Jer. 1:5–10). God promised his servants in the course of their ministry that he would providentially guide (Isa. 42:16; Jer. 10:23), succor (Isa. 40:11), and save them (63:9). God's providential protection is vividly seen in his preservation of Shadrach, Meshach, and Abednego in the fiery furnace, where not a hair of their head nor a thread of their clothes was singed by the intense heat (Dan. 3:19–27).

The prophecy of Jonah dramatically portrays God's providential working to extend his grace to the nations. The Lord's response to Jonah's disobedient flight from duty was to cause a violent storm to erupt at sea, thus prompting the mariners to throw Jonah overboard. In a further display of his control of the natural world, God miraculously "provided [piel of mānāh] a great fish to swallow Jonah" (Jonah 1:17). When Jonah prayed in desperation from within the fish, God answered by causing the sea creature to vomit the prophet onto the shore (2:1–10). The outcome of these dealings was the wholesale repentance of the Ninevites in response to Jonah's message. Finally, when Jonah wallowed in self-pity, God "provided" (piel of mānāh] a gourd, a worm, and a hot wind (4:6–8) to teach the prophet how great was his love for the pagan city.

Prominent in the prophetic books is God's control over the destiny of rulers and nations. Daniel acknowledges that "the Most High is sovereign over the kingdoms of men and he gives them to anyone he wishes" (Dan. 4:17, 25, 32; cf. 5:21). The metalic image of Nebuchadnezzar's dream (2:32–45)—interpreted as the succession of Babylonian, Medo-Persian, Greek, and Roman empires that would ultimately be crushed by the kingdom of the Messiah—further affirms God's providential direction of human history.

Isaiah prophesied that God would

send Assyria "the rod of [his] anger" (Isa. 10:5) to conquer the northern kingdom and lead them into captivity (cf. 7:20). The prophet describes the conquest of the chosen people by pagan forces as "his [i.e., God's] work" (Isa. 10:12). Moreover, God gave Egypt and its wealth to Nebuchadnezzar as a reward for the Babylonian's service to him (Ezek. 29:18–20). God later would raise up the Babylonians to punish Judah with captivity (Hab. 1:6; Isa. 39:6–7; cf. Lam. 3:37–38). In due course God stirred up the Medo-Persian Empire under Cyrus to vanquish the mighty Babylonian kingdom (Isa. 13:17). Finally, God called Cyrus "in righteousness to his service" (Isa. 41:2), designated this unbelieving ruler as his "shepherd" (Isa. 44:28), and so used him to restore the Jews to the land and to rebuild the temple (Isa. 45:1–7). Clearly the prophets depict God as actively guiding the affairs of the nations for the realization of his general and redemptive purposes.

Synoptic Gospels

Jesus affirmed God's general providence by saying that the "Father in heaven . . . causes his sun to rise on the evil and the good, and sends rain on the righteous and the unrighteous" (Matt. 5:45). Since God is Father of all by virtue of creation, he sends undeserved blessings to all humankind through the ordinary processes of nature. Jesus also upheld God's special providence in Matthew 6:25–34. As the disciple seeks God's kingdom and righteousness, he need not be anxious about material needs. Arguing from the lesser to the greater, Jesus reasoned that since God manifestly feeds the birds and adorns the flowers, so he will feed, clothe, and provide his servants with every material necessity. God's loving concern extends even to trivial matters: the Father who watches the common sparrow fall to the ground has numbered the hairs on the head of his people (Matt. 10:29–30).

The Gospels represent angels as personal, immaterial, and asexual beings that exist in great numbers (Matt. 22:30; 26:53; Luke 2:13). "Holy angels" (Mark 8:38; Luke 9:26)—those beings that retained their spiritual integrity—frequently are depicted as agents of divine providence. Thus God sent the angel Gabriel to inform Mary that she would conceive by the Holy Ghost and give birth to the Son of God (Luke 1:26–38). An angel of the Lord communicated the same message to Joseph in a dream (Matt. 1:20–21) and later commanded Joseph to flee to Egypt with his family (Matt. 2:13). During Jesus' earthly ministry, angels comforted the Lord following his temptations by the devil (Matt. 4:11) and strengthened him during his agony in Gethsemane (Luke 22:43). Jesus taught that every childlike believer has at least one ministering angel with direct access to the Father in heaven (Matt. 18:10). At the end of the age, the angels who accompany Christ at his second coming will gather up the elect (Matt. 24:31) and execute judgment upon the wicked (Matt. 13:41, 49).

The Gospels identify demons as angels who were carried away by Lucifer in his rebellion against God (Matt. 25:41). Demons frequently possess unbelievers (e.g., Mark 1:23–24; 5:2–5; 7:25–26), causing manifold physical and psychological disorders (Matt. 9:32; 12:22; 17:15). By his divine power and authority, Jesus exorcised demons from the possessed (Matt. 8:16, 32; 12:22; Luke 4:36), as did the disciples acting in his name (Luke 10:17).

The Gospels say much about prayer as an instrument of providence. By means of three imperatives—"ask . . . seek . . . knock"—Jesus enjoined believers to pray. He also taught that God delights to give good gifts to his children in response to their prayers (Matt.

7:7–11). God performs the seemingly impossible in response to prayer offered in unwavering faith (Matt. 21:22). The model prayer Jesus taught his disciples (Matt. 6:9–13) petitions God to bring to fruition his kingdom purposes and providentially to supply the physical, moral, and spiritual needs of his children.

Primitive Christianity/Acts

Paul proclaimed to pagan Athenians (Acts 17:28) what their own poets had discovered to be true from general revelation, namely, that all living things owe their existence to God's sustaining power: "in him we live [zōmen] and move [kinoumetha] and have our being [esmen]." God's general providence is seen in the wise ordering of the universe, by which he causes the seasons, rainfall, growth of crops, and food to nourish the body (Acts 14:17). Likewise, God guides the course of history, having established political boundaries and assigned the epochs in which the individual nations flourish (Acts. 17:26).

God's special providence, directed to the outworking of his redemptive purpose, is evident in the phenomena of Pentecost (Acts 2:1–41). When the disciples were gathered in the upper room, God sent a powerful visitation of the Spirit in the form of a violent wind and tongues of fire (vv. 1–4). When the disciples mingled among the multitudes assembled for the feast, the people were amazed to hear them speaking in their own languages (vv. 5–12). The upshot of it all was that in response to Peter's preaching, three thousand persons were converted and the church came into being (v. 41). The special providence that leads to Christ is seen in Philip's encounter with the Ethiopian eunuch (Acts 8:26–39). It seemed strange that an angel of the Lord directed Philip to a hot desert road. Yet enroute Philip encountered an Ethopian official who was puzzled about the meaning of the fifty-third chapter of Isaiah. Philip interpreted this prophetic text and led the Ethopian to Christ. Clearly Philip was God's man in God's place at God's time.

In relation to evil, Paul attests God's permissive providence in Acts 14:16: "In the past, he let [eiasen] all nations go their own way" (cf. Acts 17:30: "In the past God overlooked such ignorance"). What Paul declared at Lystra was that in former days, before the coming of special revelation in Christ, God in seeming complacency left the pagan world to itself. But now that Christ has come, he calls the unbelieving world into judgment through the One whom he raised from the dead (17:31). Peter attests a kind of redirecting providence in Acts 2:23–24; 3:13–15; 4:27–28. Filled with malice, the Jews, assisted by the Romans, killed the Lord's Christ. But the sovereign God redirected the evil he permitted by making atonement for the sins of the world and openly displayed the triumph by raising Jesus from the dead.

Angelic ministers of providence are prominent in the Book of Acts. In Acts 10 an angel in a vision to Cornelius ordered him to send for Peter (vv. 3–6). On the following day God supernaturally informed Peter not to judge unclean what God had made clean (vv. 9–16). Led to Cornelius by messengers, Peter preached Christ and saw that the Holy Spirit fell on all who heard the gospel (vv. 44–48). Through this course of events God opened the church to Gentile believers. Angels abetted the advance of the gospel when through miraculous occurrences they delivered Christian preachers from jail (Acts 5:18–24; 12:5–11). Prayer not only led to the miraculous release of Paul and Silas from prison but also resulted in the conversion of the Philippian jailor and his household (Acts 16:25–34).

Pauline Literature

In Colossians 1:16–17 Paul maintains that Christ is the cosmic agent of creation and preservation. The origination of the universe and its maintenance in existence are related but distinct works. The apostle's words, "in him all things hold together [*synistēmi*]," affirms that the power of Christ renders the universe a cosmos rather than a chaos. Romans 11:36 juxtaposes God's preservation and his providence: "For from him [*ex autou*] and through him [*di autou*] and to him [*eis auton*] are all things." Or as the NEB expresses it: God is "Source, Guide and Goal of all that is." Murray correctly comments that God "is the agent through whom all things subsist and are directed to their proper end."[55] Ephesians 4:6 makes the same point.

Paul affirms God's special providence in relation to believers in Galatians 1:15–16. God set Paul apart from his birth, revealed his Son to him in the Damascus experience, and made Paul the greatest missionary in the church. From a broader perspective, God causes all of life's circumstances to fall out for the ultimate good of the saint who loves him (Rom. 8:28). Things do not cooperate fortuitously, for the subject of *panta synergei eis agathon* is "he" (i.e., God), which some manuscripts rendered explicit by inserting the nominative phrase *ho theos*.[56] In Philippians 4:19 Paul encourages believers by saying, "God will meet [*plērōsai*, to "fill up"] all your needs according to his glorious riches in Christ Jesus."

In relation to evil, God's limiting providence is affirmed in 1 Corinthians 10:13. God mitigates the intensity of trials and provides a way of escape so that believers will be able to stand and not fall. Second Thessalonians 2:6–7 teaches that the anarchy to be unleashed by the man of lawlessness presently is restrained by what he describes as *to katechon* (v. 6) and *ho katechōn* (v. 7). Who or what is "the restrainer" that holds the mystery of lawlessness in check? The interpretation that best explains the neuter and masculine genders posits "the restrainer" as God-instituted government (neut.), which in Paul's day was personified by the Roman emperor (masc.). "Paul viewed established government as imposing a salutary restraint on evil (Rom. 13:3–4), and in his mission field established government was effectively the Roman Empire personally embodied in the emperor."[57]

Permissive providence is clearly seen in Romans 1:24, 26, 28. There Paul affirms of those who rejected the rudimentary knowledge of God afforded by general revelation that "God gave them over" (*paradidōmi,* to "deliver over") to the lusts of their sinful natures. In the words of C. S. Lewis, the unsaved "enjoy forever the horrible freedom they have demanded, and are therefore self-enslaved."[58] A further example of permissive providence is seen in the Corinthian church's handing over an immoral brother to Satan's influence (1 Cor. 5:5). Similarly God allowed Paul to be imprisoned in Rome for preaching the gospel (Phil. 1:12–14). Because of Paul's chains, the palace guard and other officials heard about Christ, and the Christians were encouraged to preach Christ more courageously.

Paul depicts Satan as "the ruler of the kingdom of the air" (Eph. 2:2), who holds sway over "the dominion of darkness" (Col. 1:13). In the battle between the two kingdoms, believers contend "against the rulers, against the authorities, against the powers of this dark world and against the spiritual forces of evil in the heavenly realms" (Eph. 6:12). In the last days demonic activity will increase, and many people will follow these "deceiving spirits" and deny the truth (1 Tim. 4:1). Yet Paul teaches that God's kingdom will prevail over that of the ursurper. On the cross Christ scored a victory over Satan and his legion (Col. 2:15) in anticipation of his final triumph over every alien power (Phil. 2:10–11; Eph. 1:20–21).

Johannine Writings

Jesus upheld divine preservation when he affirmed, "My Father is always at his work [*ergazomai*] to this very day . . ." (John 5:17). God's seventh-day rest is not one of inactivity, for he actively sustains the world he created and also redeems his people through mighty acts in history. See also Revelation 4:11.

God's providential activity consists in upholding believers in the faith. Jesus acknowledged before the Father: "While I was with them, I protected them [*tēreō*] and kept them safe [*phylassō*] by that name you gave me" (John 17:12). God occasionally permits affliction to strike so that through his supply of the person's need his own excelling glory might be displayed (John 9:1–34).

The course of end-time events outlined in the Apocalypse confirms God's providential control of history. "The Lion of the tribe of Judah" who opens the seven seals to the scroll will set in motion the awesome complex of eschatological events (Rev. 5:1–8:1). This symbolism of the Lion connotes that the Christ who triumphed on the cross (Rev. 5:5) is "lord of history and master of the world's destiny."[59] Seven angels will sound seven trumpets that announce the unleashing of a series of natural disasters and demonic assaults on the human race (Rev. 8:2–11:19). After that seven angels will pour out on the sinful world system seven bowls containing yet more intense plagues from the angry God (Rev. 15:1–16:21). The fall of Babylon, "the great prosti-

tute," anticipates the collapse of the God-rejecting, self-exalting nations of the world (Rev. 17:1–19:5). Finally Satan—that liar and murderer who caused the Fall (John 8:44; 1 John 3:8) and who subsequently "leads the whole world astray" (Rev. 12:9)—will be seized by an angel, bound, and cast into the abyss for a thousand years (Rev. 20:1–3). After a final brief rebellion in which he deceives the nations (vv. 8–9), Satan will be thrown into the lake of fire to be tormented forever (v. 10). Thus God's victory and his purpose for humanity will be complete.

Other New Testament Writings

Hebrews 1:3 affirms God's preservation of the universe through the agency of his Son by the phrase, "sustaining [*pherōn*] all things by his powerful word [*rhēma*]." Through his creative word Christ called the universe into existence, and through his sustaining word he maintains it in its course. Christ "upholds the universe not like Atlas supporting a dead weight on his shoulders, but as One who carries all things forward on their appointed course."[60]

God's permissive providence is seen in the disciplinary sufferings he allows his children to experience, according to Hebrews 12:5–11. This text affirms that as God used suffering to make the author of our salvation "perfect" (Heb. 2:10), so he uses hardships and persecution to lead his blood-bought children to the goal of personal holiness (Heb. 12:10–11). In a similar vein, James teaches that Christians should rejoice in the trials (*peirasmoi*) of life, for such God-permitted testings produce perseverance that leads to spiritual maturity (James 1:2–4).

Scripture affirms that angels are intelligent (1 Peter 1:12) and powerful (2 Peter 2:11) "ministering spirits [*leiturgika pneumata*] sent to serve those who will inherit salvation" (Heb. 1:14).

According to this general statement, angelic agents of providence minister to the spiritual and physical needs of believers in Christ. The General Epistles attest the fall of certain angels who, overcome with pride and not content with their God-given "positions of authority" (*archē*), rebelled against God (2 Peter 2:4; Jude 6). The Lord has consigned these malignant spirits to pits of darkness to await the day of judgment. Although *de jure* a defeated foe, Satan and his forces *de facto* oppress the saints by stalking and seeking to overwhelm them as an animal hunts down its prey (1 Peter 5:8). When overcome by trials or misfortunes or when sick, believers are to petition the God who is able to effect objective changes in their circumstances (James 5:13–18).

SYSTEMATIC FORMULATION

God's acts of creation called something into existence out of nothing and formed things into the basic "kinds." God's acts of providence enable creation to continue (in spite of sin and its consequences) and fulfill both God's uniform and special, redemptive purposes. As Charles Hatfield succinctly explained, "God not only made the world, but He manages the world and guides it productively toward worthy goals."[61] By providence we refer to God's continuous use of his great power to achieve his wise, just, and loving values in nature and history. Everything that exists in nature and takes place in history fulfills some aspect of God's wise purposes envisioned in holy love. Temporary appearances notwithstanding, evil does not have the last word in either the objective or humanly subjective worlds. Everything is ultimately relatable to God's presence and purposes in providential activity.

We noted previously five of God's revealed purposes for history, the first two being realized in God's universal rule, the last three in his redemptive rule: (1) to create self-determining beings in his image to function in the world according to uniform physical and moral laws; (2) to permit the Fall, unfaithfulness to him and his laws with the physical, moral, and spiritual consequences; (3) to send his Son to provide atonement as a just basis for universal and redemptive grace; (4) to send the Holy Spirit to call out from the kingdom of evil a people to bless the whole world not only individually, but also in their families, nations, and churches; and (5) to unite the whole of heaven and earth under Christ's kingdom (I:314–17).

To achieve these ends for his glory, we saw that God planned to use unconditional strategies apart from human agents and conditional strategies with human agents (1:317–19). In this chapter we investigate God's deployment of these strategies. To achieve the ends of the unconditional decretive will God, according to his miraculous strategy, acts either apart from any second causes or uses human agency or nature's laws in extraordinary (miraculous) ways. Thus God accompishes his unconditional ends supernaturally. Ordinarily, however, God achieves his preceptive and permissive wills through human means according to a conditional (providential) strategy. God makes known his moral requirements in the heart or in the written law (the requirements of the Ten Commandments). People may either believe and obey them or disbelieve and disobey them. When people believe and obey his revealed desires, God's preceptive will is done and he is pleased. When people disbelieve and disobey them, God's preceptive will is not done and he is displeased. In either case God achieves his preceptive ends conditionally through people. In this chapter's biblical section we found numerous illustrations of God's conditional will at work in history. Scripture repeatedly attests the fact that God not only permits evil, while sovereignly restraining or limiting it, but also redirects it, overcoming evil for goods not otherwise obtainable. We now attempt to understand more specifically God's providential working in relation to nature, time, persons, free will, and moral evil.

God Rules Universally in Space

The cosmos is not a supreme, self-existent expanse. God is the only eternal, self-existent being. He created and sustains the vast extent of the universe. And God providentially rules in space through natural laws. The laws of nature depend on the Creator's freely chosen purposes and freely exercised power to carry them out in the ways planned. What, then, is God's continuous relation to space? How is the ordinary activity of the living God related to the regular functions of the cosmos?

Creation's space and laws are not absolute or ultimate, but they depend on God. Scientifically described laws do not determine final purposes. They are means or instruments created and sustained to accomplish God's usual purposes. Nature's laws may limit human freedom, but they do not limit God's freedom. God freely made these laws what they are to accomplish his universal objectives through ordered processes and relationships. Because he is omnipresent, God is not removed from nature's laws as deists think. Because he is transcendent and changeless, God's being is not continuous with the temporal, changing being of nature as pantheists and panentheists think. The transcendent Creator remains the Lord of space and everything extended in space.

The naturalistic worldview dominant in much Western education has influenced many to imagine that the so-called laws of nature are *ultimate explanations* of natural phenomena. To respect the observations of science it is not necessary to add to one's worldview naturalistic presuppositions as did Bultmann. Naturalists simply *assume* the regularity of natural laws. Nontheists have no adequate basis, however, for their faith that the law of gravity will hold tomorrow. The observations of regularity that have been made as science has developed do not guarantee anything about the future. A turkey with naturalistic assumptions could readily assume that because every morning the farmer comes with water and feed he will do so tomorrow. Tomorrow the farmer may have a different purpose, however, such as the celebration of a holiday like Thanksgiving, and come with an axe! Mere descriptions of past regularities, important as they are, provide no guarantee of future regularities.

Theists, in contrast, have a reason for believing that nature's regularities will be the same tomorrow. The uniformity of nature depends on the sustaining power of the God who faithfully keeps his Word. God promised Noah that as long as the earth remains, he will not again destroy "all living creatures" by a flood (Gen. 8:21). "As long as the earth endures, seedtime and harvest, cold and heat, summer and winter, day and night will never cease" (8:22). Indeed we are dependent on God, "for in him we live and move and have our being" (Acts 17:28).

As the final cause of everything, God has chosen to accomplish some of his goals through both (1) material causes informed by the Logos (John 1:1–3) and (2) personal agents as efficient causes (on personal and impersonal causes, see 1:310). Natural regularities being sustained by God are not unnecessary, insignificant, nor alien to God. Rather, they are given eternal significance in God's plan. For example, God has designed physical organisms like human bodies so that, given normal circumstances, they heal themselves. Hence natural healings are ultimately divine healings through the secondary causes.

The "laws" of nature are not autonomous powers, but statistical probabilities based on our observations of the way God ordinarily chooses to accomplish his purposes through real, but dependent material entities. Some of God's purposes are achieved on earth through impersonal causes within the range of possibilities provided by the regular patterns of nature that God created and sustains. Within that range of possibilities, God also achieves his purposes through personal causes, the often unpredictable individual choices that actually do take place.

We find ourselves a long way from Eden in a world affected by humanity's sin. Since the Fall God's ways of accomplishing his purposes through nature differ. Natural evils have resulted from moral evil (Rom. 8:20). Some sinners, through what insurance people call "acts of God," justly receive some of the deserved consequences of their rebellion against God here and now, while others will receive most of the consequences after this life. For God's moral and spiritual children by faith, natural evils may also serve purposes of chastening, education, and discipline.

Unquestionably, natural evils such as hurricanes, earthquakes, and floods seem cruel, especially when they take lives. No one who dies, however, dies unjustly, for all have sinned and deserve to die physically at some time. By touching a high voltage wire an electrician can be electrocuted, and so equally can a young athlete. At a small lake at a church camp two boys broke through thin ice and drowned. So did their leader who tried to save them! The population of Pompeii was destroyed by burning volcanic ash and lava and superheated air. Natural laws are no respecters of persons. When we hear of events like these, we think that there must be a better way to run the universe. Imagine, however, how impossible life would be if nature did not function according to regular laws! Imagine, if you can, what it would be like trying to live in a world where people could be electrocuted without notice by wood or plastic, suffocated by warm air, or burned by cold water! Without the order of nature, life would not only be worse, it would be impossible! Wisely God has chosen to sustain an ordered world. With the decision to sustain an ordered world came the consequences for all who break either natural or moral laws without respect of persons.

In *Why Bad Things Happen to Good People* Rabbi Harold S. Kushner finds it impossible to attribute nature's laws to divine providence. Unfortunately he fails to take into account God's permissive will and attributes suffering to other sources like the laws of nature, "which God did not cause and cannot stop."[62] This may seem to make his child's illness easier to accept, but Kushner's God is too small. The hypothesis of a limited God does not fit the abundant data of Scripture that attributes natural laws and conditions to divine creation and providence. Our comfort may be short-lived if our God is too small to be the final cause of all things and to work through nature's regularities for wise, just, and good ends. Although God is the final cause of everything, he is not the efficient or blameworthy cause of moral evil (I:310).

Living by God's providence in a universe ordered, rather than chaotic, our building codes, driving patterns, and health guidelines need to be in harmony with nature. Confucianism and many "back to nature" movements have a part of the truth. Harmony with natural law contributes to a healthy life.

To be in harmony with nature, however, is not necessarily to be in moral and spiritual harmony with the transcendent Lord of all. God is distinct from nature and his redemptive purposes are not discovered in nature (chap. 2, vol. 1). Harmony with nature's laws may reflect harmony with God's physical purposes, though not necessarily from motives of honoring the Lord of all. Neither does harmony with God's physical purposes alone necessarily indicate harmony with God's moral rule nor with his gracious redemptive purposes for the unjust. The Christian cannot ultimately divorce any level of creation from the purposes of God. Everything in the world of space is intended to promote communion with the Lord who is present in all of nature and support his values.

God Rules Universally Through Time

Every event in time as well as everything in space speaks of the transcendent Lord of providence. Before creation apparently there was no time, other than its potential in the changeless God's plans for creation. But with creation came the changing world with its succession of events. The earth had a beginning, is dependent, and is passing away. In a biblical view, however, temporal history is neither unreal nor cyclical. On the fourth "day" of creation God appointed the sun and moon for measuring the successions of events on earth by days and nights, weeks, months, seasons, and years. Providentially God sustains the earth in its orbit around the sun for the marking out of time sequences. The Bible does not explicitly emphasize scientific time relative to the speed of light, but majors on historical time and its significance for personal decision making.

God is not limited by time, but knows and understands and sustains the temporal sequence as we experience it. The Creator provided for temporal reality by creating accountable people who, like him, have ability to transcend the present moment. We are not limited to the present moment but can remember the past and anticipate the future. So we can be conscious of meaningful successions of events in our lives. Hence humans have unique biographies, and societies have unique histories. In the temporal arena humans have unrepeatable opportunities to know love and obey the creator and the redeemer. Within the historical matrix every thought, word, and deed is known by the Lord of all. However insignificant one's life may seem, each day has significance in the light of eternity. For each opportunity we will give account to our all-knowing Judge.

God knows and sustains all that transpires in time, both history's long ages, and history's major turning points. The scriptural "age" (aiōn) refers to the Lord's managing of the great epochs of history. The aeons are not authorities in their own right (as in Gnosticism) nor emanations or delegates of God (as in pantheism). Within God's long-range purposes for the ages of human history, however, are some definite temporal turning points especially appropriate for a given undertaking. The prime turning point (kairos) for all time came at Christ's first advent.

After the creation of the first Adam, history's greatest turning point occurred at the second Adam's first advent. The end of the present age will occur at Christ's return in power and glory. The infinite qualitative disjunction between God and humans assumed by Kierkegaard, Barth, Brunner, Bultmann, and many biblical theologians tends to undermine universal providence by limiting divine acts to vertical, internal experiences. Cullmann's corrective in Christ and Time correctly puts the incarnate Christ at the center of God's continuous work horizontally in history. But Cullmann's mythological treatment of the beginning and end of history raises the possibility that all biblical events, including Christ's incarnation, may be reduced to myth.[63] The Lord of time created the first Adam and providentially guides historical opportunities from his day to this, and from this day to the end.

The great biblical themes of self-determination, responsibility, and decision, of unbelief or belief, and final judgment can best be appreciated in this concept of time as humans experience it. Persons in historical time inescapably face responsibility for moral conduct *now*. In the present moment we live life and make decisions and commitments. We cannot alter our past. No amount of regret will change the opportunities that parents or children, church officers or church members have lost. Historians cannot experiment with their material. But the most distinctive characteristic of the future is the variety of its possibilities. To humans the future seems pregnant with possibilities of all sorts. As gamblers, with their limited purviews testify, until a thing has happened, almost anything can happen and does!

To human consciousness everything in the future appears to be open and alterable. Only those events that God achieves unconditionally are not. In the ordinary conditional strategy, although God is the final cause of everything, God does not unconditionally determine the future nor become the efficient cause of ordinary human conduct. Neither preoccupation with divine foreknowledge nor the probabilities of scientific time and relativity can eliminate the existential givenness of the present moment and our consciousness of the radical distinction between the past and the future.[64] As we make choices in the openness of our futures, we do so under the knowledge of the all-seeing God and under his wise, holy, and loving influences. But in these decisions we are the responsible agents. How the great Sustainer, Teacher, and Guide is able to bring together unique convergences of real human choices in history to realize his purposes needs further consideration.

God's Universal Rule and Human Wills

Granting that God uses nature's regular operations and the unique convergences of factors at the great moments of history to accomplish his ends, it may seem more problematic for him to work ordinarily with human persons who have "free wills." In theism, in contrast to pantheism, however, God is not the only real agent. God initially gave his image-bearers the ability to examine alternatives, to choose among ends, and to do what they desired, whether moral or immoral. No human beings lack some knowledge of God's desire for communion with them (Acts 17:27) and of God's moral requirements (Rom. 2:14–15; see chap. 2, vol. 1). Some have Moses' law in addition and some have the example of Christ's fellowship with the Father and his fulfillment of God's moral demands.

It seems paradoxical or contradictory to many that, given God's moral suasion, people determine their own choices and actions and at the same time do God's will. The frequent tendency of people who lack a method of theological decision-making is to pronounce biblical emphases on divine sovereignty and human responsibility an irreconcilable antinomy, a paradox, or a mystery. In the final analysis no finite, fallen mind fully comprehends either the divine or human wills separately, let alone in relationship. But the limited information God has disclosed does make sense. An integrative approach to understanding providence seeks to display the coherence and viability of revealed truth about the activity of both the divine and the human persons in history.

In the light of the biblical evidence we cannot deny the reality of either the divine or the human factors. It does not follow that if God directs, then we have no part in a matter, or if we decide, God has nothing to do with it. It was not the case that if the Father willed the cross Jesus did not, or vice versa. Not just one will, but many wills may contribute influentially to significant personal, family, church, and national events. In any event in a personal biography or a church's history many human wills may have suggested possibilities, methods, ethical principles, and consequences of certain decisions. As other persons may influence our decisions and actions, so God's influence can be noted in a biography or any complex historical event. We will never understand divine providence in human decision-making if unrealistically we assume a single cause for each event. And it is not enough to recognize many finite factors as antecedents if God is ignored or excluded.

Seeking to be fair to all strands of evidence, we incorporate the data concerning both the divine and the human factors in history. But the cases for both are not equally strong and they are not equally ultimate. Hence in the ordinary usage of the word, people should not call them "antinomies."[65] Appeals to antinomies since Kant admit that our reasoning has come to an irrecoverable stalemate with equally good (or bad) arguments on both sides. If such an eventuality appears, however, we ought not attribute our logical difficulties taken from Scripture by our interpretive processes to God's teaching as actually given in Scripture.

Neither is it prudent to attribute to the Scriptures our psychological "tensions" about God's personal relationship to persons. No unhealthy tensions divided God's mind as the Holy Spirit inscripturated the Word! In Holy Writ human agency is not presented as an embarrassment to its creator's or sustainer's providential purposes. And it does not help to add that here we face an irresolvable "mystery." In the tragic poets *mystērion* meant "that which must not or cannot be said" and in Plato "the very negation of speech."[66] But in the New Testament it "betrays no relation to the mystery cults."[67] "Mystery in the New Testament does not deal with the unknowable, but with what is imparted by revelation."[68] The content of biblical mysteries when finally revealed, may not be understood fully, but it can be understood in part. Unlike the Buddhist koans, biblical mysteries when revealed do make sense.

With exceptional insight at this point G. C. Berkouwer explained,

> Hesitation where Paul was bold has caused the Church often to make only a problem of God's rule and man's responsibility. She thus undermines either the Providence of God or human responsibility. *They do not exist in the Scriptures as something problematic.* They both reveal the greatness of Divine activity, in that it does not exclude human activity and responsibility but embraces them and in them manifests God on the way to the accomplishment of His purposes.[69]

God created and providentially preserves humans with wills. Through their decisions he achieves his chosen *ends* in history with pleasure when they follow his precepts and with displeasure when they disobey. God made and sustains self-determining persons, not to ignore them or obliterate them, but that they might share his fellowship, values, and work. Persons with minds, emotions, and wills are a real, highly valued part of God's grand design for lived history.

What does it mean for humans to have "free will"? Two major historic definitions have been given. Free will has been defined as (1) the power of contrary or alternative choice and (2) the power of self-determination and action according to one's nature and apart from coercion. Whether one or the other of both of these major meanings is appropriate depends on the conditions of the era under consideration and the substantial differences made by the Fall, regeneration, and glorification. Hence we must consider the meaning of freedom in four distinct situations.

Before the Fall Adam and Eve experienced freedom not only as the power of responsible self-determination but also as the power of contrary choice. Adam and Eve and the angels could have chosen and determined either to love and obey God or not. But they refused God's ethical persuasion, disobeyed God's command, and so separated themselves from God's fellowship.

Since the Fall the unregenerate freely determine themselves in accord with their depraved natures. Fallen human freedom is the power of responsible self-determination, but it fails to receive redemptive truth, choosing rather motives and acts in accord with a fallen nature. By nature apart from the assistance of divine grace depraved people do not in heart and mind fully accept God's counsel, obey God's laws, believe the gospel, trust Christ, and dominantly seek to please the Lord. When the unregenerate choose objectively good acts, they do so from motives other than the honoring of God and the building of his kingdom. Hence their best acts in actuality come short of the ideal.

At present the regenerate, in addition to the old fleshly nature, have a new spiritual nature. The one self must decide between these two conflicting inclinations or motivations to evil and good. The basic power of self-determination must decide whether to yield to temptation and commit sin or not to yield to temptation and not to commit

sin. Hence the regenerate now have the power of contrary choice. For their acts to be worthy in God's sight they must not only have objective morality but also worthy motives. So they need to decide and act in the energy of the Holy Spirit, not the flesh.

In the eternal state the believer's freedom will be self-determination in accord with a fully sanctified nature like Christ's. Then Christians will consistently determine every thought, word, and action wisely, justly, and lovingly. In the new heavens and the new earth, thank the Lord, there will no longer be the freedom of contrary choice, or freedom to obey and to disobey God. In a fully sanctified freedom our self-determination will decide and act consistently in accord with a Christlike nature from motives that please God. That is a freedom like that of God, who cannot deny himself. God does not have the power of contrary moral choice or of sin. Making choices consistent with nature confirmed in righteousness will be our highest freedom!

Unfortunately many discussions of free will fail to consider these temporal differences as Augustine did.[70] This neglect makes untenable generalizations like the claim that freedom always and essentially involves contrary choice. We prefer the simplest possible hypothesis to account for the givens, but when the givens differ at different times we must avoid oversimplification. Oversimplified hypotheses do not fit as many facts as a comprehensive one that accounts for the real volitional differences before and after the Fall, before and after regeneration, and before and after glorification.

God Uses Ethical Persuasion

God used the lure of love and ethical persuasion with Adam and Eve before the Fall, warning them of the consequences of disobedience to a simple command. As necessary and valuable as ethical persuasion was, it did not prove effective for our original parents even in their unfallen state and environment. After the Fall, loving moral suasion has become even less effective because the dominant desires of the unregenerate prevent them from knowing, loving, and serving God with pure motives and with all their capacities. In the regenerate the old nature remains, rendering less than effective the mere knowing of what we ought to be and do. Even for its limited values, however, with either the regenerate or unregenerate God may work indirectly through human teachers and leaders to introduce or stimulate thoughts, feelings, and volitions. The Holy Spirit's presentation of rules, reasons, and consequences of decisions for our consideration finds biblical support.

How do the best parents and teachers work with maturing children and students? They do not make decisions for others who are past childhood, but they treat them as adults. Parents and teachers provide the opportunity for young people to decide, indicating the basic rules or methods of making good decisions in view of sound reasons. They also use ethical persuasion, pointing out the consequences of alternative courses of actions. No analogies are perfect, but another may help.

Think of the God of providence as greater than those who excel in the management of persons in large businesses. People are the manager's most important asset. Managers get things done through people. Good managers treat people with dignity and respect as adults, as partners.[71] The worth that God places on people is higher than the value an excellent manager places on his colaborers.

Managers get things done through people who share similar values. People with shared values are one of God's most important assets in the world.

God, like the leader of a business, is primarily an expert in the promotion and protection of values.[72] God who is the source and support of all values affirmed the value of people in creating them uniquely in his image and sustaining a life support system on planet earth for them. Above all else God values the love of people. God shares his wise, holy, and loving purposes and methods with people. Not mechanistically, but as a wise manager God works with people. Productivity in corporations dedicated to excellence comes through people. A manager is value-driven and so leads, organizes, evaluates, and exercises quality control. Similarly the divine manager of human history does all of these par excellence. In managing people in the world God promotes and protects values as he leads, organizes, evaluates, and exercises quality control in history. His actions, like ours, express his priorities.[73]

The quality control of God's enterprise in history called for people who shared his values. At the heart of any successful enterprise are the shared values of the people in it. Unfortunately, left to mere ethical persuasion, no depraved sinners came to live authentically by God's values! The good that the unregenerate do would be far worse if it were not for God's inner and outer persuasion to do good. But the liberal emphasis on ethical persuasion as God's only means of working with people is insufficiently realistic concerning the debilitating effects of habitual pride, selfishness, greed, lust, and hatred.

God Governs Through Families

God works not only with individuals but also with social groups. Providentially God promotes good and restrains evil through primary social institutions such as families and nations. The Lord of all established *the family* to provide for stable, structured personal relationships. In the providence of God, a male and female leave their fathers and mothers and become one flesh (Gen. 2:24). The mutual commitment of spouses is designed for lasting and healthful relations between persons in spirit and body. Jesus reinforced the creation ordinance by adding, "Therefore what God has joined together, let man not separate" (Matt. 19:4–6). Marriage is not mandatory. Jesus himself remained unmarried, and Paul recognized the validity of celibacy (1 Cor. 7:1). Generally, however, "since there is so much immorality, each man should have his own wife, and each woman her own husband" (v. 2). The wife's and the husband's bodies belong not only to themselves, but also to each other (v. 4). The author of Hebrews taught that "marriage should be honored by all, and the marriage bed kept pure, for God will judge the adulterer and all the sexually immoral" (13:4). The marriage ceremony expresses publicly and legally the spouses' mutual respect, trust, and lifelong commitment.

In God's providence faithful *marital relationships* promote several great values. Faithful, loving husbands and wives enjoy lifelong loving companionship and mutual helpfulness in their work as stewards of the earth. Marital fidelity promotes personal security, family stability, and community solidarity. The moral problem of adultery involves not only consequences of the physical act itself but the breaking of freely assumed vows and the flouting of self-determined commitments (even if in some cultures these only amount to accepting one's parents' prearranged marriage). The heinousness of breaking faith with one's spouse is analogous to the evil of God's people breaking faith with their Lord (Mal. 2:11–14). Hence the prophet Malachi exhorts, "So guard yourself in your spirit, and do not break faith with the wife of your youth. 'I hate divorce,' says the LORD God of Israel" (vv. 15–16). Nevertheless God permitted divorce where it was justified (Matt. 19:8–9), but he did so with displeasure. Breaking faith with your spouse leaves scars, not only on spouses and children, but also on other family members.

No matter how attractively adultery may be portrayed in literature, movies, and television, it compromises the integrity of the persons involved, breaks moral commitments, degrades the significance of sexual relationships, and hurts all involved, especially the children. Christian theists, in accord with God's providential order, must decisively choose between mere recreational views of sex that reduce persons to objects (as in lust-inducing pornography) and an understanding of sex as a beautiful gift of God to be enjoyed in the marital commitment for nurturing spouses in an enduring, intimate relationship. As God's gift, sexual intimacy expresses the spouses' *agapē* love for each other and so symbolizes God's faithful *agapē* for his people. Although marriage is not a sacrament that conveys saving grace, it is a beautiful sign of common grace, pointing to the greatness of God's steadfast love. For Christians the self-giving love of husbands for wives also portrays Christ's love for the church in giving himself up for her (Eph. 5:25).

Faithful marital relationships generally tend to produce children, and the *parent-child relationship* is crucial in God's management of the world for the upbringing of the coming generation. God gives parents not only the privileges and joys of parenthood but also its responsibilities. Some of these responsibilities are the following:

1. Parents respect their children's inalienable rights and value children highly, for they also bear the image of the Creator. The "qualities of the child as image-bearer of God—intrinsic significance, possession of gifts and capa-

bilities, and heavenly foundation for identity—speak eloquently to parents. They declare that the child has the right to be respected; they assert the child's unique individuality and worth; and they trace our children's origin to God."[74] For such reasons believers in creation and providence consecrate their children to the Lord of all (Luke 2:23).

2. In divine providence parents ought to exhibit God's love for them in parental *love* (Eph. 5:1). With unconditional love parents will provide for their imperfect children's need for acceptance and for necessities, such as food and clothing. Even non-Chistian parents give their children good gifts (Luke 11:11–13). "After all, children should not have to save up for their parents, but parents for their children" (2 Cor. 12:14). "If anyone does not provide for his relatives, and especially for his immediate family, he has denied the faith and is worse than an unbeliever" (1 Tim. 5:8).

3. Loving parents also are responsible to *teach* their children what they need to know spiritually. Parents may be helped in this responsibility by church teachers, youth leaders, and ministers, but parents who delegate the entire task to others will be dissappointed. It is their joy to teach their own children about the truths of divine revelation. Children coming to an age of accountability for their actions need to learn the lessons of universal revelation first. They need to realize that they depend on God and are accountable to God. They need to know that there is a real, objective difference between right and wrong (in the mind of God) and that they have the potential for doing both great good and great evil. Parents need to teach their children honestly to admit it when they have distorted the truth, coveted the gifts and possessions of others and dishonored their Sustainer. One of the best ways to do this is for parents to exhibit confession of the wrongs they have done to their children and seek their forgiveness as well as God's. After children can appreciate their own moral and spiritual sinfulness before God they can helpfully grasp the redemptive significance of God's mighty acts like the deliverance of his people from Egypt (Exod. 12:26–27; Deut. 4:9) and Christ's bearing of their penalty for them. God's great commandments (Deut. 5:6–21) are to be taught morning, noon, and night (Deut. 6:4–6; 11:18–19).

4. Loving parents know that they will need to *discipline* their children to avoid hurting themselves and others. Fathers ought not exasperate or embitter their children, but lovingly and justly bring them up "in the training and instruction of the Lord" (Eph. 6:4; Col. 3:21). Parents ought to discipline the children they love for their good, following God's example (Heb. 12:5–11). In our times it is not easy to know how to do this, but several methods of helping your child develop more acceptable behavior patterns with suggestions for applying them have been developed.[75] In spite of the home-shattering moral, economic, and educational pressures of recent years, the faithful, loving husband-wife and parent-child relationships serve as God's established means for providentially accomplishing in the home the ends of peace with justice. Then as children mature and leave home, they should carry these values with them.

As members of families we may be implicated in the moral choices of the solidarity of the family. Collectively we often enjoy the blessings of a family that made wise and good choices. Unfortunately we may also experience the effects of unwise and morally unjust choices of our families. In addition to individual guilt, collective guilt and its temporal consequences for the family members may be experienced for up to three or four generations (Exod. 20:5; 34:7).

God Governs Through Nations

As the descendants of fallen families encountered each other, there arose the need for an additional institution to arbitrate disputes between families, to restrain and punish evil, and to reward the good. The descendants of Noah were fruitful and multiplied, and their family's descendants developed into nations (Gen. 10:1–32). To scatter the nations over the earth geographically God used linguistic differentiations at the tower of Babel (Gen. 11:5–9).

A nation is a people, race, or tribe usually having the same descent and history, occupying the same country, united under the same government, and usually speaking the same language. "Nation" may also be used in Scripture to refer to heathen nations or Gentiles in contrast to the Jewish nation with the gracious advantage of the oracles of God. Members of the Jewish nation in addition to all the commonalities for other nations uniquely received the blessings of a divine covenant with Abraham (Gen. 12:2–3; 15:9–21; 17:1–16). Although nations that cursed Israel would be cursed, through Israel "all people on earth will be blessed" (Gen. 12:3). God, in his providence among all the nations, ultimately desired that people seek him, reach out for him, and find him (Acts 17:27). Even though they would not, Israel's descendant, Christ, would finally bring blessing to the whole world.

God authorized national governments to protect a nation's citizens, promote justice, and restrain evil by wise legislation and equitable judicial decisions (Rom. 13:1–5). In God's general purposes for humanity he rules all the nations, permitting the evils that ensue, and using one nation to judge another for its evil. For example, God promised the land of Canaan to Abraham many years before Joshua led the Israelites into that land. "In the fourth generation your descendants will come back here, for the sin of the Amorites has not yet reached its full measure" (Gen. 15:16). Not until the corruption of that Canaanite nation was so pervasive that its people deserved death, did God allow their destruction by Israelite armies under Joshua. In New Testament times Paul observed that "from one man he made every nation of men, that they should inhabit the whole earth; and he determined the times set for them and the exact places where they should live" (Acts 17:26).

In the outworking of his providential justice God is no respecter of nations. God warned Israel that if they did the same evils as the Canaanites, they would receive the same penalties. "If you ever forget the LORD your God and follow other gods and worship and bow down to them, I testify against you today that you will surely be destroyed. Like the nations the LORD destroyed before you, so you will be destroyed for not obeying the LORD your God" (Deut. 8:19–20). Eventually both Israel and Judah suffered the agonies of captivity as the divided groups at different times were providentially dispersed.

In the order of justice God does not show favoritism for persons' positions in nations—whether dictators, prime ministers, presidents, legislators, judges, law-enforcement people, or mere citizens. All are accountable before divinely revealed moral norms for the good of themselves and those they influence. As a result of their involvement in any nation, however initially blessed, citizens, like those in Canaan and Israel, may incur a measure of collective guilt and so collectively suffer deserved punishment. If there were ten righteous people in the midst of the wicked of Sodom God would have preserved the city (Gen. 18:20–32).

Thankfully with Abraham we have good reason to believe that the judge of all the earth does right (v. 28).

God Permits but Redirects Moral Evil

God abhors responsible rebellion against his physical, moral, and spiritual laws by individuals, parents, and civil leaders. Nevertheless the longsuffering Lord of history permits moral evil. Admittedly a concept of God's permissive will construed to imply that human freedom is on a par with divine sovereignty, or as an ultimate threat to God's sovereign purposes, fails to account for the Scriptures on the ultimacy of the divine nature and rule. If the concept of God's permissive will is sovereignly granted by God and is "within his ruling for human freedom and responsibility," as Berkouwer has said, "then the line of Biblical thinking has not been wholly abandoned. For this freedom, this creaturely freedom, receives a place *in* God's rule of the world."[76] As enterprising as God's enemies may be, they are unable to undermine his divine supremacy. They owe their very ability to act against God to God and their uses of that ability to God's permissive will.

How, then, does God relate to the moral evil permitted to self-determining parents and children, rulers, and citizens? As the scriptural section shows, God sometimes restrains or limits sin, sometimes judges sinners for what they are in history, and sometimes redirects and overrules evil for values otherwise unobtainable. In the final judgment God will correct any injustices not adequately vindicated in history.

Even when God permits moral evil, however, he does not initiate it. God is not the efficient or blameworthy cause of rebellion against himself. He is the final cause, for without him no one would exist to disbelieve and disobey his holy and loving desires for them.

Although Satan owes his existence to the Creator, the determination to rebel against his source is wholly his own. The will of the creature is the final explanation of the rebellion. The creature was not influenced by the Creator to rebel but, if anything, to know, love, and obey. The creature chose to question God's Word, love himself more than God, and go his own way.

An objective difference between good and evil exists (Isa. 5:20; Amos 5:14–15). Evil is not relative, nor is it illusory. It is not eternal but began with the rebellion. It is not traced ultimately to matter, nor to the body or its reproductive organs (1 Tim. 4:1–5). Sin originated with the misuse of the creature's will (Rom. 5:12–18; 2 Cor. 11:3). God is not the author or blameworthy cause of evil. No more ultimate blameworthy cause can be found than the self-determination of angels and humans. God has not only permitted moral evil but has also done some highly significant things about it. Sometimes he judges it in history, sometimes in the future life. The culmination of history will see a major battle with the demonic powers of the world.

Initially the supralapsarian strategy of the execution of God's purpose (vol. 1, chap. 8) seems best to exalt God's sovereignty. However, we have found extensive evidence that God does not relate in the same way to the evil events in the world as to the good. To assign evil to the God's sovereign initiation contradicts the fact that God is so pure as not even to tempt people to evil (James 1:13–14). In contrast an Arminian strategy leaves God no more involved in the redemptive acts of people in history than in the evil acts. In this scheme, after restoring ability to believe and obey to sinners, God appears as a spectator who observes people trying to exercise their evil-oriented wills toward the good. He simply foreknows what people will do, whether they believe or disbelieve, obey or disobey.

An Augustinian or sublapsarian Calvinistic hypothesis provides a more adequate account of the biblical data. It is the outworking of the sublapsarian (or infralapsarian) doctrine of God's purposes that sees the divine initiative active in the production of good and simply foreknowing and permitting the creature's sinful acts. God may actively answer intercessory prayer in accord with his holy and loving purposes in ordinary or extraordinary ways. God may test his people and actively judge moral evil with natural evils, but he does not literally initiate moral evil or sinful rebellion against himself.

The primary purposes of God's universal rule are to preserve and govern human life and activity in a fallen world subject to self-destruction and acts of demonic terrorism, as in the life of Joseph. Because depraved and condemned sinners deserve the benefits of neither the universal nor the redemptive kingdoms, both kingdoms are a result of unmerited favor. The benefits of both realms can ultimately be traced to God's mercy and grace. And the primary end of preservation is to allow for the outworking of the redemptive goals. So in a sense both common and special grace rest ultimately on the salvific purposes in Jesus Christ.

God's Rule Under Attack by the Satanic Kingdom

A kingdom of deception and destruction fights against God's kingdom of light (Col. 1:12–13). The kingdom of darkness (metaphysically, intellectually, morally, and spiritually) is headed by the Devil, who among the created angels initiated and headed up the insurrection of creatures against the Creator's sovereignty. Unable to create, he enviously seeks to destroy. Unable ultimately to rule all things, this jealous creature rebels in every way possible, especially by deceiving humans.

The deceived followers of Satan are not thankful to God, do not glorify God, and exchange his glory for images of birds and beasts and reptiles. Followers of the evil kingdom may degrade their bodies in sexual impurity. They exchange the truth of God for the lies of the great Deceiver (Rom. 1:21–27). Their depraved minds become filled with every kind of wickedness, evil, greed, envy, murder, strife, deceit, and malice. They become gossips, slanderers, God-haters, insolent, arrogant, and boastful. They invent ways of doing evil, disobey their parents, and are senseless, faithless, heartless, and ruthless (vv. 28–31). In ways like these the ruler of darkness instigates acts of terrorism against the kingdom of light.

Given the evils of history, including the holocaust, it seems increasingly difficult for naturalistic theologians to account for humanity's inhumanity to mankind apart from the reality of Satan. Two Sunday school youths allegedly argued about the reality of the Devil. One believed in a personal devil. The other sought to demythologize the biblical teaching. He said to the other, "The Devil isn't another personal being. The Devil is like Santa Claus, he turns out to be your father!" Unfortunately, the distinct reality of Satan cannot be so lightly dismissed. Jesus recognized the reality of Satan and cast out demons. Paul made it clear that "our struggle is not against flesh and blood, but against the rulers, against the authorities, against the powers of this dark world and against the spiritual forces of evil in the heavenly realms" (Eph. 6:12). Hence a realistic view of history must reckon not only with humanity's inhumanities, but also behind the scenes with evil principalities and powers.

As the spiritual conflict of the ages continues, Christian leaders not only in animistic cultures but also in all others do well to discern direct as well as indirect demonic terrorism. People who deny the reality of the demonic labor under the false assumption that all that is supernatural is of God. Unfortunately, as the scriptural writers knew, this is not true. Not all that is supernatural is of God! False Christs and false prophets will appear and perform great signs and miracles to deceive even the elect—if that were possible (Matt. 24:24). God's people "do not believe every spirit, but test the spirits to see whether they are from God" (1 John 4:1). Not everyone may have a special gift of discernment any more than the gift of evangelism. But just as every Christian needs to evangelize, every Christian needs to distinguish the supernatural that is demonic and far from divine.[77] Christians need not live in fearfulness, however, for the power of Christ's name is greater than any other name in heaven or earth.

In the great conflict with Satan, God is still supreme. The Lord Jesus Christ heads God's government of all things in heaven and earth, visible and invisible, whether thrones or powers or rulers or authorities (Col. 1:16). In Him "all things hold together" (v. 17). The Lord of creation and preservation, Jesus Christ also governs history. The Christ who is preeminent in creation and providence is also supreme in the redemptive kingdom. "For he has rescued us from the dominion of darkness and brought us into the kingdom of the Son he loves, in whom we have redemption, the forgiveness of sins" (vv. 13–14).

Christ's Redemptive Rule Through Believers

God is now retrieving from the fallen world a people to share his fellowship, values, and work. To provide the just basis for this the Son of God became incarnate, suffered, died, and rose. The Savior is the Logos by whom all things were created (John 1:1–3) and hold together (Col. 1:17). So the Lord heads all things in heaven and earth, visible and invisible, whether thrones or powers or rulers or authorities (1:16; 2:10). He reconciles all in the church as well as the world, making peace through the blood of his cross (1:20). It is Christ who has "disarmed" the demonic powers and authorities, making "a public spectacle of them . . . by the cross" (2:15). Jesus Christ came supremely to bear the just wrath of the Creator on the destroyer of his magnificent work. Allowing the evil designs of Satan, Jews, and Roman Gentiles against Jesus Christ, the heavenly Father overruled their betrayal, false accusations, mistrials, scourging, and crucifixion to satisfy justice while providing for their reconciliation, redemption, and forgiveness.

In the future God will bring Satan's acts of terrorism to an abrupt end, judge the unrepentant, and establish a reign of justice and love. In eternity the joys of sharing divine knowledge, love, and service will outweigh comparisons with the suffering of the present evil world. At present God works with people not only by providential ethical persuasion but also by miraculously regenerating their hearts. Shared values are central to God's creative purposes. Unlike some human managers, God did not just fire the whole human race for having rejected his values. God anticipated and planned for the first people who rebelled against justice, love, and wisdom. Anticipating the need of sinners from before the foundation of the world, God showed how adroit he could be in responding to the change in them. While remaining just, God devised a constructive response to the change, a liberating plan that is just, loving, and wise. So now at the heart of God's activity in the world are not only creative values but also redemptive covenants and mighty renewing acts. God's regenerative activities do more than satisfy legal justice, they restore the sinners' lost ability to see, desire, and follow spiritual values.

The companies that excel in business are "brilliant on the basics." In those companies "tools didn't substitute for thinking. Intellect didn't overpower wisdom. Analysis didn't impede action."[78] Divine providence is also "brilliant on the basics." In an increasingly complex world, God highly regards all people, but works redemptively with those who by his enabling now share his values. God, as well as others, may influence us, but tools do not substitute for thinking. God restores our lost abilities to know, love, and serve him. But knowledge needs to be used wisely. Unethical modes of coercion are as unworthy of God as they are of cultic programers or anticult deprogramers.

In thinking of the Holy Spirit's work with believers, we must avoid impersonal and mechanical analogies. How does one person influence another? Think of the best pastors you have ever known. If the best pastors can achieve certain worthy, prechosen goals without reducing regenerate people to robots, cannot God do so? If the best pastors may have goals for their churches and work toward them in, with, and through thinking, decisive people, cannot God? If effective orators, apologists, and counselors can be ethically persuasive, so can God. "It is no more subversive of human free agency for God to influence effectively a man's volitions and secure a certain course of action than it is for one ethical person effectively to influence another."[79] As Charles Hodge has pointed out, "It is in vain to profess to hold the common doctrines of Theism, and yet assert that God cannot control rational creatures without turning them into machines."[80]

Christ's Redemptive Rule Attested by Miracles

In removing the tragic effects of sin and defeating demonic hordes God may choose to act in supernatural or miraculous ways. A miracle, or a supernatural act, (1) is an extraordinary phenomenon transcending natural law, a "mighty act," so extraordinary that it (2) elicits awe as a "wonder" and (3) serves as a "sign" indicating that either God or Satan are acting in extraordinary ways for either good or evil purposes.

Too many definitions of miracle attribute all supernatural events to God. We must challenge that very influential and disastrous presupposition. Many assume that if a person seems to be supernaturally healed the healing must be a miracle of God, and the healer is therefore confirmed as a servant of God. Because such mighty acts may be performed by false christs, false prophets, and false apostles, the occurrence of a miracle does not guarantee that every wonder worker is of God (Matt. 24:24; 1 John 4:1–3; Rev. 13:13). Only if a miracle worker's character and his concepts of God, Christ, and salvation are sound is he to be regarded truly of God. We need to be alert to counterfeit miracles (2 Thess. 3:9).[81]

Although God ordinarily achieves his purposes through real secondary agents (providentially), at times of crisis the redemptive rescue operation has called for his extraordinary, once-for-all direct acts (miracles). Divine miracles occurred in clusters at Creation; the Flood, supporting the integrity of Noah; the Exodus, supporting the leadership of Moses; the Baal crisis, supporting the ministries of prophets Elijah and Elisha; the Incarnation, attesting the claims of Jesus of Nazareth to be the Messiah; and the beginning of the Christian church, attesting the claims of the apostles in the hostile environment of the Romans and many Jews, such as the Pharisees and Sadducees.

When God performs "miracles," natural laws are not obliterated or even temporarily suspended. Neither does the God who acts unusually "intervene" in an otherwise independent and alien cosmos. Rather, while sustaining the world's regularities, God may perform "mighty acts" to correct irregularities resulting from sin. Miracles may take place in two ways. First, God may achieve his startling ends independently of second causes. When a leper cried out for help, Jesus simply touched him and said, "Be clean," and the leper was healed (Matt. 8:2–3). On other occasions God uses secondary causes in an extraordinary way. Jesus asked the man who had been blind from birth and on whose eyes Jesus had placed mud mixed with saliva to wash in the Pool of Siloam (John 9:6–7). Such mighty acts evoked "wonder" and provided a "sign" confirming his special messianic claims.

Miracles in Scripture are closely related to God's redemptive program. By his mighty acts God may either (1) overcome counterproductive forces of evil, as in preserving the line of the coming Messiah; (2) supernaturally authenticate the claims of the incarnate Messiah; (3) confirm the teaching of his spokesmen, prophets, and apostles; and (4) build the church in a hostile environment (Acts). God can, of course, perform miracles for other reasons at other times, but he has chosen primarily to do so for these reasons. We ought not look for miracles constantly. If they happened every day, we could not recognize them. Only against the background of natural law can we recognize extraordinary mighty acts. The constant desire for miracles may reflect disregard for God's wisdom in providence or a failure to share God's ordinary values.

Take physical healing as an example. God customarily heals through ordinary providential means over a period of time. In contrast to providential healings, miraculous healings are complete and quick and not only help the person healed but also strengthen God's redemptive program at the time. The majority of biblical miracles occurred during times of crisis in the battle with the kingdom of darkness. Clusters of miracles happened as Moses led God's people out of Egyptian slavery, as Elijah and Elisha defeated the prophets of Baal, as Christ became incarnate and provided atonement for the sin of the world, and as the apostles planted the church.

God's Redemptive Rule Advanced by Prayer

God has chosen to work powerfully and effectively in the world for good through the prayers of righteous people (James 5:16). Prayer involves far more than petition. Persons relate to God in different ways. We may contemplate his purposes and the blessings of universal grace and of special grace. In prayer we respond in awe to his mighty redemptive acts. Included in the prayer life may be elements of faith, worship, confession, adoration, praise, thanksgiving, and dedicated action.

Christian prayer also may include requests ideally offered in faith and motivated by love for God and others. Intercessory prayer is not a means of compelling an unwilling God to do our bidding. It is not magic that compels impersonal powers to do what we want when we want it. In prayer we express our desires to God as requests to a person. Requests to persons do not have predictable responses. The responses of persons to requests are not automatic. God may give us what we ask, or grant us something better. But he may also keep us waiting or in wisdom respond negatively.

What then is the connection between asking and receiving? C. S. Lewis has suggested some helpful illustrations. Ask a neighbor to feed the cat, an employer to give you a raise, or a woman to marry you. "Your neighbor may be a humane person who would not have let your cat starve even if you had forgotten to make arrangements. Your employer is never so likely to grant your request for a raise as when he is aware that you could get better money from a rival firm, and he is quite possibly intending to secure you by a raise in any case. As for the lady who consents to marry you—are you sure she had not decided to do so already? Your proposal, you know, might have been the result, not the cause, of her decision. A certain important conversation might never have taken place unless she had intended that it should." So it is that as we come to know more of God and his purposes we have greater confidence that his nature and purposes are such as to grant our requests.[82]

In summary, the God of providence ordinarily achieves his decretive or permissive purposes for the world by governing space, time, laws of nature, and human decisions through ethical persuasion via families, nations, and churches, as well as intercessory prayer. But when God's rule is under direct demonic attack, God may act in extraordinary (supernatural, or miraculous) ways to serve his redemptive program.

APOLOGETIC INTERACTION

Wolfhart Pannenberg, like many other recent theologians, has despaired of defending the classical doctrine of providence for this scientific generation. According to Pannenberg, "the idea of a divine providence that not only conserves the world but also guides the course of history is admittedly so problematic to the modern mind that any return to it, at least in its traditional form, can hardly be expected."[83] It is important to examine some of the perspectives that seem to make divine guidance of nature and history unreasonable to our contemporaries.

Not Merely a Mechanistic (Clockwork) World

Science seems to support a world that runs on its own like a self-winding watch. Naturalists hypothesize that the universe is "self-existent, self-explanatory, self-operating and self-directing . . . the world process is purposeless, deterministic, and only incidentally productive of human life . . . and human values, compulsions, activities, and restraints can be justified . . . without recourse to supernatural sanctions."[84] For religious naturalists values are just another dimension of nature and a byproduct of a system of physical laws closed to any supernatural influence. Human actions are determined by impersonal factors in all decision making. Not only divine but also distinctively human "interventions" become problematic. In a mechanistic universe persons are reduced to unaccountable, impersonal cogs.

God's providential activity is not to be left to the unexplained gaps in scientific descriptions; it underlies everything observed by scientists and underlies the scientists themselves. Artists are not one more object in a scene to be painted. Persons are self-conscious, creative, self-determining, morally accountable agents. Naturalistic scientists have overlooked important elements of the evidence—the scientists themselves and the absolutes that make their lives and work meaningful! In short we must reject a reductive naturalistic hypothesis as anthropogically depersonalizing and ethically demoralizing. Intellectual honesty is nonnegotiable in any situation if scientific conclusions are to be trusted. Since persons with inherent value and nonnegotiable values are part of reality, scientific persons (*sic!*) have not "proved" that "the cosmos is all that is, or ever was, or ever will be."[85]

The naturalists' explanations are fallaciously reductive. They insist that humans and values are "nothing but" by-products of physical processes. Have they forgotten how difficult it is to confirm universal negative propositions? And dogmatic naturalists overlook the fact that scientific conclusions are tentative and probable because the scientific method has self-imposed limits and is always open to new evidence. The scientific method tests hypotheses by observed evidence and at best arrives at highly probable conclusions in circumscribed areas. So the very general "laws of nature" need not be regarded as all that is or as alternatives to divine activity. Rather, scientific laws are "our codification of that activity in its usual manifestations."[86]

We do not adequately portray the values of a scientific text if we ignore its author. We have missed something in literature if we reduce a poem to electrical processes in a poet's brain. If we try to reduce the just causes of oppressed minorities to cranial secretions, have we not overlooked the value of persons, the importance of justice, and accountability for human conduct? By adding literary, ethical, and spiritual values persons do not destroy scientific description but complement it. The complexity of human experience does not support a reductive idealism any more than it supports a reductive materialism. Both scientific and providential explanations include what is confirmed by observation and by analysis of personal and ethical significance.

The naturalists' addition of the hypothesis of *blind fate* does not supply a more coherent account of human experience. The hypothesis that the operative forces of the universe are merely mechanistic does not fit the biblical data on God's nature and providential activity nor the broad teleological accomplishments of history, particularly in Israel. Disraeli was asked to explain in a word why he believed in God. He replied, "The Jew." Jesus' detailed fulfillment of predictions hundreds of years in advance reflects an intelligence at work to accomplish overarching purposes in the flux of human history.

Again, a *mere chance* cannot coherently account for events apart from the sustaining and governing activity of God. Chance must not be considered a distinct agent that causes these unique events. To attribute a human decision and action to chance means that given a set of causative influences, the operations of history are incalculable to human forecasters. The scriptural data allow for no ungoverned or irresponsible factors. Even the casting of lots is under the supervision of the Lord of all (Prov. 16:33). Within the possibilities and probabilities of creation's natural laws, "histories" and biographies with their unique sequences of events that actually occurred are not fortuitous. So far as the laws of nature and logical possibilities are concerned, the universe *could* have had many histories other than the one it had.[87] But the particular events that happened only once as distinct from repeated events may be said to involve "chance" and "accident" but can be traced to volitional decisions for which persons are responsible. And persons are instruments or means of accomplishing God's purposes.

Indeterminacies in history may also be attributed to *accidents*. Accidents are those "situations in which two or more chains of events that have no causal connection with each other coincide in such a way as to decide the course of events."[88] From that perspective, the history of the planet could have been quite different had it not been for Eve and Adam's disobedience, Cain's killing of Abel, the deliverance of Noah, the scattering of people by diverse languages at Babel, Moses' courage to lead the people out of Egypt, Paul's journey to Rome, and the Allies' victory over Hitler. But other logical possibilities do not rule out empirical decision making on the basis of divinely revealed principles or the overruling of human decisions by providence. Putting our confidence in divine providence, we do not take an uncertain leap into the dark but trust in the all-knowing One for whom not even the humanly unpredictable, exceptional, once-for-all events in history are surprises.

Deists deny divine providence and miracles even though they affirm the reality of a Creator. The divine source of persons and values makes no difference in ongoing historical events. The deists' God is like a business person who started a company and left it to run on its own. Like the naturalists, deists reduce the cosmos to a closed system of observable effects determined by observable causes, and no miracles are possible. Having regarded God an alien to their scientific world, many recent thinkers faced an insuperable problem of how God could act in the world except by "intervention." God has become a stranger to his own world! When God acts in extraordinary ways in creation, he is not "intervening" in someone else's world, but engaging in a redemptive operation in his creation.

Not Merely a Subjective Response to a Meaningless World

Existentialists and many biblical theologians assume such a closed naturalistic system of natural law and so their view of providence asserted nothing about the activity of a transcendent God in an objective world. For existentialists, belief in God's providence simply reflects the subjective attitudes of people toward the conundrum of the cosmos. Bultmann naïvely accepted the world picture of nontheistic scientists, and regarded a biblical view of creation and providence to be crude and prescientific.[89] For Paul Tillich providence "is not a theory about some activities of God: it is the religious symbol of the courage of confidence with respect to fate and death. For the courage of confidence says 'in spite of' even to death."[90] In effect existentialists say that even though there is no objective basis for belief in divine providence, they will heroically cultivate an inner faith, hope, and love as if there were.

Talk of faith and courage seems hypocritical if the Lord of all does not transcend nature and have qualities distinct from those of the cosmos (vol. 1, chaps. 5–6). God is self-existent and eternal; the universe is dependent, having a beginning in the finite past. And to say that nature is self-directed attributes intelligence to the nonintelligent. Apart from a transcendent God, the impersonal physical world has no mind or will and hence no wisely chosen "direction." Any lasting meaning of historical existence has lost its foundation if the case for an objectively real God and accountability are not accepted.

Talk of divine sovereignty and lordship is empty also if God exists but does not have a relationship to our environment as well as to our hearts. God's redemptive rule is now primarily in the hearts of believers, but God's providential rule is over all of nature. The failure to distinguish between the universal and the redemptive rules may be at the base of the existentialist difficulty. To regard nature as objectively meaningless and yet talk about the mighty acts of the Lord of history (as in some biblical theology) creates an artificial bifurcation. Langdon Gilkey has said, "Contemporary views are left with an action that is a mere inward influence which leads man, as in existentialism, to make decisions in an alien, meaningless world, and to have 'faith' in a God who is sovereign only elsewhere."[91]

The data noted in the scriptural section showed that divine providence cannot be relegated to the hearts of believing people. The doctrine affirms the activity of God in the objective world and the events of history. For example, providence was not just an internal belief in the mind of Joseph; he believed it internally because God actually redirected the the betrayal of his brothers and the Egyptian government by leading a Jew to become prime minister! God also permitted the famine that brought Joseph's jealous brothers and grieving parents to him for food. An informed view of providence must fit the multitudes of instances like this in the biblical section above. God achieves his purposes objectively through the laws of nature and specific historical events beyond individual control, as well as the inner attitudes of human beings. In respect to evil, God's will is accomplished permissively; in respect to good, God's will is accomplished through his revealed precepts, ordinary guidance, and miraculous acts.

Not Occult Manipulation

Divine providence is not to be confused with "The Age of Aquarius." The amazing thing is not that people at times find belief in God's righteous providence difficult to understand and accept but that they find it possible to believe almost everything else! Although alleged to have "come of age," people now spend millions of dollars on horoscopes with their astrological generalities. However, to turn to the counsel of astrologers is to turn one's back on a biblically based divine guidance through responsible decision and action. For many people the astrologer has replaced the pastor or counselor.

The hypothesis that our characters and destinies are in some mysterious way determined by the positions of the stars at our births lacks both clear meaning and adequate support. Consider the following points:

1. In reality it is impossible for people to know what their astrological sign is. The "sign" for a given birth date in the Eastern lunar calendar differs from that in the Western solar calendar.

2. The meanings of astrological "signs" are derived from meaningless ancient, primitive traditions. Leo, for example, derived its name from the coincidence of lions arriving at the riverside and the position of the visible stars in the sky. Astrological meanings must be read into the sky; they are not read in it.

3. In the ancient world about nine thousand stars were visible to the naked eye. If the visible stars had some hidden influence, what about the power of millions of other stars recently discovered with the help of telescopes?

4. The advice of the horoscopes is often so general as to be applicable in some sense to anyone. What one horoscope predicted of then Republican President Nixon anyone could have "predicted": in August and September of that year Nixon would experience Democratic opposition!

5. Astrological predictions that become more specific, often err, as newspaper articles point out annually.

6. If that is not enough, read the advice of different astrologers for the same sign on the same day. They may contradict each other.[92]

7. People who cannot accept responsibility for their conduct may wish to blame it on alleged cosmic influences or vibrations. As responsible agents, how-

ever, Christians accept responsibility for their choices and actions.

8. We challenge astrologers to come with a message to save people destined for divine judgment as did the prophets of old. Like stubble, the astrologers are unable to save themselves or others from the flames (Isa. 47:13–15). Fearing the signs in the sky, in Jeremiah's view, is a worthless heathen custom (Jer. 10:1–3). The only dependable revealer of mysteries, Daniel showed, is God who worked through accredited prophets (Dan. 2:27–28). With mediumistic channelers, astrological diviners must be called "to the law and to the testimony! If they do not speak according to this word, they have no light of dawn" (Isa. 8:20). Confidence in astrologers discloses a lack of confidence in God's inspired prophets and apostles or a lack of courage to take responsibility for one's own decisions in accord with biblical principles.

9. What about the Magi seeing the star over Bethlehem at the time of Christ and thinking that it signified the birth of a ruler of the Jews (Matt. 2)? An isolated event like this is no endorsement of astrology. It may have been a nova; a comet; a conjunction of planets such as Jupiter, Mars, and Saturn; or a supernatural light in the sky. At Jesus' death the sun was darkened and at his second coming there will be signs in the sun, moon, and stars (Luke 21:25). Why should there not have been a supernatural sign in the heavens at his first coming?[93]

Also, belief in divine providence ought not be confused with belief in *magic*. Magicians seem to have the ultimate powers of the universe at their disposal. However, in the world of entertainment magicians may be simply sleight-of-hand artists. Some magicians practice a deceptive "con game" in which they merely seem to use hypnosis, extrasensory perception, telepathy, clairvoyance, and precognition. Acceptance of the supernatural by the undiscerning creates a power base and wealth. People who trust in magic imagine that the forces of the universe orbit around their desires or prayers. The ends served by magical manipulation of hidden knowledge and power are at best temporary and limited, and at worst, fraudulent or demonic. To the extent that people rely on the secrets of occultists, they do not rely on public revelations from God. Magicians seek to manipulate the "principalities and powers" of the cosmos for their own ends rather than trusting the wisdom of God. Here is another major difference between the people of God and the people of the world. By this you can discern who are of God and who are not. The people of God use the world to honor God's wise and good purposes; the people of the world use hidden powers to serve their own often unwise and evil ends.

Scripture attributes any supernatural occult powers ultimately to Satan, but theists need to be careful not to consider more to be supernatural than in fact is. Much entertainment that takes place in the name of magic is nothing more than a con game. The remarkable phenomena are achieved by sleight of hand or illusions. They are pseudo-occult happenings. "Pseudo-occult phenomena are events which appear to be caused by secretive, supernatural powers and yet are brought about by physical or psychological means."[94]

Christians need to develop discernment in spying out activities primarily stimulated by channelers of the satanic hosts. Before concluding that any person or event is demonized, however, we must examine, test, try, prove, and eliminate naturalistic fraud. The magicians of Egypt were able to duplicate some of the plagues that came upon them by divine judgment at the time of the Exodus. But others were beyond their powers, and these magicians could not save the Egyptians from punishment.

Satan's unholy angels or demons are engaged in a centuries-long warfare with God and the holy angels. And Christians specifically may be targets of demonic schemes (Eph. 6:11-12). Hence Christians need to arm themselves with truth, righteousness, the gospel of peace, faith, salvation, and the Word of God (vv. 13-17). Christians also need to pray in the spirit in all situations and keep on praying for all the saints (v. 18).[95]

Problems in Relating Prayer to Providence

A spiritual life will be permeated with prayer to God rather than manipulations of hidden cosmic vibrations or the powers of dead spiritual masters. But if God has planned everything and is working in everything that comes to pass, why do Christians need to pray? For one thing, God wants our fellowship. Prayer is more than making requests, it includes loving personal response to the Lord of all in faith, worship, confession, adoration, praise, thanksgiving, and dedicated action. But God also wants us to express our requests to him. God asked us to bring to him our petitions for our own needs and intercessions for those of our friends and our enemies. Jesus prayed for all his followers and those who through them will believe. Jesus taught us to pray for the fulfillment of the Father's will on earth, for the establishment of his kingdom, the supply of necessary food, the forgiveness of sins, deliverance from temptations, and the final triumph of his kingdom over evil.

Since God plans and governs all things, why do we have to present our requests? We pray because God asks us to, and God asks us to pray because he chose to accomplish certain things through the intercession of his people.

Prayer is not magic, so we should not expect to compel greater powers to do our bidding and have invariable "success." Prayer is not just using impersonal spiritual laws or powers of the righteous kingdom as we will. Rather, prayer with all the variables of our personal desires, loyalties, understandings, and purposes asks God to do as he wills in accord with his wisdom, justice, and love.

Several fallacies or misconceptions often contribute to unnecessary difficulties about the role of petition in providence. The *predestination fallacy* reasons that prayer is pointless because God has predestined all things. This overlooks God's two distinguishable strategies, the conditional and the unconditional. Although prayer will not change those events that God predestined to be accomplished by his own power unconditonally, many aspects of our lives are not unconditionally determined. Most are envisioned in God's conditional strategy. "*If* my people . . . will humble themselves and pray and seek my face and turn from their wicked ways, *then* will I hear from heaven and will forgive their sin and heal their land" (2 Chron. 7:14). In accord with God's conditional strategy, he forgives and revives only in answer to prayer. Although prayer that asks God to act contrary to his nature or unconditional purposes is of no avail, our petitions in other matters have great and eternal significance.

Others struggle in thought about prayer because of the *foreknowledge fallacy*. Since God foreknows our needs, does that not render our requests meaningless? A medical doctor's foreknowledge of requests from patients recovering from heart surgery does not make them meaningless. Rather, a wise physician prepares to answer those needs in advance of the requests. Analogously God's foreknowledge of our requests from the beginning of history

111

does not make them pointless. Rather, God has wisely built the answers to our prayers into the structure of the universe and developments in history. From the beginning he planned the world for significant personal relationships with his people and so for significant communion in prayer. Having been away from home for a long time, our foreknowledge of a coming reunion with a spouse and children does not lessen the warmth of the embraces when one finally arrives. Anticipation actually enhances the joy! Similarly God's anticipation of those times in history when we finally express our love does not detract from them. We ought, then, to overcome the foreknowledge roadblock to prayer that imagines that if some eventuality is foreknown it is in vain to pray.

The *single-cause fallacy* attributes historical events in our lives either to God or to humans, but not to both. It assumes that if God does something, then human agency has no part, or if we do something, it is not of God or an answer to prayer. Most significant events in our lives are the product of complex antecedents, not a single factor. We need to understand that among the many contributing factors to events in our lives in the course of history is "presenting our requests to God" (Phil. 4:6). Intercessory prayer can serve as one factor in receiving certain blessings without being the sole and sufficient condition of some of God's good gifts. Disciplined memorization of Scripture and meditation upon it may be important also.

The *punctiliar fallacy* in thinking about prayer imagines that if God answers, his answer will be identifiable at a single, dramatic point in time. Immature as we are, we want what we want when we want it. Some answers to prayer may indeed be complete and sudden. But other answers to prayer may develop gradually over a long period of time. We have become so used to instant coffee and tea that we imagine we can receive instant spirituality. Prayers for Christlike maturity will not be answered instantly. We do well to avoid imagining that if our prayer is not answered instantaneously it is not answered.

The *sufficient-cause fallacy* in thinking about prayer assumes that if intercession is important it must be the sole and sufficient cause of the result requested. Many necessary conditions of results are not sufficient causes of effects. A light bulb is a necessary condition of artificial illumination in a room, but it is not the sufficient cause. It must be connected to a properly wired light fixture. And the wiring in the building must be connected to the generating source of the public service company. In addition the utility bills must be paid! Prayer is one of many necessary factors in God's providential interweaving of many factors contributing to states of affairs. Intercession may be a necessary condition of certain things happening, even though it may not be a sufficient condition in and of itself. The Scriptures mention several associated factors: praying in the Holy Spirit (Eph. 6:18), according to God's revealed will (1 John 5:14), in faith (James 1:5–7) while remaining in Christ, with Christ's words remaining in us (John 15:7), and in Jesus' name (John 14:13–14; 16:24) or as he would pray for the sake of his kingdom. Hence in our thinking about prayer and providence in general we need to avoid thinking of praying as a sufficient cause of divine acts but still realize that it is a necessary factor among many in divine providence.

God has chosen not only the ends of the redemptive rule but also the strategies, using human means for their accomplishment. God chose to accomplish many of the ends of redemption through the prayers of his people. *Any view of God's predestination or provi-*

dence that keeps people from praying indicates something out of line with the Bible's teaching.

RELEVANCE FOR LIFE AND MINISTRY

Since God is working out all things in the universe according to a wise, holy, and loving plan, events do not happen to us without a reason in God's design or permission. However absurd and pointless things may seem on the surface, everything is related teleologically. Human minds have been created in God's image to know reality and assess it responsibly. Hence some knowledge is possible from nature and history about the universe and about God from universal and special revelation. From these sources we grow in appreciating many values. We list a few of them here.

A Sense of Reality and Adventure in Life

For Christian theists life is no mere illusion or dream. Theists have a sense of the reality of both physical and spiritual realms. God has endowed us with real capacities and has sustained their real, not merely apparent, efficiency as second causes. So healthy Christian theists are not autistic; they are not removed from intellectual reality, emotional reality, or volitional reality. Rather, they have a sense of knowing reality (in part) by a conceptual revelation. Theists respond emotionally to the reality they face in God's providence with gratitude and praise. They need not seek to escape reality, but, as God's stewards, they make decisions and accept responsibility for their attitudes, words, and actions.

When former secular scientist William G. Pollard became a Christian, he found that, "Life in a world which is consciously apprehended as the expression of the will of its Creator is not a sequence of baleful incidents thwarting human purposes, but a meaningful and joyous adventure."[96]

Humility to Accept What Is Not Within Our Power

Being limited creatures in a huge universe, we know that there are factors beyond our control. God works through an ordered cosmos. The laws of nuclear energy are not going to bend to our personal wishes. God's laws of justice and morality are not respecters of persons. And neither are the laws of meaningful thought (logic). Being fallen creatures and facing the ravages of selfishness, injustice, political power, arrogance, and sensuality, we know that some evils are beyond our power to prevent and correct.

There are innumerable aspects of the world and the shaping of history about which, in the nature of things, we can do nothing. True humility is simply the recognition and acceptance of this primary reality of our finite status in creation. But secular man does not dare admit to any such predicament. How can he? In a world without God there is nothing short of an act of defeat, a giving up of struggle. He can see in it nothing beyond an unnecessary self-imposed resignation, a forfeiture of man's right to use and change the world as he thinks best, and an attitude of submission which sits back and merely lets things happen.[97]

Knowing that God accomplishes many of his purposes independently of us, and some through us, we may appropriately pray the serenity prayer:

God give me the serenity
  to accept the things I cannot
    change,
  the courage to change the things
    I can,
    and the wisdom to know the one
      from the other.

Commitment to Improve What We Can

The Christian doctrine of providence does not produce a Stoic resignation nor a fatalistic submission to the status quo. In our finite, fallen world many things need to be changed. What God has put within our power to change for the better, Christians dedicate themselves to improve. Far from passivity, the ideal of theists, as J. I. Packer said in *Knowing God,* is an "active yieldedness." God has chosen to accomplish many things through peoples' decisions, determinations, and actions. In areas such as health care, family fulfillment, education, the nation, transportation, communication, and safety theists may be in the forefront of invention and creative contribution.

Stewardship of Health

Given God's use of orderly patterns as means to accomplish his ends in history, people who want health will not neglect needed nourishment, rest, and exercise. Except in extraordinary cases connected with his redemptive program, God grants healthy eyes, teeth, and lungs to those who take care of them. When Christians claim to be too busy in God's service to take care of themselves, they suffer the consequences.

Notwithstanding the best of diets, rest, and exercise, we sometimes face illness and accident. In cases of injury and disease believers in divine providence strongly favor medicine, physicians, nurses, and paramedics. The prescribed medicines and certified persons that are available for healing are there in the providence of God. Understanding God's guidance in the development of every good thing, including medicine, Christians do not refuse the medical provisions God has made possible in preventive and corrective ways.

Total dependence on miraculous healings may express faith in God's supernatural power, but it may also express a tragic failure to understand and accept God's ordinary ways of working with mature people through medical means that are available providentially.

Christian theists eat and drink and do whatever they do to the glory of God (1 Cor. 10:31). We recognize that God created a multitude of foods with a rich variety of tastes for our good. So for balanced nutrition we eat a variety of vegetables, legumes, fruits, nuts, and meats. God has shown kindness by giving rain from heaven and crops in their seasons (Acts 14:17). We feed and care for our own bodies (Eph. 5:29). Deceiving spirits forbid people to marry and command them to abstain from certain foods that God created to be received with thanksgiving (1 Tim. 4:1–3). Anorexia is not the spiritual ideal, even in the name of spiritual discipline. Scripture recommends temporary fasting but not starvation.

Given the continued influence of our depraved natures, we often find that the good that we would do (in diet and exercise) we do not in fact do. And what we would not do, on holidays and under all kinds of imagined and real pressures, we end up doing (Rom. 7:15, 20). "Now if I do what I do not want to do, . . . it is sin" (v. 20). The inclination to sin wages war against the law of the mind, making us prisoners (v. 23). But God has provided an antidote for slavery to self-destructive, sinful behavior. God forgives our guilt and empowers us to counteract and overcome temptations of all sorts. In place of a lack of self-control, the Spirit enables believers to develop self-control (Gal. 5:22–23).

Overcoming the world by faith in Christ (1 John 5:4–5) and by quoting Scripture (1 John 3:6), Donna Platt found her life changed from the inside out. What she needed, she said, was not another diet plan, but power to do the good she knew. Committing herself to eat to honor God and consciously depending on Christ living in her, she changed from a dress size of 22 to size 10. When she realized that Christ lived in her she said no to compulsive eating and junk food. She realized she could do nothing without Christ (John 15:5) but that she could do everything through him who gives strength (Phil. 4:13). "Most important," wrote Donna, "keep an awareness of Christ's presence with you continually."[98]

Fidelity to the Family

The providentially authorized institution of the *family* survived throughout biblical history across varied cultures to the present day. In spite of contemporary attacks on it, the family structure ought to be sustained. Through years of loving relationships, instruction, and discipline a family becomes a unified whole composed of members who function in structured interrelationships. Family members become interrelated not only genetically and legally but also by a sense of oneness morally and spiritually. In God's providential strategy faithfulness to spouse and children supports several values: overcoming loneliness, avoding promiscuity, populating the earth, and educating and disciplining children.

As important and valuable as the family with its ethical persuasion is, however, since the Fall the best of filial relationships come short of the divine ideal. The family of dependent, fallen members ought not usurp the prerogatives of God. Allegiance to the family can be required only under God. If and when family members, however well-meaning they may be, would coerce a Christian to break God's precepts, believers ought to follow the higher authority. Parents should not usurp the place of God in the lives of children nor

should children occupy the place of God in the lives of parents. The highest value and ultimate concern of all family members should be to please God. When we put God's kingdom and his righteousness first, however, he often grants us the blessings of food and clothing (Matt. 6:33), and we may add rewarding family relationships.

Some ask, "Is AIDS a special judgment of God upon sinful individuals or a natural consequence of certain behavior?" When the first-century media reported that Pilate took the lives of some people from Galilee, Jesus replied, "Do you think that these Galileans were worse sinners than all the other Galileans because they suffered this way? I tell you, no! But unless you repent, you too will all perish" (Luke 13:1–3). Jesus then recalled eighteen who died when the tower in Siloam fell on them; he said, "Do you think they were more guilty than all the others living in Jerusalem? I tell you, no! But unless you repent, you too will all perish" (vv. 4–5). So to ask if God particularly judges homosexuals is like asking if Legionnaire's disease is a special judgment on the American Legion. Sexually transmitted diseases may be natural consequences of certain kinds of human conduct rather than special judgments of God on individuals. Disease, accidents, earthquakes, and war—all can be used by God to bring any or all of us as sinners to repentance. Just as we would relate to alcoholics with compassionate treatment of support groups for psychological, physical, and spiritual needs, so we ought to minister to people with AIDS. If, however, entire communities should rebel against God's institution of the family, the possibility of divine judgment may have a precedent in the judgment that occurred long ago at Sodom and Gomorrah (Gen. 19:24–29).

Those who would seek leadership in the church should begin with their own homes. Before they attempt to lead the church, there should be sufficient evidence of their marital fidelity and ability to lead their own children in worthy directions (1 Tim. 3:5; Titus 1:6). Presumably a reasonably demonstrated ability to bring up one's own children to live morally while serving God and others constitutes a necessary qualification also for leadership in church. We might infer that those who would seek to promote a just and lasting peace throughout the world should begin in their own families.

Patriotism Under God

Knowing that God has providentially worked with nations to promote justice, theists obey the laws of their *nation,* pay their taxes, and actively participate in its drama. Theists are generally loyal to their governments. "Everyone must submit himself to the governing authorities, for there is no authority except that which God has established" (Rom. 13:1). This passage does not teach that God is responsible for misuses of governmental authority, but that God is the final cause of all governmental authority as a providential means of restraining evil and promoting justice. With Paul we "urge, then, first of all, that requests, prayers, intercession and thanksgiving be made for everyone—for kings and all those in authority, that we may live peaceful lives in all godliness and holiness" (1 Tim. 2:1–2).

We seek to be worthy citizens of our temporal nations because we are involved in a higher spiritual kingdom or "holy nation" (1 Peter 2:9). Christians seek first the kingdom of God and his righteousness. But God's righteousness requires justice for all, especially the unfortunate. God is a jealous God, and we dare not value our national leaders idolatrously. Thoughtful theists evaluate their governments, opposing them whenever they demand allegiance due

only to God or take over the role of the church. Revelation 13 stands in stark contrast to Romans 13. God's people cannot support the government of a leader who demands worship. No government should take the place of God in the obedience of its citizens. Christ and the apostles generally obeyed the Roman government even though that government was far from ideal. However, when the government forbade preaching the gospel, they chose to obey God rather than men (Acts 4:17–20). Christians ought not subscribe to slogans like "My country, right or wrong" if by that they mean they are willing to condone what is wrong, but as far as possible they should support only what is right. And theists will not submit to governmental leaders who abandon their God-given responsibilities to preserve life and to maintain order and justice.[99]

In the light of Revelation 13 Christian theists ought to look even more critically on movements toward a world government. New Age politics alleges that the primary source of evil in the world is found in the conflicts of the different governments. We are told that we will never have peace until we escape the prison of nationalism. Nationalism allegedly encourages national chauvinism and leads inevitably to war. So New Age hope lies in giving up our national citizenships for global citizenship with a planetary consciousness. That hope lies not in divine regeneration but in transformation by world citizenship under a world tribunal and law enforcement agency.[100] However, Jesus explained that evil arises from within people (Mark 7:20–23), and so power would very likely corrupt the hearts of leaders in a global government. New Age meditation techniques are not adequate to change human nature. The diversity of governments has its disadvantages, but may provide more checks and balances on people in power than could be possible in a global government. Not until the Prince of Peace himself returns to reign in righteousness will nationalism be dissolved and a lasting planetary guidance system be established with justice for all.

Encouragement to Pray

The doctrine of providence stimulates prayer as Christians understand that the transcendent Lord of all accomplishes many ends through praying people and has answered many prayers providentially in the past. Some people think that prayer makes a difference only in the minds of those who pray. Indeed it does that. Petitioners themselves receive freedom from anguish and fear (Ps. 118:5–6), strength of soul (138:3), guidance and satisfaction (Isa. 58:9–11), wisdom and understanding (Dan. 9:20–27), deliverance from harm (Joel 2:32), reward (Matt. 6:6), good gifts (Luke 11:13), fullness of joy (John 16:23–24), peace (Phil. 4:6–7), and freedom from anxiety (1 Peter 5:7).

Can prayer make a substantial difference also in the lives of others? Moses cried, " 'In accordance with your great love, forgive the sin of these people . . .' The LORD replied, 'I have forgiven them as you asked' " (Num. 14:19–20). Although the responsible adults did not enter the Promised Land, the children did, and Israel was not put aside for another nation. The apostle Paul believed prayer could result in greater wisdom and power (Eph. 1:15–19), strength in the inner person, knowledge of the love of Christ, and filling with the fullness of God (3:16–19). To another church Paul wrote that prayer could contribute discernment, approval of what is excellent, filling with the fruits of righteousness (Phil. 1:9–11), knowledge of God's will, spiritual understanding, a life pleasing to God, fruitfulness, endurance, patience, and joy (Col. 1:9–12). Paul considered prayer effective in others for love for one another, holiness

before God (1 Thess. 3:10–13), worthiness of God's call, and fulfillment of every good resolve (2 Thess. 1:11, 12; see also Philem. 6; Heb. 13:20–21).

Some have held that prayer can change people, but not things. Prayer also changes things, such as conditions in nature and the human body. Elijah prayed for the cessation of rain, and it did not rain for three and a half years. Again he prayed, and the heavens gave rain (1 Kings 17:1; 18:41–45; James 5:15–16). From the belly of the great fish Jonah prayed and was delivered (Jonah 2:7–10). The prayer of faith may heal the sick (James 5:17–18). Jesus prayed for daily bread (Matt. 6:11), and Paul for the sound and blameless keeping of body as well as soul and spirit (1 Thess. 5:23). Indeed in God's providence, "the prayer of a righteous man is powerful and effective" (James 5:16).[101]

Appreciation for Every Good Thing

"Every good and perfect gift is from above, coming down from the Father" (James 1:17). Whether coming directly from God's activity or indirectly through his creature's human instrumentality, everything is ultimately from God. Since God's creation reflects his broad interests in the kinds of experience he has made possible, Christians develop broad interests, especially those who would lead others. This important quality is often overlooked by pulpit committees. An elder is not only one who is not overbearing, quick-tempered, drunk, violent, or dishonest, but he is also one who is hospitable and who "loves what is good" (Titus 1:8). Lovers of goodness revere all that comes from God, as appreciated in varied fields of music, art, business, sports, science, psychology, philosophy, and theology. The "world" is theirs so long as their interests in everything are dedicated to God's kingdom (1 Cor. 3:22).

Christians, then, thank God from whom all blessings flow! Anyone with a theistic understanding of whatever comes to pass has the basis for living doxologically! We are not ungrateful for life itself and the lives of our loved ones. Our dependent lives come from the eternal One who has life in himself.[102]

We may gratefully meditate, for example, on the blessings of our God-given five senses, or as many as we have. To the sighted vision brings the great variety of sights enjoyed during a walk along a seashore or mountain trails. We praise not only the artists but the ultimate source of aesthetic values when we see the exceptional beauty of the sculptures in Athens, the Louvre in Paris, the Sistine Chapel ceiling in Rome, and the cathedrals of Florence. Although *The David* of Michelangelo is one of the greatest of sculptures, it does not think or create. It remains motionless. With all the regard Christian theists have for Michelangelo's art, they have far more for the Creator of Michelangelo, who thought and moved!

Christians also thank God for the blessing of hearing, as some of us did at the dedication of a beautiful new electronic organ at Denver Seminary. Thank the Lord of providence for its capacity and the skill of a world-class organist who dedicated it with classics from Bach! But most of all, thank the Lord of all for the sense of hearing and for the gift of music with its varieties and enriching affects on our lives.

Theists also thank God for the sense of taste. What a great variety of tastes in foods await hungry people. Before or after a delicious meal it is appropriate that we thank the skillful and dedicated cook. Gratitude is in order also for the Sustainer of the unbelievably complex life-support system that makes the growth of foods possible. To his creative and providential work we owe the joys of eating and the opportunities for fellowship and respite from work it provides. So theists appropriately express their gratitude at meals and other times of regular worship, adoration, and praise.

Theists also express gratitude for the sense of smell. Recall a walk through a rose garden or a pine forest. Remember coming home after a busy day and walking in the door to smell a delicious meal cooking! Perfumes enrich many experiences in life. And what would life be without the sense of touch? We would greatly miss the warmth of friendships communicating common interests in a meaningful handshake or embrace. What joy the embrace of a baby brings to its parents and grandparents! Theists thank God for the feeling of relaxation after a vacation. Consider even the smoothness of a sanded piece of fine furniture. Summing up, theists thank God for the combination of delights through all the senses—as for example in the consummation of a married couple's mutual expression of their faithful love!

Patience in Adversity

We may suffer in many ways in a temporally limited and fallen world full of conflict with the powers of evil. Those who love God, his moral values, and his redemptive program will gladly suffer when necessary to serve his holy and loving purposes. At any cost they will seek first his kingdom among their physical and spiritual relatives and neighbors. If they suffer the loss of health, they may struggle initially, but they will learn to trust the Lord of all for sufficient grace each day. And although struggling with acceptance at the loss of a loved one, theists eventually discover sufficient grace to say with Job, "The LORD gave and the LORD has taken away; may the name of the Lord be praised" (Job 1:21).

Faith in Uncertainty

Having good and sufficient evidence for believing that the ultimate power with which we have to do is sovereign, wise, holy, and good, and has a reason for all that he does and allows, we trust God even in those baffling times when we cannot appreciate what has happened.

Those who are called by God can be confident that God is working in all the circumstances of their lives. "And we know that in all things God works for the good of those who love him, who have been called according to his purpose" (Rom. 8:28). God works all things together not so much for our ease as for our education, not so much for our comfort as for our discipline, not so much for our pleasure as for our chastening. Through suffering we ought to develop patience. In God's providence all things, however initially shocking, paradoxical, or disturbing, are teleologically related. God has a wise, just, and loving purpose in either his permissive, perceptive, or unconditional purposes and strategies. Knowing God, knowing his purposes and strategies, and knowing his power to bring them to pass in history in the way he has chosen, theists trust God even when in agony they cannot fathom what that purpose can be.

Hope for the Future

We cannot now understand why God has permitted the kingdom of darkness to do battle so long and inflict such anguish on so many lives in so many ways. In times of potential nuclear bribery and massive destruction, none of us knows what the future may hold. But theists do know who holds the future. And they know that the Lord of all is wise, just, and loving. Prophecy assures us that when Christ returns, there will be humans on earth. Although the spiritual battle of the two kingdoms will intensify, theists know that the ultimate future will be one of which they can approve. For they know that God's great power can bring his wise philosophy of history to a victorious conclusion. Knowing God's wisdom, power, and love, we find sufficient courage in our present time of need. With Job we can say, "Though he slay me, yet will I hope in him" (Job 13:15). Death itself cannot separate us from the love of God (Rom. 8:38–39). Even though we walk through the valley of the shadow of death, we will fear no evil (Ps. 23:4).

REVIEW QUESTIONS

To Help Relate and Apply
Each Section in This Chapter

1. *Briefly state the classical problem* this chapter addresses and indicate reasons why genuine inquiry into it is important for your worldview and your existence personally and socially.

2. *Objectively summarize the influential answers* given to this problem in history as hypotheses to be tested. Be able to compare and contrast their real similarities and differences (not merely verbal similarities or differences).

3. *Highlight the primary biblical evidence* on which to decide among views—evidence found in the relevant teachings of the major divisions of Scripture—and decide for yourself which historical hypothesis (or synthesis of historical views) provides the most consistent and adequate account of the primary biblical data.

4. *Formulate in your own words your doctrinal conviction* in a logically consistent and adequate way, organizing your conclusions in ways you can ex-

plain clearly, support biblically, and communicate effectively to your spouse, children, friends, Bible class, or congregation.

5. *Defend your view* as you would to adherents of the alternative views, showing that the other views are logically less consistent and factually faced with more difficulties than your view in accounting for the givens, not only of special revelation but also of human experience in general.

6. *Explore the differences the viability of your conviction can make in your life.* Then test your understanding of the viability of your view by asking, "Can I live by it authentically (unhypocritically) in relation to God and to others in my family, church, vocation, neighborhood, city, nation, and world?"

MINISTRY PROJECTS

To Help Communicate This Doctrine in Christian Service

1. *Memorize one major verse or passage* that in its context teaches the heart of this doctrine and may serve as a text from which to preach, teach, or lead small-group studies on the topic. The memorized passages from each chapter will build a body of content useful also for meditation and reference in informal discussions.

2. *Formulate the major idea of the doctrine in one sentence* based on the passage memorized. This idea should be useful as the major thesis of either a lesson for a class (junior high to adult) or a message for a church service.

3. *State the specific purpose or goal of your doctrinal lesson or message.* Your purpose should be more than informative. It should show why Christians need to accept this truth and live by it (unhypocritically). For teaching purposes, list indicators that would

show to what extent class members have grasped the truth presented.

4. *Outline your message or lesson in complete sentences.* Indicate how you would support the truth of the doctrine's central ideas and its relevance to life and service. Incorporate elements from this chapter's historical, biblical, systematic, apologetic, and practical sections selected according to the value they have for your audience.

5. *List applications of the doctrine* for communicating the difference this conviction makes in life (for sermons, lessons, small-group Bible studies, or family devotional Bible studies). Applications should make clear what the doctrine is, why one needs to know it, and how it will make differences in thinking. Then show how the difference in thought will lead to differences in values, priorities, attitudes, speech, and personal action. Consider also the doctrine's possible significance for family, church, neighborhood, city, regional, and national actions.

6. *Start a file and begin collecting illustrations* of this doctrine's central idea, the points in your outline, and your application.

7. *Write out your own doctrinal statement on this subject in one paragraph* (in half a page or less). To work toward a comprehensive doctrinal statement, collect your formulations based on a study of each chapter of *Integrative Theology*. As your own statement of Christian doctrine grows, you will find it personally strengthening and useful when you are called on for your beliefs in general and when you apply for service with churches, mission boards, and other Christian organizations. Any who seek ordination to Christian ministry will need a comprehensive doctrinal statement that covers the broad scope of theology.

CHAPTER 3

HUMAN BEINGS IN GOD'S IMAGE

Human Beings in God's Image

THE PROBLEM: HOW SHALL WE VIEW THE NATURE OF PERSONS IN TERMS OF THEIR INTRINSIC BEING AND CAPACITIES?

Having considered in chapters 1 and 2 God's creation and providential control of the cosmos and humanity, we now investigate the nature of the highest expression of God's handiwork—namely, persons as male and female. This is a central question for faith, since Scripture tells the inspired story of how the triune God once created and now relates to human persons.[1] To understand aright the drama of Scripture we need to understand the nature of persons as God created them.

God endowed the human race, as the pinnacle of his creative activity, with special dignity and honor. Because God constituted human persons as he did, Augustine acknowledged that "a weeping man is better than a happy worm."[2] Yet history and experience tragically confirm that persons are an enigma to themselves and others. Their behavior and actions span the spectrum between brilliance and decadence. Pascal pointed out this antithesis between the person's greatness and his meanness or wretchedness: "What sort of freak then is man! How novel, how monstrous, how chaotic, how paradoxical, how prodigious! Judge of all things, feeble earthworm, repository of truth, sink of doubt and error and refuse of the universe!"[3] Calvin, however, rescues us from despair on the subject when he insists that the human person does have meaning and dignity, but only in the light of the prior reality of God. Christians, then, can make sense of what human persons are from the reliable data of God's revelation.

Many modern authorities deny that Scripture discusses the ontological structure of persons and claim that traditional statements about persons' being and nature represent the fruit of Greek rationalism. Some contemporary thinkers insist that in lieu of the being and nature of persons we must speak only of their existential situation, i.e., of their self-understanding, decisions, and guilt. Traditionally, however, Christians have affirmed that the Bible levies no embargo against viewing the person ontologically. The axiological worth of man depends on man's ontological nature. Believing that God has answered the question posed by the psalmist, "What is man?" (Ps. 8:4; cf. Job 7:17), we follow Christian history in exploring several issues concerning persons as they came from the creative hand of God. The most important matter in Christian anthropology concerns the meaning of the proposition that God created the human person in his own image and likeness (Gen. 1:26–27). Modern non-Christian opinion regards the person as an advanced animal. What is it, we ask, that distinguishes the human person from the lower animals? Moreover, must we think of the person as an undifferentiable whole, as much contemporary thought suggests, or can we identify material and immaterial aspects of man? Does Scripture indicate that the person ontologically is monistic, dichotomous, or trichotomous? If we find that the person possesses a separate reality called the soul, the question arises as to how the soul came into existence. Since Scripture identifies the human person as an image-bearer of God (cf. vol. 1, chaps. 5–6), our task in this chapter is to examine the nature of the person metaphysically, intellectually, ethically, emotionally, volitionally, and relationally.

One's understanding of humanness ontologically has a direct bearing on many crucial issues in the contemporary world. For example, when does human life begin to exist? Whether or not the fetus is a person, or when it becomes human, lies at the heart of the abortion controversy. Remarkable advances in medical technology raise urgent ethical questions. Among these is, when and under what conditions ought the life of an ill or aged person be terminated? In the realm of Christian outreach and mission, should the church focus strictly on the spiritual side of the person, i.e., the immortal soul? Or ought the church minister to both the person's spiritual and material needs?

ALTERNATIVE INTERPRETATIONS IN THE CHURCH

One is not surprised that the nature of God has been subjected to a variety of interpretations. It is equally true that the nature of the human person, the image-bearer of God, has been widely debated throughout the history of the church. To these alternative interpretations of what it means to be human we now turn.

Early Church View Emphasizing Rationality

Many early Fathers, influenced in part by Greek philosophy, defined the *imago Dei* chiefly in terms of the natural faculties of reason and free will. Justin Martyr wrote: "When he [God] created man, he endued him with the sense of understanding, of choosing the truth, and of doing right."[4] Athenagoras identified the distinctive of the human person as follows: ". . . whose nature involves the possession of mind and who partakes of rational judgment."[5]

Irenaeus, the first Father to discuss the *imago* systematically, posited a distinction between "image" and "likeness" (Gen. 1:26). He defined the former as the endowments of a rational mind and a free will[6] retained after the Fall, and the latter as the gratuitous life of the Spirit lost at Eden but restored by grace. By so arguing, Irenaeus laid the foundation for the medieval differentiation between the person's natural endowments and the superadded gift of righteousness. By implication, Irenaeus held that the unsaved person ontologically is dichotomous (consisting of body and soul), but that the believer quickened by the indwelling Spirit becomes trichotomous (consisting of body, soul, and spirit). He wrote, "The perfect man consists in the union of the soul receiving the spirit of the Father, and the admixture of that fleshly nature which was moulded after the image of God."[7] Clement of Alexandria similarly distinguished between "image" and "likeness," defining the former as the powers of reason and free will and the latter as moral excellence that may grow or diminish.[8]

Gregory of Nyssa likewise located the *imago* chiefly in the intellect. "The form of man was framed to serve as an instrument for the use of reason."[9] Similarly, "the soul finds its perfection in that which is intellectual and rational."[10] John of Damascus claimed that the image consists of the person's "reasoning and thinking soul," or his "mind and free will."[11]

Gordon Clark, a modern Idealist, also identifies the image of God as reason. Appealing to such Scriptures as Job 32:8; Isaiah 33:6; John 1:9 (where *phōs* is "the light of logic");[12] and Colossians 3:10, Clark interprets the *imago* as "knowledge," or "the innate equipment for learning."[13] Clark argues that fellowship with God, right moral conduct, personal responsibility, and having dominion over the animals all require thinking and understanding. Thus Clark concludes that "the distinction between truth and falsehood . . . is the basic element in the image of God."[14]

As for the dichotomy-trichotomy issue, most Western theologians, such as Ambrose, Jerome, and Augustine, favored a twofold division of human nature. Athenagoras claimed that the person is a unity consisting of body and soul: "The whole nature of man in general is composed of an immortal soul and a body which was fitted to it in the creation."[15] Leading Greek Fathers, including Clement, Origen, and Gregory of Nyssa, followed Plato in upholding trichotomy. The person consists of an immortal spirit, a rational soul, and a material body. The theory of trichotomy lost favor following the Council of

Constantinople's condemnation of Apollinarius (A.D. 381), who had constructed a heretical Christology on the basis of a trichotomous nature of man.

The Fathers discussed at length the question of the genesis of the human soul. Guided by the preexistence philosophy of Plato, Origen held that God created all human souls, or rational natures, before the formation of Adam. After sinning in the heavenly realm, these souls sought redemption and so united with physical bodies by ordinary generation.[16] Scotus Erigena adopted this theory of the soul's preexistence in the ninth century. Creationism, the Aristotelian theory that God brought the soul of each person into existence simultaneous with the body, was held by most authorities in the East and by a few in the West (e.g., Hilary, Ambrose, Jerome). Hilary wrote, "Every soul is the direct work of God."[17] Traducianism, the view that both body and soul are begotten by natural generation, gained wide acceptance in the West through the writings of Tertullian. The latter claimed that by the joining of two seeds, one soulish and one physical, the entire human race propagated naturally.[18] Tertullian insisted that the embryo or fetus is a genuine human being. In his essay *On the Soul* he vividly describes the procedure physicians used to do an abortion. Tertullian denotes abortion "murder within the womb" and calls the aborting physician a child-killer. He observes that all the doctors "were convinced that a living thing had been conceived" and "that they all felt pity for the poor child who must be killed in the womb."[19]

The Traditional Roman Catholic View

Medieval Catholic theologians enlarged on Irenaeus' distinction between "image" and "likeness" to create a distinctive anthropology. They identified the "image" as the natural powers of reason and free will and the "likeness" as the added endowment of righteousness (*donum superadditum*). Catholic authorities claim that the Fall left the original natural endowment untarnished but destroyed the supernatural endowment. Constituted in God's image, the sinner retains considerable intellectual power and is capable of choosing freely and of actualizing the good. Fashioned in God's likeness, the person is given the resources to curb fleshly desires and to merit eternal life. This common distinction between "image" and "likeness," or between natural and supernatural endowments, undergirds the Roman nature-grace distinction and provides the basis for a far-ranging natural theology. In the light of these considerations, Catholics conclude that by the exercise of their intellect persons can learn much about God and moral duty, short of heavenly blessedness.

Peter Lombard endorsed this position by saying, "Man is made . . . to the *image* according to memory, intelligence, and love and to the *likeness* according to innocence and justice which are naturally in the rational mind. Or, *image* may be considered in the cognition of truth, and *likeness* may be considered in the love of virtue."[20] The Franciscan Bonaventure argues similarly. Insofar as the person is a likeness to God, he "is related to God as to a gift infused into it." Thus "every creature which knows God is an image, and every creature in which God dwells is a likeness."[21]

Thomas Aquinas likewise posits a distinction between "image" and "likeness," the latter signifying "a certain perfection of the image."[22] The image, according to Aquinas, consists chiefly in the person's intellectual nature. Inherent in the rational mind is not only the capacity for virtue, but also the aptitude for understanding and loving God. Aquinas boldly states that all

persons by nature love God more fully than they love themselves.[23] Such powers common to humanity cannot be forfeited. Furthermore, the "likeness" represents a "supernatural endowment of grace," the content of which is actual love for and obedience to God.[24] This grace was lost at the Fall, but when restored by baptism, it enables the person to love and serve God meritoriously. Aquinas clearly consolidated a two-tiered theology of the natural and the supernatural.

The *New Catholic Encyclopedia* articulates this same position:

Man, in the whole of his being, was created; his soul by immediate (first) creation; his body in a manner that has not been precisely revealed, i.e., the possibility of evolution is not excluded. In addition, man received supernatural gifts of grace and virtue that made him a partaker of the nature of God (2 Peter 1:4) and other prerogatives and powers transcending ordinary human nature.[25]

Most Catholic theologians uphold the Western twofold material-immaterial division of human nature. Following Augustine, Anselm argued that the real person is not a bodiless soul but is a composite being that includes a corporeal as well as a spiritual-rational-volitional affective nature. Guided by Aristotle rather than Plato, Aquinas judged that the human person is a complex union of body and soul, the soul uniting to the body as its "form." As for the origin of the soul, traditional Catholicism upholds creationism. Anselm, Lombard, and Aquinas, the encyclical *Humani Generis,* and other Catholic authorities affirm that God creates each individual soul at its infusion into the human body.

The Lutheran Postulate of Righteousness and Holiness

Whereas the Reformers as a whole repudiated the Roman distinction between image and likeness with its sub-biblical implications, the Lutheran wing of the Reformation claimed that the *imago* consists chiefly of moral likeness to God. Commenting on Genesis 1:26, Luther rejects both Augustine's thesis that the image resides in the triad of memory, intellect, and will and the dualistic medieval schema involving natural and supernatural endowments. Luther believed that such theories painted too optimistic a picture of humanity under sin. Moreover, "if these powers are the image of God, it will follow that Satan was created according to the image of God, since he surely has these natural endowments, such as memory and a very superior intellect and a most determined will, to a far higher degree than we have them."[26] Troubled by the semi-Pelagianism of the Roman definition—whereby the person works for salvation by his natural powers—Luther insists that the *imago* consists of the righteousness, holiness, and wisdom God gave to Adam, but which subsequently were lost at the Fall. Comments Luther, "My understanding of the image of God is this: that Adam . . . not only knew God and believed that He was good, but that he also lived a life that was wholly godly; that is, he was without the fear of death or of any other danger, and was content with God's favor."[27] The wisdom, moral uprightness, freedom of will, and fitness for eternity (the content of the *imago*), forfeited by sin, is restored to the believer in this life by the Gospel (1 Cor. 15:48; Eph. 4:21–24).

Melanchthon agrees that the *imago* consists of the wisdom and righteousness with which Adam was originally endowed: "Through the Holy Spirit God kindled in Adam and Eve the wonderful light of wisdom, through which they knew God, number, order, virtue, and vice, and their hearts and members were pure and in true order, and obedient to the light in the under-standing, and their hearts glowed with love and joy to God."[28]

The Lutheran doctrinal standards concur that the *imago* resides in Adam's original righteousness and capacity to know God. Thus the Formula of Concord states: "Man was created of God in the beginning pure and holy and free from sin."[29] The Lutheran dogmatician Quenstedt typically defines the *imago* as "an entire conformity with the wisdom, justice, immortality, and majesty of God, which was divinely con-created in the first man, in order that he might perfectly know, love, and glorify God, his Creator."[30]

Lutheran anthropology largely upholds an essential dichotomy. The doctrines of creation, redemption, and the resurrection of the dead confirm that within the unity of the person one may posit material (i.e., body) and immaterial (i.e., soul/spirit) realities.[31] Luther, however, appears to have favored an essential dichotomy and a functional trichotomy. He observed that analogous to the temple with its Holy of Holies, Holy Place, and outer court, we may speak functionally of the human person's spirit (the faculty for comprehending God), soul (the instrument of reason and the emotions), and the body (the material vessel that houses the immaterial self).[32] On the other hand, Delitzsch and a few Lutheran contemporaries argued for an essential trichotomy. Concerning the origin of the soul, Luther and his followers favored traducianism. They claim that it is most consistent with original sin and that it avoids implicating God in the creation of a sinful soul. Quenstedt, for example, teaches, "The soul of the first man was immediately created by God; but the soul of Eve was produced by propagation, and the souls of the rest of men . . . are propagated, *per traducem,* by their parents."[33]

The Functional View of Pelagians, Socinians, and Others

Pelagians in the patristic era, Socinians at the time of the Reformation, rationalistic Arminians in the seventeenth century, and certain mediating theologians in recent times interpret the *imago* functionally as the person's exercise of dominion over the earth. The argument proceeds by declaring that as God reigns over the universe as Lord, so the human person as image-bearer rules the earth in God's stead. Pelagius identified the *imago* as the endowment of reason whereby the person knows God, of free will whereby he chooses to do the good, and of power to rule the lower creation. Pelagius also placed emphasis on the person acting responsibly to fulfill his God-given tasks. The Socinians denied that original righteousness was lost in Eden, and defined the *imago* as the person's exercise of dominion over the earth. According to the *Racovian Catechism*, the image of God "properly imports the authority of man, and his dominion over all inferior creatures, which result from the reason and judgment communicated to him."[34] The rationalistic Arminians, or Remonstrants, in Holland held a similar view.

According to Gerhard von Rad, the *imago* has nothing to do with the being of a person: "The divine likeness is not to be found in the personality of man, in his free Ego, in his dignity or in his free use of moral capacity, etc."[35] Rather, the Old Testament focuses on the task or mission of the person. Von Rad notes that in the ancient world a king set up images of himself throughout the empire in order to establish his claim to dominion. The author of Genesis appropriated this ancient sense of *ṣelem* to indicate that "man is placed upon earth in God's image as God's sovereign emblem. He is really only God's representative, summoned to maintain and enforce God's claim to dominion over the earth. The decisive thing about man's similarity to God, therefore, is his function in the nonhuman world."[36] D. J. A. Clines, who follows von Rad, begins with the common non-evangelical judgment that the person is not a composite of various parts, but is a psychosomatic unity. Thus the whole person, not merely some higher reality, is the image of God. Clines interprets the *imago* in terms of man's functioning as God's representative or vizier over the lower creation: "The image is to be understood not so much ontologically as existentially: it comes to expression not in the nature of man so much as in his activity and function. This function is to represent God's lordship to the lower orders of creation."[37]

Leonard Verduin, the Calvinist scholar, argues that God created the human person in his image to exercise sovereignty and to subdue the rest of creation. Man is the divinely appointed "dominion-haver" and "conquerer" of the created order. Concerning God's creation of the person as *imago*, "the idea of dominion-having stands out as the central feature. That man is a creature meant for dominion-having and that as such he is in the image of his Maker—this is the burden of the creation account given in the book of Genesis."[38]

The Relational View of Neoorthodox and Theistic Existentialists

Neoorthodox authorities generally follow the existentialist indifference to questions pertaining to human nature and focus rather on the the person's relation to God and others. Thus Dietrich Bonhoeffer claims that the *imago* pertains not to an *analogia entis* (analogy of being) but to an *analogia relationis* (analogy of relation). The likeness between Creator and creature resides chiefly in the experience of being free for the other. God, as the prototype, is free for man. Correspondingly, the human person enjoys a threefold freedom that constitutes him the image of God. (1) The person, by means of the Word of God, is free to worship the Creator. (2) The person is free to relate to his fellow creatures. In this regard Bonhoeffer sees the male-female relation as paradigmatic. "Man is free for man, *Male and female he created them*. Man is not alone, he is in duality, and it is in this dependence on the other that his creatureliness consists."[39] And (3) the person enjoys freedom vis-à-vis the lower creation. The person is not enslaved to the cosmos, but is free to rule over it as lord. Bonhoeffer concludes thus: "Man's being-free-for God and the other person and his being-free-from the creature in his dominion over it is the image of God in the first man."[40]

Karl Barth's mature thinking on the *imago,* stimulated by Bonhoeffer's seminal ideas, appears in volume 3 of his *Church Dogmatics.* The key to understanding the being of God and thus the being of man is the plural pronoun in Genesis 1:26—"Let *us* make man . . . ." Barth observes that God is not a solitary being; rather, he exists in unbroken face-to-face relationship. That is, within the triune God there exists a profound "differentiation and relation between the 'I' and the 'Thou.' "[41] On the human side of the analogy, in what proves to be a relation of nature, Barth finds that "the coexistence and cooperation in God himself is repeated in the relation of man to man."[42] Since the Genesis statement of the person's creation in God's image is immediately followed by the reference to man as "male and female" (Gen. 1:27; 5:1–2), Barth judges that the differentiation and relationship of male and female is the great paradigm of the relation between the person and God and between the person and his fellow. Thus fundamentally Barth defines the

imago in terms of the polarity of the sexes, i.e., as the "juxtaposition and conjunction of man and man which is that of male and female."[43] But this "I-Thou" relation between the sexes can be extended to the person's "I-Thou" confrontation with his fellow human being. In each case, Barth claims, a face-to-face relationship constitutes human personhood.

Barth continues that man as *imago* is capable of personal relations with God. In what proves to be a relation of grace, Barth views the person as a being whom God addresses as "Thou" and who can answer as "I." The exact nature of man's relation with God is seen in terms of the incarnate Christ's relation to God. But Jesus of Nazareth, the true Man, is the Elected One. Consequently, Barth argues, the image defined in terms of the person's relation to God consists in his eternal election or in his being God's covenant partner— i.e., in hearing the Word of God and in obedient service to God. For the person to forsake this relationship and persist in godlessness would be to forfeit his humanity. But the divine will to save ensures that ultimately this will not occur. Barth's explication of the *imago* thus relates to his doctrine of universalism: "To be a man is to be in the sphere where the first and merciful will of God toward his creatures, his will to save and keep them from the power of nothingness, is revealed in action."[44] We conclude that for Barth persons are image-bearers of God because they are capable of sustaining a broad range of "I-Thou" relationships.

Brunner likewise argues that the ontological definition of the *imago* must be replaced by a relational one. Thus it is necessary "to interpret the *imago Dei* as *relation* and not as *substance,* as something which is part of man's nature."[45] Brunner argues that as in all theological statements, so here we must begin with Jesus Christ, namely, with the Logos of John's Gospel. Thus Brunner states that human personality is constituted by an "I-Thou" relation to the Logos of God, even in those who do not explicitly acknowledge Christ. In the Bible, Brunner continues, the rubric "image of God" is used in two senses. The first relation, the *formal image,* is that which distinguishes the person from the animal. By virtue of his relation to the Light—i.e., the Logos—the person is endowed with understanding, freedom, self-determination, and moral responsibility. Uniquely the person is an "I" that can respond to and glorify God, the supreme "Thou." As Brunner expresses it:

> The heart of the creaturely existence of man is freedom, selfhood, to be an "I," a person. Only an "I" can answer a "Thou," only a Self which is self-determining can freely answer God . . . . Thus the formal aspect of man's nature, as a being "made in the image of God," denotes his being as Subject, or his freedom; it is this which differentiates his specifically *human* quality; it is this which is given to him.[46]

The foregoing relation, which establishes a point of contact between God and the human person, is universal and cannot be forfeited.

The second relation, the *material image,* exists where the preceding is actualized in faith, i.e., where the person concretely trusts, loves, and glorifies God. In Brunner's language, the material aspect of the *imago* "is identical with 'being-in-the-Word' of God;" it is "existence in Jesus Christ, the Word made flesh."[47] This relationship was lost at the Fall and can be restored only through a saving experience with Christ. This second aspect of the *imago* is peculiar to the believer; the sinner has no share in the material image.

According to existentialist philosophy, thinking that deals abstractly with the person or objectifies him truly depersonalizes him. Rather, this school focuses on the person as a conscious self in the concrete situations of life. John Macquarrie, a Scottish existentialist theologian, insists that one cannot talk of a substantial self or an implanted soul that at death separates from the body. Christian anthropology deals rather with the authentic self that is actualized in community through an open-ended process of decision and commitment. Thus "the self is not given ready-made but has to be made in the course of existence . . . . What is given at the outset is not a fixed entity but a potentiality for becoming a self."[48] Macquarrie regards the *imago* as a function of existence rather than essence. "We must think of the *imago Dei* more in terms of a potentiality for being that is given to man with his very being, than in terms of a fixed 'endowment' or 'nature.' Man is a creature, but as the creature that 'exists,' he has an openness into which he can move outward and upward."[49] A constellation of factors constitute authentic selfhood. These include, in addition to openness to others, self-giving love and the capacity for letting others be. In the Christian life, however, the person "gains his true being, and the intention of the Creator is realized."[50]

Most neoorthodox, theistic existentialists, and so-called "biblical theologians" view the person as a psychosomatic unity. Biblical words such as "spirit," "soul," "heart," "flesh," and "body" are nontechnical terms, each of which is said to connote the whole person. Edmond Jacob, writing in Kittel's *Wordbook,* claims that Greek speculation significantly influenced the traditional Christian formulations. Consequently, "older distinctions between dichotomy and trichotomy must be abandoned so far as Old Testament anthropology is concerned. Israelite anthropology is monistic. Man is always seen in his totality, which is quickened by a unitary life."[51] In teaching that the whole person is annihilated by death just as he is restored to life by the Resurrection, Cullmann upholds the radical unity of the person. "The Jewish and Christian interpretation of creation excludes the whole Greek dualism between body and soul."[52] J. A. T. Robinson, similarly concerned with the whole person in relation to God, affirms that the Hebrew mind knew nothing of the Greek antithesis between a mortal body and an immortal soul. The biblical terms *sarx, sōma, pneuma,* and *psychē* fail to support a dichotomy or trichotomy of distinctive elements. "The parts of the body are thought of, not primarily from the point of view of their difference from, and interrelation with, other parts, but as signifying or stressing different aspects of the whole man in relation to God."[53] G. C. Berkouwer, Dale Moody, and Richard H. Bube likewise uphold monism and refuse to posit any essential differentiation in the human person.

The View of Augustine and Some Reformed and Evangelical Authorities

Augustine viewed the human person as a unity of soul and body, where the soul is "the whole life of the body."[54] Thus "man is a noble being created to the image and likeness of God, not insofar as he is housed in a mortal body, but in that he is superior to brute beasts because of the gift of a rational soul."[55] Statements such as this lead some to conclude that Augustine posits a rationalistic view of the *imago.* But Augustine's holistic interpretation makes the person's intellectual and rational capacities inseparable from one's desires and will. The person metaphysically is a soul (*anima*) in a body. The one person thinks, feels, and wills. Augustine insists that these three capacities of the human soul cannot be divorced from one another, just as the three persons of

the Trinity cannot be separated.[56] Thus the mind does not function apart from the feelings, nor the will apart from the mind, etc. The soul's thinking capacities consist of *intellectus,* the intuitive cognizance that knows changeless wisdom (*sapientia*), and *ratio,* the rational cognizance that knows facts (*scientia*). Love, which Augustine views as the "weight" of the soul,[57] consists, positively, of desire for God above the creation, and, negatively, as sinful lust (*libido*) for the creation rather than the Creator. Finally, the will refers to the self-moving or self-determining power of the soul. The exercise of the will produces the emotions, such as joy, fear, and sadness. As created, the human will was free to choose between good and evil. How the will is exercised determines the person's ethical condition.

As the preceding suggests, Augustine viewed the human person holistically as an essential dichotomy. Each human "unites in one person a rational soul and a body."[58] He affirmed that the soul is superior to the body in that the former gives life to the latter. Without the soul the body would cease to exist. Augustine appears, however, to make a subtle distinction between a higher set of capacities independent of the body (*spiritus*) and a lower set of capacities related to the body (*animus*). "The entire nature of man is certainly spirit (*spiritus*), soul (*anima*), and body (*corpus*)."[59] While not dogmatic on the issue of the soul's origin, Augustine appears to favor the traducian hypothesis. This view is preferable because Augustine judges it more consistent with the Bible's teaching on original sin.

John Calvin claims that "the likeness of God extends to the whole excellence by which man's nature towers over all the kinds of living creatures."[60] The proper seat of the image, however, is the soul, although Calvin grants that the image shines forth in the person's corporeal being. "The primary seat of the divine image is in the mind and heart, or in the soul and its powers, yet there is no part of man, not even the body itself, in which some sparks do not glow."[61] The integrity of soul that constitutes the *imago* includes both natural and supernatural endowments. What these consisted of prior to their corruption in Eden is seen in the restoration of the image effected by Christ's redemption. Exegeting 2 Corinthians 3:18; Ephesians 4:24; and Colossians 3:10, Calvin identifies the natural gifts included in the *imago* as "perfect intelligence," "right judgment," free-will, sound affections, and properly ordered emotions.[62] Calvin emphasizes not only the possession of these faculties, but also their proper use vis-à-vis God and the neighbor. From these same Pauline texts Calvin identifies the supernatural gifts that form the *imago* as "faith," "love of God," "righteousness," and "zeal for holiness."[63] Not content with the functional definition of dominion over the creation, Calvin prefers a comprehensive definition of the *imago* that does justice to persons as God intended them to be and to live. Thus Calvin concludes, "God's image was visible in the light of the mind, in the uprightness of the heart, and in the soundness of all the parts."[64]

The Reformed Confessions reaffirm Calvin's explication. The Belgic Confession states that God formed man "after his own image and likeness, good, righteous, and holy, capable in all things to will agreeably to the will of God" (art. XIV). According to the Heidelberg Catechism, "God created man good, and after his image—that is, in righteousness and true holiness; that he might rightly know God his Creator, heartily love him, and live with him in eternal blessedness, to praise and glorify him" (Lord's Day 3, q. 6). The Westminster Confession similarly affirms, "[God] created man, male and female, with reasonable and immortal souls, endued with knowledge, righteousness, and true holiness, after his own image, having the law of God written in their hearts, and power to fulfill it" (ch. IV.2).[65]

Reformed theologians generally preserved Calvin's formulation of natural and supernatural features that constitute the *imago,* some adding the notion of dominion over the lower creation. So John Wolleb writes, "The image of God consists partly of natural gifts—the simple, invisible substance of angels and of human souls, life, intellect, will, and immortality; and partly of supernatural ones—original blessedness, rectitude and majesty of intellect and will, and majesty and dominion over other creatures."[66]

Later Reformed theologians referred to the broader and narrower dimensions of the *imago,* the first retained in the sinner, and the second lost. Bavinck, for example, identifies three aspects of the broad sense of the *imago*: (1) Unlike the animals, humans possess a spiritual nature or immortal soul, by virtue of which we transcend the earth. (2) Persons are characterized by self-conscious existence that expresses itself in thinking, willing, and feeling (emotions). And (3) even the body is not excluded from expressing the image of God. "To the extent that the body serves as tool and instrument of the spirit, it exhibits a certain resemblance to, and gives us some notion of, the way in which God is busy in the world."[67] The narrower dimension of the *imago* includes knowledge of God, righteousness, and holiness, not as superadded gifts, but as intrinsic to humanity created by God. In order to escape dualism, Bavinck integrally relates the broader and the narrower dimensions of the *imago* in what he calls the "organic" view of the image.

Berkhof posits five aspects to the image of God in persons.[68] (1) The *spiritual image*: the person is a spiritual being, which means that one is endowed with the qualities of simplicity, spirituality, and immortality. (2) The *rational image*: the person is a rational and moral being, which means he has intellectual power, volitional freedom, and natural affections. (3) The *moral image*: the person was created in true knowledge, righteousness, and positive holiness. These qualities are being restored in the believer through the saving work of Christ. (4) The *corporeal image*: Scripture affirms that the whole person, not just the soul, was created in God's image. The body functions as the proper organ of the soul. And (5) the *functional image:* dominion over the lower creation forms part of the essence of the person.

Most Reformed theologians and many evangelicals favor dichotomy, although a few support the trichotomous theory. Calvin believed that a person consists of two parts, an immaterial soul or spirit and a material body. The soul, as an incorporeal substance distinct from the body, forms the nobler part of the person. It animates the body and blends its many members into a harmonious whole. The Reformed Confessions (i.e., Heidelberg, Second Helvetic) and post-Reformation theologians consistently viewed the person as an intimate union of soul and body. W. G. T. Shedd typically appeals to Genesis 2:7 to argue that God formed the person by infusing an immaterial rational spirit into a material body. L. Berkhof advances the theory of "realistic dualism," whereby soul and body mysteriously interact on each other in an organic union of life.[69] Strong favors the theory of essential dichotomy and functional trichotomy. Ontologically the person consists of an immaterial soul/spirit and a material body. But functionally *psychē* describes the person's immaterial part in its horizontal relations (i.e. those powers common with the animals), whereas *pneuma* describes the immaterial part in its Godward relations (i.e., its capacity to appropriate the Holy Spirit).[70] L. S. Chafer, *The Scofield Reference Bible* (1909), Watchman Nee, and other evangelical sources uphold trichotomy. *The Scofield Reference Bible* relates the *imago* to the person's triune structure as soul, spirit, and body.[71] Thus the spirit is the seat of God-consciousness (i.e., knowledge, morality), the soul the seat of self-consciousness (emotions, affections, desires), and the body is the seat of world-consciousness (the senses).

Most Reformed scholars follow Calvin in upholding the creationist theory of the soul's origin. Calvin views the notion that souls are passed on from parents to children as untenable.[72] John Wolleb states boldly, "The human soul is not reproduced by transmission of semen, but is put into the body as immediately created by God."[73] H. Heppe, the two Hodges, Kuyper, Bavinck, and L. Berkhof also uphold the creationist position. Other Reformed and evangelical scholars, such as Edwards, Hopkins, Shedd, Strong, Buswell, Thiessen, and G. Clark find the evidence for traducianism convincing. Shedd, whose treatment is most exhaustive, comments, "God created two human individuals, one male and the other female, and in them also created the specific psychico-physical nature from which all the subsequent individuals of the human family are procreated both psychically and physically."[74] Dabney suggests that the solution to this difficult problem may involve elements from both positions. Thus "it may be true that divine power (in bringing substance out of *nihil* into *esse*) and human causation may both act, in originating the being and properties of the infant's soul!"[75]

Other helpful evangelical discussions on the nature of the human person include works by J. Orr,[76] A. A. Hoekema,[77] and M. J. Erickson.[78]

BIBLICAL TEACHING

We now undertake a study of the relevant biblical materials to determine which of the several historical proposals concerning the nature of human persons is most accurate.

Pentateuch

The creation account addresses the nature of the human person with the brief but profound saying of God, " 'Let us make man in our image, in our likeness . . .' " (Gen. 1:26). The Hebrew word for "image," ṣelem (LXX, eikōn), means literally a statue or idol (Num. 33:52; Dan. 2:32) and metaphorically some kind of representation (Ps. 73:20). The word for "likeness," dᵉmût (LXX, homoiōsis), signifies a resemblance (Gen. 5:3; Ezek. 10:1, 22). Linguistic data and usage suggests that there is little difference in meaning between these two Hebrew words. Their equivalence is further established by the fact that (1) no conjunction "and" appears between the two words in the Hebrew text; (2) in Genesis 1:27 and 9:6, when the image is discussed, only ṣelem is used; and (3) in Genesis 5:1 only dᵉmût is used. Significantly the LXX of Genesis 5:1 translates dᵉmût by eikōn rather than the usual homoiōsis. In sum, then, "The words image and likeness reinforce one another: . . . Scripture does not use them as technically distinct expressions."[79] Since the two words connote the same thing, one is not justified in applying "image" and "likeness" to separate aspects of the person as does traditional Roman Catholic theology. Furthermore, the prefix bᵉin bᵉṣalmēnû, is likely a bêt of essence meaning "as," or "in the capacity of" (cf. Exod. 6:3)—hence God says, "Let us make man as our image" or "to be our image."[80] The point is that persons do not have the image; they are the unique representation of God (cf. 1 Cor. 11:7). The general statements concerning the imago in Genesis 1:26–27, 5:1, and 9:6 suggest that in the broadest sense (i.e., metaphysically, intellectually, morally, emotionally, volitionally, and relationally) persons closely resemble God their Maker.[81] Genesis 9:6 mandates death as the penalty for murder, given the special dignity of human persons as God's image-bearers.

Scripture depicts the person metaphysically as a complex material-immaterial unity. Genesis 2:7 describes the twofold action of God that corresponds to the human person's physical and spiritual aspects. Materially God formed Adam's body "from the dust of the ground" ('āpār min-hā'ᵃdāmāh). Concerning the immaterial dimension, God "breathed into his nostrils the breath of life" (nišmat hayyîm; see Gen. 6:17 and 7:22 for animals endowed with the breath of life). As a result of this twofold creative activity, "man became a living being" (lit. a "living soul," nepeš hayyāh). Here nepeš is not a constituent part of the person, but the person or self in the totality of his being (applied to animals in the sense of living creatures, see Gen. 1:20, 30; 2:19; et al.). This complex unity breaks down at death when the breath of life departs the body (Gen. 35:18; 49:33), the latter returning to the ground whence it was formed (Gen. 3:19).[82] The divine command in Deuteronomy 6:5 hardly supports trichotomy: "Love the Lord your God with all your heart (lēbāb) and with all your soul (nepeš) and with all your strength (mᵉ'ōd)." Rather, in this text "heart" connotes the center of the person's inner being,[83] "soul," the whole self with its aggregate of thought, affections, emotions, and will,[84] and "strength" the idea of total commitment. Thus the verse brings together three quasi-synonyms for the purpose of enjoining total and unqualified love for God.

Of further relevance to the person metaphysically, Scripture provides some hints concerning the origin of the human soul. Genesis 1:28 indicates that God created both the male and the female as a body-soul unity and commanded them to propagate the species. Likewise Genesis 2:21–23 relates that Eve as a body-soul unity was produced from Adam, no mention being made of the creation of her soul. A further argument for traducianism is the fact that God completed his creativity on the sixth day and then rested (Gen. 2:2). Although God is now active in preservation and providence, "there is no hint that God ever created anything again."[85] Likewise Genesis 5:3 teaches that Adam (a body-soul unity) fathered a son "in his own likeness, in his own image." The language of Numbers 16:22 (cf. 27:16), describing '*ēl* as the "God of the spirits of all mankind," in context affirms only that God is the giver of all life, and thus he is able also to destroy life in judgment. Hence this verse does not address the issue of the soul's origin.

The early chapters of Genesis shed light also on the relational dimension of the *imago*. Immediately following the statement of man's creation as God's image the text adds: "male (*zākār*) and female (*neqēbāh*) he created them" (Gen. 1:27). These two less commonly used words for the man and woman (cf. Gen. 5:2; Num. 5:3) stress the sexual distinction that underlies the male-female relation in marriage. This relational aspect is made clearer in Genesis 2:18, where God says, "It is not good for the man to be alone. I will make a helper suitable for him." Hence there is truth in the neoorthodox emphasis on the relational aspect of the *imago*. Scripturally the human person was not made for existence in isolation, but is most human in community with his mate, with other human beings, and with God. Kidner is right when he observes that the person "will not live until he loves, giving himself away to another on his own level."[86]

The creation of humanity as male and female (Gen. 1:27), the fact that man and woman were created to help each other (Gen. 2:18), and the fact that the woman (*'iššāh*) shares the same nature of the man (*'îš*) all argue for the ontological equality of the sexes. Yet the fact that the woman was created from the man (Gen. 2:21–23) suggests that fully consistent with this equality of personhood there nevertheless existed prior to the Fall a functional ordering of male and female within the marriage relation. The Lord's statement "He will rule over you" indicates the functional relation for unity in the family after the Fall. One authority comments, "Eve, standing for all wives, was given to understand that in the home the husband 'shall rule over thee.' Such leadership as is appropriate—and it varies greatly—for a man to give his family is meant."[87]

Given the juxtaposition of our being created as God's image and our investiture with dominion over the lower forms of life (Gen. 1:26, 28), the question arises whether dominion-having is an intrinsic part of the *imago*. In Genesis 1:26 the existence of a simple *wāw* ("and") between the statement of the person's creation as image and the command to exercise dominion suggests that the latter is a consequence of the former. God purposed that the human person, as the unique representation of God, should exercise stewardship over the lower forms of earthly life. That is, by virtue of his ontological status as God's image, the person is divinely entrusted with the special function of dominion-having.

Poetry and Wisdom

Psalm 8 vividly contrasts the greatness of God and the smallness of humans. Compared with the majesty of God and the magnitude of the universe, the human person appears highly insignificant (vv. 1–4). The rhetorical question, "What is man ['$enôš$]?" highlights the human person's frailty and mortality (cf. Pss. 39:4–6; 90:10). Nevertheless (according to a possible reading of v. 5), the person is clothed with dignity and honor by virtue of his creation in the divine *imago*. As a unique being constituted in the image of God, the human person exercises dominion over the lower creation (vv. 6–8; cf. Heb. 2:6–8). Therefore, the smaller man is in relation to the rest of the created universe, the greater he is because of his being a creature of God's special care and consideration. For this reason we can read the question of Psalm 8:4 as an exclamation: "What is man!" The sum of the matter is that "Psalm 8 gives no identification of *dominion* and image, even though the meaning of man's dominion and the special place which man occupies in the created world are strongly expressed."[88]

Metaphysically, the poetic literature confirms the body-soul/spirit unity of the person. When the psalmist exclaims to God, "My soul thirsts for you, my body longs for you" (Ps. 63:1), both *nepeš* and *bāśār* signify the whole person. Yet the phrase in Job 4:19 "how much more those who live in houses of clay" distinguishes between the immaterial and the material aspects of the person. A number of texts speak of the spirit (*nešāmāh* and *rûah*) from God that animates the physical body (Job 27:3; 32:8; 33:4; 34:14). Ecclesiastes 12:7 attests the twofold nature of the complex unity that is the person: "The dust returns to the ground it came from, and the spirit returns to God who gave it" (cf. 3:19–21). Here *rûah,* as we have seen, denotes the principle of life and consciousness that quickens and controls the physical body (cf. Pss. 77:3; 143:7). With the words "You created my inmost being; you knit me together in my mother's womb" (Ps. 139:13; cf. Isa. 44:24), the psalmist confesses that God is Creator of both the psychological and the physical aspects of the person. Also from this text we may infer that the fetus is properly a living human being.

Ecclesiastes 7:29 affirms the human person's moral likeness to his Creator: "God made man upright, but men have gone in search of many schemes." This text teaches that the person was created neither sinful nor morally neutral, but in a condition of moral rectitude. The adjective "upright" (*yāšār*), predicated of God in Deuteronomy 32:4; Psalm 111:8, et al., here refers to "the state of the heart which is disposed to faithfulness or obedience."[89] Conscience, that faculty that attests a person's compliance or noncompliance with the implanted moral law, is described under the figure of a lamp in Proverbs 20:27: "The lamp of the LORD searches the spirit (*nešāmāh*) of a man; it searches out his innermost being."

The Prophets

Some scholars cite texts in the prophets to support the creationist hypothesis for the soul's origin. But Isaiah 42:5, far from teaching the specific doctrine of creationism, affirms that God's power, manifest in his creation of heaven, earth, and earth's human inhabitants, is capable of bringing salvation to the nations. Mention of God's endowment of persons with life is subordinate to the primary emphasis on his unlimited power. The same comment applies to Zechariah 12:1, where mention of the Lord as Creator of heaven, earth, and "the spirit of man within him," highlights the totality of God's sovereign power that is competent to direct history to its goal. The prophet's use of the verb *yāṣar* in relation to the soul, with its nuance of shaping or forming, might be seen as supporting the traducian position. But again, the issue of the soul's origin is nowhere in view. Isaiah 57:16, with its phrase "the breath of man that I have created," affirms only that God breathed into the person the life-force that animates his body (cf. Gen. 2:7).

Summary of Old Testament Terminology

A precis of the principal Old Testament anthropological terms follows. *Rûaḥ,* "spirit" (cf. *nᵉšāmāh,* "breath") denotes the God-given breath of life that animates the body (Gen. 7:22; Job 12:10; Eccl. 12:7). The spirit is the center of rationality (Deut. 34:9), spiritual understanding (Job 20:3), the emotions (Ps. 77:3), volition (Dan. 5:20), jealousy (Num. 5:14, 30), etc. *Nepeš,* "soul," on the other hand, generally connotes the whole person or "I" (Gen. 36:6; Pss. 104:1; 119:175; of God, see Isa. 42:1). Thus Berkhof comments that in general "man *has* spirit, but *is* soul."[90] But in not a few texts *nepeš* signifies the immaterial principle of life that departs the body at death (Gen. 35:18; 1 Kings 17:21–22). As such the soul is the locus of the intellect (1 Sam. 2:35), the religious life (Pss. 42:1; 84:2), the emotions (Job 7:11; Ps. 6:3), the will (Gen. 23:8), and various drives and passions (Ps. 10:3; Prov. 21:10). In this sense, *nepeš* and *rûaḥ* overlap significantly (Job 7:11; Isa. 26:9; cf. Exod. 6:9 with Num. 21:4).

The heart, *lēb* or *lēbāb,* connotes the center of the inner life of the person (Exod. 7:3, 13; Ps. 9:1; Jer. 17:9). Scripture represents it as the locus of the intellect (Deut. 15:9), the emotions (Ps. 45:1; of God, see Gen. 6:6), and the will (Exod. 35:26). Thus frequently spirit, soul, and heart denote the same immaterial center of the person's being. As such, these three terms are differentiated not from one another but from the physical body. In sum, the Old Testament words describing the person are not technically precise by modern standards. Considerable flexibility in usage and overlapping of meanings occurs. The data indicates, however, that the Old Testament views the human person as a complex immaterial-material unity, where the link between soul/spirit and body is exceedingly intimate.

The Synoptic Gospels

The three Synoptic Gospels emphasize the fact that metaphysically the human person is dichotomous. In Matthew 6:25 Jesus exhorts the disciples not to be anxious about the needs of the "life" (*psychē*) and the "body" (*sōma*). Reflecting the general Jewish concept of *nepeš,* "*psychē* embraces the whole rational life of man for which he concerns himself and of which he takes constant care."[91] The immaterial life principle that is soul animates and directs the person's physical body. Jesus also upheld dichotomy when he said, "Do not be afraid of those who kill the body but cannot kill the soul [*psychē*]. Rather, be afraid of the One who can destroy both soul and body in hell" (Matt. 10:28; cf. Luke 12:5). Moreover, the Gospels indicate that shortly before Jesus died he cried out: "Father, into your hands I commit my spirit [*pneuma*]" (Luke 23:46; cf. Matt. 27:50). Here the word "spirit" bears the Hebrew meaning of the immaterial life-force that quickens the mortal body. The parable of the rich man and Lazarus (Luke 16:19–31) teaches the continued conscious existence of the immaterial self after the demise of the body. Quoting Deuteronomy 6:5, Jesus taught in Matthew 22:37 that the human person's highest duty is to "love the Lord your God with all your heart [*kardia*] and with all your soul [*psychē*] and with all your mind [*dianoia*]." Mark 12:30 and Luke 10:27 add a fourth word, "strength" (*ischys*). Each of these Greek words signify different aspects of the person's inner life—the aggregate of terms underscoring the totality of love due to God.

Primitive Christianity/Acts

Consistent with its evangelistic purpose, Acts says relatively little about the ontological nature of the person. Luke, however, attests dichotomy when he relates in Acts 7:59 that Stephen at his martyrdom prayed, "Lord Jesus, receive my spirit [*pneuma*]." At death the immaterial self separates from the body, leaving the latter lifeless and subject to decay. Likewise metaphysically, a statement of Paul at Athens would appear to support the traducian theory for the soul's origin: in Acts 17:26 Paul affirms of God: "From one man he made every nation of men, that they should inhabit the whole earth." The apostle here upholds the biological unity of the human family, of which Adam is the natural head. This suggests that both the material and the immaterial aspects of the human person are transmitted by procreation, since the solidarity of the race hardly pertains only to physical bodies. Acts furthermore reflects awareness of the nature of the person morally when it records Paul's claim to a good conscience (Acts 23:1; 24:16). The conscience (*syneidēsis*, "co-knowing") is the faculty of the soul that dialogues between the implanted moral law and the self, indicating compliance or noncompliance with God's unchanging standards. Paul's conscience did not condemn him, because of the rectitude of his life.

The Pauline Literature

Concerning the *imago* metaphysically, Paul consistently infers that human nature is dichotomous. The person is a complex unity consisting of "spirit" and "body" (Rom. 8:10; 1 Cor. 5:3, Col. 2:5), the "inner being" and the "body" (Rom. 7:22–23; cf. 8:23), and the inner and outer person (Rom. 2:28–29; 2 Cor. 4:16). Two principal Pauline doctrines, namely, the doctrine of redemption and the intermediate state, establish dichotomy. According to Romans 8:23, salvation in this life is applied to the inner or immaterial self, whereas in the life to come it will be applied to the outer self or the body. Philippians 1:22–24 attests Paul's longing to leave this earthly body (*sarx*) to be with Christ in the disembodied state.

Second Corinthians 5:1–10 warrants more extensive comment. Scholars such as J. A. T. Robinson interpret the text corporately as the body of Christ, the church.[92] But since believers already "have [been] . . . clothed with Christ" (Gal. 3:27), we judge that in this text Paul discusses the resurrection body of the believer. In verses 2–4 the apostle teaches that believers long to receive the resurrection body at the Parousia, rather than "to be unclothed" or "be found naked." The latter expressions signify the disembodied state of the soul at death. In what may be a veiled polemic against incipient Gnosticism, Paul states that the Christian hope includes being "clothed" (*ependysasthai*, v. 2) with a resurrection body suited for the life to come (cf. Phil. 3:21). Yet if the choice were between living or dying, Paul would elect the latter: "We . . . would prefer to be away from the body and at home with the Lord" (v. 8). In conclusion, "by his use of the word *gymnos* ['naked'] in 5:3 and by what he says in vv. 6–8, Paul shows that he was aware of the concepts both of a disembodied soul and the intermediate state."[93]

Does 1 Thessalonians 5:23 contradict the preceding? In the first half of the verse Paul prays for the sanctification of the whole person; and in the second half he repeats that concern in other words: "May your whole spirit, soul and body be kept blameless at the coming of our Lord Jesus Christ." That Paul emphasizes the whole person and not specific constituent parts is further indicated by the fact that the verb "kept" and the adjective "whole" are singular, even though they govern all three nouns. With F. F. Bruce we conclude, "It is precarious to try to construct a tripartite doctrine of human nature on the juxtaposition of the three nouns, *pneuma, psychē* and *sōma*."[94] Neither is trichotomy upheld in 1 Corinthians 2:14–3:4, where Paul distinguishes between the *psychikos anthrōpos* (2:14), *ho pneumatikos* (2:15; 3:1), and *ho sarkinos/ho sarkikos* (3:1, 3). Rather, the first expression ("the natural man," AV) denotes the person endowed with a human soul (Gen. 2:7) who lacks the Holy Spirit; the second ("the spiritual man," NIV) the Christian who lives in the realm of the Spirit; and the third pair of terms ("worldly," NIV; "carnal," AV) denote with slight shades of emphasis the believer who remains controlled by the flesh.

Paul sheds further light on the nature of the *imago* by pointing to the restoration through Christ of that which was tarnished by the Fall. Thus the apostle refers to the intellectual dimension of the *imago* when in Romans 12:2 he commands believers to "be transformed by the renewing of your mind [*nous*]." The *nous* that is being renewed by the Spirit is "mind, the thinking power, reason in its moral quality and activity."[95] Paul makes the same point in Colossians 3:10 when he commands: "Put on the new self, which is being renewed in knowledge [*epignōsis*] in the

image of its Creator." The end of this process is the attainment of perfect knowledge in the age to come (1 Cor. 13:12): "Now I know in part; then I shall know fully *epiginōskō*)." Paul speaks of the renewal of the imago morally in Ephesians 4:22–24, where he urges the Ephesian Christians "to put on the new self, created to be like God in true righteousness and holiness [*en dikaiosynē kai hosiotēti tēs alētheias*]." Paul implies that originally the person possessed moral rectitude, but lost the same at the Fall. Nevertheless, by Holy Spirit sanctification, the primal purity and devotion to God is being restored in those who believe. As Berkouwer observes, "Grace brings about a historical transition from the old to the new man, to that man who is created after God's image in true righteousness and holiness."[96] The apostle further attests the moral dimension of the *imago* in Romans 2:14–15, where he claims that God has implanted the moral law on each person's heart so that even the pagan "by nature" (*physai*, i.e., instinctively) is guided by its precepts. In addition, the faculty of conscience communicates to the person not only a sense of moral oughtness or obligation, but also the extent to which one obeys the law of God.

For Paul the restoration of the *imago* means that the believer progressively becomes like Christ, who in a unique sense is the image eikōn) of God (2 Cor. 4:4; Col. 1:15; cf. Heb. 1:3, which uses the stronger word, *charaktēr*). The link between Christ and the renewed *imago* is that the Son, who shares God's very nature, is the head and prototype of the new humanity God is bringing into existence. The Christian's conformity to Christ is a process that begins in this life. So Paul affirms that "we, who with unveiled faces all reflect the Lord's glory, are being transformed into his likeness eikōn) with ever-increasing glory" (2 Cor. 3:18; cf.

Gal. 4:19). But complete moral conformity to Christ (Rom. 8:29) will be realized at the resurrection, when the believer will be clothed with a spiritual body. Thus, "just as we have borne the likeness [eikōn] of the earthly man, so shall we bear the likeness [eikōn] of the man from heaven" (1 Cor. 15:49).

Concerning the relation between the sexes, Paul in 1 Corinthians 11:11 argues for the full spiritual equality of male and female "in the Lord." The apostle makes this point of absolute spiritual equality most explicitly in Galatians 3:28: "There is neither . . . male nor female, for you are all one in Christ Jesus." Yet alongside this indisputable fact of spiritual equality, the apostle repeatedly affirms a functional ordering in the family and in the church for the sexes. Thus in 1 Corinthians 11:3 Paul teaches that God is the head (kephalē) of Christ, who is the head of the man, who is head of the woman. "Head" here signifies "a relationship of superior authority."[97] That "the woman is the glory of man" (v. 7) and that she was created for man (v. 9), appear not to be a local cultural perspective, given the apostle's appeal to the creation account of their respective origins: "for man did not come from woman, but woman from man" (v. 8). The notion of submission is made more explicit in Ephesians 5:22–24. Within the Christian society, Paul states generally that believers are to "submit to one another out of reverence for Christ," in the snse of mutual consideration and deference. He then proceeds to discuss specific examples of divinely ordained submission: wives to husbands, children to parents, and servants to masters. In particular, the wife's duty is to be subject (pass. of hypotassō) to her husband, "for the husband is the head of the wife as Christ is the head of the church" (v. 23). The passive of hypotassō, "be subject to," "be under the authority of," is used of the submission

of the boy Jesus to his parents (Luke 2:51) and of the submission of citizens to the governing authority (Rom. 13:1). With respect to 1 Corinthians 11:3 and Ephesians 5:22–24, if Christ's submission to the Father's headship and the man's submission to Christ's headship are not culturally relative, neither is a wife's submission to her husband (cf. Col. 3:18; Titus 2:5; 1 Peter 3:1). Thus it appears true that "the subjection of wives to husbands . . . is according to a divinely willed order."[98]

Yet Paul lifts the male-female relation far beyond the standard of the pagan world with his insistence that, analogous to Christ's love for the church, the wife's submission to her husband must be matched by his love for her (Eph. 5:25, 28, 33). First Corinthians 14:34; 1 Timothy 2:12–14; and Titus 2:5 further attest the functional ordering of male and female. Foulkes sums up the matter as follows: "In the family, for its order and its unity, there must be leadership, and the responsibility of leadership is that of the husband and father, and his authority must be accepted."[99]

The Johannine Literature

Metaphysically, John differentiates between the material and immaterial aspects of the person. Thus in 3 John 2, the apostle prays that Gaius might prosper in health and in external circumstances, even as his soul (psyche) flourishes. Here again, psyche connotes the true immaterial self that departs the body at death. Revelation 6:9 speaks of the souls of the martyrs in heaven awaiting reunion with their bodies at the resurrection. Jesus' saying in John 3:6 tends to support the traducian proposal rather than the creationist: "Flesh gives birth to flesh [sarx], but the Spirit gives birth to spirit [pneuma]." Sarx here connotes not the material body, but the whole of human nature apart from God with its consciousness, determinations, and drives. As Plummer expresses it: "What man inherits from his parents is a body with animal life and passions; what he receives from above is a spiritual nature with heavenly capabilities and aspirations."[100]

The volitional aspect of the *imago* is indicated in John 7:17, where Jesus said that "if anyone chooses to do God's will [*ean tis thelē to thelēma autou poiein*], he will find out whether . . . I speak on my own." The Lord assumes that persons created by God are capable of making responsible decisions and commitments. The text further teaches that one attains authentic existence not merely by theoretical reflection or detached observation, but by concretely doing the truth. Responsible personhood, in other words, consists in authentic decision making. But John affirms that the full restoration of the image awaits the Parousia. Even though unaware of the full nature of this transformation, we who are believers have the confidence that "when he appears, we shall be like [*homoios*] him, for we shall see him as he is" (1 John 3:2). "It is enough for us to know that on the last day and through eternity we shall be both with Christ and like Christ."[101]

The descriptions of the operation of the Logos in John 1:4 ("that life was the light of men") and John 1:9 ("The true light that gives light to every man") impinge on the issue of the humanness ontologically. As indicated in volume 1, chapter 2, these two texts teach that the Logos is the personal power that sustains and energizes a person's intellectual, moral, emotional, volitional, and relational faculties. The Logos is the divine energy that enables people in a sinful order to function as the full-orbed beings God created them to be.[102]

Other New Testament Literature

In terms of the human person metaphysically, James concurs with the rest of Scripture by positing a material-immaterial dichotomy. Simply stated, "The body without the spirit is dead" (2:26). "The author likely refers to the concept rooted in the creation narrative of Genesis 2:7—the person is composed of body and breath (which could equally well be termed soul or spirit)."[103] Hebrews upholds dichotomy when it differentiates between a person's heart and his body (Heb. 10:22). Hebrews 4:12—"The word of God is living and active. . . . it penetrates even to dividing soul and spirit, joints and marrow; it judges the thoughts and attitudes of the heart"—makes no metaphysical distinction between soul and spirit. Rather the text reflects a literary technique in which the author used four pairs of quasi-synonyms to stress the all-inclusive power of the Word in a person's life. "That the Word of God probes the inmost recesses of our spiritual being and brings the subconscious motives to light is what is meant."[104]

The argument of Hebrews 7:9–10 points in the direction of the traducian hypothesis for the soul's origin. Upholding the superiority of Christ's priesthood to that of the Levitical order, the author states that "when Melchizedek met Abraham, Levi was still in the body of his ancestor" (v. 10). That is, he viewed Levi as genetically present in his great-grandfather Abraham, as to both his material and his immaterial self. Hebrews 12:9 offers no proof for creationism. The plain contrast in the Greek between "the fathers of our flesh" (KJV) and "the Father of our spirits" (NIV) distinguishes between earthly fathers who discipline on the human level and God who exacts discipline at the spiritual level. "To try to trace metaphysical implications in the phrase is unwarranted."[105]

James points out the shameful inconsistency of using the tongue both to praise God and to curse man "made in

141

God's likeness" (*kath homoiōsin*, James 3:9). Quoting from the LXX of Genesis 1:26, James affirms that Christians should respect the intrinsic dignity of the person as the highest replication of God on earth. Jude is somewhat more specific as he contrasts the human person with "unreasoning animals" *aloga zōa*) that operate "by instinct" (Jude 10; cf. 2 Peter 2:12). Jude assumes that the human person, as opposed to lower forms of life, is a rational being capable of weighing alternatives, choosing a plan, and acting responsibly. Concerning the male-female relation, Peter concurs with the Pauline explication. Thus Peter acknowledges the functional ordering between the sexes by observing that holy women of old "were submissive to their own husbands, like Sarah, who obeyed Abraham and called him her master" (1 Peter 3:5–6; cf. Gen. 18:12). Yet Peter was quick both to uphold the spiritual equality of the two sexes before God and to urge the husband to treat his wife, "as the weaker partner," with kindness and consideration (1 Peter 3:7).

Summary of New Testament Terminology

The New Testament anthropological terms follow the meanings of their Old Testament equivalents with some significant developments. Thus *psychē*, "soul," (1) in its broadest meaning connotes the entire person (Matt. 20:28; Acts 15:26; Rom. 2:9). More commonly, *psychē* (2) signifies the immaterial life-principle in the person and is frequently translated "life" (Matt. 10:28; Luke 14:26; James 1:21). This natural principle of life is the seat of the intellect, memory, emotions, and volition. And, given the new reality of the Holy Spirit, *psychē* (3) occasionally denotes that aspect of the immaterial self that relates to God and to spiritual concerns (Luke 1:46; Heb. 6:19; 1 Peter 2:25).

Pneuma, "spirit," (1) occasionally bears the common Old Testament meaning of the immaterial life-force that animates the physical body (Matt. 27:50; Acts 7:59; James 2:26). But with the advent of the Holy Spirit, *pneuma* (2) assumes the primary meaning of the immaterial self in relation to God and the spiritual realm. *Pneuma* is used in this extended sense in John 11:33; Acts 17:16; 1 John 4:2; et al., but it is most common in Paul (Rom. 8:16; 1 Cor. 14:14; Gal. 6:18). New Testament usage suggests that occasionally *psychē* approaches the meaning of the *pneuma*, i.e., the immaterial self in relation to God, so that here and there the two words are used interchangeably (Luke 1:46; cf. John 12:27 with 13:21; cf. Heb. 12:23 with Rev. 6:9). For Paul the *pneuma* of the believer returns to God at death (1 Cor. 5:5).

Kardia, "heart," corresponds to the Old Testament notion of the governing center of the person (Matt. 18:35; Rom. 6:17; Heb. 3:8). *Nous*, "mind," connotes the mind or the faculty of judgment (Rom. 1:28; 1 Tim. 6:5), particularly the power of spiritual understanding or discernment (Luke 24:45; 1 Cor. 14:14–15; Phil. 4:7).

SYSTEMATIC FORMULATION

We now organize the biblical data on humanness in the image of God (as we did the data concerning God) metaphysically, intellectually, morally, emotionally, volitionally, and relationally. In doing so we find sufficient reason to integrate what several of the alternative historical views of humanity affirm and differ with what they deny.

Human Beings Metaphysically

Intimidated by Kant's inability to know any reality in itself, many people have hesitated to speak of what persons *are*. Instead they speak only about what undefined "persons" *do*. The effect on psychology has been expressed in a semihumorous anecdote. Psychology began as the science (*logos*) of the soul (*psychē*). Then psychology lost its soul and became the science of mind. When psychology lost its mind, it became the science of human behavior! Theology followed a similar nonmetaphysical route.

From God's cognitive revelation, however, we discovered some truth, not only about what God does, but who God is. The Trinitarian distinctions are not merely in revelation to humans, but in God's being. God's great tri-personal essence and being make possible his great personal acts in history and relationships with humans. Similarly, given a cognitive revelation (which Kant in his metaphysical agnosticism did not utilize philosophically or theologically), we may discover some truths about humanness that make significant actions and personal relationships possible.

Humans are *real beings*. Critically interpreted Scriptures on creation, providence, and humanness, as well as the data of human experience in general, indicate that persons in their distinctness are neither ephemeral illusions (as Hinduism and Buddhism teach) nor mere bundles of impressions (as David Hume believed). Persons are substances because they are real subjects of change or subjects of predication characterized by existence as well as essence.[106] A person's essential attributes and capacities inhere in something. Linguistically, adjectives qualify nouns (substantives). Distinctively human qualities inhere in real individuals, entities who are self-conscious, active, and responsible causes of events.

What a person *is*, is not merely what a person *does*. What a person *does*, according to Christ, expresses what a person *is*. This point is explicit in moral contexts. Jesus said, "Make a tree good and its fruit will be good, or make a tree bad and its fruit will be bad, for a tree is recognized by its fruit" (Matt. 12:33). The moral condition of the heart determines the moral quality of a person's speech and actions. "For out of the overflow of the heart the mouth speaks. The good man brings good things out of the good stored up in him, and the evil man brings evil things out of the evil stored up in him" (vv. 34–35). Jesus did not say that we are what we do. Rather, our moral "fruit" discloses our moral character. To be responsible morally, we must be agents with the power of self-consciousness and self-determination. We must be ontologically real to remain accountable morally in this life and the next.

Humans are *distinct from the being of God*. People are not emanations from God's being, but creations of God's free will. God's being and energy are independent; ours are dependent. But to hold that we are dependent is not to hold that we are unreal or have no being as creatures. We are real creatures made like God. We are not gods ontologically. Our being is not continuous with God's being. To say that a person is *like* a tiger (in some respects) differs radically from saying that somehow a person *is* a tiger (in all essential respects). To blur the distinction between the Creator and human creatures is idolatrous and sinful (Rom. 1:25). Indeed, for mere humans to regard themselves as divine is blasphemous (John 10:33).

Humans are *distinct personal beings*. Each person is not a manifestation of one World Soul. There is more than one spirit or agent. Adam was one distinct, responsible person, and Eve was another. Cain and Abel, with all their similar heredity and environment, were distinct subjects of different kinds of moral actions and were accountable agents. Neither is a person an invention each of us is charged to create existentially without the help of God (Sartre). In their essence as human all persons share the same physical and spiritual qualities. But no persons are the same, for each has a unique, irrepeatable individuality, as existentialists insist. The truth in individualism, like all other truths, may be abused. It is abused when by it we rationalize loneliness and selfishness and use it to justify a neglect of relationships and responsitilities to others. To realize their fullest potential individual persons need relationships with others in society and most of all with the triune God. Without real individuals with whom to relate, however, relationships amount to empty abstractions. People are not mere relationships. Meaningful personal relationships are made possible by the existence of real human beings.

Each human is metaphysically *one being*. The oneness of a person is not like that of a mathematical abstraction, however. The oneness of an individual is like that of other existing beings, *a unity involving a multiplicity of factors*. A scriptural word study of "one" shows that husband and wife become one, a family is one, and a nation is one. Our study of the Trinity showed that God's oneness involves complexity in unity (1:270–72). Since the oneness of God's being involves the complexities of trinitarianism, it ought not be surprising that the wholeness or oneness of a human also involves complexity. That complexity may involve multiple personalities phenomenologically, or possession by other spirits, but metaphysically a person is an indivisible individual.

A person's complex oneness includes both an *outer material body* and an *inner immaterial spirit*. Paul distinguishes between the outward physical and inward spiritual aspects of a person (2 Cor. 4:16). The outward and inward aspects differ radically in this context, as radically as the momentary and seen differs from the eternal and the unseen (vv. 17–18). So in Paul's inspired teaching, the outward is a visible, temporal body; the inward is an invisible, everlasting spirit. Each has qualities not attributable to the other. The body has its publicly observable qualities, and a nonphysical spirit has its private, nonobservable qualities. Although they are related intimately in the present life, neither set of qualities can be reduced to the other. Each set of qualities must inhere in distinct kinds of substance.

The unity of the two physical and spiritual natures in humans is analogous in thought pattern to the oneness of two (divine and human) natures in Christ's person. The incarnate Christ has a human nature with its attributes and a divine nature with its attributes. Because of the unity of Christ's person he may be referred to either as God or as man. In the unity of the one person both natures are retained and neither is reduced to the other. So also, because of the unity of the two entities in us, the whole human person may be designated by either "body" or "spirit." The psalmist can say to God, "*I* seek you" emphasizing the oneness; he can also say, "*my soul* thirsts for you," or "*my body* longs for you" (Ps. 63:1).

Outwardly, humans exist in *visible physical bodies*. Although either body or soul may be used for the whole, the "body" does not refer exclusively to the whole person in relation to God. At birth Esau's "body" in itself was red and like a "hairy garment" (Gen. 25:25). The linen undergarments "as a covering for the body" of the priests reached from the waist to the thigh (Exod. 28:42). The psalmist spoke of the body in itself when he said, "My knees give way from fasting; my body is thin and gaunt" (Ps. 109:24). When John the Baptist was beheaded, his disciples "came and took his body and laid it in a tomb" (Mark 6:29). When Judas died, his "body burst open and all his intestines spilled out" (Acts 1:18). Some passages speak of the body in itself. Paul could testify, "I bear on my body the marks of Jesus" (Gal. 6:17). "Body" often refers to the entity in itself, not to a nonentity's relation to God or alienation from God.

The body in itself is to be distinguished from the "fleshly" desires of fallen people. The body is not meant for sexual immorality (1 Cor. 6:13), and anyone who sins sexually sins against one's own body (v. 18). The body is intended to be the temple of the Holy Spirit (v. 19). God designed male and female anatomical differences for an intimate, faithful relationship of mutual love and trust as well as for reproduction. As created, the physical aspects of male and female were created "very good" (Gen. 1:31). But sinful uses of sex may need to be disciplined in order that the spirit may be saved on the day of the Lord (1 Cor. 5:5).

As important as the human body is scripturally, in itself it *does not mirror the image of God,* who is spirit. The human spirit, however, can manifest God's likeness through the instrumentality of the body. Attempts to find the divine likeness in the body fail for lack of clarity of content and they contradict the teachings that God is invisible and entirely unique and that we are not even to imagine a physical likeness to him. The second commandment forbids any idols or images replacing or representing God (Exod. 20:4). Neither male nor female bodies in themselves reflect God's being. "God is spirit" (John 4:24). Although the statues of Greek gods and goddesses portray some of the greatest attempts of gifted artists to visualize a god in human likeness, they are not like the God of the Bible. We ought not make God after our image. God, who is spirit, makes us in his image. Hence the likeness of God in

humanity is to be sought, not in the outward, but in the inward self.

Inwardly a human is a *spirit in the image of God.* Like God's spirit, human spirits are *invisible, personal, indivisible, living, and active* (see 1:195–97). We differ from the divine being in that we are not self-existent, eternal, and immutable. Human spirits have a dependent existence, begin to exist in time, and, although changeless in essence, are not changeless in purpose and act. So God's attributes of aseity, eternity, and immutability as such are not communicable to humans. Like God as invisible, human spirits cannot be immediately verified by positivistic and empirical methods of knowing that begin with the physical senses exclusively. Since they are personal, human spirits think, feel, will, and relate to others. As indivisible, human spirits have an underlying metaphysical unity and a continuing identity. Because they are like God as living after their origin, human spirits are conscious and survive death and continue to exist endlessly. Since they are active as God is, human spirits initiate movement as subjects of action (not being passive objects of others' actions), and so are morally accountable agents. The biblical writers often figuratively call the spirit the *heart.* Colin Brown's word study concludes, "The heart is the whole inner man, the center of the personality."[107] Since the word "center" is figurative, for more precise purposes we ask the point and referent of the analogy. The primary nonfigurative biblical term for the "center" of the inner person is "spirit."

Inwardly a person may also be called a *soul* when the term does not refer merely to the life of the body. "It is noteworthy that the term *spirit* is commonly applied to God, while the term *soul* is only rarely so used."[108] It would be confusing to use the word *soul* to describe God, because in some contexts it may simply mean the organic life of the body, like that of the animals: a "living being" (Gen. 2:7). Or it may include that and the human spirit in reference to our having been created in the image of God. In many biblical texts *"soul" and "spirit" are often used interchangeably for the same functions.* Either "soul" or "spirit" may refer to the inner capacities such as thought, desire, or will. Some uses of "spirit" are listed first. The human spirit can be revived (Gen. 45:27), can be obedient or disobedient (Num. 14:24), may be stubborn and obstinate (Deut. 2:30), may be filled with wisdom (34:9), or it may be an evil attitude of distrust or bitterness (Judg. 9:23; 1 Sam. 30:6). Jonathan became one in spirit with David whom he loved as himself (1 Sam. 18:1). The spirit of king David longed to go to Absalom (2 Sam. 13:39), suffered anguish (Job 7:11), was broken (17:1), and crushed (Ps. 34:18). The human spirit gives understanding (Job 32:8) and compels one to speak (v. 18). Morally the human spirit may have no deceit (Ps. 32:2).

The "soul" functions intellectually, emotionally, and volitionally in the same way as the spirit. People love God with all their soul (Deut. 6:4–5). In bitterness of soul Hannah wept because of her barrenness (1 Sam. 1:10). Job also suffered from bitterness of soul (7:11). The perfect law of the Lord revives the soul (Ps. 19:7). The soul rejoices in the Lord (35:9). The soul thirsts for God (42:2). The soul finds rest in God alone (62:1). The soul may refuse to be comforted (77:2) or it may praise the Lord (146:1). The soul that sins will die (Ezek. 18:4, 20). The fruit of the body does not pay for the sin of the soul (Mic. 6:7). The body may be killed by humans, but the soul cannot be killed (Matt. 10:28). John prays that his friend's body may enjoy good health even as his soul was getting along well (3 John 2). A comparison of the uses of "spirit" and "soul" indicates that both may designate the inner person who thinks, emotes, wills, and relates.

People in most of the cultures of the world believe in the reality of the human spirit or soul from reflection upon their experience. Those who think about life merely from general revelation have pointed to distinctive human capabilities not meaningfully attributed to the body or to an empty human "wholeness." We are not mere objects, but *subjects who initiate action and agents accountable for it.* Grammatically sentences need subjects to initiate the action expressed by the verbs. Grammar indicates the fact that actions require subjects. Similarly distinctively human actions require subjects. Human acts are most coherently explained as the products of self-moving spirits. Far from being mere observers of life's drama from the balcony of a theater, we are creative actors on stage. We are self-starters, self-movers possessing the powers of self-determination. If we are living, personal spirits, like God metaphysically, we can understand why we are the unique subjects who, as existentialists insist, should act authentically or unhypocritically.

Humans also have a distinctive capacity of *self-transcendence.* The capabilities of "standing outside ourselves," "judging ourselves," and "controlling ourselves" indicate that in our spirits we are not limited to our bodies or to the present moment. Jesus said to a crowd, "Why don't you judge for yourselves what is right?" (Luke 12:57). Before partaking of the Lord's table a person "ought to examine" himself or herself (1 Cor. 11:28). Paul explained, "If we judged ourselves, we would not come under judgment" (1 Cor. 11:31). Prophets appealed to peoples' ability to transcend themselves. Rather than complain when we are punished for our sins, "Let us examine our ways and test them, and let us return to the

LORD'' (Lam. 3:40). Isaiah warned, "Woe to those who call evil good and good evil" (Isa. 5:20). The wise control themselves. "Better . . . a man who controls his temper than one who takes a city" (Prov. 16:32; 25:28). Paul exhorted the elders from Miletus, "Keep watch over yourselves and all the flock of which the Holy Spirit has made you overseers" (Acts 20:28). In likening his life to that of a runner competing for a prize, Paul said, "I do not run like a man running aimlessly; I do not fight like a man beating the air. No, I beat my body and make it my slave" (1 Cor. 9:26–27). Because Paul was capable of self-transcendence, he—as distinct from his body—disciplined his body to achieve his chosen purposes.

As humans we are not prisoners of our bodies, nor of our own past habits or conditioning, for we have a reflexive ability to criticize ourselves and by God's universal or special grace to change some of our fundamental patterns of thought. Predicatability of human behavior has some limits. We can act differently, spontaneously. "We are *spirit* in so far as we can *change our minds,* in the strongest sense of that phrase."[109] We will trace the outworking of the view that we are self-transcendent subjects and accountable agents more fully when we discuss our capacities intellectually, morally, emotionally, volitionally, and relationally.

Once the human spirit exists, it has *a continuous, everlasting identity.* Our spirits have not always existed, for God alone is eternal or "immortal" in the past, as well as future (1 Tim. 6:16). But human spirits exist everlastingly, and that fact has several implications: (1) Personal identity persists throughout repeated complete changes of physical cells, including those of the brain, at least every seven years during this life. (2) Our spiritual being unites both the conscious and the unconscious aspects of our beings throughout our lives. (3) Death itself cannot separate a believer from the love of God that is in Christ Jesus our Lord (Rom. 8:38–39). Death is the humanly irrecoverable *separation of the spirit from the body* (James 2:26). The finality of death must be distinguished from the near-death experiences of people who have recovered with the help of God and modern medicine. The biblical figure of "sleep" refers to body sleep, not soul sleep. Death does not change the personal relationship of believers and unbelievers to God. Death changes only our relationship to the physical world. Jesus said to the dying thief who believed, "I tell you the truth, today you will be with me in paradise" (Luke 23:43). Furthermore, believers in Christ have already received eternal life in the sense of possessing unbroken fellowship with God the Father. Eternal life is a present reality (John 5:24; 1 John 5:13). If conscious fellowship with God were to cease between death and the resurrection, eternal life would not be eternal.

Additional implications of the everlastingness of the human spirit are these: (4) Personal identity continues in the intermediate state before the resurrection. Although God alone has life (John 5:26) or immortality in himself (1 Tim. 6:16), God has given both life and immortality to human beings. By God's works of creation and providence he has given all humans dependent, immortal souls. At Jesus' transfiguration to his state in glory Moses and Elijah appeared, talking with the Lord (Matt. 17:3). After death and before the resurrection believers are in Abraham's bosom ("gathered to their fathers" [2 Chron. 34:28] in paradise) and unbelievers are in torment (Luke 16:19–31).[110] To live is to be at home in the body, to die is "to be away from the body and at home with the Lord" (2 Cor. 5:8). This intermediate state is no limbo of flitting shades or shadows of the real person; it is a state that is "better by far" (Phil. 1:23). Until the resurrection of our bodies, we must consciously exist, for we are able to feel "naked" (2 Cor. 5:3) or "unclothed" (v. 4). (5) Personal identity continues after the resurrection of the body, not as in another "tent," but in an "eternal house in heaven" (v. 1). In that new body we in ourselves face final judgment, where each of us will give account of himself to God (Rom. 14:12; 2 Cor. 5:10). (6) Personal identity continues in the eternal states.

The matter-energy of the body cannot be reduced to the spirit and its energy, for each has a *mutually exclusive set of attributes*. The qualities of the matter-energy of the body include visibility, extension in space, build or figure, weight, color, measurable temperature, tangibility, and the predictable regularities. None of these serve as attributes of spirit. Jesus said that a spirit does *not* have flesh and bones (Luke 24:39). All *materialistic monisms*, on the one hand, make matter more than matter is. Biblical evidence does not support the hypothesis that a personal spirit is visibly extended in space with a figure or build, weight, a tenor voice, a certain skin color and texture, and a scent of cologne. The apparent physical manifestations of spirit in visions and temporary theophanies are irrelevant to spirit in itself. All *idealistic* monisms, on the other hand, make spirit more than spirit is. The body and the spirit have two mutually distinct and real sets of attributes, functions, and destinies after death; therefore metaphysical monisms and antimetaphysical holistic hypotheses oversimplify the data.

What then is the *relationship between the spirit and the body?* How such different entities as the body and soul can relate to one another is one of the most problematic issues for dualists or dichotomists.

1. The human spirit or inner self *abides in the body.* The physical organism is the spirit's temporary, fragile dwelling place. A person, who lives in "a jar of clay," receives his or her all-surpassing power from God (2 Cor. 4:7). "We [our spirits] who are alive are always being given over to death for Jesus' sake, so that his life may be revealed in our mortal body" (v. 11). We remain "in" the body so that in it we may visibly display the power and life of the Savior. "Though outwardly we are wasting away, yet inwardly we are being renewed day by day" (v. 16). Paul also speaks of the body as the spirit's "earthly tent" (2 Cor. 5:1, 4). A person dwelling in this "tent" is said to be "at home in the body" (v. 6). Although Paul would like to have gone to be with Christ, which is better by far, he said, "It is more necessary for you that I remain in the body" (Phil. 1:24). In this life Paul's spirit lived in and through his body. But he distinguished himself from his body and taught that he himself was separable from his body.

2. The human spirit as an agent acts through its body as its instrument. A moral person transcends the body's conditioning to distinguish right from wrong and do what is just. Persons (apparently addressable as moral agents distinct from their bodies) are exhorted not to let sin reign in their mortal bodies (Rom. 6:12). Paul asks Christians not to offer the parts of their bodies as "instruments" of wickedness, but as instruments of righteousness (v. 13). Thus spirits are agents who accountably use bodily capacities as means of accomplishing their good or evil purposes. Paul exhorts, "Offer your bodies as living sacrifices, holy and pleasing to God—this is your spiritual act of worship" (12:1). Having spoken of orgies, drunkenness, sexual immorality, and debauchery, Paul exhorts us not even to consider how to gratify the desires of the sinful nature in bodily acts (13:14). Again, because the body is the temple

of the Holy Spirit, Paul enjoins Christians at Corinth, "Honor God with your body" (1 Cor. 6:20). Like a professional athlete, Paul said, "I beat my body and make it my slave" (9:27). According to James, mature followers of Christ keep the "whole body in check" (James 3:2). The tongue needs special control. As small as it is, the tongue, like a spark, can set the whole course of one's life on fire, corrupting the whole person (vv. 5–6). Neither the tongue nor even the entire body is the whole self, but both are instruments the self as spirit uses for good or ill. In these and similar passages the inward spiritual self is addressed as distinct from the body as the agent responsible for controlling the body.

3. *The body also interacts on the spirit.* We daily experience the counterproductive influence of the body's fatigue on the accomplishment of inward purposes, and this calls for repeated refreshment breaks, exercise, and rest. The disciples had intended to watch and pray with Jesus in Gethsemane. Instead they fell asleep. That happened, Jesus explained, because though "the spirit is willing, . . . the body is weak" (Matt. 26:41). Paul's physical limitation kept him from becoming conceited (2 Cor. 12:7). Although the spirit has radically different qualities from those of the body, the condition of the body affects the spirit in different ways. The taking of drugs, for example, can affect the consciousness in varied ways as it functions through the brain and nervous system in this life. In at least the above three ways the spirit and body *interact* with each other in the unity of one person.

To sum up the doctrine of humanness ontologically, a person inwardly is like God, an invisible, personal, living, and active spirit, a conscious subject with a sense of presence and a continuing identity. A person outwardly is unlike God as an extended, visible, tangible physical organism. The whole person is a complex unity composed of two distinct entities, soul and body, intimately interacting with one another. Neither of them is the whole person, yet either part can stand figuratively for the whole person. While they are alive the two natures (physical and spiritual) are neither divided nor confused. A whole person has attributes of spirit and attributes of body. Although body and spirit are separate entities ontologically, in this life they are intricately united. For metaphysical purposes, then, we propose that a human being is composed of an *interacting dichotomy* of spirit and body.

The nature of humanness, as here outlined, is not to be confused with the views of Platonic or gnostic dualists. Just as there are different varieties of monism (materialistic, idealistic, pantheistic), there are different brands of dualism. In our interacting dichotomy the following facts should be noted: (1) Both body and spirit are equally real. The body is not less real than the spirit, nor is it a mere shadow of the more real world of invisible ideas. (2) Neither the human spirit nor matter existed eternally apart from divine creation. Both have a beginning and are dependent on God. (3) Self-transcendent human spirits are not "imprisoned" by bodies; rather, bodies are generally effective instruments of the spirit. (4) The body is not the blameworthy cause of human evil, the inner self is. (5) The existence of the naked spirit after death is an intermediate and incomplete state, not the eternal state. (6) In the eternal state humans are not immortal souls only, but spirits united with resurrected bodies. Granting these significant differences in content, most of the typical objections to the Greek philosophers' dualism do not apply to our interacting dichotomy.

The primary basis of our view is not the writings of Greek philosophers, but

Scripture (illustrated with everyday experience). No categories have been used for this concept of humans that have not already been used to fit the Scriptural teaching concerning God. Biblical thought need not be totally different from Greek thought. Some of the categories utilized in the koine Greek of the New Testament, of course, are common to the classical Greek of the ancient philosophers. Not everything the philosophers said was wrong! Surely God providentially prepared not only the Roman roads for the dispersing of the gospel, but also the Greek language for its preservation in the New Testament. But general similarities of thought and wording aside, the biblical view of humanness that is developed here differs from the Greek in six definitive ways.

Humans Intellectually

Consider now some of the capabilities of spiritual-physical persons as created. Those who abandon substantives also reject a faculty psychology, for they have nothing with which to possess or exercise abilities. Finding evidence for the reality of human spirits, we can speak meaningfully not only of their attributes but also of their abilities. Although we list the mental, emotional, and volitional capacities separately, all three are activities of every person. And they interrelate in all our conduct. We *will* to know and love. We *love* to know and will. And we *know* what we will and love. Together they make possible moral accountability and meaningful relationships. Even though intimately interrelated, they are not synonymous capacities, so we will consider each separately.

One of the distinctive abilities of the human spirit is a *capacity to know itself*, as we noted above. We can become healthfully *self-conscious*. Because we are spirits, our knowledge is not limited to the centimeters of our brains or even to ideas that begin with the data of the five senses. We are conscious of the reality of our own inner existence. Augustine reasoned, "I doubt, therefore I am" (*dubito ergo sum*). Paul said, "Who among men knows the thoughts of a man except the man's spirit within him?" (1 Cor. 2:11). Only a human spirit can know distinctively human thoughts. Like other gifts, our knowledge of ourselves as spirits needs to be developed. As self-transcending spirits we are morally responsible to know, examine, and judge ourselves. We can "search our hearts" (Ps. 4:4). "Examine yourselves to see whether you are in the faith; test yourselves" (2 Cor. 13:5). To the Galatians Paul wrote, "Each one should test his own actions" (6:4).

Human spirits also have an *ability to know their bodies and the physical world*. We can develop a healthy world consciousness through our five senses: sight, hearing, taste, touch, and smell. "Ears that hear and eyes that see—the LORD has made them both" (Prov. 20:12). God has not retracted the great cultural mandate to fill the world and subdue it (Gen. 1:28). Humans under God, Erich Sauer has written, are kings of the earth.[111] For that purpose God gave us reliable senses by which to know it. The general reliability of healthy senses in an ordered world has made possible truth about the temporal world whether expressed in everyday language or in scientific technicalities. The God who created the earth and mankind to know and rule it used similar categories in both, a point overlooked by Kant. With Augustine we may call all knowledge of temporal, changing things science (*scientia*). Although each of us may have a different perspective on other people and things, no one of us thereby exhausts the knowledge of reality. Other personal agents and things exist to be perceived and thought about. But different observers approach them with different preunderstandings, starting points, and emphases. The fact that tourists surrounding a statue each see it from a different angle, however, does not mean that no statue exists in reality.

We overcome our loneliness in the midst of our limited (I-that or I-it) experience of the impersonal world by becoming acquainted with *other persons*. Our knowledge of others' invisible spiritual presence is not immediate, however. It is mediated through observable signs, including the facial expressions, bodily gestures, words, and actions of these other persons. Hence personal knowledge requires faith in the genuineness of the signs. All personal knowledge involves belief in the credibility of the others' visual indicators such as treaties, contracts, and marriage licenses. The trustworthiness of others' signs in turn depends on the sincerity of their intention (not to deceive) and our ability critically to distinguish the authentic from the deceptive. After sifting out the con artists, how rich we are to have minds capable of authentic person-to-person relationships! From them we receive comfort, encouragement, stimulation, instruction, correction, and refreshment. Since all personal relationships involve discernment and trust, we should not be surprised that personal relationship with the living God (in the midst of countless idols) also requires careful discernment of visible signs and a reflective commitment to their invisible source.

We may also know *historical events*. Knowledge of the past is not immediate; it also must be mediated through extant evidences such as tombs and tools or credible written documents. Hence the importance of criteria and a method for determining genuine from spurious documents. Since the Bible mediates much information about his-tory, our knowledge of scriptural history, like any history, involves faith. Any knowledge of the past is conditioned on belief in the reliability of the sources and of the historian who interprets them for us. Since much of the Bible records historical events, it is not surprising that we need to discriminate which are the genuinely prophetic and apostolic sources and then put faith in their inspired teaching.

As spirits in God's image, furthermore, we can transcend our consciousness of self, the world, and others and become *God-conscious*. The divine presence is not far from any one of us. All humans may have some consciousness of the higher being, however suppressed (I:75–76). To perceive God's redemptive presence we have good reason to trust the spoken, written, and acted signs of his authentic love. Through faith in these signs from God Christians can commune with God the Father, Christ, and the Holy Spirit! God said to Moses, "I will meet with you" over "the ark of the Testimony" (Exod. 25:22). Paul wrote, "[God] has called you into fellowship with his Son Jesus Christ our Lord" (1 Cor. 1:9). The believers at Corinth, Paul reported, enjoyed not only the grace of Christ and the love of God, but also "the fellowship of the Holy Spirit" (2 Cor. 13:14). John wrote his account of the first-century facts that he saw and heard, giving this as his purpose: "so that you also may have fellowship with us. And our fellowship is with the Father and with his Son, Jesus Christ" (1 John 1:3).

Persons as created in the divine image may also have immediate cognizance of *God's changeless moral principles*. Self-conscious, self-determining spirits clearly see God, and the requirements of his moral law are written on their hearts (Rom. 2:14–15). Although we are not able to invent eternal truths, we can mentally see some of them from God's universal revelation. In contrast to *scientia,* we may, with Augustine, call the immediate perception of moral norms "wisdom" (*sapientia*).[112] Two of the most prominent of these assert that we ought to love God with our whole being and our neighbor as ourselves. The Ten Commandments develop the details further as well as the exhortations of Christ to his disciples and of the apostles.

More is needed for knowledge of changeless intangibles than an intuitive capacity. The ability to see spiritual principles is closely related to our receptivity to them and our readiness to act upon them. Unfortunately these abilities and desires may be decimated by sinful desires. Nevertheless a general illumination enables all to know God's existence, power, and righteous demands. Given the capacity for *sapientia,* we can think about ultimate questions of individual morality and social ethics. Wisdom in harmony with God's mind is indispensable in the use of observed data for worthy ends. We need sapiential insights, for they provide logical principles and moral norms such as justice and love to help all in making wise choices in the use of scientific inventions. Human wisdom in applying moral principles to actual states of affairs has not kept up with the developments of human technology. In times of rapid change and culture shock we need leaders with well-founded moral guidelines and the experience to apply them to life situations.

Another distinctive function of the human spirit is its ability to know God's *freely chosen plans and purposes* when communicated in linguistic symbols. Through language, thoughtful spirits commune with spirits. The persons of the divine Trinity communicate with each other and with people created in their image. The first use of human language occurred when God gave Adam the cultural mandate to fill the earth, subdue it, and rule over it (Gen.

1:26–28). In order to do that, God created Adam with the senses to observe what is on earth and the rational capacity to judge what is true and distinguish what is false in matters of fact. We can also receive inner plans and purposes of others who speak. The human mind transcends sense data by envisioning objectives and communicating them through audible or visual *linguistic signs*. Although abstract thoughts are difficult to communicate effectively, one of the most distinctive human capacities is the ability to think of many similar things by the shorthand of general concepts.[113] Without the ability to abstract universals from particulars, our knowledge would be limited to each physical thing (one grain of sand after the other)! Like any other ability, the ability to abstract may be abused. Abstractions about human authenticity and morality may be confused with being authentic and moral as a particular person.

In the face of conflicting claims humans have the ability to *think critically*. We can distinguish objectively valid truth from erroneous rumors and counterfeit opinion. Three major methods of justifying our beliefs are used in pluralistic societies: (1) We may reason inductively from observed particulars to the probability of general conclusions. But often our experience is too limited and our time too short. Furthermore, empiricists may be insufficiently conscious of their own preunderstandings that make complete objectivity impossible. (2) Others emphasize reasoning deductively from universals to particular instances of them when we have evidence of their existence. If the universals are alleged to be self-attesting, they remain unjustified. (3) On a third method we propose hypotheses for verification and disverification. The verificational method most effectively follows the scriptural admonitions to examine, test, try, and prove. It is the most reliable method because it provides the most checks and balances on truth claims.[114]

Because we are, like God, transcendent spiritual beings, we have some ability and responsibility to work, think, speak, and write with *creativity.* We can compare and combine things differently, and imagine and propose new ways of doing things. We ought not think of ourselves as co-creators insofar as that involves a pantheistic or panentheistic equality with God. But God has given us the ability to conceive of alternative possibilities, select from among them, and move toward actualizing one or more of them. Any of these capacities can be misused and abused. We can worry unduly about the future and in the present frighten ourselves with imagined dangers. When humans wisely use these cognitive capacities, they produce cultures and subcultures with their distinctive types of art, music, architecture, horticulture, literature, religions, and mores.

The capacity for *rational intuition* may be a source of effable ideas, but it is not a reliable test of their truth. Although the intuitive capacity supplies sudden ideas sometimes accompanied by feelings of indubitable certainty, psychological certitude is not a guarantee of truth about reality. Intuitions sometimes contradict each other, fail to fit the relevant evidence, or prove to be impossible to embrace in life without hypocrisy. In those cases they turn out to be untrue. The psychological certitude that often accompanies intuitions ought not be confused with epistemological confirmation. So intuition is not a sufficient method of knowing by itself and does not take priority over other methods of justifying beliefs. Ideas suddenly "seen" to be true are to be regarded, like all otherwise derived ideas, as hypotheses to be either confirmed or disconfirmed by the same criteria of truth used throughout this text. Although not a reliable test of truth, intuition is one of several welcome sources of creative ideas to be tested.

Although Eastern mystics and Western devotional writers often say that the peak religious experience is an ineffable *mystical intuition,* God does not seek to erase the minds he created to make meaningful fellowship possible. If nothing can be known even in part about such alleged experiences, then they unsuccessfully claim to be ways of knowing. In Christian experience the ultimate goal is not mindless spirituality (Matt. 22:37; 1 Cor. 14:13–15), but a renewed mind (Rom. 12:2; Col. 3:10). Sound theological guidelines lead our nonrational desires away from unholy spirits and to experience with the God who is, hears, speaks, and acts in holy love.

Although self-conscious, world-conscious, and God-conscious, we cannot keep all that we have ever known before our conscious attention at any given time. Our spirits with their continuing identity store much of our knowledge (and associated emotions and motivations) in the *memory.* The retaining and influence of mental processes of which we are no longer aware seems to justify the widespread belief in the *unconscious.* Freud held that ideas and emotions of which we are now unaware, significantly influence our behavior. The recognition of the spirit's unconscious storage capacity need not lead to the conclusion, however, that human conduct is largely determined by unconscious factors.[115] Neither common human conduct need be attributed to a "collective unconscious" (Carl Jung). The common symbolism of people from diverse cultures can be attributed to the nature each person shares universally and to the similarity of natural laws. God will finally judge each individual, not an alleged collective unconsciousness.

153

In summary, humans intellectually are agents capable of knowing some truth about themselves and others, the cosmos, and God.

Humans Morally

As important as it is to have an adequate epistemology and ontology, the deepest problems of humans are neither physical nor metaphysical. The finite, limited, and conditioned nature of life in time and space prior to moral rebellion was "very good" (Gen. 1:31). It was not the corruptible body that made the soul sinful, Augustine said, but the sinful soul that made the flesh corruptible. Our most basic problems are ethical, and our moral condition affects our relationships with God and all others.

The ultimate human quest is not fulfilled merely in harmony with nature, but in harmony with the living God transcendent to the universe. Our greatest need is not for becoming as transcendent as God is, or attaining a divine level. What we *are* is not what we *ought to be*. We need to be forgiven and become holy as God is holy. In referring to God as personal, Christians (contrary to Hegel and Evelyn Underhill) are not just stating the truths of metaphysics in terms of personality: thus offering a third term, a "living mediator between the unknowable God, the unconditioned Absolute and the conditioned self."[116] The purpose of Christ was not to symbolize the fact that humans can come immediately into communion with God apart from a mediator. Christ came as actual mediator to provide the just basis on which the Father could remain morally just while justifying sinners and restoring them to fellowship.

Our ability to discern our own evil and feel guilt for it comes through our *conscience*. Our conscience may judge, not only ourselves but also our family, church, and society. More specifically it refers to a capacity for second-level awareness of right and wrong, an ability to judge conduct by moral standards, and to sense our obligation to follow just values personally and socially.[117] It is a court of appeal that cannot make moral laws, as God has done, but does deliver judgments on the cases before it.[118] A sensitive conscience can be poorly or well educated in God's revealed wisdom. Since the conscience can operate effectively only in relation to moral principles outside itself, a clear conscience is not a guarantee that we are right. We are commanded to have love "which comes from a pure heart and a good conscience . . ." (1 Tim. 1:5). But the reality is far from the ideal. The conscience is not the product of environment, habit, or education, but it may be influenced by all of these factors. The sin that affects every part of our nature can also scar the conscience. So Paul warned of being influenced by those whose consciences "have been seared as with a hot iron" (1 Tim. 4:2). Paul exhibited the transcendence of moral irresponsibility when he said to the Sanhedrin, "I have fulfilled my duty to God in all good conscience to this day" (Acts 23:1). Like Paul when he was on trial before Felix, we should strive always to keep our consciences clear before God and mankind (Acts 24:16). Even when we have a clear conscience to eat meat offered to idols, for example, we may choose not to eat it for the love of one whose conscience differs. Conscience serves as a red light coming on when a course of action is wrong and so serves only negatively; the positive influence on our moral judgment comes from Christ's loving fulfillment of the law.

To sum up, humans morally are agents capable of distinguishing God's normative counsel from the deceptive counsels of evil beings and from the ambiguous results of descriptive surveys of human conduct.

Humans Emotionally

Personal human spirits not only think and judge but also *experience and evoke feelings.* The inner human spirit, like the divine Spirit, has affections or feelings. God experiences righteous anger and pleasure. Human emotions cannot simply have resulted from the Fall. Undoubtedly Adam and Eve experienced emotions in their unashamed relationships with each other and with God, in the power to control the animals, and in the freedom to enjoy the fruit of every tree in the garden save one. Eve found the forbidden fruit also "pleasing to the eye" and "desirable" (Gen. 3:6). Since the Fall the Bible frequently describes the emotional states of people. "In fact, Scripture not only speaks about emotions, it also speaks to and through our emotions. The Bible itself is emotional literature, filled with emotional expression and designed not just to communicate with our rationality but also to stir us emotionally, thus affirming our emotionality."[119]

Humans evidently have the capacity for feelings of many sorts, closely associated with what they know, will, and do morally. Our good or evil conduct may include intense inner feelings that may produce tears or smiles. But we cannot reduce all the tensions and joys that we feel merely to smiles or tears, for these outward manifestations express deeper inner feelings. We are far from impassive. To list a few emotions, we may feel admiration, adoration, concern, empathy, love, elation, power, depression, distress, fear, anxiety, embarrassment, disgrace, scorn, neglect, shame, inadequacy, insecurity, inferiority, insignificance, anger, and hostility. When pleased, we may say, "Aha!" When displeased we may say, "O no,

not again!" Strong feelings of enticement and attraction accompany temptation.

Our emotions, like our intellects and wills, can be used wisely or unwisely in conjunction with good or evil ends. The answer to wrong desires, however, is not desirelessness as in Buddhist prescriptions. Rather than to try unsuccessfully to suppress all desires, the Christian overcomes evil desires by cultivating worthy loves, esteeming values in harmony with God's nature and purposes above others. So, for example, Christians prize love, not mere sex.

We must get rid of our sinful rage and not let the sun go down on our selfish anger (Eph. 4:26, 31), for these grieve the Holy Spirit (v. 30). But Christ was righteously angry at stubborn hearts (Mark 3:5). "Jesus' anger in cleansing the temple was not merely the seamy side of his pity; it is the righteous reaction of his moral sense in the presence of evil."[120] Those who love human beings must hate all that wrongs them. How can we be both good and angry? At least three conditions must be met. (1) Righteous indignation is morally motivated. It boils over more at wrong done to others than to oneself. (2) Righteous anger is wisely focused and directed. It is not directed against persons but against evil deeds, situations, and institutions. (3) Justifiable anger is ethically implemented. It is followed by positive and constructive action to end the wrong that occasioned it.[121] "Anger, if consecrated to righteousness, may sometimes be an ethical duty," Carl Henry explained, "but it must appear in Christian experience against a background of God-tempered life, and not as a flareup of short temper which lives constantly near the borderline of sudden flight into rage."[122]

Is it possible to love people and hate their sin? Although our neighbor's sin stirs us to wrath, we can oppose it because we love our neighbor. C. S. Lewis thought this a silly hair-splitting distinction until he realized he had been regarding it crucial in regard to himself. "The very reason I hated things was that I loved the man. Just because I loved myself, I was sorry to find that I was the sort of man who did these things. Consequently, Christianity does not want us to reduce by one atom the hatred we feel for cruelty and treachery. We ought to hate them." Lewis then explained that Christianity wants us to hate them in the same way in which we hate such things in ourselves, being sorry that we should have them, and hoping, if it is in any way possible, that somehow, sometime, somewhere, we can be cured and made human again.[123]

In other words, as fallen persons in a fallen world we need to control our emotions by developing the virtue of patience, more aptly called *longsuffering*. Those who are slow to anger are patient with those who do evil to them, not condoning their sin, but hoping that mercy will lead them to repentance and reconciliation. The endurance of longsuffering provides emotional stability to endure in spite of unjust attacks on ourselves, our rights, and our possessions. Christians are longsuffering for several reasons: (1) God is longsuffering. (2) Christians are part of a community of concern and action, so the church will act in their behalf providentially. (3) When Jesus Christ returns, justice will triumph over the worst evils. So Christians do not take vengeance on others who have done wrong to them. They do not become judge, jury, and executioner all in one. Christians with Holy Spirit-aided control of their emotions do not render evil for evil, but forgive those who unjustly treat them and graciously return good for evil.

Our highest emotions will never be fulfilled by the finest people or things in this world, nor by the whole of the world (as pantheists imagine). Our emotional needs can be satisfied only by a personal relationship with God. God made us to share not only his world and the truth about it but also to have fellowship with him. With all of our emotional experiences with others, we are still restless until we find our rest in God—that is, until we experience a transcendent joy. C. S. Lewis felt an intense longing (*Sensucht*) for an Object that is never fully given and cannot be fully present in the subjective experience of persons in the space-time existence. His desire for the transcendent was not fulfilled by aesthetic experience, sexual experience, or pantheistic or occult religious experiences. No mere feeling appeases us. We desire not a state of ourselves, but Something Other and Outer. This longing for the transcendent is similar to the attraction of faraway places, mountains, fantasies, magic, and occultism. But C. S. Lewis confesses, "I have myself been deluded by every one of these false answers in turn, and have contemplated each of them earnestly enough to discover the cheat."[124]

Essentially humans are capable of loving God and the good and detesting evil.

Humans Volitionally

The capacity for human volition involves (1) a choice of an end and (2) an ability to move toward its fulfillment. Freedom of the will may mean both power to choose among options and ability to move toward realizing the one chosen. First, human freedom involves a *capacity of choice among ends*. We choose wisely when we select goals in accord with God's revealed values and purposes, for they are for our best. There may be several specific options that do not violate revealed moral guidelines, so we may have alternative choices that are moral. Freedom does not require ability to choose contrary to God's will. But we have that power also. When we choose courses of action inconsistent with God's universally or specially revealed will, we choose unwisely. At our disposal is an awesome potential for either good or evil.

Second, the human will also includes *a capacity for self-determination*. Having chosen an alternative, we are not free if we do not have ability to move toward that goal and do what we want to do. We are free volitionally when we have both freedom of alternative choices and ability to attain the selected end. Instead, we may frustrate ourselves by choosing objectives we are unable to attain. Because God is omnipotent, he can perform what he chooses in the way he chooses to do it. But often the things we decide to do, we cannot carry out (Rom. 7:18). Hence even when we are most sincere in seeking to fulfill a chosen course of action, we may find ourselves lacking in ability to complete it as planned. People are not only objects of investigation by others, but also active subjects who choose and perform actions. Since persons are causal agents, not all causes are impersonal factors. Persons may be efficient causal agents who determine and initiate actions. As subjects people decide on problems worth researching, initiate inquiries, decide on a reliable method of justifying beliefs, evaluate the work of others, and arrive at conclusions. When we are subjects who initiate action, we are accountable to God and others for those words or deeds. As dependent creatures of God, we are free, but without divine providence, of course, we could do nothing.

Persons are also like God in using their powers of self-determination with *creativity*. Like God, persons have a capacity for creative imagination, goal-setting, strategies, and actions. Artists, sculptors, architects, writers, and many others have enriched our lives by creatively developing fresh approaches. We may need courage to exercise our creative capacities to develop different strategies and methods for advancing God's universal and redemptive kingdoms. Like any other capacity, *imagination* can be either misused or properly used. Imagination is misused if we visualize ourselves as having infinite potential or as being wiser than God, independent of God, or equal with God. The most imaginative creations in literature have some relation to truth about reality. Constructively we can use imagination in several important coherent ways. It can propose new hypotheses for us to confirm or disconfirm, different ways of serving others on behalf of Christ, and stimulating plans for uses of leisure time that will refresh the human spirit. Beyond that, it may awaken and foster a degree of emotional sensitivity and personal engagement that is highly compatible with the life of faith, and in doing so it affirms the significance of spiritual values, personal commitment, beauty and love.[125] C. S. Lewis's fresh ways of formulating and communicating truth with feeling in his imaginative literary works is consistent with his more closely reasoned verificational approach to Christianity's truth. Persons think and write, mere minds do not.

The will also is a distinguishable capacity, but it does not choose and act with total independence of mind, emotions, desires, and relationships. Our choices and consequent actions are not made by a will sporting about in a vacuum. Persons, not mere wills, select among options and initiate actions. When choosing among ends and moving toward their realization, we may be attracted by the nonvolitional aspects of our natures, such as our *desires*. Free will gives to love its precious value, but right love gives will its freedom and fulfillment. Unfortunately, our wills may be moved also by evil desires to evil options. While we may be conscious of being free from external coercion, our wills may be influenced by unconscious habitual desires or moral natures. Hence even when most convinced that we are exercising our wills freely, we need to consider critically the hypothesis that our choices are influenced by our desires and basic moral nature.

Our wills, although free from external coercion, do not act independently of our *motives*. Motives are thoughts or feelings that influence us to choose certain ends and to act in certain ways. Our motivations may be either conscious or unconscious. Even though we may consciously choose to be intellectually honest, for example, we may be motivated to act in accord with a greater momentary desire to impress a friend or get some advantage for ourselves. Frequently, even when our primary motive is to give gratitude, obedience, and glory to God, there is not just a single motive, but our motives may be mixed. At the same time we may be seeking to fulfill biological needs, earn some recognition from peers or superiors, and serve some ideals. Then we may ask ourselves, "Which is our ultimate concern?" Singleness of purpose in life refers to everything that is done ultimately for the Lord.[126]

The freedom of our wills may be limited by the habitual moral inclinations of our *depraved natures*. Hence even when we are conscious of our freedom to choose and have the ability to do what we choose, we may be overwhelmed by our sinful desires. Fallen people have the power of self-determination, but their choices may be influenced not only by evil desires and motives, but also by good desires without the highest motivation. The best deeds of sinful people may not be done for the glory of God. "Free will," then, may be used in different ways. In reference to humans it cannot mean entirely what it means for God. For God, freedom means no external coercion and the ability to do anything he has chosen (in accord with his nature) in the strategy chosen. For human beings, free will may mean (1) no specific external coercion, (2) the ability to select among alternatives for morally mixed reasons, and (3) limited ability to move in the direction chosen. The ability to choose contrary to our own natures is not essential to human freedom any more than to divine freedom. What is essential to free will is the ability to choose and act according to the deepest desires or loves of one's moral nature.

Whatever the internal influences, when without external coercion, normal, mature persons act with premeditated intent; they are *responsible for their choices and their conduct*. Empirical scientists and behaviorists in psychology in their quest for impersonal antecedents may overlook a person's own choices and acts. History is not totally explained in terms of impersonal causes. To account for the history of a culture we must also recognize the reality and impact of personal causes (1:310–11). Brothers and sisters with similar heredity and environmental influences are personal spirits who may think, feel, will, and act very differently in their moral conduct. When two people have the same influences toward immoral conduct, one may participate with others in a life of crime, the second may choose to rebel against his environment and obey the laws. Regenerate persons become like God when they use their volitional abilities in harmony with God's nature and purposes.

Our most valuable freedom "is not the psychological freedom to do what we will, not the physical, social or political freedom which exempts us from illegitimate interference from others, not the Stoic freedom of following the law of nature nor the Kantian freedom of doing what we ought, but the Divine freedom described by Augustine of wanting to do what we ought because we love God and take delight in Him."[127]

Volitionally, humans are self-determining agents, responsible to decide and act wisely, lovingly, and virtuously.

Humans Relationally

Talk of relationships, contrary to neoorthodox theology, need not exclude information about the nature of personal agents capable of relating to one another. Significant relationships can develop only among real personal beings who initiate and sustain them. Relational categories are vitally important to Christian theology because the persons involved, being ontologically real, have inherent worth. No follower of Christ can fail to appreciate the supreme value of loving God with one's whole being because of who God is and one's neighbors as oneself because of who our neighbors are.

Real person-to-person relationships are possible because of the ontological reality of persons as spiritual and physical beings. Humans can relate to things and technology, but the most interesting, varied, and fulfilling relationships are with other persons. We relate to one another through physical "signs" or body language. Essential to lasting relationships is careful observation of physical signs and wise discernment of their significance. On the basis of the evidence seen we trust the others' invisible sincerity and faithfulness. Faithfulness results as both adhere to such moral conditions of meaningful relationships as those characterized by justice, love, and relatedness to reality and consistency.

Relationships should mutually enrich the participants rather than depersonalize one or more of them. The unique-

ness of persons is a value that should not be destroyed by social relationships. Family solidarity in Judaism in biblical times was strong because individuals were strengthened by them, not reduced to impersonal cogs in a machine. National solidarity may seem strong also in countries under communism. But in the midst of the strongest collectives, persons remain distinguishable and accountable as individuals. Individuals will stand alone before the final Judge to account for their response to the pressures of their families, gangs, athletic teams, unions, tribes, and political or religious leaders.

In the West, insofar as there is deficient social regard and commitment under God to others in the family, the nation, and the church, people may suffer from an unhealthy individualism. In the East, insofar as there may be a lack of regard for the value of the individual, people may suffer from unhealthy collectivisms. In general the Bible recognizes the reality of accountable individuals in their common social loyalties and institutional commitments. Collectives should strengthen persons, and persons should strengthen collectives. In this reciprocal relationship, which is intended to benefit both, neither need destroy the other. We are not merely formed by these social relationships, we act and by acting help to form the character of these societies. Not only are we constituted by them, but we ourselves constitute them, modifying their quality for better or worse.[128]

The individual also is in a reciprocal relationship with the Lord of providence. In Scripture there is no such thing as an autonomous individual. Even the attempt to live as an atheist is regarded as utter folly (Ps. 14:1). In common grace the Creator-Sustainer provides the life support system on planet earth and gives life with all its opportunities. The grateful recipients in turn respond in love and service for their Source. Much more will be said about relationships in all the chapters to follow. Here we emphsize the truth actually communicated by trichotomists. Indeed humans have three levels of conscious relationships: to God, to others, and to the physical world.

To sum up, the whole person metaphysically is a complex agent, a unity of an inner (spiritual) and outer (physical) being with a multiplicity of capacities for developing excellence and ruling the world (Gen. 1:26, 28) intellectually, morally, emotionally, volitionally, and relationally. In other words, a human person is an accountable agent made up of an interacting dichotomy of spirit and body with a trichotomoy of three relationships—to the earth, others, and God. The truth in dichotomy is in two substances; the truth in trichotomy is in three major relationships. In Scripture the whole inner person relating to God is most frequently designated spirit. The whole inner person relating to oneself, others, and things is most frequently called soul. But the *one* inner person thinks, feels, wills, and relates, whether "vertically" or horizontally." Humans in themselves do have great (but not infinite) potential for sharing God's vital fellowship, relationships, and work. In the next chapter we investigate the effects of sin on the greatness of God's image-bearers.

APOLOGETIC INTERACTION

Persons Are Not Mere Bodies

We have concurred with materialists that the body is real but also deny that it is the ultimate reality. Even though our understanding of matter and atoms has changed as a result of nuclear studies, an element of truth remains in materialism. Solid material bodies are real. Unfortunately, however, materialism reduces all human spirituality and psychology to physics and its epiphenome-

nal by-products. The brain secretes thought, one says, as the liver secretes bile! Jacob Bronowski alleges that humans are "a part of nature, in the same sense that a stone is, or a cactus, or a camel."[129] Indeed our lives are dependent on the laws of creation, but such statements fail to reflect the uniqueness or value of the human spirit in the image of God. A Marxist dialectical materialism has an element of truth but oversimplifies the complexity of human existence and depersonalizes human agents. But as interacting dualist Karl Popper argues, inexplicably for materialists, matter somehow "transcends itself by producing mind, purpose, and a world of products from the human mind. One of the first products of human mind is human language."[130]

Behaviorism also denies that humans are constituted of two distinct interacting realities. According to behaviorists, all mental functions can be analyzed in terms of physical behavior.[131] The great riddle is how the physical universe created life, mind, and consciousness which illuminates the universe and itself becomes creative and self-transcendent! There is no evidence that atoms have conscious inner states. On a behaviorist hypothesis human conduct is not determined as much by the inner conscious agent as from without. Hence human behavior could theoretically be totally controlled by regulating the environment. Who then would decide which behaviorists will govern our environment and on what (nonphysical) principles shall that decision be made? In *The Abolition of Man* C. S. Lewis "insisted that man was not a thing, but an essence, a soul, and that it ill profits a man to gain the whole material world at the expense of the elementary self-knowledge that tells him that he is a soul qualitatively distinct from and superior to those things."[132]

Is the human spirit a mere emergent from bodily processes? Defending a theistic evolution, Richard H. Bube suggests not only that the body originated through an evolutionary process but also that the human spirit "results from the interaction between his bodily parts. . . . Just as flame bursts suddenly into being as a qualitatively new entity due to the interaction of wood and oxygen, so the spirit of man can be envisioned coming into being under the guidance of God." Again, "the spiritual nature of reality need not be imposed from the 'outside' upon the material, but may have its origin within material interactions in themselves."[133] Analogies, of course, do not prove anything, and Bube's analogy even fails to illustrate a sufficient qualitative difference, unless he regards the soul a physical epiphenomenon. Fire as qualitatively visible and tactual is not as different qualitatively as a personal, responsible agent.

The fact that persons may be *in some sense* identical with their bodies, C. Stephen Evans argues, is no more cause for alarm than the fact that a poem may be *in some sense* identical with a set of ink marks.[134] Several levels of description of poems may be distinguished: (1) a chemical description of the paper and ink, (2) a description of the poor or legible writing, (3) a description of the language used, (4) a description of the meanings of key words and of their sentences, and (5) a description of the entire poem in terms of its author's preplanned purpose and intended meaning, including the emotive impact and possible contribution of the poem to a new outlook and way of life. All these levels may be necessary for a comprehensive description of a poem. Similarly, for a comprehensive view of humans we need a description of the physical aspects of the body and its observable environment, but we also need descriptions of the person as a conscious, accountable agent.[135]

As materialism, behaviorism, and scientism have developed, many lament, wisdom seems not to be keeping pace. Both kinds of knowledge are important. As *homo sciens* we know *scientia:* matters of fact and quantity in the material world. As *homo sapiens* we should know *sapientia:* qualities of meaning, purpose, and value. "Enthusiasts of scientism fail to see that *scientia* is utterly dependent on *sapientia* for direction and meaning; their fervent attempts to pursue *scientia* in isolation from *sapientia* amount to a tragic rush into meaninglessness—the very antithesis of a genuine search for knowledge."[136] The exclusive use of *scientia* "is the great modern religion, our established church, with a whole panoply of priests, evangelists, saints, and bishops, and massive means of publicity and propaganda. It has the power, if it is allowed to grow uncontested in enough human minds, to bring about the end of *homo sapiens*. It may indeed prove to be the abolition of man."[137]

Scientific knowledge by perception involves more than perception itself. The mere presentation of publicly observable sense data to the mind does not constitute knowledge. Some animals perceive things we do not. Scientific conclusions involve interpretations of the data and judgments of the truth or falsity of allegations based on it. Judgments of truth or falsity involve the import of validity or invalidity, a factor quite distinct from the data received from the physical world. In making cognitive claims for their own views behaviorists or positivists either contradict themselves or lapse into absurdity. Do they really have minds or are they automata? "Philosophical behaviorists seem to be able to draw on unsuspected dialectical resources in meeting criticism. But in so doing they seem to purchase impregnability at the expense of those very features of the behaviorist outlook that attracted theorists to the position in the first place."[138]

The *human mind cannot be reduced to the physical brain*. The mind is more than an automatic telephone exchange or a computer. The brain cannot observe itself, but the mind is self-conscious (in varying degrees) and thinks about its own thinking. The brain occupies space, but the mind transcends space, imagining many other places in the world than one's skull. The brain is limited by time, but the mind can transcend the present to learn from the past and anticipate the future. We observe the brain as a physical thing; we conceive of the mind's meanings and values in nonphysical ways. The brain receives audio, visual, olfactory, and tactual signals, but the mind interprets the wave lengths or vibrations and makes assertions on the basis of this evidence that may be true or false, right or wrong. Awareness of ourselves is indispensable to our moral and spiritual accountability for our conduct in the use of our spiritual and physical capacities. We can overcome our perfectionism and pride and examine ourselves.[139]

Eccles dismisses the term "substance" because of atomic theory but nevertheless concludes that the mind is an independent "entity." The mind as an entity is actively engaged in reading out from the multitude of active centers in modules of liaison areas of the dominant cerebral hemisphere. The self-conscious mind selects from these centers in accord with its attention and its interests and integrates its selection to give the unity of conscious experience from moment to moment.[140] In memory the self-conscious mind commands, as it were, retrievals from the data of the storage banks in the cerebral cortex.[141] The dualist-interactionist hypothesis has the recommendation of its great explanatory power.[142] Our unity comes not from the neural system but from the self-conscious mind. Persons respond to the world of time and sense through the body and brain, and at the same time they respond to mental, aesthetic, and spiritual concepts, which are real, even though they are beyond the reach of the physical sciences. So the most probable explanation of human self-transcendence mentally, morally, teleologically, and in self-government is a spirit like God's that transcends matter and is moral, purposeful, and well controlled.[143]

Persons Are Not Mere Minds

In contrast to the reductive materialism stands reductive idealism. Both unwisely truncate reality to one kind of being. On the arguments above, idealists tend to regard only the inner soul or spirit real and the body unreal or illusory. Also in the reductive monism of multitudes in Vedanta Hinduism as well as its Bhakti tradition represented by Hare Krishna, the body is *maya*. The body is illusory also for many who see life from New Age pantheistic perspectives.

The idealist hypothesis, however, does not fit the fact that God created the earth and the first human body out of dust. The body cannot be reduced to nothing but idea or spirit any more adequately than the spirit can be reduced to nothing but matter. The complexity of human persons is no more adequately accounted for by the limited idealists' level of description than by that of the reductive materialist. Even in cultures where the body is regarded as illusory (*maya*), people are concerned about what they eat, get innoculations against hepatitis, and look both ways before crossing a busy street. Daily human experience indicates the reality of physical bodies beyond reasonable doubt. Bodies are fed, dressed, exercised, relieved, rested, weighed, medically examined, hospitalized, and buried.

Comprehensive scriptural descriptions of experience as well call for a recognition not only of humanity's inner spiritual reality, but also of our *outward reality as bodies*. One topical index of the Bible, besides giving ordinary references to the senses, lists passages on (are you ready for this?) manly beauty, female beauty, diminutive stature, giants, dexterity, appetites, the countenance, the hair, the beard, the forehead, stooping, prostration, sighing, tears, saliva, excretions, food, cooking, feasting, gluttony, fasting, famine, drink, sleep, the folly of anxiety about dress, the material, color, and seemliness of dress, ornaments, perfume, disguises, grief exhibited by dress, removal of dress, afflictions, sickness, weakness, restlessness, pain, consumption, fever, palsy, leprosy, cutaneous disorders, sores, boils, mutilation, wounds, lameness, sunstroke, blindness, pestilence, physicians, prescriptions, apothecaries, sickness caused by sin, recovery, old age, duties to the aged, death, preparing for death, instances of death, burying the dead, grief for the dead, corruption, nonburials, bodies devoured, and bodies burned! The Bible hardly minimizes the physical side of humanness! The resurrection body, furthermore, will be an even more marvelous reality.

Persons Are Not Mere Relationships, Functions, or Wholes

Relationships are connections between things, persons, or ideas. Unless we know something about the connected terms in themselves our knowledge of the alleged relationship may not hold in actuality. All relations are between terms or entities. What gives human and religious relationships great value is the nature of the persons involved in them. Given the reality of human spirits and their consequent inherent worth, personal relationships are of great value. The worth of personal relationships is enhanced, not displaced, when we recognize the inherent values and rights of persons. Knowing what was in humans, Jesus Christ said a person's soul is of greater value than the whole world. Why? Because persons have inalienable value.

Created persons always depend on God for life and breath and must always be seen in that dependent relationship. But who or what is the whole that always depends on God? G. C. Berkouwer claims that to speak of the mystery of persons *in themselves* at all is to speak abstractly.[144] In defining the ontological nature of humans as both spiritual and physical, however, we do not change their dependent status. We find some meaning to their continuous identity and responsibility under God. Berkouwer contradicts himself. On one hand he claims that he is not choosing relation over reality or the relational over the ontological, or choosing one horn of any such dilemma.[145] On the other hand Berkouwer says, "In Scripture we hear no ontological explanations, but rather religious affirmation."[146] The Scriptures cannot both include ontological truth in religious relationships and contain no such ontological truth. We agree that we never encounter in the Bible an "*independently existing* abstract, ontological, structural interest in man,"[147] but that does not mean that we never encounter ontological and structural implications concerning dependent humans. Initially Berkouwer allows the ontological in the relational, but does not supply the ontological with any content and later inconsistently excludes it from consideration.

Berkouwer claims "that Scripture never pictures man as a dualistic or pluralistic being, but that in all its varied expressions the whole man comes to the fore."[148] Such a claim in general fails to answer the question of what "the whole man" is composed and to fit the facts indicated in the scriptural section of this chapter. Specifically it overlooks Christ's clear distinction between the body and soul: "Do not be afraid of those who kill the body but cannot kill the soul" (Matt. 10:28). Correctly Berkouwer says that Paul's thought is far removed from gnostic dualism in which the soul is imprisoned in the body and longs for its escape,[149] but that does not exclude a dualism in which Paul is either at home in the body or at home with the Lord (2 Cor. 5:6, 8–9) and seeks in his soul (as distinguishable from his body) to exalt Christ in his body whether by life or by death (Phil. 1:20). Although Paul desired to depart (from his body) and be with Christ, he considered it more necessary to remain in the body for ministry at Philippi (vv, 23–24). Paul's distinctions between himself and his body are not adequately accounted for by the hypothesis of an undefined whole person or an unidentifiable whole mass of relationships.

Mistakenly Berkouwer says that in the Bible, not immortality, but mortality characterizes humans. He says, "The witness of the whole Bible is so clear on this point that no denial is possible"[150] However, his interpretation does not determine the limits of possibility because he has overlooked important evidence. Paul attributes mortality explicitly to the *body* (Rom. 6:12; 8:11; 2 Cor. 4:11). Concerning death Jesus and Paul teach body sleep, not soul sleep. Berkouwer acknowledges that a relation is always between two things and that his stress on relationalism does not dissolve reality.[151] But he has no distinguishable spirit to return to God when the body is buried and so he leaves the intermediate state an impossible muddle rather than a profound mystery. Although the body is in the grave, it is not a part of man but the "whole" that lives on![152] He finds no help for a solution in the Bible[153] but has no doubt that the church from the

most ancient times was convinced of continued existence after death![154] The church's view of human nature allowed a meaningful assertion of life after death; Berkouwer's does not.

Berkouwer fails to see that a belief in the continued existence of the spirit need not entail the illicit connotations of Gnostic thought. Before accusing the whole historic Christian church of a Greek philosophical view of immortality, he should have paused to consider whether the view of immortality in Christendom entailed the notions of the body as the source of moral evil and as a prison of the soul, or the soul as complete before the resurrection. We cannot accept a merely functional hypothesis that fails to provide a coherent account of the biblical and experiential data above. The view of an interacting dichotomy provides the more coherent view of the whole person's constitution with fewer difficulties.

Persons Are Not Mere Fields of Energy

Some writers of the New Age movement reduce persons to small energy fields in the vast field of all energy. The psychological aspect, like our physical structure, may be "nothing more nor less than a configuration of energies."[155] W. Brugh Joy suspects that the *chakra* system interrelates the gross physical body and the subtle, etheric bodies, but he has only one basic energy operating in both bodily and spiritual systems called by various names such as chi, vital force, and prana.[156] Marilyn Ferguson claims to have discovered that the separate self is an illusion. The self is not an encapsulated individual. Instead Ferguson proposes that the self is "a field within larger fields."[157] She finds linkage with others "as if they were one self and merged with a another Self yet more universal and primary."[158] That transcendent universal self (indistinguishable from the Hindu Brahman) provides a new (to her in the West) view of the self as part of the whole of society and the world.

The hypothesis that reduces humanness to impersonal energy dehumanizes persons. Why not fold, mutilate, and spindle bits of energy that do not cooperate with the New Age world plan? Who makes the distinctions between cooperation and noncooperation if no individuals exist in reality? If there are no personal agents, who communicates with whom and who is responsible for moral conduct? And to what? To what field of energy shall we assign responsibility for the view that persons are nothing but their actions or relationships?

The hypothesis that personal agents are unreal fails to fit the facts of the great cast of characters in the jury system and the law courts. The hypothesis that we are mere *maya* cannot provide a coherent account of the scriptural data above. *Ex hypothesi* it does not leave responsible persons with whom to communicate.

Persons Are Not Mere Phenomena (Barth and Others)

Barth does not think of a person as a soul in a body. A person is a "bodily soul" or a "besouled body."[159] The spirit, according to Barth, is not something that the person *is,* in the sense that a person is both body and soul. Rather, a person *has* spirit, or, "spirit has him."[160] For Barth a person has "double determination"[161] toward creatures and toward God, but not two ontological natures. Descriptively this has value in terms of the relation between the body and the life or soul of the body in this life.[162] But it carries little explanatory power as to who we *are.* Just as some knowledge of God's "isness" ("I am who I am" [Exod. 3:14]) is basic to understanding divine

acts in history, so some understanding of human "isness" is necessary to understanding our physical and nonphysical determinations.

Another phenomenological description of human experience portrays its twofold character psychosomatically. As Anthony Hoekema explains, "Man is *one* person who can, however, be looked at from *two* sides." Hoekema's work does not explain what it is that we have two sides of. He prefers to speak descriptively of a "psychosomatic unity."[163] Hoekema does not want to say what a person is ontologically. Hoekema's reference to the psychosomatic unity of a person also is useful descriptively for the present life but provides no account of what the *pneuma, psyche,* or *soma* actually are. The uniting of the two unknown factors in the word "psychosomatic" seems to have no real referent. To call it the one human person is circular. Definitions do not repeat the word to be defined. To the extent that his work fails to define the mental and physical aspects in some meaningful and distinguishable manner his view fails to accommodate the biblical indications of their distinct attributes and separability as well as their interaction.

Arthur Koestler may be thought to have answered a dichotomous view of humanity in his *Ghost in the Machine.* Instead he has shown that neither "ghost" nor "machine" are appropriate concepts. Koestler proposes that humans are "a multileveled hierarchy." On the one hand he mentions levels of matter: macroscopic, molecular, atomic, and subatomic. On the other hand he distinguishes levels of consciousness: unconsciousness, dreamless sleep, dreaming, day-dreaming, drowsiness, epileptic automatisms, and so on, up to bright, wide-awake states with shifts of attention and control from rather mechanical to mindful behavior.[164] Koestler claims that one level emerges into the other but fails to confirm a continuity between the highest level of matter-energy and the lowest level of consciousness. He openly admits, "I am aware that in this chapter I have indulged in some momentous question-begging."[165]

None of the no-subject, no-agent, no-soul views of human functions and relationships provide adequate accounts of the data of human experience and Scripture to the extent that interacting dualism does. That a person is a spiritual agent (a spirit) accounts for his identity, continuity, self-transcendence, self-consciousness, purposive and moral responsibility for his behavior. In spite of modern opposition to the use of "substance," "entity," or "being," no better concept has been proposed for "what stands under." As complex as the levels of matter-energy may be, it is matter-energy that accounts for the unity of attributes and capacities in our bodies. And as multifaceted as spirit-energy may be, the soul unifies a person's nonphysical qualities and capacities. Together they compose the whole person. A person may be angry, brilliant, or hopeful, but he or she is more than a bundle of those qualities at any given time. The term *substance* expresses one's reluctance to say that one quality is sadness. We predicate the set of invisible qualities of the soul or spirit as subject and the set of visible qualities to the material body as home and instrument in this life.[166]

Because God created humans in his image ontologically an analogy of being holds between God and humans as well as an analogy of act. We agree with what Stuart Barton Babbage affirms—we are like God in acts and relationships. But we differ insofar as Babbage denies an analogy of being between God and his image-bearers.[167] The image of God in man includes more than relationships and acts. God made our dependent spirits like his infinite Spirit for his fellowship and service.

How Can Two Different Substances Interact?

Granting the holistic reality of soul and body, how can entities with such radically different qualities interact with each other? This has been the major concern of those who oppose an interacting dualism in humanity. Consider the following:

1. The fact is that the interaction of spirit and body takes place constantly. Daily the human soul interacts with the body and is morally accountable for its acts in this life and in the life to come. Every time we decide to go or stay, walk or run, drive through or stop, eat or fast, pray or exercise, the decision of the inner, invisible person moves the body. Even if there is no explanation of how the interaction takes place, the fact remains that interaction takes place constantly. For example, the inner person, while driving, decides to speed up and so moves the foot to the accelerator, and the car moves faster. Again, the inner self decides to stop and moves the foot to the brake, and the brake stops the car. Apparently the spirit is able by a kind of trigger action to release the energy stored up in the healthy body. As the conscious purpose releases the physical energy of the nervous system and the muscles, the foot moves from the accelerator to the brake. A spirit's conscious purpose in this change does not violate natural laws, but uses them. And the inner person of the driver is morally and legally accountable for avoidable accidents.

2. Believers in creation and providence have already accepted the interaction of spirit on the physical, just as God, who is a transcendent Spirit, created and providentially acts in, through and upon the material world.

The eternal spirit created matter and works in the physical world either through nature's laws or independently of them. Any who have followed the doctrines of divine creation and providence should not have any essential difficulty with the fact that a real spiritual being can act upon real physical beings. So, if our natural bias against being accountable for all our actions to the all-knowing Spirit can be overcome, we should be able to admit that a human spirit can act upon its human body.

3. Unfortunately, mechanical explanations are inappropriate to the actions of spirit, whether divine or human. If the "how" questions require complete mechanical answers, they are seldom provided by either Scripture, sociology, or psychology.

4. The problem should not be exaggerated, for as different as soul and body are, they have some things in common: (1) Both are *real entities,* real beings or substances created to interact in a world of both physical and spiritual realities. (2) Both substances have *distinct sets of qualities* attributed to them and sustained by them in divine providence without forming a hybrid. Because both body and spirit are realities in God's world, it need not be thought impossible that different kinds of real beings can make an impact on one another in a world created and sustained by God for that purpose.

The lack of a detailed explanation of *how* God acts in the physical world providentially does not diminish the conclusiveness of the evidence that the divine Spirit does in fact hold it all together. Analogously, if a lack of a full mechanical explanation of how the human spirit acts on the human body remains, it is a lesser difficulty than the problems faced by reductive monisms and all nonsubstantial skepticisms. Monistic hypotheses, whether materialistic or spiritistic, must reduce half of human experience to something it is

not! Nonsubstantialist and nonagent views of humanity lose an adequate basis for continued identity in time and eternity, and for moral responsibility for all of our conduct. Wisdom chooses the hypothesis with the greatest coherence and the fewest difficulties—a holistic view of humanity involving an interacting dualism of soul and body.

Dichotomoy of Substances, Trichotomy of Conscious Relationships

Since the issue between monists and dichotomists is one of the number of substances making up a human being, one would expect trichotomists to propose that a human being is composed of three *substances*. Their diagrammatic illustrations often do suggest three spatially distinct entities. Some trichotomists visualize the spirit in a small circle encompassed by a larger circle of the soul within an even larger circle of the body. Others draw the circle of a person's being like a pie cut in three pieces. Each part or substance is said to have distinctive capacities, making possible distinct relationships and even fruitfulness and victory in the Christian life.

The trichotomists' definitions and explanations fail, however, to distinguish soul substance in itself from spirit substance in itself. Instead, trichotomists speak of the three capacities enabling humans respectively to have God-consciousness, self-consciousness, and world-consciousness.[168] Until this confusion of categories is clarified, progress in research or discussion will remain futile. If there is to be significant progress, both dichotomists and trichotomists must be addressing the same issue—the number of substances. Dichotomists believe as fully as trichotomists that humans can have relationships with God, humans, and the earth. If a trichotomy of relationships is the question, there remains no debate! Allegedly conflicting positions should not go on endlessly with confused categories. One theological problem should be considered settled!

The capacity of a person to understand God-consciousness and self-consciousness does not require two entities. A person has both awarenesses and world-consciousness through the physical nerves and the brain. One and the same person is conscious of God, of self, and of the physical world. In contrast, Watchman Nee's analysis has the spirit relating to God and the soul to self and others. The human spirit, according to Nee, has three main functions for relating to God: intuition, communion, and conscience.[169]

Nee maintains that by *intuition,* as the first function for relating to God, a human spirit allegedly directly knows God's mind and receives divine guidance. But the sudden intuitions of Christians sometimes conflict, let alone those of people in pantheistic religions. All intuitions must be tested by the teaching of Scripture interpreted with sound hermeneutical principles, sound criteria of truth, and a sound method of decision making. All of this requires the use of the mind, so it is hard to see how intuition is superior to the mental capacity alleged of the lower "soul." Second, the spirit at an assumed "deeper" level than thought, feeling, or will allegedly experiences *communion* with God. Significant personal communion with God, according to the greatest commandment, requires the fullest devotion of the whole person—mind, emotions, and will. Jesus did not demote these to a lower level and call for a noncognitive superspirituality. Some trichotomists mistakenly attribute evil, not to the "fleshly nature," but to the soul and the use of its capacities. Third, the *conscience* then reproves sin or approves righteousness. Again, how can conscience operate without mental distinctions between right and wrong,

emotional regret for real guilt, and purposes of will to follow the Lord's revealed will? Dichotomists, as well as trichotomists, receive intuitions, have communion with God, and seek clear consciences, but they do not try to limit these capacities to different parts of a person. They are activities that, at least in their interpretation, involve other capacities and eventually the whole person.

Nee's trichotomist functions of the soul feature the *emotions,* the *mind,* and the *will.* Unworthy desires such as affections, desires, and feelings may enslave the believer. Influenced by these formidable enemies, most Christians are alleged to live "soulical" or unspiritual lives. The mind is the capacity for rational thought, and often is found in conflict with intuition. The will makes decisions for the whole person and in the spiritual life must be unshackled from the fleshly soul life so that it may freely cooperate with God. Nee's soul is alleged to be inferior to his spirit and so also is exegetical study of the Word inferior to intuitions. His mind primarily examines, explains, and develops the intuitive knowledge given by the Holy Spirit to his believing spirit.

The biblical evidence alleged for trichotomy does not attribute the intuitive and reasoning capacities to two distinctly different substances, but to the one inner person who dwells in the body. Relationships as well as substances can be distinguished by the figurative "sword," the teaching of God's Word (Heb. 4:12). The whole dichotomous person can be sanctified, including all three relationships (1 Thess. 5:23). From these two passages that mention spirit, soul, and body, we have no more basis for concluding three substances than we do four substances from the great commandment—to love God with heart, soul, mind, and strength (Mark 12:30).

The implications of three substances

lead to endless difficulties. If it is the soul that thinks, feels, and wills and the spirit that communes with God, is there no thought, feeling, or decision in communion with our Maker? If the spirit's intuitions do not involve intellectual concepts, they are contentless as well as without emotions or determinations of will. Intuitions granted some content are often wrong. The soul's mind then must distinguish which of the spirit's intuited truths are true and which are false! And whose conscience is it that is discerning right from wrong if not that of the person who thinks, feels, and wills? The conscience also is incapable of functioning independently of thinking, feeling, and willing. A person with all capacities functioning (conscience, communion and intuition, reason, emotion, and will) relates to God, others, and the physical world. Intuition is not an independent source of inerrant truth. Intuitions, if true, need to be confirmed by the reason's verificational process; and intuitions may in fact be disconfirmed or shown to be false.

Trichotomists appear to hold that a person is made up of a body and two kinds of nonphysical entities: one referred to as the spirit and the other as the soul. Although trichotomists think they oppose dichotomy, they have yet to distinguish the soul from the spirit as substances. The definitions trichotomists offer provide only functional or relational distinctions. Until trichotomists propose a substantial difference between soul and spirit, there is not a meaningful difference between trichotomists and dichotomists on the number of substances that make up a human person. At present the alleged debate between dichotomy and trichotomy, as far as entities are concerned, is merely verbal. If trichotomists were to succeed in distinguishing spirit and soul as substances, the view would then find difficulty fitting the scriptural instances displaying their interchangeability.

That persons have three primary relationships—to God, other humans, and the material world—dichotomists need not debate. On the interacting dichotomist view, the one inner person (spirit or soul) relates functionally through the brain and body to (1) God, (2) other humans, and (3) the physical world. Hence our view may be referred to as a dichotomy of substances and a trichotomy of functions. Although the three general relationships hold, more than three functions can be distinguished. The one immaterial person has the functions many trichotomists attribute to the soul, for the person thinks, feels, and wills. The same person has the functions trichotomists attribute to the spirit: intuiting possible truths, communion with God, and moral discernment and obligation (conscience). None of these functions that trichotomists attribute to the spirit would be possible without the use of the soul (intellect, emotion, and will). One and the same whole person with all his capacities either does or does not relate well to God, others, or the physical world.

The hypothesis of a trichotomy of substances raises serious difficulties for understanding all of Christian experience. In regard to creation: only a third of the person (the spirit) is created in the *imago Dei*. Only the spirit is affected by the Fall, regenerated, and sanctified. The battles in the Christian life may be considered a conflict of soul against spirit more than of two opposed desires, inclinations, or natures. Many great doctrines are altered if the implications of trichotomy are consistently developed. Since the evidence for trichotomy does not compare with the data against it, we find that God created the whole inner person in his image, the Fall affects all of a person's functions (in a holistic depravity), the Holy Spirit renews the entire inner believer and all the believer's inner functions in the image of his creator, and sanctification proceeds progressively for all functions.

How Human Spirits Originate

In the chapter on creation the evidence indicated that the spirits of Adam and Eve were specially created. How did the spirits of Cain and Abel originate? How and when do human spirits originate today? There is no biblical evidence to support the view that human spirits existed prior to conception and birth. Neither do we find adequate evidence to support the view that spirits are individually created at conception or birth. The passages teaching that spirits come from God can be interpreted providentially and ultimately rather than miraculously and proximately. "The spirit returns to God who gave it" (Eccl. 12:7; cf. Isa. 42:5; Zech. 12:1), and God is "the Father of our spirits" (Heb. 12:9). Every human being, like every other good gift, in the final analysis comes from the Father (James 1:17). But not every good thing comes from God by a miraculous creative act. Creationists raise the problem of how Christ could be without sin if souls are derived from parents along with bodies. The point is irrelevant to normal conceptions, however, because the conception of Jesus was miraculous. The conception of Jesus by a virgin involved both a biological miracle and a moral miracle so that Mary's sinful nature was not transmitted to Jesus, and he was holy (Luke 1:35).

The major problem with a creationist hypothesis is that for all normally born persons the Holy One allegedly directly creates their souls with sinful dispositions. Scriptural teaching traces sinfulness not to the body but to the inner soul or spirit (Jer. 17:9). The "flesh" refers in moral contexts only secondarily to the body as the instrument of the fallen spirit. Primarily the flesh is the sinful nature received at conception.

Since throughout Scripture God is the source of good and not of moral rebellion against himself, it seems unthinkable that he, the Holy One, should specifically create each human soul with a bent toward disbelieving and disobeying him.

The traducian hypothesis attributes the origin of the soul as well as the body to one's parents. Whole spirit-body persons reproduce after their kind. The union of physical cells produces physical bodies and simultaneously the union of spirits produces the spirits of infants. This traducian view may startle at first, but those who have recognized the reality of spirit beings and know that God who is spirit created them in his image should not find the problems insuperable. A traducian hypothesis of the origin of the soul is in harmony with the psycho-physical interaction in all of human life on earth.

The major criticism that is made against traducianism is that it fails to explain *how* souls are propagated. Again, "how" questions are seldom answered. Some hints have been suggested from the development of multiple personalities. In *Three Faces of Eve,* according to authors Corbet Thigpen and Harvey Cleckley, one person was divided into three personalities with different mental characteristics. Working with the notion that personalities may be divisible, William T. Bruner develops a realistic position metaphysically. Bruner's theory asserts that when man was created, all humanity was generically present in one person. The whole human race had one body, one soul, one mind, one will, one consciousness, one personality. The race is propagated not only through a division of cells but also through a division of souls. Hence humans are dissociated selves or multiple personalities of the original pair.[170] Whether we can accept this explanation or have none at present, the difficulty of *how* souls originate is far less severe than the difficulty of tracing all sinful human natures to God.

Although there is not much explicit evidence on the origin of human souls in Scripture, traducianism is the more probable explanation, based on the following considerations:

1. The derivation of all persons from Adam and Eve accounts for the unity of the entire human population (Acts 17:26). The unity of human beings is not merely physical, but also moral and spiritual. Humanity is not a company of individually created spirits such as the angels are. The fact that human persons comprise a single race is crucial theologically as well as socially and politically (Rom. 5:12–14).

2. God is ultimately the "Father of our spirits" by establishing marriage, commanding Adam and Eve to populate the earth, and providentially sustaining mothers and infants through the birth process.

3. The hypothesis of unborn persons doing a deed when their fathers did that deed is not alien to Scripture. The family and national solidarity in Old Testament days is well known. Against that cultural background we can understand that "one might even say that Levi, who collects the tenth, paid the tenth through Abraham, because when Melchizedek met Abraham, Levi was still in the body of his ancestor" (Heb. 7:9–10). Analogously, when Adam sinned, the entire race was in his loins and from him receives sinful hearts.

4. Traducianism, furthermore, most coherently accounts for the Bible's teaching on the sinfulness of human nature from birth. Creationists have a more difficult time with the reality that what is born of flesh is flesh (John 3:6). Jesus explicitly attributes the fleshly nature of children to parents. The characteristics of the evil heart (Matt. 15:18–19) or sinful nature (Eph. 2:3) can hardly be the creation of a God who

is of purer eyes than to look with favor upon sin (Hab. 1:13). Hereditary factors that pass along family and national characteristics from generation to generation are the highly probable sources of our bent toward evil.

5. A traducian view does not contradict divine justice in condemning all mankind for the one act of Adam (Rom. 5:16, 18). On this view Adam is not merely the legal or federal representative of the race as creationists maintain. God may have made a covenant of works with Adam as the legal head of the race, though biblical evidence for this is minimal. If we were not in some sense in Adam generically, physically, and spiritually, however, the covenant of works appears to be a legal fiction without basis in reality. From a traducian perspective (with or without a covenant of works) God can justly regard the race generically in Adam. So "in Adam all die" (1 Cor. 15:22), for in Adam all "sinned" (Rom. 5:12, Greek aorist tense). Hence a traducian view of the origin of the soul provides the more coherent position with the fewer difficulties. The difficulty of explaining how the soul originates is less than explaining how a holy God can create depraved souls.

RELEVANCE FOR LIFE AND MINISTRY

"The chief end of thought and action," said secular humanist Corliss Lamont, "is to further this-worldly human interests. . . . The watchword of Humanism is happiness for all humanity."[171] So that humans can be happy Lamont affirms the unity of the body and personality, holding that "the exterior of man reflects his essential being."[172] He reduces the soul to the brain to attain a monistic metaphysics and stimulate people in the direction of those human-centered ends and values that he thinks are supremely worthwhile, desirable, and for the common good.[173]

Happiness is also the by-product of Christian humanitarianism under God. The Christian's chief end is "to glorify God by enjoying him forever," as John Piper spells out in *Desiring God*.[174] The triune God enjoys himself, his creation, and especially his image-bearers, much as parents enjoy themselves, their work, and especially their children and grandchildren. Christ exhibited joy when he was united to a human spirit and body on earth. Consider the ways in which this Christian understanding of humanity can bring great significance and lasting joy to your life.

What is worthwhile, desirable, and for the common good of humans as spirits-in-bodies? Is an interacting dualism viable? Indeed it is. Viewing humans as spirits in the image of the divine Spirit provides for human values in a better way than agnostic, secular, pantheistic humanisms. Christians can live by this doctrine with authenticity while increasingly ruling the world as good stewards accountable to God.

Prize Persons for Their Intrinsic Value

Those who live by an interacting dualism *value humans highly for their inherent worth.* Because humans are real spiritual beings who will relate to God forever in loving fellowship or will be alienated from God, each person is of inestimable temporal and eternal value and significance. Persons have this inward worth inalienably as creatures of God made in the image of God. Their value goes far beyond that of their amazing bodies or that of being the highest animal on earth. Their value is not diminished when for some reason and for some time they are not useful to society in the form of their family, church, or nation. Every living human being is of instrinsic worth—poor or

rich, female or male, educated or not, lighter or darker—because he or she is an endlessly existing active spiritual person like God.

Interacting dichotomists who live consistently with their view *treat humans as subjects, not objects.* Persons as spiritual beings are not things to be folded, mutilated, or spindled. As self-transcendent spirits humans are self-conscious and self-determining subjects and moral agents. Christians see in all other persons active beings who should be free from coercion to think, feel, will, and relate. Christians know that social regulations (like that of the Sabbath) are made for humans' health and well-being, not humans for social regulations of institutions (such as the Sabbath).

Interacting dichotomists appreciate also the inherent *dignity of human presence.* While walking in a park it is one thing for a person to pass bushes and squirrels; it is quite another to encounter persons. As souls, humans have inherent dignity and worth beyond the physical. Spirits in the presence of other spirits for any length of time (traveling on a bus or plane) find it difficult not to communicate. Paul could be "present . . . in spirit" though absent in the body (Col. 2:5; cf. 1 Cor. 5:3–4). Sometimes we sense the presence of others even before they come into sight or hearing. A sense of the presence of human spirits should not seem strange to those who have a sense of the presence of the divine Spirit. Even during tragedy the biblical writers did not yield to despair. They did not pronounce God dead but realized that they could not go anywhere to escape God's omnipresence (Ps. 139). Through universal revelation all people have some sense of the presence of God who is Spirit. Beyond that, Christians have a sense of the presence of the personal God as Redeemer. Followers of Christ sense the Holy Spirit witnessing with their spirits that they personally are children of God! Having consciousness of the divine Spirit, Christians may sense the presence of human spirits.

Respect Inalienable Human Rights

Along with the gift of existence as spirits God gave his image-bearers certain inalienable rights. Human rights have not been given by governments and ought not be taken by any national authority in any culture anywhere in the world. The rights of God's image-bearers ought not to be taken away by parents, educators, capitalists, communists, or charismatic religious leaders. The rights of human beings to fair treatment by other humans come from the Lord of justice and so are nonnegotiable; they are superior to any policy. No social goals of any collective can outweigh the intrinsic authority of a human spirit's rights. God-given rights are universal and obligatory everywhere, always. No pragmatic ends justify violating the changless principles of just relationships to God and others.

In a fallen world God also graciously gave ten commandments to protect people from violations of their rights. Our rights to life and liberty while relating to God and others are supported by those ten basic responsibilities. They constitute a universal declaration of our most basic rights and freedoms. The first four responsibilities protect our rights in relation to God: (1) the right freely to value above all the Source who liberates us from enslavement to others (Exod. 20:1–3), (2) the right freely to worship the transcendent Lord of all (vv. 5–6), (3) the right and responsibility to bear God's name without hypocrisy (v. 7), and (4) the right to a day a week for rest and worship (vv. 8–11). The last six responsibilities protect human rights in relation to each other: (5) the right of parents freely to live long on the earth with the esteem of

their children (v. 12), (6) the right of all to life without the threat of murder (v. 13), (7) the right of all to marital fidelity without suspicions of lust and adultery (v. 14), (8) the right of all to private ownership of property without threat of theft (v. 15), (9) the right of all to intellectually honest representation by others (v. 16), and (10) the right to a simple or different life-style free from coveting any person, animal, or thing belonging to neighbors.

We may not all agree on precisely how such just principles apply in any given situation, but do we not all agree that we ought to be treated justly? An equal right of all to justice is not relative to equal abilities. People with few talents have as much right to exist and freely pursue their goals as those with greater capacities. Life built on just normative commitments provides for meaningful human existence. In a sea of relativities all can cling to these lifesavers.

All people are entitled to the freedoms of religion, speech, and pursuit of goals while exercising these rights with responsibility to God and others. As moral agents we enjoy our freedom to swing our arms so long as we do not injure or offend others. All people deserve respect, whether they are female or male, students or teachers, rich or poor, owners or laborers, prisoners or free, church members or vocal atheists, secular humanists or New Age pantheists. Even in democracies with majority rule the inherent rights of minorities ought to be defended. To recognize these basic values as absolute rights is at the same time to admit that violations of them are absolute wrongs.

Similar human rights are spelled out in the American State Papers and the United States Bill of Rights. And on December 10, 1948, the United Nations adopted a Universal Declaration of Human Rights. Since that time all members of the United Nations recognize rights to life, liberty, security of person, equality before the law, and equal protection of the law without discrimination. These rights open the door to universal competition for benefits, entitling all to make the most of themselves, but not guaranteeing that any one person will make as much of himself or herself as others. Christians everywhere should respect pre-Christians' rights as they would have non-Christians respect theirs.

Develop a Healthy Self-Image and Sense of Reality

Our view of the worth of others may be low because of a low view of ourselves. Men and women who affirm the reality and dignity of God's image-bearers universally ought to see the implications of that truth for their own *self-image*. We ought to cease considering ourselves naked apes or meat machines. We are not mere victims of class interests, economic aggrandizement, genetic programming, cultural conditioning, or historical necessity. Like other persons, we ourselves have inestimable worth as self-transcendent subjects and moral agents. Our inherent value cannot be taken away by any mistake or failure. Because of what we *are* spiritually and physically, our lives are of greater value than any impersonal project in the whole world. People struggling to "find themselves" may be helped to realize who they are ontologically. One's sense of one's own identity and dignity begins with awareness of ourselves as real spirits who creatively initiate action as responsible moral agents.

An interacting dichotomy supplies a base for a healthy *sense of reality*. To strengthen this sense of our dichotomous reality in the image of God we may need to exercise all of our capacities. Intellectually, we need to accept ourselves as spiritual-physical beings.

This may take time if we have been strongly influenced by naturalistic or pantheistic views. Morally, we may need to develop a sense of our reality as agents initiating great good or evil. This may be difficult if we viewed ourselves as victims of conditioning by others. Emotionally, we may need to joyfully accept ourselves for what we are in our essential spiritual-physical being with all of our distinctively human capabilities. What a privilege it is to be a person and not wallpaper! Volitionally, we may need to reaffirm our worth and dignity under God, make our own decisions, act upon them, and maturely accept our share of the responsibility for their consequences. Relationally, we will cultivate friendship with God and other humans. God and others can appreciate what it is like to be a self-critical spirit and understand our problems intellectually, morally, emotionally, volitionally, and relationally. Our highest joys in time and eternity result from fulfilling person-to-person experiences.

Apparently few people are totally satisfied with their bodies. Most of us feel some physical limitations in appearance or in coordination of athletic, musical, or artistic talents. If so, whether male or female, we may well meditate for twenty minutes on the fact that whatever the real or imagined defects may be, we can learn to be "at home" in our bodies. And we may improve our self-regard by strengthening our hearts through aerobic exercises and our basic muscle groups with guided weight lifting. Regular training programs for both purposes contribute to the effective use of our bodies as instruments of our spirits. Then we may feel well enough about ourselves to take up music, art, or theology!

One reason for a lack of self-esteem among women may stem from the dearth of recent preaching and teaching on the equality of women and men ontologically. Studies have indicated that in some churches women have suffered from a lack of self-esteem more than men. In view of that, although this entire chapter applies to women, an explicit application of an interacting dualism to their ontological status seems relevant. If women have unrealistic views of themselves, they may have concluded with most recent philosophy and theology that they cannot know anything about who they are in themselves (metaphysically). So they may have reduced their significance to that of fragile phenomena, pragmatic functions, or changing relationships. In such an intellectual climate it is little wonder that women have difficulty recognizing their identity and value. Since the evidence in this chapter indicates that women are real physical beings and more than that, real self-conscious, self-determining spiritual subjects and moral agents, they have solid reasons to respect themselves. One woman, whether single or married, young or old, educated or not, is of far more value than the whole nonhuman world. Women have inestimable intrinsic worth because they, not a whit less than men, are spirits made in the divine image for fellowship with God and service for God throughout time and eternity.

Tragically the metaphysical foundation of female dignity and inherent worth has been destroyed by the anti-metaphysical spirit of the age. Ontologically a woman's human nature is not in any way inferior to a man's. Men ought to respect women because their essential human nature is as significant as theirs. Whatever differences remain functionally or relationally should in no way alter this basic reason for self-respect and self-esteem. By way of illustration, the distinct offices of Father, Son, and Holy Spirit are no basis for failing to esteem all three as equally divine in essence and being. (I:279). Analogously, since male and female are equally spiritual-physical be-ings, it follows that there ought be mutual respect. In the context of ontological equality, people need not be overly sensitive about the Bible's generic use of "man" for male and female in the image of God (Gen. 1:27).

Because we are spirits-in-bodies, both women and men may improve their self-esteem not alone by training their bodies, as indicated above, but also by a regular program for *training their spirits*. In order for the implications of an interacting dualism to become part of our consciousness we may need to meditate on its implications repeatedly, change inconsistent attitudes and habits, and act with new self-esteem and new respect for others. As important as is the disciplined training of our bodies, we should be even more concerned with training our spirits. Jesus, who sees the sparrow fall and counts the hairs of your head, said, "Don't be afraid; you are worth more than many sparrows" (Matt. 10:28–31). The human body is of great value for roughly seventy years, but Jesus viewed the soul as of far greater value. "What good will it be for a man if he gains the whole world, yet forfeits his own soul? Or what can a man give in exchange for his soul?" (Matt. 16:26). Our value does not consist in the amount of our earthly possessions (Luke 12:15). A person's worth is finally calculated by omniscience in heaven (Matt. 6:20, 25). So a development of the spiritual disciplines of Bible study, meditation, prayer, and fasting may be used by the Holy Spirit to strengthen our sense of well-being.

Overcome Fear of Death

Being told that they cannot know anything about their souls or spirits in themselves, people, fearing the unknown, fear death. Nonmetaphysical views of the inner person provide few answers; so people turn for information away from theologians and philosophers to mere descriptions of near-death experiences and to unreliable messages allegedly from the dead through mediums or channelers. Jesus emphatically distinguished the reality of the soul from that of the body and used his metaphysical dichotomy to help his disciples face persecution and death for his sake. Jesus said, "Brother will betray brother to death, and a father his child; children will rebel against parents and have them put to death" (Matt. 10:21). Then, "Do not be afraid of those who kill the body but cannot kill the soul" (v. 28). No terrorist on earth can kill your soul! We can know this about the soul in itself (apart from its relation to the body): it exists everlastingly. Hence Christian believers do not fear death as others do. Although Christians' bodies are buried, their spirits will go to be with Christ. That is great comfort also when the spirit departs from the body of a loved one.

Overcome Racial Prejudices

We must confess the sin of *racial discrimination* because all humans of whatever racial background are chidren of Adam and Eve, who are children of the Creator metaphysically. The Bible represents mankind as *one human race* derived from common original parents, not a company of individuals separately created like the angels. Adam and Eve were to be fruitful and multiply and fill the earth (Gen. 1:28), and Eve is "the mother of all the living" (3:20). "From one man he made every nation of men, that they should inhabit the whole earth" (Acts 17:26). All are one in Adam for moral and theological considerations (Rom. 5:12–18). "For as in Adam all die, so in Christ all will be made alive" (1 Cor. 15:22). Differences of pigmentation and culture should never be allowed to overshadow our basic human oneness. Red and yellow, black and white, all need to overcome biases and consciously emphasize equal human worth in the others.

Care About the Unborn

Abortion is not merely a private religious issue between individuals and God. It is also a universal human issue—among all human beings. Because a human soul has inherent value if it originates at conception, people ought not take the life of a growing human infant before birth. Admittedly the Bible does not explicitly teach that the soul originates at conception. So other suggestions have been made and may be regarded with some tolerance. Consider these alternative ideas for the time when life begins in the womb: (1) The soul originates with implantation in the uterus (starts the 7th or 8th day, completed by the 12th day), (2) when the blood system is formed (third week), (3) at quickening (motion felt at about four months), or (4) when the baby is able to survive outside the womb (six months).

The origin of the soul at conception seems more probable because we found that the whole child originates from the union of both parents. The entire RNA and DNA genetic potential is received at conception. And because the body and soul are inseparable throughout life, both most likely originate together. So from conception, a potential person, a human person in the most elementary form exists (Ps. 139:13–16). Hence from the moment of conception more than the mother's rights are involved. The rights of mother, father, and infant need to be respected. The general rule says no to aborting a life with inherent worth and human rights for the sake of convenience.

In rare exceptions in which the survival of the mother is endangered, however, she has the more fundamental claim. With limited wisdom, at times people fail to discover a good alternative action and resort to what seems the lesser of two evils (aborting the life of a child). In so doing, they sin, for even the lesser evil can never be called good. But those who minister to persons who have had abortions need to assure them that they have *not* committed the unforgiveable sin. God has forgiven premeditated murderers like Moses, David, and Paul. By the same divine mercy, people who have aborted unborn humans can be forgiven! God forgives their sin if they confess their sin for what it is (1 John 1:9).

Help Others

We may show our high regard for human life by helping those who are not able to improve their situations, such as *the hungry, orphans, widows, and prisoners.* Their inherent value as persons is not diminished by their circumstances. How can we do more, you say, than we are already doing? Whatever the limitations of the outer jar of clay, believers can receive the treasure of the all-surpassing power from God within (2 Cor. 4:6). Christians, like Paul, may be "hard pressed on every side, but not crushed; perplexed, but not in despair; persecuted, but not abandoned; struck down, but not destroyed" (v. 7). God has not promised believers perfect health and physical prowess in this life, and he did not answer Paul's prayers to remove his "thorn in the flesh." The Lord answered Paul's prayer in another way, saying, "My grace is sufficient for you, for my power is made perfect in weakness" (12:9).

Help *children and adolescents.* Infants and children are no less human just because they are young and economically unproductive. They should be wanted, loved, and cared for in spite of their apparent lack of utility! Infants and children are inwardly little people with inner spiritual natures of inestima-

ble worth. The ugly reports of child abuse by Satanists and others may be in part attributed to the loss of a view of a child's inherent worth. There is also a failure to follow the example of Christ. Our Lord respected and loved children during his brief ministry on earth. And Jesus warned, "If anyone causes one of these little ones, who believe in me to sin, it would be better for him to have a large millstone hung around his neck and to be drowned in the depths of the sea" (Matt. 18:6).

Care for the *elderly.* The aged are no less human for outwardly "wasting away" (2 Cor. 4:16). Elderly persons should be wanted and loved because of their inherent worth, quite apart from what they can do for others. For their own self-esteem they should be aided in caring for themselves as long as possible. When they are unable to care for themselves, we should care for them as we would wish to be cared for when we are in a similar condition. Loving relationships should be sustained as normally as possible.

Care as well for the *sick and handicapped.* In his day Jesus cared about the lepers; we today must care about people with AIDS and other diseases. One who believed more in every human's right to life above the quality of life said, "The moral question for us is not whether the suffering and the dying are persons but whether *we* are the kind of persons who will care for them without doubting their worth."[175] In a fallen world people face debilitating injuries, allergies, and diseases. They remain persons with inherent worth and deserve our respect and esteem. They need to be treated, not as curiosities, but as persons.

Care for *your neighbors.* Who are our neighbors? They are those who have an urgent need like that of the man helped by the good Samaritan (Luke 10:25–37). Even though the Samaritan did not know that person before, he knew that he had not only a need but also great worth. Because a person in need is not a thing, we will do all in our power with our abilities and resources to help. We will treat our neighbors as we would be treated (Matt. 7:12). Care also for your *enemies*. Our political, social, ecclesiastical, and other opponents have inherent worth as persons. Because they are image-bearers of the Creator we should show them respect and love. Insofar as it is in their power to do so Christians will pray for those who oppose them because of their faith, and they will do so just as Christ prayed from the cross, "Father forgive them, for they do not know what they are doing" (Luke 23:34).

Secular and cosmic humanists talk about loving humanity in general, and they do many fine things. But Christ exhibited the greatest concern for human well-being, and his teaching remains unequalled. It is now crucial for Christian humanists to demonstrate their Master's superior values in every aspect of human existence.

Achieve Your Highest Human Potential

After a bad day at school a small boy in a televsion commercial reported, "My teacher says I am not living up to my full potentiality." Having pronounced the last word with difficulty, he complained, "I don't even know what 'full potentiality' means." Others have a similar problem. Is the highest human potential a fulfilling sex life (Freud)? fulfilling our social conditioning (Skinner)? freedom from nature's laws or anything outside ourselves? or transcendence of our humanness to become divine (like Maslow)? Have we unlimited potential (Fromm, May, Rogers)? In our development can we draw from the collective unconscious of all humans (Jung)? Have we infinite

potential for spiritually evolving into gods (New Age writers)?

Participants in the most practical personal, business, and social programs for self-improvement need to know whether self-realization programs aim toward the goals of humanness as seen by naturalists, by pantheists, or by theists. People who understand that all humans are by nature an interacting dichotomy ought not give themselves to leaders or programs that either reduce them to mere animals or claim to help them realize their inner divinity. As creatures who bear the image of God we will seek to be the best we can be in reflecting God's communicable characteristics. We will be the best we can be both spiritually and physically. As spirits we will seek our highest potential, not through the guidance of channelers or magical coercion of occult powers, but through Holy Spirit-illumined guidance of Scripture and Holy Spirit-endued service. As real physical beings we will develop our aerobic capacity so that our hearts can achieve their fullest potential and regularly exercise each major muscle group in our bodies so that our physical instrument will serve its highest usefulness.

We have the privilege of relating in personal and fulfilling ways, not only to loved ones, friends, and associates each day, but to the Designer and Creator of the universe! Our highest potential goes beyond married love, parental love, and love of achievement, to love of God. Although our astounding relational potential can be used for evil, by grace we can creatively serve loved ones, friends, and associates each day, and in it all help establish the kingdom of the Most High. Our highest potential is not achieved in our excellent work in our homes, schools, or businesses as such, but in our labor for God's rulership in these relationships. So we keep ourselves in the best condition we can physically and spiritually to develop to the fullest our potential as stewards accountable above all to the Creator whose image we bear.

REVIEW QUESTIONS

To Help Relate and Apply Each Section in This Chapter

1. *Briefly state the classical problem* this chapter addresses and indicate reasons why genuine inquiry into it is important for your world view and your existence personally and socially.

2. *Objectively summarize the influential answers* given to this problem in history as hypotheses to be tested. Be able to compare and contrast their real similarities and differences (not merely verbal similarities or differences).

3. *Highlight the primary biblical evidence* on which to decide among views—evidence found in the relevant teachings of the major divisions of Scripture—and decide for yourself which historical hypothesis (or synthesis of historical views) provides the most consistent and adequate account of the primary biblical data.

4. *Formulate in your own words your doctrinal conviction* in a logically consistent and adequate way, organizing your conclusions in ways you can explain clearly, support biblically, and communicate effectively to your spouse, children, friends, Bible class, or congregation.

5. *Defend your view* as you would to adherents of the alternative views, showing that the other views are logically less consistent and factually faced with more difficulties than your view in accounting for the givens, not only of special revelation but also of human experience in general.

6. *Explore the differences the viability of your conviction can make in your life*. Then test your understanding of the viability of your view by asking, "Can I live by it authentically (unhypocritically) in relation to God and to others in my family, church, vocation, neighborhood, city, nation, and world?"

MINISTRY PROJECTS

To Help Communicate This Doctrine in Christian Service

1. *Memorize one major verse or passage* that in its context teaches the heart of this doctrine and may serve as a text from which to preach, teach, or lead small-group studies on the topic. The memorized passages from each chapter will build a body of content useful also for meditation and reference in informal discussions.

2. *Formulate the major idea of the doctrine in one sentence* based on the passage memorized. This idea should be useful as the major thesis of either a lesson for a class (junior high to adult) or a message for a church service.

3. *State the specific purpose or goal of your doctrinal lesson or message*. Your purpose should be more than informative. It should show why Christians need to accept this truth and live by it (unhypocritically). For teaching purposes, list indicators that would show to what extent class members have grasped the truth presented.

4. *Outline your message or lesson in complete sentences*. Indicate how you would support the truth of the doctrine's central ideas and its relevance to life and service. Incorporate elements from this chapter's historical, biblical, systematic, apologetic, and practical sections selected according to the value they have for your audience.

5. *List applications of the doctrine* for communicating the difference this conviction makes in life (for sermons, lessons, small-group Bible studies, or family devotional Bible studies). Applications should make clear what the doctrine is, why one needs to know it,

179

and how it will make changes in thinking. Then show how the change in thought will lead to differences in values, priorities, attitudes, speech, and personal action. Consider also the doctrine's possible significance for family, church, neighborhood, city, regional, and national actions.

6. *Start a file and begin collecting illustrations* of this doctrine's central idea, the points in your outline, and your application.

7. *Write out your own doctrinal statement on this subject in one paragraph* (in half a page or less). To work toward a comprehensive doctrinal statement, collect your formulations based on a study of each chapter of *Integrative Theology*. As your own statement of Christian doctrine grows, you will find it personally strengthening and useful when you are called on for your beliefs in general and when you apply for service with churches, mission boards, and other Christian organizations. Any who seek ordination to Christian ministry will need a comprehensive doctrinal statement that covers the broad scope of theology.

CHAPTER 4

GOD'S IMAGE-BEARERS IN REBELLION

God's Image-Bearers in Rebellion

THE PROBLEM: HOW DO WE ACCOUNT FOR THE IMPERFECTIONS AND FAILURES OF PERSONS CREATED IN GOD'S IMAGE TO BE THE NOBLEST BEINGS IN GOD'S WORLD?

One prominent European scholar affirms that "the church's anthropology revolves around the two concepts of 'the image of God' and 'original sin.' "[1] The previous chapter considered persons as God's image, the highest and noblest of living beings. It presented persons ontologically as created for fellowship with God and ordained to function as his vice-regents over the world and lower forms of life. The present chapter considers persons in rebellion against God and spoiled by sin. It draws out the implications of the fall of humans from their high estate and seeks to account for their conduct, which at times rivals that of the beasts. How one understands the problem considered this chapter will influence one's views of the purpose of Christ's coming to earth (vol. 1, chap., 5), the import of his death on the cross (vol. 2, chap., 7), and the meaning of salvation (vol. 3, chaps. 1–4).

Undeniably human persons are capable of extraordinary accomplishments. They can investigate the smallest particles of the atom and can propel themselves into space to search out the planets. Yet even the casual observer recognizes persons' capacity for horrible forms of brutality and inhumanity. Right-minded people are repulsed by the incidence of murder, rape, drug trafficking, highjackings, and white-collar crimes in our most enlightened societies. Human persons, as we know them, are an enigma of greatness and degradation bundled into single conscious beings.

How did humans become evil? Did their descent from grandeur begin with a Fall, a moral defection of the first man and woman? Can we point to the Fall as the greatest tragic episode in the history of the human race? We inquire further whether the historical reality of the Edenic drama, widely denied by critical scholars, can be factually sustained. Moreover, we must trace the consequences of what happened in Eden upon the mind, the will, and the emotions of Adam's descendants. To what extent has the Fall damaged human persons as image-bearers of God? Has the image of God in sinners been destroyed? Moreover, we must address the difficult question of how and to what extent Adam's sin has affected every individual born into the world. How could persons be held guilty for deeds perpetrated before they were born? Is it just of God to condemn all for the sins of one pair? Does the classical notion of imputed guilt and penalty negate *my* personal responsibility for crimes committed? How, then, should Christians view the relation between Adam's sin and the spiritual condition of the human race?

Next we explore the nature and effects of sin. Is the *fundamental* human problem childhood psychic traumas (Freudianism)? Or inequitable economic arrangements (Marxism)? Or the realities of anxiety and inauthentic existence (existentialism)? Or is the basic human problem what the church has called sin? Can the saying be sustained that "the heart of the human problem is the problem of the human heart"? The issue of sin is of the utmost importance, for the Bible suggests that all the physical diseases, mental disorders, and crimes, all the barbarism, brutality, and bureaucratic manipulation are the consequences of the malady called sin. Furthermore, we must as a matter of pastoral care for grieving parents address the question of the spiritual condition of infants. Are infants and small children afflicted with the scourge of sin and the guilt that arises from it? What should Christians believe concerning the standing of these little ones before God if they should die before an age of moral accountability?

ALTERNATIVE INTERPRETATIONS IN THE CHURCH

The leading answers to the problems concerning the Fall and sin will now be identified as hypotheses to be tested against the primary data of Scripture.

Pelagians, Socinians, Unitarians, and Modernists

Pelagius, Julian of Eclanum, Celestius, and others proceeded from the assumption that if persons are truly human they must possess the freedom to choose responsibly. Since persons are born into the world capable of willing and actualizing the good, it is perverse, these thinkers argued, to view men and women as fallen and depraved. Rather, the Pelagians insisted that each person who enters the world is by nature innocent and free from proclivity to evil. Pelagius acknowledged the rather obvious fact that persons do transgress God's law. He explained the fact of evil, however, not on the basis of imputation or inheritance but by the power of bad examples that persons tend to imitate. Some people, Pelagius argued, perfectly obey God and thus live sinless lives. Furthermore, the Pelagians rejected the idea that death represents God's punishment for original sin. On the contrary, they claimed that God created people mortal; they were destined to die irrespective of any sin committed. The church condemned Pelagianism at the Synod of Carthage (418) and again at the Council of Ephesus (431).

The sixteenth-century Socinian movement represented a revival of the old Pelagian heresy. Like their humanistic forebears, the Socinians denied original sin, the transmission of depravity and guilt to posterity, and the sentence of death as punishment for sin. "The fall of Adam, as it was but one act, could not have power to deprave his nature, much less that of his posterity."[2] Individuals sin through a combination of unfavorable circumstances and negative examples. Sin when committed does not eliminate free will or the person's ability to obey God, and certainly it does not vitiate the *imago,* which the Socinians defined functional-

184

ly as the exercise of dominion over the world.

Unitarians such as William E. Channing and Henry Ware argued that the doctrines of original sin and total depravity are repugnant to the moral character of God. They judged it inconsistent with the divine goodness that a child should enter the world disposed to evil and subject to damnation. Said Ware, "Man is by nature . . . innocent and pure; free from all moral corruption. . . . He has natural affections, all of them originally good, but liable by a wrong direction to be the occasion of error and sin."[3] Channing, in fact, spoke of the "essential sameness" of human beings and God. Consequently, the person is not depraved, for he is intrinsically like God, even as Christ is like God.

Theological modernists likewise deny the fall of the race from a higher condition and uphold, rather, human ascent from an animal past to new heights of moral achievement. In the words of W. N. Clarke, "Humanity certainly is by nature a slowly rising race, with a native tendency to outgrow faults."[4] Liberals generally believe that persons were created as children of God, their potential for sonship needing only to be awakened. Thus the tradition consistently denies original sin, claiming that a sudden incursion of sin in the evolutionary ascent is psychologically impossible. According to W. A. Brown, "Sin is not a foreign intruder making its appearance in the universe suddenly at a moment of time, and bringing about an abrupt transformation in human nature as a whole."[5] Denying total depravity, he defined sin as sensuality, i.e., as the inevitable conflict between the person's residual animal impulses and the impulses of the spirit. Thus "sin is a necessary stage in the evolution of humanity—an essential element in God's training of mankind for higher things."[6] Brown argues that persons succumb to temptations and so sin as a result of parental influences and social environment.

Semi-Pelagians and Roman Catholic Theologians

Theologians such as John Cassian, Vincent of Lerins, and Faustus of Riez, reacting in the fifth and sixth centuries against the teachings of Augustine, affirmed that Adam's sin caused his posterity to be spiritually weak rather than radically fallen. The moral corruption transmitted to the human family is not total, does not constitute sin and guilt, and does not merit the wrath of God. As born into the world, persons remain capable of willing and performing the good. Each person, however, actualizes his weakened moral nature in the performance of specific sins and so becomes morally culpable before God. We may sum up as follows: according to the Pelagians, the person is spiritually well; according to the Semi-Pelagians, spiritually sick; and according to the Augustinian tradition, the unregenerate person is spiritually dead.

Medieval and modern Roman Catholic theology is predominantly Semi-Pelagian. As noted in the previous chapter, Catholic thought holds that to the person's more or less morally neutral human nature God subsequently added the gift of righteousness, which served as a check on sensuous impulses. At the Fall, the *donum superadditum* was lost, whereupon Adam reverted to his original condition, which involved conflict between flesh and spirit. Since Adam was the head of the race, his privation of righteousness and his tendency to concupiscence were passed on to the human family. Adam's posterity therefore suffers a spiritual deficiency, but not actual sin and guilt. Sin is not committed and legally reckoned until each individual willfully acts contrary to God's law. Thus Catholicism views sin not as a condition whose consequence is spiritual inability, but as a series of discrete acts that constitute the perpetrator sinful and guilty. Gregory the Great, the Franciscans, and Abelard adhered to these tenets.

The Council of Trent reiterated the judgment that as a result of sin Adam lost the superadded gift of righteousness. Moreover, by propagation, not merely by imitation, Adam's sin "injured" the entire human race, Mary excepted. It appears, however, that the Tridentine reference to racial "sin" does not connote sin in the strict sense of the word.[7] Thus, although Trent did not specify what Adam transmitted to his posterity, the best inference seems to be a nature devoid of righteousness, morally wounded, and inclined to sin. Trent clearly states that in spiritual matters free will was weakened but not lost. Thus "if anyone saith that, since Adam's sin, the free-will of man is lost and extinguished; . . . let him be anathema."[8] Trent commanded that infants be baptized for the remission of the contagion inherited from their parents.[9]

Not entirely consistent with Catholic formulations on sin and depravity, Pope Pius IX in 1854 promulgated the dogma of the immaculate conception of Mary. Many in the church argued that unless Mary was free from the pollution of sin, Christ would not have been born sinless.

McBrien acknowledges that "the doctrine of Original Sin does not play a very large part in contemporary Catholic theology."[10] Thus the Catholic manual of doctrine, *A New Catechism*, denies that the Fall was a historic event. The claim that "Adam is Man" means that Adam's experience in the scriptural myth portrays the experience of each person. Repeated mention of the sin of "one man" in Romans 5 is viewed as literary embellishment and not the true meaning of the text. *The New Catechism* rejects the notion that the race became depraved and guilty as a result of Adam's sin. Rather, with the loss of the supernatural gifts and the resultant exposure to concupiscence, each person freely violates God's law and so becomes corrupt. "Hence no one is condemned for original sin 'alone,' but only for the personal decisions by which he ratified original sin, so to speak, and stood over it."[11]

Piet Schoonenberg reinterprets the doctrine of hereditary sin from an evolutionary and existentialist perspective. The old view that sin passes down to the human race by propagation violates human responsibility. Schoonenberg argues that the genesis of sin resides not in Adam but in the world. That is, due to the collective pressure of the social situation and the power of negative examples, individuals transgress God's law and so incur condemnation. We must not "overlook the specific nature of original sin, which consists in this, that it comes to us from others, thus besetting our existence from the very start."[12] According to Schoonenberg, the sinner is afflicted not with total depravity, but with a wounded moral nature.

As suggested above, Catholicism emphasizes less the sinful nature or disposition than specific sins. It distinguishes between sins that are venial and those that are mortal. Venial sins are sins of lesser importance or sins of greater gravity done without full knowledge. Catholicism judges that venial sins hinder a person's access to God. They are said to be removed by prayer, fasting, and almsgiving. Mortal sins, on the other hand, are willful transgressions of a serious nature, such as apostasy, murder, or adultery, and they merit eternal punishment. Catholic theology maintains that mortal sins are forgiven only by the sacrament of penance, which involves confession, absolution by a priest, and satisfaction that might include the payment of indulgences.

Arminian Interpreters

Arminian theology focuses on the effects of the Fall on Adam's posterity and the mitigation of the consequences of it by prevenient grace. Two broad classes of opinion prevail. The first—espoused by Arminius, Wesley, and Wiley—holds that Adamic sin brought depravity, guilt, and punishment on the race as a whole. But through prevenient grace, which is said to flow universally and unconditionally from Christ's atonement, guilt and punishment are nullified and depravity is alleviated to such an extent that the sinner is able to cooperate with saving grace. The second class of Arminians—including the Remonstrants, Finney, and Miley—approximates the Semi-Pelagian position. According to this view, Adam's sin brought guilt and punishment on himself, but not on his posterity. The pollution inherited from Adam gives rise to specific sins, which God in turn reckons to each person as guilt and penalty. Once again, prevenient grace nullifies the effects of depravity, enabling the unregenerate person to cooperate with God.

According to John Wesley, God imputed to the human race Adam's sin and the depravity, guilt, and condemnation of it. Wesley believed that the polluted nature inherited from Adam ("We were all born with a sinful, devilish nature."[13]) is properly sin and that it renders the human family guilty before God. Said Wesley, "The sin of Adam, without the sins which we afterward committed, brought us death."[14] With great passion Wesley upheld "that entire depravity and corruption, which by nature spreads itself over the whole man, leaving no part uninfected."[15] Thus far Wesley was generally Augustinian. Believing, however, that a person is responsible only for deeds that he or she commits, Wesley insisted that inherited guilt and penalty are cancelled by "preventing grace," so that in reality each person born into the world is innocent until the perpetration of actual sins. Furthermore, Wesley claimed that the same prevenient grace alleviates inborn depravity. With the mind thus enlightened and the will freed, all persons are enabled to repent and exercise faith toward God.[16]

Wiley, who subscribes to both the natural and the federal headship of Adam, claims that Arminianism

> holds to the unity of the race in Adam, that "in Adam all have sinned," and that all men "are by nature the children of wrath." But over against this, it holds that in Christ, the second Man who is the Lord from heaven, the most gracious God has provided for all a remedy for that general evil which was derived to us from Adam, free and gratuitous in His beloved Son Jesus Christ.[17]

Wiley adds that on the basis of prevenient grace no person who enters the world is guilty of inbred sin. Each person, however, becomes guilty and subject to judgment when he follows his lower nature and commits actual sins. The *Beacon Dictionary of Theology* attempts to clarify the uncertainty surrounding the ascription of guilt with the following observation. "It is helpful to make a distinction between guilt as *culpability,* or personal blameworthiness; and guilt as *liability* for consequences. The former was Adam's guilt alone, the latter belongs potentially to the race, if the remedy in Christ is rejected."[18]

The position of these Arminians with regard to the spiritual condition of infants is as follows. Infants theoretically are afflicted with Adamic depravity, guilt, and punishment. But through the benefit of prevenient grace, guilt and punishment are removed such that no child of Adam is condemned eternally. "Where all were born sinful, they were also born in grace."[19] Each child at the age of moral accountability determines his or her destiny by a personal decision for or against Christ.

The second class of Arminians, introduced above, maintains that the only connection between Adam and his race is a polluted moral nature that predisposes each person to transgressions. This inherited condition involves neither sin, guilt, nor condemnation. Thus the Remonstrant theologians argued that prior to the actualization of the will the person is blameless before God. God reckons to each person sin and guilt only when he consciously actualizes his inborn propensities by specific transgressions.

John Miley, a Methodist theologian, affirms that by natural generation Adam transmitted to his posterity depravity—i.e., loss of original righteousness, corruption of the moral and sensuous nature, and a tendency toward evil. Miley emphasizes that, since it is a natural inheritance, depravity is not a penalty inflicted by God. Furthermore, humanity did not participate in Adam's *sin,* for native depravity is not a transgression of any law of God. Moreover, humanity did not inherit Adam's *guilt,* for a mere tendency toward evil is not blameworthy. And finally, humanity did not inherit Adam's *punishment,* for one cannot be justly condemned except for his own sin. In sum, "native depravity is a part of the Arminian system, and entirely consistent with its principles; native demerit is discordant and contradictory."[20] Miley concludes that in real life each person actualizes the tendencies of his corrupt nature and so sins, thereby incurring personal guilt and condemnation. In practice, however, prevenient grace mitigates the effects of depravity thus enabling the sinner to repent.

Charles Finney's position borders on Pelagianism. He vigorously denies that sin pertains to a person's moral state. More preposterous still, he believes, is the notion that one can inherit a sinful nature from his ancestors. "Man is not born sinful or virtuous, but innocent and acquires his sinful nature by his choices."[21] Finney judges that sin is wholly a willful violation of a known law of God. Furthermore, the supposition of inherited sin and guilt contravenes God's justice. "It is a monstrous and blasphemous dogma, that a holy God is angry with any creature for possessing a nature with which he was sent into being without his knowledge or consent."[22]

Neoorthodox Interpretation

Neoorthodoxy sought to uphold the seriousness of humanity's alienation from God, while rejecting aspects of the Fall and sin that classical theology judged important. Karl Barth denies the existence of Adam as a historical person and rejects the notion that there existed a morally upright couple in a pristine Garden environment. Barth views the Genesis account of the Fall not as history, but as a saga (a tale with symbolic features) that belongs to the realm of suprahistory (*Urgeschichte*). Sin originated in the Fall, but the when, where, and how of the event transcends human comprehension. According to Barth, the Fall of Adam describes an event that happens to everyone, so that each person "constantly reenacts the little scene in the garden of Eden."[23] Barth believes that the doctrine of hereditary sin (*Erbsunde*) is mistaken; we must not think of sin as a disease that passes from one person to another. Rather, "original sin" (*Ursunde*) is the radical, prideful departure of every person, and thus of the race, from the will of God. How does Barth interpret the relation between Adam, Christ, and humanity in Romans 5:12–21 and 1 Corinthians 15:22, 45? He begins, not with Adam, but with Christ and insists that as humanity is joined with Christ in redemption, so the race is linked with Adam in condemnation. In other words, Paul envisages Adam's act as the negative side of the work of Jesus Christ. Beyond that nothing can be affirmed.

By virtue of the universal Fall, God places all persons under the sentence of sin and guilt. Barth's description of the sinner's depraved moral condition is unequivocal. The person "is totally perverted and ruined by his sin and guilt."[24] He adds that "the realization of the total and radical corruption of human nature must not be weakened."[25] The will of the sinner is in bondage, and his mind is sinfully distorted. Yet contrary to his earlier stance in dialogue with Brunner,[26] Barth's mature view was that in spite of human degeneracy, the image of God has not been altogether effaced. Barth, however, concludes that this radical godlessness of the sinner is not final by virtue of election and status in the covenant of grace. Sin, in other words, is overcome in a world reconciled to Jesus Christ. "The sinful No of man has been matched and opposed and destroyed by the divine Yes spoken by Jesus Christ."[27]

Brunner's views about the Fall and sin are similar to those of Barth. The account of Adam and Eve, which Brunner calls a myth or parable, must be rejected on scientific grounds. The doctrine of sin must be developed "without this mythical idea of a Fall."[28] Since Adam means "man," what Genesis 3 relates about Adam and Eve describes the history of every person. That is, in one's determined quest for freedom, each person rebels against the authority of the Creator and sins in discrete acts. Like Barth, Brunner claims that the notion of inherited sin eliminates personal responsibility for one's actions. "The theory of Original Sin . . . is completely foreign to the thought of the Bible."[29] The New Testament teaches both that each person sins individually and that the race as a solidarity is under sin. How the sin of one person becomes the sin of the race Brunner believes is an impenetrable mystery. He hints, however, that the universality of sin results from the limitations imposed by human creatureliness; human persons as finite, contingent beings have an inherent tendency to defect from the sovereign God.[30] Since Brunner believes that sin is never a state but always a concrete act, he polemicizes against the notion of total depravity. "The expression 'the total depravity of man,' which in later Calvinism has become a slogan, is not biblical."[31] As for its effects, sin has damaged the formal image (natural likeness to God), but has destroyed altogether the material image (moral likeness to God).

Reinhold Niebuhr inveighs against modernists who fail to treat the story of Eden seriously and against so-called fundamentalists who interpret it literally. Although the Fall, as myth, belongs to the realm of suprahistory rather than history, it nevertheless enshrines important truths about the human condition. The Genesis 3 story, argues Niebuhr, conveys the fact that persons stand in the paradoxical relation of freedom and finitude. As spirit, persons transcend nature and so are free. But as creatures, they are part of nature's order and so are bound. As those both free and bound, persons inevitably experience anxiety (Matt. 6:31)—the internal precondition of sin. In this state of anxiety Satan tempts persons to deny their limitations through pride or to violate their freedom through sensuality. "When anxiety has conceived, it brings forth both pride and sensuality. Man falls into pride when he seeks to raise their contingent existence to unconditioned significance; he falls into sensuality when he seeks to escape from his unlimited possibilities of freedom . . . by losing himself in some natural vitality."[32]

Niebuhr, like Barth and Brunner, denies that original sin transmits to the race by generation. The myth of Adam proclaims the universal truth that every person inevitably falls into sin. "Original sin is not an inherited corruption, but it is an inevitable fact of human existence. . . . It is there in every moment of existence, but it has no history."[33] Moreover, the fact that each person sins inevitably and yet bears personal responsibility for his sins represents an insoluble paradox of the faith. Finally, Niebuhr claims that the assertion of total depravity is unduly pessimistic. If persons were totally corrupted, they could not be sinners at all. Thus sin has not destroyed essential human nature; the divine *imago* endures despite the reality of sin.

Liberation Theology

Included in this category are the so-called political theologians, third-world liberation theologians, and proponents of radical black and feminist theologies. The movement as a whole denies (1) that sin is individualistic, in the sense of personal enmity against God or violation of a divine law, and (2) that sin is an interior reality, such as a polluted moral nature. Rather, it argues that sin is a collective reality manifested in specific socio-political situations. In the words of Dorothy Sölle, a political theologian, "Sin is not to be understood in a special religious sense as the lack of love for God or as rebellion against a master, but it must be thought of in worldly and political categories."[34] James H. Cone, a leading proponent of black theology, makes the same point: "Sin is not primarily a religious impurity, but rather it is the social, political, and economic oppression of the poor. It is the denial of the humanity of the neighbor through unjust political and social arrangements."[35]

Liberationists claim that persons are naturally endowed with freedom, creativity, and the capacity to transform the world. Yet by virtue of political oppression, economic deprivation, social exploitation, and sexual domination, the person "falls," or is reduced to the status of a nonperson. As a result of these dehumanizing forces, the world becomes filled with poverty, hunger, illiteracy, and crime. Such a line of reasoning prompts liberation theologians to speak, not of a "state of sin" in the human heart, but of the "praxis of sin," that is, the practice of oppressive behavior that exploits and despoils the human race.

Liberation theologians extend the notion of sin to include the apathy of the despoiled toward oppression or active collaboration with the oppressor. The sinner is one who lacks the courage to oppose the exploiter. Thus, according to Cone, one sins when he attempts to love or even accept the agent of injustice. For many feminist theologians, sin represents the cowardly failure to affirm the female self. Evil is the false humility that passively resigns itself to masculine domination.

Many Fathers, Reformers, and Reformed Evangelicals

Authorities in this tradition maintain that God implemented his purpose for the race by an initial moral probation. Persons in a state of childlike innocence could become perfect only through a process of right moral decision making. Following a successful probation, Adam and Eve would have been confirmed in love for God and in holiness of life. Possessing the power both to persevere in holiness and to disobey God, they tragically chose the latter. This original sin of Adam and Eve brought on themselves and their posterity guilt, a depraved nature, and the sentence of condemnation. The tradition maintains that by virtue of total depravity, sinners apart from grace can do nothing to please God. Their sinful wills are unable to perform what God requires. Nevertheless, fallen persons are morally responsible for their sin-induced incapacity to fulfill God's law. Concerning the means whereby Adamic sin transmitted to the race, three main interpretations are proposed: (1) The natural headship or seminal view, holding to the traducian view of the soul's origin, maintains that the entire race was present in Adam in seed form and so participated in his original sin. (2) The representative headship or federal school, positing Adam as the covenant head of the race, maintains that God immediately imputed Adam's guilt, depravity, and punishment to the race he represented. (3) Others, like Berkouwer, Thiessen, and Ramm, insist that Scripture merely relates the fact of the Fall of humanity in Adam, not the how of it. As distinct from Arminianism, the broadly Reformed tradition insists that sin includes not only overt acts but also the underlying thought life and the evil disposition of the human heart.

Augustine made the doctrine of original sin the cornerstone of his theological system. Adam's self-determined sin of rebellion against God brought upon each person born into the world guilt, depravity, and liability to punishment. Augustine taught that the depravity of Adam and the entire human race is pervasive. In the first place, the intellect of the sinner is blind to *sapientia*, or the eternal, changeless truth about God. Augustine wrote that the mind "dulled by sins, blinded, enfeebled by infirmity" cannot of itself see God.[36] Only as the mind is illumined by the Logos in general grace can the sinner apprehend modest truths about God's character and moral demands. And only as the mind is illumined by the additional light of special grace by the same Logos can he attain saving wisdom. Second, Augustine believed that the will of the sinner is able only to oppose God and the purpose for which he or she was created. "The will is truly free only when it is not a slave to sin and vice. God created man with such a free will, but . . . that kind of freedom was lost by man's fall from freedom."[37] Whereas in Eden Adam was *posse non peccare et mori* (able not to sin and die), now as sinner man is *non posse non peccare et mori* (not able not to sin and die). Through the practice of sin, the person's God-given freedom has been turned into sinful necessity. Wrote Augustine, "A man's free-will, indeed, avails for nothing, except to sin, if he knows not the way of truth."[38] And third, concerning the emotions, Augustine held that in place of love for eternal things (the city of God), the sinner possesses a yearning or desire (*libido*) for fleeting, temporal things (the city of the world). Overcome by carnal lusts, the sinner experiences restlessness of soul rather than rest in God. Although sin erased the spiritual gifts of faith and holiness, it corrupted but did not destroy the natural capacities of the soul that constitute the *imago*. "God's image has not been so completely erased in the soul of man by the stain of earthly affections."[39]

Augustine believed that as the biological head of the race Adam transmitted original sin to his progeny by the process of natural generation. Since the race as a whole was in Adam seminally when he sinned, each member of it at birth receives the sin and guilt of the head. "We all existed in that one man. . . . Although the specific form by which each of us was to live was not yet created and assigned, our nature was already present in the seed from which we were to spring."[40] Augustine went beyond the notion of a corrupted seed

191

to suggest that sin also pertains to sexual procreation. Augustine also claimed that infants contract hereditary sin from Adam. Unless their guilt and concupiscence are removed by Holy Spirit regeneration and baptism, infants will endure a just damnation.

Luther judges that as a result of Adam's Fall the human race became totally corrupted, inclined toward evil, guilty before God, and exposed to divine wrath. Luther's explication of original sin (*Erbsunde*) is bleak. The sinner is *curvatus in se* (bent in on himself), habitually seeking selfish ends. He is filled with avarice, lust, anger, hatred, and a host of other vices. Having forsaken God, the sinner's nature is wholly corrupted. "All our faculties are leprous, indeed, dull and utterly dead."[41] Moreover, the sinner exists in a condition of spiritual servitude; apart from grace one is unable to do anything good spiritually. In relation to God, the will is hopelessly bound in its sinful orientation. Thus, "he that will maintain that man's free-will is able to do or work anything in spiritual cases be they ever so small, denies Christ."[42] Yet Luther admitted that in secular matters the will is free to perform what he called deeds of "external" or "civil righteousness."

Luther concludes that the Fall totally destroyed the *imago Dei*, defined as righteousness and wisdom. The human person's dominion over the animals represents but a "relic" of the lost image. In fact, Luther maintains that the sinner exists in the image of the Devil. The natural endowments of intellect, will, and emotions (not constitutive of the *imago*) remain severely corrupted in the sinner. Luther, the traducianist, followed Augustine in postulating that guilt, depravity, and condemnation were transmitted to the human race by procreation. "The human seed, this mass from which I was formed, is totally corrupt with faults

and sins. The material itself is faulty."[43]

Calvin similarly affirms that Adam's sin brought upon his posterity guilt, a depraved nature, and liability to punishment. "All of us, who have descended from impure seed, are born infected with the contagion of sin."[44] Thus all persons participate in original sin, which Calvin defines as "depravity and corruption of our nature, diffused into all parts of the soul, which first makes us liable to God's wrath, then also brings forth in us those works which Scripture calls 'works of the flesh.' "[45] For Calvin this depravity is total in that sin corrupts every part of the person. "The whole man is overwhelmed—as by a deluge—from head to foot, so that no part is immune from sin."[46] In particular, Calvin affirms that the will is so vitiated by sin that, although free in everyday matters, it is not able to respond positively to God. The sinner's will is not compelled by any external force but is driven by a contrary internal compulsion, namely, by the promptings of his fallen nature. As for the *imago*, Calvin argues that the sinner's natural endowments (intelligence, will, and emotions) are corrupted by sin. His spiritual endowments (faith, love of God, holiness), however, are altogether lost. How does Calvin interpret the relation between the sin of Adam and that of the race? He appears to approximate the representative position; God ordained that the fate of Adam—the legal head of humanity—should be the fate of each member. "The contagion does not take its origin from the substance of the flesh or soul, but because it had been so ordained by God that the first man should at one and the same time have and lose, both for himself and for his descendants, the gifts that God had bestowed upon him."[47] Calvin maintains that infants experience the baneful consequences of original sin, which effects nevertheless are uniquely their own.[48] Elect infants are regenerated by a secret work of the Holy Spirit.

The Reformed Confessions likewise speak to the issue of original sin. The Belgic Confession, article XV states:

> We believe that through the disobedience of Adam original sin is extended to all mankind; which is a corruption of the whole nature and a hereditary disease, . . . and which produces in man all sorts of sin, being in him as a root thereof, and therefore is so vile and abominable in the sight of God that it is sufficient to condemn all mankind.

A similar view is affirmed by the French Confession of Faith (art. XI), the Heidelberg Catechism (Lord's Day 3, Q. & A. 7), the Second Helvetic Confession (chap. 8), and the Thirty-Nine Articles of Religion (art. IX). The Westminster Confession of Faith (chap. 6) unites the Augustinian theory of natural headship with the federal notion of Adam's representative headship.

The Westminster Confession (chap. 9) reiterates the Reformed position on the bondage of the will in matters spiritual. "Man, by his fall into a state of sin, hath wholly lost all ability of will to any spiritual good accompanying salvation." Similarly, the French Confession of Faith (art. IX), the Heidelberg Catechism (Q. & A. 8, 9), and the Second Helvetic Confession (chap. 9).

W. G. T. Shedd was a leading advocate of the seminal or natural headship theory for the imputation of Adam's sin. Shedd maintains that God imputed to each of Adam's descendants guilt, depravity, and the punishment of death, for the reason that the race was in Adam in undistributed form. That is, the entire psychico-physical human nature, not yet individualized, existed in Adam and Eve when they perpetrated the first sin. Shedd claims the active verb *hēmarton* in Romans 5:12 denotes the work of the common human nature in Adam rather than the countless deeds of individuals in subsequent history. Because all persons are guilty co-agents with Adam, the following holds: "The individual Adam and Eve were no more guilty of this first act . . . than their descendants are; and their descendants are as guilty as they."[49] Shedd guards against Christ's involvement in sinful Adamic nature by arguing that the Logos assumed only a part of humanity, namely, that flesh and blood derived from Mary.[50]

A. H. Strong, who holds to the same natural headship theory of sin's transmission, advanced a popular view of the spiritual condition of infants. Infants participate in the common guilt and depravity of Adamic sin and so need to be saved by Christ. But as opposed to those who have personally transgressed, infants prior to the age of moral accountability are characterized by "a relative innocence,"[51] i.e., by absence of premeditation, naïveté, and trustfulness. For this reason infants are the objects of divine compassion and receive a special application of the atonement, Strong surmises, at the soul's first view of Christ in heaven.

The covenant theology of Cocceius (d. 1669) gave rise to the federal headship theory of sin's imputation. Espoused by Owen, the Westminster Standards, and the old Princeton School, the federal headship or representative theory is typically set forth by L. Berkhof. Like the seminal theorists, federalists insist that the effects of the Fall to Adam were guilt, depravity, and punishment in the form of spiritual and physical death. Indeed, from Adam "sin flows on as an impure stream to all the generations of men, polluting everyone and everything with which it comes in contact."[52] Berkhof explains the spread of Adam's sin to his posterity not in terms of natural headship, but in terms of his status as head of the race in the covenant of works. Thus when Adam sinned as federal head, God imputed his guilt to all humanity, by virtue of which every person is born with a depraved and sinful soul. Adam's posterity did not directly participate in his sinful act, but through the forensic (i.e., judicial) imputation of guilt based on legal unity, "God adjudges all men to be guilty sinners in Adam."[53] This representative theory for the transmission of sin is usually linked with the creationist position for the soul's origin. The view also judges that infants are afflicted with original sin and need salvation through Christ. Infants born into a Christian family have the promise of salvation by virtue of their status in the covenant of grace. When the parents are not Christians, an infant may be the object of God's secret election.

Other valuable evangelical discussions of the Fall and sin are provided by G. C. Berkouwer,[54] Bernard Ramm,[55] and Millard J. Erickson.[56]

BIBLICAL TEACHING

Which historical explication concerning the Fall and the condition of persons in sin we choose to accept depends on the teachings of inspired Scripture, to which we now turn.

The Pentateuch

If the first great epic drama recorded in Scripture is creation (see chap. 1), the second is the Fall of the human race into sin. It is possible that the Genesis accounts of creation and the Fall originated by what Ramm calls "divinely inspired reconstruction."[57] But whereas Barth considers the account of the Fall to be saga and Adam the paradigm for the moral experience of every person, Ramm focuses on "generic Adam," "generic Fall," and "generic sin."[58] Later biblical attestation of Adam (Rom. 5:14; 1 Cor. 15:22, 45; 1 Tim. 2:13–14), the serpent (2 Cor. 11:3; Rev. 12:9), and the Fall (1 Tim.

2:14) as historical realities suggest that we should view the Genesis 3 narrative both as historically valid and as paradigmatic of the spiritual experience of each person coming into the world. That is, every man and woman replicates Adam's and Eve's experience of sin, alienation from God, and punishment.

The history of humankind begins in a paradisiacal setting in Eden. In the Garden environment God made provision for all the person's physical, social, and spiritual needs. In the center of Eden God placed two trees, the tree of life and the tree of the knowledge of good and evil (Gen. 2:9). The first, the tree of life, played a special role in sustaining human life. Thus after sinning, the first pair was driven from the Garden, since partaking of the fruit of this tree was alien to their fallen condition (cf. Gen. 3:22–24). The tree of the knowledge of good and evil, whose fruit God had forbidden to be eaten (Gen. 2:17), symbolized the full range of ethical knowledge that the partaker would come to experience. That is, by disobediently eating of the fruit of the second tree Adam would come to know good by the loss of it, and evil by personal, painful experience.[59] God's purpose in placing Adam and Eve in the Garden with the prohibition against eating the fruit of the second tree was one of testing. That is, in a condition of innocence where the will and affections were capable of inclining either to good or evil, humans could move to a state of confirmed righteousness only by a process of testing and moral decision making. In the divine plan, Adam and Eve must determine whether they would live righteously under God's liberating authority or whether they would pursue meaning independently of their Creator. Confronted with the second tree and the divine command in respect of it, Adam and Eve faced the fundamental issue of obedience to God, the Lord of life.

The inspired account of the Fall of

the human race occupies but twenty-four verses. "The serpent [who] was more crafty than any of the wild animals the LORD God had made" (Gen. 3:1), should be viewed as a reptile that Satan employed as his mouthpiece. The Genesis 3 record and its interpretation by Jesus (John 8:44) and John (1 John 3:8; Rev. 12:9) indicates that the real tempter was Satan himself. The serpent, in dialogue with Eve (vv. 1–4), first cast doubt on the word God had spoken ("Did God really say?") and then expressly denied that same word ("You will not surely die"). Lack of confidence in God's truth (unbelief) thus constitutes the first step in spiritual defection. Moreover, Satan falsely suggested to Eve that God forbade the eating of the fruit for the selfish reason that he did not want them to be like himself (v. 5). In addition to the promptings of Satan, Eve experienced in the tree itself a threefold temptation (v. 6). She first sensed that the tree was "good for food" (material temptation), then that it was "pleasing to the eye" (aesthetic temptation), and finally that it was "desirable for gaining wisdom" (intellectual temptation). John similarly speaks of the threefold enticement that comes from the world order ruled by Satan: "the lust of the flesh and the lust of the eyes and the pride of life" (1 John 2:16 RSV). Jesus experienced a similar threefold temptation in Matthew 4:1–11.

The Fall consisted of the inner defection of the soul from God outwardly manifested in the act of eating the forbidden fruit: Eve "took some and ate it. She also gave some to her husband . . . and he ate it" (v. 6). A classical interpretation that identifies the eating with sexual intercourse is mistaken, for, among other reasons, Adam and Eve each partook independently. Rather, via an inner attitude of unbelief and self-exaltation—not through any magical potency within the tree—Eve and

then Adam willfully disobeyed the clear command of God. We readily add that each subsequent sin in the world replicates that of our first parents. "It begins with the darkening of the understanding, continues with the excitement of the imagination, stimulates desire in the heart, and culminates in an act of the will."[60]

More than two-thirds of Genesis 3 is devoted to explicating the far-ranging results of the spiritual defection of our first parents. Thus Adam and Eve (1) were afflicted with a profound sense of guilt, for the text says (v. 7) that their eyes were opened to their nakedness, even as the serpent had foretold. That is, now they knew evil experientially in the form of shame and a sense of the unworthiness of the flesh. Moreover, the first pair (2) experienced *estrangement,* a broken relationship with God, or spiritual death (vv. 8–10). Thus whereas formerly they had sweet communion with God in the Garden, following their defection Adam and Eve hid themselves from God's presence. So the sinner's habitual experience is one of flight from God, motivated by fear of his holiness and power (v. 10). In addition, (3) they were overcome with *depravity,* or a fallen, sinful heart (vv. 11–13). Adam and Eve's spiritually twisted nature is reflected in the evasive answers they gave to God. Adam blamed the helper God had given him for his misdeed, whereas Eve blamed the serpent. Clearly evident here is the sinful human tendency to transfer personal responsibility for transgressions to another. And finally, (4) Adam and Eve were punished with *physical death* by being banished from the garden lest they should eat of the tree of life and live forever (vv. 22–24). From the cradle, all sinful human beings begin to die.

As a result of the fall of Adam and Eve, God cursed the serpent that Satan indwelt (v. 14). The repulsive form and movement of snakes is a consequence of the divine curse upon these reptiles. The fact that the serpent was cursed "above . . . all the wild animals" concurs with Paul's declaration that God judged the entire animate and inanimate order in consequence of Adam's sin (Rom. 8:20–21). Verse 15 records God's judgment on Satan. "I will put enmity between you and the woman, and between your offspring and hers; he will crush your head, and you will strike his heel." This text predicts the agelong conflict between the people of God and the forces of evil. The head of each side would do spiritual battle with the other. Satan would wound the Messiah, but "he," the principal seed of the woman (Gal. 4:4), would crush the Devil altogether. The church rightly designates this verse the *Protoevangelium* (the first announcement of the Gospel).

As a consequence of sin, God punished the woman with the pain of multiplied conceptions (v. 16). Now women experience suffering in their fundamental role of bearing children. The sentence "Your desire will be for your husband, and he will rule over you," we saw in chapter 3 anticipates the sinful struggle for power between the sexes. The woman sinfully seeks to control the man, and the man responds in kind by exceeding the God-instituted ordering relation (1 Cor. 11:3, 7–8; Eph. 5:22–25; 1 Tim. 2:12–14; Titus 2:5) to dominate selfishly the woman. Genesis 3 continues by relating that God punished the man in his calling as a man. Thus (1) God cursed the ground that man must work (vv. 17–18), so that both man and his environment are on the same fallen basis. Moreover, (2) the strenuous labor to which God consigned him (v. 19) both retards his physical deterioration and serves as a restraint against sin. This sentence God pronounced leads many unsaved to conclude that life is weariness and vanity (Eccl. 1:8; 4:8, 10). Finally,

(3) God condemns man to death: "Dust you are and to dust you will return" (v. 19; cf. vv. 22–24). This punishment underscores the repetitive litany in the genealogy of Genesis 5:5, 8, 11, et al.—"and then he died."

Genesis 4–11, which covers more than two thousand years of history, is a highly condensed narrative whose purpose is to highlight humankind's spiritual condition subsequent to the Fall. Adam's immediate family demonstrates the harsh consequences of sin in the human race (Gen. 4:1–16). When Cain's offering was not accepted by the Lord and his heart was filled with jealousy and hatred toward his brother, Cain brutally beat Abel to death. Man against God thus became man against his fellowman. When confronted by God, Cain added to the sin of murder the sin of lying. Yahweh pronounced a curse on Cain, and the latter wandered across the earth without finding rest for his sinful soul. From the line of Cain came Lamech, the first polygamist, who not only killed a man that had inflicted a lesser wound on him but also proudly boasted about his excessive revenge (Gen. 4:23).

A new chapter in the progress of moral evil occurred when "the sons of God" (*bᵉnê-'ᵉlōhîm*) took as their wives "the daughters of men" (Gen. 6:1–3). It is preferable to interpret "the sons of God" as the descendants of godly Seth (cf. Hos. 1:10), who grieved the Lord by polygamously marrying unbelieving women. The intensiveness of moral evil in the antediluvian era is expressed in the words "The Lord saw how great man's wickedness [*raʿ*] on the earth had become" (Gen. 6:5), and its extensiveness is expressed in the latter part of the same verse, "and that every inclination [*yēṣer*] of the thoughts of his heart was only evil [*raʿ*] all the time" (cf. v. 11). This same verse affirms the inward nature of sin; the noun *yēṣer*, from the verb *yāṣar*, to "create, devise," connotes a plan deliberately fashioned in the mind (cf. Gen. 8:21). Vriezen comments concerning Genesis 6:5, "A more emphatic statement of the wickedness of the human heart is hardly conceivable."[61] These evil intentions inevitably gave way to deeds of violent degradation (vv. 11–12). Since the whole earth had become morally corrupt, God became angry (v. 3) and resolved to destroy the people with the Deluge (vv. 7, 13). Even after the awesome judgment of the Flood, the inspired writer attests the pervasive sinfulness of the human heart: "Every inclination [yēṣer] of his heart is evil [ra'] from childhood" (8:21).

The experience of Noah following the flood reveals the endemic character of sin. Noah appears as "a righteous man" (Gen. 6:9), with whom God made a gracious covenant (9:8–17). Yet in spite of such character and privilege Noah became drunk and shamefully exposed himself before his son (vv. 20–23). Notwithstanding the Fall and the horrible expressions of sin, Scripture attests that, however blemished, the sinner retains his status as image-bearer of God (9:6). God's command that the penalty of death be exacted for murder is linked to wanton destruction of the *imago Dei*. The account of the building of the tower at Babel dramatizes the vanity of societal existence without God (11:1–9). The desire of the people to crowd together rather than disperse throughout the earth (cf. Gen. 1:28) reflects the sinner's fundamental insecurity. Their plan to build a tall tower so as to "make a name for ourselves" (v. 4) discloses the prideful quest to attain autonomy vis-à-vis God. The fact that the project was abandoned before completion (v. 8), suggests that human aspirations sought apart from God are never fully realized.

Even specially chosen people were not exempt from sin. Abram in Egypt deliberately lied to Pharaoh, telling him that Sarah was his sister, and this led Pharaoh to take her as his wife (Gen. 12:11–20; cf. 20:2–13). The account of the destruction of Sodom and Gomorrah (Gen. 19:1–29) relates that all the male inhabitants of Sodom, both young and old, practiced homosexuality (vv. 4–5). Moreover, Lot, Abraham's nephew offered the Sodomites his two virgin daughters for their sexual pleasure (v. 8). The attempt by evil men to break into homes to molest the occupants (v. 9) attests the violence rampant in Sodom. God's anger toward such raw depravity is seen in the supernatural judgment meted out on the cities of the plain (vv. 24–26).

The subsequent history of God's dealings with the chosen people likewise discloses the horrible faces of human sin. Jealous over their father's special love for Joseph, the brothers plotted to kill the lad (Gen. 37:18–20), threw him into a cistern (v. 24), sold their brother to Midianite merchants (v. 28), and then lied to Jacob, telling him that Joseph had been killed by a wild animal (vv. 31–33). Moreover, Moses, the great deliverer of Israel, began his career by killing an Egyptian and burying him in the sand (Exod. 2:12). Moses and Aaron sinned at Kadesh by smiting the rock and so were not allowed to enter the Promised Land (Num. 20:6–13; 27:14). God consigned Israel to forty years of wilderness wandering because of their persistent stubbornness, provocation, and idolatry (Num. 14:20–35). Aaron's comment to Moses sums up the condition of the human heart: "You know how prone these people are to evil" (Exod. 32:22).

The moral laws God gave Israel highlight the complex character of sin. Whereas God condemned the volitional perpetration of crimes such as stealing, lying, and defrauding one's neighbor (Lev. 19:11–16), he also proscribed hidden thoughts or intentions such as bearing a grudge or hating a brother in the heart (vv. 17–18). The same distinction between sins conceived in the mind and sins volitionally committed occurs in the Ten Commandments (Exod. 20:3–17).

When God consigned most of Israel to death in the wilderness, he made an exception in regard to their children: "Your children who do not yet know good from bad—they will enter the land" (Deut. 1:39). We may infer that since they lacked moral discernment and personal responsibility, God judged the children innocent of the rebellion in the wilderness and so did not subject them to the common judgment (cf. Num. 14:29–31).

Poetry and Wisdom

We find an allusion to the Fall in the statement of the Teacher: "God made man upright [yāšār], but men have gone in search of many schemes" (Eccl. 7:29). The Psalter acknowledges the reality of inherited sin with unusual candor: "Even from birth the wicked go astray; from the womb they are wayward and speak lies" (Ps. 58:3). David's admission "Surely I was sinful at birth, sinful from the time my mother conceived me" (51:5) indicates that underlying his adultery with Bathsheba was a sinful nature that he acquired at conception from a sinful father and mother. With good reason one could say that "this is the Old Testament's greatest statement of original sin."[62]

The literature freely acknowledges the darkness of moral depravity. Eliphaz describes the sinner as "vile and corrupt, who drinks up evil like water" (Job 15:16; cf. 25:4). Depravity is universally ingrained in human life. So the psalmist writes, "They are corrupt, and their ways are vile; there is no one who does good. . . . Everyone has turned away, they have together become corrupt; there is no one who does good, not even one" (Ps. 53:1, 3; cf. 14:1, 3;

Prov. 20:9). When compared with the righteous God, the sinful person is a "maggot" and a "worm" (Job 25:6). God's response to humans' sinful orientation is "anger," "indignation," and "wrath" (Ps. 90:7, 9, 11; cf. Job 20:23). Human depravity expresses itself in hardness of heart (Ps. 95:8), hatred of God (Ps. 139:21), and slavery to sin (Prov. 5:22). The last text suggests that sin exerts a paralyzing power; it captures and binds those who embrace it. The Teacher, moreover, emphasizes that the sinner finds life futile or "meaningless" (hebel; Eccl. 1:14; 2:11, 17; 3:19, et al.). Nothing can bring permanent satisfaction; not philosophy (1:12–18), not sensual pleasure (2:1–3), and not wealth (2:4–9; 5:10–17). To persons alienated from this Creator, life is frustration, anxiety, and enigma. All that sinners can anticipate is death (2:14–15; 7:2) and judgment (12:14). The spiritual condition of sinners, furthermore, is one of objective guilt. For failure to live up to the demands of the law God reckons sinners blameworthy before the bar of divine justice (Ps. 69:5). In addition, the Psalms provide insight into the spiritual and psychological effects of guilt on persons. In Psalm 38 David describes guilt ('āwôn) as a crushing burden that he can scarcely bear (v. 4). It produces a range of psychosomatic symptoms (vv. 5–7). Guilt torments the mind (vv. 8–9), destroys the person's zest for life (v. 10), and causes social isolation (v. 11). In a word, guilt produces a thoroughgoing sense of dis-ease (Ps. 32:3–4).

Original sin, in addition, incurs a just penalty. Scripture testifies that in the present time sin brings its own retribution. "The trouble he causes recoils on himself; his violence comes down on his own head" (Ps. 7:16). In a moral world, the sin a person commits inevitably returns to haunt him (cf. Ps. 9:15; Prov. 26:27). God may execute punishment by cutting short the life of a wicked person (Ps. 55:23). So the psalmist confesses, "Like sheep they are destined for the grave, and death will feed on them" (Ps. 49:14; cf. 9:17). But beyond death lies the day of judgment, when "the heavens will expose his guilt" (Job 20:27) and the sinner will face the wrath of an offended God (20:26, 28–29).

The literature represents sin as a complex reality that encompasses both the person's inner life and the wicked acts he commits. In Proverbs 6:16–19 sinful deeds such as lying and brutality arise from ungodly attitudes and intentions, which in turn arise from a corrupt "heart" or nature. Psalm 58:2 teaches that behind specific acts of injustice lies a perversely calculating heart (*lēb*). Cf. Prov. 24:8–9.

The Prophetic Literature

Isaiah 53:6 attests both sin's universality ("We all, like sheep, have gone astray") and sin's individuality ("each of us has turned to his own way"). Sin in the Prophets is both collective ("Ah, sinful nation, a people loaded with guilt," Isa. 1:4) and personal ("I am a man of unclean lips," Isa. 6:5). Jeremiah 17:9 powerfully portrays the depravity of the human heart: "The heart is deceitful [*'āqōb*, crooked] above all things and beyond cure [*'ānuš*, sick]. Who can understand it?" At the personal level depravity manifests itself in sinful pride and arrogance (Isa. 14:11–14; Dan. 5:20), in conceit (Isa. 16:6), in stubbornness (Jer. 5:23; 16:12), in rebellion against God (Isa. 30:9; Ezek. 12:2), in moral uncleanness (Isa. 64:6; Jer. 2:23), and in impulsively wicked behavior (Jer. 2:24–25; cf. 6:7). Sinners are intellectually darkened in their minds (Isa. 42:7) and volitionally paralyzed in their wills (Isa. 61:1). Apart from grace sinners are incapable of altering their dispositions. Thus Jeremiah 13:23 reads: "Can the Ethiopian change his skin or the leopard its spots? Neither can you do good who are accustomed to doing evil." One authority comments, "Here is a classic example of loss of freedom of the will through persistent sinning. Sin becomes natural."[63]

The prophets also powerfully accentuate the social dimensions of sin. Israel's rulers oppressed the foreigner and mistreated the fatherless and widows (Ezek. 22:7). The powerful and wealthy exploited and defrauded their neighbors (Ezek. 22:12; Mic. 3:1–3). The rich lived luxurious and degenerate lives at the expense of the poor (Amos 4:1; 5:11). Judges sold verdicts to the highest bidder (Mic. 3:11), and corrupt priests taught for a price what people wanted to hear (v. 11). The poor, moreover, were deprived of justice in the courts (Amos 5:12). Micah sums up the state of affairs in Israel. "All men lie in wait to shed blood; each hunts his brother with a net. Both hands are skilled in doing evil; the ruler demands gifts, the judge accepts bribes, the powerful dictate what they desire—they all conspire together" (Mic. 7:2–3).

Sin, both individual and corporate, relationally separates persons from God (Isa. 59:2) and incurs the sentence of objective guilt (Isa. 53:6; Jer. 2:22; Ezek. 22:4; Hos. 12:14; 13:12, 16). Guilt emotionally experienced brings loss of peace (Isa. 48:22), misery (Mic. 7:1), and self-hatred (Ezek. 20:43). The fundamental symptom of guilt is inner restlessness: "The wicked are like the tossing sea, which cannot rest, whose waves cast up mire and mud. 'There is no peace,' says my God, 'for the wicked'" (Isa. 57:20–21).

Sin kindles God's jealousy and anger (Jer. 7:20; Hos. 12:14; Nah. 1:2), and this results in inevitable punishment (Jer. 2:19; Ezek. 28:22; Hos. 12:2). Simply put, "the LORD . . . will not leave the guilty unpunished (Nah. 1:3). God's righteous judgment took many forms: drought (Jer. 14:1–6; Amos 4:7), famine (Jer. 14:12–15; Amos 4:6), plagues (Jer. 14:12; Joel 1:4), military defeats (Jer. 5:15–17; Ezek. 5:12), and, finally, dispersion and exile into foreign lands (Isa. 5:13; Jer. 25:8–11).

Old Testament Words for Sin

In large measure the Old Testament explicates its theology of sin by means of several descriptive words. A primary Hebrew word is the verb *ḥāṭā'*, whose root means to "fall short" or "miss the mark." Thus *ḥāṭā'* connotes "to sin" in the sense of missing God's standard (Lev. 5:5, 16; Ps. 51:4; Zeph. 1:17) and, there being no separate word in Hebrew for guilt, the extended meaning of "to bear blame" (Gen. 43:9; 44:32). The cognate noun *ḥēṭ'* connotes (1) sin as failure to measure up to God's standard (Ps. 103:10), (2) guilt (Lev. 20:20), and (3) punishment (Lam. 3:39). Similarly the common feminine noun *ḥaṭṭā't* (used 290 times) signifies (1) sin or disobedience (Exod. 10:17), (2) guilt (Ps. 32:5), and (3) liability to punishment (Lam. 4:6; Zech. 14:19). The noun *'āwôn*, whose root idea is crookedness, likewise bears multiple meanings: (1) perverse behavior or iniquity (Gen. 15:16; Isa. 43:24), (2) guilt (Gen. 44:16; Ps. 32:5), and (3) consequent punishment (Gen. 4:13; Lam. 4:22). The noun *peša'*, the correlate of the verb *pāša'*, to "rebel" or "transgress" (Isa. 1:2; Hos. 8:1), denotes deliberate rebellion or revolt against God's law or covenant. The verb *'ābar*, the root idea of which is motion across, bears the theological meaning of transgressing stipulations laid down by God. Thus Numbers 22:18 reads, "I could not . . . go beyond the command of the LORD my God" and *'ābar* is variously translated "violate," "disobey," "break," etc. (Josh. 7:15; Isa. 24:5; Hos. 8:1).

The noun *reša'*, from the verb *rāša'*, to "act wickedly" (1 Kings 8:47), "incur guilt" (Job 40:8), is commonly translated "wickedness" (Ps. 45:7; Ezek. 3:19). The noun *šeqer* is variously rendered "falsehood,'''"lie," and "deceit" (Ps. 52:3; Jer. 27:10; Hos. 7:1). The noun *ma'al*, which has the fundamental idea of breach of trust, is translated in the NIV as "unfaithfulness" and "treachery" (Lev. 26:40; 1 Chron. 9:1; Ezek. 18:24). The masculine noun *'āwel* (Deut. 32:4; Job 34:32) and the feminine noun *'awlāh* (Ps. 92:15; Hab. 2:12) derive from the root meaning to "deviate," and so connote "an act or deed that is against what is right."[64] The verbs *šāgāh* (Lev. 4:13; Job 19:4) and *šāgag* (Lev. 5:18; Num. 15:28), to "err," "go astray," denote the committing of unintentional sins that nevertheless require atonement. The verbs *mārad* (Isa. 36:5; Dan. 9:5) and *mārāh* (Num. 27:14; Hos. 13:16) and the noun *mᵉrî* (Deut. 31:27; Ezek. 2:5–8) signify rebellion against God or his commandments. The verb *'āšam* denotes the act of sin that brings guilt and punishment (Ps. 34:21–22; Isa. 24:6; Hos. 5:15). Correspondingly, the nouns *'āšam* (Num. 5:7; Jer. 51:5) and *'ašmāh* (2 Chron. 28:10; Ezra 9:6–7) are commonly translated "sin" and "guilt."

The Synoptic Gospels

Luke the historian attests the reliability of the Genesis account of human origins by identifying Adam (Luke 3:38) as a historical person like Abraham, David, or Jesus. Our Lord, furthermore, acknowledges inherited sin by describing unregenerate persons as intrinsically "evil" (*ponēros*, Matt. 7:11; Luke 11:13) and "sinful" (*hamartōlos*, Luke 24:7). Jesus, moreover, viewed sin comprehensively in terms of (1) persons' underlying disposition, (2) the thoughts or intentions of their hearts, and (3) the resultant acts or deeds. Thus in the first place Jesus employed the analogy of a tree and its fruit (Matt. 7:17–19; 12:33) to teach that the fundamental disposition of persons' hearts directs the course of their lives. "The good man brings good things out of the good stored up in him, and the evil man [ho ponēros] brings evil things [ponēra] out of the evil stored up in him [ek tou ponērou thēsaurou]" (Matt. 12:35; cf. Luke 6:45). Second, Jesus affirmed that the thought or intent that arises from the fallen nature is properly sinful and incurs divine judgment. Thus he who is angry against a brother is guilty of murder (Matt. 5:21–22), and he who lusts after a woman in his heart is guilty of adultery (vv. 27–28). According to Jesus, the inner determination to sin is as culpable as the overt act. Jesus unites the three dimensions of sin in Matthew 15:18–19: "the things that come out of the mouth come from the heart [kardia], and these make a man 'unclean.' For out of the heart come evil thoughts [dialogismoi], murder, adultery, sexual immorality, theft, false testimony, slander" (cf. Mark 7:20–23).

Matthew 18:1–4 records our Lord's attitude toward children. When the disciples asked who is greatest in the kingdom, Jesus chose a child and commended the child's qualities of teachableness, humility before evidence, and complete trust. Jesus concluded with the words, "your Father in heaven is not willing that any of these little ones should be lost" (v. 14). The phrase "little ones" likely refers to both children and those who become like children in the spirit of their minds. Jesus' saying in Matthew 19:14, "Let the little children come to me, and do not hinder them, for the kingdom of heaven belongs to such as these," suggests that infants become the object of his special saving care.[65]

The Pauline Literature

By juxtaposing Adam with Moses and Jesus Christ in Romans 5:12–19, Paul attests the validity of the Genesis Fall narrative. The apostle, furthermore, certifies the historicity of Adam and Eve and their seduction by the serpent in 2 Corinthians 11:3 and 1 Timothy 2:13–14. Although sin is universal in the human family—"All have sinned [hēmarton] and fall short of the glory of God" (Rom. 3:23)—Paul nevertheless views persons as retaining in some significant measure their status as image-bearers of the Creator (1 Cor. 11:7).

In the key theological passage, Romans 5:12–19, the apostle contrasts the effects of the one sin of Adam with the one redemptive act of Jesus Christ. Given the repeated appeal to "one man" and "one trespass" (vv. 12, 15–19), Paul clearly regards the initial disobedience of the first pair as the cause of all the sorrows inflicted on the human race. By using the words "sin" (hamartia, vv. 12–13, 21), "transgression" (parabasis, v. 14), "trespass" (paraptōma, vv. 15–18, 20), and "disobedience" (parakoē, v. 19), the apostle views Adam's act as sinful in all respects. In this text Paul argues (1) that Adam's disobedience in Eden involved his posterity in sin. Verse 12 teaches that the whole of the race sinned, not subsequently, but in the first man Adam; the sin of one was the sin of all.[66] Thus Paul writes, "Sin entered the world through one man, and death through sin, and in this way death came to all men, because all sinned." We note in this verse first that the phrase ep hō should be interpreted causally in the sense of "for this reason," or "because" (cf. 2 Cor. 5:4).[67] And second, the constative aorist hēmarton signifies the particular historical event in which humanity sinned collectively in the primal sin of Adam. Furthermore, verse 19 states, "Through the disobedience of the one man the many were made sinners." The aorist passive of kathistēmi ("appoint," "make") may simply mean "became." "Here there is hardly any linguistic or material difference between *katestathēsan* and *egenonto*. The meaning is that 'as the many became sinners through the disobedience of the one man, so the many became righteous through the obedience of the one.' This does not imply that the forensic element is absent."[68] (2) Adam's sin brought upon all persons the curse of physical death. Verse 12, cited above, teaches that universal death is the consequence of universal sin (cf. v. 14). Paul's further statements, "the many died [*apethanon*, aorist tense] by the trespass of the one man" (v. 15) and "by the trespass of the one man, death reigned through that one man" (v. 17) clearly indicate that persons experience death not because of acts of their own, but by virtue of their participation in the sin of Adam. First Corinthians 15:21–22 makes the same point: "death came through a man"; "in Adam all die." Finally (3), Paul teaches that Adam's primal sin resulted in condemnation for all. Thus "the judgment [*krima*] followed one sin and brought condemnation" (*katakrima*, Rom. 5:16), and "the result of one trespass was condemnation (*katakrima*) for all men" (v. 18). *Krima* here signifies the judicial verdict, and *katakrima* the result of it, namely, the execution of condemnation that issues in damnation.[69] "Here the emphasis is on the judicial sentence of God, which on the basis of the act of the head determines the destiny of all."[70] In conclusion, Romans 5:12–21 affirms that Adam's one trespass constitutes all persons guilty sinners, subject to death, and liable to eternal damnation. The ground of God's righteous judgment is the real solidarity of the human family. Consequently when Adam sinned, the entire race sinned and so suffers the awesome consequences of his rebellion.

The section Romans 1:18–3:20 sets forth the moral bankruptcy of human-kind in order to establish the sinner's need for Christ. Thus Paul argues that humanity's rejection of the light of the knowledge of God afforded by general revelation results in sin-darkened minds and hearts: "Their thinking became futile and their foolish hearts were darkened" (1:21). Sinful thoughts and imaginations (*dialogismoi*) then give way to sinful behavior, specifically, to false religion and idolatry (v. 23) and to homosexual acts (vv. 26–27). God judges fornication a grievous sin (v. 24), but homosexuality is particularly odious, since it represents a perversion of his purpose for the race as male and female. Having excluded God from their lives, sinners "become filled with every kind of wickedness, evil, greed and depravity. They are full of envy, murder, strife, deceit and malice. They are gossips, slanderers, God-haters, insolent, arrogant and boastful; they invent ways of doing evil; they disobey their parents; they are senseless, faithless, heartless, ruthless" (vv. 29–31). This selective list depicts the depths of moral ruin to which unregenerate humanity has sunk.

In Romans 3:9–20 Paul portrays the entire human race as wholly depraved. In spiritual matters, all sinners are (1) *blind*—"there is no one who understands" (v. 11a), (2) *rebellious*—"all have turned away, they have together become worthless" (v. 12a), (3) *lawless*—"there is no one who does good, not even one" (v. 12b), and (4) *errant*—"no one . . . seeks God" (v. 11b). Human depravity expresses itself in corrupt speech (vv. 13–14) and in perverted deeds (vv. 15–16), with the result that sinners lack peace of mind (v. 17). The experience of humanity under sin thus is one of pervasive depravity—*non posse non peccare*.

Elsewhere Paul locates depravity in the *"sarx"* (Rom. 8:4–5; Gal. 5:16–17, 24), which the NIV often translates as "sinful nature." "*Sarx* is man's unrenewed nature . . . his whole nature ethically viewed as under the dominion of sin."[71] It is that inclination toward sin and self from which specific sins flow (Gal. 5:19–21). Central to depravity is an anti-God bias or an ingrained hostility toward God (Rom. 8:7; Col. 1:21). Depravity, moreover, blinds the mind in relation to spiritual concerns (2 Cor. 4:4; Eph. 4:17–18). First Corinthians 2:14 teaches that depravity results in epistemic inability in the sinner: "The man without the Spirit does not accept [dechomai] the things that come from the Spirit of God, for they are foolishness [mōria] to him, and he cannot understand them, because they are spiritually discerned." The verb dechomai connotes the idea of welcoming (Luke 16:4, 9) and suggests that sinners reject spiritual realities because they appear to be nonsense (mōria). Paul, furthermore, represents sinners as volitionally dead in the spiritual realm, or incapable of making any response honoring to God: "You were dead [nekros] in your sins and in the uncircumcision of your sinful nature" (Col. 2:13; cf. Eph. 2:1, 5). "Man's sinful condition is lifeless and motionless as far as any Godward activity is concerned."[72] Lacking spiritual power, sinners are enslaved by Satan (2 Tim. 2:26), by the sin principle that rules their lives (Rom. 6:6, 16–20), and by numerous lusts and passions (Titus 3:3). Thus the apostle depicts sinners as helpless bondslaves in the service of sin and Satan. Contaminated by sin in their bodies and spirits (2 Cor. 7:1), sinners morally are assailed by consciences that are "corrupted" (Titus 1:15) and "seared" (1 Tim. 4:2).

By virtue of universal sin and depravity, Paul indicts humanity as guilty and culpable before God. The apostle states that since both Jews and Gentiles have violated God's standards, "the whole world [is] held accountable [hypodikos, 'under judgment'] to God" (Rom. 3:19).

Elsewhere Paul states, "Cursed [epikataratos, "under penalty"] is everyone who does not continue to do everything written in the Book of the Law" (Gal. 3:10). Again, "Scripture has shut up all men under sin" (Gal. 3:22 NASB), which means that all persons languish under the guilt and condemnation that follows from sin. God's response to depravity and guilt is wrath, that righteous displeasure of the Holy One that results in punishment. "The wrath [orgē] of God is being revealed from heaven against all the godlessness and wickedness of men who suppress the truth by their wickedness" (Rom. 1:18; cf. Eph. 5:6; 1 Thess. 2:16). The most fearful aspect of retribution is the eschatological wrath that God will mete out against sinners on the last day (Rom. 2:5; 1 Thess. 1:10). The penalty prescribed for sin is death (Rom. 6:23), both physical (Rom. 8:10), spiritual (Eph. 5:14), and eternal (2 Thess. 1:9).

The Johannine Literature

By describing Satan as "the father of lies" and a "murderer from the beginning" (John 8:44; cf. 1 John 3:8), Jesus certifies the historical facticity of the Genesis account of the Fall. When John the Baptist addressed Jesus as "the Lamb of God, who takes away the sin [hamartia] of the world!" (John 1:29), he acknowledged that the human family languishes under the burden of a common corruption and guilt. Jesus appears to have taught inherited depravity with the words "Flesh gives birth to flesh" (John 3:6). As Plummer observes, "what is born of sinful human nature is human and sinful."[73] Jesus further taught (John 5:42) that sinful and depraved persons lack the love for God the Law demands (Deut. 6:5). Indeed, sinners emotionally hate Jesus and the Father (John 15:18, 24). The perfect tense of the verb miseō in the preceding verses suggests that the animosity is a permanent rather than a fleeting emotion. Depravity, moreover, results in intellectual blindness (Rev. 3:17) and volitional inability (John 6:44) in spiritual matters. When Jesus taught that "everyone who sins is a slave [*doulos*] to sin" (8:34), he meant that the condition of the habitual sinner is one of volitional servitude to the lower nature and malignant powers. John perceives that "the whole world is under the control of the evil one" (1 John 5:19).

The inevitable response of the holy God to moral depravity is fierce anger (*thymos*, Rev. 14:10, 19; 15:1, 7) and wrath (*orgē*, John 3:36; Rev. 16:19; 19:15). Thus by virtue of their unbelief and God's righteous judgment, sinners legally suffer the sentence of condemnation. "Whoever does not believe stands condemned already" (John 3:18). Here and now the penalty of sin is death, both physical (1 John 5:16–17) and spiritual (John 5:24; 1 John 3:14). Hereafter the penalty will be eternal death, or endless exclusion from the presence of God (John 5:29; Rev. 20:13–15).

Other New Testament Literature

James teaches not only that evil desire is the root of particular sins but also that the human heart is fundamentally sinful: "Each one is tempted when, by his own evil desire [*epithymia*], he is dragged away and enticed. Then, after desire has conceived, it gives birth to sin" (1:14–15). "This verse, in fact, so far from being opposed to the doctrine of original sin, substantiates it."[74] Sin and depravity result metaphysically in the separation of the spirit from the body (2:26), morally in licentious conduct (1 Peter 4:3; 2 Peter 2:14; Jude 7) and a guilty conscience (Heb. 9:9, 14; 10:2), emotionally in crippling inner conflicts (1 Peter 2:11) and the gnawing fear of death (Heb. 2:15), relationally in enmity

toward God (James 4:4) and others (4:1), and volitionally in hardness of heart (Heb. 3:8, 15) and bondage to sinful passions (2 Peter 2:19). Failure to fulfill the law of God, even at one point, results in guilt (*enochos,* James 2:10), the punishment of which is physical death (Heb. 9:27; 1 Peter 4:6) and spiritual death (James 1:15; 5:20). In spite of human depravity, God views persons as constituted in his image (James 3:9). The perfect form of the verb (*gegonotas*) in the phrase "men, who have been made in God's likeness" underscores persons' continued status as divine image-bearers.

The intricate argument of Hebrews 7:4–10 illumines the issue of how Adam's sin affected the entire human family. Verses 9 and 10 are most relevant for our discussion: "One might even say that Levi, who collects the tenth, paid the tenth through Abraham, because when Melchizedek met Abraham, Levi was still in the body [literally, 'in the loins,' [*osphys*] of his ancestor." F. F. Bruce observes that "an ancestor is regarded in biblical thought as containing within himself all his descendants"[75] If we take verse 10 in its literal sense—"loins" being the source of physical generation (cf. v. 5)—then the notion of racial solidarity and the seminal theory, in particular, is supported.[76]

New Testament Words for Sin

Negatively, the New Testament describes sin as *harmartia,* a missing of the mark or a failure to attain God's standard (Matt. 1:21; Rom. 5:12–13, 20–21; 1 John 1:9); compare *hamartēma,* which focuses on the consequence of such failure or fault (Mark 3:28; Rom. 3:25; 1 Cor. 6:18). The word *anomia,* that connotes departure from God's law, is commonly translated by the NIV as "lawlessness" or "wickedness" (Matt. 23:28; Titus 2:14;

1 John 3:4). The noun *adikia* (Rom. 1:18, 29; 2 Peter 2:15; 1 John 5:17) possesses the root idea of absence of righteousness and is frequently translated "wrongdoing" or "wickedness." *Apeitheia*, which fundamentally signifies lack of faith, is often rendered "unbelief" or "disobedience" (Rom. 11:30, 32; Eph. 2:2; 5:6; Heb. 4:6). The noun *asebeia*, from the verb *sebomai*, to "worship," signifies impiety or irreligion and is translated "godlessness" (Rom. 1:18; 11:26) or "ungodliness" (Titus 2:12). Finally, the nouns *agnoia* (Acts 3:17; 17:30; Eph. 4:18) and *agnoēma* (Heb. 9:7) connote "ignorance" of God's holy requirements.

Positively, *parabasis* constitutes a breach of the law or a violation of a commandment, and so is translated "transgression" (Rom. 4:15; Gal. 3:19) or "violation" (Heb. 2:2). *Paraptōma*, from the verb *parapiptō*, to "fall away" (Heb. 6:6), signifies a fault or offense, and so is commonly rendered by the words "trespass" (Matt. 6:14–15, KJV; Rom. 5:15–18, 20) and "transgression" (Rom. 11:11–12; Eph. 2:1). *parakoē*, from the verb *parakouō* meaning "fail to hear," signifies overt "disobedience" to God (Rom. 5:19; 2 Cor. 10:6; Heb. 2:2). The noun *ponēria*, whose root idea is evil or ill-natured, connotes human character as wicked and depraved (Luke 11:39; 1 Cor. 5:8; Eph. 6:12). The adjective *ponēros* describes persons as morally evil or wicked (Matt. 7:11; 12:35; 2 Thess. 3:2). The noun *epithymia*, from *thymos* meaning "passion," signifies the evil desires and lusts that reside in the heart (Rom. 1:24; Gal. 5:16; James 1:14–15; 1 Peter 2:11; 1 John 2:16–17). The reality of guilt that follows the various sins of omission and commission is indicated by the noun *opheilēma* ("debt" or obligation, Matt. 6:12) and the adjective *enochos* ("guilty" or liable to punishment, Matt. 5:21–22; 1 Cor. 11:27; James 2:10).

SYSTEMATIC FORMULATION

Which elements of the historical views of the human moral condition cohere in a systematic doctrine that makes sense of the extensive evidence available in Scripture and human experience? A systematic discussion must begin with the status of humans before and after the Fall.

Our First Parents in God's Image

Ontologically in the image of the eternal God, the souls of Adam and Eve (after their creation) have an unconditional *everlasting existence*. Others hold that they had only a conditional immortality. Their souls would live forever only if they partook of the fruit of the tree of life. Physically we may agree that the body would live on and on only if they had eaten of the life-giving tree. Conditional immortality applies, however, only to the body. The human spirit had more than a conditional existence. [77] The day Eve and Adam ate the forbidden fruit, they experienced the potential for physical death and its processes began. What was conditional was the morality of their existence and their fellowship with God. Their spirits exist forever, as we argued in the previous chapter.

Our first parents also reflected a likeness to the sovereign God *functionally* in the faithful use of their personal intellectual, emotional, and volitional capacities. Adam and Eve knew, loved, and served God and each other. Their thoughts, desires, and actions were relationally loving but also morally just. In their work they were able effectively to maintain dominion over other creatures on earth. As stewards accountable to God, they were faithful. Adam and Eve were joyful vice-regents in the providential kingdom of God on earth (Gen. 1:26, 28; Ps. 8:6–8; Heb. 2:6–8). *Morally*, Adam and Eve were originally righteous like God. Adam and Eve before the Fall were upright in character and used all of their capacities to worship the Creator and serve his purposes in Eden. They were motivated by love for God and each other so that their actions were in accord with God's revealed will. Hence the consequences of their sin affected the well-being of themselves and of God's kingdom on earth. They portrayed God's moral character as revealed subsequently by the incarnate Christ. In essence humankind is not evil, but good. Goodness or righteousness is not something distinct from them that was added to them, but a quality of human existence created in the divine image. Humanness as created is not merely morally neutral nor is it evil; on the contrary, it is good.

Relationally, prior to the Fall Adam and Eve enjoyed unbroken fellowship with their Creator and Sustainer. Apparently it was common for them to consciously encounter their Maker morning and evening (Gen. 3:8). The first pair enjoyed also faithful loving relationships with each other. No evidence of suspicion, envy, jealousy, or hatred occurred before the Fall. Male and female were like God (Gen. 1:27; 5:1–2) in having mutual relations of respect, love, and trust (Gen. 2:18, 20; 1 Cor. 11:11–12). God created Eve out of Adam, differentiating female from male in the unity of mankind. Their marriage relationship as "one flesh" restores the unity. "Mankind" equals male and female. The biblical account of the creation of man, and then of woman from man, provides a basis both for the essential unity of male and female as human and the relational unity of one husband and one wife. "When God created man, he made him in the likeness of God. He created them male and female and blessed them. And when they were created, he called them 'man' " (Gen. 5:1–2).

So the whole original internal and external context of human life was one of *peace (shalom)*. Both Old and New Testament terms for peace indicate rest, safety, freedom from care, trustfulness, security, understanding, and ease. The peace that comes from God is not so much the opposite of war as of any disturbance in communal well-being. Hence the original *shalom* covered human well-being in the widest sense of the word.[78] The original human state was not one of evolving from a brute type of existence through the survival of the fittest to a more "human" existence. Humanity's deepest struggles are not those of animals evolving to a higher form of existence, but of unique kinds of beings in God's image suffering from the loss of peace. Adam and Eve lost their loving and trustful relationship with God; their former moral uprightness; and their intellectual, emotional, and volitional integrity.

The Factual Fall

Instead of continuing to trust, love, and enjoy their Creator with their whole beings, at a point in time and space Eve and Adam disbelieved and disobeyed God. Their sinful rebellion occurred at a point in human history as an *actual fact.* The narrative in Genesis 3 is not merely a mythical illustration of how all men and women sin. It records the actual beginning of moral evil among humans. After presenting informative "accounts" of the origins of the earth, vegetation, animals and man, the author presents the origin of moral evil and the consequent natural evils. Although the biblical narrative has some symbolic aspects, the symbols occur in a literal framework. Bernard Ramm calls the events of the Fall "datable historical events," but he joins Barth in denying that they are "actual history."[79] Ramm apparently hesitates here because he does not regard the record complete. But no historical records exhaustively duplicate every detail of an event. Brief reports, we maintain, can nevertheless be accurate. From inspired revelation we can *know* in part.

The *temptations* of our first parents involved temptations much like our own. They gave attention to an inherently wrong possibility, felt its enticement, and desired to do it. Such temptations by themselves are not sin. They sinned when they continuously coveted the forbidden fruit, deliberately decided to eat it (possibly planning to pick it unobtrusively), and finally ate it. Inwardly they sinned, when yielding to the enticements, by questioning the truth of God's word (Gen. 3:1), denying the reality of death for sin, desiring forbidden pleasures, and seeking to know as God knows. Outwardly they sinned when they finally partook of the fruit. Also today men and women are tempted to (1) question God's Word, (2) seek to know evil as well as good experientially, (3) deny the reality of death, and (4) seek divine powers. New Age occult emphases like these are far from new. They are as old as the race. As at the beginning, the ultimate source of these ideas today is the ultimate deceiver, Satan.

Adam's and Eve's first sins *symbolize the fall of all men and women.* Genesis 3 not only describes the literal fall of our first parents but also vividly illustrates how all men and women yield to temptation. Realistically, Adam and Eve stand for all human beings because at the time they constituted the entire human population. (We noted the unity and solidarity of the race in the previous chapter.)

Our reference to our first parents as symbols in no way denies their literal significance. *Symbols* involve three factors: (1) the factually existent symbol itself, (2) something other than itself that it denotes, and (3) a point of similarity between the two. Additional considerations make it highly probable that

Genesis 3 contains a real symbolism embodied in actual things. Just as Adam was both the first literal man and symbolic of all humanity, so two literal trees symbolized life and knowledge, and a literal serpent symbolized Satan. If the account of Eve's and Adam's sins was not factual, then at what point in the history of Genesis does the text suddenly begin to speak about actual humans on this actual earth? Our Lord and his disciples who were inspired to write the New Testament took the Fall and surrounding events literally and factually. Hence those who accept Jesus' lordship today interpret Genesis as he did. The biblical account of the Fall explains not only how human sin originated, but also by way of illustration how every person sins. The literal significance need not be denied to support the universal symbolism; neither need the universal symbolism be denied to support the literal significance.

Furthermore, Adam, as the first human being, represents every human being morally and legally. Adam's sin may justly and legally implicate all Adam's human descendants as a consequence of God's solemn promise to him that if he even touched the tree in the middle of the garden he would die (Gen. 3:3). Covenant theologians think this teaches a "covenant of works" specifying the parties to the agreement, the condition, and the results if the condition is not met. The parties to the covenant were God and mankind's first representative (Adam), the covenant was conditioned on obedience, and the penalty for disobedience was death. Although the context does not explicitly call this a "covenant," the text has the elements of a solemn promise or legal agreement made by God made with Adam. In Paul's theology Adam's sin implicated his descendants. Adam has a relationship to the fallen race parallel to Christ's relation to the redeemed (Rom. 5:12–18). Adam's one sin brought condemnation to all generated in the fallen human family (vv. 16, 18); Christ's one sacrifice brings justification to all who have been regenerated in his moral and spiritual family. The theological value of Christ's death for all, furthermore, depends on the literalness of his incarnation in human flesh (1 John 4:1–3; 2 John 9). It follows that in Paul's parallel the theological effect of Adam's sin also depends on the literalness of his one act of sin. Because Adam literally sinned, he can really represent all his descendants. Adam's representation of all humans is not an arbitrary legal fiction, however. His legal representation is justified by the fact that each descendant has an Adamic nature not only as human but also as depraved. As Jesus taught, "Flesh gives birth to flesh" (John 3:6).

Consequences of the Fall for Adam and Eve and All Humans

Inwardly, by falling into the foul whirlpool of temptations, both Adam and Eve developed a strong desire for sin's seductiveness in general, and love for specifics not resisted led to habitual sins. Even if their words and acts appeared externally to adhere to God's revealed will, their motives were not for his glory. So struggle with fleshly loves tainted every aspect of their natures. Their inward hearts became inclined to sin. Inwardly Adam and Eve were now lawbreakers and rebels against the Lawgiver. Their hearts, the very centers of their natures, had become deceitful and desperately wicked. Instead of being loving creatures in reflecting God's likeness, they had become insolent. Their essential inclinations were changed from those of believing and obedient children of God to those of believing and obedient children of the Devil.

Functionally, Adam and Eve's use of their capacities to think, feel, and will became misdirected, misused, and terribly complicated in the fallen world. Eve's distinctive roles in childbirth and in her marriage were no longer to be free from trouble (Gen. 3:16). And Adam's activities also began to entail pain, perspiration, and frustration. The Fall debilitated all their distinctively personal capacities to think, feel, and act with conduct and motivations that please God.

Morally, also as sinners they brought on themselves a verdict of guilty as the efficient causes of their sins (*reatus culpae*). The all-knowing divine Judge found them to blame for abusing the marvelous self-determining capacities he gave them and violating moral principles of a healthful life that flow from his nature. So they received the sentence deserved for the heinousness of their crime. And they lived their remaining time on earth in fear of physical and eternal punishment that justly follows (*reatus poenae*). What Adam and Eve *were* morally was far from what they *ought to have been.* From descriptive accounts of each other as psychologists and sociologists they might not have appeared far out of line with each other's moral discernment. But their originally righteous natures had become prone to sin.

Spiritually, although dependent on the Holy One for their existence, Adam and Eve no longer had unbroken fellowship with God or each other. Having knowingly and deliberately rebelled against God's rule of their lives, enmity arose between Satan and Eve and between the offspring of the Devil (John 8:44) and of the woman (the Messiah and his regenerate followers (Gen. 3:15). Our first parents became alienated from fellowship with the Holy One and strangers to his spiritual blessings. Instead of enjoying communion with their Maker, they found themselves trying to hide.

Ecologically and environmentally,

God banished Adam and Eve from the Garden of Eden and judged their environment. God judged the ground "because of" Adam, who then found his work to require "painful toil" (Gen. 3:17). The ground produced thorns and thistles for Adam and he was to eat of the plants "by the sweat of his brow" (vv. 18–19). As Paul later explained, "the creation was subjected to *frustration,* not by its own choice, but by the will of the one who subjected it, in hope that the creation itself will be liberated from its *bondage to decay* and brought into the glorious freedom of the children of God. We know that the whole creation has been *groaning* as in the pains of childbirth right up to the present time" (Rom. 8:20–23). Natural evils (such as hurricanes, volcanos, floods) in general are a part of the penalty for moral evils. Even so we may not trace a specific occurrence to a specific sin.

Relationally, or socially, the very next generation openly exhibits the outward evidence of inner jealousy and hatred. Cain's murder of his brother Abel typified the family, social, and political problems that follow in human history individually and collectively.

Ontologically, in spite of the loss of communion with God and the impairment of their natures, fallen people remain in God's likeness as living and active personal spirits. Human beings continue to be of great value in themselves. No human should be murdered, because every man and woman remains in God's image metaphysically (Gen. 9:6). And because everyone remains in the image of God, we ought not even curse people (James 3:9). Luther overstates the effect of the Fall when he says, "Man who was little different from the angels is now little more than a brute."[80] Although at times sinners may act like beasts, human beings remain everlasting spirits like God. So the worst criminals deserve our respect for what they are, even when we must legally oppose what they have done. And because humans remain in the *imago Dei,* God is not "totally other." We cannot agree with Kierkegaard, Barth, Bultmann, and their followers, who deny any analogy of being between God and humans, for humans remain in God's likeness. An analogy of being continues between God, who is spirit, and humans, who are physically clothed spirits, even though God's being is noncontingent and ours is contingent.

Not only did Adam and Eve suffer these consequences of sin, but so have all their descendants, whom they represented. All their offspring, for example, have lived in environments far from Edenic. In the present state of restlessness and longing for lost fellowship with God, we may try to find peace in less-demanding gods. We fail to find lasting peace, however, in materialism, hedonism, humanism, mystical unions with nature, science, education, and political action. Such idols leave us alienated from ourselves, from God, and from others and leave us troubled with anxiety. "The wicked are like the tossing sea, which cannot rest, whose waves cast up mire and mud. There is no peace, says my God, for the wicked" (Isa. 57:21). Our depraved hearts are restless, as Augustine well knew, until they find their rest in God. Because of liberal, unitarian, and other views that deny the biblical support and the moral justice of any transmission of either Adamic depravity or Adamic guilt, it is important to explore the meaning and support of these hypotheses.

A Tendency to Insolence Inherited by All

Adam's sins were not entities like books that could be passed on to his children, but Adam and Eve reproduced after their kind, not only ontologically, but also morally. For that reason every one of their Jewish and Gentile descendants actually commits sins (Rom. 1:18–3:20). From the fountainhead of the race everyone has received an inherent propensity to defy God's ways. Adam's first rejection of God not only corrupted his unsullied ability to believe and obey God but also affected the nature of all his offspring. All descendants of Adam have evidently received a perverse nature with impaired abilities to know, love, and serve God. All, when informed of God's righteous demands, tend to become insolent.

As Jesus taught, "flesh gives birth to flesh" (John 3:6). "Flesh" sometimes refers to physical life in itself without moral implications (Phil. 1:22–24), sometimes to the next of kin (Lev. 18:12), and sometimes human ancestry (Rom. 4:1). But in emphasizing the necessity of regeneration to Nicodemus, Jesus Christ indicated that morally perverse parents beget children with inclinations to moral perversity. When used morally, the "flesh" refers to an aversion to God and his righteousness. So Paul exhorts, "Do not . . . indulge the sinful nature" (Gal. 5:13), or "gratify the desires of the sinful nature" (v. 16). "For the sinful nature desires what is contrary to the Spirit, and the Spirit what is contrary to the sinful nature" (v. 17). In moral contexts, then, "flesh" designates the the degenerative tendency of personal agents to use the power of contrary choice in opposition to the will of God. The "flesh" involves a general inclination to think, feel, choose, and act in ways contrary to God's pleasure. It may be illustrated in the life of Zedekiah, when he was a twenty-one-year-old king of Judah. He did not humble himself before Jeremiah the prophet when Jeremiah spoke the Word of the Lord; he rebelled against King Nebuchadnezzar, became stiffnecked, hardened his heart, and would not turn to the Lord, the God of Israel (2 Chron. 36:11–13).

By nature the "heart" of a human is "deceitful above all things and beyond cure" (Jer. 17:9). Just as the evil tree brings forth evil fruit, the aversion of the human heart to God's ways issues in sinful deeds. The general influence of depraved human nature leads self-determining human agents to specific acts of unwillingness to open ourselves to God's wisdom and insensitivity to our neighbors' needs. The specific sins may include thoughts, emotions, attitudes, motives, words, and acts. The "flesh" exhibits itself in "sexual immorality, impurity and debauchery; idolatry and witchcraft; hatred, discord, jealousy, fits of rage, selfish ambition, dissensions, factions and envy; drunkenness, orgies, and the like" (Gal. 5:19–21). In other instances the flesh may produce more "splendid vices," but they are vices nevertheless! These include pride of accomplishment, self-worship, self-aggrandizement, fear, child abuse, employee abuse, prisoner abuse, and abuse of members by cult leaders. Religious people may also defy God's righteousness under the pretense of conformity to it! Pharisaically we may add to biblical standards, pray and tithe to be seen of men, and despise people who do not adhere to our traditions. Whether in sensuality, materialism, intellectualism, emotionalism, voluntarism, scientism, or cultism, defiant cravings dominate the minds and enslave the bodies of the unregenerate (Eph. 2:3) and continue to harass children of God by grace.

"I tell you the truth," Jesus said, "everyone who sins is a slave to sin" (John 8:34). In our fallen condition, Paul explains, we are "controlled by the sinful nature" (Rom. 7:5). Sin has dominion over the unregenerate. Regularly yielding to the flesh, they become dominated by a fleshly mind set (8:5, 7). Because of this inherent inclination of motive as well as thoughts, words, and acts, their hardened, stubborn hearts are unable to obey God's law (8:3) or to please God (v. 8). Everything is tainted in life according to the flesh and nothing is good without qualification (7:18). Like Paul, by nature we have within ourselves the inability to do the good that we desire (vv. 18–20).

The Bible also refers to people dominated by fleshly or evil natures as the "world" (*kosmos*). The term "world" sometimes has no moral connotation in references to the heavens and earth as the dwelling place of humanity and the theater of history. In other contexts "world" refers to the unregenerate people who dwell on the earth. The people of the world are ruled by demonic powers (1 Cor. 2:6; Eph. 2:2) and in irreconcilable conflict with God's rule.[81] Jesus charged the disciples to take the gospel to the whole world (Mark 16:15), clearly referring to all people struggling with fallenness. Again the field is the world (Matt. 13:38) and Christians are to be the light of the world (5:14). Christians are in the world but not of the world system. Believers are to love those who dwell on the earth for Christ but they are not to love "the cravings of sinful man" (1 John 2:16) and the desires of the world that pass away (v. 17). Christians are not to let evil desires dominate or rule them. By the Spirit of grace believers in Christ no longer let their sinful propensity dominate their lives.

Depravity Is Holistic

The fleshly desires of the human heart affect *every human capacity of the whole person*. But a person, not a part of a person, thinks about the possibility of disbelief and disobedience, imagines the emotional pleasures of going his or her own way, and deliberately decides to yield to peer pressure (or other temptations). A person created to know, love, and serve God knows, loves, and serves self, others, or something in creation more. Our sins have corrupted all our personal capacities and relationships. The taint of idolatrous passions affects us holistically. The mind is not exempt, as some rationalists imagine. The conscience is not exempt, as some moralists think. The emotions are not exempt, as some romanticists might wish. And the will is not exempt from the taint of sin, as some activists might hope. It is no mere addition to our essential humanity that is lost in the Fall (as in the traditional Roman Catholic view): our essential nature is corrupted and our essential relationships are broken.

"Holistic depravity" conveys better than "total depravity" the fact that all our abilities and our best achievements are tainted by evil without implying that we are all as bad as we could possibly be. No capacity of our unrenewed nature escapes the taint of our sinful hearts. What the older Reformed writers called a person's "agencies" and their "excellencies," we are calling a person's "capacities" and their "uses" or "functions." The mental capacity remains, but the mind has become unreceptive ("blind") to truth about divine spiritual realities. The desires and emotions no longer find their fulfillment in the Holy Spirit. And the will is predisposed to sinful motivations, choices, and actions. Instead of using our capacities to know, love, and obey our Creator, we prefer to know, love, and serve God's creatures. As sinners we tend to be preoccupied with untrue thoughts, impure desires, and unjust conduct. Having desired forbidden knowledge, illicit love, and irresponsible power, we became inclined toward unwise, unfair, and unloving acts. Hence we fail to enjoy all the excellent by-products that could have been ours from a use of our intellects, emotions, and wills for God's glory. So our best attempts to fulfill the cultural mandate tend to be tainted with unworthy motives. Our best efforts in religion, philosophy, the sciences, the fine arts, personal religion, or social reform fail to please the most High. We either tend to pride of achievement in the development of our skills or in claiming premature finality in our thinking, or we immerse ourselves in an unprincipled hedonism and sensuality. The Romans before the fall of their empire desired only bread and circus; our ultimate concerns may be bread and television.

Sinful acts, on an Augustinian analysis, may not appear to be wicked. On the other hand, "worship and service" may be sinful when the humanistic creatures displace the Creator (Rom. 1:25). If our concerns for our families, business, or nation become more ultimate than our concern for God, we sin. Our acts may appear to others to be splendid. If we do not seek first the kingdom of God, however, they are "splendid vices." As Isaiah said, "All our righteous acts are like filthy rags" (64:6). Jesus observed that the Pharisees, though outwardly fasting, praying, and tithing, were inwardly uncaring.

How does the depravity of our hearts affect the varied aspects of human existence?

Depravity of Heart and Human Emotions

Emotions are not inherently wrong, and our original tendency may not directly affect their expression in relation to ordinary interests and relationships. But because of our deceitful hearts they do not delight supremely in God and his righteousness. Our emotional lives become detrimental when they delight in evil rather than good. In our unregenerate condition we gratify the "cravings of our sinful nature" (Eph. 2:3). Repeatedly we give priority not only to bad thoughts but also to harmful words and deeds. As a habitual tendency becomes compulsive (like an addiction) we discover our inability to change our fleshly cravings. But we ourselves, like Adam and Eve, have begun the habits that become compulsive. As a result, even the good that we still choose, we find ourselves unable to do with consistency and purity of loving motives.

The root of all evil, Augustine concluded from his scripturally informed interpretation of his own experience, is wrongly directed desire, affection, or love. When we divert our highest love from the Creator to the creature, we become idolatrous. By seeking our emotional fulfillment in what cannot last and yet what demands more and more from us, we sin. *Lust (libido)* for creatures (like lust for money) we can lose in this changing, temporal world, is the deepest root of evil. Lust for things leads to *vice*—the corrupting of one's own soul and body. Personal vices then lead to *crime*—injuring others. In contrast, *the deepest root of all good is love for the Creator* (whom we cannot lose since he is eternal). Love for the eternal Lord of all leads to *prudence*—conduct to one's own advantage or edification. Prudence in turn leads to *benevolence*—conduct with a view to a neighbor's advantage or upbuilding.[82]

As persons with deceitful hearts we bring sinful desires with us to any environmental structures. The most radical diagnosis of the human predicament does not trace the roots of our difficulties to our environment, our parents, the other sex, or to the party in power in our nations at the moment. The deepest roots of evil in the contemporary world can be traced to our own inner selves. The tendency "to mess everything up" artistically, economically, nationally, and internationally lies within ourselves. When theological writers speak of "original sin," they generally do not refer to the first sin of humans chronologically, but to the fact that sinful proclivities are as original in each new baby as a tendency to cry. To change the analogy, by "original equipment" for an automobile we mean the water pump, brakes, etc., included with each new model of automobile. Similarly, each new human being since the Fall has an *original tendency* to moral evil (often called original sin [sing.]). This is not to say that anyone is born with *original sins* (pl.). All self-determining personal agents responsibly commit sins when they displease God by doing what is counterproductive to their wellbeing either knowingly or in inexcusable ignorance.

If the desires of our hearts are persistently evil, they further fix the hereditary *perversity of character* received by nature. (1) By valuing the word of others above the Word of God we break the relationship of mutual trust with God, and this leads to mistrust of one another. (2) By desiring our own way above his rule we become estranged, and by misusing God-given abilities to disregard God's moral directives we rebel against his lordship. (3) Repetition of these sins becomes customary; custom not resisted becomes necessary; and necessity becomes enslaving. Thus the inclination becomes inherent in human nature to habitually disbelieve God's words, alienate one self from God, and use God-given capacities in ways counterproductive to God, others, and creation. Hence fallen people not only commit sins but *are* sinners. Humans since the Fall must realistically be concluded to have *sinful natures*.

Depravity and Reason

Fallen human thinking may be highly developed in many areas of research and skill, but it is unreceptive to God's revealed redemptive plans. Depraved people of themselves stubbornly refuse to repent genuinely of their sins. The resurrected Jesus rebuked even the eleven disciples for their lack of faith and their stubborn refusal to believe those who had seen him after he had risen (Mark 16:14). Paul spoke of those who show contempt for the riches of God's kindness, tolerance, and patience because of "stubbornness" and an "unrepentant heart" (Rom. 2:4–5). "The man without the Spirit does not accept the things that come from the Spirit of God, for they are foolishness to him, and he cannot understand them, because they are spiritually discerned" (1 Cor. 2:14). "The god of this age has blinded the minds of unbelievers, so that they cannot see the light of the gospel" (2 Cor. 4:4). Although the light of the sun shines into their very eyeballs the blind cannot see it! Because they are preoccupied with the visible things, their ability to see the invisible atrophies. Hence human mental efforts in the direction of spiritual experience and religion are plagued by error and resist the clear evidence of truth.

This inability of the intellect (*intellectus*) to receive God's redemptive plans (wisdom, *sapientia*) does not necessarily imply limitations on the rational capacity (*ratio*) to investigate changing, material things (*scientia*). Quite the contrary, sinners prefer to make idols of the scientific method, logic, psychology, sociology, even the biblical languages, and other accomplishments in career or family. Thus, however apparently sagacious, the wise of the world are involved in pride and a curious itch for learning the delights of the flesh. They may become experts in rationalizing inherently wrong conduct. Their sins may be splendid, but they are "splendid vices." What about those in the world (in religions, education, etc.) who seek God? Apparently they are only hypothetical persons. In reality, as Paul concludes, "there is no one who understands, no one who seeks God. All have turned away, they have to-

213

gether become worthless; there is no one who does good, not even one" (Rom. 3:11).

For several years Ludwig Wittgenstein realized that he expended his mental abilities on petty and self-destructive concerns. Although study with Bertrand Russell seemed to provide some respite, he left for seclusion in Norway and often thought of suicide. Wittgenstein explained that he thought "he had no right to live in a world where he constantly felt contempt for other people and irritated them by his nervous temperament." He broke off his friendship with Russell primarily because of his own weaknesses and confessed, "My life is *full* of the most hateful and petty thoughts and acts (this is no exaggeration)." Again, "Perhaps you think it is a waste of time for me to think about myself, but how can I be a logician if I am not yet a man! Before *everything else* I must become pure."[83] This outstanding philosopher acknowledged the fact that his great mental abilities were selfishly enslaved and recognized the need for moral purity to set them free.

Depravity and Free Will

A sinful person's capacity of self-determination is fully free when he has both (1) an uncoerced ability to choose among available alternatives (apart from spiritual things) and (2) an ability to do what he desires. Sinners act freely when they choose and act according to their natures. Since the Fall human natures are both finite and depraved, both dependent on God for their life and disposed to rebellion against God's moral rule. The basic conflict is not between the soul and the body, but between the diverted nature of the sinner and his Sustainer.

Both human ontological and depraved natures are logically prior to our existential choices. Atheistic existentialist Jean-Paul Sartre claims that "there is no human nature, since there is no God to conceive it."[84] So he thought that existence (with unlimited choices) logically precedes essences or natures. The existentialists' alleged unlimited human freedom to define ourselves in any way at all seemed to critics a "dreadful" or "a nauseous freedom." In such a total relativism there are no givens for points of reference. Life by the existentialists' totalistic relativism was like traveling in space without any fixed reference point (nothing like a compass, a uniform law of gravity, or a regular speed of light). Totally free existential decisions preceded any patterns.

A total relativist buys freedom in a vacuum by denial of a human nature. Given the reality of God, that dream of freedom is unrealistic, and given the truth of an inscripturated revelation, it is unbiblical. The Old Testament teaches that the moral nature of the human heart determines the morality of the sacrifices, ceremonies, fasts, and feasts. Christ Jesus teaches that the nature of the tree determines the fruit, denying that the fruit determines the nature of the tree. A free choice is not made by a will abstracted from the whole person acting in a vacuum. Whole persons are free when they make uncoerced moral choices and act in accord with their creaturely potential and fallen natures. Realistically, the great freedoms of God's image-bearers must be viewed within the limits of both our finiteness and our fallenness.

Since God sustains us as humans—not gods, angels, or animals—it is pointless to seriously claim free will to choose to be another kind of being. Our dependence on divine providence sets some limits to our meaningful choices, and our God-given finite abilities set some limits to realizing them. Similarly, our fallenness not only blinds our minds and diverts our desires, but also limits our abilities to perform. So we have some limits to our free choices morally. We have numerous alternatives within the range available to our depraved minds, emotions, and wills. But in regard to a whole range of higher spiritual values, motives, and ends we are blinded to them, disenchanted with them, and in rebellion against them.

When choosing and acting according to our sinful natures (doing what comes naturally) we still have *free choice* among the alternatives available to persons unable to receive spiritual things and *self-determination* within the limits of a world curved in upon ourselves. The choices available to fallen "selves" are limited by their fallen inclinations. The unregenerate are "free" when not coerced by an outside force against their wills, but inwardly they are slaves to sin in general and may become addicted to specific unworthy cravings and acts. Alcoholics, for instance, may be unable to change drinking habits that have become compulsive, but as responsible agents they could have stopped before the habit that led to physical dependency. Humans are not the pawns or mere victims of alcohol or other kinds of substances in their environments. Personal agents are responsible also for their responses to the influences of their peers, subcultures, and cultures. "No matter how powerful the external forces," Bernard Ramm argues, "there is a strip of responsibility in every such psyche that cannot be negotiated away."[85]

Freedom of choice and freedom of ability must be distinguished. Sinners may still have some unsuppressed knowledge of God's law by common grace and general illumination. So they may choose not to covet, bear false witness, or get drunk, but they lack the ability to achieve the chosen objective. Depravity does not mean that sinners never have morally worthy ideals that please God. Rather, it means that they

lack the proper motivation (the love of God) and that they cannot sustain that conduct perfectly in the strength of the flesh.

It is always important not to make generalizations about human freedom because of the difference that the Fall made, the difference regeneration makes, and the difference glorification will make. Consider now the range of alternative choices available in each situation, whether or not choices contrary to God's pleasure are possible. (1) *Before the Fall* Adam and Eve had the power of contrary choice to please or displease God in motive and act. (2) *Since the Fall* however, unregenerate humans' alternative choices are within a range in which they all come short of pleasing God. The unsaved do not have the contrary choice of loving and serving him above all else, and if they had they would not have the ability to do it. Their ability to achieve the worthy ends chosen is severely limited by their fleshly natures. (3) *After regeneration* believers in Christ have not only the old fallen nature but also a new spiritual nature, and thus they have both the full range of alternatives pleasing and displeasing to God in contrary choice, and the full range of contrary abilities as they walk either in the flesh or in the Holy Spirit. (4) *In the glorified state,* when they are finally made fully like Christ, believers will have only one nature. Finally, when they are glorified with Christ, believers will be confirmed in righteousness and will be like their Lord in being unable to sin. Then they will freely determine themselves according to their glorified natures. Thus human freedom always involves self-determination according to one's nature, but it does not always involve morally good or evil options. At present for the unregenerate, the options are all evil in some degree within the evil kingdom; in the future for the glorified, the options are all righteous in the righteous kingdom.

Depravity and Religion

Holistic depravity results in a total inability to justify ourselves before the Most High. Our repeated idolatrous uses of our abilities to know, love, and serve God leave us alienated from the source of all meaning and purpose in life. With that break in faith we place ourselves at the center of the universe. Attempting to become autonomous, we make ourselves, our family, or our group our "god." There follows the need for endless material acquisition to defend one's self and one's security against all opponents.

So the holistically depraved persistently suppress the truths of theism in universal revelation and of the gospel in special revelation. Or worse, they do so while hypocritically advertising an adherence to them. Countless suppressions of revealed truth are disclosed in the theological diversity of the new religions and cults, and even in the major divisions of christendom. As commendable as these movements may appear to be, no amount of devotion to humanly devised educational, economic, political, moral, or religious causes can by themselves renew anyone's personal fellowship with a holy God. The fact that people do not love God as they ought does not mean that they are irreligious. What is remarkable is what they will worship and serve! After relativizing the Absolute, they may absolutize any relative loyalty. They may place ultimate value in any created thing—spouse, children, business, political party, animals, and endless idols. Both making God small and exalting created things are obviously evil and apparently worthy icons.

Regenerate leaders with the best of motives (love for God) and chosen ends (the glory of God) may choose fleshly strategies or unjust means for attaining them. Not only corruption in the papacy throughout its history but also corruption in high Protestant echelons, even among groups standing for separation from the unbelieving religious and secular world, disclose the need to be aware of subtle temptations in handling finances, maintaining marital fidelity, and keeping the centralities of the Christian faith central.

Depraved People in Society

Sinners fail not only to love God above all, but also to love others as themselves. Sooner or later these delinquencies lead to isolation and loneliness. So sinners miss the mark socially as well as individually. Having alienated themselves from God, sinners alienate themselves also from relatives, in-laws, neighbors, church members, other citizens of their nation, and others of other countries and races and cultural levels. Young sinners, for example, may need to accept responsibility for their own decisions and no longer blame their parents. Like the prodigal son, they may need to come to their senses and confess, "Father [and mother], I have sinned against heaven and against you" (Luke 15:21). Parents as sinners also may need to confess to their children that they have sinned against them by failing in their calling to love faithfully, to educate morally, and to discipline them wisely.

The effects of self-centeredness and injustice have hurt not only the hungry, the poor, and minorities of all sorts but also divinely established institutions of the family, the nation, and the church. So human history has missed the privileges attendant upon authentic caring for others.[86] Those who have no more ultimate concern than themselves become estranged from others and tend toward the idolatry of narcissistic self-worship. To center our highest values on ourselves is sin. Made for God, the human self finds its security, peace, and hope in God and not in itself. Without that foundation, sin shatters the most fundamental relationships we have.

The deceitfulness of fallen human nature may occasion special relational temptations for people with *economic status or power*. The excitement to turn out bigger and better products in greater quantities can be for the good of the users, but it may entail a waste of the earth's limited resources. It may also entail excessive pollution of the air or nearby water supplies. It may needlessly waste coal or gas. If we allow this to happen, we sin against the Creator, his commands, our greedy selves, our neighbors, our descendants, and the creation of the greatest of all designers, architects, artists. Exploitive abuses pervert, waste, and ultimately destroy God's great creation. Whatever new energy sources we may develop we cannot pursue ideals of affluence, comfort, mobility, and leisure indefinitely. The "basic cause of the energy crisis," Wendell Berry insists, "is not scarcity; it is moral ignorance and weakness of character."[87]

Quite apart from theological premises, Berry argues:

> We don't know *how* to use energy, or what to use it *for*. And we cannot restrain ourselves. Our time is characterized as much by the abuse and waste of human energy as it is by the abuse and waste of fossil fuel energy. Nuclear power, if we are to believe its advocates, is presumably going to be well used by the same mentality that has egregiously devalued and misapplied man- and woman-power. If we had an unlimited supply of wind power, we would use that destructively, too, for the same reasons.[88]

Board members, administrators, and managers of businesses ought to avoid possibilities of sinfully exploiting the talents and energies of employees. Employees also need to consider the possible effects of their sinful nature on the quality of their work.

The outworkings of depravity may also be writ large in a city, state, county, province, nation, or the United Nations by those in *political positions of power*. The "powers" (*dynameis*) of this world are distinguished from angels and demons (Rom. 8:38–39). Their philosophies are based on the "basic principles of this world" rather than on Christ (Col. 2:8). The powers were created by Christ (Col. 1:16) and so are not inherently evil. But the great powers of the world and society, though beyond the control of individuals, may come under the control of demons. If and when human or demonic powers are involved in destroying God's creation, Christians must contend against them. Paul exhorts us to contend against the powers of this dark world (Eph. 6:12). Whether they be intellectual, moral, economic, or political forces destructive of humans, they are powers with which we must reckon.[89]

Leaders with power in any type of government may disregard the equality of all people before the law and defraud poor citizens and tourists of their inalienable rights. The temptation to pretensions of unreal power, wisdom, and virtue are far greater for political leaders than for most of us. The poor in spirit, the humble, and the tax collectors receive the benediction of Scripture, not because they are not also evil, but for the reason that they are generally more willing to admit their sinful condition. Governmental leaders are also sinners and should not forget that theirs should be a rule of just principles and values that respect freedom of conscience. The lust for more and more power has defrauded many people of their right to own property. The right to property implied in the commandment not to steal should be protected even against the state. The security of property leads to the propensity to save and to invest. Wendell Berry proposes "that as many as possible should share in the ownership of the land and thus be bound to it by economic interest, by the investment of love and work, by family loyalty, by memory and tradition."[90]

Individual and corporate ownerships may create a multiplicity of power centers to rival that of the state. Thus they need a self-correcting mechanism—the consciences of the individuals who are accountable finally to the divine Judge. When many hold property, political power cannot as easily become a monopoly. Hence with informed, critically thinking citizens a democratic capitalism has the potential to be self-correcting. It can change things other than by force with many consciences appealing to objective moral standards. Add to this the sense of constant readiness to meet our Judge, the greater value of investments in eternity, the need for regular proportionate giving to those in need, and the impetus for regular accounting of vice and virtue in preparation for the final audit of our individual stewardship. The innate selfishness and corruptibility of every human being calls for a system of checks and balances to transform selfishness and corruptibility of people with power into a modicum of creativity, virtue, efficiency, and decency.[91]

Collectively, a peoples' policies may be unjust in business, in society, or in government. Although it is common to blame the evils of the world on certain economic structures, the problem is not that the structures (whether capitalist, socialist, or communist) are inherently evil. In any form of economic system or government sinners can abuse other sinners and flout their attempted independence from God. Nevertheless some economic systems and governments are better than others because they have more checks and balances against sinful misuses of power and provide greater freedom for worship

and service of God. As Reinhold Niebuhr put it, "Man's capacity for justice makes democracy possible; but man's inclination to injustice makes democracy necessary."[92]

When any state usurps divine prerogatives, even those who deny the reality of demons call it demonic. Christian theists ought not give to their nations the same degree of allegiance given to God. Our pledge of allegiance to any other power must always be *under* our pledge of allegiance to a personal, transcendent God. We are subject to rulers and authorities in order "to be ready to do whatever is good" (Titus 3:1).

Total Inability

Although fallen people can do many wonderful things, as a consequence of holistic depravity sinners face a *total inability* to change their moral natures or achieve perfect justice in society. So they cannot justify themselves before God. Every aspect of human existence is so selfishly oriented that the best persons in any type of endeavor come short of the ideal. Always in all situations, none of us in ourselves do or can live up to any moral principles we propagate, let alone live up to God's *law*. We are glad for all the elements of truth in religious and philosophical ethical systems. But the higher our moral standards, the farther short even the most sincere fall.

All the good deeds or karma we can possibly accumulate will never suffice for the evils we have done. In fifty years as a missionary to India holding conversations with Hindus and Buddhists, E. Stanley Jones did not find one who had attained release from the bondage of countless reincarnations or rebirths. No Eastern pantheistic-occult or Western secular humanist programs can enable sinners to achieve their highest *human potential*. No naturalistic self-esteem or self-realization programs can change the basic perversion of our moral natures. Neither can any New Age spirits of alleged ascended spiritual masters or spirit-guides forgive sins against the Most High, reconcile people to the Lord of all, or regenerate their natures. Realistically we must acknowledge our *total inability* to save ourselves from our self-centeredness and creature centeredness by any type of individual or collective human, creaturely effort. As fallen people, we are unable to change our natures and so free ourselves from poorly motivated and poorly directed uses of our abilities. As fallen, we are unable to justify ourselves from our objective moral guilt before God's moral law. As fallen, we are unable to reconcile ourselves to a God of holy love.

A Comprehensive Concept of Sin

Comprehensive notions of sin ought not limit human sin to *discrete* willed acts or deny the reality of the sinful nature. Finney called such a denial of the deep-seated nature of sin an abomination. In agreement with Finney we have sought to avoid the idea of sin as an ontological entity or thing. But a biblically informed view of sin must include its pervasiveness from our hearts to our attitudes, thoughts, words, and deeds. A full-orbed view of humanness morally encompasses at least an insolent heart with its consequences for every human function and relationship.

No more can comprehensive concepts of sin limit it to *intentional* acts. The Old Testament makes explicit provision for anyone who unintentionally does what is forbidden in any of the Lord's commands (Lev. 4:2), whether the high priest (vv. 3–12), the whole Israelite community (vv. 13–21), a leader (vv. 22–26), or a member of the community (vv. 27–35). Once a year the high priest offered sacrifice for "the

sins the people had committed in ignorance" (Heb. 9:7). Since the law was available, ignorance of it was inexcusable, and infractions were still morally wrong and detrimental. Offerings are stipulated for unintentional sins of the community or individuals (Num. 15:22–29), but the penalty for defiant sins was much more severe, the offender being cut off from the people (vv. 30–31).

Our culpability for our morally evil acts is greater according to our degrees of knowledge and intention. We are most culpable when knowingly and deliberately we sin against ourselves, God, others, and creation. There may be less culpability when we do the same things in ignorance, but that does not make them good. It follows that there are degrees of guilt. Jesus said, "To whom much is given much will be required." Our obligations depend on our intent relative to the extent of the number and importance of moral principles knowingly violated, and the number and quality of the relationships broken, and the amount of human and natural energies used up counterproductively. Fortunately God is the final Judge of the degrees of knowledge and intentionality. We do well to judge ourselves that we be not judged. In relation to the culpability of others, no one person ought to become the accuser, jury, judge, and executioner.

Comprehensive concepts of sin, furthermore, cannot be limited to overt deeds. We may sin not only by acting wrongly, but also by failing to act. So a concept of sin must be broad enough to include acts of omission as well as commission. "Anyone, then, who knows the good he ought to do and doesn't do it, sins" (James 4:17). Jesus had said, "That servant who knows his master's will and does not get ready or does not do what his master wants will be beaten with many blows. But the one who does not know and does things deserving punishment will be beaten with few blows'' (Luke 12:47).

How can we define *sin* (sing.)? Sin, or the sinful nature, refers to the common tendency of human hearts since the Fall to disbelieve God's Word, to become disenchanted with God's presence, and to disobey God's revealed moral principles whether by action or inactivity. In short, when we speak of sin, we generally refer to our rebellious nature or inclination.

How, then, can we define *sins* (pl.)? Sins in thought, word, and deed are self-determined, responsible acts or in-attentions of morally accountable people who (1) yield to the selfish, evil desires of their depraved natures; (2) inexcusably misuse their intellectual, emotional, and volitional abilities; (3) disrespect others' inalienable rights by treating them unfairly, inconsiderately, or uncaringly; (4) violate revealed moral principles necessary for meaningful human existence; or (5) otherwise reject God's wise rule of their lives by seeking to live autonomously.

Every Human Sins

Can any truth claim ever be more fully confirmed by overwhelming empirical evidence than the claim that human beings are not morally what they ought to be? All ordinarily born persons who come to an age of moral accountability misuse their abilities, break relationships, and fail to please God by obeying moral principles. Those who have no special revelation sin against the truth about God that can be known in nature and against his moral requirements in their hearts. The Jews, who received the ministry of the Old Testament prophets, sinned also against that additional revelation. So did the people who heard and saw the ministry of Jesus Christ and the Gospels. And those who also had the revelation of the apostles and the rest of the New Testament have failed to live up to it. All Jews and Gentiles are sinners (Rom. 1:18–3:20). All people sin, whether poor or rich, male or female, older or younger, activists or researchers, politicians or scientists, students or professors, seminarians or veteran missionaries. ''As it is written: 'There is no one righteous, not even one; there is no one who understands, no one who seeks God' '' (3:10).

What about the ''innocence'' of children and adolescents? Recalling his childhood after he became morally accountable, Augustine wanted to love his Creator, but did not. He could not remember a time when he was innocent. He knew that, like David, he must have been conceived and born in iniquity (Ps. 51:5). He asked God, Suppose I don't love you, is it all that important? More than God he loved leisure play for its own sake, disliked his studies in school, and hated the discipline of parents and teachers. Many destructive delights pulled him away from God. As a student of rhetoric he sought a reputation for eloquence. He would be very careful not by a slip of the tongue to ''murder'' a word like ''human being.'' If the fury of his feeling succeeded in actually bringing about the murder of his enemy (a human being), he would not give it a second thought. He told many lies to his teachers and parents and stole things he did not need, just for the love of stealing. Augustine loved sports and plays and ''itched'' to imitate the actors in the spectacles. When he was outplayed in sports, he tried to win games by cheating; yet when he was caught, he would start an argument rather than admit he was wrong. Meanwhile if he caught someone else cheating, he became furious and accused that person in no uncertain terms. Is this the innocence of childhood? Summing up his youth, Augustine confesses, ''I sought for pleasure, honor, and truth, not in God, but in his creatures, including myself and others, and so fell into sorrow, confusion, and error."[93]

Why Every Last Person Sins

It is not enough to say with Reinhold Niebuhr that sin is inevitable. That simply moves the problem back a step. Then we must ask, Why is moral evil inevitable? *Why* does every morally accountable person sin?

Surely if by nature we were morally and spiritually good, or even neutral, there would be some people who would not yield to the influences of a poor environment. The most adequate account of the universality of sin traces it to our inheritance of an inner propensity to misuse our abilities by worshiping and serving ourselves more than our Creator. In the words of our Lord, "Flesh gives birth to flesh" (John 3:6). Jesus explained that evil fruit is produced because the tree is evil. He viewed humans as by nature inclined to desire, think, and do evil.

At its headwaters the stream of the human race went astray—in the space-time Fall. Granting the unity of the race and a traducian origin of the soul, each person receives from fallen parents, and they from theirs, back to Adam and Eve, an inherent tendency to sin. That is why every last human being inevitably sins. Everyone sins because everyone has an innate disposition to sin. We are sinners by choice because we are sinners by nature, and we are sinners by nature because we are sinners by choice. We are self-determined, but the nature of the self is inclined to rebel against moral norms. We cannot blame our sin on others or on circumstances. Circumstances provide only the occasion to yield to temptations or resist them. As self-determining agents we freely choose according to our natures. Hence our best activities are acknowl-

edgments of the deceitfulness of our hearts (Jer. 17:9). As one sophomore put it, we are "primordial stinkers." We bring with us to our environments an inherent tendency to mess up everything.

Justice for All, Guilt for All

Because the Scriptures teach that God as the final Judge is just and that God's purposes involve moral laws, it is impossible to eradicate legal terminology from an understanding of sin. The loving and righteous Judge finds human sinners *morally guilty* (Rom. 1:18–3:20). On evidence beyond any reasonable doubt God finds us guilty of rebellion against the Source of life and the principles for sustaining meaningful life on earth. Having undermined the bases of life with its values, we receive the deserved sentence, we are *destined to die* (Rom. 6:23). All face the physical death of separation of the spirit from the body (James 2:26). All sinners are spiritually dead or alienated from God's fellowship (Eph. 4:18). And, apart from receiving the atonement of the Messiah, all will continue to be estranged from God eternally (John 3:36).

What are the *grounds* of judgment, guilt, and punishment? Is God's entire judgment system just? Consider the following points:

1. We are accountable for breaking faith with the Creator (who has life in himself), defecting from the values indispensable to meaningful life as God's image-bearers. On these grounds alone all fallen people are indeed objectively guilty, whether or not they have guilt feelings. Before God himself we find ourselves repeatedly guilty of illicit desires, relationships, words, and acts. Guilt feelings that are not rooted in such sinful desires, relationships, and acts may be dismissed by friends and counselors with ease. But real guilt is incurred from idolatrous desires, the

221

breaking of relationship with God, and defecting from God's kingdom.

2. God's image-bearers are specifically accountable for moral excellence as disclosed in God's moral law. God revealed his changeless moral nature and its norms for life in relation to himself and others in three major formulations: (1) the basic moral requirements implanted in human hearts (Rom. 2:14–15), (2) similar principles disclosed for the commonwealth of Israel (Exod. 20:1–17), and (3) nine of the Ten Commandments repeated in the New Testament for the guidance of believers in churches. Not one of Adam's depraved race has measured up to the moral law in any of its formulations every day of his life. All who have come to an age of responsibility for decisions between right and wrong are accountable for their behavior. All who inexcusably sin are under condemnation (Rom. 1:18–3:20).

3. Another ground of divine judgment is deliberate disbelief of the gospel and rejection of Christ (John 3:36; Heb. 2:2–4). Although all are under the sentence of separation from God for time and eternity and await its execution, not all have the sentence executed. Believers in Christ do not face that punishment, because their substitute suffered it in their place. To reject Christ's atonement is to reject the one basis on which God can remain just and with integrity justify the ungodly (Rom. 3:25). Those who never heard of Christ are not said to be punished on the basis of rejecting him but on the basis of the revelation they did have (Rom. 1–3). The unevangelized are responsible for the moral law they did know and inexcusably failed fully to keep. "Whoever does not believe stands condemned already because he has not believed in the name of God's one and only Son" (John 3:18).

The general principle of judgment is that to whom much is given, of them much is required (Luke 12:48). We have degrees of responsibility according to the amount of truth revealed to us. A just judge gives a person exactly what is deserved. The Judge of all the earth will not punish anyone more than he or she deserved or merited. Although all are guilty in some measure, there are different degrees of premeditated disbelief and disobedience. As there are degrees of light and responsibility, so there are degrees of punishment (Matt. 11:20–24; Heb. 2:2–3).

4. God also judges the entire race for the one sin of Adam (Rom. 5:12, 16, 18). On what basis can we be guilty for the sin of another? Although Paul does not make the basis explicit in Romans 5, he emphasizes elsewhere a realistic solidarity of the race. From the Judeo-Christian point of view, humans are not a mere company of individuals like angels. God apparently created each angel, for angels do not marry or procreate. All humans, in contrast, compose a single race, for God commanded the original parents to be fruitful, increase in number, and fill the earth (Gen. 1:28). Eve is the "mother of all the living" humans (Gen. 3:20). The genealogies trace all humans back to Adam (Gen. 5; 1 Chron. 1:1; Luke 3:38). Paul could say to the Athenians, "From one man [God] made every nation of men, that they should inhabit the whole earth (Acts 17:26).

The oneness of the human race, thoughtful Christians recognize, is supported also by the natural fatherhood of God and brotherhood of all mankind. Even though not morally or spiritually children of God in Christ by the new birth, all men and women have physical life and breath by the providence of our Father who is in heaven. The providential unity of humanity also provides a basis for viewing all the descendants of Adam as organically one with their forefather. Although Paul did not explicitly refer to Adam's natural headship of humankind in Romans 5, he simply assumed a natural headship of Adam in his theological argument. On the same assumption he wrote that "in Adam all die" (1 Cor. 15:21–22).

What about the moral and legal standing of infants who die? Infants born of flesh are flesh (John 3:6; cf. Ps. 51:5; Eph. 2:3); they are included in the universal sentence of the race in Adam (Rom. 5:16, 18) and physically die (v. 12). Nevertheless infants who die do not suffer the eternal penalty, for *that penalty falls only on those who themselves responsibly sin.* Parents who responsibly sinned in the wilderness died there and did not enter the Promised Land. But children who did not yet "know good from bad" were not punished for their parents' sins; they entered the Promised Land (Deut. 1:39). The age of responsibility here indicated was twenty years for inclusion in the census of adult citizens (Num. 14:29–31). Other passages show that children may suffer the natural consequences of their parents' sins until the third and fourth generations (Exod. 20:5; 34:7), but their spiritual relation to God, whether good or bad, was not determined by their parents. "The soul who sins is the one who will die" (Ezek. 18:20). Children are not capable of responsibly committing the sins attributed to those who eternally alienate themselves from God. For reasons like these, minors who die before reaching moral accountability, will not suffer the execution of the penalty of imputed condemnation.

Since infants cannot repent and believe to receive the benefits of Christ's atonement, they must receive them by a special application. Theirs is not a different ground of salvation, but a different mode of application.[94] Punishment in Scripture is always merited and fits the crime. Infants who die, not knowing right from wrong, are not punished eternally for their parents' sins. That principle is operative when parents who sinned in the wilderness would not go in to the Promised Land, but their children who did not know good from bad would go in (Deut. 1:39). Children may suffer temporal consequences of their parents' sins to the third and forth generation, but the eternal welfare of each soul is determined by itself irregardless of whether the parents were wicked or good (Ezek. 18). So, although under the sentence of eternal death by reason of the solidarity of the race, infants who have not themselves responsibly sinned, will not suffer eternally.

Other indications that children will be saved in addition to those from the general principles of divine judgment come from Christ's special concern for them. Jesus said that children exemplified the humility of his kingdom (Matt. 18:2–5). They should not be caused to stumble (vv. 6–9) and should not be looked down on (v. 10). Furthermore, "the Father is not willing any of these little ones should be lost" (vv. 12–14). "Let the little children come to me," Jesus said, "for the kingdom of heaven belongs to such as these" (19:14). Although these passages are not as explicit as we might like, they may justify a special application of the provisions of Christ's atonement to children. Since they have not responsibly committed any sins and have no sins of which to repent, and since they could not consciously believe on Christ to deliver them from their innate inclination to sin, surely Christ will pardon them of their sinful natures and welcome them to his kingdom, whether or not the parents are in the covenant, whether or not they have had the child undergo infant baptism or last rites.

It can be of considerable comfort to grieving parents to assure them that a child's death is a sure sign of his or her election. This doctrine of justification at death for infants who have not become moral agents can be extended to others whose development has not ever attained a state of moral accountability. It cannot be extended, however, to any who have themselves responsibly sinned. That would contradict other express principles of moral judgment.

APOLOGETIC INTERACTION

Should Theology's Starting Point Be Human Need?

Ludwig Feuerbach's theology is an illustration of what happens when one begins theology with anthropology under the assumption that one can know nothing in itself. Emphasizing human experience with Schleiermacher, he concluded that all his alleged knowledge of God is merely an enlargement of ideas about human experience. His "theology" turned out to be nothing but an abstraction and externalization of humanism. His "knowledge of God" turned out to be merely his knowledge of humanity.[95]

Rudolph Bultmann also started with interpretations of humanity's needs. Considering Heidegger's existentialist philosophy the closest to the heart of the New Testament message, he assumed that our selfhood is not the expression of a pregiven nature but rather that it is created in personal choices. Subjectivity became subjectivism when he found it impossible to talk about God's transcendence and his action in history. Lacking any ontological referent for God, statements about God again turned out to refer to humans (except for a contentless "faith"). Bultmann's thought was more anthropology than theology.[96]

Paul Tillich's method of correlation also began with an analysis of the human situation. Tillich sought to give Christian answers to the existential questions stimulated. Human existence, he felt, is filled with anxiety and meaninglessness. It is estrangement. Reconciliation is a matter of anticipation, expectation, and an unfounded faith, but not of reality.[97] He ruled out all but one cognitive statement about God in himself: "The statement that God is being-itself is a nonsymbolic statement."[98] Tillich experienced the healing power of symbols that point to "the ground of being." He considered the Fall to symbolize the human situation universally. Tillich's analysis of human need can contribute in some measure to an understanding of our need, but it fails to acknowledge a personal God to whom we are to be reconciled, the reality of sinful human nature, and objective guilt before God's law. Although Tillich knows one cognitive assertion about God, most of his "theology" turns out to be anthropology.

Reinhold Niebuhr supplies another example of beginning theology with an existentialist analysis of human needs. As a result of the paradox of nature and spirit, he thought, we are anxious about our existence. Anxiety is not sin, but it leads inevitably either to sinful pride or to sensuality. To meet these needs Niebuhr offers faith in Christian myths. He thought cognitive knowledge of God impossible because of an alleged dialectic between eternity and time. With only paradoxical metaphysical knowledge and few criteria for selection among human mythologies, some have wondered why he chose Christian myths over those of the attractive mythologies of the Greeks or Hindus. Niebuhr's most important work begins, "Man has always been his own most vexing problem." After a study of Niebuhr's trenchant analysis of the human predicament in *The Nature and Destiny of Man,* one becomes convinced that if his mythological prescription is all we have, man will continue to be "his own most vexing problem."[99]

Well-meaning theologians who start with descriptions of human needs but have no cognitive revelation find difficulty getting beyond human experience to the living God who thinks, feels, wills, speaks, and relates in holy love. Without a cognitive revelation from God, the finest finite, fallen minds distort the truth of general revelation and know neither God nor themselves in themselves. Having sold the birthrights to truth in order to be relevant at their times, these theologians come short of a biblical diagnosis of human need itself. None of them soundly concluded that our deepest problems involve more than estrangement from ourselves and anxiety about the meaningfulness of our lives, fate, and death. None discovered that humans have real guilt before God's objective, moral law and a depraved nature that explains why all inevitably alienate themselves from their Creator.

We do better to include among our initial hypotheses a biblically disclosed assessment of our deepest need and see if without contradiction it accounts more coherently for the givens of inner and outer human existence. A comprehensive classical doctrine of sin as developed in the Systematic Formulation above proposes a more adequate and viable explanation of our moral experience than contradictory options. Our view makes sense of our goodness, for the *imago Dei* has not been totally destroyed, and of our depravity, for we lack ability to do the good we envision. The doctrines of creation in the *imago Dei* and the factual fall provide the most coherent accounts of humankind's awesome potential for great good or inestimable evil. The explanatory power of a biblical assessment of our moral and spiritual need fits human social experience also, including corruption in high places, oppression of the poor, countless efforts to justify oneself (in philosophies and religions before moral law or karma), and an inner longing not filled by anything in creation.

Convinced of both the truth and relevance of a biblical diagnosis of human fallenness, the doctrine of humanness as fallen provides a beneficial conversational point of contact with people anxious about human destiny. With the nuclear threat to a third of the population on earth, humanistic concerns are understandable! According to the Book of Revelation, however, not all life will be destroyed before Christ returns. Points of contact with non-Christians include more than our humanness as persons, they include also our unfaithfulness to the source of all being, values, and beauty, and our unethical conduct toward God's creation and especially toward his image-bearers.

Are Monistic Diagnoses Coherent or Viable?

The Neoplatonic hypothesis that moral evil is a mere *privation of being*—a lack of being and goodness—or *finiteness,* helped Augustine overcome the Manichaean notion that sin is a distinct material substance, but it did not for long adequately explain his experience. His problems did not stem from a lack of being, but from a perverse use of his own capacities. He struggled with the aversion of his will against God's desires. The hypothesis that sin was a rebellion of the will against its Creator made more sense of Augustine's own experience. He admitted that he had stolen pears, not for the sake of need, but for the sheer delight of getting away with it. Sin as rebellion also best accounted for the crumbling Roman Empire in Augustine's time. It remains the most coherent view of personal and social corruption today. Our deepest problem is not what we lack in ourselves but our failure to use to their full potential the abilities God gave us.

Many Hindu, Buddhist, and New Age monists today think that humans

225

are holographic manifestations of God and that evils stem from a lack of consciousness of our infinite potential. In their imagined reality we are small fields of energy in one all-encompassing field of energy. By considering our spirits metaphysically distinct from God, they feel, we suffer from many illusions. Humans are not individual persons; there is but one world soul. Humanity's deepest problems stem from a lack of knowledge of our own pantheistically conceived inner divinity. Evil is an illusion that can be overcome by visualizing things as divine or imagining that we can evolve beyond moral evil.

Resurgent monistic diagnoses of the human predicament come short in all three criteria of truth. Let us consider the serious flaws that monism suffers:

1. Monistic explanations of evil are *self-contradictory*. If there were but one world soul or divine causal agent, then who is it that suffers the illusion of evil's reality? No other "mortal mind" exists to be deceived into accepting the reality of physical bodies or sin. Paradoxically a New Age ad said, "It is a sin to call a person a sinner!" Furthermore, in a monistic worldview there are no distinct other persons to persuade of pantheism, for all persons (sic) are one.

The monistic hypothesis not only is self-contradictory; it also flatly contradicts biblical teaching. The Scriptures never blur the bifurcation between the being of the eternal Creator and the being of created image-bearers. Any functional, moral, or reflectional likeness to God in contingent beings ought not be confused with continuity with the noncontingent being of God. Although limited, physical, and distinct from God, humans as created were "very good." Since the Fall humans experience a real difference between good and evil, between uprightness and unrighteousness.

Monists who regard contradictions acceptable abort any meaningful thought and communication. If two contradictories may both be true, then we may affirm not only that "all is one" but also that "some beings are not one." Again, we may affirm both that "all evil is unreal," and that "some evil is real." If we may assent to contradictories as true, then all statements are true. In that case "true" has lost all significance, and we may as well hold that all statements are false. All meaning and communication become impossible if we can affirm and deny the same thing at the same time and in the same respect.

2. Monistic explanations of morality and immorality also lack explanatory power. A mere illusion of our distinctness fails to account for our personal self-consciousness and accountable self-determination. No person ever advances beyond the real differences between good and evil. Humans everywhere and always are accountable moral agents. Any hypothesis that regards humans divine fails to explain adequately humanity's pervasive envy, jealousy, bitterness, hatred, covetousness, lust, terrorism, drug abuse, spouse abuse, child abuse, and murders. A far more probable proposal is that humans in every generation have an inherent inclination to destructiveness. The alleged unreality of sin, sickness, and death is also counteracted experientially by the pervasiveness of churches, hospitals, and funeral homes. The Bible's teaching never minimizes the sinfulness of evil, even in the lives of the heros. Realistically Scripture asserts that humans are *not what they ought to be*. The deepest human problem is not ignorance, but insolence.

3. A monistic view of injustice is not only logically inconsistent and factually inadequate, it also *lacks existential viability*. No finite, fallen person can live unhypocritically with belief in his or her own divinity. Devotion to hatha yoga

exercises, or mindless meditations cannot fundamentally change our ontological reality or our moral perversity. Persistence in disciplined self-mortification to produce sensory deprivation or altered states of consciousness may seem to attune adherents to the cosmos, but they are not transcendent enough. They do not provide a just basis on which to reconcile sinners to the Holy One. No imagined paranormal activities or quantum leaps in our spiritual evolution can ever make us ontologically divine or morally as righteous as Christ. We agree with Marilyn Ferguson that human beings need personal and social transformation.[100] But *self*-transformations, however sincere and sustained, are insufficiently radical. Beliefs that monistic visions will save humanity are unfounded. Where such visions have flourished, as in India, they have not approached utopia. "The problem is human perversity, not human perception."[101]

Monistic views are not viable insofar as they think that our unique personalities are unreal appearances and that a belief in their reality is the source of evil. Transpersonal psychologist Ken Wilbur imagines that

> mankind will never, but never, give up this type of murderous aggression, war, oppression, and repression, attachment, and exploitation, until men and women give up that property called personality. Until, that is, they awaken to the transpersonal. Until that time, guilt, murder, property, and personality will always remain synonymous.[102]

In contrast, we have presented evidence that humanity's deepest predicament arises, not from being distinct persons, but from our faithless and unprincipled use of our abilities to think, feel, will, discern, and relate. Each person in God's creation is of inestimable worth. What God wants to take from us is not our ontological uniqueness, but our unjust desires! Holistic depravity means that no repetitious visualizations can ever satisfy justice, change our own natures, or put ourselves right with God. We fallen people need Jesus Christ's satisfaction of justice in our place, the Holy Spirit's regeneration of our inner natures, and the Father's gracious acceptance of us as repentant believers into his fellowship.

Is Human Nature Morally Neutral?

Unitarianism strongly opposed the doctrines of depravity and condemnation (even more than it attacked Trinitarianism).[103] Unitarians alleged that the original nature of human persons was *morally neutral.* Human conduct becomes "sinful" when it becomes antisocial. To act contrary to accepted social customs or mores is wrong. Antisocial conduct, furthermore, could become psychologically unhealthy. Immoral behavior is maladaptive rather than adaptive behavior. It violates relatively useful laws for a modicum of social decorum. From a biblical perspective, however, the adjustment given top priority is adjustment to God. Maladjustment to God and his moral rule is far more devastating than maladjustment to an established society or to its reformers and revolutionaries.

According to secular humanist Corliss Lamont, human nature is neither morally good, nor depraved, but morally neutral. "What the scientific study of human motives shows is that human nature is neither essentially bad nor essentially good, neither essentially selfish nor essentially unselfish, neither essentially warlike nor essentially pacific."[104] Because Lamont finds human nature "essentially flexible and educable," he rejects the "hoary half-truth" that "you can't change human nature." How does he expect to change it? "One of the great aims of Humanism is the transformation and socialization of human motives. This is a sector where human nature can be drastically reconditioned and reshaped."[105] To do so he appeals to an unending debt to the collective culture of mankind and a corresponding obligation to serve the common good. Apparently, the most prominent scientific humanists of each generation define for the rest what the collective culture and the common good requires. Lamont lists their "doctrinal statements" in an appendix that includes "Humanist Manifesto I, 1933," and "Humanist Manifesto II, 1973").

Lamont laments the fact that propaganda and cultural conditioning spur on "selfish, and violent impulses."[106] He does not say where "selfish and violent impulses" come from. The admission of evil impulses seems contradictory to Lamont's theory of essential moral neutrality. The function of the community (school) for this humanist is "to guide and redirect emotional life; to replace antisocial passions, motives, ambitions, and habits by those that are geared to the common good."[107] Humanism's naïve confidence in education to solve humanity's problems arises from its unrealistic optimism about the pliability of the human moral condition. And with no absolute right or wrong, Lamont's humanism replaces good and evil in view of God's revelation with social and antisocial behavior in the eyes of influential humanists. Secular humanism has had a powerful influence on the teachers and administrators of our tax-supported public schools, and some of these leaders of today's youth are now open to pantheistic and occult cosmic humanisms. Even if Christian schools are proposed as an alternative, moral theists ought not abandon public education to naturalistic and pantheistic philosophies of education. In pluralistic societies academic freedom should give equal opportunity to a view of humanity in the moral context of a theistic world-view.

Is Human Nature Essentially Good?

Confucianism claims that by nature human persons are *inherently good.* Mencius taught that human nature is essentially good. Any evil in it results from changes made on it by external influences.[108]

Liberal theology in the first half of the twentieth century also denied an inherited moral depravity, affirming instead humanity's inherent goodness and inevitable progress.

In the liberal tradition theologian L. Harold DeWolf rejects the Augustinian doctrine of hereditary sinfulness and imputed guilt. The liberal theologian does admit that sin came into the world through one man and that sin begets sin, both within the sinning individual and in those he or she influences. Sin is so influential that "all human beings who who have long lived at a responsible level of development are actual sinners."[109] Why do all intrinsically good people inevitably sin? All persons suffer temptations to sin and disabilities in resisting temptations, DeWolf claims, as a result of the sins of past generations.[110] The influence of previous generations has so effectively counteracted our essential goodness that

> we do not find it equally as easy to be true to our duty and to be false to it. To relax moral effort and "let nature take its course" is to drift into indolence, sensuous indulgence, cowardice and selfishness. We do not drift into industry, purity, courage and loyal generosity. Movement toward moral perfection is upstream.[111]

Liberalism's confidence that education and other influences would result in inevitable progress has been shattered by the Nazi holocaust, by repeated wars, and by many acts of terrorism.

But having admitted the universality and inevitability of sin, the liberal doctrine of humanity's inherent goodness can apply only to the time before the Fall. Liberals need a literal, historical fall to account for the radical change in humanity's moral condition. Instead of their earlier naïve faith in inevitable human moral and cultural evolution, liberals now have a pessimistic view, sensing a devolution from humanity's original goodness to its universal corruption. Early historical indications are that it did not take centuries for the Fall to occur.

Edward Wilson's attempt to articulate a socio-biological rationale for the pervasiveness of evil traces moral evil to *our gene pool*. It is our genes that make us what we are. In the light of the evidence above for both the inner spirit and the body, this physical explanation appears to be oversimplified, though it may be helpful as far as it goes. Wilson's prescription for humanity's problems through the gene of altruism also seems insufficient. A biological basis of all social behavior cannot account for the fact that in recorded history the human species has been at war forty-eight percent of the time.[112]

Sigmund Freud's explanation of human fallibility suggests that it can be traced, not to a sinful nature, but to *childhood traumas* that produce conflicts within the self between the drives, impulses, and determinations (the id); the conscience (superego); and the socially acceptable self (the ego). As descriptively accurate as this view of such inner conflicts may be and as helpful for counseling purposes, it fails to explain the source of the universally acknowledged higher values and, particularly for present purposes, the universal and inevitable antagonism to them.[113]

B. F. Skinner attributed human immorality to parental and societal *punishment*. Denying freedom and blaming punishment for creating more evils, he has not accounted for the origin of evil. Many have lived with little punishment during a permissive generation in wonderful environments controlled by many scientific advancements. But sin continues to multiply in its subtlety and extent.[114] The truth in the diagnoses of these writers may help in recognizing and alleviating symptoms, but their diagnoses fail to identify the underlying cause of universal and inevitable sinfulness.

Are Society's Structures the Source of Human Evil?

Karl Marx explained human evil as *economic maladjustment*. In *Das Kapital* he attributed the inevitable injustices of humans to one another to dialectical conflicts between two classes, the bourgeois (the haves) and the proletarians (the have nots). But such a dialectical determinism does not do justice to the evidence above for personal self-determination. The continued power of individual choice may be seen in the dissidents' refusal to conform to the Soviet's "classless society."[115] Alexander Solzhenitsyn and others have demonstrated that moral decisions come from within and are not imposed on us even by a coercive society. Class conflicts contribute to much human evil, and as far as possible ought to be justly avoided. But apart from an intrinsically sinful disposition, class conflicts do not account for all the evils of mankind. A Marxist diagnosis does not explain the evils done by people of the same class to one another, nor does it explain evils that persist in "socialist" efforts toward classless societies.

Liberation theologians also attribute the root of human evil to economic oppression of the poor by unjust *social structures*. Jose Miranda, in *Marx and the Bible,* argues that for Paul, sin has supraindividual dimensions. Sin has characteristics, he claims, not reducible to the sum of individual sins. Miranda quotes Romans 7:17, 20: "As it is, it is no longer I myself who do it [evil], but it is sin living in me." A "supraindividual force," he claims, gains control over whole peoples and becomes incarnated in social structures. The power of sin increases its own power and control over people and "forces" us to act in a certain way even while we try to be conscientious observers of the law and think we are struggling against sin.[116]

Although Miranda apparently considers these coercive forces demonic, he does not appear to attribute them to literal demons. He extends Paul's references to "the law" beyond the laws of Israel to those of all civilizations and attributes evils to the oppression of all social orders, and he understands deliverance from "the present evil age" (Gal. 1:4) to be synonymous with deliverance from "the law" (4:5). Law as the primary structural focus of societies is sin incarnate, the institutional condensation of sin created to control humans. Sin, he thinks, is identical to civilization as specified or codified in its laws.[117] Miranda seems to attribute all human evil to oppressive social orders or to all the laws of civilization.

"Christ has redeemed us from the curse of the law by becoming a curse for us" (Gal. 3:13). As Christ became a curse for us, Miranda explains, "he was incarnated into the incarnation of all the human injustice which has been accumulated in civilization and the law."[118] Marxists believed that dialectics would produce justice in the world. Miranda believes that faith in Christ will produce justice in the world—real justice, not merely imputed justice.[119] Marx, Miranda says, is on the same side as the biblical authors, for he does believe there is hope for our world.[120] Authentic justice is justice for all peoples, for humans, not as abstractions, but as working, struggling persons[121] Early

liberal thinking attributed human evil to antisocial behavior; liberationists now attribute evil to acceptance of the social status quo.

As challenging and relevant as Miranda's interpretation of structural sin seems, there are several debatable points: (1) We are not justified in making generalizations about all human laws from Paul's references to Old Testament Jewish laws given by special revelation or even Pharisaic interpretations of them. The Ten Commandments and other biblical laws cannot be regarded as the incarnation of evil. We must distinguish those laws that accurately express principles of God's moral nature from those that do not. Believers in an inscripturated revelation concerning the law of Israel cannot accept generalizations about all laws as sin incarnate and oppressive. Miranda's approach hopefully will increase our sensitivity to unjust social structures, unjust administrators, and enforcement personnel wherever they are found. But Jesus and Paul did not attack all the laws of civilization. They opposed superficial interpretations of revealed principles by inauthentic Pharisees. God's revealed laws are still to be reflected in society to restrain outbreaks of evil among depraved people.

The problems with lawful societies did not stem from laws, for the law Paul spoke about is holy, just, and true (Rom. 7:7, 12). The problems with the law, Paul taught, resulted from the fact that it "was weakened by the sinful nature" (8:3). Miranda's diagnosis fails to pierce to the hearts of those in power in any social structure. His diagnosis is not sufficiently radical. He needs to challenge, not all civilization, but the moral depravity in the hearts of oppressive political leaders. The deepest problems with the law Paul talked about were more personal than structural. Paul himself, in his inner being delighted in the law of God (7:22). But he found another principle in his fallen nature: the "flesh" (v. 18) waging war against that delight. The most important battle Paul fought was between two natures within himself. In the final judgment, God judges, not social structures or legal codes, important as these are, but individuals responsible for formulating, administering, and enforcing just laws and living by them.

The best way to liberate the oppressed is to deliver the dynamite of the gospel to the oppressors to regenerate their hearts to renew their abilities to think, feel, and act justly. Every other legal and moral means toward justice should also be utilized. But no other will be as effective as the power that turned an oppressor named Saul into an evangelist-theologian named Paul. Surely some cultures are to be preferred to others, but in the power centers of every culture oppressive evils may come to dominate. With apologies to Lord Acton (who said that power corrupts and absolute power corrupts absolutely), it is not legal power that corrupts humans, but corrupt human natures that abuse legally given powers. It is not absolute power that corrupts humans, but fallen humans corrupt any situation in which they are unaccountable to others. Because humans are the source of evil, no one is good enough or wise enough, as Plato concluded in his *Republic*, to be given unaccountable, absolute power. Without a doctrine of original sin, Miranda lacks an explanation of the inherent evil of every culture, subculture, and institution.

The failure of all of these views to explain the problem of evil indicates that acts of sin do not originate with the social or structural environments. Sinful acts are not merely conditioned responses to inherited cultural givens or unfortunate social situations. External temptations presented by the great deceiver provided occasions for our original parents to sin, but the act of yielding to the temptations came from within them. They deliberately sinned in a most positive context before the curse. Personal sin is not caused by the environment, nor by the tempter. Moral decisions and actions originate, after all, in the hearts of morally accountable human agents (Prov. 4:23–27; Matt. 12:33–37; Mark 7:14–23). Persons, not situations, are the efficient, culpable causes of moral evil.

Our environment today is far from that before the Fall. The different degrees of difficulties in our environments came about as a result of divine judgment on personal sin. Environmental and structural hypotheses emphasize occasions of evil that we ought to avoid when possible. Not every human being inevitably responds to situational factors (injustice) in unethical ways: unjust and oppressive acts of enemies may be occasions either to lure us toward sinful acts in turn or to return good for evil. Even the characters of unregenerate self-determined spirits are not determined by the circumstances. The unregenerate make their own choices and exercise their own abilities in accord with their own desires. Unless we are forcefully coerced, we are not mere victims of an evil society. Under identical conditions (such as those at the stock exchange on Wall Street) one person may yield to temptation to dishonesty, another may not. Or the same person may yield to the attendant temptations at one time and not at another. Motives also may vary, and those of the fallen and unregenerate may never be for the glory of God. But occasions of sin must not be confused with the efficient or blameworthy personal causes of sin.

Why Do All Humans Sin?

What accounts for the universal and inevitable sin of human beings? We have set forth above a biblical case for receiving from our sinful parents an *inclination to desire and do* what is contrary to the Spirit (Gal. 5:16–17) involving a traducian view of the origin of souls and the solidarity of the human race. Here we seek to point up the adequacy of the biblical view to account for human experience.

The view that humans have endemic sinful tendencies accounts for the *universality of evil* better than the view that blames infinitely variable external influences. It indicates why humans of any cultures invariably (1) desire to be like God, (2) challenge the wisdom of God's revealed truth, (3) rebel against God's rule by moral law, and (4) tend to reject the gracious offer of the gospel concerning Christ's atoning provisions. In all of our mature stages of growth, more blameworthy than any influences of our peers, parents, or teachers in our lives are our own fallen desires, purposes, and distorted interpretations.

Overwhelming evidence that humans bring a sinfully inclined nature to their environments can be found in any cultural context. Sin breaks out and bears its bitter fruit in communist, socialist, and capitalist economies. People bring sinful tendencies with them to all areas of society, not only to the inner cities but also to the suburbs and rural farms and castles. Education is no cure, for the highly educated struggle with sinful inclinations as well as those not formally educated. Immoralities and injustices occur among prominent educators, legislators, law-enforcement personnel, and prison officials.

Thus the Christian doctrine that we are sinfully inclined at the control center of our thoughts, desires, and wills provides the most coherent way to account for humanity's moral experience. Those holding to the hypothesis of an original tendency to sin can understand why people of all levels are, according to one author, chronic, systematic, and hypocritical liars.[122] We can understand why literature portrays the story of human existence as one of a conflict between good and evil and why philosophies and systems of ethics that do not face up to human endemic evil lack realism, relevance, and explanatory power.

The Christian doctrine of depraved tendencies helps us understand why every psyche is to some degree a disordered psyche. We can understand why all of us can use physical, psychological, and spiritual counsel and help. Given a view of inherited fleshly desires, we can understand political and economic unrest and the need for accountability and as many checks and balances as possible in order to achieve as much justice as possible. The doctrine of a universal, inherent tendency to sin accounts also for actual sins by religious people in religious organizations: mainline, evangelical, separatist, and cultic. In all honesty before God, others, and ourselves, we must admit our own sinful tendencies. Until we acknowledge our sinful desires, we cut ourselves off from the possibility of radical forgiveness, regeneration, and reconciliation.

Has Prevenient Grace Removed Inherited Depravity?

Although people are by nature depraved, Wesleyans and Arminians suggest that the Holy Spirit in a universal ministry of grace (based on Christ's universal atonement) removes from all people hereditary corruption and guilt for Adam's sin.[123] As a result of this alleged prevenient grace, our inherent depravity becomes only a hypothetical condition already universally alleviated.

We have been able to find no explicit scriptural basis for this presalvation work of the Holy Spirit enabling all human beings to respond to moral law or the gospel. John 16:8–10 makes it clear that the Spirit convicts the world of guilt for sin because the world remains in unbelief, but that passage does not say that the Holy Spirit changes the fleshly desires and abilities of all fallen people. An appeal to Titus 2:11 also fails to support a doctrine of prevenient grace. It was Christ, not the invisible Holy Spirit, who "appeared" for all (2 Tim. 1:10) and will appear again (Titus 2:13). Whatever Paul teaches in Titus 2:11 does not contradict the condition he described a few verses earlier: "to those who are corrupted and do not believe, nothing is pure. In fact, both their minds and consciences are corrupted. They claim to know God, but by their actions they deny him. They are detestable, disobedient and unfit for doing anything good" (Titus 1:15–16). In Paul's mind the prior advent of Christ for all people had not in fact changed the unbelievers' inability to respond to spiritual things mentally, morally, or volitionally. For that change a special work of the Holy Spirit is needed.

All the passages on the human condition refer to actual depravity of human desires and acts, not simply to a hypothetical condition already removed on the ground of Christ's universal atonement. As born of the flesh, pre-Christians *are* flesh (John 3:6). The fleshly human nature has nothing good in it (Rom. 7:18). Unregenerate human nature is set on its own desires and hostile to God, meriting his displeasure and spiritual separation from God (Rom. 8:5–8). The fleshly person gratifies his own thoughts and desires and follows the ways of the spirit at work in the disobedient (Eph. 2:1–3). The pre-Christians' minds are darkened and their hearts are hardened, separating them from God (Eph. 4:18). By nature people are slaves to the law of sin (John 8:34; Rom. 7:25). (See also Gen. 6:5; Ps. 51:5; Isa. 48:8; 64:6; Jer. 17:9). An overwhelming amount of explicit biblical teaching refers to humans as depraved after Christ completed his work on the cross. These and similar passages cannot be reinterpreted on behalf of a supposition that lacks scriptural support.

Can Sinfully Inclined People Be Responsible?

If the desire and tendency to sin is hereditary, can we be responsible for committing sins? Can people be justly accountable for doing what comes naturally?

May we ask another question? If a God of truth did not call the deceitful heart what it is, would God be intellectually honest? Would God be morally just if he said our selfish inclination was not evil, but good? Would God be genuinely caring if he did not inform us of our terminal moral condition? Our sinful choices, desires, and acts are not coerced from outside ourselves. Freely and habitually we determine our behaviors according to our own natures.

It is contradictory, Emil Brunner thought, to say, "Humans are slaves to sin" and "Every sin is an actual decision."[124] But we have not found it insoluble to say, "God cannot sin, or, in effect, God is a slave to righteousness" and "Every act of God is an actual decision." God is free always to choose according to his nature and always does what is righteous. Freedom does not always involve contrary choice, but it always involves self-determination (see vol. 1, chap. 8). So it is not contradictory to say that the moral nature of moral agents is enslaved to sin and that every self-determination made according to that nature is freely, and so responsibly, sinful (in motivation if not in external act).

In no way can God with integrity call these self-determined acts of disbelief and disobedience "good." If there is to be any justice in history, the divine Judge can never call evil inclinations or the habitual sins that result from them "good."

Can Others Be Justly Condemned for Adam's Sin?

Some who accept an inherited inclination to sin consider it unjust to find all humans guilty for the one sin of Adam. Can the guilt of one person be justly transferred to others? We consider it unfair to be blamed for another's crime or to have the alien guilt of another held against us. Liberals and others rightly find the transference of sins meaningless. Sins are not entities that can be passed along to others. Sins are attitudes and actions of persons. And in ordinary circumstances it is unjust to attribute to anyone the injustices of someone else.

How then can a just God find us guilty and sentence us for Adam's sin? As Ramm says, the Scriptures do not answer this problem explicitly but from them we may gather the elements for an inferred answer.[125] Adam alone was guilty in the sense of being culpable or personally blameworthy for his first sin, Ramm thinks, and Adam's descendants are guilty only as liable for the sin's consequences. Indeed the children suffer from the consequences of an alcoholic parent. Ramm's view is true in what it asserts of consequences, but it fails to account for imputed guilt.

Paul teaches explicitly that God passed judgment on Adam's sin and found all guilty. "The judgment followed one sin and brought condemnation" (Rom. 5:16), "death reigned" (v. 17), and "the result of one trespass was condemnation for all men" (v. 18). *Condemnation* is a judicial term for judging a person guilty and deserving of punishment. Although sins as such cannot be transferred, these verses teach the transfer of the legal guilt of one person to others he represents. How can that be just?

One can voluntarily accept another's moral standing with its consequences. Paul voluntarily asked for a slave's obligations to be put on his account. He told Philemon to receive a runaway slave as himself, and, he added, "if he has done you any wrong or owes you anything, charge it to me" (Philem. 17–18). Paul asked that the slave's indebtedness be put to his account, or imputed to him.

Two other imputations in Scripture may help to understand the principles at work. First, although our sins as such are not literally laid on Christ, he voluntarily assumed human sinners' guilt and as their substitute suffered the penalty for their sins (Isa. 53:6; 2 Cor. 5:14, 21; 1 Peter 2:24; 3:18). A second imputation occurs when Christ's perfectly righteous standing before God's law and its rewards is put into the accounts of those who accept it by faith (Rom. 4:3, 6, 9, 24). In this case imputation involves the gracious transfer of righteousness of one person (a sinless substitute) to the legal standing of those who believe and are reborn into God's family.

The third scriptural imputation is the most problematic. It is the imputation of Adam's guilt and penalty to all human beings apparently without their choice. "The judgment followed one sin and brought condemnation" (Rom. 5:16), and "the result of one trespass was condemnation for all men" (v. 18). Every human being does come under the sentence passed on the father of all, for all will receive from him a sinfully inclined nature that must be called what it is. The fact of imputed guilt is simply affirmed in Scripture. To deny that fact is to deny the authority of the inspired Word. However, what is recorded is authoritative for good reasons. We ought to do our best to discover what those reasons may be.

How can God justly find all people guilty for the sin of the first man? Some

Augustinians have argued that a just basis of imputing alien guilt is based on a legal relationship of all to Adam. Inferring a covenant with Adam for all his descendants in Genesis 3, Adam knowingly and legally acted for all humanity. Hence covenant theologians refer to the federal headship of Adam. They illustrate forensic headship by pointing out that the legal head of a country acts for its citizens. When the legal President or Prime Minister acts ceremonially and officially, he or she acts for all that country's citizens. If the leader legally implicates the people in war, all are at war and suffer the consequences. If it is an unjust war, the citizens are collectively implicated. Whatever validity there may be to theories of collective guilt should make more understandable covenant theology's concept of the covenant of works and collective guilt for the sin of Adam.

A second Augustinian school of thought finds the justification of the collective sentencing of the race in Adam on the basis of Adam's natural headship of a unified race. A hint of how we could have sinned in Adam may be indicated by the statement that Levi, before he was conceived, paid tithes in the body of his forefather Abraham as the latter paid tithes to Melchizedek (Heb. 7:4–10). This reflects the realism with which the solidarity of the chosen people in Old Testament times was understood. Assuming the solidarity of the human race, the guilt of Adam is not entirely "alien" to us. Adam's guilt and penalty was that of the entire "kind" generically. On this realistic unity of all in Adam's natural headship, the forensic headship is no mere legal fiction. We can well hold both the natural and the legal headship of Adam, since the two concepts are not mutually exclusive and some evidence can be found for both.

God must call our moral condition and consequent status what they are.

The closest thing to an explanation of Paul's meaning comes in Romans 5:12. Through the one person sin and death came to all because all have sinned. Commenting on this passage, Alford found that death passed on all because of both original and actual sin. We all sinned "in the *seed,* as planted in the nature by the sin of our forefather; and in the *fruit,* as developed by each conscious responsible individual in his own practice"[126]

Part of the difficulty here is understanding the point of the parallel Paul draws between the condemnation for the one act of Adam and the justification by the one act of Christ. The attribution of guilt, to be just, must be merited, but the attribution of righteousness in justification must be unmerited. Retaining this distinction, the point of the parallel may be this: all born of Adam are condemned and all born again by faith in Christ are justified. Or in another way of explaining the parallel between Adam and Christ: in Adam the sentence of condemnation passed upon the whole human race, but it is effectually executed only upon those who responsibly sin; in Christ the verdict of justification is provided for the whole race, but is effectual only for those who trust him and are born again. This last formulation is especially important, for although all are justly under the sentence of their natural and legal head, none will suffer the execution of the penalty who have not themselves responsibly sinned. Hence responsible sinful choice and action of a person must have taken place before that person suffers the penalty of eternal death. None will suffer eternally for being born in Adam's fallen race alone.

RELEVANCE FOR LIFE AND MINISTRY

Check Up on Your Ultimate Concern

What is your ultimate concern? What do you value most of all? Is your

235

highest value pleasing God in the way his Word makes clear? Or is it getting your own fleshly way, achieving success, and receiving praise? Our *raison d'etre* is not self-aggrandizement. Neither should our highest goal be living for others. Allocentricity, good and important as it may be, if not done for the glory of God is idolatrous service of the creature more than the Creator. We must not substitute the second greatest commandment for the first. Nor should we give the last six commandments priority over the first four. The Christian has not been redeemed to serve things. Neither is our supreme good centered in the things we can accumulate. Tacentricity, (to coin another word from the Greek *ta* for "things") can be deceptively appealing when many of these things can be greatly used for the glory of God. How subtle is the temptation to make automobiles or houses of greater value than they serve under Christ's *sapiential* rule.

The ultimate concern in our world of values should be the triune God and the values of God's kingdom. The ultimate concerns and excitements of theists should be theocentric. If your life is under the lordship of Christ, your values will also be kyriocentric. Since his lordship comes to expression in the written revelation, Christians ought also be revelation-centered, not worshiping the Bible but following its informative teaching. In terms of the revealed content Christians ought to be doctrinally centered, as was their Lord. The doctrinal framework supplies the skeleton for the flesh of morality.

Never Call Evil Good

In reality all Christians must face up to an ultimate difference between good and evil. Moral reality is not monistic but dualistic. What we are is not what we ought to be. A radical difference exists between satanic injustice and divine justice as revealed by Christ and the Scriptures.

If our loyalties are with the kingdom of God, we will detest the kingdom of Satan, which subtly seeks its destruction. We live in the midst of a moral and spiritual war undertaken by Satan against Christ. By natural birth we find ourselves loyal slaves of the evil forces in the cosmos. To enter the kingdom of God we must be born again. Then believers face a lifelong spiritual exercise program to build up their moral and spiritual immune systems to resist the forces that attack their well-being as individuals, families, churches, and nations.

"Woe to those who call evil good and good evil, who put darkness for light and light for darkness, who put bitter for sweet, and sweet for bitter (Isa. 5:20). One of the factors leading to the Charles Manson murders was his belief in monism. Since all was one, he reasoned, there was no ultimate difference between helping Sharon Tate and murdering her. From a monistic perspective all actions are relative, and nothing is either right or wrong. From a biblical perspective God is absolutely just, and Satan, who fights against God's righteous kingdom, is inherently evil.

Insofar as we bear the image of God we have loyalties to our holy Creator; insofar as we are depraved we value the deceptions of the great destroyer. Naturally inclined toward selfishness and the self-destructive, we need divine revelation to revise our thinking and we need divine illumination to enable us to receive and obey its instruction.

Candidly, we must call moral evil "sin." The biblically informed avoid euphemisms for sins such as lying, lust, or covetousness. Excusing themselves for such sins, people often say, "That was only human." We should be honest and say, "That was only sinful." Sin is not part of the essence of humanness. People were fully human without sin before the Fall; Christ was fully human on earth without sin; and believers will be fully human in glory without sin. Sins express, not the essence of humanity, but fallen peoples' fleshly desires, designs, and actions.

We ought not call the purchase of slaves, for example, "merely human." Uses of our freedom that deprive others of theirs are "sin." Charles Hodge, for example, as a leading Presbyterian theologian at Princeton Seminary in the years prior to the American Civil War, at first saw no sin in the institution of slavery as he narrowly defined it, and at one time he bought a slave. But his theoretical support of an abstract idea of slavery must be judged against his outspoken and increasingly intense disapproval of American slavery (from 1836 to 1849). Hodge became a strong spokesman for the abolition of slavery.[127]

Recently black theologians have questioned whether Christians are in effect calling racist attitudes and practices human or sinful. And Latin American liberation theologians have recently called on Christians to consider to what extent the evils of endemic unemployment, hunger, and disease are the result of sin. Have we failed to discern the evil of others' landlessness when a handful possess most of the land? By condoning capitalist, socialist, and communist abuses of power in neocolonialism, international cartels, and dictatorial governments are we in effect calling evil good? Have we a need to develop our moral discernment as Charles Hodge did his?

Respect and Love Sinners

The *imago Dei* ontologically remains undestroyed in all persons, however dominated they may be by the works of the flesh. However overtly depraved, all humans in their being remain constitutionally image-bearers. All of them remain persons, and none ought to be treated like things (such as pornographic commodities). All are potentially recoverable, as far as we know. If Paul "the chief of sinners" could become Paul the apostle, then we must not give up hope for our relatives and neighbors, nor for leaders of cults or gangs. It is not a waste of time to relate wisely and lovingly to sinners.

Following the example of Jesus, Christians ought to makes friends of sinners while separating themselves from the sinful practices of pre-Christian people. Jesus was the friend of tax collectors and sinners (Matt. 11:19) while remaining morally and spiritually separate from sinners. Believers in whom the moral and spiritual image of God is being renewed remain in the world, but Christ wants his followers to be set free from enslavement to sin by the truth he taught and exhibited. The Lord prayed, not that the Father take us out of the world, but that he would protect us from the evil one (John 17:15). We are here to exhibit God's *agape* love for the unrighteous. We must not let "moral" termites quietly eat away the foundation of our relationships with God, relatives, friends, employees, employers, church members, and other fellow citizens by the abuse of God-given abilities.

Feel Toward Sin What God Feels

To deal effectively with morally counterproductive behaviors we need to feel toward them as God does. With the help of descriptive anthropological, psychological, sociological, and historical analyses we may understand better than those before us the multiplicity of factors predisposing people to sin. But we cannot thereby rationalize away its atrociousness. Descriptive understanding of antecedents provides background for caring relationships but does not change the need for moral discernment of sin's infamy. The Creator knows better than all the rest of us together how understandable sin is in a fallen world. But God hates the insolence that destroys his creative, providential, and redemptive work. "There are six things the LORD hates, seven that are detestable to him: haughty eyes, a lying tongue, hands that shed innocent blood, a heart that devises wicked schemes, feet that are quick to rush into evil, a false witness who pours out lies and a man who stirs up dissension among brothers" (Prov. 6:16–19). Such sins shatter the peace of God's creation and of persons God so highly values. Sin is to the spirit what cancer is to the body. "To fear the LORD is to hate evil; I hate pride and arrogance, evil behavior and perverse speech" (8:13).

Of the Lord's anointed it was said, "You love righteousness and hate wickedness; therefore God, your God, has set you above your companions by anointing you with the oil of joy" (Ps. 45:7). To follow the moral paradigm of Christ is to hate wickedness (Heb. 1:9). "Let those who love the LORD hate evil" (Ps. 97:10). Business success, movies, and television make self-destructive sin so appealing that we may need to step back in order to evaluate and despise broken promises, greed, envy, covetousness, theft, jealousy, short tempers, anger, murder, covetousness, theft, lust, and harmful sexual conduct. Let us say with the psalmist, "I will set before my eyes no vile thing. The deeds of faithless men I hate, they will not cling to me" (Ps. 101:3) and "I gain understanding from your precepts; therefore I hate every wrong path" (Ps. 119:104). Until sin is the stench in our nostrils that it is in God's, we will not grasp the seriousness with which he takes it. Hatred of sin is necessary if one is to have the determination to overcome it.

Fight Temptation

We must be clear that temptation is not sin. Jesus was tempted as we are, but without sin. But we ought not use the distinction between temptation and sin to rationalize repeated entertainment of temptation. We sin when we lack fidelity to what is right and pleases our Creator. A temporal advantage may seduce us away from pleasing our eternal Creator. A desire to go beyond the bounds of temperance may entice us into gluttony or covetousness.

Sin should be distinguished also from appreciation of the beauty of God's creation in its highest forms. We may admire the beauty of nature, the great works of art, the build or figure of a person of the other sex. This, however, must not become a rationalization for a prurient interest in pornography. Aesthetic admiration is one thing, lust is another. What is morally wrong is to lust for a person who has belonged, belongs, or will belong to another. One who has given himself or herself in a lifelong commitment to a spouse and lusts for another violates the covenant in the marriage commitment with that person and loses integrity before God as well as humans. Analogously, we may appreciate the valuable acquisitions of others so long as we do not covet for ourselves what belongs to them.

Because of the consequences of sin for time and eternity Jesus taught in the strongest figurative language that Christians should take action to correct or avoid the sources of their own temptations: "And if your hand or your foot causes you to sin, cut it off and throw it away from you; it is better for you to enter life maimed or lame than with two hands or two feet to be thrown into the eternal fire. And if your eye causes you to sin, pluck it out and throw it from you" (Matt. 18:8–9 RSV). "Because of the temptation to immorality, each man should have his own wife and each woman her own husband. . . . Do not refuse one another . . . lest Satan tempt you through lack of self-control" (1 Cor. 7:2, 5, RSV). Young church members and leaders like Timothy should make every effort to "treat younger men like brothers, older women like mothers, and younger women like sisters, in all purity" (1 Tim. 5:1–2, RSV).

With media advertisements tempting us to spend our money for what rusts, gets worn out, and perishes, good stewards must develop Holy Spirit–enabled self-control of their finances. We should learn to be content with food and clothing, for "people who want to get rich fall into temptation and a trap and into many foolish and harmful desires that plunge men into ruin and destruction. For the love of money is a root of all kinds of evil. Some people, eager for money, have wandered from the faith and pierced themselves with many griefs" (1 Tim. 6:9–10).

Such are the subtleties of temptation that we can so defend our individual rights as to make society defenseless against unprincipled individuals. When every neighbor becomes a potential adversary in court, we have lost ordinary selflessness. Christians ought to fight the temptation to go to court. The backlog of litigation threatens the right to a speedy trial and discriminates against the poor, who cannot afford prolonged legal battles. Citizenship not only protects rights, but also demands that we put the good of others ahead of our advantage.

One way to fight temptation is by keeping eternity's values in view. Follow the example of Moses, who "chose to be mistreated along with the people of God rather than to enjoy the pleasures of sin for a short time" (Heb. 11:25). We also do well to quote relevant Scripture as did the Lord Jesus Christ. He effectively fought the tempter by quoting God's authoritative Word (Matt. 4:1–10). We should avoid tempting others. "Temptations to sin are sure to come," Jesus said, "but woe to him by whom they come!" Insofar as it is within our control, we ought not tempt others. "It would be better for [the person who causes another to sin] to be thrown into the sea with a millstone tied around his neck than for him to cause one of these little ones to sin" (Luke 17:1–2, RSV). Hence Christians do everything in their power not to tempt others to gossip, lie, cheat on examinations, steal, or fail to keep their word.

In a time when you are tempted, turn to Old Testament examples intended to keep us from "setting our hearts on evil things" as they did—idolatry, sexual immorality, testing the Lord, and grumbling. "These things happened to them as examples and were written down as warnings for us. . . . So, if you think you are standing firm be careful that you don't fall!" (1 Cor. 10:6–12). In countertemptation warfare wield the sword of God's Word as Jesus did (Matt. 4:4–10). Memorize and quote Paul's encouragement to the Corinthians: "No temptation has seized you except what is common to man. And God is faithful; he will not let you be tempted beyond what you can bear. But when you are tempted, he will also provide a way out so that you can stand up under it" (1 Cor. 10:6–13).

Entertain Realistic Expectations of Yourself and Others

In our youth, particularly, we may expect more of *ourselves* than is possible for us to accomplish in a fallen world. Political individualism or self-government, even with a return to nature's surroundings, will not result in utopia. Nature remains under a curse, and sinners in themselves are not capable of faithfully practicing austere self-denial of the fleshly nature throughout life. And if any could for a time continuously overcome their fleshly inclinations, that would not be redemptive for sins already committed. A less severe type of self-government provides a commendable ideal. To the best of our ability we may wisely guide our conduct toward worthy ends.[128] But even with our best efforts, the bent of our sinful nature means that we will come short of the ideal of self-control and wise self-management in every aspect of life.

In a fallen world we must overcome perfectionist expectations of *spiritual leaders*. B. B. Warfield has traced the tragic results of several perfectionistic movements among Christians—those of the so-called higher life, Keswick, and victorious life.[129] The ideal, as Jesus taught, is to be perfect as God is perfect (Matt. 5:48), and Christians should aim for nothing short of moral perfection. It is beneficial to strive for a grade of 100 on a theology paper, but the perfect paper has yet to be written. Similarly, in morality we strive for total Christlikeness, but the reality is that none of us can achieve that in this life. Until we do, we ought not to expect its accomplishment in others. Pelagians reason that if perfection is commanded it must be possible. But Augustinians know that human nature has been so corrupted by the Fall that the ideal of perfection cannot be attained in this life.[130]

Human depravity necessitates some form of government and also keeps any type of *government* from perfection. A well-constructed union, James Madison believed, would have the advantage of controlling the violence of faction. As long as reason continues fallible and people are at liberty to exercise it, different opinions will be formed. As long as the connection subsists between reason and self-love, opinions and passions will have a reciprocal influence. The effects are seen in the unequal faculties for acquiring property. So the latent causes of faction and the propensity of mankind to fall into mutual animosities are thus sown in the nature of humanity. Neither an individual nor a group can be the judge and the parties of their own causes. Not even an enlightened diplomat can adjust these clashing interests. Since political power cannot remove the causes of faction, "relief is only to be sought in the means of controlling its effects. Relief from the effects of depravity is at best what the American government was explicitly formed to provide."[131]

Realistic expectations must also be held in relationships of the sexes and *family* life. A naïve optimism is not possible for one acquainted with the subtleties of fallenness among men and women. We must keep our critical faculties about us as we hear the fantasies about "love" in popular music and novels. Similarly the biblically informed should have realistic expectations for parent-child relationships. Here also we tend to give our own interests greater importance than they deserve. Selfish desires and inclinations have serious consequences in families. Since all are fallen, we will not expect to be perfect spouses, parents, or children.

Realism ought also to characterize our expectations for *religious organizations*. We will not find a perfect church, mission station, denomination, interdenominational organization, or small-group Bible study. Critical discernment and accountability are as imperative in religions as elsewhere, because (1) not all supernatural persons and experiences are of God; (2) Satan masquerades as an angel of light (2 Cor. 11:1–4, 15); (3) temptation presents evil in its most favorable light, even as a good; (4) worship is not always of God; (5) humanitarian service is not always for building God's kingdom; (6) prayer meetings are not always directed to the triune God; (7) biblical quotations are not always used as God intended them;

(8) Bible studies may be twisted to one's own destruction (2 Peter 3:16); (9) prophets and apostles may be deceived or false; (10) fine-appearing people may falsely claim to be Messiahs, and dedicated founders of religious groups may not be of God; (11) the best of fallen human beings in this life come short of God's standards; (12) spiritual disciplines and devotional methods may be directed toward idols as well as the true God; and (13) God's social institutions (families, nations, and churches) can be used for evil purposes as well as good.

Remind All of Their Moral Accountability

As self-determining agents humans are responsible for their choices and actions. We tend, however, to blame others or situations for our sins. In self-pity we may develop an ethic of irresponsibility. We say something like this: "Blame it on God, the government, heredity, the environment, parents, economic changes, peer pressures, or being unloved and unwanted; but don't blame it on me, the very center around which the whole universe revolves!" However, self-analysis and self-pity may lead to self-hate and finally the obsession to be rid of the self. That is one of the appeals of the Eastern and New Age religions. From a Christian perspective, however, the self is not absorbed; it is renewed (Eph. 4:24; Col. 3:10).

It is often alleged, "You can't teach morality." On the contrary, if you can teach and exemplify immorality, you can teach and exemplify morality, though because of sinful inclinations it will be more difficult. The old rules on safe sex make more sense than ever. That person is chaste who limits sexual contact to his or her lifelong partner. The sexual revolution promised unlimited fun but overlooked the disastrous consequences that have followed. Survivors from the front lines of the revolution return leaving a trail of broken marriages, increased teenage prostitution, hard-core pornography, child abuse, and epidemic diseases like AIDS.

The Ten Commandments represent the basic elements necessary for the most minimal well-being of any society. Advocates of chastity on moral and religious grounds do so for very positive, not negative reasons. The Judeo-Christian revelations place a very high value on healthy sexuality, emphasizing the deep joys and lasting fulfillment found in intimacy with faithfulness. When Scripture advocates exclusive, committed, and lifelong monogamous relationships, it does so, not from a sense of Victorian prudery, but because God knew that the sort of freedom and loving abandon necessary to true sexual enjoyment are by-products of faithful relationships, and not of extracurricular sexual activity. Attempts to be value-free or value-neutral in sex education imply that values are so relative as to be meaningless. A society that has no shared values one day will discover that it is not a society at all.

Radically Diagnose the Human Plight

Superficial diagnoses of the human predicament result in superficial resolutions. The body is essential to full humanness but is not the blameworthy cause of evil, and so the punishment of the body in asceticism is not sufficiently radical. "Radical" proposals for educational advancement, economic fairness, psychological adjustment to the environment, and self-improvement, valuable as they may be, are not sufficiently radical. They are cover-ups of our deepest moral and spiritual disease.

The most profound human predicament is rooted in the inner person. The fallen human heart has a basic tendency to turn away from God's ways. Until the inner self is born anew all the education, culture, and environmental improvements, like aspirin, may remove symptoms, but they do not address our most radical need. Until a provision is made for reconciliation to the transcendent, personal God, all other spiritual disciplines will serve only like band-aids. We are glad for them, but unless there is a healing process underneath the surface, we have only covered up our problem. Until sinners are divinely acquitted of their objective guilt, redeemed, and reconciled the efforts of counselors, educators, and ministers may remove certain guilt feelings, but they will fail to address the deepest need. Humans universally are depraved, alienated, and condemned. Only those with the gospel of Christ have the resources to address these radical needs.

Even evangelicals need to rediscover the poignant truth of human lostness. Jesus was clear on his major purpose for coming into the world. "For the Son of Man came to seek and to save what was lost" (Luke 19:10). Many of Christ's alleged followers are unclear about their primary *raison d'etre* because pastors and teachers have neglected the unpopular doctrine that sinners are lost. Although evangelicals deny being universalists, many appear to be universalists by their neglect of teaching on the tragic nature of sin and its awesome results. If we imagine that lost sinners are already in the kingdom of God, we are deceived. Jesus said to Nicodemus, a member of the Jewish ruling council: "I tell you the truth, no one can see the kingdom of God unless he is born again" (John 3:3). Since church members hear so little about the plight of unbelievers, it is not surprising that in general they seem to lack motivation for evangelism. Jude said, "Snatch others from the fire and save them" (v. 23).

In what ways can we bring the doctrine of lostness back into the life of the church? It may help to recall what we were before our conversions. Remembering our depravity, guilt, and alienation, we can marvel at our redemption, forgiveness, and reconciliation. We do not suggest preaching and teaching lostness alone. Always preach and teach divine grace for lost humans. Presenting a combination of need and the grace to meet it overcomes the abuses of communicating either without the other. "Consider therefore the kindness and sternness of God: sternness to those who fell, but kindness to you" (Rom. 11:22).[132]

Deliver the Divine Indictment to the Lost

Acutely aware of the divine indictment of all human beings even in high places (Rom. 1:18–3:20), we, like the prophets and apostles, must deliver to every human the divine summons (Jer. 15:19; Ezek. 18:30, 32). As Paul told the distinguished Aeropagus court at Athens, the university center of the ancient world: "[God] . . . now commands all people everywhere to repent" (Acts 17:30). Some people may be highly sensitive to their sins, but others may need to be reminded that they are not all what they should be.

What approaches may be used to help people deeply realize their sinfulness? With traditional Lutheran and Reformed preachers, declare the standards of the moral *law*. Like Christ we may give prominence to the summation of the first four commandments. Love God with your whole being. Ask anyone who is hesitant to confess his sinfulness: "Have you always loved God with all your abilities?" Then ask a question based on Jesus' summation of the last six commandments: "Have you always loved your neighbor as yourself?" If necessary point up some everyday failings of your listeners. In addition you can suggest that their need may be indicated psychologically by guilt feelings, a lack of a healthy self-image, and failures in close relationships.

With the Old Testament Prophets we may underline the subtleties of hypocrisy spiritually, relationally, and vocationally. The wisdom of Proverbs may help point up lacks in personal character, functions, and relationships. Or the Spirit may use a study of James to convict a person of the sins of the tongue that like a fire produce a whole world of evil and point out the failure of our deeds to measure up to our words. From James we may expose favoritism, quarrelsomeness, spiritual unfaithfulness, pride, slander, boasting, oppression, and wandering from the truth. Like James, Jesus and existentialists particularly expose hypocrisy.

Helmut Thielicke helps people realize their sinfulness by presenting existential analyses of *gospel stories*. Many people today are able to identify with the Samaritan woman at the well, the prodigal son, and Zaccheus. And we can learn from Jesus' approach to them.

Some have realized their lostness when face to face with the converging eschatological *signs of the end of the age* and the return of Christ. Others may need an existential shock treatment from accounts of near-death experiences of their peers and of the deaths of some. Indeed, they may begin to realize that though "crime does not pay," sin does. The wages of sin is *death* (Rom. 6:23)—physical, spiritual, and eternal. Along with subjects neglected in recent preaching and teaching add that of *judgment* to come (Heb. 9:27).

Most tellingly we may see our sinfulness, not by comparisons with what the majority may be doing, but with the sterling life of Jesus Christ. To show people their sin, Ramm (following Barth) recommends preaching *Christ as the ideal human*.[133] Surely the Savior is the exemplar of righteousness par excellence. In his upright presence we sense how far short we come from the divine righteousness. Christ fulfilled the law and the prophets, loved his heavenly Father and his neighbors, taught the importance of readiness in view of the signs of his return, and disclosed people's everyday, psychological, and existential shortcomings. Hence in referring to Christ as the paradigm of humanness, we incorporate elements of the other approaches. Jesus himself used the other ways to remind people of their moral and spiritual need. Upon occasion he exposed failures to fulfill the law. He also warned of the signs of the end of the age, no doubt evoking fear in some people. In talking with individuals, Jesus used psychology wisely, identifying with others' interests and needs. He also presented parables with vital existential significance. By portraying the sterling character of the Messiah, we help people realize that they are not all that they ought to be, and that they need to repent.

REVIEW QUESTIONS

To Help Relate and Apply Each Section in This Chapter

1. *Briefly state the classical problem* this chapter addresses and indicate reasons why genuine inquiry into it is important for your worldview and your existence personally and socially.

2. *Objectively summarize the influential answers* given to this problem in history as hypotheses to be tested. Be able to compare and contrast their real similarities and differences (not merely verbal similarities or differences).

3. *Highlight the primary biblical evidence* on which to decide among views—evidence found in the relevant

teachings of the major divisions of Scripture—and decide for yourself which historical hypothesis (or synthesis of historical views) provides the most consistent and adequate account of the primary biblical data.

4. *Formulate in your own words your doctrinal conviction* in a logically consistent and adequate way, organizing your conclusions in ways you can explain clearly, support biblically, and communicate effectively to your spouse, children, friends, Bible class, or congregation.

5. *Defend your view* as you would to adherents of the alternative views, showing that the other views are logically less consistent and factually faced with more difficulties than your view in accounting for the givens, not only of special revelation but also of human experience in general.

6. *Explore the differences the viability of your conviction can make in your life.* Then test your understanding of the viability of your view by asking, "Can I live by it authentically (unhypocritically) in relation to God and to others in my family, church, vocation, neighborhood, city, nation, and world?"

MINISTRY PROJECTS

To Help Communicate This Doctrine in Christian Service

1. *Memorize one major verse or passage* that in its context teaches the heart of this doctrine and may serve as a text from which to preach, teach, or lead small-group studies on the topic. The memorized passages from each chapter will build a body of content useful also for meditation and reference in informal discussions.

2. *Formulate the major idea of the doctrine in one sentence* based on the passage memorized. This idea should be useful as the major thesis of either a lesson for a class (junior high to adult) or a message for a church service.

3. *State the specific purpose or goal of your doctrinal lesson or message.* Your purpose should be more than informative. It should show why Christians need to accept this truth and live by it (unhypocritically). For teaching purposes, list indicators that would show to what extent class members have grasped the truth presented.

4. *Outline your message or lesson in complete sentences.* Indicate how you would support the truth of the doctrine's central ideas and its relevance to life and service. Incorporate elements from this chapter's historical, biblical, systematic, apologetic, and practical sections selected according to the value they have for your audience.

5. *List applications of the doctrine* for communicating the difference this conviction makes in life (for sermons, lessons, small-group Bible studies, or family devotional Bible studies). Applications should make clear what the doctrine is, why one needs to know it, and how it will make differences in thinking. Then show how the difference in thought will lead to differences in values, priorities, attitudes, speech, and personal action. Consider also the doctrine's possible significance for family, church, neighborhood, city, regional, and national actions.

6. *Start a file and begin collecting illustrations* of this doctrine's central idea, the points in your outline, and your application.

7. *Write out your own doctrinal statement on this subject in one paragraph* (in half a page or less). To work toward a comprehensive doctrinal statement, collect your formulations based on a study of each chapter of *Integrative Theology.* As your own statement of Christian doctrine grows, you will find it personally strengthening and useful when you are called on for your beliefs in general and when you apply for

service with churches, mission boards, and other Christian organizations. Any who seek ordination to Christian ministry will need a comprehensive doctrinal statement that covers the broad scope of theology.

PART TWO

CHRIST'S ATONING PROVISIONS

CHAPTER 5

GOD'S ETERNAL SON INCARNATED

God's Eternal Son Incarnated

THE PROBLEM: HOW COULD THE ETERNAL WORD OF THE DIVINE SPIRIT (JOHN 1:1) BECOME A TEMPORAL CHILD OF HUMAN FLESH (JOHN 1:14)?

The name of Jesus has become a household word in our day. In popular magazines, billboards, and bumper stickers the life and teachings of the carpenter of Nazareth have become the subject of ordinary conversation. Should we follow popular thought and view the One about whom history is divided merely as a noble prophet, teacher, or moralist? Or, as Christendom traditionally has affirmed, is the Jesus attested in history the divine Spirit himself manifested in a human life? If he is the second person of the Trinity (cf. vol. 1, chap. 7), in what sense did the Son of God empty himself in becoming a man (Phil. 2:7)?

Christian faith, by definition, centers on the person of Jesus Christ. The Anglican theologian W. H. Griffith Thomas appropriately entitled one of his books *Christianity Is Christ*. Emil Brunner similarly stated that "the Christian religion is summed up in the revelation of God in Jesus Christ."[1] Moreover, according to orthodox Christianity, the heart of Christology is the coming of the Logos into time and space by birth through Mary. The focus of Christian confession, then, is the Christmas event—the fact that the transcendent God has visited and redeemed his people in Jesus of Nazareth.

Given the centrality of Christ in the Christian scheme of things, it is not surprising that Jesus Christ is profoundly related to other doctrines of the faith. We established in volume 1, chapter 7, that within the essential unity of the Godhead the Logos exists eternally as the second divine person begotten of the Father. In volume 2, chapter 4, we confirmed that the human race is justly condemned and, without divine intervention, will perish eternally. Furthermore, how we answer the question in this chapter will influence our understanding of the reality of Jesus Christ (chap. 6), the significance of his death on the cross (chap. 7), and the meaning of his resurrection (chap. 8).

A number of issues surround the study of the person of Jesus Christ. Methodologically, does Christian reflection begin with Jesus as God and move to think about him as man? Or does it begin with Jesus as man and consider what it means to call him God?

Expressed in other terms, is Christology more responsibly done "from above" or "from below"? Classical theology has generally taken the former approach (the metaphysical), whereas modern critical thought has pursued the latter approach (the ethical). Furthermore, does Christ's person inform his work as most orthodox Christians have insisted, or does the work he performed explicate his person? Some theologians such as G. C. Berkouwer suggest that Christ's person and work ultimately are inseparable. Moreover, was Jesus of Nazareth conscious of being the Messiah? For what purposes did Jesus live and die? Why was Jesus Christ a stumbling block to Jews and foolishness to Greeks? (1 Cor. 1:23). An additional issue to be faced is the historic Christian claim that Jesus was supernaturally conceived of the virgin Mary. Was the virgin birth necessary for the incarnation of the God-man and for the begetting of a man free from sin? Or could Christ be the Savior of the world independently of his virginal conception? Is it possible for a person to be saved without assenting to the miracle of the virgin birth? Furthermore, was Mary herself sinless? If not, was Jesus without sin? Could Mary be said to be the "mother of God"?

The present chapter explores the meaning of Christ's preexistence, and the humiliation of his incarnation and birth of Mary.

ALTERNATIVE INTERPRETATIONS IN THE CHURCH

Kenotic Theologians

A number of theologians in Germany and later in England developed so-called kenosis theories of the incarnation. The term *kenosis* comes from the Greek text of Philippians 2:7, which refers to the fact that the One eternally in the form of God (or equal with God)

emptied himself to become a man. These theologians attempted to do justice both to the claims for the second person of the eternal Trinity and to the growing interest in the human figure of Jesus portrayed in the Gospels. The kenotic theories thus sought to mediate between theological orthodoxy and liberalism. In general, "kenoticism interprets the incarnation as the transformation of God into man, or the exchange of divinity for humanity."[2]

Here we mention two major types of kenotic Christology. The first, championed by Thomasius and Delitzsch in Germany and by Gore and Fairbairn in England, was the less radical of the two. Thomasius distinguished between God's relative attributes (omnipotence, omnipresence, omniscience) and his immanent attributes (holiness, power, truth, love). In an act of self-limitation, the eternal second person of the Trinity was said to have divested himself of the relative attributes when he assumed the limitations of space and time. Having given up the divine form of existence for a creaturely form of existence, Jesus acquired a genuinely human consciousness and passed through all the stages of normal human development. Thomasius insisted that if the Son of God had retained the so-called relative attributes, he could not have lived a truly human existence. At his exaltation to heaven, Christ reassumed the relative attributes that he had temporarily set aside. Delitzsch similarly maintains that the Logos gave up the relative attributes without surrendering the identity of his divine being.

The incarnate Logos is not in possession of the eternal *doxa*, for he looks back longingly after it (John 17:5). He is not omniscient, for he knows not . . . the day and the hour of the end (Mark 13:32). He is not almighty, for the power over all things is given to him . . . after his resurrection (Matt. 28:18). He is not omnipresent, for he ascended up, that he might fill all things (Eph. 4:10).[3]

The second group of kenotic theories, advanced by Gess, Godet, Clarke, and Mackintosh, took the kenosis doctrine to its logical extreme. They interpreted Philippians 2:7 in the sense that at the incarnation the Logos gave up *all* the divine attributes, laid aside his deity, and so was transmuted into a man. Gess insisted that when the Son became a man, not only did he lay aside all the divine perfections but, initially at least, he had no consciousness of his Logos-nature, no longer experienced the mutual indwelling of the Father and the Spirit, and ceased to govern the universe. At the incarnation the Trinity of God was profoundly altered. When Christ later returned to the Father in heaven, he regained the divine life he possessed prior to his incarnation. Godet upholds a similar incarnation by divestiture. He insists that in John 1:14 ("The Word became flesh") the verb "became" signifies a profound alteration in the subject's mode of being, and the predicate "flesh" connotes complete human nature. Thus the incarnation means not "two natures or two opposite modes of being coexisting in the same subject, but a single subject passing from one mode of being to another."[4] In his essential being, the Logos depotentiated himself into the form of a man, although his personal subject or ego remained the same. Following the ascension, the Son regained his original divine state. All these kenotic theologians upheld Christ's preexistence and deity, and most subscribed to his virgin birth.

Progressive or Gradual Incarnationists

I. A. Dorner, together with a few other European theologians, sought to do justice to critical opinion about Jesus by propounding the theory of progressive incarnation. According to this proposal, "the incarnation is not indeed to be conceived as finished from the beginning, but as gradually developing."[5] Progressive incarnationists rejected the notion that the Logos assumed human nature and a human mode of existence at the moment of Jesus' conception or birth. Rather, Dorner explicates the incarnation developmentally as a moral union of the Logos and the humanity of Jesus. That is, by a gradual moral process that respects Jesus' human development, the Logos became more fully joined to the representative head of humanity. At the beginning of his life, Jesus was not the God-man. But as Jesus yielded himself to the Father in submission and prayer, the Logos progressively penetrated his humanity. The theory postulates that as a result of Jesus' self-surrender to the Father, the separate divine and human egos gradually united into perfect God-manhood. As expressed by Dorner: "The incarnation is not to be conceived as finished at one moment, but as continuing, even as growing, since God as Logos constantly grasps and appropriates each of the new facets that are formed out of the true human unfolding, just as conversely the growing actual receptivity of the humanity joins consciously and willingly with ever new facets of the Logos."[6] The divine and human natures united indissolubly at Jesus' resurrection and ascension to heaven.

Whereas the orthodox view of the incarnation postulates the humiliation of the divine Son of God, the present view upholds the gradual deification of the human Jesus. Moreover, whereas according to the traditional view the incarnation occurred at the beginning of the process, Dorner located the incarnation at the end of Jesus' life. Orthodox authorities charged the progressive incarnationists with following the Nestorian error, in that they posited a nonessential union between the divine and human *hypostases*. Although Dorner upheld Jesus' virgin birth, he severely compromised Christ's deity and preexistence.

Liberal Theologians

The liberal view of Jesus was shaped by at least three assumptions: (1) A growing antipathy to the supernatural and miracles. These theologians viewed the incarnation of a heavenly being as a primitive "myth" unacceptable to the modern scientific mind. (2) The supplanting of ontological concerns by ethical interests. Kant's polemic against knowledge of God in himself in the *Critique of Pure Reason* paralyzed discussion of Christ's preexistence and incarnation. For Kant, the old notion of the Son coming down from heaven is best understood as the embodiment of the eternal ideal in a human life. (3) Emphasis on the divine immanence rather than transcendence. From a pantheistic or panentheistic perspective, liberal scholars focused on the presence of God in the man Jesus, who by word and example functioned as the revealer of God.

Ritschl, following Kant, eliminated metaphysics from theology. Christology, in particular, concerns itself not with ontology, but with value-judgments made in respect of the historical Jesus. Thus Ritschl abandoned theoretical questions about the Logos and the two natures in favor of practical judgments of value, namely, the function Jesus performed in establishing the kingdom. Hence Ritschl maintains, "The origin of the person of Christ— how his person attained the form in which it presents itself to our ethical and religious apprehension—is not a subject for theological inquiry, because the problem transcends all inquiry."[7] Ritschl judges that the notion of Christ's preexistence, in addition to being an illegitimate ontological question, is a semideistic concept that would compromise Jesus' identification with human beings. Preexistence, as reinterpreted by Ritschl, denotes Christ's election as founder of the kingdom of God in the world. Moreover, the incarnation for Ritschl signifies that Jesus was the bearer of an ethico-religious ideal. Ritschl is uncertain whether the incarnation, so defined, occurred once-for-all in Jesus or whether it has been replicated in other noteworthy religious figures.

Adolf Harnack insists that the doctrines of Christ's preexistence and incarnation represent the intrusion of Greek religious philosophy into the sphere of Christianity. Harnack identifies the Greek Logos doctrine as the entry-point for what he calls the acute Hellenization of the faith. That is, early Christian authorities, particularly the apologists, identified Christ with the preexistent Logos who allegedly came down from heaven, united with a man, and performed supernatural works. "The identification of the Logos with Christ was the determining factor in the fusion of Greek philosophy with the apostolic inheritance."[8] This process of Hellenization tragically perverted the simple ethical message of Jesus into "a philosophy of religion." Harnack insisted that we must get behind the Christ of the creeds to Jesus the ethical prophet, who preached the fatherhood of God, the brotherhood of man, and the infinite value of the human soul.

Henry P. Van Dusen maintains that God is incarnate, or immanent, in the experience of every person. He grants, however, that a distinctive incarnation occurred in Jesus Christ in the sense that God uniquely indwelt the soul of the Nazarene. For Van Dusen, the incarnation means that Jesus is "a genuine human person who shared, as freely as is possible for a truly human life, the Vision and Purity and Purpose of God."[9] Van Dusen cautions that the incarnation represents not a total, but only a maximal, indwelling of God in Jesus. "It is mistaken to claim that in Jesus, the whole being of God was present, that God's purpose was fully expressed through him."[10]

The volume entitled *The Myth of God Incarnate,* edited by John Hick,[11] summarizes the contemporary liberal attitude toward the incarnation. Hick and his colleagues insist that the doctrines of Christ's preexistence and incarnation represent ancient myths, where myth is an event, not literally true, that evokes a particular religious meaning in its hearers. How did the so-called myths of preexistence and incarnation make their way into Christian theology? The essayists respond that the early Christians lived in a world where preexistent beings and divine visitations to earth were commonplace. Thus it was natural that believers should have used supernatural, i.e., mythical, categories to represent the significance of Jesus. Since "the present [scientific] climate is alien to the whole Christian position as traditionally conceived,"[12] modern believers must abandon the incarnation as a metaphysical reality, yet retain it as a religious claim. The traditional incarnation language and imagery, the essayists insist, express the truth of God's self-giving love to the world. For modern people who no longer believe in divine visitations, the incarnation means, "I see God in Jesus." Hick interprets the incarnation in adoptionist categories: "Jesus was a 'man approved by God' for a special role within the divine purpose, and the later conception of him as God incarnate, the second Person of the Holy Trinity living in a human life, is a mythological or poetic way of expressing his significance for us."[13]

Most liberal theologians reject Christ's virgin birth for the following reasons: (1) The doctrine is said to be derived from prescientific pagan myth-ology. Thus Frances Young insists that the virgin birth "as a literal statement of Jesus' origins . . . is virtually inconceivable in the light of modern knowledge of genetics and reproduction."[14] (2) The doctrine is irrelevant to the adoptionist view of Jesus. Russell Aldwinckle reinterprets the virgin birth as a sign pointing to "the new creative and saving activity which now begins in this man Jesus."[15] (3) The virgin birth is said to be inimical to Jesus' full humanity and solidarity with persons. And (4) The virgin birth is viewed as not essential to the church's message of salvation. Some liberals retain the traditional language of virgin birth, while reinterpreting its meaning, e.g., "God is the source of his life," or "Jesus' reality is due to the initiative of God."

Existentialist and Neoorthodox Authorities

This tradition sharply criticizes the liberal caricature of Jesus as a mere man adopted by God. Authorities identify the enfleshment of the transcendent God in the form of a man as a mystery beyond the grasp of human reason. Theologians aligned with the movement minimize the historical aspects of the incarnation while emphasizing the existential. The focus of the incarnation is said to be the meeting of divine and human subjects.

Søren Kierkegaard viewed the incarnation and virgin birth as the absolutely unique event by which the Wholly Other entered time. "The historical assertion is that the Deity, the Eternal, came into being at a definite moment in time as an individual man."[16] By virtue of his assumed infinite qualitative distinction between God and man and eternity and time, Kierkegaard regards the incarnation as offensive to conceptual thought—indeed, as "the absolute paradox." The fact that the Eternal became temporal, that the Absolute became relative, that Being-in-Itself became history is for Kierkegaard an intellectual scandal. "The absurd is— that the eternal truth has come into being in time, that God has come into being, has been born, has grown up, and so forth, precisely like any other individual human being."[17] This rational uncertainty represents a significant gain for Kierkegaard, since he insists that only in the face of so great a paradox can a person truly and passionately "believe."

Guided by Kierkegaard's dialectic between heaven and earth, Brunner denies the existence of any connecting links between the Christ-event and history. The meaning of history, according to Brunner, is ambiguous. Thus, "we are bound to oppose the view that the Christian faith springs out of historical observation, out of the historical picture of Jesus of Nazareth."[18] Brunner here distinguishes between "Christ *after* the flesh" and "Christ *in* the flesh." The former, the Christ known by the historian, because it deals with the realm of relativity, is carnal knowledge. The latter, the Christ known in the divine-human encounter, is properly spiritual knowledge. Brunner thus insists that the incarnation, an event in the primal history (*Urgeschichte*), connotes the encounter between the divine "I" and the human "thou" in which God addresses the person with the divine claim and elicits a decision of faith. Thus defined existentially, incarnation is synonymous with personal revelation. Revelation "is the coming of God in the Word, which is a personal advent, the Incarnation of the Word."[19] Brunner concedes that Christ did assume our humanity. The real focus of the incarnation, however, is not historical, but existential or suprahistorical; it resides in the personal meeting between divine and human subjects.

In view of the foregoing, Brunner regards the historical claim of the virgin birth as "useless speculation." Indeed, "The majesty wonder of the Incarnation of the Son of God is not made greater but smaller by the biological theory of the procreation through one sex alone."[20] Brunner believes that the dogma of the virgin birth is untenable for several reasons: (1) It is lacking in the *kerygma* of the early church. (2) The Matthew 1 and Luke 1 narratives on which the doctrine is based are said to be historically unreliable. (3) The parents of Jesus, who alone knew the facts, gave no report on the subject. (4) The virgin birth affords no security against Christological heresy, for Adoptionists, Arians, and Socinians all accepted it. (5) The doctrine is closely linked with the Docetic heresy and Greek asceticism. And (6) the dogma was derived from the mistaken Septuagint translation of Isaiah 7:14.

Barth started with Kierkegaard's assumption that God is totally other than man. Consequently only God could speak about God. All revelation is Christomonistic, or located in Christ alone. Reacting sharply against the immanentalism of liberal theology, Barth develops a Christology from above. Thus he speaks of "the miracle of Jesus Christ's existence, this descent of God from above downwards."[21] Furthermore, Barth approaches the incarnation from the perspective of the two states, which he views dialectically rather than successively and to which he adapts the two natures. Barth finds in the parable of the Prodigal Son a paradigm of Christ's humiliation and exaltation. The journey of the son into a far country speaks of Christ's condescension and solidarity with sinful humanity. "It is He who descends so deep down to men in order to lift them up so high. It is He who goes into the far country in order that man may return home."[22] Barth argues dialectically that the incarnation is precisely a veiling; Christ conceals himself by the manner in which he reveals himself. That Christ was manifest in folly and weakness—i.e., incognito—rather than in power and glory, places persons before an unavoidable decision. Barth insists that the flesh Christ assumed was not neutral human nature, but Adamic nature, i.e., humanity in the state of disobedience, sin, and enmity against God. Although Christ did not commit particular sins, he nevertheless became a man with a sinful nature like each one of us. Thus Barth writes of Christ: "If He really entered into solidarity with us—and that is just what He did do—it meant necessarily that He took upon Himself, in likeness to us, the 'flesh of sin' (Rom. 8:3)."[23] The other side of Christ's humiliation is his exaltation, which corresponds to the return of the son to the father's home. Here Barth argues that in this movement God raised up humanity into himself. The statement "The Word became *flesh*" (John 1:14) means that Christ became not a man, but humanity as a whole. Thus when Christ returned to heaven in the flesh, he incorporated humankind into the life of God. "In Jesus Christ it is not merely one man, but the *humanum* of all men, which is posited and exalted as such to unity with God."[24]

Barth staunchly defended the virgin birth of Christ. The miracle of Christ's virgin birth for Barth possesses noetic rather than ontic significance. Whereas God could have brought about the incarnation in another way, the virgin birth serves as a "sign" of the fact that *God* has bridged the abyss between eternity and time. The phrase in the Apostles' Creed concerning Jesus' conception—"conceived of the Holy Ghost"—signifies that Christ's existence is due to God's special decision and initiative. The phrase "born of the virgin Mary" connotes that Jesus Christ is the real son of a real woman.

Process Theologians

Followers of Whitehead reject as crassly prescientific the claim that the second person of the triune Godhead literally assumed human flesh. Modern minds must reject "as incredible and impossible the Greek idea of a god who comes down to earth and walks about as a human being."[25] The process worldview renders impossible the idea of an intrusion from outside the natural order. Instead, the incarnation must be interpreted solely in terms of the cosmic world process. The neoclassical vision of the incarnation is rooted in its special understanding of the Logos. Not an eternally divine person, the Logos is identified as the impersonal and timeless principle of order and purpose in the universe, or as the instrument of novelty and the lure for feeling. The Logos, Whiteheadians argue, is immanent in the world *nexus,* luring all entities toward optimal creative transformation. In the Whiteheadian scheme, broadly speaking, the incarnation represents the immanence of the Logos in the man Jesus.

John B. Cobb, Jr., argues that the substantialist model of the incarnation must give way to an experiential relation in which societies of past experiences or events merge in creative synthesis. The incarnation, Cobb insists, describes the indwelling of the Logos, or the power of creative transformation, in the historical Jesus. To be sure, the Logos is incarnate and operative in all persons and religious traditions. But the indwelling of the Logos in Jesus was so complete that it shaped his very being. "In Jesus there is a distinctive incarnation because his very selfhood was constituted by the Logos."[26] In other words, for Cobb, "Christ" designates the incarnate Logos, that is, the power of creative transformation operative in the world.

Professor Pittenger argues that a God

who is so remote and unrelated that he can intrude into nature only from without represents a deistical concept. The catastrophic view of the incarnation disrupts the regular workings of nature and so must be rejected. Consistent with the evolutionary vision, Pittenger claims that God continually incarnates himself in nature and history, thereby energizing the cosmic process. Yet the God who is immanent in the world process is eminently operative in the man Jesus—the latter becoming through this indwelling the special personal agent through whom God acts. "At every point in the existence of Jesus, the divine activity is operative—in teaching, preaching, healing, comforting, acting, dying, rising again. . . . He is indeed the personalized instrument for the Self-Expressive Activity of God."[27]

J. A. T. Robinson claims that as "a genuine product of the evolutionary process,"[28] the man Jesus was divinely raised up to represent the race before God. The notion that God become man should not be regarded as a "bolt from the blue" or a "Christ comet," by which a celestial visitor lands on earth, stays for a while, and then takes off after completing his mission. The old mythological concept of the God-man must be replaced by the functional notion of "God-in-man."[29] Thus Robinson concludes that Jesus "is not a divine or semi-divine being who comes from the other side. He is a human figure raised up from among his brothers to be the instrument of God's decisive work."[30] Jesus is distinctive (not unique or final) in that he emerged from the historical process to serve as the exemplary instrument of God's self-expression.

Process thinkers likewise disavow the virgin birth as mythological and thus meaningless to modern minds. The carpenter of Nazareth was the humanly conceived son of Joseph and Mary.

Pittenger speaks for the tradition: "The stories told in the first two chapters of Matthew and Luke are apologetic, or christological, in content, and they cannot be taken as historical narratives. Insistence on a biological virgin birth has been a mistake."[31]

Modern Roman Catholic Authorities

The so-called "progressive" Roman Catholic theologians uniformly approach Christology "from below" (i.e., beginning with Jesus' authentic manhood) and seek to reinterpret traditional Christological language in terms of Christian experience. The classical doctrines of Christ's preexistence, virgin birth, and incarnation are viewed nonhistorically as "poetic imagery" (Hellwig) or as "mythological discourse" (Carmody). Such Roman Catholic authorities, moreover, shift the focus of concern from Christmas to Good Friday and Easter, i.e., not on who Christ was in the beginning, but what he did at the end. In sum, recent critical Catholic scholarship claims that the old ontological way of representing Jesus must be replaced with functional and personalist perspectives. One recent study, for example, gives the following definition of the incarnation: "God chose to take one man's capacity or orientation and so fill it that that man uniquely 'incarnated' God's Word."[32]

Piet Schoonenberg insists that God was initially an undifferentiated being, and thus there was no transcendent, preexistent person called the Son of God. But at a specific moment in time, the second person of the Godhead came into being in the human figure of Jesus (likewise the third person in the Holy Spirit). Thus God changes, indeed, he *becomes* triune through his salvific self-communication. This means, for Schoonenberg, that Jesus is the *natural* Son of God, a single, undivided human being (i.e., the two-natures dogma does not hold). The incarnation, on this showing, means God's whole presence and working in the man Jesus. The focus of Christology is not an alleged Word from eternity who became flesh. Rather, it is "the self-identification of God's being with the human person of Jesus."[33] Schoonenberg calls this pattern, which he judges to be less mythical and more human, "a christology of God's presence" or "a christological humanism."[34]

Hans Küng works a Christology from below by beginning with the life and deeds of the man Jesus and then inquiring about his relation to God. According to Küng, the doctrines of the Son's preexistence, conception by the Spirit, and assumption of human flesh are Hellenistic myths chosen to set forth the meaning of Jesus for faith. The result of this development is that the historical Jesus of Nazareth was overshadowed by the mythical Son of God. But such language, Küng insists, is incomprehensible today and should be avoided in the church's proclamation. "We can no longer accept the mythical ideas of that age about a being descended from God, existing before time and beyond this world in a heavenly state."[35] This mythical "descending" Christology must be replaced by an historical "ascending" Christology, which views Jesus as a man gradually elevated to the status of revealer of God.

Küng observes that the ancient world was replete with myths depicting the miraculous birth of heroes and gods. He holds that the early church utilized the virgin-birth mythology to highlight Jesus' functional role as Son of God and Messiah. But since a supernatural conception adds nothing to Jesus' role as a human spokesman for God, "No one can be obliged to believe in the biological fact of a virginal conception or birth."[36] Raymond Brown, a Catholic biblical scholar, adds that the virgin birth stories are of questionable historicity and extraneous to the Christian message. McBrien identifies the dogma of the virgin birth as an unhistorical *"theologoumenon,"* that is, "a theological belief that is read back into the historical life of Jesus in order to make a point of faith."[37] According to the Notre Dame theologian, the early church fabricated the virginal conception doctrine to communicate the truth that Jesus was one with God from the moment of his conception.

A brief summary of Catholic opinion regarding Mary follows. From the fourth century onward many Catholic authorities expanded the virginal-conception doctrine to affirm the doctrine of Mary's perpetual virginity. Thus it was held that Mary was a virgin not only *before* birth but also *in* birth (Jesus did not pass through the birth canal) and *after* birth (Mary had no marital relations with Joseph and hence no natural children). The name of Augustine[38] could be mentioned in this regard. The generally accepted view was that Mary was miraculously conceived and lived a sinless life. The Council of Ephesus (431) promulgated the dogma of Mary's divine motherhood. Against the Nestorians, Mary was given the title "Mother of God." But throughout the patristic era and beyond, Mariology remained subservient to Christology.

In the medieval era, however, when theology became increasingly divorced from Scripture, Mary herself gradually became a channel for saving grace. Thus many Catholic authorities viewed Mary as mediatrix between Christ and humankind. This conviction possessed the status of a thesis (a pious belief) rather than a dogma (a binding doctrine). According to Bernard of Clairvaux, persons need "a mediator with that Mediator, and there is no one more efficacious than Mary."[39] Bonaventure, Duns Scotus and others, envisaged Mary as co-redemptrix of the human race. A cult of Mary arose in which prayers were made and worship offered to the "Mother of the Redeemer" and the "Queen of heaven." Many Roman authorities upheld Mary's immaculate conception, a dignity that was said to be commensurate with Christ's choice of Mary to be his mother. Other authorities such as Thomas Aquinas rejected the notion of Mary's immaculate conception as inconsistent with the doctrine of universal sin.

By the nineteenth century Mariology had acquired a separate theological status. In 1854 Pope Pius IX, in the bull *Ineffabilis Deus*, promulgated as a dogma of the faith the Immaculate Conception of Mary. As the "God-Bearer" Mary was declared to be free from the stain of original sin from the moment of her conception. In the mystery of sin, however, Mary endured sin's consequences in the form of sickness and death. In 1950 Pope Pius XII certified longstanding legends by promulgating the bull *Munificentissmus Deus*, which dogmatized the Heavenly Assumption of Mary. Instead of succumbing to death, Mary allegedly was translated bodily to heaven and was seated at the right hand of Christ to mediate the prayers of the faithful.

The Second Vatican Council and much contemporary Catholic theology posits Mariology squarely within ecclesiology. That is, while retaining devotion to Mary as advocate and mediatrix, recent Catholic thought subordinates Mary to Christ in the scheme of redemption by relating her to the church. Thus "Mary is, by means of her faith and obedience to the Word of God, a model of the Church and is its preeminent member."[40] Many recent Catholic scholars find little biblical justification for Mary's perpetual virginity, that is her virginity *in partu* (in birth) and *post partu* (after birth). The same scholars deny that belief in the dogmas of the Immaculate Conception and Heavenly Assumption are necessary for good standing in the church.

Many Fathers, Reformers, and Evangelicals

Ignatius, the bishop of Antioch, speaks for the subapostolic age when, against the docetists, he upholds the objective reality of the incarnation. The Son of God or Word, who was with the Father from eternity, became a man in the line of David and thereby revealed the Father. "There is one God, who has manifested Himself by Jesus Christ His Son, who is the eternal Word."[41] The miracle of the virgin birth attested the union of Deity with human nature. Thus typically, Ignatius claims that Christ "was begotten by the Father before all ages, but was afterwards born of the Virgin Mary without any intercourse with man."[42] The confessional type of language used by Ignatius indicates that belief in Christ's preexistence, incarnation, and virgin birth was widely held early in the second century.

The Apologists consistently identified Christ as the enfleshment of the eternal Logos who, by becoming man, revealed and interpreted the Father. Thus Justin Martyr affirmed that the personal Word "preexisted and submitted to be born a man of like passions with us, having a body, according to the Father's will."[43] The disseminated Word illumines the minds of all persons, whereas the incarnate Word saves all who believe. "The Word . . . became man for our sakes, that becoming a partner for our sufferings, he might also bring us healing."[44] Justin expounds the virgin birth doctrine by relating Mary to Eve. As Eve, the virgin believed and obeyed the serpent and thus became the mother of sin, so Mary, also a virgin, believed and obeyed the angel and thus became the mother of the sin-Bearer.[45]

In his important essay *On the Incarnation of the Word*, Athanasius argues that the race languished in a state of moral corruption, death, and impending judgment. The curse and ruin that afflicted sinners' corporeal existence could be undone only as the Word, the image of the Father, assumed the body of our humiliation. "Man would not have been freed from sin and damnation if the Logos had not taken upon himself our natural, human flesh. Neither could man have become Godlike if the Word which became flesh had not come from the Father—if he had not been his own true Word."[46] Thus, having been conceived of a virgin, the Savior made his abode in a body like ours, capable of death. Opposing the notion of a mere functional immanence of the Logos in Jesus, Athanasius insisted that "he became man and did not just come into man."[47] In this state of humiliation, the Word initially performed the work of revelation. By many signs he showed himself to be the Ruler and King of the universe. Then he performed the work of reconciliation by offering his body as a sacrifice for sinful souls. Athanasius believed that the incarnation would not have occurred had the race not fallen into sin. But since humankind did lie under the curse, "He was made man that we might be made God."[48]

Augustine viewed the Word as the preexistent second person of the Trinity who became man in the carpenter of Nazareth. The coeternal Word of God "took on human nature, and thereby became the one Jesus Christ, Mediator between God and man, equal to the Father in his divinity, less than the Father according to the flesh, that is, as man."[49] Following Irenaeus and Athanasius, Augustine insisted that because the human race languished under sin and condemnation, "a mediator was required, that is to say, a reconciler, who by offering a unique sacrifice . . . should allay that wrath."[50] Thus through a miraculous conception wrought by the Holy Spirit, the only

Son of God clothed himself with sinless human nature. Said Augustine, "I believe that Christ was born of a virgin because I have read it in the Gospel."[51]

As for the church's early creedal affirmations, the Apostles' Creed, which originated from a second-century Roman baptismal confession, describes Jesus Christ as "conceived by the Holy Spirit, born of the virgin Mary." Plainly, early candidates for Christian baptism were required to assent to the validity of our Lord's virgin birth. Since only essential tenets of the faith were included in the Apostles' Creed, the importance of the virgin birth to the early church is established. The Nicene Creed of 325 and its revision of 381 attest Christ's incarnation and virgin birth: "Who for us men and because of our salvation came down from heaven, and was incarnate by the Holy Spirit and the Virgin Mary." Furthermore, the Chalcedonian Definition of 451 attests Christ's incarnation and virgin birth, and the so-called Athanasian Creed certifies the incarnation (art. 29) as a belief necessary for salvation.

Anselm, in his classic essay, *Cur Deus Homo,* observed that Adamic disobedience disturbed God's design for the universe. God's justice was such that either the debt must be paid or divine punishment must fall. But to punish all persons everlastingly would defeat God's purpose of creation. The only viable alternative was that the debt of sin must be paid and many humans saved. Anselm notes that human persons could not make the needed satisfaction by virtue of their sinful and impotent condition. Only God himself could make amends. But since sinners owe the debt, the satisfaction must be offered by a man. Thus, concludes Anselm, "it is necessary that the same being should be perfect God and perfect man, in order to make this atonement."[52] In the divine plan the eternal Son of God was conceived by the virgin

Mary, was born a man free of Adam's guilt, and surrendered his life as the perfect offering for sin.

Calvin's approach to the incarnation followed that of the Fathers. Since our iniquities estranged us from the righteous God, a mediator was needed who was capable of bridging the gulf between God and sinners. "The situation would surely have been hopeless had the very majesty of God not descended to us, since it was not in our power to ascend to him."[53] The mediator must be God, for only God could conquer sin, defeat death, and make us children of the Most High. On the other hand, the mediator must also be human, for only thus could human flesh be presented as satisfaction to God's righteous judgment. Consequently, "God's natural Son fashioned for himself a body from our body, flesh from our flesh, bones from our bones, that he might be one with us."[54] Calvin attributes Christ's sinlessness (necessary for a perfect sacrifice), not to the absence of a human father, but to a miraculous conception wrought by the Holy Spirit. To the question whether the incarnation would have occurred if Adam had not sinned, Calvin responds negatively and insists that Adam's sin and Christ's coming to earth were united in God's eternal decree. Calvin notes that Scripture closely links Christ's humiliation with the shedding of his blood for the remission of sins.

B. B. Warfield insists that Christ the Son, eternally abiding with the Father, took into his divine personality a human nature and so came into the world for the purpose of saving sinners. The Messiah is "a divine being who has entered the world on a mission of mercy to sinful man."[55] Scripture represents Christ's humiliation as a miraculous event: a supernatural Christ begotten via a supernatural birth effects a supernatural salvation. In Warfield's opinion, Christ's virginal conception by the Holy Spirit is an essential element of biblical faith: "The supernatural birth of Jesus . . . is the expression of Christianity's supernaturalism, the safeguard of its doctrine of incarnation, and the condition of its doctrine of redemption."[56]

Machen claims that one's attitude toward the virgin birth turns on one's view of Jesus Christ. If Jesus is understood to be the incarnate Son of God and Savior, then the New Testament teaching concerning his supernatural conception makes eminently good sense. "Only one Jesus is presented in the Word of God; and that Jesus did not come into the world by ordinary generation, but was conceived in the womb of the virgin by the Holy Ghost."[57]

Additional helpful studies on the incarnation and virgin birth are provided by James Orr,[58] and Millard J. Erickson.[59]

THE BIBLICAL TEACHING

To determine which historical proposal or integration of elements best fit the data, we turn to the primary teachings of Scripture on the subject of Christ's incarnation and birth.

Pentateuch

Immediately following Adam and Eve's disobedience in Eden, God pronounced a series of judgments against the parties that participated in the first sin. In the theologically pregnant Genesis 3:15 text God responded to the serpent, as follows: "I will put enmity between you and the woman, and between your offspring and hers; he will crush your head, and you will strike his heel." Since "seed" (*zera'*) in Scripture designates both posterity collectively and a single offspring, the focus of the text is twofold. The first of these is the hostility that would persist throughout history between the unbelieving followers of Satan and the believing offspring of the woman. Ultimately, however, this divine pronouncement anticipates the struggle between the two personal representatives of the rival parties, namely, Christ ("he," *hû'*) and Satan ("you"). Eve's principal seed, though wounded by Satan, would in the end vanquish the leader of the kingdom of darkness. The point of interest in this Protoevangelium (i.e., first announcement of the Gospel) is that the future Messiah, who would destroy Satan, is described as the "offspring" of *Eve*. The identification of the triumphant Messiah as the *zera'* of the woman remained enigmatic until the New Testament explication of Christ's supernatural conception without male agency (Matt. 1:23; Gal. 4:4). "Not until the virgin birth would the full implication of the promise be understood."[60]

During Israel's wilderness wanderings God ordered Moses to strike a rock at Horeb. When the leader of Israel did as the Lord had commanded, water flowed from the rock, providing refreshment for all (Exod. 17:5-7). The apostle Paul explicates the meaning of this remarkable event in 1 Corinthians 10:4, when he writes that the people of Israel all "drank the same spiritual drink; for they drank from the spiritual rock that accompanied them, and that rock was Christ." "Rock" (*ṣûr*) is a common name for God in the Old Testament (Deut. 32:4, 15; Ps. 18:2, 31; etc.). Thus the meaning of this Exodus text is that the Christ who eternally preexisted his birth in Bethlehem was present with Israel in their wilderness journey as the providential provider of their needs. Juxtaposing Exodus 17:5-7 and 1 Corinthians 10:4, what emerges is an "explicit reference to Christ as preexistent, and his being the source of the people's blessings at all times."[61]

Prophetic Literature

Volume 1, chapter 7 shows that texts such as Psalms 2:7; 45:6-7; and 110:1 attest the real existence of the Messiah prior to his birth at Bethlehem during the reign of Caesar Augustus. The prophet Isaiah likewise confirms Messiah's preexistence with the phrase "Everlasting Father" (*'abî-'ad*) (Isa. 9:6), which literally describes Messiah as the "father [i.e., possessor] of the ages." Micah makes the same point, when he describes the royal Messiah as one "whose origins are from of old, from ancient times" (*mîmê 'ôlām*, Mic. 5:2). These two texts, Unger argues, convey "the strongest assertion of infinite duration of which the Hebrew language is capable."[62] Many scholars believe that the incident involving God's miraculous preservation of the three devout Hebrews in the Book of Daniel may also attest Christ's preexistence. When king Nebuchadnezzar looked into the blazing furnace, he saw a fourth person who looked "like a son of the gods" (Dan. 3:25). With many Christian interpreters both ancient and modern, we suggest that in this text "more likely we have to do with a preincarnate manifestation of the Son of God."[63]

Isaiah undoubtedly anticipates the kingly Messiah's incarnation with the words, "to us a child [*yeled*] is born, to us son is given" (Isa. 9:6). The seventh chapter of the same prophecy prophetically speaks of the instrumentality of the incarnation, namely, the virgin birth. By way of background to Isaiah 7:14, Syria (Aram) and Israel waged war against Judah, striking fear into the heart of corrupt king Ahaz. In the hour of national calamity, the Lord directed Isaiah to urge Ahaz to be calm and trust in God. The Lord, moreover, invited Ahaz to ask for a sign of divine protection in the present crisis. Wicked Ahaz, however, had already determined not to accept God's provision but to secure military assistance from Assyria (cf. 2 Kings 16:7–8). The prophet thus declared that since Ahaz had turned his back on this particular sign of divine assistance, God would give a greater sign (*'ôt*) to the entire house of David ("you," pl., v. 14). This greater sign, set in the context of God's covenant with David (2 Sam. 7:12–16), would guarantee the perpetuity of the threatened line of David through the promised child. The substance of the new sign forms one of the great prophecies of Scripture: "The virgin will be with child and will give birth to a son, and will call him Immanuel" (Isa. 7:14). This exceptional sign proclaimed the miraculous birth of the Messiah by a virgin. ("While the king calls in an army, God looks to the birth of a child."[64])

The woman who would give birth to the Messiah is described as "the virgin" (*hā'almāh*), and is so rendered by the AV, RV, and NIV. The vast scholarly discussion surrounding the meaning of *'almāh* is best summed up in the article on the word in *Theological Wordbook of the Old Testament,* the heart of which follows: "It seems reasonable to consider that the feminine form of this word is not a technical word for a virgin but represents a young woman, one of whose characteristics is virginity." The article continues: "There is no instance where it can be proved that *'almāh* designates a young woman who is not a virgin."[65] The fact that the Holy Spirit guided Matthew (Matt. 1:23) to employ *parthenos,* the Greek word for a virgin, to translate *'almāh,* clinches the argument that Isaiah predicted the Messiah's incarnation by means of a virginal conception. Orr offers this summation of the import of Isaiah 7:14. "The vision of the prophet sweeps far beyond present events . . . and he beholds in this Son that should be born, this child that should be given . . . the security for the fulfillment of the promise to David,

and the hope for the future of the world."[66]

The Synoptic Gospels

The New Testament offers explicit testimony to Christ's eternal preexistence. Jesus states in Matthew 11:27: "All things have been committed [*paredothē*] to me by my Father. No one knows [*epiginōskei*] the Son except the Father, and no one knows [*epiginōskei*] the Father except the Son and those to whom the Son chooses to reveal him." In the midst of his earthly ministry Jesus claimed a profound knowledge of his Father in heaven. Such knowledge and ability to reveal the Father fully could not have been acquired during his lifetime but is best explained on the hypothesis of the eternal communion of the Father and the Son within the life of the triune Godhead. Moreover, as Plummer notes, the aorist tense of *paradidōmi* ("committed") "points back to a moment in eternity, and implies the preexistence of the Messiah."[67]

The birth narratives of Matthew and Luke attest the incarnation of our Lord. Matthew observes that, in fulfillment of the promise of Isaiah 7:14, the infant son born to Mary would be named " 'Immanuel'—which means, 'God with us' " (Matt. 1:23). In Luke's narrative, the angel Gabriel informed Mary that her newborn child would be none other than "the Son of the Most High," the royal Messiah of David (1:32–33). Luke further relates that the Holy Spirit informed the devout Jew Simeon that he would not die before he had seen the Messiah. When Simeon found the infant Jesus in the temple and cradled him in his arms, he thanked God for the privilege of beholding the Lord's salvation incarnate in the child Jesus (Luke 2:25–32). Simeon's song of praise indicates that God's purpose relative to the incarnation was to provide deliverance and salvation (vv. 30–32). Later Luke related Christ's coming into the world to the reality of human sin: "The Son of Man came to seek and to save what was lost" (Luke 19:10; cf. Matt. 20:28; Mark 2:17).

The same birth narratives explicitly attest the reality of our Lord's virgin birth. The patent differences between the two accounts can be explained partly by the thesis that Matthew recounts the birth of Jesus from the perspective of Joseph, whereas Luke formulated his narrative from the angle of Mary's experience. In Matthew's account (Matt. 1:18–25), attention focuses on Joseph who was informed by an angel of the Lord that Mary, his fiancé who was yet a virgin, would bear a child without male agency: "what is conceived [to gennēthen] in her is from the Holy Spirit" (1:20). Matthew makes clear that Joseph had no marital relations with Mary "until" (heōs) she bore the child (1:25; cf. v. 18). Thus the Roman Catholic postulate of Mary's perpetual virginity is without biblical foundation. Matthew presents the episode as a direct fulfillment of the prophecy of Isaiah 7:14—namely, that a virgin would bear a son whose name would be Immanuel. Finally, Joseph took Mary into his home and legitimized the marriage (short of sexual relations) in obedience to the heavenly command.

In the second account (Luke 1:26–38) Luke, the physician and historian, relates that the angel Gabriel announced to Mary, a humble "virgin" (v. 27, parthenos) who delighted in the Lord, that she would be the mother of Israel's Messiah. The Greek word parthenos, according to Marshall, "means a young, unmarried girl, and carries the implication of virginity."[68] This is clear from Mary's astonished response to the angel: "How shall this be, seeing I know not a man?" (v. 34, AV). To this the angel responded: "The Holy Spirit will come upon [epeleusetai] you, and the power of the Most High will overshadow [episkiasei] you. So the holy one to be born [to gennōmenon] will be called the Son of God" (v. 35). While not informing Mary precisely how the conception would occur, the heavenly messenger declared that she would conceive miraculously through the special energy of the Holy Spirit.

Contrary to the charges of skeptical critics, the Matthean and Lukan birth narratives agree on a number of significant points: (1) Joseph and Mary were engaged to be married (Matt. 1:18; Luke 1:27). (2) In the betrothed state Mary was a virgin (Matt. 1:23; Luke 1:27, 34). (3) The child was conceived by the Holy Spirit without male agency (Matt. 1:18; Luke 1:35). (4) The name of the son born to Mary was "Jesus," which means, "the Lord is salvation" (Matt. 1:21, 25; Luke 1:31). (5) The child would be the promised messianic Redeemer (Matt. 1:21; Luke 1:32). (6) Jesus would be a uniquely divine person (Matt. 1:23; Luke 1:32, 35). (7) Jesus was born in the town of Bethlehem (Matt. 2:1; Luke 2:4). And (8) Mary and Joseph had a normal married life and begat other children (Matt. 1:25; Luke 2:7–prōtotokas, "firstborn"). Indeed, specific mention of Jesus' brothers (James, Joseph, Simon, and Judas) and sisters (Matt. 13:55–56; Mark 6:3; cf. Acts 1:14; Gal. 1:19) contravenes the theory of Mary's perpetual virginity. "It is natural to suppose that the brothers and sisters of Jesus were children of Joseph and Mary."[69]

The fact that both Matthew's and Luke's genealogies of Jesus include Joseph does not disprove the doctrine of our Lord's virginal conception. On the contrary, the round-about manner in which they mention Joseph confirms his role as Jesus' legal rather than natural father. Thus Matthew 1:16 refers to "Joseph, the husband of Mary, of whom was born Jesus, who is called Christ." Similarly Luke 3:23 states that "Jesus . . . was the son, so it was thought, of Joseph."[70] References in the Gospels to Joseph as Jesus' father (Luke 2:27; 33, 41, 48; 4:22; cf. John 1:45; 6:42) merely uphold the importance in Jewish culture of adopted fatherhood.

The Pauline Literature

In order to demonstrate the unrivaled supremacy of Christ, Paul describes the Lord as "the firstborn [*prōtotokos*] over all creation" (Col. 1:15). The text offers no support for the Arian view that *prōtotokos* depicts Christ as the most eminent created being. Rather, according to Lightfoot, the term connotes two main ideas: (1) Christ's priority to creation as eternally preexistent, and (2) Christ's sovereignty over all creation as its Creator and Ruler.[71] The apostle's main point in Colossians 1:15–17 is that as the eternally preexistent One ("He is before all things," v. 17), Christ exercises lordship over the entire universe. In other words, Jesus Christ is "sovereign Lord over all creation by virtue of primogeniture."[72]

When Paul speaks of Christ as God's "Son, who was descended from David according to the flesh" (Rom. 1:3, RSV), he clearly contemplates the Lord's eternal preexistence and incarnation. When Paul adds, "designated Son of God . . . according to the Spirit of holiness by his resurrection from the dead" (v. 4, RSV), he gives a rounded presentation of Christ's three stages of preexistence, humiliation, and exaltation. The apostle's reference in Romans 8:3 to God "sending [*pempsas*] his own Son in the likeness of sinful man to be a sin offering" tersely depicts the enfleshment of Christ and the inauguration of his earthly mission. Bengel observes that the aorist participle *pempsas* "denotes a sort of separation, as it

were, or estrangement of the Son from the Father, that He might be the Mediator."[73] A further text, "But when the time had fully come, God sent [*exapesteilen*] his Son, born of a woman, born under the law, to redeem those under law" (Gal. 4:4–5), once again describes Christ's preexistence, incarnation, and saving mission.[74]

The primitive hymn preserved in 1 Timothy 3:16 explicates the heart of the Christian "mystery," namely, the person and history of Jesus Christ. The six rhythmic lines summarize the career of our Lord from his incarnation to his resurrection and ascension. The first line of the hymnodic piece, *hos ephanerōthē en sarki,* clearly affirms Christ's bodily manifestation on earth. The New Testament frequently employs the verb *phaneroō* to describe the incarnation (Rom. 3:21; 2 Tim. 1:10; cf. Heb. 9:26; 1 Peter 1:20; 1 John 1:2). The passive form of the verb here implies the existence of Christ prior to his appearance in the space-time continuum. The phrase *en sarki* denotes that Christ appeared on earth as a real man, a fact attested elsewhere in Paul (Rom. 8:3; Eph. 2:15; Col. 1:22) and in other New Testament writings (John 1:14; Heb. 5:7).

In the context of a discourse on Christian giving, Paul recalled the extraordinary liberality of Christ and interjected a succinct statement on the incarnation: "You know the grace of our Lord Jesus Christ, that though he was rich, yet for your sakes he became poor, so that you through his poverty might become rich" (2 Cor. 8:9). The pregnant phrase *plousios ōn* clearly signifies the Son's preexistence clothed with the glory of the Godhead (1 Cor. 2:8; 2 Thess. 2:14). The words *di hymas eptōcheusen* (note the ingressive aorist of *ptōcheuō,* to be "reduced to poverty") affirm our Lord's transition to the state of humiliation at the incarnation. Christ entered this abject condition when he laid aside the wealth of heaven's glory, assumed our lowly condition, and died a cruel death. The concluding clause of the verse plainly links Christ's incarnation with the atonement; for Paul Christ's person and work constitute an indissoluble whole.

The crowning jewel of incarnational texts is Philippians 2:6–11, an early Christian hymn in praise of Christ that Paul appropriated when writing to the church at Philippi. Just as the previously discussed ethical exhortation to sacrificial giving led Paul to reflect on Christ's voluntary impoverishment (2 Cor. 8:9), so here the apostle's enjoinder to Christian humility prompted the recollection of Christ's incomparable self-renunciation for us. In this text Paul contemplates three states or stages in the existence of the church's Lord: (1) his preexistent condition (v. 6), (2) his incarnation and death, or humiliation, (vv. 7–8), and (3) his triumphant resurrection, or exaltation, to the heavenly realm (vv. 9–11). The opening phrase of the hymn, *hos en morphē theou hyparchōn* ("though he was in the form of God," v. 6a, RSV), speaks of Christ's participation in the divine essence prior to his historical manifestation. One authority translates *hyparchōn* as "being essentially" and adds, "It is said of this divine mode of existence that Christ existed in it in the past. . . . It refers to his preexistence prior to the Incarnation."[75] The hymn continues by declaring that the preexistent Lord "did not consider equality with God [*to einai isa theō*] something to be grasped" (v. 6b). That is, the eternal Christ chose not to regard existence-in-a-manner-of-equality-with-God a treasure to be greedily hoarded. Instead, he voluntarily stripped himself (*ekenōsen*) of his prerogatives as the divine Son (his God-equal position) by "taking the very nature of a servant" (*morphē doulou*, v. 7)—namely, by assuming the form and exhibiting the condition of a common slave. The text indicates that while renouncing participation in the heavenly glory, Christ retained the divine form or *morphē*. "Paul does not teach that our Lord was once God but had become instead man; he teaches that though he was God, he had become also man."[76] The hymn unfolds further the dynamic of the enfleshment of the heavenly Lord: he was "made in human likeness" (*homoiōma*, v. 7b). Christ became in every respect a man like us, sin excepted. The relation is said to be one of "likeness," for in regard to his intrinsic being he was both God *and* man. Lest the reader be misled by the preceding "likeness" relation in a docetic direction, the hymn immediately adds that as to outward appearance (*schēma*) Jesus was, indeed, an authentic man. The One who from eternity possessed the essence and glory of God, and who in an act of supreme self-renunciation assumed the existence of a lowly servant was in truth an authentic man among men.

In opposition to proto-Gnostic teachers who held that the divine emanations and energies were distributed among numerous aeons, Paul insists in Colossians 1:19 that "God was pleased to have all his fullness [*pan to plērōma*] dwell [*katoikēsai*] in him" (i.e., Christ). The "fullness" likely denotes the totality of the divine being and attributes.[77] Far from being parceled out among many intermediaries, the total reality of God made its abode in Jesus of Nazareth. The verb *katoikēsai* may be an ingressive aorist signifying to "take up a permanent abode." In the related text, Colossians 2:9, Paul states that "in Christ all the fullness [*pan to plērōma*] of the Deity lives [*katoikei*] in bodily form [*sōmatikōs*]." The adverb *sōmatikōs* refers to Christ's human body and underscores the fact that at the incarnation the divine essence took upon himself our human nature.

Paul repeatedly affirms that Christ came into the world for the explicit purpose of making amends for sin. "Christ Jesus came into the world to save sinners" (1 Tim. 1:15). The apostle speaks, in addition, of "the appearing [*epiphaneia*] of our Savior, Christ Jesus, who has destroyed death and has brought life and immortality to light through the gospel" (2 Tim. 1:10). Other texts such as Romans 8:3 and Galatians 4:4–5 plainly teach that the chief motivating factor for the incarnation was the salvation of doomed sinners.

The New Testament reader is mildly surprised to find no explicit discussion of the virgin birth outside Matthew's and Luke's gospels. *Prima facie* one might have expected Paul, theologian *extraordinarius,* to have expounded this important theme. The fact, however, that Luke failed to mention the virgin birth in Acts indicates that the argument from silence carries little weight. Given Luke's close relationship with Paul in the ministry of the early church, it is highly probable that the latter knew about the virgin birth, but because of the circumstantial nature of his writings chose not to expound the theme directly. One might also argue with Barth and others that since the virgin birth was not disputed by the early church, Paul felt no need to develop the theme in his letters that primarily dealt with pressing practical problems. Many interpreters have noted that the manner in which Paul discusses the coming of God's Son (e.g., Rom. 8:3; Gal. 4:4) differs from the language customarily used to describe a natural birth. Thus it seems fair to conclude with the judgment of Machen: "The virgin birth is not explicitly mentioned in the Epistles, but is does seem to be implied in the profoundest way in the entire view which Paul holds of the Lord Jesus Christ."[78]

The Johannine Literature

John's gospel is unique in that its opening verses describe the Logos in his supratemporal existence with the Father. The first statement, "In the beginning was the Word" (*En archē ēn ho logos*), signifies that before time or anything else came to be, the Word absolutely *was* (cf. 1 John 1:1). As Westcott observes, "The imperfect tense suggests in this relation . . . the notion of absolute, supratemporal existence."[79] Not only does John affirm the Word's eternal preexistence (cf. 1 John 2:13–14) but also his eternal communion with God: the Word "was with God in the beginning" (*houtos ēn en archē pros ton theon,* v. 2). When nothing but God had being, the Word enjoyed an intimate "I-Thou" relation with the Father (cf. 1 John 1:2). Clearly the first three verses of John's Gospel refute the notion that Christ first became personal either at creation or in the incarnation.

John 8 also explicitly affirms Jesus' timeless preexistence. During a ceremony of the Festival of Tabernacles, four great candelabra were lit to commemorate the pillar of fire that guided Israel through the wilderness. In the midst of the solemn ceremony, Jesus proclaimed to the gathered throng, "I am the light of the world" (John 8:12). Jesus proceeded to assert both that he had a prior existence with the Father in heaven (v. 23) and that Abraham, Israel's revered patriarch, rejoiced to see his day (v. 56). Jesus concluded his dialogue with the Jews with the startling statement: " '. . .before Abraham was born, I am!' " (*egō eimi,* v. 58). By appropriating this self-designation of Yahweh (cf. Exod. 3:14; Isa. 41:4), Jesus boldly claimed that he was the timelessly eternal God.

The Apocalypse presents further evidence of Christ's eternal preexistence. The Savior represented himself to the church at Laodicea as "the beginning [*hē archē*] of God's creation" (Rev. 3:14, RSV), namely, as the originator and sovereign of the cosmos. Christ, moreover, described himself to John with the words "I am [*egō eimi*] the first and the last" (Rev. 1:17; cf. 2:8). In the final chapter of the prophecy, where Christ consummates the course of history, he bears the character of the timeless Sovereign: "I am the Alpha and the Omega, the First and the Last, the Beginning and the End" (Rev. 22:13).

John 1:14, the most complete Johannine statement concerning the incarnation, may be considered from four perspectives. (1) The *subject* of the incarnation is "the Word" (*ho logos*), that is, the divine Logos who existed in communion with the Father from eternity (cf. John 1:1–2). (2) The *substance* of the incarnation: the Word "became flesh" (*sarx egeneto*). The noun *sarx* here connotes human nature without moral disparagement (cf. John 1:13; 3:6; 8:15). John states, not that the Word ceased to be what he was before (i.e., God), but that the Logos assumed our nature and our human mode of existence (sin excepted). "He took the whole nature of man, including its frailty; all that nature in which He could grow, learn, struggle, be tempted, suffer, and die."[80] (3) The *scene* of the incarnation: "and lived [*eskēnōsen*] for a while among us." The verb is the ingressive aorist of *skēnoō,* which means to take up a temporary dwelling place. Just as the divine Presence made its abode in the tabernacle (2 Sam. 7:6), so John claims that God dwelt among us for a season in the man Jesus. And finally, (4) the *substantiation* of the incarnation: "We have seen his glory, the glory of the One and Only [Son], who came from the Father, full of grace and truth" (John 1:14). John and others observed the glory of the majestic God shining through Jesus' human flesh. Thus eyewitnesses testified that the eternal God had indeed become a man

in Jesus of Nazareth. John additionally states that Jesus Christ embodies the fullest revelation of the invisible God: "No one has ever seen God, but God the One and Only [Son], who is at the Father's side, has made him known" (*exēgēsato,* 1:18). The aorist middle of *exēgeomai* indicates that Jesus has uniquely "expounded" or "interpreted" the reality of God to finite persons. Christ uniquely reveals the Father to men and women (John 14:8–9).

Opposing the Docetic heresy, which denied that Christ came in genuine human flesh, John affirms in his first letter: "The life appeared [*ephanerōthē*]; we have seen it and testify to it, and we proclaim to you the eternal life, which was with the Father and has appeared to us" (1 John 1:2). Referring here to "the life" rather than to "the Word," John attests the same historical event of the incarnation that he expounded in John 1:14. John adds, "Every spirit that acknowledges that Jesus Christ has come in the flesh [*en sarki*] is from God, but every spirit that does not acknowledge Jesus is not from God" (1 John 4:2–3). John's specification that Jesus came "in flesh" rather than "into flesh" rules out the hypothesis that the Christ descended upon the man Jesus at his baptism. According to John, those who fail to acknowledge that Jesus Christ has come in human flesh (*en sarki*) embody the spirit of the antichrist (2 John 7).

Jesus also spoke of the glory (*doxa*) he shared with the Father from eternity past (John 17:5). Furthermore, Jesus describes himself as one whom God sent into the world on a mission of saving mercy (John 4:34; 5:24, 36). The Lord affirms his eternal preexistence and incarnation by representing himself as the Son of Man who came down from heaven (John 3:13, 31). He is the true bread that descended from the heavenly realm to impart spiritual life to all who will receive him (John 6:32–33, 38, 41,

51). John possessed the unshakeable conviction that Jesus Christ is God's gift of life to the world (John 3:16). He was not a man raised up to represent God, but the divine Son who had come from the Father's presence (John 16:27–28).

John concurs with Paul that the express purpose of the incarnation is the salvation of sinners: "We have seen and testify that the Father has sent his Son to be the Savior of the world" (1 John 4:14; cf. vv. 9–10). Equally directly, John states that Christ "appeared so that he might take away our sins" (1 John 3:5) and "to destroy the devil's work" (1 John 3:8). In a profound sense, Jesus was born and lived that he might die (John 12:27).

Although John does not explicitly mention the virgin birth, it is likely that "the beloved disciple" had some knowledge of Jesus' unique entry into the world. John 8 offers hints that support this hypothesis. At the Festival of Tabernacles the Pharisees raised questions about Jesus' paternity (v. 19) and suggested that he was illegitimately born (v. 41), perhaps of mixed Jewish-Gentile blood (v. 48). Jesus' consistent response throughout this dialogue with the Jews was that his paternity lay with God (vv. 19, 27–28, 38, 49). Indeed, Jesus insisted that the One whom the Pharisees claimed to be their God was none other than his Father (v. 54).

Other New Testament Writings

The opening verses of Hebrews describe the incarnation as the consummation of all God's previous revelations in history: "In these last days he [i.e., God] has spoken [elalēsen] to us by his Son" (Heb. 1:2). Christ came forth from heaven and lived as a man to be the final and definitive disclosure of God (cf. Heb. 3:1, which denotes Jesus as "the apostle"). Peter attests Christ's eternal sonship and incarnation with similar imagery: "He was chosen before the creation of the world, but was revealed [phanerōthentos] in these last times for your sake" (1 Peter 1:20). The verb is the aorist passive participle of phaneroō, to "make plain," or to "manifest," and denotes the historic revelation of God in Christ at Bethlehem. The writer of Hebrews did not doubt, however, that Christ eternally preexisted his manifestation as a man (Heb. 1:10; 7:3; 13:8).

In constructing his case for the superiority of Christ's priesthood, Hebrews teaches that Christ became a man and lived a truly human life, participating in all humanity's experiences, sin excepted (Heb. 4:15). To this end, in Hebrews 2 the author makes several statements about the *nature* of Christ's humiliation. (1) At the incarnation God "made [him] a little lower than the angels" (v. 9). We understand the word "lower" (brachy) in the sense of degree rather than of duration, in keeping with the text of Psalm 8:5. The expression may be a Hebraism meaning simply "became man." (2) Christ "shared in their humanity," i.e., he fully participated in our "flesh and blood" (v. 14). In order to attain true solidarity with those he came to save, Christ voluntarily became a human as we are. (3) Christ entered the stream of "Abraham's descendants" (v. 16). The Christ who came to save mortals, not angels, became a member of a particular people, the family of Abraham (Matt. 1:1). Finally, (4) At the incarnation, Christ "had to be made like his brothers in every way" (v. 17). To redeem people, it was necessary (note the verb opheilō, expressing obligation) that Christ should become all that we are, and that he should share our pain, sorrows, and trials.

From this discussion of the nature of the incarnation, the author passes to a consideration of the *purpose* for which God became man. His exposition here is even more extensive. (1) Christ left heaven and became a man "so that by the grace of God he might taste death for everyone" (v. 9). The overarching purpose of the incarnation was the concrete fact that Christ should die for sinners (cf. Heb. 9:26). (2) Christ entered time and space in order "to bring many sons to glory" (v. 10). As the pathfinder of salvation, Christ descended to earth that he might direct many believers upward to heaven. (3) Christ became man so that both he and they might be "of the same family" (v. 11). The incarnation opened the door to a new relationship between God and persons. Through faith aliens and enemies now become privileged members of his household. (4) Christ entered the world and died so that "he might destroy him who holds the power of death—that is, the devil" (v. 14). Paradoxically, the death of Christ destroyed Satan and the grip of death the evil one holds over the human race. The Puritan writer John Owen developed this motif in his classic essay *The Death of Death in the Death of Christ*. (5) Christ lived and died to "free those who all their lives were held in slavery by their fear of death" (v. 15). Christ means liberation from the prince of terrors, the fear of death and nothingness. Lastly, (6) Christ became man "that he might make atonement for the sins of the people" (v. 17). Here again, the express purpose of the incarnation is stated to be the propitiatory sacrifice Christ offered on the cross.

SYSTEMATIC FORMULATION

In accord with the redemptive plan (vol. 1, chap. 8), the Father sent his unique Son into the world to do for the lost what they could not do for themselves. In understanding the incarnation what elements of the alternative views may be integrated in a coherent doctrine accounting for all the lines of relevant scriptural data? Consider first the incarnation's visible indicator.

The Sign of Jesus' Virgin Birth

Beyond any reasonable doubt in the first century in Bethlehem a woman named Mary conceived and gave birth to an actual baby named Jesus. Bultmann's view that we can know almost nothing about the historical Jesus has been discredited. The continued discovery of early evidence renders less and less probable the hypothesis that the story of Jesus' birth was a later church invention. The evidence does not support a naïve belief in everything handed down by tradition, but a historical realism.[81] The Gospel accounts are written by contemporaries who investigated what happened (Luke 1:1–4). Those who considered Jesus a literal baby included not only Mary, but also his foster father Joseph, the shepherds, the angels, the Magi, and King Herod. Other evidence for the historicity of Jesus remains to this day—the change in the day of worship from Saturday to Sunday, the change in the calendar, the writing of the New Testament, and the origin of the Christian church. To these critical considerations for the historical Jesus we may add the theological case that Matthew 1 and Luke 1 are part of the informational revelation supernaturally inspired by the all-knowing God (volume 1, pages 115–16; 146–64, supports an informational revelation and supernatural inspiration of the Bible as a whole, including Matthew 1 and Luke 1). The interpretive issues of the birth narratives being minimal, the Bible clearly teaches the fact of Jesus' actual birth.

Mary's conception of Jesus was a biological miracle. Matthew's record indicates that her conception of Jesus was not the result of ordinary sexual intercourse. Mary's pregnancy was extraordinary, according to Matthew, for at least three reasons: (1) She conceived prior to union with Joseph (Matt. 1:18). (2) Joseph, being "a righteous man," acted as an honorable fiancé would under the circumstances. He "did not want to expose her to public disgrace . . . [and] had in mind to divorce her quietly (v. 19). (3) After he had considered divorce, an angel of the Lord appeared to him in a dream and said, "Joseph son of David, do not be afraid to take Mary home as your wife, because what is conceived in her is from the Holy Spirit" (v. 20).

Doctor Luke's investigative report confirms the miraculous conception of Jesus for similar reasons. After the angel Gabriel's announcement of Jesus' coming birth to Mary, she exclaimed, "How will this be, since I am a virgin?" (Luke 1:34). Luke records the angel's explanation: "The Holy Spirit will come upon you, and the power of the Most High will overshadow you. . . . For nothing is impossible with God" (vv. 35, 37). Explicitly both Matthew and Luke deny any role of a man in Mary's conception of Jesus, and both attribute her pregnancy to an extraordinary creative act of the Holy Spirit. The virgin conception and birth of Jesus was indeed a "mighty act" of God, a "wonder," and a "sign."

Why is the rest of the New Testament silent about the virgin birth? Some find allusions to the virgin birth in Matthew 1:16; Luke 3:23; John 1:13; and Galatians 4:4. These passages are marvelously consistent with the fact once it is granted on more explicit evidence, but they are not the best texts for establishing the fact. The silence of the gospels of Mark and John does not contradict the teaching of Matthew and Luke but presupposes them. Mark makes no reference even to Jesus' childhood but begins with Jesus' baptism, and so reference to the birth is not part of his purpose. John's later emphasis on the incarnation could assume the explicit teaching on the conception and birth of Matthew and Luke. It seems clear that the major reason for a lack of other references in the recorded messages in Acts is that this information was not part of the apostles' initial message (kerygma) for unbelievers. As J. V. L. Casserley concluded, "The New Testament evidence is not as strong in the case of the virgin birth as it is in that of the resurrection. There is, however, no evidence at all for any other alternative."[82] If we are to judge importance by the number of verses on a topic, then we should note that there is more specific material about the virgin birth than about the creation of mankind in the divine image or the Lord's Supper. Clearly the number of verses on a subject does not determine its importance.

No serious textual difficulties with the extensive passages in Matthew and Luke are found. Matthew's and Luke's accounts of the virgin birth are unquestionably genuine parts of their respective gospels. And "the gospels containing these narratives are genuine documents of the Apostolic Age. The texts of these narratives have come down to us in their integrity."[83] More affirmatively, as J. Gresham Machen said, "it is perfectly clear that the New Testament teaches the virgin birth of Christ; about that there can be no manner of doubt. There is no serious question as to the interpretation of the Bible at this point. . . . The only question is whether in making that representation the Bible is true or false."[84] An initial skepticism of such a miracle may be expected. We ought not invent miracles where evidence for them is lacking. It is healthy to ask for explicit biblical evidence. But an initial skepticism is not a good reason for ignoring or denying a conclusive case from two extensive passages.

Although a virgin conception is an impossibility for reductive naturalists and pantheists (except as myth), for theists it is genuinely *possible*. Creation's regular laws do not form a closed system (as we found in studies of creation and providence). The Creator and Sustainer of the ordinary processes can, for purposes of recovering his lost people, work in extraordinary ways. God worked miraculously to deliver his people from Egyptian oppressors. A virgin conception and birth may sound like a mere myth to people who assume the absolute uniformity of nature and who think nature is God. But the Lord of nature is not bound by nature. The sustainer of nature can choose to act unusually through it or independently of its usual processes.

The virgin birth is *not an isolated miracle* but one of a series of mighty acts for redeeming God's people. The series of redemptive acts are the specific messianic predictions of the Old Testament made hundreds of years in advance, and specifically, the prediction of his supernatural birth as a "sign" (Isa. 7:14). Supernaturally Jesus healed the blind, the lame, and the lepers. Supernaturally he raised the dead and calmed the storms. Supernaturally he was transfigured before his disciples. Supernaturally he was raised from the dead, and supernaturally he ascended into heaven. As Ramm has said, "The virgin birth is part of a complex of doctrines (rooted in events) where each doctrine supports the rationale of the other."[85] Since the Messiah's ministry concluded with a miraculous resurrection and ascension, it is appropriate that he entered the world miraculously.

The Significance of Jesus' Virgin Birth

Christ's virgin birth provides a case study in the impossibility of totally separating the historical events from their theological meanings. The sign of the virgin conception (Isa. 7:14) signifies the once-for-all supernatural incarnation of God's eternal Word or Son. We need not decide whether the writers of the Gospels were either historians or theologians. They were both historians and theologians. Their accounts of miracles in general were not only "mighty acts" of God and "wonders" but also "signs" pointing to spiritual truths. So the uniqueness of Jesus' birth was a "sign" that he was not only a human son but also the long-awaited God-sent Messiah on a special mission. Consider several aspects of the significance of Jesus' virgin conception.

1. Jesus' virgin conception and birth signify the *moral miracle* of his *unique holiness*. The angels' announcement of the Spirit's overshadowing added, "So the holy one to be born will be called the Son of God" (Luke 1:35). From conception Jesus was set apart from sinners for the redemption of sinners. It is true, as Ramm suggests, that people who are not sinless may be called holy. But the designation can also refer to God who is sinless, and the context bears out the divine holiness involving sinlessness. Any naturally born person since the Fall has sins (1 John 1:8–10) because a bad tree (heart) brings forth bad fruit (Matt. 12:33–35). But Jesus challenged anyone to prove him guilty of sin (John 8:46). John, who may have known him best, could write, "You know that he appeared so that he might take away our sins. And in him is no sin" (1 John 3:5). A person born of a fallen woman, although tempted for many years as we are, never yielded to the enticements! At the beginning of his human existence Jesus' supernatural conception draws attention to his supernatural sinlessness.

The fact that Jesus had no fallen human father does not mean that he lacked humanity. There is no reason to deny that Mary was fully human or that her child was fully human. To imply that the Holy Spirit could not supernaturally supply the male contribution to the conception of the child is unjustifiable, since the Spirit was involved in the creation of human life in the beginning. Because he is Spirit no physical process is appropriately imagined in the Holy Spirit's "overshadowing" of Mary. The chaste biblical narrative differs greatly from pagan myths of "gods" having intercourse with women.

2. Jesus Christ's virgin conception also serves as a sign of his *deity*. "So the holy one to be born will be called *the Son of God*" (Luke 1:35, italics mine). He would also be called "Immanuel—which means God with us" (Matt. 1:23). An ordinarily born person did not have a previous existence, let alone exist as a member of the Godhead. Had Jesus been born in the usual way, he might have symbolically represented some aspects of God's nature, but he would not have actually been the eternal second Person of the Trinity. The sign of his supernatural birth indicates the supernaturalness of his Person.

3. Jesus Christ's virgin birth draws attention to the eternal Son's *incarnation*. The assertion that the invisible God became flesh cannot be entirely verified by the senses—God cannot be seen. The supernatural aspects of the conception and birth signify Jesus' extraordinary eternal existence; the natural aspects point to his actual involvement with humans in literal flesh and blood. The gestation, birth, and growth processes are *indicii* that here was no mere mythical figure but a literal person in an actual human body. The possibility of full humanness without sin is indicated by Adam and Eve before the Fall and by believers' future glorified state.

4. Jesus' virgin birth from his beginning points up his *redemptive mission*. The angel said, "She will give birth to a son, and you are to give him the name

Jesus, because he will save his people from their sins" (Matt. 1:21). Had Jesus been ordinarily born, he would have been a sinful member of the fallen race and represented by its first head, Adam, in whom he would be judged guilty of sin (Rom. 5:16, 18). Jesus came, however, to save the people whom God called out of the world, and he did so by becoming their head. Jesus' supernatural birth indicates that he is not one more member of the depraved, condemned, and alienated Adamic race, but the head of a new order composed of those who have become new creatures by God's grace.

5. The fact of the virgin birth also *confirms the reliability of the prophetic word*. "All this took place to fulfill what the Lord had said through the prophet: 'The virgin will be with child and will give birth to a son' " (Matt. 1:22–23; cf. Isa. 7:14). One's belief in Christ's virgin birth is a test case of one's conviction that "nothing is impossible with God" (Luke 1:37) and of one's belief in God's promises of the supernatural. Faith in the coming birth of a son in elderly Abraham's case involved "being fully persuaded that God had power to do what he had promised" (Rom. 4:21). Similarly Mary became fully persuaded of the prophetic word issued before Jesus' birth that the messianic servant would be born of her though she was a virgin. After the marvelous fulfillment, Christians should not be less fully persuaded that God demonstrated his power to do what he had promised!

The Importance of Jesus' Virgin Birth

Because of its rich significance, the teaching of Christ's virgin birth is *indispensable* to a biblically based Christology and soteriology. Although we can imagine other ways by which God could supernaturally have kept Jesus sinless, in historical actuality the sign of the virgin birth is nonnegotiable. Furthermore, as a highly significant part of divine revelation the story of the virgin birth is inspired and profitable. As such it needs to be taught faithfully to each generation.

Although the doctrine of the virgin birth of Christ is necessary for understanding the implications of salvation, it is *optional evangelistically*. The truth of Jesus' birth of a virgin need not be highlighted in the initial gospel message to unbelievers. No passage of Scripture says explicitly that if you believe in Jesus' virgin birth you will receive eternal life. Each doctrine revealed in Scripture is important and profitable for its respective purposes, but not all are equally important for an initial evangelistic purpose. We need not explain every doctrine in presenting the gospel to the lost.

What, then, does the New Testament affirm that sinners must believe to be saved? This will be discussed and documented further under the subject of the verbal call. Briefly, explicit passages assert that to be saved people must believe, in fulfillment of the (Old Testament) Scriptures, that: (1) Jesus is the Christ, the Messiah, (2) he died for our sins and was buried, and (3) he rose again from the grave (1 Cor. 15:3–4). Although the Scriptures mention those doctrines many times, not one verse asserts that those who believe in the virgin birth will be saved. In all of his conversations with sinners, Jesus did not ask them to accept this doctrine in order to receive eternal life. In all the recorded evangelistic messages of the apostles in Acts, none call for belief in the virgin birth for justification. None of the epistles, furthermore, include the doctrine in summations of the heart of the gospel. Hence we conclude that we need not include teaching on the virgin birth in our initial evangelistic presentations.

Furthermore, to make acceptance of Christ's virgin birth a condition of salvation is to hinder little children from coming into the kingdom of heaven. By way of illustration, at a minister's meeting in Denver in the 1960s a noted preacher declared vehemently that no one could be saved who did not believe that Christ was born of a virgin! He went on to label any seminary that did not teach that truth "liberal." Later in the message the pastor told of his own conversion at the age of six. When he sat down in a pew just ahead of us, a colleague leaned over to ask him, "At the age of six did you know what a virgin was?"

Although one who has not heard of Jesus' virgin birth need not believe it to be saved, it would seem improbable that an adult who has received Jesus as Lord and has become aware of the explicitness of the biblical support and its theological importance would persist in denying its truth. Before the New Testament was available there were no doubt Christians who had not heard of the virgin birth. This fact, however, provides no excuse for rejecting the biblical evidence for the virgin birth. A Christian does not knowingly and deliberately reject an explicit biblical teaching without accountability to divine judgment.

Mary, the Mother of Jesus

No biblical or other evidence gives us reason to believe that Mary was immaculately conceived or miraculously born. Hence we may conclude that she, like all other persons, had a fallen father and mother and from them received a sinful human nature. The biblical teaching indicates that the moral miracle at his conception by the Holy Spirit freed Jesus, not her, from a sinful nature. The child, not Mary, is "the holy one" (Luke 1:35).

Mary, nevertheless, was "highly favored" by God (Luke 1:28) and "found favor with God" (v. 30). She was "blessed" (v. 42) to be chosen from among all the women of the world to be the mother through whom God's eternal Word would become flesh. As the one highly favored to be the mother of the long-awaited Messiah, she was not a bestower of divine grace but the recipient of divine grace. A recipient of grace receives favors that are undeserved. She did not merit the privilege of giving birth to the Messiah; rather, she was chosen among women by sheer grace. Elizabeth too felt favored that the mother of her Lord should come to visit her (v. 43). Elizabeth clearly thought of Mary as a human woman, not a divine mediatrix. As a woman Mary was the mother of the Messiah to whom these godly women looked in faith for salvation. Hence Mary may be honored as the most favored woman in history but not worshiped as sinless or divine. For the real humanity of her Son, it was essential that Mary be fully human. If she were in some sense divine, that would not in any way enhance his deity. But she was indispensable to his being truly human. Since Mary was only human, we ought not worship her.

No Scripture calls Mary "the mother of God." God, being eternal and self-existent (see 1:198–200), can have no mother. Similarly God's eternal Word can have no mother, for he was with God and was God (John 1:1). Mary was the mother of Jesus' humanness, begotten supernaturally from the Holy Spirit. Because Jesus was the long-awaited Messiah, Elizabeth was able to speak honorifically of Mary as "the mother of my Lord" (Luke 1:43). Warfield explains, "Clearly she intends to express by the designation the height of at least Messianic glory; but it does not seem obvious that her thought went beyond the delegated glory of the divine representative."[86] Mary rejoiced in her privilege (vv. 46–47), but she also recognized her "humble state" as God's servant (v. 48).

Although the Scriptures emphasize Mary's virginity until Jesus' birth, scriptural support cannot be found for the Roman Catholic tradition of her perpetual virginity. We have good reason to believe that after the birth of Jesus Joseph and Mary lived together as man and wife and had a family. Jesus' "brothers" are mentioned several times (Matt. 12:46–50 and parallels). Four brothers are named (James, Joseph, Judas, and Simon), and his sisters (plural) are also indicated (Mark 6:3). A document, "History of Joseph the Carpenter," written in Egypt in the fourth century to glorify Joseph and foster his cult, alleges that Joseph was a widower with children at the time of his engagement to Mary, a girl of twelve.[87] The reliable scriptural accounts could easily have mentioned this fact if it were true, so it seems improbable. At any rate, even if Joseph had been a widower with some children by a previous marriage, he and Mary apparently had other children of their own.

In Protestant churches and homes Mary can appropriately be honored—not only on Mother's Day but also on other occasions. Her favor and blessedness among women need not be ignored because of Roman Catholic tendencies to exalt her to a mediatrix. "When the time had fully come, God sent his Son, born of a woman, born under law, to redeem those under law, that we might receive the full rights of sons" (Gal. 4:4). As we exalt the Redeemer, we ought not forget that in the Father's timing the Messiah was "born of woman," and that he was born of this woman, Mary. "After all," Paul Jewett has observed, "if their [Roman Catholic] theology of the Virgin is too high, maybe ours is too low—if indeed we have any theology of Mary at all."[88] An effective Protestant corrective to an unbiblical Roman theology of Mary is not lack of thought about her. The antidote is a biblically founded theology of Mary!

Negatively, a biblically informed Protestant theology of Mary will not allow attention to be taken away from the centrality of Jesus as the incarnate Son of God, the Savior, and the one Mediator. In patristic tradition from Ignatius to Aquinas, "The virgin birth of Jesus gradually became separated from Christology and became attached to Mariology."[89] Because of the popularity of pagan sources the church leaders felt a necessity to Christianize the "Lady," the "Queen," and the "Mother."[90] Faced with similar pressures from some radical feminists today who virtually worship Mary as a goddess, contemporary Protestants need to resist paganizing the faith.

Affirmatively, a Protestant theology of Mary incorporates several points: (1) It regards her as a primary example of the God-given dignity of women. (2) She provides a prime exhibit of a pure, thoughtful, believing, and spiritually vital daughter of Abraham. Her marvelous song of praise reflects Spirit-illumined receptivity to God's Word and a personal relationship with the living Lord of all (Luke 1:46–55). (3) She exemplifies God's strategy of using human agents and women in particular in the accomplishment of his holy and loving purposes. (4) She also exhibits human willingness to accept God's Word and do God's bidding at great personal risk. (5) Mary was betrothed, indicating the importance of a family and home in which to bring up Jesus. (6) With a devout engaged couple, God worked a miracle, signifying the sanctity of conception and birth in the security of the marriage commitment. Synthesizing all of these factors, a Protestant theology of Mary emphasizes God's great esteem for a devout woman in bringing to pass the greatest event in history—the incarnation of God's eternal Word.

Joseph, the Foster Father of Jesus

To complete the family picture we need also to formulate a brief theology of Joseph. Mary was "pledged to be married to Joseph, but before they came together, she was found to be with child through the Holy Spirit" (Matt. 1:18). Even though there were no sexual relations during a Jewish betrothal period, the betrothal could be broken only by divorce. Upon hearing of Mary's pregnancy, Joseph was distressed. He was a righteous man, but he was also considerate and did not want to expose Mary to public disgrace; therefore he sought to divorce her quietly (v. 19). Joseph received the message from the angel of the Lord explaining that the baby was conceived by the Holy Spirit and that he should name him Jesus, because he would save his people from their sins (vv. 20–21). Joseph did what the Lord had commanded and took Mary home as his wife. He had no union with her until she gave birth to a son (vv. 24–25). The family went from Nazareth to Bethlehem to register in his hometown for the census of Quirinius (governor of Syria) because Joseph belonged to the line of David (Luke 2:1–2). Jesus had the right to the throne of David through his legal father, Joseph. When the shepherds came to Bethlehem to see the newborn baby, they found Joseph with Mary and Jesus (v. 16). Luke's genealogy, emphasizing the line of Mary, the blood relative, notes that at the beginning of Jesus' ministry when he was thirty years of age, "he was *the son, so it was thought, of Joseph*" (Luke 3:23, italics mine).

Although he was not the natural father of Jesus, Joseph served as his foster father. Joseph and Mary together served as faithful spiritual parents. Both Joseph and Mary took Jesus to Jerusalem and consecrated him to the Lord (vv. 22–24). When Simeon blessed them and spoke of Jesus' coming greatness (vv. 28–32), the child's "father and mother marveled at what was said about him" (v. 33). Joseph and Mary did everything at his dedication that was required by the Law of the Lord (v. 39). The genealogy in Matthew shows that Jesus was the legal son of Joseph and so was in the line of descent from David and Abraham (Matt. 1:1, 16). When an angel warned Joseph in a dream to flee to Egypt to avoid Herod's attempt to kill the Jewish Messiah, Joseph, sensitive to the Lord's leading, obeyed and moved to Egypt (2:13–14). Again at the leading of the Lord he moved the family back to Israel. For the safety of the child he was led not to settle in Judea but went to Galilee and settled in Nazareth (vv. 19–23). At the Lord's direction Joseph moved the family three times.

Every year Joseph took the whole family to Jerusalem for the Feast of the Passover (Luke 2:41). When at twelve years of age after the Feast Jesus did not leave Jerusalem with his parents, they returned to find him in dialogue with the teachers at the temple. Joseph and Mary had been anxious about him, and when they saw him in the temple, they were astonished at his knowledge (vv. 45–48). After Jesus' baptism he taught in the synagogues, and when he read from the scroll of Isaiah and spoke of its fulfillment in Nazareth, people were amazed at his wisdom and miraculous powers. Understandably they asked, "Isn't this the carpenter's son? . . . Where did this man get all these things?" (Matt. 13:55–56). From these brief indications, the carpenter-father exhibited a sensitivity to the Lord's leading and a faithfulness in worship that contributed to Jesus' early development physically and spiritually. Theologically, Joseph furnishes for all fathers, and especially foster fathers, a worthy example of spiritual faithfulness and unquestioning obedience to the

Lord's leading. Together, Joseph and Mary exemplify the values of raising children in a home characterized by spiritual fidelity.

In sum, although the fact that Christ was born of the virgin Mary need not be included in every tract for the lost, our biblical and systematic research has shown that his birth was indeed a mighty act of the Holy Spirit, a wonder, and a sign bearing great theological significance. The actuality of the virginal conception dramatically signifies Christ's sinlessness, deity, incarnation, and mission to save the lost. The fact also exhibits the reliability of one of the most astounding predictions in the prophetic Word. The favoring of Mary to bear and nurture the Messiah displays God's esteem of women and one of their crucial roles in the coming of the divine kingdom on earth. In addition, the account reflects Joseph's character as spiritually perceptive, just, and considerate. Partly as a result of the providential spiritual influence of both Joseph and Mary, Jesus "grew and became strong; he was filled with wisdom, and the grace of God was upon him" (Luke 2:40). The fact that "Jesus grew in wisdom and stature and in favor with God and men" (v. 52) cannot be entirely unrelated to his parents' loving care and spiritual example.

Challenges to Understanding the Incarnation

We turn attention now from the "sign" of the supernatural birth of a baby boy to the even more dramatic event it primarily signified—the incarnation of the second person of the Trinity! The term "incarnation" can be traced to the Latin version of John 1:14 and has been commonly used since the fourth century. In the narrow sense "incarnation" refers to the initial event in which the eternal Word "became flesh," the beginning of his first advent to earth. In a broader sense "incarnation" may refer to the entire experience of human life into which he entered, including the facts of his resurrection and his ascension with his human nature to heaven. In this chapter we generally use the term in its narrower sense, the beginning of his life on earth. The rest of Jesus' life will be in view in the three chapters that follow.

Understanding how God could become a human has presented a great challenge, as pointed up by the number of alternative views. How did a member of the invisible Godhead become visible? How could the eternal even enter time let alone experience time? Could the eternal Son of God be born a human infant? Could the omniscient One grow in knowledge and wisdom? Answers to questions like these are complex because they involve many factors, such as one's grasp of the relevant implications of trinitarianism, the eternal God's relation to all temporal events, whether the accounts of a divine being in history can be interpreted literally or must be taken figuratively, and the compatibility of the divine archetype with a human image-bearer.

At first the case seems strong for a figurative interpretation of the incarnation. It seems impossible for the infinite to become literally finite, the omnipotent to become a weak baby, the omniscient to grow in knowledge as a child, and the omnipresent to walk from one town to another. Immersed in a naturalistic scientific mentality, we are suspicious of the paranormal and of any claims to be in touch with it. Even those who believe in a tri-personal God often restrict the members of the Trinity to their regular activities through nature and take figuratively or mythically some aspects of what the Bible reports that God in fact did. Furthermore the story of God's becoming man through a virgin may seem reminiscent of Hindu and Greek mythology. It sounds like the appearance of springtime, the rising again of life in nature, or a handsome prince coming from above to rescue a sleeping princess.

The Cognitive Significance of the Incarnation

Christmas is first of all a story about God the Father and secondly a story about Jesus. God has not left us to our fallenness and deserved judgment. God mercifully withholds deserved punishment and graciously gives the world's greatest gift. The heavenly Father sent us his unique eternal Son. "Thanks be to God for his indescribable gift!" (2 Cor. 9:15).

The eternal person of the Son took on himself a real human nature. Christ's primary purpose in coming to earth to visit us was to save the lost. The redemptive action seems so important that some relationalists and functionalists have lost sight of the One who accomplished it. The crucial point, they maintain, is what Jesus did, not who he was (in his metaphysical or ontological being). They seem to overlook the fact that the value of Jesus' dynamic work depends on who he *was*. The question Jesus asked must still be answered: "Who do people say the Son of Man is?" Surely he would have been unsatisfied with the reply, "An unknown 'X'."

Essential to the concept of the incarnation is the Father's sending of his precious Son. This implies Jesus' preexistence as the eternal second person of the Trinity (see I:272–75). Although everything is made *by* God, and all humans are made *in* God's image, only Jesus of Nazareth is eternally begotten *of* God. So the coming of the eternal Word into the literal world of Mary in the literal flesh of a baby exhibits God's actual loving presence with us in spite of our sin. "For what the law was powerless to do in that it was weakened by the sinful nature, God did by sending his own Son in the likeness of sinful man, to be a sin offering" (Rom. 8:3; cf. Gal. 4:4). As Wolfhart Pannenberg said, "Jesus was always one with God, not just after a certain date in his life. . . . Were it otherwise, Jesus would not be in person the one revelation of the eternal God."[91] At the beginning of his life Jesus descended from his preexistent trinitarian state and at the end of his advent to earth the glorified One ascended back to the Father.

Although in thought we can distinguish the eternal Son from the man Jesus, "the eternity of the Sonship and the earthly human mode of Jesus' existence are parts of a single, concrete existence."[92] Jesus is the Christ in human flesh. Christology involves the conjunction of the two. And it involves the order of movement from God to man. Christology cannot be adequately done from "below." It must coherently account for the evidence both for his humanness below and for his divinity from "above."

Prophetic Anticipation of the Incarnation

The preparatory movement for the incarnation began centuries before with the Old Testament messianic predictions. The eternal antecedents (in Logos Christologies) must not obscure the historical antecedents in the prophetic writings. The incarnation is the eschatological fulfillment of specific predictions and varied allusions to the effect that God would send the Messiah through the line of Eve, Abraham, and David. The incarnation is also a fulfillment of a Jewish philosophy of history. Thinkers who do not have the Old Testament hope for the last days can easily consider the descent and ascent of Christ a myth from a fantasy world, and a rift may be imagined between the eternal Christ and the historical Jesus. Apart from Israel's messianic hope, the birth and ascension of Jesus become merely illustrations of the significance of life in general. From within the context of Old Testament eschatological promises, however, the announcement that the Son of God became man in Jesus of Nazareth becomes a dramatic fulfillment. Divine promise and fulfillment permeates biblical history coherently with a view of revelation in both information and act.

The damaged divine image in mankind after the Fall still included an obscure consciousness of his original happy condition and an earnest desire to regain it. This was insufficient of itself, however, to effect the great end of his being—fellowship with his Creator. Why did God not send his Son immediately after the Fall? Apparently there needed to be a cultivation of a state in which at least some people would be receptive to him. Gentiles were driven to see their need by the law written on their hearts, and the Jews by Moses' law. By the law the sinner became aware of sin, desired freedom from it and felt the need for redemption. After the earlier illustrations of judgment and grace, God called Abraham to be the father of the people through whom his Son would appear at the appointed time. He strengthened their faith by visible signs of his gracious appearance in many wonderful works. And he sent messages in varied ways by his prophets one after another. "Frequent new revelation kept the expectation alive and rendered it continually more and more definite. "And thus," Hengstenberg argued, "the doctrine of a coming Redeemer, even when partially misunderstood, became the soul and centre of all theocratic expectations."[93]

Summarizing the messianic predictions discussed in the Scripture section, a descendant of Eve would defeat Satan (Gen. 3:15). Then one in the line of

Abraham would bring blessing to the whole earth (Gen. 12:3; 18:18; 22:18). As a son of David, furthermore, he would rule on David's throne forever (2 Sam. 7:12–16; Isa. 9:6–7; 11:1; Jer. 23:5–6). And he would be born in Bethlehem (Mic. 5:2). He would be called Immanuel and would be born of a virgin (Isa. 7:14). The Septuagint Greek translation, compiled during the second and third centuries B.C., used the Greek word for virgin (*parthenos*) to translate the Hebrew ' *almāh,* as do the Dead Sea Scrolls, and some of the rabbis from before the time of Christ.[94]

What of those who with Schleiermacher and others find in the Old Testament only indistinct longings and feelings of the need for redemption? Hengstenberg argues that the Lord Jesus Christ and his apostles, although they referred to the Old Testament in different ways (direct quotations, allusions, and similar principles and events), believed the Old Testament Scriptures to contain genuine predictions. Although even after the resurrection the minds of the disciples on the road to Emmaus were kept from recognizing Jesus, he said to them, " 'How foolish you are, and how slow of heart to believe all that the prophets have spoken! Did not the Christ have to suffer these things and then enter his glory?' And beginning with Moses and all the Prophets, he explained to them what was said in all the Scriptures concerning himself" (Luke 24:25–27).

Earlier Jesus had pointed out how people diligently study the Scriptures that testify about him, yet refuse to come to him to have life (John 5:39–40). "If you believed Moses," Jesus said, "you would believe me, for *he wrote about me*" (v. 46, italics mine). Jesus added, "But since you do not believe what he wrote, how are you going to believe what I say?" (v. 47). When Jesus was about to be arrested, he said, "It is written: 'And he was numbered

with the transgressors' [Isa. 53:12]; and I tell you that this *must* be fulfilled in me. Yes, what is written about me is reaching its fulfillment" (Luke 22:37, italics mine). "But the Scripture *must* be fulfilled" (Mark 14:49, italics mine). To appreciate the extent of the Old Testament materials, see Hengstenberg's 699-page exposition and defense of Old Testament messianic predictions in his classic *Christology of the Old Testament.*[95] The righteous, devout, and Spirit-illumined Simeon, who waited for the consolation of Israel before his death, saw the infant Messiah in the temple, took him in his arms, and exclaimed, "My eyes have seen your salvation . . . a light for revelation to the Gentiles and for glory to your people Israel" (Luke 2:25–32). Anna also "gave thanks to God and spoke about the child to all who were looking forward to the redemption of Jerusalem" (v. 38).

Was Jesus Conscious of His Incarnation?

Did Jesus believe himself to be the Messiah? Some naturalists deny that he was conscious of his incarnate nature and messianic mission. Some allege that the idea developed in his mind gradually, and some think he used the suggestion as a literary device to gain acceptance for his views. But Jews, Muslims, and others who deny that Jesus ever claimed to be essentially one with the Father, lack a coherent interpretation of the evidence to be laid out in the following paragraphs.

Jesus used unique *messianic titles* for himself. He spoke of himself as "the Christ," "the Lord," "the Son of God," "the Son of Man," and "the Savior." The detailed significance of these self-designations as developed by Geerhardus Vos in *The Self-Disclosure of Jesus* supports his unique identification of himself with his heavenly Father.[96]

Jesus of Nazareth referred to his uniquely divine origin and nature. As "the Son of Man" he claimed that he alone had "[come] from heaven" (John 3:13) and that God "gave his one and only Son" (v. 16). As God's Son he was begotten (of the same nature as the Father), not a creation out of nothing. Jesus said to the Samaritan woman at the well, "If you knew the gift of God and who it is that asks you for a drink, you would have asked him and he would have given you living water" (4:10). She said, "I know that Messiah is coming. When he comes, he will explain everything to us." Then Jesus confessed, "I who speak to you am he" (4:25–26). The Jews tried to kill him because "he was even calling God his own Father, and making himself equal with God" (5:18). Again the Jews understood the import of Jesus' claims for himself and grumbled among themselves saying, "Is this not Jesus, the son of Joseph, whose father and mother we know? How can he say, 'I came down from heaven'?" (6:42). But Jesus continued to say, "I am the living bread that came down from heaven" (vv. 50–51, 58). "The living Father sent me" (v. 57). "What if you see the Son of Man ascend to where he was before!" (v. 62). When the Jews said they knew where he was from, Jesus replied, "I am not here on my own, but he who sent me is true. You do not know him, but I know him because I am from him and he sent me" (7:28–29). The Father "sent me" (8:16, 18). "You are from below; I am from above. You are of this world; I am not of this world" (v. 23). "I came from God" (v. 42).

The Jesus of history spoke of his *preexistence as God.* Jesus said, "Before Abraham was born, I am!" (v. 58). What his first-century hearers understood him to mean became evident quickly. They sought to stone him for blasphemy, "because you," they said, "a mere man, claim to be God" (10:33). From these relatively few passages from the Gospels it becomes evident that Jesus was conscious of being uniquely incarnate and not of this world (not born of the flesh—John 3:6), but virgin-born. His conscious understanding of himself is not what developed in time; only progressively did he choose to disclose his divine nature and mission.

Jesus taught his disciples about his unique *messianic mission.* He said, "The Father judges no one, but has entrusted all judgment to the Son, that all may honor the Son just as they honor the Father. He who does not honor the Son does not honor the Father who sent him" (John 5:22–23). "I seek not to please myself but him who sent me" (v. 30). "I have testimony weightier than that of John. For the very work that the Father has given me to finish, and which I am doing, testifies that the Father has sent me" (v. 36). "I have come down from heaven not to do my will but to do the will of him who sent me" (6:38). Confidently he sets his teaching above that of all others when he says, "But I tell you" (Matt. 5:22, cf. 26, 28). He came to be more than a great prophetic teacher and a sterling example of what he taught: he said he had come into the world "to seek and to save what was lost" (Luke 19:10) by giving his life "as a ransom for many" (Mark 10:45). Early in his ministry he anticipated his death for the lost (Matt. 9:15; Mark 2:20; Luke 5:35). After Peter's recognition of Jesus' messiahship, "Jesus began to explain to his disciples that he must go to Jerusalem and suffer many things . . . and that he must be killed and on the third day be raised to life" (Matt. 16:21). On two other recorded occasions Jesus prepared them for his betrayal and death (Matt. 17:22–23; 20:17–19). Christ envisioned not only the event but also its meaning: "For even the Son of Man did not come to be served, but to serve, and to give his life as a ransom for many" (Mark 10:45). He gave his life not simply as an example of altruism, but as the price of purchasing our freedom from sin. Jesus anticipated not only the fact of the atonement but also a "theory" of its meaning.

In sum, throughout his ministry Jesus applied messianic titles to himself, spoke of his divine origin, taught his divine nature and preexistence with God, and explained his messianic mission. We cannot with intellectual integrity redate and rewrite all these converging lines of evidence to fit a naturalistic denial of Jesus' messianic consciousness. The most adequate account of the historical evidence is that Jesus did indeed exhibit a consciousness of both his divine origin and his messianic mission.

The Incarnate Son's Self-Limitations

To report that God's eternal Son became human is for Paul to say that he "made himself nothing" (Phil. 2:7). Theologians seem to find it easier to discover what the emptying (kenōsis) does not mean than what it did mean for the One equal with God to make himeelf "nothing." A spectrum of proposals deserve consideration.

1. In becoming a mere human and a servant, the Son of God gave up *all* of his divine attributes (Godet, Clarke, Mackintosh). But had Christ given up his divine attributes, he would have had no continuing identity and would have been a mere human. The eternal Son left his position in glory, but did not abandon his essential equality with God (v. 6). The reductive hypothesis that he became merely human does not account for the evidence that he remained essentially one with the Father. Our view of the kenōsis must account for the

indications that he continued to be equal with the Father and "was God" (John 1:1) with all the divine attributes that make up that essence.

2. The eternal Son gave up *some* of his divine attributes—that is, the relative—while retaining the essential (Thomasius, Delitzsch). Or he gave up the natural while keeping the personal, moral, and spiritual (A. B. Bruce and D. G. Dawe). Although this understanding seems to lessen some of the problems initially, it fails to account for Jesus' continued identity as the eternal Son of God. The hypothesis fails to grasp the fact that all of the divine "attributes" are essential qualities, not accidents. By definition, attributes constitute the essence of anything. Without any attributes a thing can no longer be what it is. As essential qualities, God's attributes are not accidents that may come and go. Other evidence indicates that Christ remained the Son of God, so he must have retained all the attributes essential to his sameness of nature with God the Father. His sonship would no longer be what it was if he gave up even some of his divine characteristics.

3. In becoming a man, some suggest, the Son of God covered his divine characteristics so that to others they were completely veiled. Although he appeared as a man, his divine nature was *incognito* (Kierkegaard, Barth, and Brunner). Clearly there is a measure of truth in the statement that unillumined Israelites, having a single glimpse of Jesus walking down the street, would not be likely to exclaim, "There goes God incarnate!" But people who over a period of time heard Jesus teach, came to know his spotless character, and saw his miraculous signs were responsible for concluding that Jesus was what he claimed to be. Peter by divine enablement finally overcame his natural, fleshly resistance to Jesus' authority and affirmed, "You are the Christ, the Son of the living God" (Matt. 16:16).

At other appropriate times the veil of Jesus Christ's human nature was lifted and people saw the progressive revelation of his divine glory. Had Jesus revealed his deity all at once, he would (speaking from the human point of view) have been put to death before completing the training of the Twelve. At Cana, where he gave the sign of turning water to wine, "he revealed his glory, and his disciples put their faith in him" (John 2:11). The death of Lazarus was permitted "so that God's Son [would] be glorified through it" (John 11:4). When Jesus was about to raise Lazarus from the dead he said, "Did I not tell you that if you believed, you would see the glory of God?" (v. 40). Peter, James, and John saw Jesus transfigured and heard the Father say, "This is my Son, whom I love; with him I am well pleased. Listen to him!" (Matt. 17:2–5). So in his high priestly prayer Jesus could say, "I have given them the glory that you gave me" (John 17:22).

Had Jesus' divine nature been totally veiled, he would not have denounced the cities in which most of his miracles had been performed. Those cities will be more accountable in the day of judgment than Tyre and Sidon and Sodom (Matt. 11:20–24). Hence they must have been able to see enough signs of his messianic authority to be justly accountable and judged for their response to them! In view of this evidence, what the Gospels portray is not a totally incognito Christ, but a human disclosing progressively visible indications of his invisible deity.

4. Some have proposed that a merely human Jesus gradually became conscious of his *progressive incarnation* (e.g., I. A. Dorner). To what degree does that hypothesis fit the data? The biblical evidence noted above indicates, not a progressive incarnation, but a progressive revelation by Jesus of his deity and messianic mission. It also shows the disciples' progressive realization of the truth of that increasing revelation.

5. Although the Son did not give up his divine powers in order to experience growth as a human, he gave up *all use* of his divine attributes (Martensen and Gore). All of his miracles on this position were done solely by the power of the Holy Spirit, in much the same way that the prophets and apostles had performed miracles. According to that reasoning, however, the "signs" would have indicated no more than they did for the prophets or apostles. They would not have pointed to his unique divine origin and messianic mission. The view does not fit instances like the transfiguration where his inherent glory was unquestionably revealed.

6. To accentuate Jesus' harmonious relationship to the Father, A. H. Strong emphasized that Jesus relinquished the *independent exercise of his divine attributes*.[97] But his use of his divine powers had always been in harmony with the Father and the Spirit. To say that Jesus gave up a contrary use of his powers seems like reporting that a husband quit beating his wife when in fact he had never beaten her. Jesus could not give up a power of contrary choice in the use of his divine capabilities if he never had acted contrary to the Father and the Spirit. And in a providential sense no human can do anything totally independent of the Father.

7. In addition to giving up his position of equality with the Father in glory (Phil. 2:6), the Son voluntarily gave up *the continuous use* of his divine powers and any *contrary uses of his human capabilities*. Humans can and do use their capabilities in ways contrary to the Father's desires. So when the Messiah adds human capabilities, it makes sense for him to choose not to exercise his human powers contrary to the Father's pleasure. Not only as he came to earth,

but throughout his ministry, he faithfully surrendered to the Father's will and yielded to the Spirit's power. "And being found in appearance as a man, he humbled himself and became obedient to death—even death on a cross!" (Phil. 2:8). Peter exclaimed about "how God anointed Jesus of Nazareth with the Holy Spirit and power, and how he went around doing good and healing all who were under the power of the devil, because God was with him" (Acts 10:38). Hence in agreement with Strong, but in a different way, we underline the harmony of Jesus' acts with the Father's pleasure and the Spirit's enablement.

Much of the time Jesus' unique divinity and messianic mission may not have been dramatically displayed, although it should have been evident in his wisdom, holiness, and love. But it seems probable that when he healed the sick, revealed what was in people, and raised the dead, he considered those appropriate occasions for revealing more of his divine capabilities. Each of these revelations of his divine nature was carried out in harmony with the leading of the Holy Spirit and in fulfillment of the Father's purposes. However, in conjunction with his claims for himself, they signified more than ordinary enablement of a human by the Holy Spirit. Jesus' signs and wonders indicated that he was more than a prophet—that he was God's unique Son. Progressively, then, he revealed his divine nature and messianic mission, and his followers realized progressively that he was exhibiting not merely prophetic but also divine power and authority.

We have not answered all questions and do not claim full comprehension of the incarnation by proposing a view that makes sense of the varied lines of evidence—an intermittent visible use of his divine attributes and a progressive revelation of his deity and mission in harmony with the Father and the Spirit.

Exactly how Jesus could choose not to use his omniscience to know the time of his return (Mark 13:32) remains unexplained. We may suggest one possibility that much of the content of his omniscient knowledge (such as the time of his return) was stored in his unconscious, while he grew in wisdom and knowledge as humans do. Although this speculation may remove some unnecessary concern about a way in which the *kenōsis* could be accomplished, many questions remain (e.g., about omniscience having unconscious memories in storage).

However much Scripture reveals of the incarnation, no human mind will be able to fully comprehend it. "Beyond all question, the mystery of godliness is great: He appeared in a body, was vindicated by the Spirit, was seen by angels, was preached among the nations, was believed on in the world, was taken up in glory" (1 Tim. 3:16). We seek to remove only unnecessary roadblocks to understanding and assenting to the incarnation. By affirming this mighty act we highlight its awesomeness and wonder. We simply adopt the interpretive hypothesis that makes the most sense of the converging lines of data. Those include Jesus' continuous sense of identity before and after Bethlehem, his essential deity, his growth as a human in body and spirit, the responsibility of those who heard and saw him to realize who he was, the progressively conclusive "signs," and the disciples' developing realization that he was indeed the eternal *Logos* on a messianic mission in human form.

We conclude, then, that what the eternal Word did *not* give up during his messianic mission was his divine essence and personal identity. What he *did* give up was his heavenly position or glory and the constant use of his divine attributes and consciousness in order to be able to grow in knowledge, obedience, etc. What he *added* was a human nature with a human consciousness that grew and became strong. Our view that Jesus limited the use of his divine attributes, except when appropriate for the accomplishment of his purposes as planned by the Father and led by the Holy Spirit, provides the most probable explanation of the givens with less severe difficulties than those faced by the other hypotheses. On our method we remain open to consider the case for any hypothesis that can account for all the relevant data with greater coherence. More on the human and divine natures of Christ will be found in the next chapter.

No illustrations of the one and only God or his unique acts are perfectly analogous at all points, but Addison Leitch suggested a useful one of the *kenōsis*.[98] When an athletic father plays softball with his young son, he plays on the boy's level. The father will throw at a speed and distance the boy can manage. Dad will hit easy grounders and run just fast enough to make the play interesting for the son. For the purposes of enjoyment and teaching his son to play ball the father gives up, not his more mature abilities, but their unrestrained exercise. Although the father could throw the ball farther and harder, he chooses to suppress his abilities in order to adapt to his son's capacities. Similarly, Jesus' divine powers were not given up but were generally not used or purposefully restricted in their use, so that he could know the human experiences of growth, learning, temptation, suffering, and even death.

By the incarnation we mean, then, that there is a personal divine absolute in history. The transcendent second person of the Trinity actually entered history as a human. At Bethlehem God's eternal Word humbled himself to became incarnate once-for-all, as confirmed by the irrepeatable sign of his virgin birth. Hence relativists need to understand that we have not only an

Absolute beyond history, but also an Absolute in history! Humans in history are not left in a sea of relativism without an anchor! God has actually entered history and progressively made himself known in the person and teaching of Christ. God spoke in history as well as in the teaching of his prophetic and apostolic spokespeople. In the inspired Scriptures, then, we have a third absolute. Evangelicals affirm faith in the transcendent God disclosed supernaturally in the Jesus of history and the teaching of Scripture.

Some Purposes of the Incarnation

In several different explicit ways the Scriptures state the varied purposes of the Son's incarnation. We will not here repeat the evidence of Jesus' own consciousness of his own nature and purposes. Consideration of other passages may strengthen the focus on his multifaceted mission. Although we have focused on the beginning of the incarnation in this chapter, the significance of the Messiah's birth can be appreciated only in the light of his entire ministry, atoning death, and triumphant exaltation.

1. The eternal Son became flesh as the great *prophet* to reveal the Father (Heb. 1:2), to make him known (John 1:18), and to manifest the divine being and characteristics in the flesh (1 Tim. 3:16). Jesus came to his own (Jews) on behalf of the truth and through their rejection he came to confirm God's promises, especially those about the inclusion of the Gentiles (Rom. 15:8–9). Jesus came to teach and personally to exhibit God's love for sinners of the whole world as well as of Israel (John 3:16). He came to fulfill the Father's mission by discipling those who would call sinners of every nation to repent, believe the gospel, develop in the church, and then reach others.

2. The eternal Word became flesh

also to become the *priest* to offer himself as the final sacrifice. He came to taste death for everyone (Heb. 2:9), to identify as a brother with the human race, and to make us holy (vv. 11–12). He came to destroy the Devil, who holds the power of death (v. 14), and to free those who all their lives were held in slavery by their fear of death (v. 15). As John put it, "The reason the Son of God appeared was to destroy the devil's work" (1 John 3:8). Christ came "as an atoning sacrifice for our sins (4:10) to satisfy the justice of God (Rom. 3:25–26). In providing for our justification, reconciliation, and redemption he came as the merciful and faithful high priest to make atonement for the sins of the people (Heb. 2:17–18).

3. The eternal second person of the Trinity also came as *king* to rule in a kingdom of inner spiritual vitality and righteousness. Christ came to reveal the grace of God, destroying death and bringing life and immortality to light through the gospel (2 Tim. 1:10). God sent his Son "that we might live through him" (1 John 4:9). So although sinners depend on the heavenly Father as their sustainer, they must be born again to have eternal life and enter Christ's spiritual kingdom (John 3:3–6). God sent his Son to redeem sinners under the law that we might receive the full rights of sons (Gal. 4:4–5). Further development of Jesus' work as prophet, priest, and king will be found in that order in each of the next three chapters.

APOLOGETIC INTERACTION

Why a "Stumbling Block" to Jews?

For many first-century Jews the problems with believing that the Messiah had come from God and that his name was *Yēšua'* (Hebrew) were neither ontological nor moral, for they believed in a living, omnipotent, and holy God. He who created the first Adam could create a second head of the race. But the incarnation contradicted influential Jewish interpretations of Messianic predictions. They had anticipated that the heir of David's throne would be a powerful king anointed by God to deliver Israel from the yoke of the heathen and establish universal peace and endless prosperity from his world capital in Jerusalem. Instead, Jesus was born in the lowliest surroundings and lived in relative obscurity. Although he performed many miracles, he did not perform the "signs" for which the Jews looked. They anticipated "miraculous signs" (1 Cor. 1:22) on a broader social and political scale.

Jews, like Gentiles, wanted the global kingdom of justice, peace, and plenty without first dealing with their iniquities. But Joseph named the baby *Iēsous* (Greek) because he would save his people from their sins (Matt. 1:21). When John the Baptist called them to repentance, the chosen people found it difficult to acknowledge their insolence along with proselyte Gentiles. So for Jews who were seeking a material kingdom but did not feel the need of justification, the Messiah's lowly birth, life, and crucifixion seemed "a stumbling block" (1 Cor. 1:23).

A more careful study of the context of the birth accounts should have prepared Jewish readers for Jesus' humble birth. From Matthew's genealogy (chapter 1) they might have expected the unexpected in God's program for his people. That genealogy lists several women, whose names would not have been required in any legal account. Three of these women were morally of bad repute—Tamar, Rahab, and Bathsheba—and three were foreigners—Rahab, Bathsheba, and Ruth. Knowing how unusually God worked with women as well as men in the past, Jewish readers might have anticipated something extraordinary when they then read, "This is how the birth of

Jesus Christ came about'' (Matt. 1:18). Admittedly, however, that fact is much easier to see afterward than it must have been at the time.

In presenting the truth of the incarnation to people with Jewish backgrounds, it is important not to compromise the primary atoning purpose of the incarnation and its provision for Jesus' spiritual kingdom. All of the Old Testament messianic prophecies would be fulfilled, but not all at once. *Yēšua'* read from Isaiah 61:1–2, and said, "Today this scripture is fulfilled in your hearing" (Luke 4:16–21), He stopped with his purpose "to proclaim the year of the Lord's favor." Note the predictions given hundreds of years in advance that were fulfilled in his first coming to restore *shalom* with God. Jesus of Nazareth not only claimed to be the Messiah or Christ (Mark 14:61–62), his claim was also confirmed by many factors beyond his human control. We mention just a few of the predictions he fulfilled: (1) He was born of a woman (Gen. 3:15). (2) He was a descendant of Abraham, who brought blessing to all peoples on earth (Gen. 12:2–3). (3) Jesus also descended from the line of David (2 Sam. 7:12–16; Isa. 9:6–7; 11:1; Jer. 23:5–6; Matt. 1:1–17). (4) He was born in Bethlehem (Micah 5:2). (5) And he was born of a virgin (Isa. 7:14). He preached good news to the poor; bound up the broken-hearted; and proclaimed freedom for the captives, release for the prisoners, and the year of the Lord's favor (Isa. 61:1–2). Although despised and rejected, he was pierced for our transgressions, the punishment that was upon him brought us peace, and by his wounds we are healed (Isa. 53:3–5). These and many other prophecies came to pass in the first century in ways beyond the control of any human to manipulate.

The Messiah's work will be fully completed at his second advent to earth. In his first advent the Messiah came to offer himself as a just basis for the justification, redemption, and reconciliation of all (Jews and Gentiles). In his second advent the mighty Conqueror will return for "the day of vengeance of our God" and to "provide for those who grieve in Zion—to bestow on them a crown of beauty instead of ashes" (Isa. 61:2–4). Then he will establish his universal social and political rule with lasting justice for all. Those who imagine that Jesus failed in his first coming adequately to confirm his claims to be the Messiah miss the tremendous import of numerous signs such as his virgin birth, sinless life, miracles, teaching, ministry to the poor, and resurrection. Jesus did not fail to train his Jewish disciples to preach the Gospel and to plant churches. At the cross the Messiah tore down the great wall between Jews and Gentiles so that both could be united in one spiritual body (Gal. 3:28). People in the Jewish tradition ought not miss the invaluable provisions of the Messiah's atoning death and triumphant resurrection and ascension—personal redemption, justification, and reconciliation. These blessings have powerful social implications as the recipients permeate their respective cultures. Jewish pre-Christians may need to examine again the Messiah's triumphant resurrection, return to heaven, and sending of the Holy Spirit at Pentecost to build the church. They may need to consider afresh Christ's present lordship of believers and his spiritual rule as king of all Jews and Gentiles, not on the basis of race, but of grace. No more coherent account of the first-century phenomena has appeared. And no more viable hope for individual peace or world peace (for Jews and Gentiles) can be found. So many Jews have put their faith in Jesus as their long-awaited Messiah.

Why "Foolishness" to Greeks?

The claim that the eternal Word who was God become a man (John 1:1, 14) was particularly difficult for admirers of Greek culture and its philosophers' worldviews. Paul did not oppose philosophy, but only philosophies opposed to God's revealed wisdom. He disclosed his understanding of Greek philosophy not only in addressing the Stoics and Epicureans at Athens (Acts 17:16–34) but also when he wrote to the Corinthians of the incarnation as "foolishness" to the Greeks (1 Cor. 1:23). Paul could understand the problematic nature of his claims for people who thought the flesh evil and whose God could not move.

Still today there are Greekophiles and those with other philosophies whose version of moral dualism suggests that all spirits are good and that all matter is evil. Hence it becomes morally unthinkable that God should become flesh. The goodness of a spirit would be morally contaminated by inhabiting a human body. For people who believe that matter is our basic problem, presentation of the Messiah's actual incarnation seems to be nonsense and grossly offensive. So before claiming that the eternal Son of God has come in the flesh, we need to point out that the battle between good and evil is not between spirit and matter but between two tendencies of a spirit's thoughts, desires, and volitions. The body is not the basic source of evil, the body is simply the instrument of fallen people's insolence. A divine spirit or a regenerated spirit with good desires and purposes can bring forth good fruit through the body. An understanding of the body as created by God and in itself good may remove one moral roadblock to Christ's assumption of a human body.

The Greeks also upheld a metaphysical dualism in which eternal Being is totally unchanging and inactive and temporal existence is totally changing. On that hypothesis it became impossible for them even to imagine that a truly eternal and immutable person could act or change in any way, and so could not be born, mature, and die. Because of the difficulty of relating their interpretation of the eternal to their interpretation of the temporal, some Greeks denied one or the other. *Heraclitus* denied any changeless reality, considering any changeless being or truth about it as a mere appearance. He maintained that everything is changing, or in flux; nothing is changeless. He said that one cannot step into the same river twice. Greeks influenced by this totalistic relativism might agree that Jesus was a developing human, but they could not consent to his eternal existence in the Godhead.

In contrast, *Parmenides* had said that in spite of kaleidoscopic appearances, nothing changes in reality; all that is, is. "Being doth be." Greeks of this school of thought could agree that the Word *was* (Greek imperfect tense) continuously God (John 1:1), but could not concur that the eternal Word could ever actively change by entering history in human flesh (John 1:14). Meaningfully to present the truth of Christ's incarnation to total relativists or absolute idealists today, Christians must challenge their underlying presupposition concerning reality and appearance. The physical, changing world God created and sustains is real. The body is real. On the presupposition of only one unchanging reality, incarnation will always appear foolish. Adherents need to realize that the ultimate being, though immutable in nature and purpose, has changeless plans for changing events in time. They also need to consider that, as living and active, the God of the Bible can providentially achieve these worthy temporal intentions either conditionally or unconditionally. Then the eternal, second personal subsistence of the Trinity can meaningfully become incarnate in time.

Plato distinguished an eternal, changeless world of universal ideas transcendent to the changing temporal order of particular things. An intermediate Maker (*demiurge*) constructed matter as far as possible after the pattern of these eternal forms or blueprints of things. But the observable world is a faint replica or shadow of the eternal realities. So the ultimate form of the Good could never become mere flesh. Admirers of Plato today need to realize with Augustine that Plato's world of ideas is not above God and they need to identify changeless principles with the Logos. The Word is God (John 1:1). The second person of the Trinity can live and act in time with wisdom, justice, and love, because he *is* wise, just, and loving.

Aristotle held that God, the eternal thinker, is occupied with only the highest objects of contemplation. Hence he thought, not of finite, changing particulars in history, but only of himself! Aristotle's followers might agree with the eternality of the Christ, but could not imagine the eternal Logos even thinking of flesh, let alone becoming flesh. Admirers of Aristotle today need to realize that their Creator not only has an encyclopedic concern for concrete, observable things but is also personally concerned with his creatures because of his self-giving and outgoing love. Until people overcome a deistic notion of God as unknowing and uncaring, the incarnation will remain "foolishness."

Philo, the Jewish philosopher-theologian contemporary with Christ, sought to combine Plato's (Gentile) philosophy with Old Testament (Jewish) theology. Philo stressed that the unchanging God is so transcendent to all human qualities and classifications as to be ineffable. Philo's God sustains the world through intermediate (angelic) powers, the highest of which he called the Logos. According to Philo's view, the Logos was the first created being, but probably impersonal (though at times personalized) and never incarnate. God himself, Philo thought, could never directly contact the world.[99]

To Greeks with such metaphysical and moral presuppositions about God and matter, it seemed nonsensical for a tentmaker to insist that the Son of God had come into time. The most basic absurdity derived from two different views of God. Christians did not start with an impersonal, inactive Principle when they affirmed that he who was God had taken up flesh. Rather, they began with the living God of the Old Testament, the personal, covenant-making God of Abraham, Isaac, and Jacob. Although he is active, Yahweh is immutable in character and purposes. The logical starting point for understanding the incarnation is not the impersonal absolutes (of the Greeks and others today) but the living God of the Bible, the creator of matter. So matter is not inherently evil, removing the moral difficulty. God is also the active creator of man; he made male and female in his image so that ontologically humans, although dependent, are not totally other than God. Having defended the existence of the God of the Bible in apologetics, the claim that the Word became flesh makes sense ontologically and morally. It is not unthinkable that God could adapt himself to the level of his image-bearers for the supreme revelation of the grand plan of redemption.

People continue to find difficulty in grasping the concept of the incarnation because they start with a static Being who is more like that of the Greek thinkers than the living God of Adam and Eve, Abraham and David, and Mary and Jesus. For this basic reason Kierkegaard's and Barth's views of the incarnation and all God's relationships with humans, as J. Oliver Buswell, Jr. pointed out, are beset with numerous unnecessary "paradoxes." Unfortunately these are not merely apparent contradictions, they are alleged to be irresolvable contradictions in the Bible.[100] People today who, like Kierkegaard, find the incarnation an "absurdity" ought to consider whether they are starting with Greek philosophical speculations about God or biblical revelation concerning God's nature and relation to creation.

The problem of the Greeks illustrates the difficulty of defending Christianity piecemeal and the need for the defense of its whole worldview. The specific doctrines of the incarnation and virgin birth make sense in the Judeo-Christian theistic worldview and Trinitarian doctrines. What, then, is the logical starting point for defending a Christian case for the incarnation in a crosscultural context? It is the hypothesis of the God disclosed in the Jesus of history and in the teaching of Scripture.[101] The message of the incarnation is not nonsense, it is the wisdom of God. The wisdom Paul challenges is the wisdom of men like the Greek philosophers who distort the universal revelation. Paul praises the wisdom that comes from God by Spirit-illumined interpretation of special revelation. "The foolishness of God is wiser than man's wisdom, and the weakness of God is stronger than man's strength" (1 Cor. 1:25).

Not a Mere Myth, as Bultmann Claimed

Rudolph Bultmann presupposed a naturalistic worldview with a cosmos closed to any extraordinary activity by a transcendent God. Hence he relativized the absolute in history by interpreting the virgin birth of the incarnate Son of God as an unscientific or unrealistic myth. In the Gospels, however, there is a pervasive testimony to the fact that Jesus was involved with the miraculous. And from the time of the events to their recording there was *insufficient time* for myths to develop.

Furthermore, between the pagan myths and the account of Jesus' virgin birth several *significant differences* stand out. The mythological stories of gods becoming human occur frequently and repeatedly, whereas the virgin birth of Christ occurs only once and once-for-all. The purposes in mythology are immoral, whereas the purpose of the virgin birth is the fulfillment of justice in providing for redemption. The mythological invasions are not historically confirmed, whereas the virgin birth was investigated and recorded by Luke the physician and takes place in a series of many historically confirmed events.

Bultmann's attempt to explain the New Testament concept of incarnation as a redeemer-myth derived from Gnostic sources fails also for *lack of evidence*. Evidence of myths at the time of the New Testament events, not only in the apostolic age but also in pre-Christian times, is lacking. As F. F. Bruce concludes, "Until more positive evidence of the pre-Christian date of this elaborate myth is forthcoming than hypothetical reconstructions from late Mandaean texts can supply, theses like Bultmann's and Schlier's cannot be regarded as having adequate foundation."[102]

Although no specific non-Christian myths may be cited as the source of Jesus' birth narratives, *myths* in general may have *prepared the way for Christ's actual incarnation*. F. F. Bruce explains:

Quite different is the approach of C. Williams, C. S. Lewis and others, who have maintained that in Christianity the ancient myths have come true, that when God became Man, as Lewis put it, "Myth became fact," so that the aspirations and insights of the human soul which have from ancient times found mythological expression have been given a satisfying answer in the historical events of the gospel.[103]

As Clark Pinnock put it, "These ancient tales tell us of mankind's dreams and aspirations; Christmas tells us about God's mighty act to fulfill them all. In Jesus Christ the myths are not so much abrogated as fulfilled."[104]

After a critical examination of mythical interpretations of incarnation, Charles C. Anderson concludes that they are incompatible with the authors' general purpose:

> (1) any attempt to interpret the Bible accurately must begin by taking seriously its self-witness to being the special revelation of God; and (2) in accordance with the divine purpose of special revelation, the Scriptures must be interpreted literally. . . . This is what we should expect if God wished to make himself known to man. He did not conceal that revelation in allegories and myth. To be sure, the communication of divine truth to man had its problems. The necessity of figurative language, metaphor, analogy, etc., could not be avoided. But these devices were used to clarify, not to obscure the message.[105]

First-century eyewitnesses to the life of the Messiah deny a mythological interpretation. "We did not follow cleverly invented stories [myths] when we told you about the power and coming of our Lord Jesus Christ, but we were eyewitnesses of his majesty" (2 Peter 1:16). Paul was equally emphatic. "For the time will come when men will not put up with sound doctrine. Instead, to suit their own desires, they will gather around them a great number of teachers to say what their itching ears want to hear. They will turn their ears away from the truth and turn aside to myths. But you, keep your head in all situations" (2 Tim. 4:3–5). Paul's concern for a sound conceptual base for faith excluded even myths that belonged to his Judeo heritage. "Therefore, rebuke them sharply, so that they will be sound

in the faith and will pay no attention to Jewish myths or to the commands of those who reject the truth" (Titus 1:13–14; cf. 1 Tim. 1:4; 4:7).

Were these biblical writers using "myth" in a manner that was relevant to Bultmann and other recent writers? "In each [New Testament] instance it signifies the fiction of a fable as distinct from the genuineness of the truth."[106] Hughes finds the New Testament use "in complete harmony with the classical connotation of the term [Gr. mythos], which from the time of Pindar onward always bears the sense of what is fictitious, as opposed to the term logos, which indicated what was true and historical."[107] Hence we can understand the view of John in using "Word" as a name for Christ (John 1:1, 14) and Paul's use of it as a synonym for the Gospel. Hughes documents a similar distinction between a true logos and a fictitious mythos in Plato, Philo, and Pseudo-Aristeas. And after finding Bultmann, Barth, and Brunner lacking in clarity on this most basic difference, Hughes concludes that their concepts of myth, legend, the poetic, etc., are "incompatible with the classical doctrine of Holy Scripture. The Christ of the Bible is the Logos, not a mythos; he needs no demythologization at the hands of human scholars."[108]

More Than a Mighty Act of God, as D. M. Baillie Taught

An influential work reflecting the antimetaphysical temper of thought since Kant, Donald M. Baillie, in his book *God Was in Christ,* claims that the New Testament tells us "nothing about who or what Jesus was or did" in himself, but only about the nature of God and God's activity. Whatever Jesus was or did, "it is really God that did it in Jesus."[109] Rather than allegedly "static" terms such as two "natures" in Christ, Baillie prefers "dynamic terms'' such as ''God acts in Jesus Christ or is revealed in the Christ event.'' John Knox, similarly limited himself to ''dynamic'' categories in his *Jesus Lord and Christ*.[110] These writers claim that God's essence was not distinguishable in a theistic worldview prior to the life of Jesus; what Baillie and Knox know of God is reduced to what God *does* in Christ. They know nothing of who God is in himself or who Jesus was in himself. Jesus was merely what he did, or better, Jesus was what God did in him. Although Baillie has no difficulty in affirming the humanity of Jesus, he nowhere affirms his ontological deity. But we emphatically affirm that there is no incarnation unless the one born at Bethlehem was the eternal Son of God.[111]

The mightiness of the mighty act of God at the birth of Jesus depends on the nature of the one born. Long before Chalcedon Jesus asked, ''Who do men say that I am?'' As a result of what Jesus did they should discern who he was. We must still press that question today. John wrote his gospel in support of the thesis that Jesus is the Christ (the eternal Word of 1:1) so that believers might find spiritual life (John 20:31). The test of counterfeit spirits is their denial that the Christ (the eternal Word) has come in the flesh (1 John 4:1–3). ''He who has the Son has life; he who does not have the Son of God does not have life'' (1 John 5:12). ''Anyone who . . . does not continue in the teaching [this critical doctrine of who Christ is contextually] . . . does not have God.'' (2 John 9). To support (by giving them hospitality) teachers who can affirm only what Jesus does, and cannot affirm who Jesus is, implicates us in their deceptive work (vv. 10–11). The church did not read changeless metaphysical concepts of the divine being or nature into the Bible, the church read them out of the New Testament. But Baillie has failed to exegete the Christo-logical texts in their cultural context without a modern antimetaphysical bias. So he reduces the message to ''dynamic events'' among unknown participants.

More Than One of Many Avatars to Hindus and Buddhists

Pantheistic thinkers who regard God as part of the cosmic process claim to believe in the incarnation, not only of Jesus Christ but also of many other ''avatars.'' Avatars are alleged to be human souls of deceased spiritual masters who descend to the earth to carry out a mission. So avatars may be either (1) naturally born, literal humans who in their life on earth realize their own inner divinity or (2) the spirits of dead spiritual masters mythically returning to earth to guide others in a time of crisis. Any person, it is alleged, can become conscious of oneness with God (as Jesus is alleged to have done). However the concept of an avatar or incarnation to help ignorant souls is inherently inconsistent, as an Indian scholar has pointed out: ''If there is only one Soul, i.e., God, and the human soul is God, then it does not make any sense for God to get into the bondage of ignorance, forget that he is God and send God [guru or avatar] to enlighten himself [God] from this ignorance, which exists in his own mind!''[112]

Before presenting the incarnation of a personal God's Son to monists, we must, like Paul in addressing the Stoics at Athens, declare the truth about the God they ignorantly worship. In a theistic worldview all things are made by God, but God is not incarnate in everyone or everything. The world is the creation of God's free will and distinct from God ontologically. It is not the automatic emanation of God's being.

How then does the Messiah differ from avatars? (1) Monists worship a man, Jesus, who allegedly became God (or was enlightened) at his baptism (or subsequently); Christians worship God who became man. (2) Avatars allegedly appear repeatedly in countless reincarnations; Jesus Christ came once-for-all. (3) Hindu avatars differ only in degree from other humans; Jesus, although fully human, is also fully divine and differs in kind, from other spiritual leaders. (4) Mythical avatars do not have literal bodies, for the body is considered evil; Jesus lived in a literal body without sin. (5) Returning avatars are not literally born, for a human body would contaminate them with evil;[113] Jesus was literally born of Mary in Bethlehem. According to a Hindu myth of Krishna's birth, for example, "under auspicious skies, transcendental sounds and an overjoyous moon (although not a full moon) a baby was born with four hands, holding a conch shell, club, disk and lotus flower, wearing a jeweled necklace, dressed in yellow silk, wearing a helmet, bracelets, earrings and similar other ornaments all over his body and an abundance of hair on his head."[114] This lavish legend stands in stark contrast to the chaste biblical accounts of Jesus' actual birth to Mary in a literal city, Bethlehem. (6) Hindu and Buddhist "holy men," in contrast to the avatars, are born in an ordinary way and so have sinful natures; Jesus was supernaturally born and sinless. (7) Eastern sages pass on wisdom from the past; Jesus taught wisdom from above. (8) Gurus offer varied kinds of experiences: altered states of consciousness (e.g., Rajneesh's nude marathons and free sex), inner peace and creativity, psychic and occult experiences in the advanced siddhis (e.g., Maharishi Mahesh Yogi's Transcendental Meditation), and ecstatic mystical unions with cosmic consciousness personified as Krishna. In contrast, Jesus calls people to inner regeneration, redemption, and fellowship with the living God, who transcends not only the self but also the entirety of the cosmos.

The difference between an avatar and Jesus Christ became important for me one day at the Christmas season. In a mall in 1980 Santa Claus offered me some candy canes for my children. I accepted them for the fun of it, even though my children were grown. Then Santa Claus requested a donation! I asked, "For what?" After much evasion the contributions turned out to be for the local Hare Krishna temple. I expressed my desire that the costumed Santa should give his time to telling people about the birth of Jesus Christ. "Santa" responded that Krishna is the Christ. As a larger and larger crowd gathered around us, I argued that Christ is unique and Krishna differs from the Messiah in the several ways listed above. In the market places, at the Christmas season and at other times, Christians need to be prepared to set forth the case for Jesus Christ's uniqueness.

More Than an Instance of Universal Incarnation, as Hegel Taught

Theologians, in Hegel's opinion, express in figurative language what philosophers assert literally. So when Christians assert that "God's Son became incarnate," Hegel claims that they mean figuratively that the Absolute is being progressively realized in all of history. He held that the infinite mind (which alone is real) cannot be distinct from, or beyond, the finite and partial. Hegel held to a kenōsis of God in all creation and providence. For him art is the embodiment of Absolute Mind in material things. All individual minds are actively developing their potential in increasingly complex forms and are in a sense realizing the Absolute, or God. God is manifested in all the world in the artist's external vision and the mystic's internal vision. And thus Hegel takes the incarnation figuratively for a kind of pantheistic immanence in all human thought.[115]

Absolute idealists like Hegel will not understand the literal, once-for-all incarnation until Christians challenge their basic assumptions concerning the Absolute and its relation to the world. The world is not an emanation of the Absolute, and God is not incarnate in everything. Universal providence is never to be confused with a progressive incarnation. Again, our reason for our hope in the incarnate Christ must be presented as part of the entire Christian belief system involving all our previous doctrines. Through an informational revelation and biblical inspiration we know that the Absolute is a personal God distinct from the cosmos and the minds created in his image. God created the world, not out of his own being, but out of nothing. Although the Lord of all works out his wise, holy, and loving purposes providentially, his being is not continuous with the processes of historical development. In historical reality Jesus of Nazareth uniquely and once-for-all enfleshed the eternal Word. Christ differs in kind (morally and metaphysically as well), not just in degree, from all mere creatures.

More Than a Paradigm of Indwelling

The case is similar in relation to Whiteheadian process theology's figurative interpretation of Christ's incarnation. Dale Moody follows Norman Pittenger in denying that the presence of God in Jesus was different in kind from a panentheistic incarnation (*sic*) of God in creation, the church, and individual Christians. The indwelling of God in the man Jesus differs in degree from God's indwelling in others, Moody says, because it was perfect. Moody revives Pittenger's marital model of unity between husband and wife who become one in will and love. God is the great cosmic Lover who lured Jesus on to do his will in every word and deed. Jesus can be called the incarnation of God because of his free surrender and love in response to the gracious indwelling of God. The condescension of the Logos in becoming human, according to Moody's view, does not feature an emptying of divine glory (a *kēnōsis*), but an emptying of the human will and a divine indwelling (a *skenōsis*). Instead of God's becoming man, a man is united with God! Pittenger, Moody thinks, comes nearest to keeping Christ's humanness and divineness in balance and is alleged to be "Chalcedon in a contemporary setting."[116] But Moody fails to see that having dismissed the ontological referents, he has lost the reality of both Jesus' humanness and his divineness. In losing the ontological categories Moody has lost any substantial connection with the Chalcedonian formulation.

John B. Cobb, Jr., sees the implications of this view more clearly than Dale Moody does. If the deity of Jesus is not different in kind from that of other men, Jesus differs only in degree from Gautama, the Buddha. This is not the result of Cobb's "preoccupation with Buddhism," as Moody argues *ad hominem*. Rather, it is the implication of his indwelling model of the incarnation. In *Christ in a Pluralistic Age*, Cobb does not take the referent of "Christ" to be a permanent entity or concept, but an "image" by which life is ordered and energy directed. What "Christ" names or images is "creative transformation."[117] "To assert that the Logos was incarnate in Jesus in itself, therefore, is true, but insufficient. The Logos is incarnate in all human beings and indeed in all creation." It follows that Jesus is merely "a paradigm case of incarnation" that can be followed by all. Cobb calls Jesus "unique" in degree but not in kind.[118] By way of contrast, the evidence above strongly

295

indicates that Jesus is more than a great teacher and example. He is a divine-human Savior whose once-for-all incarnation confirms the fact that although ontologically human, Jesus is also ontologically divine. Jesus is different in kind both morally (as a sinless human) and metaphysically (as one in essence with the Father).

In view of these varied interpretations of Christ's incarnation it is not enough for communicating the faith to the next generation to receive mere verbal agreement that "Jesus is the Christ." We must ask what interpretation of those words people hold. Do they mean that Jesus is merely the paradigm of the highest yieldedness of a human to God? Do they mean that Jesus was filled with "Christ spirit" as all of us may be (even though in greater degree)? Or do they mean that he is ontologically the eternal Son of God (the second person of the trinity) who became flesh? With an ontological interpretation of Jesus' being, we may also consider him the supreme paradigm of humanness yielded to God the Father in his wise teaching, authentic love, and powerful deeds for the poor and despised. Only an ontological interpretation of his deity as the second person of the Trinity, however, adequately accounts for the scriptural teaching on his essential oneness with God the Father, the uniqueness of the incarnation, and its infinite provisions for the salvation of all human beings.

RELEVANCE FOR LIFE AND MINISTRY

Value Sinful Persons Highly

In the darkest hours of our experience we know that God cares about us. Although transcendent to humans both metaphysically and morally, God has taken the initiative to reach out to us. The incarnation demonstrates in fact that it is no mere myth that God loves sinners in spite of the fact that they are holistically depraved, personally estranged, and deservingly guilty. "This is how God showed his love among us: He sent his one and only Son into the world that we might live through him" (1 John 4:9). God the Son valued lost humans so greatly that he willingly left heaven's glories to seek and to save them! And God the Holy Spirit so prized human rebels that he performed the miracle making possible Jesus' conception by Mary. Abiding with Jesus throughout his life, the Holy Spirit guided and enabled him in the accomplishment of his redemptive mission. The ministries of each person of the Trinity reveals the Triune God's evaluation of sinners as being of inestimable worth.

Not everyone in the ancient world esteemed humans of such great value. Thales thought we were essentially water vapor; others, a combination of fire, air, earth, and water. Some thought the body evil, and others declared it a prison house of the soul. Plotinus despised his parents and wanted to have nothing to do with them. In more recent history the inhumanity of people to one another has led to despair of human worth. During Dietrich Bonhoeffer's imprisonment by the Nazis, he felt personally the enormity of extreme and cruel tortures. So brutal was the punishment Bonhoeffer witnessed in the concentration camps that many prisoners despaired. They asked, "Are humans any more than beasts?" Yes, said Bonhoeffer in *Letters and Papers from Prison*. The martyr could not despise even those who would take his life! "God Himself did not despise humanity," he wrote, "but became man for man's sake." If God did not despise sinful humanity, how could a Christian pastor-teacher?[119]

The eternal Word so valued his fallen image-bearers that he took human form, humbled himself as a human child, became a carpenter's helper, and washed dirty feet. Christ esteemed sinners enough to leave heaven's riches and become poor. Do we his followers prize sinful people enough to leave behind the riches of earth and become poor? Christ gave up being served to serve others. Do we who take his name as Christians seek more to be served than to engage faithfully in servant ministries to sinners? To save the lost the Messiah gave up his life and bore the penalty fallen humans deserved. Even though humanity's functional *imago* is impaired and the relational image lost, Christ did not consider humans mere beasts. To Christ humans are worth living for! Humans are worth dying for!

Not only are fallen humans in general of value to God, persons are of value in particular. You may consider yourself the chief of sinners, but you have worth to God. If you were the only wayward human in the world, we may be assured, Christ would have come into the world for you.

Be Assured That Human History Has Meaning

Although human history does not manifest God's incomparable being, it does realize his awesome plans for his fallen creatures. In God's grand design, linear history has two irrepeatable stupendous climaxes that give meaning to all the rest—the first and second advents of the eternal Word.

At the first advent the one who holds all things together in the entire cosmos (Col. 1:16–17) came to earth as a baby! Many of our contemporaries can find no abiding person or principle to give meaning to their worldview or purpose to their lives. Since Copernicus' discoveries the earth can no longer be considered the physical center of the universe. The sun, as the center of our solar system, seems unanchored in the expanse of endless galaxies. But the cosmos is not a pointless field of diminishing energy destined eventually to burn itself out in the vastness of empty space. And the value of God's image-bearers does not depend on the comparative size or location of their planet. Because he values human lives the transcendent sustainer of the galaxies has come to visit us! The coming to earth of the infinite Sustainer of all matter-energy provides an absolute in nature. So Christians prize not only the personal Absolute transcendent to nature, but also one personal Absolute incarnate on earth! "For God was pleased to have all his fullness dwell in him" (Col. 1:19). The birth of Jesus Christ, then, is more significant than the election of our preferred candidate for president, the meriting of a doctoral degree, or even the discovery of the Salk vaccine to prevent polio. The winning of gold medals at the Olympics, and the victory of one's favorite team in football's superbowl do not compare. And the incarnation stands far above the outstanding productions of actors, musicians, and artists.

The desires of mankind for an ethical hero or a just deliverer have come to realization in Christ. God's Anointed One came into history at the appointed time, at the appointed place, and in the appointed manner. God's eternal Word came into our world as lost mankind's Messiah! God's Son became human flesh on planet earth to exhibit God's nature and teach God's truth. He came to save both Jews and Gentiles from philosophies based only on the principles of this world (Col. 2:8), from blind fate, pointless chance, and unholy spirits. Of all the wonders of history and the world, this is by far the greatest! The incarnation of the Son of the living God is incomparably greater than any of the wonders of the ancient world. God's enfleshment is far more wonderful than the amazing pyramids, Phidias' forty-foot statue of Zeus carved in gold and ivory for the original Olympic games, or the four-hundred-foot-long marble temple of Diana at Ephesus. The greatness of Christ's advent far exceeds that of such natural wonders as Mount Everest, Victoria Falls, or the Grand Canyon. For all the fullness of deity (Col. 1:19) to dwell in a human on earth carries far greater significance than the discovery of wireless communication, atomic power, a computerized information age, or successful round trips to the moon. The Lord of all came to seek and to save us!

In contrast to totalistic relativists for whom history has no center, no purpose, and no abiding meaning, *all history centers in the birth of God's eternal Word*. Oscar Cullmann in *Christ and Time*, seeks to let the Bible speak for itself; so he does not start with a speculative concept of eternity (God totally other than humans), but with God's revelatory actions in history. Cullman feels that God sovereignly works not only in individual encounters but also in a series of happenings. The creative Word, without whom nothing exists, works in every age (*aiōn*), but achieves his redemptive purposes in the fullness of time (*kairos*). Human history may be pictured as an hourglass on its side with all prior happenings leading to the center at Bethlehem, and all events subsequently flowing out from the incarnation.

Cullmann did not do as well in letting the Scriptures speak for themselves on the nature of revelation. God not only acts but also speaks about who he is. In limiting knowledge of Jesus to what he does, Cullmann failed to appreciate the importance of who Jesus was and what he taught. But Cullmann's stress on the mid-point of God's activity in history helpfully focused attention on the once-for-all incarnation.[120] Appropriately, then, Christians mark all events as before Christ's birth (B.C., before Christ) or after Christ's birth (A.D., from the Latin *anno domini*, the year of our Lord). From the time of the focal point of all history (Christ's birth at about 4 or 5 B.C.), then, we live in the "last days" (Heb. 1:2). And we eagerly await the glorious return of our great God and Savior, Jesus Christ (Titus 2:13). The perspective of the Messiah's birth supplies a holistic perspective of all human history.

Rejoice That Your Life Has Significance

The coming of Christ to die for sinners and rise again supplies not only the center of history in general, but also *the crux of our own personal histories!* Although many of our contemporaries think their lives or biographies to be pointless, a personal acceptance of the incarnation of the eternal Lord of the cosmos can provide lasting significance to our own historical experiences. The difference between our lives before and our lives after accepting Jesus as Messiah and Lord can be as great as the difference between Saul the enemy of the faith and Paul its apostle. Acceptance of the Lord of all brings focus to all of the events in our lives both before and after receiving him. Although busy with varied activities, those preparing to minister in Christ's stead consciously center their desires, thoughts, and actions on him. By regular meditation on the incarnation we center our lives on Jesus Christ rather than ourselves or others.

The centrality of the Messiah ought to be reflected in our celebrations. To honor the greatest of all persons ever to live on earth, our celebrations of Christmas should be carefully planned to give the transcendent sustainer of the cosmos, the mid-point of history, and the supreme paradigm of humanness our greatest of honors. Prizing the birth of

God's unique Son above all others, our commemorations of Christmas should reflect the greatest of tributes we can ever give. Our children should realize from our celebrations that the birthday of Jesus is of far greater importance than the birthdays of our spouses, children, or parents. Our jubilation over the greatest event in history should surpass that of our marriage, the births of our children, and the inheritance of a fortune. The indescribable significance of Christ's coming to seek and to save the lost ought never be overshadowed in the commercialism and tinsel of Christmas. Rather, parents should appropriately teach and exhibit the inestimable value of Christ's condescension and self-giving love. And Christian leaders in every church should discerningly plan fitting ways to commemorate God's mercy and love to the undeserving population of our planet. It is understandable that through a liturgical season of six weeks in the East and one of four weeks in the West Christians prepare for Christmas as they prepare for Easter in the Lenten season.[121]

While celebrating Christ's first advent, Christians also anticipate the celebration of his second advent. The fact that Jesus actually came in literal fulfillment of prophecy gives us solid reason for taking literally his promise, "I will come back" (John 14:3). Jesus said that the nations would see "the sign of the Son of Man . . . coming on the clouds of the sky, with power and great glory" (Matt. 24:30). For centuries people of many religions and utopian visions have longed for someone to bring peace to the world. In country after country hopes for new deals and great societies have failed. The utopian hopes of economic determinists and free-market devotees have been shattered in the East and the West by fallen human nature. Similarly unrealistic and destined for disillusionment are visionary utopian hopes by which we assume

that we have only consciously to realize our inner divine potential to produce global peace. In contrast, Jesus already came, lived without sin and began his spiritual kingdom on earth. So Christians have well-founded, realistic reasons for anticipating his return as Prince of Peace to rule the world in social and political righteousness. How sad that many in the first century missed the profound point of Jesus' birth, life, death, and resurrection! May those who today call themselves Christian not miss it. And when the Lord Christ comes again, may every reader be watching and working for him!

Believe the Doctrine of the Incarnation

Christians believe in more than theism and moral values. Christians get their name from believing something about Jesus Christ. And what Christians believe about Jesus nontheists and pantheists do not affirm. Christians affirm the eternal Word's incarnation and virgin birth. Christianity focuses on what the eternal Word of God did for all who are not what they ought to be. A *sine qua non* of a Christian statement of faith affirms that the historical Jesus *is* the incarnate Son of God. Christians do not divorce the Jesus of history from the Christ of faith. Rather, they believe that the Jesus of history *is* the Christ. The life-changing story of Christianity centers in who Jesus was as well as what he was able to do for people unable to save themselves. The point of distinctively Christian faith is not that Jesus represents the eternal Christ spirit (or the cosmic spirit of love) as well or even better than other spiritual leaders do or have done. The confession given by Peter and the Jewish and Gentile converts in Acts alone continues among their successors in Christianity today. Christians today, as in the first century, believe that Jesus of Bethlehem, Egypt,

Nazareth, and Calvary, *is* both Lord and Christ (Acts 2:36).

John wrote his gospel "that [we] may believe that Jesus is the Christ, the Son of God, and that by believing [we] may have life in his name" (John 20:31). To receive eternal life one believes in Jesus. But which Jesus? Not the first created angel (Jehovah's Witnesses), not an adept psychic (spiritualists), not a practitioner of divine science (Christian Scientists), not a great avatar (Hindus), not an enlightened one (Buddhism), nor merely "a marvelously good man" (Harry Emerson Fosdick), but the eternal Word (John 1:1) who became flesh and made his dwelling among us (John 1:14, 18). "Here is a trustworthy saying that deserves full acceptance: Christ Jesus came into the world to save sinners" (1 Tim. 1:15). Any Jew or Gentile who believes in the truth of that proposition and "trusts him will never be put to shame" (Rom. 9:33; 10:11). Faithfulness in guarding the truth of the incarnation will keep the most sincerely committed people from devotion to false Christs, who will fail. The Holy Spirit uses the sharp sword of this truth to direct our devotion away from unreal idols to the Christ of reality.

The first Christians determined whether people had the spirit of Christ or the spirit of Antichrist (1 John 4:1–3) by their assent or dissent to the literal meaning of the assertion that God's eternal Word or Son has come "in the flesh." By this doctrine the early church also determined whether candidates for church membership were salvifically related to God. "Anyone who runs ahead and does not continue in the teaching of Christ does not have God; whoever continues in the teaching has both the Father and the Son" (2 John 9). The "teaching of Christ" that John had in mind is clear in his gospel and first epistle. In these contexts, adherence to "the teaching of Christ" does

not specify here all that Jesus taught, but the doctrine that John emphasized in his gospel and epistles—that Jesus was the eternal Word who had become flesh (John 1:1, 14; 20:31; 1 John 1:1–3; 4:1–3).

The true story of God's actual incarnation was affirmed from heaven by the Father at Jesus' baptism and transfiguration, claimed throughout his life by Jesus himself, and is subjectively attested by the witness of the Holy Spirit. As a major part of his ministry, the Holy Spirit attests the truth of the good news of Christ's incarnation (1 Cor. 12:3). You "have an anointing from the Holy One, and all of you know the truth. . . . Who is the liar? It is the man who denies that Jesus is the Christ. Such a man is the antichrist—he denies the Father and the Son. No one who denies the Son has the Father; whoever acknowledges the Son has the Father also" (1 John 2:20–23). It is indeed crucial, then, that every member of every Christian home and every Christian church confess that Jesus is the Christ. This is not to say that each must be able to explain the incarnation in technical theological language. Even a child, however, can understand that Jesus, as he said, was "from above," from God, whereas all the rest of us are from beneath, from sinful parents.

Why is belief in the incarnation so important? Athanasius saw clearly that Jesus must be God's eternal Word to be able to provide salvation for all. In *The Incarnation of the Word of God* Athanasius noted that the Father effects the renewal of creation by the same Word who made it in the beginning. The Word became flesh out of the goodness of his Father, for the salvation of humans. The incorporeal and incorruptible Word of God entered our world, stooped to our level in his self-revealing love to keep creation's purpose from coming to naught and to die as a sufficient exchange for all. Jesus' real deity is necessary to the sufficiency of his atonement for all. It is also necessary to renew the debilitated *imago Dei* in mankind so that through it people might once more come to know him. Jesus' real humanity is necessary to put an end to human corruption by his resurrection. For by man death gained its power over men and by the Word made man death has been destroyed and human life raised anew. Christ's body, for him, was not a limitation, but an instrument. In a human body Jesus accomplished two things: he banished death and made us anew.[122]

Belief, as Athanasius knew, does not save us. The faith of sinners for salvation is no more efficacious than its object. No amount of positive thinking about themselves can transform the holistically depraved. People have sincerely trusted a bridge that collapsed. And people have been totally committed to a Rajneesh who has now said, "The joke is over." The incarnate Word alone has the infinite wisdom, power, and righteousness to save all. Belief in the incarnation is necessary to salvation, furthermore, because in a pluralistic world the Holy Spirit's major instrument is truth. The Spirit uses truth about the incarnation to direct our commitments away from humanistic antidotes and pantheistic idols to the one real divine-human person who can save from sin. If the metaphysically real Word of God has not become flesh, Christians have no good news.

Trust the Incarnate Christ

Christians are those who not only believe the doctrine of the incarnation, but also trust the One of whom the doctrine speaks. John wrote his gospel not only that we might believe, but "that by believing [we] may have life in his name" (John 20:31). He proclaimed that the Word of life had appeared, and what John saw and heard he proclaims

to us so that we also may have fellowship with other believers, with the Father, and the Son (1 John 1:1–3). The religious experience of the first Christians and of all Christians since has been, not of their own divinity, but of Christ's. The distinctively Christian life involves more than the mere remembrance of him or of imitation of him. Spiritual life involves experience of him through the living, personal Holy Spirit with and in the spirit of the believer. This was Christ's own conception: "Remain in me, and I will remain in you. No branch can bear fruit by itself; it must remain in the vine. Neither can you bear fruit unless you remain in me. I am the vine; you are the branches . . . apart from me you can do nothing" (John 15:4–5). The life-changing spiritual experience of Paul began a personal experience with Jesus Christ. So Paul wrote, "Christ lives in me" (Gal. 2:20) and "To me to live is Christ" (Phil. 1:21).

A person can be a Hindu without trusting Krishna, or a Buddhist without commitment to Gautama, but not a Christian without commitment to Jesus the Messiah. In other world religions one commits oneself to a type of yoga or a noble eightfold path for human achievement, to moral law and spiritual disciplines. A person can be a devout Muslim without devotion to Mohammed. A Muslim does not joyfully sing, "Mohammed, lover of my soul!" The founders of other religions charged people to follow their religious teachings and the practices of human sages and even to follow their examples. But human religious leaders sooner or later reveal their depravity, as did Jim Jones. Christ charged people not only to follow his example, but to believe him, honor him, pray to him, receive his forgiveness of their sins, and abide in him. In following him they did receive his teachings and imitated his life. More than that, however, they believed *on* him as God's Word incarnate. He said, "Trust in God, trust also in me" (John 14:1). If he had not been God in human flesh, their worship would have been idolatrous. Christianity is not merely a religion focusing on the teachings and practices of Christ. Rather, as W. H. Griffith Thomas wrote, *Christianity Is Christ*.[123] A personal relationship to the scripturally revealed Lord Jesus Christ is of the essence of the Christian religion.

Personal communion with Christ leads to love for his heavenly Father. Those who receive the incarnate Son of God find fellowship with the Father. Our "fellowship is with the Father and with his Son, Jesus Christ" (1 John 1:1–3). A spiritual life of communion with Christ and the Father also results in love for others. Those who believe in the divine love expressed in the incarnate Christ do not love only God but also other believers. "And this is his command: to believe in the name of his Son, Jesus Christ, and to love one another as he commanded us. Those who obey his commands live in him, and he in them. And this is how we know that he lives in us: we know it by the Spirit he gave us" (1 John 3:23–24).

The good news of God's gift of his Son still authorizes sinners who will receive him to become children of God (John 1:12) and joint heirs with him of all the riches in glory. "Now if we are children, then we are heirs—heirs of God and co-heirs with Christ, if indeed we share in his sufferings in order that we may also share in his glory" (Rom. 8:17). "If you belong to Christ, then you are Abraham's seed, and heirs according to the promise" (Gal. 3:29). For the Gentiles are heirs together with Israel, members together of one body, and sharers together in the promise in Christ Jesus (Eph. 3:6). To join the people of God one needs, like Mary, to accept God's gracious promises and

relate to the Savior of whom they speak.

Have you personally a trustful and loving relationship with the eternal Christ who became flesh?

> Though Christ a thousand times
> In Bethlehem be born,
> If He's not born in thee
> Thy soul is still forlorn.
> —Angelius Silesius

Like Christ, Be in the World but Not of It

The incarnate Word identified with the fallen people of the world in their humanness, but not in their evil. Like our spiritual Master, we are to identify with our human friends in the world, but not to the extent of committing their private sins or public crimes. Jesus said, "They are still in the world" (John 17:11), but he added, "They are not of the world" (v. 14). "My prayer is not that you take them out of the world but that you protect them from the evil one" (v. 15). Among the evils of the world from which Jesus delivers people are materialism, covetousness, hedonism, sensuality, pride, and waste.

Exhortations to separate ourselves from the evils of worldly people may be misconstrued to mean isolation from non-Christians. A Christlike separatism means not waging war as the world does or using worldly weapons (1 Cor. 10:3–5). It means to be poor in the eyes of the world but rich in faith (James 2:5). It means not to crave the things the unbelieving world desires and of which it boasts (1 John 2:15–17). But separation from the world does not mean withdrawal from the world like a celibate monk (1 Cor. 7:9–10). That would not solve all of our problems, for we would take our fallen natures with us into a monastery. Christians involve themselves in the lives of those who most need them. So our Christlikeness can be tested by checking our relationships to others. Jesus did not spend so much time training others for ministry that he had no time for evangelism and service to those in need. Until church leaders not only teach but also exhibit Christlikeness in relating to the world, church people will not gain new converts as Christ commissioned them to do. Again, until leaders challenge church members to use some of their time and energy outside the church with non-Christians, they will have missed much of the relevance of Christ's incarnation.

A spiritual life not only separates from the evils of the world and reaches out to the people of the world, but it also *overcomes* the world's evils. "Who is it that overcomes the world? Only he who believes that Jesus is the Son of God" (1 John 5:5). With spiritual weapons like Christ's "we demolish arguments and every pretension that sets itself up against the knowledge of God" (2 Cor. 10:5). Believers can overcome temptations and addictions because Christ's name is above every other name that can be named in heaven and earth. And believers together can made a difference in the social evils around them.

After discussing separation from the unbelieving world in Anabaptist and community traditions; accommodation to it in the Constantinian, Lutheran, and civil-religion trends; and the transformational model in Augustine, Calvin, and liberation theology, Robert E. Webber integrates elements of truth from each in an incarnational model. He writes:

> My conclusion is that the Incarnation is the center point from which to reflect on the role of the Christian in the world. As a revelation of the Father, Christ was *identified* with the natural and social order, He was separate *from the powers of evil that rule the course of the world, and He began the transformation* that will be

completed in His second coming. *This three-sided view of reality points to the relationship that exists between the Christian and the world.*[124]

Like Christ, Give Yourself to Reach the Lost

The Father's sending of the Son into the world is a great motive for evangelistic and missionary service. "As you have sent me into the world, I have sent them into the world" (John 17:18). Our Lord commissions us to go to a lost world, not wait for the world to come to us. The Christian missionary mandate is no mere appendage to theology. The heart of the Christian message contains good news to share with the whole world. The long-awaited Messiah has come! To accept Jesus Christ as the unique and only Son is to accept the need for taking that message to the ends of the earth. Every Christian teacher, pastor, and leader needs to participate in outreach to non-Christians. Outreach is crucial for the essentially Christlike nature of a church. Involvement in missions is not optional, it is required. All church officers should exemplify self-giving love to reach out and touch the unreached with the gospel of God's grace. The church elders should be good witnesses whether or not there is some other committee or group devoting special attention to sending forth laborers into the harvest field.

Although Christians "flesh out" God's purposes personally in the world and in the church, we are not literally extensions of the incarnation. Aware of the uniqueness of Jesus Christ, Christians ought never claim to be extending the incarnation literally. Christ alone and Christ once-for-all is God's unique Son who perfectly fleshed out his purposes in the history. His uniqueness ought never be blurred. We are not kings but ambassadors of the one Mediator. Although we are regenerated, we are at best merely human, and we continue Christ's relationship to the world only in lesser ways. At best, our attempts to identify with humans, separate ourselves from their sins, and transform people individually and collectively are incomplete and tainted.

Nevertheless, "The test of 20th century Christianity," said Sargent Shriver, former President John Kennedy's Director of the Office of Economic Opportunity, "is not how much the poor enter into the life of the church, but how much the church enters into the life of the poor."[125] We need also to care for those of other races. Jesus went out of his way to meet the Samaritan woman at the well and help her believe that he was the Messiah. A black seminary professor, William E. Pannell, observed, "On the one hand, I really do not expect a pagan to act like a Christian toward me. It seems reasonable, on the other hand, to expect those who say they love God to love their brothers. . . . The Christian is practicing a kind of love which is content to relate to people at a comfortable distance. Hence, the presence of the missionary in Sierra Leone, West Africa and the absence of his sponsoring denomination among Afro-Americans."[126]

Like Christ, Humbly Serve Others

Although the eternal Word was spiritually rich beyond description, "yet for your sakes he became poor, so that you through his poverty might become rich" (2 Cor. 8:9). "Your attitude should be the same as that of Christ Jesus: Who . . . made himself nothing, taking the very nature of a servant, being made in human likeness. And being found in appearance as a man, he humbled himself and became obedient to death—even death on a cross!" (Phil. 2:5–8). Like Jesus, we need to exemplify the servant ministry we teach.

"Whoever wants to become great among you must be your servant, and whoever wants to be first must be slave of all. For even the Son of Man did not come to be served, but to serve, and to give his life as a ransom for many" (Mark 10:43–45). Those who understand the basics of Christ's kenōsis and incarnation understand that they take marching orders from the master of self-giving service. Jesus exemplified a simple life of self-denial and self-discipline in order to reach the poor in spirit, the poor in health, the poor in friends, and the poor in purse.

Above all, Christians put loyalty to the kingdom of God and his righteousness first. In this changing world, however, our priorities are easily scrambled. Disciples of the Messiah, ask not only what the world can do for you, but ask what you can do for the starving, the ill, the poor, and the lonely of the sinful world. Furthermore, followers of Christ, ask not only what the church can do for you, but what you can do for the church in its ministries to the world around it. Like Christ, Christians minister to those who know they need a physician. "Blessed are the poor in spirit, for theirs is the kingdom of heaven" (Matt. 5:3). As Jesus came in poverty of spirit, so must we.

Christ's incarnation has not yet had its full effect on those who are now born again, let alone on the world. But the incarnation indicates that in spite of the ugliness and pervasiveness of sin, creation is open to its Maker and full of spiritual significance. The incarnation gives us reason to be believing participants in Christ's present spiritual kingdom. And the incarnation gives us reason to hope for the future fulfillment of the rest of the prophets' highest visions.

REVIEW QUESTIONS

To Help Relate and Apply Each Section in This Chapter

1. *Briefly state the classical problem* this chapter addresses and indicate reasons why genuine inquiry into it is important for your worldview and your existence personally and socially.

2. *Objectively summarize the influential answers* given to this problem in history as hypotheses to be tested. Be able to compare and contrast their real similarities and differences (not merely verbal similarities or differences).

3. *Highlight the primary biblical evidence* on which to decide among views—evidence found in the relevant teachings of the major divisions of Scripture—and decide for yourself which historical hypothesis (or synthesis of historical views) provides the most consistent and adequate account of the primary biblical data.

4. *Formulate in your own words your doctrinal conviction* in a logically consistent and adequate way, organizing your conclusions in ways you can explain clearly, support biblically, and communicate effectively to your spouse, children, friends, Bible class, or congregation.

5. *Defend your view* as you would to adherents of the alternative views, showing that the other views are logically less consistent and factually faced with more difficulties than your view in accounting for the givens, not only of special revelation but also of human experience in general.

6. *Explore the differences the viability of your conviction can make in your life*. Then test your understanding of the viability of your view by asking, "Can I live by it authentically (unhypocritically) in relation to God and to others in my family, church, vocation, neighborhood, city, nation, and world?"

MINISTRY PROJECTS

To Help Communicate This Doctrine in Christian Service

1. *Memorize one major verse or passage* that in its context teaches the heart of this doctrine and may serve as a text from which to preach, teach, or lead small-group studies on the topic. The memorized passages from each chapter will build a body of content useful also for meditation and reference in informal discussions.

2. *Formulate the major idea of the doctrine in one sentence* based on the passage memorized. This idea should be useful as the major thesis of either a lesson for a class (junior high to adult) or a message for a church service.

3. *State the specific purpose or goal of your doctrinal lesson or message*. Your purpose should be more than informative. It should show why Christians need to accept this truth and live by it (unhypocritically). For teaching purposes, list indicators that would show to what extent class members have grasped the truth presented.

4. *Outline your message or lesson in complete sentences*. Indicate how you would support the truth of the doctrine's central ideas and its relevance to life and service. Incorporate elements from this chapter's historical, biblical, systematic, apologetic, and practical sections selected according to the value they have for your audience.

5. *List applications of the doctrine* for communicating the difference this conviction makes in life (for sermons, lessons, small-group Bible studies, or family devotional Bible studies). Applications should make clear what the doctrine is, why one needs to know it, and how it will make differences in thinking. Then show how the difference in thought will lead to differences in values, priorities, attitudes, speech, and personal action. Consider also the doc-

trine's possible significance for family, church, neighborhood, city, regional, and national actions.

6. *Start a file and begin collecting illustrations* of this doctrine's central idea, the points in your outline, and your application.

7. *Write out your own doctrinal statement on this subject in one paragraph* (in half a page or less). To work toward a comprehensive doctrinal statement, collect your formulations based on a study of each chapter of *Integrative Theology*. As your own statement of Christian doctrine grows, you will find it personally strengthening and useful when you are called on for your beliefs in general and when you apply for service with churches, mission boards, and other Christian organizations. Any who seek ordination to Christian ministry will need a comprehensive doctrinal statement that covers the broad scope of theology.

CHAPTER 6

THE MESSIAH'S DIVINENESS AND HUMANNESS

The Messiah's Divineness and Humanness

THE PROBLEM: HOW COULD DEITY WITH ALL ITS PERFECTIONS UNITE WITH HUMANITY WITH ALL ITS LIMITATIONS IN A SINGLE INTEGRATED PERSON WHOM WE KNOW AS JESUS CHRIST?

The present chapter continues reflection on the person of Jesus Christ, whom all persons acknowledge to be not only the founder of Christianity but also one of the central figures of human history. Here we focus on how we should understand the person of Jesus Christ, who is said to be the subject of some sixty thousand books written in the past one hundred years alone.

Classical Christian theology traces three stages in the formulation of its understanding of Jesus Christ. The first stage of Christological investigation deals with the Trinitarian problem. As the second person of the eternal Trinity, Christ fully participates in the being and attributes of God. The second stage focuses on the authentic humanity of Jesus Christ. Here most Christians acknowledge that Jesus was a human being as we are (sin excepted). The third and final stage directs attention to the question of how deity and humanity could unite in a single, integrated person. The first stage of the Christological problem was treated in the discussion of the Trinity in volume 1, chapter 7. It was shown that in his intrinsic being and perfections Christ is ontologically God. The transition from the first to the second stages was dealt with in volume 2, chapter 5, where it was demonstrated that the Logos, who existed in eternal communion with the Father, voluntarily entered time and space and became a man in Jesus of Nazareth. The second and third stages in the Christological development—the question of the complete humanity of Jesus Christ and how humanity and deity united in the one person—are investigated in this chapter.

Some within the church have denied the genuineness of Christ's humanity, claiming that he was some sort of heavenly phantom. Others, though they accept the full reality of his human nature, ask how he who was also God could grow emotionally and spiritually and how he could participate in the suffering and death common to our condition. Was Jesus Christ fully tempted as we are? Did he or could he succumb to sin? Could Jesus be fully human if he had no experience of sin?

Other problems surround the issue of the union of deity and humanity in the one person of Jesus Christ. Is the claim that God and man united in a single person logically absurd, as some modern scholars claim? If we emphasize the unity of Jesus Christ, can we at the same time maintain the integrity of his deity and humanity? On the other hand, if we uphold the reality of his two natures, can we posit a union that is entire and complete? If Jesus Christ is an integrated personality, does he possess one will or two? Furthermore, what is the relationship between the divine-human Christ and his fitness to be a sufficient Savior from sin? If Jesus is our example or model, in what respects should believers strive to become like Christ?

Other questions will be addressed in this chapter: Did Jesus Christ in his ministry perform the functions of a prophet? If so, what did his prophetic ministry involve? Furthermore, how important for Christian faith is a body of reliable historical data concerning the life of Jesus of Nazareth? Must the claims and deeds of Jesus be verifiable by the usual criteria of historical research, or does faith rest primarily on certain nonhistorical ideas the church associated with the Christ? Expressed in other terms, which is of greater importance, the Jesus of history or the Christ of faith?

G. C. Berkouwer observes that high points or "crescendos" in the church's reflection on Jesus Christ occurred in four time periods, namely, in the fourth, fifth, nineteenth, and twentieth centuries.[1] Given this fact, our survey of principal interpretations in the church will concentrate largely, but not exclusively, on these great periods of Christological debate.

ALTERNATIVE INTERPRETATIONS IN THE CHURCH

The following four Christological interpretations are the principal ways in which leading figures within the church have sought to explicate the person of Jesus Christ. These groups represent the major ways that human minds have related the deity and humanity in the one person, Jesus of Nazareth.

Docetic, Marcionite, Monarchian, and Bultmannian Reductions of Christ's Humanity

Docetism, which denied the reality of Christ's humanity, was one of the earliest and simplest Christian heresies. Widespread from the end of the first century into the latter half of the second, Docetism was refuted by the apostle John (John 1:14; 1 John 2:22; 4:2–3; 2 John 7), by Ignatius, and by Justin Martyr. Whereas Ebionism was influenced by Judaism, Docetism was shaped by Greek thought. Centuries earlier Plato had postulated a hierarchy of reality from the heavenly Ideas or Forms, that were completely real, to the physical world, which possesses only relative reality. Aristotle contributed in some measure to this outlook by his thesis that God, the Unmoved Mover, is beyond suffering and change. Further influenced by incipient Gnosticism, the early outlook known as Docetism (from *dokeō*, to "seem," "appear"), postulated a rigorous metaphysical and moral dualism between God and matter, or between God and the world. Thus the docetists asserted that the good God cannot be joined to evil flesh. The upshot of this assumption was that Christ's manhood was regarded as only a mirage or a phantasm of some kind but not truly real. Christ's birth of Mary, his sufferings, and his death were mere illusions.[2] The apocryphal Gospel of Peter testifies to the illusory nature of his flesh when it says that the Savior on the cross "kept silence, as feeling no pain" (4:11). The docetists found it impossible to postulate that the divine Christ was properly united to the body of Jesus' flesh. Their solution to the Christological problem was to deny the reality of our Lord's proper humanity. Although the docetic tendency has been less powerful than the opposite denial of Christ's full deity, some medieval theologians, Anabaptists, and conservative Christians so stressed Christ's deity as to lose sight of his authentic humanity.

Marcion's view of Christ was broadly docetic. He believed that Christ came forth as a revelation of the Redeemer God of the New Testament, and thus he had nothing to do with the material world that was the creation of the vengeful demiurge or creator. According to Marcion, Christ was not born of a woman. Rather, he descended directly from heaven as a phantom and appeared suddenly in an illusory body in the Capernaum synagogue in A.D. 29. Since Christ's flesh was a mirage, the events of his daily life, his miraculous works, death at the instigation of the demiurge, and resurrection from the grave were all illusory. Tertullian summed up Marcion's position as follows: "His Christ . . . was not what he appeared to be, and feigned himself to be what he was not—incarnate without being flesh, human without being man, and likewise a divine Christ without being God!"[3]

Monarchianism in its two forms also compromised the true humanity of Jesus Christ. Patripassianism, which claimed that the Father himself was born of the virgin and died on the cross, acknowledged that Christ was fully God. The Savior, however, only appeared to be a man. Sabellianism, which claimed that the three "persons" are merely three names for the three different manifestations of the one God, likewise forfeited the distinction of persons within the Godhead and so postulated a Christ who was a man in external appearance only.

The Bultmannian school, reacting against the certitude with which the liberal *Lives of Jesus* reconstructed the history of the Nazarene, so stressed the kerygmatic Christ that it seriously neglected the Jesus of history. Since the Gospels were viewed as the free creations of the Evangelists, Bultmann claimed that our knowledge of the personality, the words, and the deeds of Jesus is minimal. All we know about the founder of Christianity is the "thatness" of Jesus Christ, his passion, and what the early church (reflecting on its own needs) believed him to be. For Bultmann this is no loss, since the gospel is concerned not with knowledge of the historical Jesus but with a person's encounter with the apostolic kerygma through which one discovers authentic existence. Given Bultmann's disinterest in Jesus as a historical personage, his writings reflect a docetic tendency. "I do indeed think that we can now know almost nothing concerning the life and personality of Jesus, since the early Christian sources show no interest in either, are moreover fragmentary and often legendary; and other sources about Jesus do not exist."[4] Schubert Ogden takes the final step that Bultmann was reluctant to take, namely, to demythologize the "thatness" or the event of Jesus Christ. Thus, according to Ogden, nothing in the Gospels is historical; everything is mythical. This means that the Jesus of history is completely irrelevant to the attainment of self-realization. A person moves from inauthentic to authentic existence solely by his own personal decision.[5]

Ebionite, Adoptionist and Liberal Reductions of Christ's Deity

Ebionism, which Hippolytus and Tertullian linked with one Ebion,[6] the alleged founder of the sect, but which other authorities claim derived from the Hebrew word for "poor" ('ebyôn),

311

arose from a Judaizing form of Christianity similar to that which assailed the churches in Galatia in Paul's day. The Ebionites struggled with the problem of how to reconcile strict Jewish monotheism with devotion to Jesus of Nazareth. The heretical Christian sect "solved" the Christological problem by upholding Jesus' humanity but denying his essential deity. Jesus, they insisted, was a genuine man naturally born to Joseph and Mary. By virtue of his strict observance of the law, the Holy Spirit came upon Jesus at his baptism and constituted him the Son of God and Messiah. The Spirit empowered Jesus to serve as a prophet and teacher of the law. At the crucifixion, the Holy Spirit departed Jesus' life, thereby forfeiting his messianic dignity.[7] The Nazarenes were a branch of Ebionites who accepted the reality of Jesus' miraculous virgin birth. Ebionism, which was the earliest humanitarian heresy, represents the *apotheōsis* of a man. It anticipated the adoptionist and Arian views of Christ and was a factor in the rise of Islam.

The Adoptionism championed by Theodotus of Byzantium and Paul of Samosata, concerned to preserve the unity and indivisibility of the Godhead, denied that in Jesus Christ deity personally had united with humanity. Although their formulations were similar, Greek adoptionism and the Jewish oriented Ebionism were not historically related. Paul of Samosata, bishop of Antioch, insisted that the man Jesus, born of a virgin, was indwelt by the Logos of God at his baptism and was thereby equipped with power (*dynamis*) for the exercise of his messianic ministry, hence the name "Dynamic Monarchianism." The bishop claimed that the Logos, the attribute of reason or wisdom in God, had indwelt Moses and the prophets. Yet this impersonal Logos indwelt and energized Jesus more fully than any other man. Through this spe-

cial presence of the Logos, God adopted Jesus as his Son (Mark 1:11; cf. Ps. 2:7). For Paul of Samosata, the bond between the human Jesus and the indwelling Logos was moral only, being a unity of will and purpose. As a reward for his obedience, Jesus was exalted to heaven at the end of his life to a state of perfect fellowship with God. Paul of Samosata's denial of the proper union of God and man in Jesus Christ was condemned by the Synod of Antioch in 268.

Arius, presbyter of Alexandria (d. 336), maintained with the Monarchians the uniqueness and indivisibility of the one God. As the one absolute Monad, Arius insisted that God's essence cannot be communicated to another. Thus God created the Logos or Christ a finite spirit, albeit the first and highest of all created beings. Plainly not *alēthinos theos,* the Logos was a demigod or subordinate deity. Through the instrumentality of the virgin birth Christ took upon himself a human body. The incarnate Christ therefore was not ontologically God, neither was he fully man, for in assuming flesh the Logos replaced the human soul (*nous*) in Jesus Christ. Although the depreciation of Jesus Christ's deity was more prominent, Arius actually viewed the Savior as half God and half man. The church formally condemned the Arian formulation as unbiblical at the councils of Nicea (325) and Constantinople (381).

The Socinians in the Reformation era believed that Christ was a human prophet of God distinguished from other men in several important respects: (1) Jesus was supernaturally begotten of a virgin; (2) his life was free of sin; (3) he was baptized by the Spirit and endowed with special wisdom and power; (4) he was caught up into heaven and given special revelations from God; and (5) he exercised a ministry as prophet (teaching the divine will), priest (interceding for the saints), and king (protecting and ruling over the church). Thus Jesus was not God, but a man of extraordinary wisdom and power.[8] The rationalistic Socinians dismissed the doctrine of the two natures in Christ as logically absurd. Socinianism later gave way to Unitarianism and exercised a profound impact on nineteenth-century skepticism regarding the divine-human Christ.

Liberal theologians, guided by an antisupernaturalist bias and an antipathy to claims that transcend bare reason, pursued a Christology "from below" and upheld a Jesus who was an inspired human teacher of morality. The English deists, who rejected all divine interventions in history, repudiated the doctrine of the two natures in Christ. Although professing reverence for Jesus, they viewed the Nazarene as the prophet of an ethical religion, contrary to the Pharisees, who commended a ritualistic religion. According to John Locke, Jesus was the Son of God, not ontologically, but by reason of his moral superiority to other men. Thomas Woolston, on the other hand, had doubts whether Jesus was even a good man.[9] H. S. Reimarus, the German deist who launched the quest for the historical Jesus, actively opposed Jesus' divinity and viewed him instead as a Galilean teacher of natural religion. Reimarus claimed that Jesus became involved in politics, failed to win the masses to his messianic vision, and died a defeated man. Jesus' followers fabricated the stories of his resurrection and future return to establish a messianic kingdom.

F. D. E. Schleiermacher stands in the vanguard of the nineteenth-century assault on the two-natures doctrine. Since the essence of religion for Schleiermacher was feeling, he judged the classical Christological formulae that expound the two natures of Christ to be invalid. Employing the categories of German idealism, Schleiermacher directed attention away from the ontological dimension to the ethical. Christ was special because of his unique God-consciousness; i.e., because his inner awareness of God controlled every aspect of his life. Furthermore, due to the strength of Christ's God-consciousness, Schleiermacher could speak of a special indwelling of God in him: "To ascribe to Christ an absolutely powerful God-consciousness, and to attribute to Him an existence of God in Him are exactly the same thing."[10] By virtue of the undisturbed character of his God-consciousness, Christ was absolutely sinless. In view of the foregoing development, Schleiermacher viewed Christ as an absolutely religious man—the ideal man who functioned as revealer of God.

In his rationalistic life of Jesus, the Heidelberg theologian H. E. G. Paulus explained away all the miracle accounts traditionally used to substantiate Christ's deity. Thus Jesus did not walk on the surface of the Sea of Galilee; he strolled along the edge of the shore. Likewise, Jesus never multiplied bread and fish to feed the multitude; rather, when Jesus and the disciples shared their lunch with the poor, onlookers became convicted and did the same. Jesus' so-called healing miracles were performed by means of native medicinal agents. Paulus believed that Jesus was the noblest teacher of humanity that history has ever seen. "The truly miraculous thing about Jesus is himself, the purity and serene holiness of his character, which is genuinely human."[11]

D. F. Strauss, in his influential book *Das Leben Jesu* (1835–36), carried the mythical interpretation of the Gospels to an extreme. The only events of Jesus' life that Strauss judged historical were his baptism by John, preaching in Galilee, rejection at Nazareth, and trial and crucifixion. Everything else Strauss regarded as mythical. Nevertheless, the myths and legends created by the community enshrine the absolute truth that the infinite Spirit has united not with a particular individual but with the entire human race. Thus the message of Christianity is the Hegelian notion that by the union of the Infinite with the finite, humanity suffers, dies, rises from the grave, and lives forever. Jesus, according to Strauss, was a human teacher of morality and a social reformer. His distinctiveness resides in the fact that he grasped most clearly the idea of this union of the Infinite with humanity.

Ernst Renan wrote his *Vie de Jesus* (1863), not from the perspective of Hegelianism but under the impulse of Romanticism. Predisposed against the miraculous, Renan represented Jesus as a man from Galilee, a gentle teacher whom John the Baptist transformed into a religious revolutionary. Quickened by an apocalyptic vision, Jesus assumed the role of Messiah and strove to foster a moral revolution in the then-known world. So great were the achievements of this messianic reformer that his followers called him "God" and fabricated numerous legends to perpetuate his memory. In time Jesus came to cross purposes with the Jewish authorities and, in the course of the struggle, paid the ultimate price. Renan's Jesus, although a religious genius, never rose above the level of a man endowed with a highly developed God-consciousness.

Albert Schweitzer, whose book *The Quest of the Historical Jesus* (1906) propounded a "thoroughgoing eschatology," shifted the focus from the ethical to the eschatological or from the prophetic to the apocalyptic. Jesus, according to Schweitzer, lived in an era aglow with messianic fervor. At his baptism Jesus understood himself to be the heavenly Son of Man who was commissioned to usher in the eschatological kingdom. Jesus sent out the Twelve, expecting that before they returned from their tour of Israel the world would end. When this did not happen, Jesus decided to challenge the political powers and thereby force God to bring in the kingdom. Jesus later was betrayed by Judas and was put to death on the cross, being crushed by the very historical forces he sought to orchestrate. Although Jesus died disillusioned and discredited, his "spirit" lives on to inspire posterity. In Schweitzer's famous words, Jesus

lays hold of the wheel of the world to set it moving on that last revolution which is to bring all ordinary history to a close. It refuses to turn, and he throws Himself upon it. Then it does turn; and crushes him. . . . The wheel rolls onward, and the mangled body of the one immeasurably great Man, who was strong enough to think of himself as the spiritual ruler of mankind and to bend history to his purpose, is hanging upon it still. That is his victory and his reign.[12]

Schweitzer judges that as a man who mistakenly believed himself to be the Messiah, Jesus must be viewed from our perspective as mentally unbalanced. Least of all was he ontologically God.

Post-Bultmannian Christology reexamined the historical parameters of the life of Jesus. Pursuing a Christology from below, many post-Bultmannian theologians viewed Jesus as a Spirit-filled man. According to Jeremias, Jesus was a human prophet in whom the Spirit, quenched by the sins of Israel, returned with power. Jeremias concluded from a study of the prologue to John's gospel that Jesus as Logos was the man in whom God was uniquely present and through whom God decisively spoke. "As bearer of the spirit, Jesus is not only one man among the ranks of the prophets, but God's last and final messenger. His proclamation is an eschatological event. . . . God is speaking his final word."[13]

Apollinarian, Nestorian, and Eutychian Formulations of the Union

Before considering specific attempts to relate deity and humanity within the one person of Jesus Christ, we summarize two historical tendencies in Christology that were quite different from each other. The first, the Alexandrian school, focused on the metaphysical side of theology. It was concerned to preserve the deity of Christ and so focused on the unity of the Word and Jesus' humanity. Guided by John 1:14, the Alexandrian tradition formulated a *Logos-sarx* (Word-flesh) Christology. A weakness of this approach, however, was that Jesus' humanity was overshadowed by or even absorbed into his deity. The Cappadocian theologians Gregory of Nazianzus (d. 390), Gregory of Nyssa (d. 394), and Cyril of Alexandria (d. 444) reflect the Alexandrian emphasis. Objecting to Nestorianism, Cyril so emphasized the unity of Christ's person that Cyril was (unjustifiably) claimed by the later Monophysite party.[14] Apollinarianism and Eutychianism were extreme expressions of the Alexandrian emphasis.

The Antiochene school emphasized not only the grammatico-historical interpretation of Scripture but also the historical implications of theology. Thus theologians in the tradition focused primarily on the genuine humanity of Jesus and secondarily on his deity, while seeking to preserve the distinctive properties of the two natures. The Antiochenes appealed to Philippians 2:6–8 and so produced a *Logos-anthrōpos* (Word–human being) Christology. The deficiency of this approach was that the essential union of the two natures was minimized. Theodore of Mopsuestia (d. 428) and Theodoret (d. 457), among others, furthered the Antiochene emphasis. The former wrote concerning Christ: "He did not take a body only, but the whole man, composed of a body and of an immortal and rational soul."[15] Taken to its extreme, the Antiochene emphasis resulted in Nestorianism.

Apollinarius (d. 390), bishop of Laodicea and friend of Athanasius, believed with the latter against Arius that in order to save sinners Christ must be both divine and human. Thus his approach to the Christological problem in *Demonstration of the Divine Incarnation* (376) stressed the unity of the person of Jesus Christ. From the perspective of a Platonic trichotomy, Apollinarius maintained that the person is body (*sōma*), sensitive soul (*psychē*), and rational soul (*nous* or *pneuma*). Reflecting on the dynamics of the incarnation, he reasoned that if Christ had a rational human soul he would not be God-incarnate but merely God *in* a man or an inspired man. Moreover, if Christ had a human will, he would be mutable and thus liable to sin. Therefore Apollinarius concluded that at the incarnation the Logos replaced the rational soul (*nous* or *pneuma*) in the man Jesus. That is, the Logos took on human nature (a body and a sensitive soul), but not human personality (a rational soul) in becoming the divine-human being, Jesus Christ. For Apollinarius, the divine Logos was clearly the living center in Jesus Christ. Thus he referred to the Savior as "God-incarnate" and the "flesh-bearing God."

Orthodox theologians commended Apollinarius for upholding the unity of Christ's person without sacrificing his deity. On the other hand, they criticized his proposal by insisting that Christ's human nature would be defective without a sensitive soul (i.e., intellect and will). Moreover, opponents reasoned that if the Logos did not take on human nature in its entirety, he could not be the perfect Redeemer: "What Christ did not assume, Christ could not heal." Many authorities perceived that, although upholding the unity of Christ's person, Apollinarius depreciated the integrity of his humanity. Thus the church repudiated the views of Apollinarius at the Council of Constantinople (381) and burned his theological writings.

Nestorius (d. 451), patriarch of Constantinople, was a leading representative of the Antiochene school of theology. Nestorius objected to the mixing of Christ's two natures and the resultant depreciation of Christ's true humanity as proposed by Apollinarius and Eutyches. He stressed the fact that we must keep separate the two natures of Christ and the two sets of properties associated with those natures. Thus Nestorius insisted that only a created man (not the uncreated God) could be born, grow, suffer, and die. On the other hand, only the uncreated God (not a created man) could be eternal, omnipotent, and omnipresent. These considerations led Nestorius to conclude that at the moment of conception the divine Logos joined with a complete person in the womb of Mary. Accordingly, Jesus Christ consisted of two natures, each with its own set of personal properties bound together by a moral union to form one *prosōpon* or the appearance of one being. The important issue for Nestorius appears to have been that, lest the properties of the two natures be confused, deity and humanity must have come together in a moral and voluntary connection (*synapheia*), rather than in a vital, personal (i.e., essential) union. Nestorius' famous claim was, "I hold the natures apart, but unite the worship." Nestorius likened the union of human and divine in Jesus Christ to the union of a husband and a wife, who become "one flesh" while remaining two distinct persons. In the light of this development, Nestorius refused to speak of Mary as the "God-bearer" (*theotokos*), preferring to give her the title the "Christ-bearer" (*Christotokos*). Because Nestorius upheld the

reality of Christ's two natures, but seemingly compromised the integrity of the union of these natures, his views were condemned at the Council of Ephesus (431), and Nestorius was banished to exile in Egypt. Some modern scholarship judges that formulations of Nestorius are less heterodox than traditionally thought.[16]

Reacting against the Nestorian position, Eutyches (d. 454), a presbyter at Constantinople, carried the Alexandrian emphasis to an extreme. Seeking to uphold Christ's deity and the unity of his person, Eutyches claimed that our Lord's humanity merged into his deity and in the process was lost. The outcome, according to Eutyches, was a single person with one divine nature. Others in the tradition maintained that the resultant nature was a *tertium quid,* albeit a nature more divine than human. When Flavian, archbishop of Constantinople, asked Eutyches whether Christ possessed two natures, the latter responded: "I admit that our Lord was of two natures before the union, but after the union one nature." Contrary to Nestorius, Eutyches believed that it was God who was born of Mary, who suffered, and who died on the cross. Thus the docetic element in Eutyches' Christology is evident. Eutyches was tried at the Synod of Constantinople in 448 and excommunicated for his alleged heretical views. A council hastily convened at Ephesus in 449 (the "Robber Synod") and presided over by Dioscorus pronounced Eutyches orthodox. His teachings were repudiated shortly after that (451) by the ecumenical Council of Chalcedon.

In the years following Chalcedon, groups in Syria, Egypt, and Palestine who persisted in the error of Eutyches were called Monophysites. Since they believed that person (*hypostasis*) and nature are inseparable, the Monophysites upheld the one person of Christ with a single composite nature. Also called Theopaschites, their common liturgical formula was, "God has been crucified for us." The Monophysites were condemned at the Second Council of Constantinople (553), but Monophysitism persists in the Coptic, Jacobite, and Armenian churches. The Monothelite controversy, which erupted in the middle of the seventh century, represents the final phase of the ancient debate about Christ's two natures. Led by Sergius of Constantinople, the Monothelites claimed that will is an attribute of the person rather than of a nature. Thus although most Monothelites posited two natures in Christ, they allowed only one divine-human will in the Savior. Some within the church saw in Monothelitism a repudiation of Chalcedon and a return to Monophysitism. Thus the Third Council of Constantinople (681), undoubtedly falsely, asserted that there are two wills in Jesus Christ and that the human will is subordinate to the divine.

Lutheran theology followed the Alexandrian emphasis in upholding the *communicatio idiomatum,* or mutual interpenetration of Christ's natures in the personal union. Determined to avoid the Nestorian error, Luther claimed the full participation of Christ's divine nature in his human nature and vice versa. "Because divinity and humanity are one person in Christ, Scripture . . . ascribes also to divinity everything that happens to humanity, and vice versa. And so it is in reality."[17] Thus Luther maintained that God the Son nursed at Mary's breast, lay in the cradle, suffered, was crucified, and died.[18] On the other hand, Mary's son ascended into heaven, now sits at the right hand of God, and will return to judge the world. Taking the argument a step further, Luther claimed that the properties of Christ's divine nature penetrated his human nature. Thus with respect to his humanity Christ is properly omniscient, omnipotent, and omnipresent. "The Word of God is not separated from the flesh. Where God is, there the flesh of Christ is. But God is everywhere; therefore Christ is everywhere."[19] Given the claim that Christ's body is ubiquitous, Luther understood the Savior to be truly and substantially present "in, with, and under" the bread and the wine at the Lord's Supper. A number of authorities judge that Luther and his followers tended toward Eutychianism and so violated the spirit of Chalcedon, which insisted that Christ's two natures united "without mixture."[20] Orthodox authorities posit the complete deity and complete humanity of Jesus Christ and insist that the two natures united in a single, sinless person. Most, with the exception of some Alexandrians and Lutherans, maintain that in the union Christ's two natures did not commingle, but retained their own peculiar properties.

Most Fathers, Reformed Theologians, and Evangelicals

Early church fathers such as Ignatius and Justin opposed Gnostic and docetic denials of Christ's authentic humanity. While upholding the Lord's full divinity, Ignatius claimed that Jesus was born of Mary, was baptized by John, lived a holy life, truly suffered and died, and rose in a body from the grave. Ignatius testifies to the union of Christ's two natures in the one person as the divinely ordained vehicle of salvation. "Being impassible, he was in a passible body; being immortal, he was in a mortal body; being life, he became subject to corruption, that he might free our souls from death and corruption."[21] Irenaeus in the West likewise affirmed in biblical and nontechnical language the divine-human character of the one person, Jesus Christ. God united with man in order to recapitulate humanity, i.e., to reverse the effects of sin and restore humanity to its God-intended

317

goal. Linking Christology with soteriology, Irenaeus stressed that the efficacy of Christ's redemptive work depends on the complete integrity of his two natures as true God and true man. "If the enemies of man had not been overcome by man, they could not have been truly overcome; furthermore, if our salvation is not from God, we cannot be sure that we are saved. And if man has not been united with God, it would not be possible for him to share in immortality."[22] Tertullian, whose formulation of Christ anticipated the Chalcedonian definition, upheld the reality of the divine and human natures of Christ, while preserving the integrity of their union in the single personal subject. Thus Godhead and manhood united in the one person, Jesus Christ, without the natures being confused or their properties altered. Wrote Tertullian: "We see plainly the twofold state, which is not confounded, but is conjoined in one person—Jesus, God and man."[23]

Augustine blended emphases from both the Alexandrian and Antiochene schools to produce a balanced Christology that was Chalcedonian decades before Chalcedon. According to Augustine, the divine Person united with a complete human nature (a rational body and soul) to constitute the one person of the God-man. Noteworthy is the emphasis Augustine placed on the personal unity of the God-man: "Christ, therefore, is one; the Word, soul and flesh, one Christ; the Son of God and Son of man, one Christ; Son of God always, Son of man in time, yet one Christ in regard to unity of person."[24] Augustine's favorite illustration for the union of the Godhead with man is the union of the soul with the body in the human person. Augustine continues by saying that the Word was not altered by the assumption of humanity. The Word "did so assume a body from the Virgin and manifest Himself with mortal senses, as neither to destroy His own immortality, nor to change His eternity, nor to diminish His power, nor to relinquish the government of the world, nor to withdraw from the bosom of the Father."[25] Furthermore, in the union Christ's humanity was entire, lacking nothing. "No part was wanting in that human nature which he put on, save that it was a nature wholly free from every taint of sin."[26] Augustine notes that Christ took food, rested his body, experienced all the emotions of humanity, and finally died. Thus in the union of God with man, neither deity nor humanity was altered, but each retained its distinctive properties.[27]

The principal creeds of the church enshrine the orthodox view of Christ. The Apostles' Creed upholds the deity of Christ when it confesses faith in "Jesus Christ, His [i.e., God's] only Son, our Lord." The Creed also attests the humanity of Christ by referring to his conception and birth of the virgin Mary, his suffering and death under Pontius Pilate, and his bodily resurrection and ascension to heaven. By reciting the Apostles' Creed, Christians assented to the fact that Jesus Christ was truly God and truly man in one person. The Creed of Nicea (325), formulated to refute the teachings of Arius, and its enlargement in the Constantinopolitan Creed (381), which refutes Apollinarianism, expounds Christ's deity in nonbiblical language. Christ was begotten eternally from the being of the Father and thus is "of the same essence as the Father [homoousion tō patri]." Christ, moreover, is truly human, for the Creed adds, "who for us men and because of our salvation came down from heaven, and was incarnate by the Holy Spirit and the Virgin Mary and became human [enanthrōpēsanta]." The Creed then confesses Christ's crucifixion, burial, resurrection, and ascension to heaven.

The first Council of Ephesus (431) condemned the teachings of Nestorius, asserted that the one person Jesus

Christ is "true God of true God," and from an Alexandrian perspective designated Mary the Mother of God (*theotokos*). At the Council of Chalcedon (451), more than five hundred bishops dealt with the relation of humanity and deity in Jesus Christ and produced a statement that refuted not only Arianism and Apollinarianism but particularly Nestorianism and Eutychianism. The Chalcedonian Definition, which strikes a balance between the Alexandrian and Antiochene emphases, is commonly regarded the definitive Christological statement. Chalcedon initially reaffirmed the Nicene tradition by upholding Christ's authentic deity and authentic humanity. Then it proceeded to assert the proper union of the two natures in the one person. Accordingly, deity and humanity came together "to form one person (*prosōpon*) and subsistence (*hypostasis*), not as parted or separated into two persons, but one and the same Son and Only-begotten God the Word, Lord Jesus Christ." Finally, Chalcedon confessed the distinctiveness of the two natures in the union. Thus it refers to Christ as "recognized in two natures, without confusion, without change, without division, without separation; the distinction of natures in no way annulled by the union, but rather the characteristics of each nature being preserved."[28]

The last third of the so-called Athanasian Creed, a document formulated in the West in the fifth century, sets forth what one must believe concerning Jesus Christ in order to be saved. This third ecumenical creed upholds the union of deity and humanity in the one person of Jesus Christ, in which both natures retain their unique characteristics. The most important statements concerning the person of Christ follow:

(30) The right faith is that we believe and confess that our Lord Jesus Christ, the Son of God, is God and man. (31) God of the substance of the Father, begotten before the worlds; and man of the substance of His mother, born in the world. (32) Perfect God and perfect man, of a reasonable soul and human flesh subsisting. (34) Who, although He is God and man, yet He is not two, but one Christ. (35) One, not by conversion of the Godhead into flesh, but by taking the manhood into God. (36) One altogether, not by confusion of substance, but by unity of person. (37) For as the reasonable soul and flesh is one man, so God and man is one Christ.

In the context of the Monophysite controversy, Leontius of Byzantium (d. 543) strove to preserve the integrity of Christ's two natures within the one person by means of the term *enhypostatos*. By this term he meant that Christ's authentic humanity had no subsistence in itself but came to subsist only in union with the Logos from the moment of the incarnation. John of Damascus refined this conceptuality in his classic work *The Orthodox Faith* (Bk. III.1–3). Every nature, John argued, must have a *hypostasis,* or center of personality. Christ's humanity realized personal existence in and through the Logos, for Scripture teaches that the Logos, as the governing principle, assumed human nature, not vice versa.

Calvin's Christology, adhering to the pattern of Chalcedonian orthodoxy, begins with the axiom "It was of the greatest importance for us that he who was to be our Mediator be both true God and true man."[29] For Calvin, everything depends on the true divinity of Christ; only God can conquer sin and restore peace to the soul. Moreover, the punishment due us must be born by a man; hence Jesus Christ must be truly man, with a human body and soul. "God's natural Son fashioned for himself a body from our body, flesh from our flesh, bones from our bones, that he might be one with us."[30] As true man, Christ is distinguished from the common lot by a humanity that is "without fault and corruption."[31] Calvin views the two-natures doctrine not as a mere theoretical construct, but as a necessary feature of God's plan of salvation: "Since neither as God alone could he feel death, nor as man alone could he overcome it, he coupled human nature with divine that to atone for sin he might submit the weakness of the one to death; and that, wrestling with death by the power of the other nature, he might win victory for us."[32] Calvin, however, is careful to insist on the unity of the two natures in the Redeemer. Against Nestorius, there can be no separation of Godhead from manhood: "Both natures are so closely bound up together that Jesus Christ is one Person only."[33] Moreover, against Eutyches, there can be no mingling or fusion of the two natures. "We affirm his divinity so joined and united with his humanity that each retains its distinctive nature unimpaired, and yet these two natures constitute one Christ."[34] Here Calvin distanced himself from the Lutheran *communicatio idiomatum,* which he perceived compromised the integrity of Christ's two natures and thus vitiated the efficacy of his saving work. Calvin does acknowledge, given the unity of the two natures in the one person, that with Scripture we may speak of the human nature as if it partook of the divine attributes, and vice versa (e.g., John 3:13; 1 Cor. 2:8). Finally, Calvin modestly posits what later came to be known as the *extra Calvinisticum;* namely, that during the incarnation the Word was also beyond or outside of (*extra*) Jesus' human nature. Whereas Luther held that the Logos was wholly contained in Jesus' body, Calvin maintained that although the Logos was "completely" present in the historical Jesus, he nevertheless was not confined to his body but filled the world with his immeasurable essence.[35]

The Reformed confessions follow Chalcedon and Calvin in affirming that deity and humanity are permanently united in the one person of Jesus Christ. Although related to one another in a dynamic union, the two natures retain their own distinct characteristics. Hence the properties of Christ's deity are not transferred to the humanity nor are the properties of his humanity transferred to his deity. The Reformed position is set forth in the Belgic Confession (1561), articles 10, 18, 19; in The Second Helvetic Confession (1566), chapter XI; in the Thirty-Nine Articles of the Church of England (1563), article II; and in the Westminster Confession of Faith (1646), chapter VIII.2.

A. H. Strong upholds the full reality and integrity of Christ's divinity and humanity. The latter, consisting of a body and a rational soul, was subject to all the laws of growth and development, yet was free from hereditary depravity and actual sin. Following several earlier authorities, Strong insists that Christ's human nature had no personality apart from its union with the divine nature. That is, "the Logos did not take into union with himself an already developed human person, such as James, Peter, or John, but human nature before it had become personal or was capable of receiving a name. It reached its personality only in union with his own divine nature."[36] Strong thus proposes not *un*personality (*anhypostasia*), but *in*personality (*enhypostasia*). Christ's human nature realized its personality only *in* union with the divine. At Jesus' conception the two natures vitally united to form one person with a single consciousness and will. Jesus' "consciousness and will . . . is always theanthropic—an activity of the one personality which unites in itself the human and the divine."[37] Strong concurs with the orthodox conviction that Christ must unite deity and humanity in one person to be a proper Mediator. "Because Christ is man, he can make atonement for man and can sympathize with man. Because Christ is God, his atonement has infinite value, and the union which he effects with God is complete."[38]

Additional helpful studies on the person of Christ include works by G. C. Berkouwer,[39] John F. Walvoord,[40] and Millard J. Erickson.[41]

THE BIBLICAL TEACHING

To determine which view of the person of Christ is valid, we now investigate the primary biblical teaching on the subject. Volume 1, chapter 7 showed that Scripture identifies Jesus Christ as God. The present chapter examines other evidence for Jesus' deity, evaluates the data for Jesus' humanity, and investigates the problem of the union of deity and humanity in the one person, Jesus Christ.

Synoptic Gospels

The most cursory reading of the Gospels indicates that Jesus of Nazareth was a genuine man. Matthew and Luke testify that Jesus did not descend from heaven full-grown, but was physically born of a young virgin in a manger in the town of Bethlehem (Matt. 1:20–25; Luke 2:6–12). The records suggest that apart from his supernatural conception (see chap. 5), Jesus' prenatal existence, birth, and childhood were indistinguishable from that of any other man. Matthew's genealogy, which traces Jesus's descent from Abraham through the royal line of Israel, establishes the Nazarene as the legal heir to the throne of Israel (Matt. 1:1–17). Luke's genealogy, in reverse order, traces Jesus' physical ancestry through David and Abraham back to Adam, the first man.

As required by the Jewish law, Jesus was circumcised on the eighth day and was consecrated to the Lord in the temple (Luke 2:21–22). Luke reports that prior to the age of twelve, Jesus experienced a perfect physical and moral development (1:80; 2:40). Luke adds that during his youth "Jesus grew in wisdom and stature, and in favor with God and men" (2:52). Thus Jesus "was completely subject to the ordinary laws of physical and intellectual development, except that in his case there was nothing of the influence of sin or shortcoming."[42] The Gospels suggest that Jesus assisted his father at the carpenter's bench (Matt. 13:55) and that after Joseph's death he continued to support his mother and family by working at his trade (Mark 6:3). At about age thirty (Luke 3:23) Jesus was baptized by John in the Jordan River (Matt. 3:13–16; Luke 3:21–22). But whereas others came to the water confessing their sins (Matt. 3:6), Jesus had no need for repentance—hence John's initial reluctance to baptize him (Matt. 3:14–15). Following the baptism, the Spirit led Jesus into the desert to be tempted by the Devil (Matt. 4:1–10; Luke 4:2–13). As a man, Jesus genuinely experienced the power of Satan's offer (1) to change stones to bread, or to satisfy his physical needs; (2) to cast himself to the ground from the pinnacle of the temple, or to seek proof of God's faithfulness; and (3) to receive the kingdoms of the world by worshiping Satan, or to attain kingdom rule without first suffering. Tempted in like manner as Eve in the garden (Gen. 3:6) and like each one of us in the course of life (1 John 2:16), Jesus responded to Satan's enticements by quoting Scripture (Matt. 4:4, 7, 10). In these temptations and others that followed, Jesus chose to obey his Father and thus continued in a perfectly upright and sinless state.

The Synoptic Gospels also relate that Jesus experienced all the normal human instincts and emotions. Physically he felt the pangs of hunger (Matt. 4:2; 21:18), of thirst (Matt. 25:35), and of physical weariness (Matt. 8:24). Spiritu-

321

ally Jesus, like other devout persons, sensed a deep dependence on the Father and so spent many hours in prayer (Matt. 14:23; 26:36–44; Mark 1:35–38; Luke 11:1–4). Emotionally Jesus experienced anger, albeit not a self-centered wrath, but a righteous and controlled indignation against injustice (Mark 3:5). Moreover, Jesus responded to human suffering with deep compassion (the verb *splanchnizomai,* Matt. 9:36; 14:14; 15:32). As Jesus viewed Jerusalem from the Mount of Olives, he recalled the unbelief of its inhabitants, and with profound emotion he wept over the city (Luke 19:41). A few days later in the city Jesus felt great pity for the Jews who spurned God's love and who refused to repent (Matt. 23:37).

The fact that on occasion Jesus' knowledge was limited confirms his authentic humanity. In Mark 5:30–33 Jesus did not know who had touched his clothing, and in Mark 9:21 (because he chose to be ignorant of the answer) Jesus asked the father of a boy convulsed by an evil spirit, "How long has he been like this?" In the Olivet Discourse Jesus himself acknowledged that he did not know the time of his return to earth: "No one knows about that day or hour, not even the angels in heaven, nor the Son, but only the Father" (Mark 13:32; cf. Matt. 24:36, where the reading "nor the Son," omitted in some manuscripts, has sufficient textual support to be retained). We observe that this self-chosen ignorance is not error, for the Gospels represent Jesus as entirely without fault or sin (Matt. 27:4; Luke 1:35; 23:41). Other texts in the Gospels (see below) indicate that on other occasions Jesus drew upon his divine power of omniscience.

The passion narratives vividly display Jesus' manhood. Matthew 26:37 relates that in Gethsemane Jesus "began to be sorrowful [present passive of *lypeō,* to 'be sad'] and troubled" [present infinitive of *adēmoneō,* to "be distressed"]. The following verse confirms that in the garden Jesus experienced intense anxiety and distress: "My soul is overwhelmed with sorrow to the point of death" (cf. Isa. 53:3). Luke adds that so great was his agony, that sweat fell from his body as drops of blood (Luke 22:44). Like any normal person, Jesus longed to avoid the impending crisis. Yet, desiring to be obedient to the Father, he prayed, "Not my will, but yours be done" (Luke 22:42). Nailed to the cross with spikes, Jesus suffered excruciating pain. But even greater than the physical agony was the spiritual pain that occurred when the Father placed on the Son the sins of the world and for a moment broke fellowship with his Beloved. This divine forsaking prompted Jesus' anguished cry of dereliction: "My God, my God, why have you forsaken me?" (Matt. 27:46). Moments later "Jesus called out with a loud voice, 'Father, into your hands I commit my spirit.' When he had said this, he breathed his last" (Luke 23:46; cf. Matt. 27:50). Thus the animating spirit left Jesus' physical body, and he died. Out of love for the Nazarene, Joseph of Arimathea took Jesus' dead body, prepared it for burial, and placed it in a tomb. Surely the Gospel accounts of Jesus' life and death reflect a powerful realism. Having participated in the experiences common to humanity, Jesus was fully a man. Yet he was so perfectly; his manhood was uncorrupted by the dark forces of sin.

On the other hand, the Gospels portray Jesus as manifestly more than a man. This is seen, first, in terms of the divine *qualities* he possessed. During his ministry Jesus frequently displayed suprahuman knowledge or omniscience. Thus he perceived the unspoken thoughts of the Pharisees and the teachers of the law (Luke 5:21–22; 6:7–8). He knew that the crowd believed he had cast out the demon by the power of Beelzebub (Luke 11:17). Also he penetrated the minds of the disciples as they reasoned within themselves who would be the greatest (Luke 9:46–47). And finally Jesus knew that Judas would betray him (Matt. 26:21–25) and that Peter would disown him three times (Matt. 26:31–35).

During his ministry Jesus also displayed the quality of superhuman power, or omnipotence. By his spoken word Jesus stilled the stormy sea, whose ragings threatened to capsize the boat in which he and his disciples were sailing (Matt. 8:23–27). The awesome forces of nature submitted to his will. Jesus' power is also seen in his multiplying five barley loaves and two fish into sufficient food to feed five thousand people, with a dozen baskets of food left over (Matt. 14:15–21; Mark 6:35–44). The same supernatural power is seen in the feeding of four thousand people (Matt. 15:32–38; Mark 8:1–9). The Gospels relate numerous instances of Jesus' power over sickness and disease. The Nazarene healed persons of their paralysis (Matt. 9:5–7), of spinal deformity (Luke 13:10–13), of leprosy (Matt. 8:2–3), of life-threatening hemorrhage (Mark 5:25–29), of fevers (1:29–31), and of blindness (Matt. 9:27–30; 20:30–34). Jesus' power was especially evident in his frequent exorcisms of demons and evil spirits from possessed persons (Matt. 9:32; 12:22; Mark 1:32–34; 5:1–20; 7:25–30). Jesus' power was supremely displayed in acts of restoring the dead to life. By means of a simple touch Jesus caused the deceased son of the widow of Nain to rise up in his bier (Luke 7:12–17), and by his spoken word he brought back from the dead the daughter of Jairus (Mark 5:35–42).

Various suprahuman *deeds* confirmed his divinity, particularly the work of forgiving sins. Jesus remitted the sins of the paralytic lowered through the roof of his home in Capernaum (Mark 2:1–12; Luke 5:17–26).

The scribes and Pharisees correctly assessed the significance of this work: "Who can forgive sins but God alone?" (Mark 2:7; Luke 5:21). Later Jesus forgave the sins of a prostitute while dining at the home of a Pharisee (Luke 7:47–50). Said the astonished guests, "Who is this who even forgives sins?" (v. 7:49). Furthermore, the Gospels relate that Jesus exercises the prerogative of judging the world. In Scripture judgment is the work of God alone (Ps. 62:12; Jer. 9:24). Yet Jesus affirms that at the end of the age *he* will execute judgment. In his explanation of the parable of the weeds, Jesus teaches that at the close of the age the Son of Man will consign the sons of the kingdom to eternal bliss and the sons of the evil one to eternal punishment (Matt. 13:41–43). Jesus' story of the sheep and the goats indicates that in the eschaton he will gather the nations before him and reward the righteous with eternal life and punish the unrighteous with eternal judgment (Matt. 25:31–46).

Jesus' identity is further unfolded by the extraordinary *claims* he made for himself. First, he claimed authority over the sacred law of Israel (Matt. 5:21–22, 27–28, 31–34, 38–39). By means of the retort "but I tell you," Jesus claimed the right to reinterpret the moral law of God. Furthermore, Jesus claimed authority over the God-ordained Sabbath (Exod. 20:8–11) when he revealed its true function in the new economy of grace (Matt. 12:8). Jesus likewise claimed authority over the covenant God established with Israel (Exod. 19:3–24:18), for he spoke of the new covenant that he would inaugurate through his shed blood (Matt. 26:28). Moreover, Jesus claimed authority over the kingdom of God itself, when he promised to delegate to Peter authority for the building of the primitive church (16:19). Indeed, Jesus made an extraordinary claim, appropriate to Deity alone: "All authority [*pasa exou-*

323

sia] in heaven and on earth has been given to me'' (Matt. 28:18). On this basis Jesus demanded the absolute loyalty of his followers. They were to choose him over all other loyalties (10:27–38), find in him spiritual refreshment and rest (11:28), follow him in obedient discipleship (4:19), and render worship to him alone (14:31–33; 28:9–10).

In terms of Jesus' *self-consciousness,* the evidence is formidable that he understood himself to be the Son of God and Messiah. After Peter's confession of Jesus' deity at Caesarea Philippi (Matt. 16:16), Jesus informed Peter that his new understanding was given by God himself, and he warned the disciples not to tell others that he was the Christ (vv. 17, 20). Later, before the Sanhedrin, Caiaphas charged Jesus to tell if he was the Christ, the Son of God. Jesus' response according to Matthew (26:64) was, ''Yes, it is as you say'' (*su eipas*), whereas according to Mark (14:62) it was, ''I am'' (*egō eimi*). Earlier in his ministry, Jesus exercised reserve about his identity. But when his hour had come, the man Jesus acknowledged before the highest Jewish authority that he was the Son of God and Messiah.

In Judaism a prophet (*nābî'*) was a chosen servant who received a message from God and communicated it to the people. The prophet warned of judgment, called people to repentance, announced salvation, and predicted future events. Deuteronomy 18:15 and Isaiah 61:1 present Old Testament intimations of the prophetic ministry of the Messiah. The Gospels indicate that Jesus' contemporaries viewed him as a prophet (*prophētēs,* Matt. 16:14; 21:11, 46; Luke 7:16; cf. John 4:19; 6:14), and the Lord himself was conscious of his prophetic mission (Luke 4:24; 13:33). Jesus exercised a prophetic ministry chiefly by the words he spoke from the Father (Matt. 17:5). With authority

Jesus taught what he had received from above by means of profound sayings, parables, proverbs, and discourses. Infallible predictions of future events were an important component of Jesus' teaching ministry (Matt. 10:26; 24:2–31; Luke 19:41–44). Moreover, substantiating Jesus' prophetic utterances was the powerful example of his prophetic life. Through his deeds of compassion, healing, and judgment Jesus effectively revealed the Father (cf. John 1:18; 17:6).

Primitive Christianity/Acts

A plain reading of Acts confirms that the early Christian preachers upheld Jesus' authentic humanity. In the first Christian sermon Peter acknowledged that Jesus was a descendant of David (Acts 2:30), a man from the town of Nazareth accredited by God (2:22), and one whom the Jewish leaders cruelly killed by impaling him on a tree (4:10; 5:30).

The apostles, however, attributed to the human Jesus *perfections* befitting God alone. Perceiving in Jesus the fulfillment of the Isaiah 53:11 servant passage, the early Christian missionaries represented him as completely righteous and holy (Acts 3:14; 4:27; 7:52). While choosing a replacement for Judas Iscariot, the apostles acknowledged Jesus' omniscience, with the prayer, ''Lord, you know everyone's heart'' (1:24). Moreover, through the authority and power of the risen Jesus the apostles performed many miraculous signs and wonders (4:30). In Jesus' name they healed a crippled beggar (3:6; 4:10), cast an evil spirit out of a woman who was a diviner (16:18), and brought Eutychus back to life (20:9–10). Evil spirits openly acknowledged the power and authority of the risen Jesus (19:15). Jesus performed these supernatural works in his state of humiliation when he was energized by the Spirit and directed by the Father (10:38).

The apostles also ascribe to Jesus suprahuman *works*. Peter describes Jesus as "the author [*archēgos*] of life" (Acts 3:15). Applied to the Nazarene four times in the New Testament (cf. Acts 5:31; Heb. 2:10; 12:2), *archēgos* denotes that Jesus is the source of life—naturally in relation to all persons and spiritually in relation to those who believe.[43] Moreover, the apostles attribute to Jesus the cosmic work of judgment. God appointed Jesus judge of the human race (Acts 10:42). Paul's statement in Acts 17:31 that God "has set a day when he will judge the world with justice by the man he has appointed" emphasizes that the divine judge will return as *man* (cf. Dan. 7:13–14) to execute his work. Paul envisages the union between Jesus' deity and his humanity as complete and unbroken. Finally, Jesus performs the supernatural work of Savior. Sins may be forgiven only on the basis of the atoning work of the divine Redeemer (Acts 2:38; 5:31; 10:43; 13:38).

Furthermore, the apostles attribute to Jesus a number of divine *prerogatives*. First, Jesus' words possess intrinsic authority (Acts 20:35). Second, devout persons invoked Jesus' name in prayer and worship (7:59–60; 9:14, 21; 22:16). In this regard, Stephen's opening words, "Lord Jesus, receive my spirit" (7:59), recall Jesus' final prayer to the Father while on the cross (Luke 23:46). Similarly, Stephen's last words on earth, "Lord, do not hold this sin against them" (Acts 7:60), approximate Jesus' first prayer to the Father on the cross (Luke 23:34). Stephen clearly understood that he was calling on the name of a divine person. Third, Acts 15:26 applies to Paul and Barnabas what could have been said of all the early missionaries: they were "men who . . . risked their lives for the name of our Lord Jesus Christ."

Acts acknowledges the proper unity of the two natures in the one person, Jesus Christ, when it predicates human characteristics to the person viewed from the divine side and vice versa. Humanity and deity are so united in the God-man that Peter could say that "the author of life" was brutalized and killed (Acts 3:15). Similarly, Paul claimed that the divine Lord bought the church with his own blood (20:28). William Neil translates the last part of verse 28 like this: "the church of God which he obtained with the blood of his Own One."[44] On the other hand, Stephen ascribed divine qualities to the God-man viewed from his human side, when he relates that in a vision he saw the man Jesus enthroned in glory at God's right hand (7:55).

Pauline Literature

Paul intimates in 2 Corinthians 5:16 (cf. 1 Cor. 2:8) that prior to his conversion he readily accepted Jesus as a human prophet but stumbled over his identity as the Son of God. As a Christian Paul acknowledged Christ's humanity as the principal seed of Abraham (Gal. 3:16) and as a descendant of King David (2 Tim. 2:8) whose birth (not conception) of Mary was quite ordinary in human experience (Gal. 4:4).[45] In his discussion of Adam and Christ as the respective heads of the old and the new humanities (Rom. 5:12–21), the apostle three times identifies Jesus Christ as an authentic man (vv. 15, 17, 19). Neither his life nor his death was a phantasm, for Paul attests that Jesus was killed by the Jews who earlier had maltreated the prophets (1 Thess. 2:15). Yet as one "who had no sin" (2 Cor. 5:21), Jesus was the paradigm of humanity as God intended it to be— the one pure man uncorrupted by the slightest moral stain.

The apostle establishes Jesus Christ's deity by ascribing to him several divine *qualities*. Christ's omnipotence is displayed in the mighty power whereby he brings all things in the universe under his control (Phil. 3:21). His immensity is affirmed as Paul writes of "the fullness of him who fills everything in every way" (Eph. 1:23). Phillips renders the latter verse as follows: "The church is his body, and in that body lives fully the One who fills the whole universe." The Christ who fills the entire universe with his Spirit Being (Eph. 4:10) is ubiquitous: Christ's presence pervades everything; there is no place in the cosmos where he is not present and available. In the words of William Barclay, "To Paul the ascension of Jesus meant not a Christ-deserted, but a Christ-filled world."[46] Paul also ascribes to Christ an incomparable *agapē* love. By referring to the "breadth and length and height and depth" of Christ's love (Eph. 3:18–19, RSV), and by claiming that it "surpasses knowledge," Paul infers that the love that flows from Christ's heart infinitely exceeds the love of even the most compassionate human being.

That Christ differs in kind, not merely in degree, from us mortals is evidenced by the *works* ascribed to him. The apostle represents Christ as the cosmic agent of creation: "For by him all things were created: things in heaven and on earth, visible and invisible, whether thrones or powers or rulers or authorities; all things were created by him" (Col. 1:16). In the following verse Paul identifies Christ as the cosmic agent of preservation. "In him all things hold together" (v. 17). The verb *synistēmi* in the latter verse means to "stand together," to "hold together," to "cohere."[47] Without the power of Christ at every moment causing the elements to cohere, the cosmos would disintegrate into a chaos. Furthermore, Paul depicts Christ as the cosmic agent of providence. In 1 Corinthians 10:1–10 the apostle describes Christ's spiritual presence with Israel during their wilderness wanderings providentially supplying all their physical and spiritual needs and even chastening when rebuke was needed to bring the wayward people back to God. Moreover, Paul represents Christ as the cosmic agent of redemption. In the Old Testament God is the One who saves from sin (Isa. 43:3, 11; Jer. 14:8; Hos. 13:4). Yet Paul affirms that under the new covenant it is Christ who delivers from sin. Thus Christ has redeemed believers from the domain of sin and Satan (Eph. 1:7), propitiated God's wrath toward us (Rom. 3:25), reconciled us to God (5:11), purified us from the defilement of sin (Titus 2:14), and destroyed death and opened the gate to heavenly immortality (2 Tim. 1:10). For those who refuse to accept God's offer of grace, Christ is the appointed cosmic agent of judgment. As "judge [of] the living and the dead" (2 Tim. 4:1), Christ will expose the hidden motives of each person's heart (1 Cor. 4:5) and mete out rewards and punishments in accordance with each one's works (2 Cor. 5:10).

Paul juxtaposes the divine and human natures of Christ in several important texts. Romans 9:5 speaks of "the human ancestry of Christ, who is God over all, forever praised!" Without question, Christ is a man descended from the distinguished Hebrew patriarchs (cf. 2 Tim. 2:8). Yet simultaneously and without compromising his authentic humanity, Christ is truly God.[48] Romans 1:3–4 makes the same theological affirmation. On one hand, Jesus Christ "as to his human nature [*kata sarka*] was a descendant of David." Since *sarx* here signifies human nature in its entirety, Paul envisages Jesus Christ as properly a man. The apostle then adds, "who through the Spirit of holiness [*kata pneuma hagiosynēs*] was declared with power to be the Son of God by his resurrection from the dead: Jesus Christ our Lord." Several exegetical comments need to be made in respect of this latter clause. (1) The expression "the Spirit of holiness" is a Hebrew idiom for the Holy Spirit. (2) The aorist passive participle of *horizō*, consistent with its meaning elsewhere in the New Testament (Luke 22:22; Acts 2:23; 10:42; et al.), means to "appoint" or "ordain." And (3) the phrase *en dynamei* ("with power") qualifies *huiou theou* ("Son of God") rather than *horisthentos* ("appointed"). Paul thus affirms that, although Christ was the Son of God in his state of humiliation, by Spirit-energized resurrection from the grave, he was appointed in his state of exaltation Son of God with *power*.[49] The bottom line is that although fully human, Jesus Christ is also in every respect fully God. Paul's discussion in 1 Corinthians 15 of Christ as the second Adam who leads the saints in victorious resurrection from the grave, registers the same point. As death came through the one man Adam, so the resurrection comes through the one man Jesus Christ (v. 21). Yet Christ is distinguished from Adam in that the latter "was of the dust of the earth," whereas the former is "the man from heaven" (vv. 47–49). Paul's identification of Jesus Christ as "the man from heaven" suggests, not that he possessed a body of air (so the Manichaeans), but that although truly human he was simultaneously the divine Son of God (v. 28)—one integrated person simultaneously both man and God.

Paul's grand hymn extolling the humiliation of Christ (Phil. 2:6–11) clearly attests the two natures in the one person of the God-man. Since the passage was exegeted in chapter 5, we need only draw out a few key points that pertain to the discussion at hand. Paul's opening affirmation about Christ Jesus is that *en morphē* he subsists as God (v. 6). Since *morphē* is "the form proper to a being in its objective reality,"[50] Paul claims that prior to the incarnation Christ shared the very being

and attributes of God; i.e., he was ontologically God. This is confirmed by the following statement that Christ subsisted in a state of "equality with God" (*to einai isa theō*), which in chapter 5 we defined as existence-in-a-manner-of-equality-with-God. Out of love for humanity and obedience to the Father, Christ laid aside the outward manifestations of his God-equal-existence, which act is explained by three participial phrases. The first, "taking the very nature of a servant" (*morphēn doulou labōn*, v. 7a), indicates that while retaining the *morphē* of God, Christ took to himself the *morphē* (i.e., the nature and characteristics) of a lowly servant. The second phrase, "being made in human likeness" (*en homoiōmati anthrōpōn genomenos*, v. 7b), explains that in the incarnate state he was similar to us but not identical, for he was both God and sinless man. Paul's point here is the same as that made in Romans 8:3: "sending his own Son in the likeness [*homoiōma*] of sinful man."[51] The third phrase, "being found in appearance as a man" (*schēmati heuretheis hōs anthrōpos*, v. 8), suggests that to the most critical human observer Christ deported himself as the man he truly was. The Greek word *schēma* bears the nuance of the "actual form or stature perceptible to the senses."[52] Implicit is the idea that Christ's outward bearing fully corresponded to his inner reality. Thus in the portion of the hymn considered, Paul teaches that at the incarnation the eternal Son of God added to himself what he did not previously possess, namely, a complete but sinless humanity. Without explaining the actual "how" of this reality Paul states that the one person Jesus Christ is both God and man.

First Timothy 2:5 reads as follows: "For there is one God and one mediator between God and men, the man Christ Jesus." Concerning this verse we note the following: (1) Paul suggests that

Jesus Christ is one person with an integrated psychology. (2) Given the emphasis in the context on Christ's representation of man, the apostle stresses the humanity of the Mediator. In addition, docetic tendencies may have prompted Paul to focus on Christ the man. And (3), this text teaches that the union of deity and humanity in Christ is permanent. The divine Son who even now intercedes for the saints is also fully man.

As we saw in the previous section, the unity of deity and humanity in Jesus Christ is so complete that divine characteristics are attributed to the person viewed from the human side (1 Cor. 15:47). More frequently, human characteristics are predicated of the person viewed from the divine side of his being (1 Cor. 2:8; 2 Cor. 13:4; Gal. 2:20).

Johannine Literature

For a writer who devoted much attention to Christ's deity, John was careful to uphold the reality and integrity of the Lord's humanity. Thus John the Baptist (John 1:30), the people of Jerusalem (7:25, 27), the Pharisees (9:16, 24), and the Jews (10:33) regarded Jesus as an authentic man. Pilate exclaimed to the mob who sought Jesus' life, "Here is the man!" (*idou ho anthrōpos,* 19:5)—by which the Roman governor may have meant: "Here he is, poor fellow!"[53] John identifies Jesus' lineage as of the tribe of Judah and the family of David (Rev. 5:5; 22:16). Moreover, Jesus represented himself as "a man" (John 8:40) with a real body (2:19, 21). Yet Jesus' manhood was as God intended humanity to be—perfectly sinless and integrated. The Nazarene flawlessly obeyed the commands of his heavenly Father (8:29; 15:10) and was conscious of not the slightest guilt (8:46; cf. 1 John 3:5).

Emotionally Jesus experienced joy (*chara,* John 15:11; 17:13), anger (the verb *embrimaomai,* 11:33a, 38), and inner distress (the verb *tarassō,* 11:33; 12:27; 13:21). When Lazarus, the brother of Mary, died of an illness, John relates that "Jesus wept" (11:35). Physically, the carpenter of Nazareth thirsted (4:7; 19:28), became hungry (4:8), and experienced fatigue (4:6). Severely weakened from severe beatings and impalement on the cross, Jesus died as any person dies: "He bowed his head and gave up his spirit" (19:30). When a Roman soldier thrust a spear into Jesus' side, water and blood flowed out of the wound (19:34), confirming that he had already expired. Moreover, Joseph of Arimathea and Nicodemus carefully prepared Jesus' body for burial and placed it in a new tomb (19:38–42).

In the light of such facts, John sternly warned against docetic and incipient gnostic denials of Jesus' authentic manhood. He said, "Every spirit that acknowledges that Jesus Christ has come in the flesh is from God, but every spirit that does not acknowledge Jesus is not from God. This is the spirit of the antichrist, which . . . is already in the world" (1 John 4:2–3; cf. 2:22; 2 John 7). Significantly, John wrote that Christ came "in the flesh" (*en sarki*), not that the Christ or an emanation entered "into the flesh," in the sense of descending upon the man Jesus as a temporary enablement. The perfect tense of the verb *erchomai* ("has come") in 1 John 4:2 emphasizes that at the incarnation flesh was permanently incorporated into the person of Jesus Christ.

But that Jesus was more than a man is evident from the divine *qualities* ascribed to him. Jesus affirmed his eternality in John 8:58: "Before Abraham was born, I am [*egō eimi*]." Hear the testimony of John, the disciple who knew Jesus intimately: "We proclaim to you the eternal life, which was with the Father" (1 John 1:2; cf. 5:20). In addition, Jesus declared his self-existence in John 14:6: "I am . . . the life" (*egō eimi . . . hē zōē*). Whereas ordinary mortals affirm, "I have life," Jesus unequivocally states that he *is* the inexhaustible source of physical, moral, and spiritual life. John agrees with Jesus' self-understanding when he declares, "For as the Father has life in himself, so he has granted the Son to have life in himself" (John 5:26). John's words "In him was life" (1:4; cf. 1 John 1:2) connote that Jesus uniquely participates in the self-existent life of the Godhead. John, furthermore, represents Jesus as "the Almighty," or the One endowed with limitless power (Rev. 1:8). One of the prominent qualities ascribed to Jesus in the Fourth Gospel is omniscience. Thus Jesus instinctively knew Nathanael's inner character (John 1:47–48), the history of the Samaritan woman (4:16–18), which of the disciples would betray him (6:64; 13:11), and the treacherous events of his last days on earth (18:4). From their life with Jesus, the disciples concluded that he was all-knowing: "We can see that you know all things" (16:30; cf. 21:17). Texts such as John 3:34 and 5:19, 30 suggest that in his state of humiliation the Lord drew on his supernatural powers only when directed by the Father and energized by the Spirit. Moreover, Jesus Christ is consummately loving (13:34; 1 John 3:16), righteous (1 John 2:1), just (John 5:30), and faithful or reliable (Rev. 3:14; 19:11).

Jesus is also more than a man by the divine *works* attributed to him, the first of which is the work of creation. John 1:3 affirms of Christ: "Through him [*di' autou*] all things were made; without him nothing was made that has been made." John believed that all things in the universe (save God himself) were created through the agency of the Word, who later became flesh (cf. Rev. 3:14). Moreover, in chapter 2 we saw that Christ is the cosmic agent of providence; he opens the seven seals to the scroll and sets in motion the awesome series of events that will consummate the present age (Rev. 5:1–8:1). Also ascribed to Jesus is the divine work of remitting sins universally (John 1:29). Through his work as the Lamb who was slain, Jesus gives eternal life to all who believe (4:14; 5:40; 17:2; 20:31). Jesus understood himself to be the bread of life which, when taken in faith, guarantees the receiver spiritual life without end (6:25–59). Ascribed to Jesus is the divine work of raising the dead on the last day (5:25; 6:39; 11:25), of which his miracle of restoring Lazarus to life (11:38–44) was an anticipatory sign (v. 47). A final divine work that Jesus will perform is that of judging the world. "The Father judges no one, but has entrusted all judgment to the Son" (5:22; cf. v. 27). In John 5:17 Jesus coordinates his working with that of the Father, which implies that he is a person ontologically equal to the Father.

Jesus also made *claims* that are appropriate to God alone. In claiming to be one with the Father (John 10:30), Jesus implied that ontologically he was God (v. 33). Because of the perfect union that exists between the Father and the Son, Jesus could say, "All that belongs to the Father is mine" (16:15). Jesus' prediction that he would rise from the grave (2:19–21) was grounded in his assertion to possess complete authority (*exousia*) over his own life (10:17–18). In relation to others Jesus claimed to be the ultimate object of a person's faith (14:1) and obedience (v. 15; 1 John 5:3). The carpenter from Nazareth, moreover, repeatedly claimed to satisfy the deepest spiritual and emotional needs of humanity (John 4:14; 7:37–38; 8:12; 14:27). He claimed to be the way to God (14:6): to see him is to see God (12:45; 14:9), to know him is to know God (8:19; 14:7), and to honor him is to honor God (5:23).

John makes several explicit statements concerning the union of deity and humanity in Jesus Christ, the most important of which is John 1:14: "The Word became flesh and made his dwelling among us." The verb "became" (*egeneto*) is an ingressive aorist, indicating entrance into a state or condition.[54] The Word, who eternally was in fellowship with the Father (John 1:1–2), entered the world and took to himself "flesh." *Sarx* here connotes complete human nature, with emphasis on its weakness and frailty.[55] John thus states, not that the Word was transmuted into a man, but that while remaining what he previously was (i.e., God), the Word assumed all the characteristics of flawless humanity in a perfect union with a single personal center. According to Westcott, the thrust of John 1:14 "lies in the recognition of the unity of the Lord's Person, before and after the incarnation. His personality is divine. But at the same time we must affirm that his humanity is real and complete."[56] In John 1:18 the apostle emphasizes that the assumption of human nature did not nullify his deity, for so the man Jesus is denoted *monogenēs theos,* "God the only Son" (RSV).

Jesus' postresurrection appearance to Thomas and the other disciples in John 20:24–30 confirms that the one person Jesus Christ is both God and man. Jesus' humanity is evidenced by the fact that the disciples witnessed the nail marks and the spear wound in Jesus' body. His deity is attested (1) by the fact that Jesus supernaturally appeared in the midst of the disciples who had assembled behind locked doors; (2) by the forthright confession of the heretofore doubting Thomas: "My Lord and my God!"[57] and (3) by the fact that Jesus did not correct Thomas but acknowledged the validity of his confession (v. 29).

In 1 John 1:1–2 the apostle also upholds the unity of deity and humanity in the single integrated person. John testifies that Jesus appeared in a human body whose reality the disciples grasped with the three higher senses of hearing ("which we have heard"), sight ("which we have seen with our eyes, which we have looked at," aorist middle of *theaomai,* connoting careful and continuous contemplation),[58] and touch ("and our hands have touched"). On the other hand, John attests Jesus' deity by ascribing to him eternal preexistence—he who appeared "was from the beginning" (v. 1) and "the eternal life . . . was with the Father" (v. 2).

The fact that deity and humanity united in the one person, Jesus Christ, is no theoretical concern, but a datum absolutely necessary for salvation. Thus John affirms, "If anyone acknowledges [*hos ean homologēsē*] that Jesus is the Son of God, God lives in him and he in God" (1 John 4:15). Grammatically this verse is a third-class conditional sentence, whereby the statement in the apodosis becomes a reality when the condition given in the protasis is met. Thus confession that Jesus is the incarnate Son of God is the necessary condition for participating in the life of God. John makes the same point in 1 John 5:5: "Who is it that overcomes the world? Only he who believes that Jesus is the Son of God."

Other New Testament Literature

Hebrews devotes more attention to Christ's humanity than any other New Testament letter. The writer upholds Christ's patient endurance of suffering as an encouragement to Jewish Christians who were being persecuted for their faith in Christ, and he focuses on the death of our Lord as that which qualifies him to be an effectual high priest forever. Thus the descendant from the line of Judah (Heb. 7:14) entered the world in a genuine human body (10:5). He shared our "flesh and blood" (2:14), which is a Hebraism for his full participation in our humanity (cf. Matt. 16:17; Gal. 1:16). The aorist active indicative of the verb *metechō* to "share" or "participate in") "points to the historical event of the incarnation when the Son of God assumed this same human nature and thus himself became truly man and accordingly truly one with mankind."[59] As a man, the Son of God was fully tempted as we are (Heb. 4:15) and experienced all the trials and sorrows common to our lot (2:18; 1 Peter 4:1). Hebrews 5:7 vividly describes Christ's emotional anguish as he faced the prospect of drinking the cup of the world's sins: "During the days of Jesus' life on earth, he offered up prayers and petitions with loud cries and tears to the one who could save him from death." The following verse— "Although he was a son, he learned obedience from what he suffered" (v. 8)—suggests that Jesus Christ, even like the son of a human father, had to learn what it means to obey God in the midst of painful trials.[60] Hebrews 2:17 affirms that in order to liberate sinners from bondage to Satan and death Christ "had to be made like his brothers in every way" (3:17). That is, in complete identification with us, Christ entered into the full range of our human experiences. Yet so that he might function as a perfect high priest, Christ's humanity was without moral taint or stain. Although sorely tempted, Jesus never gave in to sin. Thus Hebrews 7:26 describes Jesus as "holy, blameless, pure, set apart from sinners," and 1 Peter 1:19 represents him as "a lamb without blemish or defect." Hebrews 4:15; 9:14; and 1 Peter 2:22 likewise uphold the sinlessness of Jesus.

Three texts describe Jesus as having been made "perfect." Hebrews 2:10 reads: "It was fitting that God, for whom and through whom everything exists, should make the author of their salvation perfect [*teleiōsai*] through suf-

fering." Similarly, Hebrews 5:9 reads, "Once made perfect [*teleiōtheis*], he became the source of eternal salvation for all who obey him." Hebrews 7:28 employs the perfect passive participle form, *teteleiōmenon*. The verb *teleioō* used in each text means to "complete," "finish," or "perfect."[61] In these three verses it bears the specific sense, to "complete a process."[62] Thus the perfection ascribed to Jesus is not a moral perfection but a soteriological one. Through the process of suffering without sinning, of bringing the perfect sacrifice on the cross, and of being raised above all infirmity, Christ discharged his redemptive work to perfection. In short, the perfection discussed in Hebrews signifies God's "making Jesus, through his sufferings, perfectly qualified to be the Savior of His people."[63]

But the one whose humanity is so vividly described is also the eternal God. First, the writer attributes to the Son the cosmic work of creation. Thus he speaks of God's "Son . . . through whom he made the universe" (*di hou kai epoiēsen tous aiōnas,* Heb. 1:2). The words *hoi aiōnes* signify "the whole created universe of space and time."[64] Hebrews 1:10 takes a creation text directed to Yahweh (Ps. 102:25) and applies it to the Son. The writer envisages Jesus Christ as the builder of the universe in all its immensity (Heb. 3:3–4). Second, Hebrews assigns to the Son the cosmic work of preservation. So the Son is engaged in "sustaining [*pherōn*] all things by his powerful word" (1:3). The present active participle, *pherōn,* connotes Christ's task of upholding and directing the vast universe. Noteworthy is Hebrews' ascription of immutability to the church's Lord: "Jesus Christ is the same yesterday and today and forever" (13:8; cf. 1:12).

Names and Titles of Jesus
in the New Testament

Jesus' identity is made clear by names and titles attributed to him in the New Testament. In volume 1, chapter 7 we showed that New Testament writers specifically addressed Jesus as "God" (John 1:1, 18; 20:28; Rom. 9:5; Titus 2:13; 3:4; Heb. 1:8; 2 Peter 1:1; 1 John 5:20). In addition, the New Testament ascribes to Jesus the name and title of "Lord" nearly two hundred and fifty times. Prior to the resurrection, Lord was a common title of respect (Matt. 8:2; Luke 6:46). But following his resurrection and ascension to heaven, the title was conferred on Jesus, especially in the Gentile wing of the church, to designate him the absolute sovereign of the universe (Acts 2:36; 10:36; Rom. 10:9; 1 Cor. 8:6; 2 Cor. 4:5; Phil. 2:11). Thus the apostles applied to Jesus Old Testament citations originally addressed to *Yahweh* (Matt. 3:3; Acts 2:20–21) and to *'adōnay* (Matt. 22:43–45). As *kyrios* Jesus exercises the functions of deity; i.e., he creates (1 Cor. 8:6), saves sinners (Rom. 10:9, 13), and judges the world (Rom. 2:16; 2 Thess. 1:7–8). In terms of his self-understanding, Jesus applied the title "Lord" to himself (Mark 12:36–37). Paul ascribed to Jesus the title "Lord of glory," which Scripture elsewhere applies to God the Father (Acts 7:2; 1 Cor. 2:8; cf. Ps. 24:8–10; Eph. 1:17).

The New Testament represents Jesus as the "Son of God." The angel Gabriel so designated Jesus (Luke 1:35), as did Satan (Matt. 4:3, 6; note the first-class condition, which assumes that the condition in the protasis, "If you are the Son of God . . . ," is true), Peter under divine illumination (Matt. 16:16), John (1 John 3:8; 5:5, 12, 20), and most frequently the apostle Paul (Rom. 1:4; 8:3; Gal. 2:20; 4:4). Moreover, at the baptism (Mark 1:11) and the transfiguration (Mark 9:7) God the

Father certified Jesus to be his Son. Some fifty times Jesus called God his "Father," whereas on several occasions he used Son as a self-designation (Matt. 11:25–27; Mark 13:32). The Jews understood that Jesus made for himself the claim of divine sonship (John 19:7). Thus it is clear that "the synoptic Gospels present a Messiah who was fully conscious of his special relationship to God as Son."[65] The fact that the Old Testament represents Israel as God's son (Exod. 4:22; Hos. 11:1) suggests that Jesus as Son perfectly executes the messianic vocation of the chosen people. But Jesus exercises his messianic calling as the One who ontologically is the eternal Son of the Father. The Son is one with the Father in will (John 4:34; 6:38), in working (14:10), and in very being (10:30). In summary, "the title [Son] also implies a unity of being and nature with the Father, uniqueness of origin and preexistence."[66] The representation of Jesus as "the one and only Son" (*monogenēs huios,* John 1:14; 3:16, 18; 1 John 4:9) upholds the uniqueness of Jesus' sonship: the son of Mary and the Son of God is in a class by himself.[67]

The apostles ascribe to Jesus the name "Holy One" (1 John 2:20; cf. Acts 3:14), or "Holy One of God" (John 6:69). We saw in volume 1, chapter 6 that "Holy One" or "the Holy One of Israel" is a common Old Testament designation for Yahweh, especially in Isaiah. Moreover, Jesus designates himself "the First and the Last" (Rev. 1:17; 2:8) and "the Alpha and the Omega, the First and the Last, the Beginning and the End" (Rev. 22:13)—titles the Old Testament attributes to God alone (Isa. 44:6; 48:12). The title "Word of God," an important Johannine designation of Jesus (John 1:1–4, 14; 1 John 1:1; Rev. 19:13; cf. 1 Peter 1:23), chiefly designates God in his self-expressive activity. The Old Testament refers to the word by which

God creates (Ps. 33:6), reveals himself (Ps. 119:9, 105, 130), sustains the created order (Pss. 147:15–18; 148:8), and effects his will in history (Isa. 55:11). John informs us that the Word or Logos who performs these cosmic functions is the preexistent God (John 1:1–2), who in an act of extreme abasement assumed our humanity (1:14).

An important Christological title is "Messiah" (*messias,* a transliteration of the Hebrew *māšîah*) or "Christ" (*christos,* from the verb *chriō,* to "anoint"). Paul uses *christos* in his letters almost exclusively as a proper name. The title "Christ" was frequently ascribed to Jesus by others (John 1:41; 4:29; 20:31; Acts 2:36; 8:5; Rom. 9:5). Jesus accepted the title three times in the Gospels (Matt. 16:16–17; Mark 14:61–62; John 4:25–26), and this confirms that he understood himself to be the personal fulfillment of Old Testament messianic prophecies. More directly, Jesus applied Isaiah 61:1–2 to himself in the synagogue at Nazareth (Luke 4:18–19; note the aorist form of the verb *chriō*), thus acknowledging his role as the Lord's anointed servant. Whereas contemporary Israel anticipated a triumphant messianic deliverer, Jesus interpreted his role spiritually rather than politically (1 Cor. 15:25). Thus the purpose of his earthly ministry was to inaugurate the rule or reign of God in the hearts of all who would believe and only later to establish a visible, earthly kingdom in power (1 Cor. 15:24–25). Since Israel expected the Messiah to be a king in the line of David (2 Sam. 7:16; Luke 1:32), "Son of David" was a common messianic title applied to Jesus (Matt. 20:30–31; 21:9, 15; cf. Rev. 5:5; 22:16). Yet in Jesus' own mind, the human son of David was simultaneously divine (Matt. 22:42–45).

The title "Son of Man," which occurs some eighty times on the lips of Jesus in the Gospels, derives from the vision of Daniel 7:13–14. The Son of Man, who receives from the Ancient of Days a universal and eternal kingdom, is best understood as both an individual and the ideal representative of the people of God (cf. Heb. 2:6–9). In postbiblical Judaism the Son of Man was a supernatural Messiah who would come at the end of the age and rule in the kingdom of God. Contrary to Jewish expectation, Jesus used the title Son of Man in the context of his humiliation, suffering, and death on the cross (Matt. 12:40; Mark 8:31; John 6:53; 8:28). Yet Jesus also used the title in the context of his future exaltation, world rule, judgment, and second coming to earth (Matt. 16:27; 19:28; 25:31; Mark 14:61–62; John 5:27; 13:31–32; Acts 7:56—the only reference outside the Gospels). In sum, by employing the Son of Man imagery, "Jesus thought of himself in terms of a heavenly Messiah fulfilling on earth a ministry on man's behalf which would culminate in scenes of final glory."[68] The reality of Christ's divine and human natures is implicit in the title.

Paul's equivalent of the Son of Man title is "the last Adam" (1 Cor. 15:45) and "the man from heaven" (1 Cor. 15:47–49). Jesus as the perfect man is the representative of humanity (cf. Rom. 5:15, 17–19) who by his death and resurrection leads the redeemed race to the heavenly world whence he came.

SYSTEMATIC FORMULATION

Attempts to develop Christologies exclusively "from above" (revelation) or exclusively "from below" (historical evidence) are deficient in that they eliminate some of the relevant information (either from below or from above). In contrast, a verificational approach critically considers hypotheses from any source and accepts the hypothesis that accounts for the lines of relevant evidence both from above (revealed meanings) and below (observable evidence). In accord with the extensive biblical data in the previous section, we find most coherent the hypothesis that Christ Jesus was one person with both divine and human natures. Here we develop that view systematically and exhibit its coherence, including its consistency, adequacy, and viability. We begin by exhibiting the view's adequacy to account for the data from below—the observable Jesus in history.

A Person in History

The Son of God not only entered into the world in literal human flesh but also lived for about thirty-three years on earth. His historical existence was significant throughout his mature life and ministry. The above views of Bultmann and Ogden question whether we can know anything historically about Jesus as we try to reconstruct the past by a critical use of ancient records. In *Ancient Evidence for the Life of Jesus,* Gary Habermas, in addition to examining the accurate Gospel accounts, assesses numerous extrabiblical sources from secular historians (Tacitus), government officials (Pliny the Younger), religious records of Jews (Josephus, the Talmud), other Gentile sources (Lucian, Mara Bar-Serapion), Gnostic writings, and others. The seventeen non-Christian sources from within 125 years of Jesus' death are far more than for any other person from ancient times. They indicate that Jesus was a flesh-and-blood person, the brother of James, who lived in Palestine. He was known as a virtuous person who taught the need for conversion, the importance of faith and obedience, the brotherhood of believers, the need for abandoning other gods and worshiping himself, and the idea that his death was the means of life for many. He performed miracles and made prophecies that were later fulfilled. So he had many disciples from both Jews and Gentiles. Some believed he was the Messiah and some worshiped him as God. Because he led Jews astray by teaching apostasy, he would die. He was put to death by Pontius Pilate, who had him crucified during the reign of Emperor Tiberius on the eve of the Passover. After his death his teachings broke out again and witnesses claimed to have seen Jesus alive three days after his death. In addition to all this are the early creeds and other noncanonical Christian sources. Recent archaeological discoveries, furthermore, also support the historicity of Jesus' life, and the same basic view of Jesus as the New Testament does.[69]

At the same time, according to Ronald Nash, attempts to derive the life of Christ and early Christianity from Greek philosophical sources, pagan mystery religions, and Gnosticism have failed to find adequate support. In *Christianity and the Hellenistic World* Nash finds those hypotheses to depend more on naturalistic presuppositions than adequate evidence. The hypotheses of derivation from Greek philosophy, mystery religions, or Gnosticism explain everything but how there came to be a Christian church and how writers could draw from these sources and produce a mythical hero with the uniqueness of Jesus. Nash asks, "Was early Christianity a syncretistic faith? Did it borrow any of its essential beliefs and practices either from Hellenistic philosophy or religion or from Gnosticism?" And after extensive research, Nash answers, "The evidence requires that this question be answered in the negative."[70]

John Stott concludes his work *The Authentic Jesus* by saying,

> Instead of seeking to edit the New Testament witness to Christ, we should feel what Paul called a "godly jealousy" for his glory, and should have an unshakeable resolve to give him the honor which is due his name. In order to do this, we shall

have to renounce the folly of fabricating "a Jesus other than the Jesus we [the apostles] preached" (2 Cor. 11:1–4) and instead hold fast to the authentic Jesus, who is the Jesus of the apostolic witness.[71]

A Fully Human Person

Jesus' humanness is evident in many different ways. Historically, he lived during a certain historical epoch in a distinctive milieux. Physically, he was limited to a relatively small space (in a certain geographical area in which he needed to walk or ride an animal from place to place). Biologically, Jesus hungered and ate, grew tired, slept, suffered pain, eventually died, and was buried. Filially, he obeyed Mary and Joseph (Luke 2:51). Intellectually he grew in knowledge and wisdom (2:40, 52). He could express amazement at the faith of the centurion (7:9) and the unbelief of the men of Nazareth (Mark 6:6), and he did not know the time of his return. Religiously, he regularly attended public worship (Luke 4:16) and, at least in one instance, paid the temple tax (Matt. 17:24–27).

Spiritually, Jesus did not neglect private prayer. He prayed alone very early in the morning (Mark 1:35). He also prayed after ministering to the five thousand (6:46), and he sometimes prayed all night (Luke 6:12). His praying shows that he had a deep sense of felt need. Socially, he attended weddings (John 2:1–11) and banquets with sinners (Matt. 9:10–11) and he especially loved specific people such as Mary, Martha, and Lazarus (John 11:3, 5). Politically, he urged citizens to pay taxes to the state (Matt. 22:21). Psychologically and emotionally, he experienced joy (John 15:11), sorrow (11:35), and anxiety (in Gethsemane).

A Tempted Person

One of the clearest indications of Jesus' full humanity is his genuine struggle with temptations. Jesus experienced severe temptations from Satan to use his divine powers in ways contrary to the Father's redemptive purpose. Starving after forty days of fasting, Jesus could have used his divine power to turn stones into bread (Matt. 4:3). By drawing on those divine powers he could have thrown himself from the highest point of the temple and so, by escaping injury, demonstrate the Father's care (vv. 5–6). By changing his loyalty from pleasing the Father to pleasing Satan, he could have avoided the crucifixion and, insofar as Satan is to be trusted, possessed all the kingdoms of this world (vv. 8–9). Then the devil left him until another "opportune time" (Luke 4:13). No doubt Jesus was also tempted by others around him throughout his ministry. Indeed, he was tempted in every way, just as we are (Heb. 4:15).

Since Jesus was tempted in every way as we are, he must have been tempted sexually as an adolescent and also as a man in the prime of his sexual potency. God created persons male and female, and so sexual desires as such are not themselves sinful or a sign of fallen human nature. As a man, Jesus could have respected and admired women without desiring them for himself. Temptation would occur in enticements to satisfy his sexual desires in a way displeasing to the Father, that is, contrary to his or others' best interests. Undoubtedly, displeasing sexual proposals came to Jesus' attention, were considered, and had a certain allure, as all temptations do. But regularly Jesus willed not to consent to the enticements. Temptation is not sin; entertaining it in the mind and yielding to it in action is sin. And Jesus did not entertain sinful suggestions in his heart or yield to them in action. He neither lusted nor committed adultery. He did not covet what belonged to others nor steal. He did not get angry without cause, nor did he commit murder. He worshiped God only and did not take his Father's name in vain. He loved the Father with his whole being and his neighbors as himself.

Facing betrayal and agonizing death in Gethsemane, Jesus pled, "Father, if you are willing, take this cup from me" (Luke 22:42). So severe was the struggle that he was in "anguish" and prayed more earnestly, "and his sweat was like drops of blood falling to the ground" (v. 44). Although he had no sinful tendencies within himself, no doubt the appeal of sinful options presented themselves to him with even greater force because of his moral purity. As fully human, he felt the full psychological, moral, and spiritual force of severe temptations.

A Just Person
(From Human Observation)

It is one thing to be lured by a tempter and another to yield and sin. Although tempted as we are, Jesus was "without sin" (Heb. 4:15). That witness came from varied sources. He himself could say, "Can any of you prove me guilty of sin?" (John 8:46). Alerting his disciples to his approaching departure, he said, "The prince of this world is coming. He has no hold on me" (14:30). When his enemies could not sustain their accusations, Pilate concluded, "As for me, I find no basis for a charge against him" (19:6). His closest disciples, who traveled with him for three years, support his sinlessness. John could say, "In him is no sin" (1 John 3:5). Peter called him "the Holy and Righteous One" (Acts 3:14) and "a lamb without blemish or defect" (1 Peter 1:19). Peter also declared, "He committed no sin, and no deceit was

found in his mouth" (2:22) and later stated that Christ died for sins, "the righteous for the unrighteous" (3:18). The writer of Hebrews said that he "was tempted in every way, just as we are—yet was without sin" (Heb. 4:15), and as a high priest he was "holy, blameless, pure, set apart from sinners" (Heb. 7:26). Paul wrote that he "had no sin" (2 Cor. 5:21). So when Paul teaches that God sent his Son "in the likeness of sinful man" (Rom. 8:3), he speaks of the need for Christ to identify with fallen humans to save them but not to partake in their sin.

For the fully human Jesus to be tempted as we are, however, some argue that it was necessary that he have a sinful or fleshly nature. Reinhold Niebuhr and Karl Barth hold that since Jesus was tempted in all points as we are, he must have had a sinful nature like our fallen nature.[72] That Jesus had a morally defective nature is not a necessary inference from the fact that he was tempted as we were. Our problem is not one of mere sins, but a sinful nature, leading John Knox to ask, "Could one have shared in that existence and not participated in that wrongness?"[73] Several considerations make the hypothesis of Jesus' sinful nature implausible.

1. Jesus must have been tempted inwardly, but that is not to say that the temptations originated in the nature of the Holy One. He had the same types of temptations, but that is not to say that they had the same source. What, then, can we infer from his being tempted as we are? It means that he experienced all the same basic types of temptations we do. Jesus became flesh in the physical sense (John 1:14), and he was, according to his human nature, a descendant of David (Rom. 1:3). Therefore he could be tempted in all ways as we are physically.

2. Given a scriptural concept of the flesh in a moral sense, a fallen nature

involves far more than temptations. If Jesus had been fleshly in nature as fallen people are, he would have been "controlled by the sinful nature" (Rom. 7:5). Jesus would have been unable to do good, for nothing good lives in the sinful nature (7:18). If he had had a sinful nature like ours, he could not have obeyed God's law (8:3). And he would have been dominated by a mind-set contrary to the will of the Spirit (v. 5). The mind of Jesus would then have been hostile to God and would not have submitted to God's law, nor could it have done so (v. 7). Had Jesus had a sinful nature as we do, he could not have pleased God (v. 8), and he would have desired what is contrary to the Spirit (Gal. 5:13). Had Jesus been born of sinful flesh, he would have had to be born again to enter the kingdom of God (John 3:3–7). But from conception and birth Jesus was Lord! He did not need to be born again, for his virgin conception involved more than a biological miracle. It involved a moral miracle. As a result of the Holy Spirit's overshadowing Mary, "the holy one" to be born of her would be the Son of God (Luke 1:35, see previous chapter). Had he been a sinner, he would have had to die for his own sins and could not have been the sacrifice for others' sins.

3. It does not require a fleshly—that is, sinful—nature for one to be fully human. Adam's and Eve's natures were fully human and not fleshly before the Fall. And they were subject to temptations as fallen people are. In heaven believing people will be fully human without sin. So Jesus' sinlessness in nature is not logically incompatible with full humanity. We often include sin in the essence of humanity by saying, "What I did was only human!" More accurately we should say, "What I did was only sinful!" Jesus did what was human but not what was sinful. His righteous acts came from a righteous, not a depraved, heart.

4. To atone for sin Jesus came in the *likeness* of sinful man (Rom. 8:3), but he did not come as a sinful man. The term *likeness* involves sufficient similarity to humanness that Jesus could die for sinners as a sin-offering, but it indicates a limit. Paul did not say what Barth interprets him to say, that it was essential for Jesus to have existed as "man who is a sinner" or "in sin-controlled flesh."[74] Barth tends to overlook the term *likeness* in interpreting this verse. He also fails to understand that at the cross the guilt and penalty of our sins were imputed to Christ. Our sins were not transferred to the crucified Messiah. We need to keep in mind the sinless life that made his death for others possible. Jesus' likeness to us was not as an initiator of sin, but as one who could be tempted. "He was passively exposed to sin," Käsemann concludes, "but in distinction from us he did not actively open himself to it. What is decisive for such a perspective is not the susceptibility to sin, but the reality of the sin-offering which was made for us and represents us."[75] It is one thing to say in a metaphoric sense that life is *like* a vapor and another to say that life is a vapor. So it is one thing for Paul to write in Romans 8, after explaining what was involved in the sinful nature in chapters 6–8, that God sent his own Son in the *likeness* of sin-controlled flesh, and quite another to say that he sent his own Son *in* sin-controlled flesh! Jesus did not bring sin with him to his environment, all kinds of temptations came from around him, but he was not a tempter of himself or others.

The hypothesis that Jesus had a sinful nature fails to fit the Scripture's explicit teaching (above and following) that he was totally without spot, blemish, or sin. An alleged inference from his being tempted as we are does not merit greater probability than that explicit evidence. A sinful Jesus of history cannot be divorced from a sinless Christ of faith. Christology rests on both history and theology. In *Luke: Historian and Theologian,* I. Howard Marshall has presented a conclusive case that no necessary conflict rages between history and faith. Rather, "Christian faith is dependent upon historically verifiable events. This was the view taken by Luke, and we have attempted to show in adopting this view he was not taking up an individual point of view but that he was in agreement with the early church generally."[76]

A Fully Righteous Person (From the Father's Perspective)

In addition to the events attested by historical observers, however, we have the invisible meanings of the facts that God gave by special revelation. We look now at what even first-century eyewitnesses could know of Jesus Christ only by revelation from above. This content came through credentialed spokespeople: the inspired prophetic and apostolic writers of Scripture.

The ultimate standard of goodness is what pleases the Father. God the Father looks not only on the outward appearance but also on the heart. So Jesus said, "I seek not to please myself but him who sent me" (John 5:30). Jesus evidently succeeded in pleasing the Father, for both at Jesus' baptism and at his transfiguration God the Father said, "With him I am well pleased" (Matt. 3:17; 17:5). Jesus did not transgress divine law nor deviate from whatever it means to be ethically human. All that he thought, said, and did was motivated by love, energized by the Holy Spirit and was pleasing to the heavenly Father. Hence Jesus not only did not sin, he was not inwardly sinful.

Because he was sinless in the sight of God and man, the Son of God had authority on earth to forgive sins (Matt. 9:6). To the paralytic who was healed Jesus said, "Son, your sins are forgiven" (Mark 2:5). The teachers of the law, thinking this blasphemy, properly asked, "Who can forgive sin but God alone?" (2:6–7). Because he was sinless Jesus did not need to die for his own sins but could offer himself for the sins of others. "No miracle of Christ equals the miracle of his sinless life. To be holy in all thought and feeling, never to fail in duty to others, never to transgress the law of perfect love to God or man, never to exceed or to come short—this is a condition outstripping the power of imagination and almost of belief. Here is a casement opening on a Diviner world."[77]

A Fully Divine Person

In the previous chapter we proposed that although the eternal Word gave up the constant use of his divine attributes, he progressively revealed his divine nature through increasingly specific teaching attested by more and more conclusive miraculous "signs." We need here to consider further whether the view of his full deity can adequately fit the scriptural givens.

Non-Trinitarians often allege that Jesus himself never said, "I am God." Jews and Muslims especially may make a major case out of the fact that he did not explicitly say, "I am God." But in his historical context (including theism and the extensive evidence given for Trinitarianism) he could not be expected to make that claim. For Jesus to say "I am God" would mean far more than it does for monists like Shirley MacLaine, who in her television mini-series, "Out on a Limb," stood on the beach and repeated with increasing conviction, "I am God." She meant that inwardly her soul was made up of the same pervasive energy as is everything else. Her "divinity" transcends herself but not the cosmos. Jesus' God is a personal Spirit distinct from the entirety of the cosmos. In a theistic and Trinitarian perspective, for Jesus to say "I am God" would mean that he imagined himself to be either the heavenly Father or the entirety of the triune Godhead. Taking Jesus' frame of reference into account, the most that Jesus could meaningfully claim was that he was one with the Father. The questions we can reasonably ask of Jesus in context are "Did Jesus ever claim to be one with the Father not only relationally in mind and purpose, but also in essence and being?" and, "Did Jesus claim divine prerogatives and do divine works?

What did Jesus actually *claim* for himself? When he said to Satan, the tempter, "Do not put the Lord your God to the test" (Matt. 4:7), Jesus applied Deuteronomy 6:16 to himself as God. Jesus claimed to preexist with the Father. When he was asked if he was greater than Abraham, he responded, "Before Abraham was born, I am!" (John 8:58). In prayer Jesus spoke of the glory he had had with the Father "before the world began" (17:5). Jesus claimed to be more than one with the Father in mind and purpose; he claimed oneness of power. For a person is as secure in his hand, he alleged, as in the Father's hand (John 10:28–29). So when he said, "I and the Father are one" (10:30), he meant they were one in the attribute of omnipotence. The Jews understood that he was claiming to be God (v. 33); this is why they sought to stone him for blasphemy. He claimed his uniqueness among humans as "the one whom the Father set apart as his very own and sent into the world" (v. 36). Distinctively Jesus alleged, "The Father is in me, and I in the Father" (v. 38). Again the Jews understood him to imply that he was divine and again they tried to stone him for blasphemy. Jesus even claimed to be omnipresent: "And surely I am with you always, to the very end of the age"

(Matt. 28:20). In statements like these Jesus claimed that as a distinct person he preexisted with the Father eternally, was one in essence (or attribute) with the Father, and was uniquely sent by the Father into the world. Although Jesus was a person with truly human characteristics, he also taught that he was different from every other human being as ontologically one with the Father.

Furthermore Jesus claimed *divine prerogatives*. He claimed that he is the source of the necessities in an eternal life-support system including spiritual water, food, and light. He said that he was the giver of living water: "Whoever drinks the water I give him will never thirst" (John 4:14, cf. v. 10). He also alleged, "I am the bread of life" (6:48) and "The bread of God is he who comes down from heaven and gives life to the world" (v. 33). The Jews understood that by saying this he claimed for himself a supernatural origin (v. 42). Furthermore, he declared, "I am the light of the world" (8:12). Again, he said, "I tell you the truth, if anyone keeps my word, he will never see death" (John 8:51). At Bethany, where Lazarus lay buried, he said, "I am the resurrection and the life. He who believes in me will live, even though he dies" (11:25; cf. 5:21). Furthermore he encouraged and accepted the worship of the apostles before his death (14:1), and after his resurrection (Matt. 28:17) Jesus exhibited his conviction that he was God. He said, "I am in the Father and the Father is in me" (John 14:11). To Thomas who questioned where Jesus was going after his death, Jesus made this astounding statement: "I am the way and the truth and the life. No one comes to the Father except through me. If you really knew me, you would know my Father as well" (vv. 6–7). Although God alone can forgive sins, Jesus forgave sins (Mark 2:9–10). Jesus also declared that "the Son of Man is

339

Lord even of the Sabbath" (Mark 2:27). Jesus had the audacity to demand that people should love him more than their own fathers, mothers, brothers, sisters, sons, or daughters (Luke 12:53; 14:26–27). As a matter of fact he made it clear that the Father had given to him "all authority in heaven and on earth" (Matt. 28:18).

Did Jesus at any time *deny* his deity? He disclaimed being the Father, but he never denied being the Father's eternal Word who came from heaven on a mission to save lost human beings. For the purpose of saving the lost he spoke of his functional subordination to the Father and his dependence on the Father. Specifically he said, "The Father is greater than I" (John 14:28). Jesus was sent by the Father into the world to perform a task that he completed in dependence on the Father. Jesus fulfilled his distinct functions in harmony with the work of the heavenly Father and the Holy Spirit. Jesus did not view himself as a human who was deified at his baptism or transfiguration. Repeatedly he spoke of himself as the eternal Son of God or Son of Man who alone had come from above. He alone knew the Father as the Father knew him (John 10:15). When Jesus responded to the rich young ruler, "Why do you call me good? No one is good—except God alone" (Luke 18:19), he hardly denied what he had said of himself so many other times. Rather, he drew attention to who he really was and why he could ask the rich to leave all and follow him (v. 22). None of his references to himself in the state of humiliation deny his claims that he was uniquely and essentially one with the Father from before his conception and birth on earth.

By accepting the fact that Jesus was essentially God in human flesh as he claimed, we can account for much related first-century data or phenomena. The hypothesis of his divine sonship accounts for his *incomparable teaching*. As Jesus taught in the temple courts, "the Jews were amazed and asked, 'How did this man get such learning without having studied?'" (John 7:15). When the temple guards were asked why they did not arrest him, they explained, "No one ever spoke the way this man does" (v. 46). When he had finished his Sermon on the Mount, "the crowds were amazed at his teaching, because he taught as one who had authority, and not as their teachers of the law" (Matt. 7:28–29). The response to Jesus' unparalleled and authoritative teaching and the countless changed lives confirm his astounding claims.

If Jesus is what he claimed to be, we can coherently account also for his *sterling character*. No ordinary fallen person could challenge an audience of friends and enemies as Jesus did, "Can any of you prove me guilty of sin?" (John 8:46). After Jesus was condemned to death as a criminal, Judas, seized with remorse, returned the thirty silver coins to the chief priests and elders and cried, "I have sinned, for I have betrayed innocent blood" (Matt. 27:3–4). Pilate, the judge at Jesus' trial, having found that Jesus had committed no crime, washed his hands in front of the bloodthirsty crowd. "'I am innocent of this man's blood,' he said. 'It is your responsibility!'" (Matt. 27:24). The thief crucified to the right of Jesus said, "We are punished justly, for we are getting what our deeds deserve. But this man has done nothing wrong" (Luke 23:41). Jesus' closest friends with him in all kinds of circumstances for three years also confirmed the righteousness of his character. Peter likened Jesus to a sacrificial lamb "without blemish or defect" (1 Peter 1:19). John wrote, "in him is no sin" (1 John 3:5).

Granting that Jesus was what he claimed to be, we can explain his *supernatural works*. Jesus healed invalids (John 5:1–15), gave sight to the blind

(9:1–12), cured lepers (Matt. 8:1–4), raised the dead (John 11:38–44), and controlled a furious storm that had nearly sunk the disciples' boat. The disciples woke him saying, " 'Teacher, don't you care if we drown?' He got up, rebuked the wind and said to the waves, 'Quiet! Be still!' Then the wind died down and it was completely calm" (Mark 4:37–39). The terrified followers asked each other, "Who is this? Even the wind and the waves obey him!" (v. 41).

If Jesus was what he claimed to be, furthermore, we can explain his *dying grace*. During his betrayal, his unjust trial, threats of death, and the agony of crucifixion, Jesus exhibited *agapē* love—the self-giving love of God. While in agony on the cross, he prayed for his executioners, "Father, forgive them for they do not know what they are doing" (Luke 23:34). The thief on his right said, "Jesus, remember me when you come into your kingdom" (v. 42). The centurion guarding Jesus exclaimed, " 'Surely he was the Son of God!' " (Matt. 27:54).

If Jesus indeed was what he claimed to be, we can account for his empty tomb and *triumphant resurrection*. Although buried in a cave sealed with a huge rock and guarded by armed soldiers, "up from the grave he arose in a mighty triumph o'er his foes!" The risen Christ left the tomb empty and appeared to several individuals and groups including over five hundred people at once (1 Cor. 15:1–8). Indeed, Jesus "through the Spirit of holiness was declared with power to be the Son of God by his resurrection from the dead: Jesus Christ our Lord" (Rom. 1:4).

What hypothesis provides the most coherent and viable account of Jesus' claims? Was he a good man, a liar, a lunatic, or Lord of all? Good men who made anything like the claims Jesus made for himself would no longer be considered good. Unable to substantiate such claims, they would be judged to be either intentional liars or irresponsible lunatics. Of all persons, Jesus was no liar! He lived and died to stand up for the truth. And Jesus, was no raving lunatic! His teaching and conduct reflected sanity and control in the midst of even the most excruciating circumstances. Purposefully and consistently he revealed who he was, and he supported his claims with a sinless character, incomparable teaching, supernatural works for others, and supremely with his own resurrection from the dead. Since the hypotheses of a good person, a liar, or a lunatic are improbable in the light of the evidence, we need a more adequate hypothesis. Finding that the narrative of the Gospels is a coherent account of these first-century phenomena, we propose that Jesus was in fact all that he claimed to be—one in essence, power, and prerogative with the Father in heaven.

Christ's claims for himself cannot successfully be dismissed as mere projections of the church without a referent. If a group of untrained writers like the disciples could make up the fabulous character who has influenced history more than any other person, they would merit an international literary award. The import of Jesus' claims is recognized not only by friends but also by enemies. There is no mistaking the witness of the apostles who knew him best. One of his closest associates, Peter, concluded that he is "the Son of the living God" (Matt. 16:16) and wrote to "those who through the righteousness of our God and Savior Jesus Christ have received a faith as precious as ours" (2 Peter 1:1). Thomas, after making stubborn attempts to think of him otherwise, exclaimed, "My Lord and my God!" (John 20:28). Jehovah's Witnesses and others should note that the definite article (*hē*) precedes the word God (*theos*), on the Witnesses' own grammatical principle referring to the Jehovah God. And in referring to Jesus as Lord and God, Thomas was not using expletives! The account of Thomas' faith supplies the climactic evidence for believing "that Jesus is the Christ" (John 20:31). Paul speaks of Jesus as "God over all, forever praised" (Rom. 9:5). And Paul anticipates the "glorious appearing of our great God and Savior, Jesus Christ" (Titus 2:13). John thought of Jesus as the eternal Word (*Logos*) of God who became flesh (John 1:1, 14) and as "Jesus Christ, the Righteous One" (1 John 2:1). Rather than recant these convictions born of their direct experience with Christ, these apostles would rather die. They proved their convictions when they became martyrs for their belief. Their faith in Jesus' deity did not contradict God's oneness (in essence) because they recognized not only Jesus' personal distinction from the Father but also his essential oneness with the Father.

If Jesus is who he claimed to be, we can account also for the witness of even the *unholy spirits*. At Capernaum a "channeler" possessed by an evil spirit cried out, "What do you want with us, Jesus of Nazareth? Have you come to destroy us? I know who you are—the Holy One of God!" (Mark 1:23–24). The title indicates Jesus' unique origin more than his messianic mission. Similarly in Tyre and Sidon, when evil spirits saw him, "they fell down before him and cried out, 'You are the Son of God'" (3:11). By recognizing Jesus as the Son of God, demons acknowledged that he was not made like other kinds of beings, but was eternally begotten of the same nature as the Father. The Gerasene man possessed by many demons fell in front of Jesus and shouted at the top of his voice, "What do you want with me, Jesus, Son of the Most High God?" (5:7).

The deity of Jesus, then, is not a late development taught only by the church long after his life was over. It is a doctrine claimed by the Messiah himself. And that claim is confirmed by his sterling character, astounding works, unparalleled teaching, self-giving spirit even in death, and supremely his predicted death-defeating resurrection. With all of these converging indications of his actual incarnation, it is most implausible that a group of untrained writers, editors, and redactors could have invented *The Greatest Story Ever Told* about the greatest person ever to live on earth.

Observe that the Jewish writers of the New Testament do not regard the confession of the deity of Christ as a challenge to monotheism. Functionally Christ strengthened monotheism by always and everywhere championing the glory, teaching, and honor of the Father. Christ's forgiveness of sins and acceptance of worship does not displace these roles for the Father; it contributes to them. Hence adoration of Christ is the direct opposite of all blasphemy. And belief in the Father, the Son, and the Holy Spirit is completely antipolytheistic.

Note also that any denial of the ontological deity of Christ undermines an ontological Trinitarianism. A soundly biblical doctrine either of Jesus Christ incarnate or of the Father, Son, and Holy Spirit inescapably involves ontology or metaphysics. If Jesus is *not* the second person of the Trinity, then a God of undifferentiated sameness has historically revealed himself in different disguises (as Father, Son, and Spirit) to be something that he really is not in himself. It seems very pious to say that we mere humans cannot know God in himself. But to repeat that after God has revealed who he is in himself through the incarnate Christ's person and teaching is to distrust God's supreme personal revelation to mankind.

The One Person Is Both Divine and Human

It is meaningful to think successively, as we have, about the humanity and then about the deity of Christ, but in thinking about the one person concretely it is important always to relate the divine and human natures to each other. The Word came into the world as Jesus in the flesh, and so the babe of Bethlehem is eternal. We seek to understand the relationship of the divineness to the humanness in the one person in respect to each of our basic categories.

Metaphysically, in accord with our critical realism (I:36–37), we have evidence above for asserting that the one concrete person in reality possessed two natures from his conception and birth. The second person of the Trinity condescended to partake in or share our humanity (Heb. 2:14). Elizabeth called the Holy Spirit-fathered infant conceived by Mary while still in his mother's womb "my Lord" (Luke 1:43). The human nature of Christ differs from all other human natures, negatively, by not having a different human personality of its own (*anhypostasia*) and positively, by subsisting *in* the divine personality (*enhypostasia*). Jesus Christ has two natures, but is not two persons. The one person who came from God the Father added to himself a human nature. This understanding preserves the continuity in the incarnation of the divine Logos. The Logos has come in the flesh (1 John 4:1–3). Since Jesus of Nazareth had both human and divine natures, it is futile to seek a reductively human Jesus of history unassociated with the eternal Son of God. The Christ of Christian faith is both human and divine.

Involved in the personal (hypostatic) union are the *two distinct natures*. The two sets of attributes are neither mixed nor confounded. No attribute of the one nature is transferred to the other. Nei-

ther is a third hybrid produced. What unites the two natures is that both may be predicated of the one actual person. The two natures exist not merely in a functional harmony, nor are they in a nonmetaphysical way merely communicated to each other. The divine nature is not simply the indwelling Holy Spirit as is the case in all Christians. Nor did the human nature lose anything by its assumption into the person of God's Son. In the God-man we find a complex of two distinct natures, but not a confusion of the two sets of attributes.

The *union* between the divine and human, however, was "personal," but not in name only as nominalists allege. The union of the human and divine natures involved a relation between the Son and the Father, but it was not a merely relational union like the oneness of mind among friends. The union was not merely an accidental union of two entities bound together. Providence was involved, but it was not merely a providential unity similar to the way in which all things hold together (Col. 1:17). Neither is it merely a legal union by the adoption of a human into a divine status at his baptism or some other occasion. The most coherent proposal suggests a personal union of the divine and human natures in one *hypostasia*. Both natures are predicated of the one person. Some of his attributes are divine and some of them are human. Hence we speak of the *hypostatic or personal union* of the two distinct natures. Whatever may be affirmed of either nature may be affirmed of the one person. The one person may be called God or the one person may be called human, not in mere figurative or functional senses, but in a cognitive sense that is true in reality. Whatever happens to the human nature happens to the Son of God, and whatever the Son of God did on earth, he did in and through the human nature.

The actual metaphysical union remains even when in the *kenosis* the eternal Word chose not always to take advantage of his divine attributes (e.g., omnipresence) in order to exist and grow as a child who walked from place to place. At the beginning of the incarnation Jesus' potential humanness was not developed, but it grew as he grew in stature. As the human child grew, however, his personality was realized only in union with the divine nature.[78] Since he did not ordinarily use the latent divine powers, his appearance generally was that of a rather typical human person.

With the Reformed, we stress the distinctness of the natures ontologically; with the Lutherans, we also underline their functional harmony in the acts and relationships of the one person. "Luther . . . does not regard the communication of the divine attributes to the human nature as 'inflexibly physical,' but as 'dynamic.' "[79] How does this general position work out in the life of the God-man?

Intellectually, the fully divine Logos had his divine mind and a fully human rational and intellectual capacity made like God's. The divine consciousness much of the time was sublimated in accord with the progressive revelation of his divine nature. Therefore most of the time the one consciousness was that of the human nature. The divine capability of omniscience was not ordinarily drawn upon, but the human mental capabilities were used in a manner consistent with the divine. When any human mind thinks truth, it thinks thoughts that conform to God's revealed thoughts about reality. So when the growing child Jesus consciously considered truth, he thought in a manner compatible with his divine nature also. Thus he grew in wisdom and in favor with both God and man (Luke 2:40, 52).

Emotionally, as fully divine the one person had the emotional capabilities of God, and as fully human he had the capabilities of the affections of a human made in God's image. Because he humbled himself, the divine affective capacities were not ordinarily utilized. When the human emotions delighted in holiness and were provoked by evil, they were not totally other than God's emotions; they pleased the Father. When the growing child or man emotionally responded to repentant sinners or self-righteous hypocrites, his affective states as such were in harmony with the affective states of the divine nature.

Volitionally, the second person of the Trinity had a divine will and added the volitional capacity of a human divine image-bearer. In the *kenosis* the divine will was not ordinarily utilized, but the human self-determinations of Christ were taken in accord with the revealed will of the Father. So when the growing boy or man chose to respond negatively to temptations or to a need with humble service, his will acted in harmony with the divine will. When he said, "Not my will, but yours be done" (Luke 22:42), he chose to follow the Father's redemptive plan rather than escape the suffering. In no instance did he exercise his divine or human volitional powers independently of the Father's pleasure. The one God-man carried out his Father's wise desires unhypocritically.

Morally, it follows that the human and divine natures are distinguishable but united in the one person. In his condescension God's Son ordinarily chose not to draw on his divine moral strengths, but when in the human nature Jesus judged tempting thoughts to be evil and rejected them, his ethical discernment and action turned out to be in accord with that of the divine nature. So as the growing boy acted with moral accountability and responsibility, he persistently resisted temptation and fled from it. We can understand why the accounts of his life reported that "the grace of God was upon him" (Luke

2:40). Throughout Jesus' life his excellent use of his capabilities morally exhibited an authentic harmony with his divine nature in its absolute holiness.

Relationally, the eternal Son of God gave up the direct fellowship with the Father and Holy Spirit he had enjoyed in heaven. As a spiritually growing human, he spoke and acted as a human in harmony with the heavenly Father and the Holy Spirit. He loved not only the Father and Holy Spirit but also the lost people he came to save. Personally Jesus loved tax collectors and sinners, Jews and Samaritans, prostitutes and physicians, fishermen and teachers, his mother and brothers, the blind and the deaf, children and adults, the hungry and the well-fed, the introverts and the extroverts.

The acts of the one incarnate person always exhibited his human qualities and on appropriate occasions progressively revealed his divine qualities. When the human Jesus performed miracles, both natures functioned concursively and harmoniously. When he died, his human nature suffered and his body began to decay and decompose (Acts 13:35–37). But when he rose again in his glorious body, he reversed the irreversible processes of decomposition and decay. Since his conception, the one person has the two distinct natures forever. The risen and glorified God-man not only lived on earth but ascended to heaven and is now seated with the Father in glory with power over all. God has exalted humanity, not only by creating mankind in his image, but also by uniting the second Adam to the person of the eternal Son.

A Test Case of One's View of the Divine and Human in Christ

Since Jesus Christ committed no sin, the question, "Could Jesus Christ sin?" is purely hypothetical. Usually it is not worth the time to speculate about such "iffy" questions. However, in this case the discussion profits by helping people think through the issues related to Christ's two natures in one person. The discussion also brings out some implications of different interpretations of free will and the importance of taking into account as many lines of evidence as possible in one's method of theological decision making. Consider several lines of argument, all of which need to be taken together for systematic purposes before drawing a final conclusion.

If Jesus could not sin, *how could he experience genuine temptation?* The major premise of arguments that the Son of God could have sinned is that the possibility of sin is necessary to genuine temptation. Must it be possible for one to yield to temptation to be tempted? Must one be able to yield in order to feel the allure of sin? To consider it? The reality of Jesus' temptations to seek peace by occult powers rather than by suffering love should not be minimized (Matt. 4:1–11; 16:21–23; 26:36–41). At the thought of his crucifixion Jesus was "troubled" (John 12:27) and "distressed" (Luke 12:50). Jesus' obedience was not automatic but "learned" (Heb. 5:8). He could genuinely struggle with temptations because being tempted is radically different from falling into temptation. Being "dragged away" by evil desires (James 1:13) is sin. Being tempted to displease the heavenly Father while living in the world is not sin. In order to understand how Jesus could be tempted although he was unable to sin we must grasp the radical difference between temptation and sin. Because a godly person does not commit certain wrong acts, it need not mean that the appeal is not felt. Because an army cannot be conquered, can it not be attacked? Because an army is repeatedly victorious, the victories are not therefore cheap or easy. Christ's victory over temptation was not attained without overcoming suffering and anguish (Luke 22:41–44). People of high character may be attracted by wrong courses of action and have to keep a strong hold on themselves. And in doing so they know that they are making real choices. Yet being true to themselves, they cannot yield. The resistance of temptation may be torture to a person of integrity, whereas the unfaithful yield easily. A truly human Jesus was attracted by wrong courses of action and had to struggle with temptations. Yet being one person faithful to his own divine nature, he did not, and, in the final analysis, could not yield.

Why then did Jesus not yield to his numerous temptations? Did he always resist temptation because of the presence and power of the Holy Spirit? Surely he was indwelt by the Spirit and empowered by the Spirit as are all his followers. But does that constitute the whole answer in view of all the lines of relevant evidence? Is it enough to say that he could have sinned like mere humans, but by the enablement of the Holy Spirit he did not? Did he have both the ability to sin in his human nature and the ability not to sin in his divine nature? Did he never use his divine powers? This hypothesis abstracts the human nature from the divine nature. But in the concreteness of the hypostatic union one nature cannot be divorced from the other. Struggling against the Satanic inducements was not just a Spirit-filled man, but the Spirit-filled God-man. Since Jesus Christ's divine nature was inseparable from his human nature, and since God cannot sin, it becomes impossible that the God-man could actually have sinned.

If Jesus was not able to sin, *how*, it may be asked, *could he be free?* Different concepts of freedom result in different answers to the question. We have found that a power of contrary choice against the Father's will is not of the essence of freedom. There remain many alternatives that are in accord with God's moral principles. God cannot deny himself, and we will not have the power of contrary choice in heaven. In these contexts the essence of freedom is the power of self-determination. Self-determination is always present whether choice contrary to God is possible or not. After struggling, Jesus always resisted temptation because he freely determined to think and do in accord with his sinless human nature and his sinless divine nature. If the human nature could be abstracted from the divine, then like Adam he could have sinned. But the two natures are inseparable in the one Spirit-led person. And even though ordinarily he chose not to rely on his own divine abilities, in the fiercest moments of temptations he could have and may have resorted to his divine powers. Because he was holy in heart, his outward self-determinations were always without sin. What Jesus said and did expressed who he was inside. Jesus was not merely what he did; what he did expressed who he was. Because he was God's Son, in the final analysis, he could not sin.

Did not the *kenosis* make sin for Jesus a "*possibility?*" There is a logical possibility of sin only if we abstract his human nature from the divine nature. Even the *kenosis,* however, does not erase Jesus' divine nature. It meant a limited use of his divine capabilities and a use of his human powers in harmony with the Father's desires. With the limited use of the divine powers, had there been a time when the human nature would have yielded to sin, the divine nature would have prevented this. Given the personal union of the two natures, the one nature cannot be abstracted from the other. So long as Jesus' divine nature was present, his yielding to temptation was not possible actually or empirically. God cannot even tempt people to sin and certainly cannot sin (James 1:13). Hence neither can the God-man.

Consider another relevant perspective, the view from the standpoint of *the Father's eternal plans*. Was not the outcome of the incarnation known from before the foundation of the world? Would not that prior knowledge alone justify the permission of sin? In the Father's omniscience he permitted sin and decreed the plan of salvation based on his "set purpose" (Acts 2:23) to allow wicked men to nail Jesus to the cross to die, the just for the unjust. As it was "impossible for death to keep its hold on him" (2:24), so it had been impossible for the Tempter to provoke him to sin. Decretively it was impossible that Jesus of Nazareth could have sinned and the entire eternal plan of salvation be scrapped.

The most probable conclusion is that although Jesus really struggled with temptation, in any actual sense he could not have sinned. That makes the most sense in terms of the distinction between temptation and sin, and in terms of freedom as self-determination, the enablement of the Holy Spirit, the inseparableness of the human from the divine nature, and the eternal plan of redemption.

APOLOGETIC INTERACTION

Not Contradictories but Subcontraries

According to Søren Kierkegaard, in asserting the deity and humanity of Jesus Christ we attempt the impossible. He assumed "an absolute difference between God and man."[80] Because Kierkegaard thought he was talking about two infinitely different things in every quality, the merging of incommensurables such as time and eternity seemed like merging ice and fire. On his understanding of God and of humanity, no resolution of the paradox of the incarnation was possible. "That God

has existed in human form has been born, grown up, and so forth, is surely the paradox *sensu strictissimo,* the absolute paradox."[81] As the supreme offense to human reason, Kierkegaard thought, the incarnation is no mere apparent contradiction. It is an irresolvable paradox or contradiction that can be accepted only by a noncognitive "faith." Although it was objectively uncertain, he could embrace it with a passionate subjectivity and so apparently with a psychological certitude in spite of its absurdity.

Although the present writers do not presume to have full comprehension of the incarnation, we do not find it contradictory. Nevertheless, with all of our explanations there remains much that is not fully understood. How could Jesus voluntarily lay aside the exercise of his divine attributes? How could the divine and human factors interrelate? How could Jesus struggle so intensely with temptation? And there are many other unanswered questions. Much concerning the incarnation remains incomprehensible or mysterious. But a biblically based Christology need not involve one in denying in one paragraph what has been affirmed in another. Whatever may be the case as two actualities existentially relate to each other, a "contradiction" is a logical relationship between two propositions, one of which asserts what the other denies at the same time and in the same respect.

Contradictory propositions in Christology especially, Kierkegaard mistakenly thinks, constitute the Gospel's offense to reason. We may agree with Kierkegaard's desire to stress the uniqueness, the greatness, and the incomprehensibility of the incarnation of the Son of God, but we need not agree with him when he says that the Bible's teaching about the incarnate Christ is logical nonsense. As J. Loewenberg said, "By deft selection and emphasis isolated themes culled from any source may be made to assume contradictory shapes."[82] The Gospel is not foolishness; it is the wisdom of God. The declaration that people are sinners incapable of saving themselves and stand in need of redemption by the incarnate Messiah is offensive but not self-contradictory. It fits the realities of human moral experience all too well. It seems to be absurd, not because it is, but because our fallen intellects are intimately related to our fallen wills and emotions. Our stubborn pride will not admit our inability to justify ourselves, and it will not admit our fleshly desires to go on in the pleasures of the world.

Kierkegaard's unnecessary logical difficulties with the incarnation begin with his *extreme view of God's transcendence*. He assumed an infinite qualitative distinction between the eternal God and temporal humans. Reacting to Hegelian immanence, Kierkegaard tended to remove God from contact with matter and humans, much like the gods of the Greek philosophers. But the God of biblical revelation is not a stranger to time or to people's thought forms. The God of Abraham, Isaac, and Jacob personally relates to the ongoing states of affairs in the world. The living God, though distinct from the world, is active in it. Christ can remain holy as man, since sin is not part of the essence of humanness. By starting with an exaggerated view of divine transcendence, Kierkegaard, like the Greek philosophers whose influence he sought to avoid, manufactured unnecessary contradictions for himself.

Unnecessary logical difficulties with the incarnation also result from Kierkegaard's failure to develop in this connection the implications of God's creation of humanity *in his image*. God, who is personal, made mankind personal in his likeness. Being like God in intellect, we can receive revelation from God and think his thoughts (in part) after him. Like God emotionally, we can respond affectively (in measure) as God feels toward sin. Like God volitionally, we can share God's eternal purposes and determine to help plant his church. Like God morally, we sense an obligation to integrity an authenticity with ethical principles. And like God relationally, as whole thinking, feeling, and willing persons we can fellowship with God as well as others. With J. Oliver Buswell, Jr., we find that "since man is created in the image of God, there is no inconsistency in the concept that God has become man without ceasing to be God."[83]

Kierkegaard's logical problems with Christology also resulted from a view of Christ's *kenosis* that allowed for no real continuity between the divine Son and the Jesus of history. Neither the Father nor the Spirit became flesh, but as the Son of God assumed or added the human nature, he did not lose his divine nature. The eternal Son did not become less divine or give up his divine attributes. As God he did not experience a beginning, a growth, or a death, but in his human nature he experienced growth, temptation, suffering, and death as we do. The incarnate Jesus did not exercise his divine or human attributes except in accord with the Father's redemptive purpose. Contradictions occur only when at the same time the same thing is affirmed and denied in the same respect. Before and after the *kenosis* language about the second person of the Trinity has in view a difference of time and respect. Hence we do not contradict ourselves in what we affirm of God eternally and what we affirm of the eternal Logos in human flesh. Complexity, yes; contradiction, no.

The Jewish philosopher Spinoza likens the doctrine of the incarnation to saying that a circle had become a square, thereby losing all continuity and ceasing to be a circle.[84] A contemporary philosopher of religion, John Hick, uses the same illustration of the incarnation.[85] In response, we suggest that as a circle encompasses a square the two figures together form a more complex geometrical design. The whole complex pattern has two natures with both the attributes of the circle and the attributes of the square. We need not contradict ourselves in reference to the complex design if we affirm that some of the attributes of the complex design are those of a circle and some those of a square. The holistic unity of the design is not thereby divided. The two "natures" need not be confused. The circle remains a circle; the square within it remains a square. The one, "circle-square design" has two distinct natures. We can speak without contradicting ourselves of their essential differences as subcontraries. As such both are true of the complex design. And when such a noncontradictory interpretation of good writers is possible, responsible interpreters ought not jump to the conclusion that they have written logical nonsense.

Reinhold Niebuhr also thought that doctrines affirming the divinity and the humanity of Jesus verge on contradiction in that they ascribe both conditioned and unconditioned qualities to him. Niebuhr thought it possible for a historical person symbolically to point beyond himself to an unconditioned eternity, but considered it impossible for any person to be historical and unconditioned at the same time.[86] Again the importance of one's view of the *kenosis* is seen. The eternal Son of God remained the unconditioned second person of the Trinity, but he freely chose to limit his freedom from space and time in order to experience life in a given space, time, and culture. In speaking about the kenotic Son of God in time, then, we speak of deity in a different respect than in references to either the Father or the Son in glory. Development of Augustine's illustra-

tion may help at this point. The assertion that Jesus is both God and man is analogous to the assertion that one person is both mind (soul, or spirit) and body. Two different sets of attributes are ascribed to a person, but neither set is denied. For a contradiction to be involved, the bodily attributes would have to be both affirmed and denied or the mental attributes would have to be both affirmed and denied. The result of affirming that a person is both soul and body is complexity, not contradiction. Analogously we may affirm that the one person, Jesus, has both the divine attributes (generally unused in his ministry on earth) and the human attributes.

Although J. I. Packer allows for "antinomies" among the "facts" related to the God-man, he maintains that all the givens exist together in the same world. Packer tries to keep his irresolvable "antinomies" from becoming a basis for justifying contradictions in theological statements.[87] However, "antimony" is generally used of two opposing conclusions, each beginning from plausible premises and issuing from valid steps of inference. Kant finds four major antinomies, and Nagarjuna, a Buddhist philosopher, lists fourteen. To the extent that Packer divorces his assertions from the data on which they are based, his statements lack fitness to the givens that he thinks remain in conflict. Statements are true to the extent that they conform to the data presented to us and also conform to the revealed mind of God about what is the case. Neither in God's mind nor in divine revelation as God gave it do irresolvable antinomies remain. If in the minds of those who interpret the faithful words of Scripture antinomies appear, they ought to be attributed to the interpreter, not to the most reliable source of religious truth in the world.

"Evidence" of a famous antinomy in physics has repeatedly been alleged to justify irreconcilable antimony in religious thought. Both the wave and particle models of electron activity are alleged to have equal empirical support. Hence some wags refer to "wavicles!" But Alfred Lande, "Mr. Quantum Physics" for many years in the physics department of Ohio State University, explains, "The real fact is, the electron does not change into a wave. It simply behaves in a wavelike manner under some circumstances, while at other times it behaves as a particle. But all the time, it remains its real self—a particle."[88] The unitary wave theory of Schrodinger fails to fit the evidence, Lande reports, but "strangely enough many theorists in their idle hours still pay lip service to the archaic idea that particles and waves of matter are pictures on an equal level. Particles are the real constituents of matter, and waves are mere appearances produced by the statistical cooperation of many particles."[89] So Lande no longer needs the duality or "double talk" hypothesis. Given a coherent explanation, he writes, "Do not contrast a snake as thing with its occasional wavy shape in order to defend the duality of snake substance."[90]

Those who charge that Christology is contradictory seldom stop to define a contradiction or to distinguish it from a subcontrary relationship of assertions. For example, christological teaching would be contradictory if it asserted that "all Jesus' attributes are divine" and that "some of Jesus' attributes are not divine." Both the affirmation and the denial of the universal truth claim that all his attributes are divine could not be true. In contrast, in a subcontrary relationship neither the affirmation nor the denial is universal, hence both may be true. For example, "Some members of the class are rapid readers" and "Some members of the class are not rapid readers." Again, "Some of the attributes of a person are physical" and "Some of the attributes of a person are nonphysical." Similarly, "Some attributes of the person of Jesus Christ are divine and some are human." Neither the divine set of attributes nor the human set of attributes is said to be all that he has, and so neither affirmation is necessarily false.

Unless we keep in mind that some attributes are human and some are divine (and not being used), we may have logical muddles rather than mysteries. We may not fully comprehend how the divine and the human attributes exist together, but that is not sufficient ground for attributing logical nonsense to the focal point of God's century-spanning redemptive program! We freely acknowledge our lack of full comprehension. But in asserting that both divine and human attributes apply to the one person, we do not violate the logical law of noncontradiction. We do not assert and deny the Son's possession of either the divine or the human sets of characteristics. We acknowledge complexity and lack of full comprehension, but not contradiction or antinomy.

Admittedly also, at first hearing, the doctrine of Christ's two natures may appear to be a *paradox, a seeming contradiction*. Apparent contradictions serve as literary devices to attract further thought. If we define the key terms with some precision and think with care, apparent contradictions in Scripture are resolvable. For example, when Jesus said one must lose one's life to find it, his paradox stimulated thought. We lose our lives in one respect (as dominated by the old sinful nature) and find them in another respect (a new freedom under enablement of the Holy Spirit). The paradoxes of Scripture are not like Buddhist "koans" (contradictions or nonsense) intended to discount use of the intellect in religion. Initially the claim that Jesus was both God and man may seem contradictory. But by remembering that the Creator is not totally other and that God made humans in his image, the eternal Word could add a human nature. The two natures can be predicated of the person of Christ logically in a subcontrary relationship. With these considerations, although we do not fully understand the God-man, we can meaningfully integrate the Scriptural teaching on Christology without imputing to it absolute absurdity. With G. K. Chesterton we pursue extraordinary truths and avoid the flippancy and light sophistry of paradox. Chesterton said, "I know of nothing so contemptible as a mere paradox; a mere ingenious defense of the indefensible."[91]

Christology Both Ontological and Functional

What about the hypothesis that early church leaders under the influence of Greek philosophy escalated biblical poetry (in Christological hymns) from a metaphorical Son of God to a metaphysical Son of God? The New Testament scholar A. M. Hunter, in *Jesus, Lord and Savior,* seeks to communicate the revealed truth about Jesus in less technical terms. He explicitly tried to avoid metaphysical concepts and speak only in moral and personal categories.[92] But this led him to theories of a progressive incarnation or progressive deification that have even greater difficulties fitting the documented givens. Hunter rejects "two natures" but accepts "two personal movements."[93] Is it more meaningful for moderns to say, "The more Christ laid down his life, the more he gained his divine soul"?[94] Having dismissed all ontology, what can Hunter mean by "soul" as distinct from physical life? Hunter's chapter on the person of Christ concludes: "Christian faith is the decision to commit your whole soul and future to the confidence that Christ is not an illusion but the reality of God."[95] How can Hunter dismiss metaphysics

in one paragraph and make assertions about "reality" in the next? In a subsequent discussion of Christian paradoxes he said, "Even if we reject the implied physiological miracle [of the virgin conception], we are yet left with a metaphysical one—the coming of the divine Son of God into human life, born of a human mother."[96] Hunter, who started out to avoid metaphysics, has not succeeded, because in referring to the incarnation of Jesus Christ the Bible refers to divine and human realities metaphysically.

Leonard Hodgson similarly attempts to avoid ontological elements in discussing the person of Christ as such. "There is no person 'behind' the word; word is the event by which the person 'happens.'"[97] Flagrantly misinterpreting the facts, he alleges that "Jesus advanced no direct messianic claims on his behalf"[98] and "it is not at all clear in *what* sense Jesus spoke of the Son of Man, if at all."[99] Since Hodgson thinks a christological interpretation cannot be "based on what Jesus may have said or thought about himself"[100] he turns from the content of the Savior's words to his acts, particularly his "verbal acts."[101] What is the most characteristic and significant aspect of Jesus' person? "That he spoke a liberating, truthful, and salvific word."[102] But who "he" is, Hodgson does not know. The phenomenon of speaking, Hodgson thinks, is the important thing, not the content asserted. The "language of Jesus *is* the event of the incarnation."[103] In order to present a less abstract view of Christ, Hodgson repudiates the conjoining of the properties of two natures in one person. In place of the "one person" he substitutes "one speaking" and substitutes *homologia* for *homoousia*.[104] Instead of a conjoining of properties he has "the concurrence" of Jesus' speaking with God's speaking. But Moses and the other prophets spoke by a concursive divine-human operation, and for Hodgson Christ differs not in kind but only in degree: he affirms that in Christ "the homologous relation between the word of God and the word of man finds its completion."[105] The co-presence of God in a merely human person's acts does not account for the passages on the eternal Word's being God and equal with God. If Hodgson had been among the disciples when Jesus asked, "Whom do men say that I am?" he would have said Jesus was another prophet or the greatest of prophets, but not the eternal Son of God.

Michael Goulder also rejects a Christology of substance and replaces it with a Christology of agency. One immediately asks, Agency of what or whom? Goulder confesses, "My faith is not in the unity of substance, but in the unity of activity of God and Jesus; *homopraxis,* if a Greek word is wanted, rather than *homoousia.*"[106] God and a human called Christ acted together in actual practice on this hypothesis, but Jesus was not actually the eternal Word who became flesh. The category of "agency" does not stand on its own, however, unless it becomes a substantive. It is always the agency of someone, a being. But if we have no ontological soul or spirit to act responsibly, we have no morally accountable spiritual agent. To Jesus' question, "Whom do men say that I am?" Goulder apparently would respond, "We do not presume to know who you really are, but your acts appear to be Godlike acts." Goulder's Jesus differs only in degree from the prophets, but Jesus is uniquely the Christ, as Peter said, the son of the living God.

In response to attempts of many like Hunter, Hodgson, and Goulder, who unsuccessfully seek to formulate a Christology without metaphysics, we offer several considerations. What anti-metaphysical writers affirm concerning Christ's acts, praxis, functions, and relationships may be true. We differ with what they deny or ignore of Christ's being, for their proposals lack explanatory power to account for all the biblical evidence of who Jesus is. The Chalcedonian formulation of one person with two natures provides the more coherent account of the biblical teaching about both who Jesus was and what he did. By acknowledging the ontological import of numerous scriptural passages we are not endorsing the metaphysical views of particular Greek philosophers. Nothing comparable to the doctrine of the one person with divine and human natures can be found in Plato, Aristotle, or other Greek philosophers. But through them God providentially prepared some basic categories of thought, including some about metaphysics. They were used by the Spirit in the inspired teaching of the New Testament to convey who the triune God is and who Jesus Christ is. When opposing the errors of Greek philosophy, some biblical scholars overlook the values God gave Greek thought-forms and language in the New Testament.

Even Hebrew, which is sometimes thought so radically different from Greek, has in common with it a concern for substantives as well as verbs—for who is speaking or acting as well as the speaking and the acting. The rejection of an ontological Christology often involves a rejection of the Old Testament's explicit teaching that God is to be viewed ontologically. In Judaism from Moses onward God was the independently existent One (Exod. 3:14). In contrast, false gods did not actually exist and so could not speak or act, for there is no spirit or breath in their mouth (Pss. 115:4–7; 135:15–17). As Paul later said, the idols were nothing (1 Cor. 8:4). Only the God who *is* knows, loves, acts, makes covenants, remains faithful to his promised plans, and pursues his people in history. No primitive stage existed with a simple functional pursuit without an ontological personal Subject or holy Agent as referent. Denials of any ontological knowledge of God reflects a suppression not only of the Old Testament but also of universal revelation. "The heavens declare the glory of God; the skies proclaim the work of his hands" (Ps. 19:1). In what God made, all people "clearly see" his "eternal power and divine nature" (Rom. 1:20).

Jesus Christ himself had deep concern for ontological truth. He asked, "Who do people say the Son of Man *is*?" (Matt. 16:13). Again he pressed the issue, " 'But what about you?' he asked, 'Who do you say I am?' " (v. 15). When Nicodemus considered him simply a rabbi, a teacher come from God (John 3:2), Jesus was not satisfied. The climax of Jesus' conversation with Nicodemus emphasizes that Jesus can uniquely speak of heavenly things because "no one has ever gone into heaven except the one who came from heaven—the Son of Man" (vv. 12–13). No alleged progression from reductively poetic or functional language to ontological language occurs in Scripture or in the church. The biblical progression is from the ontological existence of the "Son" or "Word" with God to his ontological or real existence in human flesh. This great event can be expressed literally, and even when figures of speech are used, they convey by way of illustration the greatness of their literal, univocal point.

Jesus' conversation with the Samaritan woman at the well moves quickly from his functional request for a drink, to "If you knew . . . who it is that asks you for a drink, you would have asked him and he would have given you living water" (John 4:10). Not satisfied to be called a prophet (v. 19), Jesus taught the ontological basis of true worship: "God is spirit, and his worshipers must worship in spirit and in truth" (v. 24). The woman mentioned the coming Messiah, and Jesus said, "I who speak to you am he" (v. 26). To follow Jesus' example in teaching Christology, we must emphasize not only what his teachings, works, and example were but also *who* spoke, engaged in praxis, and provided the paradigm of moral and spiritual excellence for all people of all times and cultures. The normative value of his example and the infinite value of his atonement depend on the uniqueness of his inner being.

Had Jesus claimed merely a functional unity of thought and purpose with the Father the Jews would not have charged blasphemy. Nor would they have sought to stone him if he claimed divine sonship merely as a legal inheritance. Because he claimed an ontological oneness with God, he seemed to commit blasphemy. Jesus claimed an identity of divine actions (John 5:21). What was true of the Father was true of the Son, not only in the giving of life (John 5) but also in the holding of believers in his hand (John 10). Jesus himself taught that what we are in our hearts determines what we say and do. His being or character takes priority in his thought even over his deeds. " 'I tell you the truth,' Jesus answered, 'before Abraham was born, I am!' " (John 8:58; cf. 13:19).

It is anachronistic to attribute to the New Testament writers the antimetaphysical spirit of post-Kantian philosophy and theology. As in the first century Christians must continue to live in Christ Jesus as Lord. "See to it that no one takes you captive through hollow and deceptive philosophy, which depends on human tradition and the basic principles of this world rather than on Christ. For in Christ all the fullness of the Deity lives in bodily form, and you have been given fullness in Christ, who is the head over every power and authority" (Col. 2:6–10). Still today people in Third-World countries believe in real spirits (divine, demonic, angelic, and human). If we are to interpret the Scriptures in their first-century historical and cultural contexts, we cannot impose on them a discredited logical postivist notion of "literal" meaning limited to presently observable sense data. That is one of the mistakes of the contributors to *The Myth of God Incarnate*.[106] Paul's metaphysical assertions concerning Christ are well documented in the section above entitled "The Biblical Teaching." The one who humbled himself as a human and servant enjoyed a status equal with God's, for he was "in very nature God" (Phil. 2:6). No radical difference appears between the ontological concern of Jesus and that of Paul. When confronted on the road to Damascus, Paul was not satisfied with a phenomenal experience. He asked, "Who are you, Lord?" (Acts 9:5). On that occasion Paul did not receive a full answer. Later he gave the answer in no uncertain ontological terms. In Paul's thought it is because Christ is the image of the invisible God, the firstborn over all creation and before all things (ontologically) that he serves functionally as the creator, sustainer of all, and head of the church, and the world's reconciler and peace maker (Col. 1:15–20). The relational and functional values of Paul's exhortations depend for their worth on logically prior metaphysical realities. Actions are no substitute for character and being, they flow from the heart. So we need not choose against ontological categories to emphasize functional values. Rather, we utilize both ontological and functional categories as do the Scriptures. The pragmatic values of Jesus' functions on behalf of mankind depend on the nature of the one who acts.

The Augustinian and Chalcedonian doctrine of Christ's person as really divine and human rests ultimately on the claim to be a comprehensive (but not exhaustive) analysis of the biblical teaching. That has been evident in the biblical section above. "Chalcedon did not adopt philosophy; it took some basic philosophical words and forged a theology based on Scripture. Its logic is a systematization of the logic inherent in Scripture, not a philosophical corruption of primitive texts."[107] For that reason, although the Chalcedonian formulation may be popularized for mass consumption, its ontological import must not be lost. Its biblical foundation is so highly probable as to be beyond reasonable doubt. "Ontological christology is part of the biblical revelation which cannot and must not be compromised in the name of historical and/or cultural relativism."[108]

Not Orthodox Because Politically Victorious

According to Don Cupitt's contribution to *The Myth of God Incarnate*, "What we have been taught to call 'orthodoxy' was in fact merely the form of Christianity which happened to triumph over the others."[109] Apparently, in Cupitt's view of providence God does not influence developments in doctrine in the history of church councils. One view just "happened to triumph over the others" apparently for less than adequate reasons or worthy motives. Cupitt's evaluation commits the genetic fallacy in reasoning by dismissing the objective validity of an idea because of the circumstances of its origin. Pressures from persons in political authority at some of the church councils do not account for the classical acceptance of a doctrine among people of all levels of different cultures and periods of history. Because at one point the party in political power favored an idea does not make it either true or false. Similarly, the political leaders' opposition to certain doctrines in history did not determine the truth or falsity of those doctrines. Might does not make right. Neither does might at any given time make reliable tenets with classical appeal at all times and cultures.

As the above research has indicated, the classical doctrine of one person with two natures has appealed to students of the evidence in different cultures and periods of history because it proposes the most coherent account of the strands of relevant biblical and historical evidence. Reasoning like Don Cupitt's commits the genetic fallacy of thinking that certain factors culturally surrounding the origin of an idea determine its validity. To determine the objective validity of the Chalcedonian formulation, Cupitt needs to consider the consistency and adequacy of the view and evaluate its viability with those guidelines. Cupitt adds, "In retrospect the Christ of the Eastern Church looks all too like the Hellenistic king," and "the Christ of the Western Church looks like one who died to seal the authority of the patriarchal family as a model for the organization of church and state."[110] A comprehensive concept of Christ includes worthy elements of fidelity to the family and of kingship. To the degree that a view without contradiction integrates with all the relevant data, it has probability of being true, however lowly the cultural conditions and motives of the origin of the idea. To the degree that the hypothesis does not meet these criteria it lacks probability of being true, however exalted the motives in the hearts of the conveners of the church councils or contemporary scholars. The appeal of orthodox Christology classically may be appreciated when it is realized that some other views have not received the same kind of classical recognition in East and West and among Roman Catholics and Protestants. The hypotheses of Mary's sinlessness and ascension to heaven, for example, have not had the same overwhelming degree of coherence with the relevant evidence.

Jesus Is Not a Dead Spiritual Master

According to *The Aquarian Gospel of Jesus the Christ,* during his unrecorded childhood years Jesus traveled to India and studied under Hindu holy men and himself became a Hindu spiritual master. Allegedly he also traveled to Persia, Assyria, Greece, and Egypt, learning and speaking. He then returned to the Near East where he was baptized by John the Harbinger. In Egypt, supposedly, Jesus received his mystic name and number and passed seven tests of brotherhood, received the seventh and highest degree, and was crowned "The Christ" in the Great Lodge of the heavens and earth.[111]

As a boy, transcriber Levi H. Dowling (1844–1911) received a vision that he would "build a white city," and the publishers say that it was a book—*The Aquarian Gospel.* From "Visel the holy one" Dowling received a "commission" to read a message in the Akashic records for men of the New Age, the Piscean Age. "Take up your pen and write."[112] Of all the vibrations allegedly left by every person in the universe in the Akashic records, Levi became attuned to the "tones and rhythms of Jesus of Nazareth, Enoch and Melchizedec." Exercising his developed mediumistic ability between 2 and 6 A.M., he "transcribed" messages "true to the letter" received from the Universal Mind; these messages have been called by some Orientals the Akashic records.[113]

Had Jesus received years of instruction and practice in Hindu-Buddhist religion of the first century, abundant evidence of these perspectives should appear in the biblical records of his teaching. But Jesus' teaching and life, interpreted by sound principles of hermeneutics, does not disclose the assumptions of Hindu-Buddhist pantheism or occultism. Jesus' general outlook reflected the theistic worldview of

Judaism based on the Old Testament, not a pantheistic and occult worldview. His belief system did not include a pantheistic interpretation of the Father-motherhood of God and a spiritual brotherhood of all humans. Although Jesus emphasized that by creation all are naturally dependent on the heavenly Father for their existence, apart from God they are morally and spiritually not children of God but children of the Devil, the Great Deceiver (John 8:44). Because people are born of the flesh, Jesus insisted that fallen humans must be born again. By that he did not mean born in many reincarnations, but once, inwardly by the Holy Spirit (John 3:1–8).

Jesus did not teach a form of monism when he said, "The kingdom of God is within you" (Luke 17:21). With these words he referred to the way in which the kingdom comes (v. 20). Christ's rule comes to individuals by the Holy Spirit, and as he had said to Nicodemus, "The wind blows wherever it pleases. You hear its sound, but you cannot tell where it comes from or where it is going. So it is with everyone born of the Spirit" (John 3:8). And as individuals are regenerated by the Spirit, the kingdom of God is among them (plural) or in their midst. Jesus did not teach Eastern distinctives such as the divinity and infinite potential of humans, repeated reincarnations or rebirths of the soul, vegetarianism, or celibacy. The Jesus of historically attested biblical sources advocated no occult ways to manipulate the Father's will to our advantage. Quite the contrary, he repudiated occult practices as demonic. The "signs" he performed were done in public, in broad daylight; they were not occult manipulations in the dark. They were visible or verifiable signs, wonders, and mighty acts. And many times Jesus Christ demonstrated his authority over demonic powers. In contrast to mere meditation or magical manipulation of vibrations, Jesus taught his disciples to offer praise and requests to a personal God.

It is naïve indeed to accept intuited messages as from spirits (even spirits who call themselves Jesus) without subjecting them to critical testing. Some messages may be naturalistically explained as projected contents of a channeler's own unconscious mind. Even if intuited messages are not from the unconscious and actually come from spirits, not all spirits are necessarily knowledgeable or trustworthy. According to the Holy Scriptures demonic deceivers as well as angelic spirits exist. Sudden intuitions may be either true or deceptive. Hence the Bible wisely urges discernment in spiritual disclosures: "Dear friends, do not believe every spirit, but test the spirits to see whether they are from God" (1 John 4:1). What is the test? "This is how you can recognize the Spirit of God: Every spirit that acknowledges that Jesus Christ has come in the flesh is from God, but every spirit that does not acknowledge Jesus is not from God" (vv. 2–3). A crucial test of reliable and unreliable spirits is their allegiance to the incarnation of the eternal Son of the living God.

The *Aquarian Gospel,* unfortunately, fails this test. It denies that Jesus of Galilee is the eternal Christ. It says that Jesus is a pattern of the Christ spirit and that "Christ is not a man. The Christ is universal Love, and Love is King."[114] It says that the Christ does not refer to any particular person but only to a spirit of love and brotherhood with which anyone can be "christed." Other spiritists have claimed to channel messages from Jesus, but they regularly affirm pantheistic and occult views of Jesus as a human who attained mediumship or spiritual mastery. They flatly deny the explicit biblical doctrines of Christ as the eternal Word who became flesh.

Representatives of eastern and occult spirituality often allege that Christians need not give up their faith to accept a monistic belief system involving occult manipulations of spiritual forces. However, anyone who regards Jesus as one of many men who became spiritual adepts flatly denies the central doctrine of biblical revelation—the unique cosmic lordship of Jesus who was God and became flesh. Candidly Eva Dowling in the introduction to her husband's book acknowledges that an orthodox belief "is wholly at variance with the teachings of Jesus himself and of his apostles."[115] But the many lines of biblical evidence above point up their error. According to "the Aquarian [ascended] Masters in council" in typical theosophical language, Jesus was a remarkable child, qualified to be an avatar, and lived as a pattern for the sons of men to show the possibilities of man. Jesus is alleged to have said, "What I have done all men can do, and what I am all men shall be."[116] Never do occultists affirm that Jesus is the Christ. Instead, they deny that central affirmation of New Testament Christians. The spiritists' Jesus is a human who learned from the wisdom of the sages like other avatars. Jesus is little different from many others in whom the Christ spirit (of Father-Mother Love) is said to manifest itself again and again at the beginning of every age.[117]

No one can loyally follow two spiritual masters (Matt. 6:24), even though both are called "Jesus." On one hand, if we devote ourselves to a human who became divine as all others are allegedly able to do, we reject the lordship of the biblically revealed eternal person of the Trinity who became human once-for-all. On the other hand, to worship and serve the unique scriptural Lord Jesus Christ is to reject a merely human Jesus who spiritually evolved to consciousness of an impersonal cosmic spirit of love. The lines of spiritual warfare are being sharply drawn between the kingdom of spirituality as an evolutionary development humanly achieved and as a gift of perfect righteousness by sheer divine grace. Not all are teaching the same thing. Christians teach that God can remain just and accept sinners only by faith in the incarnate Christ and his atoning work. Many non-Christians in other world religions think that without the uniquely incarnate Christ they can evolve morally into higher kinds of beings. Jesus did not teach moral and spiritual evolution, but rather he taught that we reproduce after our kind morally, "Flesh gives birth to flesh" (John 3:6). Fallen humans can enter the kingdom of God only by the gift of new life from the Spirit of grace.[118]

RELEVANCE FOR LIFE AND MINISTRY

Liturgical and sermonic language generally needs to be more poetic and affective than theological language does. But to avoid hypocrisy "there needs to be at least consistency, if not an identity, between the belief expressed in worship and the belief expressed in the form of reflective theology."[119] The psalmists sang of the great actualities of creation and ordinary providence, as well, and the extraordinary deliverance of the Exodus that happened in history. Is it not insincere "worship" to repeat creeds and sing hymns if in our critical thought we cannot affirm the truths expressed? The revealed truth about Christ not only provides for worship in spirit and in truth, but also helps avoid the disillusionment that follows devotion to imperfect spiritual masters.

One young woman, after coming out of a series of several cults said she had been "spiritually promiscuous!" She finally accepted the biblically revealed Christ, and a sound Christology now enables her in spirit and truth to worship the Messiah who is God, speaks for God, and saves sinners. Christians praise the Lord Jesus Christ and sing and testify about him because of who he is. And because of his divine-human nature Christians follow him as Lord of all.

Bow to Jesus as Your Spiritual Master

We do not need to attempt the impossible task of working our way to the Father in heaven, because Christ has brought God to us (Rom. 10:6–10). Christians prize Christ above all other humans because *"God was pleased to have all his fullness dwell in him"* (Col. 1:19). No more complete resources for spirituality can be discovered in any natural or supernatural powers. In Christ are all the attributes and powers of the Almighty. So Christians value the one Mediator far above all political, educational, athletic, and entertainment greats. Christ rises in stature far above Billy Graham, any pope of Rome, any founder of any other religion, and any spirits of former spiritual masters who would channel messages to the world today. The founders of world religions were ordinarily born humans with fleshly natures who gained some insights from universal revelation. At best any truth they have is partial; the fullness is found in Jesus Christ. But none made such claims for themselves as did Jesus, and none confirmed them with years of sinlessness, such remarkable teaching, astounding works, death for the sins of the world, and a triumphant resurrection. Indeed the ascended Jesus is "both Lord and Christ" (Acts 2:36).

> No mortal can with Him compare
> Among the sons of men,
> Fairer is He than all the fair
> That fill the heavenly train.
> S. Stennett

We esteem Jesus above all because we "have been given fullness in Christ,

who is the head over every power and authority" (Col. 2:10). Having spiritual completeness in Christ, Christians do not turn from him to mere nature religions, religions of mere law, or religions of endless occult phenomena. Christ abides in the hearts of believers that they may be "rooted and established in love, may have power together with all the saints, to grasp how wide and long and high and deep is the love of Christ, and to know this love that surpasses knowledge—that you may be filled to the measure of all the fullness of God" (Eph. 3:14–19). Although we are not incarnations of God as Jesus was, we can have an abiding personal relationship with him, drawing on a love and power far beyond our own, the greatest love and power in the cosmos.

We honor Christ above all because our love for the Lord of all unites us spiritually to others who similarly love him. Those from all around the earth who bow before Jesus as Lord of all—whatever their racial, political, economic, educational or cultural differences—constitute a great family in heaven and on earth (Eph. 3:14–17). Christians bow before Jesus as Lord of all other good and evil powers in the cosmos. Jesus is Lord of the nations, Lord of our churches, Lord of our families, and Lord of our vocations.

Having begun the Christian life by faith in Christ, "continue to live in him, rooted and built up in him, strengthened in the faith as you were taught, and overflowing with thankfulness" (Col. 2:6). Paul exhorts that, as a Christian, you need to "see to it that no one takes you captive through hollow and deceptive philosophy, which depends on human tradition and the basic principles of this world rather than on Christ" (v. 8). Refrain from judging people by rites, vegetarianism, drink, festivals, New Moon celebrations, sabbath observances, and worship of angels and other spiritual masters (vv. 11–18). Since we died with Christ to the basic principles of nature worship, why should we submit to its rules and regulations? Why resort to practices that have an appearance of wisdom, false humility, and harsh treatment of the body "but lack any value in restraining sensual indulgence?" (vv. 20–23).

Honor the Lord of all in every aspect of your life. In devotion to Christ, "set your hearts on things above, where Christ is seated at the right hand of God" (Col. 3:1). Let your dominant mind-set be on things above, not on earthly things. Distance yourself from the works of the flesh, and clothe yourselves with Christlike qualities (Col. 3:1–14). Let Christ's peace rule in your heart, let the word of Christ dwell in you richly as you teach and admonish one another, and as you sing (vv. 15–16). "And whatever you do, whether in word or deed, do it all in the name of the Lord Jesus, giving thanks to God the Father through him" (v. 17). Glorify Christ in all your relationships—with your spouse (vv. 18–19), your parents, your children (vv. 20–21), your employer, and your employees (vv. 22–4:1). Pray for all who proclaim the mystery of Christ (4:2–4). "Be wise in the way you act toward outsiders; make the most of every opportunity. Let your conversation be always full of grace seasoned with salt, so that you may know how to answer everyone" (vv. 5–6).

Confidently Approach the Most High

We interrupt this program to bring you a special news bulletin! The transcendent Father sent his only Son to live as one of us! The uniqueness of the God-man makes him the one Mediator between God and man (1 Tim. 2:5). To what other founder of any world religion or cult shall we go? All were humans who became "enlightened" by some experience. At most they were

fallen sinners who came to be lauded by those who follow their examples. No others are eternally God and became incarnate. The exaltation of Christ alone as Mediator should free us from false messiahs. Our hope spiritually is not in education, a *gnosis* (knowledge or enlightenment), an organization, a spiritual discipline, or a world peace program. The one Mediator is not Eastern culture or Western technology, but a Person. A realization of this truth, as narrow as it may sound, wonderfully liberates believers from oppressions in organization-bound, human-leader-bound, and culture-bound exclusivisms.

Because he is fully human, *Jesus is a sympathetic mediator.* "For we do not have a high priest who is unable to sympathize with our weaknesses, but we have one who has been tempted in every way, just as we are—yet was without sin" (Heb. 4:15). Although the adherents of other religions regard God as an impersonal Absolute, Force, Energy, or a personification ("mother") of nature or the cosmos, Christians alone recognize that a member of the divine Trinity has lived on earth and faced exactly the kinds of frustrations and temptations that we face with close relatives, neighbors, and business associates.

Because of the marvel that Christ was tempted as we are and suffers along with us, Helmut Thielicke explained, "we have a brother in the profoundest danger in life. There is no longer any lonely point in this life. . . . We are not alone in our temptation. He suffers it with us down to the lowest depths which Satan has conceived."[120] And because of the marvel that Jesus was tempted as we are but without sin, "we are certain of his love from all eternity. Christ not only marches on our right hand against death and the devil, but he upholds us from his height, because he is the Lord. The knowledge that we are sheltered by his power gives us that peace which the world cannot give or take away from us."[121]

"Let us then approach the throne of grace with confidence, so that we may receive mercy and find grace to help us in our time of need" (Heb. 4:16, italics ours). Those who by faith identify with Christ need not approach God through countless intermediaries or dead "spiritual masters" in the next life (as Theosophists and others do). Christians need not wait for countless rebirths in order to evolve morally and spiritually to the level at which they can approach the ultimate Reality directly (as Hindus, Buddhists, and others do). In our approach to God we are not limited to having a high priest enter the Holy of Holies once a year as our representative (as in Judaism). We need not convey our heartfelt concerns to human priests or to Jesus' mother, Mary. Those whose trust is in the God-man can enter the Holy of Holies itself and pray to the heavenly Father directly in Christ's name with the Holy Spirit's enablement. At the Father's request we exalt the name of Jesus Christ above every name in heaven and on earth. In that great name we pray and because of that great name the Father hears and answers.

Seek no additional mediator. No religious leader or any hierarchy of living or dead spiritual masters ought to come between young Christians and their heavenly Father. Many insufficiently taught Christians need to hear this warning. They may be easily convinced by well-meaning but false teachers that they can continue to relate to God only through certain organizations or programs. Two interrelated features of the multiplying cults, according to Anthony Hoekema, are "the devaluation of Christ" and "the group as the exclusive community of the saved."[122] Wherever evangelistic fruit appears, faithful ministers in this shrinking pluralistic world need to help young converts devote themselves not only "to the fellowship, to the breaking of bread and to prayer," but also "to the apostles teaching" (Acts 2:42). Without a well-founded doctrine of who Christ is, untaught Christians can easily be persuaded that they need some additional ways to be acceptable to God.

Because of his deity, we may worship the Son as we do the Father. Since Jesus is truly God, we can trust him as we trust the Father (John 14:1). We may adore and value Jesus as we do God the Father. The object of our distinctively Christian worship and obedience is the one person with divine and human natures. Christians offer their highest allegiance to their great High Priest, the once-for-all Sacrifice, the resurrected and ascended Head of the church. We pray to the triumphant Lord with two natures who continues to serve as our Mediator, Advocate, and faithful High Priest. He fellowships with us and liberates us from the kingdom of evil here and now. It is he who will receive the worship of his people when he returns from heaven in glory and power.

Heed and Teach the Teachings of the Greatest Prophet

Moses predicted that after Israel would suffer years of false prophets and astrologers, God would raise up another prophet like him and put words in his mouth (Deut. 18:15–19). Like Moses, Jesus mediated a new and greater covenant. When the long-awaited Prophet greater than Moses came, Peter said, "You must listen to everything he tells you" (Acts 3:22). As the author of Hebrews put it, "In the past God spoke to our forefathers through the prophets . . . , but in these last days he has spoken to us by his Son" (Heb. 1:1).

As chief spokesman for God the Father, Jesus "came from the Father, full of grace and truth" (John 1:14). He "who comes from above . . . testifies to what he has seen and heard" (3:31–32). Again, "the one whom God has sent speaks the words of God" (v. 34). No other prophet had ever seen God, but "the One and Only, who is at the Father's side, has made him known" (1:18). The Word who was with God in the beginning (1:1–2) revealed information important to his hearers to understand the past, evaluate the present, and realistically anticipate the future. Because of the Son's unique eternal relationship with the Father, he cannot be considered one of many merely human prophets who received his message from the Father by special revelation. He declared that "the kingdom of heaven is near" (Matt. 4:17) and that salvation is received by faith in him (John 6:45–47; 8:24).

Jesus proclaimed the requirements of the law and their fulfillment in himself (Matt. 5:17–18). But his new message focused on the long-awaited new covenant, his coming to give his life as a complete atonement, and thus the gospel of grace (John 1:17). Conscious of his own uniquely predicted prophetic ministry, Jesus unrolled the scroll of Isaiah and read from it (Isa. 61:1–2), "The Spirit of the Lord is on me, because he has anointed me to preach good news to the poor. He has sent me to proclaim freedom for the prisoners and recovery of sight for the blind, to release the oppressed, to proclaim the year of the Lord's favor" (Luke 4:18–19). When he told the Samaritan woman the number of her husbands, she said, "Sir, . . .I can see that you are a prophet" (John 4:19). Jesus' prophetic ministry was confirmed by many signs recorded in the Gospels. After he fed the five thousand, the people said, "Surely this is the Prophet who is to come into the world" (John 6:14; see also 7:40). On Palm Sunday, as Jesus rode on a donkey into Jerusalem, the people inquired who he was. "The crowds answered, 'This is Jesus, the prophet from Nazareth in Galilee'" (Matt. 21:11). In his hometown the amazed people asked, "Where did this man get this wisdom and these miraculous powers?" (Matt. 13:54). Knowing his carpenter-father, mother, brothers, and sisters, the people took offense at him. "But Jesus said to them, 'Only in his hometown and in his own house is a prophet without honor'" (v. 57). On another occasion some Pharisees warned him that Herod would kill him if he remained in Jerusalem. Purposefully Jesus determined to complete his ministry there and replied, "Surely no prophet can die outside Jerusalem" (Luke 13:33).[123]

Christians value Christ's teaching above that of others because he did not invent ideas out of his own human heart, but communicated the truths the transcendent Father gave him. Jesus communicated God's changeless truths in the culturally influenced human languages of Aramaic and Greek. Jesus explained, "For I did not speak of my own accord, but the Father who sent me commanded me what to say and how to say it" (John 12:49). In the upper room he reminded his disciples, "These words you hear are not my own; they belong to the Father who sent me" (14:24). Through his teaching Jesus Christ could say to the Father, "I have revealed you" (17:6). "For I gave them the words you gave me" (v. 8). "I have given them your word" (v. 14). "I have made you known to them [the world], and will continue to make you known in order that the love you have for me may be in them and that I myself may be in them" (v. 26).

Unfortunately many people who have been influenced by recent philosophy, anthropology, psychology, and sociology seem to regard a total conceptual relativism more highly than Jesus Christ's prophetic teaching as nonnegotiable truth. One can appreciate the frailty and fallibility of the relative words of fallen and finite humans in general without exalting a totalistic relativism to the only absolute. By holding that no universal and necessary truths can be expressed in human language and that absolute truth resides only in the mind of the transcendent God, a mind that is allegedly totally different from human minds, they make Jesus' teachings (as well as their own, even about God) time-bound and relative. Previously we tried to show that the Lord taught that his own teachings in temporal languages conveyed changeless truths (1:111–12). His teachings in human words originated with God the Father, were true (coherent and viable), were authoritative for all, and give eternal life. Jesus' classical teaching was not time-bound but of relevance to every culture and subculture and of normative value not only for his day but also for all times. "Heaven and earth will pass away," Jesus said, "but my words will never pass away" (Matt. 24:35). Hence the presupposition that no changeless truth can be expressed in human language ought to be dismissed by those who call Jesus Christ their Lord.

No more reliable guidance can be found in the world's religions or philosophies than the teaching of the greatest of all prophets. Those who know and love God today, as in the first century, believe and obey all that the Messiah taught. "Why do you call me 'Lord, Lord' and do not do what I say?" (Luke 6:46). Do you love God the Father? Do you love his eternal Word? No more clear test can be found than your obedience to the Word made flesh. "If you obey my commandments you will remain in my love, just as I have obeyed my Father's commands and remain in his love. I have told you this so that my joy may be in you and that your joy may be complete" (John 15:10–11). Although no one perfectly lives up to all

the teachings of Christ, a substantial difference becomes evident between the lives of those whose deepest desire and dominant purpose is to follow Christ at any cost and those whose deepest desire and dominant purpose is selfish pleasures or acquisition of earthly goods.

Ways to Be Like the Supreme Paradigm of Humanness

In the midst of rapid developments in knowledge, immorality, violent crime, terrorism, and corruption in high places, people do well to identify with the best possible paradigm of a just and loving life. Through all the changes in history and culture, Christ remains in every age and context the paragon of human excellence. Neither the phantasms of sorcerers nor examples of other religious leaders come near possessing the beauty of his lifestyle. Mahatma Ghandi, Mother Theresa, Billy Graham, and others have done nobly in many respects but Jesus Christ remains the supreme standard of authentic humanness for those who bear the divine image. None in fields of literature, the media, or ethics can compare with Jesus Christ. And Jesus said, "A student is not above his teacher, but everyone who is fully trained will be like his teacher" (Luke 6:40).

Although we need not be like Christ in every detail, in what ways ought Christians seek by God's grace to be like our incarnate Savior? Jesus' disciples not only believe all that he taught but also become like him in exemplifying (1) God's unchanging character in the midst of change, (2) life according to universally revealed moral principles, and (3) life according to specially revealed redemptive purposes true for all who have sinned in any cultures. We can grow in Christlikeness intellectually, morally, emotionally, volitionally, and relationally.

Intellectually, we can grow in our mental ability to receive his teaching about his own character in relation to his heavenly Father's moral qualities and think his thoughts after him. Jesus' teachings about the human heart provide rich content for meaningful contemplation and application. So do his teachings about moral law and justice in the Old Testament Scriptures, which he knew and applied so well. Our mentalities may become more like his also as we grow in understanding the Gospel of mercy and grace. The Gospel was anticipated in the Old Testament and developed in the New Testament, which Christ endorsed in advance in principle. Christ's life exhibits, as will the lives of his followers, understanding of the Gospel's satisfaction of uncompromising justice, deliverance from the powers of evil on any level, and the transforming dynamic of reconciling love.

Morally, we can mature in qualities of character like the Messiah's, although we can never in this life attain perfection. When we struggle with temptation, we will follow Jesus' example of resisting its most attractive and powerful enticements. We can seek to please the Father in all that we think, say, and do and thus keep a *clear conscience* (1 Peter 3:16). As Paul, who followed Christ, said, "I strive always to keep my conscience clear before God and man" (Acts 24:16). For another thing, we ought to develop *endurance* in tribulation from the world. "Let us fix our eyes on Jesus, the author and perfecter of our faith, who for the joy set before him endured the cross, scorning its shame, and sat down at the right hand of the throne of God. Consider him who endured such opposition from sinful men, so that you will not grow weary and lose heart" (Heb. 12:2–3; cf. 2 Thess. 3:5; 1 Tim. 1:16; 1 Peter 2:23). Jesus was not masochistic, but he did not try to escape the inestimable sufferings from evil persons—sufferings he endured to provide our salvation. In the declared spiritual war of the evil against the good, we too may need to endure discrimination from sinners in our workplace (1 Peter 2:18–20). "To this [suffering] you were called, because Christ suffered for you, leaving you an example, that you should follow in his steps" (v. 21).

Emotionally, by grace we can endeavor to grow in appropriate affective expressions in relation to God, others, and ourselves. Following the example of Jesus, we will rejoice with those who rejoice and weep with those who weep. We will take pleasure in what is good and express wrath at the powers that would destroy the Father's purposes of common and special grace. Strengthened by our Savior's example, however, we will not let our emotions get out of control.

Volitionally, we will decide among courses of action in ways that would merit his approval. As busy as we may be, we will accept invitations to weddings, banquets, breakfasts, and visit with the ill and bereaved. Christ has set a consistent example of obedience to his Father's will (Heb. 5:7–9). Like him, we will pray, "Not my will, but yours be done on earth as it is in heaven" (Luke 22:42; Matt. 6:10). Such a prayer expresses the conviction that the Father's wisdom is greater and better than ours.

Relationally, we ought to live each day, as Jesus did, in communion with the heavenly Father and the Holy Spirit. By the Father's guidance and the Spirit's enablement those who are Christlike will cross barriers of racial, gender, and social prejudice to reflect the justice and love Jesus exhibited with the Samaritan woman at the well. Disciplined followers of Christ can exhibit the respect, consideration, and love he showed toward people such as Mary and Martha of Bethany, Mary the Magdalene, tax collectors, and fishermen.

Similarly in self-giving love we who call Christ Lord will cross age barriers by enjoying children as Jesus did. Like Christ, we will cross barriers of hatred to show love for our enemies. And, like Jesus, we may even lay down our lives for them (John 15:13).

Jesus' lifestyle was exemplary, Michael Griffiths shows, in the ways he related to his family as a child and as an adult. As a child he grew in favor with God and human persons. During those silent years without any spectacular miracles or ministries, he pleased the Father by living as a human being with his parents, his brothers, and his sisters in Nazareth. Apparently he grew in ability to help in the family carpentry business, and his parables show familiarity also with agriculture. We do not know when Joseph died, but when he did, leaving Jesus as the eldest son, Jesus accepted responsibility to care for his mother. Moreover, the Lord's miracles and parables exhibited his appreciation for family affections, such as he displayed in the healings of the daughter of the Syro-Phoenician woman and the daughter of Jairus, the resurrection of Mary and Martha's brother Lazarus, and the parable of the prodigal son. After the example of Jesus, who recognized the divine authorization of marriage and the family from the account of the creation (Matt. 19:1–15), his disciples highly valued their own parents, brothers and sisters, spouses and children, but always under God's rule in these relationships.

Jesus was a diligent worker and chose many working-class people as his disciples. His teachings exhibit several examples of his appreciation for the responsibilities of owners and stewards. Jesus also honored the Sabbath as a day of rest. He was also concerned that his followers get needed rest: "Because so many people were coming and going that they did not even have a chance to eat," he said to his disciples, "Come with me by yourselves to a quiet place and get some rest" (Mark 6:31). Industrious as he was, he did not endorse the overreactions of even Christian workaholics.

If time and space permitted, it would be well worth pursuing Jesus' model of enjoying nature as God's creation, of developing spiritual disciplines, of participating in the political world, and of living a simple lifestyle. Much profit would be gained from considering his working methods in teaching and training people for establishing churches. Jesus used different methods in teaching, natural approaches in personal evangelism, and varied strategies in missions to found a community that changed history.[124]

Ways Not to Be Like Christ

In saying that we should follow Christ's example, we do not mean that unregenerate people in the strength of the flesh can imitate him and so gain salvation. We do not suggest imitation of Christ as a way to self-justification. Efforts to be like Christ are no substitute for justification by belief in his atonement. Rather, in gratitude for justification and regeneration and in the spirit of biblical teaching, we want to become increasingly like him morally and spiritually. We do not suggest play-acting or pretending to be what we are not. If anything is clear in the life of Jesus it is his opposition to hypocrisy and his insistence that life change starts from the heart. Any attempt to be like Christ, therefore, must begin with proper motivation, that is, not for selfish advantage, but for glorifying our spiritual Master. We must be like him in the inner person before we can exhibit his characteristics in our outer behavior. And as millions of Christians follow his paradigm from the heart, the outward results are not all identical. We follow in his steps, not by going to the near East, but by resisting our temptations as he did his by the power of the Holy Spirit and the teaching of the Scriptures. He does not live our lives for us, but he has shown us how to face the basic moral and spiritual challenges in life. How likeness to him works out creatively in our different personalities, family, neighborhood, and cultural situations may vary greatly.

In several ways we need not seek conformity to the image of Jesus Christ. Men need not follow him in appearance with long hair and beards. Women and men need not wear robes and sandals because he did. We need not generally walk to where we want to go, or limit our transportation to donkeys and small boats. We need not shake the dust off our feet if people do not receive our message. We need not wash one another's feet. In many cultures with paved roads and sidewalks, other forms of humble servanthood may be more appropriate, such as washing another's car or polishing another's shoes. We need not always raise our hands in benediction (Luke 24:50). We need not take the Lord's Supper in a reclining position or be baptized in the Jordan River. Radical discipleship does not require that all have as simple a lifestyle as Jesus, who was single and had no family for which to provide. In general, we need not duplicate the nonuniversal cultural specifics of his situation. Some Christians may attempt to replicate such factors, but they ought not make such aspects of his life normative for others nor feel that by doing so themselves they are more holy than others.[125]

When devoted to following the example of Christ we need to avoid making him over into our image. He was not an antiestablishment revolutionary armed with weapons, nor was he an unthinking vassal of the establishment in a grey flannel suit. Jesus was a great teacher but no mere academician. He was a crusader for certain well-chosen and timely causes, but not a blind activist. Jesus was a healer and miracle worker, but he did not make miracles ends in themselves. He taught us to pray by an example—the "Lord's prayer"—but we need not always quote its words. We do not follow his teaching on prayer if we repeat memorized words meaninglessly.

Metaphysically, we can never be divine as Christ was. We should avoid encouragements by pantheistic and occult leaders to visualize ourselves to have infinite divine potential. Jesus never blurred the distinction between the Creator and the creature, or between himself as from above and all others who were from below. Ontologically Jesus is God's one and only Son. Our spiritual problem is not our finite distinctness but our moral rebellion. Hence all appropriate attempts that we make to be like Jesus Christ ought to avoid the blasphemy of claiming to be God, in the God-class, or having an infinite potential. The fullness of Christ may dwell in us, but we ought never confuse ourselves with his power. Our being is not continuous with his divine Being.

How, then, is it possible in any measure to become like the God-man? We are not advocating a hypocritical show of Christlikeness out of selfish motives in the strength of the flesh. Attempts of non-Christians to mimic Christ's outward behavior, though understandable, cannot approach his inner authenticity. The *kenotic* Christ modeled the primary motivation of faithful love and walked in the enduement of the Holy Spirit. So believers in Christ cannot expect to grow in Christlikeness in the flesh. Only as motivated above all by faithful love and as enabled by the Holy Spirit can we make significant and lasting progress in becoming genuinely like our Lord.

REVIEW QUESTIONS

To Help Relate and Apply Each Section in This Chapter

1. *Briefly state the classical problem* this chapter addresses and indicate reasons why genuine inquiry into it is important for your worldview and your existence personally and socially.

2. *Objectively summarize the influential answers* given to this problem in history as hypotheses to be tested. Be able to compare and contrast their real similarities and differences (not merely verbal similarities or differences).

3. *Highlight the primary biblical evidence* on which to decide among views—evidence found in the relevant teachings of the major divisions of Scripture—and decide for yourself which historical hypothesis (or synthesis of historical views) provides the most consistent and adequate account of the primary biblical data.

4. *Formulate in your own words your doctrinal conviction* in a logically consistent and adequate way, organizing your conclusions in ways you can explain clearly, support biblically, and communicate effectively to your spouse, children, friends, Bible class, or congregation.

5. *Defend your view* as you would to adherents of the alternative views, showing that the other views are logically less consistent and factually faced with more difficulties than your view in accounting for the givens, not only of special revelation but also of human experience in general.

6. *Explore the differences the viability of your conviction can make in your life*. Then test your understanding of the viability of your view by asking, "Can I live by it authentically (unhypocritically) in relation to God and to others in my family, church, vocation, neighborhood, city, nation, and world?"

MINISTRY PROJECTS

To Help Communicate This Doctrine in Christian Service

1. *Memorize one major verse or passage* that in its context teaches the heart of this doctrine and may serve as a text from which to preach, teach, or lead small-group studies on the topic. The memorized passages from each chapter will build a body of content useful also for meditation and reference in informal discussions.

2. *Formulate the major idea of the doctrine in one sentence* based on the passage memorized. This idea should be useful as the major thesis of either a lesson for a class (junior high to adult) or a message for a church service.

3. *State the specific purpose or goal of your doctrinal lesson or message*. Your purpose should be more than informative. It should show why Christians need to accept this truth and live by it (unhypocritically). For teaching purposes, list indicators that would show to what extent class members have grasped the truth presented.

4. *Outline your message or lesson in complete sentences*. Indicate how you would support the truth of the doctrine's central ideas and its relevance to life and service. Incorporate elements from this chapter's historical, biblical, systematic, apologetic, and practical sections selected according to the value they have for your audience.

5. *List applications of the doctrine* for communicating the difference this conviction makes in life (for sermons, lessons, small-group Bible studies, or family devotional Bible studies). Applications should make clear what the doctrine is, why one needs to know it, and how it will make differences in thinking. Then show how the difference in thought will lead to differences in values, priorities, attitudes, speech, and personal action. Consider also the doc-

trine's possible significance for family, church, neighborhood, city, regional, and national actions.

6. *Start a file and begin collecting illustrations* of this doctrine's central idea, the points in your outline, and your application.

7. *Write out your own doctrinal statement on this subject in one paragraph* (in half a page or less). To work toward a comprehensive doctrinal statement, collect your formulations based on a study of each chapter of *Integrative Theology*. As your own statement of Christian doctrine grows, you will find it personally strengthening and useful when you are called on for your beliefs in general and when you apply for service with churches, mission boards, and other Christian organizations. Any who seek ordination to Christian ministry will need a comprehensive doctrinal statement that covers the broad scope of theology.

CHAPTER 7

CHRIST'S ONCE-FOR-ALL ATONING PROVISIONS

Christ's Once-for-All Atoning Provisions

THE PROBLEM: WHAT DID JESUS CHRIST'S DEATH ON THE CROSS OF CALVARY ACHIEVE FOR SINFUL AND CONDEMNED MEN AND WOMEN?

The major religions of the world focus primarily on the life and teachings of their founder or leader. While by no means neglecting Jesus' instruction, Christianity uniquely assigns chief importance to his sufferings and death as interpreted by the Scriptures. The focal importance to Paul of Christ's passion is evident in his figurative statement to the church at Corinth: "I resolved to know nothing while I was with you except Jesus Christ and him crucified" (1 Cor. 2:2; cf. 1:18; Gal. 6:14). A growing number of contemporary liberal and mediating theologians focus attention on Christ's earthly life while minimizing the significance of his suffering and death on the cross.[1]

In this chapter we investigate the question of why biblical people view the cross of Christ as the center where many lines of Christian conviction converge. How does Calvary illumine the character of God, such as his love, holiness, faithfulness, righteousness, and abhorrence of evil (vol. 1, chap. 6)? How does the cross relate to human persons after Eden in a condition of sin and alienation against God (vol. 2, chap. 4)? Moreover, how is the cross linked with the person of Jesus Christ (chaps. 5–6)? Did the second person of the Godhead, who abandoned heaven to become a man, do for us spiritually what we sinners could not do for ourselves? How is the cross related to the Christian doctrine of salvation? What has the cross on which Christ died 1,900 years ago to do with our salvation today? Furthermore, why is the cross the major symbol of the Christian church? How does Calvary relate to the *ekklēsia* or the worldwide family of God (vol. 3, chaps. 5–6)? Finally, how does the death Christ suffered during his first advent relate to his second advent (vol. 3, chaps. 7–9)? Biblical eschatology deals with the future God has planned for the people of God who glory in the cross of Christ. Given the profound relatedness of the cross to other Christian doctrines, Warfield's comment is appropriate: "Not only is the doctrine of the sacrificial death of Christ embodied in Christianity an essential element of the system, but in a very real sense it constitutes Christianity."[2]

371

In the present chapter we enquire into several vital but debated issues associated with the death Christ died. In the context of universal sinfulness, how can alienated men and women be restored to fellowship with a holy God? Millennia ago Job posed the question, "How can a mortal be righteous before God?" (Job 9:2). Later the apostle Paul inquired how God could be perfectly just and yet justify the ungodly (Rom. 3:25–26). To answer these questions we must address the meaning and significance of the death Christ died. What does the cross Jesus bore nearly two thousand years ago accomplish for people today? Did a once-for-all transaction occur at the cross, or does it simply evoke a personal relationship to Christ? Did the cross accomplish something objectively, or is its impact only subjective? If the former, how could one person bear the guilt and penalty of all the people who have ever lived? Moreover, what is the meaning and significance of the biblical metaphors traditionally used to describe the work of Christ, such as passover sacrifice, ransom, redemption, propitiation, victor, and reconciliation?

Furthermore, is it valid to affirm that Christ functioned as a great high priest on our behalf? If so, what does the symbolism of priesthood connote in relation to our Lord? We need also to interact with the widely debated question in Christendom: For whom did Christ die? Did the Father send his Son into the world to die for all persons or only for the elect? Might there be a viable alternative to these two popular interpretations? Finally, does Scripture teach that between his death and resurrection Christ descended to the nether regions of the earth to preach to human spirits allegedly imprisoned there? How valid is the statement in the Apostles' Creed "He descended to hell"? The issues addressed in this chapter on the cross of Christ may seem complex and difficult. But as Emil Brunner has said, with some overstatement, "He who understands the cross aright . . . understands the Bible, he understands Jesus Christ."[3]

ALTERNATIVE INTERPRETATIONS IN THE CHURCH

The crucial question of what the death of Jesus Christ accomplished for persons alienated from the life of God has been variously explicated in the church. For purpose of evaluation by scriptural evidence, we will now survey the varied historical proposals for understanding the cross.

The Classic or Ransom View

Many patristic authorities to the time of Anselm and a few contemporary theologians interpret the atonement as a cosmic victory over sin, death, and Satan. This classic, dramatic, or ransom theory, which depicts God triumphing over hostile forces that enslave persons, was the dominant view in the church for a thousand years. The interpretation found considerable favor with early Christians surrounded by oppressive satanic activity in the pagan world. The theory focuses not on Christ's bearing the sinner's penalty or propitiating God's wrath but on the Savior's delivering humankind from enslaving powers. The theory assumes at least two forms: (1) Following Mark 10:45, some interpreters viewed Christ's death as a ransom paid to the Devil. The world, they argued, had fallen under Satan's dominion by virtue of sin. At the cross God delivered Christ over to Satan in exchange for the souls of those he held captive. But Satan could not hold Christ, thus the Son of God rose powerfully from the grave. (2) Guided by Colossians 2:15, other authorities claimed that God did battle with Satan, triumphed over death and the Devil once-for-all, and rescued those held captive by the powers of darkness.

Irenaeus interpreted Christ's death as a victory over sin, death, and the Devil. Through Edenic transgression, humanity fell under the dominion of Satan. By recapitulating in himself all the experiences of humankind and by rising from the dead, Christ conquered Satan, thereby freeing believing sinners from his power and giving them eternal life. Wrote Irenaeus: "Reasonably redeeming us with his blood, Christ gave himself as a ransom for those who had been led into captivity."[4]

Origen maintained that by reason of sin humanity was bound in the clutches of Satan. In exchange for the freedom of souls held under his sway, Satan demanded the blood of Christ. When God gave Christ to the Devil as a ransom (*lytron*), Satan released the imprisoned souls. Origen continues by stating that Satan was deceived in the transaction on two counts: (1) Christ's humanity hid his deity so that when Satan swallowed the bait of Christ's flesh he was caught on the hook of his deity; and (2) Satan discovered that he could not hold Christ in hell and on the third day the Savior rose powerfully from the grave. Origen summarizes as follows: "The evil one reigned over us until the soul of Jesus had been given to him as a ransom—to him who deceived himself, thinking that he could be master over Jesus, not realizing that he did not suffer the agony which he applied to hold him down."[5]

John of Damascus used the same imagery, except that he identified the enemy that was snared as death rather than Satan. "Death approaches and eagerly swallowing the bait of the body is transfixed by the hook of the divinity. And so having tasted that innocent and life-giving body, itself is destroyed, vomiting up all those whom it had previously swallowed."[6]

Gustaf Aulén claims that the sometimes crude metaphors of the Fathers convey the important truth that God in Christ triumphed over sin, death, and the Devil. In a great cosmic drama that issued in his death, Christ fought against and overcame malignant spiritual powers. As a result of that victory captive persons were freed and gained the hope of eternal life. The central theme of the classic view "is the idea of the Atonement as a divine conflict and victory; Christ—*Christus victor*—fights against and triumphs over the evil powers of the world, the 'tyrants' under which mankind is in bondage and suffering, and in him God reconciles the world to himself."[7] Aulén claims that the *Christus victor* motif, much neglected in modern theology, faithfully reflects the teachings of Scripture and of Luther. Aulén cites the prediction of warfare between Christ and Satan in Genesis 3:15, the Lord's exorcism of demons in the Gospels, and texts such as Colossians 2:15, Hebrews 2:14, and 1 John 3:8. Clearly Aulén's *Christus victor* motif emphasizes Christ's kingly rather than priestly office.

The Moral Influence Theory

This subjective view of the atonement focuses on the change of attitude Christ's death produces in sinners. Proponents claim that there were no obstacles in God that needed to be overcome in order to restore sinners to fellowship with their Creator. From the divine side no satisfaction of justice and no placation of wrath was required. The only barrier to salvation lies in estranged persons themselves, i.e., in their sinful pride and stubborn wills. This theory maintains that the love of God displayed on the cross overwhelms sinners' hostility and persuades them to repent and be reconciled to God. First advanced as a theory by Peter Abelard in the medieval era, the moral influence theory finds many adherents among modern liberal theologians.

Proceeding from a view of sin as contempt of God, Abelard claimed that Christ's death provides a compelling demonstration of God's suffering with his creatures. The spectacle of Christ impaled on the cross causes people to recognize their selfishness, melts their stony hearts, and moves them to be reconciled to God. The sufferings of the innocent Christ on the cross stir sinners to love the One who so manifestly loves them. At bottom, then, people are saved by the compelling power of God's self-giving love. "Christ died for us in order to show how great was his love to mankind and to prove that love is the essence of Christianity."[8] Abelard believed that the cross exerts the most powerful moral influence in human history.

The Socinians modified Abelard's views with themes from Renaissance humanism. Their conception of the atonement was rooted (1) in a Pelagian understanding of the essential goodness of human nature, (2) in a humanistic vision of God that allowed for no wrath against sin, and (3) in an adoptionist view of Jesus as human prophet chosen by God to be his Son. The Socinians claimed that in his life and death Jesus modeled the moral life that God expects humans to live. The enduring example of Jesus' obedience unto death inspires persons to pursue self-reformation. Said Socinus, "Christ takes away sins because by heavenly promises He attracts and is strong to move all men to penitence, whereby sins are destroyed. . . . He draws all who have not lost hope to leave their sins and zealously to embrace righteousness and holiness."[9] As sinners repent and strive to live morally, they experience God's forgiveness. Socinus believed that Christ's death was but a preliminary stage to the crucial event of his exaltation to heaven. Undertaking in the heavenly world the office of priest, Christ there offered the true sacrifice, which is his representation of believers before the Father.

Horace Bushnell, the father of American liberalism, believed that the cross displayed God suffering in love with his creatures. "It is not that the suffering appeases God, but that it expresses God—displays, in open history, the unconquerable love of God's heart."[10] Subjectively the death of Christ releases a moral power in the world that softens hardened hearts and leads sinners to repentance. Primarily Christ's death "was designed to have a renovating power in character."[11] Seeking to retain some link with orthodoxy, Bushnell suggested that concepts such as divine anger, sacrifice, blood, and expiation ("the altar form") convey the "sentiments, states, and moral effects in the worshippers, which . . . they were unable to conceive or speak of themselves."[12] Although retaining the traditional language, Bushnell viewed the atonement as the power of love that evokes repentance and transforms character.

L. H. DeWolf also subscribes to the moral view of the atonement. He claims that at the cross sinners, (1) negatively, discover the vileness of their sin vividly represented and, (2) positively, learn that God lovingly suffers with them in their alienation. Thus as men and women contemplate the cross on which God acted in Christ, "they are moved to place their hope in the Father, repent with faith, and aspire to serve him in obedient love."[13]

The Satisfaction or Juridicial Theory

This theory of the atonement, also called the Latin view, first arose in the patristic West and achieved full expression in the Middle Ages. In suggesting that the death of Christ chiefly satisfies the wounded honor of God, medieval theologians were influenced by the concept of a feudal overlord whose dignity was injured by his serfs. While reflecting a keen awareness of sin and the solidarity of the race, this theory focused largely on God's injured honor and paid less attention to the penal and substitutionary nature of Christ's death. Unlike the focus of the previous two theories, that of the juridicial theory is primarily Godward.

In his essay *Cur Deus Homo* (*Why God [Became] Man*), Anselm claims that sin is the failure to render God his due, namely, entire subjection and obedience. When a person disobeys God and sins, he offends God's honor and violates the divinely ordained order of the universe. God's nature is such that he requires either satisfaction or punishment for sin. But since God willed that sufficient persons should be saved to replace the number of fallen angels (a judgment borrowed from Augustine), satisfaction for sins must be made. In addition, the medieval mind held that the recompense must be proportional to the dignity of the offended party, in this case God. Consequently, finite persons cannot make an infinite satisfaction for the offense committed against the Lord of the universe. In any case sinners have nothing to offer God, for they already owe God everything. "Sinful man cannot at all accomplish this justification, because a sinner cannot justify a sinner."[14] Thus adequate satisfaction must come from one who is divine, that is, from God himself. On the other hand, satisfaction must be paid by one who genuinely represents humanity. Thus satisfaction must be made by one who is both God and man. "If only God can make this satisfaction and only a man ought to make it: it is necessary that a God-man make it."[15] Wherefore God was born of a virgin, and the sinless Jesus Christ voluntarily suffered and died, thereby accruing more merit than needed to pay the debt humanity owed. God accepted the surplus of Christ's passion, credited it to the account of the sinful race, and thus is disposed to restore to fellowship all who trust in Christ's saving provision.

How does Anselm's satisfaction theory differ from the view of many Reformed and Evangelical theologians? First, Anselm made the idea of satisfaction virtually the whole of his theory. And second, he "saw *satisfaction* for our sins as the offering of compensation or damages for dishonor done." Packer continues this point, saying that "the Reformers saw it as the undergoing of vicarious punishment (*poena*) to meet the claims on us of God's holy law and wrath (i.e., his punitive justice)."[16]

Several later medieval theologians modified Anselm's theory of satisfaction rendered to God's injured honor. Hugh of St. Victor combined Anselm's juridicial theory with the classic view of ransom from the dominion of Satan. Accordingly Christ rendered satisfaction to God for the dishonor sinners caused him. Now aligned with persons, God is disposed to free sinners from Satan's domination. Alexander of Hales and Bonaventura generally followed the Anselmic scheme, though both appeared reluctant to posit the absolute necessity of Christ's death as Anselm had done. The English Reformer John Wycliffe also followed the main lines of the Anselmic satisfaction motif.

The Governmental or Rectoral Theory

Hugo Grotius, the Remonstrant jurist and theologian, first expounded the governmental theory of the atonement. Grotius envisaged God as world Ruler who preserves moral government. His key scriptural text was Isaiah 42:21: "The Lord was pleased, for his righteousness' sake, to magnify his law and make it glorious" (RSV). Grotius sought to forge a middle ground between the Socinians and the Calvinist Reformers.

Against the Socinians he argued that God exacts punishment for sin, albeit not out of retribution but for the maintenance of the moral order of the universe. And against the Reformers he insisted that Christ did not bear the full penalty of human sin, nor did he propitiate God's wrath.

Objectively, Grotius maintained that the death of Christ was a real offering made to God, an offering that displays the divine justice. Although divine love modified the demands of strict justice so that God need not exact the full penalty for sin, the offering of Christ did render God favorable so that he could pardon sins and restore sinners to fellowship. God could have relaxed his law altogether and not punished Christ, but such a course would not have achieved the maximal deterrence for future sins. Here the subjective component of the atonement comes into view. For Grotius the punishment inflicted on Christ is exemplary in that it communicates God's hatred of sin and strikes fear into the hearts of persons so that they will forsake evil and seek personal reformation. Grotius argues, "God, who has supreme power as to all things not unjust in themselves, and who is liable to no law, willed to use the torments and death of Christ for the setting up of a weighty example against the immense faults of us all."[17] For Grotius, the main emphasis of the atonement is subjective: Christ's death motivates sinners to repent of their sins and reform their lives.

The older Arminians followed the viewpoint of Grotius. John Miley, a Methodist theologian, rejected the penal satisfaction theory advanced by the Protestant Reformers. Said he, "The Wesleyan soteriology . . . excludes the satisfaction theory, and requires the governmental as the only theory consistent with itself."[18] Arguing that sin and guilt could not be imputed to the sinless Son of God, Miley concludes that Christ did not bear the punishment due to our sin. "The sufferings of Christ are not, and cannot be, an atonement by penal substitution."[19] Advancing the governmental theory, Miley claims that Christ's sufferings are atoning in the sense that they uphold law and serve the interests of moral government. God exacted a penalty for human sin in the form of the death of Christ. But Christ's death fulfills justice not as a substitute of penalty, but insofar as it serves a rectoral end. The sufferings of Christ avail in that they maintain the honor of the divine Ruler, manifest the ugliness of sin, foreshadow the punishment of the unrepentant, and restrain sin by striking fear in the hearts of persons. Miley concludes, "The chief rectoral value of penalty, simply as an element of law, is through the moral ideas which it conveys, and the response which it thus finds in the moral reason."[20]

J. Kenneth Grider, a Nazarene theologian, likewise upholds the governmental view of the atonement:

> According to this theory, Christ did not pay the penalty for our sins; instead, he suffered for us. Scripture never says that Christ was punished for us, or paid the penalty, as Calvinists teach. . . . His death was of such a nature that a holy God could accept it as a *substitute* for penalty. Its merits as a substitute could provide a moral basis for forgiveness without compromising either God's holiness or the integrity of moral government.[21]

Arminian theologians consistently uphold a universal atonement: Christ died for the purpose of providing salvation for the entire world. Thus Arminius succinctly affirmed: "Christ died for all men and for every individual."[22] Desiring that none should perish in their sins, God bestows prevenient grace universally and extends salvation to all through worldwide gospel proclamation. Arminians such as Miley aver that an unconditional atonement makes universal salvation theoretically possible. But since many persons fail to respond to the gospel in faith, not all actually are saved. The Arminians press their position by asking how persons could be held guilty for refusing to believe what was not intended for them. Miley reasons that the broader the intent of the atonement, the greater the good that accrues. He suggests that a universal atonement optimally fosters the maintenance of moral government. He concludes, "The atonement, as a provision of infinite love for a common race in a common ruin of sin, with its unrestricted overture of grace and requirement of saving faith in Christ, is, and must be, an atonement for all."[23]

Neoorthodox Reconciliation Theory

Opposing liberalism's subjective understanding of the atonement, Karl Barth affirms that the death of Christ objectively reconciles the world to God. Seeking to be like God, humankind is godless, guilty, and condemned to death. To make amends, the divine Son descended into a strange land to experience rejection. In depicting the atonement Barth freely uses the language of substitution.[24] Yet Barth's view of the atonement diverges significantly from the orthodox representation. He denies that Christ by suffering propitiated the wrath of the offended God. Rather, by his incarnation and death Christ, our Representative, united human nature (humanum) to his divine nature. Said Barth of Christ's earthly experience: "He takes human being into unity with His own."[25] Thus at Calvary, in solidarity with Christ, humankind suffered and died. Barth rejects the notion that Christ bore the penalty of sin in our place. On the cross the wrath and the punishment of God fell both on him *and* on us. "In His person, with Him, judgment, death and end have come to us ourselves once and for all."[26] Fur-

thermore, united with Christ in his resurrection, humanity participates in the Lord's victory over death and the Devil. Concerning the final end of humanity, Barth affirms, "Our exaltation took place in Him."[27] Barth insisted that God pardons sinners not by means of a penal satisfaction, but simply on the basis of his determination to forgive—which act of forgiveness satisfies the requirements of his righteousness. "His forgiveness makes good our repudiation and failure and thus overcomes the hurt that we do to God, and the disturbance of the relationship between Himself and us, and the disturbance of the general relationship between the Creator and the creation."[28]

The presupposition of this act of justification and reconciliation is the eternal covenant that God made with the human race. In volume 1, chapter 8, Barth postulated that God eternally elected himself in Jesus Christ for suffering and death. In this respect the cross signifies the rejection of the Son of God. In addition, God eternally predestined sinful humanity in Jesus Christ for salvation. In this latter respect the cross signifies the election of humankind in the Son. Ontically, Barth maintains that the death of Christ achieved a cosmic victory; the entire world has been won back to the Father. "In the death of Christ both the destroying and the renewing have taken place for all men. . . . Unbelief has become an objective, real and ontological impossibility and faith an objective, real and ontological necessity for all men and for every man."[29] But noetically, Barth acknowledges that not all persons are aware of their redeemed status. The Spirit's task, he argues, is to awaken this realization of reconciliation in the hearts of every human being. Although Barth removes the event of reconciliation from history to so-called meta-history, his position is that Christ not only died for all but that in the triumph of grace Christ will bring all persons savingly to himself. Barth's position regarding the intent of the atonement is clear: through the death of Christ God willed to save all persons.

Hendrikus Berkhof, a contemporary Dutch theologian, broadly follows Barth's line of reasoning. Berkhof interprets the human dilemma as estrangement and guilt due to sin (where guilt is a relational, not a forensic concept). Christ's death should not be interpreted in terms of the old concepts of vicarious penalty or propitiation of the divine wrath, which Berkhof holds to be alien to the the modern mindset. Rather, the terms that best describe the atonement are "representation" and "reconciliation." That is, by representing a sinful race before God, Christ identified with sinners and restores them to fellowship with their Creator. Berkhof insists that Christ effected this representation not by the cross only, but through the totality of his earthly life. Berkhof summarizes his position as follows: "Representation signifies that in him the relationship is restored, that is, that which *from our side* obstructed the relationship simply does not count anymore in the light of his perfect love and obedience" (italics mine).[30] Berkhof concedes that the exact connection between the cross and reconciliation is not clear. "The NT asserts the 'that,' but has no answer to the 'why' and the 'how.' That is God's secret."[31]

Some modern theologians replace concepts of substitutionary sacrifice and penal satisfaction with the idea of representation and vicarious identification. Thus Vincent Taylor writes, "No offer of penal suffering as a substitute for his own will meet his need, but a submission presented by his representative before God becomes the foundation of a new hope."[32]

Many Fathers, Reformers, and Evangelicals

The apostolic fathers advanced no single theory of the atonement, but articulated a number of biblical motifs. Clement of Rome described the work of Christ, using the language of substitution. "Because of the love which he felt for us, Jesus Christ our Lord gave his blood for us by the will of God, his body for our bodies, and his soul for our souls."[33] Ignatius expressed the idea of our Lord's vicarious atonement: "All these sufferings, assuredly, he underwent for our sake, that we might be saved."[34] According to the *Epistle to Diognetus,* Christ's substitutionary death justifies the wicked, and his righteousness covers sins:

God gave up his own Son as a ransom for us—the holy one for the unjust, the innocent for the guilty, the righteous one for the unrighteous, the incorruptible for the corruptible, the immortal for the mortal. For what else could cover our sins except his righteousness? . . . O sweet exchange! O unfathomable work of God! The sinfulness of many is hidden in the Righteous One, while the righteousness of the One justifies the many that are sinners.[35]

In the East Cyril of Jerusalem describes the cross in terms of penal substitution, although he grounds the sentence of death in God's veracity rather than in his justice:

We were enemies of God through sin, and God had decreed the death of the sinner. One of two things, therefore, was necessary, either that God, in his truth, should destroy all men, or that in his loving-kindness, he should remit the sentence. But see the wisdom of God; he preserved the truth of his sentence and the exercise of his loving-kindness. Christ took our sins "in his body upon the tree; that we, having died to sin," by his death "might live to justice."[36]

Athanasius taught that in order to solve the problem posed by human sin and condemnation God sent the divine Word into the world. In his body the Son bore the penalty and paid the debt that sinners owed to God. Thus Christ offered "the sacrifice on behalf of all, surrendering his own temple [body] to death in place of all, to settle man's account with death and free him from the primal transgression."[37] For Athanasius Christ's death was a penal satisfaction of the divine sentence of death. By virtue of Christ's cross and resurrection, death is annulled and believers are raised to immortality.

In the West Augustine synthesized previous insights into a comprehensive view of the atonement. Original sin brought humanity under the divine sentence of condemnation and death. In love Jesus Christ yielded to the snare of the Devil and endured the punishment that sinners justly deserved. Wrote Augustine: "Christ bore for our sakes sin in the sense of death as brought on human nature by sin. This is what hung on the tree. . . . Thus was death condemned that its reign might cease, and accursed that it might be destroyed."[38] In making this sacrifice to satisfy the divine justice, Christ functioned as both priest and oblation, as both offerer and offering.[39] Christ's death achieved several significant benefits, the first of which is placation of the divine wrath. "When the Father was angry with us, he looked upon the death of his Son for us and was propitiated towards us."[40] Christ's penal sacrifice, furthermore, delivers saints from satanic bondage, cleanses sins, reconciles to the Father, and offers the church an example of humility, patience in suffering, and faith in God.[41]

Luther taught that Christ in his life and death bore the sin, guilt, and punishment of a condemned race. On the cross the Savior endured the divine wrath against transgressions and the sentence of death the law justly demanded. As a result of his propitiatory sacrifice, Christ frees trusting souls from the curse of the law; reconciles God and sinners; imparts perfect righteousness; and conquers sin, death, and the Devil. Luther sums up his position thus: "Putting on your sinful person, he [Christ] bore your sin, death, and curse. He became a sacrifice and a curse for you, in order thus to set you free from the curse of the law."[42] Although one important outcome of the cross is the destruction of sin and Satan, Aulén is not correct in asserting that Luther primarily represents Christ's work in terms of the classical theory of triumph over Satanic powers.[43]

Calvin held that for sinners to be freed from sin's curse, a fitting sacrifice must be offered. Thus the "big idea" of Calvin's discussion of the cross is the notion of vicarious sacrifice. First, Christ is our sin-bearer. Through his life and especially his death, the Savior bore our guilt, the wrath of God, and the penalty due us. "The Son of God, utterly clean of all fault, nevertheless took upon himself the shame and reproach of our iniquities."[44] Second, Christ is the believer's righteousness. God reckoned Christ's suffering to the elect as perfect moral rectitude: "We are made righteous in him . . . because we are judged in relation to Christ's righteousness."[45] Calvin elaborates the "big idea" of vicarious sacrifice by means of three key theological concepts, the first of which is *propitiation*. This depicts the work of Christ in its Godward aspect. By his substitutionary sacrifice Christ satisfied the demands of a just God and appeased the divine wrath for all who believe. So Calvin asserts, "God, to whom we were hateful because of sin, was appeased by the death of his Son to become favorable to us."[46] Calvin's second term is *redemption,* which represents the manward focus of the cross. By his sacrificial death Christ liberates elect believers from sin, guilt, and the penalty of death.[47] Calvin's third word is *reconciliation,* which represents both the Godward and the manward sides of Christ's work. Formerly hostile to sinners by reason of their unrighteousness, God for Christ's sake is now reconciled to repentant sinners. "Christ had to become a sacrifice by dying that he might reconcile his Father to us."[48] On the other hand, the cross impacts man and so reconciles sinners to God. Thus "God appointed Christ as a means of reconciling us to himself."[49] Calvin claims that Christ performs his mediatorial work by executing the three offices of prophet, king, and priest.[50] As Prophet Christ proclaimed the grace of God and assists the church in its proclamation of the gospel. As King he rules over, guides, and protects the church. And (most relevant to this chapter) as Priest he expiated sins by his sacrifice and eternally intercedes before the Father on behalf of his people.

B. B. Warfield asserts that by the complete obedience of his life Christ fulfilled the demands of the law that Adam failed to keep and that by bearing the penalty of our sin through his sacrificial death he satisfied the justice of God. "Our Lord's redeeming work is at its core a true and perfect sacrifice offered to God, of intrinsic value ample for the expiation of our guilt; and at the same time is a true and perfect righteousness offered to God in fulfillment of the demands of his law."[51] By means of his vicarious sacrifice Christ propitiated the wrath of God, secured forgiveness of sins, delivered his people from Satanic bondage, reconciled God to sinners and sinners to God, and liberated us from the burden of the law as a way of life.

Concerning the intent or purpose of the atonement, most patristic authorities held that Christ died for the sins of the world. Athanasius maintained that in the divine scheme of things "death there had to be, and death for all, so that the due of all might be paid."[52] Cyril of Jerusalem affirmed that "Jesus truly suffered for all men."[53] While not speaking clearly on the issue, Augustine seemed to suggest that Christ died for the world, although the cross is effectual only for those who believe.[54] As for John Calvin, several recent scholars believe that although Calvin held to double predestination he also taught a doctrine of unlimited atonement.[55] In his *Institutes* Calvin wrote, "It is certain that the Lord offers us mercy and the pledge of his grace both in his Sacred Word and in his sacraments. But it is understood only by those who take Word and sacraments with sure faith, just as Christ is offered and held forth by the Father to all unto salvation, yet not all acknowledge and receive him."[56] In his later commentaries Calvin more clearly postulates an unlimited atonement. With regard to Galatians 5:12 Calvin affirms: "God commends to us the salvation of all men without exception, even as Christ suffered for the sins of the whole world."[57]

Other moderate Calvinists point out that Christ's saving provision includes many racial benefits, such as the common blessings of life, the restraint of evil, an objective provision sufficient for all, the removal of every obstacle on God's side for the forgiveness of sins, and the future resurrection of the dead.[58] On the other hand, they seek to do justice to texts that indicate a special purpose for those persons given to Christ out of the world. They point out that 1 Timothy 4:10 indicates a twofold purpose in the cross, namely, general benefits for all people and saving benefits for elect believers. In a sermon entitled, "General and Yet Particular," C. H. Spurgeon maintains that Christ's death fulfilled a twofold purpose: "There is a general influence for good flowing from the mediatorial sacrifice of

Christ, and yet its special design and definite object is the giving of eternal life to as many as the Father gave him."[59] The observation of Charles M. Horne is instructive: "God's salvation is one. As applied to non-Christians, it includes their preservation in this life and the enjoyment of certain blessings which come to man by common grace. As applied to believers, however, this salvation extends into eternity. This view would seem to be the best one, because it gives the power force to the word *especially* [1 Tim. 4:10]."[60] In a similar vein Robert P. Lightner claims that Christ's saving provision reaches every member of Adam's race. Yet its redemptive benefits are applied only to those who believe, i.e., to the elect.[61] Donald G. Bloesch arrives at a similar conclusion in language colored by the thought of Barth.[62]

Scholastic Calvinism, however, narrowed the intent of the atonement and claimed that Christ died solely for the purpose of saving the elect, the exact number of whom are actually brought to salvation. Thus proponents argue that the design of the cross was not merely to provide salvation but to *secure* the salvation of those persons the Father gave to the Son. Christ allegedly died for all who were related to him, just as Adam sinned for all who were related to him. For high Calvinism the question "For whom did Christ die?" follows from God's logically prior elective decree. Since antecedent to his decree to create humanity God purposed to save some persons and to condemn others, the high Calvinist claims that Christ died solely for those predestined to life.

In the Westminster Confession the divine decree assigning people to life or death (chap. III) precedes discussion of the work of Christ (chap. VIII). It is clear that its doctrine of election controls its doctrine of the atonement (XI.4). The Confession concludes that Christ died to obtain redemption for the elect only: "The Lord Jesus . . . purchased not only reconciliation, but an everlasting inheritance in the kingdom of heaven, for all those whom the Father hath given unto him" (VIII.5; cf. VIII.8). The Canons of Dort likewise treat the doctrine of election (I.1–18) prior to the person and work of Christ (II.1–9). God willed that the efficacy of the cross should extend only to the elect. "It was the will of God that Christ by the blood of the cross . . . should effectually redeem out of every people, tribe, nation, and language, all those, and those only, who were from eternity chosen to salvation and given to Him by the Father." (II.8).

John Owen judges that none of God's intentions or purposes fail to eventuate. If Christ died for all and not all are saved, then Christ died ineffectively, which cannot be. If God loves all and not all are saved, then God loves ineffectually, which also cannot be. Thus Christ did not die for all, and God does not love all people. Says Owen: "We deny that all mankind are the object of that love of God which moved him to send his Son to die."[63] God's love is reflected in his will to save the elect, the heirs of the covenant of grace, for whose sins Christ made satisfaction on the cross. Owen concludes that if the death of Christ accomplishes all that the Father intended, "then died he only for those that are in the event sanctified, purged, redeemed, justified, freed from wrath and death, quickened, saved, etc.; but that all are not thus sanctified, freed, etc., is most apparent: and, therefore they cannot be said to be the proper object of the death of Christ."[64]

Other Calvinist authorities who uphold a limited atonement include Jonathan Edwards, Francis Turrettin, Charles Hodge, A. A. Hodge, W. G. T. Shedd, L. Berkhof, Loraine Boettner, John Murray, and R. B. Kuiper. In each of these theologians the intent of the atonement is governed by the logically prior doctrine of election. Roger Nicole prefers the concept of "definite atonement" or "particular redemption." Christ died for the specific purpose of redeeming those whom the Father had given him.[65]

Offended by what he judged to be the harsh double predestinarianism of scholastic Calvinism, Amyraut in the seventeenth century propounded the theory of hypothetical universalism. According to this view, the covenant of grace included a universal, conditional covenant and a particular, unconditional covenant. Against scholastic Calvinism, Amyraut insisted that God willed the salvation of all persons on the condition that they believe. That is, the Father appointed Christ to suffer for the sins of the entire world. God, however, foresaw that no sinners would respond in faith, hence he implemented the particular or unconditional covenant. Here, against the Arminians, who denied that God brings the redeemed to faith, Amyraut argued that since none are able to come to God on their own, God effectively creates saving faith in the elect and reprobates others. Amyraut thus upheld an ideal universalism supplemented by a real particularism. His scheme could be represented as follows: "Christ died for all persons sufficiently, but for the elect efficiently." Amyraut's position was championed by later scholars such as Cameron of the Saumar Academy, Richard Baxter, John Bunyon, Samuel Hopkins, and Heinrich Heppe.

The "Descent of Christ Into Hell"

Based on such Scriptures as Psalm 16:10; Matthew 12:40; 27:52–53; Ephesians 4:9; 1 Peter 3:18–20; and 4:6, many church authorities affirm that between his death and resurrection Christ descended to the nether regions to preach the gospel to deceased persons. According to Eastern fathers such as Clement of Alexandria, Origen, Cyril of Alexandria, and John of Damascus, Christ in hell proclaimed the gospel to evangelize unbelieving dead. Clement, for example, averred that Christ preached to Jews who strove to live according to the law and to Gentiles who sought to live according to philosophy.[66] Western fathers such as Tertullian and Augustine held that Christ descended to the lower regions to unite faithful patriarchs and prophets to himself. Mention of Christ's descent to hell appeared in a late fourth-century recension of the Apostles' Creed and in the Athanasian Creed (no. 38). Medieval theologians followed Thomas Aquinas, who held that Christ's soul went to hades to bestow the fruits of his passion upon Old Testament believers, who had been excluded from glory by virtue of original sin.[67] Roman Catholics believe that as a result of the descent into hades the souls of those who died in faith were united to God and were raised to heaven at Christ's ascension. Lutherans generally hold that by descending to hell Christ completed his triumph over Satan and passed judgment on the unsaved held there. Calvin, on the other hand, understood the descent to hell as a figurative description of Christ's penal sufferings on the cross. What could be more hellish, he asked, than for the spotless Son of God to bear the torments of sin and to be forsaken by the Father?[68] Most Reformed and evangelical authorities have followed Calvin in interpreting the *descensus ad inferna* in a figurative sense.[69]

The theory of vicarious sacrifice, supplemented by such motifs as moral example, ransom, and triumph over Satan, has also been capably expounded by A. A. Hodge,[70] W. G. T. Shedd,[71] and H. D. McDonald.[72]

BIBLICAL TEACHING

Which interpretations of the significance of Christ's death we accept will be determined by considering the various strands of the relevant biblical teaching on the subject, for Scripture is the primary source of Christian thought and commitment.

The Pentateuch

Shortly after the Fall, God said to Satan who was in the guise of a serpent, "You will strike his heel" (Gen. 3:15). This prediction indicates that the Messiah's redemptive victory would be achieved at the cost of suffering. Early in the patriarchal history sacrifices were made to deal with sins against God. According to Genesis 4:3–4, Cain brought an offering (*minḥāh*) to the Lord from his crops, whereas Abel brought an offering (*minḥāh*) from the firstlings of the flock. Although each brought offerings from his own occupation, Cain's was made in unbelief, whereas Abel's was made in sincere trust and commitment (Heb. 11:4). As a result Abel's sacrifice effectually atoned for sins that are hateful to a holy God.

The first explicit mention of an altar occurs after the Flood when Noah sacrificed burnt offerings to God for deliverance from the deluge (Gen. 8:20). Later Abraham (12:8; 13:18), Isaac (26:25), and Jacob (33:20; 35:7) established altars for sacrifice to the Lord. "How clearly the patriarchs understood the meaning of their sacrifices one cannot say, but that they had a concept of vicarious atonement seems quite clear (Job 1:5)."[73] Abraham's near slaying of his son Isaac as a burnt offering (*'ōlāh*) in the region of Moriah (Gen. 22:1–18) prefigures the substitutionary death of the Messiah two millennia later. Isaac ascended the mountain, bearing the wood on which the sacrifice would be laid (cf. John 19:17). When Isaac inquired about the lamb for the burnt offering, Abraham responded, "God himself will provide the lamb for the burnt offering, my son" (v. 8). As Abraham was about to slay his son on the altar, the angel of the Lord showed him a ram caught in a thicket. Abraham then "took the ram and sacrificed it as a burnt offering instead of his son" (v. 13). The phrase "instead of his son [*taḥat benô*]" clearly affirms the substitutionary nature of the animal sacrifice.

The key to Israel's sacrificial system was the Passover (*pesaḥ*) in Egypt (Exod. 12:1–30). God commanded each Hebrew household to slay an unblemished yearling lamb or goat at twilight and to apply the blood of the victim to the doorframe of their houses. For the Israelites who obeyed God's instructions the sprinkled blood secured exemption from the divine judgment. But in the case of the unbelieving Egyptians, who were not sheltered by the blood, the Lord struck dead all their firstborn men and animals (vv. 29–30). The Passover ritual clearly was sacrificial in nature, for verse 27 designates it as a "Passover sacrifice" (*zebaḥ-pesaḥ*). This atoning sacrifice resulted in Israel's deliverance from the land of bondage (Exod. 14). Concerning the Passover sacrifice the following may be said: "The blood has atoning power and points to the blood of the Lamb that will take away the sin of the world (John 1:29, 36)."[74]

The Levitical sacrificial system plainly sets forth the concept of penal substitution and atonement. In the burnt offering (*'ōlāh*, Lev. 1:3–17; Judg. 13:16; 1 Sam. 7:9–10), the fellowship or peace offering (*šelāmîm*, Lev. 3:1–17; 7:11–21; 2 Sam. 6:18), the sin offering (*ḥaṭṭā't*, Lev. 4:1–35; Num. 6:14–16; 2 Chron. 29:23–24), and the guilt offering (*'āšām*, Lev. 5:14–6:7; Num. 6:12; 1 Sam. 6:3–4), a sacrificial procedure was followed that generally involved the following elements: (1) An unblemished animal, connoting the idea of moral perfection, was presented at the door of the sanctuary by the offerer.

(2) The offerer placed his hands on the animal's head, signifying identification with the victim and the transfer of the penalty of sin to the substitute. (3) The animal was slain by the offerer (in later times by the priest), signifying that death is the just punishment for sin. (4) The priest sprinkled the blood of the victim on the altar and around the base of it, the blood representing the life of the victim (Lev. 17:11). And (5) the offering, in part or in whole, was burned on the altar of burnt offering, its fragrance ascending to God as a pleasing aroma. Repeatedly Scripture indicates that the purpose of these sacrifices was "to make atonement" for the offerer (e.g., Lev. 1:4; 4:20; 5:13; Num. 5:8; 8:12; 15:25). The Hebrew verb *kāpar,* commonly translated in the Piel, "make atonement," fundamentally means to "cover" or to "hide," and in a sacrificial context means to propitiate God's wrath, expiate sins, and restore fellowship between God and sinners.[75] The grain offering (*minḥāh,* Lev. 2:1–16; Num. 5:15, 18; Judg. 13:19) was a bloodless offering comprised of meal, oil, and incense. Part of the grain offering was burned on the altar, and part was given to the priests for food. "The idea of atonement is not specifically present in *minḥāh,* although that of propitiation certainly is."[76] With many scholars we judge that the offerings cited above anticipate the vicarious sacrifice of Christ. "The laws in Leviticus remind us then of Christ's death and what he has done for us. . . . The worshiper might well feel very much deprived when he had paid for a choice lamb to be sacrificed. But it reminded him that the animal was a ransom, a substitute payment instead of his own life."[77]

The annual Day of Atonement (*yôm hakkippurîm,* Lev. 23:27; 25:9) was the most important cultic celebration in the Old Testament. In preparation for the solemn event the high priest sacrificed a young bull as a sin-offering and a ram for a burnt-offering to atone for his sins and for those of the priesthood (Lev. 16:11–14). He sprinkled the blood of the bull on the front of the golden lid of the ark or the "atonement cover" (AV, "mercy seat"; *kappōret,* meaning "covering" or "expiation"; cf. Exod. 25:17). Then the high priest sacrificed the first male goat brought by the people as a sin-offering and sprinkled its blood on and in front of the "atonement cover" in the Holy of Holies, thereby expiating the uncleanness of the people (Lev. 16:15–19) and making atonement (*kippurîm*; cf. Exod. 29:36; 30:10; Num. 5:8). This act of blood shedding, according to Leviticus 17:11, represents God's ordained way of securing atonement. The high priest then laid his hands on the head of the second goat (the "scapegoat," AV, NIV) and confessed all the sins of the community, thus symbolically transferring guilt from the people to the victim. The second goat became a sin-bearer, as it irretrievably carried the sins and iniquities of the people into the wilderness. The scapegoat signifies an important result of atonement, namely, the expiation of sins.

Whereas in Judaism the prophet represented God to the people, the priest represented the people before God. The Hebrew priest offered sacrifices to Yahweh to atone for sins (Exod. 18:12), officiated in the sanctuary (Deut. 18:5), and interceded for the people (Joel 2:17). Genesis 14:18–20 refers to Melchizedek, "king of Salem" and "priest of God Most High," who performed sacerdotal functions before the Lord. The Book of Hebrews identifies this God-fearing Canaanite priest-king as a type of the eternal priesthood of Christ.

Poetical Books

Israel's hymnbook contains several vivid prefigurations of the sufferings of

Christ. The most descriptive occurs in Psalm 22. Although this song immediately refers to David's own trials, the poet's vision transcends the present moment to embrace the passion of the coming Messiah. Thus the Savior's God-forsakenness and cry of desolation are anticipated in verse 1 (cf. Matt. 27:46; Mark 15:34). The words "My God, my God, why have you forsaken me?" imply penal substitution. Indeed, they express "the punitive separation Christ accepted in our place, 'having become a curse for us' (Gal. 3:13).''[78] Furthermore, verses 7–8 depict the mocking insults that were hurled against Christ at Calvary (cf. Matt. 27: 39, 44; Luke 23:35); verses 14–15, the excruciating physical suffering he experienced; verse 16, the piercing of his hands and feet (cf. Luke 24:39–40); and verse 18, the dividing of his garments (cf. Luke 23:34; John 19:23). Additional anticipations of the Savior's passion occur in Psalms 34:20, 69:4, 9, 21; 109:25.

Psalm 40:6–8 (quoted in Heb. 10:5–7) indicates that although the animal sacrifices provided a certain benefit, they would be superseded by the coming Messiah who would do God's will and fulfill the law. "His will with regard to sacrifice would be fulfilled when a person, in the full freedom of personal moral choice and qualified so to act, would devote himself and his human life to doing God's will by offering his own body.''[79] The psalmist, moreover, was aware of the fact that "God" his "Savior" (Ps. 65:5) had atoned for the sins of the faithful. "When we were overwhelmed by sins, you atoned for our transgressions" (Ps. 65:3; cf. 78:38). David uses the piel of *kāpar*, possibly referring to the propitiation effected by the blood sacrifices on the Day of Atonement. Psalm 49:7–9 acknowledges that a mere human is incapable of redeeming himself or another from the power of death. No mortal can provide a ransom (*kōper*) powerful enough to deliver from the grave. Yet in faith the psalmist confesses that "God will redeem [the Qal of *pādāh*] my life from the grave (v. 15).'' His point is that God himself pays the ransom price and redeems the trusting soul from the grip of sin, death, and Satan. Ransom (*kōper*) elsewhere in the Old Testament denotes money paid to redeem the life of a person (Exod. 21:30), to free a murderer (Num. 35:31), and to purchase the freedom of a relative (Lev. 25:50–52).

The Psalms explicate God's redeeming work by means of the verb *pādāh*, to "rescue, deliver, ransom" (Pss. 31:5; 44:26; 69:18). The psalmist affirms of the Lord: "He himself will redeem Israel from all their sins" (Ps. 130:8; cf. 34:22). The noun *pᵉdût* connotes the redemption that God effects through the atoning sacrifices. Thus "he provided redemption [*pᵉdût*] for his people" (Ps. 111:9; cf. 130:7). Finally, God's redeeming activity is conveyed by means of the verb *gā'al*, to "redeem, avenge, do the part of a kinsman." God redeemed by delivering Israel from slavery in Egypt (Pss. 74:2; 77:15; cf. Exod. 6:6; 15:13) and by rescuing persons from the consequences of sin (Pss. 103:4; 107:2). Thus the Lord is known as Israel's "Redeemer" (*gô'ēl;* Job 19:25; Ps. 78:35).

Looking backward to the account of Melchizedek in Genesis and forward to the Messiah's advent, David identified Christ as a radically new kind of priest: "The Lord has sworn and will not change his mind: 'You are a priest forever in the order of Melchizedek' '' (Ps. 110:4). David took notice of Melchizedek, a unique, non-Aaronic priest superior to the Jewish ministrant, neither the commencement nor the termination of whose office Scripture records. It remained for the writer of Hebrews to develop the full Christological implications of Melchizedek's royal priesthood.

Prophetic Literature

The Old Testament prophets richly portray the passion of the future "servant" and "branch." Isaiah writes that when confronted with terrible physical and emotional sufferings the Messiah neither resisted nor shrank back (Isa. 50:5). The prophet Zechariah acted out a parable to dramatize the final rejection of the Good Shepherd for a mere thirty pieces of silver (Zech. 11:12–13; cf. Matt. 27:3–10). Isaiah predicted Messiah's maltreatment by the people and his patient endurance of sufferings (Isa. 53:6–7). Messiah's disfigured appearance and marred form reflect the abuse and pain he endured (52:14). Isaiah adds that the Messiah "was numbered with the transgressors," anticipating Christ's crucifixion among common criminals (53:12; cf. Luke 22:37; 23:33). At Calvary, the Messiah was judged like a criminal, and his life was cut off by a violent death (Isa. 53:8). Bewildered and guilt-stricken, the people would gaze upon the one they had pierced (Zech. 12:10; cf. John 19:34, 37). Fittingly Isaiah describes the Messiah as "despised and rejected by men, a man of sorrows, and familiar with suffering" (Isa. 53:3). Finally, after the shepherd had been smitten, the sheep (his disciples) would flee and be scattered (Zech. 13:7; cf. Matt. 26:31, 56).

Eight centuries before Christ, Isaiah foresaw Yahweh's servant bearing the burden of sin that estranged us from God. "Servant" (*'ebed*) in Scripture is used of (1) great men of God (Isa. 20:3; 37:35; 44:2), (2) the covenant people Israel (Isa. 41:8–9; 42:19; 49:3), and (3) the divine Messiah. That *'ebed* cannot be limited to contemporary human personalities but is a designation of the Christ is clear from several considerations: (1) The servant is given a mis-

sion to Israel (Isa. 49:5–6; 52:5–6); (2) the accomplishments of the servant are yet future to Israel (Isa. 42:4; 49:6; 53:11); (3) the works the servant performs are suprahuman (Isa. 42:6–7; 53:11–12); and (4) the New Testament specifically identifies the servant as Jesus Christ (Matt. 12:17–21; Acts 8:32–35).[80]

The focus of the fourth servant song (Isa. 52:13–53:12) is Messiah's substitutionary sacrifice for sins. The prophet writes, "Surely he took up our infirmities and carried our sorrows" (53:4; cf. Matt. 8:17). The verb *nāśā'* ("lift up" or "bear") and *sābal* ("carry" or "transport"), together with the juxtaposition of "he" and "our," clearly communicate the idea of substitution. Isaiah reiterates the "big idea" of substitution throughout chapter 53 of his prophecy. Thus in verse 6, "the LORD has laid on him [hiphil of *pāga'*, 'cause to fall on' or 'assail'] the iniquity ['*āwôn*] of us all." Likewise, in verse 11, "he will bear [*sābal*] their iniquities ['*awônîm*]," and verse 12, "he bore [*nāśā'*] the sin [*hēṭ'*] of many." Verse 5 affirms the vicarious nature of Christ's suffering: "He was pierced for our transgressions, he was crushed for our iniquities." Similarly, verse 8: "For the transgression of my people he was stricken." Verse 10 represents Christ's death as a "guilt-offering" (*'āšām*). "By calling it a guilt offering, the suffering of the Servant of the Lord is placed in the category of substitutionary satisfaction."[81] Verse 5 indicates the outcome of the Messiah's substitutionary sacrifice: "The punishment that brought us peace was upon him." The divine judgment he bore provided sinners peace with God and salvation (cf. Eph. 2:14–15; Col. 1:20). The only coherent conclusion that can be drawn from Isaiah 53:4–12 is the following: "The coming servant, Messiah, lifts up and takes upon himself man's sickness and bears the weight of his worrisome sorrows. Nothing could more graphically portray the vicarious sacrificial work of Christ who bore the penalty for man's sin so that man may receive God's righteousness and stand justified before him."[82] In addition, Daniel 9:24 provides a comprehensive description of the work of "the Anointed One." Some 490 years after the decree to rebuild Jerusalem the Messiah would appear "to finish transgression, to put an end to sin, to atone for wickedness [*lᵉkappēr 'āwôn*], to bring in everlasting righteousness."

The prophets elaborate Messiah's atoning work via the imagery of ransom and redemption. The verb *pādāh* alone (Mic. 6:4; Zech. 10:8) or in combination with *gā'al* (Jer. 31:11; Hos. 13:14), signifies the act of delivering or rescuing through the payment of a price.[83] The verb *gā'al,* meaning to "redeem" or "recover from bondage," places the emphasis on the release obtained (Isa. 44:22–23; 63:9; Lam. 3:58; Mic. 4:10). Thus the Lord is "the Redeemer" of Israel (*gô'ēl*; Isa. 41:14; 49:7; 60:16), and the people of God are "the redeemed" (*gᵉ'ûlîm*; Isa. 35:9; 62:12). An important work of the Messiah, then, is to liberate many who are bound by the power of sin and Satan. His task is "to free captives from prison and to release from the dungeon those who sit in darkness" (Isa. 42:7; cf. 61:1). An important concomitant of redemption is expiation—the removal of the guilt and stain of sin. Thus Yahweh declares, "I . . . am he who blots out your transgressions, for my own sake, and remembers your sins no more" (Isa. 43:25). Jeremiah 33:8; Zechariah 3:9; 13:1 also describe God's work of cleansing from sin.

Messiah's priestly work of vicarious sacrifice is represented in the fourth servant song (Isa. 52:13–53:12), discussed above. Moreover, the prophet Zechariah describes the postexilic coronation of the high priest Joshua, son of Jehozadak. Ultimately royal and priestly functions will be united in one called "the Branch," or Messiah. So Yahweh says: "It is he who will build the temple of the LORD, and he will be clothed with majesty and will sit and rule on his throne. And he will be a priest on his throne" (Zech. 6:13).

The Old Testament makes only minimal reference to the intent of Messiah's death. Isaiah 53:4–6 seems to indicate that the Messiah bore the penalty for the sin of the Jewish people. First-century Jews believed that Christ suffered for his own sins, but Isaiah states that he was afflicted for the nation. Isaiah further indicates that although Messiah bore the sin of many, his death was effectual for some—i.e., for the believing remnant of Israel. Thus Messiah bore "the punishment that brought us peace" (v. 5). The statement of verse 11—"My righteous servant will justify many"—refers to the multitude of people who in faith appropriate Messiah's atoning work. Hebrews 9:28 captures the sense: "Christ was sacrificed once to take away the sins of many people." Micah 4:2 seems to suggest that the Messiah's work would be effectual for those who believe.

Synoptic Gospels

Matthew and Luke record the angelic announcements to Mary and Joseph that the name of Mary's child would be Jesus (*Iēsous*), a transliteration of the Hebrew name Joshua (*yᵉhôšûa'*), who saved Israel from her enemies and which means "Yahweh is salvation" (Matt. 1:21; Luke 1:31). Matthew explicitly states that the purpose of Jesus' coming was to "save his people from their sins" (v. 21). The crucial event of Jesus' baptism by John in the Jordan (Matt. 3:13–17; Mark 1:9–11; Luke 3:21–22) signifies (1) the divine commission to public ministry (cf. Matt. 21:23–27), (2) Jesus' dedication to his vocation of suffering and death, and (3) his identification with those he came to save. The phenomena accompanying Jesus' baptism are significant. The descent of the Spirit in the form of a dove connotes Jesus' endowment with divine power for the fulfillment of his messianic ministry. And the heavenly voice (Matt. 3:17), which is a conflation of Psalm 2:7 and Isaiah 42:1, suggests that the divine Son would perform his messianic work in fulfillment of the Isaianic prophecies concerning the servant of the Lord.

Jesus spoke about his death in Mark 10:45 (cf. Matt. 20:28): "The Son of Man did not come to be served, but to serve, and to give his life as a ransom [*lytron*] for many [*anti pollōn*]." This saying points to Jesus' vicarious suffering and death: (1) because the Lord applies to himself Isaiah's description of the suffering servant (especially Isa. 53:10–12) and (2) because *anti* with the genitive case is a preposition of substitution signifying "instead of" or "in the place of."[84] The noun *lytron,* "price of release" or "ransom price," was widely used in classical Greek to denote the payment made to free a slave or a prisoner. The metaphor connotes that Jesus' death possesses an atoning dimension in that it wipes out guilt, and it has a liberating dimension in that it sets spiritual captives free from sin and the Devil. Jesus' saying makes no mention of the one to whom payment is made. The metaphor simply conveys the truth that it cost God dearly to free sinners from spiritual enslavement.

That Jesus' death involved substitutionary atonement is clear from his institution of the Lord's Supper. The reading of Luke 22:19, retained in the ASV, NASB, and NIV, indicates that Jesus took bread, broke it, and said: "This is my body given for you [*hyper hymōn*]." After that (v. 21) the Lord took the cup of wine, gave thanks, and said, "This cup is the new covenant in my blood,

which is poured out for you [*hyper hymōn*]." Mark's account (Mark 14:24) reads, "which is poured out for many [*hyper pollōn*]." Compare Matthew's account (Matt. 26:28), which uses the phrase *peri pollōn—peri* being equivalent in meaning to *hyper.*[85] The preposition *hyper* in these texts means "in behalf of" or "in place of" and so connotes substitution: Jesus gave his flesh and blood (i.e., his life) on behalf of sinners.[86] Furthermore, Jesus' sayings imply that his death supplanted the old Mosaic covenant sacrifices (Exod. 24:6–8) and inaugurated the new covenant promised by the prophet Jeremiah (Jer. 31:31–33). In the old covenant Moses made burnt and fellowship offerings to the Lord and sprinkled the blood of animals on the altar, thereby temporarily propitiating God's anger and expiating sins. Jesus suggests that his death rendered an atonement for sins that was perfect and permanent.

Jesus' death served not only as a ransom (*lytron*) but also as redemption (*lytrōsis*), the latter word meaning "deliverance" or "release." Thus in Luke 1:68 (cf. 2:38) Zechariah acknowledges that through Mary's child the Lord "has come and has redeemed his people." The deliverance Zechariah anticipated through the Christ includes Israel's liberation from political bondage (v. 71) as well as release from the guilt and power of sin (vv. 77–79). The word "redemption" (*lytrōsis*) in Zechariah's prophecy is equivalent to the word "salvation" (*sōtēria,* "deliverance") in verses 69, 71, 77. That Christ delivers from the bondage of sin and death is clear from the incident in the synagogue at Nazareth, where Jesus read from the servant passage of Isaiah 61:1–2. In fulfillment of this prophecy, Jesus indicated that the Lord had sent him "to proclaim freedom [*aphesis*] for the prisoners" and "to release the oppressed" (Luke 4:18). Whereas *aphesis* sometimes means "forgiveness of sins"

(Matt. 26:28), here in Luke it means "release from captivity."[87] Jesus' priestly ministry of self-oblation is discussed above under the categories of vicarious sacrifice, ransom, and redemption.

The death of Christ also exerted a moral and spiritual influence on people who viewed it. According to Luke 23:39–43, having heard Jesus petition the Father to forgive those who had crucified him (v. 34), and having observed the firm faith of the Innocent One, a criminal who hung on the cross believed that Jesus could save him. Similarly, a Roman soldier who observed Jesus' confidence in God in the face of a humiliating death became convinced that the Nazarene's claims were true; he confessed, "Surely this man was the Son of God!" (Mark 15:39).

The totality of Jesus' life as well as his death should be viewed as a sacrifice to God. In his complete obedience to the will of the Father (John 14:31; Heb. 10:7–9) and in his entire fulfillment of the law and its demands (Matt. 5:17; Gal. 4:4), Jesus "fulfilled all righteousness" (Matt. 3:15).

Concerning the intent of Christ's death, Jesus invited all persons burdened with Jewish legalism to come to him for spiritual refreshment (Matt. 11:28). On the other hand, an angel of the Lord announced to Joseph that Mary would give birth to a son named Jesus, who would "save his people from their sins" (1:21). The *laos* referred to clearly is the new Israel, the people who would believe in Christ. Mark 10:45 is relevant to the present discussion: "The Son of Man did not come to be served, but to serve, and to give his life as a ransom for many [*anti pollōn*]." Most commentators recognize that this saying reflects the thought of Isaiah 53:11–12, which we saw refers to the believing remnant in Israel. Furthermore, in the Qumran literature "the

many" commonly describes the elect within the community. Thus "many" in Mark 10:45 likely refers to the saved who have been bought from slavery by Christ's blood. "The 'many' are the redeemed community who have experienced the remission of sins in and through Jesus' sacrifice and so are enabled to participate in the salvation provided under the new covenant. . . . He freely yields his life in order that God's will to save his people may be effected."[88]

Pauline Literature

Paul frequently represents Christ's death as a substitutionary sacrifice for sins. He insists that the message transmitted to him by the earliest Christians was a matter "of first importance." The heart of this early Christian confession is that "Christ died for [*hyper*] our sins" (1 Cor. 15:3). Elsewhere Paul writes of God's "sending his own Son in the likeness of sinful man to be a sin offering" (*peri hamartias,* Rom. 8:3). Furthermore, Paul establishes a direct relationship between Christ's death and the Old Testament Passover sacrifice: "Christ, our Passover lamb [*pascha*], has been sacrificed" (1 Cor. 5:7). This reference to the Jewish Passover indicates that the blood of Christ shed on the cross propitiates the divine wrath, delivers from the guilt of sin, and secures exemption from divine judgment. Contemplating the suffering servant of Isaiah 53, Paul wrote, "God made him who had no sin to be sin for [*hyper*] us" (2 Cor. 5:21). As our substitute, Christ suffered God's wrath against sin that we might receive God's righteousness. "God placed our sins on the sinless Jesus and as our substitute in our place God punished him with death."[89] In a similar vein Paul writes, "Christ redeemed us from the curse of the law, by becoming a curse for [*hyper*] us" (Gal. 3:13). Here the curse (*katara*) is the sentence of death that hung over all persons as law-breakers. In addition, the apostle succinctly states that Christ "gave himself for [*hyper*] our sins" (Gal. 1:4; cf. Rom. 5:6, 8; 8:32; Gal. 2:20; Eph. 5:2; Titus 2:14). Once again *hyper* with the genitive connotes both representation ("on behalf of") and substitution ("in place of").

To describe the results of Christ's death Paul uses the figure of a ransom payment. In what may be an echo of Jesus' words in Mark 10:45, Paul refers to "the man Christ Jesus, who gave himself as a ransom [*antilytron*] for all men" (1 Tim. 2:5–6). The compound word *antilytron*, which literally means "substitute-ransom," denotes "what is given in exchange for another as the price of his redemption."[90] Paul's words "You were bought at a price" (1 Cor. 6:20; 7:23; cf. Acts 20:28), affirm that Christ on Calvary paid the price that sets believers free. The question, To whom was the price paid? goes beyond the main point Paul wished to make. The apostle proceeds to speak of the liberation from sin and Satan that is obtained by the costly sacrifice of Christ: "In him we have redemption [*apolytrōsis*] through his blood" (Eph. 1:7; cf. Rom. 3:24; Col. 1:14). "In the Pauline writings it [*apolytrōsis*] figures largely to designate the deliverance from sin and its penalty brought about by the propitiatory death of Christ."[91] This deliverance wrought by Christ is affirmed by the verbs *lytroomai* ("redeem," "liberate") in Titus 2:14, by *exagorazō* ("buy out of the market place," "redeem" from slavery) in Galatians 3:13; 4:5, by *rhyomai* ("rescue," "deliver") and by *methistēmi* ("remove from one place to another") in Colossians 1:13, and by *exaireō* ("rescue," "deliver") in Galatians 1:4. Elsewhere Paul teaches that Christ's death liberates from servile bondage to sin (Rom. 6:6–7, 14, 20, 22) and death (8:2).

Another significant outcome of Christ's death is reconciliation of God and sinners. The verb *katallassō* means to "effect a change," to "reconcile," and was used in classical Greek in the sense of "restoring the original understanding between people after hostility or displeasure."[92] Theologically reconciliation connotes that the relationship of enmity between God and sinners is changed to one of friendship. Paul writes in Romans 5:10 that before being reconciled to God by the death of his Son, "we were God's enemies." Does the enmity that prevents reconciliation reside on God's side or ours? The answer appears to be that it lies on both. Cranfield makes the following comment: "The enmity which is removed in the act of reconciliation is both sinful man's hostility to God (Rom. 1:30; 8:7) and also God's hostility to sinful man (this aspect is particularly clear in 11:28), though the removal of God's hostility is not to be thought of as involving a change of purpose in God."[93] With enmity on both sides abolished and the separation breached, Paul can write, "We . . . rejoice in God through our Lord Jesus Christ, through whom we have now received reconciliation" (*katallagē*, Rom. 5:11). In 2 Corinthians 5:18–21 Paul teaches that it is God who initiates reconciliation (*katallagē*). Through Christ God eliminated the chasm between himself and wayward sinners and established a communion that formerly was absent. As seen above, the event of reconciliation presupposes the removal of God's enmity vis-à-vis sinners through Christ's propitiatory sacrifice.

Moreover, reconciliation involves the nonimputation of sins or justification, for Paul in v. 21 speaks of the reconciled sinner's attaining the "righteousness [*dikaiosynē*] of God," namely, that state of being righteous in relation to the law. In Ephesians 2:12–16 Paul elaborates on the idea of reconciliation; through the work of Christ, Gentiles, "who once were far away," are united to the covenant people (vv. 12–15). With the partition between Jew and Gentile broken down, God is creating a new humanity in Christ. In addition, through Christ God is uniting both Jew and Gentile to himself: "His purpose was . . . in this one body to reconcile both of them to God through the cross" (vv. 15–16). Paul's verb in verse 16 is *apokatallassō,* which means to "turn from hostility to friendship, to reconcile."[94] The apostle mentions without elaboration reconciliation on a cosmic scale in Ephesians 1:10 and Colossians 1:20. Although not teaching universal salvation, these texts suggest that the discord and fragmentation characteristic of the fallen universe ultimately will give way to harmony and unity as Christ sovereignly rules over the created order.

Paul perceives that the life and death of Christ achieved a mighty victory over malignant spiritual powers. Thus through his public ministry and passion Christ has "destroyed death" (2 Tim. 1:10)—the aorist participle of *katargeō* indicating that through Christ death has been rendered inoperative or annulled. Elsewhere Paul asserts that by his death and resurrection Christ gained the victory (*nikos*) over the mortal adversaries—law, sin, and death (1 Cor. 15:55–57). Employing vivid images from the ancient world, Paul describes the victory Christ gained at the cross over hostile spiritual forces: "Having disarmed the powers and authorities, he made a public spectacle of them, triumphing over them by the cross" (Col. 2:15). The first verb, the aorist middle of *apekdyomai,* signifies that at the cross Christ stripped, as one puts off a garment, the evil powers that assailed him. The imagery is that of a deposed monarch stripped of the robes of his office. "The use of the double compound is probably to stress that it is a complete putting off and putting away,

which makes a falling back into the former manner of life impossible."[95] The last verb, the aorist of *thriambeuō,* connotes that at the cross Christ roundly conquered these powers, leading them in a triumphal procession, much as a victorious general would lead his captives in a public display through the streets of the city. Thus through his life and death Christ disarmed and despoiled all hostile powers that threaten the citizens of the kingdom.

Paul also views the death of Christ as a powerful example of Christian conduct. Since the cross is the supreme demonstration of divine love (Rom. 5:8), Paul summons the Ephesian Christians to imitate Christ's love by living a compassionate life (Eph. 5:1–2). Moreover, Paul enjoins the Philippians to adopt an attitude of humility and unselfish concern for others. This mindset is achieved as the believer follows the example of Christ, who, in the supreme act of self-renunciation, divested himself of the divine glory, assumed our lowly humanity, and went obediently to the cross (Phil. 2:3–8).[96] Moreover, reflection on the fact that Christ suffered and died on their behalf will compel (*synechō,* "press together," "constrain") Christians to live the rest of their lives for the good of others (2 Cor. 5:14–15). Clearly, then, one outcome of Christ's death is the stimulus to moral action it affords Christians. Yet in every instance where Christ's death is presented as an example to be followed, the fundamental truth of his death as a substitutionary sacrifice for sin is also present.

An important Pauline text on the atonement, Romans 3:21–26, deserves special consideration. The central idea of this passage is how God justifies or declares righteous both Jews and Gentiles. The apostle begins by considering the *manifestation* of justification (vv. 21–23). "But now a righteousness from God [*dikaiosynē theou*] . . . has been made known" (v. 21). The righteousness that Paul contemplates (thirty-five times in Romans and twenty-four times elsewhere) is the legal status of right-standing with God. Cranfield observes that *dikaiosynē* signifies "a status of righteousness before God, which is God's gift."[97] This righteousness is (1) conferred independently of law-keeping (v. 21a), (2) attested to by the Old Testament (v. 21b), and (3) appropriated by faith in Jesus Christ (v. 22).

Second, Paul considers the *means* of justification by faith (vv. 24–25), which is given in two word-pictures. The first is the imagery of redemption: both Jews and Gentiles "are justified freely by his grace through the redemption [*apolytrōsis*] that came by Christ Jesus" (v. 24). The noun *apolytrōsis* speaks of the liberation or emancipation that occurs through payment of an appropriate price.[98] The second word-picture is that of propitiation: "God presented him as a sacrifice of atonement [*hilastērion*], through faith in his blood" (v. 25). The meaning of *hilastērion* in this verse has been widely debated. Authorities such as Dodd, Von Rad, Richardson, and the RSV interpret *hilastērion* subjectively and translate it "expiation"—that is, as the cleansing of sin. Others such as F. F. Bruce, guided by the LXX where *kappōret* is frequently rendered by *hilastērion,* translates the word as "mercy seat," the golden cover of the ark where atonement was made. Still other authorities translate *hilastērion* as "propitiatory sacrifice" and interpret it as the self-oblation of Christ that placates the divine wrath and purges sin from the conscience.[99] The third interpretation satisfies the greatest amount of data with the least number of difficulties. Thus (1) in the Greek world *hilastērion* meant to placate the anger of an offended person or god; (2) the LXX has the verb *exhilaskomai* in several places (Zech. 7:2; 8:22; Mal. 1:9) in the sense of appeasing God; (3) in the Old Testament the verb is never used with sin as its object; (4) the *hilas-* word group often occurs in the context of the divine wrath (Rom. 3:5; 5:9); and (5) in the LXX when *hilastērion* connotes mercy seat it always has the article. In summary, when Paul describes the work of Christ he utilizes the language of the law court ("justified"), the slave market ("redemption"), and the temple ("propitiatory sacrifice").[100]

Finally, Paul refers to the *rationale* of justification (3:26): God "did it . . . so as to be just and the one who justifies the man who has faith in Jesus." By giving Jesus as a vicarious sacrifice, God was able (1) to remain true to his holy nature, which cannot overlook sin; (2) to uphold his law, which stipulates that sin be punished by death; and (3) mercifully to acquit sinners, who were deserving of death.

The preceding discussion of Christ's death as a substitutionary offering and Passover sacrifice that ransoms, redeems, and reconciles sinners to God clearly attests his completed priestly work as victim.

Concerning the intent of Christ's death, Paul indicates a twofold purpose in the cross, when he writes of "the living God, who is the Savior of all men, and especially [*malista*] of those who believe" (1 Tim. 4:10). Arguing from the universal to the particular (cf. Gal. 6:10; Phil. 4:22), the apostle indicates that the atonement conveys general benefits to all persons in the present and special benefits to believers both in the present and in the future (cf. "the present life and the life to come" [1 Tim. 4:8]). God is the Savior of all persons here and now in the sense that he preserves them in existence, provides them with the blessings of common grace, delays the execution of his judgment, removes every obstacle from his side to the pardon of repentant sinners, and provides salvation for those who die in infancy. He is the Savior of believers in the specifically redemptive sense that he ransoms, redeems, and reconciles such persons to himself.

Given this twofold purpose in the atonement, Paul sometimes refers to the universal dimension of the cross. Thus he writes of "the man Christ Jesus, who gave himself as a ransom for all men [*hyper pantōn*]" (1 Tim. 2:6). That this phrase refers to all persons and not merely to the elect is clear from verse 2, where the *hyper pantōn* includes kings and rulers. Paul's statement in verse 4 that God "wants [*thelei*] all men to be saved and to come to a knowledge of the truth," signifies God's will of desire that may be sinfully violated. On the other hand, Paul may have written these words with an eye to Gnostic teaching that viewed enlightenment or salvation as the privilege of a spiritual elite. Paul's statement "For the grace of God has appeared, bringing salvation to all men" (Titus 2:11, NASB), may support the universal dimension of the atonement, though the phrase "all men" may signify "all classes of people," given the discussion of men and women, slaves and free in the preceding context (cf. Acts 2:17; 9:35).

On the other hand, the apostle clearly affirms a special, salvific intention in the cross. Urging husbands to love their wives, Paul states that "Christ loved the church and gave himself up for her" (Eph. 5:25). Just as a man may love other people generally but his wife supremely, so Christ loves humankind with one degree of affection and his people with a still deeper measure of love. In the same category is 2 Corinthians 5:14–15. The "all" for whom Christ died are all believers who, in becoming Christians, died to their old nature and became united with Christ.

Johannine Literature

By means of several pregnant metaphors the fourth gospel presents Jesus' death as a substitutionary sacrifice for sins. Thus John the Baptist said of Jesus, "Look, the Lamb of God, who takes away the sin of the world!" (John 1:29; cf. v. 36). "Lamb" (*amnos*) signifies the animal used as a sacrificial offering and likely recollects the lamb of Isaiah 53:7 as well as the Paschal lamb, for the Passover feast was near at hand when the Baptist spoke these words (John 2:13). In the Apocalypse Christ is represented as a Lamb (*arnion*) twenty-seven times (Rev. 6:16; 7:10; 12:11; 13:8; et al.). There the Lamb takes his place on the throne of God, executes the eschatological judgment, and is worshiped. Nevertheless, he is the Lamb that was slain (5:6, 9, 12; 13:8). By representing Christ as *arnion,* Revelation indicates that the victorious Lord is also the Christ crucified for sins. "The judge of all the earth is he who died for us, and even as sovereign Lord he still bears the marks of his passion."[101] Furthermore, Jesus describes himself as "the bread of God" (John 6:33) or the "bread of life" (vv. 35, 48). In the context of his speaking about the manna given to Israel in the desert (vv. 31, 49), Jesus indicates that he is the spiritual food that sustains eternal life. Jesus' words "This bread is my flesh which I will give for [*hyper*] the life of the world" (v. 51), connote that the eternal life offered to the Jews would be secured by the sacrifice of himself. Jesus also described his work in terms of the metaphor of the shepherd: "The good shepherd lays down his life for [*hyper*] the sheep" (John 10:11; cf. v. 15). Of his own accord and in full obedience to the Father, Jesus surrendered his life on behalf of others. On the cross Jesus gave demonstration to the truth of John 15:13: "Greater love has no one than this, that one lay down his life for [*hyper*] his friends.''

Caiaphas uttered prophetic truth to the Sanhedrin when he said, ''You do not realize that it is better for you that one man die for [*hyper*] the people than that the whole nation perish'' (John 11:50). Caiaphas viewed Jesus' death as a matter of political expediency, but John interpreted this unwitting prophecy in terms of Jesus' vicarious death for both Jews and Gentiles (vv. 51–52). John further explicates the theological significance of Christ's death by affirming that he is ''the propitiation for our sins'' (*hilasmos peri tōn hamartiōn hēmōn* [1 John 2:2; 4:10, NASB]). *Hilasmos*, like *hilastērion* discussed above, connotes ''propitiatory sacrifice'' and indicates that Christ's death appeased God's anger toward sin and changed his attitude vis-à-vis sinners from displeasure to favor. Thus, ''By the *advocacy* of Christ (*paraklētos*) God is *propitiated* (*hilasmos*) and we are *reconciled to him* (*katallagē*).''[102]

In addition to writing of the vicarious sacrifice that propitiates God and effects reconciliation, John cites other implications of Christ's death. Christ's blood functions as the ransom price that purchased sinners for God (Rev. 5:9). Moreover, his sacrificial death frees believers from bondage to sin (John 8:36; Rev. 1:5). Through his work on the cross Christ overcame Satan's tyranny and destroyed his evil work (John 12:31; 1 John 3:8; Rev. 12:11). In addition, the blood of Jesus purifies lives from the defilements of sin (1 John 1:7; Rev. 7:14). And finally, John saw in Jesus' life and death the ultimate pattern of self-sacrificing love (John 15:12; 1 John 3:16).

John 3:16 affirms that God's love for sinners moved him to give his Son as a free gift to the world. At one level God's love embraces all humanity. John twice designated Jesus ''the Savior of the world'' (John 4:42; 1 John 4:14).

The Samaritans expressed the hope, later confirmed by John, that the Messiah would be given not for the Jews alone but for the benefit of the entire world. It is important to note that '' 'Savior' covers all aspects of Christ's work for men, and 'world' the totality of mankind.''[103] John's statement in 1 John 2:2 (NASB) about Jesus being ''the propitiation for our sins; and not for ours only, but also for those of the whole world,'' should be understood with the preceding texts. ''The propitiation that has availed to wipe out their [i.e., the believers'] sins is sufficient to do the same for all. Jesus is 'the general Savior of mankind' as well as the particular Savior of each believer.''[104] Concerning the Baptist's saying in John 1:29, ''Look, the Lamb of God, who takes away the sin of the world!'' the word *kosmos* does not necessarily denote every person on earth (1:10; 6:33; 12:19; 17:14; 1 John 5:19). The text indicates that the Lamb will expiate the sins of persons without regard to nationality or race.

The specifically redemptive dimension of Christ's death is evident in John 10, where Jesus states that he lays down his life for ''the sheep'' (*ta probata*, vv. 11, 15). The sheep are those given to Jesus by the Father (v. 29); they recognize Jesus' voice and follow him (v. 27), and to them the Son gives eternal life (v. 28). ''In John *probaton* denotes Christ's elect people, 'his own.' ''[105] Jesus died to bring these to God. Moreover, in his high priestly prayer Jesus prays not for the world but for those the Father has given him out of the world (17:6, 9). Elsewhere in Scripture Jesus or the Holy Spirit intercedes especially for believers (Rom. 8:26–27, 34; Heb. 7:25; 1 John 2:1). Hebrews clearly teaches that Christ's self-oblation and intercession represent the two principal components of his high priestly ministry. For those for whom Christ redemptively died he intercedes. Thus specifically Christ exercises his priestly ministry on behalf of believers. John confirms this conclusion in 1 John 3:5: "You know that he appeared so that he might take away our sins;" here *tas hamartias* plainly refers to the sins of believers.

Other New Testament Literature

The central section of Hebrews develops the work of Christ under the rubric of high priest. Hebrews 4:14–5:10 and 7:1–28 argue the superiority of Christ's *priesthood* to that of the Levitical order. Thus God appointed Aaron high priest over Israel to offer gifts and sacrifices for sins (5:1–4). Aaron's priesthood, however, was not perfect, for he first had to offer sacrifices for his own sins and he had to repeat the sacrifices year after year. Consequently by an irrevocable oath God appointed his own sinless Son (Heb. 4:15; 7:26) to be high priest of a radically new sacerdotal order typified by Melchizedek, the godly priest-king of Salem (5:5–10). This "king of righteousness" and "king of peace" exercised a priesthood that was superior to that of the Aaronic order (7:1–10) for several reasons: (1) Abraham, the ancestor of Levi, paid tithes to Melchizedek; (2) Melchizedek blessed the patriarch Abraham; and (3) Melchizedek "lives on" (NASB), whereas the Levitical priests all succumbed to death.

Hebrews proceeds to argue that Jesus' singular self-*sacrifice* was superior to the repeated offerings of the Jewish priests. The sacrifices offered by the Aaronic high priest on the Day of Atonement, effecting only ceremonial cleansing, failed to purge the inner life of the worshipers: "It is impossible for the blood of bulls and goats to take away sins" (10:4; cf. 9:9). The Day of Atonement ritual was not meaningless but served as a "shadow" (8:5) or type of the perfect sacrifice of Christ. Faith-

ful to the will of God, Jesus our "great high priest" (4:14) surrendered his life and shed his blood once-for-all as the truly efficacious sacrifice (10:5–10, 12; 7:27; 9:26, 28). The writer thus adds, "We have been made holy through the sacrifice of the body of Jesus Christ once for all" (Heb. 10:10).

Guided by the suffering-Servant imagery of Isaiah 53, Peter likewise upheld Christ's substitutionary sacrifice: "He himself bore our sins in his body on the tree" (1 Peter 2:24), and "Christ died for sins once for all, the righteous for the unrighteous" (*dikaios hyper adikōn,* 1 Peter 3:18). The perfect sacrifice of the body of Christ on Calvary purges sins (Heb. 1:3; 9:26, 28), expiates the guilt of sin (*eis to hilaskesthai tas hamartias,* 2:17), obtains divine forgiveness (9:22; 10:18), and restores sinners to fellowship with God (1 Peter 3:18). Hebrews adds that Christ's sacrifice on the cross destroyed death and the Devil (2:14) and liberates sinners from the grip of sin and Satan (2:15; 9:15; cf. 1 Peter 1:18). The second aspect of Christ's high-priestly work emphasized by Hebrews, his ministry of intercession, will be examined in chapter 8.

Although the primary emphasis of Hebrews and the Petrine letters is on the propitiatory and expiatory worth of Christ's death, both uphold the exemplary value of Christ's death for the believer. Peter reminds persecuted Christians, "Christ suffered for you, leaving you an example, that you should follow in his steps" (1 Peter 2:21; cf. 4:1–2). And the writer of Hebrews urged his readers: "Let us fix our eyes on Jesus, . . . who for the joy set before him endured the cross, scorning its shame, and sat down at the right hand of the throne of God" (Heb. 12:2).

Concerning the design of the atonement, Peter writes of false prophets and teachers who "secretly introduce destructive heresies, even denying the sovereign Lord [*despotēs*] who bought them" (2 Peter 2:1). As we have seen, in its figurative use *agorazō* means to purchase or ransom from the slave market of sin (1 Cor. 6:20; 7:23; Rev. 5:9). The probable interpretation of this text is that Peter judges the prophets on the basis of their own Christian profession, and so describes them as those who have been "bought" by Christ.[106] Second Peter 2:2 suggests that these have denied their Master and Lord by blatant immorality—Peter's word is *aselgeia* (cf. 1 Peter 4:3; 2 Peter 2:7, 18; Jude 4), which means "repeated habitual acts of lasciviousness."[107] The way Peter describes the false teachers (vv. 12, 17, 19) and the fact that they faced certain judgment (vv. 1, 3, 12) suggests that, although professing Christians, they were unregenerate. "These false teachers professed the name of Christ. . . . They made it known that Jesus had bought them, but they eventually rejected Christ and left the Christian communityy.[108] Thus Peter does not suggest that Christ's ransom work applies to all people.

The writer of Hebrews affirms that the end or purpose of Christ's incarnation and passion was that "by the grace of God he might taste death for everyone" (*hyper pantos*, Heb. 2:9). When expressing an advantage that accrues to a person, *hyper* usually means "for the benefit of."[109] Thus the writer affirms that in the broadest, nonredemptive sense Christ's humiliation and death avails for every person.

The "Descent of Christ Into Hell"

Some interpret Psalm 16:10—"you will not abandon me [*nepeš*] to the grave [*še'ôl*], nor will you let your Holy One see corruption [*šāḥat*]"—as the conviction that God would rescue Jesus' soul from hell, to which it had descended between his death and resurrection. But as we saw in chapter 11,

nepeš frequently means the entire person. Moreover, the word *še'ôl* commonly denotes the grave (Gen. 37:35; 1 Sam. 2:6; Pss. 6:5; 30:3, et al.).[110] Thus the immediate focus of the text is that God would deliver David's life from the peril of death. But prophetically (cf. Acts 2:31) it means that God would deliver the Messiah from death at the resurrection, and that his body would not decompose in the grave (note the Hebrew parallelism between the two lines of the verse).

Others cite Matthew 12:40 as proof of Christ's descent to hell between his death and resurrection: "For as Jonah was three days and three nights in the belly of a huge fish, so the Son of Man will be three days and three nights in the heart of the earth." The figurative phrase "in the heart of the earth" (*en tē kardia tēs gēs*) was prompted by the language of the Jonah story (Jonah 2:2–3). It is highly probable that " 'the heart of the earth' is not *hades,* but the grave."[111] Thus this text affirms only that Jesus to the Hebrew mind was in the grave three days and three nights.

Matthew 27:52–53 is more perplexing. The most satisfactory interpretation appears to be that the earthquake that followed Christ's death and broke open the tombs reminded Matthew of the eschatological judgment that would occur at the resurrection of the dead. From such a perspective, following Jesus' resurrection the saints rose from the grave and entered the holy city to be reunited with believers who had gone before. "The point being made is clear: with Christ the general resurrection has begun; the power of death is now vanquished."[112] The liberation of deceased saints from the netherworld as a result of the preaching of Christ appears not to be taught by this text.

Paul's main point in Ephesians 4:8–10 is that at his ascension Christ gave spiritual gifts to his church. The "captives" Christ led in his train at his exaltation are the hostile powers he defeated at the cross (cf. Col. 2:15). After mentioning Christ's ascent Paul cites the Savior's descent in order to make the point that Christ is Lord over heaven and earth and thus is competent to give gifts to believers. The phrase "descended to the lower, earthly regions" (*eis ta katōtera merē tēs gēs,* v. 9) involves an appositive genitive and should read: "descended to the lower regions, that is, the earth."[113] Thus Paul reflects awareness of the *katabasis-anabasis* (incarnation-exaltation) motif commonplace in the early church.

On balance 1 Peter 3:18–20 does not support a mission of Christ in hades. "The spirits in prison" (v. 19) are neither Old Testament saints nor fallen angels but unbelievers now deceased (cf. 1 Peter 4:6). The message Christ preached was neither the victory of his resurrection, nor final condemnation, but an appeal for repentance. And Christ preached not between his death and resurrection but during the time of Noah. The sense of the passage is as follows: Christ, in the realm of the Spirit, preached repentance through Noah while God patiently waited during the building of the ark. Christ preached to human spirits, who in the intermediate state are now in prison (hell) because of disobedience and godlessness. This interpretation fits the purpose of the context (1 Peter 3:13–22), which encourages the suffering minority, like Noah, to bear courageous witness to a hostile, unbelieving world (especially 3:15–16; cf. 2:12).[114]

Others appeal to 1 Peter 4:6 as support for the *descensus ad inferna.* The context focuses on the inevitable persecution that Christians scattered throughout the Roman Empire had to face. Mention of the preaching of the gospel to the *nekroi* is best understood as proclamation to those who had heard the message, who believed, and who

subsequently died. Opponents of Christianity objected that the faith of these believers availed for naught, since they died just as unbelievers do. Peter responds to this challenge by affirming that from a human point of view (*kata anthrōpous*) the deceased believers appear to have been judged in the body for their sins, but from the divine point of view (*kata theon*) they live eternally in the Spirit.

Our study of the preceding texts leads to the conclusion that an alleged descent by Christ into hell to preach the gospel either to the unsaved or to Old Testament saints rests on slender evidence and ought not be pressed as certain dogma.

SYSTEMATIC FORMULATION

The previous gathering of the biblical data has exhibited the substantial unity in a diversity of teaching genre on atonement throughout the centuries and in varied cultures in the progress of special revelation. We now attempt to formulate a systematic and normative statement for the present by incorporating biblically supported elements from the historical views and by seeking to avoid their weaknesses.

Humanity's Radical Need

Understanding of Christ's atonement as the basic prescription for human need requires a grasp of the *radical diagnosis* of the human predicament. If diagnoses of the human plight are environmental, the prescriptions for their improvement will start with changing structures in the surrounding society. Many diagnoses trace the human predicament to "fallout" from technology, economic or political structures (capitalist, socialist, or communist), religious institutions, or psychological conditioning by them. But we have found that humans personally are responsible agents. God's creative image-bearers can respond in different ways to the same situation. Environments occasion moral conduct but do not determine humanity's moral nature.

The deepest issues of life are from within, since *all humans are inherently disposed to evil.* In all cultural contexts the most deeply rooted issues are whether our inner attitudes and behavior are just and loving before God and neighbor. In any situation the most profound issues have to do with a self-determining person's moral integrity and spiritual faithfulness to the purposes of the God of Scripture. While all religions find something wrong between humankind and a "higher power," not all grasp the seriousness of each person's plight before the transcendent, righteous God of Scripture, who judges without respect of a persons's economic, social, or political status.

Our innate moral plight is real. It is no illusion that we have corrupted our own natures, exploited the limited resources of nature, alienated ourselves from different races, and abused every type of economic structure. In all of this and more we have been unfaithful to our Creator and Sustainer, his incarnate Son, and his written Word. The One responsible for the moral order of the universe operates according to nonnegotiable principles of justice. By his moral principles the best of us come far short of being all that we ought to be.

People who forget about the reality of our plight may ask, "Could not a loving God simply forget about our sin?" Since God is both knowledgeable and responsible, God cannot deny the reality of humanity's perversity with its tragic consequences. The absolutely just and honest One cannot tamper with the actual evidence. We humans have more than guilt feelings, we have *real guilt* before God. Repeatedly in offending others we have offended the Most High. We have violated the justice and

spurned the love of the source and support of all values. We have rejected their disclosure in our hearts and in the Scriptures. Beyond that, we have despised his incarnate Son. God's integrity does not permit him to call our moral evil "good."

Our endemic moral affliction is *humanly incurable.* We cannot transform our own natures. In our insolent rebellion we are unable to (1) provide a basis on which God can forgive us while he remains honest and just, (2) liberate ourselves from our fallen propensities to corrupting ourselves and others, (3) reconcile ourselves to God's fellowship, or (4) restore peace to all the cosmos. Nothing fallen humans can do personally, educationally, socially, economically, politically, or religiously is sufficient to attain perfect righteousness and peace (Rom. 10:1–3).

Will the Father not receive us if we just return like the prodigal son? Interpretations of the parable of the prodigal son should emphasize its primary purpose. In context (along with the parables of the lost sheep and the lost coin) the parable of the lost son primarily teaches rejoicing in heaven over one sinner who repents (see Luke 15:7, 10, 24, 32). It does not teach the grounds on which the heavenly Father can justly accept sinners in his holy presence. Hermeneutically it is unwise to base one's doctrine and hope of salvation on one parable, and it may be disastrous to rest one's eternal destiny on a parable given for a different purpose. A much sounder approach considers the numerous, extensive didactic passages on depravity (and the fact that no holistically depraved people do in fact on their own return to God) and on the necessity of the atoning work of Christ. God himself cannot welcome sinners back in a way that leaves them under condemnation, in bondage to evil, and estranged from his fellowship. The Creator's original purposes, glory, name, honor, justice, and love must be vindicated. The faithfulness of God's written Word concerning sin's consequences must be upheld: "The soul who sins is the one who will die" (Ezek. 18:4, 20; Rom. 6:23). The parable of the prodigal son illustrates the point that when any sinner repents and trusts the Savior, the Father celebrates in heaven and elder sons should rejoice on earth! It does not teach the basis on which the Father can remain just and justify the ungodly.

The basic human plight, apart from God's grace, is terminal. By violating the principles that make meaningful life possible for God's image-bearers, we have forfeited the right to life. Receiving what we deserve, all fallen people equally receive the sentence of death (Rom. 6:23)—physical, spiritual, and eternal. In sheer mercy, however, the divine Judge has freely chosen to postpone deserved punishment. It is "because of the LORD's great love we are not consumed" (Lam. 3:22).

The Just and Loving Divine Initiative

By sheer grace the heavenly Father took the initiative in unfathomable love to send his unique Son (John 6:39), and in love the Son became human to pay the just penalty for the lost (Luke 19:10). God's just and loving initiative on behalf of sinners has been illustrated by the story of two classmates who graduated from law school. One used his knowledge of law to get around it and became a noted criminal. The other used his mastery of law to support it as an attorney and later as a judge. One day the two classmates met in court. Because of their earlier acquaintance the judge was tempted to pronounce the lightest sentence possible. Instead, he decreed that his guilty former classmate must pay the highest possible fine for the offense he had committed. To the further amazement of the court, the judge stepped down from behind the bench, embraced his law-school friend, and paid the criminal's fine in full. In a far greater way than this, the Judge of the world, whose moral law was constantly violated, found us guilty and pronounced the just sentence of death. Then, leaving heaven, the Son became a man, lived without sin, and paid in full the inestimable penalty for our sins. To demonstrate how he remains just while justifying the ungodly who believe, the Father sent the Son as a sacrifice of atonement (Rom. 3:25–26). The Judge who found us guilty came in the person of his own Son to atone for our sins.

What motivated such a marvelous satisfaction of justice? The *primary motives* of the atonement were to satisfy justice and to redeem undeserving sinners in self-giving (*agapē*) love. Because God is just and loving, all of his providential and covenant activities are just and loving. But in the supreme manifestation of divine justice and love, "God so loved the world that he gave his one and only Son" (John 3:16). God the Father does not love us because Christ died for us, but Christ died for us because God the Father loved us (Rom. 5:6–8; 1 John 4:9–10). Out of self-giving love the Son came into history by the power of the Holy Spirit and died, satisfying justice for our sins according to the Father's eternal purpose (2 Cor. 5:14–15; Eph. 3:11).

The cross fulfilled the loving purpose the three divine persons had designed in their *eternal covenant* with its immutable promises justly to save sinners. God revealed that eternal covenant of just love in different ways to different people: to Eve, Noah, Abraham, Moses, David, Isaiah, and others prior to Christ's incarnation and death. Without the giving of a life (the shedding of blood) for a forfeited life, amnesty is not just (Heb. 9:22). The Old Testament versions of the covenant as revealed to Moses required the offering of animal sacrifices and ceremonies. Even though

God's repentant people offered sacrifices with faith in the messianic promises available at their point in the progress of revelation, we have the Mediator of a new (outworking of the eternal) covenant (v. 15). After Christ's crucifixion believers do not need repeated animal sacrifices, for our sins are remembered no more (10:17–18). Indeed the news concerning Christ's death signifies a better covenant based on better promises (8:6). "The 'covenants of the promise' (Eph. 2:12) are God's guarantees that he will provide salvation in spite of man's inability to keep his side of the agreement."[115]

Christ Died Willingly

From the beginning Jesus anticipated the sacrifice of his life for sinful people. In his death he was not a helpless victim of a political upheaval or a mere miscarriage of justice in the courts. He chose to give up the glory of heaven (Phil. 2:6–8) and come into the world as the Lamb of God (John 1:29). He identified himself with human "flesh and blood" (Heb. 2:14), human conditions (v. 17), and human sufferings (v. 10). After Peter confessed the deity of Jesus (Mark 8:29), Jesus spoke plainly and repeatedly of his coming suffering, death, and resurrection (vv. 31–32; 9:31; 10:32–34). He would "give his life a ransom for many" (Mark 10:45). Jesus determined also the time of his death. Earlier he had avoided enemies to prevent death from happening prematurely. Later he hastened events so that his self-sacrifice occurred on the day the paschal lamb was offered. Christ, not Judas, was Lord. To Pilate he said, "You would have no power over me if it were not given to you from above" (John 19:11). On the cross Jesus remained Lord of hatred, praying for the forgiveness of his tormentors. Jesus chose the place, time, and manner of

his death. Even in the giving of his life, Jesus was not a victim, but the victor.

Because Jesus purposefully gave up his life, his death cannot be blamed ultimately on either Jews or Gentiles. Proximately, however, both Jews and Gentiles as depraved sinners evoked his death. It was not just Jews who cried out, "Crucify him!" Both Gentiles and Jews opposed Jesus. So Peter and John prayed, "Indeed Herod and Pontius Pilate met together with the Gentiles and the people of Israel in this city to conspire against your holy servant Jesus, whom you anointed" (Acts 4:27).

The Messiah Died Physically and Spiritually

Questioning people sometimes ask, if God died, how did the world survive without him for three days? The Messiah's death did not mean his annihilation. "Death" designates, not annihilation, but separation. Separations occurred in at least two senses. First, Jesus *died physically* as his spirit was separated from his body. "The body without the spirit is dead" (James 2:26). Jesus' body was buried and his "unclothed" spirit or soul waited for the resurrection of his body. Before giving up his spirit, Jesus suffered one of the most agonizing forms of physical death.

Second, the Son *died spiritually* by being separated from the Father's fellowship. Relationally the Father and Son had enjoyed unbroken fellowship from before creation. But as Jesus bore the guilt and penalty of the world's sin, he suffered far more than physical pain. Suffering the anguish of alienation and estrangement from the Father, he cried, "My God, My God, why have you forsaken me?" (Matt. 27:46). Under the wrath of God upon all our sins he was crushed like grapes in the winepress. He experienced the hell we should have experienced. Although from the biblical evidence it is not probable that he literally descended into hell, Jesus experienced the hell of God-forsakenness and divine wrath for the sins of the world.

Jesus Could Die for Others Because He Was Sinless

Neither the life nor the death of Jesus can be understood apart from each other. The early Eastern theologians and recent relational thinkers associate the redemptive activity of our Lord with the totality of the incarnation, treating the cross as one element within it. The Western theologians increasingly emphasized the cross, almost dissociating the death of Jesus from his life. The death and the life of Christ are inseparably related. If Jesus had not actively and fully obeyed the Father's will and lived a holy life, he would have had to die for his own sins. His perfect keeping of God's law (active obedience) throughout his life enabled him to offer the perfect sacrifice (in passive obedience) on the cross.

In a sense the entirety of Jesus' life was lived for us. "Through the whole of Christ's life there ran an element of infinite humiliation, especially in his death. Every act, therefore, was in one aspect an item of vicarious suffering, and in another aspect, an item of vicarious obedience to the will of his Father."[116] From the beginning the pattern of the cross was evident in the presence of his willingness to have himself "made nothing" (*kenosis,* Phil. 2:7). And the full significance of dying to temptations reaches its consummate height at Calvary. Attempts of some thinkers to give priority to the incarnation rather than to the atonement do not account as coherently for the evidence. James Denney explained, "It is the atonement which explains the incarnation: the incarnation takes place in order that the sin of the world may be put away by the offering of the body of Jesus Christ."[117]

Christ Died in Our Place as a Sacrifice

Early in written revelation God taught sinners the need for a substitutionary *sacrifice.* "For the life of a creature is in the blood, . . . it is the blood that makes atonement for one's life" (Lev. 17:11). As the the high priest offered the blood of a healthy lamb on the altar, one life was given in place of another life. These animal sacrifices were temporary object lessons typologically illustrating the coming work of the Messiah. At the annual celebration of the Passover the Judge and Savior were the same person. Salvation was by substitution of a firstborn lamb, and the lamb's blood had to be sprinkled, indicating a personal appropriation of the divine provision. Similarly, on the annual Day of Atonement, the high priest offered two goats. One was sacrificed, and the blood sprinkled in the usual way. On the living goat's head the priest was to lay both his hands and confess over it all the wickedness and rebellion of the Israelites. It would carry all their sins to a solitary place in the desert (Lev. 16:21–22).

The sacrifices were both *representative* and also *substitutionary.* "A *representative* is one who acts on behalf of another, in such a way as to involve the other in his action. A *'substitute'* is one who acts in place of another in such a way as to render the other's action unnecessary."[118] The Christ serves as our legal representative as a result of the eternal covenant of grace or plan of salvation. The implications of Christ's representation are considered below in the "Relevance for Life and Ministry" section. If an instructor has a substitute taking the classes for her, she does not teach those classes. Since the biblical evidence indicates that Christ as the sinners' substitute received the sinners' guilt and penalty, believers do not experience them. The penalty for an infraction cannot justly be demanded twice.

As Isaiah foresaw, the suffering servant "took up our infirmities and carried our sorrows, . . . was pierced for our transgressions, crushed for our iniquities; the punishment that brought us peace was upon him, and by his wounds we are healed. We all, like sheep, have gone astray, each of us has turned to his own way; and the LORD has laid on him the iniquity of us all" (Isa. 53:4–6). Emphatically the servant's suffering is "punishment for the sins of others."[119] "It is clear from the Old Testament usage," John R. W. Stott concludes, "that to 'bear sin' means neither to sympathize with sinners, nor to identify with their pain, nor to express their penitence, nor to be persecuted on account of human sinfulness (as others have argued), nor even to suffer the consequences of sin in personal and social terms, but specifically to endure its penal consequences, to undergo its penalty."[120]

The New Testament frequently shows how Jesus fulfilled the teaching of Isaiah 53. In numerous other ways the New Testament brings out the fact that vicariously Christ accepted our guilt and suffered our penalty. Explicit passages make clear that "one died for all" (2 Cor. 5:14; Heb. 9:28; 1 Peter 2:24). The preposition "instead of" (anti) "always has the idea of equivalence, substitution or exchange present; it never has the more general meaning 'on behalf of, for the sake of' (see Matt. 20:28; Mark 10:45)."[121] Christ did more than represent our guilt and penalty, he received them. Hence believers need not live under a sense of legal guilt or experience sin's deserved penalty.

The preposition "for" or "over" (hyper) "may and often does include the stricter idea 'instead of' and if the context warrants, we may so under-stand it."[122] The substitutionary significance of hyper is clear in the context of Galatians 3:10–13. At a class in New York City, Greek scholar A. T. Robertson found the message of the cross in three prepositions: (1) All who rely on observing the law are under (hypo) a curse (Gal. 3:10). Robertson likened that to being under Damocles' sword hanging by a thread. (2) Jesus became a curse for (hyper) us (v. 13). As the sword of divine judgment dropped, Jesus interposed his body "over" or "in place of" ours, and the sword fell on him instead of on sinners. (3) So Jesus redeemed believers from (ek) the curse of the law (v. 13). He died that believers might live "out from in under" the law that can only condemn because of the weakness of our natures.[123]

Additional illustrations of substitution may help. During the civil war substitutes volunteered to fight in the place of those drafted for service. In the National Football League a substitute plays in place of another team member. In January 1975 a judge in Cleveland, Ohio, sentenced a young lady to three days in jail for possession of an unregistered gun. According to the Associated Press report, her boyfriend accepted the sentence for her because, he said, "a jail is not a good place for a lady." According to the judge, such substitutionary bearing of punishment was "unusual but legal." The young lady did not go to jail.[124] At Auschwitz, in June 1941, because a prisoner had escaped, a Nazi officer sentenced ten men to death by starvation. When Polish Sergeant Gajowniczek heard his name, he screamed that he wanted to see his wife and children. Then suddenly Father Kolbe stepped forward and offered to take the place of the man with a family. Annually Frank Gajowniczek places a wreath at Auschwitz where the Franciscan monk died in his place.[125]

Several questions about Christ's substitutionary sacrifice may arise. Did Jesus suffer exactly the same kind of punishment all sinners must have suffered? If different in kind, was his penalty equal in amount? If less in amount, did he suffer an equivalent punishment? Did he suffer the torment of the finally lost? In what sense was his punishment eternal? Some have scoffed, "How could a week-end of suffering atone for the sins of the entire human population?"

Questions like these may assume quantitative similarities based on analogies to *fair commercial transactions*. In a commercial setting satisfaction of justice requires payment of the same thing or something of equivalent value quantitatively. Clearly Christ did not suffer on the cross as long as humans have sinned. Neither did he suffer separate blows for each of the billions of humans' sins. His ransom cannot be measured quantitatively. But if a commercial analogy is demanded, we remind people of the infinite value of the God-man's sacrifice of himself. The unlimited significance of the Messiah's death is not worthy to be compared with the finite number of sins committed by finite persons.

The more frequent biblical analogy features a *just judicial transaction* in a criminal court. A convicted criminal usually satisfies the law in a way very different from that of the offense. So although Christ's penalty was quantitatively different from the offenses (in length of time), it entailed the same kind of anguish (separation from the Father). Christ's self-sacrifice satisfied the Administrator of Justice for several reasons. His death (1) had infinite value, (2) met all the demands of divine justice or moral law, (3) propitiated God's righteous indignation, (4) released believing slaves from moral evil, (5) reinforced divine honor, and (6) glorified the divine name by providing for the reconciliation of mankind to himself.

The concept of *substitution is essential* to all of the biblical analogies— passover sacrifice, ransom, redemption, propitiation, victory over Satan, and reconciliation. In each aspect of what Christ did, sinners united to him by faith cannot do for themselves. The divine substitute fully provided for sinners' liberation, forgiveness, and reconciliation. "So substitution is not 'a theory of the atonement.' Nor is it even an additional image to take its place as an option alongside the others. It is rather the essence of each image and the heart of the atonement itself."[126]

Jesus' substitutionary sacrifice completed the work of atonement "once for all" (Heb. 9:12, 25–28). What could be justly done for the salvation of sinners has been done in that unique and irrepeatable historical event. The crucifixion fulfilled all that was planned in and promised in the eternal covenant. The benefits of the cross are also everlasting. "By one sacrifice he has made perfect forever those who are being made holy" (10:10–14). As result of the completeness of that unique and irrepeatable event in history "there is no longer any sacrifice for sin" (10:18). No alleged merits from self-flagellation, penance, purgatory, fasting, praying, giving to the poor, inner-city service, preaching, teaching, evangelizing, parenting, or defending of country can add to Christ's complete provisions.

Having fulfilled the goals of the eternal covenant, the cross *completed the objective transaction* between two parties (the Father and the Son). "It is finished," Jesus declared (John 19:30). As covenanted, the crucified Messiah, so to speak, "signed in blood" his last will and testament, assuring an incorruptible, objective inheritance for its recipients. So a theology of the cross cannot limit itself to relational categories. To do justice to the cross, we need, in addition to a relational theology, a transactional theology. A transactional theology gives a better account of the objective content of covenants and promises conveyed by sentences and the historical completion of the atonement's provisions. What objective "provisions" were signed and sealed in the transaction at the cross?

Christ's Sacrifice Provides Forgiveness of Legal Guilt

In the first century Jesus Christ on the cross took upon himself our *moral guilt*. When the Bible speaks popularly of Christ "bearing sins," it refers to "sins," not as entities, but as standing for the sinners' moral guilt (by divine judgment).[127] When Jesus was "made sin," he willingly accepted our sentence of guilt. As Christ became a sacrificial lamb in our place, he assumed judicial liability for the fallenness of the human race. He willingly said, in effect, "Put the sinners' moral obligations to my account." In discussing sin in chapter 4 we considered the imputation of the legal consequences of Adam's sin to the race (Rom. 5:16, 18). The Scriptures also teach the imputation of the guilt of insolent humans to Christ on the cross (Isa. 53:6; 2 Cor. 5:14, 21; 1 Peter 2:24; 3:18).

On the cross Christ also experienced the *penalty* of our sin. He died in the place of sinners, so that they need not die. To reject substitution is to say that sinners can never be right with God. To put it bluntly, if Christ is not our vicarious sacrifice, we are still under condemnation. If our guilt was not transferred to him and he did not bear our penalty, we are destined to endless alienation from God and enslavement to our own fallen natures.

Because Christ's exchange for sinners is so complete, we can also say that in Christ *we died* to sin (Rom. 6:2). This carries over his legal representa-

tion of sinners from Romans 5. The legal significance is supported also by the fact that he died to sin's guilt (certainly not its power over him), and his once-for-all death (6:10) provides for our justification by faith from our sins' legal consequences (5:9). By faith "we were one with Christ in his obedience unto death, as we were one with Adam in his disobedience. Christ's death to sin belongs to us, and is as much ours as if we had borne the penalty."[128] So believers crucified with Christ now have the righteousness that comes from God, the righteousness of the obedient Christ, put to their account (2 Cor. 5:21). Justified by faith in the crucified Christ, believers face no condemnation (Rom. 8:1). But the Messiah's atonement provides more than forgiveness of legal guilt.

Christ's Sacrifice Provides Freedom From Enslaving Addictions

Because those in Christ legally died and were freed from sin, "we should no longer be slaves to sin" (Rom. 6:6–7). Christ paid a great *ransom* to free sinners also from the power of the slave markets of evil. It cost Christ his precious blood to set us free (1 Peter 1:18–19). Bought at such a precious price, the liberated no longer belong to themselves (1 Cor. 6:19–20). "With [his] blood [Christ] purchased men for God from every tribe and language and people and nation" (Rev. 5:9). His ransom was not a commercial transaction with the value paid to Satan; rather, it satisfied divine justice. Christ died to restore the divine image, renewing our abilities to know, love, and serve the transcendent God in creation.

Christ's death paid the inestimable price to free us from the dominion of temptations that come from the flesh, the world, and the Devil. Free from what specifically? Christ's *redemption* provides freedom from morally evil thoughts, attitudes, words, and behavior. Jesus did what the law could not do because of the weakness of our sinful natures—set us free from "the law of sin and death" (Rom. 8:1–4). He paid the awesome price that believers in any culture anywhere in the world would not be enslaved by inner desires of the old fleshly nature such as hypocrisy, covetousness, greed, sexual immorality, drunkenness, witchcraft, chauvinism, and racism. Christ also sacrificed himself that believers should no longer be dominated by pressures from external influences of "the present evil age" (Gal. 1:4), such as unjust business, political, or ecclesiastical pressures. We are freed by Christ, who stood against the world to take a stand against temptations from the powers of the world around us. "So if the Son sets you free, you will be free indeed" (John 8:36).

For what does Christ provide freedom from sin's power? He died that the liberated might build a loving, forgiving community. The Savior "loved the church and gave himself up for her to make her holy, cleansing her . . . and to present her to himself as a radiant church, without stain or wrinkle or any other blemish, but holy and blameless" (Eph. 5:26–27). Christ gave himself "to redeem us from all wickedness and to purify for himself a people that are his very own, eager to do what is good" (Titus 2:14). Those whom Christ rescued from the dominion of darkness are brought into the kingdom of the Son he loves (Col. 1:13) to help establish the rule of holy love on earth. Those legally Christ's are experientially no longer bad trees bringing forth bad fruit but good trees bringing forth good fruit (Matt. 7:17; 12:33–35).

Christ's Sacrifice Provides Victory Over Unholy Spirits

At the cross Christ won a dramatic victory over Satan, the demonic hosts, and their human dupes. The battle analogy for the cross fits the broader context of warfare between the two kingdoms. Conflict between God and Satan began on earth at the Fall and continues (Gen. 3:15). Satan attacked and tempted Christ from his birth to the cross. But what seemed like a victory for Satan turned out to be a triumph over him who holds the power of death (Heb. 2:14–15). Christ "gave himself for our sins to rescue us from the present evil age" (Gal. 1:4). On the cross Christ not only "disarmed the powers and authorities," but "made a public spectacle of them, triumphing over them" (Col. 2:13–15). Instead of meeting evil power with evil power, Christ overcame the powers of evil with good. In holy love Christ transformed history's greatest miscarriage of justice into its final fulfillment of justice. The decisive victory was confirmed by Christ's resurrection from the dead. Mopping-up operations continue until the Second Coming. Meanwhile in encounters with evil powers Christians can overcome Satan by the blood of the Lamb and the word of their testimony (Rev. 12:11).[129] Christ's first-century triumph over the forces of evil provides the base for believers to conquer them today.

Christ's Sacrifice Provides Propitiation and Reconciliation

The cross provides the just ground on which the Father's wrath can be pacified and fellowship restored. Sinners are separated from Christ, excluded from citizenship in Israel, and foreigners to the covenants of promise, without hope and without God in the world (Eph. 2:12). We deserved God's righteous indignation and divine wrath. "Why not wrath? What other possible attitude can God take toward evil and sin but righteous wrath?"[130] What else can a just and loving God do with sinners who, contrary to every benefit of grace, persistently delight in pride, injustice and hatred, but display his wrath (or as Scaer suggests, "give them hell")?[131]

Divine wrath must not be identified with petty jealousy, arbitrary vengeance, or other types of selfish vindictiveness. God's wrath is the reaction of his holy love against sin. Such righteous indignation is not the opposite of love; it is a part or aspect of faithful love.

> God's wrath is an integral constituent of his love. The wrath of God is the active manifestation of God's essential incapacity to be morally indifferent and let sin alone. It denotes the attitude of God in his holy love toward wilful sin. God's wrath is God's grace. It is his grace smitten with dreadful sorrow. It is his love in agony.[132]

Again, "In the total biblical portrayal, the wrath of God is not so much an emotion or an angry frame of mind as it is the settled opposition of his holiness to evil."[133]

How did Christ's death change the relationship between God and sinners? The cross provided for *propitiation* of God's wrath and reconciliation to God's fellowship. Propitiation is "the gracious provision made by God himself, whereby the effects of His righteous anger against sin may be averted and the sinner may receive the blessings of his paternal love without infringement of his holiness and moral government."[134] Because of the propitiatory provision of Christ's death, God can look upon believers without displeasure and believers can be reconciled to God. "God presented him [Christ] as a sacrifice of atonement [or propitiation] through faith in his blood" (Rom. 3:25).

Since God's wrath has been turned away, we can enjoy *reconciliation to God*. Christ not only removed wrath, but reconciled all things in heaven and earth, making peace through his blood shed on the cross (Col. 1:19). We who formerly feared God's wrath now rejoice in the Father's presence (Rom. 5:11). God does not impute our sins to us (2 Cor. 5:19); to believers he imputes Christ's righteousness (v. 21). "Once you were alienated from God and were enemies in your minds because of your evil behavior. But now he has reconciled you by Christ's physical body through death to present you holy in his sight, without blemish and free from accusation" (Col. 1:21–22). The reconciled ought not keep this good news to themselves! God committed to them the ministry of reconciliation (2 Cor. 5:18). So as Christ's ambassadors we implore sinners to be reconciled to God (v. 19–20).

Attempts to place the gospel emphasis on spiritual life of fellowship with God by sidestepping Christ's atonement have not sufficiently faced the varied consequences of sin, including continued alienation. It took the blood of Christ to unite Samaritans and Gentiles with Jews in the church. The way to spiritual life (fellowship with God) for sinners is through death. Through crucifixion with Christ to the old fleshly order of life, we receive the new order of life in love. Unless a grain of wheat falls into the ground and dies, it will not produce the fruit of spiritual life—fellowship with God.

Christ's Sacrifice Provides Reconciliation of Persons to One Another

Christ died also that believing sinners may enjoy also *reconciliation to each other*. Christ's sacrifice provides for a new community, a fellowship of sinners at peace with God and so at peace with one another. Because of the cross Samaritans and Gentiles could be united with Jews in Christ's body, the church. Having put to death their hostility, he made Jew and Gentile one, destroying the dividing wall by abolishing the law and giving both access to the Father by the Spirit (Eph. 2:14–18). At one time we were "uncircumcised, . . . separate from Christ, excluded from citizenship in Israel and foreigners to the covenants of promise, without hope and without God in the world" (vv. 11–12). "But now in Christ Jesus you who once were far away have been brought near through the blood of Christ." So he is "our peace" (v. 14). "Christ loved the church and gave himself up for her" (5:25). Commitment to life under the cross—not race nor economic status— reconciles sinners to one another. People living under the cross should not be expected to meet extraneous requirements for membership in a church.

Because they are forgiven by grace, church members seek to be graciously forgiving. Because they are liberated from the reign of sin (Rom. 6:12), God's people rejoice in making peace with others who have been reconciled to God through faith in Christ. The crucified Christ provides the one foundation on which to build a church (1 Cor. 3:10–15) because he bought the church of God "with his own blood" (Acts 20:28). Christian homes, churches, and organizations enjoy reconciliation and peace to the extent that they are just and loving communities. Families and churches respect members' dignity and rights, and lovingly families and churches go beyond justice in acts of mercy and love.

Christ's Sacrifice Provides for Future Cosmic Peace

Clearly believers do not now enjoy imperishable resurrection bodies, nor has nature been delivered from its thorns and thistles. Some of the provisions of the cross, such as counteracting the physical effects of sin with perfect bodies, await Christ's return. At the resurrection nature also will be "liberated from its bondage to decay" (Rom. 8:21, 23). Then Christ's atoning work will remove all the remaining consequences of sin on the race and the earth.

When the crucified and risen Christ returns, his mission of pacification will overcome Satan and his demonic powers. Our Lord will reconcile not only all things on earth but also "all things . . . in heaven" (Col. 1:20). In context that cannot mean, unfortunately, that every last individual will be in personal fellowship with God. The cosmic pacification Paul has in mind includes the reconciliation of believers and the disarming of unrepentant enemies of the cross (2:15). Having become impotent, the evil forces must submit to Christ's cosmic victory so that his peaceful purposes will be fully achieved.[135]

Atonement: A Multi-faceted Diamond

The above aspects of Christ's death are all encompassed in an integrative view of Christ's atonement. By the general term *atonement,* we refer primarily to the voluntary substitutionary sacrificial death of the divine-human Messiah to provide the just basis by which God could remain holy and restore peace by counteracting all the legal, experiential, relational, and cosmic effects of sin. Through faith in Christ's once-for-all substitutionary sacrifice, God can (1) acquit believers of their real guilt, (2) free them from domination by inherent tendencies to evil, (3) give them power to overcome evil principalities and powers, (4) reconcile believers to himself, and (5) reconcile them to one another. Future provisions of Christ's death and resurrection include (1) the provision of an incorruptible, resurrection body or the complete restoration of the divine likeness and (2) enjoyment of restored Edenic conditions in the millennium and in the new heavens and earth. The basis of such a rich salvation is not faith, but Christ's completed atonement. Faith is the means by which Christ's atoning provisions are personally received.

Illustrations of the atonement point up its different aspects. Analogies implied in biblical teaching refer to substitutionary sacrifice at an altar, acquittal in court, liberation from a slave market, victory on a battlefield, the embrace of reconciled enemies, the relationships of a new family, and inner peace. Thoughts about Christ's atonement are impoverished if they are limited to one of these models: sacrificial, judicial, experiential, or relational. Sin is not justly atoned for by a mere feeling of at-one-ment with the world or a mystical union with the cosmos. Sin is not sufficiently atoned for by a mere judicial decree of acquittal without personal reconciliation to God or experiential deliverance from bondage to unrighteousness. Neither is sin adequately atoned for by a mere liberation from the slave market of sin (in a battlefield of temptation) without divine forgiveness and reconciliation. An integrative concept of the atonement seeks to incorporate the biblically supported facets that the historical views affirm while avoiding their exclusivistic negations.

Can these figurative teachings be gathered together in one coherent doctrine? According to Leon Morris, that "cannot be done"[136] and according to John Stott it cannot be done "neatly."[137] If Morris and Stott mean that the diversity of biblical evidence cannot be adequately incorporated in any single analogy, we concur. However, the nonfigurative points of the respective illustrations are not contradictory, and the integrative synthesis above, though far from exhaustive, coherently incorporates their legal, experiential, and relational significances. In everyday life, furthermore, we combine all three major categories without confusion. Take the case of a divorced couple.

Legally they are not married, experientially they may not keep themselves for each other, and relationally they may be alienated and estranged. Then consider the unusual case of divorcees eventually being remarried. Legally their status again is married, experientially they again remain faithful to each other, and relationally they again are reconciled and living together in peace. We might well call such a reconciliation a dramatic victory!

One's doctrine of atonement surely will have as many facets as one's doctrine of sin. Legally sinners are not God's people; experientially they do not remain faithful to God; and relationally they are estranged from God. When sinners believe in Christ's atoning sacrifice, legally they become God's children, experientially they grow in faithfulness to God, and relationally they enjoy peace with God. We find in the cross a many-splendored expression of God's love. We view the cross in a way that is typical of life's experiences in which these distinguishable categories are often intertwined without contradiction. Not all of life or salvation is fully comprehended in such a formulation, but it can make sense of the varied emphases of Scripture.

An even broader term than "atonement" is *salvation*. Salvation includes the eternal plan, the Old Testament preparation, the Son's incarnation, death, resurrection, ascension, the present ministries of Christ and the Spirit, and future realizations at the second coming and in eternity. For clarity of understanding, when we are not referring to salvation in such a comprehensive way, we use the more concrete terms (such as the atoning sacrifice and its just provision for forgiveness, redemption, victory over unholy powers, reconciliation to God and God's people, justification, and sanctification.

For Whom Were the Atoning Provisions Made?

Christ could die for all people, for, because he was divine, his provisions were of unlimited value. People who subscribe to the deity of Christ do not doubt that the provisions of his atonement were of sufficient value for all. The precious blood of the God-man had unlimited value. Surely the Father planned that the sacrifice suffice for the salvation of every lost person. The primary issue does not concern the sufficiency of the atonement's objective provisions as being sufficient for the justification, redemption, and reconciliation of all. Both Calvinistic and Arminian evangelicals affirm that.

Some may ask, "If the price has been paid for all, how can any people justly be punished for their sins?" The provisions of a last will or testament, although provided by a legal transaction, must be personally received to become of personal benefit. Christ's death does not forgive, redeem, or reconcile all, but makes publicly available to all sufficient provisions of forgiveness, redemption, and reconciliation. Several years after Christ's crucifixion and resurrection John wrote, "Whoever does not believe stands condemned already" (John 3:18), and he "will not see life, for God's wrath remains on him" (v. 36). On the basis of Christ's repeated warnings and other teaching about eternity, the hypothesis of universal salvation does not fit the facts. So a distinction must be made between the atonement's provisions and their application to sinners. The Scriptures could not be more emphatic that the atonement is efficient salvifically only for believers.

Even those who remain in unbelief, however, receive the benefits of common grace on the basis of the cross. Because of Christ's death sinners are not consumed *en masse* by divine wrath. The continued blessings of sunshine and rain universally remain possible because of the redemptive plan and provisions. In divine providence the Father may use Christ's powerful example to stimulate humility, justice, and love. Believers in the atonement make a difference in the world (Matt. 5:13–17). So the outworking of evil is not as great generally as it would be without the cross. God's temporal purposes are not unrelated to Calvary. In discussing the Father's plans for history (vol. 1, chap. 8) we emphasized God's purposes for all human beings and his purposes for his people morally and spiritually by faith. In fulfillment of both those purposes the cross is the basis for God's undeserved temporal favors to all sinners and his redemptive grace to those who believe.

A twofold universal and particular purpose for the cross accounts coherently for three types of related passages. We discuss them as follows:

1. The universal purpose accounts for the passages emphasized by Arminians indicating that Christ died for all, for the world, for whoever will believe (John 3:16–17; Rom. 5:18; 2 Cor. 5:14–15; 1 Tim. 2:4; Heb. 2:9; 2 Peter 2:1; 1 John 2:2; 4:14). Passages like these underline the sufficiency of the atonement for all, the desire (but not purpose) to redeem all who sin, and the indirect blessings of common grace for all.

2. A second purpose with a special intent of the cross for the elect accounts for passages that are highlighted by Calvinists: those that teach that Jesus Christ died for the persons the Father gave to him, the many, or the church (Mark 10:45; John 17:9, 20, 24; Acts 20:28; Eph. 1:4–7; 5:25; 2 Tim. 1:9–10). Passages like these indicate that Christ died with a special end in view for those the Father gave him out of the world: the members of his body, the church.

3. A view including both distinct universal and particular purposes for the cross provides the most probable account of Paul's teaching that the living God "is the Savior of all men, and especially of those who believe" (1 Tim. 4:10). What did Paul mean? In view of Paul's teaching that the unbelieving are under the curse of God's wrath, he cannot here be supporting universalism. Furthermore, in view of Paul's emphasis on the provisions of propitiation, redemption, and reconciliation, he does not here tell Timothy that believers enjoy a higher degree of common grace. As we have seen, "salvation" may be used in two ways, more generally for preservation in this life and more specifically for justification, redemption, and reconciliation. This twofold purpose coherently fits not only Paul's frame of reference and a word study of "salvation" but also the temporal-eternal contrast in the context regarding fitness physically and spiritually (v. 8). Furthermore, the grammatical structure is similar to another of Paul's uses of "especially." Paul exhorts, "As we have opportunity, let us do good to all people, *especially* to those who belong to the family of believers" (Gal. 6:10).[138] Parallel to this in grammatical structure is Paul's teaching that Christ is the Savior of all people, but *especially* of those who believe.

The interpretation of "those who believe" (1 Tim. 4:10) turns on whether sinners in fact are able to believe. Has prevenient grace delivered all sinners from their unwillingness and inability to respond to the gospel? In our study of sin we did not find evidence for a restoration of volitional ability to all. Rather, the hypothesis of prevenient grace enabling all humans to believe is contradicted by the numerous descriptions of sinners' present slavery to sin and blindness to spiritual things. Since sinners are unwilling and unable of

themselves to believe, it would not be enough for Jesus to give his life for whoever would believe. None would believe! The "whosoever" passages do not discuss the point at issue—the *ability* of people enslaved to sin to receive Christ, any more than the giving of the Ten Commandments presupposes the ability of people to keep them. The class of all who would believe apart from a special call and enablement of the Spirit of grace is an empty class. So it would be in vain for Christ to provide forgiveness, redemption, and reconciliation "to whom it may concern." Given the present actuality of depravity, none would believe. Rather, Christ died to provide the just basis for (1) the undeserved temporal blessings of common grace and general revelation for all and (2) justification, sanctification, and glorification for God's people, those the Holy Spirit effectually calls out of the world. Some of the issues of election and the lost have been treated in volume 1, chapter 8. For more on the divine initiative in calling and the Holy Spirit's special enabling of the elect to believe, see volume 3, chapter 1.

APOLOGETIC INTERACTION

Must Human Sin Be Punished?

Much has been said recently about rehabilitating sinners who are also criminals, but little has been said about retributive justice. Retributive justice is served when criminals receive the penalties deserved for the injuries they have caused others. Rehabilitation is served when a criminal turns from a life of crime to work for a living and contributes to a peaceful society. The goals of both retribution and rehabilitation are ends sought by Christ's atonement. The cross satisfies justice in bearing our retribution and directly seeks our reconciliation to God and neighbor. The resultant process of sanctification rehabilitates a believer to a productive life in the church and the world.

Can sinners not be rehabilitated without the punishment of their sin? Since retribution at present is the most controversial issue, consider two of Leon Morris' arguments for reconsidering the value of retribution:[139] (1) Governments have no right to punish merely for reformatory and deterrent purposes. Unless a person deserves to the punished, society ought not inflict suffering. The penal system is at fault unless there is just desert. Punishment is just only when deserved. As violators of the law, we pay the penalty because we owe it, and for no other reason. Only when a government has the right to punish is it legitimate to exercise that right for rehabilitative purposes. (2) Punishment must in fact be retributive if it is to be reformatory. If people know that they are being punished unjustly it will not reform them. Of first importance it is necessary that justice be done, that sin be punished. The retributive character of punishment, A. E. Taylor argued, is a doctrine "really indispensable to sound ethics."[140]

Immanuel Kant argued at length for the importance of vindicating justice in society:

The notion of ill desert and punishableness is necessarily implied in the idea of voluntary transgression; and the idea of punishment excludes that of happiness in all its forms. For though he who inflicts punishment may, it is true, also have a benevolent purpose to produce by the punishment some good effect upon the criminal, yet the punishment must be justified first of all, as pure and simple requital and retribution; that is, as a kind of suffering that is demanded by the law without any reference to its prospective beneficial consequences; so that even if no moral improvement and no personal advantage should subsequently accrue to the criminal, he must acknowledge that justice has been done to him, and that his experience is exactly conformed to his conduct. In every instance of punishment, properly so called, justice is the first thing, and constitutes the essence of it. A benevolent purpose and a happy effect, it is true, may be conjoined with punishment, but the criminal cannot claim this as his due, and he has no right to reckon upon it. All that he deserves is punishment, and this is all that he can expect from the law that he has transgressed.[141]

In addition to the moral imperative of oughtness in itself, for theists God's integrity, God's Word, and God's moral order are at stake. As Warfield said, "Indiscriminate forgiveness of sin would be precisely the subversion of the moral order of the world."[142] If a moral order is operative, in it the consequences of sin ought to fall upon the sinner. In the human experience the consequences of sin do not always appear to fall upon the sinner, but sometimes fall upon others. In that case the sinner ought to make restitution, making good the wrong as far as possible. No one can completely undo a wrong, especially against God. Still the sinner ought to be punished in order to vindicate righteousness. The person sinned against may forgive the sinner, but in this case the one who forgives suffers for the sinner as a substitute. The guilt is not artificially transferred, but the one who forgives bears in his own person the penal consequences of the other's sin.[143]

The moral order of the world is not something distinct from God, or God's justice and love, as so-called governmental theories of the atonement imply. The principles of morality and providence are rooted in the nature of God himself. " 'Satisfaction' is an appropriate word, providing we realize that it is he himself in his inner being who needs

411

to be satisfied, and not something external to himself."[144]

Did Jesus Actually Die?

Some skeptically inclined people may ask, "Did Jesus really die?" Many lines of evidence indicate that he did. Mythical interpretations of the Gospels do not account for their historical reliability. The *cultural factors* surrounding the death fit the historical context in both method and motive. In the Roman and Jewish cultures crucifixion was common. As one of the most cruel methods of execution ever practiced, the Romans reserved it for criminals, slaves and other "nonpersons" convicted of murder, rebellion, or armed robbery. Among the Jews no distinction was made between the curse of hanging and crucifixion (Deut. 21:23). Both the Jews and Romans had motives for putting Christ onto the cross. Jesus frequently challenged the hypocrisy of the Jewish establishment, arguing that unless their righteousness exceeded that of the scribes and Pharisees, they would in no way enter the kingdom of heaven (Matt. 5:20). By speaking of his kingship and kingdom Jesus aroused enemies in the Roman tetrarchy also. Gentiles were as responsible for his death as Jews.

The primary visible *sign* of Jesus' death was his shed blood. The Messiah's shed blood, however, was not of magical value. Its significance stood out, rather, as a "visible sign" of his ultimate sacrifice, the offering up of his life for others. It was the visible indication of the invisible, new covenant. The preciousness of the Messiah's truly human blood came from its union with his divine nature. Jesus' shed blood was of inestimable worth, not because of inherent magical properties, but because it was the blood of the incarnate Logos.

Several converging lines of evidence conclusively support the fact that Jesus died. He "gave up his spirit" (Matt. 27:50) and "breathed his last" (Mark 15:37). Finding Jesus already dead, the soldiers did not break his legs as they did those on his right and left (John 19:31–33). One of the soldiers had pierced his side with a spear, bringing a sudden flow of blood and water (v. 34). Pilate questioned whether Jesus was already dead, summoned the centurion, and learned that it was so (Mark 15:43–45). Then Pilate gave the body to Joseph of Arimathea. Joseph wrapped it in a clean linen cloth and placed it in his own new tomb that he had cut out of rock and then rolled a large stone in front of its entrance (Matt. 27:57–60). The evidence from both his friends and his enemies places the fact of Jesus' death beyond reasonable doubt.

The evidence leads us to affirm that Christ's death occurred in actuality. If a distinction between *Historie* and *Geschichte* is made, he died in both respects! The testimony is not limited to believing followers of Christ. There were the unbelieving soldiers and no doubt others who had cried, "Crucify him!" Jesus' followers were hardly strong believers when he died. They struggled to maintain their faith through the experience of deep sorrow. Only after the appearances of the risen Christ did they interpret these events in faith, that is, in terms of *Geschichte,* or *Heilsgeschichte.* The belief in his death did not precede the observation of the evidence for the fact. And that evidence convinced both friends and enemies.

As an irrepeatable historical event, Jesus' death occurred *once-for-all*. To hold with Roman Catholicism that the sacrifice of Calvary is continued and made effective by its representation in the Eucharistic sacrifice amounts to an implicit denial of the historicity and uniqueness of Christ's person and death.

The once-for-all happening occurred as an *objective* event. The tendency of recent theologians to make the atonement a subjective experience or feeling within Christians does not do justice to its historicity. These things were not done in a corner but in broad daylight and before unbelievers as well as believers.

Christ's death was an *influential* event. In the preface to his book, *Great Sermons on the Death of Christ,* Wilbur Smith contrasts the preeminent place given the death of Christ in the New Testament with the insignificant references to the death of other great figures in history. Smith quotes the description of Napoleon's death and burial as given in an *Encyclopedia Britannica* article and observes, "The death of Napoleon was about the least important episode of his life, whereas it was the great event in the life of Christ."[145]

Christ's death became the *focal point* of history. As described by Albert A. Trevor in his *History of Ancient Civilization,*

> In the later years of Tiberius, probably soon after 30 A.D., occurred in Judea an event unnoticed by Romans, the crucifixion of Jesus. Yet this seemingly insignificant affair was to become the central point of future history, and the despised Galilean was destined to triumph over all the gods and emperors of the Roman world.[146]

Can Sins Justly Be Transferred to a Third Party?

The response to this question begins by challenging its assumption. The query presupposes an inadequate view of who Jesus is. Jesus is not some disinterested third party, but truly God, one with the offended party, and truly human, one with the offenders. We answer this and some other important questions briefly in view of the content in this and the two preceding chapters.

How Could One Death Atone for All?

Again the question fails to take account of who Jesus Christ was and is. He is not just one other finite human, but also the eternal Son of God. The precious blood of Christ is not that of one mere human. The death of the God-man has inestimable value, the value of the offered life of the infinite Son of God. His incarnate life is of unlimited inherent worth and with its sacrifice God the Father was well pleased.

Can Sins Be Transferred?

To restate the question, Is it not unjust to punish one person for another's sins? Sins are not substances that can be passed along from one person to another as in a bucket brigade. The word "sin" in Scripture often refers to its guilt and penalty. Indeed an innocent person considers it unjust to be blamed and punished for another's crime against his will. But no principles of justice are violated if one freely chooses to accept another's blame and take another's punishment so that the guilty person may go free.

Does a Substitutionary Atonement Make Sinners Passive?

Quite the reverse. is true. People enslaved to sin cannot redeem themselves. Atonement must be provided for them. When Christ gave his life for sinners, they were spiritually incapacitated. Although active in ways displeasing to Christ, in motives and service pleasing to him they are completely passive. However, the response of sinners to Christ's death is far from passive. The sinners' repentant, believing, and consecrated response to the cross involves active participation in new moral and spiritual life. The affirmative actions involved are considered in relation to sanctification.

Do We Place a Mythological Emphasis on Jesus' blood?

According to the Old Testament, blood was necessary to life (Lev. 17:11, 14), and the shedding of blood meant death. Since death is the just consequence of sinful living, there could be no just remission of sin without the shed blood, if not that of the sinner, that of a substitutionary sacrifice. It is "the blood that makes atonement for one's life" (v. 11). At the Passover God said, "When I see the blood [of a sacrificial lamb on the doorpost], I will pass over you. No destructive plague will touch you when I strike Egypt" (Exod. 12:13). The blood on the entrance to the house indicated that the inhabitants acknowledged their deserved judgment and by faith had offered a substitutionary sacrifice. "The OT, therefore, indicates that atonement for human sin was obtained by the death of an acceptable substitute, rather than by its life."[147]

In New Testament times rebels against moral principles still deserved to die, but Jesus shed his human blood as the sinless Lamb of God in our place. The significance of Jesus' shed blood is not life set free, but "life given up in death."[148] Jesus' shed blood had no magical effects or mythical significance. Although inseparable from his divine nature, his fully human body had fully human life that depended on fully human blood. The shedding of Jesus' blood carried great significance also as confirmation of the fact that the God-man was giving up his life in accord with the Father's covenant. Jesus said, "This is my blood of the covenant, which is poured out for many for the forgiveness of sins" (Matt. 26:28). Like a will, this new covenant had force only after "the death of the one who made it" (Heb. 9:16; 12:24). Since Jesus' life was actually given as the once-for-all sacrifice with all its rich significance, we need attach no mythological value to his blood. The preciousness of Jesus' blood (1 Peter 1:18–19) comes from his personal significance as the Son of God incarnate and from all the covenanted provisions of the atonement that his substitutionary sacrifice secured.

Because you are bought with such a price, "you are not your own" (1 Cor. 6:19–20). "You were bought at a price, do not become slaves of men" (7:23). Ministers are to "be shepherds of the church of God, which he bought with his own blood" (Acts 20:28). Eternally we will sing praise to the Lamb who with his blood "purchased men for God from every tribe and language and people and nation" (Rev. 5:9).

Is the Substitutionary Sacrifice Central to Christian Faith?

William Hordern charges that whereas evangelicalism makes atonement (and one view of it) central to Christianity, neoorthodoxy makes incarnation central and is hesitant to make any doctrine of the atonement final. The ultimate purpose of the incarnation, however, was to provide the atonement for the hopelessly lost. Hence the cross cannot be divorced either from the incarnation or from the core of Christianity.[149]

In ministry as well as thought evangelical Christians should give priority to the fact and meaning of the death of the incarnate Son of God. The experience of holistically depraved people trying to imitate Jesus, or identify with him, or take him as their representative shows that they need Christ's redemption and reconciliation first. The atonement is central to spirituality in the ministry and teaching not only of evangelists but also of pastors and theologians. Christ's substitutionary sacrifice supplies a key to the unity of Scripture, the purpose for the incarnation, the union of justice and love in God's nature, and genuinely Christian personal and social ethics.

Should We Politicize the Cross?

Jürgen Moltmann's theology illustrates how panentheistic and process assumptions can affect views of human sin and Christ's atonement. Hope for humanity's future, Moltmann says, comes from the remembrance of Christ's incarnation and death, for Christ suffers in the world's sufferings. Moltmann's immanent God exists in the living deeds of men.[150] So social action is Christian when the activists perform it as an act of identification with Christ.[151] Moltmann rejected an apathetic God unmoved by the world's suffering, but he fails to realize that biblical theism has a God who is afflicted in all the afflictions of his people (Isa. 63:9). Moltmann so identifies his "God" with suffering that unfortunately his processive God seems insufficiently transcendent, living, and active as a personal spirit to do the mighty acts necessary to correct the human plight.

Since Moltmann's God includes humanity, he includes evil. Moltmann imagines "a rebellion in God himself."[152] Essential to understanding the cross, Moltmann thinks, is his unorthodox version of trinitarianism as "an eschatological process open for men on earth, which stems from the cross of Christ."[153] Moltmann finds it impossible to grasp how Jesus could really be God and at the same time be forsaken by God.[154] Undercutting a distinction between the provisions of the cross and their reception, he writes, "All being and all that annihilates (including Auschwitz) has already been taken up in God and God begins to become 'all in all.' "[155]

Moltmann glibly labels capitalism "sin" and prescribes a democratic socialism for salvation from the circle of poverty.[156] He does not call technocracy, as an institutionalized cause of misery, sinful, but "inhuman." Similarly, Moltmann might have said that society's problem is "inhuman abuses of capitalism" rather than "capitalism." Depraved humans can and do abuse any form of economy or human government. Some forms may be more easily abused than others, however, because of fewer checks and balances on those in authority and power. Moltmann's key to liberation from the vicious circle of force is "democracy."[157] In our judgment, democracies may have many checks and balances to minimize evils of coercion, but democratic governments cannot bring the just and lasting peace that either regeneration or the actual return of the transcendent Christ will bring.

The church of the insulted, poor, and oppressed, Moltmann argues, "must take sides in the concrete social and political conflicts going on about it and in which it is involved, and must be prepared to join and form parties."[158] But the forming of Christian political parties does not follow from biblically sound teaching of the cross. Christians can misuse political power, as history has repeatedly indicated. Christians need to fulfill their responsibilities as citizens, but may not agree on full-blown economic structures or political parties and programs. The atoning provisions of God's grace at Calvary has been enjoyed by people of all different tribes and nations in history. The provisions of the cross transcend any economic or political structure. When it is necessary to take sides socially and politically, Christians ought always to remain loyal above all to the Savior of people from *all* sides.

The example of Jesus' life does not support a politicizing of his death. Jesus lived in a province of the Roman Empire in the midst of a society seething with discontent as a result of injustices. In those circumstances the Messiah opposed violence in general and refused to lead a violent revolution as a Zealot,

415

but he headed a spiritual kingdom for the poor in spirit. What was the nature of the Messiah's good news for the poor, release for the captives, and liberty for the oppressed (Luke 4:18)? He addressed evils endemic in human nature, more than the oppression of the Roman Empire. He discouraged attempts to reestablish Jewish national freedom. He did not teach socialism in a democracy. He treated the deeper root of our problem—our personal relationships to God and one another. He liberated people from the peace-shattering sins of prejudice, pride, greed, barriers of class, wealth, and hypocrisy. Apparently the evil fruit would come forth from evil trees in any economic or political system, and with new hearts God's people would work to overcome evil in any social context. Changed hearts will not change society automatically, but people with renewed abilities to discern evil, feel it deeply, and do the good that they should, will make a difference.

The liberation that in the New Testament parallels the Exodus experience (and the cross) is directly a liberation from personal sin and social evil within the control of redeemed people. Instead of destroying the present social order, Jesus sought to demonstrate a more radical way of love to God and neighbors.[159] Christ liberates the poor, not in the sense of attacking economic structures directly, but by undercutting the world's value system. The *sumum bonum* can be neither material advantage nor a different economic structure.

While, then, Jesus did not campaign directly for economic revolution, nor set out for his disciples a programme for doing so, he nevertheless preached and lived such values and attitudes that those who take him seriously can neither exploit nor ignore the plight of the exploited. Socio-economic liberation if it was not his direct aim, is the proper concern of those who accept his radical value system.[160]

As Richard J. Mouw says,

Unless human beings are willing to forsake the futile patterns of pretending to be their own lords, they will be liberated from one form of oppression only to be victimized by other forms. Political and economic restructurings are important elements in the total kingdom picture, but they are not by themselves the total picture.[161]

The basic issue facing Christians, according to Mouw, is, "What kinds of actions, if any, are compatible with commitments of those who are living in grateful response to what God did in the cross of Jesus Christ?" or, "What kinds of actions are proper effects of the cross?"[162] In considering proposed answers in different cultural contexts, Christians need to be encouraged by the assurance that eschatologically the risen Christ will not only restore creation but will also eliminate injustice and bestow both personal and institutional righteousness. Until that great *kairos*, the present age need not be considered merely a holding action. The present opportunities present a challenge to do what is within our power to overcome evil with good. That demands getting our facts straight, critically using a responsible method of decision making, willingness to take responsibility for our actions, and authenticity in living by them. In this approach we do not politicize the cross, but develop the indirect significance of identification with the crucified Christ for our relationships to others in the contexts of varieties of socialist, communist, or capitalist political structures.

Did All Actually Die With Christ in the First Century?

Karl Barth considers Christ's sacrifice more than a provision for a just amnesty, redemption, and reconciliation. Barth proposes that the cross in the first century *actually justified all fallen human beings*. The atoning work of Christ does not present a mere possibility of salvation (Thomasius). Barth insists that "this possibility has to become actuality."[163] "That Jesus Christ died for us does not mean, therefore, that we do not have to die, but that we have died in and with him, that as the people we were we have been done away and destroyed, that we are no longer there and have no more future."[164] When raised by the Father, Jesus was justified as a man and "in him as the Representative of all men all were justified."[165] So in Christ

all were justified, converted, sanctified and called.[166] In the death of Jesus Christ both the destroying and the renewing *have* taken place for *all* men. . . . Therefore objectively, really, ontologically, there is a necessity of faith for them all. . . . Unbelief has become an impossibility and faith an objective, real and ontological necessity for all men and for every man.[167]

Barth's hypothesis comes short of confirmation by all three of our criteria of truth—noncontradiction, adequacy, and viability:

1. A letter from one who attended Barth's 1961 lectures in Germany indicated that he found the theologian's *inconsistencies* on election "maddening":

God's grace is irresistible, but man can succeed in resisting it. Christ's redemptive work is all-inclusive and 100% effective, but the possibility of damnation remains (though Barth refuses to decide between particularism and universalism because to do so would be to usurp the divine prerogative of judgment—if forced to choose, Barth candidly admitted he would choose universalism). Not everyone will necessarily be saved, but no one can suffer hell (though one could possibly suffer the "shadows" of hell—whatever

that means). Christ will be in hell as well as heaven, and on and on. It is maddening.[168]

Barth correctly insisted that Christ died in the first century to provide more than a mere possibility of salvation. Christ's atonement assured the fulfillment of the redemptive plan, but that plan included not only Christ's just provision for amnesty, but also the Holy Spirit's conviction, calling, and regeneration of unbelievers. Christ's victory at this point guaranteed that the reaching of God's people would be just and would take place subsequently. But after the cross the Holy Spirit had to come to help people go out as witnesses and to help sinners receive the message, repent, and believe. People are justified and sanctified only when they hear the gospel, believe it, and trust Christ. These eventualities were foreknown in the first century but not realized then.

2. Barth's failure to distinguish the objective provisions from their actual subjective reception at the moment of faith also *fails to fit the scriptural data:* (1) Spiritually Christ himself divided humanity into two spiritual classes— the lost and the saved, but Barth has only one class, in which all humans are already justified and sanctified. Unscripturally Barth gives all humans the same spiritual status. "Thus the so-called 'outsiders' are really only 'insiders' who have not yet understood and apprehended themselves as such."[169] (2) Prior to faith, sinners, according to Scripture, are not united to Christ and are not forgiven, redeemed, or reconciled. (3) Barth minimizes the importance for redemption of the Holy Spirit's ministries of calling, regenerating, justifying, sanctifying, and glorifying the foreknown and predestined (Romans 8:28–30). (4) Barth's view of informing people that they are already in God's kingdom has none of the urgency of Christ's ministry. The apostles then

417

pled with sinners in behalf of Christ to make the decision that appropriates the provisions of the cross and settles one's eternal destiny. (5) The view that all are objectively sanctified fails to fit the facts of human experience. All too obviously, as we know from hearing or reading the daily crime news, all human beings are far from holy. The inhumanity of humans to one another remains a major problem among the peoples of the world, religious and nonreligious. Prior to regeneration people today remain actually in slavery to sin, alienated from God, and under condemnation. Apart from the distinction between the atoning provisions and their application, it seems impossible to make sense of fallen humanness.

3. Barth's view of an actualized universal justification and sanctification is not viable. Barth speaks of more than a legal status: he insists on an actual justification and sanctification. Christians honest with themselves cannot hold that they are actually as holy as God is holy. Socially Christians could not live by that view without hypocrisy in any known church or in a non-Christian business, labor union, or political party. Legally, in the first century Christ did provide a just basis for some universally experienced blessings. On the basis of his atonement divine wrath has not already consumed the whole fallen human race; instead, God bestows the benefits of common grace universally. But it is impossible to live unhypocritically with Barth's claim that all humans are now really renewed or sanctified.

Did Believers Die With Christ in the First Century?

Some people who hold to exchanged-life emphases teach a version of what Barth taught for all humans but limit it to those who are believers in Christ. Victorious-life writers may affirm that all believers actually died with Christ on the cross in the first century. The view places a believer's crucifixion with Christ (Gal. 2:20) at Calvary rather than at the point of the person's faith in the Savior. The argument is that as all humans were realistically in Adam when he sinned, so all believers were realistically in Christ when he died. Charles Solomon argues that being "in Christ" means being in him eternally and so "we were in him *at the cross.*"[170] The putting off of the "old nature," it is alleged, "was done by the operation of the Cross, according to Romans 6:6."[171] When was our old nature crucified (Greek aorist tense) with Christ (Romans 6:6)? The context indicates that when we were "baptized into Christ Jesus," we were "baptized into his death" (v. 3). So "you died" (Col. 3:3) when you identified with Christ by faith and exhibited your faith in baptism. Realistically, believers died with Christ when they were converted. Legally, or covenantally, believers were represented by Christ's once-for-all death on the cross. Decretively, of course, believers are foreknown because they were chosen in Christ from before the foundation of the world.

Although all people were "in Adam" genetically and have his nature by birth, people are "in Christ" only when by faith they are born anew and receive a new nature. At the cross our legally received Substitute suffered the guilt and penalty our sins deserved, and the good news is that we did not need to be there! The believers at Rome died with Christ (past tense) at the point of their faith, new birth, and baptism. At their regeneration believers also rose with him and received a renewed nature in his image (and all the present provisions of the cross). Both the definitive divorce from the former way of life dominated by the flesh and the definitive beginning of resurrection to a new way of life dominated by the Holy

Spirit marks the meaning of baptism that beautifully witnesses to these realities in the world. As John Stott explains,

These verses [Rom. 6:3–5] probably allude to the pictorial symbolism of baptism. When baptisms took place in the open air in some stream, the candidate would go down into the water . . . and as he went down into the water, whether partially or totally, he would seem to be buried and then to rise again. His baptism would dramatize his death, his burial, and his resurrection to a new life.[172]

We actually died and rose with Christ when we inwardly turned from former spiritual masters to Jesus Christ. Then it was that by faith we received the blessings of redemption, forgiveness, and reconciliation for which he died once-for-all. Our union with the eternal Christ does not make the succession of events of our lives in time less real. God's foreknowledge of our sinful condition and our faith at a point in time does not make the temporal event of the cross or of our reception of its benefits less temporal.

Since the provisions of the cross become ours at the crisis of conversion signified by baptism, the realization of these great blessings ought to take place then. Well-instructed believers should not need a subsequent crisis of identity to determine whether their ultimate identification is with Christ and his kingdom or with Satan and his dominion. If these teachings have not been taught, or have been misconstrued, then by the illumination of the Holy Spirit they need later to be realized and internalized. And exchanged-life emphases have helped meet this need. Apart from some realization of the believer's death with Christ, we wonder if the meaning of repentance, faith, and regeneration to a new life was understood inwardly when the person outwardly claimed to believe and was baptized to confess these very commitments publicly.

Is the Meaning of the Cross Merely Subjective?

Some interpreters find no objective provisions for sinners completed in the first century and make salvation depend wholly on one's subjective response to Christ's crucifixion. D. M. Baillie speaks for many when he says, "We are dealing with a realm of personal relationships and nothing else."[173] J. A. T. Robinson also denies any objective transaction between two parties at the cross. He finds getting saved an experience like that of the prodigal son as we "come to ourselves." He says, "It is a coming home, or rather being received home."[174] Paul Van Buren asked what Jesus' death accomplished, saying it was "not an objective ransom, substitution or redemption." By regarding people as sinners forgiven and by proclaiming their forgiveness, "Jesus convinced them that they were released from the burden of their guilt and the consequences of their acts."[175] The cross, Van Buren claims, is

a discernment situation, i.e, for those who "see." If taken as a cosmological assertion, however, this is "meaningless" in terms of a [positivistic] verifiability theory of meaning. In the form of a confession of faith the statements suggest a situation in which the history of Jesus has been or might be seen in a new way and the speaker's commitment to what he has now "seen."[176]

Surely sinners are illumined to receive the meaning of the cross, and do testify to it. The question is whether their witness is true. Is it consistent with the meaning the Holy Spirit inspired in Scripture? Do the meanings sinners read into or out of the cross hold for God as well? Interpreters of the cross will not lose heart or be disillusioned if their affirmations have objective validity. The faithful words that Jesus is the Messiah and that he died for our sins are reliable because they are true historically and revelationally. Certainly personal relationships are involved in the biblical analogies, but relationships can be based on spoken and written affirmations in objective covenants and promises. The sincerity of the personal commitment to the cross is crucial on the subjective side, but also indispensable is the objective truth of the eternal covenant and the good news of its promises.

Are the psychological benefits more important than Calvary's objective provisions? J. Norman King attempts to address human psychological and existential problems without an objectively real God, guilt, atonement, or justification! Human loneliness, despair, and death, he thinks, can be overcome by an experience of the "infinite mystery at the depth of human existence." King thinks that "the past can be redeemed by including the integration achieved in guilt within a new positive option which ratifies one's orientation to the self-bestowing infinite mystery."[177]

Healthful psychological integration of sinners is important but in itself does not displace the need for the once-for-all historical reality of the cross with all its pathos and revealed meaning. The Scriptures indicate that the subjective distinctive of the new and better covenant is that God puts his laws in believers' minds and writes them on their hearts (Heb. 8:10–11). The previous covenant with its repeated sacrifices did not cleanse once for all; it left people feeling guilty (10:2). Under the new covenant believers have been "made holy . . . once for all" (v. 10); God forgives them and remembers their lawless acts no more (vv. 17–18). Some of the greatest subjective benefits of the cross have been dismissed by denying its once-for-all objective provisions for a clear conscience. We defend the objective provisions of the cross because they are indispensable to its subjective values for God and believers.

RELEVANCE FOR LIFE AND MINISTRY

At an ugly cross the incarnate Word has made known who God really is (John 1:18), and he is far from Aristotle's unmoved and uncaring Mover. The historical cross discloses an invisible personal Spirit who knows, cares, speaks, and acts in the midst of our spiritual blindness and moral decadence. Behind the cross is an invisible God who knows all about history's public and private problems of evil. Behind the cross is a God who understands when people in the midst of the anxieties, meaninglessness, and tragedies of life think he has forsaken them or even died. Behind the cross is a living God who cares about us just as we are. Behind the cross is a God who covenants with his Son to save those who know they need a physician. Behind the cross is a faithful God who keeps his word. Behind the cross is a God who acts on planet earth in human history. Behind history's worst miscarriage of justice is a God who acts mercifully and graciously on behalf of undeserving rebels. Behind the agony of the cross is not a God of cheap grace, but a God whose grace cost him dearly. Behind the death on the cross is a God who remains just while providing for the justification of the insolent. Behind that cross is the God who turned the gross injustice of Jesus' death into a marvelous instrument of justification, redemption, and reconciliation. Behind the cross is the God who on the third day turned the enigma of Good Friday into the triumph of Easter.[178] To grasp the objective meaning of the cross in some measure is to feel poignantly its subjective impact.

Experience the Moral Impact Personally

Jesus gave up his life because of your sins and ours. The final reason for his death was not his betrayal, his first-century enemies, the religious establishment, the political establishment, but ourselves. He went through the anguish of physical and spiritual death because of the sins of all fallen humans of all times. All of us are contributors to his death whenever we disbelieve him, disobey him, deny him, betray him, follow him far off, or subject his name to public disgrace. "Before we can begin to see the cross as something done *for* us (leading us to faith and worship), we have to see it as something done *by* us (leading us to repentance)."[179] At the cross

> God overturned the judgment of the world, and with it exposed as idols its standards of righteousness, wisdom and power. The cross confronts us with the demand to turn away from the present age with its standards and values—which when greatly magnified lead to the "God of this present age"—and instead bring our thinking about God, ourselves and his world into conformity with the cross.[180]

Moved to repudiate our sinful disposition, we turn to God in gratitude. We love God because he first loved us. We want to love in a similar self-giving way (Eph. 5:2). Viewing Jesus' humility and perseverance, we humble ourselves (Phil. 2:3–8), endure opposition from sinful people (Heb. 12:2–3), emotionally suffer for doing good and make no threats or retaliate (1 Peter 2:21–23), and physically suffer in order to do the will of God (4:1–2). Like the thief on the cross at Christ's right, we are moved to receive Jesus as King. The attractive power of the cross moves us

to live no longer for ourselves but for him who died for us (2 Cor. 5:14–15). As imitators of Christ we choose to give up ourselves as fragrant offerings and sacrifices to God (Eph. 5:1–2). We acknowledge the element of truth in the moral influence and example hypotheses.

Isaac Watts expressed classically the Spirit-illumined Christian response to the cross.

> When I survey the wondrous cross
> On which the Prince of Glory died
> My richest gain I count but loss,
> And pour contempt on all my pride.
>
> Forbid it Lord, that I should boast
> Save in the death of Christ, my Lord;
> All the vain things that charm me most,
> I sacrifice them to His blood.
>
> Were the whole realm of nature mine,
> That were a present far too small;
> Love so amazing, so divine,
> Demands my soul, my life, my all.

Live Under the Sign the Cross

When archaeologists dig up a place of worship in the desert sand and find in it the sign of the cross, they can be virtually certain that it was a Christian church. From the very first the Christian faith was distinguished from the religions that surrounded it by its worship of the crucified Christ. Still today Christians portray their inner faith in Christ outwardly by a cross. If a single symbol of Christian faith is chosen, nothing is more distinctive than the cross. No founder of any of the world's religions died for his followers' justification, redemption, and reconciliation.

Christians hang crosses from necklaces, pin them to lapels, and place them on the steeples of their churches. Symbols of the cross stand primarily, not for what we do for Christ, but what the Savior did *for us*. The spiritual value of displaying the cross derives from the users' *faith* in Christ and his once-for-all sacrifice, with its marvelous provisions. Many make the sign of the cross and meditate at the stations of the cross. Even the sign of the cross becomes valueless, however, if it be regarded as a mere fetish, charm, or amulet. It ought never become a magical symbol. Neither should it become an occasion for mystics to be spiritually absorbed in Christ's sufferings. The significance of the sign of the cross does not point to the mystical sufferings and resignation of Jesus' devout followers. By believing the gospel and trusting Christ we become partners with Christ. We then no longer view ourselves separately as sinners, but as legal partners with Christ: it is now Christ and the believer incorporated. The partnership's assets include all the rich spiritual provisions of Christ. They meet all believing sinners' obligations. Some say, "It does not matter what you believe so long as you have faith, or have faith in Christ." But the Scriptures say that we receive atonement "through faith in his blood" (Rom. 3:25). The Lord's final will (testament) leaves propitiation, redemption, and reconciliation to all who will receive them.

Although other uses of the sign of the cross are optional, Christ did request his followers to give *two visible signs* of their faith in him—baptism and the Lord's Supper. *Baptism* is an initiatory rite expressing several great truths. (1) Baptism signifies one's confession of personal guilt. The baptized believe not only that all have sinned, but they also acknowledge, "I have sinned and deserve to die under the wrath of God." (2) One's baptism also indicates a personal reception of Christ's death as substitutionary. He died, not just for all people in general but for me personally, or in my place. (3) Christian baptism should signify a personal reception of the provisions of forgiveness from my guilt, redemption from the domination of sin in my life, and reconciliation to open fellowship with God and God's people. (4) In other words, baptism signifies that the candidate ceases depending on his or her own sin-tainted works and dies with Christ to fleshly achievements. The once-for-all burial in water pictures one's crucifixion with Christ and death to, or separation from, former evil masters and the dominion of sin in our lives. Rising from the water pictures resurrection to new spiritual life for the Lord of all (Rom. 6:2–3, 10–11). Inwardly by faith and outwardly by the sign of baptism Christians "have been united with him in his death" (v. 5). Having become partners with Christ by faith, his death pays our inescapable penalty. Baptism occurs once-for-all, signifying a decisive alienation to the fleshly loves of our preconversion loyalties. We "[were] crucified with him so that the body of sin might be done away with, that we should no longer be slaves to sin" (v. 6).

Experientially, however, because baptized believers do yield to temptation and sin, they need repeatedly to confess sin, realign their values, and renew fellowship at *the Lord's table*. Partaking of the bread and wine indicate that we thankfully remember his sacrifice in our place, proclaim the propitiatory, redemptive, and reconciling provisions of his sacrifice, and testify to our oneness with those who similarly express their salvation on the basis of Christ's atonement. Believers keep the feast of the Passover, not in boasting of self-justification or in malice, but with sincerity and truth (1 Cor. 5:6–8). The communion table, Protestants insist, is not an altar at which Christ is sacrificed again. God forbid! The great high priest completed the work of atonement and sits at the right hand of God the Father (Heb. 10:11–12). Hence the Reformers removed Roman Catholic references to an altar in their communion services. Instead, God's people meet at a table, the Lord's table. Believers who regularly join others at the Lord's table signify that they continue to live for the purpose for which Christ died.

Rejoice in the Security of Forgiveness (the Cross *for* Us)

A convert to an Eastern religious movement said, "As a Roman Catholic I forever felt guilty. Since my 'enlightenment' I have not felt guilt for three years." It is impossible, however, to live for years without real guilt when we become aware of the holy and loving One's revealed purposes and values. The best of us comes far short of God's righteous standards. Yet, like David, believers can exclaim, "Blessed is he whose transgressions are forgiven, whose sins are covered. Blessed is the man whose sin the LORD does not count against him" (Ps. 32:1–2). *Rejoice!* Although we were unacceptable in our fallen selves the God of the cross accepts believers!

Some of us find it hard to forgive ourselves (as children, parents, and spouses) even though God has forgiven us. What Christianity offers is not a hypocritical denial of guilt, but a candid confession of it in its reality and a just forgiveness based on Christ's atonement. All sinners who believe the gospel and trust Christ have the price of their sin paid in full. Having real guilt (against God), we need the assurance that God forgives. Psychologists as such, helpful as they are, cannot forgive sin against God. Only God can forgive sin and that on the basis of the cross. Having heard the good news and received the propitiation Christ provided, people of faith no longer live under God's wrath for their sin. In the joy of sins forgiven they know that their indictment has been erased and their justification declared.

Become an Agent of Forgiveness

Secure in God's merciful forgiveness and having died to our fleshly desires, we become free to please our Savior. Living daily in the assurance of what Christ did for us, we are free to value his kingdom above all else. So we can enjoy life as *agents of forgiving love.* To live by the forgiveness of God without being forgiving is unthinkable (Matt. 18:23–35). We have become part of a dynamically forgiving movement. Sinners receive forgiveness, not to store it up, but to pour it out like a river of life-giving water. Whether you have something against another (Mark 11:25) or another has something against you (Matt. 5:23), go at once and make peace. Do not let a "bitter root" grow up to cause trouble and defile many (Heb. 12:14–15). Christians ought to forgive as God has forgiven them (Eph. 4:32). Like God, we do not call evil good or deny its reality, but we love evildoers and remember that their sins can be cleansed by Christ's blood. Like our Savior on the cross, we pray, "Father forgive them for they do not know what they are doing" (Luke 23:34). How often must we forgive? As often as we need forgiveness (Matt. 18:21, 22). When Christians living under the cross become agents of forgiving love, our families and churches will become more than communities of the forgiven—they will be forgiving communities.

Conquer Sin's Addictions (the Cross *in* Us)

Christ died to liberate us from sin's control of us. Christians *can* overcome the desires of the old nature. Christians cannot excuse sins by claiming, "That's the way I am." Sinful desires and deeds should no longer dominate our lives. Christ did not come to take away our God-given individualities. All God

423

wants to take from us is our sin. We can embrace and esteem all that we are by creation—our intelligence, conscience, femininity or masculinity, family life, creativity, and need for relationship with others and God. But we divest ourselves of all that we are by the Fall: our moral perversity, the selfishness that spoils our family life, fascination with the ugly and the irrational, our lazy refusal to develop God's gifts, our waste of natural resources, and our antisocial tendencies. Courageously we affirm the worth of all that we are by creation and re-creation; ruthlessly we dismiss all that we have become by the Fall. The cross of Christ teaches us both attitudes. On the one hand, the cross illustrates the value of our created self, since Christ loved us while we were yet sinners. On the other hand, the cross models for us self-sacrifice, the denying of our fallen nature.[181]

Christ paid the ransom to set us free from the power of all varieties of sin. Black (and red) theology reminds us that Christ died to liberate us from racist prejudices and oppressions. Having been bought with such a price, we are not our own—we belong to our Lord. Our weapons are not those of the flesh but those of a Christlike self-giving love. Although we do not politicize the cross, we live a life crucifed to sins of prejudice, as well as other sins. There could as well be yellow and white theologies, for the power of the cross delivers from sinful prejudices in all directions. Christ shed his blood to deliver us from a sinful apathy that lives comfortably with unethical views of racially different people.

Feminist theology justifiably summons Christian men to remember that Christ died to liberate them from the sins of disrespect and exploitation of women, especially the particular women they know. Since chauvinism can work in either direction, Christian women may also need to seek the Redeemer's power to overcome unjust attitudes toward men in general, as well as particular men among their acquaintances.

Theologians from the less materially developed two-thirds of the world ask comparatively wealthy Christians whether we have been set free from covetousness and have become good stewards. Has the ransom Christ paid delivered us from unjust and unloving attitudes toward the poor? Have the followers of the cross who have economic power overcome policies and practices that exploit the poor? Those who live under the cross are not satisfied with its provisions of forgiveness and fellowship with God, important as these are. Believers in the crucified Christ join the Savior, the prophets, and the apostles in proclaiming good news to the poor.

Christ's redemption also brings good news to both young and old. The elderly may disrespect the young, and the young may despise the old. In youth-oriented cultures, especially, the elderly may be disregarded, hurriedly retired, and forgotten. However strong these pressures may be, Christians can find power and grace in the blood of Christ to overcome them.

The atonement that provides forgiveness also provides power for discipleship. Those who believe in the Redeemer's victory over Satan know that some former desires in their lives can pass away. As redemptive deliverance from sin's power progressively makes more differences for more believers it will make a difference in their relationships with others (socially). Let Americans and others who championed slavery repent of the sins of their fathers who championed slavery and instead actively champion black freedom. In any culture disciples of Jesus Christ can begin by exhibiting the power of Christ's atonement to deliver them from their own prejudicial attitudes and acts.

Then unhypocritically they can seek deliverance from the consequences of these sins as expressed in exploitive and oppressive structures. But the weapons of our warfare are not those of the (unjust, fleshly) world. On the contrary, those who know Christ and him crucified demolish strongholds with divine power (2 Cor. 10:4).

Become an Agent of Reconciliation (the Cross *Through* Us)

Do sinful attitudes alienate you from Christians who are younger or older? Of the other sex? Of another race? Of a greater or lesser economic status? Christ gave his life so that as we are reconciled to God we may be reconciled to one another. What unites the body of believers in Christ is not age, sex, skin color, economics, political party, or national loyalties, but repentance for our sins and faith in the Reconciler.

Because God made peace by the cross, those who live under the cross should be powerfully moved to be peacemakers. Peace-making patterned after the cross is quite different from appeasement at any price. The peace that God achieved was not cheap, but costly. To forgive and to ask for forgiveness are both costly exercises. Calvary love was not unprincipled nor unjust. Followers of Christ do not seek peace at the price of justice or morality. Just love requires self-discipline. The object of discipline with our children or our church members is not to humiliate, let alone to alienate, but rather to maintain integrity and to reclaim. The call of disciplinary action is the call to exhibit the tough love of the cross.

People who take the signs of baptism and the Lord's table strive not only for the *ends* of the cross (forgiveness, freedom, and peace), but also to accomplish them by *means* consistent with the cross. For strategies and means consistent with the cross consider the following points.

Never Compromise Justice in the Name of Love

The greatest service of love should not be done with less than moral means. For the great end of saving sinners God's matchless love at the cross went far beyond the demands of justice. As God's gracious plan satisfied moral demands, so must our plans and programs. Our most loving projects for others may go far beyond moral requirements, but they ought never come short of them. The Reverend Jim Jones devoted himself to helping the unreached young, the poor, and the minorities in an inner city. But in spite of his good motives initially, he yielded to unethical means of ministering to human need. Taking his followers to build an ideal society in Guyana, he commanded over nine hundred of them to drink poison and needlessly die. Less dramatically, not less tragically, numerous other people with great potential as pastors and church leaders, seminary students and professors, missionaries and television evangelists, have lost significant opportunities to serve others. Among other reasons, one stands out: often they did not learn the lesson of the cross. If God himself could not do moral evil that good might come, his moral and spiritual children ought not attempt to do so.

More positively, consider Billy Graham whose years of productive evangelistic ministry have been influential for many thousands of people. With all his fame, enabled by the Spirit, Graham maintained accountability to God, God's Son, God's written Word, and God's people. He has maintained his credibility morally and financially. Having been faithful in the seemingly little things, God gave Billy Graham greater and greater opportunities.

Lose Your Life to Find It

To be a follower of Jesus is to go with him all the way to Calvary. It is to be crucified with him. How? Usually not physically, although many martyrs have given their lives to be faithful to God's Word. Many of us may find ourselves some day choosing between faithfulness and physical death. Jesus took up the cross, not to carry it for years, but to die on it for our sin. Those who follow his example do not carry a cross as a burden for a lifetime, but die on it to their old natures. What does it mean to die? Entire books on being crucified with Christ sometimes fail to define the term. Death does not mean annihilation, as we have found, but primarily separation. To die with Christ or take up the cross means decisively to divorce ourselves from the domination of our fleshly desires and habits. To take up the cross is definitely to distance oneself from the peer pressure of worldly conformity and from Satanic deception in doctrine and practice. Some who die with Christ abandon everything, and others remain what they were. To follow Jesus as supreme spiritual master means to demote other loyalties, however good, such as loyalty to education, family, religious status, or employment. To follow Christ is above all to hunger and thirst for righteousness (Matt. 5:6) and to seek first the kingdom of God and his righteousness (6:33). "Whoever wants to save his life will lose it, but whoever loses his life for me and for the gospel will save it" (Mark 8:35). The objective provisions of Christ's cross are received by those who accept its judgment of their selfishness, greed, envy, jealousy, covetousness, and lust. To begin life in Christ's kingdom of light is to make a clean break with Satan's kingdom of darkness.

"The knowledge of the cross brings a conflict of interest between God who has become man and man who wishes to become God."[182] To die with Christ means to have away done with efforts like those of the people at the tower of Babel to rise to God through materialistic acquisitions, political influence, popularity in entertainment, or heroism in sports. To die with Christ is to bear witness to the lordship of Christ before the people of this world in all these fields. It is to experience Christ's suffering love for sinners, the lost, the abandoned, the despised, and the betrayed.

Acceptance of the blood of the covenant in both the Old and New Testaments symbolized not only forgiveness, Leon Morris found, but also consecration.[183] Forgiveness is not the one isolated result of believing in Jesus. By their faith in the crucified Christ God purifies a people for communion with him and service to the world. Only those who are cleansed from sin "may fittingly be termed God's people." The people sprinkled with the blood of the new covenant exhibit "newness of living, for God's people must be *God's* people."[184] The faith that receives forgiveness by sheer grace gratefully serves by love (Gal. 5:6, RSV).

The goal of Christ's followers is not self-absorption but self-giving love, like that of Jesus. Our self-denial is not to become lost in inner devotional or mystical experiences. Having cared for our own needs sufficiently, we can displace selfish ambition with self-sacrifice, comfort with suffering, and lust with service. Christ's priority for his followers is not prosperity, nor dominion, but self-giving service for others. He who would be the greatest in the kingdom of the crucified One would become a servant of all (Mark 10:43). The cross lies at the very heart of the Christian mission to the present world. It is significant in church growth and in crosscultural communication. As John Stott said,

Jesus first took our flesh and then bore our sin. This was a depth of penetration into our world in order to reach us, in comparison with which our little attempts to reach people seem amateur and shallow. The cross calls us to a much more radical and costly kind of evangelism than most churches have begun to consider, let alone experience. [185]

Develop Values Like Those of the Crucified Christ

Paul had many good reasons to take pride in his fleshly righteousness: "circumcised on the eighth day, of the people of Israel, of the tribe of Benjamin, a Hebrew of Hebrews, in regard to the law a Pharisee; as for zeal, persecuting the church; as for legalistic righteousness, faultless" (Phil. 3:5–6). But having received the righteousness that comes through faith in the crucified Messiah, he considered all that to be loss compared to the surpassing greatness of knowing Christ Jesus his Lord (vv. 7–9). Grateful for the gift of right standing with God, Paul said, "I want to know Christ and the power of his resurrection and the fellowship of sharing in his sufferings, becoming like him in his death" (v. 10).

In the quest for self-esteem, fallen humans need to remember that Christ was crucified by people who were conscientiously moral and religious. Sinners may have some elements of truth about God and morality from universal revelation that serve as points of contact, but, like members of Alcoholics Anonymous, all of us as sinners must look beyond ourselves and admit that divine help is needed if we are to be transformed. "Our self-confidence must be shattered so that amidst the wreckage of our self-esteem we may discover the means by which we may rebuild our understanding of God and ourselves. The cross forces us to a point where we concede our inadequacies and turn instead to God."[186] Even more succinctly, "the cross represents an act of God which is simultaneously annihilating and creative—it destroys our (fleshly) preconceptions of God and in their place allows the living God to make his entrance. The cross places a question mark against all our (fleshly) values"[187] According to our fleshly nature, we expect God to endorse our moral and religious insights, but instead at the cross God shatters them and exposes them for the caricatures that they are.

A theology of the cross humbly sees things as they are in the sight of God's revelation of himself in Christ. "Your attitude should be the same as that of Christ Jesus" (Phil. 2:5). Jesus did not cling to his equality with God, but made himself nothing, becoming a human and a servant who obeyed until death, even death on a cross (vv. 6–8). In humility God's Son faced the realities of human life. He exposed our fleshly origins, named our conduct sin, and exposed us as the slaves we are to it. He left the self-righteous hearts open to the light of truth. But then he died in our place. The incarnate life of the Logos was completed as it was offered up on the cross. Have you found life through death? Strength through weakness? Hope through despair?

By our sufferings for the crucified and risen Christ we do not add any merit to his provisions, but we exhibit our highest loyalty. To large crowds Jesus said, "If anyone comes to me and does not hate his father and mother, his wife and children, his brothers and sisters—yes, even his own life—he cannot be my disciple" (Luke 14:26). In a growing series of confrontations with the Pharisees and attorneys, Jesus castigated them for their fanatic adherence to the letter of the law while denying its heart—justice and love. Then he asked those who continued to follow him against the legalistic establishment whether they would follow when it meant putting his kingdom of justice and love ahead of their usual respect, honor, and love of relatives.

A South African pastor explained that Jesus did not mean literal hatred of close relatives, but that

> while we love them we must realize that love for the Messiah, obedience to the Messiah, comes before and above all. It is to know that a time may come when all other obedience must give way to that obedience, when all other commitments must give way to that ultimate commitment. Nothing, not love of father, mother, wife or children, brother or sister, or even one's own life, must then stand in the way of that obedience.[188]

After alluding to a revealed plan to assassinate him and Bishop Tutu, Allan Boesak added:

> If they kill us, I want you to know: it is not because we have picked up a gun. It is not because we hated them. . . . If they kill us it is not because we have planned revolution. It will be because we have tried to stand up for justice, because we have refused to accept the cheap "reconciliation" which covers up evil, which denies justice, and which compromises the God-given dignity of black people. It will be because we love them so much that we refuse to allow them to continue to be our oppressors.[189]

In that spirit Christians can oppose racism wherever it is found without endorsing either communism's truncated materialistic diagnosis of human need or its economic determinism for a prescription.

Relate to God Boldly Through the Great High Priest

Christ's interrelated and divinely commissioned servant ministries have been viewed as primarily threefold. In the previous chapter on the God-man's life we emphasized his role as the greatest of prophets, but we also mentioned his qualifications as mediator. In this chapter on his death we stress his ministry as the greatest of all high priests. In the next chapter on his resurrection and ascension we will meditate further on his ministry as King, King of kings, and Lord of lords. Thinking about these roles as "ministries" for sinners seems more fitting than the traditional three "offices," though Christ held these official positions by the Father's commission. To avoid making the three aspects of Christ's mission unrelated to each other, Erickson calls them the three "functions" of revealing, reconciling and ruling.[190] Indeed they are all interdependent functions for our sakes and no one would have succeeded without the others. But Berkouwer goes too far in speaking of Christ's "office" (singular).[191] As loving functions for the sake of others, they may be fittingly called ministries, or "servant ministries" as of prophet, priest, and king.

Keeping in mind the interrelationships of Christ's work as prophet, priest, and king, we now consider Christ's distinctive ministry as the greatest of all high priests who offered the sacrifice to end all sacrifices.

1. Jesus Christ ministers as our high priest *in the heavenly sanctuary itself.* Under the old covenant the high priest only once a year on the Day of Atonement entered the temporal replica of the Holy of Holies behind the curtain in the tabernacle to pour the blood of the sacrifice on the mercy seat. The high priest did not have direct access to the immediate presence of God in heaven, and only once a year could enter its earthly symbol. But when Jesus died, "the curtain in the temple was torn in two" (Luke 23:45), portraying the opening of the way directly to God. "For Christ did not enter a man-made sanctuary that was only a copy of the true one; he entered heaven itself, now to appear for us in God's presence" (Heb. 9:24).

2. To the heavenly Father Christ offers his *once-for-all sacrifice for all our sins*. Year after year the Old Testament priests had to offer animal sacrifices which could not make sinners perfect (Heb. 10:1–3). It was impossible for the blood of bulls and goats to take away sins (v. 4). Jesus Christ became not only our priest but also our sacrifice. By the will of God the Father, Jesus Christ sacrificed his body once-for-all (v. 10). The sacrifice need not be repeated year after year "because by one sacrifice he has made perfect forever those who are being made holy" (v. 14). The blood of bulls and goats made recipients ceremonially and outwardly clean (9:13), but "how much more, then, will the blood of Christ, who through the eternal Spirit offered himself unblemished to God, cleanse our consciences from acts that lead to death, so that we may serve the living God!" (v. 14).

3. Our high priest is *empathetic*. He understands our deepest spiritual agony better than any other priest. When we suffer without cause, we may think that we have been forsaken by others and even by God. Sometimes we think no one cares. Like the psalmist, we may question whether God is with us here and now. At times the heavens seem like brass. God appears to take away blessings previously given. But those who cry out to God in suffering echo the death-cry of the Savior. He felt, more deeply than any of us can, the agony of being God-forsaken. So "we do not have a high priest who is unable to sympathize with our weaknesses, but we have one who has been tempted in every way, just as we are—yet was without sin. Let us then approach the throne of grace with confidence, so that we may receive mercy and find grace to help us in our time of need" (Heb. 4:14–16).

4. *In heaven Christ intercedes for us, as imperfect people*. The suffering servant, Isaiah perceived, not only "bore the sin of many" but also "made intercession for the transgressors" (Isa. 53:12). On earth he interceded for the unbelievers who crucified him: "Father, forgive them, for they do not know what they are doing" (Luke 23:34). And he intereceded in special ways for believers (John 17). In heaven Jesus "always lives to intercede for them" (those who come to God through him) (Heb. 7:25). John writes his first epistle so that his readers will not sin. "But if anybody does sin, we have one who speaks to the Father in our defense—Jesus Christ, the Righteous One. He is the atoning sacrifice for our sins, and not only for ours but also for the sins of the whole world" (1 John 2:1–2).

5. *The Messiah's atonement for our sins is complete and permanent*. Like Melchizedek, Jesus is "one who has become a priest not on the basis of a regulation as to his ancestry but on the basis of the power of an indestructible life" (Heb. 7:16). On the word of the Father Jesus is a priest forever (vv. 17, 21). His eternal ministry on behalf of his people assures a better covenant (v. 22). Death prevented other priests from continuing in office, "but because Jesus lives forever, he has a permanent priesthood" (v. 24). "Therefore he is able to save completely those who come to God through him, because he always lives to intercede for them" (v. 25).

6. Christ's atonement makes possible in history *the priesthood of every believer*. On the basis of Christ's atonement all of us can come directly to the Most High for ourselves and others. "Therefore, brothers, since we have confidence to enter the Most Holy Place by the blood of Jesus, by a new and living way opened for us through the curtain, that is, his body, and since we have a great priest over the house of God, let us draw near to God with a sincere heart in full assurance of faith"

(Heb. 10:19–22). Because we have committed sins against the holy God, human priests or good works will never suffice to allow us to approach God himself. From the absolutely holy One we can receive forgiveness on the ground of Christ's completed atonement as often as needed. The priesthood of believers means that none need approach the Almighty through a hierarchy of human priests or a series of alleged Gnostic or theosophical spiritual masters as intermediaries. Only One is our spiritual master (Matt. 23:8–10). And we may approach the supreme Being in heaven itself through Christ directly!

Present the Crucifixion to Children With Care

Truth about the death of Christ is essential for everyone who becomes a Christian, but is not the first doctrine to present to children or adults unacquainted with Christianity. The constructive nurture of our children begins with parental exhibits of fairness for all people and loving and dependable provisions to meet their needs. Against that background we can teach very young children about the Creator and sustainer of all, who is fair to all and wants us to be fair to all. Children also need to learn that people with loving care for them also teach them to avoid physical and moral dangers to their well-being. So caring parents and teachers prepare their children to live in a world where moral evil is very real.

Even the children of the most godly parents are born of the flesh and must learn about the subtleties of temptations, the complexities of their motivations, and their propensity toward sin for its own sake. They will learn about evil in the neighborhood and school, from the cartoons and comics, and through the entertainment and news media. Since they cannot be sheltered

from the reality of fallenness, they can learn of the ambiguities and moral culpability of even the heroes of biblical history. From the Scriptures we ought to give them good reasons for rejecting temptations to sin. When children at their different stages come to moral accountability, they may sometimes intentionally hurt others, themselves, and God. They need to know that as much as they desire to please parents and teachers, they will do wrong. When they are old enough to realize their guilt before divine standards, they need more than further nurture in theism and morality. Children old enough to sin knowingly are old enough to hear the gospel of Christ. Loving nurture can show the need for the Messiah, but it cannot displace the necessity for receiving him.

Christians ought to tell their children and grandchildren that God cared enough for them as sinners to send his only Son as a baby. Parents and teachers ought to let children know about the life of Jesus, the supreme revelation of God. "Looking to the Gospels," James Denney observed, "we cannot fail to see that our Lord allowed His disciples every opportunity to become acquainted with Him, and to grow into confidence in Him before He began to teach them about His death."[192] In loving ways parents can help children to prize Jesus Christ, the example of faithful love, righteousness, mercy, and truth. When children understand at their levels of ability that Jesus was not only fair, but also merciful and loving to the undeserving, they are in a better position to understand the significance of his death.

Loving teaching about Christ's death for sinners reveals to young people both the consequence of sin and the cost of redemption from it. At their level of development, children can learn that by faith in the Christ who died and rose they can be forgiven of their guilt before

God's law. They can learn also to trust the crucified one for ability not to commit those sins again. And they can trust Christ for the turning away of God's righteous wrath and for reconciliation to God and others. Children can believe Christ's promises and receive eternal life. But they ought not be coerced or programed into believing by parental or peer pressures. Children need to develop their own convictions and present themselves to God by faith in the Messiah who died for them. Ultimately, their faith must be their own. When children are ready to commit themselves to the Savior, parents should not stand in their way. After their public profession of faith, parents and church leaders need to provide adequate training for their spiritual growth at each stage of their development.[193]

The more one loves, every parent knows, the more one is open to both happiness and sorrow. The more we love our children (and others), the more vulnerable we become to sorrow and disappointment at their hurts and losses. Both the Father and the Son loved greatly, and so throughout Jesus' life of temptation and agonizing death both suffered greatly. Because Father and Son are moved with a feeling of human infirmities, they are afflicted in all the afflictions of parents. Living for Christ is not one glorious television image of "success" with a dazzling flow of words and dollars. Commitment to the suffering servant calls for faithfulness while suffering in this world for his sake. Both parents and children need to view the Christian life with some realism.

Communicate the Message of the Cross Lovingly and Clearly

Any witness to the gospel must be given in love, and certainly love ought to be the primary motivation when working with pre-Christians of any age. Christ lovingly identified with those who were different and demonstrated a solidarity with those who were alien. "While we were still sinners, Christ died for us" (Rom. 5:8). Only in the practical form of love for others in the faith and outside it can Christians bear faithful witness to the One who laid down his life for those he loved. A loving spirit, however, is no substitute for the true story of Christ's death for our sins. As James Denney said,

> To preach the love of God out of relation to the death of Christ, or to preach the love of God in the death of Christ but without being able to relate it to sin, or to preach the forgiveness of sins as the free gift of God's love while the death of Christ has no special significance assigned to it, is not, if the New Testament is the rule and standard of Christianity, to preach the Gospel at all.[194]

Is it not enough lovingly to live for Christ? Some unbelieving spouses may indeed be won without a word by their mate (1 Peter 3:1–2). But no doubt they have heard the gospel from other sources. Generally we need to report the fact of the cross and explain its significance because our lives with their best deeds can be interpreted in many conflicting ways. Sinners must hear that God's Son came into the world and offered his sinless life as a sacrifice for their justification, redemption, and reconciliation. It is not, as Karl Barth claimed, that all are already reconciled to God and need only be informed of this prior fact. That Barthian view robs preaching the gospel of its urgency. For the provisions of the cross to become effective individuals must hear about them and personally receive them. "And how can they believe in the one of whom they have not heard? And how can they hear without someone preaching to them?" (Rom. 10:14). Essential to Christian communication with non-

Christians should be the good news of Christ's atoning provisions!

To preach the cross is not just to tell a story, dramatic and meaningful as stories and myths from different religions may be. To preach the cross is not even to tell this particular story as one among many moving religious stories. To preach the cross is to stand as a sworn "witness" to *this story's truth*. The Gospel, as Paul summed it up, contains assertions tested and found to be true as either historically observed facts or their divinely revealed meanings (1 Cor. 15:1–4). Which *facts* do we report in giving out the gospel? Jesus actually lived, died, was buried, and rose again from the grave. What are the *meanings* of these events included in the communication of the gospel? First, we ought to explain that these events occurred "according to the Scriptures," that is, in fulfillment of true predictions God's prophets made in his written Word. This assumes the plan of a personal God distinct from the world (Heb. 11:6) who has revealed truth to chosen spokesmen and inspired the prophetic writings. Second, proclaimers of the gospel affirm that in fulfillment of those trustworthy writings Jesus is the Christ, that is, the Lord from heaven, the promised Messiah. Third, preachers of the gospel declare that the Messiah died "for our sins." Fourth, they affirm that on the third day, Christ rose again from the dead.

The gospel is not about the human search for God, or human efforts for social justice; the good news reports God's merciful and gracious substitutionary action in Christ to save sinful people. The good news is not what we must do for Christ, but what Christ has done for us! We have shown that belief in the gospel greatly affects the relationships of the reconciled with others socially. But the social effects in human relationships and works are the fruit; the gospel message of the cross as the just basis of reconciliation is the root. Nontechnical passages of Scripture referring to the gospel do not always explicitly distinguish the message from the results of receiving it, but careful preaching and teaching do. Distinctively Christian reconciliation in society results from believing the great news of Christ's substitutionary sacrifice as its just and unifying basis. But the uncompleted responsibilities of creatures (as indicated in the law) ought never be confused with the gospel (the completed work of Christ). Those who want to make the social requirements of the law part of the gospel tragically turn it into bad news. No believers can fully live up to the commandments Christ gave his followers every day of their lives. The law is bad news not only to the unregenerate but also for the regenerate who continue to struggle with the flesh. The gospel is good news that does not focus on what we ought to do for Christ, but what our substitute has done once-for-all for us. Having received the crucified and risen Christ, however, Holy Spirit-enabled Christians do substantially fulfill the law (Rom. 8:3–4).

Give Priority to the Gospel in Your Teaching

The truths of the gospel lead our hearers away from false messiahs and to the One who can save them. By believing the truth of this message and receiving the provisions of the cross people receive eternal life and fellowship with the living God. So the facts and meanings of the gospel ought to take priority in all our oral and written communications with pre-Christians. By Paul's exaggerated statement "I resolved to know nothing while I was with you except Jesus Christ and him crucified" (1 Cor. 2:2), he asserts the central place of the atonement in Christian ministry.

To give priority to any other message

is to become cultic. In a theological context a cult is "a religious movement which claims authorization by Christ and the Bible but neglects or distorts the Gospel, the central message of the Savior and the Scripture."[195] Information about Christ's atonement is essential and central to genuinely Christian ministries. As Bernard Ramm wrote,

A cult is a religious group which places a secondary need in the position of a primary need. Any group which puts its emphasis on health, or mental hygiene, or some religio-political program is cultic. The chief enemies of man are sin and death (1 Cor. 15), and the divine remedy is Jesus Christ crucified and risen from the dead. This is the first witness of the Bible (2 Tim. 3:15). If the cultists heard the Holy Spirit, they would hear this message. The fact that they do not so speak indicates that they do not hear the voice of the Spirit, which in turn means that they have an improper principle of religious authority.[196]

In the Old Testament the foreshadowing of Christ's atonement is central. In the Gospels the incarnation, sinless life, and death in place of others stand out above all else. The New Testament epistles expound on the significance of the cross as the foundation for all the work of the church with insiders and outsiders. According to Revelation, throughout eternity we will praise the Lamb that was slain. The great confessions and creedal statements of God's people feature the centrality of Christ's atonement. Can any who consider themselves moral and spiritual children of God by receiving Jesus as the Christ focus on a higher priority for both time and eternity?

The church "must learn that external criteria of relevance imposed upon it by society should give way to its inner criterion of relevance and identity—the cross and resurrection of Jesus Christ."[197] Again, it is imperative "that the church bases her understanding of the manner in which power is to be exercised upon a God-given, rather than a secular model."[198] In engaging the forces of evil as Christ did, the church needs to "regain a sense of perspective and a sense of *excitement,* of having something exhilarating to say, as we return to face the world."[199]

REVIEW QUESTIONS

To Help Relate and Apply Each Section in This Chapter

1. *Briefly state the classical problem* this chapter addresses and indicate reasons why genuine inquiry into it is important for your worldview and your existence personally and socially.

2. *Objectively summarize the influential answers* given to this problem in history as hypotheses to be tested. Be able to compare and contrast their real similarities and differences (not merely verbal similarities or differences).

3. *Highlight the primary biblical evidence* on which to decide among views—evidence found in the relevant teachings of the major divisions of Scripture—and decide for yourself which historical hypothesis (or synthesis of historical views) provides the most consistent and adequate account of the primary biblical data.

4. *Formulate in your own words your doctrinal conviction* in a logically consistent and adequate way, organizing your conclusions in ways you can explain clearly, support biblically, and communicate effectively to your spouse, children, friends, Bible class, or congregation.

5. *Defend your view* as you would to adherents of the alternative views, showing that the other views are logically less consistent and factually faced with more difficulties than your view in accounting for the givens, not only of

433

special revelation but also of human experience in general.

6. *Explore the differences the viability of your conviction can make in your life*. Then test your understanding of the viability of your view by asking, "Can I live by it authentically (unhypocritically) in relation to God and to others in my family, church, vocation, neighborhood, city, nation, and world?"

MINISTRY PROJECTS

To Help Communicate This Doctrine in Christian Service

1. *Memorize one major verse or passage* that in its context teaches the heart of this doctrine and may serve as a text from which to preach, teach, or lead small-group studies on the topic. The memorized passages from each chapter will build a body of content useful also for meditation and reference in informal discussions.

2. *Formulate the major idea of the doctrine in one sentence* based on the passage memorized. This idea should be useful as the major thesis of either a lesson for a class (junior high to adult) or a message for a church service.

3. *State the specific purpose or goal of your doctrinal lesson or message*. Your purpose should be more than informative. It should show why Christians need to accept this truth and live by it (unhypocritically). For teaching purposes, list indicators that would show to what extent class members have grasped the truth presented.

4. *Outline your message or lesson in complete sentences*. Indicate how you would support the truth of the doc-

trine's central ideas and its relevance to life and service. Incorporate elements from this chapter's historical, biblical, systematic, apologetic, and practical sections selected according to the value they have for your audience.

5. *List applications of the doctrine* for communicating the difference this conviction makes in life (for sermons, lessons, small-group Bible studies, or family devotional Bible studies). Applications should make clear what the doctrine is, why one needs to know it, and how it will make differences in thinking. Then show how the difference in thought will lead to differences in values, priorities, attitudes, speech, and personal action. Consider also the doctrine's possible significance for family, church, neighborhood, city, regional, and national actions.

6. *Start a file and begin collecting illustrations* of this doctrine's central idea, the points in your outline, and your application.

7. *Write out your own doctrinal statement on this subject in one paragraph* (in half a page or less). To work toward a comprehensive doctrinal statement, collect your formulations based on a study of each chapter of *Integrative Theology*. As your own statement of Christian doctrine grows, you will find it personally strengthening and useful when you are called on for your beliefs in general and when you apply for service with churches, mission boards, and other Christian organizations. Any who seek ordination to Christian ministry will need a comprehensive doctrinal statement that covers the broad scope of theology.

CHAPTER 8

CHRIST'S RESURRECTION, ASCENSION, AND PRESENT EXALTATION

Christ's Resurrection, Ascension, and Present Exaltation

THE PROBLEM: HOW SHALL WE UNDERSTAND THE RESURRECTION OF JESUS, HIS ENTRY INTO HEAVEN, HIS SOVEREIGN RULE OVER THE WORLD, AND HIS INTERCESSORY MINISTRY ON BEHALF OF BELIEVERS?

Classically Christianity has been viewed as a religion of resurrection. This is to say that most authorities scattered in different countries and situations understand the Christian faith as profoundly bound up with the Easter event. Even the avant garde Roman Catholic theologian Hans Küng can affirm: "Without Easter there is no Gospel, . . . no faith, no proclamation, no Church, no worship, no mission in Christendom."[1] But the plethora of challenges to the resurrection in the modern world raises the question whether scientifically oriented people can reasonably accept the resurrection of a dead man some two thousand years ago. Modern science, philosophy, and historiography—based on naturalistic assumptions—pose numerous objections to the Christian belief concerning the resurrection of Jesus from the grave. Thus Christian faith and much

humanistic scholarship clash head-on relative to this crucial tenet of the faith.

The issue of the resurrection relates in important ways to other Christian doctrines. Many regard Christ's resurrection (variously defined) as the fitting conclusion to his descent to earth (chap. 5) and atoning death on the cross (chap. 7). How we understand the resurrection will influence our comprehension of the application of salvation to believers (vol. 3, chaps. 1–4), the nature of the church (vol. 3, chaps. 5–6), and Christ's rule over the world (vol. 3, chaps. 7–9).

In the present chapter we inquire whether reports of the resurrection of Christ from the dead two thousand years ago are historically factual or merely statements of faith. Did the bodily resurrection of Jesus engender the disciples' faith, or did the rekindling of faith in the disciples' hearts give birth to the resurrection stories? Are the accounts of the resurrection in the Gospels and the Epistles coherent, or are they difficult to resolve and thus of questionable validity? If the resurrection be granted as true, we must inquire whether it involved the literal raising of Jesus' body or only the survival of his soul. Greek philosophy anticipated much modern thought with its view of salvation as the liberation of the soul from the shackles of the body. How compelling are the evidences for the raising of Jesus' body from the tomb? Moreover, is the resurrection an event in ordinary history, like Jesus' death on the cross or the conversion of Saul of Tarsus? Or does the resurrection belong to some suprahistorical realm and therefore elude verification by the ordinary methods of historical investigation?

In addition, if Jesus literally rose from the grave, what can be said about the nature or composition of his resurrection body? How shall we understand the relation between Jesus' earthly body and the body of his resurrection? Of primary importance is the theological significance of Christ's bodily resurrection for the Christian scheme of things. Would Christian life and faith remain viable if Christ had not risen from the dead? C. E. M. Joad, a liberal churchman who became a more orthodox Christian, somewhere said that if he were able to interview any person from the past it would be Jesus of Nazareth. and he would ask Jesus the most important question in the world: "Did you or did you not rise from the dead?"

In this chapter we also investigate whether Jesus' ascension to heaven was an actual event in space and time. How compelling is the evidence for Jesus' elevation to heaven? Moreover, what is the significance of the Son's ascension to the Father for the life of the believer? In addition, we inquire into the meaning and significance of Jesus' exaltation to the right hand of God. How shall we understand this event? Furthermore, what is meant by Christ's ministry of heavenly intercession, and what does this activity accomplish for the individual believer and the church? We discuss also whether the exalted Christ performs the work of king in his stage of

exaltation. What does this royal ministry involve? In all these matters we seek to determine the difference faith in the exalted Christ makes for Christian life day by day in the world.

Finally, what light does Christ's resurrection, ascension, and present exaltation shed on the question of the uniqueness of Jesus Christ for salvation? Is the Nazarene the only way to God, or is he but one of several ways, as many modern voices allege?

ALTERNATIVE INTERPRETATIONS IN THE CHURCH

Liberal Denials of the Resurrection

Assuming that at creation God established a religion of nature that was perfect and that no supernatural events disturbed the fixed order of things, deists flatly denied Jesus' resurrection from the grave. Thomas Woolston claimed that the resurrection stories "consist of absurdities, improbabilities and incredibilities."[2] Woolston reiterated Celsus' argument that the resurrection was a deliberate fraud.[3] The disciples either bribed or intoxicated the Roman soldiers, then stole the body from the tomb and pretended that Jesus had risen from the dead. The postresurrection appearances were said to be as reliable as pagan stories of the ghosts of the dead. Peter Annet, in *The Resurrection of Jesus Considered* (1744), also attacked the trustworthiness of the resurrection narratives and claimed that on the cross Jesus did not actually die.

The eighteenth- and nineteenth-century liberal "Lives of Jesus" eliminated all traces of the supernatural from the person of Christ. Writers of the "Lives" offered naturalistic explanations for the Gospel miracles. The most popular interpretation of the resurrection was the swoon theory. According to the Heidelberg theologian H. E. G. Paulus, Jesus fell into a deathlike trance on the cross. But the cool air of the tomb, the aromatic spices, and the earthquake revived him to consciousness. Donning the garments of a gardener (John 20:15), Jesus returned to his disciples and began to teach them. When his strength began to fail, he assembled his followers on the Mount of Olives and blessed them. A cloud moved in to hide Jesus from their sight. Later on the Lord died in obscurity. In his *Life of Jesus* (1864) Schleiermacher likewise argued that Jesus merely lapsed into unconsciousness on the cross and in the cool of the tomb revived and lived for a while among his followers. What came to be known as the resurrection connotes that the believer, animated by Christ's life, achieves perfect union with God. In any case, the essence of true religion is not a dogma, such as the resurrection or ascension; rather, it is the experienced reality of the person's sense of absolute dependence on God. "The right impression of Christ can be, and has been, present in its fullness without a knowledge of these facts."[4]

Others propounded the theft or fraud theory. In *The Goal of Jesus and His Disciples,* published by Lessing in 1778, Reimarus argued that the disciples, discouraged by the failure of Jesus' political mission, conspired to steal his body. After waiting fifty days for the body to decompose, the disciples falsely claimed that Jesus had risen, that he had appeared to them several times, and that he would return in glory to inaugurate his kingdom. O. Holtzmann theorized that Joseph of Arimathea was embarrassed by having a crucified man buried in his family vault. Thus without the knowledge of the disciples, Joseph secretly removed the body of Jesus and buried it in another grave.

Other biographers of Jesus advanced the subjective-vision theory. According to D. F. Strauss, the emotionally distraught disciples hallucinated and "saw" in their minds Jesus risen from the dead. Strauss maintained that the Gospel stories of Jesus' transfiguration, miracles, resurrection, and ascension represent legendary accretions stimulated by "tales" from the Old Testament. By this means Jesus' followers elevated their human teacher into a supernatural Messiah-figure. J. Ernst Renan, in *La Vie de Jesus* (1863), argued that while in a state of profound emotional frenzy Mary Magdalene believed that she saw and heard Jesus in the garden. The poetic Renan wrote of Mary: "O divine hallucination! Her enthusiasm gave to the world a resuscitated God."[5] Like wildfire, Mary's frenzied vision spread to other friends of Jesus. Vision followed upon vision, until all the disciples believed that Jesus was alive. In due course the excitement abated, and the visions ceased to occur.

Theologians such as Fichte, Riggenbach, Keim, and Streeter, unable to affirm Jesus' bodily resurrection, propounded the objective-vision theory. As outlined by Keim, Jesus' spirit survived the death of his body (which slept on in the tomb) and was exalted to the right hand of God. In order to rekindle faith following Calvary, the glorified spirit of Christ appeared to the disciples and communicated with them by a "telegram from heaven." The God-given visions of the exalted Christ were so realistic that the disciples mistook them for a bodily resurrection. Streeter identified the communication as a kind of telepathy and added that the tomb was found empty because an unknown person removed Jesus' body to another place.

Kirsopp Lake, a Harvard theologian, rejects the bodily resurrection of Jesus and suggests that on Easter morning the women visited the wrong grave. When they arrived at an empty tomb, a young man directed their attention to a sealed tomb nearby where Jesus supposedly lay: "He is not here. See the place where they laid him" (Mark 16:6). Frightened and confused, the women fled and told the disciples of the empty tomb, which report encouraged the latter in their belief that they had seen the Lord. Concludes Lake: "The empty tomb is for us doctrinally indefensible, and is historically insufficiently accredited."[6]

Most liberals view Jesus as a human prophet and ethical reformer who labored to advance the kingdom of God. Authorities in the tradition generally rejected the biblical miracles and viewed the Gospel narratives as seriously flawed. Harnack drew a sharp distinction between the "Easter message" of the empty grave and the "Easter faith" that death has been destroyed. Faith must abandon forever the Easter message, for the traditions of the empty tomb and the appearances of Jesus are far from certain historical facts. On the other hand, "the Easter *faith* is the conviction that the crucified one gained a victory over death; that God is just and powerful; that he who is the firstborn among many brethren still lives."[7] Harnack grounds faith, not in historical evidences, such as the alleged empty tomb, nor in human reports, such as Jesus' purported appearances, but in the impression Jesus made on the hearts and minds of the New Testament writers. In fact, Harnack judges that faith has nothing to do with the question of Jesus' bodily resurrection but everything to do with the experienced reality that Jesus is the living Lord. Harnack concludes that the doctrine of Christ's literal resurrection must yield to the existential fact "that death is vanquished, that there is a life eternal."[8] Other liberals, such as Walter Rauschenbusch, W. A. Brown, and Henry Van Dusen focus on the religion of Jesus rather than on dogmas about Jesus. Since most liberals viewed Jesus as a man indwelt by God, traditional doctrines of the bodily resurrection and ascension to heaven were disallowed.

From their philosophical presuppositions, process theologians view the resurrection as the obverse of the incarnation. Whereas the incarnation signifies that God is immanently present in the man Jesus and the world, the resurrection signifies that Jesus is immanently present in God. "It is as meaningful to speak of Jesus raised into God and 'living on' in God as it is to speak of God 'prehended' into and indwelling in—'living' in—Jesus. The first is the supreme instance of resurrection, the second the supreme instance of incarnation."[9]

Process thinkers such as Hartshorne, Hamilton, Griffin, and Mellert assent, not to the objective immortality of Jesus (i.e., his conscious existence beyond death), but to his subjective immortality (i.e., the memory of him in the mind of God). That is, the resurrection is a symbol for the fact that Jesus' thoughts, actions, and experiences have been raised up and incorporated into the reality of God. But Jesus' experiences (as the paradigmatic man) were no different from those of any other human being. "We are indeed, moment by moment, likewise being taken up into the divine nature and 'resurrected' into objective immortality where we become part of the perishable data for future occasions."[10] For process theologians, the resurrection means that the inspiration and genius of a person are "continually being resurrected from the past for the edification of emerging moments of history."[11] Mellert believes that this is particularly true for the great personalities of history, such as Socrates, Buddha, St. Francis, and Jesus. In sum, many process theologians see no conscious life after death and certainly no bodily resurrection of Jesus from the grave.[12]

Neoorthodox Dehistoricizing of the Resurrection

Neoorthodox authorities remove the resurrection of Christ from the realm of verifiable history. Theologians in the tradition claim that the Easter event is not a scientifically demonstrable fact like other events in history, but is a reality to be apprehended solely by faith.

Enlightenment philosopher G. E. Lessing stimulated this emphasis by speaking of "the ugly ditch" that exists between absolute truths and the contingent events of history. Faith rests not on external historical facts, but on the certainty afforded by inner experience. Consequently, Lessing concludes, the New Testament stories of Jesus' resurrection (even if they were reliable) offer no viable basis for the absolute truths of religion. More positively, Kierkegaard accepted the miracle of Christ's resurrection.[13] Yet because of the "infinite qualitative difference" between eternity and time, Kierkegaard insisted that the resurrection cannot be grasped by the historical method. Rather, by a radical leap of faith the believer comes to know the power of Christ's resurrection in his life.

The early, dialectical Barth viewed the resurrection not as an historical event but as a symbol of God's revelatory action. Said Barth of the risen Lord: "Within history, Jesus as the Christ can be understood only as problem or myth."[14] For the early Barth the resurrection was a "nonhistorical" event that bears no essential relationship to historical concerns such as the empty tomb and the personal appearances.

In his *Church Dogmatics* Barth spoke more confidently of the resurrection as an objective event in the space-time world. Thus Christ rose from the dead "in the human sphere and in human time, as an actual event within the world with an objective content."[15] Furthermore, Barth views the resurrection as the verdict of the Father on the Son's obedient representation of the human race on the cross. Whereas on Good Friday the "No" of the Father fell on the Son and sinful humanity, on Easter the "Yes" of the Father fell on the Son and all humanity in him. In other words, the resurrection of Christ signifies that on the cross sinful humanity was irrevocably judged and forgiven. Thus, the resurrection "is the justification of all sinful men, whose death was decided in this event."[16] By such a line of reasoning Barth relates the resurrection to the notion of universal salvation.

Yet Barth adds that because of the presence of "obscurities and irreconcilable contradictions"[17] in the resurrection narratives a coherent account of the Easter event cannot be reconstructed. The mature Barth continued to deny that the resurrection can be validated by modern scientific or historical investigation. Whereas the wars of Caesar and even Jesus' crucifixion can be thought of as historical, the resurrection cannot. Seeking to shelter this extraordinary act of God from historical criticism, Barth judges the resurrection to be the same genre as Genesis 1 and 2— namely, "saga," "legend," and "a 'prehistorical' happening."[18] Said Barth of the Easter accounts: "the stories are couched in the imaginative, poetic style of historical saga, and are therefore marked by the corresponding obscurity. For they are describing an event beyond the reach of historical research or depiction."[19] Barth thinks that the historian, with his critical methods, can neither refute nor confirm the empty tomb and the postresurrection appearances to the disciples.

Furthermore, Barth denies that the ascension was an actual elevation in space observable to the disciples. Not a verifiable event in history, the ascension is "a legend," "a sign of the Easter event," or "a *pointer* to the revelation that occurred in the resurrection of Jesus Christ as the bearer of all power in heaven and earth."[20] The ascension was the last and the most concrete of all the appearances of the Risen Lord.

Emil Brunner identifies the resurrection of Christ as the cornerstone of the Christian faith: "The message of Easter is the Christian message, and the Christian Church is the Church of the Resurrection."[21] Yet like Barth, Brunner refuses to view the resurrection as an event of ordinary history. Following Kierkegaard, who permitted no direct identity between revelation and history, Brunner posits the resurrection as an event of primal history (*Urgeschichte*) that must be differentiated from ordinary history (*Historie*). "It is suprahistory, eschatological history, hence it is no longer historical at all."[22] Brunner judges that the situation would be precarious if faith rested on inconsistencies and legends in the Gospel narratives. Christian faith never arises out of historical data such as the empty tomb or the postresurrection appearances. Rather, for Brunner, faith rests on the proclamation of the apostles who experienced the resurrection as fact. Said Brunner: "In faith we are not concerned with the Jesus of history, as historical science sees Him, but with the Jesus Christ of personal testimony, who is the real Christ."[23] Since the resurrection is an event of primal history, Brunner is reluctant to affirm that Christ rose from the grave on the third day literally and bodily. The language of the bodily resurrection connotes the continuity of Christ's personality and individuality in his supramundane existence.[24] For the same reason, Brunner denies the historical actuality of Christ's bodily ascension to heaven. Spiritually interpreted, the exaltation and ascension signify Christ's "return

to the pure transcendence of his prehistorical existence."[25]

For Dietrich Bonhoeffer Christ's glorious resurrection from the dead represents God's "Yes" to Christ and his work, to the believer, and to all that God has made. Faith in the resurrection, however, is not bound up with historical concerns such as the empty tomb. If the resurrection could be verified by history, it would render faith superfluous. Bonhoeffer's bottom line concerning the resurrection is that "we cannot be sure of its historicity."[26] The reality of the resurrection is existentially certified through faith in the apostolic testimony to Christ. Since Bonhoeffer views the entire life of Christ as a stumbling block to reason, he is not surprised that the Lord should depart from this world *incognito*.

Bultmannian Demythologizing of the Resurrection

Whereas neoorthodoxy claimed that the resurrection could not be historically verified, the Bultmannian school more radically viewed bodily resurrection from the dead as an untenable prescientific notion. Bultmann's view of the resurrection was shaped by three principal factors: (1) Form criticism, which examines the oral traditions that undergird the written documents, led Bultmann to conclude that all that can be known about Jesus is that he existed and was crucified under Pontius Pilate. (2) His naturalistic view of history posited a nexus of cause and effect in a closed system. Consequently all alleged miracles, including the resurrection, cannot be accepted as historical events (*Historie*). Bultmann maintains that "an historical fact which involves a resurrection from the dead is utterly inconceivable!"[27] (3) Existentialist philosophy led him to conclude that the New Testament focuses, not on the objective facts of history (such as the bodily resurrection), but on the meaning of the resurrection for personal existence (*Geschichte*).

Thus Bultmann declares that "the resurrection is not an event of past history,"[28] but a Hellenistic cult-myth that found its way into the New Testament. From our modern, scientific perspective we must demythologize the resurrection story, that is, reinterpret it in terms of the possibilities of human existence. For the disciples the resurrection signified the rise of faith in the crucified Lord. As Jesus' followers reflected on his message, his example, and the significance of his death on the cross, they were moved to forsake their old way of life and embrace the new life of victory over sin and death. For Bultmann the resurrection is not an event that happened to Jesus, but one that happened to the disciples. The Marburg theologian thus reduced the Easter *event* to the Easter *faith* of the disciples. Moreover, the risen Christ comes to people today through the call to decision and authentic existence mediated by Christian preaching. This means for Bultmann that Christ is risen in the event of gospel proclamation, which is to say that the eschatological "now" has arrived. Affirms Bultmann: "Christ meets us in the preaching as one crucified and risen. . . . The faith of Easter is just this—faith in the word of preaching."[29] But if Christ's resurrection signifies no more than the rise of faith, where did the notion of a bodily resurrection come from? The early Bultmann suggested that this untenable corporeal view arose from subjective visions prompted by the disciples' intimate relation to Jesus during his lifetime. The later Bultmann appears to have vacillated on this matter. "How the Easter faith arose in the individual disciples has been obscured in the tradition by legend and is not of basic importance."[30]

An influential group of Bultmann's students and followers—such as Ernst Käsemann, Günther Bornkamm, Ernst Fuchs, Hans Conzelmann, Willi Marxen, and James Robinson—have pursued "the new quest for the historical Jesus." Committed to a critical reevaluation of Bultmann, the "new questers" seek to establish continuity between the historical Jesus and the kerygma of the early church. These scholars believe that identity between the earthly Jesus and the exalted Christ must be preserved lest the Easter faith collapse into pure myth. In their studies they ground the Christian message in Jesus' self-understanding or his teaching. Yet given their positivistic view of history and their antipathy to the miraculous, the "new questers" appear no more willing than Bultmann to affirm Jesus' bodily resurrection from the dead.

Günther Bornkamm believes that the Gospels are products of the faith of the Christian community. Consequently what the historian can know is not the Easter event itself but the Easter faith of the disciples. "The event of Christ's resurrection from the dead [is] removed from historical scholarship. History cannot ascertain and establish conclusively the facts about them as it can with other events of the past. The last historical fact available to them is the Easter faith of the first disciples."[31] The significant datum is that the disciples *believed* that Jesus had risen from the dead. What gave rise to their Easter faith was the revelation of Jesus' transcendent selfhood to their hearts and minds. Later the church preserved the faith of the disciples in the form of the Easter stories, including the legends of the empty tomb and the bodily appearances. Bornkamm judges that the resurrection narratives exclude the possibility of an actual corporeal resurrection of Jesus.

Willi Marxen affirms that the basis of Christology is not the post-Easter kerygma but Jesus' ministry and summons to faith. The closest one can get to the resurrection is the event of Simon Peter's faith. But the fact that Jesus calls forth faith from people, even after his death, represents the real miracle. Declares Marxen, "The miracle [of the resurrection] is the birth of faith."[32] That Jesus evokes faith even after his physical death means that the activity of Jesus in the world continues. The early Christians expressed this conviction by means of the saying "Jesus is risen!" Clearly Marxen does not believe that the resurrection was an actual event in space and time. Rather, the resurrection is a vivid pictorial image for the miraculous nature of the faith found in the lives of people even after Jesus' death. The faith Marxen envisages is commitment in response to a call—a faith that would be weakened by appeal to historical evidences. Marxen's thesis that the recorded teachings of Jesus evoke faith in the form of radical commitment does not require the survival of Jesus beyond the grave.

Influenced by logical empiricism's affirmation of the meaninglessness of anything not accessible to the five senses, Paul van Buren draws the sweeping conclusion that theological statements are invalid in a secular age. Whereas the empty tomb can be empirically verified, the claim that the invisible God raised Christ from the dead cannot be so validated. Van Buren maintains that "we would prefer not to speak of the Easter event as a 'fact' at all, not in the ordinary use of the word."[33] The radical postcrucifixion change in the disciples provides a clue to the resurrection. Precisely what happened to the disciples is not open to historical investigation. But on Easter Sunday "a situation of discernment" occurred, which is to say that "the light dawned"[34] upon the hearts of Jesus' fearful followers, providing them with a new perspective on life and death. This liberating power had always been in

Jesus; but "on Easter, the freedom of Jesus began to be *contagious*."[35] When the disciples experienced this radical inner transformation, they fabricated the story of Jesus' bodily resurrection from the dead.

Post-Bultmannian Dekerygmatizing of the Resurrection

Scholars to the left of Bultmann complain that the Marburg theologian failed to demythologize consistently and completely. Thus whereas Bultmann believed that everything must be demythologized except the saving event of Jesus Christ, more radical theologians dekerygmatize the faith by claiming that human self-understanding can be achieved without reference to Christ or the gospel. Thus the Swiss theologian Fritz Büri propounds a kind of existential natural theology that has no need of Jesus Christ and his resurrection. The important thing for Büri is that the idea of the Christ is the symbol of love. Similarly, German theologian Herbert Braun argues that the contemporary church must translate the message about Jesus into a more modern metaphor. Accordingly, Braun subsumes the person and work of Jesus under the rubric of human self-understanding. Concerning Jesus' deity and resurrection Braun writes, "In the literal sense in which these terms are used in the New Testament, I cannot accept them."[36]

Schubert Ogden likewise argues that the conditions for authentic existence "can be formulated in complete abstraction from the event of Jesus of Nazareth and all that it specifically imports."[37] Since the view that men and women are in bondage to sin and are powerless to rescue themselves is pure myth, Ogden judges that persons can actualize authentic existence by their own efforts without regard to Christ. "The premise . . . is that man is a genuinely free and responsible being, and therefore his salvation is something that . . . he himself has to decide by his understanding of his existence."[38] Hence the "myth" of Jesus' resurrection possesses no soteriological relevance. So Ogden boldly declares, "If, *per impossibile*, the corpse of a man was actually resuscitated, this would be just as relevant to my salvation as an existing self or person as that the carpenter next door just drove a nail in a two-by-four, or that American technicians have at last been successful in recovering a nose cone that had first been placed in orbit around the earth."[39] Rejecting the traditional distinctions between nature and grace, philosophy and theology, general revelation and special revelation, Ogden claims that what Jesus imparts is available to all people through science and philosophy, particularly existentialist thought. Theology must stress "that God saves man by grace alone in complete freedom from any saving 'work' of the kind traditionally portrayed in the doctrines of the person and work of Christ."[40] Ogden claims that the historic Christian teaching that Christ alone imparts salvation amounts to the heresy of works righteousness denounced by the apostle Paul. For Ogden, then, Jesus Christ and his resurrection from the dead are virtually irrelevant to the human quest for authentic existence.

More recently Ogden emphasizes that Christology must be viable both personally (i.e., existentially) and practically. Thus in *The Point of Christology*[41] Ogden supplements his existential interpretation of Christianity with a new political interpretation that seeks the transformation of the present social order. Whereas Ogden had demythologized and dekerygmatized the faith, he now seeks to "deideologize" Christian belief by interpreting Scripture politically with a view to transforming the basic structures of society.

The Historicism of the Pannenberg School

Pannenberg opposes both the neoorthodox view that relegates the resurrection to the realm of suprahistory and the existentialist view that denies the resurrection any independent reality. Only if the resurrection is a historical fact, Pannenberg argues, does the Christian faith have a stable foundation. In fact, Pannenberg claims that historical research demonstrates to a high degree of probability that God raised Jesus from the dead. "The resurrection of Jesus is an historical event, an event that really happened at that time."[42] Although he holds that the Gospel resurrection narratives are late, legendary, and contradictory, Pannenberg argues that two independent lines of historical evidence confirm the high probability of Jesus' resurrection. The first is the evidence of the empty tomb. Unwilling simply to read off the resurrection from the Gospel accounts, Pannenberg believes that the early Christians satisfied themselves that Jesus' tomb was empty. If the tomb had not been empty, the early church would not have survived as a witnessing community. The second line of evidence focuses on the appearances of the risen Lord to the disciples (1 Cor. 15:1–11). The early date and independent nature of the traditions in the Christian community validate the actual appearances of Jesus to his followers. Pannenberg claims that, rooted in the postexilic Jewish apocalyptic expectation of the end of the world, the resurrection of the dead, and the final judgment, the disciples possessed the language to express Jesus' resurrection from the grave. Pannenberg notes that the term *resurrection* is a metaphor that describes a reality unique to human experience. Jesus' resurrection should be viewed, not as the resuscitation of his former body, but as the emergence of a radically new life in a new body. As for its significance, the resurrection not only confirmed Jesus' claim to divine authority but also served as the principal sign of the irruption of the end of the world in anticipation of the goal of history.

Influenced by the Marxist philosopher Ernst Bloch, Jürgen Moltmann focuses attention on the future and hope. Against Bultmann's existentialism that collapses Christ's resurrection into human self-understanding, Moltmann interprets the resurrection as a unique historical event. "Christianity stands or falls with the reality of the raising of Jesus from the dead by God. In the New Testament there is no faith that does not start a priori with the resurrection of Jesus."[43] Moltmann insists that we cannot talk about the meaning of the resurrection apart from its historical foundation; the resurrection cannot be existentially true and at the same time historically false. Instead of defining the resurrection in terms of the modern positivistic understanding of history, Moltmann requires that we define history in terms of the resurrection. Thus the resurrection of Jesus creates history, where history is the process that presses toward the eschatological goal. "The resurrection is 'a history-making event' in the light of which all other history is illumined, called in question and transformed."[44] More particularly, "The resurrection has set in motion an eschatologically determined process of history, whose goal is the annihilation of death in the victory of the life of the resurrection."[45] Moltmann, however, is vague about the nature of Jesus' resurrection. He judges that the resurrection has no precise analogue to anything in the space-time continuum. "What 'resurrection of the dead' really is and how the rising of Jesus 'actually happened'

is something even the New Testament reports of Easter do not claim to know."[46] Both Jesus' resurrection and his appearances to the disciples belong to eschatological history and are subject to future verification. Accordingly, "the resurrection of Christ is without parallel in the history known to us."[47] By claiming that Jesus' resurrection belongs to eschatological history rather than to world history, Moltmann has made concessions to the thought of Barth.

For Moltmann the significance of the resurrection lies in its future-orientation. Thus (1) the resurrection of the crucified is primarily an event of promise. Jesus' resurrection extends to humankind the promise of life, peace, freedom, and truth. The ultimate promise grounded in Easter is, "I am making everything new!" (Rev. 21:5). (2) The resurrection is the ground of hope. Because Jesus rose from the grave, humankind is filled with hope regarding the resurrection of the body, the annihilation of death, and the coming of the genuinely new. And (3) the resurrection represents a call to action. In anticipation of the end-time transformation, the God of the Exodus and the resurrection summons the church to world-wide mission, including the struggle for justice, freedom, and peace.

Most Fathers, Reformers, and Evangelicals

Against docetist denials of Christ's corporeality, the apostolic fathers firmly upheld the Lord's bodily resurrection from the tomb. Thus Ignatius wrote of Christ: "I know and believe that he was in the flesh even after the resurrection."[48] For Ignatius Christ's resurrection was no less a historical event than his birth and death: "I believe steadfastly in the birth, passion and the resurrection, which took place during the procuratorship of Pontius Pilate."[49] The Lord's resurrection is the guarantee of his divine mission and the resurrection of Christian believers in the last day. Pseudo-Barnabas attests both the Lord's bodily resurrection and his ascension: "Jesus rose from the dead, after which he manifested himself and went up to heaven."[50] Similar is the view of Polycarp of Smyrna: "God raised our Lord Jesus Christ from the dead and gave him glory and a throne on his right hand."[51]

The apologists opposed dualistic Greek philosophy that viewed matter as inherently evil and incapable of attaining immortality. In his essay *On the Resurrection,* Justin Martyr states his conviction about Christ in the form of a question: "Why did he rise in the flesh in which he suffered, unless to show the resurrection of the flesh?"[52] To the objection that Jesus' appearances were mere phantasms and not reality, Justin responded that the disciples fully satisfied themselves of Jesus' bodily resurrection by examining his wounds and eating food with him. Irenaeus testified that on the third day Jesus rose from the grave in the flesh and ascended to the Father in heaven.[53] On the basis of Christ's victory, believers also will rise into the presence of God.

Tertullian observed that among his fellow Christians "belief in the resurrection was firmly settled."[54] Tertullian himself upheld the Latin view that the substance of Jesus' resurrection body was identical to the body of his earthly existence. According to Tertullian, Christ's post-Easter appearances confirm that his resurrection body consisted of the same bones, nerves, and veins that constituted his earthly body. However the nature of the resurrection body be defined, Tertullian insisted on the reality of the Easter event: "If the resurrection of the flesh be denied, that prime article of the faith is shaken."[55] Tertullian's perspective on the nature of Christ's resurrection body was shared by Justin Martyr, Methodius, Jerome, Gregory the Great, and most medieval theologians.

Origen in the East likewise confessed the resurrection and ascension of the Savior in a body.[56] Origen judged that Jesus' disciples could not have persevered in the dangerous task of proclaiming Christ if he had not risen from the grave. Yet from his Alexandrian perspective Origen held that the nature of Jesus' resurrection body was somewhere between the phantom view of the Docetists and Gnostics and the material view of Latin theology.[57] Thus at the resurrection Christ's body did not return to its earthly condition, but was transformed into a spiritual form capable of inhabiting the heavens. Accordingly, Origen writes, not of the resurrection of Christ's flesh, but of the resurrection of his body, which was profoundly spiritual. Origen's view on the nature of Christ's resurrection body was shared by Cyril of Jerusalem, Gregory of Nyssa, and John Chrysostom.

Augustine firmly believed that Christ's bodily resurrection, his heavenly ascension, and his session at the right hand of the Father were attested by Old Testament prophecies, by the reports of faithful eyewitnesses, by the courageous preaching of early Christians threatened with martyrdom, and by the miracles wrought by Jesus' followers. As for acceptance of the resurrection, Augustine testified, "The fact is that the whole world now believes that the earthly body of Christ has been taken up to heaven. Learned and unlearned alike no longer doubt the resurrection of his flesh and his ascension into heaven, while there is but a handful of those who continue to be puzzled."[58] Concerning the nature of the resurrection body, Augustine follows Luke 24:39 and the Western tradition; Christ's heavenly body consists of the same flesh and bones as his earthly body. "I believe that the Lord's body is in heaven in the same condition as it was on earth when he ascended into heaven."[59] Although material in substance, the Lord's body is called spiritual because it is energized by the Holy Spirit and because of its freedom of movement from place to place.

Several early Christian creedal statements attest the historical reality of Christ's bodily resurrection, ascension to heaven, and session at the right hand of the Father. The Apostles' Creed testifies concerning Christ: "The third day He rose again from the dead; He ascended into heaven, and sitteth at the right hand of God the Father Almighty." Since Jesus' birth, crucifixion, and burial immediately preceding clearly are historical, so are the parallel statements concerning his resurrection, ascension, and session. Similar convictions are contained in the Nicene Creed and the Athanasian Creed.

Luther accepted the bodily resurrection of Christ on the basis of Old Testament prophecies, reliable eyewitnesses of the event, and the testimony of true apostles. Said Luther, the resurrection "is the chief article of Christian doctrine. No one who claims to be a Christian . . . may deny that."[60] Agreeable with the Western tradition, Luther upheld the resurrection of the flesh that Jesus possessed during his earthly existence. Moreover, Christ's resurrection is profoundly related to human salvation. By rising from the grave, Christ "has destroyed sin and brought righteousness to light, abolished death and restored life, conquered hell and bestowed on us everlasting glory."[61] Luther advanced a unique theory concerning the ubiquity of Christ's resurrected body. Affirming the intercommunication of divine and human attributes (see chap. 6), Luther concluded that both during his earthly sojourn and after his ascension the body of Christ filled heaven and earth. "The right hand of God" to which Christ is said to have ascended is a symbol for the divine power. Thus "Christ's body is everywhere because the right hand of God is everywhere."[62] Later Lutheran theology likewise affirmed that in the state of exaltation the body of Christ was permanently ubiquitous. According to the Formula of Concord, "Now not only as God, but also as man, he . . . is present to all creatures."[63] Quenstedt maintained that the heavenly Christ "is present to all creatures in the universe with a true, real, substantial and efficacious omnipresence."[64]

Calvin firmly upheld the historicity of Jesus' bodily resurrection. "Scorners will treat as a fairy tale what the Evangelists relate as history."[65] Calvin cites numerous evidences that validate the resurrection as a historical event: (1) the armed Roman guard at the tomb, (2) the inability of the Jews to produce the body, (3) the several appearances of the risen Lord to his followers, (4) the fact that the disciples touched his risen body, (5) the witnesses to his ascension to heaven, and (6) Christ's glorious manifestations to Stephen and Paul. Said Calvin: "To discredit so many authentic evidences is not only disbelief but a depraved and even insane obstinacy."[66] Calvin discusses at length the spiritual benefits of Christ's bodily resurrection. Because the Lord rose from the grave (1) sin, death, and the Devil are conquered; (2) perfect righteousness is procured for believers; (3) the power of his resurrection is manifested in us; (4) believers are seated in heavenly glory with Christ; and (5) Christians are assured of bodily resurrection and immortality. While he did not debate the nature of Christ's resurrection body, Calvin does state that the substance of his heavenly body is the same as that of his earthly body. Moreover, the ascension, for Calvin, means that Christ opened for believers the doors of the heavenly kingdom sealed by Adam's sin.

Furthermore, Christ ministers in heaven as our constant advocate and intercessor before the Father. Against the Lutherans, Calvin rejected the ubiquity of the ascended Christ's human nature. Whereas Christ's body was raised up above the heavens, his spiritual presence and power are with believers always. To the question, Is Christ with us now bodily? Calvin responded, "No. There is on one hand the body raised up into heaven; and there is on the other his virtue which is diffused everywhere."[67] Christ's session at the Father's right hand is a metaphor signifying that he now exercises the government committed to him until the day of judgment. "Christ was invested with lordship over heaven and earth, and solemnly entered into possession of the government committed to him."[68]

The Reformed church's Heidelberg Catechism, Lord's Day XVII (Q. 45), asks how Christ's resurrection benefits believers. The answer (A. 45) reads: "First, by his resurrection he has overcome death, so that he might make us share in the righteousness he won for us by his death. Second, by his power we too are already now resurrected to a new life. Third, Christ's resurrection is a guarantee of our glorious resurrection." Lord's Day XVIII focuses on Christ's ascension to heaven. Question 47 deals with the Savior's promised presence with believers. The reply (A. 47) is "In his human nature Christ is not now on earth; but in his divinity, majesty, grace, and Spirit he is not absent from us for a moment." Question 49 inquires about the benefits Christ's ascension brings to believers. The reply (A. 49) reads, "First, he pleads our cause in heaven in the presence of his Father. Second, we have our own flesh in heaven—a guarantee that Christ our head will take us, his members, to

himself in heaven. Third, he sends his Spirit to us on earth as a further guarantee."

George Eldon Ladd claims, in regard to the resurrection, that historical evidences and faith must harmoniously interact. Faith is not a blind leap into the dark; neither are historical evidences of such a nature as to demand faith from those with positivistic views of the world. "No amount of evidence can persuade a mind that is closed."[69] Whereas Ladd believes that Jesus' resurrection was an event in history, he holds that resurrection to the heavenly realm cannot be established by strict scientific or historical investigation. Yet Ladd maintains that of all the hypotheses, the supposition of Jesus' bodily resurrection most adequately fits the known facts. Thus Jesus' predictions of his death and resurrection, the phenomenon of the empty tomb, the undisturbed grave clothes, the appearances of the Lord to his followers, the disciples' sudden transformation from desolation and fear to being courageous preachers of the resurrection, the conversion of Saul of Tarsus, and the explosive growth of the Christian church corroborate, for those open to the working of God in history, Jesus' bodily resurrection from the dead. "The bodily resurrection of Christ is the only adequate explanation to account for the resurrection faith and the admitted 'historical facts.' "[70]

As for the nature of Jesus' resurrection body, Ladd concludes that his mortal physical body was transformed into a glorified spiritual body suited for the life of the age to come. Thus it is a body animated by the Spirit of God and endowed with marvelous properties unknown to human experience. For Ladd the theological significance of the resurrection is enormous. If Jesus had not risen from the dead, then his victory over his enemies would be an illusion, his message of the kingdom meaning-

449

less, the doctrine of justification a figment of the imagination, the hope of our resurrection a dream, and history would have no meaning, no purpose, and no goal. "If Jesus is not raised, redemptive history ends in the cul-de-sac of a Palestinian grave."[71] Since everything hinges on Jesus' bodily resurrection from the grave, Ladd concludes that "the resurrection may be called the major premise of the early Christian faith."[72]

Other helpful studies on the resurrection include works by W. J. Sparrow-Simpson,[73] M. C. Tenney,[74] and D. P. Fuller.[75]

BIBLICAL TEACHING

Which of the several interpretations with respect to Christ's resurrection and ascension we accept is determined by the teaching of inspired Scripture on the subject. The Bible's evidence must be understood within its own assumptions according to which God is able to perform great signs and wonders at crucial times in regard to his redemptive program (see chap. 2).

Poetry and Wisdom

Luke relates that the risen Christ chided his disciples for failure to understand what was written in the Old Testament about his sufferings and subsequent glorification: "How foolish you are, and how slow of heart to believe all that the prophets have spoken! Did not Christ have to suffer these things and then enter into his glory?" (Luke 24:25–26). Then Jesus added: "This is what is written: The Christ will suffer and rise from the dead on the third day" (24:46). Similarly, Paul cites a piece of early Christian tradition that says Christ "was raised on the third day according to the Scriptures" (1 Cor. 15:4). From the preceding we should expect to find reasonably clear statements concerning

Christ's resurrection on the third day and subsequent glorification in the Old Testament. We consider first Psalm 2:7–9: "I will proclaim the decree of the LORD: He said to me, 'You are my Son; today I have become your Father. Ask of me, and I will make the nations your inheritance, the ends of the earth your possession. You will rule them with an iron scepter; you will dash them to pieces like pottery.'" The immediate focus of this text was the enthronement of David's son in Jerusalem as king. Yet Peter affirms that David's saying "You are my Son; today I have become your Father" finds its ultimate fulfillment in Jesus' resurrection from the grave (Acts 13:33). "The New Testament, revealing God's only-begotten Son as co-eternal with the Father, refers the 'today' of Psalm 2:7 to the incarnate Son's resurrection, when, like a king at his crowning, He was 'designated Son of God in power' (Rom. 1:4; cf. Acts 13:33)."[76] Verses 8–9 of Psalm 2 anticipate the world-wide dominion and victorious reign of the enthroned Messiah (Rev. 19:15; cf. 12:5).

Psalm 16:9–11 provides a clear anticipation of Christ's resurrection from the tomb. The immediate focus of the psalm is David's confidence in the hope of eternal life. But guided by the Spirit, Peter (Acts 2:24–28, 31) and Paul (Acts 13:34–37) testify that David in this psalm predicted the resurrection of Christ from the grave. These texts in Acts prove "that David was thinking and speaking of the death and resurrection of Christ, the events which then constituted the source of his own hope."[77] Psalm 118:22–23 likewise anticipates the resurrection of Christ: "The stone the builders rejected has become the capstone; the LORD has done this, and it is marvelous in our eyes." In historical context these verses describe the procession of Israel's king, priests, and people to the temple at the zenith of the nation's power and influence. But Jesus (Mark 12:10–11) and Peter (Acts 4:10–11) confirm that by these words David anticipated the rejection and triumph of "the stone" who is the Messiah.

Psalm 24:7–10 appears to be a prophetic anticipation of Christ's victorious exaltation to heaven: "Lift up your heads, O you gates; be lifted up, you ancient doors, that the King of glory may come in. . . ." Israel sang this psalm as the ark of the Lord, returning from war, approached the gates of the city (cf. 1 Chron. 15:1–16:3). However, "in its later usage it affirmed the victory achieved by Jesus Christ in death and resurrection and anticipated the ultimate and triumphant Advent of the King."[78] The Christian church traditionally has sung these verses on Ascension Day. Psalm 68:18, written in the same historical context as the previous text, anticipates the ascension of Christ, when he would lead captivity captive and share the spoils of his victory (Eph. 4:8).

The Hebrew king exercised a broad range of executive, legislative, judicial, and military powers. In the Pentateuch Jacob's blessing of Judah (Gen. 49:10) points forward to the advent of the royal Messiah who will rule the nations. An oracle of Balaam refers to royal accomplishments early in the monarchy, but this ultimately refers to the future accomplishments of the Messiah (Num. 24:17). Nathan's prediction that David's dynasty would endure forever through his offspring (2 Sam. 7:13–16) anticipates the messianic King who was both the son of David and the Son of God (cf. Luke 1:32–33).

The Psalter clearly reflects expectation of a royal Messiah. Psalm 2, which depicts the reign of the Davidic king, yet envisages the future "Anointed One" (v. 2), messianic "King" (v. 6), and "Son" (v. 12), who will vanquish the nations and rule over the earth. Psalm 45, a marriage song for a Hebrew monarch, prophetically describes the splendor of the messianic King and his righteous reign. Psalm 72, a Davidic psalm that extols the glory of Solomon's reign, likewise looks forward to the just and universal rule of the royal Messiah. Psalm 110:1 was written on the occasion of the enthronement of David as king in Jerusalem. Since the king functions as God's vice-regent, he is invited to take the place of honor: "The Lord says to my Lord: 'Sit at my right hand until I make your enemies a footstool for your feet.'" Yet Jesus (Matt. 22:44), Peter (Acts 2:34), and the letter to the Hebrews (1:13) look to the future and apply this psalm-text to the ascension, heavenly session, and world-rule of the exalted Christ. Psalm 110:4 indicates that the Messiah's throne is also a priestly throne, and as a royal priest Christ lives forever to mediate between the Father and his people (Heb. 5:6, 10; 6:20; 7:11).

After being severely tried by the Devil and falsely charged by his counselors, Job saw with the eye of faith a "witness" ('ēd), an "advocate" (śāhēd), and an "intercessor" in heaven who pleads his cause before God (Job 16:19–21). "This passionate longing for a heavenly witness on his side strikingly points forward to the Christian thought of 'an advocate with the Father, Jesus Christ the righteous' (1 John 2:1). Here faith is reaching out for a 'God for us.'"[79] We understand this "witness" to be identical with the "Redeemer" (gô'ēl) of Job's confession in 19:25: "I know that my Redeemer lives, and that in the end he will stand upon the earth." Transported to the future, Job contemplates the risen Vindicator or Advocate who faithfully pleads his cause in heaven. "No Christian can read vv. 25–27 without finding the passage a mirror of the one who 'always lives to make intercession' (Heb. 7:25), who has 'brought life and immortality to light through the Gospel' (2 Tim. 1:10).''[80]

Prophetic Literature

After describing the Servant's death as a "guilt offering" (Isa. 53:10a) that justifies many persons (v. 11b), Isaiah states that the Servant "will see his offspring and prolong his days" (v. 10b). That is, after contemplating the spiritual seed who were to gain an inheritance through his death, the Messiah will be revived back to life and live eternally. "Life in 'length of days' acquires unique significance because it is life after death, the life of one resurrected (cf. Rev. 1:8). . . . Not only the cross but also the open tomb is clearly shown in this wonderful prophecy."[81] The contrast in verse 11a between the Servant's experience of soul-suffering and his seeing "the light of life" also suggests resurrection. Verse 12, moreover, prefigures the Servant's priestly ministry of intercession: "he bore the sin of many, and made intercession for the transgressors." The hiphil of *pāga'* means to "entreat" or to "intercede" (cf. Jer. 15:11). The text anticipates Jesus' prayer for his crucifiers (Luke 23:34) as well as his postresurrection intercessory ministry.

In the light of New Testament statements that the Old Testament predicted Christ's resurrection after three days (Luke 24:46; 1 Cor. 15:4), Hosea 6:2 takes on fresh significance: "After two days he will revive us; on the third day he will restore us, that we may live in his presence." Although the immediate focus of this text is the restoration of Israel to the land (cf. v. 1), the reference to the third day prompts the Christian reader to contemplate the resurrection of Christ. Faith comprehends that the Messiah's resurrection from the dead provides the only viable ground for the resurrection of the people of God.[82] To describe the victory

Christ's resurrection wrought over sin and death, Paul quotes from the saying of the Lord in Hosea 13:14: "I will ransom them from the power of the grave; I will redeem them from death. Where O death, are your plagues? Where, O grave, is your destruction?" Furthermore, in the light of Jesus' explicit saying in Matthew 12:40, we conclude that Jonah's incarceration and deliverance from the belly of a whale (Jonah 1:17–2:10) foreshadowed the death and resurrection of Christ. With this judgment many interpreters concur.[83] Jonah's rescue from "the pit" (Jonah 2:6) recalls David's statement about deliverance from the grave (Ps. 16:10), a statement that was applied by Peter in Acts 2:27 to Christ's resurrection. Moreover, Daniel in a night vision saw "one like a son of man, coming with the clouds of heaven. He approached the Ancient of Days and was led into his presence. He was given authority, glory and sovereign power; all peoples, nations and men of every language worshiped him. His dominion is an everlasting dominion that will never pass away" (7:13–14). This appearance of the heavenly son of man (cf. Matt. 26:64; Mark 14:62) before the divine Father and his appointment as universal Judge was possible only on the basis of his resurrection and ascension to the heavenly world.

Isaiah sketched a magnificent portrait of the supernatural birth, impeccable character, and peaceful reign of the royal Messiah (Isa. 2:1–4; 7:14; 11:1–10; 32:1; 33:17; 42:1–7). Jeremiah likewise beheld the "righteous Branch" and Davidic "King" who "will reign wisely and do what is just and right in the land" (Jer. 23:5–6). Daniel in a vision saw that the "son of man" is King of all the earth. So the latter "was given authority, glory and sovereign power; all peoples, nations and men of every language worshiped him. His dominion is an everlasting dominion that will not pass away'' (7:13–14). Ezekiel prophetically contemplated the Messiah serving as a shepherd, prince, and king forever over the restored house of David (34:22–24; 37:24–25). Micah portrayed the Messiah as "one who will be ruler over Israel" (5:2), whereas Zechariah wrote of the coming Davidic prince who would unite in himself the office of ruling king and ministering priest (3:8–9; 6:12–13; 9:9–10).

Synoptic Gospels

Whereas the Gospels were written about one generation after Jesus' death, the traditions concerning his cross and resurrection were transmitted to the evangelists by reliable eyewitnesses. The Gospels indicate that on several occasions Jesus predicted his resurrection from the dead. In Matthew 12:38–40 the teachers of the law and the Pharisees demanded that Jesus provide a miraculous sign that would corroborate his messianic authority. Jesus' response—"none will be given it except the sign of the prophet Jonah" (v. 39; cf. Matt. 16:4)—suggests that confirmation of his messianic authority would be given by his resurrection from the grave as foreshadowed by the Jonah typology. Matthew's statement that the Son of Man would remain in the grave "three days and three nights" (v. 40) does not contradict Jesus' actual stay in the tomb from Friday night to Sunday morning, since Jews reckoned part of a twenty-four hour day as a whole (cf. Matt. 27:63; Mark 8:31, "after three days"; Matt. 16:21; 17:23, "on the third day"). Furthermore, Jesus spoke of his death and resurrection following Peter's confession at Caesarea Philippi (Matt. 16:21; Mark 8:31; Luke 9:22), immediately after his transfiguration (Matt. 17:9; Mark 9:9, where the transfiguration was a direct anticipation of his exaltation and parousia), to the disciples in Galilee (Matt. 17:22–23; Mark 9:31), prior to entering Jerusalem (Matt. 20:19; Mark 10:33–34; Luke 18:32–34), and immediately after the Last Supper (Matt. 26:31–32; Mark 14:27–28). Considered together, these teachings of Jesus indicate that the goal of his life was death and resurrection. Moreover, contrary to popular Jewish expectations of a human Messiah, Jesus recalled Daniel 7:13 and spoke of the session of the Son of Man in the place of highest honor at God's right hand in heaven (Matt. 25:31; 26:64).

After Jesus had been betrayed and arrested, out of fear for their own personal safety "all the disciples deserted him and fled" (Matt. 26:56). The only ones who remained close to Jesus during the last hours were a few women (Mark 15:40–41). We see the reaction of Jesus' friends to his arrest in the experience of a young man who broke free from the grasp of the police and fled naked into the night (Mark 14:51–52). By recording this incident, Mark wished "to emphasize that *all* fled, leaving Jesus alone in the custody of the police. No one remained with Jesus, not even a valiant young man who intended to follow him."[84] Even Peter, who had confidently boasted that he would never disown Jesus (Matt. 26:33–35), later, in the courtyard of Caiaphas vigorously denied three times that he knew Jesus (Matt. 26:69–75; Mark 14:66–72; Luke 22:55–62). Peter's bitter weeping indicates extreme remorse over his lack of fidelity to the Lord.

The Gospels disclose beyond any shadow of doubt that Jesus died on the cross. Jews and Romans scourged, beat, and nailed him to the cross by large nails through his hands and feet. Enduring the excruciating pain of crucifixion for six hours, Jesus remained conscious to the very end. Then he died in agony, with a cry of trust to his heavenly Father. The Roman soldiers did not break Jesus' legs as they did those of the two thieves, because they were convinced that he had already died (John 19:33). Instead, with a spear one of the soldiers pierced Jesus' side, from which flowed blood and water (v. 34). After Joseph's request to obtain the body of Jesus for burial, the centurion reported to Pilate that the Nazarene had died (Mark 15:44–45). Then Joseph and his servants took Jesus' body from the cross, wrapped the corpse tightly with fine linen, placed it in a new tomb, and closed the tomb with a large stone (15:46). Mark relates that "Mary Magdalene and Mary the mother of Joses saw where he was laid" (15:47), thus ruling out the likelihood that the women later went to the wrong tomb. Matthew records an incident that refutes the allegation of the Jews that the disciples stole Jesus' body (Matt. 27:62–66). The chief priests and Pharisees requested of Pilate that a Roman guard be posted at the tomb to insure that the body would not be stolen. "So they went and made the tomb secure by putting a seal on the stone and posting the guard" (v. 66). A later vignette shows the disciples disillusioned and despondent over Jesus' crucifixion. "Their faces downcast" (Luke 24:17), two disciples, walking on the road to Emmaus, admitted, "We had hoped that he was the one who was going to redeem Israel" (v. 21). The disciples regarded Jesus as a conquering Messiah who would free Israel from her enemies (2:38). But when the Lord died a sudden death on the cross, the hopes of his followers died also.

Since the Evangelists describe Jesus' resurrection and subsequent appearances from their unique perspectives, it is not surprising that we have different but harmonious accounts of what actually transpired. We believe that a reasonably accurate synthesis of the Easter events can be made from the Gospel narratives, as follows: Early Easter Sunday morning Mary Magdalene, Mary, and Salome visited the tomb to anoint the body of Jesus with spices. Approaching the place, the women discovered the guards struck unconscious and the stone rolled away from the entrance. Inside the tomb were two angels surrounded with dazzling glory, one of whom said to the women, "Why do you look for the living among the dead? He is not here; he has risen!" (Luke 24:5–6). After this incident was reported to the disciples, Peter and John ran to the tomb. Peter entered the tomb and found it empty and the linen shroud and head cloth neatly wrapped and lying separately (John 20:6–7). Struck by the fact that a thief would not have taken time to unwrap the grave clothes and arrange them neatly, John immediately believed in the Lord's resurrection (John 20:8). Mary Magdalene, thinking that Jesus' body had been stolen, returned to the tomb weeping. Peering inside the tomb, she saw two angels sitting where the body of Jesus had been lying. Suddenly the risen Jesus appeared to Mary, but she did not immediately recognize him. After Jesus tenderly addressed her, Mary recognized the Lord and physically grasped him. Jesus then said to her, "Do not hold on to me [*mē mou haptou*], for I have not yet returned to the Father" (v. 17). *Mē* with the present imperative of *haptomai* signifies that Jesus commanded Mary to cease clinging to his body. Then Jesus told her to report his future ascension to the disciples. Sight and touch persuaded Mary that Jesus had, indeed, risen in a body from the dead (v. 18). Thereafter, when the other Mary and Salome reached the tomb, Jesus disclosed himself to them. They too fell before Jesus and grasped his feet. The Lord ordered them to tell the disciples to meet him in Galilee (Matt. 28:10).

Meanwhile the Roman guard related to the chief priests the extraordinary events that had occurred at the tomb.

The chief priests and elders bribed the guards with a large sum of money to say that the disciples had come by night and stolen Jesus' body (Matt. 28:11–15). In this scene the Roman guards bore testimony to the fact that Jesus had miraculously risen from the grave. Luke 24:34 indicates that the first apostle to encounter the risen Jesus was Simon Peter in the region of Jerusalem (cf. 1 Cor. 15:5). Then Jesus appeared to Cleopas and another disciple on the road to Emmaus, miles from Jerusalem (Luke 24:13–32). Along the way Jesus conversed with the pair, interpreted the Scriptures concerning himself, and shared a meal with them. Then suddenly Jesus disappeared from their sight. When the ten disciples (without Thomas) were gathered behind locked doors discussing these things, Jesus suddenly appeared in their midst and said to them, "Look at my hands and my feet. It is I myself! Touch me and see; a ghost does not have flesh and bones, as you see I have" (Luke 24:39). Then Jesus ate a broiled fish the disciples had given him. The ten related to Thomas this encounter with the risen Lord, but Thomas remained unconvinced that a corpse could return to life. One week later, when the eleven were again gathered behind locked doors, Jesus suddenly appeared in their midst and said to Thomas: "Put your finger here; see my hands. Reach out your hand and put it into my side. Stop doubting and believe!" (John 20:27). Overwhelmed by the sight and touch of Jesus' wounded body, Thomas' skepticism turned to conviction, and he cried out, "My Lord and my God!" (v. 28).

Having gone to Galilee as instructed by the Lord (Matt. 28:10), seven of the disciples were fishing on the lake. Then they saw Jesus on the beach without recognizing him. The risen Lord directed the disciples to a huge catch of fish. This miracle caused John to realize that the stranger was Jesus. On the shore of the lake Jesus took food with the disciples (John 21:1–14). Later Jesus appeared to the eleven on a mountain in Galilee, gave them the Great Commission, and promised to be with them forever (Matt. 28:16–20). Paul's statement that Jesus appeared to more than five hundred of the brothers at one time (1 Cor. 15:6) may refer to the appearance on the mountain, or it may pertain to a different meeting. Back in Jerusalem, Jesus appeared to James the brother of Jesus (v. 7), an encounter that undoubtedly led to James' conversion (cf. John 7:5). At the end of the forty days Jesus instructed his disciples to wait for the enduement of the Holy Spirit that would enable them to witness to him (Luke 24:49; Acts 1:4–8). Then Jesus led his followers to the Mount of Olives and blessed them. Luke the historian writes that "while he was blessing them, he left them and was taken up into heaven" (Luke 24:51; cf. Acts 1:9). Thus from the Mount of Olives, a specific place three-quarters of a mile east of Jerusalem, Jesus physically took leave of his followers and entered the invisible world. Luke adds that two angels, dressed as men in white, assured the disciples that the Lord would return in the same manner that he went up to heaven (Acts 1:11). Thus in this final encounter with his disciples Jesus closely linked his ascension, mission, and parousia. The mission of the glorified Lord must be carried out until he returns from heaven.

With regard to the Synoptic resurrection narratives, the non-evangelical scholar J. A. T. Robinson is impressed by their credibility:

When we turn to the gospels, their evidence on the empty tomb is in substance unanimous. There are, indeed, differences of detail which at times have been given an exaggerated prominence. . . . None of these, however, is the kind of difference that impugns the authenticity of the narrative. Indeed they are all precisely what one would look for in genuine accounts of so confused and confusing a scene. . . . But details of description apart, the basic witness is extraordinarily unanimous. . . . Many in fact will continue to find it easier to believe that the empty tomb produced the disciples' faith than that the disciples' faith produced the empty tomb.[85]

The Gospel writers, particularly Matthew, teach that Jesus was the messianic King. Eastern astrologers, guided to Bethlehem by a star, inquired: "Where is the one who has been born king [*basileus*] of the Jews?" (Matt. 2:2). Prior to his entry into Jerusalem on a donkey Jesus declared that the prophecy of Zechariah 9:9 was about to be fulfilled: "See, your king comes to you, . . . gentle and riding on a donkey" (21:5). Pilate reflected popular convictions when he asked Jesus, "Are you the king of the Jews?" (27:11; cf. Mark 15:2; Luke 23:3). The Lord responded in the affirmative: "Yes, it is as you say [*su legeis*]." As Jesus hung on the cross the Roman soldiers mocked and reviled him: "Hail, king of the Jews!" (v. 29), and the inscription placed over his head read: "THIS IS JESUS, THE KING OF THE JEWS" (v. 37). Jesus himself was conscious of the fact that he was the messianic King (19:28; 22:43–45; 25:31, 34, 40) who would rule over a kingdom. The "kingdom of heaven" (7:21; 13:11) and the "kingdom of God" (Mark 12:34; Luke 17:21) synonymously refer to the redemptive rule of God in Christ that defeats malignant spiritual powers and liberates his people. The Gospels indicate that the kingly rule of the Messiah was realized invisibly and spiritually at his first advent (Matt. 3:2; 12:28–29; Luke 17:21), and will be instituted visibly and materially at his second advent (Matt. 19:28; 25:31, 34, 40; Luke 1:33).

Primitive Christianity/Acts

Luke relates in Acts 1:3 that after his passion Jesus "showed himself to these men and gave many convincing proofs that he was alive." The Greek word for "convincing" (*tekmērion*) in classical Greek meant "strict proof." Thus "Luke intends the events following the appearance of the risen Christ to be treated as infallible evidence."[86] Luke, a careful historian, was convinced that the appearances of the risen Lord to his followers were genuine rather than illusory. In his history Luke records two appearances or revelations of the glorified Lord. The first occurred after Stephen's confession of Christ before the Sanhedrin. "Stephen, full of the Holy Spirit, looked up to heaven and saw the glory of God, and Jesus standing at the right hand of God" (Acts 7:55). That Jesus was standing at the side of the Father attests his ministry of advocacy. "He is standing as advocate to plead Stephen's case before God and to welcome him into God's presence."[87] The second revelation of the ascended Lord was given to Saul, the arch-persecutor of the church, seven years after the Ascension (Acts 9:3–9). Nearing Damascus, Saul was surrounded by a bright light from heaven (the glory of God) that struck him blind for three days. In addition, Saul heard the heavenly Lord speak to him and instruct him what to do. That these were sense phenomena is confirmed by the fact that Saul's companions saw the light and heard the voice (Acts 22:9). "What is beyond question historically is that the fanatical oppressor of the Nazarenes, who left Jerusalem 'breathing threats and murder' (v. 1), entered Damascus mentally shattered and physically blinded and became on his recovery the foremost protagonist of the beliefs he set out to extirpate."[88]

Before ascending to heaven Jesus commanded his followers to wait in

Jerusalem for the descent of the Holy Spirit that would empower them for mission (Acts 1:4–5). As Peter later stated, the Spirit could be given only after Christ had conquered death and ascended to the place of honor at the Father's right hand (2:33). In preparation for that event, Luke depicts the eleven selecting an apostle to replace Judas. The primary qualification of the new apostle was that he must have observed the Lord's life and resurrection (1:21–22a). And the principal task of the newly appointed apostle was that he "must become a witness with us of his resurrection" (v. 22b). Then on the day of Pentecost, as the Father had promised, the Holy Spirit fell on the disciples and empowered them to witness to the risen Christ by their lips and their lives (Acts 2:1–4).

Filled with the Spirit, Peter addressed the crowd of Jews who had gathered in Jerusalem for the festival. The man who had thrice denied his Lord boldly proclaimed that although wicked men had cruelly nailed Christ to a cross, "God raised him from the dead, freeing him from the agony of death, because it was impossible for death to keep its hold on him" (Acts 2:24). Marshall observes that here Peter uses a powerful metaphor: "Death is regarded as being in labor and unable to hold back its child, the Messiah."[89] To substantiate Christ's resurrection Peter quotes from Psalm 16:8–11. In this psalm David wrote about the Messiah not about himself, for after David died, he was buried and suffered corruption. Peter continued the thought by declaring that Christ's resurrection was not merely a revivification but an exaltation to the heavenly realm. To prove this point Peter appealed to Psalm 110:1: "Exalted to the right hand of God, he has received from the Father the promised Holy Spirit" (v. 33). Peter concluded his message by stating, "God has made [epoiēsen] this Jesus, whom

you crucified, both Lord and Christ" (v. 36). Peter offers no adoptionist Christology; rather, he declares that via Jesus' resurrection and ascension God openly declared him to be the Lord, Christ, Prince, and Savior that he truly was (Luke 2:11).

In his second Jerusalem sermon Peter alluded to Isaiah 52:13 by saying, "The God of Abraham, Isaac and Jacob, the God of our fathers, has glorified his servant Jesus'" (Acts 3:13). Then he declared to the Jews: "You killed the author of life, but God raised him from the dead. We are witnesses of this" (v. 15). Brought before the Sanhedrin for teaching the resurrection of the dead in Jesus (Acts 4:2), Peter boldly stated that the One whom the Jews brutally killed "God raised from the dead" (v. 10). After being imprisoned for speaking in the name of Jesus (5:18), Peter and the apostles continued to proclaim the risen Lord: "The God of our fathers raised Jesus from the dead—whom you had killed by hanging him on a tree. God exalted him to his own right hand as Prince and Savior. . . . We are witnesses of these things" (vv. 30–32). Later, in the first sermon to a Gentile audience Peter declared to the household of Cornelius events that were publicly enacted— namely, that Jesus was anointed by the Spirit, worked miracles, was killed by the Jews, and that "God raised him from the dead on the third day and caused him to be seen" (10:37–40). Peter was convinced that Christ's resurrection was as much a verifiable historical event as his earthly deeds and death. Underscoring the belief that Christ's appearances were not mere visions, Peter added that he was seen "by witnesses whom God had already chosen—by us who ate and drank with him after he rose from the dead" (v. 41).

At Pisidian Antioch, in his first major sermon, Paul proclaimed the resurrection of Christ as the heart of his Gospel: "God raised him from the dead, and for many days he was seen by those who had traveled with him from Galilee to Jerusalem" (Acts 13:30–31). The former Jewish rabbi saw Christ's resurrection foreshadowed in Psalm 2:7; Isaiah 55:3; and Psalm 16:10. On Mars Hill in Athens the apostle also preached the Good News of Jesus and his resurrection (17:30–32). Paul argued that Jesus' resurrection constitutes proof that God will judge the living and the dead with justice (v. 31; cf. Acts 10:42). Later, in his defense before the Sanhedrin, Paul precipitated a controversy between the Pharisees and the Sadducees by upholding Christ's resurrection as the guarantee of the general resurrection of the dead (23:6–10). Moreover, in his defense before Festus and Agrippa, Paul related the story of his encounter with the risen Christ near Damascus (26:12–18), which was precisely what Moses and the prophets said would happen (v. 22). Rebutted by Festus as deluded, Paul responded: "What I am saying is true and reasonable [*sōphrosynē*, rational]' " (v. 25). The apostle then emphasized the empirical nature of his case by appealing to factual evidence known to the king (v. 26).

The above data confirms that Christ's resurrection was not only the cornerstone of the Christian faith but also the heart of the apostolic proclamation. The sermons of the early Evangelists reflect a common pattern: in fulfillment of prophetic Scripture David's greater Son was killed by the Jews, was buried, rose again on the third day, was exalted to the right hand of God in heaven as Lord of all, and will return on the last day to judge the living and the dead.

Pauline Literature

The letters of Paul, written less than twenty years after Jesus' death, represent the earliest New Testament documents. During his visit with Peter and James in Jerusalem (Gal. 1:18), Paul received firsthand reports of the events associated with Jesus' final days on earth. The Epistles indicate that the focus of Paul's message was the death and resurrection of Jesus Christ and his exaltation to the right hand of God. Paul recounts his own encounter with the risen Christ on the Damascus road some three years after the resurrection: "God . . . was pleased to reveal his Son in me so that I might preach him among the Gentiles" (vv. 1:15–16). Paul regarded this manifestation of Christ to him as the last of the Lord's postresurrection appearances (1 Cor. 15:8, "last of all"). Paul, moreover, states that that encounter with the risen Lord was a necessary condition for apostleship: "Am I not an apostle? Have I not seen Jesus our Lord?" (1 Cor. 9:1; cf. Gal. 1:1).

Paul records in his letters the earliest Christian confession of faith: "Jesus is Lord!" (1 Cor. 12:3; cf. John 13:13). Lordship signifies Christ's universal dominion by virtue of his resurrection from the dead. The apostle also writes: "If you confess with your mouth, 'Jesus is Lord,' and believe in your heart that God raised him from the dead, you will be saved" (Rom. 10:9). First Corinthians 15:3–5 reflects an early creed much older than the letter itself. Mention of "receiving," the fourfold use of (*kai*) *hoti,* and the non-Pauline vocabulary suggest that Paul cites an early Christian testimony to the resurrection: "For what I received [*parelabon*] I passed on [*paredōka*] to you as of first importance: that Christ died for our sins according to the Scriptures, that he was buried, that he was raised on the third day according to the Scriptures, and that he appeared to Peter, and then to the Twelve." Paul likely added verses 6–8 especially to establish that Christ's resurrection could be verified by living witnesses and secondarily to validate his own apostleship.[90] In Romans 1:3–4 Paul reproduces an early Christological creed that says of David's most eminent offspring: ". . . who through the Spirit of holiness was declared with power to be the Son of God by his resurrection from the dead: Jesus Christ our Lord." The phrase "with power" modifies the aorist passive verb "was declared" (*horisthentos*) and signifies that Christ's bodily resurrection from the grave publicly certified that he is the divine Son of God. The power that openly displayed Christ as the Son of God is "the Spirit of holiness," or the Holy Spirit, the third person of the Godhead. Paul cites an additional Christological creed in 2 Timothy 2:8: "Remember Jesus Christ, raised from the dead, descended from David." The perfect tense of the verb *egeirō* (to "raise") attests the Lord's ongoing state: Christ was raised from the dead and continues to live. The preceding citations of early Christian conviction confirm that "for Paul the resurrection of Christ was the most prominent Christian truth, containing as it does the guarantee of all other aspects of the work of Christ."[91]

In 1 Corinthians 15, the classic text on the resurrection, Paul expounds the negative consequences of denying the Easter event. If Christ is not risen from the grave, then the following prevail: (1) Christian faith and preaching is worthless: "If Christ has not been raised, our preaching [*kērygma*] is useless [*kenos*] and so is your faith" (v. 14). *Kērygma* connotes the content of the preached message, and *kenos* bears the figurative meaning, "without content, basis, truth or power."[92] (2) The apostles then would be false witnesses: "We are then found to be false witnesses about God, for we have testified about God that he raised Christ from the dead" (v. 15). (3) There would be no forgiveness of sins: "Your faith is futile [*mataios*, empty, aimless];

you are still in your sins" (v. 17). (4) The dead in Jesus have perished, and salvation is an illusion: "Then those also who have fallen asleep in Christ are lost" (v. 18). (5) Christians who now endure hardships in hope of the world to come would be objects of special pity: "If only for this life we have hope in Christ, we are to be pitied more than all men" (v. 19). (6) Life is inexplicable, and hedonism proves to be the only option: "If the dead are not raised, 'Let us eat and drink, for tomorrow we die' " (v. 32).

But the apostle asserts that "Christ has indeed been raised from the dead" (v. 20; cf. 2 Cor. 13:4; 1 Thess. 1:10). Whereupon Paul enumerates in his letters many spiritual benefits that accrue to believers on the basis of the Lord's certain resurrection: (1) Christ's resurrection guarantees the justification of his people: "He was delivered over to death for our sins and was raised to life for our justification" (*dikaiōsis*, Rom. 4:25). On Easter sin was put away and righteousness restored to those who believe. (2) The believer now participates in the new quality of life provided by the risen Christ: "Just as Christ was raised from the dead through the glory of the Father, we too may live a new life" (Rom. 6:4; cf. vv. 5, 8). Elsewhere Paul describes the believer as positionally seated with Christ and sharing his resurrection life: "God raised us up with Christ and seated us with him in the heavenly realms in Christ Jesus" (Eph. 2:6; cf. Col. 3:1). "Here it is a symbolic resurrection from the spiritual 'death' brought about by sin into a new quality of life shared with Christ. It describes a spiritual transformation available to the Christian *now* in this life."[93] (3) Christ's resurrection and ascension to heaven result in the bestowal of spiritual gifts to his church (Eph. 4:7–10). "Christ's enthronement over the universe is the guarantee that nothing needful for the church is lacking.''[94] (4) Christians participate in the power of Christ's resurrection for effective service: Paul writes of the Father's "incomparably great power for us who believe. That power is like the working of his mighty strength, which he exerted in Christ when he raised him from the dead and seated him at his right hand in the heavenly realms" (Eph. 1:19–20; cf. Rom. 7:4; Phil. 3:10). (5) Christ's resurrection is the pledge and guarantee of the bodily resurrection of all who belong to him: "By his power God raised the Lord from the dead, and he will raise us also" (1 Cor. 6:14; cf. Rom. 8:11; 1 Cor. 15:21–23; 2 Cor. 4:14; 1 Thess. 4:14). Paul refers to Christ as "the firstfruits of those who have fallen asleep" (1 Cor. 15:20, cf. v. 23) and "the beginning and the firstborn from among the dead" (Col. 1:18). (6) Christ's exaltation to heaven marks a new phase in his kingly rule over the entire universe: "God exalted him to the highest place and gave him the name that is above every name, that at the name of Jesus every knee should bow, in heaven and on earth and under the earth, and every tongue confess that Jesus Christ is Lord" (Phil. 2:9–10; cf. 1 Cor. 15:24–27; Eph. 1:20–22).

Seated at the Father's right hand, Christ exercises a mediatorial ministry on behalf of his people. "For there is one God and one mediator [mesitēs] between God and men, the man Christ Jesus" (1 Tim. 2:5). Paul represents the glorified Christ as the sole intermediary between the Father and humans. The apostle stresses the Savior's humanity because it is the human race he represents. Paul specifies Christ's heavenly ministry of intercession in Romans 8:34: he "is at the right hand of God and is also interceding [entynchanei] for us." The verb entynchanō here bears the figurative sense of "petition," "appeal to," or "entreat."[95] In secular Greek it was used of a person's bringing a petition before a king on behalf of another.[96]

Paul attests the present aspect of Christ's kingship in terms of his rule over the church as "head." So Christ "is the head of the body, the church" (Col. 1:18; cf. Eph. 1:22; 4:15; 5:23; Col. 2:19). The image of "head" (kephalē) connotes that Christ sovereignly rules and governs the community of believers who respond with submission.[97] In this regard the apostle writes of believers entering the kingdom of Christ (Eph. 5:5; Col. 1:13). In addition, Paul observes that Christ functions as Lord of all demonic spiritual agencies that enslave persons (Col. 2:10), both in the present age and in the age to come (Eph. 1:21). In consequence of his obedient death and exaltation, Christ possesses complete authority over all creation (Phil. 2:9–11). As for the future aspect of Christ's kingly rule, Paul writes of Christ's work of judgment (2 Tim. 4:1) and the unleashing of punishment on the unbelieving world (2 Thess. 1:7–10). Moreover, at his second advent believers will be ushered "into the eternal kingdom of our Lord and Savior Jesus Christ" (2 Peter 1:11). Then after Christ has vanquished every evil power he will surrender the kingdom to the Father, that the Father may be all in all (1 Cor. 15:24–28).

Comparing the believer's future body to the resurrected body of the Lord, Paul makes a few observations about the nature of the latter. In contrast with the body of flesh Christ possessed during his humiliation, Paul describes the body of the resurrected Lord as a "glorious body" (sōma tēs doxēs; Phil. 3:21). Moreover, Paul states that "the last Adam [became] a life-giving spirit" (eis pneuma zōopoioun; 1 Cor. 15:45). The apostle means by the latter phrase that the body with which Christ rose from the grave was animated by the Spirit and was thereby fitted for a new mode of existence in the heavenly realm. So Paul refers to that body as a "spiritual body" (*sōma pneumatikon*; v. 44), that is, a body energized not by mortal *psychē* but by immortal *pneuma* with all accompanying glory (cf. 2 Cor. 3:18).

Johannine Literature

The "sign" (*sēmeion*, miracle, pointer, proof) is an important concept in John's gospel. The purpose of the signs Jesus performed was to "prove Jesus' identity as the Christ of God, who brings the fullness of eschatological salvation."[98] Thus John wrote: "Jesus did many other miraculous signs [*sēmeia*] in the presence of his disciples, which are not recorded in this book. But these are written that you may believe that Jesus is the Christ, the Son of God, and that by believing you may have life in his name" (John 20:30–31). Jesus identifies his resurrection from the dead as one of the most important of these signs. When the Jews demanded of him a "miraculous sign" (*sēmeion*) that would prove his divine authority, Jesus responded with the promise: "Destroy this temple, and I will raise it again in three days" (John 2:19; cf. vv. 21–22).

Jesus' statement "I lay down my life that [*hina*] I may take it again" (John 10:17, NASB) suggests that the goal of his life on earth was resurrection from the dead. In order to impart resurrection life to others, Jesus had to die and rise from the grave. Moreover, because Jesus has within himself supernatural resurrection power, he is able to raise the dead on the last day. This is the meaning of Jesus' words at the death of Lazarus: "I am the resurrection and the life. He who believes in me will live, even though he dies" (11:25). Or as the Lord later said to his disciples: "Because I live, you also will live" (14:19).

Jesus taught not only about his resurrection, but also in diverse ways about his ascension or entry into the invisible world. Thus the Lord spoke of leaving this world (John 13:1), of going back to the Father (14:12; 16:10, 28), and of ascending to where he was before (6:62). As the reward for conquering death, the Father exalted the Son by sharing his heavenly throne with him (Rev. 3:21; cf. 22:1). An important theme in the fourth Gospel is Jesus' glorification (John 7:39; 12:16, 23; 13:31–32; 17:5). When teaching about his impending death, Jesus said: "The hour has come for the Son of Man to be glorified" (12:23). Prior to his betrayal by Judas Jesus prayed, "Father, glorify me in your presence with the glory I had with you before the world began" (17:5). Thus Jesus' glorification began at the cross but was not complete until his return to the Father.[99] The aged John on the Isle of Patmos had a majestic vision of the living, exalted, and glorified Lord clothed with a body (Rev. 1:12–18). Endued with power and glory, the heavenly Lord spoke to John saying, "I was dead, and behold I am alive for ever and ever!" (v. 18).

John also underscores the saving benefits of Christ's resurrection, ascension, and heavenly session: (1) Christ's glorification is the precondition for the outpouring of the Holy Spirit, who continues the saving work of the historical Jesus. John observes that during his earthly ministry "the Spirit had not been given, since Jesus had not yet been glorified" (John 7:39). In the final discourse with his disciples, Jesus spoke of the "Counselor" (*paraklētos*) who would be with believers forever as Revealer, Interpreter, and Helper (14:16, 26; 15:26; 16:7). So Jesus said to his followers: "It is for your good that I am going away. Unless I go away, the Counselor will not come to you; but if I go, I will send him to you" (John 16:7). (2) Jesus' exaltation guarantees the believer's ascent to the Father's home. The Lord's resurrection and ascension opened the doors to heaven that had been sealed since Adam's rebellion. Jesus comforted his disciples by saying, "I am going . . . to prepare a place for you. And if I go and prepare a place for you, I will come back and take you to be with me that you also may be where I am" (14:2–3). (3) Since he has risen and ascended to the Father's side, Jesus Christ functions as the believer's advocate and intercessor. In 1 John 2:1 the word *paraklētos* is used of the ascended Lord: "But if anybody does sin, we have one who speaks to the Father in our defense—Jesus Christ, the Righteous One." "Advocate is a term with a legal ring about it, and it often indicates the counsel for the defense. It is the friend at court."[100] And (4) Jesus' exaltation to heaven inaugurates his sovereign rule over people, kings, and nations. Citing Psalm 89:27 ("I will also appoint him my firstborn, the most exalted of the kings of the earth"), Revelation 1:5 describes the glorified Lord as "the firstborn [*prōtotokos*] from the dead, and the ruler of the kings of the earth." The slain Lamb is portrayed as conqueror; so the Lamb stands in the center of the heavenly throne and receives worship (Rev. 5:6; cf. the Lamb standing on Mount Zion, 14:1).

Other New Testament Literature

Peter observes that the flood in Noah's day signifies the water of believer's baptism, which in turn represents Christian salvation: "This water symbolizes baptism that now saves you. . . . It saves you by the resurrection of Jesus Christ, who has gone into heaven and is at God's right hand" (1 Peter 3:21–22). Peter means that salvation comes to us through the resurrection of Jesus Christ, who has ascended to heaven and is seated at the place of honor, with angels, authorities, and powers subject to him. "Not the act

[baptism] but the event that lies behind what the act symbolizes is the only meritorious basis for salvation."[101] Compared with the despair associated with his rejection of Christ, Peter declares that the resurrection provides the believer with "living hope" of eternal life and "an inheritance that can never perish, spoil or fade" (1 Peter 1:3–4). Christ's resurrection alone accounts for the dramatic change in Peter's life. Scripture indicates that during Jesus' lifetime his brothers neither understood his mission nor followed him (Mark 3:21; John 7:3–5). Yet after the resurrection James emerged as a leader in the Jerusalem church (Acts 12:17; 15:13; Gal. 1:19; 2:9). In the letter that bears his name, this brother of our Lord identifies himself as "James, a servant of God and of the Lord Jesus Christ" (James 1:1). The appearance of the risen Lord to James likely was the reason for his radical spiritual transformation (1 Cor. 15:7). The same applies to Jude, another brother of Jesus, who identifies himself as "a servant of Jesus Christ and a brother of James" (Jude 1; cf. Acts 1:14; 1 Cor. 9:5).

Hebrews' description of Christ's exaltation is unique. The two principal moments in the Old Testament sacrificial ritual were the slaughter of the victim and the presentation of its blood inside the sanctuary. In arguing the superiority of Christ, the author compares the Jewish ritual to Christ's death on the cross and his appearance in the sanctuary on high. Hence Hebrews affirms much about Christ's death and his entry into the presence of God, but little about his resurrection as such (but see Heb. 13:20). Thus Hebrews 1:3 states, "After he had provided purification for sins, he sat down at the right hand of the Majesty in heaven" (cf. Heb. 10:12; 12:2). The act of sitting (aorist of *kathizō*) signifies that Christ's work of purifying sins is completed. Furthermore, Hebrews describes

Christ's exaltation in terms of the exercise of his high priestly ministry in the heavenly sanctuary. "We do have such a high priest, who sat down at the right hand of the throne of the Majesty in heaven, and who serves in the sanctuary, the true tabernacle set up by the Lord, not by man" (8:1–2). Likewise the letter refers to "the inner sanctuary behind the curtain, where Jesus . . . has entered on our behalf. He has become a high priest forever, in the order of Melchizedek" (6:19–20).

As the believer's great high priest, the Christ who was tempted as we are is fully able "to sympathize with our weaknesses" (Heb. 4:15). In the midst of dangers or temptations, believers are assured that Christ suffers along with them. The letter also says of our high priest, "Because he himself suffered when being tempted, he is able to help [boēthēsai] those who are being tempted" (2:18). The heart of Christ's representation of the believer in the heavenly sanctuary is his ministry of intercession. Hebrews 7:25 states, "He is able to save completely those who come to God through him, because he always lives to intercede for them." The focus of eis to panteles may be both qualitative (to the uttermost) and temporal (for all time).[102] The verb entynchanō, to "intercede," upholds both Christ's presentation and his representation of the believer. Presentation connotes Christ's perpetual presence before the Father in the vigor of his completed sacrifice (cf. Exod. 12:13). So Hebrews 9:24 declares that Christ "entered heaven itself, now to appear for us in God's presence [to prosōpon tou theou]." Representation means that Christ mediates the prayers of believers and pleads their cause with the Father.

SYSTEMATIC FORMULATION

The numerous interrelated events of the great Mediator's life and work can be put in perspective in terms of the *two stages* (often called "states") that Paul describes—humiliation (Phil. 2:6–8) and exaltation (vv. 9–11). The stage of Christ's *humiliation* includes the following steps, previously considered: (1) The eternal Word left the glory of heaven, limiting the use of his divine powers; (2) was born as a human of the virgin Mary; (3) lived as a human without sin; (4) died for sinners; and (5) was buried.

From Humiliation to Exaltation

In this chapter we focus on the stage of Christ's *exaltation* with its several steps: (1) Jesus came back to life and abandoned his grave clothes; (2) left his tomb; (3) appeared visibly, audibly, and tangibly to over five hundred disciples on different occasions over a period of 40 days; (4) confirmed his universal authority by uniting Jewish and Gentile believers in the church and inaugurating a new age or dispensation ("these last days" Heb. 1:2); (5) commissioned his disciples to take the good news of his spiritual kingdom to the entire world; (6) ascended to the highest position in all reality, "the right hand of God"; and (7) began his present ministry of intercession for his people.

The teaching of the New Testament does not allow us to isolate the resurrection and ascension from the Father's eternal purpose or the Son's incarnation, life, and death. Christ's exaltation must be considered in connection with his person as the incarnate Logos with both his divine and human natures.

It is because he who lives and acts in this situation is divine and human *in one Person*, that all he does in our fallen existence has a dark side and a light side, a side of humiliation and a side of exaltation—the one is the obverse of the other, but as the Mediator he has come to overcome our darkness and baseness and to build a bridge in and through himself over which we may pass into the light and glory of God.[103]

So Christ's exaltation is considered in connection with the whole of Christ's life as he entered the arena ruled by the forces of evil. Having overcome in the battle with temptation, his eternal purpose can be fulfilled. The New Testament does not present us with isolated events, one after the other, but a connected series of events. So we not only distinguish the two stages of humiliation and exaltation, but we relate them to each other. The crucified One is the one who was raised and ascended; the exalted One is the one who became incarnate and was crucified for our sins.

Resurrection, Not Mere Revivification

What is meant by "resurrection"? It does not mean a temporary revivification like that of Lazarus or Jairus' daughter, who would again face the necessity of dying. In a secondary sense, however, Lazarus is said to have been resurrected (John 11:23–25, 43). Interpreters ought not assume a priori that they know what is meant by the unique "resurrection" of the second Adam. We may need to grow in our understanding of the Bible's teaching, avoiding oversimplification by affirming a doctrine comprehensive of all the elements in the views that find biblical support. Some defenders of a literal, bodily resurrection focus on the similarities to his previous body with little reference to its new powers, while some so emphasize the new spiritual qualities that they lose the physical continuity. From either a literal or spiritual perspective, people ought not to be so quick to defend a doctrine that they fail to define what they seek to guard.

The word "resurrection" derives from the Latin re ("again") and surgere ("to rise"). The Greek equivalent is ana ("up," or "again,") and stasis ("stand"), or egersis (a "rising" or "raising"). What rises or stands again is what was buried—the outer person, Jesus' body. The derivative meaning of "resurrection" has not essentially changed in general use. To obtain a comprehensive biblical meaning, our definition synthesizes the similar and different aspects of the relevant biblical teaching. Hence Christ's resurrection refers to the miraculous once-for-all act that not only united Jesus' buried body with his spirit again but also gave his identifiable body capabilities of transcending the limits of space, time, and natural laws, such as indestructibility and power.

What was raised from the dead was not Jesus' human soul, spirit, or inner person—which in accord with our anthropology survived death—but his human body. When the disciples had thought they saw a spirit, Jesus emphatically replied, "Look at my hands and my feet. It is I myself! Touch me and see; a ghost does not have flesh and bones, as you see I have" (Luke 24:39). The data emphasize his corporeal existence, making it impossible to interpret the event as a psychical or ectoplasmic materialization, as alleged in spiritualism. So we speak of the resurrection of Christ's body rather than of his person, against some oversimplified holistic thinking. When Jesus died, his spirit departed from his body; so his body was buried. Hence it was the body that was raised up again. Christ's raised body was visible, audible, and tangible. Specifically the corporeal characteristics are emphasized by the eyewitnesses (at the end of each Gospel) and by Paul's comparison of the corruptible body buried and the incorruptible body raised (1 Cor. 15:35, 42–44). The Scriptures explicitly refer to the resurrection of others' mortal or lowly bodies as a result of Christ's resurrection (Rom. 8:11; Phil. 3:21). Furthermore a bodily resurrection is consistent with our previous study of humanness. A holistic view of a person is oversimplified if it does not account for the difference between the body and the soul or spirit.

Christ's resurrected body manifested significant *differences* from the body that slept in Mary's arms, hungered, wept, and died. Divine power did not merely resuscitate Jesus' corruptible body, which would then experience another death. God's power transformed its nature, so that it became an incorruptible, spiritual, and glorious body (1 Cor. 15:42–44). The body that died was corruptible; his post-Easter body is imperishable. The buried body was dishonorable; the raised body honorable. The crucified body in itself was subject to natural laws; the spiritual body was not limited by them (1 Cor. 15:42–44). The evidence sufficiently emphasizes the glorified qualities as safeguards against any merely physiological or naturalistic explanation.

What did Paul mean by a "spiritual body"? "Spiritual" is an adjective, "body" is a substantive (v. 44). The apostle does not speak of a bodily spirit, but a spiritual body. A spiritual body is a resurrected physical body with greater capacities as an instrument of the spirit. Among its new powers are those of being incorruptible and giving life (v. 45). With the many new powers of his new life Jesus could leave the grave clothes, disappear from the sealed and guarded tomb, triumphantly appear to fearful disciples behind locked doors, and ascend to heaven. Unquestionably Jesus' raised body had remarkable new capacities. His resurrection was the first fruits of those who died (1 Cor. 15:20). Then when the head of the redeemed race comes to earth again, he will raise "those who belong to him" (v. 23). Christ's resurrection is the first of a unique kind (*sui generis*) of mighty acts. And that mighty act, like the cross, took place once-for-all. Christ's resurrection is irrepeatable. Hence "resurrection" in Scripture cannot mean reincarnation in a series of different corruptible human bodies.

Was Jesus' resurrected body the same body in which he died? Although it had significant differences, there were also significant *similarities*. An adequate view must account for both similarities and differences. When resurrected, Jesus' body was verifiable visibly, audibly, and tangibly. He could be recognized, and those who knew him best identified him as the same person. Speaking of his body Jesus said, "Destroy this temple, and I will raise it again in three days" (John 2:19, 21). When the risen Jesus appeared to the disciples, he said, "Look at my hands and my feet. It is I myself." (Luke 24:39). Those who had been with him for three years and were best able to identify him exclaimed, "It is the Lord!" (John 21:7). Christ's body had been temporarily glorified on the Mount of Transfiguration (Matt. 17:13). Christ's resurrection body was the former body transfigured permanently. Notwithstanding all of the new powers and glory, there remains a verifiable continuity of the resurrected body with the body on the cross.

Paul's analogy helps to unite the similarities and differences. The body that was buried is like a seed that is sown in the earth; the body that was raised is like the wheat that grows from the planted seed (1 Cor. 15:35–38). Although the full-grown wheat is very different from the seed, the point is that the buried seed has an *organic continuity* with the wheat. Who could regard a magnificent oak tree as the material reconstruction of the acorn? But there is an organic connection between the two. Without a continuity between the body buried and the body raised, as Godet argued, "we could no longer speak of resurrection. Death would not be vanquished; it would keep its prey. God would simply do something new by its side."[104] Although a long time may elapse between the death of believers and their resurrection, Paul's teaching is that the resurrection of believers will be like Christ's.

How can we hold to a physical resurrection when Paul teaches that "flesh and blood" cannot inherit God's kingdom (1 Cor. 15:50)? The point of Paul's idiom is that by natural power Jesus' untransformed body could not rise again and ascend to be with the Father. "Flesh and blood" is an idiom for unaided and unchanged natural human powers. It was Jesus' transformed and supernaturally endowed body that ascended to the throne of God's kingdom. When Peter made his great confession, "You are the Christ, the Son of the living God," Jesus replied, ". . . this was not revealed to you by man [flesh and blood], but by my Father in heaven" (Matt. 16:16–17).[105] Supernatural illumination enabled Peter to overcome his blindness to the observable supernatural indications and to affirm Christ's deity. Christ performed his miracles in the flesh, but their power and significance were not ultimately of the flesh, but of God.

We conclude that the resurrection body is an observable physical body but supernaturally incorruptible and able to enter heaven. No merely natural power could reverse the irreversible forces of decay and decomposition, transform the body, and cause it to exist at the "right hand" of God. Natural laws were not violated but overruled by their Creator for a redemptive purpose. Christ arose and ascended by a power transcending the natural powers of "flesh and blood." Passive and active aspects may be discerned in his resurrection. Christ gladly yielded to the will of the Father as the mighty act of the Father and the Spirit graciously gave him a more glorious body. The eternal

Word himself also participated in raising up again this bodily "temple" as he promised (John 2:19). When he had his incorruptible body, the glorified Christ actively moved through the burial clothing, out of the grave, and appeared to over five hundred people.

Confirmable Signs of Christ's Resurrection

Although no one saw Jesus rise and leave the tomb, evidence of his resurrection overcame the disciples' reticence to believe it. The event occurred in sharp antithesis to what they had expected theologically, and it was in genuine conflict with the framework of the secular world view at the time. To the Jew it was a stumbling block and to the Greek nonsense because the evidence required a Copernican revolution in their theology and cosmology.

The first indication from Scripture that Jesus had risen was *the empty tomb*. The possibility of Christ's resurrection presented itself as the women found the formerly well-sealed and guarded tomb open and empty. A tomb could be empty for many reasons; therefore the empty tomb's evidential value does not stand alone. But in association with other converging lines of evidence—Christ's appearances, the grave clothes, the change in the disciples, the conversion of Saul, the formation of the church, and the writing of the New Testament—it becomes strong.

Another indication that Jesus had risen from the empty grave was the *cadaver wrappings*. Probably Jesus's body was wrapped as Lazarus' body had been—"his hands and feet wrapped with strips of linen, and cloth around his face" (John 11:44). Although Lazarus came out of his grave in response to Jesus' command, others had to take off the grave clothes and let him go (v. 44). In the case of Christ, John looked in and saw the strips of linen lying there, but Peter went into the tomb, bent over, and saw the strips of linen lying there as well as the burial cloth that had been around Jesus' head. "The cloth was folded up by itself, separate from the linen" (John 20:3–7; cf. Luke 24:12). Apparently the glorified body that passed through walls and through locked doors previously had without assistance passed right through the burial clothes. In John's mind the burial clothes excluded Mary's theory that the body had been stolen, for the thieves would not have left the grave clothes as John found them. "Finally the other disciple [John] who had reached the tomb first, also went inside. He saw and believed" (John 20:8).[106]

A third immediately observable indication of Christ's resurrection involved the series of Christ's *appearances* over some forty days. The word "appeared" (1 Cor. 15:5) means "that the risen Lord takes the initiative to make himself known to the disciples. The disciples did not come into Easter Faith by some kind of process of self-recuperation."[107] The disciples did not gullibly believe Christ's resurrection. They tested other hypotheses unsuccessfully. At first they thought he was a gardener, another traveler on the way to Emmaus, or a ghost. These hypotheses did not hold up as the evidence was confirmed by more and more witnesses. On one occasion when the crucified, buried, and risen Jesus suddenly stood among the disciples, "They were startled and frightened, thinking they saw a ghost. He said to them, 'Why are you troubled, and why do doubts arise in your minds? Look at my hands and my feet. It is I myself! Touch me and see; a ghost does not have flesh and bones, as you see I have'" (Luke 24:37–39).

"When he had said this, he showed them his hands and feet. And while they still did not believe it because of joy and amazement, he asked them, 'Do you have anything here to eat?' They gave him a piece of broiled fish, and he took it and ate it in their presence" (Luke 24:40–43). "He was not seen by all the people, but by witnesses whom God had already chosen—by us who ate and drank with him after he rose from the dead" (Acts 10:41). Before he ascended, over five hundred people had seen the risen Christ, most of whom were still living when Paul wrote 1 Corinthians. In effect Paul invites his first-century readers to check his report of the resurrection with the living eyewitnesses.

Thomas would not accept the conclusion of the other disciples who had reported that Christ was alive. He said, "Unless I see the nail marks in his hands and put my finger where the nails were, and put my hand into his side, I will not believe it" (John 20:25). A week later Jesus appeared through the doors that were locked and invited Thomas, "Put your finger here; see my hands. Reach out your hand and put it into my side. Stop doubting and believe" (v. 27). Persuaded by the sight of the resurrected Christ, Thomas said to him, "My Lord and my God (v. 28)!"

Jesus did not rebuke Thomas for wanting critically to examine the evidence for himself. He had warned about counterfeit Christs and false prophets who would do many powerful works in his name. The Lord did not advocate building a house on sand. Faith should be based on conclusive evidence of confirming signs. Jesus knew, however, that he would not be continuously available for others to examine. So Jesus said, "Because you have seen me, you have believed; blessed are those who have not seen and yet have believed" (John 20:29).

The object of our faith—the risen Christ—is no longer visibly available. But strong converging lines of written testimony continue to indicate that, indeed, he rose. Although the *object* of Christian faith can no longer be seen (the ascended Christ), the *evidence* for faith in the risen Messiah can be seen in historically reliable and inspired accounts of the visible signs. It was not the disciples' "faith" that produced the idea of Christ's resurrection. The conclusiveness of the lines of physical evidence produced the disciples' faith in Christ's resurrection. Still today we accept Christ's resurrection because we are convinced by the evidence that it happened in fact and as the Holy Spirit attests that evidence, he overcomes our pride and reluctance. For additional lines of evidence and argument for the resurrection, see the section "Apologetic Interaction" below.

The Revealed Significance of Christ's Resurrection

Although the event was empirically confirmable, its meaning for God and man was cognitively (propositionally) revealed. The apostles were not only eyewitnesses, but specially chosen and gifted spokesmen for God. By the Holy Spirit they recalled and wrote what Jesus had disclosed of the significance of his life, death, and resurrection. Paul, who saw the risen Lord (1 Cor. 15:8), did not make up his gospel message. "I did not receive it [the gospel] from any man, nor was I taught it; rather, I received it by revelation from Jesus Christ" (Gal. 1:12). He could observe the fact that Christ had risen; he received information by revelation that Christ had died "for our justification," etc. According to the inspired scriptural revelation, what was the theological significance of the resurrection?

1. One after another, Christ's appearances exhibited his glorified existence and so *confirmed Jesus' earlier claims for the authority of his person.* The resurrection powerfully declared that he was what he had claimed to be, the One from above (John 8:23), *the Son of God* (Rom. 1:4). The fulfillment of the predicted sign of his resurrection also confirmed his claims to be the *Messiah* (Matt. 12:40; 16:21; 17:9; 20:19; John 2:19, 21). Jesus' claims to authority for himself do not stand alone and are not self-authenticating any more than those of the founders of other religions. Like the claims of God's prophets and apostles, they must be confirmed by the coming to pass of his signs. Facing the supreme test, Jesus predicted the verifiable sign of his resurrection. As Wolfhart Pannenberg has said, "Everything depends upon the connection between Jesus' claim and its confirmation by God."[108]

2. Christ's resurrection *confirms the Father's acceptance of his atoning sacrifice and its provisions.* The resurrection is a sign certifying the satisfaction of the Father in both justice and love. The Father's will prospered in his hand, and both Father and Son are satisfied (Isa. 53:10–11). The Father did not forsake the guilt-bearer on the cross permanently. He restored Jesus not only to physical life but also to his spiritual fellowship! The sign of Christ's resurrection assures people that the long-awaited ground of salvation has been realized.

3. Christ's resurrection *certifies that sinners through faith in Christ can now enjoy the peace of present justification* (Rom. 4:25). Now it becomes clear how sinners can with justice be called righteous. Christ's substitutionary death and triumphant resurrection make possible the just acquittal of sinners. Whether or not believers are Jews, they are justified on the ground of the risen Christ's atoning sacrifice (Acts 3:25–26; 10:46). At the point of faith justification is the legal verdict that forgives sins and imputes Christ's perfect righteousness (Rom. 3:21–26). Hence there is now no

condemnation for those who are in Christ Jesus (8:1). "Therefore, since we have been justified through faith, we have peace with God through our Lord Jesus Christ" (5:1).

4. The Messiah's resurrection *assures believers' eschatological justification.* Christ's unique resurrection stands at the beginning of the era that from the Old Testament Jewish perspective is known as the "last days." It marks the dramatic beginning ("firstfruits") of eschatological events. As such it verifies believers' acceptance before God the Father in Christ, not only in the present but also for the entire *aeon* of the last days, including the day when believers will appear before the judgment seat of Christ (2 Cor. 5:10). Christ's resurrection assures believers that the acquittal now received by faith will be confirmed by God's verdict in their final judgment (Rom. 8:33–34). That assurance is secure because neither the resurrection nor justification derive from any quality or ability of sinners. Both occur solely by God's gracious authority on the basis of Christ's atonement and resurrection.[109]

5. The Scriptures do not as explicitly state that Christ rose *for the redemption and reconciliation of sinners,* but these provisions would not be available had the story of Jesus ended at the cross. Such a termination would have been an unmitigated tragedy. It would have become the supreme evidence that injustice and irrationality have the last word in life on planet earth. But Christ has risen! He has demonstrated his power to provide emancipation from decay, freedom from addictions, restoration of broken fellowships, and communion with God the Father. All the New Testament teaching concerning redemption and reconciliation was written subsequent to, and on the basis of, Christ's resurrection. The water of baptism "now saves you," Peter writes, "—not

the removal of dirt from the body, but . . . it saves you by the resurrection of Jesus Christ, who has gone into heaven and is at God's right hand—with angels, authorities and powers in submission to him" (1 Peter 3:21–22).

6. The resurrected Christ *becomes the last Adam, the new head of the race.* The risen Christ began a new order of spiritual, life-giving existence for all who are in solidarity with him by faith. "For as in Adam all die, so in Christ all will be made alive" (1 Cor. 15:22). "The first man Adam became a living being; the last Adam, a life-giving spirit" (v. 45). The old order of being subject to death pertains to all who were born of fallen Adam's race. The new kind of existence is made up of all who are "in" the sinless Christ by faith and it anticipates eternal life, including the resurrection of the body. The invitation to believe is to be given universally, but the new order of being is entered only by those who receive Christ's redemptive kingdom and are delivered from the kingdom of darkness. Paul develops the theological importance of Christ's headship in contrast to Adam's not only in 1 Corinthians 15 but also in Romans 5. Through a generic solidarity with Adam all are condemned to die; but through a believing solidarity with Christ all are graciously given the gift of his righteousness (justification).

7. Christ's resurrection also *signifies that Jesus Christ is Lord of all.* Before he ascended, the risen Lord could triumphantly report, "All authority in heaven and on earth has been given to me" (Matt. 28:18). God the Father has put everything under him (1 Cor. 15:27–28). Jesus was Lord of the discouraged and scattered Jewish disciples, who become apostles, that is, witnesses of the resurrection. He becomes Lord also of all who have believed through their witness. The primitive Christian apostolate did not carry

out the commission of another great rabbi but of the Messiah, the one teacher who was a Savior and rose from his grave. By faith in the one who demonstrated authority over all demonic forces, the early believers turned the first-century world upside down. In Christ there is neither Jew nor Gentile, male nor female (Gal. 3:28). And one day every knee will bow to him as Lord of all. The Lord of all reality will reign "until he has put all his enemies under his feet" (1 Cor. 15:25).

8. Christ's resurrection *assures the resurrection of all.* Paul's belief that "there will be a resurrection of both the righteous and the wicked" (Acts 24:15) is clearly rooted in Christ's resurrection. Jesus had said, "All who are in their graves will hear his [the Son of Man's] voice and come out—those who have done good will rise to live, and those who have done evil will rise to be condemned (John 5:28–29). The one who raised the Lord Jesus from the dead will also raise believers with Jesus and present them in his presence (2 Cor. 4:14). Christ's resurrection was the "firstfruits" of those who have fallen asleep (1 Cor. 15:20). "For as in Adam all die, so in Christ all will be made alive. But each in his own turn: Christ, the firstfruits; then, when he comes, those who belong to him" (vv. 22–23). Another indication of the "resurrection of those who belong to him" is Jesus' reference to "the resurrection of the righteous" (Luke 14:14). As believers, we have reason to anticipate that Christ, "by the power that enables him to bring everything under his control, will transform our lowly bodies so that they will be like his glorious body" (Phil. 3:21). Christ's resurrection demonstrates the error of those who identify the Christian hope exclusively with the immortality of the soul. The whole person is redeemed. But Christ's resurrection does not by any means imply the denial of a continued existence in an intermediate state.[110] His spirit was not annihilated between his death and resurrection; it was committed to his Father's keeping.

9. Christ's resurrection *signifies that he will be the ultimate Judge of all.* Peter testified that he who rose from the dead is "the one whom God appointed as judge of the living and the dead" (Acts 10:42). Paul concluded his message to the Gentiles at Athens with a warning that the day of God's grace has its limits. "[God] has set a day when he will judge the world by the man he has appointed. He has given proof of this to all men by raising him from the dead" (Acts 17:31). Again, Christ's resurrection is a public fact that provides conclusive evidence not only for those with prior knowledge and faith but also for all human beings.

10. Christ's resurrection *assures the Lord's continuing presence in the church.* The church belongs exclusively to the Lord. It is made up of believers who are "in him" forensically, who fellowship with him relationally, and who are made new creatures by him experientially. The resurrected Lord is alive and present in the church (Eph. 1:19–23). However frail and fragile the church may be, where his people are gathered the glorified Christ is in their midst. However weak the church may appear to the world, the Lord is with her in resurrection power. If you are ever tempted to give up on the church, remember the resurrection! The living Lord will build his church. Open yourself to his presence in united worship and remembrance as you partake at his table. Believers in Christ ought not stand outside the church criticizing its acknowledged weaknesses. Believers actively participate in a church to help it become more fully what it can be by the power of the risen Christ.

The Verifiable Sign of Christ's Ascension

Jesus' ascension was God's mighty act concluding the incarnation; it took the crucified and resurrected Messiah from the earth to the Father's glorious presence in heaven. As at Jesus' other postresurrection appearances, he ascended (was raptured) bodily from his disciples, "before their very eyes" (Acts 1:9). His resurrection body, which had passed through closed doors, now passed through the atmosphere. After giving many convincing proofs for the forty days that he was alive (Acts 1:3), Jesus provided a further unforgettable signal that his earthly ministry was completed.

The fact of the Messiah's ascension is supported by predictions before the event and reports afterward.

1. *In anticipation* Jesus gave the disciples good reason to expect his ascension. When he said that he was the bread who came down from heaven (John 6:58), many of the disciples said, "This is a hard teaching. Who can accept it?" (v. 60). Aware that his disciples were grumbling about this, Jesus said to them, "Does this offend you? What if you see the Son of Man ascend to where he was before!" (v. 62). He said that he would return to his Father's house to prepare a place for his disciples (14:2–3), "I am going to the Father" (v. 12), and "I am going away and I am coming back to you" (v. 28). To Mary after his resurrection Jesus said, "Do not hold on to me, for I have not yet returned to the Father" (20:17).

2. *In retrospect,* having commissioned the disciples, the risen Christ led them to the vicinity of Bethany, and while he was blessing them "he left them and was taken up into heaven" (Luke 24:51). Again, "he was taken up before their very eyes, and a cloud hid him from their sight. They were looking intently up into the sky as he was going" (Acts 1:9–10). The apostles had witnessed his life from his baptism to "the time when Jesus was taken up from [them]" (1:22). John could report, "No one has ever gone into heaven except the one who came from heaven—the Son of Man" (John 3:13). Paul says Christ was "taken up in glory" (1 Tim. 3:16).

A literal interpretation of the event is also supported in several ways. Like Jesus' other miracles and appearances, his ascension was not limited by the laws of nature. So the necessity of life-support systems for ordinary human space travel does not make the ascension impossible. A literal rapture is impossible only if we forget the incorruptible nature of Jesus' resurrection body. Christ ascended in the powerful, spiritual body that overcame death and corruptibility. He passed through the atmosphere both without a space-suit and without ill effects because his glorified body could not be destroyed by less oxygen, radical changes of temperature, or differences of air pressure.

Does our modern knowledge that the earth is round make a literal interpretation impossible? The fact that "up" at one place on the globe is "down" on the other side of the globe does not change the observations of the disciples. From Jerusalem they saw him go "up" into the sky (Acts 1:9, 11). The primary point is not the location of heaven, but that Jesus left the observable, created world. But we cannot help asking, Where did Jesus go? He went "through the heavens" (Heb. 4:14). That may mean through (1) the earth's atmosphere and (2) the cosmic heavens of the sun and stars to (3) the transcendent abode of God.[111] Jesus "ascended higher than all the heavens" (Eph. 4:10). He returned to the place from which he came; he returned "where he was before" (John 6:62); he returned to the Father (14:12). His prayer was

471

answered as he was glorified in the Father's presence with the glory he had with him before the world began (17:5). "For Christ did not enter a man-made sanctuary that was only a copy of the true one; he entered heaven itself, now to appear for us in God's presence" (Heb. 9:24).

Since the heavens, even the highest heaven, cannot contain God (1 Kings 8:27) and since God is everywhere present in the universe, it is impossible to locate the Father or the Son at a particular place in space and time, such as some nova far out in space. Hence it has become commonplace to say that the ascension involved not a change of place but a change of state. Jesus' transformation to a glorified "state" of existence, however, had already occurred at his resurrection. The ascension in fact involved a change of place—a physical removal from the earth. So Christ's ascension involved both a change of place and a change of position and authority (to "the right hand of God").

We do not take the "right hand of God" literally, for God is a spirit. Since a spirit does not have a flesh-and-bones body, it cannot have a literal right hand. Hence the young Mormon literalist need not have worried. She thought the Father's right hand must be getting very tired because Jesus has been standing on it all these years! The figurative expression "right hand of God" refers to the position of highest authority and power given by the Father over every other power in all of reality.

Is Christ's body now in heaven? The one person, with his human nature inseparable from his divine nature, ascended to the Father. Is his body visible there? Yes, his body is with the Father. But its new spiritual powers may allow it to be invisible as well as visible. Since on earth the resurrected Christ could disappear as he chose, we ought not be surprised that neither Russian cosmo-nauts nor American astronauts have visibly seen the ascended Lord when traveling in space. With due consideration of modern cosmology, we can imagine no more meaningful sign of the culmination of the Messiah's incarnate ministry on earth and glorious return to the Father in heaven than a visible ascension into the sky (Acts 1:11).

The Revealed Significance of Christ's Ascension

The verifiable and confirmed event of Christ's ascension carries rich *theological significance*. The sign was confirmed by eyewitnesses; we derive its meaning from propositional revelation given through Jesus and the apostles as preserved in the reliable accounts of inspired Scripture. The miraculous event of the ascension is the second mighty act (with the resurrection) drawing attention to Jesus' exaltation and several important theological tenets.

1. The ascension *marked the end of Christ's incarnate appearances and revelations* (until his second coming). A dramatic event was necessary so that the disciples would not be kept in suspense, anticipating more appearances and disclosures. The ascension also kept them from wondering what finally became of their Lord. Furthermore, by ascending, Christ ended his prophetic ministry on earth for this age. He would not appear visibly to people on earth until his second coming in power and glory. Hence alleged visions of Christ during the present age need to be examined critically. Some alleged visions of Christ may be the fabrications of religious con artists, some may be deceptions from evil spirits, and some may be figurative ways of referring to contemporary applications of Christ's biblically recorded teaching. In any case the content of alleged visions must be tested to determine whether

they do or do not contradict biblically revealed truth. With his ascension the Lord Jesus Christ completed his teaching ministry on earth.

Until his second coming he sits at the Father's right hand. "After he had provided purification for sins, he sat down at the right hand of the Majesty in heaven" (Heb. 1:3). This seated position or "session" as theologians have called it indicates the completion of his incarnate work on earth and the assumption of authority as King. Clearly he has chosen not to appear visibly on earth again until his second coming. The Holy Spirit now draws attention to Christ, attests the truth of what he taught, and may act in supernatural ways as he wills. But the Holy Spirit does not now add new content to the divine revelations given through accredited prophetic and apostolic spokespeople in the Scriptures. Through the written Word a follower of Christ can be "thoroughly equipped for every good work" (2 Tim. 3:17). Christ has said what he wants to say, and the heavens remain silent until Christ returns in power and glory.

2. Christ's ascension *reversed his kenosis*. The eternal Word had "humbled himself and became obedient to death—even death on a cross!" (Phil. 2:8). Faithfully he completed all that he could do on earth to provide for salvation. "Therefore God exalted him to the highest place and gave him the name that is above every name, that at the name of Jesus every knee should bow, in heaven and on earth and under the earth, and every tongue confess that Jesus Christ is Lord to the glory of God the Father" (vv. 9–11). What God's Son did not take advantage of in coming to earth as a human he receives and freely uses again; he assumes again the full authority and power and glory that he left and adds a triumphant position. Christ no longer limits the use of all his divine attributes as he did during the

state of humiliation. Having accomplished the redemption of sinners, the second person of the Trinity remains the same ontologically, but Christ's exalted position and honor are even greater because of his accomplishments in his incarnation, crucifixion, and resurrection.

3. Christ's ascension *inaugurated his heavenly ministry as King and Lord of the cosmos*. On earth Jesus' authority over evil spirits had previously indicated that the Lord was here, that his kingdom was at hand, and that in the King the kingdom had indeed come. The fact that God exalted Jesus to his right hand, along with his resurrection, further confirmed that he is both Lord and Christ (Acts 2:33–36). The Messiah who died and rose again and is now ascended is indeed all that he claimed to be. The Lord who resides at the Father's right hand presently reigns with power and authority above every created being in heaven and earth.[112] All other powers—angels, authorities, and rulers—must now submit to him (1 Peter 3:22). The conqueror of sin, Satan, and death on earth now rules, not only over all persons and institutionalized powers on earth but also over all heavenly angelic powers and demonic powers.

4. Christ's ascension *clarified the meaning of his present rule on earth*. The ascension pronounced the final *no* to the disciples' hopes of an economic and political messianic kingdom during the present age. Many Jews were looking for military deliverance from foreign oppression and for universal peace. Legalistic interpreters of Old Testament promises of liberation unfortunately overlooked its teaching on the necessary preparations of repentance and forgiveness. But the incarnate Messiah liberated many from demonic oppression and established his present rule. "My kingdom," he said, "is not of this world" (John 18:36). His present au-

thority does not center in an earthly capital. Christians do not have an enduring city now—not Jerusalem, Rome, Mecca, Salt Lake City, Moscow, Washington, or Wheaton. He who came from above rules morally and spiritually at present in the thinking, feeling, willing, and relating of those who receive him as Savior and Lord. Christ's rule over believers can be experienced in whatever economic or political situations they find themselves. He is not satisfied with the status quo in any country, and his followers should not be. But as we work for more justice and mercy, we ought not identify the ascended Christ's kingdom with any present political, economic, educational, or religious institution. Not even institutional churches or denominations can be identified with Christ's kingdom.

5. Christ's ascension also *marked the beginning of his present ministries as head of the church.* Although the kingdom is not the church, Christ who rules the cosmos also rules the church. Christ ministers as head of the church in at least three ways.

a. From heaven the exalted Christ *sends the Holy Spirit to those who believe in him.* Previously "the Spirit had not been given, since Jesus had not yet been glorified" (John 7:39). "Exalted to the right hand of God, he has received from the Father the promised Holy Spirit and has poured out what you now see and hear" (Acts 2:33). On the day of Pentecost Christ sent the Holy Spirit to those who believed in him as the Messiah who is Lord. Ever since then, both Jews and Gentiles receive the Spirit by believing the fact that the Messiah has come and by trusting him. Christ sends the Spirit to endue people of faith with power for witnessing (Acts 2:4), to remain with them, and to lead and guide his people in their various ministries.

b. The exalted Christ *builds the church* as he planned to do (Matt. 16:18). Although now in heaven, Christ remains "head over everything for the church" (Eph. 1:20–23; Col. 1:18). He gave his Spirit to work with believers, not only individually but also collectively. Prior to the ascension the Spirit brought people into God's kingdom through the new birth (John 3:3–8). After the ascension the Spirit's new work introduces (or "baptizes") Jewish and Gentile believers into his body, the church (1 Cor. 12:13). Christ through his Spirit gives members of his body gifts (Eph. 4:7–11). He also nurtures (4:16; 5:24; Col. 2:19) and sets apart the church for service (Eph. 5:26). Although transcendently in heaven, in these and other redemptive ministries Christ fulfills his promise to be immanently present as active with his people. "And surely I am with you always, to the very end of the age" (Matt. 28:20). Believers do not now experience Christ's glorious presence in heaven, but they can never escape his presence in his universal providential activities and his particular redemptive activities in their lives. He is present in the activities Scripture attributes to him personally and in the activities Scripture attributes to the Holy Spirit (who is one in essence with him), whom he has sent to abide with us.

c. The exalted Christ *intercedes for believing members of the church* (Rom. 8:34; 1 Tim. 2:5). At the right hand of the Father Christ now pleads the case of believers who sin (1 John 2:1). We could not have a better attorney to plead our case. He is the advocate with universal authority and power who has been installed at the head of the government of heaven and earth. At the same time the Righteous One knows what it was like to be a sojourner in this world (Heb. 2:14–16). Having offered up himself for our salvation, he ever lives (9:11–28) to make intercession for us. Christ pleads our case in heaven itself, or the heavenly Holy of Holies (6:19–20; 8:1–2). The best indications of what he prays for may be seen in his prayers on earth, and especially those for his disciples and all who would believe through them (John 17). When he knew he would remain in the world no longer (v. 11), he pled with the Father, "Protect them by the power of your name . . . so that they may be one as we are one" (vv. 11, 20–23), "protect them from the evil one" (v. 15). "Sanctify them by the truth; your word is truth" (v. 17). I have made you known "in order that the love you have for me may be in them and that I myself may be in them" (v. 26).

6. The resurrected Christ's exaltation *will culminate in his powerful and glorious visible return* in the clouds of heaven as he ascended (Acts 1:11). When the Victor returns, every eye will see him, even those who pierced him (Rev. 1:7). His presence will again be manifested in his incarnate body, but he will not be the "meek and lowly Jesus" of the typical artist's imagination. He will come as the resurrected, ascended, and glorified Lord with eyes like blazing fire (1:14) and wielding a sharp double-edged sword (v. 16). He will judge those who reject the gospel and "bring salvation to those who are waiting for him" (Heb. 9:28). His spiritual kingdom will break out into the open, and visibly the glorified Messiah will rule the entire earth and cosmos. The kingdom, which has been progressively revealed and developed, will finally be consummated by the Prince of Peace.

(7) Christ's ascension *is the first instance of the rapture of a glorified body* (1 Cor. 15:20). Associated with the resurrection of saints is the rapture of those who will be alive at the time of Christ's return. When he returns, "we who are still alive and are left will be caught up together with them in the clouds to meet the Lord in the air" (1 Thess. 4:16–17). Christ has already demonstrated the possibility of a bodily rapture. That may have been foreshadowed also in the translations of Enoch and Elijah. But we have no indication that they received resurrection bodies for their departures, so Christ remains the first to be resurrected and raptured. The resurrection will occur before dead or living believers will be raptured (4:13–17). Anyone who believes in the ascension of Christ's glorified body should not have insuperable difficulties believing in the possibility of the ascension of others in glorified bodies.

8. Christ's ascension *assures the existence of a resurrected and glorified human body and spirit in the Father's immediate presence.* Leaving the earthly scene, the Lord in his glorified humanness entered the heavenly sanctuary (Heb. 6:20; 9:12, 24). Just as "the right hand of God" is figurative, so is the heavenly "sanctuary." It is another analogy for the immediate presence of the Father. Although it belongs to God to be at the place of ultimate authority, wisdom, love, and power, a human nature went there! And Christ's glorified humanness remains in the Father's immediate presence. Jesus' raptured body need not be always visible, however, for in the glorified body Jesus could appear and disappear at will. The human body and spirit interact with each other in this life and even more effectually in the glorified state. Christ's ascension secures us in the belief that when we will be resurrected and will ascend and be like him, we will be able in our wholeness directly and joyfully to relate not only to our Savior, but to God the Father and God the Holy Spirit. What higher hope could enliven the hearts of humans in this life?

APOLOGETIC INTERACTION

How Important Is the Facticity?

The importance of the factual question is momentous, for the claims of

Christ for himself and the validity of his atonement rest on his resurrection. Is it true that Jesus physically rose from the dead? The issues were clearly drawn in a formal debate at Liberty University in 1985 between atheistic philosopher Antony G. N. Flew and Christian philosopher Gary Habermas. In the debate Flew denied and Habermas affirmed a literal, physical interpretation of the accounts of Christ's resurrection. But both agreed on a literal resurrection's supreme theoretical and practical importance as a distinguishing characteristic of Christianity and not of any other world religion.[113]

If Jesus was not physically raised, the Messiah has not come and Jesus has lost his integrity. If Christ did not rise, belief in his claims for himself or anything he taught is discredited. Jesus admitted as much. After Jesus cleansed the temple, the Jews asked, " 'What miraculous sign can you show us to prove your authority to do all this?' Jesus answered them, 'Destroy this temple [his body], and I will raise it again in three days' " (John 2:18–19). Less figuratively on other occasions he explained that he would be killed "and after three days rise again" (Mark 8:31; 9:31; 10:34). If the most important sign given of his true authority did not occur, we have no reason to believe that he was even a true prophet of God. "If what a prophet proclaims in the name of the LORD does not take place or come true, that is a message the LORD has not spoken. That prophet has spoken presumptuously. Do not be afraid of him" (Deut. 18:22). If Christ did not rise, no one ought to trust him even as a prophet.

If Christ did not rise, furthermore, the gospel deceives. From the beginning the heart of the good news headlined eyewitness testimony to Jesus' resurrection. The conclusion to each Gospel affirmed in detail not only his crucifixion and burial, but also his res-

urrection. The Christian church began when Peter declared that, as prophesied, it was impossible for death to keep its hold on Jesus Christ, his body did not see decay; "God raised this Jesus to life," and, Peter added, "we are all witnesses of the fact" (Acts 2:24–32). Paul, having received the gospel from the Lord and his apostles, passed on

as of first importance: that Christ died for our sins according to the Scriptures, that he was buried, that he was raised on the third day according to the Scriptures, and that he appeared to Peter, and then to the Twelve. After that he appeared to more than five hundred of the brothers at the same time, most of whom are still living, though some have fallen asleep. Then he appeared to James, then to all the apostles, and last of all he appeared to me also, as to one abnormally born (1 Cor. 15:3–8).

Those who do not affirm that Christ rose do not preach the gospel that Paul preached.

If Christ has not been physically raised, furthermore, no one has been forgiven, redeemed, or reconciled and the Christian church has lost its *raison d'etre*. Justification, a provision of Christ's atonement, Paul taught, is conditioned upon our inner belief in Christ's resurrection (Rom. 10:9–10; cf. 3:23–25). No amount of passionate commitment to a false message can reconcile us to the God of truth. If Christ has not been raised, neither Paul, Augustine, nor Billy Graham have ever actually been born again. If Christ has not been raised, the primary basis of Christian unity has been swept away. No one ought to continue in the apostle's teaching, the breaking of bread, fellowship, or prayer. If Christ has not been raised, all the alleged theological significance of his humiliation and exaltation have collapsed, and Christians who believe the lie are to be pitied (1 Cor. 15:14–17). Without a basis in reality claims to the existential values of the Messiah's crucifixion, resurrection, and ascension are inauthentic.

So much rests on the reality of the resurrection that it is little wonder that debate swirls around its facticity. The basic questions in the debate concern its possibility, purpose, and actuality.

Could Christ's Resurrection Have Happened?

Would the first-century evening news have reported Christ's resurrection and ascension? Were they observed events at particular times and places? Could TV cameras have filmed Christ coming back to life, going through the solid rock of the still-sealed tomb, and later cooking breakfast for his disciples?

By definition, the atheist understands the miracle of the resurrection and ascension as a logical impossibility. If nature is the highest reality and its laws are invariable, no power can overrule those laws. Since no miracles are possible a priori, alleged testimony like that for the resurrection and ascension are usually ignored, reinterpreted as myth, or humorously dismissed as absurd.

Forty students laughingly dismissed Christ's ascension as a parody on Ascension Day in May 1967. They thought that their knowledge of space travel reduced Christ's ascension to nonsense. On one end of a long cord they fastened several gas-inflated balloons; on the other, a crude effigy of Christ made of tissue paper and cardboard. As high noon approached, the crowd began a hilarious countdown from 100. The volume of the shouting and the air of boisterous jollity heightened until with a mighty shout of "Zero" and "Blastoff" the crowd released the cord holding the the balloons and the effigy. A naïve bystander did not realize what the raucous crowd was mocking until, as the balloons ascended dragging behind them the paper Christ, he heard one of the men quote Scripture: "Men of Gali-

lee, why do you stand looking into heaven? This Jesus, who was taken up from you into heaven, will come in the same way as you saw him go into heaven." Who were these people? The participants in this charade were not communists taunting Christians, and they were not hecklers on drugs. They were students preparing for Christian ministry on the campus of a well-known seminary.[114]

More generally, naturalists ignore the evidence for Christ's resurrection and ascension. According to invariable natural law, dead men stay dead. Naturalists often prejudge the evidence, assuming a priori what is to be proved, that all events can be naturally explained. In this context naturalists also tend to make natural laws more than they are. Scientific laws statistically describe what generally occurs. They neither cause events nor keep any specific event from happening in human history. If nontheists are not to beg the question, then, they ought to examine carefully the indications that Christ rose from his tomb. Historical evidence cannot be erased by the fiat of philosophers. Pannenberg comments, "The weakness of Professor Flew's position in the dispute with Professor Habermas was his a priori assumption of the inconclusive character of the evidence and his reluctance to enter into a serious discussion of the historical detail."[115]

Rudolph Bultmann studied the New Testament thoroughly but reinterprets the resurrection accounts to fit his assumed closed system of natural laws. So he alleges that the resurrection accounts amount to prescientific myths of first-century people expressed in a crude "world picture." To make the reports meaningful to people with a scientific model of the universe, the New Testament scholar dismissed what he thought were the husks of literal meaning and embraced only what he considered their existential significance.

There are others who take the account of the resurrection seriously, albeit mythically, not literally. Was Christ's resurrection a myth? Myths are symbolic expressions of something beyond history—a universal, ever-existent ground of all visible phenomena. The application of the concept of myth to the resurrection meant a leveling down of the particular to the universal and the changing of a special revelation into general revelation. But Christ's resurrection is not parallel to a recurring event like the sprouting of perennials in spring. The Gospels are an expression of the religion divinely initiated by the incarnation, death, and resurrection of one unique person in the flesh, not a general nature religion. The apostles were not interested in proclaiming a general religious truth in the symbolic language of myth, but a specific truth in empirically observed facts. And the risen Lord is not presented as a new cult hero to stand alongside others. As a result of his confirmed resurrection, the apostles held that he alone is Lord. The supernatural uniqueness of Christ's resurrection, Walter Kunneth concludes, forbids any application of the concept of myth and makes impossible any analogical relationship with other myths of religious history.[116]

From the time of Bultmann's writings to the present the scientific models of the world have dramatically changed. Mechanistic models have given way following the discovery of atomic energy. The assured, predictable, closed system of natural law, which Bultmann assumed, has been shaken. Although scientific world pictures come and go, the metaphysical, ethical, and factual questions remain the same. In any century have we to do with a living God who can perform mighty acts like the resurrection and ascension of the Messiah?

A fundamental error of Bultmann was to confuse the scientific world picture of his day with a metaphysical worldview (a closed one). The God of the Bible, whom the heavens cannot contain (1 Kings 8:27), is not limited by our changing world pictures. The power of the transcendent, living, and active God brought Jesus Christ back to life. The resurrection has ineradicable significance in every culture on earth (prescientific or scientific) and at every stage of scientific knowledge of the world. It is tragic to perform open-heart surgery upon the Christian faith in an attempt to substitute for the risen and ascended King of kings one of many naturalistic spiritual masters. Christianity at its heart involves unique mighty acts in the space-time world. The most coherent view of the scriptural evidence affirms that the eternal Logos came, died, was buried, rose again, and ascended in a publicly verifiable, literal human body.

Alan Richardson examined Bultmann's view as a hypothesis to be tested by continually checking with the New Testament documents and other relevant evidence from the period. This verificational method necessarily involves a personal or subjective element but not an absolute subjectivism or historical relativism. One historical interpretation can be shown to be better (more coherent and viable) than another.[117]

Thus, for example, R. Bultmann's hypothesis that the theology of the New Testament is a mythological conglomeration of Jewish apocalyptic and Hellenistic gnostic ideas which have somehow coagulated round the name of Jesus of Nazareth, about whom little certain historical knowledge can be attained, must be studied to see whether it gives a rational and coherent explanation of the New Testament evidence.[118]

The more adequate hypothesis, Richardson finds, is that Jesus himself was the prime author of the striking reinterpretation of the Old Testament theology found in his own reported teachings and in the New Testament as a whole. Among those teachings Richardson included are the new covenant, the new Israel, the reinterpreted messiahship, and the reign of God.[119] Richardson regards Bultmann's denial of Christ's resurrection as an event in history "a compromise with post-Enlightenment historiography" and "a sign of the disintegration of contemporary Protestantism."[120] Why the early celebrations of Easter, he asks, if nothing extraordinary happened on Easter Day?

Unfortunately Barth also ascribed a reductive naturalism to all history (*Historie*), although historiography need not be limited to antisupernaturalists. Unless Christians challenge the naturalistic presuppositions, it will do little good to join Barth in calling the resurrection a "saga" or interpreted history (*Geschichte*) rather than a "fact." Ramm thinks Barth's case "the best of the options because he has most thoroughly understood the nature of the historical issue."[121] Those who defend the objectivity of the resurrection, Ramm thinks, underplay its unique character, and those who seek to guard its uniqueness shade away its historical factuality.[122] From the beginning we have emphasized both the uniqueness and the factuality of Christ's resurrection. Insofar as the body is uniquely incorruptible, powerful, and glorious, those truths come from propositional revelation; insofar as the body is continuous, visible, audible, and tangible, it was verified publicly by eyewitnesses. We integrate both the continuity and the uniqueness as a visible sign laden with invisible meanings.

If a transcendent personal God who has purposes for our world exists, ordinarily we expect regular natural laws, but there is no reason why God cannot act in extraordinary ways. If God were merely an idea within our own heads, or a formless life-force that we could tap for our purposes, a miracle like the literal resurrection would be impossible. But belief in the living God of the Bible provides the most coherent and viable explanation of why there is anything at all, why it is orderly, why there are persons, and why in conscience and history there is a difference between right and wrong.

> If we are in fact spirits, not Nature's offspring, then there must be some point (probably the brain) at which created spirits even now can produce èffects on matter not by manipulation or technics but simply by the wish to do so . . . . every time you move your hand or think a thought. And nature . . . is not destroyed but rather perfected by her servitude"[123]

He who created the body as an instrument of spirit can restore one ravaged by sin and make the body become an even more wonderful instrument (of spirit). The peak Christian experience is not a contentless mystical contemplation from which the environment and the senses are banished but a full realization of God's presence as nature and spirit are finally harmonized. Every state of Christ's resurrection body perfectly expresses his spiritual state and his spiritual state is supremely just and loving, wise and powerful. So Paul's question to Agrippa is appropriate: "Why should any of you consider it incredible that God raises the dead?" (Acts 26:8).

The living Spirit who made humans unique can also actively pursue sinners in history like a hunter, king, or husband. As C. S. Lewis found,

> There comes a moment when the children who have been playing at burglars hush suddenly: was that a *real* footstep in the hall? There comes a moment when people who have been dabbling in religion

('man's search for God'!) suddenly draw back. Supposing we really found Him? We never meant it to come to that! Worse still, supposing He had found us? So it is a sort of Rubicon. One goes across; or not. But if one does, there is no manner of security against miracles. One may be in for anything."[124]

With good reason to believe in the reality of the God of the Bible, unquestionably the miracle of Christ's resurrection could happen.

Should Christ's Resurrection Happen?

It would be pointless for God to resurrect Abraham Lincoln for an atomistic appearance to a bartender for no particular reason. But Jesus Christ is not just another person, and his resurrection is no isolated event. Why should Christ have been raised? Is it not enough that Jesus lived and died? No, it is not enough.

Christ's resurrection completes the purposes of the whole century-spanning program of salvation. It powerfully fulfills divine justice and love. It dramatically culminates the Messiah's saving mission. The purpose of Christ's resurrection is not to celebrate the joys of spring but to save the lost. The resurrection exhibits God's concern for the world of fallen people with all the literal blood, sweat, and tears their sins entail. God is not like an executive away on a trip, but more like a loving father willing to go to any length to recover a lost child. In order to reconcile sinners God transcended his usual method of working and performed miracles. By astounding signs and wonders God delivered enslaved Israelites from Egyptian bondage, brought down the walls of Jericho, and established Israel in the Promised Land. When Baal worship threatened to destroy the line of the coming Messiah, God spewed fire from heaven onto Elijah's altar. Christ's resurrection is part of a re-

demptive program that included numerous miraculous events for important redemptive purposes.

In the fullness of time the Messiah came into the world by the miracle of the virgin birth. Jesus healed the sick, gave sight to the blind, predicted the future, and quieted nature's violent storms. In this context it is not surprising that he should say, "Destroy this temple and in three days I will raise it up again." The resurrection was the grand climax of a series of mighty acts in the life of the incarnate Word of God.

Several important things were accomplished by the crucified Christ's resurrection historically and theologically. As we have documented above, it fulfilled his predictions, demonstrated the truth of his claims, and certified the Father's acceptance of his atoning provisions. It assures believers' justification, redemption, and reconciliation today. And in the world to come it guarantees their own reembodiment and acceptance with the final Judge. Indeed it constitutes God's empirical signature on the bottom line for every aspect of salvation. On the one hand, if Christ's tomb was not emptied, the faith of every Christian has been in vain. All who have trusted him were deceived and remain in their sins. On the other hand, if he came forth from the tomb, such a mighty act of God has tremendous significance for sinners of all time.

Should the resurrection happen? Indeed, it should. But many things that would be great never take place in fact.

Did Christ's Resurrection Happen?

Human knowledge of the conclusion of Christ's unique life is not totally different from the knowing of all past events. We do not learn about ancient history with an intuitive psychological certitude, but a probability based on research of credible ancient documents. The most coherent interpretation, then, has the greatest probability of conveying the truth. Some theologians, such as P. Althaus, think that intuition can open an "immediate, prescientific relationship to past history, across centuries and millennia, which bears within itself unconditional certainty about this past life."[125] But Pannenberg aptly responds, "Intuition always requires confirmation through detailed historical observation. . . . The only method of achieving at least approximate certainty with regard to the events of a past time is historical research."[126]

Insofar as the sign of Christ's resurrection was literal and physical, it can be subjected to historical research; insofar as the sign involved revealed conceptual meanings, it cannot be subjected to testing by the five senses. It is still necessary to verify as far as possible the prophetic or apostolic sources of the revealed meanings and our interpretations of their teachings. Futile is the quest for a reductively historical Jesus, in the sense of a Jesus apart from such supernatural events as the resurrection and ascension with their supernaturally revealed meanings.

Can we integrate the varied accounts of the resurrection coherently? Many think the four Gospels are full of glaring discrepancies and so find harmonies impossible (e.g., E. Brunner, W. Marxen, N. Perrin). Christian scholars were certain that this does not mean the narratives cannot be reconciled, but for a long time no one had brought forth a convincing harmony. Challenged by this problem, John Wenham, in Jerusalem in 1945, set out to determine whether a convincing harmony of the resurrection accounts was possible. After thorough examinations of the sites in and around the city, Wenham was at first impressed with the intractable nature of the discrepancies. On the first Easter morning did five women go to the tomb (Luke), three (Mark), two (Matthew), one (John), or none (Paul)?

Did they visit the tomb while it was still dark (John) or when the sun had risen (Mark)? Were the messengers who spoke to them men (Mark one, Luke two) or angels (Matthew one, John two)? Were the messengers inside the tomb (Mark, Luke, and John), or did they start outside the tomb and finish inside (Matthew)? Did Christ appear to a number of women who held his feet without rebuke (Matthew) or to one whom he forbade to touch him (John)? Did Christ appear to the eleven disciples in Galilee (Matthew) or in Jerusalem (Luke)?[127]

Wenham's insatiable curiosity motivated study of the Greek text, extensive further research, and map making. He reported:

I gradually found many of the pieces of the jigsaw coming together. It now seems to me that these resurrection stories exhibit in a remarkable way the well-known characteristics of accurate and independent reporting, for superficially they show great disharmony, but on close examination the details gradually fall into place.[128]

Although some details remained uncertain, Wenham proposes the following harmony. Of special evidential value were Christ's initial appearances for eight days in Jerusalem where Joseph's well-known garden and empty tomb could be checked by first-century friends and enemies. In the first fifteen days Christ appeared at least seven times quietly teaching individuals and groups about the kingdom of God. After this preparation he met the great gathering in Galilee. To counter their hope for a political kingdom in Jerusalem, he regathered the disciples and recommissioned them as apostles in Galilee, reconstituting the Christian movement. In the atmosphere of Galilee they were weaned afresh from the ideal of a temporal Jewish messianic kingdom until they were ready to be sent back to the city that had crucified their Lord to begin their worldwide witness. In Jerusalem the transformed apostles waited for the coming of the Holy Spirit on the day of Pentecost.[129]

The appearances occurred in a kind of progressive revelation of Christ's exaltation as people were able to receive it. The women who first saw the opened and empty tomb and heard the angels' explanation were ready before the men. Jesus met and spoke first to one of them and then to the others. Then after hearing the women's account and seeing the empty tomb and the grave cloths, the two men walking to Emmaus were joined by Jesus; he explained his mission and gradually revealed facts about the fulfillment of prophecy concerning himself. This prepared them for the commissioning of the official witnesses: Peter, the eleven, Thomas, the five hundred, and finally his own brother James, who would one day lead the Jerusalem church. There remained only the last farewell and the coming of the Holy Spirit before they would courageously preach Christ crucified and risen, turning the world upside down.[130]

> So ends an investigation which we believe has shown that the charge of irreconcilability brought against the resurrection stories has not been substantiated. Rather it has shown that these records exhibit the characteristics of accurate and independent reporting, for superficially they show great disharmony, but on close examination the details gradually fall into place.[131]

Other scholars have set forth harmonizations of the resurrection narratives confirming the possibility of a coherent integration of the Gospel records in the light of recent knowledge.[132]

Differences of detail occur in reporting emergencies today with all the instant communication facilities available for highly trained news investigators

and writers. With such a confusing flurry of untraceable, sudden appearances for forty days in the first century, it is amazing that the differences are not greater. "There may even be a virtue in the fact that the evangelists present such diverse accounts, for it shows their independence of each other and suggests that the points on which they do agree are likely to be all the more historically reliable."[133]

On what points do the records agree? The biblical records consistently present the following *data that demand explanation* from the standpoint of any worldview. We here present certain undoubted phenomena of the first century and ask how the reader proposes to account for each and all of them together.

1. *Jesus of Nazareth died and was buried.* We noted the biblical evidence for the fact of his death in the previous chapter. The claim that he was not raised because he did not die does not fit the facts. An expert on executions was not likely mistaken when he found Jesus dead and so did not break his legs to speed death. A Roman soldier pierced him with a sword. Both his loved ones and enemies concluded he had died. Joseph of Arimathea buried him in his own tomb. The tomb was a cave, the entrance to which was closed with a huge boulder. Roman soldiers sealed the tomb and stood guard over it.

According to the theory that Jesus did not really die, he, the one who had no sleep throughout the mistreatment and trial the night before and who was too weak to carry his cross, suddenly revived and became strong enough to break out of the graveclothes and the sealed cave and overpower the armed guards. Then the wounded victim overwhelmingly convinced his disciples that he had triumphantly conquered death! Jesus, in his mere humanness, would not have had the strength for such a performance. And even if he had done so, he would have deceived his followers until they too became party to a pious fraud. Whatever else may be thought of Jesus and his followers, no responsible scholar regards them premeditated deceivers. It is beyond reasonable doubt that Jesus died and his body was buried.

2. After the crucifixion *a resurrection was unexpected.* In spite of Jesus' several attempts to prepare his disciples for his death, they were not prepared for what took place. Having misinterpreted the nature of his present kingship, the disciples were disillusioned and confused. In that condition psychologically they were not capable of inventing a story of his triumphant resurrection and ascension.

3. On Easter Sunday both women and men confirmed that *the tomb was open and empty.* Before dawn an earthquake had occurred, and an angel had come and rolled the boulder back up the hill. If the tomb was not empty, how does one account for the successful emergence of Christianity in Jerusalem where belief in the resurrected Christ could have been disconfirmed by opening his grave?

4. *The grave clothes were undisturbed,* indicating that Jesus left them without unwrapping them. To the observer it was evident that Jesus' body had passed through the grave clothes, leaving them as they had been wrapped.

5. For a period of forty days the living *Jesus appeared* to individuals and to groups of up to five hundred. At first the observers tried to explain the empirical evidence in other ways. But after seeing and hearing Jesus and being invited to touch his wounds, even the most skeptical were convinced that he was alive again. Among the witnesses were those who were best qualified to recognize him—those that had been with him for three years.

6. As a result of their eyewitness experiences with the risen Christ, *the disciples were transformed.* In forty days their despair changed to hope, their disbelief to faith, their fear to courage. In just six or seven weeks from the crucifixion to the day of Pentecost, Peter, who had denied his Lord three times, boldly proclaimed Christ's resurrection a short distance from his grave. Something provoked the belief of doubting Thomas, Jesus' brother James, and Jesus' enemy Saul. If it was not Jesus' resurrection that transformed the disciples, what was it? Certainly not a legend.

7. *A new movement arose* in Jerusalem and quickly advanced throughout the region. It was based on the belief that Jesus was alive. If it were not for the resurrection, Jesus' Jewish followers might have formed a sect of Judaism, but not a distinct religion. There is nothing but the resurrection to distinguish the first Christians from any other Jews of their day. Nor would the disciples have been tenacious enough to keep up their distinctiveness over against the pious Judaism to which they otherwise belonged if it had not been for their unshakeable convictions about Jesus' resurrection. The primitive message did not limit itself to general philosophical statements but concentrated on specific happenings. Distinctively the sect of the Nazarenes reported that Christ rose. Either that belief was rooted in fact, in a serious misapprehension, or in a deliberate lie. It was not a sect with a new philosophy to propagate, nor was there a dominating personality. It was a body of people bearing witness to the alleged resurrection of a historical figure.[134]

Several observable indications of Christ's resurrection have continued to the present day:

8. The *Christian church still exists today.* Apart from this triumph of Christ, the church would not have begun or continued. As one wag put it, other businesses run like the church

would have become extinct long ago! The frailty and fallibility of church leaders has become notorious in literature and the media. Had it not been for its confidence in the One who conquered sin and death, the church would long ago have disappeared.

9. Christians generally practice *Sunday worship*. The change in the day of worship from Saturday to Sunday took place and remains evident today. If not the resurrection, what remarkable first-century event can explain that major transformation of a longstanding Sabbath tradition?

10. The first century produced the written *New Testament,* which remains to this day. If Jesus did not rise, what first-century event did motivate the written preservation of the apostles' teaching? Had Jesus not risen, few would have been interested in apostolic doctrine. Apart from the resurrection, the discouraged group after the crucifixion and burial would not have had the heart or the motivation to write the books of the New Testament.

11. *The Calendar* directs attention to what happened before Christ (B.C.) and after the birth of the Lord (A.D.). If Jesus did not rise, what event in history better accounts for the change in the dating of all events that later occurred?

In sum, if the incarnate Word did not rise, what other life-transforming, history-changing, first-century event does account for all of these eleven phenomena? Deception, mistake, bribery, hallucination, etc., are inadequate explanations. The liberals have decimated each other's proposals until most have abandoned attempts to propose naturalistic explanations. The hypothesis of hallucinations does not account for the number, the variety, and the abrupt cessation of the appearances. The swoon theory does not fit the overwhelmingly probable evidence that Jesus died (see vol. 1, chap. 7). The same kinds of evidence and method of

reasoning that conclusively support Jesus' death conclusively support his resurrection from the dead. These lines of evidence empirically confirmed by many witnesses are as significant for pre-Christians as for Christians. God "has set a day when he will judge the world with justice by the man he has appointed. He has given proof of this to *all men* by raising him from the dead" (Acts 17:31).

As a graduate student at Cornell University in a course on philosophy of religion, Gordon Lewis presented a case like this in a paper on Paul's classic religious language at Athens (Acts 17). Professor Irving Singer, a philosophical analyst, responded in the margin of the paper, "This makes the case for a bodily resurrection meaningful." It was encouraging to hear a naturalist admit the cognitive significance of the historical data. As Antony Flew admitted, a naturalistic presupposition that miracles are impossible "should not be the end of the affair. For historians, like everyone else, ought to be ever ready, for sufficient reason, to correct their assumptions about what is probable or improbable, possible or impossible. And this readiness should allow that even the qualification *secular* may, for sufficient reason, have to be abandoned."[135]

Professor Singer then raised a probing question that may be expected from any naturalist. "How do you know that it was *God* who raised him from the dead?" Briefly, an answer to that question reverts to how we know anything about a transcendent being (see vol. 1, chaps. 2–4) and what may be known about God (see vol. 1, chaps. 5–9). We found reason to believe in two supernatural powers—God and the fallen angel Satan. So the question becomes, Was Christ raised from the grave by the power of God or by the power of the devil? The need for discernment between good and evil spirits arises in interpreting any supernatural phenomenon. Whether a miracle is ultimately done by divine or by demonic power is best answered by assessing its purposes. Did it serve the ends of God's righteous kingdom or of Satan's evil kingdom? In the context of its prophetic anticipation and all of its moral and spiritual significance above, behind Christ's resurrection was the power of the Holy One. If doubt remains, many inspired biblical texts explicitly reveal the fact that it was God who raised Jesus from the dead (Acts 2:24, 32; 3:15, 26; 4:10).

What Form Does the Apologetic Take?

In drawing responsible conclusions about Christ's resurrection, we seek to avoid two extremes. We cannot dismiss history as unimportant in favor of a transcendental call to conversion or inner witness of the Spirit, nor can we dismiss the transcendent Spirit's illumination in favor of such history as can be confined within the assumptions of naturalistic presuppositions. On the one hand, attempts to discover the Jesus of naturalistic history have ended in a *cul de sac*. On the other hand, a gospel that cares only for the apostolic proclamation and denies that it either can or should be tested for its historical antecedents is only a thinly veiled gnosticism or docetism. Christian historical apologetic, if it is respectable, welcomes careful scrutiny of its method. Even Helmut Thielicke, who stresses the existential implications of the gospel, has wisely cautioned, "Nothing can be the object of our faith which stands in evident contradiction to the factual. . . . The Easter faith would then be possible only by means of schizophrenia of our human consciousness—which would be unbearable and unallowable."[136]

The verificational method of reasoning used throughout *Integrative Theology* does not imagine that anyone can be totally objective in examining this evidence or come to it with a mind free of all prior conclusions. More realistically the method simply invites readers to carefully consider the consistency and adequacy of hypothetical explanations and accept the most adequate explanation. If God exists as revealed in Christ and Scripture, we have a coherent account of all eleven lines of evidence. Several scholars have utilized variations of the hypothetical method of reasoning. C. F. D. Moule, for example, "attempts simply to display a selection of the phenomena which need to be reckoned with, and to ask, What do you make of these? Can you make sense of them as history without importing precisely the value-judgments to which the original Christians were led? Conversely, can you account for the value judgment without the historical basis?"[137] Open to alternative hypotheses, Moule invites his readers to propose a more coherent account if they can.

Having employed a verificational or critical method, George Ladd concluded,

> The only hypothesis which adequately explains the "historical" facts, including the empty tomb, is that God actually raised the body of Jesus from the realm of mortality in the world of time and space to the invisible world of God, and that Jesus was able to appear to his disciples in different ways on different occasions. Admittedly this is not a "historical" explanation; it involves *theology*—a belief in God. . . . Does such a faith mean a "leap in the dark"? By no means."[138]

Ladd did not seek by a "historical" reasoning from naturalistic assumptions and a blank mind to "prove" the resurrection in some compulsive sense. It was his purpose, he said, to exhibit the historical facts and show that the hypothesis of Christ's bodily resurrection is the most adequate explanation without self-contradiction. That is the meaning of confirmation or "proof" in most factual issues.[139] Although Ladd calls his approach an "inductive method," his starting point is not a totally objective, blank mind but hypotheses to be tested. Hence New Testament scholars who follow Ladd in this are not following an inductive method of reasoning, in spite of advertising "inductive Bible studies." When admittedly starting with hypotheses to be tested, New Testament scholars use a method more like the verificational method of reasoning (reminiscent of Edward John Carnell, Ladd's colleague for many years). New Testament scholars would avoid the naïveté of alleging a blank mind at the beginning of their research if they explicitly adopted a verificational method.[140]

Does Scientism Have All the Answers?

Often it seems that science has all the answers. For reliable knowledge about the weather, illness, and any physical or historical possibilities people do not go to the minister, but to the scientists. The attempt to empty nature of God since the Enlightenment, however, fails to account for Christ's empty tomb and appearances. On either a naturalistic or pantheistic worldview dead people stay dead. Once decomposition and decay have begun, they continue. But on one occasion this natural process did not have the last word. *A power distinct from nature and atomic energy reversed irreversible natural laws of decomposition and overcame death itself!* Christ's resurrection demonstrated *the Creator's transcendent power over nature's irreversible laws in space and time.* Although occurring in space and time, Christ's resurrection cannot be explained within space and time. Neither naturalistic nor pantheistic hypotheses can adequately account for the fact of Christ's resurrection. It confirms a divine power above or over nature. The resurrection shows that the divine power is not so far removed that God cannot act in extraordinary ways within and upon nature. The deistic hypothesis does not account for the facts of the first century. The most coherent account of the regularities of nature and history and the miracles of the first century is a theistic, biblical worldview.

Does the Problem of Evil Have an Answer?

On occasion it seems that evil gets out of control in history. Then people cry out, "Why does not God do something about it?" God has done something about it! Providentially God prevents and overrules much of the evil. But the crucifixion and resurrection exemplify God's mightiest acts to this point in response to the problem of evil. At Calvary it seemed that evil had triumphed, but evil and death did not have the last word. The resurrection and ascension did! History is not merely the arena of impersonal spatial and temporal forces. Bound up with space and time in historical events are the interactions or intentions of human agents and, above all, those of the divine Agent. Numbers of fallen human agents conspired to take the life of Jesus—Judas, Herod, Pilate, Jews, and Gentiles (Acts 4:27). God permitted their evil but overruled history's worst evil to provide salvation for all! However great a hold moral evil may have in your life, God can transform it. The resurrection has demonstrated God's power to deliver from sin's power and from its tragic consequences. *Christ's resurrection demonstrated God's ability to transform history's worst injustice into its greatest good.*

Christ's incarnation, life, death, and resurrection did not occur in some kind of suprahistory, touching our fallen world only in a tangential manner. The eternal Word came in actual, literal history. The tendency to speak of timeless events or crises in the early Barth and Brunner, and in Bultmann, Dodd, and Reinhold Niebuhr is inadequate. Far from violating or abrogating time, the risen Christ has created a new age or aeon. So the church fulfills its mission of overcoming evil in the overlap of the two times, the present evil aeon that will pass away and the new righteous aeon that has already come in the triumph of Christ. Spiritually, the end time "has telescoped itself into the present and penetrated the Church through the coming of the Spirit."[141] Because of its participation in the new creation, the church can continue to live on earth and in history only through being crucified with Christ to the present evil powers. What does the future hold from the standpoint of the centrality of Christ's incarnation, death, and resurrection in history? We expect ethical crises to the end of time, but Christ's resurrection assures our own final victory over sin and death. In the light of our coming *telos* we ought not give in to the evil of the present age, but overcome it by making responsible decisions along the way.[142]

Is Jesus Christ the Only Reconciler?

Is the crucified and risen Christ the only religious leader to have justly provided for forgiveness, redemption, and reconciliation to God? Few issues are as sensitive as this in a pluralistic world of instant communication.

To avoid an unhealthy exclusivism John Hick proposes a Copernican revolution in Christian theology, a paradigm shift from a Jesus-centered to a God-centered model. He sees the great world religions as different responses to the one divine reality. When Hick calls Jesus the Son of God, he announces that the myth of Jesus is the means by which he came to know God.[143] Many

Eastern thinkers also regard all faiths as relative ways to the one transcendent God. Paul F. Knitter rejects a miraculous resurrection and favors the disciples' subjective faith as producing Christ's resurrection, and also takes a theocentric view of Christianity and a nonnormative reinterpretation of the uniqueness of Jesus Christ.[144]

Fully aware of relativism in religion, Ernst Troeltsch argued that historical phenomena are not all the same and that they all have values that call for choices among them. He found Christianity superior to the religions of nature (Hinduism and Buddhism) and of law (Judaism and Islam) because it gives greater value to personal existence. Nature religions, by dissolving humans in the divine essence, forfeit all positive meaning and content in the divine Being. Christianity does not deny the empirical world as actually given and experienced but builds on it, transforms it, and eventually raises it to a new level. The Absolute entered history in Jesus of Nazareth, and only his crucifixion and resurrection make possible this achievement for souls ensnared in depravity and guilt. Jesus Christ represents the only complete break with the limits and conditions of nature (and process) religions. And Jesus Christ provides the only satisfaction of absolute justice for religions of law. People must make a choice between meditation on nonbeing or redemption and reconciliation through faith and growth in grace.[145]

It is important that we neither absolutize relatives nor relativize the incarnate Absolute. But if the Absolute has come into history in the Lord Jesus Christ, we must not relativize his incarnation to the level of other religious leaders. "The only reason for being a Christian," said Stephen Neill, "is the overpowering conviction that the Christian faith is true." And as Alec Vidler said of Christianity, "Either it is true for all men, whether they know it or not; or it is true for no one, not even for those people who are under the illusion that it is true." After citing these statements Elton Trueblood added, "In the long run, the best reason for dedication to the spread of the faith of Christ is the conviction that this faith conforms to reality as does no other alternative of which we are aware."[146]

Although admittedly many who have held to the exclusivity of the truth of the gospel have been arrogant, we seek to respect the right of people in other traditions to differ. Tolerance is often mistaken for agreement with others. It does not take tolerance to be kindly to those who hold similar convictions. Tolerance involves respect and consideration for those committed to contradictory views on issues of importance. Belief in the truth of some religious statements and the realities they designate need not be maintained in an intolerant attitude. Those who believe in the risen Messiah should care about those who reject him and should avoid any unethical attempts to persuade them. Although Paul and the other apostles were convinced of the uniqueness of Christ, they did not resort to coercive programing or deprograming of others. Both non-Christians and Christians in a civilized pluralistic world have the freedom to engage in dialogue and discussion in an effort to persuade one another of the truth of their views.

People must be free to conclude whether or not the Messiah has come and was crucified and raised for all humans of all times and cultures. It cannot be both ways without self-contradiction. The price of rejecting the law of noncontradiction (with Knitter and others) is forfeiture of the possibility of meaningful affirmation about anything at all. If all assertions are equally true, they are all equally false, and we are reduced to meaninglessness or silence.

The law of noncontradiction cannot be refuted, since it is the necessary condition of any intelligible communication in the East or West. Illustrating the necessity of choice, Stephen Neill says, "Whom shall we follow—eastern teachers who tell us that the world is evil or illusion? Western teachers who tell us to accept the world, because we can do no other? Jesus, who tells us that the world is God's world, and therefore essentially good and serviceable?"[147] Whom shall we follow? Eastern teachers who tell us that Jesus was one more avatar who did not physically come into the world, literally die for literal sins, or literally rise? Or shall we believe the confirmed signs and revealed significance of the Messiah's life according to inspired Scripture?

When Peter says, "Salvation is found in no one else" (Acts 4:12), he is not pronouncing a narrow-minded a priori prejudice. He is reporting that Christ has uniquely done what others neither have done nor can do. What founder of any other religious movement: (1) claimed to be the unique, once-for-all divine incarnation? (2) lived a fully human life without sin and so was worthy to die in place of sinners? (3) was God so that he could bear the penalty of all human sin? (4) could identify as fully with both God and humans as mediator? (5) died to propitiate the Father's righteous wrath, redeem, and reconcile? (6) predicted his or her resurrection and came back to life in triumph over sin and its death penalty? (7) ascended to the place of highest power over every other power in heaven and earth? and (8) was uniquely in the image of God and so able to recreate sinners in God's image and bring peace to the entire world?

We ought not confuse the issues of the objective validity of an assertion with a subjective agreement with its content, or a personal commitment to its referent in reality. A personal commitment to the Savior does not change the universal validity of the truths of the gospel. In religion we are concerned with both personal and propositional truths. Conceptual truths guide us away from counterfeit Christs to the living Christ who alone has demonstrated power over death. It is not our commitment that saves us, but the one in whom we place our trust. False beliefs do not become true simply by being internalized.

In view of the evidence in volume 1, chapter 7, we affirmed with overwhelming probability and objective validity that Jesus was both truly human and truly divine. Hence he differed from Abraham, Krishna, Buddha, Mohammed, Joseph Smith, and Mary Baker Eddy not merely in degree, but in kind. There have been many other great teachers and fine examples; but there have in fact been no other propitiators, redeemers, and reconcilers. If salvation from our moral predicament were attainable by an immediate, direct mystical experience of God the Father, the Son of God would not have needed to come or die for sinners. But since God himself acted decisively in history in order justly to save sinners, we cannot agree with those who think that by mystical intuition or spiritual disciplines they can by-pass faith in Christ's incarnation, death, and resurrection. Non-Christian mystics may experience oneness with the cosmos and its energy or even become aware of its Creator's existence, but apart from the provisions of Christ they do not enjoy personal fellowship with the Creator, who is not only distinct from the cosmos but also righteous.

The deepest question is not how we can come to God or become aware of God's existence. All religions lead to God—as Judge! Before him eventually every knee will bow. The root question is, How can sinful people come to God as Savior? What non-Christian, non-

Evangelical religion provides for a just punishment of sin and acquittal of sinners? Many today are like the Jews in Paul's day. Paul said, "They are zealous for God, but their zeal is not based on knowledge. Since they do not know the righteousness that comes from God and sought to establish their own, they did not submit [themselves] to God's righteousness" (Rom. 10:2–3). Our heart's desire and prayer to God for people trying to build up good *karma* (works) is like Paul's for the Jews—that they may be saved (v. 1). Christians need not strive for perfect *karma* through imagined endless incarnations in order to attain the perfection of heaven because by faith they have received the righteousness that comes from God—Christ's perfect *karma*.

Since Jesus is Lord of all, the highest lordship by its very nature can have no equals. Jesus cannot be added to a god shelf along with 330 million other Eastern Hindu deities or a similar number of Western materialistic idols. Every other lordship is either (1) only derived and dependent on Christ's power, or (2) a presumptuous and enslaving lordship in rebellion against Christ's authority. Christ's right to rule has been authorized by his resurrection and ascension for all people in every culture and in every situation. In the finest of human cultures followers of the Lord Jesus Christ will introduce people not to their previous cultures, but to the Lord over all cultures and world religions—the risen Lord classically revealed in the written Word.

Since God the Father has inaugurated the exalted Christ as Lord of all, Walter Kunneth argues, "where the risen Christ is, there is God. God is where the risen Christ holds sway." He then continues, "God is the God who has raised Christ: he is the God of the resurrection. Thus because of the Easter event, there can be no other [redemptive] knowledge of God than in and through the knowledge of Christ as the Lord.''[148]

On the basis of several converging lines of evidence, with Saul, who became Paul, we conclude beyond reasonable doubt that "Christ has indeed been raised from the dead" (1 Cor. 15:20). God the Father did not abandon his one and only Son! God is faithful; God kept his word! Death is not stronger than God's love! Jesus' claims for himself are true! He is the Messiah! His death provides salvation! He is not only Messiah, he is Lord! His spiritual kingdom has come! He will return to extend it! History has a goal! He is head of his church! The church is going somewhere!

RELEVANCE FOR LIFE
AND MINISTRY

Faith

On the solid basis of the confirmed evidence and revealed truth, our trust in the crucified, risen, and ascended Lord Jesus Christ will never be futile. Those united to Christ by faith are no longer under legal condemnation; believers are legally justified! Believers are no longer dominated by their own depravity, that of the peers in the world or that of the devil; believers are liberated! Believers are no longer estranged; they are reconciled to God and one another! Believers are no longer spiritually dead; believers have eternal life.

At times however, we yield to temptation, break relationships, and question our legal standing. A certain former student admired his pastor and former Bible college professor greatly. For years the alumnus served as chairman of the board of his hero's large church. Then one Sunday morning he had to do the hardest thing in his life. He had to explain to the church that his hero had resigned, effective immediately. After over two decades of ministry in that

pulpit he would not appear again, because he had committed adultery. This alumnus' most important personal relationship with a Christian leader had exploded in his face. He said he nearly lost his faith. He would have, he surmised, if he had not remembered the conclusiveness of the case for Christ's resurrection and so of the objective truth of Christianity. During his disillusionment with a Christian leader, he remembered the fact of Christ's triumph.

In the final analysis, as important as personal relationships may be, a Christian's faith does not rest in frail and fallible human disciplers, but in the risen Christ. When we face criticism, hardship, poverty, disillusionment, or sorrow, we need to remember that God is not dead. The psalmist often cried out because the heavens seemed to be like brass. If ever it appeared that God was not relevant to the human situation, it was at Calvary. Christ himself cried out, "My God, my God, why have you forsaken me?" (Matt. 27:46). But the Father was there transforming history's worst injustice into a triumph of grace! In all our private meditations, family devotions, and public teaching and preaching, church leaders ought to feature far more than is usually done the resurrection and exaltation of the Savior to the right hand of the Father.

When everything collapses around you and your work, remember Christ's death-conquering resurrection and triumphant ascension! These objective facts provide a solid base for faith and the following great subjective blessings.

Peace

The risen Christ approached his fearful and confused disciples in the first century with the words "Peace be with you." (John 20:19, 26). In anticipation of leaving them Jesus earlier said, "Peace I leave with you; *my peace I give you. . . .* Do not let your hearts be troubled and do not be afraid'' (John 14:27). Christ has provided for reconciliation and peace within ourselves as well as with God and others. He rose and intercedes for us to give us peace. "The Lord is near. Do not be anxious about anything, but in everything, by prayer and petition, with thanksgiving, present your requests to God. And the peace of God, which transcends all understanding, will guard your hearts and minds in Christ Jesus" (Phil. 4:4–7). After urging meditation on whatever is right, pure, lovely, admirable, excellent, or praiseworthy, Paul adds, "And the God of peace will be with you" (vv. 8–9).

Like Christ and Paul, we could well use "peace" as a greeting or farewell. In good times and bad it can remind us that the triumphant Lord is near. So long as the greeting does not become an empty formality, it can be refreshing and uplifting. Christians have more to say to one another than "Hi," although that may give some recognition of personal worth. So in public services (as Episcopalians do) or in private relationships, we may greet our friends with the words "The peace of the ascended Lord be with you."

"He himself is our peace" (Eph. 2:14). When estranged from themselves and others, Christians need the Messiah's peace. Even when facing prejudicial relationships like those between Jews and Gentiles, we recall that "he himself is our peace." Christ's presence with his disciples restores *shalom*. Recognition of one's personal presence is not entirely a matter of physical immediacy, effective historical influence, or psychological immediacy. We can recognize a personal presence through verbal signs or enacted signs.[149] So by continuing in the apostles' doctrine, fellowship, prayer, and breaking of bread we appreciate our risen Lord's just and loving presence with his people.

And even in the frontlines of battle with unholy spirits the Lord's peace sustains us. The gospel of peace is like well-designed footwear that enables soldiers to walk through the battles of life (Eph. 6:15). The peace of Christ, the conqueror of Satan, is part of the armor that enables us to stand in the front lines against all the devil's schemes. Christ fits our feet with the readiness for defeating the demonic by believing (continuously) the gospel of peace. Appropriation of that peace makes for good footing in warfare against evil powers.[150] Inner tranquility comes not from meditating on meaningless sounds to deny the reality of evil, but by meditating on the God of peace, who brought back from the dead our Lord Jesus (Heb. 13:20).

Purpose

Because of Christ's resurrection, Christians *live teleologically*. With Paul they say, "I want to know Christ and the power of his resurrection and the fellowship of sharing in his sufferings, becoming like him in his death, and so, somehow, to attain to the resurrection from the dead" (Phil. 3:10–11). Believers already share legal status with Christ as crucified and risen (Col. 2:12–13; 3:1). So believers desire also to know experientially what it means to suffer as Christ did for others and by the power that raised Christ from the dead to overcome temptations and testings.

As a result of the resurrection, a Christian has a distinctive goal (a *telos*) in life. As Paul put it, "He died for all, that those who live should no longer live for themselves but for him who died for them and was raised again" (2 Cor. 5:15). Our purpose in life is not to serve ourselves but our risen Lord and others in his name. Just before ascending, Jesus explained how we could serve him: fulfill his global commission by the power of the Holy Spirit. Before ascending he predicted that "repentance and forgiveness of sins will be preached in his name to all nations, beginning at Jerusalem" (Luke 24:47). World Christians live to equip the church for its global mission focused on communicating the gospel. Whatever else Christians do in meeting other needs of people, Christ's last request must be obeyed: "Therefore go and make disciples of all nations, baptizing them in the name of the Father and of the Son and of the Holy Spirit, and teaching them to obey everything I have commanded you. And surely I am be with you always, to the very end of the age" (Matt. 28:19–20).

Power

The ascension must have been a traumatic experience for the disciples. Psychologically Peter and the apostles needed to mature from a position where they expected the incarnate Christ to do things *for* them, to a position where they looked to the ascended Christ to do things *through* them. The ascension occasioned a new relationship to their Lord. No longer could they depend on the physical Jesus in the energy of their sinful natures; now they must live by faith in the no-longer-visible Christ in the strength of the Holy Spirit (Rom. 8:4).

The divine power that raised Christ from the dead raises up those buried with him in baptism to *newness of life* (Rom. 6:4). In dependence on the power of the resurrected and ascended Christ we can overcome satanic powers. Christ's resurrection revealed the Creator's ability to overrule the irreversible forces, not only of nature but also of human nature. From a natural perspective it is impossible to change human nature. The power that raised

Christ from the grave and exalted him above all can deliver us from the strongest tendencies to sin and enable us to live in justice and love. Even before the resurrection Jesus gave the Twelve power and authority to drive out all demons, to cure diseases (Luke 9:1), and to overcome all the power of the enemy (10:19). Paul could easily have torn down the problem-plagued believers at Corinth, but the risen Lord gave Paul apostolic authority for building them up rather than pulling them down (2 Cor. 10:8; 13:10).

Christians pray for resurrection power for one another. As Paul prayed for the Ephesians pray that your family and church may be enlightened to know

> his incomparably great power for us who believe. That power is like the working of his mighty strength, which he exerted in Christ when he raised him from the dead and seated him at his right hand in heavenly realms, far above all rule and authority, power and dominion, and every title that can be given, not only in the present age but also in the one to come (Eph. 1:18–21).

Do you need inner strength to cope with the pressures of life? Paul prayed "that out of his glorious riches he may strengthen you with power through his Spirit in your inner being" (Eph. 3:16).

Ability for every good work we attempt is possible because of the risen Christ. "May the God of peace, who through the blood of the eternal covenant brought back from the dead our Lord Jesus, that great Shepherd of the sheep, equip you with every good thing for doing his will, and may he work in us what is pleasing to him, through Jesus Christ, to whom be glory for ever and ever. Amen" (Heb. 13:20–21).

Communion

Fellowship with the living Christ in prayer is a blessing made possible by his exaltation. Our communion with God does not depend on our efforts or eloquence. Our heavenly Advocate expresses what we cannot utter. So, important as periodic introspection may be, we ought not be forever taking our own spiritual temperatures. Our acceptance with God the Father rests, finally, not on our internal or external achievements, but on the exalted Messiah's completed work! He serves as the attorney for believers, pleading our causes before the Father. He has never lost a client and will not lose your case, for the grounds on which he pleads for sinners are the gracious provisions of his atonement and resurrection.

Counting on our Savior's fellowship with the Father, we can commune with God with our whole being and all our capacities. "I will pray with my spirit, but I will also pray with my mind" (1 Cor. 14:15). Aware of your union with Christ by faith and the great truths of Christ's death, resurrection, and ascension for us, we may explicitly appropriate Christ's marvelous provisions as we pray. By faith we can enter into the gracious work of the cross, claiming our personal forgiveness, redemption, and reconciliation. By faith we count ourselves dead to sin but alive to God in the exalted Christ (Rom. 6:11).

Prayer

To help realize the values of being crucified and risen with Christ in your life, develop the practice of "doctrinal praying." Join pastor-author Mark Bubek in this prayer:

I enter by faith into the mighty work of the crucifixion of my Lord. Thank You that through the blood of Jesus Christ there is not only cleansing from the penalty and guilt of sin but moment-by-moment cleansing, permitting me to fellowship with You. Thank You that the work of the cross brings Satan's work to nothing. Deliberately and by faith, I bring all of the work of my Lord on Calvary directly against Satan's workings in my life. I will accept in my life only what comes by way of the cross of Christ. I chose to die to the old man. I count him to be dead with Christ on the cross. . . .

I enter by faith into the full power and authority of my Lord's resurrection. I desire to walk in the newness of life which is mine through my Lord's resurrection. Lead me ever more into a deep understanding of the power of the resurrection. I bring the mighty truth of my Lord's victory over the grave against all of Satan's workings against Your will and plan for my life. The enemy is defeated in my life because I am united with the Lord Jesus Christ in the victory of his resurrection.

By faith I appropriate and enter today into my union with the Lord Jesus Christ in His ascension. I rejoice that my Lord displayed openly His victory over all principalities and powers as He ascended into glory through the very realm of the prince of the power of the air. I rejoice that He is seated in victory far above all principalities and powers and that I am seated there with Him. Because of my union with my Saviour, I affirm my full authority and position of victory over Satan and all of his kingdom of darkness.

By faith I enter into the benefit and blessedness of my union with Christ in his glorification. It is my joy to choose to obey Him who is my Shepherd. I ask for You to lead me in Your path today. As my great High Priest, I appropriate your high priestly work into my life today. Thank You, Lord Jesus Christ, for interceding for me and being my advocate with the heavenly Father. Thank You for watching over me and leading me, that Satan may gain no advantage over me. Grant me wisdom to discern all of the devil's deceivings and temptations.[151]

Hope

After God's eternal Son had humbled himself to become human and to die on a cross, "God exalted him to the highest place and gave him the name that is above every name, that at the name of

Jesus every knee should bow, in heaven and on earth and under the earth, and every tongue confess that Jesus Christ is Lord to the glory of God the Father" (Phil. 2:9–11).

As enthusiastic as believers in the risen Christ should be, we must warn against the dangers of an unrealistic "resurrection enthusiasm" that forgets the divine order in Christ's life and ours. If humiliation preceded exaltation in Christ's life, how much more must that order be followed in ours. An emphasis on exaltation and victory with Christ that insufficiently emphasizes a prior crucifixion with Christ may lead to unfortunate consequences in several areas. It may result in an unrealistic anthropology, a naïve view of victory in the Christian life, oversimplified advice in counseling, and a triumphalistic missiology and ecclesiology.

Hope for a Christlike style of liberation and peace follows death to selfish pride, covetous greed, and debilitating jealousy. Hope for a Christlike victory over such temptations begins with a Christlike death to them. In his humiliation the Lord of our lives is Lord first of all because he was willing to die to sin's seductions. We must not make the mistake of the first-century Jews who wanted the kingdom of glory without the kingdom of suffering. Our hope of enjoying life abundant begins with our willingness to serve Christ without it. In the present life our hope is never fully realized, so we walk by faith. Hope comes from faith in the exalted Christ.

In his life, death, and resurrection Jesus lived the life of faith and spoke words of faith. At present we too must walk by faith and express words of faith as we talk with others. Our faith in the risen Christ leads to faithfulness in words and works. On the day of Pentecost Peter's thesis confirmed by Christ's recent resurrection and ascension asserted that the crucified Jesus was "both Lord and Christ" (Acts 2:36). Still today, "if you confess with your mouth, 'Jesus is Lord,' and believe in your heart that God raised him from the dead, you will be saved" (Rom. 10:9). Ascension Day services and others may well proclaim that there is no sphere in which those who confess that "Jesus is Lord" are absolved from a faith that obediently works by love.

As we weep at the graves of our loved ones, we need to remember that death cannot separate us from the love of God in Christ Jesus our Lord (Rom. 8:38–39); our spirits continue in eternal fellowship with God. But after death our spirits long to be clothed with bodies. In times of bereavement Christians also remember Christ's resurrection. The hope it evokes is stronger than death. "Christ has indeed been raised from the dead, the firstfruits of those who have fallen asleep. . . . As in Adam all die, so in Christ all will be made alive" (1 Cor. 15:20–22). When we are raised imperishable and immortal, death will be swallowed up in victory (vv. 52–54). "The sting of death is sin, and the power of sin is the law. But thanks be to God! He gives us the victory through our Lord Jesus Christ. Therefore, my dear brothers, stand firm. Let nothing move you. Always give yourselves fully to the work of the Lord, because you know that your labor in the Lord is not in vain" (vv. 56–58). The best of lives end short of their fullest promise and potential. Death, however, does not have the last word! We shall rise! And we will complete what we began here.

Given the reality of Christ's exaltation, we can never face a situation so difficult that there is "no hope." A young Bible school student was called in before the dean for some unacceptable sin. Whatever he was told, the gifted student concluded that for him there was no future. After a lengthy search for him, his body was found in a back room of his old New England church. He had hung himself in the choir robe in which he formerly sang. Pinned to the robe was a note with two words: "No hope." No situation ought to be beyond hope for those who have faith in the forgiveness of Christ's cross and the renewal of Christ's resurrection. The great High Priest and Lord of all ever lives to make intercession for us. However dark the night of your life becomes, remember the resurrection! Remember that Christ lives and can overcome the greatest evils.

"May the God of hope fill you with all joy and peace as you trust in him, so that you may overflow with hope by the power of the Holy Spirit" (Rom. 15:13).

Joy

We rejoice at the achievement of a child, the attaining of a new position, and a victory in sports. How much greater should be our rejoicing at the decisive triumph of Christ and his kingdom over Satan and all his evil powers! Our celebrations of Easter ought to stand out for the greatness of our joy.

Because Christ lives, even though we still struggle with sinful natures and physical weaknesses, we can rejoice. With Peter, "greatly rejoice" and experience an "inexpressible and glorious joy" as you internalize the reality of your new birth and living hope. To early persecuted followers of the risen Christ Peter wrote:

Grace and peace be yours in abundance. Praise be to the God and Father of our Lord Jesus Christ! In his great mercy he has given us new birth unto a living hope through the resurrection of Jesus Christ from the dead, and into an inheritance that can never perish, spoil or fade—kept in heaven for you, who through faith are shielded by God's power until the coming of the salvation that is ready to be revealed in the last time. In this you *greatly rejoice*, though now for a little while you may have had to suffer grief in

all kinds of trials. These have come so that your faith—of greater worth than gold, which perishes even though refined by fire—may be proved genuine and may result in praise, glory and honor when Jesus Christ is revealed. Although you have not seen him, you love him; and even though you do not see him now, you believe in him and are *filled with an inexpressible and glorious joy,* for you are receiving the goal of your faith, the salvation of your souls (1 Peter 1:2–9).

REVIEW QUESTIONS

To Help Relate and Apply Each Section in This Chapter

1. *Briefly state the classical problem* this chapter addresses and indicate reasons why genuine inquiry into it is important for your worldview and your existence personally and socially.

2. *Objectively summarize the influential answers* given to this problem in history as hypotheses to be tested. Be able to compare and contrast their real similarities and differences (not merely verbal similarities or differences).

3. *Highlight the primary biblical evidence* on which to decide among views—evidence found in the relevant teachings of the major divisions of Scripture—and decide for yourself which historical hypothesis (or synthesis of historical views) provides the most consistent and adequate account of the primary biblical data.

4. *Formulate in your own words your doctrinal conviction* in a logically consistent and adequate way, organizing your conclusions in ways you can explain clearly, support biblically, and communicate effectively to your spouse, children, friends, Bible class, or congregation.

5. *Defend your view* as you would to adherents of the alternative views, showing that the other views are logically less consistent and factually faced

with more difficulties than your view in accounting for the givens, not only of special revelation but also of human experience in general.

6. *Explore the differences the viability of your conviction can make in your life.* Then test your understanding of the viability of your view by asking, "Can I live by it authentically (unhypocritically) in relation to God and to others in my family, church, vocation, neighborhood, city, nation, and world?"

MINISTRY PROJECTS

To Help Communicate This Doctrine in Christian Service

1. *Memorize one major verse or passage* that in its context teaches the heart of this doctrine and may serve as a text from which to preach, teach, or lead small-group studies on the topic. The memorized passages from each chapter will build a body of content useful also for meditation and reference in informal discussions.

2. *Formulate the major idea of the doctrine in one sentence* based on the passage memorized. This idea should be useful as the major thesis of either a lesson for a class (junior high to adult) or a message for a church service.

3. *State the specific purpose or goal of your doctrinal lesson or message.* Your purpose should be more than informative. It should show why Christians need to accept this truth and live by it (unhypocritically). For teaching purposes, list indicators that would show to what extent class members have grasped the truth presented.

4. *Outline your message or lesson in complete sentences.* Indicate how you

would support the truth of the doctrine's central ideas and its relevance to life and service. Incorporate elements from this chapter's historical, biblical, systematic, apologetic, and practical sections selected according to the value they have for your audience.

5. *List applications of the doctrine* for communicating the difference this conviction makes in life (for sermons, lessons, small-group Bible studies, or family devotional Bible studies). Applications should make clear what the doctrine is, why one needs to know it, and how it will make differences in thinking. Then show how the difference in thought will lead to differences in values, priorities, attitudes, speech, and personal action. Consider also the doctrine's possible significance for family, church, neighborhood, city, regional, and national actions.

6. *Start a file and begin collecting illustrations* of this doctrine's central idea, the points in your outline, and your application.

7. *Write out your own doctrinal statement on this subject in one paragraph* (in half a page or less). To work toward a comprehensive doctrinal statement, collect your formulations based on a study of each chapter of *Integrative Theology.* As your own statement of Christian doctrine grows, you will find it personally strengthening and useful when you are called on for your beliefs in general and when you apply for service with churches, mission boards, and other Christian organizations. Any who seek ordination to Christian ministry will need a comprehensive doctrinal statement that covers the broad scope of theology.

Notes

Chapter 1

[1] Origen, *On First Principles,* III.5.3; cf. ibid., "there were ages [i.e., worlds] before our own, and there will be others after it."

[2] William Newton Clarke, *The Christian Doctrine of God* (Edinburgh: T. & T. Clarke, 1909), 287.

[3] Augustine, *On the Trinity,* III.9.16; cf.: "The hidden seeds of all things . . . are concealed in the corporeal elements of this world." Ibid., III.8.13.

[4] Augustine, *The Literal Meaning of Genesis,* IV.27.44.

[5] Lactantius, *The Divine Institutes,* III.24; cf. Augustine, *City of God,* XVI.9.

[6] Augustus H. Strong, *Systematic Theology* (Valley Forge: Judson, 1907), 392.

[7] James Orr, *God's Image in Man* (London: Hodder & Stoughton, 1905), 95. In the Tyndale commentary on Genesis, Derek Kidner affirms that "God initially shaped man by a process of evolution," having conferred his image not only on Adam, but also on Adam's near human contemporaries "widely distributed over the world." *Genesis, TNTC* (London: Tyndale, 1967), 28–29.

[8] Richard H. Bube, *The Human Quest: A New Look at Science and the Christian Faith* (Waco: Word, 1971), 199.

[9] Bube upholds this model in his article, "Biblical Evolution?" *Journal of the American Scientific Affiliation* 23.4 (Dec. 1971): 140–44. Bube explains, "With all of its admitted difficulties, some form—possibly not understood completely at present—of the General Theory [of evolution] appears to be the best scientific interpretation of the data available from the natural world." "Inerrancy, Revelation and Evolution," *Journal of the American Scientific Affiliation* 24.2 (June 1972): 83.

[10] *A New Catechism: Catholic Faith for Adults* (New York: Herder & Herder, 1967), 264.

[11] Hans Küng, *Does God Exist?* (New York: Doubleday, 1980), 648.

[12] Karl Barth, *CD,* III.1.97.

[13] Ibid., 228–329.

[14] Emil Brunner, *The Christian Doctrine of Creation and Redemption. Dogmatics,* Vol. II, (London: Lutterworth, 1952), 40.

[15] Rudolf Bultmann, *Primitive Christianity* (New York: Meridian, 1956), 18; cf. *Jesus Christ and Mythology* (New York: Scribners, 1958), 69: The only valid meaning of the Genesis account is the "personal confession that I understand myself to be a creature which owes its existence to God."

[16] Irenaeus, *Against Heresies,* V.28.3: "For in as many days as this world was made, in so many thousand years shall it be concluded. . . . For the day of the Lord is as a thousand years; and in six days created things were completed: it is evident, therefore, that they will come to an end at the six thousandth year." Cf. *Epistle of Barnabas,* 15.

[17] Cited by Richard H. Bube, "Creation and Genesis," *Journal of the American Scientific Affiliation* 32.1 (March 1980): 35, and by Robert C. Newman and Herman J. Eckelmann, Jr., *Genesis One and the Origin of the Earth* (Grand Rapids: Baker, 1981), 57.

[18] Wheaton College biologist Pattle P. T. Pun, in his article "Evolution," registers a criticism of the flood-geology school based on current scientific findings, *EDT,* 390.

[19] The *Scofield Reference Bible,* ed. C. I. Scofield (New York: Oxford University Press, 1945), 3,nn.2,4; 4,n.3.

[20] James M. Houston, *I Believe in the Creator* (Grand Rapids: Eerdmans, 1980), 59.

[21] Ronald Youngblood, *How It All Began* (Ventura, Calif.: Regal, 1980), 25.

[22] Nicholas H. Ridderbos, *Is There Any Conflict Between Genesis 1 and Natural Science?* (Grand Rapids: Eerdmans, 1957), 45.

[23] Bernard Ramm, *The Christian View of Science and Scripture* (Grand Rapids: Eerdmans, 1954), 115–16.

[24] Ibid., 116.

[25] Newman and Eckelmann, *Genesis One*, 85–86.

[26] Arthur C. Custance, *Evolution or Creation?* (Grand Rapids: Zondervan, 1976).

[27] Norman L. Geisler and J. Kerby Anderson, *Origin Science: A Proposal for the Creation-Evolution Controversy* (Grand Rapids: Baker, 1987).

[28] Davis A. Young, *Christianity and the Age of the Earth* (Grand Rapids: Zondervan, 1982).

[29] Gleason L. Archer, Jr., maintains: "Genesis 1 was never intended to teach that the sixth creative day, when Adam and Eve were *both* created, lasted a mere twenty-four hours. In view of the long interval between these two, it would seem to border on sheer irrationality to insist that all of Adam's experiences in Genesis 2:15–22 could have been crowded into the last hour or two of a literal twenty-four-hour day." *Encyclopedia of Bible Difficulties* (Grand Rapids: Zondervan, 1982), 60.

[30] Carl F. H. Henry, *God, Revelation and Authority*, 6 vols. (Waco: Word, 1976–83), 6:133.

[31] Kidner, *Genesis*, 56.

[32] As suggested, for example, by Millard J. Erickson, *Christian Theology*, 3 vols. (Grand Rapids: Baker, 1983–85), 1:382.

[33] Walter Brueggemann states that Genesis 2 "is a more intense reflection upon the implications of creation for the destiny of humanity." *Genesis* (Atlanta: John Knox, 1982), 40.

[34] *Eerdmans Concise Bible Handbook*, ed. David and Pat Alexander (Grand Rapids: Eerdmans, 1980), 43. Cf. Pattle P. T. Pun, "Evolution," *EDT*, 392; Youngblood, *How It All Began*, 134.

[35] R. K. Harrison, "Flood," *EDT*, 419.

[36] Henry, *God, Revelation and Authority*, 6:226.

[37] Francis I. Anderson, "Job," *TOTC* (Downers Grove: InterVarsity, 1976), 274.

[38] F. Davidson and R. P. Martin, "Romans," *NBCRev*, 1:144.

[39] Donald Guthrie, *The Pastoral Epistles, TNTC* (London: Tyndale, 1957), 77. Cf. H. H. Esser, "Creation," *NIDNTT*, 1:385.

[40] Alfred Plummer, *The Gospel According to St. John* (Grand Rapids: Baker, reprint 1981), 65.

[41] John Gill, *Body of Divinity* (Atlanta, Ga.: Turner Lassiter, reprint 1957), 256.

[42] For extensive argument in defense of usual translations of Genesis 1:1 see Bruce Waltke, *Creation and Chaos: An Exegetical and Theological Study of Biblical Cosmogony* (Portland, Ore.: Western Conservative Baptist Seminary, 1974), 25–32; Edward J. Young, *Studies in Genesis One* (Grand Rapids: Baker, 1964), 1–7.

[43] Thomas E. McComiskey, *bārā'*, *TWOT*, 1:127.

[44] Ibid.

[45] Ibid.

[46] G. Ch. Aalders, *Genesis* (Grand Rapids: Zondervan, 1981), 53.

[47] C. F. Keil and F. Delitzsch, *Biblical Commentary on the Old Testament* (Grand Rapids: Eerdmans, reprint 1951), *Genesis* 1:46–47.

[48] Henry Alford, *The Greek New Testament*, 4 vols. (Boston: Lee and Shepard, 1872), 4:209.

[49] Ibid.

[50] Keil and Delitzsch, *Genesis*, 46.

[51] Ibid., 49.

[52] Alan A. MacRae, "Principles of Interpreting Genesis 1 and 2," Martin J. Wyngaarden, "Phenomenal Language According to Bernard Ramm," and G. Douglas Young, "The Effects of Poetic and Literary Style on the Interpretation of the Early Chapter of Genesis," *Journal of the Evangelical Theological Society* 2.4 (Fall 1959): 1–16.

[53] Leonard Verduin, *Somewhat Less Than God* (Grand Rapids: Eerdmans, 1970), 20.

[54] Keil and Delitzsch, *The Pentateuch*, 1:45; cf. E. J. Young, *In the Beginning* (Carlisle, Pa.: The Banner of Truth Trust, 1976), 43.

[55] Some discussion of energy in relation to light may be found in F. A. Filby, *Creation Revealed* (Westwood, N.J.: Revell, 1963), 63–71.

[56] Newman and Eckelmann, *Genesis One*, 30, 72.

[57] See Filby, *Creation Revealed*, 72–75.

[58] See Archer, *Encyclopedia of Bible Difficulties*, 59–60.

[59] J. Oliver Buswell, Jr., *A Systematic Theology of the Christian Religion*, 2 vols. (Grand Rapids: Zondervan, 1962), 1:140–41.

[60] Young, *Studies in Genesis One*, 43; cf. Leonard J. Coppes, "*yôm*," *TWOT*, 1:370–71.

[61] Henry M. Morris, ed., *Scientific Creationism* (San Diego: Creation Life, 1974), iv.

[62] Ibid., 21, 215.

[63] Benjamin B. Warfield, *Studies in Theology* (New York: Oxford University Press, 1950), 244; cf. J. Oliver Buswell, Jr., *Systematic Theology* 1:325–43; Robert D. Culver, "Peculiarities and Problems of Chronological Method and Text in the Book of Chronicles" *Journal of the Evangelical Theological Society* 5.2 (Spring 1962): 35–41.

[64] William C. Duke "The American Scientific Affiliation and the Creation Research Society: The Creation-Evolution Issue" (doctoral dissertation, Southwestern Baptist Theological Seminary, Fort Worth, Texas 76122, 1982), 147.

[65] Davis A. Young, *Creation and the Flood* (Grand Rapids: Baker, 1977); Newman and Ecklemann, *Genesis One*.

[66] Richard H. Bube, "Creation (A): How Should Genesis Be Interpreted?" *Journal of the American Scientific Association* (March 1980), 32–37; cf. idem, *The Encounter Between Christianity and Science* (Grand Rapids: Eerdmans, 1968) and *The Human Quest*.

[67] Henry M. Morris, ed., *Scientific Creationism*, 217. See also idem, *The Biblical Basis for Modern Science* (Grand Rapids: Baker, 1984).

[68] Thomas S. Kuhn, *The Structure of Scientific Revolutions*, 2nd ed. (Chicago: University of Chicago Press, 1970).

[69] Gordon Clark, *The Philosophy of Science and Belief in God* (Nutley, N.J.: Presbyterian and Reformed, 1964).

[70] Charles Sanders Pierce. "The Architecture of Theories," *The Monist* 1 (January 1891): 161–76, reprinted in Max H. Fisch, *Classic American Philosophies* (New York: Appleton, Century, Crofts, 1951), 99.

[71] Paul Davies, *God and the New Physics* (New York: Simon and Schuster, 1983), 170.

[72] Robert Jastrow, *God and the Astronomers* (New York: Norton, 1978), 115–16.

[73] Sir Fred Hoyle, "The Universe: Past and Present Reflections," *Engineering and Science* (November 1981), 12.

[74] Ibid., 10.

[75] Ibid., 12.

[76] Ibid.; cf. Richard L. Purtill's argument that it is overwhelmingly more probable that intelligent life was produced by a previously existing mind than by a random process in nature. (*C. S. Lewis' Case for the Christian Faith* [San Francisco: Harper & Row, 1981), 22–27.

[77] Charles B. Thaxton, Walter L. Bradley, and Roger L. Olsen, *The Mystery of Life's Origin: Reassessing Current Theories* (New York: Philosophical Library, 1984), 144.

[78] Ibid., 183.

[79] Ibid.

[80] Ibid., 185.

[81] Ibid.

[82] Ibid., 186.

[83] Harold F. Blum, *Time's Arrow and Evolution* (Princeton: Princeton University Press, 1968), 164.

[84] Robert Jastrow, *Until the Sun Dies* (New York: Norton, 1977), 62–63.

[85] Gordon J. Van Wylen and Richard E. Sonntag, *Fundamentals of Classical Thermodynamics*, 2nd ed. (New York: Wiley, 1978), 243.

[86] Jeremy Rifkin, *Entropy: A New World View* (New York: Bantam, 1980), 46.

[87] Ibid., 231–37.

[88] Ibid., 253.

[89] Ibid., 254.

[90] Concerning the issues of classification see Mortimer J. Adler, "Evolution," in *The Great Ideas: A Synopticon of the Great Books of the Western World* (Chicago: Encyclopedia Britannica, 1952), 1:451–59.

[91] Harold T. Wiebe, "What Can Be Learned from the Evolutionist Who Takes a Hard Look at His Own Theory," *Journal of the American Scientific Affiliation* (December 1966), 116.

[92] G. A. Kerkut, *Implications of Evolution* (New York: Pergamon, 1960), 6–7.

[93] Luther D. Sunderland, *Darwin's Enigma: Fossils and Other Problems* (San Diego: Master Book, 1984).

[94] Charles Darwin, *The Origin of Species* (1859), in *Great Books of the Western World*, ed. Robert M. Hutchins, 49:42.

[95] Ibid.

[96] A. H. Clark, *The New Evolution Zoogenesis* (Williams and Wilkins, 1930); cited by Harold T. Wiebe, "What Can Be Learned From the Evolutionist Who Takes a Hard Look at His Own Theory," *Journal of the American Scientific Affiliation* (December 1966), 116.

[97] Steven M. Stanley, "Evolution of Life: Evidence for a New Pattern" in *The Great Ideas Today 1983* (Chicago: Encyclopedia Britannica, 1983), 8; cf. Stephen Jay Gould, "Darwinism Defined: The Difference Between Fact and Theory." *Discover* 8.2 ((January 1987), 64–69; idem, "The Lesson of the Dinosaurs: Evolution Didn't Inevitably Lead to Us," ibid (March 1987), 51. Gould writes, "We didn't have to evolve at all. Life is a series of complex and unpredictable events, not a straight and narrow path to progress," Gould defends a "punctuated equilibrium." See also "Enigmas of Evolution," *Newsweek* (March 29, 1982), 44–49.

[98] Ibid., 20.

[99] Ibid.

[100] Jastrow, *God and the Astronomers*, 16.

[101] T. A. Goudge, "Henri Bergson," *EP*, 1:292.

[102] Fritjof Capra, *The Tao of Physics* (Boulder, Colo.: Shamballa, 1983), 8.

[103] Ibid., 319–21.

[104] Ibid., 9.

[105] Ibid., 12.

[106] Davies, *God and the New Physics*, vii.

[107] Brunner, *Christian Doctrine of Creation and Redemption*, 8–9.

[108] Ibid., 13.

[109] Ibid., 14.

[110] A. C. Schultz, "Wine and Strong Drink," *ZPEB*, 5:934.

[111] Anderson Spickard and Barbara R. Thompson, *Dying for a Drink* (Waco: Word, 1985), 27.

[112] Ibid., 17.

[113] Ibid., 41.

[114] Ibid., 188–89.

[115] Francis Schaeffer, *Pollution and the Death of Man* (Wheaton: Tyndale, 1970), 49–50.

[116] Rifkin, *Entropy: A New World View*, 234–35.

[117] Alfred A. Glenn, *Taking Your Faith to Work* (Grand Rapids: Baker, 1980), 61–64.

[118] Paul King Jewett, *The Lord's Day: A Theological Guide to the Christian Day of Worship* (Grand Rapids: Eerdmans, 1971).

Chapter 2

[1] Martin Luther, *LW*, 17:125.

[2] Ibid., 45:331.

[3] Huldrich Zwingli, *Commentary on True and False Religion*, ed. S. M. Jackson and C. N. Heller (Durham: Labyrinth, 1981), 272.

[4] Ibid., 273.

[5] John Calvin, *Institutes of the Christian Religion*, I.16.3.

[6] Ibid., I.16.9; cf. ibid., I.16.6; I.17.2; I.18.1.

[7] Ibid., I.18.1.

[8] Ibid., I.18.2.

[9] Jacob Arminius, *The Works of Jacob Arminius*, 3 vols., ed. James Nichols (Auburn and Buffalo: Derby, Miller & Orton, 1853), 1:251.

[10] Ibid.

[11] John Wesley, *The Works of John Wesley*, 14 vols. (Grand Rapids: Zondervan, reprint, n.d.), 6:326; cf. ibid., 6:318.

[12] Charles Finney, *Finney's Systematic Theology* (Minneapolis: Bethany, reprint 1976), 6.

[13] Donald S. Metz, "Providence," *Beacon Dictionary of Theology*, ed. Richard S. Taylor (Kansas City: Beacon Hill, 1983), 428. Cf. Charles W. Carter, ed., *A Contemporary Wesleyan Theology*, 2 vols. (Grand Rapids: Zondervan, 1983), 1:161: God's providence is "based on moral and religious principles in which the action and beliefs of mankind as free moral agents play a vital role. . . . This lays great stress on the fact that God's relationship to the cosmos is one that is based on moral and religious principles. God's providence, His sovereignty and lordship, is exercised in a manner that demonstrates this. This indicates that the teleology of God's providential relationship to His creation is moral and religious."

[14] Thomas Paine, *The Great Works of Thomas Paine* (New York: Bennett & Liberal, n.d.), 151.

[15] Ibid., 29.

[16] Thomas Paine, *Classics of Free Thought*, ed. Paul Blanchard (Buffalo & New York: Prometheus, n.d.), 133.

[17] William Adams Brown, *Christian Theology in Outline* (New York: Scribner, 1911), 219.

[18] Gordon D. Kaufman, *Systematic Theology: A Historicist Perspective* (New York: Scribner, 1968), 258.

[19] Adolf Von Harnack, *What Is Christianity?* (London: Williams & Norgate, 1912), 29. "What happens in space and time is subject to the general laws of motion, and that in this sense, as an interruption of the order of nature, there can be no such thing as miracles." Ibid., 27.

20 L. Harold DeWolf, *The Case for Theology in Liberal Perspective* (Philadelphia: Westminster, 1959), 94.

21 Langdon B. Gilkey, "The Concept of Providence in Contemporary Theology," *Journal of Religion* 68.3 (July 1963): 174.

22 Nicolas Berdyaev, *The Beginning and the End* (Westport, Conn.: Greenwood, 1976), 152.

23 Ibid., 155.

24 Rudolf Bultmann, *Essays Philosophical and Theological* (London: SCM, 1955), 76.

25 Emil Brunner, *The Christian Doctrine of Creation and Redemption: Dogmatics, Vol. II* (London: Lutterworth, 1952), 184.

26 John Macquarrie, *Principles of Christian Theology* (New York: Scribner, 1977), 250.

27 Rudolf Bultmann, *Kerygma and Myth* (New York: Harper & Row, 1961), 4.

28 Heinrich Ott, *God* (Edinburgh: Saint Andrew, 1974), 81.

29 Rubem Alves, *A Theology of Human Hope* (St. Meinrad, Minnesota: Abbey, 1974), 136.

30 Albert B. Cleage, Jr., *The Black Messiah* (New York: Sheed and Ward, 1968).

31 James H. Cone, *A Black Theology of Liberation* (Philadelphia & New York: Lippincott, 1970), 27.

32 Clement of Alexandria, *Christ the Educator,* II.6.

33 Clement of Alexandria, *Miscellanies,* IV.12.

34 Augustine, *The Literal Meaning of Genesis,* VIII.9.17; VIII.24.45.

35 Augustine, *Eighty-Three Different Questions,* 24; cf. 53.

36 Augustine, *Enchiridion,* 101.

37 Carl F. H. Henry, *God, Revelation and Authority,* 6 vols. (Waco: Word, 1976–83), 6:479.

38 Bernard Ramm, *A Christian View of Science and Scripture* (Grand Rapids: Eerdmans, 1954), 90.

39 Augustine, *The Christian Combat,* VIII.9.

40 Augustine, *The Literal Meaning of Genesis,* XI.16.

41 Augustine, *Sermon on the Mount,* II.3.14.

42 Henry, *God, Revelation and Authority,* 6:482.

43 C. S. Lewis, *The Problem of Pain* (New York: Macmillan, 1944).

44 G. C. Berkouwer, *The Providence of God* (Grand Rapids: Eerdmans, 1952);

45 Colin Brown, *Miracles and the Critical Mind* (Grand Rapids: Eerdmans, 1984).

46 G. Ch. Aalders, *Genesis,* 2 vols. (Grand Rapids: Zondervan, 1981), 1:50.

47 Derek Kidner, *Genesis, TNTC* (London: Tyndale Press, 1967), 207.

48 W. H. Gispen, *Exodus* (Grand Rapids: Zondervan, 1982), 38.

49 J. D. Spiceland, "Miracles," *EDT,* 723.

50 Meredith G. Kline, "Genesis," *NBCRev,* 84.

51 J. G. McConville, *Ezra, Nehemiah, and Esther* (Philadelphia: Westminster, 1985), 8.

52 *Eerdmans' Concise Bible Handbook,* ed. David and Pat Alexander (Grand Rapids: Eerdmans, 1980), 103, elegantly expresses the central message of Ruth. God "is the One who orders all the circumstances of daily life, even for the most unimportant people. And so the new-found faith of a Moabite girl, and her sacrificial love for her mother-in-law are woven into the great tapestry of God's plan of salvation. For descended from Ruth is King David, and from the line of David comes the Messiah himself."

53 McConville, *Ezra, Nehemiah, and Esther,* 173.

54 See Hugh J. Blair, "Joshua," *NBCRev,* 244, for a discussion of the possible interpretations of the restriction of the sun's light in Joshua 10:12–14.

55 John Murray, *The Epistle to the Romans,* 2 vols. (Grand Rapids: Eerdmans, 1959–65), 2:108.

56 Cf. F. F. Bruce, *Romans, TNTC* (London: Tyndale, 1963), 175.

57 F. F. Bruce, *1 & 2 Thessalonians, WBC* (Waco: Word, 1982), 171–72.

58 Lewis, *The Problem of Pain,* 115–16.

59 F. F. Bruce, "The Revelation to John," *NLBC,* 1988.

60 F. F. Bruce, *The Epistle to the Hebrews* (London: Marshall, Morgan & Scott, 1965), 6.

61 Charles Hatfield, "Probability and God's Providence," *Journal of the American Scientific Affiliation* 17.1 (March 1965), 18.

62 Harold S. Kushner, *When Bad Things Happen to Good People* (New York: Avon, 1981), 58.

63 Oscar Cullmann, *Christ and Time: The Primitive Christian Conception of Time and History* (Philadelphia: Westminster, 1950); see also Carl Henry, "Time," *EDT,* 1,094–96.

[64] William G. Pollard, *Chance and Providence* (New York: Charles Scribner's Sons, 1958), 73–74.

[65] J. I. Packer, *Evangelism and the Sovereignty of God* (Downers Grove: InterVarsity, 1961).

[66] G. Finkenrath, "Secret, Mystery," *NIDNTT*, 3:501–2.

[67] Bornkamm, *"mystērion," TDNT*, 4:824.

[68] Walter L. Leifeld, "Mystery," *ZPEB*, 4:330.

[69] Berkouwer, *Providence of God*, 98.

[70] All four contributors to David and Randall Basinger, eds., *Predestination and Free Will: Four Views of Divine Sovereignty and Human Freedom* (Downers Grove: InterVarsity, 1986), 27–28.

[71] Thomas J. Peters and Robert H. Waterman, Jr., *In Search of Excellence: Lessons from America's Best Run Companies* (New York: Warner, 1983), 238.

[72] Ibid., 85.

[73] Ibid., 73.

[74] Bruce Narramore, *Parenting With Love and Limits* (Grand Rapids: Zondervan, 1979), 38.

[75] Bruce Narramore, *Help! I'm a Parent!* (Grand Rapids: Zondervan, 1972). See also James Dobson, *Dare to Discipline* (Wheaton: Tyndale, 1970); Haim G. Ginott, *Between Parent and Child* (New York: Avon, 1965); idem, *Between Parent and Teen Ager* (New York: Avon, 1969).

[76] Berkouwer, *Providence of God*, 140.

[77] See Gordon Lewis, "Criteria for the Discerning of Spirits," in *Demon Possession*, ed. John Warwick Montgomery (St. Paul: Bethany, 1976), chapter 23. See also Gordon Lewis, "The Bible, the Christian and Spiritualism," *Confronting the Cults* (Phillipsburg, Penn.: Presbyterian and Reformed, 1966), 163–98.

[78] Peters and Waterman, *In Search of Excellence*, 13.

[79] Wilbur F. Tillett, "Providence," *International Standard Bible Encyclopedia* (Grand Rapids: Eerdmans, 1949), 4:484.

[80] Charles Hodge, *Systematic Theology*, 3 vols. (Grand Rapids: Eerdmans, 1946), 1:169.

[81] Gordon R. Lewis, *Judge for Yourself* (Downers Grove: InterVarsity, 1974), 46–60.

[82] Gordon R. Lewis, "Prayer," *ZPEB*, 2:835–44.

[83] Wolfhart Pannenberg, *Anthropology in Theological Perspective* (Philadelphia: Westminster, 1985), 505.

[84] B. A. G. Fuller, "Naturalism," in *Dictionary of Philosophy*, ed. D. Runes (New York: Philosophical Library, 1960).

[85] Carl Sagan, *Cosmos* (New York: Random House, 1980), 4.

[86] Donald M. Mackay, *The Clock Work Image* (Downers Grove: InterVarsity, 1974), 60.

[87] William G. Pollard, *Chance and Providence* (New York: Scribner, 1958), 68.

[88] Ibid., 74.

[89] For a responsible account of what the Bible does teach about the universe in response to Bultmann see R. Laird Harris, "The Bible and Cosmology," *Bulletin of the Evangelical Theological Society* 5.1 (March 1962): 11–16.

[90] Paul Tillich, *The Courage to Be* (New Haven, Conn.: Yale University Press, 1952), 168.

[91] Langdon Gilkey, "The Concept of Providence in Contemporary Theology," *The Journal of Religion* 53.3 (July 1963): 184–85.

[92] Robert A. Morey, *Horoscopes and the Christian* (Minneapolis: Bethany, 1981); see also Gary Jennings, *A Teenager's Realistic Guide to Astrology* (New York: Association, 1971).

[93] H. F. Vos, "Astrology," *EDT*, 93.

[94] Danny Korem and Paul Meier, *The Fakers: Exploding the Myths of the Supernatural* (Grand Rapids: Baker, 1980), 15.

[95] See Mark Bubek, *Overcoming the Adversary* (Chicago: Moody, 1984).

[96] Pollard, *Chance and Providence*, 180.

[97] Ibid., 179.

[98] Donna Platt, "The Key to Weight Control," *Ministry* (March, 1986), 13.

[99] Charles Colson, *Kingdoms in Conflict* (Grand Rapids: Zondervan, 1987), 247–48.

[100] See Mark Satin, *New Age Politics* (New York: Dell, 1979), 24, 47; see also Douglas Groothuis, *Unmasking the New Age* (Downers Grove: InterVarsity, 1986), 111–30.

[101] See Gordon R. Lewis, "How Effective Is Prayer?" in *Decide for Yourself* (Downers Grove: InterVarsity, 1975), 69–73; "Prayer," *ZPEB*, 4:843.

[102] For further applications of God's presence and action in the world see Geoffrey Wainwright, *Doxology: The Praise of God in Worship, Doctrine, and Life* (New York: Oxford University Press, 1980), 79–86.

Chapter 3

[1] This appears to be the focus of Otto Weber's remark when he said, "The issue in the Bible and in the message of the Church is really [i.e., primarily] man." *Foundations of Dogmatics*, 2 vols. (Grand Rapids: Eerdmans, 1981–83), 1:530.

[2] Augustine, *On True Religion*, 12.

[3] Blaise Pascal, *Pensees* (Baltimore: Penguin, 1966), no. 131.

[4] Justin Martyr, *Apology*, 1.28. Cf. ibid., 1.10; *Dialogue With Trypho*, 102, 141.

[5] Athenagoras, *The Resurrection of the Dead*, 12.

[6] Irenaeus, *Against Heresies*, IV.4.3; IV.37.1; V.1.3.

[7] Ibid., V.6.1. Cf. ibid., II.33.5; V.6.1; V.8.1; V.10.1.

[8] Clement of Alexandria, *Miscellanies*, II.19; *The Instructor*, I.12.

[9] Gregory of Nyssa, "On the Making of Man," 9.

[10] Ibid., 15.2. Cf. ibid., 5.2; 16.17.

[11] John of Damascus, *The Orthodox Faith*, II.12.

[12] Gordon H. Clark, *The Biblical Doctrine of Man* (Jefferson, Md.: The Trinity Foundation, 1984), 19.

[13] Ibid., 14–15.

[14] Ibid., 25.

[15] Athenagoras, *The Resurrection of the Dead*, 15. The apologist adds that at death the soul separates from the body, the two to be reunited at the resurrection. Ibid., 16–18.

[16] Origen, *On First Principles*, I.7; II.1–3; II.9.6; III.3–5.

[17] Hilary of Potiers, *On the Trinity*, X.20.

[18] Tertullian, *On the Soul*, 5–9, 27, 36–38. Said Tertullian, "The soul is a seed placed in man and transmitted by him, that from the beginning there was one seed of the soul, as there was one seed of the flesh, for the whole human race." Ibid., 36.1.

[19] Tertullian, *On the Soul*, 15.5.

[20] Peter Lombard, *Book of Sentences*, II.xvi.3.

[21] Bonaventure, "Disputed Questions Concerning Christ's Knowledge," Q. IV.2, in *A Scholastic Miscellany: Anselm to Ockham* (Philadelphia: Westminster, 1956), 394.

[22] Thomas Aquinas, *ST*, 1.93.9.

[23] Ibid., 1.60.5.

[24] Ibid., 1.95.1;1.93.4.

[25] F. J. Corley, "Man," *NCE*, 9:128.

[26] Martin Luther, *LW*, 1:61.

[27] Ibid., 1:62–63.

[28] Philip Melanchthon, *Melanchthon on Christian Doctrine* (Grand Rapids: Baker, reprint 1965), 72.

[29] *Formula of Concord*, "Epitome," Art. I., Affirmative 1.

[30] Cited by Heinrich Schmid, *The Doctrinal Theology of the Evangelical Lutheran Church* (Minneapolis: Augsburg, reprint 1961), 218.

[31] For historical testimonies within the older Lutheran tradition, see Schmid, *Doctrinal Theology*, 166.

[32] See Hugh T. Kerr, ed., *A Compend of Luther's Theology* (Philadelphia: Westminster, 1966), 77–79.

[33] Cited by Schmid, *Doctrinal Theology*, 166–67.

[34] *The Racovian Catechism* (Lexington, Ky.: American Theological Library Association, 1962), 1.2.21.

[35] Gerhard von Rad, *"eikōn,"* *TDNT*, 2:391.

[36] Gerhard von Rad, *Genesis. OTL* (Philadelphia: Westminster, 1961), 60. Cf. von Rad, *"eikōn,"* *TDNT*, 2:392: "Man in his sphere of rule as God's vice-regent is summoned to represent the dominion and majesty of God."

[37] D. J. A. Clines, "The Image of God in Man," *Tyndale Bulletin* 19 (1968): 101. Clines earlier in the article posed the question whether dominion was determinative of the *imago*, or whether it was merely a consequence of it. His conclusion is that "since dominion is so immediate and necessary a consequence of the image, it loses the character of a mere derivative of the image and virtually becomes a constitutive part of the image itself." Ibid., 96.

[38] Leonard Verduin, *Somewhat Less Than God: The Biblical View of Man* (Grand Rapids: Eerdmans, 1970), 27. Cf., "Man is the image-bearer of God and that this image, this Godlikeness, evinces itself in dominion-having." Ibid., 49.

[39] Dietrich Bonhoeffer, *Creation and Temptation* (London: SCM, 1966), 37.

[40] Ibid., 39.

[41] Karl Barth, *CD*, III.1.192.

[42] Ibid., 185.

[43] Ibid., 195.

[44] Ibid., III.2.145. Cf. this statement: "Every man belongs to God, and is the object of Christ's redemptive act wrought in history. Every man is destined for the glory of God by

sharing in this redemption, and his whole being consists in the active service of God." *Kirkliche Dogmatik*, III.2.85–86, cited by David Cairns, *The Image of God in Man* (New York: Philosophical Library, 1953), 170, n.2.

[45] Emil Brunner, *The Christian Doctrine of Creation and Redemption: Dogmatics*, Vol. II, (London: Lutterworth, 1952), 69.

[46] Ibid., 56–57.

[47] Ibid., 58.

[48] John Macquarrie, *Principles of Christian Theology* (New York: Scribner, 1977), 76.

[49] Ibid., 231.

[50] John Macquarrie, *An Existentialist Theology* (London: SCM, 1955), 137.

[51] Edmond Jacob, *"psychē," TDNT*, 9:631.

[52] Oscar Cullmann, "Immortality or Resurrection?" *Christianity Today* 2.21 (July 21, 1958), 6.

[53] John A. T. Robinson, *The Body: A Study in Pauline Theology* (Chicago: Regnery, 1952), 16.

[54] Augustine, *Freedom of the Will*, 2.16.

[55] Augustine, *On Christian Doctrine*, 1.22.

[56] In terms of one of his Trinitarian analogies—the triad of memory, understanding, and will—Augustine writes, "I remember that I have memory, understanding, and will; I understand that I understand, and will, and remember; I will that I will, and remember, and understand; and at the same time I remember my whole memory, understanding, and will." *On the Trinity*, 10.11.18; cf. *Letter*, 169. Feelings, love, or desires could be substituted for memory in this quote.

[57] Augustine, *Confessions*, 13.9.10.

[58] Augustine, *Enchiridion*, 11.36. Cf. idem, *On the Trinity*, 15.7.11; idem, *Reply to Faustus the Manichaean*, 24.2.

[59] Augustine, *On the Soul and Its Origin*, 4.3.

[60] John Calvin, *Institutes of the Christian Religion*, I.15.3. Cf. *Commentaries on the Epistles to the Philippians, Colossians, and Thessalonians*, 212, where Calvin states that the image of God, according to Genesis 9:6, is "the rectitude and integrity of the whole soul."

[61] Calvin, *Institutes*, I.15.3.

[62] Ibid. Cf. *Commentaries on the Book of Genesis*, 95.

[63] Calvin, *Institutes*, I.15.4; II.2.12.

[64] Ibid., I.15.4. Cf. *Commentaries on Genesis*, 95.

[65] Cf. *The Westminster Shorter Catechism*, quest. 10, which adds the element of dominion over the lower forms of life: "How did God create man? God created man, male and female, after his own image, in knowledge, righteousness, and holiness, with dominion over the creatures."

[66] John Wolleb, *Compendium Theologiae Christianae*, V.2, in John W. Beardslee, III, *Reformed Dogmatics* (Grand Rapids: Baker, reprint 1977), 56.

[67] Herman Bavinck, *Our Reasonable Faith* (Grand Rapids: Baker, reprint 1977), 213.

[68] L. Berkhof, *Systematic Theology* (Grand Rapids: Eerdmans, 1941), 207.

[69] Ibid., 195.

[70] Augustus H. Strong, *Systematic Theology* (Valley Forge, Penn.: Judson, 1907), 483–88.

[71] *The Scofield Reference Bible*, ed. C. I. Scofield (New York: Oxford University Press, 1945), notes to Genesis 1:26 (p. 5) and 1 Thessalonians 5:23 (p. 1,270).

[72] Calvin, *Institutes*, I.15.5.

[73] Wolleb, *Compendium Theologiae Christianae*, I.5, in Beardslee, *Reformed Dogmatics*, 57.

[74] W. G. T. Shedd, *Dogmatic Theology*, 3 vols. (Grand Rapids: Zondervan, n.d.), 2:7.

[75] Robert L. Dabney, *Lectures in Systematic Theology* (Grand Rapids: Zondervan, reprint 1972), 321.

[76] James Orr, *God's Image in Man* (Grand Rapids: Eerdmans, 1948).

[77] Anthony A. Hoekema, *Created in God's Image* (Grand Rapids: Eerdmans, 1986).

[78] Millard J. Erickson, *Christian Theology*, 3 vols. (Grand Rapids: Baker, 1983–1985), vol. 2.

[79] Derek Kidner, *Genesis, TNTC* (London: Tyndale, 1967), 50.

[80] Clines, "The Image of God in Man," 80; G. Ch. Aalders, *Genesis*, 2 vols. (Grand Rapids: Zondervan, 1981), 1:70.

[81] Cf. John E. Hartley, *"ṣelem," TWOT*, 2:768: "God's image obviously does not consist in man's body which was formed from earthly matter, but in his spiritual, intellectual, moral likeness to God from whom his animating breath came."

[82] Concerning the complex unity that is the person, H. W. Hoehner, "Body, the Biblical View of," *EDT*, 165, comments, "The Scriptural dualism is not the same as Greek dualism, where the soul is the prisoner of the body, but rather the body is the instrument through which the immaterial expresses itself. The

material and the immaterial parts are on a par with each other."

[83] *Lēb* and *kardia* "refer usually to the entire man understood from the point of his governing center, the essential person, rather than the emotional nature as in current English usage." Bruce Milne, *Know the Truth* (Downers Grove: InterVarsity, 1982), 97. Cf. Andrew Bowling, *"lēb," TWOT,* 1:466.

[84] See Bruce K. Waltke, *"nepeš," TWOT,* 2:589; M. E. Osterhaven, "Soul," *EDT,* 1036.

[85] Clark, *The Biblical Doctrine of Man,* 53.

[86] Kidner, *Genesis,* 65.

[87] Robert D. Culver, *"māšal," TWOT,* 1:534. Susan T. Foh, "What Is the Woman's Desire?" *Westminster Theological Journal,* 37 (Spring 1975), offers the following convincing interpretation of the clause in Genesis 3:16 "he will rule over you": "After the Fall, the woman sinfully desires to control her husband. In the ensuing struggle for control, the husband often responds with excessive domination. In this battle between the sexes, the divine pattern (inherent in the creation order) of the husband's loving headship and the wife's faithful submission becomes corrupted and distorted."

[88] C. G. Berkouwer, *Man: The Image of God* (Grand Rapids: Eerdmans, 1962), 71–72.

[89] Michael A. Eaton, *Ecclesiastes, TOTC* (Downers Grove: InterVarsity, 1983), 116.

[90] L. Berkhof, *Systematic Theology,* 194. Berkhof adds, "The Bible, therefore points to two, and only two, constitutional elements in the nature of man, namely, body and spirit or soul." Ibid.

[91] G. Harder, "Soul," *NIDNTT,* 3:683.

[92] J. A. T. Robinson, *The Body: A Study in Pauline Theology* (Chicago: Henry Regnery, 1952).

[93] Joseph Osei-Bonsu, "Does 2 Cor. 5:1–10 Teach the Reception of the Resurrection Body at the Moment of Death?" *Journal for the Study of the New Testament* 28 (Oct. 1986): 89. In this article Osei-Bonsu refutes the thesis of M. J. Harris, *Raised Immortal: Resurrection and Immortality in the New Testament* (Grand Rapids: Eerdmans, 1983), who argues that 2 Corinthians 5:1–10 teaches that the believer is clothed with the resurrection body at the moment of death.

[94] F. F. Bruce, *1 & 2 Thessalonians, WBC* (Waco: Word, 1982), 130. Leon Morris adds, "Paul is not here concerned to give a theoretical analysis of man, but is uttering a fervent prayer that the entire man may be preserved."

[95] *1 & 2 Thessalonians, TNTC* (London: Inter-Varsity, 1956), 107.

[95] Fritz Rienecker and Cleon L. Rogers, Jr., *LKGNT,* 375.

[96] Berkouwer, *Man: The Image of God,* 45.

[97] Leon Morris, *1 Corinthians, TNTC* (London: Tyndale, 1958), 151. Cf. H. Schlier, *"kephalē," TDNTAbr,* 429: "The distinction between man and woman is seen here to have an ontological ground, having her life from man and for man." Moreover, on the basis of a computer search of more than 2,300 uses in ancient Greek literature, Wayne Grudem concludes that *kephalē* means not primarily "source" or "origin," but "authority over." See, "Does *kephalē* ("head") Mean 'Source' or 'Authority Over' in Greek Literature? A Survey of 2,336 Examples," in *The Role Relationship of Men and Women,* ed. George W. Knight, III (Chicago: Moody, 1985), 49–80.

[98] G. Delling, *"hypotassō," TDNTAbr,* 1159.

[99] Francis Foulkes, *Ephesians, TNTC* (London: Inter-Varsity, 1963), 155. Donald Guthrie comments on 1 Timothy 2:12–13: "The idea of woman's subjection . . . appears to be inherent in the divine constitution of the human race." *The Pastoral Epistles, TNTC* (London: Tyndale, 1957), 76.

[100] Alfred Plummer, *The Gospel According to St. John* (Grand Rapids: Baker, reprint 1981), 102.

[101] John R. W. Stott, *The Epistles of John, TNTC* (London: Tyndale: 1964), 120.

[102] We noted earlier in this chapter that Gordon Clark explicates the work of the Logos more narrowly in terms of intellectual enablement: "The Logos or rationality of God, who created all things without a single exception, can be seen as having created man with the light of logic as his distinctive human characteristic." *Biblical Doctrine of Man,* 18–19.

[103] Peter H. Davids, *The Epistle of James, NIGTC* (Grand Rapids: Eerdmans, 1982), 133.

[104] F. F. Bruce, *The Epistle to the Hebrews, NLCNT* (London & Edinburgh: Marshall, Morgan & Scott, 1964), 82.

[105] Ibid., 360.

[106] W. L. Reese, "Substance," *Dictionary of Philosophy and Religion: Eastern and Western Thought* (Atlantic Highlands, N.J.: Humanities, 1980), 556.

[107] Colin Brown, "Heart," *NIDNTT,* 2:181–82.

[108] R. Laird Harris, *Man–God's Eternal Creation* (Chicago: Moody, 1971), 12.

[109] Don Cupitt, *The Leap of Reason* (Philadelphia: Westminster, 1976), 112–13.

[110] Gordon R. Lewis, "Paradise," *ZPEB*, 4: 598–99.

[111] Erich Sauer, *King of the Earth* (Grand Rapids: Eerdmans, 1962).

[112] Gordon R. Lewis, "Faith and Reason in the Thought of St. Augustine," Ph.D. dissertation, Syracuse University, 1959. Available from University Microfilms, Ann Arbor, Michigan 48106.

[113] Julius Weinberg, "Abstraction," in *Dictionary of the History of Ideas*, ed. Philip P. Wiener (New York: Scribner, 1968), 1–9.

[114] Gordon R. Lewis, "Francis Schaeffer's Apologetic Method," in *Reflections on Francis Schaeffer,* ed. Ronald Reugsegger, (Grand Rapids: Zondervan, 1986), 69–104.

[115] Orville S. Walters, "Unconscious," in *Baker's Dictionary of Christian Ethics,* ed. Carl F. H. Henry (Grand Rapids: Baker, 1973), 683–84.

[116] Evelyn Underhill, *Mysticism* (Cleveland and New York: World, 1955), 104.

[117] L. I. Granberg and G. E. Farley, "Conscience," *ZPEB*, 1:949.

[118] H. C. Hahn, "Conscience," *NIDNTT*, 1:350.

[119] D. G. Benner, "Emotion," *EDT*, 352.

[120] B. B. Warfield, "The Emotional Life of our Lord" in *The Person and Work of Christ* (Philadelphia: Presbyterian and Reformed, 1950), 122.

[121] Norman Hope, "How to Be Good—And Mad," *Christianity Today* (July 19, 1968), 3–5.

[122] Carl F. H. Henry, *Christian Personal Ethics* (Grand Rapids: Eerdmans, 1957), 499.

[123] C. S. Lewis, *Mere Christianity* (New York: Macmillan, 1952), 90–91.

[124] C. S. Lewis, *Pilgrim's Regress* (Grand Rapids: Eerdmans, 1943), 8; cf. 129.

[125] Harold O. J. Brown, "Romanticism and the Bible," in *Challenges to Inerrancy,* eds. Gordon R. Lewis and Bruce Demarest (Chicago: Moody, 1984), 54.

[126] See Ronald C. Doll, "Motives and Motivation"; Murray J. Harris, "Mixed Motives"; and Stephen S. Smalley, "Singlemindedness," *Baker's Dictionary of Christian Ethics*, 437–38, 427–28, 622–23.

[127] Mary T. Clark, *Augustine, Philosopher of Freedom* (New York: Desclee, 1958), 69.

[128] C. Stephen Evans, *Preserving the Person* (Downers Grove: InterVarsity, 1977), 145; see

also George David, *The Eclipse and Recovery of Person* (Bombay: TRACI, 1976).

[129] Jacob Bronowski, *The Identity of Man* (Garden City: Natural History, 1965), 2.

[130] Karl R. Popper and John C. Eccles, *The Self and Its Brain* (New York: Springer, 1977), 11.

[131] Arnold S. Kaufman, "Behaviorism," *EP*, 1:270.

[132] Michael D. Aeschliman, *The Restitution of Man* (Grand Rapids: Eerdmans, 1983), 80. See also Ludger Holscher, *The Reality of the Mind: Augustine's Philosophical Arguments for the Human Soul as a Spiritual Substance* (New York: Routledge & Kegan Paul, 1986).

[133] Richard H. Bube, *The Encounter Between Christianity and Science* (Grand Rapids: Eerdmans, 1968), 80–81.

[134] Evans, *Preserving the Person,* 149.

[135] Ibid., 151–52.

[136] Aeschliman, *Restitution of Man,* 55.

[137] Ibid., 48.

[138] Kaufman, "Behaviorism," 271.

[139] For similar arguments see J. Oliver Buswell, Jr., *A Christian View of Being and Knowing* (Grand Rapids: Zondervan, 1960), 126–60; Bernard Ramm, *Protestant Christian Evidences* (Chicago: Moody, 1954), 58–70; Stuart C. Hackett, *The Resurrection of Theism* (Chicago: Moody, 1957), 220–29.

[140] Popper and Eccles, *The Self and Its Brain,* 355.

[141] Ibid., 378.

[142] Ibid., 374.

[143] G. Stafford Wright, "Man," *NIDNTT*, 2:568.

[144] Berkouwer, *Man: The Image of God,* 23.

[145] Ibid., 35.

[146] Ibid.

[147] Ibid, 196.

[148] Ibid., 203.

[149] Ibid., 205.

[150] Ibid., 235.

[151] Ibid., 259.

[152] Ibid.

[153] Ibid., 264.

[154] Ibid. 269; for other exclusively relational views see Bruce Larson, *The Relational Revolution* (Waco: Word, 1976) and *The Meaning and Mystery of Being Human* (Waco: Word, 1978).

155 W. Brugh Joy, *Joy's Way* (Los Angeles: J. P. Tarcher, 1979), 32.

156 Ibid., 163.

157 Marilyn Ferguson, *The Aquarian Conspiracy* (Los Angeles: Tarcher, 1980), 100.

158 Ibid., 98–99.

159 Barth, *CD*, III.2.350.

160 Ibid., 354.

161 Ibid., 361.

162 See also Ray S. Anderson, *On Being Human: Essays in Theological Anthropology* (Grand Rapids: Eerdmans, 1982), 210–11.

163 Hoekema, *Created in God's Image*, 217.

164 Arthur Koestler, *The Ghost in the Machine* (London: Hutchinson, 1967), 205–8.

165 Ibid., 219.

166 For an informed philosopher's discussion of substance see Albrey Castell, *The Self in Philosophy* (New York: Macmillan, 1965) 50–79.

167 Stuart Barton Babbage, *Man in Nature and Grace,* (Grand Rapids: Eerdmans, 1957), 17.

168 Watchman Nee, *The Spiritual Man* (New York: Christian Fellowship, 1986), 1:26.

169 Ibid., 2:67–127.

170 William T. Brunner, "A New Theory of Original Sin" *Gordon Review* (1959), 125–37 and William T. Brunner, *Children of the Devil: Fresh Investigation of the Fall of Man and Original Sin* (New York: Philosophical Library, 1966).

171 Corliss Lamont, *The Philosophy of Humanism* (New York: Frederick Ungar, sixth ed. 1982), 227.

172 Ibid., 87.

173 Ibid., 3–8.

174 John Piper, *Desiring God* (Portland: Multnomah, 1986).

175 Arthur Dyck, cited by C. Everett Koop, "The Slide to Auschwitz," in Ronald Reagan, *Abortion and the Conscience of the Nation* (New York: Thomas Nelson, 1984), 60.

Chapter 4

1 Otto Weber, *Foundations of Dogmatics,* 2 vols. (Grand Rapids: Eerdmans, 1981–1983), 1:596.

2 *The Racovian Catechism,* ed. Thomas Rees (Lexington, Ky.: American Theological Library Association, 1962), 326; sec. V., chap. 10.

3 Henry Ware, cited by H. Shelton Smith, *Changing Conceptions of Original Sin* (New York: Scribner, 1955), 76.

4 William Newton Clarke, *An Outline of Christian Theology* (Edinburgh: T. & T. Clark, 1909), 245.

5 William A. Brown, "The Old Theology and the New," *Harvard Theological Review,* 4 (January 1911): 15.

6 William A. Brown, *Christian Theology in Outline* (New York: Scribner, 1911), 273–74.

7 See Jaroslav Pelikan, *The Christian Tradition,* 4 vols. (Chicago: University of Chicago Press, 1971–1984), 4:279.

8 *The Canons and Decrees of Trent,* Session VI, canon 5.

9 Ibid., Session V, chap. 4.

10 Richard P. McBrien, *Catholicism* (Minneapolis: Winston, 1981), 162.

11 *A New Catechism: Catholic Faith for Adults* (New York: Herder & Herder, 1967), 267.

12 Piet Schoonenberg, *Man and Sin* (South Bend: University of Notre Dame Press, 1965), 198. Monika K. Hellwig argues from the same perspective: The "focus or orientation of our whole being which we cannot escape is necessarily a sinful one because of the . . . sinfulness of the world as we know it. It is a sinful one because the human community in which we are rooted . . . is out of focus and estranged from its end and purpose in God." *Understanding Catholicism* (New York: Paulist, 1981), 51.

13 *A Compend of Wesley's Theology,* ed. Robert W. Burtner and Robert E. Childs (Nashville: Abingdon, 1954), 117.

14 Ibid., 114.

15 Ibid., 120.

16 See the *Methodist Articles of Religion,* VIII. Cf. "There is no man that is in a state of mere nature; there is no man, unless he has quenched the Spirit, that is wholly void of the grace of God. No man living is entirely destitute of . . . preventing grace." *Compend of Wesley's Theology,* 148.

17 H. Orton Wiley, *Christian Theology,* 3 vols. (Kansas City: Beacon Hill, 1952), 2:107.

18 A. Elwood Sanner, "Total Depravity," *BDT,* 525.

19 Ibid., 546.

20 John Miley, *Systematic Theology,* 2 vols. (New York: Eaton and Mains, 1892), 1:521.

21 *Finney's Systematic Theology,* ed. J. H. Fairchild (Minneapolis: Bethany, reprint 1976), 429.

[22] Ibid., 180.

[23] Karl Barth, *CD,* IV.1.508.

[24] Ibid., III.4.43.

[25] Ibid., III.2.29.

[26] Karl Barth, "No!" in *Natural Theology,* trans. Peter Fraenkel (London: Centenary, 1946), 74 (cf. 20, 22). In this work Barth asserts that the *imago Dei* has been totally obliterated by sin.

[27] Barth, *CD,* I.1.145. Barth's point is that sin is a temporary betrayal of the covenant relation that ultimately will prevail. Thus the person is "the object of divine grace, the partner in the covenant which God has made with him." *CD,* III.2.32.

[28] Emil Brunner, *The Christian Doctrine of Creation and Redemption: Dogmatics, Vol. II* (London: Lutterworth, 1952), 90.

[29] Ibid., 103.

[30] Emil Brunner, *The Scandal of Christianity* (London: SCM, 1951), 56–57.

[31] Ibid., 65.

[32] Reinhold Niebuhr, *The Nature and Destiny of Man,* 2 vols. (New York: Scribner, 1951), 1:186.

[33] Reinhold Niebuhr, *An Interpretation of Christian Ethics* (New York: Meridian, 1956), 86.

[34] Dorothy Sölle, *Political Theology* (Philadelphia: Fortress, 1974), 91. Sölle adds that the notion of original sin "means that man has the capacity for guilt." Ibid., 88.

[35] James H. Cone, "Christian Faith and Political Praxis," in *The Challenge of Liberation Theology,* ed. Brian Mahan and L. Dale Richesin (Maryknoll, N.Y.: Orbis, 1981), 57. Leonardo Boff, a Latin American liberation theologian, comments, "Sin isn't something purely spiritual, something just on the inside. It's exploitation, it's injustice, it's oppression, it's chains on persons in this world, external chains, that destroy them." Leonardo and Clodovis Boff, *Salvation and Liberation* (Maryknoll, N.Y.: Orbis, 1984), 76.

[36] Augustine, *Sermons on the New Testament,* 67.15.

[37] Augustine, *City of God,* XIV.11. Cf. *Against Two Letters of the Pelagians,* I.5; *Letters,* 115.2; *On Rebuke and Grace,* XIII.42.

[38] Augustine, *On the Spirit and the Letter,* 5.

[39] Augustine, *On the Spirit and the Letter,* 48. Cf. ibid., "What was impressed on their hearts when they were created in the image of God has not been wholly blotted out."

[40] Augustine, *City of God,* XIII.14.

[41] Martin Luther, *LW,* 1:66.

[42] Martin Luther, *A Compend of Luther's Theology,* ed. Hugh T. Kerr (Philadelphia: Westminster, 1966), 90. "Godward, or in things which pertain unto salvation or damnation, he has no 'free will,' but is a captive, slave, and servant, either to the will of God, or to the will of Satan." Ibid., 88.

[43] Luther, *LW,* 25:348.

[44] John Calvin, *Institutes of the Christian Religion,* II.1.5.

[45] Ibid., II.1.8.

[46] Ibid., II.1.9.

[47] Ibid., II.1.7. Cf. Calvin, *Commentary on the Gospel According to John,* 1:113: "The corruption of all mankind in the person of Adam alone did not proceed from generation, but from the appointment of God, who has in him deprived us of his gifts."

[48] Calvin, *Institutes,* II.1.8.

[49] W. G. T. Shedd, *Dogmatic Theology,* 3 vols. (Grand Rapids: Zondervan, n.d.), 2:186.

[50] Ibid., 2:188–89.

[51] Augustus H. Strong, *Systematic Theology* (Valley Forge, Penn.: Judson, 1907), 661. Strong theorizes that the reason why Scripture does not speak more explicitly about the salvation of infants may be that some parents might then have killed their children so as to ensure their entry into the kingdom of God. Ibid., 663.

[52] L. Berkhof, *Systematic Theology* (Grand Rapids: Eerdmans, 1941), 221.

[53] Ibid. Berkhof makes the point that guilt is not transmitted seminally but is reckoned forensically to Adam's posterity.

[54] G. C. Berkouwer, *Sin* (Grand Rapids: Eerdmans, 1971).

[55] Bernard Ramm, *Offense to Reason: The Theology of Sin* (San Francisco, 1985).

[56] Millard J. Erickson, *Christian Theology,* 3 vols. (Grand Rapids: Baker, 1983–1985), 2:561–658.

[57] Ramm, *Offense to Reason,* 68. Ramm's thesis that Genesis 1–11 represents "theology by narration"—theology expressed by telling a story—has not been fully substantiated. Moreover, Jesus appears not to have understood Genesis 1–11 in this way. Thus in regard to the first eleven chapters of Genesis, we cannot follow this particular thesis of Ramm with all its theological implications.

[58] Ibid., 71–75.

[59] Herman Bavinck suggests that the second tree was so called because it would demon-

strate whether man would arbitrarily determine what was good and evil, or whether he would allow God to make that determination. *Our Reasonable Faith* (Grand Rapids: Baker, reprint 1977), 218. This explanation seems to deviate from the main thrust of the tree's name—"the tree of the *knowledge* of good and evil."

[60] Bavinck, *Reasonable Faith*, 224.

[61] Th. C. Vriezen, *An Outline of Old Testament Theology* (Wageningen: Veenman, 1960), 210.

[62] Leslie S. McCaw and J. A. Motyer, "The Psalms," *NBCRev*, 483.

[63] Charles L. Feinberg, *Jeremiah: A Commentary* (Grand Rapids: Zondervan, 1982), 110.

[64] G. Herbert Livingston, "'āwel, 'awlāh," *TWOT*, 2:653.

[65] Contrast the statement of R. E. Nixon, "Matthew," *NBCRev*, 840: This text "provides justification for treating children as members of the Christian community."

[66] F. F. Bruce comments, "The whole of mankind is viewed as having originally sinned in Adam." *Romans, TNTC* (London, Tyndale, 1963), 126. Cf. John Murray: "For some reason the one sin of Adam is accounted to be the sin of all." *The Epistle to the Romans*, 2 vols. (Grand Rapids: Eerdmans, 1959–1965), 1:185.

[67] See *BAGD*, 287; Nigel Turner, *Syntax*, vol. 3 of J. H. Moulton, *A Grammar of New Testament Greek* (Edinburgh: T. & T. Clark, 1963), 272; Fritz Rienecker and Cleon L. Rogers, Jr., *LKGNT*, 360.

[68] Albrecht Oepke, "*kathistēmi*," *TDNT*, 3:445.

[69] See W. Schneider, "Judgment," *NIDNTT*, 3:365. Cf. C. E. B. Cranfield, *The Epistle to the Romans, ICC;* 2 vols. (Edinburgh and London: T. & T. Clark, 1975), 1:287.

[70] Heinrich Oepke, "*katakrima*," *TDNT*, 3:446.

[71] John Eadie, *Galatians* (Grand Rapids: Baker, reprint 1979), 401. Cf. John Murray, *Romans*, 2:284–85: "'The flesh' is human nature as corrupted, directed, and controlled by sin."

[72] Francis Foulkes, *Ephesians, TNTC* (London: Inter-Varsity, 1963), 69.

[73] Alfred Plummer, *The Gospel According to St. John* (Grand Rapids: Baker, reprint 1981), 102. Cf. E. Schweitzer, "sarx," *TDNTAbr*, 1006: "In John 3:6 everything human is *sarx. Sarx* is the earthly sphere in which there is no knowledge of God and nothing to save from lostness."

[74] R. V. G. Tasker, *James, TNTC* (London: Tyndale, 1957), 46.

[75] F. F. Bruce, *Epistle to the Hebrews, NLCNT* (London and Edinburgh: Marshall, Morgan & Scott, 1964), 142.

[76] See Heinrich Seesemann, "*osphys*," *TDNT*, 5:496–97.

[77] Erickson, *Christian Theology*, 613.

[78] H. Beck and C. Brown, "Peace," *NIDNTT*, 2:777.

[79] Ramm, *Offense to Reason*, 82.

[80] Martin Luther, *Commentary on Genesis* excerpts quoted in Kerr, *Compend of Luther's Theology*, 79.

[81] G. W. Bromiley, "World," *ZPEB*, 5:966–67.

[82] Augustine, *On Christian Doctrine,* III.10.16; Philip Schaff, ed.,*Nicene and Post-Nicene Fathers* (Grand Rapids: Eerdmans, 1956), 2:561.

[83] Norman Malcolm, "Wittgenstein" *EP*, 8:327–28.

[84] Jean Paul Sartre, *Existentialism and Human Emotions* (New York: Philosophical Library, 1957), 15.

[85] Ramm, *Offense to Reason*, 93.

[86] Ibid., 42–43.

[87] Wendell Berry, *The Unsettling of America: Culture and Agriculture* (San Francisco: Sierra Club, 1986), 13.

[88] Ibid.

[89] Erickson, *Christian Theology*, 2:648–52.

[90] Berry, *The Unsettling*, 13.

[91] See Irving Kristol, Paul Johnson, and Michael Novak, "The Moral Basis of Democratic Capitalism" (Washington, D.C.: American Enterprise Institute, n.d.), 16–32.

[92] Reinhold Niebuhr, *The Children of Light and Children of Darkness* (New York: Scribner, 1944), xiii.

[93] Augustine, *Confessions*, Book 1, trans. Shirwood Wirt, (Grand Rapids: Zondervan , 1986), 21.

[94] Strong, *Systematic Theology*, 660–64.

[95] Mark A. Noll, "Feuerbach, Ludwig Andreas," *NDT*, 259.

[96] See J. B. Webster, "Bultmann, Rudolph," *NDT*, 16.

[97] Paul Tillich, *Systematic Theology*, 3 vols. (Chicago: University of Chicago Press, 1951–63), 2:25.

98 Ibid., 1:238.

99 See G. Lewis, "Niebuhr's Relativism, Relationalism, Contextualization and Revelation," in *Challenges to Inerrancy: A Theological Response* ed. Lewis and Demarest, (Chicago: Moody, 1984), 145–73.

100 Marilyn Ferguson, *The Aquarian Conspiracy: Personal and Social Transformation in the 1980s* (Los Angeles: Tarcher, 1980).

101 Robert J. L. Burroughs, "A Vision for a New Humanity," in *The New Age Rage*, ed. Karen Hoyt (Old Tappan, N.J.: Revell, 1987).

102 Ken Wilbur, *Up from Eden* (Boulder, Colo.: Shambala, 1981) in Frances S. Adeney, "Transpersonal Psychology: Psychology and Salvation Meet," in *The New Age Rage*, 123.

103 H. Shelton Smith, *Changing Conceptions of Original Sin* (New York: Scribner, 1955), 76–78.

104 Corliss Lamont, *The Philosophy of Humanism* (New York: Frederick Ungar, revised and enlarged 1982), 241.

105 Ibid., 241–42.

106 Ibid., 242.

107 Ibid., 247.

108 Mencius, in Ch'u Chai with Winberg Chai, *The Story of Chinese Philosophy* (New York: Washington Square, 1961), 53–60.

109 L. Harold DeWolf, *A Theology of the Living Church* (New York: Harper, 1953), 199.

110 Ibid.

111 Ibid.

112 See Edward O. Wilson, *Sociobiology: The New Synthesis* (Cambridge: Harvard University Press, 1975), and Bernard Ramm's discussion in *Offense to Reason*, 23–24.

113 See *The Major Works of Sigmund Freud, Great Books of the Western World*, ed., Mortimer J. Adler, (Chicago: Encyclopedia Britannica, 1952) vol. 54, and Ramm's discussion in *Offense to Reason*, 19–21.

114 See B. F. Skinner, *About Behaviorism* (New York: Vintage, 1974) and Ramm's discussion in *Offense to Reason*, 21–23.

115 Karl Marx, *Capital and Manifesto of the Communist Party, Great Books*, vol. 50.

116 Jose Miranda, *Marx and the Bible* (Maryknoll, N.Y.: Orbis, 1974), 181.

117 Ibid., 190.

118 Ibid., 191.

119 Ibid., 202.

120 Ibid., 17.

121 Ibid., 173.

122 M. Scott Peck, *The People of the Lie: The Hope for Healing Human Evil* (New York: Simon and Schuster, 1983).

123 Charles W. Carter, "Hamartiology," in *A Contemporary Wesleyan Theology*, ed. C. W. Carter (Grand Rapids: Zondervan, Francis Asbury, 1983), 267–68; H. Orton Wiley, *Christian Theology* (Kansas City: Beacon Hill, 1952), 352–57.

124 Emil Brunner, *Man in Revolt* (Philadelphia: Westminster, 1957), 147.

125 Ramm, *Offense to Reason*, 51.

126 Henry Alford, *The Greek Testament*, 4 vols. (Boston: Lee and Shepard, 1872), 2:360.

127 David Murchie, "From Slaveholder to American Abolitionist: Charles Hodge and the Slavery Issue" in *Christian Freedom*, ed. Kenneth W.M. Wozniak and Stanley J. Grenz (New York: University Press of America, 1986), 148.

128 J. Edmondson, *A Concise System of Self-Government in the Great Affairs of Life and Godliness* (New York: Lane and Scott, 1848).

129 See B. B.Warfield, *Perfectionism* (Philadelphia: Presbyterian and Reformed, 1958).

130 See John Passmore, *The Perfectibility of Man* (London: Duckworth, 1970).

131 "American State Papers," in *Great Books of the Western World*, ed. Robert Maynard Hutchins, 43:49–51.

132 See Ajith Fernando, "Rediscovering the Doctrine of Lostness," *World Evangelization* 13.49 (Nov.-Dec. 1987): 18–19.

133 Ramm, *Offense to Reason*, 108.

Chapter 5

1 Emil Brunner, *The Mediator* (Philadelphia: Westminster, 1947), 212; cf. ibid., 232: "The center and the foundation of the whole Christian faith is Christology, that is faith in Jesus Christ."

2 George S. Hendry, "Christology," *A Dictionary of Christian Theology*, ed. Alan Richardson (London: SCM, 1969), 60.

3 Franz Delitzsch, *A System of Biblical Psychology* (Grand Rapids: Baker, reprint 1966), 386.

4 Frederick L. Godet, *Commentary on the Gospel of John*, 3 vols. (Grand Rapids: Zondervan, reprint, 1969), 1:270.

5 I. A. Dorner, *A System of Christian Doctrine*, 4 vols. (Edinburgh: T. & T. Clark, 1880–82), 3:340.

6 Ibid., 3:328.

7 Albrecht Ritschl, *The Christian Doctrine of Justification and Reconciliation* (Clifton, New Jersey: Reference Book Publishers, 1966), 451.

8 Adolf Harnack, *What Is Christianity?* (London: Williams & Norgate, 1912), 208.

9 Henry P. Van Dusen, "The Significance of Jesus Christ," in *Liberal Theology: An Appraisal*, ed. David E. Roberts and Henry P. Van Dusen (New York: Scribner, 1942), 217.

10 Ibid., 221.

11 John Hick, ed., *The Myth of God Incarnate* (Philadelphia: Westminster, 1977).

12 Frances Young, "A Cloud of Witnesses," in *The Myth of God Incarnate*, 32.

13 Hick, *The Myth of God Incarnate*, ix.

14 Young, "A Cloud of Witnesses," 47, note 45.

15 Russell F. Aldwinckle, *More Than a Man* (Grand Rapids: Eerdmans, 1976), 197.

16 Søren Kierkegaard, *Kierkegaard's Concluding Unscientific Postscript* (Princeton: Princeton University Press, 1941), 512.

17 Ibid., 188; cf. 187, 528.

18 Emil Brunner, *The Mediator* (Philadelphia: Westminster, 1947), 158. Brunner's historical relativism led him to conclude that by the ordinary canons of historical research the existence of Jesus is not at all certain. So ibid., 187: "Even the bare fact of the existence of Christ as an historical person is not assured."

19 Ibid., 286.

20 Ibid., 325.

21 Karl Barth, *Dogmatics in Outline* (New York: Philosophical Library, 1949), 96; cf. *CD*, II.2.7.

22 Karl Barth, *CD*, IV.2.43.

23 Barth, *CD*, II.1.397. Cf. ibid., IV.1.258: "He took our flesh, that nature of man as he comes from the fall"; ibid., I.2.151–53. Barth's argument is that unless Christ assumed fallen human nature he would not be in solidarity with the race he came to save.

24 Barth, *CD*, IV.2.49. Cf. *CD*, III.1.54

25 William N. Pittenger, *The Lure of Divine Love* (New York: Pilgrim, 1979), 11.

26 John B. Cobb, Jr., *Christ in a Pluralistic Age* (Philadelphia: Westminster, 1975), 139.

27 William N. Pittenger, "The Incarnation in Process Theology," *Review and Expositor* 71 (1974), 52–53.

28 J. A. T. Robinson, *The Human Face of God* (London: SCM, 1973), 148.

29 Ibid., 115.

30 Ibid., 184.

31 Pittenger, *The Lure of Divine Love*, 114–15.

32 John Tully Carmody and Denise Lardner Carmody, *Contemporary Catholic Theology* (New York: Harper & Row, 1985), 45.

33 Piet Schoonenberg, *The Christ* (New York: Herder & Herder, 1971), 88. He adds that the incarnation "is exclusively a matter of God's presence in this Man, who thereby is God's only-begotten Son." Ibid., 90.

34 Ibid., 91.

35 Hans Küng, *On Being a Christian* (Garden City, New York: Doubleday, 1976), 446; cf. idem, *The Incarnation of God* (New York: Crossroad, 1987), 442.

36 Küng, *On Being a Christian*, 457.

37 Richard P. McBrien, *Catholicism* (Minneapolis: Winston, 1981), 542.

38 Augustine, *The Creed*, III.6: "A virgin conceived, a virgin brought forth, and after bringing forth remained a virgin." Cf. *Enchiridion*, X.34; *Sermon*, 192.1.

39 Cited by McBrien, *Catholicism*, 875.

40 Ibid., 892. McBrien adds that Mary "is an image, a model, a figure, or a type of the Church and Christian existence." Ibid., 896.

41 Ignatius, *To the Magnesians*, 8.1.

42 Ibid., 11.1. Cf. *To the Trallians*, 9: "Jesus Christ the Son of God, who was descended from David, . . . was truly begotten of God and of the Virgin, but not after the same manner."

43 Justin Martyr, *Dialogue With Trypho*, 48.

44 Justin Martyr, *Apology*, II.13.

45 Justin Martyr, *Dialogue With Trypho*, 100. For Justin, the virgin birth is an inviolable datum. Thus he states that "the Word, who is the first-born of God, was produced without sexual union." *Apology*, I.21. Cf. *Dialogue With Trypho*, 84.

46 Athanasius, *Four Discourses Against the Arians*, II.70.

47 Ibid., III.30.

48 Athanasius, *On the Incarnation of the Word*, 54.

49 Augustine, *Letters*, 137.40.

50 Augustine, *Enchiridion*, 33. Cf. *Sermon*, 192.1: "He who was God became Man in his effort to make godlike those who were men; without relinquishing what He was, He desired to become what He had made." Cf. *The Creed*, III.6: "The only Son of God . . . , so great a God equal to the Father, was born of the Holy

Spirit and the Virgin Mary that He might heal the proud."

[51] Augustine, *The Christian Combat,* XXII.24.

[52] Anselm, *Cur Deus Homo,* II.7.

[53] John Calvin, *Institutes of the Christian Religion,* II.12.1.

[54] Ibid., II.12.2.

[55] Benjamin B. Warfield, *The Person and Work of Christ* (Philadelphia: Presbyterian & Reformed, 1970), 6–7; cf. ibid, 17: "He came into the world to die."

[56] Benjamin B. Warfield, *Biblical and Theological Studies* (Philadelphia: Presbyterian & Reformed, 1968), 167; cf. ibid., 166: "The Redemptive work of the Son of God depends upon his supernatural birth."

[57] J. Gresham Machen, *The Virgin Birth of Christ* (New York: Harper & Brothers, 1930), 397. The following quotation confirms Machen's insistence that the Virgin Birth is an integral part of the Christian world-and-life view: "If Christ really rose from the dead, if He really was at all the kind of person that He is represented in the New Testament as being, then there is every reason to think that He was conceived by the Holy Ghost and born of the virgin Mary." Ibid., 268.

[58] James Orr, *The Christian View of God and the World as Centering on the Incarnation* (Grand Rapids: Eerdmans, 1948).

[59] Millard J. Erickson, *Christian Theology,* 3 vols. (Grand Rapids: Baker, 1983–1985), 2:661–81, 739–58.

[60] H. L. Ellison and D. F. Payne, "Genesis," *NLBC,* 138.

[61] Norman Hillyer, "1 and 2 Corinthians," *NBCRev,* 1064; cf. Paul W. Marsh, "The First Letter to the Corinthians," *NLBC,* 1440: "Paul's usage goes beyond a mere typological reference—and is a clear statement of the preexistence of Christ."

[62] Merrill F. Unger, *Unger's Commentary on the Old Testament,* 2 vols. (Chicago: Moody, 1981), 2:1863. J. Barton Payne agrees that the two phrases attest Messiah's eternal preexistence: *The Theology of the Older Testament* (Grand Rapids: Zondervan, 1962), 263.

[63] Edward J. Young, "Daniel," *NBCRev,* 692. Cf. idem, *A Commentary on Daniel* (London: Banner of Truth, 1972), 94. Also agreeing with this interpretation is Unger, *Unger's Commentary on the Old Testament,* 2:1624, and Ronald S. Wallace, *The Lord Is King: The Message of Daniel* (Downers Grove: InterVarsity, 1979), 68.

[64] Derek Kidner, "Isaiah," *NBCRev,* 596.

[65] Alan M. MacRae, "'almāh," *TWOT,* 2:672. According to Unger, *Commentary on the Old Testament,* 2:1161, 'almāh "denotes a virgin or young unmarried woman of good repute." So also Kidner, "Isaiah," *NBCRev,* 596.

[66] James Orr, *The Virgin Birth of Christ* (New York: Scribner, 1907), 135. Cf. Unger, *Commentary on the Old Testament,* 2:1162: "The prophet was assuring the nation that though the dynasty of David was being imperiled by foreign powers and debased by rulers such as Ahaz, it would nevertheless not be blotted out, but through the Davidic line the Lord would send a virgin-born Savior, who would save Israel and the nations and establish the promised kingdom over Israel."

[67] Alfred Plummer, *An Exegetical Commentary on the Gospel According to St. Matthew* (Grand Rapids: Baker, reprint 1982), 168.

[68] I. Howard Marshall, *Commentary on Luke. NIGCT* (Grand Rapids: Eerdmans, 1983), 64.

[69] R. E. Nixon, "Matthew," *NBCRev,* 818.

[70] The genealogies recorded in Matthew 1:2–16 and Luke 3:23–38 differ in a number of respects. Luke's register is the longer of the two, and it proceeds from Joseph through David and Abraham back to Adam. Matthew's, on the other hand, begins with Abraham and moves through David to Joseph and Jesus. Between David and Jesus the two lists present a different set of names for Shealtiel and Zerubbabel. Of the several hypotheses advanced to account for these differences, the following contains the fewest difficulties. In order to present Jesus as the legitimate Davidic Messiah and heir of the promises given to Abraham (Matt. 1:1), Matthew traces Jesus' legal descent from David to Joseph by citing the person who occupied the throne of David at any given time. Luke, whose primary concern was to uphold Jesus' solidarity with and relevance to all humankind, traces Jesus' natural descent through the Davidic branch to which Joseph belonged back to Adam, the first man. "Luke provides a pedigree of actual descent, while Matthew gives the throne-succession. Matthew's whole attempt was to show, in the face of current calumnies, that the Messiah's genealogy was divinely ordered and legally correct." David Hill, *The Gospel of Matthew,* NCBC (Grand Rapids: Eerdmans, 1981), 74. See also I. Howard Marshall, *Commentary on Luke,* 157–61; F. F. Bruce, "Genealogy of Jesus Christ," *NBD,* 410–11.

71 J. B. Lightfoot, *St. Paul's Epistles to the Colossians and to Philemon* (London: Macmillan, 1890), 144–45.

72 Ibid., 147.

73 J. A. Bengel, *Gnomon of the New Testament*, 5 vols. (Edinburgh: T. & T. Clark, 1863), 3:98.

74 Donald Guthrie, *Galatians*. NCBC (Grand Rapids: Eerdmans, 1981), 113–14, comments as follows: "The form of the verb [*exapesteilen*] . . . implies a sending out from a previous state, and must in the case imply the preexistence of the Son."

75 G. Braumann, *"morphē,"* NIDNTT, 1:706. Augustine, Lightfoot, Vincent, Gifford, Foulkes, and other authorities observe that the participle suggests a time-frame that is both past and present, i.e., "he both was and is God."

76 Warfield, *The Person and Work of Christ*, 41.

77 Cf. the NEB translation of *plērōma* in Colossians 1:19: "the complete being of God." J. Schneider, "God," NIDNTT, 2:83 defines the term as "the fullness of the being of God and Christ." J. B. Lightfoot, *Colossians and Philemon*, 225, 328, and C. F. D. Moule, *The Epistles of Paul the Apostle to the Colossians and to Philemon* (Cambridge, Cambridge University Press, 1958), 166, interpret *plērōma* as the totality of the divine powers and attributes.

78 Machen, *Virgin Birth of Christ*, 363.

79 Brooke Foss Westcott, *The Gospel According to St. John*, 2 vols. in 1 (Grand Rapids: Baker, reprint 1980), 1:4.

80 Alfred Plummer, *The Gospel According to St. John* (Grand Rapids: Baker, reprint 1981), 71.

81 See *Integrative Theology* 1:148–54; Craig Blomberg, *The Historical Reliability of the Gospels* (Downers Grove: InterVarsity, 1987), 1–268; R. T. France, *The Evidence for Jesus* (Downers Grove: InterVarsity, 1986); Stephen Neill, *What We Know About Jesus* (Grand Rapids: Eerdmans, 1972); Orr, *Virgin Birth of Christ*, 30–90.

82 J. V. L. Casserley, "Virgin Birth," in *Handbook of Theology*, ed. Marvin Halverson and Arthur Cohen, (New York: World, 1958), 370.

83 Orr, *Virgin Birth of Christ*, 227.

84 Machen, *Virgin Birth of Christ*, 382.

85 Bernard Ramm, *An Evangelical Christology: Ecumenic and Historic* (Nashville: Nelson, 1985), 70.

86 B. B. Warfield, *The Lord of Glory* (Grand Rapids: Zondervan, n.d.), 142.

87 G. F. Hawthorne, "Joseph the Carpenter, History of," ZPEB, 3:696.

88 Paul Jewett, "Can We Learn From Mariology?" *The Christian Century* (August 9, 1967), 1020.

89 Thomas Boslooper, *The Virgin Birth* (Philadelphia: Westminster, 1962), 50.

90 Ibid., 80.

91 Wolfhart Pannenberg, *Jesus—God and Man*, trans. Lewis L. Wilkins and Duane A. Priebe, (Philadelphia: Westminster, 1968), 153.

92 Ibid., 155.

93 E. W. Hengstenberg, *Christology of the Old Testament* (Grand Rapids: Kregel, reprint 1970), 8.

94 See Edward E. Hindson, *Isaiah's Immanuel* (Phillipsburg, N.J.: Presbyterian and Reformed, 1978), esp. 64–80 on "Early Interpretation of Isaiah 7:14." See also J. Skinner, *The Book of Isaiah* (Cambridge University Press, 1900), 1

95 Hengstenberg, *Christology*, 8.

96 For a full discussion of this hypotheses and the biblical data see Geerhardus Vos, *The Self-Disclosure of Jesus* (Grand Rapids: Eerdmans, 1954).

97 A. H. Strong, *Systematic Theology* (Philadelphia: Judson, 1907), 703.

98 Addison H. Leitch, *Interpreting Basic Theology*, (Great Neck, N.Y.: Channel, 1961), 81–82.

99 For discussions of the Greek philosophers see Frederick Copleston, *A History of Philosophy: Greece and Rome* (Westminster, Md.: Newman, 1953).

100 J. Oliver Buswell, Jr., "The Place of Paradox in Our Christian Testimony," *Journal of the American Scientific Affiliation* 17.1 (March 1965): 88–96.

101 See Gordon R. Lewis, *Testing Christianity's Truth Claims* (Chicago: Moody, 1976), 176–81.

102 F. F. Bruce, "Myth," NIDNTT, 2:646.

103 Ibid.; compare F. F. Bruce, "Myth and History," in *History, Criticism and Faith*, ed. Colin Brown (Downers Grove: InterVarsity, 1976), 77–100.

104 Clark Pinnock, "Demythologizing Christmas: Bultmann Had It Backwards," *Christianity Today* (Dec. 11, 1981), 74.

[105] Charles C. Anderson, *The Historical Jesus: A Continuing Quest,* (Grand Rapids: Eerdmans, 1972), 198.

[106] P. E. Hughes, "Myth," *EDT,* 747.

[107] Ibid.

[108] Ibid., 749.

[109] D. M. Baillie, *God Was in Christ* (New York: Scribner, 1948), 66–67.

[110] John Knox, *Jesus, Lord and Christ* (New York: Harper and Brothers, 1958), 225.

[111] Arthur W. Klem, "D. M. Baillie on the Person of Christ," *JETS* 7.2 (Spring 1964): 45–52.

[112] Vishal Mangalwadi, *The World of Gurus* (New Delhi, India: Nivedit Good Books, revised 1987), 251; see also Stephen Neill, *The Supremacy of Jesus* (Downers Grove: Inter-Varsity, 1984).

[113] Swami Bhaktipada, *Christ and Krishna* (Moundsville, W.V.: Bhaktipada Books, 1985), 4.

[114] A. C. Bhaktivedanta Swami Prabhupada, "The Birth of Lord Krishna," *Back to Godhead* (no. 64), 4.

[115] H. B. Acton, "Hegel, Georg Wilhelm Friedrich" *EP,* 3:436, 443.

[116] Dale Moody, *The Word of Truth* (Grand Rapids: Eerdmans, 1981), 424–26.

[117] John B. Cobb, Jr., *Christ in a Pluralistic Age,* 65, 138.

[118] Ibid., 142.

[119] Referred to by Bruce A. Demarest, *Who Is Jesus?* in *The Victor Know and Believe Series,* ed. Bruce L. Shelley (Wheaton: Victor, 1983), 47–48.

[120] Oscar Cullmann, *Christ and Time,* trans. Floyd V. Filson (Philadelphia: Westminster, 1950); 25, 65. See also D. Bruce Lockerbie, *The Cosmic Center: The Supremacy of Christ in a Secular Wasteland* (Portland, Ore.: Multnomah, 1986).

[121] John Tiller, "Advent," in *The New International Dictionary of the Christian Church,* ed. J. D. Douglas (Grand Rapids: Zondervan, 1974), 14.

[122] Athanasius, *The Incarnation of the Word of God* (New York: Macmillan, 1946), 1–45.

[123] W. H. Griffith Thomas, *Christianity Is Christ* (Grand Rapids: Zondervan, n.d.).

[124] Robert E. Webber, *The Secular Saint* (Grand Rapids: Zondervan, 1979), 195.

[125] Cited by William E. Pannell, *My Friend, the Enemy* (Waco: Word, 1968), 33–34.

[126] Pannell, *My Friend,* 120.

Chapter 6

[1] G. C. Berkouwer, *The Person of Christ* (Grand Rapids: Eerdmans, 1954), 14.

[2] So Justin Martyr writes that the Docetists believe that "since he [Christ] was the Son of God, he did not feel what was done and inflicted on him." *Dialogue With Trypho,* 103. Cf. Ignatius, *To the Trallians,* 9–10; *To the Smyrnaeans,* 2; Hippolytus, *Refutations of Heresies,* VIII.1–3; X.12.

[3] Tertullian, *Against Marcion,* III.8.

[4] Rudolf Bultmann, *Jesus and the Word* (New York: Scribner, 1962), 8. Charles C. Anderson, *The Historical Jesus: A Continuing Quest* (Grand Rapids: Eerdmans, 1972), 56, comments: "It is not true that Bultmann denied that Jesus lived, but in his denial of nearly all the history of that life as contained in the Gospels, he has run the risk of doing so in effect."

[5] "The only final condition for sharing in authentic life that the New Testament lays down is a condition that can be formulated in complete abstraction from the event of Jesus of Nazareth and all that it specifically imparts." Schubert Ogden, *Christ Without Myth* (New York: Harper & Row, 1961), 143. For the full discussion of Ogden's elimination of Jesus as necessary for salvation, see ibid., 138–64.

[6] Tertullian, *On the Flesh of Christ,* 14.

[7] Irenaeus, *Against Heresies,* I.26.1-2; V.1.3; Hippolytus, *Refutation of Heresies,* VII.2.2; Tertullian, *On the Flesh of Christ,* 14.

[8] *The Racovian Catechism,* par. 100; cf. *A Dictionary of Christ and the Gospels,* ed. James Hastings (New York: Charles Scribner's Sons, 1906–08), 2:867: "The doctrine of the God-man . . . held a truth for which Socinianism found no expression."

[9] John Orr, *English Deism: Its Roots and Fruits* (Grand Rapids: Eerdmans, 1934), 139–40.

[10] Friedrich D. E. Schleiermacher, *The Christian Faith* (Philadelphia: Fortress, reprint 1928), 387.

[11] Heinrich E. G. Paulus, quoted by Albert Schweitzer in *The Quest of the Historical Jesus* (New York: Macmillan, 1948), 51.

[12] Schweitzer, *Quest of the Historical Jesus,* 370–71.

[13] Joachim Jeremias, *New Testament Theology* (Scribner, 1971), 85; cf. ibid., 84–85: "In Matt. 5:17, Jesus is claiming to be the *eschatological messenger of God,* the promised prophet like Moses (Deut. 18:15, 18), who

brings the final revelation and therefore demands absolute obedience."

[14] See Harold O. J. Brown, *Heresies* (Garden City, N.Y.: Doubleday, 1984), 174–76.

[15] Theodore of Mopsuestia, *Catechetical Homilies*, V.19. Against Apollinarius, Theodore argued that the incarnate Word did not literally *become* flesh: "But when we read that 'he became' (John 1:14), that must not be taken literally, for he was not transmuted into flesh." *On the Incarnation*, 9.

[16] See, for example, Brown, *Heresies*, 172–75, 180, 192.

[17] Martin Luther, *WA*, 26:320; cited in *What Luther Says*, ed. Edward M. Plass (St. Louis: Concordia, 1986), 170.

[18] Martin Luther, *LW*, 45:352, 492–94.

[19] Luther, *LW*, 15:151; cf. ibid., 22:494: "The human nature in Christ shares the glory of all the properties which otherwise pertain to God."

[20] Brown, *Heresies*, 321; H. E. W. Turner, "Communicatio Idiomatum," *Dictionary of Christian Theology* (Philadelphia: Westminster, 1983), 113. For a survey of the *communicatio idiomatum* in post-Reformation Lutheran theology, see Heinrich Schmid, *The Doctrinal Theology of the Evangelical Lutheran Church* (Minneapolis: Augsburg, 1961), 309–47. See also The Formula of Concord, "Epitome," art. VIII and "Solid Declaration," art. VIII.

[21] Ignatius, *Ephesians*, 7; cf. *Trallians*, 10: "God the Word was truly born of the Virgin, having clothed Himself with a body of like passions with our own."

[22] Irenaeus, *Against Heresies*, III.18.7; cf. ibid., III.19.1.

[23] Tertullian, *Against Praxeus*, XXVII.

[24] Augustine, *On the Gospel of John*, 27.4; cf. *Enchiridion*, 35; *Letters*, 137.3; *Selected Sermons*, 7.

[25] Augustine, *Letters*, 137.2; cf. *City of God*, 11.2.

[26] Augustine, *Enchiridion*, 10.34; cf. *Expositions on the Book of Psalms*, 59.2; *City of God*, 13.23. The sinlessness of Jesus Christ is set forth in the following writings: *On Original Sin*, 33; *On Man's Perfection in Righteousness*, 21; *City of God*, 9.17.

[27] Augustine, *On the Trinity*, 1.7.

[28] For an evangelical defense of the Chalcedonian Definition against modern critical objections see Gerald E. Bray, "Can We Dispense With Chalcedon?" *Themelios* 3.2 (Jan. 1978), 2–9.

[29] John Calvin, *Institutes of the Christian Religion*, I.12.1.

[30] Ibid., II.12.2.

[31] Ibid., II.13.4.

[32] Ibid., I.12.3.

[33] John Calvin, *CR*, 46:110; cf. *Institutes*, II.14.5: "the Word begotten by the Father before all ages took human nature in a hypostatic union."

[34] Calvin, *Institutes*, II.14.1; cf. ibid.: "He who was the Son of God became the Son of man—not by confusion of substance, but by unity of person."

[35] Ibid., II.13.4; cf. ibid., IV.17.30: "Since the whole Christ is everywhere, our Mediator is ever present with his own people, and in the Supper reveals himself in a special way, yet in such a way that the whole Christ is present, but not in his wholeness."

[36] Augustus H. Strong, *Systematic Theology* (Valley Forge, Pa.: Judson, 1907), 679.

[37] Ibid., 695.

[38] Ibid., 698.

[39] G. C. Berkouwer, *The Person of Christ* (Grand Rapids: Eerdmans, 1954).

[40] John F. Walvoord, *Jesus Christ Our Lord* (Chicago: Moody, 1969).

[41] Millard J. Erickson, *Christian Theology*, 3 vols. (Grand Rapids: Baker, 1983–1985), 2:683–738.

[42] Norval Geldenhuys, *The Gospel of Luke*, *NICNT* (Grand Rapids: Eerdmans, 1983), 122; cf. Francis J. Hall, *Theological Outlines* (London: SPCK, 1934), 183: "He never grew from moral deficiency to virtue, but was at each stage of his development what He ought to be, exhibiting successively, . . . the highest perfections of a child, of a youth, and of full-grown manhood."

[43] H. Bietenhard, "Beginning," *NIDNTT*, 1:168 comments that the meaning here is "that Jesus brings men to life, and also that Jesus Christ is the author of life." Classical usage supports the meaning, "first cause," or "source" for *archēgos* in Acts 3:15. See H. G. Liddell and R. Scott, *A Greek-English Lexicon* (Oxford: Clarendon, 1940), 252.

[44] William Neil, *The Acts of the Apostles*. *NCBC* (Grand Rapids: Eerdmans, 1973), 214–15.

[45] F. F. Bruce observes in relation to Galatians 4:4 that "Paul's wording is applicable to anyone of women born." *Commentary on Galatians*, *NIGTC* (Grand Rapids: Eerdmans, 1982), 195.

46 William Barclay, *The Letters to the Galatians and Ephesians, The Daily Study Bible* (Philadelphia: Westminster, 1958), 171.

47 Fritz Rienecker and Cleon J. Rogers, Jr., *LKGNT*, 568; cf. H. Bietenhard, "Beginning," *NIDNTT*, 1:166.

48 C. E. B. Cranfield, *Romans. ICC*, 2 vols. (London: T. & T. Clark, 1975–79), 2:468–69 insists that the evidence overwhelmingly favors interpreting the latter part of Romans 9:5 in terms of Christ. He prefers the translation " . . . Christ, who is over all, God blessed forever, Amen." See also the discussion in Lewis and Demarest, *Integrative Theology* (Grand Rapids: Zondervan, 1987), 1:265.

49 So F. F. Bruce, *Romans. TNTC* (London: Tyndale, 1963), 72: "He who during his earthly ministry was the Son of God in weakness and lowliness became by the resurrection the Son of God in power." So also Cranfield, *Romans*, 1:60–64.

50 J. Behm, *"morphē," TDNTAbr*, 608.

51 "The *homoiōma* denotes likeness in appearance but distinction in essence . . . . The term *homoiōma* is clearly an attempt to overcome the difficulty of having to say that the Christ in whom human sin is condemned is not himself a sinner . . . Christ is not just a heavenly being with an external human form; he is fully and truly human, but not a sinner." J. Schneider, *"homoiōma," TDNTAbr*, 686. We take issue with Cranfield, who claims that *homoiōma* in Romans 8:3 and Philippians 2:7 extends to Christ's sharing of our sinful nature. Cranfield writes that we "understand Paul's thought to be that the Son of God assumed the selfsame fallen human nature that is ours, but that in this case the fallen human nature was never the whole of him—He never ceased to be the eternal Son of God." *Romans*, 1:381–82.

52 Schneider, *"schēma," TDNT*, 7:954.

53 F. F. Bruce, *The Gospel of John* (Grand Rapids: Eerdmans, 1983), 359.

54 James A. Brooks and Carlton L. Winbery, *Syntax of New Testament Greek* (Washington, D.C.: University Press of America, 1979), 91.

55 A. C. Thistelton, "Flesh," *NIDNTT*, 1:678–79.

56 Brooke Foss Westcott, *The Gospel According to St. John*, 2 vols. in 1 (Grand Rapids: Baker, reprint 1980), 1:19.

57 See Lewis and Demarest, *Integrative Theology*, 1:268 for an exegesis of this text in support of Jesus' deity.

58 Rienecker and Rogers, *LKGNT*, 784.

59 Ibid., 670.

60 Cf. Brooke Foss Westcott, *The Epistle to the Hebrews* (Grand Rapids: Eerdmans, reprint 1974), 128: "The Lord's manhood was (negatively) sinless and (positively) perfect, that is perfect relatively at every stage; and therefore He truly advanced by 'learning' (Luke 2:40, 52), while the powers of His human nature grew step by step in a perfect union with the divine in His one Person."

61 R. Schippers, "Goal," *NIDNTT*, 2:59.

62 Gerald F. Hawthorne, "The Letter to the Hebrews," *NLBC*, 1985.

63 F. F. Bruce, *The Epistle to the Hebrews* (Grand Rapids: Eerdmans, 1964), 43.

64 Ibid., 4.

65 Donald Guthrie, *New Testament Theology* (Downers Grove: InterVarsity, 1981), 309–10.

66 R. S. Wallace, "Christology," *EDT*, 223.

67 For further insight into Christ's unique sonship see the discussion of the eternal generation of the Son in *Integrative Theology*, 1:275–79.

68 Guthrie, *New Testament Theology*, 281.

69 Gary Habermas, *Ancient Evidence for the Life of Jesus* (Nashville: Thomas Nelson, 1984), 87–115, 152–63. See also R. T. France, *The Evidence for Jesus* (Downers Grove: InterVarsity, 1986) and F. F. Bruce, *Jesus and Christian Origins Outside the New Testament* (Grand Rapids: Eerdmans, 1974).

70 Ronald H. Nash, *Christianity and the Hellenistic World* (Grand Rapids: Zondervan, 1984).

71 John Stott, *The Authentic Jesus*, (Downers Grove: InterVarsity, 1985), 92.

72 Reinhold Niebuhr, *The Nature and Destiny of Man*, 2 vols. (New York: Scribner, 1951), 2:73–74; Karl Barth also holds that the flesh Christ assumed was fallen Adamic nature, humanness in a state of sin, but that Christ did not sin, *CD*, IV.2.43.

73 John Knox, *The Humanity and Divinity of Christ* (Cambridge: Cambridge University Press, 1967), 51.

74 Karl Barth, *CD*, IV.1.165; idem, *The Epistle to the Romans* (London: Oxford University, 1933), 278–82.

75 Ernst Käsemann, *Commentary on Romans* (Grand Rapids: Eerdmans, 1980), 217.

76 I. Howard Marshall, *Luke: Historian and Theologian*, (Grand Rapids: Zondervan, 1970), 52.

[77] Hugh Ross Mackintosh, *The Doctrine of the Person of Christ* (New York: Scribner, 1912), 403.

[78] Strong, *Systematic Theology*, 694.

[79] Francis Peiper, *Christian Dogmatics* (Saint Louis, MO: Concordia, 1951), 239.

[80] Søren Kierkegaard, *Concluding Unscientific Postscript*, trans. David F. Swenson and Walter Lowrie, (Princeton: Princeton University Press, 1941), 195.

[81] Ibid., 194.

[82] J. Loewenberg, ed., *Hegel, Selections* (New York: Scribner, 1929), xii.

[83] J. Oliver Buswell, Jr., "The Place of Paradox in our Christian Testimony," *Journal of the American Scientific Affiliation*, 17.1 (March 1965), 92.

[84] Cited in Henry L. Mansel, *The Limits of Religious Thought* (Boston: Gould and Lincoln, 1860), 319.

[85] John Hick, "Jesus and the World Religions," in *The Myth of God Incarnate*, ed. John Hick (Philadelphia: Westminster, 1977), 178.

[86] Niebuhr, *The Nature and Destiny of Man*, 2:61.

[87] J. I. Packer, *Evangelism and the Sovereignty of God* (Downers Grove: InterVarsity, 1961), 18.

[88] Alfred Lande, lecture: "Why Do Quantum Theorists Ignore Quantum Theory?" Denver University, March 2, 1966, reported in *The Denver Post* (March 3, 1966), 27.

[89] Alfred Lande, *New Foundations of Quantum Mechanics* (Cambridge: Cambridge University Press, 1965), 109–11.

[90] Ibid.

[91] G. K. Chesterton, *Orthodoxy* (Garden City: Doubleday, 1959), 11.

[92] A. M. Hunter, *Jesus, Lord and Savior* (Grand Rapids: Eerdmans, 1976), 115.

[93] Ibid., 117.

[94] Ibid.

[95] Ibid., 118.

[96] Ibid., 167.

[97] Leonard Hodgson, *Jesus, Word and Presence: An Essay in Christology* (Philadelphia: Fortress, 1971), 136.

[98] Ibid., 137.

[99] Ibid., 138.

[100] Ibid.

[101] Ibid.

[102] Ibid., 139.

[103] Ibid., 166.

[104] Ibid., 147.

[105] Ibid., 146.

[106] Michael Goulder, "Jesus, The Man of Universal Destiny," in *The Myth of God Incarnate*, 62.

[107] Bray, "Can We Dispense With Chalcedon?" 9.

[108] Ibid.

[109] Don Cupitt, "The Christ of Christendom," in *The Myth of God Incarnate*, 145.

[110] Ibid.

[111] Levi H. Dowling, *The Aquarian Gospel of Jesus the Christ* (Santa Monica: DeVorss, 1907, reprint 1972), 56-97.

[112] Ibid., 15.

[113] Ibid., 16–17.

[114] Ibid., 13, 265.

[115] Ibid., 13. For an assessment of Hindu gurus in comparison and contrast with Jesus Christ see Vishal Mangalwadi, *The World of the Gurus* (New Delhi: Nivedit Good Books, 1987).

[116] Dowling, *Aquarian Gospel*, 265.

[117] Ibid., 13.

[118] For an evangelical appraisal of recent developments in occultism see Gary North, *Unholy Spirits: Occultism and New Age Humanism* (Fort Worth: Dominion, 1986). For evaluation of another spirit message alleged to be from Jesus, see Gordon R. Lewis, *Confronting the Cults* (Nutley, N.J.: Presbyterian and Reformed, 1966), 175–79, 181–83.

[119] Geoffrey Wainwright, *Doxology: The Praise of God in Worship, Doctrine and Life* (New York: Oxford University Press, 1980), 57.

[120] Helmut Thielicke, *Between God and Satan* (Grand Rapids: Eerdmans, 1958), 75–76.

[121] Ibid., 76.

[122] Anthony Hoekema, *The Four Major Cults* (Grand Rapids: Eerdmans, 1963), 382–85.

[123] On the significance of Christ as prophet see Bruce A. Demarest, *Who Is Jesus?* (Wheaton: Victor, 1983), 70.

[124] See Michael Griffiths, *The Example of Jesus* (Downers Grove: InterVarsity, 1985), 75.

[125] For amplification of each of these aspects of Christ's example see Michael Griffiths, ibid., 136–85.

Chapter 7

[1] On the Protestant side Dale Moody devotes only half a dozen pages to Christ's death in his systematic theology, *The Word of Truth* (Grand Rapids: Eerdmans, 1981). On the Catholic side the Notre Dame theologian Richard P. McBrien devotes fewer than 10 pages out of 1,250 to the cross in *Catholicism*, 2 vols. in 1 (Minneapolis: Winston, 1981).

[2] Benjamin B. Warfield, *The Person and Work of Christ* (Philadelphia: Presbyterian and Reformed, 1970), 425.

[3] Emil Brunner, *The Mediator* (Philadelphia: Westminster, 1947), 436.

[4] Irenaeus, *Against Heresies*, V.1.1; cf. *Proof of the Apostolic Preaching*, 31: "Because death ruled in the body, it was necessary through the body that it should be done away with and man set free from its oppression."

[5] Origen, *Commentary on Matthew*, XVI.8; cf. *Commentary on Romans*, II.13; *Exodus Homily*, VI.9; *Against Celsus*, I.31; VII.17. Gregory of Nyssa proposed a similar view: "In order to secure that the ransom in our behalf might be easily accepted by him who required it, the Deity was hidden under the veil of our nature, that so, as with ravenous fish, the hook of the Deity might be gulped down along with the bait of flesh." *The Great Catechism*, 24.

[6] John of Damascus, *The Orthodox Faith*, III.27; cf. III.1.

[7] Gustaf Aulén, *Christus Victor* (London: SPCK, 1970), 4; cf. 55.

[8] Peter Abelard, *Sentences*, XXIII; cf. "Exposition of the Epistle to the Romans," *LCC*, 10:283–84.

[9] Faustus Socinus, *Praelectiones Theologia*, 591; cited by L. W. Grensted, *A Short History of the Doctrine of the Atonement* (Manchester: Manchester University Press, 1920), 287.

[10] Horace Bushnell, *God in Christ* (New York: AMS, reprint 1972), 216.

[11] Ibid., 192; cf. 212–13.

[12] Ibid., 247–48.

[13] L. Harold DeWolf, *A Theology of the Living Church* (New York: Harper & Row, 1953), 267; cf. idem, *The Case for Theology in Liberal Perspective* (Philadelphia: Westminster, 1959), 77–80.

[14] Anselm, *Cur Deus Homo*, I.23.

[15] Ibid., II.6; cf. II.7,18.

[16] J. I. Packer, "What Did the Cross Achieve?" *Tyndale Bulletin* 25 (1974): 4.

[17] Hugo Grotius, *A Defense of the Catholic Faith Concerning the Satisfaction of Christ Against Faustus Socinus*, trans. F. H. Foster (Andover: Draper, 1889), 100.

[18] John Miley, *Systematic Theology*, 2 vols. (New York: Hunt & Eaton, 1892–1894), 2:168.

[19] Ibid., 2:176; cf. ibid, 2:95: "The vicarious sufferings of Christ are a provisional substitute for penalty, and not the actual punishment of sin."

[20] Ibid., 2:179. Miley expresses the outcome of the cross in other words in ibid., 2:181: "The cross is the highest revelation of all the truths which embody the best moral forces of the divine government."

[21] J. Kenneth Grider, "Governmental Theory of the Atonement," *BDT*, 240; cf. *A Contemporary Wesleyan Theology*, ed. Charles W. Carter, 2 vols. (Grand Rapids: Zondervan, Francis Asbury, 1983), 1:502–5.

[22] James Arminius, *The Works of James Arminius*, 3 vols. (Auburn and Buffalo: Derby, Miller & Orton, 1853), 1:316. Thomas Watson, the first important systematic theologian of Methodism wrote, "Christ died for all men, so as to make their salvation practicable." *Theological Institutes*, 2 vols. (New York: Lane & Scott, 1851), 2:303.

[23] Miley, *Systematic Theology*, 2:239; cf. H. Orton Wiley, *Christian Theology*, 3 vols. (Kansas City: Beacon Hill, 1952–1953), 2:296: "Arminianism, with its emphasis on moral freedom and prevenient grace, has always held to the universality of the atonement."

[24] Karl Barth, *CD*, II.2.123; IV.1.222, 230–35.

[25] Ibid., IV.2.46.

[26] Ibid., 1.296.

[27] Ibid., 2.294.

[28] Barth, *CD*, IV.1.486. Barth immediately adds, "His forgiveness repels chaos, and closes the gulf, and ensures that the will of God will be done on earth as it is in heaven. What, then, is the guilt of man, in the light of the fact that God encounters him in this way, as the One who pardons his sin?" Ibid.

[29] Barth, *CD*, IV.1.747; cf. *The Faith of the Church* (New York: Meridian Books, 1958), 91: "There no longer exists any object under the curse after what happened at Calvary. By taking over that curse Christ accomplished our acquittal." Cf. also *CD*, II.2.774; IV.1.294; *Dogmatics in Outline* (New York: Philosophical Library, 1949), 119–20.

[30] Hendrikus Berkhof, *Christian Faith*, trans. Sierd Woudstra (Grand Rapids: Eerdmans, 1979), 305. For the full discussion of Berkhof's

position see the section "Death and Reconciliation," ibid., 299–307.

31 Ibid.

32 Vincent Taylor, *Jesus and His Sacrifice* (New York: St. Martin's, 1965), 308; cf. ibid., 309: Christ's sacrifice is "the perfect expression of his perfect penitence for the sins of men."

33 Clement of Rome, *Epistle to the Corinthians*, I.49.5; cf. ibid., I.7.4.

34 Ignatius, *To the Smyrnaeans*, 2; cf. *To the Trallians*, 2.

35 *Epistle to Diognetus*, X.2–5.

36 Cyril of Jerusalem, *Lenten Lectures*, XIII.33; cf. ibid., XIII.18: "Jesus assumed the thorns to remove the condemnation."

37 Athanasius, *Incarnation of the Word*, XX.2; cf. XX.5; *Discourse Against the Arians*, I.60.

38 Augustine, *Reply to Faustus the Manichaean*, XIV.3; cf. *On the Trinity*, IV.12–14; *On The Gospel of John*, XLI.6.

39 Augustine, *City of God*, X.20.

40 Augustine, *City of God*, XIII.11.15; cf. *Faith, Hope and Love*, 33.

41 Augustine, *City of God*, XVIII.49; cf. *On the Gospel of John*, XXV.16,18.

42 Martin Luther, *LW*, 26:288.

43 Aulén, *Christus Victor*, 101–22.

44 John Calvin, *Institutes of the Christian Religion*, II.16.6; cf. ibid., II.16.2: "Christ took upon himself and suffered the punishment that . . . threatened all sinners"; cf. ibid., III.4.26.

45 John Calvin, *Commentary on the Epistles of Paul to the Corinthians*, 2:242.

46 Calvin, *Institutes*, II.17.3; cf. ibid., II.16.10: "Christ appeased God's wrath and satisfied his just judgment." Cf. ibid., II.17.4; III.4.26; *Commentaries on the Catholic Epistles*, 171–72.

47 Calvin, *Institutes*, II.16.7; II.17.5; III.4.30.

48 John Calvin, *Commentaries on the Epistles of Paul to the Philippians, Colossians and Thessalonians*, 159; cf. *Commentaries on the Catholic Epistles*, 240–41.

49 Calvin, *Institutes*, II.17.2; cf. ibid., III.6.3; III.11.8.

50 Calvin, *Institutes*, II.15.1–6. For an analysis of Calvin's development of the three offices, which would have a profound influence on later Protestant theology, see John Frederick Jansen, *Calvin's Doctrine of the Work of Christ* (London: James Clarke, 1956).

51 Benjamin B. Warfield, "Atonement," *Studies in Theology* (New York: Oxford University Press, 1932), 278. Warfield observes that the doctrine of vicarious sacrifice has been upheld by the major branches of the Christian church—e.g., the Greek, Latin, Lutheran, and Reformed.

52 Athanasius, *On the Incarnation of the Word*, IV.20; cf. *Against the Arians*, I.60: "Suffering in the flesh [the Logos] gave salvation to all."

53 Cyril of Jerusalem, *Lenten Lectures*, XIII.4.

54 Augustine, *Enchiridion*, 49; *Homilies on the First Epistle of John*, I.8; cf. *On Nature and Grace*, 48.

55 R. T. Kendall, *Calvin and English Puritanism to 1649* (Oxford: Oxford University Press, 1979) argues that Calvin taught a universal atonement. Several recent studies maintain that Calvin held a tension between God's purpose for humankind as a whole and his purpose for the elect in particular. That is, Christ's atonement is universal in scope, but God gives saving faith only to the elect. So argue James B. Torrance, "The Incarnation and 'Limited Atonement,'" *Evangelical Quarterly* LV.2 (April 1983): 83–94; Tony Lane, "The Quest for the Historical Calvin," ibid., 95–113; M. Charles Bell, "Calvin and the Extent of the Atonement," ibid., 115–23 ; R. B. Knox, "John Calvin: An Elusive Churchman," *Scottish Journal of Theology*, 34 (1981): 147–56. The following comment from Lane is typical of the above: "Calvin was prepared to recognize *both* God's universal love for all mankind and his desire for all to repent *and* his purpose that some only should be saved. To the feeble human mind these are irreconcilable." 113.

56 Calvin, *Institutes*, IV.14.7; cf. ibid., II.16.2, 13; II.17.2.

57 Calvin, *Commentary on Galatians*, 157; cf. his comment on Romans 5:18: "Paul makes grace common to all men . . . because it is offered to all. Although Christ suffered for the sins of the whole world and is offered . . . without distinction to all men, yet not all receive him." *Commentary on Romans*, 211. See also Calvin's comments on Isaiah 53:5; John 3:16; Romans 10:16; Colossians 1:14.

58 See, for example, Herman Bavinck, *Our Reasonable Faith* (Grand Rapids: Baker, reprint 1977), 361.

59 C. H. Spurgeon, "General and Yet Particular," *The Metropolitan Tabernacle Pulpit*, 63 vols. (Pasadena, Texas: Pilgrim reprint 1969–1980), 10:233; cf. ibid., 230: "It has pleased

God to put the whole race under the mediatorial sway of Jesus, in order that he might give eternal life to those who were chosen out of the world.''

[60] Charles M. Horne, *Salvation* (Chicago: Moody, 1971), 46.

[61] Robert P. Lightner, *The Death Christ Died* (Des Plaines, Ill.: Regular Baptist Press, 1967), 46–47, 55–56. See also by the same author, *Evangelical Theology* (Grand Rapids: Baker, 1986), 209–10. Cf. the comment by Walter A. Elwell, "Atonement, Extent of the," *EDT*, 99: "Paul had no trouble saying that God could be the Savior of all, in one sense, and of those who believe, in another sense (1 Tim. 4:10).''

[62] Donald G. Bloesch, *Essentials of Evangelical Theology*, 2 vols. (New York: Harper & Row, 1978–79), 1:164–68.

[63] John Owen, *The Works of John Owen*, ed. William Goold; 16 vols. (Edinburgh: Banner of Truth Trust, 1965–1968), 10:227.

[64] Ibid., 10:214.

[65] Roger R. Nicole, "The 'Five Points' and God's Sovereignty," in *Our Sovereign God*, ed. James M. Boice (Grand Rapids: Baker, 1977), 31–33; cf. Nicole, "Particular Redemption," in *Our Savior God*, ed. James M. Boice (Grand Rapids: Baker, 1980), 165–78.

[66] Clement of Alexandria, *Miscellanies*, VI.6.

[67] Thomas Aquinas, *ST*, III.1, q. 52, art. 1–8; esp. art. 5.

[68] Calvin, *Institutes*, II.16.10–11.

[69] See *The Heidelberg Catechism*, pt. II, q. 44; L. Berkhof, *Systematic Theology* (Grand Rapids: Eerdmans, 1941), 342–43; G. C. Berkouwer, *The Work of Christ* (Grand Rapids: Eerdmans, 1965), 169–80. But Dale Moody, *Word of Truth*, 387–88, accepts the possibility of a preaching mission of Christ in hades.

[70] A. A. Hodge, *The Atonement* (Grand Rapids: Eerdmans, reprint 1953).

[71] W. G. T. Shedd, *Dogmatic Theology*, 3 vols. (Grand Rapids: Zondervan, n.d.), 2:353–489.

[72] H. Dermot McDonald, *The Atonement of the Death of Christ* (Grand Rapids: Baker, 1985).

[73] Geoffrey W. Bromiley, "Atone; Atonement," *ISBERev*, 1:353.

[74] Hywell R. Jones, "Exodus," *NBCRev*, 117.

[75] R. Laird Harris, "*kāpar*," *TWOT*, 1:452–53; cf. *BDB*, 820.

[76] G. Lloyd Carr, "*minḥāh*," *TWOT*, 1:515.

[77] Gordon J. Wenham, *The Book of Leviticus. NICOT* (Grand Rapids: Eerdmans, 1979), 65.

[78] Derek Kidner, *Psalms 1–72. TOTC* (Downers Grove: InterVarsity, 1973), 106.

[79] A. M. Stibbs, "Hebrews," *NBCRev*, 1208.

[80] For convincing discussions that identify the servant of the Lord ultimately with the Messiah, see Walter C. Kaiser, "'*ebed*," *TWOT*, 2:639–40; Jan Ridderbos, *Isaiah* (Grand Rapids: Zondervan, 1984), 366–73; and J. Barton Payne, *The Theology of the New Testament* (Grand Rapids: Zondervan, 1962), 254–57.

[81] Ridderbos, *Isaiah*, 484.

[82] R. D. Patterson, "*sābal*," *TWOT*, 2:616.

[83] William B. Coker, "*pādāh*," *TWOT*, 2:716.

[84] Murray J. Harris, "Prepositions and Theology in the Greek NT," *NIDNTT*, 3:1180; cf. F. Büchsel, "*lytron*," *TDNT*, 4:342–49; Nigel Turner, *Syntax* (Edinburgh: T. & T. Clark, 1963), 258; vol. III of J. H. Moulton, *A Grammar of New Testament Greek*.

[85] Harris, *NIDNTT*, 3:1174, 1176.

[86] Harris, *NIDNTT*, 3:1196, indicates that *hyper* simultaneously implies both representation and substitution.

[87] H. Vorländer, "Forgiveness," *NIDNTT*, 1:701.

[88] William L. Lane, *Mark. NLCNT* (Grand Rapids: Eerdmans, 1974), 501.

[89] Fritz Rienecker and Cleon L. Rogers, Jr., *LKGNT*, 471.

[90] C. L. W. Grimm and J. H. Thayer, *A Greek-English Lexicon to the New Testament* (New York: American Book, 1889), 50.

[91] C. Brown, "*lytron*," *NIDNTT*, 3:199; cf. Leslie Mitton, *Ephesians. NCBC* (Grand Rapids: Eerdmans, 1981), 52: "Its main significance is to suggest an entry into a new kind of freedom.''

[92] H. Vorländer and C. Brown, "Reconciliation," *NIDNTT*, 3:166.

[93] C. E. B. Cranfield, *The Epistle to the Romans, ICC* 2 vols. (Edinburgh: T. & T. Clark, 1975–1979), 1:267. Millard J. Erickson, *Christian Theology*, 3 vols. (Grand Rapids: Baker, 1983–1985), 2:815, affirms that in reconciliation man turns to God, "but the process of reconciliation is primarily God's turning in favor toward man." Berkhof, *Systematic Theology*, 373, observes that the subjective component of the sinner's reconciliation to God, is secondary to the objective component of God

being propitiated by the vicarious death of Christ.

⁹⁴Rienecker and Rogers, *LKGNT*, 527.

⁹⁵H. Weigelt, "Clothe," *NIDNTT*, 1:315.

⁹⁶"The Christ hymn (vv. 6–11) presents Jesus as the supreme example of the humble, self-sacrificing, self-denying, self-giving service that Paul had just been urging the Philippians to practice in their relations toward one another (vv. 1–4)." Gerald F. Hawthorne, *Philippians*, *WBC* (Waco: Word, 1983), 79.

⁹⁷Cranfield, *Epistle to the Romans*, 1:202.

⁹⁸Leon Morris, *The Apostolic Preaching of the Cross* (Grand Rapids: Eerdmans, 1965), 12, 18.

⁹⁹For developments of this interpretation see Cranfield, *Romans*, 1:216–17; Morris, *Apostolic Preaching*, 184–202; George Eldon Ladd, *A Theology of the New Testament* (Grand Rapids: Eerdmans, 1974), 429–30; Donald Guthrie, *New Testament Theology* (Downers Grove: InterVarsity, 1981), 467–70; and C. Brown, "Reconciliation," *NIDNTT*, 3:151–60.

¹⁰⁰F. F. Bruce, *Epistle to the Romans*. *TNTC* (London: Tyndale, 1963), 107.

¹⁰¹J. Gess, "Lamb, Sheep," *NIDNTT*, 2:411.

¹⁰²Alfred Plummer, *The Epistles of St. John* (Grand Rapids: Baker, reprint 1980), 35.

¹⁰³Leon Morris, "2 John," *NBCRev*, 1268. F. F. Bruce comments that "here John ascribes the widest scope to the saving purpose of God." *The Epistles of John* (Grand Rapids: Eerdmans, 1970), 111.

¹⁰⁴Bruce, *Epistles of John*, 50.

¹⁰⁵R. Tuente, "Lamb, Sheep," *NIDNTT*, 2:413; cf. H. Preisker and S. Schulz, "Probaton," *TDNT*, 6:689–92.

¹⁰⁶Berkhof, *Systematic Theology*, 397; cf. George Smeaton, *The Doctrine of the Atonement as Taught by the Apostles* (Edinburgh: T. & T. Clark, 1870), 446–47.

¹⁰⁷Rienecker and Rogers, *LKGNT*, 774. According to O. Bauernfeind, "*aselgeia*," *TDNT*, 1:490, the word means "debauchery" or "licentiousness," particularly serious sexual excesses.

¹⁰⁸Simon J. Kistemaker, *Exposition of the Epistles of Peter and the Epistle of Jude, New Testament Commentary* (Grand Rapids: Baker, 1987), 282.

¹⁰⁹M. J. Harris, "Appendix," *NIDNTT*, 3:1196; B. F. Westcott, *The Epistle to the Hebrews* (Grand Rapids: Eerdmans, reprint 1974), 47. A. M. Stibbs thus translates *hyper*

pantos as "for the benefit of all;" "Hebrews," *NBCRev*, 1197. Cf. Erickson, *Christian Theology*, 2:832, citing H. O. Wiley, who suggests that 2 Peter 2:1 teaches "that there is a distinction between those for whom Christ died and those who are finally saved."

¹¹⁰"Originally the word meant just 'the grave' and became specialized for 'hell.' " R. Laird Harris, "*šᵉ'ôl*," *TWOT*, 2:892. Harris adds, "It may be that *šᵉ'ôl* is just a poetic synonym for *qeber*." Ibid.

¹¹¹J. A. Alexander, *The Gospel According to Matthew* (Grand Rapids: Baker, reprint 1980), 344.

¹¹²David Hill, *The Gospel of Matthew*. *NCBC* (London: Olifants, 1972), 356.

¹¹³So Turner, *Syntax*, 215; cf. Rienecker and Rogers, *LKGNT*, 531. Francis Foulkes, *Ephesians*. *TNTC* (London: Inter-Varsity, 1963), 116, adds that the phrase "may mean this earth, so low in comparison with his heavenly home."

¹¹⁴See the development by Wayne Grudem, "Christ Preaching Through Noah: 1 Peter 3:19–20 in the Light of Dominant Themes in Jewish Literature," *Trinity Journal*, N.S. 7.2 (Fall 1986); cf. Augustine, *Letter 164*, 15–17.

¹¹⁵"Covenant," *Nelson's Illustrated Bible Dictionary*, ed. F. F. Bruce et al. (Nashville: Thomas Nelson, 1986), 260.

¹¹⁶A. A. Hodge, *The Atonement*, 254.

¹¹⁷James Denney, *The Death of Christ* (London: The Tyndale Press, 1951), 131.

¹¹⁸John R. W. Stott, *The Cross of Christ* (Downers Grove: InterVarsity, 1986), 276.

¹¹⁹B. Gartner, "Suffer," *NIDNTT*, 3:721.

¹²⁰Stott, *Cross of Christ*, 143.

¹²¹R. E. Davies, "Christ in Our Place—the Contribution of the Prepositions," *Tyndale Bulletin* 21 (1970): 90.

¹²²Ibid.

¹²³In the class of J. Oliver Buswell, Jr., as reported in his *Sin and Atonement* (Grand Rapids: Zondervan, 1937), 67.

¹²⁴*The Denver Post* (Jan. 3, 1975), 10.

¹²⁵Patricia Treece, *A Man for Others* (San Francisco: Harper & Row, 1982), vii.

¹²⁶Stott, *Cross of Christ*, 203.

¹²⁷A. A. Hodge, *Atonement*, 170.

¹²⁸George Smeaton, *The Apostles' Doctrine of the Atonement* (Grand Rapids: Zondervan, 1957).

¹²⁹See the historical study by Gustaf Aulen, *Christus Victor* (London: SPCK, 1970).

130 Samuel J. Mikolaski, "The Atonement and Men Today," *Christianity Today* (March 13, 1961), 3.

131 David Scaer, *What Do You Think of Jesus?* (St. Louis: Concordia, 1973), 37.

132 Robert H. Culpepper, *Interpreting the Atonement* (Grand Rapids: Eerdmans, 1966), 133.

133 W. C. Robinson, "Wrath," *EDT,* 1196.

134 Roger Nicole, "Propitiation," in *Christian Faith and Modern Theology,* ed. Carl Henry (New York: Channel, 1964), 198.

135 See Ajith Fernando, *A Universal Homecoming?* (Madras, India: Evangelical Literature Service, 1983), 146.

136 Morris, *The Cross in the New Testament* (Grand Rapids: Eerdmans, 1965), 400.

137 Stott, *Cross of Christ,* 202.

138 See Horne, *Salvation,* 46.

139 Morris, *Cross in the New Testament,* 385–86.

140 A. E. Taylor, *The Faith of a Moralist* (London: Macmillan, 1951), 183.

141 Immanuel Kant, *Praktische Vernuft,* 151, cited by W. G. T. Shedd, *The Doctrine of Endless Punishment* (New York: Scribner, 1886), 122–23.

142 Warfield, *Person and Work of Christ,* 292.

143 Buswell, *Sin and Atonement,* 80.

144 Stott, *Cross of Christ,* 123. For a critical study of a moral government theory in Youth With a Mission (YWAM) see Alan W. Gomes, *Lead Us Not Into Deception: A Biblical Examination of Moral Government Theology,* 3rd ed. (La Mirada, Calif.; Alex Gomes, P.O. Box 1464, 1968).

145 Wilbur Smith, *Great Sermons on the Death of Christ* (Natick, Mass.: Wilde, 1965), 7.

146 As quoted in ibid., 8.

147 R. K. Harrison, "Blood," *ZPEB,* 1:627.

148 Ibid.

149 For amplification see William Hordern, "The Essence of Christianity and the Cross of Christ" in Warfield, *Person and Work of Christ,* 1950, 477–530.

150 Jürgen Moltmann, *The Crucified God* (New York: Harper & Row, 1974), 15.

151 Ibid., 19.

152 Ibid., 227.

153 Ibid., 249.

154 Ibid., 228.

155 Ibid., 277.

156 Ibid., 332.

157 Ibid., 329–34.

158 Ibid., 53.

159 R. T. France, "Liberation in the New Testament," in *The Best in Theology,* ed. J. I. Packer (Carol Stream, Ill.: CTI, n.d.), 189–95.

160 Ibid., 198.

161 Richard J. Mouw, *Politics and the Biblical Drama* (Grand Rapids: Eerdmans, 1976), 73.

162 Ibid., 111.

163 Barth, *CD,* IV.1.285.

164 Ibid., 295.

165 Ibid., 306.

166 Ibid., 148.

167 Ibid., 747.

168 Personal letter from Robert Gundry to Gordon Lewis, March 18, 1961. Used by permission.

169 Karl Barth, *The Humanity of God* (Richmond: John Knox, 1960), 59.

170 Charles R. Solomon, *Handbook to Happiness* (Wheaton: Tyndale, 1971).

171 Charles R. Solomon, *Counseling With the Mind of Christ* (Old Tappan, N.J.: Revell, 1973), 29.

172 John R. W. Stott, *Men Made New* (Grand Rapids: Baker, 1966), 36.

173 D. M. Baillie, *God Was in Christ* (New York: Scribner, 1948), 198.

174 J. A. T. Robinson, *Honest to God* (Philadelphia: Westminster, 1963), 78–83.

175 Paul Van Buren, *The Secular Meaning of the Gospel* (New York: Macmillan, 1963), 151.

176 Ibid., 154.

177 J. Norman King, *The God of Forgiveness and Healing in the Theology of Karl Rahner* (Washington, D.C.: University Press of America, 1982), 90.

178 On the existential relevance of the cross see Alister E. McGrath, *The Mystery of the Cross* (Grand Rapids: Zondervan, 1988), 79–190.

179 Stott, *Cross of Christ,* 60.

180 McGrath, *Mystery of the Cross,* 151.

181 See Stott, *Cross of Christ,* 282–85.

182 Moltmann, *The Crucified God,* 71.

183 Morris, *Apostolic Preaching of the Cross,* 100.

184 Ibid., 105.

185 Stott, *Cross of Christ*, 291.

186 McGrath, *Mystery of the Cross*, 167.

187 Ibid., 168.

188 Allan Boesak, *Walking on Thorns* (Grand Rapids: Eerdmans, 1984), 44.

189 Ibid., 46–47.

190 Erickson, *Christian Theology*, 2:762–63.

191 G. C. Berkouwer, *The Work of Christ* (Grand Rapids: Eerdmans, 1965), 63.

192 Denney, *Death of Christ*, 163.

193 See the contributions of several authorities to "Building Faith: How a Child Learns to Love God," a supplement to *Christianity Today* (June 13, 1986), 3-I–16-I.

194 Denney, *Death of Christ*, 157.

195 Gordon R. Lewis, *Confronting the Cults* (Phillipsburg, N.J.: Presbyterian and Reformed, 1966), 3.

196 Bernard Ramm, *The Pattern of Authority* (Grand Rapids: Eerdmans, 1957), 35–36.

197 McGrath, *Mystery of the Cross*, 180.

198 Ibid., 177.

199 Ibid., 175.

Chapter 8

1 Hans Küng, *On Being a Christian* (Garden City, N.Y.: Doubleday, 1976), 381.

2 Thomas Woolston, *A Sixth Discourse on the Miracles of Our Saviour* (London: 1729), 1; cf. Woolston's *First Discourse on the Miracles of Our Saviour* (London: 1728), 57: the Gospel account of the resurrection "is such a complication of absurdities, incoherences, and contradictions."

3 For the position of Celsus, see Origen, *Against Celsus*, II:56; cf. Justin Martyr, *Dialogue With Trypho*, 108.

4 Friedrich Schleiermacher, *The Christian Faith* (Philadelphia: Fortress, reprint 1976), 418.

5 J. Ernst Renan, *Vie de Jesus* (Paris: Michel L'evy, 1870), 434; cf.: "Mary alone loved enough to dispense with nature, and to have revived the phantom of the perfect Master. . . . The glory, then, of the Resurrection belongs to Mary Magdalene." Renan, *Les Apotres* (Paris: Michel L'evy, 1866), 12–13.

6 Kirsopp Lake, *The Historical Evidence for the Resurrection of Jesus Christ* (London: Williams & Norgate, 1907), 253.

7 Adolf Von Harnack, *What is Christianity?* (New York: Williams & Norgate, 1912), 164.

8 Ibid., 165.

9 Peter N. Hamilton, "Some Proposals for a Modern Christology," in *Process Philosophy and Christian Thought*, ed. Delwin Brown, Ralph E. James, and Gene Reeves (Indianapolis and New York: Bobbs-Merrill, 1971), 379–80.

10 Robert B. Mellert, *What Is Process Theology?* (New York: Paulist, 1975), 85.

11 Ibid., 86.

12 David R. Griffin, *A Process Christology* (Philadelphia: Westminster, 1973), 12, writes: "Christian faith (as I understand it) is possible apart from belief in Jesus' resurrection in particular and life beyond bodily death in general."

13 *Søren Kierkegaard's Journals and Papers*, 6 vols. (Bloomington, Indiana: Indiana University Press, 1967–78), 2:252–53.

14 Karl Barth, *Epistle to the Romans* (London: Oxford University Press, 1933), 222.

15 Karl Barth, *CD*, IV.1.333; cf. III.2.441–55; IV.1.336.

16 Barth, *CD*, IV.4.1, 309; cf. ibid., 316: "In virtue of the justification which has come to them in his resurrection, they are no longer what they were but they are already what they are to be. They are no longer the enemies of God but his friends, his children."

17 Barth, *CD*, IV.1.335; cf. III.2.452.

18 Barth, *CD*, IV.1.336.

19 Barth, *CD*, III.2.452.

20 Karl Barth, *Credo* (New York: Scribner, 1962), 113; cf. *CD*, III.2.453.

21 Emil Brunner, *The Mediator* (Philadelphia: Westminster, 1947), 563.

22 Ibid., 583.

23 Ibid., 159.

24 Emil Brunner, *The Christian Doctrine of Creation and Redemption: Dogmatics, Vol. II* (London: Lutterworth, 1952), 372.

25 Ibid., 374.

26 Dietrich Bonhoeffer, *Christ the Center* (New York: Harper & Row, 1978), 112; cf. *True Patriotism* (London: Collins, 1973), 48: "It is impossible to demonstrate the resurrection by historical method."

27 Rudolf Bultmann, "New Testament and Mythology," in *Kerygma and Myth*, ed. H. W. Bartsch (New York and Evanston: Harper & Row, 1961), 39; cf. *Theology of the New Testament*, 2 vols. (London: SCM, 1965), 1:295.

28 Bultmann, "New Testament and Mythology," 42. Since Bultmann believes that the

resuscitation of a dead body from the grave is myth, he undoubtedly believes that the body of Jesus decomposed in the tomb. Ibid., 39.

[29] Ibid., 41; cf. idem, "The Primitive Christian Kerygma and the Historical Jesus, in *The Historical Jesus and the Kerygmatic Christ,* ed. Carl E. Braaten and Ray A. Harrisville (New York and Nashville: Abingdon, 1964), 42: "It is often said . . . that according to my interpretation of the kerygma Jesus has risen in the kerygma. I accept this proposition."

[30] Bultmann, *Theology of the New Testament,* 1:45.

[31] Günther Bornkamm, *Jesus of Nazareth* (New York and Evanston: Harper & Row, 1960), 180.

[32] Willi Marxen, *The Resurrection of Jesus of Nazareth* (Philadelphia: Fortress, 1970), 128.

[33] Paul M. van Buren, *The Secular Meaning of the Gospel* (New York: Macmillan, 1963), 128.

[34] Ibid., 132, 143.

[35] Ibid., 133.

[36] Herbert Braun, *Jesus of Nazareth: The Man and His Time* (Philadelphia: Fortress, 1979), 125.

[37] Schubert Ogden, *Christ Without Myth* (New York: Harper & Brothers, 1961), 143; cf. ibid., 136: "If the fulfillment of our lives as persons is dependent on our individual decisions concerning self-understanding, and so is something for which we ourselves are each responsible, then 'events' like Jesus' . . . physical resurrection, his bodily ascension, and his visible coming again in the clouds of heaven are of no relevance whatever to such fulfillment."

[38] Ibid., 136.

[39] Ibid., 136.

[40] Ibid., 145.

[41] Schubert M. Ogden, *The Point of Christology* (San Francisco: Harper & Row, 1982).

[42] Wolfhart Pannenberg, "Did Jesus Really Rise From the Dead?" *Dialogue* 4 (Spring 1965): 135.

[43] Jürgen Moltmann, *Theology of Hope* (London: SCM, 1967), 165.

[44] Ibid., 180; cf. ibid., 181: The resurrection "is to be called historic because, by pointing the way for future events, it *makes* history in which we can and must live."

[45] Ibid., 163.

[46] Ibid., 197.

[47] Ibid., 180.

[48] Ignatius, *To the Smyrneans,* 3; cf. ibid., 11: The resurrection "was both of the flesh and of the spirit."

[49] Ignatius, *To the Magnesians,* 11.

[50] *Epistle of Barnabas,* XV.9.

[51] Polycarp, *To the Philippians,* II.1.

[52] Justin Martyr, *On the Resurrection of the Flesh,* 9.

[53] Irenaeus, *Against Heresies,* V.31.2; cf. III.19.3; III.23.1.

[54] Tertullian, *On the Flesh of Christ,* 1.

[55] Tertullian, *On the Resurrection of the Flesh,* 2.

[56] Origen, *Dialogue With Heraclides,* 132–40.

[57] Origen, *Against Celsus,* II.62.

[58] Augustine, *City of God,* XXII.5.

[59] Augustine, *Letter 205;* cf. *City of God,* XXII.9; *Faith, Hope and Charity,* 23.

[60] Martin Luther, *LW,* 28:94; cf. ibid.: "Every Christian must believe and confess that Christ has risen from the dead."

[61] Hugh T. Kerr, ed., *A Compend of Luther's Theology* (Philadelphia: Westminster, 1966), 55; cf. Luther, *LW,* 24:346; 25:284.

[62] Luther, *LW,* 37:207; cf. ibid., 63, 69.

[63] Formula of Concord, "Epitome," Art. VIII, Affirmative 11; cf. Article VIII, Negative 11, 13.

[64] J. A. Quenstedt, *Didactico-Polemical Theology,* 2 vols. (Leipzig, 1715), 2:265; cf. *Formula of Concord,* "Epitome," Affirmative, 11: "Therefore now not only as God, but also as man, he . . . is present to all creatures." Cf. also "Epitome," Negative, 11, 13.

[65] John Calvin, *Institutes of the Christian Religion,* III.25.3.

[66] Ibid.

[67] John Calvin, "Calvin: Theological Treatises," *LCC,* 22:101; cf. ibid., 312: "Although withdrawn in respect of bodily presence, he yet fills all things by the virtue of his Spirit."

[68] Calvin, *Institutes,* II.16.15; cf. *LCC,* 22:312.

[69] George E. Ladd, *I Believe in the Resurrection of Jesus* (Grand Rapids: Eerdmans, 1975), 25.

[70] Ibid., 27.

[71] Ibid., 144.

[72] Ibid., 42.

[73] W. J. Sparrow-Simpson, *The Resurrection and the Christian Faith* (Grand Rapids: Zondervan, reprint 1968).

[74] M. C. Tenney, *The Reality of the Resurrection* (New York: Harper & Row, 1963).

[75] Daniel P. Fuller, *Easter Faith and History* (Grand Rapids: Eerdmans, 1965).

[76] Derek Kidner, *Psalms 1–72. TOTC* (London: Inter-Varsity, 1973), 20.

[77] J. Barton Payne, *The Theology of the Older Testament* (Grand Rapids: Zondervan, 1962), 253.

[78] Peter C. Craigie, *Psalms 1–50. WBC* (Waco: Word, 1983), 215.

[79] E. S. P. Heavenor, "Job," *NBCRev*, 431.

[80] Ibid., 432.

[81] J. Ridderbos, *Isaiah* (Grand Rapids: Zondervan, 1984), 484; cf. Leon Morris, *The First Epistle of Paul to the Corinthians. TNTC* (London: Tyndale, 1958), 206: "Isaiah 53:10–12 may fairly be held to prophesy Christ's resurrection."

[82] Cf. Payne, *Theology of the Older Testament,* 276.

[83] F. W. Grosheide, *The First Epistle to the Corinthians. NICNT* (Grand Rapids: Eerdmans, 1983), 350; M. C. Tenney, *The Reality of the Resurrection* (New York: Harper & Row, 1963), 44.

[84] William L. Lane, *The Gospel of Mark. NLCNT* (London: Marshall, Morgan & Scott, 1974), 527–28.

[85] J. A. T. Robinson, "Resurrection in the NT," *The Interpreter's Dictionary of the Bible,* 5 vols. (Nashville: Abingdon, 1962, 1976), 4:46.

[86] G. T. D. Angel, *"Tekmērion," NIDNTT,* 3:571.

[87] I. Howard Marshall, *The Acts of the Apostles. TNTC* (Grand Rapids: Eerdmans, 1980), 149.

[88] William Neil, *The Acts of the Apostles. NCBC* (Grand Rapids: Eerdmans, 1981), 128.

[89] Marshall, *Acts,* 76.

[90] Jerome Murphy-O'Connor, "Tradition and Redaction in 1 Cor. 15:3–7," *Catholic Biblical Quarterly* 43.4 (Oct. 1981): 582–89.

[91] Donald Guthrie, *The Pastoral Epistles. TNTC* (London: Tyndale, 1957), 143.

[92] E. Tiedtke and H. G. Link, "Empty," *NIDNTT,* 1:546.

[93] C. Leslie Mitton, *Ephesians. NCBC* (Grand Rapids: Eerdmans, 1981), 89.

[94] Ralph P. Martin, "Ephesians," *NBCRev,* 1116.

[95] C. E. B. Cranfield, "The Epistle to the Romans." *ICC,* 2 vols. (Edinburgh: T. & T. Clark, 1975–79), 1:423.

[96] Fritz Rienecker and Cleon L. Rogers, Jr., *LKGNT* (Grand Rapids: Zondervan, 1982), 689.

[97] C. Brown, "Head," *NIDNTT,* 2:162.

[98] O Hofius, "Miracle," *NIDNTT,* 2:632.

[99] S. Aalen, "Glory, Honor," *NIDNTT,* 2:48: "The glorification of Jesus is not accomplished merely by his entry into heaven; it becomes a reality by his sufferings, death, resurrection, and finally by the witness of the Spirit."

[100] Leon Morris, "1 John," *NBCRev,* 1262; cf. Rienecker and Rogers, *LKGNT,* 786.

[101] Robert H. Mounce, *A Living Hope: A Commentary on 1 and 2 Peter* (Grand Rapids: Eerdmans, 1982), 58.

[102] So Thomas Hewitt, *The Epistle to the Hebrews, TNTC* (London: Tyndale, 1960), 125: "Christ is able to save completely in time and for eternity." The RSV, Moffatt ("for all time") and NASB ("forever") prefer the temporal meaning, whereas the ASV, Berkeley ("to the uttermost"), NEB ("absolutely"), and NIV ("completely") prefer the qualitative sense.

[103] Thomas F. Torrance, *Space, Time and Resurrection* (Grand Rapids: Eerdmans, 1976), 46–47.

[104] Frederick Godet, *Commentary on Paul's First Epistle to the Corinthians* (Edinburgh: T. & T. Clark, 1893), 404.

[105] "Flesh and blood" stands for "perishable, corrupt, weak, sinful human beings." See note on 1 Corinthians 15:50 in *The NIV Study Bible* explaining "man" in Matthew 16:17.

[106] See J. A. Shep, "Resurrection of Jesus," *ZPEB,* 5:78.

[107] Bernard Ramm, *An Evangelical Christology* (Nashville: Thomas Nelson, 1985), 95.

[108] Wolfhart Pannenberg, *Jesus—God and Man* (Philadelphia: Westminster, 1968), 66.

[109] See Ladd, *I Believe in the Resurrection of Jesus,* 147–48.

[110] Walter Künneth, *The Theology of the Resurrection* (St.Louis: Concordia, 1965), 40.

[111] Wilbur M. Smith, "Heaven," *ZPEB* 3:60–61.

[112] Bruce M. Metzger, "The Meaning of Christ's Ascension" *Christianity Today* (May 27, 1966), 4.

[113] Terry L. Miethe, ed., *Did Jesus Rise from the Dead? The Resurrection Debate* (San Francisco: Harper & Row, 1987), Introduction.

[114] See Editorial, *The Christian Century* (May 24, 1967), 675.

[115] Wolfhart Pannenberg, "Response to the Debate," in *Did Jesus Rise from the Dead? ed. Miethe,* 134.

[116] For further critical discussion of myth see Künneth, *Theology of the Resurrection,* 47–62.

[117] Alan Richardson, "New Testament Theology," in *A Dictionary of Christian Theology,* ed. Alan Richardson (London: SCM, 1969), 229.

[118] Ibid.

[119] Ibid.

[120] Richardson, "Resurrection of Christ," in *Dictionary of Christian Theology,* 290.

[121] Ramm, *An Evangelical Christology,* 97.

[122] Ibid.

[123] C. S. Lewis, *Miracles* (New York: Macmillan, 1948), 114.

[124] Ibid., 180.

[125] P. Althaus, *Fact and Faith in the Kerygma Today* (Philadelphia: Muhlenberg, 1959), 69.

[126] Pannenberg, *Jesus—God and Man,* 99.

[127] John Wenham, *Easter Enigma* (Grand Rapids: Zondervan, Academie, 1984), 11.

[128] Ibid.

[129] Ibid., 123.

[130] Ibid., 124.

[131] Ibid.

[132] Murray J. Harris, *Raised Immortal* (Grand Rapids: Eerdmans, 1983), 69–71.

[133] See C. F. D. Moule, *The Phenomenon of the New Testament* (Naperville, Ill.: Allenson, 1967), 1–20.

[134] Ibid., 81.

[135] Antony Flew, "Negative Statement," in *Did Jesus Rise from the Dead? ed. Miethe,* 6.

[136] Helmut Thielicke, *The Easter Message Today* (London and New York: Thomas Nelson, 1964), 82.

[137] Moule, *Phenomenon of the New Testament,* 81.

[138] Ladd, *I Believe in the Resurrection,* 93.

[139] Ibid., 27.

[140] For a comparison of the methods of reasoning see Gordon R. Lewis, "Schaeffer's Apologetic Method," *Reflections on Francis Schaeffer* (Grand Rapids: Zondervan, 1986), 69–104; and *Testing Christianity's Truth Claims* (Chicago: Moody, 1976).

[141] Kunneth, *Theology of the Resurrection,* 253.

[142] Ibid., 253–54.

[143] John Hick, *God Has Many Names* (London: Macmillan, 1980), 1–5; and *God and the Universe of Faiths* (New York: St. Martin's, 1973).

[144] Paul F. Knitter, *No Other Name?* (Maryknoll, New York: Orbis, 1985), 199–200.

[145] Ideas adapted from Ernst Troeltsch, *The Absoluteness of Christianity and the History of Religions,* trans. David Reid (Richmond: John Knox, 1971), 89–112.

[146] D. Elton Trueblood, *The Validity of the Christian Mission* (New York: Harper & Row, 1972), 56.

[147] Stephen Neill, *The Supremacy of Jesus* (Downers Grove: InterVarsity, 1984), 51.

[148] Kunneth, *Theology of the Resurrection,* 136.

[149] See Mark I. Bubeck, *Overcoming the Adversary* (Chicago: Moody, 1984), 82–91.

[150] See Leonard Hodgson, *Jesus—Word and Presence* (Philadelphia: Fortress, 1971), 267.

[151] Bubek, *Overcoming the Adversary,* 98.

GENERAL INDEX

Aalen, S., 525n.99
Aaron, 81, 197, 395
'*ābar*, 200
Abednego, 85, 263
Abel, 39, 108, 143, 170, 196, 209, 383
Abelard, Peter, 186, 373–74
'*abî-'ad*, 263
Abimilech, 81
Abortion, 125, 136, 176–77
Abraham: covenant with, 100, 399; compared with Jesus, 268, 282, 328, 339, 353, 489; in genealogies, 30, 321, 512n.70; as historical, 39, 200; and Isaac, 80, 274, 383; and Jesus' heritage, 270, 280–81, 288, 321, 325; and Melchizedek, 141, 171, 204, 235, 395; mentioned, 46, 277, 290, 348, 457; as patriarch of God's people, 270, 280, 302; and providence, 80, 81, 82, 101; and Sarah, 81, 142, 197
Abraham's bosom, 147
Abram. *See* Abraham
Absalom, 146
Absolutes, 286, 294–95
Abstraction, 152
Acts of the Apostles, Book of, 33–34, 87, 138, 324–25, 456–58
Acton, Lord, 231
Adam: commission to, 28, 38, 152; creation of, 28, 29–30, 36, 42, 44, 134, 170, 498n.29; and creation of souls, 171, 221, 232; date of creation of, 22, 23, 30, 46; effects of sin of, 186, 193, 262; and evolution, 19, 42–43; and the Fall, 34–35, 82, 96, 108, 194–96, 206–9; federal or representative headship of, 187–88, 193–94, 207–8, 235; freedom of, 96, 215, 346; historicity of, 20, 21, 39, 43, 188–90, 200, 201; in Jesus' genealogies, 321,

512n.70; as literal ancestor of all humanity, 34, 38, 43; natural headship of, 171, 186–88, 191–92, 204, 235 ; and original sin, 185–88, 190–94, 201-2, 207-8, 210, 221–23, 234, 418; parallels to Jesus, 43, 201–2, 274, 325, 404, 418; personal history of, 46, 127, 143, 290; status of before the Fall, 205–6, 274, 337; and unity of the human race, 176, 221, 234, 469; and universal death, 201–2, 327, 469, 494
Adam, second. *See* Jesus Christ
'*dāmāh*, 29, 134
Addictions, 60–62, 404, 423–25
adēmoneō, 322
adikia, 205
adikōn, 395
'*dōnay*, 332
Adoptionist view of the Incarnation, 255, 256, 312–13
Adultery, 98, 198, 201
Advent of Christ, first, 93
Adversity, 118–19
Aeropagus, 242
Africanus, Julius, 22
agapē, 58, 61, 98, 326, 341, 399
Age of Aquarias, 109
Agrippa, 458, 479
agnoēma, 205
agnoia, 205
agorazō, 396
Ahaz, 263–64, 512n.66
aiōn, 93, 298
AIDS, 115, 177
Akashic records, 355
Alcohol, 60–62
Alcoholics Anonymous, 61, 427
Alcoholism, 115
Aldwinkle, Russell, 255

SCRIPTURE INDEX

555

Proverbs

INTEGRATIVE
THEOLOGY

INTEGRATIVE THEOLOGY

To
Edward John Carnell
a major contributor
to the resurgence of evangelicalism
in the last half of the twentieth century
and to the method of research
in this theology

CONTENTS

CONTENTS

Preface

In a cartoon picturing workers laying the foundation for Italy's famous Leaning Tower of Pisa one workman said to the others: "No one will ever notice if on this one side we do not build it according to code." But so many have taken note of the mistake that the leaning tower is considered one of the seven wonders of the modern world! Some Christians preparing for leadership imagine that no one will ever notice if they take shortcuts in laying a theological foundation for their lifetime of ministry. But the most gifted Christians can profit from the historical, biblical, systematic, apologetic, and practical considerations of each major doctrine of the faith by which they will live, minister, and die.

The goal of dialogue with alternative views, according to Socrates and Plato, is neither mere opinion nor even true opinion. It is *well-founded* true opinion. Our goal has been to help readers through interchange with alternative views to arrive at well-founded, true conclusions concerning Holy Spirit-given life. On the basis of the big picture we have sought to stand for truth against error where the primary biblical evidence supports it but also to avoid unnecessary polarities where possible.

In *soteriology* the approach integrates forensic justification, experiential regeneration, and relational reconciliation, whereas contemporary theologies often opt for one of these categories to the exclusion of others. Faith is not viewed as either belief or trust, but both. Through belief of the Gospel (information in human language asserting that Jesus is the Messiah who died and rose) one's personal commitment is directed away from idols to trust in the living person of the Christ who hears, justifies and sanctifies. The holistic treatment of sanctification incorporates emphases from several different Christian traditions.

Beyond personal transformation the world's need for social transformation is addressed in a distinctive system of *spiritual-institutional theology*. As a *spiritual theology* of God's people collectively, we include veracious elements from covenant theology, promise theology, kingdom theology, and dispensationalism. Concerned about people in permanent relationships as well as individually, an *institutional theology* develops out of the relation of the church to Israel. It focuses on the distinctive social

9

structure of the present age, the church and its relation to the previous institutions of the family and the church and the coming institution of the Christ's personal rule on earth. Readers are encouraged to rise above divisive labels and think through these specific proposals.

Regarding *last things*, our research supports the return of the Lord to the earth to rule in a premillennial sense (both spiritually and institutionally). On the time of the rapture of the church we represent both pre- and post-tribulational views while exemplifying the fact that the issue need not be divisive.

Wasted energy on schisms continues to undermine the contribution of Christianity at a time of exceptional global opportunity and need. A tragic tendency to divisiveness cannot permanently be ignored or sidestepped. It is the prayer of the authors that these volumes will help Christians relate with respect to those from different traditions, find greater levels of agreement in the multiplex theology here set forth, and expend more energy in an effective ministry to a world in need of Spirit-given life.

For the roots of the epistemological method and criteria employed throughout the series we are indebted to Edward John Carnell. His short but highly influential career in apologetics and ethics did not allow him to produce an extensive work in theology. This attempt to integrate conceptual and existential considerations using a method like his, is gratefully dedicated to his memory. Our thanks go also to Denver Seminary for sabbaticals and to our colleagues, who have made constructive suggestions, especially Craig Blomberg and a former adjunct, Charles Moore. Student Darius Panahpour has helped in matters of style as did Jeanette Freitag and Rebecca Barnes in word processing. For the remaining limitations in their respective sections the authors bear responsibility.

The Discussion Topics at the end of each chapter and the Review Questions and Ministry Projects on pages 501–2 are intended to clarify issues either individually or in small groups. Please refer to them as you finish studying each chapter.

Abbreviations

BAGD *A Greek-English Lexicon of the New Testament*, ed. William F. Arndt and F. Wilbur Gingrich; rev. by F. Wilbur Gingrich and Frederick W. Danker. (Chicago: University of Chicago Press, 1979)

BDT *Beacon Dictionary of Theology*, ed. Richard S. Taylor. (Kansas City, Mo.: Beacon Hill, 1984)

CD *Church Dogmatics*, ed. G. W. Bromiley and T. F. Torrance. (Edinburgh: T. & T. Clark, 1936–77)

CGTC *The Cambridge Greek Testament Commentary*, ed. C. F. D. Moule.

CR *Corpus Reformatum*. (Berlin, et al.: C. A. Schwetschke, 101 vols., 1834–1956)

EBC *The Expositor's Bible Commentary*, ed. Frank E. Gaebelein. 12 vols. (Grand Rapids: Zondervan, 1976–93)

EDT *Evangelical Dictionary of Theology*, ed. Walter A. Elwell. (Grand Rapids: Baker, 1984)

EP *Encyclopedia of Philosophy*, ed. Paul Williams. 8 vols. (New York: Macmillan, 1967)

HNTC *Harper's New Testament Commentary*, ed. Henry Chadwick.

ICC *The International Critical Commentary*, ed. J. A. Emerton and C. E. B. Cranfield.

ISBERev *The International Standard Bible Encyclopedia*, revised, ed. Geoffrey W. Bromiley, 4 vols. (Grand Rapids: Eerdmans, 1979–88)

JETS *Journal of the Evangelical Theological Society*.

LCC *Library of Christian Classics*, ed. J. A. Baillie, John T. McNeill, and Henry P. Van Dusen. 26 vols. (Philadelphia: Westminster, 1953–69)

LKGNT *A Linguistic Key to the Greek New Testament*, ed. Fritz Rienecker and Cleon L. Rogers, Jr. (Grand Rapids: Zondervan, 1982)

LW *Luther's Works*, ed. J. Pelikan and H. T. Lehman. 55 vols. (St. Louis: Concordia; Philadelphia: Fortress, 1955–76)

NBCRev *The New Bible Commentary*, revised, ed. D. Guthrie and J. A. Motyer. (London: Inter-Varsity, 1970)

NBD   *New Bible Dictionary*, ed. J. D. Douglas. Revised by N. Hillyer. (Wheaton, Ill.: Tyndale House, 1982)

NCBC   *The New Century Bible Commentary*, ed. R. E. Clements and M. Black.

NCE   *New Catholic Encyclopedia*, ed. F. J. Corley. 15 vols. (San Francisco: McGraw-Hill, 1967)

NDT   *New Dictionary of Theology*, ed. Sinclair B. Ferguson, David F. Wright, and J. I. Packer. (Downers Grove: InterVarsity, 1988)

NICNT   *The New International Commentary on the New Testament*, ed. Ned B. Stonehouse and F. F. Bruce.

NICOT   *The New International Commentary on the Old Testament*, ed. R. K. Harrison.

NIDNTT *The New International Dictionary of New Testament Theology*, ed. Colin Brown. 3 vols. (Grand Rapids: Zondervan, 1975–78)

NIGTC   *New International Greek Testament Commentary*, ed. I. Howard Marshall and W. Ward Gasque.

NLBC   *The New Layman's Bible Commentary*, ed. G. C. D. Howley, F. F. Bruce, and H. L. Ellison. (Grand Rapids: Zondervan, 1979)

NLCNT   *New London Commentary on the New Testament*, ed. F. F. Bruce.

SCG   Thomas Aquinas, *Summa Contra Gentiles*. 4 vols. in 5. (Notre Dame: Notre Dame University Press, 1975)

ST   Thomas Aquinas, *Summa Theologica*. 22 vols. (London: Bums, Oates and Washbourne, 1927–35)

TDNT   *Theological Dictionary of the New Testament*, ed. G. Kittel and G. Friederich. 9 vols. (Grand Rapids: Eerdmans, 1965)

TDNTAbr *Theological Dictionary of the New Testament*, abridged by G. W. Bromiley. (Grand Rapids: Eerdmans, 1965)

TDOT   *Theological Dictionary of the Old Testament*, ed. G. Johannes Botterweck and H. Ringgren. 6 vols. (Grand Rapids: Eerdmans, 1977)

TI   Karl Rahner, *Theological Investigations*. 21 vols. (New York: Seabury, 1947–88)

TNTC   *Tyndale New Testament Commentaries*, ed. R. V. G. Tasker.

TOTC   *Tyndale Old Testament Commentaries*, ed. D. J. Wiseman.

TWOT   *Theological Wordbook of the Old Testament*, ed. R. Laird Harris, Gleason L. Archer, Jr., and Bruce K. Waltke. 2 vols. (Chicago: Moody, 1980)

WA   *D. Martin Luthers Werke: Kritische Gesamptausgabe*. (Weimar, 1883–)

WBC   *Word Biblical Commentary*, ed. David A. Hubbard and Glenn W. Barker.

ZPEB   *Zondervan Pictorial Encyclopedia of the Bible*, ed. Merrill C. Tenney. 5 vols. (Grand Rapids: Zondervan, 1975–76)

PART ONE

PERSONAL TRANSFORMATION

CHAPTER 1

THE HOLY SPIRIT'S CALLING OF THE CHOSEN

The Holy Spirit's Calling of the Chosen

**THE PROBLEM:
DOES THE FATHER APPLY
THE BENEFITS OF CHRIST'S
ATONING PROVISIONS
ON THE CROSS
TO THE ELECT BY MEANS OF
THE SPIRIT'S EFFECTUAL
CALLING IN TIME?**

In volume 1, chapter 8, we investigated God's eternal decree or purpose and its relation to human decision making and responsibility. In the present chapter we consider the doctrines of (1) *grace*—the disposition of God underlying his entire saving activity, (2) *election*—that planned salvation for the heirs of grace, and (3) *calling*—the work of the Holy Spirit that brings some sinners who hear the Gospel to Christ. God's purpose in creating humans was that the Creator and creatures might enjoy rich fellowship together. But through Adamic sin (vol. 2, chap. 4) the entire race became alienated from God, crippled with guilt, and exposed to divine wrath. The God whose character is holiness, justice, and anger against sin is also a God of love, mercy, and grace (vol. 1, chap. 6). Thus the Father sent his Son into the world to suffer and die that sinners might be saved (vol. 2,

chap. 7). The church (chap. 5) represents the body of those who celebrate God's grace and forgiveness and await the return of the Savior (chap. 7) to consummate their redemption (chap. 8). God's purpose to save thus lies at the very heart of the Christian faith. Although Barth's own doctrine appears flawed, the following statement by him is close to the truth: "The doctrine of election is the sum of the Gospel."[1]

In the present chapter we inquire broadly into the nature of the salvation God offers. Should salvation be interpreted primarily in psychological (internal), social (horizontal), or spiritual (vertical) categories? Is salvation chiefly a matter of personal integration, social wholeness, or a new spiritual relationship with God? Moreover, we ask how salvation is mediated to sinners. Is it imparted morally by personal merit and good works? mystically by the immediate engagement of the soul with absolute Mystery? sacramentally by the rites of baptism or penance? or spiritually by personal faith in Christ whose person and deeds are described in the Word of God?

Furthermore, we wish to determine what sinners are capable of contributing to their salvation. Can unbelievers come to God savingly on the basis of

17

natural, human ability? Does salvation involve a synergistic cooperation between God and sinners? Or is it true that sinners contribute nothing to the attainment of salvation? Furthermore, can a legitimate distinction be made between common grace given to all people and special grace granted only to some? Does God bestow on all the unregenerate so-called "prevenient grace," which allegedly reverses the effects of sin and enables every person to accept the Gospel?

An additional issue is whether God has willed the salvation of all people or only a privileged few. Is election conditional, based on a person's faith response to the Gospel; or is it unconditional, grounded solely in God's sovereign purpose? Is election to salvation individual, corporate, or perhaps both? In this regard we need to define the relationship between God's foreknowledge and his elective activity.

We must ask, furthermore, What is the role of Jesus Christ in God's elective program? What does election "in Christ" mean? At a practical level is the doctrine of unconditional election unjust and unworthy of God? Does election engender complacent living and undermine the quest for a holy life? In addition—analagous to the distinction between common and special grace—may we differentiate between a general, external call to all persons and a special, internal call to some? If so, is God's special call resistible, irresistible, or perhaps effectual? The present chapter directs attention to these several issues of crucial importance to the Christian doctrine of salvation.

ALTERNATIVE INTERPRETATIONS IN THE CHURCH

The theological issues of grace, election, and calling have been diversely interpreted and even passionately argued throughout Christian history. The following represent the principal views on these subjects articulated within professing Christendom.

Pelagian and Liberal Interpretations

The British monk Pelagius (d. 419) believed that the Augustinian views of moral inability and sovereign grace would undermine Christian morality. Thus he argued that humanity exists in the same morally neutral condition as Adam did in Eden. Free will (defined as the power to choose between good and evil) is a reality, since people must be able to perform all that God commands. Because the Ten Commandments are addressed to all people, everyone must be able to keep them perfectly. Said Pelagius, "Man is able to be without sin, and he is able to keep the commandments of God."[2] Pelagius defined grace as the natural faculties of free will, reason, and conscience with which all persons are endowed at their creation. Whereas grace represents the God-given capacity (*posse*) for doing good, the actual willing (*velle*) and the being or result (*esse*) of it is the responsibility of persons themselves. In addition, God supplied external inducements to virtuous living, such as the Law of Moses and the example of Christ. Pelagius believed that even the heathen by willing and doing the good could please God and achieve salvation.

Opposing Augustine's doctrine, Pelagius defined predestination as the divine prevision of a person's free deeds and the ordination of rewards and punishments commensurate with one's actions. Predestination is totally conditional: by sheer volition persons freely determine their own fate. Pelagius likewise repudiated the notion of a special calling to salvation. God need not exert any internal power on a person to do good, since the power of right living naturally resides within. If God were to exert such a power, it would destroy human freedom and responsibility. Pelagius's position on the attainment of salvation could be expressed by the phrase *"I came by myself."* Reflecting the outlook of a Christianized paganism, Pelagianism postulated that persons save themselves by their own effort. "This was the first purely autosoteric scheme published in the church."[3] Pelagianism was condemned at the councils of Carthage (418) and Ephesus (431), but the spirit of self-salvation has lingered on throughout the ages.

Modern liberal theology denies the doctrine of original sin and so mutes the need for a supernatural salvation. At the individual level, salvation denotes moral renewal facilitated by the principles and ideals of Jesus, the revealer of God. At the collective level, salvation represents the gradual transformation of humanity into a truly ethical society known as the the kingdom of God. Individually or collectively, salvation by following Jesus' example is self-salvation. Furthermore, theological liberals commonly allege that since the doctrines of sovereign grace and individual election violate human freedom and violate the character of God they are repugnant and immoral. At most, election signifies selection to service. The doctrine of calling, liberals allege, means that the responsibility for beginning and continuing the Christian life lies with persons themselves.

Emphasizing the collective aspect of sin, Walter Rauschenbusch (d. 1918) focused on social salvation or the "christianizing" of the human community. He said that a theology that promotes individual salvation fosters personal egotism and a false godliness. Thus Rauschenbusch thoroughly dismissed the doctrines of sovereign grace, unconditional election, and special calling. The doctrine of election, stimulated by medieval despotism, is characterized by "autocratic power and monarchical self-assertion"[4] and finds no place in the modern world where socialist sensibilities prevail. Added Rauschenbusch, "The old 'scheme of salvation' seems mechanical and remote."[5]

W. A. Brown (d. 1943) averred that salvation is not deliverance from guilt and punishment but the process of transformation whereby the lower animal impulses give way to the ideals of Christ. Such transformation occurs both at the individual level ("the substitution of the outgoing for the self-centered life"[6]) and the social level (the organization of the human community according to the spirit of Christ). Brown claimed that Calvinism falsely narrowed the meaning of grace from God's free love for all to the arbitrary choice of some persons to be saved. Brown turned from what he judged the tyrannical "Nietschian" doctrine of election (i.e., "might makes right") to a social and historical view: "By election is meant God's choice of individuals or of nations for special service connected with his redemptive work."[7]

In the 1960s so-called secular theology promoted a worldview that left little room for God. Theologians claimed that God saves not by the traditional means of conversion and regeneration but through responsible living in the midst of the secular reality. Christians must view secularization positively as the God-ordained means of salvation. According to Paul Van Buren in *The Secular Meaning of the Gospel*,[8] linguistic analysis shows that the word "God" has lost meaning in a world of sense verification. Since belief in God is problematic, Jesus, not God, becomes the focus of religion. Van Buren claimed that in his life and death Jesus was a man totally free for others. As one reflects on this reality a "discernment situation" occurs in which people see themselves and the world in a new light. "Salvation" results as individuals exercise their Jesus-inspired freedom and maturity by living responsibly for others.

Thomas J. J. Altizer claimed that on the cross God actually negated himself and ceased to exist in his original form. Thus the remote, transcendent God became immanent in the world as Jesus—universal humanity. Since Jesus neither bore our sins on the cross nor rose from the grave, faith in his death is of no effect. A person attains salvation both by denying that a sovereign God exists and by abandoning every external authority and transcendent norm. Altizer wrote, "The radical Christian knows that God has truly died in Jesus and that his death has liberated humanity from the oppressive presence of the primordial Being."[9] One realizes salvation, on the other hand, by redirecting all the powers once bestowed on the Beyond to the concerns of our temporal existence. "The 'good news' of the death of God . . . frees us for a total participation in the actuality of the immediate moment."[10]

For liberation theology the soteriological starting point is the human situation rather than biblical revelation, the assumption being that all persons are in Christ. Liberation theologians define sin *corporately* rather than individually as institutional exploitation that breeds poverty, ignorance, and general misery. Negatively, salvation involves the elimination of oppressive social, political, and economic structures by violence if necessary. Positively, salvation means the creation of a just and fraternal social order in which people can live freely. In the liberationist scheme people save themselves through revolutionary action. Gutièrrez maintains, "By working, transforming the world, breaking out of servitude, building a just society, and assuming his destiny in history, man forges himself."[11]

Believing in the instrinsic goodness of every human being, process theologians define salvation in terms of one's cooperation with the divine lure to novelty and aesthetic creativity. Whiteheadians allege that God is constantly luring or influencing persons toward maximum fulfillment consistent with the good of the entire creation. Argues Pittenger, "God's manner of working . . . is not by coercive control but by persuasive lure and appeal."[12] Those who respond to the novel initial aims presented by God at every moment experience "salvation."[13] That the onus for salvation rests with people themselves is seen in Griffin's statement that God "loves all his creatures for what they are, yet urges them on to become what they can be."[14] Process thinkers roundly dismiss the biblical teaching on sovereign grace and election; they believe that a God who arbitrarily decides whether or not a person will be saved would be an absolute despot. They allege that persuasion, not coercion, lies at the heart of the creative process.

Semi-Pelagian and Roman Catholic Interpretations

Mediating between Pelagianism and Augustinianism, fifth-century theologians such as John Cassian, Vincent of Lérins, and Faustus of Riez held that sinners are morally weak, not spiritually dead. Rejecting Augustine's doctrine of sovereign grace, the semi-Pelagians insisted that grace does not compel the will to obey God. Since there are seeds of goodness in all people, special grace is not needed for sinners to turn to God. The semi-Pelagians claimed that sinners make the first move toward salvation by choosing to repent and believe. With this sincere first desire established, God then supplies the grace of justification and citizenship among the redeemed. Judging Augustine's doctrine of unconditional election novel and fatalistic, the semi-Pelagians claimed that God desires the salvation of all people. Their position was that God ordained to life all those he foresaw would believe and persevere to the end. With the initiative for salvation posited in man rather than God, the semi-Pelagians defined calling as the spiritual enlightenment and moral persuasion offered through the Law. Since free agents may resist all inducements to salvation, the latter involves a synergism of human and divine working. The semi-Pelagian scheme of salvation thus may be described by the statement *"I started to come, and God helped me."*

Traditional Roman Catholicism claimed that although the gift of superadded righteousness (see vol. 2, chaps. 3–4) was lost at the Fall, unbelievers retain the capacity for willing and doing the good. In the state of nature, sinners both aspire to grace (*desiderium naturale*) and have the capacity for receiving grace (*potentia obedientalis*). God responds to this spiritual longing at baptism by bestowing sanctifying grace, which remits original sin and unites the soul to Christ's body, the Roman church. Where a person cannot receive water baptism (through ignorance or lack of opportunity), the "baptism of desire" suffices. God provides additional grace through the sacraments of penance and the Eucharist and through church teachings, but such grace is resistible. As persons cooperate with the preceding means of grace they are enabled to perform good works (rosary prayers, fastings, alms-giving, etc.) that effect moral improvement and thus contribute to their salvation. Catholicism believes that "man really cooperates in his personal salvation from sin."[15] Mary plays a significant role in the Roman scheme of salvation. As a result of her sufferings and exemplary life, Mary merits grace for the faithful. Moreover, Mary persuasively intercedes with her Son before the heavenly throne. To a lesser degree deceased saints abet human salvation by their accumulated treasury of merit and their face-to-face intercession before God in heaven.

Traditional Catholicism believes that God wills the salvation of all human beings (1 Tim. 2:4). Beyond this Catholics articulate differing views of predestination. The following position appears to predominate: Predestination involves two aspects. (1) God predestines to heaven all who die in a state of grace, and (2) he consigns to hell all who die in a state of mortal sin. In the process of salvation human free will remains intact, so that the "elect" have full power to fall from grace and the "nonelect" have power to rise to salvation on their deathbed. Predestination thus signifies the divine prevision of a person's free choices and meritorious works. "Heaven is not given to the elect by a purely arbitrary act of God's will, but it is also the reward of the personal merits of the justified."[16]

The Council of Trent (1545–63) anathematized those who denied that Christ's saving merits are applied to adults and infants via the sacrament of baptism (Sess. V.3). Moreover, Trent affirmed that persons are justified by cooperating with God's offer of sacramental grace. Those "who by sins were alienated from God may be disposed through his quickening and assisting grace to convert themselves to their own justification by freely assenting to and cooperating with that said grace" (Sess. VI.5). The grace-inspired works persons perform of their own free will are meritorious before God (Sess. VI.16; cf. canons 7, 9). Since grace can be lost through mortal sin, no assurance of predestination to salvation is possible in this life (Sess. VI.12; cf. canon 15). Finally, Christians render to God satisfaction for sins by punishments voluntarily undertaken or as prescribed by a priest (Sess. XIV.9).

The Second Vatican Council (1962–65) reiterated the traditional view that the church's sacraments mediate salvation. People, however, contribute to their salvation by doing adequate penance ("penitential expiation") and by performing works of charity.[17] The Virgin Mary facilitates the salvation of humankind by her piety and prayers: "She cooperated by her obedience, faith, hope and burning charity in the work of the Savior in restoring supernatural life to souls."[18] But by broadening its concept of revelation, Vatican II explicitly claimed universal salvation. Merging general and special revelation, the Council stated that God's "providence, evident goodness, and saving designs extend to all men."[19] People discover God experientially in their lives and thus are imbued with a deep religious sense (i.e., "implicit faith"). All who follow their consciences and strive to do right are united to Christ's mystical body. Vatican II added that salvation extends to all non-Catholic Christians, Buddhists, Muslims, atheists, etc., who live by the light of God within. "Those who through no fault of their own, do not know the Gospel of Christ or his Church, but who nevertheless seek God with a sincere heart, and moved by grace, try in their actions to do his will as they know it through the dictates of their conscience—those too may achieve eternal salvation."[20] The God of creation will be satisfied only when all are saved through the uniting of humanity in the body of Christ. By this line of argument the Council rejected the Augustinian doctrine of sovereign election and effectual calling of some for salvation as inconsistent with divine love.

Karl Rahner (d. 1984), the German Jesuit theologian who modified Thomism by modern philosophy, insists that since grace permeates nature, humans are orientated to the saving life of God. The dynamic impulse that drives persons toward the immediate presence of God Rahner calls the "supernatural existential." Thus, "this 'supernatural existential,' considered as God's very act of self-bestowal which he offers to men, is universally grafted into the roots of human existence."[21] Semi-Pelagianism surfaces when Rahner claims that all who cooperate with the transcendent Mystery by accepting their new freedom are Christians. Non-Chistian religionists or atheists who obey their consciences are "anonymous Christians." In reality, the entire world proves to be an "anonymous Christendom." Rahner insists that non-Christian faiths and ideologies play an important role in God's plan for the redemption of the world. "The history of the world, then, means the history of salvation. God's offer of himself, in which God communicates himself absolutely to the whole of mankind, is by definition the history of salvation."[22]

The Arminian Tradition

Arminians begin with the philosophical premise that in regard to human destiny God's sovereign choice is incompatible with human freedom. Christ died for all, and God wills that all persons be saved (1 Tim. 2:4; 2 Peter 3:9). Furthermore, personal obligation is limited to ability to perform. Since the command to obey Christ is universal, Arminians claim that all persons are able to respond to the Gospel. They hold that God restores to sinners universally the ability to believe through prevenient grace, which mitigates depravity. The tradition insists that general or prevenient grace differs from special grace in degree not in kind, and that both forms of grace are soteriological. Arminians define election as that general purpose of God to save those he foresaw would of their own accord respond to prevenient grace, repent, and believe. They speak of God's electing the *class* of people who exhibit a certain kind of character. "The basis for this divine choice is in the moral character which they have been enabled, through God's transforming grace, to embody and experience."[23] In the Arminian scheme, salvation is synergistic: both divine grace and the human will are causes of salvation. In the words of one authority, "There is a cooperation, or synergism, between divine grace and the human will. The Spirit of God does not work irresistibly, but through the concurrence of the free will of individuals."[24] The Arminian view of salvation could be represented as follows: *"God started the process and I cooperated."*

James Arminius (d. 1609), a professor at Leiden, formulated his views in reaction to the supralapsarianism of Beza and Gomarus. Arminius charged that the Calvinistic doctrine whereby God gives saving grace to some while withholding it from others is unjust. How could God be just, he reasoned, if he condemns persons who are powerless to change their lives because they are not blessed by special grace? Moreover, Arminius alleged that the Calvinist's denial of free will dehumanizes persons. Sinners do retain a measure of free will, which he defined as the power of contrary choice. Arminius held that God established four decrees concerning salvation. The *first* focuses on the election of Jesus Christ. God unconditionally appointed Jesus Christ to be the Savior of mankind. The *second* concerns the election of the people of God. God decreed unconditionally that the class of people who repent and believe would be saved. "He decreed to receive into favor those who repent and believe, and, in Christ . . . to effect the salvation of such penitents and believers as persevered to the end."[25] The *third* relates to the provision of prevenient or "exciting" grace, which mitigates the effects of the Fall and enables sinners to respond to the gospel call. Whereas it is God who gives the ability to believe, humans bring forth the faith

that saves. The *fourth* decree concerns the election of individuals on the basis of foreknowledge. God elects to life those he knows will believe and persevere and punishes eternally those who refuse to do so. "This decree has its formulation in the foreknowledge of God, by which he knew from all eternity those individuals who would, through his preventing grace, *believe,* and through his subsequent grace would *persevere."*[26] According to Arminius, then, the determining factor as to whether individuals respond to the call of the Gospel and are saved is their own free decision.

John Wesley (d. 1791) was influenced by contemporary Anglicanism that had moved from Calvinism to a more Arminian stance. Wesley vigorously opposed Reformed views on predestination as follows: (1) He judged that unconditional election necessarily implies reprobation, a doctrine he held to be unbiblical. "Election cannot stand without reprobation. Whom God passes by, those he reprobates. It is one and the same thing."[27] (2) Sovereign election renders preaching vain, for the elect would be saved with or without preaching and the nonelect could not possibly be saved. And (3) the Calvinist doctrine of unconditional election undermines holiness, for it removes the chief motive to righteous living, which is the hope of rewards and the fear of punishment. Wesley insisted that Christ died for all and his grace is available to all, otherwise there would be no Gospel to proclaim. Wesley viewed grace as a seamless garment; no difference exists between general and special grace. Divine grace provides for basic human needs, restrains evil, maintains civil justice, removes the guilt and penalty of original sin, implants the first wish to please God, convicts of sin, and grants all people the power to turn to God in faith. To each person who responds to prevenient grace God grants justifying grace followed by sanctifying grace. Wesley saw two elections in Scripture. The first is the unconditional election of individuals (e.g., the apostles) and nations (e.g., Israel) to service in the world. The second is the conditional election to eternal destiny. In eternity past God elected those persons he foresaw would believe and persevere in holy living. Wesley's view of salvation as a series of moments in which God offers people resistible grace resembles the classical Catholic rather than the Reformation view.[28]

Forster and Marston propose a passive corporate election in their book *God's Strategy in Human History*.[29] They argue that Scripture does not teach sovereign election to salvation; people's eternal destiny depends on *their* moral response to the universal offer of the Gospel. Jesus Christ is the chosen One, and Christians are said to be elect because they are in Christ.[30] Through the free responses of repentance and faith, people become part of Christ's body, the church, and thus may be described as *chosen*. Forster and Marston write:

> The prime point is that the election of the church is a corporate rather than an individual thing. It is not that individuals are in the church because they are elect, it is rather that they are elect because they are in the church, which is the body of the elect One. . . . A Christian is not chosen to become part of Christ's body, but in becoming part of that body [by free will, exercising faith] he partakes of Christ's election.[31]

In other words, predestination points to the future and refers to the heavenly heritage of the people of God (Rom. 8:28–30). "Predestination does not concern who should be converted; it concerns our future destiny. It is not that we are predestined *to be* Christians, it is rather that *as* Christians we receive a glorious destiny."[32] In summary, God did not choose any individual to be saved; rather, he has chosen the church in Christ to be the heir of heavenly glory. Robert Shank, in his book *Elect in the Son,* advances a similar view of the conditional corporate election of the people of God (the *ekklēsia*), together with a single universal and resistible call to salvation.[33]

William Klein, in *The New Chosen People,* avers that the Reformed doctrine by which God from eternity chose some individuals to be saved and passed by others is "to most of us, a cause of bewilderment or frustration."[34] "Such a claim . . . seems so arrogant, so exclusive."[35] God does not select some sinners to be saved; he wills to save all who believe (1 Tim. 2:4; 2 Peter 3:9). Election to salvation is a *corporate* reality; God has chosen to save the *body* of believers, i.e., the people of God who have come to believe. "God has chosen the church as a body rather than the specific individuals who populate that body."[36] Since Jesus Christ is God's Elect One, and those who exercise saving faith are "in Christ," Klein concludes that the latter group constitute God's chosen people, or the "elect." He claims that this view of election agrees with the biblical concept of corporate solidarity, whereby God regards Israel and the church not as so many individuals but as collective entities. Whereas under the old economy God chose corporate Israel to be his people, under the new economy he chose the people who believe in Christ, i.e., the church, to be his elect. "God's foremost choice encompasses a people or nation."[37] As for the place of *individuals,* God chooses them to *service* not to salvation or eternal destiny. Klein claims that Paul's testimony in Galatians 1:15–16 deals with his call to apostleship, not his election to salvation. Likewise the opening of Lydia's heart that facilitated her response to the Gospel (Acts 16:14) was caused, not by the effectual work of the Spirit, but by her own belief in the Gospel.[38]

Klein continues by saying that *foreknowledge* pertains to God's cognizance of his people prior to their corporate existence. This divine knowledge is neither selective nor elective. Klein defines *election* as God's determination of the *benefits* that accrue to the people who believe, i.e., adoption into God's family, conformity to Christ's image, and future glory. "Paul's concern in predestination is not *how* people become Christians nor *who* become Christians, but to describe *what* God has foreordained on behalf of those who *are* (or *will be*) Christians."[39] Finally, *calling* describes the act whereby God *names* or *labels* believers "saints" or "holy ones." It "specifies the divine act when God names or designates people from among Jews and Gentiles to become his own people."[40]

Neoorthodox Views

Given the destruction of the *imago,* Karl Barth (d. 1968) asserted that sinners can do nothing to facilitate their salvation. Through grace alone God makes people what they cannot become by their own strength. Rejecting any general grace through creation and preservation, Barth identified *Jesus Christ* himself as the grace of God.[41] God manifested grace chiefly through his eternal electing activity. Barth rejected the classical Calvinist view of election for several reasons. (1) It postulates a hidden, antecedent will of God independent of Jesus Christ. (2) It regards election as a static, fixed decision rather than a dynamic history between God and man. And (3) it suggests that God is for some persons and against others, whereas the Gospel is Good News for all.

Barth developed his view of election under three headings, the first of which is "the election of Jesus Christ." The cornerstone of his doctrine is that Jesus Christ "is both the electing God and elected man in One."[42] As the electing God, Christ is the divine freedom in action. "Before him and without him and beside him God does not, then, elect or will anything."[43] Jesus Christ is also elected man. Negatively, this means that the Son of God was elected to rejection. On the cross God said "No" to himself as Christ bore the sentence of man's rejection. Positively, Christ's being elected man means that God has chosen humankind for fellowship with himself. At Calvary God said "Yes" to his Son and to humanity in him. "His election carries in it and with it the election of the rest."[44] Christ's election thus includes the election of the human race in him.

The second heading of Barth's development is "the election of the community." The people of God, Barth argued, exist in the twofold form of Israel and the church. On one hand, Christ is the crucified Messiah of Israel, which signifies the judgment Christ has taken upon himself. On the other hand, Christ is the risen Lord of the church, which denotes the new man accepted and received by God. The task of the believing community is to witness to the divine election of the race and to summon the world to faith in Christ.

The third heading is "the election of the individual." Individual election takes place in Jesus Christ and with the community. Barth reiterated that the individual is already elected in Jesus Christ, the elected man who bore his rejection. Thus objectively each person is eternally loved, justified, and sanctified in God's Son. Even if a person does not personally receive the Gospel, his or her unbelief is overcome by Christ's election. "This choice of the godless man is void; he belongs eternally to Jesus Christ and therefore is not rejected, but elected by God in Jesus Christ."[45] Although Barth provided a theoretical framework for universal salvation, he claimed that to conclude that every person will be saved amounts to limiting God's freedom. Since universal salvation is an affirmation of faith and hope, Barth confidently anticipated the salvation of all. In the end, grace will triumph over every form of sinful opposition.

W. Pannenberg rejects the classical formulation of an individualistic elective decree from eternity. Alternatively he proposes "a concretely historical concept of election,"[46] which affirms that through history God fulfills his purpose to bring humanity to eternal communion with himself. God has been accomplishing this salvific purpose for the race through the election and history of Israel and the Christian church. Not an exclusive community, the church functions as a sign and symbol of the destiny of humankind in the future kingdom of God. Writes Pannenberg, "The community of the church symbolizes the eschatological Kingdom of a new mankind in communion with God."[47] Comprising people from all nations, the church witnesses to the fact that God willed through Christ the reconciliation of the race. "The liberation from the power of sin and death to the enjoyment of freedom in communion with God is not meant for the Christians as the happy few. It is meant for the whole world."[48] Pannenberg believes that God's purpose could be none other than the salvation of the world, given persons' creation as image-bearers and their investiture with eternal dignity.

Some Fathers and Medieval Authorities, and Many Reformers and Evangelicals

As noted in volume 1, chapter 8, most pre-Augustinian fathers reacted against Stoic and Gnostic fatalism and determinism by stressing human freedom. Beginning with Justin (d. 165) most early church authorities stated that God's saving will is conditioned on foreseen human responses. Yet as Thomas F. Torrance argued, many early fathers succumbed to Hellenistic naturalism. "The converts of the first few generations had great difficulty in apprehending the distinctive aspects of the gospel, as for example, the doctrine of grace. It was so astonishingly new to the natural man."[49] Hence Torrance rightly referred to "the urge toward self-justification in the second century fathers."[50] Influenced by Greek humanism, many early fathers judged that God gives saving grace to those who worthily strive after righteousness. For at least two reasons, the doctrines of sovereign grace and election prior to Augustine were significantly muted.

Belief in the divine initiative in salvation was not entirely absent. Tertullian (d. 220) noted that, contrary to those born in a pagan home, "the children of believers were in some sense destined for holiness and salvation."[51] Ambrose (d. 397) wrote that "God calls those whom he deigns to call; he makes him pious whom he wills to make pious, for if he had willed he could have changed the impious into pious."[52] Likewise Athanasius on occasion spoke the language of unconditional election. Commenting on Ephesians 1:3–5 and 2 Timothy 1:8–10, he observed that whereas the Fall was "foreseen," the salvation of some people was predestined or "prepared beforehand."[53]

Augustine (d. 430) conceded that his early position on election (his exposition of Romans) was synergistic: God predestined those he foreknew would respond to his call. Shortly after becoming bishop in 395, Augustine changed his views markedly and described the synergism he once held as the "pest of the Pelagian error." The bishop insisted that although the unregenerate possess psychological freedom, they lack the moral freedom (i.e., the ability or power) to do the good. Thus sinners cannot come to Christ unless God graciously illumines their darkened minds and quickens their dead wills. "The human will does not attain grace through freedom, but rather freedom through grace."[54] Put otherwise, God's commands will be fulfilled only as God himself gives the ability to perform them. Thus Augustine's prayer to God was, "Give what you command, and command what you will."[55]

Augustine believed that by virtue of inherited sin the unsaved justly deserve judgment. Thus if God through unmerited mercy chose to save some sinners, none can charge him with acting unrighteously. Wherefore, according to the good pleasure of his will and to the praise of his grace, God in eternity past chose out of the "mass of perdition" a certain number of people to be saved. "Grace came into the world that those who were predestined before the world may be chosen out of the world."[56] Why God elected one person and not another is a mystery hidden in his unscrutible will. Moreover, Augustine observed that God wisely furnishes the means and arranges the circumstances that will lead the elect to convert to Christ. Foreknowledge, according to Augustine, connotes God's gracious foreordination of some persons to salvation. Human inability rules out the equation of foreknowledge with prescience. "Had God chosen us on the ground that he foreknew that we should be good, then would he also have foreknown that we would not be the first to make choice of him."[57] Moreover, if God chose individuals because he foresaw that they would respond to Christ (a form of human merit), grace would cease to be grace. "For it is not by grace if merit preceded: but it is of grace; and therefore that grace did not find, but effected the merit."[58]

Augustine continued by arguing that those whom God elected in eternity past he effectually calls in time. Although a general call through the preached Word goes out to many, God issues a special, effectual call to the elect. "There is a certain sure calling of those who are called according to God's purpose, whom he has foreknown and predestinated before to be conformed to the image of his Son."[59] The special call consists of a secret working of the Spirit that makes the sinful heart willing and able to repent and believe in Christ.

John Calvin (d. 1564) stressed that every good that sinners experience derives from God's grace. He distinguished between God's common grace to all and his special grace bestowed on the elect. Common grace refers to God's universal goodness in supplying the necessities of life, restraining evil, and maintaining the moral order of the universe. Special grace is salvific; it frees the wills and enlightens the minds of the elect enabling them to respond to the Gospel. Calvin insisted that without saving grace sinners cannot be freed from their spiritual corruption. "Free will is not sufficient to enable man to do good works, unless he be helped by grace, indeed by special grace, which only the elect receive through regeneration."[60]

With an eye to the works-righteousness of Rome, Calvin identified sovereign election as the cornerstone of the Christian faith. Calvin noted that the Gospel has not been preached equally to all persons, and where it has been proclaimed it has not been equally received. Such phenomena corroborate God's secret, elective purpose. "It is plain that it comes to pass by God's bidding that salvation is freely offered to some while others are barred from access to it.[61] Calvin viewed election and reprobation as two aspects of the single will of God. "We call predestination God's eternal decree, by which he compacted with himself what he willed to become of each man. For all are not created in equal condition; rather, eternal life is foreordained for some, eternal damnation for others.''[62] He spoke first of a general election of a people (Israel) for himself, which choice could be revoked by national disobedience. More fundamentally God eternally chose particular individuals among Israel and the Gentiles for an irrevocable spiritual heritage in Christ. ''The general election of the people of Israel does not prevent God from choosing in his most secret counsel those whom he pleases.''[63] Calvin deliniated the nature of God's sovereign election in Christ thus: (1) Election is according to God's sovereign will and good pleasure. It is God's sovereign choice of a man or woman, not a man or woman's choice of God. (2) Election is founded on freely given mercy. God is not obliged to save any sinner, but in sovereign grace he does save some. (3) Election is not based on foreseen faith or holiness. Although God knows all things in advance, biblical foreknowledge is a divine determination to save specific persons. ''The foreknowledge of God . . . is not a bare prescience . . . but the adoption by which he had always distinguished his children from the reprobate.''[64] (4) Election is absolutely certain as to its outcome. Since the omnipotent God accomplishes his purposes, all the elect will be saved. And (5) God's purpose is that the elect should bring forth good works. Humbled by the divine gift of grace, believers strive to live lives honoring to the Father.

Calvin continued by asserting that the special call, or the Spirit's inner persuasion of the truth of the Gospel, confirms the individual's eternal election. A general call goes out into all the world through the preaching of the Word. But by a special, internal illumination the Holy Spirit causes the Word to take root in the hearts of the elect.

''The [special] call is dependent upon election and accordingly is solely a work of grace.''[65]

The old Waldensian Creed, prepared by persecuted twelfth-century French believers who sought to recover the apostolic faith, upheld sovereign election: ''God saves from corruption and damnation those whom he has chosen from the foundations of the world, not for any disposition, faith, or holiness that he foresaw in them, but of his mere mercy in Christ Jesus his Son, passing by all the rest according to the irreprehensible reason of his own free-will and justice.''

The Belgic Confession (1561), prepared for the Reformed churches in the low countries, reads as follows: God is ''merciful and just: *merciful*, since he delivers and preserves from this perdition all whom he in his eternal and unchangeable counsel of mere goodness has elected in Christ Jesus our Lord, without any respect to their works; *just*, in leaving others in the fall and perdition wherein they have involved themselves'' (art. XVI). The Thirty-Nine Articles of the Church of England (1571) opposed a synergistic view of election. ''Predestination to Life is the eternal purpose of God, whereby (before the foundations of the world were laid) he hath constantly decreed by his counsel secret to us, to deliver from curse and damnation those whom he hath chosen in Christ out of mankind, and to bring them by Christ to everlasting salvation, as vessels made to honour. Wherefore, they which be endued with so excellent benefit of God, be called according to God's purpose by his Spirit working in due season'' (art. XVII).

The Westminster Confession of Faith (1647) states concerning election: ''Those of mankind that are predestined unto life, God, before the foundation of the world was laid, according to his eternal and immutable purpose, and the secret counsel and good pleasure of his will, hath chosen in Christ, unto everlasting glory, out of his mere free grace and love, without any foresight of faith or good works, or perseverance in either of them, or any other thing in the creature, as conditions, or causes moving him thereunto; and all to the praise of his glorious grace" (ch. III.5). Concerning the calling of sinners, the Confession refers to the Word and Spirit "enlightening their minds, spiritually and savingly, to understand the things of God; taking away their heart of stone, and giving unto them an heart of flesh; renewing their wills, and by his almighty power determining them to that which is good, and effectually drawing them to Jesus Christ; yet so as they come most freely, being made willing by his grace" (ch. X.1).

The Baptist preacher Charles Haddon Spurgeon (d. 1892) explained divine election as follows: (1) Election arises from the sovereign will of God. Salvation occurs not because humans will it, but because God in the eternal past planned it. "The whole scheme of salvation, from the first to the last, hinges and turns on the absolute will of God."[66] (2) Election is entirely of grace. Like condemned criminals, sinners deserve only wrath and punishment. But in his great love God granted life to many hell-deserving souls. And (3) election is personal. If it be unjust of God to elect a person to life, it would be far more unjust to elect a nation, for a nation is but an aggregate of individuals. "God chose that Jew, and that Jew, and that Jew. . . . Scripture continually speaks of God's people one by one and speaks of them as having been the special objects of election."[67]

Spurgeon believed that Scripture teaches two kinds of calling, general and special. The general call goes out to all the world by virtue of Christ's universal mediatorship. Although this general call is sincere, persons dead in sins and corrupted with lusts are unwilling and incapable of responding to the offer. But to the elect sovereign grace cries out through the Word applied by the Spirit, "Come forth!" and so the chosen ones receive new life. "There is a fountain filled with blood, but there may be none who will ever wash in it unless divine purpose and power shall constrain them to come."[68] At the pastoral level Spurgeon observed that people who sincerely desire to be saved can be sure they are called. And if called, they can be sure that they are elected. Every seeking soul who comes to Christ shall be a finder. Behind each seeking soul is the all-powerful God who infallibly enables that person to trust Christ for salvation.

A. H. Strong (d. 1921) defined election as "that eternal act of God, by which in his sovereign pleasure, and on account of no foreseen merit in them, he chooses certain out of the number of sinful men to be the recipients of the special grace of his Spirit, and so to be made voluntary partakers of Christ's salvation."[69] Election is not based on any activity of sinners, including faith, since human depravity ensures that without special grace the unregenerate refuse to respond to the Gospel. The divine foreknowledge connotes not merely "to know in advance," but more specifically "to regard with favor" or "to make an object of care." The biblical words "know" and "foreknow" bear the same meaning. The biblical teaching on election asserts that the initiative in salvation is entirely with God.

Strong went on to say that God's general or external call is that sincere offer of life extended to all people through divine providence, the Word, and the Spirit. This general call, however, is rendered ineffectual by sinners' settled opposition to the things of God. Whereupon God graciously issues a special or effectual call to the elect that both restores spiritual ability and infallibly leads them to trust Christ and accept his salvation. In sum, the Reformed position on calling could be expressed by the phrase, *"God brought me to Christ."*

Other helpful studies on election and calling from a Reformed perspective include works by Harry Buis,[70] R. C. Sproul,[71] and C. Samuel Storms.[72]

BIBLICAL TEACHING

In this section we examine the topics of God's grace, election, and calling to salvation as they appear in each major portion of Holy Scripture.

Pentateuch

The literature reflects God's purpose to create a special people for himself through the structure of institutional Israel. God called Abram out of Ur of the Chaldees and made a covenant with him (e.g., Gen. 12:1–3; 13:14–17), promising Abram an abundant "seed" (Gen. 22:7) and a mission of blessing the nations (Gen. 12:3; Gal. 3:8). The chosen people formally became a nation at the Exodus from Egyptian bondage (Exod. 20:2; Deut. 4:20, 37–38). Deuteronomy 7:6 describes this corporate election of the nation: "You are a people holy to the LORD your God. The LORD your God has chosen you out of all the peoples on the face of the earth to be his people, his treasured possession." God chose the Israelite people not because of any merit on their part, for they were a "stiff-necked people" (Exod. 32:9; Deut. 9:6), but solely on the basis of his own love (cf. Deut. 4:37; 10:15; 23:5). By virtue of this corporate election Israel gained the status of God's "holy people" (Deut. 7:6; 14:2, 21), "flock" (Ps. 78:52; Isa. 40:11), "servant" (Isa. 41:8; Mal. 1:6), "bride" (Isa. 49:18; Jer. 2:2), adopted offspring (Exod. 4:22; Deut. 32:19), and "trea-sured possession" (*segulāh,* Exod. 19:5; Deut. 14:2).

God's election of ethnic Israel for temporal blessings was conditional; its privileges could be forfeited by national disobedience. Thus after Aaron had made the golden calf, God threatened to destroy Israel and choose another nation, beginning with Moses (Exod. 32:9–10). Clearly by choosing Israel for present and future blessings God exercised a certain *selectivity;* promises and privileges were extended to Israel that were not offered to other peoples (Ps. 147:19–20; Amos 3:2).

Abram's election was not only corporate, it was also individual unto salvation. God's choice of Abram (Gen. 12:1) was made, not on the basis of any foreseen virtue, but solely according to his sovereign purpose. Descended from a family of idol-worshipers (Josh. 24:2, 14), Abram did not seek after God; rather God sought out Abram, called him, and made a covenant of grace with him. Only after that did the Chaldean respond with faith (Gen. 15:6). God's promise clearly involved *personal,* saving blessings for Abraham ("I will bless you," Gen. 12:2). The sevenfold "I will" (vv. 1–3, 7) indicates that God himself would guarantee the performance of the promises. Later (Gen. 18:19) God acknowledged that he had "chosen" Abraham for himself. The verb (*yāda',* to "know" or "regard with favor") signifies that God set his affection on Abram or sovereignly elected him to salvation.[73] Similarly God "knew" or elected Moses (Exod. 33:17).

As for Abraham's two sons, Isaac and Ishmael, God chose the former to be heir of the promise (Gen. 17:19–21; 21:12). The Lord's determination that the promise would be fulfilled through Isaac constitutes the latter's personal election to salvation and destiny, as Paul argued in Romans 9:6–9. God would take note of Ishmael and his seed

(Gen. 25:12–18), but the special blessing was given to Isaac and his seed. Mention of the descendants of the two sons indicates that the author regarded Ishmael and Isaac as *individual* heads of their respective families (Edom and Israel). Of the two unborn children of Isaac and Rebekah, God made a sovereign choice of Jacob over Esau to inherit the covenant promise (Gen. 25:23). God's choice was independent of the cultural rule of primogeniture and of Jacob's character or works, for Jacob schemed to get the birthright (vv. 27–34) and gained Isaac's blessing by deception (27:5–40). *In spite of* his scheming nature, Jacob was the object of God's elective purpose, as confirmed by Paul's argument in Romans 9:10–13.[74] "By sovereign election, God declared that the promised line would belong to Jacob, the younger son. Jacob thus owed his supremacy not to natural order or to human will but to the divine election."[75] God later told Moses that he sovereignly extends saving mercy to whom he wills: "I will have mercy on whom I will have mercy, and I will have compassion on whom I will have compassion" (Exod. 33:19; cf. Rom. 9:16, 18a).

The Historical Books

The historical books attest corporate election by stating that God chose ethnic Israel for earthly privileges and spiritual benefits. Solomon observed that God had fulfilled his promise to the patriarchs concerning a posterity, prompting him to say to God: "Your servant is here among the people you have chosen, a great people, too numerous to count or number" (1 Kings 3:8). David identified the offspring of the patriarchs as God's "chosen ones" (*be ḥîrîm*, 1 Chron. 16:13). Historically national Israel broke the covenant by forsaking the Lord and worshiping foreign gods. Thus not all of institutional Israel was the true Israel of God.

This portion of the Old Testament also attests individual election, the first aspect being individual election to service. God clearly chose certain persons for specific tasks or ministries. He selected Moses for leadership in Israel (Num. 16:5–7), his elder brother Aaron for priestly service (Ps. 105:26), Eli's father to perform priestly functions (1 Sam. 2:28), Saul to be king over Israel (1 Sam. 10:24), David the shepherd to be Israel's premier monarch (1 Sam. 16:7–12; 2 Sam. 6:21; 1 Kings 8:16), and Solomon to rule as king and build the temple (1 Chron. 28:4–6; 29:1).

But allusions of individual election to salvation are not lacking. During the renewal of the covenant at Shechem, Joshua reminded Israel of God's grace to their forefathers. Abraham was born to a polytheistic people and likely would have persisted in paganism had God not intervened. But the Lord visited Abraham, called him by grace, and made him the father of the nation (Josh. 24:2–4). Nehemiah 9:7–8 reiterates God's special grace to Abraham by citing the themes of election, deliverance, change of name, covenant, and gift of the land. Joshua added that God chose Isaac and Jacob to inherit the promise. "By stating that the Lord gave to Isaac *Jacob and Esau*, Joshua's prophetic summary of past events brings into clear focus the divine choice that was operative in the distinction made between these twins. . . . This was another reminder to the Israel of Joshua's day of the unmerited choice underlying their national existence."[76] In Elijah's day God preserved a *remnant* of seven thousand faithful in Israel who had not bowed the knee to Baal (1 Kings 19:18). Paul stated that by sovereign decision God reserved for himself (*katelipon emautō*) the chosen remnant (Rom. 11:4).

31

Poetry and Wisdom

The Psalms extol God's universal benevolence or common grace to all persons: "The LORD is good to all; he has compassion on all he has made" (Ps. 145:9). His power sustains all creatures in existence (104:27–30), and he indiscriminately blesses all people with rain, fructification of the soil, and abundant crops (65:9–13; 67:6). So David said of God: "You . . . satisfy the desires of every living thing" (145:16).

Psalm 147:19–20 describes God's choice of the nation Israel: "He has revealed his word to Jacob, his laws and decrees to Israel. He has done this for no other nation; they do not know his laws." The Lord uniquely favored Israel above all other nations with his gracious word and promises. It is clear, however, that by choosing ethnic Israel for present and future blessings God exercised a certain selectivity vis-à-vis other nations. Thus the question of God's "unfairness" must be faced precisely at this level. In the wilderness Israel, however, turned away and refused to heed God's word. Thus the Lord swore by an oath: "They shall never enter my rest" (Ps. 95:11). Again we must posit a distinction between God's choice of national Israel and his election of a spiritually faithful minority within the nation.[77]

The Psalms give some indication of God's choice of individuals for salvation. Consider their use of the verb *bāhar*. Psalm 65:3–5 describes the unregenerate as overwhelmed by transgressions but certain ones chosen and brought near by forgiving grace. David wrote, "Blessed are those you choose and bring near to live in your courts" (v. 4). The choosing clearly is soteriological (cf. "live"), and the Piel of *qārab* ("bring near") stresses God's gracious initiative in drawing sinful souls to himself. Psalm 78:70 and 105:26 seem to embrace God's choice both to

salvation and to service. The adjective *bāhîr* ("chosen") also occasionally denotes a person (Pss. 89:3; 106:23) or persons (105:6, 43; 106:5; Isa. 65:15, 22) chosen comprehensively to salvation and to a task.

The Prophetic Literature

This body of writings attests the premundane election of the Christ. Yahweh identified the Servant of the Lord or Messiah as "my chosen" (*beḥîrî*, Isa. 42:1)—one called of the Lord long before his birth (Isa. 49:1, 5). The Christ is elect and called in the sense that the Father ordained him to messianic vocation, chiefly to suffering and death as Mediator of the new spiritual creation. Smedes comments as follows concerning the election of Christ: "He was elect as the *concrete* individual doing the specific task that He was chosen to do."[78] Believers are brought into a redemptive relationship with God on the basis of Christ's election.

The prophets frequently cited the election of ethnic Israel effected in time by God's calling of Abraham (Isa. 51:2). The Lord ordained Israel for a relationship with himself not enjoyed by any other nation (41:8–9). By virtue of the national covenant, Israel became God's "chosen" people and his "servant" (43:10; 44:1–2; Ezek. 20:5). Hosea 11:1 expresses this special relationship between Yahweh and Israel thus: "When Israel was a child, I loved him, and out of Egypt I called my Son." The purpose of this election was that Israel might glorify and praise God (Isa. 43:7, 21). Isaiah 14:1 suggests that the original election of Israel came to an end with the Babylonian exile. Later God would make a new beginning with a new election.[79]

The prophets also attest the election of individuals. Yahweh chose Jeremiah before his birth both for salvation and for prophetic ministry: "Before I formed you in the womb I knew [yāda'] you, before you were born I set you apart" (Jer. 1:5). That yāda' here means "choose" is clear from Amos 3:2, where Yahweh said of Israel, "You only have I chosen [yāda'] of all the families of the earth." "The word to 'know' in this covenantal context had nothing to do with recognition or acknowledgment of one's deeds; it had to do with God's gift of choice—an unmerited choice as Deuteronomy 7:8 passim had made plain."[80] See also Hosea 13:5. Concerning Jeremiah 1:5, "the emphasis is on the divine initiative and sovereign choice."[81] We conclude that God's "knowledge" of a person is his choice, and vice versa. Election to salvation and election to service are complementary, not contradictory, issues; the former in no wise excludes the latter.

Individual election is implied in Malachi 1:2–3. Although Esau was Jacob's elder brother, Yahweh declared, "I have loved Jacob, but Esau I have hated." The Hebrew verb to "love" ('āhēb) here means to "prefer," while the verb to "hate" (śānē') signifies to "value less highly" (cf. Deut. 21:13, 16–17; cf. Matt. 6:24; Luke 14:26; John 12:25). "When Yahweh says, 'I have loved Jacob,' he means, 'I chose Jacob,' and when he says, 'I hated Esau,' he means, 'I did not choose Esau.' "[82] Thus God loved the younger son Jacob more intensely and the elder son Esau less so, which means that in his sovereign wisdom God elected Jacob. The initiative in salvation resides entirely with God: "Salvation comes from the LORD" (Jonah 2:9). Salvation eventuates as God pours out his Spirit upon sinners (Isa. 44:3; Ezek. 36:26–27; 39:29). The mystery of grace is seen in the fact that God savingly revealed himself to Israelites who did not seek him (Isa. 65:1).

Individual election finds further support in the Isaianic concept of "a remnant" in Israel. Isaiah 10:20–22 indicates that whereas the majority of Israel would perish in captivity, a "remnant" (śe'ār) would put their trust in the Lord. Yahweh designated this believing remnant, "my people" (v. 24; cf. Jer. 31:7). "Śe'ār . . . had a technical (perhaps cultic) meaning of the authentic and integral core of the people who were the genuinely elect, the genuine Israel. . . . They are 'the pious remnant,' the 'righteous remnant,' the 'faithful remnant.' "[83] The synonym śe'ērît ("remnant," "posterity") likewise affirms the existence of a believing minority within ethnic Israel (Isa. 37:32; Jer. 31:7; Micah 2:12). In Isaiah 65:8 Yahweh described national Israel as a bunch of grapes and the believing remnant as its sweet juice. The faithful within ethnic Israel Yahweh further represented as his "servants" (Isa. 65:9, 13–14), his "disciples" (8:16), and his "chosen ones" (65:15, 22). The remnant, sometimes viewed as "a tenth" of the people (6:13), are heirs of the new covenant (Jer. 32:37–40; 50:4–5). They are called of the Lord (Joel 2:32), they are gathered by the Lord (Micah 2:12), and they bear spiritual fruit (Isa. 37:31). In short, the remnant are forgiven and saved (Jer. 50:20). This phenomenon of the saved remnant implies an individual election to salvation within the corporate election of ethnic Israel to earthly and spiritual privileges.[84]

A study of election in the Old Testament leads to the conclusion that corporate election to earthly and spiritual privileges is the major theme and individual election to salvation a minor theme. God's purpose in the Old Testament was to differentiate the *nation Israel*—chosen, blessed, and set aside for mission—from her godless neighbor nations. An analogous phenomenon was the revelation of God's nature; in the Old Testament the unity and uniqueness of Yahweh was stressed and his triune nature muted. Thus the casual reader of the Old Testament might be inclined to hold a Unitarian view of God as well as a doctrine of conditional election. Not until the New Testament revelation would the Trinity of God and unconditional, personal election come into clearer light.[85]

In the name of God, the prophets gave a universal invitation or *general call* to all people to be saved (Isa. 45:22; 55:1, 6–7), but their summons to repentance often were not heeded. So the Lord said of Israel: "I spoke to you again and again, but you did not listen; I called you, but you did not answer" (Jer. 7:13; cf. Isa. 50:2; 65:12). The unregenerate in Israel did not respond because they were spiritually incapable of doing so on their own (Jer. 13:23; 17:9; 30:12). By failing to obey God's word, Israel rendered the old covenant null and void (31:32), wherefore Yahweh rejected them as a nation (Hosea 9:17). With the old covenant abrogated, God promised that he would inaugurate a new covenant with his people—an inward covenant that effects a changed mind and heart and an intimate, personal knowledge of God (Jer. 31:31, 33–34). When God brings his grace to bear on a heart by issuing his *effectual call,* sinners respond positively. Thus the remnant are not only the elect, they are the effectually called: "There will be deliverance . . . among the survivors whom the LORD calls" (Joel 2:32).

The Synoptic Gospels

Jesus acknowledged the reality of God's common grace or nonredemptive goodness to all people. He taught that the Father causes the sun to rise and the rain to fall on both the righteous and the unrighteous (Matt. 5:45). In addition, universal common grace enables sinners to perform a variety of salutary deeds, or acts of civil decency, such as loving others, doing good, and lending money to others (Luke 6:33–34).

Although God is good to all persons, the parable of the workers in the vineyard (Matt. 20:1–16) teaches that God is not obliged to deal with everyone in the same way. To the objection of those who labored all day but received the same wage as those who worked but one hour, Jesus implied that none get less than they deserve (justice) but some do get more than they deserve (grace). It is not unfair of God to give some more than their due. Elsewhere Jesus taught that in former times God favored certain persons with his grace while passing others by. Thus there were many needy widows in Israel at the time of Elijah, but the prophet was sent to minister only to the widow of Zarephath (Luke 4:25–26; cf. 1 Kings 17:8–24). In addition, there were many lepers in Israel in Elisha's time, but only one was healed of the disease, Naaman the Syrian (Luke 4:27; cf. 2 Kings 5:1–14).

The Gospels apply the concept of election to the Messiah, Jesus. Reciting Isaiah 42:1 (cf. 49:7), a heavenly voice from the enveloping cloud said concerning Jesus: "This is my Son, whom I have chosen [*eklelegmenos*]; listen to him" (Luke 9:35; cf. Matt. 12:18). Later the rowdy crowd hurled insinuations at Jesus impaled on the cross: "He saved others; let him save himself if he is the Christ of God, the Chosen One" (*ho eklektos,* Luke 23:35). Christ is "chosen" in the Old Testament sense of the Servant-Messiah ordained by the Father to suffer and atone for sins.

The concept of the corporate election of the people of God appears in the Gospels. Upholding the revocable nature of the national covenant, Jesus said to Israel's chief priests and elders: "I tell you that the kingdom of God will be taken away from you and given to a people who will produce its fruit" (Matt. 21:43). The church is the faithful "people" or true remnant of Israel who inherit the kingdom promises given to the patriarchs. This great truth is captured in the line from the famous hymn by Perronet, "All Hail the Power of Jesus' Name": "Ye chosen seed of Israel's race . . . ."

The Gospels also attest individual election to service. At the beginning of his ministry Jesus chose twelve apostles to preach and to drive out demons (Mark 3:13–15; Luke 6:13). Jesus also "appointed seventy-two others and sent them two by two" to preach the gospel of the kingdom (Luke 10:1). The Lord, however, referred to the "elect" by the plural *eklektoi* (Matt. 24:22, 24, 31; Mark 13:20, 22, 27; Luke 18:7; cf. other New Testament usage in Rom. 8:33; Col. 3:12; 2 Tim. 2:10; Titus 1:1; 1 Peter 1:1), which suggests that Jesus viewed the righteous in Israel as chosen individuals. The elect are not an empty class, for as individuals they cry out to God, obey Christ, are faithful to him, and manifest the fruit of the Spirit. Elsewhere the Gospels attest the divine choice of some persons to be saved (Matt. 1:21; 25:34). Jesus, moreover, acknowledged the Father's sovereign right to reveal or conceal the significance of the Son's words and works as he pleases. So he prayed in Matthew 11:25–26: "I praise you, Father, Lord of heaven and earth, because you have hidden these things from the wise and learned, and revealed them to little children. Yes, Father, for this was your good pleasure [*eudokia*]." "*Eudokia* expresses independent volition, sovereign choice, but always with an implication of benevolence."[86] Jesus then added: "No one knows the Father except the Son and those to whom the Son chooses [present subjunctive of *boulomai*, to "will"] to reveal him" (Matt. 11:27). The point is that God sovereignly extends his enlightening and saving influence to some persons while justly withholding it from others

(cf. Matt. 13:11). A universal invitation to receive Jesus (v. 28) is not inconsistent with God's purpose to reveal his Son to some.

The divine choice in salvation is also evident in Jesus' encounter with Zacchaeus (Luke 19:1–10). The latter's primary motive in wanting to see the friend of tax collectors was curiosity. Since it was undignified for a wealthy publican to be seen in a tree, Zacchaeus hid himself in its branches. Approaching the tree, Jesus called out to the despised publican: "I must stay [*dei*] at your house today" (v. 5). The verb *dei* signifies that God's plan of salvation for Zacchaeus was being worked out through Jesus' overture. "The selection of Zacchaeus is an act of sovereign grace as much as the physical healing in the previous episode."[87]

The parable of the wedding banquet (Matt. 22:1–14; cf. Luke 14:16–24) distinguishes between God's universal, general call and his particular, effectual call. The king's servants initially sent to the invited guests represent the prophets who bore God's offer of salvation to the Jews. Matthew emphasized the (universal) call in verse 3 with a twofold use of the verb *kaleō*: the king "sent his slaves to call those who had been invited" (NRSV, *kalesai tous keklēmenous*). Consumed with worldly interests and indifferent to their spiritual need, the invitees rejected the offer and were punished with death (v. 7). Hence the king sent his servants to invite the unfit and unworthy to the banquet, an act that signifies Jesus' and the apostles' preaching to outcast Jews and Gentiles (Luke). This latter summons achieved its purpose, in that a crowd joined the king for the wedding feast. Jesus concluded the parable with the words, "For many are called [*klētoi*], but few are chosen" (*eklēktoi*, v. 14, RSV). "The calling must refer to the gospel message to which they [the first group] made a merely outward response, not being chosen by God."[88] The "chosen" were those who responded to the second invitation. Jesus made it clear in Luke 14:24 that none of those who received only the general call (*ton keklēmenon*) "will get a taste of [his] banquet" (i.e., will be saved). In sum, God extends a general call to many via gospel preaching (Matt. 11:28–30; Luke 24:47) that may be sinfully rejected (Matt. 23:37). But the special call issued by the Spirit effectually accomplishes the Father's salvific purpose (Luke 14:21–23).

Primitive Christianity/Acts

Addressing educated Athenians at Lystra, Paul and Barnabas acknowledged the reality of universal, common grace. They noted that God blesses all people with rainfall, the cycle of the seasons, crops that sustain existence, and a sense of satisfaction with life (Acts 14:17). This grace is qualitatively different from the grace that produces faith resulting in salvation (Acts 16:14).

At Pisidian Antioch Paul attested God's corporate election of national Israel: "The God of the people of Israel chose our fathers; he made the people prosper during their stay in Egypt" (Acts 13:17). A saying of James at the Jerusalem Council confirmed the corporate election of the Gentile church: "God at first showed his concern by taking from the Gentiles [*ex ethnōn*] a people [*laos*] for himself" (Acts 15:14). Under the old covenant God chose one people from among many nations; under the new covenant he chose many individuals to form one new people for himself.

At the conclusion of Paul and Barnabas' ministry in Pisidian Antioch, Luke observed that "all who were appointed for eternal life believed" (Acts 13:48). The verb of special interest is the perfect passive participle of *tassō,* to "order," "appoint," "ordain." F. F.

Bruce suggested that the verb might be translated "enrolled" or "inscribed," i.e., in the Lamb's Book of Life (cf. Luke 10:20; Phil. 4:3; Rev. 13:8; 17:8).[89] The text clearly indicates that God's sovereign action, be it ordaining or enrolling, occurred prior to the people's believing; this confirms that Luke contemplated God's sovereign election of certain persons for salvation.[90] During his second missionary journey, Paul received a vision in which God encouraged him to continue preaching in Corinth in the face of strong opposition. Paul had to persevere in sharing the Gospel, God said, "because I have many people [*laos*] in this city" (Acts 18:10). God had chosen many persons in Corinth as his own, and Paul's preaching was the divinely ordained means to bring the elect to savation. Concerning the "people" at Corinth, Morris comments, "They had not yet done anything about being saved; many of them had not even heard the gospel. But they were God's. Clearly it is he who would bring them to salvation in due course."[91]

Acts records many examples of an external call to repentance that was resisted by stubborn hearts (Acts 7:51; 13:46). The conversion of Saul of Tarsus, however, resulted from a specific summons by the risen Christ that was powerfully effective. Saul, who regarded the Christian movement as blasphemous heresy, went to extraordinary lengths to terrorize the fledgling church (9:1–2; 22:4–5; 26:10–11) and "to do all that was possible to oppose the name of Jesus of Nazareth" (26:9). Near Damascus Christ appeared to Saul in the form of a glorious, heavenly light which, while blinding his physical eyes, opened his spiritual eyes to Jesus' true significance (9:1–9; 22:8–10). Driven by a darkened mind Saul had fought against Christ (vv. 4–5). But the Savior powerfully pursued Saul and overcame his raving, sinful heart through grace.[92]

Paul later testified that Christ's summons to salvation was completely effectual (26:19). As Ananias said to Paul: "The God of our fathers has chosen you to know his will and to see the Righteous One" (22:14). Paul's conversion testimony in Galatians 1:15–16 upholds God's sovereign purpose and initiative as the basis for his radically altered life. Acts 16:14 records a similar effectual call issued to Lydia: "The Lord opened her heart to respond to Paul's message." Luke used the same verb, *dianoigō* (to "open"), to describe Jesus' illumining the minds of the disciples to recognize him (Luke 24:31) and understand the Scriptures (Luke 24:45). The opening of Lydia's heart by the Spirit was the efficient cause of her conversion.

The Pauline Literature

Briefly let us set God's gracious salvific work in the context of the spiritual condition of sinners. In Romans 3:10–18 the apostle Paul detailed the spiritual bankruptcy of the unsaved: "There is no one who understands, no one who seeks God" (v. 11). He added, "All have turned away, . . . there is no one who does good, not even one" (v. 12), and "There is no fear of God before their eyes" (v. 18). Elsewhere Paul claimed that sinners are spiritually lifeless: "You were dead in your transgressions and sins" (Eph. 2:1; cf. 2:5; Col. 2:13). Even the liberal Bultmann affirmed, "The whole pre-Christian life is dead because sinful."[93] Romans 8:7 adds that "the sinful mind is hostile to God. It does not submit to God's law, nor can it do so." Moreover, sinners' minds are darkened, their spiritual hearts are hard as stone (Eph. 4:18; cf. 5:8), and their wills are enslaved to the power of sin (Rom. 6:20). Being spiritually bound and spiritually dead, sinners cannot of themselves respond positively to the Gospel.

Paul further explained the spiritual inability of sinners in 1 Corinthians 2:14: "The man without the Spirit does not accept the things that come from the Spirit of God, for they are foolishness to him, and he cannot understand them, because they are spiritually discerned" (cf. 1 Cor. 1:18). The unregenerate person (*psychikos anthrōpos*) does not "welcome" (*dechetai*) the things of the Spirit for, lacking the spiritual faculties to understand them, he or she judges them to be nonsense (*mōria*). Concerning the unregenerate, "in the noetic sphere there is no understanding; in the conative [volitional] there is no movement towards God."[94] The spiritual condition of sinners contradicts the hypothesis that prevenient grace has universally overcome the deleterious effects of original sin and depravity.

Paul distinguished between God's universal, nonsalvific goodness to all people and his special, salvific grace to some. As suggested in volume 2, chapter 7, 1 Timothy 4:10 differentiates between these two aspects of grace when it affirms that Christ "is the Savior of all men, and especially of those who believe." By virtue of his universal mediatorship, Christ conveys nonsaving benefits to all persons everywhere. The universal blessings that constitute common grace include moral discernment (Rom. 2:14–15), the delay of divine punishment (2:4), and the institution of government whose task is to promote civil good while restraining the forces of evil (13:1–6; cf. 1 Peter 2:14).

Since sinners lack the spiritual resources to find God on their own, the whole movement of salvation must originate with God. Special grace is God's unmerited favor that brings sinners to salvation. Paul wrote, "By grace [*charis*] you have been saved, through faith—and this not from yourselves, it is the gift of God—not by works, so that no one can boast" (Eph. 2:8–9).

This text indicates that sinners attain salvation independently of any ability or merit on their part; redemption is wholly a divine gift. If sinners were saved on the basis of anything within themselves, there would be ground for boasting. Paul acknowledged the effectual nature of this grace when he wrote, "His grace to me was not without effect" (1 Cor. 15:10). This unmerited heavenly gift transformed Saul, the hateful persecutor, into Paul, the passionate missionary, preacher, and theologian.

In Romans 8:28–30 Paul delineated the full circle of salvation, that clinched his argument concerning Christians' hope of future glory (Rom. 8:18–27):

> And we know that in all things God works for the good of those who love him, who have been called according to his purpose. For those God foreknew he also predestined to be conformed to the likeness of his Son, that he might be the firstborn among many brothers. And those he predestined, he also called; those he called, he also justified; those he justified, he also glorified.

Observe that the basis of the Christian's calling to salvation is God's *prothesis*, i.e., "purpose," "resolve," or "decision" (Rom. 9:11; Eph. 1:11; 3:11; 2 Tim. 1:9). Hope of future glory is grounded in the sovereign, pretemporal purpose of God. The first of the aorist verbs in the text—*proginōskō*, to "foreknow," "choose beforehand"—[95] indicates that election to salvation is rooted in God's foreknowledge. Elsewhere Paul wrote that "the man who loves God is known by God" (1 Cor. 8:3). Again, "But now that you know God—or rather are known by God" (Gal. 4:9). Given the relational dimension of the corresponding Hebrew verb *yāda'*, *proginōskō* means more than mere prescience; it also signifies "foreloved," or "chosen." As Cranfield noted: "The -*egnō* is to be understood in the light of the *yāda'* in such passages as Gen. 18:19; Jer. 1:5; Amos 3:2, where it denotes that special taking knowledge of a person which is God's electing grace. The thought expressed by the *pro-* is . . . that God's gracious choice of those referred to . . . took place before the world was created (cf. Eph. 1:4; 2 Tim. 1:9)."[96] F. F. Bruce agreed: "The words 'whom he did foreknow,' have the connotation of electing grace which is frequently implied by the verb 'to know' in the Old Testament. When God takes knowledge of his people in this special way, he sets his choice upon them."[97] Note that what God consistently "foreknows" is persons themselves, not any decision or action on their part (Rom. 8:29; 1 Cor. 8:3; Gal. 4:9; 2 Tim. 2:19). Thus divine election is according to *foreknowledge* (properly defined), not according to *foresight*.

Continuing with Paul's thought, those whom God foreknew "he also predestined to be conformed to the likeness of his Son" (v. 29). The verb *proorizō*, "decide upon beforehand," "predestine,"[98] occurs three other times in the New Testament (1 Cor. 2:7; Eph. 1:5, 11) in the sense of God's gracious election to life. The point of the present text is that God did not predestine those he knew would respond to the Gospel and be conformed to his Son. On the contrary, before time God predestined those he foreknew (i.e., foreloved) and called them to be conformed to the likeness of Christ.

Return to the the golden chain of salvation detailed in Romans 8:29–30. The aorist verbs "foreknew," "predestined," "called," "justified," and "glorified" imply the certain occurrence of these events by God's prior determination. Grammatically the verbs occur in perfect sequence. Thus if the election and calling were exclusively corporate, so also must be the justification and the glorification. But God does not justify an empty class; he justifies individuals *within* the class who are moved to saving faith in Christ. Similarly, *individuals* possess the Spirit (v. 23), "groan inwardly," awaiting the day of glorification (v. 23), exercise "hope" (v. 24), and display patience (v. 25). Thus the focus of the circle of salvation is both corporate and individual.[99]

Three times in 1 Corinthians 1:27–31 Paul used the verb *eklegomai*, "pick out," "select," "choose for oneself,"[100] to denote God's gracious election to salvation. God did not call to salvation many who are "wise," "influential," or "noble." Rather, he chose "the foolish . . . the weak . . . the lowly . . . and the despised" of this world to confound human self-sufficiency. Because saving grace in its entirety comes from God, every ground of human boasting is cut away: "Let him who boasts boast in the Lord" (v. 31).

In Galatians 1:15–16 Paul wrote, "God, who set me apart from birth and called me by his grace, was pleased to reveal his Son in me so that I might preach him among the Gentiles. . . ." Prior to his conversion Paul hated the church and did his utmost to destroy it (cf. Gal. 1:13, 23; 1 Tim. 1:13). But Paul testified that God graciously took the saving initiative in his life. The Father separated him from birth—the word *aphorisas* ("set apart") being related to *proorisas* ("predestinate")—and revealed his Son to him (cf. 2 Cor. 4:6). Only then did Christ commission Paul for ministry. The text thus confirms God's separation of Paul in eternity past for salvation and his separation in time for service. By the fourfold use of the first person pronoun in Galatians 2:20 Paul stated that God's saving action toward him was profoundly personal. Paul saw himself (1) personally *loved* by Christ ("who loved me"), (2) personaly *justified* ("I live by faith in the Son of God"), (3) personally

regenerated ("Christ lives in me"), and personally *united with Christ* ("crucified with Christ").[101] God had a plan for Saul and worked efficiently in his life to bring him to Christ. The same could not be said for God's relation to Judas, Pilate, or Herod.

To encourage severely persecuted Thessalonian Christians, Paul wrote that the God who had chosen and called them to eternal salvation would sustain them in their earthly trials (2 Thess. 2:13–14). Sorely tempted to renounce Christ, the believers would have found little consolation in the reminder that it was *they* who had chosen God. Rather, their supreme encouragement was that God had chosen *them* for an unshakable salvation. Paul wrote, "We . . . thank God for you, brothers loved by the Lord, because from the beginning God chose [*eilatō*] you to be saved through the sanctifying work of the Spirit and through belief in the truth." The middle voice denotes a subject acting with respect to itself. Here the aorist middle of *haireomai* "emphasizes . . . the relation of the person chosen to the special purpose of him who chooses. The 'chosen' are regarded . . . as they stand to the counsel of God."[102] See also 1 Thessalonians 1:4–5, where the saints' response to the Gospel was evidence of their prior election. Election in eternity past was actualized in time by the sanctifying work of the Spirit and the Thessalonians' belief in the Gospel preached by Paul. Verse 13 (NRSV) indicates that God chose them specifically "for salvation" (*eis sōterian*). So also 1 Thessalonians 5:9: "God [appointed] us to receive salvation" (*eis peripoiēsin sōterias*).[103] To the Christian's searching question, "Why am I a Christian?" the biblical answer is, "Because God chose me."

The most comprehensive text on election is Ephesians 1:3–14, which we summarize as follows:

1. The *source* of election: "the God

and Father of our Lord Jesus Christ" (v. 3). Election is a monergistic operation of God, not a synergism.

2. The *fact* of election: "We were also chosen, having been predestined according to the plan of him who works out everything in conformity with the purpose of his will" (v. 11; cf. vv. 4–5, 9). Paul's election words in these verses are powerfully active and descriptive of what *God* himself did: *eklegō*, "choose out," "select;" *kleroō*, "choose," "destine;" *proorizō*, "foreordain," "predestinate;" *protithēmi*, to "purpose," "intend;" *prothesis*, "purpose," "resolve," "decision;"[104] *boulē*, "intention" or "deliberation (with emphasis on the deliberative aspect of the decision);[105] *thelēma*, "will," "intention,"—i.e., "God's eternal and providential saving will"[106]—(with emphasis on the volitional aspect, or God's will in exercise); and *eudokia*, "good pleasure," "act of the will"—a choice grounded in God's sovereign purpose.[107]

3. The *time* of election: from eternity past, i.e., "before the creation of the world" (v. 4; cf. 2 Thess. 2:13; 2 Tim. 1:9). "The Scriptures say that God chose us in Christ from before the foundation of the world, not that he saw us from before the foundation of the world as choosing Christ."[108]

4. The *objects* of election: "we" (v. 7) or "us" (vv. 3–6, 8–9). Paul envisaged the elect both in their corporate standing as the church and in their individuality. The latter is clear in Romans 16:13: "Greet Rufus, chosen [*ton eklekton*] in the Lord," and in 1 Peter 1:1: "To God's elect . . . scattered throughout Pontus, Galatia, etc." Paul commonly viewed the people of God both in their individuality and in their unity (Rom. 12:4–5; 1 Cor. 12:12, 20; Eph. 4:25). Berkouwer correctly observed: "We are repeatedly struck by the lack of tension between the election of the individual and the election of the

church. . . . The life of the individual does not dissolve into the community."[109] The New Testament designates Christians as "believers," "saints," and the "elect." Ultimately it is the individual who believes and is sanctified; likewise it is the individual who is loved and chosen by God. Luther captured this individual dimension of salvation with the comment: "You must do your own believing, as you must do your own dying."[110]

5. The *sphere* of election: "in Christ" (vv. 3–7, 9, 11; 3:11; cf. 2 Tim. 1:9b). Arminians interpret "in Christ" as elect according to one's quality as a believer. Predestination "in Christ," however, affirms God's purpose to effect salvation through the person and work of Christ (vv. 5, 7; cf. Rom. 6:23; 2 Tim. 1:9b). The phrase "in Christ" positively excludes salvation based on human works or merit.

6. The *motive* of election: "in love he predestined us" (vv. 4–5). God's foreloving, foreknowing, and choosing are all of one piece.

7. The *impartiality* of election: "in accordance with his pleasure and will" (v. 5; cf. Rom. 2:11).

8. Finally, the *goal* of election: that believers might "be holy and blameless in his sight" (v. 4), and that they might live "to the praise of his glorious grace" (v. 6). The *outcome,* not the *condition,* of election is righteousness of life.

Romans 9–11 is an important passage dealing with God's saving purpose for Jews and Gentiles. Paul began by recalling Israel's glorious spiritual heritage: "Theirs is the adoption as sons; theirs the divine glory, the covenants, the receiving of the law, the temple worship and the promises" (Rom. 9:4; cf. v. 5). Given these high privileges, why are so few Jews saved? Has God's purpose for his people failed? Paul responded with a firm "No!" He then added: "For not all who are descended from Israel are

Israel. Nor because they are his descendants are they all Abraham's children" (vv. 6–7). The existence of a believing remnant—a circle of elect ones—within ethnic Israel proves that God's saving purpose has not failed.

Paul then pointed to the fact that God chose Isaac over Ishmael (vv. 7–9) and Jacob over Esau (vv. 10–13) before they were born or had done good or evil "in order that God's purpose [*prothesis*] in election [*eklogē*] might stand" (v. 11). To support this argument he quoted from Malachi 1:2–3: "Jacob I loved, but Esau I hated." According to Cranfield, "loved" and "hated" here "denote election and rejection respectively."[111] God's election of Isaac and Jacob is individual unto salvation and not merely corporate (Israel and Edom) in respect of earthly privileges, since in verses 9–13 each of the children—their birth and their deeds—is in the foreground. A further factor is the flow of Paul's argument. He sought to show that in spite of the unbelief of ethnic Israel God's saving purpose has not failed, as confirmed by the election of a believing remnant exemplified by Isaac and Jacob. To say that God's purpose for Israel remains valid, notwithstanding the unbelief of ethnic Israel, because God chose the line of Isaac and Jacob for temporal blessings is merely to restate the historical problem and to solve nothing.[112]

Paul's critics raised two objections to his affirmation of the election of a remnant within ethnic Israel:

1. God then would be *unjust* in his dealings (vv. 14–18). (Note that this objection would lose its force if the issue at hand were merely the choice of ethnic Israel to earthly priviliges!) Paul's response to this objection is emphatic—"Not at all!" (v. 14). Although humans do not fully comprehend the rationale of sovereign election, God reserves the right to exercise mercy and compassion upon whom he chooses. So Paul cited Yahweh's words to Moses: "I will have mercy on whom I will have mercy, and I will have compassion on whom I will have compassion" (v. 15). Concerning the divine election of a remnant Paul added, "It does not, therefore, depend on man's desire or effort, but on God's mercy" (v. 16). The decisive factor in salvation is not human volition but God's sovereign will.

2. If God is sovereign in election and hardening *no one could be blameworthy* (vv. 19–24). Paul responded to the arrogance of the objector sternly: "Who are you, O man, to talk back to God?" (v. 20). Citing a familiar Old Testament image (Jer. 18:2–6), Paul argued that as a potter has the right to mold the clay as he wills, so God has the sovereign right to bestow more grace on one person than on another (v. 21). Paul's reference to "the objects of his mercy, whom he prepared in advance for glory" (v. 23) depicts his sovereign, pretemporal election of some for heavenly destiny.[113] Verse 22 refers to God's permitting—not ordaining—unbelievers to remain in their sin, thereby demonstrating his severe wrath against sin.

In the second section, Romans 9:30–10:21, of our extended text Paul argued that his doctrine of sovereign election, drawn from the Old Testament, preserves the individual's responsibility to believe. "Everyone who calls on the name of the Lord will be saved" (10:13). The Gospel has been published widely and to Jews first. "But not all the Israelites accepted the good news" (v. 16). Why? Because they sought righteousness by law-keeping rather than by faith in the crucified and risen Messiah. Consequently the Lord holds unbelieving Israel morally responsible for their unbelief.

The third section, Romans 11:1–29, explains God's future purpose for Israel and the Gentiles. Paul again repudiated

41

the notion that God has rejected Israel (v. 1a): "God did not reject his people, whom he foreknew" (v. 2). What God "foreknew" is stated to be his *people,* not any action or deed of theirs—which agrees with the interpretation that God's foreknowing equals his foreloving or choosing. The close relationship between God's loving and choosing is common in the New Testament (Eph. 1:4; Col. 3:12; 1 Thess. 1:4; 2 Thess. 2:13). God has not forsaken his people, as evidenced by the fact that "at the present time there is a remnant chosen by grace" (v. 5). The existence of an elect remnant within the chosen nation represents the outcome of God's sovereign purpose. God formed the remnant by a *personal election within the corporate election* to produce *a spiritual seed within the institutional people.* Thus: "Israel was elect in a double sense: in an outward and temporal sense, the nation, as a nation, was elect; in an inward, personal, and eternal sense, a faithful remnant was elected."[114]

To illustrate this choice of an elect remnant, Paul pointed to himself (v. 1b) and to seven thousand faithful souls in Elijah's day who would not bow to Baal (vv. 2b–4). Israel at large failed to obtain spiritual blessing, "but the elect [*eklogē*] did [obtain it]" not by works but by grace (v. 7). But what God has planned for the future is even more wonderful; the hardening of Israel will not last forever. Israel's temporary obduracy will issue in the salvation of many Gentiles. "Israel has experienced a hardening in part until the full number of the Gentiles has come in" (v. 25). We concur with Cranfield's judgment that the phrase *to plērōma tōn ethnōn* "is probably explained as meaning the full number of the elect from among the Gentiles."[115] God's blessing of the Gentiles then will provoke Israel to jealousy (vv. 11, 14; 10:19), whereupon a large number of Jews will be converted: "And so all Israel will be saved" (v. 26). As used by the rabbis of Paul's day, the phrase "all Israel" meant Israel as a whole, without comprehending every individual within the group.[116] Thus Paul envisaged God's elective purpose issuing in the future salvation of a multitude of Jews who will trust Christ as Messiah and Savior.

Paul concluded this discussion of God's sovereign, elective purpose for Jews and Gentiles with a hymn of praise (vv. 33–36). The salvation of the remnant is the result of the "wisdom," "knowledge," "judgments," and "mind" of the Lord.[117] God's sovereign purpose of mercy and grace is so exalted and wonderful that the only fitting response on the part of humans is humble adoration. "For from him and through him and to him are all things. To him be the glory forever!" (v. 36).

Effectual calling to salvation figures prominently in Paul's writings. According to Romans 8:29–30, those whom God in eternity past foreknew and elected in time he effectually called to himself. A universal, external gospel call is not in view here, for God neither works all things for good (v. 28) nor justifies (v. 30) all hearers of the Gospel. Furthermore, Paul wrote to Timothy about the Father "who saved us and called [*kalesantos*] us with a holy calling [*klēsis*], not according to our works but according to his own purpose [*prothesis*] and grace" (2 Tim. 1:9 NRSV). Moreover, the apostle addressed the Corinthians as those whom God "has called . . . into fellowship with his Son Jesus Christ" (1 Cor. 1:9). Jews and Gentiles who receive only the external call regard the Gospel as "a stumbling block" and "foolishness" (1 Cor. 1:23). But when drawn by the Spirit, the same people judge the Gospel "the power of God and the wisdom of God" (v. 24), and to this call they respond positively.

Paul envisaged those enlightened in their minds, quickened in their wills, and drawn to Christ not as an empty class but as individuals who collectively constitute the church. For other examples of God's special call to salvation see Romans 1:6–7; 1 Corinthians 7:18, 21, 22; Galatians 1:6, 15; 5:8, 13; Ephesians 1:18; 1 Thessalonians 5:24; and 2 Thessalonians 2:14. The verb *kaleō* in these verses indicates that the internal call is not a human achievement but the result of God's sovereign purpose and initiative. In the words of Cranfield: "As used by God, *kalein* denotes God's effectual calling: the *klētoi* are those who have been called effectually, who have been summoned by God and have also responded to his summons."[118] This calling cannot be restricted to summons to service, for often the outcome is explicitly stated to be salvation: e.g., "called to belong to Jesus Christ" (Rom. 1:6) and "called to be free" (Gal. 5:13). Also the weaker sense of "naming" fails to make good sense in most of these verses.

Paul added that the special calling comes to people through the Gospel message (2 Thess. 2:14) applied by the Spirit. The Holy Spirit's operation in the hearts of the elect always accomplishes his purposes. Paul upheld the effectual nature of God's calling as follows: "For we know, brothers loved by God, that he has chosen you, because our gospel came to you not simply with words, but also with power, with the Holy Spirit and with deep conviction" (1 Thess. 1:4–5). The Spirit's inner calling, however, does not eliminate personal responsibility to answer the external call (1 Tim. 6:12b). Finally, Paul often stated that God's purpose in calling a person to Christ (like that of election) is holiness of life: "For God did not call us to be impure, but to live a holy life" (1 Thess. 4:7; cf. Eph. 4:1; 2 Tim. 1:9).

Does 1 Timothy 2:3–4 contravene the doctrine of unconditional election? "This is good, and pleases God our Savior, who wants [*thelei*] all men to be saved and to come to a knowledge of the truth." The verb *thelō* means to "wish, desire, take pleasure in."[119] The text likely refers to one aspect of God's will, namely, his conditional will of pleasure that may be sinfuly violated by misused freedom. Paul's point is that God takes no pleasure in the perdition of sinners (cf. Ezek. 18:23, 32; 33:11). Or as Wisdom of Solomon 1:13 expresses it: "because God did not make death . . . he does not delight in the death of the living." A sensitive human judge takes no delight in sentencing a criminal to death; nevertheless his office requires that he order that penalty justly. Alternatively, Paul had just requested prayer for all persons, especially for kings and those in authority (2:1–2). Thus "all men" may refer to all classes of people whom God desires to save.[120] Scripture, indeed, uses "all" or "every" to denote "all kinds of" (Luke 11:42; John 12:32; Acts 2:5; 10:12; Col. 1:23; 1 Tim. 6:10).

The Johannine Literature

Jesus taught that the unregenerate are spiritually bound by their lower sin nature: "I tell you the truth, everyone who sins is a slave to sin" (John 8:34). Only those spiritually liberated by the Son through regeneration are free to exercise contrary choice spiritually (v. 36). In John 12:39 Jesus flatly said of Jews who were rejecting him: "They could not believe [*ouk ēdynato pisteuein*]." This spiritual inability was due to their hatred of the light and their love of darkness (John 3:19–20; cf. John 8:43; 14:17). That spiritual ability comes from God is confirmed by Jesus' words to his disciples "Apart from me you can do nothing" (John 15:5).

In the prologue to his gospel (1:1–18) the apostle John described Christ as the *logos,* which in the Greek world signified the principle of reason and order in the universe. The *logos* mediates the original act of creation, the continuing work of preservation, and the new work of spiritual regeneration. John 1:4 (cf. v. 9)—"in him was life, and that life was the light of men"—suggests that both prior to and following Bethlehem Christ is the source of all physical, intellectual, moral, and spiritual life. The preceding texts attest the reality of common grace universally. Christ is the source of all life, truth, beauty, and goodness. This general grace can be resisted, however, by sinful human wills (vv. 10–11).

Although John affirmed God's love for the entire world, the fourth gospel, more thoroughly than the Synoptics, emphasizes God's sovereign choice of individuals to be saved. This is clear in John 5:21, where Jesus said to the Jews: "Just as the Father raises the dead and gives them life, even so the Son gives life to whom he is pleased to give it." Likewise in John 13:18 Jesus said to his disciples: "I am not referring to all of you; I know those I have chosen." The Lord chose the Twelve as a group for ministry, but prior to that he chose each one, Judas excepted, for salvation.

In John 10 Jesus figuratively identified himself as the shepherd and his elect people as the "sheep."[121] John recorded several instructive statements about the relation between the shepherd and the sheep.

1. *The sheep are those people whom the Father specifically has given to the Son* (v. 29). The repetition of this concept in John 17:2, 6, 9, 24 and 18:9 reveals its importance to the apostle. Jesus said more pointedly in John 6:37, "All that the Father gives me will come to me" (i.e., will believe and be saved). Concerning the sheep, the Father "chose them out of the world for the possession and the service of the Son."[122] See also John 15:16, 19: Christ chose (*eklegomai*) the disciples out of the world both for salvation and ser-

vice. Compare John 15:19 ("I have chosen you out of the world") with John 17:6 et al. ("those whom you gave me out of the world"). Carson rightly concludes that "they are Christ's sheep in his salvific purposes before they are his sheep in obedient practice."[123]

2. *The shepherd laid down his life for the sheep* and not for the salvation of the unbelieving world (vv. 11, 15). Jesus reveals himself redemptively to those the Father gave him out of the world (John 14:6, 8), and for these he intercedes in heaven.

3. *The shepherd "knows" his sheep and "calls" them by name* (vv. 3, 14, 27). Packer comments concerning the shepherd's knowledge of the sheep: "Here God's knowledge of those who are his is associated with his whole saving purpose of saving mercy. It is a knowledge that implies personal affection, redeeming action, covenant faithfulness, and providential watchfulness towards those whom God knows. It implies, in other words, salvation now and forever."[124]

4. *The sheep know the voice of the shepherd and follow him* (vv. 4, 27). Jesus said of the others, not his sheep, "You do not believe because you are not my sheep" (v. 26). We might have expected Jesus to say, "You are not my sheep because you do not believe," but he said precisely the opposite. A sinner, then, does not become a "sheep" by believing in Jesus; rather he or she believes in Jesus because designated by God as one of his "sheep."

5. Jesus' saying, "I have other sheep that are not of this sheep pen. I must bring them also" (v. 16), implies that specific Gentiles in theory belonged to Christ (by divine election) even though they had not yet come to personal faith. In the preceding Johannine texts the sheep are not an empty class, for they are said to "hear," "know," "believe," "trust," "follow," and "love"

the shepherd—all of which are actions of *individuals*.

The Johannine literature offers examples of a general, external call that may be sinfully resisted (John 7:37–38; Rev. 22:17). Yet we find examples of a special, internal call that issues in salvation. John believed that no person comes to Christ unless quickened by the summons of the sovereign God. Thus Jesus said, "No one can come to me unless the Father has enabled him" (John 6:65, cf. v. 44). This led F. F. Bruce to comment: "None at all would come unless divinely persuaded and enabled to do so. . . . Those who come to Christ come to him by the 'secret constraint' of grace."[125] The effectually called respond with faith to the internal summons of the Spirit (John 6:29, 35, 40, 47). Jesus' saying in John 12:32 does not contravene the preceding conclusion: "But I, when I am lifted up from the earth, will draw all men to myself." Certain Greek Gentiles (v. 20) questioned the significance of Jesus' life and mission. The Lord himself responded that he would draw to himself "all men"—i.e., both Gentiles and Jews (see John 10:16; 11:52; 12:24). Distinctions of nationality, ethnicity, or social status were irrelevant to Jesus' redemptive mission.

Other New Testament Literature

Peter viewed the body of Christ, the church, as the analogue of the believing remnant in Israel ("a chosen poeple, a royal priesthood, a holy nation, a people belonging to God," (1 Peter 2:9). Yet Peter saw within this new people the election of certain individuals to salvation. Thus he addressed his first letter (1:1) to chosen ones (*eklektoi*) "scattered" throughout Asia Minor. The dispersed saints are elect "according to [*kata*] the foreknowledge of God the Father, through [*en*] the sanctifying work of the Spirit, for [*eis*] obedience to

Jesus Christ and sprinkling by his blood" (v. 2). Note the following regarding this verse: (1) The preposition *kata* states the basis of divine election, namely, the divine foreknowledge (*prognōsis*). *Prognōsis* denotes the divine foreloving or foreordaining, or as Selwyn stated, "knowing or taking note of those whom He will choose."[126] That God's foreknowledge of Christians connotes more than mere prescience is confirmed by Peter's statement that Christ "was chosen [perfect passive participle of *proginōsko*] before the creation of the world" (1 Peter 1:20; "He was destined," RSV, NRSV). First Peter 1:2 says nothing about Christians being chosen on the basis of foreseen faith. (2) The preposition *en* signifies the instrument by which eternal election was actualized in time, namely, by the powerful working of the Holy Spirit. And (3) the preposition *eis* denotes the goal or outcome of the divine election, namely, obedience to Christ and the application of his atoning benefits. Peter stated not that those who obey Christ are elect, but that the elect go on to obey Christ.

James 1:18 affirms that the initiative in salvation lies entirely with the sovereign God: "He chose [*boulētheis*] to give us birth through the word of truth. . . ." James 2:5 states that God sovereignly chose those the world judges poor to believe and to inherit the kingdom. Jude affirmed the same in his description of Christians as people "called," "loved," and "kept" by Christ (v. 1).

Hebrews acknowledges a general call or hearing of the Word of God that may be sinfully resisted (Heb. 4:6–7; 12:25). Yet several texts teach a call of God that is effectually heeded unto eternal life. Thus Hebrews 3:1 speaks of the Jewish believers as "holy brothers, who share in the heavenly calling." God gave ethnic Israel a resistible call to earthly privileges and blessings, but he extended to some an effectual call to an heavenly inheritance in Christ (Heb. 9:15). Similarly Peter urged Christians, "Declare the praises of him who called you [*hymas kalesantos*] out of darkness into his wonderful light" (1 Peter 2:9). God's effectual calling to salvation in Christ is also affirmed in 1 Peter 1:15; 2:21; 3:9; 5:10; 2 Peter 1:3; and Jude 1. The language and context of these verses exclude the notion of a general call. Thus not all those addressed by the Gospel belong to God (1 Peter 2:9), not all know Christ and his power (2 Peter 1:3), and not all are "kept by Jesus Christ" (Jude 1). Neither does redefining "calling" as "naming" fit these texts (e.g., try substituting "named" for "called" in 1 Peter 2:9, 20–21 and 3:9). Second Peter 1:10 links calling and election by a common pronoun (*tēn klēsin kai eklogēn*). It urges Christians to demonstrate publicly their divine election and calling by living out the virtuous deeds cited in verses 5–7.

Some allege that 2 Peter 3:9 refutes the doctrine of unconditional election: "The Lord . . . is patient with you, not wanting [*mē boulomenos*] anyone to perish, but everyone to come to repentance" (cf. Ezek. 33:11). Taken in context, however, this verse teaches that God delays the execution of his final judgment and extends the opportunity for people to repent for the reason that he takes no pleasure in the death of the wicked.[127] Thus the delay in reality is a manifestation of God's grace.

The cumulative evidence leads us to conclude that the New Testament plainly teaches individual election to life as a major theme. Considering all the data, Scripture sets forth "an election within the election," namely, an election of individuals to life within the corporate election of the people of God (Israel and the church) for earthly privileges and eternal destiny. God first elected the group, the new humanity or spiritual people of God, and then the individuals who would constitute that group. With respect to the doctrine of election to life we concur with the carefully measured conclusion of Jewett: "In my judgment [the] Augustinian approach reflects a much more impressive biblical and exegetical effort than does the Pelagian and Arminian view."[128]

SYSTEMATIC FORMULATION

Having focused on the Father's gracious plan of salvation and the Son's costly provisions in previous chapters, we here present a coherent topical account of the rich biblical material on the soteriological ministries of the Spirit of grace. The great salvation the Spirit brings to condemned sinners begins in the gracious character of the triune God.

The Unfathomable Riches of God's Grace

In classical usage the word *grace* referred to a person's attractiveness or charm. A gracious person was kind and of generous disposition. The relational quality of willing good for another was not a requirement but a "favor." As Aristotle said, grace was "helpfulness towards someone in need, not in return for anything nor that the helper may get anything, but for the sake of the person who is helped."[129] Those treated graciously by others felt gratitude and expressed thanks.[130] In scriptural usage the idea of grace points to God's kindness toward sinners who are unable in their fleshly natures to return anything of merit.

Some understanding of grace is basic to appreciating the Spirit's redemptive work with God's chosen people. God's undeserved acts of mercy and grace stand in contrast to his merited acts of justice. Justice is merited, grace is unmerited. As *just,* the Judge of the entire earth gives all persons exactly what they deserve according to their works. As *merciful,* God withholds punishment from the guilty. As *gracious,* God bestows on them unmerited blessings.

Some common misunderstandings of grace warrant attention. Grace does not undermine justice but fulfills it. The gracious acts of the Holy Spirit do not violate justice by bringing any undeserved punishment upon anyone. Grace, furthermore, is not a "thing" to be hypostatized by itself. Grace is misunderstood if it is confused with an impersonal power or energy that can neither satisfy justice nor grant mercy. It is not like magic or manna. Grace is a quality of persons. Only morally accountable persons can understand a just moral indictment, mercifully withhold judgment, and confer undeserved blessings. Since mercy and grace deal with distinctively person-to-person relationships, mechanical illustrations of humans under the power of the Spirit as puppets or robots are irrelevant.

All three persons of the Trinity act out of undeserved love in distinct but harmonious ways. By grace *the Father* chose to call out of the world a people to be his moral and spiritual children. The ultimate initiative in divine actions of mercy and grace come from the Father's eternal purposes. His purposes of grace rule out any appeal to human merit. Fallen humans have no natural endowments or moral achievements that merit acceptance. By incomprehensible grace *the Son* entered the world as an undeserved gift when the planned time had fully come. While we were yet sinners Christ entered the world to die for us. "Christ did not come to supplement man at his best," said H. D. MacDonald, "but to redeem man at his worst."[131] Graciously, *the Holy Spirit* on the day of Pentecost came to the Jews (Acts 1:4; 2:38) and later to Gentiles (10:45; 11:17). The Spirit who raised Christ from the dead acts with grace and power in all believers' lives. The Spirit's work is so closely associated with grace that N. P. Williams mistakenly held that "Grace" and "Holy Spirit" are synonyms.[132] As closely associated as that quality is with the third Person of the Trinity, the latter is not synonymous with a quality. The Spirit is the divine person who bestows the benefits of the Father's special love provided by the Son's Atonement.

What the Spirit of Grace Does for All

God's general or common grace is administered by the Spirit in the illumination of general revelation. The Spirit of God blesses believers and unbelievers alike with water, food, sunshine, and rain. Are these unmerited blessings the product of "common" grace, which Reformed theologians distinguish from another brand of "special" or redemptive grace? Or are they an aspect of the one "prevenient" brand of grace, which Arminians insist leads to salvation? Just as we distinguished universal revelation from special revelation and providence from miracle, so a realm of universal grace needs to be distinguished from a realm of special grace. Because of God's common grace creatures on planet earth enjoy a beautiful life-support system and normative values of truth and goodness. Although God does good to all, distinctively redemptive grace is experienced by those God the Father decides to give to Christ.

What then is the *relationship of common to special grace?* Jesus prayed: "For you granted him [your Son] authority over all people that he might give eternal life to all those you have given him" (John 17:2). The general authority of Christ serves his special, redemptive ends. God in Christ the one Mediator "is the savior of all men, and especially of those who believe" (1 Tim. 4:10). To get Mary to Bethlehem for the Messiah's birth, God providentially used a general census of the Roman world ordered by Caesar Augustus (Luke 2:1). In miraculously freeing Paul and Silas from prison, God loosed all the prisoners' chains and opened all the prison doors (Acts 16:26). God preserves the life support system on earth for all in order to keep the elect alive for salvation and service.

The *distinctive purposes* of common grace need to be noted. The Spirit withholds penalties and confers many undeserved natural blessings universally. The Spirit's works of universal grace include: (1) sustaining nature's resources for earthly life providentially, (2) enabling people to receive truths universally revealed or available so that all truth is ultimately God's truth, (3) stimulating all people to goodness, so that every worthy value in any culture is from above (James 1:17), (4) restraining moral evil, and (5) maintaining civil justice. Mercifully, the Spirit has postponed the deserved death penalty. It is because of God's great love that the entire prodigal race has not already been consumed (Lam. 3:22).

The Spirit's *general illumination* of universal moral values convicts the pre-Christian conscience of sin and evokes a sense of need for a Savior from above. But any indications of a "peace child" providing a substitutionary atonement or any openness to receive the Gospel of the incarnate Christ indicate the beginnings of the Spirit's special redemptive operations. The first hints of lasting repentance for sins and faith in Christ are not the fruit of general revelation. What the Spirit's general illumination produces from universal revelation is a preparatory awareness of (1) one's dependence upon God, (2) obligation to God, and (3) guilt before God. The best of us comes far short of divine holiness. If after sensing the need for salvation sinners show signs of turning from the service of idols to God's gift of Christ's righteousness, these are indications of the Spirit's special redemptive ministries.

The universal grace of illumination does *not lead to salvation*. Knowledge of God's existence, power, and moral demands is not enough. All members of the kingdom of darkness, although enjoying the provisions of common grace, habitually suppress its moral laws. Hence arises the world's selfishness, ungodliness, and injustice. Many persist in their opposition to the divinely created physical and moral order throughout their lives. The *results* of the Spirit's universal grace nevertheless are of indispensable benefit. But they must not be inflated (as liberals contend) into a way of salvation. Arminians tend not to limit salvation to those who have heard and received the Gospel because they consider all grace as leading to redemption. Since we did not find God's redemptive plan in general revelation, we do not have adequate evidence for the soteriological ministries of the Spirit (in prevenient grace) with all nations or with all people.

The Spirit Uses Believers' External Calls to All

The omnipotent Spirit has freely chosen to invite the world to Christ through human ambassadors. "How can they hear [about the Cross] without someone preaching to them?" (Rom. 10:14). Today Christians are emissaries of reconciliation to God through the historically incarnate, crucified, and risen Christ. Under orders from the Lord of all, they take the Good News to everyone everywhere. By the external or *verbal call* we mean the believers' activity through audible or visual signs imploring sinners to acknowledge their moral guilt before a holy God, to repent, believe the

Gospel, and so trust Jesus Christ for salvation. Since the call comes to sinners through believers' speaking or writing, it may be contrasted with the Spirit's invisible and inaudible, internal influences by the designation, the "external call" or "verbal call."

The primary *content* the Spirit uses in calling sinners to Christ is primarily a story of events with their revealed meanings conveyed by the linguistic signs in the gospels. The story and its significance comes from certified prophets and apostles, and so it is a true story. The account of Jesus is not one of thousands of myths but is *revealed truth* conveyed by inspired *Scripture,* the Spirit's primary instrument or sword. As we endeavor to bring sinners to Christ the Spirit desires to illumine the teaching of the truth inspired over some 1,500 years for this primary purpose. Unfortunately, William James, in *Varieties of Religious Experience,* and other past "psychologists, without exception, have overlooked *the absolutely decisive element* of Christian conversion: the hearing of the Word of God."[133] When the French atheist, Emile Cailliet, came to belief in God and Christ's atonement, for example, the decisive factor was the reading of the Bible.[134]

How should Christians present the Good News of God's grace to sinners? As important as the biblical truth is, we ought not just quote the Bible. Jesus conversed with each sinner differently. In the history of the church the Spirit of grace has presented the truth about Christ in a variety of ways. Consider, for example, the numerous factors the Spirit used in the conversion of Augustine. Augustine's *Confessions* portray the progression of his life from that of a skeptic to a materialist, a neoplatonist, a dabbler in the occult, a theist, and finally a born-again Christian. The Spirit providentially worked in the following ways: (1) The faithful *prayers* of his mother Monica were answered. (2) What we might call philosophical *apologetics* of the neoplatonist case for the reality of spirit led Augustine away from Manichean materialism. (3) The *biblical* preaching of Ambrose helped Augustine see that the interpretive objections he aimed against the Old Testament were misdirected. (4) The pastor's employment of *historical evidences* also removed roadblocks and convinced Augustine of the truth of events that occurred more than five centuries earlier.

Although Augustine's intellectual roadblocks to faith were removed, he still struggled with the emotional and moral issues related to living with mistresses. (5) The *counsel of older Christians* helped him. (6) The *testimonies of gifted peers* who gave up finances and professions to devote themselves to Christ influenced him to exclaim, "I burned to do likewise." Finally, (7) he opened the *Scriptures* and read, "Let us behave decently, as in the daytime, not in orgies and drunkenness, not in sexual immorality and debauchery, not in dissension and jealousy. Rather, clothe yourselves with the Lord Jesus Christ, and do not think about how to gratify the desires of the sinful nature" (Rom. 13:13–14). Augustine testified that immediately after reading that passage he was "born again."[135]

Since the Spirit uses various forms of outreach to bring people like Augustine to Christ, it is wise to avoid oversimplifications. Thus it may be tragic to say to young Christians: "All you need is prayer," or "All you need is Christian evidences," or "All you need to do is quote the Bible." We may be thankful that people in Augustine's day did not limit themselves to any one of these strategies. What approaches does God's Spirit use to bring modern Augustines to Christ? All of the above, through many different types of personalities like those of Paul, Apollos, Cephas, and Timothy. Today's Christians can learn from and use all of these strategies, for "all are yours, and you are of Christ, and Christ is of God" (1 Cor. 3:21–23).

Who is privileged verbally to call sinners to Christ? Everyone who has believed through the apostolic message. All believers, like Paul, are "obligated both to Greeks and non-Greeks, both to the wise and the foolish" (Rom. 1:14). The first believers, the disciples, were all indebted to carry the message. Said the risen Lord, "The Christ will suffer and rise from the dead on the third day, and repentance and forgiveness of sins will be preached in his name to all nations, beginning at Jerusalem. You are witnesses of these things" (Luke 24:46–48). Again he said to all the assembled believers prior to his ascension: "All authority in heaven and on earth has been given to me. Therefore go and make disciples of all nations" (Matt. 28:19). Believers of all ages beyond the Twelve are to become disciple makers (John 17:23). The Holy Spirit has chosen to use not only professional "ministers" and "missionaries" but *all believers* as ministers and missionaries. Some may emphasize pre-evangelism, some evangelism, some nurturing, and some training for global outreach. But all believers have a responsibility not just to state the Gospel but to do so persuasively in order to make disciples.

Christians are privileged to carry out the Great Commission because God has chosen to work through human means. As an aphorism puts it, "The Holy Spirit alone can save a person, but the Holy Spirit has chosen not to save a person alone." Paul explained: "Everyone who calls on the name of the Lord will be saved. How, then, can they call on the one they have not believed in? And how can they believe in the one of whom they have not heard? And how can they hear without someone preach-

ing to them? And how can they preach unless they are sent?" (Rom. 10:13–15). Although all people possess the witness of nature (v. 18), they have failed to receive its message. (vv. 16, 19, 21). Consequently, faith comes from hearing the word of Christ (v. 17). If you would help sinners come to the Savior, then expound the Gospel, defend it, and exhibit the reality of your commitment to the living Christ. Summon all people everywhere to repent (Acts 17:30) of unfaithfulness to God and neighbor.

To what ends do we invite pre-Christians to convert? Often Christians call sinners out of the sinful world but fail to make clear to what they are calling them. In Scripture God's servants seldom called people to prepare for heaven, as important as that is. Rather, their messages called people to believe, repent, and trust the living Christ as Lord and Savior in order to (1) begin a new way of life as a disciple of Jesus Christ, the spiritual master revealed in Scripture and (2) begin a vocation of loving service for Christ and his church in the world. Too many conscientious young people hear of little they can do to make a difference in the world. But desperately wanting to make a difference, they often respond to the appeals of New Age cultic leaders who seek to transform people and society without the Gospel.

The verbal call *should go to everyone.* "For many are invited, but few are chosen" (Matt. 22:14). The verbally called comprise a larger group than the internally called. Nevertheless, with whatever emphasis and in whatever style, a universal verbal presentation of the Gospel is necessary. Why? Because the crucified and risen Lord Jesus Christ provided the only just way to forgiveness, reconciliation, and redemption. But the Christ has ascended back to heaven. Thus if sinners are to hear about the provisions of his atonement, Christians must tell them. How else will they hear about the just basis of God's justifying, reconciling, and redeeming work? Christ sent the Counselor to guide and empower world Christians in that great task.

Why Some Do Not Repent, Believe, and Trust

Why do not all who hear the Gospel believe and accept Christ? Several scriptural passages imply that the Holy Spirit permits some sinners to harden their sinful hearts. Several times during the plagues in Egypt Pharaoh "hardened his heart and would not listen to Moses and Aaron, just as the Lord had said" (Exod. 8:15, cf. v. 32). So Pharaoh's heart "became hard and he would not listen to them" (7:13; 8:19; 9:35). See also Exodus 9:7. Pharaoh's refusal to listen to God's servants and their signs is also attributed to God, we take it, permissively. "But the Lord hardened Pharaoh's heart" (9:12; 10:20, 27; 11:10). We interpret this in the sense that God allowed the natural resistance of Pharaoh to persist and so indirectly hardened his heart. This is consistent with the fact that God does not tempt to evil or initiate moral evil against himself (James 1:13). By contrast God did not allow Moses to defect permanently. God similarly permitted the Canaanite nations to harden their hearts (Josh. 11:20). Informed by the biblical evidence it seems impossible to say that the internal work of the Spirit was the same in Pharaoh as in Abraham or Moses.

John's gospel, written that sinners might believe (20:31), indicates why many do not. Even after Jesus had performed many public, miraculous signs many did not believe in him (John 12:37). The issue of why some believed and some did not sets the stage for what follows in this Gospel. The reason is not their own failure to use an equal ability the Holy Spirit allegedly gave to all in prevenient grace. "For this reason they could not believe, because, as Isaiah says elsewhere: 'He has blinded their eyes and deadened their hearts, so they can neither see with their eyes nor understand with their hearts, nor turn— and I would heal them'" (Isa. 6:10 cited in John 12:39–40). "Isaiah said this because he saw Jesus' glory and spoke about him" (v. 41). The hypothesis that the Spirit calls all equally does not fit the facts stating that God allows some people to continue in increasing unbelief and disobedience (blinding their eyes) while effectually calling others.

It is difficult to support the hypothesis that the Spirit gives all persons equal ability to respond, since the Scriptures teach that God allows some hearts to harden. We interpret the hardening action permissively, rather than efficiently (as in supralapsarian Calvinism) for several reasons. In the case of Pharaoh, the Bible first mentions that he hardened his own heart. Furthermore, God as holy cannot even tempt to sin; he is the efficient cause of good gifts only. God does not strive with sinners forever, but gives some up to their uncleanness. Hence when we read that the Spirit blinds sinners' minds to the Gospel or hates Esau we understand those passages in a manner consistent with God's inability to cause moral evil. The relevant passages teach that the Spirit permits some sinners to go on hardening their hearts, for they are not among those given to Christ by the Father. Although they do not become the recipients of unmerited mercy and grace, God does not relate to them unfairly. They receive what they actually deserve according to their works, neither more nor less.

Why Others Do Convert—the Father's Election

God never promised that all would believe. "The promise is for you and your children and for all who are far off—for all whom the Lord our God will call" (Acts 2:39). Whom does God "call"? The Father calls persons "in accordance with his pleasure and will—to the praise of his glorious grace" (Eph. 1:5–6; v. 4). Those who converted did so in accord with the Father's will, because the Spirit graciously "lavished" on them "all wisdom and understanding" (v. 8) and made known "the mystery of his will" (v. 9).

Disabled sinners are not elected conditionally, because none can meet the conditions. Sinners are not chosen because of their foreseen good works (Pelagians), for none keep all the law. Holistic sinners are not chosen on the basis of their foreseen faith (Arminians), for none by themselves will believe. Salvation is *by* or *through* faith, but not *on account of* foreseen faith. No holistically depraved sinner will of himself or herself repent and believe. So unconditionally God designated many to receive the free gift of salvation. God foreknew who would believe because he knew those he had given to Christ and those are the ones the Spirit will effectually call and enable to believe and repent.

The Father elects and the Holy Spirit calls *persons* who together make up the body of Christ. The Spirit does not convict an empty class of their unbelief but specific persons who make up the class of the elect. John's gospel repeatedly calls them "those whom the Father has given to the Son." Those the Father gives him look to the Son and believe (v. 40). Sinners cannot come to Christ unless the Father draws or enables them (vv. 44–45, 65). Some do not believe because they are not Jesus' sheep, but those the Father gives to Jesus listen to his voice, receive eternal life, and can never be snatched from the Father's hand (10:26–29). The Father did not give all persons to Christ, for

Jesus said, "I am not referring to all of you; I know those I have chosen" (13:18) and "You did not choose me, but I chose you and appointed you to go and bear fruit" (15:16). Christ possesses authority over all so that he might give eternal life to those the Father gave him (17:2). To the sheep Jesus revealed the Father (v. 6) and for them he prayed (v. 9). Jesus also protected them (v. 12), therefore they will be with him in glory (v. 24). When God chose the children of Abraham from among all the nations, the choice was particular. And the choice is not all the natural children of Abraham but believers. It is the children of promise who are Abraham's offspring redemptively (Rom. 9:8):

> Yet before the twins were born or had done anything good or bad—in order that God's purpose in election might stand: not by works but by him who calls—she was told, "The older will serve the younger." Just as it is written: "Jacob have I loved, but Esau have I hated." What then shall we say? Is God unjust? Not at all! For he says to Moses, "I will have mercy upon whom I will have mercy, and I will have compassion on whom I have compassion." (Rom. 9:11–15)

The persons the Father gave to Christ are "in Christ" and collectively form *the body of Christ*. It is not a question of either individuals or a class, as assumed by those who make the object of election a corporate body devoid of individuals. As called individuals repent of their sins and believe they constitute the corporate people of God foreknown both personally and collectively. Together, those the Spirit unites to Christ by faith form one body with many individual members. The Spirit of grace works with elect sinners to bring each into the body of Christ through personal faith. When Paul wrote Romans in A.D. 57, many Gentiles were receiving the Good News. Thus the question about corporate Israel arose: "Did God reject his people? By no means!" (Rom. 11:1). As God preserved a remnant of faithful people in Elisha's day, "so too, at the present time there is a remnant chosen by grace" (v. 5). Not all, but some were chosen and saved by grace not by works. Otherwise "grace would no longer be grace" (v. 6). "What then? What Israel sought so earnestly it did not obtain, but the elect did. The others were hardened, as it is written, 'God gave them a spirit of stupor, eyes so that they could not see and ears so that they could not hear, to this very day'" (vv. 7–8). Scripture teaches that God gave spiritual sight to some in Israel and not to others. While God allows some to continue in unbelief during the times of the Gentiles, elect Jews are being saved. Corporate election does not exclude individual election. Some might prefer to leave the ultimate choice for salvation with themselves; but the hypothesis that best fits the biblical data posits the ultimate choice with the grace of God.

God loves all people, but exercises his love in different ways. C. S. Lewis identified four loves humans may have for each other: affection (*storgē*), friendship (*philia*), erotic love (*eros*), and charity (*agapē*). "The primal love is gift love." [136] The concept of God's love exegeted from the Scriptures indicates a variety of ways in which God expressed his love for sinners. God provides for the well-being of all in common love that illuminates general revelation. But the Lord manifested a special love for Israel distinct from his love for other nations. It was not because Israel was larger than other nations or because of any virtue in them, but simply because he loved her (Deut. 7:7–8). The people of Israel in Old Testament times received directly some gracious gifts that other nations obtained only indirectly, if ever. God loved Jacob in a way that he did not love Esau. The greatest example of God's primal gift love (*agapē*) is seen in his giving of his Son. God is not obligated to give the gift of Christ's perfect righteousness to any. That he has chosen to impute righteousness to any is awesome.

The notion that unmerited grace and love should be the same for all people is an unrealistic Platonic idea read into Scripture and experience. It confuses characteristics of love with those of justice. Acting in justice, God is obligated to judge everyone in the same way. But matters of love are not matters of obligation. We ought to treat all people justly, but we need not love all in the same way. We experience many different kinds of love: love for God, love for parents, married love, love for children, and love for neighbors. The idea that love ought to be the same for all persons is not derived from Scripture or experience but from a categorical confusion of love with justice. As just, God is obliged to relate to all humans in the same way. But the sovereign Lord can choose lovingly to extend mercy and grace to whom he will.

God's chooses "his people" for *both salvation and service*. At times the Lord of providence selected unbelievers for a given task, but those God calls to become his people participate in both his fellowship and his work. Christ chose his disciples for both eternal life and disciplined servant ministries. Saul on the road to Damascus was chosen for both salvation and service as the apostle to the Gentiles. The hypothesis that God predestines to service but not to salvation is difficult to harmonize with the theological interrelationship between the Spirit's works of regenerating, giving gifts to, and sanctifying every member of the body of Christ for service. All who are chosen to receive Christ's righteousness are gifted to serve others. God lovingly predestines and draws to salvation in order to serve the church and the world.

Why the Elect Convert—the Spirit's Effectual Call

It is *necessary* for the Spirit internally to renew lost capacities for knowing, loving, and serving God because depraved sinners are both persistently unwilling and unable to respond to spiritual things. By the internal calling we mean that effectual ministry of the Holy Spirit that persuades chosen sinners of the truth of the claims made in the verbal or external call. The Spirit's calling effectually enables sinners personally to believe the Word, repent of sin, and trust Jesus Christ as Savior and Lord. The last act does not mean that the penitent will obey perfectly every aspect of Christ's will. Salvation is never based on obedient works. If it were, grace would no more be grace (Rom. 11:5–6). Among the indications of the new gracious gift of life, however, is the new and growing desire of maturing converts to do all that their Lord commands (John 15:10).

The Holy Spirit's *inner call* is distinct from the Christians' *verbal call*. Although Paul spoke to many who did not believe, he addressed believers at Corinth and elsewhere (1 Cor. 1:2) as those whom God "called . . . into fellowship with his Son Jesus Christ" (v. 9). The message of the cross is foolishness to those who are perishing (v. 18), but "to those whom God has called, both Jews and Greeks, Christ [is] the power of God and the wisdom of God" (v. 24). Not all whom we call regard Christ as the power and wisdom of God, but those whom God calls do. Later in the chapter Paul argued that not many whom God called were wise, influential or noble, but God chose the foolish things of the world to shame the wise so that no one may boast. It is because of him (the Father) that you (in contrast to the others) are in Christ Jesus (vv. 26–30). God's gracious, effectual call of people to be in Christ, then, is not universal, but particular.

Although Christians persuasively present the Gospel of grace to sinners, the latter's response to the verbal call is not uniform. Many are called (by words externally), but few are chosen (enabled internally). In response to the apostle Paul's message, some Athenians mocked, some put off a decision, and some believed. Why, in the final analysis, do some believe assertions conveyed by words and others not? Since inability to respond to spiritual things is true of all sinners, no unregenerate people left to themselves would believe. We have found no scriptural support for a renewal of all sinners' ability to believe the Gospel prior to the special work of the Spirit with the elect. To avoid the possibility that no one would receive the provisions of the Cross, the Father and Son sent the Spirit to illumine the minds, attract the affections, and enable the wills of people chosen by sheer grace.

The Spirit begins *providentially* by presenting to the consciousness biblical information through preevangelists, pastors, teachers, and missionaries. The Spirit appeals to the conceptual understanding through the teaching and example of others, especially of Christ. The Spirit led Cornelius and Peter to each other so that Cornelius, a religious Gentile, might be converted and added to the church (Acts 10). The Spirit's soteriological activity cannot be limited to a single point in time. Paul wrote that "God has poured out his love into our hearts by the Holy Spirit, whom he has given us" (Rom. 5:5). The perfect continuous tense of the verb "poured out," indicates that the Spirit's soteriological work is not just a single, momentary act. So the Spirit's saving activity should not be limited to occasions of receiving the "sacraments" from a "priesthood" (Roman Catholicism). Neither should it be reduced to certain supernatural phenomena (charismatic thinking). The Spirit has chosen to help some sinners to Christ in church services when baptism and the Lord's Supper are observed by ordained ministers who read from the Bible. The omnipresent Spirit, however, has no limited office hours. He works with people prior to and after church services (as well as during them).

The Spirit also works *supernaturally* or by a direct influence, renewing the sinner's capacities to know, love, and act upon spiritual things. The Spirit graciously enables the sinner's *mind* to apprehend the good, her *desires* to love the good, and her *will* to do the good. Paul explained, "It is God who works in you to will and to act according to his good purpose" (Phil. 2:13). If the Spirit must aid born-again church members to receive spiritual things (1 Cor. 2:14), how much more is the Spirit's ministry imperative in the depraved state before regeneration? With the Reformers we stress an inward exercise of love awakened by the Spirit's free, efficacious impact. The Spirit's calling involves an *immediate* Person-to-person activity. A songwriter correctly wrote, "It took a miracle to save my soul."

As noted in the historical section, Pelagius denied any direct operation of the Holy Spirit on human wills. He maintains only an indirect influence through the conscience. With no Fall and no human depravity, Pelagianism limited the Spirit's ways of working to external providential teachers and examples of law-keeping. Human obligation to keep the law, Pelagius reasoned, implied ability to keep it. A merely indirect approach through moral influence, however, is not sufficiently radical because of the weakness of the flesh. Analogously, a reductively indirect approach through the Gospel fails because of the weakness of the old

nature. For this reason Arminians fallaciously infer *from* the invitation *to* ability to believe. We assert, rather, that with the invitation, the Spirit of truth grants to some the ability to believe. To the paralyzed Jesus said, "Take up your bed and walk." And to Lazarus in the grave he said, "Come forth." So Augustine prayed, "Give what you command and command what you will."

The Spirit of grace helps sinners overcome their spiritual inabilities by an initial *renewing of the depraved mind, desires, and will*. Thus the inwardly called and illumined sinner begins to comprehend spiritual truths (1 Cor. 1:18–25; 2:10–14). The Spirit pours God's love into hearts (Rom. 5:5), convicts of moral guilt (John 16:8–11), and persuades of the truth of the Gospel. Believers understand the truths of Scripture by an internal divine-human operation. Ideas that suddenly burst upon our minds may be intuitions from ourselves or demons as well as from the Holy Spirit. Satan "prompted" the mind of Judas (John 13:2). Hence it is crucial not to believe immediately every idea that bursts intuitively upon the mind but to test them (1 John 4:1). However timely sudden flashes may seem, they need to be verified before being considered true and acted upon. We know ideas are from God not because they occur suddenly but because of their consistency with the teachings of Christ. Attempts to follow the Holy Spirit untested by the Word may lead us astray; attempts to follow the Word unattested by the Holy Spirit may abort.

The Spirit's internal call is *effectual,* but not irresistible. Prior to the Spirit's calling, slaves to sin not only *can* resist special grace but invariably *do* so. The point of effectual grace is that the Holy Spirit lovingly overcomes insolence in the elect and delivers them from bondage to sinful unbelief. The spiritually dead, like Lazarus, cannot come forth from their tombs, but the Holy Spirit grants the beginnings of spiritual life. Although efficacious for salvation and service, the Spirit's modes of operation are not irresistible in an impersonal, automatic way. Since the word "irresistible" often connotes a mechanical coercion, it is inapplicable to personal relationships. If a good parent, teacher, or pastor can effectively accomplish preestablished goals without breaking a person's will, how much more can God's Spirit? If human lovers can win the affections of mates who formerly disregarded them, how much more can God? The Spirit who raised Christ from the grave raises from among the spiritually dead those who are his. In this way the Spirit achieves the Father's purposes by enabling sinners to receive the Son's provisions. The "hound of heaven" never ceases to strive with the elect. The Spirit's effectiveness in Augustinian thought, as N. P. Williams noted, "is always described as proceeding by way of infallible attraction, not of overmastering compulsion."[137]

Of what does the Spirit convict? In calling sinners out of the world to become people of God the Spirit *convicts of deserved judgment for their moral and spiritual guilt.* Jesus said, "When he comes, he will convict the world in regard to sin and righteousness and judgment" (John 16:8). For amplification of this passage see the biblical section above.

In summary, the Spirit's mission in internal calling involves (1) convicting a worldly person of sin, righteousness, and judgment; (2) illumining the mind to understand the observed facts and revealed meanings of the Gospel message; (3) persuading of the Gospel's objective validity for all; and (4) witnessing to the Gospel's applicability for one's repentant self.[138]

Relating the Factors Logically (*Ordo Salutis*)

A basic issue in formulating a doctrine of soteriology is, Who makes the first move—the Spirit or the sinner? Does the Holy Spirit take the initiative in drawing sinful persons to Christ so that the effectual call and/or regeneration precedes conversion? Or do sinful persons who hear of Christ take the initiative to believe such that conversion precedes the Holy Spirit's regeneration? It may be impossible to determine the temporal priority because the factors related to salvation appear to occur simultaneously (calling, conversion, regeneration). For that reason the issue is *not* the chronological order of the factors in our conscious experience but their logical order in the *ordo salutis* (plan of salvation).

Previously we considered the logical order of God's decrees in eternity (vol. 1, chap. 8). On the related issue of the logical order of the divine and human factors *three major options* need consideration: (1) Some find the Scriptures to teach that God's calling of all in prevenient grace and their response in conversion precedes regeneration (Arminians). (2) Others find the Scriptures to teach that the special call and regeneration precede conversion (traditional Calvinists). (3) A third view finds that the special call precedes conversion and conversion precedes regeneration (Millard Erickson and ourselves).[139]

Having found abundant support for the present reality of universal human enslavement to sin and a lack of evidence for prevenient grace, the ultimate and decisive factor is election. God foreknew that none would seek him or trust Christ. Hence the Father predetermined that many would be enabled by the Spirit to repent and believe the Son. The choice was not of an empty class but of particular people. These by sheer grace would be called personally out of the world and brought by the loving Spirit into the corporate body of Christ. That corporate body was never envisioned as empty of members; rather, it was inclusive of persons who would receive redemptive love.

Consider whether the following order is the more probable account of the data of Scripture and experience: (1) In eternity past, after foreseeing the fall of all, the Father graciously *elected* many depraved sinners to conversion, sanctification, and service. (2) In temporal history human witnesses *verbally called* those given to Christ and (3) the Holy Spirit specifically issued to the same an *efficient, internal call.* (4) As a Spirit-enabled response to their effectual calling, sinners genuinely *convert* (believe, repent, and trust Christ). (5) The converted who are *justified, regenerated,* and *sanctified* then *persevere* and are *glorified.* A listing of the *ordo* looks like this: election, verbal calling, effectual calling, belief of the Gospel, repentance from sin, trust in the living Christ, regeneration, justification, reconciliation, sanctification, perseverance, and glorification.

This modified Calvinistic hypothesis (designated infralapsarianism in vol.1, chap. 8) best coheres with the Bible's teachings of (1) the unwillingness and inability of sinners to receive the Good News and (2) the *need* to receive it to be born again. For example, after Jesus had emphasized to Nicodemus that people must be born again, the Lord explained that he "must be lifted up, that everyone who believes in him may have eternal life" (John 3:15). "Eternal life" in context can be shown to refer to the new birth more specifically than can the more general term "saved" in Acts 16:31. The teaching that regeneration must precede faith seems to contradict the teaching that we must believe in Christ to receive eternal life, justification, and adoption as children of God.

This moderately Reformed scheme agrees with Arminianism in holding that human conversion precedes divine regeneration (Miley, Wiley) and disagrees with high Calvinism in its claim that the Spirit's regeneration takes logical precedence over conscious, human conversion (Strong, Berkhof, Murray). In contrast to Arminianism, however, the only sinners who convert to Christ are effectually called by the Spirit. Whereas theologians such as L. Berkhof seem to equate special calling and regeneration, we distinguish the one from the other; they are as distinct as conception and birth. It is one thing to conceive the truth of the Gospel by the Spirit and another to be born of the Spirit, although the one leads to the other. Indications of conception are initial belief, repentance, and faith (conversion); an indication of the new birth is persevering growth in the grace of Christ.

Let us develop the biblical analogy of conception and birth further. The Spirit's effectual call provides fertile ground for the initial sowing of the seed of God's revealed truth. Those who conceive—as indicated by belief in the Gospel, repentance, and faith in Christ—are then reborn or regenerated. The internal call of the Spirit renews the sinner's abilities (mind, emotions, and will) and secures a positive response to the Gospel. The Spirit then brings about the new birth, permanently changing atrophied abilities and giving eternal life. Some who appear to have received the Spirit's effectual call and to have been converted fall away, as in the parable of the sower (Matt. 13:1–23). Teaching that the Spirit's redemptive call leads to justification and glorification (Rom. 8:30) rules out permanent rejection of the Father's effective purpose.

Another way to relate the components in soteriology focuses on three distinct categories: (1) our legal standing before God's law, (2) our unconscious experience, and (3) our conscious experience. (1) On the first *forensic* or *positional* level sinners who were (a) under condemnation receive (b) justification and (c) a positional sanctification. (2) On the level of *unconscious experience* the Spirit (a) effectually calls sinners to faith, (b) regenerates believers, and (c) enables the regenerate to persevere. (3) On the level of *conscious experience* sinners (a) hear the Gospel, (b) repent and believe, and (c) grow in grace and knowledge. If in discussions of these issues some speak of conscious experience and others unconscious experience or legal status, merely verbal controversies may multiply. It is important not to attempt to verify from conscious human experience what takes place in the unconscious (except by outward results). As Jesus emphasized, no one can put human conditions or control on the Spirit's work of regeneration: "The wind blows wherever it pleases. You hear its sound, but you cannot tell where it comes from or where it is going. So it is with everyone born of the Spirit" (John 3:8).

APOLOGETIC INTERACTION

Is Not Election of Only Some Unfair?

For God to choose to save some and not others to many seems unjust. We are not defending a double predestination but a view that places priority on the Fall and depravity of all. Not some, but all are foreknown to be fallen and under a just sentence of condemnation. Some are left to receive what they justly deserve; others are chosen to receive the Spirit's gracious effectual call. God owes grace to no one. That God relates to any insolent people mercifully and graciously is amazing. The complaint may stem from confusing the ethical demand of justice for equal treatment before the law with the freedom of judges to pardon whom they will. No pardons are obligatory. That any are given is astounding. Those who do not receive amnesty will doubtless wish that they did, but they have no right to complain that it is unfair or unjust not to pardon them because someone else was pardoned.

The charge of unfairness in the gift of salvation may stem from a failure to define grace and justice under the proper categories. We confuse categories if we think of a lemon as a vegetable rather than a fruit. We compound the problem when we complain that it is not a good vegetable. We confuse categories if we apply to things that are *unmerited* the qualities of the things that are *earned*. We may also confuse *what is obligatory* with *what is not owed, but freely given*. To complain of unfairness when God does extend mercy and grace is to confuse the mutually exclusive categories of obligatory justice with free grace.

Jesus illustrated the fact that gracious gifts need not always be equal. As discussed in the biblical section, the parable of the workers (Matt. 20:1–16) teaches that those who worked shorter periods of the day received the same pay as those who worked in the vineyard all day. The parable does not lay down a new system of economics but illustrates the principle of grace at work in God's kingdom. The owner met the requirements of justice for every worker, for no one received less than agreed upon. To those who thought they should have received more, Jesus said, " Friend, I am not being unfair to you" (v. 13). Regarding those who worked a much shorter time and received as much as those who worked all day, Jesus said, "Don't I have the right to do what I want with my own money? Or are you envious because I am generous?" (v. 15).

No one is obliged to extend undeserved blessings to any. If some receive undeserved gifts, the benefactor is not bound to give the same gifts to all. It is not unjust if the Spirit does not give the same spiritual gifts to every believer. Justice is not at issue here. We may wish we had other gifts or more gifts, but to complain that the Spirit distributes the gifts in the body of Christ unfairly shows an inability to understand the difference between a requirement of justice and a gift of grace. Although justice must treat everyone equally, the beneficence of free grace need not.

A complaint about the injustice of God's saving grace is an oxymoron. It uses words of opposite meaning as if they were not categorically exclusive concepts (Rom. 11:5–6). God's grace is not in the same ball game as fairness. The obligations to justice are met at the Cross and in divine judgment according to works. The charge of unfairness does not apply to the Holy Spirit's freedom to be magnanimous with tax collectors, adulterers, and dying thieves rather than respectable Pharisees. Never did Jesus relate to a Pharisee unfairly. But gracious treatment of them was a free choice not an obligation. Those who defend the free will (i.e., power of contrary choice) in humans ought give greater priority to defending the freedom of the triune God of grace. The Spirit may freely choose to transform a persecutor like Saul into an apostle like Paul, rather than choose a hundred self-righteous ones. "It is his [Christ's] prerogative to do as he wishes with what he has to give. We stand in his debt, not he in ours."[140]

Can Calvinists Honestly Invite "Whosoever Will"?

A universal invitation is valid because it is descriptively true. It reports the fact that trust is essential to a personal relationship with God as well as others. Fellowship with Christ involves faith in him. Reformed theology does not say that God elects sinners to heaven without themselves becoming believers. It states the truism that any who will turn from idols to Christ will be saved. John wrote that "everyone who believes in him may have eternal life" (3:15), "shall not perish" (3:16), and "is not condemned" (3:18).

Pelagius reasoned that ability to keep the Ten Commandments may be inferred from the commands to keep them. If humans were unable to keep them, the moral law would be inauthentic. From that Pelagius illicitly concluded that the effects of sin did not seriously enslave the human will. The fact is that even though the depraved cannot keep the entire law all the time, moral principles remain normative. The law is holy, righteous, and good (Rom. 7:12). The problem lies with the weakness of fallen human nature (Rom. 8:3–4). Obligation is not limited by inability to believe. Wesleyans agree with the criticism of Pelagius but argue analogously that the validity of the Gospel invitation to believe assumes the ability of sinners to respond to it. And they claim that all the depraved receive that ability by an alleged prevenient grace. But we have not found any biblical indications of a work of the Holy Spirit enabling every person to believe. The problem is not with the invitation to "whosoever will," but with the weakness of the fleshly nature of the people receiving it (Rom. 8:3).

The necessity of faith is not the issue between Arminians and Reformed, but whether sinners are *able* to believe apart from a special work of the Spirit. Biblical passages describing the means to acceptance with God do not speak to depraved sinners' ability or lack of ability to repent and believe. So the question remains whether the depraved are willing or able to convert. We should not build a view of fallen humanity's *ability* to repent and believe by inference from an *invitation* to believe. We must turn to explicit passages on the actual condition of the sinful mind, desires, and will. And we find that these do not support an ability to believe as a result of prevenient grace. Depraved sinners in fact do not correctly perceive Gospel truths if left to themselves (1 Cor. 2:14).

In the *Chronicles of Narnia,* book IV, C. S. Lewis depicts Jill as puzzled about the task for which the Lion called her out of her world. " 'I was wondering—I mean—could there be some mistake? Because nobody called me. . . . It was we who asked to come here. Scrubb said we were to call to—to Somebody—it was a name I wouldn't know—and perhaps the Somebody would let us in. And we did, and then we found the door open.' 'You would not have called to me unless I had been calling to you,' said the Lion."[141] Less poetically, R. B. Kuiper explained that

> the decree of election is not secret in the sense that none can be certain of belonging to the elect, but that, on the contrary, faith in Christ being the fruit and also the proof of election, one can be just as sure of being numbered among the elect as of being a believer; that the house into which they are invited has an eternal, unmovable foundation, so that he who enters, though all hell should assail him, cannot possibly perish but will most certainly inherit everlasting life.[142]

What About "Prevenient Grace"?

Wesleyans acknowledge an originally sinful nature but find both its guilt and power removed by prevenient grace. For Wesley the Spirit's activities in prevenient grace are displayed universally not only in divine providence (which restrains evil and enhances cultural values) but also in (1) "setting aside the penalty for the guilt inherited from Adam," (2) giving every person "a fresh start" (like Adam's and Eve's before the Fall), (3) aiding everyone to make the first wish to please God, (4) giving all the first dawn of light concerning God's will, (5) initiating the first transient conviction of having sinned against him, and (6) providing some degree of salvation, in the form of the beginning of deliverance from a blind, unfeeling heart that is insensible to God and the things of God.[143]

These Wesleyan hypotheses amount to a universal restoration of spiritual and moral ability in unrepentant sinners—proposals difficult to reconcile with scriptural teaching concerning pre-Christians' blindness, enmity, and alienation. The spiritually enslaved conditions of fallen humans (vol. 2, chap. 4) appear in Scripture as actual conditions of people encountered by prophets, Christ, and apostles, not merely as hypothetical conditions. The human depravity the biblical writers taught in such strong language has an actual referent in actual persons. It does not apply only to a hypothetical condition from which all have been delivered. Such a prevenient grace hypothesis does not fit the facts of Scripture or the general experience of pastors and counselors.

The original human freedom *for* God was changed by the Fall into a freedom *from* God. Sinners do not have the power to reverse this change.[144] The restoration of our relation to God involves the sacrifice of a broken and contrite spirit and the special call of the Holy Spirit. In calling us, "The Holy Spirit does not annihilate our spirits, but bears witness with our spirits. And the Holy Spirit does not destroy the freedom of our spirits, but restores it by changing their false freedom from God into that true freedom for God, which is 'the glorious liberty of the children of God.' "[145]

Why Pray for the Lost?

A typical charge is that belief in election and effectual calling makes prayer unnecessary. But Christians ought to follow the example of Paul. A major source of the doctrines of election and the special call, Paul prayed for the salvation of his Jewish friends out of a deep, heartfelt passion (Rom. 10:1). Similarly, those who believe in the effectual calling of sinners by the Spirit should pray for the lost they seek to reach directly and through their missionaries. Like Jesus who wept over Jerusalem, Christians have a deep compassion for the lost in their region. It is both reasonable and sincere, then, to cast such a burden upon the Lord in prayer.

In fact, prayer seems pointless, not from a Reformed position, but from an Arminian perspective. According to the latter, the Spirit in prevenient grace has already done all that he can justly do for all persons equally. Thus prayer for the Spirit to work in special ways to bring unsaved relatives to Christ would be asking God to act unfairly. However, from before Creation God had taken the *means* to salvation (e.g., prayer) into account as well as the *end* of salvation. Few Christians dispute the fact that "everyone is a Calvinist on his knees."

Why Bother to Present the Gospel to Sinners?

If the Holy Spirit assuredly will convert the elect, why should we witness to the unreached throughout the world? If the Holy Spirit must take the initiative, why go to the trouble of bringing the Gospel to all sinners? Some important reasons need consideration:

1. We must begin with the command of Jesus Christ. As Donald McGavran has said, "The great issues in Christian mission are theological. The question is: What does God command the Church to do in regard to the multitudes who have no knowledge of Christ?"[146] The risen and glorified Christ positively commands his followers to make disciples in every nation (Matt. 28:18–20). No longer sending his disciples to "the lost sheep of the house of Israel" (Matt. 10:6), he orders now that repentance and remission of sins should be preached to all people (Luke 24:46–48; cf. Acts 1:8). So Christians obediently take the Good News to sinners in the power of the Holy Spirit to obey and glorify God.

2. Such God-honoring obedience fits harmoniously with God's twofold purpose—universal and particular. The Father granted Christ authority over all people so that he might give eternal life to all those given him (John 17:2). Because Christ is the Savior and mediatorial Lord of all, especially of those who believe, we authentically take to all the message of his providential mercy as well as his atoning grace. In the name of the one, universal Mediator between God and men, we offer an honest and sincere invitation to any who will drink of the water of life. The focus of our witness is upon God's gracious plans for fallen humans in order that the chosen may recover their potential as his image-bearers.

3. Although our communication of the Gospel is not a sufficient condition of anyone's salvation, it is a necessary means in the divine plan. The external call of the evangelist is not efficacious in itself; it cannot enable any sinner to believe. Nevertheless, the Holy Spirit sovereignly has chosen to use the prayerfully presented message as an occasion for producing new life from above. In other words, the Spirit of grace is pleased to do the work of evangelism through faithful witnesses. Christians are like "servants" or gardeners who sow the seed, water it, and cultivate the ground; but it is the life-giving Spirit alone who makes the seed grow (1 Cor.

3:5–7). Since the Spirit works through human instruments such as evangelists, preachers, and teachers, Christians have courage to call Muslims, Hindus, Buddhists, and New Age occultists to bow before Jesus Christ.

4. Furthermore, since no human knows that any given unrepentant person is not among the elect, we must present the Gospel to all (Acts 1:8; 17:30). We do not know that any given person is not among those whom the Holy Spirit will call redemptively. We do not lose heart in witnessing because we know that the Spirit of grace will use the universal verbal call to save many "sheep." Arminians often suggest that Reformed teaching eviscerates the passion to witness; on the contrary it encourages witnessing. It assures Christians facing people with an incorrigible aversion to Christ that God uses them to bring sinners to salvation. Missionaries facing the challenge of witnessing to passionate devotees of the world's religions and cults can take comfort in the fact that the Spirit has chosen to use them to reach the elect.

5. We bring the Gospel to sinners by following the example of Christ and the apostles. As models for us, they faithfully and courageously witnessed in spite of minimal responses and even in the face of strong opposition.

6. God has called all Christians to preevangelism and evangelism as a way of life.[147] God called Paul not only to personal justification but also to a life of Gospel outreach. Thus he wrote, "God, who set me apart from birth and called me by his grace was pleased to reveal his Son in me so that I might preach him among the Gentiles" (Gal. 1:15). Paul by God's grace became "the apostle to the Gentiles" (Rom. 11:13). Does it follow that God calls everyone to the same kind of service as the apostles? No, but the Spirit gives gifts to everyone for some ministry to the body of Christ and for some form of verbal witness and service to the world.

7. Finally, why God desires all to hear the Gospel even though he has not purposed to save all is a question mortals do not fully comprehend. One reason that may be offered is that the hearing of Christ's selfless sacrifice stimulates certain temporal benefits, such as the demonstration of love and the restraint of evil.

What Message Must Pre-Christians Hear?

Humans conveying God's call of sinners out of the world to be his people should communicate several important elements of the message of general and special revelation. Posttheistic humanists and other sinners need consciously to realize that they are (1) dependent on a personal, transcendent God, (2) morally obligated to God, (3) guilty before God, (4) alienated from God, and (5) enslaved to sin. Some concepts of the apostolic *kerygma* make sense only in the larger belief system of the apostles' *didachē*. Their first Jewish hearers were people who shared their belief in one personal God transcendent in being and immanent in activity. The Gospel makes sense in the apostles' biblical *world-and-life-view*. In a pluralistic world we must be prepared to discuss a Christian view of God and the world, humanness and sin as Paul did with the Athenian Epicurean and Stoic philosophers. Then the meaning of the Incarnation, how miracles can happen, and how Jesus relates to God make better sense. To avoid a total relativism concerning world religions built on other worldviews, Christians must be able to justify their claims concerning God and God's relation to people in the world. Pre-Christians need reasons to believe in our diagnosis of human need, Christ's saving provision, and fellowship with God free from guilt.

Pre-Christians do not need a technical theological understanding of God's justice and grace but some knowledge of how these are exhibited in the *kerygma*—the account of the unique incarnation, life, death, and resurrection of Jesus Christ. They need to receive Christ's atoning provisions personally in order that they themselves may receive a new nature, justification, and reconciliation. Christians need a way of expressing Gospel essentials for the unreached mission field of new religions and cults that claim to believe the Bible. Seven questions have been used by many Christians to explain the Gospel of grace and identify false gospels: (1) "Do you base your teachings on sacred writings other than the Bible?" (1 Cor. 15:3–4). (2) "Is your primary task the communication of the Gospel?" (Gal. 1:8–9). (3) "Do you believe that Jesus is the Messiah, the eternal Word who became flesh?" (John 1:1, 14; 1 John 4:1–3). (4) "Do you believe that Christ's death is the only basis for the forgiveness of your sins?" (Rom. 3:25). (5) "Do you believe that Jesus rose bodily from the dead?" (Rom. 10:9–10). "Are you personally trusting Jesus Christ as your own redeemer?" (Acts 16:31). (7) "Are you depending on your own achievements for your justification or wholly on God's grace?" (Eph. 2:8–9). These seven questions, based on explicit statements of Scripture, are designed to help nonevangelicals like Jehovah's Witnesses, Latter-Day Saints, Christian Scientists, and Spiritualists (channelers) understand the Gospel of grace.[148]

Skeptics need to be persuaded that the Gospel is *true*. The best reason for one to receive the faith of Christ is the conviction that it conforms to reality. Should evidences like those to which the New Testament appeals in fulfilled prophecy and miracles be included in preevangelism and evangelism? Yes, for people need to know not only *that* we believe it true, but also *why*. The apostles presented the facts of the Gospel as distinct from myths. And they supported their claim with eyewitness testimony confirming its objective validity. Since absolute proof is not possible, the best approach to objective confirmation is cumulative and converging lines of evidence. The enduring Christian church is a fellowship of verification as the experiences of one generation support those of another. The Spirit's inner illumination confirms one's subjective appropriation of the Gospel's objective provisions. Bernard Ramm explains, "The *testimonium* validates one's personal participation in redemption; evidences validate the objective religion of the Gospel. A cavalier treatment of Christian evidences is therefore a failure to understand the total complex of the Christian revelation."[149]

Is God's Call to Service Different From the Call to Salvation?

Arminians affirm that God predestines to service but not to salvation. Wesleyans emphasize the universal Christian mission as a divine mandate,[150] but the predestination and call to salvation is conditional.[151] Calvinists agree that God predestines Christians to make disciples universally; no people of God can escape that claim of the sovereign Lord upon their lives. Both Arminians and Reformed agree that predestination to service does not violate the free will of Christians. Since divine choice predetermines what the human will ought to do after regeneration without violating human integrity, can it not do so prior to regeneration?

The divine initiative calls people to *be* something in order that they may *do* something. It is impossible to delete calling and justification from the series secured by predestination in Paul's teaching: "Those he predestined, he also called; those he called, he also justified; those he justified, he also glorified'' (Rom. 8:30). A word study suggests that ''Paul understands calling as the process by which God calls those whom he had already elected and appointed, out of their bondage to this world, so that he may justify and sanctify them (Rom. 8:29f.), and bring them into his service.''[152] Faith in Christ and grateful service for Christ are intimately associated in Scripture. Upon occasion the Father chose a nonbeliever for a special service (e.g., Cyrus). But when God calls sinners out of the world to be his people, he calls them to both fellowship and service. Thus Christ chose and called his disciples to both salvation and service. Before God called Saul to become an apostle to the Gentiles, he called him to faith in the Messiah. Paul's letters to the churches assume that those who believe will also serve.

RELEVANCE FOR LIFE AND SERVICE

Are You Among God's Chosen People?

Unfortunately some sensitive souls harbor real fears that they are not numbered among God's elect. To such distressed persons and others we offer the following comments. First, as far as the individual is concerned, election is an *a posteriori* rather than an *a priori* doctrine. That is, teaching about election should be presented to a person *after* he or she comes to Christ, not before. The Bible offers no encouragement whatsoever to speculate about an individual's status as elect or nonelect. Election is a precious biblical truth to be shared with the person who already has made his or her decision for Christ and who demonstrates this reality by the fruit of a changed life. We see this in 2 Thessalonians 2:13, where Paul celebrated the fact of divine election with

persecuted believers who had converted to Christ from paganism. The apostle wrote, ''We ought always to thank God for you, brothers loved by the Lord because from the beginning God chose you to be saved through the sanctifying work of the Spirit and through belief in the truth'' (cf. also 2 Tim. 1:9). Preachers and teachers expound the biblical doctrine of divine election in order to help *saints* understand that it is *God* who has blessed them with eternal salvation. This teaching gives saints great comfort and encourages them to persevere in their trials. The doctrine of election, then, is not a doctrine to be proclaimed to the world. We must take issue with the belief of the great C. H. Spurgeon (with whom we agree on many other points) that election should be preached to the unsaved because it destroys all hope in self-will and good works. Spurgeon wrote,

> If the potent hammer of electing sovereignty dashes out the brains of all a man's works, merits, doings, and willings, while it pronounces over the dead carcass this sentence: ''It is not of him that willeth, nor of him that runneth, but of God that showeth mercy;'' then the best thing is done for a sinner that can be done as a stepping-stone to the act of faith. When a man is weaned from self, and totally delivered from looking to the flesh for help, there is hope for him: and this the doctrine of divine sovereignty does through the Holy Spirit's power.[153]

Second, instead of harboring gnawing fears about election the distressed soul should accept Christ's offer of life. We have Jesus' firm promise ''Whoever comes to me I will never drive away'' (John 6:37). The person who in truth forsakes sin and receives Christ not only has the Lord's *promise* of acceptance but will *experience* the witness of the Spirit in her heart and know a peace of soul that is entirely new. Such a person will keep God's commands; she will have a deep love for God and his Word, for God's people and his church, and for works of "light" rather than darkness (see, e.g., 1 John 2:27; 3:1, 7, 18–19, 21). By such evidences the anxious person can *know* with certitude that he or she is a child of God and thus among the number of the elect. Thus the person agitated with concerns of his or her election should turn away from idle speculation and accept the invitation to life that Christ lovingly proffers.

Are You Experiencing the Quality of Life to Which God Called You?

A survey of biblical passages on God's "call" indicates that this reality is for every Christian in a number of rich senses. We are called not just to future glory but to an abundant life here and now. God's acts of wholly unmerited generosity are not merely reported events to which we assent intellectually; they are also continuing acts of the Holy Spirit's unmerited love to be *experienced,* as follows.[154]

1. God calls every Christian to *a new identity*. By grace the estranged become God's friends and the guilty receive pardon. We who were aliens become God's new people. Does your self-image include thinking of yourself as "among those who are called to belong to Jesus Christ" (Rom. 1:6)? Are you clear that the Spirit of grace has called you to be a saint (v. 7)? Do you view yourself as an object of God's mercy prepared in advance for glory (Rom. 9:24)? Join with John in exclaiming, "How great is the love the Father has lavished on us, that we should be called children of God! And that is what we are!" (1 John 3:1).

2. God calls us to experience the reality of his *special love*. As the Lord said through Paul, "I will call them 'my people' who are not my people; and I will call her 'my loved one' who is not my loved one" (Rom. 9:25). Imagine a person waiting for a call from a lover and finally hearing the phone ring. What a joy to hear those great words, "I love you!" God himself calls people who have sinned and says, "My loved one!" Jude wrote "to those who have been called, who are loved by God the Father and kept by Jesus Christ: Mercy, peace and love be yours in abundance" (Jude 1–2). When it seems that few people love you, think of yourself as one truly loved by the Lord of heaven and earth.

3. God has called us to *fellowship* with his Son. Paul makes this clear in 1 Corinthians 1:9. The unsaved regard the Messiah as a stumbling block or foolishness (1 Cor. 1:23), but to the divinely called he is an intimate friend. If your life has become routine and meaningless, remember you received an invitation, not to meet the sovereign head of your country, but to unbroken fellowship with the eternal Word who incarnated himself into our midst.

4. The Holy Spirit calls every Christian to *a holy life*. Paul wrote to a young minister: "Join with me in suffering for the gospel by the power of God, who has saved us and called us to a holy life—not because of anything we have done but because of his own purpose and grace" (2 Tim. 1:8–9). Peter exhorted his readers: "Just as he who called you is holy, so be holy in all you do" (1 Peter 1:15). Does your self-image include a sense of being called to be distinct from those who are not the people of God? Are you conscious of your call to be morally upright (1 Cor. 1:2)?

5. God's Spirit calls every Christian to *a free life*—liberation from bondage to sinful passions. The freedom of Spirit-enabled self-determination according to the new nature delivers from sin's mastery. Jesus said, "If the Son sets you free, you will be free indeed" (John 8:36; cf. Gal. 5:13). Slaves to sin have no permanent place in God's moral and

spiritual family, but a child belongs to it forever (John 8:35). The effectually called discover a new sense of liberty to fulfill God's revealed will in a spirit of love and freedom (Rom. 8:2, 4, 15; 2 Cor. 3:17).

6. God calls Christians out of a hostile world to lives of *perseverance through suffering* that they may know and do what is good. "To this you were called, because Christ suffered for you, leaving you an example, that you should follow in his steps" (1 Peter 2:21). "Finally, all of you, live in harmony with one another; be sympathetic, love as brothers, be compassionate and humble" (3:8). "And the God of all grace, who called you to his eternal glory in Christ, after you have suffered a little while, will himself restore you and make you strong, firm and steadfast" (5:10). God does not call his people to a pain-free existence but to do battle in the age-long moral and spiritual war of the two kingdoms.

7. God calls us to a life of *peace* in the body of Christ. "Let the peace of Christ rule in your hearts, since as members of one body you were called to peace" (Col. 3:15). Although wars may rage around us, we can face moral decisions and spiritual battles knowing that our troubled hearts can be overruled by God's matchless grace. As a fruit of the presence of the Spirit of grace Christians can enjoy inner peace and serenity.

8. Christians are called to a life founded on assent to *truth*. Paul was grateful for the Thessalonians, "because," he told them, "from the beginning God chose you to be saved through the sanctifying work of the Spirit and through belief in the truth. He called you to this through our gospel, that you might share in the glory of our Lord Jesus Christ. So then, brothers, stand firm and hold to the teachings we passed on to you, whether by word of mouth or by letter" (2 Thess. 2:13–15).

Among the blessings God's divine power has given us "for life and godliness" are "his very great and precious promises" (2 Peter 1:3–4). We hold them fast not merely by carrying a Bible in our hands, but by holding biblical principles in our memories and conducting our lives by them.

9. God calls us from a merely temporal life to *life everlasting*. "Take hold of the eternal life to which you were called when you made your good confession in the presence of many witnesses" (1 Tim. 6:12). "For this reason Christ is the mediator of a new covenant, that those who are called may receive the promised eternal inheritance" (Heb. 9:15). As God's children our names are in the will along with the name of Jesus Christ. As joint heirs with Christ we now enjoy eternal life.

In inquiring whether people are ready to join their church elders or deacons do well to determine if candidates have experienced God's call to the above qualities. Not everyone can recall the date of his or her conversion, but all should be able to testify to these spiritual realities. Instead of emphasizing the past, put questions in the present tense. "Do you believe the Gospel? Are you repentant for your sins? Are you trusting Christ for acceptance with the Father? Do you have the witness of the Spirit that you are a child of God? Are you called by God to a life of holy love and praise in fellowship with Jesus Christ?"

Extend the Verbal Call Creatively

We should present the truth of special revelation in varied ways to those who do not know they are God's moral and spiritual children. When working with theists who assent to the truth of the Old Testament, follow Peter's pattern; quote messianic prophecies and show how Jesus fulfilled them. Then call people to repentance and faith in Jesus as Lord and Messiah (Acts 2:22–40). Paul did this after reading the Scriptures in the synagogue (Acts 13:23–41). Many evangelicals, however, imagine that quoting the Scriptures as Peter did is the only way to reach non-Christians from any worldview or culture.

When witnessing to diverse people in a pluralistic world, review the many factors the Spirit used in bringing Augustine to Christ. Follow also the example of Paul who said,

> Though I am free and belong to no man, I make myself a slave to everyone, to win as many as possible. To the Jews I became like a Jew, to win the Jews. . . . To the weak I became weak, to win the weak. I have become all things to all men, so that by all possible means I might save some. I do all this for the sake of the gospel, that I may share in its blessings. (1 Cor. 9:19, 22–23)

God specifically chose and prepared Paul for work with people untutored in the Old Testament faith. Most non-Christians today, even among the Jews unfortunately, are in this group. The most extensive example of the apostle's ministry to Gentiles is his message at Athens. A number of points are worth observing. Like Paul, we should do the following: (1) Be observant (Acts 17:16, 23), knowing the thinking of the people we seek to reach. (2) Feel deep concern for them (v. 16). Although Paul recognized the beauty of the statues of Greek gods and goddesses, he was stirred inwardly at the people's idolatry as Yahweh was when the Israelites worshiped the golden calf.[155] (3) Engage the people in conversation daily in the marketplace (v. 17). In this way we will earn the right to be heard by others.

(4) Address with respect the leaders you seek to reach. Paul did not begin by saying, "You apostate philosophers and idol worshipers!" Neither did he begin by saying, "My dearly beloved brethren!" He used the standard, respectful way of addressing the distinguished members of the Areopagus: "Men of Athens!" (Acts 17:22). (5) Find something to commend honestly. Thus Paul said to the idol worshipers: "I see that in every way you are very religious" (v. 22).

(6) Help Gentiles (nontheists) understand who God is before talking about Christ's Atonement. Utilize any common ground possible. Paul quoted approvingly a Stoic poet who said, "We are his [God's] offspring" (Acts 17:28). (7) Make it clear that the God of whom you speak is the living Lord of every thing (vv. 24–25), every nation (v. 26), and every person (v. 27). (8) Explain that the Source of persons is not himself impersonal (v. 28) and that they are living inconsistently with their understanding of God. As Paul said, "Since we are God's offspring, we should not think that the divine being is like gold or silver or stone—an image made by man's design and skill" (v. 29).

(9) Emphasize that all are not only dependent on God but are morally accountable to God and guilty before him (v. 30). (10) Deliver the divine summons to all to repent, whether they are idol worshipers, secular humanists (like the Epicureans) or New Age pantheists (like the Stoics), politicians, or educators (v. 30). (11) Announce the day of judgment for all (v. 31). (12) Disclose the name of the Judge—the Lord Jesus Christ, and (13) cite the evidence God gave to all by raising him from the dead (v. 31).

No doubt Paul amplified these points, or his message was one of the shortest in history. Surely he emphasized Christ's unique nature and death for our sins. But with those unfamiliar with the Lord of the old covenant Paul first made clear what he meant by "God." In our posttheistic age we need to help people understand who God is "because anyone who comes to him must believe that he exists and that he rewards those who earnestly seek him" (Heb. 11:6).

Trust the Lord of the Harvest for Spiritual Fruit

As we issue the external call, we may expect responses similar to Paul's at Athens. Some sinners will sneer and others will postpone their decision (Acts 17:32). But, thank God, some will repent and believe. Two of Paul's converts, well enough known to be named (Dyonisius and Damaris) and several others believed! (v. 34).

Paul's ministry did not fail at Athens, for several people were saved. A church began there, and tradition suggests that Dyonisius became its first pastor. The hypothesis that Paul changed his apologetic approach after his alleged failure at Athens does not fit well with the facts, for at Corinth he "reasoned in the synagogue, trying to persuade Jews and Greeks" (Acts 18:4). In Ephesus also he "reasoned with the Jews" (18:19). For three months he "spoke boldly . . . arguing persuasively about the kingdom of God" (19:8). When some publicly maligned "the Way," Paul did cease to defend the faith among the Jews. He left the synagogue with his disciples and "had discussions daily [the same Greek verb 'argued'] in the lecture hall of Tyrannus" (v. 9). Later at Troas Paul "spoke to [or reasoned with] the people" (Acts 20:7). Never did Paul reflect any sense of failure at Athens. Luke considered his preaching there exemplary enough to give it a lengthy report as he wrote Acts 17 under the Spirit's inspiration.

Christians are mere servants (farmers, gardeners) who sow the seed of the Word and water it. God the Holy Spirit makes it grow! If there is any new spiritual life and fruitfulness, it comes from the Spirit of grace (1 Cor. 3:6–9). As we faithfully extend the verbal call to the world, we do so confidently, not in the strength of our fleshly natures. Our confidence is in the Holy Spirit, who has chosen to bring the world to Christ through his people's sowing and watering of the seed, God's truth.

Faithfully Support the Objectives of God's Common Grace

As noted in the Systematic Formulation section, above, the Spirit of grace who illumines special revelation also illumines general revelation. Granting that people's deepest problem is their own moral depravity, the primary work of the Holy Spirit is to regenerate sinners, and the primary task of every Christian is to communicate the Gospel to sinners. Believers, however, are not exempt from meeting people's other needs. We are servants of God's kingdom not only in its redemptive aspect but also in its providential aspect.

Just as the Spirit works through humans to achieve some purposes of special grace, so he works through human agents to achieve other purposes of common grace. For example, Christians should care for the created order. "The earth is the Lord's, and everything in it, the world, and all who live in it" (Ps. 24:1; cf. 50:12b). The older generation feared the hydrogen bomb, but the younger generation fears an ecological Armageddon. Christians should not unnecessarily pollute the environment, extinguish species, or waste natural resources—all of which tragically have occurred in our generation. Christians ought to support programs for clean air and the conservation of resources such as forests, coal, and oil for future generations. As Ronald Sider has well said, "Nature is not divine. Biblical faith desacralizes nature. God offers it to us to use for our good. But it is not a trifle to be wasted. It is a good garden, to be treasured and preserved as it is tended and used."[156] Sider makes an observation that even believers need to heed: "Joy comes through right relationships with the Creator, other persons, and then the earth."[157] Sider rightfully laments the fact that "we have failed to articulate this biblical vision in a compelling way."[158] Evangelicals need to enunciate the fact that our expectations of nonbelieving society in general are founded on the moral values imparted by universal revelation and common grace. This does not mean, however, that Christians will impose on non-Christian society the distinctive values of God's special revelation.

DISCUSSION TOPICS

1. Does Scripture support the distinction between universal or common grace and particular or special grace? If so, what is the contribution of each? Which mode of grace is salvific?

2. Show from Old and New Testament Scriptures that God purposed to form a special people for himself.

3. Does the biblical record suggest that God sovereignly chose *individuals* to be saved, who collectively would form the new humanity? Consider data from both Old and New Testaments.

4. Does the New Testament make a distinction between an external, general call and an internal, special call to salvation? Discuss the nature of each.

5. From Scripture how would you relate the several doctrines of soteriology into a coherent whole? Indicate where the relationship between doctrines is logical and where it is chronological.

6. If sinners are incapable of choosing Christ because of holistic depravity and if unconditional election is true, is it hypocritical to preach the Gospel to every creature and to proclaim, "Whosoever will may come"?

See also the Review Questions and Ministry Projects on pages 501–2.

CHAPTER 2

THE SINNER'S CONVERSION AND REGENERATION

The Sinner's Conversion and Regeneration

THE PROBLEM:
WHAT IS THE NATURE
AND OUTCOME OF
CONVERSION AND
THE NEW BIRTH?

In this chapter we continue consideration of the application of the atoning work (vol. 2, chap. 7) of the resurrected Christ to sinners. In chapter 1 of this volume we saw that in eternity past God sovereignly chose out of the lot of fallen humanity some persons to be saved. Moreover, in historical time the Holy Spirit, through the message of the Gospel, effectually calls or draws elected individuals to Christ. We now take up those events that follow in the process of salvation, namely, individual conversion (belief, repentance, and faith) and regeneration (the new birth).

We investigate the biblical concept of repentance. What must a person forsake in order to become a Christian? Does insistence on repentance itself involve a works-righteousness that confounds grace? Additionally, what is the nature of saving faith? Is it primarily intellectual assent to revealed truths, or trust in a person, or a certain mode of existence? Does true faith rest on historically verifiable evidences, or is faith a commitment that transcends empirical

considerations? Furthermore, do all persons to some extent possess a faith that saves? Must saving faith be explicit, or can it be implicit, in the sense of a vague assent to the transcendent dimension of life? As a matter of practical ministry strategy, must a person confess Christ as Lord as well as Savior in order to become a Christian? Here we assess the contemporary so-called Savior-Lord debate.

We investigate also the relationship between repentance and faith. Does Scripture teach that one response precedes the other either logically or chronologically? Or are both part of the sinner's one act of turning to God from idols? Moreover, do repentance and faith lie within the capability of the pre-Christian, or are they in some significant sense enablements of God? On what basis can unconverted people bring forth the responses of repentance and faith?

We also consider the commonly discussed "born-again" phenomenon. What is involved in this experience? When a person is regenerated, is the fallen, sinful nature radically changed or even obliterated? At the new birth is a new metaphysical nature added? Can a person be born again more than once, as many Eastern teachers affirm? A further issue is whether God effects regeneration through human instrumentalities, such as baptism or membership in a Christian family or church. Moreover, is regeneration the work of God alone (monergism), or does the individual cooperate in the event (synergism)? Finally, we inquire into the relationship between conversion and regeneration. Do repentance and faith in some sense precede regeneration, or is regeneration necessary in order to enable depraved pre-Christians to repent and believe?

ALTERNATIVE INTERPRETATIONS IN THE CHURCH

The meaning of conversion and the new birth have been widely discussed throughout the church's history. A summary of the main interpretations of these soteriological doctrines follows.

Roman Catholic, Lutheran, and Anglo-Catholic Sacramentalism

Appealing to texts such as John 3:5 and Titus 3:5, authorities claim that God gives regenerating grace via the sacrament of baptism. Baptism confers cleansing of sins, union with Christ, and the infusion of sanctifying grace. In children baptismal regeneration generally turns on the faith of the sponsor, whereas in adults the good disposition of the recipient is necessary for baptism to be valid. The Roman Catholic McBrien asserts that "the Church has always taught that Baptism is necessary for salvation."[1] Romanism defines faith chiefly as intellectual assent to truths commended on ecclesiastical authority. Traditionally reason (especially in the laity) has limited capacity in the spiritual realm, hence the need for assent to the Magesterium's teaching. Moreover, in Catholicism the personal trust (*fiducia*) aspect of faith is secondary to mental assent (*assensus*). Later Roman Catholic thought distinguished between

"explicit faith" (personal assent to known truths) and "implicit faith" (trust in the church and its teachings without specific knowledge). In Roman Catholicism faith is equivalent to submission to the church and its teachings.

The apostolic fathers and apologists drifted toward ceremonialism by associating regeneration with baptism. Justin Martyr (d. 165) described baptism as "the washing that is for the remission of sins and unto regeneration."[2] Irenaeus (d. 200?), who marked the beginning of historic Catholicism, claimed that Naaman the leper's washing in the Jordan River (2 Kings 5) was a type of baptism. "We are made clean by means of the sacred water and the invocation of the Lord from our old transgressions, being spiritually regenerated as newborn babes."[3] According to Cyril of Jerusalem (d. 386), baptism is "a remission of offenses, a death to sin, a new spiritual birth, a chariot to heaven, the delight of paradise, a passport to the kingdom."[4] Only martyrs can be saved without baptism.

Augustine (d. 430) asserted that God's gift of effectual grace regenerates, creates faith, and works repentance. The Word of God applied to the water of baptism creates new spiritual life and unites to Christ. So Augustine flatly stated, "The sacrament of baptism is undoubtedly the sacrament of regeneration."[5] At the baptismal font ("the saving laver of regeneration")[6] the elect receive both the external sign (the water) and the spiritual reality (regeneration); the nonelect receive only the physical sign. Augustine held that at baptism infants die to original sin, adults to original sin and sins personally committed. Thus God through baptism "cleanses even the tiny infant, although itself unable as yet with the heart to believe unto righteousness and to make confession with the mouth unto salvation."[7] Unbaptized infants are lost and under the control of the Devil. In the case of elect infants, Augustine claimed that personal conversion will follow the regeneration effected by baptism. In the case of adults the candidate following conversion gladly receives (i.e., does not resist) the water of baptism. For Augustine, then, salvation consisted of both baptism and conversion. In baptism we die to sin and "live through being reborn at the [baptismal] font."[8]

Scholastic Catholicism solidified the idea that the sign of the sacrament accomplishes what it signifies. According to Thomas Aquinas (d. 1274), baptism effects spiritual generation; confirmation, spiritual growth; eucharist, spiritual nourishment; and penance and extreme unction, spiritual healing.[9] Assuming the recipient imposes no obstacle, baptism regenerates because administered by authority of the Roman church (the *ex opere operato* concept). Thus Thomas claimed that the visible sign of water imparts to the baptized infant invisible, regenerating grace. "Through baptism, which is a spiritual generation, not only are sins taken away . . . but also every guilt of sin. For this reason, baptism not only washes away the fault, but also absolves from all guilt."[10] In short, "baptism opens the gates of the heavenly kingdom to the baptized."[11] Where the sacrament was not available or when a person died prior to baptism, Thomas upheld the efficacy of the so-called baptism of desire: "Such a man can obtain salvation without actually being baptized, on account of his desire for Baptism, . . . whereby God . . . sanctifies man inwardly."[12] For simple folk who have not developed an explicit faith, implicit faith suffices for salvation.[13] Thomas also held that to *fides informis* (intellectual assent to the truth, James. 2:17) must be added for salvation *fides formata caritate* (faith that works by love, Gal. 5:6). Any act proceeding from human free will and directed to God is meritorious. Hence Thomas regarded faith as a meritorious act.[14]

Regeneration, which Catholicism confused with justification and sanctification, came to be viewed as a process whose outcome was not assured until the end. According to the Council of Trent (1545–63), regeneration commences at baptism: "If anyone . . . denies that the said merit of Jesus Christ is applied, both to adults and to infants, by the sacrament of baptism rightly administered in the form of the Church, let him be anathema" (Sess. V.3). "Even infants, who could not as yet commit any sin of themselves, are for this cause truly baptized for the remission of sins, that in them that may be cleansed away by regeneration, which they have contracted by generation" (Sess. V.4). In the Tridentine scheme infants are baptized in the faith of the church. In the case of adults, penitence for sins and faith augmented by hope and love precede baptism (Sess. VI.6). "For faith, unless hope and charity be added thereto, neither unites man perfectly with Christ, nor makes him a living member of his body" (Sess. VI.7).

The Second Vatican Council (1962–65) held that for Roman Catholics Christ presented the necessity of faith and baptism for salvation. But given its panentheistic worldview—in which all humankind is oriented to the life of God—it asserts that all people are saved by the "baptism of desire." The baptism of desire is equivalent to the nonspecific implicit faith that all human beings possess. The Council affirmed:

> Those who, through no fault of their own, do not know the Gospel of Christ or his Church, but who nevertheless seek God with a sincere heart, and, moved by grace, try in their actions to do his will as they know it through the dictates of their conscience—those too may achieve eternal salvation. Nor shall divine providence deny the assistance necessary for

salvation to those who, without any fault of theirs have not yet arrived at an explicit knowledge of God, and who, not without grace, strive to lead a good life.[15]

Gregory Baum similarly commented, "One may seriously wonder whether baptism of desire is not the way of salvation for the great majority of men in this world, chosen to be saved."[16] In the same vein McBrien writes, "Everybody does not strictly 'need' baptism to become a child of God and an heir of heaven. Every human person, by reason of birth and God's universal offer of grace, is already called to be a child of God and an heir of heaven."[17] What, then, is the saving relevance of the sacraments? McBrien answers that "the sacraments signify, celebrate, and effect what God is, in a sense, doing everywhere and for all."[18]

While rejecting the synergistic idea of human cooperation in salvation via meritorious works, Luther (d. 1546) retained the Catholic doctrine of baptismal regeneration. God's usual way of regenerating a life is at the baptismal font. Thus baptism remits sins, justifies, imparts the Spirit, and recreates in the divine image. Luther wrote that God "himself calls it [baptism] a new birth by which we are . . . loosed from sin, death, and hell, and become children of life, heirs of all the gifts of God, God's own children, and brethren of Christ."[19] In the customary infant baptism, regeneration occurs at the moment the Word of God unites with the sign (water) and as the infant responds to the Gospel with simple faith. Baptism does not regenerate simply because performed (the old Catholic *ex opere operato* concept); for Luther, baptism without faith is useless. Rather, the infant truly believes the word of the Gospel presented in the sacrament. "In baptism children themselves believe and have faith of their own. God works this within them through the intercession of the sponsors who bring the child to the font in the faith of the Christian Church."[20] Upon coming of age children must ratify their new birth by repentance, mature faith, and obedience. In rare cases of adult baptism, the individual is made new by the word received in faith (*regeneratio prima*) and by strengthening of the new life through baptism (*regeneratio secunda,* or *renovatio*).

In *The Small Catechism* (1529) Luther wrote, "Baptism is not merely water, but it is water used according to God's command and connected with God's Word" (IV). To the question, "How can water produce such great effects?" Luther responded, "It is not the water that produces these effects, but the Word of God connected with the water, and our faith which relies on the Word of God connected with the water. . . . When connected with the Word of God [the water] is a Baptism, that is, a gracious water of life and a washing of regeneration in the Holy Spirit" (IV).

Post-Reformation Lutheranism upheld Luther's view of baptismal regeneration. The statement of the Lutheran theologian David Hollaz (d. 1713) is typical: "The intellect of infants in regeneration is imbued with a saving knowledge of God by the Holy Spirit in Baptism, and their will is endowed with confidence in Christ."[21] Dietrich Bonhoeffer also stated that baptism incorporates one into the body of Christ. "In baptism man becomes Christ's own possession. . . . From that moment he belongs to Jesus Christ. He is wrestled from the dominion of the world, and passes into the ownership of Christ."[22]

The Church of England officially teaches the regeneration of infants via baptism. Thus The Thirty-nine Articles (American revision, 1801) states: "Baptism is . . . a sign of Regeneration or New-Birth, whereby, as by an instrument, they that receive Baptism rightly are grafted into the Church; the promises of the forgiveness of sin, and of our adoption to be the sons of God by the Holy Ghost, are visibly signed and sealed" (art. XXVII). As prescribed by *The Book of Common Prayer*, prior to baptism the priest prays, "Give thy Holy Spirit to this child, that he may be born again, and be made an heir of everlasting salvation." Following baptism, the priest gives thanks that God was pleased "to regenerate this infant with thy Holy Spirit, to receive him for thy own child, and to incorporate him into thy holy Church."[23]

The Covenant Reformed View

This view, although rejecting the high sacramentalism of Roman Catholicism and Lutheranism, yet posits a close connection between baptism and regeneration. Some advocates of covenant theology insist that infants of believing parents are baptized not to become regenerated but because in some important sense they already possess the seeds of faith and regeneration. That is, the sacrament of baptism is a sign or promise of the saving work God is doing in the elect, including infants born into a Christian family. Accordingly, this tradition holds that the unconscious divine work of regeneration precedes the conscious human responses of faith and repentance.

John Calvin (d. 1564), a precursor of covenant theology, viewed regeneration broadly as the whole process of spiritual vivification, inclusive of the new birth, conversion, and sanctification. Calvin held that the Spirit's work of regeneration often commences at the beginning of life in the womb, as illustrated by the yet-unborn John the Baptist (Luke 1:15). Whether in the womb or in earliest infancy, God can give regenerating grace to his elect by the Spirit's inner illumination apart from the preached Word.[24] According to Calvin, Christ instituted baptism as an external sign of a person's election within the covenant community and of future faith and repentance. Calvin posited an anagogic relationship between Old Testament circumcision and New Testament baptism. Although differing in external details, both signify spiritual regeneration. Thus in the case of infants of believing parents (the usual subjects of baptism), the sacrament signifies forgiveness of sins, union with Christ, and Spirit regeneration. Calvin insisted that infants are not capable of faith and repentance, but as members of the covenant family they are able to receive the seed of regeneration and sanctification.[25] In response to the question, What does baptism signify? Calvin responded, "It has two parts. There is remission of sins; and then spiritual regeneration is symbolized by it (Eph. 5:26; Rom. 6:4)."[26] For Calvin, baptism "is like a sealed document to confirm to us that all our sins are so abolished, remitted, and effaced that they can never come to his sight, be recalled, or charged against us."[27] Elect infants who come to maturity will exhibit the fruit of their baptism (i.e., their election, forgiveness, regeneration, and union with Christ) by the personal responses of faith and repentance.

Calvin asserted that faith, which consists of knowledge of the Gospel, persuasion of its truth and trust in Christ, is the conscious human response to the divine work of regeneration. Repentance, defined as mortification of the old nature (the flesh) and quickening of the new nature (the spirit) unto holiness, is born of faith. Repentance, or living in the reality of the new nature, is a process that continues throughout the Christian's life. Calvin understood by repentance what later divines would call sanctification. For Calvin, both faith and repentance are free gifts of the sovereign God.

According to The Westminster Confession of Faith (1647), baptism is "a sign and seal of the covenant of grace, of his ingrafting into Christ, of regeneration, of remission of sins, and of his giving up unto God, through Jesus Christ, to walk in newness of life" (ch. XXVIII.1). Not only may adult believers be baptized, "but also the infants of one or both believing parents are to be baptized" (ch. XXVIII.4). In chapter XXVIII.5 the Confession added that it is possible to be regenerated without being baptized, and that not all those baptized are regenerated.

W. G. T. Shedd (d. 1894) insisted that regeneration, the genesis of spiritual life, precedes conversion, the effect of spiritual life. Persons are not regenerated because they first believe and repent; rather they believe and repent because they are first regenerated. "The Holy Ghost is not given as a converting and a sanctifying Spirit, until he has been given as a regenerating Spirit."[28] Moreover, faith must precede repentance, for the existence of repentance prior to faith would involve an impossible legalism. Shedd added that infant regeneration is taught *scripturally* in Luke 1:15; 18:15–16; Acts 2:39; and 1 Corinthians 7:14 and *symbolically* via Old Testament circumcision and New Testament infant baptism. In an adult, "regeneration immediately exhibits its fruit in the converting acts of faith and repentance. In the case of infant regeneration, there is an interval of time between regeneration and conversion."[29] Added Shedd: "The regenerate infant believes and repents when his faculties will admit of the exercise and manifestation of faith and repentance. In this . . . instance, regeneration is *potential* or *latent* faith and repentance."[30]

Virtually all Reformed covenant theologians uphold the logical priority of regeneration to conversion (faith and repentance). John Murray (d. 1975) typically asserted, "Without regeneration it is morally and spiritually impos-sible for a person to believe in Christ, but when a person is regenerated it is morally and spiritually impossible for that person not to believe."[31] Louis Berkhof boldly added, "A conversion that is not rooted in regeneration is no true conversion."[32]

The Arminian Tradition

The usual order of elements in the Arminian tradition is prevenient grace, repentance, faith, the new birth, and continued obedience. Primarily *human* works, *repentance* is defined as a voluntary separation from sin and *faith* as intellectual assent to the truth and personal trust in God. Regeneration—viewed by some Arminians as a change of moral purpose, but by many as a change of nature from sin to holiness—occurs through a synergism of human willing and divine working. God regenerates when the pre-Christian believes by a free act of the will, which involves ceasing to resist the moral influence of the truth presented to persons universally. Since divine grace can be resisted, ultimately it is the pre-Christian's will that determines the outcome. The saved are those who choose to cooperate with the (resistible) grace of God; the unsaved are those who fail to cooperate. Some Arminians view regeneration as inclusive of everything from conversion to sanctification, or what the Wesleyan-holiness tradition calls the first and second works of grace. The movements of repentance, faith, and regeneration are enabled by universal prevenient grace, which proponents claim frees sinners spiritually to respond to the Gospel. "This grace will shepherd one to repentance, regeneration, entire sanctification, and final perseverance if not resisted somewhere along the way."[33] Most Arminians affirm assurance of present acceptance by God but deny assurance of one's final destiny, since regenerating grace may be lost.

John Wesley (d. 1791) subscribed to the doctrines of original sin and depravity. The unregenerate are morally and spiritually corrupted, lacking knowledge of and love for God. As indicated in the previous chapter, this depraved condition is only hypothetical, since the "preventing grace" that flows from the Cross reverses the debilitating effects of original sin from birth onward. "Preventing grace [includes] the first wish to please God, the first dawn of light concerning his will, and the first slight transient conviction of having sinned against him. All these imply some tendency toward life; some degree of salvation."[34] Pre-Christians cooperate with this prevenient grace to work out their own salvation (Phil. 2:12), i.e., to repent of sin and believe in Christ. Thus for Wesley the enlightened human will is one of the causes of the new life breathed into the soul at regeneration. Wesley added that renewal in the image of God (the new birth) can be lost by willful sin. Thus the assurance of forgiveness of sins extends no further than the present moment.

John Fletcher (d. 1785), the first Wesleyan systematic theologian, opposed the notion that saving faith is a sovereign gift of God. Like Wesley, he argued that universal prevenient grace (John 1:9; Titus 2:11) frees the human will to believe aspects of the Gospel presented to it. Wrote Fletcher, "We have all *some* gracious power to believe *some* saving truth."[35] As unbelievers have the power of sight in the physical realm, so they have the power of faith in the spiritual realm. Using the analogy of a ladder, Fletcher explained the possibility of an ascent of faith on the part of all pre-Christians, provided that the divine influences are not resisted. "If the foot of the ladder is upon the earth, in the very nature of things the lowest step is within their reach, and by laying hold on it they may go on 'from faith to faith,' till they stand firm even in the Christian faith."[36] According to Fletcher, sinners cooperate with God in the work of salvation. Human free will and divine grace exist in a synergistic relation to bring about the new birth, which consists of justification and sanctification.

Charles Finney (d. 1875) rejected the Reformed tenet that regeneration is wholly a work of God in which the human subject is passive (monergism). He insisted that both God and sinners are active in regeneration (synergism). The Spirit presents God's truth to the soul, and sinners change the disposition of their hearts and turn themselves to God. In this process, faith "is the will's closing in with the truths of the Gospel."[37] His view approximating Pelagianism, Finney defined regeneration as a change in the attitude of the will, a change of moral character, or setting a new spiritual direction. "Regeneration consists in the sinner changing his ultimate choice, intention, preference; or in changing from selfishness to love or benevolence."[38] Regeneration, so defined, is synonymous with conversion. Finney's view of pre-Christians actively engaged in regeneration flows from his rejection of human depravity. Non-Christians possess a natural ability to choose God, alter their fundamental affections and obey all God's commands. Finney made the following observation about the duty of preachers: "Ministers should . . . aim at, and expect the regeneration of sinners, upon the spot, and before they leave the house of God."[39]

The Ethical View of Pelagians and Liberals

As explained in volume 2, chapter 4, Pelagians and liberals repudiate original sin and depravity and so envisage little need for radical, spiritual rebirth. They maintain that each person born into the world is a child of God indwelt by the divine principle. Pelagians and liberals identify regeneration as the process of ethical development stimulated by the ideals of Jesus. Liberal authorities at the turn of the twentieth century focused on social regeneration—i.e., the collective renewal of humanity in the kingdom of God. Liberals both old and new identify regeneration as a process of self-improvement achieved by self-effort and the example of Christ.

Pelagius (d. 419) claimed that every person born into the world is free from the taint of inherited sin. Thus he opposed the early church practice of infant baptism for the remission of sins. Many persons sin when, following the example of Adam, they choose to violate the law of God. According to Pelagius, salvation occurs as persons forsake sins and obey the divine law. The stimulus for this change comes from the illuminating power of the truth upon the mind and from the example of Jesus. Faith lies within the free will of each person. The soteriological agenda of Pelagius, then, was not supernatural regeneration but personal, moral reformation. Pelagius "made God only a spectator in the drama of human redemption."[40]

Walter Rauschenbusch (d. 1918) rejected original sin and depravity and claimed that by birth men and women fundamentally are children of God. Since sin is a social force (i.e., denial of human fraternity), so also is salvation. Thus Rauschenbusch envisaged "the salvation of the collective life of humanity, the fulfillment of the theocratic hope."[41] Faith is akin to hope—the hope of a just and fraternal social order. And regeneration is the gradual transformation of the social order—namely, "the spread of the spirit of Christ in the political, industrial, social, scientific, and artistic life of humanity."[42]

Norman Pittenger, who also embraced process motifs, opposed the notion of "individual salvation," which he called "a parody of genuine Christian faith and practice."[43] Proceeding from a Pelagian perspective, Pittenger asserted that social obstacles must be removed so that benign human nature may mature unimpeded. He wrote, "The aim is to secure such an ordering of social existence, in its every aspect, as shall make this maturing possible. This is why slavery, deprivation, rejection because of race or color or sexual orientation or family background or situation, as well as anything else which interferes with healthy and sound growth, is to be condemned."[44]

The literature of liberation theology contains few references to original sin, individual conversion, or regeneration. Advocates allege that people are spoiled by political, economic, racial, and sexual oppression born of the capitalist system. Thus salvation, or the recovery of human wholeness, unfolds as dehumanizing injustices are swept away by social revolution (sometimes violent). Liberationists allege that following the overthrow of oppressive social structures a new and freed humanity will emerge in the kingdom of God, and so God's universal salvific will is realized. Here liberationists follow the Hegelians in viewing history as the process whereby humans free the divinity within and pursue the utopian goal. Specifically, liberationists identify conversion collectively as the process of revolutionary social transformation. Regeneration is the creation of a more humane and humanizing society. Thus Gutièrrez affirms, "By working, transforming the world, breaking out of servitude, building a just society, and assuming his destiny, man forges himself."[45] Leonardo and Clodovis Boff insist that the goal of liberation theology is "a fuller and more humane society, freed and liberated, a society of the freed."[46] According to the radical black theologian James Cone, salvation involves the black Christ liberating oppressed blacks from the shackles of white racism. Continues Cone: "Faith is the response of the community to God's act of liberation. It means saying yes to God and no to oppressors."[47]

From a panentheistic worldview (in which the world is seen as a part of God), process theology asserts that the divine Eros provides the "lure" or "initial aim" to all persons for their maximal fulfillment. Thus Ford asserts, "Everywhere God's creative urging toward the establishment of increased levels of intensity is present, but only with intelligent life can there be any awareness of this."[48] The presentation of novel initial aims can come through Jesus, Plato, the Buddha, or other gurus or philosophers. According to process thinkers, "salvation" occurs when intelligent creatures respond positively to the novel initial aims God presents at every moment. Reflecting on John 3:3, Ford makes the following observation about the new birth: "In terms of the perishing occasions of our temporal life, we are being born anew and from above as we receive novel initial aims from God originating our subjectivity from moment to moment."[49] According to Pittenger, human response to the divine lure "ennobles and enriches, vitalizes and makes new."[50] Since the novel initial aims offered by the cosmic Lover are persuasive and not coercive, regeneration is self-salvation. So Pittenger asserted that as persons respond to the divine lure constantly presented, we "make ourselves."[51] Whiteheadians define faith as the human *perception* of the initial aims presented by God, involving a sense of novelty, refreshment, and love. Thus faith is an affective and experiential reality and not intellectual assent to formal doctrines. "Faith," argue Cobb and Griffin, "is fundamentally a mode of existence."[52] All people possess varying degrees of "saving" faith.

Existentialist Authorities

Existentialist theologians reverse the classical ordering to assert that existence precedes essence. Humans are nothing until they freely define themselves by responsible decisions and actions. Judging the biblical cosmology mythological, proponents focus not on life hereafter but on concrete human existence here and now. They insist that faith has little to do with formal beliefs and everything to do with passionate commitment. Regeneration, or the new birth, involves exchanging the new self for the old self. Authentic existence is realized through enhanced self-understanding of personal existence mediated through the mythical kerygma.

Against the abstract system of Hegel and the complacent orthodoxy of Danish Lutheranism, Kierkegaard (d. 1855) stressed the personal, inward, and passionate dimension of faith and salvation. Seeing few indications of vital faith in Danish Lutherans who had been baptized in the church, Kierkegaard concluded that "baptism cannot be the decisive factor with respect to becoming a Christian."[53] Rather, a person becomes a Christian as the human "I" existentially engages the divine "Thou" through a radical decision of faith. The faith Kierkegaard envisaged involves a risk or a "leap" of spiritual passion that contravenes rational arguments and historical evidences. He held that if persons could grasp the Gospel objectively, they would not have to believe. For Kierkegaard the proper object of faith is the rationally absurd. "Faith is the objective uncertainty due to the repulsion of the absurd held fast by the passion of inwardness, which in this instance is intensified to the utmost degree."[54] In this God-inspired act of

81

inner passion and objective uncertainty the individual in fear and trembling decisively engages the absolute Paradox (God become a man). By so doing the person moves from a state of nonbeing to being, which is to say, he or she becomes a new creature.

According to Paul Tillich (d. 1965), the fundamental human problem is not disobedience or rebellion but estrangement from the Ground of Being, from other beings, and from oneself. This estrangement or split did not result from a historical fall (Tillich viewed the Edenic drama as "myth"), but is the necessary concomitant of a created world as such. Sin, in other words, is an existential category rather than a moral one. The results of this universal estrangement are unbelief, *hybris* (pride), concupiscence, and psychological anxiety.

Salvation, for Tillich, is the conquering of anxiety and estrangement through transformation by New Being, that is, by Christ-power, *eros*-urge, or the power of creative transformation. According to Tillich, New Being may be mediated through Jesus or other charismatic personalities. Salvation, healing, or reintegration is by faith. Faith in the God above the God of theism is the state of being ultimately concerned. Tillich did not specify the *object* of faith, since faith transcends the subject-object relation. One has faith when he is "ultimately concerned about his state of estrangement and about the possibility of reunion with the ground and aim of his being."[55] Regeneration represents the initial entry into this new reality, namely, the unification of what was estranged. Thus "regeneration is the state of having been drawn into the new reality manifest in Jesus as the Christ."[56] Who, according to Tillich, will be saved? Everyone and everything! "The reunion with the eternal from which we come, from which we are separated, to which we shall return,

is promised to everything that is. We are saved not as individuals, but in unity with all others and with the universe."[57] Hamilton summed up Tillich's view in this manner: "Salvation is participation in a power-reality which is suprafactual."[58]

Bultmann (d. 1976) insisted that biblical teaching about a historical Fall in Eden, blood atonement for sins via the Cross, and Jesus' bodily resurrection are myths. He argued that one must demythologize the mythical husk to get at the existential kernel of Christian reality. God addresses persons through the preached word about the human prophet Jesus (the *kerygma*), thereby extending the possibility of salvation. For Bultmann salvation is not a once-for-all divine declaration of innocence but the transition from inauthentic to authentic existence. The former involves attachment to objective, historical facts and the quest for self-autonomy and worldly security. The latter involves the inner realities of enhanced self-understanding, personal freedom, and openness to the future. Thus salvation, or the new birth, is "an act of God through which man becomes capable of self-commitment, capable of faith and love, of his authentic life."[59] Faith, the instrument of this change, is not assent to formal doctrines but an act or a decision. Thus faith "is neither more nor less than the *decision . . . against the world* for God."[60] Bultmann denied the need for personal confession of sins. "It is an error to think that belief in the grace of God requires a sense of sin or a confession of sin, in the sense that a man must admit to himself how much or how often and grievously he has sinned and continually is sinning. . . . He is to consider the reason for his being, and to ask himself whence his life comes."[61]

Evangelicals in the Reformed Tradition

Most Reformed evangelicals hold that all responsible people, afflicted with inherited sin and depravity, must receive a new spiritual nature and be united with Christ to receive eternal life. Authorities in the tradition uphold the monergism of regeneration; the new birth is entirely the work of the sovereign God. The Spirit regenerates not on the basis of the faith of godly sponsors, church membership, or participation in the sacraments. Rather, God graciously grants new spiritual life by virtue of the individual's conscious decision to repent of sins and appropriate the provisions of Christ's atonement. Given the reality of holistic depravity, repentance and faith are viewed as gifts of God's grace. Some authorities see regeneration as occurring logically before conversion. Others identify the first wish to please God as the result of effectual calling and so place conversion prior to regeneration in the *ordo salutis*.

George Whitefield (d. 1770), the Calvinistic Methodist, protested the nominal Christianity of his day that sought salvation in baptism or church membership. In his sermon "The Nature and Necessity of our New Birth in Christ Jesus," which played a crucial role in the evangelical awakening in England, Whitefield wrote, "It [is] too plain, beyond all contradiction, that comparatively but few of those who are 'born of water' are 'born of the Spirit' likewise; or, to use another scriptural way of speaking, many are baptized with water which were never, effectually at least, baptized with the Holy Ghost."[62] For Whitefield, regeneration is that instantaneous creation wrought on the heart and soul by the Holy Spirit producing new inclinations, desires, and habits. As God spiritually quickens people dead in sins, they become partakers of the divine nature and are renewed in the image of God. He added that in the new birth "our souls, though still the same as to essence, yet are so purged, purified and cleansed from their natural dross, filth and leprosy, by the blessed influence of the Holy Spirit that they may properly be said to be made anew."[63] This dramatic change known as the new birth results from a person's conscious and deliberate act of repentance and faith. Yet by virtue of total depravity the human responses of repentance and faith must be gifts of God's grace. Thus Whitefield declared that we sinners could not come to God until "God . . . put his faith in us."[64]

C. H. Spurgeon (d. 1892) argued against the view that baptism regenerates. In his sermon "Baptismal Regeneration," he wrote, "Facts all show that whatever good there may be in baptism, it certainly does not make a man 'a member of Christ, the child of God, and an inheritor of the kingdom of heaven,' or else many thieves, whoremongers, drunkards, fornicators, and murderers are members of Christ."[65] Moreover, he inveighed against the view that birth in a Christian family regenerates: "There can be no such thing as sponsorship in receiving Christ or in faith. If you are an unbeliever, your father and your mother may be the most eminent saints, but this faith does not overlap and cover your unbelief. You must believe for yourself."[66] Spurgeon held that each person must be born again by the Spirit of God. Regeneration involves the spiritual renovation of one's entire being, the implantation of the divine life, and mystical union with Christ.[67] It is "a change of the entire nature from top to bottom in all senses and respects."[68] Saving faith involves knowledge of the Gospel, assent to its truths, and personal trust in Christ as sin-bearer. Repentance involves sorrow for transgressions and a forsaking of all known sins. As the fruits of regeneration, both faith and repentance are gifts of divine grace.

A. H. Strong (d. 1921) viewed regeneration and conversion as chronologically simultaneous events, although logically the former precedes the latter.

"Regeneration, or the new birth, is the divine side of that change of heart which, viewed from the human side, we call conversion. It is God turning the soul to himself—conversion being the soul's turning itself to God, of which God's turning it is both the accompaniment and cause."[69] Conversion, consisting of repentance and faith, is the human act that attests the prior regenerating work of the Spirit. According to Strong, the resuscitation of Lazarus in John 11 illustrates the relationship between the new birth and conversion. God made Lazarus alive; in this event his soul was passive. But Lazarus came forth from the tomb; in this his soul was active. Strong continued by saying that conversion, the human side of regeneration, consists of repentance and faith. *Repentance* signifies the sinner's determination to turn from all known sin. It involves an intellectual element—recognition of sin, an emotional element—sorrow for sin, and a voluntary element—abandonment of sin. *Faith* connotes the sinner's determination to turn to Christ. It too involves an intellectual element—knowledge of the gospel, an emotional element—feeling the sufficiency of Christ's grace, and a voluntary element—trusting Christ as Savior and Lord.

Millard J. Erickson's position is similar to Strong's, with the exception that conversion logically precedes regeneration. Repentance, the negative side of conversion, consists of godly sorrow for sin plus the determination to forsake sin. Faith, the positive aspect of conversion, consists of assent to gospel truths together with trust in the person of Christ. Temporally, conversion and regeneration occur simultaneously, but logically repentance and faith represent the condition for God's work of regeneration. Erickson attributes the enablement to repent and believe not to regeneration but to the Spirit's effectual calling:

In the case of the elect God works intensively through a special calling so that they do respond in repentance and faith. As a result of this conversion, God regenerates them. The special calling . . . is not the complete transformation which constitutes regeneration, but it does render the conversion of the individual both possible and certain. Thus the logical order of the initial aspects of salvation is special calling—conversion—regeneration.[70]

Against competing hypotheses, Erickson insists that regeneration is not a process, but an instantaneous work wrought in the soul by the Holy Spirit as God applies salvation to elect believers.

Other helpful evangelical discussions on conversion and regeneration include works by H. D. McDonald,[71] David Wells,[72] and Peter Toon.[73]

BIBLICAL TEACHING

In this section we gather the relevant biblical evidence by which to test any historical or contemporary view of conversion and regeneration.

The Pentateuch

Concerning the offspring of Adam and Eve, Genesis 4:4–5 states that "The Lord looked with favor on Abel and his offering, but on Cain and his offering he did not look with favor." Outwardly the two brothers performed similar works; both presented to the Lord offerings from the firstfruits of their respective occupations. God was pleased with Abel's offering but not with Cain's because the former, unlike the latter, brought his gift with an attitude of trust in God. Hence the inspired writer of Hebrews commented, "By faith Abel offered God a better sacrifice than Cain did. By faith he was commended as a righteous man, when

God spoke well of his offerings" (Heb. 11:4).

Abram evidenced a more specific faith in Yahweh. In Genesis 12:1–3 we read that the Lord called Abram and promised him a posterity and a land (cf., e.g., Gen. 13:14–17; 15:4–5). The record indicates that Abram obediently moved from Haran to Canaan, built an altar, and called on the name of the Lord. Later God renewed the covenant and promised Abram and Sarah a son in their old age (Gen. 15:4). Moses recorded Abraham's response to God's promise as follows: "Abram believed [Hiphil of 'āman] the LORD, and he credited it to him as righteousness" (Gen. 15:6). The patriarch's faith was both propositional and personal; he believed God's word (cf. Heb. 11:8–12, 17–19) and committed his soul to the God who had revealed himself. The New Testament upholds Abraham as the paradigm of the faith that saves (Rom. 4:16–22; Gal. 3:7). From Genesis 15:6 and 17:10–14 we note that the patriarch was justified fourteen years before he was circumcised. The order of events in Abraham's life was faith, justification, then circumcision (cf. Rom. 4:9–11).

Genesis 15:6 is the first biblical citation of the verb "believe." The Qal form of 'āman means "nourish," "support," or "rear," whereas the Niphal connotes "be established" or "be faithful" (2 Sam. 7:16; 1 Chron. 17:23). The Hiphil signifies "believe in" or "trust" (e.g., Exod. 14:31; Num. 14:11; Deut. 9:23; Ps. 106:12). The Septuagint translates the Hiphil of 'āman by the Greek verb pisteuō. The Hiphil of 'āman with ki signifies belief in certain facts, whereas with the preposition be it connotes trust in a person or promise. The noun "faith" is rare in the Old Testament. The primary meaning of 'emûnāh is "faithfulness" or "loyalty." Yet according to Romans 1:17 and Galatians 3:11, Paul understood 'emûnāh in Habakkuk 2:4 as the "faith" that justifies and saves (ASV, RSV, NIV).

In the Pentateuch Yahweh issued repeated warnings against profaning the covenant he made with Israel. Yet the loving God also identified the path of return that makes amends for willful covenant violations. Thus after sinning, Israel had to acknowledge their "treachery" and "hostility" (Lev. 26:40b), confess it to the Lord (v. 40a), and humbly repent of all known offenses (v. 41b). After Israel turned to the Lord, he would renew his covenant and bless them (v. 42). Moses commended the need for repentance via the metaphor, to "circumcise" (mûl) the heart (v. 41; cf. Deut. 10:16; 30:6; Jer. 4:4). Whereas physical circumcision represented the external sign of membership in the covenant community, spiritual circumcision signified regeneration or "the spiritual life God creates in his people" (cf. Rom. 2:28–29; 4:9–12; Col. 2:11).[74] Repentance, moreover, is the theme of Deuteronomy 30. Moses commanded Israel to "return [Qal of šûb] to the LORD your God and obey him with all your heart and with all your soul" (v. 2). According to verse 6, circumcision of the heart is a work of God himself. "God will transform the wills of his repentant people, bringing them once again in line with the covenant ideals."[75]

The common Hebrew word for conversion or repentance is the verb šûb, which occurs more than 1,050 times. Its basic meaning is to "turn" or "return" in a physical sense (Gen. 18:33; Lev. 22:13). The primary theological meaning, however, is to turn to God in repentance. The verb bears this meaning some 130 times in the Qal form (Deut. 4:30; 30:2; Isa. 19:22) and eleven times in the Hiphil (Neh. 9:26; Ezek. 14:6; 18:32). The Scriptures represent šûb some seventy-five times as a human act, but several times as a sovereign work of God (e.g., Jer. 31:18; Lam.

1:13; 5:21). In its theological sense, *šûb* "includes repudiation of all sin and affirmation of God's total will for one's life."[76] The Septuagint translates *šûb* by the Greek verb *epistrephō*.

The Old Testament incident of the brazen serpent attested the reality of saving faith. God commanded Moses to place a bronze snake on a pole so that "when anyone was bitten by a snake and looked at the bronze snake, he lived" (Num. 21:9). The serpent fixed to the pole symbolized Christ, who took the form of a man and was cursed for us. For the healing to occur, no work was involved; a person simply looked in faith and lived (cf. John 3:14–15). Faith is inherent in the concept of "the fear" (*yir'āh*) of God (Gen. 20:11) or in the command to "fear" (*yārē'*) the Lord (Deut. 5:29; 6:2; 10:12). Fear on the part of a saint involved trust, awe, reverence, and righteous living. In this sense God is "the Fear [*paḥad*] of Isaac" (Gen. 31:42).

The Historical Books

A prominent theme in these writings is Israel's repeated spiritual defection from Yahweh and consequent chastisement. The Lord faithfully raised up leaders to summon the covenant people to repentance. Toward the end of his life Joshua led Israel in a renewal of the covenant with Yahweh. Central to this event was a call to repentance: "Throw away the foreign gods that are among you and yield your hearts to the Lord, the God of Israel" (Josh. 24:23). Later, amidst widespread idolatry, Samuel urged Israel to repent: "If you are returning [Qal of *šûb*] to the Lord with all your hearts, then rid yourselves of the foreign gods and the Ashtoreths and commit yourselves to the Lord and serve him only" (1 Sam. 7:3). In addition to rejection of idols and a return to the Lord, repentance involved mourning, fasting, and prayer (v. 6). In his prayer of temple dedication Solomon anticipated Israel's idolatry and prescribed the path of repentance (1 Kings 8:33–50). The repentant soul must "have a change of heart" (v. 47a), confess wrongdoing (v. 47b), pray and make supplication (v. 33), turn from known wickedness (v. 35), and return to the Lord with one's entire being (v. 48). Then Yahweh would hear from heaven and forgive their sins (vv. 49–50). The verb *šûb* ("turn" in repentance) occurs six times in Solomon's prayer. The Lord set forth the essence of repentance in 2 Chronicles 7:14: "If my people, who are called by my name, will humble themselves and pray and seek my face and turn [*šûb*] from their wicked ways, then will I hear from heaven and will forgive their sin and will heal their land."

The literature also records that righteous persons exercised faith in Yahweh. Second Kings 18:5 states that "Hezekiah trusted in the Lord, the God of Israel." The verb *bāṭaḥ* occurs nine times in 2 Kings 18–19 alone. Frequently used with *be* ("in") or *'al* (upon), *bāṭaḥ* signifies to "confide in," "lean upon," or "trust." The verb connotes confident reliance upon God and the sense of attendant well-being. See also 1 Chronicles 5:20. The Hiphil of *'āman* ("believe in," "have faith in," or "trust") occurs in 2 Kings 17:14 and 2 Chronicles 20:20.

First Samuel 10:9 suggests a dynamic work of the Spirit upon the heart of Saul: "God changed [*hāpak*, transitive, to "bend"] Saul's heart" (cf. v. 6). Although Saul did not fully obey God and acted wickedly at times, it appears that he had a genuine spiritual experience with the Lord (cf. 1 Sam. 28:9). Thus A. R. S. Kennedy commented: "Saul's is the first conversion recorded in sacred Scripture."[77]

Poetry and Wisdom

According to Proverbs 28:13 (cf. Ps. 32:3–5) repentance begins with confession of known sins followed by forsaking them: "He who conceals his sins does not prosper, but whoever confesses and renounces them finds mercy." The volitional element of repentance is present in the verb *šûb*. Thus Eliphaz replied to Job: "If you return [Qal of *šûb*] to the Almighty, you will be restored" (Job 22:23; cf. 36:10). The emotional element of repentance occurs in the verb *nāḥam,* to "be sorry," "regret," "repent"—where the root idea means to breathe deeply. After gaining a fuller knowledge of God and himself, Job exclaimed: "Therefore I despise myself and repent [Niphal of *nāḥam*] in dust and ashes" (Job 42:6; cf. Jer. 31:19). Here Job expressed regret or sorrow for the careless words he spoke to God (cf. 40:4–5). The literature suggests, however, that the initiative in conversion or repentance lies with God. Thus the psalmist uttered the petition: "Restore [Qal of *šûb*] us again, O God our Savior" (Ps. 85:4; cf. 80:3–7). And in verse 6 he inquired of the Lord: "Will you not revive us again, that your people may rejoice in you?" The psalmist's desire was that God's people would turn to him rather than "return [Qal of *šûb*] to folly" (v. 8).

In the Psalms faith is expressed by *bāṭah,* a verb that occurs fifty times in Israel's hymnbook. David said to the Lord: "I trust in your unfailing love; my heart rejoices in your salvation" (Ps. 13:5; cf. 22:4; 26:1; 33:21). And Solomon wrote: "Trust [Qal of *bāṭah*] in the LORD with all your heart and lean not on your own understanding" (Prov. 3:5; cf. 16:20; 28:25; 29:25). The fear of God is a common theme in the poetic and wisdom literature (e.g., Job 6:14; Ps. 86:11; 112:1; Prov. 3:7; Eccles. 3:14; 7:18). As noted above, the fear of God connotes faith, awe, and reverence for the Lord.

Psalm 51, a penitential psalm David composed after his sin with Bathsheba, outlines God's pattern of repentance: (1) David expressed *awareness of his sins* (vv. 1–3). He refused to face up to his sins until the prophet Nathan's charge pricked his conscience. (2) He offered heart-felt *confession of sins* (vv. 4–5). He acknowledged to the Lord both the specific sins of which he was guilty (vv. 3–4) and his inherently sinful condition (v. 5). (3) David showed a true *attitude of contrition,* reflected by his mention of "a broken spirit" and "a broken and contrite heart" (v. 17). (4) He uttered a *prayer for pardon of sins* (vv. 7–9), beseeching God to "cleanse" and "wash" him and to "blot out" all his iniquities. (5) David sought profound *inner renewal* (vv. 10–12). So he prayed, "Create in me a pure heart, O God, and renew a steadfast spirit within me" (v. 10). The verb *bārā'* ("create," cf. Gen. 1:1, 21, 27) suggests that the radical change of heart is God's work alone (cf. Ezek. 11:19; 36:26). Finally (6) David experienced the joy that comes from deliverance from sin and its consequences (v. 12).

The Prophetic Literature

The theme of repentance, expressed by *šûb,* is one of the dominant motifs in the prophets (e.g., Isa. 31:6; 44:22; Ezek. 18:30, 32; Hos. 3:5; Zech. 1:3), especially in Jeremiah (e.g., Jer. 3:14; 18:11; 25:5; 26:3; 35:15; 36:3). Yahweh declared to his people through Isaiah: "In repentance [*šûbāh,* "returning"] and rest is your salvation, in quietness and trust [*biṭḥāh,* "confidence," "hope"] is your strength" (Isa. 30:15). Jeremiah 4:4 uses the figure of circumcision to summon Israel to conversion and a changed heart: "Circumcise yourselves to the LORD circumcise [lit., "remove the foreskins of"] your hearts, you men of Judah and people of Jerusalem." Verse 14 amplifies the meaning of the figure of circumcision: "O Jerusalem, wash your heart from wickedness, that you may be saved" (RSV).

The prophets repudiated perfunctory, ritual forms of repentance (Isa. 1:11; 29:13; 58:5; Jer. 14:12; Hos. 7:14). True repentance consists of acknowledging one's guilt (Jer. 3:13), remorse for sins (Jer. 31:19; Ezek. 36:31; Jonah 3:8a), forsaking evil thoughts and deeds (Isa. 55:7; Ezek. 14:6; Jonah 3:8b), turning to the Lord with the whole being (Isa. 55:6; Joel 2:12), and bringing forth fruits reflective of a changed heart (Hos. 12:6; 14:2). In response to genuine repentance the Lord would withhold punishment (Jer. 26:3), forgive the sins of the penitent (Isa. 55:7), and grant life (Ezek. 33:15–16). Those who failed to repent genuinely could expect divine judgment in the form of death (Ezek. 33:8–11, 14).

The prophets indicated, however, that repentance is an enablement of God; the unsaved of themselves cannot turn from sins and produce saving faith. Thus Ephraim petitioned God: "Restore me, and I will return, because you are the LORD God" (Jer. 31:18). This verse contains a play on words, for it literally reads: "Turn me back [Hiphil of *šûb*], and I will be turned" (Qal of *šûb*). A similar play on words occurs in Lamentations 5:21. Jeremiah added that because sin is so ingrained, unbelievers (short of special grace) cannot repent, any more than an Ethiopian can change his dark skin or a leopard his spotted coat (Jer. 13:23).[78] Because of pervasive sinfulness, Yahweh said of Israel: "Their deeds do not permit them to return to their God" (Hos. 5:4). Thus God must grant a spirit of prayerful repentance, as Zechariah 12:10 plainly teaches.

Genuine conversion also involves the movement of faith. In response to Jonah's preaching, "the Ninevites believed [Hiphil of *'āman*] God. They declared a fast, and all of them, from the greatest to the least, put on sackcloth" (Jonah 3:5). Note that here faith and repentance are closely linked. With a play on words Isaiah (7:9) exhorted wavering Ahaz: "If you do not stand firm in your faith [Hiphil of *'āman*], you will not stand at all" (Niphal of *'āman*). Compare the RSV: "If you will not believe, surely you shall not be established." According to Isaiah 28:16, "the one who trusts [Hiphil of *'āman*] will never be dismayed." This verse identifies the *object* of trust as "a tested stone, a precious cornerstone for a sure foundation"—which the New Testament identifies as Christ, the Messiah (cf. Rom. 9:33; 1 Peter 2:6). Emphasizing the idea of confident reliance, Jeremiah wrote: "Blessed is the man who trusts [*bāṭaḥ*] in the LORD, whose confidence [*mibṭāḥ*] is in him" (Jer. 17:7).

The prophets also reflect the hope of spiritual rebirth. Yahweh promised that he would create in the Jewish exiles a new heart: "I will give them a heart to know me, that I am the LORD" (Jer. 24:7). The main Old Testament text on regeneration, however, is Jeremiah 31:31–34, where the Lord stated that in coming days he would make a "new covenant" (v. 31) with his people that would be far superior to the old covenant. The old covenant instituted at Sinai was (1) a *national* covenant (made with "the house of Israel and with the house of Judah," v. 31); (2) an *external* covenant, inscribed on stone or in a book; and (3) a *conditional* or *violable* covenant that Israel and Judah repeatedly broke (v. 32). Sealed by circumcision, the old covenant did not give life (Gal. 3:21). Hence many within national Israel, although physically circumcised, were not spiritually converted. But God promised that the new covenant would change the human heart in radical ways: "I will put my law in their minds and write it on their hearts. I will be their God, and they will be my people" (v. 33). The new covenant would be an agreement not of the letter that kills, but of the Spirit that gives life (2 Cor. 3:6). And it would be written not externally on stone but internally on believers' hearts. The latter anticipates the work of regeneration in the age of the Spirit. "The entire transformation implies the new birth set forth in the gospel."[79] Jeremiah added that as a result of the Spirit's regenerating work Yahweh would "forgive their wickedness" and "remember their sins no more" (under the old covenant sins were remembered). Moreover, many will know Yahweh intimately without human mediation (v. 34). In sum, the law inscribed within by the Spirit "gives intimate knowledge of and fellowship with God, forgiveness of sins, and peace of heart."[80] These promises came to realization through the cross and resurrection of Jesus Christ, the believer's great High Priest (Heb. 8:3–13).

The promise of regeneration further appears in Ezekiel 36:24–27. Consistent with the comprehensive nature of biblical prophecy, Yahweh's promise to restore Israel to the land also included spiritual renewal. The text holds out (1) the promise of purification of sins: "I will sprinkle clean water on you . . . ; I will cleanse you from all your impurities and from all your idols" (v. 25; cf. Jer. 31:34). There follows (2) the promise of a new heart: "I will give you a new heart and put a new spirit in you; I will remove from you your heart of stone and give you a heart of flesh" (v. 26; cf. Ezek. 11:19; 18:31). God would replace the unregenerate heart with a regenerate heart. The "new spirit" refers to the new disposition and affections that constitute the new nature. The text includes (3) the promise of a permanent bestowal of the Holy Spirit in the gospel era (v. 27a; cf.

Ezek. 39:29; Joel 2:28–29). And finally, (4) the result of the Spirit's work is instinctive obedience to the law in a God-honoring life (v. 27b; Jer. 31:33).

The prophetic vision of Ezekiel 37:1–14 anticipated, proximately, Israel's restoration to the land and, ultimately, the regenerating work of the Spirit under the new covenant (cf. Jer. 31:31–34; Ezek. 11:19). God gave the prophet a vision of a valley filled with dry bones. Like the dry bones in the vision, Israel in Babylon was spiritually dead. Yet at God's first word through Ezekiel the bones came together (vv. 7–8), signifying Israel's national restoration (vv. 12–14). At God's second word "the breath [$h\bar{a}r\hat{u}ah$] came into them" (v. 10, RSV), and the lifeless forms came alive and stood on their feet. The latter aspect of the vision anticipates the spiritual renewal of all believers in the gospel era and the end-time conversion of multitudes of Jews (Rom. 11:25–32).

The Synoptic Gospels

According to Mark's gospel, John the Baptist went about "preaching a baptism of repentance [$metanoia$] for the forgiveness of sins" (Mark 1:4; cf. Luke 3:3). From Matthew's perspective the essence of the Baptist's message was: "Repent [present imperative of $metanoe\bar{o}$], for the kingdom of heaven is near" (Matt. 3:2). $Metanoia$ here and elsewhere in the New Testament means "not just a change of inward disposition but a complete turn-about of one's life, with all that such a re-direction implies of the need for God's help on the one side and of ethical conduct on man's side."[81] This suggests that John's baptism was closely linked with the expectation of divine judgment and the need for forgiveness of sins.[82] John's additional saying recorded in Matthew 3:11—"I baptize you with water for repentance [$en\ hydati\ eis\ metanoian$]"—is instructive. The preposition *eis* is causal and should be translated "because of."[83] John's baptism was a sign of prior repentance and a new life of righteousness.

Jesus began his Galilean ministry with a call to conversion identical to that of the Baptist (Matt. 4:17). The parallel in Mark's gospel—"Repent and believe [*pisteuete en*] the good news" (Mark 1:15)—places repentance before faith. So also a later saying of Jesus to his adversaries, "Even after you saw this [i.e., the ministry of the Baptist], you did not repent and believe him" (Matt. 21:32). Here the phrase *tou pisteusai* is epexegetic, giving the content of *metemelēthēte*.[84] The Lord also said, "I have not come to call the righteous, but sinners to repentance" (Luke 5:32). Jesus gave an object lesson on repentance by placing a little child among his disciples and saying,"Unless you change [aorist subjunctive of *strephō*] and become like little children, you will never enter the kingdom of heaven" (Matt. 18:3). Jesus contrasted the trust and humility of a child with pride and self-seeking. The Lord clearly taught that failure to repent would result in judgment and death (Matt. 3:10; 11:20–24; Luke 13:3, 5). Yet certain sayings of Jesus suggest that (apart from special grace) the unsaved cannot bring forth the positive responses necessary for salvation (Matt. 7:17–18).

In the parable of the lost son (Luke 15:11–32) Jesus explained the meaning of conversion. The younger son's journey into a far country with his share of the family wealth signifies humankind's rebellious departure from God and sinful self-indulgence (vv. 13–16). The steps in conversion consist of (1) awareness of one's lost condition (v. 17), (2) honest confession of personal sins and guilt (vv. 18, 21), (3) acknowledgment of one's utter unworthiness before a righteous God (v. 19), and (4) the determination to return to the Father's house (vv. 18–

20a). The Father anticipated the wayward son's homeward journey and responded with undeserved mercy (vv. 20b–24). In sharp contrast with this was the incomplete repentance of Judas. The latter was filled with remorse for betraying Jesus, but he failed to turn wholeheartedly to God and exchange failure for divine forgiveness (Matt. 27:3–5).

In the Gospels the notion of faith as believing assent to divinely revealed truths is not absent (e.g., Luke 24:25). The chief object of faith, however, is Jesus himself in his miracle-working power. After healing blind Bartimaeus, Jesus said to him: "Go . . . your faith has healed [perfect of *sōzō*] you" (Mark 10:52). The fact that Mark used *therapeuō* (cf. 1:34; 3:2), *iaomai* (cf. 5:29), and *sōzō* ("save") indicates that faith effects deliverance that is physical and spiritual. For further examples of faith and Jesus' miracle-working power, see Matthew 9:22, 29; 15:28; Mark 5:34; 9:23–25; Luke 17:19.

The verb *epistrephō* ("turn back," "return") is the Greek equivalent of the Hebrew *šûb*. It occurs several times in the Gospels in the sense of spiritual conversion (Matt. 13:15; Mark 4:12; Luke 1:16–17). The last text suggests that sinners require a superior energy not their own to cause their conversion to Jesus. The story of Jesus' anointing by a sinful woman (Luke 7:36–50) outlines the steps of genuine conversion. The woman's tears (vv. 38, 44) attested her contrition vis-à-vis past sins; her visit to Jesus with a gift of perfume (vv. 36–37) was a sign of her faith in him as Messiah; and her lowly service (v. 38) was evidence of genuine love for Jesus. As a result of her repentant heart and genuine trust, Jesus forgave her sins (v. 47) and declared, "Your faith has saved you; go in peace" (v. 50).

Mark 16:16 indicates that after people believe in Jesus they should receive baptism. Textual considerations indicate that the order of faith followed by baptism was (at least) a firm conviction of the second-century church. Does Luke 1:15 suggest that regeneration commenced in John the Baptist from infancy? There the angel announced to Zechariah, "He will be filled with the Holy Spirit even from birth." The correct interpretation may be as follows: The ministry of John the Baptist anticipated the new era of the Spirit. Whereas the Spirit descended sporadically upon Old Testament saints, John's endowment with the Spirit would be permanent. Hence the Gospels describe John the Baptist, the forerunner of Christ, in the same terms as the Lord himself (Luke 4:1).

Primitive Christianity/Acts

Paul spoke of conversion when he said to the Ephesian elders, "I have declared to both Jews and Greeks that they must turn to God in repentance and have faith in our Lord Jesus" (Acts 20:21). Early on the word "conversion" (hē epistrophē) became a technical term in the mission vocabulary of the apostolic church (Acts 15:3). Genuine conversion involves belief in the truth (Acts 11:21; 15:11), a turning from evil (Acts 8:22), and trust in Christ (Acts 20:21). Several texts specify both the turning from and the turning to that is conversion (Acts 14:15; 26:18; cf. 26:20). The results of conversion are forgiveness of sins (Acts 2:28; 3:19; 10:43), the gift of the Spirit (Acts 2:38; 3:19), and inclusion in the people of God (Acts 26:18). In agreement with other Scriptures, repentance is presented as a gift and enablement of God. In Acts 5:31 — "that he [God] might give repentance and forgiveness of sins to Israel" — Peter claimed that repentance is fully as much a gift of God as is remission of sins. In Acts 11:18 the apostles reported, "God has even granted the Gentiles

repentance unto life." See also Acts 13:48 and 16:4. From the preceding texts Harrison concluded: "We are accustomed to think of 'repentance' as a humanly inspired act that prepares the soul for faith that leads to 'life.' But in the last analysis both the possibility and the actuality of this turning away from sin and turning to God is His gracious work."[85]

In Acts faith is belief in the truths of the Gospel joined with trust, commitment, and obedience to Christ. The object of faith most often was the person of Jesus Christ (Acts 11:17; 14:23; 16:31); but it was also the preached word (4:4; 17:11) and the corpus of saving doctrine (6:7; 13:8; 14:22; 16:5). Hence Christians were designated "the believers" (hoi pisteusantes, 2:44; 4:32). Acts 8:13 states that Simon the Sorcerer, the heretical founder of Gnosticism, "himself believed and was baptized." Yet Simon's faith was superficial (see John 2:23–24), for verse 6 indicates that he was impressed with Philip's miraculous healing powers, and verses 18–20 suggest that he saw in the Christian movement opportunity for financial gain. The text gives no indication that Simon genuinely repented; indeed, Simon's heart was not right with God (v. 21) and was captive to sin (v. 23). Perhaps thinking of the reprobate Judas (cf. Acts 1:18), Peter declared that if he did not repent, Simon would perish along with his money (vv. 20–22).

Consider also the account of Saul's conversion (Acts 9:1–18). Saul was a zealous Jew who lived an exemplary moral and religious life (Acts 26:4–5; Gal. 1:14; Phil. 3:4–6). He was also a violent persecutor of the early Christian church (Acts 9:1–2; 26:9; 1 Tim. 1:13). As Saul was en route to Damascus on a terrorist mission against the Christians, the living Christ revealed himself to him with such power and brilliance that he was rendered blind (vv. 3, 8–9). Saul's being cast to the ground suggests that he was stripped of all self-sufficiency. Moreover, Jesus' words from heaven— "Saul, Saul, why do you persecute me?" (v. 4)—aroused his awareness of sin and alienation. Overcome by the power and grace of Christ, Saul undoubtedly repented and trusted Christ at this time. After Ananias had laid hands on Saul, he was filled with the Holy Spirit (v. 17) and was baptized (v. 18). Shortly thereafter he began to preach Christ in the synagogues (v. 20) and upheld the Christian way against the Jews (v. 22) as a faithful servant of the risen Lord.

Instructive is the account of the conversion of the Philippian jailor. When the jailor in *extremis* inquired of Paul and Silas, "What must I do to be saved?" the missionaries responded, "Believe in the Lord Jesus, and you will be saved—you and your household" (Acts 16:30–31). The jailer and his household then were instructed in the faith, were baptized, and experienced great joy in believing (vv. 32–34). Scripture reflects a high regard for the family unit. But children and servants must come to Christ individually. They must hear the Word of God (v. 32) and believe the Gospel (v. 34) for themselves. Marshall correctly asserts that "the jailer's own faith does not cover them [children and servants]."[86]

A superficial reading of Acts 22:16 might suggest that baptism works regeneration. Ananias said to Saul, "What are you waiting for? Get up, be baptized and wash your sins away, calling on his name." The first two aorist verbs literally could give us this translation: "Permit yourself to be baptized and have your sins washed away." The final verb is the aorist middle participle of *epikaleō*, to "call upon," the tense signifying that Saul's invocation of the Lord temporally preceded the two previous verbs. Thus Saul should allow himself to be baptized and have his sins forgiven by first calling on the Lord in faith.[87]

The Pauline Literature

Paul spoke of conversion when he wrote that the Thessalonians "turned [aorist of *epistrephō*] to God from idols to serve the living and true God" (1 Thess. 1:9). Christian conversion thus is a turning from evil (cf. 2 Cor. 12:21) to God in devotion and service (cf. 2 Cor. 3:16). The apostle taught that true repentance (turning from sin) involves the emotional element of sorrow for misdeeds. Thus Paul's painful letter to the Corinthians stimulated a "godly sorrow" that led to repentance unto salvation (2 Cor. 7:9–11). Paul distinguished "godly sorrow" (*lypē kata theon*) from "worldly sorrow" (*lypē tou kosmou*)—the latter characterized not by sadness for offending God (the root of repentance), but by self-pity and self-anger (the root of depression). Yet Paul, like other biblical writers, insisted that repentance is a gift and enablement of God (Rom. 2:4; 2 Tim. 2:25).

The theme of faith occupies a prominent place in the Pauline writings. The apostle used the noun *pistis* 142 times and the verb *pisteuō* 54 times. Similar to Acts, in Paul's writings faith means belief in the truths of the Gospel and wholehearted trust in Christ. Essential to saving faith are correct beliefs concerning the person and work of Christ: e.g., "saved . . . through belief in the truth" (2 Thess. 2:13; cf. Titus 1:1). To become a Christian one must assent to the reality of Jesus' atoning death (1 Cor. 15:3; 1 Thess. 4:14), resurrection (Rom. 10:9; 1 Cor. 15:4, 17; 1 Thess. 4:14), and divine lordship (Rom. 10:9). There can be no saving faith without hearing and understanding the Gospel (Rom. 10:14, 17; 1 Cor. 15:1–2, 11). Thus Paul wrote of "the faith" (*hē pistis*), namely, the entire body of Christian doctrine one must believe in order to be saved (Gal. 1:23; Eph. 4:5; Phil. 1:27; often in the Pastorals: 1 Tim. 3:9; 4:1, 6; 6:10, 21; 2 Tim. 4:7; Titus 1:13).

The faith that saves is also trust in or commitment to the person of Christ (Col. 2:5) or God (1 Thess. 1:8). Faith is intellectual assent to truths (see above), but it also involves total surrender of the self to Christ manifested in obedience (Rom. 1:5; 16:26), love (1 Cor. 13:2; Gal. 5:6), and good works (1 Thess. 1:3; Titus 2:14; 3:8). In this respect Paul was in agreement with James's definition of faith (James 2:14–26). Moreover, faith is a mode of living before God that should grow extensively and intensively (2 Cor. 10:15; 2 Thess. 1:3). Finally, Paul recognized that saving faith is a sovereign gift of God. It is likely that in Ephesians 2:8, "by grace you have been saved, through faith—and this not from yourselves, it is the gift of God," the antecedent of "this" (touto, neuter) is salvation in its totality, of which faith is one element. Elsewhere Paul explicitly attributed the rise of faith to God himself. "No one can say, 'Jesus is Lord,' except by the Holy Spirit" (1 Cor. 12:3). And, "it has been granted to you on behalf of Christ not only to believe on him, but also to suffer for him" (Phil. 1:29).[88] See also 1 Corinthians 3:6, Ephesians 6:23, and 2 Thessalonians 2:13.[89]

Paul explained the meaning of regeneration by a variety of figures. (1) The new birth is a re-creation, a radical inner change wrought by God's power whereby one becomes a new spiritual being. So the apostle wrote, "If anyone is in Christ, he is a new creation [kainē ktisis]; the old has gone, the new has come!" (2 Cor. 5:17; cf. Gal. 6:15; Eph. 2:10). (2) It is a spiritual vivification or a quickening from death to life by identification with the risen Christ. "When you were dead in your sins and in the uncircumcision of your sinful nature, God made you alive [the verb syzōopoieō] with Christ" (Col. 2:13; cf. Eph. 2:4–6; in Gal. 2:20 the new self is constituted by the risen Christ living his life in the believer). (3) It is a circumcision of the heart or an inner spiritual renewal, not a cutting of the flesh. "In him you were also circumcised, in the putting off of the sinful nature, . . . with the circumcision done by Christ" (Col. 2:11). (4) It is a washing, signifying the cleansing of former sins: "But you were washed [aorist of apolouomai], you were sanctified, you were justified in the name of the Lord Jesus Christ and by the Spirit of our God" (1 Cor. 6:11; cf. Eph. 5:26). And (5) it is a baptism in Christ. Spirit baptism speaks of regeneration and mystical union with Christ and his body: "For we were all baptized by one Spirit into one body . . . and we were all given the one Spirit to drink" (1 Cor. 12:13; cf. Rom. 6:3–8; Gal. 3:27). The preceding Scriptures underscore the monergism of regeneration: God gives the new birth independently of human agency.

Paul wrote of the effects of Spirit-regeneration upon people as image-bearers of God: (1) Intellectually, regeneration enables minds once blind to spiritual truths to comprehend the things of God (1 Cor. 2:12, 14–16; 2 Cor. 4:4, 6; Col. 3:10). Regeneration renews the mind's capacity to know God's will, thus fulfilling the divine purpose. (2) Volitionally, the new birth renews believers' wills, thus enabling them to choose and pursue godly goals (Phil. 2:13; 2 Thess. 3:5). (3) Emotionally, regeneration begins the reintegration of disordered affections (Rom. 8:15). (4) Ethically, regenerate believers progressively become more Christlike in thought and deed. Paul wrote, "Put on the new self, created to be like God in true righteousness and holiness" (Eph. 4:24; cf. 5:26–27). And

(5) *relationally*, the new birth establishes genuine fellowship with the triune God (1 Cor. 1:9; Eph. 2:22) and with other believers (Rom. 12:5; Eph. 2:15).

How did Paul view the relation between baptism and regeneration? In 1 Corinthians 7:14 he wrote that "the unbelieving husband has been sanctified through his wife, and the unbelieving wife has been sanctified [perfect passive of *hagiazō*] through her believing husband." Also when at least one partner is a believer, the children of the marriage are "holy" rather than "unclean." Since the unbelieving husband or wife is not born again by virtue of living with the believing spouse, the sanctification is not a matter of being cleansed from sin. Rather the sense is that the godly life of the believing partner exerts a salutary influence on the unbelieving mate, making it more likely that the latter will become a Christian. Analogously, the children of a mixed marriage (or even of two Christian parents) are not thereby regenerated and saved. Rather the godly life of the believing parent brings spiritual influences to bear, making it more possible for the child to trust Christ in a mature decision of faith.[90]

Does Titus 3:5 support the doctrine of baptismal regeneration when it says that Christ in mercy "saved us through the washing of rebirth and renewal by the Holy Spirit"? Consider first the phrase "through the washing of rebirth" (*dia loutrou palingenēsias*). Those to whom Paul wrote personally had "trusted in God" (v. 8). Analogous to the cleansing action of water specified in 1 Corinthians 6:11 and Ephesians 5:26, the phrase in question undoubtedly refers to the cleansing of sins effected at the new birth by the Word of God. In a secondary sense Paul may have contemplated baptism as the outward sign of this inward cleansing. The second phrase, "through . . . renewal [*anakainōsis*] by the Holy Spirit," does not refer to the subsequent process of sanctification. Rather it is an amplifying description of the new birth in terms of a making new (cf. 2 Cor. 5:17 and Gal. 6:15, which use *kainē*). Jesus similarly linked water and the Spirit in his teaching on regeneration in John 3:5. Titus 3:5 thus offers no support for the notion that baptism effects the regeneration of the person baptized.

The Johannine Writings

In the context of incipient Gnosticism, which exalted knowledge and depreciated faith, John repeatedly emphasized the faith that saves. John preferred the verb *pisteuō* (98 times in the Gospel, 10 times in 1 John) to the noun *pistis* (only in 1 John 5:4; Rev. 2:13, 19; 13:10; 14:12). Fourteen times John used *pisteuein hoti* (e.g., John 6:69; 8:24; 16:27, 30; 20:31; 1 John 5:1, 5) to denote revealed truths that must be believed. Faith for John had a solid intellectual basis. He commended belief in Jesus' preexistent deity (John 8:24), ontological unity with the Father (John 14:11), identity as the Son of God (John 11:27; 1 John 4:15) and promised Messiah (John 6:69; 1 John 5:1), incarnation at the Father's initiative (John 11:42; 17:8, 21), and authentic humanity (1 John 4:2). The cognitive dimension of faith is further reflected in John's use of *pisteuein* with the dative (John 2:22; 4:50; 5:47). Faith involves believing assent to Old Testament teachings or the words of Jesus himself. John stated that the purpose of his Gospel is "that you may believe that [*hoti*] Jesus is the Christ, the Son of God" (John 20:31). While absolutely necessary, correct beliefs are not sufficient for salvation. Thus John stated that "many people saw the miraculous signs he was doing and believed [*episteusan*] in his name" (John 2:23). Since many onlookers were awestruck at Jesus' miracles but lacked commitment to his person, John added, with a play on words, that "Jesus would not entrust [*episteusen*] himself to them, for he knew all men" (v. 24).

John's focus of faith, however, was on wholehearted trust and commitment to the person of Christ. While occasionally expressing this by *pisteuein en* (John 3:15), John's favorite expression is *pisteuein eis*, "to believe into" or "on" Christ (John 1:12; 2:11; 3:12, 16, 18, 36; 4:39; 6:29, 35, 40, 47; 8:30; 12:11). This aspect of personal trust or appropriation of Christ is evident in John 1:12: "To all who received [*elabon*] him, to those who believed in [*pisteuousin eis*] his name, he gave the right to become children of God." The aorist of *lambanō* signifies the personal act of receiving Christ into one's life, whereas the present participle of *pisteuō* with *eis* implies the continuous exercise of faith in the Savior. The appropriational element of faith is strikingly clear in John 6:53–56, where the vivid imagery of eating Christ's flesh and drinking his blood signifies making the benefits of Christ's atoning death a profound part of one's being.

The consequences of genuine faith are likewise profound. Authentic faith results in the verdict of noncondemnation (John 3:18), the overcoming of death (John 10:28; 11:26), possession of eternal life here and now (John 3:15–16, 36; 6:40, 47; 1 John 5:13), and future resurrection from the grave (John 6:40, 54). Although Jesus repeatedly enjoined faith, he made clear that ultimately faith is an enablement of God: "The work [*ergon*] of God is thus: to believe in the one he has sent" (John 6:29).[91] Certain Johannine texts suggest that the decision of faith logically precedes regeneration. John 1:12–13 indicates that receiving Christ in faith results in the new birth and inclusion in the family of God. In John 7:37–39 faith precedes the gift of the Spirit in regenerating and sanctifying power. According to 1 John 5:1, everyone who truly believes in Jesus as Messiah can be assured that he or she has been born of God. The foregoing indicate that saving faith is a specific, knowledgeable decision to trust Christ as sin-bearer. John knew much about "explicit faith" but little about so-called "implicit faith."

John represented regeneration by the figure of a spiritual birth: "children born not of natural descent, nor of human decision or a husband's will, but born of God" (John 1:13). The aorist passive of *gennaō*, to "be born," denotes that instantaneous event whereby the believer receives the new nature—an event qualitatively different from ordinary physical birth. In dialogue with Nicodemus, an orthodox Jew, Jesus explained the meaning of the new birth (John 3:3–8). The Lord began by astutely shifting the discussion from the inquirer's materialistic understanding of the kingdom to his need for a radical, spiritual transformation. "I tell you the truth, no one can see the kingdom of God unless he is born again" (John 3:3). Does the phrase *gennaō anōthen* mean "born again" or "born from above"? An antonym of *katō*, *anō* means "up" or "above" (John 8:23; 11:41; Acts 2:19; Col. 3:1). Elsewhere in John *anōthen* clearly conveys the spatial meaning "above" (John 3:31; 19:11; cf. 19:23). In addition, John envisaged believers as born of God (John 1:13; 1 John 3:9; 4:7; 5:1, 4, 18). As Ladd noted, the fourth gospel reflects "the tension between the above and the below, heaven and earth, the sphere of God and the world" (John 3:12–13, 31; 6:33, 62; 8:23).[92] Thus Jesus probably meant that Nicodemus had to be "born from above," which includes the idea of rebirth.

To Nicodemus, who could not understand this teaching, Jesus delineated the nature of this birth from above: "No one can enter the kingdom of God unless he is born of water and the Spirit [*ex hydatos kai pneumatos*]" (John

3:5). The Greek closely links the agencies of water and the Spirit. Historically several interpretations of the "water" have been proposed: (1) water as a symbol of purification (Lightfoot, Murray, Bruce, Carson); (2) the water of John's baptism (Bengel, Hendriksen, Godet); (3) the water of Christian baptism (Luther, Cullmann, Barrett, Guthrie); (4) water as a symbol for the Word of God (Ironside, Pink, Boice); and (5) the water that accompanies physical birth (popular view). We favor the first interpretation for the following reasons. As a studious Jew Nicodemus was familiar with the Old Testament use of water as a symbol of purification from sin's defilement (Lev. 14:8–9; 2 Kings 5:10; Ps. 51:2–3; Zech. 13:1). Moreover, the purifying function of water and the renovating power of the Spirit are juxtaposed in the prophecy about the new covenant in Ezekiel 36:25–27. Hence by speaking of "water and the Spirit" Jesus made it clear that in order to enter the kingdom of God Nicodemus had to be purified from sin and be spiritually renewed. Note that John's baptism also involved water and the Spirit; the Baptist applied the water, and the Messiah would baptize with the Spirit (John 1:33). Jesus' further statement—"flesh gives birth to flesh, but the Spirit gives birth to spirit" (3:6)—pointed up the radical distinction between a natural, human birth and supernatural rebirth by the Spirit. Thus Jesus insisted that not only Nicodemus but all Jews "must be born again" (v. 7). Finally (v. 8), Jesus taught that the Spirit's work in effecting the new birth is analogous to the operation of the wind. It is (1) invisible and mysterious: "you cannot tell where it comes from." Spirit regeneration is not bound to any external rite such as baptism. And (2) it is sovereign: "the wind blows wherever it pleases." God causes regeneration monergistically as he sovereignly wills.

Other New Testament Literature

Hebrews and James present distinctive meanings of faith. The author of Hebrews, who used *pisteuō* twice but *pistis* thirty-one times, viewed faith as patient endurance and hope in the face of persecution. Writing to believers tempted to revert to the safety of Judaism, Hebrews contemplated faith as the confidence that God will fulfill his promises and uphold his people (3:6; 10:23; 11:11). Faith enables Christian converts to go beyond present, visible trials to apprehend future, invisible realities promised by God. So Hebrews 11:1 affirms, "Now faith is being sure of what we hope for and certain of what we do not see." Hebrews 11:4–40 catalogs many examples of this kind of faith by great heroes of Israel. The writer invited wavering saints to "believe that [*pisteuein hoti*] he [God] exists and that he rewards those who earnestly seek him" (Heb. 11:6).

James opposed the view held by a party of Christians that faith defined as assent to truths can stand alone, i.e., without being validated by good works. The NIV translation highlights the issue with the rhetorical question: "Can *such* faith save him?" (James 2:14, italics added). James responded that right beliefs, if not accompanied by loving works are useless and dead (v. 17). He added that, like his orthodox opponents, the demons believe in the unity and uniqueness of God (v. 19). But right beliefs alone possess no saving potency. Whereas Paul appealed to Abraham's faith in the divine promise given before Isaac was born, James pointed to the evidence of Abraham's faith manifested by his willingness to sacrifice his beloved son (vv. 21–23). Thus James concluded, "You see that a person is justified by what he does and not by faith alone" (v. 24). Paul and James thus held complementary views of justification. The former used the verb *dikaioō* in the sense of a secret vindication by God, the latter in the sense of a public vindication by man. "For both Paul and James 'justify' means to *declare righteous*. In Paul's writings, it is God who declares the believer righteous. In James's epistle, it is a man's works which declare him righteous by showing that he is a man of faith."[93]

Hebrews 6:1 suggests that repentance from evil deeds logically precedes faith directed to God. Moreover, consistent with other Scriptures cited above, the General Epistles regard faith as a gift and enablement of God. Thus 2 Peter 1:1 addresses those "who through the righteousness of our God and Savior Jesus Christ have received a faith as precious as ours." The juxtaposition of "faith" and "righteousness" and the fact that Peter's readers had been given a faith of the same value or quality as his indicates that *pistis* is trust in Christ. Hebrews 12:2 describes Jesus as "the author and perfecter of our faith." Christ begins the work of faith in the believer, and he will bring it to a triumphant conclusion.

James 1:18 depicts the new birth by the verb *apokyeō*, to "give birth" or "bear," whereas 1 Peter 1:3, 23 employs the verb *anagennaō* (only here in the NT), "cause to be born again." The instrument of the new birth, according to these verses, is the Word of God or the truth of the Gospel (cf. 1 Peter 1:22). Hebrews 10:22 describes regeneration using the familiar Old Testament imagery of sprinkling and purification: "having our hearts sprinkled to cleanse us from a guilty conscience and having our bodies washed with pure water." Sprinkling of the heart ultimately refers to the spiritual cleansing wrought by Christ's blood, whereas the washing of the body with water represents the outward, visible sign given in baptism. The literature nowhere suggests that water baptism saves the soul. The intri-

cate argument of 1 Peter 3:18–22 (see vol. 2, chap. 7) teaches that the flood, by cleansing the world of wickedness and delivering the faithful in the ark, is a picture of salvation—which salvation is symbolized by the rite of baptism. What saves is not the external rite, but the completed work and resurrection of Christ (vv. 21b–22) appropriated by faith.

Second Peter 1:4 further describes the new birth as a participation "in the divine nature" (*theia physis*). Using current Hellenistic language, Peter described regeneration as spiritual union with Christ involving impartation of the life of the triune God to the soul. The outcome of this transaction between Christ and the believer is a new disposition, new moral qualities, and a new set of affections. Participation "in the divine nature" is Peter's way of describing the reality Paul set forth in Romans 6:4 and Galatians 2:20 and what the writer of Hebrews related in Hebrews 3:14 ("share in Christ"); 6:4 ("shared in the Holy Spirit"); and 12:10 ("share in his holiness"). Peter certainly did not contemplate any pantheistic notion of absorption into the whole.

SYSTEMATIC FORMULATION

We now seek to integrate the strengths of the alternative views of conversion and regeneration into a coherent account faithful to the primary scriptural data. In response to the effectual call of the Spirit (previous chapter), sinners consciously convert by (1) believing the Gospel, (2) repenting of their idolatries, and (3) trusting Jesus Christ alone. Then converts are (4) regenerated by the Holy Spirit.

Belief: Mental Assent to the Truth of the Gospel

Believe what you know to be true. Some people think that in religion it does not matter what one believes. Others imagine that knowledge leads us part of the way and that faith takes over from there. Neither sincere Gentile worship of an unknown God (Acts 17) nor zealous Jewish spirituality without knowledge (Rom. 10:1–4) is acceptable. Believers do not make a mindless leap into the dark of the cosmos or the totally transcendent. Christians know what they believe and why; they give assent to the truth of the Gospel.

Augustine, often misunderstood as teaching a blind faith prior to knowledge, insists that we could not believe at all if we could not think:

> Who cannot see that thinking is prior to believing? For no one believes anything unless he has first thought what it is to be believed. For however suddenly, however rapidly, some thoughts fly before the will to believe . . . , it is yet necessary that everything which is believed should be believed after thought has preceded; although even belief itself is nothing else than to think with assent. For it is not everyone who thinks that believes, since many think in order that they may not believe; but everybody who believes, thinks—both thinks in believing, and believes in thinking. . . . If faith is not a matter of thought, it is of no account.[94]

Many assume that since the object of Christian faith is unseen, there is no rational basis for it. Rather, on the ground of visible promises guaranteed by the Lord of all, "we fix our eyes not on what is seen, but on what is unseen. For what is seen is temporary, but what is unseen is eternal" (2 Cor. 4:18). In the first century knowledge was necessary to belief. People heard and observed Jesus. Then they heard the apostles' eyewitness testimony to him as Savior and Lord. Since the departure of the apostles, their witness is carefully preserved for us in the New Testament. The reliable medium through which we learn about God's plan of salvation is

inspired apostolic teaching attested by the Spirit of truth (1 John 5:6–7).

Trusting and loving personal relationships are still based on truth. We cannot love a person of whom we are totally ignorant. Slaves to sin need to know who can redeem them and why. They need to know about Christ's atonement. Beliefs provide the guidelines directing commitment away from idols to the living Lord who can hear, answer, and save (Rom. 10:2–3, 14). As New Testament scholar J. Gresham Machen accentuated, "Christian doctrine, according to Paul, was not something that came after salvation, as an expression of Christian experience, but it was something necessary to salvation. The Christian life . . . was founded upon a message."[95]

Accepting mediated information on the authority of the apostles is often rejected as an uncritical authoritarianism. "But reason is not entirely absent from authority, for we have got to consider whom we have to believe."[96] Historians determine the credibility of sources through documents, copies, and any surviving evidence. So do Christians studying the Scriptures. Scientists depend on the reliability of eyewitness reports to experiments they have not themselves repeated. In a pluralistic world of conflicting messianic claims, belief is strengthened by *converging lines of verifiable evidence* that Jesus was who he claimed to be. If every person were divine, we might be able uncritically to believe religious leaders. But since the creation, all is not God; and since the Fall, all is not good. Hence the Bible frequently urges people to be critically discerning, not profligate, in their spiritual beliefs. It even tells readers at times *not* to believe certain spirits (1 John 4:1).

Which specific revealed doctrines must one believe to begin the Christian life? In order to relate redemptively to the God who is, people must believe in

(1) the existence of the one personal, moral God distinct from the world but active in it (Heb. 11:6; James 2:19; 1 Peter 1:21). Aware of their sin, people must also believe in (2) the deity and unique sonship of Jesus the Messiah (John 1:1, 14; 16:30; 17:21; 20:31; 1 John 5:1, 5). Sinners must assent to (3) Christ's death as the complete atonement for their sins (Rom. 3:25; 1 Thess. 4:14). To be saved people also believe in (4) Christ's bodily resurrection from the dead (Rom. 10:9–10; Acts 4:2; 1 Peter 1:21). In summary, acknowledging their guilt before God people with a theistic worldview accept the Gospel (*kerygma*), the Good News of the kingdom brought by Christ (Mark 1:15; Acts 8:12). In other words, Christians believe the basic truths about God, sin, and salvation (Gal. 1:8–9). This central message of the Scriptures was anticipated in the Old Testament Scriptures (Luke 24:25; John 2:22; 1 Cor. 15:3–4) and developed in the New. A child's level of understanding of these truths is sufficient; an expert's grasp of alternative ways to God is not.

Adherents of different ways of salvation often charge: "That is just *your* interpretation!" An interpretation of the New Testament's apostolic doctrine is reliable if it meets the standard criteria of truth. (1) It needs to be logically consistent with the all the data of the Old and New Testaments. (2) It must conform to the phenomena of first-century history, for "this salvation, which was first announced by the Lord, was confirmed to us by those who heard him. God also testified to it by signs, wonders and various miracles, and gifts of the Holy Spirit distributed according to his will" (Heb. 2:3–4). (3) We can test our understanding of the Gospel by its existential viability. Does it encourage hypocrisy or demand authenticity? (4) For another check against subjective interpretation we can compare our view with the conclusions of the confessions in the church from many different cultures and times.[97]

In summary, belief of the Gospel is necessary but not sufficient for conversion. Conversion also entails repentance and trust or commitment. As we come into God's holy presence, we are overwhelmed by our own sinfulness.

Repentance: The Repudiation of Lesser Lords

The necessity for repentance is universal. Jesus made that emphatic in response to those who told him that Pilate had mixed the blood of humans with their sacrifices. Were these worse than other sinners because they suffered this way? "I tell you, no! But unless you repent, you too will all perish" (Luke 13:3). Were the eighteen crushed by the tower that fell in Siloam more guilty than all the others living in Jerusalem? "I tell you, no! But unless you repent, you too will all likewise perish" (v.5). William Fitch concludes, "There is no area in all the Bible to support the belief that man can find God without first having turned from his sins. The kingdom of God is opened only to those who truly 'repent and believe the gospel.' "[98]

In the Old Testament the prophets called for a radical transformation of mind and purpose regarding God and their own spiritual condition. They summoned Israel to repent of personal and relational sins. Repentance involved the whole spirit or heart, affecting its capacities to think, will, feel, and relate. In the New Testament repentance almost exclusively involved regretting or "having remorse."[99] As such, however, it involved a change of mind and feeling that leads to a change of determination, action, and relationships. "The goal of authentic spirituality is a life which escapes from the closed circle of spiritual self-indulgence, or even self-improvement, to become absorbed in the love of God and other persons."[100]

Because of many misunderstandings, the nature of repentance needs to be considered carefully. A repentant spirit is not just an Oriental sense of shame for disappointing family or others. It is not merely a fear of getting caught, judged, and punished. Neither is repentance a matter of doing penance to obtain merit or purchase forgiveness. It is not an annual attempt at self-reform (beginning on New Year's Eve). Repentance is not giving up an external pleasure during Lent while continuing to satisfy inner passions. It is not merely a conviction of one's sinfulness, valid as that is. Repentance is more than feeling sorry for our sins; it means feeling bad enough about them to quit. Before the supreme disclosure of God in Christ we cry out like Isaiah, "Woe is me! . . . I am ruined" (Isa. 6:5). Repentance, as H. A. Ironside held, "is a recognition of the need of grace, not an act of merit opposed to grace."[101]

The repentant *repudiate good works* as a way of self-justification. The rich ruler (Luke 18:18–27) claimed to have kept the law from his youth. Jesus' line of reasoning pointed out that the man failed to keep the true spirit of the law. His selfish accumulation of riches violated the loving intent of morality. Jesus said to the ruler, in effect, that if he could keep the law perfectly he would not need salvation (v. 20). But he was unwilling to repent of his greed, sell what he had, and give to the poor. Neither the rich ruler then nor we today can perfectly fulfill the law. The moral law is not a vehicle for salvation. At a practical level the law helps people become aware of their sin and prompts them to repent. All of us need to repent of the false belief that we can please God by the performance of virtuous deeds.

The repentant *renounce all other spiritual masters* and regard Jesus alone as supreme. An initiate in Transcendental Meditation said she was a born-again Christian and that the Eastern disciplines enhanced her devotional life. At the initiation (*puja*) ceremony she brought sacrifices and bowed to the Maharishi Mahesh Yogi's guru, Brahmananda Saraswati, as "the supreme teacher." No one who receives Christ for who he is can regard another person a "supreme" teacher. Jesus is not another mere human to be added to a Theosophist's list of ascended masters. He will not be subordinated to Mohammed, the Buddha, or Joseph Smith. The Lord Jesus Christ will not be added to many other deities on an ancestral god-shelf. The conqueror of sin, death, and the Devil will not be subordinate to the entertainment or sports heroes *du jour*.

The repentant *renounce illusory and immoral fantasies and return to reality*. Much counterfeit spirituality is a rejection of God's creation and kingdom purposes in history. The world of space and time is dismissed as unreal, as *maya*. That denial opens a person to all kinds of fantasies from Hindu, Greek, and other cultures. Those who receive the Gospel receive truth about reality. Paul asked Timothy to "command certain men not to teach false doctrines any longer nor to devote themselves to myths" (1 Tim. 1:3–4). Again he wrote, "Have nothing to do with godless myths" (4:7). Repentance means a holistic aversion to the outlook and attitudes dominated by the flesh and its works, including witchcraft (Gal. 5:19–21).

Repentance *transforms one's highest moral values*. The assumption of the repentant is that God knows what is best for us and wisely sets the rules. The early Christians did not relativize Christ's character or his virtues. Rather than continuing to challenge the moral principles flowing from the divine nature, the repentant acknowledge their absolute validity. And before those objectively just norms they acknowledge that all fall far short. The sins they dearly loved they now detest. Like the family gardener, the repentant not only love flowers, they hate weeds. They despise what destroys the lives God formed and redeemed. Discerningly they disown the old fleshly mentality by repudiating former rationalizations of their sins. The truly repentant refuse to conform to the prevailing ethos in the face of peer pressure and refuse to cower at the world's disapproval.

The repentant no longer suppress or dismiss the truth but *bow before God's revealed truth*. The biblical mandate to cleave to the truth of God is impressive. The God of the Bible is the "God of truth" (Ps. 31:5), who "desires truth in the inner parts" (51:6). Many times Jesus emphatically said, "I tell you the truth" (e.g., Matt. 5:18; 6:5, 16). Before Pilate he stated, "For this reason I was born, and for this I came into the world, to testify to the truth. Everyone on the side of truth listens to me" (John 18:37). Christ sent the "Spirit of truth" to guide the apostles and those who hear their message (John 14:17; 15:26; 16:13). Paul also warned of those who would distort the truth in order to lure away people after them (Acts 20:30). The apostle did not impose Jewish cultural customs on Gentiles but criticized both groups when "he saw that they were not acting in line with the truth of the gospel" (Gal.2:14). Unrepentant people in the last days "perish because they refused to love the truth and to be saved, . . . but have delighted in wickedness" (2 Thess. 2:12). The Thessalonians were "saved through the sanctifying work of the Spirit and through belief in the truth" (2 Thess. 2:13). For all cultures the Gospel is "the word of truth" (Eph.1:13). Today we need to fill the cavities resulting from truth decay. The message to the church at Sardis was "Remember,

therefore, what you have received and heard; obey it, and repent" (Rev. 3:3).

The repentant need the *humility* to admit that they have been fundamentally wrong in the direction of their moral life and must begin anew as little children. Jesus said, "I tell you the truth, unless you change [convert] and become like little children, you will never enter the kingdom of heaven. Therefore whoever humbles himself like this child is the greatest in the kingdom of heaven" (Matt. 18:3–4). Again, "Blessed are the poor in spirit, for theirs is the kingdom of heaven. Blessed are those who mourn for they shall be comforted. Blessed are the meek, for they will inherit the earth. Blessed as those who hunger and thirst after righteousness, for they will be filled" (Matt.5:3–6). In short, repentance is a drowning person's desperate cry: "Help! 'God be merciful to me, a sinner!' "

Repentance requires that we remove the masks and become *radically honest with ourselves*. People trying to "find themselves" may need a metamorphosis of mind, desire, will, and relationships.[102] Our fallen selves are not the persons God created us to be. Having yielded to temptation, we may say, "But I wasn't myself"; "I hate myself when I do that"; or "I was almost out of my mind." By such statements we acknowledge that we are at war with ourselves and with our Creator. The repentant need to cut through superficial concerns and get to the heart of the problem by repenting of actual sin and wickedness.

Faith: Trusting the Living Christ Without Reservation

Faith is not a synonym for belief. We believe in propositional truth; we have faith in or trust the glorified person of Christ. Having rested one's mind on the sufficiency of the evidence and having

101

repented of the perversity of one's desires, one comes to the point of holistic commitment. The object of belief is propositions; the object of faith is a person.

What, then, is *faith*? One trusts an unseen person on the basis of sound evidence that has been seen or heard. Faith in persons requires knowledge just as does faith in things. Faith is not belief without evidence, but *trust without reservation*. Through belief of the Good News we come to trust the Spirit-filled Messiah. We must drop all futile attempts at self-justification and depend on Christ alone for justification.

Anything less than wholehearted commitment and loyalty is inappropriate. A small tip for One who did not spare his own Son would hardly be fitting. A simple "thank you" to a person who gave his life to save yours would be insufficient. A small fine would not suffice for a lifelong involvement in pride and covetousness. An apology could hardly satisfy for a lifetime of habitual disbelief and disobedience. No attempted bribery can buy the favor of an absolutely holy God. We depend entirely on the mercy of the divine court.

Well-founded commitment continues in the midst of present sufferings. During Paul's many trials and testings his full-orbed faith or trust in God kept him faithful. While undergoing suffering he was not disenchanted or ashamed, nor did he go back to his former ways. Why such steadfastness? Attributing his patient endurance to his faith, he wrote, "I know whom I have believed, and am convinced that he is able to guard what I have entrusted to him for that day" (2 Tim. 1:12). Paul's knowledge (*notitia*) led not only to persuasion (*assensus*) but also to a new relationship of trust (*fiducia*).

The fiducial trust of Abraham is often portrayed as a leap in the dark totally divorced from evidence. Although Abraham did not know where he was going when he left Ur of the Chaldees, he knew whom he trusted—the personal, living covenant-making Lord of all! Later when beyond the age of begetting children, Abraham was "fully persuaded that God had power to do what he had promised" (Rom. 4:21; cf. Heb. 11:11–12). The God who promised countless descendants in due course gave him Isaac. Then when tested by the agony of sacrificing Isaac, Abraham reasoned that God could raise the dead (Heb. 11:19). Abraham, like Paul, knew whom he believed and was confident that he was able to fulfill his promises. Hence Abraham's faith was not a blind leap into the void, but was much like Paul's reasoned faith. Being committed to the name above every name of the living or dead, Christians confidently face losses, disappointments, and even death itself.

Conversion: Conscious Belief, Repentance, and Trust

Conversion is the general term encompassing conscious belief of the Gospel, turning from sin in repentance, and trusting Christ. We *define* conversion to Christ as that conscious experience of sinners who believe the truth of the Gospel, repent of their sins, and rely on the crucified and risen Messiah for justification and newness of life. Conversion's "about face" has *two inseparable aspects*. The positive side includes belief of the Gospel and faith in Christ; the negative side involves repentance for sin and renunciation of other spiritual masters.

Although belief and repentance are not synonymous, they are inseparably related to one another like two sides of the same sheet of paper. Sometimes the Bible summons sinners to "repent," sometimes to "believe" or "trust." Sometimes it refers to both in either order when it commands sinners to "convert." Whether speaking of the "turning from" or the "turning to," one term implies the other and the whole act of conversion. You can no more have faith without repentance than you can have a coin without both sides.

Conversion is not all of God nor all of sinners; it is a divinely enabled *conscious human determination*. When referring to this divine-human synergism, the Bible more frequently refers to the human agency. Sacred Scripture refers to conversion almost 140 times as being an act of humans and only six times as an act initiated by the Holy Spirit.[103] Avoiding the single-cause fallacy, we must say that conversion is not exclusively of God nor exclusively of humans; it is a divine-human concursive operation. The first signs of spiritual life, however, are enabled by the Spirit's power. The biblical section identified many texts supporting this claim. The prophet, for example, prayed: "Restore us to yourself, O LORD, that we may return" (Lam. 5:21; cf. Ps. 85:4). In the New Testament God "even granted the Gentiles repentance unto life" (Acts 11:18; cf. 2 Tim. 2:25). Paul identified faith as a gift of the Spirit (1 Cor. 12:9). Thus he wrote that you should "think of yourself . . . in accordance with the measure of faith God has given you" (Rom. 12:3; cf. Eph. 6:23). Faith at the beginning of salvation as well as faith throughout life is the gift of God (Eph. 2:8). The ability to will and the willingness itself ultimately come from the Author of every good gift. It follows that conversion is not a merely human condition that sinners must meet before God acts, but a divine-human means to salvation.

Conversion involves a *conscious struggle* of the whole person, usually over a period of time. Any habitual sinner faces a conscious struggle with believing the Gospel, repenting of idolatry, and trusting Christ (as the spiritual "embryo" begins to move). C. S. Lewis recalls a turbulent time in his life when he came "kicking and screaming" into the kingdom. We suggest that belief and repentance are the first signs of life (kicking) during the spiritual gestation period (in the spiritual "womb"). During the span of the spiritual pregnancy the prenatal life-signs (analogous to detecting a heartbeat) are a radical change of mind, affection, and purpose with respect to one's sin and the Messiah. *Emotions* are involved, but "the thinking introvert is incapable of experiencing or displaying the emotion shown by the feeling extrovert."[104] The internal struggle eventually comes to a decisive *volitional* commitment.

Converts commit themselves in their entirety to a holy God. People who by nature were reluctant to identify themselves with God and his kingdom now commit themselves to the Lord and his rule. The Old Testament word for such turning (*šûb*) refers to the "return" of the spiritually "unfaithful wife." It was never a superficial matter for Israel to turn away from servitude to other gods and to turn back to their rightful Redeemer and spouse. The call to convert in Old Testament times often was accompanied by announcement of the Lord's coming judgment. Sinners were told to prepare to meet their God (Amos 4:12). For Amos, Hosea, and Isaiah "returning" meant giving up false piety and confidence in political arrangements while freeing the land from injustice. For Jeremiah "returning" meant turning away from false prophets in a pluralistic society. Returning

does not mean responding to the needs of the hour nor to the needs of a changed world. It was not the expansion of the power of Assyria, Babylon or Persia that made the return of the people of God necessary. The 'return' or 'conversion' offered is in no sense an adaptation to a changed world (*aggiornamento*). It is 'the ever new response to God's mighty acts among man' (Loffler). For Israel events and developments in world history never have this character or weight of acts of God. But every event always reminds Israel through the words of the prophets of 'the mighty acts of God'—those acts whereby Israel realizes that it is called to be the people of God.[105]

The conscious experience of conversion itself may be *momentary or gradual*. Some fall in love at first sight. Others realize their love over a longer period of time. Whether quickly or slowly, the new allegiance and commitment of the whole person clearly occurs when both say "I do." However gradual one's conversion may have been, any holistically depraved sinner makes a dramatic change from natural proclivities to affirm that Jesus is Lord. However long it may take, there remains no reasonable doubt if a prodigal son or daughter truly returns to his or her spiritual home.

Conversion to the crucified and risen Messiah begins *a new orientation of life*. The center around which believers orbit is no longer themselves but their exalted Lord. William Barclay wrote that "the genuine convert finds these attitudes [repentance and faith] the steadily dominant factor in life."[106] If converts do not continue in allegiance to Christ but later permanently reject him, the seed of the Word unfortunately fell on poor soil or was crushed by thorns (Matt. 13:19–22). In contrast, the dominant loyalty causes the authentically converted to forsake other gods and cleave to Christ alone. There may be temporary lapses of faith and obedience, but in the long term "godly sorrow brings repentance that leads to salvation and leaves no regret" (2 Cor. 7:10). There are instances of converted people yielding to sin; but the first instance of genuine belief, repentance, and faith leads to the irrevocable gift of everlasting life.

Regeneration: God's Gift of Eternal Life

Conversion (spiritual gestation) differs from regeneration (spiritual birth) in several respects: (1) Conversion is primarily a human act; regeneration is exclusively an act of God the Holy Spirit. (2) In conversion the Holy Spirit works indirectly or mediately through human witnesses; in regeneration the Spirit works directly and immediately, wherever he pleases, like the wind (John 3:8). (3) Whereas conversion involves conscious travail, regeneration occurs beneath the level of consciousness. (4) Conversion takes a longer or shorter period of time; the gift of new life is received at a specific point in time (though we may be unable to identify it). (5) Conversion expresses an initial response to Christ; regeneration permanently renews the moral image of God and provides for a lifelong perseverance.

Are we regenerated in order that we may convert? Or do we convert in order to be regenerated? The usual Calvinist view maintains that a conversion that does not logically follow regeneration is not a true conversion.[107] In place of regeneration in that statement we would insert the Spirit's effectual calling. This better fits the biblical passages indicating that sinners convert in order to become children of God (John 1:12–13) and to receive eternal life (John 3:16, 18, 36; 5:24). As John later explained: "By believing you may have life in his name" (20:31). So in our moderately Reformed *ordo salutis,* sinners who convert are regenerated. Spiritual conception (calling and conversion) precedes the spiritual birth of a child of God (1 Cor. 3:6).

Morally and spiritually people are in one of *two classes*. Humans are either among the children of God or the children of Satan (1 John 3:10). By physical birth we are children of the Devil

(John 8:44), however proud we may be of our religious heritage. New spiritual life is "not of natural descent" (John 1:13). No human "decision" or determination of the "will" of a wife or husband before, during, or after conception can produce a child of God morally or spiritually (v. 13). Talking with Nicodemus, a Jewish leader with reason to be proud of his roots, the Messiah emphasized: "I tell you the truth, no one can enter the kingdom of God unless he is born again" (John 3:3).

The once-born *of Adamic flesh* have a corrupt heart that pollutes thoughts, desires, willing, relationships, and religion. How can we become children of God? Negatively, we do not change human nature through the unfolding of the potential born in us. Nor do we become regenerate as the result of a gradual cultural evolution. Regeneration is not the product of a lengthy period of education, even of Christian education. Education is an important preliminary step in making the Gospel clear, but it cannot change human nature. Economic, social, and political forces cannot alter human dispositions. Not even a decision for Christ can change our natures. Neither is the regeneration of human nature affected by baptism sanctioned by a religious organization. Since in Acts 2:28 regeneration precedes baptism, the latter cannot be the cause of regeneration.[108] Baptism is a proclaiming not a procuring ceremony.

Affirmatively, birth to spiritual vitality comes from above, from beyond all our religious resources. Jesus taught this emphatically and repeatedly: "I tell you the truth, no one can see the kingdom of God unless he is born again" (John 3:3; cf. vv. 5, 7). Those controlled by the sinful nature cannot please God (Rom. 8:8). Only by the Spirit's life-giving power can we who were evil trees bringing forth evil fruit become good trees producing good fruit

(Matt. 7:16–20). Only the Spirit of God can renew the basic orientation of the morally depraved and relationally dead human spirit.

We become children of God by a *supernatural* regenerative work of God. The action of the transcendent Holy Spirit is as dramatic as a new birth (John 3:3–8), a new creation (Eph. 2:10; 2 Cor. 4:6; 5:17), and a resurrection from the dead (Eph. 2:1; Col. 2:13). What did you have to do with creation, your birth, or Christ's resurrection? Certainly nothing! Since we cannot give ourselves spiritual life, it must come from the transcendent Source. If human nature morally is to be significantly changed, substantial change must come directly from above.

Regeneration by the Spirit of life renews the *heart and life*. It does not impart a new metaphysical entity, for our basic problem is not metaphysical finiteness but moral insolence. Hence the change that occurs is not in our ontological constitution but in our abilities to function as morally responsible persons vis-à-vis God's wise, holy, and loving program. As fallen we did not cease to be human beings, and through redemption we do not become superhuman. Regeneration does not produce a change in substance by giving a sinner a spirit, a missing third to one's being (as in trichotomy). The Spirit does not simply put a new part in a person. Rather, the same person who was addicted to the selfish kingdom is renewed with a disposition to love God and others.

The Spirit's work of regeneration renews the heart (spirit), restoring the use of all one's debilitated spiritual capabilities. The *imago Dei,* impaired and enslaved by the Fall, is rejuvenated. Regeneration is more than the "enlightenment" of ancient and modern gnosticism. It is not merely a new emotion or volition of romanticism. Regeneration does not change just a single capacity of a person but the whole sinner, beginning with the innermost self. We are said to become "partakers of the divine nature" (2 Peter 1:4), not by an infusion of the being of God making us divine beings or some *tertium quid* (third kind of thing). Rather, with renewed capacities we share the values of the divine moral nature by living in fellowship with Christ.[109]

The renewal of the regenerate person's capacities to know, love, and serve God is *holistic*. The mind-set of the twice-born is freed from enslavement to fleshly passions and is renewed in the image of the Creator (Col. 3:10). The dominant longing of the affections is released from the magnetism of sin and freed to love God, lay up treasure in heaven, and seek the well-being of others (Col. 3:1–2). The will of the regenerate is freed from all kinds of bondage in order to dedicate itself to ultimate concerns pleasing to God. Ethically, in all their relationships, the regenerate seek to honor the highest values as did Christ (1 John 1:5–10). Relationally, regeneration results in a fulfilling life directed to love of God (1 John 1:3), love of God's people, and love of the lost.

Morally the regenerative work of the Holy Spirit *breaks the dominance of sin:*

> In regeneration man's will remains. But now it is a will obedient to a higher will which it recognizes. So also in regeneration the mental powers remain. But now the mind of man finds a higher mind and discovers that the truth he has been seeking has been seeking him all the time. His own mind finds its true self in God. The heart of man remains in regeneration, but now the affection finds its true Object in the Supreme Companion. All lower loves give way to the highest of all. . . . Paul the apostle was the same as Saul the persecutor. Yet the change in him was so great that he described himself as an

entirely new creature. Thus in regeneration man finds himself, comes to himself, realizes his own potentialities and possibilities as he can do in no other way.[110]

The event of regeneration *marks a lasting break with what happened in the past.* Church members addressed along with Titus once were "enslaved by all kinds of passions and pleasures" (Titus 3:3). Without presumption Paul referred to the fact that his readers were "saved . . . through the washing of rebirth and renewal by the Holy Spirit" (past tense, v. 5). Regeneration may always seem to be mere development to people presupposing evolution. "However, it is never a development of what is naturally present, but always takes a person through a fundamental break which sooner or later becomes clearly visible."[111]

The newness of heart and life is *a gracious gift* from God's Spirit; it is never earned. Regeneration is freely given as the Spirit wills (James 1:18). New life is not of works but is entirely unmerited, for we have seen that there is no merit in the human responses of repentance and faith. God saved us "not because of righteous things we had done, but because of his mercy . . . through the washing of rebirth and renewal by the Holy Spirit, whom he poured out on us, generously . . . so that having been justified by his grace, we might become heirs having the hope of eternal life" (Titus 3:5–7).

The Holy Spirit's work of regenerating our natures *occurs in the unconscious* recesses of one's being internally. Whereas conversion is a conscious act of turning from sin to God, regeneration is an unconscious transformation by the Holy Spirit in the unconscious.[112] The biblical metaphors for the Spirit's supernatural work of regeneration could not be more vivid or pointed. Like the wind the Spirit works unpredictably (John 3:8), producing a change of moral and spiritual capabilities, which we become aware of through their effects. As we were not conscious of our natural creation or natural birth, so we are not conscious of our second birth.

Regeneration *takes place once for all*. We may repent again and again, but we are born into spiritual life and the spiritual kingdom only once. The analogies to birth, creation, and resurrection illustrate this point. Unique persons are not born, created, or resurrected many times. So also, regeneration occurs once at a specific date in time. Although many providential factors may lead up to it, regeneration is not a long process of evolutionary development. After new life is given, there is growth and development, but the giving of life is analogous to birth and happens when the new life and nature are received through faith. Regeneration is the unrepeatable, once-for-all historical beginning of both justification and sanctification. This radical change lasts for eternity.

Life-signs will eventually exhibit the *outward effects* of the new nature from God. In some cases they are immediately visible; in other cases time may elapse before observable changes are evident. In either case the good tree will bring forth good fruit. Spiritually speaking, God has no still-born children.

Enduring spiritual life is not easy to define, but in the twice-born it includes at least a sensitivity and responsiveness to the greatness of God's love, truth, moral norms, and kingdom purposes. Regeneration may be *defined* as that recreative act of the Holy Spirit graciously establishing the permanent propensity of a convert to become like Christ in fulfilling moral law and fellowshiping with the heavenly Father forever. How shall we define a Christian? A Christian is a theist who through mental assent to the truth claims of the Gospel personally repents and trusts the exalted Christ of the apostolic writings. A believer concurs that Jesus of Nazareth is the eternal Word who became flesh, lived without sin, died to atone for our sins, and rose bodily from the dead. The people of faith in Old Testament times received these truths in figure and type, but twice-born followers of Christ accept them in the clear light of day.

Assurance of salvation varies with the degree of mental assent to converging lines of evidence supporting the truth of the Gospel. These lines of evidence strongly support one's intellectual perception of the probability that the Gospel is true, leading one on to *psychological certitude*. That settled conviction of resting on the sufficiency of the evidence brings *moral responsibility* for life in accord with belief. By the illumination and conviction of the Holy Spirit Christians rest their hearts on the sufficiency of the evidence. Christians trust the living Christ in heaven and receive the permanent gift of the Holy Spirit, who attests the truth of the Gospel. The Spirit's work in our lives (1 Cor. 12:3) becomes a *deed of trust* for eschatological salvation. That function of belief is described in the words of the author of Hebrews: "Now faith is being sure of what we hope for and certain of what we do not see" (Heb. 11:1).

APOLOGETIC INTERACTION

This section interacts with live options challenging the necessity of conversion and regeneration. It tests the conformity of the systematic formulation in terms of its logical consistency and adequacy to account for the relevant external and internal data of Scripture and experience.

Is "Once-Born" Sufficient for the Well-Adjusted?

Are there some people who do not need regeneration? In *The Varieties of*

Religious Experience William James described people who are congenitally happy and psychologically well-adapted to their environments as "once-born." Theirs is thought to be the religion of "healthy mindedness."[113] In contrast, James referred to "sick souls" who are at odds with their environments and divided in their moral and intellectual constitution. In these people their divided selves become united through the process of conversion. Limiting himself to observations as a psychologist and philosopher, James sees no reason to expect that the reported experiences of all people should show identical religious elements. He believes that sick souls require a religion of deliverance and that the healthy-minded do not need conversion.[114]

Long before William James, Jesus said something similar: "It is not the healthy who need a doctor, but the sick" (Matt. 9:12). Again, "I have not come to call the righteous, but sinners" (v. 13). By such statements Jesus assumed that the religious Pharisees needed the new birth; so he highlighted their unwarranted moral egotism. The basic human issue is not adjustment to this world but adjustment to God and his nonnegotiable righteousness. "To some who were confident of their own righteousness and looked down on everybody else" (Luke 18:9), Jesus told the parable of the Pharisee and the tax collector, both of whom went to the temple to pray. Because he acknowledged his moral obtuseness in crying out, "God, have mercy on me, a sinner" (v. 13), the tax collector rather than the "healthy-minded" Pharisee went home justified.

Knowing that human nature universally is an evil tree that brings forth evil fruit, Christ said to Nicodemus the Pharisee, "I tell you the truth, no one can see the kingdom of God unless he is born again" (John 3:3). Not even those children who have had the best of

human nurture in a Christian home and church escape that universal necessity. After Nicodemus raised a question, Jesus explained, "No one can enter the kingdom of God unless he is born of water and the Spirit. Flesh gives birth to flesh, but the Spirit gives birth to spirit" (vv. 5–6). Human nurture is a means the Spirit may use, but however skillfully done, nurture is no substitute for the Holy Spirit's transformation of the human heart.

Were All Saved at the Cross?

Karl Barth proposed that the Messiah's death was more than a *provision* that sinners may or may not choose to accept. He held that Christ *realized salvation objectively* for all humans generically in the first century (see vol. 2, chaps. 7–8). Since everyone after the Cross is depraved in nature, however, each sinner needs to receive Christ's provisions for redemption, reconciliation and forgiveness. And every depraved person needs to respond to the Spirit's call, to convert, and be regenerated. God chooses people who will not deny their sin but who will repent of it and believe. Human potential and psychological renewal programs may alleviate symptoms, but something more radical is needed to change our inner natures, our personal relationship to God, and our status before God's moral law.

The hypothesis of theoretical universalism is difficult to accommodate to the abundant data in the biblical section concerning sinners' urgent need to believe, repent, and trust Christ to be saved. God has purposed in history to make the children of the Devil (John 8:44) his children by their conversion and regeneration. Since conversion is necessary for one to become a child of God (John 1:12), the status of sonship was not realized at the Cross. Although Christ's atonement "brings life for all men" (Rom. 5:18) as a gift, Gentiles as well as Jews personally must receive it.

Were the Elect Saved at the Cross?

Some suggest that the salvation of *the elect* was realized at the Cross. They appeal to texts such as Romans 8:29–30 that guarantee the salvation of the elect from eternity past. But God's people chosen from before the foundation of the world are destined to receive the provisions of the Atonement through their conversion and regeneration in time. The Father's eternal purposes for the "sheep" given to the Son in no way render their historical participation meaningless. God realizes his sovereign purposes successively in history through our responsible Spirit-enabled decisions and commitments.

A variation of the hypothesis that salvation was realized at the Cross was developed by Neal Punt. He suggests that all persons are elect in Christ and that salvation was achieved in the first century for *all* universally *except* for those the Bible explicitly states are lost—i.e., murderers, liars, etc.[115] Punt's primary proof text is Romans 5:18: "just as the result of one trespass was condemnation for all men, so also the result of the one act of righteousness was justification for all men." But the immediate context of this verse indicates that the blessings of Christ's cross are experienced by those who "*receive* God's abundant *provision* of grace" (v. 17). Sinners receive the provisions of the Cross at conversion during their lifetimes, expressed visibly in the enacted sign of baptism (6:3–4). (This is not to mention the repeated emphasis on belief and faith throughout Romans 4 and 5.) The context of other Scriptures to which Punt appeals apply only to believers who have become united to Christ by faith. The interpretation of Paul's parallel between Adam and Christ (Rom. 5:12–18) that fits the

context most coherently claims that all born of Adam's race are condemned in his one act, and all who are born again as children of God's family are justified by the one act of Christ.

Can Naturalists Adequately Account for Christian Conversion?

The logical positivist, A. J. Ayer said, "If the mystic who asserts that he is seeing God is merely asserting that he is experiencing a peculiar kind of sense-content, then we do not for a moment deny that his assertions may be true."[116] If, however, the mystic speaks of something beyond sense content (presumably like moral transformation) the mystic "simply supplies material for the psycho-analyst!"[117] Other naturalistic explanations of religious conversion abound. The German romantic writer Goethe said that mystical experience is simply the infusion of strong and over-mastering feeling into the operations of the intellect. J. B. Pratt expressed his naturalistic position thus: "Imitation, social education, and individual suggestion furnish quite a sufficient explanation for all the phenomena of mysticism"[118] (and we might add conversion and regeneration). Other naturalists speak of the emergence of a more unified or higher sense of selfhood, the resolution of conflict, intensity of emotional involvement, and the displacement of one belief system by another. There may be some truth in these explanations of religious experience. But Lit-sen Chang, a Zen Buddhist who converted to Christ, concluded, "I should say now that what Zen offered me was merely a technique of self-intoxication and a sense of false security."[119]

In reducing all conversions to Christ to physical or psychological factors, naturalists reason fallaciously. "The genetic fallacy is committed when the latter stages of a process are evaluated only in terms of its earlier stages."[120] Some circumstances attendant to the origin of the experience of conversion to Christ may be similar to ordinary conversions from one philosophy or religion to another. Fair scholarly evaluations of religious experiences, however, seek to do justice to both similarities and differences.

The *differences* in Christian and non-Christian conversion may not reside so much in the observable psychological symptoms as in other unique factors. The object about whom the personality is integrated is not a mere human witness or a human Christian institution, but Jesus Christ himself. Robert O. Ferm observed that "the difference between the Christian and non-Christian turns out to be, not a difference in psychological symptoms, but rather in the object about which the new personality is integrated. The thing that makes Christian conversion different, then, is Christ."[121] The Christ to whom we refer is the Jesus of history and of Scripture attested by the Holy Spirit.

People who arbitrarily exclude the possibility of unverifiable acts of God's Spirit speak not in terms of all the relevant external and internal data but as presumptive, reductive secularists. Flo Conway and Jim Seigelman, in *Snapping: America's Epidemic of Sudden Personality Change,* fail to do justice to the spiritual differences by pointing to an alleged common quest for intense ecstatic moments and a sudden profound conversion.[122] They illicitly associate the experience of twice-born Christians with the trancelike states of Transcendental Meditators. Some superficial similarities may exist, but the radical differences between Christian and Hindu religious experience have been documented elsewhere.[123] Conway and Siegelman also irresponsibly classify evangelical conversions with the ecstacies and bizarre trancelike states that characterize many cult activities.[124] Referring to the conversion of Charles Colson as told in his book *Born Again,* these authors cite his involvement in the Watergate crimes, the physical sensations he felt, and the tears of release that flowed. But they report nothing of Colson's reading of C. S. Lewis's *Case for Christianity,* the witness of peers to the Gospel, or the power of the Holy Spirit in his life.

In *The Battle for the Mind,* William Sargant concerns himself "not with the immortal soul which is the province of the theologian . . . but with the brain and nervous system, which man shares with the dog and other animals."[125] His experimentation with dogs showed how stimuli such as electric currents of varying strength produced responses like an anxiety state and eventual collapse. Observing some examples of religious conversion he noted similar stimuli and responses. He claimed that a subject's emotions must be worked up by "brain washing" to abnormal degrees of anger, fear, and exaltation. Having initially limited his treatment to the physiological, it is not surprising that he reduced all conversions to physiological conditioning and response.[126] Ian Rammage in *The Battle for the Free Mind* shows the factual inaccuracies in Sargant's treatments of the allegedly identical "breakdown under external stress exhaustion" and of "abreaction of internal stress leading to healing."[127] Apart from the conviction and witness of the Spirit, people can make a number of other changes in their lives. An adequate hypothesis, however, must account not only for changes of symptoms but also for the most radical moral transformation of the perverted human heart.

Does Psychotherapy Explain Away Regeneration?

It is popularly thought that all belief in God through Christ is a psychological projection of a father image by someone who feels the need of assistance amid the pressures and turmoil of life. If that were the case, one could also say that all atheism and antiregeneration talk is a mere projection of one's hatred for one's father. Granting that these conflicting projections cancel one another out, we need to test the hypotheses by meaningful evidence.

Paul Tournier observed that psychotherapy justifiably rejects the trap of pharisaic legalism sometimes found in Christian churches, but it irresponsibly dismisses Christianity's radical honesty, confession, and repentance.[128] Actual guilt before God for premeditated moral evil can be handled in two ways. First, the weight of real guilt may become so intolerable that there is the natural tendency to repress it and to justify oneself by blaming our problems on spouses, friends, society, religion, or God. Second, this inner lack of peace may lead to casting one's repentant self on the mercy of the divine court and receiving the gift of forgiving grace. The first route leads to disaster. "It is natural for man to project his guilt upon other people and upon God. But he does not thereby get rid of it, and the rebellion against others and against God which results becomes in its turn a source of fresh impulsions to evil, and therefore of more guilt."[129] It is such moralism and pharisaic legalism that psychology opposes, not the honest recognition of our evil desires, acceptance of responsibility for ourselves, repentance, and the joy of forgiveness. Jesus Christ also opposed the proud Pharisees knowing that the sequence of guilt-anger-crime-guilt can lead only to despair.

Irritation, obduracy, aggressiveness: this is the law of unconscious and repressed guilt. Conversely, pardon and grace produce joy, relaxation and security, an atmosphere in which guilt can become conscious, mature, be openly acknowledged, and in its turn, lead on to pardon and grace. So the enemy, guilt, becomes a friend, because it leads to the experience of grace.[130]

God gave the moral law not to crush sinners but to drive them to Christ for forgiveness and deliverance from the vicious circle of self-justification. In communion with the living God the sense of guilt, so far from being blunted, is sharpened. Sinners feel their wretchedness vis-à-vis the holiness of God to whom all are accountable. "But instead of petrifying us, this sense of guilt is stimulating and revivifying because it leads to a true and personal relationship with God."[131] The mentality of self-justification must be radically transformed into a mentality of grace. That calls for a radical change of mind, a *metanoia*.

Is Conversion to Christ a Mystical Experience?

Aldous Huxley designated pantheism "the Perennial Philosophy."[132] In the pantheistic experience of feeling one with the All, William James found that monists (1) lost a sense of distinctness from the One, (2) neglected history, (3) were passive, and (4) had a sense of psychological certitude.[133] The Chicago investigative reporter William Braden found that drug-induced experiences also resulted in (1) a loss of a sense of personal ego with no dualities, and (2) a sense that time stopped and words lost all meaning—although people felt they had experienced ultimate reality.[134]

The New Age mystic Marilyn Ferguson thinks that God is totally immanent and that consequently "human nature is neither good nor bad but open to continuous transformation and transcendence."[135] She imagines that we are "spiritually free" and the stewards of our own evolution; thus she seeks to "communicate the vision and the

111

infinite possibilities of human potential."[136] Her first great challenge is "to create a consensus that fundamental change is possible."[137] Mystical experiences of the divine energy within us come to consciousness as we meditate, chant, visualize, repeat positive affirmations, etc.

A Christian view of fallen human nature is more realistic. Although God created his image-bearers with high potential in fellowship and service, sin has kept us from sustaining fellowship with God and others by even the most disciplined devotional techniques. Our perversity also keeps us from serving God and others with pure motives. Complete peace with justice and love will be realized only when the Prince of Peace returns. Meanwhile we overcome our evil inclinations by being born again and receiving from God's Spirit a new nature. Fallen humans do not achieve their fullest potential apart from a special, supernatural divine grace.[138]

The characteristics of Christian conversion are radically different from those of pantheistic mystics. Instead of an ecstatic "I-That" experience, Christians enjoy a personal "I-Thou" experience of fellowship with God. According to the latter, time does not stop but history gains fresh significance in the kingdom of God. Neither do words lose meaning; rather, scriptural teaching becomes more precious. Christians possess not only a psychological certitude but also sound reasons for believing they are children of God. The Christian experience of conversion is inaccurately classified with mystical experiences in pantheistic world religions.

Is Faith Nonconceptual?

Many people regard faith as little more than sincerity. Friedrich Schliermacher defined faith as *a feeling of dependence* upon a higher power. According to Søren Kierkegaard, faith is exclusively a matter of *passionate commitment*. Emil Brunner viewed faith not as a response to propositions or evidence but as a nonpropositional *personal encounter* with the living Christ. Karl Barth held that faith does not involve assent to propositions and doctrines but is the freedom to affirm the Word (the living Christ) as binding and absolutely valid for the world, the community, and oneself.[139] Faith, he judged, is a person-to-person experience of the contemporary Christ, not a matter of information about the Jesus of *historie*. Paul Tillich said that faith is accepting our acceptance in spite of evidence to the contrary indicating that we are unacceptable.[140] And W. T. Stace held that faith did not call for assent to the truth of any propositions, but declared that faith is a synonym for an ineffable, mystical intuition.[141]

Surely there are religious feelings, encounters, and crises that we humans do not fully understand. Nevertheless, insofar as the preceding hypotheses do not judge essential the hearing of assertions that Jesus is the eternal Word who became flesh, died for our sins, and rose again, they are all inadequate to account for the early Christians' faith in the teachings of Christ and Scripture. We may incorporate into our view elements of truth concerning engagement and commitment; but genuinely Christian encounter and commitment are directed to the transcendent Christ by hearing and assenting to the truth of the Gospel.

Are Nonbelievers Implicit Converts?

May an atheist who opposes unworthy concepts of God and the values of justice and love be considered an implicit theist? May a non-Christian who repents but does not receive the Good News have implicit faith in Christ? Given the effectiveness of the Spirit's ministries in the lives of those who decisively repent, the issue is extremely hypothetical. If missionaries meet people already repentant and ready to believe when they hear the Gospel, they may be considered *prepared* for belief but not implicit believers. Our position is that the Spirit who began this preparatory work will bring the Gospel to them, and then they will become explicit believers.

Roman Catholicism suggested the idea of implicit faith to soften the doctrine of "no salvation outside the church." Protestants are not overjoyed with the idea that they have implicit faith in the authority of the pope. Neither are non-Christians comforted to discover that unknowingly they are believers in Christ or in God. The idea of someone else suggesting that persons have a faith that they do not consciously affirm could easily be abused by coercive communist programmers and religious deprogrammers. It raises serious ethical issues, such as, Is it intellectually honest?

All who have God's moral norms written on their hearts (see vol. 1, chap. 2) disobey them to some extent. Why then should we assume that if they had the Gospel they would adhere to it? Even if an affirmative response to the law could be demonstrated, that would not serve as a good analogy of acceptance of the Gospel. The fact that one does good for oneself may not indicate that one will humbly accept what another has done on his behalf.

Belief and faith lose their meaning if regarded as implicit or unconscious. Belief is a *conscious* act of assent to the truth of an affirmation. A person cannot give personal assent to the truth of unknown propositions. Faith also involves a conscious act of holistic commitment to the living Christ. If words have meaning, it is fallacious to claim that a person without belief or faith in Christ has genuine assent and commitment. The many effects of faith, such as a new desire to pray and praise God or lead others to Christ cannot be done by a proxy. The concept of implicit faith is as self-contradictory as proxy faith. It is as impossible for one person to believe the Gospel, repent of sin, and trust Christ for others as it is for someone else to eat food for others. The notion that unbelievers have implicit faith may be thought comforting. But comfort that fails to conform to reality will not last. The Bible knows of no salvation apart from faith in Christ.

Should We Call for Repentance in This Dispensation?

According to L. S. Chafer, the evangelistic message invites Gentile sinners only to believe. He claims that it is erroneous to require repentance prior to the act of believing. Chafer argues that a separate call to repentance is addressed only to Israel (Matt. 10:5–6) and to Christians (2 Cor. 7:8–11). But the sole message that should be brought to unsaved Gentiles is "believe." Belief includes abandoning all other grounds of hope, and so Chafer considers repentance an unspoken element of saving faith.[142] Chafer even considers repentance a synonym for believing in Bible passages addressed to Gentiles. He cannot distinguish repentance from faith because he finds that some 150 Scripture texts condition salvation on believing only. And he adds that the gospel of John and the epistle to the Romans fail to mention the word repentance in relation to salvation. Covenant people in Israel and the church may be called upon to repent, not in order to be saved, but to restore a former relationship with God.[143]

Certainly God commands all people everywhere to repent (Acts 17:30). Repentance is not something separate from conversion, for a turning *to* Christ necessarily involves turning *from* other masters. The term "repentance" need not be mentioned for the concept to be implicit in the command to first-century Gentiles to turn from their idols to receive Christ. To receive Christ as the light of the world is to turn from darkness (John 8:12). One who receives Christ and becomes a child of God (1:12) rejects his previous father, the Devil (8:44). To live like the one father is not to live like the other. If Jesus is just added as one more of many finite gods on a "god shelf," the exalted Jesus is not the one Mediator. In the first century, conversion to Christ involved a radical break with moralistic legalism, pride of status, idolatry, and occultism. In that setting texts in John that simply call people to "believe" point up the need for knowledge, assent, and a commitment to Christ that repudiate bondage to the Deceiver.

Must Christ Be Acknowledged as Lord to Be Savior?

One does not *make* Jesus Lord but *confesses* that the crucified Jesus is Lord of creation and redemption. Christ's lordship is inherent in the *apostolic Gospel*. The early Christians confessed that Jesus is Lord (Acts 2:21, 36; 16:31; Rom. 10:9–10, 12). Thomas, after finally seeing the risen Christ for himself exclaimed, "My Lord and my God!" (John 20:28). To believe the truth about Jesus is to assent to claims that the eternal Logos became flesh, atoned for our sins, rose from the grave, and ascended to the right hand of the Father, where he reigns as Lord of all. Those who believe the Gospel believe in Christ as Savior and Lord.

Christ's exclusive lordship is inherent in the meaning of *repentance*. The change of mind concerning Christ means a change of mind concerning previous masters. Repentance is not a synonym of a positive belief, as Ryrie maintains;[144] repentance is the negative side of the same conversion. No one

can be committed to two ultimate masters morally or spiritually. Christ's lordship is also integral to the meaning of *faith* as unreserved trust in Jesus for life eternal. No one less than the eternal Lord of all could grant eternal life to believers. Those who follow the Lord of all leave activities that are displeasing to him. With renewed abilities they begin to function in a new moral direction. According to the parable of the sower, the seed that falls on good ground brings forth spiritual fruit. And, according to Paul, the faith that justifies (Gal. 2:16) is the faith that expresses itself by love (Gal. 5:6). Works that are good in God's sight are motivated by love and energized by the Spirit, not the flesh. We are not born again because of our good works, but we are born again to do good works. The new life produces evident life-signs.

Belief in the lordship of Christ is *indispensable when facing moral and spiritual conflicts*. Christ commissioned Paul not only to tell Gentiles about justification and adoption but also to "turn them from darkness to light" and also "from the power of Satan to God" (Acts 26:18). The objective of conversion is a powerful regeneration that overcomes evil powers within and without. Christ died and the Holy Spirit came to deliver believers from domination by fleshly desires, words, and deeds. Converts do not initially comprehend all that the Messiah's truth and power mean for their living in present or future situations. And the most committed may not always obey what they do understand. Growth in understanding and applying Jesus' wise and loving instruction develops progressively throughout believers' lives. But from the beginning believers ought to know that the Jesus who died for them is the Head of the body of believers, the King under whose rule they have become subjects, the Owner for whom they work as stewards, and the Judge to whom they are ultimately accountable. Conversion, however, marks the Spirit-enabled initial reception of Christ's work for us, not our work for him.

RELEVANCE FOR LIFE AND SERVICE

What Major Problem Faces the Church Today?

One of the most crucial problems of the Christian church is not a lack of marketing skills or church growth techniques. The more penetrating problem is its members' lack of moral and spiritual commitment to Christ. Apparently many have believed the Gospel, but evidence of repentance for sin and trust in Christ is not as apparent. Too easily the unconverted may call themselves Christians and church members. Many members and leaders do not seem to be authentically converted from a life driven by the flesh to one controlled by the Spirit. Either people are alive to God or they are not. C. S. Lewis graphically illustrated the point: "It may be hard for an egg to turn into a bird; it would be a jolly sight harder for it to learn to fly while remaining an egg. We are like eggs at present. And you cannot go on indefinitely being an ordinary decent egg. We must be hatched or go bad."[145]

Rather than judging others who show few spiritual life-signs, invite them to take a candid look at their lives. Leaders must ask church members to make an exacting self-examination: "Examine yourselves to see whether you are in the faith; test yourselves" (2 Cor. 13:5; cf. 1 Cor. 11:28). But before asking church members to examine themselves, leaders must search their own hearts. Both leaders and members must determine if Christ and his life are central. Consider Robert E. Coleman's diagnosis of "The Principle Issue Today" in *The Master Plan of Evangelism:*

> The whole thing revolves around the Person of the Master. Basically his way was his life. And so it must be with his followers. We have his life in us by the Spirit if we are to do his work and practice his teaching. Any evangelistic work without this is as lifeless as it is meaningless. Only as the Spirit of Christ in us exalts the Son are men drawn unto the Father.
>
> Of course, we cannot give something away which we do not possess ourselves. The very ability to give away our life in Christ is the proof of its possession. Nor can we withhold that which we possess in the Spirit of Christ, and still keep it. The Spirit of God always insists on making Christ known. Here is the great paradox of life—we must die to ourselves in order to live in Christ, and in that renunciation of ourselves, we must give ourselves away in service and devotion to our Lord. This was Jesus' method of evangelism, seen at first only by His few followers, but through them it was to become the power of God in overcoming the world.[146]

Make Clear the Theology of the Cross

The Cross rightly interpreted must remain central to our evangelism. The way to new life is the way of the Cross. The way to Christlikeness is the way of death to un-Christlikeness. We do not make the Gospel clear if we fail to point out its negative, as well as its positive, implications. Disciples must both uphold the meaning of the Cross and expose the powers and values arrayed against it. Christ drew attention to negative demands of the Gospel when he asked the rich young ruler to sell all that he possessed. Had Paul, Augustine, or Luther preached only the positive side of the message, we would have a very different world today. An unrealistic treatment of our sin and its consequence does not make tough disciples for tough times. "Cheap grace," said Bonhoeffer, "is the preaching of forgiveness without requiring repentance, baptism without Church discipline, Communion without confession, absolution without contrition."[147]

How can God fill the deep emptiness of our lives and give us identity, meaning, and purpose? Job cried, "If only I knew where I might find him!" (Job 23:3). The Great Eternal One answered Job's cry and told us that we may find him redemptively in his Son. Resolution of the human dilemma comes only through the Gospel, the message of the cross of Jesus Christ. Thus Jesus said, "Come to me, all you who are weary and burdened, and I will give you rest. Take my yoke upon you and learn from me, for I am gentle and humble in heart, and you will find rest for your souls" (Matt. 11:28–29). Before assuring people of soul-rest, however, we must be sure they have authentically "come" to the Lord Jesus Christ, taken up his yoke, and pursued the path of disciplined learning from him. Faithful disciples need to hold fast to that eternal Gospel and clearly expound its meaning for lost and forlorn souls today.

Do the Work of an Evangelist

What is the best way today to communicate the Gospel and call forth belief from unbelievers? If we simply inform them of the Gospel's facts and meanings, the bottom line then becomes: How many people heard the message? If we use a manipulative monologue, the bottom line becomes: How many people said yes? For many hearers the temptation is to be courteous and respond positively to please the evangelist. For example, some African cultures consider it rude to refuse a sincere offer. Thus when the preacher (usually from the West) forcefully invites people to "receive Christ," virtually all raise their hands. But not all

these trusted Christ in saving faith. Preferably the evangelist engages in a nonmanipulative dialogue (Acts 17:17), sharing honest concern for his hearers in order to help them discover their basic moral and spiritual needs. We may seek a decision as one important step, but the goal of evangelism is not mere decisions but disciples in the body of Christ. Furthermore, an evangelistic process that does not build relationships with a local church may persuade people who show no signs of new spiritual life that they are Christians.

Grace is free, but it is not cheap. Evangelism is not a project but a relational process involving one's entire lifestyle. Among the early believers in Acts, evangelism was the constant outflow of experience with Christ. But there are "seasons" like cultivating of caring relationships, sowing the seeds of relevant truth, and harvesting by persuading the will to respond with total commitment. We ought not judge success only from the final step of the evangelistic process; it needs to be considered also in its cultivating, caring, relating, and communicating stages. The greatest number of people are won to Christ, not by the clergy or church programs, but by a friend or family member who demonstrates truth, life, and love from the Spirit of Christ.

The faithful evangelist will ensure that those to whom he ministers repent of moral and spiritual slavery and trust Christ alone. As Christian disciples talk with those who profess to have accepted Christ, it is not a matter of how much they *remember* about their earlier conversion. The issue, rather, is whether they can sincerely testify to *being* a regenerate person. Do they now believe the objective truth of the gospel message? Are they now trusting the living Christ for acceptance with God eternally? Do they experience deliverance from the dominion of darkness?

Are their highest value and concern self and sinful pleasures or the triune God?

Deal Openly with Honest Doubts

Before and after conversion people may be assailed by doubts under the influence of alternative ideas from many sources. "Doubt is a state of mind in suspension *between* faith and unbelief." [148] Doubters ought not think themselves unique, for doubt is everyone's problem. A person who struggles with doubts is not a disbeliever but one humbly willing to follow evidence where it leads. A doubter is open to belief when evidence and argument become conclusive. "Doubt acts as a sparring partner both to truth and error. It keeps faith trim and helps to shed the paunchiness of error." [149] Some Christians constantly talk about their doubts, others give the impression that all their beliefs are assured. The fact is that every Christian's faith will be tested at one time or another.

Intellectual questions deserve intellectual answers. The invitation to faith is not an invitation to irrationality, for Christianity is founded on assent to truth. Christians should think through *what* they believe and *why* throughout their lives. The Bereans "examined the Scriptures every day to see if what Paul said was true" (Acts 17:11). What is knowable can be critically checked and verified to some degree of probability. Knowledge without data from experience is empty; data from experience without knowledge is blind. We ought not dismiss genuine questions to make room for faith. Knowledge is not mere feeling or opinion, nor a leap into the dark. Christians believe in the invisible Messiah on the basis of visible evidence from history and Scripture. Without genuine understanding of truth to guide commitment, what passes for faith may be a counterfeit confidence. The Gospel of Christ is not just a ticket to heaven, it is a set of convictions to live by and die for.

Some doubts, although presented as intellectual difficulties, result from having had a bad experience. While a student of an influential naturalistic philosopher in New York City, Ralph Keiper discovered in a discussion after class that his noted professor was still fighting his father's faith. "It is not a sign of weakness to have wounds, but to keep wounds from being healed is sheer stupidity." [150] Os Guinness offers a prescription for those troubled with doubts rooted in moral rebellion:

> The best long-term remedy lies in remembering that God is light and that we are called to "walk in the light as he himself is in the light" (1 John 1:7). We should practice a style of openness in our relationships that will mean constant forgiveness for our sins, healing for our wounds, comfort in our sorrow. If this is our practice, if we make this the disciplined set of our mind, then we will be letting God be God over our sins, over our wounds and over our sorrows—in short, over all our problems. [151]

Address the Deepest Need for Repentance

In his farewell report to the Ephesian elders Paul said, "I have declared to both Jews and Greeks that they must turn to God in repentance and have faith in our Lord Jesus Christ" (Acts 20:21). To the leaders of the city-state in the Areopagus he said, God now "commands all people everywhere to repent" (Acts 17:30). Faithful disciples understand that their call for sinners to convert requires a summons to repentance. In considering repentance, sinners should heed Paul's injunction: "A man ought to examine himself" (1 Cor. 11:28). Honest self-examination requires looking at one's thoughts, motives, aspirations, and actions in the light of God's law. It means asking the

117

following questions: Are my purposes in the world aligned with those of the kingdom he rules? How do I measure up before God's nonnegotiable moral standards? Above all, self-examination means comparing oneself not with other humans but with Jesus Christ. "Do not begin ever considering what is wrong with you without first being quite sure your mind is directed towards the glory of God as it has shown forth in Jesus Christ."[152] John's words relate to the need for repentance: "If we claim to be without sin, we deceive ourselves and the truth is not in us" (1 John 1:8; cf. v. 10). God promises, however, that "if we confess our sins, he is faithful and just and will forgive us our sins and purify us from all unrighteousness" (v. 9).

Penitent sinners also need to face up to the matter of personal guilt. How honestly we handle our sense of guilt likely will affect our mental and spiritual health. It is abundantly clear that no man or woman lives totally free from sin and guilt. Paul Tournier observed that as our sense of guilt "is repressed or recognized"

> it sets in motion one of two contradictory processes: repressed, it leads to anger, rebellion, fear and anxiety, a deadening conscience, an increasing inability to recognize one's faults, and a growing dominance of aggressive tendencies. But consciously recognized, it leads to repentance, to the peace and security of divine pardon, and in that way to a progressive refinement of conscience and a steady weakening of aggressive impulses.[153]

True repentance will be expressed in heartfelt confession. Until David confessed his conspiracy to murder and commit adultery his sin was always before him (Ps. 51:3), his bones were crushed (v. 8), his heart was unclean, his spirit not steadfast (v. 10), and his communion with God was broken (v. 11a). The ministry of the Spirit in

his life was quenched (v. 11b). With guilt unresolved David had lost the joy of his salvation (v. 12). Only after he confessed his sins with radical candor was his guilt eased and blessed fellowship with God restored.

Christian leaders in each generation and culture need to remember the warning of English scholar R. E. O. White, who wrote,

> We assume too readily that because forgiveness is free it must be easy. We emphasize peace more than purity, comforting rather than cleansing, relief of guilty souls more than regeneration of sinful hearts. Thus we sometimes heal the hurt of sin too slightly, and evangelical experience and evangelical piety are often shallow in consequence.

White's additional words also need to be emblazoned indelibly on every evangelical Christian's mind and heart:

> Upon the meaning that we give to repentance turns the inmost truth and power of all evangelical Christianity, and the meaning of the Protestant Reformation. . . . Luther saw that penance and true penitence were miles apart. The penitent heart . . . must turn with loathing from the sin itself, crying out in broken pride for mercy, and casting oneself by faith upon the grace of Christ. With that realization Protestantism was born, and New Testament Christianity returned to Europe.[154]

New converts find it beneficial to *become radically honest with a support group*. Even if confession to God and others were not necessary for forgiveness, it would be necessary for relationships with other persons. Jesus said that we will be forgiven as we forgive others (Matt. 6:14–15; cf. Eph. 4:32; James 5:16). The fact that some confession to a priest is done in a legalistic spirit does not rule out the possibility of sincere and honest confession of sins to one another. Given the priesthood of every believer, we can confess our sins not merely to a spiritual leader but to spiritually earnest brothers and sisters. For some time Paul Tournier's religious life was characterized largely by assent to the Apostles' Creed until he met men who honestly confessed their sins to one another. From their example began the regular practice of confession. In Tournier's words, "The whole climate of my life changed. I was at last experiencing what I had known for a long time. 'Now I understand,' I said, 'what the action of the Holy Spirit, the conviction of sin and the experience of grace really are.' "[155] Soon thereafter a spiritual ministry opened up for Tournier: "I have seen men come to me in large numbers and find true freedom as the result of an absolutely concrete confession of their faults."

To avoid *abuses* of public confession it is wise to consider how widely sins should be confessed. As a general rule the confession should be as extensive as the knowledge and injury of the sin. Private sin thus calls for private confession to God. Sin against one's spouse requires confession to God and one's husband or wife. Sin against the church mandates confession to God and the church. When planning *evangelistic and worship* services, allow significant opportunity for the collective confession of sins, including at the Lord's Table. In more liturgical contexts ensure that repetition of the confession does not become routine and meaningless.

Inward repentance further expresses itself in making restitution where possible. Like the Gentiles in Paul's day, we must "prove" our repentance by our deeds (Acts 26:20). Restitution is the return to the rightful possessor of what has been misappropriated, or reparation made for an injury done. Restitution is based on the principle that a right has been violated. The Old Testament set forth an elaborate system of compensation. In general the reparation should be equivalent in value to the loss, but in some cases it was to be four, five, or even seven times that (Exod. 21:18–36; Prov. 6:31). In the New Testament, Zacchaeus, the converted tax collector, said he would restore four times the amount he had cheated others out of (Luke 19:8). In making restitution, do for others as you would have them do for you. Speedy reconciliation with those who have something against us precedes acceptable giving to God (Matt. 5:23–26).[156]

Rejoice in Forgiveness (Absolution)

Sinners who have come to repentance and faith rejoice in the assurance of divine absolution. To be "absolved" (from the Latin *absolvo*) is to be "set free." In the final analysis our sin is against God; thus only God the Father and his unique Son can set believers free from their sins (Luke 7:47–50; Rev. 1:5b). Absolution assures repentant believers of the Father's forgiveness on the ground of Christ's atonement and Spirit-inspired promises. Both privately and publicly, Protestants emphasize confession directly to God and offer assurance of divine absolution on the basis of faithful Gospel sayings.

The resurrected Messiah said to his disciples gathered on the first day of the week: " 'Peace be with you! As the Father has sent me, I am sending you.' And with that he breathed on them and said, 'Receive the Holy Spirit. If you forgive anyone his sins, they are forgiven; if you do not forgive them, they are not forgiven' " (John 20:21–23; cf. Matt. 18:18). In statements like these Christ delegated to his Spirit-empowered witnesses the joy of conveying assurance of forgiveness to other penitent persons.

As ambassadors in Christ's stead and on the authority of faithful promises, believer-priests may assure other converts of their absolution. Those who announce God's reprieve should be accountable to a church, but that joyful privilege need not be limited to ordained clergy. However hesitant unordained Christians may feel about pronouncing a sinner forgiven, all believers have been given the Holy Spirit, and with his presence comes the joy of assuring penitents who trust Christ that they also are forgiven![157]

Trust the Holy Spirit to Produce the Fruit of Regeneration

No self-help seminars, no new schemes of education, no otherwise helpful social programs can alter human nature and permanently change society. As Jesus plainly said, "What is born of the flesh is flesh, and what is born of the Spirit is spirit" (John 3:6, NRSV). The "theology that contemplates nothing higher than moral suasion and free-will, and which repudiates the supernatural," George Smeaton warned, "is soon divested of all evangelical power as well as of all permanence and strength."[158] Smeaton also insisted that "the essential feature of Christianity, according to our Lord's own delineation, is the new birth; and so indispensable is it that without the new nature there can be no evangelical health or progress."[159] However intensely evangelicals become sensitized to egregious injustices resulting from economic and political forces, ministers must continue to focus on the necessity of new spiritual life. The health and progress of evangelicalism in the final years of the twentieth century and in the twenty-first will improve only as the necessity of conversion and regeneration is given first priority.

Christian conversion is not merely a change of association, culture, or religion;[160] it also involves a transformation of human nature. Apart from the Spirit no Christian can give sinners life from above. On the day of Pentecost Peter preached to convince sinners that Jesus was both Lord and Messiah (Acts 2:36); three thousand people were converted because he was filled with the Holy Spirit. However well qualified otherwise, ministers and missionaries who seek to bring others into God's kingdom need to be led and empowered by the Holy Spirit. However thorough our training, however extensive our experience, we all need the Spirit's working in evangelistic endeavors.

Jesus Christ himself began his public ministry by receiving the Holy Spirit (Matt. 3:16–17; Luke 3:21–22). The Lord said to his followers: "You will receive power when the Holy Spirit comes on you, and you will be my witnesses" (Acts 1:8) in your community, throughout your region, and to the ends of the earth. Following Pentecost the Spirit came upon Samaritan and Gentile believers when they believed (Acts 8 and 10). The Spirit directed Philip to the Ethiopian eunuch whom he led to Christ (Acts 8:29–39). The Spirit had to overcome Peter's reluctance to witness to Cornelius, a Gentile (Acts 10:19). It was the Spirit who directed the church at Antioch to set apart Barnabas and Paul for crosscultural witness (Acts 13:2, 4). The Spirit restrained them from going to Asia or Bithynia and instead directed them to Macedonia (Acts 16:6–10), where the Lord opened Lydia's heart to receive the Gospel (v. 14) and brought their jailer to faith (vv. 30–34). Leighton Ford observed:

> The Holy Spirit was working at both ends of the evangelistic encounter. He prepared and directed the evangelists, and he also prepared and opened the hearts of the evangelized, enabling them to seek. Through prayer and intuition, through the study of situations, societies and people, through inner promptings and outer promptings, the Spirit is the master strategist, and the church must seek to be sensitive to him and his promptings.[161]

The responsibilities of preaching the Gospel as a message of life to some and a message of death to others may seem too much to bear. "Who is equal to such a task?" (2 Cor. 2:16). Paul found strength in the knowledge that his Corinthian converts were the fruit of the divine Spirit working in human hearts (2 Cor. 3:3). Like Paul, we confess, "Not that we are competent in ourselves . . . but our competence comes from God. He has made us competent as ministers of a new covenant—not of the letter but of the Spirit; for the letter kills, but the Spirit gives life" (vv. 5–6). As human servants we cannot coerce anyone into the kingdom of God. But through the gentle yet powerful ministry of the Spirit God can change lives eternally.

Help Converts Enjoy a New Sense of Identity

Many people spend years trying to find themselves, and some never do. But by grace the converted can discover who they really are. Believers may enter into a rich and multifaceted existence that opens up to them. Consider the following ways in which new converts may grow in their Christian identity:

1. Recognize yourself as a moral and spiritual child of God. The true convert is no longer holistically corrupted but is renewed by the Spirit in the image of God. John wrote, "To all who received him, to those who believed in his name, he gave the right to become children of God—children born not of natural descent, nor of human decision or a husband's will, but born of God" (John 1:12–13). The saints' ultimate concern is no longer autonomous pleasure but pleasing the Savior and Lord who seeks their best. As good as it is to celebrate annually the birthdays of our family members, we should celebrate with greater joy the full significance of our spiritual birthdays. An approximate date will do for those who can no longer recall the event.

2. Enjoy the experience of belonging to God's family. We all like settings where we belong, feel comfortable, and where everyone knows our name. The good news is we don't have to wait for heaven to enjoy these delights. Here and now we can enjoy our personal acceptance by the Lord. In addition, we can delight in the blessed fellowship of other twice-born people in Christ's church. The saints enjoy each other's love (John 15:12), fellowship in worship (Acts 2:42), spiritual and emotional encouragement (Gal. 6:2, 10), and practical support (Acts 20:35) in the oneness of the body (1 Cor. 12:13). This means that new converts will identify with a local church and participate fully in its life and ministry. Since our new identity has a corporate component, absenting oneself from the local form of the body will have deleterious effects.

3. Develop new meaning, values, and purposes. People of faith are loyal to a new object of ultimate devotion. The exalted Lord of all becomes their new spiritual, intellectual, and moral standard of reference. To love Christ is to love what he has said in his Word. The radical change of heart means that radically new desires, new purposes in life, and new loves become dominant. New methods of decision making will result in new short-term objectives and long-term goals. The conversion of the whole person to Christ made a holistic difference for Jews in the first century and ought to do so for Jews and Gentiles today. Conversion, including both repentance and faith, will bring about a major reorientation of our personalities with reference to God, his character, and his purposes as disclosed in the Christ of the Scriptures.

4. Celebrate the new life by being baptized. All who have heard the Gospel, exercised repentant faith, and been

121

born again should follow their Lord's command to be baptized. By God's Spirit one is baptized into the mystical body of Christ; by the hands of a minister one is baptized into the local expression of Christ's body, a church. Although baptism in water does not convey the benefits of Christ's atonement nor regenerate, baptism declares one's death to the old life and resurrection to the new. Baptism also publicly represents the person's openness to the Spirit's ministries. It unites new believers with others in a gathered community for fellowship, teaching, discipline, observance of the Lord's Table, and ministry.

5. Give priority to personal versus social transformation. Shortly after the deaths of John F. Kennedy, Robert Kennedy, and Martin Luther King, Jr., in the 1960s, America faced an unparalleled social crisis. Some thought the greatest need of the hour was structural changes brought about by social and political legislation. Others thought the nation needed better education and law enforcement. Some traced the problems back to the need for better housing and employment. About that time some in the World Council of Churches—anticipating its Fourth Assembly on the theme "Behold I Make All Things New"—realized that "neither the renewal of the world nor of the church can be adequately understood apart from the reorientation of people as persons."[162] Here an organization noted for its emphasis on social and political change acknowledged the need for radical conversion and a change of heart. Paul Tournier observed that Western societies possess a plethora of values from religious faith, philosophy, and literature. But "these values no longer have any decisive influence upon the destiny of culture."[163] If scriptural values are to impact the world at large, evangelicals must continue to call individuals to belief, repentance, trust, and the new birth.

DISCUSSION TOPICS

1. What constitutes true belief in the Gospel, genuine repentance, and sincere faith in Christ? How can you as a personal worker know whether a person has genuinely repented and trusted Christ?

2. To what extent is repentance an enablement of God? Is faith likewise a divine enablement? Are sinners capable of repenting and exercising faith in Christ in and of themselves?

3. Does the rite of baptism regenerate the soul? Discuss the meaning of key Scriptures on the subject, such as Titus 3:5 and 1 Peter 3:21.

4. Explain the logical (not chronological) relation that exists between belief, repentance, and faith and between conversion and regeneration.

5. What minimal biblical beliefs must a pre-Christian assent to in order to be saved?

6. Were Old Testament saints regenerated by the Spirit in the same way as New Testament believers? Can we speak of the Old Testament faithful as new creatures in Christ? In what way were they transformed?

7. In what sense do believers at the new birth "participate in the divine nature" (2 Peter 1:4)? Explain the meaning of this enigmatic phrase.

8. To be a true Christian disciple must an unbeliever accept Christ as the Lord of his life as well as Savior from sin? Interact with the dangers of works righteousness and cheap grace.

See also the Review Questions and Ministry Projects on pages 501–2.

CHAPTER 3

THE BELIEVER'S JUSTIFICATION AND RECONCILIATION

The Believer's Justification and Reconciliation

THE PROBLEM:
WHAT DOES SCRIPTURE MEAN WHEN IT AFFIRMS THAT THE RIGHTEOUS GOD JUSTIFIES AND RECONCILES CONDEMNED AND ALIENATED SINNERS?

The doctrine of justification deals with fundamental issues of how guilty sinners are acquitted and restored to favor with a righteous God. Justification is related to other theological concepts such as forgiveness of sins, reconciliation to fellowship, the gift of eternal life, and adoption into the family of God. Reformation Protestantism regards the doctrine of justification as a crucial article of the faith on which the Gospel absolutely stands or falls. One historical authority rightly describes the doctrine of justification as "the chief doctrine of Christianity and the chief point of difference separating Protestantism and Roman Catholicism."[1] Not a few modern theologians, however, regard justification as a doctrine encrusted with hoary Jewish legalism and thus irrelevant to the modern mind. Dale Moody, for example, did not hesitate to call the Reformation doctrine of forensic justification "this Latin legalism."[2] Is the doctrine of justification by faith an indispensable part of the Good News about Christ, or is it a dispensable relic from an earlier age?

Justification by faith is related to other Christian doctrines. Earlier we examined the character of God in its diverse aspects (vol. 1, chap. 6). There God was seen to be absolutely righteous, in that his nature is the perfect standard of right and truth. Moreover, God is absolutely just, in that he consistently rewards good and punishes evil. As "the righteous Judge" (2 Tim. 4:8) the Lord cannot simply acquit the guilty (Exod. 23:7). We also considered the background of justification—humanity guilty, condemned, and alienated from God (vol. 2, chap. 4). We also discussed the ground of justification—the death of Christ on the cross as he took the sinner's place, bore his guilt, and suffered the just penalty for sins (vol. 2, chap. 7). Moreover, the first half of the present volume deals with the implementation of justification—the application of Christ's atoning provisions to condemned and alienated sinners. The doctrine of election (chap. 1) concerns God's gracious choice of some persons among the sinful race to be saved. Regeneration (chap. 2) discusses the event by which God imparts new spiritual life to persons dead in trespasses and sins. And sanctification (chap. 4) deals with the transformation of believers morally and ethically into the image of Christ.

A number of problems cluster around the doctrine of justification. Is justification an instantaneous event or an ongoing process? If the latter, is justification merely another name for moral improvement? If the former, is justification chiefly a matter of restoration of fellowship with God without reference to legal categories? Is justification an event whereby God objectively *declares* a person righteous or by which he subjectively *makes* a person righteous? If the former alternative, does God reckon a person righteous simply on the basis of faith acceptance of Christ's work on the cross, or on the ground of the imputation of Christ's righteousness received by faith? If the latter alternative is true, is the notion that God pronounces sinners to be what they actually are not—i.e., righteous— a legal fiction? Does the forensic view encourage a life of moral laxity (antinomianism)? Furthermore, what is the meaning of the phrase, so essential to a correct understanding of justification, "the righteousness of God" (Rom. 3:21–22)? Is it a description of how God acts in saving sinners, or is it a quality in God that may be attributed to sinners? Is justification something to which individuals can contribute by moral deeds or acts of love? What about the so-called surplus of merits allegedly possessed by Mary and other noteworthy saints?

Moreover, what benefits does justification impart to believing sinners? In the event of reconciliation, who is reconciled to whom? Do the obstacles to reconciliation reside on God's side or on the sinner's side? Can justifying grace be lost by moral lapses or willful sins? Related to this is the issue of assurance of present and future justification. Can believers in Christ be confident of permanent forgiveness of

sins and reconciliation with God? These and other important issues will be examined in the sections that follow.

ALTERNATIVE INTERPRETATIONS IN THE CHURCH

A number of divergent views of justification and reconciliation have appeared in the history of the church. To the most important of these interpretations we now turn.

The Roman Catholic Interpretation

Catholics have traditionally spoken of both the inception and the increase of justification. Concerning the first: God, on the basis of the merits of Christ and via the sacrament of baptism infuses into the soul new habits of grace and forgives past sins. Although this first stage involves making the person inherently righteous by the infusion of a just nature, "concupiscence" (desire that is the seedbed of sin but not itself sin) remains in Christians. It is inconceivable for Catholic authorities that the holy God would accept into his family those who remain contaminated by indwelling sin. Moreover, they insist that imputed righteousness would destroy human moral effort. Concerning the second aspect of justification, baptized persons work for eternal life by means of love-inspired virtues that are the fruit of the divine grace infused in the soul. Here Rome upholds the "merit of worthiness" (*meritum de condigno*)— namely, the merit wrought by free moral acts performed in the state of grace. It may be fairly stated that according to Rome persons are justified not on the basis of what Christ has done *for* them but what God is doing *in* them. Roman Catholics trust God's infusion of a new nature and plead the worth of their God-enabled works.

Rome has traditionally taught that surplus merits earned by Christ and saints can be applied to ordinary way-farers. Mary, in particular, contributes to the justification of the faithful: (1) By her holy life and good works on earth, Mary earned excess merit that can be transferred to others. (2) Mary shared in the pain and sufferings of her Son on the cross. And (3) Mary, as "Mother of God," effectively pleads with the Father in heaven. As stated by one Catholic source, Mary contributes "her share to the justification of the human race, beginning with herself and extend-ing to everyone ever justified."[3] Catho-lics believe that justifying grace, defined as the infusion of righteousness in the soul, can be forfeited by mortal sin but may be restored by the sacrament of penance (involving contrition, confes-sion, satisfaction, and absolution). If the process of justification (i.e., attain-ing righteousness or transformation) is not completed in this life, the individual must endure the purifying sufferings of purgatory for varying lengths of time (see chap. 8, below).

Justification in Roman Catholicism is a comprehensive term that includes, among other things, what Protestants understand by regeneration and sanc-tification. For Rome justification is not an objective *pronouncement* of right-eousness but a lifelong *process* of mak-ing righteous. The Catholic interpreta-tion, furthermore, pays little attention to the satisfaction of divine justice and to the removal of sin's guilt. And since the process of justification can be lost by mortal sin, no assurance of final salvation normally is possible.

Augustine (d. 430), the first postbibli-cal theologian to explore justification in depth, offered the following summa-tion: "Justification in this life is given to us according to these three things: first by the laver of regeneration by which all sins are forgiven; then by a struggle with the faults from whose guilt we have been absolved; the third, when our prayer is heard, in which we say, 'For-give us our debts.' "[4] For Augustine justification is both objective and sub-jective; God not only *declares* sinners righteous, he *makes* them so. Thus "we are justified, but righteousness itself grows as we go forward."[5] The bishop, however, emphasized the subjective dimension of justification more than the objective. "What else does the phrase 'being justified' signify than 'being made righteous.' "[6] Thus justification for Augustine is that gracious work whereby God makes baptized Chris-tians righteous by renewing their inner beings and filling them with love for him (*amor Dei*). Justification progresses as the Spirit gradually supplants the con-cupiscence (evil desire) that remains in baptized believers with love. As a result of this infusion of divine grace and love, believers are enabled to work righteous-ness and fulfill the law.[7] Augustine added that God views the righteous deeds of Christians as meritorious. Yet he insisted (against the Pelagians) that since the inspiration for the good will and work comes from God, the merit derives entirely from grace.[8] The bishop concluded that if Christian love is per-fected in this life believers will go directly to heaven. If not, justification will be completed after death by the purifying sufferings of purgatory (1 Cor. 3:13–15).[9]

Augustine clearly subsumed under justification what Protestants under-stand by regeneration and sanc-tification.[10] We could say that since Augustine represented the *ordo salutis* as predestination, calling, justification, and glorification,[11] he envisaged jus-tification broadly as the entire move-ment of salvation from regeneration through sanctification. This is support-ed by the fact that he employed the terms *regeneratio, vivificatio, renova-tio,* and *sanctificatio* as synonyms for justification. When describing salvation Augustine preferred these terms to jus-tification. Later Roman Catholic theology expanded on the Augustinian notion that justification is the process that actually makes a person righteous.

Thomas Aquinas (d. 1274) asserted that justification begins at baptism on the basis of the merits of Christ. Justification includes the infusion of grace, the movement of the will toward God in faith and against sin, and the remission of sin.[12] The primary factor in justification is the unmerited infusion of grace (*gratia infusa*) that changes sinners from a state of sin to a state of justice, or from a condition of corrupt nature to a condition of habitual grace. Thomas emphasized that justification involves an actual change in the soul: "In the infusion of justifying grace there is a certain transmutation of the human soul."[13] Justification does not guarantee eternal life, since it can be lost through mortal sin. Moreover, since no person knows when he or she has performed sufficient good works, certainty of salvation normally is impossible. By virtue of the infusion of habitual grace, which engenders love, the Christian obeys God's law and performs good works. Because performed by the person's will, good deeds are counted as meritorious (*meritum de condigno*) and ultimately render the person worthy of eternal life. "By every meritorious act a man merits the increase of grace, equally with the consummation of grace which is eternal life."[14] The greater the work, Thomas argued, the greater the merit that accrues. If perfection is not attained in this life the individual must endure purgatory. "The punishment of purgatory is intended to supplement the satisfaction which was not fully completed in the body."[15] The pope or priests can apply the excess merit earned by exceptional persons on earth (the "treasury of superabundant merits") to souls in purgatory to diminish their punishments.

The canons and decrees of the Council of Trent represent the authoritative statement of the Counter-Reformation. Session six of the Council (1547) affirmed that justification occurs in three stages: (1) The *preparation* for justification. Blessed by prevenient grace and addressed by God's call, the individual "is able by his own free will . . . to move himself to justice in His sight" (chap. 5). In adults this preparation includes faith, repentance, and the intention to accept baptism. (2) The *beginning* of justification. Through the regenerating work of the Spirit God infuses grace, hope, and love into the soul at baptism thereby remitting past sins and making the person righteous. Thus justification "is not only a remission of sins but also the sanctification and renewal of the inward man through the voluntary reception of the grace and gifts whereby an unjust man becomes just" (chap. 7). (3) The *increase* of justification. Because Trent (following Roman tradition) defined justification as the process of becoming righteous, justification must be augmented if the *viator* would attain heavenly glory. Thus "through the observance of the commandments of God and the Church, faith cooperating with good works," believers "increase in that justice received through the grace of Christ and are further justified" (chap. 10). Justification can be forfeited by mortal sins but can be recovered by the sacrament of penance (chap. 14). Since justification can be lost, the pilgrim possesses no certainty of present and future pardon. The realistic attitude of the pious is hope mixed with "fear and apprehension" (chap. 9). Following tradition, Trent maintained that God regards the good works individuals perform as meritorious (Matt. 10:42; 2 Tim. 4:8; Heb. 6:10). Such God-enabled merit increases righteousness and prospects for eternal life (chap. 16).

In the Canons that follow, Trent polemicized against justification by faith alone. "If anyone says that the sinner is justified by faith alone, meaning that nothing else is required to cooperate in order to obtain the grace of justification . . . , let him be anathema" (Canon 9). The Council, moreover, placed the ban on Protestants who insisted that justification is not increased by good works. "If anyone says that the justice received is not preserved and also not increased before God through good works, but that those works are merely the fruits and signs of justification obtained, but not the cause of its increase, let him be anathema" (Canon 24). Canon 32 added an anathema against the Reformers who denied that a person's good works merit eternal life.

From a panentheistic perspective, much post-Vatican II Catholic theology claims that justifying or divinizing grace is universal. Richard P. McBrien, for example, denies that Christ died to bear sins and expiate offenses against the divine majesty. The notion of Christ as "a curse" is strictly metaphorical. The blood Christ shed on the cross was not a literal payment for sins; rather, it was a peace offering that unites God and humans. "It was not that God was so enraged by the world's sin that a price was to be exacted (the prevalent idea of God among the pagans), but that God 'so loved the world that he gave his only Son.'"[16] McBrien upholds the traditional Catholic definition of justification as "the event by which God, acting in Jesus Christ, makes us holy (just) in the divine sight."[17] But because revelation and grace are universal, justification or divinization extends to all people everywhere. Thus, "Every human person, by reason of birth and of God's universal offer of grace, is already called to be a child of God and an heir of heaven."[18]

Pelagian and Liberal Interpretations

This tradition is characterized by the naïve optimism that says God is a God of love not wrath and that pre-Christians are inherently upright. God's relation to people is not that of lawgiver and judge who exacts the demands of penal law but of loving Father who seeks the rehabilitation of prodigals. The tradition firmly denies the legal imputation of the alien righteousness of Christ to sinners. Rather, God regards as just and worthy of fellowship those who, inspired by Jesus' example, improve themselves morally. The tradition replaces the Reformation doctrine of justification by faith with the agenda of justification by personal virtue.

Pelagius (d. 419) viewed persons as free moral agents unimpaired by Adam's fall. He defined grace as enlightenment provided by the law of Moses and the teachings and example of Christ. The latter enable people to discern the will of God and stimulate them to perform it. People could live morally and please God without grace, but with greater difficulty. Baptism in adults connotes a break with the past and actually remits past sins. Thereafter assisted by divine grace, people attain righteousness and merit eternal life by moral action. Justification thus involves overcoming sinful habits, pursuing worthy ethical goals, and fulfilling the law of God. Pelagius claimed that people are capable of achieving their own justification and many, in fact, do so.

Sixteenth-century Socinianism, the forerunner of Unitarianism, held a view of justification similar to that of Pelagius. The Socinians denied that Christ's death was a satisfaction rendered to the divine justice. "That Christ by his death has *merited* salvation for us and has *made satisfaction* freely for our sins . . . is fallacious and erroneous and wholly pernicious."[19] The Socinians appealed to the following arguments to support this rejection: (1) Righteousness is not a quality in God but a description of how God acts. (2) Since wrath is antithetic to goodness, there is

129

no anger in God that needs to be appeased. (3) Moral qualities such as guilt and righteousness are nontransferrable; hence each person must make amends for himself. And (4) since humans can forgive wrongdoing by a simple determination, so also can God. The Socinians thus viewed justification as a process of ethical improvement effected by free moral agents. God forgives and raises to immortality all who repent, who follow the precepts and example of Christ (a human prophet whose death was the supreme display of obedience), and who strive to live virtuously.

Albrecht Ritschl (d. 1889), the father of modern liberal theology, viewed justification and reconciliation as the fundamental datum of Christianity. The context for justification is not God's holiness or wrath but his love. "The conception of love is the only adequate conception of God."[20] God as loving Father stands ready to forgive all persons unconditionally and to restore them to fellowship with himself. But people in sin (defined as ignorance and weakness) construct a false picture of God as unapproachable holiness and wrath. Thus the human attitude toward God is one of fear and mistrust. To correct this false conception God disclosed himself in Christ. As human founder of the kingdom Christ demonstrated loving fellowship with God, revealed God as a gracious Father disposed to forgive, and through word and deed inspires persons to return to God. Ritschl described as "altogether false"[21] the view that justification is the judicial act whereby God imputes the righteousness of Christ to sinners. Ethically interpreted, justification involves the forgiveness of sins, the eradication of *consciousness* of guilt, and removal of mistrust of God. Ritschl concluded that those who experience justification and reconciliation will replicate the ethical life of Jesus and collectively hasten the coming of the kingdom.

Shailer Mathews (d. 1941) likewise opposed the imputational view of justification. Modern man's "fundamental conception of the universe makes it difficult for him to respond to the forensic conception of God as a monarch who establishes days of trial and passes individual sentences upon millions of lives. His idea of law makes it hard for him to think of a remitted penalty in a moral world, where relations are genetic and only figuratively to be conceived of in terms of the law court and a king."[22] Mathews reasoned that the loving God who conceived the plan of salvation does not need to be placated or appeased. Salvation represents the triumph, via social evolution, of the higher spirit of Jesus over lower, vestigial animal impulses. As humans emulate the ideals of Jesus (the human revealer of God), they attain a higher level of moral and spiritual development, are reconciled to God and one another, and forge a true human brotherhood in a renewed social order. Argued Mathews: "To be saved is to be so transformed by new relations with spiritual forces both human and divine that past mistakes and sins have their effects offset by new life."[23]

We saw in previous chapters that liberation theology views salvation as this-worldly and socially rather than other-worldly and individually. It defines faith as practical commitment to the revolutionary struggle, and justification as personal participation in the battle for human freedom. Liberation theologians often link justification and sanctification under the practical rubric of "discipleship." From a liberal black perspective, James Cone argues that "God's act of reconciliation is not mystical communion with the divine; nor is it a pietistic state of inwardness bestowed upon the believer."[24] Objectively, justification is God's righteous deliverance of the oppressed from socio-political bondage.[25] And subjectively, justification is the participation of the liberated in the social struggle for justice.

Process theology judges the traditional doctrine of justification by faith to be irrelevant to the modern vision of reality. According to Pittenger, the classical formulation of justification "seems to make little or no sense to our contemporaries."[26] Pittenger insists that we cannot accept as literally true Paul's teaching of a forensic imputation of Christ's righteousness. The seedbed of justification is not the offended justice of the heavenly Lawgiver or Judge but the spurning of divine love. Pittenger assimilates justification into sanctification and redefines it according to the Whiteheadian conceptuality. Thus justification is the divine approval of positive human responses to the divine lure, optimally displayed in Jesus, that leads to the vanquishing of lovelessness, the overcoming of estrangement, and personal transformation.[27]

The Arminian View

Consistent with the governmental theory of the Atonement (see vol. 2, chap. 7), seventeenth-century Remonstrants and many Arminians explain justification as the forgiveness of sins that enhances God's wise governance of the universe. Many Arminian authorities reject the Calvinist view whereby God reckons Christ's obedience to believers and accepts said obedience as if it were their own, as "fictional."[28] Arminians claim that the notion that God regards persons as holy when, in fact, they are not holy encourages antinomianism. Negatively, justification connotes the forgiveness of sins on the basis of Christ's passive obedience on the cross and release from the guilt and penalty of transgressions committed. Positively, justification signifies God's

actually constituting believers as new creatures with initial righteousness. Usually this righteousness is not a forensic imputation but involves the transformation of believers' moral character (renovation). Some Arminians hold that faith is not merely the *instrument* of justification but the *ground* on which justification rests. Thus, "any righteousness created by the act of justification is real because of the ethical or moral dimension of faith."[29] Arminians generally hold that obstacles to reconciliation reside on the human side rather than on God's side. The loving God is always disposed to the restoration of fellowship with sinners. Most Arminian authorities, furthermore, hold that justification can be forfeited by willful sin; thus certainty of final justification is not possible.

John Wesley (d. 1791) defined justification as "present forgiveness, pardon of sins, and, consequently, acceptance with God."[30] The *source* of justification is the grace of God, the *cause* the merits of Christ who satisfied the divine justice on the cross, and the *condition* the free response of faith. Because holiness is indispensable to salvation, Wesley rejected Luther's notion that the believer is *simul justus et peccator*. "Least of all does justification imply that God is deceived in those whom he justifies; that he thinks them to be what, in fact, they are not; that he accounts them to be otherwise than they are. It does by no means imply that God . . . believes us righteous when we are unrighteous."[31] It follows that justification has nothing to do with the imputation of the alien righteousness of Christ to the believer.[32] Rather, in "the moment a sinner is justified, his heart is cleansed in a low degree. But yet he has not a clean heart, in the proper sense, till he is made perfect in love."[33] All of this suggests that Wesley could not resist assimilating justification into *sanctification* (his preeminent interest).

Wesley insisted that Christian experience provides the believer with assurance of *present* salvation. But there can be no assurance of *final* salvation, since it is not certain whether the believer will persist in good works.

Richard Watson (d. 1833) defined justification as the sentence of pardon and the exemption from the penalty of sins. Watson denied as "fictitious" both the imputation of Adam's sin to his posterity and the imputation of Christ's righteousness to believers. "For this notion, that the righteousness of Christ is so imputed as to be accounted as our own, there is no warrant in the word of God."[34] Watson perceived in the Reformational view the danger of antinomianism; the imputation of Christ's righteousness implies that believers need not seek righteousness in daily living. The only imputation Watson allowed is God's act of reckoning the human act of faith as righteousness. In the final analysis Watson set the scheme of justification within the context of God's moral governance of the universe. "The fruit of the death and intercession of Christ," he argued, "renders it consistent with a righteous government [for God] to forgive sin."[35]

Charles Finney (d. 1875) also regarded justification (i.e., pardon of sins and acceptance by God) as a governmental rather than a judicial or forensic act. To uphold the moral order of the universe God substituted Christ's death for the punishment required by the law. "The Godhead desired to save sinners, but could not safely do so without danger to the universe, unless something was done to satisfy public, not retributive justice."[36] To support this conclusion Finney denied (1) the imputation of Adam's sin to his posterity, (2) the imputation of the sins of the elect to Christ, and (3) perpetual justification by imputation of the righteousness of Christ to believers.[37] Since Christ owed full obedience to the law like any other person, he had no surplus of obedience that could be applied to us. Finney boldly stated, "For sinners to be forensically pronounced just, is impossible or absurd."[38] He affirmed that the one *ground* or *procuring cause* of justification is the benevolence of the Godhead in the interests of moral government. The several *conditions* of justification include Christ's vicarious sufferings, repentance, faith in the Savior, present sanctification (entire consecration to God), and perseverance to the end (manifested by complete obedience to the moral law). Finney insisted that justification can be forfeited by forsaking "full-hearted consecration."

The Neo-orthodox Perspective

Karl Barth (d. 1968) rooted his objectivist view of justification in God's eternal election of humanity in Christ, which is identical to God's eternal covenant with the race. Mankind, however, broke the covenant by virtue of sin and the Fall. For Barth, God has bound himself to his image-bearers as Creator and Lord and thus cannot tolerate disruption of the covenant. God must be just (Rom. 3:26); he must act consistently with his nature to overcome this impediment to fellowship. Therefore, "He does not renounce the grace of election and the covenant."[39] For Barth justification represents God's "affirmation and consummation of the institution of the covenant between Himself and man which took place in and with the creation."[40] Justification is that decision of God regarding humankind made before time but given historical expression through Jesus Christ. In order to reveal the eternal, justifying decision of God and restore the covenant relation broken by sin, God became a man in Christ, died on the cross and rose from the grave. Through Christ's death God said No! to himself and through Christ's resurrection said

Yes! to humanity, thereby negating sin and condemnation. For Barth justification is not a subjective reality that can be experienced (contra Schleiermacher); it is God's eternal verdict enacted in time through Christ that forgives sins, accepts sinners into sonship, and grants the inheritance of eternal life. Küng, in his definitive study of Barth, affirms that for the latter "justification [is] the accomplishment and revelation of God's verdict upon man."[41]

Since God's covenant with humankind is universal in scope (cf. the covenant with Noah), Christ, our representative, became a man, died, and was resurrected for the justification of all. "Jesus Christ died totally for the reconciliation of every man as such."[42] God's eternal verdict objectively (*de jure*) has justified the entire human family. Thus it is impossible for humankind not to be elected, restored to covenant relation, and justified. Even resolute human unbelief cannot thwart God's gracious covenant purpose. Thus "there has to be a reconciling of the world, and this has already taken place."[43] However, subjectively (*de facto*) many people have not yet come to personal knowledge of this justification by faith reception of the Holy Spirit.

In explaining the doctrine of justification, Barth focused on Christ's repairing the broken relation between God and humans rather than on God's imputing Christ's righteousness to believers. The core of Barth's doctrine of justification is the loving God achieving his sovereign right as Creator by reestablishing the broken covenant relation with humans. Moreover, in Barth's scheme persons do not believe the Gospel in order to be justified. Rather, having been justified in eternity past by the divine verdict, individuals in time respond to the Gospel, thereby making justification a conscious reality for them.

Gustaf Aulén (d. 1977), the Swedish neo-orthodox theologian, minimized wrath and retributive justice in God in deference to the divine *agapē*. According to Aulén, God's attitude toward persons is not governed by legal categories; Christ did not bear sinners' punishment, and God does not impute Christ's righteousness to believers. "The Christian conception of atonement is obscured if it is interpreted . . . as a compensation to divine righteousness rendered by Christ as Man."[44] Aulén added that the hostile powers of sin, death, and the Devil and the tyrannical powers of the law and divine wrath have created a separation between God and humankind. But on the cross divine love triumphed over the enslaving forces of evil and subdued sinners in their alienation from God (the "classic" theory of the atonement). "The sole purpose of God's loving will is to realize the dominion of love."[45] Justification, grounded entirely in the divine *agapē*, involves forgiveness of sin, the reestablishment of fellowship between God and sinners, and the blessing of eternal life. Aulén observed that justification is not an event that marks the beginning of the Christian life; it is a process that continues throughout the entire journey of faith. Thus "forgiveness [or justification] is both the essential foundation of the Christian life and its continually active power."[46] Aulén was uncertain whether all or only some persons are justified, though he frequently referred to the reconciliation God effects between himself and the world.[47]

The Perspective of Lutherans, Reformed, and Many Evangelicals

The early fathers of the church, occupied with pressing Christological and Trinitarian controversies, did not explore in depth the doctrine of justification by faith. The first serious study of justification was undertaken by Augustine in the fourth century (see above). Not until the personal discovery that Martin Luther made was the forensic interpretation of justification developed in detail.

The Reformation tradition interpreted justification as God's judicial declaration whereby sins are freely pardoned and believers are accounted righteous and worthy of eternal life. It distinguished justification from sanctification, insisting that the former involves a change in the believer's *standing* before God rather than a change of *nature*. Justification thus is an instantaneous event that marks the beginning of the Christian life rather than a life-long process of moral and spiritual renewal. Reformational theology holds that the *ground* of justification is Christ's righteousness imputed to the believer, whereas the *means* or *instrument* of justification is God-given faith in the Redeemer. Most authorities hold that obstacles to reconciliation exist on the side of both God and sinners. With respect to God, enmity against sin must be assuaged. With respect to sinners, fear of God's righteous judgment must be neutralized. Authorities hold that persons who trust in the finished work of Christ can be *assured* that they have passed from a state of condemnation to one of favor and life.

Martin Luther (d. 1546) was a pious Augustinian monk who sought peace with God through good works and monastic disciplines. In spite of earnest striving, his troubled soul found no repose. In pursuit of the question, "How can I find a gracious God?" he turned to the letters of St. Paul. Initially he understood the phrase "the righteousness of God" (Rom. 1:17) actively as that quality in God that punishes unrighteous sinners. After considerable prayer and reflection Luther came to understand the phrase passively as the inestimable gift God grants to sinners through faith in Christ. It is "the righteousness with which God clothes us when he justifies us."[48] As a mother hen covers her chicks with her wing, so God covers sinners with the perfect righteousness of his Son. Thus Luther understood justification to mean that God imputes Christ's alien righteousness to those who trust in the Savior's atoning death. Indeed, justification is that imputation, whereby for the sake of Christ, "God reckons imperfect righteousness as perfect righteousness and sin as not sin, even though it really is sin."[49] Christ's righteousness imputed to believers is "alien" because it is external and because no sinners could possibly merit it. Having been justified by faith, believers receive forgiveness of sins, union with Christ, and the gift of eternal life.

Essential to Luther's forensic view is his contention that the justified believer is "righteous and a sinner at the same time" (*simul iustus et peccator*).[50] Extrinsically believers are righteous, but intrinsically they are sinful, even though the remnants of sin are not charged to their account. "The righteous are not wholly perfect in themselves, but God accounts them righteous and forgives them because of their faith in his Son Jesus Christ."[51] Against Rome Luther firmly believed that, notwithstanding spiritual struggles, believers possess assurance of this new standing. "We must by all means believe for a certainty . . . that we are pleasing to God for the sake of Christ."[52] Although good works contribute nothing to justification, they serve as a litmus test of whether people have been justified by faith. "True faith is not idle. We can, therefore, ascertain and recognize those who have true faith from the effect or from what follows."[53] Luther differentiated between the "inward righteousness" before God that is born of justification and the "outward righteousness" before men that takes form through faith and love.

Philip Melanchthon (d. 1560) challenged the Roman view by insisting that justification is not a *making* righteous but a forensic *declaration* of righteousness. "All of our righteousness is a gracious imputation of God."[54] Justification signifies that God clothes believers with the alien righteousness of Christ so that sins are forgiven, we are made pleasing to God, and his wrath is averted. Although God views believers as clothed with Christ's righteousness, the sinful nature and its passions endure. The *ground* of justification is the righteousness of Christ, acquired by his total obedience in life and death. The *means* of justification is the believer's faith. Melanchthon distinguished between the instantaneous event of justification and the ensuing process of sanctification. Apprehending by faith the biblical teaching that God justifies believers on the basis of Christ's obedience and merits, Christians ought not doubt their reconciliation with God. Melanchthon summed up his view as follows:

> The Mediator's entire obedience, from his incarnation until the resurrection, is the true justification which is pleasing to God, and is the merit for us. God forgives us our sins, and accepts us, in that he imputes righteousness to us for the sake of the Son, although we are still weak and fearful. We must however, accept this imputed righteousness with faith.[55]

Calvin (d. 1564) regarded justification as "the principle of the whole doctrine of salvation and the foundation of all religion."[56] Against Rome Calvin developed a forensic interpretation of justification: God justifies guilty sinners by imputing to them the righteousness of Christ. The *material cause* of justification is Christ's entire obedience in life and death, whereas the *instrumental cause* is faith apart from all works.

"Justified by faith is he who, excluded from the righteousness of works, grasps the righteousness of Christ through faith, and clothed in it, appears in God's sight not as a sinner but as a righteous man."[57] God imputes the righteousness of Christ, and believers receive forgiveness of sins past, present, and future, removal of guilt and condemnation, reconciliation with God, and the gift of eternal life. The obstacles to reconciliation chiefly lie on God's side. Sin turns "God's face away from the sinner; and . . . it is foreign to his righteousness to have any dealings with sin. For this reason . . . man is God's enemy until he is restored to grace through Christ."[58] Calvin steadfastly upheld believers' assurance of final salvation, *objectively,* as faith lays hold of the biblical promises concerning the Father's elective purpose and the Son's atoning work and, *subjectively,* by the ministry of the Spirit in the heart. Assurance, like faith, admits of degrees. Calvin held that believers may not always sense this assurance of final salvation:

> Surely, while we teach that faith ought to be certain and assured, we cannot imagine any certainty that is not tinged with doubt, or any assurance that is not assailed by some anxiety. On the other hand, . . . we deny that, that in whatever way they are afflicted, believers fall away and depart from the certain assurance received from God's mercy.[59]

More carefully than Luther, Calvin distinguished between the external event of justification and the subsequent internal process of sanctification. "To be justified means something different from being made righteous."[60] Yet sensitive to the Roman charge that the Reformers denigrated good works, Calvin held justification and sanctification in close relation. From 1 Corinthians 1:30 (Jesus Christ is "our righteousness, holiness and redemption") Calvin reasoned that "you cannot possess Christ without being made partaker in his sanctification." In the same section he observed that "in our sharing in Christ, which justifies us, sanctification is just as much included as righteousness."[61] We mention what some Calvin scholars call his doctrine of "double justification." God not only justifies the sinner, he also justifies the *works* of the justified. Because Christians remain empirically sinful, their works are defiled in God's sight. God, however, adorns Christians' works with Christ's righteousness, covering any unrighteousness so that both they *and* their works are pleasing and acceptable. "As we ourselves, when we have been engrafted in Christ, are righteous in God's sight because our iniquities are covered by Christ's sinlessness, so our works are righteous and are thus regarded because whatever fault is otherwise in them is buried in Christ's purity, and is not charged to our account."[62] This insight of Calvin undergirds his understanding of the place of works in the Christian life. No sinner is justified by works. But God justifies believers' works—which works demonstrate obedience to God and accumulate heavenly rewards.

The Heidelberg Catechism (1563), poses the question, "How are you right with God?" (Lord's Day 23, Q. 60). The answer follows that in spite of gross sin "without my deserving it at all, out of sheer grace, God grants and credits to me the perfect satisfaction, righteousness, and holiness of Christ, as if I had never sinned nor been a sinner, as if I had been as perfectly obedient as Christ was obedient for me. All I need to do is to accept this gift of God with a believing heart." The Westminster Shorter Catechism (1647), in the answer to Question 33, "What is Justification?" replies: "Justification is an act of God's free grace, wherein he pardoneth all our sins, and accepteth us as righteous in his sight, only for the righteousness of Christ, imputed to us, and received by faith alone." The Westminster Confession of Faith (1646) states that God freely justifies "not by infusing righteousness into them [the effectually called], but by pardoning their sins, and by accounting and accepting their persons as righteous: not for any thing wrought in them, or done by them, but for Christ's sake alone . . . ; but by imputing the obedience and satisfaction of Christ unto them, they receiving and resting on him and his righteousness by faith" (ch. XI.1). The Confession adds that although assurance of justification can be dulled by sin, believers in Christ "may in this life be certainly assured that they are in a state of grace, and may rejoice in the hope of the glory of God, which hope shall never make them ashamed" (ch. XVIII.1).

J. I. Packer offers a concise summary of the Reformation-evangelical view of justification. The biblical verbs (*ṣādēq* and *dikaioō*) possess the forensic meaning to "pronounce," "accept," or "treat as righteous." God's act of justification means, negatively, that sinners are freed from the penalty of the law and, positively, that they are reinstated into divine favor and privilege. The former involves remission of all sins, removal of guilt, and the end of the divine enmity and wrath. The latter involves bestowal of a righteous status, fellowship with God, and the gift of eternal life. The problem posed by justification is how the immutably just Lawgiver and Judge can remain righteous in himself while acquitting sinners (Rom. 3:21–26). The heart of the Gospel is that "the claims of God's law upon them have been fully satisfied. The law has not been abated, or suspended, or flouted for their justification, but fulfilled—by Jesus Christ, acting in their name."[63] Jesus Christ in his life perfectly obeyed the law and in his death bore its penalty. Thus on the ground of Christ's perfect satisfaction of the law, God imputes righteousness to all who believe. God "reckons righteousness to them [i.e., sinners], not because he accounts them to have kept his law personally (which would be a false judgment), but because he accounts them to be united to the one who kept it representatively (and that is a true judgment)."[64] Faith is the instrumental means whereby Christ and his righteousness are appropriated; it is "the outstretched empty hand which receives righteousness by receiving Christ."[65]

Other valuable works on justification and reconciliation include monographs by A. W. Pink,[66] Peter Toon,[67] and Alister McGrath.[68]

BIBLICAL TEACHING

To ascertain which of the preceding historical interpretations of justification is valid we now turn to the teachings of authoritative Scripture on the subject.

Pentateuch

We find a hint of justification in the antedeluvian period in the statement that "Noah found favor (*māṣā' ḥēn*) in the eyes of the LORD" (Gen. 6:8; cf. Exod. 33:17). "The idea [of the phrase] obviously is to gain acceptance or to win approbation."[69] Although subjectively Noah was not without sin in his life (see Gen. 9:20–23), objectively God regarded his servant as "righteous" (*ṣaddîq*) and "blameless" (*tāmîm*, Gen. 6:9).

Genesis 15:6 lives up to its reputation as the seedbed of the doctrine of justification: "Abram believed the Lord, and he credited it to him as righteousness [*ṣᵉdāqāh*]." The New Testament quotes this key text in Romans 4:3, 9, 22; Galatians 3:6; and James 2:23 as the basis for the doctrine of justification by faith. The Hebrew verb *ḥāšab* ("cred-

ited") means to "make a judgment," "count," or "impute" (cf. Lev. 7:18; 17:4; Num. 18:27, 30; Ps. 32:2).[70] The noun *ṣᵉdāqāh* implies conformity to the nature and the will of God.[71] The Genesis text thus teaches that Abram gave God wholehearted confidence in the latter's covenant promise, whereupon God gave Abram right standing with himself. Aalders comments, Abram's "faith, his childlike trust did not justify Abram, nor did it make him righteous. His believing trust was 'credited to him' by God as righteousness. The faith of this sinful person placed him in a position where the Judge of heaven and earth declared him to be righteous."[72] Abram was justified in the sense that, although he was empirically sinful, God accepted his faith in the covenant promise as righteousness.

In the Old Testament the Qal form of *ṣādaq* means to "be just" or "be righteous" (Gen. 38:26; Job 9:15; Ezek. 16:52). The Hiphil form in legal contexts means to "vindicate," "acquit," or "declare to be in the right." This is evident in Exodus 23:7, where in a judicial setting involving a guilty party and an innocent party Yahweh said: "I will not acquit ['*aṣdîq*] the guilty." Similar is the sense of Deuteronomy 25:1: "When men have a dispute, they are to take it to court and the judges will decide the case, acquitting the innocent and condemning the guilty." The Hiphil of *ṣādaq* is parallel to the Hiphil of *rāša'* (to "condemn," "declare guilty"), thus establishing the legal or forensic sense of the main Old Testament verb to "justify" (cf. 1 Kings 8:32). In justification God does not *make* a person righteous, any more than a judge makes a defendant innocent or guilty.

Poetry and Wisdom Literature

Job posed the fundamental question of human existence: "How can a mortal

137

be righteous before God?'' (Job 9:2). God is so holy, righteous, and just—and sinners so unworthy—that it is not possible by human means to gain his favor. If Job were to plead personal righteousness in the divine court, God would pronounce him guilty (v. 20). Bildad reiterated this sentiment: "How then can a man be righteous before God? How can one born of woman be pure?" (Job 25:4). Bildad concluded that he could never achieve these goals, for man is "a maggot" and "a worm" (v. 6).

Amidst this pessimism Psalm 103:10 states that God in grace does not recompense people according to their deserts: "He does not treat us as our sins deserve or repay us according to our iniquities.'' Thus David exulted in God's justifying grace: "Blessed is the man whose sin the Lord does not count against him" (Ps. 32:2). Joyful, indeed, is the person to whom God does not impute (lo'-ḥāšab, cf. Gen. 15:6) 'āwôn—a comprehensive word meaning iniquitous behavior (Gen. 15:16), the resultant guilt or blameworthiness (1 Sam. 25:24; Ps. 51:2), and the inevitable divine punishment (Jer. 51:6). David affirmed that through God's gracious declaration the debt of sin is no longer reckoned to his (or our) account, the separation between Creator and the believer is breached, and the deserved penalty is averted. Elsewhere the psalmist affirmed that "love and faithfulness meet together; righteousness and peace kiss each other" (Ps. 85:10). God's covenant love (ḥesed) and faithfulness ('emet) unite to effect Israel's salvation. His covenant attribute of righteousness (ṣedeq) vis-à-vis believers results in a settled state of peace and reconciliation (šālôm). When David prayed to God, "In your faithfulness and righteousness [ṣᵉdāqāh] come to my relief" (Ps. 143:1), he asked that God would set him, a sinner, right with himself. A clearer delineation of how the righteous Judge would make right the ungodly had to await the cross and resurrection of Christ.

The legal or forensic intent of the Piel and Hiphil forms of ṣādaq is attested in several biblical texts. Thus, "Elihu . . . became very angry with Job for justifying [Piel infinitive of ṣādaq] himself rather than God" (Job 32:2). Job declared himself to be in the right in his dispute with God (cf. Job 40:8). Moreover, in facing up to his sin, David acknowledged the validity of God's perspective: "You are proved right when you speak and justified when you judge" (Ps. 51:4, quoted in Rom. 3:4). Furthermore, Proverbs 17:15 indicates that God hates the perversion of justice that involves judges' "acquitting the guilty and condemning the innocent.'' The parallelism between the verbs "acquit" (Hiphil of ṣādaq) and "condemn" indicates that the Old Testament justification language is forensic and declarative in nature. Nevertheless believing Jews—forgiven and restored to God's favor—were acutely conscious of indwelling sin. God's justifying decision had not made them subjectively free of sin in disposition, in thought-life, or in deeds of omission and commission (Job 31:33; Ps. 51:1–9; 130:3–4: Prov. 20:9).

Prophetic Literature

Against endemic human unrighteousness (Isa. 6:5; 46:12; 64:6), the prophets upheld the perfect righteousness of the Messiah (53:11). In both word and deed he would fully comply with the law of God (53:9). As the royal Messiah, Christ would rule the nations with equity and justice (9:7; 32:1; Zech. 9:9). Thus Jeremiah described Messiah as "a righteous Branch" (ṣemah ṣaddîq, Jer. 23:5; 33:15), and Isaiah claimed that "righteousness [ṣedeq] will be his belt and faithfulness the sash around his waist" (Isa. 11:5).

The prophets caught glimpses of the fact that through the righteous Messiah God reckons righteousness to unclean sinners (Isa. 45:25; cf. Jer. 23:6; 33:16—"the Lord our Righteousness"). Thus Yahweh said to rebellious Israel, "Though your sins are like scarlet, they shall be as white as snow; though they are red as crimson, they shall be like wool" (Isa. 1:18). The repentant sinner (v. 19) comes to God with a sin-stained soul but departs pure and blameless in his sight. Young writes, "The doctrine of a forensic justification is found in these words."[73] Isaiah 32:15–17 teaches that the outpoured Spirit effects "justice" and "righteousness" (ṣᵉdāqāh) in the earth, and that the fruit of this righteousness will be "peace," "quietness," and "confidence forever." Isaiah further testified (Isa. 61:10) that God covers the redeemed with his righteousness: God "has clothed me with garments of salvation and arrayed me in a robe of righteousness" (ṣᵉdāqāh). The same imagery occurs in Zechariah 3:1–5. There Joshua the high priest, as representative of the people, stood before the judging angel of the Lord. The "filthy clothes" Joshua wore (v. 3) symbolize the iniquity of the people; the command of the angel to remove the defiled garments connotes the pardoning of iniquity (cf. v. 9; 13:1); and the command to put on white festival garments suggests the clothing of sinners with divine righteousness. The ground of Joshua's and the people's acceptance clearly was no righteousness of their own but the perfect righteousness of another imputed to them. Isaiah explicitly attested forensic justification in 53:11: "By his knowledge my righteous servant will justify [Hiphil of ṣādaq] many, and he will bear their iniquities." The people of Judah were unrighteous, but on the ground of the righteous Messiah God pronounced them blameless. Young observed that "if the verb is not taken as forensic and if it is held that it refers to *iustitia infusa,* it would follow that the servant, in bearing the iniquities of the many, is himself infused with these iniquities and himself becomes sinful."[74]

The New Testament found an important basis for its doctrine of justification by faith in Habakkuk 2:4: "The righteous will live by his faith ['ᵉmûnāh]." Whereas the prophet saw in 'ᵉmûnāh the faithfulness or steadfastness that springs from faith, Paul (Rom. 1:17; Gal. 3:11) and the author of Hebrews (Heb. 10:38) linked justification with the underlying faith itself. Both Habakkuk and the New Testament writers understood that persons are judged righteous and thus live spiritually through their faith relation to the Lord. "Faithfulness or a life of faith is characteristic of the justified in God's sight."[75]

Many scholars (Dodd, Käsemann et al.) interpret "the righteousness of God" as a subjective genitive, namely, as an attribute of God by which he acts to save Israel. It is true that in texts such as Isaiah 45:8; 46:13; 51:5–8; 56:1; and 62:1 "righteousness" and "salvation" are juxtaposed. But the Old Testament does not restrict ṣedeq and ṣᵉdāqāh to the narrow meaning of "salvation" or "victory." God has displayed his righteousness in salvation in the sense that those without any righteousness of their own receive his righteousness. Young argued that "the concept *justify* is here about equivalent to *salvation.* . . . At the same time it is not a precise equivalent, for it also stresses righteousness. In saving Israel God has shown himself to be just."[76] Young continued, "Quite possibly the prophet anticipates Paul, and the righteousness of which he speaks originates with God and comes to man from Him, and in it man may stand before him."[77]

The prophets employed the Hiphil of ṣādaq (which the LXX translated by the verb dikaioō) in a forensic and declarative sense. Thus ostensibly in a legal context Isaiah pronounced a woe on judges "who acquit [Hiphil participle of *ṣādaq*] the guilty for a bribe, but deny justice to the innocent" (Isa. 5:23). Moreover, the Servant of the Lord declared, "He who vindicates [Hiphil participle of *ṣādaq*] me is near. Who then will bring charges against me? Let us face each other! Who is my accuser? Let him confront me!" (50:8). Parallel to the verb "condemn," "vindicate" means to pronounce or declare just. In this case God proclaimed his Servant just because he is completely righteous in himself.

Synoptic Gospels

In the Gospels *dikaiosynē* assumes the basic meaning of conformity to the will and law of God (Matt. 3:15; 5:20; 21:32; Luke 1:75). However, no man or woman can claim to be *dikaios* save Jesus Christ himself (Matt. 27:19; Luke 23:47; cf. Luke 1:35; 4:34; 23:41). In the words he spoke, the deeds he performed and the death he died, Jesus was fully committed to the Father and obedient to his word.

Justification, broadly conceived, is evident in the parable of the unmerciful servant (Matt. 18:23–35). One servant of a king incurred a debt so large that he was unable to pay it (vv. 24–25). Moved by generosity the king freely canceled his servant's substantial obligation (vv. 27, 32). The king's action in the parable signifies that God in mercy cancels all the debt of our sins. The parable of the lost son (Luke 15:11–24) also teaches the pardoning and justifying love of the heavenly Father. The younger son who took his inheritance and left home to engage in riotous living in a distant country (vv. 12–13) signifies the estrangement of the unconverted. The son's return home to his father's embrace and joyous celebration (vv. 20–24) signifies reconciliation with

God, restoration to favor, and adoption to the status of a beloved child. The wayward son petitioned his father to "make" or treat him as a hired hand (v. 19), but the father in grace treated him as a beloved son.

In the waning moments of his life the repentant thief on the cross was justified before God (Luke 23:40–43). A profound sense of his own sinfulness and Jesus' ability to save prompted his faith-petition, "Jesus, remember me when you come into your kingdom" (v. 42). Jesus' reply to the man, "today you will be with me in paradise" (v. 43), indicates that the criminal at that moment was reckoned right and introduced to fellowship with the heavenly Father. The closest synoptic teaching to Paul's doctrine of justification by faith, however, occurs in the parable of the Pharisee and the tax collector (Luke 18:9–14). The Pharisee lauded his own righteousness, carefully sought by punctilious observance of the law (vv. 9–12). All his religious endeavors, however, failed to make him acceptable to God. The tax collector, in striking contrast, acknowledged his inability to please God with the plea "God have mercy on me, a sinner" (v. 13). The aorist passive of the verb *hilaskomai* ("be merciful") suggests that the idea of propitiation lies in the background. Jesus then concluded, "I tell you that this man, rather than the other, went home justified before God" (v. 14). The perfect passive participle of *dikaioō* is an intensive perfect, pointing to the existing state of being declared righteous. The tax collector pleaded no works of his own. But by virtue of his contrite cry to Jesus for help, God forgave his sins and set him in a right relation with himself.

The parable of the sheep and the goats (Matt. 25:31–46) might suggest at first blush justification by virtuous deeds—namely, feeding the hungry, clothing the naked, and caring for the stranger (vv. 35–40). Yet Matthew focused on those "who are blessed by [the] Father" (v. 34), namely, the disciples and their conduct in the community of Jesus. The Lord encouraged such deeds of mercy not in order to earn justifying grace but as outer demonstrations of the disciples' inner faith and love. The perspective here is similar to the relation of faith and works in James. Furthermore, the parallelism between the ones "blessed by my Father" (v. 34) and "the righteous" (hoi dikaioi, v. 37) suggests that a forensic and declarative view of justification pertains.

Several nontechnical usages of dikaioō in the Synoptic Gospels confirm the forensic and declarative sense of the verb, the meaning of which is to "declare righteous, to recognize as righteous, proved to be in the right and accepted by God."[78] Jesus' saying that "wisdom is proved right [aorist passive of dikaioō] by her actions" (Matt. 11:19) means that God's wise, saving purpose was vindicated by Jesus' miracles. Luke's report that "all the people and the tax collectors justified [aorist of dikaioō] God" (Luke 7:29, RSV) means that they acknowledged God to be in the right. Luke's observation that the lawyer "wanted to justify [aorist infinitive of dikaioō] himself, so he asked Jesus, 'And who is my neighbor?' " (Luke 10:29) indicates that dikaioō here means to "acquit." Jesus' words in dialogue with the Pharisees "You are the ones who justify [present participle of dikaioō] yourselves in the eyes of men" (Luke 16:15) also confirms that the verb means to "acquit" or "vindicate." Finally Jesus' saying to the Pharisees—"By your words you will be acquitted, and by your words you will be condemned"— (Matt. 12:37), demonstrates that dikaioō, being parallel to the verb "condemn," has a forensic connotation.

Primitive Christianity/Acts

As described in Acts, pre-Christians are sinful and unrighteous and need to be converted (Acts 22:16). But in sharp contrast to human unrighteousness, Acts depicts Jesus Christ as "the Righteous One" (Acts 7:52; 22:14) and "the Holy and Righteous One" (Acts 3:14). The Messiah is so described not only because he was blameless before God and man, but also by virtue of his entire dedication to God's service (cf. Acts 4:27, 30) and his complete fulfillment of God's Law.

Peter, addressing Gentiles at the house of Cornelius, proclaimed "the good news of peace through Jesus Christ, who is Lord of all" (Acts 10:36). The chief effect of the Gospel is spiritual peace (eirēnē) or reconciliation with God (cf. Isa. 52:7). Notice that the ground of reconciliation is Jesus Christ (dia Iēsou Christou), the peace-maker. Rehearsing his conversion and call to ministry before King Agrippa, Paul stated that Christ commanded him to preach the Gospel so that his hearers might "receive forgiveness of sins and a place among those who are sanctified by faith in [Christ]" (Acts 26:18). The perfect passive participle of hagiazō, to "sanctify," indicates the condition of being positionally sanctified or justified (cf. 1 Cor. 6:11). The verb does not endorse a process of ethical development but attests, positively, the decision of God that declares believers just and constitutes them members of his holy family. Negatively justification includes forgiveness of sins and the removal of guilt.

Paul's sermon at Pisidian Antioch in Acts 13 contains an explicit reference to the doctrine of justification by faith alone, which the apostle would develop at length in his letters. The heart of his message is recorded in verse 39: "Through him [Christ] everyone who believes is justified [aorist passive infinitive of *dikaioō*] from everything you could not be justified from by the law of Moses." The results of justification are, negatively, forgiveness of sins and acquittal from condemnation (v. 38; cf. Acts 2:38; 10:43) and, positively, the declaration of right standing with God. Paul insisted that people attain justification by faith alone and not by the futile venture of law keeping.

The Letters of Paul

Paul, the former rabbi, understood that God can regard people righteous only as they perfectly obey his law. "For it is not those who hear the law who are righteous [*dikaioi*] in God's sight, but it is those who obey the law who will be declared righteous" (future passive of *dikaioō*, Rom. 2:13; cf. Rom. 10:5; Gal. 3:12). Since no human being keeps the law in its entirety (Rom. 3:5, 10–18, 23), no one is justified by works required by the law (Rom. 3:20; Gal. 2:16–17; 3:11; 5:4). Against Judaizers who claimed that justification comes by the law, Paul argued, "If righteousness [*dikaiosynē*] could be gained through the law, Christ died for nothing!" (Gal. 2:21). The fact is that since no one renders the perfect obedience demanded by the law, "All who rely on observing the law are under a curse" (*katara*, Gal. 3:10).

But amid universal human unrighteousness and guilt, Paul in Romans 1:17 (cf. Rom. 3:5; 10:3) pointed to a righteousness that comes from God, the revelation of which constitutes the Gospel. "For in the gospel a righteousness from God [*dikaiosynē theou*] is revealed, a righteousness that is by faith from first to last, just as it is written: 'The righteous will live by faith.'" The righteousness in view has its origin in God, satisfies the demands of divine justice, and effects the justification of the unrighteous. Significantly Paul linked the impartation of the divine righteousness to sinners with Christ and his substitutionary sacrifice on the cross (2 Cor. 5:21). Jesus Christ is righteous in that he completely obeyed the Father's will. During the course of his life he perfectly fulfilled the law (Rom. 10:4), and at Calvary he obediently and willingly died the death of a criminal (Phil. 2:8). Hence Paul wrote, "Christ Jesus . . . has become for us wisdom from God—that is, our righteousness [*dikaiosynē*], holiness and redemption" (1 Cor. 1:30). Through the obedience of his life and death Christ earned righteousness that God would credit to those who believe.

Paul expressed his confidence in this matter as follows: ". . . that I may gain Christ and be found in him, not having a righteousness of my own that comes from the law, but that which is through faith in Christ—the righteousness that comes from God and is by faith" (Phil. 3:8–9). He acknowledged that he could never generate sufficient righteousness of his own to please God. Instead, by an act of faith in Christ he freely received righteousness (*dikaiosynē*) from God himself. On the basis of this gift of Christ's alien righteousness, God justifies believers—that is, he pronounces them righteous in his sight. Paul clearly attested that justification is a forensic and declaratory act. Appealing to Genesis 15:6, he wrote concerning Abraham: "He believed God, and it was credited to him as righteousness" (*elogisthē autō eis dikaiosynēn*, Rom. 4:3). Abraham gave God faith, and God reckoned to Abraham righteousness or right standing with himself. Other Pauline texts confirm that the verb *dikaioō* means to "declare righteous" (e.g., Rom. 2:13; 3:20). Furthermore, in 1 Timothy 3:16 the statement that Christ "was vindicated [aorist passive of *dikaioō*] by the Spirit" makes clear that the Holy Spirit pronounced righteous the rejected Christ via his resurrection from the dead. And in Romans 8:33–34 the verbs "justify" and "condemn" are parallel to each other and thus represent two opposing judicial verdicts.

Paul taught that the ground of justification is the perfect obedience of Christ that culminated in his shed blood (Rom. 5:9). The *instrument* of justification is the individual's faith in Christ. Thus the apostle affirmed that justification is mediated "by" or "through faith": *pistei* (instrumental dative, Rom. 3:28), *ek pisteōs* (Rom. 3:30; 10:6; Gal. 2:16; 3:24), *dia pisteōs* (Rom. 3:30; Gal. 2:16; Phil. 3:9), and *epi pistei* (Phil. 3:9).

The results of justification, according to Paul, are several. Negatively, God's declaration of righteousness results in the nonimputation of sins (Rom. 4:8; 2 Cor. 5:19), cleansing from the defilement of sins (1 Cor. 6:11), annulment of condemnation (Rom. 8:1, 34), and deliverance from the divine wrath (5:9). Positively, justification bestows reconciliation with God, inner peace (5:1), adoption as children into the family of God (8:17; Gal. 4:5–7; Eph. 1:5), and the gracious gift of eternal life (Rom. 5:18, 21; Titus 3:7).

Of all the New Testament writers, Paul most fully developed the theology of personal reconciliation. (1) He first highlighted the *need* for reconciliation with God. Prior to legal acquittal sinners are "separate from Christ" (Eph. 2:12; cf. v.13), "foreigners and aliens" (v. 19), and "God's enemies" (Rom. 5:10; cf. Col. 1:21). Spiritually and psychologically enmity exists between God and sinners. (2) The *agent* of reconciliation is God. Reconciliation is an act and a gift of the Father. The initiative in healing the breach comes from God (Rom. 5:10–11; 2 Cor 5:18–19; Col. 1:20, 22). (3) Paul explained the *relation* between justification and reconciliation. By virtue of the divine acquittal achieved on the cross (i.e., justification), God offers sinners personal reconciliation. Consider the following pairs of texts: "justified by his blood" (Rom. 5:9) and "reconciled to him [God]" (v. 10); "the righteousness of God" (2 Cor. 5:21) and "God was reconciling the world to himself in Christ" (v. 19; cf. v. 18); "not counting men's sins against them" (v. 19b) and "God was reconciling the world to himself in Christ" (v. 19a); finally "the blood of Christ" (Eph. 2:13b) and "you who once were far away have been brought near" (v. 13a). And (4) Paul cited the *results* of personal reconciliation. By faith in Christ's finished work and reception of the Father's acquittal, enmity is transformed into friendship (Rom. 5:10), hostility into peace (Rom. 5:1; Eph. 2:17; Col. 1:20), and estrangement and alienation into fellowship (Col. 1:21–22). Wherein lies the obstacle to personal reconciliation? It seems to be both on God's side and on man's side. As Martin observes:

> To Paul the estrangement which the Christian reconciliation has to overcome is indubitably two-sided; there is something in God as well as something in man which has to be dealt with before there can be peace. . . . It is God's earnest dealing with the obstacle on His own side to peace with man which prevails on man to believe in the seriousness of His love, and to lay aside distrust. It is God's earnest dealing with the obstacle on His own side which constitutes the reconciliation.[79]

Paul, like John, maintained that believers should possess assurance of justification and salvation. *Doctrinally,* assurance is rooted in Christ's victorious resurrection from the dead. Paul wrote that Christ "was raised to life for our justification" (*dikaiōsis,* Rom. 4:25). Christ's victorious resurrection serves as the guarantee of the believer's justification. Furthermore, in the "grand circle of salvation" (8:29–30) Paul grounded assurance in the saving purpose of God delineated by the five verbs, "foreknew," "predestined," "called," "justified," and "glorified." On the basis of God's effectual saving action, believers in Christ know that nothing can separate them from the divine love. Experientially, the ministry of the Holy Spirit in the heart provides inner certitude of justification and adoption. Thus Paul wrote, "Because you are sons, God sent the Spirit of his Son into our hearts, the Spirit who calls out, 'Abba, Father'" (Gal. 4:6; cf. Rom. 8:15). Moreover, "The Spirit himself testifies with our spirit that we are God's children" (Rom. 8:16). Also relevant here is the subjective experience of peace and hope God gives to justified believers (5:1–2).

We turn attention to three important Pauline texts that deal with justification, the first being Romans 3:21–26. In the beginning of the chapter (vv. 5–18; cf. v. 23) Paul argued that both Jews and Gentiles are unrighteous and guilty before God. In vv. 21–26 Paul developed his doctrine of justification, as follows: (1) The *announcement* of justification in the Gospel disclosed a way, other than the futile venture of law keeping, whereby sinners can be made acceptable to God. The radical solution to the problem of the justification of sinners resides in the phrase "righteousness from God" (vv. 21–22). *Dikaiosynē theou*—as in Romans 1:17—connotes a righteousness that comes from God that provides right standing with him.[80] (2) The *instrument* by which God applies justification is faith directed toward Jesus Christ. "This righteousness from God comes through faith [*dia pisteōs*] in Jesus Christ to all who believe" (v. 22, cf. v. 25b). Paul never said that justification is *dia pistin* ("on account of faith")—which would posit faith as the basis of justification. (3) The *ground* of God's gracious act of justification is the propitiatory sacrifice (*hilastērion*) of Christ, who bore the just punishment for our sins and so averted the divine wrath (vv. 24–25a). Finally,

(4) Paul spoke of the *demonstration* of justification in verses 25c–26. By virtue of Christ's penal sacrifice God vindicated his own character by remaining *dikaios* (a) by in punishing his Son and (b) by finding a just way to acquit guilty sinners and pronounce them righteous.

In Romans 4 Paul produced scriptural support for the doctrine of justification by faith by appealing to the examples of Abraham (vv. 1–3, 9–24) and David (vv. 6–8). In Romans 4 the apostle used the verb *logizomai* ("reckon to one's account" or "credit") eleven times (vv. 3–6, 8–11, 22–24) to prove that a believer is justified not by works but as God credits righteousness to his or her account. By appeal to Genesis 15:6 (vv. 3, 9, 22) Paul again (cf. Gal. 3:6) argued that God reckoned Abraham's faith in the divine promise to him as righteousness (*dikaiosynē*). Hence Abraham is the father of all those who are justified by faith. "The words 'it was credited to him' were written not for him alone, but also for us, to whom God will credit righteousness—for us who believe in him who raised Jesus our Lord from the dead" (vv. 23–24). The forensic nature of justification is particularly clear here. From the history of David, Paul concluded that justification involves, negatively, the nonimputation of sin and guilt: "Blessed is the man whose sin the Lord will never count against him" (*ou mē logisētai*, v. 8). And positively, justification involves the imputation of divine righteousness to believers: "David . . . speaks of the blessedness of the man to whom God credits righteousness [*ho theos logizetai dikaiosynē*] apart from works" (v. 6).

Paul further attested the forensic nature of justification in Romans 5:16–19. According to verse 16 Adam's sin incurred the divine "judgment" (*krima*), the nature of which is "condemnation" (*katakrima*). But the gracious "gift of God . . . brought justification" (*dikaiōma*). The Hebrew-like parallelism in verse 16 sets the divine decisions of "judgment" and "justification" in antithetic relation. Thus *dikaiōma*, no less than *krima*, represents a judgment of God—specifically "the gift of righteousness" (v. 17) that God graciously bestows on believers in Christ. Continuing the parallel structure pattern, verse 18 teaches that just as Adam's one trespass led to "condemnation" (*katakrima*), so Christ's "one act of righteousness" (*henos dikaiōma*) resulted in "justification (*dikaiōsis*) that brings life for all men." The "one act of righteousness" (v. 18; cf. "the obedience of the one man," v. 19) highlights the ground of justification, namely, Christ's obedient submission to death that crowned his entire life of fidelity to the Father. The parallelism between the work of Adam and Christ concludes in verse 19: "For just as through the disobedience of the one man the many were made sinners [aorist passive of *kathistēmi*], so also through the obedience of the one man the many will be made [future passive of *kathistēmi*] righteous [*dikaioi*]." The verb *kathistēmi* means to "constitute" or "establish." Thus "this constitutive act consists in our being placed in the category of righteous persons by reason of our relation to Christ."[81] Clearly, the nature of justification is not moral or ethical but legal and declaratory.

The Johannine Literature

The righteousness of Christ was an important theme for John. Jesus Christ is righteous because he always sought to please the Father (John 5:30; 8:29, 46) and he unfailingly spoke truth from the Father (John 12:49–50). In addition, Jesus made it his purpose to do the Father's will and to finish his work (John 4:34; 6:38; 17:4). In life and in death Jesus was completely obedient to the Father's commands (John 14:31; 15:10). By virtue of his perfect adherence to the will of God, John described Jesus Christ as "the Righteous One" (1 John 2:1; cf. 1 John 3:7). As Jesus himself said to his disciples: "On him [the Son of Man] God the Father has placed his seal of approval" (John 6:27).

While not using the verb *dikaioō*, 1 John 1:8–2:2 nevertheless speaks the language of justification. All persons everywhere are afflicted with sin and unrighteousness (1 John 1:8, 10; 2:2). But on the ground of Jesus' shed blood and on the basis of his faithfulness and justice God does three things: (1) He pardons sins, thereby liberating believers from sin's punishment (1 John 1:9a). (2) He frees believers from the pollution of sins committed (1 John 1:9b). As an aside, the preceding demonstrates the close link that exists between God's works of justification and sanctification (cf. 1 John 2:29). "The one effects our peace, the other our character. The forgiveness is the averting of God's wrath; the cleansing is the beginning of holiness."[82] And (3) on the basis of Christ's atoning sacrifice God is propitiated and believers are reconciled to him (1 John 2:2).

Did John teach that a person's good works justify? Jesus said to his disciples, "The work [*to ergon*] of God is this: to believe in the one he has sent" (John 6:29). The disciples were thinking of many works (*erga*) of the law they must perform to please God (v. 28). But Jesus affirmed that there is but one work or one moral act they must do—namely, adopt an attitude of faith toward himself as the one sent by the Father. Furthermore, 1 John 3:7 reads, "He who does what is right is righteous" (*ho poiōn tēn dikaiosynēn dikaios estin*). The verse teaches that the person who has been declared righteous (*dikaios*) and who therefore possesses right standing with God will continue to perform deeds of righteousness (*dikaiosynē*). The proof of one's secret justification is the public performance of righteous works. Here again John established a close link between justification and sanctification.

John understood that God in love legally adopts justified believers into his family. Thus 1 John 3:1 (cf. v. 2) reads, "How great is the love the Father has lavished on us, that we should be called children of God [*tekna theou*]! And that is what we are!" According to John 1:12–13, people are born with the capacity to become children of God. But only justification by faith gives them the right or authority (*exousia*) to become his adopted children. We note that John, unlike Paul, never referred to Christians as *hyioi theou* ("sons of God"). John reserved the title "Son of God" exclusively for Jesus Christ (John 20:31; 1 John 5:13).

Confidence in the believer's *assurance* of justification was a precious reality to John: "I write these things to you who believe in the name of the Son of God so that you may know that you have eternal life" (1 John 5:13). Believers in Christ obtain assurance at several levels: (1) *Doctrinally* they can be assured of justification on the basis of scriptural teaching concerning Christ's deity, incarnation, and atoning death (John 4:14–16; 5:24; 1 John 5:20). (2) *Morally*, Christians gain assurance as they obey God's commands (1 John 2:3, 5; 3:24). (3) *Relationally*, they acquire assurance as they spontaneously perform loving deeds to others (1 John 3:18–19; 4:7). And (4) *experientially*, believers gain assurance of salvation through the powerful presence of the Spirit within (1 John 4:13). John firmly believed that the normal Christian experience, in an age of doubt and uncertainty, is assurance of final salvation. John Stott sums up the matter thus: "Putting together the purpose of Gospel and Epistle, John's purpose is in four stages, that his readers should hear, hearing should believe, believing should live, and living should know."[83]

Other New Testament Literature

The writer of Hebrews and Peter both placed considerable emphasis on Christ's righteousness as the foundation of salvation. Peter wrote, "Christ died for sins once for all, the righteous [*dikaios*] for the unrighteous, to bring you to God" (1 Peter 3:18). During the course of his life Christ was tempted in every way, "yet was without sin" (Heb. 4:15; cf. 1:9; 1 Peter. 2:22). Hebrews 5:7–9 speaks of Jesus' "reverent submission" (*eulabeia*, godly fear), his perfect obedience at every stage of life (cf. Heb. 10:7), and his "being made perfect" (RSV). "His perfection consisted in the retention of his integrity, in the face of every kind of assault on his integrity, and thereby the establishment of his integrity."[84] Thus the writer of Hebrews described Jesus as "one who is holy, blameless, pure, set apart from sinners, exalted above the heavens" (Heb. 7:26). Moreover, Christ went to the cross submissive, obedient to the will of the Father, and with a nonretaliatory attitude vis-à-vis his enemies (1 Peter 2:23). His passion on Good Friday was the supremely righteous act of his earthly existence. "Christ . . . offered himself unblemished to God" (Heb. 9:14).

Hebrews 11:7 links righteousness with faith in a manner reminiscent of Paul, when it says of Noah: "By his faith he . . . became heir of the righteousness [*dikaiosynē*] that comes by faith." Here faith (*pistei, kata pistin*) is the instrument by which righteousness reaches a person. With the suffering servant of Isaiah 53:5 in mind, Peter wrote, "by his wounds you have been healed" (1 Peter 2:24). Through the scourgings inflicted on Jesus, believers receive spiritual healing. The figurative term "healed" in 1 Peter 2:24 "denotes the restoration of divine fellowship through the forgiveness of sins, and all the saving benefits which accompany it."[85] Jesus' atoning death makes believers acceptable in God's sight and establishes a right relationship between the Creator and the creature (1 Peter 3:18). Finally, Hebrews 7:22 affirms that "Jesus has become the guarantee of a better covenant." Through the virtue of his person, the sufficiency of his sacrifice, the power of his resurrection, and the efficacy of his eternal priesthood, Christ is the sure pledge of the new relationship between the Father and believers. Concerning this new covenant, "as His people's representative, He satisfies its terms with perfect acceptance in God's sight."[86]

The Scriptures affirm the close relation that exists between justification and sanctification. First Peter 2:24 states of Christ: "He himself bore our sins in his own body on the tree, so that we might die to sins and live for righteousness." Moreover, 2 Peter 2:21 describes the Christian life as "the way of righteousness" (cf. Matt. 21:32). The purpose of justification is that believers might be liberated from the bondage of sin and live a righteous life (cf. Rom. 6:11, 13, 19; Phil. 1:11). James's unique presentation of justification (2:21–25) was considered in the previous chapter in the context of his view of faith (2:14–26). We concluded that for both Paul and James *dikaioō* meant to "declare righteous." Whereas for Paul and other New Testament writers justification signified *God's* gracious act of declaring believers positionally righteous, for James justification was a matter of *believers'* virtuous works offering public attestation of underlying faith and righteousness of life.

The literature indicates that *assurance* of justification and salvation ought to be the normal experience of every healthy Christian. The author of Hebrews wrote, "We desire each of you to show the same earnestness in realizing the full assurance of hope until the end" (Heb. 6:11, RSV; cf. 1 Peter 1:3). Similar is the exhortation of Hebrews 10:22: "Let us draw near to God with a sincere heart in full assurance of faith." Christians know that the way into God's presence is open because two conditions have been satisfied: the sinful heart has been cleansed and the defiled conscience purified.

SYSTEMATIC FORMULATION

The gift of eternal life that transformed (1) our condition (regeneration, chap. 2) also makes a dramatic difference in (2) our forensic standing (justification) and (3) our relationships (reconciliation). The richness of salvation may be appreciated as these complementary categories are distinguished.

The Need for Forensic Justification: Universal Condemnation

Consider first our legal standing vis-à-vis the moral laws of God, the Source of all values. All of us are objectively guilty before the bar of divine justice. A great gap exists between what we are and what we ought to be. The gap, judicially viewed, seems irreparable. The courtroom context provides a useful analogy for the vivid display of God's mercy and grace through a verdict won by the exalted Advocate who pleads our case.

The legal verdict of condemnation does not *make* one guilty, it simply *declares* the finding of the divine court. The pervasiveness of inherent moral evil at all levels of society means there is no contest. What we *are* and *do* incurs the divine sentence. As those who do not live up to universal moral virtues, we all merit the verdict "Guilty." Ethicists and others who seek to live by moral laws invariably come short of the standards they require of others. Although the Lord keeps his promises and everlasting covenants, we lack fidelity to ours. All await the execution of God's righteous wrath, the result of the loving One's settled opposition to evil.

The guilty cannot justify themselves. Whether for Jews or Gentiles, self-justification is not a viable possibility. An expert in the law answered Jesus correctly on the matter of the first and second greatest commandments, but "he wanted to justify himself, so he asked Jesus, 'And who is my neighbor?'" (Luke 10:29). In reply Jesus told the story of the Good Samaritan. The moment religious persons depend on what they deserve, they become legalistic and miss the meaning of grace. Many ethicists assume that because they "ought," therefore of themselves they "can." But we cannot justify ourselves through self-affirmation (Sartre) if the self is corrupt. So all humans remain accountable to and guilty before God (Rom. 1:18–2:16). No one "will be declared righteous in his sight by observing the law; rather, through the law we become conscious of sin" (3:20). Outward acts may appear worthy, but are our inner motives? After Jesus said, "No servant can serve two masters. . . . You cannot serve God and Money," the money-loving Pharisees sneered at him. Jesus replied, "You are the ones who justify yourselves in the eyes of men, but God knows your hearts" (Luke 16:13–15). We may not have a criminal record at the local police station, but we have one in the court of heaven.

Impotent to conform fully to moral norms ourselves, we all need to *cast ourselves on the mercy of the court.* Paul Tournier's medical counseling disclosed that "there are only endless torments and a vicious circle of misfortunes if one represses one's guilt and denounces the guilt of others. The only peace lies in accepting one's guilt and confessing it."[87] If any of Adam's race are to receive a moral status acceptable in a sinless heaven, it must be by the mercy of the Judge; it must be on the ground of a righteousness not our own. We aspire to be better spouses and parents, but our families are far from what they ought to be. Our best educational efforts do not change human nature. Paul Tillich tried to accept himself in spite of his unacceptability by feeling united with the Ground of Being.[88] But he, like the rest of us, was not acceptable. Whatever their religious experience, the guilty cannot drop the charges against themselves.

The Final Judge: The Just and Gracious God

Justification is the prerogative of God alone: "It is God who justifies" (Rom. 8:33; cf. 4:5). Only the divine legislator and administrator of justice whose moral norms have been broken can grant acquittal. Our sin has infinite consequences because it offends the infinite Source of values to whom we are ultimately accountable. Job addressed the basic question, "How can a mortal be righteous before God?" (Job 9:2).

God cannot call evil good, for that would be to condone our rebellion. How can one who knows every unworthy thought, desire, and motive ethically change a just verdict from "Guilty" to "Not Guilty"? Neither a human judge nor the divine Judge can retain moral integrity and reverse such a verdict arbitrarily. God cannot regard action or inaction that is self-destructive or harmful to others as good. One who is holy and just must pronounce the verdict each person deserves. If there is to be moral health in the world, sin must be called what it is; it cannot be arbitrarily dismissed. If justice is not to be mocked, intentional evil deserves retributive punishment.

In spite of our death sentence, *love found a way* to remain just, to acquit the guilty, and bestow the gift of Christ's righteousness. In unfathomable love the divine Judge himself stepped from behind the bench to satisfy the demands of justice for the unworthy! Hebrews tells us that Jesus Christ is the high priest of the new covenant embracing both Jews and Gentiles (Heb. 8:8–11). Among the blessings of the new covenant that Jeremiah foresaw was a merciful pardon and a gracious gift of righteousness. "I will forgive their wickedness and will remember their sins no more" (v. 12; Jer. 31:34). "And where these have been forgiven, there is no longer any sacrifice for sin" (Heb. 10:18). Since Jesus paid the penalty for all, sinful people come to God empty-handed to receive the free gift. Although under no compulsion to save any, the divine Judge may choose to acquit and declare righteous whom he will.

The Ground of God's Verdict: Christ's Work Alone

The basis of a right moral standing with God is not anything we can do. No fallen Gentiles are justified by recognizing the Creator or by trying to keep the moral law in clear conscience (Rom. 1:18–32; 2:12–15). Moreover, no Jews are justified by striving to keep the written laws, sacrifices, and ceremonies of the Old Testament (2:1–3:8). However sincere and committed we may be, the best of us fall short and stand before God's holiness condemned. To break the law at one point is to reveal the fact that we are lawbreakers.

The exclusive ground for acceptance with the Holy One is the *atoning sacrifice of the sinless Christ*. To satisfy divine justice the impeccable Christ offered himself as the sacrifice for our sins (Rom. 3:25). It is he who turns away divine wrath. By the Father's oath, "Jesus has become the guarantee of a better covenant" (Heb. 7:22). Because he lives forever his priesthood is permanent; thus he is "able to save completely those who come to God through him, because he always lives to intercede for them" (v. 25). Unlike priests under the old covenant, Jesus was "holy, blameless, pure, set apart from sinners [and] exalted above the heavens" (v. 26). He had no need to offer repeated sacrifices for his own sins. But living without sin the Messiah could sacrifice himself for his people's sins once for all (v. 27). So a Christian's righteousness is an alien righteousness; it is the right standing of another—even our great high priest, Jesus Christ—that is put to one's account. On the ground of the Messiah's death for sins the Father pardons those who believe from all guilt and imputes to them Christ's righteousness.

The basis for acceptance with God is *not our faith but its object*. Justification by faith does not mean that God accepts us because of our knowledge, assent, or commitment. Our faith does not make us acceptable. Belief may be poorly founded or well-founded. And faith may be properly placed or misdirected. Faith in our faith does not provide a just basis for God to pardon our sin or to impute to us Christ's righteousness. What does make persons acceptable to God is not faith per se but the one we trust. If our faith is in the one and only Christ, we are justified because of his atonement. As sinners summoned by the Spirit actively believe the Gospel, they accept the free gift of righteous standing before God that Christ actively provided. The Holy Spirit then assures believers of the truth of the objective offer of the Gospel and of their actual personal appropriation of it. Essential to the Good News is the exclusively Christological ground of justification.

Try a true-or-false quiz with church members to disclose their understandings of the ground of acceptance by the heavenly Father. Does God accept us as legal children because: (1) God is putting Christ's goodness into our hearts? (2) our character has been transformed by regeneration? (3) the Spirit indwells our bodies and is making us good? (4) Our faith has become active in love? (5) the Spirit enables us to follow Christ's example? (6) Christ will live out his life of obedience in us? (7) we have done better than others in obeying the Ten Commandments? All these options are false. Not until we radically sever all works from consideration can we appreciate the perfect righteousness that comes from God by sheer grace.

The Means of Becoming Justified: Faith Alone

How does a person actually receive justification? Through Christ "everyone who believes is justified" (Acts 13:39). The offer of justification initially appears to be based on *conditional* formulations. If a sinner exercises his or her ability to believe, he or she will be made right with God. We are invited to believe in order to be justified. "Believe and be saved" seems to follow the scriptural order. But if humanly exercised faith were a condition sinners must meet, none would be saved. Scripture teaches the pre-Christian's inability to believe the Gospel or trust Christ. No evidence was found for the Arminian hypothesis that prevenient grace alleviates the inability to convert (chap. 1). The biblical descriptions of sinners after the blessings of universal grace teach their actual, not hypothetical, inability to receive spiritual truths (1 Cor. 2:14).

In other formulations justification is *unconditional,* as the culminating verdict of unmerited love and grace. From the biblical perspective the justified receive the gift of Christ's perfect right-

eousness. If God pardoned those who met a condition, forgiveness would not be a gift but an obligation. That holds for the condition of believing as well as working. "Now when a man works, his wages are not credited to him as a gift, but as an obligation" (Rom. 4:4). Prior to believing in Christ Luther was proud of his achievements as a Roman priest. Finally after a protracted struggle he learned that righteousness is a gift not a reward for performance. God's justifying love must be unconditional, for enslaved, alienated sinners cannot meet the law's demand of perfect righteousness.

Conversion precedes justification in scriptural presentations, but it is not therefore the "condition" of the legal settlement. To argue that because conversion is "before" salvation it is therefore the "cause" of salvation is to commit a logical fallacy (*post hoc, ergo propter hoc*). Repentance preceding justification is simply "the recognition of guilt, and it is the sense of guilt which drives us to God and reveals to us the love and forgiveness of God."[89] Those who are justified by faith are not justified as innocent persons but as guilty. Hence a repentant acknowledgment of guilt is involved in the faith that justifies.

A counselor of seekers, Paul Tournier, concluded, "I do not think that in the mouth of Jesus Christ repentance has the force of a condition, but rather of a route."[90] The faith that precedes justification is the avenue or means of receiving the free gift. As noted in the biblical section, when referring to the relation of justification to faith, Scripture uses the terms "by faith" and "through [*dia*] faith" but not "on account of faith." Faith must be directed to Jesus Christ (Rom. 3:22) who brought redemption (v. 24). It is "through faith in his blood" that his death becomes our sacrifice of atonement (v. 25). Berkouwer explains that "faith is only an instrument with which we embrace Christ, who is our justification"[91] The preposition "by" or "from" (*ek*) faith (v. 30) shows that faith occasions and logically precedes our personal justification. Accepted by Christ as legal partners, believers receive Christ's perfect standing credited to their account. They become as righteous as he and so enjoy the same legal status as he. As Paul wrote, Abraham's faith was "credited to him as righteousness" (Rom. 4:22), and "the words 'it was credited to him' were written not for him alone, but also for us, to whom God will credit righteousness—for us who believe in him who raised Jesus our Lord from the dead. He was delivered over to death for our sins and was raised to life for our justification" (vv. 23–25). Clearly justification is based exclusively on what our Lord has completed for us, not on what we do.

The Meaning of Justification: Perfect Legal Standing in Christ

God's declaration of a sinner's justification accomplishes several important things:

1. Divine justification *pardons* those who believe from the guilt and penalty of all sins past, present, and future. Paul wrote, "In him we have redemption through his blood, the forgiveness of sins, in accordance with the riches of God's grace that he lavished on us" (Eph. 1:7–8). What about our future? Jesus said, "I tell you the truth, whoever hears my word and believes him who has sent me has eternal life and will not be condemned" (John 5:24; cf. 3:18). "Since we have now been justified by his blood," Paul reasoned, "how much more shall we be saved from God's wrath through him!" (Rom. 5:9). See also Romans 8:30.

2. Justification also *imputes to believers the perfect righteous standing of Jesus Christ*. The gift of imputed right-

eousness does more than simply restore to believers a prefallen innocence. God bestows on them the tested, proven, and perfectly righteous standing of Christ. In writing to the Romans Paul wanted to be sure, not that they had attained a relative righteousness by their faith or efforts, but that they had received "the righteousness that comes from God" (Rom. 10:3). Sinful humans were identified with Adam and so condemned by their legal representative's one sinful act (5:16a, 18a). But God reckons to believers the perfect righteousness of "the second Adam" (vv. 5:16b, 18b). Those who are forensically identified with Christ by faith are justified by the one sacrifice of their legal representative. So believers discover that Christ is "our righteousness, holiness, and redemption" (1 Cor. 1:30). "God made him who had no sin to be sin for us, so that in him we might become the righteousness of God" (2 Cor. 5:21).

3. Justification *legally unites believers to Christ*. Through faith sinful men and women are juridically "in Christ." Being united to Christ in the context of justification designates a legal agreement in virtue of which Christ's righteousness is made ours (Phil. 3:9).[92] So believers are joint heirs of all the assets of Christ in glory. Justification by faith is like that exciting transaction that occurs when an alien becomes a citizen by a naturalization ceremony.

4. By the declaration of justification God also *adopts* believers into his soteriological family. By the same faith and on the same ground of Christ's atoning righteousness God grants believers the right to be called children of God (John 1:12). A couple who have fulfilled all the requirements for adopting a child do not regard the final decision that the child is legally theirs a fiction.

Since justification does not impart

holiness, some describe it as a *legal fiction*. But justification is a once-for-all ruling by the divine Judge concerning a person's moral status that provides for fellowship with God (reconciliation) and progressive growth (sanctification). A criminal on death row does not consider the governor's pardon from all charges a legal fiction. Similarly condemned recipients of the imputed righteousness of Christ do not consider their great gift a fiction. Psychologists know that the difference consciousness of identification with Christ makes to one's self-concept is no mere fiction.

By way of *definition,* then, justification is the gracious verdict of the divine Judge granting sinners united to Christ by faith a complete pardon from the guilt of all their sin and imputing to them Christ's perfectly righteous moral status.

Justification Does Not Make Righteous

Most ethical and religious teachers assume that we must strive to become completely upright in order to come to God. So multitudes of sincerely ethical and religious people wonder if they are good enough—as Hans Küng said—"really and truly, inwardly and outwardly, wholly and completely."[93] But those who try to earn acceptance with God by just deeds will never attain the ideal. Works righteousness or complete existential authenticity must be differentiated from the Good News of justification. If God accepted only those who attain perfect authenticity, none would be received. Those God does accept admit their sin, believe the Gospel, turn from their wicked ways, and receive the perfect provisions of Christ their substitute.

Justification does not make one righteous, any more than condemnation makes one wicked. In justification the divine Judge acquits believers of moral charges. Although justification changes one's legal status, it does not transform the heart; regeneration and sanctification do that. Justification is not to be confused with other provisions of Christ's atonement or other ministries of the Spirit. The teaching of Roman Catholics, Mormons, and others concerned about the perils of lawlessness make justification a matter of infused righteousness. We agree that imputed righteousness is not the whole of the practical Christian life, but is the developmental process of sanctification the point of scriptural teaching on justification? The basic issue is not whether sanctification inevitably follows from and is continually rooted in justification, but whether sanctification is to be included in the concept of justification.

Justification is distinct from sanctification, although the former leads to the latter. Justification is a complete provision of Jesus Christ's atonement; sanctification is a progressive enabling by the Spirit's ministries. That is, justification is once-for-all; sanctification is continuous. Justification is the Good News of pardon from condemnation; sanctification deals with the difference that objective legal transaction makes to the whole Christian lifestyle. If we imagine that our pardon depends on our acts of penance, we will be forever unpardoned. If we make our acceptance in God's family a matter of works, we will never be free as redeemed children of God to grow into the family likeness. As Berkouwer observed, "The Reformation, in its defense of the forensic, declarative justification that points us always to the free favor of God, has not endangered, but rescued the confession of true sanctification."[94]

Contrast the differences between justification and sanctification as adapted from a list by Kenneth Prior.[95]

Justification	Sanctification
1. Concerns guilt	1. Concerns pollution
2. Legal, external, objective	2. Experiential, internal, subjective

3. Relates to our position	3. Relates to our condition
4. Righteousness imputed	4. Righteousness imparted
5. Has no degrees, complete	5. Has degrees, progression
6. Once-for-all, not repeated	6. A gradual process
7. By declaration of the Father	7. By operation of the Spirit
8. No place for our works	8. Our concurrent operation by moral exertion and personal discipline

The Relationship of Reconciliation to Justification

The transition from justification to reconciliation involves a change from forensic to relational categories. Once the Judge to whom we answer no longer counts sin against repentant believers, freedom of personal fellowship is restored. John Oman explains, "Justice must be put first, as a condition to be fulfilled, before love can be suffered to exercise its mercy, and God, like man, must be just before He is generous."[96] Justification removes the moral and legal impediments to fellowship, but alienated persons still need to respond to God's loving advances. Reconciliation involves a change of one's internal attitude and a restoration of relationship to a former enemy.[97] It involves both the initial restoration of a broken relationship and its continuous maintenance.[98]

Neither reconciliation nor justification should be considered the whole of salvation. A holistic soteriology cannot be expressed in either relational or legal categories alone. The richness of biblical teaching on salvation requires an integration of both the legal and relational categories supplemented by the experiential categories of conversion-regeneration (chap. 2) and sanctification (chap. 4).

Our Need for Reconciliation: Alienation

The violation of God's will at the Fall led humans into estrangement from him. Like Adam and Eve we all try to hide from God. "In practice, therefore, enmity against God comes to be just the spirit which resents discipline and evades duty."[99] Ultimately, our disciplines and duties are not from legal codes but from their tripersonal Source. Having come short of these values, we have separated ourselves from God. We were "separate from Christ, excluded from citizenship in Israel and foreigners to the covenants of the promise, without hope and without God in the world" (Eph. 2:12). We were separated from the life of God because of the ignorance in us, due to the hardening of our hearts (4:18). Having become "hostile to God" (Rom. 8:7), like the people at Colosse, we have been "enemies" in our minds (Col. 1:21).

Tournier notes that "real life is life directed by God. Sin means to lose contact with God, and to be guided by Him no longer."[100] Christ, like many other religious teachers, taught renunciation ("Deny yourself, take up your cross, and follow me"). "But," says John Oman, "renunciation, in other religions, is first and is for reconciliation; in Christianity, reconciliation is first and renunciation of value only as it is from reconciliation."[101] Before trying to follow Jesus in discipleship we need to be reconciled to God. Oman adds, "After we have laboured our hardest to love God, we are no nearer our goal, for the simple and sublime reason that love is not love as it deliberately fans its emotion, but only as it forgets itself in what it loves."[102] We have a desperate need to find a way to break out of the vicious circle of sin, alienation, and estrangement. We need peace with God.

The Initiative in Reconciliation: God's Gracious Condescension

Initially reconciliation concerns an act of God in Christ and not a change in us or our status. The fact of the divine initiative that provided for the restoration of fellowship through the Cross remains true, whatever our response. God has done in Christ what is necessary to fulfill all the demands of righteousness and to recover our friendship. Making atonement is not something sinners do to reestablish relationship to God; it is the expression of God's love to reestablish relationships with sinners.

When we speak of the reconciliation between a criminal and his victim, we do not mean that the offender simply changes his mind but that the victim no longer prefers charges against the lawbreaker. God properly brought charges against us when we were dominated by sinful passions and deeds. The end result of such charges was the divine wrath. Reconciliation commenced when God the Father chose to drop the charges against those who believe in his Son. God reconciles sinners to himself by bridging the difference, not between his eternal existence and our temporal existence, but between his holiness and our sinfulness. The Spirit then delivers us from our moral and spiritual inability to return to the Father. Some think that reconciliation applies to human alienation, and that God was never alienated from fallen humans. But not only did our sin cause us to hide from God; our unfaithfulness also brought God's wrath on us (Gen. 6:57). God has taken the initiative to propitiate his own righteous wrath against our injustices and also to expiate our sinful attitudes toward himself. "God demonstrates his own love for us in this: While we were still sinners, Christ died for us" (Rom. 5:8).

God also takes the initiative in the effectual call. The Spirit calls elect sinners to fellowship with God as loving children. Through the prophet Hosea God said, "I will call them 'my people' who are not my people; and I will call her 'my loved one' who is not my loved one,' and, It will happen that in the very place where it was said to them, 'You are not my people,' they will be called 'sons of the living God' '' (Rom. 9:25–26; cf. Hos. 2:23). As God promises in the new covenant, "I will be their God and they will be my people" (Jer. 31:33). A loving horizontal relationship develops among the reconciled, but the priority in reconciliation is the vertical relationship with a promise-keeping God.

The Ground of Reconciliation: Christ Alone

Right relationships with God can occur because of Christ's sacrifice. "God was pleased . . . through him [Christ] to reconcile to himself all things, whether things on earth or things in heaven, by making peace through his blood shed on the cross" (Col. 1:19–20). God's love turned his own wrath to peace by Christ's atonement. Neither persuasive reasoning nor mystical experiences independent of faith in Christ yields peace. The most effective preaching, counseling, or education apart from the Cross cannot reconcile a holy God to holistically depraved humans. A mere moral influence or example is not enough to bring enemies to the peace table permanently. Justice must first be done in our place. And justice was fully satisfied by Christ our substitute.

Reconciliation rests on justice being satisfied by Christ's substitutionary atonement. "God was reconciling the world to himself in Christ, not counting men's sins against them. And he has committed to us the message of reconciliation. We are therefore Christ's ambassadors, as though God were making his appeal through us. We implore you on Christ's behalf: Be reconciled to God" (2 Cor. 5:19–20). He who had no guilt and deserved no penalty became our substitute, bearing our guilt and penalty. Karl Barth captured the basis of reconciliation in substitution, although he applied it to "us men" generically, as in universalism, instead of to "us believers," as in the context of Paul's teaching.

> For the fact that God has given Himself in His Son to suffer the divine judgment on us men does not mean that it is not executed on us but that it is executed on us in full earnest in all its reality—really and definitively, because He Himself took our place in it. That Jesus Christ died for us does not mean, therefore, that we do not have to die, but that we have died in and with him, that as the people we were we have been done away and destroyed, that we are no longer there and have no more future.[103]

When Barth says, "We are no longer there and have no more future," his concept of death appears more like annihilation than separation. But he is right in saying that reconciliation requires more than a mere subjective change in people's attitudes. The definitive event of the Cross cannot be sidestepped by nontheistic existential or psychological approaches that concentrate on restoring relationships. Reconciliation presupposes a personal, living God active in the historical event of Christ's substitutionary atonement to satisfy the demands of justice and open the door to justification. Christ "himself is our peace." Paul continued: "For through him we both [Jews and Gentiles] have access to the Father" (Eph. 2:14, 18).

The sacrifice of the Cross replaces divine wrath with human joy:

> Since we have now been justified by his [Christ's] blood, how much more shall we be saved from God's wrath through him! For if, when we were God's enemies, we were reconciled to him through the death of his Son, how much more, having been reconciled, shall we be saved through his life! Not only is this so, but we also rejoice in God through our Lord Jesus

Christ, through whom we have now received reconciliation." (Rom. 5:9–11)

In Christ believers have been given the fullness of a new peaceful relationship (Col. 1:20; 2:9).

No appeal to the parable of the lost son (Luke 15) contravenes the central biblical emphasis that without the shedding of blood there is no restoration. Reconciliation to God becomes possible on the same basis as justification, namely, the atonement of Christ (2 Cor. 5:19, 21). Only the divine person Jesus Christ is able to reconcile alienated sinners to a holy God. The Lord Jesus Christ is the one and only Mediator between God and man (1 Tim. 2:4). He is the Advocate who thoroughly understands both sides.

The Means of Reconciliation: Faith Alone

Reconciliation comes by the same means as justification, namely, by belief and trust in Christ. Barth held that the "possibility has become the actuality," for sinners need only to be informed that they are already in fellowship with God.[104] This is hard to relate to all the biblical texts dealing with the urgency of belief, repentance, and faith. Christ's provision is sufficient for all in the world, but it must be received one by one. Since Jesus paid it all, nothing remains but for sinners to receive the access he provided and to grow in fellowship with their Savior.

Our faith, indispensable as it is, does not reconcile us. It is the *object* of our faith, the one mediator between God and estranged sinners, who reconciles. Trust in the eternal Word (who became flesh, accepted our guilt, bore our penalty, and rose again from the dead) opens the way not only to justification but also to authentic, lasting communion with God. So Christ's ambassadors implore people to believe in order

155

to be justified and reconciled to God (2 Cor. 5:20).

The Ultimate Goal: Personal Communion With the Most High

Negatively, the goal of reconciliation is not metaphysical union with the Absolute. Reconciliation does not mean absorption into the being of God like the dewdrop in the shining sea. Nor does it does mean the loss of personal consciousness as in ecstatic mystical experience. Christ's provision for reconciliation contributes not to the loss of personality but to its enrichment. Being reconciled to God does not make history or moral evil unreal; both are as real and significant as the death of Christ. John testified as an eyewitness to the importance of empirically verifying the historical Jesus by seeing, hearing, and touching so that we might have fellowship with the Father and with his Son Jesus Christ (1 John 1:1–3).

Affirmatively, the reconciling work of Christ and the Holy Spirit nullifies moral enmity and restores sinners' communion with the triune God. "God is light; in him there is no darkness at all. If we claim to have fellowship with him yet walk in the darkness, we lie and do not live by the truth. But if we walk in the light as he is in the light, we have fellowship with one another, and the blood of Jesus Christ purifies us from all sin" (1 John 1:5–7). "Fellowship" (*koinōnia*) implies persons in association, participation, and communion with one another or with the divine persons.

The highest values in life are experienced not in "I-it" relationships but in loving "I-You" relationships with the living, personal, and holy Source of all. Reconciliation restores a relationship of mutual, participatory love with God the Father (1 John 1:3, 6), with God the Son (1 Cor. 1:9) symbolized by the Lord's Supper (10:16), with God the Holy Spirit (2 Cor. 13:14), and with one another (John 13:34; 1 John 1:7). Estrangement gives way to joyful fellowship; distrust turns into faith; hostility is overcome by love; and rebellion is displaced by active yieldedness. Life in the natural sphere is responsiveness to light, heat, nutrition, etc.; so eternal life is responsiveness to the living, knowing, loving, acting, and relating God. Life is eternal fellowship with the most fulfilling persons of all—Father, Son, and Holy Spirit.

Through Christ converts have eternal reconciliation with God, just as a married couple are in association for life. But our conscious communion with God may be broken by sin, just as spouses for some reason may not speak to each other for a short time. We may become spiritual adulterers by loving, worshiping, and serving other gods. When that happens, we need to be honest before God and confess our sins. Then we can enjoy making up! But as we mature in relational fidelity we should have fewer of these temporary estrangements. Both our legal status (justification) and relational status (reconciliation) are secure on the ground of Christ's work. Analogously, children in stages of teen-age rebellion remain legally children of their parents though temporarily estranged from them. When they mature, they typically restore the personal fellowship they had previously enjoyed.

The believer's personal relationship with God may be called "eternal life" (John 3:16). Life in its deepest and richest sense consists of faithful, loving fellowship with other persons and supremely with God. Spiritual life is essentially relational and everlasting. It begins here and now at the point of one's conversion. We have fellowship with a living God who is Lord of his kingdom and head of the church—a God who decides, acts, does good, meets needs, makes peace, and gives joy. While the goal of meditation and worship in some forms of Buddhism is emptiness, in Christianity it is a personal, relational life lived to the full (John 10:10). Christians seek first God's kingdom and righteousness, knowing that "all these things will be given to [them] as well" (Matt. 6:33).

The Penultimate Goal: Restored Friendship with Enemies

In the Sermon on the Mount Jesus stressed the importance of reconciliation with an estranged brother. He taught that if a person should bring an offering to the altar and remember that a brother is offended, his gift should be left at the altar. "First go and be reconciled to your brother; then come and offer your gift" (Matt. 5:24). It was important to Paul that, if possible, a separated wife should be "reconciled" to her husband (1 Cor. 7:11). "The need for human reconciliation is parabolic of man's need of reconciliation with God."[105]

Christ's provision of reconciliation is for the entire multiethnic world, including people like Jews and Gentiles torn by centuries of racial, religious, and political prejudice. As alienated Gentiles and Jews are brought near to the Father and the Son by one Spirit, they are brought near to each other (Eph. 2:13, 17). Christ "himself is our peace, who has made the two one and has destroyed the barrier, the dividing wall of hostility, by abolishing in his flesh the law with its commandments and regulations. His purpose was to create in himself one new man out of the two, thus making peace, and in this one body to reconcile both of them to God through the cross, by which he put to death their hostility" (vv. 14–16). In the one body of Christ—the Pharisee of the Pharisees—Gentiles (heathen) and Samaritans (half-breeds) are no longer enemies; they are friends and fellow citizens as God's people and members of God's family built on the common foundation of Christ and indwelt by God's Spirit (vv. 19–22).

Summation

Through the declaration of our new legal status before God and assured of legal adoption in God's spiritual family, believers can experience open, loving relationships. Christ provided for the restoration of relationships through his reconciling Atonement at Calvary. Thus the sting has been taken out of loneliness—the feeling of not being related to God and others. The realization of Christ's just and loving provision for reconciliation comes to the regenerate through the illumination of the Word and the Spirit's witness with our spirits. Humanistic attempts at reconciliation prove inadequate. To gain sufficient motivation and energy for love of neighbor we must first be restored to the love of God. In later discussions of sanctification, the church, and the future we will develop further the outworking of new relationships.

APOLOGETIC INTERACTION

Thoughtful people since Schleiermacher came to a continental divide on the doctrine of salvation, said David Wells. The central issue was: "Is theology and in particular the doctrine of salvation to be written in terms of modern self-understanding, or is it to be written in terms of God's revelation in Scripture?"[106] Christians concerned for the unreached in this world of conflicting truth claims will prepare to assess the most influential options arising from modern self-understanding.

Justification Based on Humanistic Works or Good Karma?

A humanistic works-righteousness is one of the primary opponents of the

Gospel of grace in the church today. According to successors of Pelagius, secularists and ethicists as well as most world religions and cults, sinners become acceptable to God on the basis of their good works. But in both Old and New Testaments justification means bringing a person into a right (just) standing with God and consequently into harmonious relationships (reconciliation) with others.

Through the ages alienated people needing the wholeness and justice that reconciliation brings have advocated spiritualities and ethics based on "good works." Recall the controversies of Jesus with the Pharisees, Paul with the Galatian legalists, Augustine with the Pelagians, and Luther with the Roman system of indulgences. "Paul, Augustine, and Luther insisted that man pleases God and releases His transforming power into society only through simple trust in God's powerful grace."[107] All who accept Christ's atonement are justified only by faith. Their works are an expression of the life of the Spirit within them. The New Testament brand of activism is a far cry from the hate-filled, impatient, humanistic variety often seen in today's world. It is loving, sacrificial, and humble. It is as compassionate and effective as the good works of Paul, Augustine, Luther, Wesley, or Billy Graham.

Jesus taught us to pray, "Your kingdom come, your will be done on earth as it is in heaven" (Matt. 6:10). John Oman laments,

How often is that order reversed! Let us do Thy will, that Thy Kingdom may be gradually brought in, and, in the end, every heart inspired by the true reverence! The result is striving and crying, with the perpetual menace of defeat and the increasing shadow of despair. But the servant of the Lord should not strive, nor be, after that fashion, morally strenuous. An essentially apocalyptic hope . . . and the ground of it lies in beginning with our relation to God, and, only through it passing to man's achievement. The order is first reverence, then surrender, then obedience, yet always one and indivisible, even when successive in their manifestation.[108]

We cannot compel the unbelieving world to accept a perfect righteousness that comes only through faith. But we can proclaim the joys and exemplify the good works of justified and reconciled people. God's love in Christ liberates saints from past sins and prejudices thereby enabling them to serve others in Christ's name. Believers do not work to be saved, but labor in the power of the Holy Spirit to bring reconciliation to the whole world. Good works occupy a prime place in the service of the saints.

Justification by Ignorance ("Faith")?

Recent existentialist thinkers, in properly emphasizing total commitment, have tended to misinterpret the Protestant principle of faith alone. They substitute their noncognitive epistemological stance for belief in objective truth. Faith then becomes an unreflective commitment to an unknown "God." By adopting this position they transform justification by grace apart from works into justification independent of Gospel truth and the historical evidences supporting its claims. This confusion of soteriological and epistemological categories involves a misunderstanding of the meaning of belief and its relationship to faith.

This misunderstanding of justification by faith stems from a nonconceptual doctrine of *revelation,* as in Barth and Bultmann. Barth maintained that God disclosed himself savingly not in information about the redemptive plan that could be accepted or rejected. "Faith," the early Barth said, "is a void."[109] Barth thought that clear concepts to be believed and an evidential base for believing them would foster human security before God that is incompatible with grace. No doctrine or evidence could provide an escape from our "disturbance and tension, the insecurity and questionableness."[110] Later, Barth allowed for revelation in the person of Christ, but the Gospels remained for him paradoxical human witness to revelation and not divinely originated truth. The human efforts of biblical writers to point to God were distinct from God's Word (Christ). Barth added, "Religion is the possibility of the removal of every ground of confidence except confidence in God alone."[111] This Barthian view does not adequately account for the data of revelation and faith. In the natural world God has revealed information about himself that one can acknowledge or suppress. Christ's own teachings could be received favorably or rejected. And the prophetic and apostolic writings can be believed or disbelieved (vol. 1, chaps. 3–4). However revealed truths are presented, they may be refused as well as received.

Holding a contradictory view, Bultmann wrote, "Indeed, demythologizing is the radical application of the doctrine of justification by faith to the sphere of knowledge and thought. . . . There is no difference between security based on good works and security built on objectifying knowledge."[112] Such a dialectical misunderstanding of justification by faith alone stems from the unfounded assumption of an infinite qualitative distinction between God and humanity. Neglect of the cognitive image of God in us (Col. 3:10) in turn leads to the view that all religious concepts and language equivocate. Hence revelation becomes a contentless encounter. Bultmann's commitment without evidence is allegedly addressed to the living Christ of the Christ-event, but it is not guided by the teaching of the Jesus of history. Hence Bultmann lacks a test by which to determine whether the spirits are from God (1 John 4:1–3).

His theological statements are true only as existential statements about his own experience. His faith amounts to nothing more than authentic self-understanding. Bultmann imagines that confidence in divinely disclosed truths becomes a meritorious basis for claims upon God. On the contrary, belief in assertions of Scripture is a divinely enabled reception of revealed truth. One is justified on the basis of the Christ revealed in Scripture.

Abraham's faith is the most prominent biblical example of the kind of faith that God reckons for righteousness. But his faith is often misunderstood by existentialists as being without content. The authentic faith by which Abraham was justified was not an unsupported existential leap into the unknown. Abraham's *faith* included (1) *knowledge* of the covenant-making Lord and his promises. Abraham believed the informative promise that he would be the father of a great nation and have countless offspring (Rom. 4:18). Although he was some one hundred years old and Sarah's womb was barren, he did not waver through unbelief. Abraham's faith also involved (2) *persuasion* that God has the power to do what he promised (v. 21). Furthermore, (3) Abraham's faith culminated in entire soul *commitment* guided by truth. He did not have extensive knowledge, but he knew what he believed and why he believed it. God's propositionally revealed promises that he heard and received directed his commitment to significant action. "This is why 'it was credited to him as righteousness'" (v. 22).

Justification by Self-Acceptance Without Acceptability?

Paul Tillich thought that we overcome anxiety and are justified at the moment when we accept ourselves in spite of being unacceptable. It is true that God accepts us in spite of being unacceptable; but he accepts only those sinners who come on the basis of Christ's atonement. Tillich's understanding of human sin was much too restricted. Sin is more than metaphysical separation from the ground of our being; it is moral rebellion against God. Furthermore, Tillich's doctrine of acceptability lacks a moral basis. He quoted these words of Paul: "Where sin increased, grace increased all the more" (Rom. 5:20). But Tillich ignored the context of the passage, which explains the provision of grace—i.e., the reality of Christ's atoning sacrifice. Christ does not ignore righteousness or destroy moral standards; he fulfills them. Although "sin reigned in death," grace reigns "through righteousness to bring eternal life" (v. 21). The categories of justification are moral and not merely psychological or metaphysical. Tillich's "Being itself" cannot accept anyone; only a personal God can do that. But the biblical heavenly Father accepts us "just as we are" when we receive Christ's sacrifice in our behalf.

Reinhold Niebuhr noted that sinful human pride infects every society leading people to direct their lives and history by their own plans, programs, and panaceas. In pride (*hybris*) people seek to obscure the conditioned character of their existence and rise to the infinite. But Niebuhr emphasized that humans in society cannot be justified by their own achievements, institutions, or traditions. Hope lies, he said, not in our own self-justification but in God who justifies even the things that are not that no flesh may glory in his presence.[113] Our only hope individually or collectively resides in justification by the transcendent God of the scriptural promises.

Some regard the doctrine of justification as a mere legal fiction. But justification is based on several historic realities: the eternal Word who became flesh, lived a sinless life, actually accepted our guilt, suffered our penalty as our substitute, and rose bodily from the grave. The Cross was not a fabrication but a dreadful actuality. The sacrifice of our real substitute supplied the just basis for the verdict of the divine Judge. Because the verdict was grounded on actual facts, charges of myth do not fit. The person who judges biblical statements about God and the world as mythical should examine the case for Scripture's reliability in volume 1. What the Bible teaches is truth about reality. The means of justification is also real. God declares *righteous* those sinners who actually repent and believe. As we have seen, habitual sinners who hear, understand, receive, and turn from lesser gods to the Lord of all undergo a real struggle of thoughts, desires, and wills.

Are Legal Categories Essential to Justification?

With an eye to many nonevangelical and even a few evangelical theologians who reject the legal character of justification, Packer makes the following observation:

The validity of forensic categories for expressing man's saving relationship to God has been widely denied. Many neo-orthodox thinkers seem surer that there is a sense of guilt in man than that there is a penal law in God, and tend to echo this denial, claiming that legal categories obscure the personal quality of this relationship.[114]

Legal aspects of salvation may seem problematic when difficulties with justice on the human level are transferred to God. At least three guidelines may help us interpret the legal analogies of God as Judge: (1) Delete any finite limitations and unjust operations of any human court. (2) Overcome the present gap between ideal and real justice by thinking of a perfectly just Judge whose decisions are perfectly fair. (3) Contemplate the fathomless love of the same Judge who at great cost to himself acts on behalf of the guilty with unparalleled mercy and grace.

Concerns about legal status may arise because it may be coldly abstracted from persons. The heavenly Judge who determines the verdict is personal, knowing, and caring. There can be no legal verdict of justification without a living, personal God. And the suspects in this courtroom are persons. When justice is satisfied, broken relationships may be restored. Is not the person who is released from criminal charges personally grateful to the Judge who grants the pardon? The legal realities of justification no more hurt one's relationship to God than the marriage license and ceremony hurt the personal relationship of a committed couple.

Legal aspects add *objectivity* to the moral and spiritual transaction. Objective assessment is essential to justice for people against whom charges are brought. "The Rabbinic doctrine of justification postpones the judicial act until the last judgment. It should be noted, however, that to think of *dikaiousthai* one-sidedly in terms of experience is to imperil the forensic objectivity of the process."[115] Berkouwer explains:

> Reconciliation through Christ's cross broadcasts God's righteousness. For this reason, we can speak of justification only forensically. And for this reason, Paul's thought suggests the atmosphere of the *tribunal Dei*. It is not as though he wants to circumscribe the mystery of salvation in juridical categories. It is simply that in justification pardon appears in the context of accusation and guilt.[116]

Are the legal categories of justification valid for *God in himself*? Alister McGrath helpfully incorporates existentialist implications of justification, but fails to show their consistency with propositional truth from God about himself. McGrath claims that the doctrine of justification by faith does not concern objective knowledge of God in himself, but only of God for us.[117] But in himself God remains just (Rom. 3:25) while justifying the ungodly. God has revealed propositional truth about himself as well as his plans and purposes for history. So we need not choose between whether God is just in himself or whether he is just in relation to believers only. The God who is for us is the One who, independent of his relationship to us, can say "I am." "Who will bring any charge against those whom God has chosen? It is God [himself] who justifies" (Rom. 8:33). As a result, believers are justified, not just for time, but for eternity.

Legal categories and verdicts are *not foreign to biblical revelation* about God. Leon Morris observes that although the verb "justify" in both Greek and English is used in more general senses, "that does not alter the fact that the verb is essentially a forensic one in its biblical usage, and it denotes basically a sentence of acquittal."[118] And the word study in Kittel concludes that "in Paul the legal usage is plain and indisputable."[119] Notions of accountability to God as Judge, a day of judgment, and justification pervade much of special revelation. Scripture is replete with moral and legal terms, such as moral laws, guilt, condemnation, pardon, imputation, citizenship, judgment according to works, and justification. Judicial justice and mercy find their source in the attributes that inhere in God's very being.

Moral and legal justice must be taken seriously because God is the ultimate administrator of justice for both the evil and the good. God holds every human being accountable for living by moral guidelines that make life possible and significant. All are accountable in a heavenly courtroom before the omniscient and righteous divine Judge. Without a day of accountability the administration of moral law would be a sham. So God has appointed a Judgment Day to assess our standing before the moral principles that make significant human life possible. Every religion and philosophy leads to God—as Judge. The question is how unrepentant and unbelieving moralists can stand before an omniscient and righteous Judge and be found morally upright.

Forensic "justification" is integral to Paul's argument in Romans. Its theme is the revelation of "a righteousness from God" (1:17). The lack of righteousness by moral law-keeping among both Jews and Gentiles leads to the condemnation of all (1:18–3:20). Christ's propitiation (3:21–16) is received by faith (3:27–4:25); a faith that not only bears fruit (5:1–11) but also justifies by imputing the righteousness that comes from God as a gift to believers (5:12–21). Whoever presents a testimony or tract on salvation that omits forensic forgiveness and the gift of Christ's perfect righteousness, misses a major aspect of the Bible's Good News. People need to know how they stand before the values of their ultimate Judge either in themselves or in Christ.

Can Christ's Righteousness Be Transferred to Others?

We have previously discussed the principles of substitution and representation in the imputation of Adam's guilt and penalty to the race he represented as natural and legal head. The same principle was at work on the cross where human guilt was imputed to the Lamb of God who bore its penalty.

Granting the validity of imputation in principle, is it realistic and fair for the righteousness of Christ, our Substitute, to be transferred to believers with the

gift of eternal life? The question confuses categories. The issue at this point is not a matter of *justice* but of *grace*. At issue is God's right to give unmerited blessings as he wills. No one deserves to be pardoned and reckoned as righteous as Christ. Every human has chosen to go his own way rather than God's way. All are guilty, and left to themselves all would continue eternally in separation from God. Since justice has been satisfied and our penalty already paid by Christ, who can say that God the Father could not on that basis freely pardon whom he will?

Are All Universally Justified?

If Christ's righteousness may be imputed to many, why not to all? Much as we would like to find universalism supported by the Scriptures, this is not the case. Justification as presented in the Bible is always by grace through faith. And without faith no one is accepted by God. Neither Christ nor the apostles affirmed universalism. Karl Barth's view that Christ died for the human race generically and so all are justified does not fit the repeated and urgent summons in Scripture to be saved. According to Barth's proposal, repentance and faith are not required for the implementation of justification; people simply need to be *informed* that God has reestablished the broken covenant relationship for them. Faith simply makes justification a *conscious* reality for us. All of us would like to think that every human being is a child of God. But realistically, this hypothesis does not cohere with the reality that some harden their hearts, some sneer, and others put off a decision for Christ.

Christ's provisions are sufficient for all universally, but God has given some up to their own unrighteousness (Rom. 1:24, 26, 28). God treats humans as responsible persons, not as things. If people distort and suppress the benefits of *common grace,* is there any reason to think that they will humble themselves to receive *special grace*? Their rejection of God's ways may continue not only throughout this life but also the life to come. "Universalism perverts the gospel of the love of God into an obscene scene of theological rape quite unworthy of the God whom we encounter in the face of Jesus Christ."[120]

As we have seen in chapter 1, those whom the Father has given to the Son from every tribe and nation *do come* to him. By sheer grace they will be justified, sanctified, and glorified. In strict justice, however, those who are permitted to continue in their own sinful ways can not justifiably say that they have been unfairly judged. None will be punished more than they deserve.

All who believe need not doubt that they have been justified. Apart from the Spirit of God none can become persuaded that Jesus is Lord and commit themselves to him (1 Cor. 12:3). Justification comes via that faith. If you believe, like Abraham, you are persuaded that God can do what he promised. He promised to justify all who come to him through faith in Jesus as the eternal Word who became flesh, died for their sins, and rose again.

Does James Contradict Paul?

Throughout Romans and Galatians Paul insists that sinners are justified by faith alone and not by works. James, however, wrote, "What good is it, my brothers, if a man claims to have faith but has no deeds? . . . Faith by itself, if it is not accompanied by action, is dead" (2:14, 17).

James appealed to a strand of Jewish teaching that "complements, rather than contradicts" Paul on justification by grace. "In both Paul and James *dikaioō* means to pronounce righteous, though in the case of James it concerns evidence that can be seen by men,

whereas in Paul it is the eschatological verdict pronounced by God on the unrighteous."[121] When Paul addressed a situation like the one James addressed, he too preached the need for obedience and action. When alleged believers are indifferent to the starving and ill-clad, content with their own spirituality and given to gossip and slander, Paul, like James, upholds a faith that expresses itself in love (Gal. 5:6). Both refer to Abraham's faith, which was credited to him as righteousness (Gen. 15:6). Although Paul illustrated his point from this verse itself, James supported his point from the story in the context of the offering of Isaac (James 2:21; Gen. 22:1–14). Paul opposed self-righteous legalism by emphasizing the importance of faith; James opposed self-righteous indifference by emphasizing the resultant indications of faith in life.

James said that Abraham's faith and actions worked together, or that his faith was made complete by what he did (2:22). So when James wrote, "You see that a person is justified by what he does and not by faith alone" (v. 24), he had in mind not just the legal status but the *result* of it in experience. When Paul viewed the total picture of salvation, he wrote in ways similar to James. But Paul restricted (as we have done) the word justification to the narrower usage of legal standing rather than its broader use in James, which includes the results of that status.

Does a Forensic View of Justification Foster Unfaithfulness?

Since the faith that justifies accepts Christ's work as sufficient and considers human religious achievements "rubbish" (Phil. 3:3-9), shall we not sin that grace may abound?

Raising this question shows that we uphold a view much like Paul's. The same question was asked of him: "What shall we say, then? Shall we go on sinning so that grace may increase?" (Rom. 6:1). Paul responded, "By no means! We died to sin; how can we live in it any longer?" (v. 2). A change of attitude toward sin in those who are repentant and committed to Christ makes a substantial difference. Consider an illustration. Does a human expression of unconditional love and commitment at a marriage ceremony lead to unfaithfulness? At the legal ceremony the bride and groom publicly declare their death to other sexual relationships. That public expression of mutual trust need not, and ought not, contribute to infidelity. With God and others as witnesses, a bride and groom publicly pledge their faithfulness to each other. Similarly, confessing Christ as Savior does not contribute to infidelity to him. The great love of the triune God ought not lead the saint to disloyalty and disaffection. The effectual wooing of the Spirit continues through the lifelong process of sanctification.

The fruit of justification and reconciliation is good works. "For it is by grace you have been saved, through faith—and this not from yourselves, it is the gift of God—not by works, so that no one can boast" (Eph. 2:8–9). Too often we stop quoting the Scripture at that point. The thought continues: "For we are God's workmanship, created in Christ Jesus to do good works, which God prepared in advance for us to do" (v. 10). The purpose and end of conversion, regeneration, justification, and reconciliation is a dramatic transformation that makes a difference in life in terms of good works. Having been accepted by sheer grace apart from works, we are recreated, regenerated, and resurrected from the dead. Thankful for acceptance in God's family and experiencing renewed abilities to know, love, and serve God, believers mature in developing worthy motives and actions.

RELEVANCE FOR LIFE AND MINISTRY

What bearing do justification and reconciliation have on how Christian people think of themselves and how they act? What difference does the objective meaning of justification make in our relational lives with God, our families, our neighbors, and our churches?

Gratefully Accept Your New Righteous Status

Consider Jesus' parable of the Pharisee and the tax collector (Luke 18:10–14):

> Two men went up to the temple to pray, one a Pharisee and the other a tax collector. The Pharisee stood up and prayed about himself: "God I thank you that I am not like other men—robbers, evildoers, adulterers—or even like this tax collector. I fast twice a week and give a tenth of all I get."
> But the tax collector stood at a distance. He would not even look up to heaven, but beat his breast and said, "God, have mercy on me, a sinner."
> I tell you that this man, rather than the other, went home justified before God. For everyone who exalts himself will be humbled and he who humbles himself will be exalted.

Illegal tax collectors did not become acceptable to God on the basis of religious rituals, tithes, or social activism. Even world-class players lose the game of self-justification. Like the tax collector in Jesus' story you become acceptable to God by possessing the righteousness that God himself gives (Rom. 3:21–5:21). God accepts you by sheer grace and clothes you with the righteousness of his Son. Be grateful to God that though formerly you were filled with selfish desires and insatiable pride he has blessed you with the gift of Christ's perfect righteousness.

Also celebrate the fact that God has constituted you a legally adopted child in his soteriological family. Christ is God's only-begotten Son, but believers are adopted children. Thus Paul wrote that in "love" the Father "predestined us to be adopted as his sons through Jesus Christ" (Eph. 1:5). In this new status the Holy Spirit witnesses with human spirits that we are adopted children of God. "For you did not receive a spirit that makes you a slave again to fear, but you received the Spirit of sonship. And by him we cry, 'Abba, Father.' The Spirit himself testifies with our spirit that we are God's children. Now if we are children, then we are heirs—heirs of God and co-heirs with Christ" (Rom. 8:15–17). John adds, "To all who received him, to those who believed in his name, he gave the right to become children of God" (John 1:12). This legal authority comes to us from the transcendent God, not from human priesthoods. In daily devotions cultivate gratitude to God that you are a forgiven child of the faithful, covenant-making God of truth. Rejoice that your name is legitimately registered in the Lamb's book of life (Rev. 3:5; 20:12, 15; 21:27).

Take heart that you are a lawful heir to the Abrahamic promises (Gal. 3:16, 29). You are no longer an outsider, a slave, or a mere friend. You are an adopted child of the owner of all real estate and a legal heir (4:1–7). The Father sent his Son to redeem those under the law "that we might receive the full rights of sons" (v. 5). In times of heightened consciousness of human rights, it may be helpful to raise our awareness of our spiritual rights. We have direct access to our transcendent Father (Rom. 5:2). We partake of the benefits of members in the body and bride of Christ, the church. Changing the analogy to that of a nation, we may celebrate also becoming legal citizens of heaven (Phil. 3:20).

Because of our forensic and relational union with Christ we constantly seek to be faithful. As God's children we love regularly to meditate on our standing and utilize our access to the throne of grace. Before God's Law we are as righteous as the Messiah. Christ's moral status does not simply restore an innocence like that of Adam and Eve before the Fall. Justification provides his tested, proven, and perfect righteousness. "Therefore, since we have been justified through faith, . . . we rejoice in the hope of the glory of God" (Rom. 5:1–2).

A celebration of the reality of our legal worth and relational value frees us from concerns for ourselves to care about others. Whether we are Jew or Gentile, employer or employee, woman or man, to the divine Judge we were worth creating and we are also worth salvaging. To the inherent value of our human spirits as image-bearers of God we can add enhanced value because of the divine Judge's pardon. Since our justification was of such importance to the Father that he sent his only Son to die for us and his Spirit to renew us, know that our justified and reconciled selves are of significant value. Our new status as God's children ethically and spiritually gives significance to our lives and relationships.

The Justified Can Deal Decisively with Guilt Feelings

When we were justified, God dealt once-for-all with our objective guilt. The believing are "justified freely by his grace through the redemption that came by Christ Jesus" (Rom. 3:24). Converts who occasionally feel under condemnation need to deal conclusively with those feelings. Since the all-knowing Judge now finds us "Not guilty!" feelings of guilt do not come from him. When they occur, we need to forgive ourselves, for we have been acquitted of all the charges resulting from our sins by the heavenly judiciary. When we have difficulty forgetting our sins, recall that we have the righteous standing of Jesus Christ himself!

We can rejoice over deliverance from our death sentence as Barabbas did from his (Matt 27:16–26). Imagine how this guilty criminal felt when the guards came to his prison cell to execute him at Golgotha. But they opened the prison door, not to take him to the cross, but to set him free! Why? Because at the request of the crowd Pilate agreed that Jesus would die in place of Barabbas at Calvary. Barabbas must have celebrated his new lease on life for the rest of his years. And so should believers. Jesus voluntarily took our guilt and penalty at Calvary, vindicating divine justice. Thank your Substitute and celebrate your forgiveness! Since God forgives you on the basis of Christ's sacrifice, on that same foundation you should be able to accept yourself. Free from the guilt and penalty of moral laws, live as a liberated child of a loving God.

If our guilt feelings persist from unrealistic expectations of ourselves, they may need to be dismissed as childish. Affirm with Paul, "When I became a man, I put childish ways behind me" (1 Cor. 13:11). Childish ways in 1 Corinthians 13 appear as the opposite of love's reconciling ways. Mature love (of self and others) "keeps no record of wrongs" and "does not delight in evil but rejoices with the truth" (1 Cor. 13:5–6).

Also forgive self and others as you recall that God overrules evil for good. In his book *Guilt and Grace*, Paul Tournier explains the following to his guilt-ridden clients: "Fulfillment of God's plan is happily not dependent on the faultless obedience of men! That God does make use of the obedience of those who give heed to Him is obvious enough. What is amazing is that He also

uses their faults and their hardness of heart."[122] Joseph understood that aspect of divine providence when he met the brothers who had tried to kill him and said, "I am your brother Joseph, the one you sold into Egypt! And now, do not be distressed and do not be angry with yourselves for selling me here, because God sent me ahead of you . . . to save your lives by a great deliverance" (Gen. 45:4–5, 7).

A depressed client once said to physician Paul Tournier, "I have come to the conclusion by reading one of your books, that all the principal decisions of my life, which I believed I had freely made, were in fact no more than evasions. So my entire life has been false; I have lost a sense of God's plan, and I shall not find it again." Tournier wrote, "Just think how guilty I felt at that statement!" But, replying to his client, he explained, "You are still within God's plan. He reigns over our lives, and our flight cannot prevent Him reigning. And He also guides us, in a mysterious way, even through our evasions; otherwise the whole world would be lost, for everyone is evasive, myself included on scores of occasions."[123]

Guilt feelings are inescapable in a fallen world, Tournier claims. "To speak with more precision, all of us are at the same time guilty and obdurate. We all experience guilt feelings, and we also continually seek to escape from them, not by the pardon of God but by the mechanism of self-justification and the repression of conscience."[124] What is Tournier's answer? "We ourselves have need at one and the same time of both aspects of the biblical inversion. We need the assurance of grace to meet our conviction of guilt, and we need the severity of God to drive us back upon ourselves, to the recognition of our guilt and misery, and to make us entrust ourselves still more ardently to the divine grace."[125]

Unlike those governed by mere moralism, God's justified and adopted children develop a confident assurance of forgiveness. Experientially, when that harmonious relationship is broken, they honestly acknowledge their sins, confess them to God, accept his forgiveness, and enjoy reconciliation. Others "attempt—vainly, and unconsciously to be sure—to make expiation, to 'pay.' And they do pay, quite literally, with their health. The dreadful agony of this inexhaustible guilt to which the neurotics are martyrs is a kind of expiatory sacrifice which they are rendering."[126] To help guilt-ridden people we also need some act or public ritual implying solidarity in our guilt and marking our faith and repentance. Those are functions of the communion ceremony.[127] God himself wipes away human guilt; we do not have to atone for it ourselves. God forgives us when we honestly acknowledge our guilt, not when we try to pay for it.

Good News for Failed Perfectionists

Several ways of achieving perfection apart from God's grace have intrigued great minds. (1) Many think of perfection as *keeping the moral law,* and they hope for perfect karma through spiritual evolution in millions of existences. (2) Some view perfection as fully *realizing our inner potential* individually or in communities. (3) Others view perfection as completely *modeling Godlikeness* as exhibited by Jesus Christ or another. These concepts are not mutually exclusive and so may be combined when we seek to achieve our fullest potential as Christ did throughout his life.

But in this life the best of us fall far short of the ideal. Perfection remains a goal of Christian living, but it is not a precondition of divine forgiveness. We work for 100 percent in a theology course, while knowing that no fallen person achieves perfection in scholar-

ship. Paul's polemic against "the works of the law" applies not to those whose goal is perfection, but to those who think they earn membership among God's people through works. We not only start the Christian life by faith, we also continue in it by faith. If salvation could have come by the law, furthermore, Jesus would not have needed to die. The commandments are like a mirror in that they show us our sins; but they do not cleanse us from our unrighteousness. If we insist on achieving perfection, we will be plummeted into despair daily. For all failed perfectionists, whether Jew or Gentile, perfectly righteous status comes from God as a gift of grace through faith in Jesus as both Lord and Messiah (Rom. 3:21–31). Our standing with God depends, however, not on what we do, but on what the sinless Christ has perfected for us![128]

Be at Peace About Your Eschatological Acceptance With God

"Therefore, since we have been justified through faith, we have peace with God through our Lord Jesus Christ" (Rom. 5:1). The verdict issued *in the present* on the basis of Christ's work through faith (Rom. 3:21–26) accurately anticipates the verdict to be issued in the future at the final judgment (Rom. 2:1–10). Since faith itself is the product of the Spirit's life-giving ministry (1 Cor. 12:3; 2 Thess. 2:13), what God has begun he will complete (Phil. 1:6). Justification and reconciliation set believers free, not only from anxieties arising from guilt feelings concerning the past and present, but also from phobias connected with their final destiny.

"Since we have now been justified by his blood," the apostle continued, "how much more shall we be saved from God's wrath through him!" (Rom. 5:9). This age of grace one day will

167

come to an end, and Christ will return in blazing fire to punish those who are ignorant of God and disobedient to the Gospel (2 Thess. 1:6–9). Judgment has already begun with the acts of condemnation and justification. Believers now have eternal life; those who are in Christ need never fear the fury of his eschatological wrath. Packer explains that "the background of Paul's doctrine was the Jewish conviction universal in his time, that a day of judgment was coming in which God would condemn and punish all who had broken his laws. That day would terminate the present world order and usher in a golden age for those whom God judged worthy.[129]

The eschatological verdict of the last days has already been pronounced for those who by faith have died and risen with Christ. We cannot be judged twice for the same sins. With our citizenship already in heaven we eagerly wait for his return when everything will be brought under his control (Phil. 3:20–21). Whether troubled by specific phobias or general anxiety, recipients of Christ's perfectly righteous standing can strengthen their inner sense of assurance: "Anyone who believes in the Son of God has this testimony in his heart. . . . And this is his testimony: God has given us eternal life, and this life is in his Son. He who has the Son has life; he who does not have the Son of God does not have life" (1 John 5:10–12).

Although intermittently doubting and unfaithful, the called, converted, and regenerate have a status that is permanently fixed. Legally we are members of God's moral and spiritual family, joint heirs of the riches that are Christ's, and in fellowship with God. Although communion with God may be temporarily interrupted, we remain twice-born children by creation and regeneration. Officially we have a birth certificate in heaven dated from the time of our conversion and regeneration. This reali-

zation brings to the justified and reconciled great peace, as the Protestant Reformers emphasized. McGrath observes that

> For Luther and Calvin alike, the question of how the believer can rest assured that he is justified was of central importance. . . . The believer is able to rest secure in the knowledge that he has been justified because justification does not depend on him in any way. . . . Forensic justification was seen as the foundation of the Christian life.[130]

Become an Agent of Reconciliation to Lonely People

Loneliness in a crowded world is felt as a lack of open relationship with God and others. Curved in upon ourselves (Luther), we feel a profound longing for free, honest, and loving relationships with our Creator and those he has created. The worst punishment of prisoners or hostages is total isolation or unrelatedness. The beginning of the end of persistent loneliness, of course, is for a person to be reconciled to God. Then those legally justified and adopted into God's family can forge meaningful relationships with others, both Christian and non-Christian.

Forgiven disciples should be agents of reconciliation to unbelieving *people at large.* God's justification opens the door to the kingdom of the reconciled.[131] Forgiven for the skeletons in our closets and liberated from unfounded fears of estrangement forever, we devote attention to our present relations with others. Christians must accept all those whom God created and over whom he providentially rules. For these reasons we respect the human rights of all. However unacceptable they may be to us personally, all people have the inalienable right from the Creator to life, liberty, and the pursuit of happiness. Pre-Christians' most urgent need, however, is to enjoy a saving relation with their creator and sustainer God. Using a natural form of friendship evangelism, the forgiven help lonely people at large to a relationship with God through Christ.

A good place to start is by becoming agents of reconciliation to our *immediate neighbors*. Urban and suburban life in America and elsewhere is characterized by significant isolation. Many Christians have no relations with their closest neighbors. Imagining ourselves rugged individualists, we travel from office to home isolated in our automobiles. Once at home, we draw the curtains, turn on the air-conditioners, and focus in on our television sets. In spite of all these modern inventions a feeling of gnawing loneliness persists. The forgiven should creatively strive to build relationships with their unsaved neighbors. The justified should have a vision and a burden to see their neighbors on the avenue or cul-de-sac reconciled to God. After gaining their friendship and confidence, we should trust God to use our word and life to bring them into relationship with him.

The justified seek to be reconciled to all other imperfect *members of their local church*. As God has accepted you, accept apparently unacceptable Christians on the same ground—Christ's atonement. "You are all sons of God through faith in Christ Jesus. . . . There is neither Jew nor Greek, slave nor free, male nor female, for you are all one in Christ Jesus" (Gal. 3:26, 28). In the first century believing Jews needed to accept believing Gentiles as equal spiritual partners in the church. Today Gentile church members may need to accept Jewish believers. Believing employers need to relate to their believing employees as spiritual peers in the church. In short, believing men and women must be reconciled to other believers in the local community and esteem them as brothers and sisters in Christ. Remember that a Christian without a church is like a person without a country.

Justified by Christ, younger and older Christians belong to one another! Young people often go astray spiritually because they feel rejected by their families and churches. Many feel that they do not "fit in" anywhere. Lonely and disillusioned, they meet a charismatic personality urging them to join a new religious group. At introductory sessions they are "love bombed" and conclude that finally they have found a new "family." So from a counterfeit spirituality they gain a sense of significance. How tragic that they did not first find a sense of identity and belonging to the body of Christ locally. In working with these and other church absentees, the more radical the cause of their alienation, the more sensitive our methods of reconciliation need to be.

Finally, the forgiven should be agents of reconciliation to *the church universal*. The divine Reconciler is head of the whole body of Christ. Acceptance of believers who have sinned against us may be difficult, given prejudices surrounding differences of color and ethnicity. But our common acceptance by God through Christ should form the basis for developing fellowship with saints around the world. It is a striking fact that peoples around the world are deeply divided by factors of race, nationality, and gender. Consider ethnic and religious strife among Croats, Serbs, and Bosnians in the former Yugoslavia. The camaraderie of Christian brothers and sisters living and working together in harmonious relations can be a powerful testimony to a world fractured by discord. The objectively justified therefore should strive to overcome racial, ethnic, and gender gaps. In a highly diverse world may we realize the vision of the psalmist, who wrote, "How good and pleasant it is when brothers live together in unity" (Ps. 133:1).

169

In all of these relationships, disciples help the lonely to become children of God who develop a growing and expanding relationship with him. McGrath writes in this regard:

> Personal relationships are not static—they are dynamic, they develop, they *change individuals*. And so our relationship with God, once established, forms the context within which we develop. It is the starting point for becoming more like the God who has entered into this gracious relationship with us. All of us know how two parties in a relationship become closer as the relationship matures and develops. And so it is with our personal relationship with God. It is a transformational relationship, in which our knowledge of God deepens and we become more like him.[132]

SUMMATION

Our understanding and offer of salvation should embrace at least three mandates: (1) Proclaim the legal transaction of justification, but do not define the ministries of the Spirit as a simple assent to a mere legal agreement. (2) Call for the transformation of character that conversion brings, but do not truncate salvation to little more than a new experience. And (3) witness to restored personal relationships with God and others, but do not reduce salvation to mere relational ups and downs. In calling sinners to conversion disciples present the need for experiential regeneration (chap. 2), legal justification, and relational reconciliation. Our teaching of new converts to Christ should strengthen all three facets of soteriology.

DISCUSSION TOPICS

1. Examine the Hebrew and Greek words for justification. Does the language in biblical context bear the legal meaning to "vindicate" or "declare in the right"?
2. What is the meaning of the phrase "the righteousness of God"? Can this righteousness be transferred from God to unclean and unworthy sinners? If so, how?
3. Study the key New Testament text on justification—Rom. 3:21–26. What does this text teach concerning the meaning and the outcome of God's justifying work?
4. Explain and illustrate the difference between the *ground* or *basis* of justification and the *instrument* of justification. Why is it important that these two not be confused?
5. Explain the emphasis on justification by works recorded in James 2:14–26. Does this teaching of James contravene the Pauline doctrine of justification by faith?
6. Where do the obstacles to reconciliation reside—with God, with the sinner, or with both? How has God brought about personal reconciliation with sinners alienated from himself?
7. What is meant by the biblical doctrine of adoption? Discuss the several spiritual privileges that follow from the Christian's new status as an adopted child of the Father.
8. Ought the trusting and obedient Christian possess assurance of eternal pardon, acceptance by God, and adoption into the heavenly family? What factors might hinder awareness of assurance?

See also the Review Questions and Ministry Projects on pages 501–2.

CHAPTER 4

THE SANCTIFICATION AND PERSEVERANCE OF THE JUSTIFIED

The Sanctification and Perseverance of the Justified

THE PROBLEM:
HOW DO CHRISTIAN
BELIEVERS GROW SPIRITUALLY
AND PERSEVERE IN THE FAITH
TO THE ATTAINMENT OF
ETERNAL LIFE?

Because God is infinitely holy and righteous he can have no fellowship with unrighteousness in any form. Consequently those who constitute God's new society must themselves be holy. But having rebelled against God's authority all persons are sinful and defiled (vol. 2, chap. 4). The Fall stripped image-bearers of the holiness required for fellowship with their Creator. But God in love provided for the salvation of sinners by sending his Son into the world (vol. 2, chap. 5) to atone for sins (vol. 2, chap. 7) and to vanquish sin and death by his resurrection (vol. 2, chap. 8). To all who repent of their sins and put faith in the Savior the Father gives new spiritual life (vol. 3, chap. 2), imputes the righteousness of Christ, and declares them guiltless before the bar of divine justice (vol. 3, chap. 3). The present chapter considers how the Spirit makes those who are righteous in principle (i.e., regenerated and justified) holy in fact (i.e., sanctified). Furthermore, it inquires

whether God preserves all true believers unto final salvation. The doctrines of sanctification and perseverance involve a number of important theological and practical concerns, the most important of which follow.

In personal sanctification what is the relation between the Spirit's working and human activity? Is sanctification primarily a work of God or a work of the human will? Moreover, do converted Christians attain a state of holiness by a single act of faith and surrender—the so-called "second blessing" experience? Or is the Christian life characterized by a lifelong struggle between the old and new natures? What is meant by the important Pauline doctrine of baptism in the Holy Spirit? Is tongues-speaking the necessary initial sign that one has been baptized in the Spirit? Another debated issue is whether sanctification is brought to completion in this life. Can the child of God attain the condition known as "entire sanctification" or "Christian perfection"? Should the dedicated Christian expect to be freed from all sinful thoughts and impulses and even consciousness of sin in the present life? Moreover, can we differentiate between the "carnal Christian," who fails to live a victorious life, and the "spiritual

Christian," who through the Spirit's power experiences victory over indwelling temptation and spiritual unrest?

In addition, we discuss the nature and importance of the gifts of the Holy Spirit as presented in the New Testament. Specifically, what was the character of New Testament prophecy and tongues? Are the so-called supernatural gifts of the Spirit (e.g., working of miracles, prophecy, healing, tongues) valid in the present age? Or were they the unique possession of believers in the apostolic era and thus unavailable to present-day Christians? Are these gifts received in some postconversion crisis experience? What relationship, if any, is there between the Spirit's gifts in the New Testament and their representation in the modern charismatic movement?

Finally, can the regenerated, justified, and Spirit-sealed believer fall from the state of grace and be condemned to hell? Is saving grace conditioned upon the Christian's continued faith and obedience, or does God's saving purpose ensure the perseverance of the elect to the end? Does the doctrine of eternal security lull Christians into a condition of inactivity and moral laxity? To determine how these questions have been answered in the history of the church, we now turn to the principal interpretations advanced through the centuries.

ALTERNATIVE INTERPRETATIONS IN THE CHURCH

The historical views that follow are important proposals to be compared and critically evaluated by those seeking new life in Christ.

Pelagians, Socinians, and Liberals

The liberal tradition adopts a low view of sin and a high view of human free will and its moral accomplishments. The upward ascent of the human spirit is hindered, according to older views, by the weight of the animal nature or, in more recent thought, by inhibiting political, social, and economic structures. Theological liberals generally interpret sanctification as personal reformation and moral improvement facilitated by the ideals of Christ. The traditional Protestant distinction between justification and sanctification is weakened and loses its importance. The tradition's general consensus on universal salvation, of course, implies universal perseverance.

The British monk Pelagius (d. 419) denied the reality of inherited sin and claimed that infants are born in the same condition as Adam's prior to the Fall. Most people sin individually by following the negative example of Adam's disobedience. But since people possess the power of free will and self-determination, God expects them to use these powers for moral improvement. Jesus demonstrated how one overcomes fleshly passions and negative habits and advances toward moral perfection. By volitionally following Christ's precepts and example, converts can fulfill God's moral requirements and live sinless lives. Pelagius firmly denied that converts need the Spirit's inner enablement to advance in holiness. The grace of God, which merely facilitates what persons can do for themselves, is wholly external. For Pelagius, then, salvation is by faith and self-improvement (perfectionism).

In the spirit of rationalism the Socinians denied original sin and upheld human freedom and ability. Even when persons sin, there is no diminution of moral power; like Adam, all are capable of obeying God's commands. Endowed with sufficient moral ability, all that sinners require to please God and advance in righteousness is enlightenment in the form of additional knowledge.

Christ met this human need as a human prophet who revealed God's will. He prompts persons to holiness by promises and threats and by serving as an example of total obedience to God. Christians progress in holiness and receive justification as the outcome by obeying the commandments and by imitating Christ. "What is the imitation of Christ? It is the composure of our life according to the rule of his life. Wherein doth it consist? In the exercise of those virtues which the Lord Jesus proposed to us in himself, as a living pattern."[1]

W. A. Brown (d. 1943) viewed sanctification as the renewal of personality and transformation of character achieved by following Jesus' example of filial trust and brotherly love. Sanctification represents the exchange of self-gratification for the service of one's fellows or the adoption of the outgoing life for the self-centered life. In concert with other liberals Brown held that the gradual growth of all persons toward perfection (i.e., maturity and wholeness) will continue beyond the grave and be completed in the future life.[2]

Consistent with their definition of theology as praxis, liberation theologians view sanctification as love-generated transformation wrought by commitment to the cause of the oppressed. Bonino typically insists, "Our sanctification must not be measured by some idealistically conceived norm of perfection or by some equally unreal purity of motivation, but by the concrete demand of the present *kairos*. There is an action, a project, an achievement that is required of us now; there is an action that embodies the service of love today. . . . It is *perfection*—the mature, ripe form of obedience."[3] Persons become radically transformed and humanized as they struggle against injustice and forge a better future for the oppressed. Liberationists claim that human deeds of love on behalf of the marginalized and powerless possess redeeming virtue. Gutièrrez explains this reality in terms of "the sacrament of our neighbor." By moving out of oneself in an attitude of concern for one's neighbor the activist comes closer to God, advances in wholeness, and is transformed. "The encounter with Christ in the poor man constitutes an authentic spiritual experience. It is a living in the Spirit, the bond of love between Father and Son, God and man, man and man. Christians . . . find the love of Christ in their encounter with the poor and in solidarity with them."[4]

Roman Catholic Interpretation

As outlined in the previous chapter, Catholicism designates the increase of justification as sanctification.[5] By the sacrament of baptism God infuses into the soul justifying grace that remits original sin and imparts the habit of righteousness. This initial justification is augmented by the grace of Christ mediated through other sacraments (confirmation, eucharist, penance, last anointing), love-inspired works, and the so-called surplus merits of Mary and the saints. Since baptism removes all sin (leaving behind only "concupiscence" that is not itself sin), the good works performed by the Christians are said to be perfect. Hence Christians can entirely fulfill the law—a condition necessary for attaining eternal life. Some faithful, however, perform more than the law requires. In the medieval era, for example, Rome drew a distinction between "precepts" (or "commandments") and "counsels" (or "advices"). The former designate specific injunctions of the law that bind the conscience and that issue in rewards or punishments. The latter signify virtues not specifically imposed by God but that warrant excess merit. Specific counsels include poverty (Matt. 19:21), celibacy (Matt. 19:12), and monastic obedience (Luke 14:26). The alleged excess merit of those in religious orders (i.e., monks, priests, nuns) who perform such counsels can be transferred to those who lack merit. Thus there arose a hierarchy of holiness and spirituality—the clergy superior in spiritual graces to the laity. According to Rome, the church consists of three classes of people: sinners, penitents, and saints.

If the process of transformation (making righteous) is not completed in this life, Christians must endure the purifying sufferings of purgatory. Catholics find support for purgatory in the early practice of prayers for the dead and in such texts as 2 Maccabees 12:46; Matthew 5:26; 12:32; and 1 Corinthians 3:11–15. The duration of purgatory depends on the number and gravity of one's sins. Following the cleansing work of purgatory, sanctification (or justification) is said to be complete. Rome holds that in this life baptized Christians can fall from grace by committing mortal sins. The guilt of such sins may be forgiven and saving grace restored by the sacrament of penance (involving contrition, confession, absolution, and works of satisfaction). Since perseverance is dependent on the continued obedience of the baptized, no certainty of salvation is possible. "It is the defined teaching of the Church that actual perseverance to the end is impossible without a special grace; it remains uncertain whether this latter will be granted."[6]

The sixth session of the Council of Trent (January 13, 1547) discussed sanctification under the heading of justification. The infusion of justifying grace remits sins and effects inner transformation. The baptized "through the observance of the commandments of God and of the Church, faith cooperating with good works, increase in that justice which they have received through the grace of Christ, and are still

further justified."[7] Baptized persons progress in sanctification unto eternal life by faith, good works (which are perfect), and endurance to the end. Thus, "the good works which he performs through the grace of God and the merits of Jesus Christ . . . merit increase of grace, eternal life, and the attainment of that eternal life."[8] The baptized can lose justifying grace by apostasy or other mortal sin (1 Cor. 6:9–10). This said that grace can be restored only by the sacrament of penance. The guilt and eternal penalty of mortal sin is removed by sacramental absolution, whereas the debt of temporal penalty is removed by works of satisfaction (Matt. 3:18). Hence Trent referred to "satisfaction by fasts, alms, prayers, and the other pious exercises of a spiritual life."[9] For Trent, progress in sanctification (justification) requires complete obedience to the commandments. Thus the church prays, "Give unto us, O Lord, increase of faith, hope, and charity."[10] Christians not perfected in this life must endure purgatory, where they are assisted by "the sacrifices of masses, prayers, alms, and other works of piety . . . performed by the faithful for other faithful departed."[11]

The Dutch theologian F. G. L. Van Der Meer explained how God works sanctification (or justification) through the church's sacraments:

1. Sanctification begins with *baptism,* which purifies from original and actual sin and imparts a holy life. In the early church catechumens were clothed with white garments to signify their baptismal sanctification.

2. *Confirmation,* by way of anointing with oil, signifies the gift of the Spirit as the enablement for growth toward maturity.

3. The *Eucharist* is the sacrament of spiritual nourishment. As Christians partake of the body and blood of Christ in the Mass they feed on Christ himself.

Concerning Eucharist, "the state of grace is maintained by it, preserved from ruin, strengthened and augmented."[12] The preceding three sacraments effect the state of "sanctifying grace." In this state Christians cooperate with grace by obeying God's commands—and this obedience conveys actual merit. Thus "the Church has declared emphatically that we can earn an increase of grace and glory."[13] Van Der Meer affirmed three things about the state of grace in which the baptized dwell: (1) It is unequal. "Some are more intimately united with God than others and grace is increased in some more abundantly than in others."[14] (2) It can be forfeited. "It can be lost, since divine life does not perish only through unbelief but through every mortal sin."[15] And (3) it is not secure. "No one knows for certain that he has received the grace of God [and] it is impossible to know whom God has chosen, except by means of a special revelation."[16]

4. The sacrament of *penance*, or "second pardon," restores the baptismal righteousness when forfeited by mortal sin. As fallen Christians repent, receive absolution, and perform works of satisfaction, they experience anew the mystery of justification. Van Der Meer held that one Christian can do penance for another, and the treasury of merits accumulated by the saints can be applied to those in want.

5. The *last anointing*, or extreme unction, is the sacrament that equips the *viator* for the final conflict with death. Van Der Meer upheld the church's view that the souls of the righteous are purged of venial sins through the sufferings of purgatory. "The decisive element in these punishments is the temporary privation of the vision of God."[17] A soul's experience in purgatory may be ameliorated by the prayers, alms, and offerings of living believers.

Wesleyan and Holiness Traditions

The above teachings opposed the Lutheran and Reformed belief that holiness is only imperfectly achieved through a lifelong process. Rather, sanctification begins at justification and the new birth ("initial sanctification") and is perfected by an instantaneous, transforming work of the Spirit called the "second work of grace" or the "second blessing." The condition of Christians following this decisive experience is variously called "entire sanctification," "Christian perfection," "perfect love," or "fullness of the blessing." The second blessing experience, which most modern Wesleyans equate with the baptism of the Holy Spirit, removes inherited sin, eradicates the carnal nature, enables Christians to live without willful sin, and fills the heart with pure love for God and others. The Lutheran and Reformed view that the presence of residual sin in Christians is a normal state of affairs is said to breed moral laxity and antinomianism. Advocates also argue that perseverance in grace is contingent upon continued obedience. Christians may fall away from Christ totally and finally. Holiness advocates thus postulate three classes of people: sinners, the saved, and the entirely sanctified.

John Wesley (d. 1791) was influenced both by older Arminianism and by Catholic mysticism that stressed themes of pure love and perfect conformity to Christ. The doctrine of sanctification was the centerpiece of Wesley's theology. Appealing to Hebrews 12:14, Wesley concluded that sanctification is a prerequisite for final justification at the last judgment. Thus Christians should fervently seek moral perfection, which God graciously gives by faith via an instantaneous crisis experience (the "second grace" or "second blessing"). Wesley held that there are two great moments in the

177

Christian life: (1) justification, which includes forgiveness of sins, regeneration, and initial sanctification, and (2) "entire sanctification," which Wesley also called "Christian perfection," "perfect love," or "full salvation." Some believers are entirely sanctified shortly after conversion, others later in life, and still others at death. Wesley explained that the crisis of entire sanctification, negatively, involves the elimination of all sinful desires from the heart (e.g., pride, envy, jealousy), the destruction of inbred moral depravity, and deliverance from outward transgressions of the law. Positively, entire sanctification includes complete purity of intentions, tempers, and actions and perfect love of God and neighbor.

Wesley concluded that "a Christian is so far perfect, as not to commit sin."[18] Again, "so long as he believes in God through Jesus Christ and loves Him and is pouring out his heart before Him, he cannot voluntarily transgress any command of God, either by speaking or acting what he knows God has forbidden."[19] Entire sanctification involves complete freedom from "pride, self-will, anger [and] unbelief."[20] The perfection of the Christian believer is not the absolute perfection of God, but a relative perfection that represents freedom from willful transgression of a known divine law (which is the essence of sin).[21] Hence perfected Christians, while not committing deliberate sins, remain subject to ignorance, mistakes, infirmities, temptations, and involuntary transgressions. Moreover, Christian perfection admits of degrees and is capable of increase. Wesley believed that the typical pattern of the Christian life is one of process-crisis-process. Following justification and the new birth the Christian dies to self and grows in grace. Then occurs the crisis of entire sanctification, followed by continued growth in holiness.[22]

Wesley believed that the "extraordinary gifts" of the Spirit (i.e., healings, prophecy, tongues, and interpretation of tongues) died out in the church by the time of Constantine. He personally laid claim to none of the miraculous gifts,[23] noting that tongues-speaking has been a particularly divisive force in the church. Believers ought rather to cultivate the "ordinary gifts" of the spirit and, more important, the way of love (1 Cor. 12:31).[24]

Wesley added that believers through neglect can lose the grace of Christian perfection and by deliberate, willful rebellion against God can lose their salvation. Those who today are children of the Father tomorrow may become children of the Devil. Wesley found no biblical support for the idea that God keeps Christians from apostatizing and losing the first experience of justification. God's grace is not unconditional or invincible; it is conditional in that it depends on Christians' continuing in faith, love, and obedience to the moral law. Wesley claimed that the doctrine of eternal security lulls Christians into a sense of false security. The believer who takes eternal security for granted "grows a little and a little slacker till ere long he falls again into the sin from which he was clean escaped. . . . So he sins on, and sleeps on till he awakes in hell."[25] Justifying grace, however, may be recovered by a fresh act of repentance and faith.

Charles Finney (d. 1875), a Congregationalist who adopted the Wesleyan doctrine of entire sanctification, argued that as the gratification of the lower nature (i.e., sin) involves an action of the will, so holiness resides in the right exercise of the will. "Entire sanctification" or "Christian perfection" consists of (1) total volitional consecration of the person to God, (2) uninterrupted communion with the Father, (3) unswerving love of God and neighbor, and (4) perfect and continued obedience to God's law—adjusted to human knowledge and ability. "Entire sanctification implies the complete annihilation of selfishness in all its forms."[26] Finney learned from Wesley that entire sanctification is achieved instantaneously by an act of faith. God calls Christians to complete sanctification, hence it must be attainable in this life by natural human powers assisted by grace. Entire sanctification was *promised* in the old dispensation (Jer. 31:31–34; Ezek. 36:25–27) and became *possible* in the new (2 Cor. 7:1; 1 Thess. 5:23–24; Jude 24). The apostle Paul, according to Finney, testified to his entire sanctification (Acts 24:16; 2 Cor. 6:3–7; Gal. 2:20; 1 Thess. 2:10). Galatians 2:20 "strongly implies that he [Paul] lived without sin and also that he regarded himself as dead to sin in the sense of being permanently sanctified."[27] Finney said about Paul: "He nowhere confesses sin after he became an apostle."[28] Romans 7:14–25 describes people who live in sin under the law, whereas Romans 8 depicts persons in a state of entire sanctification through the Gospel. Finney believed that continued growth in grace ought to follow the experience of entire sanctification.

Although vacillating on the issue of final perseverance of believers, in the end Finney upheld it. He drew his conclusion not as a logical consequence of the doctrines of sovereign election or union with Christ, but on the basis of the divine influences exercised by scriptural promises, warnings, and threatenings. "Their conversion, perseverance, and salvation are secured by means of the grace of God in Jesus Christ, prevailing through the gospel, so as to influence their free-will as to bring about this result."[29]

J. Kenneth Grider explained salvation under the rubric of two instantaneous works of grace. "The first work of grace"—which occurs at conversion—consists of justification, regeneration, initial sanctification (Titus 3:5),

and reconciliation. The outcome of this first work is forgiveness of actual sins. "The second work of grace"—which may occur any time between conversion and death—effects the believer's entire sanctification. This second crisis experience is also called the "second blessing," "Christian perfection," "Christian holiness," or "heart purity." Scripture describes this second experience as a baptism with the Holy Spirit (e.g., Acts 1:5–8; 2:2–4; 8:4–25), sealing (Eph. 1:13; 4:30), and circumcision (Col. 2:11). (As an aside, Wesley did not equate the crisis of entire sanctification with the Pentecostal experience recorded in Acts.) According to Grider, entire sanctification radically cleanses one from Adamic sin, eradicates depravity, removes the inherited inclination to acts of sin, creates wholehearted love of God and neighbor, and empowers for service. Wrote Grider, "Entire sanctification is a sanctification, a cleansing that is entire. No carnality, or original sin, remains to deprave our faculties, to incline us to acts of sin."[30] The crisis of entire sanctification does not preclude growth in grace and continued cleansing of the heart. Christians, however, who refuse to follow God's leading toward entire sanctification will lose their justification. Grider held that although entire sanctification greatly strengthens Christians ("establishing grace"), it is possible for recipients of second grace to sin willfully and be eternally lost: "The Christian who has been sanctified wholly can fall completely from saving grace. But just as surely, such a person is wonderfully enabled not to fall from grace."[31]

Pentecostal Perspectives

Pentecostal theology divides into two main branches. The earlier, minority wing influenced by the Wesleyans is represented by the Holiness Pentecos-

179

tals. The later, majority wing that is more baptistic includes the Assemblies of God, the Church of the Foursquare Gospel, and the Elim Pentecostal Church. In recent years neo-pentecostalism has flourished in mainline Protestant denominations and in the Roman Catholic church.

Holiness Pentecostals, represented by the Church of God (Cleveland, Tennessee), the Pentecostal Holiness Church, the Church of God in Christ, and the Pillar of Fire Church, trace their roots to the nineteenth-century Wesleyan-Holiness revival. They posit three instantaneous works of grace: (1) The *regenerating* work of grace includes justification and the new birth. Here God forgives sins and imputes righteousness to believers. (2) The *sanctifying* work of grace eradicates the old, Adamic nature and completely purifies the heart and mind. Following Wesley, the state of the Christian following the second blessing is known as "entire sanctification," "Christian perfection," or "perfect love." This second definite work of grace renders believers purified vessels fit for the Holy Spirit's abiding. So the Pentecostal Holiness Church affirms: "We believe that entire sanctification is an instantaneous, definite second work of grace, obtainable by faith on the part of the fully justified believer."[32] (3) The *empowering* work of grace represents the Pentecostal experience of baptism in the Spirit. Here the Holy Spirit takes full possession of perfected believers. Tongues-speaking, or utterances in an unlearned language, represents the initial *sign* of Spirit baptism. Thereafter believers may cease to speak in tongues, or they may exercise the *gift* of glossolalia. The Church of God (Cleveland, Tennessee) sums up the sequence as follows: "We believe . . . in sanctification subsequent to the new birth . . . and in the baptism of the Holy Ghost subsequent to a clean heart."[33]

Other Pentecostal groups independent of Wesleyanism arose. The Assemblies of God and similar groups (Elim Pentecostal Church, Church of the Foursquare Gospel) deny the separate experience of entire sanctification following conversion that destroys inbred sin. These hold to the following sequence:

1. *Positional sanctification.* At justification and the new birth God imputes righteousness to believers. Thus positionally, although not experientially, believers are wholly sanctified through the work of Christ.

2. *Baptism in the Holy Spirit.* Through this second work of grace Christians by faith are baptized in the Holy Spirit (Mark 1:8; Acts 2:1–4; 8:15–17; 11:15–17). This crisis experience of Spirit baptism allows for subsequent fillings of the Spirit. Spirit baptism does not completely purify, for in Christians the old nature and its passions persist. Rather, its principal function is enduement with power for service and witness. Thus each believer should seek and expect this second-blessing experience. Pentecostals assert that speaking in other tongues is the initial *sign* that a person has been baptized in the Spirit (Acts 2:4; 10:45–46; 19:6). It also serves as a rebuke to unbelievers. Another sign or evidence of Spirit baptism is the bestowal of spiritual gifts (1 Cor. 12:8–10, 28–30; Rom. 12:6–8; Eph. 4:11). Pentecostals claim that all the spiritual gifts—including prophecy, healing, glossolalia, and interpretation of tongues—are applicable in the present age. "Just as the gift of the Spirit, the baptism of the Spirit, is for us, so all the gifts are for us. Why not claim them, exercise them, depend on them?"[34] As a gift, tongues are useful for private worship, and when interpreted they edify the church. The preceding suggest that Pentecostals place greater importance on spiritual gifts than on purity of heart. "The

baptism in the Holy Spirit . . . leads to a life of service marked by gifts of the Spirit that bring power and wisdom for the spread of the Gospel and the growth of the church."[35] The Spirit-baptized Christian lives on a higher spiritual plane than the believer lacking this post-conversion experience.

3. *Progressive sanctification.* This involves the gradual process whereby holiness is made actual in daily life. This goal is achieved as believers cooperate with the Spirit in the work of sanctification. Christians grow in holiness by identification with Christ in his death and resurrection, by separation from the sinful world, and by consecration to God's service. Final perfection is not attainable in this life, since the sin nature remains in believers. Horton sums up as follows: "The Scriptural pattern is first new life by the Spirit, then the empowering experience of the baptism in the Holy Spirit, then a life of spiritual growth that makes progress in both sanctification and service."[36]

4. *Entire sanctification.* Provided they do not fall away, Christians attain moral perfection in the glorified state. Entire sanctification thus awaits transformation into the image of Christ at the resurrection. Pentecostals as a whole maintain that believers can lose their salvation by walking after the flesh. Horton comments, "We recognize that all [Christians] have carnal moments, but we would say that Christians who continue to sin are in danger of losing their salvation."[37] Mainstream Pentecostals thus identify three groups of people: the unconverted, the converted, and the Spirit-baptized.

Ernest S. Williams (d. 1981), an Assemblies of God theologian, says that sanctification is both positional and progressive: "Each believer in Christ is sanctified positionally when he accepts Christ."[38] From the Acts record Williams believes that a definite crisis experience of Spirit baptism subsequent to conversion is normative for all believers. The principal evidences of immersion in the Spirit are enduement with power for witness, speaking in other tongues, and bestowal of spiritual gifts. Williams avers that all the New Testament spiritual gifts are valid for the church today—including the dramatic gifts of miracle-working, healing, prophecy, glossolalia, and interpretation of tongues. Glossolalia, in the first place, enhances private worship: "Those who have spoken in tongues in private worship can testify to the enriching, spiritual rest, and refreshing to the soul that results from such communion with God."[39] And second, when interpreted, glossolalia edifies the church in its experience of corporate worship. Concerning progressive sanctification, Williams insists that eradication of the Adamic nature does not occur in this life. Sanctification is a gradually unfolding reality that involves mortification of the deeds of the flesh and appropriation of Christ's grace that yields the fruit of righteousness. Williams observes that God has made ample provision for the Christian's perseverance to the end. Yet the scriptural warnings against apostasy suggest that the believer is capable of willfully forfeiting salvation. "When a person leaves holiness and begins to walk after the flesh, he has lost his sanctification."[40]

Neo-pentecostalism, or the charismatic movement, represents the extension of the Pentecostal spirit in the mainline Protestant denominations. Championed by David de Plessis, John Sanford, Larry Christenson, Michael Harper, J. Rodman Williams, and others, neo-pentecostalism holds that the Acts 2 Pentecost experience is breaking out in churches today. It identifies "baptism in the Spirit" as an experience distinct from and subsequent to conversion. "There are two distinct moments: conversion and baptism with the Spirit. They may be separated from each other by years, although both belong to the full life of the Christian."[41] The release or outpouring of the Spirit via this second blessing provides spiritual revitalization, power for service, and church renewal. An important fruit of the Spirit's baptism is the bestowal of spiritual gifts, of which prophecy, healing, and glossolalia are most important. The Roman Catholic renewal movement regards the baptism in the Spirit as the conscious actualization of spiritual benefits received at baptism. This event deepens a person's relationship with Christ and offers a heightened sense of the Spirit's presence and gifts. Many Catholic charismatics do not consider tongues to be a necessary sign of the Spirit's baptism but a "prayer gift" helpful for personal devotion.

The Keswick and
Victorious Life Movements

Stimulated by holiness emphases, Keswick began meetings in England in 1875 as a "Convention for the Promotion of Practical Holiness." The North American counterpart of Keswick is the so-called Victorious Life movement. The broad tradition features such names as W. E. Boardman, Robert Pearsall Smith and his wife Hannah Pearsall Smith, F. B. Meyer, H. C. G. Moule, Andrew Murray, Robert C. McQuilken, and W. Graham Scroggie. Keswick teaching is similar to the holiness movement, although it does not hold to sinless perfection. According to Keswick teaching, sanctification occurs in three stages: (1) *Positional sanctification,* or accepting Christ as Savior, is attained through the experiences of forgiveness of sin, justification, and regeneration. (2) *Experiential sanctification,* commencing with a decisive surrender subsequent to conversion to Christ as Lord, produces victory over

indwelling sin and enjoyment of a higher level of Christian living. It involves both a crisis event and a process. (3) *Complete or final sanctification* occurs when the Christian is transformed into the likeness of Christ in the life to come.

Fundamental to Keswick thought is the distinction between two types of believers, the "carnal Christian" and the "spiritual Christian." The first, or *average* Christian, fails to abide in the Spirit's power and lives a defeated life under the control of the flesh. Some Keswick advocates depict the carnal Christian as "only partially Christian."[42] The second, or *normal* Christian, lives a life of continual victory in the power of the Spirit. The born-again person becomes a "spiritual Christian" by a postconversion, crisis experience of unconditional surrender or complete abandonment to Christ. One receives fullness of the Spirit not by a protracted spiritual struggle, but simply by a decision of the will to dethrone self and enthrone Christ. "Faith throws the switch, releasing the current of divine power."[43] God works sanctification in believers to the extent that they permit him to work. As a result of this crisis experience, inbred sin is overwhelmed and rendered powerless by the greater power of the indwelling Spirit. In relation to sin, whereas Wesleyanism is "eradicationist," Keswick theology could be called "counteractionist." Spirit-filled Christians, moreover, are freed from the desire for sin, from the power of sin, and even from the consciousness of sin. Believers who have experienced this second blessing live in a state of complete victory over known sin and enjoy a life of spiritual rest on the highest plane. "Keswick does not teach the perfectibility of human beings prior to the eternal state, but it does teach the possibility of consistent success in resisting the temptation to violate deliberately the known will of

God."[44] Or as Barabas expressed the Keswick view, "We believe the Word of God teaches that the *normal* Christian life is one of uniform sustained victory over known sin."[45] Since Keswick teachers define sin at the level of motive or intentionality, when the struggle with conscious sin ceases believers experience the victorious life.

Keswick emphasizes that growth in holiness normally follows this crisis experience. The act of total consecration represents "a decision which initiates . . . sanctification in real earnest."[46] According to many Keswick adherents, Romans 7:7–25 describes the failure of carnal Christians who struggle to overcome sin in their own strength. In contrast, Romans 8 describes the victory experienced by spiritual Christians by a volitional act of total surrender to Christ. Since positional sanctification involves the legal imputation of holiness to believers, most Keswick advocates uphold the doctrine of eternal security. In sum, Keswick proponents identify three kinds of people: non-Christians, carnal Christians, and spiritual Christians—or the unconverted, the converted, and the wholly consecrated.

Neo-orthodox Interpretations

In the *Church Dogmatics* Karl Barth (d. 1968) retreated from his earlier view that sanctification is identical to justification. Nevertheless Barth did not view justification and sanctification as two successive steps in the *ordo salutis*. Rather they represent two movements in the one act of God's reconciliation in Jesus Christ. "The *simul* of the one redemptive act of God in Jesus Christ cannot be split up into a temporal sequence, and in this way psychologized."[47] To eliminate all human merit and pride, Barth insisted that sanctification is God's doing and work: "His action is man's sanctification."[48] Consistent with his Christocentrism, Barth related the sanctification of the Christian to Jesus Christ, who is both the holy God and the sanctified man. Jesus Christ was in need of sanctification because he had a sinful human nature and a sinful essence (cf. *IT,* vol. 2, chap. 6). Christ's sanctification consists in the fact that he committed no sinful act and that his humanity was raised by divine power to a new level of existence. Christians, Barth argued, are sanctified as they participate in the sanctification of the Son of Man. "The sanctification of man which has taken place in this One is their sanctification. But originally and properly it is the sanctification of Him and not of them."[49]

Barth continued by declaring that by virtue of the divine decision *objectively* all persons are justified and sanctified. The entire world in principle has died in Christ and renounced its sin. "The sanctification of man . . . is actually accomplished in the one Jesus Christ in a way which is effective and authoritative for all, and therefore for each and every man, and not merely for the people of God, the saints."[50] But *subjectively* not all are sanctified, since only some of the elect have appropriated and confessed their sanctification. Barth wrote, "The sanctification of man, his conversion to God, is, like his justification, a transformation, a new determination, which has taken place *de jure* for the world and therefore for all men. *De facto,* however, it is not known by all men, just as justification has not *de facto* been grasped and acknowledged and known and confessed by all men, but only by those who are awakened to faith."[51] What, according to Barth, is the practical difference between the two classes of sanctified Christians? Those who subjectively acknowledge justification and sanctification are sinners *disturbed* out of their spiritual slumber by the ministry of the Spirit.[52] Those who are sanctified objectively but not subjectively remain *undisturbed* in their sleep. On the individual level, the former enter a new form of existence as *faithful* covenant partners of God. While muting the quest for perfection in holiness, Barth insisted that awakened sinners should live a life of love, cross-bearing, and praise to God. On the corporate level, the church is the provisional, *de facto* representation of the *de jure* sanctification of all humanity in Jesus Christ. The church's task is to serve as "the revelation of the sanctification of all humanity and human life as it has already taken place *de jure* in Jesus Christ."[53]

Concerning the issue of the perseverance of the saints, Barth held that although Christians stumble and even draw back, God will sustain them spiritually to the end. The eternal covenant, the sacrifice of Christ, and the ministry of the Holy Spirit "ensure the continuity of the Christian life, the perseverance of the saints."[54]

Reinhold Niebuhr (d. 1971), a leader in the American school of dialectical theology, like Barth stressed the objective rather than the subjective aspect of sanctification; sin is overcome in principle rather than in fact. Also like Barth Niebuhr minimized the goals of Christian perfection and the victorious life, emphasizing rather Christians' existential predicament in their lifelong conflict with sin. Justified believers, Niebuhr held, struggle to the grave with the contradictions of freedom and finitude, of being justified in principle but not in fact, of being holy but troubled by sin. "The conquest of sin in the heart of man . . . is never entirely overcome in any human heart."[55] The goal of the Christian conflict is the rule of *agapē* in human relationships, which (given the Christian's existential predicament) Niebuhr called an "impossible possibility." *Agapē* (although never perfectly attainable) manifests itself in acts of forgiveness, reconciliation, and justice both individually and socially.

Certain Church Fathers, Most Reformers, and Reformed Evangelicals

This broad tradition posits a clear distinction between justification and sanctification while affirming that the two are inextricably related. In terms of differences, justification is a legal declaration of right standing before God (imputed righteousness), whereas sanctification makes the believer existentially holy (inherent righteousness). Moreover, justification is an instantaneous event, whereas sanctification is a lifelong process. Finally, justification allows for no degrees, whereas sanctification admits of degrees. In terms of their inner unity, justification issues in sanctification, thereby eliminating the error of cheap grace. And sanctification is grounded in justification, thereby avoiding the error of works-righteousness.

Authorities maintain that sanctification is not an autonomous human work but a divine-human (concursive) operation initiated by God. At every moment of the Christian life God graciously enables believers to respond to the Spirit's promptings toward Christlikeness. Moreover, the divine work of Spirit baptism occurs simultaneously with regeneration and union with Christ. Yet filling with the Spirit happens continuously as believers yield to God's will moment by moment. Christians are positionally holy by virtue of being in Christ (1 Cor. 1:2; 6:11; Heb. 10:10), but empirically they remain sinful. The tradition generally identifies two "natures" in the believer. The old nature ("the flesh") represents the believer's tendency to serve self, sin, and Satan, whereas the new nature ("the spirit") signifies the indication to serve God and others and follow after righteousness. In the present life Christians experience struggle between the old nature and the new (Rom. 7:13–25). But by Holy Spirit sanctification they enjoy freedom from the dominion, albeit not from the presence, of sin. By daily yielding to God's will in faith, Christians cooperate with the Spirit's initiative to mortify sinful inclinations and to bring forth holy dispositions and good works. Sanctification "is nothing less than the progressive uprooting of sin within him by the conquering energy of the Spirit of God."[56] Motivated by gratitude rather than fear, believers seek to fulfill the moral law. Christians realize entire sanctification or moral perfection not in this life but in the life to come when they behold Christ (1 John 3:2). Many Reformed and dispensationalist theologians maintain that the miraculous gifts of healing, prophecy, tongues, and interpretation of tongues certified the apostles' credentials as bearers of new revelations and founders of the church. Hence these miraculous sign gifts ceased with the close of the apostolic age or with the demise of the disciples on whom the apostles had laid hands.[57]

Augustine (d. 430) taught that sovereign grace instantaneously changes human hearts (regeneration) and then gradually conforms believers into the image of Christ (sanctification). Sanctification involves both God's provision and Christians' participation. God initiates sanctification as grace breaks the dominion of sin and heals the will so that it may freely love God and fulfill his law. Although the initiative in sanctification is with God, believers' decisions and effort are necessary. "It is he who makes us will what is good; . . . it is he who makes us act by supplying efficacious power to our will."[58] The Christian's two natures are not essences but two sets of inclinations. The old nature or "flesh" (not eradicated by the new birth) represents the will or inclination to sin, whereas the new nature or "spirit" signifies the inclination to glorify God. The two contend with each other throughout the Christian's earthly life. Although God urges believers toward the goal of perfection, because of indwelling sin no one actually attains moral perfection this side of heaven. Wrote Augustine, "There is not a man living in the present life who is absolutely free from sin."[59] Nevertheless as believers (cooperating with grace) resist temptations and cultivate the fruit of the Spirit, they grow progressively like Christ. The Christian, then, advances in sanctification "insofar as he does not yield to evil concupiscence," but overcomes it by his "desire to live according to the Law."[60]

Eternal security flows from the unmerited gift of perseverance. Augustine taught that some who are baptized and become church members are changed for the better but only appear to be Christians. Such people are not given the gift of perseverance and so fall away and are damned. But to the elect God bestows both the gift of saving faith and perseverance in holiness. "See how foreign it is from the truth to deny that perseverance even to the end of this life is the gift of God. . . . He makes the man to persevere to the end."[61] This latter benefit means that God endues the elect both with the will and the strength to repudiate evil and actually to persevere to eternal life. If the elect should deviate from the path of righteousness, God will faithfully restore them or take them home via death.

John Calvin (d. 1564), called "the theologian of sanctification,"[62] held justification and sanctification in close relation: "Christ justified no one whom he does not at the same time sanctify."[63] Sanctification consists of mortification and vivification. The former means that God breaks the dominion of sin, subdues the flesh, and weakens carnal desires. The latter means that the

185

Holy Spirit enables the Christian to put on the "new man," be renewed in the image of Christ, and perform works pleasing to God. Calvin stressed that sanctification is gradual and progressive:

> This restoration does not take place in one moment or one day or one year; but through continual and sometimes even slow advances God wipes out in his elect the corruptions of the flesh, cleanses them of guilt, consecrates them to himself as temples, renewing all their minds to true purity that they may practice repentance throughout their lives and know that this warfare will end only at death.[64]

The goal of sanctification, to which Christians must strive, is conformity to God's will in thought and deed. The law facilitates sanctification in two ways: (1) It enables Christians to understand the nature of God's will, and (2) it arouses them to obedience and draws them back from the slippery slope of transgression.[65] In the process of sanctification Christ is the believer's example of righteous living. Calvin emphasized that however earnestly Christians strive for perfection they never attain the ideal of perfect conformity to the moral law in this life. "We teach that in the saints, until they are divested of mortal bodies, there is always sin; for in their flesh there resides that depravity of inordinate desiring which contends against righteousness."[66]

Calvin believed that God gave the apostolic church miraculous gifts for two purposes: (1) to advance the spread of the Gospel and (2) to support the church in its infancy. Following the death of the apostles the supernatural gifts no longer were needed, and God withdrew them. Calvin wrote, "That gift of healing, like the rest of the miracles, which the Lord willed to be brought forth for a time, has vanished away in order to make the new preaching of the gospel marvelous forever."[67]

Reformed and dispensational theology generally followed Calvin's belief concerning the withdrawal of the miraculous gifts.

Calvin insisted that God brings his saving work to completion by confirming the saints in perseverance. Perseverance is both a gift and a work of God.[68] From the divine side, believers persevere to the end by virtue of the Father's elective purpose, the Son's sacrifice and intercession, and the Spirit's sealing and empowering. From the human side, perseverance involves believers' active appropriation of divine grace. "Does not the Spirit of God, everywhere self-consistent, nourish the very inclination to obedience that he first engendered, and strengthen its constancy to perseverance?"[69] Whereas Christians occasionally fall into sin, Calvin insisted that God allows none of his elect finally to perish. Ultimately the stability of the Christian life depends on God, not on us mortals. Concerning Hebrews 6:4–6, Calvin maintained that the "enlightened, who have tasted the heavenly gift, [and] who have shared in the Holy Spirit" (v. 4) are not believers who subsequently fell away. Rather, they are "reprobates" and "apostates" who gained some knowledge of the gospel and some taste of God's grace, but who refused to repent and surrender to Christ.[70]

The Heidelberg Catechism (1563) states, "To be washed with Christ's Spirit means . . . that more and more I become dead to sin and increasingly live a holy and blameless life" (Lord's Day 26, Q. 70). The Christian life involves a struggle with the "'sinful nature" (Lord's Day 21, Q. 56), hence no perfection is possible in this life. The Catechism refers to "the sins we do" and "the evil that constantly clings to us" (Lord's Day 51, Q. 126). Indeed, "the longer we live the more . . . we come to know our sinfulness and the more eagerly look to Christ for forgiveness of sins and righteousness" (Lord's Day 44, Q. 115). The Catechism affirms the perseverance of true believers to eternal life; it refers to Christ "who governs us by his Word and Spirit, and keeps us in the freedom he has won for us" (Lord's Day 12, Q. 31).

The Westminster Shorter Catechism (1647) provides the following answer to Q. 35, "What is Sanctification?": "Sanctification is the work of God's free grace, whereby we are renewed in the whole man after the image of God, and are enabled more and more to die unto sin, and live unto righteousness" (cf. The Westminster Confession of Faith, XIII.1–3). The answer to Q. 36, concerning the benefits that flow from justification, adoption, and sanctification, reads: "assurance of God's love, peace of conscience, joy in the Holy Ghost, increase of grace, and perseverance therein to the end." The Westminster Confession of Faith upholds perseverance in XVII.1–3.

L. Berkhof (d. 1957) defined sanctification as "the gracious and continuous operation of the Holy Spirit, by which He delivers the justified sinner from the pollution of sin, renews his whole nature in the image of God, and enables him to perform good works."[71] Berkhof identified the two contemporaneous parts of sanctification as mortification of the "old man" (human nature controlled by sin) and quickening of the "new man" (human nature renewed by the Spirit). Although the work of strengthening holy dispositions is chiefly a divine and not a human work, believers must cooperate with grace by the proper use of spiritual means. These include the Word of God, the sacraments, prayer, the constant exercise of faith, confession of sins, and providential discipline. Berkhof held that the flesh and the Spirit do battle in all Christians and that the process of sanctification is not completed in this life. "Believers must contend with sin as long as they live."[72] Although Christians are delivered from the curse of the law as a rule for attaining salvation, "the law as the standard of our moral life is a transcript of the holiness of God and is therefore of permanent validity also for the believer."[73]

Berkhof defined perseverance as "that continuous operation of the Holy Spirit in the believer, by which the work of divine grace that is begun in the heart, is continued and brought to completion. It is because God never forsakes His work that believers continue to stand to the very end."[74] Believers persevere by God's grace as they pursue constant vigilance, watchfulness, self-examination, and prayer.

Other helpful studies on the subject include works by J. I. Packer,[75] G. C. Berkouwer,[76] and R. Lovelace.[77]

BIBLICAL TEACHING

To understand which perspectives on sanctification and perseverance fit the primary evidence best, we now turn to the teachings of Scripture.

The Pentateuch

The notion of holiness lies at the heart of the biblical doctrine of sanctification. The verb *qādaš* ("be consecrated," "be holy"), the noun *qōdeš* ("apartness," "holiness"), and the adjective *qādôs* ("holy," "pure") derive from the Hebrew root that means to "cut" or "separate." Thus the fundamental Old Testament idea of holiness is separation or consecration. Persons, places, or objects are ceremonially holy because they are separate from what is profane and devoted to God. In this sense persons are declared holy, such as the Jewish priests (Lev. 21:8), prophets (2 Kings 4:9; Jer. 1:5), the firstborn male (Exod. 13:2), and Israel itself (19:6; Deut. 14:2; Ezek. 37:28). Places also are designated holy, such as

INTEGRATIVE THEOLOGY

Mount Horeb (Exod. 3:5), Mount Zion (Zeph. 3:11), and Israel's territory (Zech. 2:12). Likewise, objects are holy, including the tabernacle (Exod. 40:9), the altar (Exod. 29:37), and the sacrifices (Exod. 18:17). Supporting the root idea of the word holiness is the fact that the Hebrew word for prostitute (qᵉdēšah) derives from the same root (a prostitute is one set aside for that nefarious activity: Genesis 38:21–22; Deuteronomy 23:18; 2 Kings 23:7). The Old Testament recognizes a moral aspect of holiness, namely, the condition whereby persons are separated from what is defiled or evil. In this sense God himself is said to be holy (Lev. 20:26; Ps. 99:5), as are his people (Lev. 19:2; Num. 15:40).

In the covenant context God summoned Abraham to holiness of life: "walk before me and be blameless" (Gen. 17:1). Later, before entering the land, Moses urged Israel to "be blameless [tāmîm] before the LORD your God" (Deut. 18:13). Whereas the KJV translates tāmîm as "perfect" and the LXX renders it by teleios (giving rise to perfectionist interpretations), the Hebrew word group fundamentally means completeness, soundness, and integrity.[78] Morally a person described as tāmîm is "wholehearted in commitment to the person and requirements of God,"[79] without being entirely free from sin. Thus Genesis 6:9 states that "Noah was a righteous man, blameless [tāmîm] among the people of his time. . . ."Relatively Noah was "blameless" in that he obeyed God's commands, offered sacrifices, and kept the Sabbath. Yet Noah was not free from sin, as his drunkenness and sexual misconduct clearly indicate (Gen. 9:21). How candidly the Pentateuch records the sins of mature servants of the Lord! The saintly Abraham urged Sarah to lie to the Egyptians that she was his sister (Gen. 12:11–13), thereby violating the ninth commandment and exposing

Sarah to disobedience to the seventh commandment. Isaac was a man of faith (Heb. 11:20) and prayer (Gen. 25:21), but, motivated by fear, he lied to Abimelech, saying that Rebekah was his sister (26:7). Jacob deceived his father Isaac that he might inherit the birthright blessing (27:18–29). Moses' disobedient striking of the rock twice at Meribah highlighted his rebellion against God (Num. 20:24), his sinful anger against the people (v. 10), and his disbelief of God's word (v. 12). Moses failed to do what he was commanded and did what he was not commanded (cf. Rom. 7:15, 19). For this he and Aaron were excluded from entering the Promised Land (v. 12).

God's preceptive will was that Israel should demonstrate God's choice of them as a unique people by reflecting his holy character. Thus God said to the Israelites, "I am the LORD your God; consecrate yourselves and be holy, because I am holy" (Lev. 11:44; cf. 19:2; 20:7–8, 26). Israel was formally holy because they were set apart from unbelieving nations to be God's peculiar people (the "indicative" of holiness). But Israel had to become morally and spiritually holy (the "imperative" of holiness) by refraining from the sinful practices of her pagan neighbors (Deut. 18:9–14) and by obeying God's commands (28:9, 14). Although Israel was commanded to seek holiness, Yahweh was Israel's "sanctifier" (Exod. 31:13); he was the one who made the covenant people holy (Lev. 21:8, 15; 22:32).

The Poetic Literature

To the questions "Lord, who may dwell in your sanctuary? Who may live on your holy hill?" (Ps. 15:1), the psalmist responded that it is those whose life is characterized by righteous character (v. 2), righteous speech (v. 3a), righteous relations (v. 3b), and righteous dealings with others (v. 5).

The word "blameless" (*tāmîm*) in verse 2 (cf. Pss. 37:37; 119:1) indicates, as noted above, not sinless perfection but moral soundness and integrity. Psalm 24:3 poses related questions: "Who may ascend the hill of the Lord? Who may stand in his holy place?" They worship God truly whose thoughts, motives, and deeds are pure and noble (v. 4). The literature portrays the life of the godly as one of progressive moral and spiritual development. Proverbs 4:18 likens the devout life to the path of the sun. As the sun progresses from the dim glow of first light to the full brilliance of its midday zenith, so the believer advances in knowledge of God and spiritual virtue.[80]

Scripture describes Job as "blameless [*tām*] and upright [*yāšār*]" (Job 1:1, 8; 2:3) and as "righteous [*ṣadîq*] and blameless [*tāmîm*]" (Job 12:4). *Tām* connotes one who is "complete, innocent, having integrity."[81] Moreover, *yāšār* (cf. Ps. 33:1; Prov. 14:9) signifies one who is "straightforward, just, upright."[82] The Lord himself said of Job: "There is no one on earth like him; . . . a man who fears God and shuns evil" (Job 2:3). These testimonies do not imply sinless perfection, for the following reasons: Job himself acknowledged his sins (Job 9:20; 13:26; 14:16–17); he admitted that he was not innocent but guilty (9:28–29); he needed God's mercy and forgiveness (7:20–21; 9:15); and at the end of the book he repented wholeheartedly for his imperfections (42:6).

Scripture likewise represents David as "righteous and upright in heart" (1 Kings 3:6). David described his intention as that of living a "blameless [*tāmîm*] life" and possessing a "blameless [*tām*] heart" (Ps. 101:2). Yet David candidly admitted not only his overt and heinous sins, including adultery (Pss. 32:1–2, 5; 51:1–5, 7–9), but also the seemingly trivial sins of ignorance or inadvertence buried in the depths of his heart. Thus he cried out to God, "Who can discern his errors? Forgive my hidden faults" (Ps. 19:12). David knew full well that not even the most devout believer measures up to the standards of God's holy Law (Pss. 130:3; 143:2). Solomon likewise asserted that no mortal is free from sin: "Who can say, 'I have kept my heart pure; I am clean and without sin'?" (Prov. 20:9). Even godly saints commit sins of omission and of commission: "There is not a righteous man on earth who does what is right and never sins" (Eccles. 7:20).[83]

The poetic literature reflects confidence in the faithful God who preserves trusting believers to the end. Psalm 37 teaches God's trustworthy guardianship of the saint: "Though he stumble, he will not fall, for the LORD upholds him with his hand" (v. 24). Moreover, "the LORD . . . will not forsake his faithful ones. They will be protected forever" (v. 28). Similar is the statement of Psalm 125:1: "Those who trust in the LORD are like Mount Zion, which cannot be shaken but endures forever." Job 17:9; Psalm 55:22; Psalm 73:23–24; and Proverbs 18:10 also teach the believer's security amid the trials of life.

Prophetic Literature

Isaiah, a faithful believer and a devout servant of the Lord, had a vision in the temple of God's awesome glory and holiness that led him to cry out, "Woe to me!. . . I am ruined! For I am a man of unclean lips" (Isa. 6:5). Having beheld the Lord, Isaiah realized that he was unclean and his heart had to be purified if he would worship and serve God (cf. Isa. 64:6). Isaiah's experience suggests that the closer believers come to God the more conscious they are of ingrained sinfulness. Daniel, another devout prophet of God, in a moving prayer confessed the wickedness and guilt both of himself and of the people (Dan. 9:4–16). Daniel's greatness, in part, lay in his keen sensitivity to his innate, sinful impulses.

Old Testament prophets predicted a future outpouring of the Spirit as the principal sign of the messianic age (Isa. 42:1; 44:3; Ezek. 36:27; 39:29). Yahweh said, "Afterward, I will pour out my Spirit on all people. Your sons and daughters will prophesy, your old men will dream dreams, your young men will see visions" (Joel 2:28). Peter interpreted the phenomena of Pentecost as the fulfillment of Joel's prophecy (Acts 2:16–21). God's visitation in the messianic age would include radical cleansing from sin (cf. Isa. 4:4); so the Lord said, "On that day a fountain will be opened to the house of David and the inhabitants of Jerusalem, to cleanse them from sin and impurity" (Zech. 13:1). Cleansing from sin's penalty (justification) and defilement (sanctification) would occur through Messiah's blood shed on the cross. Similarly the Lord, through Malachi, foretold the coming of "the messenger of the covenant" (Mal. 3:1), who is Jesus Christ the Messiah (Mark 1:2–3). The images of a "refiner's fire" and a "launderer's soap" indicate that Messiah, at his first coming, would radically sanctify his people for effective worship and service (Mal. 3:2–3).

The prophets repeatedly chronicled the spiritual defection of Israel and Judah. The noun mᵉšûbāh ("backsliding") occurs twelve times in the Old Testament, nine in Jeremiah. The Lord said of Judah: "Their rebellion is great and their backslidings many" (Jer. 5:6; cf. 2:19; 3:22; 14:7; Hos. 14:4). Isaiah indicted the sinful nation thus: "They have forsaken the LORD; they have spurned the Holy One of Israel and turned their backs on him" (Isa. 1:4). The covenant people refused to listen to the Lord's instruction (Isa. 30:9), exchanged the glory of Yahweh for worthless idols (Jer. 2:11), and engaged in ritual prostitution (Hos. 4:10–11, 14). God indicted his people, saying, "Like Adam, they have broken the covenant" (Hos. 6:7). Concerning Israel's backsliding, in every instance save one (Prov. 1:32), mᵉšûbāh refers to the nation; the people collectively had turned from the Lord and violated the covenant. Moreover, in spite of their faithlessness Yahweh would not abandon his covenant people. So the faithful Lord said, "How can I give you up, Ephraim? How can I hand you over, Israel?" (Hos. 11:8). "I will heal their waywardness and love them freely" (Hos. 14:4). True to his promise Yahweh will restore Israel and Judah to Jerusalem and join them to himself "in an everlasting covenant that will not be forgotten" (Jer. 50:5). God himself will ensure the perpetuity of his covenant with the elect (Isa. 55:3; Jer. 31:31–33; Ezek. 16:60).

The Synoptic Gospels

Holiness advocates appeal to Jesus' beatitude "Blessed are the pure in heart, for they will see God" (Matt. 5:8) as support for the doctrine of sinless perfection. The notion of "seeing God," however, figuratively describes the believer's experience of engaging God in worship (cf. Heb. 12:14). This privilege extends to the katharoi in heart—i.e., those whose life, while not absolutely holy, is free from deceit and falsehood and is marked by sincerity of purpose. The holiness tradition also appeals to these words of Jesus to his disciples: "Be perfect, therefore, as your heavenly Father is perfect" (Matt. 5:48). The adjective teleios (cf. Matt. 19:21) "does not mean 'sinless,' 'incapable of sinning,' but 'fulfilling its appointed end, complete, mature.' "[84] That the meaning is spiritual maturity rather than absolute moral perfection is clear from the use of teleios in 1 Corinthians 2:6; Ephesians 4:13; Philippians 3:15; Colossians 4:12; and James 1:4. The context of Matthew 5:48 (i.e., vv. 43–44, 46) suggests that God's purpose for Christian disciples is maturity in love. Jesus' followers are to pursue the love wherewith God himself loves. Jesus' command to the Pharisees and Sadducees—"Love the Lord your God with all your heart and with all your soul and with all your mind" (Matt. 22:37; cf. Deut. 6:5)—indicates that love for God must be wholehearted and undivided.

According to Mark 16:17–18 Jesus said of his believing servants: "They will drive out demons; they will speak in new tongues; . . . they will place their hands on sick people, and they will get well." Since the "longer ending" of Mark likely was a second-century addition, the preceding saying was not part of the *ipsissima verba* of Jesus. The text indicates, however, that glossolalia, exorcisms, and healing were practiced in certain second-century Christian communities. Ultimately the legitimization of these miraculous gifts for the contemporary church must be established by canonical New Testament texts.

Jesus urged Peter to prayer and watchfulness so as to avoid yielding to temptation. He then added, "The spirit is willing, but the body [*sarx*] is weak" (Matt. 26:41). Here *sarx* connotes (sinful) human nature that is morally and spiritually weak. The thoughts and impulses that arise from the old nature resist obedience to God's will. Similarly, Jesus taught his disciples to pray: "Forgive us our debts [*opheilēma*], as we also have forgiven our debtors" (Matt. 6:12). *Opheilēma* here means a moral debt owed to God, hence the parallel text in Luke 11:4: "Forgive us our sins [*hamartia*]." Jesus recognized that even committed disciples commit sins that require God's forgiveness.

Concerning believers' perseverance, Jesus in the Olivet Discourse said that "false prophets will appear and perform great signs and miracles to deceive even the elect—if that were possible [*ei dynaton*]" (Matt. 24:24). The phrase *ei dynaton* (cf. Mark 13:22), though elliptical (i.e., lacking a verb), is a second-class condition indicating remote possibility of fulfilling the condition. Jesus seemed to indicate that Satan's ultimate deception of God's elect is not possible.

To some the parable of the sower (Matt. 13:3–8, 18–23) suggests the possibility of believers lapsing from faith. With its focus on four kinds of soils, the parable highlights the reception the Gospel meets in people's hearts. Consider the four types of soil. (1) The seed of the word that fell on "the path" only to be devoured by birds (v. 4) describes people who are spiritually *indifferent and unresponsive*. These hear the good word but, deceived by Satan, fail to understand and so reject it (v. 19). (2) The seed of the word also fell on "rocky places." Shoots soon sprang up, but for lack of subsoil they withered and died (vv. 5–6). This soil describes people who are spiritually *shallow and superficial*. They hear the word and make an initial overture to it, but when trouble or persecution come, they quickly fall away (vv. 20–21). (3) Some seed furthermore fell among "thorns" (v. 7). Young plants grew from the seed, but they were choked by the more virile thorns. This describes people who are *worldly and disinterested*. They respond to the Gospel, but worldly concerns prevent their lives from developing spiritually (v. 22). (4) The seed of the word fell on "good soil," which in time produced a rich harvest of grain (v. 8). This signifies people who are truly *responsive*. They understand the Good News, personally appropriate it, and bring forth abundant fruit (v. 23). Only in the fourth type of individual is the word of truth properly understood, received, and disposed to grow. The first three kinds of people never were genuinely converted.

According to some, "the blasphemy against the Spirit" (Matt. 12:31–32; cf. 1 John 5:16) describes a sin that causes loss of salvation. In response to Jesus' healing of a demon-possessed man, the Pharisees alleged that he had performed the miracle by the power of Beelzebub, the prince of demons (v. 24). By attributing the healing power of God's Spirit to Satan, the Pharisees demonstrated their resolute hostility to God's purposes. Such deliberate resistance to divine grace, Jesus taught, precludes the genuine repentance and trust in God necessary for salvation. Such self-chosen "blasphemy against the Spirit" places the individual beyond the reach of forgiveness, and in this sense is unpardonable. Thus this incident focuses on Christ-rejecters who were not believers rather than on any sin of believers.

Peter's denial of Jesus in Luke 22:55–62 illustrates a believer's backsliding rather than loss of salvation. After Jesus' arrest three people claimed that they recognized Peter as a follower of Jesus. Three times Peter denied that he knew the Lord or was his disciple. When Jesus "looked straight at Peter" (v. 61), Peter recalled the Lord's prediction of his threefold denial (vv. 31–34), was overcome with grief for his failure to confess Christ, and "went outside and wept bitterly" (v. 62). Spiritually immature and weak, Peter succumbed to the temptation to deny his Lord. But stricken with genuine sorrow for his failure, Peter repented of his sin and was restored to leadership among the disciples. Peter's turning back to Christ was due to Christ's prayer for his continued perseverance in faith (v. 32).

Some suggest that Judas, one of the Twelve (Luke 22:3), was a believer whose willful sin resulted in his fall from grace. Judas objected to Mary's anointing Jesus with expensive oil because, as keeper of the purse, he had stolen money belonging to the disciples (John 12:1–6). Later, having come under the control of Satan (Luke 22:3; cf. John 13:2, 27), Judas negotiated with the high priests to hand Jesus over for thirty silver coins (Matt. 26:14–16)— the price of a common slave (Zech. 11:12). In the upper room (John 17:12) Jesus prayed to the Father: "None has been lost except the one doomed to destruction [*ho huios tēs apōleias*]"— a phrase used of the man of sin in 2 Thessalonians 2:3. Matthew wrote that Jesus with deep sorrow pronounced Judas's doom: "Woe to that man who betrays the Son of Man! It would be better for him if he had not been born" (Matt. 26:24). After Judas had handed Jesus over to the crowd (Matt. 26:47–49), the following morning he was filled with remorse and returned the thirty pieces of silver to the chief priests and elders (Matt. 27:3–4). Judas may have displayed sorrow for his sin, but he failed to repent and change his behavior. Thus consumed by despair, Judas left the temple and hanged himself (v. 5; cf. Luke's account of Judas's death in Acts 1:18).

It is clear that Judas never possessed saving knowledge of Christ. Jesus said to the Twelve: " 'You are clean, though not every one of you.' For he knew who was going to betray him, and that was why he said not every one was clean" (John 13:10–11; cf. 6:64). All the disciples except Judas were "clean" in the sense that their sin and guilt had been removed (cf. 1 John 1:7, 9). Jesus, moreover, pronounced Judas "a devil" (*diabolos*), a word used of Satan in John 8:44; 13:2; and 1 John 3:8, 10. Luke referred to the "apostolic ministry, which Judas left to go where he belongs" (Acts 1:25). Judas turned aside from following Christ to depart to the place that was uniquely his own—

namely, hell. John MacArthur writes the following about Judas:

> Judas is a prime example of a professing believer who fell into absolute apostasy. For three years he followed the Lord with the other disciples. He appeared to be one of them. . . . Yet, while the others were growing into apostles, Judas was quietly becoming a vile, calculating tool of Satan. Whatever his character seemed to be at the beginning, his faith was not real (John 13:10–11). He was unregenerate, and his heart gradually hardened so that he became the treacherous man who sold the Savior for a fistful of coins. In the end, he was so prepared to do Satan's bidding that the devil himself possessed Judas (John 13:27).[85]

Primitive Christianity/Acts

According to Acts 1:5, the resurrected Jesus gave the following promise to the Eleven: "John baptized with water, but in a few days you will be baptized with the Holy Spirit." Compare the Baptist's earlier prediction of Jesus' activity: "He will baptize you with the Holy Spirit and with fire" (Matt. 3:11; cf. Mark 1:8; Luke 3:16; John 1:33). Baptism here is a metaphor that describes the outpouring of the Spirit on believers. The fact that the eleven disciples believed for some time before being baptized by the Spirit may be attributed to the unique historical situation. The promised Spirit of prophecy could not be poured out (Ezek. 36:27; 39:29; Joel 2:28) until Christ had risen from the dead and ascended to heaven (Acts 1:2; John 7:39).

Holiness people claim that the fulfillment of this promise of Spirit-baptism, realized in Acts 2, 8, 10, and 19, depicts the postconversion crisis experience of entire sanctification each believer should pursue. *Pentecostals* interpret the Spirit-baptism (attended by tongues-speaking) as a crisis experience that provides power for service. Let us examine these four accounts of the Spirit's outpouring in Acts. On the day of Pentecost (Acts 2:1–13) the disciples witnessed extraordinary manifestations of wind and fire, symbols of the Spirit's purifying and judging ministry. Suddenly, "all of them were filled with the Holy Spirit and began to speak in other tongues as the Spirit enabled them" (v. 4). The Spirit's activity is variously described as a baptism (Acts 1:5; 11:16), a filling (2:4), and an outpouring (2:17). The "other tongues" (*glōssa,* "tongue," "language," "utterance") the disciples spontaneously spoke represents xenolalia, or foreign languages not previously learned. This is so, for Luke thrice stated (vv. 6, 8, 11) that the crowd heard them speak in their own languages. In verse 11 Luke used the word *glōssa;* but in verses 6 and 8 he used the word *dialektos,* which in Acts 1:19 refers to the Aramaic language. This outpouring of the Spirit at Pentecost, accompanied by wind, fire, and tongues, represents the definitive sign of the dawning of the messianic age (Joel 2:28–32). The disciples were believers in Jesus prior to Pentecost, but the promised effusion of the Spirit occurred only then. Concerning the disciples at Pentecost, Packer correctly comments: "Their two-state experience must be judged unique and not a norm for us."[86]

According to Acts 8:12–17 certain Samaritans believed Philip's message and were baptized in water in the name of the Lord Jesus. Hearing of this development, the Jerusalem apostles dispatched Peter and John, who laid hands on them and prayed that they might receive the Holy Spirit. Forthwith the Spirit descended on the believing Samaritans. The record does not explicitly mention tongues-speaking. The excited response of Simon the sorcerer (v. 19) may be due to his observing Philip's miracles (v. 13). Should the time interval between the

Samaritans' act of believing and their Spirit-baptism be explained as a subsequent second-blessing experience? Undoubtedly not. We view this scenario not as a normative pattern for all believers but as a special situation in the life of the early church. The bestowal of the Spirit after some delay publicly certified that the Samaritan believers were true Christians and full-fledged members of the church.[87]

Acts 10:44–48 records the Spirit's outpouring on representative Gentiles in Caesarea. Although the Roman centurion Cornelius and his family were "God-fearing" (vv. 1–2), they were not converted and thus had not been baptized by the Spirit into the body of Christ. Led by the Spirit, Peter proclaimed Christ to the household of Cornelius. The latter believed (cf. v. 43), were endued with the Holy Spirit (v. 44), spoke in tongues (v. 46, glōssai), and were baptized (v. 48). Concerning this "Gentile Pentecost," there was no time interval between their believing in Christ and receiving the Spirit. Since all who believed Peter's message spoke in tongues, the latter activity is not the grace gift of 1 Corinthians 12–14. What happened to these Gentiles at Caesarea was similar to what happened to the disciples at Pentecost (Acts 10:47; 11:15, 17; 15:8–9). It was a supernatural sign certifying to the Jerusalem church that believing Gentiles were not second-class citizens but spiritual equals with believing Jews in the body of Christ.

Acts 19:1–7 recounts the outpouring of the Spirit on disciples of John at Ephesus. The recipients were Old Testament-type believers who knew only John's baptism of repentance (Acts 18:25; 19:3) and who did not know that the Spirit could be received—i.e., they were ignorant of Pentecost (Acts 19:2). After being instructed by Paul, the followers of John believed in Jesus, were baptized in his name, received the Spirit, spoke in tongues (glōssai), and prophesied (vv. 4–6). The experience of John's disciples, like that of the believing Samaritans in Acts 8 and the believing Gentiles in Acts 10, was a unique historical occurrence. "Somehow knowledge of Jesus separate from the Christian message about his resurrection and outpouring of the Spirit seems to have spread to Ephesus and probably elsewhere."[88] Concerning the tongues-speaking, Marshall adds, "Some unusual gift was perhaps needed to convince this group of 'semi-Christians' that they were now fully members of Christ's church."[89] Since all John's disciples spoke in tongues, the phenomenon likely was not Pauline charismata. In summary, Acts records the centrifugal movement of the Gospel geographically (Jerusalem, Samaria, Caesarea, Ephesus) and ethnically (Jews, Samaritans, and Gentiles) attested by recognizable signs.

Concerning the claim that Acts 2, 8, 10, 19 describes a crisis, second-blessing experience attested by tongues and normative for Christians of all ages, note also the following: (1) Luke clearly stated that new converts received the gift of the Holy Spirit at the moment they trusted Christ and were regenerated (Acts 2:38; 5:32; 19:2, 5–6). All believers experience their own "Pentecost" (short of tongues-speaking) at the time of conversion to Christ. (2) Acts records numerous instances in which persons who came to Christ apparently did not speak in tongues (e.g., 3:7–8; 4:4; 5:14; 6:7; 8:36). (3) Luke cited many cases where persons were filled with or full of the Holy Spirit with no reference to tongues (e.g., 4:8, 31; 6:3, 5; 7:55; 9:17; 11:24). And (4) those who did speak in tongues did not petition or tarry for the experience (2:1–4; 10:44–46; 19:2–6). In many cases (Corinth excepted) tongues-speaking and other "miraculous signs and wonders" (5:12; 14:3) served an evidential purpose in the early church. As J. I. Packer correctly observes, "Luke seems to have understood his four cases of 'Pentecostal manifestations' as God's testimony to having accepted on equal footing in the new society four classes of folk whose coequality might hereto otherwise have been doubted—Jews, Samaritans, Gentiles, and disciples of John."[90]

The Pauline Literature

Paul acknowledged the *positional* dimension of sanctification in 1 Corinthians 6:11. Even though many Corinthian believers were empirically sinful, Paul could say of them: "But you were washed, you were sanctified, you were justified in the name of the Lord Jesus Christ and by the Spirit of our God" (cf. Rom. 15:16; 1 Cor. 1:2). Because they had been cleansed of past sins and set apart for God, the apostle designated them "saints" (*hagioi*, Rom. 1:7; 2 Cor. 1:1; Eph. 1:1; et al.). Paul understood that at the outset of the Christian life (simultaneous with regeneration) the believer is Spirit-baptized into the body of Christ: "For we were all baptized by one Spirit into one body . . . and we were all given the one Spirit to drink" (1 Cor. 12:13). Paul's words "all . . . all" indicate that at the new birth *every* Christian receives the Spirit's baptism. Yet clearly not all the Corinthians spoke in tongues, nor were they expected to do so (1 Cor. 12:30). Whereas believers experience but one Spirit-baptism (cf. Rom. 6:3–4; Gal. 3:27), they experience many fillings of the Spirit (Eph. 5:18).

Concerning the *experiential* dimension of sanctification, God purposed that believers should be conformed to Christ's image (Rom. 8:29; cf. Eph. 1:4). God's work of effecting Christlikeness in saints is gradual and progressive rather than instantaneous. So Paul wrote, "We, who with unveiled faces all reflect the Lord's glory, are being transformed [present passive of *metamorpheō*] into his likeness with ever-increasing glory" (2 Cor. 3:18). Similarly, "speaking the truth in love, we will in all things grow up into him who is the Head, that is, Christ" (Eph. 4:15). Ephesians 4:13 and Galatians 4:19 also teach a gradual growth in Christlikeness. Numerous other texts affirm the progressive nature of sanctification. "Inwardly we are being renewed [present passive of *anakainoō*] day by day" (2 Cor. 4:16). And again, "Let us purify ourselves from everything that contaminates body and spirit, perfecting holiness out of reverence for God" (2 Cor. 7:1). The present tense of *epiteleō* (to "complete" or "finish") connotes the Christian's gradual advance in holiness. See also Romans 12:2 and 2 Thessalonians 1:3. Whereas *hagiosynē* in 1 Thessalonians 3:13 indicates the *state* of being holy, *hagiosmos* in 4:3, 7 signifies the *process* of making holy— so the rendering of the NIV.

Whereas Romans 5 discusses believers' justification, Romans 6 explains the nature of their sanctification. Since Christians have been set right with God, why not sin boldly that grace might abound (Rom. 6:1)? Using the symbol of baptism, Paul inveighed against this suggestion, as follows. Sanctification *negatively* signifies the mortification of the old nature. In conversion believers were united with Christ in his death and burial (vv. 4a, 5a). In its Godward aspect this means that Christians died to the old life of sin (vv. 6–8a; cf. Gal. 5:24); in its manward aspect it means that they must reckon themselves dead to sin (v. 11a) by allowing sin no place in their lives (vv. 12–14). Sanctification *positively* means the vivification of the new nature. In conversion believers were united with Christ in his resurrection (vv. 4b–5). In its Godward aspect this means that Christians have come alive in Christ (v. 8b), whereas in its manward aspect it signifies that they must reckon themselves alive to God (v. 11b) and become servants to righteousness (vv. 13b, 18b, 19b, 22).

Similarly Ephesians 4:22–24 teaches that sanctification negatively involves the decision to put off the "old self" (*palaios anthrōpos*) and positively, through the continual process of the mind's renewal to put on the "new self" (*kainos anthrōpos*). The two verbs specifying mortification and renewal are present tenses, denoting a continual process. For sanctification as a progressive putting off of the "earthly nature" and a putting on of the "new self," see Colossians 3:5–10. We understand the old nature as that capacity to serve Satan, sin, and self acquired through Adam, whereas the new nature is the capacity to serve God and righteousness acquired through regeneration. Against most "victorious life" emphases, Paul affirmed that the normal Christian life involves struggle against vestiges of indwelling sin. Within believers the "sinful nature" (*sarx*) and the "Spirit" (*pneuma*) do battle and hinder the other's working (Gal. 5:17). As a result, "you do not do what you want."

Paul stated in Romans 7:1–6 that Christians are free from law-keeping as a means of attaining salvation. Does this mean that the law is sin? Not at all, Paul responded, for the problem rests not with the law but with the human propensity to sin. The apostle explained the meaning of this claim in verses 7–25. It is clear that verses 7–13 describe Paul's preconversion experience and verses 14–25 his postconversion experience, for the following reasons. (1) The first section employs past tenses, whereas the second employs the present tense throughout. (2) The first section shows absence of inner tension, the subject being at ease with sin. The second section reflects a powerful inner tension between good and evil (vv. 15,

18b, 20a). And (3) in the second section the subject wills the good (vv. 15a, 18b, 19a, 21a), delights in the law of God (vv. 22, 25b), and hates evil (vv. 15b, 16a)—all responses of a regenerate person. Thus Paul the mature Christian acknowledged, "I am unspiritual [*sarkinos*], sold as a slave to sin" (v. 14). In 1 Corinthians 3:1, 3 Paul described believers in that church as *sarkinos*, "made of flesh" and as *sarkikos*, "characterized by flesh," which the NIV renders "worldly." Moreover, "I know that nothing good lives in me, that is, in my sinful nature" (*sarx*, Rom. 7:18). The presence of residual sinful impulses means that "there is something in man—even regenerate man—which objects to God and seeks to be independent of Him."[91] The sin that yet dwells within (v. 20b) hindered Paul from fulfilling the law and urged him to do what the law forbids. This tension between the law of the mind and the law of sin (v. 23) lingers with Christians as long as they live. As Horne observed, "Sanctification does not mean the abolition of sin in regenerate and sanctified persons. Though the saints do not live in sin, it still lives in them, and sometimes it becomes very active and powerful."[92]

Elsewhere Paul acknowledged that he had not yet "been made perfect" (Phil. 3:12). He added, "straining toward what is ahead, I press on toward the goal to win the prize for which God has called me heavenward in Christ Jesus" (vv. 13–14). The verb *epekteinomai* in this context depicts a racer bent forward and straining toward the goal. The present tense of *diōkō* indicates ongoing action; Paul pursued that which he had not yet attained—i.e., moral and spiritual perfection. Indeed, the Christian's sanctification is completed only at Christ's return (1 Thess. 3:13). In 1 Thessalonians 5:23 Paul prayed that believers' sanctification might be completed "at the coming of our Lord Jesus Christ.'' The aorist verb in the phrase "sanctify you through and through," does not attest a crisis experience of entire sanctification prior to death. Rather, the verb is a "culminative aorist," that focuses on the conclusion or end result of the sanctifying action.[93]

We turn now to Paul's teaching on the nature and distribution of spiritual gifts. The word *charisma* signifies both a spiritual benefit in general (Rom. 5:15; 6:23) and a particular endowment of the Spirit to specific believers for ministry to the church and world (e.g., Rom. 12:6; 1 Cor. 12:4, 9, 28, 30). There are four main passages on the subject, which cite some twenty-two gifts. The gifts listed appear to be representative rather than exhaustive of the grace gifts God bestows.

The earliest list of spiritual gifts occurs in 1 Corinthians 12:7-11. Whereas certain Corinthians believed that possession of supranormal gifts rendered them more spiritual, Paul taught that the Spirit sovereignly dispenses the *charismata* for the enrichment of the entire body (vv. 4-7). (1) The gift of the message of wisdom (*logos sophias,* v. 8a) and (2) the gift of the message of knowledge (*logos gnōseōs,* v. 8b) may concern the ability to apply and understand spiritual truths, respectively. (3) The gift of faith (*pistis,* v. 9) concerns the ability to claim the promises of God in the face of seeming impossibilities. (4) The gifts of healing (*charismata iamatōn,* v. 9; cf. vv. 28, 30) may not represent a permanent endowment—such that persons become "healers"—but specific gifts for specific occasions of healing (James 5:14-15). (5) The gift of miraculous powers (*energēmata dynameōn,* v. 10; cf. vv. 28-29) refers to other supernatural workings such as exorcisms of evil spirits (cf. Acts 8:6-7; 19:11-12). Healings and other miracles done by Jesus and early Christians not only attested

the inbreaking of the eschatological kingdom (Luke 10:9-11) but also were an inherent part of the holistic Gospel message (Acts 10:38).

(6) The gift of prophecy (v. 10) follows. The messages of Old Testament prophets came from God, possessed infallible authority, and when written down constituted canonical Scripture. The counterpart of the Old Testament prophets were the apostles (Luke 11:49; 2 Peter 3:2), who also delivered infallible messages from God that became authoritative Scripture. There were in New Testament times prophets (cf. Acts; 1 Cor. 12:28-29; Eph. 2:20; 3:5; 4:11) who delivered Spirit-inspired messages for the edification of the church. Prophecy involved spontaneous, Spirit-prompted communications (*apokalyptō,* 1 Cor. 14:30) expressed in human words. Prophecy served the purposes of prediction (Acts 11:28), instruction (Acts 13:1-2), and exhortation (Acts 21:4). As an *order of ministry,* prophets, like apostles, died out with the close of the apostolic era (1 Cor. 15:8). Some of the *functions* of the prophet (like that of the apostle) continue in the form of the gift of prophecy (Rom. 12:10; 1 Cor. 12:10; 13:2, 8; 14:1-39). The purposes of prophecy as an ongoing gift include edification of the saints (1 Cor. 14:3), encouragement (Acts 15:32), and convicting unbelievers of sin (1 Cor. 14:24-25). Not possessing infallible authority, later prophetic messages must be carefully evaluated by the church (1 Cor. 14:29; 1 Thess. 5:21). (7) The ability to distinguish between spirits (*diakriseis pneumatōn,* v. 10) concerns the power to judge whether claims and works are from God or from evil powers (cf. Acts 13:9-11; 16:16-18; 1 John 4:1-3). (8) The gift of tongues (*glōssai,* v. 10; cf. 12:28, 30) and (9) the interpretation of tongues (*hermeneia glōssōn,* v. 10; cf. 12:30) will be discussed in the study of 1 Corinthians 14, below.

The second text, 1 Corinthians

12:28–31, relates certain gifted ministries to the *charismata* (v. 31). (1) The ministry exercised by apostles (*apostoloi,* v. 28; cf. Eph. 2:20; 4:11). In the narrow sense apostles denote those who saw the risen Christ and who were commissioned by him. They include the Twelve and Paul, together with a few others such as Barnabas (Acts 14:14), James the brother of Jesus (Gal. 1:19), Andronicus and Junias (Rom. 16:7). As Christ's special ambassadors, the apostles transmitted revelation, preached the Gospel, and planted churches. The *office* and authority of the apostles passed away, but some of their *functions* continue in the form of evangelism, church-planting, teaching, leadership, and administration. (2) The ministry of "prophets" (v. 28) was discussed under 1 Corinthians 12:10, above, and that of (3) "teachers" (v. 28) will be considered under Romans 12:7, below. Paul's use of "first," "second," and "third" in reference to apostles, prophets, and teachers highlights their importance in establishing and edifying the church (cf. 1 Cor. 12:31; 14:5).

Paul continued by mentioning (4) workers of miracles (v. 28; cf. v. 10) and (5) gifts of healing (v. 28; cf. v. 9). There follows (6) the gift of helps (*antilēmpsis,* v. 28; cf. Acts 20:35) that concerns giving assistance to those in need. (7) The gift of administration (*kybernēsis,* v. 28; cf. Rom. 12:8) deals with managing the affairs of the local church, a function that may have become formalized in the office of the elder/pastor. Finally (8) Paul cited the gift of "kinds of tongues" (*genē glōssōn,* v. 28; cf. v. 30; 1 Cor. 14). In Corinth certain spectacular *charismata,* particularly tongues and prophecy, had been abused. Hence in the following chapter (1 Cor. 13) the apostle argued that the charismatic gifts are worthless unless exercised in love for the church's edification.

Because the spiritually immature Co-rinthians (1 Cor. 14:20) caused confusion and disorder with their tongues-speaking and prophesying (vv. 33, 40), Paul in chapter 14 regulated their use. He urged the believers to seek the spiritual gifts (*ta pneumatika*), particularly the gift of prophecy (v. 1; cf. under 1 Cor. 12:10). Prophecy is superior to tongues (*glōssai*) because, expressed in intelligible speech, it immediately instructs and edifies the church (vv. 2–5). While commending the value of prophecy, Paul did not forbid speaking in tongues (v. 39). Tongues-speaking in Acts 2, at least, represented known human languages or zenolalia. But "tongues" in 1 Corinthians 12–14 likely meant glossolalia, or Spirit-prompted verbal patterns containing cognitive content employed in prayer and worship.[94] Thus Paul referred to "tongues . . . of angels" (13:1); the tongues-speaker addressed God, not humans (14:2, 28); glossolalia involved the spirit not the mind (14:14–16); and glossolalia was unintelligible to the speaker's congregation (14:2); hence there was the need for interpretation (14:5, 11, 13).

The apostle affirmed the legitimacy of the tongues gift that was abused at Corinth. Paul himself spoke in tongues more than others (v. 18), and he urged others to employ the gift responsibly (vv. 5, 39). Tongues, as verbal utterances of praise and prayer, were primarily used in the believer's private worship experience (vv. 2, 4a, 28b). In addition, when exercised in public and explained by one with the gift of interpretation, glossolalia edifies the church (v. 5b, 13, 27). Thus as explained by Paul, "the gift of tongues was a genuine supernatural *charisma.*"[95] It is clear, however, that the apostle tempered the importance some Corinthians assigned to tongues-speaking. As a public exercise glossolalia is deficient since it lacks intelligibility and uninterpreted it does not profit hearers. Hence Paul concluded, "In the church I would rather speak five intelligible words to instruct others than ten thousand words in a tongue" (1 Cor. 14:19).

The third text, Romans 12:3–8, specifies (1) the gift of prophecy (*prophēteia*, v. 6), see 1 Corinthians 12:10 above. (2) The gift of serving (*diakonia*, Rom. 1: 7; cf. 1 Peter 4:11) designates the grace that enables Christians to minister to human needs, both physical and spiritual. (3) The gift of teaching (v. 7; cf. 1 Cor. 12:28; Eph. 4:11; cf. 2 Tim. 2:2) refers to the ability to instruct others in apostolic doctrine. (4) The gift of encouragement or exhortation (v. 8) concerns the ability to persuade others to follow the way of godliness. (5) The gift of contributing (v. 8) deals with the grace of sharing material resources with others in the name of Christ. (6) The gift of leadership (v. 8) refers to the ability to rule and provide direction to the church. And (7) the gift of showing mercy (v. 8) concerns acts of compassion directed to the needy.

In Ephesians 4:11–13 Paul identified several endowments of "grace" (v. 7) that edify and equip the body for service. These gifted ministries focus on leadership and teaching and include the work of (1) apostles (see 1 Cor. 12:28, above); (2) prophets (see 1 Cor. 12:10, above); (3) evangelists such as Philip (Acts 21:8) and Timothy (2 Tim. 4:5), who win the lost to Christ; (4) pastors (*poimenēs*), who patiently nurture the flock spiritually (cf. Acts 20:28; 1 Peter 5:2); and (5) teachers (Rom. 12:7; 1 Cor. 12:28–29), who edify the saints by instructing them in the faith. As noted above, the foundational ministries of the apostles and prophets ended with the close of the apostolic era, although certain apostolic and prophetic functions continue to the present.

Our survey of the spiritual gifts leads to the conclusion that, with the excep-

tions of the offices of apostle and prophet, Paul made no distinction between extraordinary ministries and gifts that have been rescinded and ordinary ministries and gifts applicable to the entire church age. To the question, "Are supernatural gifts of the Spirit available in the present era," Lovelace responds, "The plain import of the New Testament gives no hint that they are limited to the first century" (1 Cor. 14:39; 1 Thess. 5:19–21).[96] All the gifts are valid in the present age when exercised in love (1 Cor. 13:1–3). In 1 Corinthians 13:8 Paul states that "prophecies . . . will cease," "tongues . . . will be stilled," and "knowledge . . . will pass away." He adds, "when perfection [*to teleion*] comes, the imperfect disappears" (v. 10). The context of this statement (vv. 8–12) has a strong eschatological focus. Hence the "perfection" denotes the exchange of immortality for mortality at the Second Advent (cf. v. 12). "'The perfect' means the future world, in which everything imperfect (v. 9) which distinguishes our present world is overcome."[97] Turner concludes that "the New Testament does not envisage the cessation of the prototypical gifts; on the contrary, every indication suggests that Luke and Paul expected them to continue."[98]

As to whether true Christians can fall from salvation and be lost, consider the following. Paul's unbreakable circle of salvation in Romans 8:29–30 consists of a series of aorist verbs signifying past action—"foreknew," "predestined," "called," "justified," and "glorified." The final verb ("glorified") is a proleptic aorist, indicating that the action is so certain of occurrence that it is viewed as past. Salvation is a "package deal" embracing the whole of God's action from election in eternity past to glorification in eternity future. The following verses (vv. 31–39) ground the believer's eternal security in the Father's verdict of justification (cf. Rom. 5:1–2; Titus 3:7) and in the Son's atoning death, resurrection, and advocacy in heaven. Thus both with respect to the privileges of national Israel and Christian believers, "God's gift and his call are irrevocable" (Rom. 11:29).

Paul further grounded believers' final salvation in the Spirit's sealing ministry. The Holy Spirit grafts Christians into the body of Christ and steadfastly maintains them in this relationship to the end (Eph. 4:30). Paul added that God objectively "set his seal of ownership on us" and subjectively "put his Spirit in our hearts as a deposit [arrabōn], guaranteeing what is to come" (2 Cor. 1:22; cf. 5:5; Eph. 1:13–14). The Greek word arrabōn connotes a deposit that serves to guarantee the full payment at a later date. Thus "the Spirit as the present earnest of our future inheritance guarantees our complete, final salvation."[99]

Furthermore, believers are preserved to the end by God's perfect knowledge (2 Tim. 2:19a), unswerving faithfulness (1 Cor. 10:13; Phil. 1:6; 2 Thess. 3:3), and limitless power (1 Cor. 1:8–9; 2 Tim. 1:12). Hence Paul wrote to Corinthian believers: "Now it is God who makes both us and you stand firm in Christ" (2 Cor. 1:21; cf. 2 Tim. 4:18). This prior working of God motivates and strengthens Christians to persevere in the Way. Believers, for their part, exercise God-given faith (2 Cor. 1:24) and endurance (Rom. 2:7; Col. 1:23) and persist in the quest for holiness (1 Tim. 5:22; 2 Tim. 2:19b). The various warnings in Scripture to believe and stand firm are important means God uses to ensure believers' perseverance to the end.

Paul united these two strands of divine preservation and human perseverance in Philippians 2:12–13, where he urges believers, "Continue to work out your salvation with fear and trembling." The context plus the present imperative of katergazomai suggests the meaning "keep on working." But Paul recognized that believers' working is made possible by God's prior working in them. Thus he added, "For it is God who works in you to will and act according to his good purpose." The conjunction gar ("for," "since") indicates that "because God works and has worked, therefore men must and can work."[100]

But did not Paul teach that Christians can forfeit salvation in Christ? Did he not write to the Galatian Christians: "You have fallen away from grace" (Gal. 5:4)? Paul clarified the meaning of this statement by the immediately preceding: "You who are trying to be justified by law have been alienated from Christ." Paul's addressees were weak believers who, under the influence of Jewish legalists, lapsed in their understanding of God's plan of salvation by grace through faith. What the erring believers did was to defect from a theology of justification by grace to a theology of justification by law-keeping. Paul expressed confidence that the erring saints would soon return to the truth (v. 10).

Other Pauline texts that prima facie might suggest loss of salvation actually teach potential loss of heavenly rewards. The believer's eternal rewards are not carnal objects like gold and silver coins, but degrees of noble employment in heaven and the capacity to enjoy God (Matt. 25:21, 23; cf. Matt. 16:27; 1 Cor. 3:8; Rev. 22:12). Paul wrote concerning the Christian's works in the day of judgment: "If what he has built survives, he will receive his reward. If it is burned up, he will suffer loss; he himself will be saved, but only as one escaping through the flames" (1 Cor. 3:14–15). Having built on the proper foundation, which is Jesus Christ (v. 11), believers will inherit eternal life, even if the works that follow are of inferior quality (v. 13).

Similarly, "I beat my body and make it my slave so that after I have preached to others, I myself will not be disqualified for the prize" (1 Cor. 9:27). Paul buffeted his body, thereby restraining sinful impulses, so that when the fruit of his service is examined in the judgment he will not be *adokimos*, or "unapproved."

Other problematic texts attest Christian *backsliding* rather than loss of salvation. Paul wrote, "Demas, because he loved this world, has deserted me and gone to Thessalonica" (2 Tim. 4:10). Earlier Demas was one of Paul's close associates (Col. 4:14) and "fellow-workers" (Philem. 24). Overcome by a worldly spirit, Demas the believer set his heart on possessions rather than on Christ's service. Other texts teach the *apostasy* of professing Christians who were unconverted. "By rejecting conscience, certain persons have suffered shipwreck in the faith; among them are Hymenaeus and Alexander, whom I have turned over to Satan, so that they may learn not to blaspheme" (1 Tim. 1:19–20 NRSV). The two persons cited willfully rejected *tēn pistin*, the essentials of the Christian faith. According to 2 Timothy 2:17–18 (NRSV), Hymenaeus and Philetus "swerved from the truth" (*tēn alētheian*) by claiming that the resurrection had already taken place: "They are upsetting the faith of some." Hymenaeus was an unconverted false teacher, whose teaching was "godless" and "ungodly" (v. 16). Paul added that Alexander "did . . . a great deal of harm" (2 Tim. 4:14)—perhaps by testifying against Paul in Rome—and that he "strongly opposed" their message (v. 15). Because Hymenaeus and Alexander showed themselves to be unbelievers by blaspheming the truth (cf. Rev. 13:6; 17:3), Paul removed them from the church. The apostle was acutely aware of demonically inspired false teachers in the churches who would lead many professing Christians astray. "In later times some will abandon the faith and follow deceiving spirits and things taught by demons" (1 Tim. 4:1). The verb *aphistēmi* is a strong verb meaning to "fall away," or "become apostate."

The Johannine Literature

John's statement "We know that when he appears, we shall be like him, for we shall see him as he is" (1 John 3:2) indicates that sanctification will be completed only at the resurrection when believers behold Christ and become like him. Only then will Christians experience moral purity (v. 3), absence of sins (v. 5), and actual righteousness (v. 7). In the meanwhile, believers further their sanctification by abiding in Christ (John 15:4,7), walking in the light of God's presence (1 John 1:7), holding fast to their Christian profession (Rev. 2:25; 3:11), turning from sin (1 John 3:3), continuing in Christ's teaching (John 14:23; 15:7), and submitting to providential discipline (John 15:2). Realistically Christians do commit sins, for as Jesus said to his disciples: "A person who has had a bath needs only to wash his feet; his whole body is clean. And you are clean" (John 13:10). The disciples were "clean" in the sense that past sins and guilt had been canceled; hence they had no need to be entirely bathed (*louō*, v. 10). Nevertheless their feet needed to be washed (*niptō*, vv. 5–6, 8, 10), signifying the forgiveness of sins that arise daily from our fallen nature. Moreover, 1 John 1:8 states that those who deny the reality of sin (*hamartia*) deceive themselves. First John 1:10 adds that those who claim that they have not committed sinful acts make God out to be a liar. John, in his old age, acknowledged sins in his life and sensed the need for divine forgiveness (1 John 1:7, 9). Concerning the preceding verses, Plummer wrote of "that constant cleansing which even the holiest Christians need.''[101] Yet John stated that the believer who abides in Christ does not live a life of habitual sin (1 John 3:6). John reasoned that ''no one who is born of God will continue to sin, because God's seed [*sperma*] remains in him; he cannot go on sinning because he has been born of God'' (v. 9). Since believers possess a new ''nature'' through regeneration, sin does not rule their lives.

The claim of the churches in the Holiness Movement that Jesus' act of enduing his disciples with the Holy Spirit (John 20:22) represents the second-blessing gift of entire sanctification is exegetically weak. What happened in the Upper Room was a unique and nonrepeatable event. The Spirit could be given only after Jesus was glorified. After he had risen from the grave Christ infused his Spirit into the disciples and sent them into the world in his name. ''What John records is no mere anticipation of Pentecost but a real impartation of the Spirit for the purpose specified. The Pentecostal outpouring of the Spirit was more public, and involved the birth of the Spirit-indwelt community, the church of the new age.''[102]

Concerning whether a true believer can forfeit salvation, consider Jesus' allegory of the vine and the branches (John 15:1–8). Jesus said, ''My Father . . . cuts off every branch in me that bears no fruit, while every branch that does bear fruit he prunes so that it will be even more fruitful'' (vv. 1–2). The dry and fruitless branches cut off signify professed believers whom Christ rejects because their relation to him was not genuine. ''The absence of fruit in the branch of the vine casts grave doubt upon its real union with the central stem, however attractive it may appear. Such useless members must be cut off; perhaps Judas is the outstanding example.''[103] Does Jesus' exhortation ''Remain in me, and I will remain in you''

(v. 4) suggest that the disciples' salvation is conditioned upon unbroken abiding? Certainly believers' security can never be divorced from faith, obedience, and perseverance. But, as Beasley-Murray observes, ''The emphasis in the passage is on *Jesus,* the Vine, hence it is more likely that a note of encouragement is intended here, 'and be assured, I am remaining in union with you.' In the divine relationship grace is alike the source and support of faith.''[104]

Does 1 John 5:16 (''There is a sin that leads to death'') teach that a Christian may forfeit salvation? Here John encourages Christians to pray for a fellow believer when he is guilty of wrongdoing, described as a ''sin that does not lead to death'' (v. 17). In response to prayer God will renew that brother's spiritual life. But not every sinner can be given spiritual life through an intercessor's prayer. The ''sin that leads to death,'' for which prayer is not commanded, refers to the deliberate denial of the Son of God on the part of false teachers (cf. 2 John 7, 9–10). Their persistent opposition to Christ puts them beyond the reach of God's gift of spiritual life (John 8:24). Thus Jesus' teaching in Matthew 12:31–32 is corroborated by 1 John 5:16.

John, indeed, affirmed that those who withdrew from the believing community never were saved in the first place. ''They went out from us, but they did not really belong to us. For if they had belonged to us, they would have remained with us; but their going showed that none of them belonged to us'' (1 John 2:19). God grants those who are saved the grace to endure; those who fail to endure do so because they never possessed regenerating and preserving grace.

Positively, those who believe in the Son immediately possess eternal life (John 3:15–16, 36; 5:24; 6:40, 47; 1 John 5:11–13). The life Jesus bestows on believers is eternal (*aiōnios*) both qualitatively (a radically new kind of life) and quantitatively (life without end). Moreover, Jesus taught that true believers never will be condemned or come into judgment (John 3:18; 5:24); judgment is forever behind those who are united to Christ. In addition, Christians are those who have successfully completed the passage from a state of death to a state of life (John 5:24; 1 John 3:14). The perfect tense of *metabainō* in the last two texts upholds the irreversibility of the believer's new status.

John further taught the certainty of the believer's final salvation in 1 John 5:18: "We know that anyone born of God [perfect passive participle of *gennaō*, to bear] does not continue to sin; the one who was born of God [aorist passive participle of *gennaō*] keeps him safe, and the evil one cannot harm him." Believers do not persist in a life of sin, for the uniquely begotten Son preserves and keeps them safe from the deadly attacks of Satan (cf. John 10:28; 17:12, 15). The Evil One is not able to "take hold of" (present middle indicative of *haptō*) Christians in the sense of inflicting spiritual harm on them.

After stating that he gives his sheep eternal life, Jesus in John 10:28–30 promised that "they shall never perish" (*ou mē apolōntai eis ton aiōna*). The Greek emphatic double negative indicates that the sheep assuredly will not be forever lost. The Lord then added, "No one can snatch them out of my hand," affirming that no power can seize the elect from his secure grip. Finally, the Father and the Son guarantee the security of the sheep in the unity of their being and purpose. Jesus stated in John 6:39–40 that believers as a whole and each believer individually will be kept by the Father's purpose and the Son's power, and so will be raised to heavenly glory. "In this perfect unity of will and purpose the Father

and the Son stand engaged for the salvation of all believers."[105] God secures the final salvation of every true believer by effecting his free perseverance in faith and obedience (cf. Rev. 12:11).

Jesus' effectual prayers to the Father enable Christians to endure in faith. According to John 17:6–19, Jesus interceded for his disciples, petitioning the Father to protect them from the Evil One (v. 11, 15) and consecrate them from worldly to holy purposes (v. 17, 19). In verses 20–26 Jesus prayed for believers of all times, petitioning the Father that they might be spiritually one (vv. 21–23), that they might know the love of the Father for the Son (v. 26), and that they might be with Christ in heavenly glory (v. 24). By virtue of the Son's perfect obedience in life and death, his prayers to the Father are effectual: "I knew that you always hear me" (John 11:42). Thus the Father faithfully honors the Son's prayers for the preservation of his chosen people. First John 2:1 teaches that God's provision for postconversion sins is the advocacy of the "Righteous One," who presents the believer's case before the Father in heaven and secures from the latter forgiveness and cleansing.

Other New Testament Literature

Although the literature teaches positional sanctification (Heb. 10:10, 29), it focuses more on the process of growth toward Christlikeness (2 Peter 3:18; cf. Heb. 10:14; 1 Peter 2:2). Hebrews uniquely portrays Christ as high priest who sanctifies his people by purifying their consciences of guilt, cleansing them from inner defilement, and making them fit to approach God in worship (Heb. 9:14; 10:22). Although God takes the initiative in sanctification, believers must put forth effort in the quest for holiness (2 Peter 1:5–7; cf. Heb. 12:14). Given the fleshly lusts that war against the soul (1 Peter 2:11; cf. Heb. 12:14), the Christian life involves real struggle. James flatly denied that saints attain sinless perfection in this life: "We all stumble in many ways" (James 3:2). The present iterative of *ptaiō*, means that believers repeatedly err morally and spiritually. Yet in obedience to God's command to be holy (1 Peter 1:15) believers press on toward spiritual wholeness or maturity (*teleiotēs*, Heb. 6:1; cf. James 1:4). Believers are made perfect only at death when they attain blessedness in heaven (Heb. 12:23).[106]

As to whether salvation can be forfeited, the lot of those who trust Christ is said to be an "eternal redemption" (Heb. 9:12), an "eternal inheritance" (Heb. 9:15), and an "eternal glory" (1 Peter 5:10). From the divine side believers are said to be "kept by Jesus Christ" (Jude 1:1; cf. 1 Peter 1:4), "shielded by God's power" (1 Peter 1:5), and guarded by God's faithfulness and strength (Jude 24). Yet on the human side believers must persist in doing God's will (Heb. 10:36) and diligently maintain a love relationship with him (Jude 21). Christians *persevere* by virtue of God's effectual *preservation*.

How shall we understand the debated Hebrews 6:4–6 text? The Jewish Christian addressees lacked assurance of their position in Christ (Heb. 6:11) and so had become spiritually sluggish (Heb. 6:12; cf. 5:11). In this immature condition (Heb. 5:12–13) and under the pressures of persecution (Heb. 10:32–34) they were tempted to revert to Judaism. Those warned are described by four aorist participles: (1) They "have been enlightened" (*phōthisthentos*, v. 4), which signifies the spiritual illumination they received at their new birth (cf. Heb. 10:32; cf. Eph. 1:18). (2) They "have tasted the heavenly gift" (*geusamenous*, v. 4), where tasting metaphorically connotes personal spiritual experience (Ps. 34:8;

1 Peter 2:3). This phrase suggests that the readers had firsthand knowledge of God's grace in Jesus Christ (cf. Eph. 3:7). "*Tasted the heavenly gift* . . . refers to those who, through repentance and faith, have had a definite spiritual experience of Jesus Christ."[107] (3) They "have shared in the Holy Spirit" (*metochous genēthentas*, v. 4), where the noun *metochos*, "one who shares in" (cf. Heb. 3:1, 14, 12:8) signifies a genuine participation in the Spirit who is the seal of the new birth.

Furthermore, (4) they "have tasted the goodness of the word of God and the powers of the coming age" (*geusamenos*, v. 5). This additional tasting (cf. v. 4) denotes personal experience of God's Word (*rhēma*) and mighty works (*dynameis*) characteristic of the new age. The "once" (*hapax*, cf. 9:26–28; 10:2; 12:26–27) points to an experience that is complete. Thus the addressees likely were genuine believers in Christ. The writer continues by saying that "it is impossible" for these "if they fall away, to be brought back to repentance" (vv. 4, 6). The word *adynaton* signifies an actual impossibility (cf. 6:18; 10:4; 11:6). The aorist participle of *parapiptō* (to "fall away") probably is conditional and refers to repudiation of Christ. The writer thus argued that if the wavering Jewish believers forsake Christ they forfeit all possibility of repentance unto life, since they abandon the only basis for salvation, which is Jesus Christ, our effectual high priest. The fact that the writer shifted from the first person (vv. 1, 3) to the third person ("those," "they," vv. 4, 6) and the words "in your case" (v. 9) suggest that he was confident the actual defection of the "*agapētoi*" would not occur.[108] Their good works, love, and service to the saints (v. 10) confirm their perseverance. This stern warning issued to wavering Jewish Christians (cf. 3:12–13; 12:25) represents an important divine strategy for achieving believers' perseverance in the faith. This text focuses on the side of *human* responsibility in the preservation-perseverance relation. Others who do apostatize were not Christians in the first place (cf. Heb. 3:14; 1 John 2:19).[109]

In Hebrews 10:26–31 the author again warned Jewish Christian believers against spurning Christ, the covenant, and the Christian assembly. That the readers had "received the knowledge of the truth" (*epignōsis tēs alētheias*, v. 26; cf. 6:4) and had been sanctified by the blood of the covenant (v. 29) suggests that they were genuine Christians. Abandonment of God's truth and reversion to Judaism amounts to contemptuous rejection of Christ, a profane attitude to his sacrifice, and insolent spurning of the Spirit of grace (v. 29). The penalty for forsaking the only effectual sacrifice for sins (v. 26b) is fiery judgment (vv. 27–31). Hebrews 10:26–31 should be understood in the same sense as 6:4–6, namely, as a stern warning against forsaking Christ and reverting to the ineffectual religion of Judaism. In both texts the author is confident that his readers will not abandon Christ but will continue in faith unto final salvation (v. 39; cf. 6:9).

Second Peter 2:1 describes "false prophets" who "secretly introduce destructive heresies, even denying the sovereign Lord who bought them," and then mentions the "swift destruction" that is their end. Peter's further description of them as "brute beasts, creatures of instinct" (v. 12), "springs without water" (v. 17), and "slaves of depravity" (v. 19) suggests that the false prophets were unregenerate. According to verses 20–21 they had gained some knowledge of Christ and the Gospel, broke with the world, and entered the church. But later they turned their backs on Christ, returned to the world, and taught abominable heresies. Their actions reminded Peter of two prov-

erbs: (1) "A dog returns to its vomit" and (2) "A sow . . . goes back to her wallowing in the mud" (v. 22). These facts, together with no mention of repentance and faith, suggest that 2 Peter describes apostasy proper—i.e., deliberate rejection of the Gospel by persons with a knowledge of Christ that was superficial rather than genuine.[110] Jude described similar (proto-Gnostic?) apostate teachers in Jude 4, 8, 10–13, 16–19.

SYSTEMATIC FORMULATION

We now attempt to integrate the historical perspectives on sanctification and perseverance, insofar as they conform to Scripture, into a valid and coherent whole.

The Meaning and Mandate of Sanctification

Having entered God's kingdom by the new birth, we continue in it as ambassadors under Christ's dominion. Christians are not isolated spiritual hermits but agents of a great spiritual kingdom. So the converted seek to develop characteristics like those of their King. Consider the following two aspects of the believer's sanctification:

1. Sanctification assumes that the *forensic status* of justification is permanent. The completeness of Christ's imputed righteousness continues throughout this life and beyond. "By one sacrifice he has made perfect forever those who are being made holy" (Heb. 10:14). Christ is "our righteousness" (1 Cor. 1:30). By virtue of Christ's tested and confirmed righteous status before the law, the believing may be called "saints" (1 Cor. 1:2), though still far from becoming in experience what they are legally in Christ.

2. Sanctification also involves a *liberating process to be actively pursued* in order that we may become experiential-

ly what we are forensically. Freed from the guilt of sin, we seek to be liberated from its power. God enjoins us to "make every effort to . . . be holy" (Heb. 12:14). An active, Spirit-enabled pursuit of holiness frees one from domination by the world to become an agent of God's redemptive kingdom. The process of sanctification involves growth both in spiritual relationships and in ethical behaviors in a progressively realized redemption.

> Redemption is the deliverance from the power of an alien dominion and enjoyment of the resulting freedom. . . . It often involves the idea of restoration to one who possesses a more fundamental right or interest. The heart of the Biblical message of redemption is the deliverance of the people of God from the bondage of sin by the perfect substitutionary sacrifice of Jesus Christ and their consequent restoration to God and his heavenly kingdom.[111]

What does it mean for Christians to seek first the kingdom of God and his righteousness? It means wholly placing their lives within the Father's will under Christ's lordship through the power of the Holy Spirit. By renewing and strengthening abilities to know, love, and serve God, the Spirit enables Christians to overcome addictions. Saints can stand fast in their Christian liberty and not to be "burdened again by a yoke of slavery" (Gal. 5:1). Christians stand firm against the perversion of healthy desires. The sanctified spirit calls also for freedom from ecclesiastical tyrannies such as those faced during the Reformation by Martin Luther as described in his essay *Christian Liberty*. The maturing will not be dominated by the unprincipled feelings of modernity or authoritarian cult leaders. Growing Christians also demand liberation from political tyrannies like those of communism. They demand freedom to worship God by tearing down Berlin walls.[112]

The *objective* of this liberating pursuit of moral integrity is to be holy as God is holy (1 Peter 1:15–16). God's holiness involves his awesome transcendent uniqueness and unapproachable moral excellence. As holy, the living God is incomparably transcendent in being and completely righteous in character. The goal of the Christian life is nothing less than uniqueness from the world, ethical perfection of character, and spiritual perfection in communion with the divine Spirit and all others (Matt. 5:48; Col. 1:28). To grow in sanctification is to recover godlike qualities of character and restore lost relationships.

The *paradigm* of transcendent holiness in history is Jesus Christ. In his worldview not all was God and not all was good. He did not worship the totality of creation. His critical discernment directed devotion away from idols to the Creator, the covenant-making God of Abraham. He resisted repeated Satanic temptations and daily consecrated himself to purity of heart and self-giving love. Christ's decision making for God's redemptive kingdom was directed, furthermore, by universal and necessary moral principles of law. So Jesus exhibited *par excellence* the sanctified life characterized by a discerning growth in biblical knowledge as well as growth in the graces of the Spirit (Gal. 5:22–26). The sanctified Christian life progressively involves critical thought, worthy desires, kingdom purposes, moral character, and loving relationships. In other words, sanctified spirituality involves maturation in "the whole measure of the fullness of Christ" (Eph. 4:13).

The truth that edifies the believer in this context is not an irrational fascination with secretive, neo-gnostic mysteries. In *The Idea of the Holy*, Rudolph Otto depicted holiness as an experience beginning with nonconceptual fascination with the sacred, called the "numinous." The literature on spirituality in alternative religions indicates that this mysterious feeling is without a rational aspect altogether and beyond moral valuation.[113] But Otto wrote that in the New Testament "we must no longer understand by 'the holy' or 'sacred' the merely numinous in general, nor even the numinous as its own highest development; we must always understand by it the numinous completely permeated and saturated with elements signifying rationality, purpose, personality, morality."[114] But Otto seems to contradict this statement with his claim that in knowing the "peace that passes all understanding" we return to a way of "knowing" that is not merely incomprehensible; it is exclusive of conceptual understanding.[115] Again he wrote, "The mysterious, on the other hand, is that which lies altogether outside what can be thought, and is, alike in form, quality, and essence, the utterly and 'wholly other.' "[116] It is, rather, that the Creator has made us capable of thinking true thoughts about his being, activities, and relationships in order that we might relate significantly to him and serve his kingdom.

The truth that leads to godliness is conceptual, and its promises have been conveyed in human languages. The "faith and knowledge" of which Paul spoke rested on "the hope of eternal life, which God, who does not lie, promised before the beginning of time" (Titus 1:2). God's "divine power has given us everything we need for life and godliness through our knowledge of him" (2 Peter 1:3). The context specifies that the knowledge in view comes from the prophetic Word (vv. 12–21). Wisdom for maturing in Christlikeness is found in the Spirit-inspired and Spirit-illumined Word of God.

In a fallen world not all spiritual experiences are of God. Given the reality of evil spirits and our own sinful inclinations, we need to grow in moral and spiritual discernment. If all were God, as in pantheistic worldviews, one could uncritically worship anything or anyone. But the Creator is distinct from creation; thus to avoid idolatry we must discern what we worship (Rom. 1:25). Since Satan is the ultimate father of lies and since evil powers sometimes appear as angels of light, many sincerely devoted people have experienced the evil Deceiver rather than the Author of truth and goodness.

Two basic steps are involved in a discerning pursuit of holiness by the way of the Cross. We sanctify ourselves (1) by dying to, or separating ourselves from, the morally evil lifestyles of our culture and (2) by rising anew, or dedicating ourselves to knowing, loving, and serving the values of the Lord of providence and redemption. Motivated existentially by gratitude and love, committed converts refuse to be merely average Christians; they identify themselves as unique people of God dedicated to holistic intellectual, moral, and spiritual excellence (1 Thess. 5:23). Separating ourselves from the dominance of the desires of the old nature, we develop the desires of a new nature. The experience of growth is not so much one of an exchanged life as exchanged moral and spiritual inclinations.

The Holistic Results of Sanctification

Consider the effects of sanctification on the believer's total person. *Ontologically,* the process of sanctification involves developing control of the *body and spirit.* Paul commands the repentant regularly to mortify evil temptations and to offer their bodies "as living sacrifices, holy and pleasing to God— which is [their] spiritual worship" (Rom. 12:1). Citizens of God's kingdom avoid immorality because they belong to Christ. "It is God's will that you should be holy; that you should avoid sexual immorality; that each of you should learn to control his own body in a way that is holy and honorable, not in passionate lust like the heathen, who do not know God" (1 Thess. 4:3–5). Through regular exercise saints develop growing self-control over their physical capabilities and use them for kingdom values (1 Cor. 6:19). The body is good when received with thanksgiving, consecrated to uses consistent with the Word, and dedicated by prayer (1 Tim. 4:3–5). Avoiding myths, we should train ourselves, above all else, to be godly. "For physical training is of some value, but godliness has value for all things, holding promise for both the present life and the life to come" (v. 8). The health of the soul, likewise, is developed by disciplined exercise of its intellectual, emotional, volitional, and relational capacities as follows:

Intellectually, Christians develop control of their *thought life.* In a fallen world we cannot control every thought as it enters our minds, but the twice-born need not be mastered by unworthy considerations. Christians have available the resources to "take captive every thought to make it obedient to Christ" (2 Cor. 10:5). "The weapons we fight with are not the weapons of the world. On the contrary," we "have divine power to demolish strongholds" (v. 4). Annihilating unworthy thoughts we contemplate in their place what is "true . . . noble . . . right . . . pure . . . lovely . . . admirable . . . [and] praiseworthy" (Phil. 4:8). Growth in conceptual knowledge is not an end in itself; it should lead to developing *wisdom,* which is the use of knowledge for Christlike ends in being, relating, and serving our culture. Some students of theology fear that they may learn too much. But Jesus was omniscient, and his vast knowledge was no hindrance. Rather, his understanding enhanced his spirituality. It is a little knowledge that "puffs up" (1 Cor. 8:1). The greater occupational hazard is making theology an *end* in itself. Studying *about* God is no substitute for relating effectively *to* God. Faithfulness in thought is indispensable to Christlikeness, but in itself it is insufficient for sanctification.

Emotionally, the justified mature as the outward expression of inner *feelings and desires.* The Christian's goal is not desirelessness; *evil* desires alone are sinful. God the Father is not apathetic but is afflicted with all the afflictions of his people (cf. Isa. 63:9). Jesus had strong emotions and was far from dispassionate. He wept with those who wept at the grave of Lazarus, and he celebrated at weddings and feasts. At the prospect of an agonizing death he struggled with a heavy heart. But the Lord's emotions always were appropriate and controlled. Similarly our hearts should be set on things above (Col. 3:1). It need not be selfish to desire eternal fellowship with God, but it is wrong to desire to exist independent of God. Negatively, Christians will not fan the flames of fleshly desires. Affirmatively, they fan the flames of holy desires through regular praise, petition, and meditation on God's character and purposes. Our problems do not begin with our environments, families, neighbors, or even Satan. Our problems come from within us (James 4:1). "Each one is tempted when, by his own evil desire, he is dragged away and enticed" (1:14). Our sanctification cannot be provided by parents, church, or school. A health club cannot *give* a person health; one must work out regularly. A godly life starts from within—from a single-minded, humble thirst for righteousness.

Volitionally, in the power of the Spirit converts make *Christlike moral decisions* and keep them. The freedom to decide on what we know and love as right is one aspect of the inner person; the ability to do this is another. Believers need not remain enslaved to sinful ways. People with Spirit-renewed wills need not yield to sin's enticements. Their "No" can mean "No!" As the disciplined exercise good choices and acts, holy habits are formed. They grow in acting, not according to the flesh, but according to the Spirit. So converts are divinely enabled to overcome evil desires within, temptations from worldly associates, and demonic assaults. Many members of first-century churches had power to persevere in overcoming temptations (e.g., Rev. 2:7, 11, 17). "The difference between unfreedom and freedom is not the difference between being bound and unbound, but rather between false and true bondage."[117] Christians are freed from sin to determine actions in harmony with their new moral nature. Although we may be temporarily influenced by our old natures, evil people, or demonic aspects of our cultures, we are not wholly and permanently controlled by our evil inclinations, circumstances, or other people. Believing men and women are not mere victims of their families, schools, churches, or communities. They are responsible agents to determine their own activities in accord with the desires exemplified in the life of Christ and explained in the moral teaching of Scripture.

Relationally, for the believer love is the primary *motivation* of distinctively Christian associations. Since love is a settled purpose of will as well as a feeling, Spirit-led Christians overcome tendencies to self-centeredness and release their ability to minister to others, particularly the poor. Is caring for one another a mark of a Christian or an empty ideal? Among the ruins of Germany following World War II, Helmut Thielicke said, "Love for the ideal can be controlled and made whole only if the ideal grows out of love. Therefore the excesses of false idealism cannot be removed by rationalistic attack; they can be fought only with the power of idealizing which is bestowed by love."[118] With volitional freedom to honor God and his kingdom, Christians should obediently develop loving relationships with God and others, especially the destitute.

Our pursuit of holiness will be completed when Christ returns to rule on earth. It is unrealistic and unbiblical to anticipate complete Christlikeness during our lifetimes. "But we know that when he appears, we shall be like him, for we shall see him as he is" (1 John 3:2). Meanwhile this hope motivates the present process. "Everyone who has this hope in him purifies himself, just as he is pure" (v. 3).

Divine Initiatives in the Process of Sanctification

Sanctification is *a response to the Holy Spirit's initiatives* much as conversion is. In the continual moral and spiritual warfare against our integrity, we need the enablement of the Spirit's multiple ministries. Contrary to Wesleyanism, the Spirit does not annihilate the old desires (Gal 5:16–17; cf. Rom. 7). But what in the weakness of the old fleshly nature we cannot do, we can realize through the Spirit (Rom 8:3–4). We need to rely on the Spirit of grace in order to grow progressively through life's challenging stages. People with sinful inclinations need more than secular counsel, as valuable as it may be in alleviating symptoms. We need the wisdom, love, and power of the all-holy Lord of the universe. Although Christian spirituality occasionally engages in introspection, in contrast to pantheistic spiritualities it does not simply look for needed resources within the self. Christian growth in spirituality ultimately derives from responsiveness to the transcendent Spirit's transforming ministries. We have already considered the activity of the Spirit in internal calling, conversion, regeneration, and reconciliation. It remains to contemplate such ministries of the Spirit as baptizing, gifting, indwelling, filling, leading, and guiding:

1. The Holy Spirit *baptizes all believers into the body of Christ*. While water baptism introduces believers to a local church, Spirit baptism incorporates all converts into the universal body of Christ (1 Cor. 12:13). In 1 Corinthians Paul addressed all church members at Corinth and everywhere who call on the name of Christ (1:2)— including erring and disobedient saints. Paul recognized that *every Christian* has been baptized by the Spirit. Paul followed Jesus, who acknowledged only two classes of people: those baptized by the Spirit and those who will be baptized by the unquenchable fire of divine judgment (Matt. 3:11–12).

The Spirit unites people to the body of Christ at the *time* of their conversion. Christians need not seek the baptism of the Spirit as a crisis experience or second work of grace after salvation. Believers may properly wait for the *filling* of the Spirit, for as Jesus said to his disciples: "Stay in the city [Jerusalem] until you have been clothed with power from on high" (Luke 24:49). Two ministries of the Spirit occurred at Pentecost: the baptism of believers into Christ's body, the church (Acts 1:5), and the filling of the Spirit-bestowing power for service (v. 8).

Like water baptism, the baptism of the Spirit *occurs but once* in a person's life. The figure of "baptism" makes the point of an initiatory rite that occurs once-for-all. For the believers present at Pentecost, Spirit baptism was not repeated; but the Spirit's filling did occur several times. Their experiences of the Spirit's filling are recorded in several different contexts (Acts 2:4; 4:8, 31; 9:17; 13:9).

The distinguishing *function* of the Holy Spirit's baptism is to unite all believers to their Head and to one another in one body, removing impediments to fellowship among the reconciled. Both believing rich and poor, black and white, parents and children are under the one Head of the church. All believers are spiritually equal by sheer grace. For "all of you who were baptized into Christ have clothed yourselves with Christ. There is neither Jew nor Greek, slave nor free, male nor female, for you are all one in Christ Jesus (Gal. 3:27–28). In Christ by the Spirit all have the "full rights" of God's children and are heirs of heavenly riches (4:4–7). Members of the one universal church have equal rights, whether male or female, whether white, yellow, red, or brown.

> In this strange initiatory rite called baptism, all the old, rather silly distinctions get washed away. We find ourselves in a new community that is accountable to a new story. . . . This makes it all the more incomprehensible that the church, of all societies, should now be found attempting to order its life on the basis of distinctions (quotas) that belong to the old order rather than the new.[119]

What is the *evidence* of being baptized by the Spirit? It is not necessarily tongues-speaking. Although the sign of speaking in other tongues was given when the church began at Pentecost and when Gentiles were added to the one body (Acts 10:46), tongues-speaking was not an invariable *evidence* of participation in the one body for the Samaritans (Acts 8:1–8), Paul (9:1–19), or Lydia (16:11–15). Neither do all believers have the *gift* of speaking in tongues (1 Cor. 12:30). All are baptized by the Spirit into the one body at their conversion; but all need not speak in tongues.

The distinctive *ministry of the Spirit in the New Testament* is baptism into the one body of Christ. At Christ's ascension Spirit baptism was still future (Acts 1:5). At Pentecost the Spirit formed the church as one organism that would include Jewish, Samaritan, and Gentile believers. The forming of a church from every tribe and nation previously had been a mystery (Eph. 3:6). The distinctive work of the Spirit in the New Testament is not grace, for grace was operative in Old Testament times. It is not regeneration, for Nicodemus should have understood that from the Old Testament (John 3: 1–8). It is not the fruit of the Spirit (Gal. 5:22–23), for Old Testament saints exhibited these characteristics. It is not the filling of the Spirit, for people were filled with the Spirit in Old Testament times for specific ministries. It is not the Spirit's presence with believing Jews or Gentiles individually. It is *the Spirit's presence with them collectively and permanently in the church* (John 14:16–17).

2. The Holy Spirit graciously *bestows gifts* upon each believer in the body "just as he determines" (1 Cor. 12:11). Not all saints are given the same gifts. More gifts mean more responsibility, not more reasons to boast. All are to discover and faithfully use their gifts as good stewards to strengthen the body and to make it a blessing to the whole world. For these ends the Spirit does two things: (1) He renews and redirects basic capacities (which he gave with foresight providentially), and (2) he may also bestow some new distinctive abilities. All gifts are the results of grace, temporal or redemptive, and provide no grounds for boasting. For a listing of the gifts see the Biblical Teaching section (Rom. 12:3–8; 1 Cor. 12:28–31; Eph. 4:11–13).

Some gifts were unique to the first century, and so ought to not be sought or expected today. Verified *apostles* were given gifts for their unique foundational ministries. In the strict sense of eyewitnesses to the incarnate Messiah and his resurrection, apostles ceased after the deaths of the first-century eyewitnesses (Acts 1:21–22). If we define an apostle more broadly as one sent by God to bring the Gospel to unreached peoples, some exercise that function today. But no one in our day is an apostle in the strict sense of a spokesman for Christ who is Spirit-inspired to write books with canonical authority. *Prophets,* similarly, were spokesmen for God inspired to write books of the Old Testament. In that foundational sense none today should claim to be prophets. Only in a looser sense can those who communicate God's Word for strengthening, encouragement, and comfort do the work of prophets (1 Cor. 14:2). Such prophetic speaking and teaching are the better gifts to be eagerly desired (1 Cor. 12:28, 30).

Today's Spirit-given abilities are intended to be as *permanent* as the Christian's life of service. Although they are always dependent on the Spirit's power for fruitfulness, they do not appear to be temporary "gracelets" for each need that arises. The gifts are to be developed by regular, disciplined use. The gift of pastor-teacher, for example, is not given and removed at each worship service or class session, but remains while the recipients live what they teach. It is the Spirit's filling and enduement with power for fruitfulness that comes and goes, not the gifts.

3. The Holy Spirit's *indwelling* is a figure of speech indicating the permanence of the redemptive relationship beginning at conversion. Since the Spirit does not have extension in space, we do not think of his indwelling literally (physically) at a location in the body (such as the heart or brain). The latter were figurative expressions for the inner person who thinks, feels, wills, and relates. Nevertheless, our bodies are now the temples of the Holy Spirit individually (1 Cor. 6:19–20) and corporately (3:16–17). We no longer need travel to the most holy place of a

portable tabernacle or a permanent temple (Heb. 13:11–14). Now God manifests his holy presence most awesomely in his people personally and as gathered in the church. The Spirit manifests his presence insofar as believers progressively redirect their desires and commitments, depart from evil, and dedicate themselves to what honors the Lord.

4. The Holy Spirit's *witness* to the truths of the Gospel assures believers that they are children of God and that they personally belong to the body of Christ (Rom. 8:15–16; Gal 4:6–7). The Spirit stimulates receptivity to inspired teaching in order to relate life to the realities designated. As a result of the Holy Spirit's presence we are "sealed for the day of redemption" (Eph. 4:30). The *seal* of the Spirit's continuous presence and ministries assures believers not only that they are God's children but also that they will persevere in their newfound faith and life.

5. Closely associated with the Spirit's witness to the Gospel is his *illumination* of all that the Scriptures teach. This ministry of the Spirit enables converts to assent to revealed teaching as objectively true to reality, subjectively receive it for themselves, and relate to the realities designated. (See *IT*, 1:167–68).

6. The Counselor's *guidance or leading* stimulates believers to apply wisely the moral principles of the Word to specific life situations. The divine Counselor helps Christ's followers to remember his teachings (John 14:26), thus supplanting fear with peace (v. 27). How can we know God's desires for our lives? The Spirit's method of leading frees us from occultists' guidance via ouija boards, crystal balls, and mediums. The wise divine Counselor guides his maturing people by suggesting their active application of biblical principles toward making decisions and following through in action. Since the completion of the New Testament, Christians do not need additional special revelation to live up to; the sixty-six books of Scripture are sufficient for us to become "thoroughly equipped for every good work" (2 Tim. 3:17). Our great need personally is to *receive* the publicly revealed guidelines and wisely *apply* them to the specific areas of our own accountability. We do the will of God when, as God's new covenant people, we behave like Christ, actively yielded to the purposes of his kingdom within and around us (see also *IT*, 1:332–34).

7. Our repeated *fillings* with the Holy Spirit enable us to become more consciously aware of his communion and more bold in witness to the world. Although the Spirit continuously abides with all believers, no one always consciously experiences the Spirit's fellowship or relies on his power. Hence we need repeatedly to "be filled with the Spirit" (Eph. 5:18). We are not filled with power but with the Spirit. The power of God ought not be separated from the Holy Spirit and made an entity we can manipulate. How is one person filled with another person? We do not, like a ventriloquist's dummy, require every thought and word to be put in our mouths by another. But we may be greatly influenced by others and particularly by our peers. We are in considerable measure the products of the values and attitudes we hear from others. But our communion with the Spirit should be such that the dominant factor influencing our attitudes, expressions, and actions is the Holy Spirit. The Spirit fills God's people when, in response to his persuasion of the truth, they increasingly overcome the dominion of the fleshly attitudes and yield more fully to the Spirit's leading toward inner moral integrity and outward servant leadership.

What are the explicit *biblical indications* of the Spirit's filling (Eph. 5:18)? When the apostles were filled, they spoke the Word of God boldly (Acts 4:31) and experienced freedom in the exercise of their gifts. Peter never was more free than when he was filled with the Holy Spirit (Acts 2). The evidence of filling is not in a single sign like tongues or miracles; rather, Christians indicate the repeated fullness of the Spirit by expressing their joyful gratitude in singing (Eph. 5:19) and in words of thanksgiving (v. 20). They are also mutually submissive to others in Christ's body (v. 21), particularly to their spouse (vv. 22–32). The filled are maturing in their relationships as parents and children (6:1–4) and as employers and employees (vv. 5–9). Saints filled with the Spirit are strong enough to stand against the rulers, authorities, and powers of this dark world and against the spiritual forces of evil in heavenly realms (vv. 10–12). They exhibit the "armor" of truth, righteousness, faith, and assurance of salvation (vv. 13–17). Those filled with the Spirit pray in the Spirit on all occasions (v. 18).

The Spiritual Life a Dynamic Adjustment to the Holy Spirit

The ethical qualities and spiritual relationships of sanctification develop as converts *actively commune with* the awesome indwelling presence of the Holy Spirit and *respond to his dynamic ministries* to them. Christians do not perform ceremonies or spiritual disciplines to find God in their own consciousness or Jüng's alleged collective consciousness. Having turned within, Christians move beyond themselves to the Holy Spirit who transcends their thoughts and perceived needs. The Holy Spirit and the Word also transcend the present state of any self-appointed guru's individual consciousness and alleged insights into the cosmos. Self-realization movements in monistic contexts do not have an Other

to whom to relate and so end up in an idolatrous worship of the inner self.

One's inner self is not only finite but also *morally depraved*. Christians looking within find that they are unclean and in themselves unworthy of surviving in the presence of the Holy One. *Pelagians* and liberals think the Fall did not affect the human moral condition and tend to make spiritual growth an achievement of human self-development. *Semi-Pelagians* in traditional Catholic approaches to spirituality do not regard sin's effect as wholly pervasive and so tend to place the human initiative ahead of the divine in the development of Christian spirituality. Even after regeneration, *evangelical Protestants* affirm that the inner self struggles with two moral inclinations or natures. So Christians mature spiritually, not by cultivating the old nature within but by continuously putting it off (Col. 3:5–11). Then they clothe their ontological being with the fruits of the Holy Spirit's ministries (vv. 12–17). Made for relationship with God, we cannot achieve our highest potential apart from dependence on the Spirit of grace.

Although the spiritual life both begins and continues in personal response to the Holy Spirit, it is *not all of God*. The Buddhist goal of egolessness sounds spiritual, but is not the Christian goal. The Holy Spirit's ministries are renewing. The Spirit's ministries do not reduce a person to total passivity nor lead to a mere resignation to fate as in some types of Islam. All God wants to take from us is our sinfulness! The Spirit does not eradicate one's distinct ontological being but rejuvenates the powers of informed and loving self-determination to overcome the old nature. The Spirit revitalizes the ego in Christ's likeness. Christians do not just "let go and let God" (do it), nor do they claim, "The Devil made me do it." The spiritual life does not mean total placidity.

213

The Holy Spirit renews our power of self-determination. Although the Holy Spirit is its ultimate causal agent, he is not the only causal agent. Christians are ontologically real agents who actively work together with the Spirit. Insofar as some Calvinists and some exponents of the exchanged life give the idea that the Christian life is all of God they sound pious, but they are unbiblical and unrealistic.

How then are the saints involved in sanctification? Human participation in the spiritual life and disciplines, according to Roman Catholicism, at all times requires *human cooperation* in three ways: (1) purgation, cleansing, purification; (2) illumination, enlightenment, knowledge; and (3) union, contemplation, and ecstasy. Peter Toon says, "Much traditional material on meditation is structured to lead the beginner through exercises which help to get started and then to deepen the experience of being made aware of sin and purged of it. . . . Delight in the presence of God must be preceded by a process of cleansing and spiritual enlightenment."[120] Toon continues:

> In contrast the primary way in which Protestant spirituality is presented is that of the dual process of mortification and sanctification. There is to be constant putting to death of the thoughts and activities which spring from the old nature (the self in its own strength and inclinations); and there is to be constant inflowing of the Spirit to illuminate, guide, strengthen the believer to love, and to obey the will of God and thus be sanctified, made holy and conformed to the model of Jesus Christ.[121]

In evangelical Protestant spiritual experience, the wills of Christians are renewed, but they are not on a par with God's will. Arminian synergism acknowledges our need for the Spirit's enablement in general, but seems to place human ability on a par with the Spirit's by making the Spirit's love and ministries conditional: they will be exercised only to the extent that humans cooperate. Some place the Spirit under the control of human power, holding that the Spirit cannot work until the human will, like a light switch, turns the Spirit's operations on, or off. The merciful or gracious work of the sovereign Spirit in sanctification is not conditioned on the human "cooperation" but stimulates it.

The divine initiative in sanctification produces behavioral fruit in the repentant and believing. The good tree brings forth good fruit. The Spirit creates us in Christ Jesus "to do good works" (Eph. 2:10). Paul exhorted the saints, "Continue to work out your salvation with fear and trembling" (Phil. 2:12). He did not suggest that we *earn* cleansing through our spiritual disciplines but lovingly *express* our justification and reconciliation through them. Our growth in grace personally and relationally in the church is made possible through "God who works in you to will and to act according to his good purpose" (v. 13). We owe both our initial faith and our continued obedience in spiritual disciplines ultimately to the One who graciously gave us life and renews it.

The divine-human synergism in the Christian life, in the words of J. I. Packer, is a Spirit-prompted activity, not Spirit-prompted passivity."[122] "We know that in all things God works [*synergei*] for the good of those who love him, who have been called according to his purpose" (Rom. 8:28). Romans 8:28 does not teach a pantheistic fusion of the divine and human spirits. Neither does it teach a semi-Pelagian or Arminian cooperation. Rather, in this divinely initiated synergism, God works all things together for the good of actively yielded agents who work them out, not in the flesh, but motivated by a loving response to the Spirit. Like the authors of Scripture, Christians are not passive, but active. And as in the production of the Bible, the fruit or product originates with the divine initiative rather than the human.

In the dynamic relationship with the Spirit of truth, believers regularly *mortify un-Christlike characteristics*. If we want to find ourselves, we must lose ourselves. What we lose is not our ontological identities but the dominance of our old, fleshly natures. By faith a believing man or woman develops a new moral and relational identity. Since one's former moral and spiritual nature has been "crucified with Christ" at conversion-regeneration, it must not be allowed to dominate one's ontological self. One's new identity by faith in Christ now lives (and rules) in one whose life is not identified with bodily lusts but with the Son of God who loved us and gave himself for us (Gal. 2:20). Christians responsive to the Spirit *intentionally surrender to Christ* as Lord. They regard him the supreme paradigm of virtue. Like him, they pray, "Not as I will, but as you will" (Matt. 26:39). Surrendering human autonomy to the transcendent Christ means submission to his creative power, love, and freedom. Having made this commitment, one is not cabined in. Rather, one finds oneself empowered, loving, and free from all the tyrannies in creation.[123] So Christians in love regularly *draw on the energy of the Spirit*. On a long trek in the rugged terrain of the Rocky Mountains it takes much energy to keep placing one foot ahead of the other. While rising to the challenges of life, we find that the putting of one foot ahead of the other as Christ did takes more energy than we have in ourselves. Step by step each day, Christians walk in the strength of the Spirit not the flesh (Rom. 8:4). Good works are not only done according to God's revealed will and motivated by love but also energized by the Holy Spirit.[124] Seekers of holiness heed the following injunction:

"Let us cry out to our Father to so fill us with Spirit that our lives brim over, spilling His life and joy like refreshing rain on a tired and cynical planet."[125]

APOLOGETIC INTERACTION

Consistent with our method throughout, we seek to show that a distinctively evangelical view of spirituality makes the most sense of the relevant lines of evidence in Scripture and experience. Like Oliver Barclay, who started with the framework of the ethical formulation drawn from the entire Bible, we argue that it is uniquely convincing as an explanation of the phenomena of life, both intellectual and experiential.[126]

Is Christian Spirituality Anti-Intellectual (Eastern Mysticism et al.)?

Do spiritual people get beyond moral distinctions between *good and evil*? Testimonies to ecstatic experiences by mystics in world religions convince many that they have moved beyond all conceptual distinctions, including that between right and wrong. One Buddhist lecturer alleged that "enlightenment has nothing to do with ethics." The Hindu guru Rajneesh thought he was beyond distinctions of good and evil. His followers were not kids, but well-educated professional people who sang "Joy to the World" and "Love Is a Beautiful Feeling."[127] One said, "It feels so good to be here with my family."[128] A few months later the guru charged his former aide with theft and attempted murder and ended the promised free-love utopia with the announcement that "the community is no longer viable."[129] Wherever theft and murder are permitted for professing spiritual people the community is threatened. The amoral spirituality of ancient and modern gnosticism radically differs from Christianity's essentially moral spirituality.

Much Western anti-intellectual devotional literature also suggests that in spiritual experience we transcend doctrinal discriminations between *truth and error*. Monistic Christian mystics may imagine themselves able to progress beyond all conceptual guidelines. But although our spiritual experiences are beyond full comprehension, the claim of total ineffability does not fit with the truths of general or special revelation. The primary instrument the Holy Spirit utilizes in bringing sinners into fellowship with God the Father is conceptual truth expressed by Jesus Christ and the Scriptures in intelligible human languages. Spiritually minded people need biblical truths to teach, rebuke, correct, and train them in righteousness (2 Tim. 3:16). According to a major point in Calvin Miller's poetry, a spiritual inwardness that only feels may be warm but intellectually misleading. And a spiritual inwardness that thinks but does not feel is void of hope and compassion.[130]

Do spiritual giants get beyond conceptual distinctions of *reality from unreality*? Even the monists distinguish reality from illusion, maya. But the realms of the senses also are part of reality. And some Christians imagine that the Holy Spirit and the believer's spirit are "mingled" in reality. According to Watchman Nee,

> the Holy Spirit and our spirit have become so mingled; while each is distinctive, they are not easily distinguished. . . . they can be distinguished only in name, not in fact. . . . others can touch the Holy Spirit whenever they touch our spirit. Thank God that inasmuch as you allow people to contact your spirit, you allow them to contact God. Your spirit has brought the Holy Spirit to man. . . . So God's Spirit is imprisoned within man's spirit.[131]

The hypothesis that the Holy Spirit is indistinguishable from our spirits blurs the distinction between the Creator and creatures. No excitement about the Holy Spirit's abiding in our bodies must blur the basic theological reality that God's being is distinct from ours. If God is not clearly other, we approach the blasphemy of claiming to be God. In Christian spiritual experience a person's identity is not absorbed in God or the leader. Hindu mystics want a devotee to "come to the point where his individuality is lost."[132] But in biblical history not even the family and national solidarities of Old Testament times erased people's individuality and moral accountability to God. Persons interrelated in families, churches, gangs, and tribes remain distinct, accountable moral agents.

The Eastern Orthodox doctrine of human "deification" is sometimes understood to involve an ontological oneness of humans and God. An Orthodox writer explains that deification "does not mean human beings are able to become God in his essence. But it does mean that they can become 'gods' by grace even as they remain creatures of a human nature."[133] Judges in Israel were not God but could be figuratively called "gods" (John 10:35) as representatives determining people's destiny. Since God's infinite being transcends the finite beings of people in both East and West, we are not God however spiritually mature we may become.

Is spiritual knowledge beyond critical examination because it is *intuitive and self-authenticating*? No truth claim is self-authenticating. Moral statements require a critical use of the mind using standard criteria of truth. But mystics tend to discount critical knowing as unspiritual, favoring intuitive knowledge. Intuition may be a useful source of possibly true ideas, but the suddenness and persuasiveness of an idea does not justify assent to it as true. It does not help for trichotomist Watchman Nee to attribute the intuitive capacity to the spirit (intuition, conscience, and communion) and so regard it "higher" than the capacities of the soul (reason, emotion, and will).[134] In Watchman Nee's influential thinking reason is contaminated by association with the lower body. Sanctification then occurs as the outward person (soul and body) is broken or "slain in the light" releasing the spirit.[135] Television speaker Kenneth Hagin maintains, "One almost has to bypass the brain and operate from the 'inner man,' which is our heart or spirit."[136] And the charismatic televangelist Benny Hinn alleges that "a man with an experience is never at the mercy of a man with an argument."[137] But he overlooks the fact that experiences do not come with tags interpreting them. In a world of deception, critical thinking must interpret and evaluate spiritual intuitions and experiences.[138]

Several responses to the above are crucial: (1) Contrary to the presupposed trichotomy, relevant biblical evidence does not support the belief that the soul and spirit are ontologically distinct entities. Rather, they are often synonyms for the one inner self. (2) Sin comes from the desires of the spirit or heart, not the influence of the body or soul on the spirit. (3) The functions of the inner person are not inherently higher or lower, but equally useful for their respective purposes. (4) Intuitions may be a source of truth but must be tested by responsibly exegeted Scripture. (5) Intuited ideas may contradict each other, and so intuition is not a reliable criterion of truth or a self-authenticating norm of faith and practice. (6) A spirituality based on Christ's cross fulfills the conceptually stated moral law of God. Motivated by gratitude and love and energized by the Holy Spirit, the fulfilling of the law is not a mere "conformity to a set of rules," L. S. Chafer said, nor "a major hindrance to the Christian life."[139]

Is Justification Alone Sufficient (Lutheranism)?

With deep indebtedness to Martin Luther and Lutheranism, we emphasized forensic justification in the preceding chapter. We need to grow in "the art of getting used to unconditional justification" and put to death the idea that we can be accepted by God through works.[140] Indeed, we live in joy of acceptance, not in fear of nonacceptance. Moreover, we are simultaneously just and sinners. Salvation is oversimplified, however, when reduced to justification only. Sanctification does not "appear in Scripture to be roughly equivalent to other words for the salvation wrought by God in Christ."[141] A reduction of salvation to Christ's legal provisions fails to account for the personal relationships of reconciliation or the existential aspects of redemption and sanctification. Regeneration does not make us perfect, but it makes a substantial difference in our lives from the inside out. The new heart produces new fruit; the new relationship to God produces new relationships to others. The faith that justifies apart from works (Gal. 2:16) is the faith that expresses itself through works of love (5:6). The Christian life is not merely a cruise on Kathryn Ann Porter's *Ship of Fools*. From her experience Porter concluded wrongly that all simply sail through life's joys and crises to disembark fundamentally unchanged.[142] Believers are substantially changed by their new legal status and by their new loyalty to the purposes of the Father, the lordship of Christ, and the ministries of the Spirit.

Is Our Ultimate Concern One of Inner Authenticity Alone (Existentialism)?

A great contribution of Kierkegaard's existentialism has been its powerful unmasking of "the prodigious illusion" of Christendom.[143] Everyone born in Denmark became not only a citizen but also a "Christian." But, like Kierkegaard early in life, most lived for aesthetic pleasure. Others tried living moral lives legalistically. But Kierkegaard concluded that neither way of life was Christian. A mere admirer of Christ is not automatically a Christian. An admirer fails to recognize that Christ makes a claim on him to be what he admires. Christ's life was one of suffering, and to be a follower of Christ is to suffer for his kingdom. For Kierkegaard, Christian existence is essentially a life of suffering like Christ's against the world.[144]

Kierkegaard insisted that Christian spirituality demands consistency of life with Christ's life and teachings. But Kierkegaard did not appreciate a similar demand for consistency in one's own teaching. By undercutting the law of noncontradiction in doctrine by dialectic and paradox, some Kierkegaardians have sought to destroy the very ground on which they stand while calling for authentic living. If Christians can glory in the paradox of one "totally other" relating personally (sic!) to humans, what principle hinders Christians from exulting in the paradox of hypocritically teaching Christ and living for personal pleasure?

Kierkegaard undercut the distinctive meaning of faith in Christ. He made faith indistinguishable from passionate commitment to anyone by removing it from logical and factual truth about the Jesus of history. There is more to Christian spirituality than feelings of intense devotion and more to sanctification than emotional upheavals. It takes reliable information from God to direct passionate commitment away from idolatrous relationships. Laws of moral conduct and laws of thought are indispensable to sanctification in a fallen world. We have found reason to affirm the objective validity of the laws of noncontradiction and morality in the nature of God, the trustworthy divine revelation, and the imago Dei. The power of Christ's biblically recorded challenges to dedicated hypocrites stems from the assumption that God's revealed truths cannot be contradicted. Only on the foundation of that absolute ideal of consistency in preaching and practice can Christians authentically hold that hypocritical living ought not be accepted in any culture or subculture.

Have Christians Become a Different Self (Needham)?

David C. Needham in Birthright helpfully emphasizes that it is important to know who we are in Christ. Needham claims that "a Christian is a person who has become someone he was not before."[145] He insists, "It is correct to say that when a person has passed through the death and resurrection described in Romans 6, the person he used to be has ceased to be and the person he now most deeply is will be forever."[146] Similarly, John Stott writes, "The 'old self' denotes, not our old unregenerate nature, but our old unregenerate life. . . . Not my lower self, but my former self."[147]

Needham mistakenly claims that those who hold the two-nature view "understand that their 'old sin nature' is really their most fundamental nature."[148] But our most fundamental reality is our ontological being created good not inherently evil. Christ died to meet our legal, moral, and relational needs not to replace parts of our ontological being. If the formulation of two moral inclinations seems to contribute to a split personality, how much more does a doctrine of two persons? Of the theory's earlier adherents Horatius Bonar asked a series of questions: Who was saved? Not the old self, for it died with Christ and no longer exists; not the new self, for as a member of a "new species" it does not need salvation.[149] A reviewer of Needham's book concludes, "All these word games are played without 'rules' defining what is meant by such basic concepts as 'person,' 'nature,' 'regeneration,' 'death,' etc."[150]

We maintain that a person has two natures because the identity of the person is existentially important (as Needham well says). He writes, "You are not two 'you's.' "[151] But in his concern to emphasize existential meaning, he fails to explain adequately the underlying identity of the "You" before, during, and after conversion. Needham's view makes one's co-crucifixion with Christ (Rom. 6:6) not a representative judicial transaction (5:15–19), but a realistic event that actually took place in the first century for all believers. In contrast, we find that the "snapshot" (aorist) reference point for crucifixion with Christ was our baptism (vv. 3–4). Needham's view that at regeneration our old self "ceased to exist"[152] fails to fit the experience of Paul (Romans 7; Phil. 3:12–14) and other Christians. If the fleshly nature (evil inclinations) does not continue, why does it need to be counted "dead" repeatedly?

The view of a Christian as one ontological person with two moral inclinations (natures) provides the more coherently realistic and viable account of the relevant biblical data and the struggles in the Christian life. The same person who was condemned has now satisfied the law in Christ (Rom. 6:1–6a, 11). The same ontological person who lived in sin finds newness of life (vv. 4b, 6b–7, 11–14) and faces final judgment. So believers count themselves dead (dominantly unresponsive) to their sinful inclinations and alive (dominantly responsive) toward righteous inclinations. Christians are progressively sanctified by refusing to rejoin their sinful natures and continuously offering their renewed capacities as slaves to righteousness (vv. 15–22). It is most important to know who you are in Christ!

Can a Christian Achieve Complete Sanctification (Wesleyanism)?

Humanistic and mystical approaches assume no depravity and so sometimes anticipate perfection.[153] Charles Wesley and his followers reason that since we can be sanctified progressively in this life, we can be sanctified entirely or completely. They maintain that there is a second work of grace understood as a crisis experience subsequent to justification by faith.[154] Wesleyan Wilber T. Dayton explains that to receive perfect sanctification by faith does not mean absolute, divine perfection. Rather,

> Christian perfection is a matter of the heart—of love, attitude and relationship. It accepts human limitations and leans on the perfect Savior and Lord. . . . Christian perfection has none of the pride and boasting of a humanistic quest of perfection, which seeks the absolute and dreams of a goal beyond which there can be no further development or improvement. The perfection of the people of God is a growing, changing, and improving life.[155]

Dayton's synonyms for perfection are full-grown, mature, fully up to standard in a certain respect, expert and fully developed.[156] He adds that perfection does not make a person infallible. It is improvable, capable of being lost, and is constantly both preceded and followed by a gradual work.[157]

Wesleyanism lowers the biblical ideal of the Christian life. A gradually developing maturity that does not claim to attain absolute perfection fits experience, but lowers the revealed ideal. Jesus said, "Be perfect, therefore, as your heavenly Father is perfect" (Matt. 5:48). Paul wrote, "We proclaim him

[Christ], admonishing and teaching everyone with all wisdom, so that we may present everyone perfect in Christ" (Col. 1:28). And Peter exhorted, "Just as he who called you is holy, so be holy in all you do [holistically]; for it is written: 'Be holy, because I am holy'" (1 Peter 1:15–16). If the Wesleyan ideal is not absolute perfection, possibly another term such as "holistic maturity" would be less misunderstood. The uncompromised ideal of Scripture needs to be kept in its pristine beauty. A holistic sanctification substantially affecting every capacity affected by sin is scriptural (1 Thess. 5:23).

A holiness advocate writes, "Quantitatively, the lure of divine love was so immeasurable that the lifestyle of the sanctified believer was always that of a pilgrim and not that of a settler. There was no stopping place in the constant quest for personal spiritual growth and witness in love—in relationship with God and others."[158] But stopping places *have* occurred in the history of perfectionists, as B. B. Warfield amply documents. The complexity of fallen human motives complicates the issue as well as the subtlety of sins of omission and commission.[159] Addressing those who have fellowship with God, John wrote, "If we claim to be without sin, we deceive ourselves and the truth is not in us" (1 John 1:8). John also firmly commended the regular confession of sin (v. 9).

Are There Two Classes of Christians, Spiritual and Carnal?

C. I. Scofield divided people into three categories: people who are lost ("natural"), believers who live under the power of the Adamic nature ("carnal"), and believers who walk in the Spirit ("spiritual").[160] Lewis Sperry Chafer also divided Christians into two classes:

By various terms the Bible teaches thus that there are two classes of Christians: those who "abide in Christ" and those who "abide not," those who are "walking in the light" and those who "walk in darkness," those who "walk by the Spirit" and those who "walk as men," those who have the Spirit *in* and *upon* them, those who are "spiritual" and those who are "carnal," those who are "filled with the Spirit" and those who are not. All this has to do with the quality of daily life in saved people, and is in no way a contrast between the saved and the unsaved.[161]

Does the Bible contrast classes or characteristics of Christians? By identifying one respect in which the Corinthians were carnal, Paul did not intend to say they were carnal in all respects. First Corinthians 3:1–4 may be interpreted coherently in terms not of classes but of respects. By asserting that some at Corinth were carnal at that time (1 Cor. 3:1–4) Paul did not teach that "brothers" who were "in Christ" (v. 1) would remain in a total state of carnality the rest of their lives. Rather, he assumed their carnal attitude toward certain ministers would be changed. So he challenged them to grow up in their attitudes toward teachers and ministers with different personalities and gifts (1:7). He considered them sanctified in the name of the Lord Jesus Christ and by the Spirit of our God" (6:11). All of these phrases teach more than a legal standing of justification. Every Christian develops some degree of holiness, for "without holiness no one will see the Lord" (Heb. 12:14). The hypothesis of two permanent classes of Christians is not drawn from 1 Corinthians 3 but read into it.

It is counterproductive to sanctification to place some Christians in a higher class than others. Those considered to be on the higher plane may be misled by imagining that they are beyond temptation and have attained the full stature of Christlikeness. Those on the lower plane may imagine that they do not need to grow in Christ. But all believers are on the spiritual journey in the same spiritual kingdom. All who are born again will struggle with aspects of carnality in different, subtle ways at different stages of life. None have attained perfection. The claim also disrupts Christian unity to divide a church into two mutually exclusive "classes." Harm comes whether the division is made on the basis of a second work of grace, the baptism of the Spirit, speaking in tongues, fasting, or "victory" over a besetting sin. No growing Christian actually has "victory" if this means being on a plane beyond spiritual struggle with subtle temptations. Throughout this life believers must be overcomers.

Is a Primary Concern Exorcising Demons From Christians (Some Charismatics)?

The practice of casting demons out of Christians in some charismatic deliverance ministries is hard to square with the ministries of our Lord or his apostles. The Gospels contain no example of Jesus casting a demon out of a child of God. The Lord's exorcisms delivered people from the kingdom of Satan to demonstrate the coming of his redemptive kingdom (Matt. 12:28). In Acts those delivered from demonic powers likewise were non-Christians. Nowhere in the Epistles is there an example of elders being told to deliver members of churches from inhabitation by demons.

The practice of delivering Christians from demons is also difficult to square with biblical soteriology. Christians no longer belong to the Devil's family (John 8:44) but to God's. The redeemed have been liberated from the slave market of moral evil and transferred from the kingdom of darkness into the kingdom of light (Col. 1:12–13). Baptized by the Spirit once-for-all into the body of Christ, Christians are permanently indwelt by the Holy Spirit. The Holy Spirit who abides with them forever continues his work in them until the day of Christ (Phil. 1:6).

Although demons cannot actually *possess* Christians, we dare not take their guerrilla warfare lightly. Satan can do many other horrible things to Christians. To minister to believers under demonic assault the Scriptures suggest strategies other than exorcism. The ministry depends on the type of attack. For example, when Christians believe demonic doctrines, such as forbidding to marry and abstaining from meat (1 Tim. 4:1–3), the antidote is not exorcism but instruction. If deceived by the great signs and wonders of false Christs and false prophets toward the end of the age, God's people need discernment (Matt. 24:24). After Satan tried to seize Peter (Luke 22:31), Jesus asked Peter if he loved him and sent him back to feed his sheep (John 21:15–19). When the young widows followed Satan in idleness, gossip, and sensuality (1 Tim. 5:11–15), they needed to care for others so that their relatives would not become a burden to the church (vv. 4, 8, 16). The member of the church at Corinth who slept with his father's wife did not have the demon of adultery cast out but was subjected to church discipline (1 Cor. 5). Later, when the church members failed to forgive this repentant one, they were "outwitted by Satan" because they were unaware of his schemes (2 Cor. 2:5–11).

Unholy spirits may influence Christians to give Satan a "foothold" by continuing in unrighteous anger (Eph. 4:26–27). Again, the approach is not for a deliverance ministry to drive out the demon of anger; rather, the individual must quickly "get rid of all bitterness, rage and anger, brawling and slander, along with every form of malice" (v. 31) so as not to grieve the Holy Spirit (v. 30). To remove demonic footholds Christians must "be kind and

221

compassionate to one another, forgiving each other, just as in Christ God forgave [them]" (v. 32). Although Christians cannot be *possessed* by Satan, they can yield to various demonic enticements. To repel Satan's onslaughts, Christians need more than one strategy and more than one tactic. Every Christian needs to utilize the whole armor of God. Protection starts with girding oneself with revealed truth as a weight lifter dons a belt (Eph. 6:14). Every Christian also needs the protection of righteousness in character, readiness for reconciliation through the preaching of the Gospel of peace (v. 15), skill in fending off flaming arrows with the shield of faith (v. 16), and assurance of final salvation (v. 17). To stand against the Devil's schemes we also need to handle the Spirit's sword of the Word with the facility of a fencer. In addition to the armor and sword, Christians stand against the Devil and recapture surrendered ground by praying "in the Spirit on all occasions with all kinds of prayers and requests" (v. 18). With all of these resources at their disposal, Christians need not become preoccupied with the demonic.

Must Christians Obey God's Moral Law?

This is another troubling issue. *Liberated* from bondage to the evil kingdom to serve God's holy kingdom of love, we want to please the King, but we may not be clear about his will. We may confuse what is inherently right and wrong by divine command with actions not commanded and morally indifferent (*adiaphora*) (e.g., Rom. 14). Surrendered to the Commander-in-chief, we may wonder if God expects his people to keep the law of Moses. Jesus did not destroy Moses' law but *fulfilled it* (Matt. 5:17–18). What Jesus shattered was the Pharisees' additions (Matt.

5:43–47) and hypocritical interpretations of the law (vv. 21–28).[162] Fulfillment of the Mosaic law at Jesus' death did away with the present need to observe *ceremonial laws, priesthoods, and animal sacrifices* (Heb. 9:11–28). Jesus also abolished the necessity of churches' trying to administer *Moses' civil laws* by establishing an institutional church distinct from Israel's national structure.[163] Churches should not endeavor to implement Israel's civil laws any more than its sacrifices. They ought not legislate taxes, drafts for military service, or capital punishment for blasphemy, sorcery, adultery, homosexuality, or disobedient children!

Christ also abolished Moses' particular formulation of God's *moral laws* for national Israel. Contrary to some Reformed thinking, we are not now under the Mosaic expression of the Ten Commandments. The "law written on tablets of stone" faded away in the first century (2 Cor. 3:3, 7, 11). Moses' law was added to the Abrahamic promise "until the Seed to whom the promise referred had come" (Gal. 3:19). "Now that faith has come, we are no longer under the supervision of the law" (v. 25). Although God's moral nature is unchanged, Moses' expression of it for the commonwealth uniting religion and state has been changed. The failure to recognize this fact causes Seventh-day Adventists, Seventh-day Baptists, and others to think that they must now observe the Sabbath on the seventh day. On the first day of the week that law was fulfilled by the resurrection of the crucified Messiah. Under the new covenant, therefore, the Mosaic formulation of the law has faded away (2 Cor. 3:7–11).

To be free from keeping the Mosaic expression of God's moral law for a particular nation prior to the Cross is not *antinomianism*. To keep apostolic formulations of God's moral law is to keep nine of Moses' Ten Commandments. Since Christ's incarnation, death, and resurrection, God has reformulated moral virtues through teachings of Christ and the apostles as recorded in the New Testament. The apostolic commandments are similar to Moses' Ten Commandments, with one exception, the Sabbath command is not repeated.[164] Jesus went out of his way to break details of the Old Testament Sabbath requirements. But Christians are now obligated to keep the New Testament expression of God's moral law. Without the nine commandments, we would not know sin (Rom. 7:7). The commandments remain "holy, righteous and good" (v. 12).

God's moral law transcending the ages remains unchanged whether in the wording of Moses, Christ, or the New Testament writers. It is an illumined mirror helping us to become conscious of our sin (Rom. 3:20; 7:7). It gives freedom if we abide by its provisions (1:23–25). The person who fulfills the law lives in the context of its myriad benefits (Ps. 119). "Righteousness is alignment with reality, and the one who is out of alignment with reality will finally destroy himself. But to be true and right, in alignment with ultimate reality, will make a person free, fulfill the purpose of his existence."[165] This surrender to God's will should proceed from a loving heart. Pharisaic legalism never pleased and satisfied God, who knows the heart. Abraham's faith, not his outward works, was credited to him for righteousness (Rom. 4:3–5). Like him. we must have an "obedience that comes from faith" (Rom. 1:5; cf. 16:26). That is not an obedience of pride to secure merit but to express one's gratitude for the gift of Christ's perfect righteousness.[166] Our sanctification as well as our justification is by grace, not meritorious works. The Galatians mistakenly thought that they began the Christian life by faith but advanced in it by meritorious acts (Gal. 3:1–3). "Any

teaching that good works are done alongside of and coordinately with faith, instead of as a result of faith, is Galatianism."[167]

Do Christ's Disciples Persevere (Arminianism versus Calvinism)?

From the standpoint of observed experience the hypothesis that people can lose their salvation seems to fit certain facts. But the question remains whether these ever were authentic believers. The Scripture section contains warnings of *permanent apostasy* from the Gospel and Christ. Some soil is not good ground, and the planted grain does not survive (Matt. 13:1–23). Some professions of faith from the beginning were inauthentic. Judas seems to be a case in point (John 13:10–11). Although appearing to be a follower of Christ, Judas turned against Christ in a deliberate and permanent way. Since no other just ground for acceptance with God can be found, Judas remained under condemnation. John concluded concerning first-century people who apostatized from the Gospel: "They went out from us, but they did not really belong to us" (1 John 2:19). Peter said that those who deny the sovereign Lord who bought them "bring swift destruction on themselves" (2 Peter 2:l). Both Arminians and Calvinists concur that those who deliberately and permanently reject the Gospel and spurn Christ's love were never true Christians.

Experience and biblical teaching support the possibility of *temporary lapses* among genuine believers. Peter was a disciple who temporarily denied his faith but returned to feed Christ's sheep because he genuinely loved the Lord (John 21:15–17). To help us avoid the embarrassment Peter faced, we must remain faithful to Christ, to his teachings, and to the moral integrity he exhibited. Believers experience temporary lapses into sin, but they will come to loathe it, repent, and find restoration. During Peter's defection, however, he was justified by faith and was therefore, from God's standpoint, secure (Rom. 8:29–30). Both Arminians and Calvinists who affirm a forensic view of justification should recognize temporary lapses in faith and obedience that do not change one's legal status.

The hypothesis of *the perseverance of the saints* in spite of loathsome, temporary lapses is grounded in many great doctrinal convictions. (1) The faithful and inspired *teachings of Scripture* can be relied on: "There is now no condemnation" for those in Christ Jesus (Rom. 8:1). We are "free from the law of sin and death" (v. 2). If "we are children, then we are heirs—heirs of God and co-heirs with Christ" (v. 17). The Holy Spirit intercedes for us (vv. 26–27). Those who have been called and justified will be glorified unconditionally (vv. 29–30). All the redeemed are included in these statements, not just some of them (see Eph. 1:4; 1 Peter 1:1–2). Furthermore nothing, such as death or demonic powers in the present or future, can separate believers from the love of Christ (vv. 38–39). Those who are given to Christ hear his voice, and no one can pluck them out of his or the Father's hands; as Jesus said, "I give them eternal life, and they shall never perish" (v. 28).

Reflect also on these additional *doctrinal considerations:* (2) the completeness of Christ's atoning provisions, (3) your pardon from all sin and reception of Christ's righteousness, (4) the supernaturalness of Holy Spirit regeneration, (5) your awareness of the presence, witness, and sealing of the Spirit abiding with you, (6) the confirming marks of the Spirit's transforming ministries such as love for God and the brothers and sisters in Christ, (7) the efficacy of your Advocate's intercession before the throne of grace, and (8) the reality that God will never rescind the unconditional gift of everlasting life.

In view of such forceful, converging lines of scriptural and doctrinal teaching, believers in Christ need not live in a continual paradox of possible perseverance and possible failure to persevere, as argued by I. Howard Marshall.[168] Rather, as Marshall himself concludes, "the main emphasis of the New Testament is on confidence and assurance of final salvation." Marshall also acknowledges that as one "grows in trust, he is able to proclaim with the voice of faith that nothing can separate him from the love of God."[169]

Scriptural *warnings to believers* may be interpreted as reminders not to be overconfident in ourselves (1 Cor. 10:12). "God is faithful, he will not let you be tempted beyond what you can bear. But when you are tempted, he will also provide a way out so that you can stand up under it" (v. 13). Although the legal status of the justified is secure in the mind of God, sanctification is a progressive process involving conscious human self-determinations against conformity to a depraved society. At each stage of our lives scriptural exhortations remind us to discipline ourselves in godliness. Surely the peace of forensic acceptance, the joy of fellowship with God and others, and the experience of relying on God's faithful promises should produce an inner strength that makes a substantial difference in life. When relationships fail and experience seems dismal, our unchanging legal status remains a solid base for hope. In the midst of life's changes, God's justification does not waver.

Concern about security in Christ is often a good sign. It may indicate the new Spirit-illumined sensitivity to sin. All of us see examples of permanent apostasy and temporary lapses doctrinally and morally. Given our limited knowledge, it is not easy for us to determine whether one not living for

Christ is permanently apostate. We ought not assure people that they are saved when flagrant disobedience dominates their lives. Hope, like faith and love, contribute an abiding essential to Christian morality and spirituality. How do we retain hope in the face of disillusionment? How can we encourage hope in our relatives, church members, students, and colleagues? Assured of justification, we can cope with the pain of the present because we have the abiding presence of the Spirit of grace. Although there is no such thing as perfection, hope sets us free to grow in knowledge and love.

RELEVANCE FOR LIFE AND MINISTRY

Is the doctrine of sanctification viable? Can one live it authentically without hypocrisy?

No Single Secret of a Spiritual Life

"What is the secret of a victorious or happy life?" In answering that trick question, students often mention Bible reading, prayer, witnessing, the baptism of the Spirit, the exchanged life, obedience, the filling of the Spirit, and speaking in tongues. This question falsely assumes that the way to sanctification is singular and instantaneous. Most of the items cited may be among the essentials of a full-orbed Christian life, but no single secret produces spiritual health any more than a single vitamin guarantees bodily health. No rite such as baptism or tongues-speaking creates instantaneous Christlikeness. Neither can sudden realization of identification with Christ or teaching about the exchanged life. Growth in Christ involves disciplined learning by experience with multiple occasions of grace throughout our lives. Additionally the essentials of Christian spirituality are no secret! They are publicly disclosed in the world's best seller. And Christ illustrated them in the broad daylight of history. Mature Christian spirituality is not based on any hidden, deeper *gnōsis* available only to a select few.

Too often the foundations of moral courage and spiritual faithfulness are sidestepped in favor of pragmatic shortcuts or popular fads. Christians need to ground individual understanding of their experiences in a fully developed theology, including the purposes of God in the Atonement, the lordship of Christ, and the ministries of the Spirit.[170] Created for holy living, we are unfulfilled by anything less than growth in a viable ethic and spirituality. God's active image-bearers sooner or later find life unfulfilling if they live for material acquisition, titillation of the senses, intellectual achievement, or political power. We may become slaves to these ends rather than to the fundamental values of God's kingdom. The process of sanctification in God's redemptive kingdom involves maturation in the disciplined exercise of all the convert's Spirit-renewed abilities.

The Priority of Self-Giving Love in the Kingdom

Of all the many qualities of life lived for Christ, what is the highest good (*summum bonum*)? More than anything else God desires self-giving love. The first and second commandments enjoin holistic *agapē* love for God and neighbor (Matt. 22:37–38). Jesus said that the person who understood the priority of love was "not far from kingdom of God" (Mark 12:34). Jesus exhibited the priority of gift-love by leaving his heavenly position and privileges in order to be born, live, and die as a human. "Above all," said Peter, "love each other deeply, because love covers over a multitude of sins" (1 Peter 4:8). Without love all our communicative skills, gifts, faith, and benevolence profit nothing (1 Cor. 13:1–3). Paul wrote, "And over all these virtues put on love." Why? Because love "binds them all together in perfect unity" (Col. 3:14).

How does love integrate other virtues? John Burnaby sums up Augustine's answer in part:

> *Courage* is love enduring for God's sake all pain and hardship, resisting especially the fear of death which is innate in the embodied soul, and increased by ignorance of the body's true nature and destiny. *Justice* is love serving God only, and in the strength of that service ruling over all that is properly in subjection to the soul. *Prudence* is love alert and watchful to discern between what promotes our journey to God, and what hinders it. (italics added)[171]

The habitual desires of love or lust, Augustine maintained, constitute the "weight" of the soul, propelling it upward or downward. Thus "oil poured under the water is raised above the water; water poured upon oil sinks under the oil. They are propelled by their own weights, they seek their own places. Out of order they are restless; restored to order, they are at rest. My weight is my love; by it am I borne whithersoever I am borne."[172] The people of the city of God and the city of the world are distinguished by their respective loves. The good use the world to enjoy God, while the wicked simulate use of God to enjoy the world.[173] Lifelong learning and service of God's people should be motivated by love. The will to love ought to motivate the life focused on the King and service of his kingdom (Rom. 14:17).[174]

"Love is not measured by the intensity of feeling but by the sacrifice it stands ready to make."[175] Greater love has no one than this: to lay down one's life for a friend. God's people plead the cause of those who have been treated unjustly (Ps. 82:3–4). Our attitude to the less fortunate reflects our attitude to God. "He who oppresses the poor shows contempt for their Maker, but whoever is kind to the needy honors God" (Prov. 14:31). Christians "speak up for those who cannot speak for themselves, for the rights of all who are destitute" (31:8). They "judge fairly" and "defend the rights of the poor and needy" (v. 9). The subjugated would not need to seek vengeance if those who love them and their Creator would come to their aid.

The career of Henri J. M. Nouwen, who for many years taught divinity courses at Notre Dame, Yale, and Harvard, illustrates this kind of self-giving love. With remarkable candor he confessed, "After twenty-five years of priesthood, I found myself praying poorly, living somewhat isolated from other people, and very much preoccupied with burning issues. Everyone was telling me that I was doing really well, but something inside me was telling me that my success was putting my own soul in danger." Facing burnout, Nouwen said, "I began to ask myself whether my lack of contemplative prayer, my loneliness, and my constantly changing involvement in what seemed most urgent were signs that the Spirit was gradually being suppressed."[176]

"Go and live among the poor in spirit," the founder of the *L'Arche* communities for mentally handicapped people told him, "and they will heal you."[177] So Nouwen resigned from Harvard and began his ministry at L'Arche. He found that the people there could not read and were not impressed by his books. Nouwen wrote, "Not being able to use any of the skills that had proved so practical in the past was a real source of anxiety. I was suddenly faced with my naked self, open for affirmations and rejections, hugs and punches, smiles and tears, all dependent simply on how I was perceived at the moment."[178] Nouwen remembered Christ's words to Peter, "Do you truly love me?" (John 21:15–16). He then concluded that the basic question is not, "How many people take you seriously? How much will you accomplish? But are you in love with Jesus?"[179] Nouwen wrote, "In our world of loneliness and despair, there is an enormous need for men and women who know the heart of God, a heart that forgives, that cares, that reaches out and wants to heal."[180] Nouwen found that "Christian leaders cannot simply be persons who have well-informed opinions about the burning issues of our time. Their leadership must be rooted in the permanent, intimate, relationship with the incarnate Word, Jesus, and they need to find there the source for their words, advice, and guidance."[181] Christian leaders should not seek upward mobility so much as the downward-moving way of Jesus. "Here we touch the most important quality of Christian leadership in the future. It is not a leadership of power and control, but a leadership of powerlessness and humility in which the suffering servant of God, Jesus Christ, is made manifest." This is not a psychologically weak leadership, but one in which "power is constantly abandoned in favor of love."[182]

Loving Obedience to the King's Directives

Although Christians no longer are under the curse of Pharisaic legalism, they are not unprincipled but should lovingly *obey their Lord's will*. Even Jesus strove to fulfill the law. Moral expressions of God's nature remain "holy, righteous and good" (Rom. 7:12). The Lord of all requires obedience leading to justice in every situation, be it public or private. God's ethical expectations are not lowered for his moral and spiritual children! Categorical imperatives admit of no exceptions, however complex our life situations may be. The kingdom comes when saints do the Father's will on earth (Matt. 6:10), when Christ is lived out as Lord, and when people are anointed by the Spirit as was Christ to "preach good news to the poor" (Luke 4:18).

Personal and corporate spiritual renewal begins with acknowledgment of the loss of our first love for God and for obedience in the service of justice. We may not be able to keep the identical emotional expression of our first love decades later, but we can keep the same loving determination. When we become aware of the loss of that determination, we must repent and cultivate our love for the Holy One again. Richard Lovelace wisely observed, "The 'law' comes to us again and again, not only in the pages of Scripture, but also in the warnings or protests of people close to us who can see our failings, however much they may remain in the dark about their own. Parents, teachers, the police, and other authorities are all personalized forms of the law."[183] Lovelace adds:

> A husband or wife also functions in the same way, serving God as an agent of our sanctification. He or she can see the patterns of sin which are hidden from our own vision by spiritual darkness, and from the world because it sees only the surface of our lives. Most divorces among Christians probably occur because the parties have not realized that *marriage is a contract to aid one another's sanctification.* Without this realization, we become experts at what is wrong with one another, without recognizing that the information our spouse is giving us is an essential aid to spiritual growth. (italics his)[184]

We may also grow in Christlike righteousness by *keeping a clear conscience.* Conscience is the activity of the inner self that perceives the measure of agreement between our conduct and the divinely revealed virtues for which we are accountable.[185] Our ability to judge whether our conduct is right or wrong bears witness to the universality of moral law and our accountability to the God who gave it (Rom. 2:15). To violate our conscience is to be at war with general revelation in our hearts or with special revelation in Scripture. Paul asked Timothy to command certain men not to teach false doctrine or myths but to love from a pure heart and a good conscience (1 Tim. 1:3–5). Timothy should fight the good fight by "holding on to faith and a good conscience" (v. 19). Paul exemplified what he taught, for he said to the Sanhedrin: "My brothers, I have fulfilled my duty to God in all good conscience to this day" (Acts 23:1). To Felix Paul later said, "I strive always to keep my conscience clear before God and man" (Acts 24:16).

Unfeigned obedience expresses love even when it induces *suffering* for Christ's kingdom. To live for Christ and serve others in his name often arouses opposition from the fallen world order. Followers of Christ may be called upon to suffer unjustly (1 Peter 2:19) "for the Name" (Acts 5:41), "for what is right" (1 Peter 3:14), "for the kingdom of God" (1 Thess. 1:5), and for the "gospel" (2 Tim. 2:8–9). Like Christ's early followers, growing Christians may suffer in various ways from political, social, and even religious authorities. We may be called upon literally to die for the kingdom of God, as some martyrs have done. Catholicism has made saints and mediators of martyrs—some of whom provoked their own deaths; however, Protestants need not therefore dismiss the Bible's teaching about witnessing for Christ even through death (Rev. 12:11).

While complying with the requirements of God's moral nature, growing saints should not expect adherence to their personal views on matters of moral indifference, *adiaphora*. Obedient Christians will not divide families or churches over dietary matters such as vegetarianism (Rom. 14:2–3) or sacred days (vv. 5–6). Accountable for our own actions, we cease "passing judgment on one another" and putting stumbling blocks in their way (v. 13). Rather, we "make every effort to do what leads to peace and to mutual edification" (v. 19). Centered on God as the ultimate reality, we allow for differences in the application of Scripture to different social, economic, or political situations. Christians build up those who are weak (Rom. 15:1), exhibit a spirit of unity (v. 5), and accept one another as Christ has accepted us (v. 7). When we have sinned against another on matters of indifference, we exhibit growth in holy love by always being ready for reconciliation.

Mature in Self-Control

Control of oneself in accord with moral law results in the byproduct of freedom from control by other humans. Self-government, or self-control, is a fruit of the Holy Spirit's ministries (Gal. 5:23). Having put off deceitful desires, Christian people "put on a new self [nature] created to be like God in true righteousness and holiness" (Eph. 4:24). The discipline of self-mastery is one facet of the new nature that needs to be developed through active yieldedness to the Spirit. As infants and children we require much control by others, as teenagers less control, but as adults we are responsible for our own decisions and actions. In our Christian development there may be three similar stages. As we grow we need not be mastered by our circumstances or programmed by others. Maturing Christians develop self-discipline not only for personal well-being but also to serve God and others.

Christians possess the resources to *control their sex drives*. As Paul introduced a discussion of sexual immorality he wrote, " 'Everything is permissible for me'—but not everything is beneficial. 'Everything is permissible for me'—but I will not be mastered by anything" (1 Cor 6:12). In the midst of cultures obsessed by sexual expressions contrary to God's purposes, self-control is possible. Moral evil is more a matter of immoral desires of the heart than physical acts. Lust is "out of control thinking."[186] Lust may take the form of obsessions with masturbation, voyeurism, promiscuity, pornography, homosexuality, or sexual abuse of children. But Christ has made it possible to overcome these habits as we keep in step with the Spirit. Earl D. Wilson wrote, "Deliverance does not come automatically with salvation but with obedience; not with justification but with sanctification. It is not usually a once-for-all event, but an everyday process. Deliverance is a . . . series of choices that I make. Deliverance from sexual obsession results from choosing to focus on real life and not on fantasy."[187] Applying Romans 8:5–6, Wilson adds, "Those who live according to the sinful nature have their minds set on *sexual fantasies and obsessions,* but those who live in accordance with the Spirit have their minds set on enjoying their sexuality as God intended us to enjoy it."[188] According to Paul, there are three things Spirit-filled Christians can do to control sex drives. We can (1) present our bodies as living sacrifices to God, (2) resist conformity to the world's norms and standards, and (3) experience transformation by the renewing of our minds (see Rom. 12:1–2).

The self-controlled can *love even their enemies.* More than self-controlled love of friends is expected of a person saved by grace. "I tell you," Jesus said, "love your enemies and pray for those who persecute you, that you may be sons of your Father in heaven" (Matt. 5:44–45). Augustine understood the difficulty of that task, admitting that nothing dies so hard in the human heart as hate. As he interpreted the command, "in your enemy, you are called to love not what he is but what he may be—and that is how God loves the sinner."[189]

Self-disciplined people seek the joys of other moral and spiritual challenges. As dentists say, "You don't have to clean all your teeth, only those you want to keep!" We do not have to discipline all our capacities, just those we wish not to deteriorate! Another challenge is the disciplined use of our time. A pastor asked D. Elton Trueblood how he found time to write so many books while teaching and preaching. He took out his date book and showed the pastor a typical week, pointing out the blocks of each day he had reserved for writing. "This is the idea of the fuller date book," Dr. Trueblood said, "Nature abhors a vacuum, and if I don't mark out times for writing, for study, and for my family, others will demand it. To prevent this, I beat them to the punch."[190]

James Newby suggests the following covenant to make with yourself. *Physically:* (1) I will be careful as to what I eat, recognizing that what I consume directly affects how I feel. I will not overeat! (2) I will exercise at least twenty minutes each day. (3) I will receive a physical checkup at least once a year. *Mentally:* (4) I will read at least two hundred pages per week of Christian literature and one hundred pages per week in secular fields. (5) I will join a study group where I can share my ideas and test my conclusions regarding what I have read. (6) I will attend at least two continuing education events per year to keep abreast of new developments in the field of pastoral work. *Spiritually:* (7) I will read a portion of Scripture and pray daily, preferably at the beginning of each day. (8) I will study the great spiritual models of

Christendom by reading the classics of Christian devotion. (9) I will consciously moderate or abstain from practices that inhibit my relationship with God: for example, television, idle conversation, and negative criticism. And (10) I will meet with two friends weekly in a spiritual support group where I can openly share my personal concerns without fear of ridicule or breach of trust.[191]

Practice the Rewarding Discipline of Christian Meditation

A spiritual discipline of particular benefit is Christian meditation (CM), which is not to be confused with Transcendental Meditation (TM). The latter is a spiritual discipline (yoga) of pantheists in which one repeats a meaningless sound (mantra) for twenty minutes before breakfast and dinner. The purpose is to remove the conscious mind from preoccupations with rational concepts (including biblical teachings) so that one can "float" back to union with the impersonal, nonrational Source, Brahman. The widely advertised benefits of yoga may not be specific to TM but can be replicated, e.g., by resting twice a day. Dangers may also be involved in the practice of TM.[192]

Christian meditation should be distinguished also from Herbert Benson's secularized *Relaxation Response*. This Boston physician found that his heart patients overcame the "fight or flight" response to crisis by his secular relaxation response. This involves four elements: a quiet environment, a comfortable position, a passive attitude, and an object to dwell on.[193] Benson suggests a relaxation break two hours after meals (instead of a coffee break), repeating the word "one" once or twice daily for ten to twenty minutes. As a result his heart patients show less inner tension, lower blood pressure, and improved emotional health.

A working definition of Christian meditation is a spiritual discipline of believers in a quiet environment and a comfortable position (when possible) who ponder God's great qualities and works in nature and biblical history with alert minds, grateful affections, and actively yielded wills. "Meditation," as Packer defined it, "is the activity of calling to mind, and thinking over, and dwelling on, and applying to oneself, the various things that one knows about the works and ways and purposes and promises of God."[194]

The practice of CM has some *similarities* to other kinds of meditation. Christians usually need a quiet place; practice the discipline regularly; and derive certain spiritual, mental, and physical benefits from it. The similarities between Christian and non-Christian forms of meditation, however, should not obscure several important *differences*:

1. *The Source* to which we return is personal, transcendent in being, and immanent in activity. Peter Toon concluded,

> The simplest way to highlight the difference is to say that for the one meditation is an inner journey to find the centre of one's being, while for the other it is the concentration of the mind/heart upon an external Revelation. For the one revelation/insight/illumination occurs when the inmost self (which is the ultimate Self, the one final Reality) is reached by the journey into the soul, while for the other it comes as a result of the encounter with God in and through his objective Revelation to which Holy Scripture witnesses.[195]

2. The *problem* of being accepted by God is moral and relational, not metaphysical as in most eastern systems.

3. CM differs in its *goal*. The objective of each period of meditation is not metaphysical union but personal communion. Christian meditators do not pursue the beatific vision here and now but seek inward renewal day by day.

4. The role of the *affections* differs in CM. Christians exhibit active charity, not apathetic detachment. The Christian priority on gift-love takes wholesome desires beyond oneself to others. God's people often express their meditative feelings in *music*. "I will sing to the LORD all my life; I will sing praise to my God as long as I live" (Ps. 104:33). After urging the Ephesians to be filled with the Spirit, Paul wrote, "Speak to one another with psalms, hymns and spiritual songs. Sing and make music in your heart to the Lord" (Eph. 5:19).

5. In a teleological creation, furthermore, the *will* is not passive but is actively yielded to the Lord's purpose. Informed Christians meditate, not to abandon responsibilities, but to experience renewal for the battle with evil forces (Rom. 12:1–2).

6. CM differs from nonconceptual forms of meditation in its role for the *mind*. A mindless meditation is understandable in a meaningless world without an informational revelation. The mind, as Guru Maharaj Ji of the Divine Light Mission taught, is a demon to be exorcised so that one may receive "spiritual knowledge." So he said, "Let's get rid of that concept maker!" Zen Buddhists use koans to destroy confidence in logical sense; but the Father of Christ renews minds. Seeking to love God without using the mental abilities God has given breaks the first and great commandment. So even in meditation Christians test the spirits by sound doctrine verified by reliable criteria of truth.[196] Paul wrote, "Finally, brothers, whatever is true, whatever is noble, whatever is right, whatever is pure, whatever is lovely, whatever is admirable—if anything is excellent or praiseworthy—think about [meditate on] such things" (Phil. 4:8).

7. Christian meditators have distinctive *objects to dwell on*. CM may focus on universal revelation in creation and providence, such as a glistening snow-capped mountain range. Before any part of the Bible was written, Isaac "went out to the field one evening to meditate" (Gen. 24:63). We may surmise that in the twilight he pondered not only the Creator's wisdom and power, but also the woman his servant would bring for him to marry in fulfillment of the Lord's promise of a "seed" to Abraham. But the prime object to dwell on in CM is the triune God of special revelation. In meditation Christians focus on the covenant-making God's attributes and his mighty acts. Preeminence is given to the Messiah's incarnation, atonement, and exaltation. The Gospel of Christ is enrichingly re-presented for meditation in services of baptism and the Lord's Table.

Growing Christians meditate primarily on Scripture content. To Joshua, who needed courage in leadership, God said, "Do not let this Book of the Law depart from your mouth; meditate on it day and night" (Josh. 1:8). Blessed is the one whose "delight is in the law of the LORD, and on his law he meditates day and night" (Ps. 1:1–2). The psalmist said, "I meditate on your precepts and consider your ways. I delight in your decrees; I will not neglect your word" (119:15–16). "Oh, how I love your law! I meditate on it all day long" (v. 97). "I have more insight than all my teachers, for I meditate on your statutes" (v. 99; cf. 148). The objective truth of God's Word is far from cold and lifeless when it is the object of the believer's Spirit-assisted meditation.

If your life seems empty, you may be missing CM. No discipler or shepherd can do your meditating for you. Like the psalmist, we must do it for ourselves. Without CM we become spiritually vulnerable. Consider, by contrast, the "highest insight" in Buddhism: "The true mode of existence is empty."[197] Jesus said, "I have come that they may have life, and have it to the full" (John 10:10). So like Paul, "discipline yourself for the purpose of godliness" (1 Tim. 4:7 NASB). And like the psalmist, pray this prayer: "May the words of my mouth and the meditation of my heart be pleasing in your sight, O LORD, my Rock and my Redeemer" (Ps. 19:14; cf. 104:34).

A Method of Contemplative Bible Study

You can use the Bible devotionally in many different ways. One approach involves the following steps:[198] (1) *Feel the need,* not for bread alone, but for "every word that comes from the mouth of God" (Matt. 4:4). (2) *Enjoy the quest.* Capture the expectation and excitement of discovering for yourself a scripturally guided experience with God. "Blessed are those who hunger and thirst for righteousness" (Matt. 5:6). (3) *Study a paragraph* or one unit of thought in the original language. Longer sections of Scripture may contain too many ideas for adequate response. A single verse without its context may too easily be misinterpreted and misapplied. It will be helpful to compare different translations. (4) *Write out the text's basic meaning* in your own words. Does it imply or illustrate a general principle that held when it was written and holds today? Do not search for hidden, "deeper" meanings. Each paragraph should be interpreted consistently with other passages on the subject, i.e., with scriptural doctrine in general.

(5) *Apply the truth to yourself today.* Although the original meaning of the text was one, its applications are many. Apply the universal principle to your own life by using personal references (I, me, my), immediate time references, (this morning, today, now), and specific roles you fill (friend, spouse, child, or parent). For example, "I today, as a spouse, parent, teacher, and citizen will

seek to live thankfully in Christ because all the fullness of the Deity lives in him and in him I am complete" (Col. 2:6–10). Memorize the verse that conveys the major thought most fully to be able to meditate on it when possible throughout the day. (6) *Commit yourself to the referent* in nonsymbolic reality. Meditate not just on words and ideas but on the living Christ himself. Recognize no higher power or authority in your life, family, or congregation. Offer Christ the affection he properly evokes. Having the fullness of spiritual knowledge and power in Christ, rejoice that you need no other Mediator. The fullness of authentic spiritual experiences is ours in the Christ of the Word attested by the Spirit. (7) *Pray for wisdom in applying the truth.* Let doctrinal praying become natural. Finally, (8) *act on the truth.* By the Spirit of grace be a doer of the Word and not a hearer only (James 1:22). Seize opportunities each day to put the principle into operation.

The printing press and Bible translations in the vernacular languages centuries ago opened the Book to ordinary laypeople. Some today, however, such as Pastor Earl Paulk, think that the unity of his church will be shattered if people study the Bible for themselves.

Another cloak of spirituality is when pastors say that every Christian needs to take his Bible and judge truth for himself. This is not the instruction of God's Word. God gives the five-fold ministry for the "equipping of the saints" and the "edifying of the body" (Eph. 4:12). Man has no right to private interpretation of the Word of God apart from those whom God sets in the Church as spiritual teachers and elders. . . . Many Christians are encouraged to be their own biblical authorities. But how will the body of Christ ever be "fitly joined together" with such independence of spirit?[199]

Christians should respect their church officers, but even the apostle Paul commended the Bereans for checking his teaching by the Scriptures (Acts 17:11). What Peter disavowed was a human *origin* of Scripture, not a personal study and interpretation of it (2 Peter 1:12–21). Peter did not invite his readers to duplicate his once-for-all mountain-top experience. But he did urge them to pay attention to the Scriptures that originated with God through Spirit-carried writers (vv. 19–21). When members of the Roman Church are at last recovering the value of personal Bible study, let not Protestant shepherds remove it from their people!

Faithfully Utilize All Spiritual Disciplines (Occasions of Grace)

Prayer is an essential discipline of the spiritual life. After his exhortation to put on all the armor of God to stand against the fiery arrows of the Devil, Paul commanded that we "pray in the Spirit on all occasions with all kinds of prayers and requests" (Eph. 6:18). Jude similarly enjoined saints to "pray in the Holy Spirit" (Jude 20). Prayer on "all occasions" includes times of attack by "the powers of this dark world" and "the spiritual forces of evil in the heavenly realms" (Eph. 6:12). The phrase "all kinds of prayers and requests" (v. 18) includes personal and family prayer, spoken and unspoken requests, joyful praise, adoration, painful confession, petition, and intercession. To "pray in the Holy Spirit" does not signify speaking in tongues, which are not mentioned in the context of Ephesians 6 or Jude. Praying in the Spirit more likely involves (1) intimate conversation with the Father (*Abba*) as we are assured by the witness of the Holy Spirit within us (Gal. 4:6–7), (2) intercession energized not by the flesh but by the Spirit (Rom. 8:2–4), and (3) petitions prompted by the Spirit's suggestions and intercessions through scriptural meditation (Rom. 8:23, 26–27).

Prayer in Christianity is not mere reflection on a situation by secularists whose faith excludes a transcendent God. Neither is prayer an ecstatic union with an impersonal Ground of Being (Tillich). And for evangelicals prayer cannot be reduced solely to *communion* with a personal, transcendent God (Barth and Brunner). Prayer involves personal response to the initiatives of the tri-personal God, including confession, worship, praise, thanksgiving, and dedicated action. An evangelical understanding of prayer also emphasizes the offering of requests based on promises recorded in inspired Scripture (an aspect missing in Barth and Brunner's view of prayer).[200] Assured by Scripture that God hears and answers petitions and intercessions, evangelicals bring their requests to God with thanksgiving (Phil. 4:6).

Persevere in utilizing other resources for spiritual vitality and power both private and public. *Privately,* Christians need to develop personal ways of thinking, listening, memorizing, and meditating upon revealed truths. Such spiritual disciplines are *necessary* but *not sufficient* conditions for Spirit-illumined growth. They are not ends in themselves but important means by which the Spirit accomplishes his sanctifying work in our lives. Alone before God and in the light of his revealed will we need to question, examine, and admonish ourselves. When we are in free fellowship with God, we can share more effectively with others and respond appropriately to them.

Publicly and corporately, Christians grow through the preached Word, worship, fellowship, and the Lord's Supper. Together with others of like mind and purpose, we gain fresh insights into the apostles' foundational doctrines and their application to our standing and our relationships. Baptism and the Lord's Supper are sacred ordinances, not sacraments conveying growth. Only as

233

observed in faith will they be set apart from refreshments in general to signify our union with the crucified and risen Son. Because of the suffering and anguish we experience in the world, we recognize the joy of fellowship with others who build on the same apostolic principles in God's written Word.

For more specific goals and incentives for Christian living, the reader may well integrate what has been said in the final section of each chapter in these three volumes. Every doctrine of God's Word is profitable for "training in righteousness" (2 Tim. 3:16). The Relevance for Life and Ministry sections will enable saints to arrive at a deeper "knowledge of the Son of God, to maturity, to the measure of the full stature of Christ" (Eph. 4:13 NRSV).

Persevere in Faith, Not Fear

"Love . . . always trusts, always hopes, always perseveres" (1 Cor. 13:7), for there is a higher reality behind the scene. Jesus said to his followers in a boat during a storm: "You of little faith, why are you so afraid?" (Matt. 8:26). One reason we fear the storms of life is a lack of faith in the divine reality that does not meet the eye. "Why are you so afraid? Do you still have no faith?" (Mark 4:40). The psalmist said, "I sought the LORD, and he answered me; he delivered me from all my fears" (Ps. 34:4). Faith in Christ delivers from fear of a *lack of forgiveness*. After the first sin, Adam's first recorded word to God was "I was afraid" (Gen. 3:10). But the believer who anticipated the coming of the suffering Servant said, "Surely God is my salvation; I will trust and not be afraid" (Isa. 12:2).

We need not fear the *pressures of life*. We need not respond to external stressors with internal stress. We need not be enslaved to what others think and say. We can be delivered from such timidity by trusting the Lord of all.

"For God did not give us a spirit of timidity, but a spirit of power, of love and of self-discipline" (2 Tim. 1:7). Being afraid of what others think or say about us may keep us from serving freely and joyously. Timothy and Paul were timid, but when filled with the Spirit they became bold. "Fear of man will prove to be a snare, but whoever trusts in the LORD is kept safe" (Prov. 29:25). John wrote, "Everyone born of God has overcome the world. This is the victory that has overcome the world, even our faith. Who is it that overcomes the world? Only he who believes that Jesus is the Son of God" (1 John 5:4–5). Conquer life's pressures by relying on the Spirit—your Caller, Regenerator, Sustainer, Counselor, and Guide.

You need not fear *the future*. Jesus told his disciples, "Do not worry about your life, what you will eat or drink; or about your body, what you will wear. Is not life more important than food . . . ? Who of you by worrying can add a single hour to his life?" (Matt. 6:25, 27). Those who trust Christ need not waste emotional energy on worry about tomorrow. Most of what we worry about never happens. The psalmist said, "I was young and now I am old, yet I have never seen the righteous forsaken or their children begging bread" (Ps. 37:25). The "fight and flight" syndrome serves an important function in emergencies such as a bear attack, but fears that become routine waste emotional energy, and constantly high levels of stress may lower the immune system and lead to depression.

By God's grace Christians can respond to *life-threatening situations* as did the heroes of faith in Hebrews 11. By faith Moses chose to be mistreated with the people of God rather than enjoy the pleasures of sin; he regarded disgrace for the sake of Christ of greater value than the treasures of Egypt; he did not fear the king's anger but persevered in an alien country (Heb. 11:25–27). Why? "Because he saw him who is invisible" (v. 27). You can become preoccupied with visibly impossible circumstances, or by faith you can behold the risen Lord's exalted power over all. Whatever your circumstances, you can trust Christ for the present and the future just as you trusted him for forgiveness and the gift of righteous standing before the Father. Jesus juxtaposed fear and faith when he entreated his disciples, "Do not let your hearts be troubled. Trust in God; trust also in me" (John 14:1). Courageously decide to exchange fear for trust in Christ.

We need not be afraid of what happens *after death*. The Messiah came, among other reasons, to "free those who all their lives were held in slavery by their fear of death" (Heb. 2:15). Our faith is in one who defeated death and rose to live eternally. Neither need we be afraid of divine judgment. Having made peace with God (Rom. 5:1), we cannot come again into condemnation (John 3:18; Rom. 5:1; 8:1). We no longer stand under the curse of the law (Gal. 3:10–13). Our eternal life is like God's, not only in its marvelous qualities but also in its extent. The saints have crossed over from eternal death to eternal life (John 3:18, 36; 5:24).

Fear is like the red light on the car's dashboard indicating that the alternator is not working. "When you experience fear, it is a reliable indicator that your faith is down.... Every time fear appears within us, we should stop and deal with our faith. Like the warning signal in a car, it is cause for alarm and calls for immediate action."[202] When the light of fear comes on in your life, remember that Christ promised to be with you every day until the end of the age (Matt. 28:20). "The Lord's unfailing love surrounds the man who trusts in him" (Ps. 32:10; cf. 27:1–3). Repeat these words from the Shepherd Psalm: "I will fear no evil, for you are with me" (Ps. 23:4). Choose not to be anxious about anything, but "by prayer and petition, with thanksgiving, present your requests to God. And the peace of God, which transcends all understanding will guard your hearts and your minds in Christ Jesus" (Phil. 4:6–7). Freedom from fear is contingent on faith, not on material possessions, one's situation, or other people.

Rejoice in the security of your positional justification and sanctification. Believers "were sanctified" (1 Cor. 6:11; Heb. 10:29), "have been made holy" (Heb. 10:10), and "are sanctified" (Acts 20:32; 26:18). Jesus suffered "to make the people holy through his own blood" (Heb. 13:12). Walk by faith in your forensic position in the glorified Christ, not by sight. By faith look beyond all the physical, emotional, and spiritual struggles of this pilgrimage. Hold fast the truth that God has wedded true believers in Christ to himself forever!

DISCUSSION TOPICS

1. Were great Old Testament saints of God free from the awareness, power, and reality of sin in their lives? Illustrate by appeal to four individuals.

2. Do Scriptures cited in support of sinless perfection (e.g., Matt. 5:48; 2 Cor. 3:18; 1 Thess. 5:23; Heb. 12:14) actually teach that Christians can be free from the presence and power of sin? Is "sinless perfection" an attainable goal for Christians this side of eternity?

3. Does the New Testament indicate that all believers should seek and experience a postconversion crisis experience that decisively elevates them to a higher plane of Christian living?

4. Can normal, growing Christians expect to experience spiritual struggles in their lives with the lower nature,

sin, and Satan? What can we do as Christians to achieve victory in the midst of such struggles?

5. What positive functions does the Law of God exert in the life of the growing Christian? How can you as a believer avoid the twin errors of legalism and antinomianism?

6. How convincing is the case in the New Testament for God's preservation of true believers to the end? What responsibility do you as a Christian bear in the area of Christian living?

7. Discuss the value of the spiritual disciplines (Scripture meditation, prayer, solitude, service, fasting, journaling, etc.) in the quest for spiritual maturity and sanctification. What criteria distinguish Christian spirituality from non-Christian spirituality?

See also the Review Questions and Ministry Projects on pages 501–2.

PART TWO

SOCIAL TRANSFORMATION

CHAPTER 5

THE CHURCH SPIRITUALLY AND INSTITUTIONALLY

The Church Spiritually and Institutionally

THE PROBLEM:
WHAT DO WE BELIEVE
ABOUT THE NATURE
OF THE CHURCH, ITS
MEMBERSHIP AND POLITY, AND
ADDITIONALLY ABOUT ITS
SACRED RITES, DISCIPLINE, AND
MISSION IN THE WORLD?

The church represents the fulfillment spiritually and institutionally of the Father's grand design (vol. 1, chap. 8) for believers in world history. Men and women, as image-bearers of God (vol. 2, chap. 3), are spoiled by sin and alienated from their Creator and from one another (vol. 2, chap. 4). By his vicarious death (vol. 2, chap. 7) and triumphant resurrection (vol. 2, chap. 8), Christ provided for the restoration of believing sinners to God. Through the Holy Spirit's effectual calling of the "sheep" given by the Father to the Son (vol. 3, chap. 1) individuals trust Christ, are supernaturally born from above (vol. 3, chap. 2), and are legally justified and personally reconciled to the Father (vol. 3, chap. 3). By this divine initiative God has gathered to himself a new and holy people.

In God's wise purpose believers in Christ exist as an ordered and purposeful community with a pattern of leadership, a common life of worship and fellowship, a set of sacraments or ordinances, and a defined mission in the world. In this chapter we consider the nature of the church, its polity, ministry leadership, sacraments or ordinances, community life, and task in the world. In the following chapter we will examine the relation of the church to Israel vis-à-vis the kingdom. Finally, chapter 8 will explore the ultimate realization of God's purposes for his chosen people in the heavenly New Jerusalem.

As we consider the collective reality known as the church, a number of issues arise. Is it valid to describe the church by such qualifiers as "universal," "local," "invisible," or "visible"? Moreover, when did the Christian church begin—at some point in the Old Testament, during the ministry of Jesus, or at Pentecost? Is membership in the church restricted to believers in Christ, or may it include sincere seekers of the truth? Does Scripture suggest that each congregation is self-governing, or may superior bodies such as a presbytery, synod, or general assembly be invested with authority over the local church? What kind of leadership pattern does the New Testament reflect? Is this apostolic pattern normative for all times and cultures? Moreover, what functions do the bishop, elder, pastor, and deacon(ess) perform in the church? Is the local church led by a plurality of elders, or does one pastor shepherd each congregation? What authority do individual church members have in the decision-making process? Is the biblical model of church leadership hierarchical, proceeding from deacon to elder to bishop to pope? History poses the question of the role of Peter in the church. Did Christ delegate supreme and infallible authority to Peter and the succession of bishops centered in the Roman See?

Moreover, in what respects does a sacrament differ from an ordinance? How many sacraments or ordinances should the church celebrate? How valid are the seven sacraments historically enumerated by Rome? Moreover, what does the ordinance of baptism signify, and what spiritual benefits does it convey? Should children of Christian parents be baptized, or only professing believers in Christ? Is sprinkling, affusion (pouring), or immersion the biblical mode of baptism? Should a believer sprinkled as an infant in one of the historic Christian churches (Roman Catholic, Episcopal, Lutheran, et al.) be rebaptized? Furthermore, what spiritual realities did Jesus intend that the Eucharist should signify? How are we to understand the presence of Christ at the Table? Is Christ present in the bread and wine in a way that he is not present elsewhere? And finally, what task did Christ entrust to his church in the present age? What balance should Christians strike between evangelism and social concern, between preaching the Gospel and caring for the poor?

ALTERNATIVE INTERPRETATIONS IN THE CHURCH

The history reflects a variety of interpretations concerning the topics introduced above. We present the following schools of interpretation under the primary category of the nature and government of the church, with explanation of the sacraments as a further issue.

Roman Catholicism

Traditional Roman Catholicism views the church as a visible and external institution organized heirarchically as episcopate, presbyteriate, and diaconate. The mystical body of Christ is identical with the institutional Roman church. The church is said to be the continuation of the incarnation of Christ, the visible and material form of God on earth. Jesus' saying to Peter, "You are Peter [Petros], and on this rock [petra] I will build my church" (Matt. 16:18) identifies Peter as the foundation of the Roman church. Catholicism posits the doctrine of apostolic succession, whereby the church's duly consecrated bishops are the legitimate heirs of Peter and the apostles. The church is Roman in that the bishop of Rome possesses primacy over other bishops. The argument goes that since Peter was prince of the other apostles (cf. Matt. 16:18–19; Luke 22:32; John 21:15–17) and since he founded the church at Rome and was martyred there, the bishop of Rome enjoys supremacy over all other bishops. In the medieval era the infallibility of the pope and the college of bishops was proposed. On the basis of Christ's promise to guide the apostles into all truth (John 16:13–15), Rome claims that its official teachings in matters of faith and morals are infallible. The church, moreover, is catholic in that it claims to be the universal congregation of the faithful throughout the entire earth. The Roman Catholic church traditionally claimed to be the exclusive vehicle of salvation for the human race; outside the institutional church founded on Peter there is no salvation.

Rome views the sacraments as outward, visible signs of an inward, invisible grace. Translating the Greek word *"mystērium"* (1 Tim. 3:16) by *"sacramentum,"* the church regards a sacrament as a visible enactment of the Gospel that brings the participant within the sphere of divine grace. The sacraments, Rome avers, were instituted by Christ and are necessary for salvation. Assuming the recipient imposes no obstacle, the sacraments are effectual simply because they are properly administered (*ex opere operato*). For the first twelve or thirteen centuries there was no fixed number of sacraments. Some Roman authorities posited only two sacraments, whereas others affirmed as many as twelve. Abelard (d. 1142) acknowledged five sacraments; Hugo of St. Victor (d. 1141), six; and Peter Lombard (d. 1160) and Thomas Aquinas (d. 1274), seven. The Council of Florence in 1439 officially sanctioned the church's seven sacraments.

Rome regards baptism as the sacrament of regeneration and initiation into the church. Infant baptism works *ex opere operato,* since infants offer no resistance to divine grace. Whenever faith was judged important, the faith of the sponsor or the church itself was cited. Adults must possess faith or at least the desire to receive the sacrament. Baptism, according to Rome, (1) remits the guilt of all prior sins, (2) removes the pollution of sin but not "concupiscence," (3) delivers from eternal punishment, and (4) regenerates through the infusion of sanctifying grace. Traditional Catholicism claimed that unbaptized persons suffer perdition in hell. Hence in the absence of a priest, a person may be baptized by a midwife, a layman, or even an unbeliever. If circumstances render baptism impossible, the mere desire to receive baptism is said to suffice. The mode of baptism is not an important issue in Catholicism, although sprinkling is universally practiced.

Rome interprets literally Christ's words at the Last Supper—"this is my body" and "this is my blood" (Matt. 26:26, 28). When consecrated by a priest, the substance of the bread and wine are miraculously changed into Christ's body and blood, although the external characteristics of the elements (texture, color, taste, etc.) remain the same. Rome understands John 6:50–58 to teach that participants in the Mass feed upon Christ not merely spiritually but physically with the mouth. Lest the blood of Christ in the chalice be spilt, the church traditionally withholds the cup from the laity. The view of the Eucharist as a repetition of Christ's sacrifice arose at the time of Gregory the Great (d. 604). In the Mass the priest offers the transubstantiated elements (the body and blood of Christ) as an unbloody sacrifice to God. As a *sacrament* the Mass mediates grace that strengthens and refreshes the soul. As a *sacrifice* it communicates to the living the expiation of venial sins and reconciliation with God. Masses said for souls in purgatory allegedly remit sin and guilt and thereby facilitate the salvation of the departed.

We briefly mention the remaining five sacraments and Rome's interpretation of them. *Confirmation,* performed by a bishop by laying on of hands and anointing with oil (Acts 8:17; Heb. 6:2), confers on those baptized in infancy the power of the Spirit. *Penance* (John 20:22–23; James 5:16) imparts absolution from the guilt and eternal punishment of mortal sins committed after baptism. It involves contrition, confession, works of satisfaction, and priestly absolution. *Matrimony* (Gen. 2:24; Eph. 5:32) confers on baptized partners grace to fulfill marital responsibilities. The sacrament creates a bond that is indissoluble. *Holy Orders* (1 Tim. 4:14; 2 Tim. 1:6) imparts authority to exercise the functions of the priesthood, chiefly the consecration of the host in the Mass. Finally, *extreme unction* (Mark 6:13; James 5:14) involves anointing with oil persons in danger of dying so that souls are strengthened to resist the final assaults of Satan.

Cyprian (d. 258), bishop of Carthage, planted the seeds of the Roman church in its hierarchical and sacerdotal aspects. Against schismatics such as the Novatians, Cyprian asserted the unity of the Catholic church. The one true church is founded on the college of bishops, who are invested with final authority in spiritual matters. "There is one church throughout the world . . . , likewise one episcopate diffused in a harmonious multitude of many bishops."[1]

The bishops, organized as the episcopate, constitute the church's unity and ensure continuity of doctrine and sacramental practice. Cyprian attributed to the See of Peter special prominence. He referred to Rome as the *"matrix et radix"* ("womb and root") of the church.[2] Outside the one true church there is no salvation: "You cannot have God for your Father if you have not the church for your mother."[3] Cyprian commanded that infants be baptized for remission of sins and regeneration. Baptism within the sphere of the church was more important than the mode of baptism, though Cyprian favored sprinkling.[4] Although his thought is not fully systematized, Cyprian used sacrificial language to describe the Eucharist. The priest "imitates that which Christ did [on the cross] and offers the true and full sacrifice in the church."[5] The Eucharist is valid only when performed within the Catholic church by a legitimate priest.

Augustine (d. 430) distinguished between the invisible church (the mystical body of Christ) and the visible church (the external organization). The former consists of the elect from the beginning of history who are known only to God. The latter consists of the institutional

Catholic church, some of whose members belong to Christ and others who do not. Augustine described the visible church as "a net full of fish both good and bad."[6] The visible church is the kingdom of God on earth: "The church in her temporal stage" is "the kingdom of Christ and the kingdom of God."[7] The marks of the true church are its *unity* (as the body of Christ joined in love), *catholicity* (its worldwide scope), *apostolicity* (its unbroken succession of bishops from Peter in the Roman See), and its *sanctity* (but not in the rigorous sense of the Donatists, who made purity the chief mark of the church). Against schismatics Augustine claimed that salvation is peculiar to the Catholic church, since it alone possesses Christ and the sacraments.[8] Yet, against Cyprian, some of the elect are found outside the Roman church.

Augustine defined a sacrament as "a sign of something sacred."[9] "The word is added to the element and there results the sacrament, as if itself also a kind of visible word."[10] The sign not only bears a resemblance to what it signifies (e.g., baptismal water and spiritual cleansing), but it also accomplishes what it signifies. Augustine used the word *sacramentum* in connection with baptism, the Eucharist, penance, holy orders, matrimony, and other rites. With his theology of original sin, Augustine prescribed the baptism of infants. In the latter baptism works *ex opere operato*, whereas adults require faith and a good disposition. Baptism cleanses from original sin, infuses sanctifying grace, unites with Christ, and imparts eternal life. Since Christ is the real minister of baptism, its validity does not depend on the worthiness of the administering priest. Heretical baptism is ineffectual, but when the lapsed return to the true church their baptism becomes effectual for the remission of sins. Thus, against Cyprian, rebaptism is unnecessary. "The definitive theology of infant baptism in Roman Catholicism as well as in the Protestant Reformation was formulated by Augustine."[11] Augustine judged that the bread and wine of the Eucharist symbolize Christ's body and blood. "He set before and entrusted to his disciples his own body and blood under a figure."[12] But the sacrament is more than an empty sign, for it spiritually refreshes the souls of the living and alleviates the condition of the baptized dead in purgatory.[13] To eat Christ's flesh and drink his blood (John 6:50–58) signifies to believe, to be indwelt by Christ, and to be quickened by his Spirit.[14]

Cyril of Jerusalem (d. 368), Gregory of Nyssa (d. 394), Chrysostom (d. 407), and John of Damascus (d. 749) upheld the belief that the bread and wine in the Eucharist changed into the body and blood of Christ. Paschasius Radbert (d. 865), a French Benedictine monk, wrote *The Lord's Body and Blood,* a major contribution to the dogma of transubstantiation. Radbert claimed that as the priest consecrates the elements of the Eucharist the substance of the bread and the wine are supernaturally changed into the body and blood of Christ, although the outward appearance remains unchanged. "The Spirit . . . from the substance of bread and wine daily creates the flesh and blood of Christ by invisible power through the sanctification of his sacrament, though outwardly understood by neither sight nor taste."[15] Radbert held that persons of great faith actually detect the change in the elements. Thus daily Christ is sacrificed in the Mass for the sins of the world, as once he was sacrificed at Calvary. Interpreting John 6:50–58 strictly literally, Radbert claimed that at the table Christians eat Christ's flesh and drink his blood. For those who partake worthily, the Eucharist remits venial sins, strengthens faith, and imparts eternal life.

Since the Cyprianic view of the church changed little up to the time of Trent, we direct attention of the sacraments in the medieval era. Authorities such as Peter Lombard (d. 1160), Alexander of Hales (d. 1245), and Bonaventura (d. 1274) upheld the belief that there are seven sacraments. The Fourth Lateran Council (1215), the most important medieval council, first gave transubstantiation dogmatic status. It referred to "Jesus Christ . . . whose body and blood are truly contained in the sacrament of the altar under the figures of bread and wine, the bread having been transubstantiated into His body and the wine into His blood by divine power."[16] For Thomas Aquinas (d. 1274) the sacraments rightly administered are efficacious signs of grace that work *ex opere operato.* Judging baptism the sacrament of regeneration, Thomas wrote, "Baptism opens the gate of heaven."[17] Children "believe, not of their own act, but by the faith of the Church, which is applied to them."[18] The baptized who impose no obstacle receive remission of original sin, sanctifying grace, the gifts of the Holy Spirit, and access to the heavenly kingdom. Since baptism imparts an indelible character to the soul, it need not be repeated. As long as the water flows over the body, sprinkling, immersion, or pouring are legitimate modes of baptism. For those who wish to be baptized but lack opportunity to do so, the "baptism of desire" (a notion related to implicit faith) suffices.[19] Thomas upheld the classical doctrine of transubstantiation. The instantaneous conversion of the elements occurs in such a way that the whole Christ is present in each. Thus even though the cup is withheld from the laity, the latter partake of both Christ's body and blood in the wafer. Insofar as the Eucharist is *offered,* it is a sacrifice; insofar as *received,* it is a sacrament. The Eucharist removes venial sins and nourishes spiritual life.

The Council of Trent (1545–63)

defined the church as "the body of all the faithful who have ever lived on earth, under the authority of the invisible head, Christ, and the visible head, the successor of Peter, who occupies the Roman See." By divine ordination the church is a hierarchy consisting of bishops, priests, and deacons who exercise its ministry. Trent insisted that not all Christians are priests, the bishops as successors of the apostles are superior to the priests, and the bishop of Rome (or the pope) is the sovereign pontiff. The Profession of the Tridentine Faith (1564) states: "I acknowledge the holy Catholic Apostolic Roman Church for the mother and mistress of all churches; and I promise and swear obedience to the Bishop of Rome, successor to St. Peter, Prince of the Apostles, and Vicar of Jesus Christ."[20]

According to Trent the seven sacraments contain the grace they signify and work *ex opere operato* for those who impose no obstacle. Baptism is effectual in infants on the basis of the faith of the church, whereas adults must come to baptism with a contrite spirit. For infants and adults, baptism regenerates and incorporates into Christ. Concerning the Eucharist, Trent affirmed, "By the consecration of the bread and of the wine, a conversion is made of the whole substance of the bread into the substance of the body of Christ our Lord, and of the whole substance of the wine into the substance of his blood; which conversion is, by the holy Catholic Church, suitably and properly called Transubstantiation."[21] In the Eucharist Christ is immolated in an unbloody manner under the visible signs and offered to God as a propitiatory sacrifice. Thus appeased, God grants to the recipient remission of venial sins, increase of sanctifying grace, preservation from mortal sins, and hope of eternal salvation. Masses also assist the souls of the departed in Christ who are not yet purified.

On the basis of Matthew 16:16–19 and John 21:15–17 the First Vatican Council (1869–70) upheld Peter's primacy over the other apostles. Moreover, the keys of the kingdom were entrusted to Peter's successors in the holy Roman See. Thus "the Roman Pontiff possesses the primacy over the whole world, and the Roman Pontiff is the successor of blessed Peter, Prince of the Apostles, and is the true vicar of Christ, and head of the whole Church, and father and teacher of all Christians; and that full power was given to him in blessed Peter to rule, feed, and govern the universal Church by Jesus Christ."[22] Appealing to Christ's ordination of Peter (Luke 22:32), Vatican I dogmatized the notion of papal infallibility. "The Roman Pontiff, when he speaks *ex cathedra*, . . . when by virtue of his supreme apostolic authority he defines a doctrine regarding faith or morals . . . , is possessed of that infallibility with which the divine Redeemer willed that his Church should be endowed for defining doctrine regarding faith or morals."[23]

The Second Vatican Council (1962–65) made significant changes in Roman ecclesiology. The Council stated that the church, with its visible social structure, possesses the nature of a sacrament. As "the universal sacrament of salvation,"[24] the church represents, vertically, the pledge of union with God and, horizontally, the union of all humankind. The Council stated, on one hand, that church is both "a visible organization and a spiritual community"[25] and, on the other, that the church is both universal and local. The Council reiterated papal infallibility, but set it within the larger context of the infallibility of the entire church.[26] Vatican II ascribed considerable importance to the ministry of the laity. Through baptism all the faithful "are made sharers in the priestly, prophetic, and kingly functions of Christ."[27] Thus there exists both the "apostolate of the hierarchy" and the "apostolate of the laity."[28] The laity exercise apostolic ministries formerly restricted to the ordained priesthood. These include teaching Christian doctrine, various liturgical actions, and the care of souls. In effect the Council upheld a triumvirate of pope, bishops, and laity working in concert. The Council, in addition, adopted a more positive attitude toward non–Roman Catholic Christians. Concerning the Protestant churches (previously called "communities") the Council stated, "All who have been justified by faith in baptism are incorporated into Christ; they therefore have a right to be called Christians, and with good reason are accepted as brothers by the children of the Catholic Church."[29] More radically, non-Christian religions such as Judaism, Islam, Hinduism, and Buddhism are said to mediate salvation to their adherents.[30] The basic structure of the sacraments remained intact in Vatican II. Yet with respect to the Eucharist, the emphasis shifted from what happens to Christ to what happens to the worshiping community. In the Mass the participant experiences the transforming power of Jesus and communion with other believers in the body.

Lutheranism

Lutherans hold that the visible church consists of all who make a profession of faith and who observe the sacraments. Within this external body is hidden the invisible church—the spiritual communion of all justified believers. The marks of the church in its earthly pilgrimage are broadly two: Word (i.e., ordained ministry, preaching, worship, discipline, etc.) and Sacrament (i.e., baptism and the Eucharist). Concerned chiefly with the pure teaching of the Word and right administration of the sacraments, Lutheranism evidences flexibility in matters of church government. In Europe the episcopal and territorial (state-church) system prevailed, whereas in America congregational independence with synodal association for ministry and fellowship was adopted.

Concerning the sacraments, Lutherans hold that baptism and the Lord's Supper are instruments of grace. The Word of God added to the water of baptism remits sins, regenerates, and imputes the righteousness of Christ. The evangelical Lutheran O. Hallesby wrote, "Baptism is the means whereby the little one is regenerated. From the moment of baptism the child has life in God."[31] To avoid the *ex opere operato* position, Lutherans link baptism with faith. Some maintain that when confronted with the Word pronounced over the water infants actually believe. David Scaer, for example, upholds the reality of "infant faith" and insists that the expression "believer's baptism" is a fair description of the Lutheran paedobaptist position.[32] Others claim that infants are baptized on the basis of the faith of parents or sponsor.

Because of Christ's perfect sacrifice, Lutherans reject the Roman doctrine of transubstantiation and the notion of the Eucharist as a propitiatory sacrifice. They interpret Christ's words of institution, "This is my body," and "This is my blood," literally. Given the communication of Christ's divine properties to his human properties (the *communicatio idiomatum*) and the belief that the "right hand of God" is everywhere, Lutherans posit the *ubiquity* of the Lord's glorified body. Hence the real flesh and blood of Christ are present "in, with, and under" the consecrated wine (consubstantiation). Thus all who partake worthily eat and drink Christ's body and blood and so experience forgiveness of sins and strengthening of faith.

In light of certain dubious doctrines and questionable practices on the part

247

of Rome, Martin Luther (d. 1546) was reluctant to use the word "church" (*Kirche*), preferring instead the words "community" (*Gemeinde*) and "communion" (*Gemeine*). Luther delineated the two aspects of the Christian community as (1) an internal, spiritual Christendom and (2) an external, physical Christendom. Concerning the former, the church is the spiritual communion of all persons throughout history who believe on Christ. Luther further described this aspect of the church as an "organism," a "spiritual assembly of souls," and the "holy Christian people of God." The holy Catholic church is "the spiritual gathering of believers wherever they may be in the world."[33] Moreover, the church began with believing Adam: "there has always been a people of God from the time of the first person Adam to the very latest infant born."[34] Against the visible Roman church, Luther insisted (analogous to his concept of the "hidden God") that the church is the believing community concealed from the world. Only God knows those who belong to the spiritual, inner Christendom. But secondly, as the visible, historical reality from the apostles to the present, the church is a mixture of true Christians and hypocrites.[35] The visible church is recognized by its several marks: proclamation of the Word of God, baptism, the Lord's Supper, the office of the keys, and the public ministry. Against Rome, Luther upheld the priesthood of all believers through the grace of baptism and the Holy Spirit's anointing. "We are all priests, as many of us are Christians."[36] Each believer exercises all the functions of the priesthood: proclamation of the Word, administration of the sacraments, prayer, etc. Yet to facilitate order, the congregation sets aside certain gifted believers for *public* ministry. Ordination does not endow Christian ministers with an indelible character; clergy may forfeit the office of public ministry for a variety of reasons.

Luther located the efficacy of the two sacraments in the recipient's faith: "It is not the sacrament, but faith in the sacrament, that justifies."[37] Against the Anabaptists, Luther insisted that a sacrament is not a sign of a person's faith but the assurance of God's activity, to which the recipient assents. Luther upheld infant baptism, arguing that God would not have permitted its widespread practice in the church if it were not true. He preferred the mode of immersion because it best suits the meaning of the word *baptismos* and because it symbolizes the death of the old person and the resurrection of the new (Rom. 6:3–5). The Word of God pronounced over the water causes it to become a gracious washing of regeneration (John 3:3, 5; Titus 3:5). Thus baptism "effects forgiveness of sins, delivers from death and the devil, and grants eternal salvation to all who believe."[38] At first, Luther argued that infants were baptized on the basis of the faith of the sponsor, but later he insisted that infants respond to the Word in the sacrament with faith. "We say and conclude thus: In baptism children themselves believe and have faith of their own."[39] Ultimately, however, the sacrament's efficacy resides in God's Word and commandment (Mark 10:13–15; 16:16).

In *The Babylonian Captivity of the Church* (1520), Luther rejected withholding the cup from the laity, the doctrine of transubstantiation, and the Mass as a propitiatory sacrifice. He interpreted Christ's words of institution—"This is my body" and "This is my blood"—in the realistic sense that the Lord's body and blood are "in, with, and under" the bread and wine (consubstantiation).[40] Thus in the Eucharist a proper eating of Christ's body and blood occurs: "I confess that in the sacrament of the altar the true body and blood of Christ are orally eaten and drunk in the bread and wine."[41] Those who eat worthily receive forgiveness of sins, strengthened faith, and eternal life. Those who partake unworthily heap upon themselves condemnation. Christ's bodily presence in the Eucharist was important for Luther, for it guarantees the resurrection of the believer's body. "The body will live eternally because it has partaken of an eternal food which will not leave it to decay in the grave and turn to dust."[42]

John T. Mueller (d. 1967), a Missouri Synod Lutheran, similarly defined the church in its invisible and visible aspects. The former connotes all people of all times who trust Christ and thereby are justified. "The church [is] the communion of true believers who adhere to the Scriptural doctrine of justification of faith."[43] The latter aspect points to professing Christians, regenerate and unregenerate, organized in local congregations. The bishop (*episkopos*) or elder (*presbyteros*) or shepherd (*poimēn*) exercises the public ministry of the local assembly. Given the priesthood of all believers, public ministers are ordained on the authority of the local congregation. On baptism, Mueller judged that as the Word of Christ is added to the water the sacrament becomes an effectual means of grace that remits sins and unites the soul to Christ. The subjects of baptism are believing adults and infants. According to Mueller, infants personally believe the promises offered to them in baptism (Matt. 18:6; Luke 18:16; 2 Tim. 3:15). "Faith is engendered in that moment when the water is applied to the infant in the name of the triune God."[44] Mueller upheld the traditional Lutheran view of the Eucharist. "Lutherans . . . regard the sacramental union between the bread and body and between the wine and the blood as so real and intimate that in the sacramental act the communicant receives Christ's true body and

blood in, with, and under the bread and wine, the bread and wine indeed in a natural manner, but the body and blood in a supernatural, incomprehensible manner."[45]

Presbyterians and Reformed

This tradition broadly follows Augustine and Luther in differentiating between invisible and a visible aspects of the church. The invisible church represents the spiritual communion of believers of all ages who constitute God's elect. Contrary to Rome, Presbyterians and Reformed hold that the unity and catholicity of the church are rooted in its invisible nature rather than in its visible, institutional structure. The marks that distinguish the true church from heretical sects are the pure preaching of the Word, authentic celebration of the sacraments, and the exercise of biblical discipline. Presbyterians generally hold that the principles of church polity are set forth normatively in the New Testament. The ministry of the local church consists of a plurality of elders and deacons chosen by the congregation. Elders include a preaching elder, teaching elder, and lay ruling elders who direct the affairs of the congregation. The governing body of the local church, called the session (Presbyterian) or council (Reformed) consists of ordained and lay elders. Over the sessions of local congregations is the presbytery, or classis, comprised of ordained ministers and ruling elders. The presbytery exercises general oversight of the church and its elders and administers pastoral care. Over the presbyteries is the general assembly, or synod, which deliberates matters of concern to all the churches. Berkhof comments that "such a wider organization undoubtedly imposes certain limitations on the autonomy of the local churches, but also promotes the growth and welfare of the churches . . . and serves to give fuller expression to the unity of the church."[46] Presbyterians hold that church and state each has its peculiar responsibilities. The state in no wise dominates the church; rather, it maintains the peace, protects the church, and follows biblical principles in civil matters.

Presbyterians view the sacraments as signs and seals of the covenant of grace that mediate spiritual benefits when received in faith. They claim that New Testament baptism fulfills the Old Testament rite of circumcision. As the Jewish infant was incorporated into national Israel by the rite of circumcision, so the child of Christian parents is received into the church by the sacrament of baptism. For a few theologians baptism is a sign signifying that regeneration has begun prior to birth ("presumptive regeneration"). For most, however, baptism is a sign of future new birth ("promissory regeneration"). Under the covenant of grace baptism signifies forgiveness of sins (Acts 2:38), regeneration (Titus 3:5), and incorporation into Christ. When the child (as heir of the covenant of grace) comes to maturity, it is expected to ratify its baptism by openly confessing Christ. Since baptism primarily symbolizes cleansing from sins, the mode may be pouring, sprinkling, or immersion.[47] How baptism is administered does not determine its efficacy.

As baptism is the fulfillment of the Old Testament rite of circumcision, the Lord's Supper is seen as the fulfillment of the Jewish Passover. Theologians in the tradition uphold a realistic view of the Eucharist, insisting that Christ is present in the Supper not corporeally (his body is located in heaven) but spiritually as a life-giving influence. As a sign and seal of the covenant of grace, the Eucharist actually conveys to the worthy recipient the benefits of Christ's redemption. The Eucharist must be administered to believers by pastors or elders.

John Calvin (d. 1564) distinguished between invisible and visible aspects of the church. The invisible church includes all God's elect from the beginning of time, i.e., from Adam and the patriarchs to the last believer. The visible church, as the aggregate of local churches, comprises all professing Christians who are baptized and observe the Lord's Supper. Calvin had a high view of the empirical church, which in its unity and catholicity is the mother of all believers. "Away from her bosom one cannot hope for any forgiveness of sins or any salvation."[48] The marks of the visible church are the pure preaching of the Word, the faithful administration of the sacraments, and the exercise of spiritual discipline. As for the church's ministry, Calvin identified three "extraordinary" offices relevant only for the early church: namely, apostles, prophets, and evangelists (Eph. 4:11). The church's "permanent" offices are four in number: (1) pastors or preachers, who proclaim the Gospel, administer the sacraments, and engage in pastoral care; (2) doctors or teachers, who expound the truths of the faith and train future ministers; (3) presbyters or elders, who govern and administer discipline; and (4) deacons, who care for the poor and needy. According to Calvin, the task of civil government is to lend broad support to the church in its earthly mission. Such a view paved the way for the territorial church in Europe.

Calvin defined a sacrament as "a testimony of divine grace toward us, confirmed by an outward sign."[49] God's word of promise added to the material element constitutes a sacrament. Calvin believed that since we are creatures of flesh God gave his promises under tangibly palpable things such as water, bread, and wine. In other words, via the sacraments God communicates with us by senses other than hearing. Calvin added that the sacraments do not merely suggest spiritual realities; they also effectually *convey* grace to those who believe. Thus the sacraments "sustain, nourish, confirm, and increase our faith."[50] The two sacraments must be administered by legitimate ministers of the church.

Calvin taught that believing adults should be instructed in the faith and then baptized. "Baptism is like a sealed document to confirm to us that all our sins are so abolished, remitted, and effaced that they can never come to his sight, be recalled, or charged against us."[51] Once adults are in the fellowship of the faithful, the covenant promise of salvation extends to their children also (Gen. 17:7). Given this covenant blessing, whereby the offspring of at least one Christian parent is "holy" (1 Cor. 7:14), infants may be baptized. Calvin saw a relationship between the Old Testament sign of circumcision and the New Testament sign of baptism. Both signify entry into the covenant community, and both mediate saving grace. Since God commanded that children of the patriarchs be circumcised, so children of one or more Christian parents should be baptized (cf. Mark 10:14–15). Calvin not only held that baptized children are "part of the family of the church,"[52] but he used language descriptive of regeneration. "We deny . . . that infants cannot be regenerated by God's power, which is as easy and ready for him as it is incomprehensible and wonderful to us."[53] As support Calvin appealed to John the Baptist's quickening by the Spirit in his mother's womb (Luke 1:15,44). Calvin's bottom line was that "infants are baptized into future repentance and faith, and even though these have not yet been formed in them, the seed of both lies hidden with them by the secret working of the Spirit."[54]

Believing that Christ's resurrected body is in heaven, Calvin upheld the real and spiritual (not bodily) presence of Christ in the Eucharist. Christ's words, "This is my body," and "This is my blood," is a figure of speech known as a metonymy, whereby the name of the sign is given to the thing signified (e.g., "rock" for "Christ" in 1 Cor. 10:4). In this sense Christ called his body "bread" and his blood "wine." The eating and drinking in the Eucharist do not merely recollect what Christ has wrought; rather, through faith the Spirit actually communicates the whole Christ to believers in the Supper and nourishes them through this act of communion with the crucified and risen Mediator (1 Cor. 10:16). In a profound sense the Eucharist becomes for believers "a spiritual banquet."[55] That is, "our souls are fed by the flesh and blood of Christ in the same way that bread and wine keep and sustain physical life."[56] Because the ungodly receive the elements without faith, the Eucharist imparts no grace to them.

Reformed confessional statements explain the nature of the church and the sacraments as follows: According to the Westminster Confession (1647),

> The catholic or universal Church, which is invisible, consists of the whole number of the elect, that have been, are, or shall be gathered into one, under Christ the head. . . . The visible Church, which is also catholic or universal under the gospel . . . consists of all those, throughout the world, that profess the true religion, and of their children. . . . Unto this catholic visible Church Christ hath given the ministry, oracles, and ordinances of God for the gathering and perfecting of the saints. (ch. XXV.1–3)

Concerning the sacraments, the Confession (ch. XXVIII.1, 3–4) states that

> baptism is . . . a sign and seal of the covenant of grace, of his ingrafting into Christ, of regeneration, of remission of sins, and of his giving up unto God, through Jesus Christ, to walk in newness

of life. . . . Dipping of the person into the water is not necessary; but baptism is rightly administered by pouring or sprinkling water upon the person. . . . [Moreover], not only those that actually do profess faith in and obedience unto Christ, but also the infants of one or both believing parents are to be baptized.

Concerning the last point the Heidelberg Catechism (1563) states, "Infants as well as adults are in God's covenant and are his people. They, no less than adults, are promised the forgiveness of sins. . . . Therefore, by baptism, the mark of the covenant, infants should be received into the Christian church" (Lord's Day XXVII, A. 74; cf. Westminster Shorter Catechism, Q. and A. 95). The Reformed confessions aver that the Lord's Supper is not a mere memorial but a spiritual feast by which Christ communicates the benefits of his atoning death. According to the Heidelberg Catechism, when I as a believer receive the elements, Christ "nourishes and refreshes my soul for eternal life with his crucified body and poured-out blood" (Lord's Day XXVIII, A. 75; cf. Westminster Confession, art. XXIX.7).

Charles Hodge (d. 1878) held that a candidate may be excluded from church membership only if demonstrated to be unworthy by overtly evil behavior. Since the commonwealth of Israel comprised both righteous and unrighteous persons, "it is not the purpose of God that the visible church on earth should consist exclusively of true believers."[57] In fact, "the attempt to make the visible church consist exclusively of true believers must not only inevitably fail of success, but it must also be productive of evil."[58] Hodge continued by declaring that as circumcision was the sign and seal of membership in Israel ("the Hebrew church"[59]), baptism represents the sign and seal of membership in the visible church under the New Testament economy. For Hodge the subjects of baptism include children of the cove-

nant. Infant baptism (1) procures membership in the visible church, and (2) it may confer the benefits of redemption, i.e., cleansing of sin and guilt, imputation of Christ's righteousness, Spirit regeneration, and reconciliation with God. "Baptism . . . assures them of salvation if they do not renounce their baptismal covenant."[60] Immersion, affusion, and sprinkling are all legitimate modes of baptism. Regarding the Eucharist, Hodge taught that although absent from the Supper bodily, Christ is present operationally in the sense that he infuses spiritual life into worthy recipients. Consistent with his conviction that no person may judge another's heart, Hodge claimed that the church should not be overly restrictive as to whom it permits to partake of the Lord's Supper.

Anglicans and Episcopalians

Anglicans regard the church as the visible society on earth united with its bishops. Although the Church of England consists of factions such as Anglo-Catholics ("high church"), latitudinarians ("broad church"), and evangelicals ("low church"), generally Canterbury has forged a middle way between Rome and Geneva. The English Reformers viewed the Church of England as the Catholic Church in England freed from Roman jurisdiction. Anglicans uphold episcopacy as the essence of the church; Christ committed spiritual authority to the bishops as the legitimate successors of the apostles. The Anglo-Catholic wing upholds the principle of "apostolic succession," whereas the evangelical wing affirms "the historic episcopate"—there being no "mechanical" conveyance of the Spirit by the laying on of hands.[61] The three orders of ministry include (1) bishops, who guard the faith, ordain other clergy, and exercise discipline in their jurisdiction. The bishop is the visible symbol of the unity and catholicity of the church. Thus (upholding the conviction of Ignatius), "where the bishop is there is the church in its fullness."[62] (2) *Presbyters* or priests, who preach the Word and administer the sacraments (evangelicals stress the former, Anglo-Catholics the latter). And (3) *deacons,* who constitute both a permanent order of service and a temporary order as preparation for priesthood. The Church of England traditionally upheld the Erastian principle,[63] by which the monarchy exercises temporal jurisdiction over the church. Thus the king or queen calls general assemblies, appoints bishops, and makes ecclesiastical laws, but refrains from the ministry of Word and sacraments.

The Church of England distinguishes between the sacraments of Baptism and the Eucharist as ordained by Christ and Confirmation, Reconciliation, Marriage, Unction, and Orders as "rites and states of life." As effectual signs the sacraments quicken, strengthen, and confirm faith. To varying degrees baptism and the Eucharist *give* what they signify. Anglo-Catholics (as reflected in the American Prayer Book) insist that baptism actually conveys saving grace (baptismal regeneration). Low-church Anglicans, on the other hand, generally follow Calvin's covenant view of baptism. In both cases baptism looks forward rather than backward. Believing adults and infants are proper subjects of baptism. With regard to the Eucharist, Anglo-Catholics hold to a ritualistic view that emphasizes the substantial presence of Christ in the Supper, if not transubstantiation. Low-church Anglicans subscribe to a real presence, whereby believers spiritually commune with the crucified and risen Christ in the Supper.

Although Irenaeus (d. 200) fits into no neat category, he sowed the seeds of the monarchial view of the church. Whereas the Gnostics claimed to have received a secret tradition from the apostles, Irenaeus argued that the apostles transmitted the "rule of faith" to the bishops they appointed over the churches. Thus, with a view to preserving the doctrinal purity and unity of the visible church, Irenaeus upheld "the succession of the bishops" from the apostles.[64] His view of apostolic succession concerned primarily the faithful transmission of apostolic teaching and secondarily governing authority in the churches. Thus Irenaeus wrote of the apostles "delivering up their own place of government to these men [i.e., the bishops]."[65] The bishops, who occupy the place of the apostles, possess a special *charisma* for the preservation of the truth and pastoral care of the churches. Since Irenaeus occasionally used "bishop" and "presbyter" interchangeably,[66] the bishop may have been the prominent elder in the local congregation. Irenaeus noted that the church at Rome most faithfully preserves the apostolic tradition and so possesses "preeminent authority."[67] As for the sacraments, Irenaeus attested the baptism of children of professing believers. Baptism effects cleansing from sins, regeneration, and infusion of the Spirit. Concerning the Eucharist, Irenaeus claimed that at the prayer of dedication the Spirit unites the body and blood of Christ with the elements. Thus when believers partake of the Supper they are nourished by the body and blood of Christ and thereby are fitted for resurrection and eternal life.[68]

The Thirty-nine Articles (1563), the official doctrinal standard of the Church of England, focuses on the visible rather than the invisible church. According to the American Revision (1801), "the visible Church of Christ is a congregation of faithful men, in which the pure Word of God is preached, and the Sacraments be duly administered according to Christ's ordinance" (art. XIX). The sacraments are not merely badges of Christian profession; they are also "effectual signs of God's grace, and God's good will towards us, by the which he doth work invisibly in us, and doth not only quicken, but also strengthen and confirm our Faith in him" (art. XXV). Thus baptism is "a sign of Regeneration or New-Birth, whereby, as by an instrument, they that receive Baptism rightly are grafted into the Church; the promises of the forgiveness of sins, and of our adoption to be the sons of God by the Holy Ghost, are visibly signed and sealed." Furthermore, "The Baptism of young children is . . . to be retained in the Church, as most agreeable with the institution of Christ" (art. XXVII). The Articles reject the Roman doctrines of transubstantiation and the sacrifice of the Mass. The statements concerning the Lord's Supper approximate the Calvinist position: "The Body of Christ is given, taken, and eaten, in the Supper, only after an heavenly and spiritual manner. And the means whereby the Body of Christ is received and eaten in the Supper, is Faith" (art. XXVIII).

H. B. Swete (d. 1917) affirmed that as Jesus Christ is both invisible and visible, "so His mystical body the Church is one, invisible on one side of its life, visible on the other."[69] Swete stressed the visible dimension of the church, namely, the Christian society on earth instituted by Christ with its ministry, sacraments, membership, and liturgy. The church is both catholic and apostolic—the latter in that it was founded by the apostles, adheres to apostolic teaching, and perpetuates apostolic ministry. The church's ordained ministry is threefold, consisting of (1) the *episcopate,* that unbroken continuity of bishops from the apostles (Acts 15; 21:18). The Church of England, by virtue of "the succession of the historical Episcopate,"[70] is the exemplar church. Swete refused to call non-Episcopal communities "churches."

Rather, "they are voluntary associations of baptized Christians, religious societies which have shown themselves capable of doing much admirable work; but they lack that note of unity which characterizes the historical Church. 'Churches,' in the strict and Scriptural sense, they are not."[71] The ordained ministry of the church, furthermore, includes (2) the *presbyteriate* (Acts 14:23; 20:17), which administers the Word and the sacraments, and (3) the *diaconate* (Acts 6), which engages in works of service. A nonordained ministry, on the other hand, is exercised by the common priesthood of all believers conferred at baptism. Swete's discussion of the relation between church and state reflects Erastianism: "The alliance of Church and State is an ideal which for the sake of the State is to be preserved even at considerable sacrifice." Furthermore, "a breach between Church and State would be deplorable."[72]

According to Swete, the incarnation of God in Jesus has made the physical the vehicle of the spiritual. The sacrament of baptism, which marks the beginning of the spiritual life, is a putting on of Christ and an entrance into his body, the church. "Baptism is a second birth which admits us into the supernatural life of the Body of Christ."[73] The Eucharist, which represents the perfecting of the spiritual life, is the chief means of deepening fellowship with Christ and with one another. In the Eucharist Christ comes to worthy participants with a special sacramental presence. "The Eucharistic Presence is . . . a constant source of refreshing grace."[74]

Adherents of a Congregational Form of Government

Some early Fathers, the Anabaptists, Congregationalists, Baptists, and some Independents—although differing somewhat on the sacraments—hold common convictions regarding the nature and governance of the church. Sixteenth-century "evangelical" Anabaptists did not seek reformation of the church (as did Lutherans and Calvinists) but its radical reconstruction along apostolic lines. They viewed the *ekklēsia* as a voluntary society of regenerate people, governed by locally elected leaders in independent churches, purified by strict discipline, and separated from higher ecclesiastical and political powers. The Anabaptist concept of the church as a voluntary fellowship of baptized believers separated from the world differed significantly from the magisterial Reformers' vision of a territorial church. Congregationalists in England (e.g., John Owen, Philip Dodderidge) and America (e.g., Jonathan Edwards), while generally following the Westminster Confession, stressed the "gathered" nature of the church and the autonomy of the local congregation. The church is the believing fellowship of disciples led by the Spirit. Church members choose their ministers and elect their officers.

Baptists regard the church as the spiritual body of which Christ is head. The universal or invisible church finds local and visible expression in congregations of professing believers who submit to the Word of God and observe the ordinances of baptism and the Lord's Supper. The word "church" in the New Testament always refers to the body of Christ in its universal (invisible) or local (visible) aspects, never to regional, national, or international organizations. Membership in Christ's church is limited to born-again, baptized believers who, though differing in gifts, are all equally priests before God. Concerning local church polity, the broad tradition maintains that each congregation is autonomous and self-governing. Responsible only to Christ, the members choose ministers, elect officers, regulate worship and discipline, send missionaries, and allocate funds. Local churches may enter into voluntary associations or fellowships, but the latter have no control over local congregations. Ministry leadership is exercised by ordained pastors or elders, who preach, teach, and administer the ordinances, assisted by lay deacons and deaconesses. "The pastor and deacons are the spiritual leaders of the church, and there are no officers over them in the exercise of that leadership."[75] Baptists hold that God ordained the church and the state as two distinct institutions that function in two different spheres. On the basis of the principle of separation of church and state, civil authorities may not interfere in the operation of the churches or the beliefs of individual Christians.

Recently leaders such as Earl Radmacher, Ray Steadman, Gene Getz, and John MacArthur, Jr., have advocated a multiple-elder polity or system of collegiality in ministry. They suggest that, following the model of the Jewish synagogue, the early church adhered to a system of several elders who shared leadership in ministry. A board of elders consisting of those who manage, shepherd, preach, and teach makes maximal use of the Spirit's diverse gifts, offers a system of checks and balances, and avoids the "benevolent dictator" syndrome occasionally seen in single-pastor churches. MacArthur writes, "all the biblical data indicates that the pastorate is a team effort. . . . The norm in the New Testament church was a plurality of elders. There is no reference in all the New Testament to a one-pastor congregation."[76] Getz adds, "The Bible definitely teaches multiple leadership. . . . A group of godly elders and pastors serve as a multiple model of Christlikeness."[77] Some advocate that elders are selected by fellow elders (a self-perpetuating system), others that elders be chosen by congregational vote. Radmacher, a Baptist, advocates the principle of "congregational authority" rather than "congregational government."[78]

Regarding the sacraments, Baptists and some others prefer the term *ordinance* to *sacrament,* since baptism and the Lord's Supper were ordained by Christ and mediate no special grace or spiritual power. The ordinance of baptism is a visible sign demonstrating the believer's identification with Christ in his death and resurrection. The subjects of baptism, therefore, are responsible persons who repent of sin and trust Christ. "Believers' baptism" is regarded as the only legitimate form of baptism; infant baptism is no baptism at all. Moreover, converts to Christ baptized in infancy must be rebaptized upon a credible profession of faith. The mode of baptism, both from the meaning of the word *baptizō* and the symbolism of death and resurrection, is said to be immersion in water.

Baptists and others uphold the commemorative view of the Lord's Supper. Christ instituted the ordinance to serve as a continual reminder of his passion and atoning death on the cross. Thus the bread and wine are symbols of Christ's body broken and blood shed for believers' salvation. According to this view, the Lord's Supper communicates no special efficacy not available through the word of preaching or prayer. The spiritual utility of the ordinance resides not in the sacrament but in the *faith* of its born-again participants.

Seeds of this view of the church occur in the postapostolic era. Ignatius (d. 117), like Clement, attested both universal and local aspects of the church. Faced with schisms within the body and heresies without, Ignatius stressed the unity, holiness, and universality of Christ's church. To preserve the apostolic tradition and thus maintain church unity and doctrinal purity,

each local congregation was led by a bishop assisted by presbyters and deacons.[79] "Let all follow the bishop as Jesus Christ did the Father, and the presbyters as you would the apostles. Reverence the deacons as you would the command of God."[80] Vis-à-vis the presbyters and deacons, the bishop functioned as *primus inter pares* in the local congregation. The episcopate, in other words, was still congregational. The notion of apostolic succession does not occur in Ignatius. Significantly Ignatius made no mention of a bishop in his letter to the church at Rome. Ignatius viewed baptism as the rite of initiation into the church. Its validity depends on the right disposition of the baptized. He described the Eucharist figuratively as the flesh and blood of the Savior who died for our sins and was raised from the dead. The Eucharist is the "medicine of immortality and the antidote against death, enabling us to live forever in Jesus Christ."[81]

The *Didache* (c. 120–180) specified the following ministers: apostles (itinerant missionaries), prophets (anointed spokespersons in the churches), teachers (catechists), bishops (identical with elders), and deacons (ministers to the poor). The basic pattern of ministry appeared to be that of bishops (or elders) and deacons, both of which were chosen by the local congregation: "Elect . . . for yourselves bishops and deacons worthy of the Lord."[82] Concerning baptism, the document reads, "Baptize . . . in running water. But if you have no running water, baptize in any other; . . . But if the one is lacking, pour the other three times on the head 'in the name of the Father, and Son, and Holy Spirit.' "[83] The *Didache* was the first Christian writing to designate the Lord's Supper a "Eucharist." The latter was celebrated in the evening as part of the *agapē* meal or love feast. [84] When the church grew larger, the Eucharist and the love feast separated, the latter eventually dying out as a regular practice. The document describes the bread and wine as "spiritual food and drink and eternal life."[85] Only baptized believers should participate in the Lord's Supper.

Against the Catholics and Luther, Zwingli (d. 1531) upheld a broadly memorial view of the Lord's Supper. The latter is a pictorial representation of Christ's broken body and shed blood. "The Eucharist . . . is the commemoration, festival, or celebration of our redemption."[86] Jesus' words "This is my body" and "This is my blood," imply that the elements "signify," "represent," or "are a reminder of" his atoning sacrifice. If the words were intended literally, "then Christ is a vine, or a silly sheep, or a door, and Peter is the foundation-stone of the Church."[87] Zwingli emphasized that Christ's presence in the Eucharist is not corporeal, according to his human nature, but spiritual, according to his divine nature. This is so because the body in which Christ ascended to heaven is not ubiquitous (otherwise it would be infinite and eternal). Zwingli interpreted 1 Corinthians 10:16 as follows: The word koinōnia (translated "communion" [KJV] or "participation" [NIV]) means "community." Paul, in other words, taught that by partaking of the Eucharist Christians attest that they are the "community of the body and blood of Christ" rather than a company of idol-worshipers.[88]

One authority notes that "it is with the appearance of the evangelical Anabaptists that the Believers' Church movement as such actually began."[89] Ecclesiology was a central concern of the Anabaptists. They emphasized the priesthood of all believers, the purity of the visible church, and the separation of church and state. The Anabaptist Schleitheim Confession (1527) depicted the church as "God's little flock and people" (art. 5), the temple of God, whose citizenship is in heaven and which separates itself from the evil world system. Concerning the ordinances, "Baptism shall be given to all those who have learned repentance and amendment of life, and who believe truly that their sins are taken away by Christ, and to all those who walk in the resurrection of Jesus Christ. . . . This excludes all infant baptism, the highest and chief abomination of the pope" (art. 1). Only baptized believers are admitted to the Lord's Table, which serves as a memorial of Christ's supreme sacrifice on the cross (art. 3).

The New Hampshire Baptist Confession (1833) states:

> We believe that a visible Church of Christ is a congregation of baptized believers, . . . observing the ordinances of Christ; governed by his laws, and exercising the gifts, rights, and privileges invested in them by his Word; that its only scriptural officers are bishops, or pastors, and deacons (art. XIII). [Concerning the ordinances:] We believe that Christian baptism is the immersion in water of a believer, into the name of the Father, and Son, and Holy Ghost; to show forth, in a solemn and beautiful emblem, our faith in the crucified, buried, and risen Saviour, with its effect in our death to sin and resurrection to a new life; that it is prerequisite to the privileges of a Church relation; and to the Lord's Supper, in which the members of the Church . . . are to commemorate together the dying love of Christ. (art. XIV)

The Baptist A. H. Strong (d. 1921) distinguished between the invisible or universal church and the visible or local church. Concerning the former, he wrote, "The church of Christ, in its largest signification, is the whole company of regenerate persons in all times and ages, in heaven and on earth."[90] Concerning the latter, "the individual church may be defined as that smaller company of regenerate persons, who, in any given community, unite themselves voluntarily together, in accordance with Christ's laws, for the purpose of receiving the complete establishment of his kingdom in themselves and in the world."[91] The church began at Pentecost; only the "germ" or "bud" of it existed prior to Calvary. Prerequisites for local church membership are a credible confession of regeneration and believer's baptism. Concerning church government, from God's side the church is an absolute monarchy under Christ. But from the human side the church "is an absolute democracy, in which the whole body of members is entrusted with the duty and responsibility of carrying out the laws of Christ."[92] Each member having one vote, the church elects its officers and chooses its ministers, the latter consisting of pastor (or elder/bishop) and deacons. "The gifts of teaching and ruling belonged to the same individual."[93] Larger New Testament churches had a plurality of elders; others had but one elder.

According to Strong, ordinances are external rites commanded by Christ as visible signs of gospel truths. By way of baptism the born-again believer "professes his death to sin and resurrection to spiritual life."[94] Infant baptism, Strong argued, lacks biblical warrant. The Lord's Supper is a memorial celebration that symbolizes (1) Christ's death for our sins, (2) our appropriation of its benefits through union with Christ, (3) the believer's continuous dependence on the Savior for spiritual life, and (4) the coming perfection of the kingdom of God. Those who would partake of the Lord's Supper must be (1) regenerated, (2) baptized, (3) members of that particular church, and (4) living upright lives.

Other useful studies on this subject include works by Robert Saucy,[95] Howard Snyder,[96] and John MacArthur.[97]

BIBLICAL TEACHING

We now test the historical hypotheses by turning to the primary data of Scripture to determine which understandings of the church and its ministry, sacraments, and mission best fit the revealed data.

Old Testament Backgrounds

The genesis of important ecclesiological concepts can be found in the Old Testament, particularly in the organization of Israel for religious purposes. Old Testament material in the present chapter focuses on the cult, whereas in the next chapter it will focus on the people of the covenant. The Hebrew noun qāhāl ("assembly," "company," "congregation") is related to qôl ("voice") and signifies an assembly summoned for a particular purpose. The Septuagint translates qāhāl primarily by ekklēsia but some thirty-six times by synagōgē. In a nontheological sense qāhāl denotes an assembly of any sort, e.g.: (1) an Israelite civic assembly (1 Kings 12:3; Job 30:28), (2) a company of evildoers (Ps. 26:5), (3) an assembly for war (Judges 20:2; 1 Sam. 17:47), (4) a company of returning exiles (Neh. 7:66; Jer. 31:8), (5) a group of foreigners (Ezek. 17:17; 27:34), and (6) a community of nations (Gen. 35:11). In a theological sense qāhāl denotes (1) the congregation of Israel as an organized body (Num. 16:3; Deut. 31:30; Neh. 13:1), (2) the assembly to establish the covenant on Sinai (Deut. 9:10; 10:4), (3) an assembly for covenant renewal (Deut. 31:30; Josh. 8:35), and (4) an assembly for feasts, fasts, and worship (2 Chron. 20:5; 30:2; Neh. 5:13; Joel 2:16).

The Hebrew word 'ēdāh ("congregation," "assembly") derives from the verb yā'ad, which in the Hiphil means to "appoint" or "come together." Of its 147 occurrences in the Hebrew Bible, 123 are in the Pentateuch, and of these 81 are found in the book of Numbers. The Septuagint consistently translates ʿēdāh by the Greek noun synagōgē. In Scripture ʿēdāh is used exclusively of Israel, the word emphasizing the unity of the congregation of Israel especially in relation to its religious life. Thus ʿēdāh denotes "the people as a community in all its functions," particularly "the community centered in the cult or the law."[98] The first occurrence of the word in Exodus 12:3 points to the formation of the fledgling nation.

Zāqēn ("old person," "elder") designates the head of a family, a town, a tribe, or Israel as a whole. The zāqēn formed a council to regulate community life in the political, judicial, religious, and military spheres. At various times in Jewish history the elders enforced the Mosaic Law, administered justice, officiated at the sacrifices, and exercised administrative oversight of their communities. Israel had elders during the Egyptian period (Exod. 3:16, 18; 4:29), the sojourn in the wilderness (24:1, 9, 14; Deut. 5:23), the conquest of Canaan (Josh. 8:33; 20:4; 23:2), the monarchy (2 Sam. 19:11; 1 Kings 12:6; 21:8), and the Babylonian captivity (Jer. 29:1). They also had elders upon their return to Palestine from exile (Ezra 10:8, 14), and at the time of Jesus (e.g., Matt. 16:21; 21:23; 26:47). In the first century, the Sanhedrin in Jerusalem was the most important council of elders. The synagogue ("house of assembling") likely came into existence following the destruction of the first temple (586 B.C.) and during the Babylonian exile (cf. Ezek. 11:16). The elders of an Israelite town or city normally managed the affairs of the synagogue (John 12:42). The council of elders usually chose one of their number to be "synagogue ruler" (Mark 5:22; Luke 8:41, 49; 13:14); however, Acts 13:15 indicates that sometimes several officials served in this capacity. The synagogue ruler cared for the synagogue building and administered the public services.

At the first Passover (Exod. 12:1–30) in Egypt God commanded each household to slay a male lamb or kid and sprinkle the blood on the lintel and doorposts of the house. The houses marked with the blood were spared judgment by the destroying angel. Thus the Passover (pesah) was a memorial of the greatest redemptive event in the Old Testament, i.e., Israel's deliverance from four hundred years of Egyptian bondage. The Passover prefigured the death of Christ; hence Calvary's victory over sin and death is the perfect fulfillment of this Old Testament event (John 1:29; 1 Cor. 5:7; 1 Peter 1:18–19; Rev. 5:12). Commemorating Christ's atoning sacrifice, the Eucharist represents the New Testament counterpart to the Old Testament Passover. Thus Christians rightly observe the Lord's Supper in place of the Passover.

The Old Testament records a variety of ceremonial washings. Some of Israel's purification rites involved sprinkling water or blood. The Levites were sprinkled prior to their consecration to render them ceremonially clean (Num. 8:6–7). Persons who touched a corpse were sprinkled to make them fit for worship (Num. 19:11–22). Other purification rites involved bathing in water. Aaron and his sons were ceremonially washed at their ordination to the priesthood (Lev. 8:5–6). The high priest on the Day of Atonement bathed in water prior to entering the holy place (16:1–28). The New Testament refers to these Jewish ceremonial washings (perhaps also proselyte baptism) as baptismoi (Heb. 6:2; 9:10). Yet since these external Jewish washings rendered people at most ceremonially clean, Yahweh promised a future, internal cleansing: "I will sprinkle clean water on you, and you will be clean; I will cleanse you from all your impurities and from all your idols" (Ezek. 36:25).

259

The Jewish washings found their perfection in the spiritual cleansing Christ wrought through his shed blood (John 13:10; 1 Cor. 6:11). Thus despite the differences, the Jewish purification rites provided some of the inspiration for the baptism of John and Christian baptism. The former were related to the latter as shadow to substance.

Synoptic Gospels

The word *ekklēsia* ("assembly," "meeting," "congregation")[99] occurs 114 times in the New Testament with three primary meanings: (1) an assembly of citizens (Acts 19:32, 39, 41), (2) an assembly of Israelites (Acts 7:38; Heb. 2:12), and (3) the church of Jesus Christ (109 times). The word *ekklēsia* occurs three times in two verses of the Gospels (Matt. 16:18; 18:17). In the latter text Jesus taught that if an erring brother refused to listen to those whom he has offended they should "tell it to the church." Matthew envisaged the local community of Jewish-Christian believers viewed as the true Israel headed by the Messiah, Jesus. In the former text (Matt. 16:18), following Peter's faithful confession of Jesus' identity, the Lord said, "I tell you that you are Peter [*Petros,* i.e., stone], and on this rock [*petra*] I will build my church, and the gates of Hades will not overcome it."

Interpreters variously explain the meaning of "rock" (*petra*): (1) The *papal system* (Peter and the succession of bishops in the Roman See) upon which Christ founded his church (so Cyprian, Cajetan, Vatican I). But it is highly unlikely that Jesus' disciples would have understood *petra* in this institutionalized sense. (2) *Christ* himself (cf. Ps. 118:22; Rom. 9:32–33; 1 Peter 2:6–8). For Jesus said that he is the foundation of the church (so Augustine, Jerome, Luther, Scofield Reference Bible, Thiessen). (3) *Peter as pri-mary proclaimer* of Christ in the early chapters of Acts (cf. Gal. 2:9; Eph. 2:20). Protestants claim that Peter's foundational role in the early church was only temporary (Cullmann, Guthrie, Saucy). (4) *Peter's confession* of Christ in the preceding context (Matt. 16:16). Peter's confession thus constituted the foundation upon which Christ would build his church (Origin, Calvin, Bruce). And (5) *Jesus' own teaching* (cf. Matt. 7:24, "these words"). In Matthew 16:18 the Lord identified his teachings as the bedrock upon which the church would be built (Gundry). We understand the "rock" in Jesus' play on words as Peter's role in the early chapters of Acts as primary confessor of Christ. For Jesus said further to Peter— "I will give you the keys of the kingdom of heaven; whatever you bind on earth will be bound in heaven, and whatever you loose on earth will be loosed in heaven" (v. 19). "Keys" is a figure connoting the authority delegated to Peter to admit or refuse entry to the kingdom (cf. Luke 11:52), and the binding and loosing refer to the remitting or nonremitting of sins (cf. John 20:23). The fact that the access granted is to the *kingdom* and not to the *church* rules out the idea of ecclesiastical office. Moreover, Jesus delegated such authority to Peter and the other disciples (Matt. 18:18).[100] Evidence is lacking for the hypothesis that Peter possessed a unique authority that was transferred to the other successor apostles. Furthermore, it is clear from Jesus' promise to Peter in verse 18 that the *ekklēsia* was not yet in existence but was a future entity.

The verb *baptō* (to "dip in or under") occurs four times in the New Testament (Luke 16:24; John 13:26; Rev. 19:13), none in the technical sense of baptism. The verb *baptizō*, an intensive form of *baptō* meaning to "dip, immerse, submerge, baptize,"[101] occurs seventy-six times in the New Testament. In secular usage it signified the act of drowning a person or sinking a ship. The notion of immersion in water appears to be the primary meaning of *baptizō*. The noun *baptismos* ("dipping" or "immersion") occurs four times in the sense of a ritual Jewish cleansing by immersion (Heb. 6:2; 9:10). The word *baptisma* ("baptism") in the New Testament describes both the baptism of John (Matt. 3:7; 21:25; Mark 1:4; Luke 7:29) as well as Christian baptism (Rom. 6:4; Eph. 4:5; Col. 2:12; 1 Peter 3:21). The verb *rhantizō* (to "sprinkle") occurs four times concerning Jewish rituals of sprinkling blood (Heb. 9:13, 19, 21; 10:22) but never of Christian baptism.

Consistent with Matthew's sense of the new fulfilling the old (*plēroō*, 1:22; 2:15, 17, 23; 3:15; 5:17 et al.), John's baptism served as a link between the Old Testament purification washings and Christian baptism. John's baptism functioned (1) as a sign of a Jew's sincere repentance with assurance of forgiveness of sins and (2) as an anticipation of the coming Spirit-baptism in grace and with the fire of judgment. Jesus' baptism by John in the Jordan (Matt. 3:13–17; Mark 1: 9–10) served as the model for the early church's baptisms. The significance of the baptism of the sinless Lord is threefold: (1) It was an act of identification with those he came to minister to (cf. Isa. 53:12); (2) Jesus' words "It is proper for us to do this to fulfill all righteousness" (Matt. 3:15), suggest that he accepted God's calling for his life; and (3) it marks the commencement of his messianic ministry (cf. Luke 3:23).

Concerning the subjects of baptism, John the Baptist required repentance (Matt. 3:2) and confession of sins (Mark 1:5) in those he baptized. The longer ending of Mark's gospel (an early Christian addition to the text) records the following words of Jesus: "Whoever believes and is baptized will be saved, but whoever does not believe will be condemned" (Mark 16:16). Thus faith—not baptism—saves, and unbelief—not lack of baptism—leads to condemnation. In the Great Commission (Matt. 28:19–20) Jesus enjoined the sequence of disciple making (which includes repentance and faith), baptism, and Christian instruction.

Some appeal to Matthew 18:2–6 as support for infant baptism. The disciples had been selfishly preoccupied with their rank in the kingdom, whereupon Jesus summoned a small child (*paidion*) and appealed to its qualities of humility and instinctive trust. If the disciples wished to be great in the kingdom of God they would have to emulate these virtues of the child. Since the text says nothing about baptism, it is not wise to construct a sacramental theology from it. In what sense do children "believe" (*pisteuontōn*) in Jesus (v. 6)? Because of their unpretentious and receptive spirit (prior to the age of moral accountability) they belong to Jesus. On another occasion (Matt. 19:13–14; Mark 10:13–16; Luke 18:15–17) little children (*paidia*) were brought to Jesus; he blessed them, and said to his disciples, "Let the little children come to me, and do not hinder them, for the kingdom of God belongs to such as these" (Mark 10:14). Here Jesus taught the Jewish rabbis (who frequently blessed children) that if they would attain the kingdom they must possess a childlike spirit characterized by humility and trust. Thus "the basic thought is that of the sheer receptivity of children, especially infants, who cannot do anything to merit entry into the kingdom."[102]

As for the mode of baptism, John baptized "in [*en*] the Jordan River" (Matt. 3:6; Mark 1:5). Jesus likewise was baptized by John "in [*eis*] the Jordan" (Mark 1:9), the preposition signifying "entry into." John's choice of the Jordan River suggests the need for considerable water. Following his baptism, Jesus "went up out of the water" (*anebē apo tou hydatos,* Matt. 3:16). Compare Mark 1:10, which reads, "As Jesus was coming up out of the water . . ." (*anabainōn ek tou hydatos*). The language of these texts favors immersion in the Jordan, although affusion (pouring) cannot be positively ruled out.

The time when Jesus and his disciples observed the Last Supper is widely debated. The Day of Preparation for the Passover was 14 Nisan (March–April), which began on Wednesday at 6 P.M. The Synoptic Gospels indicate that on 15 Nisan, the first day of Unleavened Bread, which began on Thursday at 6 P.M., Jesus ate the Passover meal with his disciples (Matt. 26:17–19; Mark 14:12–16; Luke 22:7–16) on the day when the lambs were killed. During the night of the fifteenth Jesus was arraigned before the Roman and Jewish authorities, about noon of Passover Day he was crucified, and about three that afternoon he died. John 18:28, however, indicates that when Jesus was brought before Pilate the Jews had not yet eaten the Passover. John's *pascha* likely refers to another meal associated with the week of Passover and Unleavened Bread, perhaps the noon *chagigah* meal eaten after the first evening of Passover.[103] Moreover, John 19:14 states that the day of Jesus' crucifixion was "the day of Preparation of Passover Week." The latter undoubtedly signifies the day of preparation for the weekly Sabbath, i.e., on Good Friday (cf. Mark 15:42).

Notwithstanding problems of calendar, the Last Supper clearly bore the significance of a Passover meal. The Jewish Passover looked backward to God's deliverance from Egyptian slavery and forward to a still greater deliverance (cf. Luke 22:16). All three Synoptics record Jesus' institution of the Last Supper (Matt. 26:26–29; Mark 14:22–25; Luke 22:17–20). During the meal Jesus took a loaf of bread, gave thanks, broke it, distributed pieces to the disciples, and said, "Take and eat; this is my body" (*touto estin to sōma mou,* Matt. 26:26). Consistent with Jesus' frequent use of symbolism elsewhere (e.g., Matt. 13:38; Luke 8:11; John 10:9; 15:1), the verb *estin* here means "signifies" rather than "is identical with." Jesus then said, "Do this in remembrance [*anamnēsis*] of me" (Luke 22:19). The word *anamnēsis* (cf. 1 Cor. 11:24–25; Heb. 10:3) means "remembering" or "reminder." After that, Jesus took the cup of wine, gave thanks to God, offered it to his disciples, and said, "This is my blood of the covenant, which is poured out for many for the forgiveness of sins" (*touto estin to haima mou tēs diathēkēs,* Matt. 26:28). These words of Jesus also are to be taken figuratively, because the Cross was yet future and Jesus' blood had not yet been shed. Moffatt translated Jesus' words of inauguration thus: "Take this, it means my body," and "This means my covenant blood."

The Supper Jesus instituted corresponds to the Jewish Passover (Exod. 12:1–30). Analogous to the original Passover, which signified exemption from divine judgment (through the blood of a lamb) and deliverance from bondage in Egypt, the Lord's Supper points to spiritual redemption by the blood of Christ (1 Cor. 5:7). The significance of the Lord's Supper as an enduring observance is threefold: (1) It involves remembrance of Christ's sacrificial death on the cross ("my body given for you," "my blood, which is poured out for you," Luke 22:19–20). (2) It describes the new covenant Jesus would inaugurate via his death ("This cup is the new covenant in my blood," Luke 22:20; cf. Jer. 31:31–34). And (3) it anticipates Christ's return to celebrate the messianic banquet with his people in the kingdom of God ("I will not drink again of the fruit of the vine until that day when I drink it anew in the kingdom of God,'' Mark 14:25).

Primitive Christianity/Acts

On the Day of Pentecost the 120 disciples assembled in Jerusalem experienced a supernatural outpouring or baptism (Acts 1:5; 11:16) of the promised Spirit (Acts 1:4; cf. Isa. 32:15; Joel 2:28–29) and spoke in "other tongues" (*heterai glōssai*). Following Christ's resurrection and this outpouring of the Spirit, the band of disciples formed the Christian church as a distinct institution. At the end of Peter's sermon explaining the significance of this Spirit-baptism, three thousand Jews believed and were baptized (Acts 2:41). The fact that the new converts "were added to their [i.e., the disciples'] number" suggests that the church institutionally had become a reality. This is further supported by the fact that Luke used *ekklēsia* not once in his gospel but twenty-four times in Acts.

Luke described the life and ministry of the fledgling church in the verses that follow: (1) The believers in Christ gathered for fellowship, (Acts 2:42), a common meal (v. 46), and prayer (v. 42). (2) They were "together" (v. 44) in the sense of being "one in heart and mind" (cf. 4:32), thus fulfilling Jesus' prayer for unity (John 17:21–26). (3) They possessed a doctrinal standard—"the apostles' teaching" (v. 42). (4) They observed two ordinances or sacraments, i.e., baptism (v. 41) and the "breaking of bread" (v. 42). (5) They had a regular time and place of worship (v. 46; 3:1). Within a few years the Lord's Supper and the love-feast (cf. Jude 12) were held on the first day of the week, i.e., Sunday (Acts 20:7; cf. 1 Cor. 16:2). (6) They shared their material possessions so that none suffered want (2:44–45; cf. 4:32–35). And (7) the young church in Jerusalem had a vital evangelistic outreach (v. 47b).

Within a short period of time the 120 had grown to a "multitude" (4:32 KJV) of believers.

Following persecution in Jerusalem, Acts 8 onward records the expansion of the young church into Samaria and Judea (primarily through the ministry of Philip and Peter) and throughout the wider Roman Empire (chiefly through Paul, Barnabas, Mark, Silas, and Luke). With the rapid numerical growth of the church, persons were chosen to assist the apostles in leadership and ministry. Acts 6:1–6 records the selection of seven men who would relieve the apostles of the routine tasks of distributing food to needy widows and waiting on tables so the latter could devote themselves to ministry of the Word and prayer. Spiritual qualifications of the seven include faith, wisdom, and enduement with the Holy Spirit (vv. 3, 5, 10). Although the word *diakonos* (deacon) is not used here, the noun *diakonia* (service) and the verb *diakoneō* (to "serve," "wait on") are. The functions of the seven are similar to those exercised by persons later identified as deacons (Phil. 1:1; 1 Tim. 3:8–13). We may regard the twelve in Acts 6 as prototype deacons. Their ministry was not limited to administrative tasks, for Philip (8:5–40; 21:8) and Stephen (6:8–7:60) became effective evangelists.

At Antioch the disciples were first called "Christians" (11:26). In the church's outreach prophets exercised an active ministry in Jerusalem and Antioch. It appears that the prophets, though attached to a local church, engaged in an itinerant ministry (11:27; 15:30–32). The functions of the prophet included words of edification and comfort from the Scriptures (15:32), charismatic utterances (11:28, through Agabus), and foretelling the future (11:28; 21:10–11). Their ministry was closely related to that of the teachers. Thus the church at Antioch had men who were both prophets and teachers, five of whom are mentioned (13:1).

The first mention of church "elders" occurs in Acts 11:30. Following the prediction of famine (v. 28), disciples at Antioch sent gifts with Paul and Barnabas to the elders of the Jerusalem church. The office of elder (*presbyteros*) likely was appropriated from the Jewish synagogue. Later during their first missionary journey, Paul and Barnabas set the newly founded churches on a stable basis by appointing elders (plural) in each fellowship in the Greek world (14:23). It appears that a plurality of elders ministered in the local churches in Acts. As Carson observes, "A plurality of elders, if not mandated, appears to have been common, and perhaps the norm."[104] A single elder may have presided over a house church or smaller subunit within a larger Christian community (cf. Rom. 16:5; 1 Cor. 16:19; Col. 4:15; Philem. 2; 2 John 1). According to Acts 15, the church in Antioch sent Paul and Barnabas to Jerusalem to deal with the claim of certain Judaizers that Gentile believers must be circumcised and obey the Law of Moses. In the meetings that followed, the apostles and elders of the church directed attention to this potentially divisive issue (vv. 2, 4, 6, 22–23; 16:4).

According to Acts 21:18, the leadership of the Jerusalem church was in the hands of James and "all the elders." As an aside, by reason of the appearance of the risen Lord to him (1 Cor. 15:7), his personal spirituality, and his kinship to Jesus, James emerged as the leading elder in the Jerusalem church, albeit as *primus inter pares* (cf. Acts 12:17; 15:13–21; Gal. 2:9). It would be unwarranted to conclude that James held the office of bishop in the sense of possessing superior authority to that of the other elders. On his third missionary journey while at Miletus, "Paul sent to Ephesus for the elders [*presbyteroi*] of

the church" (Acts 20:17) and said, "Keep watch over yourselves and all the flock of which the Holy Spirit has made you overseers [*episcopoi*]. Be shepherds [present active infinitive of *poimanō*] of the church of God" (20:28). Verses 17 and 28 indicate that elder, bishop, and pastor/shepherd refer to identical ministries. Elder (*presbyteros*) likely refers to the office, whereas bishop (*episcopos*) and pastor (*poimēn*) describe its functions. Paul's words that Christ "bought [the church of God] with his own blood" (v. 28) indicate that the church is rooted in the Cross and thus came into existence subsequent to Calvary.

Luke stressed the unanimity of the early church in selecting its leaders. The 120 proposed two men for selection as successor to Judas (Acts 1:23). According to Acts 6:3–6 the whole body of disciples chose the seven deacons and presented them to the apostles for the laying-on of hands. Members of the church appointed Paul and Barnabas to missionary work (Acts 13:2–3; cf. 14:27). The church sent Paul and Barnabas to the Jerusalem assembly (Acts 15: 2–3), whereupon the apostles, elders, and the whole church sent representatives back to Antioch with a letter (vv. 22–23). The picture that emerges is that of ordinary Christians making crucial decisions in the life of the church.

Peter in his Pentecost sermon declared that repentance followed by baptism "in the name of Jesus Christ" results in forgiveness of sins and the gift of the Holy Spirit (2:38). Peter added, "The promise is for you and for your children and for all who are far off" (v. 39). The *tekna*—the recipients of the promise—are old enough to prophesy (v. 17); hence they are the hearers' descendants in future generations.[105] Some three thousand persons who heard Peter's message believed, were baptized, and were added to the church (v. 41). The order of faith in Christ followed by baptism is also seen in the conversion of certain Samaritans (8:12–13) and the Ethiopian eunuch (8:35–38). Concerning the latter, Luke stated that "both Philip and the eunuch went down into the water [*eis to hydōr*] and Philip baptized him" (v. 38); then "they came up out of the water [*anebēsan ek tou hydatos*]" (v. 39). The account is not sufficiently specific to indicate whether the mode of baptism was by immersion or by affusion while they were standing in the water.[106] Saul of Tarsus was dramatically converted when confronted with a vision of the risen Christ en route to Damascus (9:3–6; cf. 1 Cor. 9:1; 15:8; Gal. 1:15–17). Later Saul was baptized by Ananias, a layman, and filled with the Holy Spirit (Acts 9:17–18; cf. 22:16). According to Acts 16:14–15 Lydia was born again and then baptized. So also the Philippian jailer (16:31–33). A similar order prevailed according to Acts 18:8: "Many of the Corinthians who heard him [i.e., Paul] believed and were baptized."

Whether household baptisms in Acts involved infants and children is widely debated. On one side of the argument G. R. Beasley-Murray writes, "The conviction that household baptisms included infants is strengthened by the contention that the term *oikos* had gained an almost technical significance among Jews and had special reference to little children."[107] On the other hand, members of Cornelius's family (10:2, 24) are described as "devout and God-fearing" (v. 2). Those who were baptized heard the Word and received the Holy Spirit (v. 44, 47b). Members of his household then spoke in tongues and praised God (v. 46). Concerning the baptism of Lydia and her household (*oikos*, 16:15), it may be that Lydia the businesswoman was single or widowed. Lydia's conversion and baptism took place near the river Gangites (16:13–15) with its supply of water. On another occasion Paul and Silas said to the Philippian jailer: "Believe in the Lord Jesus, and you will be saved—you and your household" (*oikos*, 16:31). It is important to note that "*kai ho oikos sou* does not mean that [the jailer's] faith would save his household, but that the same way was open to them as to him."[108] Verse 32 indicates that the missionaries spoke the Word to all persons in the house that they might believe along with the jailer. The manner by which the household was baptized within the prison or its court is not clear.

The Pauline Letters

Of the 109 usages of *ekklēsia* in the technical sense of the "church," 61 occur in Paul (22 in 1 Corinthians alone) with the following meanings: (1) The word is used of believers gathered in a house church (Rom. 16:5; 1 Cor. 16:19b; Col. 4:15). (2) Always in the singular, it refers to the church in a given city (Rom. 16:1; 1 Cor. 1:2; 2 Cor. 1:1; Col. 4:16; 1 Thess. 1:1). (3) In the plural it designates Christian assemblies in a Roman province (1 Cor. 16:1, 19; 2 Cor. 8:1; Gal. 1:22; 1 Thess. 2:14). (4) It refers to local churches without geographical qualification (Rom. 16:16; 1 Cor. 7:17; 11:16; 2 Cor. 12:13). And (5) it denotes the universal fellowship of believers gathered in local assemblies (Acts 20:28; 1 Cor. 15:9; Gal. 1:13; Eph. 1:22; 3:10; Col. 1:18, 24; cf. Heb. 12:22–23, which depicts the entire assembly of saints as enrolled in heaven).

Paul developed his theology of the church largely by expounding pictorial images from the human realm.[109] Paul's favorite image of the church is that of the human *body* (Rom. 12:4–5; 1 Cor. 12:12–27; Eph. 4:12–16; Col. 1:18, 24). The image of the body (*sōma*) fundamentally connotes *unity*. As the human body is one, so believers are baptized by the Spirit into the one body of Christ

(Rom. 12:4–5; 1 Cor. 12:12–13; Col. 3:15). "There is one body and one Spirit . . . one hope . . . one Lord . . . one baptism; one God and Father of all" (Eph. 4:4–6). From God's perspective the church as social reality cannot be divided by nationality, race, social standing, or economic status (Gal. 3:28; Col. 3:11). The body image, second, connotes *diversity*; as the human body possesses many parts, so the church of Christ consists of many members with differing gifts and functions (Rom. 12:4–8; 1 Cor. 6:15; Eph. 5:30). By virtue of natural abilities and spiritual gifts members of the body differ in identity (1 Cor. 12:17), in function (vv. 17–18), in utility (vv. 21–22), and in honor (v. 23). Thus the many members, each with unique ministries, form a harmonious whole under the headship of Christ (Eph. 4:15–16). Paul's identification of Christ as Head of the body (Col. 1:18) signifies the Savior's sovereign authority over the church (Eph. 1:19b–22; 5:23–24; Col. 2:10). Moreover, as Head he is the source of the church's unity (Col. 2:19), its life, and its growth (Eph. 4:16; Col. 2:19).

Paul further depicted the church as a *building*, specifically a temple: "You yourselves are God's temple [*naos*] and . . . God's Spirit lives in you" (1 Cor. 3:16; cf. 2 Cor. 6:16). The church is the *naos* or inner sanctuary where God through the Spirit uniquely dwells (Eph. 2:22), rather than the *hieron*, the total structure. As the temple of God the church is "sacred" (*hagios*) in the sense of being set apart for God and indwelt by him (1 Cor. 3:17; cf. Col. 3:12). Paul laid the foundation (*themelios*) of the building by proclaiming Christ (1 Cor. 3:10–11), whereas Christians invest their lives completing the edifice (v. 10b, 12). In Ephesians 2:20–22 Paul identified Jesus Christ as "the chief cornerstone" of the temple, the apostles and prophets as "the foundation," and the church itself as the "building" (*oikodomē*). Thus "in him the whole building is joined together and rises to become a holy temple [*naos*] in the Lord . . . a dwelling in which God lives by his Spirit" (vv. 21–22).

The apostle, moreover, depicted the church as the *bride* of Christ, drawing on the Old Testament imagery of Yahweh's marriage to Israel initiated by the covenant relation (Isa. 54:5–6; Ezek. 16:8–14; Hos. 1–3). The bride symbolism signifies moral purity, devotion, and exclusive allegiance to Christ (2 Cor. 11:2–3). Hence the church constitutes the *people* of God (Rom. 9:25–26), enhancing the image of Israel as God's special people (Hos. 1:10; 2:1, 23). In addition, based on the Old Testament imagery of Israel as Yahweh's "house" (Num. 12:7; Hos. 8:1), the church is "God's household" or *family* (*oikos*, 1 Tim. 3:15). Thus Paul represented Christians as "members of God's household" (Eph. 2:19) and the church as "the family of believers" (Gal. 6:10).

Paul suggested that the church institutionally began its existence at Pentecost. Only after Christ's resurrection and heavenly enthronement did God appoint him head of the body, the church (Eph. 1:20–22). As God's new creation, the church is founded on the person and redemptive work of Christ on the cross (Eph. 2:15–16). Moreover Paul taught that the church was constituted when its members were baptized into the body of Christ by the Holy Spirit (1 Cor. 12:13). This teaching points to the outpouring of the Holy Spirit at Pentecost as the inauguration of the church as a distinct institution (cf. Mark 1:8; Acts 1:5; 11:16).

Concerning offices or gifted ministries in the church, 1 Corinthians 12:28 states that God appointed in the church "first of all apostles, second prophets, third teachers" as most important. According to Ephesians 4:11 the ascended

Christ gave to the church "apostles," "prophets," "evangelists," "pastors," and "teachers." Luke's "apostle" more narrowly designates the Twelve who were chosen by Jesus, accompanied the Lord during his earthly ministry, and constituted the foundation of the church (e.g., Luke 6:13; 9:10; 11:49; 17:5). Acts relates that the Twelve (Matthias now added to the Eleven) witnessed Christ's resurrection, evangelized, performed miracles, received revelation, taught converts, and established churches. Paul emerged prominently as the thirteenth apostle (1 Cor. 9:1; 15:8–10). As those who laid the foundation of the church, the Twelve plus Paul no longer exist. But the New Testament enlarges the concept of apostleship beyond the original thirteen to include all those divinely commissioned for mission. Hence Barnabas (Acts 14:14), Titus (2 Cor. 8:23), Silas and Timothy (1 Thess. 1:1; 2:7), James the brother of Jesus (Gal. 1:19), Andronicus and Junias (Rom. 16:7), and Epaphroditus (Phil. 2:25) are all designated apostles. In this Pauline sense (1 Cor. 12:28; Eph. 4:11; 1 Thess. 2:6) "apostle" approximates what we today call a "missionary"—a spiritually gifted person who establishes and strengthens churches.

The New Testament attests the succession of apostolic doctrine (2 Tim. 2:2) but not of apostolic office. Little support exists for the Roman dogma of the universal and infallible authority of Peter. Paul claimed that whereas Peter was God's "apostle to the Jews," he [Paul] was God's "apostle to the Gentiles" (Gal. 2:7–8). God worked equally through Paul and Peter, although in different spheres of responsibility. Paul gave the order of the three pillars in the Jerusalem church as "James, Peter, and John" (v. 9). Moreover, Peter was not without fault in the exercise of his ministry. Because Peter refrained from eating with Gentiles (v. 12), Paul charged Peter and other Jews with "hypocrisy" (v. 13) and rebuked them publicly (v. 14). Paul wrote, "When Peter came to Antioch, I opposed him to his face, because he was clearly in the wrong" (v. 11).

The work of *prophet* (*prophētēs*) was a second foundational ministry in the church. New Testament prophets uttered direct messages from God through the Spirit. These included prediction of the future (Acts 11:28; 21:10–11) and the application of divine truths to life situations (1 Cor. 14:3). The ministry of the *teacher* (*didaskalos*) was added for the instruction of persons brought to Christ by the apostles. Thus Paul enjoined Timothy to entrust the apostolic doctrine "to reliable men who [would] also be qualified to teach others" (2 Tim. 2:2). A body of teaching was in place that served as the basis for the teacher's ministry (1 Tim. 1:10–11; 2 Tim. 1:13). The *evangelist* (*euangelistēs*) supplemented the ministry of the apostles by preaching the Gospel to unbelievers. Philip (Acts 8:4–40; 21:8) and Timothy (2 Tim. 4:5) served as evangelists in the early church. The absence of an article before *euangelistou* in the latter text ("do the work of an evangelist") might suggest a gifted ministry rather than an office.

The final ministry is that of *pastor* (*poimēn*, Eph. 4:11). Paul had pastors of a local assembly in mind when he wrote, "Respect those who work hard [present participle of *proistēmi*, to "preside, lead, direct"] among you, who are over you in the Lord and who admonish you" (1 Thess. 5:12). The latter exercised ministries of leadership, pastoral care, and teaching. That these leaders were also known as elders is clear from 1 Timothy 5:17, where the identical verb *proistēmi* describes the ministry of the *presbyteroi*. "The elders who direct [perfect participle of *proistēmi*] the affairs of the church well are worthy of double honor, especially those whose work is preaching and teaching." Paul may have meant that whereas the basic task of the *presbyteros* was oversight and care of the church, those who excelled in teaching and preaching deserve double "honor" (*timē,* i.e., added respect and remuneration, cf. v. 18).

That the "elder" also bore the designation of "bishop" (*episkopos*) is clear from the juxtaposition of the two words in Titus 1:5–7 and from the similar lists of moral and spiritual virtues in 1 Timothy 3 and Titus 1. Both 1 Timothy 3:2 and Titus 1:6 mandate that the elder or bishop must be "the husband of but one wife" (i.e., a one-woman man). Given the prevalence of sexual promiscuity in the Roman world, the elder or bishop must be one who is faithful to his wife in the covenant of marriage (cf. 1 Tim. 5:9). The word "elder," borrowed from Judaism, denotes the office, whereas "overseer" (bishop) designates the function. The idea of a monarchial bishop superior to elders is nowhere in view. Against Lightfoot, Timothy was not bishop of Ephesus, and Titus did not serve as bishop of Crete in the heirarchical sense. Rather Timothy, left by Paul in Ephesus to organize the church (1 Tim. 1:3), was a lead pastor-elder in the local congregation. Consider the following facts: (1) Timothy was relatively young (1 Tim. 4:12); (2) his primary ministries were reading the Scriptures, preaching, and teaching (1 Tim. 4:13); and (3) he ministered to all kinds of people—older men, younger men, older women, younger women, widows, children, grandparents, the rich, etc. (1 Tim. 5:1–16). Similar considerations suggest that Titus was a lead pastor-elder in Crete (see Titus 1:5; 2:1–10, 15; 3:1–2, 10). Paul consistently endorsed a plurality of elders or overseers in the local assembly (Phil. 1:1; 1 Tim. 5:17; Titus 1:5). Noteworthy is the phrase in 1 Timothy 4:14: "when the body of elders [*presbyterion,* cf. Luke 22:66; Acts 22:5] laid their hands on you."[110]

The qualifications of deacons (*diakonoi*) set forth in 1 Timothy 3:8–13 chiefly concern spiritual maturity. Similar to the elder, the deacon "must be the husband of but one wife" (v. 12). The focal point of diaconal ministry are works of service (cf. the verb *diakoneō,* vv. 10, 13) rather than oversight or teaching. Paul described Phoebe as a *diakonos* ("deacon" or "servant," Rom. 16:1) in the church at Cenchrea, although it is debated whether this constituted the formal office of deaconess. In Paul's letters church members make decisions affecting the whole body. Thus they exercised discipline in the case of a morally defective member (1 Cor. 5:4–7, 12–13). Discipline of an offender was administered by a "majority" of the members (2 Cor. 2:6).

According to Romans 6:3–8 (cf. Col. 2:12), the primary significance of baptism is union with Christ in his death and resurrection. When Christians are plunged into water in baptism (note the threefold use of *baptizō* and *baptismos*) they are symbolically incorporated into Christ in his death. When brought up from the water, they are raised with Christ in newness of life. Baptism, however, is not only a spiritual event, it is also a profoundly social event. At baptism believers not only put on Christ individually (Gal. 3:27) but also enter into a new relationship with other believers in the body. Such a unity transcends social, sexual, and ethnic distinctions (Gal. 3:28; cf. 1 Cor. 12:13). This is especially forceful if Galatians 3:27–28 was part of the baptismal liturgy of the early church.[111] Secondarily baptism signifies a washing or cleansing from sins; so 1 Corinthians 6:11—"you were washed." As explained in chapter 2 of this volume, Titus 3:5 (Christ "saved us through the washing of rebirth and renewal by the Holy Spirit") does not teach baptismal regeneration, but the fact that baptism is an outward sign of inner cleansing effected by Holy Spirit regeneration.

Covenant theologians see in Colossians 2:11–12 a link between circumcision and baptism. Circumcision as applied to Christians in verse 11a appears to be a spiritual circumcision (cf. Deut. 10:16; 30:6; Jer. 4:4) rather than the Jewish circumcision of the flesh. Similarly the circumcision cited in verse 11b with respect to Christ (*hē peritomē tou Christou*) symbolically represents the stripping of his entire body (*sōma*) in death. Paul taught, then, that the death of Christ (his experience of circumcision) works in believers a spiritual circumcision, i.e., a new birth and a life of victory over sin. These realities are symbolized by Christian baptism. Some interpreters judge that Israel's being "baptized into Moses in the cloud and in the sea" and their eating "spiritual food" and drinking "spiritual drink" are types of Christian baptism and the Lord's Supper (1 Cor. 10:1–4). But if passage through the Red Sea and eating spiritual food and drink meant such, then even unbelieving adults ("all," vv. 2–3) should be baptized and partake of the Lord's Supper. The import of the text is not sacramental but the recollection of Israel's experience of grace, idolatry, and divine judgment. In the light of Israel's Red Sea and desert experiences, Christians should avoid idolatry and immorality (vv. 6–12). "It is not intended to be a typological statement of sacramental theology but a Midrashic exposition of Old Testament stories for the elucidation of Christian ethics."[112]

Concerning the Lord's Supper, 1 Corinthians 10:16 reads, "Is not the cup of thanksgiving for which we give thanks a participation [*koinōnia*] in the blood of Christ? And is not the bread that we break a participation in the body of Christ?" The word *koinōnia* means "association, communion, fellowship,

participation."[113] The big idea of the context (vv. 14–22) is that sharing in the Lord's table is incompatible with eating food offered to idols. Paul argued his case as follows. By eating its sacrifices the Israelites were *koinōnoi* (i.e., "companions, partners, or sharers") in the spiritual realities the sacrifices denoted (v. 18–20). Likewise, as Christians partake of the bread and wine, they are participants in the benefits won by the sacrifice of Christ (vv. 16–17). "The participation in the blood and body of Christ are not a sharing in corporeal elements, but in an experience of Christ in terms of his sacrifice."[114] Thus believers should have no part in pagan sacrifices, for such practices involve association with, or participation in, the realm of demonic powers. The intent of the 1 Corinthians 10:16 text, then, is not to explain the precise nature of the Christian's participation in Christ in the Lord's Supper.[115]

In 1 Corinthians 11:23–35 Paul restated and interpreted Jesus' institution of the Lord's Supper. Jesus' words with respect to the breaking of the bread and the pouring of the wine—"do this" (present continuous, vv. 24–25)—signify an ordinance of perpetual observance. Likewise the following words— "in remembrance of me" (vv. 24–25)—suggest that the purpose of the Lord's Supper is primarily commemorative. The noun *anamnēsis*, "remembrance," is a strong word that means recalling to mind with sufficient intensity to make the benefits of the Cross effectively present. The significance of the Lord's Supper is at least fourfold: As a visibly enacted Word it involves (1) spiritual fellowship with the living Christ (cf. 1 Cor. 10:16), (2) present fellowship with other believers in the unity of the body (1 Cor. 10:17), (3) proclamation (not reenactment) by word and symbol of Christ's vicarious death (1 Cor. 11:26), and (4) anticipation of Christ's return and the eschato-

269

logical banquet (1 Cor. 11:26b; cf. Matt. 26:29). Paul indicated that the Lord's Supper (*kyriakon deipnon*) was part of a larger common meal (the love feast) that wealthier believers provided for poorer brothers and sisters (1 Cor. 11:20–22). Not until the mid-second century did the Eucharist separate from the *agapē* meal.

The Johannine Literature

John's Gospel contains no explicit discussion of the *ekklēsia*. Prior to the emergence of the church John focused attention on Jesus as the Son of God and the salvation he brought. Nevertheless John presented several images of the prospective community known as the church. In the parable of the good shepherd (John 10:1–18) Jesus likened the people of God to a flock, analogous to the shepherd-sheep relationship between Yahweh and Israel (Jer. 23:1–4; Ezek. 34; Zech. 11:4–17). Jesus described himself as the "good shepherd" (*poimēn*), believers of Jewish descent as "this sheep pen" (*aulē*), and Gentile believers as "other sheep" (*probata*) whom he must gather. Those who obey his voice, both Jews and Gentiles, "shall be one flock" (*poimnē*) under one shepherd (v. 16). This description of the flock attests the universality and unity of the prospective Christian community.

In the allegory of the vine and the branches (John 15:1–8) Jesus depicted the community as *many branches* vitally united to the vine, an image that corresponds to Israel as the vine of God's planting (Ps. 80:8–16; Isa. 5:1–7; Jer. 2:21). In the story Jesus is "the true vine" (*ampelos*), the Father is "the gardener" or vinedresser (*geōrgos*), and the disciples are "the branches" (*klēmata*). The image of many branches united in one vine points to the vital, organic unity of believers in Christ. Membership in the new people of God depends on a genuine spiritual relationship to Christ the vine (vv. 5–6). And fruitfulness (answers to prayer, Christlike character, and effective discipleship) depends on believers' maintaining life-giving contact with the vine (vv. 7–8). The Apocalypse represents the church as the *bride* of Christ, only here the future aspect of the relationship is in view. The church is a bride presented to her groom at the *Parousia*—both parties celebrating the union at the marriage banquet in heaven (Rev. 19:7–9; cf. 21:2, 9).

Concerning the founding of the Christian community, John's interpretation of Caiphas's prophetic utterance suggests that the uniting of a scattered people must await Christ's vicarious death on the cross (John 11:50–52). Thus the high priest "prophesied that Jesus would die for the Jewish nation, and not only for that nation but also for the scattered children of God, to bring them together and make them one." Here the unity of the future church clearly is in view. In his high priestly prayer Jesus prayed that his followers may be one as he and the Father are one (John 17:20–26). Since the unity of believers with one another and with God is likened to the unity of the Father and the Son (v. 21), the oneness envisaged is a supernatural reality. The "complete unity" Jesus prayed for must be evident to the unbelieving world (v. 23). Revelation 5:9 attests the catholicity of the church, for the heavenly beings sang the following words in praise to Christ: "With your blood you purchased men for God from every tribe and language and people and nation." The church is catholic in that it transcends all political, cultural, and ethnic boundaries. John's acknowledgment that the citizens of heaven are those "whose names are written in the Lamb's book of life" (Rev. 21:27) attests the invisible character of the church. Not all who profess allegiance to Christ are members of his body; the true church is hidden and known to God alone.

Roman Catholics insist that Jesus' charge to Peter, "Feed my sheep" (John 21:17), constituted Peter the supreme vicar of Christ on earth, and that Peter transmitted this unique authority to his successors. Erasmus, for example, interpreted Jesus' command to Peter as "You shall *govern* my sheep." The biblical data suggests otherwise. In 1 Peter 5:1–3 Peter, an elder, commanded his fellow elders, "Be shepherds of God's flock that is under your care, . . . not lording it over those entrusted to you, but being examples to the flock." Peter's use of the verb (aorist imperative) *poimainō* (to "shepherd") in verse 2 is identical to Paul's use of *poimainō* in his charge to the Ephesian pastor-elders recorded in Acts 20:28—"Be shepherds of the church of God." The evidence indicates that Jesus commissioned Peter to provide pastoral care to the people of God as the first of a long line of pastor-shepherds. Peter's relation to succeeding ministers was that of *primus inter pares*.

John 3:23 states that "John also was baptizing at Aenon near Salim, because there was plenty of water." The place-name Aenon literally means "springs," suggesting an abundance of water for baptism. John 3:22 (cf. 4:1) records that, concurrent with John's baptizing activity, Jesus baptized in the countryside. Yet John 4:2 indicates that Jesus baptized through the hands of his disciples. Jesus' baptizing work was not yet Christian baptism but an extension of the baptism of John. We observed in chapter 2 that John 3:5 does not support the doctrine of baptismal regeneration. The water in Jesus' words "unless he is born of water and the Spirit" symbolizes the cleansing from sin. The emphasis in the dialogue is on the Spirit (vv. 6, 8); no further mention is made of water.

Thus Jesus taught that Nicodemus must be purified of sin and be spiritually renewed if he would enter the kingdom of God. At most baptism is a symbol of this new spiritual beginning.[116]

Roman Catholics appeal to John 6:25–59 as support for the Mass. Jesus informed the crowd that he is "the bread of God" (v. 33) and "the bread of life" (vv. 35, 48) who came down from heaven. Continuing to speak in metaphors he said, "My flesh is real food and my blood is real drink" (v. 55). Jesus made clear that the act of eating his flesh and drinking his blood (vv. 35, 50, 53–57) does not imply devouring his body with the mouth. Rather, it is a figure for *believing* in him (vv. 29–30, 35–36, 40, 47, 64), appropriating his work on the cross, and abiding in him (v. 56). Augustine correctly commented, "To believe on him is to eat the living bread. He that believes eats."[117] This feeding on Christ (i.e., believing and abiding) results in eternal life (vv. 40, 51, 57). Jesus, moreover, insisted that what imparts life is not partaking of his physical flesh but participating in the Spirit through the words he spoke (v. 63). Whereas John 6 does not explicitly refer to the Lord's Supper (the listeners were mainly unbelievers), the Eucharist beautifully represents the feeding and abiding of which Jesus spoke.

Other New Testament Literature

The word *ekklēsia* occurs but three times in this portion of Scripture, twice with respect to the local church (Heb. 2:12; James 5:14) and once concerning the universal church (Heb. 12:23). Hebrews 12:22b–23 reads, "You have come to . . . the church of the firstborn [*prōtotokoi*], whose names are written in heaven." The *prōtotokoi* undoubtedly are those who have been reborn through faith in Christ. For the author of Hebrews, the earthly church has its analogue in heaven, the latter being more important than the former. The only use of *synagōgē* as a designation of a Christian assembly occurs in James 2:2: "Suppose a man comes into your meeting. . . ." The common word for the religious gatherings of the Jews or the buildings where they assembled for worship (Matt. 4:23; Acts 13:43; Rev. 2:9), *synagōgē* translates both the Hebrew *qāhāl* and *'ēdāh* (assembly, congregation).

The Bible uses several images to describe the church, the first being the *new people of God.* First Peter 2:9 reads, "You are a chosen people [*genos eklekton*], . . . a holy nation [*ethnos hagion*], a people [*laos*] belonging to God." The following verse adds, "Now you are the people [*laos*] of God" (cf. Heb. 4:9; 11:25). The foregoing link the church spiritually with the Old Testament covenant people (cf. Exod 19:6; Deut. 7:6; Isa. 43:20-21; Jer. 32:38). The church is also represented as the *house* or temple of God, i.e., a fellowship of believers who offer spiritual sacrifices to God. So 1 Peter 2:5 (cf. Heb. 3:3-6) reads, "You also, like living stones, are being built into a spiritual house [*oikos pneumatikos*] to be a holy priesthood, offering spiritual sacrifices acceptable to God through Jesus Christ." Jesus Christ is the cornerstone of the building (vv. 6-8), Peter explaining that not he but Christ is the church's foundation. Moreover, believers are the building blocks of the structure (v. 5). The present tense of *oikodomeō* (to "build," "erect a building") in the phrase "you . . . are being built into a spiritual house" indicates that the church of Jesus Christ is still under construction. First Peter 2:5 also depicts the church as a "holy priesthood" (*hierateuma hagion*), that is, the new mediatorial community (cf. Exod. 19:5-6). In this capacity the church offers to God spiritual sacrifices (v. 5), such as praise (Heb. 13:15), witness

(v. 9), intercession (James 5:14-18), and sharing with the needy (Heb. 13:16). Employing the imagery of Israel as a flock of sheep (Ps. 78:52; Isa. 63:11; Jer. 31:10), Peter pictured the church as "God's flock" (*poimnion*, 1 Peter 5:2-3; cf. Acts 20:28-29) and Jesus Christ as the "Chief Shepherd" (1 Peter 5:4; cf. Zech. 13:7).

First Peter 5:1-2 suggests the identity of the pastor, elder, and bishop. To the elders (*presbyteroi*), Peter wrote, "Be shepherds [aorist imperative of *poimainō*] of God's flock that is under your care, serving as overseers" (present participle of *episkopeō*, to "oversee," "superintend"). Peter thus commanded elders to function as spiritual shepherds while they serve as overseers of the community. First Peter 2:25 indicates that shepherding and exercising oversight are two functions of Christ's ministry. Peter's designation of Christ as "the Shepherd and Overseer of your souls" (cf. 5:4) demonstrates that Christ, not any earthly primate or pope, is the principal Overseer of the church. The literature also recognizes a plurality of leaders in the local community. Those charged with pastoral care and proclaiming the Word in the local church are referred to as "leaders" (*hēgoumenoi*, Heb. 13:7, 17, 24) and "elders" (*presbyteroi*, James 5:14; 1 Peter 5:1,5). Yet the literature supports the priesthood of all believers when it teaches that every Christian has direct access to God through the merits of Christ (Heb. 4:14-16; 10:19-22; 1 Peter 2:5, 9).

Hebrews 10:22 ("having our hearts sprinkled . . . and having our bodies washed with pure water") indicates by way of allusion that baptism signifies the cleansing of the inner and outer person. The picture of the flood waters bringing deliverance to Noah's family (1 Peter 3:19-21) reminded Peter of the spiritual deliverance wrought by Christ's death (cf. v. 18) and symbolized by Christian baptism. Peter made clear, however, that the efficacy of baptism resides not in the washing of water but in the individual's faith in the resurrected Christ (v. 21). Jude 12 refers to the love feast (*agapē*) or fellowship meal during which the Lord's Supper was observed and which served as the focal point of the early Christian community (cf. 1 Cor. 11:20–22; 2 Peter 2:13). Texts such as Hebrews 7:27; 9:25–28; 10:10, 12, 14, 18 affirm that the one sacrifice of Christ was sufficient to purify from sins, provide access to God, and maintain believers in right relation to God. No further sacrifice for sin is required—a fact that undercuts the traditional Roman doctrine of the Mass.

SYSTEMATIC FORMULATION

The Father calls repentant believers into a new community headed by the Son and created by the Spirit. Converts are renewed for fellowship with the Triune God and with one another. It is neither good nor healthy that people rejuvenated in the divine likeness should be alone. Without association we are restless and unfulfilled. Christians express the shared values of their "partnership in the gospel" in a local church (Phil. 1:5).

The definition of the church in historical studies may encompass all groups claiming to be Christian. But we must distinguish a church from a Bible study or Koinonia group, a specialized parachurch ministry, or a counterfeit body that has strayed from the Gospel. Systematics seeks normative decisions as to what a church ought to be according to apostolic doctrine. When pioneer missionaries plant a church, what essentials should they incorporate into its structure and life?

A church should be made up of people related spiritually to God and organizationally to one another. The inner authenticity and outer institutionalized structure are both essential to the well-being of Christ's body in a given place. The distribution of the church locally and universally is not meaningful until we have defined just what is distributed. A church has two essential elements: (1) an inner and personal, spiritual relationship to Christ its head, and (2) an outward, institutional structure relating the members to each other in their ministries.

A Church Is Composed of Spiritual People

A church is composed of sinners who have responded to God's effectual *call* out of the world, have been converted to Jesus as Lord and Messiah, and have been initiated into one body by the Spirit. The first church came into existence when the regenerate at Pentecost were baptized by the Spirit into Christ's body (Acts 1:5; 2:4). Others were added to the church when Peter preached a message of repentance, water baptism, and reception of the Holy Spirit (2:38). Even the despised Samaritans later believed and received the Holy Spirit (8:15–17). So did pagan outsiders, the Gentiles (10:43–48). Paul addressed the church in Corinth "together with all those everywhere who call on the name of our Lord Jesus Christ" (1 Cor. 1:2). All believers in the Gospel form a community that is like a spiritual bride and bridegroom (Eph. 5:21–33), a family (Gal. 6:10), a body (1 Cor. 12:12–27), and a temple (1 Cor. 3:16–17; 2 Cor. 6:16). A church that is Christian is one that is indwelt by the Holy Spirit (1 Cor. 3:16; Eph. 2:22).

A church is made up of converts with *equal spiritual standing*. Because all saints are united by faith to Christ (Gal. 3:28), membership and opportunities in a church are not based on political affiliation, economic status, or educational attainment. Believing women and men in a church are all *priests* enjoying equal access to God through Christ (1 Peter 2:5, 9). All can come immediately into the Father's presence on the ground of Christ's atonement and through the Spirit's enablement (Heb. 10:19–22). All members enjoy equal access to God's throne of grace (4:16). The priesthood of all believers means that no leaders (bishops, ministers, or elders) can demand that others confess sins to them for divine forgiveness. No leader can add to the mediatorial provisions of Jesus Christ as implemented by the Holy Spirit. As priests, church members have not only equal privileges but also equal responsibility to exercise in love their different spiritual gifts for the good of all. Packer sums this up as follows: the church is "a divinely created fellowship of sinners who trust a common Savior and are one with each other because they are all one with him in a union realized by the Holy Spirit."[118]

The unity believers share with Jesus and one another is *a diversity of unique persons* who love each other and with their varied gifts serve common values. Human love is directed to other persons for their worth in themselves; but those who have spiritual love care for church members for Christ's sake. Christ and believers remain distinct persons in loving, personal (I-Thou) relationships even in their peak experiences of communion. Members of a church ought not lose their identity to a leader or an organization; rather, they should be personally enriched by just and loving personal relationships. As they are edified, they in turn contribute to the well-being of the whole body.

Church members are *distinct from people of the world*. Church members in allegiance to Christ are no longer under the control of the Evil One (1 John 5:19). Although God is the Father of all providentially, not all are in fellowship with Christ. The once-born are not spiritually children of God; they are descendants of the fallen "world" that rebels against the moral laws of the Providence that sustains them. The weeds and the wheat grow together in the mission field of the "world" (Matt. 13:38), not the church. As far as humanly possible we ought never give weeds the impression they are wheat. Although all human beings are children of God's providence, not all are children of God's moral and spiritual family.

A church is *distinct from the state*. Citizenship in a country does not make one a member of Christ's body. People may be Hindus because they are born in India of Hindu parents, but people are not Christians because they are born in a so-called Christian nation of Christian parents. To enter the kingdom of God each person must, as Jesus emphasized, be born again (John 3:3–7). A prime minister, president, or other political leader is not a Christian because he is dedicated to good causes rooted ultimately in general revelation. The church is made up of individuals from varied families, tribes, and nations responsive to special, salvific revelation.

A church, of course, is *distinct from the building* in which it meets. A church is not a house, a storefront, or a cathedral but a community of the called and forgiven who have come to faith union with Christ. Euphemistically, a building in which believers gather may be called a church. But ministers and members could avoid misunderstanding by referring to their building as their training center. Within the building the church is protected from the elements while being edified in the faith and trained to minister to the world.

However the outward appearance of the church members may vary throughout this multicultural globe, their *inner spiritual reality is the same* universally. To become members of a church, sinners in the East as well as the West need to respond to the Father's call, the

Son's atonement, and the Spirit's baptism into Christ's body. A church will undoubtedly be culturally influenced and culturally relevant, but it ought never be culturally bound. The inner spiritual nature of the church has been highly relevant in countless cultures for twenty centuries. Its classical spiritual essence is from above, transcending every culture but meeting needs in every culture. The external, institutional structure of the church will be considered following discussion of the ends it exists to serve.

A Church Has Numerous Objectives

The *raison d'etre* of a church in a community is to carry out God's purposes for the well-being of its members and the world. What objectives ought a Christian church pursue by the enablement of the Holy Spirit?

1. A church should work for the reconciliation of everyone under the headship of Christ. In the future God will unite all creatures in heaven and earth under their Lord (Eph. 1:9–10, 22–23). The church, not the United Nations or a new world order, is the prime earthly agent of the cosmic reconciliation God wills.[119] Those who seek to serve the primary community of reconciliation will serve a church that manifests God's redemptive program for this age.

2. To reach the lost, the "found" in each generation ought to recruit, train, and deploy evangelists to make disciples in the unreached areas of the world (Matt. 28:18–20; Luke 24:47). Every young person trained by the educational ministries of the church and every adult church member, after a reasonable time, should know how to present the Gospel of God's grace to people sensing their guilt and need.

3. A church ought to baptize its new disciples to mark their decisive divorce from the old, fleshly lifestyle and celebrate their commitment to a new, spiritual lifestyle under the lordship of Christ in his church (Acts 2:38–41). It should also regularly serve the Lord's Supper (v. 42) to represent the members' continued repentance from sin and trust in Christ's atonement. Church members need more than an annual revival, they also need regular recommitment to kingdom obligations.

4. A church, furthermore, should stimulate enriching fellowship within the membership (Acts 2:42). It should encourage mutual caring among all its members intergenerationally, irrespective of gender, marital status, and socioeconomic standing. The church is not a community of lonely people.

5. Since God's truth can never be exhausted, a church ought to provide for every member's lifelong learning in teachings consistent with apostolic doctrine (v. 42). A church should support parents in teaching children as well as young people to understand, apply, and communicate basic Christian beliefs. In a culture where values are garbled, church worship and teaching services cultivate loyalty to the highest virtues in God's kingdom (Matt. 6:33). In an undisciplined world a church must also responsibly discipline members who fail to keep its doctrinal and moral standards (1 Cor. 5:13; 2 John 10).

6. A church exists to ordain, commission, and send church planters to evangelize and establish churches where none exist (Acts 13:2–3). One denomination requires those who desire to attend seminary to have won a number of sinners to Christ and started a church. And its seminary graduates who desire ordination must have begun more than one church! A church ought to prepare all its members for their ministries by helping them discover, develop, and deploy their gifts for strengthening the church and blessing the world (1 Cor. 12:7; Eph. 4:11–12).

7. Churches need to communicate

with one another. Because members may move from one locality to another, letters of reference should be prepared with care (Acts 18:27; 2 Cor. 3:1). Doctrinal issues resolved in a church ought to be shared with other churches responsibly (Acts 15:23–30).

8. Such multiple services and ministries involve financial costs, hence churches ought to encourage, receive, and accountably use offerings for the support of local and distant ministries (1 Cor. 16:2; 2 Cor. 8:1–9).

9. A church should minister to the needs of single people, such as widows (1 Tim. 5:9–10), orphans, and others. Since countless other needs arise in the world, a church ought to do good to all people, especially those of the household of faith (Gal. 6:10).

A church serves these and many other important purposes in the lives of its members from birth to death. In order to minister to so many lifelong needs of its own members and the world a band of Christians must organize. A well-organized community of believers provides ministries that are not effectively accomplished by individuals, families, nations, or specialized parachurch religious organizations.

A Church Needs to Be Organized Institutionally

To succeed in fulfilling these kingdom purposes, a group of sincere believers needs structured relationships and shared responsibilities. No one leader can discharge all the challenging responsibilities of a church. To overcome the discouragement that often results from isolated efforts, every member's ministry is urgently needed. To avoid duplication and accomplish all their multitudinous tasks, spiritual people of like mind need organization. The members of a church cannot adequately achieve their multiple objectives without some social structure.

A church inevitably becomes *an organized social institution.* An institution is a social organization for the promotion of particular objectives. Organizations, like other instruments, have been used not only for the good objectives announced but also for evil ends. Anti-institutionalism may arise for worthy reasons. For example, power corrupts, and the resources of many organizations have been diverted to unjust purposes. Anti-institutionalism also results from the mind-control abuses of some religious cult leaders. A perceived lack of spiritual vitality in hierarchical religious structures has resulted in a backlash among independent churches. Mystics may regard organizational structures a roadblock to spirituality. The power of religious leaders has been dreadfully misused in church history, but communities of Christians cannot achieve their goals without leadership. We ought to decry abuses by church officers without becoming totally anti-institutional.

For a group to work together efficiently some organization with qualified officers accountable to fulfill the distinctive ministries is indispensable. To provide for regular worship and prayer a church functions as *an agency of spiritual renewal.* To train every age level in the apostles' doctrine it must organize as *an educational agency.* To persevere in stimulating fellowship among people from diverse backgrounds, ages, and interests, Christians need to organize their fellowship as *a social agency* called a church. As *an evangelistic association,* it needs officers to train members to reach out to non-Christians near and far. As *a mission board,* organization is required to send the gifted and committed to the ends of the earth. Christians need to be organized according to the laws of a state or province as *a legally recognized entity.* As *a businesslike community* a church also needs to organize responsibly to be financially accountable. As *a communications center,* it needs people competent to operate and maintain equipment for the dissemination of messages important to its goals.

To maintain its distinctive nature and fulfill its unique purposes a church also needs *standards for membership* and hence *a membership list.* Only with an up-to-date membership list can churches write letters of reference, discipline members, conduct business, and elect officers in a responsible manner. The membership standards should be doctrinal, moral, and geographical. All members ought to subscribe to the *doctrinal* convictions set forth in its constitution. The standards are also *moral.* Church members ought to exhibit a repentant spirit when they sin, even when not publicly exposed. The standards for a gathered community are also *geographical.* In order to participate in church activities regularly a member ought also to live within commuting distance of the meeting place for regular involvement in fellowship and service.

Organization is also needed to remove people from the membership list. The ultimate purpose of church discipline is first of all restoration. If that becomes impossible, it may be necessary to dismiss people for several reasons: (1) moving permanently beyond commuting distance, (2) transferring to another church, (3) remaining unrepentant for verified public moral violations, (4) lack of participation in its ministries for a long period of time, or (5) not affirming items in the doctrinal statement of the church or contradicting them. Every effort at reconciliation ought to be made before removing names from church membership.

Two Church Offices Are Functionally Necessary

To lead the membership in the achievement of its purposes, an institutional church develops a constitution describing its organization in terms of certain *offices.* And it needs to make their job descriptions and qualifications clear. Then a church can identify members with gifts for leadership in those tasks as *officers* (Acts 14:23; 1 Tim. 3:1; Titus 1:5). Church officers are not different from other Christians, except in the disciplined use of their abilities and gifts. Howard Snyder argues that in the New Testament the church is *a charismatic organism, not an institutional organization.*[120] The church is a charismatic organism because the Holy Spirit bestows on every member gifts called the *charismata* (e.g., 1 Cor. 12:4, 9). And because every member is spiritually gifted, he or she is a minister of the church. But the fact that every member is a servant minister does not exclude the need for structured decision-making procedures for official action.

A contrasting view of church officers stresses the authority of the offices to the neglect of their holder's gifts. L. Coenen concludes that in the New Testament "the concept [of the church] also takes on an organizational aspect. It is related to the role of offices, clearly underlining the significance of the apostolic tradition and displaying institutional and hierarchical features (Eph. 4:11)."[121] We concur that the New Testament supports institutional features but not an alleged *"hierarchal"* structure. A hierarchical order, a Roman Catholic explains, requires "the distinction between clergy and laity," excludes "the acceptance of a charismatical structure," and considers the church "a sacrament."[122] The New Testament does not adequately support any of these factors.

277

A hierarchical view of the clergy is also based on an alleged succession of apostolic leaders from Christ to the present. But this hypothesis also lacks adequate historical support. The New Testament distinguishes the apostles from other Christians as those who had been with the Lord from the beginning and had seen his resurrected body (Acts 1:21–22). The Twelve have had no successors with the same qualifications, position, or authority. The apostolic eyewitnesses to the Messiah's incarnation had a unique foundational ministry. But after the first century there were no eyewitnesses of the incarnate, crucified, and risen Messiah.

Although a charismatic community, the church also has an organized social structure with designated offices. The officers of the institutional church are chosen for public leadership and have a *functional* authority, not a hierarchical or apostolic authority. Assuming maturity of character, their right to lead depends on personal gifts and the faithful, loving use of them. The leaders' job description includes the responsibility "to prepare [or train] God's people for works of service, so that the body of Christ may be built up" (Eph. 4:12).

Who selects the officers? Since there are no more apostles, biblical qualifications are best assessed by those who have known candidates for the office of elder for some time—i.e., members of their church. A church elects certain experienced members to the *office* of elder. The "brother" (probably Luke or Barnabas) sent with Titus "was chosen [*keirotoneō*] by the churches" to accompany Paul (2 Cor. 8:18–19). The term "chosen" means to select by raising hands, and so may mean elected by the congregation.[123] The same term is used when they "appointed" or "ordained" elders in every church with prayer and fasting (Acts 14:23). Titus was left in Crete to "appoint" elders in every town (Titus

1:5). In the most explicit instance (2 Cor. 8:19), the appointment was probably made by the choice of the members indicated by the raising of the hand (*cheir*). Churches request recommendations of others, but final choice by the church provides for the greatest measure of accountability to the whole body.

The Pastor-Elder-Bishop

The term "elder" has an instructive background. In Old Testament times elders as *representatives of their families* were given instructions about the Passover as those who had authority over kinfolk (Exod. 12:21–27). Elders also appear as *representatives of the nation.* Thus Moses chose seventy men to be "elders of Israel" (Exod. 18:13; cf. Deut. 1:13). This process eventually led to the formation of the Sanhedrin as a council of seventy members. An elder in Israel at first derived his authority and status as well as his name by reason of his age and success in his family, community, and nation.[124]

In New Testament times some men who met the qualifications—in terms of character, personality, and experience in managing their own families—were appointed elders in the local church (1 Tim. 3:2–7; Titus 1:6–9). Paul addressed the "elders" in Philippi as "overseers" (Phil. 1:1). He invited the "elders" at Ephesus to meet him (Acts 20:17), and he spoke of their pastoral responsibilities to the flock over which the Holy Spirit had made them "overseers" (bishops) (v. 28). Returned missionaries reported to James and the "elders" at Jerusalem (Acts 21:18–19). The elders in Jerusalem received the funds as Paul delivered the gift from the church at Antioch (Acts 11:30). Elders were capable of teaching believers sound doctrine and refuting those who opposed it (Titus 1:9).

The highest servant ministry (office) in a church requires a person capable of modeling Christlike maturity in a threefold way. The individual must exhibit in his own family the maturity of an *elder,* the caring and nurturing abilities of a shepherd (*pastor*), and successful experience in administration as a *bishop.* Although the three designations are not synonyms, they specify distinct roles or responsibilities of one and the same person. This was seen as Paul urged the elders (Acts 20:17) from Ephesus to guard the people over whom they were overseers (bishops) (v. 28), and to function as shepherds or pastors (v. 28). Peter exhorted the persons called "elders" to be "shepherds" (pastors) of God's flock under their care, and to serve as "overseers" (1 Peter 5:1–2). The qualifications of elders (Titus 1:6) and those of bishops are essentially the same (vv. 7–9; 1 Tim. 3:27). Lake concludes his study of the biblical usage of the term as follows: "An elder is, therefore, an older, spiritually more mature male member of the Church who is responsible for the administration of the congregation. . . . The office of pastor or bishop and elder were the same (Didache 10:6)."[125]

The New Testament evidence favors *a plurality of elders,* but that does not exclude the predominant leadership of one elder or the participation of the whole church. Wallace observes that "there may have been elders who were not *episkopoi.*"[126] However, early evidence is lacking for elders who were not also overseers or bishops. One elder usually is recognized as senior pastor, but as churches grow, a larger representative body may be necessary. Paul and Barnabas ordained "elders [pl.] for them in each church" (Acts 14:23) and in every town (Titus 1:5). Paul addressed a plurality of deacons at Philippi and also a plurality of bishops (Phil. 1:1). James instructed a sick person to call for "the elders of the church to pray for him" (James 5:14). In Ephesus, where Timothy served, there was a plurality of elders (Acts 20:17). In the only singular uses of elder, Paul writes generically of qualifications expected of anyone appointed as elder (Titus 1:6–7; cf. 1 Tim. 3:1).

A plurality of elders responsible for the church does not mean that all have identical responsibilities or equal remuneration (1 Tim. 5:17). "It does, however, avoid the concept of a single ruler of a congregation and distributes authority as well as responsibility among several, thus corresponding to the Jewish community from which the office of elder was adopted."[127] Among the elders, some may have been better teacher-preachers for equipping the saints for ministry, and others may have been better administrators. But evidence for a clear-cut distinction between ruling and teaching elders is lacking in the one proof text (1 Timothy 5:17). Every elder must be "able to teach" (1 Tim. 3:2).

Ordination to pastoral ministry professionally should be limited to those elders with gifts for teaching apostolic doctrine and refuting those who oppose it (Titus 1:9). Elders are accountable for leading their people well by their preaching and teaching, as well as their faith and godly way of life (Heb. 13:7). The authority of elders is not inherent in themselves but is derived from the Lord's teaching as recorded and developed in inspired Scripture. Those who administer a church well by faithful preaching and teaching of the Scriptures are worthy of greater financial support (1 Tim. 5:17–18). Members of the church pastoral staff should be appropriately paid for their labors.

Deacons/Deaconesses

Although all church members are lovingly to serve others, not all are appointed to the office of deacon or deaconess. First-century "servants" served others like waiters at a meal (John 2:5, 9). The office of deacon in the church is usually traced to Acts 6:1–6; deacons were appointed by the elders as servants to minister to the special needs of widows. Later Paul underlined the importance of that ministry and some of its principles (1 Tim. 5:3–16). Stephen was chosen to be a deacon because he was full of the Spirit, wisdom, grace, and power (Acts 6:3, 8). Stephen's opponents "could not stand up against his wisdom or the Spirit by whom he spoke" (v. 10). The requirements of deacons are similar to those of elders (1 Tim. 3:8–13). The significance of their role is recognized by Paul, for he specifically addressed them as well as all the saints and the overseers at Philippi (Phil. 1:1).

Deaconesses may have been the wives of deacons who served with them, for the qualifications of wives of deacons are listed along with those of the deacons. These qualifications included being "worthy of respect, not malicious talkers, but temperate and trustworthy in everything" (1 Tim. 3:11). Phoebe, a servant of the church, may have held the office of a deaconess (Rom. 16:1). Euodia and Syntyche contended for the Gospel at Paul's side. As co-workers and possibly deaconesses, it was important that they agree with each other in the Lord (Phil. 4:3). The service of women to meet the needs of widows is particularly appropriate. All should help relatives who are widows so that the church can help those widows who have genuine need (1 Tim. 5:16).

It is certain that women served actively as deacons. This is clear not only in Rom. 16:1, where the deaconess Phoebe of Cenchrea is commended by Paul, but in 1 Tim. 3:11. Here the best exegesis would view the reference to women as meaning another order of deacons (*gynaikas hōsautōs*), namely women deacons. . . . A parallel development is found in 1 Tim. 5:3–16, where a women's order of widows was recognized for its ready service. Nevertheless, the patristic church enjoyed the service of an independent order of women deacons, as witnessed to in the Syriac *Didascalia.* . . . From the fourth century on, their common title was "deaconess."[128]

The unique paradigm of servanthood is none other than Jesus Christ. He became "a servant to the Jews on behalf of God's truth, to confirm the promises" (Rom. 15:8). Our Lord, indeed, willingly became a slave (*doulos,* Phil. 2:7). In contrast to Gentile authority and his disciples' selfish ambitions, "the Son of Man did not come to be served, but to serve" (*diakonēsai,* Mark 10:45). Jesus said, "Who is greater, the one who is at the table or the one who serves? Is it not the one who is at the table? But I am among you as one who serves" (Luke 22:27). If Jesus considered himself a servant minister (or a deacon) of his disciples and washed their feet, what higher role can any Christian seek? All Christians, and *a fortiori* all leaders, are to be servant-ministers. J. Stam wrote, "Indeed the whole of the Christian life is a participation by grace in the Servanthood of the Son of man. This diaconate-in-Christ marks the entire Church; we are partakers in the communal life and in the corporate servanthood and suffering of the suffering Servant."[129]

For the sake of a functional unity and order, elected deacons and deaconesses serve under the leadership of the elders. As in the Trinity and the family there are distinct functional (not hierarchical) roles. The responsibility in human leadership under Christ is through the congregation led by its appointed elders and deacons/deaconesses fulfilling their functions. Deaconesses have no greater obligation to the elder board than the deacons. Women who are not officers have no greater accountability to the elders than the men who do not hold office. Women may utilize their gifts as fully as men who are not elders. Women evangelists have led many boys and girls and men and women to Christ. All women (as well as men) are needed to exercise their gifts creatively as servant ministers in accord with the guidelines laid down by our Lord.

If trustees are required by the state, this responsibility can be filled by the holders of the two biblical offices, or another office can be formed for these responsibilities. Any other office required in different cultural contexts, however, should be in close communication and cooperation with the elders. Offices remain in the church constitution even when they may not be filled for some reason. In summary, then, the New Testament teaches two levels of offices. The one office is held by the elder, bishop, or pastor; the second is exercised by the deacon and deaconess.

A Flow Chart for Decision Making in a Church

In any social institution with two or more persons, unity requires a flow chart of responsibilities. "God is not a God of disorder but of peace" (1 Cor. 14:33).

1. Preeminently the exalted head of the church is *Jesus Christ*. His teachings have first priority on any matter of which he has spoken. His example of servant ministries is normative for all. Those gathered in fellowship recognize his presence and ruling authority in their midst.

2. The authority of the exalted Christ now comes to expression on earth through the *Spirit-illumined Scriptures*. The twice-born discover the mind of Christ, God's living Word, by personally receiving the teaching of the written Word. The Bible possesses unique authority because it was written by personally trained and Spirit-inspired, apostolic spokesmen for Christ. Hence all normative beliefs and practices must be subject to scriptural pronouncements. The major doctrines of Scripture hold greater weight than all ministers, creeds, confessions, and church councils.

3. In the conduct of church business under Christ and the Scriptures, the *congregation* is the final human authority. In disputes among members, after going directly to the person and to the elders, the final court of appeal is the entire membership (Matt. 18:15–17). The congregation participated in choosing the first deacons (Acts 6:2–3). The church at Antioch sent Paul and Barnabas to discuss the issue of Gentile obedience to Moses' Law with the apostles and elders (Acts 15:1–3). The church at Jerusalem welcomed them (v. 4) and listened to their report (v. 12). After James spoke, "the apostles and elders, with the whole church, decided to choose some of their own men and send them to Antioch" with a letter (vv. 22–23). At Antioch the church gathered to hear the encouraging message (vv. 30–31). "Apparently there was unanimous agreement with the choice of messengers and with the contents of the letter (vv. 23–29)."[130] The church leaders worked with the people in coming to a decision.

Of course church officers should take the lead in addressing major issues. But officers do not lord it over their people. Elders rule by the power of persuasion from the written Word and faithful experience. A congregational polity seems more consistent with a regenerate church membership and the priesthood of every believer. The fact that church boards are not infallible may be disappointing in some ways, but it also means that they can change. Members can revitalize a church, but not without effort enabled by the Holy Spirit. As those who desire constructive change, members themselves must be open to change.

4. To satisfy the need for leadership,

church members elect qualified and gifted *elders* to administer congregational activities for the achievement of its objectives. The senior shepherd or elder shares public ministry with the other elders. All the elders are accountable to the people for the faithful exercise of their responsibilities. The eldership is not a self-appointed, self-perpetuating body. Elders can be replaced at the end of the term designated in the church constitution. Elders may suggest names and serve on a nominating committee to propose future candidates for the office. Ultimately elders will give account of their stewardship to the Lord Jesus Christ, the head of the church. The difference between the elders and other members is not a matter of inherent hierarchical authority nor an insupportable apostolic succession through generations of church history. The elder's authority is merely functional. It depends on spiritual gifts recognized by the congregation and the faithful use of these gifts for the good of the entire body.

5. The elders delegate certain ministries to *deacons/deaconesses* chosen by the congregation. As stewards of specified ministries, the deacons/deaconesses give account first to the elders. They also are accountable to the congregation. Ultimately, of course, all members, elders, deacons, and deaconesses will give account of their stewardship to the Lord Jesus Christ.

The apostles, as Carnell said, "rendered a normative interpretation of Christ's messianic office as Son of Man and Son of God," but "did *not* legislate a specific polity on the church."[131] Its "organization is the servant of fellowship" and "polity is good or bad to the degree that it promotes or hinders the fellowship."[132] Admittedly, the scriptural evidence is not as abundant as we would like, but some guidelines for church organization seem clear. Under Christ and the Word a congregational

government appears to be the most conducive to fellowship of spiritual equals in Christ (Gal. 3:28). It also seems most consistent with the priesthood of every believer and the ministerial responsibilities of every member rather than a special class. All members are accountable to the whole body for edifying it by the faithful use of their abilities in the power of the Holy Spirit. Apart from repeated fillings of the Spirit, furthermore, a hierarchical organization has no inherent sacramental power to convey forgiveness or redemption. No humanly appointed priesthood exclusively mediates God's grace to others. A congregational polity provides the greatest number of checks and balances to an officer who might seek to abuse a position. A democratic pattern of government may not be the most efficient, but in the final analysis it best preserves the members' joint participation with freedom and responsibility.

What is a Christian church? In summary, a local church is a distinctive community both spiritually and institutionally. *Spiritually* a church is made up of men and women who are personally responsive to the Father's call, receptive to the Son's atoning provisions, and actively yielded to the Spirit's life-giving ministries. *Institutionally* a church is composed of believers who are organized with the two biblical offices responsible for leading all the members in ministries to fulfill its numerous purposes.

A Church Is Related to Other Churches

Apparently Christ's followers initially met together in house churches. Believers assembled in houses, as in the home of Priscilla and Aquila (Rom. 16:5) and of Nympha (Col. 4:15). House churches exemplify what we today call *local churches*. Several house churches may have been related to each other in larger municipalities, as the New Testament refers to *"the church"* at Jerusalem (Acts 2:41–42) and at Antioch (13:1). Paul addressed letters to several churches in cities. For example, he wrote "to the holy and faithful brothers in Christ at Colosse" (Col. 1:2).

The house and city churches in a larger area were viewed as a *regional church*. Under great persecution the church (singular) was scattered throughout Judea and Samaria (Acts 8:1). Later "the church throughout Judea, Galilee and Samaria enjoyed a time of peace" (Acts 9:31). In these uses the church seems to refer, not to a distinct ecumenical government superior to local churches, but to the associated churches and their members in that area. More typically, the New Testament refers to the churches (plural) in a larger area. For example: "The churches in the province of Asia send you greetings" (1 Cor. 16:19).

The concept of the church quickly came to include all believers in all the churches on earth at the time, *the universal church*. Paul addressed believers in Corinth "together with all those everywhere who call on the name of our Lord Jesus Christ—their Lord and ours" (1 Cor. 1:2). The apostle also spoke of a practice "in all the congregations of the saints" (1 Cor. 11:16; 14:33). Moreover, Paul stated that his way of life agreed with what he taught "everywhere in every church" (1 Cor. 4:17) and to "the rule" he laid down "in all the churches" (7:17). As Stephen Neill observed,

Jews in the diaspora never ceased to think of themselves as part of the one people of God; each Jewish community *was* the Israel of God manifest at that particular point in space. Since the Church thought of itself as the new Israel, and inherited precisely that sense of unity, the oneness of the Body of Christ was the starting point of thought, and not the goal of conscious endeavor.[133]

The universal church must not be identified with any one contemporary organization. It is *catholic*, but not to be identified with Roman Catholicism, for the Roman Catholic Church has departed from apostolic doctrine in many of its traditions. Neither is the universal church to be identified with Protestant associations like the World Council of Churches or the World Evangelical Fellowship. Fortunately, manifestations of the universal church become evident here and there globally, affording us the opportunity to see glimpses of its multicultural beauty. But the universal church is never entirely visible to humans on any given day in any locality.

The one body of Christ includes not only all living believers at any given moment on earth but also all believers in the Messiah of all times. This is often called *the invisible church* or *the church triumphant,* although its living members are very visible on earth. We would prefer to call it *the spiritual body of Christ*. This doctrine is not based solely on a word study of "church" but on the believers' relationship to the Messiah and other saints justified by faith. Death cannot separate those "in Christ" from God's love or from the risen Lord's body (Rom. 8:38–39). The redeemed belong to him, for they have been bought with a price.

The church triumphant includes members already in *the heavenly city* (Heb. 11:13–16; 13:14; cf. Phil. 3:20). "But you have come to Mount Zion, to the heavenly Jerusalem, the city of the living God. You have come to . . . the church of the firstborn, whose names are written in heaven" (Heb. 12:22–23). The designation "firstborn" suggests believers' privileged position as heirs together with Christ, the "heir of all things" (Heb. 1:2). The "church of the firstborn" does not include angels but all who, like Abraham, believed that what God promised he could do (Rom. 4:21). Their names are written in heaven and even though "spirits," they are now righteous by faith in Christ. Thinking of the church spiritually as "the people of God" (the justified by faith from all times, including Abraham and David), we must deal with an even larger invisible reality. Only the tip of the iceberg is present on earth at any given moment.

Belief in the invisibility of the total spiritual body of Christ offers Christians no excuse to neglect obligations to its local expression in their community. The reality of the spiritual body must not be an excuse for abandoning local church responsibilities. Any argument against the doctrine of the spiritual oneness of God's people of all times applies equally to the universal church, which is never visible in its entirety. The fact that the major part of the latter is invisible does not make it less real or significant. The response to people who neglect commitment to a local church because they are members of the invisible church is not to deny the latter's spiritual reality, but to point up their fallacious inferences. Analogously, the response to the myopic who are concerned only with their own local work is not to deny the reality of the local church; it is to point out the values of the catholicity of Christ's multicultural body from the beginning. We may rejoice that Christ's work has been triumphant in defeating much opposition globally, but we have no reason to manifest an arrogant triumphalism in ourselves or our ministries. Christ is Lord of the church, and the Holy Spirit gives the fruit.

The observant will note that the systematic formulation integrate biblically supported elements from several of the historical views. Theology is not done by labels but by research.

APOLOGETIC INTERACTION

Does Baptism Regenerate (Roman Catholicism, Lutheranism)?

Is water baptism a sacrament that conveys the Spirit's regeneration and baptism? Or is the Spirit's baptism logically prior to water baptism, giving baptism its meaning? The historical section (above) explains that the *Church of Rome* views the sacraments in general, and baptism in particular, as rites that have the power of efficiently conveying grace. Such a view makes water baptism the prior condition for receiving regeneration and Spirit baptism. It also seems to consider grace an *entity* that can be conveyed by water and controlled by the rite of an authorized priest with proper intentions. One Roman priest pictured God's grace as a liquid in a container with seven outlets that could be opened to people only as seven approved priests turned a faucet. Many contemporary Catholics no longer limit the mediation of the Spirit's saving grace to the priestly sacraments. As shown in the historical section, those who posit a "baptism of desire" think the Spirit works redemptively apart from the sacraments. The hypothesis of baptismal regeneration is difficult to integrate with the fact that regeneration is a work of the Holy Spirit who moves sovereignly when and where he will (John 3:8). Only by the supernatural re-creation of the Spirit can a sinner be born again and enter God's redemptive kingdom. Baptism logically follows, not precedes, the new birth.

The historical section also documents the *Lutheran view* that water baptism is a sacrament that effects conversion and sanctification. Lutherans have criticized Billy Graham for failing to use baptism as a means to conversion. "If we have been baptized, we are already in the road of conversion even before our first decision. . . . [Baptism] is a genuine means of grace and veritable door to salvation."[134] A Lutheran reflecting on the theme "What My Baptism Means to Me," explained, "It was more than a symbol of God's grace. It was a God-given means of grace through which my sins were 'washed away.' I was born again of water and the Spirit into a life of faith. I became a child of God, loved by Him, and destined for eternal fellowship with Him in heaven."[135]

In the extensive didactic passages on justification, however, *faith* rather than baptism is the means of being saved (e.g., Rom. 3–4; Gal. 3–4). Baptism outwardly expresses a person's inner faith. No human rite can determine whom the Holy Spirit will regenerate. A church can no more impart the regenerative power of the Spirit by a ceremony than it can control the wind (John 3:8). The kingdom of God is not so much like a school at this point, but a family. Converts must be born into the kingdom. Prior to receiving the initiation ceremony and education in an organized church, holistically depraved and condemned people need to be born of the Spirit into God's kingdom and baptized by the Spirit into Christ's body.

Does Baptism Remit Sins and Bestow the Holy Spirit (Christian Church)?

The Disciples of Christ and the Christian Church deny teaching baptismal regeneration, but they do affirm baptismal remission of sins and consequent reception of the Spirit. Faith and adult immersion become the necessary conditions for receiving forgiveness and the Holy Spirit. But God grants justification, redemption, and reconciliation by sheer grace unconditionally because (as our research showed) the lost are unwilling and unable to meet the conditions.

Moreover, in the temporal order the Holy Spirit came to some before they were baptized. The Spirit restored Paul's sight prior to his baptism (Acts 9:12–18). The Spirit came on Gentiles before being baptized in water (Acts 10:44–48; 11:15–17). People who heard and believed by the Spirit's inner call were then baptized in water (Acts 16:14–15; 18:8). Conversion is the means of receiving the benefits of the Cross, especially in Galatians (2:16) and Romans (3:22, 25–26; 4:3, 9–24; 5:1; 10:9–11, 13). The logical priority of Spirit baptism to water baptism is based not so much on brief historical allusions as on major didactic passages concerning salvation by faith.

What about the texts often cited for baptismal remission of sins and reception of the Spirit? Jesus' reference to "water and Spirit" (John 3:5) is not to Christian baptism. Discussion in the biblical section of chapter 2 concluded that that phrase, recalling Jewish imagery, refers to natural man's need to be purified from sin and spiritually renewed. Concerning Peter's challenge, "Repent and be baptized. . . . And you will receive the gift of the Holy Spirit" (Acts 2:38), F. F. Bruce commented, "Baptism in water continued to be the external sign by which individuals who believed the gospel message repented of their sins and acknowledged Jesus as Lord, were incorporated into the Spirit-baptized fellowship of the new people of God."[136] Bruce continued, "It is against the whole genius of Biblical religion to suppose that the outward rite had any value except insofar as it was accompanied by true repentance within."[137] Instead of the usual translations of Acts 2:38—"be baptized for [*eis*] the remission of sins"—Bruce would translate it "be baptized because of the forgiveness of your sins." The preposition *eis* in the context is causal. The same preposition in Romans 6:3 signifies that all of us who were baptized into Christ Jesus were baptized "because of" his death.

Similarly, we ought not make the "laying on of hands" by officials in a church a necessary condition of salvation. That ceremony welcomed believers who had received the same Spirit into the body of Christ's followers. The laying on of hands by the apostles, Beasley-Murray holds, "was added to baptism, not in order to convey a *donum superadditum* that could not be associated with baptism as such, but to strengthen this element inherent in baptism itself."[138]

Does Baptism "Seal" One's Salvation (Presbyterian and Reformed)?

Presbyterians deny that baptism is a sacrament "conveying" saving grace but regard it as more than a symbol of conversion and regeneration. It is both "a sign and a seal" of the Spirit's redemptive work. As John Murray argues, "The tenet of baptismal remission/regeneration reverses the order inherent in the definition which Scripture provides."[139] Charles Hodge maintained that the sacraments are real means of grace. But the efficacy of baptism does not reside in the water, the sacramental action, the person who administers it, or the leader's office or character; it resides in the work of Holy Spirit in adults who believe. Hodge adds, "God has promised that his Spirit shall attend his Word; and He thus renders it an effectual means for the sanctification of his people. . . . The sacraments are effectual as means of grace only, so far as adults are concerned, to those who by faith receive them."[140]

Do not the same arguments that undercut the Roman hypothesis that baptism conveys salvation undermine the Presbyterian argument for the alleged efficacy of a sacrament to "seal" salvation? The scriptural "seal" of a person's union with Christ and his church is the presence of the Holy Spirit (2 Cor. 1:22; Eph. 1:13). Also, it is the Spirit's continued work that enables one to persevere (Phil. 1:6). The washing with water does not of itself seal the believer to Christ; rather, it signifies the presence of the Spirit who unites believers to Christ. An application of water by ordained leaders does not replace or control the Spirit's sealing ministry. Baptism depicts the Spirit's ministries in the convert's life.

Is Baptism a Sacrament or a Sacred Ordinance (Baptists)?

Sacramental viewpoints agree that baptism is a sign ordained by our Lord. Its marvelous *significance* could not be greater. (1) *Ontologically,* baptism signifies that the Holy Spirit has already renewed the human spirit's capacities to know, love, and serve God. (2) *Intellectually,* baptism declares one's assent to the Gospel's objective truth for all and one's subjective reception of it as true personally. (3) *Volitionally,* baptism manifests the person's entire soul commitment to the crucified and risen Messiah. (4) *Emotionally,* baptism expresses one's deep desire to love God with one's whole being. (5) *Ethically,* baptism marks the transfer of one's ultimate loyalty from the kingdom of darkness to the kingdom of light and to Christ as King. (6) *Relationally,* by being baptized, a person gives visible testimony to an invisible communion with the crucified and exalted Christ and to other members of the institution Christ heads, universally and locally. Through baptism a person expresses an initial public acceptance of both the privileges and the responsibilities of membership in that church.

Seeking to make baptism more meaningful, some Baptists now call it a sacrament, a faith sacrament, or a dynamic sacrament.[141] Although Cook and Walton admit that a sacramental concept was not characteristic of the Baptist tradition, they call baptism "an *effective sign* of our entrance into Christ"[142] a "sacrament" in which God acts through the church,[143] and a channel of grace and unique divine power.[144] R. E. O. White argues for a "dynamic sacramentalism," imagining that considering baptism a mere ordinance leads to the Quaker view of dispensing with the symbol. White emphasizes that as a means of grace any value in baptism is conditioned on faith. Since it conveys grace only for genuine believers, he calls it a "faith sacrament."[145]

Other Baptists agree that baptism is not effective apart from faith and that it ought to be administered with more meaning than is often done. But those who find difficulty believing that the Holy Spirit's summons is an effectual call face overwhelming complications in making the human act of baptism an effectual agent of grace. Faith itself is no more effective than its object. Similarly, the rite of baptism is not more effective than what it represents. Designating an application of water a sacrament adds nothing to the magnificent significance of its referent—the crucified and exalted Christ.

A missionary to a Catholic South American country debated in a class whether baptism was an ordinance or a sacrament. He found it impossible to redefine "sacrament" in a country dominated by a Roman view of baptismal regeneration. The missionary wisely referred to baptism not as a sacrament but as *"a sacred ordinance."* It is, indeed, an ordinance commanded by our Lord, and for sincere followers of Christ its meaning is not secular but sacred. Indebted to him for his suggestion and integrating the elements of agreement with alternative ideas, we here view water baptism as an ordained sign with sacred significance.

The term *ordinance* has considerable biblical precedent. In the Old Testament, as J. A. Wharton explains, "the ordinances are grounded in the vital command of God (Deut. 4:5, 14; 5:31ff.; 6:1–2, 24–25) based upon his gracious activity (Deut. 4:32–40; 6:20; 7:6–8; 29:2–9), and therefore may not be understood in terms of mere legalism."[146] The New Testament warns against being enslaved to the ordinances of the previous age foreshadowing the coming of Christ (Heb. 9:9–10) because they were abolished at the Cross (Eph. 2:15; Col. 2:14). Nevertheless, we are to keep the civil ordinances of national leaders to contribute to a lawful and decent society (Rom. 13:2) and the ordinances of God delivered by the apostles for the church (1 Cor. 11:2). Baptism is included in our Lord's command to make disciples among all nations (Matt. 28:19).

As an ordinance that Jesus personally exemplified, water baptism of new converts is *imperative* when humanly possible. The Quaker denial of the visible sign must be regarded as disobedience. The fact that a ceremony can be hypocritically performed is not a valid reason against its meaningful use motivated by love of Christ. Like any other good work, baptism must be prompted by a loving obedience and not considered a means to attain merit. Rather than a means of grace, then, baptism is a *manifestation* of grace. By seeking baptism a candidate confesses publicly what has already occurred in private by the Spirit's power.[147] The ceremony then becomes an important occasion for celebrating the Spirit's ministries of grace. During times of war, displacement, or extreme drought, new believers may be regenerated and have their sins remitted although unable to join a church and visibly express their faith in baptism. As important as church observances are, God's grace and power are not within the control of the institutional church. God's gracious activity is not suspended until a church makes all the arrangements for a public service of baptism. But as soon as feasible a new convert should obey the Scriptures and be baptized as an outward indication of inward faith.

Should Infants Be Baptized?

Infant baptism makes sense only if the rite is a sacrament that in some way conveys or seals saving grace. Paedobaptists appeal also to the unity of God's people in the old and new covenants and the covenant of grace in eternity. The latter was made not only with Christ and all believers but also allegedly with their descendants. "Believers and their seed," Berkhof claims, is "an organic idea."[148] This does not mean salvation in the case of every individual, he admits, but refers to the seed of the covenant collectively.[149] "From the preceding it follows that even unregenerate and unconverted persons may be in the covenant."[150] But the church, our research found, is composed of those called out of the world, namely, the converted and reconciled.

The case for infant baptism also is based on the continuation of an Old Testament concept of family and national solidarity and the unity of the covenant signs. Although the outward ceremonies have changed, Bromiley argues, the functions of baptism and circumcision are exactly parallel.[151] Infants shared in the benefits of the family and nation under the old covenant and received circumcision as a sign and seal. So infants must share in the new covenant and its rite of baptism. Baptism is said to be the replacement for circumcision as the sign and seal of the covenant of grace (Col. 2:11–12). Bromiley concedes, "To be sure, there is no explicit command to baptize infants."[152] But close approximation to it occurs in household baptisms. Infants of Christian parents have a "seed" of faith, and infant baptism may be a means of grace for the parents. But the operation of baptism "may in some mysterious way increase the grace of God in the heart."[153]

The covenant of redemptive grace indeed is one in all ages, and in Old Testament times there was a strong concept of family and national solidarity. Nevertheless, an individual's relationship to God was determined by no one but himself (Ezek. 18). The New Testament also emphasizes the need for personal conversion and regeneration. Granting the unity of the covenant, in no age was a child saved by another's faith or a proxy rite. People were justified by grace through faith before Abraham and the rite of circumcision. Even after Abraham, circumcision was not the initiatory rite into the covenant of grace but into the *nation* institutionally. As Presbyterian theologian Charles Hodge wrote, "There cannot be a greater mistake than to confound the national covenant with the covenant of grace, and the commonwealth founded on the one with the church founded on the other."[154] If a comparison is intended between circumcision and baptism in Colossians 2:11–12, an analogy proves nothing, it only illustrates; and nothing about infants or the age of the baptized appears in the context. If in biblical times the true descendants of Abraham are not the children of the flesh but adult believers (Gal. 3:26, 29), how much more is that the case at present?

Since the effectiveness of baptism is not in the administrator, the water, or the parents but in the faith and obedience of the one baptized, infant baptism lacks efficacy. Its ineffectiveness has been documented in the Church of England. "Out of every 100 children born, 67 are baptized at fonts of the Church of England, 26 are subsequently confirmed, only 9 remain faithful even to the extent of making their communion . . . at Easter."[155]

What is the significance of household baptisms in the New Testament? The contexts indicate that they occurred where each member was old enough to assent to the Gospel, receive the Spirit, and participate in ministry. Henry Alford's *Greek Testament Commentary* suggests translating Acts 16:31 as: "Believe and thou shalt be saved: and the same of thy household."[156] When Peter spoke to Cornelius, the Holy Spirit came on "all who heard the message" (Acts 10:44). These were old enough to make a response, speak in tongues, and praise God (v. 46). The baptized members of the household of Stephanas were mature enough to devote themselves to service of the saints and so earned recognition for their ministries (1 Cor. 16:15–18).

With typical sarcasm, Søren Kierkegaard lamented the lack of authentic existential spirituality (or "subjectivity") in infant baptism. According to Carnell's interpretation of Kierkegaard, while universally practiced in the Danish churches, infant baptism "is based on such a mechanical, objective ritual that no spiritual inwardness is aroused."[157]

After surveying the case for infant baptism, Karl Barth concluded, "These things prove neither the legitimacy nor the necessity of infant baptism."[158] There is not a divine work in, with, or under the human ceremony duplicating or adding to Christ's death and resurrection. As Barth observed, "Baptism takes place in active recognition of the grace of God which justifies, sanctifies and calls. It is not itself, however, the bearer, means or instrument of grace."[159] The New Testament neither designates baptism a mystery or sacrament nor regards it a causative vehicle of salvation. Baptism does nothing for an infant that Christ has not already done. In the New Testament no one was ever brought to be baptized, but adults came to be baptized. Freely one chooses to accept Christ and identify with Christ. "It is a dangerous thing to believe in Christ and water."[160] In calling for action against the state church tradition at this point Karl Barth felt alone:

> But how can the Church be or become again, as is said to-day on many sides . . . , an essentially missionary and mature rather than an immature Church, so long as it obstinately, against all better judgment and conscience, continues to dispense the water of baptism with the same undiscriminating generosity as it has now done for centuries?[161]

Many suggest an alternative ceremony to dedicate new Christian parents for their crucial task. Moltmann proposes that "infant baptism should be replaced by the blessing of the children in the congregation's service of worship and by 'ordination'—the public and explicit commissioning of parents and congregation—for their messianic service to the children."[162] If the true meaning of a service does not guarantee the salvation of the infant, it should be accurately named a parental dedication service. New parents are at that time especially sensitive to their responsibilities to become paradigms of the faith and teachers of moral principles. Church leaders can minister to them in preparation for such a dedication ceremony.

What Form of Baptism Did Jesus Exemplify and Ordain?

Although all Christian denominations recognize the validity of immersion as a form of baptism, many who sprinkle argue that the Greek terms *baptō* and *baptizō* do not require that one form invariably. What was the public sign Jesus instituted as initiatory? In his historical and cultural context several lines of evidence support immersion:

1. Jewish proselyte baptism was by

289

immersion in water. Baptism does not replace circumcision, for Judaism requires three distinct rites: circumcision, baptism, and sacrifice. Immersion as the form of baptizing Gentile converts into Judaism was indicated by the amount of water required to fill the pools (about one hundred gallons), provisions for modesty (implying nudity), and discussions of complete contact with the water. Jewish proselyte baptism is still done by immersion.

2. John the Baptist's ceremony required immersion. The difference was that he called upon Jews, not just Gentiles, to repent and be baptized. John baptized at Aenon "because there was plenty of water" (John 3:23).

3. John immersed Jesus into (*eis*) the Jordan (Mark 1:9). Hence in Jesus' context *baptizō* designated immersion, and he expected his followers to practice it (Matt. 28:18–20).

4. The early church practiced immersion. "Philip and the eunuch went down into the water and Philip baptized him. When they came up out of the water . . ." (Acts 8:38–39). "In New Testament times baptism was by a single immersion, preferably in running water."[163]

5. Immersion continues to be the form of baptism in the Eastern Orthodox Church.

6. The primary meaning of *baptizō* is to dip, plunge, or immerse. Although *baptizō* may have a few other meanings, its predominate usage is to immerse. In classical Greek the meanings are to dip, plunge, dye, draw wine by dipping a cup in a bowl, to be drowned, immersed.[164] In New Testament Greek the meanings of *baptizō* are to "dip, dip oneself, wash, immerse."[165] The Greek language had words for pouring and sprinkling, but these are not used in contexts of baptism.

7. In order to exhibit rather than conceal what the New Testament authors said, the term should be *translated* ("immerse") rather than transliterated ("baptize"). So argued T. J. Conant, a member of the American Bible Union's translation committee in a book containing an exhaustive word study citing hundreds of early uses of the term.[166]

The important issue, many still insist, is not the *form* but the *fact* of baptism. The seven converging lines of evidence listed above show that the scriptural "fact" of baptism when translated is believers' immersion. Although we ought not alter the essence of immersion, its forms are not so important. Immersion may be in water that is running or still. A candidate clothed or naked may be dipped forward or backward once or three times. None of these variables alters the fact of baptism. But a change to sprinkling or pouring does alter our Lord's command. Jesus, who did away with scores of ceremonies, asked his followers to observe two simple ones. People who advertise that the Bible's teaching is their norm of faith and practice are not free to change the Lord's requirement of immersion.

The Lord's Supper, an Ordained Sign With Sacred Significance

The second outward sacred ceremony Jesus asked his followers to observe is the Lord's Supper. The simple essence of the *sign* our Lord ordained is the eating of bread, symbolizing Christ's broken body, and the drinking of wine, symbolizing his shed blood. Again the form may vary as long as it does not alter the designated reality. Believers may use unleavened or leavened bread and may drink grape juice or wine from one common vessel or from separate glasses. More important than such details of form is the purpose that believers eat and drink in remembrance of the One who died that they might live.

The Lord's Table is repeated to signify the participant's continued repentance from sin and faith in Christ. It is *not a sacrament* alleged either to convey or seal salvific grace. Nor is the bread changed into the literal substance of Christ's body. When Jesus said after taking bread, "This is my body given for you" (Luke 22:19), he spoke metaphorically of his coming death, as the biblical section makes clear. Jesus spoke prior to his death not in Aristotelian philosophical technicalities but in ordinary language. At the first observance of the Lord's Table the substance of the bread the disciples ate was not literally transformed into the inner substance of Christ's body, for he was still among them. Neither was the drink transformed into the actual blood of Christ, otherwise they would have crucified him prior to Calvary!

The signs of eating broken bread and drinking red wine at the Lord's Table are important not in themselves but as *vivid reminders*. Repeatedly, Jesus said, "Do this in remembrance of me" (1 Cor. 11:24–25). These two symbols refresh our memories concerning the Messiah's sinless life and atoning sacrifice in our stead. They vividly recall the unjust accusations and personal suffering he bore to deliver us from the power of evil. They recollect something of the agony of the Father's wrath Jesus felt to effect our pardon. They recollect the precious blood he shed that we might be reconciled to God. For all who remember the greatest act of love in history, the Lord's Table does not become an empty ritual. Signs bearing such extraordinary significance can hardly become routine. Those who doubt the truth of the Gospel may have little to remember, but those who believe the Bible are overwhelmed with memories of the greatest act of love ever offered.

Do believing participants in the Lord's Table experience Christ's "real presence"? Christians remain ever conscious of the Lord's redemptive presence with them until the end of the age (Matt. 28:20). Also they are cognizant of his presence in the church whenever members gather in his name. In both these cases his presence is real. Is there some additional divine presence when the gathered community partakes of the signs of his broken body and shed blood? The fact is that his presence can be made no more objectively "real" by a human observance in a communion service. Rather, as participants examine themselves (1 Cor. 11:28) and intentionally partake (10:16), they become more consciously aware of their needs and of the presence of the Savior who sacrificed himself for them.

The signs of the broken bread and poured-out wine carry a cargo of rich significance to be freshly appreciated at each observance: (1) *Ontologically,* the Holy Spirit faithfully strengthens the participant's capacities to know and serve the values of Christ's kingdom. (2) *Intellectually,* participation in the Table declares one's continuing assent to the Gospel's objective truth and its subjective application for one's life. (3) *Volitionally,* responsible participation in the Supper manifests a person's continued commitment to Christ as Lord in all relationships. (4) *Emotionally,* the bread and cup express one's renewed desire to love the Savior with one's whole heart. (5) *Ethically,* partaking exhibits one's continual dismissal of other masters and the giving of ultimate allegiance to Christ above all else. (6) *Relationally,* at the Lord's Table a person gives visible testimony to abiding fellowship with the crucified and exalted Christ and to the members of the institution he heads. So this observance may appropriately be called "communion." "Is not the cup of thanksgiving . . . a participation [*koinōnia*] in the blood of Christ? And is not the bread that we break a participation [*koinōnia*] in the body of Christ?" (1 Cor. 10:16). At the Lord's Table

291

people of faith experience not metaphysical union but relational communion (v. 17). Furthermore, believers together present a public *proclamation* of Christ's death until his return (1 Cor. 11:26).

In order to assure that its rich meaning be maintained, the Lord's Supper ought to be observed publicly under the leadership of the church. For those unable to gather, it should be celebrated under the auspices of the church by its appointed representatives. The observance is administered responsibly by the church, but it is not the church's supper; it is the *Lord's* Supper. It was ordained by our Lord for all his followers, not for one particular church or denomination. Hence a church invites to participate all who owe their spiritual life to the crucified and risen Lord. And participants are to examine themselves, rather than be examined by the officers of the church (v. 28).

What About Parachurch Organizations?

God instituted the church as a missionary agency to minister to peoples' needs in all cultures and subcultures from the cradle to the grave. Unfortunately the Western church has limited itself almost exclusively to suburban middle-class families. Because of this narrow vision, parachurch groups have arisen to minister to other target groups, such as college students, international students, singles, seniors, street people, prisoners, single parents, etc. The structure of the local church in Scripture is sufficiently flexible that it can include many of these special target groups in its ministries.

If we build specialized ministries into our churches as the parachurch is doing, we will have a great advantage with those we evangelize and disciple. When we in the local church reach that unchurched teenager for Christ we don't have a *transition*

problem. We don't have to try to get him into another group because someday he will turn twenty and no longer fit in with us. We are designed to minister to him through all the stages of his life.[167]

One writer calls for a "wedding ceremony" uniting the local church body with parachurch target-group ministries. Then the senior pastor must be willing to share the home base ministry with others and trust volunteer members with ministry. He will not be threatened by others' gifts but will rejoice in their successes. The unleashing of the laity for ministry helps solve serious people problems. While continuing to reach middle-class families with traditional services, all members are challenged to use their God-given abilities to meet the needs of some target group or groups. In this way money may be channeled into many different ministries rather than in larger buildings for the home base. Christian ministries need to be performed in the world, not simply in a church building. Only then will the church become the missionary agency the Lord intended it to be.[168]

Which Is the One True Church?

Some fundamentalists, after withdrawing from liberal denominations, have mistakenly viewed their separatist movements as the only remnant church. Some sects and cults have done the same. Anthony Hoekema observed that one of the distinctive traits of a cult is the claim that its group is the exclusive community of the saved. It absolutizes itself as the only organization approved by God. "There is among the cults no appreciation for the Biblical doctrine of the 'one holy catholic Church'—that is, of the universal church of Christ composed of Christ's true people of all the ages and from all the nations."[169] Cults claim an abrupt break with historic Christianity after the first century, propose an extrascriptural source of authority, devalue Christ, deny justification by grace alone, and then absolutize the organization itself.

For centuries the Roman Church made the cultic claim that there was no salvation outside its particular organization. Many recent Catholic scholars no longer affirm this, but it seems inescapable where the traditional views of the hierarchy and the sacraments remain. The founder of Mormonism, Joseph Smith, allegedly was told by an angel that all other churches are false. According to Smith, the institutional church was in a state of apostasy until 1830 when God allegedly made revelations to him. Hence he perceived the Church of Jesus Christ of Latter-day Saints to be the one true church. Some Mormons, however, now claim to be Christians, implying the extension of the body of Christ beyond the ministries of their priesthood.[170] Jehovah's Witnesses claim that the Watchtower Bible and Tract Society constitutes God's true organization and that all other religious groups are agents of Satan. Rather, an institution without the essentials of the Gospel relating a person to Christ spiritually is not a Christian church. No absolutist claim for a single institution fits the scriptural doctrine of the universal church. The latter reality precludes any single organization or denomination from thinking itself the only true remnant church serving God's purposes.

If one's church or denomination fails to maintain classical Christian doctrinal standards by failing to discipline contradictory teaching, what is one's responsibility? In the Roman Catholic Church sound doctrinal statements remained on the books, but the church became so encrusted with tradition that the Gospel was not preached. Under such conditions Martin Luther took his stand against the Roman church. Seeking to restore apostolic doctrine, he found himself outside it spearheading the sixteenth century Protestant Reformation. John Calvin, also against Rome, believed that the church was the community of saints justified by faith. In response to serious charges against the new movement, Calvin wrote that "all union which is formed without the word of the Lord, is a faction of the impious, and not an association of believers." He added, "It is sufficient for me that it was necessary for us to withdraw from them, in order to approach to Christ."[171]

Earlier in the twentieth century J. Gresham Machen withdrew from the liberal Presbyterian church, and Westminster Seminary separated from Princeton Seminary. In the 1940s Regular Baptists and Conservative Baptists withdrew from the American Baptist Convention to train, send, and support ministers in America and abroad who believed the Gospel. After trying for many years to call for adherence to an orthodox doctrinal statement in the Presbyterian Church USA, John Gerstner concluded in 1990 that it no longer had even an orthodox statement of faith on the books and regretfully withdrew.

Separation from those publicly denying distinctive doctrines of Christian faith does not violate the unity of the church but preserves it. The bases of church unity are apostolic doctrine and brotherly love. Schism breaks the bonds of love in the body of Christ. It violates love over lesser matters of policy. The unity of a church presupposes that the members and leaders are believers in the personal God who is distinct from the world and active in it as disclosed in the Scriptures. Where theism, sin, the Incarnation, Atonement, and Resurrection are no longer required, a community of the saints no longer exists. Jesus said, "Everyone who is on the side of truth listens to me" (John 18:37).

Is it not unloving to separate from

293

unbelievers? Love for God may be tested by our willingness to listen to false prophets and failure to discipline them (Deut. 13:3). John, who stressed the importance of love for other Christians, reminded us that not all people with "prophetic" ministries are of God (1 John 4:1). Those "spiritual" people who do not teach that the eternal Word became literal (not mythical) flesh are antichrist (vv. 2–4). They may claim to be Christians and function in Christian schools and churches, but they do not possess God (2 John 9).

Paul, who judged love the supreme virtue, urged the church at Rome, "Watch out for those who cause divisions and put obstacles in your way that are contrary to the teaching you have learned." He continued, "Keep away from them. For such people are not serving our Lord Jesus Christ, but their own appetites" (Rom. 16:17–18). Paul alerted Titus to the fact that "there are many rebellious people, mere talkers and deceivers," who "must be silenced because they are ruining whole households by teaching things they ought not to teach—and that for the sake of dishonest gain" (Titus 1:10–11). Paul added, "Rebuke them sharply, so that they will be sound in the faith and will pay no attention to Jewish myths or to the commands of those who reject the truth" (vv. 13–14). In contrast, Titus was to "teach what is in accord with sound doctrine" (2:1).

The obligation to defend the Gospel and separate from those who reject biblical essentials is abused when made the excuse for petty quarrels with other Christians on secondary matters. "Avoid foolish controversies and genealogies and arguments and quarrels about the law, because these are unprofitable and useless" (Titus 3:9; cf. 2 Tim. 2:23). Because some separatists have appeared unloving does not invalidate a biblically required discipline or separation from unbelievers. On major issues of theism, Christology, and soteriology, Paul urged, "Warn a divisive person once, and then warn him a second time. After that, have nothing to do with him" (Titus 3:10).

The nature of the church as God's called-out people here is at stake. Essential to the unity of the church is the truth revealed to God's people. When someone preached another gospel, Paul said, "Let him be eternally condemned" (Gal. 1:8). To stand for the great truths of the Gospel of Christ is not nit-picking. Renowned Christians like Athanasius, Augustine, and Calvin labored for years to establish doctrinal essentials. Shall we undo all the centuries of labor that these great theologians invested in the cause of truth and orthodoxy? Those who get their theology from Christmas cards and bumper stickers may not appreciate the need for careful thought. But the faith that avoids theological argument on behalf of Christianity's distinctive doctrines is not the faith of the New Testament.

RELEVANCE FOR LIFE AND MINISTRY

Although religion for many is merely a private matter, Jesus viewed his disciples as a social institution alternative to Judaism. In the new community called the church the Holy Spirit's presence produced bold witnessing, generous giving to the poor, freedom from social barriers, and togetherness in mutual service.[172] "The person whose overreaching desire is for his own personal liberty will naturally be anti-church, because he cannot fail to see that genuine church membership involves heavy responsibilities which limit one's personal whims."[173] But what a privilege it is to make disciples and plant churches in company with the redeemed!

Participate in a Church With Spiritually and Institutionally Vibrant Purposes

As brothers and sisters in a church we need to function as a loving spiritual community founded on an evangelical belief system to foster authentic spiritual goals. To believe that one is forgiven and accepted by God is a great blessing. But these realities need to be lived out in the life of a community. One of the most rewarding spiritual experiences is to be genuinely accepted by the church just as you are. Believing that a spiritual church begins with a regenerate membership, leaders will carefully examine the testimony and life of proposed members. Acceptance by the leaders and the congregation corroborates the Spirit's inner witness that one is accepted by God. This frees people to work without regard to acclaim, to be willing to receive criticism, and to acknowledge the need for continued growth.

The antidote for ailing churches today, says Ralph Martin, is similar to that which Paul offered the first-century Corinthians.[174] The latter were divided over leadership and blighted by party rivalry. They perverted biblical standards of sexual morality. Their worship disfigured even the Lord's Supper. Their attitudes of pride and unbridled freedom bordered on license amid claims to esoteric knowledge and flamboyant manifestations of power. At the root of these maladies was a selfish pride expressed in a belief system that failed to affirm the lordship of the crucified and risen Messiah. In contrast, align yourself with a healthy church that views the *charismata* as gifts of grace for the well-being of the entire community, that preaches the whole Gospel, and that practices self-giving love.

One should commit oneself to a church with *institutional goals* supportive of God's universal *providential purposes*. On the basis of God's general revelation and providential kingdom, churches should (1) respect the rights and duties of all people to life, justice, and liberty as image bearers of God; (2) actively support moral and political causes to build up one's neighborhood, city, and nation; (3) teach, support, and obey universal norms of intellectual honesty and moral decency; (4) reprove injustice in business, education, the media, and entertainment; and (5) assist victims of oppression, crime, terrorism, and natural disasters.

One should also commit oneself to a church devoted to God's specially revealed *redemptive purposes* achieved on the ground of the Messiah's atonement by the ministries of the Holy Spirit. In God's gracious redemptive kingdom, dynamic churches (1) communicate the Gospel by all ethical means to all persons in their locality, nation, and the world; (2) promote ministry involvement to edify others and evangelize the globe; (3) manifest both the gifts and the fruit of the Spirit in the church and the world; and (4) cooperate with others who believe the same Gospel for the realization of kingdom purposes.

Believers should support a church with biblical offices designed to accomplish its multiple theological purposes. The constitution of the church ought to include an official doctrinal statement that does not replace redemptive objectives by providential goals, or vice versa. The pastor, elders, diaconate, and members ought to embrace these aims and implement them. Members of a church regularly need to refresh their vision of the institutional *raison d'etre*. The members should be involved in formulating goals and objectives so that they will own them and live by them. As members articulate the objectives, they can participate wisely in choosing appropriate strategies, programs, and methods for achieving them.

Help Develop Creative Strategies and Methods

After generating attainable purposes consistent with biblical doctrine, church leaders need creatively to design *strategies* and *methods* for achieving them. The strategies and methods, like the church's nature and purposes, should be set by well-founded convictions concerning the church's nature and purposes, not by the world. Our medium as well as our message must target more than people's hedonistic felt-needs. As Christ's unique people, we must address also the deeper revealed-needs of the human spirit.

One pastor implemented a college preparatory strategy for his high school seniors. The semester or summer before graduation he asked them to read three books, one on theology, one on apologetics, and one on ethics. After each was read he would discuss it with his seniors and answer questions they had. By doing this he established, not only a stronger foundation for a persevering faith, but also a good personal relationship for future contacts.

A similar strategy emphasizing ethics in the marketplace could well be devised for high school seniors about to enter the commercial world. The resources of mature employers and employees in the church could be used to help with this. Popular business seminars from secular or New Age self-realization approaches are attracting many of our people. Christian leaders with business experience ought creatively from a Christian theistic world-and life-view to develop refreshing seminars for people among the pressures of competitive production and sales.

An exemplary strategy has been developed for training church members to reach unchurched people and spiritual seekers with difficult questions. At Willow Creek Community Church in South Barrington, Illinois, Mark Mittelberg, Director of Evangelism, ministers with this goal:

All people matter to God and therefore to us. But they are lost without Christ and must be reached with the message of the gospel . . . along with answers to their questions and objections. This must be done in a relevant way, realizing that it will generally take a period of time for them to go through the process of coming to the point of trusting Christ.

To implement that objective, staff strategy sessions identified four groups of people who matter: (1) the non-churched, (2) the spiritual seekers who need Christ, (3) all believers, and (4) those led to become evangelists and pre-evangelists. To reach the unchurched and the seekers, Pastor Bill Hybels designs the topic of each weekend service to show the target audience the relevancy of Christ, the Bible, and the Gospel message in their daily lives. "A general tone is set that says, in effect, 'It's okay to doubt and ask questions; we take your questions seriously, and we want you to take the time to investigate Christianity carefully.'" Some messages deal explicitly with alternatives to Christianity or reasons for faith, but others with more everyday issues. A Foundations class has been designed for seekers and Christians with skeptical friends who have similar questions. Its midweek sessions are reminiscent of John Stott's "Agnostics Anonymous" groups that met in homes in London a few years ago. The twofold approach both answers challenges to the faith and presents and defends the positive alternative. Other midweek classes provide advanced teaching for Christians.

For church members who think evangelism is not "their thing," Willow Creek has another strategy in place. An

Impact Evangelism Seminar over a four-week period seeks to free them from stereotypes, show how to communicate the story of Christ in everyday language and to cope with questions. Research identified the ten questions members were most often asked by seekers in their community, and in a role-playing session a church member talks with a seeker who raises these issues. The seminar seeks to help people see that Christianity has answers and that numerous other resources are available. Some are so motivated by these sessions as to want to specialize in evangelism and pre-evangelism. So a monthly Defenders Ministry equips those Christians with a passion for giving seekers and skeptics solid evidence and valid arguments in leading them to Christ. Members are motivated by "field trips" to such places as Muslim mosques, Hindu or Buddhist temples, etc. In time some of these people develop expertise in various areas and become a referral team for the church staff and members. Any church in the midst of the conflicting truth claims of an increasingly pluralistic culture could enhance its outreach by implementing apologetics with strategies like this.

Lifelong church education also calls for an enterprising plan for training members to teach. Christians can love, serve, and teach only One who is known. If a nearby Bible college or seminary has relevant lay training courses, a selection of those might be required or recommended. Or, qualified Christian teachers may be brought in for classes on the church campus. Capitalize on the use of audio- and video-taped materials available for credit or audit at such places as the Institute of Theological Studies. Qualified and experienced teachers may be able to teach younger persons to teach. Some elders can train younger deacons and deaconesses. Certificates of achievement might be awarded for those who complete board-approved training programs with qualified teaching.

An annual evaluation, as in any business, may be scheduled to measure the success of present strategies for achieving both spiritual and institutional goals. Secondary objectives ought not be inflated to the neglect of matters of top priority. And church members need to know that their personal spiritual growth and institutional service is important to the leaders. They would do well annually to discuss with members in a non-threatening way their spiritual growth, their role in their family, their service in the church, and their outreach in the world.

A young Canadian pastor, after a seemingly fruitless year of preaching, had a serious question about the strategy of weekly sermons. He asked: "Why preach every Sunday?" The basic answer is that private worship and Bible study are not enough. We all need public learning and accountability. Revealed truth is the Holy Spirit's primary means of instruction (Eph. 6:17; Heb. 4:12) for uniting God's people in mind, desire, and purposes. Such shared values determine the conduct of both individuals and institutions. Through the Spirit-filled applications of these principles church members receive strength, encouragement, and comfort (1 Cor. 14:3). Only by effectively communicating such foundational truths will a church continue into the next generation. A pastor needs to preach weekly to resist the tendency to become more a manager than a theologian, more an administrator than a spiritual leader, more a master of ceremonies than a master of worship.

Each church meeting, like each ministry, should have a creatively formulated, distinctive approach to reach its goal. Members cannot be expected to gather simply because others do or it has been traditional. Church leaders cannot remain satisfied with maintenance of the status quo. The faith once-for-all given to the saints does not essentially change, but the strategies and methods for presenting and defending it vary with the times. The detailed strategies and methods used a century ago are not necessarily the best for today. Our innovative God has worked creatively through ordinary people, Jewish and non-Jewish kings, shepherds, a physician, children, tax collectors, prostitutes, a huge fish, and a donkey. Why should not his servants find creative ways to minister? The paralytic would not have gotten to Jesus for healing if his friends had not broken a hole in a roof and let the man down in Jesus' presence. Review again the purposes of the church in the Systematic Formulation section of this chapter and use your imagination to upgrade ways of accomplishing them more effectively. Meanwhile, additional suggestions for strategies and methods follow.

Promote Deacon/Deaconess Led Support Groups

Elders should identify and train gifted and caring people as deacons and deaconesses. The family unit has fragmented as people move from the neighborhoods where they grew up, commute many miles to work, and pursue sundry recreational outlets. Loneliness has become one of the greatest afflictions of the modern age. People want us to buy something or do something; but who cares for us as individuals? Too often the church appears to be one more organization that wants to use us. "Often, it shows more contrivance than compassion, more social prestige than spiritual power, more concern with statistics than with salvation."[175]

Christian helpers, like Stephen, need to be filled with the Holy Spirit—and so with wisdom, grace, and power (Acts 6:5, 8, 10) to lead support groups. Spirit-endued deacons and deaconesses

led groups such as those that ministered to widows in the early church (Acts 6:1–5). Spiritually mature deacons/deaconesses could lead a group for singles or single parents. Many different needs suggest other target groups, such as drug addicts, parents of children with learning disabilities, and unwed mothers. Other groups might focus on leaders in education, health services, politics, etc. The twelve steps popularized by Alcoholics Anonymous, originally developed out of Pastor Sam Shoemaker's concern for people outside the traditional ministries of the church, may be adapted to the needs of people with all sorts of counterproductive addictions.[176]

Eventually support groups become *ministry groups* that focus on outreach. Leaders train others who in turn may become deacons and deaconesses. In this way many more qualified people could be involved in ministry than is often the case. Support and ministry group leaders should be authorized by the elders in consultation with the members. The elders may appoint a person or couple for leadership on the basis of experience, qualifications, and abilities. Is there not a danger that these small groups might divorce themselves from the church? The regular accountability of the group leaders to an elder or elders should keep these ministries from becoming schismatic entities. With appropriate accountability to the elders, the support and ministry groups could richly contribute to the unity and mission of the entire church.

Elton Trueblood sums up the value and power of small groups in the church for support and ministry:

> Much of the uniqueness of Christianity, in its original emergence, consisted of the fact that simple people could be amazingly powerful when they were members one of another. As everyone knows, it is almost impossible to create a fire with one log, even if it is a sound one, while

several poor logs may make an excellent fire if they stay together as they burn. The miracle of the early Church was that of poor sticks making a grand conflagration. A good fire glorifies even its poorest fuel.[177]

Cultivate an Honest, Forgiving Fellowship

Our vision for our church must be candidly realistic because in this fallen world a perfect church does not exist. Churches do not last long if built on perfectionist dreams alone. "The sooner this shock of disillusionment comes to an individual and to a community the better for both. . . . He who loves his dream of a community more than the Christian community itself becomes a destroyer of the latter even though his personal intentions may be ever so honest and earnest and sacrificial."[178]

The existing church, as distinct from an ideal church, is a fellowship, not just of the forgiven but of forgiving friends. Having been forgiven countless times themselves, members are forgiving of others. Sin contributes to loneliness and alienation as Christians miss the mark in life. A few secular psychologists may acknowledge sin, but they lack the just ground on which it can be forgiven. Members of a church, having found the way to forgive themselves and others through Christ's atonement, can uphold righteousness while being forgiving. The great Head of the church, the friend of sinners, called his disciples into a new relationship, not as servants but as friends (John 15:13–15). Friends of Jesus do not limit their friends to their own age, race, or political party. They call other Adams and Eves out of hiding from God to reconciliation with the Father and the Son and with the community of reconciliation. Church members confess their faults to one another (James 5:16) because, while aiming at perfection, they do not reach it. Bonhoeffer comments:

In confession the break-through to community takes place. Sin demands to have a man by himself. It withdraws him from the community. The more isolated a person is, the more destructive will be the power of sin over him, and the more deeply he becomes involved in it, the more disastrous is his isolation. Sin wants to remain unknown. It shuns the light. In the darkness of the unexpressed it poisons the whole being of a person. This can happen even in the midst of a pious community. In confession the light of the Gospel breaks into the darkness and seclusion of the heart. The sin must be brought into the light. The unexpressed must be openly spoken and acknowledged. All that is secret and hidden is made manifest. It is a hard struggle until the sin is openly admitted. But God breaks the gates of brass and bars of iron (Ps. 107:16).[179]

To receive forgiveness a church member need not always make public confession of sin before the entire congregation. "I meet the whole congregation in the one brother to whom I confess my sins and who forgives my sins. . . . In this matter no one acts in his own name nor by his own authority, but by the confession of Jesus Christ. This commission is given to the whole congregation and the individual is called merely to exercise it for the congregation."[180]

Develop Church Members With Well-founded Convictions

As Elton Trueblood has concluded, "The best insurance against falling away is the development of a profound and well-grounded set of convictions."[181] Wherever we find a vital, effective congregation we find at its center vibrant teaching and preaching. Christian leaders must continually resist the tendency to soft-pedal biblical truths in order to palliate prospective members. We do not help secular hedonists, pious pantheists, or other autosoteric enthusiasts by watering down Christian beliefs. Leaders must so present apostolic doctrine that members will appreciate its truth and relevance for their lives as well as defend it. Elders as player-coaches need to exhibit daily personal discipline in study. Leaders should guide members in the regular study of the Scriptures and secondary Christian literature. "The renewed church must be the disciplined fellowship of disciplined persons."[182] Meditation on biblical convictions may helpfully be done morning and evening.

The teaching of a church needs to be multigenerational. To meet the needs of the coming generation, leaders must teach parents to train their children in important biblical convictions. Spiritually mature Christians should instruct their elders who are babes in Christ. Resources are available for overcoming generation gaps in contemporary Sunday school literature. If the coming generation is to advance the kingdom, young people particularly must become committed to its belief system, values, and way of life. The whole congregation needs a worldview and lifestyle that are balanced and functional at home and in the world—in all their activities and relationships.

Convictional truth must be communicated in love. Love, the prime motivator of personal sanctification, is also the prime motivator in church instruction and growth. Elders and deacons should lovingly exemplify growth in knowledge and gracious servant leadership. The church gathers to renew love in the inner person; it scatters to bring temporal and eternal life to the world. Christ called people out of the world, renewed them, and sent them back into the world to change it. Your church may be small, but like a little leaven, its message of truth spoken in love can make a great difference in the world. The church has a dynamitelike message to proclaim and a humble service to perform globally. The entire Christian enterprise expands, according to Augustine, as one loving heart sets another on fire. The fires of loving devotion led Jesus to wash dirty feet, forgive adultery, and preach repentance to white collar criminals who lied and stole (e.g., Zacchaeus). As it preached the Gospel in love, the early church braved persecution and martyrdom and turned the first-century world upside down.

Free Church Members to Meet Crosscultural Needs

On one hand, "the Gospel says, 'Go,' but our church buildings say, 'Stay.' The Gospel says, 'Seek the lost,' but our churches say, 'Let the lost seek the church.' "[183] Small support groups and Bible studies are not enough; the individual cells of Christ's body need to experience their unity with the larger body. Ingrown renewal groups eventually confront the same basic people-problems that ingrown institutional churches face. In groups small and large we need people redirected and renewed by the Cross. "Someone has said that there are three things true about a man on a cross. 1) He has no further personal plans; 2) He can look in only one direction; and 3) He is never going back where he came from."[184]

Churches need to become centers for recruiting, training, and equipping a breed of spiritual pioneers competent to evangelize and edify multicultural people. This is the way to true apostolic succession. A church program limited to the vision and insight of one type of person is destined to remain one-sided and ineffective. Members should learn from missionaries serving in different cultures. They should establish networks of communication with students and businesspeople from other lands. Both suburban and inner-city churches may strengthen each other by developing close relationships and sharing needs and resources.

To serve a variety of people a church needs to implement a well-formulated and well-founded philosophy of ministry. An institution will always fail when it is bent on saving itself. It cannot save the world if it demonstrates an obsession with its own material enrichment and comfort. It may be less difficult to plant a church than through the years to keep its salt from losing its savor. More difficult still is the challenge of restoring the savor to the salt once it is lost! God calls pastors to develop a philosophy of ministry that draws out the abilities and gifts of others. The effectiveness of the minister is tested primarily by changed lives and their effectiveness in servant ministries. A church is a society of friendly ministers who gather to strengthen one another and who scatter to serve the needs of people of all races and classes. Leaders should encourage people to identify their own ministry and to develop their strategies and methods. Leaders should not always protect them from failure nor be surprised when they serve creatively and effectively.

Church buildings should not be larger or more elaborate than necessary for worship and the training of disciples for ministry. Simply to pay the interest on loans for church buildings, one denomination in one year spent more than 50 million dollars. More money that year went to incomes of bankers than to the incomes of all of their home and foreign missionaries![185] Jesus' vision for his disciples was world-shaking, but not in terms of real-estate holdings.

Whatever else our Lord had in mind, it is clear he envisioned something very big. He did not propose a slight change in an existing religion! . . . A small venture would not have aroused such fierce opposition, but neither would it have been worth the trouble. The Christian Movement was initiated as the most radical of all revolutions! [186]

Encourage Church Members to Minister to the Poor

In the loving ministry of Christ and the church a concern for the poor stands out. Jesus made the virtue of compassion one (albeit, not an exclusive) test of authentic discipleship (Matt. 25:34–40). His apostles urged compassion for the poor first to one's own *family* members (1 Tim. 5:4, 8). When families care for their own, they do not become an unnecessary burden to the church. Then compassion should extend beyond our families to members of the *church* (Gal. 6:10). Finally, compassion moves beyond the household of faith to care for the poor *around the world*. Disciples recognize that not all poverty is the responsibility of the poor themselves. Although some in a fallen world who disregard physical and moral laws suffer poverty as a consequence, others may become poor for reasons beyond their control.

Christian compassion, like God's, uses only just means to serve the needy. Followers of the prophets, Christ, and the apostles should not be Robin Hoods who steal from others to give to the poor. Rather, Christians work that they may have something (private ownership) to give to the poor who are willing but unable to work (Eph. 4:28). Christians work to become advocates and supporters of the genuinely needy. Jesus' followers become mediators between the oppressors and the oppressed, not guerrilla soldiers. Faith in Christ brings no guarantees of material betterment, but accountable stewards develop virtues of industry and thrift and tend to diminish costly vices. In ways like these a by-product

301

of authentic faith may be economic improvement.

The Gospel is not a message about redistributing wealth, nor does it assure material abundance. It is Good News to rich and poor alike as they become poor in spirit (Matt. 5:3). Church members who have received the Good News love not only one another but also outsiders who have inadequate incomes to sustain their families. God sent the Messiah "to preach good news to the poor" (Luke 4:18). Although the Messiah made it clear that in the present age the Good News was not about material abundance, he did seek to meet people's physical needs. He was not on the side of the arrogant poor any more than he was on the side of the arrogant rich. The transcendent Lord of all does not "take sides" in our conflicts.

Rather than seeking to get the Lord on our side, we should be concerned that we are on his side! Whatever their economic status, Jesus served people honest and humble enough to admit their need. Like our Lord, we minister to both the illegally wealthy tax collectors and impoverished beggars. The Messiah's message was not Good News to those like Pharisees who prided themselves on their almsgiving; it was Good News to the publicans and sinners who cried out: "God, have mercy on me, a sinner" (Luke 18:13). To illustrate the spirit of those who receive the Gospel, Jesus said, "Anyone who will not receive the kingdom of God like a little child will never enter it" (Luke 18:17). One enters God's kingdom as a child by repentant faith, not by seeking the bread and fish of this world. Hence we ought not confuse the mission of the church to the economically poor with its mission to the poor in spirit (Acts 17:30).

Like Jesus, we should minister to the poor and needy unobtrusively. Only incidentally do we learn of Jesus' gifts to the poor when he was seen talking with Judas. Apparently the Lord so often gave to the poor that onlookers thought he was urging Judas to give to the poor (John 13:29; cf. 12:5). Church leaders following Christ's example will not champion the plight of the poor to advance their own personal eminence. Neither will followers of Jesus claim that wealth justly earned is morally evil. Christian leaders will teach that wealth justly earned is an opportunity for greater stewardship. Christians will also teach that poverty through no fault of one's own is not morally evil, but a greater opportunity to trust the providence of God.[187]

Charity to those in need is not a matter of obligation, but it is encouraged by God's gracious gift of his Son. Charity is not simply a value of Christian individuals; Christian churches also ought to be known as beneficent centers of charity. Churches materially blessed should give to help other churches in need. Rather than considering other churches competitors or ignoring the need of small churches trying to obtain an adequate home base, affluent churches should give to new-church programs. In some instances churches have kept their resources to themselves, whereas parachurch organizations have found the joy of charitable giving. If families and churches were more charitable, nations could devote their resources more fully as agents of justice in common grace.

What Officers Owe Their Church and a Church Owes Its Officers

In the seemingly small decisions of life elders need to build character traits worthy of leaders of Christ's church. Elders should "be above reproach, the husband of but one wife, temperate, self-controlled, respectable, hospitable, able to teach, not given to drunkenness, not violent but gentle, not quarrelsome, not a lover of money" (1 Tim. 3:2–3;

cf. Titus 1:7–8). An elder ought to develop a personality balanced between being respectable or dignified and being hospitable. One merits respect by being authentic and develops hospitality by helping outsiders feel at home in one's house. Elders also owe a church their ability to manage their own families well and to disciple their own children at various age levels (1 Tim. 3:4–5; Titus 1:6). They improve skills of teaching and encouraging adults with sound doctrine (Titus 1:9), of resolving disputes (Acts 15; 16:4), and of refuting opponents of the faith. An elder will not be a new convert but a mature Christian who has a good reputation with outsiders (1 Tim. 3:6–7). Because elders must give account for their care of the flock (Heb. 13:17), they will keep a clear conscience and live honorably in every way (v. 18). When responsibilities become too great for the elders to attend to the Word and prayer, they need to appoint deacons and deaconesses to assist in the ministry. Elders owe their church faithful work, but not overwork. They ought to keep busy, but they ought not have so many irons in the fire that they burn out.

As a mature Christian, an "elder" owes it to the church to model Christlike wisdom. As a "pastor," an elder gives of himself in the care and feeding of the people. As a "bishop," an elder represents the whole church and leads it in fulfillment of its goals without lording it over the members. Some elders may be stronger in administration, some in relating to people's needs, and some in exhibiting Christian character. But all these emphases should be present to some degree in the elder and can be developed. In a given church, hopefully, the strengths of the elders will be complementary.

Not all elders are equally proficient in preaching and teaching, but those who devote themselves to these functions vocationally should be ordained and receive remuneration for their service (1 Tim. 5:17). Such pastor-teachers dedicate themselves to serving members by teaching the truth, warning of error, and doing the work of an evangelist. Elders, like Epaphroditus, may risk their lives for work the church could not do itself (Phil. 2:25, 30). Elders and deacons have nothing they have not received from God's grace and so nothing of which to boast. The work of church officers ought not be merely problem-oriented, but task-oriented as they focus on prayer, teaching, and facilitation (administration).

Elders should covenant to pray for one another and the whole body (1 Thess. 5:17), consider others better than themselves (Phil. 2:3), maintain unity in mind and purpose (1 Cor. 1:10), develop love for one another (1 John 4:7–13), and grow in trust and appreciation for one another (2 Cor. 1:14). In addition they should seek divine wisdom to distinguish scriptural convictions from personal preferences (Rom. 14). They should be "quick to listen, slow to speak and slow to become angry" (James 1:19). They will pursue agreement with others in the Lord and harmony in the church (Eph. 4:3; Phil. 4:2). As Means correctly observes,

> Scripture does not emphasize the rights, privileges, and authority of the church's elders; rather, Scripture emphasizes their qualifications, responsibilities, and obligations. Failure to note this has caused much dissent over appropriate leadership authority. Although the Bible does not specifically say how much authority church leaders should have, it explicitly opposes attitudes of demagoguery in the church.[188]

What do members owe church officers? The members of a church ought to treat elders with respect (1 Thess. 5:12) and "hold them in highest regard in love because of their work" (v. 13). The author of Hebrews wrote to wavering Christians: "Obey your leaders and submit to their authority. They keep watch over you as men who must give an account. Obey them so that their work will be a joy, not a burden, for that would be of no advantage to you" (Heb. 13:17). Members also are to "imitate their faith" (v. 7) and support them financially (1 Cor. 9:7–14). Faithful church members defend the leaders' reputation by nipping gossip in the bud. "Do not receive an accusation against an elder unless it is brought by two or three witnesses" (1 Tim. 5:19). If, however, elders have sinned as confirmed by several witnesses, they may need to be rebuked publicly so that others may be warned (v. 20).

Church members need consideration for their elders and particularly for the senior pastor, who must exercise so many functions. The senior elder or pastor serves as loving educator, evangelist, defender of the faith, preacher, leader of his family, hero for children and youth, statesman, administrator, director of spiritual growth, publicity director, budget director, burden bearer, and counselor. Consideration of your pastor's need for some privacy, family life, relaxation, and vacations is appropriate and needful. Church members should also take seriously the directive to pray for their church leaders and to care for their spiritual and physical well-being.

DISCUSSION TOPICS

1. What is the relationship of the bishop (*episkopos*), elder (*presbyteros*) and pastor/shepherd (*poimēn*) in a New Testament church?
2. Develop a flow chart of authority in the local church that you feel best represents the relevant New Testament data.
3. What is your understanding of the role of women in the ministry of the local church? Explain the meaning of key Scriptures to which you appeal in support of your position.
4. Discuss the scriptural and theological evidence for the validity of baptizing infants. How persuasive is the evidence?
5. Discuss the spiritual efficacy of the Lord's Supper. Does the rite convey special grace to the worthy participant, or does it function chiefly as a remembrance of Christ's saving work?
6. Under what circumstances is it appropriate for a local church to separate itself from its parent denomination that appears to be going liberal?

See also the Review Questions and Ministry Projects on pages 501–2.

CHAPTER 6

THE CHURCH AND ISRAEL IN GOD'S KINGDOM

The Church and Israel in God's Kingdom

THE PROBLEM: WHAT IS THE INTERRELATIONSHIP BETWEEN ISRAEL, THE CHURCH, AND THE CONNECTION OF BOTH TO THE KINGDOM OF GOD?

The topics considered in this chapter look both backward and forward. In chapter 5 we examined the nature, government, ordinances or sacraments, and world mission of the Christian church. In the present chapter we relate the church to the nation Israel and then both of these institutions to the kingdom of God. Chapter 7 will examine the hope of Israel and the church, namely, the return of Christ to earth and the place of the people of God in the Messiah's future kingdom. Chapter 8 will consider the condition of the people of God after death and their final estate in the new heavens and new earth.

This present topic raises a number of important questions. Can the varied data of the Old and New Testaments be integrated systematically under a single rubric? Is there a central theme in Scripture, such as covenant, dispensation, kingdom, or promise, that unites the whole of biblical revelation? To address this issue we explore the main features of the systems of theology created from a single biblical concept—namely, covenant theology, dispensationalism, kingdom theology, and the theology of promise-fulfillment. We inquire how these major systems of theology understand the relation between Israel and the church and the place of each in the kingdom of God.

With respect to the system known as covenant theology, can the twofold division of Scripture into the covenant of works and covenant of grace be substantiated? With regard to dispensational theology, does Scripture set forth God's dealings with the human race under seven time periods or schemes of administration? Does the concept of kingdom do full justice to the teaching of both Testaments on Israel and the church? To what extent does the concept of promise fulfill the same objective? More particularly, does God have one plan for Israel and another plan for the church? Is the way of salvation in the two Testaments different or the same? Is it true that the Old Testament is chiefly a book of law and the New Testament a book of grace? Moreover, are Israel and the church identical, each being the people of God in different eras and under different names? If they are identical, in what respects? Is it more accurate and helpful to identify similari-

307

ties and differences between Israel and the church spiritually and institutionally? Did the church begin, as some suggest, with Abraham or some other Hebrew patriarch? Were believing Jews under the old covenant proper members of the church, as defined in the previous chapter?

What precisely is meant by the kingdom of God? Is it a material or political entity, a spiritual entity, or both? Does the kingdom manifest itself in the past, the present, the future, or a combination of these? Furthermore, what was the nature of the kingdom Jesus offered to Israel, a kingdom they rejected? What role do believers play in the growth of the kingdom? Finally, what functions do political and social action play in the building of the kingdom?

ALTERNATIVE INTERPRETATIONS IN THE CHURCH

Historically the interrelation of Israel and the church and the connection of both to the kingdom has been expounded in quite different ways. We now summarize the principal systems of theology relative to this important issue of theology.

The Perspective of Covenant Theology

The system designated covenant or federal (from the Latin *foedus,* "covenant") theology was unknown prior to the Protestant Reformation.[1] Preliminary steps toward a covenant theology were made in the sixteenth century by Zwingli, Calvin, Bullinger, and Olevianius. In reaction to Reformed scholasticism and Arminianism, federal theology was developed in the seventeenth century by Wollebius and Cocceius and by the English Puritans Perkins, Ames, Owen, and Baxter. Authorities such as Turretin, Dabney, the Hodges, Shedd, Vos, Kuyper, Bavinck, and L. Berkhof have refined covenant theology subse-

quently. Federal theology asserts that the covenant motif is the hermeneutical key and organizing principle of the entire Bible. Covenant in Scripture (Hebrew *berît,* Greek *diathēkē*) is that agreement or pact God sovereignly makes with his creatures. Classically covenant theology identifies two or three different covenants, and each of the covenants reflects a fixed form analogous to covenants between kings in the ancient world.

It is claimed that in the covenant of works or Edenic covenant God, the moral Governor of the universe, submitted Adam as a free moral agent to a test of obedience in Eden. The *parties* to the covenant of works were God and Adam, Adam being the representative head of the race. The *promise* God made to Adam (and to humanity in him) was eternal life and favor. The *proviso* was obedience to God's command relative to the tree of knowledge. And the *penalty* for disobedience was physical and spiritual death. The seal connoting ratification of the covenant of works is identified as the Tree of Life. The covenant of works is said to remain binding for all unsaved persons.

Many, but not all, Reformed theologians also speak of a covenant of redemption. Advocates (e.g., Turretin, the Hodges, Shedd, Vos, L. Berkhof) maintain that the covenant of redemption provides the necessary basis for a third covenant, i.e., the covenant of grace. The *parties* to the covenant of redemption, made in eternity past, are said to be God the Father and God the Son. The *promise* is that Christ would become the head of the new humanity consisting of all people the Father gives to the Son. The *proviso* of the covenant of redemption is the Son's perfect obedience unto death.

Given the failure of humankind in Eden under the covenant of works, God in grace purposed to redeem the elect on the condition of faith. The *parties* to the covenant of grace are God and the chosen "seed." The *promise* is eternal life and favor. The *proviso* is faith in Christ, albeit a faith given by God himself. And the *penalty* for covenant-breaking is death. The covenant of grace, made with the elect, is a particular covenant. Moreover, it is unconditional in the sense that God will not violate the covenant, but conditional in the sense that individual faith is required for its fulfillment. Covenant theologians maintain that although the covenant of grace and the truth revealed in it is one, it includes several dispensations or differing modes of administration. With some variations, covenant theologians describe the old covenant God made with Adam, Noah, Abraham, Moses, and David, and the new covenant inaugurated by Jesus with the attendant manifestations of the Spirit.

The unity of the covenant of grace, being essentially *the same from Genesis 3:15 through Revelation 22:21*, has several important theological outcomes. Covenant theologians affirm (1) a unity of soteriological purpose. Both Testaments set forth identical promises, the same spiritual life, and the same means of salvation, namely, faith in God's promises. Advocates uphold (2) the identity of Israel and the church. In spite of certain institutional and administrative differences, they focus on the church as the covenant people of God in all ages (cf. Gal. 6:16, "the Israel of God"). Hodge boldly affirmed that "the commonwealth of Israel was the church."[2] Covenant theologians variously date the beginning of the church with Adam, Abel, or Abraham. Furthermore, (3) the seals or sacraments of the old covenant—Passover and circumcision—find their analogies in the sacraments of the new covenant, namely, the Eucharist and baptism. In this relation lies the justification for infant baptism. (4) Externally the Old Testa-ment church (Israel) and the New Testament church both contain a mixture of regenerate and unregenerate members. Furthermore, (5) since God established the covenant of grace with believers and their offspring, children of Christian parents are members of the visible church. According to Hodge, "If the church is one under both dispensations; if infants are members of the church under the theocracy, then they are members of the church now."[3]

Covenant theology views the kingdom as a broader concept than either Israel or the church. The kingdom signifies the rule of God, as a spiritual and invisible reality, initially over believing Israel and subsequently over the New Testament community. In the future age the kingdom will appear concretely and visibly as the absolute reign of God over the renewed order in heaven.

John Calvin (d. 1564), while not strictly a covenant theologian, enunciated certain principles developed by later covenant theologians.[4] Calvin's teachings are similar to later covenant theology in the following respects: (1) The covenant God contracts with his people is rooted in his sovereign elective purpose. In the divine plan the covenant is the means by which God adopts his elect.[5] (2) The old and new covenants constitute a unity. Although differing in external form and manner of disposition (i.e., ceremonies, sacrifices, and political structures), the two covenants are one and the same in substance. Calvin argued that the old covenant had the same Gospel, the same hope of eternal life, the same justification by faith, and the same Mediator (Christ) as the new covenant. "God has never made any other covenant than that which he made himself with Abraham and at length confirmed by the hand of Moses."[6] While minimizing differences between old and new covenants, Calvin acknowledged that the relation between the two may be described as shadow versus substance, as literal doctrine versus spiritual doctrine, and as nationalistic focus (Israel) versus universalistic focus (the nations). In the progress of divine revelation, the new covenant contains a fuller and clearer disclosure of the covenant given to Abraham. Calvin added that the Mosaic covenant confirms the covenant God made with Abraham.[7] All the Old Testament promises of salvation through Christ have their basis in God's covenant with the patriarchs. (3) Calvin clearly stated that the church existed in the Old Testament.[8] All Old Testament saints constituted the church, albeit the church "yet in its childhood."[9] Because of his privileged covenant position Abraham was the premier member of the Old Testament church. And (4) the old and new covenants possess analogous signs or sacraments. In particular, an "anagogic relationship" exists between circumcision and baptism.[10] As circumcision inaugurated Jews into the old covenant, so baptism initiates infants and adults into the new covenant. Jewish circumcision and Christian baptism differ only in external details.

But Calvin's teachings differ from covenant theology in the following important respects: (1) The Genevan Reformer identified no covenant prior to Abraham that promised salvation blessings. Calvin made no mention of a gracious covenant with Adam representing the race.[11] (2) Calvin made a distinction, not between the covenant of works and the covenant of grace (as do later covenant theologians), but between the old covenant and the new covenant, or between the Old Testament and the New Testament. The covenant under the Abrahamic-Mosaic economy he called "the covenant of the law."[12] The new arrangement inaugurated by Jesus and characterized by the life of the Spirit Calvin called "the covenant of the gospel."[13] In this im-

portant respect the framework of Calvin's theology differed from that of later covenant theology with its covenant of works–covenant of grace scheme.

Like Augustine before him, Calvin came close to identifying the kingdom of God with the church (in both its Old and New Testament forms). The kingdom, for Calvin, represents the realization of God's rule among the redeemed in and through Christ. In the *present* age the kingdom manifests itself in theocratic societies (Israel and Geneva as the model for the new order). Calvin, however, strenuously insisted that the spiritual kingdom of Christ ought not be confused with God-ordained civil government. In the *future* age the kingdom represents God's absolute rule over the renovated and gloriously new order.

In the Westminster Confession (1647) the covenant of works–covenant of grace scheme was elevated to creedal status. "The first covenant made with man was a covenant of works, wherein life was promised to Adam, and in him to his posterity, upon condition of perfect . . . obedience" (ch. VII.2; cf. XIX.1; Shorter Catechism, Q. & A. 12, 16). When Adam violated this covenant by sin, "the Lord was pleased to make a second, commonly called the covenant of grace: wherein he freely offered unto sinners life and salvation by Jesus Christ, requiring of them faith in him that they may be saved, and promising to give unto all those that are ordained unto life his Holy Spirit" (ch. VII.3; cf. Shorter Catechism, Q. & A. 20, 93). The Confession notes that the one covenant of grace was administered differently through history: under the *law* "by promises, prophecies, circumcision, the paschal lamb and other types and ordinances," and under the *gospel* by "the preaching of the word and the administration of the sacraments of baptism and the Lord's supper" (ch. VII.6). "There are not, therefore, two covenants of grace differing in substance, but one and the same under various dispensations'' (ch. VII.6). No mention of the covenant of redemption between the Father and the Son can be found in the Westminster Confession.

According to L. Berkhof (d. 1957), God inaugurated the covenant of works in Eden with Adam as the representative head of the race. The *promise* extended was eternal life for Adam and his descendants based on the *proviso* of perfect obedience to the command concerning the Tree of Knowledge of Good and Evil. Adam was able to keep the covenant of works by his unfallen, natural endowments. The *penalty* for disobedience was physical, spiritual, and eternal death. Berkhof identified the seal of the covenant of works as the Tree of Life (Gen. 2:9; 3:22). The single covenant of grace consists of two aspects, the covenant of redemption and the covenant of grace proper—the former providing the eternal basis for the latter.

Berkhof defined the covenant of redemption as "the agreement between the Father, giving the Son as Head and Redeemer of the elect, and the Son, voluntarily taking the place of those whom the Father had given him."[14] He developed the covenant of redemption chiefly as an inference from the idea that salvation is grounded in an eternal decree of God, which assumes a voluntary agreement among the persons of the Trinity to accomplish the work. The *parties* of the covenant of redemption are the Father and the Son, who as the last Adam is the Surety and Head of it. The *promises* made to Christ include grace for the performance of his task, deliverance from death, a redeemed people as his reward, and sovereign rule over all things. The *proviso* includes the Son's perfect fulfillment of the law and obedience unto death. Berkhof observed that, insofar as Christ committed himself to fulfilling the law, the covenant of redemption was for him a covenant of works rather than a covenant of grace.[15]

Concerning the covenant of grace proper, the contracting *parties* are God and the elect (adults and children). The *promises* include justification, the gift of the Spirit, and final glorification. The *proviso* is faith in Christ. And since some people choose to violate God's solemn compact (as deliberate covenant-breakers), the *penalty* for disobedience is death. Berkhof affirmed that the covenant of grace, in addition to being gracious and particular, is also "unbreakable" and "inviolable."[16] The covenant is unconditional in that God himself faithfully fulfills its conditions in the elect. The covenant is conditional in the secondary sense that it requires faith. Berkhof addressed the problem raised by the claim of the unconditionality of the covenant of grace with the reality that some children of the covenant do not receive Christ, as follows: "God undoubtedly desires that the covenant relationship shall issue in a covenant life. And he himself guarantees by his promises pertaining to the seed of believers that this will take place, not in the case of every individual, but in the seed of the covenant collectively."[17] On one hand, the covenant of grace with believers and their children is unconditional and inviolable. On the other, it can be freely violated. As an aside, covenant theology places considerable emphasis on the notion of promise within the several covenants.

Berkhof added that although the same *essentially* in all dispensations, the covenant of grace does undergo a change of *form*. He posited two dispensations or administrations of the covenant of grace: the Old Testament and the New Testament. The former involves four stages of the revelation of the covenant: the revelation to Adam (the *Protoevangelium* of Gen. 3:15), the revelation to Noah (the covenant of common grace), the revelation to Abraham (which marked the beginning of the institutional church), and the revelation to Moses at Sinai (where the covenant became a national covenant). Several theological outcomes of Berkhof's covenant scheme ensue: (1) The way of salvation, by grace through faith, remains the same from Adam to the end of the church age. (2) The church commenced prior to Abraham as "the church in the house"[18] and subsequent to Abraham as a defined institution. At the Exodus Israel became both a nation and a church. In the New Testament the church became divorced from Israel's national life and assumed a universal character. And (3) the seal of the old covenant (circumcision) is analogous to the seal of the new covenant (baptism), thus providing the theoretical basis for infant baptism.

Berkhof rejected the definition of the kingdom as the reign of God over restored, theocratic Israel ("a kingdom of Israel").[19] The kingdom of God is the spiritual and invisible rule of God established in the hearts of sinners by Spirit regeneration. This rule is realized in principle on earth, but it attains fullness only at the return of Christ, who will consummate the process of salvation.

The Perspective of Dispensational Theology

Dispensationalists claim that God manages the world through a series of dispensations, initially defined as time periods (Ironside, Scofield, Chafer) but later as stewardship arrangements (Ryrie). "These periods are marked off in Scripture by some change in God's method of dealing with mankind . . . in respect of the two questions: one of sin and of man's responsibility."[20] Rudimentary dispensational ideas appeared in the eighteenth-century writings of Pierre Poiret, John Edwards, and Isaac Watts. Dispensationalism was systematized in the nineteenth century by J. N.

Darby and furthered in the twentieth century by A. C. Gaebelein, C. I. Scofield, L. S. Chafer, J. Walvoord, and C. Ryrie. Dispensationalists traditionally identified seven time periods wherein God dealt in unique ways with the human race: (1) A dispensation in Eden in which God tested Adam and Eve's obedience via the Tree of Knowledge. (2) A dispensation prior to the giving of the law in which persons were tested with respect to the moral law written on their hearts. (3) A dispensation after the flood in which man was tested by the administration of just laws administered by human government. (4) A dispensation following the call of Abraham in which humans were tested with regard to the promises made to Abraham and his seed. (5) A dispensation subsequent to the giving of the law in which people were tested with respect to the Ten Commandments. (6) A dispensation in the church age in which individuals are tested with respect to the Gospel offer. And (7) a dispensation in the millennial age in which Christ will reign over the restored Davidic kingdom. Dispensationalists note that every dispensation save the last ends in radical failure, hence the note of pessimism that characterizes the system.

While claiming a unity of the plan of salvation, dispensationalists sharply differentiate between law and grace and between Israel, the church, and the kingdom. Appealing to John 1:17, advocates claim that the law dominated from Moses to Calvary, whereas grace prevails from Christ's resurrection onward. "Scripture never, in *any* dispensation, *mingles* these two principles. Law always has a place and works distinct and wholly diverse from that of grace."[21] In recognition of God's different administrations Chafer added: "With the call of Abraham and the giving of the Law . . . there are two widely different, standardized, divine provisions whereby man, who is utterly fallen, might stand in the favor of God."[22] Moreover, although a people of God existed in the Old Testament, the faithful there never constituted the church. The church was uniquely formed at Pentecost by the Spirit's baptism of believers into the body of Christ. Concerning scriptural teaching about Israel and the church, "all is contrast."[23] Consequently (against covenant theology) none of the Old Testament promises to Israel apply to the church. In fact, through the ages God has pursued two distinct purposes: "one related to the earth with earthly people and earthly objectives involved, which is Judaism; while the other is related to heaven with heavenly people and heavenly objectives involved, which is Christianity."[24]

Traditional dispensationalists, moreover, differentiated between the phrases "kingdom of God" and "kingdom of heaven." The former refers to God's spiritual reign over the entire creation, whereas the latter pertains to the earthly reign of Messiah in the restored Davidic kingdom. Jesus preached the gospel of the kingdom, whereas Paul preached the gospel of grace. At his First Advent Jesus offered Israel not a spiritual kingdom but the earthly, political kingdom, which, after the Jews rejected it, was postponed. At the Second Advent the earthly Jewish kingdom (the "kingdom of heaven") will be established, thereby fulfilling God's unconditional covenant with David. In the present age the kingdom exists in "mystery" form as the Christian church, which God instituted as an interim arrangement following the Jewish rejection. By adhering to a rigorously literal interpretation of prophetic Scripture, dispensationalism consistently upholds a premillennial eschatology with particular emphasis on the Jewish character of the messianic kingdom.

So-called ultradispensationalism posits two distinct churches in Acts—a Jewish church from Pentecost to Paul and the body-of-Christ church (comprising Jews and Gentiles) that began with the ministry of the apostle (Acts 9, 13, or 28).[25] Anglican clergyman E. W. Bullinger (d. 1913) founded ultradispensationalism with his thesis that the church age began at Acts 28:28, where God revealed to Paul in Roman confinement the mystery of the body of Christ. Thus the only New Testament documents addressed to the church are Paul's prison letters. And since water baptism and the Lord's Supper are not mentioned in this corpus, these two ordinances are judged irrelevant for the church age. Bullinger was followed by C. H. Welch and A. E. Knoch. More moderate ultradispensationalists identified the beginning of the church with the conversion of Paul in Acts 9 or the commencement of Paul's ministry to Gentiles in Acts 13. The latter regard all thirteen Pauline letters as relevant to the church. The church observes the Lord's Supper but not water baptism, which is applicable to Jews only. Advocates of the more moderate form of ultradispensationalism include C. R. Stam, J. C. O'Hair, and C. F. Baker.

The Scofield Reference Bible, edited by C. I. Scofield (d. 1921), a lawyer become Congregationalist theologian, defines a dispensation as "a period of time during which man is tested in respect of obedience to some *specific* revelation of the will of God."[26] *The Scofield Bible* identifies seven dispensations, as follows: (1) *Innocency,* from the creation of Adam and Eve to their expulsion from Eden (note to Gen. 1:27); (2) *Conscience,* from Eden to the flood (note to Gen. 3:23); (3) *Human Government,* from the flood to the call of Abram (note on Gen. 8:20); (4) *Promise,* from the promise given to Abraham to the giving of the law (note on Gen. 12:1); (5) *Law,* from Sinai to

313

Calvary (note on Exod. 19:8); (6) *Grace,* from the resurrection of Christ to his second advent (note on John 1:17); and (7) *Kingdom,* from the Second Advent through the Millennium (note on Eph. 1:10). The work also identifies eight covenants in Scripture, "which condition life and salvation, and about which all Scripture crystallizes:"[27] (1) the Edenic Covenant, (2) the Adamic Covenant, (3) the Noahic Covenant, (4) the Abrahamic Covenant, (5) the Mosaic Covenant, (6) the Palestinian Covenant, (7) the Davidic Covenant, and (8) the New Covenant. What is the relation between a dispensation and a covenant? "The *dispensation* must be distinguished from the *covenant.* The former is a mode of testing, the latter is everlasting because unconditional."[28] For example, the Abrahamic Covenant did not abrogate the dispensation of law, which served as an interim arrangement until Christ came.

The Scofield Reference Bible posits a sharp antithesis between law and grace. Grace is "constantly set in contrast to law. . . . Law is connected with Moses and works; grace with Christ and faith."[29] In statements such as the following *The Scofield Reference Bible* has been accused of affirming salvation by works under the administration of law: "The power of testing is no longer legal obedience as the condition of salvation, but acceptance or rejection of Christ, with good works as a fruit of salvation."[30] The notes, moreover, differentiate between two kinds of Israel, the Israel after the flesh and those who through faith are Abraham's spiritual children.[31] Israel in both forms is carefully distinguished from the church.[32] The work devotes four notes to the "kingdom of God," which it defines as God's eternal spiritual reign over angels, saints, and the church.[33] Yet it discusses the "kingdom of heaven" in some twenty notes, defining it as the

political, Davidic rule of the Messiah in the Millennium centered in Jerusalem.[34] The primary application of Jesus' Sermon on the Mount (which is "pure law") is to the restored Davidic kingdom in the Millennium.[35] When the Jews rejected Jesus' offer of the kingdom of heaven, God instituted the church as the "mystery" form of the kingdom in the interadvental period. "Upon his return the King will restore the Davidic monarchy in His own person, re-gather dispersed Israel, establish His power over all the earth, and reign one thousand years."[36]

The New Scofield Reference Bible[37] posits the same seven dispensations (although the name of the sixth is changed from "Grace" to "Church") and the same eight covenants. The definition of a dispensation has been enlarged to include three concepts: "(1) a *deposit* of divine revelation concerning God's will," "(2) man's *stewardship* of this divine revelation, in which he is responsible to obey it," and "(3) a *time-period* . . . during which this divine revelation is dominant in the testing of man's obedience to God."[38] The antithesis between law and grace has been softened somewhat—chiefly in the change of the sixth dispensation from "Grace" to "Church."[39] The work states that in every dispensation salvation comes by grace through faith in Christ.[40] The distinction between Israel and the church is preserved; the church nowhere is found in the Old Testament. Another important change from the original edition is the admission that "the kingdom of heaven is similar in many respects to the kingdom of God."[41] However, the principal focus of the kingdom of heaven remains the future, political, millennial reign of Christ centered in Jerusalem. "The kingdom of heaven is the earthly sphere of the universal kingdom of God."[42]

Charles Ryrie defines the biblical dispensation as a stewardship arrangement rather than a time period. "A dispensation is a distinguishable economy in the outworking of God's purpose," and includes a distinctive revelation, a testing, human failure, and divine judgment.[43] Ryrie lists seven dispensations, as follows: *Innocency* or *Freedom, Conscience* or *Self-determination, Civil Government, Promise* or *Patriarchal Rule, Mosaic Law, Grace,* and *Millennium*.[44] The absolute essentials of dispensationalism are three: (1) the distinction between Israel and the church, (2) a consistently literal hermeneutic, and (3) the glory of God as the basic theme of his dealings with humankind. Whereas law and grace are fundamentally antithetical (John 1:17), the dispensation of law incorporates and displays divine grace. Thus there are not two ways of salvation—one by legal obedience under the law and the other by grace through faith; rather, salvation in every age has the same *basis* (the death of Christ), the same *means* (faith), the same *object* (God). The *content* of faith, however, changes in every dispensation. Ryrie adds that "to affirm a sameness of the content of faith would of necessity deny progressiveness in revelation."[45]

Ryrie identifies four aspects of the kingdom theme in Scripture:[46] (1) "the universal kingdom," which focuses on God's rule over the entire world; (2) "the Davidic Kingdom," which involves the rule of Messiah on the throne of David; (3) "the mystery form of the kingdom," which pertains to the church between Christ's first and second advents; and (4) "the spiritual kingdom," which involves God's rule over believers in the church age. Constituted Christ's body by the baptizing work of the Spirit, the church is distinct both institutionally *and* spiritually from Israel. God has one purpose for the church and quite another purpose for Israel. The kingdom proclaimed by Old Testament prophets, preached by Jesus, and

offered to the Jews was the earthly Davidic kingdom which, when rejected, was postponed to the millennial age. Ryrie insists that the church is not the present form of the Davidic kingdom; the latter's purview is solely Israel. "It was this Davidic kingdom which Jesus offered and not the general rule of God over the earth or His spiritual reign in individual lives."[47]

Recently scholars such as Craig A. Blaising, Darrell L. Bock, David L. Turner, Robert L. Saucy, William R. Foster, and others have revised the system of Scofield, Chafer, and Ryrie into what is being called "reconstructed" or "developing dispensationalism."[48] Among the changes made to traditional dispensationalism are the following:

1. The *dichotomy of law and grace* as principles of salvation for Israel and the church, respectively, has been rejected. Advocates clearly affirm that there is but one way of salvation in both Testaments—salvation by grace through faith.

2. The idea of *two new covenants,* one for Israel (Jer. 31:31–34) and the other for the church (Luke 22:20; 1 Cor. 11:25), is set aside. The new covenant discussed by Jesus, Paul, and Hebrews is not different from that spoken of by Jeremiah. The one new covenant, however, is fulfilled in two different ways relative to the church and Israel.[49]

3. A new understanding of *the kingdom* has emerged. The traditional distinction between the kingdom of heaven and the kingdom of God has been abandoned in favor of the unity of the redemptive kingdom in the progress of divine revelation. The kingdom is said to be both present and spiritual ("already") and future and institutional ("not yet"). The new conviction is that the Old Testament promises concerning the messianic kingdom began to be fulfilled in the ministry of Jesus and the apostles. In language reminiscent of

Ladd, Bock comments: "What emerges is a two-stage rule: a kingdom now, and a future manifestation of judgment authority. . . . The current phase of the kingdom has continuity with the kingdom to come, because it shares the call to reflect the activity and presence of God's righteousness in the world."[50] Saucy adds, "This age [is] the first phase of the fulfillment of the promised messianic kingdom. The present age involves the spiritual aspects of that messianic kingdom, that is, the blessings of the New Covenant (i.e. regeneration, the indwelling Spirit, etc.)."[51] Between Christ's two advents the kingdom is being extended by worldwide Gospel proclamation. Many now deny that the messianic kingdom announced by Jesus was postponed until the Second Advent. "The present age is not an historical parenthesis which is not unrelated to the history which preceded it. Rather it must be viewed as an integral phase in the development of the mediatorial kingdom."[52]

4. The absolute *distinction between Israel,* as God's earthly people, *and the church,* as God's heavenly people, has been set aside. These scholars no longer speak of the church as "the mystery form of the kingdom." Whereas they allow a distinct earthly future for Israel in fulfillment of the promises to David, significant continuity exists between believing Israel and the church as the one people of God.[53] In other words, God has a unified plan for Israel and the church within his historical kingdom program. Barker sees this new development as "a mediating position between traditional dispensational premillennialism and traditional covenant theology."[54]

The Perspective of Kingdom Theology

J. Jeremias, H. Ridderbos, and W. Kümmel articulated elements of king-dom theology prior to its fuller development by G. E. Ladd for the Anglo-Saxon world. The kingdom of God, a soteriological term, denotes the future reign of God beyond history as anticipated by Old Testament prophecy. This eschatological rule of God has invaded the historical present with saving power through the life and ministry of Jesus. In the broad sweep of redemption the reign of God was operative in Israel, is now a reality in the church, and will come with glory for salvation and judgment in the Millennium and the New Jerusalem. Kingdom theology stresses both the similarities and differences between Israel and the church. Spiritually the redemptive rule of God embraces a single people of God—believing Israel and the church—organized as distinct institutions. The church comprises those who accept Jesus' offer of the kingdom and who are Spirit-baptized into the body of Christ. Kingdom theology generally is premillennial with emphasis on the redemptive character of the future kingdom. Christ's millennial rule has a mixed Jewish-Gentile character, analogous to the church in the present age.

W. G. Kümmel defines the kingdom in terms of the eschatological order of salvation. Jesus expected the future consummation and the last judgment to come with power during his disciples' lifetime. "Jesus did indeed count on a shorter or longer period between his death and the Parousia, but he equally certainly proclaimed the threatening approach of the Kingdom of God within his generation."[55] The future eschatological consummation, however, became a present reality in Jesus of Nazareth. Through his person, deeds, and message the Old Testament promise of the future, glorious aeon began to be fulfilled.[56] The burden of Jesus' message was to summon his contemporaries to prepare for the imminent inbreaking consummation. Kümmel denies that the kingdom of God was manifested in the community of his disciples between his death and the Parousia. "Jesus saw the Kingdom of God to be present before the Parousia, which he thought to be imminent, only in his own person and his works; he knew no other realization of the eschatological consummation."[57]

George Eldon Ladd (d. 1982) maintained that "kingdom of heaven" and "kingdom of God" are Semitic and Greek linguistic variants of the same idea. The kingdom is a complex reality with abstract and concrete poles. The abstract side denotes God's sovereign rule or reign over creation (Ps. 103:19; John 18:36; Rev. 16:10), whereas the concrete side specifies the domain over which this rule is exercised (Matt. 4:8; Rev. 16:10). Ladd observed that the kingdom is both present and future. God's rule is present, inward, and spiritual, being realized as people repent and believe the Word of God (Matt. 6:33; 12:28; Luke 17:21). God's rule is also future, outward, and apocalyptic, to be revealed in power and glory when the King returns to judge and reign (Matt. 8:11; 2 Peter 1:11).

Ladd noted that, as a dynamic concept, God's kingdom manifests itself in four stages in and beyond history. "The redemptive rule of God creates realms in which the blessings of the divine reign are enjoyed."[58]

1. The kingdom of God formerly was operative over *Israel*. In Old Testament times God's sovereign rule initially was offered to the family of Abraham and was known through the law (Matt. 21:31). In olden times God's rule was only partially and imperfectly realized; Israel perverted the truth of God and hindered access to his rule. Ladd held that God offered Israel not a political kingdom collectively but a spiritual rule individually, which kingdom offer Jews consistently refused (Luke 4:16–29). Because of this rejection God withdrew

the kingdom from Israel and gave it to a believing people (Matt. 21:43).

2. The kingdom of God presently operates over the *church,* the true Israel (Col. 1:13). Through Jesus' life and mission, God's redemptive reign has dealt Satan a preliminary but decisive defeat (Matt. 12:29; Luke 11:21–22). As individuals submit to Christ's rule they inherit the blessings of the messianic salvation—i.e., forgiveness of sins and right standing with God. The "mystery" form of the kingdom (Mark 4:11) connotes the entry of the eschatological kingdom in advance of the final consummation, not as a political but as a spiritual power. The salvation promised by the prophets (Isa. 35:5–6; 61:1) has entered the world in a totally unexpected form. What was Ladd's perception of the relation between Israel and the church? He emphasized the spiritual continuity between believing Israel and the church as successive instruments of the kingdom. He wrote, "The fellowship established by Jesus stands in direct continuity with the Old Testament Israel."[59] Here Ladd appealed to Paul's image of the olive tree in Romans 11:16–24. The tree represents the one people of God, the unbroken natural branches the believing remnant of Israel, and the ingrafted shoots of a wild olive believing Gentiles. "It is impossible to think of two peoples of God through whom God is carrying out two different redemptive purposes without doing violence to Romans 11."[60] On the other hand, he alluded to the discontinuity existing between Israel and the church institutionally. "Historically the activity of the kingdom of God effected the creation of the church and the destruction of Israel."[61]

3. A further manifestation of the kingdom will occur at the end of the age with *Christ's millennial reign* on earth (Matt. 19:27–30; Acts 1:6; Rev. 20:4–6). Then Satan will be bound, Israel will be converted, and believers will

celebrate the messianic banquet in the kingdom of God.

4. Finally, the kingdom will come with great power and glory in the *New Jerusalem* (Isa. 65:17; 66:22; Rev. 21–22). As sin and death are destroyed and Satan consigned to hell, the kingdom of God will be realized in ultimate perfection.

The Perspective of Promise-Fulfillment Theology

Theologians such as Willis J. Beecher, G. Von Rad, W. Zimmerli, and Walter C. Kaiser, Jr., envisage the relationship between Old and New Testaments as one of promise to fulfillment. The relation between Israel and the church and the place of each in the kingdom unfolds from this premise. Beecher (d. 1912), the Princeton scholar, viewed the one, eternal and irrevocable promise given to Abraham and unfolded to Moses and David as the theme of the Old Testament. "God gave a promise to Abraham, and through him to mankind; a promise eternally fulfilled and fulfilling in the history of Israel; and chiefly fulfilled in Jesus Christ, he being that which is principal in the history of Israel."[62] Beecher held the continuity (not identity) of Israel and the church within the larger people of God. Thus he wrote of "Israel the church, gathered from the nations and abiding in the Christ."[63] Beecher observed that the kingdom of God operates in the present world but has its consummation in the world to come. In the *present age* the kingdom promise is being fulfilled in a threefold way: (1) in racial Israel with its sufferings and brilliant achievements throughout history; (2) in the religion of Israel and its daughter religions, Christianity and Islam; and (3) ultimately in the person and work of Christ.[64] In the *future age* the kingdom promise will be fulfilled as the absolute rule of God in heavenly blessedness. Beecher ex-

cluded from kingdom fulfillment the rule of Christ over a restored Israel for two principal reasons: (1) he applied "directly to Jesus Christ whatever the prophets say concerning Israel the promise-people,"[65] and (2) he understood the kingdom chiefly "as a body of spiritual forces for the social and ethical elevation of men."[66]

Kaiser asserts that the biblical writers consciously wrote with "an inner plan" in mind communicated by God himself.[67] The "focal point," "material center," or "central theme" of the Old Testament canon is the concept of "promise."[68] Subsumed under the promise motif are related themes such as "oath," "blessing," "rest," "seed," and the tripartite formula: "I will be your God and you shall be my people." Kaiser sees the promise theme unfolding in eleven stages, as follows.[69] (1) "Prolegomena to the Promise: Pre-patriarchal Era." In Eden the promise is given of a victorious Seed who would crush Satan (Gen. 3:15). (2) "Provisions of the Promise: Patriarchal Era." God graciously (Gen. 12:1–3) promised Abraham and his descendants an *heir* ("seed"), an *inheritance* ("land"), and a *heritage* ("all the nations of the earth shall be blessed"). (3) "People of the Promise: Mosaic Era." God promised that the descendants of Abraham would become a people and then a separate nation (Exod. 19:6). (4) "Place of the Promise: Premonarchical Era." God promised to plant his people in the land of Canaan and give them "rest" (Josh. 21:44–45). (5) "King of the Promise: Davidic Era." God promised Israel a King from the house of David, a dynasty, and a kingdom (2 Sam. 7). (6) "Life in the Promise: Sapiential Era," where the key concept is "the fear of the Lord" (Prov. 1:7; Eccles. 12:13–14). (7) "Day of the Promise: Ninth Century," where the principal motif is "the day of the Lord" (Joel

2:28–32). (8) "Servant of the Promise: Eighth Century," where Isaiah predicted the vicarious death and future rule of the "Servant of the Lord" (Isa. 49–57). (9) "Renewal of the Promise: Seventh Century." The prominent idea here is the promise of the "new covenant" God would make with all believers, both Jew and Gentile (Jer. 31:31–34). (10) "Kingdom of the Promise: Exilic Prophets." Here God promised the restoration of Israel in the everlasting kingdom of the Son of Man (Dan. 7:13–14). And (11) "Triumph of the Promise: Postexilic Times," where the victory of God's plan achieved by Israel's conquering King is given (Zech. 14).

Kaiser observes that the single promise given to Abraham, Isaac, Jacob, and David (Acts 26:6; Rom. 4:13, 16; Gal. 3:29; Eph. 2:12; Heb. 6:13, 15, 17) had many specifications—hence the plural "promises" (Rom. 9:4; 15:8; 2 Cor. 1:20; Heb. 7:6). The specifications inherent in the one promise, fulfilled in the New Testament era, include the following: (1) the Advent and mission of the Messiah (Acts 3:25–26; 13:23, 32–33;); (2) the offer of the Gospel to Gentiles (Gal. 3:8, 14, 29; Eph. 2:12; 3:6–7); (3) the coming of the Holy Spirit in new fullness (Luke 24:49; Acts 2:33, 39; Gal. 3:14); (4) redemption from sin and its consequences (Rom. 4:2–5; James 2:21–23); (5) resurrection unto eternal life (Acts 26:6–7; 2 Tim. 1:1; Heb. 9:15); and (6) the second coming of Jesus Christ (2 Peter 3:4, 9).

The promise motif, according to Kaiser, embraces a variety of "longitudinal themes," one of the more important being "covenant." Analogous to the ancient promise and the recent fulfillment is the relationship between the old covenant and the new covenant. Between the two covenants exists *continuity*, in the sense that both affirm the same covenant-making God, the same law, the same promised fellowship, the same "seed" and "people," and the same forgiveness of sins.[70] Yet in the progress of revelation the new covenant brings several *new features,* such as universal knowledge of God, universal peace and prosperity, and a perpetual sanctuary in the midst of Israel. "Thus the New is more comprehensive, more effective, more spiritual, and more glorious than the Old."[71]

Another important longitudinal theme subsumed under the Old Testament promise-plan is "kingdom." Kaiser asserts that as "the rule, reign and realm of God over all beings, all nations, and all creation,"[72] God's kingdom is one. Yet this one kingdom contains two significant aspects: (1) The kingdom is *present* and *spiritual* (a soteriological category), being the reign of God in the hearts of believers in both Testaments. Kaiser here observes that there is but one people of God. Yet under the new covenant Gentile believers are being grafted into the Jewish olive tree (Rom. 11:17–25; cf. Eph. 3:6). "The NT writers add to the emerging thesis of the OT that there was just one people of God and one program of God even though there are several aspects to that single people and single program."[73] (2) The kingdom is *future* and *national* (an eschatological concept). The kingdom will be consummated when God's promised "Anointed One" rules over a restored Israel in an age of peace, prosperity, and universal worship. By the above line of reasoning Kaiser steers a course between dispensationalism and covenant theology and explains the meaning of the kingdom in ways similar to those of George Ladd.

The Perspective of Liberal Theology

Modern liberal theologians ascribe great importance to the kingdom concept in the teaching of Jesus, while indifferent to the relation of Israel and the church. Influenced by the Enlightenment, with its high view of human nature and its vision of evolutionary social progress, the tradition stresses the present, ethical dimension of the kingdom. It radically depreciates the future, eschatological dimension of the kingdom as the product of first-century, Jewish apocalyptic fervor. The kingdom of God thus represents a new and Christianized social order on earth achieved by human effort and guided by the ethical teachings of Jesus.

A. Ritschl (d. 1889), the father of modern liberal theology, identified the kingdom of God as the human community striving for the common good via benevolent social action. The kingdom represents "the moral unification of the human race, through action prompted by universal love to our neighbor."[74] Ritschl held that the kingdom must not be equated with the church. The former is an ethical community committed to social action, whereas the latter is a worshiping community organized on a legal basis. Although Jesus was the founder and inspiring force of the kingdom, "the moral perfection of man in the kingdom of God" will be achieved by human action impelled by love.[75] Since the human spirit is destined for God, the entire world is progressing via moral education toward the kingdom. Ritschl's development of the kingdom theme provided a powerful impetus to the twentieth-century social gospel in America.

Walter Rauschenbusch (d. 1918) claimed that the kingdom of God is the quintessential doctrine of Christianity. For him the kingdom is human society Christianized by education and social legislation. The futuristic interpretation of the kingdom, which he claimed obscures the ethical sense, originated from the crude apocalypticism of late Judaism and early Christianity. "The kingdom is not a matter of saving human atoms, but of saving the social organism. It is not a matter of getting individuals to heaven, but of transforming the life on earth into the harmony of heaven."[76] Rauschenbusch explained the nature of the kingdom as follows. (1) The *domain* of the kingdom is not heaven (the other-worldly Greek outlook) but the earthly social situation (the this-worldly Hebrew outlook). "The faith of the Kingdom of God . . . is a religion for this earth and for the present life."[77] (2) The *enlargement* of the kingdom occurs via the forces of evolutionary development. "Translate the evolutionary theories into religious faith and you have the doctrine of the kingdom of God."[78] (3) The *task* of the kingdom is not saving souls or establishing churches but Christianizing social customs and institutions. (4) *Membership* in the kingdom is not restricted to a select minority but embraces the whole of humanity. And (5) the *goal* of the kingdom is the unity of all mankind. Rauschenbusch claimed that often in history the church has been an impediment to the kingdom, in that it diverted energy and resources from this-worldly problems to other-worldly interests.

Liberation theology represents a politically radicalized form of the social gospel. Believing that concern for a future kingdom of God in heaven seriously blunts commitment to social problems, liberationists view the kingdom as a present historical reality. Jesus' message of the kingdom centered on liberation from political, economic, and social oppression. The movement claims that the kingdom of God arrives when the poor and oppressed become liberated human beings. Since God has a special regard for the disenfranchised, *they* are the unique citizens of the kingdom. Transformation of the world into the kingdom is achieved by struggle against all forms of tyranny, by the social emancipation of the oppressed, and by opposition to the capitalist system. Some liberationists condone violence as a necessary means of introducing the kingdom.

Gustavo Gutièrrez warns against adopting a spiritualized view of the kingdom of God. Rather, the kingdom is primarily an interhistorical, social phenomenon: "The coming of the Kingdom and the expectation of the Parousia are necessarily and inevitably historical, temporal, earthly, and material realities."[79] Gutièrrez envisages the kingdom as "a new, just and fraternal society,"[80] indeed, as an earthly utopia. The sign of the inbreaking of the kingdom of God is the elimination of human misery and exploitation. The forging of history toward the kingdom will be achieved chiefly by human efforts. Radical disciples of Jesus will introduce the kingdom via struggles against all forms of oppression, by transformation of unjust social structures, and by the punishment of oppressors of the poor.

Dissolving eschatology into history, black theologian James Cone regards the kingdom of God as this-worldly. Cone concurs with Marx that interest in the afterlife diverts attention from the present sufferings of the exploited. "Black Theology is an earthly theology! It is not concerned with the 'last things' but with the 'white thing.' "[81] Cone interprets the kingdom theme vis-à-vis the American situation, as follows: White American society constitutes the oppressive, racist antichrist. But the black Christ conquers the white oppressor and liberates the black community so that the latter may realize its unique black dignity, black unity, and sense of black nationhood. Thus in the process of salvation history, "the kingdom of God is a *black* happening."[82] Cone condones the use of human violence, as a necessary evil, in the realization of these kingdom goals.

See also helpful studies on the subject by G. R. Beasley-Murray[83] and John Feinberg.[84]

BIBLICAL TEACHING

To understand the relationship between Israel and the church in Christ's redemptive kingdom we test the secondary historical sources by the teachings of the primary biblical doctrine. Essential to this goal will be to examine the scriptural development of the themes of kingdom, covenant, promise, and dispensation.

The Pentateuch

From its opening chapter the Bible depicts God as the sovereign, all-powerful Creator who rules over the entire cosmos. Although the phrase "kingdom of God" is not found in the Old Testament, the language of divine dominion is abundantly evident. Several Hebrew words set forth God's kingdom rule. The verb *mālak* means to "reign" (Exod. 15:18; Pss. 47:8; 97:1; Isa. 24:23; Micah 4:7). Given the existence of the *molek* cult early in Israel's history (Lev. 18:21), the noun *melek*, "king," did not emerge as a title for Yahweh until later in the Old Testament (Ps. 47:2; Isa. 6:5; Jer. 46:18; cf. Num. 23:21). The noun *malkût* connotes God's "kingdom," "dominion," "reign," (Pss. 45:6; 103:19; 145:11–13), *melûkāh* his "kingship" or "royalty" (Ps. 22:28; Obad. 21), and *mamlākāh* his "sovereignty" or "kingdom" (1 Chron. 29:11 and often with respect to earthly kingdoms). God is sovereign over the entire earth (Ps. 29:10), the nations thereof (2 Kings 19:15; Pss. 47:8; 99:1–2), and the chosen people Israel (Exod. 15:18; Num. 23:21; Deut. 33:5; Isa. 43:15; 44:6). The Old Testament also affirms that in the future God's authority will be openly manifest in a dominion unrivaled and universal (Isa. 24:23; 52:7; Zech. 14:9).

The loving and gracious ruler of the earth entered into covenant relations with his creatures. The noun *berît*, "covenant" (almost three hundred times in the Old Testament) is "a compact or agreement between two parties binding them mutually to undertakings on each other's behalf." The expression "make a covenant" (Gen. 15:18; Exod. 24:8) literally means "cut a covenant," from the practice of cutting the covenant sacrifice in halves and the parties walking between the pieces (Gen. 15:10, 17; Jer. 34:18). God, being superior to humans, initiated the covenants and stipulated their terms. If a biblical covenant between God and humans were a relation between equals, the LXX would have translated *berît* by *synthēkē* rather than *diathēkē*. The major covenants in Scripture are the Abrahamic, the Mosaic, the Davidic, and the new covenant.

Covenant theologians see in Genesis 2:16–17 the so-called covenant of works. God's interchange with Adam in the garden centered on the command. "You are free to eat from any tree in the garden; but you must not eat from the tree of the knowledge of good and evil, for when you eat of it you will surely die." The word "covenant" does not appear in the text until Genesis 6:18. Moreover, the typical covenant structure is not clearly delineated, particularly the promise of life on condition of obedience. Thus it may be preferable to interpret this as a probationary injunction or trial command rather than a formal covenant. But does not Hosea 6:7 confirm the existence of a covenant of works with Adam? "Like Adam [*ke'ādām*], they have broken the covenant." Two interpretations of this text are possible: (1) "Like men they [Israel] transgressed covenant" (cf. Hosea 8:1). And (2) "At Adam they transgressed covenant." The following words, "they were unfaithful to me there" (v. 7b) suggest that Adam may be a place. This interpretation is favored by Moffatt, RSV, other modern versions, and the NIV margin. Hindley favors a double sense: "Hosea picks

the place-name, Adam, out of the Joshua narrative to show that at the very time of covenant renewal (Josh. 3:16; 5:1–12) the sin of Achan revealed the unchanged heart of Israel. At the same time he subtly pointed back to Adam, the father of all self-seeking sin."[86] The hypothesis that Genesis 2:16–17 is a formal covenant of works thus falls short of proof.

How valid is the claim that Genesis 3:15 inaugurates the so-called covenant of grace? God's words to the serpent announce (1) the perpetual conflict between the powers of darkness and the children of light; (2) the suffering of Christ, the principal seed (*zera'*) of Eve; and (3) the promise of Christ's ultimate defeat of Satan and the powers of evil. The text does not explicitly mention a covenant. Moreover, as above, no identifiable covenant structure exists: i.e., no explicit promise of eternal life, no condition of faith, and no explicit penalty of death for unbelief. The hypothesis that Genesis 3:15 represents the initial declaration of the covenant of grace likewise appears improbable. Rather, the verse is a prophetic promise of the sufferings of Christ and the defeat of Satan.

The first formal statement of a covenant occurs at God's call and blessing of Abraham (Gen. 12:1–3; 15:7–21; 17:1–21). The sovereign Lord, in an act of gracious election, pledged himself to Abraham and his descendants to be their God (Gen. 17:7; cf. Exod. 6:7; 19:5–6; Deut. 29:13). Covenant theologians commonly posit the Abrahamic covenant as the beginning of the church as a formal organization.[87] The *parties* to this covenant are God and Abraham (Gen. 12:1; 15:18) and his descendants (Gen. 17:19; Exod. 2:24). The *promise* God gave to Abraham was severalfold.[88] The Lord pledged to Abraham (1) a *seed* or offspring (collective noun, *zera'*, Gen. 12:2a; 13:16; 15:5; 17:2, 6; 22:17; 26:4), (2) a great *name* or reputation (Gen. 12:2c), (3) a *land* that is both a present, material home (Gen. 12:1, 7; 15:18; 17:8; 26:3; Deut. 1:8; 6:10) and a future, heavenly habitation (cf. Heb. 11:9–10, 13–14, 16), and (4) *spiritual blessings*—to Abraham and his descendants (Gen. 12:2; 22:17; 26:3) and through them to all people on earth, both Jews and Gentiles (Gen. 12:2d, 3b; 22:18; 26:4; 28:14). The latter promise of blessing is to be fulfilled in Christ, the principal male "seed" (Gal. 3:16, 19). The essence of the covenant was God's promise to be the God of Abraham and his offspring (Gen. 17:7–8). The covenant *obligation* God placed upon Abraham and his seed was faith (Gen. 15:6; 22:16–18; cf. Heb. 11:8a, 17a) evidenced by obedience (Gen. 12:4; 26:5; cf. Heb. 11:8b, 17b). The *penalty* for breaking the covenant (Gen. 17:14; Isa. 24:5) was personal forfeiture of the promised blessings. On God's side the covenant was unconditional (Heb. 6:13–18). God's promises will come to pass; no human power can frustrate his plan (Gen. 17:7; 28:15; Exod. 2:24; Lev. 26:42, 44–45; Ps. 105:8–11). But on the human side the covenant was conditional. The promised benefits would accrue to those who respond positively (Exod. 15:26; 19:5). When Abraham embraced the covenant promises with faith and obedience (Gen. 12:4; 15:6), spiritual Israel began to exist. The existence of a spiritual remnant within the broader nation is seen in the fact that only Joshua, Caleb, and young children were permitted to enter the promised land (Num. 14:21–30; Deut. 1:35–36; Ps. 95:8–11).

The covenant promises given to Abraham were repeated to Isaac (Gen. 26:2–5) and later to Jacob (Gen. 28:13–15). At Bethel (Gen. 35:9–10; cf. 32:28) God changed the name of Jacob ("deceiver") to Israel ("one who wrestles with God"). The descendants of Jacob were known as "the Israelites" (Exod. 1:7; 6:5; Lev. 1:2; Judg. 2:4), "the people of Israel" (Exod. 16:31; 1 Sam. 7:2), and "the sons of Israel" (Gen. 45:21; 50:25; Exod. 1:1). Out of fidelity to his covenant with Abraham God delivered the fledgling people from four centuries of Egyptian bondage (Exod. 2:24–25; 6:4–6). Following the Exodus God constituted the descendants of Jacob a socially structured nation at Sinai (Exod. 19:3–6). "The house of Israel" (Exod. 40:38), now a "nation" (*gôy*, Exod. 32:10; 33:13; Num. 14:12; Deut. 4:7–8) possessed a specific national identity, ethnic character, defined territory, governmental structure, and institutional leadership.

God's promise to Moses (Exod. 19:3–8), sealed by sacrificial animals (Exod. 20:24; Heb. 9:18, 22), inaugurated the "first covenant" (Heb. 9:15) or the "old covenant" (2 Cor. 3:14) with Israel spiritually and institutionally. Covenant theologians envisage the Mosaic covenant, like the Abrahamic covenant, as a further stage in the development of the covenant of grace. The *parties* to the Mosaic covenant were God and "the people of Israel" (Exod. 19:3). The *promise* of the covenant was twofold: the worshiping people of God would become a political entity or nation ("a kingdom of priests and a holy nation," v. 6). Moreover, they would be a very special nation among the nations of earth (God's "treasured possession," v. 5). The *obligation* laid upon Israel was obedience (Exod. 19:5, 8; 24:7; Deut. 4:23) to God's law—both to the Decalogue (Exod. 20:3–17) and to its elaboration in the "Book of the Covenant" (Exod. 20:22–23:33; see 24:7). Obedience to the covenant would result in blessing (Exod. 19:5; Lev. 26:3–12; Deut. 29:9), whereas the penalty for disobedience would be manifold curses (Lev. 26:14–39; Deut. 28:15–68; 29:18–28). Unlike the Abrahamic covenant, the Mosaic covenant was a temporary arrangement (cf. Gal. 3:19, 24–25). Israel could and did violate the covenant. Her history was characterized by covenant disobedience (Judges 2:20; Ps. 78:37; Jer. 11:10; Hos. 8:1), hence the need for a new and effectual covenant (Jer. 31:31–33).

Historical Books

God's covenant with David represents an enlargement of the covenant with Abraham. The word *berît* does not occur in the texts that record the covenant with David (2 Sam. 7:12–16; 1 Chron. 17:11–14), but the connection is made elsewhere (2 Sam. 23:5; Pss. 89:3, 28; 132:12; Jer. 33:21). With a play on words, Yahweh forbade David to build a house (temple) because he was a man of war (1 Chron. 22:8). Rather, the Lord would build David a house or a dynasty that would endure forever. The *parties* of the Davidic covenant are God and David (2 Sam. 7:5–9). The *promises* to David are threefold: (1) an eternal seed (*zera'*: vv. 12a, 14; Ps. 89:4a, 29a, 36a), (2) an eternal throne (*kissē'*: vv. 13, 16b; Ps. 89:4b, 29b, 36b, 37), and (3) an eternal kingdom (*mamlākāh*: vv. 13b, 16a). Similar to the promise given to Abraham, God pledged to be a God to his people (vv. 23–24). God's promise in verse 14 to be a "father" to David (the "son") speaks the language of kingdom rule (cf. Ps. 2:7–9; 89:26–29; Jer. 3:19). In the ancient Near East the relation between a superior king and a subject king was one of "lord" to "servant" and "father" to "son." The burden of the arrangement is that the covenant obligations rest on Yahweh alone; no conditions are imposed on David. Thus the Davidic covenant is unconditional in the sense that the divine promise, rooted in covenant love (*ḥesed*, v. 15), assures the perpetuity of the Davidic dynasty (2 Sam. 23:5; 1 Kings 8:25; Ps. 89:28, 34–37; Jer. 33:17, 20–21). The line of Davidic kings literally fulfilled this promise for four hundred years (*'ad-'ôlām* in the sense

of "for a long time"). But the ultimate fulfillment of the promise is future, namely, in the eternal (*'ad-'ôlām*) reign of Jesus Christ, who was born of the house of David (Isa. 9:6–7; Jer. 23:5–6; Luke 1:32–33, 69; Acts 2:29–31; Rev. 22:16). Of course, faithfulness and obedience were required for a particular Davidic king to remain on the throne (1 Kings 2:4; Pss. 89:30–32; 132:11–12). In summary, "even if David's son or any of his future successors were to fail in his obedience, God would punish him severely, but he would not be cut off from the succession as Saul had been."[89]

In fulfillment of his promise to David, God placed Solomon on the throne to rule over Israel in his (God's) stead (2 Chron. 9:8). But the throne of the Davidic king was God's throne (1 Chron. 28:5; 29:23). This is made clear by the saying of Abijah: "The kingdom of the Lord . . . is in the hands of David's descendants" (2 Chron. 13:8). Thus in a peculiar sense Israel in the Old Testament is the socialized institution over which Yahweh exercised his sovereign rule.

The Poetic Literature

The Psalter celebrates God's eternal kingship over the heavens and the earth in the so-called enthronement psalms (Pss. 47, 93, 95–99). The literature attests both the abstract sense of God's kingdom as rule or reign and the concrete sense of domain: "The LORD has established his throne in heaven, and his kingdom rules over all" (Ps. 103:19; cf. 145:11–13). God exercises his rule over the entire earth (Pss. 24:1–2; 47:2, 7–8; 96:10) by right of creation and over Israel (Pss. 24:7–10; 59:13) by right of sovereign election. The phrase "great King" (Pss. 47:2; 95:3) suggests a covenant treaty context, indicating that the *berît* with Israel is a particular outcome of Yahweh's kingly rule.

Covenant theologians support the covenant of redemption idea by appealing to several poetic texts. The first, Psalm 2:7–9, depicts David's enthronement and adoption as God's son (cf. 2 Sam. 7:14). The ultimate fulfillment of the text is Jesus Christ, who was acclaimed "Son" by virtue of his incarnation (Heb. 1:5), entry into high priesthood (5:5), and resurrection (Acts 13:33). The historical context of the second text, Psalm 40:7–9, likely was David's commitment to Yahweh's will on the occasion of his enthronement. The text finds future fulfillment in Christ's obedience to the Father by leaving heaven's glory (cf. Phil. 2:5–8) and by doing his will on earth (cf. John 4:34). God's words in the third text, Psalm 89:3—"I have made a covenant with my chosen one"—clearly refer to David not Christ (cf. vv. 4, 34–37). Verses 38–39 indicate that God has renounced this covenant, which would be a wholly inappropriate act if Christ were the promisee. The phrase "covenant of redemption" does not appear in any of these texts.

Prophetic Writings

The prophets acknowledged that by virtue of creation Yahweh is king over the nations (Jer. 10:7, 10; Dan. 4:37), and by reason of both creation and redemption is sovereign over Israel (Isa. 43:15; 44:6; Zeph. 3:15). King Darius confessed the dynamic character of God's eternal and invincible kingdom with these words: "He rescues and saves; he performs signs and wonders in the heavens and on the earth. He has rescued Daniel from the power of the lions" (Dan. 6:27). Yet the prophets anticipated a future time when God will rule gloriously over the earth openly and without rivals (Isa. 24:23; Obad. 21; Zech. 14:9).

Cocceius (d. 1669) and other covenant theologians saw in Zechariah 6:12–13 the covenant of redemption: "The Branch . . . will be a priest on his throne. And there will be harmony between the two." This text rather asserts that the messianic Branch (the royal shoot of David) will build the temple and will harmoniously unite the offices of king and priest. The prophet disclosed that the future Davidic king will also be a priest (cf. Ps. 110:4). The prophets acknowledged that the divine King enters into covenant relations with his people, and that the Sinaitic covenant (Exod. 6:7; Lev. 26:12) is summed up in the promise "I will be your God and you will be my people" (Jer. 7:23; cf. 11:4; 30:22; 32:38). The people of Israel thought themselves secure under the blood of the covenant. They believed they had satisfied the covenant obligations by observing feasts and sacrifices. But they erred by externalizing the covenant. Wherefore Yahweh said, "I desire mercy, not sacrifice, and acknowledgment of God rather than burnt offerings" (Hos. 6:6; cf. Isa. 1:11–14). Because Israel violated the sacred covenant (Isa. 24:5; Jer. 11:10), it became for them a covenant of death (Isa. 28:15, 18)—i.e., "a covenant that carried death in it."[90]

The zenith of Jeremiah's prophecy was Yahweh's announcement of "a new covenant" he would make with Israel and Judah (Jer. 31:31–34; cf. Isa. 59:21; Ezek. 11:19–20; 36:25–28; Hos. 2:18–20), otherwise denoted an "everlasting covenant" (Isa. 55:3; Jer. 32:40; Ezek. 37:26) and a "covenant of peace" (Isa. 54:10; Ezek. 34:25; 37:26). Thus the "everlasting covenant" and the "covenant of peace" likely are not to be identified with the covenant of redemption between the Father and the Son. The phrase "the time is coming" (Jer. 31:31), points to the messianic future as the time of the new covenant's implementation.

Earlier we concluded the following concerning the old or Sinaitic covenant:

Made with the "house of Israel" and the "house of Judah" (1) it was a *national* covenant. (2) It was an *external* covenant inscribed on stone. (3) From the human side it was a *conditional* or violable covenant, for Israel repeatedly broke the Mosaic arrangement (cf. Jer. 31:32) prompting its replacement. (4) The old covenant required a *human mediator* (Exod. 20:19). And (5) the Mosaic covenant of law *failed to impart life* (cf. Gal. 3:21). "The old covenant did not, could not, and was never intended to save anyone."[91]

The spiritual benefits afforded by the *new covenant* (Heb. 8:6–13; 10:16–17) far exceed those of the old. These include (1) the law inscribed on the mind and heart (Jer. 31:33; Ezek. 36:25–26), (2) intimate knowledge of and communion with the Lord (Jer. 31:34a), and (3) a new ability to live according to God's law (Jer. 31:34a). The prophets foretold the inclusion of Gentiles under the new covenant (Isa. 11:10; 42:1, 6; 49:6; 55:4–5; Amos 9:1–11) in fulfillment of the promise to Abraham (e.g., Gen. 12:3; 18:18). The preceding highlight the *dissimilarities* institutionally and spiritually between the two arrangements. Yet significant *similarities* also exist between them, chiefly, the reality of salvation by grace (Jer. 31:34b). Moreover, the new covenant fills out the old covenant in the sense that it brings to fruition promises made in the covenant at Sinai, not the least of which is the promise ("I will be their God, and they will be my people": Jer. 31:33; cf. Exod. 6:7; Lev. 26:12). Truly "covenant" (*berît*) is a fundamental concept in the life and history of Israel.

Yahweh's words to the Servant "I . . . will make you to be a covenant for the people and a light for the Gentiles" (Isa. 42:6) suggest that the Spirit–filled Servant would impart the blessings of the new covenant to all people. In fulfillment of the promise to Abraham the new covenant spiritually will convey "showers of blessing" to many (Ezek. 34:26). That the blessings of the new covenant would extend to Gentiles is made explicit in Isaiah 55:3–5. Yahweh's promise to inaugurate an everlasting "covenant of peace" (*berît šālôm*, Ezek. 34:25; 37:26) under the Davidic "king," "prince," "servant," and "shepherd" ultimately refers to the new covenant. The new arrangement will prove effectual in that the old promise will be fully realized: "I will be their God, and they will be my people" (37:27).

The idea of a faithful "remnant" in Israel is a common theme in the prophets (Isa. 10:20–22; 37:31–32; Jer. 31:7; Joel 2:32; Micah 2:12; Zeph. 3:12–13; Zech. 8:11–12). In the midst of Israel's apostasy a minority of Jews remained loyal to the covenant (cf. 1 Kings 19:18). The Jewish remnant represents the called of the Lord (Joel 2:32). They trust in the Lord (Zeph. 3:12), they are "forgiven" (Jer. 50:20; Micah 7:18), they are "holy" (Isa. 4:3; 45:25), and they receive the promised inheritance (Zech. 8:12). From this remnant the promised seed of David would come. The prophets envisaged (in fulfillment of the promise to Abraham) that under the new covenant in the messianic age many believing Gentiles would be added to the remnant of Israel to constitute the new people of God (Isa. 19:19–25; 25:6–7; 49:6; Zech. 2:11). The incorporation of Gentiles within the new covenant community known as the church (cf. Acts 2:39; Eph. 2:11–13) would occur in the messianic age ("afterward") through a mighty outpouring of the Holy Spirit (Joel 2:28–29). The preceding promises affirm the spiritual unity of the people of God in the two dispensations.

In fulfillment of the promise made to David (2 Sam. 7:12–13, 16), the prophets foresaw a future, earthly kingdom under the just rule of the Messiah (Isa. 9:6–7; 16:5; 33:17; Jer. 23:5–6; Amos 9:11–12). Following the subjugation of all earthly powers (Pss. 2:9; 72:9–11; 110:5–6) and as the ultimate fulfillment of the Abrahamic promise of world blessing (Gen. 12:3), the Messiah will inaugurate an era of universal worship where the weapons of mass destruction will be abolished and peace will prevail (Isa. 2:2–4; 11:6–9; Micah 4:1–3; Zech. 9:10). In that future era the Messiah's rule will be unrivaled and complete (Pss. 2:8–9; 22:27–28; Isa. 52:10). Daniel's apocalyptic vision of the "son of man," who was given power and authority by the "Ancient of Days," attests in different imagery the kingly rule of the Messiah at the Second Advent, through the earthly Millennium, and into the eternal state (Dan. 7:13–14).

The Synoptic Gospels

The kingdom of God was a dominant theme in Jesus' teaching. The nouns *basileia* ("kingly rule," "kingdom") and *basileus* ("ruler," "king") and the verb *basileuō* (to "be king," to "rule") occur 18 times in Paul but 180 times in the Synoptic Gospels. The phrase "kingdom of heaven" occurs only in Matthew ("kingdom of God" occurs in Matthew four times). The phrases "kingdom of God" and "kingdom of heaven" are linguistic variants of the same idea (cf. Matt. 4:17 with Mark 1:15; Matt. 13:11 with Mark 4:11 and Luke 8:10; Matt. 19:14 with Mark 10:14 and Luke 18:16). Matthew undoubtedly employed "kingdom of heaven" as a circumlocution for the divine name out of respect for his Jewish audience. The evidence suggests that for the Gospel writers the word "kingdom" refers to the dynamic reign of God over a particular domain, i.e., Israel or individual hearts.

With his summons, "Repent, for the kingdom of heaven is near" (Matt. 3:2), the Baptist affirmed that God's eternal rule anticipated in the Old Testament was about to break into history in a new way. The perfect active of the verb *engizō* indicates that the kingdom has drawn near but has not yet arrived (Matt. 21:34; 26:45). Jesus preached the same message of the kingdom as did John (Matt. 4:17; Mark 1:15; cf. Luke 10:9, 11). Yet the Lord undoubtedly knew that the irruption of God's rule in time would occur uniquely through his own person and ministry. The center of Jesus' ministry was the proclamation of "the good news of the kingdom"—which is the redemptive rule of God realized by repentance and faith (Matt. 4:23; 9:35; cf. Luke 4:43; 8:1; 9:11). The Lord commanded the Twelve (Matt. 10:7; Luke 9:2) and the seventy-two (Luke 10:9) to proclaim the same message of the kingdom.

Jesus taught that the kingdom is a present realm of blessing into which the humble believer may enter (Matt. 21:31; cf. 23:13; Luke 11:52). When he affirmed, "Do not be afraid, little flock, for your Father has been pleased to give you the kingdom" (Luke 12:32), he meant that believers in the present enjoy kingdom blessings and that at the end of the age they will receive the kingdom in fullness. The works of healing and exorcism Jesus and his disciples did (Matt. 11:5; 15:30–31; cf. Isa. 35:5–6; 61:1) were signs that the messianic age had dawned (Matt. 12:28; Luke 11:20) and that the disarming of Satan had occurred (Matt. 12:27, 29; Luke 10:18). Although defeated in principle, Satan and his cohorts assail the kingdom powerfully. Hence Jesus said, "From the days of John the Baptist until now the kingdom of heaven has suffered violence, and men of violence take it by force" (Matt. 11:12 RSV). The thrust of Matthew 11:12–13 is that the Old Testament spoke about the coming kingdom, but with the appearance of

John the kingdom had arrived in a new way. With Gundry, Mounce, Hill, and the RSV, we interpret the verb *biazetai* not as a middle voice but as passive, meaning "to be violently treated." Accordingly, "ever since the days of John the Baptist the kingdom of heaven has been under assault by violent men who are trying to overcome it by force."[92]

According to dispensationalists, the kingdom Jesus offered to Israel and which was later rejected was the Jewish theocratic kingdom. The biblical data appears not to support this view. Jesus' Jewish contemporaries expected a victorious political Messiah who would conquer their foes and establish a material kingdom (Luke 19:11). This is further supported by the response of the populace at Jesus' Palm Sunday entry into Jerusalem (Mark 11:9–10). Confirming that his mission was spiritual, Jesus immediately went not to the seat of civil power in Jerusalem, but to the temple (v. 11). Even Jesus' disciples shared the popular expectation that he was a political Messiah who would defeat Israel's foes and establish an earthly kingdom. Hence they argued among themselves who would be greatest in Messiah's reign (Luke 9:46; 22:24). James and John petitioned the Lord to give them places of prominence in his earthly kingdom (Matt. 20:21–26; Mark 10:35–40), but Jesus took pains to correct their misunderstanding. When it became clear that Jesus must suffer and die and that his followers likewise must suffer, many forsook the Lord altogether (Mark 14:50).

When quizzed by the Pharisees when the kingdom would come, Jesus explained its true character: "The kingdom of God does not come visibly, nor will people say, 'Here it is,' or 'There it is,' because the kingdom of God is within you" (Luke 17:20–21). The phrase *entos hymōn* admits of two possible interpretations: (1) "in the midst of you" and (2) "within you" (cf.

Matt. 23:26). The first interpretation, favored by Marshall, D. Moody, and the NEB is preferred. Jesus made the point that the kingdom had drawn near in his own person; hence its saving benefits were available to all. Either interpretation, however, confirms that the kingdom Jesus offered was the spiritual rule of God that persons enter in the present by faith. The "mystery of the kingdom" (*mystērion tēs basileias*, Matt. 13:11; cf. Mark 4:11; Luke 8:10) should be understood as follows: The Old Testament anticipated a single appearance of the kingdom at the end of the age when the glory of God would fill the earth. The mystery is that this rule of God had entered history furtively through Jesus' person and ministry in advance of the end. "It is the secret that in Jesus the Kingdom of God has begun to penetrate the experience of men."[93] Jesus' parables in Matthew 13 and Mark 4 describe the nature and working of the kingdom in its advance enactment and the demands the kingdom imposes on all persons (note Mark 4:26; cf. v. 30: "This is what the kingdom is like").

In addition to the kingdom as a present, internal reality brought near in Jesus' person, the Gospels testify to the future, external manifestation of the kingdom. This glorious and eternal kingdom of the Father or the Son (Matt. 6:10; 8:11; 26:29; Luke 14:15; 22:29–30) is equivalent to "eternal life" in the age to come (Mark 10:17, 23, 30). It will be introduced at our Lord's future Parousia (Matt. 25:6, 31; Luke 21:31). Jesus' reference to the coming of the kingdom with power (Mark 9:1; cf. Matt. 16:28; Luke 9:27) likely refers to the Transfiguration, which was a dramatic preview of Messiah's future coming with kingdom glory (2 Peter 1:16–17).

The Greek word for covenant (*diathēkē*) occurs thirty-three times in the New Testament, almost half in quotations from the Old Testament. As opposed to the word *synthēkē* (an agreement among equals), *diathēkē* signifies a unilateral arrangement, involving promises, initiated by the sovereign God which humans cannot annul. As for the covenants inaugurated under the Jewish economy, the words of the angel Gabriel to Mary indicate that the Davidic covenant was still in force. The promise to David that Messiah "will reign over the house of Jacob forever" had not been wholly realized (Luke 1:32–33; cf. 2 Sam. 7:12–13, 16; Ps. 132:11; Isa. 9:6–7; 16:5). Similarly, Christ's first coming, with the resultant national security (Luke 1:71, 74a) and spiritual salvation (vv. 68b, 69a, 77–79), represents a fulfillment of the promise made to Abraham (v. 73). Moreover, during Jesus' lifetime the Mosaic covenant remained in force. Jesus was circumcised on the eighth day, Mary herself was purified, and the parents dedicated the infant to the Lord as required by the law (Luke 2:21–24).

The Last Supper prefigured Jesus' impending death and the inauguration of the new covenant (Matt. 26:26–29; Mark 14:22–25; Luke 22:17–20). Jesus' words of consecration contain allusions to two important Old Testament texts. The first, "the blood of the covenant, which is poured out" recollects the sprinkling of blood that ratified the Sinaitic covenant (Exod. 24:5–8). The second, "the new covenant" and "the forgiveness of sins," recalls Jeremiah's prophecy (Jer. 31:31–33). Jesus' words over the elements indicated that his death and resurrection would inaugurate the "new covenant" with the "many." This new covenant fulfills the old covenants and launches a dramatically new phase of redemptive history. The Lord's Supper at once looks back to Israel's deliverance from Egypt and forward to the messianic banquet in heaven (Matt. 26:29). The Eucharist, not baptism, represents the sign of the new covenant (1 Cor. 11:25).

Primitive Christianity/Acts

Stephen's rehearsal of the history of God's dealings with Israel confirms that the promise was an integral part of the Abrahamic covenant (Acts 7:5–8; cf. 7:17). The book of Acts envisages the ancient promise fulfilled in several ways: (1) Israel's possession of Palestine (7:4; cf. Gen. 17:8; 26:3), (2) the coming of the Messiah who would bless the nations (3:25–26; 13:23; cf. Gen. 12:3; et al.), (3) his resurrection from the dead (13:32–37; 26:6–8; cf. Ps. 16:10), (4) the forgiveness of sins (13:38–39; cf. Jer. 31:34), (5) the gift of the Holy Spirit (1:4; 2:33, 38–39; Luke 24:49; cf. Ezek. 36:26–27; Joel 2:28–29; Zech. 12:10), and (6) Messiah's eternal dominion (13:22–23; cf. 2 Sam. 7:12–16; Ps. 89:29, 36–37).

Luke wrote that following his resurrection Jesus "appeared to them [the apostles] over a period of forty days and spoke about the kingdom of God" (Acts 1:3). In obedience to the Lord the apostles preached the identical message of the kingdom (19:8; 20:25), the heart of which was the person and redemptive work of Jesus Christ (8:12; 28:23, 31). For the apostles the kingdom—in the sense of the dynamic, saving action of God through the risen Christ and the Spirit—was already present. The content of the "good news of the kingdom of God" (Acts 8:12) was not the immediate restoration of the theocratic kingdom to Israel; rather, central to Jesus' thought was the spiritual kingdom regnant in those who believe (Acts 1:6–7). Marshall correctly comments that early in the church's existence "the disciples . . . had not yet realized that Jesus had transformed the Jewish hope of the kingdom of God by purging it of its nationalistic elements."[94]

Acts suggests that Israel and the church are *different* ethnically and institutionally. It might be expected that the early Christian community which

329

emerged out of Judaism would have adopted the word *synagōgē* ("assembly," "synagogue"). Yet the absence of *synagōgē* in Acts and the rest of the New Testament (except James 2:2, "meeting") suggests that the early church distanced itself from institutional Israel. Indeed, Acts consistently preserves the distinction between the nation Israel and the multiethnic community known as the church. Thus at the Jerusalem council James declared that God had taken "from the Gentiles [*ethnē*] a people [*laos*] for himself" (15:14). With the dawning of the messianic era the church is a community of believing Jews and Gentiles, where race or national identity is spiritually irrelevant. Moreover, although Israel was the people of God (Exod. 19:5; Deut. 7:6), the nation was unsaved (Acts 5:31; 9:15) and was a chief enemy of the Messiah (4:10, 27).

Acts also highlights *differences* between Israel and the church spiritually. Luke viewed the Holy Spirit as a special gift of the ascended Christ to the apostles (Acts 2:33). According to Acts 2:17, 18, 33 and 10:45, the Holy Spirit was "poured out" (*ekcheō*) upon those who believed. *Ekcheō* is the same verb used by Jesus with regard to the cup during the Lord's Supper (Matt. 26:28; Mark 14:24; Luke 22:20, which inaugurated the new covenant relationship with God. The Spirit poured out upon the fledgling church in fullness equipped them with supernatural power for service (Acts 1:8; 4:8, 31, 33), which included miraculous signs and wonders (2:43). As the prophecies and promises of the Old Testament came to fulfillment, life under the new covenant became life in the Spirit.

Pauline Literature

Paul wrote concerning spiritual Israel or the believing remnant of Abraham: "Theirs is the adoption as sons; theirs the divine glory, the covenants, the receiving of the law, the temple worship and the promises" (Rom. 9:4). The covenants undoubtedly were the Abrahamic, Mosaic, and Davidic agreements. The promises were primarily those made to Abraham, David, and Jeremiah (concerning the new covenant) and secondarily the many other messianic promises in the Old Testament. Paul argued in Romans 11:1–10 that by virtue of Israel's rejection of the Gospel, the covenant promises were being realized in the believing Jewish remnant ("the elect," v. 7). Moreover, the inviolability of the covenant promises ensures a future conversion of many Jews at the end of the age (vv. 25–27, 31–32). Israel's unfaithfulness cannot annul God's covenants (cf. Ps. 94:14). Thus Paul wrote, "God's gifts and his call are irrevocable" (Rom. 11:29; cf. Gal. 3:15–18).

For the apostle the essence of the covenants made with the fathers is *promise*. Covenant and promise in Paul are virtually interchangeable concepts (Rom. 4:13–16; Gal. 3:17), thus his reference to "the covenants of the promise" (Eph. 2:12). The covenant relationship, in fact, is summed up in the divine promise "I will be their God, and they will be my people" (2 Cor. 6:16, 18; cf. Lev. 26:12; Jer. 32:38; Ezek. 36:28; 37:27). The promises given to the fathers are fulfilled as follows: (1) Christ's first advent and earthly ministry (Rom. 15:8), (2) the gift of the Holy Spirit (Gal. 3:14; Eph. 1:13), (3) the offer of the Gospel to Gentiles (Gal. 3:8, 14; Eph. 2:12; 3:6–7), (4) righteousness or right standing with God (Gal. 3:21–22, 29), (5) adoption into the family of God (2 Cor. 6:18; cf. 7:1), and (6) eternal life in Christ (2 Tim. 1:1; Titus 1:2; 1 John 2:25). All God's promises to the patriarchs and prophets find their fulfillment in Jesus Christ (2 Cor. 1:20).

The new covenant fulfills the promise

made to Jeremiah (Jer. 31:31–33; 32:38–40). Paul's record of the institution of the Lord's Supper on the eve of the Crucifixion attests the reality of this new covenant (1 Cor. 11:25), which replaced the inferior Mosaic covenant. Paul differentiated between the old covenant and the new in the Hagar–Sarah allegory (Gal. 4:24–31). Hagar signified the legal covenant given to Moses on Sinai, whereas Sarah represented the new covenant in which God's promises to Abraham are realized. Ishmael, born to Hagar after the flesh, is a son of bondage (law), whereas Isaac, born to Sarah as a result of promise, is a son of freedom (grace). By virtue of sinful weakness the law could not impart life; its purpose was to drive sinners to the life promised in Christ Jesus (Gal. 3:21–22). The apostle, in fact, distinguished old and new covenants by a series of antitheses: "the letter [that] kills" vs. "the Spirit [that] gives life," etc. (2 Cor. 3:3–11). Paul's fundamental distinction, therefore, was not between the so-called covenant of works and the covenant of grace, but between the old or Mosaic covenant and the new covenant inaugurated by Christ's blood. The Mosaic economy was chiefly (but not exclusively) one of law, whereas the new covenant economy is chiefly one of grace (Rom. 5:20–21; 6:14).

The word "dispensation" (*oikonomia,* found nine times in the New Testament) means (1) a management scheme or administration (Eph. 1:10; 3:9) and (2) in the case of one under authority, a stewardship or commission (Luke 16:2–4; 1 Cor. 9:17; Eph. 3:2). It is the first usage of *oikonomia* that concerns us here—i.e., the management or administration of the *oikos* ("household, family, race"). In Ephesians 1:9–10 (NRSV) Paul wrote that God "has made known to us the mystery of his will, according to his good pleasure that he set forth in Christ, as a plan (*oikonomia*) for the fullness of time, to

gather up all things in him. . . ." F. F. Bruce observes that "the 'administering' of God's good pleasure is the manner in which the purpose of God is being worked out in human history."[95] Paul further wrote that "grace was given to me to bring to the Gentiles the news of the boundless riches of Christ, and to make everyone see what is the plan [*oikonomia*] of the mystery hidden for ages in God who created all things"(Eph. 3:8–9 NRSV). *Oikonomia* thus is God's plan or management scheme being worked out in social institutions by his servants for the realization of his redemptive purposes.[96]

Although Paul discussed the kingdom of God relatively infrequently, his teaching permits no equation of the kingdom and the church. The kingdom is the future sphere of eternal glory to which believers are called (1 Thess. 2:12; 2 Thess. 1:5; 2 Tim. 4:18). The apostle envisaged a reign of Christ in a future, visible, kingdom on earth (cf. 2 Tim. 4:1). After all alien powers are vanquished, Christ will surrender the kingdom to the Father (1 Cor 15:24–28). This glorious, eternal kingdom represents the Christian's final inheritance at the resurrection (1 Cor. 15:50–54; cf. negatively, 1 Cor. 6:9–10; Gal. 5:21; Eph. 5:5). However, believers in Christ enter into the reality of God's rule or reign presently through the Spirit (Rom. 14:17; 1 Cor. 4:20; Col. 1:13). The saints' present experience of the kingdom is equivalent to participation in the dynamic new life in Christ.

Similarity between Israel and the church spiritually is seen in the fact that Abraham (Rom. 4:1–3) and David (4:6–8) experienced the same justification by faith as do Christians under the new covenant. Both Old and New Testament saints equally experienced right-standing with God (vv. 23–24). Further similarity between Israel and the church spiritually is found in Paul's discussion of the olive tree and branches (Rom.

11:17–24). The "olive root" (v. 17–18) connotes the patriarchs, the "cultivated olive tree" (v. 24) the people of God, the "natural branches" broken off (vv. 20–21, 24) unbelieving Jews, and the wild olive shoots grafted in (v. 17) believing Gentiles who thereby share in the ancient promises. Similarity between Israel and the church spiritually is seen in their status as branches of the same tree (the people of God). At various times God worked with one people, then with the other. All believers are spiritual children of Abraham (Gal. 3:7), being part of his "seed" (vv. 28–29). Abraham "is the father of all who believe but who have not been circumcised" (Rom. 4:11; cf. Gal. 3:16). By claiming that Abraham is the father also of the believing circumcised, Paul upheld the unity of faithful Jews and Gentiles in the one people of God. Paul's point is that both Jews and Gentiles who belong to Christ by faith are the spiritual offspring of Abraham and thus heirs of the promise (Gal. 4:28, 31). Unbelieving Gentiles "were excluded from citizenship in Israel and foreigners to the covenants of the promise" (Eph. 2:12). But upon trusting Christ they participate fully in the covenantal promises made to Abraham, which remain in force to the present time. Paul frequently designated believing Jews and Gentiles by the term "the saints" (e.g., Rom. 1:7; 1 Cor. 6:2; Eph. 1:15).

In the New Testament "Israel" often refers to the physical descendants of Jacob that formed the Jewish nation (Rom. 9:3–5; 10:1; Phil. 3:5). Some dispensationalists, seeking to separate the two communities, insist that "Israel" always connotes physical descendants of Jacob and never the church as the new community of believing Jews and Gentiles.[97] In Romans 9:6 "Israel" is used not only of the nation as a whole (institutional Israel) but also of the spiritual remnant within the nation (spiritual Israel)—otherwise described in verse 8 as "God's children," "children of the promise," and "Abraham's [true] offspring." But what about Galatians 6:16—"Peace and mercy to all who follow this rule, even to the Israel of God"? Many dispensationalists claim that "the Israel of God" signifies the believing remnant within Israel—spiritual Israelites in contrast to carnal Judaizers. With Meyer, Lenski, Cole, Guthrie, and the NIV, we view *kai* in the text as explicative. Thus the "Israel of God" are those "who follow this rule," namely, circumcised and uncircumcised (cf. v. 15) believers who share the faith of Abraham, who thus constitute the true seed of Abraham, and who are heirs of the promise (Gal. 3:14, 29; cf. Phil. 3:3: "For it is we who are the circumcision, who worship by the Spirit of God").

Dissimilarity spiritually between Israel and the church is seen in the permanent indwelling of the Holy Spirit in Christians individually (1 Cor. 6:19) and collectively (1 Cor. 3:16; Eph. 2:21–22). Likewise the Spirit's effectual gifting of all believers in Christ for ministry in the church (Rom. 12:6–8; 1 Cor. 12:7–11, 28–30). Dissimilarity ethnically is seen in the fact that, unlike racial Israel, the people of God in the present constitute a unity of Jews and Gentiles. Paul affirmed as much when he wrote to Gentile Christians, "You are no longer foreigners and aliens, but fellow citizens with God's people and members of God's household" (Eph. 2:19; cf. Titus 2:14). The *ekklēsia* is the new post-Pentecost reality identified as the "body of Christ." This *sōma Christou* is the new creation constituted by the Spirit's baptism of believing Jews and Gentiles into a single reality in which the old distinctions disappear (Rom. 12:5; 1 Cor. 12:13; Eph. 2:15–16; 4:4, 12, 16; 5:30; cf. Gal. 3:28). "The church of God is neither Jewish nor Gentile; it is a new society comprising former Jews and Gentiles alike, a 'new race' or a 'third race,' as later Christian writers liked to call it."[98] It is not true, therefore, that there was no essential difference between the people of God in the Old and New Testaments.[99]

Johannine Literature

Covenant theologians appeal to texts such as John 5:30, 43; 6:38–39; and 17:1–12 as support for the so-called covenant of redemption, even though the phrase is not found in these texts. Rather, Jesus' consciousness of having come from the Father, his dependence upon the Father's power, and his obedience to the Father's will are explained on the basis of his filial relation. Jesus revealed the Father's person (John 17:6), communicated his message (v. 8), and completed the work entrusted to him (v. 4) not necessarily by virtue of a formal pretemporal covenant but as the obedient Son.

Should we interpret John 1:17—"the law was given through Moses; grace and truth came through Jesus Christ"— as two administrations of the one covenant of grace or as two different economies? It appears clear that by "law" and "grace and truth" (i.e., the Gospel) John contemplated two contrasting orders. Grace and truth were not entirely absent in the Mosaic administration (cf. Exod. 34:6–7), but God's unmerited kindness (grace) and spiritual reality (truth) were uniquely manifest in Christ. It was he who brought the fuller and richer experience of salvation. John's statement is consistent with the distinction between the old (Mosaic) covenant and the new covenant (inaugurated by Jesus).

Jesus clearly understood himself as king (John 12:15; 18:37; 19:21). Yet his consciousness of kingship was antithetic to that of his Jewish contemporaries.

Believing that Jesus would liberate Israel from Roman oppression, the people of Galilee sought by force to make him king (John 6:15). Yet Jesus rejected their overtures, knowing that his was a spiritual kingdom that must be realized via the Cross. During Jesus' entry into Jerusalem the pilgrims acclaimed him the conquering Davidic Messiah (John 12:12–13). But whereas they viewed Jesus' kingship in political and military terms (cf. their appeal to Ps. 118:25–26), his selection of a donkey on which to ride demonstrated that his rule was one of peace. Finally, Jesus himself said, "My kingdom is not of this world. If it were so, my servants would fight. . . . But now my kingdom is from another place" (John 18:36). The kingdom he envisaged was different from the kingdoms of this world. Thus the data fail to support the hypothesis that Jesus offered Israel a theocratic kingdom, which the Jews ignorantly rejected. Quite the opposite appears to be the case. Israel expected Jesus to inaugurate a political kingdom, whereas the kingdom he offered his contemporaries was a spiritual one. John's description of Christ's future kingdom will be discussed in the next chapter.

A notable *difference* between Israel and the church spiritually is evident in the ministry of the Counselor. John affirmed that the coming of the Spirit would expand Jesus' ministry (John 16:7) as he testified to the Lord's words and deeds (John 15:26). The same Spirit would enlarge the body of revelation by guiding the disciples into the truth of Jesus' teachings (John 14:26; 16:13–15). Moreover, believers collectively would enjoy the permanent indwelling of the Counselor as a controlling power (John 14:16–17). In relation to the world, the Spirit would bring profound consciousness of guilt and impending judgment (John 16:8–11).

Other New Testament Literature

No portion of Scripture expounds the new covenant more fully than does the book of Hebrews. The *parties* to the new covenant are God and "those who are called" (Heb. 9:15), both Jews and Gentiles. The *promises* inherent in the new covenant are manifold: (1) forgiveness of sins (8:12), (2) the law of God inscribed on the mind and heart (v. 10), (3) a knowledge of God that is personal and experiential (7:19b; 8:11; 9:8), (4) an intimate relationship between God and his people ("I will be their God and they will be my people" 8:10), (5) righteousness of life (12:10, 14; 2 Peter 1:4), (6) an eternal inheritance (Heb. 9:15; cf. 11:13, 16), otherwise known as spiritual "rest" (4:1–11), (7) Christ's second advent to earth (2 Peter 3:4, 9), and (8) a new heaven and a new earth (2 Peter 3:13; cf. Heb. 11:10; 12:22; 13:14). The *proviso* is faith in Jesus Christ (Heb. 3:12, 19; 4:2; 6:1, 12), obedience (5:9; 13:17), holiness of life (12:14), and perseverance (3:6, 14; 10:36; 12:1–3). The *penalty* for noncompliance with the covenant requirements is eternal judgment (2:2; 6:8; 10:27–31, 39).

According to Hebrews *continuity* spiritually exists between old and new covenants, as evidenced by the following *similarities*. (1) The same God initiated the two covenants. (2) Both covenants embraced the same law (cf. Exod. 24:12 and Deut. 17:18–19 with Jer. 31:33). (3) Both covenants were inaugurated by the shedding of blood (Heb. 9:18–22; 10:29; 12:24; 13:20). (4) Both covenants center about God's promise to be the God of his people (Heb. 8:10; cf. 2 Cor. 6:16–18; Rev. 21:2–3). And (5) both hold out the promise of salvation through Christ (John 8:58; Rom. 9:3–5; 1 Cor. 10:1–4). More noteworthy, however, is the *discontinuity* institutionally and spiritually between the old (Mosaic) covenant and the new covenant inaugurated by Christ, as evidenced by the following *differences*. (1) The new covenant was enacted on better promises (Heb. 8:6), chiefly the promise of Jeremiah 31:31–34. (2) The new covenant was inaugurated by a better mediator (Heb. 9:15; 12:24a), for Christ is presented as one greater than Moses (3:1–6). (3) The new covenant involves a better sanctuary, which is no man-made tent but heaven itself—the very presence of God (9:11–12, 24). (4) The new covenant is administered by a better priest, who is sinless and undying, perfectly empathetic, and who is seated at the right hand of the Father (2:17; 4:14–15; 6:19–20; 7:16; 10:12). (5) The new covenant is based on a better sacrifice, even the single sacrifice of Jesus Christ (7:27; 9:12–28; 10:1–18; 12:24). (6) The new covenant mediates a better salvation, indeed, an eternal redemption that involves forgiveness of sins, justification, and sanctification (5:9; 9:12, 14–15; 10:10, 14, 17–18). The ritual system of the old covenant provided only ceremonial cleansing (9:9–10, 13) and not spiritual renewal (7:11; 10:1–4, 11). And (7) the new covenant provides a better ministry of the Holy Spirit, chiefly in the spiritual ability to perform the will of God (8:10; 10:16; 13:20–21).

Hebrews further observed that the Old Testament saints to whom the promises were made received only a partial fulfillment (Heb. 11:13, 39). Moreover, there was something "wrong" with the old covenant (8:7). The Mosaic economy was "obsolete," "aging," and "will soon disappear" (8:13). Thus to make the promised salvation a reality, Christ replaced the old covenant with the new covenant in his blood (10:9). The conclusion is unavoidable, therefore, that significant discontinuity exists between the old and new covenants—more than the system of covenant theology generally allows.[100]

Hebrews closely links the two covenants with two ages or dispensations by its reference to "the past" and "these last days" (Heb. 1:1-2). The former designates the old era prior to Christ's coming (the world of shadows), whereas the latter (cf. 9:26; 1 Peter 1:20) signifies the messianic age inaugurated by Christ's first advent (the world of reality). Through the gracious provisions of the new covenant—actualized by Christ's exaltation to the right hand of the Father—believers participate here and now in the blessings of the future age, when Christ's kingdom will be realized in perfection (Heb. 6:5; 2 Peter 1:11). As in the case of the two covenants, the dawning of the new age has decisively terminated the former age. This portion of Scripture knows nothing of the "postponed kingdom" idea. Peter wrote that through prophets of old "the Spirit of Christ . . . predicted the sufferings of Christ and the glories that would follow" (1 Peter 1:11). The parallelism between "the sufferings of Christ" and "the glories that would follow" suggest that both Christ's passion and his glorification were divinely foreordained. The purpose of Christ's coming to earth was to die for sins and found the church, not to offer ethnic Israel a political kingdom.

The literature offers insight into the relationship between covenant, promise, and kingdom and between Israel and the church. God the *King* sovereignly entered into covenants with his chosen people. The key feature of the *covenant* between God and persons is the *promise* (Heb. 6:13-18). Furthermore, the overarching content of the promise is the *kingdom of God*—namely, "a kingdom that cannot be shaken" (12:28). The latter phrase refers to the future, eternal kingdom, the good of which believers in Christ enter by faith here and now. "It is the new quality of life, the new existence, made possible through the fulfillment of the promises

of a new covenant."[101] Thus through the Old Testament covenants God the King gave promises that were enlarged and perfected in the new covenant, the chief of which was participation in the kingdom both in its present and future forms.

Since national Israel was constituted by the Mosaic covenant in the former age and the church by the new covenant in Christ's blood in the present age, a fundamental structural *dissimilarity* exists between Israel and the church. Yet the relation between the two evinces significant spiritual *similarities*. First Peter 2:9 describes the church by a series of phrases descriptive of Israel in the Old Testament: "a chosen people" (cf. Deut. 10:15; Isa. 43:20), "a royal priesthood" (cf. Exod. 19:6), "a holy nation" (cf. Exod. 19:6; Deut. 28:9), and "a people belonging to God" (cf. Deut. 4:20; 14:2; Mal. 3:17). In this text in 1 Peter (cf. Rev. 1:6) Christian believers are described in language used of faithful Jews under the old economy (*laos*, used of Israel in Acts 26:17, 23; *ethnos*, used of Israel in Rom. 15:10). This continuity prevails because believers in Christ are heirs of the old covenant and one spiritually with believing Israel. Peter asserted that "the Christian community . . . is to be understood as the fulfillment of the promises and hopes given to Israel."[102]

SYSTEMATIC FORMULATION

Continuities and discontinuities between the church and Israel identified in the biblical section now need to be coherently related to each other in the kingdom of God. Controversial discussions of the relationship of the church to Israel often miss the mark because of a failure to define them adequately. A church was defined both spiritually and institutionally in the previous chapter. Here it is important to define Israel, not only ethnically but also spiritually and institutionally.

The Meaning of "Israel"

Nation-states had arisen prior to Israel. With the multiplication of families (Gen. 5) came disputes between them and the need for governments (Gen. 10) and kings (Gen. 14). Life in the condition of nature (since the Fall) is not some South Sea fantasy but, as political philosopher Thomas Hobbes said, can be "nasty, brutish and short." So God instituted civil government to achieve his purposes for the race including civil order and justice. Admittedly, the state is imperfect and its power often abused. But on a theistic worldview the state is "the servant of eternal justice."[103]

Ethnically, Israel includes Abraham, Isaac, and Jacob, whose twelve sons produced twelve tribes. *Spiritually,* Israel includes all ethnic or proselyte Jews who believed the messianic promises as did Abraham (Rom. 4:3, 21). "A man is not a Jew if he is only one outwardly. . . . No, a man is a Jew if he is one inwardly; and circumcision is circumcision of the heart" (Rom. 2:28–29). In certain periods of history only a remnant of individuals composed spiritual Israel (Isa. 28:5; Rom. 9:27) and personally loved God (Deut. 6:5). God's promises to Abraham's spiritual children are different from those to the faithless in the nation.[104] Thus the Lord said, " 'I gave you my solemn oath and entered into a covenant with you,' declares the Sovereign Lord, and 'you became mine' " (Ezek. 16:8). "I will be their God, they will be my people" (Ex. 6:7; cf. Ezek. 11:20; 36:28). Abraham's spiritual children, like Simeon and Anna, believed in the messianic significance of sacrifices and feasts and genuinely longed for the coming Messiah. See Luke 2:25–38. The spiritually illumined understood that God's beneficent reign could be realized only in the coming of the long-awaited Messiah.[105]

Institutionally, "Israel" may refer to a national social structure or institution. God said to the childless Abraham: "I will make you into a great nation" (Gen. 12:2) with a "land" (15:7–21). The nation was organized under Moses through whom God promised, "If you obey me fully and keep my covenant, then out of all nations you will be my treasured possession. Although the whole earth is mine, you will be for me a kingdom of priests and a holy nation" (Exod. 19:5–6). God initially chose the Levitical priests to lead the nation in repentance from sin and faith in the promises. Political leadership passed from Moses to Joshua, the judges, and finally numerous kings. To King David God promised a great name (2 Sam. 7:9), rest from enemies (v. 11), and the establishment of his kingdom and throne (vv. 12–16). The term "nation" signifies "the people occupying the same country, united under the same government, and usually speaking the same primary language."[106] The ethnic children of Abraham eventually occupied the same Promised Land under the same government and spoke the same Hebrew language. The Old Testament gives relatively more space to the history of a nation than any sacred book in non-Christian religions. Anyone familiar with the Old Testament history of the kings of Israel and Judah needs no further documentation of the prominence of its national structure.[107] The notion of institutional Israel is a missing link in much systematic theology.

Inwardly, Israel is composed of ethnic or proselyte believers in the promised Messianic deliverer (as revealed to their time). *Outwardly,* Israel is organized in a national social institution led at its height by a king. When exploring the relation of the church to Israel, then, we compare and contrast the church and Israel both *spiritually* and *institutionally*.

Similarities Between Israel and the Church Spiritually

What similarities exist between the spiritual people of God in the nation Israel and in the church? Abundant Scriptural data confirms the spiritual *oneness* of God's people in Israel and the church. (1) Members of both institutions have been saved by faith in the work of the same *Messiah* through the same *Abrahamic promise* (Rom. 4). (2) Believers in both Israel and the church accept the same *Gospel* (Rom. 10).[108] (3) Old Testament people of God exercised the same kind of *faith* (Rom. 4; Heb. 11). (5) Depraved sinners in both Testaments needed the same *new birth,* for before the Cross Jesus expected Nicodemus to understand through Old Testament teaching that he must be born again (John 3:1–7). (6) Both Israel and the church, as branches in the same tree, received the same *spiritual life* in the same illustrative olive tree (Rom. 11:17–24). (7) Both Old and New Testament believers enjoyed a *fellowship with God* in confession, adoration, prayer, and meditation (recall the Psalms and other recorded prayers). (8) Old Testament heroes of faith (Heb. 11) *exuded the Spirit's fruit* such as "love, joy, peace, patience, kindness, goodness, faithfulness, gentleness and self-control" (Gal. 5:22–23). Hence (9) the people of God must have overcome their holistic depravity by the enablement of the Holy Spirit, not only in the providential realm of the kingdom but also in the redemptive realm.

The Old Testament prayer "Do not . . . take your Holy Spirit from me" (Ps. 51:11), did not contradict this basic relation of Old Testament believers to God, but expressed David's concern about losing the gifts and position as king for which the Spirit's presence had made him qualified (1 Sam. 16:13). Commonly the Spirit came upon people for special craftsmanship (as in building and furnishing the tabernacle or temple), and for the kingship of Israel. At issue was not the personal standing of the just who lived by faith, but their particular gifts and offices in service to the nation.

A remarkable *agreement* exists among contemporary schools of theology that acceptance with God in both Israel and the church was by grace through faith in the promised Messiah. *Covenant theology* distinctively focuses on the covenant of grace or redemption in both Israel and the church. The different covenants or promises to Noah, Abraham, Moses, and David express a single covenant in eternity between the Father and the Son. Herman Hoeksema calls it the counsel of peace *("pactum salutis")* arranged to save fallen humanity.[109] M. E. Osterhaven explains the relation of the different historical covenants and promises to the eternal covenant:

Although the covenant of grace includes various dispensations of history, it is essentially one. From the promise in the garden (Gen. 3:15), through the covenant made with Noah (Gen. 6–9), to the day that the covenant was established with Abraham, there is abundant evidence of God's grace. With Abraham a new beginning is made which the later, Sinaitic covenant implements and strengthens. At Sinai the covenant assumes a national form and stress is laid on the law of God. This is not intended to alter the gracious character of the covenant, however (Gal. 3:17–18), but it is to serve to train Israel until the time would come when God himself would appear in its midst. In Jesus the new form of the covenant that had been promised by the prophets is manifest, and that which was of a temporary nature in the old form of the covenant disappears (Jer. 31:31–34; Heb. 8). While there is unity and continuity in the covenant of grace throughout history,

337

the coming of Christ and the subsequent gift of the Holy Spirit have brought rich gifts unknown in an earlier age.[110]

Promise theology with a similar emphasis on the unity of covenant promises finds a unity of the people of God in believing that the Lord would do what he promised (Heb. 11). What did Habakkuk mean when he wrote that "the righteous will live by his faith" (Hab. 2:4)? Habakkuk meant, Walter Kaiser explains, that a believer "put an immovable confidence in the God who had promised His salvation and the coming Man of promise. It was a steadfast, undivided surrender to Yahweh, 'a childlike, humble and sincere trust in the credibility of the divine message of salvation.' "[111]

Kingdom theology concurs with the fact that there is one way of salvation by grace. "Jesus did not teach a new doctrine of forgiveness; he brought to lost sinners a new experience of forgiveness."[112] How different the experience of forgiveness was in New Testament times may be questioned, but not the fact that "Jesus did not teach a new doctrine of forgiveness." George Eldon Ladd explained, "The kingdom of God is the redemptive rule of God in Christ defeating Satan and the powers of evil and delivering men from the sway of evil. It brings to men 'righteousness and peace and joy in the Holy Spirit' (Rom. 14:17). Entrance into the kingdom of Christ means deliverance from the power of darkness (Col. 1:13) and is accomplished by the new birth."[113] Israel's task was not to bring in the kingdom or to become the kingdom but to proclaim and exhibit kingdom values to a lost world. Kingdom theology teaches that all who are saved by grace through faith form one spiritual people of God in one redemptive kingdom.

Some *earlier dispensational theology* taught salvation by works ("obedience") during the dispensation of the law.[114] In contrast, the note to John 1:17 in *The New Scofield Reference Bible* (1967) states that "prior to the cross man's salvation was through faith (Gen. 15:6; Rom. 4:3), being grounded on Christ's atoning sacrifice, viewed anticipatively by God (Rom. 3:25)." According to Roy Aldrich, "there is only one way of salvation throughout all Bible history since the Fall. The erroneous teaching of some ultradispensationalists at this point should not be attributed to dispensationalists as a whole."[115] Charles Ryrie explains that "the basis of salvation is always the death of Christ; the means is always faith; the object is always God (though man's understanding of God before and after the incarnation is obviously different); but the content depends on the particular revelation God was pleased to give at a certain time."[116]

The four theologies concur, as we do, that the biblical evidence indicates several *important spiritual continuities* between believers in Israel and the church. By grace both alike put faith in the Messiah, accepting the revealed promises, and so are justified by faith. It follows that believers in Israel and the church, both Jews and Gentiles, are one spiritually (Gal. 3:28). Institutional and functional differences may remain for Israel and the church, but "if you belong to Christ, then you are Abraham's seed, and heirs according to the promise" (v. 29). It also follows that believers in Israel and the church serve others under the one redemptive order (the realm of the kingdom) extending through all ages. Jesus came and preached the Good News of the kingdom (Matt. 4:23; Mark 1:14). "The manifestation of Christ being finished, the kingdom is already begun. Those who receive *him* entered into *it*."[117] They became "agents of the personal administration of Jesus Christ."[118]

Dissimilarities Between Israel and the Church Institutionally

Having compared the church and Israel spiritually, we now contrast them institutionally. In addition to possessing many similarities spiritually, it will be seen that Israel and the church are very different social structures or institutions. An *institution* in God's redemptive kingdom is a community of believers organized with distinctive offices for promoting temporally appropriate ends among God's unique people. Attention to the social structures involved makes more specific what the other theological systems called the kingdom's "phases," "administrations," or "economies."

What are the *differences* between Israel and the church *institutionally?* We briefly cite the contrasts as follows: (1) The nation Israel resulted from the old covenant with Moses; the church from the new covenant based on the completed ministries of the Messiah and new baptizing ministry of the Holy Spirit. (2) People born in an ethnic line were citizens or had to become proselytes of national Israel; the reborn from any ethnic background may become members of institutional churches. (3) The nation occupied a land or country with a capital city; the church has no country or capital. (4) Members of a nation spoke primarily one language; members of the church speak any of the world's languages. (5) The nation of Israel legislated taxes; the church does (or ought) not. (6) The nation of Israel had armies; the church does (or ought) not have forces for waging war. (7) The nation legislated and enforced both civil and religious laws on all its citizens; the church does (or ought) not. (8) The chief executive officer in Israel was a king; in the church it is a senior pastor–elder–bishop. (9) The mission of God's people under the old covenant called for a political structure to implement Mosaic legislation in one state; the mission under the new covenant calls for an ecclesiastical structure to implement the discipleship of people in all nations.

How then shall we categorize the above differences? *Covenant theology* speaks of them as different *administrations* or *dispensations* of the one covenant of grace. Where Osterhaven refers to "dispensations" of the one covenant (above), many other covenant theologians speak of its different "administrations." Long before the system of dispensationalism, the Baptist covenant theologian John Gill (d. 1771) called the different historical periods "manifestations," "exhibitions," and "dispensations" of the covenant of grace.[119] The concept of "administration" or dispensation (without specifying the structural changes) is too vague to be a clear criterion for classifying periods of history. A distinctive difference marked by Pentecost brings more than an administrative change; it brings a new institutional structure.

Kingdom theology refers to Israel and the church as different *stages* in God's kingdom. George Eldon Ladd wrote, "God's reign expresses itself in different stages through redemptive history."[120] But Ladd failed to spell out criteria by which to detect a new "stage." The organized church seems to be more than a stage of the redemptive kingdom expressed in national Israel. The church is a completely new institution.

Dispensationalism distinguishes Israel and the church as historical *economies*. Charles Ryrie identified a dispensation as "a distinguishable economy in the outworking of God's purpose."[121] The tendency of dispensationalists to transliterate *oikonomia* as "economy" helps only if we know who is accountable to whom in which institutional structure. As the Greek term for house (*oikos*) expands in meaning, it may refer to a king's palace, a prison house,

339

occasionally a city, a nation, a spiritual house, and God's house.[122] Note that each of these was organized. The Greek noun (*oikonomia*) behind the English "dispensation" means "management" of a given institution, and *oikonomos* designates its "steward" or "manager."[123] The verb (*oikonomeō*) means to manage, regulate, plan, and administer the affairs of the organized social institution. Although all members of the household were equally image-bearers of God, the stewardship of a household's resources required a functional order of the members. With more than one person in a permanent social structure, the legal and functional responsibility for the whole operation terminates with the steward. In the families of the Pentateuch it was the husband, in national Israel a king, and in the church the senior elder or pastor, who bears final responsibility.

As we shall see more fully below, God has given prominence in the redemptive order to three different institutions in three different eras. R. E. O. White observes, "Biblical religion is faithful . . . to its concept of the religious community. At first the family, then the nation, forms the unit-group; later the covenant people is seen as a selected group within the nation, united by their acceptance of prophetic ideals."[124] With the coming of John the Baptist and Jesus, White notes, a corporate conception of religious life was still maintained. "Even in its most individualistic expressions, biblical thought never conceives of the saved man out of relation with the rest of his group—nation, remnant, kingdom, church."[125] Holding that the nation and the covenant people were intended to be the same, our overview of the Bible's believing communities points up the fact that God's redemptive program gives prominence to different social structures at different historical periods. So we may speak of three

dispensations of the family, the nation, and the church, so long as a "dispensation" is defined as *the stewardship of God's redemptive purposes collectively through a distinctive institution prominent during a given era of biblical history*. So the dispensations underline families, a nation, and churches. For responsible stewardship in the present age a church has distinctive offices for accountable stewardship. Without specification of the organizational structures and officers ultimately responsible for management, an "economy" is too vague a principle for clear classifications of the differences in biblical history.

Summing up the institutional differences between Israel and the church, the latter are very different organizations under different divine covenants with different offices for strengthening God's people and blessing the world. In the organization of institutional Israel, the highest office was that of king; in a church the highest office is that of elder-bishop-pastor. The spiritual purposes of the former were administered through an ethnic, national social structure, and the latter through a multiethnic ecclesiastical social structure separate from the state. Recognition of the differences in the organization, offices, and purposes of these institutions gives specificity to the covenant or promise theologian's "administrations," the kingdom theologian's "stages" and the dispensationalist's "economies or stewardships."

Spiritual-Institutional Theology

The scheme we designate spiritual-institutional theology carefully considers the relation between Israel and the church spiritually and institutionally. We have seen above that major *similarities* exist between Israel and the church *spiritually* and major *dissimilarities* exist structurally or *institutionally*.

The very significant points of continuity spiritually between Israel and the church do not mean total similarity on everything spiritual before and after the Cross. Some important *spiritual differences* occur primarily as a result of the differences between the old and new covenants (Jer. 31:31–34).

1. Under the new covenant *all believing men and women are priests* having direct access to God the Father and spiritual gifts for serving the church and the world (1 Peter 2:9). Under the old covenant priestly ministries belonged only to a few men, the Levites. Believers now approach the Most High, not through human priests, but through the one risen Mediator, Jesus Christ. With Protestantism in general we affirm the priesthood of every believer.

2. By a different initiating ministry, Spirit baptism (outwardly expressed in water baptism), the Holy Spirit unites believing men and women of all ethnic backgrounds in *one community*. The Spirit's baptism in Acts overcame racial and political prejudices against Samaritans (Acts 8) and Gentiles (Acts 10). Prior to Pentecost, Gentiles had to become proselyte Jews to be numbered among the children of Abraham. Now without any racial or national requirements (Acts 15), Gentile believers are baptized by the Holy Spirit directly into one multiethnic body for which Christ died. The requirement for membership is nothing other than conversion to Christ. Spirit baptism forms one spiritual-institutional organism of Jews, Samaritans, and Gentiles who accept the Messiah (1 Cor. 12:13).

3. *The Spirit's permanent dwelling* is no longer in a temple at a capital city but among the gathered members of this prejudice-shattering community. Bearing the disgrace he bore, Christians need make no pilgrimages to any sacred city (Heb. 13:13–14). The universal or catholic church recognizes no capital city like Rome, Mecca, or Salt Lake City. Under the new covenant God puts "his law in their minds and writes it on their hearts" (Jer. 31:33). So the gathered community is now the temple or dwelling place of the Holy Spirit (1 Cor. 6:19). As women and men repent and believe, they become living parts of this temple (1 Cor. 3:16). Jesus said, "[the Counselor] will be in you [pl.]" (John 14:17). The plural "you," as the subsequent historical context shows, refers to the gathered men and women at Jerusalem (Acts 1–2). When 120 of Christ's followers met for worship on the Day of Pentecost, the Holy Spirit not only endued them with power but also created a new community by baptizing them into one new body. The new work of the Spirit from Pentecost onward is more collective than individual. Together all believing men and women from any ethnic background form the holy temple where God's Spirit abides (Eph. 2:21–22).

4. *The New Testament* is now added to the Old Testament as the church's primary source of faith and practice. Illumined by the Spirit who inspired the completed revelation, believers "receive" the apostolic doctrine for themselves (1 Cor. 2:14). Like its central figure, Christ, the New Testament does not destroy the teachings of Moses and the prophets (Matt. 5:17–18); it fulfills them. The *telos* of the law was to direct people to the Messiah (Rom. 10:4). Hence each believer receives both the Old and New Testaments as teaching originating not with humans (2 Peter 1:12–21) but breathed out by God (2 Tim. 3:16). The Holy Spirit now illumines all new-covenant believers as they are instructed in righteousness through their study of Scripture.

On the other hand, the significant points of dissimilarity between Israel and the church institutionally do not mean that they share no commonalities. Rather, as sociological structures both Israel and the church have some *institutional similarities*. Both social structures are instruments by which God manages and leads his people collectively.[126] Both national Israel and the institutional church are instruments of God's redemptive rule. But neither national Israel nor the institutional church is to be confused with God's redemptive kingdom. Neither institution could bring in the kingdom nor become the kingdom. Both in their respective ages are instruments of God's rule to further the kingdom by edifying their people collectively and serving the world. But both have communal objectives to fulfill and officers responsible to lead in their achievement. But both the social structures of Israel and the church are intended for the benefit of believers and the service of the fallen world. But in particular epochs of history both have woefully failed.

Spiritual-institutional theology develops out of a comparison of similarities and differences between Israel and the church in the redemptive realm of the kingdom. The biblically based system affirms the many spiritual continuities (and differences) between Israel and the church and also institutional discontinuities (and similarities). Moreover, it focuses on a major integrating idea of special revelation. "The center of theology" in the Old Testament, as Kaiser affirms, is "God's word of *blessing* or *promise . . . to be* Israel's God and *to do* something for Israel and *through them* something for *all the nations* on the face of the earth."[127] Similarly, central to the New Testament is the Messiah's promise to be the Savior of believers and by his Spirit to build his church and thus bring Good News to all people. Consolidating the big ideas of both Testaments, *the Father has promised to be faithful to believers in the Messiah, graciously blessing his Spirit-renewed people personally and institutionally so that they may lovingly bless one another and the world.*

How does this spiritual-institutional theology integrate the covenants, promises, kingdom, and dispensations of the four major single-theme theologies? We give logical priority to agreement among the Trinity in eternity to redeem sinners (as in covenant theology). That gracious, eternal plan was temporally revealed in the promise to Abraham repeated to others (as in promise theology). Believers in the Messiah both before and after his advent constitute one people of God called out of a world dominated by evil powers to live under the spiritual rule of Christ (as in kingdom theology). Since the Messiah's advent the primary institution for edifying believers is the church with duly appointed officers (an element of dispensationalism). This unique New Testament institution (the church) based on the former covenant and serving the one redemptive kingdom is Christ's special instrument fitted to the post-Pentecost situation. Although there has been one people of God saved by grace throughout the Old and New Testaments, their organization as a church is a uniquely New Testament phenomenon instituted by Christ. It displaces the theocratic temple organization of the Sinaitic covenant and meets the need of the new situation since Pentecost.[128]

When Did the Institutional Church Begin?

Given the similarities and differences in the church and Israel, it is important to ask when the church began. *According to covenant theologians, the church began with the first believer in the Old Testament.* Hanke argued effectively for the spiritual unity of God's redeemed people of all times.[129] But he misapplied the text "Jesus Christ is the same yesterday and today and forever" (Heb. 13:8) as indicating institutional continuity. This verse teaches the changelessness of Christ's divine nature not the sameness of his program in all periods of history. Hanke's covenant theology fails to distinguish the different social institutions through which God's people were edified and commissioned to witness to the world prior to Pentecost and afterward. The nation of Israel still had prominence in the social purposes of the redemptive order following the captivity of northern and southern sections when only a remnant of Jewish believers remained. The old covenant was fulfilled and the new covenant established when the eternal Logos became flesh and trained his followers to disciple all nations and established the church. From the beginning of Jesus' ministry in the first century the nation of Israel became less prominent as a social structure for redemptive purposes. After the destruction of Israel's temple in A.D. 70, the church stands alone as the preeminent social structure distinctive of the present age.

Dispensational, promise, and kingdom theologies hold that the church began at Pentecost (Acts 2). Then both Jewish and Gentile believers were incorporated into the Jerusalem church by Spirit baptism (Acts 2:1–4, 38–39). Prior to Pentecost the Spirit's baptism was still future (Acts 1:5). The first evidence of a church organized was at Jerusalem (2:41–47). Peter explicitly designates the event of Pentecost as "the beginning"; when the Gentiles were saved the Holy Spirit came on them as he had come on the 120 "at the beginning" (Acts 11:15). Then uncircumcised Gentiles were admitted to the social structure that began at Pentecost.

Some ultradispensationalists place the beginning of the church in Acts 28. Toward the end of his ministry Paul referred to Israel's rejection of the kingdom and the sending of God's salvation to the Gentiles (Acts 28:26–28).[130] E. W. Bullinger (d. 1913) found three dispensations in the New Testament. In the first, Christ offered the kingdom only to Jews; entrance was marked by water baptism (the Gospels). In the second dispensation the apostles offered the Jews participation in the "bride church" and practiced two baptisms—in water and in the Spirit (Acts and the earlier Epistles). In the third dispensation Paul taught the oneness of Jew and Gentile by Spirit baptism in the body of Christ (the Prison Epistles, 1 and 2 Timothy and Titus). We note that Bullinger based some of his arguments on dichotomies of words that did not refer to incompatible realities. For example, he argued that the ordinances of baptism and the Lord's Supper dealt with the flesh only and so had no place in the body of Christ alleged to be of the Spirit only. Bullinger failed to understand that just as the inner and outer self constitute one person, so the inner Spirit baptism and outer water baptism can constitute one baptism.

Other ultradispensationalists claim that the church began when Paul began his mission to Jews and Gentiles (Acts 13:2). Spokesmen include J. C. O'Hair, C. R. Stam, and Charles F. Baker. Baker noted that Paul's statement in Acts 28:28 does not mark the beginning of the body of Christ but should be understood in the past tense: i.e., the Gospel *has been* sent to the Gentiles (RSV, NIV, and others). Baker found support in Paul's letters for the practice of the Lord's Supper (1 Cor. 11) but not water baptism. Paul's transitional use of water baptism for Jews (he assumed) was not normative for Gentiles (1 Cor. 1:13–17). Baker interpreted baptism in Romans 6:3–4 as Spirit baptism, although most adequately it may be understood as both inner Spirit baptism and outer water baptism.

When did the church begin, according to spiritual-institutional theology? We call for division of the question to avoid confusion of categories. (1) *Spiritually,* all God's people by faith are "in Christ" and in his redemptive kingdom, and they have a similar eternal destiny. The risen Messiah heads one body in which there is neither Jew nor Gentile. Abraham and David were in "spiritual Israel" which is indistinguishable from the "spiritual church" in regard to justification by faith in the Abrahamic promise and its fulfillment in Jesus. (2) *Institutionally,* however, the church began at Pentecost when believers under the new covenant were baptized into the risen Christ and also into the organized transethnic and transnational church with officers responsible for teaching apostolic doctrine, leading in worship, and administering the two ordinances. In summary, the most coherent account of the evidence is as follows: In some important *spiritual* respects the church existed in the Old Testament; but as a multiethnic *organization* distinct from the family and the state the church began at Pentecost.

The organized church began when Jewish believers in the crucified and risen Christ were baptized by the Spirit into one body (Acts 2:38, 41, 44, 47; cf. 1 Cor. 12:13). To that same community the Spirit added Samaritans (Acts 8:17) and Gentiles (Acts 10:28, 34–35, 45–48; 11:18). The fact that Paul most fully received, understood, and explained the mystery of uniting Jew and Gentile in one body need not imply that Peter, Cornelius, and the Jerusalem church grasped nothing of this truth (Acts 10:30–38; 11:2–17). Jesus Christ laid the one foundation for the church and prepared his disciples to establish it. Saucy shows that the church is built upon the entire work of Christ's first coming and is sustained through his present leadership.[131] But he also finds that the actual historical formation of the church occurred in Jerusalem on the day of Pentecost.[132] Indeed it was after Pentecost that God's people made disciples and established churches in Jerusalem, Judea, Samaria, and beyond (Acts 1:8). In summary, the belief that the church began previous to Pentecost (as in covenant theology) has a half truth *spiritually,* but the belief that the church began at Pentecost (as in dispensationalism and the other theologies) is a half truth *institutionally.* Both halves need to be integrated to form a more adequate theology.

Prior to Israel What Social Institution Had Prominence?

Spiritual-institutional theology asks what social structure had prominence in God's redemptive program prior to the founding of Israel as a nation? Before institutional Israel the basic social structure was the *family.* It was rooted in the creation of male and female to leave mother and father, cleave to one another, and multiply. Marriage "is an order of creation in the *real* sense, . . . an order 'before the fall.' "[133] A "family" consists of a married husband and wife and their children in a shared residence. A family could be diminished by such factors as childlessness, death, and divorce or extended into a household by adding children's spouses, grandchildren, and other relatives and employees.

God's redemptive rule focused on *believing families* of *patriarchs* such as Noah, Shem, Ham, Japheth, Abraham, Isaac, Jacob, and Jacob's twelve sons. Other families who exhibited faith in the redemptive revelation given to their time came to be included (Gen. 3:15–50:26; Heb. 11:7–22). With his family Noah "became heir of the righteousness that comes by faith" (Heb. 11:7). God raised up families like those of Noah and Abraham for both the providential purposes of teaching moral values and the redemptive purpose of urging faith in Eve's victorious descendant. These "households" provided far more than rest and leisure; they were centers of education and worship. Often located on the land they all worked, the children received moral, spiritual, and vocational instruction while on the job. The family provided health care, financial aid, insurance, and welfare for travelers.[134] The Bible does not certify economic or educational institutions in any age as distinct institutions for redemptive purposes. For that reason we do not add them to the three featured institutions of the family, nation, and church.

To this day the family remains an important primary social structure for teaching biblical justice and grace to future generations. Thus two institutions are featured in the redemptive program of the present age, but the church stands out as the more distinctive institution in God's redemptive program. Families and churches are also important in the providential realm, and they in turn depend on the protection of their national government. Providential roles assigned to the nation of Israel may apply to any other nation, but references to Israel redemptively designate Israel as the unique preparer of the way for the Messiah.

In spiritual-institutional theology the *institutions are not necessarily mutually exclusive*. In an age when another institution gains prominence, the earlier institution continues to serve providential purposes and may also contribute to the redemptive program. After Israel became the prominent institution, godly families still served the providential and redemptive kingdoms. After the church became prominent, Israel as a nation no longer served prominently as a social institution in the redemptive order, but has taken its place since 1948 in the providential kingdom along with all other nations. Families are still crucial for both providential and redemptive purposes.

Each of the three institutions should *be free from, but supportive of, the others.* Christian families and churches should be free from the state to pursue their objectives. The state should be free from an established religion to pursue its objectives. Leaders of one of these institutions should not seek to usurp the prerogatives of the others. Rather, they ought to encourage the others to fulfill their distinctive objectives. A purpose of Israel's king was to provide for God's people a safe, just, and productive nation in which the priests could educate believers in divine revelation and lead them in worshipful sacrifices. The purposes of leaders in the church as distinct from the state include educating believers in applying divinely revealed truths in their lives and ministries, leading them in fellowship and worship, and equipping them to take the Gospel to the world.[135] Both the church and the state may assist the family, but neither the state nor the church assume the ultimate educational and vocational responsibilities God gave to the family.

Spiritual-Institutional Theology Fits the Facts Coherently

Several considerations may further clarify and justify spiritual-institutional theology:

1. A spiritual-institutional theology emphasizes the fact that *God's eternal purposes and temporal rule have been not only personal but also relational and corporate.* For our enduring social needs God established the organized communities of the family, the nation, and the church. As image-bearers of God, people have a capacity for morally responsible action, and this makes institutional accountability feasible. "Our capacity for social justice makes government possible; our tendency to injustice makes it necessary."[136] The three social structures are necessary to help people overcome their tendencies

toward self-centeredness. An international journal on social justice points out that "institutions are needed to give justice ordered expression."[137] Love as well as justice is given ordered expression in the primary social structures of spiritual-institutional theology.

2. Spiritual-institutional theology *furnishes a coherent account of similarities and differences between Israel and the church.* Before addressing the relationship of the church to Israel we called for a division of the question. Has the question to do with people individually or collectively? Individually, members of the remnant in Israel and the church have the same spiritual status and constitute one people of God with the same promises, faith, and spiritual life. Collectively, both are divinely ordained social institutions with different organizations and different officers. A major difference between Old and New Testament saints, then, is in relation to the revealed mystery of the transnational church and the Holy Spirit's distinctive ministries to produce it. Neither national Israel nor the institutional church is to be confused with the kingdom of God, but both are structures in which God rules his people collectively for their good and the blessing of the world.[138]

3. Spiritual-institutional theology *integrates the multiple themes of the Old Testament.* Gerhard Hasel argues that the varied data of the Old Testament cannot be forced into a single "center" such as covenant (Eichrodt), the holiness of God (Sellin), God's lordship (Kohler), kingdom (Gunther Klein, George Ladd), kingdom and communion with God (Fohrer), or the functioning of the Word of God in salvation history (Von Rad).[139] The concept of promise contributes an important element (Kaiser), but it is not adequate. So Gerhard Hasel calls for a "multiplex" approach in Old Testament theology because it

leaves room for indicating the varieties of connections between the Testaments and avoids an explication of the manifold testimonies through a single structure or unilinear point of view. The multiplex approach has the advantage of remaining faithful to both the similarities and dissimilarities as well as the old and new without in the least distorting the original historical witness of the text in its literal sense and its larger kerygmatic intention nor falling short in the recognition of the larger context to which the OT belongs. Thus both Testaments will finally shed light upon each other and aid mutually in a more comprehensive understanding of their theologies.[140]

4. Spiritual-institutional theology *synthesizes also the multiple motifs of New Testament.* Hasel also concludes that a "multi-track" theology accounts for the richness of the New Testament data and avoids artificial and forced unilinear approaches. Hasel warns of the difficulty of finding an inner unity that binds together the various theologies and longitudinal themes, concepts, and motifs. He urges that an integration not be performed hastily, but rightly insists that *"integration is the final aim and ultimate object of theology"*[141] (italics added). Unfortunately, Hasel did not integrate the different strands of content in a meaningful multiplex theology for either Old or New Testaments. His preoccupation with methodology has kept him from answering his own important call. The categories of spiritual-institutional theology incorporate multiplex factors brought out in biblical theologies of both the Old and New Testaments. In the "spiritual" category it includes the concepts of God's eternal purposes, covenants, promises, kingdom, and God's responsive people. In the "institutional" category it integrates structural relationships as a family member, a citizen of a nation, and a member of a church.

5. Thus spiritual-institutional theology *incorporates the strengths of sin-*

gle-theme theologies. With covenant theology, spiritual-structural theology emphasizes the unity of the covenant of redemptive grace for people individually and collectively. With promise theology, it is built on the New Testament fulfillment of God's great promises for individuals and communities. With kingdom theology, it emphasizes the one redemptive kingdom and hence the one people of God through history. But spiritual-institutional theology makes explicit kingdom requirements for God's people both personally and collectively. In his several books on the kingdom Ladd focuses on the Gospels rather than the Epistles. Hence he more adequately explains the spiritual rather than the institutional form of the kingdom. Inclusive of a major theme in dispensational theology, spiritual-institutional theology identifies three economies or stewardships in the structures of the family, Israel, and the church.

6. Featuring the roles of God's people collectively in the redemptive realm of the kingdom, spiritual-institutional theology *sharpens the focus of Christianity's philosophy of history*. The great news is that the Father eternally purposed to do gracious things through his Son and Spirit for redeemed people both individually and collectively in order to bless the whole world! This thought supplies a coherent account of the varied lines of relevant evidence concerning the primary sociological relationships of the family, church, and state. It furnishes a philosophy of history in which all human beings may live authentically as responsible family members and citizens under God's providential kingdom. It also adds a viable theology of redemption from oppression as converts to Christ authentically advance God's redemptive kingdom in their families and churches.

7. Spiritual-institutional theology *avoids confusion concerning social justice and the Gospel by distinguishing the providential realm from the redemptive realm of God's kingdom*. In harmony with the rest of Scripture Jesus sometimes spoke of God's program for all people in the providential realm of the kingdom. At other times he spoke of God's special program for his disciples in the redemptive realm of the kingdom. The purposes disclosed in general revelation and common grace are not to be confused with God's collective purposes of special revelation and redemptive grace.[142] The distinction between the providential and redemptive realms of divine rule is crucial in decisions about a believer's responsibilities to all human beings and especially to other Christians (Gal. 6:10).

8. Spiritual-institutional theology *provides the theological foundation for both personal and social ethics*. On one hand, much theology has targeted almost exclusively individual justification and personal ethics. Worthy aspects of these concerns are integrated in the "spiritual" designation of this theology. On the other hand, many recent theologies have focused almost exclusively on structural evil, social justice, and liberation from oppression. Worthy aspects of these concerns are integrated in the "structural" expression of this theology. Authentic personal spirituality is necessary to beneficial social structures, and healthy social structures exist to strengthen, not eradicate, personal growth. The individual and collective purposes are mutually enriching. From the infrastructure of this multiplex theology one can develop both Christian personal ethics and Christian social ethics.

9. Finally, spiritual-institutional theology *holds the inner spiritual and outer structural realities together* in this life. The relation of the spiritual to the structural (in the institutions of the family, Israel, and the church) is analogous to the relationship of the spirit to the body in temporal human life. Soul

and body are two interacting entities necessary to the one life in space and time. Similarly, the spiritual and institutional realities are indispensable interacting entities in these historical institutions. Moral and spiritual issues have priority and ought to guide uses of institutional power in the kingdom. They ought not become independent of each other. On one hand, when institutional power becomes unconstrained by moral and spiritual realities, its operations become tragically unjust and fruitless. On the other hand, when mystical aspirations uproot one from accountable fellowship and ministry with others in a church, God's rule on earth is not realized as it is in heaven.

APOLOGETIC INTERACTION

The god of Plato anticipated some forms of things in the shadow world but provided few purposes for persons and communities in history. In contrast, the God of the Bible who created people according to a prior plan had significant personal and communal purposes for them in his rule of history. How do these purposes work out in space and time among God's people from the standpoint of spiritual-institutional theology?

The Redemptive Kingdom Is Primarily, But Not Exclusively, Spiritual

Is God's redemptive rule at present limited to the *changed hearts of the regenerate and their inner relationship to God?* Harold Hoehner, responding to theonomists, said, "I just cannot buy their basic presupposition that we can do anything significant to change the world. And you can waste an awful lot of time trying."[143] Hoehner suggested that our time would be better spent on evangelism. That view of some dispensationalists correctly emphasizes the priority of the spiritual nature of the realm one enters by the new birth. But it does not follow that God's redemptive kingdom is exclusively spiritual. "Dispensationalists," said Mennonite Thomas Finger, "from my point of view are far too spiritualist."[144] Finger might have said more accurately that some dispensationalists view the redemptive kingdom as too exclusively spiritual.

Eastern mysticism also makes God's work in the world independent of matter and the body. Advocates often cite out of context Jesus' saying, "the kingdom of God is within you" (Luke 17:21). Editors of *The New Age Journal* write, "Each of the major mystical systems has its own way of expressing this [pantheistic] idea. The Hindus or Vedantists say that the Atman, or immanent eternal Self, is one with Brahman. Christians might say, 'The kingdom of God is within you.' Buddhists sometimes say, 'You are Buddha.' "[145] Jesus' statement does not limit the kingdom to the heart nor teach that all are divine. Rather it affirms that God's rule had come near and was in the midst of his people. Jesus made a radical distinction between the Father above and all else beneath, and for entry into God's kingdom he requires regeneration.

McClain, a dispensationalist, argued that the kingdom is *basically spiritual but not reductively so.* He reasoned, "Whenever and wherever we find God establishing a direct and personal relationship between Himself and other personalities, whether as individuals or as a group, regardless of the place or conditions, such a relationship must be regarded as basically *spiritual* in nature."[146] Foundational to the kingdom is relationship with God. But "we must understand that such a spiritual relation and control is not inconsistent with considerations which are mundane and material in character."[147] He added, "From its beginning at Sinai the historic kingdom of Israel was truly an 'organized system of government' with a definite polity, both internally and externally."[148] McClain then explored ways in which the basically spiritual kingdom under the first covenant manifests itself politically, economically, religiously and physically.[149]

McClain averred that "the Kingdom of God is primarily a spiritual kingdom, always, and wherever it exists. But a spiritual kingdom in biblical parlance can manifest itself and produce tangible effects in a physical world; or to be more precise, in the world of sense experience."[150] McClain's view rejects, among other things, a merely earthly program for Israel. "It should hardly be necessary to point out that, in the Word of God, it is nothing new to find a *spiritual cause* producing tangible effects in the area of sense experience. On this point the personal testimony of the late Ananias and his wife Sapphira would be very impressive. . . . They learned by bitter experience that a *spiritual* force can operate in the *physical* world."[151] Thus the primary biblical contrast is not between the material and the spiritual, but between two inner inclinations toward good and evil.

At all periods of history spiritual agents have made a difference in the observable world. The deepest dynamic in history is not economic, structural, or sexual but spiritual. God's image-bearers, however, express themselves for good or evil through their bodies in all kinds of relationships in the family and in society. Physical acts are not unreal or indifferent (*adiaphora*) but express one's ultimate loyalties either to the kingdom of light or the kingdom of darkness. The evil tree brings forth evil fruit. The good tree bears good fruit in relationships with others in their families and churches, their places of employment, and their nations.

Jesus demonstrated the outer effects of his kingdom's power. The victorious power of Jesus over Satan in the temptations (Matt. 4:1–11), the miraculous works done to deliver individuals from illness and death (Matt. 12:28), the proclamation of the good news which resulted in fruitfulness (Matt. 13:1–2) were all illustrations of the powers of the kingdom at work in the world, and looked forward to the consummation of that divine purpose for which Jesus prayed—"your kingdom come, your will be done on earth as it is in heaven" (Matt. 6:10). The powers to be expressed in the future eschatological kingdom entered into history in the person and work of Jesus in order to work toward its realization.[152]

The Redemptive Kingdom Is Present, Not Merely Future

According to classical dispensationalism, Jesus Christ offered a global, political kingdom that was rejected and postponed until his return. A future consummation of the redemptive kingdom fits a number of passages teaching that the saints will reign and rule with him (Luke 22:29–30; 1 Cor. 6:2–3; 2 Tim. 2:11–12; Rev. 5:10). But the hypothesis that the redemptive reign was postponed and is exclusively future does not cohere well with the biblical data concerning Christ's present rule. Christ did offer his rule first to the lost sheep of Israel (Matt. 10:5–6), and most did not receive him (John 1:11). But that does not mean that the kingdom in its entirety was postponed until his second advent. William Foster explains, "The consummation of the kingdom purpose is indeed associated with the second advent, but the concept of postponement does not seem to be appropriate in light of abundant evidence of the continuing proclamation and presence of the kingdom in some particular sense."[153]

Jesus said, not only, "I tell you that the kingdom of God will be taken from you," but also that it would be "given to a people who will produce its fruit" (Matt. 21:43). So Jesus referred to the present age as "the times of the Gentiles" (Luke 21:24), and Paul observed that Israel has experienced a hardening in part until the full number of Gentiles has come in" (Rom. 11:25). The present kingdom is not exclusively Gentile, however, as Craig Blomberg shows:

> In retrospect, and in light of the use of the term elsewhere, it is easy to assume that the *ethnos* (a "people" or "nation") . . . was exclusively Gentiles, but the context nowhere demands this assumption. The New Testament regularly conceives of the community of God's people who produce "good fruit" as a combination of Jewish and Gentile followers of Jesus. Even the most universalist text in Matthew's Gospel, the Great Commission (Matt. 28:18–20), with its call to preach to all the *ethne* ("nations"), does not exclude the Jews from its purview. . . . In essence, Matthew highlights what Paul would later encapsulate in the formula: "to the Jew first and also to the Greek."[154]

The future aspects of the kingdom do not preclude its present aspects. John the Baptist announced that God's rule was near (Matt. 3:1) and required personal repentance. By driving out evil spirits Christ demonstrated that his kingdom had come (Matt. 12:28). After his triumphant resurrection, Jesus spoke of the kingdom (Acts 1:3) and told his disciples of their Pentecostal endowment with power to become his witnesses, not just in Israel but to the ends of the earth (vv. 6–8). God's Spirit now reigns in any life personally related to God and seeking to become morally like the Holy One.

The present redemptive kingdom is entered by new birth from above (John 3:3–7). Its ethics are set forth in the Sermon on the Mount (Matt. 5–7), and its "secrets" are disclosed in the Messiah's parables (13:11, 16–17). The one who is least in the present age of the kingdom is greater than John the Baptist in the previous age (11:11). But the greatest in the kingdom enters with the humility of a child (18:1–4). Regenerate members of the redemptive kingdom now exercise their dominion by overcoming the tempting powers from their own evil nature, the fallen world system, and the spiritual forces of evil. The kingdom, as R. E. O. White maintains, requires spiritual individuals, but is not individualistic, and it calls for historic and contemporary continuity with other agents of the King.[155]

We note that Philip preached the Good News of the kingdom of God (Acts 8:12). Paul wrote that Christ "has rescued us from the dominion of darkness and brought us into the kingdom of the Son he loves" (Col. 1:13). To the church at Rome Paul explained that "the kingdom of God is not a matter of eating and drinking, but of righteousness, peace and joy in the Holy Spirit" (Rom 14:17). Throughout the course of his ministry Paul preached the kingdom of God (Acts 19:8; 20:25; 28:23, 31).[156] Merrill Tenney rightly argued,

> Since the new birth relates to the present state of believers, the kingdom must also have a present existence. Its fundamental character is spiritual; it is not primarily a social or a political organization. Essentially it consists of regenerate disciples of Christ, though the sphere of sovereignty may extend beyond their number. It is the nucleus of those who have pledged complete allegiance to Christ in this world, and on whom he can depend for support in the exercise of His authority.[157]

Although the total redemption of the body and nature is future (Rom. 8:21–23), the Savior is also redemptively at work in creation in the present. The Messianic kingdom that will be consummated in the future was inaugurated at the suffering Messiah's first advent and holds dominion over believers here and now!

Our Task Is Not to Reconstruct Nations After the Image of Israel (Reconstructionists, Theonomists)

Reconstructionists insist that Christians must impose the Old Testament law across the spectrum of religious and civil authority. As a result of this action it is alleged that the majority of peoples will be converted and governments will be restructured according to the Old Testament pattern. This allegedly will produce the rule of divine law (a theonomy) in which the kingdom of God will prevail on earth. According to Greg Bahnsen:

> Central to the theory and practice of ethics, whether personal or social, is every jot and tittle of God's law as laid down in the revelation of the Older and New Testaments. The Christian is obligated to keep the whole law of God as a pattern of sanctification, and in the realm of human society the civil magistrate is responsible to enforce God's law against public crime.[158]

Certain points of agreement with reconstructionism could be enumerated, but it is difficult to concur with its overall agenda in several important respects. Does God command Christians to *impose* Old Testament civil legislation uniformly on the unsaved? Will a majority in every nation become Christians and so achieve the dominion of theistic principles in the spheres of education, communication, and the arts? Will the imposition of biblical law bring world peace and justice and extend the human life span? The belief that the church should work to produce an Old Testament type of theonomy encounters numerous difficulties:

1. *Theonomy does not adequately distinguish God's kingdom from the nation-state of Israel.* The kingdom is broader than the family, Israel, or the church. With all its legislation, Israel was a unique instrument of the kingdom under the old covenant, but not the ideal for all times except as it exhibits principles universally revealed. The uniquely chosen nation (Deut. 7:7–9) served special purposes in preparation for the Messiah's first advent. But that does not make it the paradigm for other political institutions in which religion and state are distinct. Gary DeMar said, "I challenge those who don't believe [Old Testament laws] apply anymore to provide a good hermeneutical model that explains why."[159] One answer is that in God's present redemptive kingdom the political institution of Israel has been replaced by churches whose polity is distinct from any one ethnic people or national government.

2. *"Law" in Scripture does not always imply the entirety of Old and New Testament legislation.* Law may mean the Ten Commandments (Exod. 20:2–17), the Book of the Covenant (Exod. 20–24), all the laws of Exodus and Leviticus, the entire Pentateuch (Luke 24:44), or all three sections of the Hebrew Old Testament (John 10:34–35). Churches may learn principles from the Old Testament disclosure of God's unique purposes for the Jewish nation at any given time, but the explicit outworking of God's moral law for the church age is found in the teachings of Christ and his apostles. Although every jot and tittle of the Old Testament is inspired truth, not all the laws God commanded for the nation Israel are required of nations or churches today. Just as Israel's ceremonial laws and priesthood were terminated by Christ (in that they failed to pass through the "grid" of his teaching), so its institutional laws were abrogated by the formation of the transnational church at Pentecost.

3. *Theonomy gives inadequate place to the motive of love in law keeping.*

351

The Pharisees "kept the law" but infuriated our Lord because they missed its foundational driving force—love for God and others. Only two allusions to motivation can be found in more than six hundred pages of Bahnsen's *Theonomy in Christian Ethics*. The section "Love and Law" claims that love is inseparable from law and, indeed, is "*identical* with lawful obedience."[160] Love fulfills the law, but it is not a synonym for keeping it. Love involves at least the desire and determination to act morally for God's glory and others' well-being. Apart from the primacy of self-giving love, the best moralizing efforts are doomed to fail (Matt. 22:37–40; 1 Cor. 13:1–3).

4. If any nation were to become predominantly Christian, *it would be unwise to try to enforce all of Israel's Old Testament laws today*. What present "Christian" nation would require capital punishment for a rebellious son (Deut. 21:18–21), for witchcraft (Exod. 22:18), bestiality (Exod. 22:19), adultery (Lev. 20:10), homosexuality (v. 13), or blasphemy (24:16)? Theonomy gives permanent value to arrangements designed for a particular national institution with a distinctive mission during the period prior to Messiah's advent. If Christians do not want distinctively Hindu, Buddhist, or Islamic beliefs and practices required of them in countries where these religions are dominant, Christians should not seek a state-church patterned after ancient Israel.

5. *Reconstructionism misinterprets God's command to exercise dominion.* God commanded Adam and Eve before there was a nation to subdue the earth and "rule over . . . every living creature that moves on the ground" (Gen. 1:28). The context of the chapter applies the command explicitly to managing plants, fish, birds, and land animals. This mandate provides a basis for people to serve as God's stewards in areas of ecology, agriculture, and animal husbandry. In its historical setting prior to the birth of other humans, dominion over the "earth" did not explicitly signify ruling over people politically.

6. *The means of attaining reconstructionists' objectives may become coercive.* Most would try to accomplish their goals by ethical persuasion and revival, but some would resort, if necessary, to revolutionary coercion (Gary North). Following the Old Testament paradigm, it would appear consistent for postmillennial reconstructionists to use arms to overthrow a corrupt nation. Others would resort to civil disobedience, not armed revolt, if God's law were violated. But the fact is that God's redemptive kingdom is not something *imposed* upon persons or minorities. "The crucial question," Ron Sider observes, "is one of *methodology,* of how to translate biblical truths to public policy prescriptions."[161] The best of legislative strategies and methods must be developed in harmony with God's purposes for political institutions in the present age. Spirit-enabled Christians need to correct social injustices without blurring the distinction between the church and Israel or the world of unbelievers.

7. *Christians ought not identify God's redemptive kingdom with a political party* any more than with a nation. As important as government is in the providential realm of the kingdom, it is not wise to identify God's redemptive kingdom with a political party. Even if the political party were made up of believers only, they would subscribe to more than one political strategy. The fact that we cannot identify Christ's redemptive rule with any political organization, however, ought not mean noninvolvement in the moral issues of our culture. The contribution of our individual voices, parties, and denominations should play an important part providentially. With their varied per-

sonalities, gifts, and expertise, Christians will pray and work across social and political structures for the ends of basic morality and world peace (1 Tim. 2:1–4).

Christ's Kingdom Is Not to Be Identified With a Global Government

The ability to receive pictures and sounds from satellites in space brings global issues to every television set. Vivid images of planetary crises lead people to contemplate a single world community. The unimaginable horror of nuclear weaponry in many countries increases the sense of urgency for one world government. Mark Satin's *New Age Politics* considers peace possible only if we break out of the "prison" of nationalism.[162] Among larger nations, nationalism encourages chauvinism, he thinks, and among smaller nations, feelings of inferiority. So the nation-state system inevitably leads to war. Satin's prescription for the illness of nationalism is a planetary consciousness of the oneness and interdependence of all of life. He advocates complete military disarmament and a decentralization of each nation. Furthermore, all individuals should give up their national citizenships and become world citizens.

Karl Marx's dream of a global government of the people proved unrealistic. Peace, Marx thought, could be attained only in an economically classless society when the last vestiges of capitalism had been eradicated from the earth. History painfully showed, however, that the dictatorship itself was affected by depravity (enjoying certain capitalist advantages). The "temporary" dictatorship did not foster liberty and would not wither away. So people overthrew the communist dictatorships of eastern Europe and the Soviet Union in 1989 and 1990.

No more should the union of world religions with a global government be identified with the kingdom of God. In our day we confront Hindu pantheistic and occult movements, such as the Maharishi Mahesh Yogi's World Plan. Full page ads in papers and magazines invited government leaders to bring their problems to the Maharishi for solutions. How would he accomplish this? According to the "Governor of the Age of Enlightenment" at the Denver TM Center, the great teacher would invite hundreds of faithful Transcendental Meditators to surround government offices. The effect of the vibrations of their mantras would solve the world's social, political, and ecological problems. Having targeted New York City and Washington, D.C., their meditative vibrations have admittedly not made a noticeable difference.

No syncretism of world religious and economic powers will bring a lasting and just peace to the globe. The Lord Jesus Christ said, "My kingdom is not of this world" (John 18:36 KJV). God's kingdom in the present age is no more to be identified with a union of nations than with a single political party or a church. Although Christ knew the human tendency to make idols of government leaders, Christ did not ask his followers to give up their national citizenships. The variety of nations in a fallen world serves as a check and balance on each other's pretensions to power over others. If some kind of global democracy could be structured with adequate checks and balances, ideally it might be advantageous. But even with such assurances a worldwide democracy would not produce a just and lasting peace.

Spiritual-Institutional Theology and Covenant Theology

We now undertake a brief summation of the deficiencies of the major single-theme theologies. Covenant theology in general stresses similarities between

Old Testament Israel and the church while minimizing differences. Spiritual-institutional theology seeks to do justice to both similarities and differences. The latter recognizes spiritual similarities based on the one covenant of grace but does not assume that spiritual oneness implies *institutional oneness*. The covenant theologian's hypothesis of "two dispensations or administrations, namely, that of the Old, and that of the New Testament"[163] (with different "stages" in the Old Testament) does not as explicitly account for the structural differences between the Jewish nation and the church. The spiritual oneness of God's people in all times does not of itself justify inferences from the polity of a nation to the government of a church, nor from the rite of circumcising infants in Israel to the baptism of infants in a church. Given the differences between Israel and the church, inferences from the polity and practices of Israel to the polity and practices of the church are illicit. An adequate theology (1) must not confuse spiritual and institutional categories and (2) must account not only for similarities but also for differences.

Spiritual-Institutional Theology and Promise Theology

Our assessment of promise theology is similar to that of covenant theology because God's promises are so closely related to his covenants. In making a promise one gives one's word to another; in making a covenant two or more people give their word on a given matter to each other. Promise theologian Walter Kaiser, in his book *Toward an Old Testament Theology*, appeals to covenants as well as promises.[164] Both covenant and promise schools of thought emphasize the promises to Abraham with their Old Testament reaffirmations and New Testament fulfillments. Continuities are noted as well as the fact that there are some new features.[165] Kaiser helpfully contends,

> Paul's claim is that Gentile believers have been "grafted into" the Jewish olive tree (Rom. 11:17–25) and made "fellow heirs of the same body and partakers of his *promise* in Christ by the gospel" (Eph. 3:6). Since "salvation is of the Jews" (John 4:22), and since there is only one fold (John 10:16), it should not be too surprising to see that NT writers add to the emerging theses of the OT that there was just one people of God and one program of God even though there are several aspects to that single people and single program.[166]

Promise theology well emphasizes the spiritual continuity of the one olive tree, but it does not as adequately explain how its two branches are distinct.

In a chapter entitled "Kingdom Promises as Spiritual and National,"[167] Kaiser finds that "it is this national and spiritual kingdom, then, about which our Lord came preaching (Mark 1:14–15). It is the same kingdom which Paul proclaimed and associated with the 'gospel of God's grace' or 'the whole will [plan, counsel] of God' (Acts 20:24–27). Herein lies the Bible's own claim to its line of continuity."[168] Kaiser does not agree that there are two offers of the kingdom; rather, he sees one purpose of God for history and one kingdom with different aspects. Kaiser does not adequately define "aspect" in this context.

We concur that the kingdom theme is just one model of the all-embracing plan God promised—a plan encompassing both the *material land* and *spiritual blessings* (Gen. 12:3; Gal. 3:8).[169] By not heeding the offers of John the Baptist and Jesus, the Jews missed their priority on the internal feature of the kingdom of God.[170] But Christ also came to build the church as the distinctive institution through which he would accomplish his collective purposes in the present age. Our emphasis on the social structure of the church in the present age is consistent with Kaiser's thought. But the church's social structure does not appear to have received sufficient emphasis in promise theology.

Spiritual-Institutional Theology and Kingdom Theology

We agree with much in George Eldon Ladd's view of the *redemptive kingdom* as the dynamic rule of God, as follows: (1) The kingdom is not the church but is God's redemptive rule in human hearts before and after the church. (2) The kingdom creates the church. (3) The apostles preached the kingdom (not the church), and people entered the kingdom by the new birth. (4) The kingdom works through the church. The disciples preached the kingdom and displayed the power of its "keys," thereby binding people or loosing them from their sins. "The Kingdom is God's reign and the realm in which the blessings of his reign are experienced; the church is the fellowship of those who have experienced God's reign and entered into the enjoyment of its blessings."[171] Spiritual-institutional theology would make similar points concerning *institutional Israel*. Thus (1) Israel was not the kingdom, (2) the kingdom created Israel, (3) Israel witnessed to the kingdom, and (4) Israel was the instrument of the kingdom. Moreover, similar points may be made of the earlier *godly families:* (1) The households of faith were not the kingdom, (2) the kingdom created the families, and (3) godly families witnessed to the kingdom and were instruments of the kingdom.

Kingdom theology helpfully features the one people of God in all times, but it is not as clear on the distinction between Israel and the church. How does kingdom theology differentiate Israel from the church? God's reign is said to express itself in "different stages."[172]

Exactly what denotes a stage? What marks its beginning and end? Until "stage" is defined, it is too vague to classify periods of history adequately. We need to know more specifically what a stage is to distinguish "two stages in the single redemptive purpose of God."[173] Moreover, Ladd overstated the lack of evidence for an organized church. He wrote, "In any case, the idea that the unity of the church found expression in some kind of external organization or ecclesiastical structure finds *no support in the New Testament*"[174] (italics added). Ladd himself contradicted this statement both before and following it. Just before, he had noted some organization at Jerusalem: "The final decision was made by the 'apostles and the elders, with the whole church' (Acts 15:22ff.)."[175] Ladd also failed to see the implications in Acts of gathering elders, sending missionaries, taking offerings, and writing official letters. Ladd admitted, "The organization of the church appears in clearer outline in the pastoral epistles. . . . Both the qualifications and duties of elders are set forth in 1 Timothy 5:17–22. They exercise a threefold function: ruling, preaching, and teaching."[176] We acknowledge that the New Testament does not spell out church polity in detail, but we do find evidence of two offices in each church to indicate that it was organized to carry out its many God-ordained purposes.

Ladd did not provide a comprehensive (connotative) definition of the church. He referred to a "fellowship" of Christians[177] and "groups of believers,"[178] and "a meeting of Christians for worship."[179] Such designations without the necessary offices, however, are too broad, for they would qualify any collection of Christian youth or business people as a church. A church is more than a fellowship in a group or meeting; it is also an institution distinc-

355

tively organized to serve its multiple goals.

Spiritual-Institutional Theology and Dispensational Theology

Dispensationalists properly criticize covenant theologies for claiming that the church completely fulfills the Old Testament institutional promises to Israel. How and when does the church take over the realm of Caesar? The church, Robert Saucy argues, "has been unable to consistently live out a theology in which it makes claim to Israel's position."[180] Saucy well emphasizes the fact that God now works with all nations, not just one nation. He notes that the church differs from Israel as multinational.[181] In the present age the church is the heir of the promises to Israel spiritually in reaching non-Jews from all nations, but it is not the heir *materially* (e.g., of the land or the capital city).

Dispensationalists call for a "sharp" distinction between Israel and the church, but they fail to produce one. The church and Israel are both composed of sinners saved by grace and so are not distinct peoples spiritually with different eternal destinies.[182] Dispensational distinctions have to do with stewardships in history. A parenthetical view of the church in relation to God's redemptive program with Israel reflects an inadequate view of the overarching redemptive plan to include the spiritual unity of Jew and Gentile in the one kingdom. From eternity the Father foreknew in what respects Christ's teaching on the kingdom would be rejected. And from eternity God planned for the formation of a multi-ethnic community. That plan envisioned not only one people of God in one kingdom but also the social structure of the church. Its organization may have been a mystery to people prior to its revelation by Paul, but it is as much

God's purpose for this age as the nation was for the previous age. Although he acknowledged the same salvation by grace through faith, in his book *Dispensationalism Today* Ryrie needs to give a clearer account of the respect in which the church differs from Israel and the purpose of the church in the present and future.[183]

Saucy helpfully perceives Israel and the church as two outworkings of God's plan for the redemptive kingdom. The church is not merely an extension of Israel, nor is Israel incorporated into the church. Neither is the church parenthetical. Rather, each is "an integrated phase of the mediatorial kingdom."[184] We are left wondering, however, what specifically demarcates these "phases." Saucy writes, "The broad outline portrayed in Scripture suggests that there is no basis for a reductionist interpretation which levels Israel and the church in a total continuity. Rather, the picture is one of the basic unity of the people of God, yet with functional distinction in the historical outworking of the salvation of God's kingdom."[185] Distinctive "functions," however, are determined by one's place in an organization, and because dispensationalists do not spell out the distinct offices as institutions, the reasons for the "phases" and "functional" divergences are not clear.

We also find dispensationalists' definition of a dispensation lacking in precision. "God's way of dealing with man" (Scofield I) was so general any historical change in God's activity could have constituted a dispensation. The definition of Scofield II is little better. "A dispensation is a period of time during which man is tested in respect to his obedience to some specific revelation of the will of God."[186] In his omniscience God foreknew that depraved humans would never meet the requirements of such tests. Disobedience and judgment is similar throughout history and not sufficient for clearly classifying distinct periods of history. Several dispensationalists (Charles Ryrie, Robert Saucy, John Feinberg, and Earl Radmacher) have removed the testing-failure-judgment scenario from the headlines.

The principle of "testing humanity by some specific rule of conduct" was difficult to apply. The seven "dispensations" listed in Scofield II (innocence, conscience, human government, promise, law, church, and kingdom) do not test obedience in the way law does. The dispensation of "promise" (to Abraham) tests faith. The dispensation of the "church" does not primarily test obedience. The notes in Scofield II helpfully changed the dispensation of grace to that of the church, but it failed to change the dispensation of law to that of Israel. The major contrasts are not between periods of law and grace or between law and church. Grace is the same in both, and 90 percent of the Ten Commandments are reaffirmed in the New Testament. The relevant contrast is between the two institutions, the nation and the church.

The dispensationalist's principle of classification, furthermore, is too negative in significance to serve as the major integrating concept of biblical revelation. The overarching negative concept in the Bible may be the testing of humanity by some specific rule of conduct, but the outcome of depraved human behavior by any moral standard is easily predicted and confirmed. God's law does show sinners their need for the Savior; but the primary emphasis of redemptive revelation more appropriately should be on the new life that the Messiah provided and the Spirit imparts to sinners both personally and communally.

RELEVANCE FOR LIFE AND MINISTRY

Whenever and wherever problems arise, whether in families, churches, or nations, spiritual-institutional theology is pertinent. But we need not wait for problems to appreciate its amazing relevance preventatively.

Approaches That Render the Institutional Church Dysfunctional

Os Guinness imagines a gravedigger who seeks to neutralize the Western church by subversion from within. He considers ways to inflict damage on Christian institutions. For the gravedigger the issue is not whether Christianity is true, but how to make it seem implausible as an institution disengaged from the public world except for ceremonial formalities. A faith that has withdrawn from central areas of modern society will not be taken seriously, and whatever is left of Christianity in public the gravedigger can either manipulate or mock. So the gravedigger tempts leaders of Christian institutions to withdraw from public life and to restrict religion to the private sphere. If some decide to reenter the public sphere, he convinces them to do it in the wrong ways, such as following media stars, appealing to masses of consumers, or building monuments to parachurch structures whose leaders have moved on. Copying cultural institutions, leaders put local churches, not themselves, out of a job.[187]

How can Christians avoid the first error of *withdrawing from the public sphere?* We overcome privatism by intentionally supporting the values of God's providential and redemptive kingdoms in our families, churches, and country. Guided by insights from spiritual-institutional theology, Christian activists will focus their agendas not merely on media-identified issues but on the classically relevant family, church, and national institutions. Christian social ethics may dispense with other social structures in the present age, but not these. Admittedly many tragically abuse these God-given institutions and hurt people they ought to help. Antifamily and antichurch movements today call for entirely new paradigms, but they have yet to come up with better ones. What needs radical changing today is *people,* including husbands, pastor-manager-elders, and national leaders. The foundational elements of the family, church, and nation ought not be altered, though in their means of functioning they need to keep abreast of the times.

How can Christian activists avoid Guinness's second error of *engaging social issues in unethical ways?* By common grace the most reticent among us can overcome the weaknesses of our fleshly natures and fulfill God's will on earth in our families and nations. And by special grace we can fulfill the mandates of redemptive mercy and grace revealed in special revelation in our families and churches. Christian social activists today, like God's people in all ages, adhere to uncompromising justice and self-giving love in all relationships, not only spiritually but also institutionally. We live by our Lord's teaching and example. The following sections contain further elaborations of these issues.

Prize the Spiritual Values of the Messiah's Kingdom

Christ came as the "King" of the Jews, and in fulfillment of predictions concerning the Davidic dynasty he spoke frequently of the kingdom (in the Gospels). Paul referred to the kingdom occasionally, but he more often spoke of Christ as the Lord of all (in his epistles). Paul's frequent references in non-Jewish cultures to Jesus as Lord are equivalent in connotation to those among Jews to Jesus as King.

Having entered God's kingdom by regeneration, we display *loyalty to its virtues* as summed up in the Sermon on the Mount. Whatever our view of the future, we are not pessimistic regarding the powers of Holy Spirit-enriched salt and light in the present tasteless, dark world (Matt. 5:13–16). It is encouraging that most dispensationalists now view the Sermon on the Mount as applicable to Jesus' day and throughout the present age.[188] In this discourse Jesus declared, "Unless your righteousness surpasses that of the Pharisees and teachers of the law, you will certainly not enter the kingdom of heaven" (Matt. 5:20). This means more than legalistic righteousness in our relationships with others (or our social ethics). Followers of Jesus avoid even the thought of murder and adultery. They shun divorce, oaths, vengeance, judgment of others, worry, and laying up treasures on earth. Instead, they love their enemies, give to the needy, pray meaningfully, fast, accumulate treasure in heaven, and wisely build their lives on the solid foundation of all Jesus' teachings (Matt. 5:21–7:29).

Christians who would make a difference in the world also practice the principles presented in Jesus' parables of the kingdom. Saints learn from the parables the kingdom's inestimable value and that gaining it is worth sacrificing everything (Matt. 13:44–46). Summing up the teaching of the parables, Blomberg adds,

> The citizens of the kingdom persevere in prayer, boldly requesting the speedy completion of God's kingdom building activity (Lk 11:5–8; 18:1–8). They avoid the idolatry of materialism, while using money shrewdly (Lk 12:13–21; 16:1–31) and counting the cost of discipleship (Lk 14:28–33). Failure to obey key commands of God, finally, may lead to the forfeiture of temporal privileges of leadership in the kingdom (Lk 13:6–9; Mk 12:1–9 pars; Lk 14:16–24).[189]

The values Christ taught in his parables are eminently important, not only for individuals but also for the permanent relationships of family and church.

Social activists ought not lose the "keys to the kingdom" that Jesus delegated to his followers (Matt. 16:19). So his Spirit-endued ambassadors have authority on earth to forgive sins, deliver the repentant from the dominion of darkness, and make disciples of unreached peoples everywhere. The one to whom cosmic authority has been given did not intend, as Karl Barth said, to found "a pious little Jewish club."[190] All efforts of preevangelism and evangelism of unconverted people everywhere constitute missions. Let no Christian use social concern as an excuse for evading responsibility to implement the Great Commission. The call to new birth from above is the key that opens the door to a spiritual life characterized by kingdom ethics.

The unfortunate dichotomy often imagined between preaching the Gospel and meeting temporal needs is illustrated by a criticism of Luis Palau's evangelism in Latin America. Since Palau did not publicly criticize institutionalized sin, some thought that he fully supported existing social structures.[191] Palau's Evangelistic Association published the following helpful response:

> It should be noted that Luis Palau grew up in South America and personally lived in poverty. He has seen—and felt—the results of injustice. As a young man, he dreamed about becoming a lawyer and defending the poor and oppressed, but became disillusioned with that dream after recognizing what little direct influence he could have on people's lives as a lawyer. Later, Luis became convinced that evangelism is the deepest, most profound and most important social action in the world.[192]

Palau added, "What we have found is that the typical Latin American effectively doubles his income by embracing the Gospel and rejecting gambling, alcoholism and immoral relationships. The Gospel transforms both rich and poor alike and especially benefits the poor in the here and now."[193] The task of building spiritual values in God's kingdom begins but does not end with the new birth.

Magnify Kingdom Values in Your Household

As an agent of God's kingdom, treasure spiritual values in your household. Family values are kingdom values. A family begins with a husband and wife and is enlarged by children. "In the OT family relationships are concentric, that is the married couple—husband and wife—form the nucleus of the circle, the children lie in the next circle, the grandparents, cousins, and the like on a further circle."[194] Partnerships of homosexuals are not a legitimate form of marriage. People support family values by opposing casual sex, out-of-wedlock births, abortion on demand, and recreational drug use. If God has given you a spouse and children, incorporate in your family the values of both the providential and redemptive realms of the kingdom.

Tragic consequences follow the loss of fidelity to the family. All eight young men arrested for the serial rape of a Central Park (New York City) jogger in 1990 came from broken homes. A perceptive observer of American culture, Bill Moyers, concludes, "The demise of our family life is the largest challenge facing our society, financially and emotionally. But I don't see the problem given any priority on local or national levels."[195] The growing crime rate in America, particularly among young people in fatherless households, led the secretary of Health and Human Services to issue an urgent plea to shore up the family, "the first transmitter of the habits and values that sustain communities."[196]

God gave parents the final responsibility for their children's *vocational training*. Our first parents' task of gaining dominion over the earth involved training their household to work for the good of the home. Christian parents should take final responsibility for preparing their children for productive work. The basics of God's plan for labor and management flow from the nature of creation in the divine image and the environmental commission to rule nature (Gen. 1:28–31). The New Testament develops the importance of respect for God's image-bearers in labor relationships: "Slaves, submit yourselves to your masters with all respect, not only to those who are good and considerate, but also to those who are harsh" (1 Peter 2:18; cf. Eph. 6:5–9; Col. 3:22–4:1).

God also entrusted to parents the final responsibility for their children's *moral and spiritual education*. God chose Abraham to "direct his children and his household after him to keep the way of the LORD by doing what is right and just" (Gen. 18:19). The Lord commanded Moses to teach his children spiritual truths (Exod. 10:2). Fathers as well as mothers were to teach their offspring the ways of God (Prov. 1:8; 6:20). Parents began to teach them at an early age (Prov. 22:6; Isa. 28:9) when moral patterns are formed. Growing children should grasp the outlines of a theistic worldview and an ethical way of life. Because God revealed himself in mighty acts, Christians teach their children biblical history that illustrates moral and doctrinal principles. Succeeding generations ought not to forget the fulfilled promises, exemplary prayers, and spiritually significant events that brought God's people to their present situation.

The distinctive *goal* of Christian education needs to be clear. It is not the obliteration of the individual in the service of the state (as in Sparta), nor the service of the culture (as in Athens), nor devotion to the state (as in Rome).[197] It is not socialization to relativistic community standards (as in contemporary humanism), nor divinization (as in pantheism). In the Old Testament holy love was the primary aim, not self-interest (Exod. 19:6). The aim of parents in God's kingdom is to train each child to believe the covenant-maker's messianic promises, love the Father and the Son, and think and act with moral responsibility in the family, church, and nation.

Those with *extended families* have additional responsibilities to strengthen the values of more distant relatives. Christians ought to do more than the heathen do; they should love and forgive relatives even when they seem to be adversaries. Care enough to write, telephone, and meet with all your relatives as far as possible. Principles of fairness and love apply beyond the immediate family. Singles and couples should plan and participate in family reunions and other meaningful times together. Family gatherings ought to include a time for relating one's spiritual experiences. A newsletter may help people keep in touch on occasions of graduations, weddings, births, promotions, and career changes.[198]

Champion Kingdom Values in and Through Your Church

We misread the Gospel if we think it the way to a nonrelational salvation. Rather, as Hauerwas argues, it is "the good news of the creation of a new community of peace and justice formed by hope that God's kingdom has and will prevail."[199] God's kingdom produces more than loosely knit people groups. "Those who attempt to establish authentic Christian corporate life in the midst of a technological society must recognize two fundamental aspects of the Christian communal lifestyle: Christian personal relationship within Christian social structures."[200]

Church membership calls for a dynamic ethical character exhibited in Spirit-enabled conduct. Christians seek justice based on truth not on violence. "Because Christian community is founded solely on Jesus Christ, it is a spiritual and not a psychic reality. In this it differs absolutely from all other communities."[201] We need not become total pacifists to appreciate the reminder of Hauerwas: "The church must learn time and again that its task is not to *make* the world the kingdom, but to be faithful to the kingdom by showing to the world what it means to be a community of peace."[202]

Church members should not let the world set their agenda by replacing theological imperatives with ideological causes. Is it not unwise, some ask, to criticize theologically an Operation Rescue or an exit counseling program that appears to be working? But Myers observes that this allows ideology to replace theology and the pursuit of power to eclipse truth.[203] Because evangelical subculture tends to be more concerned with doing than knowing, the world mistakes it for more than an interest group intent on seizing political power. "The problem is not so much the specifics of this or that political agenda, but with the subversion of theology by any ideology that eclipses the Christian witness."[204] The death of Christendom does not mean the death of those churches that are essentially spiritual and well-organized institutions.

A Christian approach to social structures differs from both a traditionalist [formal] approach and a socialist approach. The body of Christ is intended to be a diverse people of committed love, structured as a relational grouping according to the principle of equal care.[205] The caring of this community is led by qualified elders assisted by dea-cons and deaconesses to equip other members to serve one another and the destitute. The potential of believing men and women trained by qualified leaders as agents of change for God's kingdom has yet to be plumbed in many churches. Informed efforts for global justice will not abandon the biblically given structure of the servant church. In the present age the church takes preeminence over any national or international institution. The gates of hell have overcome many political powers, but they have not yet destroyed the church. "Thanks be to God! He gives us the victory through the Lord Jesus Christ. Therefore, my dear brothers, stand firm" (1 Cor. 15:57–58).

Churches do well to celebrate their spiritual unity with Israel. In God's spiritual kingdom we have discovered a century-spanning unity with the believing children of Abraham in the covenant promises concerning the Messiah. Although churches are institutionally distinct from national Israel, they are enriched by recalling Israel's great spiritual victories. Kaiser, following North, suggests services celebrating our shared values with the believing in ancient Israel and re-presenting them at the Lord's Supper:

> In the festivals of the Passover, Unleavened Bread, and the Feast of Tabernacles, God's gracious acts in the past (such as His deliverance of Israel from Egypt, His giving the Law on Sinai, His help to Israel in the wilderness) were annually presented as present, contemporaneous happenings which called for a corresponding action of love and service to the God of Israel.[206]

By reliving these great events, church leaders emphasize ancient covenant commitments in the present tense. As Moses said, "You are standing here in order to enter into a covenant with the LORD your God, a covenant the LORD is making with you this day and sealing with an oath" (Deut. 29:12). Rehearse such mighty acts with your children (cf. 6:20–21). Let the entire community feel as the captives did: "The Egyptians mistreated us and made us suffer, putting us to hard labor. Then we cried out to the LORD, the God of our fathers, and the LORD heard our voice and saw our misery, toil and oppression. So the LORD brought us out of Egypt with a mighty hand and an outstretched arm" (26:6–7). When we use our imaginations in this way, Kaiser warns, we should be careful not to elevate our reinterpretation to a level above the written Scriptures. Authority should not be shifted from the Scriptures to the work of dramatic or homiletical interpreters, however moving they may be.[207] It remains true, however, that the covenants and promises of God's Old Testament people are an important context for grasping God's spiritual kingdom under the new covenant.

Christians should strive to ensure that their churches (and parachurch groups) identify and implement kingdom values in their communities of faith. Only so can we effectively counter the forces of secularism, occultism, and hedonism rampant in the land.

Uphold Spiritual (Kingdom) Values in Your City, Province, and Nation

Although God is not now working redemptively through one nation as he did in Israel, Christians serve the providential realm of God's kingdom by taking a responsible role as citizens. By caring for their neighbors, citizens of the spiritual kingdom can do for a community and nation what no government can do. Like the Creator, we need to be pro-life in the broadest sense. We will not impose distinctively evangelical Christian virtues on unbelievers, but we will remind them of the theistic values they know from creation. On the basis of general revelation and common grace we can work together with people of other philosophies and religions for basic morality. We can support any effort to preserve a healthy environment, conserve natural resources, and keep harmful drugs and weapons from children in schools. Such activities as these are not a substitute for witnessing to Christ, but they may produce a climate conducive to presenting the Gospel.

Christians ought to obey their government's laws and leaders insofar as they are agents of universal justice (Rom. 13:1–2; Titus 3:1; 1 Peter 2:13–14). Jesus said, "Give to Caesar what is Caesar's" (Matt. 22:21; cf. Rom. 13:6–7). Such a biblical exhortation is to be understood and applied in a manner consistent with the broader context of God's revealed will. When leaders in power forbid us from preaching the Gospel, we ought to obey God rather than men (Acts 5:29). If antichrists use their political/religious authority like beasts, we will resist them (Rev. 13). "Have nothing to do with the fruitless deeds of darkness, but rather expose them" (Eph. 5:11). Unless we care enough to pray for our leaders (1 Tim. 2:1–3) and take a stand against injustice, we may not live to proclaim the Gospel.

When Hitler's Nazi totalitarianism was on the rise, Charles Colson observed, the clergy in Germany "failed to provide an independent moral voice for the country."[208] Colson continues,

> The church's authority, deeply rooted in the lives of the German people, could not be erased by a simple directive from Berlin. It was the only institution in Germany that offered any enduring or meaningful resistance. But it was not enough. Eventually alone, divided from within, with large numbers of its membership capitulating and even supporting Hitler's schemes, the church failed to hold the state to account. The roots of

World War II were in a sense theological. In England and in Germany, the state and the church failed to fulfill their God-ordained mandates. And whenever that happens, evil triumphs.[209]

Christians in every nation must develop a deep desire for justice like that of the God they value above all else. Biblical teaching is completely clear on this. "The LORD reigns forever. . . . He will govern the peoples with justice" (Ps. 9:7). "Righteousness and justice are the foundation of his throne" (97:2). The servant of the Lord "will not falter or be discouraged till he establishes justice on earth" (42:4). The two-edged sword of justice "brings joy to the righteous but terror to evildoers" (Prov. 21:15). "The righteous care about justice for the poor, but the wicked have no such concern" (29:7). "Woe to those who make unjust laws, to those who issue oppressive decrees, to deprive the poor of their rights and withhold justice from the oppressed of my people, making widows their prey and robbing the fatherless" (Isa. 10:1–2).

Our striving for justice should not be based on the perennial heresy of utopianism. "From time to time the belief spreads among men that it is possible to construct an ideal society. . . . Despite its attractiveness, this is a delirious ideal . . . and its key problems can never be solved by social engineering. . . . The dream—utopia leads to the denial of God and self-divinization—the heresy."[210] The attitude of Christian leaders in conflicts with evil powers is neither naïve optimism nor hopeless pessimism; it is a confident realism. "Human nature being what it is, the Christian witness will be advised always to be a hopeful, prayerful realist rather than a utopian enthusiast."[211] "This is the crucial point. While human politics is based on the premise that society must be changed in order to change people, in the politics of the Kingdom it is the people who must be changed in order to change society."[212]

God's three great institutions exist for people, not people for them. They were designed not to consume persons but to build them up. No one of them is to become an end in itself or an idol. Loyalties to one ought not preclude fulfillment of basic responsibilities to the rest. Each institution needs the others. Families educating children in moral values need the support of their church and nation. And governments can survive only on the basis of virtues transcending their own existence.

DISCUSSION TOPICS

1. Does explicit biblical evidence adequately support the covenant of works–covenant of grace scheme?

2. What was the nature of the kingdom Jesus offered to Israel? Discuss the results of Israel's rejection of that kingdom offer.

3. How would you correlate in a meaningful way the biblical themes of covenant, kingdom, promise, and dispensation within a multiplex scheme?

4. List the similarities and differences between Israel and the church at the spiritual level. What are the implications of this?

5. List the similarities and differences between Israel and the church institutionally or corporately. What implications do you draw from this?

6. Does spiritual-institutional theology integrate more adequately than other single-theme theologies the pertinent biblical data concerning God's redemptive purposes throughout history?

See also the Review Questions and Ministry Projects on pages 501–2.

PART THREE

FUTURE CULMINATION

CHAPTER 7

CHRIST'S SECOND ADVENT AND MILLENNIAL RULE

Christ's Second Advent and Millennial Rule

THE PROBLEM:
HOW SHALL WE UNDERSTAND THE SECOND ADVENT OF CHRIST, THE RAPTURE OF THE CHURCH, AND MESSIAH'S KINGLY REIGN?

The term "eschatology," by definition, connotes the study of last things. Judaism and Christianity, in contrast to Eastern cyclical systems, affirm that history is moving purposefully toward a divinely ordained goal. The two theistic faiths traditionally claim that God will inaugurate a new world order where evil is abolished and righteousness and peace prevail. Christian thought maintains that the whole of theology is eschatological in orientation, hence the importance of this topic. In the present chapter we consider such important issues as the return of Jesus Christ to earth to claim his church, the era of intense trial known as the Tribulation, and the thousand-year period designated the Millennium.

The significance of Christ's second advent is so central that it relates to numerous other topics in Christian theology. We previously learned that the providential Ruler of history (vol. 2, chap. 2) has a purposeful plan for human life and history that cannot be thwarted (vol. 1, chap. 8). Moreover, the resurrection and ascension of Jesus Christ to heaven (vol. 2, chap. 8) provide the basis for a future visitation when God's purposes for human history will be consummated. As Oscar Cullmann has shown, the "decisive battle" won via the Cross and Resurrection ensures "Victory Day" at Christ's second coming.[1] The studies on salvation in the present volume (chaps. 1–4) anticipate the final perfecting of the saints in God's future, heavenly order. The Christian salvation is an eschatological salvation. The study on Israel, the church, and the kingdom (chap. 6) concluded that the rule of God is both present and future. This chapter examines the issues involved in Christ's future coming to reign. Conclusions drawn in chapter 6 concerning the relation between Israel and the church will shed valuable light on key eschatological issues. Finally, the next chapter will examine matters of personal eschatology, such as the intermediate state, resurrection of the body, future judgment, and the destinies of the saved and the unsaved.

Discussion of Christ's coming to reign involve a number of important questions. *How* will Jesus Christ return? Will the Lord come back to earth physically and visibly or spiritually and invisibly? *When* will Christ's second advent occur? Is this event past or present, or will it eventuate in the future? If in the future, could Christ's glorious return to earth occur at any moment? Must any observable signs take place prior to his coming? What shall we say about some well-meaning Christians who set specific dates for the Rapture? Since the apostolic church believed in Christ's imminent return, is the claim of his second coming discredited altogether? And *under what circumstances* will Christ return in the future? How much time will there be between the Rapture and Christ's return to earth (2 Thess. 2:1): a very short time, three and one-half years, or seven years?

Furthermore, what will the future tribulation period be like? Is the Tribulation the time of God's wrath, or the wrath of Satan and the Antichrist, or both? Although not a crucial issue of orthodoxy, will the church be on earth during the Tribulation, or will it be raptured to heaven prior to this unparalleled time of woe? The interpretations of pretribulationists, midtribulationists, and posttribulationists will be evaluated in the light of Scripture. Moreover, what is the nature of the golden era known as the Millennium? Is the millennial reign of Christ primarily present and spiritual or future and material? The perspectives of amillennialists, postmillennnialists, and premillennialists will be carefully considered. What place will national Israel have in Christ's millennial kingdom? Will the Jewish nation be reconstituted as a prominent political entity? Will the Jewish temple worship and sacrificial system be reinstituted? Finally, what are the practical outcomes of Christ's second advent for Christian faith and living? How can this future hope become a present, dynamic reality in the lives of every believer?

ALTERNATIVE PROPOSALS IN THE CHURCH

The issues associated with Christ's return to earth to reign have been widely interpreted in the history of the church, as the following survey shows.

Liberal Denials of Christ's Literal Second Advent

Most liberals claim that Scripture paints no clear and consistent picture of things to come. In any case, what modern people should believe is not the same as what is written in the Bible. Since humans have no certain knowledge of future events, eschatology does not occupy a prominent place in liberal theology. "Theologians of liberal views are brief or apologetic when they reach eschatology."[2] Liberals typically assert that the idea of a personal and bodily return of Christ—the husk of eschatology—arose from crude Jewish apocalypticism and must be set aside. The kernel of the doctrine—the spiritual presence of Christ in the church and the world—is to be retained. Liberals reject a cataclysmic inauguration of the Millennium in favor of the gradual realization of the kingdom of God through evolutionary forces and the power of Jesus' ethical teachings. Thus the outlook of most liberal theologians is secular and optimistic.

W. N. Clarke (d. 1912) claimed that the traditional Second Coming doctrine, couched in Jewish apocalyptic language, should not be taken literally. Christ's second advent should be understood as a spiritual *process* inaugurated by the coming of the Holy Spirit at Pentecost and by his coming at the destruction of Jerusalem in A.D. 70. "The real coming of Christ is not an event by itself, but a spiritual process, long ago begun and still continuing."[3] Clarke likewise dismissed a literal millennial reign of Christ on earth as an apocalyptic anachronism. What some call the Millennium connotes Christ's present and invisible governance of the church and the world.

Shailer Mathews (d. 1941), the Baptist proponent of the social gospel, held that notions of Christ's return from the sky, Messiah's battle with evil at Armageddon, and the establishment of a Jewish state centered in Jerusalem derived from the apocalypticism of pre-Christian Judaism. According to Mathews, modern science and evolutionary social theory compel us to reject Paul's futurist, catastrophic view of eschatology and to accept Jesus' realized, social perspective. Jesus taught that the Jewish millennial hope would be realized as people practice brotherly love and justice in the new social order known as the kingdom of God. Mathews concluded, "This is the Modernist's eschatology—an uplifting hope for a social order in which economic, political and all other institutions will embody the cosmic good will which Jesus taught and revealed."[4]

H. E. Fosdick (d. 1969) claimed that miracles, demons, and Jesus' return from heaven to earth are notions unacceptable to scientific minds: "I believe in the victory of righteousness on this earth, . . . but I do not believe in the physical return of Jesus on the clouds of heaven."[5] From the fourth gospel Fosdick interpreted the Second Coming as Jesus' indwelling believers' hearts. Similarly, he viewed the notion of a glorious messianic kingdom on earth to be a fantastic Jewish dream. Jesus "never indulged in fanciful pictures of the established kingdom, as the Jewish apocalyptists did. He had no interest in their carnal materializations of the coming era of God's sovereignty over man; he made the kingdom thoroughly moral."[6] Fosdick stressed the realized, denationalized and ethical character of God's kingdom, the essence of which is purity of heart, poverty of spirit, and self-renouncing love.

L. H. DeWolf (b. 1905) similarly rejected the notion of a future bodily return of Jesus Christ from heaven. The failure of Christ to return quickly (as taught by New Testament letters) confirms "the deluded and escapist character of the current apocalypticism."[7] Christ comes to reign spiritually in the hearts of the faithful here and now. The kingdom will not be inaugurated by cataclysmic intervention but by a process of spiritual evolution. Thus "the community of the divine Spirit already known to many [will] grow in purity and extent until it is here in all its fullness."[8] In a final sense, DeWolf concludes, Christ comes to each person at the hour of his or her death.

According to J. A. T. Robinson (d. 1983) the Parousia, Millennium, Antichrist, and Last Judgment are all myths fabricated by the early church. Eschatology is "inaugurated," in the sense that Christ's coming to his own in power following the Resurrection is *the* eschatological event. Christ taught only a single coming; he "did not look . . . to a second act in history after an interval, a 'part two' of his coming, incorporating elements . . . not introduced by the first."[9] From the perspective of inaugurated eschatology, "the myth of the Parousia universalizes and clarifies . . . what must happen, and is already happening, whenever the Christ comes in love and comes in power."[10] How did the early church conclude the idea of two comings of Christ separated by a time interval? When a crisis arose as to whether the messianic event had occurred or not, the early church agreed on a compromise: Christ had already come, and he would come again.

Amillennial Interpretations of Christ's Second Advent

This position upholds the personal, bodily return of Christ at the end of the age, but denies that Messiah will establish a visible, political kingdom on earth prior to the Last Judgment. The amillennial order of events is: Christ's present, spiritual reign over the church; increasing apostasy on earth; the Great Tribulation; Christ's second coming with deceased saints; the destruction of evil powers; the general resurrection of believers and unbelievers; the Last Judgment; and the eternal state. Amillennialism thus affirms that at the end of the age there will be one return of Christ, one resurrection, and one judgment. This view was advanced by the Alexandrian fathers Clement and Origen, by Augustine and many medieval Roman Catholics, by the Reformers Luther and Calvin, and following the twentieth-century decline of postmillennialism by A. Kuyper, H. Bavinck, W. Hendriksen, G. Vos, G. C. Berkouwer, L. Berkhof, J. Murray, T. Torrance, A. A. Hoekema, and L. Morris.

Amillennialists insist that the covenants and promises made to Israel are being fulfilled spiritually in the church. They interpret Scripture more figuratively than do premillennialists. Furthermore, sections of the Apocalypse are not strictly chronological; each covers the interadvental period in a scheme of progressive parallelism. Moreover, amillennialists view Revelation 20:1–6 as fulfilled spiritually during the interval between Christ's two advents. Thus the binding of Satan (Rev. 20:2–3) is interpreted as the limitation of Satan's power in the present age by virtue of Christ's resurrection victory (cf. Matt. 12:29). The first resurrection and thousand-year reign with Christ (Rev. 20:4–6) denote either (Warfield, F. Hamilton) the reign of Christian martyrs with Christ in heaven during the church age (Rev. 17:6) or (Augustine, Allis, Berkhof) sinners coming to spiritual life (Eph. 2:1–6; Col. 3:1). The symbolic number "one thousand" signifies the completeness of Christ's victory over Satan. Being "posttribulational," Christ's coming is judged not imminent (in the sense of an any-moment coming), but must await observable signs such as the evangelization of the Gentiles (Matt. 24:14), the conversion of Israel (Rom. 11:26), the Great Tribulation (Matt. 24:15–26), and the revelation of the Antichrist (2 Thess. 2:3–10).

The Alexandrian fathers, with their Greek aversion to matter and their allegorizing exegesis, opposed millenarianism. Believing that the Christian's hope is heavenly, not earthly, and that the object of God's promises is the soul, not the body, Origen rejected the chiliasm of his day. He said that those who posit a carnal kingdom centered in Jerusalem interpret the Old Testament overly literally "in a sort of Jewish sense."[11] The kingdom of God is not a physical realm to be savored by the carnal faculties; it is Jesus Christ himself. "He is absolute kingdom, reigning in every thought of the man who is no longer under the reign of sin."[12] Origen interpreted the prophecies concerning the future kingdom spiritually in terms of the eternal state.[13]

In the West Augustine initially held to chiliasm. But, offended by crude claims of physical eating and drinking in the Millennium, Augustine interpreted the latter spiritually as the reign of Christ over the church. The "thousand years" (ten cubed)—the number of perfection—denotes the entire Christian era. Since the *church* is the kingdom,[14] there is no need for a future reign of Christ on earth. "The church begins its reign with Christ now in the living and in the dead."[15] Augustine interpreted the binding of Satan spiritually as the limitation of his power to deceive during the church age (Mark 3:27). The first resurrection (Rev. 20:4–6) symbolizes sinners coming alive in Christ via the new birth (John 5:25). At the close of the church age Satan will be loosed for three-and-a-half years to test the elect and purge the nonelect; thereafter he will be defeated by Christ. Then will follow the second (or physical) resurrection unto eternal life and eternal death for the righteous and the unrighteous, respectively. "There are two resurrections, the first of which is temporal and spiritual and allows no second death, while the other is not spiritual but corporeal and is to be at the end of time."[16] Augustine's amillennialism prevailed from the fifth to the fifteenth centuries and represents the official Roman Catholic view.

Calvin distanced himself from the sometimes radical apocalypticism of the Anabaptists by not writing a section on eschatology in the *Institutes* and no commentary on the book of Revelation. Nevertheless here and there in his writings Calvin modified Augustine's amillennialism with certain postmillennial motifs. Calvin applied many Old Testament prophecies of a golden age (Isa. 11:1–9; Amos 9:13) to Christ's reign over the church. The First Advent inaugurated the eschatological kingdom in a spiritual sense within history. This side of eternity "the kingdom of Christ is spiritual."[17] Again, "the saints began to reign under heaven when Christ ushered in his kingdom by the promulgation of his gospel."[18] This kingdom progressively is being established through the warfare of the church and the defeat of the Antichrist (the papacy). "The kingdom of God is continually growing and advancing to the end of the world."[19] Until Christ returns to earth at the general resurrection, "God rules in the world only by his gospel."[20] Calvin added that the church's lot on earth in its warfare with Satan is one of trial and suffering. The kingdom now in process of realization will be perfected not in an earthly millennium of opulence but in the eternal state following Christ's second advent. Of believers he wrote, "If their blessedness is to have

an end [i.e., in a millennium], then Christ's kingdom, on whose firmness it depends, is but temporary."[21] With an eye to Anabaptist excesses, Calvin wrote that the "fiction" of "the chiliasts who limited the reign of Christ to a thousand years . . . is too childish either to need or to be worth a refutation."[22]

Anthony A. Hoekema (d. 1988) posited a single (not two-stage) coming of Christ following the fulfillment of certain signs: the worldwide preaching of the Gospel, spiritual apostasy, the revelation of the Antichrist, and persecution of the church in the Great Tribulation. When Christ returns following man's wrath in the Tribulation, the general resurrection will occur. Then transformed believers will meet the Lord in the air and will accompany Christ back to earth to execute the Last Judgment. Hoekema maintained that the Parousia is "impending" rather than imminent. In large measure his amillennialism is based on his understanding of the structure of the Apocalypse. Following Hendriksen's commentary on Revelation,[23] Hoekema posited a "progressive parallelism" whereby each of seven parallel sections depicts history from Christ's first advent to his second advent.

1. Revelation 1–3 (the letters to seven churches) describes events of the first century A.D.
2. Revelation 4–7 (the vision of seven seals) describes the church suffering trial and persecution against the background of the victory of Christ.
3. Revelation 8–11 (the vision of seven trumpets) describes the church avenged, protected, and victorious.

The preceding three sections depict the struggle between Christ and the forces of evil from the beginning of the church.

373

4. Revelation 12–14 describes the birth of Christ and opposition directed against the church by the Dragon (Satan) and the two beasts.
5. Revelation 15–16 (the vision of the seven bowls of wrath) describes the final outpouring of God's wrath on the impenitent wicked.
6. Revelation 17–19 describes the fall of Babylon (the forces of secularism and godlessness), the Beast, and the False Prophet. Christ's second advent occurs at Revelation 19:11–16.
7. Revelation 20–22 describes the doom of the Dragon, the final judgment of the wicked, and the final triumph of Christ and his church.

The preceding four sections depict deeper aspects of the struggle from the beginning of the church.

According to this scheme of progressive parallelism, Revelation 20 depicts events from Christ's first advent through the history of the church. Verses 1–3, which go back to the beginning of the Christian era, describe the binding of Satan figuratively in the sense that "Satan cannot prevent the spread of the gospel during the present age, that he cannot gather Christ's enemies together to attack the church, and that this binding takes place during the entire era of the New Testament church."[24] Following Augustine, the events of verses 4–6 transpire in heaven. The "thousand years" concurrent with the gospel era (vv. 2–3 and 5–6) is a symbolic number signifying "a very long period of indeterminate length."[25] Believers' coming to life (v. 4b) in a "first resurrection" connotes their reign with Christ in heaven during the state between their death and resurrection (cf. Rev. 6:9–11). Hoekema rejected a restoration of national Israel in a literal Millennium for several reasons: (1) Since there is but *one* olive tree (Rom. 11:17–24), Israel has no future distinct from that of the church.

> To suggest that God has in mind a separate future for Israel, in distinction from the future he has planned for Gentiles, . . . is like turning the clock of history back to Old Testament times. It is imposing Old Testament separateness upon the New Testament, and ignoring the progress of revelation.[26]

(2) The Old Testament does not teach a future earthly kingdom. Texts commonly cited in favor thereof (Isa. 2:1–4; 11:6–10; 65:17–25) describe the new earth at the consummation (Rev. 21). (3) Scripture does not teach a millennial return of Israel to the land. Some land promises have been fulfilled literally during Israel's history, whereas others are being fulfilled figuratively vis-à-vis the church both in time and in eternity. Canaan, e.g., is a figure for the eternal state.

Hoekema upheld what he called a "realized millennium."[27] "The millennium is now, and the reign of Christ with believers during this millennium is not an earthly but a heavenly one."[28] Moreover, he understood the coming to life of the rest of the dead at the end of the thousand years (Rev. 20:5a) to describe the unbelieving dead who did not participate in the first resurrection. The condition of the latter is opposite that of faithful saints. "The unbelieving dead . . . did not live or reign with Christ during the thousand-year period."[29] At the end of the thousand years unbelievers will experience the second death (Rev. 20:11–15). Thus neither the first nor the second resurrection is a bodily resurrection.

Postmillennial Interpretations of Christ's Second Advent

This viewpoint locates Christ's second coming *after* the formation of a golden age of indefinite length via the Christianization of the world. Citing texts such as Psalms 47; 72:1–11; Isaiah 45:22–23; Daniel 2:44; and Zechariah 9:10, as well as the parables of the mustard seed and the yeast (Matt. 13:31–33), advocates claim that gospel preaching will transform the world religiously, economically, and politically. Not all persons will be converted and not all evil will be eliminated; but the world to which Christ returns will be largely Christian. The order of events in the postmillennial scheme is as follows: a golden age of increasing righteousness; a brief apostasy followed by the rise of the Antichrist; three-and-a-half years of Great Tribulation; the personal return of Christ; the general resurrection of believers and unbelievers; the Last Judgment; and the eternal state. Postmillennialists interpret the binding of Satan in the same figurative manner as amillennialists. The "first resurrection" (Rev. 20:4–6) signifies the elevation of faithful martyrs to heaven to reign with Christ.

Postmillennialists generally hold that Old Testament prophecies about Israel's future apply to the church. Since Messiah has come, God has no special purpose for national Israel distinct from the church. Postmillennialism flourished during the eighteenth and early nineteenth centuries stimulated by the scientific revolution, the age of revivals, and the beginning of modern missions. Two devastating world wars caused a decline of interest, but in recent years a revival of postmillennialism has occurred. The long list of postmillennialists includes Eusebius; St. Benedict; Cocceius; the Puritans Thomas Brightman, John Owen, and Samuel Rutherford; Philip Spener; Isaac Watts; Jonathan Edwards; the Methodists John Wesley, Adam Clarke, and Richard Watson; Charles Finney; Matthew Henry; Charles Hodge; A. A. Hodge; W. G. T. Shedd; Robert L. Dabney; A. H. Strong; J. Orr; B. B. Warfield; L. Boettner; H. Berkhof; and J. J. Davis.

Eusebius (d. 340) interpreted the establishment of Christianity during the reign of Constantine I as the beginning of the kingdom of God. He judged that the chiliasm of the early fathers was "mythology" and interpreted the Old Testament kingdom promises "mystically" or spiritually.[30] Jonathan Edwards (d. 1758) identified the forty-two months of Antichrist's reign with twelve hundred and sixty years of the papacy's domination—namely, from A.D. 606 (when universal episcopacy was established) to 1866 (when the papacy would be dethroned).[31] Before history's end there would occur a "latter day" age of the Spirit brought about by gospel preaching and the progress of the church. Edwards believed that the First Great Awakening (1735–43) was a sign that this age of the Spirit, involving a weakening of Satan's power, had dawned. When Antichrist finally is destroyed about A.D. 2000, the Millennium will begin. Interpreting the "islands" of Isaiah 60:9 as the American colonies, Edwards judged that the Millennium would originate in America. This golden age will be characterized by peace and prosperity on earth, the destruction of false doctrines, and the conversion of one-third of the world's population. The first resurrection (Rev. 20:4–6) is spiritual and denotes the heavenly ascent of believing souls martyred by Antichrist. Edwards' eschatology is postmillennial because the thousand years will be inaugurated not by Christ's second advent but by "the glorious revival of religion."[32]

A. H. Strong (d. 1921) wrote that there "is abundant evidence that there is no interval of a thousand years between the second coming of Christ and the resurrection, general judgment, and end of all things."[33] Prior to Christ's bodily return at the end of the age to judge the dead, his kingdom will prevail throughout the earth. The Millennium will come not catastrophically but progressively via the conquest of evil forces and mass conversions to Christ. According to Strong, Revelation 20:4–6 teaches in figurative language an "invisible and spiritual coming" of Christ to reign and a spiritual "resurrection of faith and love in the hearts of his people."[34] Thus the first resurrection of the saints is spiritual, whereas the second resurrection of all people is physical.

Loraine Boettner, who said that much biblical language is figurative (e.g., "the cattle on a thousand hills" [Ps. 50:10], the "dragon" [Rev. 20:2], the "Lamb" with "seven horns and seven eyes" [Rev. 5:6]), envisaged the Millennium as the gradual realization of the spiritual kingdom in human hearts through gospel preaching. During this golden age of indeterminate length believers will constitute the majority, Christian principles of conduct will be the rule, peace and prosperity will prevail, evil will be reduced to negligible proportions, and poverty and ignorance will be eliminated. "Possibly we can look forward to a great 'golden age' of spiritual prosperity continuing for centuries, or even for millenniums, during which time Christianity shall triumph over all the earth, and . . . the great proportion even of adults shall be saved."[35] Signs of the Millennium's approach are now evident in the form of progress in the *social* arena (the abolition of slavery and polygamy and the rising status of women and children), in the *educational* arena (the knowledge explosion and gradual elimination of ignorance), in the *technological* arena (advances in transportation and communication), in the *political* arena (foreign aid to developing nations), and in the *spiritual* arena (progress in foreign missions, Bible translations, evangelical mass communications, and the decline of non-Christian religions). Hence the present age gradually will merge into the golden age of the Millennium.

As for exegetical details, Boettner claimed that Revelation 19:11–12 describes, not the battle of Armageddon and Christ's second advent, but the *age-long* struggle between the forces of good and evil and promise of final victory. The text presents "a picture of the victorious career of the gospel of Christ in the world."[36] The thousand-year binding of Satan (Rev. 20:1–3) describes the limitation of his power during the interadvental period facilitating Christianization of the world. The reign of the saints for a thousand years (Rev. 20:4–6) depicts their presence in heaven in the intermediate state. Boettner insisted that the thousand years of verses 1–3 and 4–6 do not refer to the same thing (the first being the church age, and the second the intermediate state of each believer). Moreover, the first resurrection is spiritual whereas the second is physical.

The theonomy movement, represented by R. J. Rushdoony, Greg Bahnsen, Gary North, David Chilton, and the *Journal of Christian Reconstruction,* advocates postmillennialism from a unique perspective. It insists that the precepts and penalties of the Old Testament Mosaic laws have never been annulled and so must be enforced today by civil magistrates (the modern equivalent of Israel's kings). Proponents appeal to Matthew 5:17–19 and interpret *plērōsai* as "confirm" rather than "fulfill." As the church persuades the state to conform to biblical (especially Old Testament) laws, a universal theocracy—the Millennium—will be established on earth. Theonomists understand that prophecies concerning the Israelite theocratic kingdom are being fulfilled literally among the nations of earth prior to Christ's second advent.[37]

David Chilton, in *Paradise Restored,* sets forth an "eschatology of dominion,"[38] by which God destined his church for victorious conquest. Chilton boldly states, "The Christian goal for the world is the universal development of biblical theocratic republics, in which every area of life is redeemed and placed under the Lordship of Jesus Christ and the rule of God's law."[39] As the Gospel is preached and the nations discipled, strongholds of evil will be dismantled and Christ's rule established. The church age, then, is the Millennium, its characteristics being the conversion of the majority of humanity, the cessation of war, the reversal of the curse, and the restoration of earth to Edenic conditions. "The garden of Eden, the mountain of the Lord, will be restored *in history,* before the second coming, by the power of the gospel; and the desert will rejoice and blossom as the rose (Isa. 35:1)."[40]

In Chilton's scheme the Apocalypse describes contemporary, not future, events. The Great Tribulation occurred in A.D. 70 with the Roman invasion. The "coming of the Son of Man" (Matt. 24:26–31) describes Christ's enthronement in heaven to rule the nations. The Son of Man sending his angels to gather the elect (Matt. 24:31) denotes the worldwide conversion of the nations following upon the destruction of Israel. The thousand-year Millennium (Rev. 20:3–6) denotes the vast interadvental period: "This world has tens of thousands, perhaps hundreds of thousands of years of increasing godliness ahead of it, before the Second Coming of Christ."[41] Finally, Revelation 21–22 is a highly symbolic description of earth restored to Edenic conditions in the Millennium (the present age). Hence we now live in the "new heavens and new earth."

Bahnsen interprets the Old Testament prophecies of future kingdom prosperity in terms of the rule of Christ during the church age. Christ's kingly rule will be brought about by the success of the Great Commission and the conversion of the majority of humankind. He is confident that the nations "will become disciples of Christ, and [that] the church will grow to fill the earth, and that Christianity will become the dominant principle."[42] The present discipling of the nations in the power of the Spirit will effect the Christianization of the world, material prosperity, and international peace. In summary, "the millennium or kingdom of Christ is a present reality spanning the interadvental age."[43]

Premillennial Interpretations of Christ's Second Advent

Premillennialists believe that Christ's literal second advent will precede his physical, thousand-year reign on earth. Interpreting Scripture more literally than amillennialists or postmillennialists, premillennialists affirm a personal, bodily, and glorious return of Christ to inaugurate a political millennial kingdom on earth prior to the Last Judgment. The land promises in the Abrahamic and Davidic covenants have not been realized in the church but will be fulfilled in Messiah's future earthly reign. Premillennialists regard the binding of Satan as a literal incarceration in the bottomless pit during the Millennium. The first resurrection, preceding the Millennium, and the second resurrection, following it, are both physical. During the thousand years Christ will reign as King in an era of unparalleled righteousness, peace, and prosperity. Since nature itself will be renewed, the earth will become remarkably productive. Significant differences exist between *historic premillennialism* and *dispensational premillennialism,* as indicated below.

Historic premillennialism seems to have prevailed for some three centuries in the postapostolic church. It is distinguished from the later dispensational form by its single plan embracing Israel and the church in God's unfolding kingdom. Some historical premillennialists assert that no future exists for *national Israel;* in the Millennium Jewish and Gentile believers will enjoy equal privileges as co-members of Christ's body. Others suggest that when interpreting the Old Testament prophecies one must distinguish between predictions directed to Israel *as a nation* and those directed to Israel *as the people of God* (a people that includes the church).[44] Historic premillennialism also believes that the church will remain on earth during the seven-year Tribulation. Proponents distinguish between the wrath (*orgē, thymos*) of *God* directed against sinners and the vengeance (*thlypsis*) of *Antichrist* meted out against the saints. Since several events must occur before Christ's return (world evangelization, the rise of Antichrist, the Great Tribulation, etc.), his coming is not strictly imminent.

The order of future events according to historic premillennialism is as follows: increased apostasy toward the end of the church age; the seven-year Tribulation and the rise of the Antichrist; the persecution of the church; Christ's second coming to destroy the forces of evil at Armageddon; the resurrection of deceased saints and rapture of living believers; the marriage feast of the Lamb; Christ's millennial reign on earth; Satan's release from the pit and destruction at the end of the Millennium; the resurrection of the unjust dead; the Last Judgment of believers and unbelievers; and the new heavens and the new earth. Historic premillennialism claims the following adherents in the early church: Papias, Pseudo-Barnabas, Justin Martyr, Irenaeus, Tertullian, Hippolytus, Methodius, Lactantius, and Apollinaris of Laodicea. Under the influence of Augustine the view lost favor until the seventeenth century. Modern adherents include J. H. Bengel; J. Gill; J. Priestly; the biblical scholars Delitzsch, Zahn, Lange, Godet, Trench, and Alford; A. Reese; O. J. Smith, G. Ladd; J. B. Payne (with variations); G. R. Beasley-Murray; and M. J. Erickson.

Papias (d. 120), who tradition says was taught by the apostle John, was the first major postapostolic chiliast. Eusebius quoted Papias as saying that "there will be a millennium following the resurrection of the dead, when the kingdom of Christ is to be established physically on the earth."[45] The latter's description of the Millennium's bounty is vivid. "The days will come, in which vines shall grow, each having ten thousand branches, and in each branch ten thousand shoots, and in each one of the shoots ten thousand clusters, and on every one of the clusters ten thousand grapes, and every grape when pressed will give twenty-five metretes [one metretes = forty liters or nine gals.] of wine."[46] Justin Martyr (d. 165) believed there will be two resurrections separated by a physical Millennium: "I and others . . . are assured that there will be a resurrection of the dead and a thousand years in Jerusalem, which will then be rebuilt, adorned, and enlarged, as the prophets Ezekiel and Isaiah and others declare."[47] Justin viewed the church as the true Israel. "We, who have been quarried out from the bowels of Christ, are the true Israelite race."[48] Thus the Millennium is not Jewish in character but Christian. Justin apparently judged that millenarianism was held by all second-century authorities except the Gnostics.[49]

Irenaeus (d. 200) set forth a full-fledged premillennial scheme. While favoring a literal hermeneutic, he held that the millennial blessings promised to Abraham and his seed will be fulfilled in the multiracial church (Gal. 3:16).[50] Irenaeus saw in the Millennium several purposes: (1) demonstration in history of Christ's victory, (2) the training of Christians in the vision of God, and

(3) the rewarding of believers in the material world for their sufferings. Tertullian (d. 230) defended chiliasm against Marcion:

> We confess that a kingdom is promised to us upon the earth before heaven, only in another state of existence; inasmuch as it will be after the resurrection for a thousand years in the divinely-built Jerusalem, 'let down from heaven.' . . . After its thousand years are over . . . there will ensue the destruction of the world and the conflagration of all things at the judgment.''[51]

Church fathers such as Barnabas, Irenaeus, Methodius, Hippolytus, and Lactantius found chiliasm corroborated by the scheme of six days of creation and one day of rest. On the basis of 2 Peter 3:8, the latter believed that the six days of creation correspond to six thousand years of world history, whereas the seventh day of rest corresponds to the Millennium. Lactantius wrote, "When Christ shall have . . . made the great judgment and restored to life those who were just from the beginning, he will stay among men for a thousand years and will rule them with a most just dominion."[52]

Many early authorities upheld a posttribulational return of Christ. The *Didache* states that at the end of the age Antichrist will rule the world and inflict severe persecution on living believers, after which Christ will return to resurrect the righteous. So the document exhorted believers: "The whole time of your faith shall not profit you except you be found perfect at the last time."[53] The Epistle of Barnabas states that although the church will endure the Tribulation, God will shorten the time and deliver his people. At the end of this trial Christ will return to destroy Antichrist and usher in the millennial rest.[54] The Shepherd of Hermas records a vision of a large beast (a symbol of the great persecution to come) with a head

of four colors: *black,* signifying the fallen world in which the church dwells; *red,* indicating that the world must perish by fire and blood; and *gold,* signifying purification by trial. "Just as gold casts off its dross, so you will cast off all sorrow and tribulation, becoming pure and useful for the building of the tower" (i.e., the church).[55] The fourth color *white* signifies the age to come. That writer was confident that God will preserve the church in the midst of tribulation. Justin Martyr wrote that before Christ's return to inaugurate the Millennium Antichrist will blaspheme the Most High and persecute the saints. Christ "shall come from heaven with glory when the man of apostasy . . . shall venture to do unlawful deeds on the earth against us the Christians, who . . . have fled for safety to the God of Jacob."[56] For Justin the Great Tribulation represents an intensification of the distress Christians have endured throughout the ages.

Irenaeus believed that the end was not strictly imminent. Rome must yet fall and the empire be divided among ten kings. The Antichrist must appear, control ten kingdoms, and persecute the church. Irenaeus claimed that God will use the persecution by the Antichrist to purify the church and prepare it for glory. "Tribulation is necessary for those who are saved, that having been after a manner broken up, rendered fine, sprinkled over by the patience of the Word of God, and set on fire [for purification], they may be fitted for the royal banquet."[57] Irenaeus described Antichrist's persecution as "the last contest of the righteous, in which, when they overcome, they are crowned with incorruption."[58] Christ will return at the end of the Tribulation to destroy Antichrist and raise deceased saints. "The resurrection of the just . . . takes place after the coming of Antichrist and the destruction of all nations under his rule."[59] Tertullian observed that after the restrainer is removed (the Roman state, 2 Thess. 2:7) and ten kingdoms take its place, the Antichrist will arise to persecute the church. In that time of unparalleled anarchy "the beast Antichrist with his false prophet will wage war on the church of God."[60] Following the Tribulation Christ will return to destroy Antichrist and rapture the saints.

Hippolytus (d. 235) saw in the account of the woman (the church), the male child (Christ), and the dragon (Antichrist) in Revelation 12:1–6 "the tribulation of the persecution which is to fall upon the church from the adversary."[61] That period will consist of "one thousand two hundred and three score days during which the tyrant is to reign and persecute the church, which flees from city to city and seeks concealment in the wilderness among the mountains."[62] Following the abomination of desolation Christ will descend from heaven to avenge the unrighteous and raise the saints. Lactantius (d. 340) presented a vivid description of the horrors of the Great Tribulation. Antichrist "will persecute the righteous people,"[63] and two-thirds of living believers will perish.[64] Surviving saints will flee to the mountains in search of safety, but Antichrist will pursue and surround them. In that crisis the saints will call upon God, who "shall hear them and send from heaven a great king to rescue and free them and destroy all the wicked with fire and sword."[65]

Such testimony from the Ante-Nicene fathers leads Gundry to conclude that "the early church was as explicitly posttribulational as it was premillennial."[66] Clouse expands the time-frame: "Until the early nineteenth century those believers who discussed the rapture believed it would occur in conjunction with the return of Christ at the end of the tribulation period."[67]

As indicated in chapter 6, George Eldon Ladd (d. 1982) distinguished between a present inbreaking of the kingdom within history through the ministry of Jesus and the consummation of the kingdom in the eschaton. A plain reading of Revelation 20–21 led Ladd to claim that the kingdom will come in two stages: the reign of Christ in the Millennium and then in the eternal state. Since Scripture depicts the church as "the new Israel, the true Israel, and the spiritual Israel" (Rom. 4:11–12, 16; Gal. 3:7),[68] many prophecies made in respect of Israel are being fulfilled in the one people of God, the Jewish-Gentile church (cf. Hos. 1:10 with Rom. 9:26; Hos. 2:23 with Rom. 9:25). The Millennium will not involve a renewed Jewish order with a rebuilt temple and reinstituted sacrifices, for the Mosaic covenant and its elaborate cult has been abolished forever by Christ's finished work (Heb. 8:6–7; 10:1, 16–18). "It is inconceivable that God's redemptive plan will revert to the age of shadows."[69]

Ladd added that "nowhere does the Word of God affirm that the rapture and the resurrection of believers will precede the Tribulation."[70] There is only one Second Advent (not two or two parts), for the parousia, apokalypsis, and epiphania are one and the same. Moreover, there are only two resurrections (not three or three parts), for "Revelation speaks explicitly of a first resurrection at the beginning of the millennium, and . . . a second resurrection at the end of the millennium (Rev. 20:4–15)."[71] At the Second Advent the righteous dead and living saints will be caught up to join Christ (the Rapture) and will accompany him as he continues to earth. Revelation 20:4–6 (not at 4:1) describes this event. Furthermore, Christians in the Tribulation will suffer, not the wrath of God, but persecution and distress from evil forces. Such has been the lot of the saints throughout history (John 16:33; Acts 14:22). "When we contemplate the history of martyrdom, why should we ask deliverance from what millions have already suffered?"[72] Thus the "blessed hope" is not the prospect of deliverance from tribulation; it is the glorious appearing of the Savior himself (Titus 2:13). Ladd claimed that the Second Coming is not strictly imminent, for certain prophesied events must yet occur, e.g., the Tribulation signs, the rise of Antichrist out of the European political scene, and persecution of the Jewish nation. The Christian's responsibility is to be spiritually alert and to watch expectantly for Christ's coming.

J. Barton Payne's (d. 1979) "imminent posttribulationism"[73] sought to reconcile the imminency of pretribulationism with a posttribulational Second Advent. Payne taught that there will be a single Second Coming of Christ following the Tribulation (Matt. 24:29–31; 2 Thess. 1:6–8; Rev. 20:4–5). Payne argued for an *imminent* posttribulational coming of Christ, as follows: The church at the end of the apostolic period believed that all the events predicted to precede Christ's return had occurred; viz., Paul's imprisonment and death (Acts 27:24; 2 Tim. 4:6), the death of Peter (John 21:18–19), the fall of Jerusalem (Luke 21:24), worldwide Gospel preaching (Matt. 24:14), and the persecution of the Asian churches (Rev. 2:10). Since the church has always been persecuted, the Great Tribulation may be in progress. Furthermore, the seven years may be symbolic, hence the Tribulation may be rather short. Since all necessary antecedents to Christ's return have occurred, we can affirm the "imminence" or "potential immediacy" of his coming;[74] Christ *could* come at any moment, with no need for additional intervening signs. In building his case Payne denied the "double fulfillment" of Old Testament prophecy (i.e., both a near *and* a distant future fulfillment). In other words, he interpreted prophetic Scripture (including the Apocalypse) in preterist fashion. Thus the fall of the Roman Empire in A.D. 476 fulfilled the prediction of Rome's overthrow by the ten horns (Rev. 17:12–16). The fall of Jerusalem exhausted the travail described in Matthew 24:4–22. Daniel's seventieth week (Dan. 9:24–27) extends no further than A.D. 70. Moreover, the Antichrist (2 Thess. 2:6–8) may have already appeared. Payne surmised that "an unusually apt candidate for the Antichrist is Nikita Khrushchev right today."[75] By such a line of reasoning "the last times *could* be the historical present,"[76] hence Christ could come today.

Robert H. Gundry sees himself as a dispensationalist (one distinguishing Mosaic and church economies) who holds to a posttribulational rapture. According to Gundry, Scripture frequently asserts that Christ will return *after* the Tribulation to accomplish the "first resurrection." Gundry sees a transition period between old and new dispensations in the ministry of the Baptist and the apostles wherein God dealt simultaneously with Israel and the church. Similarly there will be a transition period involving both Israel and the church during the Tribulation. "This future period of transition might well be the tribulation, during which God finishes His dealings with the Church and prepares Israel and the nations for the millennial kingdom of Christ."[77] In the tribulation believers will experience not divine wrath (*orgē, thymos*) but satanic distress (*thlypsis*)—which will be an intensification of the troubles Christians have endured throughout history. The *divine wrath* does not cover the entire seventieth week but commences at the sixth seal, the fourth trumpet, and the first bowl—i.e., at the close of the Tribulation during Armageddon. God will rapture the church (in the Day of the Lord) immediately prior to this outpouring of divine wrath. Unconverted Jews (the 144,000) who survive the Tribulation will believe on Christ when he returns and will enter the theocratic kingdom as descendants of Abraham to populate the earth. Gundry claims that because specific signs must precede Christ's return (Matt. 24:32–25:13; 2 Tim. 3:1–7) the Second Advent is not imminent. We should replace strict imminence with the concept of "suddenness, unexpectedness or incalculability, and a possibility of occurrence at any moment."[78] "A tribulational interval no more destroys expectancy than did necessary delays during the apostolic age." [79]

Dispensational premillennialism arose in the nineteenth century under the impetus of Edward Irving (d. 1834), a church of Scotland minister, and John N. Darby (d. 1882), the Anglican founder of the Plymouth Brethren. Promoted by H. A. Ironside, C. I. Scofield, A. C. Gaebelein, R. A. Torrey, J. M. Grey, L. S. Chafer, J. D. Pentecost, J. Walvoord, A. J. McClain, and C. C. Ryrie, the movement pursues (1) a thoroughly literal interpretation of Scripture and (2) a rigorous distinction between God's program for Israel and his program for the church. According to Chafer, "the dispensationalist believes that throughout the ages God is pursuing two distinct purposes: one related to the earth with earthly people and earthly objectives involved, which is Judaism; while the other is related to heaven with heavenly people and heavenly objectives involved, which is Christianity."[80] The Tribulation woes concern unbelievers, not the church. "The purpose of the tribulation is to judge unbelieving Gentiles and to discipline disobedient Israel (Jer. 30:7). The church does not have purpose or place in the Tribulation."[81] Dispensationalists hold (cf. chap. 6) that through the Davidic covenant God unconditionally assured Israel that a descendant of David would rule over the promised land. Classically it was held that Jesus offered the theocratic kingdom to contemporary Israel, and, when the offer was rejected, God instituted the church as a parenthesis arrangement within his primary purpose for Israel. In the Millennium God will return to the heart of his earthly plan by fulfilling vis-à-vis Israel the unfulfilled covenants and prophecies. Thus not only will Israel be exalted above the nations in the promised land, but the temple will be rebuilt and animal sacrifices reinstituted as a memorial to the sacrifice of Christ.

The order of end-time events, according to dispensational premillennialism, is as follows: increasing apostasy in the church age; an any-moment, secret coming of Christ for deceased and living saints (the "Rapture" in "the day of Christ," 1 Thess. 4:13–18), which removes the Holy Spirit from the earth (2 Thess. 2:7); the marriage feast of the Lamb in heaven; the seven-year Tribulation on earth (Daniel's seventieth week), which involves divine wrath upon unbelieving Gentiles and disobedient Israel; the terrible reign of Antichrist; the conversion of a remnant of Israel (the 144,000, Rev. 7:3–8); the widespread conversion of Gentiles (Rev. 7:9); and the Battle of Armageddon. There follows the glorious return of Christ with his saints in "the day of the Lord" (Matt. 24:29–31; Rev. 19) to destroy his enemies at Armageddon; the conversion of the vast majority of Jews; the incarceration of Satan in the abyss; the resurrection of tribulation martyrs and Old Testament saints who join the raptured church in heaven; the judgment of individual Gentiles based on their treatment of the Jews during the Tribulation; the judgment of Israel (Ezek. 20:33–38); the establishment of the theocratic kingdom (Millennium) centered in Jerusalem, which will be populated by believers living at the Second Advent who will marry, reproduce, and die; a final rebellion by Satan and the unsaved toward the close of the

Millennium, followed by their defeat, Satan's confinement in the bottomless pit, and the resurrection of believers who died in the Millennium; after the Millennium the unbelieving dead will be raised, judged at the great white throne, and cast into the lake of fire.

John Darby (d. 1882), reacting against nineteenth-century postmillennialism, taught that the return of Christ would occur in two stages: a secret coming *for* the saints at the Rapture and a glorious coming *with* the saints at the close of the Tribulation. Darby held that the Great Tribulation is exclusively Jewish and thus does not concern the church. God "does not make us pass through that hour of temptation which is to sift out those who have their home here."[82] With the church (the "mystery" economy described by Paul) in heaven during Daniel's Seventieth Week, God will resume his dealings with Israel. During the seven-year tribulation period Antichrist will make a covenant to protect the state of Israel, break the agreement, and demand that the Jews worship him. This embodiment of evil will violently persecute Jews who do not worship him. The final assault on the chosen people will prompt the widespread conversion of Jews to Christ. Following the ensuing battle of Armageddon, Christ will return to earth to bind Satan for a thousand years and inaugurate a Millennium of peace and prosperity. Thereby the theocratic kingdom postponed during Christ's First Advent will be realized in fulfillment of the land prophecies made long ago to Israel.

The *Scofield Reference Bible* notes teach that near the end of the church age a ten-kingdom empire possessing ancient Rome's authority will arise, the professing church will become apostate, and the Man of Sin will be revealed. Then, with no predicted events intervening, Christ will descend to rapture the church and remove the res-

trainer (2 Thess. 2:7), the Holy Spirit, from the earth. The ensuing tribulation period is "distinctively 'the time of Jacob's trouble' (Jer. 30:7)."[83] Antichrist will covenant with the Jews to restore the temple sacrifices. But in the middle of the week he will terminate the sacrifices and demand to be worshiped as God. In this half week of Great Tribulation a remnant of Israel and a great multitude of Gentiles will be saved. The Jewish remnant will preach the Gospel of the kingdom; some will be martyred, but others will live to enter the Millennium in physical bodies. When the lawless one and his allies seek to destroy the saints, Christ will return to consume his enemies at the Battle of Armageddon. Then the theocratic kingdom, earlier offered to Israel but rejected, will be set up by David's greater Son. "The kingdom is to be established first over regathered, restored, and converted Israel, and then is to become universal."[84] In this era of justice, peace, and prosperity, "the enormous majority of earth's inhabitants will be saved."[85] The Sermon on the Mount—the divine constitution of the Millennium—describes the righteousness that will prevail during this golden age. According to the Scofield notes there are *two comings of Christ* and *four resurrections* (of bodies following the resurrection of Christ [Matt. 27:52–53], of Old Testament saints at the Rapture [1 Cor. 15:53], of Tribulation martyrs at the close of the seven years [1 Cor. 15:52], and of the wicked at the close of the Millennium [Rev. 20:12–13]). There are *five principal judgments* (of believers following the Rapture [2 Cor. 5:10], of the nations at Christ's return [Matt. 25:32], of Israel at Christ's return [Ezek. 20:37], of angels after the thousand years [Jude 6], and of the wicked dead at the end of history [Rev. 20:12–15]).

Walvoord insists that "the rapture question is determined more by ecclesiology than eschatology.''[86] God has distinctive purposes for Israel, for believers in the church age, for Tribulation saints, and for the godly in the Millennium. Daniel's Seventy Weeks concern Israel, not the church. The extended time period between Daniel's sixty-ninth and seventieth weeks constitutes a parenthesis in God's dealings with Israel, the focus of which is the church. In the Seventieth Week (the seven years of Tribulation) God's attention will return to Israel. "God will fulfill His program for the church by translating the church out of the earth before resuming His program for dealing with Israel in the period of tribulation.''[87] The purpose of the Tribulation is to judge and purify Israel and to punish unbelieving Gentiles. Walvoord affirms that the Rapture is not found in the Synoptic Gospels but appears in John 14 and in the Pauline letters (1 Cor. 15:51–58; 1 Thess. 4–5; 2 Thess. 2). Moreover, "many pretribulationists find in the catching up of John [Rev. 4:1] a symbolic presentation of the rapture of the church.''[88] Whereas New Testament saints will be raised at the imminent Rapture, Old Testament saints and Tribulation martyrs will be raised at Christ's second coming following the Tribulation.

Walvoord cites further considerations for a pretribulational rapture: (1) the church is not mentioned in any Tribulation passage (Jer. 30:4–11; Matt. 24:15–31; Rev. 4–19); (2) the church is promised deliverance from the time of divine wrath (1 Thess. 5:9; Rev. 3:10); (3) before the lawless one is revealed the "restrainer," the Holy Spirit, must be removed from the earth ("the removal of the Spirit would involve a dispensational change and the removal of the church as well");[89] (4) the Rapture is an imminent event (1 Thess. 4:13–18; 1 Cor. 15:51–52), whereas the Second Advent is not; and (5) an interval of time is needed between the Rapture and the Second Coming for certain events to take place: viz., *in heaven,* the marriage feast of the Lamb and the reward of believers at the judgment seat of Christ and, *on earth,* the conversion of Jews and Gentiles who will enter the Millennium in natural bodies and the judgment of unbelieving Israel (Ezek. 20:34–38) and the Gentile nations (Matt. 25:31–46).

Walvoord regards the Millennium (the kingdom of heaven) as the literal fulfillment of the unconditional promises contained in the Abrahamic and Davidic covenants. The establishment in 1948 of the modern state of Israel confirms that the ancient land promises are being fulfilled. In the Millennium Satan will be bound, Christ will rule as universal King, Israel will be reconstituted and exalted above the other nations, and earth will enjoy unparalleled righteousness, peace, and prosperity. The majority of earth's population in the Millennium will be converted. Furthermore, a new temple will be rebuilt in fulfillment of Ezekiel 40–46, and Jewish worship and animal sacrifices will be reinstituted as memorials to the sacrifice of Christ. In the Millennium resurrected saints will mingle with humans in natural bodies. Consistent with his sharp distinction between Israel and the church, Walvoord claims that the prophecy of the new covenant in Jeremiah 31:31–34 will be fulfilled vis-à-vis Israel as universal knowledge of the Lord in the *Millennium.* "The new covenant is with Israel and the fulfillment in the millennial kingdom after the second coming of Christ.''[90] This latter new covenant differs from the new covenant inaugurated by Christ's blood (1 Cor. 11:25).

Midtribulationism is held by N. Harrison, H. J. Ockenga, J. O. Buswell, Jr., M. Tenney, R. Culver, R. Longenecker, and G. L. Archer. Distinguishing between the Rapture (1 Thess. 4:14–18) and the Second Advent

(1 Thess. 5:1–9), advocates assert that the church will be caught up at the midpoint of the Tribulation following the appearance of Antichrist but before the severe judgments of the last half. The first half of the week (Matt. 24:10–26), highlighted by numerous signs, constitutes the preliminary phase of the Tribulation. By virtue of the preceding signs—especially the covenant between Antichrist and Israel—the Rapture is said to be not strictly imminent. Nevertheless, "even if the fulfillment of signs must precede the Rapture, the interval of three and a half years fits better with the idea of imminence than does the full span of seven years posited by the posttribulationist."[91] The rapture of the saints in the middle of the week (Matt. 24:27) is not secret, for it involves a great shout and the trumpet blast (1 Thess. 4:15–16; Rev. 10:7; 11:15). Some midtribulationists claim that the Rapture will occur with the sounding of the seventh trumpet of Revelation 11:15 (which is identical with that of Matt. 24:31; 1 Cor. 15:52; and 1 Thess. 4:16). The visible Rapture will startle the unconverted and lead to the salvation of multitudes (Rev. 7:9, 14). The second half of Daniel's week, or the Great Tribulation (Matt. 24:29), involves the reign of the Antichrist and the outpouring of divine wrath against the forces of evil. The church, raptured in the middle of the week, will experience the fury of man but will be delivered from the wrath of God.

J. O. Buswell, Jr. (d. 1977), interpreted the seals, trumpets, and bowls sequentially. The seven *seals* describe the tribulation that has befallen saints throughout church history. The seven *trumpets* (six of which precede the Rapture) warn of judgment to come. The seven *bowls* (during the last half of the week) signify the outpouring of divine wrath. The "sign" of Christ's coming and the close of the age (Matt. 24:3) will be the revelation of the Beast (Rev. 11:7), or the Man of Sin (2 Thess. 2:3), and the abomination of desolation (Matt. 24:15). A short but violent tribulation (not divine wrath) will follow, driving the saints into the wilderness. For the sake of the elect this time of intense distress will be shortened to three-and-a-half days (Rev. 11:9–10). In the middle of the Tribulation week the seventh trumpet will sound (Rev. 11:15–19; cf. Matt. 24:30–31; 1 Thess. 4:16) and the church will be raptured visibly ("like a flash of lightning throughout the entire horizon of the world").[92] "The two witnesses," slain by Antichrist, "are caught up into heaven 'in the cloud' at the same moment that the elect of God are caught up together in clouds to the meeting of the Lord in the air (Rev. 11:11–12)."[93] For forty-two months the beast will exercise dominion on earth, but when Antichrist and his armies gather at Armageddon to conquer Jerusalem, Christ will return with his saints and vanquish them. With Satan cast into the abyss, Christ will reign for a thousand years in "an age somewhat analogous to the Garden of Eden before the fall of man."[94]

The partial-rapture theory has been held by a few pretribulationalists, such as R. G. Govett, J. A. Seiss, G. H. Pember, and G. H. Lang. Citing texts that emphasize personal worthiness and preparedness (Matt. 20:40–51; Luke 20:34–36; Rev. 3:3,10), advocates of this view judge that only believers who are seriously watching for Christ will be raptured before the Tribulation. Deliverance from the Great Tribulation and participation in the millennial kingdom are seen as rewards for unflinching commitment to Christ. Unprepared saints will be raptured at the end of the Tribulation or following the Millennium (along with all unbelievers). Robert G. Govett (d. 1901), the apparent founder of this theory, claimed that spiritually unfit Christians will not be raptured until after the Millennium. Eternal life is

God's unconditional gift of grace; but "the participation of believers in the kingdom of God depends upon their conduct after they begin to believe."[95] He added, "The kingdom of God is a time of *reward:* and . . . entrance into it will turn upon the conduct of the believer."[96] G. H. Pember similarly envisaged carnal believers not being raptured until the close of the Millennium: "To those who believe on Christ but go no further, the Lord does, indeed, give eternal life; but the fruition of it will not begin . . . until the thousand years of the millennial reign are ended."[97] As a result, "the Last Day will witness the resurrection of many that are saved and of all the lost."[98] G. H. Lang, a leading twentieth-century proponent, posited prior to the Tribulation "the removal of a portion of the church of God, not to the air, but to Christ, at the throne of the Father."[99] He explained, "The Lord does not come for the Firstfruits. They are simply taken away as were Enoch and Elijah."[100] This escape from the Tribulation is the reward for spiritual maturity and service. Following the Great Tribulation, Christ will descend and rapture the rest of the saints (1 Cor. 15:51–52; 1 Thess. 4:15–17).

For other helpful works on this subject see the volumes by R. Ludwigson,[101] Robert Clouse,[102] and Millard Erickson.[103]

BIBLICAL TEACHING

To decide between the several historical proposals concerning the return of Christ to reign we now turn to the teachings of inspired Scripture.

Poetry and Wisdom

The first explicit teaching on the return of Christ to reign occurs in the Psalms. Psalm 2, frequently applied by New Testament writers to Christ,[104] ultimately attests Messiah's enthronement and rule over the nations. Following the prideful rebellion of earthly kings (vv. 1–3), God installs David's greater Son as King in Jerusalem (vv. 4–7) and announces his mandate: "I will make the nations your inheritance, the ends of the earth your possession. You will rule them with an iron scepter; you will dash them to pieces like pottery" (vv. 8–9). These words cannot be limited to Jesus' earthly ministry or the church, but find fulfillment in Christ's future, universal reign on earth (Rev. 12:5; 19:15). "The Revelation . . . contains an anticipation of the ultimate rule and triumph of the man born to be king in the language and imagery of Psalm 2."[105]

Psalm 110 proximately celebrates the coronation of the Davidic king but eschatologically is fulfilled in Christ, the triumphant priest-king. In its future application, Messiah will rule from Zion in worldwide dominion: "The LORD will extend your mighty scepter from Zion; you will rule in the midst of your enemies" (v. 2). As the universal King, Christ will subdue his enemies in battle and execute judgment on the nations (vv. 5–6; cf. Isa. 13:9, 13; Zeph. 2:3). "The theocratic king, as the earthly representative of Jehovah, . . . was the embodiment . . . of God's purpose to establish His kingdom on earth."[106] Psalm 45 (which late Judaism and Christianity applied to the Messiah, cf. Heb. 1:8–9) characterizes Christ's triumphant reign in history (vv. 5, 17) by the words "truth," "humility," "righteousness," and "justice" (vv. 4, 6). Psalm 72 (not quoted in the New Testament) is a prayer for the Davidic king that finds fulfillment in Christ and his kingdom. Messiah's universal (v. 8) and enduring (v. 5) kingdom will be characterized by "righteousness" and "justice" (v. 2), "prosperity" (v. 3), compassion (vv. 12–14), natural fertility (v. 16), abundance of peace (v. 11), and unparalleled blessings (v. 17).

Prophetic Literature

In texts announcing the fall of Israel and Babylon, the prophetic vision merged into a time of catastrophic judgment on the earth in "the Day of the Lord." Isaiah announced the terror of that day thus: "See, the day of the LORD is coming—a cruel day, with wrath and fierce anger—to make the land desolate and destroy the sinners within it" (Isa. 13:9; cf. v.6). The scope of the divine vengeance will be worldwide (v. 11) and its implications cosmic (vv. 10, 13; cf. Matt. 24:29). Joel predicted that the divine judgments in that "great and dreadful day of the LORD" would have dramatic, universal effects (Joel 2:30–31). Jesus and John used Joel's language to describe the terrible judgments in the Day of the Lord (Matt. 24:29; Rev. 6:12; 8:8–9; 16:4, 8–9). Jeremiah stated that the Day of the LORD "will be a time of trouble for Jacob, but he will be saved out of it" (Jer. 30:7). The judgments of that day will be unparalleled in severity, but God's people will be converted (v. 9) and gathered to a place of safety (vv. 10–11). The theme of Zephaniah's prophecy is the coming of the Day of the Lord. God will pour out terrible judgments (Zeph. 1:14–18) against Judah (1:4–13; 3:1–8) and the nations (ch. 2); but afterward he will cause the scattered remnant of God's people (both Jews and Gentiles, 3:9–10) to be redeemed and restored, and to dwell in safety (3:9–20).

Certain Old Testament references to "Israel" and "Judah" envisage spiritual Israel or the more inclusive people of God. For example, the prophecy concerning the new covenant (Jer. 31:31–34; Ezek. 11:19–20; 36:25–28) finds fulfillment in the multiethnic, spiritual people of God (Matt. 26:28; 1 Cor. 11:25; Heb. 8; 9:15; 10:15–17). Other texts depicting the salvation of Israel and Judah may refer to the more inclusive people of God (Isa. 40:9; 49:5–6;

Jer. 23:6). Similarly, reference to the priestly ministrations of "the Levites" (Mal. 3:3) and the offerings of "Judah and Jerusalem" (v. 4) may describe the ministry of spiritual Israel, the new people of God. "Verse 4 . . . does not mean that descendants of Levi and Aaron will function in any NT temple; it is, rather, symbolic of a cleansed and sanctified church" (1 Peter 2:5, 9; Rev. 1:6; 5:10; 20:6).[107]

Other texts concerning a return from exile and future regathering and restoration in the Day of the Lord pertain to the Jewish nation. In the distant future Israel will be regathered and restored in the Promised Land (Ezek. 11:17–18; 36:24, 28–36) in fulfillment of the promises to the fathers. Ezekiel's apocalyptic dream-vision of the valley of dry bones (Ezek. 37) teaches that Yahweh's Spirit will cause Israel to be reconstituted. The fact that the predicted national restoration (vv. 12, 25) is linked with spiritual renewal (vv. 6, 14, 24) in fulfillment of the promised new covenant (vv. 26–27) suggests that the vision will be fully realized in the messianic age. The promise to the returning exiles embraces the blessings of the Millennium under the coming Son of David (vv. 21–26) and merges into the New Jerusalem where the tabernacle of God will be with his people (vv. 27–28; cf. Rev. 21:3).

Hosea's prophecy of the regathering of Judah and Israel under "one leader" (1:10–11) points to the future messianic age ruled by the Son of David. Hosea 3:5 paints a similar picture: "Afterward the Israelites will return and seek the LORD their God and David their king. They will come trembling to the LORD and to his blessings in the last days." The context (2:18–23) contains a graphic picture appropriate to the future messianic age: viz., harmony in nature, peace in human affairs, the elimination of war, and temporal prosperity. God will plant Israel in the land and confirm her as his special people (2:23). Romans 9:25 and 1 Peter 2:10 apply the latter verse to Gentiles entering the church. Amos 9:11–15 vividly describes the reestablishment of national Israel ("David's fallen tent," v. 11) and the worldwide rule of the Messiah in an era of Edenic prosperity (vv. 13–14). Other texts that may point to a final regathering of the nation Israel include Isaiah 43:1–8; 49:8–16; Jeremiah 16:14–15; 23:7–8; Ezekiel 20:33–44; 34:11–16; 37:25–29. Thus prophetic Scripture seems to anticipate a future for national Israel. When interpreting Old Testament prophecy we need to distinguish between Israel institutionally and Israel spiritually as the broader people of God.[108]

Scriptures such as Isaiah 2:2–5 (cf. Micah 4:1–3) point to a future age of universal peace and prosperity. The phrase "In the last days" (v. 2), refers to the period embracing Messiah's First Advent (Acts 2:17; Heb. 1:2) and Second Advent (James 5:3; 1 Peter 1:5). "Mountain" (v. 2) in the Old Testament often connotes the future kingdom of the Messiah (Isa. 11:9; 65:25; Dan. 2:35, 45). The kingdom of Isaiah 2, centered in Jerusalem (v. 3), will be universal in scope and superior to all earthly kingdoms (v. 2). In this kingdom many Gentiles will come to worship the Lord (v. 3; cf. Isa. 56:7; 66:20; Micah 4:2; Zech. 2:11), Yahweh will adjudicate all disputes (v. 4a), and weapons of war will be eliminated (v. 4b). These remarkable conditions transcend anything in the present age; hence its focus is not Christ's rule over the church. Isaiah 9:6–7 clearly portrays the messianic Son of David ruling forever in a reign of "justice," "righteousness," and "peace." Messiah's kingdom will vastly surpass the greatness of David's reign (v. 7a). Isaiah 11:4–9 records the promise of a coming Davidic king (cf. v. 1) in whom the ancient promises will be fulfilled and surpassed. Messiah's worldwide rule will be characterized by "righteousness" and "justice" (v. 4–5; cf. 9:7). Other features of this age include harmony in the natural order (vv. 6–8), peace and safety (v. 9a), and universal knowledge of God (v. 9b). References to "the earth" (vv. 4, 9), "peoples" and "nations" (v. 10) suggest that this kingdom is not heavenly or spiritual.

Isaiah 33:17–24 presents a further description of the earthly messianic kingdom. Verse 22 portrays Messiah invested with the functions of government: "The LORD is our judge, the LORD is our lawgiver, the LORD is our king." What about Isaiah 65:17–25? Since verse 17 ("Behold, I will create new heavens and a new earth. The former things will not be remembered nor will they come to mind") is cited in the context of the New Jerusalem (Rev. 21:1, 4), verses 17–19 likely describe the eternal state. Verses 20–25, however, offer a graphic description of Messiah's millennial reign. Human longevity (v. 20), material abundance (v. 21), harmony in the natural order (v. 25a), and peace and security (v. 25b) characterize the Millennium. Isaiah 65:17 represents an elaboration of Isaiah 11:6–9, which is a millennial text. The juxtaposition of Millennium and eternal state may be explained thus: "A restored Jerusalem after the exile and in the Messianic kingdom pointed toward this greater Jerusalem."[109]

Isaiah 24:1–21 ultimately refers to God's judgment poured out upon the unbelieving world in the Tribulation. Verse 22 teaches that evil powers will be bound and *afterward* judged: "They will be herded together like prisoners bound in a dungeon; they will be shut up in prison and be punished after many days [*mērōb yomîm*]." The text suggests a time interval between the incarceration of the powers and their destruction, in agreement with Revelation 20:1–3, 7–10. Verse 23 describes the glorious reign of the Lord of Hosts in the New Jerusalem (Rev. 21:22–24; 22:5).

Jeremiah 23:5–6 envisages "a righteous branch" from the line of David who would reign wisely and justly in the land ("land," *'eres* locates the scene on earth). The benefits provided by the messianic King will be spiritual ("be saved") and material ("live in safety"). Jeremiah 33:14–22 affirms that, in spite of captivity, the monarchy and priesthood will endure. Yahweh's saying "David will never fail to have a man to sit on the throne of the house of Israel" (v. 17) has been fulfilled by Jesus, the Davidic King. Verse 18 continues, "Nor will the priests, who are Levites, ever fail to have a man to stand before me continually to offer burnt offerings, to burn grain offerings and to present sacrifices." The latter does not support the reestablishment of Jewish sacrifices in the Millennium; rather, it affirms, proximately, that dynasty and priesthood would not become extinct as a result of the captivity and, ultimately, that kingship and priesthood will be united in the Davidic Branch (Ps. 110:4; Heb. 5:6–10; 7:11–25). Mention of the countless descendants of David and the Levites who minister to the Lord (v. 22) likely refers to the vast multitude of the people of God who will reign with Christ. Other texts that describe a future messianic age on earth are Isaiah 16:5; 32:1, 15–18; 35:1–10; Micah 4:1–4; and 5:2–5. Boice's judgment concerning the book of Isaiah is perceptive: "The idea of a golden age is repeated again and again, almost as a leitmotif throughout the prophecy."[110]

According to many dispensationalists, Ezekiel 40–48 describes the rebuilt Jewish temple and reconstituted Levitical worship in the Millennium. Since Ezekiel's valley of dry bones is highly symbolic (see chap. 6), so likely is his vision of the temple. Proximately Ezekiel 40–48 describes the rebuilding of

the temple following the Exile. But ultimately it figuratively depicts the perfected worship of the Millennium and eternal state. The following considerations argue against a rebuilt temple and reinstituted Levitical cultus: (1) Three times the stated purpose of the sin, grain, burnt, and fellowship offerings is to "make atonement" (Piel of *kāpar*, Ezek. 45:15, 17, 20). The Pentateuch uses identical language to describe the propitiatory nature of the Jewish sacrifices (e.g., Lev. 6:30; 8:15; 16:6). If one interprets the Levitical sacrifices literally, they must perform atoning functions. But the New Testament teaches that these sacrifices have been abolished forever by Christ's sacrifice (Heb. 8:13). (2) John interpreted Ezekiel 40–48 figuratively in terms of the spiritual inheritance and worship of the redeemed in heaven (Rev. 21:1–27). (3) A *new reality* introduced into the familiar Jewish scheme is the life-giving river flowing from the throne of God and bordered by trees, whose fruit is good for food and whose leaves heal (Ezek. 47:1–12; cf. Joel 3:18). John cited this vision in Revelation 22:1–2. (4) Ezekiel's vision ends with the words of an angel: "And the name of the city from that time on will be: THE LORD IS THERE" (Ezek. 48:35), which perfectly describes the glory of the New Jerusalem. In sum, Ezekiel 40–48 "is to be regarded as a true prediction of the kingdom of God under the forms with which the prophet was familiar, viz., those of his own (Jewish) dispensation."[111]

The events of Zechariah 12–14 occur in the future Day of the Lord (e.g., 12:3–4, 6, 8–9, 11; 13:1–2, 4). Zechariah 12:1–9 looks forward to the future trial when Israel will be invaded by hostile nations (v. 2; cf. 14:2) but strengthened by God to resist (v. 3). This Satanic onslaught will kill two-thirds of Israel (13:8–9). Following the Tribulation, the Messiah will return to rescue his surviving people and destroy the nations at Armageddon (14:3–9). By the Spirit's power Israel will be converted at the sight of him whom they killed (Zech. 12:10–14), and both the nation and the land will be cleansed from sin's defilement (13:1–6). Zechariah 14:4–5 adds that Christ will return with "all the holy ones" (*qᵉdôsîm*, departed saints and perhaps angels, cf. Matt. 25:31; 1 Thess. 3:13; 2 Thess. 1:7; Jude 14, Rev. 19:14), whose arrival will split the Mount of Olives in two. The universal messianic kingdom (cf. 9:10) that follows, centered in Jerusalem (8:3; 14:10), will be one of spiritual vitality (14:8), monotheistic religion (14:9), peace (9:10), security (14:11), universal worship (14:16–18), and holiness (14:20–21).

According to Daniel 2:31–45, Nebuchadnezzer saw in a dream a large statue made of four metals—a head of gold, chest and arms of silver, belly and thighs of bronze, and feet and legs of iron and clay. The four parts denote the Neo-Babylonian, (2:37–38), Medo-Persian (8:20), Grecian (8:21), and Roman empires. Some suggest that the toes of iron and clay (vv. 41–43) signify a later confederation, occupying the same territory as Rome, characterized by conflict and division. In a decisive act of judgment the Messiah will destroy the God-rejecting world system: "A rock was cut out, but not by human hands. It struck the statue on its feet of iron and clay and smashed them" (v. 34). By a climactic, supernatural act of God Messiah's kingdom will supplant the godless kingdoms of this world: "the rock that struck the statue became a huge mountain and filled the whole earth" (v. 35; cf. v. 44). "The fifth kingdom is the eternal kingdom of God, built on the ruins of the sinful empires of man. Its authority will extend over 'the whole earth' (v. 35) and ultimately over 'a new heaven and a new earth' (Rev. 21:1)."[112]

Daniel's dream in 7:2–14 depicts the same four world powers under the figures of a lion, a bear, a leopard, and a "terrifying and frightening and very powerful" beast (vv. 4–7). The fourth beast (the Roman Empire) had ten horns (cf. the ten toes of the fourth kingdom, 2:40–42) that may signify a future, ten-power confederation. A proud and profane "little horn" (v. 8, the Antichrist) will conquer three of the horns (v. 8, 24) and lead a coalition of the remaining rulers. The little horn will blaspheme the sovereign God, reject international law, and oppress the "saints of the Most High" for three and one-half years in the Great Tribulation: "The saints will be handed over to him for a time, times and half a time" (7:25; cf. v. 21). Then the Ancient of Days will send the Son of Man (the Messiah, v. 13) to execute judgment (vv. 9–10) and rule over the earth in an everlasting kingdom (vv. 14, 27b). The "saints" oppressed by the Antichrist are the same loyal subjects of the Most High who share in the rule of the messianic kingdom (v. 18, 21–22b, 27a); they are true believers, the people of God. Analogous to the first four kingdoms, the kingdom of the Son of Man is literal and earthly involving a certain structure. Daniel's vision of the kingdom of the Messiah likely merges into the perfected rule of God in the eternal state.

The vision of Daniel 9:24–27 has been interpreted in two main ways. Amillennialists (e.g., Augustine and Young), claim that the "sevens" are symbolic and the "seventy 'sevens'" consecutive, terminating in the earthly ministry of Christ (v. 24). According to Young[113] God decreed the accomplishment of the messianic salvation for "your people" (i.e., Israel and the church). Two segments of time ("seven 'sevens'" and "sixty-two 'sevens'") will pass from the decree to rebuild Jerusalem to Christ's First Advent (v. 25). "The Anointed One, the ruler" is the Christ. In the midst of the final "seven" the Jews will reject the Messiah and kill him (v. 26). After that Jerusalem and the temple will be destroyed by Titus, "the ruler who will come." Verse 27 reads, "He will confirm a covenant with many for one 'seven.' " The "he" refers back to Christ, "the Anointed One" of verses 25–26. The verb *higbîr* is said to mean "cause to become effective" rather than "originate," indicating that Messiah's death will cause the covenant of grace to become effectual. The words "he will put an end to sacrifice and offering," imply that Christ's death will terminate the Jewish sacrificial system; hence the temple will become desolate—i.e., will no longer have a place in God's redemptive plan.

The more coherent interpretation is as follows:[114] God ordained "seventy 'sevens' " (a group of seven years) to complete the salvation of his covenant people. The numbers seven, sixty-two, and one suggest that specific time periods are in view. The purpose of the "seventy 'sevens' " is twofold (v. 24): (1) The abolition of sin by atonement and the introduction of righteousness, which will occur at Christ's First Advent, and (2) the fulfillment of prophecy and the anointing of "the most holy," which will occur at his Second Advent. Sixty-nine "sevens" pass from the edict to rebuild Jerusalem to the coming of "the Anointed One, the ruler" (*māšîaḥ nāgîd,* v. 25). Of the several *termini* proposed the following may be preferable: The sixty-nine "sevens" commence with the decree of Artexerxes I in 458 B.C. (Ezra 7:11–16) and end with Jesus' baptism in A.D. 26. After a short interval Messiah will be crucified (v. 26a). "The people" of the coming ruler (i.e., the Romans under Titus) will destroy Jerusalem and the temple during the Jewish revolt in A.D. 70 (v. 26b). "The ruler who will come" is the Antichrist, the "little horn,"

perhaps the leader of the revived Roman confederacy (cf. 7:8, 23–25; 11:36–45). After a lengthy interval the Antichrist ("he" refers to the nearer antecedent, "the ruler who will come") will make a covenant with the Jews for seven years (v. 27a—*higbîr* means to "make firm" a covenant). In the midst of this seven-year Tribulation Antichrist will break the covenant by abolishing the Jewish worship and launching a terrible persecution (v. 27b). This future abomination of desolation (Matt. 24:15; Mark 13:14; 2 Thess. 2:4; Rev. 13:1–10) represents the less intense and widespread desecration by Antioches Epiphanes, who in 168 B.C. ended the daily sacrifices and killed a sow on the altar (1 Macc. 1:45–54; 2 Macc. 6:2; cf. Dan. 8:11–13; 11:30–32; 12:11). Christ's second coming to judge Antichrist concludes the prophecy (v. 27c).

Daniel 12 describes the Great Tribulation, the resurrection, and final judgment. As in Daniel 7:21, 25, the Antichrist will exhaust the power of "the holy people" (v. 7). The archangel Michael, however, will deliver (thereby purifying, v. 10a) God's suffering people. The "people" in view may be larger than ethnic Israel, for verse 1 describes them as "everyone whose name is found written in the book" (cf. Rev. 20:12, 15), verse 2 envisages the resurrection of *all* the saints, and verse 3 contemplates the reward of *all* "wise" believers in the Last Judgment. The text posits the resurrection of the "multitudes" after the Tribulation. Concerning the promised deliverance (v. 1b), escape from the Great Tribulation by prior rapture is a possibility. But (cf. "protect," v. 1a),

It is also possible to construe this deliverance from the time of distress in the sense of remaining steadfast in faith and triumphant in witness through it all, as Daniel and his three comrades did in the days of Nebuchadnezzar and Darius. In other words, deliverance *from* despair and fear

391

could mean the ability to stand successfully in the face of adverse pressures.[115]

The designation of the persecuted faithful ("the holy people") recalls "the saints of the Most High" in 7:18, 21, 22, 25 and likely describes all "true believers of the end time."[116] The God of the saints will powerfully intervene and destroy the Beast at Armageddon (cf. 11:40–45; Joel 3:1–16). Following that great victory all the dead will be raised bodily: "Multitudes who sleep in the dust of the earth will awake: some to everlasting life, others to shame and everlasting contempt" (v. 2).

Amillennialists argue that Daniel describes the resurrection of the just and the unjust in one breath. But the text likely reflects a compression of the prophetic vision. Thus the verse may be translated, "And many from among the sleepers of the dust of the earth shall awake; these shall be unto everlasting life; but those, the rest of the sleepers, those who do not awake at this time, shall be unto shame and everlasting contempt."[117] The lot of the righteous will be one of inestimable blessing as they receive the "inheritance" (v. 13). They will "become citizens of the most wonderful society governed by the most wonderful ruler in all human history—the millennial kingdom of our Lord Jesus Christ!"[118]

A summary of Old Testament teaching concerning the Day of the Lord follows. "The day of the LORD" (Isa. 13:6, 9; Amos 5:18, 20), "that day" (Isa. 5:30; Joel 3:18), "those days," "that time" (Joel 3:1), etc., often has a near focus in history (Isa. 13:6; Joel 1:15–2:11; Zeph. 1:14–2:15). But the phrase also connotes God's decisive intervention at the end of the age. The Day of the Lord embraces, not necessarily in chronological order, (1) God's end-of-the-age judgment on wicked Gentile nations (Isa. 2:6–22; 13:9–16; Joel 3:18–19; Zeph. 3:8; Obad. 15–17),

(2) end-of-the-age judgment on Israel (Jer. 30:7; Amos 5:18–20; Zech. 14:1–2), (3) judgment on fallen angels (Isa. 24:21–23), (4) the battle of Armageddon (Joel 3:11–16; Zech. 12:4–9; 14:3), (5) Messiah's Second Advent (Zech. 14:4–5; Mal. 3:2), (6) Israel's conversion (Zech. 12:10–14), cleansing (Joel 3:21; Zech. 13:1; Mal. 3:2–3), restoration to the land (Isa. 49:8–16; Jer. 30:3–11; Amos 9:11–15; Zech. 10:6–10) and spiritual prosperity (Joel 3:18; Obad. 17), (7) the consummation of salvation for believers (Isa. 25:9; Isa. 27; Joel 2:28–32; Mal. 4:2), (8) Messiah's millennial reign (Isa. 2:2–5; 4:2; 24:22; Hos. 2:18–23; Micah 4:1–5), culminating in (9) the new heavens and new earth (Isa. 65:17–19; 66:22; Zech. 14:6–11, 20–21). To sum up the Old Testament picture: the eschatological day of the Lord represents a dark period ("retribution," "disaster," "doom," "destruction") against a bright background (salvation for the people of God).

The Synoptic Gospels

The Olivet Discourse (Matt. 24; Mark 13; Luke 21) is the major source of Jesus' eschatological teaching. In response to the disciples' questions about the destruction of the temple (Matt. 24:3), Jesus taught the following matters regarding eschatology:

1. He described the character of the present age prior to the end (vv. 4–14). Signs that must precede his coming include false Christs (v. 5), wars and rumors of wars (v. 6–7a), famines and earthquakes (v. 7b), persecution and martyrdom (v. 9), religious apostasy (v. 10), deceiving prophets (v. 11), spiritual apathy (v. 12), and worldwide preaching of the Gospel (v. 14). The last sign is the implementation of the Great Commission (Matt. 28:18–20) to all nations.[119] In addition, there will be "the abomination that causes desolation" (v. 15) and occult signs and won-

ders (v. 24). The preceding is hardly a picture of a world transformed by the Gospel.

2. Jesus then described the Great Tribulation to follow (vv. 15–26). Verse 15 (cf. Dan. 9:27; 11:31; 12:11) *retrospectively* describes the desecration by Antiochus Epiphanes in which a pagan alter to Zeus was erected in the temple (cf. 1 Macc. 1:54) and swine were sacrificed (cf. 1 Macc. 1:47). But *prospectively* the verse refers to Antichrist's covenant-breaking activity in the end time. In Mark 13:14 *to bdelygma tēs erēmōseōs* ("the abomination that causes desolation") governs a masculine participle, suggesting that a person is in view. Since the affliction meted out upon the saints in the present age is described by the word *thlipsis* (v. 9) and that of the Great Tribulation by *thlipsis* (v. 29) and *thlipsis megalē* (v. 21), the Tribulation woes may represent an intensification of present distresses. The travail of that period will be such that unless God shortens the days none would survive (v. 22). Who are the persecuted "elect" (*eklektoi*) in the Tribulation (vv. 22, 24) whom Christ will gather at his coming (v. 31)? Dispensationalists aver they are elect Jews. Yet since Matthew and Mark were written after the Pauline letters, the "elect" in the Gospels likely are the same as those described in Romans 8:33; Colossians 3:12; and 2 Timothy 2:10 (cf. 1 Peter 1:2; 2:4). But the Roman and Colossian churches were primarily Gentile communities, and Peter wrote to Gentile believers scattered throughout Asia. Furthermore, Jesus distinguished between "you" (the disciples as representatives of all believers, vv. 6, 9, 15) and "they" (Jews, v. 30). Verse 30 literally reads, "all the tribes [*phylai*] of the earth will mourn" when they see the Son of Man whom they pierced return in glory (cf. Zech. 12:10–14). Matthew, indeed, was directed to Jewish Christians, but Mark,

who also employed the word "elect" (13:20, 22, 27) was written to Gentile believers. For these reasons *hoi eklektoi* likely describes the redeemed of all ages (cf. v. 31).[120]

3. Verses 27–31 depict the glorious, sudden (like a lightning-bolt), and universally visible return of Christ. The descriptions of Christ's posttribulational Second Advent in verses 27 (*parousia*) and 31 ("angels," "loud trumpet call," "*episynagō*") are linguistically similar to phrases in 1 Thessalonians 4:16–17 ("voice of the archangel," "trumpet call of God") and 2 Thessalonians 2:1 (*"parousia," "episynagōgē"*). Christ's coming, accompanied by cosmic disturbances (v. 29), results in the destruction of the Gentile world powers (v. 28). The meaning of Jesus' words "This generation [*genea*, "generation," "contemporaries," "period"] will certainly not pass away until all these things have happened" (v. 34; cf. Mark 13:30) is difficult to ascertain with confidence. It is most natural to interpret the saying in terms of Jesus' own generation and the fall of Jerusalem forty years later. If so, Jesus regarded the latter as a preview of the ravages of the Antichrist. In summary, Jesus made no mention of a "rapture" prior to the Tribulation and subsequent Second Advent. Dispensationalists respond that the Rapture was not the subject of discussion because Jesus answered the disciples' question about his coming to restore the kingdom to Israel.

The time of Christ's return in glory (Matt. 16:27; 25:31) is not known by the Son or by angels, but only by the Father (Mark 13:32, 33b, 35). Hence every attempt to date his coming is futile. Jesus' saying to the Twelve "You will not finish going through the cities of Israel before the Son of Man comes" (Matt. 10:23) establishes a continuing mission to Israel (along with a mission to the Gentiles) until the Second Advent. Then the Lord will return sud-

393

denly and unexpectedly (Matt. 24:44, 50), his Parousia catching people unaware as the flood did Noah's contemporaries. Thus believers must "be ready" (Matt. 24:44), "be on guard" and "be alert" (Mark 13:33), and "keep watch" (v. 35; cf. v. 37). Luke 18:8— "when the Son of Man comes, will he find faith on the earth"—opposes postmillennialism by teaching that life on earth when Christ returns will be one of spiritual declension and persecution (cf. 17:26–30). How shall we understand Luke 21:36: "Be always on the watch, and pray that you may be able to escape all that is about to happen, and that you may be able to stand before the Son of Man"? If the verb *ekpheugō* (to "escape out of the midst of"; cf. Acts 16:27; 19:16) implies physical removal from the end-time trials, then pretribulationism is supported. But if the text is taken as a prayer for strength to escape by persevering to the end (cf. v. 35), then posttribulationism is indicated.[121]

Jesus taught that the Parousia will effect a dramatic separation of the righteous and the unrighteous (Matt. 24:40–41). The parable of the weeds depicts both weeds (unbelievers) and wheat (believers) growing together until the end (Matt. 13:24–30, 36–43). Since the main point of this parable is God's judgment on false disciples (vv. 40–42), the final disposition of the evildoers is mentioned first. The parable hardly supports the postmillennial view of a converted world in the present age. The parable of the net also teaches God's judgment on false disciples (Matt. 13:47–50). According to Matthew 25:31–46, the end will entail the separation of righteous and unrighteous and their respective destinies in heaven or hell. In the story Jesus again telescoped into a single event his coming for reward and his coming for judgment (cf. John 5:28–29). In Luke 20:34–35 Jesus contrasted "the people of this age" with "those who are considered worthy

of taking part in that age and in the resurrection from the dead [*hē anastasis tēs ek nekrōn*]." The latter phrase suggests a prior resurrection of believers from among unbelieving humanity (cf. Phil. 3:11). Such an interpretation supports a premillennial Second Advent.

The Gospels present allusions, at least, of Christ's millennial kingdom. Concerning the son to be born to Mary, the angel Gabriel predicted, "The Lord God will give him the throne of his father David, and he will reign over the house of Jacob forever; his kingdom will never end" (Luke 1:32b–33). Mary would have understood this saying literally in terms of the messianic inheritance of David's throne. Jesus' saying to his disciples is equally pertinent: "at the renewal of all things, when the Son of Man sits on his glorious throne, you who have followed me will also sit on twelve thrones, judging the twelve tribes of Israel" (Matt. 19:28; cf. Luke 22:29–30). The "renewal" (*palingenēsia*) signifies the restoration of the world order in fulfillment of the Old Testament kingdom promises. The disciples who share Christ's sufferings will in the future, messianic kingdom participate in his rule (cf. Dan. 7:27; 2 Tim. 2:12; Rev. 2:26). It is difficult to decide whether the objects of this rule are national (cf. Luke 2:32) or spiritual Israel, the church (cf. James 1:1, "To the twelve tribes scattered among the nations . . ."). Luke 12:32 may also pertain: "Do not be afraid, little flock, for your Father has been pleased to give you the kingdom." Jesus' disciples already shared in the blessings of his rule; but at the end of the age they would possess it completely.

Primitive Christianity/Acts

In Acts 1:11 (cf. 3:20) two angels informed the perplexed apostles that the ascended Christ would return to earth personally, bodily, visibly, and gloriously. Jesus himself said that the time of his coming to inaugurate the kingdom was God's secret (Acts 1:7). Rather than speculate about the time of the Parousia, Jesus' followers must witness to him faithfully throughout the world. In obedience to their calling, Paul stated that Christians "must go through many hardships to enter the kingdom of God" (Acts 14:22). The Greek word *thlipsis* ("affliction, "tribulation") is used both of present trials (John 16:33; Acts 11:19; 20:23) and of the future distress of the Great Tribulation (Mark 13:19, 24; Rev. 7:14).

James' words to the Jerusalem Council (Acts 15:13–18) have been interpreted in two ways. According to many dispensationalists, the passage teaches the following sequence: (1) the calling out of Gentiles (v. 14), (2) Christ's return (v. 16a), (3) the establishment of Israel in the Millennium (v. 16b), and (4) the final salvation of Gentiles in the kingdom (v. 17). Historic premillennialists and amillennialists aver that James quoted Amos 9:11–12 to make the single point that God intended from the beginning to save Gentiles and include them in the church (cf. Acts 15:14–15). Amillennialists argue that verses 16 ("David's fallen tent") and 17 ("all the Gentiles") refer to the same event—i.e., the salvation of Gentiles. Thus Harrison comments, "The introduction of a whole panorama of prophecy at the Jerusalem Council goes far beyond the demands of the situation. . . . The one item James was concerned to validate from Scripture was the inclusion of the Gentiles in the Christian fellowship (v. 14)."[122]

The Pauline Writings

The series of resurrections in 1 Corinthians 15:22–24 may point to a literal millennium. "For as in Adam all die, so in Christ all will be made alive" (v. 22).

"But each in his own turn [*tagma*]: Christ the firstfruits; then [*epeita*], when he comes [*parousia*], those who belong to him" (v.23). *Tagma*, a military term, means "band," "group" or "class," and *epeita*, "next in order, "afterward," indicates a temporal sequence (cf. vv. 6–7, 46). Verse 23 states that Christ's resurrection is followed some time later by believers' resurrection at the Second Advent. Note that the text affirms a single coming of Christ and (contra amillennialism) that the Parousia effects the resurrection of believers only. "Then [*eita*] the end [*telos*] will come, when he hands over the kingdom to God the Father after he has destroyed all dominion, authority and power" (v. 24). *Eita* (a temporal adverb synonymous with *epeita*) means "next," "after that" (Mark 4:17; John 19:27; 1 Cor. 15:5), and *telos* connotes the end of the resurrection process involving the unrighteous dead. The point is that, analogous to the preceding interval, *eita* marks a period of indefinite duration between the raising of the saved at the Parousia and the raising of the unsaved at the end of the Millennium.[123] The kingdom (*basileia*) cannot be Christ's reign present over the church, for everything is yet future (the resurrection of the dead [v. 21], the Parousia [v. 24], the kingdom [vv. 24–25a], and the destruction of Satan and death [vv. 25–26]).

Elsewhere Paul hinted at two resurrections by writing that he aspires "somehow, to attain to the resurrection from the dead" (*tēn exanastasin tēn ek nekrōn,* Phil. 3:11)—literally "the out-resurrection out from among the dead ones." Second Timothy 3:1–5, 13 argues against postmillennialism by teaching that as the present age progresses godlessness and moral decadence will increase. The forceful language hardly paints a picture of a world transformed by the Gospel.

Paul appears to have anticipated a

future for institutional Israel. God has not totally rejected his chosen people (Rom. 11:1), for true to his promises God will graft the natural branches (ethnic Israel) back into the parent olive tree (the kingdom of God). His statement "Israel has experienced a hardening in part until the full number of the Gentiles has come in. And so all Israel shall be saved" (Rom. 11:25b–26) suggests that when the full complement of believing Gentiles is achieved the nation will experience God's salvation. Israel's blindness during the church age will be followed by national restoration and salvation (see the numerous Scriptures under the prophetic teaching, above). The occasion of Israel's conversion may be the Parousia, when the chosen people behold the promised One whom they rejected. Paul here "is dealing with nations: with the Gentile nations, and the Jewish nation. And thus dealing he speaks of the 'fullness of the Gentiles' coming in, and of 'all Israel' being saved."[124]

Concerning the Rapture, consider 1 Corinthians 15:51–52. Pretribulationists aver that, since the Old Testament taught only a general resurrection, the "mystery" (v. 51) is the secret rapture of the saints. Posttribulationists identify the "mystery" as new teaching about the resurrection body—namely, that at Christ's return believers will receive transformed, imperishable bodies suited for heavenly existence ("the perishable must clothe itself with the imperishable," v. 53; cf. v. 50). Paul's words "we will all be changed" (v. 51) discredit the partial-rapture thesis. Paul located the raising of deceased saints and the transformation of living saints "at the last trumpet" (v. 52). Pretribulationists identify this trumpet with the rapture trumpet of 1 Thessalonians 4:16. Most midtribulationists identify it with the seventh trumpet of Revelation 11:15. Posttribulationists, however, equate it with the trumpet of Matthew 24:31 and the anticipatory seventh trumpet of Revelation 11:15 that signals the end of the present world-order and the final judgments. The resurrection of 15:51–52 is the same as the resurrection of 15:21–23, i.e., of the righteous at the Second Advent. In summary, Paul's concern here is not to present a systematic eschatology (citing events that precede the Second Coming) but to uphold the believer's inheritance of an imperishable body at Christ's return.

First Thessalonians 4:13–17 is an important Rapture text, which we examine verse by verse. Verse 14: "We believe that God will bring with Jesus those who have fallen asleep in him." When Christ returns to earth he will bring believers now in heaven with him (cf. 1 Thess. 3:13). Verse 15: "We who are still alive, who are left till the coming [parousia] of the Lord, will certainly not precede those who have fallen asleep." Deceased saints will not be deprived for having died prior to his return. Verse 16: "For the Lord himself will come down from heaven, with a loud command, with the voice of the archangel and with the trumpet call of God, and the dead in Christ will rise first." Christ's return will be literal and personal, and the believing dead will be physically raised before living believers are transformed. Pretribulationists envisage Christ meeting the saints in the air and taking them to heaven. Posttribulationists maintain that the verb "descend" (katabainō) means a complete descent to the earth (cf. Matt. 3:16; John 3:13; 6:33, 38, 41–42). Pretribulationists regard verses 16–17 as the secret Rapture, but posttribs observe that the event—accompanied by "a loud command," "the voice of the archangel," and "the trumpet call of God" (cf. Matt. 24:31; 1 Cor. 15:52; Rev. 11:15)—is very open and public. Some pretribulationists identify "the dead in Christ" as church age believers (Old Testament saints being raised after the Tribulation), whereas posttribulationists identify them as all the believing dead.

Verse 17: "After that, we who are still alive and are left will be caught up together with them in the clouds to meet [*eis apantēsin*] the Lord in the air. And so we will be with the Lord forever." The verb *harpazō* means to "snatch up, seize, carry off by force, rapture."[125] Posttribulationists claim that raised and transformed saints will meet Christ in the air as he descends and will accompany him back to earth. They observe that the Greeks used *apantēsis* for a delegation that went out to meet an approaching dignitary and returned with him to his destination (cf. Matt. 25:6; Acts 28:15). "When a dignitary paid an official visit (*parousia*) to a citizen in Hellenistic times, the action of the leading citizens in going out to meet him and escort him back on the final stage of his journey was called the *apantēsis*."[126] Pretribulationists ask, why need the church rise at all? Why not remain on earth for Christ to separate them from the unsaved?[127] Verse 18: "Therefore encourage each other with these words." Pretribulationists explain the "comfort" in terms of the pretribulational rapture, though the Thessalonian Christians had experienced "severe suffering" (1:6), "trials" (3:3), and "distress and persecution" (3:7). According to posttribulationists, deceased believers are not disadvantaged by having died before Christ's Second Advent.

Viewing *peri de* (1 Thess. 5:1) as adversative, pretribulationists distinguish between 1 Thessalonians 4:13–18—the Rapture or Christ's coming *for* the saints in the day of Christ—and 5:1–11—Christ's coming *with* the saints for judgment in the Day of the Lord. Posttribulationists hold that *de* is a transitional particle by which Paul moved from the status of the dead at the Parousia (chap. 4) to the responsibilities of the living in light of that awesome event (chap. 5). Paul's mention of "times and dates" (5:1) without further elaboration suggests that the principal event discussed in chapter 5 is the same as that of chapter 4. "The day of the Lord" (5:2; cf. 1 Cor. 5:5; 2 Thess. 2:2) is identical to the day of Jesus Christ (1 Cor. 1:8; 2 Cor. 1:14; Phil. 1:6, 10; 2:16). That day would come suddenly like a thief and catch unbelievers unawares (5:2–4). Believers are to be "alert," "self-controlled," and "watchful" (vv. 5–8; cf. Matt. 24:42–44) so they will not be caught off guard by this event. Verse 9 reads as follows: "God did not appoint us to suffer wrath [*orgē*] but to receive salvation [*sōtēria*] through our Lord Jesus Christ." Pretribulationists interpret this as deliverance from the wrath of the Great Tribulation, the concern of the context (1:10; 4:16–17). Posttribulationists note that the verse follows Paul's mention of the future aspect of "salvation" (v. 8) effected "through our Lord Jesus Christ" (v. 9) and conclude that the "wrath" is meted out in the Final Judgment. That the wrath is perdition in hell is made clear in Romans 2:5–8, where the final judgment is specified, and in Romans 5:9, where deliverance from *orgē* is accomplished by Christ's justifying work. See also 1 Thessalonians 1:10.

This side of eternity believers do not experience *orgē* (eschatological wrath on the unsaved), but they will experience *thlipsis* ("oppression, affliction, tribulation").[128] *Thlipsis* commonly describes the future tribulation distress (Matt. 24:21, 29; Mark 13:19, 24; Rev. 2:22; 7:14). Yet Paul repeatedly used the word to teach that, in solidarity with Christ's sufferings (2 Cor. 1:5; Phil. 3:10; 1 Peter 4:13), believers must endure oppression from enemies of the Gospel (Rom. 5:3; Eph. 3:13; 1 Thess. 3:7). In several texts the *thlipsis* that believers must endure now is exceedingly severe (2 Cor. 8:2; 1 Thess. 1:6; 2 Thess. 1:4).

Paul stated in 2 Thessalonians 1:6–10 that in the Day of the Lord God will punish those who afflict the saints (v. 6) with everlasting destruction and separation from his presence (vv. 8–9). In addition to punishing the wicked, God will provide relief for afflicted believers (v. 7). It is important to note that the saints' deliverance from affliction and the eternal destruction of the wicked occur together in the Day of the Lord (vv. 9–10) or at the Parousia (1 Thess. 2:19; 3:13; 4:15; 5:23; 2 Thess. 2:1, 8). The latter is the *apokalypsis* of the Lord Jesus (v. 7; cf. 1 Cor. 1:7; 1 Peter 1:7, 13; 4:13) when he comes to be glorified in his saints (v. 10), which is also his *epiphaneia* (2 Thess. 2:8).

Second Thessalonians 2:1–8 requires close examination. Paul responded to the believers' concern that the Day of the Lord had come by identifying three events that must precede that day: (1) the apostasy, (2) removal of "the restrainer," and (3) the revelation of the man of lawlessness or the Antichrist. Consider the text verse by verse.

Verses 1–2: "Concerning the coming [*parousia*] of our Lord Jesus Christ and our being gathered [*episynagōgē*] to him, we ask you, brothers, not to become easily unsettled or alarmed by some prophecy, report or letter supposed to have come from us, saying that the day of the Lord has already come." *The Scofield Reference Bible* replaced "the day of the Lord" (v. 2) with "the day of Christ" to argue that the event is the pretribulational coming of Christ *for* his saints.[129] Other pretribulationists acknowledge that the Day of the Lord is a period that begins with the rapture of the church.[130] Posttribulationists hold that the *parousia* (v. 1, cf. v. 8) and the *episynagōgē* (v. 1, posttribulational in Matt. 24:31 and Mark 13:27), concern the single second advent of Christ (cf. 1 Thess. 5:1–9, 23)

within the period of "the day of the Lord." Verse 3: "Don't let anyone deceive you in any way, for that day will not come until the rebellion [*hē apostasia*] occurs and the man of lawlessness is revealed, the man doomed to destruction." Some pretribulationists affirm that *apostasia* signifies the Rapture, the verse teaching that the Tribulation will not occur until Christ removes the church from earth. Posttribulationists observe that *apostasia* ("falling away, rebellion, revolt, apostasy")[131] primarily connotes religious apostasy and civil disorder. They note that *apostasia* in the LXX (Josh. 22:22; 2 Chron. 10:19; 33:10; Jer. 2:19), in the Apocrypha (1 Macc. 2:15; 2 Esdras 5:1–12), the Pseudepigrapha (Jub. 23:14–21; 1 Enoch 91:7; 93:9), and rabbinic writings (b. Sanh. 97) consistently denotes rebellion against God. Moreover, the only other use of *apostasia* in the New Testament (Acts 21:21) describes departure from the teaching of Moses. And, whereas the verb *aphistēmi* occurs ten times in the sense of physical separation (e.g., Luke 4:13; Acts 12:10; 19:9), it is used four times of religious defection (Luke 8:13; 1 Tim. 4:1; 2 Tim. 2:19; Heb. 3:12).

Robert H. Gundry has done a detailed study of *apostasia* in this text. He notes that the meaning of a New Testament word is determined from (1) other uses of the word in Scripture, (2) the Septuagint, (3) *koinē* Greek, and (4) classical Greek. Gundry observes that "at the time the NT was written, *apostasia* had acquired the limited meaning of departure in the spheres of religion and politics, i.e., political revolt and religious apostasy."[132] Moreover, "*apostasia* and its cognate . . . appear over forty times in the LXX . . . —every time with the meaning of religious or political defection. In matters of vocabulary and style the LXX strongly influenced the NT writers, whose Bible for the most part was the LXX."[133] He continues: "The *koinē* . . . offers several examples of political rebellion and religious apostasy, but not one example of simple spatial departure. No wonder, then, that NT lexicons uniformly give *apostasia* the special sense of religious apostasy and political rebellion— BAGD, Kittel, Cremer, Abott-Smith, Thayer, and others. No wonder also that scholarly commentators on 2 Thessalonians interpret *apostasia* as bearing this meaning—Alford, Ellicot, Moffatt, F. F. Bruce, Frame, Milligan, Morris, and others."[134] Gundry adds that classical Greek usage is the least determinative. "But even in classical Greek simple departure by no means predominates."[135] In summary:

> *apostasia* had acquired the special sense of religious apostasy or political defection. Whereas *aphistēmi* very many times carries the simple meaning of spatial departure, *apostasia* appears elsewhere in the NT and many times throughout the LXX *solely* with the special meaning. Such usage counts far more than etymology. We should take the meaning which a word had during the time and in the culture in which it was written instead of making recourse to a literal definition of the root. Thus, the terms "apostasy," "falling away," and "rebellion" do not overlay the Greek word with a questionable interpretation. They rather represent a valid and necessary recognition of the *usus loquendi*—i.e., they are true translations.[136]

This being the case, Paul wrote that the day of the Lord would not precede the end-time spiritual declension and the manifestation of the Antichrist.

Verse 4: "He will oppose and will exalt himself over everything that is called God or is worshiped, so that he sets himself up in God's temple [*naos*], proclaiming himself to be God." The lawless one will invade the most holy place and demand to be worshiped as God (cf. vv. 9–11). Verse 4 thus culminates the spiritual apostasy mentioned in verse 3. Verse 5: "Don't you remember that when I was with you I used to tell you these things?" Verse 6: "And now you know what is holding him back, so that he may be revealed at the proper time." Pretribulationists identify the restraining force (*to katechon*, neuter) as the power of the Holy Spirit, whereas posttribulationists identify it either as the principle of law and God-ordained government[137] or the power of God.[138] Verse 7: "For the secret power of lawlessness is already at work; but the one who now holds it back will continue to do so till he is taken out of the way." Pretribulationists interpret the restraining person (*ho katechōn*, masc.) as the Holy Spirit in the world through the church.[139] Posttribulationists, noting that the Spirit's removal from earth is cited nowhere else in Scripture, identify the restrainer as either the principle of government personified in human rulers (Tertullian and many church fathers) or as God himself. Marshall observes that the presence of both the *neuter* and the *masculine* participles "suggests that Paul is thinking of some entity which can be regarded both as a principle and as a person."[140] F. F. Bruce gave an insightful rationale for Paul's reticence to identify the restrainer: "This can best be explained if more explicit language was liable to cause trouble should the letter fall into the wrong hands."[141] Were the restrainer the Holy Spirit, Paul likely would have said so more directly. Thus at the end of the age when God-ordained government collapses a great Satan-inspired anarchy will break loose.

Verse 8: "And then the lawless one will be revealed, whom the Lord Jesus will overthrow with the breath of his mouth and destroy by the splendor of his coming [*hē epiphaneia tēs parousia autou*]." This refers to Christ's second advent to gather the church, destroy Antichrist, and establish the Millennium. *Epiphaneia* in all but one occurrence (2 Tim. 1:10) denotes Christ's second advent (1 Tim. 6:14; 2 Tim. 4:1, 8; Titus 2:13). Posttribulationists insist that the *parousia* of 2 Thessalonians 2:8 is identical with the *parousia* of verse 1, and thus the text envisages no prior rapture of the saints. Additionally verses 9–10 indicate that during the last half of the Tribulation the counterfeit Christ "deceives those who are perishing" by supernatural signs. Implied is the conviction that believers who are alert will not be so deceived.

Did Paul teach that Christ's return for the church is strictly imminent (i.e., an any-moment event)? Romans 13:11–12, often said to teach this, reads, "Our salvation is nearer now than when we first believed. The night is nearly over; the day is almost here." Scripture affirms that Christ's First Advent nearly two thousand years ago set in motion the "last days" (Acts 2:17). "Since the next great event in God's redemptive plan is the Second Coming of Christ, 'the night,' no matter how long chronologically it may last, is 'nearly over.' "[142] Other texts may be understood in similar fashion: 1 Corinthians 7:29 ("the time is short"), Philippians 4:5 ("the Lord is near"), as well as James 5:8–9, 1 Peter 4:7, and 1 John 2:18. In light of Christ's certain return, Paul enjoined attentive watching (Rom. 8:23, 25; 1 Cor. 1:7; Gal. 5:5; Phil. 3:20). The verb in each of the preceding texts is *apekdechomai,* to "await expectantly but patiently."[143] That for which believers patiently wait is the redemption of the body (Rom. 8:23) and acquittal at the Last Judgment (Gal. 5:5), which will occur at the *apokalypsis* of our Lord (1 Cor. 1:7) or in "the day of our Lord Jesus Christ" (1 Cor. 1:8; cf. Phil. 1:6).

Johannine Literature

John's statement "this is the last hour" (1 John 2:18) indicates that the church age is the final era before Christ's second advent. Even though the duration of the interadvental period may be long, believers are to be alert and watchful for his return. Prior to the end many antichrists will appear who will deny Christ (1 John 2:22; 4:3) and the faith (2 John 7). Because the spirit of Antichrist is at work in the world (1 John 4:3), Jesus said to his disciples (John 16:33), "In this world you will have trouble [*thlipsis*]." Indeed, their time of "anguish" (*thlipsis*, v. 21) and "grief" (*lupē,* v. 22) had already begun. As Jesus declared, "If they persecuted me, they will persecute you also" (15:20). Thus Jesus prayed to the Father, ". . . not that you take them out of the world but that you protect them from the evil one" (John 17:15). Also verse 11: "Holy Father, protect them by the power of your name." The verb *tēreō* in the preceding verses means to "keep under guard." Jesus did not seek the disciples' removal from the hostile world; rather, he prayed for their protection and sanctification in the midst of the fallen world order (v. 17). "The Lord specifically disavows a prayer that the disciples may escape the evil one by their removal from the world."[144]

The Second Advent is not a major theme in the fourth gospel. However, in John 14:3 Jesus said to his disciples, "If I go and prepare a place for you, I will come back and take you to be with me that you also may be where I am." The present tense of *erchomai* may suggest that Christ comes to his people in various ways: (1) via his postresurrection appearances (John 14:19; 16:22), (2) through the gift of the Paraclete (14:18–23), and (3) at the believer's death. The primary focus in 14:3, however, is his Second Advent, the consummation of all other comings. Some pretribulationists claim John 14:3 as a major Rapture text, arguing that the verse teaches Christ's coming in the air *for* his saints to take them directly to the Father's house.[145] According to posttribulationists, the verse states that at his single Second Advent Jesus will cause dead and living saints to be with him, beholding his glory (John 17:24). This presence with Christ begins in the earthly Millennium and continues forever in the Father's house. In his High Priestly Prayer the Lord did not present a systematic eschatology; rather, he shared his heart's burden with the Father at a very intimate level. "Jesus does not touch on the cosmic dimensions of the Lord's return; it is introduced here as the consummation of the personal fellowship between him and his disciples."[146]

John wrote the Apocalypse amidst a wave of severe persecution against Christians. Many were suffering affliction (Rev. 2:9–10) and some were martyred for their faith (2:13). John wrote to assure believers that in spite of the mounting evil Christ is Lord of history. Moreover, he will return from heaven (1:7) shortly (1:3; 22:10) or without delay (tachy, 3:11; 22:7, 12, 20) to destroy opponents of the Gospel. Therefore believers must patiently endure hardships and persevere in faith (1:9; 2:3, 19; 3:10a; 13:10; 14:12). Consider the following overview of the Apocalypse.

Following [I] the Introduction and Greetings (1:1–8), John recalled [II] his Patmos Vision of Christ (1:9–20), which contains a three-point outline of the book (1:19): "what [is] seen" (ch. 1), "what is now" (chs. 2–3), and "what will take place later" (chs. 4–22). There follows [III] a section dealing with Christ and the Churches (chs. 2–3) that contains messages from the risen Lord to seven congregations in Asia Minor relevant to churches today. It is doubtful that the messages offer a summary of the history of the church in its downward course as some dispensationalists affirm. To the church at Philadelphia, Christ said, "I will also keep you from the hour of trial that is going to come upon the whole world" (3:10). Pretribulationists interpret *tērēsō ek tēs hōras tou peirasmou* as deliverance from the time-period of tribulation by rapture (cf. John 12:27; Heb. 5:7).[147] Posttribulationists hold that *tēreō ek* signifies divine preservation in the midst of trials (cf. John 17:5, which teaches protection within the sphere of trouble; also Rev. 7:14), and that "hour" denotes the trials themselves (Mark 14:35). They note also Jesus' words that the Philadelphians "have kept [his] command to endure patiently." On balance the text offers conclusive support for neither view.

The major portion of Revelation concerns [IV] Christ and the Tribulation (chs. 4–19). The Introductory Vision (chs. 4–5) begins with a trumpetlike summons to John from an angel in heaven: "Come up here, and I will show you what must take place after this" (4:1). Many pretribulationists see in this verse the rapture of the church.[148] Since there is no hint of any descent of Christ and since John is on earth in the Tribulation sections of Revelation (see 10:1; 13:1; 18:1), the verse likely describes the apostle caught up in an ecstatic vision to see the future from a heavenly perspective. John saw in heaven "twenty-four elders [*presbyteroi*]" seated on twenty-four thrones (4:4; cf., e.g., 4:10–11; 5:5–14). Pretribulationists interpret these glorified and enthroned elders as representatives of the raptured church and so approve of the Textus Receptus (and KJV) reading, "Thou . . . hast redeemed *us* to God" (5:9). Posttribulationists note that the elders are juxtaposed with "four living creatures" (see the previous texts) and *both offer up the prayers of the saints* (5:8). They follow the NIV (cf. NRSV) reading: "You purchased *men* for God," and judge that the elders are heavenly beings similar to seraphim or cherubim who worship the Lamb and execute the divine order of the universe. "These may constitute the order of angel-princes called 'thrones' in Col. 1:16; . . . they discharge priestly functions before the throne of God."[149] The seven-sealed scroll that Christ will open (5:1-7) contains the eschatological judgments of the seals, trumpets, and bowls of wrath (chs. 6-19).

The Opening of the Seven Seals (6:1-8:1) represents the unleashing of preliminary judgments. The first four seals describe armed invasion, famine, and death. The fifth seal prefigures persecution and martyrdom, and the sixth—using Day of the Lord language (cf. Ezek. 32:7-10; Joel 2:31; cf. Mark 13:24-25)—describes the end of the Great Tribulation. The seventh seal—accompanied by silence in heaven—awaits the Last Judgment. The parenthetical Vision of the Tribulation Saints (ch. 7) follows. Pretribulationists interpret the 144,000 from the tribes of Israel (7:4-8; cf. 14:1-5) as the Jewish remnant saved during the Tribulation. Posttribulationists view these "servants of our God" (v. 3) as symbolic of spiritual Israel, the church, who are *sealed*, thus sparing them from God's Tribulation wrath (7:3; cf. 9:4, 20; 14:9-10; 16:2; 18:4). F. F. Bruce concluded, "The followers of Christ are here viewed as the true 'Israel of God'; and the number [12,000 times 12] indicates the sum total of the faithful."[150] The result of this sealing is the deliverance and final glorification in heaven of this "great multitude . . . from every nation, tribe, people and language" who "have come out of the great tribulation" (vv. 9-17).

The Sounding of the Seven Trumpets (8:2-11:19) depicts judgments more severe than those of the seals. They bring us to the sober events of the latter half of Daniel's Seventieth Week. The first four trumpets (8:7-12) represent judgments that affect one-third of the earth. The last three trumpets are especially deadly. The fifth announces demonic activity that plagues only the "unsealed" (9:1-12), and the sixth is a demon-inspired force that massacres one-third of humanity (vv. 13-21). A parenthesis (11:1-14) describes the ministry of two godly witnesses who prophesy for 1,260 days (or 3½ years). The beast kills them, and their bodies lie in the streets as a public spectacle. After a short time God raises them to heaven in a cloud. Pretribulationists identify the pair as *converted Jews* who are witnesses of Christ during the "time of Jacob's trouble." Posttribulationists see the witnesses as a symbol of the *church* bearing courageous testimony during the Great Tribulation and raised at the end.[151] Some midtribulationists identify the raising of the witnesses as the rapture of the church (11:11-15). The seventh trumpet (11:15-19), however, proleptically announces the end of the Tribulation, the establishment of Christ's millennial kingdom (vv. 15, 17), and God's final judgment (v. 18).

A parenthesis (12:1-14:20) describes the nature of the age-long conflict between God and Satan and prepares for the vision of the seven bowls of wrath (16:1-21). Pretribulationists view the scene of the woman who gave birth to a male child and who fled into the wilderness to escape the dragon as the believing remnant of Israel. Posttribulationists regard the woman (12:1) as spiritual Israel, the messianic community, and "the rest of her offspring" (12:17) as Christian believers who testify to Jesus (12:11) and "obey God's commandments" (12:17). The Dragon is Satan, the male child is Christ, and Michael is the preserving angel of God's people. The fact that the woman is spared for 3½ years (12:6; cf. the "sealing" of God's people, above) suggests to posttribulationists that the saints are kept safe during Antichrist's reign of terror.[152] The conflict continues with the account of the two beasts. The ten-horned beast from the sea (13:1-8; cf.

11:7; 17:8–11; Dan. 7:7) represents the Roman Empire, personified in the persecuting emperor who anticipates the end-time Antichrist. The beast is empowered by Satan (13:2, 5–7) to make war against the saints (13:7) and is worshiped by the unbelieving world (13:4, 8, 12, 15). The two-horned beast from the earth (13:11–18), who performs miraculous signs and exercises economic dictatorship, is the False Prophet or lieutenant of Antichrist's (16:13; 19:20; 20:10). He bears the enigmatic number 666 (13:18). There follows a series of anticipatory visions portraying the fall of Babylon (14:8), the wrath of God against the followers of Antichrist (vv. 9–11), and the final conflict of Armageddon (vv. 14–20).

The Seven Bowls of God's Wrath (16:1–21) are poured out at the end of the Great Tribulation (16:1–2). The contents of the bowl judgments are similar to those of the trumpets. Intensively the bowls are more severe than the trumpets, and extensively they afflict the entire earth, not just a part of it. The seventh bowl (16:17–21) signifies the final execution of God's terrible judgment against the evil alliance at Armageddon in the Day of the Lord. The seals, trumpets, and bowls are not strictly consecutive but overlap considerably.

The Vision of the Fall of Babylon (17:1–18:24) previews the effects of Christ's coming in judgment. The woman on the scarlet beast is described as "BABYLON THE GREAT THE MOTHER OF PROSTITUTES AND OF THE ABOMINATIONS OF THE EARTH" (17:5). John added that "the woman . . . is the great city that rules over the kings of the earth" (17:18), which proximately was pagan Rome (17:9, 18; 18:10). Ultimately, however, "Babylon the Great" (cf. 14:8) denotes not the revived Mesopotamian city,[153] but the fallen political, economic, and religious system at the end of the age. The view of the *Scofield Reference*

Bible (the original and revised editions) identifying Babylon as apostate Christendom headed up by the papacy is also too restrictive. We saw in 13:1–10 that the beast on which the woman sits is the Roman Empire personified in the persecuting emperor, which symbolizes the end-time Antichrist. This suggests that godless society, in its disordered and demonic behavior, is impelled by the Evil One. The collapse of Babylon— i.e., civilization organized apart from God—which has brutalized the people of God throughout history, is graphically described in 18:1–24.

Pretribulationists observe that the word *church* (*ekklēsia*), although used in chapters 1–3 and in 22:16, is absent from the Tribulation section of the Apocalypse (chs. 4–19). Posttribulationists respond that since many scenes in chapters 4–19 are set in heaven (4:1– 5:14; 7:9–8:5; 11:15–12:12; 15:2–16:1; 19:1–10) the argument is unconvincing. In addition, as Moo notes, "John . . . *never* uses *ekklēsia* other than as a designation of a local body of believers."[154] In five texts Tribulation believers are designated "saints" (*hoi hagioi*, 13:7, 10; 16:6; 17:6; 18:24). Revelation 12:17 identifies them as "those who obey God's commandments and hold to the testimony of Jesus." The beast has power to conquer them (13:7). Yet the saints overcome him by the blood of the Lamb (12:11; cf. 15:2), an experience that is the lot of all Christians (1:5b).

Analysis shows that God's *orgē* ("settled state of wrath") falls on the unsaved worshipers of the beast and the evil world system (6:16–17; 11:18; 14:10; 16:19; 19:15). God's *thymos* ("violent outburst of anger") likewise strikes only the wicked, i.e., the armies of the Beast, Babylon, and the unbelieving nations (12:12; 14:8, 10, 19; 15:1, 7; 16:1, 19; 19:15). The outpouring of God's wrath thus is selective (9:4; 16:2) and is clustered toward the end of the

Great Tribulation. John, however, used *thlipsis* ("trouble, distress, suffering") to designate tribulations directed against God's people by evil powers both in the present (John 16:21, 33; Rev. 1:9; 2:9–10, 22) and in Daniel's Seventieth Week (Rev. 7:14). All agree that true believers do not experience divine wrath.

Christ's Second Coming and associated events are described in 19:1–21. The heavenly hosts rejoice greatly over Babylon's destruction (vv. 1–6) and over the wedding supper of the Lamb— the union of Christ and his church (vv. 7–10). Pretribulationists aver that the latter occurs during the interval between the Rapture and Christ's return to earth with the saints. Posttribulationists locate it following the Second Advent. The "KING OF KINGS AND LORD OF LORDS" returns to vanquish his foes, followed by "the armies of heaven" (v. 14). The latter may designate angels and risen saints (cf. 17:14). Christ descends to destroy the forces of the Antichrist and the False Prophet at the final great battle of Armageddon (vv. 17–21). Thereafter the two beasts are "thrown alive into the fiery lake of burning sulphur" (v. 20).

The next major section [V] concerns Christ and the Millennium (20:1–15). Having disposed of Antichrist and the False Prophet, God next deals with Satan, the power behind the two beasts. God's destruction of the evil triumvirate is evidence that the casting of Satan into the Abyss for a thousand years (vv. 2–3) is a literal, future event (premillennialists) rather than a figurative description of the church age (amillennialists). Moreover, Satan's binding in Matthew 12:29 restrains his ability to control individuals, whereas the binding in Revelation 20:2 restricts his ability to deceive the nations. Verse 4 describes the coming to life (*ezēsan*) of those seated on thrones (apostles and saints) and of martyrs (those who did not worship the beast) to reign with Christ for a thousand years. "This is the first resurrection" (v. 5b). "The rest of the dead [i.e., the unsaved] did not come to life [*ezēsan*] until the thousand years were ended" (v. 5a). Since the second resurrection involves a literal bodily raising from the dead, so also likely does the first resurrection.[155] Moreover, since verses 2–3 deal with the earth, so also do verses 4–6 that describe the resurrection of the saints and their reign with Christ. Posttribulationists add that since "first" and "second" are *temporal* in force, a prior large-scale rapture is excluded. Thus the "first resurrection" following the Tribulation and prior to the Millennium concerns all the righteous dead, including church saints (cf. 5:9–10).[156]

It is likely that Israel will turn in faith to their Messiah at his glorious Second Advent (Zech. 12:10–13:1). At the close of the thousand years Satan will be released from the Abyss, muster his allies in a final rebellion against God, be devoured by fire from heaven, and be cast into the lake of fire and eternal torment (20:7–10; cf. Matt. 25:41). There follows the Great White Throne judgment of the wicked dead (20:11–15), who are brought before this final great assize at the second resurrection (v. 13). Amillennialists interpret this as a general judgment of the saved and the unsaved. Then the unrighteous of all ages, together with death and Hades, will be cast into the lake of fire.

The last event in the apocalyptic calendar concerns [VI] Christ and the Eternal State (21:1–22:5). The following chapter will examine the nature of the "new heaven and [the] new earth" (21:1) and the "new Jerusalem" (21:2–22:5). Revelation closes with Jesus' promise "Yes, I am coming soon [*tachy*]"—and John's response "Amen. Come, Lord Jesus" (22:20).

Other New Testament Writings

Pretribulationists cite 2 Peter 2:5–9 to illustrate that God's sparing the families of Noah and Lot confirms the deliverance of saints from the wrath of God against unbelievers. Posttribulationists maintain that Noah's family was not removed from the flood but was "protected"—the verb *phylassō* meaning to "guard, watch over, protect."[157] Also God "rescued" (*hryomai*) Lot in the sense that angels grasped his and his family's hands and led them safely out of the city (Gen. 19:16). The summary statement follows: "the Lord knows how to rescue godly men from trials" (2 Peter 2:9). Posttribulationists claim that the act of rescuing (*hryomai*) should be understood in the sense of Matthew 6:13— "deliver [*hrysai*] us from the evil one"—(cf. 2 Tim. 4:18). The "trials" (*peirasmoi*) Peter envisaged describe the troubles the righteous suffer in an evil world (Acts 20:19; James 1:2; 1 Peter 1:6). These historical analogies likely do not settle the issue concerning the time of the church's rapture.

James 5:8 states that "the Lord's coming [*parousia*] is near [*engiken*]." The verb in the perfect tense literally means "has drawn near." So also 1 Peter 4:7: "The end of all things is near [*engiken*]." Christ's second advent is "near" because we now live in the "last days" (Heb. 1:2; James 5:3; 2 Peter 3:3)—i.e., in the period between Christ's two comings. Hence James wrote, "The judge is standing at the door!" (James 5:9). Perhaps New Testament teaching about Christ's imminent return should be understood in this sense, that "The end has drawn near because the last days *have begun*."[158] That Christ's coming (*parousia*) has not occurred after considerable time (2 Peter 3:4) is due to the fact that God's time-frame differs radically from ours (v. 8). Although from a human perspective delayed, "the day of the Lord will come like a thief" (v. 10; cf. Matt. 24:43–44; 1 Thess. 5:2). Christ will come suddenly and unexpectedly in that day to judge (cf. 2 Peter 2:9, 10b–12; 3:7) and consummate salvation (3:13). Hence believers should await his coming with patient but eager expectancy (Heb. 9:28b), even as a farmer patiently waits for the rains to fall and crops to grow (James 5:7–8).

The New Testament expressions "the day of the Lord" (Acts 2:20; 1 Thess. 5:2; 2 Thess. 2:2; 2 Peter 3:10), "the day of God" (2 Peter 3:12), "the great Day" (Jude 6), "that day" (Matt. 7:22), "the Day" (1 Cor. 3:13; Heb. 10:25), "the day of our Lord Jesus Christ," and variants (1 Cor. 1:8; 2 Cor. 1:14; Phil. 1:6) all describe the same set of events associated with Christ's return. Undoubtedly "the day of the Lord" and "the day of Christ" are identical.[159] According to the New Testament, the following events (not necessarily in chronological order) comprise the day of the Lord/God/Christ: (1) The battle of Armageddon (Rev. 16:14), (2) Christ's second advent (1 Cor. 1:7–8; 1 Thess. 5:2, 4; 2 Thess. 2:2; 2 Peter 3:10), (3) the first resurrection and perfecting of believers' salvation (Eph. 4:30; Phil. 1:6), (4) the radical transformation of the material universe by fire (2 Peter 3:10, 12), (5) judgment and rewards for Christians (1 Cor. 3:13–15; 2 Tim. 4:8), (6) Christ's millennial reign (not explicitly stated), (7) the second resurrection and judgment of unbelievers and evil spirits (Matt. 7:22; Rom. 2:5; 2 Peter 2:9; Jude 6), culminating in (8) the new heaven and the new earth (2 Peter 3:13). In the New Testament, then, the day of the Lord/God/Christ will be an event of salvation and blessing for believers but one of retribution and punishment for unbelievers. With the coming of Christ that day represents a bright picture against a dark background.

Parousia, Apokalypsis, and Epiphaneia in the New Testament

Parousia, which means "presence, appearing, coming, advent,"[160] was used in the Hellenistic world for the arrival of a king or other dignitary. In the New Testament it is sometimes used as a technical term for Christ's future return in glory. In Matthew 24:27 (cf. vv. 3, 37, 39) the *parousia* is a single event that follows Antichrist's end-of-age activity. In 1 Corinthians 15:23 the word is used of Christ's single coming to raise dead believers and rapture living saints. Pre- and posttribulationists interpret the *parousia* in 1 Thessalonians 4:15 as the secret Rapture and the single Second Advent, respectively. Christ's *parousia* is the object of the believer's hope (1 Thess. 4:13) and patient expectation (James 5:7–8). Hence holiness of life must be actively pursued (1 Thess. 3:13; 5:23; 2 Peter 3:12a; 1 John 2:28). *Parousia* in 2 Thessalonians 2:8 denotes the single second advent of Christ to crush the lawless one. Peter regarded the Transfiguration as a preview of Christ's glorious parousia to establish his kingdom (2 Peter 1:16). The scoffers understood Christ's promised *parousia* (Matt. 24:48) as his Second Advent (2 Peter 3:4). Peter further specified the *parousia* as the time of judgment upon the ungodly (2 Peter 3:7), the total renovation of the universe (vv. 10–12), and arrival of the new heavens and new earth (v. 13)—which suggests the single Second Advent.

Apokalypsis is used five times in the New Testament for the return of Christ. In 1 Corinthians 1:7 *hē apokalypsis tou kyriou hēmōn Iēsou Christou*—synonymous with "the end" and "the day of our Lord Jesus Christ" (v. 8)—refers to his glorious Second Advent with resurrection and rapture implied. Here Christ's *apokalypsis* is the object of the Christian's eager expectation. At the *apokalypsis* God will give relief to suffering believers (2 Thess. 1:7) and punish enemies of the Gospel (vv. 6, 8–9). These events seem to describe a single Second Advent. First Peter 4:13 reads, "But rejoice that you participate in the sufferings of Christ, so that you may be overjoyed when his glory is revealed" (lit., "at the revelation of his glory"). Christ's unveiling also marks the moment when salvation comes in its fullness (1 Peter 1:13; cf. v. 5).

Except for one reference to Christ's First Advent (2 Tim. 1:10), *epiphaneia* in its five other occurrences denotes Christ's Second Advent at the end of the age (2 Thess. 2:8; 1 Tim. 6:14; 2 Tim. 4:1, 8; Titus 2:13). *Epiphaneia* signifies Christ's coming to overthrow the Antichrist (2 Thess. 2:8), execute judgment on the living and the dead (2 Tim. 4:1), reward believers (v. 8), and establish his kingdom (vv. 1, 18). Guthrie concludes that "*epiphaneia* is in the Pastorals a characteristic description of the second advent."[161] Christ's *epiphaneia* is presented as the object of the believer's expectation and obedience (2 Tim. 4:1, 8). Paul held out the possibility that Timothy would live to see Christ's *epiphaneia* or Second Advent (1 Tim. 6:14–15). In Titus 2:13 Paul urged believers to live disciplined and godly lives in light of the "blessed hope," i.e., the *epiphaneia* of Christ, which will consummate the purposes of his first advent (*epiphainō,* 2:11; 3:4).

SYSTEMATIC FORMULATION

Since so much of Scripture is devoted to eschatology, church leaders ought not ignore it but help people understand it. To help our families and churches face the future with hope we need to develop the most coherent view possible of future events.

Messianic Prophecies Fulfilled in Two Distant Advents

Old Testament prophets often anticipated the work of the Messiah as a whole, not distinguishing the accomplishments of two Advents separated by millennia. From the Old Testament perspective the "last days" began in the first century (Heb. 1:1). During Jesus' ministry his disciples became convinced of his messiahship, but they were disturbed at the revelation of the necessity of his death (Matt. 16:21). At that time the Lord promised that he would come again in glory and judgment. "For the Son of Man is going to come in his Father's glory with his angels, and then he will reward each person according to what he has done" (v. 27). The idea of two separate comings had not been openly revealed before his death became imminent and questions arose about his identity as the messianic King. At his transfiguration the disciples saw a preview of his future, unveiled majesty (Matt. 17:1–9). Thus "in the New Testament we . . . find the realization that what the Old Testament writers seemed to depict as one movement must now be recognized as involving *two stages*: the present Messianic age and the age of the future."[162] The "last days" had in part already begun and in part were not yet. Although inaugurated at the Messiah's first coming, they will be culminated on earth at his return. Therefore Old Testament references to him may have two applications, separated by at least two millennia.

Christ's Return Understood Literally

Although Old Testament messianic predictions included figurative language, the First Advent occurred in literal fact. The eternal Logos came to earth in verifiable flesh (John 1:1, 14, 18; 1 John 1:1–3). To deny his literal enfleshment, resurrection, and ascension is to be against the Messiah and not have God (1 John 4:2–3; 2 John 9). Christianity is not a belief in mythology but in historical events and their meanings. It is in that crucial context that Christians interpret their Lord's return. (1) Christ will return *personally*. "For the Lord himself" will come down from heaven (1 Thess. 4:16). (2) The Lord Jesus Christ will return to the earth *physically*. "This same Jesus, who has been taken from you into heaven, will come back" (Acts 1:11). Since his first advent was not an ephemeral manifestation, neither will his second advent be. (3) He will return in the same way he ascended, *verifiably*. At his ascension two angels stated that Jesus "will come back in the same way you have seen him go into heaven" (Acts 1:11). So his returning body will be visible, audible, and tangible. (4) He will return *publicly*. As his resurrection and ascension were viewed by more than five hundred at once, so at his return "every eye will see him, even those who pierced him" (Rev. 1:7). All the nations will mourn as they "see the Son of Man coming on the clouds of the sky" (Matt. 24:30). (5) He will return with the new characteristics of his resurrection body, *powerfully, incorruptibly, and gloriously* (1 Cor. 15:42–44; cf. Matt. 24:30b).

It follows that the same basic *hermeneutic* for understanding the events of the First Advent with their revealed theological meanings is appropriate to discover the observable events of the Second Advent and their revealed significance. Normal literal, cultural, and critical principles of interpretation do not radically change just because the Apocalypse and other prophetic passages use more figures of speech than texts with a different literary genre. Figures of speech illustrate the nonfigurative points. A literal return is the most natural interpretation of such statements as "He will appear a second time'' (Heb. 9:28) and ''They will see the Son of Man coming on the clouds of the sky, with power and great glory'' (Matt. 24:30). Old Testament people misinterpreted many details of the first coming, but not the basic fact that the Messiah would appear on earth in literal flesh. Similarly, whatever details of the Second Coming people now may misunderstand, they are not mistaken who look for his literal return.

> We cannot call in question what stands so plainly in the pages of the NT—what filled so exclusively the minds of the first Christians—the idea of a personal return of Christ at the end of the world [or age]. If we are to retain any relation to the New Testament at all, we must assert the personal return of Christ as Judge of all.[163]

Christ Will Return to Rule Globally

The Lord of all will reenter the space-time world finally to reverse the effects of the Fall and complete his redemptive program on earth. He will liberate creation from bondage to decay (Rom. 8:21), redeem believers' bodies (Rom. 8:22–23), and judge the dead. He will ''destroy all dominion, authority and power. For he must reign until he has put all his enemies under his feet'' (vv. 24–25), including agents of the Antichrist (Rev. 19:11–21). ''The last enemy to be destroyed is death'' (1 Cor. 15:26). Then he will make his blood-bought people a kingdom to serve God and reign with him on earth (Rev. 5:10). Christ will return to *feed the poor* who ''will eat and be satisfied'' (Ps. 22:26). He will return to *restore dysfunctional families* as ''all the families of the nations will bow down before him'' (Ps. 22:27). Christ will return to *engender global peace* universally in all its physical, mental, emotional, and relational facets. He will return to *evangelize and teach* so that ''the earth will be full of the knowledge of the Lord as the waters cover the sea'' (Isa. 11:9).

Then ''no longer will a man teach his neighbor, or a man his brother, saying, 'Know the Lord,' because they will all know me, from the least of them to the greatest'' (Jer. 31:34). Such purposes present a prophecy, ''The realization of which is to be expected on this side of the boundary between time and eternity . . . when the Son of David enters upon the full possession of his royal inheritance.''[164]

The church is not presently mediating all these blessings of Christ's future reign. Christ's present form of ruling through the church addresses some of these needs to a degree, but the most effective church ministries collectively cannot produce the diverse benefits listed above. The aforementioned characteristics of the coming kingdom cannot be completely spiritualized. After two thousand years of ministry the church has not produced obedience in every believer, harmony in every home, food for all the hungry, or a lasting and just peace among all the nations. Given the work of modern missions, nature remains cursed, wars multiply, and death remains our greatest enemy.

Scripture promises *a distinct, future reign with Christ on earth.* Jesus said that those who stood by him in his trials would ''eat and drink at [his] table in [his] kingdom and sit on thrones, judging the twelve tribes of Israel'' (Luke 22:30). To the early churches Paul said, ''Do you not know that the saints will judge the world?'' (1 Cor. 6:2). Again: ''If we endure, we will also reign with him'' (2 Tim. 2:12). John taught that those who now suffer with Christ will in the future ''reign [with him] on the earth'' (Rev. 5:10). Note that the reigning takes place on the ''earth''; the new heavens and earth are not in this context. Christ's present redemptive rule mediated through Christians in various spheres does not preempt a more direct, universal rule of Christ following his return.

Christ's Global Reign Follows His Return

The future reign with Christ *follows his return* according to the Apocalypse. Christ will return from heaven, defeat the forces of evil in the Battle of Armageddon (Rev. 19), and then establish a thousand-year reign with those raised in the first resurrection (Rev. 20:4–5). The return recorded in Revelation 19 precedes the millennial reign of Revelation 20 because the destruction of rampant opposition is logically prior. New Testament scholar Merrill C. Tenney identifies the chronological order of events in Revelation 17:1–21:8 thus: Christ's return, the first resurrection, the reign with Christ for a thousand years, the second resurrection, the loosing and final doom of Satan, the Great White Throne judgment and the new heaven and new earth.[165] A Reformed premillennialist, D. H. Kromminga, argues that since the binding and loosing of Satan are consecutive, the thousand years that intervene must be in sequence. Thus Revelation 20 completes the story begun in chapter 12 of the great delusion of the nations by the two Beasts. In order to deny a future Millennium, Kromminga argues, the amillennialists disrupt the story of satanic deception as it unfolds in chapters 12–20 and shift his activity from accusing the children of God in Christ's heavenly presence to the earth and its inhabitants.[166]

Two resurrections separated by a thousand years (Rev. 20:4–5) are most coherently accounted for by premillennialism. The resurrection of believers occurs in connection with the rapture of the living at his return (1 Thess. 4:13–18). So at Christ's return and the first resurrection martyrs come to life to reign with Christ for a thousand years. As the first resurrection precedes their thousand-year reign with Christ, Christ's return precedes the Millennium. The doctrine of a single resurrection and judgment of the righteous and unrighteous is based on passages like John 5:28–29 that identify an impending day of resurrections for the just and the unjust. But the point of such passages is to teach a universal judgment, not a chronology. In the context of Revelation 20:4–5 dealing with chronological matters, the two resurrections are separated by a thousand years. The view of a resurrection before and after the Millennium, furthermore, fits Jesus' reference to the resurrection of the righteous (Luke 14:14) and the resurrection from among (*ek*) the dead ones (Luke 20:35). The first apostles also proclaimed the resurrection from among (*ek*) the dead (Acts 4:2); and Paul sought to attain to the resurrection from among (*ek*) the dead ones (Phil. 3:11).

What is the *duration* of Christ's coming universal reign? Six times in Revelation 20:2–7 John specified one thousand years. Satan will be bound for a thousand years. Martyrs who did not worship the Beast will be resurrected and reign with Christ for a thousand years. After the thousand years the rest of the dead will come to life. The period separating the two resurrections in the round numbers of ordinary speech is one thousand years; but we need not count precisely the days, hours, and minutes. Even if figurative, the number represents a long or complete period of time, a significant age of history on earth. We do violence to the context to interpret the thousand years as an ethical virtue, such as perfection.

Christ Will Reign Both Spiritually and Institutionally

Historical premillennialism assumes that the social structure in the Millennium is continuous with the present church. It thus fails to acknowledge the connection between the thousand-year reign of Revelation 20 and the Old

Testament predictions of Israel's role in global peace from Jerusalem. This system does not anticipate Israel's restoration in the Millennium as a national institution, or when it does, it fails to give institutional Israel a distinctive role. *Dispensational premillennialism* tends to give Israel exclusive institutional prominence in Christ's future millennial reign and has no place for the continuation of the church. *Spiritual-institutional premillennialism* anticipates Christ's millennial rule as being continuous with that of the present age spiritually but discontinuous institutionally.

Morally, the premillennialism of spiritual-institutional theology anticipates no change of ethical principles in the providential realm of Christ's coming kingdom. The eternal Logos on earth will continue to support the moral values rooted in the divine nature and implanted in God's image bearers as essential to meaningful human life. Justice will be administered without favoritism, even to the poor. Crime will be substantially eradicated, and there will be no more wars. As Christ and those who reign with him administer justice universally, all people will live in peace and safety.

Spiritually, unrepentant survivors of Armageddon and sinners born during the Millennium will still break the two great commandments concerning love for God and neighbor and will need to be saved by grace through faith in the Messiah. Among the justified by faith in Christ—be they Jews or Gentiles, males or females—there will be no difference of status spiritually. United in Christ, believers personally will enjoy unbroken fellowship with God and all other believers! *Intellectually* all will know the Lord. *Volitionally* and *emotionally* all will treasure Christ's kingdom over all other values. *Ethnically,* Jews and other ethnic peoples will remain distinct; but every tribe and nation will enjoy unbroken cooperation and fellowship. *Physically,* Christ will renew adequate resources in a curse-free environment of pure water, sunshine, unpolluted air, and arable land. The Lord's people will distribute abundant harvests where they are needed so that all people on earth will have adequate food. Those raised from the dead and reigning with Christ will enjoy the new powers of their resurrected bodies.

Institutionally, Christ will not destroy but fulfill the *raison d'être* of the three prior institutions. The *family* will not be dissolved but will be enhanced. Even though there will be no marriage relationships (Matt. 22:30), the future life will be even better. Since people will be recognizable, present family relationships will not be erased but enhanced. National Israel, furthermore, will not be destroyed but fulfilled. The promises to the Israelite *nation* concerning the rule of the Davidic King in Zion, Jerusalem, and the entire land will be fulfilled in a way far superior to the social structure under the old covenant. The institutional *church,* furthermore, will not be destroyed but will be enriched. The countless members of Christ's body will exercise their gifts superbly and work together as never before in evangelism, edification, worship, and service.

To the three previous dispensations of spiritual-institutional theology, then, premillennialists may add a fourth social structure. What form will Christ's unmediated millennial reign take? The global millennial kingdom appears to incorporate the strengths of a believing "family," a healthfully functioning multiethnic church, and a wise and beneficent monarchy. As the chief executive officer, Christ will head an ethical-spiritual-economic-political government on this earth.

Although we have little explicit biblical detail about the structure of Christ's coming kingdom, it may include *com-*

plementary roles for both institutional Israel and institutional churches. This suggestion is based on the continuation of the family in the ages of the nation and the church, the unfulfilled predictions for Israel as a nation, and the principle that Christ will come not to destroy but to fulfill his work from the previous age. A servant-leadership role may be in view for those governing with Christ from Israel's twelve tribes and for the twelve disciples representing the multicultural church age. In the Millennium many promises to Israel and the church will be fulfilled not only individually (Rom. 4–8) but collectively and institutionally (Rom. 9–11). Is it not possible that God's people from each dispensation may have complementary roles in the Millennium? Analogously, there may also be a servant-leadership role for the offices of a transfigured family. As a government Christ's millennial rule may appear more like national Israel than like the church. But it will not be a return to the Old Testament government through one nation; rather, Christ on earth will rule all nations and in a way that preserves and enhances family and church values.

What primary *offices* will mark the millennial leadership? The highest office is that of king, which will be filled by the glorified Christ. Other distinct offices observed in the previous ages may be elevated in function. Officers are necessary in any institution, and many may be anticipated in the new global one. Those who suffered as faithful stewards of the family, the nation Israel, or the church may be given greater governing and religious roles. Christ will not rule then as he did in early Old Testament times through one ethnic line. Neither will he work through literal churches in the same way he does in the present age. So the responsible representatives from each tradition (family, nation, church) are not likely to continue in the univocal

sense. But a division of labor will undoubtedly lead to some distinctive responsibilities in the social structure of the global kingdom. Their designations have yet to be revealed.

Will Israel Have a Distinctive Role in the Millennium?

Since in Christ Israelites and church members are one, the nation will not have a unique role *spiritually*. But several texts point to a future role for Israel *institutionally*:

1. "The Lord God will give him [Jesus] the throne of his father David, and he will reign over the house of Jacob forever; his kingdom will never end" (Luke 1:32–33). The "throne" indicates the office of a king for a descendant of David in institutional Israel. "Forever" would include Christ's present spiritual rule over believers and his future institutional rule on the earth in the Millennium as the vestibule to eternity. Since the oneness of Jew and Gentile in the church was not disclosed when the angel spoke those words, only by an anachronism can a completely nonliteral meaning based on the "mystery" be read back into the time of Christ's birth.

2. The night before the Crucifixion Jesus assured his disciples that they would judge the twelve tribes of Israel (Luke 22:29–30). Does this activity not presume the future restoration of the twelve tribes in institutional Israel? Persevering believers will also judge the unbelieving world (1 Cor. 6:2–3) and will reign alongside Christ (2 Tim. 2:12). The latter refers to a future reign following the church age, because 2 Timothy was written well into the present era after Paul's fourth missionary journey.

3. After Christ rose from the dead, the disciples asked when the kingdom would be restored to Israel (understood at that time as institutional as well as

spiritual Israel). Christ's reply did not challenge the fact that it would be restored, but only the wisdom of knowing the time (Acts 1:7).

4. Israel collectively will be restored after the times of the Gentiles at Christ's return. At the Jerusalem conference James assured the Jewish believers that: (1) God was taking from the Gentiles a people (the church) for himself, (2) Christ will return and rebuild David's fallen tent (collective institution) and (3) the more complete salvation of Gentiles will occur (Acts 15:13–18). James interpreted Amos 9:11–12 in terms of a present and future application at Christ's return.

5. Paul taught that Israel will believe *en masse* when Jesus returns (Rom. 11:25; Rev. 1:7). The context requires a collective and then an institutional interpretation of Israel. A remnant of individual Jews are being saved now (Rom. 11:1–6), while the Jewish people (collectively) are now hardened in unbelief (vv. 7–10). But Israel is not beyond recovery (v. 11), even though the natural branches of the olive tree have been broken off (v. 17) and unnatural branches grafted in (vv. 19–21). God is able to graft the branches of Israel (unbelieving Jews) back in again (vv. 22–24). Israel's hardening is temporary—until the full number of Gentiles have come in (v. 25). Then Christ will return and turn godlessness away from Jacob (v. 26). God's call of Israel as a structural future branch is irrevocable (11:25–29).

6. The connection of Revelation 20 with Israel's Old Testament hope must not be overlooked. John was familiar with Isaiah 11:4 when he wrote that "out of his [Christ's] mouth comes a sharp sword with which to strike down the nations" (19:15) and that the Antichrist, the False Prophet, and their followers are "killed with the sword that comes out of the mouth of the rider on the horse" (19:21). Paul also wrote

that the Lord Jesus would overthrow the lawless one with the "breath of his mouth" (2 Thess. 2:8). These statements are reminiscent of the descendant of Jesse who "will strike the earth with the rod of his mouth; with the breath of his lips he will slay the wicked" (Isa. 11:4). In Isaiah's contextual teaching the animal kingdom will be at peace, children will be safe, and the knowledge of the Lord will fill the earth (11:6–9). The descendant of Jesse will reclaim the remnant of his people (vv. 10–11), gather the exiles of Israel, and assemble the scattered people of Judah from the ends of the earth (v. 12) to the land around Jerusalem (cf. Isa. 2:2; 27:13; 66:20). This allusion to Isaiah 11 in Revelation 19 and 2 Thessalonians 2 is overlooked by historical premillennialists who find no connection between the thousand-year reign of Revelation 20 and the Jews' hopes for a universal kingdom and who think there is only the one passage on the Millennium.

7. At that time the Lord's house will be exalted in Jerusalem on Mount Zion. Although some will interpret the Lord's holy mountain (Isa. 2:2–3; 11:9) figuratively as the church, that hypothesis does not fit well with the context of the parallel passage in Micah 4:1–7. The mountain to be exalted is the same mountain that was destroyed in the preceding paragraph, Micah 3:8–12. It was the literal leaders of institutional Israel that sinned (3:8), despised justice (3:9), and filled Jerusalem with wickedness (3:10). Even her priests taught for a price, and her prophets told fortunes for money (3:11). As a result literal Israel, Jerusalem, and the temple were severely judged (3:12). When the next verse says that "the mountain of the Lord's temple will be established as chief among the mountains . . . and people will stream to it" (4:1), the meaning is Mount Zion that was devastated. With such continuity, responsible interpreters can hardly take the destruc-

tion of the location literally and its restoration merely spiritually. The Mount Zion that was destroyed is the Mount Zion that will be rebuilt for the King of Kings in a period of universal peace and safety.

In summary, the fact that Gentiles now are spiritual children of Abraham does not fulfill the teaching of Old Testament references to the future of institutional Israel. The institutional distinctives of the Jewish and Gentile branches of the same olive tree have not deleted their spiritual oneness. Neither has their spiritual unity obliterated their outward institutional differences. Confusion of spiritual oneness with institutional sameness in Israel and the church has led to strained nonliteral interpretations by those who see no future for institutional Israel.

A spiritual-institutional perspective of the millennial reign *following* Christ's return, provides the background for comprehending what takes place *before* his return.

The Last Antichrist

Before Christ's return and millennial rule the Antichrist will arise. The prefix "anti" indicates that he is both "against" Christ and exalts himself "instead of" Christ. As Christ is a person, so *he is a person*. A series of false Christs has plagued the church since the first century (Matt. 24:23–25; 1 John 2:18, 22; 4:1–3). The last of these, the Antichrist, is called "the *man* of lawlessness" (2 Thess. 2:3), i.e., of sin or unrighteousness.[167] He is a human agent who opposes God and exalts himself (v. 4), who takes his seat in the temple, and who will be revealed in his time (v. 6). Beyond reasonable doubt this is the person elsewhere called the Antichrist.

The Antichrist's *personal assistant* becomes another "beast" in the use of political authority. A false prophet, he

will coerce worship of the Antichrist (Rev. 13:11–12), perform great miraculous signs (vv. 13–14), and demand that people worship Antichrist's image on pain of death (vv. 14–15). Without his mark on their forehead none can buy or sell (vv. 16–17).

The Antichrist will become a *powerful political leader*. Utilizing satanic power and authority (Rev. 13:2) he is healed from a fatal wound, astonishing the world (v. 3), and so will be worshiped as unconquerable (v. 4). He will openly blaspheme God for three and one-half years (vv. 5–6), ruling all the world's people who are not faithful to Christ (vv. 7–8). Like a beast Antichrist will make war against the saints (v. 10). His politically powerful global government is called Babylon (Rev. 17:1). The mother of the spiritually promiscuous (Rev. 17:5), Babylon will control all the world's commerce and rule over the kings of the earth (v. 18).

The Antichrist becomes *the global leader of this counterfeit spirituality*. Babylon will be "a home for demons, a haunt for every evil spirit, a haunt for every unclean and detestable bird" (Rev. 18:2). She sells not only all luxuries but the bodies and souls of humans (v. 13). By her magic spell she leads all the nations astray (v. 23). She sheds the blood of the prophets and saints (v. 24). One of her ruses will be witchcraft and worship of the mother goddess, a sign of unfaithfulness to God, or spiritual adultery. The Antichrist will set himself up in the holy place in Jerusalem (Matt. 24:15; 2 Thess. 2:4), demand worship, and perform "counterfeit miracles, signs and wonders" (2 Thess. 2:9). The clever deceptions of the "man of lawlessness" at first will delude many into believing that he is divine (v. 11) and that Jesus was not (2 John 7). Only later will his diabolic nature be revealed.

The Antichrist, as predicted twice in

Daniel, will *commit the abomination that causes desolation.* "His armed forces will rise up to desecrate the temple fortress and will abolish the daily sacrifice. Then they will set up the abomination that causes desolation" (Dan. 11:31). Earlier prototypes, like Antiochus Epiphanes, profaned the temple by dedicating it to Zeus and substituting sacrifices of swine on a pagan altar above the altar of burnt offerings (1 Macc. 1:45–46, 54; 2 Macc. 6:2). But this had already occurred when Jesus spoke. A second application of Daniel's prophecy occurred in A.D. 70 when the Roman emperor Titus and his legions entered Jerusalem with banners displaying the emperor's image as an object of worship. But in the Olivet Discourse Jesus warned of the primary fulfillment just before his coming again in power and great glory (Matt. 24:29–30). Daniel predicted the Antichrist's open rebellion against God and continual harassment of the saints, who will be handed over to him for "a time, times and half a time" (Dan. 7:25). Daniel's fourth kingdom will arise from the earth (7:17) just before the Ancient of Days comes to pronounce judgment. With Hoekema, "we conclude that New Testament teaching about the antichrist does indeed have Old Testament antecedents, and that both Antiochus Epiphanes and Titus were types of the Antichrist who is to come."[168]

The Coming Unique Period of Tribulation

Through the centuries God's people have suffered greatly for their faith. But beyond this suffering Jesus predicted a period in which the *Devil's fury* will be unleashed: "Then there will be great distress, unequaled from the beginning of the world until now—and never to be equaled again" (Matt. 24:21). The Great Tribulation will bring unparalleled distress in two ways: (1) The *time* is unique, as the Antichrist will mount a global opposition to God's kingdom in every way possible; and (2) the *period* is unique as God's unrestrained wrath falls upon the unjust Jews and Gentiles who worship and serve the Antichrist.

Antichrist's activities (above) represent the time of Jacob's trouble. The extent of his global stranglehold on economics, politics, and religion will be incomparable. The intensity of the all-out war perpetrated by the demonic and human hordes loyal to the Beast has never been equaled. Every demonic terrorist attack that the Adversary can devise will be unleashed against people who will not submit. His fiery arrows and subtle deceptions will wound believing people everywhere. First-century persecution through Roman emperors and twentieth-century devastation through communist leaders cannot compare with it.

In the Great Tribulation *divine wrath* will be executed on the Antichrist and his unrighteous followers as never before in history. The purpose of this "hour of trial that is going to come upon the whole earth" is to "test those who live on the earth" (Rev. 3:10). "The inhabitants of the earth" are the unbelieving whose names are not written in the Book of Life, who delight in the death of two prophets, and who worship the Beast (11:10; 13:8, 14). The rich and mighty of the earth will beckon the mountains to fall on them to escape the wrath of the Lamb (Rev. 6:16–17). The sun and moon will change color, stars will fall to the earth, and mountains and islands will be dislocated. Babylon will be split into three parts by an earthquake more severe than any that has ever occurred (Rev. 16:18–19). Huge hailstones (about 100 pounds each) will fall from the skies (v. 21). This is the time for "destroying those who destroy the earth" (11:18). Finally, Christ will strike down the nations who bow to the Beast (Rev. 19:15). At the end of the Great Tribulation Christ will defeat the forces of the Antichrist at Armageddon and throw him and his assistant into the fiery lake of burning sulfur (v. 20). Hoekema thinks that the final, climactic distress just before Christ returns "will not be basically different from earlier tribulations which God's people have had to suffer, but will be an intensified form of those earlier tribulations."[169] If so, as Jesus emphasized, it will be incomparable in intensity and unique in its global extent. Never in history has God's wrath been poured out like this.

This age-ending period of unparalleled global distress will last seven years if not shortened. According to Daniel's interpretation of his vision, seventy sevens or weeks of years from the decree to restore and rebuild Jerusalem are required for the completion of the several purposes listed (Dan. 9:24). Seven weeks and sixty-two weeks (i.e., sixty-nine weeks, or 483 years) from the command to rebuild the city follow before the Anointed One comes and rebuilds the city in a time of trouble. This works out to the time of Jesus' ministry in his first advent. But after the sixty-nine weeks, the Anointed One is cut off (v. 26a) or crucified. Then a coming ruler (the Antichrist) will destroy the city and the sanctuary (typified in A.D. 70). Wars and desolations will continue to the end (v. 26b). Satan's animosity for Israel will come to a climax for a "a time, times and half a time" (Rev. 12:14). This is the equivalent of three and one-half years or forty-two months (Dan 7:25; Rev. 12:6). The Beast is allowed authority for forty-two months, closely paralleling Daniel 7:24–25.

The coming ruler will confirm a covenant with many for one "week" (seven years), but will break it. In the middle of the week he will put an end to sacrifice and offering and will set up an abomination that causes desolation until his decreed end (Dan. 9:27). Although some think the Seventieth Week was fulfilled during Christ's first advent, a future fulfillment is more probable. It was separated from the previous sixty-nine sevens (weeks) by a period of wars and desolations that continue. And Jesus predicted the abomination that desolates just prior to the culmination of his second advent (Matt. 24:15). An interval (like that between the sixty-ninth and seventieth weeks) is not unusual in Old Testament prophecy. Many passages make no chronological distinction between the Messiah's first and second comings already separated by approximately two thousand years. Daniel did not mention four rulers (2:26, 38–39); he left a gap in chapter 7, (omitted 150 years in 11:2–3), and moved straight to the resurrection (12:2). The setting of dates on the basis of the seventy weeks is ruled out because no one knows how long the gap may be. Jesus also said, "If those days had not been cut short, no one would survive, but for the sake of the elect those days will be shortened" (Matt. 24:22).

Christ's Second Advent

The Second Advent is a period of time long enough to encompass (1) Messiah's descent from heaven (1 Thess. 4:16a), (2) the resurrection of the believing dead (v. 16b), (3) the rapture of living and dead saints (v. 17), (4) the resurrection and rapture of two witnesses (Rev. 11), (5) the celebration of the Marriage Supper of the Lamb with the church (Rev. 19:1–10), (6) the execution of the judgments of the seven seals (7) the seven trumpets, (8) the seven bowls of wrath, (9) the return of Christ for the climactic war with evil forces, (10) the final defeat of Antichrist at Armageddon (19:11–21), (11) the binding of Satan (Rev. 20:3),

(12) the resurrection of martyrs (v. 4), and (13) Christ's reign for a thousand years (Rev. 20:4b–6). The Second Advent, like the First Advent, begins in a twinkling of an eye, but continues for a considerable period of history.

"The Day of the Lord" encompasses all the events outlined in the previous paragraph. It is not a technical term for the final Tribulation as Rosenthal argues.[170] Neither is it a twelve- or twenty-four-hour period at the beginning of Armageddon as Gundry holds. In earlier uses days of the Lord are foretastes of decisive acts of God at Messiah's coming, the outpouring of the Spirit, and Christ's return in glory for judgment.[171] In the Old and New Testaments "the Day of the Lord" refers to God's execution of just judgment on the unrighteous and the bestowal of blessings for God's faithful people. In the day of universal retribution Israel will not escape (Amos 8:8–9:5). The New Testament adds that Christ's second coming (or Parousia) will hallmark the Day of the Lord. It will be a day of Christ's revealing (1 Cor. 1:7; 2 Thess. 1:7; 1 Peter 1:13) and thus may be termed "the day of the Lord Jesus" (2 Cor. 1:14) or simply "the day of Christ" (Phil. 1:10; 2:16). While in some respects the values of the Day of the Lord were accomplished during the First Advent, its more complete fulfillment will be realized throughout Daniel's Seventieth Week. Some biblical passages on the First Advent speak of the entire thirty-three years, and others refer particularly to Jesus' conception and birth. Similarly, some passages on the Second Advent may refer to the whole period of seven years, or three and one-half years, or the rapture of the church, or his return to the Battle of Armageddon.[172]

Just as the First Advent encompassed thirty years, the Messiah's second advent involves a *period of time,* involving two aspects: (1) an ascension of church members to meet Christ in the air and (2) their descent with Christ to defeat the idolatrous in the Battle of Armageddon and begin the millennial reign. The time between our gathering to be with Christ and return with him to Armageddon, whether a few hours, three-and-a-half years, or seven years is relatively insignificant. A seven-year interval between the two aspects is not a long period compared to a thousand-year Millennium or two thousand years of church history to this point. It is ludicrous for either pre- or posttribulationists to imply two Second Comings because of a seven-year or three-and-a half-year span between the Rapture and the descent to Armageddon.

The Book of Revelation Teaches Several Raptures

Much debate about the time of the saints' catching-up mistakenly assumes that the Bible teaches a once-for-all rapture at a single point in history. That assumption oversimplifies the evidence. Revelation 4–20 supports elements of truth in post- mid- and pretribulational views. The "first resurrection" (Rev. 20:5) is not only chronologically first, it is also first in rank. It encompasses an order of all resurrections and raptures of the just. The "firstfruits" (1 Cor. 15:20, 23) included Christ, who rose and ascended together with others raised at that time. The first resurrection also includes the two witnesses who were raised in the middle of the Tribulation and the martyrs who were raised toward the end of it. The controversial issue is the time of the *church's* rapture.

The posttribulational case for the rapture of the church on the same day as Armageddon (Rev. 19) builds in part on an analogy. As noted in the biblical section, in the ancient Greek world a delegation would leave a city to greet a returning victor's armies, turn around on the same day, and march back into the city with the conquerors. Analogies, however, only illustrate a point if other evidence holds. No reference to the timing of the Rapture on the same literal day as the Battle of Armageddon can be discovered in Revelation 19, save for mention of the arrival of the "wedding of the Lamb" (v. 6–8). One may infer from the chapter that the church has been caught up to be with the Lord at this time. If it is assumed to be the same day, the posttribulational view would require an extremely hasty celebration of the centuries-awaited consummation of union with Christ before descending to the bloodiest battle in history (Rev. 19:1–10). If the "wedding" is a symbol for the union of Christ and his church, and not an event, there are better texts for that.[173]

There may be a *midtribulational ascension of 144,000 Jews,* but it is debatable whether that refers to the church. Archer thinks the "more likely" point of identification of the rapture of the church is in Revelation 14:14. One like the Son of Man is seated on a cloud with a gold crown on his head holding a sickle in his hand. With the sickle he brings God's wrath upon the ungodly of the earth (vv. 14–20). Before his throne the 144,000 learn a new song, and the dead are said to be blessed who die in the Lord and rest from their labors (v. 13).[174] But Revelation 7 identifies the 144,000 as 12,000 Jews from each of the twelve tribes of Israel contrasted with a Gentile multitude. The 144,000 Jews from the twelve tribes have died and been resurrected and raptured, but it is difficult to identify this reference to Israel's twelve tribes with the church.

J. Oliver Buswell, Jr., finds a *midtribulational rapture of two witnesses* in Revelation 11:15–18.[175] Two prophets were dead three-and-a-half days. Then they were resurrected and caught up in a cloud while their enemies looked on. There is a truth in this mid-tribulationalism. Two people are raised from the dead and raptured as an installment of the first resurrection. But this does not imply the rapture of all in the church age. A primary reason for associating the rapture of the whole church with them is the mention of the "mystery" that is accomplished (10:7). But John's "mystery" is not the Pauline inclusion of Jews and Gentiles in one body; it is that "There will be no more delay!" (10:6). Although there is a resurrection and rapture of two persons in Revelation 10 or 11, the passage does not give adequate indication of the rapture of the church.

There may be a *prewrath rapture prior to the opening of the seventh seal* (Rev. 7:9–17), but is it of the institutional church? A great multitude from every nation and tribe, people, and language stand in white robes before the throne of the Lamb. This anticipatory vision apparently takes place at his judgment after the Great Tribulation, but before the great and terrible "Day of the Lord"—the period of unleashed wrath against the lawless followers of the Antichrist.[176] Rosenthal's view that the rapture of the church precedes the outpouring of divine wrath has support. All concur with the promise of exemption from retributive divine wrath. But the church is also promised deliverance from the *time* of divine wrath (Rev. 3:10).[177] It is difficult to limit God's wrath to the end of the Tribulation. On Rosenthal's view the events prophesied in the seals must occur before we need be always watching for our gathering to Christ. But the first six seals are opened by the wrathful Lamb and convince the leaders of the earth that the day of the Lamb's wrath has come (6:16–17). The destructive aspects of war, inflation, famine, and plague express his righteous indignation. If the multitudes saved "out of" the Tribulation are caught up after the period of Tribulation started, that does not preclude the rapture of people in the age of the

417

institutional church prior to the start of Daniel's Seventieth Week.

A pretribulational rapture seems indicated when Christ promised faithful members of the church at Philadelphia: "I will keep you from the hour of trial that is going to come upon the whole world to test those who live on the earth" (3:10). This promise to one church applies to others in the same way that Paul's teaching to the church at Rome applies to churches throughout this age. Jesus gave assurance to all Christians who endure increasing abuse as the signs of Christ's return multiply. Does his promise apply to the Great Tribulation? Those "who live on the earth" is a technical phrase in the context of Revelation 3–17 for unbelievers at the time of greatest distress. They receive God's judgment (3:10), gloat over the death of God's two prophets (11:10), worship the Beast (13:8, 12), and are deceived by the Beast (13:14). The purpose of the global Tribulation is to "test" these ungodly people. Is Christ's promise to "keep [them] from [*tēreō ek*] the Great Tribulation" the same in meaning as his prayer "not that you take them out of the world but that you protect them from (*tēreō ek*) the evil one" (John 17:15)? Christ's petition is not a good parallel to his promise in Revelation 3:10 for two reasons. It does not promise deliverance from a period of time, for it has no grammatical equivalent for an "hour" from which to be kept. And the tribulation Jesus referred to is not to be compared with the future period of satanic wrath and consequent divine wrath "unequaled from the beginning of the world until now" (Matt. 24:21). Jesus promised the church deliverance from the period of history with the purpose of testing the followers of Antichrist. There are only two ways to be kept from a period of history, death and rapture. Christ did not promise death.

The Apocalypse, then, indicates a pretribulational rapture of the institutional church as well as post- and midtribulational raptures of God's people subsequently. The primary social institution through which God is working could change at the beginning, in the midst, or toward the end of the Tribulation. The fact that no evidence of officers or practices of the institutional church can be been found in chapters 4–19 provides further support that the church will ascend to meet Christ in the air at the beginning of the Tribulation. An argument from silence is not weak, but strong when a topic (elders and churches) that has been prominent in the writer's thought (Rev. 1–3) is completely dropped (chs. 4–19). The only ones said to be sealed for protection from the Antichrist's wrath are 144,000 Jews from the twelve tribes of Israel (chap. 7). There is no reason churches should suffer from this outpouring of divine wrath upon the ungodly. In Revelation 4–19, the most extensive passage on the Tribulation, the institutional church no longer appears to be the primary institution in God's redemptive program.

Christ's Teaching on the Time of the Church's Rapture

Seeking a coherent account of all the relevant data, we must give special consideration to what Christ taught concerning the time of the rapture of the institutional church. Negatively, our Lord repeatedly insisted that the end of the present (church) age and the beginning of the Second Advent is *undeterminable*. "No one knows about that day or hour, not even the angels in heaven, nor the Son, but only the Father" (Mark 13:32). Christ warned against setting a date for his return because, with all of the signs mentioned, the timing is unforeseeable and unpredictable. He forbade not only the specifics of day or hour, but also more general designations like months or years: "It is not for you to know the times or dates" (Acts 1:7). Christ's teaching assumed that his return was as unpredictable as "the day of the Lord" in Old Testament times.

Affirmatively, Christ taught that his followers should be in *constant readiness* for his return. Their meeting him in the air was potentially at hand morning, noon, or night of any day. Since no one can know this time, church members must be alert with a constant, joyful expectation. Whether in the first century, the tenth, or the twenty-first, the obedient are to be always ready: always watching, always praying, and always working (Matt. 24:42–44; 25:13). In order not to be found asleep when the Master returns, his followers need constant watchfulness (Mark 13:37). Christ emphasized, "Be always on the watch, and pray" (Luke 21:36). Perpetual readiness involves a chronological nearness as well as a "salvation-history" nearness. In both senses the Rapture is always near.[178] So Hoekema concluded, "The believer should live in constant joyful expectation of Christ's return; though he does not know the exact time of it, he should always be ready for it."[179]

The typical posttribulational interpretation of Christ's teaching on imminency urges constant "preparation" in view of "signs" giving the "expectation" of his coming several years hence. The most explicit sign, "the abomination that causes desolation," removes the Rapture by some three-and-a-half years. Only after that blasphemous event will there be need for constant readiness to meet Christ. Readiness will need to be constant then, for the time of the Tribulation may be shortened. Granting some diminution of time, posttribulationalism involves the saints in a three-and-a-half-year countdown from the Antichrist's abomination to the time of the church's resurrection.

Such an approximate predictability contradicts Christ's emphases on their unpredictability and thus the need for constant readiness. A pretribulational interpretation avoids any such countdown and is consistent with Christ's teaching. Other signs are sufficiently vague that Christians at several points in church history have assumed that they were about to be raptured. In summary, Christ's teaching has called his followers from the first century to the present to be ready *always* for the Rapture and to avoid even approximate date-setting for it. Our Lord's instructions are most coherently affirmed in a pretribulational context.

The Time of the Rapture of the Church in 1 and 2 Thessalonians

Both Thessalonian epistles have spoken explicitly about the rapture of the church. These teachings ought to be understood in their historical contexts and as consistent with Christ's teaching.

Paul's first letter taught faithful church members "to wait for his Son from heaven . . . Jesus, who rescues us from the coming wrath" (1 Thess. 1:10). They are assured that God did not appoint them to suffer God's wrath but to receive salvation (5:1–11). In some contexts (cf. 1:9) it is possible that "wrath" and "salvation" may refer only to the final judgment and eternal state, but the context of the teaching concerning the historical Day of the Lord here includes the Tribulation climaxed by Armageddon. The fact of the Rapture is clearly affirmed when the believing dead are raised (1 Thess. 4:13–18). That their ascension is the method of deliverance from the day of wrath is made clear in context (1:10; 4:13–18). Therefore they are to "encourage one another and build each other up" (5:11).

Paul wrote his second letter to remind Thessalonian believers that although their suffering for the faith was intense, Christ would return "to be glorified in his holy people" (1:10) and to "punish those who do not know God," temporally (v. 8) and eternally (v. 9). Believers need not be alarmed because of "the coming of our Lord and our being gathered to him" (2:1–2), supposing that the day of wrath had already begun. Suffering in the present age for one's faith may be expected and will be rewarded (1:5–7). But the day of the Lord's vengeance on the ungodly will not come on earth until "the rebellion" (NIV, NRSV) or "the falling away" (KJV) (hē apostasia) occurs first (2:3). Given the historical setting and purpose of the letter, does Paul refer to moral collapse in society or to the people's felt need concerning the time of the departure to meet Christ? Is this a figurative departure (from moral and spiritual standards) not mentioned in the first Epistle or a literal departure (from a place on earth)?

1. Checking the usage of apostasia in classical Greek, the literal and spiritual meanings are both possibilities. Liddell and Scott's Greek-English Lexicon lists as the second meaning of the term "departure or disappearance" and cites an example of the stiffening of a material caused by the apostasia of water from it.[180] Evaporation provides a fitting analogy to the apostasia of the Rapture.

2. Although the majority of commentators favor a figurative meaning, their dogmatism goes beyond the one other New Testament usage of the noun. In Acts 21:21 Paul is charged with apostasy from the teaching of Moses. One other use of the noun in the New Testament does not provide sufficient data for a dogmatic conclusion to a word study. So we turn to the fifteen New Testament uses of the verb (aphistēmi). Four refer to a figurative departure morally or spiritually (Luke 8:13; 1 Tim. 4:1; 2 Tim. 2:19; Heb.

3:12). Other uses of the verb convey the literal meaning of departing from: e.g., iniquity (2 Tim. 2:19), ungodly men (1 Tim. 6:5), the temple (Luke 2:37), the body (2 Cor. 12:8), and a person (Acts 12:10; Luke 4:13). The angel who delivered Peter from prison departed from him (Acts 12:10) and Paul prayed that his thorn in the flesh might depart from him (2 Cor. 12:8). These New Testament uses make it clear that to apostatize most often means to "depart" or "go away from." Only in specialized instances does it mean to depart from the faith.

3. A literal departure fits best the purpose for which Paul wrote—to correct the idea that the day (period) of the Lord's wrath had already begun (2 Thess. 2:2). Apostasy and persecution had already set in during the first century and so would not provide a discernible new sign that the day of vindicating justice had not already started.

4. A literal departure is indicated by the function of the definite article. The definite article "the" serves "to point out an object or draw attention to it. Its use with a word makes the word stand out distinctly" and one of its purposes is "to denote a previous reference."[181] Commenting on 2 Thessalonians 2:3, A. T. Robertson said, "The use of the definite article (hē) seems to mean that Paul had spoken to the Thessalonians about it."[182] The departure Paul previously referred to was "our being gathered to him" (v. 1) and our being "caught up" with the Lord and the raptured dead in the clouds (1 Thess. 4:17).

5. Some early English versions appear to take the literal meaning. Apostasia in 2 Thessalonians 2:4 is translated "departynge" by William Tyndale (c. 1526), Coverdale (1535), Cranmer (1539) and the Geneva Bible (1557). Beza (1565) translates it "departing." Their translation, like the Greek term,

allows for a physical departing as well as a spiritual one. Although a minority of translators and exegetes hold that the *apostasia* is spatial, the norm of truth is not majority vote, but biblical usage. Such scholars as MacRae, English, Wood, Lineberry, and Wuest have maintained a literal interpretation of the departing.[183]

6. A literal, spatial departure provides a *better parallel with the supporting argument that follows* (2 Thess. 2:5–8). Paul reminded his readers the things he taught when with them (v. 5) and added some details. Some*one* (masc., v. 7) or some*thing* (neuter, v. 6) is holding back the outbreak of lawlessness until it will be taken out of the way. The church throughout its history has held back lawlessness. The restrainer cannot refer to the Holy Spirit, since the omnipresent Spirit cannot be removed from creation. It seems more probable that the restrainer of evil in the present is the church (enabled by the redemptive ministries of the Holy Spirit). After the body of Christ is "taken out of the way" the lawless one will then be revealed. Furthermore, the other alternatives do not fit as well with the purpose of the Epistle—to comfort the Thessalonians regarding the day of the Lord's vengeance.

7. Only a literal physical departure (*apostasia*) coheres with constant watchfulness and avoiding date setting. On the posttribulational interpretation constant watchfulness for Christ is unnecessary until after a future global apostasy and the appearance of the man of lawlessness. From the time of his revelation church members could count three and a half years to the approximate date of the Rapture (allowing for some shortening of the time). But this would contradict Jesus' admonition to be constantly watching for his return. Even after Christ listed the signs, including the abomination of desolation, he emphasized the need for constant watchfulness (Matt. 24:36–50).

Taken together, these points indicate that a physical departure is more probable than a doctrinal defection. After the removal of the restrainer (v. 7)—the rapture of the church—the man of lawlessness will be revealed (2:3, 8), set himself up in the temple and call himself God (2:4), and finally will be overthrown (2:8). Although the church will continue to suffer from the evil world until the Rapture, we are promised deliverance from the period of divine wrath on the ungodly.

The Importance of Theological Method and Attitudes

The evidence in this section has indicated several raptures (e.g., two witnesses in the middle and martyrs at the end of the Tribulation). In all the views of the time of the Rapture there may be some truth. When it comes to *the rapture of the church*, all views concur that it is pre-Armageddon (the culmination of the Tribulation). The evidence further indicates that it is prior also to earlier manifestations of divine wrath, otherwise called the Day of the Lord and the hour of trial designed to test devotees of the Antichrist. Such a pretribulational view of the rapture of the church fits Christ's teaching regarding our inability to predict the times or seasons of his return and preserves his teaching on constant readiness. This view also conforms to the teaching of Paul that the Thessalonians need not think they have missed the Rapture, for that will occur before the revelation and destruction of the man of lawlessness.

That there remain differences in putting together such diverse hints as we have in the Gospels, the Thessalonian epistles and Revelation should not be considered strange. Since there is no explicit biblical statement affirming that the rapture of the church is pre-, mid-, or posttribulational, each view is at best inferential. The spiritual-institutional theology developed in the previous chapter does not of itself resolve the problem of the time of the rapture of the institutional church, but it does make a pretribulational view possible without the usual criticisms of dispensationalism. Holding the spiritual oneness and institutional distinction of Israel from the church, people may adhere to different views of the time of the Rapture. And we do!

On the time of the rapture of the church the co-authors represent the diversity among evangelicals and illustrate the fact that even with agreement on method in general, differences in exegesis and application of the approach to an issue may result in different conclusions. To test the coherence of a posttribulational hypothesis, review Bruce Demarest's exegesis in the historical and biblical sections of this chapter. With most of his case against traditional dispensational arguments for pretribulationalism, Gordon Lewis concurs, but they do not answer pretribulationalism on other grounds. A difference between the co-authors on the time of the rapture of the institutional church of about six years does not affect their personal or professional work together. Thus we recommend that such a difference not divide the fellowship or work of other Christians or churches. (For more on the significance of this issue see the section "Relevance for Life and Ministry" in this chapter.)

APOLOGETIC INTERACTION

The Book of Revelation Is Divinely Inspired Prophecy

Often Revelation is considered Jewish apocalyptic literature because of a number of *similarities*. Like noncanonical Jewish apocalyptic writings, Revelation refers to the end of the age, using many dramatic images and figurative expressions. It dramatizes the battle between good and evil and the triumph of justice in vivid figures of speech and symbols. With graphic language the Jewish author records his dreams and visions. But there are also very significant *differences*:

1. *The ultimate source* of John's book is God's special revelation. Like other canonical books, it originated not with man but with God. Its title, "The Apocalypse [*apokalypsis*] of John," refers to its origin as information divinely revealed.[184] For example, Paul received his Gospel "by revelation" (*di' apokalypseōs,* Gal. 1:12) and the mystery of the church similarly (*kata apokalypsin,* Eph. 3:3). So John received from Jesus Christ revelation (*apokalypsis,* Rev. 1:1) of what would take place in the future. The author classified the book as prophecy both at the beginning and at the end (Rev. 1:1, 3; 22:7, 10, 18–19).

Characteristic of apocalyptic literature is its *esoteric source*. Taylor explains: "the secrets of the universe and of the last days are revealed to the author or chief character of the book in a series of visions, often through angelic mediation."[185] Through the influence of fallen angels, some Jewish apocalyptic literature tried to predict what God had not revealed (cf. Dan. 12:9). It transmitted occult knowledge secretly preserved from antiquity (2 Esdras 12:35–38) or derived from Sibylline channelers. Mathews called the Sibylline Oracles "the most important illustration of the extra-Palestinian-Hellenistic apocalyptic hope."[186] Sibyl was "One of the those women in the classic period reputed to possess powers of prophecy. Hence, a fortune-teller; a witch."[187] In contrast to occult secrets for the initiated, Mounce observes, the book of Revelation is an "open declaration of eschatological truth."[188] To the extent that apocalyptic means drawing on *oc-*

cult traditions, the ultimate source of Revelation is not apocalyptic.

2. Classifying Revelation as Jewish apocalyptic literature overlooks also important differences in its *human authorship*. Jewish apocalyptic literature was not written by identifiable and accredited prophets but by anonymous writers after the school of the Old Testament prophets had ceased (200 B.C. to A.D. 100). Because some of their prophecies rewrite the Old Testament and are "imitative and artificial," Ladd called Jewish apocalyptic literature *"pseudoprophecy."*[189] These include such books as 1 Enoch, 2 Enoch, the Apocalypse of Baruch, Book of Jubilees, the Testament of the Twelve Patriarchs, the Martyrdom and Ascension of Isaiah, and the Apocalypse of Peter.[190] In contrast, the author of Revelation is a well-known apostle who immediately identified himself so that his apostolic credentials could be verified. The true apostle does not appeal to a common tradition of ancient saints for his authority; he appeals to what he saw and heard through immediate visions of the Lord through the Spirit.

3. The different sources are reflected in different *content*. Revelation implies that God is not through with this world but will vindicate his moral purposes in history. When evil seems to have the upper hand, God's people do not seek ecstatic escape from space, time, and responsibility. Rather, they repent of moral and spiritual unfaithfulness and persevere in righteousness. The result of the Spirit's action is not a paralyzing mysticism but a powerful impulse to a moral life. The reading of Revelation evokes, not contentless delirium, but wonder and awe at God's truths foreseen and fidelity to Christ's teachings.

4. Revelation centers on *the Messiah's second advent* to consummate redemption, whereas apocalyptic literature does not. Many of the yet-to-be fulfilled prophetic passages emphasize

God's sovereignty in history, Satan's opposition, and the suffering of God's people culminating in a triumph of justice over unjust forces at Christ's glorious revelation. Biblical apocalyptic is not *ultimately* concerned with the evils developing in the world, nor even with the signs of Christ's return. Its focal point is the glorified Christ—the Victor who comes to conquer the wicked, judge the unrighteous, and rule with his people. John was *realistic* about the forces of evil, but he did not think history—present or future—is meaningless. Jewish apocalyptic literature is generally pessimistic regarding the present age and expects the righteous to suffer passively. According to John, the present age is not abandoned to evil; the enduring saints actively resist and overcome its injustices. Apocalyptic literature contains nothing parallel to the remarkable pastoral letters to the churches with their stimulus to present faithfulness (Rev. 2–3).

In view of these serious differences, Revelation should be regarded not as a species of mere Jewish apocalyptic but as canonical *prophecy*. The book of Revelation, as Ladd observes, reflects the revival of the prophetic word with divine authority. Integrating both similarities and differences, Ladd more accurately considers Revelation as "prophetic-apocalyptic."[191]

Hermeneutical Principles for Understanding Prophecy

The standard literal-cultural-critical principles applicable to all prophetic Scriptures (2 Peter 1:20–21) apply to Revelation (Daniel, et al.) as a species of divinely revealed prophecy. Since books like the Apocalypse have many figures of speech, it is important to ask the following questions: What is literal and what is figurative?[192] Does the passage teach a chronological order of events or not? Is the prediction conditional or unconditional? What aspects were of immediate significance to the writer, and what aspects were future?

One also needs to ask: What did New Testament writers mean when they said an Old Testament passage was fulfilled? Various answers have been given to this question: Some passages have been fulfilled in intention, such as the law (Matt. 5:17–18). Some are realized in literal detail at Christ's first advent, e.g., Bethlehem (Micah 5:2; Luke 2:4–7). Others draw upon an apparent incidental point of similarity between past and future events, like Rachel's mourning for her children (Matt. 2:17–18). And still others refer not to a single fulfillment but, according to the principle of multiple applications, to one instance at the time of the prophet and one or more in the future. For example, the statement "They will reign on the earth" (Rev. 5:10) may come to pass in some respects in the present age, in more complete respects in the Millennium, and even more fully in the new heaven and new earth.

In view of spiritual-institutional theology (developed in the previous chapter), readers need also to ask: Does a passage refer to God's people individually (spiritually) or collectively (institutionally)? For example, do predictions concerning Israel refer to spiritual Israel including believers today or to a restored and organized nation? In many passages we must ask, How does the spiritual unity in the Messiah and their differences institutionally relate to Israel's future both spiritually and institutionally? Are future functional differences indicated between Israel and the church though they are one in Christ?

Non-Literal Attempts to Explain Christ's Return

One basic hermeneutical question determines one's view of Christ's return: Are the predictions to be taken figuratively or literally? Is his return a symbolic myth about our present experience or a literal, future event in space and time?

Assuming the uniformity of natural law and evolution, liberal theologies did not interpret Christ's return literally. They regarded the first man, Adam, as symbolic, and on similar grounds dismissed a literal view of the Second Adam in both his Advents. They alleged that the kernel of truth in Christ's message about his return nevertheless was fulfilled. That is, Christ's kingdom came in the first century and continued among those who accepted the fatherhood of God and brotherhood of man. The future was envisioned to be much the same as the present, assisted by evolutionary optimism. A liberal theologian, Delwin Brown, now says, "Maybe we should never be so presumptuous as to announce progress, but we must be bold enough to believe it possible and work for it."[193] Brown thinks that conservatives who await the literal return of Christ are too content with the status quo. There is justification for that comment in some cases; but while waiting for Christ's return we are to be working for the purposes of God's providential and redemptive kingdoms. Furthermore, a liberal view fails to do justice to the facts and meanings disclosed by special revelation concerning Christ's first and second advents.

Albert Schweitzer's *The Mystery of the Kingdom of God* (1901) and *The Quest of the Historical Jesus* (1906) posit that in his original teaching Jesus' coming and kingdom would be supernatural and discontinuous with present human society before his generation passed away (Matt. 24:34). Schweitzer could not make Jesus into a modern evolutionist, and Jesus, as a literalist, seemed a mistaken child of his times! In spite of Jesus' supposedly errant literalism, Schweitzer advocated following his example. Knowing Jesus, he thought, did not depend on reliable histories of the Nazarene but on mystical encounters with him. But Paul said, "If Christ has not been raised, our preaching is useless and so is your faith" (1 Cor. 15:14).

C. H. Dodd held that the Parousia would not occur in the future, for it is already *realized*. The last days began when Christ entered history, overthrew evil, brought new life to believers, and granted his Spirit. Today as the Gospel is received, the kingdom is realized. "There is no coming of the Son of Man 'after' his coming in Galilee and Jerusalem, whether soon or late, for there is no before and after in the eternal order. . . . So far as history can contain it, it is embodied in the historic crisis which the coming of Jesus brought about."[194] But the meaning of history was not fully achieved in the First Advent, nor is it exhausted in the present experience of Christians. A completely realized eschatology does not account for the pervasive New Testament expectation that the present age will end with the Son of Man's return.

Emil Brunner's *Eternal Hope* advocates a paradoxical approach to texts on Christ's return within a generation. Assuming an infinite qualitative distinction between God and humans,[195] Brunner could not speak of God acting in history without paradox. So he spoke of Christ's return as both present and future, already and not yet, a possession and an anticipation. Christ's return figuratively pictures "the fathomless meaninglessness of history."[196] For Brunner, the Parousia is not an event verifiable in future history, for the eternal breaks into the temporal whenever persons sense the utter otherness of the present. But Brunner did not accept a fully realized eschatology for the present age because Christians inevitably sin and all attempts to introduce the kingdom have failed. Christ's return to rule, for Brunner, is not literal but a mere symbol of Christian hope and progress.

Reinhold Niebuhr and Paul Tillich also interpreted Jesus' references to his own return symbolically. Niebuhr thought that "it is important to take the Bible seriously, but not literally."[197] He said that the symbol of Christ's second coming informs us that we are always troubled with moral ambiguity and cannot find our purpose in history. Tillich similarly suggested that the Second Coming points to no future event but reminds us now that our happiness is transhistorical in the Ground of Being. The kingdom of God is the symbolic answer to the ambiguities of history.[198]

Rudolph Bultmann neither accepted nor rejected as erroneous Jesus' references to his return, but he reinterpreted them in terms of existentialist philosophy. In *Jesus Christ and Mythology* he claimed that one must not take prescientific biblical teachings as factual explanations of the cosmos or history. To make the Second Coming meaningful to naturalists, Bultmann held, it must be demythologized while highlighting its existential significance. Does the existential import hold, however, if the events on which they are based will not take place? The existential values of Christ's return derive their significance from its actuality. One cannot maintain a naturalistic worldview and reap the benefits of a theistic world-and-life view.

Jürgen Moltmann developed his theology of hope when he despaired of his homeland while he was a British prisoner in World War II. Communism seemed to provide a hope, while Christianity seemed irrelevant. Then he came to see that Christ's resurrection builds on promises yet to come. As a result, Moltmann makes eschatology central to every other doctrine. Salvation is the firstfruit of the future in Christ. The coming kingdom of Christ is no mere private vision, for it challenges all social structures that absolutize themselves. Moltmann does not passively await the kingdom; the future depends on our efforts as God works through us. So his theology of hope demands social action to bring about the object of faith, the coming kingdom. Without imagining that we can bring in the millennial kingdom, however, we are to do what we can to improve relationships here and now.

Conflicting interpretations of the Second Advent do not turn on whether we take figurative language figuratively, for most language contains figurative elements. Rather, the issue is whether the entire framework of a text is to be taken in a manner beyond the bounds of a normal use. The phenomena associated with Jesus' second coming are not fulfilled by the "comings" to cities during his First Advent (Matt. 10:23), his resurrection appearances (John 16:16), or his Spirit's coming at Pentecost. Jesus spoke of the Holy Spirit as "another Counselor" (John 14:16) and said that he himself would return at the end of the age to vindicate justice. Furthermore, the Second Coming does not mean our going to be with Christ at death, his judgment on Israel in A.D. 70, or his alleged reincarnation as some other person. In such cases divine wrath is not executed on all unbelievers, the dead are not raised, and living believers are not raptured. Christ must return in the body that lived, died, rose, and ascended. In that *glorified body* he will return. For similar reasons the Second Coming is not fulfilled by Sung Myung Moon or any alleged messianic figure (Maitreya), who was not crucified in the first century for our sins and who did not rise from the grave.

The philosopher Hegel, who earlier advocated a symbolic interpretation of Christ's advents, must face Harald Hoffding's criticism. It applies equally to others who do not take literally Christ's teaching on his second coming. "In his speculative zeal Hegel overlooked the fact that to the believers in revelation the whole point is that dogma is more than a figure. Every positive religion must assume that, at certain points, the difference between symbol and reality disappears—only under this condition can the concept of revelation possess validity."[199] If what symbolic interpreters affirm is true, let those who propound it tell us so plainly. Surely the Good News of the Gospels is more straightforward than alleged profundities that contradict the literal meaning and that are said to be beyond our ability to grasp. A. E. Murphy asked nonliteral interpreters to "bring their teaching to the level at which we can know what it is that they are saying and what evidence there is that what is said is true."[200]

Postmillennialism Insufficiently Realistic

The optimism of postmillennialists like David Chilton may serve as a healthy corrective to the pessimism of some premillennialists. Stemming from their pessimism about the present world, some dispensationalists have tended to disregard the world's needs other than for the Gospel. But we ought both to preach the Gospel and do good to all people, especially those of the household of faith (Gal. 6:10). But this text does not justify Chilton's hope for the "social transformation of the entire world."[201] Events in this fallen world have a way of exploding utopian dreams. We concur that we are not to despair of the world or flee it in defeat. We may expect victory for the Gospel in the present and future.[202] The Christian's great hope, however, focuses, not on the global success of *our* mission but on the success of the returning *Christ's mission.*

We rejoice with the postmillennial emphasis on universal preaching of the Gospel[203] and agree that acceptance of the Good News extends the kingdom's redemptive realm. Indeed, we are to be salt and light in the world (Matt. 5:13–16); but Chilton goes beyond those statements to claim, "This is nothing less than a mandate for the complete social transformation of the entire world."[204] Even if the saved outnumber the lost at any point in history, that does not assure their majority permanently. With population explosions it seems *unrealistic* to think that every generation of evangelicals will Christianize the entirety of the fallen world. Given all the benefits derived from Gospel preaching, the results do not compare with those predicted for the future Millennium. The hypothesis that the world will be Christianized before Christ returns is not only difficult to fit with the history of missions but also with the developing signs of Matthew 24: e.g., apostasy, idolatry, false Christs, and false prophets. Loraine Boettner's optimism in 1977 is hard to imagine today. Said he, "All of the false religions are dying. Christianity alone is able to grow and flourish under the modern civilization, while all of the others soon disintegrate when brought under its glaring light. . . . They await only the *coup de grace* of an aroused and energetic Christianity to send them into oblivion."[205] On the contrary, since the 1960's resurgent Eastern religions have invaded the Western world and permeated its culture.

With views reminiscent of Dodd's realized eschatology, Chilton writes,

The Biblical prophecies that Christ would reign as King were fulfilled in Christ's enthronement at His Ascension. . . . Daniel's prophecy of the Son of Man 'coming in the clouds' was fulfilled in the ascension of Christ. . . . Jesus Christ definitively defeated and bound Satan and the demons in his Atonement, Resurrec-

tion, and Ascension. . . . The Kingdom was established during the First Advent of Christ (including the Judgment of A.D. 70); it is now in progress and will increase until the end of the world. . . . Ethnic Israel was excommunicated for its apostasy and will never again be God's Kingdom. The Kingdom is now made up of all those (Jew and Gentile) who have been redeemed by Jesus Christ. The Olivet Discourse (Matt. 24, Mark 13, Luke 21) is not about the Second Coming of Christ. It is a prophecy of the destruction of Jerusalem in A.D. 70. . . . The Great Tribulation took place in the Fall of Israel. . . . Although Israel will someday be restored to the true faith, the Bible does not tell of any future plan for Israel as a *special* nation. . . . *Antichrist* is a term used by John to describe the widespread apostasy of the Christian church prior to the Fall of Jerusalem. . . . The Great Apostasy happened in the first century. We therefore have no Biblical warrant to expect increasing apostasy as history progresses; instead, we should expect the increasing Christianization of the world. . . . *The Last Days* is a Biblical expression for the period between Christ's Advent and the destruction of Jerusalem in A.D. 70; the "last days" of Israel.[206]

In view of the exegesis in the biblical and systematic sections above, it is difficult to concur with postmillennialists that many predictions usually related to Christ's Second Advent are fulfilled in Christ's First Advent. Also debatable historically is the claim that "the hope of worldwide conquest for Christianity has been the traditional faith of the Church through the ages."[207]

Chilton's "key" to Revelation 20 is his interpretation of "the first resurrection" as a spiritual resurrection—i.e., our justification and regeneration in Christ. Hence the born-again are now partakers of the first resurrection. He fails to mention that the raised in the first resurrection are "those who had been beheaded because of their testimony for Jesus. . . . They had not worshiped the beast or his image'' (Rev. 20:4). The new birth is not a subject in the context of Revelation 20, although in other passages it is referred to figuratively as a resurrection from the dead.

From the faulty premise that the first resurrection is occurring now, Chilton reasons that "of necessity, . . . *the Millennium is taking place now as well.*"[208] "The 'Millennium' is the Kingdom of Jesus Christ, which He established at His First Advent. . . . The 'thousand years' of Revelation 20 is symbolic for a vast number of years—most likely *many* thousands."[209] We may not deny that the thousand years may represent a long period of time, but it seems questionable that the period said six times to be one thousand has "lasted almost 2,000 years and will probably go on for many more."[210] Although a present sense of Christ's kingdom is now inaugurated in believers' lives, we have yet to see his rule bringing lasting peace and justice to the entire globe. Yes, Jesus definitively defeated and bound Satan and the demons in his atonement, resurrection, and ascension, but the mopping-up operations will continue until his return. About the only event Chilton does not regard as already having occurred is Christ's second coming. Since that is future, the associated events must also be future. Furthermore, it is hard to reconcile the glories of the Messiah's reign in the Millennium with Boettner's statement that "the golden age will not be essentially different from our own so far as the basic facts of life are concerned."[211] Marked differences have yet to occur. Nature still longs to be delivered, many remain poor, weapons have not been destroyed, and death remains our greatest enemy. Although Christ's present rule is inaugurated and implemented in substantial ways among believers and those they influence, it is far from achieving the predicted global revolution. It is difficult to reconcile postmillennialism with either the scriptural data or the experience of the church.

Amillennialism Circular and Inadequate Institutionally

We concur with Hoekema that great evil will occur before Christ's return in spite of the fact that he is Lord of history. We agree that the kingdom of God is central and that history is moving toward a goal—the redemption of the universe. Also we agree that there is a spiritual oneness of believing Jew and believing Gentile. Indeed, there is one olive tree, one spiritual life, and one way of salvation by grace through faith. We have agreed with amillennialists who find the unity of the Old and New Testaments in one covenant of grace (one plan of salvation or one spiritual kingdom) and who posit one people of God (spiritually). Amillennialism fails, however, to develop the significance of the structural differences between the two branches of the olive tree. The institutional prophecies about the Jewish nation are not fulfilled in the Jewish-Gentile church.

Hoekema's cyclical interpretation of Revelation is hard to square with the progression of thought in chapters 19–20, and it presumes the point to be established. The cyclical interpretation presupposes only one resurrection and judgment at the end of history based on passages about the fact of resurrection, but it misreads the chronological factors. Those are discussed in Revelation 20, that explicitly separates two resurrections by the thousand years (vv. 4–7). Adherents of a cyclical view also assume that after one final judgment there is no more history. So they interpret the millennial account (Rev. 20) in terms of the beginning of the church. If the period between the resurrections dealt with Christ's present reign mediated through the church, John should have been inspired to extend it to at least two thousand years. But that would contradict Christ's prohibition of setting dates. Christ's present mediated rule between his comings to earth does not exclude a direct rule after his return. As Ladd taught, chapters 19 and 20 are continuous and describe "the destruction of the evil triumvirate: first the beast, then the false prophet (19:20–21) and then the power behind these two—the devil. There is absolutely no hint of any recapitulation in chapter 20."[212] We considered on page 409, above, Tenney's argument that the events of Revelation 17:1–21:8 are successive[213] and Kromminga's conclusion that the development in Revelation 12–20 is chronological.[214]

Where do believers rule with Christ? Not in heaven but "on the earth" (Rev. 5:10), which is the present globe. The new heavens and new earth are not in view until Revelation 21:1. *When* do Christians rule with Christ? Jesus said that the one who will rule is the one who serves as he did. Then, after Jesus' ascension and the advance of the church, Paul said, "Do you not know that the saints will judge the world?" (1 Cor. 6:2). Again: "If we died with him, we will also live with him; if we endure, we will also reign with him" (2 Tim. 2:11–12). These passages teach a *future* reign with Christ. Although at present we share in the redemptive kingdom, Satan (though disarmed) is not bound (Rev. 20:1–3) and the church is not close to reigning universally as it will in the Millennium (Rev. 20:4). Christ may now rule in substantial ways over our persons, families, and churches, but the saints can hardly be said to be judging Israel or the world.

Amillennialists, like postmillennialists, interpret the referent of the first resurrection (vv. 4, 6) to be the new birth. Yet they take the second resurrection literally. If in this context the literal meaning holds for the second resurrection, it is far more likely that a literal meaning holds also for the first. In other contexts the transformation of people coming to faith can be figuratively denoted a resurrection from spiritual deadness, but the context in Revelation 20 follows the return of Christ, the Battle of Armageddon, and the literal coming to life again of those beheaded for Christ. "The rest of the dead did not come to life until the thousand years were ended" (v. 5). Dying and going to be with Christ is wonderful, but for all the blessings of the intermediate state it is not resurrection. In summary, amillennialism helpfully emphasizes the spiritual kingdom between the Advents; but it fails to detect the significant change of social structure that will occur when Christ returns and reigns between the two resurrections.

The Hazards of Predicting the Date of Christ's Return

Some have predicted Christ's return within *a generation*. Hal Lindsey, who authored the best seller *The Late Great Planet Earth*,[215] later published *Hope for the Terminal Generation*. This book implied that within one generation (20, 30, or 40 years?) Christ would return. He wrote, "It is my unwavering conviction that this is the Terminal Generation. By this I mean that this generation is witnessing the coming together of all the prophetic signs into the exact pattern that Jesus and the other prophets predicted would immediately precede His return."[216] Although Lindsey did not propose a specific date for Christ's return, the book's title suggested that it would be within a generation. Later he published *The 1980's: Countdown to Armageddon* (1980). Although he did not predict a date, the title implies that the Parousia would occur within the decade of the 1980s.

Others have predicted Christ's return to *the year*. Before World War I Jehovah's Witnesses predicted Armageddon would occur in 1914. When this did not happen, they suggested that "the last days" or the last "generation" began in 1914. Later they predicted Armageddon for September, 1975. They revived the patristic argument that there would be six thousand years of human history followed by a thousand years of rest in the Millennium. The six thousand years of human existence, they said, began with Adam's creation in 4026 B.C. Others predicted Christ's return in 1982 because of the so-called "Jupiter Effect." At that time the positioning of the planets in relation to the sun was said to cause cosmic disturbances. But no such disturbances happened, and Christ did not return.

Some have even predicted *the year, month, and day* of the church's ascension. Edgar Whisenant, a former NASA rocket engineer, specified September 11, 12, or 13, 1988, for the Second Advent. His two titles in one cover are *88 Reasons Why the Rapture Could Be in 1988* and *On Borrowed Time?*[217] He claims that his view agrees perfectly with every verse in the Bible and particularly with the 886 end-time prophecies and all seven feasts of Israel and their dates.[218] Where did Whisenant go wrong? According to Dean Halverson he took verses out of context, misinterpreted symbols, and built on unwarranted dates.[219] He read meanings into many numbers and used forty years for a generation. For example, he claimed Jesus (Matt. 24:34) meant that the wicked generation from 1948 to 1988 will certainly not pass until all these things have happened.[220]

Whisenant's major mistake is instructive, because others tend to repeat it in one way or another. Whisenant's booklets find ways around Jesus' statements forbidding the setting of dates. Jesus said, "No one knows about that day or hour, not even the angels in heaven, nor the Son, but only the Father" (Matt. 24:36). Whisenant boldly claims that this "does not preclude or prevent the faithful from knowing the year, month and the week of Christ's return."[221] Furthermore, by misconstruing the meanings of "know" (*oida* and *ginōskō*), he concludes that Jesus said we could not know intuitively the time of his coming, but that with effort believers could research the year, month, and week.[222] But that is precisely the opposite of our Lord's instruction.

Whisenant also misinterprets the parable of the ten virgins (Matt. 25:1–13). He asks, "Would this book or some similar event just before the end let the faithful church . . . at least know the week, the month and the year a short time in advance to allow the bride to get ready to meet the bridegroom?"[223] But Jesus made the point that the wise virgins should prepare *before* the cry announcing the coming of the groom was heard. After that it was too late to prepare. Jesus' point was that we should keep watching for him always (v. 13).

He similarly mistakes another verse. When the disciples asked, "Lord, are you at this time going to restore the kingdom to Israel?" he replied, "It is not for you to know the times [*chronous*] or dates [*kairous*] the Father has set by his own authority" (Acts 1:7). Whisenant quotes the New American Bible—"the exact time is not yours to know"—and again makes the verse teach the opposite of its intention. We can know the time down to a three-day period, he thinks, but not the day or the hour. But the intent of Jesus was far broader here, as in the other passages. *Chronos* means time, a long time, a considerable time, the whole time, all the time, etc.[224] And *kairos* means not only a point of time but a period of time, a time of crisis, the last times.[225] Hence Jesus banned predictions of even more general times—weeks, months, and years—as well as days and hours.

Repeatedly and in different ways, Jesus emphasized that awareness of the signs should result in constant readiness.

Some postribulationalists think that people observing the signs and the Tribulation events will be able to predict an approximate date for the Rapture. Assuming that the church will be in the Tribulation, Robert Gundry writes,

> We shall not know exactly. But the delineation of preceding signs, including especially if not exclusively tribulation events, shows that we will know approximately. The shortening of the tribulation thus enables us to resolve general predictability and specific unpredictability without rending the exhortations to watch from their postribulational context and without minimizing the function of signalling events by resorting to the historical view with its vagaries. We are to watch, both because we cannot know exactly and because we must be alert to the signs which will enable us to know approximately.[226]

What was said in response to Whisenant's view applies also to Gundry. The signs, other than the revelation of the man of lawlessness, are sufficiently vague as to forbid even approximate date setting. Moreover, throughout this age Jesus would have his followers always watching. But Gundry writes, "Concerning NT exhortations to watch, we are led to the conclusion: until tribulational events have taken place, New Testament expectancy does not mean to look for the return of the Lord as a present possibility, but to look *forward* to His return after the events of the tribulation."[227] Christ enjoins us always to be looking for him. What are the parameters of knowing "approximately"? To what extent would posttribulationalists agree with Whisenant that people in the Tribulation can know not the day and hour but the year, month, and week? Since the Antichrist has not revealed himself, we can know now that it will be at least seven, or at very least three and a half years. If we are alive when the Man of Sin is revealed, we can know the year, even if the Great Tribulation were shortened by six months.

Which hypothesis best fits Christ's teachings? Did he teach that his return was always to be anticipated by his disciples throughout the church age or anticipated only after the revelation of the Man of Sin and the Great Tribulation? The Lord taught that his return would be *unexpected:* "The Son of Man will come at an hour when you do not expect him" (Luke 12:40). Hence we should always be ready when the master returns so that we can welcome him (Luke 12:36). When his disciples asked, "When will these things happen?" Jesus replied, "Watch out that you are not deceived. For many will come in my name . . ." (Luke 21:7–8). With all the signs given to indicate that his return was "near" (vv. 20, 28), Jesus said, "Be *always on the watch*" (v. 36). Again, "Be on guard! Be alert! You do not know when the time will come. . . . Therefore keep watch because you do not know when the owner of the house will come back. . . . What I say to you, I say to everyone: Watch!" (Mark 13:33, 35, 37). Jesus did not suggest that we need to watch only after certain events come to pass. According to Hoekema, "the very unexpectedness of the Second Coming means that we must always be watching for it. Jesus himself indicated certain signs of his coming. . . . Watchfulness for his coming, therefore, includes being alert to these signs. But, above all, watchfulness means readiness—being always ready for Christ to return."[228] What did Paul teach about the time of Christ's return? Hoekema summed it up this way: "Like Jesus, Paul taught that though the time of the Second Coming is uncertain, the fact of that coming is certain. The believer should live in constant joyful expectation of Christ's return; though he does not know the exact time of it, he should always be ready for it."[229]

Since the Tribulation is not entirely different from the present age but continues with signs observed from the first century, Christians are not able to compute when the intensity will become sufficient to say the period of Tribulation has actually begun. Doctrinal apostasy has always been with us, and an increasing degree will not be evident on any given day. And the "revelation" of the Antichrist may not be as evident as many posttribulationalists suppose. The revelation of the Messiah in the First Advent was not acknowledged by most of his own (John 1:11). Similarly, the apocalypse of the Antichrist may be undetected and thus consistent with the command to watch constantly. Jesus' statements forbid a countdown to the approximate time of the Rapture or Armageddon. Our Lord prohibits computations concerning the beginning of his Second Advent in favor of always looking for his return.

The warning of Michael Green applies to both post- and pretribulationalists. "Those who think they can map out a detailed program of what will happen at the second coming of Christ should remember that, despite the prophecies of the Scripture, nobody got the details of the first coming right."[230] Hence it seems foolhardy to identify detectable events that must necessarily occur prior to the Rapture. We do not know how much apostasy from the faith or how evident the revelation of the Man of Sin will be. Thus a pretribulational rapture seems more consistent with our Lord's teaching on constant watchfulness and his warnings against setting even approximate dates for his return.

What Did Jesus Mean When He Said That "This Generation" Would Not Pass Away?

After listing signs of his return, Jesus said, "I tell you the truth, this generation will certainly not pass away until all these things have happened" (Matt. 24:34; Mark 13:30; Luke 21:32). Understanding of his second coming appears inseparably related to the meaning of "this generation." Various interpretations of the verse call for consideration.

1. Because Jesus had just spoken of the Roman siege and destruction of Jerusalem (Luke 21:5–6, 20–24), "all these things" refers to the fall of Jerusalem in A.D. 70. "This generation" then would refer to people living at the time Jesus spoke these words. The fall of Jerusalem, within the lifetime of his hearers, would be a picture of Antichrist's future destruction.[231]

2. Jesus spoke of his physical return within the lifetime of his hearers, but made a mistake. This is most improbable since it implies that he set a date for his return—the very thing he himself said he could not do (Matt. 24:36; Mark 13:32).

3. He may have meant that humankind in general will not pass away before he returns. "All these things" would include all the signs of his coming as they were developing in the first century, but not the coming itself. Jesus implied that human life will survive on earth until the end.

4. Others suggest that *unbelieving* people (Jewish and Gentile) will not pass away. Jesus' use of "generation," Hoekema suggests, may be qualitative rather than quantitative. In other places he spoke of an evil and adulterous generation (Matt 12:39; 16:4) and an unbelieving and perverse generation (17:17). So Jesus meant that this evil kind of generation will not pass away until he returns.

5. Jesus may have envisaged that the

unbelieving Jewish people ethnically as a generic kind (*genera*) will not pass away until all is fulfilled and he returns. Although the biblical section takes an alternative view which readers will want to weigh, an integration of views 3, 4, and 5 appears to fit most adequately the historical and cultural context of Jesus' statements. Jesus had left the temple and predicted its destruction. Later he sat on the Mount of Olives while responding to the question "Tell us, when will this happen, and what will be the sign of your coming and of the end of the age?" (Matt. 24:3). After his resurrection, the disciples still asked, "Lord, are you at this time going to restore the kingdom to Israel?" (Acts 1:6). Their concern was for the Jews collectively and institutionally. Jews asked the question, and they were hardly concerned with Gentile issues. This would come up later (Acts 10). After considering all these views, Hoekema concluded:

By "this generation," then, Jesus means the rebellious, apostate, unbelieving Jewish people, as they have revealed themselves in the past, are revealing themselves in the present, and will continue to reveal themselves in the future. This unbelieving and evil generation, though they reject Christ now, will continue to exist until the day of his return, and will then receive the judgment which is their due. Interpreted in this way, Jesus' statement comes as a logical conclusion to a discourse which began with the proclamation of the destruction of Jerusalem, as a punishment for Israel's obduracy.[232]

RELEVANCE FOR LIFE AND MINISTRY

"What oxygen is for the lungs, such is hope for the meaning of human life."[233] Christians face the future not with fear and anxiety but with joyful confidence and expectation. Our ability to shape the future is limited, being dependent on factors beyond our control. But those factors are not beyond the control of Christ, the exalted Lord of history. Although the future is unknown to us, we confidently believe that evil will not have the last word. In the face of all the injustices we observe and experience, our ultimate confidence is that the just and loving Lord will make all things right. A reliant expectancy of the risen Messiah's actual second coming provides believers with life-sustaining hope here and now. "Set your hope fully on the grace to be given you when Jesus Christ is revealed" (1 Peter 1:13).

General Douglas MacArthur, when he was forced to leave the Philippines during World War II, said dramatically: "I shall return." In due course he did return, and with the U.S. military he liberated those islands from the invaders. With far greater authority and power, Jesus Christ said, "I shall return." The Lord will return to earth, and he will liberate the world from its satanic invaders.

Be Alert to Multiple Signs of Christ's Return

In the Olivet discourse (Matt. 24; Mark 13; Luke 21), Jesus gave his disciples a number of signs for which to watch. Some of the signs were realized (in part) before the New Testament was completed. For example, John wrote, "Dear children, this is the last hour; and as you have heard that the antichrist is coming, even now many antichrists have come. This is how we know it is the last hour. They went out from us, but they did not really belong to us. For if they had belonged to us, they would have remained with us" (1 John 2:18–19).

The intensification of several of the signs prompted attention in every century, and people frequently have thought they were at the end of the age.

Lecturing at Denver Seminary in 1967, Wilber Smith asked, Is our situation different from that of previous generations? Are the signs different today? Satellites have made possible instant *global communication*. If previously it would have seemed impossible for one person to rule the entire world, satellites now make pictures and words thousands of miles away instantly available. We also have a global *financial market*: the condition of the stock market in one country impacts markets in other countries. We also have growing global *political power* as the United Nations assumes a greater role in enforcing its resolutions. Trends like these make more possible than in any previous generation the fulfillment of the predictions concerning the universal power of the Antichrist economically, politically, and religiously.

The growth of a *global apostasy* since the 1960s has skyrocketed in the direction of pantheistic idolatry. In 1967 Wilbur Smith said he could observe no false messiahs. Since that time the Western world has been inundated with Eastern gurus and New Age leaders who claim to be enlightened avatars (incarnations) of deity. The number of counterfeit prophets, apostles, and miracles is multiplying (Matt. 24:5, 11, 23–26). "Having a form of godliness but denying its power" (2 Tim. 3:5), religious pluralism is moving toward a syncretism of world religions. In the West as well as the East Jesus' uniqueness is denied as he is viewed as only one of many spiritual masters.

In recent decades *lawlessness* has become increasingly pervasive (2 Thess. 2:7–12). The "secret power of lawlessness" (v. 7) was already at work in the first century, and today it threatens democratic societies globally. One in three high school boys in America goes to school armed. One in twenty carries a gun; 20 percent of the major city school systems use metal detectors

to discover them.[234] Relativists hold that no acts are morally wrong or sinful. There is no accountability because society is to blame and no judgment because there is no Judge. The spiritually "enlightened" (as in pantheism) imagine themselves evolving beyond distinctions of good and evil. Although the overwhelming majority of Americans in Gallup polls claim to believe the Ten Commandments, most could not even name them. The revolt of humanity at large against moral absolutes saturates all levels of society and it is sinful (1 John 3:4; cf. 2 Tim. 3:1–7, 13; 4:3–4).

Wars and rumors of wars recur as nations rise against nations (Matt. 24:6–7a). In 1986, designated by the United Nations "the International Year of Peace," an Associated Press survey counted at least forty-three countries at war, and only two conflicts had subsided by the date of the report, October 19, 1986. As nuclear weapons proliferate, renegade nations led by demented dictators threaten universal blackmail. Soon after we felt relieved that the cold war with communist countries was over, armed conflicts broke out regionally. And where there are no live wars, terrorism places life and property in jeopardy.

Famines (Matt. 24:7b) take the lives of thousands in Africa, India, and other areas. A large part of the continent of Africa is turning to dust as the ravages of years of drought expand the Sahara Desert, sometimes at the rate of ninety-three miles a year.[235] In half a century an estimated quarter of a million square miles (650,000 square kilometers) of farming and grazing land has been swallowed up by the Sahara. Much fertile farm land in the United States has been abandoned for lack of water along Interstate 10 between Tucson and Phoenix, where dust storms now often sweep the highway.[236]

Earthquakes are occurring in more

varied locations around the globe. Jesus predicted them "in various places" (Matt. 24:7b). In the first fifty years of the twentieth century major earthquakes (registering over 5.5 on the Richter scale) causing hundreds and thousands of deaths occurred in eight countries (the United States, Chile, Italy, China, Japan, India, Turkey, and Ecuador). In the next forty years (1951–90) similarly destructive earthquakes occurred in twenty-one additional countries (Turkey, Afghanistan, Iran, Morocco, Chile, Yugoslavia, the United States, China, Peru, Nicaragua, Pakistan, Turkey, Guatemala, Italy, New Guinea, the Philippines, Romania, Indonesia, Argentina, Japan, Colombia, Ecuador, Algeria, Yemen, Mexico, India, Nepal, Burma, and Armenia).[237]

"All these," (apostasy, lawlessness, wars, famine, and earthquakes), Jesus said, "are the beginning of birth pains" (Matt. 24:8). The Lord added further signs of the end: *the hatred, betrayal, and persecution* of Christians (vv. 9–11). Anti-Christian attitudes are escalating in the media, public education, and politics. "In this world," Jesus said, "you will have trouble" (John 16:33). Further documentation can be added by each reader. Belief in a pretribulational rapture provides no escape from the wrath of non-Christians during the present age.

After many centuries *the reinstatement of Israel* as a national institution (1948) makes the "abomination that causes desolation" possible in the holy place (Matt. 24:15). Jesus also said, "Jerusalem will be trampled on by the Gentiles until the times of the Gentiles are fulfilled" (Luke 21:24). Jerusalem is now under Jewish control, although Mount Zion is still "trampled on" by Muslims meeting at the Mosque of Omar. If this is the return of the Jews of which Amos spoke, they will not be uprooted. "I will bring back my exiled people Israel; they will rebuild the ruined cities and live in them. . . . I will plant Israel in their own land, never again to be uprooted from the land I have given them" (Amos 9:14–15).

The proclamation of the Gospel to "the whole world" is occurring now as in no previous generation (Matt. 24:14). Christians utilize transistor radios, television sets, and satellites to convey the Gospel to jungle and city. Many millions of Bibles are now being distributed along with countless pieces of other Christian literature in lands where communist leaders previously prohibited them. Believers excited about the future teach and preach the timeless Gospel of the kingdom in the midst of antagonistic environments. "The preaching of the gospel," said G. C. Berkouwer, "is the focal point of all the signs."[238] Taking seriously all the signs, our primary concern should be about the *one sign* for which we have a major responsibility. In this "information age" it is crucial that missionaries do not become mere global researchers rather than global evangelists. What church planters do with their global information is the important thing. As Paul said to Timothy to whom he had committed his commission: "I charge you to keep this command without spot or blame until the appearing of our Lord Jesus Christ" (1 Tim. 6:13–14).

Always Be Ready for Christ Himself

While we must plan for the possibility that the Parousia may be far off, we must be prepared for its possibility any morning, afternoon, or night. We are like the student who comes to class not knowing when she will be called on to recite. So she prepares every day to be always ready. The reason Christ's sudden, thieflike appearance will not take believers by surprise (1 Thess. 5:4) is not that they can predict even the approximate time, but that they are *always* looking for him. A group of ministers was asked, "How many of you think that Jesus could come today?" None raised their hands. The speaker then quoted Christ: "the Son of Man will come at an hour when you do not expect him" (Luke 12:40). Are there not *signs* yet to be fulfilled? There may be, but we do not know them because we can not determine the degree of their frequency. For example, we do not know when the Gospel may have been preached sufficiently throughout the world. No one can identify the number of wars and rumors of wars, earthquakes, famines, and false prophets there are. Such signs will intensify up to and during the Tribulation. Hence no one should even try to predict the date of its beginning.

We should not become preoccupied with the signs to the neglect of the Savior. For whom should Christians *watch*? For the master (Luke 12:37), the owner of the house (Mark 13:35), the Son of Man (Matt. 24:44), and the bridegroom (25:1–13). Who is *near*? "The Lord is near" (Phil. 4:5; cf. James 5:8). For whom do Christians *wait*? The Corinthian Christians eagerly waited for "our Lord Jesus Christ" (1 Cor. 1:7). The Thessalonians waited for God's "Son from heaven, . . . who rescues us from the coming wrath" (1 Thess. 1:10; cf. Phil. 3:21). Again: "He will appear a second time . . . to bring salvation to those who are waiting for him" (Heb. 9:28). Joyfully, then, "we wait for the blessed hope—the glorious appearing of our great God and Savior, Jesus Christ" (Titus 2:13).

Anyone who has had a loved one away for a length of time has experienced a longing for return and reunion. Similarly, those who love Jesus Christ with their whole being long to see him face to face. Like a bride, the members of the church desire to meet their Bridegroom. Our *present* fellowship with Christ is mediated through the Word illumined by the Spirit. We now

see a reflection of him as in a mirror (1 Cor. 13:12). But our *future* experience of the Messiah will be immediate and direct. We shall see him as he is in power and great glory, and we shall shout "Hallelujah!" (Rev. 19:1). "Let us rejoice and be glad and give him glory! For the wedding of the Lamb has come, and his bride has made herself ready" (v. 7). "Blessed are those who are invited to the wedding supper of the Lamb" (v. 9).

Rather than concentrating on the multiplying evils of the ungodly, let us, like John, meditate on the exalted Messiah. Adapting Merrill Tenney's outline of Revelation, let us contemplate Christ Communicating (1:1–8), Christ as Lord of the Church (1:9–3:22), Christ on the Throne of the Cosmos (4:1–16:21), Christ in Conquest, over the nations of the earth (17:1–21:8), Christ in Consummation, as the glorious center of the new creation (21:9–22:5), and let us personally respond to Christ's Challenge (22:6–21).[239] As Berkouwer reminds us, "The very days of catastrophe—of wars, famines, and earthquakes—can draw attention away from the eschaton and plunge us deep into defeatism or perspectiveless determinism."[240] He adds, "Like a tightly stretched bow, the eschaton stands above the times in which one talks about the *corpus Christianum* and above times of apostasy, secularization and persecution. It must be related as much to the 'golden ages' as to apocalyptic periods."[241]

Thus the Christian's anticipation differs from the pessimism of Jewish apocalypticists, who, in their concern about many details of the future, missed the central, messianic focal point. In contrast, Christian futurists capture a Christocentric vision of the last days. All other signs and Tribulation events should be subordinate to Christ. A lively expectation of Christ's Parousia, like that of the early church, does not mean a passive, unproductive, waiting for the life to come. Pretribulationalists who excuse themselves from responsibilities in the present age abuse the doctrine. "The eschatological motive, the consciousness of the coming of the Lord as near at hand, has not a negative, but a positive significance for life in the present time. It does not make the responsibility for that life relative, but rather elevates it."[242]

Be Understanding of Those Who Differ on the Time of the Rapture

We have found sufficient reasons to believe two things: (1) that Christ will literally return to rule the nations and (2) that only God knows when the rapture of the church will occur.

The *literal return* of Christ is the most important issue in eschatology, for our Lord's credibility is at stake. The issues of the Millennium are next in importance to fulfill the hope of the prophets, the predictions made at Christ's birth, his own teaching about Israel's restoration, the significance of Revelation 20, and the culmination of a Christian philosophy of history. The time of the rapture of the church in relation to the Tribulation wrath is not the most important item; neither is it unimportant. One's view of it exhibits one's belief in the way in which promises of deliverance from divine wrath are fulfilled. It also reflects on Christ's teaching concerning constant readiness. Alan A. MacRae worked out a calibration of the degrees of importance of these topics:

> It impresses me as very important to stress the fact that the differences between the pretribulation and posttribulation views are not one-fifth so vital as the difference among premillennialism, postmillennialism and amillennialism; and that these latter differences in turn, are not one-tenth so vital as the differences between those who accept the Scriptural

statements about the substitutionary atonement of Christ and his visible return and those who deny these statements. Among Christians who believe in the return of Christ there should be true fellowship regardless of their views on the millennium, and among premillennialists there should be closest fellowship regardless of their conclusions as to the time of the rapture.[243]

Every view of the time of the Rapture is *inferential,* for no Scripture teaches one view explicitly. (1) A posttribulationist, Douglas Moo admits, "the *time* of the Rapture with respect to the Tribulation is *nowhere plainly stated.*"[244] A mid-tribulationist, Gleason Archer, states, "As we draw this discussion to a close, we must confess that the data of Scripture do not lend themselves to any clear and unambiguous pattern which is completely free of difficulties."[245] Pretribulationalists must be as candid. Answers to this issue would not be so varied among Bible believers if it were more explicitly addressed in Scripture.

Although the question of the time of the church's rapture is not all-important, students should not leave it unanswered. Rather, they should have the freedom and courage to take a position. It is, of course, not a simple matter to integrate our Lord's emphasis on watching, Paul's teaching in the Thessalonian epistles, and John's teaching in Revelation. On some doctrinal issues the scales weighing evidence are heavily tipped in one direction, on others one has to decide even though the scales favor one view only slightly. Where the evidence seems less than conclusive, interpreters may be more heavily influenced by their view of the relation of the church to Israel and consequent system of theology: covenant, promise, kingdom, dispensational, or spiritual-institutional.

Some posttribulationalists seem to exude the dogmatism often attributed to earlier pretribulationalists. Representatives of both need mutual understanding. In reviewing Ladd's posttribulational *Blessed Hope,* pretribulationist John Walvoord wrote,

> Though Dr. Ladd presses his argument beyond the Scriptural facts, undoubtedly he is correct that posttribulationalism in itself does not remove missionary incentive and pretribulationalists should not assume the role that they are the only ones who are concerned with the Lord's return in a practical way. Many will agree with Dr. Ladd's closing plea in this chapter for more tolerance in this matter of pre-, mid-, and posttribulation rapture.[246]

Charles Ryrie early pointed out that "premillennialism as a system is not dependent on one's view of the rapture." "Let it be said again that one's attitude toward the tribulation or the rapture is not a decisive factor in premillennialism."[247] Leon J. Wood, for a faculty group at Grand Rapids Baptist Theological Seminary, wrote, "It should also be said, however, that each felt that continued fellowship with those who had come to accept the opposing view was possible and, more so, highly desirable. . . . They respect the view of these others, realizing that their position is likewise based in the Scriptures, as they understand them."[248] In an irenic case for pretribulationism, E. Schuyler English, *Rethinking the Rapture,* emphasized that

> diverse views concerning what the Scriptures teach, as to the time of the translation of the Church in relation to the Tribulation, do not involve heresy. Our fellowship with our brethren in Christ is not in the order of eschatological events but in the crucified, risen, ascended, and seated Son of God, our Lord Jesus Christ, who is coming again for His Blood-bought saints, and with them also, to judge and to reign.[249]

The three main contributors to *The Rapture: Pre-, Mid-, or Post-Tribulational?* exhibited this same spirit:

> The authors write as members of this denomination [Evangelical Free], as colleagues on the faculty of its seminary [Trinity Evangelical Divinity School], and as personal friends. We write with charity and respect for one another but with no less conviction with regard to our own views. . . . For some, the advocacy of differing positions on the Rapture among colleagues on the same faculty may seem incongruous. All three of us are wholeheartedly devoted to upholding the clear truths of Scripture but we do not believe that the relative time of the Rapture is one of these "clear truths."[250]

We suggest that the time of the Rapture should not be included in the doctrinal statement of a church, and that Christians should learn to live with such differences. Tolerance does not mean regarding every opinion equally true and relevant or having no opinion at all. It does require those who have convictions to respect the freedom of others to hold differing opinions on secondary matters.

Keep the Faith

In concluding his letter on the Day of the Lord and our gathering to him, Paul wrote, "So then, brothers, stand firm and hold to the teachings we passed on to you, whether by word of mouth or by letter" (2 Thess. 2:15). We may not be fully persuaded of the *time* of the Rapture, but Christ's *return* in judgment on sinners and deliverance of the church needs to be preached and taught. As busy as Paul was in crosscultural evangelism, he took time to instruct new churches on the fact of the Rapture and the global judgment of the unrepentant. Those who live in the light of Christ's return remain steadfast in these as in other apostolic doctrines. Those who would lead others dare not neglect teaching and preaching on eschatology because of differences among evangelical scholars. The lack of information on eschatology in many churches leaves people open to unbiblical emphases. Jehovah's Witnesses capitalize on the ignorance of church members concerning things to come. We ought not be so preoccupied with the present as to neglect the future, nor so absorbed in the future as to neglect the present.

The Christian faith includes not only love for Christ's incarnation, death, and resurrection, but also a longing for his visible return to judge and rule in righteousness. Paul provided the paradigm of fidelity to the faith. He left Timothy with these moving words concerning the past and future: "I have fought the good fight, I have finished the race, I have kept the faith. Now there is in store for me the crown of righteousness, which the Lord, the righteous Judge, will award to me on that day—and not only to me, but also to all those who have longed for his appearing" (2 Tim. 4:7–8).

Actively Serve As an Agent of Christ's Kingdom Here and Now

"The end of all things is near," Peter said. But he did not conclude that believers should lose their heads. Rather, he taught:

Therefore be clear-minded and self-controlled so that you can pray. Above all, love each other deeply, because love covers over a multitude of sins. Offer hospitality to one another without grumbling. Each one should use whatever gift he has received to serve others, faithfully administering God's grace in its various forms. If anyone speaks, he should do it as one speaking the very words of God. If anyone serves, he should do it with the strength God provides, so that in all things God may be praised through Jesus Christ. To him be the glory and the

power for ever and ever. Amen. (1 Peter 4:7–11)

Until our Lord returns he desires that we put our resources and talents to work (Luke 19:13). William F. Allman wrongly alleges that "the allure of the Apocalypse may lie in the very human trait of wanting simple solutions to complex problems. For some it might be easier to make the single, big decision to abandon the world for the next than to make the countless smaller, tougher choices necessary to make this one better."[251] Christ's future rule, with all that it entails, is not simple but profound. Agents of the kingdom must make a significant difference in the world. But the best we can do now is insufficient to establish the universal faith, love, peace, and plenty that Christ's return will bring. By faithful stewardship now we model readiness for the day when Christ returns to complete the task. As Alan Johnson wrote, "Premillennialists really ought to have the greatest involvement in society because they believe very firmly that redemption takes place within history."[252]

In our lives of service we *avoid the vices* that Christ the King deplored in the seven churches of first-century Asia Minor (Rev. 2–3). Shun the behaviors the glorified Christ hates, the primary one being forsaking your first love (2:4). Then do not fear the suffering, persecution, or imprisonment the Devil uses to tempt God's people (v. 10). Do not fail to discipline people holding the corrupt and deceiving teaching of Balaam, who enticed Israel to sin by eating food sacrificed to idols and by committing immorality (v. 14). Similarly, do not fail to discipline the doctrinal and ethical aberrations of the Nicolaitan types (vv. 15–16). Do not tolerate a Jezebel who calls herself a prophetess, but who by her teaching misleads God's people into immorality, pagan practices, and

"Satan's so-called deep secrets" (vv. 20–24). Do not cultivate the reputation of being spiritually alive when in fact you are dead, asleep, or unrepentant (3:1–3). Having acquired wealth, do not become lukewarm in devotion to Christ. Resist the tendency to become spiritually "wretched, pitiful, poor, blind and naked" (vv. 15–18).

Rather, here and now *exhibit the righteousness of the kingdom.* Respond to temptation by bringing spiritual resources to bear. "Put aside the deeds of darkness and put on the armor of light. Let us behave decently, as in the daytime, not in orgies and drunkenness, not in sexual immorality and debauchery, not in dissension and jealousy. Rather, clothe yourselves with the Lord Jesus Christ, and do not think about how to gratify the desires of the sinful nature" (Rom. 13:12–14). "The grace of God that brings salvation . . . teaches us to say 'No' to ungodliness and worldly passions, and to live self-controlled, upright and godly lives in this present age, while we wait for the blessed hope—the glorious appearing of our great God and Savior, Jesus Christ, who gave himself for us to redeem us from all wickedness and to purify for himself a people that are his very own, eager to do what is good" (Titus 2:11–14). Servants of the kingdom, cleanse yourself from evil thoughts, fantasies, words, and deeds, and resolutely think, speak, and do what is good. Live a life separated from evil and dedicated to God. "You ought to live holy and godly lives as you look forward to the day of God and speed its coming" (2 Peter 3:11–12). "Everyone who has this hope [of the Parousia] in him purifies himself, just as he is pure" (1 John 3:3).

Whatever crises you face in your life, seek to exhibit the qualities of Christ's present and future kingdom. "For the kingdom of God is not a matter of eating and drinking, but of righteousness, peace and joy in the Holy Spirit" (Rom. 14:17). In some churches there seems to be more eating and drinking than justice, harmony, and gladness. As a Spirit-empowered agent of God's kingdom commit yourself to personal *righteousness* like that of your King. Add to foundational justice a *peace* like God's in your own heart and relationships. Then the by-product will be *joy* over what can be realized in the present, mediated kingdom and what will be achieved in the future, immediate reign of Christ.

Rejoice, the Lord's Prayer Will Be Answered!

At present we rejoice in great answers, as we pray, "Your kingdom come, your will be done on earth as it is in heaven" (Matt. 6:10). Premillennialists have reason to rejoice even more because the Lord's prayer will be answered even more fully in the future. The best is yet to come! The perennial quest for a just and lasting peace on earth will be fulfilled. God will gain the final victory. Although it may seem that evil is out of control, eventually justice will triumph. Christ's rule on earth will no longer be mediated through others, but will be open and direct. Plato's dream of a philosopher-king finally will come to fruition.[253] The One who governs will be not merely the most just, wise, and strong; he will be so absolutely. Under Christ's direct rule, his wise and loving purposes for institutions as well as individuals will be completely realized. The resurrected agents of God's immediate kingdom will perfectly follow his ways and impart spiritual and physical blessings to all.

Thus we hope for a lasting and just global *peace.* As the realization of redemption from enslavement to evil depended on the First Advent, so the realization of deliverance from social and political evils globally depends on the Second Advent. The creation that was subjected to frustration by the Fall will be liberated from its bondage to decay and brought into the glorious freedom of the children of God (Rom. 8:20–21). God will restore everything to its original condition at Messiah's return (Acts 3:21). God's purposes for his people collectively in the family, church, and Israel will be realized in a broader and more effective, universal social structure. Envision global justice in every capital of every nation. The age-long hopes of utopian visionaries and hardbitten realists for a new world order will be realized in ways far beyond their fondest dreams. The *legislative* branch, if such be needed, in Christ's global government will implement moral and just laws. They will be inscribed on the renewed hearts of all the governed. The *executive* branch of Christ's global government will administer the world's problems and disputes in accord with these just laws wisely. The *judicial* branch of Christ's global government will treat people with justice and grace. The motives and methods of those who rule with Christ in the new world order will be worthy and fair. However much you suffer now, be optimistic about the future. However far short our best efforts may come at present, history has a goal (*telos*) of unsurpassed glory.

Having suffered for Christ, anticipate *ruling with him*. In the future the redeemed will be a kingdom of priests to serve our God, and "they will reign on the earth" (Rev. 5:10). For the present be a faithful steward in your dual citizenship in heaven and in God's institutions on earth. Accept your responsibilities and blessings in both spheres. Do your assigned work diligently and faithfully, but leave to God his work of redeeming, judging, and making new.

Trust the Realities That Cannot Be Shaken

Communist utopian dreams, thought to be guaranteed by an inevitable dialectic, have been shattered. Darwinian utopias held to be assured by evolution are being undermined. Visionary utopias considered guaranteed by channeled messages from "spiritual masters" will collapse. But the exalted Messiah has given his faithful word. He will return! He will not let his people down.

When Satan attacks and your world seems to cave in, trust the things that will never be shaken. Strengthen your belief in God's *immutable revelation*. "The grass withers and the flowers fall, but the word of our God stands forever" (Isa. 40:8). Jesus said, "Heaven and earth will pass away, but my words will never pass away" (Matt. 24:35). Develop greater confidence in the *unshakable Christ* for whom all things were created and by whom all things hold together (Col. 1:15–20). Be reassured by your *inviolable justification*. No extent of suffering from antichrists can alter the completeness of your pardon and imputed righteousness. Nothing can change your status as a joint heir with Christ of all God's blessings. Keep on cultivating an *unshakable relationship* with the Christ who promised never to leave or forsake you (Heb. 13:5). For the future as well as the present we are securely "in Christ." Nothing can separate us from his love (Rom. 8:38–39). Finally, rely on your *unshakable redemption*. Christ has paid the price in full. With confident expectation, patiently wait for the redemption of your body and soul (vv. 25).

DISCUSSION TOPICS

1. What is the theonomist or Christian reconstructionist vision for human history? Is this adequately supported by scriptural teaching? By historical experience?
2. Do Old Testament kingdom texts (e.g., Ps. 72; Isa. 2, 11; Jer. 23; Micah 4) more adequately de-

scribe Christ's future millennial reign on the earth or his present spiritual rule over the church?

3. Which of the two main interpretations of 2 Thessalonians 2:1–8 outlined in the biblical section has greater exegetical and historical support? Give reasons for your conclusion.

4. Does the New Testament teach that Christ's coming is imminent, in the sense of an any-moment event? Reflect on biblical teaching regarding observable signs, watchfuilness, and the immediacy of Christ's second coming. What should be the Christian's response to this in terms of practical life-style?

5. Where does the rapture of the church occur in the structure of the Apocalypse? What implications, if any, does this have for your understanding of the return of Christ vis-à-vis the Tribulation?

See also the Review Questions and Ministry Projects on pages 501–2.

CHAPTER 8

LIFE AFTER DEATH, RESURRECTION, AND THE FINAL JUDGMENT

Life After Death, Resurrection, and the Final Judgment

**THE PROBLEM:
IS THERE LIFE BEYOND
THE GRAVE, AND IF SO,
WHAT IS THE NATURE
OF THE FUTURE EXISTENCE
FOR BELIEVERS AND
FOR UNBELIEVERS?**

The previous chapter indicated that all theology is eschatological. In it we considered the End from the perspective of the human race as a whole and the cosmos. The present study examines the End from the perspective of the individual believer and the unbeliever. This division is fitting, for God ordained a conclusion both for humanity in general and for individuals in particular.

Discussion of the future of the individual relates significantly to the nature of God (vol. 1, chs. 5–6). Who God *is* as a righteous, just, holy, and loving person has an important bearing on the destiny of believers and unbelievers. Moreover, issues of personal eschatology will be profoundly influenced by the nature of persons as image-bearers of God (vol. 2, ch. 3). Our judgment concerning the fate of individuals is inextricably linked to the question of whether the human person is an indissoluble whole or a complex, material/immaterial dualism. The issue of whether Adam and his descendants are responsible souls that survive death obviously is crucial to the subject at hand. Moreover, the present chapter looks forward to the eternal consequences of the death that came on all by virtue of original sin (vol. 2, ch. 4). The future fate of unbelievers must be evaluated in the light of human sin and depravity. In addition, the prospect of human fellowship with God beyond the grave represents the rationale for Christ's incarnation, atoning death, and bodily resurrection (vol. 2, chs. 5–8), as well as the outcome of the plan of salvation (vol. 3, chs. 1–4).

The issue of life beyond death involving personal accountability to God raises a number of important questions. What is the nature of the death we all die? Woody Allen once commented, "I am not afraid of death; I just don't want to be there when it happens." To pose the question whether humans were born mortal or immortal is to inquire whether they possess an undying essence that survives the grave. Relevant today is the question posed in patriarchal times: "If a man dies, will he live again?" (Job 14:14). Furthermore, how coherent with biblical teaching is Plato's notion of the immortality of the soul? Can we agree with Kant's postulate of three primary truths that serve the interests of practical morality: namely, God, freedom, and immortality? Is the soul's immortality a natural endowment for all, or is it a gift of redemptive grace granted to some?

In addition, if there is life beyond the grave, what is the nature of the so-called intermediate state for believers and unbelievers? Is the condition of the deceased between death and resurrection one of conscious existence in heaven or hell? Or does the soul sleep in a state of unconsciousness following death of the body (psychopannychy)? A number of modern theologians and psychologists explain the intermediate state on the assumption of holism—that the person is an inseparable unity of soul or mind and body. Others uphold a belief in the continued existence of the soul or mind independent of the body by appeal to "out-of-the-body" experiences (e.g., Raymond A. Moody, Jr., and Elisabeth Kübler Ross). A growing number of people in our day subscribe to reincarnation.

If existence beyond the grave is established, does this include the material body? What need is there for a resurrection body if believers go to be with Christ or unbelievers are consigned to hell immediately at death? If there is a resurrection body, what is its nature? Is the present, mortal body transformed into the new resurrection body (continuity), or does a new body totally replace the old body (discontinuity)? Moreover, is divine judgment primarily a present process, or will God judge all persons in a great, end-time assize? Will God give the unsaved opportunity beyond the grave to be saved? Will the unrighteous suffer everlasting, conscious torment? Or will the finally impenitent be annihilated? What is the nature of the final punishment? Is the "fire" of hell literal or symbolic? Would a good and loving God subject any of his creatures to endless, conscious tor-

ment in hell? Would God or believers enjoy heavenly bliss knowing that multitudes of people were suffering endless torment in hell? If hell is not a reality, where lies the urgency for worldwide missionary preaching?

ALTERNATIVE PROPOSALS IN THE CHURCH

The issue of life after death is widely debated in our day. The following survey of options shows how the problem has been understood in the broad history of the church.

Immortality of the Soul

Some liberal theologians, guided by Plato and Neoplatonism, posit the immortality of the soul while depreciating the resurrection of the body. Since the human spirit is part of the bodiless Eternal, the self is said to pass to the next life as an immortal spirit. Proponents of this view insist that the present physical body is not reconstituted as *sōma,* often defined as "the whole personality" (e.g., Bultmann, Robinson). Advocates thus view personal immortality as the consummation of the evolutionary process that began in man's animal past. "Immortality in the Christian sense . . . means a new birth upward; a new advance, a new stage of human evolution; a freer and more complete spiritual personality."[1] This evolution of the human spirit allows for continuous moral growth and development for all in the life to come. Most affirm that this evolutionary process ensures the salvation of the race.

The Baptist theologian W. N. Clarke (d. 1912) held that at death the immortal spirit exits the mortal body and lives on. Neither Jesus nor Paul taught the resurrection of the physical body in the life to come. Since Christ's kingdom is spiritual and not carnal, there is no rationale for physical bodies in the hereafter. Thus "the present body, belonging wholly to the material order, has no further use or destiny after death has detached the spirit from the material order, and is abandoned, to be known no more."[2] Clarke allowed for an ill-defined "spiritual body." He suggested that "the spiritual body is now forming itself within the physical body, being built up by moral action, every deed of right or wrong contributing to some beauty or deformity to its proportions and its features."[3] Moreover, since the Parousia is a present, spiritual process and not an end-time event, "resurrection" occurs at the moment of death. "Each human being's resurrection takes place at his death, and consists in the rising of the man from death to life in another realm of life. . . . According to this view resurrection is not simultaneous for all, but continuous, or successive."[4] Clarke added that a person's destiny at death is not irrevocably settled. Since the loving God's judgments are disciplinary, it is hoped that in the life to come the Father will bring all souls to fellowship with himself.

The Baptist preacher H. E. Fosdick (d. 1969) upheld the view of the immortality of the soul in lieu of the resurrection of the body: "I believe in the persistence of personality through death, but I do not believe in the resurrection of the flesh."[5] He claimed that notions of an intermediate state, a general resurrection, general judgment, and final states of eternal felicity and torment entered exilic Judaism from Zoroastrianism.[6] Unfortunately Christian thinkers borrowed these pseudo-views from Judaism. Fosdick believed that the truth about human destiny was accurately grasped by Greek philosophy and was faithfully mediated to the church by Origen.

For the Presbyterian W. A. Brown (d. 1943), the essence of the Christian hope is the survival of the individual personality at death. Because the soul is more real and enduring than the body, "it is the spirit which is the subject of the Christian hope."[7] The biblical language of a "spiritual body," being contradictory and ambiguous, conveys no clear meaning. Whatever its reality, it is not a physical body that is continuous with the body of this life. Since at death people pass directly from the present to the future life, the intermediate state is without basis. Moreover, he held that via the evolutionary process people will continue their growth toward moral perfection in the life to come. The future life, no less than the present, will be characterized by "moral struggle and moral victory."[8] In addition, since God is the divine Father and we are his children, Brown envisaged the salvation of all. "Man is an immortal spirit capable of communion with God and meant for fellowship with him throughout all eternity."[9]

The View of Purgatory

Roman Catholics and Anglo-Catholics affirm that souls that die in a state of grace but short of Christian perfection experience penal and purifying sufferings. Following the process of purgation the righteous souls enter heaven to await the resurrection of the body. Persons who die in a state of moral perfection or mortal sin go directly to heaven or hell, respectively. Since some sins are more grievous than others, the duration and intensity of purgatorial suffering varies. Catholicism links purgatory with the notion of satisfaction for sins, whereas Eastern Orthodoxy views the purifying fire mystically as a means of spiritual growth. Catholics claim that souls in purgatory are assisted by prayers of the saints, masses, payment of indulgences, and papal absolutions. Advocates of purgatory find support for the doctrine in 2 Maccabees 12:39–45; Malachi 3:2–3;

Luke 12:59; 1 Corinthians 3:11–15; and Jude 23. Roman Catholics also affirm the reality of *limbus patrum,* a place on the edge of hell where the souls of pre-Christian saints were held until Christ's resurrection (Luke 16:22; 1 Peter 3:18–22). They also posit *limbus infantum,* the abode of the souls of unbaptized children, who, neither depraved nor justified, do not experience either punishment or heavenly bliss.

Seeds of the purgatorial doctrine were planted in the early church. Alexandrian theologians spoke of the soul's gradual purification in the intermediate state as preparation for heaven. Guided by Platonic philosophy, Origen (d. 254) held that preexistent souls infused into bodies would be released from corporeal bondage and restored to unity with God. But this would occur only after the souls first were purified by the remedial fires of hell. Origen believed that there would be a series of eons involving creation, fall, judgment, and purgation. The series would end when all souls are purified from sin and united with God (the doctrine of *apokatastasis*).[10] Origen's restorationism was condemned by the Council of Constantinople in A.D. 543. Gregory of Nyssa likewise maintained that the sinner "cannot be admitted to approach the Divinity until the purifying fire shall have expiated the stains with which his soul was infected."[11]

In the West, Augustine (d. 430) held that carnal Christians must endure purifying fire between death and entry into heaven. Malachi 3:1–6 and 1 Corinthians 3:15 "seem to make it clear that in the last judgment there are to be purgatorial pains meted out to some of the faithful."[12] Many early Christian authorities (e.g., Cyprian, Tertullian, Augustine) cite the practice of praying for the believing dead. The doctrine of purgatorial fire prior to entering heaven was firmly established by the thirteenth century. Thomas Aquinas viewed purgatory as a place in the underworld where souls undergo cleansing between death and resurrection. Christians cannot experience the vision of God and enjoy heavenly bliss without being purified of venial sins.[13] Thomas said that the souls of unbaptized children are held in *limbus infantum*—a neutral place involving neither bliss nor torment.

The Council of Trent, Session VI (1547), Canon 30 reads, "If anyone says that after the grace of justification has been received the guilt is so remitted and the debt of eternal punishment so blotted out for any repentant sinner, that no debt of temporal punishment remains to be paid, before access can be opened to the kingdom of heaven, 'let him be anathema.' " Session XXV, "The Decree on Purgatory" (1563), adds, "The Catholic Church . . . has taught in the holy Councils and most recently in this ecumenical Council that there is a purgatory and that the souls detained there are helped by the acts of intercession of the faithful, and especially by the acceptable sacrifice of the altar."

The Catholic Encyclopedia defines the doctrine succinctly. "Purgatory is the intermediate state of unknown duration in which those who die imperfect, but not in unrepented mortal sin, undergo a course of penal purification, to qualify for admission into heaven. They share in the communion of the saints and are benefited by our prayers and good works."[14] The contemporary Oxford Catholic Roderick Strange writes,

> The Church has perceived a gap between our state at death and the perfect state we must achieve for heaven. We need to be purified, and that process is expressed in the doctrine of purgatory. It is not a second chance, a second death; rather we work out the consequences of our decision for Christ, which have previously been impeded, but not annulled, by our sins. . . . But for those who have died in

Christ perfectly, for the martyrs, there is no purgatory.[15]

Other contemporary Catholics have modified the doctrine of purgatory as the instantaneous encounter with Christ at death that burns away imperfections.

Conditional Immortality and Annihilationism

Many monistic non-Christians, insisting that mind or soul is but a function of the brain, claim that at death the entire person ceases to exist. This view of the dissolution of the whole person is held by empiricists (Hume), materialists (Feuerbach, d'Holbach, Vogt), pantheists (Spinoza, Fichte, Hegel, Strauss), humanists (Lamont, Sagan), and Marxists. The position boasts only a few adherents in Christian circles.

Those who hold to a belief in *conditional immortality* assert that God created persons *mortal* and therefore subject to the law of death. Believers, however, become immortal via God's gift of regenerating grace. Adherents of this view claim that alien notions of body-soul dualism, the soul's immortality, and the endless punishment of the wicked entered the church through Greek philosophy. The unsaved face extinction of existence at death or following the resurrection of the body at the Last Judgment. Conditionalists deny the eternal torment of the wicked as inconsistent with God's love. Whereas certain early fathers made suggestive statements in this direction, conditionalism was fostered by some Anabaptists, Seventh-day Adventists, and Jehovah's Witnesses. It gained popularity in the nineteenth and early twentieth centuries through scholars such as R. Whately, C. F. Hudson, E. White, A. Sabatier, W. R. Huntington, H. Bushnell, and E. S. Brightman. In recent years conditional immortality has found growing acceptance in con-servative evangelical circles (e.g., J. W. Wenham, E. W. Fudge).

Certain fathers used language that *prima facie* might suggest conditionalism. Irenaeus (d. 200) held that mortal persons become immortal by their obedience and the grace of God.[16] In the same vein Theophilus (d. 181) wrote: "God made man capable of becoming either mortal or immortal; so that by keeping the commands of God he might attain immortality as his reward and become divine."[17]

C. F. Hudson, an American Methodist, denied that God created the soul immortal: "We maintain that the guilty failure of eternal life brings the penal forfeiture of immortality."[18] In the last day all will be raised: the saved to eternal life in a spiritual body and the unsaved to "destruction," "dissolution," or "extinction" of being. Termination of existence is what is meant by the "second death," and loss of spiritual blessings forever constitutes eternal punishment. The British scholar Edward White wrote that Scripture "never once places the eternal hope of mankind on the abstract dogma of the immortality of the soul or declares that man will live forever because he is naturally immortal."[19] At Christ's return the souls of the saved and the unsaved will be united with their bodies. Believers will become immortal by the grace of regeneration and bodily resurrection, whereas unbelievers will be judged and destroyed (Pss. 21:9; 92:7; Mal. 4:1; Matt. 10:28). The New Testament, conditionalists allege, knows nothing of endless torment in hell. According to White, "all finally impenitent sinners, persistently choosing evil, shall be 'miserably destroyed.'"[20]

Upholding psychosomatic unity, Edward Fudge states that death affects the entire person. Concepts of a conscious soul apart from the body, the soul's indestructibility, and eternal torment in hell are "pagan parasites"[21] that have infiltrated Christian theology from Greek thought. Fudge insists that God will endow the righteous with immortality in the age to come. But the unrighteous will be raised body and soul, judged by God, and experience conscious punishment for as long as justice requires. Thereafter the unsaved will be annihilated. Scripture "emphatically teaches the *nature* of that everlasting punishment to be utter extinction into oblivion forever."[22] The fate of the unsaved is not one of conscious torment. "Not one time in all of Scripture does God say that any human being will be made immortal for the purpose of suffering conscious everlasting torment."[23] The lake of fire or gehenna are symbols signifying "utter, absolute, irreversible annihilation"[24]—which is what Scripture means by the "second death." But did not Jesus himself speak of "eternal punishment" (e.g., Matt. 25:46)? Fudge replies that when *aiōnios* modifies acts or processes the emphasis is on the *result* of the action rather than on the action itself. "Eternal punishment" thus involves a single act of destroying, which results in a ruin that never will be reversed.

Annihilationism proper claims that God created all persons *immortal,* in that everybody survives death and will be resurrected. The unrepentant wicked, however, finally will be destroyed. Extinction will occur as a result either of sin's natural effects or God's decisive action. Annihilationists, like conditionalists, feel constrained to soften the biblical teaching of endless torment in hell. If hell is a reality, it lasts only a short while before the reprobate are annihilated. Appealing to texts like Psalm 6:5 and Jeremiah 51:57, annihilationists such as Anglicans L. Abbott, W. Temple, O. C. Quick, and G. B. Caird and a few evangelicals press their case.

William Temple (d. 1944) claimed that individuals who persistently repu-diate God and resist heavenly communion face eternal loss as extinction of being: "There is nothing that Almighty Love can do with such a soul except to bring it to an end. That, no doubt, constitutes a failure in God."[25] Focusing on God's omnipotence might lead to the Greek view of eternal hell. But focusing on God's love leads to the conclusion that the Father of Jesus will not inflict on his creatures endless torment. The coming of God's perfect kingdom further excludes the imperfection of suffering souls in hell.

John R. W. Stott claims that the soul's immortality or indestructibility is a Greek rather than a biblical concept. Evangelicals must be open-minded "to the possibility that Scripture points in the direction of annihilation, and that 'eternal conscious torment' is a tradition which has to yield to the supreme authority of Scripture."[26] Stott inclines to the total annihilation of the wicked for at least three reasons: (1) *Explicit biblical teaching.* The fire of hell (Matt. 5:22; 25:41; Rev. 20:15) does not connote endless conscious torment, for the purpose of fire is to consume rather than to inflict pain. Moreover, Jesus' language about destroying body and soul in hell (Matt. 10:28; cf. James 4:12) must be taken seriously. "If to kill is to deprive the body of life, hell would seem to be the deprivation of both physical and spiritual life, that is, an extinction of being."[27] (2) The *concept of justice.* Punishment that is eternal would invoke "a serious disproportion between sins consciously committed in time and torment consciously experienced throughout eternity." Stott adds, "I question whether 'eternal conscious torment' is compatible with the biblical revelation of divine justice."[28] And (3) the eternal existence of the impenitent in hell is difficult to reconcile with *God's ultimate victory over evil* and his uniting all things under Christ's headship (Eph. 1:10; Phil. 2:10–11).

Clark Pinnock writes that the traditional doctrine of the eternal, conscious punishment of the wicked is "morally and spiritually flawed" and thus is a pseudo-gospel.[29] "Death" in Scripture means cessation of existence. Pinnock interprets Jesus' language in Matthew 10:28 literally as the extermination of the sinner's being in the Last Judgment. The fire of hell does not torment the unrepentant dead eternally; it consumes them. In other words, God's judgment upon the wicked is condemnation to eternal extinction, which is the "second death" (Rev. 20:11–15). "How can one imagine for a moment that the God who gave his Son to die for sinners because of his great love for them would install a torture chamber somewhere in the new creation in order to subject those who reject him to everlasting pain?"[30]

Soul-Sleep View

According to this view persons at death remain in the grave in a state of unconsciousness until the resurrection. Early Christians called churchyards *coemeteria* or "sleeping places" for the deceased. Proponents of this view typically appeal to three considerations. (1) The person is a unitary being, the soul possessing no separate existence apart from the body (monism). (2) Scripture often depicts death as an unconscious state of "sleep" (Jer. 51:39, 57; Acts 7:60; 13:36; 1 Cor. 15:6, 18, 20, 51). And (3) if people went to their reward at death it would obviate the need for Christ's second coming, the general resurrection, and the Final Judgment. This view frequently is linked with that of conditional immortality. It has been held by Psychopannychians in the Middle Ages, Socinians, some Anabaptists, Seventh-day Adventists, Jehovah's Witnesses, O. Cullmann, and B. F. C. Atkinson.

Reacting to the Roman doctrine of purgatory, Luther on occasion described the intermediate state as a kind of sleep. At death the believer sleeps in the grave awaiting the Last Judgment rather than enduring purgatory. Wrote Luther, "The nether region (*infernus*) designates the pit, or the grave (*sepulchrum*). According to my judgment, it really designates that hidden recess in which the dead sleep beyond this life."[31] Moreover, in that state the soul is less than fully conscious: "When man dies, the body is buried and wastes away, lies in the earth and knows nothing."[32] Luther further described the intermediate state as follows: "We shall sleep until He comes and knocks on the little grave and says, 'Doctor Martin, get up!' Then I shall rise in a moment and be happy with Him forever."[33] Luther was not dogmatic on this issue, and in later writings he appears to have softened this position.[34]

Insisting that the person is an integral unity, Seventh-day Adventists conclude that there is no conscious entity such as soul or spirit that survives the body's demise. At death the *whole person* goes to the grave (*sheol* or *hades*), where it sleeps in unconsciousness to await the resurrection. "Death is really and truly a sleep, a sleep that is deep, that is unconscious, that is unbroken until the awakening at the resurrection."[35] Moreover, "While asleep in the tomb the child of God knows nothing. . . . One who serves God closes his eyes in death, and whether one day or two thousand years elapse, the next instant in his consciousness will be when he opens his eyes and beholds his blessed Lord."[36] Seventh-day Adventists are concerned that belief in the consciousness of the deceased has led to spiritualism: the occult practice of communicating with deceased souls.[37] Seventh-day Adventists also uphold the annihilation of the wicked.

O. Cullmann argued that the Greek view of the soul's immortality is irreconcilable with the Jewish (i.e., biblical) view of the body's resurrection. The soul possesses no existence independent of the body. "According to the Christian view . . . it is the inner man's very nature which demands the body."[38] Cullmann averred that in the intermediate state, as they await the resurrection body, the dead "sleep" in a dreamlike, unconscious existence. Believers in the interim state sleep in special proximity to Christ. Although the New Testament provides few details about this interim condition, those who possess the Spirit as an earnest at death "are nearer to God."[39] According to Cullmann, the substance of the believer's resurrection body (received at the End) is not "flesh" but an entirely new creation wrought by the Spirit. "This is a new creation of matter, an incorruptible matter."[40] At the general resurrection unbelievers likewise will awake to consciousness. And if the latter never had an opportunity to hear the Gospel, they will be afforded an opportunity to hear it.

Further Probation

Some theologians believe God extends the opportunity to repent beyond this life. Some argue that moral and spiritual development is a continuous process embracing life on both sides of the grave. Others insist that human destiny is not settled prior to the Last Judgment. Opinion varies as *to whom* the offer of salvation in the intermediate state will be made: viz., to those who have not understood the terms of salvation, those who have never heard the Gospel, or those who have chosen not to accept Christ in this life. Advocates of a second chance include the nineteenth-century authorities F. D. Maurice, I. A. Dorner, F. Delitzsch, and F. Godet, the twentieth-century scholars P. T. Forsyth, L. H. DeWolf, F. W. Farrar, R. Aldwinckle, D. L. Edwards, B. Hebblethwaite, and the American evangelicals D. Moody, D. Bloesch, and C. Pinnock.

P. T. Forsyth (d. 1921) claimed that death is transforming. "There are more conversions on the other side than on this, if the crisis of death opens the eyes as I have said."[41] DeWolf wrote that "there is both ethical and biblical ground for believing that God will grant to all persons renewed life of some kind after death."[42] He added, "Punishment after death must be regarded as administered in the *hope* and with the *purpose* of stirring the sinner from his complacent pride and preparing him for the redeeming work of God's love."[43] DeWolf judged that most unbelievers will be saved beyond the grave, although it is possible that truly hardened sinners will endure hell. Aldwinckle claimed that at the Last Judgment God will give all unrepentant persons opportunity to respond to his saving love. This will be a time "for spiritual growth, for deeper repentance and faith, for a first acceptance of the gospel by those who have never heard it."[44] Hebblethwaite writes that we "envisage further opportunities beyond the grave for men and women denied such opportunities on earth, to respond to God's love and realize their potential as creatures destined for eternity. . . . Salvation . . . takes effect gradually through experience and growth in spirituality both this side of the grave and beyond it."[45]

The late Southern Baptist theologian Dale Moody claimed that 1 Peter 4:6 (cf. 1 Tim. 3:16) describes the evangelizing of the unsaved dead: "There is no suggestion that they [the unsaved dead] had a 'second chance,' but it is possible that they were given a 'first chance' even after death. . . . It is difficult to believe that God would leave men forever in *Hades* simply because they never had a chance to hear the gospel."[46] Donald Bloesch, echoing Barth, emphasizes the victory of God's grace even after death. He writes, "Hell is not a concentration camp presided over by the devil, but a sanitorium for sick souls who are ministered to by Jesus Christ.''[47] Furthermore, ''We can affirm salvation on the other side of the grave, since this has Scriptural warrant (cf. Isa. 26:19; John 5:25–29; Eph. 4:8; 1 Peter 3:19, 20; 4:6).''[48] Finally Clark Pinnock writes, ''God will not abandon in hell those who have not known and therefore have not declined his offer of grace. Though he has not told us the nature of His arrangements we cannot doubt the existence and goodness of them.''[49] Elsewhere Pinnock refers to ''the hope of an opportunity to accept Christ's salvation after death, only hinted at in 1 Peter 4:6 but based on the reasonable assumption that God would not reject the perishing sinners whom he loves without ever knowing what their response to his grace would be.''[50]

Instantaneous Resurrection

Preferring monism to dualism, advocates of this view reject the idea of a disembodied condition between death and the Second Advent and claim that believers receive the resurrection body immediately at death. Proponents stress the spiritual rather than the material character of the resurrection body. Usually it is argued that 2 Corinthians 5 supplants 1 Corinthians 15 as Paul's mature view concerning the resurrection body. Advocates of this view include A. B. Bruce, R. H. Charles, W. L. Knox, A. M. Hunter, W. D. Davies, T. F. Torrance, F. F. Bruce, and M. J. Harris.

W. D. Davies insisted that Paul followed his rabbinic heritage in rejecting the Greek constructs of a body-soul dualism and the soul's immortality. Paul held that the life of the age to come was an embodied life by resurrection into corporeal form. Moreover, Paul accepted with Christian modifications the Jewish view that the age to come

had two stages: (1) a future cataclysm at the end of history and (2) an eternally existing reality that, in Christ, has invaded the world of time. In 1 Corinthians 15 Paul responded to some in the church who, under Greek influences, denied the resurrection of the body. He stated that at the Parousia a revelation of the *already embodied* saints will occur (Rom. 8:19; Col. 3:4). In 2 Corinthians 5, recognizing that he might die before the Parousia, Paul focused on what lies immediately beyond the grave: namely, a unique bodily *resurrection*. In light of the dawning of the age to come via Christ's resurrection, Christians at death are not left ''naked'' but immediately receive heavenly bodies fitted for life in the spiritual realm. ''In 2 Cor. 5:1 ff. Paul expresses the view that the dead in Christ would not be disembodied at death . . . and thus undergo an intermediate period of waiting till the general resurrection. They would, on the contrary, be embodied, and there is no room in Paul's theology for an intermediate state of the dead.''[51]

F. F. Bruce (d. 1990) set forth a similar view. Paul taught in 1 Corinthians 15 that the Parousia would effect the transformation of living believers and the resurrection of the faithful dead. But later, facing the prospect of almost certain death (1 Cor. 15:31; 2 Cor. 7:5), Paul believed that he would die before the Parousia. Hence in 2 Corinthians 5 he described his new conviction about the believer's existence between death and the Parousia. Paul judged that the resurrection principle was already at work in believers; hence some kind of embodiment was available immediately at death. At that moment the believer receives the new ''spiritual body'' (1 Cor. 15:44), which he also described as a ''building from God, an eternal house in heaven'' (2 Cor. 5:1). Paul did not expect to wait in a disembodied state for the spiritual body promised in 1 Corinthians 15, for to the Hebrew mind a body was necessary for personality. Bruce summed it up like this: "In some sense the spiritual body of the coming age is being formed . . . so that physical death will mean no hiatus of disembodiment but the immediate enjoyment of being 'at home' with the Lord."[52] Again, "So instantaneous is the change-over from the old body to the new . . . that there will be no interval of conscious 'nakedness' between the one and the other."[53]

Underlying the view of Murray J. Harris is his commitment to "the basically monistic anthropology of the New Testament."[54] Since Harris does not view the person as an undying soul, he affirms that Adam "was created *for* immortality rather than *with* immortality"[55] (a form of conditional immortality). The believer receives immortality with God at the resurrection, which occurs at death.[56] Second Corinthians 5—Paul's mature view concerning the resurrection body—states that the Christian receives the "spiritual" or "glorified body" at death. This heavenly body, however, was not formed in an instant; it represents "the acceleration and completion of a process by which the spiritual body was already being formed inwardly . . . at regeneration."[57] Harris thus denies that the believer's condition with Christ in heaven is as a disembodied soul/spirit. Concerning the nature of the believer's resurrection body, there is no material (i.e., molecular) connection between old and new forms of embodiment. Consonant with the view of the Eastern church, Harris prefers the expression "the resurrection of the (spiritual) body."[58] Continuity between the two bodies resides at the level of personality. Thus "the link between the Christian's successive forms of embodiment—the physical and the spiritual—lies in the same identifiable ego."[59] In its essential immateriality the believer's resurrection body is similar to Jesus' resurrection body. At Easter the Lord's physical body was transformed into an "immaterial," "spiritual," or "invisible body," although capable of temporary materializations. By virtue of the radical transformation that occurred at the resurrection, Christ's (as also the believer's) "resurrection body is no longer a body of 'flesh.' "[60]

By way of response, P. Toon claims that while the above views are not heretical they fail to give sufficient prominence to bodily resurrection as the great consummation of God's saving work at the end.[61]

Absorption Into the Whole

Contemporary Roman Catholics such as Karl Rahner and Monika Hellwig, stimulated by Eastern philosophy and the writings of Teilhard de Chardin, affirm that at death the undifferentiated self is united with the Infinite or absorbed into the Whole. Advocates deny that a disembodied soul survives death to exist independently in a state of conscious bliss. This view is said to be eminently Christian in that it exchanges egocentric concern for the self with concern for the human community, which is viewed as the essence of salvation.

Karl Rahner (d. 1984) exchanged individual eschatology for what he calls the "collective eschatology" of the human race. Rahner asked, "Does the soul in death strictly transcend this world or does it rather, by virtue of the fact that it is no longer bound to an individual bodily structure, enter into a much closer, more intimate relationship to that ground of the unity of the universe which is hard to conceive yet is very real?"[62] Since the person is a unity, it is untrue that there is one future for the soul and another for the body. At death the human soul becomes not "acosmic," in the sense of the survival of individual self-consciousness apart from the world; rather the soul becomes "pancosmic," in that it assumes the new "body," which is the entire cosmic reality. "The soul, by surrendering its limited bodily structure in death, becomes open towards the universe and, in some way, a co-determining factor of the universe precisely in the latter's character as the ground of the personal life of other spiritual corporeal beings."[63] On this premise Rahner explains certain parapsychological phenomena. "The spiritual soul through its embodiment is in principle open to the world and is never a closed monad without windows, but is always in communication with the whole of the world."[64] Furthermore, God's universal self-communication to the entire spiritual and material cosmos means that all humanity exists in a redeemed condition. Although each person must take seriously the *possibility* of hell, by virtue of God's universal salvific will "the history of salvation as a whole will reach a positive conclusion for the human race through God's own powerful grace."[65]

Persuaded that the soul or spirit is an epiphenomenon of the brain and nervous system, Monika Hellwig affirms that belief in the separate existence of the soul is "an absurdity, an impossibility, a 'category mistake' in our thinking."[66] Hence the traditional language about the resurrection of the body, judgment, heaven and hell is symbolic and must not be taken literally.[67] At death the human self-consciousness detaches itself from the individual body and becomes incorporated into the larger community. She writes,

The maturity and fulfillment of the process of becoming of the human individual, the human race as a whole, and even the universe as a whole, appears as movement toward community and harmony at the deepest levels of being. This understanding has inspired a way of imaging the destiny of the human person after or beyond death in which the reflexive self-consciousness that has been rooted in the single, discrete organism of one human body extends its base and becomes rooted in the totality of the community and the cosmos.[68]

This means that "what happens at death might be conceptualized in terms of a transition of consciousness from being rooted in the individual body to being rooted in the community."[69]

The Classical View of the Church

Many church fathers, Reformers, and evangelicals believed that there will be an endless, conscious existence of the souls of believers and unbelievers after death in a state of blessedness or misery, respectively. God endowed souls with immortality by virtue of creation in the divine image. Immediately at death the righteous, apart from the body, go to be with Christ in heaven, i.e., "paradise" or "Abraham's bosom" (Luke 16:22; 2 Cor. 5:8; Phil. 1:23). At death the unrighteous are separated from the presence of the Lord in hell in a state of conscious suffering. Advocates hold that the eternal destiny of all is settled at death. The saved at death receive only a partial reward, the body being in the grave. But at the Parousia believers are given a glorious, immortal body fitted for life in heaven. Proponents stress the *identity* of the earthly and resurrection bodies, although the latter is radically transformed. In the case of the unsaved, confinement in a bodiless condition in hell represents a partial judgment and not the final state of suffering. Following the Millennium the wicked impenitent will be resurrected (Rev. 20:5), judged (vv. 12–13), and consigned to the "lake of fire"—the place of everlasting, conscious punishment (vv. 12b–15; cf. Matt. 25:46)—which is the "second death" (Rev. 20:6, 14). Many hold that the "fire" of hell (Matt. 5:22; 18:9; 25:41; Rev. 20:15) is figurative (symbolizing the pain of everlasting exclusion from God's presence). Most authorities believe that there will be both degrees of reward and degrees of punishment based on the individual's response to light and truth possessed.

The Epistle to Diognetus contrasts the temporary fire of persecution with "the eternal fire which will punish [the condemned] to the end."[70] Justin Martyr (d. 165) held that at death the body dies but the soul lives on in the intermediate state. At the Resurrection all the dead will be raised and the wicked will suffer everlasting punishment in hell. At his coming Christ "shall raise the bodies of all men who have lived, and shall clothe those of the worthy with immortality, and shall send those of the wicked . . . into everlasting fire with wicked devils. . . . In what kind of punishment the wicked are to be, hear from what was said in like manner with reference to this: 'Their worm shall not rest, and their fire shall not be quenched.' "[71] Athenagoras (2d cent. A.D.) affirmed that God created persons' immortal souls destined for perpetual existence: "When we are removed from the present life we shall live another life, better than the present one, and heavenly, not earthly . . . or, falling with the rest, a worse one and in fire; for God has not made us . . . that we should perish and be annihilated."[72]

For Irenaeus (d. 200) the person is a unity of a mortal body and an immortal soul. "Souls endure forever, since God has both willed that they should exist and continue in existence [after death]."[73] At death the immortal soul separates from the mortal body. Believing souls in the intermediate state abide in Christ's presence in anticipation of the bodily resurrection and eternal bliss in heaven. The souls of the unrighteous dwell in hades awaiting the resurrection of their bodies and endless, conscious punishment in hell. "Since in this world

some . . . shun the light and separate themselves from God, the Word of God comes preparing a fit habitation in darkness, that they may partake of its calamities. . . . Those on the left hand He will send into eternal fire."[74] Tertullian (d. 230) rejected the notion of soul sleep between death and resurrection[75] and the idea that believers are resurrected at the moment of death.[76] The soul, being immortal and simple, cannot be annihilated. "We so understand the soul's immortality as to believe it 'lost,' not in the sense of destruction, but of punishment in hell."[77] For Tertullian the fate of the unsaved is eternal retribution in the fires of hell.

Augustine (d. 430) upheld the immortality of the soul as created and sustained by God.[78] In the intermediate state the soul consciously exists apart from the body. Following the Parousia, when all will rise bodily, God justly will consign the unrighteous dead to everlasting, conscious punishment in hell (Mark 9:43–48). The condition of the lost in hell, Augustine argued, is one of endless "pain," "agony," or "torment." Hereafter the unsaved will be found "miserably subsisting in eternal death, without power to die."[79] Augustine interpreted hell fire literally: "Hell, which is also called the lake of fire and brimstone, will be material fire and will torment the bodies of the damned, whether men or devils."[80] He insisted that people's decision in time determines their destiny in eternity; Scripture gives no hint that God will grant mercy after death. In hell the unsaved will experience degrees of tormenting fire proportional to their response to available light.

Believing that God bestowed immortality on the human soul, Calvin (d. 1564) held that at death all souls continue in conscious existence separated from their bodies.[81] Concerning the intermediate state Calvin wrote, "Scripture goes no farther than to say that

Christ is present with them [believers] and receives them into paradise (cf. John 12:32) that they may obtain consolation, while the souls of the reprobate suffer such torments as they deserve."[82] The saved at death give up the mortal body and enter paradise to enjoy a blessedness that is provisional. On the other hand, God sends the unsaved at death to the Abyss to experience a misery that likewise is provisional and incomplete. Calvin reproved the Anabaptists who argued that the souls of the dead sleep in their graves; the metaphor of "sleep" pertains to the body not the soul. At Christ's second coming the living and the dead will be raised in bodies and summoned before the judgment seat. Calvin stressed the continuity that exists between the believer's earthly and heavenly forms. The Christian is not clothed with a new body; rather, Christ will raise "that self-same body which began to be mortal."[83] Thereafter the saved will enter into the state of blessedness, whereas the unsaved will be cast into endless hell. For Calvin the biblical language about hell fire is symbolic. Hell, or the "second death," represents the wretchedness of being cut off eternally from fellowship with God.[84] It is not a question of extinction of existence, for God has not willed "to annihilate the temple of the Holy Spirit."[85]

The *Westminster Confession* (1647) addresses the intermediate state thus: "The bodies of men, after death, return to dust, and see corruption; but their souls (which neither die nor sleep) . . . immediately return to God who gave them. The souls of the righteous . . . are received into the highest heavens, where they behold the face of God in light and glory, waiting for the full redemption of their bodies: and the souls of the wicked are cast into hell, where they remain in torments and utter darkness, reserved to the judgment of the great day" (ch. XXXII.1). Concern-

ing the general resurrection: "At the last day, . . . all the dead shall be raised up with the self-same bodies, and none other, although with different qualities, which shall be united again to their souls forever. The bodies of the unjust shall, by the power of Christ, be raised to dishonor; the bodies of the just, by his Spirit, unto honor, and be made conformable to his own glorious body" (ch. XXXII.2–3). The *New Hampshire Baptist Confession* (1833) states, "We believe . . . that at the last day Christ will descend from heaven, and raise the dead from the grave to final retribution; that a solemn separation will then take place; that the wicked will be adjudged to endless punishment, and the righteous to endless joy; and that this judgment will fix forever the final state of men in heaven or hell, on principles of righteousness" (XVIII).

Other proponents of the classical view include Ray Summers,[86] L. Boettner,[87] and Robert A. Morey.[88]

BIBLICAL TEACHING

In order to decide amongst the disparate historical proposals presented above, we now turn to the relevant biblical teaching on the future of the individual.

Pentateuch

Our study in volume 2, chapter 3 concluded that the human being essentially is a complex interactive dualism. We affirmed that the person, as image of God, metaphysically is an immaterial soul/spirit in a material body. Thus Genesis 2:7 declares, "The LORD God formed the man from the dust of the ground and breathed into his nostrils the breath of life [nišmat hayyîm], and the man became a living being [nepeš hayyāh]."[89] The human person is a unitary being consisting of a material body from the natural order animated by an immaterial breath or spirit from God. The creation account does not explicitly state that the human soul/spirit is undying (i.e., immortal in the general sense). This silence may be because the focus of Genesis is practical rather than speculative. Yet since man is presented as image of God and God's "offspring" (Acts 17:28), the common church judgment of the soul's undying nature is a serious possibility.

As a test of their fidelity, God placed before Adam and Eve in the Garden two trees: "the tree of life" and "the tree of the knowledge of good and evil" (Gen. 2:9). The former symbolically offered (contingent on obedience) holistic eternal life (cf. Gen. 3:22), i.e., absence of spiritual and physical death and embodied fellowship with God forever. But Adam and Eve chose to eat from the forbidden tree (Gen. 2:17; 3:3), symbolizing their quest for moral independence from God. By so eating they gained experiential knowledge of good and evil, leading to death. Through disobedience the pair experienced *spiritual death* in the sense of consciousness of guilt and alienation from God (Gen. 3:7–10). This was followed by *physical death* (Gen. 2:17; 3:19; 5:5)—being the separation of the immaterial spirit from the material body. Thus Adam died, not because he was created mortal but by virtue of the divine judgment on his sin. Although Adam and Eve were excluded from the Garden of Eden (Gen. 3:22–24), the promised Seed of the woman (Gen. 3:15) would reopen access to the tree of life for all who believe (see Rev. 2:7; 22:14, 19).

Old Testament statements indicating that the death of the righteous is a "rest" in company with the fathers (Gen. 47:30; Deut. 31:16; 2 Sam. 7:12) may anticipate the New Testament concept of the saints' death as a "sleep"— i.e., the repose of the body awaiting resurrection. Death for the righteous even early in the Old Testament was not a gloomy or a foreboding prospect.

The fact of the existence of conscious souls in the intermediate state is supported by strong prohibitions against necromancy (Lev. 19:31; 20:6,7; Deut. 18:10–11; cf. Isa. 8:19). "Mediums" and "spiritists" sought to call up persons from the realm of the dead and communicate with them. Whereas some of this activity was fraudulent and other forms demonic, the severe warnings may suggest that communication with departed souls belongs to God alone. In 1 Samuel 28:1–19 it is possible that God caused the spirit of Samuel to appear both to the medium at Endor and to Saul. Not only was the latter convinced that it was Samuel (vv. 14, 20), but Samuel's predictions fully came to pass (vv. 18–19). Even if the event involved demonic impersonation, the passage demonstrates Israel's belief in the conscious existence of the deceased.

Yahweh's saying to Moses, "I am ... the God of Abraham, the God of Isaac and the God of Jacob" (Exod. 3:6) indicates that the God who revealed himself to the patriarchs is the same God who made himself known to Moses in a new way. Jesus later appealed to this incident as proof for the resurrection of the dead: "In the account of the bush, even Moses showed that the dead rise, for he calls the Lord 'the God of Abraham, and the God of Isaac, and the God of Jacob.' He is not the God of the dead, but of the living, for to him all are alive" (Luke 20:37; cf. Mark 12:26). A clearer statement of bodily resurrection is found in the incident on Mount Moriah (Gen. 22:1–14). Confident of God's covenant with Isaac (Gen. 17:19, 21), Abraham believed that Yahweh would restore his son to life (cf. 22:5). When God provided the substitute ram, *in a figure* he raised Isaac from the dead. "Abraham reasoned that God could raise the dead, and figuratively he did receive Isaac back from death" (Heb. 11:19).

The word *še'ôl* occurs sixty-five times in the Old Testament and is translated by the KJV as "grave" (31 times), "hell" (31 times), and "pit" (3 times) and by the NIV as "grave" or "realm of the dead." The original and common meaning is "grave" (Gen. 37:35; 42:38; 1 Kings 2:6, 9; Ps. 49:15; Isa. 14:11, 15 [cf. *qeber*, v. 19]; Ezek. 31:15–17 [cf. *qeber*, 32:22–23, 25–26]; Hos. 13:14). The word developed into the specialized sense of the realm of the wicked dead (Deut. 32:22; Prov. 15:11; Amos 9:2)—i.e., that foreboding place of gloom and punishment where departed evil-doers are punished. The word *'abaddôn*, "destruction" or "ruin," occurs six times in the Old Testament. It is coupled with *še'ôl* three times (Job 26:6; Prov. 15:11; 27:20), whereas in Revelation 9:11 it is transliterated into Greek and used as a name for the Devil. Perhaps *'abaddôn*, designates "the depths" (Isa. 14:15) of *še'ôl* reserved for the most wicked. If this is so, we are brought close to the concept of hell. The Hebrew *šāmayim*, "heights," "heaven," "sky," is used in three ways: (1) the atmospheric region of clouds, rain, thunder, etc. (Gen. 8:2; Deut. 11:11; 33:13; Isa. 55:10), (2) the region of the celestial bodies (Gen. 15:5; Exod. 20:4; Ps. 19:1), and (3) the dwelling place of God (Deut. 26:15; Job 22:12; Ps. 123:1). Phrases such as "the highest heaven/heavens" (1 Kings 8:27; Deut. 10:14) describe the abode of God in superlative form.

Poetry and Wisdom

Some writers appeal to texts such as Psalms 6:5; 30:9; 88:10–11; and 115:17 to support the notion of death as a state of unconsciousness. These Scriptures affirm only that those in the grave no longer celebrate God's goodness with the living people of God on earth. The preacher in Ecclesiastes 9:5, 10 similarly stated that when people die the opportunity for meaningful activity with the living has ended and they are forgotten. Believers, however, live purposefully and energetically, knowing that they must give account to God.

Others cite texts such as Job 7:9, 21; 10:21; and 14:10 in support of annihilationism. These, however, affirm no more than the inevitability and finality of death. Other texts speak more directly about the wicked perishing or being destroyed (Ps. 1:6; 2:12; 37:20; 49:10; 73:27; Prov. 11:10; 28:28). The Qal form of the verb *'ābad* ("be lost," "perish") in the preceding sometimes denotes physical death and other times spiritual loss or ruin, but never extinction of being. In Scriptures that speak of the wicked being "cut off" (Ps. 37:28, 34, 38; cf. Jer. 11:19) the verb *kārat* should be taken metaphorically as "root out, eliminate, remove or destroy,"[90] the sense being that the wicked are removed by death from the sphere of the living.

Positively, texts such as Job 26:5; Proverbs 2:18; and 21:16 (cf. Isa. 26:14) describe *rᵉpā'îm* ("spirits of the dead") inhabiting the dark netherworld (*še'ôl*). The deceased cease from their labors in a state of unconscious existence (Job 3:13, 17). Ecclesiastes 3:18–21 addresses the issue of life after death. The teacher asserted that humans and animals are similar in that both die and return to dust (vv. 19–20; cf. Ps. 49:10–12), but they are dissimilar in their ultimate destinies. Verse 21 correctly reads, "Who knows the spirit of man which goes upward, and the spirit of the beast which goes down to the earth?" (KJV, RV marg., NASB, Berkeley). Following death the human *rûaḥ* ascends to God, whereas the animal *rûaḥ* ceases to be. The teacher emphasized this contrast to remind people that as eternal beings they must live uprightly. He then added, "The dust returns to the ground it came from, and the spirit returns to God who gave it" (Eccles. 12:7). Death involves the separation of the immaterial spirit from the material body and the decay of the latter (cf. Gen. 3:19b). Being indestructible, the human *rûaḥ* returns to God to continue in a new mode of existence, the nature of which is not specified here.

To the question posed earlier (Job 14:14), Job (19:26–27) responded, "After my skin has been destroyed, yet in my flesh I will see God; I myself will see him with my own eyes." Job expressed confidence that death would not terminate his personal existence; rather, by virtue of the work of his heavenly "Vindicator" (*gô'ēl*, v. 25; cf. 16:19–21), he would be reclothed through bodily resurrection (cf. "skin," "flesh," "eyes"). Job expressed the same conviction in 14:14–15. Clearly "the hope of resurrection lies at the very heart of Job's faith."[91] David in Psalm 16:9–11 testified that as God provided for him in life (v. 11a), so God would also care for him beyond the grave (vv. 10, 11b; cf. 23:6). *Še'ôl* will not be able to claim him; David will pass from the grave directly into God's presence to enjoy spiritual pleasures forever. In Psalm 17:15 David wrote that he would awake from death to enjoy the eternal vision of God: "In righteousness I will see your face; when I awake I will be satisfied with seeing your likeness." This same hope is set forth in Psalm 49:15: "But God will redeem my soul from the grave; he will surely take me to himself." The verb *lāqaḥ* ("take") is used in Genesis 5:24 of God "taking" Enoch into heaven. It also occurs in David's expectation of passing into God's presence when life ends, as in Psalm 73:24: "You guide me with your counsel, and afterward you will *take* me into glory."

Prophetic Literature

Texts cited in support of purgatorial suffering affirm rather historical judgments upon Judah and Jerusalem (Isa. 1:25; 4:4; 48:10), deliverance from Babylonian exile (Zech. 9:11), and the purifying effect of Messiah's future coming upon people and priests (Mal. 3:2–3). Other texts allegedly teaching soul sleep prove unconvincing. God's intention vis-à-vis the Babylonians— "they will sleep forever and not awake" (Jer. 51:57; cf. v. 39)—states that in wrath he will intoxicate the Babylonians, i.e., cause them to sleep the sleep of death. If the "sleep" of the Babylonians be understood literally, then also should be their "destruction" (v. 54; cf. v. 55)—which events are incompatible. Neither does Isaiah 38:18–19 depict death as a state of unconsciousness. Rather, it affirms that, having recovered from physical illness, Hezekiah could praise and glorify God, whereas the deceased in the grave could not do so. Language affirming the destruction of sinners (Isa. 13:9) teaches not annihilation of souls but divine judgments upon Babylon and Assyria in the Day of the Lord (cf. 14:25). Moreover, mention of persons being brought to ruin (26:14) indicates only that the oppressive foreign rulers of Israel, having died, will not return to further afflict God's people. Language of "devouring fire" (Isa. 29:6) and "consuming fire" (Isa. 30:27, 30; 33:14) indicates not annihilation of being but God's judging action in history that materially reduces the wicked to ashes.

The prophet anticipated the future abolition of death and the resurrection of Israel's holy dead: "He will swallow up death forever. The sovereign Lord will wipe away the tears from all faces" (Isa. 25:8). Paul appealed to the first half of the verse to affirm the bodily resurrection of the righteous dead (1 Cor. 15:54). In contrast to Israel's oppressors who are gone, the righteous within Israel will experience blessed bodily resurrection: "Your dead will live; their bodies will rise. You who dwell in the dust, wake up and shout for joy" (Isa. 26:19). The general resurrection of the dead, the eternal blessedness of the just, and the eternal doom of the unjust are explicitly taught in Daniel 12:2: "Multitudes [rabbîm] who sleep in the dust of the earth will awake: some to everlasting ['ôlām] life, others to shame and everlasting ['ôlām] contempt." Here again "sleep" is a figure for bodily death, whereas to "awake" is a figure for bodily resurrection unto life (cf. Job 14:12; Ps. 17:15). The word 'ôlām here denotes endless existence (cf. Ps. 90:2). The fact that the unjust are the object of unending "contempt" refutes opportunities for repentance beyond the grave.

The final fate of the unrepentant wicked is divine judgment (Isa. 66:15–18; Zeph. 3:8). "Fire," "chariot," and "sword" are symbols connoting the unleashing of God's awesome judgments. Isaiah described the condition of the unrighteous dead as everlasting torment. In words quoted by Jesus to the same effect (Mark 9:48), the prophet wrote, "Their worm will not die, nor will their fire be quenched, and they will be loathsome to all mankind" (Isa. 66:24). On the other hand, Isaiah struggled to describe in words the glories of the New Jerusalem: "The sun will no more be your light by day, nor will the brightness of the moon shine on you, for the LORD will be your everlasting light, and your God will be your glory" (Isa. 60:19; cf. 65:17–18). John in Revelation 21 drew freely from Isaiah 60 for his picture of the heavenly Jerusalem. Joel 3:17–18 records the promise of God's abiding presence with his people forever. Agricultural fruitfulness symbolizes the rich spiritual blessings of God's people in eternity, and the flowing fountain symbolizes the river of Paradise that imparts eternal refreshment in the New Jerusalem (cf. Zech. 14:8; Rev. 22:1–2).

The Old Testament provides few specific details concerning the condition of the dead in the intermediate state. Such reticence likely was due to Canaanite and other pagan cults of the dead, which the Hebrew writers assiduously sought to avoid.

The Synoptic Gospels

Hades (hādēs), the usual translation of šᵉ'ôl in the LXX, occurs ten times in the New Testament (Matt. 11:23; 16:18; Luke 10:15; 16:23; Acts 2:27, 31; Rev. 1:18; 6:8; 20:13–14). It signifies both the grave all persons enter at death (Acts 2:27, 31; 1 Cor. 15:55) and the specific place or state of the wicked dead in provisional torment (Luke 16:23; Rev. 20:14). Concerning the latter, (1) Hades is prisonlike in nature (Rev. 1:18; cf. 1 Peter 3:19; Rev. 20:7); (2) only the spirits of the unjust are there (Luke 16:23–26; Rev. 20:12–15); and (3) it is a place of preliminary suffering (Luke 16:23; Rev. 6:8) where the unrighteous dead await the final judgment and consignment to gehenna.[92] Often hādēs is translated "hell."

Gehenna (geenna) occurs twelve times in the New Testament (Matt. 5:22, 29, 30; 10:28; 18:9; 23:15, 33; Mark 9:43, 45, 47; Luke 12:5; James 3:6). It is the Greek form of the Hebrew words (gē hinnōm) "valley of Hinnom," located south of Jerusalem, where children were burned by fire and sacrificed to the god Molech (2 Kings 23:10; 2 Chron. 28:3; 33:6). Israel's prophets identified the valley as the place of God's judgment (Jer. 7:31–33; 19:6–7). In Jesus' day the place was the city garbage dump recognized by fire, smoke, and maggots. In particular, (1) gehenna is the place of eschatological punishment (Matt. 23:33; 25:41); (2) after the general resurrection the unrighteous will be present there in soul and body (Matt. 10:28; 18:9; Mark 9:43–47); (3) gehenna is a place of conscious torment (Matt. 5:22; 18:9; Mark 9:43); (4) the duration of its fiery punishment is everlasting (Matt. 25:41, 46; Mark 9:43, 48); and (5) Satan, demons, the beast, and the false prophet will be consigned to it in the end (Matt. 8:29; 25:41; Rev. 19:20; 20:10, 14). *Abyssos* ("the Abyss," literally, "bottomless") is another word for the place of confinement reserved for Satan and demons (Luke 8:31; cf. Rev. 9:1–2, 1; 11:7; 17:8; 20:1–3).

Paradise (*paradeisos*), a Greek loanword from the Persian, meaning "garden" or "park," occurs three times in the New Testament (Luke 23:43; 2 Cor. 12:4; Rev. 2:7). In the writings of the rabbis and in 4 Maccabees 13:17 the righteous at death are welcomed there by Abraham, Isaac, and Jacob. In the New Testament paradise denotes two realities: (1) The intermediate state of the righteous between death and resurrection (Luke 23:43); another word for the intermediate state of blessedness enjoyed by the righteous in Christ's presence is Abraham's bosom (Luke 16:22–23). (2) The final estate of the righteous, or heaven itself. Paul was caught up into "paradise" or "the third heaven" in an ecstatic experience of unspeakable glory (2 Cor. 12:2–4). According to Revelation 2:7, "the paradise of God" contains "the tree of life" and is the New Jerusalem of Revelation 21:1–22:5. This meaning is explained more fully by the word *ouranos* (272 times). Similar to the Hebrew *šāmayim*, *ouranos* signifies (1) the atmospheric region (Matt. 6:26; 8:20; Luke 8:5), (2) the stellar region (Mark 13:25; Rev. 6:13; 9:1), and (3) the abode of God. The New Testament describes in some detail the third meaning. From heaven Christ descended at the Incarnation (John 6:33, 38, 41, 51), to heaven he ascended following his death (Luke 24:51; Eph. 4:10; Heb. 4:14; 9:24), and from heaven he will return a second time (Mark 14:62; 1 Thess. 1:10; 4:16). Heaven is the believer's homeland (Phil. 3:20; Heb. 11:16), even their New Jerusalem (Heb. 12:22; Rev. 21:2, 10). Scripture suggests that heaven is a *state,* because God is pure spirit. But heaven also is a *place,* because it houses Jesus' resurrection body and because John 14:2–3 requires a spatial interpretation.

Christ taught that immediately following the death of the body the righteous are with him in a state of conscious fellowship. He said to the penitent thief on the cross, "Today you will be with me in paradise" (Luke 23:43). "The criminal's petition (v. 42) expresses the hope that he will attain to life at the Parousia; Jesus' reply (v. 43) assures him of immediate entry into paradise."[93] Jesus also exclaimed at the moment of his crucifixion, "Father, into your hands I commit my spirit [*pneuma*]" (Luke 23:46; cf. Ps. 31:5). At death Jesus' spirit separated from his lifeless body and remained so for three days until his resurrection. Jesus' dialogue with the Sadducees concerning the resurrection (esp. Matt. 22:31–32; Mark 12:26–27; Luke 20:37–38) attests the conscious existence of believers in the intermediate state. The Sadducees erred in denying the continuance of the soul after death, for at the burning bush God identified himself as "the God of Abraham, the God of Isaac, and the God of Jacob" (Exod. 3:6, 15). Jesus further added, "He is not the God of the dead but the living," thus intimating that the patriarchs enjoy fellowship with God as they await bodily resurrection. Similarly at the Transfiguration Moses and Elijah appeared in heavenly glory and spoke with the Lord about his redemptive work (Matt. 17:3; Luke 9:30–31). These two Old Testament figures appear fully conscious in the afterlife.

Although Jesus' parable of the rich man and Lazarus (Luke 16:19–31) cannot be pressed at every point, three theological implications can be drawn from the story: (1) After death Lazarus was conveyed to "Abraham's side" (v. 22), where he enjoyed comfort and rest in Christ's presence (v. 25). (2) After death the rich man found himself in "hell" (*hādēs*) in a state of conscious torment (vv. 23, 28). Since the rich man's brothers were still living and the final judgment had not occurred, the identification of *hādēs* with the intermediate state is confirmed.[94] The story portrays a clear reversal of roles. The faithless rich man is eternally deprived, whereas the faithful poor man is eternally blest. And (3) after death the condition of the wicked is forever fixed (v. 26). A person's destiny is irrevocably settled by one's decisions and actions in this life. Following Christ's return, the door to heaven will be permanently shut (cf. Matt. 25:10–12).

Jesus used two images to describe the eschatological fate of the wicked: (1) a tree cut down by an axe and then thrown into the fire (Matt. 3:10; cf. 7:19) and (2) chaff separated from the wheat, the former being burned "with unquenchable fire" (Matt. 3:12). Matthew frequently used fire as a symbol of judgment (e.g., 13:40, 42; 18:8). How shall we understand these words of Jesus to his disciples: "Do not be afraid of those who kill the body but cannot kill the soul. Rather, be afraid of the One who can destroy [aorist infinitive of *apollymi*] both soul and body in hell" (Matt. 10:28)? Luke's account of the saying (12:4–5) suggests that Jesus meant the following: "Do not fear human persecutors who can cause physical death. Rather, fear God who has the power to terminate the life of the body and thereafter to condemn the entire person to eternal hell" (cf. Matt. 23:33; Mark 9:43–47). On another occasion

Jesus said, "Wide is the gate and broad is the road that leads to destruction" (Matt. 7:13). Here, as elsewhere (cf. John 17:12; Rom. 9:22; Phil. 1:28; 3:19; 2 Thess. 2:3; 1 Tim. 6:9; Heb. 10:39; 2 Peter 2:1; 3:7), *apōleia* should be understood metaphorically as the ultimate "loss" or "ruin"—the tragic opposite of salvation and eternal life (v. 14). *Apollymi* and *apōleia* signify "definitive destruction, not . . . in the sense of the extinction of physical existence, but rather of an eternal plunge into Hades and a hopeless destiny of death."[95] Thus none of the above texts support annihilation of being.

Jesus asserted that every human being will stand before God on the Day of Judgment (Matt. 10:15; 11:22, 24; 12:36). The righteous will be resurrected (Luke 14:14) to inherit heaven— its joys are described as a rich banquet (Matt. 8:11; Luke 14:24; 22:30) and a lavish wedding feast (Matt. 22:1–14; 25:10). Heaven is a place, not of idleness or inactivity, but of satisfying service (Matt. 25:21, 23; Luke 22:29– 30). Following their resurrection and judgment the unrighteous will be cast into hell (gehenna). Jesus, in fact, spoke more of the sorrows of hell than of the joys of heaven; thus the former is as real as the latter. The compassionate Lord described hell as a place of "darkness" (Matt. 8:12; 22:13), as a fiery furnace (Matt. 13:42, 50; cf. Matt. 5:22; 13:30; 18:8–9; 25:41; Mark 9:43, 48), and a place of the undying worm (Mark 9:48). The fact that darkness and a burning fire are mutually exclusive suggests that both may be understood figuratively,[96] perhaps for the indescribable horror of exclusion from God's presence (Matt. 7:23). In hell there will be "weeping and gnashing of teeth" (Matt. 8:12; 13:42, 50; 22:13; 24:51; 25:30; Luke 13:28), which suggests the despair of those who forever have missed life's purpose. Moreover, the subjects of hell will be cut in pieces

(Matt. 24:51)—the verb *dichotomeō* (to "cut in two") being a figure for extremely severe punishment.[97] The preceding texts plainly affirm (1) continued existence after death in hell, (2) punishment that is consciously experienced, and (3) torment that is everlasting (*aiōnion*). On the judgment day degrees of punishment will be meted out based on one's moral and spiritual response to knowledge possessed (Matt. 10:15; 11:21–24; Luke 12:47–48). The fact of gradations of punishment argues against the uniform annihilation of the wicked. Jesus' saying in Matthew 25:46 that the unrighteous "will go away to eternal punishment [*eis kolasin aiōnion*], but the righteous to eternal life [*eis zōēn aiōnion*]" confirms that the punishment in hell is everlasting (cf. Matt. 18:8). The same adjective that modifies two nouns in the same context must be understood in the same sense.[98] In summary, Jesus offered no support for the doctrine of the annihilation of the wicked.

Primitive Christianity/Acts

The account of Stephen's martyrdom attests the reality of the intermediate state. "When they were stoning him, Stephen prayed, 'Lord Jesus, receive my spirit' " (Acts 7:59; cf. Luke 23:46). At death Stephen's immaterial spirit (*pneuma*) separated from his material body and passed immediately into the presence of Christ. Luke's words "he fell asleep" (v. 60) signify the sleep not of the soul but of the body. Sleep, in other words, is a Christian metaphor for physical death (cf. 1 Cor. 15:18, 51; 1 Thess. 4:15; 5:10). Luke later recorded Paul's words to the same effect: "When David had served God's purpose in his own generation, he fell asleep; he was buried with his fathers" (Acts 13:36).

Expounding Daniel 12:2, the apostles upheld a general resurrection of both the righteous and the unrighteous. Paul proclaimed to skeptical Saduccees the universal, end-time resurrection of the dead: "there will be a resurrection of both the righteous and the wicked" (Acts 24:15). See also the apostolic claim of general resurrection in Acts 4:2; 17:32; 23:6; and 26:6–8. After the general resurrection, God will execute judgment on all through his Son. So Paul declared that God "has set a day when he will judge the world with justice by the man he has appointed. He has given proof of this to all men by raising him from the dead" (Acts 17:31; cf. 10:42).

Does Acts teach that all persons will be saved? Some appeal to Peter's statement in Acts 3:21 concerning "the time of universal restoration that God announced long ago through his holy prophets" (NRSV). The *apokatastasis* ("restoration") deals with the realization of God's promises to the prophets concerning the establishment of his rule and kingdom. H. G. Link wrote,

> The *apokatastasis pantōn* does not mean the conversion of all mankind, but the restoration of all things and circumstances which the OT prophets proclaimed, i.e., the universal renewal of the earth. While the "times of refreshing" [v. 19] mean the coming in of the change and the subjective effects of this event, the 'times of restoration' emphasize the objective side and the permanent condition of the world renewed.[99]

Acts 3:23 rules out universalism: "Anyone who does not listen to him will be completely cut off from among his people."

The Pauline Writings

Some within the Corinthian church, guided by Greek philosophy, denied the future resurrection of the body (1 Cor. 15:12). In response Paul explained the inconsistency and futility of this false belief (vv. 13–19). Central to Paul's gospel was the claim that God raised Christ from the dead as "the firstfruits of those who have fallen asleep" (v. 20; cf. 1 Thess. 1:10). Since Christ's resurrection is the pledge and guarantee of the saints' future resurrection, believers in him will be raised at his *parousia* (vv. 21–23; cf. 1 Cor. 6:14). So Paul wrote, "For as in Adam all [i.e., humankind] die, so in Christ all [i.e., believers] will be made alive" (v. 22). The latter verse, as an aside, offers no support for the doctrine of universalism. At the end of the Second Advent complex Christ will abolish (*katargeō*) all malignant powers including the "last enemy," which is "death" itself (vv. 24, 26).

When someone in the community replied, "With what kind of a body will they come?" (v. 35), Paul responded with a series of dramatic antitheses. At the Parousia believers' mortal (i.e., "flesh and blood") bodies will be significantly transformed, as follows. (1) The "perishable" (*en phthora,* "in decay, corruption, ruin") body will be raised an "imperishable" (*en aphtharsia,* "with immortality") body (v. 42; cf. vv. 52–54). The verbs *speiretai* ("sown") and *egeiretai* ("raised") indicate that the apostle envisaged bodies, not mere spirits. (2) The dishonorable body will be raised an honorable body (v. 43a): "It is sown in dishonor (i.e., characterized by death and decay), it is raised in glory" (cf. Phil. 3:21). (3) The weak, natural body will be raised a powerful body (v. 43b): "It is sown in weakness, it is raised in power" (cf. Phil. 3:10). At the resurrection believers will be delivered from all physical maladies caused by sickness and old age. (4) The "earthly" body will be transformed into a body "of heaven" (vv. 48–49). "As we have born the likeness of the earthly man, so shall we bear the likeness of the man from heaven."

The sum of the above is that (5) the believer's "natural body" (*sōma psy-chikon*) will be raised a "spiritual body" (*sōma pneumatikon,* v. 44). The "natural body" is from the dust of the ground and is animated by the human *psychē* (Gen. 2:7); it is a body characterized by sin (Rom. 6:6; Phil. 3:21a). The phrase "spiritual body" does not suggest incorporeality; it suggests a body changed and animated by the Spirit of God. "The *sōma pneumatikon* is a body transformed by the life-giving Spirit of God adapted for existence in the new and redeemed order of the age to come."[100] The analogy of the seed and the plant (vv. 37–38) indicates that this transformation involves both continuity and discontinuity. The believer's personal identity will remain the same, but the substance and form of the body will change.[101] Since Paul in 1 Corinthians 15 used *sarx* two times (vv. 39, 50) but *sōma* ten times (vv. 35, 37–38, 40, et al.), his concern was with the resurrection of the *body.*

Let us examine more closely Paul's understanding of "immortality" (vv. 53–54). He wrote in verses 53–54: "For the perishable [*phthartos*] must clothe itself with the imperishable [*aphtharsia*], and the mortal [*thnētos*] with immortality [*athanasia*]. When the perishable [*phthartos*] has been clothed with the imperishable [*aphtharsia*], and the mortal [*thnētos*] with immortality [*athanasia*], then the saying that is written will come true: 'Death has been swallowed up in victory.'" *Phthartos,* as we have seen, means "subject to decay, perishable, mortal"; *aphtharsia* signifies "imperishability, immortality"; and *athanasia* means "deathlessness or immortality." Thus Paul affirmed that the resurrection body is "imperishable" or "immortal" in the sense that in heaven (negatively) it is immune from corruption, decay, and death and that (positively) it enjoys perpetuity of life. The contrary conditions prevail in the present in respect of the believer's mortal body. Paul thus

465

enlarged his discussion of immortality beyond the Greek fascination with the soul to the blessed future of the believer's total being.

Second Corinthians 5:1–9 provides further insight into the intermediate state. In verses 1–4 Paul wrote that he would rather be clothed with the resurrection body rather than experience "nakedness" at death. "The earthly tent" (vv. 1, 4) is the physical "body" (vv. 6, 8, 10) which is "mortal" (*thnētos*, v. 4). Paul added that after the earthly body is dismantled (v. 1), believers anticipate "a building [*oikodomē*] from God, an eternal house [*oikia aiōnia*] in heaven, not built by human hands" (v. 1; cf. v. 2). Scholars variously identify the latter as (1) heaven itself, (2) the spiritual body received at death, or (3) the resurrection body received at the Parousia. Paul longed to receive the "heavenly dwelling" (v. 4) while yet alive so that he would not "be found naked" (v. 3b) or "unclothed" (v. 4a). The new dwelling Paul envisaged likely is the resurrection body received at the Parousia (option 3), for the putting on of the "heavenly dwelling" will occur when our mortality is "swallowed up by life" (v. 4), i.e., at Christ's return from heaven (1 Cor. 15:21–23, 44–49, 51–52). Since the two Corinthian letters were written in the same year, it is unlikely that Paul markedly changed his eschatological view in the interim. Thus the thesis of "instantaneous resurrection" (Davies, Bruce, Harris) appears weak. Shrinking from dying naturally and thereby becoming "unclothed," Paul found attractive the option of being clothed with the resurrection body at the Parousia. But given the choice of living (without the resurrection body) or dying (and being immediately in Christ's presence), Paul favored the latter: "We . . . would prefer to be away from the body and at home with the Lord" (v. 8). Paul's assertion here of conscious fellowship with Christ in the intermediate state (cf. Phil. 1:23) argues against the soul-sleep hypothesis. Both texts indicate "an intermediate state between death and resurrection and, apparently, a disembodied state; but it is not a limbo of oblivion, for the believer who has died is at home with his Lord, and that is preferable to our present life in the body."[102]

Paul frequently used the imagery of "sleep" to describe the condition of believers between death and resurrection (1 Cor. 11:30; 15:6, 18, 20, 51; 1 Thess. 4:13–15; 5:10). A defeated foe, death is described benignly as temporary repose. Roman Catholics often cite the following Scripture in support of the doctrine of purgatory: "hand this man over to Satan, so that the sinful nature may be destroyed and his spirit saved on the day of the Lord" (1 Cor. 5:5). But these words have a historical rather than an eschatological focus. That is, Paul enjoined the Corinthian church to expel the immoral brother from the fellowship that he might be afflicted by Satan and thus either be restored or be taken in death. First Corinthians 3:12–15 describes the fire of final *judgment,* not a fire of *purgation*. These verses describe a *proving* of the lasting good rather than a *purging* of residual evil.

The apostle understood that the bodily resurrection of believers would occur at Christ's second advent, or Parousia (1 Thess. 4:14–17; cf. 1 Cor. 15:23, 51–54; Phil. 3:20–21). This clear teaching opposes the hypothesis of "instantaneous resurrection" at the moment of death. The fact that Philippians (A.D. 61) was written later than 2 Corinthians (A.D. 55) suggests that Paul had no change of mind as to when believers will receive the resurrection body. All resurrected saints will stand before God and be judged according to their works (Rom. 14:10–12; 2 Cor. 5:10). Faithful words and deeds will withstand the day of judgment and bring rewards, whereas faithless words and deeds will result in forfeiture of reward (1 Cor. 3:14–15). The unsaved will be judged according to their response to the measure of truth possessed (Rom. 2:6–15).

Graphic Pauline language prompts some to assert that the apostle taught the annihilation of the wicked following the Last Judgment. Consider (1) Paul's use of the verb *phtheirō* (to "defile, corrupt, spoil, ruin"). Thus: "If anyone destroys God's temple, God will destroy him; for God's temple is sacred, and you are that temple" (1 Cor. 3:17). Note that the people addressed are believers. Moreover, *phtheirō* in all other New Testament usages (1 Cor. 15:33; 2 Cor. 7:2; 11:3; Eph. 4:22; Jude 10; Rev. 19:2) means to corrupt or ruin rather than to extinguish existence. (2) The corresponding noun *pthora* ("decay, corruption, ruin"). Thus: "The one who sows to please his sinful nature, from that nature will reap destruction; the one who sows to please the Spirit, from the Spirit will reap eternal life" (Gal. 6:8). The opposite of *zōēn aiōnion* is *pthora*, i.e., spiritual ruin. Elsewhere *pthora* conveys the idea of decay (Rom. 8:21). (3) The verb *apollymi* (active, to "destroy, ruin"; passive, to "perish, be lost"). Thus: "If Christ has not been raised, . . . you are still in your sins. Then those also who have fallen asleep in Christ are lost" (1 Cor. 15:17–18). Paul hardly meant that if Christ were not raised deceased believers would be annihilated. The verb rather means to "irretrievably perish," "experience final perdition," or "be lost in hell" (Rom. 2:12; 2 Thess. 2:10).[103] Other usages clearly exclude the sense of annihilation or extinction of being (cf. 1 Cor. 1:18; 2 Cor. 2:15; 4:3).

(4) The noun *apōleia* ("destruction, ruin") figuratively denotes the antithesis of eternal life, namely, eternal perdition in hell (Rom. 9:22; Phil. 1:28; 3:19;

1 Tim. 6:9). Finally consider (5) the noun *olethros* ("ruin, destruction"). For example: "They will be punished with everlasting destruction and shut out from the presence of the Lord and from the majesty of his power" (2 Thess. 1:9; cf. 1 Thess. 5:3). Both *olethros* and *apōleia* occur in 1 Timothy 6:9 as near synonyms ("ruin and destruction"). "We are probably right in refusing to see in it [*olethros*] anything approaching annihilation. Rather the term is to be understood as denoting loss of fellowship with God, the loss of that life which is really life. . . . It is the opposite of life and not simply the cessation of existence."[104] All the above words denote spiritual ruin, perdition, or existence in hell rather than extinction of being. Paul's statement that "all of us must appear before the judgment seat of Christ, so that each may receive recompense for what has been done in the body, whether good or evil" (2 Cor. 5:10) suggests that a person's eternal destiny is predicated upon decisions and deeds made in this life. Opportunity to repent after death thus appears to be ruled out.

Inherently immortality belongs to God alone. Thus Paul characterized God by the noun *athanasia* ("incorruptibility, immortality") in 1 Timothy 6:16 and by the adjective *aphthartos* ("imperishable, incorruptible, immortal") in Romans 1:23 and 1 Timothy 1:17. God, the author of life, is immortal in the sense that he had no beginning and has no end, being immune to decay and death. In what sense can immortality be attributed to humans? In Romans 2:7 Paul wrote that believers "by persistence in doing good seek glory, honor and immortality [*aphtharsia*]." Again, Jesus Christ "has destroyed death and has brought life and immortality [*aphtharsia*] to light through the gospel" (2 Tim. 1:10). Here Paul considered the believer in Christ holistically as a unity of body and soul. Whereas in this life the body is "mortal" (*thnētos*) and "corruptible" (*phthartos*) and so experiences decay and death, raised at Christ's coming the total person is transformed and becomes impervious to decay and death. "As generally used, immortality means the unending, conscious existence of man after his earthly life is terminated."[105] Compare Paul's use of *aphtharsia* and *athanasia* in 1 Corinthians 15:53–54.

The Johannine Literature

John's vision of the disembodied souls of martyrs positioned under the altar (Rev. 6:9–11) suggests that between death and resurrection they exist consciously in a place of safety until their number is complete.[106] The "white robe" given to each martyr likely signifies the pledge of future immortality. For persevering saints who were not martyred, death means entry into eternal blessedness and rest (Rev. 14:13). In the case of Lazarus, mention of his having "fallen asleep" (John 11:11) is a poetic euphemism for cessation of physical life (cf. v. 14). John 8:21, 24 appears to exclude further opportunity for salvation following death, for Jesus taught that if the Pharisees did not believe in this life they could not follow him to heaven. Indeed, they would perish in their sins and forfeit the kingdom.

Jesus taught the future bodily resurrection of all the dead at the end of the age followed by the distribution of rewards and punishments (John 5:28–29). The righteous, negatively, "will never see death" (*eis ton aiōna*, John 8:51; cf. 11:25) and, positively, will enter into the full realization of eternal life (John 3:15–16, 36; 6:40, 47, 54; 10:28; 1 John 2:25). The latter explains what is meant by personal immortality. Furthermore, the unrighteous dead will come alive bodily in the second resurrection (Rev. 20:5, 13) and be judged at

the Great White Throne according to their deeds (Rev. 20:11–13). Their God-appointed fate is the "second death" (Rev. 2:11; 20:6), which John identified as consignment to the lake of fire (Rev. 20:14–15; 21:8; cf. 14:10), or hell, otherwise known as gehenna (cf. Matt. 5:22). The lake of fire also will be the place of final punishment for Satan, the Beast, and the False Prophet (Rev. 19:20; 20:10).

What is the duration of the final torment of the unsaved? According to Revelation 14:11, "The smoke of their torment rises for ever and ever [*eis aiōnas aiōnōn*]." A similar statement is made concerning Babylon (Rev. 19:3): "The smoke from her goes up for ever and ever [*eis tous aiōnas tōn aiōnōn*]." The Beast and the False Prophet (who suffer the same fate as the unsaved) will endure torment in the lake of fire *eis tous aiōnas tōn aiōnōn* (Rev. 20:10). But John described the eternal life of God (Rev. 4:9; 5:13; 11:15; 22:5) by the phrase *eis tous aiōnas tōn aiōnōn*. The conclusion follows that the conscious torment of the unsaved in hell is *everlasting*. "In Hebraic usage, when *aion* or *aionios* is used to speak of the final order of things, they always meant an eternity of duration or endlessness."[107] Eternal punishment, at the least, involves agonizing exclusion from the presence of God (Rev. 22:15). Since the context of the preceding verse is the blessedness of the saved in the New Jerusalem, we infer that the separation of the unsaved from God likewise is everlasting. None of the above texts suggest that the unsaved will have further opportunity to be saved or that their being will be extinguished. The song of the twenty-four elders (Rev. 11:18) speaks of "destroying those who destroy the earth." The verb *diaphtheirō* (to "corrupt, destroy") here signifies complete ruin, not extinction of being (cf. Rev. 19:2). Neither is annihilation warranted by the verb *apollymi* ("be lost, perish, be ruined") in John 3:16, 10:28; 17:12a or the noun *apōleia* ("destruction, utter ruin, hell") used in respect of Judas (John 17:12b).

Jesus' use of the terms "house" (*oikia*), "dwelling places" (NRSV, *monai*), and "place" (*topos*) in reference to heaven (John 14:2–3) suggests that the latter is a place. The bodily presence of Jesus and believers with the Father (John 17:24) leads to the same conclusion. Revelation 21:1–22:5 presents a symbolic description of the eternal state. The first event to occur is the replacement of the present world with "a new heaven and a new earth" (21:1; cf. Isa. 65:17; 2 Peter 3:10–13). This realm, new in kind (*kainos*), serves as a setting for the heavenly and eternal state, which John described by several familiar images. The *first image* is that of a *city,* the "new Jerusalem," which comes down "out of heaven from God" (21:2–21). The "city" has been interpreted in several ways. The "new Jerusalem" is (1) a symbol for the church in its eternal and perfected state (Calvin, Ladd)—this is inferred from the reference to the "bride" (vv. 2, 9), "the twelve apostles of the Lamb" (v. 14); and "the twelve tribes of Israel" (v. 12); (2) a description of heaven, since Jerusalem in Scripture is the homeland of God's people (D. Moody); and (3) a symbol of the eternal blessedness of the redeemed (Mounce). After the new Jerusalem has descended to the renewed earth, John relates that "the dwelling place [*skēnē*] of God is with men, and he will live with them" (v. 3). The sorrows of the old order will be gone forever; with sin abolished, there will be no more death, mourning, crying, or pain (v. 4). The *second image* is that of a *temple* (Rev. 21:22–27): "I did not see a temple in the city, because the Lord God Almighty and the Lamb are its temple" (v. 22). Since the Jewish temple uniquely was the place of God's presence, *naos* here symbolizes the

saints' eternal worship of God in the eternal order (see a discussion of Ezekiel's temple, Ezek. 40–48, in ch. 7).

The *third image* is that of a *garden* (Rev. 22:1–5). Recalling the Garden of Eden (Gen. 3), this image symbolizes the unsurpassing vitality and beauty of the eternal state after decay and death have been forever abolished. "The river of the water of life" that flowed "from the throne of God and of the Lamb" (v. 1) signifies the live-giving stream that refreshes the glorified saints. "The tree of life," bearing abundant fruit (v. 2; cf. Rev. 2:7; 22:14), denotes believers' immortality, when the perishable becomes imperishable and death itself dies (cf. 1 Cor. 15:52–54). This glorious condition of the saints in the eternal state means that "his servants will serve him. They will see his face, and his name will be on their foreheads" (vv. 3–4). A *fourth image* is the *"wedding supper of the Lamb"* (Rev. 19:9; cf. Matt. 22:1–14). Since this image is presented in a proleptic vision of the end (cf. Rev. 17:1–19:10), it is best understood as describing the perfected union of Christ the Bridegroom and his church, commencing at the Rapture (cf. Hos. 2:19 and the "bride" figure in Rev. 21:2, 9).

Other New Testament Literature

Hebrews 12:23 describes the blessed condition of deceased saints in the intermediate state: "You have come . . . to the spirits [*pneumata*] of just men made perfect." The "spirits" are not angels, for the latter were just mentioned in verse 22. Alford correctly observed that the saints "are not sleeping, they are not unconscious, they are not absent from us: they are perfected, lacking nothing . . . but waiting only for bodily perfection."[108] First Peter 4:6 (discussed in vol. 2, p. 397) refers to the *nekroi,* who believed the Gospel when alive and who later died. Opponents of the Gospel claimed that these had believed in vain, for they suffered the same fate as non-Christians. Peter responded that from the divine perspective these deceased believers live eternally in the Spirit in the intermediate state and will receive the full inheritance of life at the resurrection.

Having pictured the fate of wicked angels (2 Peter 2:4), 2 Peter 2:9 alludes to the interim punishment of the unrighteous in the intermediate state (i.e., hades) as they await resurrection and the final assize: "The Lord knows how . . . to keep the unrighteous under punishment until the day of judgment" (NRSV). This latter teaching is consistent with the picture set forth in Luke 16:23–28. The literature appears to exclude further opportunity to be saved after death. According to Hebrews 9:27, "Man is destined to die once, and after that to face judgment [krisis]." As in the present death is inevitable and final, so also hereafter is the final judgment (cf. Heb. 2:3). Some allege that 1 Peter 3:18–20a teaches that Christ preached to spirits in hades, giving them further opportunity to respond to the Gospel. However, in volume 2, page 397 evidence supported the interpretation that the preexistent Christ, via the Spirit, preached a message of repentance through Noah to his godless contemporaries. These human "spirits" (pneumata) presently are in prison (phylakē), i.e., in hades, awaiting the coming judgment, of which Noah's flood was a historical sign. The New Testament nowhere explicitly states that the Gospel will be preached to people beyond the grave.

Peter wrote that in the Day of the Lord "the heavens will disappear with a roar; the elements will be destroyed by fire, and the earth and everything in it will be laid bare" (2 Peter 3:10; cf. vv. 11–12). Peter thus described a great conflagration whereby the present physical order will disintegrate (note the three uses of luō, to "dissolve"). He added, "But in keeping with his promise we are looking forward to a new heaven and a new earth, the home of righteousness" (v. 13). Out of the old order will emerge a reconstituted universe, as anticipated by Isaiah (34:4; 65:17; 66:22) and later by John (Rev. 21:1). A. A. Hodge observed, "As there is to be a 'spiritual body,' there may be in the same sense a spiritual world, that is, a world adapted to be the theatre of the glorified spirits of the saints made perfect."[109] This renovated universe will serve as the setting for what Hebrews called the coming "city" built by God (11:10, 16; 13:14) or "Mount Zion . . . the heavenly Jerusalem, the city of the living God" (12:22). In that future home believers will find their ultimate rest (Heb. 4:9–11).

On the other hand, the literature attests the reality of endless, conscious punishment for the unsaved in hell. Jude 7 teaches that the fire and brimstone God rained on the plain of Jordan warned of the "eternal fire" God will mete out on the ungodly. Second Peter 2:6 makes the same point: God "condemned the cities of Sodom and Gomorrah by burning them to ashes, and made them an example of what is going to happen to the ungodly." Fire in Scripture is a symbol of the painful torments of hell. Jude 13 states that the final end of the immoral false teachers is the "blackest darkness" of eternal hell (cf. 2 Peter 2:17). The same fate will come upon fallen angels: "God did not spare angels when they sinned, but sent them to hell (tartarōsas), putting them into gloomy dungeons to be held for judgment" (2 Peter 2:4; cf. Jude 6). The verb tartaroō (to "consign to Tartarus") acknowledges the view of Greek mythology and Hellenistic Judaism (1 Enoch 20:2) that Tartarus is the place where fallen angels await final judgment.

Will the unsaved suffer extinction

from being in hell? Certain texts cited in support of annihilationism use the noun *apōleia* ("ruin, damnation, perdition"—Heb. 10:39; 2 Peter 2:1, 3; 3:7, 16) and the verb *apollymi* (to "ruin, perish, destroy"—James 4:12; 2 Peter 3:9; Jude 5, 11). The fact that *apōleia* appears in 2 Peter 2:1 twice as "destructive heresies" and "swift destruction" suggests that the word is used figuratively for "ruin" or "ruinous." Similarly, in Jude 5 and 11 *apollymi* is used figuratively for physical death. Hebrews adds that persistent rejection of the truth leads to "a fearful expectation of judgment and of raging fire that will consume the enemies of God" (Heb. 10:26–27; cf. Isa. 26:11). The word "consume" (*esthiō*) means to "eat," which suggests that the "consuming" should be understood figuratively. Likewise the statement, "our God is a consuming fire" (Heb. 12:29; cf. Deut. 4:24). We understand the latter as a figure referring to God's zeal for holiness and against sin;[110] hence believers must worship God with profound reverence and awe. In 2 Peter 2:12 the adjective *phthora* ("corruption, destruction") is used of animals, and the verb *phtheirō* (to "corrupt, decay, destroy, devastate") is used of the false teachers. Peter meant that as animals are hunted and killed so apostate teachers will experience a sudden and violent death. Moreover, the degrees of punishment meted out upon the unrepentant (Heb. 10:29) exclude annihilation (which admits of no degrees).

SYSTEMATIC FORMULATION

We now develop the essentials of personal eschatology by integrating elements of the alternative views that cohere with the biblical data.

The Meaning of Death

Life is not an entitlement but a gift of common grace. The moral order of the universe dictates that life is a consequent of righteousness, and death is the outcome of sin. Sin "entered the world through one man, and death through sin, and in this way death came to all men, because all sinned" (Rom. 5:12; cf. 6:23). God permits death both as part of the consequence of forfeiting the conditions of life and as its just penalty. Death is an instrument of Satan, who holds its power (Heb. 2:14–15). Satan's power over death is the last enemy to be destroyed (1 Cor. 15:26).

The word "death" has several different meanings. (1) *Physical death* is the irreversible cessation of all heart and circulatory functions, all lung and respiratory functions, and all brain functions, including those of the brain stem.[111] Confirming the complete loss of responsiveness in these three ways guards against premature pronouncements of death for persons in a coma or with partial brain damage. The threefold criterion also helps prevent euthanasia—premature "harvesting of the dead"—and experimentation on the sick and dying. In Scripture physical death does not mean annihilation but the *separation of the spirit from the body* (James 2:26). This understanding is derived not from philosophy but from teachings of prophets and apostles and preeminently Jesus Christ—who knows the other side directly. At death a Christian's unresponsive body is buried, decomposes in the grave, and returns to dust. There the body "sleeps" until it is resurrected. The spirit, however, is not sleeping or nonexistent but feels "unclothed" when the body is dismantled like a tent (2 Cor. 5:1).

(2) *Spiritual death* is the *separation of the spirit from communion with God* resulting in unresponsiveness to God's revealed will. The outcome is loss of fellowship with the Creator, or spiritual alienation, enmity, and estrangement. (3) *Eternal death* refers to *separation from God that is endless*, or the

perpetuation of spiritual death. (4) *Ethical death,* as believers are "crucified with Christ," refers to their *separation from the lure of the world,* the flesh, and the Devil—that is, unresponsiveness to temptations.

Several *misconceptions* need the corrective of a biblically informed view of death. Physical death is not natural but, as a judgment on sin, is a stinging enemy of life. Death is far from illusory; it is a real enemy. Death may be postponed by modern technologies, but it is inevitable (apart from rapture). Death is not a collective experience, even though many die in group catastrophes; it is an individual experience. Although one may be supported by relatives or friends, each person experiences this dramatic physical severance of soul and body personally. Yet in that once-for-all experience Christians are not ultimately alone, for the omnipresent Redeemer remains with them through the valley of the shadow of death (Psalm 23).

Death brings to an end opportunity for moral or spiritual development. At the point of death all the evidence is complete for the Last Judgment (Heb. 9:27). Death is not a desirable "graduation" to the next reincarnation and to millions of further occasions for spiritual evolution. The rich man's destiny was determined at death with no hint of possible change (Luke 16). As Paul wrote, what we have done "while in the body, whether good or bad," determines divine judgment (2 Cor. 5:10). God holds the unrighteous for their Day of Judgment (2 Peter 2:9). Believers face their final judgment with confidence, however, because they are no longer under condemnation (John 3:18; 5:24).

Human Spirits Survive Death

One of the most significant questions ever asked is, "What happens after death?" Some think the reports of people who had *near-death experiences* tell us what occurs after death.[112] At best they give glimpses of what the experience of dying may be like. But they do not tell us anything about what happens *after* death, not even that the soul survives it. What they do indicate is that the experience of releasing the body may be peaceful.

The doctrine of *soul sleep* is held by those who deny a unified duality of body and soul or who think they can know nothing of humanness ontologically. But our study of humanness concluded that an interacting dualism best accounts for the data of Scripture and experience. Cullmann, imagining that all dualism is Greek dualism, regarded the resurrection as the next conscious experience after death.[113] But the hypothesis of soul sleep or unconsciousness between death and the resurrection contradicts several facts. Believers enter paradise or Abraham's bosom the day they die (Luke 23:43). They live on (Matt. 22:32), approach God's glorious presence (Heb. 12:23), feel conscious longings of being unclothed spirits (2 Cor. 5:4), and wait for the resurrection of the body.

Scripture does not provide as much information as we would like about the disembodied soul, for it was not written to satisfy our curiosity. Nevertheless, the biblical writers may have assumed the survival of the soul as in traditional Judaism. The Bible gives sufficient reasons to believe in a soul that survives death. Bromiley sums it up like this:

Man has a physical side and he has a spiritual side. Both are from God. Both belong together in a psychosomatic unity. Both are integral to human life. Man is not a soul imprisoned in a body. He is certainly not a pure soul in an evil body. Nor is he a body that has of itself, and as part of itself, produced the rudiments of mental, emotional and spiritual life. Man is rather a body-soul, in which the soul is the vital principle.[114]

"Immortality" is not synonymous with "eternal life." The first by common grace makes it possible to receive the second by special grace.[115] Some (like Cullmann) deny the conscious survival of the human spirit after death because they confuse a biblical view of providentially given immortality with a Greek view of natural immortality. We listed six contrasts between the Greek and the biblical views of the soul or spirit earlier (vol. 2, p. 149). The fact that one type of dualism is unscriptural does not mean that another is. The Bible explicitly ascribes immortality to God alone (1 Tim. 6:16) because only he has eternal life in himself (John 5:26). But God created human spirits in his likeness with a contingent endless existence.

Disembodied Believers Dwell With Christ Until the Resurrection

The intermediate state of the saved is not entirely different from their present spiritual or eternal state. Personal identity continues, as the presence of Moses and Elijah at the Transfiguration confirms (Matt. 17:3). At death a Christian's spirit departs from the body (Phil. 1:23; cf. 2 Cor. 5:8), the saint feels "unclothed" (2 Cor. 5:3–4) and consciously "longs" for the resurrection body (2 Cor. 5:2).

The incomplete state at death is not the final state following the resurrection of the body. Although the disembodied condition between death and resurrection is called the intermediate state, there is nothing intermediate or purgatorial about it morally. Shedd explains, "The so-called 'intermediate' state is not intermediate in respect to the essential elements of heaven and hell, but it is a part of the final and endless state of the soul. It is 'intermediate,' only in

reference to the secondary matter of the presence or absence of the body."[116] The terms "heaven" and "hell" can be used of the disembodied and the resurrected states. Shedd adds "that the intermediate state for the saved is Heaven without the body, and the final state for the saved in Heaven with the body; that the intermediate state for the lost is Hell without the body, and the final state is Hell with the body."[117]

The believing dead are conscious of being *with Christ* (Phil. 1:23) safe in the heavenly kingdom (2 Tim. 4:18). "I am always with you; you hold me by my right hand. You guide me with your counsel, and afterward you will take me into glory" (Ps. 73:23–24). Although death separates believers from their bodies, it does not separate them from divine love (Rom. 8:38–39). The psalmist wrote, "Surely goodness and love will follow me all the days of my life, and I will dwell in the house of the LORD forever" (Ps. 23:6). As Jesus said to the dying man on the cross: "I tell you the truth, today you will be with me in paradise" (Luke 23:43).

Believers will enjoy a relationship that is far better because they become the "spirits of just men made perfect" (Heb. 12:23). Ramm has shown that the Father, a God of glory, and Christ, the Lord of glory, purpose to share their glory with believers.[118] When the justified who are legally perfected go to be with Christ, they become morally perfected, beyond satanic temptation, free from the law, and free from sin. In the present life the regenerate progressively reflect the Lord's glory as they are transformed into his likeness (2 Cor. 3:18).

After death, believers are conscious of being *with God's people* in glory. Biblical writers speak of the experience following death as one of being "gathered to their people." Abraham "breathed his last and died . . . ; and he was gathered to his people. His sons

Isaac and Ishmael buried him in the cave . . . with his wife Sarah" (Gen. 25:8–10). As Kidner says, "The expression 'gathered to his people,' which could hardly refer to the family sepulcher where only Sarah was buried as yet, must point, however indistinctly, to the continued existence of the dead."[119] The soul is taken into glory to be united with the faithful patriarchs in paradise (Ps. 73:24). One ministry of angels is to guide the deceased believer's spirit to Abraham's side (Luke 16:22). In Jewish teaching at the time of Jesus heaven was sometimes called paradise and sometimes Abraham's bosom; it was understood as a place of blessedness and bliss. In the New Testament, paradise is the presence of Christ.

With Christ and his people believers feel *at home, at peace, at rest*. Believers, like Stephen, receive the answer to their prayers: "Lord Jesus, receive my spirit" (Acts 7:59). Disembodied believers feel consciously "at home with the Lord" (2 Cor. 5:8), are spared from evil, and enter into peace (Isa. 57:2). We will no longer battle temptations from the flesh, worldly associates, or demonic powers. People justified by faith enter more fully into "God's rest" from labor as described by the author of Hebrews (4:1–11). Feeling at home and at peace, believers find life in Christ's immediate presence great "gain" (Phil. 1:21) and "better by far" than the rewarding life of faith here (Phil. 1:23). Although the body "sleeps" in the grave, the soul rests in Christ's loving presence. Death cannot separate believers from Christ's love (Rom. 8:38–39). After death they enjoy more completely the fellowship with the Savior that began at their conversion.

The Lost Suffer After Death

Moral distinctions endure in the intermediate state. After death, as now,

real differences remain between good and evil. Moral distinctions are not temporal but eternal, flowing as they do from the nature of the eternal God. Not all who die are Christians. Those who have not received Christ's righteousness remain dominated by sin and face its deserved consequences. Jesus' description of the rich man's suffering in contrast to the blessing of the beggar (Luke 16) cannot be dismissed. Even if the language is highly figurative, the figures convey two radically different situations of conscious joy and conscious torment after death. A realistic, biblical view of humans after death requires a moral dualism.

On *the nature of sufferings* after death we are given few details, but what Jesus explained is poignant: "In hell, where he [the rich man] was in torment, he looked up and saw Abraham far away, with Lazarus by his side. So he called to him, 'Father Abraham, have pity on me and send Lazarus to dip the tip of his finger in water and cool my tongue, because I am in agony in this fire'" (Luke 16:23–24). Here Jesus taught the prevailing Jewish view of conscious existence after death either in torment or bliss. If the text be a parable, it is the only one in which Christ referred to a person by name (Lazarus), and it illustrates the postmortem possibilities of irreversibly good and unalterably evil fates. Blomberg believes that it teaches these truths: "(1) Like Lazarus, those whom God helps will be borne after their death into God's presence. (2) Like the rich man, the unrepentant will experience irreversible punishment. And (3) through Abraham, Moses, and the prophets, God reveals himself and his will so that none who neglect it can legitimately protest their subsequent fate."[120]

The Resurrection Unites Body and Soul

Old Testament Judaism affirmed the resurrection of the body (Job 19:25–26;

Isa. 26:19; Dan. 12:2–3). The Sadducees wrongly assumed that life after the resurrection would be identical with the present life. Jesus also upheld the resurrection of the body, but explained that it would be significantly different in respect to marriage. Hence the Saducees were "badly mistaken," not knowing the Scriptures (Mark 12:18–27). Paul refuted the notion of those who denied a resurrection by exhibiting the evidence that Christ has been raised from the dead, the firstfruits of those who have fallen asleep (1 Cor. 15:3–8, 12–20).

Paul wrote, "We eagerly await a Savior from [heaven], the Lord Jesus Christ, who, by the power that enables him to bring everything under his control, will transform our lowly bodies so that they will be like his glorious body" (Phil. 3:20–21). Just as Jesus' resurrection body exhibits both similarities and differences with its former state, so will ours. His resurrection body could be seen, heard, and touched. In his resurrected state he walked dusty roads, ate food, and conversed with people. Jesus' resurrected body was continuous with the body that died as evidenced by the scars, but it had gloriously new spiritual powers. His body was different, however, in that he could appear in rooms with doors locked, disappear from view, and ascend into heaven.

In humans, how can bodies that have completely decomposed be raised? Paul taught that our death is like a seed that is sown and our resurrection like the bringing forth of its distinctive head of grain (1 Cor. 15:35–41). Between the seed and the full grown head exists organic continuity. There will be a similar continuity between our present body and its resurrected form. Not only does the spirit continue, the resurrected body does also. The buried body is perishable, the one raised is imperishable: "It is sown in dishonor, it is raised in glory; it is sown in weakness, it is raised in power; it is sown a natural body, it is raised a spiritual body" (vv. 43–44). The mechanics of the transformation we leave with Christ who has the wisdom and power to bring everything under his control (Phil. 3:21). The Creator who first made the body from dust will find no difficulty in *recreating* it from dust.

After being resurrected, what will it be like to exist in *spiritual bodies* (1 Cor. 15:44)? In this phrase "body" is the noun and "spiritual" the adjective describing the physical entity. Our organically continuous body of flesh and bones will enjoy new spiritual characteristics. The text does not support a mere spiritual continuity received at death with occasional bodily manifestations. The resurrection of the body occurs at the return of Christ (1 Thess. 4:16–17). Against the view of Davies, Bruce, Harris, and others that the spiritual body is received at death, see the discussion in the historical and biblical sections, above. J. A. Schep correctly concludes, "Since Paul's chief emphasis is clearly on the resurrection hope (Rom. 8:11, 23) it seems better to say with A. Nygren that 'Paul is reaching forward in hope toward the time when the perishable puts on the imperishable, and the mortal puts on immortality.' "[121] At the "first resurrection," not at death, God makes believers like the risen Christ both physically and spiritually (1 John 3:2–3).

The eternal state of resurrected people ought not be reduced to a world identical with the present one, nor a world of mere spirits. It will be a new world with a new heaven and a new earth. In the intermediate state we experience "heaven" as mere spirits; after Christ's return in the Millennium and in the new earth we will experience "heaven" in physical bodies with new spiritual powers.

Christ, the Final Judge of Both the Saved and the Lost

The future divine judgment will be *universal*. All must appear before the judgment seat of Christ that each one may receive their due for deeds done in the body, whether good or bad (2 Cor. 5:10). Liberals think that judgment is unnecessary, for evil (viewed as extrinsic) can be overcome by social action. But when ingrained evil taints all our functions and relationships, we forfeit the gift of life.

The *ultimate issue* is not whether all religions and philosophies lead to God. They do; all lead to God—as Judge! Not all people are acceptable to divine righteousness. The pressing issue is how sinners, when they finally meet God, can be accepted. God's requirement of perfect moral character and conduct cannot be relaxed. To have broken his moral law in one point is to be a guilty law-breaker. The only hope anyone has of acceptance with the God who knows all our motives, words, and deeds is the gift of Christ's righteousness.

The identity of the ultimate Judge of humanity has been made known. It will not be Plato, Aristotle, Kant, or Jung. Our thoughts and works will not be examined by Krishna, Buddha, or Maharishi Mahesh Yogi. The final Judge of all in the world is the eternal Logos who became flesh, Jesus Christ. The supreme Father has given him that authority (John 5:27), as attested in the Scriptures and by his resurrection from the dead (Acts 17:31). Christ alone has the omniscience necessary to carry out such judgment, the righteousness to make it just, the love to make it caring, and the power to administer it.

Judgment (*mišpāt*) "signifies the administration of righteousness" (*ṣedeq*).[122] Divine judgment presupposes the righteousness that has its basis in God's nature. When judging, the omniscient Judge does more than discriminate between good and evil. "Basically judgment is the process whereby one discerns between the right and the wrong *and takes action as a result*. . . . It is an activity of discrimination and vindication. He who does *mišpāt* seeks out the wrongdoer to punish him, and the righteous to vindicate his cause."[123] So Christ's judgment sets in motion the administration of the verdicts. "Out of his mouth comes a sharp sword with which to strike down the nations. 'He will rule them with an iron scepter.' He treads the winepress of the fury of the wrath of God Almighty. On his robe and on his thigh he has this name written: KING OF KINGS AND LORD OF LORDS" (Rev. 19:15–16).

Christ administers judgment *at different times*. (1) He judges some people in part during this life. (2) All are judged at death to determine whether they will be with Christ in the intermediate state. (3) At Christ's second coming he will judge and defeat the wicked (Isa. 11:3–5; Rev. 19:11), raise the just (the first resurrection), and finally judge his people. When Christ comes, he "will bring to light what is hidden in darkness and will expose the motives of men's hearts" (1 Cor. 4:5; cf. Rom. 2:16). (4) At the end of the Millennium and following the resurrection of the wicked (the second resurrection), the judgment of the Great White Throne will occur when Christ consigns the lost to their eternal state (1 Cor. 4:5; 2 Thess. 1:5–10). All will face intermediate judgments and a final day of judgment; but that "day" (singular) for the wicked and the righteous will not be a day of twenty-four hours.

God *judges each person individually*. The issue is not whether one's parents, peers, or tribal leaders trusted Christ. It is not whether a person attended a Christian church or lived in a "Christian" country, but whether each has personally received Christ's salvation. John the Baptist demanded individual repentance. "In the Old Testament whole nations are frequently addressed, and judgment falls on them. In the New Testament, while social and communal responsibility is not overlooked, the emphasis in judgment is on what the individual does or does not do."[124] Although Jesus did not come to judge the world but to save it (John 12:47), his offer of salvation is segregating. It separates those who accept the Gospel of grace from those who do not. But God also judges *nations* (Joel 3:2–3; Zeph. 3:6, 8). In addition to receiving the natural consequences of their corruption, those gathered against God's covenant people in Jerusalem will be judged by Christ at Armageddon. Since nations are made up of citizens and leaders, their judgment falls also on individual abusers of God's people.

On what *grounds* are people finally judged? Jesus Christ will judge people based on their response to divine revelation available to them. (1) All the wicked will be found inexcusable for not worshiping and serving the Creator (Rom. 1:18–22) and for not keeping the requirements of the moral law within (2:14–15). (2) Those who had also the Old Testament revelation but have fallen short of living consistently according to its laws will be condemned (2:5, 12–13; 2:17–3:10). (3) Those who heard the Gospel of God's grace through Christ will be accountable for having failed to receive the Savior (Heb. 2:2–3). These standards cannot be lowered. No Jews or Gentiles have always loved God with their whole being or their neighbors as themselves. They have not always been holy as God is holy. Thus they cannot enter the heavenly city, in which there is no sin and moral guilt. Sins of omission as well as commission will be taken into account. As depraved but responsible, humans *know* better than they *do*. All

have some knowledge of God and morality from general revelation; but sadly all give ultimate allegiance to idols and yield to immoral desires inwardly and immoral practices outwardly.

Biblical principles indicate *degrees of guilt and retribution for the lost*. Because the punishment of the lost is based on merit, and the Judge of all the earth will do right, none will receive undeserved punishment. But some are accountable for more revealed truth than others. The primary motives of some may have been less gratitude, faith, and love for God than others. Their works provide the evidence of the basic motivation of their hearts. None will be sentenced more severely than they deserve for the truth known and subsequently disbelieved or disobeyed.

The ground of the judgment for believers, in spite of all their shortcomings, is the imputed righteousness of Christ. Our hope is not in what *we* have done for Christ but what *he* did for us. The issue that determines heaven or hell is not our inadequate works but our reception of the completed Atonement. Christ has already paid the penalty for the sins of those united to him by their faith. And this penalty for sins cannot be justly extracted a second time. If Christ's perfect righteousness has been put to one's account, one need never fear being sentenced to the company of Satan.

At their final judgment believers will be evaluated not only for their legal status in God's spiritual family but also for their works as Christ's ambassadors. To church members at Corinth Paul wrote, "We must all appear before the judgment seat of Christ, that each one may receive what is due him for the things done in the body, whether good or bad" (2 Cor. 5:10). Believers' works provide verifiable *evidence* of invisible faith. The faith that justifies is the faith that produces fruit motivated by love (Gal. 5:6). The difference between works as evidence of love and legalistic works is primarily their motivation. The latter are done out of fear or necessity, but deeds that please the Father are motivated by gratitude and love in response to his grace. So Christ will assess the *motives* of our hearts (1 Cor. 4:5a). "At that time each will receive his praise from God" (v. 5). Hearing Christ say, "Well done, good and faithful servant," will be reward enough. Christ will recognize especially those who have suffered for his kingdom (vv. 11–13). The lives of many were cut short in martyrdom. "Their rewards were not described as consolation prizes for those who met premature death, but were a celestial recovery of lost benefits."[125]

The quality of a believer's service in building on the foundation laid by Christ will be tested by the fire of the Lord's judgment (1 Cor. 3:13). The divine Judge will justly assess the durability of the building materials. Some shown to be undependable will be consumed and the person saved, "but only as one escaping through the flames" (v. 15). The faithful stewardship of the justified will be rewarded (v. 14). It seems unlikely that the Creator would bestow the same recognition on those who have faithfully used their talents and those who have not. Christ will give honor to whom honor is due. He will discriminate between pharisaic works for merit and Spirit-enabled works of gratitude and love. It may be that those Christians who have been faithful will be honored with greater opportunities in millennial communities. Then, as now, we will have not reason to boast, for any good deeds ultimately are done by grace. Blomberg argues that Christians' rewards will not be evident throughout the eternal state, but will be recognized at our final judgment.[126] Sanctification, like justification, is by grace, but this does not mean that we are sanctified to the same degree. The

nature of the rewards and their results we cannot now determine. But those who have not been as faithful as others in using their gifts will be mature enough in heaven to express gratitude for those such as the martyrs whose rewards may be greater.

The Unbelieving Suffer Eternally

"The knowledge of hell comes almost exclusively from the teachings of Christ, who spoke emphatically on the subject on a number of occasions."[127] The context of Jesus' teaching was John the Baptist's warning of coming wrath (Matt. 3:7) and his telling the people that the Messiah would burn up the chaff with "unquenchable fire" (v. 12). Later in the Sermon on the Mount Jesus warned that one who is angry with another is in danger of "the fire of hell" (Matt. 5:22), that it is better to lose a part of the body than for the whole body to go to hell (5:29–30; cf. 18:8–9), and that those who do not bear fruit will be cast into the fire (7:19). After the centurion believed, Jesus said that those without true faith "will be thrown outside, into the darkness, where there will be weeping and gnashing of teeth" (8:12).

More to be feared than those who can kill the body, Jesus warned, is the One who can kill both soul and body in hell (10:28). Christ said it would be more tolerable for Tyre, Sidon, and Sodom in the judgment than for those who had seen his mighty works and rejected him (11:22–24). At the end of the age his angels will throw the sons of the Devil "into the fiery furnace, where there will be weeping and gnashing of teeth" (13:42; cf. vv. 49–50). Those not invited to the wedding banquet who try to enter by force will be thrown "outside, into the darkness, where there will be weeping and gnashing of teeth" (Matt. 22:13; cf. 25:30). Jesus' parable of the sheep and goats concludes, "Then they shall go away to eternal punishment, but the righteous to eternal life'' (25:41). Luke added Jesus' story of the rich man and Lazarus, that affirms judgment after death, conscious suffering, and an unbreachable chasm between heaven and hell.

Even if we take much of this language figuratively, Jesus taught that the destiny of the unbelieving, whether religious or nonreligious, is an endless, agonizing exclusion from his presence. But degrees of retributive suffering are involved, depending on the degree of light for which persons are accountable. Shedd sums up:

> The strongest support of the doctrine of Endless Punishment is the teaching of Christ, the Redeemer of man. Though the doctrine is plainly taught in the Pauline Epistles and other parts of Scripture, yet without the explicit and reiterated statements of God incarnate, it is doubtful whether so awful a truth would have had such a conspicuous place as it always has had in the creeds of Christendom. . . . The Apostles enter far less into detailed description, and are far less emphatic upon this solemn theme. . . . And well they might be. For as none but God has the right, and would dare, to sentence a soul to eternal misery for sin; and as none but God has the right, and would dare, to execute the sentence; so none but God has the right and should presume, so to delineate the nature and consequences of this sentence. This is the reason why most of the awful imagery in which the sufferings of the lost are described is found in the discourses of our Lord and Saviour. He took it upon himself to sound the note of warning.[128]

So Jesus Christ, the person primarily responsible for the doctrine of eternal perdition is the one with whom all opponents of this theological tenet are in conflict. To disagree with the teaching of Scripture is to undermine the integrity of Christ's personal character, atoning work, and explicit teaching.

The *meaning* of hell includes both the intermediate and eternal states separated from Christ's presence with degrees of retributive justice proportional to unforgiven sins. Christ sometimes expressed the *duration* of hell (Matt. 25:46) by the same term (*aiōn*) used of God and translated "the King eternal" (1 Tim. 1:17) and the "eternal God" (Rom. 16:26).

> The concept of endless duration could not be more strongly conveyed; the use of these expressions for the eternity of God shows conclusively that they do not mean limited duration. It is important that the same adjective is used of eternal punishment as of eternal life (Matt. 25:46 has both). The punishment is just as eternal as the life. The one is no more limited than the other.[129]

Jesus warned of the "hell, where the fire never goes out" (Mark 9:43) and "where their worm does not die, and the fire is not quenched" (v. 48). Such references to eternal punishment designate its unending duration. Several times Jesus spoke of unquenchable fire, which would have no purpose if at some point God annihilated the inhabitants. Similarly Paul wrote, "They will be punished with everlasting destruction" (2 Thess. 1:9). "Destruction" here does not mean annihilation, for that would not be everlasting. Rather, destruction is the opposite of salvation, as Paul immediately explains. It is being everlastingly "shut out from the presence of the Lord" (v. 9). So long as there are unrepentant rebels against divine grace, they must receive their due. Everlasting insolence against the Most High brings everlasting consequences.

What is the *nature* of eternal punishment? If not agnostic about the fact of eternal punishment, many seem agnostic about its character. But our Lord's teaching, whether literal or figurative, conveys vivid truth about significant realities. We need not add the wild, imaginative pictures of hell that go beyond biblical revelation from Dante's *Inferno* or from overly eloquent preaching. It is enough to envision endless existence separated from the beneficent presence of the Creator and Sustainer of all that is of value. Death, as portrayed in Scripture, is not annihilation, but separation. Spiritual death involves the alienation of the sinner from God in the present life. Eternal death is the continuation of the present enmity and estrangement from the Giver of every good gift. Charles Hodge gave one of the more complete lists of the consequences of persistent rejection of God's grace:

> The sufferings of the impenitent, according to the Scripture, arise: (1) From the loss of all earthly good. (2) From utter expulsion from the presence and favor of God. (3) From utter reprobation, or the final withdrawal from them of the Holy Spirit. (4) From the consequent unrestrained dominion of sin and sinful passions. (5) From the operations of conscience. (6) From despair. (7) From their evil associates. (8) From their external circumstances; that is, future suffering is not exclusively the natural consequences of sin, but also includes positive inflictions. (9) From their perpetuity.[130]

Not all are equally unbelieving and rebellious, so the hell Christ described involves *degrees of suffering* (Matt. 11:22–24; Luke 10:12, 14). Our Lord taught, "That servant who knows his master's will and does not . . . do what his master wants will be beaten with many blows. But the one who does not know and does things deserving of punishment will be beaten with few blows. From everyone who has been given much, much will be demanded; and from the one who has been entrusted with much, much more will be asked" (Luke 12:47–48). Hypocritical teachers of the law will be punished most severely (Mark 12:38–40). Paul explained that "all who sin apart from the law will also perish apart from the law, and all who sin under the law will be judged by the law" (Rom. 2:12). Degrees of responsibility are also indicated in Hebrews 2:2–3. After summarizing the exegetical studies of Moses Stuart on several words relating to future punishment, Vernon Grounds concludes, "Because the biblical disclosure of hell stands on the same ground logically and exegetically as its disclosure of heaven, . . . it is impossible to anticipate the bliss of heaven without at the same time asserting the terror of hell."[131]

Some Joys of Heaven

Whereas in the intermediate state the saved are at rest, in the eternal state resurrected believers are actively involved in a new heavenly world. Life there will be anything but boring, as some imagine. Think of the most joy-filled moments in your life. Subtract the sadness that comes when we realize how fleeting our temporal pleasures are. Add the immediate presence of God. Multiply by infinity, and that yields something of what heaven will be like!

1. Believers will experience *the joy of a newly created environment* unsullied by moral evil (Rev. 21:8, 27; 22:15). The eternal environment after the resurrection and Millennium is new—"a new heaven and a new earth" (2 Peter 3:13). The new world will be redeemed from the curse upon the present earth. There will be no physical darkness; the Lamb will be the light (Rev. 21:23–25; 22:5). In glorified bodies we will enjoy a restored and improved Eden, a place of pristine beauty and unbroken fellowship—a joyful existence with no pain, death, or sorrow (21:2–4). The new heaven and earth will provide an environment conducive to the most precious values we now know—just and

loving relationships, fellowship, beauty, and significant activity.

2. Believers will enjoy the new Jerusalem, called by John Gilmore "*the ultimate model city.*" "Those cities which have been winning their fight over crime, crumbling housing, and declining quality education become known as 'model cities.' One city, devoid of detractions, perpetually clean, eternally nonthreatening, will be the holy city. John called it 'the new Jerusalem.' "[132] Coming down from heaven, it owes its existence to the grace of God rather than the labors of men (Rev. 21:2). "Cities are more than masses of population, they are citadels for mutual safety, conduits of commercial enterprise, and centers of artistic and scientific creativity. The representation of heaven as a city was intended to suggest 'intensity of life, variety of occupation, and closeness of relation to each other.' "[133]

> The joy of heaven will be a group experience. With pain, sorrow, and suffering being eliminated, heaven's joys will be undiluted and unending. The beatitudes of Jesus will be fulfilled. The pure will see God, the poor will possess the imperishable, the persecuted will have losses restored, the deprived will have immediate access to all parts of the renovated earth.[134]

In the heavenly city we will experience just and loving social relationships. Social justice and *shalom* will no longer be a mere dream; it will have become a lasting reality. Life will be exciting as together we reign with the Lord in the permanently peaceful kingdom (22:5). The fulfillment of the utopian dreams of the centuries will be fulfilled. Camelot will become a reality.

3. Believers will experience *the joy of deathless existence in resurrection bodies.* There will be an end to all physical, emotional, and intellectual decline when we experience new, imperishable capabilities in the final triumph over death. Our bodies will become all that God created them to be. There will be no diseases, no surgery, and no pain. The disabled will be restored to a lasting wholeness. Our resurrection bodies will be imperishable. Imagine activity without physical or mental fatigue. Anticipate the joy of freedom from temptation, sin, and the fear of death!

4. We will experience the joy of *knowing and loving God maximally.* Our ultimate aspirations will be realized when we are at home with our heavenly Father, his Son, and his Spirit. Our highest desires will be satisfied as we love God with our various renewed capacities. Our quest for unmediated experience of the ultimate reality will be satisfied. The joy of unbroken, fulfilling fellowship with our Creator and Redeemer will motivate authentic worship, adoration, and praise (Rev. 21:22). The chief end of sin-dominated humans at present seems to be to enjoy themselves forever.

> But of course that is ridiculous. The closer we come to the essence of heaven, the less we'll be aware of ourselves, our surroundings, and our activities; the more there will be of our love, worship, and communion with him. There is another place for those who would forget God for themselves. And this is what Dante is saying: in heaven all our activity will be directed toward God; our enjoyment will be in him. Heaven will be Immanuel—God with us. And that will be the best.[135]

5. We will experience also *the joy of fellowship with all other believers.* As we love God we are not absorbed into the divine being, losing our identity in the process (as Eastern and process thought supposes). Communion does not mean union. In the heavenly reunion we will recognize one another; but we will no longer be afflicted with egocentricity or pride. The glorious beatific vision of God in heaven will not

exclude the communion of the saints. Our distinctness as humans is not accidental nor illusory. God created us for fellowship with himself and for fellowship with other believers in his kingdom eternally.

6. As distinct, recognizable persons, we will retain our *gender and ethnic characteristics.* Jesus did not say that we would cease to be male or female when he taught that resurrected people would not marry or be given in marriage (Luke 20:35–36). Gender is part of who we are as persons. Male characteristics helped to identify Moses and Elijah at the Transfiguration (Matt. 17:3). Jesus' appearance and voice in his resurrected body were recognizably male. Since both female and male spirits and bodies are created in the image of God, it is not odd that both will be renewed at the recreation into his image. Our maleness or femaleness will be necessary to our recognition of one another in heaven. Concerning ethnic qualities, the resurrected Jesus was recognized as the same Jewish person. And non-Jewish people from the East and West will relax for a feast with Abraham, Isaac, and Jacob (Matt. 8:11). The God who loves variety in rocks, flowers, and animals will not reduce the saints to an unrecognizable mass. Racial characteristics will be recognizable as part of our identities, but our fleshly pride in them will be transcended. We will experience the joy of loving our ethnically different neighbors as ourselves and the joy of endlessly multiplying friendships.

7. Saints will populate heaven with *renewed intellectual, emotional, and volitional abilities.* Our lifelong pursuit of truth will find gratifying fulfillment. "Now I know in part; than I shall know fully, even as I am fully known" (1 Cor. 13:12). In heaven self-knowledge and self-assessment will fully function. Since we will then experience God's presence *immediately,* second-hand learning of God will not be needed

(v. 8b). "Now we see but a poor reflection as in a mirror; then we shall see face to face" (v. 12). First-century mirrors gave mediocre portrayals of the real thing. But with transformed minds sharpened, emotions heightened, and wills harmoniously controlled, we will learn from the Supreme Teacher himself. In heaven we will no longer need teachers or Bibles. We will not be limited to brief accounts about Jonah, David, Peter, or Paul; we will be able to talk to these godly heroes directly. And better still, we will be able to visit and share with our Lord Jesus Christ!

APOLOGETIC INTERACTION

Does Physical Death End Human Existence?

In *A Philosophy of Humanism* Corliss Lamont has a chapter entitled, "This Life Is All and Enough." On his view of humanness there remains an "unbreakable unity of body and personality, including the mind and consciousness. . . . The monistic or naturalistic psychology stands today as one of the greatest achievements in the history of science."[136] "The monistic relation, then, between body and personality has the standing of a proved psychological law and makes untenable any theory of worthwhile personal survival after death."[137]

Many Christian psychologists also subscribe to a monistic view of humanness and so cannot escape its inferences for life beyond the grave. David Myers finds a holistic view of anthropology from Old and New Testaments consistent with the emerging scientific picture. Although he does not flatly deny an intermediate state, he reduces the option to absurdity: "To talk of the continuation of mind or soul after death of the body is like talking of the continuation of running after the amputation of one's legs."[138] If, however, the human spirit is not merely an epiphenomenal function of the body, Myers' analogy does not fit. Typically Myers regards all Greek thought as Platonic, not recognizing alternative dualistic views of the soul and body. His view of death as the cessation of life in its totality requires that he anticipate a re-creation of the whole person rather than a bodily resurrection.

In response to James Beck's rejoinder, Myers admits that "psychology's womb-to-tomb time frame limits the range of its concerns." He adds that "theology frames different questions, and yes, 'the differences between the disciplines must be respected.'"[139] But Beck's article raises important methodological issues for those who would place monistic interpretations of psychological data above theological data on issues beyond the grave.[140] A monistic hypothesis oversimplifies the qualitative differences between body and soul. In all the evidence from actual things that we call one, even as small as an atom, we find diversity in the unity. We illustrated this in relation to the oneness of God and the Trinitarian distinctions. Concerning humanness, an undifferentiated sameness or a mere epiphenomenalism fails to do justice to the Bible's teaching on the distinctness of the inner from the outer person.[141]

Is the Intermediate State Remedial (Purgatorial)?

After death can those who "died truly penitent in the love of God before satisfying for their sins through worthy fruits of penance" realize final cleansing in purgatory?[142] The Roman Church has maintained that it is not enough to feel sorry for one's sins, for that only removes their *guilt*. To make satisfaction for sins the forgiven must still pay a *penalty* for their sins. Sins violate the church as well as God, and so the church is involved in the process of reconciliation. The indulgences of the Roman Church were intended to provide remission of a punishment in Purgatory still due for sins already forgiven.[143]

Purgatory is not taught in Scripture. The Catholic theologian McBrien admits that "there is, for all practical purposes, no (clear) biblical basis for the doctrine of purgatory."[144] That is understandable since Christ's atonement completely satisfies the requirements of divine righteousness. Purgatorial works cannot add to the completed atonement of the one Mediator (1 Tim. 2:5). Purchases of indulgences from the hierarchy or prayers for dead loved ones can do no more for them than Christ has already done. With Luther we find indulgences contradictory to the teaching of justification by grace through faith alone.

"Another way of putting it is to say purgatory is required, but it is past. . . . There is no need for purgatory in the future because purgatory is past. . . . The place was Calvary, where Jesus died for our sins. He became our purgatory and took our hell."[145] As Scripture says, "After he had provided purification for sins, he sat down at the right hand of the Majesty in heaven" (Heb. 1:3). Christ did not rest until he had "brought about the purgation of sins" (NEB). Our just standing and purgation are completed by the one act of Christ, who "entered the Most Holy Place once for all by his own blood" (Heb. 9:12). By "one sacrifice he has made perfect forever those who are being made holy" (Heb. 10:14).

Forensic justification frees from sin's penalties as well as its guilt. To realize these benefits, Luther concluded, we need to relinquish all forms of self-reliance, including indulgences and prayers for the dead. Purgatory is inconsistent with the fact that on the cross Christ bore the penalty of our ancestors' sins as well as the guilt. On that basis Luther also called into question the appropriateness of prayers for the dead.

Roman Catholic and similar views fail sufficiently to distinguish the *declaration of justification* from the *process of sanctification*. McBrien thinks that "purgatory is best understood as a process by which we are purged of our residual selfishness so that we can really become one with the God who is totally oriented to others, i.e., the self-giving God." He adds, "A calculating, egocentric approach to Christian destiny, where an individual is concerned primarily with the accumulation of spiritual credits, is so antithetical to sound theological and doctrinal principles that the disappearance of that sort of interest in indulgences can only be welcomed."[146] Admittedly the process of sanctification is not completed in this life, but justification is.

Views of postmortem purgation tend to contradict the Bible's teaching on the intermediate state of Christians. Given the doctrine of purgatory, the intermediate state is not very different from the present, for it continues existing moral and spiritual battles. Instead, Scripture pictures the intermediate state of believers as one of rest from struggle with temptation and of joy in the presence of Christ. The doctrine of purgatory suggests that after death salvation is by works. Views of a purgation after death are not viable, for they make the completion of sanctification a matter of human works to enter the kingdom of God rather than acts of praise impelled by love for being in the kingdom.

Are There Opportunities for Salvation After Death?

Clark Pinnock advocates the possibility of a postmortem encounter with the Savior prior to meeting Christ as Judge for those who encountered neither Jesus nor his message during their lifetime. Admittedly the biblical evidence for an opportunity to accept Christ after death is not abundant, but "its scantiness is relativized by the strength of the theological argument for it."[147] Regarding the one passage alleged, 2 Peter 3:19–20, we concluded elsewhere (vol. 2, p. 397) that the people in prison to whom Christ ministered were not the dead but the living of Noah's day waiting for the flood.

What shall we say about Pinnock's arguments for postmortem opportunities to be saved? God does not cease to be gracious to sinners, Pinnock reasons, just because they are no longer living. "Surely the God who loves the world will *always* love it, even loving those who reject the gift of his love."[148] But whereas God's holy love in its varied aspects is eternal, opportunities during the day of grace in history do have an end (Rev. 4–19). The Scriptures emphasize the urgency of decisions in this life: "Now is the time of God's favor, now is the day of salvation" (1 Cor. 6:2). Jesus' account of the rich man and Lazarus portrayed one's future state as unalterable, based on one's commitment in the present life.

Pinnock argues that those thought to be seeking God in this life will continue to do so in the next. But do these people seek to bow to the Lord of all or to their own inner divinity? Granting human depravity, none seek the sovereign God of the Bible with all their hearts (Rom. 3:11–12). We agree with Pinnock that "no one who really wants it will be deprived of salvation."[149] Any holistically depraved people, however, who truly want salvation will give evidence of the special work of the Holy Spirit in their lives. The Spirit will lead Christ's witnesses to seeking sinners in this life. Pinnock adds that "God's enemies and not the inculpably ignorant are rejected."[150] But does not Romans 1:20 teach that no accountable persons are inexcusable or inculpable?

Is the Final Judgment a Myth?

The final judgment is not a mythical way of speaking about an impersonal law of *karma*. We can agree that moral actions have moral consequences in this life. The hypothesis that justice is always inevitably and automatically done, however, does not fit the facts of history or personal experience. And if an absolute, impersonal law does not take care of those who suffer unjustly in this life, we have no reason to think it will in the next life (or a series of lives). If moral values are to be meaningful, all of us must be ultimately accountable to the personal Administrator of justice.

Dodd's realized eschatology regards a final judgment by a personal God "no more than a *fiction* designed to express the reality of teleology in history."[151] But God's eschatological judgment is not fully realized in the present life. Unconverted criminal types often prosper, and the converted often suffer. Bultmann thought a final judgment for all by a personal God a *myth*. Within his existentialist assumptions, he found no more information in the Bible about last things than he did about first things (Creation). Bultmann thought that judgment is nothing more than a present activity of sundering faith from unfaith, the spiritually sighted from the blind. His attempts to demythologize a final event of judgment for all do not account adequately for the biblical data in context. Such a subjective existentialist interpretation, as Morris says, "gives us a good deal of information about the ideas of Bultmann but little about the New Testament teaching."[152]

In the matter of criminal behavior we admit that there are standards of right and wrong and that people should be penalized for evil actions. But divine judgment is far from complete in the present age. So "man is destined to die once, and after that to face judgment" (Heb. 9:27). Judgment is as inevitable as death. Carnell pointed out that "analytically included in culpability is the obligation to answer a lawfully established tribunal."[153] "Whenever we judge others, therefore, we reveal our belief in the administrator of justice, for apart from the obligation to appear before a duly authorized tribunal, there is no meaning to culpability."[154] To be meaningful, laws must be enforced. Unless there is a personal, transcendent, and all-knowing Administrator of justice to whom we are finally accountable, all our concerns for justice, truth, and mercy are of no lasting significance. Given the reality of the scriptural God who is holy and loving, justice eventually will be done. Our final status will be assessed by the righteous, transcendent Judge.

Is Retributive Justice Fair?

In *rectoral justice* God instituted righteous laws with their penalties and rewards for humans. Injustice is heinous because it is ultimately against the character of the infinite Creator-Redeemer who is just in himself and in his judgments. "The LORD is a God of retribution; he will repay in full" (Jer. 51:56). Retributive penalties are a direct result of moral evil (Ezek. 7:3, 8, 27; Rom. 2:12; Jude 14–15) and so are deserved (Ps. 94:2; Ezek. 18:30–31) and just (Ezek. 33:20; 1 Peter 2:23). According to what they have done, the Lord will repay wrath to his enemies and retribution to his foes (Isa. 59:18). Jesus' view of retribution is similar to that of the prophets. He said, "Will not God bring about justice for his chosen ones. . . . I tell you, he will see that they get justice, and quickly" (Luke 18:7–8).

The dispensing of rewards for obedience is called *distributive justice;* it seems to raise few objections and needs no defense. The meting out of penalties for disobedience is known as *retributive*

485

justice, and it raises many protests. The supreme Judge justifiably punishes those who have responsibly violated the moral principles necessary to life on earth and who have rejected the Gospel—the way to eternal life. A major purpose of retributive penalties is to rescue the oppressed from the destructiveness of injustice.[155] God's determination of just penalties is not capricious. Penalties for injustice and the spurning of divine love are necessary to vindicate the King's righteousness, defend the moral order of his kingdom, and highlight the preciousness of the Servant who died to make us just. If God did not vindicate unjust acts in his kingdom, its values would be destroyed. But God's administration of retributive justice is no mere expression of personal spitefulness or revenge. Rather, it is the response of positive holiness reasserting the moral order of the world against all that is evil.[156]

The Scriptures forbid private vengeance for offenses against oneself but encourage the judicial vindication of others unjustly oppressed. "By such careful distinctions Christianity effectively eschews all personal vengeance, without sentimentally destroying the moral basis of social order."[157] When the best human efforts to uphold justice fall short of the ideal, it becomes necessary for *God to administer justice without respect of persons.* God's ultimate purpose is to sustain the integrity of his people against the powers of the demonic kingdom. Those who support the heinous kingdom of darkness eventually will face the consequences.

This temporal age of divine patience vis-à-vis evil people will come to an abrupt end. God's Spirit will not always strive with the rebellious. Only retributive justice remains for the devotees of the last Antichrist. How can retribution be fair if it is *everlasting*? God respects the everlastingness of the human spirit and its self-determination though fallen.

Given the creation of spirits with a contingent immortality and freedom, the possibility of rebellion with its consequences is endless. "Once admit what seems evident, that the created will has the power of rebelling against its Maker," wrote Oxenham, "and there is absolutely no ground or reason for assuming that the rebellion, and therefore the chastisement, must sooner or later necessarily have an end."[158] If self-determined persons will not repent amidst all the opportunities of this life, why should we expect them to do so in the next life? "This freedom involves in itself the terrible possibility of an endless resistance, which equally endlessly punishes itself."[159]

To comprehend punishments that are eternal, one must recall the enormity of sin. Sin ultimately is against God, who is infinite. Does sin against the infinite Lord of all deserve only a finite vindication? If anything less than eternal punishment is sin's just penalty, why was an infinite sacrifice needed to deliver from that punishment? Did Jesus shed his blood to liberate us from merely temporal mischief? Those who endlessly neglect or reject the Source of eternal life will suffer endlessly. After life's opportunities have passed, the purpose of punishment will not be reformation or rehabilitation. The lake of fire was prepared for undying angels who followed Satan in rebelling against the divine kingdom. Since the lake of fire was prepared for creatures with derived immortality—the devil and his angels (Matt. 25:41), its eternality cannot be limited to the *result* but also includes its *extent*. No one will endure a greater degree of affliction than is deserved. But our gracious Lord repeatedly warned that the punishment is as certain and eternal as eternal life. "Why have we not one word from the lips of the Great Teacher to indicate the possibility, if not the certainty of escape or deliverance? If there was a door of hope, how unlike the Loving Lamb to conceal it!"[160]

Does God Eventually Annihilate the Wicked (Stott)?

As noted in the historical section, John Stott believes that hell is real and terrible but not everlasting. Rather than a conscious torment forever he believes there will be total annihilation of the being of the impenitent. Stott does not hold the hypothesis of conditional immortality in which no one survives death except those to whom God gives immortality by special grace. Everyone survives death and will be resurrected and judged, but the impenitent will be finally destroyed.[161] Emotionally Stott finds the concept of eternal punishment intolerable, but he admits that ultimately the issue is what Scripture teaches. Stott thinks that annihilationism best fits biblical terms such as "destruction." Jesus warned concerning the One who could destroy both body and soul in hell (Matt. 10:28). Stott takes this to mean extinction of being.[162] But we have seen that death means separation of soul from body or the self from God, not annihilation. Eternal destruction metaphorically means eternal separation from the Source of values.

In nature nothing is totally annihilated. Scientist Werner von Braun wrote, "Science has found that nothing can disappear without a trace. Nature does not know extinction. All it knows is transformation!"[163] For example, at death the body returns to dust. If God applies this fundamental principle to minute parts of the creation, does it not make sense that he applies it also to the masterpiece of his creation—the human soul? If nothing from our present bodies disappears without a trace, how much more of resurrected bodies and spirits made in God's image?

Stott admits that Christ spoke of eternal or unquenchable fire, but thinks it odd if what is thrown into it proves indestructible. But one wonders why the lake of fire continues after its inhabitants are thought to no longer exist. The worm will not die, Stott writes, at least until the work of destruction is done. Can worms ever finish the job on a resurrected body? Jesus said that they never die. Stott thinks that "what Jesus said [in Matthew 25:46] is that both life and the punishment would be eternal, but he did not in that passage define the nature of either. . . . Jesus is *contrasting* the two destinies: the more unlike they are, the better."[164] Indeed, there is a tremendous contrast between spiritual life and spiritual death, but a point of similarity remains. Although Jesus did not say much about their nature, he did say both had the same duration.

How does Stott interpret the torment by burning sulfur of the worshipers of the beast in the presence of the angels and the Lamb (Rev. 14:10)? He refers this torment to the moment of judgment not to the eternal state. He says that "the smoke of their torment rises for ever and ever" as a symbol of the completed burning (v. 11a).[165] But that interpretation does not fit the next sentence, that reads, "There is no rest day or night for those who worship the beast and his image, or for anyone who receives the mark of his name" (v. 11b). Does this not imply a perpetual rather than a momentary restlessness?

Justice, Stott argues, requires the penalty to be commensurate with the evil done. "Would there not be a serious disproportion between sins consciously committed in time and torment consciously experienced throughout eternity?" The answer depends on what is a just penalty for continuous sin committed against the infinite God. Stott hastens to add, "I do not minimize the gravity of sin as rebellion against God our Creator, . . . but I question whether 'eternal conscious torment' is compatible with the biblical revelation of divine justice, unless perhaps . . . the impenitence of the lost also continues throughout eternity."[166] Indeed, the impenitence continues throughout eternity, and so does its penalty.

Finally Stott avers that the eternal existence of the impenitent in hell would be hard to reconcile with Christ's drawing all men to himself (John 12:32), God's uniting all things to himself through Christ (Col. 1:20), and bringing every tongue to confess his lordship (Phil. 2:10–11)—so that in the end "God may be all in all" (1 Cor. 15:28). Although these passages are consistent with the final pacification of the cosmos when Satan is disarmed and judged, Stott concludes, "It would be easier to hold together the awful reality of hell and the universal reign of God if hell means destruction and the impenitent are no more."[167] But Stott never answers the question, Who finally exterminates the wicked? He sidesteps the issue by using the passive: they "are finally destroyed." The wicked do not eradicate themselves. Then who does? It cannot be the Devil, for he is bound and cast into the lake of fire forever. Apparently, Stott finds it more tolerable that God annihilates his rebellious image-bearers than to respect their freedom and allow them to endure the consequences. Annihilationists are left with the unthinkable proposal that the *author* of life becomes its *exterminator*. He who cannot be tempted to sin becomes the blameworthy cause of an incredible holocaust.

David Wells effectively responded to Pinnock's earlier case for annihilationism:

> Pinnock has tried to revive the old argument that the judgment of God raises moral problems. I assert the opposite: God's judgment settles all moral problems. Specifically, it addresses the question as to how God can still be powerful and just if there is evil in the world. It sees this present life as an interim period at the end of which God will publicly vindicate his character. This vindication (which cannot be "vindictive" as Pinnock claims) will set truth forever on the throne and error forever on the scaffold. This will be the moment of final liberation and the cause of endless praise (Rev. 6:10; 11:17–19; 19:1–8).[168]

Will God Eventually Save All People (Universalism)?

It seems axiomatic to universalists that none will be annihilated, because all will be won and hell emptied by the magnetism of divine love: "As in Adam all die, so in Christ all will be made alive" (1 Cor. 15:22). Universalism, Barth and others argue, is necessary to the eschatological triumph of God's grace. It is the outcome of omnipotent love. Proponents recall that God is greater than his evil creatures. "God is the Perfect Pedagogue and ultimately He has no problem children," said Nels Ferré. He added, "Heaven will never be fully heaven until it has emptied hell."[169]

This attractive theory has elements of truth. God is gracious, loving, and great—far greater than his rebellious creatures. God will triumph over the kingdoms of darkness finally. But no evidence indicates the conversion of Satan, Antichrist, or their devotees. Unfortunately universalists become unrealistic and lose what they seek to protect. When humanitarians dismissed hell, they soon lost heaven. Not long after universalists deleted Satan, they thought God "died." After relativists removed the absolute distinction between good and evil, anything became acceptable. Now that every action is good, good has lost its meaning. If we are to maintain a realistic worldview, we cannot dismiss the eternal difference between good and evil.

Universalism, appealing as it is, is not only naïvely unrealistic; it is also blatantly unscriptural in other ways. The powerful triumph of mercy, grace, and love taught in Scripture recognizes the reality of permanent disbelief and disobedience. A God deserving of worship cannot issue an arbitrary amnesty for humanitarians or pantheists who persist in worshiping and serving themselves more than their personal Creator. Even an omnipotent God who remains honest and just cannot call unforgiven, self-centered people good.

Brunner argued in *Eternal Hope* that universalism is necessary to the eschatological triumph of God. But abandonment of principle and integrity is no triumph over the insolent self-determination of creatures who refuse the just and loving provisions of the Gospel. The biblically described eschatological triumph comes when Satan and his tormented followers are finally disarmed and put in their chosen place, removed from all contact with God's creation. The one just ground on which omnipotent love can justify sinners is Christ's atonement. Without that, Omnipotence itself cannot transfer unrepentant murderers and child abusers to the place of perfect righteousness.

What About "Biblical Universalism" (Punt)?

Both Arminian and Calvinist evangelicals consider all persons outside of Christ under condemnation except those the Bible expressly declares will be saved. In contrast, Neal Punt presupposes that "all persons are elect in Christ . . . except those who the Bible expressly declares will be finally lost."[170]

With several of Punt's tenets we are in *agreement*. There is a vast difference in being under the sentence of death and the actual implementation of it. No one suffers eternally for Adam's sin alone. The basis for the just execution of punishment is always a responsible refusal to follow divine revelation, general or special.[171] Punt well says that no one rejected on the Judgment Day can attribute his or her damnation to our union with Adam in original sin, to the insufficiency of Christ's atonement, or to the fact that the Gospel was never presented. The condemnation of everyone who is lost will be wholly attributable to himself or herself for having disregarded God's revealed will.[172] Furthermore, the election of the saved and lost is not logically symmetrical since the one is based on grace and the other on works.[173]

But several *differences* with Punt's "biblical universalism" must be noted. Although he correctly regards the Atonement a sufficient provision for all, he insufficiently reckons with the reality of depravity and the universal inability of non-Christians to respond to the Gospel. At times Punt seems to regard the Atonement effective universally apart from a response; at other times he thinks it requires a response but admits that not all are actually delivered from condemnation.

Punt's fundamental assumption—that all are elect except . . . —does not fit scriptural data (Rom. 1–3). "It is the universal assumption of the New Testament," said Ramm, "that men without Christ and without God are lost and need a Saviour."[174] Scripture refers to the unconditional determination of God to save many so that Christ's atoning sacrifice is not in vain. None of the elect are like sheep doomed to destruction, but all the justified will be glorified. All that the Father has given to Christ will be saved (John 10:17). If all were elect as Punt assumes, all would be justified and glorified.

What about the universalistic texts to which Punt and others of like mind appeal? Many of those passages teach (1) God's universal desire that none should perish, not a universal plan to save every responsible person in sin. (2) Some universal texts also teach God's universal purpose through the Atonement to provide the blessings of common grace for all. (3) Others teach the global sufficiency of Christ's atonement for all varieties of Gentiles as well as Jews, but not the salvation of Satan, the many antichrists, or their followers. (4) Some of the universalistic passages predict a final, universal pacification that disarms the forces of evil but does not lead them to Christ (Col. 2:15). At the eschatological victory every one will bow to Christ as Judge, both the saved and the lost (Phil. 2:9). The final "fulfillment—to bring all things in heaven and on earth together under one head, even Christ" (Eph. 1:10) teaches not the salvation of all people but God's final, universal victory in Christ when all creation acclaims him Lord. As a result of this universal pacification, Satan and his devotees no longer will engage in spiritual warfare against the kingdom of God: "For he must reign until he has put all his enemies under his feet" (1 Cor. 15:25).

(5) Many texts used by universalists support the fact that Christ is the Savior of the world, i.e., of all kinds of Gentiles irrespective of their ethnic backgrounds (John 3:16; 4:42; 6:33, 17:21; 1 John 4:14). But these texts do not teach Christ's actual saving of every last individual, nor do they contradict his doctrine of eternal punishment. Christ the divine reconciler was also the divine divider. Jesus was like a sword set for the fall as well as the rising of many in Israel (Luke 2:34; cf. Matt. 10:34; 2 Cor. 2:15–16). Although the salvation he provided is sufficient for all, its realization is limited to those who respond in repentance and faith. "Whoever rejects the Son will not see life, for God's wrath remains on him" (John 3:36). Even some who claim to follow Jesus have not received him.

"Not everyone who says to me, 'Lord, Lord,' will enter the kingdom of heaven . . . . I will tell them plainly, 'I never knew you. Away from me, you evildoers!'" (Matt. 7:21, 23). "Then they will go away to eternal punishment, but the righteous to eternal life" (Matt. 25:46). Dogmatic universalists either reject such passages on endless punishment or reinterpret them in ways that do not fit the Bible's historical, cultural context. The apparently universalistic passages must be interpreted in a manner consistent with Christ's teaching on eternal punishment.

Is Reincarnation Compatible With Christianity?

Geddes MacGregor, formerly of the University of Southern California, thinks that reincarnation takes care of injustices and frees us from the arbitrariness of judgment and the dangers of hell. MacGregor abuses language by alleging that the early Christians' hope of resurrection "is itself a *kind* of reincarnationism"[175] and by calling each reincarnation a "resurrection."[176] He is right in saying that our dying souls still have many impurities, but not that the karmic principle makes reincarnationist doctrine morally acceptable. His is plainly a salvation-by-works religion. "I alone am responsible for my condition. I alone can redeem myself from it."[177] Reincarnation is very much a moral-law concept, so he reasons that it corresponds with the moral principles that the Christian Way has always sought to encompass. More than works righteousness, he fears a lazy-minded and immoral antinomianism in the church. One finds in MacGregor's writings on this subject no understanding of justification by faith, regeneration, or other biblical doctrines.

Christians agree with reincarnationists that life has a moral purpose and death does not end human existence.

Still a number of *theological problems* remain. In Christianity the inherent value of a single life is inestimable, but from the perspective of millions of reincarnations "one brief lifetime is seen not as the beginning of our existence but as nothing more than a flash in time."[178] Individuals are of little more value than an ant or cow.[179] In contrast Christians maintain that individual human beings differ in kind from animals, plants, and rocks. God made mankind distinctively *in his image*. The Lord Jesus Christ placed more value on one human life than on the whole world of matter, plants, and animals (Mark 8:36).

According to reincarnationists, we live in this present physical world trillions of times; according to Christianity unique persons live just once on earth. MacGregor has further to go spiritually than he can hope to attain in this life, so he interprets purgatory reincarnationally: "The purificatory process takes a far longer time than we are likely to imagine. . . . It may have already taken trillions of lives at various evolutionary stages to reach my present situation and trillions more may lie ahead of me."[180] But according to the Bible, "man is destined to die once, and after that to face judgment" (Heb. 9:27). The "once" in this passage cannot mean one death for each incarnation, for in the previous verse and the following one (vv. 26, 28) the same term affirms that Jesus died "once for all."

Reincarnationists also teach that death is illusory. In April 1977 a reincarnationist in lotus position burned himself to death in a cave near Boulder, Colorado. He left a note that read, "I am getting on with it. The time is ripe and the proof of the pudding is in the tasting. . . . Salvation is not to be won through the grace and will of some supreme deity, guru, or savior, but in virtue of self-directed effort." One of his friends told *Denver Post* reporters, "I knew what he was gonna do, and I wasn't about to talk him out of it. I don't feel that what he did was incongruent with life. He didn't die as far as I'm concerned."[181]

In reincarnationism the ultimate tribunal is the impersonal moral law of karma, whereas in Christianity the final Judge is Jesus Christ. "If righteousness could be gained through the law, Christ died for nothing!" (Gal. 2:21). Perfect righteousness is a gift of grace received by faith. Reincarnationists, like Jews in Paul's day, may be sincere and zealous, but they are ignorant of the righteousness that comes from God.

Reincarnationism also suffers from several *philosophical difficulties*. The concept of reincarnation involves an inherent contradiction. If there is one world soul (since all is one or nondual), individual souls cannot be distinct in any number of reincarnations. But the impression is given that one's personal identity goes through millions of reincarnations. One's identity cannot be a bodily identity either, for the body completely changes. Nor can one's self be identified with memory, for that is lost in most cases and undemonstrable in all cases.[182]

The hypothesis of reincarnation is unacceptable because it *lacks adequate supporting evidence*. Alleged memories of past incarnations are inconclusive. Hick estimates that "perhaps some 99.9% have no memory of any such previous lives."[183] When people claim to recall previous existences several other explanations need to be tested. *Memories* of the present life may be mistaken for those of a previous life. Any recollection of stories heard in childhood, books read in the past, or purely imaginary episodes can be mistaken for past life experiences, as seen in *The Search for Bridey Murphy*.[184] The author, a skilled hypnotist "regressed" a middle-aged American subject, Virginia Tighe, to her "last incarnation" in which she claimed to be a girl named Bridey Murphy. Murphy was born in Ireland in 1798, lived there her whole life, and died in Belfast at the age of sixty-four. The names and details allegedly associated with that life could not be confirmed by the efforts of researchers. A second group of investigators found several parallels between Mrs. Tighe's actual American childhood and her Bridey Murphy accounts. When Tighe was four her parents were separated, and she went to live with her aunt. Across the street from her aunt lived an Irish woman named Mrs. Anthony Corkel, whose maiden name was none other than Bridey Murphy. The facts Tighe attributed to a past incarnation were forgotten episodes heard in her present life, which she produced under hypnosis.[185] Hypnotic talk about past lives may be the product of research, projection, imagination, fantasy, and suggestions by a hypnotist. If any reincarnationist's detailed past recall or future knowledge cannot be explained naturally, it may come from *demonic deception*. Instances of the latter have been documented.[186]

Devotees claim that reincarnation accounts for the inequalities of life. But the proposed explanation never comes to light. Consequences in the present life are explained by reference to another before that, and another before that, in infinite regress. The answer has not been presented but only postponed to infinity. Shirley MacLaine appeals to a long list of distinguished people who have believed in repeated lives.[187] But many more distinguished authorities have held that one life on earth determines a person's eternal destiny. The numbers of famous adherents cannot establish the truth one way or the other.

What can Christians say to reincarnationists they encounter, as in an airport? In India beggars think they are doing people a service by their contributions, for in this way those who give earn good karma. The Christian may say, "Thanks for wanting to help me earn good karma [by purchasing your magazine or making a contribution]. Do you know that I have perfect karma? I received Christ's perfect righteousness by faith [Rom. 3:21–22]. And you can have Christ's perfect karma today. You do not have to merit it through millions of lives but simply trust the perfect spiritual Master who died for your sins and rose again. Christ liberates from enslavement to legalistic efforts here and now. Simply repent of your attempts at good works, believe the Gospel, and trust Christ." Reincarnationists need to know that they can be loved and accepted just as they are in their present bodies. Introduce them to Jesus, said former missionary to India Robert Brow, and their ideas of reincarnation will be gone within a month.[188]

RELEVANCE FOR LIFE AND MINISTRY

Some people who think about what follows death become agnostic. W. R. Inge, the famed "Gloomy Dean" of St. Paul's Cathedral, at age 93 told a *London Daily Express* interviewer:

> I have tried to solve three problems: the problem of eternity, the problem of human personality and the problem of evil. I have failed. I have solved none of them, and I know no more now than when I started. And I believe no one ever will solve them . . . . I know as much about the after life as you—nothing. I don't even know that there is one—in the sense in which the church teaches it. I have no vision of "heaven" or a "welcoming God." I do not know what I shall find. I must wait and see.[189]

Dean Inge did not have long to wait; eight months later he died.

Karl Marx ridiculed those who become preoccupied with "pie in the sky bye and bye" while ignoring oppressed people here and now. But the greater danger at present is preoccupation with present injustices to the neglect of the quality of our lives after death. "If only for this life we have hope in Christ, we are to be pitied more than all men" (1 Cor. 15:19).

Face the Reality of Your Own Death

Although we prefer not to think about our own death, insurance agents remind us of our projected demise. Approximate estimates found the average life span of people in ancient Rome to be 22 years; in the Middle Ages, 35; a century ago in England and Wales, 41; in the United States in 1900, 49 and in 1945, 65.8.[190] Now life expectancy is much longer, but no one knows that he or she will attain the average. The brevity and uncertainty of life and the fear of death are existential realities that must be faced.

It is easier to envision someone else's body being buried than one's own. As difficult as it may be to imagine your spirit leaving your body at death, the failure to do so may be detrimental. A Menninger Foundation psychologist reported that "the effort to escape the facing of death may constitute a deep source of ill health."[191] Existentialists tell us that we have not learned to live well until we have realistically faced our own death.

The values of preparing for death have been appreciated in one family. A father of four boys was diagnosed with a malignancy on his arm. The cancerous growth was surgically removed, but an agonizing week passed before the report came back that there was no evidence of other malignancies. During that week the man considered his death an imminent possibility. So he cut hours from his two jobs to enjoy more time with his wife and four boys. His relationship with his wife and children as a result is deeper and more precious.

Christians need not despair as those who have no hope. We can face death with realistic confidence. Jesus died "so that by his death he might destroy him who holds the power of death—that is, the devil—and free those who all their lives were held in slavery by their fear of death" (Heb. 2:14–15). You can experience freedom from the fear of death today. With your past forgiven and your future assured, you are free to live fully in the present! You need not be the slave of any power or phobia, whether economic, political, religious, cultic, or familial. "Though outwardly we are wasting away, yet inwardly we are being renewed day by day" (2 Cor. 4:16). Wesley said of the early Methodists: "They die well!" The just not only live by faith; they die by faith.

This is not to suggest that you should be preoccupied with your death. Rather, having faced your own body in a casket realistically, give yourself to what you want most to achieve in the family, church, and world. Because Christ lives, death will not have the last word. Therefore, anticipate also your resurrection. Leave the mechanics of it with the Creator who raised Christ from the grave. But envision your own body's deliverance from the grave and its glorious presence with the Savior you love. Then for you death will be swallowed up in victory (v. 54) and will have lost its sting (1 Cor. 15:55–56).

Comfort the Sorrowing

Having overcome some of the deep emotions connected with our own death, we are better prepared to help others deal with theirs. Like Jesus, we weep with those who weep. In contrast, a Stoic consoling a father who had lost a son was permitted to groan outwardly provided he did not groan inwardly. "Here an essential distinction between the Stoic and Christian conceptions of life, and of the significance of the individual, is obvious. The Stoic doctrine of impersonal universal reason robs the whole dimension of human life of love."[192]

Visit the bereaved simply to *be there at the right time*. As I talked with a former student of some fifteen years before, he admitted he could not recall many of my lectures, but he had not forgotten the day I came to visit. He and his wife had lost their newborn child, and they needed someone to share their grief and try to explain what happens to an infant who dies. I assured them of Christ's love for children and that their infant had done none of the things for which people are justly punished. According to scriptural principles, punishment is always merited by morally accountable agents. Although inheriting from their parents a sinful nature and so under condemnation (Rom. 5:16, 18), a morally unaccountable child is not *punished* for the sins of another. A special application of Christ's atonement would free their infant from Adamic guilt and punishment. Would personal identity continue? Yes, as it did for Abraham, Moses, and Elijah. Although uninformed of many details of the afterlife, I assured the couple that their child's present experience with Christ is better by far. We read Scripture and prayed for the Comforter and Counselor to give them hope.

Minister to the Dying

One tends to avoid calls on the terminally ill in hospitals and hospices because of the emotional drain involved. Unresolved problems of the minister, physician, or family may lead them to evade discussions related to dying. So ministers may serve the family more than the patient. With death and grief near, loved ones may find it difficult to talk with the incurable about their deepest concerns. As a result, the person desiring to prepare for the unex-perienced future may feel forgotten in the hours of greatest need. At such times Christians must demonstrate that love is stronger than death. They must be there for the incurable in their hour of deepest need.

In God's providence one evening I "happened" to visit a colleague in a hospital who was losing his battle with lung cancer. The physician informed his wife and children that he was not expected to live through the night. His wife and children having asked me to stay, I grieved with them as their husband and father calmly drew his last breath. James Cummings, an outstanding missionary and seminary professor, peacefully went to be with Christ. A few minutes after that deeply moving experience I was asked to lead in prayer. The quotation of Romans 8:38–39 helped. Then, I expressed gratitude to God that Jim's suffering was over, that my friend was with Christ, and that God would care for his loved ones left behind. Several years later there remains a special bond with that family. More crucial than what was said was the timeliness of *being there* to help them bear their loss.

Where appropriate, it may be helpful to talk with the terminally ill and their loved ones about an *evangelical theology of death*. This includes the following points: (1) Our departure from this world is the portal into the presence of the Christ we love (Phil. 1:21–23). Death means the sleep of our body, but not the end of our conscious existence. (2) Christ died for us so that, whether we are awake or asleep, "we may live together with him" (1 Thess. 5:10). When dying, we may pray like Stephen, "Lord Jesus, receive my spirit" (Acts 7:59). (3) Since Christ already experienced our spiritual death, we may die physically but not spiritually. Eternal life with God begins here and now (John 3:16; 10:28; Rom. 6:23; 8:1). Therefore death can not separate us from Christ's love (Rom. 8:38–39). (4) Even physical death will not have the last word for, like Christ the victor over death, we will rise again (1 Cor. 15:42–44; Rev. 1:18; 20:4). (5) Whether young or old, Christians facing death have sufficient resources for comfort and hope (Pss. 23, 90, 91, 139; John 14:1–7; Rom. 5:1–5; 8:31–39; 1 Cor. 15:20–28, 42–44; 2 Cor. 4:16–5:10; 1 Peter 1:3–6).

Because of the rise of the occult in our day, the minister should emphasize that a Christian theology of death does not allow for communication with dead loved ones. We should rest in the fact that their destinies are with the Judge of all the earth who does right. Our desires for supernatural guidance from those on the other side are understandable, but they ought never lead to seeking out spirit-guides. The Bible invariably diagnoses the deceptive phenomena connected with divination as demonic. Any who consult mediums or channelers for knowledge of the future turn their backs on God and deny the sufficiency of his Word. God took Saul from the throne of Israel and put him to death for consulting with the witch of Endor. Well did the Reformation protest not only indulgences but also the magical practices of spiritualism.[193]

Prepare for Your Final Judgment

Just as through years of study you prepare for examinations in school and college, so through the years of your accountable life you need to prepare for your ultimate comprehensive examination by God concerning the spiritual and moral quality of your life on earth.

While preparing for that great assize, let no philosophers of evolutionary progress deceive you into thinking that the highest human good is found on earth. Heaven is the Christian's home, and your highest fulfillments will be experienced there. Devote yourself here and now to the joys of your future home. In the details of life honor the Son as you honor the Father (John 5:23). Accountability to Christ in eternity imparts significance to the smallest actions in time. Pragmatists usually define what "works" in the short term. They should also ask whether a given mode of conduct will "work" for eternity. Our choices and actions bear an import far beyond their temporal consequences. Given the coming end of the age and the coming judgment, "what kind of people ought you to be? You ought to live holy and godly lives as you look forward to the day of God" (2 Peter 3:11–12). "For we must all appear before the judgment seat of Christ, that each one may receive what is due him for the things done while in the body, whether good or bad" (2 Cor. 5:10). The outward evidences of what lies in the heart will be examined and judged for exactly what they are.

Judge yourself that you be not judged. God will not need to judge you in the future for those sins you deal with here and now. When we confess our evils, repent of them, and make restitution for them, we will not need to be judged for them (1 Cor. 11:31). But we bring judgment on ourselves when we do not keep our commitments to Christ with moral integrity (1 Tim. 5:12). We are vulnerable also if we rebel against divinely appointed authorities (Rom. 13:2). Self-examination, self-control, and self-judgment are fruits of the Spirit that can reduce the list of charges at the final judgment.

Keep a clear conscience. A guilty conscience can lead believers to evaluate their stewardship (1 John 3:19–21), but it ought not lead them to condemn themselves. If we trust Christ, we cannot come again under the curse of damnation. And with our limited knowledge of deeds and motives we ought not condemn others. "May the Lord judge between you and me" (Gen. 16:5) is a way of maintaining one's innocence, not calling down destruction on another. None of us is the final judge of other persons. Because Christ is the Judge and he alone has sufficient knowledge of motives and acts, the self-righteous should avoid condemning others to hell (Job 32:3; Luke 6:37; Rom. 8:34; 14:3). Quickness to judge may return like a boomerang (Job 15:6; Ps. 7:16; Luke 6:37). Of course, it is utter folly for presumptuous people to damn their wise and just Creator (Job 34:17; 40:8).

Compassionately help people in need. "Learn to do right! Seek justice, encourage the oppressed. Defend the cause of the fatherless, plead the case of the widow" (Isa. 1:17). Determining what is just is a matter for objective consideration by a Judge in a court, but its implementation for those mistreated is a matter of passionate concern. Judgment "may take its origin from a legal matrix, but it makes its home with qualities like lovingkindness, faithfulness, righteousness, mercy (or mercies), truth, and glory."[194]

Prepare for divine judgment by being a faithful steward of God's gifts and resources. Be assured that Christ will acknowledge your unheralded faithfulness in this life. The secret fasting and sacrificial giving to others will be recognized. "God is not unjust; he will not forget your work and the love you have shown him as you have helped his people and continue to help them" (Heb. 6:10). Justice will reward one who gives even a cup of cold water in Jesus' name (Matt. 10:42).

Do not fear condemnation while preparing for judgment. Believers have imputed to their accounts once for all Christ's perfect righteousness. Forever justified by grace, they cannot be sentenced to the lake of fire. "God's solid foundation stands firm, sealed with this inscription: 'The Lord knows those who are his' " (2 Tim. 2:19). "Who will bring any charge against those whom God has chosen? It is God who justifies. Who is he that condemns? Christ Jesus, who died—more than that, who was raised to life—is at the right hand of God and is also interceding for us" (Rom. 8:33–34). Fortify assurance by being reminded that your names are already written in the heavenly book of life (Luke 10:20; Rev. 21:27).

Anticipate rewards for faithfulness in discipleship. C. S. Lewis distinguished two kinds of rewards. One type has no natural connection to the things you do. Money is not the natural reward of love, so we call a person "mercenary" who marries for money. But marriage is the proper reward of one who truly loves, and one is not mercenary in desiring it. "The proper rewards are not simply tacked on to the activity for which they are given, but are the activity itself in consummation."[195] The natural reward of a general who leads troops well in battle is not money but victory. The natural reward for learning *koinē* Greek is enjoyment in reading the New Testament in the original language. The final rewards to be given believers by Christ are "no mere bribe, but the very consummation of their earthly discipleship."[196]

Think More of Your Neighbor's Destiny Than Your Own

In *The Weight of Glory*, C. S. Lewis advised that "it may be possible for each to think too much of his own potential glory hereafter; it is hardly possible for him to think too often or too deeply about that of his neighbor." This is so because of the exceeding worth of the human soul made in God's image.

Christians can hardly overestimate the value of one soul made in God's image. Lewis went on to say,

There are no *ordinary* people. You have never talked to a mere mortal.

Nations, cultures, arts, civilization—these are mortal, and their life is to ours as the life of a gnat. But it is immortals whom we joke with, work with, marry, snub, and exploit—immortal horrors or everlasting splendours. . . . Next to the Blessed Sacrament itself, your neighbor is the holiest object presented to your senses. If he is your Christian neighbor he is holy in almost the same way, for in him also Christ *vere latitat*—the glorifier and the glorified, Glory Himself, is truly hidden.[197]

The pain of thoughts of souls in eternal punishment is almost unbearable. If we are to weep with those who weep here and now, how much more should we weep with those who will be weeping and gnashing their teeth eternally. Like Jeremiah, we cry out, "Oh, that my head were a spring of water and my eyes a fountain of tears! I would weep day and night for the slain of my people" (Jer. 9:1). Jesus wept over the impenitent and unbelieving in Jerusalem, knowing the destruction that would come upon them (Luke 19:41–44). Moved like his Lord, Paul "with great sorrow and unceasing anguish in [his] heart" was willing to trade places in hell if that would help his Jewish kinfolk to know Christ (Rom. 9:1–4). His "heart's desire and prayer to God for the Israelites was that they may be saved" (10:1).

Paul had no less compassion for the Gentiles. For three years in Ephesus, he recalled, "I never stopped warning each of you night and day with tears" (Acts 20:31). John Stott said, "I long that we could in some small way stand in the tearful tradition of Jeremiah, Jesus and Paul. I want to see more tears among us. I think we need to repent of our nonchalance, our hard-heartedness."[198] With deep emotion we identify with Rodin's famous statue "The Thinker" sitting in mute awe as he watches lost souls entering hell. "Once upon a time, Roman Catholic missionaries traveled around the world risking their lives to win converts to Christianity. They were steadfast in the belief that they were rescuing souls from hell. Today, most American Catholics wouldn't walk around the block on such a mission." Why? The Rev. Paul Mankowski, a Harvard Jesuit, added that there can be only one explanation: "Many modern Catholics—including theologians and bishops—no longer believe that eternal damnation is a possibility. The modern church seems more interested in 'aiding human development' than in 'saving souls.' "[199] What is true of Catholics, unfortunately, is true of many Protestants. Apparently some evangelicals consider temporal social problems a deeper concern than people's eternal destiny.

Deliver People From the Illusion of Multiple Opportunities After Death

Demand truth in advertising concerning one of the most damaging notions to the Christian faith—that of a moral and spiritual evolution through 8,400,000 lives, as the Indian Vedic scriptures teach! God requires a Christian minister not only to teach truth but also to refute error (Titus 1:9).

What more effective untruth could Satan use to counter the value of a single life than to propose a series of millions or trillions of them? What more diabolical deception could be invented to dissipate the urgency of making a decision for Christ than the notion that we have countless other opportunities to get right with God? What better deception could be devised to dismiss the claims for the unique incarnation of God in Christ than to believe that God (Brahman) is incarnate in thousands of gurus and, in fact, in everyone? What better fabrication could the author of lies spin than to encourage people to please God by their own spiritual development apart from Christ? Do-it-yourself spiritual journeys could well be the Antichrist's propaganda to turn people from the completed work of our Lord. What more deceptive alternative could be contrived to counter entrance to God's kingdom than the claim of multiple new births? Christ said that all must be born again, *once for all,* by the Holy Spirit. Reincarnationists can no more give themselves another life than they can regenerate themselves. If naturalists and pantheists are to receive eternal life as the unmerited gift of God's Spirit, they must be helped to realize this truism:

Only one life, 'twill soon be past; only what's done for Christ will last.

Be a Faithful Evangelist to the Perishing

Theories of universalism and the dispensability of trusting Christ for salvation are tragically undermining evangelism and missions. The Scriptures never speak of unconverted people as being already saved. Jesus considered unbelievers to be lost (Luke 19:10) and perishing (John 3:16). And his followers must know this with the mind and emotions. Jesus cared enough for the lost to suffer the righteous wrath they deserved. According to early Christians taught by Christ and inspired by his Spirit, unbelievers were not implicit believers; they were "separate from Christ, excluded from citizenship in Israel and foreigners to the covenants of the promise, without hope and without God in the world" (Eph. 2:12).

Saints who cherish inspired Scripture as their standard of faith and practice will give liberally, pray fervently, and go with the Good News to reach the lost. The truth in universalism is that all kinds of people from every tribe and nation can and will be saved. The crucial causes of global evangelism, church planting, and family values must

not be neglected for lesser causes, however good. A generation that finds commitment to world Christianity difficult must be transformed by renewed commitment to Christ. Having received the infinite blessings of the Cross, we must do what we can to take the Good News to all who have not heard. We must be willing to sacrifice to obtain the necessary educational and ministerial credentials to minister the Gospel effectively in different cultures. Those who cannot do so will support those who can train for crosscultural missions and serve in a fruitful field.

Because of the serious implications of a right standing with God in this life, Christians ought to present the true way of salvation persuasively to as many as possible. As long as Christians have life and breath, they must give themselves to living and teaching the truth of the written Word exhibited by living Word. "If the message spoken by angels was binding, and every violation and disobedience received its just punishment, how shall we escape if we ignore such a great salvation?" (Heb. 2:1–3).

In *The Great Divorce,* C. S. Lewis reminds us that "There are only two kinds of people in the end: those who say to God, 'Thy will be done,' and those to whom God says, in the end, 'thy will be done.' "[200] Lewis also noted that heaven is more, rather than less, solid or real than the present life. But to those who do not love God heaven would be hell. What will revive compassionate prayer meetings for the lost and giving to missions? One of the most important factors will be a return to our Lord's teaching on endless punishment. It is only against the background of this, the worst possible news, that the Gospel of Christ stands out as the best possible News. The Great Commission and the spiritual condition of the lost should impel believers to minister to the unreached with holy passion.

498

DISCUSSION TOPICS

1. Where are the righteous and the unrighteous immediately following death? Is there adequate biblical evidence to support the view that the souls of the deceased "sleep" in the grave?
2. When do believers in Christ receive their resurrection bodies? What does Scripture teach about the nature of these new bodies?
3. Do the biblical words "destroy," "consume," "perish," etc., and the imagery of fire signify the annihilation of the unrighteous following the Last Judgment? If not, what do these biblical terms mean?
4. What answer would you give to a skeptic who posed the question, "How could a loving and merciful God consign any of his image-bearers to everlasting torment in hell?"
5. What was the lot of the Old Testament saints at death? Before the coming of Christ did their souls descend to some lower region, or, like New Testament believers, were they immediately elevated into the presence of the Lord?

See also the Review Questions and Ministry Projects on pages 501–2.

Review Questions
and Ministry Projects

REVIEW QUESTIONS

How to Relate and Apply Each Section Chapter by Chapter

1. *Briefly state the classical problem* the present chapter addresses and indicate reasons why genuine inquiry into it is important for your worldview and your existence personally and socially.

2. *Objectively summarize the influential answers* given to this problem in history as hypotheses to be tested. Be able to compare and contrast their real similarities and differences (not merely verbal similarities or differences).

3. *Highlight the primary biblical evidence* on which to decide among views—evidence found in the relevant teachings of the major divisions of Scripture—and decide for yourself which historical hypothesis (or synthesis of historical views) provides the most consistent and adequate account of the primary biblical data.

4. *Formulate in your own words your doctrinal conviction* in a logically consistent and adequate way, organizing your conclusions in ways you can explain clearly, support biblically, and communicate effectively to your spouse, children, friends, Bible class, or congregation.

5. *Defend your view* as you would to adherents of the alternative views, showing that the other views are logically less consistent and factually faced with more difficulties than your view in accounting for the givens, not only of special revelation but also of human experience in general.

6. *Explore the differences the viability of your conviction can make in your life.* Then test your understanding of the viability of your view by asking, "Can I live by it authentically (unhypocritically) in relation to God and to others in my family, church, vocation, neighborhood, city, nation, and world?"

MINISTRY PROJECTS

To Help Communicate This Doctrine in Christian Service

1. *Memorize one major verse or passage* that in its context teaches the heart of this doctrine and may serve as a text from which to preach, teach, or lead small-group studies on the topic. The memorized passages from each chapter will build a body of content useful also for meditation and reference in informal discussions.

2. *Formulate the major idea of the doctrine in one sentence* based on the passage memorized. This idea should be useful as the major thesis of either a lesson for a class (junior high to adult) or a message for a church service.

3. *State the specific purpose or goal of your doctrinal lesson or message.* Your purpose should be more than to give information. It should show why Christians need to accept this truth and live by it (unhypocritically). For teaching purposes, list indicators that would show to what extent class members have grasped the truth presented.

4. *Outline your message or lesson in complete sentences.* Indicate how you would support the truth of the doctrine's central ideas and its relevance to life and service. Incorporate elements from this chapter's historical, biblical systematic, apologetic, and practical sections selected according to the value they have for your audience.

5. *List applications of the doctrine* for communicating the difference this conviction makes in life (for sermons, lessons, small-group Bible studies, or family devotional Bible studies). Applications should make clear what the doctrine is, why one needs to know it, and how it will make differences in thinking. Then show how the difference in thought will lead to differences in values, priorities, attitudes, speech, and personal action. Consider also the possible significance of the doctrine for family, church, neighborhood, city, regional, and national actions.

6. *Start a file and begin collecting illustrations* of the central idea of this doctrine, the points in your outline, and your applications.

7. *Write out your own doctrinal statement on the subject in one paragraph* (half a page or less). To work toward a comprehensive doctrinal statement, collect your formulations based on a study of each chapter of *Integrative Theology.* As your own statement of Christian doctrine grows, you will find it personally strengthening and useful when you are called on for your beliefs in general and when you apply for service with churches, mission boards, and other Christian organizations. Any who seek ordination to Christian ministry will need a comprehensive doctrinal statement that covers the broad scope of theology.

Notes

Introduction

[1]For an account of Carnell's life and thought see Gordon R. Lewis, "Edward John Carnell," *Evangelical Theologians* (Grand Rapids: Baker, 1993).

Chapter 1

[1]Karl Barth, *CD*, II. 2.3.

[2]Pelagius, *On Nature and Grace*, 49.

[3]Benjamin B. Warfield, *The Plan of Salvation* (Grand Rapids: Eerdmans, 1942), 35.

[4]Walter Rauschenbusch, *A Theology for the Social Gospel* (New York: Macmillan, 1917), 172.

[5]Ibid., 140.

[6]William Adams Brown, *Christian Theology in Outline* (New York: Scribner, 1911), 320.

[7]Ibid., 321.

[8]Paul Van Buren, *The Secular Meaning of the Gospel Based on an Analysis of its Language* (New York: Macmillan, 1963).

[9]Thomas J. J. Altizer, *The Gospel of Christian Atheism* (Philadelphia: Westminster, 1966), 71. Altizer added, "It is the Christian God who has enslaved man to the alienation of 'being' and to the guilt of 'history.'" "Theology and the Death of God," in Thomas J. J. Altizer and William Hamilton, *Radical Theology and the Death of God* (Indianapolis: Bobbs-Merrill, 1966), 110.

[10]Altizer and Hamilton, *Radical Theology*, 145.

[11]Gustavo Gutièrrez, *A Theology of Liberation* (Maryknoll, New York: Orbis, 1973), 159. Gutièrrez identifies salvation, or the act of political liberation, as the "self-creation of man." Ibid., 155.

[12]Norman Pittenger, *Freed to Love: A Process Interpretation of Redemption* (Wilton, Connecticut: Morehouse-Barlow, 1987), 65.

[13]See, for example, Lewis S. Ford, *The Lure of God* (Philadelphia: Fortress, 1978), 93–95.

[14]David R. Griffin, *A Process Christology* (Philadelphia: Westminster, 1973).

[15]A. J. Maas, "Salvation," *The Catholic Encyclopedia*, 16 vols. (New York: Encyclopedia Press, 1913), 13:408.

[16]J. Pohle, "Predestination," ibid., 12:380.

[17]"The Constitution on the Sacred Liturgy," I.9, in Austin P. Flannery, *Documents of Vatican II* (Grand Rapids: Eerdmans, 1975), 6. "Apostolic Constitution on the Revision of Indulgences," I.2, in Flannery, *Documents*, 63; cf. II.5, p. 65.

[18]"Dogmatic Constitution on the Church," VIII.61, in Flannery, *Documents*, 418; cf. VIII.56, p. 416.

[19]"Declaration on the Relation of the Church to Non-Christian Religions," 1, in Flannery, *Documents*, 738.

[20]"Dogmatic Constitution on the Church," II.16, in Flannery, *Documents*, 367.

[21]Karl Rahner, "Church, Churches and Religions," *TI*, 10:36.

[22]Karl Rahner, *Foundations of the Christian Faith* (New York: Seabury, 1978), 143.

[23]Ross E. Price, "Elect, Election," in *BDT*, ed. Richard S. Taylor (Kansas City: Beacon Hill, 1983), 182.

[24]R. Larry Shelton, "Initial Salvation," in Charles W. Carter, ed., *A Contemporary Wesleyan Theology*, 2 vols. (Grand Rapids: Zondervan, 1983), 1:485.

[25]*The Works of James Arminius;* 3 vols. (Auburn and Buffalo: Derby, Miller and Orton, 1853), 1:247.

[26]Ibid., 1:248.

[27]"Predestination Calmly Considered," *The Works of John Wesley*, 14 vols. (Grand Rapids: Zondervan, 1958), 10:207.

[28]See Colin W. Williams, *John Wesley's Theology Today* (New York & Nashville: Abingdon, 1960), 46.

[29]Roger T. Forster and V. Paul Marston, *God's Strategy in Human History* (Wheaton: Tyndale House, 1974).

[30]Ibid., 145. Cf. Alan Richardson, *Introduction to the Theology of the New Testament* (New York: Harper & Row, 1958), 279: "If Christians are the 'elect,' it is because they are 'in Christ,' because they are baptized into the person of him who alone may with complete propriety be called the Elect of God."

[31]Forster and Marston, *God's Strategy*, 136.

[32]Ibid., 131.

[33]Robert Shank, *Elect in the Son* (Springfield, Missouri: Westcott, 1970).

[34]William W. Klein, *The New People of God: A Corporate View of Election* (Grand Rapids: Zondervan, 1990), 19.

[35]Ibid. Klein acknowledges that his explanation of election and calling is more like the Arminian than the Reformed tradition, 122.

[36]Ibid., 259.

[37]Ibid., 43.

[38]Ibid., 123.

[39]Ibid., 185.

[40]Ibid., 212.

[41]Karl Barth, "No!" in Emil Brunner, *Natural Theology* (London: Geoffrey Bles, 1946), 74, 83.

[42]Karl Barth, *CD*, II. 2, 3.

[43]Ibid., 94; cf. ibid., 54.

[44]Ibid., 117; cf. ibid., 167.

[45]Ibid., 306. Cf. ibid., 322: "In Jesus Christ his rejection, too, is rejected, and his election consummated."

[46]Wolfhart Pannenberg, *Human Nature, Election, and History* (Philadelphia: Westminster, 1977), 59.

[47]Ibid., 31; cf. 99.

[48]Ibid., 25.

[49]Thomas F. Torrance, *The Doctrine of Grace in the Apostolic Fathers* (Grand Rapids: Eerdmans, 1959), 136.

[50]Ibid.

[51]Tertullian, *On the Soul*, 39.4.

[52]Ambrose, *Exposition of the Gospel of Luke*, 7.27.

[53]Athanasius, *Discourse Against the Arians*, 2.75–76.

[54]Augustine, *Admonition and Grace*, 8.17. Cf. *The Spirit and the Letter*, 52: "Grace breaks the will whereby righteousness may be freely loved."

[55]Augustine, *Confessions*, 10.29.40.

[56]Augustine, *Against Julian*, 6.2.5. Cf. idem, *Predestination of the Saints*, 37: "God chose us in Christ before the foundation of the world, predestinating us to the adoption of children, not because we were going to be of ourselves holy and immaculate, but he chose and predestinated us that we might be so."

[57]Augustine, *On the Gospel of St. John*, 86.2.

[58]Ibid.

[59]Augustine, *On the Predestination of the Saints*, 32.

[60]John Calvin, *Institutes of the Christian Religion*, II.2.6. Calvin continued by polemicizing in this section against prevenient grace: "For I do not tarry over those fanatics who babble that grace is equally and indiscriminately distributed."

[61]Ibid., III.21.1.

[62]Ibid., III.21.5.

[63]John Calvin, *Commentaries on the Epistle of Paul to the Romans*, 345.

[64]Ibid., 317; cf. Calvin, *Institutes*, III.22.1–9.

[65]Calvin, *Institutes*, III.24.1; cf. ibid., III.24.3: "We are illumined according as God has chosen us."

[66]Charles Haddon Spurgeon, "God's Will and Man's Will, in *The Metropolitan Tabernacle Pulpit*, 63 vols. (Pasadena, Tex.: Pilgrim Publications, 1969–1980), 8:183; cf. ibid., 8:189: "Every blessing we receive hangs upon the absolute will and counsel of God, who gives these mercies even as he gives the gifts of the Spirit according as he wills."

[67]Spurgeon, "Election," in *Metropolitan Tabernacle Pulpit*, 1:318.

[68]Spurgeon, "God's Will and Man's Will," in *Metropolitan Tabernacle Pulpit*, 8:185.

[69]A. H. Strong, *Systematic Theology* (Valley Forge, Penn.: Judson, 1907), 779.

[70]Harry Buis, *Historic Protestantism and Predestination* (Philadelphia: Presbyterian & Reformed, 1958).

[71]R. C. Sproul, *Chosen by God* (Wheaton: Tyndale House, 1986).

[72]C. Samuel Storms, *Chosen for Life* (Grand Rapids: Baker, 1987).

[73]J. Barton Payne, *The Theology of the Older Testament* (Grand Rapids: Zondervan, 1962), 179. Here Payne also observed, "To 'know'

carries the idea of electing grace and is equivalent to saying 'choose' (cf. Exod. 1:8; 33:12; Hos. 13:5; Amos 3:2; Rom. 8:29)." E. D. Schmitz, "Knowledge," *NIDNTT*, 2:400, concluded that *yāda'* in this sense signifies "God's loving, electing knowledge of men." Schmitz added, "When God knows a person (Jer. 1:5) or a people (Amos 3:2) he chooses or elects him. This knowledge, understood as election, is gracious and loving, but it demands a personal response," *NIDNTT*, 385. D. A. Carson, *Divine Sovereignty and Human Responsibility* (Atlanta: John Knox, 1981), 4, concurs that *yāda'* here speaks the language of election. Jewett, *Election and Predestination*, 118, observed that the election of Abraham and Sarah (cf. Isa. 51:2) was not only corporate but also individual.

[74]See *The NIV Study Bible*, ed. Kenneth Barker (Grand Rapids: Zondervan, 1985), p. 1719, n. on Romans 9:13.

[75]Allen P. Ross, *Creation and Blessing* (Grand Rapids: Baker, 1988), 439.

[76]Martin Woudstra, *The Book of Joshua*, NICOT (Grand Rapids: Eerdmans, 1981), 345.

[77]Payne, *Theology of the Older Testament*, 185: "The wilderness wanderings went on to demonstrate that though many are called, only a remnant are really chosen."

[78]Lewis Smedes, *Union With Christ* (Grand Rapids: Eerdmans, 1983), 87.

[79]Cf. R. E. Clements, *Isaiah 1–39*, NCBC (Grand Rapids: Eerdmans, 1980), 139.

[80]Walter C. Kaiser, Jr., *Toward an Old Testament Theology* (Grand Rapids: Zondervan, 1978), 194.

[81]Charles L. Feinberg, *Jeremiah* (Grand Rapids: Zondervan, 1982), 27.

[82]Ralph L. Smith, *Micah–Malachi*, WBC (Waco, Tex.: Word, 1984), 305; cf. Joyce G. Baldwin, *Haggai, Zechariah, Malachi*, TOTC (London: Tyndale, 1972), 222–23. Th. C. Vriezen, *An Outline of Old Testament Theology* (Wageningen: Veenman & Zonen, 1960), 167, comments, "The Hebrew word for 'to hate' often means to scorn, or to rank something lower than something else, while 'to love' may mean to choose something and rank it higher than something else."

[83]John D. W. Watts, *Isaiah 1–33*, WBC (Waco, Tex.: Word, 1985), 153–54.

[84]Payne, *Theology of the Older Testament*, 186–87, argues: "Fundamentally, the saved status of this remnant group was due to their individual election . . . , for our Lord Himself spoke of them saying, 'Behold, I and the children whom Yahweh hath given Me' (Isa. 8:18)."

[85]As expressed by Jewett, *Election and Predestination*, 48: "It is especially in the NT that the individual aspect of election becomes prominent, and it is largely in terms of individual election that the doctrine has been discussed by theologians."

[86]Joseph Addison Alexander, *The Gospel According to Matthew* (Grand Rapids: Baker, reprint, 1980), 319; cf. H. Bietenhard, "Please," *NIDNTT*, 2:819.

[87]E. Earle Ellis, *The Gospel of Luke*, NCBC (Grand Rapids: Eerdmans, 1981), 221.

[88]R. E. Nixon, "Matthew," *NBCRev*, 843.

[89]F. F. Bruce, *The Acts of the Apostles* (Grand Rapids: Eerdmans, 1952), 275.

[90]Agreeing with this judgment are, among others, Donald Guthrie, *New Testament Theology* (Downers Grove: InterVarsity, 1981), 618, and J. I. Packer, "Determine," *NIDNTT*, 1:476.

[91]Leon Morris, *New Testament Theology* (Grand Rapids: Zondervan, 1986), 154.

[92]Lewis B. Smedes affirms concerning Christ's elective grace: "It is a gift. Paul ran from Christ; Christ pursued and overtook him. Paul resisted Christ; Christ disarmed him. Paul persecuted Christ; Christ converted him. Paul was an alien; Christ made him a member of the family." *All Things Made New* (Grand Rapids: Eerdmans, 1970), 119.

[93]Rudolf Bultmann, "Nekros," *TDNT*, 4:893; cf. Francis Foulkes, *The Epistle of Paul to the Ephesians*, TNTC (London: Inter-Varsity, 1963), 69: "Man's sinful condition is lifeless and motionless as far as any Godward activity is concerned."

[94]John Murray, *The Epistle to the Romans*, NICNT, 2 vols. (Grand Rapids: Eerdmans, 1959–65), 1:103. J. Goetzmann, "Reason," *NIDNTT*, 3:132, wrote, "Man in his deepest being rejects God. . . . Insight is always seen as a gift of God."

[95]P. Jacobs and H. Krienke, "Foreknowledge, Providence, Predestination," *NIDNTT*, 1:693. John Murray, *Romans*, 1:317, affirmed that *proginōskō* means to "forelove." According to *BAGD*, " *proginōskō* ," 710, the verb in Romans 8:29 means to "choose beforehand."

[96]C. E. B. Cranfield, *The Epistle to the Romans*, 2 vols., ICC (Edinburgh: T. & T. Clarke, 1975–79), 1:431.

[97]F. F. Bruce, *Romans*, TNTC (London: Tyndale, 1963), 176. Similarly, Fritz Rienecker and Cleon L. Rogers, Jr., *LKGNT*, 743:

"God's knowledge is much more than knowing what will happen in the future; it includes as it does in the language of the LXX (e.g., Num. 16:5; Judges 9:6; Amos 3:2), His effective choice." Cf. Jacobs and Krienke, "Foreknowledge," *NIDNTT*, 1:693: "In Paul the verb *proginōskō*, foreknow, choose beforehand, demonstrates the character of God's activity among men. It assumes the aspect of a personal relationship with a group of people which originates in God himself." Cf. R. Bultmann, "*Ginōskō*," *TDNT*, 1:715: "In the NT *proginōskō* is referred to God. His foreknowledge, however, is an election or foreordination of his people (Rom. 8:29; 11:2) or Christ (1 Peter 1:20)."

[98]Jacobs and Krienke, "Foreknowledge," *NIDNTT*, 1:695.

[99]Jewett, *Election and Predestination*, 47, underscores this important point. "The doctrine of election . . . has not only a corporate but also an individual aspect. The elect are not only all those together whom God has chosen to be the objects of his grace and favor, *but each one in particular*" (italics added).

[100]Rienecker and Rogers, *LKGNT*, 389; cf. L. Coenen, "Elect, Choose," *NIDNTT*, 1:539–42, who affirms that *eklegomai* means to "elect."

[101]Jewett, *Election and Predestination*, 48, again offers an instructive comment: "The individual quality in God's electing love is reflected in the use of the singular personal pronoun in Scripture. . . . To be elect is to be aware that God has fixed his love on *me*, called *me* by name, given *me* a new name (Rev. 2:17), and inscribed *my* name in the Book."

[102]B. F. Westcott, *Saint Paul's Epistle to the Ephesians* (Grand Rapids: Baker, reprint, 1979), 8; cf. G. Nordholt, "Elect, Choose," *NIDNTT*, 1:534; Rienecker and Rogers, *LKGNT*, 610.

[103]Yet Klein, *The New Chosen People*, 44, asserts that "election and salvation are separate issues."

[104]Jacobs and Krienke, "Foreknowledge," *NIDNTT*, 1:697, remark, "The word *prothesis*, 'plan,' serves to characterize God's activity in Christ as the fulfillment of an eternal purpose. It is one in which men do not have a say, either in time or in its intentions."

[105]D. Mueller, "Will, Purpose," *NIDNTT*, 3:1016, refers to "the free decision of [God's] will which is prepared to carry it out."

[106]Ibid.

[107]H. C. G. Moule, *Commentary on Ephesians, Cambridge Bible for Schools and Col-*

leges (Cambridge: Cambridge University Press, 1884), 48, defines *eudokia* as God's "deliberate, beneficent resolve."

[108]Jewett, *Election and Predestination*, 73.

[109]Berkouwer, *Divine Election*, 309–10. See also Jewett, *Election and Predestination*, 47.

[110]*Martin Luther's Basic Theological Writings*, ed. Timothy F. Lull (Minneapolis: Fortress, 1989), xiv.

[111]Cranfield, *Romans*, 2:480. Vriezen, *Outline of Old Testament Theology*, 167, comments: "The Hebrew word for 'to hate' often means to scorn, or to rank something lower than something else, while 'to love' may mean to choose something and rank it higher than something else."

[112]For further evidence in support of the view of individual election to salvation see John Piper, *The Justification of God: An Exegetical and Theological Study of Romans 9:1–23* (Grand Rapids: Baker, 1983), 34–54; Storms, *Chosen for Life*, 79–85; Matthew Black, *Romans*, NCBC (Grand Rapids: Eerdmans, 1981), 131–32; Murray, *Romans*, 2:13–21. F. F. Bruce, *Romans*, 188, affirmed, "Paul implies [that] when some receive the light and others do not, the divine election may be discerned, operating antecedently to the will or activity of those who are its objects."

[113]The verb *proetoimazō* (here in the aorist tense) signifies "God's work of preparation arising from his free elective choice." S. Sölle, "Ready, Prepare, Gird," *NIDNTT*, 3:118.

[114]Jewett, *Election and Predestination*, 43.

[115]Cranfield, *Romans*, 2:575.

[116]See ibid., 2:576; Sanday and Headlam, *Epistle to the Romans* (Edinburgh: T. & T. Clark, 1950), 339; F. Davidson and Ralph P. Martin, "Romans," *NBCRev*, 1039.

[117]Cranfield interprets "knowledge of God" in Romans 11:33 ("Oh, the depth of the riches of the wisdom and knowledge of God!") as implying "God's elective love and the loving concern and care which it implies." *Romans*, 2:589–90.

[118]Cranfield, *Romans*, 1:69. F. F. Bruce, *The Epistle to the Galatians*, NIGTC (Grand Rapids: Eerdmans, 1982), 80, agrees: "The verb *kaleō* is part of Paul's vocabulary for emphasizing the divine initiative in salvation."

[119]D. Mueller, "Will, Purpose," *NIDNTT*, 3:1018.

[120]See Jewett, *Election and Predestination*, 104. Donald Guthrie, *The Pastoral Epistles*, TNTC (London: Tyndale, 1957), 71, observes that 1 Timothy 2:3–4 "speaks of God's consis-

tent mercy towards all, without distinction of race, color, condition or status."

121See R. Tuente, "Lamb, Sheep," *NIDNTT*, 2:413.

122George R. Beasley-Murray, *John, WBC* (Waco, Tex.: Word, 1987), 298. Carson, *Divine Sovereignty and Human Responsibility*, 188, observes in John 17 a "heavy emphasis on soteriological predestination."

123Carson, *Divine Sovereignty and Human Responsibility*, 192.

124J. I. Packer, *Knowing God* (Downers Grove: InterVarsity, 1973), 37.

125F. F. Bruce, *The Gospel of John* (Grand Rapids: Eerdmans, 1983), 153, 156.

126Edward Gordon Selwyn, *The First Epistle of St. Peter* (Grand Rapids: Baker, reprint, 1981), 119. *BAGD*, 710, translates 1 Peter 1:2 as chosen "according to the predestination of God the Father."

127See Buis, *Historic Protestantism and Predestination*, 123.

128Jewett, *Election and Predestination*, 78. Jewett adds, "Few, indeed, are those who today speak as these Scriptures do, so far have we drifted from the biblical moorings of our faith regarding the doctrine of election," 25.

129Aristotle, *Rhetoric* II:7.

130See H. D. MacDonald, "Grace," *ZPEB*, 2:799.

131Ibid., 803.

132N. P. Williams, *The Grace of God* (London: Hodder and Stoughton, 1966), 120.

133Sverre Norborg, *Varieties of Christian Experience* (Minneapolis: Augsburg, 1937), 176.

134Emile Cailliet, *Journey Into Light* (Grand Rapids: Zondervan, 1968), 18.

135See Augustine's classic *Confessions*, which are available in many editions.

136C. S. Lewis, *Four Loves* (New York: Harcourt, Brace, 1960), 175.

137Williams, *Grace of God*, 40.

138See Bernard Ramm, *The Witness of the Spirit* (Grand Rapids: Eerdmans, 1959).

139See Millard J. Erickson, *Christian Theology* (Grand Rapids: Baker, 1985), 932–33.

140John F. Crosby, *From Religion to Grace* (Nashville: Abingdon, 1967), 48.

141C. S. Lewis, *The Silver Chair* (New York: Collier, 1970), 19.

142R. B. Kuiper, *God-Centered Evangelism* (Grand Rapids: Baker, 1963), 39.

143John Wesley, *The Works of John Wesley* (London: The Wesleyan Conference, 1872), 6:509; cited in Leo G. Cox, "Prevenient Grace—A Wesleyan View" *JETS* 12, 3 (Summer 1969): 146–47.

144George S. Hendry, *The Holy Spirit in Christian Theology* (Philadelphia: Westminster, 1956), 117.

145Ibid.

146Donald McGavran, "Foreword," to Peter Beyerhaus, *Missions: Which Way?* (Grand Rapids: Zondervan, 1971), 7.

147See Rebecca Manley Pippert, *Out of the Salt Shaker and into the World* (Downers Grove: InterVarsity, 1979).

148See Gordon R. Lewis, *Confronting the Cults* (Nutley, N.J.: Presbyterian and Reformed, 1966), chapter 1.

149Ramm, *Witness of the Spirit*, 119.

150Carter, ed., *A Contemporary Wesleyan Theology*, 2:633–62.

151Ibid., 1:63.

152L. Coenen, "Call," NIDNTT, 1:275.

153Spurgeon, "Election No Discouragement to Seeking Souls," *Metropolitan Pulpit*, 10:82.

154James D. G. Dunn, *Jesus and the Spirit* (Philadelphia: Westminster, 1975), 201–5.

155The Septuagint uses the same verb for God's response to the golden calf that Paul uses for the idolatry of the great city-state of ancient Greece.

156Ronald J. Sider, "Green Politics: Biblical or Buddhist?" *Spiritual Counterfeits Project Newsletter* (Fall 1985), 9.

157Ibid., 11.

158Ibid.

Chapter 2

1Richard P. McBrien, *Catholicism*, 2 vols. in 1 (Minneapolis: Winston, 1981), 752.

2Justin Martyr, *Apology*, I.66; cf. ibid., I.61.

3Irenaeus, *Fragments*, 34.

4Cyril of Jerusalem, *Prologue to the Lenten Lectures*, 16.

5Augustine, *On Forgiveness of Sins, and Baptism*,II.43.

6Augustine, *Sermon*, 213.8; cf. *Enchiridion*, 120, which refers to baptism as "the sacrament of rebirth."

7Augustine, *On the Gospel of St. John*, 80.3; cf. idem, *On Marriage and Concupiscence*, I.22.

[8]Augustine, *Enchiridion*, 42; cf. *Sermon*, 259.2: "We are born again in baptism so that we may receive the image of the Creator."

[9]Thomas Aquinas, *SCG*, IV.58.4.

[10]Ibid., 59.3.

[11]Thomas Aquinas, *ST*, Pt. III, q. 69, art. 7. Cf. *SCG*, IV.59.4.

[12]Thomas Aquinas, *ST*, Pt. III. q. 68, art. 2.

[13]Ibid., II.2, q. 2, arts. 6–7.

[14]See ibid., II.2, q. 2, art. 9.

[15]Second Vatican Council, *Dogmatic Constitution on the Church*, II.16.

[16]Gregory Baum, "Baptism," *Encyclopedia of Theology: The Concise Sacramentum Mundi*, ed. Karl Rahner (New York: Crossroad, 1982), 77.

[17]McBrien, *Catholicism*, 738.

[18]Ibid.

[19]Martin Luther, *LW*, 53:103.

[20]*What Luther Says*, compiled by Edward M. Plass (St. Louis: Concordia, 1959), 53. Luther added, "The fact is that just because they are unreasoning and foolish, they are better fitted to come to faith than the old and reasoning people whose way is always blocked by reason, which does not want to force its big head through the narrow door," ibid., 51.

[21] Cited by Heinrich Schmid, *The Doctrinal Theology of the Evangelical Lutheran Church* (Minneapolis: Augsburg, reprint, 1961), 463; cf. ibid., the statement of Martin Chemnitz (d. 1586): "Although we do not sufficiently understand . . . what the action and operation of the Holy Spirit is in infants who are baptized; yet that it exists and is effected through the Word of God, is certain. We call that action and operation of the Holy Spirit in infants faith, and assert that infants believe."

[22]Dietrich Bonhoeffer, *The Cost of Discipleship* (London: SCM, 1959), 206.

[23]*The Book of Common Prayer* (New York: Church Pension Fund, 1945), 276, 280.

[24]John Calvin, *Institutes of the Christian Religion*, IV.16.19.

[25]Ibid., IV.16.17–20. Calvin added that "the truth of baptism is in them (i.e., infants of Christian parents)." *Treatises Against the Anabaptists and Against the Libertines*, ed. B. W. Farley (Grand Rapids: Baker, 1982), 52.

[26]John Calvin, "Catechism of the Church of Geneva," in *Calvin: Theological Treatises*, LCC, Vol. XXII, trans. J. K. S. Reid (Philadelphia: Westminster, 1954), 133; cf. *Treatises Against the Anabaptists*, 49: "Baptism entails repentance, or the renewing of life, with the promise of the remission of our sins. Circumcision entails the same, no more, no less."

[27]Calvin, *Institutes*, IV.15.1.

[28]W. G. T. Shedd, *Dogmatic Theology*, 3 vols. (Grand Rapids: Zondervan, reprint, n.d.), 2:514.

[29]Ibid., 508.

[30]Ibid., 528.

[31]John Murray, *Redemption Accomplished and Applied* (Grand Rapids: Eerdmans, 1955), 106.

[32]Louis Berkhof, *Systematic Theology* (Grand Rapids: Eerdmans, 1941), 485.

[33]Richard S. Taylor, "Historical and Modern Significance of Wesleyan Theology," in *A Contemporary Wesleyan Theology*, 2 vols., ed. Charles W. Carter (Grand Rapids: Zondervan, 1983), 1:65.

[34]John Wesley, "Working Out Our Own Salvation," *The Works of John Wesley*, 14 vols. (Grand Rapids: Zondervan, 1958), 6:509.

[35]John Fletcher, "An Essay on Truth," *The Works of John Fletcher*, 4 vols. (Salem, Ohio: Schmul, 1974), 1:582.

[36]Ibid., 528.

[37]Charles Finney, *Finney's Systematic Theology*, ed. J. H. Fairchild (Minneapolis: Bethany, 1976), 310.

[38]Ibid., 224. Finney's assertion, ibid., 221, that "Regeneration . . . implies an entire change of moral character" supported his claim that the human subject is active in regeneration.

[39]Ibid., 235.

[40]S. J. McKenna, "Pelagians and Pelagianism," *NCE*, 11:58.

[41]Walter Rauschenbusch, *Walter Rauschenbusch: Selected Writings*, ed. Winthrop S. Hudson (New York: Paulist, 1984), 85.

[42]Ibid., 75.

[43]Norman Pittenger, *Freed to Love: A Process Interpretation of Redemption* (Wilton, Conn.: Morehouse-Barlow, 1987), 80.

[44]Ibid., 83.

[45]Gustavo Gutièrrez, *A Theology of Liberation* (Maryknoll: Orbis, 1973), 159.

[46]Leonardo Boff and Clodovis Boff, *Introducing Liberation Theology* (Maryknoll: Orbis, 1987), 93.

[47]James H. Cone, *A Black Theology of Liberation* (Maryknoll: Orbis, 1986), 48.

[48]Lewis S. Ford, *The Lure of God: A Biblical Background for Process Theism* (Philadelphia: Fortress, 1978), 64.

[49]Ibid., 86.

[50]Norman Pittenger, "Bernard E. Meland, Process Thought and the Significance of Christ," in *Process Theology,* ed. Ewert H. Cousins (New York: Newman, 1971), 215.

[51]Norman Pittenger, "The Divine Activity," *Encounter,* 47.3 (Summer 1986), 262.

[52]John B. Cobb, Jr. and David Ray Griffin, *Process Theology: An Introductory Exposition* (Philadelphia: Westminster, 1976), 31.

[53]Søren Kierkegaard, *Kierkegaard's Concluding Unscientific Postscript,* trans. David F. Swenson (Princeton: Princeton University Press, 1941), 539.

[54]Ibid., 540; cf. ibid., 188: Faith is "absurdity held fast in the passion of inwardness." Cf. Kierkegaard, *Fear and Trembling and the Sickness Unto Death,* trans. Walter Lowrie (Garden City, N.Y.: Doubleday, 1955), 10: Faith operates "by virtue of the absurd, not by virtue of human understanding, otherwise it is only practical wisdom, not faith."

[55]Paul Tillich, *Systematic Theology,* 3 vols. (Chicago: University of Chicago Press, 1951–63), 3:223; cf. "Faith is the concern about our existence in its ultimate 'whence' and 'whither.'" *Biblical Religion and the Search for Ultimate Identity* (Chicago: University of Chicago Press, 1955), 51.

[56]Tillich, *Systematic Theology,* 2:177; cf. ibid., 3:222: Regeneration is "the state of being grasped by the Spiritual Presence."

[57]Paul Tillich, *The Eternal Now* (New York: Scribner, 1963), 121.

[58]Kenneth Hamilton, *The System and the Gospel* (New York: Macmillan, 1963), 161.

[59]Rudolf Bultmann, *Kerygma and Myth,* ed. Hans Werner Bartsch (New York and Evanston: Harper & Row, 1961), 33.

[60]Rudolf Bultmann, *Theology of the New Testament,* 2 vols., trans. Kendrick Grobel (New York: Scribner, 1951–55), 2:76.

[61]Rudolf Bultmann, *Essays Philosophical and Theological,* trans. James C. G. Greig (London: SCM, n.d.), 48.

[62]George Whitefield, "The Nature and Necessity of Our Regeneration or New Birth in Christ Jesus," in Timothy L. Smith, *Whitefield and Wesley on the New Birth* (Grand Rapids: Zondervan, Francis Asbury, 1986), 67; cf. "There are numbers that have been baptized when grown up or when very young that are not regenerated by God's Spirit, who will all go to one place [i.e., hell]." "All Men's Place," in *20 Centuries of Great Preaching,* ed. Clyde E. Fant, Jr., and William M. Pinson, Jr.; 13 vols. (Waco, Tex.: Word, 1971), 3:119.

[63]Cited by Peter Toon, *Born Again: A Biblical and Theological Study of Regeneration* (Grand Rapids: Baker, 1987), 159.

[64]George Whitefield, "Neglect of Christ the Killing Sin," cited in Stuart C. Henry, *George Whitefield: Wayfaring Witness* (New York and Nashville: Abingdon, 1957), 108.

[65]Charles Haddon Spurgeon, "Baptismal Regeneration," in *The Metropolitan Tabernacle Pulpit,* 63 vols. (Pasadena, Tex.: Pilgrim Publications, 1969–80), 10:319; cf. ibid., 15:403. Spurgeon shared his own testimony in "The Necessity of Regeneration," ibid., 54:583–84. "I was sprinkled when I was a child, but I know that I was not thereby made a member of Christ, a child of God, and an inheritor of the kingdom of heaven. I know that nothing of the kind took place in me, but that, as soon as I could, I went into sin, and continued in it. I was not born again, I am sure, till I was about fifteen years of age, when the Lord brought salvation to my soul through the regenerating work of the Holy Spirit, and so I was enabled to trust in Jesus as my Savior."

[66]Spurgeon, "The Simplicity and Sublimity of Salvation," in *Metropolitan Tabernacle Pulpit,* 38:266.

[67]See Spurgeon's sermons, "Regeneration," in *Metropolitan Tabernacle Pulpit,* 3:185–92 and "The Believer a New Creature," in ibid., 15:397–408.

[68]Spurgeon, "The Believer a New Creature," in ibid., 15:401.

[69]Augustus H. Strong, *Systematic Theology* (Valley Forge, Penn.: Judson, 1907), 809.

[70]Millard J. Erickson, *Christian Theology,* 3 vols. (Grand Rapids: Baker, 1983–85), 3:933.

[71]H. D. McDonald, *Salvation* (Westchester, Ill.: Crossway, 1982).

[72]David F. Wells, *The Search for Salvation* (Downers Grove: InterVarsity, 1978).

[73]Toon, *Born Again.*

[74]Elmer B. Smick, *"Mûl," TWOT,* 1:495; cf. Peter E. Cousins, "Deuteronomy," *NLBC,* 293.

[75]R. K. Harrison, "Deuteronomy," *NBCRev,* 226.

[76]Victor P. Hamilton, *"Šûb," TWOT,* 2:909.

[77]A. R. S. Kennedy, *1 & 2 Samuel, Century Bible* (Edinburgh: Jack, 1904), 85.

[78]So J. A. Thompson observes, "In the case of Judah, deep-seated wickedness caused by centuries of schooling and repeated excursions into idolatry had made evil virtually a fixed feature of her life and behavior." *The Book of Jeremiah, NICOT* (Grand Rapids: Eerdmans, 1980), 374.

[79]Charles L. Feinberg, *Jeremiah: A Commentary* (Grand Rapids: Zondervan, 1982), 220.

[80]Ibid., 218.

[81]Hugh Anderson, *The Gospel of Mark, NCBC* (Grand Rapids: Eerdmans, 1981), 70.

[82]Cf. ibid., 71.

[83]James A. Brooks and Carlton L. Winbery, *Syntax of New Testament Greek* (Lanham, Md.: University Press of America, 1979), 55–56; cf. Robert Hanna, *A Grammatical Aid to the Greek New Testament* (Grand Rapids: Baker, 1983), 14.

[84]James H. Moulton, *A Grammar of New Testament Greek,* 4 vols. (Edinburgh: T. & T. Clark, 1949–76), 1:216.

[85]Everett F. Harrison, *Interpreting Acts: The Expanding Church* (Grand Rapids: Zondervan, 1986), 189.

[86]Ibid., 273. George Eldon Ladd added, "The references to the baptism of households (11:14; 16:15, 31; 18:8) may . . . well designate only those of mature age who confessed their faith in Christ. It is difficult to believe that such passages mean that the faith of the head of the household sufficed for his children any more than it did for his relatives and slaves." *A Theology of the New Testament* (Grand Rapids: Eerdmans, 1974), 350.

[87]"The calling upon the Lord effects the washing away of sin." Fritz Rienecker and Cleon L. Rogers, Jr., *LKGNT,* 324.

[88]Note especially the aorist passive indicative of *charizō,* to "give graciously." H. C. G. Moule commented as follows: "Faith in Christ is here incidentally viewed as a gift of Divine grace." *The Epistle to the Philippians* (Grand Rapids: Baker, reprint, 1981), 31.

[89]Second Thessalonians 2:13 reads: ". . . saved through the sanctifying work of the Spirit and through belief in the truth." I. Howard Marshall comments, "The mention of the divine action first may well imply that it is this which gives rise to faith." *1 and 2 Thessalonians, NCBC* (Grand Rapids: Eerdmans, 1983), 207.

[90]See Robert B. Hughes, *First Corinthians, Everyman's Bible Commentary* (Chicago: Moody, 1985), 78.

[91]Brooke Foss Westcott commented concerning the response of faith: "there is a true sense in which this 'work' is 'a work of God,' as inspired and sustained by him." *The Gospel According to St. John,* 2 vols. in 1 (Grand Rapids: Baker, reprint, 1980), 1:225.

[92]Ladd, *A Theology of the New Testament,* 216.

[93]O. Michel, "Faith," *NIDNTT,* 1:605. Similarly, R. V. G. Tasker, *The General Epistle of James, TNTC* (London: Tyndale, 1957), 68; cf. Colin Brown, "Righteousness, Justification," *NIDNTT,* 3:370.

[94]Augustine, *On the Predestination of the Saints,* 1.5.

[95]J. Gresham Machen, *What Is Christianity?* (Grand Rapids: Eerdmans, 1951), 277–78.

[96]Augustine, *On True Religion,* 24.45.

[97]For these criteria review vol. 1, chap. 1; or see Gordon R. Lewis "Three Sides to Every Story: Relating the Absolutes of General and Special Revelation to Relativists" ed. R. Laird Harris et al., *Interpretation and History* (Singapore: Christian Life Publishers, 1986), 201–10.

[98]William Fitch, *Enter into Life* (Grand Rapids: Eerdmans, 1961), 44.

[99]C. G. Kromminga, "Repentance," *EDT,* 936.

[100]Richard F. Lovelace, *Renewal as a Way of Life* (Downers Grove: InterVarsity, 1985), 18.

[101]H. A. Ironside, *Except Ye Repent* (New York: Loizeaux, 1937), 10.

[102]See W. D. Chamberlain, *The Meaning of Repentance* (Philadelphia: Westminster, 1943), 31.

[103]Abraham Kuyper, *The Work of the Holy Spirit* (Grand Rapids: Eerdmans, 1956), 349.

[104]Ernest White, *The Christian Life and the Unconscious* (New York: Harper & Row, 1955), 57.

[105]Christoph Barth, "Notes on 'Return' in the Old Testament," *The Ecumenical Review* 19, 3 (July 1967): 310–11.

[106]William Barclay, *Turning to God* (Philadelphia: Westminster, 1964), 20.

[107]Berkhof, *Systematic Theology,* 485; cf. 471.

[108]See W. E. Best, *Regeneration and Conversion* (Grand Rapids: Baker, 1975), 33.

[109]See Carl F. H. Henry, *Christian Personal Ethics* (Grand Rapids: Eerdmans, 1957), 389.

[110]Edgar Y. Mullins, *The Christian Religion in Its Doctrinal Expression* (Philadelphia: Judson, 1917), 380.

[111]Helmut Burkhardt, *The Biblical Doctrine of Regeneration*, trans. O. R. Johnston (Downers Grove, InterVarsity, 1978), 29.

[112]White, *Christian Life and the Unconscious*, 30.

[113]William James, *The Varieties of Religious Experience* (New York: Modern Library, 1902), 77–78.

[114]Ibid., 477.

[115]Neal Punt, *Unconditional Good News* (Grand Rapids: Eerdmans, 1980), 6.

[116]A. J. Ayer, *Language, Truth and Logic* (New York: Dover, 1946), 119.

[117]Ibid., 120.

[118]J. B. Pratt, *The Religious Consciousness* (New York: Macmillan, 1920), 443.

[119]Lit-sen Chang, *Zen Existentialism* (Phillipsburg, N.J.: Presbyterian and Reformed, 1969), 206.

[120]W. L. Reese, *Dictionary of Philosophy and Religion* (Atlantic Highlands, N.J.: Humanities Press, 1980), 188.

[121]Robert O. Ferm, *The Psychology of Christian Conversion* (Westwood, N.J.: Revell, 1959), 225.

[122]Flo Conway and Jim Siegelman, *Snapping: America's Epidemic of Sudden Personality Changes* (Philadelphia: Lippincott, 1978), 194.

[123]Gordon R. Lewis, *What Everyone Should Know about Transcendental Meditation* (Glendale, Calif.: Regal, 1975), 39–67.

[124]Conway and Siegelman, *Snapping*, 102.

[125]William Sargant, *The Battle for the Mind* (New York: Doubleday, 1957), 12.

[126]Ibid. See also an evaluation by James Bjornstad, "Cultic and Christian Conversion: Is There a Difference?" *Update: A Quarterly Journal on New Religious Movements* 6, 1 (March 1982): 50–64.

[127]Ian Rammage, *The Battle for the Free Mind* (London: George Allen & Unwin, 1967), 5.

[128]Paul Tournier, *Guilt and Grace* (New York: Harper & Row, 1962), 128.

[129]Ibid., 141.

[130]Ibid., 150.

[131]Ibid., 167.

[132]Aldous Huxley, "Introduction," *The Song of God: Bhagavad-Gita*, trans. Swami Prabhavananda and Christopher Isherwood (New York: Mentor, 1951), 12.

[133]James, *Varieties of Religious Experience*, 370–72.

[134]William Braden, *The Private Sea: LSD and the Search for God* (Chicago: Quadrangle, 1967), 30–37.

[135]Marilyn Ferguson, *The Aquarian Conspiracy: Personal and Social Transformation in the 80s* (Los Angeles: Tarcher, 1980), 29.

[136]Ibid., 46, 130–31.

[137]Ibid., 40.

[138]See Charles R. Wilson, "Self-Realization," in *Baker's Dictionary of Christian Ethics*, ed. Carl F. H. Henry (Grand Rapids: Baker, 1973), 613.

[139]Karl Barth, *Evangelical Theology* (New York: Holt, Rinehart and Winston, 1963), 98, 100–101.

[140]Paul Tillich, *The Courage to Be* (New Haven: Yale University, 1952), 171–78.

[141]W. T. Stace, *Time and Eternity* (Princeton, N.J.: Princeton University, 1952), 152. See also idem, *Mysticism and Christianity* (Philadelphia: Lippincott, 1960).

[142]Lewis Sperry Chafer, *Salvation* (Chicago: Moody, 1917), 48–51.

[143]Lewis Sperry Chafer, *Systematic Theology* (Dallas: Dallas Seminary, 1948), 7:265–66.

[144]Charles C. Ryrie, *So Great Salvation: What It Means to Believe in Jesus Christ* (Wheaton: Victor, 1989), 100.

[145]C. S. Lewis, *Mere Christianity* (New York: Macmillan, 1942), 154–55.

[146]Robert Coleman, *The Master Plan of Evangelism* (Old Tappan, N.J.: Revell, 1969), 71–72.

[147]Dietrich Bonhoeffer, *The Cost of Discipleship* (New York: Macmillan, 1958), 38.

[148]Os Guinness, *In Two Minds* (Downers Grove: InterVarsity, 1976), 27.

[149]Ibid., 48.

[150]Ibid., 181.

[151]Ibid.

[152]William Temple, *Christian Faith and Life* (London: SCM, 1931), 74.

[153]Tournier, *Guilt and Grace*, 152.

[154]R. E. O. White, *They Teach Us to Pray* (New York: Harper, 1957), 73–74, 80.

[155]Tournier, *Guilt and Grace*, 202.

[156]See Frank B. Stanger, "Restitution," *Bakers Dictionary of Christian Ethics*, 581–86.

[157]See W. C. G. Proctor, "Absolution," *EDT*, 7–8.

[158]George Smeaton, *The Doctrine of the Holy Spirit* (London: Banner of Truth Trust, 1958), 203.

[159]Ibid., 199.

[160]Gordon R. Lewis, "A Conservative Evangelical View of the Call to Conversion," *The National Institute for Campus Ministries Journal* 1, 3 (Summer 1976): 6–15.

[161]Leighton Ford, "The 'Finger of God' in Evangelism," *The Best in Theology*, ed. J. I. Packer, vol. 1 (Carol Stream, Ill.: *Christianity Today* and Word, n.d.), 295.

[162]Paul Loeffler, "Conversion," *The Ecumenical Review* 19, 3 (July 1967): 250.

[163]Paul Tournier, *The Whole Person in a Broken World* (New York: Harper & Row, 1964), 76.

Chapter 3

[1]Jaroslav Pelikan, *The Christian Tradition: A History of the Development of Doctrine*, 5 vols. (Chicago: University of Chicago Press, 1971–89), 4:139.

[2]Dale Moody, *The Word of Truth: A Summary of Christian Doctrine Based on Biblical Revelation* (Eerdmans: Grand Rapids, 1981), 328.

[3]John A. Hardon, *The Catholic Catechism* (New York: Doubleday, 1975), 169.

[4]Augustine, *Against Julian*, II.8.

[5]Augustine, *Sermon*, 158.5. Augustine viewed the "righteousness of God" (Rom. 3:21) as an objective genitive, i.e., "the righteousness, whose origin is in God, given to the sinner."

[6]Augustine, *On the Spirit and the Letter*, 45; cf. idem, *On Nature and Grace*, 29. At the end of his essay *On the Spirit and the Letter*, 45, Augustine attested the objective dimension of justification: "The term 'They shall be justified' is used in the sense of, They shall be deemed, or reckoned as just, as it is predicated of a certain man in the Gospel, 'But he wanted to justify himself' " (Luke 10:29).

[7]Augustine, *On the Spirit and the Letter*, 18–20. Cf. idem, *On Grace and Free Will*, 14.27: Justification includes not only the remission of sin, but also "that grace which makes it possible to fulfill the Law so that our nature is set free from the dominion of sin."

[8]So Augustine, *Letter*, 194.14: "When God rewards our merits, he is actually rewarding his own gifts."

[9]Augustine, *City of God*, XX.25; XXI.13, 16, 26; idem, *Enchiridion*, 69.

[10]Hendrikus Berkhof, *Christian Faith* (Grand Rapids: Eerdmans, 1979), 435, commented, "Though Augustine does not deny the imputation, all the emphasis for him (unlike Paul) is on the inner renewal that rests on it, thus on what we are accustomed to call 'sanctification.' This has become the common meaning in Roman Catholic theology." Alister E. McGrath, in his exhaustive study of justification, refers to "the misleading interpretation given to the term 'justification' by Augustine." *Iustitia Dei*, 2 vols. (Cambridge: Cambridge University Press, 1986–87), 1:60.

[11]Augustine, *Admonition and Grace*, 9.23; idem, *On the Gospel of John*, XXVI.15.

[12]Thomas Aquinas, *Summa Theologica*, Pt. II.1, q. 113, arts. 6, 8.

[13]Ibid., art. 2.

[14]Ibid., q. 114, art. 8. This development led Otto W. Heick to observe that "the religious life of Roman Catholicism does not center in faith but in love and good works." *A History of Christian Thought* (Philadelphia: Fortress, 1965), 289.

[15]Aquinas, *ST*, Part III (Supplement), q. 71, art. 6. For further discussion of Thomas' doctrine of purgatory, see *SCG*, IV.91.6–7.

[16]Richard P. McBrien, *Catholicism* (Minneapolis: Winston, 1981), 423.

[17]Ibid., 1248.

[18]Ibid., 738.

[19]*The Racovian Catechism* (1605), ch. V.8, cited in *The Polish Brethren*, 2 vols., ed. and trans. G. H. Williams (Missoula, Mont.: Scholars Press, 1980), 1:222.

[20]Albrecht Ritschl, *The Christian Doctrine of Justification and Reconciliation*, ed. H.R. Mackintosh and A. B. Macaulay (Clifton, N.J.: Reference Book Publishers, 1966), 274.

[21]Ibid., 70.

[22]Shailer Mathews, *The Gospel and the Modern Man* (New York: Macmillan, 1912), 182.

[23]Shailer Mathews, *The Faith of Modernism* (New York: Macmillan, 1924), 91; cf. idem, *The Gospel and Modern Man*, 184: "The loving God of the universe will save a man who tries to live as Jesus did."

[24]James H. Cone, *God of the Oppressed* (New York: Seabury, 1975), 229.

[25]Olin P. Moyd, *Redemption in Black Theology* (Valley Forge, Penn.: Judson, 1979), 153, writes, "Justification in Black Theology is Black folks coming to know the impact of the justice of God in an unjust world-life situation."

[26]Norman Pittenger, *Cosmic Love and Human Wrong* (New York: Paulist, 1978), 102.

27Norman Pittenger, *Freed to Love: A Process Interpretation of Redemption* (Wilton, Conn.: Morehouse-Barlow, 1987), 68–71.

28Willard H. Taylor, "Justification," *BDT*, 298.

29Ibid. R. Larry Shelton adds, "God pronounces believers righteous and justifies them when they fulfill by faith-obedience the requirements of the covenant relationship." "Initial Salvation: The Redemptive Grace of God in Christ," in *A Contemporary Wesleyan Theology*, 2 vols., ed. Charles W. Carter (Grand Rapids: Zondervan, 1983), 1:494.

30John Wesley, "A Farther Appeal to Men of Reason and Religion," *The Works of John Wesley*, 14 vols. (Grand Rapids: Zondervan, 1958), 8:46.

31Wesley, "Justification By Faith," *Works*, 5:57.

32Wesley, "Minutes of Some Late Conversations," *Works*, 8:277: "We do not find it expressly affirmed in Scripture that God imputes the righteousness of Christ to any." What God does is reckon their faith as righteousness, namely, forgiveness of sins and the removal of guilt.

33Wesley, "An Answer to the Rev. Mr. Church," *Works*, 8:403.

34Richard Watson, *Theological Institutes*, 2 vols. (New York: Lane & Scott, 1851), 2:226. Cf. ibid., 2:215.

35Ibid., 2:211; cf. 2:214. Watson defines "the righteousness of God" as God's "rectoral justice in the administration of pardon," which, of course, is not capable of imputation.

36Charles Finney, *Finney's Systematic Theology*, ed. J. H. Fairchild (Minneapolis: Bethany Fellowship, 1976), 322; cf. ibid., 320.

37Ibid., 333.

38Ibid., 320.

39Karl Barth, *CD*, IV.1.563.

40Ibid., 36.

41Hans Küng, *Justification: The Doctrine of Karl Barth and a Catholic Reflection* (Philadelphia: Westminster, 1981), 80.

42Barth, *CD*, IV.1.492.

43Ibid., 74.

44Gustaf Aulén, *The Faith of the Christian Church* (London: SCM, 1954), 223; cf. 297.

45Ibid., 172–73.

46Ibid., 292; cf. Gustaf Aulén, *Reformation and Catholicity* (Philadelphia: Muhlenberg, 1961), 63, where justification by faith is presented as a continuing redemptive activity of God mediated by the Word and sacraments.

47Ibid., 224–25, 228, 231, and passim.

48Martin Luther, *LW*, 34:337; cf. 25:151.

49Ibid., 26:232.

50Ibid.; cf. 25:260.

51Ibid., 27:228; cf. 25:258.

52Ibid., 26:377–78.

53Ibid., 34:183.

54 "Baccalaureate Theses," 10, in *Melanchthon: Selected Writings*, trans. C. H. Hill (Westport, Conn.: Greenwood, 1978), 17.

55Philip Melanchthon, *Melanchthon on Christian Doctrine: Loci Communes* (1955), ed. Clyde Manschreck (Grand Rapids: Baker, reprint, 1982), 161.

56John Calvin, "Sermon on Luke 1:5–10," *CR*, 46:23.

57John Calvin, *Institutes of the Christian Religion*, III.11.2.

58Ibid., 11.21.

59Ibid., 2.17; cf. 4.27.

60Ibid., 11.6.

61Ibid., 16.1; cf. 11.1: By partaking of Christ we "receive a double grace," namely, we are "reconciled to God through Christ's blessedness" and we are "sanctified by Christ's spirit."

62Ibid., 17.10; cf. 17.5.

63J. I. Packer, "Justification," *EDT*, 595.

64Ibid., 596.

65Ibid.

66Arthur W. Pink, *The Doctrines of Election and Justification* (Grand Rapids: Baker, reprint, 1974).

67Peter Toon, *Justification and Sanctification* (Westchester, Ill.: Crossway, 1983).

68Alister E. McGrath, *Iustitia Dei: A History of the Christian Doctrine of Justification*, 2 vols. (Cambridge: Cambridge University Press, 1986–87). See also his more popular treatment, *Justification by Faith: An Introduction* (Grand Rapids: Zondervan, 1988).

69Victor P. Hamilton, *"Māṣā',"* *TWOT*, 1:521.

70Leon J. Wood, *"Ḥāšab,"* *TWOT*, 1:330.

71Harold G. Stigers, *"Ṣādēq,"* *TWOT*, 2:752–55.

72G. Ch. Aalders, *Genesis*, 2 vols. (Grand Rapids: Zondervan, 1981), 1:293; cf. Allen P. Ross, *Creation and Blessing: A Guide to the*

Study and Exposition of Genesis (Grand Rapids: Baker, 1988), 310.

[73] Edward J. Young, *The Book of Isaiah*, 3 vols. (Grand Rapids: Eerdmans, 1965–72), 1:77; cf. J. Ridderbos, *Isaiah* (Grand Rapids: Zondervan, 1984), 47.

[74] Young, *Isaiah*, 3:358.

[75] Jack B. Scott, "*ᵉmûnāh*," *TWOT*, 1:52. F. F. Bruce, *The Epistle of Paul to the Romans, TNTC* (London: Tyndale, 1963), 80, commented that *ᵉmûnāh* (LXX *pistis*) "means 'steadfastness' or 'fidelity' based on a firm belief in God and his Word, and it is this firm belief that Paul understands by the term."

[76] Young, *Isaiah*, 3:218.

[77] Ibid., 3:389.

[78] Fritz Rienecker and Cleon L. Rogers, Jr., *LKGNT*, 33.

[79] Ralph P. Martin, *2 Corinthians*, *WBC* (Waco, Tex.: Word, 1986), 154; cf. John Eadie, *Ephesians, GTC* (Grand Rapids: Baker, reprint, 1979), 182.

[80] According to C. E. B. Cranfield, *The Epistle to the Romans, ICC*, 2 vols. (Edinburgh: T. & T. Clark, 1975–79), 1:202, *dikaiosynē theou* signifies "a status of righteousness before God which is God's gift."

[81] John Murray, *The Epistle to the Romans*, 2 vols. *NICNT* (Grand Rapids: Eerdmans, 1959–65), 1:205.

[82] Alfred Plummer, *The Epistles of St. John* (Grand Rapids: Baker, reprint, 1980), 30.

[83] John R. W. Stott, *The Epistles of John, TNTC* (London: Tyndale, 1964), 185.

[84] Rienecker and Rogers, *LKGNT*, 679.

[85] Albrecht Oepke, "*iaomai*," *TDNT*, 3:214.

[86] F. F. Bruce, *The Epistle to the Hebrews, NLCNT* (London: Marshall, Morgan & Scott, 1964), 151.

[87] Paul Tournier, *Guilt and Grace* (New York: Harper & Row, 1962), 212.

[88] Paul Tillich, *The Courage to Be* (New Haven: Yale University Press, 1952), 164.

[89] Tournier, *Guilt and Grace*, 173.

[90] Ibid., 190.

[91] G. C. Berkouwer, *Faith and Justification* (Grand Rapids: Eerdmans, 1954), 45.

[92] Robert L. Dabney, *Lectures in Systematic Theology* (Grand Rapids: Zondervan, 1972), 613.

[93] Hans Küng, *Justification: the Doctrine of Karl Barth and a Catholic Reflection* (Burns and Oates, 1964), 68; cited by Robert M. Horn,

Go Free! (Downers Grove: InterVarsity, 1976), 24.

[94] Berkouwer, *Faith and Justification*, 100.

[95] Kenneth Prior, *The Way of Holiness* (Downers Grove: InterVarsity, 1982), 67.

[96] John Oman, *Grace and Personality* (New York: Association Press, 1961), 116–17.

[97] R. E. O. White, "Reconciliation," *EDT*, 917.

[98] Barth, *CD*, IV.1.22.

[99] Oman, *Grace and Personality*, 109.

[100] Tournier, *Guilt and Grace*, 172.

[101] Oman, *Grace and Personality*, 104.

[102] Ibid., 113.

[103] Barth, *CD*, IV.1.294–95.

[104] Ibid., 285.

[105] H. Vorländer and Colin Brown, "Reconciliation," *NIDNTT*, 3:173.

[106] David F. Wells, *The Search for Salvation* (Downers Grove: InterVarsity, 1978), 166.

[107] Charles S. MacKenzie, "Justification by Faith in the Seventies," *Christianity Today* (September 24, 1971), 6.

[108] Oman, *Grace and Personality*, 78–79.

[109] Karl Barth, *Epistle to the Romans* (London: Oxford University, 1933), 88.

[110] Ibid.

[111] Ibid.

[112] Rudolph Bultmann, *Jesus Christ and Mythology* (New York: Scribner, 1958), 84.

[113] Reinhold Niebuhr, *The Nature and Destiny of Man*, 2 vols. (New York: Scribner, 1951), 2:148–49.

[114] Packer, "Justification," 597.

[115] G. Schrenk, "*dikaiōsis*," *TDNT*, 2:216.

[116] Berkouwer, *Faith and Justification*, 93.

[117] McGrath, *Justification by Faith*, 95.

[118] Leon Morris, *The Apostolic Preaching of the Cross* (Grand Rapids: Eerdmans, 1956), 260.

[119] Schrenk, "*dikaiōsis*," *TDNT*, 2:215.

[120] McGrath, *Justification by Faith*, 106.

[121] Colin Brown, "Righteousness," *NIDNTT*, 3:370.

[122] Tournier, *Guilt and Grace*, 157.

[123] Ibid., 156–57.

[124] Ibid., 158.

[125] Ibid.

[126] Ibid., 175.

127Ibid., 177.

128For an extensive exposition of classical attempts to understand and attain perfection, see John Passmore, *The Perfectibility of Man* (London: Duckworth, 1970).

129J. I. Packer, "Justification," *EDT*, 594.

130McGrath, *Justification by Faith*, 53.

131F. W. Dillistone, "The Recovery of the Doctrine of Justification by Faith," *Theology Today* (July 1954), 209.

132McGrath, *Justification by Faith*, 106.

Chapter 4

1*The Racovian Catechism*, V.2, cited in *The Polish Brethren*, ed. and trans. George Hunston Williams, 2 parts (Missoula, Mont.: Scholars Press, 1980), 1:215.

2William Adams Brown, *Christian Theology in Outline* (New York: Scribner, 1911), 420–23.

3José Miguez Bonino, "Wesley's Doctrine of Sanctification From a Liberationist Perspective," in Theodore Runyon, ed., *Sanctification and Liberation* (Nashville, Abingdon, 1981), 63.

4Gustavo Gutièrrez, "Liberation Theology and Proclamation," in *The Mystical and Political Dimensions of the Christian Faith*, ed. C. Geffri and G. Gutièrrez (New York: Herder and Herder, 1974), 67.

5According to Karl Adam: "Justification is not . . . a mere external imputation of the righteousness of Christ. It is the communication of a true inward righteousness, of a new love which re-makes the whole man; it is sanctification." *The Spirit of Catholicism* (New York: Macmillan, 1955), 208.

6Karl Rahner and H. Vorgrimler, eds., "Perseverance," *Theological Dictionary* (New York: Herder and Herder, 1965), 351.

7Council of Trent, VI.10.

8Council of Trent, Sixth session, canon 32; cf. IV.16.

9Ibid., VI.14; cf. XIV.9.

10Ibid., VI.10.

11Session XXV (December 1563), "Decree Concerning Purgatory."

12F. G. L. Van Der Meer, *The Faith of the Church*, trans. John Murray, S.J. (London: Darton, Longman & Todd, 1966), 391.

13Ibid., 407. On page 405 Van Der Meer adds that the works of the Christian "are good works, pleasing in God's sight and meritorious because of an adequacy that belongs really to Christ but which becomes ours as well as his."

14Ibid., 408.

15Ibid.

16Ibid.

17Ibid., 515.

18John Wesley, "Christian Perfection," in *The Works of John Wesley*, 14 vols. (Grand Rapids: reprint, 1958), 6:15; cf. 6:19.

19Wesley, "The Great Privilege of Those That Are Born of God," *Works*, 5:227–28.

20Wesley, "The Scripture Way of Salvation," *Works*, 6:46.

21Wesley wrote in "The Great Privilege of Those That Are Born of God," *Works*, 5:227: "By sin I here understand outward sin . . . ; an actual, voluntary transgression of the law; of the revealed, written law of God; of any commandment of God, acknowledged to be such at the time that it is transgressed." Cf. "On Perfection," *Works*, 6:417.

22Wesley wrote, "I believe this perfection is always wrought in the soul by a simple act of faith; consequently in an instant. But I believe in a gradual work both preceding and following that instant." *A Plain Account of Christian Perfection* (London: Epworth, reprint, 1952), 112; cf. "The Scripture Way of Salvation," *Works*, 6:46.

23John Wesley, "Letter to Dr. Warburton (Nov. 26, 1762)," *The Letters of John Wesley*, ed. John Telford, 8 vols. (London: Epworth, 1931), 4:340–46.

24Wesley, "The More Excellent Way," *Works*, 7:26–28.

25Wesley, "Predestination Calmly Considered," *Works*, 10:257; cf. "A Call to Backsliders," *Works*, 6:526.

26Charles G. Finney, *Principles of Sanctification*, ed. L. G. Parkhurst (Minneapolis: Bethany, 1986), 52.

27Charles G. Finney, *Finney's Systematic Theology*, ed. J. H. Fairchild (Minneapolis: Bethany Fellowship, 1976), 362.

28Ibid., 368.

29Charles G. Finney, *Systematic Theology*, ed. J. H. Fairchild (Whittier, Calif.: Colporter Kemp, 1946), 554.

30J. Kenneth Grider, *Entire Sanctification* (Kansas City, Mo.: Beacon Hill, 1980), 112.

31Ibid., 31.

32*Discipline of the Pentecostal Holiness Church* (Franklin Springs, Ga.: Board of Publication, Pentecostal Holiness Church, 1953), 13.

[33]"Baptism in the Holy Spirit," *Dictionary of Pentecostal and Charismatic Movements* (Grand Rapids: Zondervan, 1988), 43.

[34]Ibid., 283.

[35]Stanley M. Horton, "The Pentecostal Perspective," in Melvin Dieter et al., *Five Views on Sanctification* (Grand Rapids: Zondervan, 1987), 131.

[36]Ibid., 193.

[37]Ibid., 192. Horton believes that "even children of the kingdom can be cast out" (p. 96).

[38]Ernest S. Williams, *Systematic Theology*, 3 vols. (Springfield, Mo.: Gospel Publishing House, 1953), 2:258.

[39]Ibid., 3:50; cf. 3:74.

[40]Ibid., 2:259.

[41]J. Rodman Williams, *The Pentecostal Reality* (Plainfield, N.J.: Logos International, 1972), 25.

[42]See Steven Barabas, *So Great Salvation: The History and Message of the Keswick Convention* (London and Edinburgh: Marshall, Morgan and Scott, 1952), 55–56.

[43]J. Robertson McQuilken, "The Keswick Perspective," in Dieter et al., *Five Views on Sanctification*, 167. Barabas, *So Great Salvation*, 107, described the Keswick position as "the doctrine of sanctification by faith." Fearful of "works," Keswick advocates make sanctification entirely a matter of faith.

[44]McQuilken, "The Keswick Perspective," 155.

[45]Barabas, *So Great Salvation*, 84; cf. 99: "A life of victory over conscious sin is the rightful heritage of every child of God."

[46]Ibid., 115.

[47]Karl Barth, *CD*, IV.2.507; cf. 505: "Justification and sanctification must be distinguished, but they cannot be divided or separated."

[48]Ibid., 511.

[49]Ibid., 514.

[50]Ibid., 518.

[51]Ibid., 511.

[52]Anthony A. Hoekema raised the question why in Barth's view God gives the Holy Spirit only to some Christians and not to all God's elect (or his covenant partners). Hoekema argued that in Barth's representation the Trinity is divided against itself. "Do the Scriptures give us the impression that there are elect people to whom the Holy Spirit is not given?" *Karl Barth's Doctrine of Sanctification* (Grand Rapids: Calvin Theological Seminary, 1965), 22.

[53]Barth, *CD*, IV.2.620.

[54]Karl Barth, *The Christian Life*, trans. Geoffrey W. Bromiley (Grand Rapids: Eerdmans, 1981), 94.

[55]Reinhold Niebuhr, *The Nature and Destiny of Man*, 2 vols. (New York: Scribner, 1951), 2:100.

[56]J. I. Packer, " 'Keswick' and the Reformed Doctrine of Sanctification," *Evangelical Quarterly* 27 (July-September 1955): 27.

[57]For example, B. B. Warfield, *Miracles: Yesterday and Today* (Grand Rapids: Eerdmans, 1953), 3–6, 23–28.

[58]Augustine, *On Grace and Free Will*, 17.32.

[59]Augustine, *On the Spirit and the Letter*, 65; cf. *Against Two Epistles of the Pelagians*, III.7.19: "When we call the virtue of the saints perfect, to this very perfection also belongs the recognition of imperfection, both in truth and humility."

[60]Augustine, *Faith, Hope and Charity*, 31.118.

[61]Augustine, *On the Gift of Perseverance*, 41.

[62]Klaus Bockmuehl, "Sanctification," *NDT*, 615.

[63]John Calvin, *Institutes of the Christian Religion*, III.16.1; cf. 11.1: "Being partakers of Christ we grasp a double grace."

[64]Ibid., III.3.9.

[65]Ibid., II.7.12; cf. 7.14: "By teaching, admonishing, reproving, and correcting, it [the law] forms us and prepares us for every good work." Cf. III.19.2.

[66]Ibid., III.3.10; cf. 3.14; 17.5.

[67]Ibid., IV.19.18.

[68]Ibid., II.5.3.

[69]Ibid., 3.11.

[70]John Calvin, *Commentaries on the Epistle to the Hebrews*, 135–40.

[71]L. Berkhof, *Systematic Theology* (Grand Rapids: Eerdmans, 1941), 532.

[72]Ibid., 537.

[73]Ibid., 543.

[74]Ibid., 546.

[75]J. I. Packer, *Keep in Step With the Spirit* (Old Tappan, N.J.: Revell, 1984).

[76]G. C. Berkouwer, *Faith and Sanctification* (Grand Rapids: Eerdmans, 1952) and idem, *Faith and Perseverance* (Grand Rapids: Eerdmans, 1958).

77Richard Lovelace, *Dynamics of the Spiritual Life* (Downers Grove: InterVarsity, 1980).

78*The New Brown-Driver-Briggs-Gesenius Hebrew and English Lexicon* (Peabody, Mass.: Hendrickson, 1979), 1070–71.

79J. Barton Payne, *"tāmam," TWOT,* 2:974.

80Charles Bridges, *A Commentary on Proverbs* (London: Banner of Truth, reprint, 1968), 50, wrote, "It is not necessary that every thing should be perfect at once. There may be an occasional cloud, or even (as in the case of David and Peter) a temporary eclipse. . . . Religion must be a shining and progressive light."

81*New Brown-Driver-Briggs-Gesenius Lexicon,* 1070.

82Ibid., 449.

83Bridges said concerning those who claim to be without sin: "Vain boasters these are, who proclaim their good hearts. But the boast proves, not their goodness, but their blindness. That man is so blind that he cannot understand his own depravity." *Proverbs,* 342.

84R. E. O. White, "Sanctification," *EDT,* 971. Or according to R. Schippers, "Goal," *NIDNTT,* 2:65, "*teleios* signifies the undivided wholeness of a person in his behavior."

85John MacArthur, *The Gospel According to Jesus* (Grand Rapids: Zondervan, 1988), 99.

86J. I. Packer, *Keep in Step With the Spirit,* (Old Tappan, N.J.: Revell, 1984), 205.

87Cf. Everett F. Harrison, *Interpreting Acts* (Grand Rapids: Zondervan, 1986), 146; Michael Green, *I Believe in the Holy Spirit* (Grand Rapids: Eerdmans, 1975), 136–39; D. A. Carson, *Showing the Spirit: A Theological Exposition of 1 Corinthians 12–14* (Grand Rapids: Baker, 1987), 145; Packer, *Keep in Step With the Spirit,* 204.

88Marshall, *Acts of the Apostles,* 306–7.

89Ibid., 308; cf. Harrison, *Interpreting Acts,* 307–8.

90Packer, *Keep in Step With the Spirit,* 206. Grant R. Osborne concludes that the manifestation of tongues in Acts "authenticated the addition of new groups to the church . . . for the sake of the Jewish Christians in Jerusalem." "Tongues, Speaking in," *EDT,* 1101.

91F. F. Bruce, *The Epistle of Paul to the Romans,* TNTC (London: Tyndale, 1963), 153.

92Charles M. Horne, *The Doctrine of Salvation* (Chicago: Moody, 1984), 73.

93Cf. F. F. Bruce, *1 and 2 Thessalonians,* WBC (Waco, Tex.: Word, 1982), 129.

94H. Haarbeck, "Word, Tongue, Utterance," *NIDNTT,* 3:1080, concludes that whereas in Acts 2 tongues represented unlearned foreign languages or dialects, in Corinth, at least, "it was probably a case of praise and worship addressed to God in articulate tones. What is common is . . . that these phenomena are rooted in . . . the work of the Holy Spirit, and that it is to the glorification and worship of God that they contribute." Carson, *Showing the Spirit,* 85, suggests that tongues at Corinth represent "speech patterns sufficiently complex that they may bear all kinds of cognitive information in some coded array, even though linguistically these patterns are not identifiable as human language."

95F. F. Bruce, *I & II Corinthians,* NCBC (Grand Rapids: Eerdmans, 1980), 130.

96Richard F. Lovelace, *Dynamics of Spiritual Life* (Downers Grove: InterVarsity, 1979), 125–26. Conversely, the termination of supernatural gifts is argued by John F. Walvoord, "The Holy Spirit and Gifts," *Bibliotheca Sacra* (April-June 1986): 109–21, and Robert L. Thomas, "Tongues . . . Will Cease," *JETS* 17, 2 (Spring 1974): 81–89.

97R. Schippers, "Goal," *NIDNTT,* 2:62. Carson, *Showing the Spirit,* 69–70, defines "perfection" as "the state of affairs brought about by the arrival of the parousia." So also F. W. Grosheide, *Commentary on the First Epistle to the Corinthians,* NICNT (Grand Rapids: Eerdmans, 1953); 310; Bruce, *I & II Corinthians,* 128; Max Turner, "Spiritual Gifts Then and Now," *Vox Evangelica* 15 (1985): 38–39.

98Turner, "Spiritual Gifts Then and Now," 41.

99O. Becker, "Gift, Pledge, Corban," *NIDNTT,* 2:40; cf. Mitton, *Ephesians,* 62–63.

100H. N. Ridderbos, *Paul: An Outline of His Theology* (Grand Rapids: Eerdmans, 1975), 255.

101Alfred Plummer, *The Epistles of John* (Grand Rapids: Baker, reprint, 1980), 27.

102F. F. Bruce, *The Gospel of John* (Grand Rapids: Eerdmans, 1983), 397, n. 18.

103David J. Ellis, "The Gospel According to John," *NLBC,* 1325; cf. Donald Guthrie, "John," *NBCRev,* 959.

104George R. Beasley-Murray, *John,* WBC (Waco, Tex.: Word, 1987), 272.

105Bruce, *Gospel of John,* 154.

106According to Thomas Hewitt, *The Epistle to the Hebrews,* TNTC (London: Tyndale House, 1960), 201, " 'the spirits of just men made perfect' signifies the faithful departed, including the saints of both covenants, who have already been led by the Captain of their salvation to the higher state of blessedness."

[107]Ibid., 107; cf. Rienecker and Rogers, *LKGNT,* 681.

[108]This interpretation—that Hebrews 6:4–6 represents a warning to believers against reverting to a Judaism incapable of conveying salvation—is upheld by interpreters such as Westcott, Manson, Berkouwer, Guthrie, Hewitt, G. Thomas, and H. Kent.

[109]The other leading interpretation held by Calvin, Owen, Grosheide, Hughes, Nicole, and other Reformed is that the experiences and qualities cited in Heb. 6:4–5 and 10:26 describe people who were thoroughly exposed to the Gospel, who made a Christian profession, who looked outwardly like Christians, but who were not regenerated. Their renunciation of the Gospel and opposition to Christ put them beyond the sphere of repentance. What Hebrews describes, it is claimed, is similar to "blasphemy against the Spirit" (Matt. 12:31–32) or the "sin that leads to death" (1 John 5:16). Judas is cited as a prime example of the professing believer who finally apostatized. This interpretation, in addition to assigning to unbelievers the fairly clear language of Christian experience, must ascribe the complementary words in 6:9–10 and 10:39 to a group (of believers) different from the people (unbelievers) described in 6:4–6 and 10:26–29.

[110]For a convincing interpretation of this text see Simon J. Kistemaker, *Exposition of the Epistles of Peter and of the Epistle of Jude, New Testament Commentary* (Grand Rapids: Baker, 1987), 311–13.

[111]R. D. Knudsen, "Redeemer, Redemption," *ZPEB,* 5:49.

[112]Peter Kuzmic from the former Yugoslavia, speaking at a consultation of the Theological Commission of World Evangelical Fellowship on the topic "Theological Issues in the 1990s" at Wheaton College, Wheaton, Illinois, June 19, 1990.

[113]Rudolph Otto, *The Idea of the Holy* (New York: Oxford, 1958), 6.

[114]Ibid., 109.

[115]Ibid., 135.

[116]Ibid., 141.

[117]Helmut Thielicke, *The Freedom of the Christian Man* (New York: Harper & Row, 1963), 14–15.

[118]Ibid., 55.

[119]William H. Willimon, "Stag Spirituality," *Christianity Today* (April 23, 1990), 26–27.

[120]Peter Toon, *Meditating as a Christian* (London: Collins, 1991), 41.

[121]Ibid.

[122]J. I. Packer, *Knowing God* (Downers Grove: InterVarsity, 1973), 226.

[123]On the meaning of surrender in Christianity in contrast to other religions see E. Stanley Jones, *Victory Through Surrender* (Nashville, Tenn.: Abingdon, 1966), 33.

[124]See "Does Love Alone Make an Act Good?" Gordon R. Lewis, *Decide for Yourself* (Downers Grove: InterVarsity, 1975), 129–33.

[125]Vernon Grounds, *Radical Commitment: Getting Serious About Christian Growth* (Portland, Ore.: Multnomah Press, 1984), 36.

[126]For a development of this approach to ethics see Oliver Barclay, "The Nature of Christian Morality," in *Law, Morality and the Bible,* ed. Bruce Kaye and Gordon Wenham (Downers Grove: InterVarsity, 1978), 125–29.

[127]Frances FitzGerald, "A Reporter at Large (Rajneeshpuram Part 1)," *The New Yorker* (September 22, 1986), 46.

[128]"7,000 Drawn to Oregon Hills to Meditate at Feet of Guru," *The Denver Post* (July 7, 1982).

[129]*Newsweek* (December 9, 1985), 30.

[130]Calvin Miller, *The Table of Inwardness* (Downers Grove: InterVarsity, 1984), 13–14.

[131]Watchman Nee, *Release of the Spirit* (Cloverdale, Ind.: Sure Foundation, 1965), 21.

[132]Acharya Rajneesh, *Meditation, the Art of Ecstasy* (New York: Harper & Row, 1978), 75–76.

[133]Vigen Guroian, "The Shape of Orthodox Ethics," *Epiphany Journal* (Fall 1991), 9.

[134]Watchman Nee, *The Spiritual Man,* 3 vols. (New York: Christian Fellowship, 1968), 1:27.

[135]Nee, *Release of the Spirit,* 78.

[136]Kenneth Hagin, *Right and Wrong Thinking* (Tulsa, Okla.: Hagin Ministries, 1986), 27.

[137]Benny Hinn, *Good Morning Holy Spirit* (Nashville, Tenn.: Thomas Nelson, 1990), 98.

[138]For a more complete evaluation of Christian mysticism see Gordon R. Lewis, *Testing Christianity's Truth Claims* (Lanham, Md.: University Press of America, 1990), 151–75.

[139]Lewis Sperry Chafer, *Systematic Theology,* 8 vols. (Dallas, Tex.: Dallas Seminary Press, 1947–48), 6:72.

[140]See Gerhard O. Forde, "The Lutheran View," in *Christian Spirituality,* ed. Donald L. Alexander (Downers Grove: InterVarsity, 1988), 13–14.

[141]Ibid., 17.

[142]Kathryn Ann Porter, *The Ship of Fools* (Boston: Little, Brown and Co., 1962).

[143]Søren Kierkegaard, *The Point of View for My Work as an Author*, trans. Walter Lowrie (New York: Harper, 1962), 22.

[144]For a helpful exposition of Kierkegaard's view of the Christian life, see Reidar Thomte, *Kierkegaard's Philosophy of Religion* (Princeton, N.J.: University Press, 1948), 83–84, 90–92, 170–89.

[145]David C. Needham, *Birthright* (Portland, Ore.: Multnomah Press, 1978), 47.

[146]Ibid., 255.

[147]John Stott, *Men Made New: An Exposition of Romans 5–8* (Downers Grove: InterVarsity, 1966), 45.

[148]Needham, *Birthright*, 77.

[149]Horatius Bonar, *God's Way of Holiness* (Chicago: Moody, n.d.), 83.

[150]See Charles Smith's review of David C. Needham, *Birthright; Grace Theological Journal* (Fall 1982), 287.

[151]Needham, *Birthright*, 80.

[152]Ibid., 56.

[153] For a critical assessment of these approaches see philosopher John Passmore, *The Perfectibility of Man* (London: Duckworth, 1970).

[154]Wilber T. Dayton, "The Divine Purification and Perfection of Man," in *A Contemporary Wesleyan Theology*, ed. Charles W. Carter (Grand Rapids: Zondervan, 1983), 541–44, 564–65.

[155]Ibid., 537.

[156]Ibid., 538.

[157]Ibid., 544.

[158]Melvin E. Dieter, "The Wesleyan Perspective," in Dieter et al., *Five Views on Sanctification* (Grand Rapids: Zondervan, 1987), 41.

[159]For an extensive examination of Mahan, Oberlin, Charles G. Finney, the "Higher Life" Movement, and the Victorious Life Movements see Benjamin Warfield, *Perfectionism* (Philadelphia: Presbyterian and Reformed, 1974).

[160]*The Scofield Reference Bible*, ed. C. I. Scofield (New York: Oxford University Press, 1945), 1200, n. 1 on Romans 7:14.

[161]Chafer, *Systematic Theology*, 6:170.

[162]See Carl F. H. Henry, *Christian Personal Ethics* (Grand Rapids: Eerdmans, 1957), 420–36.

[163]See Robertson McQuilkin, *An Introduction to Biblical Ethics* (Wheaton: Tyndale, 1989), 61.

[164]Roy L. Aldrich, "The Mosiac Ten Commandments Compared to Their Restatements in the New Testament," *Bibliotheca Sacra* (July 1961), 251–58.

[165]McQuilkin, *Biblical Ethics*, 52.

[166]See Daniel Fuller, *Gospel and Law: Contrast or Continuum?* (Grand Rapids: Eerdmans, 1980), 105–20.

[167]Ibid., 115.

[168]I. Howard Marshall, *Kept by the Power of God* (London: Epworth, 1969), 206–7.

[169]Ibid., 207.

[170]See Canadian scholar William R. Foster's book *The Discipline of Godliness* (Burlington, Ont., Canada: Welch, 1983).

[171]John Burnaby, *Amor Dei: A Study of the Religion of St. Augustine* (London: Hodder and Stoughton 1947), 87.

[172]Augustine, *Confessions*, XIII.9.10.

[173]Augustine, *City of God*, XV.7.

[174]For additional emphasis on a God-centered and kingdom-centered Christian life see Richard F. Lovelace, *Renewal as a Way of Life: A Guidebook for Spiritual Growth* (Downers Grove: InterVarsity, 1985), 13–62.

[175]McQuilkin, *Biblical Ethics*, 37.

[176]Henri J. M. Nouwen, *In the Name of Jesus: Reflections on Christian Leadership* (New York: Crossroad, 1991), 10.

[177]Ibid., 11.

[178]Ibid.

[179]Ibid., 24.

[180]Ibid.

[181]Ibid., 31.

[182]Ibid., 63.

[183]Lovelace, *Renewal as a Way of Life*, 145.

[184]Ibid.

[185]See L. I. Granberg and G. E. Farley, "Conscience," *ZPEB*, 942.

[186]Earl D. Wilson, *Sexual Sanity* (Downers Grove: InterVarsity, 1984), 84.

[187]Ibid., 129.

[188]Ibid., 130.

[189]Cited by Burnaby, *Amor Dei*, 135.

[190]Cited in James R. Newby, "Learn to Love the Difficult," *Ministry* 63, 9 (September 1990): 12–13.

191Ibid. James R. Newby is executive director of the D. Elton Trueblood Academy for Applied Christianity and the Yokefellow Institute, Earlham School of Religion, Richmond, Indiana.

192See Gordon R. Lewis, *What Everyone Should Know About Transcendental Meditation* (Glendale, Calif.: Regal, 1975), 63–67.

193Herbert Benson, *The Relaxation Response* (New York: William Morrow, 1975), 78–79.

194J. I. Packer, *Knowing God*, 18–19.

195Peter Toon, *Meditating as a Christian* (London: Collins, 1991), 19.

196See Gordon R. Lewis, "Criteria for the Discerning of Spirits," in *Demon Possession*, ed. John W. Montgomery (Minneapolis: Bethany Fellowship, 1976), 346–63.

197Jeffrey Hopkins, *Emptiness Yoga* (Ithaca, N.Y.: Snow Lion Press, 1989), publisher's catalog quote.

198Adapted from an alternative approach to TM from Lewis, *What Everyone Should Know About Transcendental Meditation*, 58–60.

199Earl Paulk, *That the World May Know* (Atlanta: K Dimension, 1987), 10.

200For amplification of each of these points see Gordon R. Lewis, "Prayer," *ZPEB*, 4:835–44.

201Charles D. Bass, *Banishing Fear from Your Life* (Garden City, N.Y.: Doubleday, 1986), 59.

Chapter Five

1Cyprian, *Letter*, 55.24.

2Ibid., 48.3; cf. 52.2: "Plainly, because of its greatness, Rome ought to precede Carthage."

3Cyprian, *On the Unity of the Church*, 6; cf. *Letter*, 70.2: "We know that the remission of sins is not given except in the church."

4Cyprian, *Letter*, 69.13.

5Ibid., 63.14. In 63.4 Cyprian speaks of "the sacrament of the sacrifice of our Lord."

6Augustine, *Discourses on the Psalms*, 10.5.

7Augustine, *City of God*, 20.9.

8Augustine echoed Cyprian when he wrote, "You are safe, who have God for your Father and his Church for your Mother." *Answer to Petilian*, 3.10.

9Augustine, *Letters*, 138.1.

10Augustine, *On the Gospel of St. John*, 80.3.

11Paul Lehman, "The Anti-Pelagian Writings," in Roy W. Battenhouse, ed., *A Companion to the Study of St. Augustine* (New York: Oxford University Press, 1955), 215.

12Augustine, *Discourses on the Psalms*, 3.1.

13For Augustine's belief that the Eucharist avails for the souls of deceased saints when offered on their behalf, see *Faith, Hope and Charity*, 110; *Confessions*, 9.12; *Letter*, 98.9; *Sermon*, 172.2.

14Augustine, *On the Gospel of St. John*, 26–27.

15Paschasius Radbertus, *The Lord's Body and Blood*, III.4, cited in *Early Medieval Theology*, ed. George E. McCracken, *LCC*, vol. 9 (Philadelphia: Westminster Press, 1957), 101.

16Fourth Lateran Council (1215), Canon I, cited in John H. Leith, ed., *Creeds of the Churches* (Atlanta: John Knox, 1982), 58.

17Thomas Aquinas, *SCG*, IV.59.4.

18Thomas Aquinas, *ST*, q. 69, art. 6.

19Ibid., q. 68, art. 2.

20See Philip Schaff, ed., *The Creeds of Christendom*, 3 vols. (Grand Rapids: Baker, reprint, 1977), 2:209.

21The Canons and Dogmatic Decrees of the Council of Trent, Session XIII, chap. 4 (Oct. 11, 1551), in Schaff, *Creeds of Christendom*, 2:130.

22Dogmatic Decrees of the Vatican Council, Session IV, chap. 2, in Schaff, *Creeds of Christendom*, 2:262; cf. 267–68.

23Ibid., Session IV, chap. 4, in Schaff, *Creeds of Christendom*, 2:270.

24*Dogmatic Constitution on the Church*, VII.48; cf. *Decree on the Church's Missionary Activity*, 1.

25*Pastoral Constitution on the Church in the Modern World*, VII.40.

26Ibid., III.25.

27Ibid., IV.31.

28Ibid., IV.33.

29*Decree on Ecumenism*, I.3.

30*Declaration on the Relation of the Church to Non-Christian Religions*, 2–3; *Dogmatic Constitution on the Church*, II.16.

31O. Hallesby, *Infant Baptism and Adult Conversion* (Minneapolis: Augsburg, 1924), 60.

32David P. Scaer, "The Conflict Over Baptism," *Christianity Today* (April 14, 1967), 8, 10.

33*What Luther Says*, ed. Ewald M. Plass (St. Louis: Concordia, 1959), 257.

34Martin Luther, *LW*, 13:88.

35Martin Luther, *Small Catechism*, par. 182; cited in *A Short Explanation of Dr. Martin*

Luther's Small Catechism (St. Louis: Concordia, 1943), 135.

36Luther, *LW*, 36:113; cf. 116: "We are all equally priests, that is to say, we have the same power in respect to the Word and the sacraments." Cf. 40:19.

37Ibid., 31:107.

38Luther, *Short Explanation*, 174; cf. Luther, *LW*, 35:35: "In baptism a person becomes guiltless, pure, and sinless."

39*What Luther Says*, 53; cf. Luther, *Small Catechism*, par. 251, in *Short Explanation*, 174.

40Luther, *Small Catechism*, par. 299, in *Short Explanation*, 195.

41Luther, *LW*, 37:367.

42Ibid, 93–94; cf. 71.

43John Theodore Mueller, *Christian Dogmatics* (St. Louis: Concordia, 1955), 546. Mueller's work is a summary of the larger theology of Francis Pieper, *Christian Dogmatics*, 4 vols. (St. Louis: Concordia, 1950–57).

44Ibid., 503.

45Ibid., 528.

46L. Berkhof, *Systematic Theology* (Grand Rapids: Eerdmans, 1941), 584.

47Cf. B. B. Warfield, "How Shall We Baptize?" in *Selected Shorter Writings II* (Philadelphia: Presbyterian and Reformed, 1973), 345–48.

48John Calvin, *Institutes of the Christian Religion*, IV.1.4.

49Ibid., 14.1.

50Ibid., 14.7; cf. 14.19.

51Ibid., 15.1; cf. 14.22: "Baptism attests to us that we have been cleansed and washed."

52John Calvin, *Treatises Against the Anabaptists and Against the Libertines*, trans. and ed. Benjamin Wirt Farley (Grand Rapids: Baker, 1982), 47–48.

53Calvin, *Institutes*, IV.16.18.

54Ibid., 16.20.

55Ibid., 17.1.

56Ibid., 17.10.

57Charles Hodge, *Systematic Theology*, 3 vols. (Grand Rapids: Eerdmans reprint, 1975), 3:548.

58Ibid., 572. Hodge adds, "It is to be feared that many have come short of eternal life, who, had they been received into the bosom of the church and enjoyed its guardial and fostering care, might have been saved" (p. 576).

59Ibid., 553.

60Ibid., 590.

61The evangelical wing of the church thus rejected the high-church "'pipeline theory' of power" in which "grace was thought to have been poured like a liquid into a pipe by our Lord and each ordination of a bishop . . . added another section of the pipe to the line." Urban T. Holmes, III, *What Is Anglicanism?* (Wilton, Conn.: Morehouse-Barlow, 1982), 53.

62Holmes, *What Is Anglicanism?* 56.

63The Swiss-born Thomas Erastus (d. 1583) is associated with the term "Erastianism," which posits that the church is governed by the state. Church leaders teach and preach but do not rule. The state governs, exercises discipline, and excommunicates unworthy members.

64Irenaeus, *Against Heresies*, IV.33.8; cf. III.3.1.

65Ibid., III.1.1.

66Ibid., 2.2.

67Ibid., 3.2. In 3.3 Irenaeus listed the succession of twelve Roman bishops from Linus to Eleutherus.

68Ibid., IV.18.5; V.2.2.

69Henry Barclay Swete, *The Holy Catholic Church: The Communion of Saints* (London: Macmillan, 1916), 50.

70Ibid., 41; cf. 22.

71Ibid., 19; cf. 16: "The societies known in England as 'the free churches' have little in common with the local churches of the Apostolic age."

72Ibid., 137.

73Ibid., 68; cf. 12.

74Ibid., 189; cf. 70: "The Eucharist is the appointed means of receiving . . . the spiritual or heavenly food."

75Paul R. Jackson, *The Doctrine and Administration of the Church* (Des Plaines, Ill.: Regular Baptist Press, 1968), 158.

76John F. MacArthur, Jr., *Answering Key Questions About Elders* (Panorama City, Calif.: Word of Grace Communications, 1984), 27.

77Gene A. Getz, *Sharpening the Focus of the Church* (Wheaton: Victor, 1984), 177. Getz adds that the church will designate one staff elder as the primary leader who in practice functions as "an elder to the elders, a pastor to the pastors" (p. 179).

78Earl D. Radmacher, "The Question of Elders," (Portland, Ore.: Western Baptist Press, 1977), 13.

79Ignatius, *To the Ephesians*, 4; *To the Magnesians*, 6, 13; *To the Trallians*, 2–3, 7; *To the Philadelphians*, 4, 7; et al.

80Ignatius, *To the Smyrnaeans*, 8.

81Ignatius, *To the Ephesians*, 20.

82*Didache*, 15.1.

83Ibid., 7.1–3.

84Ibid., 9.5.

85Ibid., 10.3.

86Ulrich Zwingli, *Commentary on True and False Religion*, ed. S. M. Jackson (Durham, N. C.: Labyrinth, 1981), 233; cf. 228: "The Lord's Supper . . . is a commemoration of Christ's death, not a remitting of sins."

87Ulrich Zwingli, "On the Lord's Supper," *LCC*, 24:192.

88Ibid., 236–37.

89Donald F. Durnbaugh, *The Believers' Church* (New York: Macmillan, 1968), 38.

90Augustus H. Strong, *Systematic Theology* (Valley Forge, Penn.: Judson, 1907), 887.

91Ibid., 890.

92Ibid., 903.

93Ibid., 915.

94Ibid., 941.

95Robert L. Saucy, *The Church in God's Program* (Chicago: Moody, 1972).

96Howard A. Snyder, *The Community of the King* (Downers Grove: InterVarsity, 1977) and *Liberating the Church* (Downers Grove: Inter-Varsity, 1983).

97John MacArthur, *The Church, the Body of Christ* (Grand Rapids: Zondervan, 1973).

98L. Coenen, "Church, Synagogue," *NIDNTT*, 1:294.

99Ibid., 291.

100Cf. Robert H. Gundry, *Matthew: A Commentary on His Literary and Theological Art* (Grand Rapids: Eerdmans, 1982), 368–69.

101G. R. Beasley-Murray, "Baptism, Wash," *NIDNTT*, 1:144.

102I. Howard Marshall, *The Gospel of Luke*, *NIGTC* (Grand Rapids: Eerdmans, 1978), 682–83.

103See Craig L. Blomberg, *The Historical Reliability of the Gospels* (Leicester: Inter-Varsity, 1987), 176–78.

104D. A. Carson, "Church, Authority in," *EDT*, 229; cf. Lawrence O. Richards, "Church," in *Expository Dictionary of Bible Words* (Grand Rapids: Zondervan, 1985), 167: "It is most likely that elders in the NT church served as a team to oversee the life of a wider community" (i.e., a number of congregations in a city) "and were not 'pastors' of a home-sized congregation."

105Cf. I. Howard Marshall, *The Acts of the Apostles*, TNTC (Grand Rapids: Eerdmans, 1980), 81–82: "The point of the phrase is rather to express the unlimited mercy of God which embraces the hearers and subsequent generations of their descendants."

106Cf. ibid., 165.

107Beasley-Murray, "Baptism, Wash," *NIDNTT*, 1:148–49.

108G. R. Beasley-Murray, *Baptism in the New Testament* (London: Macmillan, 1962), 319; cf. Henry Alford, *Alford's Greek Testament*, 4 vols. (Grand Rapids: Baker, reprint, 1980), 2:184.

109Paul S. Minear, *Images of the Church in the New Testament* (Philadelphia: Westminster, 1960) explains some ninety-six images of the church in the New Testament under five principal headings: "the people of God," "the new creation," "the fellowship in faith," "the body of Christ," and "minor images of the church."

110With respect to the New Testament and subapostolic periods, Robert Saucy observes, "Each time the term [*presbyteros*] appears it is a plural." *The Church in God's Program*, 148.

111As argued by Richard N. Longenecker, *New Testament Social Ethics for Today* (Grand Rapids: Eerdmans, 1884), 32–33.

112Beasley-Murray, *Baptism in the New Testament*, 181.

113J. Schattenmann, "Fellowship," *NIDNTT*, 1:639.

114Donald Guthrie, *New Testament Theology* (Downers Grove: InterVarsity, 1981), 758.

115Leon Morris, *The First Epistle of Paul to the Corinthians*, TNTC (London: Tyndale, 1958), 146, states, "Paul says that the faithful receive Christ. But he says nothing as to the 'how' of it. . . . All that the passage asserts is the fact of a participation, the nature of that participation must be determined from other sources."

116Thus F. F. Bruce, *The Gospel of John* (Grand Rapids: Zondervan, 1983), 85, observes "the baptismal allusion in these words of Jesus."

117Augustine, *Lectures on the Gospel of St. John*, 26.1.

118J. I. Packer, "The Nature of the Church," *Christianity Today* (June 8, 1962), 22.

119Howard A. Snyder, *The Problem of Wineskins* (Downers Grove: InterVarsity, 1975), 156.

120Ibid., 157.

121Coenen, "Church, Synagogue," *NIDNTT,* 1:302.

122Klaus Mörsdorf, "Hierarchy," *Encyclopedia of Theology: The Concise Sacramentum Mundi,* ed. Karl Rahner (New York: Seabury, 1975), 615–16.

123*BAGD,* 881.

124L. Coenen, "Bishop," *NIDNTT,* 1:194.

125Donald Lake, "Elder," *ZPEB,* 2:268.

126R. S. Wallace, "Elder," *EDT,* 347.

127Saucy, *The Church in God's Program,* 150.

128Gary M. Burge, "Deacon, Deaconess," *EDT,* 296.

129J. Stam, "Deacon, Deaconess," *ZPEB,* 2:48.

130See *The NIV Study Bible* note on Acts 15:22, representing the judgment of numerous Greek scholars from different denominations.

131Edward John Carnell, *The Case for Orthodox Theology* (Philadelphia: Westminster, 1959), 20, 22.

132Ibid., 22.

133Stephen Neill, *The Christian Society* (New York: Harper, 1952), 39.

134Editorial on Billy Graham, in "Theology and Life," *Concordia Theological Monthly* 32, 1 (January 1961).

135From the *Bulletin* of a local Lutheran Church.

136F. F. Bruce, *Commentary on the Book of Acts* (Grand Rapids: Eerdmans, 1955), 77.

137Ibid.

138Beasley-Murray, *Baptism in the New Testament,* 124.

139John Murray, "Baptism (Reformed View)," *ZPEB,* 1:469.

140Hodge, *Systematic Theology,* 3:499–500.

141Henry Cook, *What Baptists Stand For* (London: Carey Kingsgate, 1961), 89–94; Robert C. Walton, *The Gathered Community* (London: Carey, 1946), 155–67.

142Walton, *Gathered Community,* 159.

143Ibid., 161.

144See ibid., 171–72.

145R. E. O. White, *The Biblical Doctrine of Initiation* (Grand Rapids: Eerdmans, 1960), 263–64, 270.

146J. A. Wharton, "Ordinance," *Interpreters Bible Dictionary,* ed. G. A. Buttrick, 4 vols. (New York: Abingdon, 1962), 3:607.

147See Norman Waring and Winthrop Hudson, *A Baptist Manual of Polity and Practice* (Valley Forge: Judson, 1963), 131.

148Berkhof, *Systematic Theology,* 276.

149Ibid., 287.

150Ibid., 288.

151G. W. Bromiley, "Baptism, Infant," *EDT,* 116.

152Ibid., 116.

153Berkhof, *Systematic Theology,* 641–42.

154Charles Hodge, *The Church and Its Polity* (London and New York: T. Nelson, 1879), 66–67.

155White, *Biblical Doctrine of Initiation,* 296, note 1.

156Henry Alford, *Greek Testament Commentary,* 4 vols. (Grand Rapids: Baker, reprint, 1980), 2:184.

157Edward John Carnell, *The Burden of Søren Kierkegaard* (Grand Rapids: Eerdmans, 1965), 123.

158Karl Barth, *CD,* IV.4.176.

159Ibid., 102.

160Karl Barth, *The Teaching of the Church Regarding Baptism* (London: SCM, 1948), 15.

161Barth, *CD,* IV.4.xi.

162Jürgen Moltmann, *The Church in the Power of the Spirit* (New York: Harper & Row, 1977), 241.

163C. C. Richardson, "Worship in the New Testament," *Interpreters Dictionary of the Bible,* 4:891.

164"*Baptō*," Liddell and Scott, *Greek-English Lexicon* (Oxford: Clarendon, 1968), 305–6.

165*BAGD,* 131.

166T. J. Conant, *The Meaning and Use of Baptizein Philologically and Historically Investigated or Appendix to the Revised Version of the Gospel by Matthew* (New York: American Bible Society, 1861), v–vi, 158.

167Frank Tillapaugh, *The Church Unleashed* (Ventura, Calif.: Regal, 1982), 24.

168See Tillapaugh, *Church Unleashed,* for an explanation of this philosophy of ministry.

169Anthony Hoekema, *The Four Major Cults* (Grand Rapids: Eerdmans, 1963), 384.

170See Stephen E. Robinson, *Are Mormons Christians?* (Salt Lake City: Bookcraft, 1991).

171Calvin, *Institutes,* IV.2.5–6.

[172]See Gerhard Lohfink, *Jesus and Community: The Social Dimension of Christian Faith,* trans. John P. Calvin (Philadelphia: Fortress, 1984).

[173]Elton Trueblood, *The Incendiary Fellowship* (New York: Harper & Row, 1967), 22.

[174]Ralph P. Martin, *The Spirit and the Congregation* (Grand Rapids: Eerdmans, 1984).

[175]R. Eugene Sterner, *Being the Community of Christian Love* (Anderson, Ind.: Warner, 1971), 12.

[176]See Tim Stafford, "The Hidden Gospel of the 12 Steps," *Christianity Today* (July 22, 1991), 14–19; also Michael G. Maudlin, "Addicts in the Pew," *Christianity Today* (July 22, 1991), 19–21.

[177]Trueblood, *Incendiary Fellowship,* 107–8.

[178]Dietrich Bonhoeffer, *Life Together* (New York: Harper and Brothers, 1954), 27.

[179]Ibid., 112.

[180]Ibid., 113.

[181]Trueblood, *Incendiary Fellowship,* 46.

[182]Ibid., 74.

[183]Snyder, *Problem of Wineskins,* 70.

[184]Ralph Neighbour, *The Seven Last Words of the Church* (Grand Rapids: Zondervan, 1973), 128.

[185]Ibid., 164.

[186]Trueblood, *Incendiary Fellowship,* 100.

[187]For many biblical references regarding thoughtful care for the poor, see Gordon R. Lewis, *Judge for Yourself* (Downers Grove: InterVarsity, 1974), 94–112.

[188]James E. Means, *Leadership in Christian Ministry* (Grand Rapids: Baker, 1989), 27.

Chapter Six

[1]Donald Bridge and David Phypers conclude that covenant theology "cannot be found in any form in any of the writings of the early Fathers." *The Water That Divides: The Baptism Debate* (Downers Grove: InterVarsity, 1977), 42.

[2]Charles Hodge, *Systematic Theology,* 3 vols. (Grand Rapids: Eerdmans, reprint, 1973), 3:548; cf. 349: "The church under the new dispensation is identical with that under the old."

[3]Ibid., 555.

[4]"Calvin was not a covenant theologian, but many of the implications of covenant theology . . . are present in Calvin's teaching." Everett H. Emerson, "Calvin and Covenant Theology," *Church History* 25 (1956): 141.

[5]John Calvin, *Institutes of the Christian Religion,* II.6.4.

[6]John Calvin, *Commentaries on Jeremiah and Lamentations,* 127.

[7]Calvin, *Institutes,* II.7.1.

[8]Ibid., II.6.2; idem, *Commentaries on Romans,* 421.

[9]Calvin, *Institutes,* II.11.2.

[10]Ibid., IV.16.3–6.

[11]See John Calvin, *Commentaries on Galatians and Ephesians,* 97.

[12]Calvin, *Institutes,* II.11.5.

[13]Ibid.

[14]L. Berkhof, *Systematic Theology* (Grand Rapids: Eerdmans, 1941), 271.

[15]Ibid., 268.

[16]Ibid., 278; cf. this statement on the same page: "God remains true to His covenant and will invariably bring it to full realization in the elect."

[17]Ibid., 287; cf. 288: "The promises of God are given to the seed of believers collectively, and not individually. God's promise to continue his covenant and to bring it to full realization in the children of believers, does not mean that he will endow every last one of them with saving faith. . . . The mere fact that one is in the covenant does not carry with it the assurance of salvation."

[18]Ibid., 295.

[19]Ibid., 568.

[20]C. I. Scofield, *Rightly Dividing the Word of Truth* (New York: N. P. Scofield, n.d.), 18.

[21]Ibid., 51.

[22]L. S. Chafer, *Dispensationalism* (Dallas: Dallas Seminary Press, 1936), 41. Chafer adds, on page 51, that in the millennial kingdom the basis for acceptance with God will not be grace but the Mosaic Law. Clarence B. Bass responds that dispensationalism's rigorous distinction between law and grace "when carried to its logical conclusion will inevitably result in a multiple form of salvation—that men are not saved in the same way in all ages." *Backgrounds to Dispensationalism* (Grand Rapids: Eerdmans, 1960), 33–36.

[23]Scofield, *Rightly Dividing,* 9.

[24]Chafer, *Dispensationalism,* 107.

[25]For a more detailed discussion see Gordon R. Lewis, "Ultradispensationalism," *EDT,* 1120–21.

²⁶*The Scofield Reference Bible,* ed. C. I. Scofield (New York: Oxford University Press, 1909/1917), note to Genesis 1:27–28, p. 5.

²⁷Ibid., note on Genesis 1:28, pp. 5–6.

²⁸Ibid., note on Genesis 12:1, p. 20.

²⁹Ibid., note on John 1:17, p. 1115. The note on Exodus 32:10, p. 113, attests the "striking contrast between law and grace." Cf. note on Isaiah 61:2, p. 766.

³⁰Ibid., note on John 1:17, p. 1115. But the work makes the opposite claim: "Law neither justifies a sinner nor sanctifies a believer," note on Galatians 3:24, p. 1245. Cf. note on Exodus 19:3, p. 93.

³¹Ibid., note on Romans 9:6, p. 1202.

³²See ibid., note on Matthew 16:18, p. 1021.

³³See ibid., notes on Matthew 6:33 and 21:43.

³⁴See, for example, ibid., notes on Isaiah 11:1; Daniel 2:44; Matthew 3:2; 5:2; 1 Corinthians 15:24.

³⁵See ibid., note on Matthew 5:2, pp. 999–1000.

³⁶Ibid., note on 1 Corinthians 15:24, p. 1003.

³⁷*The New Scofield Reference Bible,* ed. C. I. Scofield and rev. by E. Schuyler English et al. (New York: Oxford University Press, 1967).

³⁸Ibid., note on Genesis 1:28–28, p. 3.

³⁹But much of the language concerning the law-grace antithesis is preserved from the 1909/1917 edition. See *The New Scofield Reference Bible,* notes on John 1:17, p. 1124, and Galatians 3:24, p. 1268.

⁴⁰See ibid., notes on Genesis 1:27–28, p. 3, and John 1:17, p. 1124.

⁴¹Ibid., note on Matthew 3:2, p. 994; cf. note on Matthew 6:33, p. 1002.

⁴²Ibid., note on Matthew 6:33, p. 1002.

⁴³Charles C. Ryrie, *Dispensationalism Today* (Chicago: Moody, 1965), 29.

⁴⁴Ibid., 57–64.

⁴⁵Charles C. Ryrie, "Dispensation, Dispensationalism," *EDT,* 322.

⁴⁶Charles C. Ryrie, *Basic Theology* (Wheaton: SP Publications, 1986), 536.

⁴⁷Ryrie, *Dispensationalism Today,* 173.

⁴⁸See especially, Craig A. Blaising, "Developing Dispensationalism by Contemporary Dispensationalists," *Bibliotheca Sacra* 145, 579 (July–Sept. 1988): 254–80; Craig A. Blaising and Darrell L. Bock, eds. *Dispensationalism, Israel and the Church* (Grand Rapids: Zondervan, 1992).

⁴⁹See Bruce A. Ware, "The New Covenant and the People(s) of God," in Blaising and Bock, *Dispensationalism,* 96.

⁵⁰Darrell L. Bock, "The Reign of the Lord Jesus Christ," in Blaising and Bock, *Dispensationalism,* 61, 66.

⁵¹Robert L. Saucy, "Contemporary Dispensational Thought," *TSF Bulletin* 7 (Mar.–April 1984): 10.

⁵²Robert L. Saucy, "The Crucial Issue Between Dispensational and Non-dispensational Systems," *Criswell Theological Review* 1 (Fall 1986): 165. William R. Foster, *The Promise of a Kingdom* (Burlington, Ont.: Welch, 1985), 197, adds, "The concept of postponement does not seem to be appropriate in light of abundant evidence of the continuing proclamation and presence of the kingdom in some particular sense." Carl. B. Hoch, Jr., "The New Man of Ephesians 2," in Blaising and Bock, *Dispensationalism,* 126, concurs: "The church is no accident or substitute for a failed kingdom program."

⁵³Ware, "The New Covenant," 97: "Israel and the church are in fact one people of God, who together share in the forgiveness of sins through Christ and partake of his indwelling Spirit with its power for covenant faithfulness." Kenneth L. Barker, "The Scope and Center of Old and New Testament Theology and Hope," *Dispensationalism,* 303, candidly adds: "As I perceive the grand sweep of what God is doing, the old sharp distinction between Israel and the church begins to become somewhat blurred."

⁵⁴Barker, "The Scope and Center," 294.

⁵⁵Werner Georg Kümmel, *Promise and Fulfillment* (Naperville, Ill.: Alec R. Allenson, 1956), 87; cf. 152.

⁵⁶"Through Jesus' activities the future consummation is brought into the present." Ibid., 114; cf. 121, 127, 153–54.

⁵⁷Ibid., 140. To arrive at this conclusion Kümmel, 139, judged that Matthew 16:18 ff. "cannot be considered to belong to the oldest Jesus tradition." Ladd, on the other hand, argued that the kingdom of God was operative both through Jesus and the community he founded.

⁵⁸George Eldon Ladd, "Kingdom of Christ, God, Heaven," *EDT,* 611.

⁵⁹George Eldon Ladd, *The Presence of the Future* (Grand Rapids: Eerdmans, 1974), 260.

⁶⁰George Eldon Ladd, *The Gospel of the Kingdom* (London: Paternoster, 1959), 118.

⁶¹Ladd, "Kingdom of Christ," *EDT,* 611.

[62]Willis J. Beecher, *The Prophets and the Promise* (Grand Rapids, Baker, reprint, 1963), 178.

[63]Ibid., 382.

[64]See ibid., 382–83. On page 418 Beecher affirms that the Old Testament kingdom promise is being fulfilled "in Israel the people," "in the great religions in which men worship Yahweh," and "in the peerless personality of Jesus."

[65]Ibid., 379.

[66]Ibid., 298.

[67]Walter C. Kaiser, Jr., *Toward an Old Testament Theology* (Grand Rapids: Zondervan, 1978), 11.

[68]Ibid., 12, 15. Kaiser adds, on page 69: "The OT does possess its own canonical unity which binds together the various emphases and longitudinal themes. This not a hidden inner unity. It lies open and ready for all: The Promise of God."

[69]See ibid., 52–54, for a concise outline of the development of the promise theme in the Old Testament canon.

[70]Ibid., 233.

[71]Ibid., 234.

[72]Walter C. Kaiser, Jr., "Kingdom Promises as Spiritual and National," in *Continuity and Discontinuity: Perspectives on the Relationship Between the Old and New Testaments,* ed. John S. Feinberg (Westchester, Ill: Crossway, 1988), 307.

[73]Kaiser, *Old Testament Theology,* 269.

[74]Albrecht Ritschl, *The Christian Doctrine of Justification and Reconciliation,* ed. H. R. Mackintosh and A. B. Macaulay (Clifton, N.J.: Reference Book Publishers, reprint, 1966), 280; cf. 12, 290.

[75]Ibid., 320, 610.

[76]Walter Rauschenbusch, *Christianity and the Social Crisis* (New York: Macmillan, 1913), 65. In *Christianizing the Social Order* (New York: Macmillan, 1914), 67, Rauschenbusch similarly defines the kingdom as "the social redemption of the entire life of the human race on earth."

[77]Rauschenbusch, *Christianizing the Social Order,* 96.

[78]Ibid., 90.

[79]Gustavo Gutièrrez, *The Theology of Liberation* (Maryknoll, N.Y.: Orbis, 1973), 167.

[80]Ibid., 15.

[81]James H. Cone, *Black Theology and Black Power* (San Francisco: Harper & Row, 1989), 123.

[82]James H. Cone, *A Black Theology of Liberation* (Maryknoll, N.Y.: Orbis), 124.

[83]George R. Beasley-Murray, *Jesus and the Kingdom of God* (Grand Rapids: Eerdmans, 1986).

[84]John S. Feinberg, ed., *Continuity and Discontinuity: Perspectives on the Relation Between the Old and New Testaments* (Westchester, Ill.: Crossway, 1988).

[85]Gleason L. Archer, Jr., "Covenant," *Baker's Dictionary of Theology,* ed. Everett F. Harrison (Grand Rapids: Baker, 1960), 142.

[86]For this third interpretation see J. B. Hindley, "Hosea," *NBCRev,* 710.

[87]See, for example, Morton H. Smith, "The Church and Covenant Theology," *JETS* 21, 1 (March 1978): 55.

[88]*Epangelia* ("promise") like *euangelion* ("Gospel") has no Hebrew equivalent. Yet the concept of promise is set forth by the Hebrew verbs *dāhar* (to "speak," Deut. 1:11; 6:3; 9:28; 15:6) and *šāba'* (to "swear," Gen. 22:16; 26:3; 50:24; Exod. 13:5; Deut. 1:8) and the nouns *dāhār* ("word," "speech," and derivatively "promise," Gen. 15:1, 4; Exod. 20:1; 24:3–4, 8; 34:1, 27–28; Deut. 9:5) and *šᵉbû'āh* ("oath," Gen. 26:3; Deut. 7:8; Ps. 105:9).

[89]Laurence E. Porter, "1 and 2 Samuel," *NLBC,* 409. Walter C. Kaiser, Jr., likewise argues for "*individual* and *personal* invalidation of the benefits of the covenant" within the unconditionality of the covenant itself. See "The Blessing of David: Humanity's Charter," in John H. Skilton, ed., *The Law and the Prophets* (Philadelphia: Presbyterian & Reformed, 1974), 307.

[90]Arvid S. Kapelrud, "The Prophets and the Covenant," in *In the Shelter of Elyon,* ed. W. Boyd Barrick and John R. Spencer (Sheffield: JSOT Press, 1984), 179.

[91]Charles L. Feinberg, *Jeremiah: A Commentary* (Grand Rapids: Zondervan, 1982), 221.

[92]Robert H. Mounce, *Matthew, Good News Commentary* (San Francisco: Harper & Row, 1985), 103.

[93]William L. Lane, *The Gospel of Mark, NLCNT* (London: Marshall, Morgan & Scott, 1974), 158.

[94]I. Howard Marshall, *The Acts of the Apostles, TNTC* (Grand Rapids: Eerdmans, 1980), 60.

[95]F. F. Bruce, *The Epistles to the Colossians, to Philemon, and to the Ephesians, NICNT* (Grand Rapids: Eerdmans, 1984), 262.

[96]See Ernest F. Kevan, "Dispensation," *Baker's Dictionary of Theology*, ed. E. F. Harrison (Grand Rapids: Baker, 1960), 168.

[97]Thus Paul Enns, *The Moody Handbook of Theology* (Chicago: Moody, 1989), 389, states: "The term *Israel* refers to the physical posterity of Jacob; nowhere does it refer to the church."

[98]F. F. Bruce, *I & II Corinthians, NCBC* (Grand Rapids: Eerdmans, 1980), 101.

[99]As argued, for example, by Berkhof, *Systematic Theology*, 267.

[100]G. R. Beasley-Murray writes as follows concerning the differences between old and new covenants: "The difference between the two 'administrations' is cataclysmic, for they are separated by a gulf and an unscalable height, the death of the Christ and the glory of his Easter, with the age of the Spirit ensuing. . . . This attempt to reduce to uniformity the old and new covenants and their respective sacraments belongs to an unrealistic mode of exegesis that fails to distinguish between shadow and substance, that fails to understand New Testament eschatology and that fails to take into account the significance of the resurrection of Christ and the coming of the Holy Spirit." *Baptism in the New Testament* (London: Macmillan, 1962), 338.

[101]Donald A. Hagner, *Hebrews, Good News Commentaries* (San Francisco: Harper & Row, 1983), 217.

[102]L. Coenen, "Church, Synagogue," *NIDNTT*, 1:305. Ernest Best, *I Peter, NCBC* (Grand Rapids: Eerdmans, 1982), 108, added, "The Christians who come from many races and nations are now one people in continuity with the people of God in the Old Testament; the history of Israel is now their history."

[103]Carl F. H. Henry, *Aspects of Christian Social Ethics* (Grand Rapids: Eerdmans, 1964), 89. See also Robert D. Culver, *Toward a Biblical View of Civil Government* (Chicago: Moody, 1974), 61–83.

[104]See Charles Hodge, *Church Polity* (New York: Charles Scribner's Sons, 1878), 743–45.

[105]See Jakob Jocz, *The Covenant: A Theology of Human Destiny* (Grand Rapids: Eerdmans, 1968), 1–78.

[106]"Nation," *The World Book Dictionary* (Chicago: Field Enterprises Educational Corp., 1977), 2:1383.

[107]See J. Alexander Thompson, "Israel, History of," *ZPEB* 3:335–54.

[108]See references to Old Testament allusions in Romans 10 in Eberhard Nestle, *Greek New Testament*. Other thorough cross reference Bibles also may be used.

[109]Herman Hoeksema, *Reformed Dogmatics* (Grand Rapids: Reformed Free Publishing Association, 1966), 285.

[110]M. E. Osterhaven, "Covenant Theology," *EDT*, 280. See also Herman Witsius, *The Economy of the Covenants Between God and Man: Comprehending a Complete Body of Divinity* (London: 1822; reprint Escondido, Calif.: The den Dulk Christian Foundation, 1990). See also Charles Hodge, *Systematic Theology*, 3 vols. Grand Rapids: Eerdmans, 1946), 2:366–73.

[111]Kaiser, *Toward an Old Testament Theology*, 227.

[112]George Eldon Ladd, *A Theology of the New Testament* (Grand Rapids: Eerdmans, 1974), 79.

[113]Ladd, "Kingdom of Christ, God, Heaven," *EDT*, 608.

[114]See the note on John 1:17 in *The Scofield Reference Bible*, 1115.

[115]Roy L. Aldrich, "A New Look at Dispensationalism," *Bibliotheca Sacra* 120 (January 1963): 44.

[116]Ryrie, *Dispensationalism Today*, 131.

[117]Thomas D. Bernard, *The Progress of Doctrine in the New Testament* (London: Macmillan, 1879), 112.

[118]Ibid., 110.

[119]John Gill, *Body of Divinity* (London, 1839; reprint, Atlanta: Turner Lassiter, 1957), 348–67.

[120]Ladd, *Gospel of the Kingdom*, 22; cf. 120.

[121]Ryrie, *Dispensationalism Today*, 29; cf. Robert P. Lightner, *Evangelical Theology* (Grand Rapids: Baker, 1986), 240: "Dispensational theology may be defined as that system of theology which sees the Bible as the unfolding of the distinguishable economies in the outworking of God's purpose."

[122]*BAGD*, 560–61.

[123]Ibid., 559–60.

[124]R. E. O. White, *The Biblical Doctrine of Initiation* (Grand Rapids: Eerdmans, 1960), 266.

[125]Ibid.

[126]See George Eldon Ladd, "Israel and the Church," *Evangelical Quarterly* 36, 4 (Oct.–Dec. 1964): 207, or Millard J. Erickson, *Christian Theology*, 3 vols. (Grand Rapids: Baker, 1983–85), 3:1042.

[127]Walter C. Kaiser, Jr., *Toward an Exegetical Theology* (Grand Rapids: Baker, 1981), 139.

[128]See the agreement of Fred H. Klooster, "The Biblical Method of Salvation: A Case for Continuity," in Feinberg, *Continuity and Discontinuity*, 159.

[129]Howard A. Hanke, *Christ and the Church in the Old Testament* (Grand Rapids: Zondervan, 1957), 109.

[130]This material on dispensationalism is adapted from Gordon R. Lewis, "Ultradispensationalism," *EDT*, 1120–21.

[131]Robert L. Saucy, *The Church in God's Program* (Chicago; Moody, 1972), 58–64.

[132]Ibid., 64–66.

[133]Helmut Thielicke, *The Ethics of Sex*, trans. John W. Doberstein (New York: Harper & Row), 1964.

[134]Stephen B. Clark, *Man and Woman in Christ* (Ann Arbor, Mich.: Servant Books, 1980), 49.

[135]For a more complete consideration of the purposes of the church see the previous chapter.

[136]As Reinhold Niebuhr said, "We have both capacity for justice and an inclination toward injustice. The former makes democracy possible; the latter makes it necessary." *The Children of Light and the Children of Darkness* (New York: Scribner, 1944), xiii.

[137]Rajah Chellah, "Economics and Christian Faith: A Personal Pilgrimage," *Transformation: An International Dialogue on Evangelical Social Ethics* 7, 2 (April/June, 1990): 21.

[138]See George E. Ladd, "Israel and the Church," *Evangelical Quarterly* 36, 4 (Oct.–Dec. 1964): 207, and Erickson, *Christian Theology*, 3:1042.

[139]Gerhard F. Hasel, *Old Testament Theology: Basic Issues in the Current Debate* (Grand Rapids: Eerdmans, 1972), 49–63, or (1975 ed.), 117–43. Although Hasel seems to favor a single theme in this chapter, his concluding chapter calls for a multiplex theology.

[140]Ibid., 95.

[141]Gerhard H. Hasel, *New Testament Theology: Basic Issues in the Current Debate* (Grand Rapids: Eerdmans, 1978), 217–220.

[142]See the chapter on Providence in IT, 2:97–106.

[143]Harold Hoehner, cited by Randy Frame, "News," *Christianity Today* (March 5, 1990), 43.

[144]Thomas Finger, cited by Frame, "News," 43.

[145]Rick Fields et al., *Chop Wood Carry Water: A Guide to Finding Spiritual Fulfillment in Everyday Life* (Los Angeles: Jeremy P. Tarcher, 1984), 12.

[146]Alva J. McClain, *The Greatness of the Kingdom* (Grand Rapids: Zondervan, 1959), 66.

[147]Ibid., 67–68.

[148]Ibid., 68.

[149]See ibid., 68–90.

[150]Ibid., 520.

[151]Ibid., 521.

[152]Foster, *Promise of a Kingdom*, 204.

[153]Ibid., 197.

[154]Craig Blomberg, *Interpreting the Parables* (Downers Grove: InterVarsity, 1990), 108–9.

[155]White, *Biblical Doctrine of Initiation*, 267.

[156]G. R. Beasley-Murray extensively documents present and future aspects of God's kingdom in an "inaugurated eschatology," in *Jesus and the Kingdom of God* (Grand Rapids: Eerdmans, 1986).

[157]Merrill C. Tenney, "The Glorious Destiny of the Believer," in *Fundamentals of the Faith*, ed. C. F. H. Henry (Grand Rapids: Zondervan, 1969), 286.

[158]Greg L. Bahnsen, *Theonomy in Christian Ethics* (Nutley, N.J.: Craig Press, 1977), xiii.

[159]Gary DeMar, cited by Frame, "News," 43.

[160]Greg L. Bahnsen, *Theonomy in Christian Ethics* (Phillipsburg, N.J.: Presbyterian and Reformed, 1984), 241.

[161]Ronald Sider, cited by Frame, "News," 42.

[162]Mark Satin, *New Age Politics* (New York: Dell, 1979).

[163]Berkhof, *Systematic Theology*, 293, wrote, "It is preferable to follow the traditional lines by distinguishing just two dispensations or administrations, namely, that of the Old, and that of the New Testament; and to subdivide the former into several periods or stages in the revelation of the covenant of grace."

[164]The index to *Toward an Old Testament Theology* lists 35 pages in which Kaiser discusses "covenant" in relation to his promise theology.

[165]Ibid., 234.

[166]Ibid., 269.

[167]Kaiser, "Kingdom Promises as Spiritual and National," in Feinberg, *Continuity and Discontinuity*, 289–307.

168Ibid., 293.

169See ibid., 299.

170Ibid., 300.

171George Eldon Ladd, *Jesus and the Kingdom*, (Waco, Tex.: Word, 1970), 273; idem, *The Gospel of the Kingdom* (Grand Rapids: Eerdmans, 1959), 262–70.

172Ladd, *Gospel of the Kingdom*, 22.

173Ibid., 120.

174Ladd, *Theology of the New Testament*, 532.

175Ibid., 531–32.

176Ibid., 533.

177Ladd, *Jesus and the Kingdom*, 273.

178Ladd, *Theology of the New Testament*, 531.

179Ibid., 537.

180Robert L. Saucy, "Israel and the Church: A Case for Discontinuity," in Feinberg, *Continuity and Discontinuity*, 258–59.

181Ibid., 259.

182Although a major emphasis in earlier dispensational writings, the heavenly/earthly division has been omitted by McClain, Walvoord, Pentecost, and Ryrie.

183Ryrie, *Dispensationalism Today*, 154–55.

184Saucy, "The Crucial Issue," 165.

185Saucy, "Israel and the Church," 259.

186*The New Scofield Reference Bible*, 3.

187Os Guinness, *The Gravedigger's File: Papers on the Subversion of the Modern Church* (Downers Grove: InterVarsity, 1983), 141–57.

188Saucy, "The Crucial Issue," 153, addresses the question of whether Christ's teaching should be interpreted strictly literally. "Most interpreters see Jesus using some extreme examples designed to teach fundamental principles rather than strict actual cases. If this is, in fact, the better understanding, then the argument for the impossibility of a primary application for the present age loses its force."

189Blomberg, *Interpreting the Parables*, 298.

190Karl Barth, "An Exegetical Study of Matthew 28:16–20," *The Theology of the Christian Mission*, ed. Gerald H. Anderson (New York: McGraw-Hill, 1961), 64–65.

191Bryan Gilling, "Mass Evangelistic Theology and Methodology and the 1987 Luis Palau Mission to Auckland," *Transformation* (January/March 1991), 9–14.

192David L. Jones, "A Response from the Luis Palau Evangelistic Association," *Transformation* (January/March 1991), 14.

193Ibid., 11–12.

194William White, Jr., "Family," *ZPEB* 2:496.

195Bill Moyers, cited in the *Rocky Mountain News* (January 14, 1991), 48.

196Louis Sullivan, cited in the *Rocky Mountain News* (January 14, 1991), 35.

197A. W. Morton, "Education in Biblical Times," *ZPEB* 2:207.

198For additional ideas, see Cheri Fuller, "Drawing a Family Circle," *Focus on the Family* (March 1991), 2–4.

199Stanley Hauerwas, *The Peaceable Kingdom* (Notre Dame: University of Notre Dame Press, 1983), 105.

200Clark, *Man and Woman in Christ*, 578.

201Dietrich Bonhoeffer, *Life Together* (New York: Harper and Brothers, 1954), 31.

202Hauerwas, *The Peaceable Kingdom*, 103; cf. Clark, *Man and Woman in Christ*, 115: "The Church, therefore, as a community based on God's kingdom of truth cannot help but make all rulers tremble."

203Kenneth A. Myers, "A Better Way: Proclamation Instead of Protest," in *Power Religion: The Selling out of the Evangelical Church?* ed. Michael S. Horton (Chicago: Moody, 1992), 47.

204Ibid., 50.

205Clark, *Man and Woman in Christ*, 595.

206Kaiser, *Toward an Exegetical Theology*, 39.

207Ibid., 40.

208Charles Colson, *Kingdoms in Conflict* (Grand Rapids: Zondervan; New York: William Morrow, 1987), 173.

209Ibid., 174–75.

210Thomas Molnar, *Utopia, the Perennial Heresy* (New York: Sheed and Ward, 1967), Preface.

211Robert D. Culver, *Toward a Biblical View of Civil Government* (Chicago: Moody, 1974), 287.

212Colson, *Kingdoms in Conflict*, 94.

Chapter 7

1Oscar Cullmann, *Christ and Time*, trans. Floyd V. Filson (Philadelphia: Westminster, 1950), 84.

2Walter Rauschenbusch, *A Theology for the Social Gospel* (Abingdon: Nashville, reprint, 1978), 210.

[3]William Newton Clarke, *An Outline of Christian Theology* (Edinburgh: T. & T. Clark, 1909), 443. Clarke, 444, adds, "No visible return of Christ to the earth is to be expected, but rather the long and steady advance of his spiritual kingdom."

[4]Shailer Mathews, *The Faith of Modernism* (New York: Macmillan, 1924), 167.

[5]Harry Emerson Fosdick, *The Modern Use of the Bible* (New York: Macmillan, 1924), 104, 110.

[6]Ibid., 107.

[7]L. Harold DeWolf, *The Case for Theology in Liberal Perspective* (Philadelphia: Westminster, 1959), 178.

[8]L. Harold DeWolf, *A Theology of the Living Church* (New York: Harper & Brothers, 1953), 305.

[9]John A. T. Robinson, *Jesus and His Coming* (London: SCM, 1957), 151.

[10]John A. T. Robinson, *In the End God* (New York: Harper and Row, 1968), 80.

[11]Origen, *On First Principles*, II.11.2.

[12]Origen, *Commentary on Matthew*, 14.7.

[13]Origen, *On First Principles*, II.11.1–7.

[14]Augustine, *The City of God*, 20.9; cf. *Sermons on New Testament Lessons*, 7.5: "All the faithful, redeemed by the blood of his only Son, will be his kingdom." Cf. *Sermon*, 214.11.

[15]Augustine, *City of God*, 20.9.

[16]Ibid., 20.6.

[17]John Calvin, *Commentaries on the Epistles to the Philippians, Colossians, and Thessalonians*, 328.

[18]John Calvin, *Commentaries on the Prophet Daniel*, 2:75.

[19]John Calvin, *Commentary on a Harmony of the Evangelists*, 1:320.

[20]John Calvin, *Commentaries on the Epistle of Paul to the Romans*, 502.

[21]John Calvin, *Institutes of the Christian Religion*, III.25.5.

[22]Ibid. Cf. *Commentaries to the Philippians, Colossians, and Thessalonians*, 284: "To assign to Christ a thousand years, so that he would afterward cease to reign, were too horrible to make mention of."

[23]William Hendriksen, *More Than Conquerors* (Grand Rapids: Baker, 1940).

[24]Anthony A. Hoekema, "Amillennialism," in *The Meaning of the Millennium*, ed. Robert G. Clouse (Downers Grove: InterVarsity, 1977), 160; cf. idem., *The Bible and the Future* (Eerdmans, 1979), 228-29.

[25]Hoekema, *Bible and the Future*, 227.

[26]Ibid., 201.

[27]Hoekema, "Amillennialism," 169.

[28]Hoekema, *Bible and the Future*, 233; cf. idem., "Amillennialism," 181: "As far as the thousand years of Revelation 20 are concerned, we are in the millennium now."

[29]Hoekema, "Amillennialism," 170.

[30]Eusebius, *Ecclesiastical History*, 3.39; 7.24; 10.4.

[31]Jonathan Edwards, "Notes on the Apocalypse," *The Works of Jonathan Edwards*, 9 vols. (New Haven: Yale University Press, 1957–89), 5:129.

[32]Jonathan Edwards, "An Humble Attempt," *Works*, 5:207.

[33]Augustus Hopkins Strong, *Systematic Theology* (Valley Forge, Penn.: Judson, 1907), 1012.

[34]Ibid., 1014.

[35]Loraine Boettner, *The Millennium* (Philadelphia: Presbyterian and Reformed, 1957), 29.

[36]Ibid., 32.

[37]For a helpful survey of the theonomy school and its eschatology see Thomas D. Ice, "An Evaluation of Theonomic Neopostmillennialism," *Bibliotheca Sacra* 145 (July–Sept. 1988): 281–300.

[38]David Chilton, *Paradise Restored: A Biblical Theology of Dominion* (Tyler, Tex.: Reconstruction Press, 1985), 156, 189.

[39]Ibid., 226.

[40]Ibid., 46.

[41]Ibid., 222.

[42]Greg L. Bahnsen, "The Prima Facie Acceptability of Postmillennialism," *Journal of Christian Reconstruction* 3, 2 (Winter, 1976–77): 68.

[43]Ibid., 63.

[44]See Douglas J. Moo, "The Case for the Posttribulational Rapture Position," in *The Rapture: Pre-, Mid-, or Posttribulational?* (Grand Rapids: Zondervan, 1984), 207.

[45]See Eusebius, *Ecclesiastical History*, III.39.12.

[46]As recorded by Irenaeus, *Against Heresies*, V.33.3.

[47]Justin Martyr, *Dialogue With Trypho*, 80.

[48]Ibid., 135.

[49]See Russell B. Jones, *What, Where, and When Is the Millennium?* (Grand Rapids: Baker, 1975), 13.

50Irenaeus, *Against Heresies*, V.32.2.

51Tertullian, *Against Marcion*, III.25.

52Lactantius, *The Divine Institutes*, VII.24.

53*The Didache*, 16.2.

54*Epistle of Barnabas*, 4.3–4; 15.5.

55*The Shepherd of Hermas*, Vision 4(24).

56Justin Martyr, *Dialogue With Trypho*, 110.

57Irenaeus, *Against Heresies*, V.28.4.

58Ibid., 29.1.

59Ibid., 35.1.

60Tertullian, *On the Resurrection of the Flesh*, 25.

61Hippolytus, *Treatise on Christ and the Antichrist*, 60.

62Ibid., 61. Hippolytus wrote (p. 59) concerning the Tribulation period: "But we who hope for the Son of God are persecuted and trodden down by those unbelievers."

63Lactantius, *Divine Institutes*, 7.17.

64Ibid., 7.16.

65Ibid., 7.17.

66Robert H. Gundry, *The Church and the Tribulation* (Grand Rapids: Zondervan, 1973), 178.

67R. G. Clouse, "Rapture of the Church," *EDT*, 908; cf. J. Barton Payne, *The Imminent Appearing of Christ* (Grand Rapids: Eerdmans, 1962), 36: "Prior to the rise of Irving and Darby a century and one-quarter ago, all premillennialists were post-tribulational."

68George Eldon Ladd, *The Last Things* (Grand Rapids: Eerdmans, 1978), 23; cf. George Eldon Ladd, "Is There a Future for Israel?" *Eternity* (May 1964), 25–28, 36: "Believers are the true sons of Abraham the true seed, the spiritual circumcision—the spiritual Israel."

69Ladd, *Last Things*, 25.

70George Eldon Ladd, *The Blessed Hope* (Grand Rapids: Eerdmans, 1956), 88.

71Ibid., 81.

72Ibid., 158.

73Payne, *Imminent Appearing of Christ*, 159.

74Ibid., 98.

75Ibid., 121.

76Ibid., 42.

77Gundry, *Church and the Tribulation*, 21; cf. 14: "Dispensationally speaking, if the Church presently occupies the predicted time of Israel's dispersion, she may also occupy the predicted time of Israel's final tribulation."

78Ibid., 29.

79Ibid., 43; cf. 37.

80Lewis Sperry Chafer, *Dispensationalism* (Dallas, Tex.: Dallas Seminary Press, 1936), 107.

81Paul Enns, *The Moody Handbook of Theology* (Chicago: Moody, 1989), 390.

82*The Collected Writings of J. N. Darby*, ed. William Kelly, 34 vols. (London: G. Morrish, 1867–1900), 2:521; cf. 561: "Israel is the scene of God's righteous judgments; the church is the scene of God's sovereign grace."

83*The Scofield Reference Bible*, ed. C. I. Scofield (New York: Oxford University Press, 1917), note on Revelation 7:14, p. 1337.

84Ibid., note on Zechariah 12:8, p. 977.

85Ibid.

86John F. Walvoord, *The Rapture Question* (Grand Rapids: Zondervan, 1957), 16.

87Ibid., 39.

88John F. Walvoord, *The Blessed Hope and the Tribulation* (Grand Rapids: Zondervan, 1976), 136.

89Walvoord, *Rapture Question*, 88; cf. idem., *Blessed Hope*, 126.

90John F. Walvoord, *The Millennial Kingdom* (Grand Rapids: Zondervan, 1959), 209; cf. idem., *Major Bible Prophecies* (Grand Rapids: Zondervan, 1991), 181: "The [new] covenant is made specifically with the nation Israel, and the detailed provisions of this covenant do not relate to anyone who is not a descendant of Jacob. . . . The major provision of the new covenant will be fulfilled after Israel's time of trouble, specifically the Great Tribulation described in many OT passages and in Revelation 6–18. . . . The new covenant will feature great spiritual blessing for the people of Israel and their exaltation to a place of prominence when God will be identified with them (Jer. 31:33)." Concerning the citation of the Jeremiah text in Hebrews 8:7–12, he adds, 186: "The passage does not state nor is it the purpose of the author of Hebrews to state that Jeremiah's prophecy is being fulfilled today."

91Gleason L. Archer, Jr., "The Case for the Mid-Seventieth-Week Rapture Position," in *The Rapture: Pre-, Mid-, or Posttribulational?* 117.

92J. Oliver Buswell, Jr., *A Systematic Theology of the Christian Religion*, 2 vols. (Grand Rapids: Zondervan, 1962–63), 2:387.

93Ibid., 2:456; cf. 390–91.

94Ibid., 2:501.

[95]Robert G. Govett, *Entrance Into the Kingdom: Or Reward According to Works* (Miami Springs, Fla.: Conley & Schoettle, reprint, 1978), 2.

[96]Ibid., 4.

[97]G. H. Pember, *The Great Prophecies of the Centuries Concerning Israel, the Gentiles, and the Church of God* (London & Edinburgh: Oliphants, 1941), 215.

[98]Ibid., 206.

[99]G. H. Lang, *The Revelation of Jesus Christ* (London & Edinburgh: Oliphants, 1945), 243.

[100]Ibid.

[101]R. Ludwigson, *A Survey of Bible Prophecy* (Grand Rapids: Zondervan, 1975).

[102]Robert G. Clouse, *The Meaning of the Millennium: Four Views* (Downers Grove: InterVarsity, 1977).

[103]Millard J. Erickson, *Contemporary Options in Eschatology* (Grand Rapids: Baker, 1977).

[104]Psalm 2:1–2 is fulfilled in Christ's crucifixion (Acts 4:25–28). Psalm 2:7 ultimately is realized in Christ's incarnation (Heb. 1:5), baptism (Matt. 3:17), transfiguration (Matt. 17:5), resurrection (Acts 13:33), and eternal priesthood (Heb. 5:5).

[105]Peter C. Craigie, *Psalms 1–50, WBC* (Waco, Tex.: Word, 1983), 69.

[106]A. F. Kirkpatrick, *The Book of Psalms* (Grand Rapids: Baker, reprint, 1982), 661.

[107]Robert L. Alden, "Malachi," *EBC* (Grand Rapids: Zondervan, 1985), 7:719.

[108]"What is important . . . is to distinguish carefully between prophecies directed to Israel *as a nation* (and which must be fulfilled in a national Israel) and prophecies directed to Israel as *the people of God* (which can be fulfilled in the people of God—*a people that includes the church!*). Such an approach is not allegorical or nonliteral; it simply calls upon the interpreter to recognize the intended scope of any specific prophecy!" Douglas J. Moo, "The Case for the Posttribulation Rapture Position," in *The Rapture: Pre-, Mid-, or Posttribulational?* 207.
William W. Klein, Craig L. Blomberg, and Robert L. Hubbard, *Introduction to Biblical Interpretation* (Dallas: Word, 1993), 310, comment: "We follow the pattern that the NT writers set out in their use of the OT. In most cases such prophecies find their fulfillment spiritually in the Church. Those that seem more physical in scope may anticipate literal fulfillment."

The occasional reading of "Israel" spiritually as the people of God is justified by a number of Scripture texts discussed in the preceding chapter 6. E.g., (1) Abraham is the father of the believing uncircumcised (Rom. 4:11); (2) Gentile believers are "children of Abraham" (Gal. 3:7; cf. 3:28–29; Gal. 4:28–31); (3) they are heirs of Abraham's blessing (Gal. 3:14); (4) New Testament believers are "the circumcision" (Phil. 3:3; cf. Rom. 2:28–29) and "the Israel of God" (Gal. 6:16); (5) Gentiles believers are "fellow citizens with God's people and members of God's household" (Eph. 2:19); and (6) Christians are described in language commonly used of Israel: "a chosen nation, a royal priesthood, a holy nation, a people belonging to God" (1 Peter 2:9; cf. "the people of God," v. 10).

[109]*The NIV Study Bible,* ed. K. Barker (Grand Rapids: Zondervan, 1985), 1112.

[110]James M. Boice, *The Last and Future World* (Grand Rapids: Zondervan, 1974), 17.

[111]G. R. Beasley-Murray, "Ezekiel," *NBCRev,* 684. I. Howard Marshall, *1 and 2 Thessalonians, NCBC* (Grand Rapids: Eerdmans, 1983), 191, states that an end-time rebuilding of a Jewish temple "rests on an over-literal interpretation of apocalyptic imagery."

[112]*The NIV Study Bible,* 1302; cf. Gleason L. Archer, Jr., "Daniel," *EBC,* 7:48: "This fifth realm is the kingdom of God, ruled over by Christ and enduring eternally, even after its earthly, millennial phase is over."

[113]Edward J. Young, *A Commentary on Daniel* (London: Banner of Truth Trust, 1972), 195–221.

[114]For a representative treatment see Leon Wood, *A Commentary on Daniel* (Grand Rapids: Zondervan, 1973), 247–63.

[115]Archer, "Daniel," *EBC,* 7:151; cf. Joyce G. Baldwin, *Daniel, TOTC* (Leicester: InterVarsity, 1978), 203: "Michael . . . does not prevent them [God's people] from enduring the suffering; rather he delivers them in the midst of it (cf. chapters 3 and 6)."

[116]Archer, "Daniel," 155.

[117]See John C. Whitcomb, *Daniel, Everyman's Bible Commentary* (Chicago: Moody, 1985), 163.

[118]Archer, "Daniel," 156–57.

[119]"And this gospel of the kingdom will be preached in the whole world [*oikoumenē*] as a testimony to all nations [*tois ethnēsin*], and then the end will come" (Matt. 24:14). The Greek word *ethnos* means "nation, people, pagan, Gentiles." In the LXX *'ām* usually is

translated by *laos*, signifying Israel as the chosen people, and *gôyim* is translated by *ethnē*, connoting the Gentiles. In the New Testament, however, *ethnē* is widened to include all peoples, whether Jews or Gentiles (Matt. 24:9; 28:19; Mark 11:17; Luke 21:24; Rom. 15:11). Undoubtedly this verse envisages church-age preaching to the nations of the earth. "Only when the church has completed its worldwide mission of evangelization will the Parousia no longer be delayed." Robert H. Mounce, *Matthew, Good News Commentary* (San Francisco: Harper & Row, 1985), 231.

[120]*The NIV Study Bible*, 1478, n. on Matthew 24:22, defines "the elect" as "the people of God."

[121]Walvoord, *Rapture Question*, 142, 194, avers that Christ promised believers deliverance from the period of this future trouble. I. Howard Marshall, *The Gospel of Luke, NIGTC* (Grand Rapids: Eerdmans, 1983), 783, argues that "*ekpheugō*, 'to escape,' (1 Thess. 5:3, et al.) has the force of coming unscathed through the terrible events of the last days and not giving up the faith in view of them."

[122]Everett F. Harrison, *Interpreting Acts* (Grand Rapids: Zondervan, 1986), 249; cf. the interpretation of Walvoord, *Millennial Kingdom*, 204–7.

[123]So F. F. Bruce, *1 and 2 Corinthians, NCBC* (Grand Rapids: Eerdmans, 1980), 147.

[124]Henry Alford, *The Greek New Testament*, 4 vols. (Grand Rapids: Baker, reprint, 1980), 2:435.

[125]Fritz Rienecker and Cleon L. Rogers, Jr., *LKGNT*, 599.

[126]F. F. Bruce, *1 and 2 Thessalonians, WBC* (Waco, Tex.: Word, 1982), 102. Marshall, *1 and 2 Thessalonians*, 131, agrees with this as the probable interpretation of *eis apantēsis*.

[127]Walvoord, *Blessed Hope and the Tribulation*, 100.

[128]R. Schippers, "Persecution, Tribulation, Affliction," *NIDNTT*, 2:807.

[129]*The Scofield Reference Bible*, n. 1 (on 2 Thess. 2:3), p. 1272.

[130]Walvoord, *Rapture Question*, 163, writes, "There seems to be some evidence that the Day of the Lord begins at once at the time of the translation of the church (cf. 1 Thess. 5:1–9). The same event which translates the church begins the Day of the Lord." So also his book *Major Bible Prophecies*, 272–73.

[131]Rienecker and Rogers, *LKGNT*, 608.

[132]Gundry, *Church and the Tribulation*, 115. Bruce, *1 & 2 Thessalonians*, 167, concludes,

"It appears more probable from the context that a general abandonment of the basis of civil order is envisaged. This is not only rebellion against the law of Moses; it is a large-scale revolt against public order, and since public order is maintained by the 'governing authorities' who 'have been instituted by God,' any assault on it is an assault on a divine ordinance (Rom. 13:1–2). It is, in fact, the whole concept of divine authority over the world that is set at defiance in '*the* rebellion' par excellence." W. Bauder, "Fall, Fall Away," *NIDNTT*, 1:607, concludes, "The absolute use of *apostasia* in 2 Thess. 2:3 is a common expression in Jewish apocalyptic, with its prophecy of a period of apostasy shortly before the appearance of the Messiah."

Walvoord, *Rapture Question*, 71–2, noting that the verb *aphistēmi* more often signifies physical departure, sees in 2 Thess. 2:3 the Rapture of the church. So also does E. Schuyler English, *Rethinking the Rapture* (Traveler's Rest, S.C.: Southern Bible Book House, 1954), 67–71. Moo, "The Case for the Posttribulation Rapture Position," in *The Rapture: Pre-, Mid- or Posttribulational?* 189, responds, "The *apostasia* is best understood as a *religious* rebellion against God. Although some have argued that it should be translated 'departure' and have seen in it a reference to the Rapture, such a translation is most improbable in light of the meaning of the term in biblical Greek."

[133]Gundry, *Church and the Tribulation*, 115.

[134]Ibid., 115–16.

[135]Ibid., 115.

[136]Ibid., 116.

[137]Bruce, *1 and 2 Thessalonians*, 171: "Paul viewed established government as imposing a salutary restraint on evil (Rom. 13:3–4), and in his mission field established government meant effectively the Roman Empire (*to katechon*), personally embodied in the emperor (*ho katechōn*)"; cf. J. B. Lightfoot, *Notes on the Epistles of St. Paul* (Grand Rapids: Baker, reprint, 1980), 112, identified the restrainer as "some intermediate power . . . which, without being directly Christian, acts as a check upon Antichrist; such as the power of law or order, civil government and the like." See also Lewis and Demarest, *Integrative Theology*, 2:88.

[138]Ladd, *Blessed Hope*, 95. In Ladd's view, "till he is taken out of the way" (v. 7) refers not to "the restrainer" but to Antichrist.

[139]See Walvoord, *Rapture Question*, 84–87, and *Major Bible Prophecies*, 275–76; Enns, *Moody Handbook of Theology*, 113, 333–34; *The New Scofield Reference Bible* (New York: Oxford University Press, 1967), 1295.

[140]Marshall, *1 and 2 Thessalonians*, 193. So also Lightfoot, *Notes on Epistles of Paul*, 112.

[141]Bruce, *1 and 2 Thessalonians*, 176. Similarly, Leon Morris, *The First and Second Epistles to the Thessalonians*, NICNT (Grand Rapids: Eerdmans, 1959), 225.

[142]*The NIV Study Bible*, 1727; cf. Hoekema, *Bible and the Future*, 126: "The nearness of the Parousia is not so much a chronological nearness as a 'salvation-history' nearness. . . . Because the return of Christ is so certain, it is in a sense always near."

[143]Rienecker and Rogers, *LKGNT*, 366.

[144]G. R. Beasley-Murray, *John*, WBC (Waco, Tex.: Word, 1987), 300.

[145]So *The Scofield Reference Bible*, n. 1 (on John 14:3), p. 1135: "This promise of a second advent of Christ is to be distinguished from His return in glory to the earth; it is the first intimation in Scripture of 'the day of Christ' (1 Cor. 1:8). Here He comes for His saints, there (e.g., Mt. 24:29, 30) He comes to judge the nations." Cf. Walvoord, *Major Bible Prophecies*, 267–68.

[146]F. F. Bruce, *The Gospel of John* (Grand Rapids: Eerdmans, 1983), 297–98.

[147]Cf. Walvoord, *Major Bible Prophecies:* 278. "If the Philadelphia church can be taken as a type, or illustration, of a true church, then this is an implication that the true church also will not go through this hour of trial."

[148]See the *New Scofield Reference Bible*, p. 1356, n. 1: ". . . the catching up of John from earth to heaven has been taken to be a symbolic representation of the translation of the Church as occurring before the events of the tribulation described in chs. 6–19."

[149]F. F. Bruce, "The Revelation to John," *NLBC*, 1688.

[150]Ibid., 1691. Klein, Bomberg, and Hubbard, *Introduction to Biblical Interpretation*, 373, comment: "One hundred forty-four thousand is 12 times 12 times 1000—the number of the tribes of Israel raised to the second power and multiplied by a large round number. So this great company of the redeemed may in fact picture the Church as the fulfillment of the promises to Israel in a grand and glorious way." Charles C. Ryrie advances the literalist dispensationalist interpretation in *Basic Theology* (Wheaton: Victor, 1986), 468–69, 490–92.

[151]Bruce, "The Revelation to John," 1695, appealing to Zechariah 4:2–14 and 13:7, argued, "The original reference is to the ministry in Jerusalem of a latter-day Moses and Elijah . . . which is terminated by their martyrdom at the hands of the occupying Roman power. . . .

The two witnesses now become symbolic figures for the church in its royal and priestly functions (11:4)." See Ryrie's interpretation in *Basic Theology*, 470–71; also Walvoord, *Rapture Question*, 181.

[152]G. R. Beasley-Murray, "The Revelation," *NBCRev*, 1295: "The picture well illustrates the spiritual security of believers against all that the devil can do in his attempts to destroy them."

[153]So Walvoord, *Major Bible Prophecies*, 357–58 and 322: "Revelation 17 and 18 present a prophetic picture of Babylon in the future. . . . Probably the simplest and most effective approach is to regard chapter 17 as a prophecy of the ultimate end of Babylon as a religion and chapter 18 as the end of Babylon as a city." This interpretation further illustrates what we judge to be an excessively literal interpretation.

[154]Moo, "The Case for the Posttribulation Rapture Position," 201.

[155]See the classic statement of Alford, *The Greek New Testament*, 4:732–33.

[156]Moo, "The Case for the Posttribulation Rapture Position," 201. Pretribulationists such as Walvoord, *Major Bible Prophecies*, 378, and Ryrie, *Basic Theology*, 514, argue that Revelation 20:4–6 describes only the resurrection of Tribulation martyrs just prior to the Millennium.

[157]Rienecker and Rogers, *LKGNT*, 775.

[158]Robert H. Mounce, *A Living Hope: A Commentary on 1 and 2 Peter* (Grand Rapids: Eerdmans, 1982), 68; cf. *The NIV Study Bible*, note on James 5:9, p. 1885.

[159]Bruce, *1 and 2 Thessalonians*, 109: "In early Christian usage, with the acknowledgment of Jesus as Lord, Jesus was viewed as the *kyrios* whose day it was." Cf. Marshall, *1 and 2 Thessalonians*, 133.

[160]G. Braumann, "Present," *NIDNTT*, 2:898.

[161]Donald Guthrie, *The Pastoral Epistles*, TNTC (London: Tyndale, 1957), 198.

[162]Hoekema, *Bible and the Future*, 18.

[163]James Denney, *Studies in Theology*, (London: Hodder and Stoughton, 1894), 239.

[164]Franz Delitzsch, *Biblical Commentary on the Prophecies of Isaiah* (Grand Rapids: Eerdmans, 1950), 1:285.

[165]Merrill C. Tenney, *Interpreting Revelation* (Grand Rapids: Eerdmans, 1962), 88–89.

[166]D. H. Kromminga, *The Millennium* (Grand Rapids: Eerdmans, 1948), 28–31.

[167]W. Gutbrod, *"nomos,"* TDNT 4:1086.

168Hoekema, *Bible and the Future*, 156.

169Ibid., 150–51.

170Marvin Rosenthal, *The Pre-Wrath Rapture of the Church* (Nashville: Thomas Nelson, 1990), 141, 147.

171Colin Brown, "Day of the Lord (Yahweh)," *ZPEB*, 5:47.

172See Erickson, *Christian Theology*, 3:1190–92

173See *The NIV Study Bible*, 1947, n. on Revelation 19:7.

174Gleason L. Archer, Jr., "The Case for the Mid-Seventieth-Week Rapture Position," in *The Rapture: Pre-, Mid-, or Posttribulational?* 142–44.

175J. Oliver Buswell, Jr., *Systematic Theology*, 2:450, 456.

176Rosenthal, *The Pre-Wrath Rapture of the Church*, 227.

177See the argument of Paul D. Feinberg, "The Case for the Pretribulation Rapture Position" in *The Rapture: Pre-, Mid-, or Posttribulational?* 50–72.

178Hoekema *Bible and the Future*, 126–27.

179Ibid., 126.

180Alan A. MacRae's translation of Olympiodorus Philosophophus, *Aristotelis Meteora commentaria* (a commentary on Aristotle's *Meteora*) cited in Liddell and Scott, *A Greek-English Lexicon* (Oxford: Clarendon, 1951), 218 (for abbreviations see xxxi).

181H. E. Dana and J. R. Mantey, *A Manual Grammar of the Greek New Testament* (New York: Macmillan, 1957), 137, 141.

182A. T. Robertson, *Word Pictures in the New Testament*, 6 vols. (Nashville: Broadman, 1985), 4:49.

183Alan A. MacRae, a pretribulational Presbyterian scholar and professor; E. Schuyler English, *Rethinking the Rapture*; Leon J. Wood, *Is the Rapture Next?* (Grand Rapids: Zondervan, 1956); John Lineberry, *Vital Word Studies in 2 Thessalonians* (Grand Rapids: Zondervan, 1961); and Kenneth Wuest, *The New Testament: An Expanded Translation* (Grand Rapids: Eerdmans, 1972).

184*BAGD*, 91.

185 John B. Taylor, "Apocalyptic Literature," *The New International Dictionary of the Christian Church* (Grand Rapids: Zondervan, 1974), 52.

186Shailer Mathews, "Apocalyptic Literature," *Dictionary of the Bible*, ed. James Hastings, 1 vol. (New York: Scribner, 1951), 41.

187Julian Franklyn, ed., *A Dictionary of the Occult* (New York: Causeway Books, 1973), 212.

188Robert H. Mounce, *The Book of Revelation* (Grand Rapids: Eerdmans, 1977), 24.

189George Eldon Ladd, *Jesus and the Kingdom* (Grand Rapids: Eerdmans, 1964), 81.

190For a summary of these books, see J. L. Koole, "Apocalyptic Literature," *The Encyclopedia of Christianity*, ed. Edwin H. Palmer (Wilmington, Del.: The National Foundation for Christian Education, 1964), 301-4.

191George Eldon Ladd, "Apocalyptic," *EDT*, 64. Klein, Blomberg, and Hubbard, *Introduction to Biblical Interpretation*, 371, argue that "Revelation is prophetic as well as apocalyptic."

192Klein, Blomberg, and Hubbard, *Introduction to Biblical Interpretation*, 312, conclude from their study of prophetic-apocalyptic literature: "It is best to take the symbolism and numbers seriously but not literally. Symbolism and imagination fascinated ancient peoples more than statistical accuracy." Cf. 371-72: "Revelation employs highly symbolic and figurative imagery that we dare not interpret too literally." They cite as examples from the Apocalypse: "seven lampstands" (Rev. 1:20), "the bowls of incense" (5:8), "the dragon" (12:9), "the great prostitute" (17:18), etc.

193Clark H. Pinnock and Delwin Brown, *Theological Crossfire: An Evangelical/Liberal Dialogue* (Grand Rapids: Zondervan, 1990), 237.

194C. H. Dodd, *The Parables of the Kingdom* (London: Nisbet, 1935), 107–8.

195Emil Brunner, *Eternal Hope* (Philadelphia: Westminster, 1954), 141, 145.

196Ibid., 86.

197Reinhold Niebuhr, *The Nature and Destiny of Man*, 2 vols. (New York: Scribner, 1951), 2:50.

198Paul Tillich, *Systematic Theology*, 3 vols. (Chicago: University of Chicago Press, 1951–63), 3:356–57.

199Harald Hoffding, *A History of Modern Philosophy*, 2 vols. (New York: Humanities, 1900), 2:191.

200A. E. Murphy, "Coming to Grips with *The Nature and Destiny of Man*," in *Religious Liberals Reply* (Boston: Beacon, 1947), 31–33.

201Chilton, *Paradise Restored*, 12.

202Ibid., 223.

203Loraine Boettner, "Postmillennialism," *Meaning of the Millennium*, 123–25.

204Chilton, *Paradise Restored,* 12.

205Boettner, "Postmillennialism," *Meaning of the Millennium,* 129.

206Chilton, *Paradise Restored,* 224–25.

207Ibid., 5.

208Ibid., 197.

209Ibid., 226.

210Ibid., 199.

211Boettner, "Postmillennialism," *Meaning of the Millennium,* 120.

212George Eldon Ladd, "A Response" (to Amillennialism), *Meaning of the Millennium,* 190.

213Tenney, *Interpreting Revelation,* 82–89.

214Kromminga, *The Millennium,* 28–31.

215Hal Lindsey with C. C. Carlson, *The Late Great Planet Earth* (Grand Rapids: Zondervan, 1970).

216Hal Lindsey, *Hope for the Terminal Generation* (Old Tappan, N.J.: Revell, 1971), 173.

217Edgar Whisenant, *88 Reasons Why the Rapture Could Be in 1988/On Borrowed Time* (Nashville: World Bible Society, 1988).

218Ibid., 1.

219Dean Halverson, "88 Reasons, What Went Wrong?" *Christian Research Journal* (Fall, 1988), 14–18.

220Whisenant, *88 Reasons,* 10.

221Ibid., 3

222Ibid., 4–5.

223Ibid., 24.

224*BAGD,* 896.

225Ibid., 395–96.

226Gundry, *Church and the Tribulation,* 43.

227Ibid., 43.

228Hoekema, *Bible and the Future,* 121.

229Ibid., 126.

230Michael Green, *2 Peter & Jude, TNTC* (Grand Rapids: Eerdmans, 1987), 141.

231See *The NIV Study Bible,* 1581, n. on Luke 21:32.

232Hoekema, *Bible and the Future,* 117.

233Brunner, *Eternal Hope,* 7.

234Mona Sharen, "Moral Dry Rot Destroying Nation's Foundation," *Rocky Mountain News* (Dec. 5, 1991), 87.

235Michael Hanlon, "Famine: A Race Against Time," *World Press Review* (February 1985), 37.

236"Earth's Creeping Deserts," *Time* (September 12, 1977), 58.

237*World Almanac and Book of Facts: 1992* (New York: World Almanac/Phonos Books, 1992), 546.

238G. C. Berkouwer, *The Return of Christ* (Grand Rapids: Eerdmans, 1972), 251.

239Tenney, *Interpreting Revelation,* 117–34.

240Berkouwer, *Return of Christ,* 254.

241Ibid., 255.

242Herman Ridderbos, *Paul: An Outline of His Theology,* trans. John R. DeWitt (Grand Rapids: Eerdmans, 1975), 495.

243Alan A. MacRae, "Second Coming," *His* (February 1960), 43.

244Moo, "The Case for the Posttribulation Rapture Position," in *The Rapture: Pre-, Mid- or Posttribulational? 211.*

245Archer, "The Case for the Mid-Seventieth-Week Rapture Position," 144.

246John Walvoord, Review of Ladd's *Blessed Hope* in *Bibliotheca Sacra* 113 (1956): 306.

247 Charles Ryrie, *The Basis of Premillennial Faith* (New York: Loizeaux, 1953), 143, 145.

248Leon J. Wood, *Is The Rapture Next?* (Grand Rapids: Zondervan, 1956), Preface.

249English, *Rethinking the Rapture,* 25–26, 122–23.

250Gleason L. Archer, Jr., Paul D. Feinberg, Douglas J. Moo, Richard R. Reiter, *The Rapture: Pre-, Mid-, or Posttribulational?* Preface.

251William F. Allman, "Fatal Attraction: Why We Love Doomsday," *U.S. News and World Report* (April 30, 1990), 13.

252Alan F. Johnson, "Our Future Hope," *Christianity Today* (February 6, 1987), 11.

253See Plato's dialogue, *The Republic* (many editions).

Chapter 8

1Shailer Mathews, *The Gospel and the Modern Man* (New York: Macmillan, 1912), 235.

2William Newton Clarke, *An Outline of Christian Theology* (Edinburgh: T. & T. Clark, 1909), 457.

3Ibid., 456.

4Ibid., 458.

5Harry Emerson Fosdick, *The Modern Use of the Bible* (New York: Macmillan, 1924), 99; cf. idem, *The Living of These Days* (New York: Harper: 1956), 240–41.

6Fosdick, *Modern Use of the Bible,* 100.

[7]William Adams Brown, *The Christian Hope* (New York: Scribner, 1912), 15.

[8]Ibid., 174.

[9]Ibid., 200; cf. 201.

[10]Origen, *On First Principles*, II.3.5; 10.6.

[11]Gregory of Nyssa, *Oratio de Mortuis, Works* (Paris, 1615), 2:1066–68; cited by Charles Hodge, *Systematic Theology*, 3 vols. (Grand Rapids: Eerdmans, reprint, 1973), 3:755.

[12]Augustine, *City of God*, 20.25; cf. 16.24; 21.13, 16, 26; idem, *Faith, Hope and Charity*, 69, and *On the Psalms*, 37.3.

[13]Thomas Aquinas, *SCG*, 4:91; cf. *Nature and Grace*, ed. A. M. Fairweather (Philadelphia: Westminster, 1954), *LCC*, 11:308.

[14]P. J. Toner, "Eschatology," *Catholic Encyclopedia*, 5:533.

[15]Roderick Strange, *The Catholic Faith* (Oxford and New York: Oxford University Press, 1986), 163–64.

[16]Irenaeus, *Against Heresies*, 2.34.3–4.

[17]Theophilus, *To Autolychus*, 2.27.

[18]C. F. Hudson, *Christ Our Life: The Scriptural Argument for Immortality Through Christ Alone* (Boston: John P. Jewett, 1860), 3.

[19]Edward White, *Life in Christ* (London: Elliot Stock, 1878), 77.

[20]Ibid., 346.

[21]Edward William Fudge, *The Fire That Consumes* (Fallbrook, Calif.: Verdict Publications, 1982), 410.

[22]Ibid., xiii. Fudge adds that the wicked "will disappear like smoke" and "Nothing will remain of the wicked but ashes" (pp. 116–17).

[23]Ibid., 434.

[24]Ibid., 304.

[25]William Temple, *Christus Veritas* (London: Macmillan, 1924), 208.

[26]John R. W. Stott, in *Evangelical Essentials: A Liberal-Evangelical Dialogue*, ed. David L. Edwards (Downers Grove: InterVarsity, 1988), 315.

[27]Ibid., 315.

[28]Ibid., 318–19.

[29]Clark H. Pinnock, "Fire, Then Nothing," *Christianity Today* (March 20, 1987), 40.

[30]Ibid.

[31]Ewald M. Plass, ed., *What Luther Says*, (St. Louis: Concordia, 1959), 385, no. 1130.

[32]Martin Luther, *Commentary on Peter and Jude*, 312ff., quoted in *A Compend of Luther's Theology*, ed. Hugh T. Kerr (Philadelphia: Westminster, 1966), 238; cf. 242.

[33]Martin Luther, *Sermon*, September 28, 1553. Cited by T. A. Kantonen, *The Christian Hope*, 37, in LeRoy Edwin Froom, *The Conditionalist Faith of Our Fathers*, 2 vols. (Washington, D.C.: Review and Herald, 1965), 2:74–77.

[34]See *What Luther Says*, 385–86, nos. 1131–34.

[35]Carlyle B. Haynes, *Life, Death and Immortality* (Nashville: Southern Publishing Association, 1952), 202; cf. "Immortality," *Seventh-day Adventist Encyclopedia* (Washington, D.C.: Review and Herald, 1966), 559: "Death is a state of complete unconsciousness."

[36]*Questions on Doctrine* (Washington, D.C.: Review and Herald, 1957), 523–24.

[37]See Froom, *Conditionalist Faith of Our Fathers*, 2:1051–1276.

[38]Oscar Cullmann, *Immortality of the Soul or Resurrection of the Body?* (New York: Macmillan, 1958), 33; cf. 36.

[39]Ibid., 57. E. F. Harrison, "Soul Sleep," *EDT*, 1037, comments concerning this view: "It is not a heresy in the narrower sense, due to the paucity of Scripture teaching on the intermediate state, but it may be called a doctrinal aberration."

[40]Cullmann, *Immortality of the Soul*, 39.

[41]P. T. Forsyth, *This Life and the Next* (New York: Macmillan, 1918), 34.

[42]L. Harold DeWolf, *The Case for Theology in Liberal Perspective* (Philadelphia: Westminster, 1959), 174.

[43]Ibid., 175.

[44]Russell Aldwinckle, *Death in the Secular City* (London: Allen & Unwin, 1972), 145.

[45]Brian Hebblethwaite, *The Christian Hope* (Grand Rapids: Eerdmans, 1985), 218–19.

[46]Dale Moody, *The Hope of Glory* (Grand Rapids: Eerdmans, 1962), 61.

[47]Donald G. Bloesch, *Essentials of Evangelical Theology*, 2 vols. (New York: Harper & Row, 1978–79), 2:225.

[48]Ibid., 2:227.

[49]Clark H. Pinnock, "Why Is Jesus the Only Way?" *Eternity* 27, 12 (December 1976): 34.

[50]Clark H. Pinnock, "Toward an Evangelical Theology of Religions," *JETS* 33, 3 (September 1990): 368.

[51]W. D. Davies, *Paul and Rabbinic Judaism* (Philadelphia: Fortress, 1980), 318.

[52]F. F. Bruce, "Paul on Immortality," *Scottish Journal of Theology* 24 (1971): 469.

[53]Ibid., 470.

[54]Murray J. Harris, *Raised Immortal: Resurrection and Immortality in the New Testament* (Grand Rapids: Eerdmans, 1983), 140; cf. 120.

[55]Murray J. Harris, "Immortality," *NDT*, 332.

[56]Harris, *Raised Immortal*, 196–98.

[57]Ibid., 129–30; cf. Murray J. Harris, *From Grave to Glory: Resurrection in the New Testament* (Grand Rapids: Zondervan, 1990), 204.

[58]Harris, *Raised Immortal*, 133.

[59]Ibid., 126. Cf. Harris, *From Grave to Glory*, 200.

[60]Harris, *Raised Immortal*, 132; cf. 53: "After his resurrection *his essential state was one of invisibility and therefore immateriality.*" In his second book, *From Grave to Glory*, 44, Harris modifies his language somewhat: "The resurrection body of Christ . . . was '*customarily immaterial*' in the sense that in *his customary mode of existence* during the forty days, he did not have a material body of 'flesh and bones.'" Norman L. Geisler has vigorously challenged Harris's view of Christ's resurrection body in *The Battle for the Resurrection* (Nashville: Thomas Nelson, 1989) and *In Defense of the Resurrection* (Lynchburg, Va.: Quest Publications, 1991).

[61]Peter Toon, *Heaven and Hell: A Biblical and Theological Overview* (Nashville: Thomas Nelson, 1986), 127.

[62]Karl Rahner, *On the Theology of Death* (New York: Seabury, 1973), 19.

[63]Ibid., 22; cf. idem., "Death," *Sacramentum Mundi*, 6 vols. (New York: Herder & Herder, 1968–70), 2:59.

[64]Rahner, *Theology of Death*, 22.

[65]Karl Rahner, *Foundations of the Christian Faith* (New York: Seabury, 1978), 435; cf. 444.

[66]Monika K. Hellwig, *What Are They Saying About Death and Christian Hope?* (New York: Paulist, 1978), 26.

[67]In ibid., 64, Hellwig writes that "heaven is . . . a circumlocution for God." Moreover, "Gehenna . . . was an established metaphor for ultimate human frustration and disaster." *Understanding Catholicism* (New York: Paulist, 1981), 180.

[68]Hellwig, *What Are They Saying About Death?* 66.

[69]Ibid., 27.

[70]*Epistle to Diognetus*, 10.7.

[71]Justin Martyr, *First Apology*, 52; cf. *Second Apology*, 2, 7–9; cf. *Dialogue With Trypho*, 5: After death "the souls of the pious remain in a better place, while those of the unjust and wicked are in a worse, waiting for the time of judgment. Thus some who have appeared worthy of God never die; but others are punished so long as God wills them to exist and to be punished."

[72]Athenagoras, *A Plea for the Christians*, 31. Cf. idem, *The Resurrection of the Dead*, 13, 20, 24.

[73]Irenaeus, *Against Heresies*, 2.34.4.

[74]Ibid., 5.28.1.

[75]Tertullian, *On the Soul*, 58.

[76]Tertullian, *On the Resurrection of the Flesh*, 22.

[77]Ibid., 34. In ibid., 35, Tertullian strongly refuted those who "suppose that the destruction of the soul and the flesh in hell amounts to a final annihilation of the two substances [i.e., body and soul] and not to their penal torment."

[78]Augustine, *City of God*, 13.2: "The human soul is in a true sense . . . immortal because it can never, in the least degree, cease to live and perceive." Cf. ibid., 21.3: "The fact is that the soul . . . cannot die." Cf. idem., *Soliloquies*, 2.3,13; *The Immortality of the Soul*, 4, 6, 8.

[79]Augustine, *Enchiridion*, 111; cf. idem, *City of God*, 11.11; 19.28; 21.3.

[80]Augustine, *City of God*, 21.10; cf. 16.24; 20.16; 21.2–3, 7–9; idem, *Enchiridion*, 68–69. Augustine takes "'fire' in the literal sense as punishment for the body, and the 'worm' as a metaphor for spiritual anguish.'" *City of God*, 20.22.

[81]John Calvin, "Psychopannychia," in *Tracts and Treatises in Defense of the Reformed Faith*, vol. 3, trans. Henry Beveridge (Grand Rapids: Eerdmans, 1958), 419–20: The human soul "is a substance, and after the death of the body truly lives, being endued both with sense and understanding." Cf. 427–28.

[82]John Calvin, *Institutes of the Christian Religion*, III.25.6.

[83]Ibid., 25.7.

[84]Ibid., 25.12; cf. idem, *Commentary on a Harmony of the Evangelists*, 1:200; 2:124.

[85]Calvin, *Institutes*, III.25.6; cf. idem., *Commentaries on the Philippians, Colossians, and Thessalonians*, 279.

[86]Ray Summers, *The Life Beyond* (Nashville: Broadman, 1959).

[87]L. Boettner, *Immortality* (Philadelphia: Presbyterian and Reformed, 1967).

88Robert A. Morey, *Death and the Afterlife* (Minneapolis, Bethany House, 1984).

89G. Ch. Aalders comments, "Christian theology has generally found a basis here for the two-sided nature of human beings. . . . We can properly speak of human beings as being both physical and spiritual, or, more simply, as being body and soul." *Genesis,* 2 vols., *Bible Student's Commentary* (Grand Rapids: Zondervan, 1981), 1:86.

90R. Laird Harris, *"kārat,"* TWOT, 1:457.

91Francis I. Anderson, *Job,* TOTC (London: Inter-Varsity, 1976), 194.

92Dale Moody, *Hope of Glory,* 101, writes, "Hades is the intermediate place of punishment for wicked men (Rev. 1:18; 6:8; 20:13ff.)."

93I. Howard Marshall, *The Gospel of Luke, NIGTC* (Grand Rapids: Eerdmans, 1978), 873.

94So Marshall, *Luke,* 636. Harris, *Raised Immortal,* 134, comments, "The least that the parable indicates is that the intermediate state is one in which there is consciousness of surroundings (vv. 23–24), memory of the past (vv. 27–28), and rational thought (v. 30)."

95A. Oepke, *"apollymi,"* TDNT, 1:396. J. H. Thayer, *A Greek-English Lexicon of the New Testament* (New York: American, 1889), 64, states that *apollymi* figuratively means "to 'devote' or 'give over to eternal misery.' " *Apollymi* is used in a variety of metaphorical ways in the Gospels: i.e., to "kill" (Matt. 2:13; Mark 9:22; 11:18), "lose" (Matt. 10:39, 42; Luke 15:4, 8), "die" (Matt. 26:52), "ruin" (Mark 2:22; Luke 5:37), and "drown" (Mark 4:38; Luke 8:24).

96Norval Geldenhuys, *Commentary on the Gospel of Luke, NICNT* (Grand Rapids: Eerdmans, 1983), 430, comments regarding the "darkness" and "fire" of hell: "In such biblical expressions we have the symbolical description of the hopeless plight of the lost."

97So Robert H. Gundry, *Matthew* (Grand Rapids: Eerdmans, 1982), 497.

98Leon Morris, noting that *aiōnios* describes the eternity of God (1 Tim. 1:17; Rom. 16:26) writes, "The concept of endless duration could not be more strongly conveyed; the use of these expressions for the eternity of God shows conclusively that they do not mean limited duration." "Eternal Punishment," EDT, 369.

99H. G. Link, *"apokatastasis,"* NIDNTT, 3:148.

100George E. Ladd, *I Believe in the Resurrection* (Grand Rapids: Eerdmans, 1975), 117.

101F. F. Bruce, *I and II Corinthians, NCBC* (Grand Rapids: Eerdmans, 1980), 151, comments that the analogy signifies "the combination of identity with difference."

102*The NIV Study Bible,* 1768, n. to 2 Corinthians 5:8.

103According to F. F. Bruce, the phrase "those who are perishing" signifies "those on the way to perdition." *1 & 2 Thessalonians, WBC* (Waco: Word, 1982), 173.

104Leon Morris, *The First and Second Epistles of the Thessalonians, NICNT* (Grand Rapids: Eerdmans, 1959), 153–54.

105William M. Arnett, "Immortality," *BDT,* 275.

106So Robert H. Mounce, *The Book of Revelation* (Grand Rapids: Eerdmans, 1977), 157–58; E. F. Harrison, "Soul Sleep," *EDT,* 1038; Murray J. Harris, "Intermediate State," *NDT,* 340; Moody, *Hope of Glory,* 75.

107Morey, *Death and the Afterlife,* 137.

108Henry Alford, *The Greek New Testament,* 4 vols. in 2 (Chicago: Moody, 1958), 4:255.

109A. A. Hodge, *Outlines of Theology* (London: Banner of Truth, reprint, 1972), 578.

110A. M. Stibbs, "Hebrews," *NBCRev,* 1215.

111John Jefferson Davis, *Evangelical Ethics Today* (Phillipsburg, N.J.: Presbyterian and Reformed, 1985), 175–76.

112Raymond A. Moody, Jr., *Life After Life* (Harrisburg, Penn.: Stackpole, 1976); Robert A. Monroe, *Journeys Out of the Body* (Garden City, N.Y.: Anchor, 1973).

113Oscar Cullmann, *The Immortality of the Soul or the Resurrection of the Dead?* (London: Epworth, 1959), 1–60.

114Geoffrey W. Bromiley, "Anthropology," *ISBERev.* 1:134.

115See J. G. S. S. Thomson, "Death and Immortality," *Christianity Today* (August 3, 1962), 19.

116W. G. T. Shedd, *The Doctrine of Endless Punishment* (New York: Scribner, 1886), 99.

117Ibid., 59–60.

118Bernard Ramm, *Them He Glorified* (Grand Rapids: Eerdmans, 1963), 62.

119Derek Kidner, *Genesis, TOTC* (London: Tyndale, 1967), 150.

120Craig Blomberg, *Interpreting the Parables* (Downers Grove: InterVarsity, 1990), 206.

121J. A. Schep, *The Nature of the Resurrection Body* (Grand Rapids: Eerdmans, 1964), 105.

[122]Robert B. Girdlestone, *Synonyms of the Old Testament* (Grand Rapids: Eerdmans, 1953), 101, 251.

[123]Leon Morris, *The Biblical Doctrine of Judgment* (Grand Rapids: Eerdmans, 1960), 17.

[124]Ibid., 49.

[125]John Gilmore, *Probing Heaven* (Grand Rapids: Baker, 1989), 273.

[126]See Craig Blomberg, "Degrees of Reward in the Kingdom of Heaven," *JETS* 35, 2 (June 1992): 159–72.

[127]Harry Buis, "Hell," *ZPEB*, 3:115.

[128]W. G. T. Shedd, *Dogmatic Theology*, 3 vols. (Grand Rapids: Zondervan, reprint, n.d.), 2:675.

[129]Morris, "Eternal Punishment," *EDT*, 369.

[130]Hodge, *Systematic Theology*, 3:868.

[131]Vernon Grounds, "The Final State of the Wicked," *JETS* 24, 3 (September 1981): 215.

[132]Gilmore, *Probing Heaven*, 111.

[133]Ibid., citing Twain, *Letters*, 17.

[134]Ibid., 113.

[135]L. A. King, "So You Say You're Going to Heaven . . . What Do You Expect?" *Eternity* (February 1983), 27.

[136]Corliss Lamont, *The Philosophy of Humanism* (New York: Ungar, 1982), 94.

[137]Ibid.

[138]David G. Myers, *The Human Puzzle: Psychological Research and Christian Belief* (New York: Harper & Row, 1978), 80.

[139]David G. Myers, "Are We Body and Soul? A Response to James Beck," *Journal of Psychology and Christianity* 10, 1 (Spring 1991): 38.

[140]James R. Beck, "Questioning the Intermediate State: A Case Study in Integrative Conflict," *Journal of Psychology and Christianity* 10, 1 (Spring 1991): 24–34.

[141]See Gordon R. Lewis and Bruce A. Demarest, *Integrative Theology*, 3 vols. (Grand Rapids: Zondervan, 1987–94), 2:123–80.

[142]Elmar Klinger, "Purgatory," *Encyclopedia of Theology: The Concise Sacramentum Mundi*, ed. Karl Rahner (New York: Seabury, 1975), 1320.

[143]Richard P. McBrien, *Catholicism* (Minneapolis: Winston, 1980), 633.

[144]Ibid., 1143.

[145]Gilmore, *Probing Heaven*, 141.

[146]McBrien, *Catholicism*, 1147.

[147]Clark Pinnock, *A Wideness in God's Mercy* (Grand Rapids: Zondervan, 1992), 169.

[148]Ibid., 170.

[149]Ibid., 174.

[150]Ibid., 175.

[151]C. H. Dodd, *The Apostolic Preaching and Its Developments* (New York: Harper, 1951), 82, 96.

[152]Morris, *Biblical Doctrine of Judgment*, 59.

[153]Edward John Carnell, *Christian Commitment* (New York: Macmillan, 1957), 102.

[154]Ibid., 103.

[155]José Miranda, *Marx and the Bible* (Maryknoll, New York: Orbis, 1974), 114.

[156]R. E. O. White, "Vengeance," *EDT*, 1138.

[157]Ibid.

[158]H. N. Oxenham, *Catholic Eschatology* (London: Pickering, 1876), 45.

[159]J. J. Van Osterzee, *Christian Dogmatics*, 2 vols. (New York: Scribner, 1887), 2:809.

[160]M. Randles, *Forever* (London: Wesleyan Conference Office, 1878), 61.

[161]Edwards and Stott, *Evangelical Essentials*, 316.

[162]Ibid., 315.

[163]Werner von Braun, "Immortality," "This Week Magazine" in *The Denver Post* (January 24, 1960).

[164]Edwards and Stott, *Evangelical Essentials*, 317.

[165]Ibid., 318.

[166]Ibid., 318–19.

[167]Ibid., 319.

[168]David Wells, "Everlasting Punishment," *Christianity Today* (March 20, 1987), 40–42 in response to Clark Pinnock, "Fire, Then Nothing."

[169]Cited by Peter Gowing, "Unwholesome Tendencies in Philippine Evangelical Theology," *The Silliman Christian Leader* 5, 1 (September 1962): 16.

[170]Neal Punt, *What's Good About the Good News?* (Chicago: Northland, 1988), 2.

[171]Neal Punt, *Unconditional Good News* (Grand Rapids: Eerdmans, 1980), 23–24.

[172]Ibid., 30.

[173]Punt, *What's Good About the Good News?* 42.

[174]Bernard Ramm, "The New Universalism in Missions," *World Vision Magazine* (August 1964), 3.

[175]Geddes MacGregor, *Reincarnation as a Christian Hope* (Totowa, N.J.: Barnes and Noble, 1982), 8.

[176]Geddes MacGregor, *Reincarnation in Christianity* (Wheaton, Ill.: Theosophical, 1978), 171.

[177]Ibid., 114.

[178]A. C. Bhaktivedanta Swami Prabhupada, *Coming Back: The Science of Reincarnation* (Los Angeles: Bhaktivedanta, 1982), 104.

[179]Ibid., 4.

[180]MacGregor, *Reincarnation as a Christian Hope*, 72.

[181]*The Denver Post* (June 6, 1977).

[182]Ninian Smart, "Transmigration," *EP* 7:122–24.

[183]John Hick, *Death and Eternal Life* (New York: Harper & Row, 1976), 305.

[184]Morey Bernstein, *The Search for Bridey Murphy* (New York: Lancer, 1965).

[185]Prabhupada, *Coming Back*, 112–15.

[186]Norman L. Geisler and J. Yutaka Amano, *The Reincarnation Sensation* (Wheaton, Ill.: Tyndale, 1987), 78–82.

[187]Shirley MacLaine, *Out on a Limb* (New York: Bantam, 1983), 216–19.

[188]Robert Brow, "Reincarnation," *His* (March 1975), 17–18.

[189]*Time*, July, 1953.

[190]*Statistical Bulletin* Metropolitan Life Insurance Co., vol. 28, no. 10 (October 1947). Cited by Carl F. H. Henry, *Christian Personal Ethics* (Grand Rapids: Baker, 1957), 46–47.

[191]*Time* (January 11, 1960), 52.

[192]Henry, *Christian Personal Ethics*, 77.

[193]For scriptural documentation see Gordon R. Lewis, *Confronting the Cults* (Phillipsburg, N.J.: Presbyterian and Reformed, 1966), 163–95.

[194]Morris, *Biblical Doctrine of Judgment*, 21.

[195]C. S. Lewis, *The Weight of Glory* (Grand Rapids: Eerdmans, 1949), 2.

[196]Ibid., 3.

[197]C. S. Lewis, *The Weight of Glory*, 1965 ed., 5.

[198]Edwards and Stott, *Evangelical Essentials*, 313.

[199]Reported by Terry Mattingly, "Eternal Damnation Put on Back Burner" *Rocky Mountain News* (October 6, 1991), 142.

[200]C. S. Lewis, *The Great Divorce* (New York: Macmillan, 1975), 72.

Scripture Index

Romans

561

General Index